ENCYCLOPEDIA OF

POP, ROCK & SOUL

Revised Edition

IRWIN STAMBLER

ST. MARTIN'S PRESS   NEW YORK

The author gratefully acknowledges the following sources of photographs that appear in this book (photos are listed by photo number; MOA = Michael Ochs Archives): Columbia/Epic, 1, 21, 38, 41, 47, 49, 80; Columbia/Epic/MOA, 18, 33, 44, 64, 68, 81; Atlantic, 2; Atlantic/MOA, 22; Capricorn/MOA, 3; MOA, 4-7, 8A, 26, 28, 30, 37, 42, 43, 48, 52, 54-57, 59, 61, 63, 73, 74, 78, 87, 89; RSO/MOA, 9, 17; Chrysalis, 10; Chess, 11; RCA, 34, 46; RCA/MOA, 12; Elektra/Asylum/ MOA, 14, 27, 76; Elektra/MOA/Debra Myers, 62; York/Pala. Atco/MOA, 15; ABC-Paramount/MOA, 16; Motown/MOA, 19; MCA, 20, 50; MCA/MOA, 91; Warner Bros., 23, 92; Warner Bros/MOA, 35, 77, 82, 88; Capitol, 24, 25; Capitol/MOA, 85; Harvest/MOA, 29; Elektra/Jacqueline Sallow, 31, 32; Fantasy/MOA, 36; Mercury, 39; Mercury/MOA, 66; United Artists/MOA, 40; Casablanca, 51; Geffen, 53; Sire, 58; Sire/MOA, 72, 83; Island/MOA, 59; Island/MOA/Sheila Rook, 86; Philadelphia Intl./MOA, 65; Shelter/ABC/MOA/S.M.H. Braitman, 67; A&M/MOA, 69; Grelun Landon, 70, 71; Rolling Stones/MOA, 75; Arista/MOA, 79; Gordy/MOA, 85; Solar/MOA, 90; Discreet/MOA, 93.

Design by Judith Stagnitto

Library of Congress Cataloging-in-Publication Data

Stambler, Irwin.
    The encyclopedia of pop, rock & soul.

    1. Popular music—Dictionaries.   2. Popular music—Bio-bibliography.
3. Rock music—Dictionaries.   4. Rock music—Bio-bibliography.   5. Soul music
—Dictionaries.   6. Soul music—Bio-bibliography.   I. Title.
ML102.P66S8   1989   784.5'0092'2 [B]   88-29860
ISBN 0-312-02573-4
ISBN 0-312-04310-4 (pbk.)

ENCYCLOPEDIA OF

POP, ROCK & SOUL

Revised Edition

To Connie, Lyndon, Barrett,
Bobbie (Regan) & Benjamin (''Jamey'')
the Seidmans (Alice, Abe,
Adam, Shoshana, Ari, Lila)
and the Spragues (Amy,
Leigh, Casey, Jim)

Contents

Introduction and Acknowledgments

As this book goes to press, the "rock revolution" that took over the popular music mantle in the U.S. and the world soon after World War II is a minimum of thirty-five years old. At least it was roughly thirty-five years ago that recordings by artists like Bill Haley, Elvis Presley, and Jerry Lee Lewis first appeared at the top of the hit lists—and that the music received the designation of rock & roll. (Disc jockey/concert promoter Alan Freed claimed to have invented the term and applied for a copyright on it; certainly it was through his efforts that the phrase stuck. But actually, the words can be found in earlier jazz and blues material. In 1938, for instance, Ella Fitzgerald recorded a song with Chick Webb's band—still played occasionally on jazz stations—that had the line "Won't you satisfy my soul with a rock & roll.")

In truth, rock didn't appear out of the blue in the mid-1950s. Precursors of rock had been performed by black artists in earlier years; rock-flavored material, for instance, was recorded by such artists on 78 rpm discs made for juke boxes in ghetto areas. But it was not until the mid-1950s that mainstream (mass audience) pop music began to be pushed aside by rhythm & blues, rock, and later, soul. By the 1960s, the "popular" music forms that had flourished in the 1930s and '40s—ballad/novelty numbers and big band material—either were relegated to a minor role in American culture or, as in the case of big bands, moved almost to extinction. (As R&B pioneer Johnny Otis pointed out in the first edition of this Encyclopedia, R&B evolved from the melding of roots blues and swing band elements.)

Still, some artists bucked the trend and retained or built up sizeable audiences with older type stylings, as recognized here by the inclusion of such major stars as Frank Sinatra and Tom Jones.

When rock first came to the fore in the mid-1950s, many observers dismissed it as just another fad among the many that came and went from the late nineteenth century to the early 1950s. But rock—and, in time, soul—proved to have staying power. To this day, rock & roll and R&B/soul remain the bellwethers of mass audience music, embraced in turn by each succeeding generation of teens and young adults.

Rock and soul have maintained their dominance to a great extent by spawning new and vibrant offshoots. In addition to rockabilly and R&B, major new artists have gained star status in such subgroupings as folk rock, country rock, heavy metal, speed metal, punk rock, reggae and rap/hip hop. The aim of this Encyclopedia is to reflect all of the pivotal influences in the evolution of today's popular music spectrum through the selection of appropriate artist entries. Almost every category noted above (and other variations besides, such as doo-wop) could fill a volume by itself. Given the limitations in time and space it would be impossible to detail the careers of all the thousands of individual performers and groups who have impacted the overall field from the 1950s through the 1980s in a single book.

The process of assembling this volume, then, began first with choosing the relatively small number of acts that merit the title of superstar or supergroup. From the remaining list of candidates, the criteria for selection included (1) choosing performers who managed to make some kind of mark in pop music history and (2) ensuring the inclusion of representatives of the various subcategories of pop music. It is recognized, of course, that categories are things writers use to try to give signposts to readers. Artists, who often like to range far afield in choice of material, don't like to be typecast—and, indeed, in individual entries this overlap is indicated. A group may perform hard rock much of the time, yet sometimes segue into ballads or softer rock offerings.

In the final analysis, the music is the thing, and one role of this book is to interest the reader in listening to material he or she might not have been acquainted with in the past—or perhaps to offer more insight into a performer's career, giving added meaning or emphasis to familiar songs.

Assembling the mass of material required for a book of this kind naturally calls for input and assistance from many organizations and individuals. Among those who have been particularly helpful are: Grelun Landon; Jeff Cohen; Michael Ochs; Shelly Selover and Diane Bluck of Columbia Records; Bob Merlis and Meryl Zukowsky of Warner Brothers Records; Paula Batson and RCA Records; Bob Garcia and A&M Records; Kathy Acquaviva and Atlantic Records; Jane Ayer; Ida Langsam and Private Eye; Vicki Rose; the National Academy of the Recording Arts & Sciences (NARAS); the Recording Industry Association of America (RIAA); MCA Records; Capitol Records; Geffen Records; EMI England; EMI America; Rhino Records; Chrysalis Records; Island Records; Epic Records; Arista Records; and Solar Records.

I also would like to express my gratitude to the editorial staffers at St. Martin's Press for their yeoman work in preparation of this volume, including former editor Bob Miller, editor Stuart Moore, editorial assistant Gordon Van Gelder, managing editor Amelie Littell, and Curt Alliaume of the production department. I also would be remiss if I didn't thank copy editor Bruce Sylvester for his careful checking of grammar and accuracy and for his thoughtful suggestions for improving the book's content.

—Irwin Stambler
Beverly Hills, California

ENCYCLOPEDIA OF

POP, ROCK & SOUL

Revised Edition

THE ABC's of POP, ROCK & SOUL

ABBA: *Vocal and instrumental group from Sweden. Members, Bjorn Ulvaeus, born Gothenburg, Sweden, April 15, 1945; Agnetha Faltskog, born Jankoping, Sweden, April 5, 1950; Anni-Frid Lyngstad, born Narvik, Norway, November 15, 1945; Benny Andersson, born Stockholm, Sweden, December 16, 1946.*

During the 1970s, the Swedish group ABBA proved that a rock band could achieve enormous success even though it was based in a relatively small country and had no major concert appearances in the main bastion of rock, the U.S. For most of its career, the band mainly made token appearances in that country, yet achieved record sales in excess of many of the most successful American bands. In fact, ABBA's annual concert totals were always relatively low, though the band did tour Europe and western Pacific nations such as Australia and New Zealand from the mid-1970s on.

ABBA depended on judicious use of TV, radio, and print exposure to build its image with record buyers.

The plan worked exceedingly well. As its manager and sometime song collaborator and co-producer Stig Anderson (sometimes called the group's fifth member) told John Rockwell of *The New York Times* (May 5, 1978): "It is possible to say that we are the most successful band in the world, because we have sold more records than anybody else. We have sold between 75 and 100 million singles, albums, cassettes, and eight-tracks [as of the end of 1977]. We know that we have sold more than the Beatles or Elvis Presley."

The four members, whose first initials provided the acronym, ABBA, all had considerable experience in the entertainment field before they formed the band.

Agnetha (Anna) Faltskog was born in central Sweden to a show business–oriented family. Her father, who produced amateur revues, encouraged her performing interests. By her teens, she had demonstrated a fine singing voice and also had tried her hand at writing songs. In 1965, she became a vocalist with a dance band, which she left in 1967 to start a solo career. Her initial solo recording of her own composition, "I Was So in Love," became a number one hit in Sweden in 1968.

In the mid-1960s, her path crossed that of Anni-

Frid (Frida) Lyngstad, who also possessed a striking pop soprano voice. Anni-Frid had been born in northern Norway, but had moved to Sweden with her family when she was two. She too showed performing talent early, making her public debut in 1956 at the age of ten. In her teens, she earned a living as lead vocalist for her own band. In 1967, she gained recognition throughout Sweden with a breakthrough appearance on the country's "Hyland's Corner" TV program.

In similar fashion, the male side of ABBA carved notable careers in Swedish pop music before their ABBA phase. Bjorn Ulvaeus was born in western Sweden and at the age of 11 moved to the east coast town of Vastervik with his parents. In his teens, he already showed skills as a singer and instrumentalist. After playing in a skiffle band for a while, he went on to play banjo and guitar in a Dixieland band and dance orchestra in the early 1960s. He also was enthused about folk music and in 1963 gained the national spotlight as leader of a group called the Hootenanny Singers, which over the next few years became one of Sweden's most popular folk organizations.

Benny Andersson became proficient as a pianist at an early age and also showed ability on other instruments, including guitar. He too was involved in pop music by his teens. His interests leaned toward rock and pop, and by the early 1960s, he was one of the mainstays of a band called the Hep Stars, the most successful Swedish pop band of the period. He was an important contributor of the Hep Stars' original songs, including the hit "Sunny Girl."

In 1966, tours of Benny's and Bjorn's groups coincided and the two became acquainted. Finding that they had similar tastes in songwriting, the two kept in contact and soon were collaborating on songs; "Ring Ring" and others later were recorded by ABBA.

Besides writing new material, Bjorn and Benny added to their income by doing session work as instrumentalists and backup singers. This brought them in contact with other young pop artists, including Agnetha and Anni-Frid. After a while, the four developed a close rapport that led to the formation of ABBA in 1972. During much of ABBA's history, the rapport became even closer. Bjorn and Agnetha married and had three children before running into marital problems. Benny and Anni-Frid lived to-

1

gether for a number of years; both had been married previously, with two children each.

The new quartet already had considerable knowledge of the Swedish pop industry and good contacts that helped them gain exposure to the public through radio and TV guest appearances. However, the primary catalyst to their fame was victory in the 1974 "Eurovision Song Contest" in Brighton, England, a show closely watched by millions of music fans throughout Europe.

It didn't harm the group's chances that it sang its contending song, "Waterloo," in English. In the Scandinavian countries, many people learn English as a second language. Considering the importance of the British and U.S. markets, ABBA had decided early in the game to write and sing all its songs in that language.

Benny and Bjorn pointed out later to John Rockwell that they felt they would have become stars with or without Eurovision. Benny said: "Everybody looks on us as a product of the Eurovision thing, but we're not . . . [however] It was a fantastic experience. Everybody's watching it and everybody's into it—in Europe, at least."

Bjorn said: "Eurovision helped us. It was a way to make it quickly on the outside, but we were on our way anyhow."

But things happened rapidly after ABBA took first place on the live telecast on April 6, 1974, a program estimated to have been seen by a half billion viewers in 32 countries. The Benny-and-Bjorn–penned song had, after all, placed ahead of some 7,000 other entries. ABBA already had a recording arrangement for Europe on Polar Music Records and it soon had a U.S. pact with Atlantic Records, which issued "Waterloo" in May 1974. Two months later, the group's debut LP, *Waterloo*, came out in the U.S. By then, the single of "Waterloo" was a top 10 hit in England, Sweden, Germany, France, and a number of Spanish-speaking nations. Although the song was written in English originally, ABBA saw to it that versions came out in the languages of the other countries.

Two more singles from the debut album proved worldwide hits as the year went by. "Honey Honey" was a number one hit in various countries. "Ring Ring" also made a number of top 10 lists.

The band backed its growing prominence with carefully chosen appearances in Europe as it prepared its second album. Issued in advance of the LP, a single from that collection, "SOS," made the top 10 in many countries, with many weeks at number one in West Germany. Album number two, *ABBA*, came out in August 1975 and it too was eagerly snapped up in Australia, and most European countries. The group still restricted its live concert ap-

pearances to nations other than the U.S., though it did come to America for a number of TV interviews and to perform "SOS" on several network programs, including "Saturday Night Live."

More hit singles followed from ABBA, including "I Do, I Do, I Do, I Do, I Do, I Do" and "Mamma Mia," both number one hits in many places, with "Mamma Mia" staying atop Australian charts for ten straight weeks (and remaining in the top 100 for nine months). Both already had been major hits overseas by the time they were released by Atlantic. ("I Do, I Do . . ." was issued December 9, 1975; "Mamma Mia" came out May 3, 1976.)

The group had done reasonably well with U.S. fans, but not as sensationally as in other countries. It made up a considerable amount of ground with its third LP, *Greatest Hits*. Besides previous best-selling singles, the album contained a new song, "Fernando," which became a worldwide best-seller in advance of the LP's release in mid-1976. Both releases did well in the U.S., with the album eventually earning RIAA platinum-record certification.

In the fall of 1976, the band could point to an even more dramatic achievement as the new single "Dancing Queen" shot up on charts around the world. Before its momentum peaked, the song rose to number one in the U.S. (the week of April 9, 1977) England, Holland, Australia, Germany, Belgium, Sweden, Norway, Denmark, Switzerland and Austria.

The album that included "Dancing Queen," *Arrival*, picked up gold and platinum records easily around the world after its release in late 1976 and was high on U.S. charts for a good part of 1977. A second single from the album, "Money, Money, Money," also was a major hit overseas before showing up on U.S. charts in 1977.

In its rise to the top, the band had surprisingly good support from critics around the world, though some complained about the almost invariably upbeat tone to most of the group's music, which emphasized ear-catching melodies and lyrics and only occasionally focused on the darker side of existence. In concert, the band also capitalized on its "wall of sound" approach (à la Phil Spector), which particularly emphasized a ringing amalgam of synthesizers, guitars, and the women's high-pitched vocals.

Australia, one of ABBA's strongest support areas, was the locale for the band's first full-length film, which was actually a concert film with a weak plot. The story involved a Sydney disc jockey assigned to interview the group, whose efforts (sandwiched in between live concert numbers) don't work out except for a supposed dream sequence in which he actually gets to talk to band members. The film (a big hit in Europe after its release in 1978) was one element of a massive promotional program involving, besides the film *ABBA—The Movie*, a paperback biography *ABBA—The Book*, published by Stafford Pemberton, and a new album, *ABBA—The Album*.

By 1978, the group ranked as a miniconglomerate, with Sweden's *Business World* magazine tabbing them the nation's fastest-growing corporation. Their yearly gross was over $16 million. The band had achieved that position without touring the U.S. to that point, though the members regularly came over to appear on U.S. talk shows and had videos on MTV and other outlets. Ulvaeus told Steven Gaines of *Circus* magazine (March 30, 1978): "We're sorry that we can't come over to perform yet, but in all the other countries we've performed in we've already been big as a record act. We'd all feel better if we could break the same way here. So far this system has worked in other countries through TV exposure and interviews. We know we're big in America, but not the way we want. We don't figure we've made it there until we've had five hit albums. If this new album puts us over we could headline a tour instead of doing a long tour as an opening act for little money." Besides, he and other members stressed, they no longer had to worry about money. It was the challenge that mattered.

Also contributing to that hesitation was the band's emphasis on having some time to itself. More than most rock stars, ABBA members spent considerable time away from the furor of the music industry in out-of-the-way retreats. Andersson told a *Newsweek* reporter: "We don't feel we have to live up to the rock image of getting drunk in public and smashing hotels. We're grownups. We work a lot," he said, "but also like to have a reasonable amount of time away from the spotlight."

Benny and Bjorn also wanted time to write new material, not only for ABBA, but for other projects as well. From time to time, the women also did separate projects. Both turned out solo albums in the middle and late 1970s. While they tended to leave the writing work for ABBA to the male members, they had more of a hand in the writing for their solo recordings.

Discussing their writing approach with Gaines of *Circus*, Bjorn and Benny stated that when not on the road, they tried to meet regularly at the ABBA offices in Sweden from 9 to 5. Bjorn reported: "Most of the time we find it practical that way. It's not a question of inspiration, it's more work. If you sit around and wait for the muse, it never happens. Using a guitar and a piano, we play around with different chords and rhythms. Sometimes a hook [a musical phrase able to catch a listener's attention] comes pretty fast and sometimes we can work for hours and nothing happens. Usually we have some

small idea left from all the years we've been writing and use it in a new thing. But we never write it down or record it with tape. We figure that if we can remember it two years later, it's good enough."

ABBA eventually did do some U.S. tours at the end of the '70s and in the '80s, but by then the foursome seemed to be losing its creative edge. It had, in fact, little left to prove as a group and there were internal strains making them look toward new creative opportunities.

The group continued to retain a massive following worldwide and it added to its commercial laurels with new albums and singers into the early 1980s. Albums included *Voulez-Vous* and *Greatest Hits, Volume 2* in 1979, *Super Trouper* in 1980, *The Visitors* in 1981, *ABBA—The Singles* in late 1982, and *Thank you for the Music* in 1983.

Increasingly in the 1980s, Bjorn and Benny sought separate writing and producing projects. One of Ulvaeus and Andersson's efforts was a musical called *Chess*—a collaboration with Andrew Lloyd Webber, of *Jesus Christ, Superstar*, *Evita*, and *Cats* fame. The show premiered on Broadway in New York City in April 1988.

AC/DC: *Vocal and instrumental group from Australia. Members in late 1970s: Bon Scott, born 1948, died February 1980; Angus Young, born Scotland, early 1950s; Malcolm Young, born Scotland, early 1950s; Cliff Williams; Phil Rudd. Scott replaced by Brian Johnson in 1980. Rudd replaced by Simon Wright in mid-1980s.*

When the Little River Band established a foothold with American fans in the mid-1970s, Australian music writers suggested there was plenty more where they came from, including AC/DC, which many of them considered the country's best rock band. The two groups, of course, had different styles: Little River Band offered middle-of-the-road rock, while AC/DC was a power-packed heavy metal–type group. Still, their releases vied for top spot on Australian charts of the 1970s and, when AC/DC gained entry to the U.S. market, predictions of its impact with young rock fanciers proved accurate.

The founding members of the group—the guitar-playing Young brothers, Angus and Malcolm—were Scottish born but Australian bred. After playing with various local groups, they assembled the first AC/DC complement in the early 1970s, working the local bar scene in their home area. By 1974, they had moved out to tour the Australian pub circuit, building up a sizable following by intensive performing activities that year and the next. This led to success with their first two LPs on an Australian label. Those albums, *High Voltage* and *T.N.T.*, rose to the

3

number one slot on Australian charts and earned the group gold and platinum records (based on smaller sales totals than those required for gold and platinum awards in the much larger U.S. market).

The success of the Little River Band in the U.S. and U.K. whetted record industry interest in Australian talent and helped bring the group a worldwide contract from U.S.-based Atlantic Records. For the group's international debut album on Atlantic's Atco subsidiary, tracks from the Australian *High Voltage* and *T.N.T.* discs were combined to form the late 1976 release also titled *High Voltage*.

The new record company affiliation cleared the way for the band to expand its live appearances beyond the Pacific Basin. On one of its first U.K. trips, it opened in a small London pub called the Red Cow in early 1976. The sparse crowd at the first set was so impressed that its members called friends to hear the band the second time around. Word of the group's pyrotechnics spread, including the menacing tones of lead singer Bon Scott and the wild corner-to-corner cavorting of lead guitarist Angus Young (typically wearing short pants and a boys' school shirt). With the second Atco LP, *Let There Be Rock* (spring 1977), and a debut U.S. tour that summer, followed by another group of shows in the fall, the band began to make its presence felt on the heavy metal scene in America as well.

The group returned to its home base in Sydney, Australia, to record its next LP at the end of 1977 and in early 1978 at the Albert Studios. That album, *Powerage,* issued by Atco in the spring of 1978, made the U.S. and U.K. charts almost immediately. The band started its 1978 world tour in the U.K. and moved over to the U.S. and Canada from June through October, headlining major venues drawing crowds of 15,000 or more.

During those appearances, tapes were made for the band's first live album on Atlantic, *If You Want Blood—You've Got It,* issued in late 1978. The songs included "The Jack," "Problem Child," "Whole Lotta Rosie," "Rock 'n' Roll Damnation," and "Rocker." The album spent much of 1979 in upper regions of the U.S. charts and was a major hit in the U.K. and in Europe.

For the next studio album, the group for the first time agreed to use a locale outside Australia—London's Roundhouse Studios. The *Highway to Hell* LP was issued in the U.S. in July 1979. Among the featured songs were the title track, "Girls Got Rhythm," and "Touch Too Much," co-written by the Young Brothers and Bon Scott. The LP was one of the most consistently exciting the band had produced and it became its best-seller worldwide to that point. It stayed on U.S. charts well into 1980 and was certified platinum by the RIAA.

Before the band could move on to a new LP to start the 1980s, it suffered the loss of lead singer Scott, who died in 1980 apparently from acute alcoholism. He was replaced by Brian Johnson, who sang and helped write some of the songs for the *Back in Black* LP. Released in mid-1980, by year-end it had been certified platinum by the RIAA. The title track, co-written by the Youngs and Johnson, also provided a U.S. charted single from late 1980 until early 1981.

1981 proved to be the high water mark of AC/DC's saga. Early in the year, *Back in Black* was joined on U.S. charts by *Dirty Deeds Done Dirt Cheap,* a compilation of earlier recordings featuring Bon Scott. That album was still on the charts at year-end and was certified platinum by the RIAA. Late in the year, the group's new and most effective album, *For Those About to Rock, We Salute You,* came out and quickly moved into the top 10, standing at number one on *Billboard* lists at the end of 1981. The band closed out the year with no fewer than five LPs on the *Billboard* top 200—*For Those About to Rock*, *Back in Black*, *Dirty Deeds*, and two "oldies" pulled back onto the lists, *Highway to Hell* and *High Voltage*. The band also could point to two worldwide best-selling singles in 1981, "Back in Black" and "You Shook Me All Night Long."

In *Billboard*'s year-end Number One Awards compilation, AC/DC finished second in the Top Group LP and Duos/Groups Hot 100 & Top LPs Combined categories, edged out by REO Speedwagon.

After that, things seemed to slow down for the band. Though it remained a concert favorite, its albums seemed to lose some of the freshness and urgency of previous releases. *Flick of the Switch*, issued on Atco in mid-1983, was only moderately successful, as was *'74 Jailbreak*, issued in late 1984. In 1984, some of the band's shows drew less than full houses.

The band had to fight negative publicity in 1985 because of news stories about the preliminary hearings for the alleged Los Angeles–area mass killer known as the Night Stalker. That individual, who professed a belief in satanism, also proclaimed his enthusiasm for AC/DC music. That guilt-by-association stigma—coupled with growing public uneasiness about the drugs and sexual promiscuity in rock lyrics—caused some people to boycott AC/DC shows.

In the long run, the furor, which had essentially died out by early 1986, seemed to help rather than hinder the band, whose members vigorously denied assertions they had anything to do with influencing aberrant behavior by the Night Stalker or anyone else. The group's 1986 concert tours were generally well attended and its *Fly on the Wall* album, released in mid-1985, was certified gold by the RIAA by the year's end.

In reviewing an AC/DC concert at the Inglewood Forum in the October 21, 1985, *Los Angeles Times*, a writer suggested antirock spokesmen were overstating their case. "Certain factions would like to make a Satan connection since all the Night Stalker business, but AC/DC continues to sing not about hell, but about the 'Highway to Hell'—substance abuse and (especially) indiscriminate sex. These guys are far too libidinously minded to devote much time to a higher—or lower—power."

In early 1988, Atlantic released the album *Blow Up Your Video*, the twelfth LP to the band's credit. Atlantic noted that the previous eleven albums had sold some 13 million copies in the U.S. alone.

AEROSMITH: *Vocal and instrumental group from Boston, Massachusetts, area. Personnel from early 1970s to start of 1980: Steve Tyler, born March 26, 1948; Joe Perry, born September 10, 1950; Brad Whitford, born February 23, 1952; Tom Hamilton, born December 31, 1951; Joey Kramer, born June 21, 1950. Perry left in 1979, replaced in 1980 by Jimmy Crespo. Whitford left in 1981, replaced by Rick Dufay in 1982. Original group reformed in 1984 with Crespo and Dufay replaced by Perry and Whitford.*

Without a doubt, one of the best U.S. heavy metal groups of the middle to late 1970s was Aerosmith. The band's no-frills, all-out rock had massive crowds shouting for more during standing-room–only concerts. More to the point, the band consistently demonstrated finely honed musicianship that showcased exciting lead singer Steve Tyler.

The band came into being in the summer of 1970, playing for $30 a night in a vacation club called The Barn in New Hampshire. In the fall, the group picked up bar and college one-nighters, sometimes playing gratis on the street outside Boston University. Gradually it built up a core of local devotees and found more impressive jobs in clubs around New England. By the end of 1972, Aerosmith ranked as one of the most popular rock bands in the Beantown area.

The band signed with Columbia Records during 1972. Its debut LP, *Aerosmith*, released in early 1973, did well in the group's home region. Its debut single, "Dream On," issued in June 1973, also was a regional hit, as was its next album, *Get Your Wings*, issued in early 1974. The band embarked on several national tours in 1974 that made converts of rock fans in many other parts of the U.S. *Get Your Wings* went gold in April 1975. Album three, *Toys in the Attic*, came out in early 1975. On August 11,

it too went gold and later passed the platinum level. In May 1976, now a headline group, Aerosmith picked up a third straight gold record with *Rocks*. "Dream On" was reissued in January 1976 and became the band's first top 10 national single. In May, the band had another single ("Last Child") on the charts and at the end of the year scored its second top 10 single with "Walk This Way," a reissue originally included in *Toys in the Attic*.

By this time, many of the group's followers in the U.S. touted it as the U.S. answer to Led Zeppelin, an apt comparison in that both bands favored no-holds-barred all-out rock with a strong blues underpinning. Another similarity was that the British group was given short shrift by most critics for much of its early existence.

When reviewers did "discover" Aerosmith, for a time the emphasis was on showing that the quintet from Boston lacked originality or sounded like another group. However, no two critics seemed to agree on just what band Aerosmith was copying. *Billboard* at one point said it sounded like Black Sabbath, several publications naturally suggested the Led Zeppelin connection, and still others said the band reminded them of Mountain or .the Rolling Stones.

Suggestions that lead singer and main lyricist Tyler was in the tradition of Mick Jagger and Robert Plant hardly put him in undesirable company. But Tyler complained to one reporter: "A comparison like that is ridiculous—not because it can't be seen—but because it has nothing to do with the music. Jagger and I have two different singing styles, but because we resemble each other physically, that's what they write about."

This was echoed by lead guitarist Perry, who provided most of the music to Tyler's words of the 1970s. He suggested that reviewers were spending too much time comparing physical resemblances instead of "listening to what we're playing."

Still, a critic always has to do a certain amount of categorizing in order to try to get across in words to the reader what a group of performers is doing. But when the similes cover such a wide range, the conclusion has to be that the object of those attentions must be doing something relatively unique. At any rate, rock fans didn't need the similes. They listened to records and attended concerts, and a good many liked what they heard. During the mid-1970s, Aerosmith could fill the largest arenas to capacity across the U.S., Canada, and elsewhere.

The band continued to make upper chart levels in the late 1970s with the albums *Draw the Line* (December 1977), *Live! Bootleg* (November 1978), and *Night in the Ruts* (November 1979). Besides its own LPs, the group also was represented on the *Califor-*

nia Jam II concert compilation on Columbia (July 1978), and the RSO Records soundtrack LP for the *Sgt. Pepper's Lonely Hearts Club Band* movie (July 1978).

The group was beginning to show signs of wear at the end of the 1970s, as reflected in part by Joe Perry's decision to try for a solo career in December 1979. After auditioning a number of possible candidates, the remaining members chose guitarist Joe Crespo, previously with the band Flame, to take Perry's place. Crespo joined the band on tour during 1980, when the only new album release was the retrospective *Greatest Hits*.

Meanwhile, Perry's new group, the Joe Perry Project, was represented on the charts in 1980 with its Columbia debut *Let the Music Do the Talking*, issued in March. Neither that LP nor the follow-up, *I've Got the Rock 'n' Rolls Again* (issued June 1981) became best-sellers and Perry moved for a while to MCA Records, which issued the LP *Once a Rocker, Always a Rocker* in September 1983. He was joined in the Aerosmith alumni society in 1981 by Brad Whitford, who teamed with guitarist/vocalist Derek St. Holmes to record the *Whitford/St. Holmes* LP issued on Columbia in August 1981.

After Whitford's departure, the band became inactive while Steve Tyler was sidelined following a motorcycle accident. For a while in 1981–82 the group remained a foursome of Tyler, Hamilton, Kramer, and Crespo. In the spring of 1982, it went back to a quintet with the addition of guitarist Rick Dufay. That band recorded an LP for Columbia, *Rock in a Hard Place* (issued August 1982). Columbia also issued the band's first single in three years, "Lightning Strikes," in October 1982. The band remained popular with large numbers of fans, as concert attendance indicated, but its new recordings didn't seem of the same caliber as in its 1970s glory years.

During that period, Whitford left St. Holmes and joined with The Joe Perry Project for a number of concert dates while also doing some session work. It seemed as though the separate parts of the earlier Aerosmith added up to less than the whole. On Valentine's Day 1984, Perry and Whitford visited their old bandmates after an Aerosmith show at Boston's Orpheum Theater and this led to further meetings that culminated in a decision to reform the 1970s band. From late spring to year-end, the reunited Aerosmith traveled the country in its "Back in the Saddle" tour, which drew respectable crowds even though the band had no new album or video.

The band's Columbia contract expired and in 1985, it signed a new pact with Geffen Records. The debut release on the new label, *Done with Mirrors*, came out in November 1985 and was on the charts well into 1986. Like all the group's previous albums, the new one received gold-record certification from the RIAA. The youthful faces that made up much of the audience at 1986 concerts indicated that the band's music still found favor with a new generation of fans. The band's second LP on Geffen, *Permanent Vacation*, was released during the summer of 1987 and amassed sales of over 1.3 million by January 1988. *(See Run–D.M.C.)*

ALLMAN BROTHERS, THE: *Vocal and instrumental group. Duane Allman, born Nashville, Tennessee, November 20, 1946, died Macon, Georgia, October 29, 1971; Gregg Allman, born Nashville, Tennessee, December 8, 1947; Dicky Betts, born West Palm Beach, Florida, December 12, 1943; Butch Trucks, born Jacksonville, Florida, May 11, 1947; Jai Johanny Johanson, born Ocean Springs, Mississippi, July 8, 1944; Berry Oakley, born Chicago, Illinois, April 4, 1948, died Macon, Georgia, November 11, 1972; Chuck Leavell and Lamar Williams added in 1972–73.*

In a few short years, the Allman Brothers Band established an awesome reputation for their playing skills. Duane Allman, in particular, was singled out again and again for his amazing slide guitar work in support of the *Layla* album by Eric Clapton's Derek and the Dominoes. By mid-1971, when rock fans were coming around to the view that the Allman Band might be America's best answer to the British supergroups, Duane died in a motorcycle accident.

The Allman group is considered to be a product of Florida, but the boys spent their early years in Tennessee, where Howard Duane Allman and Gregory Lenoir Allman were born. Their father died when they were young and their mother had to work to support the family. In 1959, she moved her family to Daytona Beach, Florida, to get a better job. Up to this time, the boys hadn't paid too much attention to music. However, at the start of the '60s, as Duane told interviewer Tony Glover, "One year, Gregg got a guitar for Christmas and I got me a Harley 165 motorcycle. I tore that up and he learned to play. He taught me, and I traded the wrecked bike parts for another guitar. Then just the regular apprenticeship thing, playing for anybody that'll listen, building up your chops."

In 1961, the boys started their own band. Their first public appearances were at Y-Teens dances at the local youth center, as they stated in a Capricorn bio. "Doing Hank Ballard and the Midnighters stuff, Chuck Berry tunes—and trying to get the Beatles harmonies down . . . 'yeah, yeah, yeah.' It was fun, man, it's never stopped being fun." The brothers loved the blues and learned many of their early songs by listening to late night R&B shows, particularly the powerful signals sent out by station WLAC in Nashville. Among their favorites were Muddy Waters, Bobby Blue Bland, J.B. Hutto, Little Walter, Robert Johnson, and Blind Willie Johnson.

As the '60s passed, the brothers played in a succession of bands. In 1963, they were in an integrated group called the House Rockers before organizing their own group, the Allman Joys. With this band, they worked go-go and liquor bars in such southern cities as Jacksonville, Florida; Atlanta, Georgia; and Mobile, Alabama. They made their first single with that group, placed on the Dial label by Joe Tex's manager, Buddy Killen. The song was a remake of "Spoonful" by R&B writer-performer Willie Dixon.

Later, they began writing some of their own songs and took them to Killen. As Duane recalled for Capricorn, Killen said, "No man, you cats better look for a day gig; you're never gonna make it. You're the worst I ever heard."

In the second half of the '60s, the brothers decided to try their luck in Los Angeles. They became part of a studio group called Hourglass that put together two albums, *Hourglass* and *Power of Love*, on the Liberty label. The band members had no control over their material, though. Duane said: "They'd send in a box of demos and say, 'Okay, pick out your next LP.' We'd try to tell them that wasn't where it was at. Then they'd get tough and say, 'You gotta have an album, man. Don't buck the system. Just pick it out!' So okay, we were game. We tried it, figured maybe we could squeeze an ounce or two of gold out of all this crap—we squeezed and squeezed—but were squeezing a rock. There was no warmth, no feeling at all in anything we were associated with—and the albums reflect that feeling to me entirely."

The Allmans grew disgusted and returned to Florida, where they started working in a group called the 31st of February, headed by drummer Claude Hudson ("Butch") Trucks, Jr. On many occasions, the group's path crossed that of a band led by guitarist Forrest Richard ("Dicky") Betts that included bassist Raymond Berry Oakley. Oakley had played with a number of groups, including the early back-up band for Tommy Roe, the Romans. Some of them also knew another drummer, Johnny Lee Johnson (who called himself Jai Johanny Johanson), a sideman in a number of bands that toured the R&B circuit supporting such performers as Clifton Chenier, Joe Tex, Percy Sledge, and Otis Redding.

Many recording executives in the South were now aware of the Allmans' ability as session men; one of them, Dick Hall, wired Duane to come to Muscle Shoals, Alabama, to play behind Wilson Pickett. (See *Pickett, Wilson*). Hall was so enthused about Duane's work on Pickett's track of "Hey Jude" that he asked him to move to Muscle Shoals and be a regular. For eight months, Duane did that, providing accompaniment for such stars as Clarence Carter, Aretha Franklin, Arthur Conley, and King Curtis. (See *Franklin, Aretha*).

He still went back to Florida occasionally and on one visit he got together with what was to become the Allman Brothers Band for a jam session. The session was outstanding, all the musicians knew. Duane went back again and again until he decided to give up session work and help organize the new band. They sought out Phil Walden in Macon, Georgia, manager of such artists as Clarence Carter and Percy Sledge, to handle them. He agreed and soon after got them a recording contract with Capricorn Records (which was initially distributed by Atlantic Records and then by Warner Brothers). Their debut LP, *The Allman Brothers Band*, was recorded in 1969 and won excellent reviews. It also sold reasonably well, expanding the group's reputation to the national scene. One result was the first of a number of tours of major cities throughout the U.S.

Duane kept up his session work because, as he put it: "It's good therapy, it keeps you from getting stale." Among the artists he played dobro and/or slide guitar for were Boz Scaggs, John Hammond, Ronnie Hawkins, Delaney & Bonnie, Laura Nyro, and Clapton. (See *Clapton, Eric*; *Hawkins, Ronnie*; *Nyro, Laura*; *Scaggs, Boz*). In response to whether he did all the slide work on *Layla*, he noted that "Eric gets more of an open, slidy sound. But the way to really tell: he played the Fender and I played the Gibson—the Fender is a little bit thinner and brighter, a sparkling sound, while the Gibson is just a full tilt screech."

By 1970, the Allman Brothers Band was gaining attention as one of the best in the rock and blues field. The group's second LP, *Idlewild South*, became a hit. The band found plenty of work, moving from one one-nighter to the next in the U.S. and Canada in a Winnebago trailer-bus. The band also was featured at the British Isle of Wight Festival during the summer of 1970 and was warmly welcomed on visits to other parts of Europe.

In their appearance at the Fillmore East in December 1970, they were in such rare form that they went on for encore after encore, not giving up the stage to the headline group, Canned Heat, until 3:30 am. During their next Fillmore engagement in March 1971, tapes were made for their third album released in mid-1971. "*The Allman Brothers Band at Fillmore East*, easily breached the million-dollar sales level needed for RIAA gold-record certification.

Though the LP had four sides, it included only seven songs, including the band's versions of two old blues, ("You Don't Love Me Baby" and "Statesboro Blues") and the Allmans' "Whipping Post" and "In Memory of Elizabeth Reed."

The band seemed on the way to pop music heights when its members were shocked by the loss of Duane. He apparently lost control of his motorcycle on a Macon street while trying to avoid hitting a tractor-trailer. Three hours after the accident, he died on the operating table at Middle Georgia Medical Center. A similar accident, not three blocks from the scene of Duane's collision, took the life of bassist Berry Oakley in November 1972.

After Duane's death, the band regrouped behind Gregg Allman and Dicky Betts. *Eat a Peach*, the first LP to come out after Duane's passing, included new material and some tracks made prior to the tragedy. The band's fortunes then declined and subsequent albums never reached the peak achieved in the late 1960s and early 1970s. There were several breakups and reunions with different rosters after the mid-1970s, while releases of LPs with both new and old material continued on various labels. Those included, on Capricorn, *Brothers and Sisters* (1973), *Beginnings* (1973), *Win, Lose or Draw* (1975), *The Road Goes on Forever* (1975), *Wipe the Windows, Check the Oil, Dollar Gas* (1976), and *Enlightened Rogues* (1979); on Arista, *Reach for the Sky* (1980) and *Brothers of the Road* (1981); and, on Polygram, *The Best of the Allman Brothers Band* (1981). Reissues of Duane Allman recordings included *An Anthology* (1972) and *Anthology, Volume 2*, (1974) both on Capricorn, and *Best of Duane Allman* (1981) on Polygram. Solo discs by Gregg Allman included *Laid Back* (1973), *The Gregg Allman Tour* (1974), and *Playin' Up a Storm* (1977), all on Capricorn. During 1977, Gregg gained more headlines from his marriage to Cher (which lasted only a short time) than for his music. The two did do a joint album on Warner Brothers, *Two the Hard Way*, issued in the fall of '77. (See *Cher*.)

After putting together a new version of the Allman Brothers Band with some of the group's previous members in 1979, Gregg was little heard from for most of the 1980s. His difficulties, he said in 1987, came from alcohol, a problem he noted he had fought for nine years. "People don't realize how insidious a disease alcohol can be," he told a *Los Angeles Times* reporter. "The stuff is legal . . . you can't watch a ballgame without someone shoving something in your hand. I've fallen off the wagon a few times, but finally I got to the point where I said, 'Man, what do you want to do with the rest of your life? Keep going into rehab centers or play your music?'"

By 1986, he seemed to have turned a corner, resulting in a 1987 top 30 LP, *I'm No Angel*, and a solo concert tour. During a stop in Los Angeles, he told Robert Hilburn: "Sure, there have been [difficult times], but I've had lots of good times, and that's what I think of when I look back . . .

"There's a great comfort in the music itself. It's a shame that everybody in life doesn't have something like that . . . so that if [you] fail in business or get your heart broken . . . you can still play your music. It helps you get through the darkest times. I hope on my death bed I'm learning a new chord or writing a new song."

ALPERT, HERB: *Vocalist, trumpeter, band leader, composer, record company executive. Born Los Angeles, California, March 31, 1935.*
The saga of Herb Alpert demonstrates that no matter what form of music dominates the charts at any given time, there is always room for something new and different. It also shows that some popular music variants depend on the style of an individual. Many artists and groups tried to emulate the musical approach of the Tijuana Brass, but no one but Alpert succeeded in making this particular sound a competitor to the ever-present rock beat.

Alpert began studying the trumpet at age eight, mainly because his parents wanted him to take up some form of musical instrument. It fitted the family style, because all the Alperts played one instrument or another. His father played the mandolin, his mother the violin, his sister the piano. His brother became a professional drummer. Alpert rebelled for a time, trying to escape to play football and baseball, practicing only because he was forced to. "But after that," he recalls, "as I grew older, it became a kind of habit, like brushing my teeth—a discipline that I appreciate very much today."

While attending Fairfax High School in Los Angeles, Alpert thought he would like to become a jazz musician. However, he also studied classical music with several teachers, including the first trumpeter of the San Francisco Symphony Orchestra. Alpert started college, but left after his sophomore year for a two-year hitch in the Army as a trumpeter-bugler at San Francisco's Presidio garrison.

Once his military service was completed, Alpert returned to try for a career in pop music. He spent a year with Keen Records in Los Angeles as an apprentice artist and repertoire man. He then went out on his own as an independent record producer. He handled the first record session of Jan and Dean, one of the top rock singing teams of the early 1960s. He also composed the song "Wonderful World," recorded first by the late Sam Cooke and later turned into another hit single by Herman's Hermits. (See

Cooke, Sam; Jan and Dean). On weekends and in spare weekday hours, he performed as a studio sideman and organized pickup groups for weddings, dances and bar-mitzvahs.

In mid-1962, married and with an infant son, Alpert earned a livable income from music, but seemed far from making a name for himself. He had a tape recorder set up in his garage for experimenting with various song ideas. One day, he went into the garage to play "Twinkle Star," a song written by a musician friend, Sol Lake. The song had a Spanish flavor to it. Experimenting with it, Alpert came up with a version that had some of the intonations of Mexican mariachi music.

He liked the playback version and asked a friend, Jerry Moss (five years Alpert's senior and a promotion man in the music industry), for his opinion. Moss was enthusiastic and the two agreed to chip in several hundred dollars apiece for a full-scale studio recording. They retitled the song "The Lonely Bull" and prepared a flip side called "Acapulco 1922." The finished studio tape, says Alpert, "felt good. It felt very good, but we both knew it needed another dimension. After all, you're competing with 250 other records which show up at the radio stations every single week."

They decided to take a sound engineer to the Tijuana, Mexico, bull ring and tape several hours of band sounds and crowd noises. These were dubbed onto the completed track of "The Lonely Bull." Because Tijuana had been the source, in part, for Alpert's musical inspiration (he enjoyed an occasional visit to the bull ring there), the record went out with the group name listed as the Tijuana Brass. The label also announced a new record firm, A&M, for Alpert and Moss. The odds against such an independent venture hitting paydirt are easily several hundred thousand to one. In this case, everything worked. Soon after the record's release in August 1962, it was on the charts. The same thing happened with the LP of that title, issued that December.

The follow-up LP, *Marching through Madrid*, fell far short of the top 40, though, and things looked grim, mainly because distributors began to tell Alpert he had a "regional sound." Alpert demurred, saying it was lack of exposure that was hurting him. His third LP, *Herb Alpert's Tijuana Brass* and the fourth, *South of the Border*, did a little better, but the turning point was a single on the latter called "Mexican Shuffle." The song won the attention of the Clark Teaberry Gum Company, which bought rights to it as the theme for a saturation ad campaign. Under the new title of "The Teaberry Shuffle," the song made Alpert's sound known in all corners of the U.S.

Now distributors and disc jockeys began to get be-

hind the TJB and Herb's LPs moved up the charts. *Whipped Cream and Other Delights*, the next LP, shot to number one soon after it was issued. The album's version of "A Taste of Honey" made number seven in *Billboard*'s Hot 100 in 1965. At this point, Alpert formed his first in-person band; all the earlier recordings were pickup sessions in studios. With the band setting attendance records on concert dates and gaining additional attention on TV programs, both the TJB and A&M were in the big time. The November 5 issue of *Billboard* showed five Alpert LPs in the top 50 with some of them having been numbers one, two, and three on occasion. In 1966, the TJB outsold the Beatles two to one, and A&M Records sales zoomed 800% from 1965 to over $32 million. This volume was partly due to a growing roster of other featured acts, including the Baja Marimba Band, Sergio Mendes and Brazil 66, and Burt Bacharach. (See *Bacharach, Burt*). Alpert's impact won him *Billboard*'s award as Record Man of the Year.

In the late 1960s, the TJB slowly went down in total output, though continuing to make good showings with their record sales. The main reasons for the decline included the usual satiation of the mass audience with even the best of groups, as well as the success of A&M Records, which called for Alpert's spending more time on business and production matters than on TJB sessions and concerts. By the early 1970s, A&M was among the top 10 U.S. record companies and had its own complex of three new recording studios and offices in a Hollywood location that had once had been the site of Charlie Chaplin's studio. Although Alpert performed very little during 1971–72, he still appeared on the charts with the LPs *Summertime* (1971) and *Solid Brass* (1972) and the single "Jerusalem."

As to the secret of Alpert's success, he has noted it was not based on presenting American-style music in mariachi form, but rather on synthesizing two different forms. "I just hit on this idea of using a mariachi sound together with American jazz. I was playing like I felt —and I still do." He credits the wild, happy sound of TJB arrangements as being responsible for public interest in all age groups. "It's not a protest and not a putdown. I think people were bugged with hearing music which had an undercurrent of unhappiness and anger, even sadism."

Nonetheless, not all of his material is happy. "There are some things which have definitely sad overtones, like the tune we wrote in memory of the matador, Carlos Arruza, who was such a big influence upon my whole idea for the Brass's sound. He was fighting in Tijuana on the day I got the inspiration for the sound. Thinking of how tragically he died, in a head-on automobile collision, after fighting bulls for 25 years, that music didn't come out too happy.''

Although Alpert broke up the Brass at the end of the 1960s, he reformed it in 1973. In 1975, the Tijuana Brass was phased out again and Alpert concentrated on management duties at his A&M Records. He helped shape the careers of other artists on the firm's roster and contributed to the selection of new A&M recording acts. But the lure of making his own music eventually proved too much. In 1979, at the urging of his nephew, Randy Badazz, he recorded a single of Badazz's song ''Rise'' (co-written with Andy Armer), and the disc made number one in *Billboard* the week of October 20, 1979, and remained there for a second week. By 1982 he was back in action with a new album and a number of concert dates backed by a nine-man group with his wife, vocalist Lani Hall, also part of the show. In 1984, as part of its presentations for the Olympic festivities in Los Angeles, The Greek Theatre management asked Herb to put together a new version of the Tijuana Brass for several August shows. The nine-man band for those appearances included four of the seven original Brass members—Alpert, guitarist John Pisano, trumpeter Bob Edmondson, and drummer Nick Ceroli. In connection with that, Alpert co-wrote and co-produced a new Brass LP, *Bullish*. Herb didn't go all out for a Tijuana Brass revival, but he remained active as a recording artist, playing his trumpet on his subsequent *Wild Romance* (July 1985). In the spring of 1987, his A&M album *Keep Your Eye on Me* showcased Alpert on some excellent funk-flavored numbers.

ALVIN, DAVE: *See The Blasters.*

ANIMALS, THE; ERIC BURDON AND THE ANIMALS: *Vocal and instrumental group. Personnel as of 1964: Alan Price, born Fairfield, County Durham, England, April 19, 1942; Eric Burdon, born Newcastle-on-Tyne, England, April 5, 1941; Bryan Chandler, born Heaton, Newcastle-on-Tyne, England, December 18, 1948; John Steel, born Gateshead, England, February 4, 1941; Hilton Valentine, born North Shields, England, May 21, 1943. Price replaced in 1965 by Dave Rowberry, born Newcastle-on-Tyne, England, December 27, 1943. Steel replaced by Barry Jenkins in 1966.*

Much of the attention paid to the centers of rock in England in the 1960s has centered on Liverpool, the spawning ground for such talents as the Beatles, Tommy Steele, and Cilla Black. However, examination of the important groups of the era indicates clearly that similar ferment went on in cities all over England, including the northern coal center of New-castle-on-Tyne, whose most important natives included Eric Burdon and the Animals. (See *Burdon, Eric*).

All of the original members were born and raised in the Newcastle area in working-class families. A number of them came from broken homes. Lead guitarist Hilton Valentine, for example, grew up in a run-down section of North Shields, a shipbuilding and coal-mining town near Newcastle. His father left home when Hilton was 15 and his mother died the next year. At 17, he was adopted by the parents of a friend. As he put it, ''I chose me own parents.''

By then, Valentine was working at odd jobs to earn a living and playing guitar with other teenage musicians from his home area. This evolved into a group assembled by Alan Price called the Alan Price Combo that included, besides Valentine, Eric Victor Burdon on vocals, Bryan ''Chas'' Chandler on bass guitar, and John Steel on drums. When the group began playing small clubs and dances, Price was working as an income tax collector, Chandler as a ship's instrument maker, and Steel as an illustrator and salesman. Burdon, who attended college for a while, worked at various times as a postman, draftsman and designer.

The inspiration was the rhythm & blues and rock arrangements of the early and middle '50s. Most of the group had been ardent followers of such American artists as Ray Charles, Bo Diddley, Chuck Berry, Bill Doggett, and Bill Haley. Their modifications of the music of those performers quickly found favor with Newcastle audiences. During 1962 and 1963, the band became the number one pop music group in that port city, with standing-room–only crowds jamming the Club à Go-Go, where the group had become the featured act.

The group changed its name from Alan Price Combo to the Animals because of audience reaction to their playing. Some of the members overheard onlookers agreeing that the band played like a bunch of wild animals and decided this had more impact than their original billing.

The main thing lacking at this point was a manager. As Burdon later recalled, he and his associates asked the club owner, a friend of theirs, to take the job. ''We're capable of making a lot of money,'' they told him. His reply was, ''You must be out of your skull!'' However, after Graham Bond (a well-known London-based band leader) came to hear the group and enthused over them, the club owner drew up a contract with the band.

He arranged for the Animals to make demonstration recordings that he took with him to play for booking agents in other English cities. This resulted in engagements outside Newcastle for much of 1963 that helped pave the way for their London debut late in the year and the band's decision to move to that city. This decision was aided by the highly favorable response to their debut radio appearance on the BBC's "Saturday Club" on December 27, 1963.

In early 1964, the group became one of the most popular rock bands playing London clubs. British Columbia signed them and their second single release on the label, "House of the Rising Sun," became a major hit, first in England, then in the U.S., where it was released by MGM Records and gained the number one spot for three weeks. The recording, a modification by Alan Price of a traditional Negro folk song often performed by Leadbelly and Josh White, sold over a million copies in England and the U.S. during the year.

Now one of the best-known pop bands in the world, the Animals won standing ovations from massive crowds on a British tour in the spring of 1964 with Chuck Berry and, in August and September, on a debut tour of the U.S. By 1965, the group was on the way to battling the Beatles for top honors, but internal strains were beginning to show up, partly due to the emergence of Eric Burdon as the central figure rather than Price. By mid-1965, organist Price had stepped down and was replaced by Dave Rowberry. Whereas Price was self-taught, Rowberry had eight years of classical organ training to his credit; he also was a capable pianist.

The group continued to be one of the major attractions on the rock circuit in the mid-1960s, going on several tours each year of England, Europe, the U.S., and the Far East.

The Animals turned out a series of best-selling singles during 1965, 1966, and 1967. ("Don't Let Me Be Misunderstood," "It's My Life," "We Gotta Get Out of This Place"). LPs included *The Animals* (October 1964); *Animals on Tour* (March 1965); *Animal Tracks* (September 1965); *Best of the Animals* (February 1966); *Animalization* (September 1966); *Animalism* (December 1966); *Eric Is Here* (March 1967); *Best of Eric Burdon and The Animals* (June 1967) and *Winds of Change* (October 1967).

By the end of 1966, group affairs had reached a low ebb. Part of this was due to personality conflicts. However, another factor was some members' self-destructive drug taking. For example, as a result of constant use of LSD, Hilton Valentine began to imagine he was Jesus Christ. His fantasizing reached the point that he not only quit music for a while, he retreated to his room for many months in 1967, never going out, and speaking only to grocery store owners. (He later overcame his problems and turned out some original material, including the late 1969 Capital Records release, *All in Your Head*.)

The upshot was disbanding before the late 1960s, despite the still-great popularity of the group. (The album, *The Twain Shall Meet*, issued in early 1968, was a best-seller through the summer. Its single, "Sky Pilot," hit the top 10). Burdon moved to California soon after, where he eventually organized a new group, War, going on from there to various solo activities in the 1970s and '80s. (*See War*).

After the Animals' departure from active performing, reissues of the group's material continued to appear from time to time. Those collections included *Best of Eric Burdon and the Animals, Volume 2* (issued by MGM in 1967), *The Greatest Hits of Eric Burdon and the Animals* (MGM, 1969), *Best of the Animals* (Abkco, 1973), *Best of the Animals* (Springboard, 1973), *Before We Were So Rudely Interrupted* (Jet, 1977) and *Night Time is the Right Time* (Springboard). In the mid 1980s, some of the original members reformed the group and took part in rock revival shows.

ANKA, PAUL: *Singer, songwriter, record producer. Born Ottawa, Canada, July 30, 1941.*

Paul Anka became a star at an age when most boys still have no idea of what they will do with their lives. His single "Diana," which he also wrote, was a solid hit in the U.S. and in England when he was only 15. He became a reigning teen idol for half a decade, then segueing into a less frenetic, but still successful career as a nightclub-style vocalist.

The oldest son of Ottawa restaurateur Andrew Anka and his wife Camy, Paul astonished friends and his family with his mimicry of them from the time he was able to talk. He made his first public appearance at the age of ten. At first, his father was aghast at the idea of his son's eagerness for show business. Andrew was doing quite well since immigrating to Canada from Syria; he had worked his business up from a small sandwich shop to a sizable restaurant and had been elected president of the Junior Chamber of Commerce. He wasn't impressed by Paul's debut at ten or the fact that, at 13, Paul had formed a trio of schoolmates that was earning as much as $45 a date. That opinion wasn't changed much by the failure of Paul's first single, which the boy had placed with a small West Coast label while working in Los Angeles in the summer of 1956. But after attending the 14-year-old's first solo nightclub engagement and seeing Paul win the hearts of the audience, Andrew's feeling began to change.

In March 1957, Fats Domino played Ottawa. Paul fought his way into the theater to talk to the R&B star and give him some pointers. The show's manager, Irvin Feld, went into Fats' dressing room to escort the 15-year-old lumberjacketed and blue-jeaned Paul out to the street. Later in the year, when Paul hit with "Diana," Feld found himself eagerly seeking Anka out.

Paul had gone to New York during his Easter vacation and talked his way into the inner sanctum of a record firm. An executive later remembered (*Life*, August 29, 1960): "Can you imagine this 15-year-old kid bouncing into the office and playing ten of his songs. He leapt at the piano like it was a steak dinner and he hadn't eaten for months."

The record firm officials liked "Diana" and called Anka's dad to fly to New York to sign the contracts. Andy Anka became an ardent backer of his son's musical career after that to the exclusion of his restaurant business. Released during the summer, "Diana" hit number one on *Billboard* lists the week of September 9, 1957. In the U.K., it was number one for nine straight weeks. By fall, Feld had added Paul to one of his tours and soon became Paul's personal manager.

Paul rapidly became the breadwinner for ABC-Paramount Records, turning out a string of best-sellers that made him an international star. He was a favorite in Europe before he caught on as strongly in the U.S. He attributed that to the fact that his song stylings, which partly reflected his Near Eastern ancestry, were more familiar to European ears. At 16 and 17, he toured England, France, Belgium, Australia, Hawaii, and Japan. His enthusiastic reception everywhere bordered on idolatry. In Japan, where he had five songs at once on the Tokyo hit parade, 2,000 fans waited all day in a typhoon to buy standing room-tickets. At the Olympia Music Hall in Paris, he outdrew Marlene Dietrich and Maurice Chevalier.

His charted singles included such original compositions as "You Are My Destiny," "Lonely Boy" (number one on *Billboard* charts for three weeks beginning July 13, 1959),"Put Your Head on My Shoulder," "Puppy Love," "Crazy Love," "Don't Gamble with Love," and "My Home Town." From the late '50s on, singers such as Buddy Holly ("It Doesn't Matter Anymore"), Tom Jones ("She's a Lady"), Frank Sinatra ("My Way"), Bobby Rydell, Johnny Nash, and Patti Page gained hit records with his songs.

After he signed with RCA Victor in 1963, he remained an important figure on the pop scene, though less of a teenage idol than in earlier years. During the mid-1960s, he was more of an album than a singles artist in the U.S., although he achieved a number of singles hits in Europe in that period. An example was his "Ogni Volta," which he introduced at the 1964 San Remo Festival. The song took second place and, released on the RCA Italiano label, sold a million copies in Italy alone by the end of that May. Total sales throughout Europe went over the two-million mark.

Anka toured widely throughout the 1960s, appearing in prestige nightclubs the world over such as the Copacabana in New York and Coconut Grove in Los Angeles. At his debut at the Copa in 1960, he was the youngest performer to star at the club and his success there was a harbinger of his future status as a major attraction on the hotel circuit of Las Vegas, a city he made his permanent residence during the '60s. His appeal by the late 1960s was primarily to "mature" audiences. By then, he had virtually stopped touring, performing mainly in Las Vegas and devoting the rest of his time to songwriting and record production for other artists.

At the start of the 1970s, he again expanded his recording and stage activities. After finishing his contract with RCA Records with the LP *'70s*, he signed a new agreement with Buddah Records, for whom he provided a top 40 single in 1971 and a charted LP, *This Is Paul Anka*, in 1972. He recorded some additional material on that label before shifting again, this time to United Artists. His debut on UA, *Anka*, was issued in 1974. During that year, Paul scored his first number one singles hit in 15 years with his composition "(You're) Havin' My Baby," presented as a duet with Odia Coates. The disc hit number one in *Billboard* the week of August 24, 1974, and stayed there for two more weeks. During his stay with UA, which ended in 1978, Paul had several more chart hits such as "I Don't Like to Sleep Alone," "(I Believe) There's Nothing Stronger Than Our Love," and "Times of Your Lives." After UA, he went to RCA again before signing a contract with Columbia Records.

Among album releases of new and old material during the 1970s were, on UA, *Feelings* (1975), *Times of Your Life* (whose title song provided a hit single in 1975), *The Painter* (1976), and *The Music Man* (1977); on RCA, *Remember Diana* (1975), *She's a Lady* (1975) *Paul Anka Sings His Favorites* (1976), and *Songs I Wish I'd Written* (1977); on Camden, *My Way* (1975); on Buddah, *Essential Paul Anka* (1976); and on Sire, *Paul Anka Gold* (1974) and *Vintage Years 1957-1961* (1977). In 1980, UA issued the retrospective *Paul Anka—His Best*.

In the 1980s, Paul maintained his routine of concerts in Vegas, occasional TV appearances, plus new album and singles releases. His name continued to show up on the charts from time to time, an example being the 1983 top 40 single "Hold Me 'til the Morning Comes."

ANTHONY AND THE IMPERIALS: *See Little Anthony and the Imperials.*

ANT, ADAM: *Singer, guitarist, band leader (THE ANTS), songwriter, record producer. Born*

London, England, mid-1950s. Members of the Ants, early 1980s: Marco Pirroni, Kevin Mooney, Terry Lee Miall, and Merrick, all from the U.K. Mooney was replaced by Gary Tibbs in the spring of 1981.

With a concert format that depended more on the shock value of unusual costuming and special effects than musical content, Adam Ant and his band, the Ants, struck paydirt with younger rock enthusiasts, first in his English homeland in the late 1970s and then in the early 1980s in the U.S. and other nations.

The head Ant, though he learned to play guitar in his teens, initially seemed headed for a career in graphic design. He was attending Hornsey College of Art in London in the mid-1970s when his focus shifted from that field to the expanding punk movement in England. In mid-1976, he got together with bass guitarist Andy Warren to found a band they called B-Sides. At various times the group included such musicians as Bid on guitar and keyboards, Lester Square on guitar, and Paul Flanagan, Bob Hip, or David Tampin on drums. The band made a demo of a rock version of Nancy Sinatra's old hit, "These Boots Are Made for Walking," before breaking up prior to the end of 1976.

By now convinced that his future lay in pop music, Adam worked with Warren to assemble a new group in early 1977. The first Ant lineup was put together at London's Roxy Club that April. By May, it had a debut engagement as a support band for X Ray Spex at the Man in the Moon Club. From then on, the group opened for a spectrum of London punk and new wave rock bands, leading up to its first date at the city's best-known rock club, the Marquee, in the fall, supporting the Buzztones.

By early 1978, Adam and the Ants were beginning to come into their own, headlining shows at a number of London clubs, including the Marquee, Roxy, and Hard Rock Cafe. Though the band was winning friends among club goers, critics were decidedly negative. Rock writer Pete Scott, who later became a strong supporter of the band, recalled in the "Adam Ant Catalogue" savaging the band after seeing it perform in April 1978. "I wasn't at all sure what to make of them. I reviewed the gig for *Sounds* and . . . gave them pretty short shrift. I conceded that Adam himself was a lovely mover, albeit as faggy as hell. I was dismissive of both his image and his musical policies."

Undeterred, Adam persisted in developing a style of music he called Antmusic. In 1980, when U.K. critical favor had swung Adam's way, Adele-Marie Cherrison wrote in *Sounds*: "Adam and the Ants . . . are a talented, innovative and conscientious band. Antmusic is the exciting alternative; it's fresh, entertaining and NOT rock 'n' roll. [A conclusion that was a bit overdone, however.] It's Antmusic for Sexpeople; you either like it or you don't, but you just try stopping it."

After making demos of some of his material, Ant and his group made an initial breakthrough: a two-song contract with English Decca. The result was "Young Parisians" backed with "Lady," issued in August 1978 with quick entry in the U.K. top 30.

Despite the singles' relative success, not much happened immediately from a recording standpoint. Meanwhile, the band continued to play local London clubs the latter part of 1978 and began 1979 with its first U.K. tour. All of this helped demonstrate the group's growing popularity with English fans and brought a new contract arrangement with Do-It Records. To try the waters, a single was issued on Do-It in June 1979: "Xerox" backed with "Whip in My Valise." When that quickly moved up the U.K. charts to the top 10, the okay was given for a more ambitious project.

In August 1979, the group began recording its debut album at Sound Development Studios in London. Besides Adam Ant and Warren (with Ant handling production and lead vocals), the other musicians on the album were Dave Barbe and Matthew Ashmans. In October, soon after a sold-out show at London's Electric Ballroom, Warren left and was replaced on bass guitar by Lee Gorman.

The debut album on Do-It, *Dirk Wears White Sox*, was released in January 1980, but hardly had it reached the record stores when everyone but Adam departed from the Ants. Adam seized the opportunity to contact Marco Pirroni, who was between bands. Pirroni had an excellent reputation in London as a guitar player and writer. He first had gained attention for his performance with Siouxsie and the Banshees, whose members included drummer Sid Vicious of Sex Pistols notoriety, at the 100 Club Festival in 1977. Later in the decade Pirroni was a featured guitarist with the bands Models and Rema-Rema.

Marco and Adam huddled at a cake shop in Covent Garden on January 28 and reached agreement on a songwriting partnership in support of a new Antmusic group. One of their first projects was to re-record some earlier songs, "Cartrouble Part II" and "Kick," for a second Do-It single. Released in February, the single "Cartrouble/Kick!" provided another top 10 hit for Adam. By now, larger record firms were bidding for the revamped Ants. After leaving Do-It, Adam and Marco began recording their first collaborative numbers, "Kings of the Wild Frontier" and "Press Darlings." Released by CBS U.K. in April, "Kings of the Wild Frontier" provided Adam and Marco with their first number one U.K. hit. In support of the new releases on the

"Ant's Invasion" tour, Adam came on stage in a flamboyant costume to the beat of the twin drums the band now featured, played by Terry Lee Miall and Merrick. As described by Danuta Wisniewska of the *Record Mirror*, Adam appeared "like a Cherokee Indian brave . . . with the image complemented aurally by his tom tom sounding drummers. Adam's voice is so intense in portraying the emotion that he is mesmerizing."

Satisfied by now that the Ants could have a hit, CBS Records signed the band to a multialbum contract announced on July 25. The band proceeded to record the remaining tracks needed for its debut album on the label over the summer. The finished collection, *Kings of the Wild Frontier*, was issued in England in September. Supported by wide-ranging concerts, the album opened at number four on U.K. charts, moved up a bit, and briefly dipped to number ten only to start progressing upward again at year-end. In January 1981, the LP went up to number one, displacing John Lennon and Yoko Ono's *Double Fantasy*. Besides being a hit in the U.K., the album also went platinum in Australia.

The disc also provided a steady stream of hit singles, some supported by wild videos that eventually helped make the group a success in the U.S. These included "Dog Eat Dog" (issued in the U.K. in October 1980 and eventually a number two entry on British charts) and "Antmusic" (number one in the U.K. in early 1981).

Airplay of some of the band's recordings received in the U.S. as imports had already started to build an audience for it, aided by magazine reports of the unusual shows Adam put on. *Kings of the Wild Frontier* was released in the U.S. by CBS on its Epic Records subsidiary in February 1981 and it was helped up the U.S. charts by Adam and the Ants' first U.S. tour, which got under way in the spring. Besides Adam and Pirroni, the band included Miall and Merrick on drums and former Roxy Music member Gary Tibbs on bass. (See *Roxy Music.*) A new single, "Stand and Deliver," came out on CBS U.K. in May 1981 and on Epic in the U.S. in June and made its way into charts in both countries, reaching number one in England.

Adam already was making plans for an even more lavish stage presentation to back a new LP, *Prince Charming*. The single of that title was issued by CBS U.K. in September 1981 and reached number one there. During the summer of 1981, the band recorded tracks for the *Prince Charming* album, which was issued simultaneously in the U.S. and U.K. in November. The album, co-produced by Adam and Marco, entered U.K. charts at number two and soon was nestled in the top spot. However, while it spent several months on the U.S. charts at the end of 1981

and early 1982, it fell far short of the top positions.

The "Prince Charming Revue" planned and designed primarily by Adam, proved much too expensive an enterprise for presentation in the U.S. But British fans were enthralled, including one special concert attendee, Princess Margaret.

Commenting on the endeavor, Adam stated in Epic bio notes: "It was a thank-you to the fans that cost me 250,000 pounds. I wanted to help revive the music industry, take it away from the traditional rock & roll show. In doing this, I was throwing down the gauntlet to other groups; I wanted to make people feel the way I did when I saw Roxy Music at the Rainbow, or the New York Dolls supporting the Faces. The Prince Charming Revue was a cameo—very visual but, in terms of clothes, very hindering to my movements, and I felt I had to stop heading in that direction. I'd gone about as far as I could with that makeup. It's a bit like Bowie after *Aladdin Sane*; you have to stop, though you know that may be a dangerous move. It was a necessary step, because I felt my integrity was being threatened. I wanted to get more basic again, a bit more savage, like the initial *Kings of the Wild Frontier* idea."

Though Adam had to limit performances of that show, the single, album, and video of *Prince Charming* were all hits at home and in many other countries, if not the U.S. He also could savor the success of another single, "Ant Rap" (issued in the U.K. in December 1981), a top three hit in 1982.

The new road Adam took after that project was toward solo performing. For much of 1982, collaborating with Pirroni on production chores and new songs, he recorded tracks for his debut solo LP, *Friend or Foe*. The album was released simultaneously in the U.K. and U.S. in October 1982. As expected, it debuted high on the U.K. charts, entering at the number five position. More to Adam's satisfaction, the LP did considerably better with U.S. record buyers than the earlier releases. It showed up on *Billboard's* list soon after release and by year-end it was at number 37 and moving higher. The album remained on U.S. charts well into 1983. The single "Goody Two Shoes" (released in the U.S. along with an accompanying video in October 1982), also appeared on American singles charts. (Previously issued in England in advance of the LP in April, it reached number one in England, Australia, and Belgium.)

Ant's tour of the U.S. to back the album in 1983 drew good-sized crowds in major cities, though critical comments were considerably mixed. He was making progress in the U.S. market, it appeared, though he wasn't accepted as a superstar as was the case in his homeland.

Adam's second solo album, *Strip*, was released in

14

the fall of 1983. It did not have the massive U.K. response of earlier releases, but moved up U.S. charts at year-end. His mid 1980s work included the 1985 Epic LP release, *Vive Le Rock*, and movie roles such as the 1988 black comedy "Trust Me." (In the late 1970s he had gained attention for his acting work in "Jubilee with the Slits." For that film he provided the soundtrack songs "Plastic Surgery" and "Deutscher Girls.")

APRIL WINE: *Vocal and instrumental group. Members, late 1970s to mid-1980s: Myles Goodwyn, born Woodstock, New Brunswick, Canada, June 23, c. 1951; Jerry Mercer, born Montreal, Canada, April 27; Gary Moffet, born Ottawa, Canada, June 22; Steve Lang, born Montreal, Canada, March 24; Brian Greenway, born Hawkesbury, Ontario, Canada, October 1.*

One of Canada's best-known rock bands for most of the 1970s, April Wine was virtually unknown south of the border. It took a well-publicized live concert pairing with the Rolling Stones in a small Toronto venue in 1977 and a record company realignment the following year to finally start to bring the band popularity in the coveted U.S. market.

Even so, it took another four years before the band scored a major album hit in the U.S. with the 1981 *The Nature of the Beast* and was able to begin seeking headline concert opportunities in the states. Founder and band mainstay Myles Goodwyn told Andy Secher of *Hit Parader* magazine: "I'd be lying through my teeth if I said that it wasn't nice to finally get the attention I always thought we deserved. We were making a very nice living by touring Canada and the Midwest, but if you're a professional musician, you want to reach as many people as possible."

For Goodwyn, the saga had begun in Nova Scotia, where he first began singing and playing guitar with school bands. In 1969, he and three others formed what was to become April Wine and, soon after, moved to Montreal, where there was more opportunity for aspiring rock artists. Through the usual route of playing local clubs and passing demo tapes around, the band got a record contract from Canadian-based Big Tree Records in 1970, which issued the group's debut LP that year. When the band's second album, *On Record*, came out on the Big Tree label in 1971, it began to draw attention from many parts of Canada. The group members in the early 1970s included Goodwyn on guitar and lead vocals, Jim Clench on bass guitar, and brothers David and Richie Henman on guitar and drums. The brothers left for another band in 1973 and were replaced by guitarist Gary Moffet and drummer Jerry Mercer, who both had worked with other Canadian groups.

Mercer had been a member of Mashmakhan March 1 and also played on the Wackers' hit album *Shredder*. While Goodwyn remained the main writer, others contributed too, an example being Clench's "Oowatanite," one of the songs Canadian fans favored in the 1970s.

Clench left in the mid-1970s and was replaced on bass by Steve Lang in September 1975. That year, April Wine scored a first in Canadian record annals when its fifth album, *Stand Back* (on Big Tree) became the first Canadian-English LP to reach platinum status in that country. The album provided the group with a number one hit single in Canada, "I Wouldn't Want to Lose Your Love." Other Canadian hits from the LP were: "Oowatanite," "Tonite's a Wonderful Time," and "Cum Hear the Band." The band's position as one of Canada's superstar rock aggregations was underscored by public acceptance of its new album, *The Whole World's Going Crazy*, which shipped platinum in 1976—again a first for a Canadian-English rock band. That album was issued on the major London label, which also released its 1977 album *April Wine Live at the El Mocambo*.

The El Mocambo, a small club in Toronto, was the setting for the much-reported incidents involving the Rolling Stones. The Stones were looking for a place to complete recordings for a new live album and decided to do two successive nights at the El Mocambo while April Wine was in residence there. The event made worldwide headlines, but not because of the recording activities. Rumors about a Stones romance involving Margaret Trudeau, then the wife of Canada's prime minister, brought attention to her presence in the El Mocambo audience. Added publicity resulted when Keith Richards of the Stones was arrested by Canadian police (See *Rolling Stones*.)

Discussing the way the joint shows came about, Moffet told reporter Pat Higgins of the University of Nebraska *Daily Nebraskan*: "The Stone's management came to us with the idea of their making a surprise appearance. It was advertised as an April Wine show. The first night they seemed nervous, but the second night was incredible. The funny thing is that it wasn't even that weird to be playing with the Stones. It was sitting around watching 'The Gong Show' [on TV] with them that seemed crazy."

The April Wine live album did well in Canada, but again gained little response in the U.S. Meanwhile, the band solidified its roster with addition of Brian Greenway in 1977. Vocalist, keyboards player, and guitarist, he had been featured in other top Canadian rock groups, including Mashmakhan and the Dudes.

Up to this point, though April Wine had played

15

some U.S. dates as opening act for bands such as Rush and Styx, its hoped-for rapport with American fans had failed to materialize. Moffet told Dale Adamson of the *Houston Chronicle* (February 22, 1981): "We established our initial reputation, not only through our records, but by doing concerts every year and putting on good shows. . . . Then for the longest time we were expecting to break into the U.S. market. But we were waiting until a record did it for us and that was just not happening.

"So we finally had to come to the decision that we were just going to come down here and tour on whatever level we have to— just so that we could start to play and start to show people what we could do in concert."

Actually, part of the problem had been that the group's record companies hadn't pushed for too much U.S. exposure. Big Tree had arranged for distribution of only two of the first five Canadian LPs: *On Record* in the summer of 1971 on the basis of the Canadian hit single, "You Could Have Been a Lady," and *Stand Back* in 1975.

The London Records association, Lang told Roger Kaye of the *Fort Worth [Texas] Star Telegram* (March 15, 1981), brought little improvement. "Although we didn't realize it at the time, it was kind of an experiment for them. They wanted to try some rock but they were basically into a classical catalogue. So it didn't work out and we ended up tied to that deal. Finally we were able to sign with Capitol and finally [got] the exposure we wanted."

Capitol issued the band's label debut in the U.S., *First Glance*, in the fall of 1978. Backed by an intensive touring schedule for the band in the U.S. (mainly as opening act for better-known groups), the album provided April Wine's first American top 40 single on Capitol, "Roller." Though not a blockbuster, the album did make U.S. charts for some months. With Goodwyn handling production and providing most of the original songs, the band's next Capitol release, the 1980 *Harder . . . Faster*, stayed much longer on the charts and earned the group its first U.S. gold-record certification from the RIAA. The next album, issued in early 1981, established April Wine's credentials as a band respected in America just as had been the case for almost a decade in its homeland. The 1981 album, *The Nature of the Beast*, provided the top 30 single "Just between You and Me" and also proved the band's most successful release to that point. It was a bestseller not only in the U.S. and Canada, but in many European nations, easily passing the levels required for gold and platinum certification.

It was a much more confident Myles Goodwyn who went to work on final production of the early 1982 Capitol release, *Power Play*. (The title re-flected Goodwyn's love for hockey, where the term *power play* refers to a situation where one team has an advantage of one or more players over the other.) During a long night of work on mixing tapes for the album tracks, Goodwyn told Andy Secher ("April Wine—In From the Cold with Big Hot Hit, "*Hit Parader*), "We get all the basic tracks done, and then it boils down to me sitting here all by myself trying to do some guitar overdubs and vocal work. It's really fun, though. It's such a basic fight—man vs. machine. It's the challenge that makes rock and roll so fascinating.

"If I get disgusted with the way things are going, I just think back on all the work we've done to get this far. There was a point not too long ago when I seriously wondered if we'd ever really make it. You reach a position after you've been recording and touring for a long time when you just say to yourself, 'This is as good as it's ever gonna get.' I thought we had reached that point, but I was wrong."

Power Play contained a blues-tinged version of the Beatles' "Tell Me Why" that made U.S. singles charts for a while. At this point, the band had regained the status of Canadian headliner it had been forced to abandon for a time after concentrating on performing in the U.S. and overseas. As was true for all rock artists of the 1980s, a major element in continued success lay in well-produced videos. For its fifth Capitol LP, *Animal Grace*, issued in February 1984, the video of the track "This Could Be the Right One" contributed to that single making the charts.

Asked about his approach to songwriting, Goodwyn said he could only do that at home in Montreal. "I make a demo [tape] of all the pieces and play all the instruments, then I take it to the group, who are able to understand quite easily what I'm thinking of."

Asked about whether he had any rules for writing, he responded: "There's only one rule to songwriting and that is that there are no rules at all. Success takes 3½ minutes—the length of a hit record—so that's the time it takes to be known universally. There are so many ways to approach songwriting. Sometimes inspiration takes over. Other times everything is premeditated and I know in advance I must find a certain chord. Some start with words stored in my head, others become clear in a melody. I wrote 'Just between You and Me' in 45 minutes while other songs take three years to write. There are no rules."

ARGENT: *See Zombies, The.*

ARMATRADING, JOAN: *Singer, guitarist, keyboards player, band leader, songwriter. Born December 9, 1950, St. Kitts Island.*

An underrated artist, Joan Armatrading has always had an excellent reputation with fellow performers, critics, and a loyal, if not overwhelmingly large, band of fans. She can point to a fine body of recorded work and her status as an entertainer who almost always presents exciting, professional concerts. Her artistic integrity—a refusal to water down her material for purely commercial reasons—has not prevented her from achieving a secure niche in the rock music scene, but has probably stood in the way of superstar status.

In albums such as *Joan Armatrading*, she demonstrated that she could do it all: sing with feeling and emotion, play excellent acoustic guitar, and, most of all, write well-matched words and music. Though she spent her early years in the West Indies, her material typically had the rhythmic intensity of Afro-American blues, jazz, and rock with a flavor of sophistication different from West Indies folk music. In her LPs, where nearly all the songs were written or co-written by her, almost every track has contributed to the overall effect. An example of her lyrical ability from *Joan Armatrading* are these lines from "Somebody Who Loves You": "Mistaken shyness can be costly/Too hasty a goodbye/And then you've lost me." While most of her songs over the years have dealt with personal relationships, some probe the general human condition, as in "People": "I got no place to hide/Nowhere to go/People all around me/Singing out of tune."

Joan was born on the Caribbean island of St. Kitts in 1950. In 1958 the family moved to England, settling in the industrial city of Birmingham, where Joan completed her formal education. One of six children, she was left on her own a good part of the time. Shy by nature, she recalled hanging back and watching other children at play, something "that went into my writing."

After a while, she became a radio addict back in the days when there was no Walkman available. She spent hours listening to whatever pop music was being broadcast in a period where the transition from old-style pop to the new rock style was affecting a generation of young Britons. As her interest in music grew, she began to teach herself to play instruments, first a piano, later a guitar. She credited that with giving birth to her percussive style of guitar performance. She told Barbara Graustark of *Newsweek* (February 11, 1980): "I was trying to be all the musicians in a band and my weird tempo changes came from not knowing what I was doing."

At the age of 14, she wrote her first song, "When I Was Young." She had Marianne Faithfull in mind when she wrote it, but had no idea of how to present the material to her. As her playing and singing improved, her brother and friends urged her to think of becoming a performer. She had already had some experience in school concerts when she finally did decide to take that step at 15. She still was hesitant, she recalled, because "I've always thought of myself as a songwriter first. I write all the time. The last thing I think about is how to sing it."

For a while she got work at local clubs, singing songs by people such as Bob Dylan and Paul Simon as well as some of her own compositions. She gained a local following, but wasn't thinking of becoming a major artist at the time. Later she moved to Bristol and at the end of the decade successfully auditioned for a U.K. touring company of the musical *Hair*.

At the start of the 1970s, she took up residence in London and slowly began to build up contacts in the music field. She still wanted to make her way mainly as a writer, staying "famous but faceless."

In London, she became friends with poet/lyricist Pam Nestor and soon the two were collaborating on new material. With Armatrading's unique guitar style and powerful voice, it made sense for her to make the demonstration records needed to sell the songs; it was only a step from that to her being offered a recording contract.

Her debut LP came out on A&M Records in 1973. It only sold about 12,000 copies, but more than a few observers could detect something very promising in the neophyte recording artist. A&M was interested in releasing another album, but Joan took a two-year hiatus, in part due to a restrictive management contract. Her next LP, *Back to the Night*, did much better than her debut collection. In the year-end poll of English music critics, it was voted one of the top 10 releases of the year. She also added to her luster with her opening-act work on concert tours with Supertramp and Nils Lofgren (See *Lofgren, Nils*.)

Her next album, *Joan Armatrading*, issued by A&M in July 1976, brought even more accolades on both sides of the Atlantic. English reviewers considered it one of the best collections of the mid-1970s. Phil Sutcliffe of England's *Sounds* magazine called it the number one album of 1976, writing: "We need Joan Armatrading like we need Bob Dylan and the Beatles. You'll play this record once in a while forever." In the U.S., *Rolling Stone* voted it runner-up Album of the Year.

Joan wasn't quite as consistent in follow-up albums of the late '70s, but all of them contained a sizable number of gems, for most of which Joan wrote both words and music. Her late '70s releases were *Show Some Emotion* (1977), *To the Limit* (1978), and *Steppin' Out* (1979). As a whole, her output from 1973 to 1979 made her a major influence on pop and rock almost everywhere but in the U.S. By 1980, she had earned 18 gold records in seven countries, but none in the U.S. Some of her releases made U.S. charts, but none rose to top levels.

She asked American interviewers, smiling but with some frustration: "Why aren't I famous?" The question remained valid in the mid-1980s, when she still was a cult favorite in the U.S., but an acknowledged star at home.

Some of the problem might have been the macho nature of rock music when she was getting started. She recalled that people enthused over the guitar licks on her albums, but were sure it was a male lead guitarist. "I'm used to people thinking it's a guy playing guitar on my albums when it's actually me. I suppose a lot of girls think they're expected to just strum along—to get by—but it annoys me that people should automatically think that's the extreme of my capabilities, too. I've always had a different approach, concentrating on writing songs and playing the guitar rather than thinking in terms of being a singer."

A&M continued to release new Armatrading LPs in the 1980s, starting with *Me Myself I* in 1980, followed by *Walk Under Ladders* in 1981. The latter was one of her more successful efforts during the winter of 1981-82. In support of the album, she made well-received tours of the U.S., parts of Europe, and several countries in the Far East.

In 1983, A&M issued two more albums, *The Key* and a best-of compilation called *Track Record*, which also contained two new songs by Joan. Following *The Key*, it was two more years before another LP of all new songs by her came out.

Commenting on whether that album, *Secret Secrets*, represented any change in musical outlook, she told an interviewer in early 1985: "It's always difficult to answer that. . . . I can only say that if you listen to [*The Key*] and then listen to this one, you'll hear what the changes are. It can be something as simple as using different chords. For example, you can pick a chord as simple as a D; you've always used one particular inversion of the chord and you suddenly decide to use a different shape for it. That can make a huge difference. I've changed the shape of my chords quite a bit this time."

The album credits indicated she also had assumed new duties, naming her as coarranger for horns and strings backing tracks. She responded: "I did all the arrangement on *The Key* and *Me Myself I*. I just didn't put it down on the album."

In 1986, A&M issued another Armatrading LP, *Sleight of Hand*.

ASHFORD & SIMPSON: *Vocal duo, songwriting team . Nickolas Ashford, born Michigan, c. 1942; Valerie Simpson, born New York, New York, August 26, 1948.*

The team of Ashford and Simpson was an important part of the rise of soul and soul-based rock music to major prominence worldwide in the 1960s. This was due to their remarkable songwriting talents, not their performing skills. Indeed, when they decided to concentrate on singing and recording their own material in the 1970s, it took some time before the songs they wrote for themselves could compete with the classic hits they had composed for others, such as "Ain't No Mountain High Enough" for Marvin Gaye and Tami Terrell plus Diana Ross's trademark concert song, "Reach Out and Touch (Somebody's Hand)." In truth, their singing abilities were somewhat less than superstar caliber, but with time, they developed a duo style that made their recordings and concerts memorable events.

The two originally crossed paths in New York's Harlem. Ashford, a native of Michigan, had moved to Manhattan in the early 1960s with thoughts of trying to find work as a singer or jazz dancer. He wasn't making much progress when he happened upon his future collaborator and eventual bride. "It all started in church," he recalled in the mid-1970s for a record company bio, "the White Rock Baptist Church in Harlem where we lived and still do. I was standing there when I looked and saw Valerie. She put me in a spin. She was such a beautiful girl. There was something about the way she moved and sang. I had to get to know her."

As good as his word, he soon made the acquaintance of 17-year-old Valerie and before long joined her as a choir member. As they got to know one another, they began to trade off words and melodies, first working out different gospel song styles and finally collaborating on original secular music. They completed their first songs in 1964 and managed to find a buyer. Valerie told a Warner Brothers interviewer, "We sold our first batch of songs to some guy for $75. We were pretty excited that we could make $75 just by sitting down and writing songs. Actually we were taken, but we didn't feel that way at the time."

That small amount of money did serve as a spur for further assaults on the music industry. The duo got their start as recording artists with three singles on the small Glover Records label: "I'll Find You"/"Lonely Town" and "Don't You Feel Sorry"/"Somebody's Lying on Love" in 1964; and "It Ain't Like That"/"You Don't Owe Me Anything" in 1965. Their work was beginning to open some doors, resulting in a songwriting contract with Scepter Records in 1965. One of their songs was accepted by the great Ray Charles. Called "Let's Go Get Stoned," it provided Ray with a top 10 hit on the soul charts and rose to number 31 on pop lists.

18

One reward Ashford & Simpson gained from that was a songwriting contract with Motown Records. Among the material they came up with was "Ain't No Mountain High Enough," which they also arranged for recording by Marvin Gaye and Tammi Terrell. The song rose to number three on soul charts and made the national pop top 20 in 1967. Three years later, Diana Ross recorded her version of it; that single made it all the way to number one on both soul and pop charts in the U.S. and also was a bestseller in many other nations. During that period, Ashford & Simpson turned out such hits for Gaye and Terrell as "You're All I Need to Get By" and "Ain't Nothin' Like the Real Thing" and, for Diana, "Reach Out and Touch (Somebody's Hand)" and "Remember Me." (See *Gaye, Marvin; Ross, Diana.*)

In the late 1960s and early 1970s, both Nick and Valerie kept their hands in as performers. Valerie worked a number of Motown recording sessions as a backup vocalist, including performing on Quincy Jones albums. She recorded two solo albums, produced by Nick on Motown's Tamla label (*Exposed*, issued in 1971, and *Valerie Simpson*, released in 1972). Not much happened with those recordings, though Tamla took advantage of Ashford & Simpson's growing reputation later in the decade by issuing the compilation LP *Keep It Comin'*. Nick was represented on some solo singles during those years, including "When I Feel the Need" backed with "Young Emotions" in 1967 on Verve and "Dead End Kids" backed with "Let's Go Get Stoned," on ABC in 1970.

By 1973, the duo had come to the conclusion they could succeed as a performing act and moved on to sign a long-term recording contract with Warner Brothers Records. Their debut on that label seemed to prove their point. Called *Gimme Something Real*, it rose into the top 20 on both soul and pop charts. They also got healthy airplay for the first Warner's single, the 1973 "(I'd Know You) Anywhere" backed with "I'm Determined." They had reasonable, if not blockbuster success with their next series of albums: *I Wanna Be Selfish* (1974), *Come as You Are* (1976), and *So So Satisfied* (1977). The hiatus between their 1974 and 1976 LPs occurred in part because of Valerie's temporary retirement for the birth of their first child in 1975. Their singles releases during that time span included "Have You Ever Tried It," "Main Line," and "Everybody's Got to Give It Up" backed with "Over to Where You Are" (1974); "Bend Me" (1975); "It'll Come, It'll Come, It'll Come" backed with "Caretaker," "Somebody Told Me a Lie" backed with "It Came to Me," and "Tried Tested and Found True" backed with "Believe in Me" (1976); and "So So

Satisfied" backed with "Maybe I Can Find Out" and "Over and Over" backed with "It's You" (1977).

Though Ashford & Simpson by then were devoting most of their time to supporting their original material with concert tours and recordings, they did find time for some other projects. Hit 1970s singles of their songs were gained by the Dynamic Superiors with "Shoe Shoe Shine," Ben E. King with "I Had a Love," Chaka Khan with "I'm Every Woman," and the Brothers Johnson with "Ride-O-Rocket." They worked as producers on Ray Simpson's LP *Tiger Love*, Diana Ross's gold LP *The Boss*, and Gladys Knight & the Pips' top 10 *About Love*. They also produced two songs on Teddy Pendergrass's *T.P.* album. In 1978, Nick & Valerie were part of the writing team for the movie version of *The Wiz*, which won a Grammy nomination. (See *Khan, Chaka; King, Ben E.; Knight, Gladys & the Pips.*)

Nick and Valerie's career soared in 1977 with the release of their fifth Warner Brothers album, *Send It*. Tracks such as the title number caught the spirit of the disco craze. Both the album and the single (backed with "Couldn't Get Enough") were among the year's best-sellers. "Send It" made the top 20 on the pop charts, as did "Don't Cost You Nothing" (backed with "Let Love Use Me"), another 1977 single release.

From then on, their albums of the late 1970s and early 1980s were certain to place on soul and pop charts soon after being unveiled to the public. Their 1978 release, *Is It Still Good to Ya*, won a gold record award, as did the 1979 LP *Stay Free*. Top 20 singles in the late 1970s included "It Seems to Hang On" backed with "Too Bad" (1978), "Is It Still Good to Ya" backed with "You Always Could" (1979), and "Nobody Knows" backed with "Crazy" (1979). Other singles issued during those years by Warners were "By Way of Love's Express" backed with "Too Bad" (1978) and "Ain't It a Shame" backed with "Flashback" (1979).

In 1980, their last studio album for Warners, *A Musical Affair*, was released. In 1981, Warners issued a live album, *Performance*. Warner Brothers singles in the early 1980s included the top 20 hit "Love Don't Make It Right" backed with "Finally Got to Me", "Happy Endings" backed with "Make It to the Sky," and "Get Out Your Handkerchief" backed with "You Never Left Me Alone" (1980); and "It Shows in the Eyes" backed with a medley "You're All I Need"/"Ain't Nothing Like the Real Thing"/"Ain't No Mountain High Enough" and "I Need Your Light" backed with "It's the Long Run" (1981).

During 1981, the duo made another record-label change, signing with Capitol. Their debut on that label was the concept album *Street Opera* (May 1982). One side of the LP comprised a group of songs that Ashford characterized as "a contemporary love story, but also involving a commentary on life in the 1980s." It opens with "Working Man" in which the male protagonist expresses both love and frustration for his woman. In "Who Will They Turn To," the woman responds, wondering, in part, what will become of their children should the two separate. In "Street Corner" (issued as the first single with "Make It Work Again" on the B side), the theme of individual survival in the concrete jungle of the inner city is expressed. The final track, "Times Will Be Good Again," has the woman coming to terms with separation. Nick noted: "It's semitragic, because she understands his problems and that they must leave each other, but there is hope in the end because she understands . . . why he must leave." The album made the top levels of black music charts and also had a good stay on pop lists. The single "Street Corner" also was well received by record buyers.

The team continued to maintain its position as one of the top acts on the concert circuit through the mid-1980s, appearing before capacity crowds throughout the U.S. and Canada and overseas. In 1984, their Capitol LP *Solid* moved onto pop charts in November, remaining well into 1985 and earning the duo another gold-record award. The title single "Solid" also was a chart hit in late 1984–early 1985 on both pop and black music lists. On black charts, it was in the top 4 during 1985. In August 1986, Capitol issued the LP *Real Love*.

Throughout their writing careers, they stated in 1985, they almost always followed the same routines with Nick providing all the lyrics and Valerie the music. Typically, she would work out melodies on the piano while Nick improvised lyrics with the help of a tape recorder.

ASSOCIATION, THE: *Vocal and instrumental group. Original members, 1965: Jules Alexander, born Chattanooga, Tennessee; Terry Kirkman, born Salinas, Kansas; Brian Cole, born Tacoma, Washington, 1944, died Los Angeles, California, August 2, 1972; Ted Bluechel, Jr., born San Pedro, California; Jim Yester, born Birmingham, Alabama; Russ Giguere, born Portsmouth, New Hampshire, October 18, 1943. Larry Ramos, born Kauai, Hawaii, added in 1967; Richard Thompson, born San Diego, California, replaced Giguere, in 1970.*

The Association was a beloved group with soft rock fans for the last half of the 1960s and fared quite well while its original roster remained essentially intact. After the death of Brian Cole, the loss of momentum was noticeable and the group broke up for a time in the 1970s, later reforming to resume touring though without new record successes.

The group evolved from discussions between Jules Alexander and Terry Kirkman in Los Angeles in early 1965. Both had considerable background in the music field and were looking for ways to develop their talent further. Alexander had dropped out of school in the tenth grade to work as a musician, spending a number of years as vocalist and guitarist with various bands before his travels brought him to Los Angeles. Kirkman had moved to the coast from his native Kansas in his teens. He spent two years as a music major in Chaffey College and two in journalism at California State College at Fullerton.

By the time Kirkman left school, he had many years' experience playing such varied instruments as brass, reeds, percussion, recorder, and harmonica. Before joining forces with Alexander, he had played with numerous rock groups, from minor ones to such heralded ones as Frank Zappa's Mothers of Invention. (See *Mothers of Invention; Zappa, Frank*.)

After deciding to organize a band, Alexander and Kirkman recruited Brian Cole and Jim Yester to begin with. They soon expanded again, adding Russ Giguere (pronounced *jig-air*) and Ted Bluechel, Jr. Cole had learned bass guitar in his teens and also developed his bass voice as he proceeded slowly to Los Angeles by way of Seattle and Portland. Along the way, he studied theater and speech in college for one year. Bluechel, raised in San Pedro, California, considered singing (baritone), playing drums, and picking guitar as sidelines, but when the opportunity arose to earn a living from music, he left college.

Giguere, though originally from New Hampshire, grew up in San Diego, where he sang in the junior high school chorale. He dropped out of high school to try to enter show business. He started singing with a group called the Men, but left when the Association started. Jim Yester, a brother of Jerry Yester of Lovin' Spoonful fame (*See Lovin' Spoonful*) grew up in the South, but later moved to Southern California. While taking business administration at Los Angeles Valley College, he put his tenor voice to good use with such combinations as the Yester Brothers and Los Conchos.

Satisfied that the group was complete, Alexander supervised an intensive rehearsal schedule that took the better part of six months of 1965. In November, the group debuted at the Ice House in Pasadena for what was to have been a one-week engagement, but audience response was so good, they were held over for many more weeks. In early 1966, they were signed by a small record firm, Valiant. Soon after, their first single, "Along Comes Mary," was released. It stayed on the hit charts for much of 1966.

Soon after, their reputation was consolidated with the smash hit, "Cherish," which sold well over a million copies and was rated on many industry charts as the number one record for the entire year. Still another 1966 success was "Pandora's Golden Heebie Jeebies," an original arrangement with psychedelic undertones.

By mid-1966, the group ranked as one of the most important in the music industry. It was featured on many major TV shows, a pattern that continued with regularity for many years.

The group's in-person appearances included many noteworthy engagements at places ranging from rock's famed Fillmore in San Francisco (where they first appeared in August 1966) to the Coconut Grove and Greek Theatre in Los Angeles; Blossom Music Center in Cleveland, Ohio; Tanglewood Music Festival in Lenox, Massachusetts; and Saratoga Performing Arts Center in Saratoga Springs, New York. In appearances at such places as the Nebraska and Illinois State Fairs and the Chicago Opera House, the group set new attendance records for rock-oriented groups.

The Association's first LP, *And Then Along Comes the Association*, issued in 1966, won a gold record. Most of the songs in the album, like most of the material in their later recordings, were originals by members of the group. (There were exceptions, such as their hit single "Windy.") Their second LP, *Renaissance*, featured only songs written by group members. Through mid-1971, the group's output totaled nine LPs, all of which made the charts. The others are *Inside Out, Birthday, The Association's Greatest Hits, Goodbye Columbus* (soundtrack), *The Association, The Association—Live*, and *Stop Your Motor*.

"Cherish" won three Grammy nominations in 1967: Best Performance by a Vocal Group, Best Contemporary Single and Best Contemporary Group Performance Vocal or Instrumental. In 1967, they had two more gold singles, "Windy" and "Never My Love," in addition to the million-selling album, *Inside Out*. All of these won Grammy nominations in the 1968 voting.

At the beginning of 1968, Jules Alexander decided he was tired of the road grind and took a leave of absence to go to India. His place was taken by Larry Ramos, originally from Hawaii, but since his teens a resident of Los Angeles, where he attended East Los Angeles and Cerritos colleges. Ramos, with his tenor voice and the ability to play lead guitar and bass, came to the Association from the New Christy Minstrels.

Besides two chart albums in 1968, the group had such successful singles as "Everything That Touches You," "Time for Living," and "Six-Man Band." (By then, Valiant Records had been purchased by Warner Brothers Records.)

In January 1969, the group was asked to provide the score for Paramount Pictures' *Goodbye Columbus*. Though on tour in the East, they agreed and a print of the film was delivered to them to work from. Alexander, who had rejoined the band, helped work on the music, which was completed by mid-February. Ramos was retained, making the Association a seven-man group.

In 1970, Giguere left to work as a solo performer on Warner Brothers. His replacement was Richard Thompson, who had attended grade and high school in San Diego. By the time Richard entered Los Angeles City College as a music major, he had learned the basics of piano, organ, reeds, brass, and percussion. His credits were impressive, including considerable experience as a jazz musician with Gabor Szabo and John Klemmer plus a stint with the Cosmic Brotherhood and his own Richard Thompson Trio.

As of early 1972, the group could point to such milestones as over 15 million records sold, total audience played to of close to 5 million, and over 750 concerts, including close to 600 at colleges and universities.

During the summer of 1972, charter member Brian Cole died of a drug overdose. It was a bad year for the Association in other ways. Warner Brothers released what proved to be the band's last album for almost a decade. By the mid-1970s, the group not only had no new records, but had seemingly faded from the music scene altogether.

In the early 1980s, with nostalgia about pop music of previous decades becoming stronger, the band was assembled again with a number of new faces. It still had a hold on a number of fans, as indicated by a warm reception at its first L.A. area show in years in January 1981 at the Ice House in Pasadena, where it had debuted 15 years earlier. The sextet could report to the audience that it had signed a new recording contract with Elektra/Asylum Records. From then through the mid-1980s, the group continued to perform in many parts of the U.S., often as part of a pop/rock revival package.

AVALON, FRANKIE: *Singer, trumpeter, actor. Born Philadelphia, Pennsylvania, September 18, 1940.*

Though performers from the South and Southwest played the main role in the rise of rock during the 1950s, the city of Philadelphia produced more than a few of the early stars, including Bobby Rydell, Fabian, and Frankie Avalon.

Avalon, whose original surname was Avallone, showed a flair for music at an early age. He took up the trumpet before he was in his teens and already was a local celebrity before he reached high school. Not yet 13 in the summer of 1953, he was a professional musician in a teenage group in Atlantic City, New Jersey. His reputation increased rapidly as he starred on radio and TV on Paul Whiteman's programs that were then being produced in Philadelphia. In the mid-1950s, his trumpet playing was featured on other TV shows, including Jackie Gleason's and Ray Anthony's.

By then, Frankie was demonstrating a good singing voice as well. His vocal talent came to the attention of music industry executives Bob Marcucci and Peter de Angelis. Both experienced songwriters, they also had their own music publishing firm and the Chancellor Records label. They became young Avalon's managers and signed him for Chancellor. Frankie's renditions of their songs gained some notice in 1957, and provided a major national hit in 1958, "Dede Dinah." Even before that, Frankie had already gained enough of a following for his first movie contract, the 1957 *Disc Jockey Jamboree*. From then into the early 1960s, Avalon was one of the top performers in the pop music field.

Frankie closed out the 1950s with his most successful year in 1959. He had two songs that sold over a million copies (combined totals, in the U.S. and England), "Just Ask Your Heart," and the number one hit "Venus." In 1960, he gained another gold record with "Why" (written by the Marcucci-De Angelis team). It was his last top 10 hit.

In the 1960s, Frankie became increasingly involved as a movie actor, a career choice that led to his making the Los Angeles area his home base. (Eventually he settled in the San Fernando Valley, where he raised a brood of four boys and four girls.) His 1960s credits included *Guns of the Timberland* in 1960, *The Carpetbaggers* in 1962, and a series of beach-bikini films produced by American International Pictures. In the latter group he was paired with Annette Funicello (a graduate of Walt Disney's "Mickey Mouse Club" TV shows) in many films.

By the late 1960s, while he continued to make personal appearances in clubs and theaters, Avalon had essentially phased out of popular music. His only recording still available at the time was the 1964 United Artist LP, *Hits of Frankie Avalon*. He made a number of TV appearances in the late 1960s and early 1970s, including a nonmusical acting role in a 1971 segment of the comic series "Love, American Style."

Frankie's interest in the record field never completely disappeared, though. In late 1975, he made top 40 once more with a disco version of his old hit "Venus" on De-Lite Records. But Frankie wasn't able to follow it up with additional chartmakers. In 1978, he had a cameo role in the movie version of the musical *Grease*, during which he sang "Beauty School Dropout."

In the late 1970s and in the 1980s, Avalon found increasing opportunities in the burgeoning pop/rock revival show circuit. In 1987, he and Annette Funicello were reunited in the film *Back to the Beach*, in which he sang a few old favorites.

AVERAGE WHITE BAND: *Vocal and instrumental group from Scotland. Original members, 1972: Alan Gorrie, born Perth, Scotland, July 19, 1946; Owen McIntire, born Lennox Town, Scotland, September 5, 1945; Roger Ball, born Broughty Ferry, Dundee, Scotland, June 4, 1944; Malcolm Duncan, born Montrose, Scotland, August 24, 1945; Robbie McIntosh, born Dundee, Scotland, died, Los Angeles, California, September 1974; Mike Rosen. Mike Rosen replaced in 1973 by "Hamish" Stuart, born Glasgow, Scotland, October 8, 1949. McIntosh replaced in January 1975 by Steve Ferrone, born Brighton, England, April 25, 1950.*

For a good part of the 1970s, the Average White Band, sometimes called AWB, ranked as one of the United Kingdom's better contributions to pop music. The band managed to overcome some significant obstacles in laying claim to a sizable audience in the U.S., drawn to a great extent from the college and young-adult population. Obstacles included the death of a key member under rather lurid circumstances and critics' reservations about an (originally) all-white group stressing black-style music.

Not only did founding members Alan Gorrie (lead vocals, guitar, and bass guitar) and Owen "Onnie" McIntyre (guitar and vocals) defy the odds by putting together a Caucasian group to play American-style soul/R&B-flavored rock, they weren't even from the States.

Gorrie stressed to an interviewer that the band played soul music simply because all the members loved it and could empathize with it. Most of the bandsmen had backed various American blues and soul artists during their U.K. or European tours in the '60s and early '70s before AWB was formed. When AWB came into being, Gorrie noted in a Los Angeles press conference, "We did a lot of American bases in Germany and we played a lot of black clubs. We never had any trouble in those black clubs because of being white. Blacks dig our music. They were most of our audience when we got started."

The founding members all had considerable experience in jazz or rock bands in Scotland and England before joining AWB. Gorrie had been a member of Forever More; McIntyre played with that band and the Roy Young Band before becoming an AWB artist. Ball and Duncan worked together in the Dundee Horns and Mogul Thrash prior to AWB. McIntyre had backed Ben E. King and Garnett Mimms and had been a sideman with Brian Auger's Oblivion Express. Stuart was an alumnus of Dream Police and Logo.

The original six (with Rosen) had come together by chance and, after jamming a bit, decided to start a group. The band worked up its own versions of classic soul/R&B songs and also added originals, most of them written by Ball and Gorrie. The band went through the usual start-up phase of trying to find the right management support while also working on demos to gain a record contract. Slowly the group made headway with club work in the U.K. and Continental Europe, finding chances to open for other artists. In 1973, its credits included taking part in Eric Clapton's comeback concert in London and a brief trip to Los Angeles, where the group played on Bonnie Bramlett's first solo album.

The band did get a contract from MCA Records, which led to its 1973 debut album, *Show Your Hand*. A fine LP showcasing a number of above-average original tracks emphasizing stirring rhythmic patterns laid down by Gorrie on bass and McIntosh on drums, it received little attention either in the U.K. or the U.S. In fact, the mass audience in England never really warmed up to the band's music, perhaps because, once the members' Scottish roots were evident, they lost "authenticity." This may have been a blessing in disguise, since it forced AWB to focus its hopes on the more lucrative U.S. market early in the game. After the disappointment of *Show Your Hand*, AWB signed with a new label, Atlantic, which set up U.S. recording sessions in 1974 with veteran arranger/producer Arif Mardin.

The Average White Band/Mardin association provided the label debut *Average White Band* from which the single "Pick Up the Pieces" was culled. Both came out in the latter part of 1974 and quickly made their mark with U.S. fans. The album and single both moved up rapidly. In February 1975, each reached number one on U.S. charts with the LP moving on to receive RIAA platinum-record certification.

One thing that helped was the timing—the album had strong disco-style tracks at a time when the new disco craze was just starting to burgeon. Gorrie told a reporter: "The album is full of disco music. That's the kind of music we're into. We go to discos ourselves. I would hate to think of an album of ours that wasn't funky enough to be played in the discos."

When Gorrie made that statement, there wasn't too much reason for members to feel like dancing. Some months earlier, in September 1974, drummer Robbie McIntosh had died from inhaling a lethal mixture of morphine and heroin at a Hollywood party. Gorrie, also in attendance, had similar exposure and collapsed, but was saved by the prompt action of singing star Cher, who kept him awake, preventing him from falling into a fatal coma, until the crisis passed. (*See Cher; Sonny and Cher.*)

McIntosh's replacement was his good friend Stephen Ferrone, who had known McIntosh from Oblivion Express days. Of English and West African heritage, he filled in on several concert dates and, in January 1975, left his previous group, Bloodstone, to become a full-time AWB member. With Ferrone's addition, some observers wondered if the band would change its name, but Gorrie indignantly objected, noting the name had no racist connections. In fact, he characterized the original members musically as black men in white skins.

At any rate, the band, if anything, achieved a tighter sound with Ferrone's addition, as demonstrated on such follow-up best-sellers as *Cut the Cake* album (1975) and the single "If Ever I Lose This Heaven." Then the group seemed to lose momentum with a series of LPs that often sounded like rehashes of what went before, such as *Person to Person* and *Soul Searching*, issued by Atlantic in 1976, *Benny and Us* (recorded with long-time friend Ben E. King) (*See King, Ben E.*) in 1977, and *Warmer Communications*, released on Atlantic in 1978. (MCA also issued an LP of older recordings, *Put It Where You Want It*, in 1975.) Moreover, the band's stage shows of 1976-77 seemed to catch fire only sporadically.

However, there were signs AWB was starting to reverse the trend with some of the songs on *Warmer Communications* and the 1979 *Feel No Fret*, reflecting efforts toward more experimentation while maintaining the infectious beat that had made AWB's reputation. There also was evidence of better pacing in the band's shows of the late 1970s.

However, the taste of the pop music audience was changing again, away from disco toward mainstream rock and such intellectual styles as new wave. The band's commercial status began to fade in the 1980s, reflected by Atlantic's decision to sever ties with AWB after the 1980 release, *Volume VIII*. The band signed with Ariola Records, which issued its label debut, *Shine*, in 1980, an album that did not recapture the group's glory of the mid-1970s.

B-52's, THE: *Vocal and instrumental group. Members, early 1980s: Cindy Wilson, born Athens, Georgia, c. 1957; Ricky Wilson, born Athens, Georgia, c. 1953, died 1986; Kate Pierson, born Weehawken, New Jersey, c. 1948; Fred Schneider III, born Belleville, New Jersey, c. 1952; Keith Strickland, born Athens, Georgia, c. 1954.*

Backed by appealing videos and offering a new wave disco sound that won approval from many dance-club disc jockeys, the B-52's flew high at the end of the '70s and start of the '80s. (The name, members of the Georgia-nurtured group hastened to add, was not derived from the U.S. bomber, but rather from southern slang for a smooth, high bouffant hairdo, a style affected by the two female B-52s in the band's early stages.) By the mid 1980s, however, it seemed that the group's momentum was slowing a bit, although it continued to release new albums.

The band came into existence in the mid-1970s in the university town of Athens, Georgia, where most of its members grew up. Sister and brother Cindy and Ricky Wilson were natives of Athens as was friend Keith Strickland. The other two founding members, Fred Schneider III and Kate Pierson, had lived a good part of their lives in Athens.

For the Wilsons, the band essentially was their first foray into the professional music field, though both had been rock fans from their early years and had taken part in school musical activities. Strickland, who had been a member of a rock band in high school, listed among his influences such diverse artists as the Beatles, Captain Beefheart, and Perez Prado. Kate Pierson's credits included membership in a folk group called Sun Donuts and some classical piano work. By far the most experience was claimed by Fred Schneider, who had been in Bridge Mix and Night Soil before becoming involved with the B-52's.

The future band members' paths crossed a number of times in the 1970s before a get-together one evening in October 1976 at a Chinese restaurant in Athens. They decided to meet later that night to match up their musical skills and party. They went to a friend's house and jammed, after which they concluded that they should work up an act. The group that evolved was made up of Cindy Wilson on lead vocals, percussion, and guitar; Ricky Wilson on guitars; Kate Pierson on vocals, keyboards, and guitar; Schneider on vocals, keyboards, and guitar; and Strickland on drums and percussion. The first public performance was at some friends' Valentine party in 1977—a free appearance, as were any other local dates the group could line up in the Athens area. Actually, at their start during 1977-78, the members didn't have the money to buy the professional equipment they needed for club or theater work. Schneider told Pete Silverton of England's *Sounds* magazine: "For a lot of that period we were just experimenting, we weren't performing. At first we didn't play our instruments live. We had everything taped except the voices." That was fine, except that one time during a performance, the Wilsons recalled, someone pulled the plug on the tape recorder.

Ricky Wilson commented that at some dates "I'd play something on guitar over it [the tape]. . . . I think I mimed it a couple of times."

For much of that period, the band members worked at other jobs while keeping music as a sideline. Cindy worked as a waitress in a luncheonette, Keith and Ricky were baggage handlers at a local bus terminal, Kate was a paste-up artist on an Athens newspaper, and Fred worked as a waiter in a vegetarian restaurant.

As the quintet became more confident of their performing skills, they expanded their taping activities to songs for possible record-company exposure. At one point, they decided to press some singles on their own, turning out "Rock Lobster," a disco rock number about an underwater dance party. The 2,000 copies made were sent to reviewers and sold to friends or attendees at the group's occasional local sets. The return address for anyone wanting to contact the band was care of the El Dorado Restaurant in Athens.

The single did bring the band some good feedback from reviewers and it encouraged it to try for some exposure in the center of new wave activity, New York. In 1978, the group drove up to take part in audition night at Max's. The payment they received—$17—made it their first salaried performance. After that, the group came back from time to time to appear at Max's and other spots such as CBGBs, winning attention after a while from both fans and some record-industry executives. By the time they came back for a featured set at the uptown Manhattan disco Hurrah in the spring of 1979, they were in line for a contract with Warner Brothers for U.S. distribution with overseas commitments to be handled by England's Island Records.

Word of the band's potential had reached many members of the music media, including *Sounds'* Silverton, who described his initial concert impressions for the May 26, 1979, issue. "They look like they picked up their clothes in an Acturian Oxfam shop. Their music is light and witty with discordant shafts of trembling organ or rumbling, manic rhythm guitar. . . .

"A music for kids of all ages. Cindy Wilson in a pink bouffant so high you could use it to sweep the ceiling in most houses. [Before long, she gave that up in favor of a short hairdo and omnipresent shiny black derby.] Kate Pierson in what looks like a blue lurex bouffant so high you could think she'd topple over. Fred Schneider in a blue shirt and a darker blue bow-tie looks like an intelligent and healthy Robert Gordon.

"Props and gadgets onstage, like a toy piano and a

telephone—Fred grasps it and starts normally enough ('Is that you baby?') but ends up swinging Mr. Bell's finest around like it was an odd-shaped yo-yo."

By the time Silverton's writeup appeared, the band was ensconced in Bermuda, where the head of Island Records, Chris Blackwell, supervised recording of its debut LP. That album, titled *The B-52's*, was released by Warner Brothers in late 1979; an early single from it, naturally, was "Rock Lobster." It took hard promotion and an enticing video to build nationwide interest in the band, but the rewards began to show in early 1980. The album moved onto U.S. charts in February and remained on them straight through to early 1981. By the end of 1980, the band had its first gold-album from the RIAA.

By the fall of 1980, that album was joined on the hit lists by the band's second LP, *Wild Planet*, which stayed on the U.S. charts into 1981. But its impact was less dramatic than the debut collection, reflecting in part the failure of the group to come up with a song to match the freshness of "Rock Lobster." Many of the tracks received considerable play in discos, however. The lack of new direction was noticeable in the band's third release, *Party Mix*, which was also on the charts for a number of months during 1981. The band could point to having had three charted LPs during that year as well as several singles on lower chart levels. Though its momentum seemed to be slowing, the band continued to release new material on Warner Brothers into the mid 1980s, including a new album issued in mid-1986. Its concert work included a set at the massive Rock in Rio concert in Brazil. But the year proved a traumatic one for the group due to the death from natural causes of Ricky Wilson.

BACHARACH, BURT: *Singer, pianist, songwriter, arranger, record producer. Born Kansas City, Missouri, May 12, 1928.*

One of the most prolific composers of the years after the mid-1950s, Burt Bacharach is presently spoken of with such famous names as Cole Porter and Richard Rodgers. A product of his age, he has demonstrated the ability to write material that runs the gamut from rock and soul to highly polished Broadway scores. In terms of top 10 success, few writers could match his track record in the mid and late '60s.

Bacharach might have been expected to be talented in writing, being the son of a famous nationally syndicated columnist, Bert Bacharach. From an early age, though, he demonstrated more ability with musical notes than with words, with the result that most of his songs have been collaborations, particularly with lyricist Hal David, though he has also worked with Mack Davis, Bob Hilliard, Jack Wolf, and Carole Bayer Sager.

Burt started piano lessons in elementary school. By then, though born in Missouri, he was living in New York, where he spent most of his youth. He showed ability with the piano, but rebelled briefly at 12, wanting to stop his lessons so he could play football. His parents insisted that he continue, a requirement he was willing to thank them for later on. During his high school years in the mid-1940s, he became an avid fan of bebop music, despite his youth managing to get into mid-Manhattan shows featuring such artists as Dizzie Gillespie and Charlie Parker, two musicians he now credits as having a major impact on his career. He organized his own band at this time and, after playing for local parties and Army installations, took his group on a USO tour of service hospitals.

After high school, Bacharach studied at McGill University in Montreal, Canada, the New School for Social Research in New York, and Mannes School of Music, in New York. He also won a scholarship to the Music Academy of the West in Santa Barbara, California. His training included grounding in the classics and music theory from such famous teachers as Darius Milhaud, Boguslav Martinu, and Henry Cowell.

Bacharach began his music career in earnest after serving in the Army from 1950 to 1952. He found work as a conductor and arranger for various record companies. During the 1950s, his services were requested by many major stars, including Vic Damone, Polly Bergen, Steve Lawrence, and the Ames Brothers. He also toured widely during a three-year period as accompanist-conductor for Marlene Dietrich's nightclub act.

Burt was already writing songs in his teens. By the early 1950s, he had a number of tunes published. He became a member of ASCAP in 1955. By the late 1950s, some of his songs were showing up on the hit charts in performances by artists from different segments of the popular music field. There were country rock successes written for Gene Pitney ("The Man Who Shot Liberty Valance," "24 Hours From Tulsa"). (*See Pitney, Gene*.) Marty Robbins gained a hit with Burt's "The Story of My Life" as did Perry Como with "Magic Moments."

In the 1960s, by then based in Los Angeles area, Burt was writing an increasing number of songs for the movies. He also continued to arrange material for many artists, including middle-of-the-road and rock bands. In 1964, he received the assignment that was really to move him into the big leagues—the score for the movie *What's New Pussycat?* Partly responsible for this was actress Angie Dickinson, a friend of *Pussycat* director Charlie Feldman. Angie was then dating Burt, prior to becoming Mrs. Bacharach. The title song for the film was given to a young Welsh singer, Tom Jones. (*See Jones, Tom.*) This move helped bring Jones national attention in America and laid the groundwork for Bacharach's first Academy Award nomination. Bacharach didn't win then, but the steady stream of requests for him to do movie scores eventually resulted in a dual-Oscar victory for the song "Raindrops Keep Falling on My Head" and the score of the 1969 hit film, *Butch Cassidy and the Sundance Kid.*

Between 1965 and 1969, Bacharach also received Oscar nominations for the songs "Alfie" in 1967 and "The Look of Love" in 1968. Both became top 10 hits for singer Dionne Warwick (*See Warwick, Dionne*), for whom the Bacharach-David team provided a continuing series of gold-record songs and albums in the late 1960s and early 1970s starting with "Don't Make Me Over" in 1962. Others included "I Say a Little Prayer" in 1967-68 and "This Girl's in Love with You," "Do You Know the Way to San Jose?" "There's Always Something There to Remind Me," and "Promises, Promises," in 1969. Other major Warwick successes from Bacharach included "Walk on By" (1964), "What the World Needs Now Is Love," "Trains and Boats and Planes," and "You'll Never Get to Heaven."

Bacharach turned almost all the bids for film scores down in favor of working on his first Broadway musical with Hal David during 1967-68. The show, *Promises, Promises*, was adapted by Neil Simon from his comedy hit, *The Apartment*. It opened to rave notices on November 23, 1968, and was still running on Broadway in 1971.

Though Bacharach is an excellent stage performer, he has tended to play this down in favor of his composing work. When he has made in-person appearances, the audience response has been highly favorable. As an example, in June 1970, a single concert in St. Louis sold out all 11,000 seats in advance to fans ranging in age from teens to sixties. A second concert was then added to which tickets were placed on sale 10 hours before show time. All 11,000 sold out in three hours. In the same way, standing-room—only audiences attended his occasional appearances at the Greek Theatre in Los Angeles, Riviera Hotel in Las Vegas, and other leading music halls in the U.S. and Europe.

Bacharach has attributed much of his success to his willingness to try new harmonic patterns. He credits the rock revolution with helping modern songwriters achieve a new degree of artistic freedom. As he told Bob Shayne of the *Los Angeles Times* (September 1, 1968): "The company Artists & Repertoire men used to be really omnipotent. They'd say, 'That's a three-bar phrase. You can't

have a three-bar phrase. Make it a four-bar phrase and I'll get so-and-so to record your song.' And I ruined some pretty good songs that way, because I believed them. They made the rules.''

Now Bacharach makes his own rules, particularly because he produces and arranges most of the hit versions of his songs. "I don't try to break the rules consciously, because most of them come from a harmonic source. It just happens. Like, we were finishing a song with Dionne the day before a date and she was counting the eighth-note flow. She said, 'Gee, this only comes to seven notes.' I said 'You're kidding. Count it again.' So we did it as a 7/8 bar. It felt good that way.''

In the late 1960s, Bacharach became a featured recording artist in his own right. His *Reach Out* album for Herb Alpert's A&M Records was on the hit charts for most of 1968. His A&M LP, *Close to You/One Less Bell to Answer* issued in spring 1971, turned up in the top 20 by mid-June.

At that point, Burt seemed on top of the world, but it proved an illusion. The composer of 22 previous top 10 singles didn't come close to having another one in 1971, when his career went into a decade-long tailspin. Adding to—or perhaps causing—the situation were the breakup of his marriage and falling outs with his long-time associates, cowriter Hal David and singer Dionne Warwick. Harbingers of things to come were the poor buyer response to his 1973 A&M LP *Living Together* and the disastrous 1973 film musical *Lost Horizon*, which he scored. He recalled for Paul Grein (*Los Angeles Times*, July 13, 1986): "I just went down to the beach at Del Mar and sort of hid. It was such a giant bust. I didn't want to be seen walking around the community.''

A&M continued to issue new LPs in the mid-1970s, including *Burt Bacharach's Greatest Hits* (1974), *Futures* (1977), and *Woman* (1979). None of his new songs were hits. *Woman*, which he recorded with the 100-piece Houston Symphony Orchestra, was his prime hope for a rebound, but it was a flop that made Bacharach despair for his future.

Of the long rupture with Warwick, which finally was repaired in 1986, he told Grein: "There was a 10-year period when we not only hadn't been in the studio, but we weren't even speaking more than 'hello.' When Hal David and I started to come apart, we weren't able to be there in the studio for Dionne. So she sued us and Hal sued me and I sued Hal. It was all very messy. It's great to leave all that stuff behind you, to clean out that excess baggage.''

Things started to turn around for him in the early 1980s, when he formed a close relationship with songwriter Carole Bayer Sager, whom he married in 1982. The two joined forces with Peter Allen to write "Arthur's Theme," which became a number one hit for Christopher Cross in October 1981. Later, Bacharach and Sager provided still more hit songs for other artists, such as Roberta Flack's "Making Love" and Neil Diamond's "Heartlight." In 1982, they wrote "That's What Friends Are For" which was sung by Rod Stewart over the closing credits for the movie *Night Shift*. (*See Cross, Christopher; Diamond, Neil; Flack, Roberta; Stewart, Rod.*)

In 1986, when the Bacharachs were considering material for a Dionne Warwick session now that she and Burt had made up, they brought "That's What Friends Are For" to Dionne's attention. She loved it and recruited Stevie Wonder, Elton John, and Gladys Knight to help record it. The song became a number one hit in the U.S., with the profits of several hundred thousand dollars donated to the American Foundation for AIDS Research. That wasn't the only reward in a banner year for Burt; he and Carole also gained still another number-one single hit with "On My Own," recorded by Patti LaBelle and Michael McDonald.

BACHMAN-TURNER OVERDRIVE: *See Guess Who, The.*

BAILEY, PHILIP: *Singer, percussionist, conga player, songwriter, record producer. Born Denver, Colorado, May 8, 1951.*

Among the high points of an Earth, Wind & Fire concert were the high-pitched, falsetto vocal passages rendered by Philip Bailey, who shared lead singing responsibilities with EW&F's driving force, Maurice White. In the mid-1980s, when EW&F activities slowed down considerably, Bailey took the opportunity to develop a solo career, while maintaining that he would remain a part of the EW&F "family" (*See Earth, Wind & Fire.*)

Born and raised in Colorado, Bailey exhibited performing skills at an early age and contributed soprano-like tones to local church choirs before he reached his teens. When he was 13, he won a music award that helped him decide on his future field. Music, he said, was his first love and remained so through his formative years into adulthood. During his teens, he learned about music theory, arranging, and composing, all of which he applied for a while in the late 1960s as musical director for a gospel-rock group, the Stovall Sisters.

Unlike many of his contemporaries in teenage vocal groups, Bailey's voice did not change dramatically when he grew up. He could hit upper-register notes with ease, which helped win him a job with the revamped version of Earth, Wind & Fire that Maurice White and his brother Verdine assembled in

the early 1970s. (The first EW&F band, which the Chicago-born Whites organized at the end of the 1960s, had not had the musical scope they had envisioned for their new group.) Bailey performed on EW&F's first album for Columbia Records, *Last Days and Times*, issued in mid-1972, and took part in recording all the EW&F LPs for that label through the late 1980s.

During that period, he also shared in the many gold and platinum awards earned by the band for its albums and singles. On a good many of the singles, such as "Devotion," "Shining Star," "After the Love Is Gone," and "Fall in Love With Me," Bailey handled lead vocal assignments. "Shining Star," which was certified gold by the RIAA in June 1975, brought the band its first of six Grammy Awards. The 1975 trophy was for the Best R&B Vocal Performance by a Duo, Group or Chorus. Through 1988, Bailey's name appeared on credits for more than a dozen EW&F albums as both a performer and a songwriter.

In late 1982, Bailey got an okay from Columbia to start work on a solo album. "This project was naturally the next step for me. There was a lot of music brewing inside of me that I wanted to hear on record," he stated in a Columbia press release. That LP, *Continuation*, for which Bailey handled arrangements and writing on many numbers, came out in July 1983.

The response to the LP and Bailey's tour dates in support of it demonstrated he had good potential as a solo artist. This was further reinforced by his next project, the album *Chinese Wall*, produced by versatile singer/drummer Phil Collins. (*See Genesis.*) Released in the fall of 1984, the LP was a chart hit on both black music and general pop lists into early 1985. It also spawned "Easy Lover," a duet between Bailey and Collins that rose to number 2 on U.S. charts. The promotional video of that song received an MTV award for Best Performance by a Duo or Group.

Both "Easy Lover" and *Chinese Wall* were certified gold by the RIAA and brought Grammy nominations for 1985—one in the Best Male Vocal Performance category, the other (with Collins) for Best Vocal Performance by a Duo or Group.

Bailey's third Columbia solo album, *Inside Out*, was released in April 1986. Overall production was done by Nile Rodgers (who had produced LPs for Madonna, Duran Duran, and David Bowie), with Bailey acting as co-producer for two numbers, "Because of You" and "Back It Up." Both featured all-star rock/jazz backing groups. On "Because of You," Bailey's support included Phil Collins on drums, Nathan East on bass, George Duke on keyboards, and Ray Parker, Jr., on guitar. On "Back It

Up,'' that same group was joined by rock guitar legend Jeff Beck.

First single release was "State of the Heart," which made hit charts in the spring. The new album also was a chart entry in the spring and summer.

Until that point, Bailey had continued to reaffirm allegiance to Earth, Wind & Fire. Bailey said, "I've been working with Maurice White for more than a dozen years. We've built something special and I have no intention of walking away from that." True to his word, in 1987–88 he worked with EW&F on a new LP and concert tour.

BAKER, GINGER: *See Cream, The; Korner, Alexis.*

BALDRY, JOHN: *Singer, guitarist, songwriter, band leader. Born England, c. 1940.*
Throughout the 1960s, John Baldry was one of the important influences on the English pop music scene, for which he received due credit from English and Continental European fans. But these people often did not realize how many of the major blues and rock performers of the '60s and '70s (including Rod Stewart, Elton John, and Brian Auger) gained their first major professional experience as members of Baldry-led groups. As for U.S. audiences, few were aware of Baldry's existence until the start of the '70s.

Baldry was born during World War II and reached his teens about the time rock was just finding favor in the U.S. He already had gained the nickname of Long John, for his height—a full growth of 6 feet 7 inches. Though aware of the rising popularity of Elvis Presley and Bill Haley, young John was mainly interested in such American art forms as the blues and folk music. By the mid-1950s, he had mastered the guitar and played and sang in small folk clubs in England.

During this period, he became close friends with an American folk singer, Brooklyn-born Ramblin' Jack Elliott. (*See Encyclopedia of Folk, Country and Western Music.*) Elliott was visiting England when he met Baldry and the two teamed up on a number of tours of England and Continental Europe between 1957 and 1961.

By the start of the 1960s, many English pop musicians were increasingly playing material based on American country blues and rhythm & blues. Baldry found much of this to his liking and turned away from more traditional folk singing in favor of blues-rock. In 1961, he was instrumental in the organization of Alexis Korner's Blues Incorporated, a group that included Mick Jagger and Charlie Watts (later the founding members of the renowned Rolling Stones). However, Baldry only stayed a short time

before transferring his activities to Germany, where he spent most of 1962, playing with various groups in major German rock centers.

He returned to England late in the year to join another pioneering British blues-rock group, the Cyril Davies All Stars. (Harmonica virtuoso Davies had been co-founder of several blues groups with Korner previously.) Baldry stayed with the group until 1964, when it dissolved after Davies' untimely death. After this, Baldry formed his own band, the Hoochie Coochie Men, which featured a young London-born vocalist named Rod Stewart. Baldry recorded a number of songs with this group, some of which were released in the U.S. in 1964 by United Artists under the title *Long John's Blues*.

This group remained together for only a year before folding. Baldry quickly lined up a new roster, retaining Stewart and adding Brian Auger, Julie Driscoll, drummer Mickey Waller, and guitarist Vice Briggs. Later, Auger and Driscoll formed two-thirds of the group known as the Trinity, while Waller starred with a number of major bands, including Jeff Beck's. Briggs, after leaving Baldry's band, became guitarist for Eric Burdon's Animals. Called the Steam Packet, the new Baldry band gained favorable comment from a number of critics, but was unable to generate enough of a following to survive.

In 1966, Baldry again reformed his band, this time organizing it under the name Bluesology. Among the sidemen were a young pianist-organist-singer named Reg Dwight (later known as Elton John) and saxophone player Elton Dean. Bluesology lasted a little longer than earlier Baldry groups, but finally dissolved in 1968.

At this point in his career, Baldry took a 180-degree turn. He gave up group work in favor of singing middle-of-the-road ballads backed by a large orchestra. This quickly provided him with a series of chart hits, including "Let the Heartaches Begin," which stayed in the number one position on English charts for weeks, only being displaced by the Beatles' "Lady Madonna." Baldry earned a gold record for the single and was featured on almost all major British TV variety shows. He also sang at a Royal Command Performance. Baldry denied that his singing success was on the order of Perry Como or other pop stars of the 1950s. "I never really left my blues-rock roots," he stated. Instead, he insisted his ballad technique was closer in form to the soul singing of such U.S. performers as O.C. Smith and Brook Benton.

After achieving success in the late 1960s, Baldry started the 1970s by going back to his earlier type of performing. In 1971, *It Aint Easy*, his first LP in seven years, was issued by Warner Brothers. One side was produced by Baldry's friend Rod Stewart, and the other by Elton John. The album became an American chart hit in the summer of 1971, but Baldry wasn't able to maintain U.S. momentum afterward. *(See Animals, The; Beck, Jeff; Burdon, Eric; Jagger, Mick; John, Elton; Rolling Stones; and Stewart, Rod.)*

BALLARD, HANK: *Singer, instrumentalist, songwriter, band leader (THE MIDNIGHTERS). Born, November 18, 1936, Detroit, Michigan.*

Time was out of joint for Hank Ballard, one of the great rhythm & blues talents. His career peaked while R&B was still mainly relegated to a ghetto audience. He wrote a number of songs that became popular hits, but for other artists, with the result that his name has never become well known to the majority of popular music fans. He was still active when the color bar in pop music was fading out, but ironically received little credit for his blockbuster creation, "The Twist," which became an international craze for Chubby Checker instead of Hank.

Although born in Detroit, Hank was raised in Bessemer, Alabama, by a devoutly religious aunt and uncle. They only let him sing gospel, so he would climb out a back window at night to go hear the blues. As a teenager, he ran away from home, making his way back to Detroit.

In 1951, Johnny Otis came to the Motor City and set up auditions for local talent. *(See Otis, Johnny.)* Otis was deluged with eager performers and found a great many who impressed him, including close to a dozen who later became famous. Of those he recommended for contracts, only a few were signed, but one of these was Ballard and his backup group, the Midnighters. (Like most backup groups of enduring acts, the Midnighters' personnel changed many times over the years.) In 1954, Ballard moved into the spotlight in the R&B field with four top 10 hits: "Work with Me Annie," "Annie Had a Baby" and "Annie's Aunt Fanny," and "Sexy Ways" on King Records' Federal subsidiary.

The first two of these reached number one on U.S. R&B lists. They also became hits in England, which was then deeply interested in the American blues idiom. The overseas sales made these records million-sellers even though they never appeared on the general hit lists in the U.S. The "Annie" series (derived from the writing team of Henry Glover and Lois Mann) were among the relatively few songs recorded by Ballard that he didn't write himself. Ballard told Robert Hilburn ("Ballard: Reviving '50s R&B," *Los Angeles Times,* July 3, 1982): "When we recorded the song ('Work With Me Annie') in 1954, we couldn't even get it on the radio. We tried to tell the radio people . . . that 'work with me' just meant dancing, but they didn't believe us. The head

of the record company even got in trouble with the FCC over the song. And now they're playing it on television. It just shows you how people's attitudes have changed."

Other releases that did well for him in the R&B market in the 1950s were "Sexy Ways," "Dance with Me Henry," and "Henry's Got Flat Feet."

During the middle and late 1950s, Ballard and his group were major attractions on the R&B circuit, playing the "name" theaters (such as the Howard in Washington, D.C., and Apollo in New York) as well as clubs in almost every urban area of the country. He added two more top 10 R&B hits during those years: "It's Love Baby" on Federal in 1955 and "Teardrops on Your Letter" on King in 1959. In addition, he placed many other songs in the top 40 or top 20. Many of these were included in his LP of 1958, *Greatest Juke Box Hits.* Another of his King Records LPs of the 1950s was *Singing and Swinging,* issued in June 1959.

Hank started the 1960s with a rush, gaining two King singles high on the U.S. and English hit lists: "Finger Poppin' Time" and "Let's Go, Let's Go, Let's Go." The former sold over a million copies worldwide. Hank also wrote and performed "The Twist," a number that went over well with theater and nightclub audiences. It was not until two years later that the song and the in-place dance associated with it became an international craze with Chubby Checker as its best-known exponent. *(See Checker, Chubby.)* Ballard did gain some recognition as the twist's originator, but nowhere near that achieved by Chubby. Hank had another top 10 R&B hit in 1961, "The Float," but his career slowed down from that point on.

He remained an important album artist for a time, with new releases coming out regularly on King. These included *Mr. Rhythm & Blues* (October 1960), *The One and Only Hank Ballard with the Midnighters, Sing Along with the Midnighters* (December 1961), *Spotlight on Hank Ballard, Let's Go Again, Twistin' Fool* (May 1962), *Jumpin'* (February 1963), *1963 Sound* (April 1963), *Greatest Hits,* and *Hank Ballard.*

By the mid-1960s, though, Hank had hit hard times. He broke up his band and worked as a solo performer, usually in the smaller clubs on the soul circuit with an occasional date at a major nightspot. To younger musicians, black and white, he remained an important influence. The Allman Brothers, for instance, recall how their early bands often played Hank Ballard songs in Florida clubs in the early and middle-1960s. Quite a few other groups that were to spawn the most successful rock bands of the late 1960s similarly used Ballard material as an important part of their repertoires.

Toward the end of the decade, things began to look up somewhat for Hank. He placed several songs on the soul charts, including "How Can You Say You're Free (When You Ain't Cut Your Process Yet)" and the early '70s King LP *You Can't Keep a Good Man Down.* (A "process" is a treatment used by a black person to slick down and straighten out normally curly hair.) However, this upsurge proved temporary. By the start of the 1980s, even R&B fans had largely forgotten him. Only true buffs treasured such out-of-print LPs as *Finger Poppin' Time* on Power Records and *20 Original Greatest Hits* on the King label.

In the early 1980s, fans' renewed interest in earlier periods of rock and R&B brought new opportunities for Hank, including well-received shows at places such as the Club Lingerie in Los Angeles. When his agent had contacted him about touring again, Ballard told a *Los Angeles Times* reporter, the then Miami-based artist was dubious. "I didn't know about these shows. In fact, it was kind of a turn-off at first—the idea of singing all the old stuff again. I was more interested in getting a new recording contract and writing something new. But that feeling went away as soon as I saw how enthused the audience was. I couldn't believe it. I'd look out at the audience and see all those people and wonder what the hell they were doing at the show. My songs were big before most of them were born. But they loved it. They sang along, and they even had copies of the albums for me to sign. It made me feel great again."

He estimated that as of the mid-1980s, he had sold some 20 million records in his career, a total that could have been far greater had he scored with "The Twist." He told a reporter: "I knew the song could be a monster. But my record company didn't have any faith in it so they put it on the back side of the single. If I had had a real strong manager in those days and a record company that believed in promotion, we could have had the hit ourselves."

Still, he told the *Los Angeles Times,* despite all the disappointments, he wasn't bitter. "I'm too positive a person to think about things like that. A lot of people tell me I've been cheated and that I should feel hostile, but it's just not me. For one thing, I don't feel like a loser. I may have felt like the business passed me by at times, but I never felt out of it. I always felt I'd be back someday."

BAND, THE: *Vocal and instrumental group. Robbie Robertson, born Toronto, Canada, July 5, 1944; Richard Manuel, born Stratford, Ontario, Canada, April 3, 1943, died Winter Park, Florida, March 4, 1986; Garth Hudson, born London, Ontario, Canada, August 2, c. 1943;*

Rick Danko, born Simcoe, Ontario, Canada, December 9, c. 1943; Levon Helm, born Marvell, Arkansas, May 26, c. 1942.

When *Music from Big Pink* became a best-selling album months after its August 1968 release, it was truly the pot of gold at the end of the rainbow for the Band, a group that had almost literally wandered in the wilderness, unknown and often booed, for more than a decade. The event was an important milestone, not only for folk and rock'n'roll, but for country music as well. For the orientation of many of their compositions, such as "The Weight," was toward country music, a trend continued in later hit LPs.

Outwardly it seems strange that a group composed mainly of Canadians should become known for southern soul music. As some critics noted, the lyrics of the Band's classic "The Night They Drove Old Dixie Down" sounded as if the song were traditional from Civil War days: "Virgil Cane is the name/And I served on the Danville train/'Til Stoneman's cavalry came/And tore up the tracks again/In the winter of '65, we were hungry, just barely alive."

Almost all the members had been fans of country music in their early years. They received additional exposure to country music when they were the backup group for country-rock artist Ronnie Hawkins in the early '60s. (*See Hawkins, Ronnie.*)

Lead guitarist and songwriter Robbie Robertson recalls listening to country music when he was five years old. Not long after that, he started to learn guitar and almost simultaneously began writing music. His interests switched as he grew up, from country to big bands to rock. He left high school to play with rock groups, including one of his own, in his home area of Toronto. In the late '50s, he met Ronnie Hawkins and joined his band, the Hawks, for several years of touring through eastern and northern Canada.

Richard Manuel also grew up in a family that enjoyed country music. He started learning piano at nine, got into an argument about lessons and dropped it, and then picked it up again at 12. He had a good voice and became popular at local parties in Stratford, Ontario. He formed a band, the Revols, during high school years. Ronnie Hawkins took a liking to his style when the Revols shared a bill with the Hawks and later asked him to join the group.

Garth Hudson, born and raised in London, Ontario, recalls that his father "used to find all the hoedown stations on the radio, and then I played accordion with a country group when I was 12." He also became an excellent organist and used the organ as the central instrument in a rock group he formed in Detroit in the early 1970s after graduating from high school in Canada. In 1962 there was an opening

30

for a keyboards player with the Hawks and he moved back to Canada to take it.

Rick Danko, bass guitarist and vocalist with the Band, played guitar, mandolin, and violin before starting high school and performed with local groups before he was in his teens. Like the others, he had been a country music fan for a long time. He began listening to the Grand Ole Opry when he was five. Midway through high school, he dropped out to concentrate on music and, at 17, joined the Hawks.

The only member from the United States was drummer/vocalist Levon Helm. He listened to country stations as a boy in Arkansas, but he also liked to play blues records, particularly those of Sonny Boy Williamson, another native of Marvell, Arkansas. In high school, he formed a rock group called the Jungle Bush Beaters. Afterwards, he joined fellow Arkansan Ronnie Hawkins as a member of the backup group that worked with Hawkins at the end of the '50s. When Ronnie decided to make Canada home base, Helm agreed to remain with him.

As Robertson recalled about his days with the Hawks in Capitol bio notes, "There were only three kinds of rock then: rhythm & blues, corny white rock, and rockabilly. We played rockabilly." But the group members tired of the format. One by one, they left the Hawks and drifted south of the border to look for new directions in the United States. Their previous association caused Robertson and the others to get together to form a new group that played in small clubs along the U.S. eastern seaboard. In 1965, they got their first big break when Bob Dylan (*see Dylan, Bob*) chose them to tour with him as his backing band.

"I don't remember exactly how it happened," Robertson said. "I think we were in Atlantic City at the time. Dylan had heard of us, I guess. And we'd heard of him, but we weren't into that kind of music and I didn't really know who he was or that we could play with each other at all. Then we jammed together and a lot of things happened. We've had a great effect on each other. Dylan brought us into a whole new thing and I guess he got something from us."

The group toured all over the world with Dylan. Sometimes, though, it was a trying experience. Often, Dylan fans who hated the thought of his abandoning folk music for folk-rock took out their frustration, not by booing Dylan, but by booing and heckling his supporting musicians.

In 1966, those engagements ended abruptly when Dylan suffered serious injuries in a motorcycle accident. The band moved to Woodstock in upstate New York to be near his home. Part of their efforts included working on some new songs with him and helping him to complete *Don't Look Back,* a film

started in Europe. The Band also went to work on some new material of its own, recording it in the Woodstock Playhouse during 1967–68. Those songs formed the basis for the 1968 debut LP on Capitol.

The success of the album in late 1968 gave them a chance to be featured performers in their own right. In 1969, they gave memorable concerts in such places as San Francisco's Winterland, New York's Fillmore East, and (with Dylan, who approved of their solo efforts) in a Tribute to Woody Guthrie at New York's Carnegie Hall. The Band also was featured in the English Isle of Wight pop festival.

The group's reputation grew with each new album. Its second LP, *The Band,* was issued by Capitol in November 1969 and its third, *Stage Fright,* in midsummer 1970. The latter two included songs that became Band classics, such as "Up on Cripple Creek," "The Night They Drove Old Dixie Down," "The Rumor," "The Shape I'm In," "Strawberry Wine," "All the Glory," "Just Another Whistle Stop," and "W.S. Walcott Medicine Show."

Both LPs easily went over gold-record levels. During 1971, the group's fourth LP, *Cahoots,* was released and quickly shot up to the national top 20. Though it stayed on the charts many months it did not match the success of earlier LPs. In the fall of 1971, the Band was warmly greeted on one of its increasingly rare in-person tours. Its first California concert in a year and a half took place in San Francisco's Civic Auditorium in late November. It was one of a series of concerts that served as warm-ups for appearances at New York's Academy of Music around New Year, the source for their first live album, *Rock of Ages.* Issued in August 1972, the two-disc set earned a gold record by year-end.

During the summer of 1973, the Band was one of the featured groups at the rock concert held in Watkins Glen, New York, attended by an estimated 600,000 people, an even vaster audience than had gone to Woodstock four years earlier. On October 29, Capitol issued album number six, *Moondog Matinee,* which stayed on the charts well into 1974. The LP presented Band versions of songs made famous by such artists as The Platters, Fats Domino, Clarence "Frogman" Henry, and other "roots" performers.

At the beginning of 1974, Dylan and the Band teamed up once more for one of the landmark concert series of the '70s. The coast-to-coast tour took them to 40 cities across the U.S., where they played to standing-room–only crowds in every venue. Starting in Chicago on January 7 and ending in the Forum in Los Angeles on February 14, they played to 658,000 fans, but promoter Bill Graham announced that that only represented a tenth of the over 6 million ticket requests that came in by mail. *Before the*

Flood, the live LP made during the tour, came out on Dylan's label at the time, Arista Records, in the summer and received a gold-record award on July 8, 1974.

The Band, however, grew increasingly weary of touring after that. In fact, members were becoming restless about the restrictions of group work. They turned out new LPs from time to time, such as *Northern Lights/Southern Cross,* issued by Capitol in late 1975, and *Islands,* also on Capitol, issued in 1977 after the group's breakup.

In mid-1976, the group announced it would go out on the road once more for one last tour and then disband. The cross-country series began in the East in the fall and ended with a gala banquet and concert in San Francisco on Thanksgiving Day, 1976. The series was titled "The Last Waltz," also the title of the LP issued by Warner Brothers in spring 1978, drawn from the music of the final concert. Besides the Band, it featured a galaxy of guests, including Dylan, Van Morrison, Joni Mitchell, Dr. John, and Muddy Waters. During the summer of 1978, *The Last Waltz* movie, which Robbie Robertson helped assemble from films of the concert, came out. It still ranks as one of the most influential pop music documentaries.

After the group's breakup, Capitol continued to release LPs, mostly reissues of earlier material: the retrospective *The Best of the Band* (December 1976), *Anthology* (1978), and *Rock of Ages, Volumes 1 and 2* (both 1982), repackaged versions of the earlier releases of that work.

The members went on to new projects of their own after disbanding. Levon Helm initially toured with the RCO All-Stars and later with the Cate Brothers Band. He cut a number of solo LPs, including *Levon Helm and the RCO All-Stars* (ABC, 1977), *Levon Helm* (ABC, 1978), *American Son* (MCA, 1980), and *Levon Helm* (Capitol, 1982). He also showed impressive acting talent in such roles as Loretta Lynn's father in the hit film *Coal Miner's Daughter;* an unsuccessful country singer on *Seven Brides for Seven Brothers;* and a fighter pilot in *The Right Stuff.*

Danko did some solo work and also performed in shows with other well-known artists, in one case with Paul Butterfield and another with Band alumnus Richard Manuel and guitarist Blondie Chaplin. For a while after the Band's breakup, Manuel took treatment for alcoholism, but seemed to be coping with his problems well by the mid-1980s. Hudson's activities included composing (including the synthesizer piece "Our Lady Queen of the Angels"), session work, and production of recordings by other artists.

Robertson, acknowledged as the creative leader of The Band, became involved in writing new music and working on film projects. In the 1980 release, *Carny,* he not only acted, but also produced the movie, co-wrote the script, and assembled most of the music. Later in the decade, he worked on the score for Martin Scorsese's *The King of Comedy* and supervised production of its soundtrack album issued in early 1983.

At about the same time, most of the original Band members announced plans to reform the group and tour. Robertson, however, demurred. He told a reporter he felt that step was "probably a business decision, not an artistic one" and commented he'd "feel like a fool" to rejoin. The remaining foursome, backed by the four-member Cate Brothers Band, toured widely in the second half of 1983 and through much of 1984, playing all over the U.S. and Canada plus doing a series in Japan. On New Year's Eve 1983, the group appeared with the Grateful Dead in a radio concert from San Francisco.

The Band's numbers were certainly listenable but, perhaps due to Robertson's absence, the group couldn't recapture the magic of its earlier days. That realization may have contributed to the despondency that resulted in Richard Manuel's suicide by hanging in a motel room in Florida following a show in March 1986.

Robertson continued to add to his credits in the mid 1980s in both movies and recordings. He composed the score and co-wrote (with Eric Clapton) the song "It's in the Way That You Use It" for the soundtrack LP of the 1986 movie *The Color of Money.* He acted as creative consultant for the 1987 film *Chuck Berry: Hail, Hail Rock & Roll.* In October 1987, Geffen Records issued his first album of new songs since The Band breakup. The core band backing him on the LP *Robbie Robertson* comprised Bill Dillon on guitar, Tony Levin on bass, Abraham Laboriel on bass, Larry Klein on bass, and Manu Katche and Terry Bozzio on drums. Also sitting in on some tracks were Peter Gabriel, U2, Maria McKee, the BoDeans, and former Band musicians Garth Hudson and Rick Danko.

BANGLES, THE: *Vocal and instrumental group, all from Los Angeles, California. Original members, 1981: Debbi Peterson, born c. 1965, Vicki Peterson, born c. 1961, Susanna Hoffs, born c. 1961, Annette Zalinskas. Zalinskas replaced by Michael Steele, born c. 1960, in 1983.*

While some all-girl rock bands (as opposed to female vocal groups) surfaced in the 1970s, none were able to achieve star status, a situation many female musicians attributed to the macho attitude of much of the rock establishment. Whether because of the impact of the women's movement or simply greater skill and determination of women in rock, this taboo changed at least a little in the 1980s with the success of groups such as the Go-Gos and the Bangles.

The Bangles coalesced in Los Angeles at a time when local punk and new wave bands were dominant on the club circuit. But its music from the beginning had strong overtones of the 1960s, with critics detecting echoes of such bands as the Beatles, Byrds, Buffalo Springfield, and Mamas and the Papas. As Vicki Peterson told an interviewer: "The '60s music is the music we grew up with. We're not consciously trying to have a Buffalo Springfield or Beatles sound; it just comes out that way."

She stressed, though, that while those were influences, the group's music still reflected other impacts, both old and new. Part of the '60s interest was dissatisfaction with the rock and soul of the 1970s, when the girls were teenagers. Vicki told Divina Infusino of the *San Diego Union* (January 20, 1986): "There has been good music in every period. But there was a point in the '70s when things were pretty dismal. So you turn your radio off and your record player on. . . . Debbi and I found ourselves in groups with people who were kind of outcasts in high school. We used to get together at night at each other's house, stay up all night, and listen to Beatles records. It sounds silly. But that was the music we really liked."

Bangles members grew up in reasonably affluent middle class homes. Debbi and Vicki came of age in L.A.'s San Fernando Valley. During teen years all the eventual members were developing skills as instrumentalists and vocalists and all worked as professional musicians before the band was formed in the early 1980s. In fact, prior to that, all had been backing members of basically male rock bands. One reason why they decided to form an all-female band, Vicki said, was that "It was hard for the men, at least the ones we encountered, to accept any kind of direction or instruction from a female."

By 1981, the Peterson sisters had decided to form their own band with Debbi handling vocals and guitar and Vicki doing vocals and drums. After reading an ad placed in a Los Angeles weekly by singer/guitarist Susanna Hoffs, they contacted her to complete the group's nucleus. Later, bassist Annette Zalinskas was added. Under the name "the Bangs," the new quartet slowly worked up a following in the local bar and club circuit. Later, when a New Jersey–based band called the Bangs threatened a lawsuit over the name, the group came up with the Bangles designation.

As the Bangles became a mainstay of a movement some local critics dubbed the Paisley Underground, the band released a record titled "Getting Out of Hand" on its own Downkiddie label. Once they signed a management contract with L.A. Personal Direction (which handled such other promising groups as Oingo Boingo and Wall of Voodoo), the Bangles recorded a more ambitious collection issued on the small Faulty Records. The fact that the extended-play release sold some 40,000 copies attracted attention from larger record firms, leading to a contract with CBS in the spring of 1983. Before the album was recorded, a new bass guitarist was brought on board—Michael Steele, who, unlike her predecessor, could qualify as another lead vocalist.

First results of the new label alignment was the debut LP *All Over the Place*. The group backed it with concert dates ranging from work as club headliners to opening act for Cyndi Lauper (*see Lauper, Cyndi*) and several performances in European cities. The album didn't come close to reaching the top rungs of the charts, but it won plaudits from many critics. *Rolling Stone*'s review stated: "The Bangles have emerged to recreate that quicksilver moment when Beatlesque pop commingled with American folk in a loving embrace that could give you the shivers." In early 1985, a number of critics included the album among their ten best for 1984 and *BAM* magazine even selected it as best album of the year. Robert Palmer wrote in *The New York Times* that he considered them "one of the brightest bands of the year."

In 1985, the band started work on its follow-up LP. Most of the material was written or co-written by the band members, but there was outside material from several notable writers, including Jules Shear ("If She Knew What She Wants"), and someone called "Christopher" ("Manic Monday").

Christopher was none other than rock star Prince, who had become a strong supporter of the band. (*See Prince.*) The band members noted he had attended a number of their club concerts and informed them of his enthusiasm. "We met him afterwards on a plane trip to London and he said the wanted to write a song for us." That song became the first single and video release from the 1986 collection *Different Light* and was in the U.S. top 20 in March.

The album itself indicated an evolution of style for the band that blended '60s leanings with '80s-oriented insight. The various tracks also demonstrated the vocal attainments of all four members in three- and four-part harmonies as well as in lead-vocal abilities. Thus, Susanna Hoffs provided lead vocals on "Manic Monday," Michael Steele on "September Girls," Debbi Peterson on "Standing in the Hallway," and Vicki Peterson on "Return Post."

For the LP-supporting tour that began in March 1986, keyboards player Walter Iglehart was added. They chose a man, Susanna Hoffs told a reporter, because "it avoided the problem we might have with a girl doing it; having her wanting to join and then our having to make a decision about adding a fifth Bangle or not."

While emphatically arguing against classing the band's sound as "female," Bangles members felt they had their own style. Vicki told the *San Diego Union:* "I think that most boys pick up the guitar trying to play like Jimi Hendrix or Eddie Van Halen. I learned folk guitar first. I learned to play chords. I learned how to play rhythm guitar rather than just lead. And that makes a difference. A lot of guys can play really fast licks. But ask them to play a chord progression and stay in time, and they can't do it."

During 1986 *Different Light* became a best-seller and was still on the *Billboard* top 10 in May 1987, by which time it had sold several million copies. The album also provided the 1986 hit single "Walk Like an Egyptian," which won Best Group Performance in 1987 American Video Awards. At one point the single "Manic Monday" rose as high as number 2 in *Billboard*.

In the summer of 1987, Susanna Hoffs made her feature film debut, starring in a movie called *The Allnighter*, directed by her mother, Tamar Hoffs. (Tamar Hoffs previously had directed two award-winning movie shorts.) However, Susanna did no singing nor were the other Bangles in the film.

BASSEY, SHIRLEY: *Singer. Born Cardiff, Wales, January 8, 1937.*

An excellent voice and a dynamic style helped make Shirley Bassey one of the best female vocalists produced by Britain in the post–World War II decades. Possibly reflecting the lessons in survival learned during a far from easy childhood, her career continued to progress thanks to a flexibility that permitted her to move from her early success as a ballad singer to recognition as an interpreter of rock and soul songs as well.

Shirley was born and raised in Tiger Bay, one of the seamier sections of Cardiff, Wales. It was a working class area, not a slum, but gang fights and other problems were not uncommon. To add to Shirley's early obstacles, her father died when she was only two years old. She became interested in music before she reached her teens, practicing vocals by listening to songs on the radio or an old phonograph. There was little money at home for such extravagances as singing lessons. When she was in her early teens, she had to help support her family by working in an enamel factory.

She had confidence in her musical ability and began to sing for friends at parties and to try for show business work. In 1953, she succeeded in gaining her first professional job as a member of the chorus

of a touring show, *Memories of Al Jolson.* She joined the show in Luton, Bedfordshire, and stayed with it as it moved to many outlying British towns and cities.

After singing at small clubs and gaining minor jobs in shows during 1954, she won an audition with well-known British show business executive Jack Hylton in 1955. Impressed, he helped place her in the revue *Such Is Life* playing in London's West End. Soon after this, she gained her first recording contract and became recognized as a rising star with the success of her 1956 single, "Banana Boat Song." From then on, her voice was often heard over the airwaves in England and, by the start of the '60s, most other western nations. Among her hits were "As I Love You" in 1958 and "Kiss Me, Honey, Kiss Me" in 1959. During 1959, she switched from the Dutch Philips label to Columbia records (U.K.) with even greater success following the change. In 1960, she had hits with "If You Love Me" and "As Long as He Needs Me" and in 1961 had the English hit version of "Climb Ev'ry Mountain" from Rodgers and Hammerstein's *Sound of Music.*

By the start of the '60s, Shirley was one of the top attractions in theaters and night clubs in Europe. She also had gained considerable attention as a musical comedy singer. She had slowly won a reputation in the U.S. and moved into the top ranks of performers there with a sensationally received engagement in the Hotel Plaza's Persian Room in New York in 1961. From then on, she was a regular visitor to major clubs in America from coast to coast.

During the 1960s, she was one of the most consistent pop music album artists, turning out many LPs that gained the charts at home or abroad. In the early 1960s, she was featured on several labels in the U.S., with such albums as *Shirley Bassey* (Epic, May 1962), *Golden Sound* (MGM, August 1965), and *Spectacular Shirley Bassey* (Mercury, December 1966). In the mid-'60s, she was signed by United Artists, which remained her U.S. outlet in the '70s. Among the releases on UA were *Shirley Bassey Sings the Hits from Oliver, In Person* (February 1966), *Shirley Means Bassey* (October 1966), *Shirley Bassey Belts the Best* (May 1965), and *And We Were Lovers* (April 1967). UA also issued the 1965 soundtrack album of the James Bond film *Goldfinger* in which Shirley sang the title song, a number that became a trademark for her thereafter.

In the early '70s, Shirley's efforts won an even wider audience. In the fall of 1970, for example, she had a hit on the U.S. single charts, "Something," and one on the LP lists, *Shirley Bassey Is Really Something*. Her 1971 UA release, *Something Else,* moved on to the LP hit lists in midyear and remained on them into November. She placed more singles on the charts in the first part of the '70s, such as her 1973 hit "Never Never Never." While she continued to turn out new recordings in later years, she was better known for her concerts, which included bravura performances in the '70s and '80s at such major U.S. venues as the Greek Theatre, Dorothy Chandler Pavilion, and Universal Ampitheater in Los Angeles plus New York's Madison Square Garden. Her material ran the gamut from ballads to disco-ish numbers such as "This Is My Life." For such up-tempo songs, she demonstrated her place as one of the best "belters" in the Barbra Streisand-Liza Minelli class. Among the songs in her concerts, besides the ubiquitous "Goldfinger," were "I Who Have Nothing," "New York, New York," "Big Spender," Don McLean's "And I Love Her So," the Doors' "Light My Fire," and "The Party's Over."

BEACH BOYS, THE: *Vocal and instrumental group. Original members: Brian Wilson, born Hawthorne, California, June 20, 1942; Alan Jardine, born Lima, Ohio, September 3, 1942; Mike Love, born Los Angeles, California, March 15, 1941; Dennis Wilson, born Hawthorne, California, December 4, 1944, died off Marina Del Rey, California December 28, 1983; Carl Wilson, born Hawthorne, California, December 21, 1946.*

In rock music, the U.S. has often seemed to have a definite tilt to it, with the West Coast elevated above the rest of the country so that new trends have swept down from California to engulf the popular music scene nationally. At least, it appeared that way throughout the 1960s, when first the "surfing beat" and later the San Francisco (or West Coast) sound were this country's main answers to the stylings of the Beatles, Rolling Stones, and other English groups.

The group credited with igniting the surf music craze is the Beach Boys, a quintet of Southern California native sons who spent much of their early years under the influence of sun-soaked beaches and Pacific whitecaps. The nucleus of the group was the three Wilson brothers, who grew up in a typical one-story five-room bungalow in the middle class enclave of Hawthorne. Hawthorne, part of a string of towns that merge imperceptibly into the greater Los Angeles area, is five miles from the ocean. A good proportion of its high-school–age youth became surfing addicts from the mid-1950s on. One of the many boys who rode the waves at every opportunity in the late 1950s and early 1960s was the middle Wilson brother, Dennis.

By that time Dennis's older brother, Brian, had

entered a local college. Though Brian majored in music, he was not an active instrumentalist as was younger brother Carl, who began playing the guitar in his early teens. All of the brothers enjoyed popular music and sometimes got together to listen to records or to sing vocals accompanied by friends or relatives. The Wilsons' cousin, Mike Love, had an excellent voice and had also been a track and football star in high school. (His younger brother, Stan, was the star of the University of Oregon basketball team of 1969–71.) Also sitting in on occasion for early 1961 sessions was Brian's friend from school, Alan Jardine. During his teens, Jardine had gained some professional experience as a folksinger, though by 1961, he was concentrating on earning his degree in dentistry.

By mid-1961, the five boys' efforts had coalesced into a more or less regular series of rehearsals aimed at formation of a rock band. Brian and Alan had begun to learn the chording for rock guitar playing and Dennis was becoming more accomplished on drums. The boys became increasingly convinced that they could make it in music, but they felt they needed a special angle to set them off from all the other groups already in the field. Dennis provided this when the idea for a song about surfing came to him one day at the beach. Brian and Mike Love agreed that the thought was a good one and started working on lyrics.

Before they completed it, Alan Jardine was asked to visit a Hollywood music firm to discuss a possible folk-song recording. Jardine brought the group along and convinced the publisher he should let them do their surfing song. This proved the catalyst to make Brian and Mike complete the number, "Surfin'." The group then paid for a demonstration record at a small studio with all five singing, but only Carl Wilson providing instrumental backing. The song came out on the small Candix label and moved onto the local, then the national charts in a few months. The group's name was chosen to fit the theme of their first recording.

The quintet didn't make its first in-person appearance until New Year's Eve 1961. They were part of a bill featuring many then-popular rock artists, most of whom faded into obscurity even before the Beach Boys gained national prominence in 1963. The location—the Municipal Auditorium in Long Beach, California—was near the boys home, but this didn't ease their stage fright, which wasn't helped by knowledge that they could only play three songs.

The audience applauded this limited repertoire and the psychological lift helped inspire the group to work long, hard hours increasing their range of material and learning to play more instruments. By early 1962, they were ready for a long tour that took in most U.S. cities. The high, whining, nasal sound of their vocals, featuring a rock beat but with a definable melody line, caught on with young fans everywhere they played. In those prehippie days, the group looked the part of all-American boys, clean shaven and dressed similarly in slacks and striped short-sleeve sports shirts.

The word got around that the Beach Boys had staying power and Capitol executive Voyle Gilmore was the one to reach them first with a major recording contract. Their first singles on the label, "Surfin Safari" (1962), "Surfin' U.S.A." and "Shut Down" (1963), remained on the charts for months. Their first LP, *Surfin' U.S.A.,* came out later in 1963, winning the group their first of many gold records in 1965. The group scored another hit single in 1963 with "Surfer Girl" and made their first of many recordings about cars, motorcycles, and racing, "Little Deuce Coupe." From 1963 through 1966, almost every Beach Boys single made the charts. Hits included "Fun, Fun, Fun," "I Get Around," "Little Honda," and "Hushabye" in 1964; "Help Me, Rhonda," "California Girls," and "10 Little Indians" in 1965 plus "Barbara Ann" in 1966.

While most of the group's singles sold in the hundreds of thousands, none exceeded the million total needed for a gold record except "I Get Around" (1964) and "Good Vibrations" (released in November 1966). Their album sales were another matter, with over $1 million each for *Surfin' U.S.A., Surfer Girl, All Summer Long, Beach Boys in Concert,* and *The Beach Boys Today!* (1965), *Little Deuce Coupe, Shutdown—Vol. 2,* and *Summer Days* (1966), and *Best of the Beach Boys* (1967). *Beach Boys Party* and *Pet Sounds* didn't hit gold record levels, but were among the more popular albums of the mid-1960s.

Through the mid-1960s, the group remained among the most popular in the rock 'n' roll field. Hampered by hearing problems and also wanting more time for writing, Brian gave up touring in April 1965 and Bruce Johnston took over for him. (Glen Campbell had stood in briefly before Johnston joined.) But Brian remained an integral part of the group, contributing new songs and helping with record production. By 1966, following Brian's lead, the band showed it had the flexibility to change with the times, turning out material with more sophisticated arrangements and incorporating more thoughtful lyrics than their original surfing and automotive themes. During these years, the group won acclaim on coast-to-coast U.S. tours, at engagements throughout Europe and in the Orient, and as featured artists on most network TV variety shows. In December 1966, they displaced the Beatles as the world's number one group in England's *Melody Maker* poll.

After 1966, things slowed down. Some of this was the result of the popular music audience's natural fickleness and constant desire for new sounds. However, a more important factor was the gap between the group's creative goals and its record producers'. These arguments caused the group to refuse to release new tapes of their material they prepared in their own studio nor would they work in Capitol's facilities.

In addition to the lack of a constant flow of recordings, the Beach Boys' public appearances during the last of the 1960s were rare. In 1970, the group's contractual agreements with Capitol were concluded and they were free to bring their material out on the Reprise label. During the year, many hours were spent on recording sessions and preparing for a new personal-appearance program.

Their efforts paid off with a warm welcome in Europe during a 1970 tour. In early 1971, they were ready to see if they could gain renewed attention from U.S. pop music adherents. An engagement at the Whiskey A-Go-Go was well received but, more important, a weekend appearance at the Santa Monica Civic Auditorium won standing ovations from the sell-out crowd. Whether the group could sustain this momentum for the balance of the 1970s was a question, but they had the critics with them as indicated by selection of their *Sunflower* (released in the fall of 1970 on their new label, Brother/Reprise) as one of the best of that year.

However, the indications of creative revival proved illusory. As the 1970s went by, it became apparent that the sidelining of Brian Wilson, the band's main creative force, by an increasingly severe drug problem sharply impacted available new material. In the 1960s, the band had 20 top 20 singles, all but a handful written by Brian. For almost the entire 1970s decade, Wilson was in a world of his own. He told David Felton of *Rolling Stone* during a rehabilitation period in the mid-1970s: "I was a useless little vegetable. I made everybody very angry at me because I wasn't able to work, to get off my butt. Coke every day. Goin' over to parties. Just having bags of snow around, just snortin' it down like crazy."

The band didn't stop recording or touring, but essentially it was living on past glories. With the passage of time, though, that was enough to make it a rock'n'roll institution that still retained a fond place in the affections of rock fans around the world. The other founding members remained active in the band's concert and recording efforts, though over the years, a variety of groupings of them toured with different sidemen. Other album releases of new and old material included *Surf's Up* (1971) *Carl and the Passions—So Tough* (1972), both on Brother/Reprise, *Endless Summer* (Capitol, 1974), *Spirit of America* (Capitol, 1975), *Good Vibrations: Best of the Beach Boys* (Brother/Reprise, 1975), *15 Big Ones* (Brother/Reprise, 1976), and *Beach Boys '69 (The Beach Boys Live in London)* (Capitol, 1976).

During 1976, Brian Wilson briefly came back to work with the band as part of the group's fifteenth-anniversary milestone performances. Symbolically, perhaps, the group had its first hit single in eight years with "Rock and Roll Music" (not written by Brian), which reached number five on *Billboard* lists. Brian's recovery was short-lived, however, as was the band's new chart success.

By then, some of the founding members were eager to try their hand at solo projects. First to go that route was Dennis Wilson, whose 1977 LP *Pacific Ocean Blue* (on the band's own label, Caribou), while not a smash hit, was an above-average compilation. Dennis continued to be part of the Beach Boys, though, as did Carl Wilson, Alan Jardine, and Mike Love. The group's album credits continued with *The Beach Boys Love You* (1977) and *M.I.U. Album* (1978), both on Brother/Reprise, and a new series on Caribou (distributed by CBS Records): *L.A. (Light Album)* in 1979, *Keepin' the Summer Alive* in 1980 (a reissue of the 1964 LP *All Summer Long*), and *Ten Years in Harmony* in 1981. In March 1981, Carl's first solo album, *Carl Wilson*, came out on that label, followed in April 1983 by his second solo LP, *Young Blood*.

On July 5, 1981, the band celebrated its twentieth anniversary with a live concert from a barge anchored next to the *Queen Mary* in the harbor of Long Beach, California. The concert, called "Good Vibrations over America: 20 Years of the Beach Boys," was sent worldwide via satellite on a radio/TV simulcast. The show, hosted by Wolfman Jack, also featured Jan and Dean, America, Three Dog Night, and John Sebastian.

The band continued to tour steadily during the first part of the 1980s and was happy to welcome Brian Wilson back again in 1983. This time, Brian seemed finally to have licked the demons that had troubled him, although he still didn't like the idea of traveling much beyond his home base in Los Angeles. One date the band had made somewhat of a tradition was a free July 4 concert on the Mall in Washington, D.C. When Secretary of the Interior James Watt abruptly canceled the 1983 event in favor of a more "family-oriented" show, it became a cause celebre that incurred a reprimand from President Reagan (at whose inaugural balls the Beach Boys had played) and brought a bonanza of fresh publicity for the Beach Boys. In subsequent concerts that year, there

was increased interest among younger fans that seemed to impart new vitality to the band itself.

However, the upbeat feelings came to a halt at year-end when Dennis Wilson drowned while swimming off a boat slip in Marina del Rey, California. The *Los Angeles Times* reported: "Toxicological tests showed he had a blood alcohol level of 0.26—more than twice California's legal standard for intoxication—at the time of his death."

Though mourning their loss, the band regrouped, with Brian playing a stronger role, and continued to keep scheduled dates. There was a several-year hiatus in new album releases until *The Beach Boys* came out on Caribou/CBS in 1985. During 1985, a documentary film about the group (produced and directed by Malcolm Leo) came out. *The Beach Boys: An American Band* was a fascinating film, but failed to find an audience. In 1986, the band returned to its old label, Capitol, its roster comprising Carl and Brian Wilson, Mike Love, Alan Jardine, and Bruce Johnston. During that year, Capitol issued the LP *Made in the U.S.A.* A highlight of the live concert work during 1986 was the presentation of two July 4 shows, one in Texas and one in New York City. The Texas set was part of Willie Nelson's Farm Aid II benefit show in Austin. The New York appearance was part of festivities celebrating the rededication of the Statue of Liberty, with the group performing on the deck of the battleship *U.S.S. Iowa* for the Secretary of the Navy and other dignitaries. In both shows, the band debuted a new song by Jardine, "Lady Liberty."

In early 1988, the group was inducted into the Rock'n'Roll Hall of Fame and took part in the New York concert that was part of the festivities.

BEATLES, THE: *Vocal and instrumental group, songwriters, record-company executives, actors. All born Liverpool, England: John Lennon, born October 9, 1940, died New York, New York, December 8, 1980; Paul McCartney, born June 18, 1942; George Harrison, born February 25, 1943; Ringo Starr, born July 7, 1940. Group disbanded 1971.*

How many superlatives in the English language have been used to describe the Beatles? There is no doubt that this group ruled rock'n'roll for almost the entire decade of the '60s. Their recordings, original compositions, and movies have had dramatic impact on the directions taken by the entertainment field and are likely to continue to do this even if the surviving members of the group, now going individual ways, should cease creating new material altogether.

The first step in the evolution of the group came in 1956, when 16-year-old John Lennon and 14-year-

37

old Paul McCartney met while performing with different groups at a rock concert at Liverpool's Woolton Parish Church. Both were in the early stages of learning to play rock guitar and soon spent much of their spare time together working on techniques. Before long, they added a third associate, Paul's school friend, George Harrison. Like the others, a child of a working class family (his father was a bus driver), Harrison looked to music as an escape from the usual cycle of leaving school in midteens to work at an unskilled job.

With various other additions of teenage musicians, the boys began playing at small clubs and coffeehouses whenever they could find engagements. Usually they received no pay, just the chance to perform before an audience. By the late '50s, calling themselves the Quarrymen, they were beginning to find a local following in a small club in one of the back streets of Liverpool.

By the time they gained their first relatively high paying job—$25 a week per musician—in Hamburg, Germany, in 1960, they had gone through several name changes—from Moondogs to Moonshiners to Beatles to Silver Beatles. For the Hamburg job, they went back to Beatles for their group name. At the time, they were five in number, the other two being drummer Pete Best, who already had an underground following in England, and guitarist Stuart Sutcliffe, who had attended art school with John Lennon.

The Beatles won favorable notice from German fans and were able to command a little more attention when they returned to England. One of their growing number of fans praised the group to Brian Epstein, whose father ran a TV and record store in Liverpool. Epstein went to hear them, decided they were potentially a sensational act, and gained a contract as their manager. Epstein, who is considered the main driving force behind the band's rise to fame, was nicknamed "the fifth Beatle" before he died in 1967 at the age of 32.

Under Epstein's direction, the Beatles made a demonstration record that Brian took to major English record firms. After a turndown by English Decca—certainly one of the biggest mistakes by a record company in modern history—he went to Abbey Road (since made famous by a million-selling LP title), home base for England's largest recording firm, EMI, and gained them a contract in early 1962. By then, Stu Sutcliffe had left, returning to live in Hamburg in 1961. (He died of a brain hemorrhage there the following year.) Before the group made their first EMI recording (on the Parlophone label), they changed drummers. The final cog in the Beatles machine was Ringo Starr, whom Lennon, Harrison, and McCartney had met during a return engagement

at Hamburg's Star Club in the first four months of 1962. Starr, born Richard Starkey, son of a Liverpool house painter, was playing with Rory Storm's Hurricanes at the time. In August 1962, he agreed to move from that band to the Beatles.

The group's first recording session at EMI's Abbey Road studio took place under the direction of George Martin September 4–11, 1962. On October 5, "Love Me Do," their first single, was released. The group caused tremendous excitement among rock fans when they debuted the next month on Granada TV's "People and Places" show in Manchester. Their first single moved onto the charts and was quickly joined by the next one (released on January 12, 1963), "Please, Please Me," which by February 16 was their first number one hit.

During February 1963, the Beatles went on their first national tour of Britain as part of the "Helen Shapiro Show." They also made their first national TV appearance on BBC-TV's "Thank Your Lucky Stars." The group went on one record-breaking tour of England after another that year including one in March with Tommy Roe and Chris Montez plus one in May and June with Gerry & the Pacemakers and Roy Orbison. In October, they toured Sweden. The group hit the charts regularly with such singles as "From Me to You" (released April 11), "She Loves You" (August 23), and "I Want to Hold Your Hand" (November 29). As 1963 came to a close, they were undisputed stars in their homeland and were asked to take part in a Royal Variety Performance for the queen on November 4.

In February 1964, the group repeated its European triumphs with a sensationally received first U.S. visit. Besides appearing twice on the "Ed Sullivan Show," the group performed in concert at the Coliseum in Washington, D.C., and Carnegie Hall in New York. They met an even more frantic outpouring of fans' delight in a five-week tour of the U.S. and Canada during August and September. In March, the boys started work on their first film, *A Hard Day's Night,* and John Lennon's first book, *In His Own Write,* was published. The group maintained its grip on the hit charts with such singles as "Can't Buy Me Love" (released March 20), "A Hard Day's Night" (July 10), and "I Feel Fine" (November 27) plus such LPs as *A Hard Day's Night* (July 25) and *Beatles for Sale* (November 27).

In 1965, besides tours of Continental Europe, England, and, in September, the U.S. (including a sell-out performance at New York's Shea Stadium), the group completed work on their second film, *Help!,* which had its Royal Premiere at the London Pavilion on July 29. The group's hits for the year included the singles "Ticket to Ride" (released April 9), "Help!" (July 23), and "Day Tripper" backed with

"We Can Work it Out" (December 3) plus the LP's *Help!* (August) and *Rubber Soul* (December.) On June 24, Lennon's second book, *A Spaniard in the Works,* was published.

In 1966, the Beatles slacked off a little on personal appearances, spending only the summer months on the concert circuit. The schedule, though, included shows in Germany, Japan, Manila, and, in August, the U.S. The group's output included the major singles hits "Paperback Writer"/"Rain" (released June 10) and "Eleanor Rigby"/"Yellow Submarine" (August 8) plus the LP *Revolver* (August 5).

With "Paperback Writer" and "Eleanor Rigby," the Beatles demonstrated their ability to grow in lyrical content and musical creativity. They were starting to make social commentary rather than simply sing of the conventional boy-girl romantic themes. Their earlier songs had already changed the course of rock, providing a combination of melody that could stand on its own if divorced from the driving rock beat, and words of penetrating insight, even if merely dealing with teenage romance or love in general. As their new songs provided increased subtlety (most, as before, being written by Lennon and/or McCartney, though Ringo and Harrison would occasionally contribute original songs of their own), they helped widen the intellectual boundaries of rock music and thus made it a much more flexible art medium than it had been earlier.

By 1967, the Beatles had become tired of the concert grind. There also was an increased trend toward individual work by group members. This had already started in 1966, when Lennon made his solo acting debut in the film *How I Won the War* and McCartney worked on the soundtrack music for Boulting Brothers' *The Family Way.* The group did no tours, though it was represented on the hit charts by such singles as "Penny Lane"/"Strawberry Fields Forever" (released February 17), "All You Need Is Love"/"Baby You're A Rich Man" (July 7), and "Hello Goodbye"/"I Am the Walrus," plus the LP *Sergeant Pepper's Lonely Hearts Club Band.* The latter, a million-seller before it reached dealers' shelves, was hailed by critics as one of the best LPs of the decade and one that demonstrated tremendous growth by the group.

1967 was marred by one of the Beatles' few failures—the TV show "Magical Mystery Tour," which was scripted, cast, directed, and edited by the group. Its soundtrack LP still sold in the millions, however. Ringo, accompanied by his wife Maureen, went to Rome to work on the film *Candy* starring Richard Burton and Marlon Brando. In February 1968, Ringo made his solo TV debut on Cilla Black's TV series. Harrison spent part of the 1967 summer in Hollywood with his wife, Patti. While there, he became a friend of Indian sitar player Ravi Shankar and wrote a number of songs, including "Blue Jay Way" about the house he rented there.

In early 1968, Harrison devoted his time to composing, arranging, and recording his own music for the soundtrack of the film *Wonderwall.* Later in 1968, the soundtrack album was released on Apple Records, the new recording company organized by the Beatles that year. Distribution of Apple Records was handled by EMI, with Capitol (the Hollywood subsidiary of EMI) providing U.S. marketing. Harrison also was instrumental in the much-discussed journey of the group to India to take a Transcendental Meditation course at the Maharishi's Academy.

"Hey Jude"/"Revolution," the Beatles' first single released on their Apple label (August 30, 1968) proved to be one of the major hits of the year. Besides *Wonderwall,* LPs on Apple that year included the double-LP *The Beatles* (also called "the White Album") and the controversial *Two Virgins* by John and Yoko Ono, who became a couple after the breakup of John's first marriage to Cynthia Powell.

Rumors of the impending dissolution of the group were rife in early 1969, though the members denied this and noted they were working on still more recordings. But Ringo started work on a new movie, *The Magic Christian,* starring Peter Sellers; John and Yoko went on concert tours of their own; and Paul McCartney, after marrying Linda Eastman in March, was also beginning to do separate work on his own and with his wife. March also was the month for John and Yoko's wedding on the isle of Gibraltar and for the release of the *Yellow Submarine* LP, which gained the Beatles their fourteenth gold-album award. (The animated film of that title, released July 17, 1968, was a financial and critical success in Europe and North America.)

Indicative of the separate roads of the artists was the increasing flow of individual albums on Apple. In May 1969, George was represented by *Electronic Sound* and John and Yoko by *Unfinished Music No. 2.* During the year, John and Yoko's appearances spanned "lie-ins" in Canada and the Bahamas and the debut of their Plastic Ono Band (other members being Klaus Voorman, Eric Clapton, and Alan White) at a September 13 rock'n'roll revival concert in Toronto, Canada. (*See Clapton, Eric.*) John and Yoko's 1969 recordings included the singles "Give Peace a Chance" and "Cold Turkey" and the LPs *Wedding Album* and *Live Peace in Toronto 1969.* As a group, the Beatles presented *Abbey Road* (released September 26) and the single "Something" (the first George Harrison composition to be the A side of a Beatles single) backed by "Come Together." In October, Ringo started work on his first solo LP, *Sentimental Journey.*

The year 1970 started with an exhibition of John's lithographs (called "Bag One") at the London Arts Gallery. The show caused a furor and was temporarily closed for being obscene until eight of the lithographs were removed. Ringo and wife Maureen spent much of the early part of the year in Hollywood, appearing at the U.S. premiere of *Magic Christian* and later attending the Las Vegas stage show of Elvis Presley, whose early records had greatly influenced the Beatles' style. Recordings released by the Beatles as a group were limited to the single "Let It Be"/"You Know My Name" (March 6) and the LP *Let It Be* (May 8); both sold in the millions. The LP title was that of the group's third film, which premiered in May in New York and London. In the same month, John and Paul received Ivor Novello Awards for two of their 1960s hits, "Get Back" and "Ob-La-Di Ob-La-Da." For the most part, the four artists went their own ways, with John and Yoko represented by the single "Instant Karma," Ringo by *Sentimental Journey,* and Paul McCartney by his first solo LP, *McCartney.*

In 1971, the group officially announced it had broken up, though in terms of output, it had ceased to exist in 1970. Some of the members appeared together, most notably Harrison and Starr, who worked concerts to help the Bengali refugees from East Pakistan. Ringo won favorable comments for his country-oriented LP *Beaucoups of Blues,* recorded in Nashville in June 1970 with steel guitarist Pete Drake and other session men, and released in early 1971. Meanwhile, McCartney and wife Linda came out with their debut album, *Ram,* one of the major hits of 1971. By midyear, their single "Admiral Halsey" was also a gold-record winner.

Both Harrison and Lennon won considerable critical acclaim for individual recordings in 1970 and 1971. Harrison had one of the top singles of 1970 with his "My Sweet Lord" and gained a gold record for his LP *All Things Must Pass,* released on Apple in late 1970 and still on the charts in the summer of 1971. Lennon's *Imagine* was number one in the U.S. in October 1971 and was hailed as one of the ten best LPs of the year by many reviewers. As 1971 came to a close, Harrison and Bob Dylan were featured on the three-LP *Concert for Bangladesh* recorded live with Leon Russell, Ringo Starr, and Eric Clapton at a special New York fundraising concert. (*See Dylan, Bob; Russell, Leon.*)

As the decade of the '70s went by, the chances of the four former band members abandoning their separate careers seemed increasingly remote. Beatles fans, though, continued to dream that the Fab Four still might reunite. That scenario became an impossibility with the assassination of John Lennon in front of his home on December 8, 1980.

Of course, there was no lack of new albums in the 1970s and 1980s by Capitol and EMI, most containing reissues of already available recordings, but some providing material not released before. Those LPs include *The Beatles 1962–1966* (1973), *The Beatles 1967–1970* (1973), *Rock'n'Roll Music* (1976), *Love Songs* (1977), *Live at the Hollywood Bowl* (1977), *Rarities* (1980), *Rock'n'Roll Music, Volume II* (1980) and *20 Greatest Hits* (1982). Releases on other labels included: *Live! at the Star-Club in Hamburg, Germany, 1962* (Ling, 1977) and *The Decca Tapes* (Circuit, 1979). (*See Harrison, George; Lennon, John, and Yoko Ono; McCartney, Paul; Peter and Gordon; Starr, Ringo.*)

BE BOP DELUXE: *Vocal and instrumental group. Members in mid-1970s: Bill Nelson, born in Wakefield, Yorkshire, England, c. 1948; Charles Tumahai, born New Zealand; Simon Fox, born England; Simon Andrew Clarke born England, 1957.*

Paced by lead singer Bill Nelson, one of the best new rock guitarists to come to the fore in England in the 1970s and also a superlative songwriter, Be Bop Deluxe for a while seemed destined to join bands such as Yes and Pink Floyd as supergroups of the period. The band turned out some of the finest progressive rock albums of the '70s and was a top headline group in England and Continental Europe, but fell short—by just a bit—of gaining a mass following in the U.S. Perhaps had Nelson, discouraged by some of the crosscurrents in the pop field in the late 1970s, not decided to break up his band, it might have established itself as one of rock's all-time great groups.

Nelson, who taught himself to play guitar at an early age in his northern England hometown of Wakefield, commented: "My playing is more emotional than technical, but you do have to have technique to express yourself. I don't feel limited. To me, any approach that produces something new and interesting from the instrument is valid and worthwhile.

"When I was starting out, I played in youth clubs around Wakefield for free ice cream and bottles of pop. We played Shadows, early [Rolling] Stones, Chuck Berry, Muddy Waters stuff. Then I joined the best band in the area, the Teenagers [in the mid '60s] although I was the only teenager in the group. I was at art college then and played the cabaret-club thing. I got fed up with it and started a three-piece band called Global Village. We were into multimedia stuff then with projectors, poetry, mime, dancing, costumes, and lights." During that time, the late

1960s, he played on two locally produced albums, *A to Austr* and *Astral Navigation.*

In 1970, he helped form a religiously oriented rock band called Gentle Revolution and stayed with it until mid-1971, when he decided to go out as a solo artist. Aided by some friends, he recorded his first solo album, *Northern Dream,* in a Wakefield studio. The album got enough airplay for Harvest Record executives to become interested in him and sign him to the label, a subsidiary of the large EMI organization.

By then Bill had already formed and reformed his backing group, beginning with one called Flagship, which he disbanded in favor of a new group that took the name Be Bop Deluxe. The latter comprised Nelson and Ian Parking on guitars, Rob Bryan on bass, and Nicholas Chatterton-Dew on drums. Four days after that group formed, the bid from Harvest came. The label wasn't happy with the first demo tapes and suggested the band rehearse and do live work for a while before starting to record.

Considering that Be Bop became known for its staid stage presence with Nelson typically wearing three-piece suits during concerts, the band's original visual approach was mind-boggling. At the time, the members affected weird costumes, makeup, and rouge. Nelson told Dave Schulps of the English magazine *The Music Gig:* "We were all working day jobs and thought it would be fun to try and do something outrageous in the evening. It was before the New York Dolls and things like that. A couple of guys didn't have the physical stature to pull it off, which made it weirder still. There was a very short, dumpy guy with eyeliner and space boots who looked very strange. It was just supposed to be a total assault on the audience up North. They weren't prepared for this sort of thing. And it worked. We got a reputation and people used to come just to see what we were wearing at first."

A year later, the band got the go-ahead from Harvest to record its debut album. The LP, *Axe Victim,* was issued in England in 1974. Nelson's dynamic guitar licks and a certain freshness in his original songs caught the ear of more than a few fans. That trend was helped by a U.K. tour in support of the band Cockney Rebel. Nelson seemed to pick up performing skills at a much faster rate than the rest of the band, with the result that a regrouping took place at tour's end. Initially this new team comprised Nelson, two former Cockney Rebel musicians, and drummer Simon Fox. (Fox, then a well-known session player, previously had been in the band Hackensack.)

Still dissatisfied, Nelson retained Fox and auditioned possible replacements. The only one that made the grade then was bass guitarist Charlie Tum-

ahai. Charlie, born in New Zealand of Tahitian and Maori parents, had moved to Australia and taken up surfing before joining the band Mississippi. Nelson was still looking for a keyboards player as time approached to record the second Harvest album. He decided to handle the keyboards himself, but then remembered a musician named Simon Andrew Clarke, whom he asked to join.

Though Clarke, who had impressed Nelson while with the group Mother's Pride, was available, he couldn't come aboard in time to learn the new material. Thus Nelson, Tumahai, and Fox formed the nucleus for *Futurama,* released in July 1975. That album was well received by critics in the U.K. and also won some nods in the U.S. when it became the band's debut release there on Capitol Records, EMI's U.S. affiliate.

The next album, *Sunburst Finish,* issued in January 1976, represented Clarke's debut as a recording member of the band. The quartet that was to make up Be Bop Deluxe for the rest of its life span was now complete (though rhythm guitarists such as Mickey Close often were added for concerts). The album served notice that the band was one to be reckoned with from a creative standpoint, something affirmed by the group's initial U.S. and Canadian tour in the first part of the year. In the fall, the band came back for a second North American tour in support of its third U.S. release, *Modern Music.* That album's tracks included such notable songs by Nelson as "Fair Exchange" and "Ship in the Night" (a top 20 singles hit in the U.K.) The album debuted in the U.K. top 10 and also made its way onto U.S. charts for a number of months. During 1976, the band also had a U.K. hit with its extended play album, *Hot Valves.* At year-end, many critics chose *Modern Music* as one of the year's ten best rock releases.

In 1977, Harvest/Capitol released a two-disc live set, *Live! In the Air Age.* During its third U.S./Canadian tour, now as a headline act, the group presented its special light and image-projection show that had previously made it one of the top concert acts in Europe. Though the show added dimensions to the live performances, the band itself seemed to lack the exuberance of its previous visits when it had outshone groups such as Blue Oyster cult and the Patti Smith Group. In Los Angeles appearances with Tom Petty and the Heartbreakers, the Petty band stole the spotlight itself as an opening act.

Perhaps some of the band's sluggishness reflected Nelson's restlessness with the material he had turned out in recent years. He told interviewers, in fact, that the "Live!" support tour marked the end of one phase of the Be Bop saga and he would come back with new rock directions the next time.

In truth, he kept his promise. The next album, *Drastic Plastic*, was different. Its thematic elements built on the synthesizer-aided work of artists such as Brian Eno and David Bowie. It had a new wave sound, though the science fiction, high technology aspects weren't newly adopted ones for Nelson, a fan of these subjects since childhood.

Objecting to type-casting in an article written for a British magazine, Nelson stated: "It seems quite fashionable nowadays to refer to anything remotely adventurous as 'new wave' and anything older than six months as 'old wave.' Quite a healthy attitude, I must admit, though it does have a few unpleasant side effects, one of which is the obvious division of music fans into two separate camps.

"The new wave has always been with us in one form or another, though its voice has often been too small to be heard. Musically literate and forward-thinking people such as a Brian Eno . . . John Cale, Bowie . . . Robert Fripp and even such aging luminaries as Peter Townsend, among others, have contributed in their own way to an exploratory feel in rock for quite some time now.

"The ability to change and progress is in all of us, but we're not going to extend ourselves very far musically if we restrict our listening to what is deemed fashionable. There's just too much good music to fall into that trap."

Despite *Drastic Plastic*'s excellent material and its warm critical welcome, it proved off-putting to the band's growing following, which was still becoming accustomed to the group's earlier, more mainstream rock songs.

Nelson, however, did not intend to replow old ground. In August 1978, he surprised fans and reviewers alike by announcing he was breaking up Be Bop. He gave as his reason his feeling that after recording six albums together, the band "was in danger of becoming institutionalized" and the time was right for a change. In 1979, Harvest/Capitol released a retrospective album, *The Best of . . . and the Best of Be Bop Deluxe.*

Meanwhile, Nelson formed a completely new group called Bill Nelson's Red Noise. Its debut album, *Sound-on-Sound*, was issued on Harvest in 1979. The act was billed as Bill Nelson and Red Noise into the early 1980s. Later in the decade, Nelson focused on a career as a solo artist, turning out collections such as the 1986 LP *On a Blue Wing*, issued in the U.S. on Portrait Records. In that project, Nelson performed all-original material and also was in charge of production.

BECK, JEFF: *Singer, guitarist, songwriter, band leader (Jeff Beck Group; Beck, Bogert and Appice). Born Surrey, England, June 24, 1944.*

First Jeff Beck Group, founded 1967, included Rod Stewart, born London, England, January 10, 1945; Mick Waller, born London, England, September 6, 1944; Ron Wood, born London, England, June 1, 1947. In 1968, Mick Waller left with Tony Newman and Nicky Hopkins added; Newman was later replaced by Ron Waller. Second Jeff Beck Group, formed in 1971, included Bob Tench, Max Middleton, Clive Chaman, Cozy Powell. Third Jeff Beck Group, formed fall 1972, included Max Middleton, Kim Milford, Tim Bogert, Carmine Appice. Group became Beck, Bogert and Appice at start of 1973.

In a career spanning over two decades, Jeff Beck has retained his reputation as one of the pioneering figures in English rock. Though he often took "holidays" from pop music, causing rumors that he had retired from the field, he continued to confound the critics by not only returning to the concert grind, but also drawing new fans from succeeding generations along the way. As he told Dennis Hunt (*Los Angeles times*, August 25, 1985): "The secret of longevity is staying out of this business for long periods of time. This business will consume you. The people will consume you. They'll eat you alive and spit the bones out. If you hang around long enough, they'll get you. But if you're not there, they can't get you."

Beck was interested in music from his childhood days when he sang in his local church choir and took music lessons on several instruments. He could play excellent guitar by the time he finished the British equivalent of high school and spent more than a few hours as a sideman in various English groups. Then he went on to attend Wimbledon Art College in London for four years and considered taking up something other than music for his life's work.

However, his peers in the music field respected his talent and persuaded him to spend more time playing rock 'n' roll and composing. This led to Beck's involvement as lead guitarist in the Yardbirds, who starved for a time in London, but then gained considerable attention after a six-week tour of the U.S. in early 1966. (*See Clapton, Eric; Yardbirds, The.*) Beck (who replaced Clapton) stayed with the group for about a year and recorded several albums with them. Some of these featured Beck compositions. Before, during, and after his Yardbird days, Beck sat in with other rock groups, particularly those concerned with the blues, which gained considerable attention among youthful British musicians during the 1960s. (Of course, in England, the blues had long found many adherents who followed the careers of legendary American bluesmen much more closely than the majority of nonblack American pop music fans.) Beck's guitar playing or arrangements can be discerned on 1960s recordings of such groups as the

Savoy Brown Blues Band and several of John Mayall's organizations. (*See Mayall, John.*)

Beck decided to form his own group in 1967. Lead singer Rod Stewart (*See Stewart, Rod*) cowrote several of the songs featured on the group's first LP (*Truth* on the Epic label), including "Let Me Love You" and "Rock My Plimsoul." A blues buff like Beck, Stewart reflected the importance of such artists as Sam Cooke and Richie Havens and the compositions of Holland and Dozier (founders of Invictus Records) in his musical outlook. Stewart, in addition to vocals, handled guitar and five-string banjo on some Beck Group songs.

Guitarist Waller came from the ranks of top sidemen in London. After attending Greenwood Grammar School and London University, Waller devoted most of his time to backing sessions of such acts as the Rolling Stones, Animals, Little Richard, and Georgie Fame. Bass guitarist Ron Wood started his musical career at 10 playing washboard in a "skiffle" group with his two brothers. By the time he finished Ealing Art School and Ruislip Manor Art School, Wood could also handle the guitar and harmonica in excellent fashion.

Truth was on the charts for many weeks in 1968, though it never made the very top levels. Meanwhile, the Beck Group won critical accolades for their initial U.S. appearance at New York's Fillmore East in 1968. The *Village Voice* commented: "The Jeff Beck Group caused something like a mild furor. Their full-grown English hard-rock, driving and together, caught everyone off-guard. The audience cheered and shouted, would hardly let them off, even when lead singer Rod Stewart pleaded for his voice. If their debut at the Fillmore is any indication, they're going to be one of the hottest groups around."

The praise grew more extravagant when rock piano star Nicky Hopkins (a sessionman on *Truth*) joined Beck to make it a quintet in the fall of 1968. He also played on the group's second album, *Beck-Ola* (issued in August 1969), which sold well in England and the U.S. and was generally considered one of the best albums of the year.

However, as Hopkins stated in his biographical notes for Capitol Records when he joined Quicksilver Messenger Service, things did not go as well offstage as on. "In October 1968, I joined Jeff Beck, who had then recently done an immensely successful tour of the U.S. Unfortunately, Jeff turned out to be totally unsuited to be leading a successful band and there was trouble with his management and road management, too. I quit his band in June [1969] and a couple of days later the others left one by one!"

Though rumors persisted that Beck was trying to assemble a new group to work on new album material after 1969, nothing appeared on disc as the 1970s got underway nor were any new tours scheduled. But by 1971, Jeff was in evidence again with the Jeff Beck Group II, featuring Bobby Tench on lead vocals and Max Middleton on keyboards. Playing rock with R&B and jazz elements, they recorded the LP *Jeff Beck Group/Rough and Ready,* issued in the U.S. on Epic Records in 1971. That band, whose members also included Clive Chaman on bass and drummer Cozy Powell (*See Emerson, Lake and Palmer*), toured with Jeff and helped lay down tracks for the 1972 Epic release *The Jeff Beck Group.* In the fall of 1972, Jeff again reorganized his band to what is sometimes referred to as Jeff Beck Group III with Max Middleton, Kim Milford, and two former Vanilla Fudge bandsmen, Carmen Appice and Tim Bogert. In early 1973, that was trimmed to a trio of Jeff, Appice, and Bogert, which recorded the hard-rock 1973 LP *Beck, Bogert and Appice.* Among the high-powered tracks on that album were "Why Should I Care," "Livin' Alone," and a driving version of Stevie Wonder's "Superstition."

The trio seemed to have the capability to become one of rock's landmark groups, but well-publicized problems and arguments led to its dissolution.

Again, not much was heard of Beck's whereabouts for a while, but he came forward again in 1975 with a stunning all-instrumental LP called *Blow by Blow.* In these tracks, Beck avoided the typical three-chord blues structure in favor of a polyphonic approach using multiple overdubs. He had moved from conventional rock to high-decibel hard rock to jazz-rock or fusion stylings, a direction he continued to explore in his next LPs, *Wired* (issued by Epic in 1976), *The Jeff Beck Group Live with Jan Hammer* (Epic, 1977) and *There and Back* (Epic, 1980). Hammer, whose synthesizer blended deftly with Jeff's guitar chords in both of the last-named LPs, also joined Beck on a memorable series of concerts often spotlighting the excellent musicianship of Stanley Clarke and John McLaughlin.

As the 1980s began, Beck apparently felt it was time for another hiatus. Once more he did little in the way of concertizing and had no LPs for several years. The main reason for his withdrawal from rock this time, he told Dennis Hunt, was a feeling that new wave had degraded the rock scene. "New wave was a standing joke among me and my friends, the dinosaurs. It was amazing that junk lasted as long as it did. It finally faded when everybody realized some melody was necessary. But all that took me off the scene for a while. It wasn't my time."

But by 1984, his time had come once more as he, Robert Plant and Jimmy Page of Led Zeppelin and Nile Rodgers hit *Billboard's* top 10 as the Honeydrippers, reviving Phil Phillips's soulful 1959 classic "Sea of Love" and putting out the platinum mini-LP *Volume I* on the Es Paranza label. (*See Zeppelin, Led.*)

In 1985, he recorded the solo LP *Flash*. It featured Rod Stewart on "People Get Ready," which was also issued as a single. During the year, Jeff was once more gracing concert stages across Europe and the U.S.

He told Hunt he was glad to be back. "I can't seem to stay away, can I? I'm like a junkie. I miss the insanity of this business. Being involved in it is like a constant jungle adventure. The lions are always just around the bend. But I do miss it when I'm away from it for a while. I wish I didn't.''

BEE GEES, THE: *Vocal and instrumental group. Barry Gibb, born Douglas, Isle of Man England, September 1, 1947: Robin Gibb and Maurice Gibb, both born Manchester, England, December 22, 1949.*

A recurring theme in rock music is the seemingly endless series of personnel changes during the career of almost every group, successful or not. Part of this can be traced to overfamiliarity—the tensions that arise from spending too much time together on planes, trains, or buses while moving from hotel to hotel during seemingly endless cycles of one-night stands. As the history of the Bee Gees shows, it's just as easy for closely related individuals to grate on each other's nerves under the pressures of the pop music grind as it is for musicians who started working together as casual acquaintances.

Because the core of the Bee Gees was three brothers ("Bee Gees" or "B.G.'s" stands for Brothers Gibb), it took quite a while before the almost predictable dissensions split the group apart in the late 1960s. The boys began performing together when the twins, Robin and Maurice, were seven and their older brother Barry only nine, making their first public appearance at a Saturday morning amateur talent show in the local Gaumont British Theatre in their hometown of Manchester.

The Gibb family emigrated to Australia in 1958. A few months after settling in Brisbane, they appeared on a radio show called "Talent Guest" on station 4KQ. They played a number of local dates over the next year and a half before debuting on Brisbane's ABC-TV channel. The response was good enough to win the brothers their own weekly TV series.

The country's teens and subteens quickly made the Bee Gees one of their favorites. The sound of the group, through, was much less frenetic than those of the hard-rock groups that dominated U.S. hit charts of the period. From the start, the songs of the Bee Gees were on the melodic side with more emphasis on the lyrics than in much stateside rock. (Words and lyrics were mainly composed by one, two, or all three of the brothers.)

Australia-based Festival Records signed the youngsters in late 1962 and released their first single, "Three Kisses of Love," in January 1963. The song made the top 20 in Australia. Succeeding singles, such as "Timber" in 1963 and "Peace of Mind" and "Claustrophobia" in 1964, gained the top 10. During 1965 and 1966, the Bee Gees (by then based in Sydney) became the hottest group in the country, gaining number one spots on the charts for such songs as "Wine and Women," "I Was a Lover and a Leader of Men," and "Spicks and Specks." The group won top honors in voting for best compositions of the year in both 1965 and 1966 and, in 1966, won the National 2UE Award as Australia's Best Group of the Year.

The time seemed ripe for the group to expand their reputation internationally. The decision was made to return to England in February 1967. There, they signed a management agreement with Robert Stigwood and the NEMS company. They also added a fourth member, drummer Colin Petersen (born Queensland, Australia, March 24, 1946), whom they met soon after reaching London. Petersen had started in show business as a child actor, performing the title role in the film *Smiley* when he was nine. He later starred in such movies as *The Scamp* and *A Cry from the Streets*.

The foursome spent a good part of their early months together recording a series of new songs in sessions that sometimes went around the clock. Their United Kingdom debut was a sellout week-long Easter-holiday stage show at Saville Theatre in London, where they shared billing with Fats Domino and Gerry & the Pacemakers. During this period, they expanded to a five-man group with the addition of Vince Melouney, considered Australia's best rock guitarist. Melouney had worked with the group as a sideman during some of the Bee Gees' Sydney recording sessions. Melouney, who played for a time with local Sydney group Billy Thorpe and the Aztecs left to form his own blues combination and then gave that up to move to London. Melouney didn't stay with the Bee Gees too long, but he did work on their first LP released in the U.S., *The Bee Gees' First*.

The LP was issued by New York–based Atco Records in July 1967 (Stigwood having signed U.S. distribution rights over to Atco in April of that year) as a follow-up to their first hit single in the American market, "New York Mining Disaster—1941." During 1967, the Bee Gees made a number of personal appearances in many parts of Europe and the U.S., while their record sales moved into the multimillion bracket. From mid-1967 through most of 1969, the group scored a continuing series of hits with such original compositions as "Holiday," "I Can't See Nobody," "Massachusetts," "World," "First of May," "I Started a Joke," and perhaps their biggest-selling record of all (until their *Saturday Night Fever* material), "Words."

For most of this time, the Bee Gees were a four-man combination—the three Gibb brothers and Petersen. However, as they became increasingly important in the pop music world, the members began to wrangle over the direction the group should take. In the spring of 1969, matters reached the point that the twins were outspokenly in disagreement with each other. Finally, Robin left to try for a career as a solo performer, beginning auspiciously with a well-received single, "Saved by the Bell," but making only minor progress thereafter.

The remaining threesome stayed together for a while, but they too had a hard time reconciling their varied ideas. At the end of August 1969, the Stigwood organization tersely stated: "Barry and Maurice Gibb have terminated their association with drummer Colin Petersen who will cease to be a member of the group." Petersen responded by stating he felt as much legal right to the group name as the Gibbs and that he was considering forming his own band under the Bee Gees title. (During 1969 RSO issued the group's *Odessa* LP.)

The only result of all this was the gradual reduction of the Bee Gees' influence in rock music. For most of 1970, not too much was heard from the various alumni. Finally, the three Gibb brothers agreed to combine forces again and showed they still could score as a group with the hit single "Lonely Days." In 1971, the brothers recorded a new LP and returned to the concert circuit. By then, their repertoire included another gold-record song, "How Can You Mend a Broken Heart," which reached number one on U.S. charts the week of August 7 and stayed three weeks. The group had two albums on the charts in 1971: *Trafalgar* and *2 Years On*. In 1972, there were three chart singles, "Alive," "My World," and "Run to Me," plus (on RSO, the label Robert Stigwood had started in the late 1960s) the album *To Whom It May Concern*. In August 1973, RSO's anthology *Best of the Bee Gees: Volume 2* (a sequel to Atco's 1970 top-seller *Best of the Bee Gees*) showed up on the hit lists. But then the Gibb brothers hit a dry spell. (*See Gibb, Andy.*) Their 1973 release on RSO, *Live in a Tin Can*, only rose as high as 69 on *Billboard* charts, and their 1974 album, *Mr. Naturally*, was a disaster. Despite the latter's poor sales, it contained a fine R&B-flavored track, "Down the Road," that was a departure from the soft-rock style the group had favored before.

It proved a harbinger of things to come. For the next album, *Main Course*, the brothers included a healthy leavening of R&B disco-style tracks and it paid off with a series of hit singles: "Nights on Broadway," "Fanny," and "Jive Talkin'" (number one on *Billboard* lists the week of August 9, 1975). The LP, of course, was also a best-seller. Barry told the group's authorized biographer, David Leaf: "When we got around to *Main Course*, we finally got into a way of thinking that suited the three of us, what we wanted to do, and what we were going to do all the way. We were always split about that ever since the breakup. We could never really decide where we were going after that. And that's why all the music came out wrong."

When Stigwood switched from Atlantic to Polydor Records for distribution, the group faced another potentially traumatic situation because their previous producer, Arif Mardin, was an Atlantic staffer they could no longer use. But they soon became accustomed to new producer Richard Perry and the result was another hit album, *Children of the World*, in 1976, which provided the hit single "You Should Be Dancing" that made number one on the *Billboard* list the week of September 4. Also on the charts in 1976 was the album *Bee Gees Gold, Volume I*. Compared to those, their 1977 LP, *Here At Last*, was a step backward.

During 1977, the trio was preparing to record a new studio album when Robert Stigwood asked them to write some songs for a new movie his organization was involved in that would star John Travolta. Five days later, they had come up with "Stayin' Alive" and "How Deep is Your Love," songs that were to have major impact on audiences viewing the eventual film, *Saturday Night Fever*. In coming weeks, the brothers wrote more songs for the soundtrack, some of which they would record themselves plus some intended for other artists. The results were nothing short of sensational. Both movie and soundtrack album rank among the most successful entertainment vehicles of the 1970s.

A taste of what was to come was gained with release of the first single from the soundtrack, the Bee Gees' own "How Deep Is Your Love." Issued in advance of the film, it made *Billboard* lists in late September and moved upward until it reached number one the week of December 24, 1977. It stayed in the magazine's top 10 for 17 straight weeks, the longest period of any single since *Billboard* had begun the Hot 100 in 1958. This was followed by still more number one soundtrack hits—"Stayin' Alive" reached that pinnacle the week of February 4, 1978, as did "Night Fever" the week of March 18, 1978, the latter staying at number one for eight weeks. At one point, the Gibbs had five songs on *Billboard*'s top 10—"Stayin' Alive," "Love Is Thicker Than Water" (not a soundtrack song, but written for younger brother Andy Gibb), "Emotion" (recorded for the soundtrack by Samantha Sang), "Night Fever," and "How Deep Is Your Love." Another Bee Gees song, "If I Can't Have You," provided a chart hit from the soundtrack LP for Yvonne Elliman. The *Saturday Night Fever* LP was a massive hit, staying at number one on the charts for months at the start of 1978 on the way to record sales in the neighborhood of 12 million worldwide. In the Grammy awards for 1978, the Bee Gees walked off with five trophies for their part in the movie/album project.

The years immediately after 1978 proved anticlimactic. The Bee Gees were represented on the charts by such albums as *Spirits Having Flown* (1979), *Bee Gees Greatest* (1979), and *Livin' Eyes* (1981), but their new material seemed tame compared to their ground-breaking material of the 1975–78 period.

Although they had a gold record disc in 1983 with "The Woman in You," the brothers Gibb for the first part of the '80s concentrated on solo projects. Barry, for instance, produced records by Barbra Streisand and Dionne Warwick, Robin made some solo recordings and Maurice wrote film scores. The three reunited for a new album in late 1987. Released in late 1987, *ESP* (issued in the U.S. by Warner Brothers) proved a shocking failure. It never went past 100 on the *Billboard* list and by early 1988 had disappeared from the *Billboard* 200 altogether. (The debut single, "You Win Again," never got higher than number 75). They took some solace from the fact the album did well in Europe and Australia.

Maurice told Stephen Williams of *Newsday* ("Bee Gees' New Album Stumbles Off Billboard Chart," *Los Angeles Times*, January 8, 1988, Part VI, p. 11), "We knew we'd have some resistance. But we didn't expect people completely not wanting to play a Bee Gee record. And not even hearing the record [referring to the almost complete lack of U.S. airplay] to judge it." Warner Brothers had tried hard for them, he said. "They just can't understand why they're getting this lockout on a Bee Gees record."

BENATAR, PAT: *Singer, songwriter, band leader. Born New York, New York, c. 1953.*

A rock singer with a first-rate soprano voice might seem a contradiction in terms, but Pat Benatar managed the combination well enough to become one of the superstars of the 1980s. Despite the inherently sweet qualities of her voice, she avoided ballads almost entirely, at least up to the mid-1980s, in favor of high-intensity, fast-paced rock'n'roll. In part, that reflected a lifelong self-consciousness

about her diminutive size (5 feet tall and around 90 pounds at maturity) and, as a teenager, a desire not to get pushed around by members of the opposite sex.

She told Dennis Hunt of the *Los Angeles Times* [July 12, 1981]: "I like being tough on stage. I don't like being sweet. I can't sing about love in the afternoon among the flowers and sunshine. I like to sing about things that make me mad, like bad relationships. People might think I've been treated like some of the women in some of those songs. No way. If I was treated that way, I'd inflict serious injury on the guy. There'd be blood in the streets."

Ballads, she agreed, require the performer to convey a sense of vulnerability. She told Hunt: "They make me feel like I'm exposing my whole self. I hate that feeling. That's why I sing the hard, fast stuff. You can put a wall up around yourself on those songs. You can't do that on the ballads."

Benatar came by her soprano voice naturally. She was the daughter of an opera singer and her family pointed her in the same direction even when Patricia Andrzejewski (her original name) was a child. Though she was a tomboy in school, at home she was pressured to conform to the style expected of a possible future prima donna. In her late teens, she revolted against the many hours of vocal training required for an operatic career and gave up opera in favor of marriage to Dennis Benatar. In the early 1970s, she followed her husband to Virginia, where he was serving in the U.S. Army for two and a half years. She first got a job as a bank teller. Eventually that seemed too tame and she found work as a vocalist in bars and hotel lounges.

In 1975, she moved back to New York, this time intent on finding a place in the pop music field. For several years, she gained experience as a rock singer, mostly doing cover versions of other artists' songs, but occasionally trying out original material as well. She followed the usual course of sending demo tapes around to record-company executives with little to show for it. Her fortunes took a turn for the better when she began singing at the New York night spot Catch a Rising Star. Club operator Rick Newman decided she had much more potential than a club artist and took over as her manager. Within a short time, he helped arrange a 1978 recording contract for her with British-based Chrysalis Records.

The first result of that was the 1979 debut LP, *In the Heat of the Night*. With savvy promotion by the label and the success of the singles releases "Heartbreaker" and "We Live for Love," Benatar rapidly attracted a sizable following among young rock fans. The album was on U.S. charts during the last months of 1979 and was still well within the *Billboard* top

100 at the end of 1980. The RIAA certified the album platinum during 1980, a status exceeded by all of her albums issued between 1979 and 1985.

Pat followed this with the 1980 album *Crimes of Passion*, whose songs all were written or co-written by her. The album was in the U.S. top 5 by year-end, having shipped platinum. It provided her with two of her most successful singles: "Hit Me with Your Best Shot" (number 9 in *Billboard* the week of December 20, 1980) and "Treat Me Right." In the Grammy awards for 1980, Pat won the coveted trophy for Best Rock Vocal Performance, Female, for the *Crimes of Passion* album. By now, she had established herself as both a best-selling recording artist and one of the most dynamic concert performers.

Her third Chrysalis album, *Precious Time*, certainly was a cut below her first two releases and was roundly condemned by many rock critics (some of whom suggested that she was a female counterpart of Peter Frampton and that she would fade into obscurity as he had after brief meteoric success). But her fans paid little attention to critical comment, making the 1981 LP one of the top-sellers of the year. It provided two more charted singles: "Fire and Ice" and "Promises in the Dark." At year-end, Pat had all three of her albums on the charts at once. She won a second straight Grammy award: Best Rock Vocal Performance, Female, for the single "Fire and Ice."

Pat's marriage to Dennis Benatar had broken up long ago. By 1981, she lived in a spacious home in the Los Angeles area's San Fernando Valley with eventual husband Neil Geraldo (lead guitarist of her band, its chief songwriter, and producer of *Precious Time*). She indicated to Hunt the hope that the relationship would in time be fulfilled by a family. "I would like to be a mother someday. I'm looking ahead. I try to stay straight and I don't use drugs and I don't get crazy and I don't go over the edge. When I have kids, I don't want them to think their mother is some rock'n'roll weirdo.

"I can't live for rock'n'roll. This will be all over one day and I'll have nothing to show for it but some money and some dumb memories. When I'm 50, I don't want to be sitting there with no kids, wondering about what went wrong. I think about that a lot and it scares me."

Though she expressed a few doubts about her future in some 1981 interviews, there was no evidence of a letdown in 1982. Her 1982 release on Chrysalis, *Get Nervous*, had a consistency as good as her first album's and was in the top 10 and rising by the end of the year. The debut single, "Shadows of the Night," was a top 10 hit in early winter. (Other songs released as singles from the LP were "Little

Too Late" and "Looking for a Stranger.") "Shadows of the Night" won still another Grammy for her, again as Best Rock Vocal Performance, Female.

Her 1983 album release, *Live from Earth*, was on the charts the latter part of the year into 1984. It produced one of Pat's most striking singles to that point, "Love is a Battlefield," a top 10 hit by year-end. When the 1983 Grammy winners were disclosed on network TV on February 28, 1984, that single brought Pat a fourth straight award for Best Female Rock Vocal Performance.

While recording material for her next album in 1984, Pat and Neil announced they were expecting their first child in March 1985. The 1984 album, *Tropico*, was another best-selling offspring, spawning the top 10 single "We Belong." Helping it along, as was the case with all of her previous hit singles, was a music video that received wide play on the MTV channel as well as other music video shows.

After the arrival of the Geraldos' child, named Haley, Pat suggested she didn't intend to settle for too small a family. She said: "Haley had forced us to look at life with a new perspective. At this rate, we're going to be making some pretty crazy records down the road with four or five kids running around the house writing on the walls."

Meanwhile, she and Neil were busily making plans for new musical efforts. After the child was born, they turned to completing a seventh studio album for Chrysalis and also decided to do their first would tour in over three years, starting in early 1986. The new album, *Seven the Hard Way*, came out in November 1985 and was in the U.S. top 20 in early 1986. Singles from the album were "Invincible" and "Sex as a Weapon," the latter inside the top 40 in the U.S. by the end of 1985. At the time of *Seven the Hard Ways'* release, it was estimated sales of Pat's previous recordings worldwide exceeded 25 million copies.

The band lineup for the 1986 concerts comprised (besides Neil on lead guitar) Donnie Nossov on bass guitar, Charlie Giordano on keyboards, and Myron Grumbacher on drums. During 1987, she began work on material for a new LP due out in mid-1988.

BENSON, GEORGE: *Singer, guitarist, songwriter. Born Pittsburgh, Pennsylvania, c. 1943.*

Ranked as one of the best jazz guitarists of the 1960s, George Benson through his concert work and intensive recording became a big fish in what was, unfortunately, a relatively small pond. In the mid-1970s, he combined jazz themes with elements of R&B to reach the larger pop music audience, becoming, in short order, a superstar in the mold of an earlier jazz great, Nat "King" Cole. Some jazz purists naturally cried "sellout," but Benson retained his integrity as a jazz artist while delighting countless millions of less demanding listeners and, perhaps, along the way swelling the ranks of true jazz fans.

Though George was known as essentially an instrumentalist during his jazz-only phase, his early efforts ranged from R&B to doo-wop. He showed musical talent at a very early age, learning to play his first stringed instrument, the ukelele, at eight. Soon after, he made his public debut, playing for coins in a candy store. He told an interviewer: "I'm originally from Pittsburgh, but I've been living in New York since 1963. I did my first record [for RCA] back in '54 or '53 [when he was only ten], then later I sang with a vocal singing group [that performed R&B/rock material along the lines of the hit group of that period, Frankie Lymon and the Teenagers] in the late '50s. Then I formed my own rhythm & blues group, which featured organ, baritone, and trombone. I've always had funny combinations in my groups because I've never realized a set pattern for a band. I believe if you can play, you can play with anybody. It can be a whistle, if the cat can play."

Before forming his own group, however, Benson put in a lot of dues-paying time. For a while in the early 1960s, he played guitar with a variety of amateur bands in Pittsburgh, having decided to concentrate on guitar after leaving the singing group. This was when he first became interested in jazz styles, inspired by records of a number of well-known jazz artists. "I could tell by the first records I heard by each one of them that they were very vital to music. [Grant] Green because of his lyricism, [Wes] Montgomery because of his knowledge of the instrument, his approach to harmony and theory, Hank Garland for his fire and technique and Charlie Christian because he could swing so hard and not lose his feeling."

At 20, in the mind-1960s, he joined a group led by Jack McDuff. McDuff mostly performed R&B, but did include some jazz numbers. Benson noted: "R&B was natural to me, but the jazz tunes involved a lot of chord changes and I had to be more alert to play them; I began to like the challenge of inventing something new, as opposed to playing just for feeling."

Soon after joining McDuff, Benson became a featured player and, in 1964, the LP *New Boss Guitar of George Benson with the Brother Jack McDuff Quartet* was released on Prestige Records. In 1965, he left McDuff to form his own band comprising Lonnie Smith on organ, Ronnie Cuber on baritone, and Phil Turner on drums. He soon had an agreement with Columbia Records that resulted in the albums *It's Uptown* (1965) and *George Benson Cookbook* (1966), with the latter also spotlighting Lonnie Smith.

George turned out a steady flow of new albums on a succession of labels, either as featured soloist or in collaboration with famed jazz performers such as Stanley Turrentine, Hank Crawford, Esther Phillips, and Freddie Hubbard. (*See Phillips, Little Esther.*) His 1960s solo albums included *Giblet Gravy* (1967) and *George Benson Goodies* (1968) on Verve (MGM) plus *Shape of Things to Come* (1968), *Other Side of Abbey Road* (1969), and *Tell It Like It Is* (1969) on A&M Records.

At the start of the '70s, he aligned himself with the jazz label CTI, an association lasting until the middle of the decade. His debut on that label was the widely acclaimed *Beyond the Blue Horizon* (1971), which included the number "The Gentle Rain" that had come out as a single in 1970. He followed in 1972 with the even more notable *White Rabbit*, which was arguably one of the year's best jazz releases. The album was nominated for a Grammy and, while it didn't win, the nomination was a harbinger of things to come. The lead track of the LP also came out as a single on CTI. George's remaining studio albums on the label were *Body Talk* in 1973, *Bad Benson* in 1974, and *Good King Bad* and *Benson and Farrell* in 1976. Also issued in 1976 on CTI was the LP *Live in Concert/Carnegie Hall*. CTI singles in the mid-1970s included "Supership" in 1974 and "Summertime" in 1976. Benson's joint LPs on CTI included *Giant Box* with Don Sebesky, *Sugar* with Stanley Turretine (1970), and, with Freddie Hubbard, *Straight Life* in 1970, *First Light* in 1971, and *Sky Dive* in 1972.

Up to this point, only Benson intimates knew he had once been a singer. His work on CTI, for instance, was almost totally instrumental. He recalled: "While I was at CTI, they didn't want me to sing, they just wanted me to play the guitar. A lot of people never knew I could sing, because I just wasn't given the opportunity to express myself vocally."

That all changed dramatically when he signed a recording contract with the more commercial-market–oriented Warner Brothers. The company teamed him with producer Tommy LiPuma and the two agreed there should be some vocal work by George on his label debut. Actually, there were plenty of instrumental tracks on the forthcoming album, but it was the vocal contributions that helped make *Breezin'* a sensational success. Benson said: "When we went into the studio to record tracks for *Breezin'* I never thought it would become such a great album. Tommy was easy to work with because he was open for ideas. Since he knew I wanted to sing, it was easy when I mentioned doing some vocal tracks. He said, 'Why not!'"

The album was issued in early 1976 as was the first single, "This Masquerade." Single and album became two of the unexpected blockbusters of the year. Both eventually rose to top levels of the charts, where the LP remained throughout 1976 and into 1977, achieving multiple-platinum status.

At the end of 1976, Benson was literally showered with awards, recognition that was to continue unabated for years to come. These include winning the Grammy in three categories: Record of the Year for the single "This Masquerade," Best Pop Instrumental Performance for the album Breezin', and Best R&B Instrumental Performance for the "Theme from Good King Bad," a track from a CTI album. He also was named number one artist in many polls: in Billboard for Best Jazz LP, Best Jazz Artist, and Top Pop Instrumentalist, Duo/Group; in Record World for Top New Male Vocalist and Top New Male Vocalist, R&B; in Cash Box for Top Jazz LP, Top Jazz Soloist, and Top Jazz Vocalist; and in the 1976 Rock Music Awards for Best New Male Vocalist of the Year. He also was named number one Jazz Guitarist in the 1976 down beat readers poll and Best Jazz Guitarist of the Year in the 1976 Playboy music poll as well as in the Rolling Stone music poll.

Benson followed up Breezin' with the equally successful In Flight album issued by Warner Brothers in January 1977. This too quickly passed gold-record levels, and though it didn't earn any Grammy awards, it was nominated in several categories. At year-end, Billboard called it the Most Charted Jazz Album and named Benson Jazz Artist of the Year and In Flight the Best Jazz Album. Significantly, Billboard also named Benson number one Box Office Artist for (under-6000–seat) Auditoriums. Record World voted George Top Instrumentalist and In Flight the Best Instrumental Album. Cash Box proclaimed Benson number one Jazz Crossover Artist to R&B and named George Benson and Joe Farrell as Top Duo. The 1977 Performance magazine poll named Benson Best Jazz Artist of the Year as did the Rolling Stone poll. Benson's success with Breezin' caused other labels to reissue some of his earlier recordings: Columbia issued Benson Burner and Polydor released Blue Benson.

George's first live album on Warner Brothers, Weekend in L.A., recorded at the Roxy nightclub on Los Angeles' Sunset Strip, was issued in early 1978 and was certified platinum in May. The two-disc set spawned the hit single "On Broadway" (the 1978 Grammy winner for Best R&B Vocal Performance, Male).

When the LP's RIAA certification was reported, Benson was performing before capacity crowds at the Belasco Theater in New York. Originally scheduled for five nights, the series was extended for an additional four performances to satisfy the response from New York–area fans.

At those concerts, as at all his shows, Benson presented a great deal of instrumental work, not relying on vocals as his main forte. In an interview with jazz critic Leonard Feather, Benson stressed he would not downgrade his guitar work in favor of singing, as Nat "King" Cole had done with his keyboard playing. "If my voice was as special as Nat Cole's, I suppose it would be possible. I'm glad people think so highly of my voice, but I just had the good fortune of being associated with some very good songs.

"I wouldn't stop playing for two reasons. First, it would be like a man who hooked people on a certain thing and made them happy with it and got them used to it, then suddenly took it away from them. Second, I've devoted 26 years of my life to the guitar, cultivating it and bringing people along with my instrumental ideas and they responded and said 'Hey man, give us more.' First it was 100,000 fans, then half a million, a million. I don't think I should ever chop that off. Glen Campbell did the right thing; when he got his own television show, he didn't stop playing.

"As for the people who became interested in my voice first, I think in turn I can get them involved with my playing. In any case, it breaks up the monotony. The early Nat Cole albums, when he played some and sang some, were a lot more interesting, as wonderful as his voice was. No matter how great anyone is, monotony can set in. That's why people go to sleep at classical concerts."

Benson's goal of maintaining consistently high standards on his albums appeared to pay off in continued good rapport with record buyers and concert goers. While the frenetic reception to his first Warner Brothers LPs tapered off a bit for later releases, they were still going past gold and platinum totals in the mid-1980s. The albums Livin' inside Your Love, issued in January 1979, and Give Me the Night, released in mid-1980, both were multiplatinum sellers and helped him win three more Grammy awards in the 1980 voting: Best R&B Vocal Performance, Male, for the Give Me the Night LP; Best R&B Instrumental Performance for the "Off Broadway" track; and Best Jazz Vocal Performance, Male, for the track "Moody's Mood." The track "Dinorah, Dinorah" on Give Me the Night also netted Quincy Jones and Jerry Hey a Grammy for Best Instrumental Arrangement. (See Jones, Quincy.)

The record output from Benson slowed a bit in the 1980s, but those he did turn out went over well with the pop music audience. Those LPs, all certified gold by the RIAA, were *The George Benson Connection* (issued in the fall of 1981) *In Your Eyes* (mid-1983), and *20/20* (1985). The 1983 album brought George the Grammy for Best Pop Instrumental Performance for the track "Being with You." The track "Beyond the Sea" from *20/20* was a nominee for the 1985 Best Jazz Vocal Performance, Male.

In 1986, besides working on a new solo album planned for 1987 release, Benson began discussing a collaborative effort with another famous guitarist, Earl Klugh. Most of their joint recording sessions were held in December 1986 and January 1987 and the LP came out on Warner Brother label in mid-1987.

Discussing his future goals with William Kinally of *Jazziz* magazine ("George Benson & Earl Klugh Collaboration," July 1987), Benson said, "First of all, I want an acting career. I'm not giving up the guitar; I'm adding to things I'm doing simply because people don't think I can do it and I keep saying I can."

To Kinnally's comment that he'd like to see an album of songs like Benson's version of "Beyond the Sea" on *20/20*, Benson responded, "Working on it now. Big band. Big bands!" *(See Toto.)*

BERRY, CHUCK: *Singer, guitarist, songwriter. Born St. Louis, Missouri, October 18, 1926.* *

"It's called rock now; it used to be called boogie-woogie; it used to be called blues; used to be called rhythm & blues; and it even went through a stage of what is known as funk. . . . Names of it can vary, but music that is inspiring to the head and heart, to dance by and cause you to pat your foot, it's there. Call it rock, call it jazz, call it what you may. If it makes you move, or moves you, or grooves you, it'll be here. The blues rolls on, rock steady knocks, and they all are here now and I think they all will be here from now on."

So said Chuck Berry in an interview with columnist Ralph Gleason in the late 1960s. Surely, no one had a better right to evaluate the past, present, and future of rock'n'roll. The two people who stand out head and shoulders above all the stars of the early days of rock are Berry and Elvis Presley. And, while Elvis may have had greater mass appeal, he was al-ways solely a performer, while Berry, as a songwriter, ranks as one of the greatest creative influences on modern pop music.

A number of articles have stated that Berry was born in California, but in his 1987 autobiography, Chuck claimed St. Louis as his true birthplace. Little Charles Edward Anderson Berry grew up in the Elleardsville section of town, but it was hardly a black ghetto upbringing; his boyhood was spent in a pleasant, brick, one-family house on a street with neatly tended lawns and large shade trees.

He didn't take an active interest in music until his teens, when he began to learn the guitar. Even then, it was mainly a hobby and he did little more than figure out how to play some songs for his own enjoyment. However, the range of material he got into included jazz, swing, and blues. Blues seemed well suited to young Berry's outlook in the mid-1940s, when he found himself in reform school with a three-year sentence for an amateurish try at robbery. Returning home in 1947, he worked at odd jobs and then found work as an assembler at the General Motors Fisher Body plant. Eventually, he learned to be a hairdresser and cosmetologist by taking a night course at the Poro School of Beauty Culture in St. Louis.

In the early 1950s, married and the father of two children, he devoted an increasing amount of his spare time to music as a supplement for his income from hairdressing. He started playing in small clubs, then formed a trio with two St. Louis musicians, pianist Johnny Johnson and drummer Ebby Harding. The group performed regularly at the Cosmopolitan Club in East St. Louis and, by the start of 1955, had gained a considerable reputation with black audiences as one of the best bands in town.

By then, Chuck had started writing original songs, both words and music in most cases, and was eager to improve his status in the music field. He saved money to go to Chicago, arriving in the spring of 1955 with a sheaf of songs in his pocket. He had hardly unpacked before he went to listen to some of the famous artists performing in the city's jazz and blues clubs. After hearing part of a show by Muddy Waters' group, he asked for the chance to sit in and Muddy obliged. Waters was amazed at the guitar techniques of this unknown—though it must be remembered that Chuck had been playing for pay in St. Louis for well over half a decade. Muddy promptly recommended that Chuck audition for Leonard Chess, president of Chess Records. *(See Waters, Muddy.)*

Berry brought Chess tapes of two songs, "Wee Wee Hours" and "Maybellene". Of the two, Berry thought the first was by far the best; "Maybellene" was intended as a comic take-off, based on the hair

---

* Over the years, some half a dozen combinations of day, month, year and even place of birth were ascribed to Berry, with some of that conflicting data issued on his own press releases. He was said to have been born in San Jose or St. Louis on January 15 or 18 or October 15, 16 or 18 in either 1926 or 1931. Until his sixtieth birthday celebration, he never affirmed which, if any, was correct, but in 1986 it seemed to be settled as St. Louis on on October 18, 1926.

cream of the same name. Chess liked "Maybellene" better and had Berry record it with a bigger beat, with "Wee Wee Hours" as the B side. The success of the record was achieved with the aid of Alan Freed, who played it on his New York radio show, then the most important rock program in the country. Whether Freed had a lot to do with revamping the song or whether he basically was cut in on its publishing royalties in return for his help is hard to say at this point. The official records list Freed and Russ Fratte as cowriters. Whatever the chain of events, it is certain that "Maybellene" rapidly became the most popular record Freed had ever played for his listeners. (*See Freed, Alan.*)

Within weeks, the record was rolling up impressive sales from one end of the country to the other. Chuck Berry jumped from nowhere to national stardom along with the disc. He followed "Maybellene" with an even more dynamic number, "Roll over Beethoven (and Dig These Rhythm & Blues)," which rose to the top 10 on R&B lists and also made the national charts in 1956, influencing not only millions of teens in America, but their counterparts the world over. In the 1960s, the Beatles earned one of their few gold records for a song they didn't originate when they paid homage to Chuck with "Beethoven."

Starting in 1956, Berry proved to be an even more impressive artist on stage than on records. Crowds clamored to see him in all parts of the country. He complied with a midyear tour that started and ended in New York; he was on stage 101 nights in 101 days. One of these engagements was in an Alan Freed show at the Paramount Theatre in Brooklyn, New York. Berry had always done a lot of dancing and moving around, but in that show he came up with an innovation called the duck walk in which he flashed across the stage, knees bent, with a fluid grace that left audiences breathless. The walk (performed while he played the most complex patterns on his electric guitar without missing a beat) became his trademark that was always certain to activate waves of applause and cheers from rapt onlookers.

During the second half of the '50s, Berry was the headliner on bills that featured such other greats as Carl Perkins, Bill Haley and the Comets, and/or Little Richard. And, with almost every new tour, Berry had one or two new hit compositions to add to his repertoire. In 1956, he turned out such songs as "Too Much Monkey Business" and "No Money Down"; in 1957, his name gained the charts for "School Days," "Rock'n'Roll Music," and "Oh Baby Doll"; in 1958, there were "Sweet Little Sixteen" and "Johnny B. Goode," the latter often a best-selling item for top country and western artists. In 1959, he wrote "Almost Grown." Besides these,

there were many other rock standards from Berry's pen—"Memphis" and "Reelin' and Rockin'" to name just two.

As the end of the '50s approached, it seemed everything was going Berry's way. New waves of young rock stars were playing his songs and glorifying him as one of the pivotal figures in rock history; he was a wealthy man and had moved his family into a beautiful mansion in the main part of St. Louis; and Chuck Berry's Club Bandstand was one of the centers of entertainment in St. Louis.

Then huge headlines in papers across the nation blazoned his indictment on a morals charge. The hatcheck girl in his club went to the police and accused Berry of taking her from New Mexico to St. Louis for immoral purposes. She also stated she was only 14 years old. Testimony at the trial, which dragged on for two years, indicated she had actually been working as a prostitute when Berry first met her and apparently had come with him willingly. He, in turn, maintained his main interest in her was to learn Spanish for songwriting purposes—a language the girl spoke fluently.

It was not a pretty case, but professional entertainers and athletes caught in circumstances hardly more attractive have sometimes gotten off with only a long probation period. Berry was finally sent to the federal penitentiary at Terre Haute, Indiana, in 1962. The incident had a drastic impact on Berry's life. When he was released in 1964, his family had separated from him, his Club Bandstand had closed, and the patterns of rock music had changed. He emerged in good financial shape, but he was sullen and bitter. While fellow musicians previously had commented on his relaxed mood after shows, when he would exchange banter or join in a jam session, now they talked about his aloofness and his dark moods.

Despite the scars, Chuck went about picking up the pieces of his career. He hadn't achieved many hit singles in the 1960s, but his albums continued to sell, including *After School* (October 1958), *One Dozen Berrys* (also October 1958), *On Stage* (early '64), *Greatest Hits* (June 1964), and *St. Louis to Liverpool*. His Chess albums soon included *Golden Decade* and *Golden Hits* (both April 1967). He came back to the Fillmore many times after his debut in Bill Graham's rock palace in early 1967. He had retained his ability to charm an audience, but his new songs didn't gain the response of his classics of the previous decade. He did place some singles on the charts, such as "Promised Land," but none came near the top 10.

Chuck's new project in the late 1960s was an amusement park and country club complex in the small town of Wentzville, Missouri. When he was not on the road, he stayed in a secluded house on the grounds and could often be found mowing lawns or supervising his employees. When Mercury Records offered him a lucrative contract in the late 1960s, he saw the chance to help defray expenses of his amusement park and went with them for several years. Tracks were all prepared in his own studio and delivered complete to the company for such LPs as *Concerto in B. Goode* (September 1969). He also put out *Chuck Berry in Memphis* (October 1967) and *Chuck Berry at the Fillmore Auditorium* (November 1967). After his contract with Mercury expired at the start of the 1970s, he returned to his old Chess Records alignment. His next LPs, *Back Home Again* and *San Francisco Dues*, both made the national charts.

In March 1972, Chuck passed another milestone in his career when he debuted as the featured attraction in a major Las Vegas hotel. The two week engagement met with a response easily as enthusiastic as that greeting Elvis Presley's first Las Vegas show a few years earlier. It was a good omen signalling a Berry renaissance in the '70s equal to that fashioned by Presley after his Vegas gig. Later in the year, while Chuck was performing at the Arts Festival in Manchester, England, his set was taped; one song, My Ding-a-Ling (stated to be co-written by him and Dave Bartholomew), was issued as a single in the fall. The song proved to be Chuck's first number one single, reaching that point on *Billboard's* pop chart the week of October 21, 1972, and staying there another week. It was ironic, though, that a novelty tune far inferior to dozens of classics by Berry outsold all his other singles. The song was included in the 1972 Chess LP, *The London Chuck Berry Sessions*. Mercury also got in on the action with the 1972 hit album *St. Louis to Frisco to Memphis*. Chess continued to issue Berry albums of both new and reissued material into the mid-1970s, including *Chuck Berry's Golden Decade, Volume 3* and *Chuck Berry*, both in 1974. The latter spotlighted the singing of his daughter, Ingrid. Other Chess LPs available in record stores during the 1970s were *Rockin' at the Hops* and *Chuck Berry Is on Top*, originally issued in France and previously available in the U.S. as imports.

Chuck continued to do intensive touring throughout the 1970s and into the mid-1980s, sometimes giving exuberant performances and other times drawing boos for shows that consisted of only a handful of songs. Apparently, his approach to each concert depended on financial arrangements with promoters. Reportedly Chuck had a fee structure covering all aspects of what he would do, including an extra charge for him to include his famous duck walk.

In the later 1970s, Chuck signed with Atlantic Records, which issued the LP *Rockit* on its Atco label in 1979. In the 1980s, he was represented on record racks by many reissues of his early material on various labels, including MCA, which had bought the old Chess Records catalog.

During 1986, plans were made for special celebrations in honor of Berry's sixtieth birthday, which he now stated was October 18 (*see footnote*). Two special concerts were planned, one in the Fox Theatre in St. Louis, Missouri, and another shortly after in New York City. Staging of both shows was arranged as part of the work on a documentary of Berry's career directed by Taylor Hackford (whose credits included *An Officer and a Gentleman* and *White Nights*). Titled *Hail! Hail! Rock 'n' Roll*, it was released in 1987 by Delilah Films in association with Universal Pictures and MCA Home Entertainment.

Joining Chuck for the St. Louis shows (an early and late set) were Keith Richards of the Rolling Stones and old friend Johnny Johnson, whose Johnny Johnson Trio had included Chuck in the 1950s. Johnson recalled for Bob Hilburn of the *Los Angeles Times* (October 26, 1986): "Chuck came to me one day and said, 'Johnny, what do you think about changing the name to the Chuck Berry Trio?' I said, 'Hey, you got it because you are a go-getter and I think we will go much further with you out front.' Yes sir, Chuck was a real go-getter."

St. Louis arrangements were marred by arguments between Richards and Berry about the way certain songs should be played; at one point Richards stalked off stage for a while. The two seemed to resolve their differences as the evening went by and the late-show audience cheered lustily for the finale, in which Berry was driven on stage in a red Cadillac convertible while singing his 1957 hit, "School Days."

Backstage after the concert, Chuck helped cut his birthday cake, but as usual made few comments to reporters. His daughter Ingrid told press members not to take outward appearances too seriously. "He's a dear man inside, though he doesn't often let others see it. He's very private, but very generous and I can tell he is touched by what is happening to him now even if he won't say it himself."

The film of Chuck's sixtieth anniversary concert, *Chuck Berry: Hail! Hail! Rock 'n' Roll*, won deserved praise from most critics (including those from both the *Los Angeles Times* and *The New York Times*) after its release in October 1987. In the film he brushed aside discussion of such incidents as a teenage robbery involvement, Mann Act conviction, and tax payment hassles with the IRS, but he did cover those in his 1987 book *Chuck Berry: The Autobiography*.

BETTER DAYS: *See Butterfield, Paul.*

BIG BOPPER, THE: *See Richardson, J.P.*

BIG BROTHER AND THE HOLDING COM-PANY: *Vocal and instrumental group, formed 1965. Peter Albin, born San Francisco, California, June 6, 1944; David Getz, born Brooklyn, New York, 1938; Sam Andrew, born Taft, California, December 18, 1941; James Martin Gurley, born Detroit, Michigan, early 1940s. Janis Joplin added as lead singer, mid-1966 through 1969. (See Joplin, Janis.)*

Big Brother and the Holding Company is best known for female vocalist Janis Joplin. The group, however, attained some measure of success before she joined it and was still in existence in reorganized form after she departed.

The band originally coalesced out of the hippie fermentation in the mid-1960s in San Francisco's Haight-Ashbury district. Music, particularly rock in its various forms, was an important part of the so-called counterculture and many groups formed and reformed to meet the demands of the young community—hippie and straight—in the Bay Area. One of the unofficial gathering places for young musicians in the Haight-Ashbury district was the apartment of Chet Helm at 1090 Page Street. Helm, who played with some local groups, and managed others, left his door open to performers who wanted to get together to meet other musicians to arrange playing dates or just to have pickup jam sessions.

Among those who wandered in and out of Helm's place were three young singer-guitarists: Peter Albin, Sam Andrew, and James Gurley. Albin came from a settled background, the other two from families that were on the move quite a lot of the time. Albin grew up in suburban San Francisco, the son of a magazine editor-illustrator and a mother who could play several musical instruments. He got his first guitar at 14 and learned to play in a year's time. His initial interests were slanted toward folk music, including bluegrass, traditional country music, and the country blues as personified by such artists as John Lee Hooker and B.B. King. While studying toward a teaching career at San Mateo Junior College, he switched his musical interest to rock. He still considered music mainly a hobby when he transferred to San Francisco State University to study photography, but he soon dropped out to concentrate on country blues and rock. For about a year, he played with various groups at local festivals, including several jobs with Jerry Garcia and Ron "Pig Pen" McKernan, two of the founders of the Grateful Dead. *(See Grateful Dead.)*

Andrew's father was in the Air Force, which resulted in a steady change of addresses—from San Antonio, Texas, to Okinawa—during Sam's school years. He started playing guitar at 14 and worked with a number of small-time rock groups before taking up classical guitar in 1962. In the late '50s and early '60s, he worked on a B.A. in literature at San Francisco State. He started on a master's at University of California at Berkeley, left for a European tour, and came back to work as a jazz guitarist at the Juke Box on Haight St.

Son of a thrill-show automobile driver, Gurley spent some of his early years touring with his father's show and then returned to the Midwest to finish high school. He next took up a wandering, beat-type style of living that took him to Mexico and to Big Sur, California, where, as he once noted: "I built myself a house made of trees, cardboard, and tin cans." During his travels, he taught himself guitar and improved his ability on the instrument at pickup sessions such as those at Helm's place.

Albin, Andrew, Gurley, and a drummer came together at the Page Street hangout and worked up a sound that Helm considered first-rate. With his encouragement, they gained occasional dates in the area. Late in 1965, they replaced their original drummer with David Getz, who also could play the piano and sing, and whose career included a Bachelor of Fine Arts from Cooper Union, a Master of Fine Arts from San Francisco Art Institute, and a year in Poland in the early 1960s on a Fulbright Scholarship. Getz had started playing drums at 14 while also exercising a growing talent as an artist. His interests alternated from art to music, with music winning out eventually. He had been in San Francisco studying art in 1960 before going to Poland. He returned to the Bay Area in 1965 to work as an art teacher and part-time cook.

The group, with its new name of Big Brother and the Holding Company, went to a three day rock affair called the Trips Festival in January 1966. Of the many groups that played during the almost round-the-clock event, Big Brother was singled out as having more than a little talent. Getz was among the onlookers and, impressed with the group's sound, moved in a few months later when the earlier drummer fell by the wayside. Big Brother's reputation increased rapidly and they were soon playing regularly at San Francisco's Avalon Ballroom.

Still, with an estimated 1,500 rock bands active throughout the Bay Area, Big Brother looked for something to set it apart from the rest. Since very few groups other than the Jefferson Airplane featured a female vocalist, this seemed a good way to go. Chet Helm remembered Janis Joplin and brought her back to the coast in June of that year to join the band. Big Brother became a major attraction at local festivals, culminating in their famous show-stopping act at the summer 1967 Pop Festival in Monterey, California. Their reputation was enhanced locally by the release of their first album, *Big Brother and the Holding Company Featuring Janis Joplin*, on Mainstream Records.

With Janis winning national attention, Big Brother was signed by Columbia. Their first LP for this label, *Cheap Thrills*, made well over a million dollars. As the months went by, Janis captured more of the spotlight and Big Brother faded into the role of a support group. The inevitable breakup finally occurred in 1969, when Janis went out on her own, forming a new group that included only Sam Andrew of the original Big Brothers aggregation.

It took the other members a while to get over the loss. Things were slow for a while. However, with Albin as leader, the group continued to perform, while various changes in arrangements and personnel took place. An album titled *Be a Brother* was released in January 1971 and was followed in June by a Columbia reissue of *Big Brother and the Holding Company Featuring Janis Joplin*. By 1971, Albin felt he had come up with a new band that could provide a return to hit status. Columbia agreed and a new album was taped for release later in the year (*How Hard It Is,* issued September 1971.) However, not much happened from that project and Big Brother's place in history continued as an adjunct to Janis Joplin's career, elements of which were explored in the 1982 Columbia LP *Farewell Song*, a record-documentary of Joplin's saga.

By the mid-1980s, nostalgia for the '60s was in the air. In 1985, Rhino Records put out *Big Brother and the Holding Company Live*, a tape of a 1966 concert. In 1987, some band alumni put together still another group using the Big Brother banner. *(See Thornton, Big Mama.)*

BISHOP, ELVIN: *Singer, guitarist, harmonica player, songwriter, band leader. Born Tulsa, Oklahoma, October 21, 1942.*

With a combination of blues, country-flavored rock, high spirits, and humor, Elvin Bishop carved an important niche for himself in post-1960s pop music. While his popularity never approached that of teen idols such as the Jackson 5 or even Shaun Cassidy, his guitar artistry and exuberant concert showmanship maintained a very respectable following from the 1970s through the mid-1980s.

Growing up in Oklahoma, his earliest influences were country & western music, though in his teens in the 1950s, he was certainly aware of Elvis Presley and the other stars of roots rock. A good high school student, he won a National Merit Scholarship allowing him to come to Chicago to attend college in 1960. He had an ulterior motive in going there—he knew he'd get the chance to hear blues giants such as Muddy Waters and Howlin' Wolf perform in South Side clubs. He said: "I didn't give a shit about college, but I knew the blues scene in Chicago was big." Indeed, the music that increasingly caught his interest during those years was the blues.

He quickly made friends with other young aspiring blues artists, among them Paul Butterfield. (*See Butterfield, Paul.*) At the time, Butterfield was an indifferent guitar player, but he soon developed a flair for harmonica, the instrument to bring him fame later in the decade. Elvin, who had learned some guitar as well as harmonica, teamed up with Paul, initially as a duo and later as the nucleus of the first Butterfield Blues Band. Until 1968, Bishop was a central element in that group, which attracted the atention of young fans who thronged clubs, auditoriums, and rock festivals during that era.

After leaving Butterfield in 1968, Elvin formed the first of a series of backing bands. His initial group, featuring singer Jo Baker, stressed blues material. But Elvin felt too restricted with that format and broke up the band in favor of one that could place more emphasis on rock. He also wanted to focus on an alter ego from Butterfield days called Pigboy Crabshaw that he used to convey a series of country and country-rock satires. Crabshaw, a *Rolling Stone* writer commented, was a countrified persona "who was equal parts the hick Tulsa kid Bishop might have been when he joined the Butterfield band and the laconic, blues-playing sharpie that he was when he left." Some of his Crabshaw numbers (such as "Hogbottom," "Stealin' Watermelons," and "Party 'til the Cows Come Home") were presented on his early solo albums. (While Bishop was with the Butterfield group it recorded the LP *The Resurrection of Pigboy Crabshaw*, released on Elektra in 1968.)

Those three LPs were recorded in the late '60s and early '70s on promoter Bill Graham's Fillmore Records label, and much of their material was reissued on Epic Records in the 1972 collections *Rock My Soul* and *The Best of Elvin Bishop/Crabshaw Rising*. Their tracks covered the gamut from Crabshaw humor to updated versions of '50s R&B and blues to flashy rock numbers in which Elvin was backed by Santana's percussion section.

Bishop's career seemed stalled on dead center in the early 1970s, particularly since he lacked major-record-company exposure. That was remedied after a New Year's Eve 1973 concert at San Francisco's Winterland. Long-time friend Dicky Betts (lead guitarist of the Allman Brothers band) introduced

Elvin to Phil Walden, president of Capricorn Records, then an important force in the pop music field.

Walden had known about Bishop, but had dismissed him as a roots-blues cover artist in too narrow a field for a commercial record organization. The Winterland show demonstrated Bishop's developing rock credentials. After Bishop sent some newly made demo tapes, Walden signed him.

Elvin's debut on Capricorn, *Let It Flow*, was recorded in Sausalito, California, near Elvin's home, and in Capricorn's studios in Macon, Georgia. The LP, issued during 1974, featured some songs by writers such as Lightnin' Hopkins and Merle Haggard, but most of the numbers were originals written by Bishop. Backing Elvin were such top country-rock artists as Charlie Daniels, Betts, and Toy Caldwell of the Marshall Tucker Band. The album was far from a major hit, but it gained enough sales to justify a follow-up, *Juke Joint Jump*, which came out in 1975.

Continuous touring slowly created an audience for Bishop. With the wider touring leeway his Capricorn affiliation permitted (the record company provided financial support), Bishop found life very satisfying. He said at the time: "We jes' love to play, and we love to jam. Why, if we have an early gig, let's say we're first on a bill somewhere, afterwards we'll find a club, walk in and take over the place, and cook all night."

In 1976, Bishop (who had handled most lead vocals) brought in a new lead singer, Mickey Thomas. The chemistry was there and the new aggregation quickly turned out the hit single "Fooled Around and Fell in Love." The song was included on Bishop's third Capricorn LP, *Struttin' My Stuff*, his most successful release up to that time. Bishop backed the LP with enthusiastically received concerts around the U.S. in small to medium sized venues. His band, besides Thomas, featured Johnny Vernazza on second guitar and Phil Aaberg on keyboards. Thomas and the others contributed to Bishop's next LP, the 1977 *Hometown Boy Makes Good*.

One complaint reviewers had about Bishop's studio LPs was their failure to capture the electricity of his live shows. The answer was a live album, *Raisin' Hell*, issued in July 1977. Bishop noted: "We had given some thought to a live album for a long time, so we just started recording concerts. The performances are really good, and we've added horns on some of the cuts. . . . People'd come up and tell us there was a real division between our recorded sound and our live sound, so this is a chance for us to show what we sound like in person. The sound quality ain't as good as a real carefully recorded studio album, but that has never bothered me before. Some

of my favorite records have turned out to be a recording in somebody's basement."

The live LP capsuled many elements of Bishop's shows from Crabshaw numbers to favorite songs such as "Sure Feels Good," "Travelin' Shoes," "Juke Joint Jump," and "Little Brown Bird." Also included was a 12-minute medley of Sam Cooke songs.

By the time *Hog Heaven* (Elvin's last studio album for Capricorn) came out in 1978, things were changing both for the label and Bishop's band. In the late '70s, Mickey Thomas left to share lead vocals with Grace Slick in Jefferson Starship and Capricorn ran into financial problems that led to its demise. (*See Jefferson Airplane/Starship.*)

Undaunted, Bishop reorganized his band and continued to be a solid attraction on the college and smaller auditorium circuit in the U.S. and a big favorite with rock fans in other parts of the world.

BLACK FLAG: *Vocal and instrumental group from Los Angeles. Members, mid-1980s: Greg Ginn, born Phoenix, Arizona, June 8, 1954; Chuck Dukowski, born Los Angeles, February 1, 1954; Henry Rollins, born Washington, D.C., February 13, 1961; Kira, born New Haven, Connecticut, August 13, 1962; Bill Stevenson, born Torrance, California, September 10, 1963.*

The Los Angeles punk rock scene always seemed something of an anomaly since the relatively affluent teen audience had little in common with the economically depressed young people in punk's birthplace, the U.K. Most of the L.A. bands tried to simulate the sound without incorporating the emotion. But there were exceptions—bands that played punk style while zeroing in on problems and hangups germane to the local environment—and this included Black Flag. Ironically, from its beginning at the end of the 1970s through the mid-1980s, it was largely ignored at home while building a substantial audience elsewhere.

Black Flag guitarist Greg Ginn, co-founder and, as of 1986, the only original member with the band, told Steve Pond (*Los Angeles Times*, January 1986): "There's a lot of distractions in L.A. Outside of California, people take Black Flag as a band that has released a lot of records and done a lot of touring. Inside California there's more media attention, people are more judgmental and they try to figure out our concepts instead of listening to the music.

"There's a lot of extreme cynicism in L.A., a lot of people who think that we calculate everything, make career moves and come up with concepts. We don't do real well in those kind of waters, because we don't calculate. To me, Black Flag isn't a concept—it's my total life."

Ginn admitted that another reason the band hadn't won respect at home (apart from the fact that it tended to spend most of its time during the first half of the 1980s performing outside the area) was that "Most of the time we haven't played well here." He stressed that the band planned to correct both those deficiencies in the second half of the 1980s, but by 1987 it had broken up.

After the original Black Flag was organized by Ginn (with bassist Chuck Dukowski) from the many young musicians performing punk in small L.A.–area bands at the end of the 1970s and early 1980s, the group slowly picked up experience at such places as Madame Wong's and the Troubadour. Ginn's vision was to build a band that would evolve, experiment with different rock styles within the high-decibel limits of punk, and, above all, remain independent. As part of that approach, he helped form an independent label, SST, based not in Hollywood, but in somewhat remote Torrance, California, to let members maintain artistic control. Typically, such new labels don't last very long, but Ginn and his associates (including former Black Flag bassist Dukowski) managed to hold their own in the economic arena.

The band's debut on SST, *Damaged*, issued in 1981, was a collection of all-out punk tracks, but with chord patterns and lyrics several cuts above typical music of that genre. A worthy effort, it won considerable praise from rock critics across the U.S., while the band's roof-shaking concerts secured converts among young rock fans. In the years that followed, the band turned out a steady stream of new albums that reflected continued probing in new musical directions. As the 1980s went by, the Black Flag repertoire increasingly included material that blended punk rhythms with aspects of heavy metal and even a considerable infusion of jazz. One critic described the group's later music as "thinking man's heavy metal."

This constant experimentation had the effect of confusing some of the original adherents, but at the same time it encouraged interest among new ranks of teens and college-age concert goers. This maintained the band's status as something more than a cult favorite, if not a mass-audience supergroup. The swings in direction, coupled with Greg Ginn's desire to maintain freedom of action to do other projects (including formation of an all-instrumental band, Gone, in the mid-1980s), also tended to cause many band members to leave for more settled environments.

By the mid-1980s, there had been several changes of roster behind Ginn. But the band assembled as of the mid-1980s was as good or better than any previous grouping. It included dynamic lead singer/lyricist Henry Rollins, female bass guitarist Kira, and excellent drummer Bill Stevenson. Rollins, who typically performed shirtless to bare his extensive tattooing (which led to his being dubbed "the illustrated man of rock"), lashed out at the audience vocally in searing tones that had an almost electric effect on listeners. Rollins, like Ginn, enjoyed making other uses of his talents, demonstrating considerable skill as a writer of stories and poetry. When not on tour with Black Flag, he also gave poetry readings with Exene of the avant garde band X. (Exene's outside activities also included performances with the country-folk-rock group The Knitters.) (*See X*)

The band's album releases during 1983–85 included *My War, Family Man, Slip It In,* and *Loose Nut.* At the beginning of 1986, the band had two more releases, showcasing its new stylings: *In My Head* with Henry Rollins featured on most tracks plus an all-instrumental EP without Rollins, *The Process of Weeding Out.* Both deservedly won high praise from reviewers.

Robert Palmer wrote in *The New York Times* (February 23, 1986): "On *In My Head*, Black Flag's music is intriguingly, sometimes dazzlingly, fresh and sophisticated, but the band hasn't had to sacrifice an iota of the raw intensity and directness that are punk's spiritual center. . . . How was this alchemy accomplished? The secret is in the way Mr. Ginn's guitar parts, Kira's bass and Mr. Stevenson's drums cohere in the middle and lower range of the frequency spectrum, fusing into an immense, dark, primal sound that months of practice, recording and touring, not to mention exceptional musicianship, have leavened with responsiveness and flexibility.

"*In My Head* is the sound of heavy metal rock as it could be, but almost never is, metal without the posturing, the pointless displays of fretboard prowess, the bashing rhythm sections and banal lyrics that have become endemic to the idiom. *The Process of Weeding Out*, Black Flag's instrumental EP, is what jazz-rock could have become if the best of the musicians who first crossbred jazz improvising with rock's sonic power had followed their most creative impulses. In a sense, this Black Flag disk takes up where ground-breaking jazz-rock albums like John McLaughlin's *Devotion* and Tony William's *Emergency* left off in the early 1970s."

Meanwhile, Ginn was busy thinking about still other projects with and without Black Flag. He told Steve Pond: "We may take advantage of the time we're not touring to do a record that isn't tour-oriented—maybe something electronic. I've been working on lots of things, and how it all fits together with Black Flag we'll have to wait . . . and see."

He also planned to continue his nonband activities, such as producing or playing on other artists' recordings. His credits there in the first half of the 1980s included work with bands like Tom Troccoli's Dog, Painted Willie, and October Faction.

In late 1986, Ginn suddenly announced that, despite his earlier protestations, Black Flag would play no more. He had become convinced, as he told Don Waller (*Los Angeles Times*, November 27, 1986), that punk rock was no longer viable. "As far as a cultural evolution, punk rock was co-opted into new wave after about a year. I hate to be reactionary here, but I don't see the Cars as anything more new or worthwhile than Boston.

"In the 1960s, the demographics were different for something that came out of a younger culture to impact upon society because there were more people in that younger culture. Right now the music is really conservative. Even in the [U.S.] underground community . . . people want something safe and defined. They want the Boss and they want a boss, and that's scary, y' know?"

BLACK SABBATH: *Vocal and instrumental group. Original members, all born in Birmingham, England: John "Ozzy" Osbourne, December 3, 1946; Tony Iommi, February 19; Terry Butler, July 17; Bill Ward, May 5. Osbourne left in 1978, replaced in 1979 by Ronnie James Dio, born New Hampshire, U.S., c. 1950. Dio left in 1982, replaced in 1983 by Ian Gillan. Group reorganized in mid-1980s, comprising, as of 1986: Iommi; Geoff Nichols, born Birmingham, England; Glenn Hughes, born England; Dave Spitz, born New York, New York; Eric Singer, born Cleveland, Ohio.**

An early stalwart (late 1960s) of heavy metal rock, Black Sabbath showed surprising longevity. Surviving the loss of original lead singer Ozzy Osbourne (*See Osbourne, Ozzy*) and several successors, the band retained the interest of several generations of teenagers around the world through the late 1980s, though by then only Tony Iommi of the founding members was still aboard.

The original foursome all had experience with other groups in their home area of the U.K. before they formed a band called Earth in the late 1960s. It comprised Iommi on guitar and flute, Osbourne on lead vocals and harmonica, Terry "Geezer" Butler on bass guitar, and Bill Ward on drums. Its first impact was on European audiences. While playing in Germany in 1969, the name was changed to Black Sabbath. Bill Ward recalled: "We were the same four people in the band when we called ourselves Earth, but we changed our name because another

band had the same name and they were bigger than us at the time. Also, the two bands were different. We were playin' what you'd call outrageous music and they were MOR [middle-of-the-road] rock. And people would come expectin' to hear that style and we'd plug in our amplifiers and blow 'em away."

The quartet had known each other from childhood days, Ward noted. "Ozzy and Tommy went to school together since they were kids. We all lived in the same district in England and were runnin' into each other for a long time. Truth be known, we used to fight each other in the early years. We were in different street gangs and later when we got into music, we were in different bands. We couldn't find the right people and then finally realized we had the same [musical] ideas.

"We came from a place called Aston in Birmingham. We're proud of it. Lot of people condemn it because it was a rough part of town, but that's what I knew when I was a kid and it was home. The fact it was like that when we were kids gave us aggression to succeed. It's a very heavy industrial section and when you see your fathers just workin' themselves to death, you say you want to improve yourself and the only way to do it then was to be in a band."

It was tough sledding for a while, but the four friends stuck to it (except for a few weeks in 1969 when Tommy briefly went with Jethro Tull). (*See Jethro Tull.*) Finally, they got a record contract with Vertigo. A single, "Evil Woman Don't You Play Your Games with Me," and a debut album, *Black Sabbath*, showcasing the group's raw, powerhouse blues-rock style, brought marked attention in Europe in 1970, paving the way for a series of highly successful concerts in the U.K. In June 1970, *Black Sabbath* was released in the U.S. on Warner Brothers Records and showed up on the charts in the summer and into 1971.

The band's next album, *Paranoid*, released by Warner Brothers in late 1970, was even more warmly received by fans (if not by critics). It moved into the U.S. top 10 within a few weeks of issuance on the way to gold-record certification. It was still on the charts a year later, joined by that time by the band's third album, *Master of Reality* (issued in Europe by Philips Records), which brought the group its third straight gold-record award.

Bill Ward, soft-spoken and articulate, but a seeming wildman on stage, recalled the incident that showed band members how off-the-wall behavior could trigger unexpected rapport between musicians and audience. "In the early stages of our career, we played this little theater in New York. We really went all out to capture the crowd. We played our heart out, but everyone just stood there with their

---

*Article is based partly on personal interview of Bill Ward by Irwin Stambler.

arms folded. It finally got to me. I got so mad I stood up and ripped me drum kit apart and started throwing it at the audience. I turned to this one guy at the side who'd been giving us a hard time and I said, 'If you can do any better, do it!' But something happened; suddenly everyone was on their feet applauding. We went back to playing and the crowd really came alive—cheering, clapping, enjoying themselves.

"I said to meself, 'We haven't changed our way of playing, but suddenly it's all different.' Minutes before they were out for blood and after I expressed my aggression, it touched something in them. I guess it served as a release for their tension too. But I must admit I felt really bad because it wasn't planned and some of the things I threw were like missiles and could have injured someone.

"Of course, luckily that was a rare situation. Our audiences usually come ready to get wound up in the music and respond to us from the start. In fact, I think that interchange has a lot to do with the popularity of rock. It appeals to the average guy because he or she can get rid of worries and frustrations. I think it's healthy; you can get your rocks off on it.

"And when things are going right, I get a lot out of it too. I really enjoy physically playing my drums. Performing for me is a lot more relaxing than preparing new material. It's never all that easy working up a new album. When you're writing, you don't know what comes out or when. You must take the time until eventually an idea will be there. Whereas when you're touring you know what there is to do and that you can do it.

"Of course, it's a great thing when you're coming up with a song and putting it on tape for the first time, but at the end of the day you can feel totally exhausted both physically and mentally. When you're performing, you might feel a bit tired when the gig's over, but if it goes well, you come off with a feeling of elation."

Damned or not by the critics, Black Sabbath had no trouble finding large, enthusiastic audiences from the early 1970s on. During 1972, it placed the single "Iron Man" on the charts and also claimed a fourth straight gold-record award for the LP *Black Sabbath, Volume 4,* issued on Vertigo/Warner Brothers in late 1972 and on the charts well into 1973. The pattern continued into the mid-1970s with such charted releases as *Sabbath Bloody Sabbath* in 1974, *Sabotage* in 1975, and, in 1976, the studio album *Technical Ecstasy* and a two-LP "best-of" retrospective, *We Sold Our Soul for Rock 'n' Roll.*

Then the band ran into internal problems about future directions. The group already was depressed about the failure of plans to make a concert album in 1977, caused by difficulties with taping equipment, when Ozzy Osbourne announced he was leaving in

autumn. Ward recalled: "He finally agreed to come back in January 1978, so we were on hold for four months. When he left, the rest of us said, 'Oh Gawd, we've gotta get another singer' and we found we couldn't seem to work with anyone else. And he couldn't work with anyone else; the people he got with just wouldn't jell. So he wanted to come back and we wanted him to come back and it all worked out in the end."

At any rate, it worked out for another LP, *Never Say Die,* issued in 1978, and more concert tours. But in 1979, Osbourne said goodbye for good and Iommi and company persevered in auditioning new vocalists until American-born Ronnie James Dio was selected. Dio, born in New Hampshire, but raised in upstate New York, first formed a hard rock band called Elf in the early 1970s and made several LPs with the band before joining Ritchie Blackmore's Rainbow in the mid-1970s. After three years with Rainbow, he was available to join Black Sabbath and work on several albums in the early 1980s: *Heaven and Hell* (issued by Warner Brothers in 1980), *Mob Rules* (1981), and a concert LP, *Live Evil* (1982).

Dio joined the band's alumni society in 1983, forming a new group called Dio. With Ronnie as soloist, the band turned out such LPs on Warner Brothers as *Holy Diver* (issued in May 1983 and certified gold by mid-1984), *The Last in Line* (issued in July 1984), *Sacred Heart* (1985), *Intermission* (1986), and *Dream Evil* (1987).

Meanwhile, Black Sabbath kept going with a new lead singer, Ian Gillan, for a time. The mainstays of the group to this point had continued to be Tony Iommi and Geezer Butler, who had co-written most of the band's songs over the years. But Butler was getting restless and in 1985 left to try for a solo career. Iommi then proceeded to revamp the band, bringing in three complete newcomers and making Geoff Nichols, who had done keyboard work with the band since its *Heaven and Hell* LP, a full-time member.

The other three additions were drummer Eric Singer, whose credits included time with the Lita Ford Band; bass guitarist Dave Spitz, a veteran of several groups in his New York home area; and lead vocalist Glenn Hughes. Hughes had been part of the Hughes-Thrall band, founder of the band Trapeze, and a supporting singer with Deep Purple. (*See Deep Purple.*)

For the first album by the new Black Sabbath, Iommi handled all the writing chores, providing both words and music for all the tracks. Discussing his new roster, he said: "I didn't want to work with anyone who was jaded or too comfortable. I wanted to work with musicians who had the passion to walk into a studio and play all night. The infusion of new blood is important. These players are hungry; they want to fight hard to make their mark.''

The result of the new amalgam was *Seventh Star*, issued by Warner Brothers in January 1986. The LP had many typical hard-driving metal tracks; atypically, it also contained some slower-paced blues-rock material.

BLACKMORE, RITCHIE. *See Deep Purple.*

BLAND, BOBBY "BLUE": *Singer. Born Rosemark, Tennessee, January 27, 1930.*

Sometimes called the "Sinatra of R&B singers", Bobby "Blue" Bland in the mid-1980s remained a favorite artist for much of the black community. He was still able, after more than 40 years as a performer, to place singles and albums on black charts. Over the years, his recordings had appeared from time to time on the general pop charts in the U.S., but he never achieved the status with nonblack audiences that his vocal abilities merited.

He was born in the small town of Rosemark, Tennessee, though for quite a few years, record company biographies attributed that honor to Memphis. In his early years, he was singing gospel music, but later, influenced by records by Blind Lemon Jefferson, he tended to country-style blues accompanying himself on the guitar. After his family moved to Memphis in 1944, he began to pay attention to the urban blues personified by artists such as Sonny Boy Williamson and B.B. King. (*See King, B.B.*) In high school in the mid-1940s, he formed his own R&B group and played for school dances and assemblies. During that period, he also was part of a gospel group, the Miniatures.

Seeking to improve his contacts in the music field, Bobby got a job as a valet for B.B. King and later worked as a chauffeur for bluesman Roscoe Gordon. But he didn't give up performing during those years. Among his sideline projects was singing with a Memphis-based group called the Beale Streeter, whose members included the late Johnny Ace.

By the early 1950s, Bobby had met many other artists in the dynamic R&B field, which was then helping give birth to what was to become known as rock'n'roll. One of the people impressed with his potential was Ike Turner, who produced some demos for presentation to Modern Records. (*See Turner, Ike and Tina.*) However, it was local promoter Don Robey, head of Duke Records, who gave Bobby his first big opportunity. After hearing Bland perform in a Houston, Texas, talent show, Robey signed the artist to his label. After several mid-1950s singles had small impact on the record audience, Bobby and Duke scored a major hit in 1957 with the single "Farther up the Road." He placed some records on lower chart levels in 1958 and then came back strong with a top 10 single, "I'll Take Care of You," early in 1960. He topped this with three major hits: "Cry, Cry, Cry" (1960), "Turn on Your Love Light," (1962), and "Lead Me On." Some of these not only made the R&B charts, but the pop lists as well, resulting in Bobby's gaining notice as a top rock artist.

Bland steadily increased his list of singles successes in the 1960s, starting off in 1961 with "Don't Cry No More" and the number-one–ranked "I Pity That Fool." In 1962, he had three more top 10 R&B singles: "Yield not to Temptation," "Stormy Monday," and "Ain't That Loving You." He was now one of the most important names in the R&B and rock fields and commanded top fees for in-person appearances in major cities across the U.S. He was also gaining a considerable reputation in Europe, as was underlined by the success of "Call on Me" in 1963, which was in the English top 10 and sold over a million copies in the U.S. and abroad. He also had a number one R&B hit that year, "That's the Way Love Is."

In the mid-1960s, Bland continued his steady pace. He hit with "Ain't Nothin' You Can Do" in 1964, "These Hands" in 1965, and three successes in 1966: "Poverty," "Good Time Charlie," and "I'm Too Far Gone (to Turn Around)."

Bland's career quieted down for a time in 1967 and 1968. His record sales fell and there seemed to be slightly less interest in him on the club circuit. Some observers thought Bobby might be losing rapport with the younger fans. But he came back strong in 1969 with singles hits "Gotta Get to Know You" and "Chains of Love." He continued to demonstrate his popularity as the '70s began with top 20 singles "If Love Ruled the World"/"Lover with a Reputation" in 1970, "Keep on Loving Me" in the winter of 1970–71, and "I'm Sorry" in 1971.

Bobby was more successful as a singles artist than an album performer. He did account for a reasonable sales total with such LPs as *Soul of a Man, Call on Me, Two Stops from the Blues* and *Here's the Man* on Duke, although his LPs rarely made the top chart levels. This situation began to change in the early 1970s after Duke Records was purchased by ABC Records. The additional promotion of a larger record firm gave more impetus to that side of his career. ABC and later MCA (which acquired ABC) reissued many of Bland's early LPs until, at the start of the 1980s, almost all of Bobby's albums were in print. (MCA noted that Bland was the only artist to have recorded for Duke, ABC, and MCA in succession.) His album credits from his early years with Duke to his MCA affiliation included: *Two Steps from the Blues* and *Call on Me* (1963), *Ain't Nothin' You Can Do* (1964), *The Soul of the Man, The Best of Bobby*

Bland, Volume 2, and *Touch of the Blues* (1968), and *Spotlighting the Man* and *Introspective of the Early Years* (all on Duke); *His California Album* (1973), *Dreamer* (1974), *Get on Down with Bobby Bland* (1975), *Reflections in Blue* (1977), and *Come Fly with Me* (1978) (on ABC); and *I Feel Good, I Feel Fine* (1979) and *Sweet Vibrations* (1980) (both on MCA). Reuniting Bland with his long-ago boss from his days as a valet were *B.B. King and Bobby Bland Together for the First Time . . . Live* (gold, 1974) and *Bobby Bland and B.B. King Together Again . . . Live* (1976).

In the 1980s, as in the 1970s and 1960s, Bland was constantly on the go, giving live performances all over the world at a rate of 200 or more a year. His name continued to show up on the black music charts with such albums as *You've Got Me Loving You* (MCA, 1981), *Here We Go Again* (MCA, mid-1982, on charts into 1983) and *Members Only* (Malaco, 1985).

BLASTERS, THE: *Vocal and instrumental group from Downey, California. Members, early 1980s: Dave Alvin, born Los Angeles, California, 1955; Phil Alvin, born Downey, California; Bill Bateman; John Bazz; Gene Taylor, born Ft. Worth, Texas. Reorganized roster, 1986: Phil Alvin; Bazz; Bateman; Hollywood Fats (Michael Mann), born 1954, died December 8, 1986.*

Starting in the late 1970s, one trend in U.S. pop music was the appearance of revivalist bands, new groups whose music paid tribute to rock and pop music of rock'n'roll's infancy. Among the more successful purveyors of this genre were the Stray Cats, Fabulous Thunderbirds, and Blasters. Of these, the Stray Cats briefly came closest to becoming a huge commercial success. Yet the California-based Blasters demonstrated the highest content of originality and musical innovation in the revival category, but unfortunately the rigid limitations of 1980s top 40 radio formats mitigated against its gaining the respect it deserved with the public at large.

The founding members of the band, Phil Alvin and his younger brother Dave, recalled listening to '50s rock along with pop, R&B, roots blues, and country music almost from their earliest years. Dave remembered a cousin named Donna, who would buy '50s rock and R&B records and turn them over to the Alvins when she tired of them. "So when I was three years old," he told an interviewer, "we had Sun Records at our house. We had Atlantic and Carl Perkins and Big Joe Turner and the Coasters. So when I was a kid, instead of putting on nursery rhyme records, I'd be putting on 'Blue Suede Shoes.'" His interest in the blues was further piqued when he found that '60s stars such as Cream and

John Mayall played their versions of numbers by blues veterans. He and his brother then would seek out the originals and listen to them.

During those growing-up years in Downey (an industrial suburb of Los Angeles), they began to teach themselves various instruments from playing along with records. Phil liked to play harmonica and sing, while Dave often sat in his bedroom and concentrated on matching chords and notes on his guitar with what came out of the phonograph or radio.

Discussing the artists who influenced his vocal style with Marty Racine of the *Houston Chronicle* (November 25, 1984), Phil said: "Certainly Big Joe Turner with 'Shake, Rattle and Roll.' That's not where my voice comes from, but I learned a lot of things from him. My first idol was Big Bill Broonzy. I think a lot of my vocalizations come from that. I like early Bing Crosby a lot, always did. Clyde McPhatter, Tommy Duncan, who sang for Bob Wills, Jimmie Rodgers, Jackie Wilson. I mean, Clyde McPhatter and Jackie Wilson to me are the greatest. And Elvis Presley, too, though Elvis Presley is not in the class of Clyde McPhatter and Jackie Wilson. I think that's it. Well, I kinda like Dean Martin, too."

His brother Dave was influenced musically by all of those, but others as well, including a pantheon of early rock stars. He also found music from such genres as Cajun and Tex-Mex intriguing. All of these elements can be detected in the diverse original songs he wrote during his years with the Blasters.

Those somewhat diverse musical tastes, Dave told Racine in 1983, contributed to the band's unique sound. "[Our rhythm] is pretty studied to tell the truth. Part of it comes from the two guitar styles. Phil is one of the best pickers of ragtime and country blues you're gonna hear. He's got it down pat. His two-hand and finger coordination is incredible. He spent 10 years, like, in front of Blind Blake records perfecting that. My idols are completely different. . . . I've always been impressed with the half-country, half-urban thing."

Both brothers performed with a number of local bands before deciding to assemble the Blasters in the late 1970s. The group shook down to Phil on lead vocals and guitar, Dave on lead guitar, John Bazz on bass guitar, Gene Taylor on piano, and Bill Bateman on drums. The group sought engagements in local clubs and naturally started putting together demo tapes. This finally resulted in an excellent, if ignored, debut collection called *American Music* that came out on the obscure Rolling Rock label in the late 1970s. The band became a favorite among many of the young musicians in Los Angeles' version of the new wave movement and it gained a faithful, if small, local following.

The group's material was good enough to induce Slash Records, a small but influential record company, to issue the album *The Blasters* in 1981. It deservedly won high praise from music writers around the U.S., something that in the 1980s had little impact on those who put together programming for the nation's disc jockeys. Even then, the album, which featured Dave Alvin's well-crafted song "American Music" from the earlier collection, sold over 60,000 copies, mostly by word of mouth. Slash then signed a promotional agreement with Warner Brothers Records, which provided a little more exposure, but not enough to do much more than double the album's overall sales total.

The wheels set in motion by the new album, though, did give the band the opportunity to demonstrate its considerable skills at small venues across the U.S. in fast-paced shows that delighted both critics and audiences. While much of the material the band played could be classed as rockabilly, in truth it did not sound dated or trite, reflecting an approach to the music by the Alvins that looked both backwards and forwards simultaneously. As Dave Alvin told a reporter from the *Chicago Tribune* in 1983: "Rock and roll grew out of blues, out of hillbilly music, out of ethnic fiddle songs—out of all the folk musics of the past. To a real rock-and-roll band, the sense of past is mandatory."

On the band's next album, *Non-Fiction,* issued in 1983, it continued to feature a mix of blues, swing, roots rock, and Cajun boogie in the music while Dave Alvin wrote new lyrics that dealt with modern-day problems of finding a job, coping with love under changing conditions, and the complexities of day-to-day living. Some of the "downer" themes were meshed with rocking, upbeat melodies. As Dave Alvin told one reporter: "I'm basically a pessimist, but whenever I can, I try to leave a way out for people."

The new album was ranked high on many reviewers' lists for the best releases of 1983. But again, it got a minimum of airplay and never made a dent on the hit charts. To add to the band's frustrations, another group playing in the same vein, the Stray Cats, became stars with best-selling LPs that won much less critical respect, but much more public support.

Not that the group was a failure. It had established itself with many rock fans in the U.S. and abroad. In most cities, it could draw full houses to its shows, but mostly as headliners in small clubs or theaters. During 1983 and 1984, it was hailed as one of this country's premier bands from the *Los Angeles Times* to *Chicago Tribune* to New York's *Village Voice.* Writers in major magazines such as *People* and *Newsweek* lauded them, but the group was aware that the economic facts of life in the music business called for making the hit charts.

Dave Alvin in particular felt it was getting near do-or-die time. He told *People* (December 24, 1984) that he was counting on the group's fourth album, *Hard Line,* to turn things around. "We brought our music up to date lyrically on the last album [*Non-Fiction*]. This time we wanted to bring the sound up to date." For the new LP, John Cougar Mellencamp was enlisted to write and produce one song, and one number was written by Dave's friend John Doe of the avant garde rock band X. (See *Mellencamp, John Cougar*; X) The rest were primarily written by Dave. The overall goal was to include material that for the most part retained the main thrust of the group's art form, but with a couple of tracks tailored somewhat toward winning large-scale commercial airplay.

As Phil told Racine: "There are two songs made almost specifically for radio—not that they aren't good songs. It is incredible to me that the free marketplace is so restricted like that. I would prefer to fight against that. But when your fans are coming up to you and saying, 'Too bad you can't get airplay,' well, I'm not gonna fight that."

Hard Line, released by Warner Brothers in February 1985, didn't do much better than its predecessors, however. Meanwhile, Dave Alvin had become increasingly involved in projects with John Doe and other members of X, including performing with an offshoot band the Knitters that emphasized country and folk music rather than rock. (The name is a playful tribute to the 1950s folk group, the Weavers.) With the Knitters, Dave helped record the 1984 Slash LP, *Poor Little Critters.*

While Dave was touring with the Blasters in support of *Hard Line,* X was in the throes of a reorganization caused by lead guitarist Billy Zoom's decision to leave. The remaining members of X asked Dave to take Zoom's place and, with the disappointment over the new album and some internal strains in the Blasters, he accepted the offer in early 1986.

Phil, who had not been happy about his brother's sideline activities, refused to break up the Blasters. He revamped the band to a foursome: himself, Bazz, Bateman, and, on lead guitar, 250-pound Hollywood Fats. (Fats had previously been featured in the James Harman Band, but died of an apparent heart attack that December.) Phil maintained that he saw no reason why a group couldn't do well even without its own in-house songwriter, citing Elvis Presley, Sinatra, and Jerry Lee Lewis as examples.

In fact, he told Chris Willman of the *Los Angeles Times* (June 1, 1986), that it was only music-business economics and not performing advantages that made singer/songwriters seem important. Singers "feel that they've got to write songs. They consider themselves inferior if they don't. Likewise, songwriters are told that they have to sing. For what? Because it makes a more salable package."

However, Phil (who had obtained several college degrees, and taught mathematics at California State University at Long Beach before opting for music full-time) decided that it might be wise to hedge his bets and re-enroll in school.

He told Willman: "I'm not saying farewell, but I am going back to school. I could've gotten my Ph.D. in the last seven years because nobody in this business is available for anything until 2:30 [P.M.] anyway. You call at 10 and they're either not in yet or nobody knows where they are right now; they come in at 11 or maybe 11:30, go to lunch at 1, then they're gone until 2:30.

"I'm working. I'm out on the road spitting blood, and what are these guys doing? So be at lunch till 2:30! Between 8 in the morning and 2:30 in the afternoon, I'll be at school."

After the death of Hollywood Fats, Dave Alvin agreed to take part in Blasters' concert dates to keep the band going. However, 1987 saw a continuation of diversified activities by Dave and a move in new directions by Phil. Dave could point to a debut solo LP on Epic called *Romeo's Escape,* released in August '87. Backing him was his new band, The All-nighters, comprising Greg Leisz on pedal and lap steel, six and 12-string guitars; John "Juke" Logan on harmonica and keyboards; Gil T on bass; and Jerry Angel on bass. (Dave's record credits in '87 also included *See How We Are* with X on Elektra label and *Border Radio Soundtrack* with Steve Berlin on Enigma.) In August '87, Phil's first solo album, *Un'Sung Stories,* was issued by Slash.

BLIND FAITH: *See Clapton, Eric; Traffic; Winwood, Steve.*

BLONDIE: *Vocal and instrumental group. Members, mid-1970s: Deborah Harry, born Miami, Florida, July 1, 1946; Chris Stein, born Brooklyn, New York, January 5, 1950; Gary Valentine; James Destri; Clement Burke.*

What's in a name? Sometimes, perhaps, a bit too much. Early on, Blondie was a five-person band, an exuberant new wave group with an infectious style. But as it moved from obscurity, both reporters and fans increasingly associated the name with the band's lead singer, a slender, dynamic blonde named Debbie Harry. The psychological impact on the other band members probably contributed to the group's breakup in the early 1980s.

Of the original quintet, Debbie Harry had the most professional experience. Born in Miami, but raised in New Jersey, she was influenced by the various rock genres of the late '50s and the '60s as well as the folk music boom. She was already active in the New York–area music scene in the late 1960s when she made her recording debut with the folk-rock Wind in the Willows on Capitol.

After that group disbanded, Harry worked at a number of nonmusical jobs—Playboy Club bunny, beautician, and waitress at the New York rock club Max's—while waiting for new opportunities. By the mid-1970s, the Big Apple rock scene was thriving with the appearance of a bonanza of new bands seeking alternatives to mainstream rock. Harry got the chance to perform with several of the new bands, including the Stilletoes and Angel, before Blondie came into existence.

The new band took form in the early '70s with Deborah and New York–area guitarist Chris Stein as founding members. During the usual shakedown period, with musicians being added and replaced, the group worked its way onto bills at various clubs on the local circuit. By 1976, Blondie had achieved the new wave big time with regular appearances at its centers, Max's and CBGB's. By then, the group consisted of Debbie, Stein, Gary Valentine on bass guitar, James Destri on keyboards, and Clement Burke on drums.

At that point, the group felt it was in position to try for a recording contract (unlike some new wave bands that disdained the commercialism of the music industry). It had taken longer to reach that point than the members had expected, Harry indicated to Robert Hilburn of the *Los Angeles Times* (February 15, 1977): "I think the biggest thing that held us back is that we had no one hyping us. There wasn't any Blondie machine in New York. We didn't have friends on newspapers, no big money behind us. We didn't even have a manager until a few weeks ago."

Lack of funds affected the group's early sound, Chris Stein noted. "We also had terrible equipment. I started out with a 1940-something $40 guitar. It's no wonder people thought we sounded terrible."

Destri added: "To tell you the truth, I never even knew if Deborah could sing until we went in to make [the first] record. I could never hear her on the equipment we had to use on stage."

Gary Valentine told Hilburn: "Three years ago everyone in all the New York bands was waiting and dreaming. It was like one big scene. Now it's really moving. I knew we'd all get signed. The only question was in what order."

By 1975, artists such as the Ramones and Patti Smith from that contingent had major recording agreements. Blondie's turn came in 1976, when it signed with Private Stock Records for its debut album. By early 1977, that disc, *Blondie,* had been released and the band was making its first concert appearances outside the New York area, including its debut in Los Angeles that February as opening act for the Ramones at the Whisky-A-Go-Go. As 1977 went along, the album became a chart hit with some writers suggesting the band might become the U.S. equivalent of Sweden's ABBA.

For the band's next LP, it switched to England's Chrysalis Records, which had a roster of successful rock performers and good worldwide distribution. Its follow-up album on that label, *Plastic Letters,* though it had some good tracks, did not measure up to the standards set in the first collection.

Kristine McKenna of the *Los Angeles Times* echoed many critics in her evaluation. "Harry's 'bad girl' image, responsible for much of the press that group had received, contrasted with their milk and cookies sound and the group came off as wryly provocative.

"Unfortunately, the follow-up suggests that somebody knocked the spunk out of Blondie. Sounding more tired than seductive, Harry delivers vocals there as if she's ordering lunch. Although the LP opens on a promising note with 'Fan Mail,' a commanding tune that coaxes some strange and wonderful sounds from Harry, it's generally downhill from there."

She noted, however, that the band was still young. Indeed, it proceeded to turn things around with its next release, *Parallel Lines,* issued later in 1978. The album, produced by Mike Chapman (who had once formed an extremely successful writing/production team with Nicky Chinn), focused not only on Harry, but on the performing skills of the other musicians, with notable contributions on drums from Burke. All the tracks were of consistently good quality; one, the new wave disco number, "Heart of Glass," became a runaway singles hit. Not only did it win the band a gold record in the U.S., "Heart of Glass" topped charts around the world. In April 1979, when it rose to number one on *Billboard*'s list, the single was said to be selling 100,000 copies a day in the U.K. The album itself passed gold-record levels later and received RIAA platinum certification.

With "Heart of Glass," Blondie had become a bona fide headliner and the band was featured in major auditoriums, arenas, and theaters around the world. But the press's focus on the lead singer was beginning to take an internal toll. The other band members repeatedly insisted that they were not just backing musicians. In fact, an ad campaign was instituted with the large headline, "Blondie is a group."

But the die seemed to be cast. The next album, *Eat to the Beat,* was uneven, though it did have some fine tracks such as "Dreaming." The gap between lead singer and other band people seemed to grow wider with the Giorgio Moroder production of the Blondie-recorded theme number for the movie *American Gigolo. Billboard* ranked that song, "Call Me," the number one singles success of 1980, but the bandsmen did seem to come out as essentially only backing for Harry's vocal. During 1980, two other Blondie singles—"The Hardest Part" and "Atomic"— also ranked high on U. S. charts.

The next LP, *Autoamerican,* which Chrysalis issued in late 1980, showed the band still had considerable selling power. It was in the top 20 at year-end and remained on the album charts well into 1981. Among other things, it provided the hit single "The Tide Is High," which reached number one in the U.S. the week of January 31, 1981. But *Autoamerican* was weaker creatively than most earlier albums and heralded the band's approaching demise. Later in 1981, the single "Rapture" from the LP was a chart hit, rising to number one on *Billboard*'s list the week of March 28 for a two-week stay.

In the fall of 1981, Chrysalis issued the band's sixth album, a retrospective titled *The Best of Blondie.* It made the top 10 in the U.K. that December and was on U.S. charts in late 1981 into early 1982.

While the band hadn't officially broken up at the time, the writing was on the wall. More and more, Debbie Harry was focusing on a solo career, one of the first fruits being her album *Koo Koo* on Chrysalis. Though she was joined in making the LP by Chris Stein plus Nile Rodgers and Bernard Edwards of the then noted disco group Chic, the renditions did not match some of her work with Blondie. It did begin to look that, despite her vocal prowess, the sum of that band was truly greater than its parts.

By late 1981, there seemed little doubt to Debbie and long-time boyfriend Chris Stein that internal strains among band members had essentially reached the point of no return. Still, the group did complete a last LP, *The Hunter,* issued in 1982, and began an accompanying tour. She told Robert Hilburn (*Los Angeles Times,* December 1, 1985): "I didn't go around announcing it, but I think people knew it was the end. In fact, I really didn't want to do *The Hunter* record . . . but Chrysalis persuaded me to do it."

Meanwhile, Stein had become seriously ill with what turned out to be a genetic disease called pemphigus. Oxygen had to be taken on tour for him to keep going, but the effort proved too exhausting for him. Harry told Hilburn: "It was really nightmarish. We ended up just doing the eastern half of the United States and canceling the rest of the tour. It was extremely taxing for him to go on stage and then having to go to doctors. But we still didn't know what was wrong with him. It was a mystery to everyone.''

Harry gave up all outside activities to stay with Chris. ''It was really a sad, unhappy and scary time. We had been working and living together for 11 years . . . so I really couldn't leave. When someone gets that sick, you can't carry on with your job.'' For some months at the end of 1983 and the start of 1984, Stein was hospitalized and Debbie spent almost every waking minute near his bedside.

She did have a hit disco single, ''Rush Rush,'' during that period, but otherwise, she was essentially out of the entertainment business from mid-1983 into mid-1985. Fortunately, Chris slowly began to recover and, in late 1985, Harry had her first single in two years, ''Feel the Spin'' (co-written by Harry and Jellybean Benitez), out on a new label, Geffen Records. During early 1986, she was working on additional material for her debut LP on Geffen, *Rockbird*, issued in October '86. In 1988, Harry appeared in the film *Hairspray*.

BLOOD, SWEAT AND TEARS: *Vocal and instrumental group, founded 1968: David Clayton-Thomas, born Surrey, England, September 13, 1941; Bobby Colomby, born New York, New York, December 20, 1944; Jim Fielder, born Denton, Texas, October 4, 1947; Dick Halligan, born Troy, New York, August 29, 1943; Steve Katz, born Brooklyn, New York, May 9, 1945; Fred Lipsius, born New York, New York, November 19, 1944; Lew Soloff, born Brooklyn, New York, February 20, 1944; Dick Halligan, born Troy, New York, August 29, 1943; Chuck Winfield, born Monessen, Pennsylvania, February 5, 1943; Jerry Hyman, born Brooklyn, New York, May 19, 1947. Hyman left in 1970, replaced by Dave Bargeron, born Massachusetts, September 6, 1942. In 1972 reorganization, Clayton-Thomas, Halligan, and Lipsius left. New members added were Jerry Fisher, born Dekalb, Texas, c. 1943; Georg Wadenius, born Sweden; Lou Marini, Jr., born Charleston, South Carolina; Larry Willis, born New York, New York, c. 1942. In 1973, Katz, Winfield, and Marini left. Tom Malone was added.*

In a number of ways, Blood, Sweat and Tears gave the appearance of being a throwback to the big-band era. Obviously, with an eight-to-ten-man total, BS&T was considerably larger than most rock groups. In addition, unlike most rock groups of the 1960s and 1970s, it featured a relatively large horn section consisting of two trumpeters, two trombonists, and a saxophonist. The original trombonists were Dick Halligan (who doubled on organ) and Jerry Hyman, who was replaced by Dave Bargeron. Chuck Winfield and Lew Soloff handled trumpets, while Fred Lipsius played saxophone as well as piano and organ. (By 1973, only Lipsius was still with BS&T.)

The music that brought BS&T to major-group status had a strong jazz-blues flavor, reflecting the backgrounds of many of its members. Most of the horn section enjoyed these musical forms in their early years, while drummer Bobby Colomby, who gained his first drum set at 14, came from a family of avid jazz fans. The group's lead singer for three years, David Clayton-Thomas, enjoyed the sounds of blues artists from his early years and brought this background into play with several Canadian rock groups prior to joining BS&T.

However, BS&T was still primarily a rock group, but with the flexibility of being able to combine elements of many phases of pop music, past and present. This flexibility was evident in their first block-buster hit album, *Blood, Sweat & Tears*, a challenger for the number one spot on the top 40 within a few months of its release by Columbia Records in 1968.

Because David Clayton-Thomas became lead singer on the band's second LP, much attention centered on him. However, the driving force in the founding of the group was Al Kooper, who, while a member of the Blues Project, had the idea of expanding beyond the confines of the blues through use of a horn section. (*See Blues Project, The; Kooper, Al.*) In forming BS&T, he brought another Blues Project member, Steve Katz, along with him. Bobby Colomby was the third founding member of the band. Colomby saw music only as a hobby as he gained a B.A. in psychology and started work on his Master's. At 22, though, he changed his mind and joined a semirock group that played a number of clubs in the New York area. He was lured away by folksinger Eric Andersen, but when Andersen broke up his group, Colomby received a bid from folk-blues singer Odetta to join her jazz trio. This led to engagements in all parts of the world and contacts with many other professional musicians. One of these was Steve Katz, then rhythm guitarist with the Blues Project.

Katz showed a good voice at an early age and began singing at weddings and bar mitzvahs at five. Before he was a teenager, he experimented briefly with the drums and ukelele. In his teens, Katz became engrossed in the folk music boom of the early 1960s and spent much of his time in New York's Greenwich Village listening to such artists as Bob Dylan and Dave Van Ronk. From these people, Katz learned to play guitar and later joined the Even Dozen Jug Band that had one LP and two Carnegie Hall appearances to its credit. By this time, Katz had become interested in country blues, which led to his move to the Blues Project.

In 1967, Kooper, Katz, and Colomby began to line up additional musicians for BS&T. One was Jim Fielder, Texas born, but brought up mostly in Anaheim, California. Fielder's credentials included formation of his own surf-rock band in high school and, during his stay at California State College at Long Beach, work as bass player with the Mothers of Invention and a brief stay with the Buffalo Springfield. (*See Buffalo Springfield; Mothers of Invention.*)

Colomby called several people he'd known from either recording session work or earlier band experience. Fred Lipsius had impressed Bobby with his musical skill and his promise as an arranger. He had started studying clarinet at nine, switched to alto sax a few years later, and then began on the piano during his years at the High School of Music and Art in New York. He went on to the Berklee School of Music in Boston for a year, leaving to play with Canada's Ron Metcalf Orchestra. This big-band experience didn't please him, so in 1964 he returned to New York, played with a rock band for a while in the mid-1960s, and then decided to concentrate on classical music. Colomby persuaded him to return to pop music and BS&T was rewarded with Lipsius's arrangements (or co-arrangements) of such songs as "Spinning Wheel," "You've Made Me So Very Happy," "Smiling Phases," and "More and More," which became hits for the group.

Soloff was a graduate of the Eastman School of Music in Rochester, New York, who went on to study on the graduate level at New York's Julliard School of Music. He met Colomby when both were playing band dates in New York's Catskill Mountains resort area. With his experience as a trumpeter (going back to lessons at age ten) coupled with that of Winfield, BS&T had a solid basis for its horn section. Winfield also attended Julliard, receiving both bachelor's and master's degrees. He too played trumpet in Catskills groups, moving into rock in a bill at New York's Basin Street East that featured the Righteous Brothers. He was playing with a group called the Motown Band when he heard the BS&T debut at the Cafe Au Go Go. He thought the BS&T sound sensational and, hearing there was an opening for another trumpeter, he asked in. "I didn't join the group with the idea it would be a monster success," he recalled. "I joined it to play music."

The critics weren't as enthusiastic as Winfield.

They gave the band a lukewarm reception, which may have helped influence Al Kooper to leave the group soon after. Another consideration was a lucrative offer from Columbia Records for Kooper to expand his activities as a record producer. Kooper played on the first BS&T album, *Child Is Father to the Man,* but was no longer with the group when it achieved national attention.

When Winfield heard the original group, it included Dick Halligan and Jerry Hyman. Both had been playing various instruments from early years and had classical grounding. Halligan earned his M.A. from the Manhattan School of Music, while Hyman played with chamber music groups and amateur symphonies in high school and briefly attended the New York School of Music. A friend of Halligan's, he was leading his own local jazz-rock group when Dick suggested he join BS&T.

Of all the BS&T group, Clayton-Thomas had the longest list of rock credits before joining. His mother was an English music hall entertainer; his father a Canadian serving in the British army. His family moved from England to the sparsely settled region of northern Canada when he was a boy. At 14, he left school for work "because that's what you did up there when you reached 14. Besides, it was almost impossible for anyone to go any further than that in those schools." He worked in logging and mining camps for a while, and found an interest in listening to blues in his late teens. After spending many evenings at black blues clubs, he went out on his own as a solo vocalist, starting in small towns in Quebec and eventually moving into larger clubs in the Toronto area.

With his own group, The Bossmen, he became a major attraction in Canada. Featuring his rasping, driving blues-rock vocals, the group earned five gold records on a Canadian label: "Boom Boom" (1963), "Walk That Walk" (1964), "Take Me Back" and "Out of the Sunshine" (1965), plus "Brainwashed" (which spent 16 weeks at number one in 1966). This paved the way for engagements in major cities outside Canada, including one at the Scene in New York. Judy Collins was impressed by him and tipped off the BS&T members, who were worried about their band's future after the loss of Kooper. Colomby called Clayton-Thomas in Canada in 1968 and asked him to audition, but David didn't become a regular BS&T member until March 1969.

Results of the new alignment were not long in coming. The group's second album, simply titled *Blood, Sweat & Tears,* found a ready audience and moved onto the best-seller lists in early 1969.

Over two years later, a gold-record album several times over, it was still on the charts. More gold records followed for such singles of 1969–71 as "Spinning Wheel" and "Lucretia Mac Evil" (both written by Clayton-Thomas) and the albums *Blood, Sweat & Tears 3* and *Blood, Sweat & Tears 4*. Other notable singles of 1970–71 were "And When I Die" and "Hi-De-Ho."

By mid-1971, Clayton-Thomas had considerably diversified his vocal stylings. The records bear out his contention that he could not be satisfied as simply a blues singer. The group itself also had a distinctive East Coast flavor, with a strong jazz emphasis. Says Katz: "The jazz orientation of the band had a lot to do with the jazz orientation of the city itself; the subways and the people, the beautiful people, the jive people, the funky people. This is a definite and large part of my environment; and with the capabilities of the music I am playing, the capabilities of the band I am in, and the potential of the music that we can do, my feelings as a New York person can best be expressed."

But problems of internal dissent cropped up. In early 1972, Clayton-Thomas departed to work as a solo vocalist. Halligan and Lipsius also left. In the reorganization that ensued, four new members were added: lead vocalist Jerry Fisher, guitarist Georg Wadenius, saxophonist Lou Marini, Jr., and keyboards artist Larry Willis.

Fisher, who played piano from the age of four, did not start singing professionally until he was 19. For ten years before joining BS&T, he played nightclubs, sometimes heading his own group, and did session work. By the time he moved to BS&T, he also owned his own nightclub, the Music Box in Oklahoma City. Wadenius's background included composing rock music for symphony orchestras, work on Swedish TV and radio and, just prior to BS&T, a stint with the group Made in Sweden (which won two Grammies from the Swedish record industry). Wadenius won his own Grammy for writing and performing a children's album, *Godda, Godda* (Hello, Hello). Willis, who earned a bachelor's degree in theory from the Manhattan School of Music, started playing piano in 1959 at 17 and joined Hugh Masekela's group the same year, playing with him for six years off and on. Later he served as music director for the Four Tops. Marini, interested in jazz from his early years, attended North Texas State University because of its jazz program. Among his many credits with jazz groups were stints with the Woody Herman Herd and the Joe Morello Quintet.

During the reorganization period, Columbia issued earlier BS&T tracks on the album *BS&T Greatest Hits* (April 1972). In October, the new group was featured on the album *New Blood.* By the time the next album was completed (*No Sweat,* issued in summer 1973), still more changes had taken place, with the departure in early 1973 of Katz, Winfield, and Marini and the addition of Tom Malone.

During 1973, Clayton-Thomas returned to the band and was still lead singer as of the early 1980s. The first reunion album on Columbia was *New City* in 1973, followed by *Mirror Image* in 1974 and *More Than Ever* in 1976. None of those could match the pinnacle reached when Al Kooper was handling production, so the band's following slumped markedly. Columbia declined to offer a new contract and the group moved to ABC Records. For the ABC project, the roster included Clayton-Thomas; David Bargeron on brass, congas, and synthesizer; Larry Willis on keyboards; Bill Tillman on saxophone, flute, and backing vocals; Tony Klatka on trumpet and fluegelhorn; Forrest Buchtel on trumpet and fluegelhorn; Mike Stern on lead guitar; Danny Trifan on bass; and Roy McCurdy on drums. Founding member Bobby Colomby was involved as co-producer. The ABC debut, *Brand New Day,* was issued in 1977. It was a listenable album, but BS&T's day seemed to have passed. It was not a hit; nor were later ABC recordings. In 1980, the band began the new decade with the album *Nuclear Blues* on LAX Records.

BLOOMFIELD, MIKE: *Singer, guitarist, songwriter, band leader. Born Chicago, Illinois, 1942; died 1981.*

Considered by some experts to be America's answer to Eric Clapton, Mike Bloomfield surely had as dramatic an effect on rock instrumentalists as the English superstar's. Many aspiring young guitarists watched his fingering technique. Others noted the arrangements used by the band he put together, in particular the legendary Electric Flag.

Michael Bloomfield was born and raised in Chicago. His first interest in music was aroused by the musical *South Pacific.* But his tastes shifted to rock as he became aware of the new kind of pop music pouring from radio loudspeakers in the late 1950s. When he was 13, he got his first guitar. "I got a guitar because my cousin Charles had one." Mike was considerably more adept at the instrument than his cousin and, at 15, he began playing in rock bands, discovering the blues after listening to such artists as Lightnin' Hopkins and John Lee Hooker.

Bloomfield gained experience with various small groups as he went through his teens. In the early '60s he performed in his own small coffeehouse in Chicago, the Fickle Pickle. By his early twenties, he had become well known in the industry as one of the best recording men around. During the first half of the 1960s, he backed many of the most respected names in folk music, including Bob Dylan, John Hammond, Jr., and Peter, Paul and Mary.

In the mid-1960s, he joined the Paul Butterfield Blues Band, one of the many blues groups thrust into the spotlight by the musical ferment in the Chicago area. (*See Butterfield, Paul.*) The band stopped the show in more than one rock or jazz festival and credit often went, in part, to Bloomfield's work. More and more reviews of the Butterfield aggregation hailed Mike as the most influential guitarist in pop music.

When Mike put together his own band, the Electric Flag, in 1967, he showed he was as good at judging talent as playing guitar. He not only recruited band members already considered top artists by their peers, but also played a part in the rise to stardom of such previous unknowns as Buddy Miles. Besides Miles (whose drumming ability Bloomfield detected in backup bands for Wilson Pickett and Otis Redding), the group included Barry Goldberg on organ, Nick Gravenites on lead vocals, Harvey Brooks on bass, Peter Strazza on tenor saxophone, Marcus Doubleday on trumpet, and Herbie Rich on guitar.

Goldberg joined the group after the breakup of his Chicago-based Goldberg/Miller Blues Band and brought along Strazza, who had been with him. (*See Miller, Steve.*) Before the Goldberg/Miller combine, Goldberg had performed with such luminaries as Bob Dylan and Mitch Ryder.

Born in Chicago in 1938, Gravenites knew Bloomfield from Butterfield Blues Band days. By the time he joined the Flag, he already had gained attention for some of his composing efforts, most notably "Born in Chicago" for Butterfield. During his time with the Bloomfield group, he added to his reputation as a singer and writer and, in the late 1960s and early 1970s, became one of the more important pop figures as a soloist and songwriter whose material was featured by Janis Joplin, Otis Rush, Quicksilver Messenger Service, and dozens of others. In the early 1970s, he was a member of Big Brother and the Holding Company for a time and helped them make a brief resurgence after Janis Joplin's departure. (*See Big Brother and the Holding Company.*)

Marcus Doubleday had shown considerable flexibility as a musician before joining Bloomfield. He had backed such diverse artists as Bobby Vinton, Jan & Dean, and the Drifters. Harvey Brooks also had played (mainly in session work) with many major artists, including Dylan, Al Kooper, Phil Ochs, Judy Collins, Eric Andersen, and the Doors.

The Electric Flag had an electric effect on the rock field when it began making personal appearances. Reviewers found it difficult to find enough glowing phrases to describe the driving rhythms and instrumental interplay of eight skilled artists. Paying the most attention were other musicians. Bloomfield's use of a brass section in rock helped in the evolution of such later bands as Blood, Sweat & Tears and Buddy Miles Express.

Generally acknowledged as a supergroup, the Electric Flag made its mark in a very short time and was represented only sparsely on albums: *Electric Flag—An American Music Band* (1967) and *The Best of the Electric Flag* (March 1971), both on Columbia Records. It was made up of too many highly individual artists to avoid the stresses and strains that cause bands to break up. By 1968, the group had split apart.

During 1968, Bloomfield teamed up with another great name in rock, Al Kooper, for concert appearances and recording work. (*See Kooper, Al.*) Their first effort, *Super Session* (with Steve Stills) was issued by Columbia in September 1968 and was on the best-seller lists for much of 1969. (*See Stills, Stephen.*) Also a chart hit was their second release, *The Live Adventures of Mike Bloomfield and Al Kooper* (March 1969).

In the early '70s, Bloomfield was active as a soloist while also making a number of tours with Kooper. His solo LPs included *It's Not Killing Me* (November 1969, reissued on the Harvard label, March 1971) and *My Labors* (1971).

His main idiom continued to be the blues, as it had always been. As he pointed out: "Blues is not just notes. It's a whole environmental thing with nuances of song, speech, and the whole personality of the people involved. It makes me feel good to understand it. It's a personal thing. I have a personal attachment to the music. It's absolutely part of me."

Mike continued to experiment with both his guitar stylings and artistic affiliations during the 1970s, but for a while, his personal following among blues-rock fans decreased steadily. An example of his efforts was the recording work with John Paul Hammond and Dr. John, the Night Tripper, that resulted in the 1973 Columbia album, *Triumvirate*. (*See Dr. John.*) For a while in the mid-1970s, Mike's declining record fortunes led to a lack of new releases, but a contract with the small, but well-regarded Takoma label promised new opportunities. His 1977 debut on the label, *Analine*, met only modest success. (Also issued that year on Guitar Player Records was the LP *If You Love Those Blues, Play 'Em as You Please*, essentially a teaching record in blues guitar.) In

1980, Takoma issued *Between a Hard Place and the Ground,* a workmanlike album, but one not carrying Bloomfield's creative efforts much beyond what he had done in the past.

In 1981, catalogs listed two more Bloomfield LPs. One of earlier material on Waterhouse Records was titled *Living in the Fast Lane. Cruisin' for a Bruisin'* (new tracks on Takoma) was an eye-opener, one of the best and freshest new releases in early '80s rock. The LP won glowing reviews both at home and abroad and Mike's career seemed headed sharply upward when his life came to an untimely end in 1981 from drug abuse.

BLUE OYSTER CULT: *Vocal and instrumental group from New York. Original members, 1971: Eric Bloom, Donald Roeser, Allen Lanier, Joe Bouchard, Albert Bouchard. Al Bouchard replaced by Rick Downey in 1981.*

Originally, Blue Oyster Cult essentially was a manufactured group, the brainchild of Sandy Pearlman, a rock journalist and songwriter turned music entrepreneur. Its saga might be compared to that of the Monkees, except that in this case, the idea was to start with at least reasonably competent musicians. As in the story of Frankenstein, the "creation" rebelled against its "master," though in Blue Oyster Cult's situation not to the extent of completely discarding its mentor's creative skills.

The first ideas about forming a new band came in the mid-1960s as a result of a trip to the San Francisco area by Pearlman and his friend, writer Richard Meltzer (who later became a regular contributor of songs to the band). Meltzer told Jim Green of *Trouser Press* (February 1982): "Pearlman and I went to college together at Stony Brook out on Long Island. It was the Summer of Love; we went to the Monterey Pop Festival, hung out in Haight-Ashbury, there were bands galore and when we got back Pearlman wanted a band and put out the call."

He started with bass guitarist Andrew Winter, who worked in Pearlman's father's drugstore. Winter, in turn, brought in guitarist Donald "Buck Dharma" Roeser. A friend of Meltzer's, John Wiesenthal, started out on keyboards and Roeser brought in one of his friends, Albert Bouchard, on drums. Those were the main members of a group that played psychedelic-style rock under the Pearlman-contributed name, Soft White Underbelly. While that group still was trying to find a niche, Pearlman replaced Wiesenthal with keyboardist Allen Lanier.

With Pearlman and Meltzer supplying most of the original songs, the band found performing opportunities in small New York–area clubs. Initially, there was no lead vocalist until Les Bronstein was added. It wasn't a good move, Meltzer told Green.

Bronstein "became the official lead singer mainly because he had a van they needed—exactly the same reason why Eric Bloom became the singer after Bronstein's van was repossessed."

The Underbelly got the chance to record some numbers for Elektra, but because no one was satisfied with Bronstein's vocals, Meltzer recalled, nothing was released on the label. Meanwhile, a disastrous gig at New York's Fillmore East caused Pearlman to change the band's name to Oaxaca, which recorded material for Elektra with Bloom on lead vocals. Elektra eventually decided to pass on that too. For that almost-released album, Meltzer wrote seven songs and Pearlman three. The band then got another new name from Sandy, the Stalk-Forrest Group, whose members now comprised Bloom, Roeser, Lanier, Albert Bouchard, and Albert's brother, Joe Bouchard, on bass.

Pearlman was developing a reputation as a writer for rock publications even as he kept playing with new ideas for the band. In bull sessions with other writers, he toyed with ideas of new rock mythologies, which evolved into a vision of a mythical subgroup of the Hell's Angels motorcycle club that he dubbed the Transmaniacon MC, about which he wrote the song "Transmaniacon." The roots of this fantasy went back to the unfortunate incident at the Rolling Stones' concert in Altamont, California, where a Hell's Angels "security guard" killed a member of the audience.

Pearlman's made-up club, Meltzer pointed out, was meant to embody the "true evil of Altamont." He told Green: "The way that they [Blue Oyster Cult] are to this day an expression of Pearlman is Pearlman's whole riff that life is an illusion."

By 1971, Pearlman had abandoned writing about music in favor of managing. The band played at an off-season summer camp in New York's Catskill Mountains, where a commercial jingle producer liked them enough to let them cut a demonstration album in his studio. Pearlman took the demo to Columbia Records executive Murray Krugman. Krugman didn't like it, but Sandy persuaded him to support another series of sessions at Columbia's expense. This led to the band's debut LP in January 1972 on Columbia, *Blue Oyster Cult.* The name was taken from one of Pearlman's lyrics.

The album showcased a promising group with a high-intensity rock sound that compared favorably with most other debut releases of the period. It won some critical support, though it never came close to making any hit charts. But the new name and the record-company–supported concert tour began to catch the attention of many young fans. Taking its cue from Pearlman, the band started building an outlaw image that incorporated Hell's Angel-like stage garb. Under an eerie, specially designed BOC banner featuring the symbol of Kronos (Saturn) in white on a black background, the band created a mood of tension and emotional bleakness punctuated by Bloom's driving vocals of such songs as "Cities on Flame," delivered in a leather costume with his eyes hidden behind silver-mirrored glasses.

Sensing broad commercial potential, CBS released a limited-edition 12-inch extended-play album in October 1972, *Live Bootleg.* The EP included material from the debut and planned second albums: "The Red and the Black" and "Buck's Boogie" backed with "Workshop" and "Cities on Flame." This was followed by the albums *Tyranny and Mutation* in 1973 and *Secret Treaties* in 1974, releases that were not gold records, but added fuel to the band's reputation as a rising force in the heavy metal pantheon. (When the *Secret Treaties* album appeared, Pearlman had been joined by Krugman as co-manager of the band). Among the new songs from those LPs that kept audiences stirred up were "Career of Evil" (which new wave poet Patti Smith co-wrote), "MF262," "Harvester of Eyes" (co-written by Meltzer), and "Astronomy." (*See Smith, Patti.*)

Blue Oyster Cult (nicknamed BOC) had become a headline band on the concert circuit and Columbia decided the best way to bring the group some overdue recording respect was to try to capture the flavor of those appearances. The result was the double-disc live set, *On Your Feet or on Your Knees,* released in the winter of 1975. It turned out to be considerably milder than the multipronged assault on the senses that took place in an auditorium or arena, but record buyers were satisfied. The LP proved to be a chart hit, the band's best-seller to that point.

The commercial success of the next release, *Agents of Fortune,* in early 1976 helped bring the live album gold-record certification. *Agents of Fortune* itself rose high on the charts, eventually earning RIAA platinum status. That album reflected increasing emphasis by band members on writing their own material. Roeser's composition "(Don't Fear) The Reaper," a "ballad" with rather gloomy symbolism, was a top 10 hit. The second single release, "This Ain't the Summer of Love," also did well on the charts. *Agents of Fortune* also included two Patti Smith–Albert Bouchard songs, "Debbie Denise" and "The Revenge of Vera Gemini," with Patti handling lead vocals on the latter.

The group had become restless with its outlaw image, which some critics even called neofascist or neo-Nazi (an odd label considering the ethnic makeup of the organization). Before *Agents of Fortune* was completed, the band declared their independence from Pearlman and Krugman.

Roeser commented: "I always thought the Cult was misunderstood. We were never as heinous as we were characterized. It disturbed us after a while to be characterized as this fire-and-brimstone group. Our reputation for being exciting live was accurate and well deserved, but people who weren't familiar with us seemed to have the totally wrong idea."

Bloom told *Trouser Press*: "We told Sandy that we had no more interest in this leather foolishness. We enjoyed it up to a point, but then we started seeing ads for us with, like S&M leather and zippers over the mouths preaching on pulpits and stuff, and we said, 'What the fuck?' So we started taking more of a hand in lyric writing and image or non-image–making."

Though band members originally weren't much concerned with songwriting, Roeser told an interviewer, as the group's fortunes improved, so did its creative urges. "A real inspiration came in about 1972 or 1973. I got a TEAC 4-track and was able to overdub at home and multilayer the tracks and find out what I could do. Actually everyone in the band got one of those machines. It changed the way we wrote songs—it's an example of the influence of technology on music." From the mid-1970s on, he took over the mantle of primary songwriter of the group, accounting for about 30% of all Cult lyrics.

The members didn't rule out recording future Pearlman songs they liked or banning Sandy from record-production activities. In fact, one of the singles from the next album, *Spectres,* issued in October 1977, was a Pearlman–Al Bouchard song, "R.U. Ready 2 Rock." One of the *Spectres* tracks was co-written by Bloom and English rock star Ian Hunter; in 1979, Bloom served as a backing vocalist on Hunter's album, *You're Never Alone with a Schizophrenic.*

The group continued to be a major draw on the concert circuit in the late 1970s and early 1980s both at home and abroad. Some material had been taped from the 250 shows the group performed before a half-million fans from late 1977 to mid-1978 and a second live LP, produced by Pearlman, Krugman, and BOC, titled *Some Enchanted Evening,* was issued in September 1978, proving more popular with record buyers than the earlier live release. On their next studio album, the band brought in for the first time a new outside producer, Ted Werman. Done in Southern California, *Mirrors* was the first LP recorded outside New York. It was released in 1979 while the band was completing a triumphal tour of Japan. Among the songs featured in concerts in Tokyo, Nagoya, and Osaka was one dedicated to the science-fiction monster Godzilla.

The band opened the 1980s with one of its better collections produced by Martin Birch (with Black

Sabbath and Deep Purple credits), *Cultosaurus Erectus,* issued in June 1980. Pearlman, who had again taken over as manager of Black Sabbath, set up a concert series featuring both bands called the "Black and Blue" tour. One of the shows at Long Island's Nassau Coliseum was filmed for release as a concert film titled *Black and Blue* in 1981. During 1981, Blue Oyster Cult also was one of the band's contributing to the score of the movie *Heavy Metal* and made its TV guest debut on Don Kirchner's "Rock Concert." At the end of 1981, *Performance* magazine named the "Black and Blue" tour "tour of the year."

As the 1980s passed, the band continued to turn out new chart-making studio albums, such as *Fire of Unknown Origin* in June 1981 (from which the hit single "Burnin' for You" was taken) and *The Revolution by Night* in late 1983. However, their content increasingly seemed predictably similar to what had gone before. In 1981, Al Bouchard was asked to leave because of disagreements with other members. His place on drums was taken by Rick Downey.

The desire to get new perspectives was reflected in band members' increasing outside activities, including various solo projects. One was Donald "Buck Dharma" Roeser's solo album, *Flat Out,* issued on Columbia's Portrait label in October 1982. He noted it gave him an opportunity to expand his songwriting efforts. "My inspiration in going solo also came from the example of Todd Rundgren and [Paul] McCartney—guys who've done solo projects well." But he emphasized he still planned to work with the Cult.

In 1986, the first Blue Oyster Cult LP in several years, *Club Ninja,* was issued by Columbia.

BLUES PROJECT, THE: *Vocal and instrumental group. Members, mid-1965–67: Al Kooper, born Brooklyn, New York, February 5, 1944; Steve Katz, born Brooklyn, New York, May 9, 1945; Andy Kulberg, born Buffalo, New York, c. 1944; Danny Kalb; Roy Blumenfeld. Founding members included Artie Traum and Tommy Flanders.*

An exciting band, one that combined the blues and rock in patterns no pop group had tried before, the Blues Project never quite made it during its first incarnation. However, its members remained vital factors in the rock field and the group itself influenced literally hundreds of bands, many of whom found gold in the fields originally tilled by the Project. In the early 1970s, some of the founding members revived the group—but unfortunately with little success.

The group was New York–based from the start. Most of its members were born and raised in that city's boroughs. Interest in the old country blues was at a high pitch in the early 1960s in that area, thanks to the brief folk music renaissance. In Greenwich Village, bands formed and reformed to play traditional blues in the small clubs and coffeehouses as ardent young musicians traded information on new blues discoveries gathered from research trips to remote parts of the South and Southwest.

Rhythm guitarist Steve Katz had played with such New York folk artists as Dave Van Ronk and the Even Dozen Jug Band in his late teens. He spent part of one year traveling cross-country to look for rare out-of-print recordings of old blues masters. As rock reaffirmed its dominance over the mass audience in the mid-1960s, Katz was among many blues aficionados who sought new directions through the blending of blues and rock.

Also strongly motivated by such ideas was another talented young New Yorker, Al Kooper. By late 1964, Kooper had an awesome reputation as instrumentalist, singer, and songwriter. Kooper and Katz were already toying with the idea of a new group that would try the then-revolutionary technique of improvisations within a blues-rock structure when they were approached by several other New York–based musicians with a similar idea. As Danny Kalb told columnist Richard Cromelin: "Roy [Blumenfeld] and I originally hit on the idea for this group at a New Year's Eve party in 1964. Al Kooper joined us and then Steve Katz on rhythm guitar and harmonica and things really began to happen." Kalb had worked with Katz in Van Ronk's Ragtime Jug Stompers and also had gained attention from young folk musicians for his guitar work behind such performers as Phil Ochs and Judy Collins.

Among other early recruits to the embryo band were folksinger-guitarist Artie Traum, Tommy Flanders, and bassist-flutist Andy Kulberg (then a music major at New York University). By the time the Blues Project had gained recognition as a promising addition to the rock field, Traum and Flanders had departed.

The new group rehearsed for several months and then began seeking engagements in New York clubs. By year-end, they had demonstrated their versatility in a highly entertaining stay at the Cafe Au Go Go in Greenwich Village. Students from the nearby New York University campus spread word of their skills; even more indicative of the group's potential were the growing numbers of rock musicians who flocked to hear their performances.

The group featured blues of all types—slow ones ("I Can't Keep From Crying"), fast-paced, dynamic ones ("Two Trains Running"), and what might be called boogie-woogie rock ("You Can't Catch Me"). The band wasn't afraid to break new instrumental ground in rock, as shown by the feature position of the flute in ''Steve's Song'' and ''Flute Thing.''

Though the band gained a faithful and outspoken following in 1966–67, it never was able to break through to the mass market. Thus, its recordings for Verve/Forecast won excellent reviews and respectable sales totals, but never enough sales to make the top levels of the hit charts. The LPs made by the original group are now considered classics by some rock fans. They included the initial Verve-Forecast album *The Blues Project Live at the Cafe Au Go Go* (recorded in May 1966), *Blues Project/Projections* (1966), *Goin' Down Louisiana* (May 1966), *Blues Project, Volume 2* (January 1967), and *Blues Project at Town Hall* (September 1967). Some material was issued after the band broke up, such as *The Best of the Blues Project* (September 1969).

The original band dissolved in late 1968, though Kooper had departed a year earlier, later setting the stage for a group that became one of the colossal successes of the rock field in 1969 and the early 1970s: Blood, Sweat & Tears, whose original roster included Kooper and Katz. (*See Blood, Sweat & Tears.*)

In 1971 the Blues Project was revived by Kalb, Blumenfeld, and Don Kretmar, encouraged by a new recording contract from Capitol Records. Kretmar came to the reincarnated group from Seatrain, a band that Blumenfeld and Andy Kulberg had helped assemble. Also joining up was former lead singer Tommy Flanders, who had spent a number of years out of the U.S. (particularly in Sweden) and had released an exquisite but almost unknown solo LP, *Moonstone* on Verve/Forecast in 1969. For keyboards, Kalb added David Cohen. Cohen was not a Blues Project alumnus, but had years of experience with Country Joe and the Fish.

The 1971 debut LP of the revived group was produced by Shel Talmy, who was instrumental in many hit discs by English groups, including the Who. Called *Lazarus,* the album won considerable critical praise.

By early 1972, the band had added Kalb's acquaintance, guitarist Bill Lussenden. The next album, which included Lussenden's contributions, was issued in the spring under the title *Blues Project.* However, this edition of the band could not recapture the innovative feel of the 1960s group. Before the end of the 1970s, it had become inactive.

BOLAN, MARC: *See T-Rex.*

BONDS, GARY U.S.: *Singer, band leader, songwriter. Born Jacksonville, Florida, June 6, 1939.*

One of the names that kindles memories for many who were teenagers in the early 1960s is Gary U.S. Bonds. For a few years, he was a top star. By the mid-1960s, like the vast majority of rock headliners, he was almost an unknown to a newer crop of young rock fans. But with the growth of rock revival shows in the late 1960s and early 1970s, his performing career began to rebound and he persevered at his trade until he once more had major hits in the 1980s.

Gary was only 22 when he first became famous and only in his midtwenties when he sank into relative obscurity for a time, but he had been performing professionally for almost a decade before reaching the heights. Born Gary Anderson, he was, from his early years, taken to church regularly by his family and he developed an interest in singing gospel music. His voice was a good one, and at nine he became part of his church choir. He continued singing in the local choir until he was 13, when he began to go further afield with various gospel singing groups.

A little while after this, he moved to Norfolk, Virginia, his home base until well into the 1960s. He formed a group called the Turks, which disbanded after a short career. By then, Gary had given up gospel singing in favor of rhythm & blues. As a solo artist, he began to sing in small R&B clubs in the Norfolk area and continued this activity for the rest of the 1950s. He became acquainted with local recording executive Frank Guida, who owned the Norfolk Recording Studios. Guida liked Gary's style and decided to market some of his records. Guida and shoe salesman Joe Royster had written a song called ''New Orleans,'' which they had Gary record for release on Guida's small Legrand label. Without Gary's advance knowledge, the artist name on the disc was U.S. Bonds, which with his first name became his professional title. Hitting the top 10 in 1960, the record justified more releases. One of these, ''Quarter to Three,'' rose to number one on *Billboard* charts the week of June 26, 1961, staying there for another week. The single earned Gary a gold record in 1962; the LP of the same title, also on Legrand, became a chart hit as well.

From mid-1961 to the fall of 1962, Gary added to his list of hits ''School Is In,'' ''School Is Out,'' ''Dear Lady Twist,'' and ''Twist Twist Senora.'' Also on lower chart levels in 1962 was the single ''Copy Cat.''

After 1962, Bonds' career declined. For the rest of the 1960s he performed in small clubs, but was largely forgotten until a renewed interest in earlier rock stars began in England in the mid-1960s and in the U.S. toward the end of the decade. He became a regular member of the annual ''Rock'n'Roll Revival'' shows staged by Richard Nader in major auditoriums around the U.S. beginning in 1969 and extending into the early 1970s.

In the middle and late 1970s, Gary found he had a bit more leverage in arranging club dates, though his recording career remained at a standstill. While appearing at a club called the Red Baron in 1978, he responded to audience interest in someone seated near the stage by asking the person to come up and join him. The stranger turned out to be Bruce Springsteen. (Bonds wasn't aware of his importance at the time.) Bruce joined Gary in a duet on "Quarter to Three" that brought down the house. (*See Springsteen, Bruce.*)

The meeting was a major break for Gary. Bruce with his friend and E Street bandsman Miami Steve Van Zandt expressed interest in recording an album of new Bonds tracks. As it turned out, there was a two-year delay until Bruce completed his album *The River*, but eventually Bruce kept his promise and he and Van Zandt brought Gary into the studios for the project in the early 1980s. Bruce provided three original songs for the album and Van Zandt wrote one, "Daddy's Come Home." When the LP, *Dedication,* came out on EMI in 1981, it proved an amazing success. One of Springsteen's songs, "This Little Girl," gave Bonds his first top 10 single in 19 years. Taking advantage of Bonds's new-found fame, Legrand Records issued a *U.S. Bonds' Greatest Hits* package in 1981.

Gary once more was a headliner who could draw capacity or near-capacity crowds to medium-sized halls such as the Universal Amphitheater in Los Angeles. Besides "This Little Girl" and his early 1960s favorites, his sets included such others as his 1982 hit single, "Out of Work," and his versions of songs such as Bob Dylan's "From a Buick 6" and the Box Tops' "Soul Deep." In the mid-1980s, Gary signed with Phoenix Records and produced his debut on that label himself. Among the tracks was a song he cowrote with Steve Van Zandt, "Standing in the Line of Fire," which was the first single issued from the LP of the same title.

BOOKER T. & PRISCILLA: *See Booker T. and the M.G.s.*

BON JOVI, JON: *Singer, band leader (Bon Jovi), born New Jersey.*

With a musical format that might be called soft heavy metal (which seems like a contradiction in terms), Jon Bon Jovi and his group became one of the major pop idols of 1987.

Assembled in 1983, the New Jersey–based group quickly got a record contract and its Mercury label debut, *Bon Jovi*, was released in 1984. It found particular favor with foreign fans; the U.K.'s *Kerrang!*

magazine named Bon Jovi the Best New Band of the Year. Top 40 singles from the LP included "Runaway" and "She Don't Know Me." The following year the group made charts around the world with the *7800 Fahrenheit* LP which, like the first LP, went gold.

In August 1986, the group's third Mercury album, *Slippery When Wet,* came out, catapulting the band to the status of major concert headliners. (Band roster was Jon Bon Jovi on lead vocals, Alec John Such on bass, Tice Torres on drums and percussion, Richie Sambora on guitar and David Bryan on keyboards.) The group's pseudo heavy metal style (reflected in such songs as "Livin' on a Prayer" and "You Give Love a Bad Name") caught on with a broad audience spectrum, particularly among female fans. (As one record store owner commented, "Lots of secretaries buy his album.")

In January 1987, *Slippery When Wet* moved to number one on *Billboard* charts, displacing the five-record Bruce Springsteen set. By May, when Jon was featured on the cover of *Rolling Stone's* "What's Hot" issue, the album had sold 7 million copies and the single, "Livin' on a Prayer," also was a best-seller. (Still high on the charts in early 1988, the album had sold over 8 million in the U.S.) Not exactly a shrinking violet, Jon told a *Rolling Stone* reporter, "I'll never be satisfied. I'm not happy that we have the number one album, single, CD, video, that I sold out every show . . . and that I can buy a huge mansion if I want to. Next year I plan to do better. I want a bigger record, more shows. I want to be able to buy two houses instead of one."

BOOKER T & THE M.G.s: *Vocal and instrumental group. Personnel in early 1970s: Booker T. Jones, born Memphis, Tennessee, November 12, 1944; Al Jackson, Jr., born Memphis, Tennessee, November 27, 1935, died Memphis, Tennessee, October 1, 1975; Steve Cropper, born Willow Spring, Missouri, October 21, 1941; Donald "Duck" Dunn, born Memphis, Tennessee, November 24, 1941. Reorganized group (called the M.G.s), late 1973, comprised Jackson; Dunn; Bobby Manuel, born Memphis, Tennessee, November 13, 1945; Carson Whitsett, born northern Mississippi, May 1, 1945. Jackson was replaced in 1975 by Willie Hall, born August 8, 1950.*

When rhythm & blues took its rightful place as a major element of popular music the world over, its two dominant segments were called the Detroit (or Motown) sound and the Memphis sound. The latter phrase describes a type of soul music played throughout the Memphis area, but caught in recorded versions primarily by Memphis-based

Stax/Volt Records through such artists as Booker T & the M.G.s. ("M.G." stands for Memphis Group).

Born and raised in the middle-class part of Memphis's black ghetto, Booker T. Jones showed an aptitude for music in his very early years. His mother told Phyl Garland (*Ebony*, April 1969): "I had an old upright piano and . . . he would get up there with these two fingers and actually make harmony. When I got rid of that bunglesome piano, Booker's heart was broken. We made up for it by buying him musical toys and, later, real instruments. He was so happy that it was evident music was his talent. I never really thought of him doing anything else." Booker took some lessons on piano and organ in his childhood, but really didn't receive concentrated attention until he was given a clarinet at ten. He was an excellent instrumentalist by his early teens at Booker T. Washington High School, where his father taught science and mathematics.

At 14, Booker became pianist and organist with a high school group, playing at school dances and then in small clubs. When he was 16, Booker auditioned for the newly formed Stax Record company on McLemore Street in Memphis. Started by one-time country music hoedown fiddler Jim Stewart in 1960, Stax had begun to make a name for itself from the success of its father-and-daughter recording team of Rufus and Carla Thomas. Stewart was open to promising new talent and agreed that the teenager could work on recording sessions. (*See Thomas, Carla; Thomas, Rufus.*)

As he spent his spare hours at the Stax studios in the early 1960s, Booker made friends with other session musicians, both black and white. Informal get-togethers resulted in music that caught everyone's fancy. It was decided to record the number "Green Onions," jointly composed by Booker, drummer-guitarist Al Jackson, Jr., lead guitarist Steve Cropper, and another drummer, Lewis Steinberg. The single hit pay dirt in mid-1962, rising to number one on the R&B charts, then moving over to the national pop lists. At 16, Booker had his first gold record.

From then on the members of the M.G. group (except for Steinberg) were vital cogs in the Stax operation both as a source of hit recordings and as the backup group for most of the vocalists who made Stax, Volt and other company labels steady candidates for best-seller lists. The basic group that comprised the M.G.s varied from time to time, but the three members most often associated with Booker T recordings were Jackson, Cropper, and a long-time friend of Cropper's from high school days, electric bassist Donald "Duck" Dunn. (Dunn and Cropper are white, making the M.G.s a truly integrated group.) For most of the backup sessions of the 1960s, Booker added Andrew Love on baritone saxophone, Wayne Jackson on trumpet, Joe Arnold on tenor saxophone, and Isaac Hayes on piano. (*See Hayes, Isaac.*)

Despite the success of "Green Onions," Booker T took a long view of his future. Instead of dropping everything in favor of pop music, he finished high school and enrolled as a music major at Indiana University. Though he continued to perform and record with the M.G.s, school came first until he got his B.A. in 1966. Booker made the dean's list, learned theory and harmony, and was featured as a trombonist with the university's symphony orchestra. After graduation, he turned down several jobs with established symphonies to resume full-time work in popular music.

Steve Cropper, on the other hand, gave up his engineering studies at Memphis State University to become a studio engineer with Stax/Volt. (Later he was chief recording engineer and also a close friend and producer of the recordings of Otis Redding.) (*See Redding, Otis.*) Cropper, born in rural Missouri, was weaned on country music, but after he moved to Memphis with his family in 1951, he slowly discovered R&B and soul. At 15, he bought his first guitar and taught himself to play it. In high school, he helped organize a group called the Mar-Keys (with Duck Dunn as a member), which later provided Stax Records' early hits "Morning After," "Popeye Stroll," and "Philly Dog."

Besides working with the M.G.s and producing records of company artists, Cropper wrote many hit songs. Along with collaborating on "Green Onions," he penned "Dock of the Bay" (Otis Redding's posthumous million-seller), "In the Midnight Hour" (gold for Wilson Pickett), and "See Saw" (gold for Aretha Franklin). (*See Franklin, Aretha; Pickett, Wilson.*)

Drummer Jackson started playing music at 12 with his father's jazz band, a popular group in the Southwest in the mid-1950s. He was recruited for Stax sessions by Cropper, with whom he had become friends when both played R&B dates in the Memphis area around 1960.

After "Green Onions," the M.G.s didn't taper off, but continued to turn out top-selling singles and albums. The band's song hits of the '60s included "Boot-Leg" in 1965, "Hip-Hug-Her" in 1967, "Soul Limbo" and "Hang 'Em High" in 1968, and two movie-related numbers in 1969: "Mrs. Robinson" (Simon and Garfunkel's song for *The Graduate*) and "Time Is Right" from *Uptight* (for which Booker T received his first assignment to write a screen score and made his debut as a soundtrack vocalist).

The "Green Onions" single hit was followed by an equally successful *Green Onions* album, issued by Stax in January 1963. In the mid-1960s, Booker T's LP output included *Mo' Onions, Soul Dressing, My Sweet Potato, And Now,* and *Hip-Hug-Her.* Most of those made the national U.S. charts, as did such later albums as *Soul Limbo* (October 1968), *The Best of Booker T & the M.G.s* (November 1968 to mid-1969), *McLemore Avenue* (1970), and *Melting Pot* (1971).

In addition to his composing and performing, Booker also won a formidable reputation as an arranger and record producer. During the 1960s, he handled production duties for many Stax/Volt sessions. In the early 1970s, he supervised the recording sessions of his sister-in-law, Rita Coolidge (sister of Booker's second wife Priscilla). The results caused many critics to pick her as one of the most promising new female vocalists for the '70s. (*See Coolidge, Rita.*)

Those new responsibilities, including the start of a recording duo with his wife, caused Jones to reduce his involvement with the M.G.s. His and Priscilla's debut album in 1971, *Booker T and Priscilla,* issued on A&M Records, was a best-seller as was their 1972 A&M release, *Home Grown.*

By the end of the '60s, the M.G.s had tapered off on personal appearances, though they continued to make a few special shows. In 1970, they performed at the World's Fair in Osaka, Japan, and, in 1971, were featured on the Creedence Clearwater Revival show that was taped for a TV special. Booker essentially departed from the band in 1970 after a dispute with Stax and relocated to the West Coast that year.

The band broke up in 1972, as Al Jackson had predicted it would a few years before, though with tongue in cheek. Jackson had told Phyl Garland: "We have a pact because we're such close friends as well as close musically. . . . We hope to retire within five years. Then we'll no longer exist as a group. We'd like to go out cool instead of dying slowly."

The band was inactive for a short while, but reorganized in 1973 around Jackson and Dunn. Rounding out that band, whose first album, *The M.G.s,.* was released in early 1974, were Bobby Manuel and Carson Whitsett. Because Stax had recording rights and Booker T was no longer under contract to the label, new M.G. releases had to be made without him. That roadblock ended when Stax went out of business in 1975 and in the fall, plans were made to reconstitute the original

quartet. Unfortunately, eight days after all had agreed to that, Jackson was shot and killed in Memphis. After the others had gotten over the shock, they decided to go ahead with the reunion. To take Jackson's place on drums, they brought in Willie Hall, who had been a member of the Barkays from his last year of high school in 1968 to 1970, after which he joined Isaac Hayes's band. Hall had been an admirer of Jackson's drum style since his teens and for a while had worked with Al on sessions at Stax.

By then, the band all lived in Los Angeles where Cropper and Dunn had plenty of work as session men and record producers. The new lineup signed with Asylum Records, which released the album *Universal Language* in 1977. That year, L.A.-based Booker T and Priscilla also put out a duo LP, *Evergreen,* on Epic.

In the years after that, the band continued on a relaxed arrangement, combining some performances as a group with separate activities by individual members. In the 1980s, the band recorded some new material for A&M Records. The LP *I Want You* made the R&B charts for several months in late 1981 and early 1982.

BOOMTOWN RATS: *Vocal and instrumental group from Dublin, Ireland. Members, late 1970s and early 1980s: Bob Geldof, born Dublin, October 5, c. 1953. Gerry Cott; Garry Roberts; Pete Briquette; Johnnie Fingers; Simon Crowe.*

Bob Geldof, lead singer and primary songwriter of Ireland's Boomtown Rats, has won international acclaim for organizing the 1985 trans-Atlantic Live Aid concert to help starving people in Africa, as well as other events in which rock artists did their bit for charitable causes. Ironically, while he was receiving plaudits for his idealistic work for the less fortunate, his band's longtime U.S. label, Columbia, was in the process of dropping the group from its roster. It was another case of a tremendously popular band in Europe somehow not quite following through with American audiences.

U.S. "establishment" music critics tended to downplay the Boomtown Rats as a band that was too light-hearted in its approach. These same reviewers later were very vocal in praise of Geldof's mid-1980s antihunger campaigns. In truth, in the Rats' early days Geldof usually emphasized that the band's primary goal was simply to be entertaining. "Our whole thing is geared towards playing rock'n'roll and making it the exciting thing it was when I used to go to dances when I was 13 or 14. Sure I want to be a star. I want to get rich and get laid. The only philosophy we espouse is that of the individual. All we're saying is, 'Be yourself!'"

The band was formed in mid-1975 when a group of young Dubliners got together in the kitchen of ex-photographer Garry Roberts in Dun Loaghaire near Dublin. Geldof told writer Dave Schulps (*Trouser Press,* December 1977): "Seven guys on the dole [were there]: one of us couldn't play an instrument, so he became the manager, six of us could so we became the band." At the time, Geldof agreed to manage, with Roberts as lead vocalist, but soon after, Bob became lead singer and Roberts one of two lead guitarists. The other members were Gerry Cott on guitar, Pete Briquette on bass, Johnnie Fingers on keyboards, and Simon Crowe on drums.

"The reason we got into it in the first place was that we were so fuckin' tired of hearing funk-rock, country-rock, jazz-rock—anything but rock'n'roll, tired of seeing musicians getting up on stage, tuning up, ignoring the audience who had paid them the supreme compliment of paying money out of their wages to see them, and generally being totally self-indulgent which has nothing to do with rock'n'roll. To me, rock'n'roll has to do with total excitement, visual, cerebral, physical, oral—if any of those things are missing, it's not rock'n'roll. We also heard music in our head that you couldn't hear anywhere else. . . .

"[When I was a young teen-ager at rock concerts,] I knew back then that the guy on the stage was a bank clerk during the day, but for now, at that dance, even though he lived in Flat 3B on some street in some armpit, that guy was a star. And I wanted to be him. When I was 11, I wanted to be Mick Jagger so bad; when I was 12, I wanted to be John Lennon; when I was 13, I wanted to be Peter Townshend. Now I just wanna be me. I want to revitalize the rock dream that was so essential to me."

The group started honing its act in the Dublin suburbs. For its initial show, it first called itself the Nightlife Thugs, but between sets, Geldof decreed a change to Boomtown Rats. He had been reading folksinger Woody Guthrie's biography the night before and remembered coming across the term, which had been used by a group of newcomers to the Oklahoma oil fields in Guthrie's home area.

But it was difficult to find a niche in the regular club system in Ireland. Geldof said: "What we did was go out and set up an alternative system. We played in any shithole that existed and we did, in fact, set up a rock circuit in Ireland which allowed musicians to give up their day jobs and actually make a living. It eventually got to the point where we could do no more in Ireland, so we went into the studio for four hours, recorded four songs, and brought them to England. We got six record companies to fly to Dublin to see us. One of them was Nigel Grainge at Phonogram's Ensign Records."

After catching a Rats performance in October 1976 Grainge signed the group, which then moved to London.

In 1977, the band began work on its album debut and in May made its first U.K. appearance at a club in Blackburn, Lancashire, England. By the summer, the group had the opportunity to open a series of shows for Tom Petty and the Heartbreakers. The band was beginning to get noticed by the press and rock fans, as reflected in the response to its first single release ("Lookin' after No. 1" in August), which rose to number one on U.K. charts that fall and helped win a U.S. contract with Columbia Records in October. The next month, the band had another U.K. chart hit, "Mary of the Fourth Form," which made the top 15. Its first LP on Ensign, *Boomtown Rats,* came out that month and entered U.K. lists at number 18. At year-end, the English-based Capitol Radio Awards named the band Most Promising Group and chose its debut LP as best of 1977.

The band continued to add to its luster in 1978 with a string of singles that made the charts in the U.K., Ireland, and on the Continent, with each gaining greater buyer response. "She's So Modern," issued in March, rose to number 12 in the U.K.; issued in June, "Like Clockwork" (from the band's second LP, *A Tonic for the Troops*) made it to the sixth spot; and "Rat Trap," issued in October, rose to number one. *A Tonic for the Troops* was a hit in the U.K. after its release in June 1978 and was on U.S. charts for a number of months in 1979 after being issued early that year by Columbia. After a highly successful series of concerts in the U.K. and Europe in the latter part of 1978, Geldof and Fingers joined Phil Lynott, Scott Gorham, and Gary Moore of Thin Lizzy and Paul Cook and Steve Jones of the Sex Pistols in a supergroup calling itself the Greedy Bastards that packed the crowds in for shows at the Lyceum in London in December 1978. (*See Sex Pistols; Thin Lizzy.*)

The Boomtown Rats made its first U.S. tour in the late winter and spring to support the *Tonic for the Troops* release and the U.S. issuance of the "Rat Trap" single, which spent some time on American charts. Back in England over the summer, the group basked in the glory of another massive singles hit, "I Don't Like Mondays," issued in July on Ensign and almost immediately number one in the U.K. In ten days, it was certified gold in England and in 1979 passed the platinum level. Issued in the U.S. in September, the single rose higher on American charts than any of the band's U.S. releases. The Rats' third LP, *The Fine Art of Surfacing,* which contained that single, was a top 10 hit in the U.K. and, after release in the U.S.in October 1979, had a moderately successful response from record buyers. At year-end, "I Don't Like Mondays" was voted U.K. Single of the Year in the British Rock and Pop awards.

In 1980, the band had several more charted releases on U.K. lists, including the singles "Diamond Smiles" and reggae-flavored "Banana Republic." The latter was on the band's fourth LP, *Mondo Bongo,* issued in early 1980. Despite extensive U.S. appearances in support of that LP, however, its showing among U.S. record buyers was decidedly lackluster. On the U.S. disco circuit, however, there was some interest in the song "Up All Night."

In the early 1980s, the band remained a top concert act in many European countries, though its position was imperiled by a paucity of new material, suggesting that Geldof might be looking for new ways to employ his talents. For instance, he accepted an invitation to play the role of Pink in the film version of Pink Floyd's *The Wall* concept album. (*See Pink Floyd.*) It wasn't until September 1982 that the next Boomtown Rats album, *V Deep,* came out—a release, as it happened, coinciding with the opening of *The Wall.* There was no new album in 1983, the only Rats release being a six-song "best-of" collection issued in March under the title *Ratrospective.* Two years later, in early 1985, the band's final LP on the Columbia label, *In the Long Grass,* was released.

By then, Geldof had become deeply involved in projects aimed at rallying rock artists behind fundraising efforts to alleviate suffering in drought-stricken parts of Africa. Appalled by news telecasts of dying adults and children, in November 1984 Bob organized almost 40 of the best-known names in British rock (collectively called Band Aid) to record "Do They Know It's Christmas?"—a song he and Midge Ure of Ultravox wrote.

Geldof expected there would be a small response, but to his surprise, the record became a worldwide hit. He told a reporter: "The fact that it became a pop phenomenon was something I hadn't bargained for." By May 1985, worldwide sales were over seven million copies with revenues over $10 million. That achievement led to another charity effort, the U.S.A. for Africa project that spawned the massive hit "We Are the World" as well as a best-selling LP with material provided by some of the superstars of U.S. rock.

Geldof was inspired to undertake an even more ambitious project that he called Live Aid. With his rapport with journalists and widespread contacts in the rock industry, he led the organization of a huge concert featuring many of the most famous pop stars on both sides of the Atlantic for July 13, 1985. Day-long shows were arranged in arenas in Philadelphia in the U.S. and in London, England, featuring a literal who's who of modern rock music. Besides the net

proceeds from ticket sales for the shows, worldwide telecasts gathered pledges of additional contributions from viewers. Overall, the result was collection of tens of millions of dollars to alleviate the famine.

Afterwards, Geldof was involved in decisions on how best to distribute the funds raised while also helping to arrange other special events for similar needs in 1986 and beyond.

Geldof continued to insist he wanted to try to revive his performing career. During 1985–86, he sought a new recording contract from major labels, but insisted he wouldn't sign an agreement unless the Rats were included. Most resisted on the ground that the band's best days were behind it. Finally, it looked as though this could be solved by an arrangement with Atlantic where Geldof would do a solo album, then one with the Rats. At the last moment, Atlantic too demurred from backing a new band project and Geldof finally gave in. He told Dennis Hunt of the *Los Angeles Times* in late 1986 ("Hungry for a Hit Record—A Boomtown Rat Tries it Solo, November 30, 1986), "The Rats are dead."

His first solo LP, which came out during the same month, was titled *Deep in the Heart of Nowhere.*

BOSTON: *Vocal and instrumental group headed by Tom Scholz, born Toledo, Ohio, 1947. Members, mid-1970s: Scholz, Brad Delp, Barry Goudreau, Fran Sheehan, Sib Hashian. Roster, 1987–88: Scholz, Delp, Gary Pihl, C. David Sikes, Jim Masdea, Doug Huffman.*

To say that Tom Scholz's engineering training made him a perfectionist is something of an understatement. Taking eight years between albums while millions of potential buyers champ at the bit could qualify him for a *Guinness Book of Records* entry. (The joke going round the music industry in the late 1980s was that the six years of sessions for Boston's new LP of 1986 constituted the "other Boston marathon.") Amazingly, Boston's '86 album (only its third overall) made the *Billboard* top 10 almost as easily as the two mid 1970s releases.

Scholz grew up in Toledo, Ohio, where his eventual six feet, five inch height qualified him for basketball excellence while his mental endowments resulted in good grades in technical subjects. In the second half of the 1960s, he moved east to study engineering at the Massachusetts Institute of Technology, where he eventually completed work on his master's degree. He had been a rock music fan in his teens and, without abandoning his engineering goals, he began to expand his musical interests, writing his first song in 1969 and polishing his skills on keyboards.

Guitarist Barry Goudreau of the original Boston lineup recalled for Cameron Crowe of *Rolling Stone*

("Boston: The Band From the Platinum Basement," August 10, 1978): "I was in my last year of high school and Tom had just graduated MIT. My band needed a keyboard player and placed an ad in the local paper. Scholz answered the ad. He was just starting to play guitar, too, the first month we were together. He'd say, 'Why don't I play guitar on this one?' We'd say, 'Oh, Tom, don't play guitar, just play keyboards,' One month he was learning to play guitar. The next month he was unbelievable. It wasn't long before it turned out to be his group—and we were doing his material."

As Tom moved into the rock field in earnest, he assembled the band he wanted, including Bradley "Brad" Delp who was lured away from a job at Hot Wad Industries, a firm that made heating coils for Mr. Coffee units. Also a member in the early years of the group was drummer Jim Masdea, replaced by John "Sib" Hashian in the mid-1970s, but back working with Scholz in the 1980s.

Scholz, after graduating from MIT, took a job with the engineering department at Polaroid Corporation. With his wife Cindy's approval, he poured any money he could save from his salary into a basement recording studio on which he later was to hone Boston's first demo tapes. It took several years before he was satisfied with the sounds he could obtain from his band and his 12-track recording system. In time, he and his co-workers completed a demo tape that won them a contract from CBS Records' Epic label in 1975. Though some material for the group's label debut, *Boston* (issued in June 1976), was recorded in Los Angeles, most of the final mix, including the excellent single "More Than a Feeling," came from that basement in Watertown, Massachusetts. The group at the time comprised Delp on vocals, Scholz on guitar and keyboards, Goodreau on guitar, Fran Sheehan on bass, and Hashian on drums.

The enthusiastic response to the band's debut LP (until Whitney Houston's debut album replaced it in 1986, *Boston*'s 9 million sales total ranked as the highest ever by a debut album) caused Epic to clamor for new material. Scholz went back to his studio (by now outfitted with a 24-track system), determined to take his time. Announced release dates slipped by until Scholz finally gave in to Epic's urgings and turned over tapes that became the LP *Don't Look Back* (issued in September 1978). Backed by an extensive concert tour, the album sold well, but not as briskly as the band's first. Scholz blamed part of that on Epic's nagging and decided he would finish his next collection at his own pace. He had given in, he later commented, because he was still unsure of his judgment—had included some songs that weren't fully developed or that he likely would have replaced with others.

Meanwhile, in 1980 Goodreau left for a solo career and took Hashian with him. That same year, looking for an anchor to windward, Tom set up Scholz Research & Design, Inc., to make high technology music equipment. The first product was a volume-control device called the Power Soak and the line expanded in the mid-1980s to include a relatively low-cost miniamp called the Rockman for which 3000 orders were received before the first one was available. By 1987, the company had 30 employees in its Waltham, Massachusetts, plant and had served the purpose of providing Scholz with working capital for his album work.

That had become necessary because of worsening relations between Tom and CBS/Epic. After trying unsuccessfully to entice Tom to provide another LP under a contract for five albums in a 10-year period, the record firm filed a $20 million breach of contract lawsuit against him in 1983. By then Tom, assisted by Delp and Masdea, was taping music for a new album, but had no desire to turn it over to Epic. CBS withheld further royalties while the lawsuit was in progress and got an injunction to prevent Scholz from placing material with another company.

The income from SR&D filled the financial gap while the new album slowly took form. Scholz's attorney got the injunction lifted in 1985 (though the case remained pending) and Tom then firmed up an agreement with another label, MCA. After what Scholz estimated had been 10,000 hours of preparation, the new LP, *Third Stage*, finally came out on MCA in the fall of 1986 and showed up on *Billboard* charts soon after (reaching over 4 million copies sold by mid-1987). The band that accompanied Tom on the 1987–88 concert tour, besides Delp and Masdea, included Gary Pihl on guitar, C. David Sikes on bass, and Doug Huffman on drums.

Scholz, who claimed he wasn't a perfectionist, just "picky," had this to say to Steve Morse of the *Boston Globe* ("6 years in seclusion and Scholz has an album," October 12, 1986): "Why am I so picky? I don't know. I'm not doing this for the money [noting he still lived in the same modest house from his first Boston years]. And it doesn't have anything to do even with the fact that it's a record. I'm sure a psychologist would have an answer right away, but it doesn't matter what it is or how little a project it is. If it's just writing a short letter to someone, I always end up tearing it up, doing it again and not liking it—spending hours at something that should take 20 minutes."

BOWIE, DAVID: *Singer, guitarist, songwriter, actor. Born Bromley, London, England, January 8, 1947.*

A strange figure, David Bowie—damned as degenerate by some critics and hailed as the vanguard star of the last quarter-century by others, but undeniably an artist with great vitality and creative ability. His writings, musically and lyrically, show originality on a par with Bob Dylan or the Beatles, while presenting considerable insight into the complexities of modern life. But for many, Bowie's talent tends to be overshadowed by his private life, particularly his avowed bisexuality.

Exactly where Bowie stands in the music spectrum has not been easy for critics to pin down since he first gained attention in his native England in the late 1960s. This situation satisfies him, for, as he noted: "My appearance changes from month to month. I want to change it. I don't want to be stationary. I want to make myself a vehicle, a prop for my songs. I've always been aware of how the actor must clothe himself for the role he is portraying."

Bowie's career decision came at an early age, as he told *Los Angeles Times* critic Robert Hilburn (November 5, 1972). "I saw a cousin of mine dance when I was very young. She was dancing to Elvis' 'Hound Dog' and I had never seen her get up and be moved so much by anything. It really impressed me. The power of music. I started getting records immediately after that. My mother bought me Fats Domino's 'Blueberry Hill' the next day. When I got older, I heard about Chuck Berry and that led me into r&b, jazz, and blues. I tried to open myself up to all styles."

He learned to play guitar and was writing original material before he finished his formal schooling, going on to work as a commercial artist. He began performing with local rock groups and, in 1968, recorded his first album, *Love You Till Tuesday,* for Deram Records. It made little headway. (He changed his original name of David Robert Jones to David Bowie to avoid confusion with David Jones of the Monkees.) For a time, he gave up music to concentrate on the study of Buddhism, but returned to the entertainment field as a member of a mime troupe. In 1969 he turned to popular music again, recording two more LPs, *David Bowie* and *The Man Who Sold the World. David Bowie* provided a hit U.K. single, "Space Oddity," which became the title of his 1969 album release in the U.S. on the Mercury label. Mercury released *The Man Who Sold the World* in 1970; both Mercury albums were later reissued in 1972 by RCA.

No sooner did he start attracting a following than he dropped out of the music field for a second time. "I was always running away from things," he told Hilburn. "If there was a chance it would lead me to success, I'd retreat. I was afraid of being channeled into the wrong direction. I didn't just want to be a musician. I wanted to be something more, something fuller. I didn't realize then that one thing can lead to another, that being a musician isn't necessarily a dead-end street."

But now people in the entertainment field sought him out, for he had the beginning of a reputation. Critics looked more closely at his activities, chronicling the surprising fact that he married and became father of a son while also admitting to be gay. Bowie seemed little affected by these discussions, but they helped generate public interest in someone who obviously flouted the accepted rules of morality.

In late 1971, Bowie responded affirmatively to a new management proposal from Tony DeFries. This soon resulted in a contract with RCA under which Bowie wrote and recorded *Hunky Dory*. The LP showcased his performing talent and his brilliant lyric touch. The songs dealt with such varied subjects as feelings about fatherhood, Bob Dylan's retreat from rock leadership, and the world of Andy Warhol. The LP didn't come close to gold-record status, but it made the lower rungs of the charts in April 1972 and won Bowie almost unanimous praise from reviewers. He followed with *The Rise and Fall of Ziggy Stardust and the Spiders from Mars,* a concept album detailing (sometimes obscurely) the rise and fall of a rock star. The final track, "Rock'n'Roll Suicide," became an audience-jarring conclusion to his stage act. The record quickly reached best-seller rank.

In late fall, Bowie made his first U.S. tour, winning still more encomiums from critics and audiences for his dazzling performance in which he became the incarnation of his mythical rock star, Ziggy Stardust. Wearing a tight, glittering metallic costume, with high, laced hunting boots and orange-tinted hair, he presented an almost unreal appearance as though he had come from outer space. Onlookers were impressed with the feeling of psychological change that seemed to flow from Bowie's act, the sensation of a glimpse into the perhaps unwelcome world of the future.

These reactions underlined Bowie's ability to project his own mood as expressed in this statement: "What frightens me . . . is that people are holding onto a century that is fast dying . . . a lot of young people as well; those, for example, who are into the idea of communal living. I think that things are going to change so incredibly and so drastically that we should really start developing our ideas along a different tangent. I don't know which way we should go, but what with the pill and sperm banks and all those trimmings, things have got to change very drastically. It's going to be a brave new world and we either join it or we become living relics."

New and old recordings continued to illuminate different creative facets of Bowie over the next few years. Some of his early work was repackaged by London Records on the 1973 release *Images 1966–67*, while his 1970s persona was presented in such RCA albums as *Aladdin Sane* and *Pin-Ups* in 1973, *Diamond Dogs* and *David Live* in 1974, and *Young Americans* in 1975. The last named provided Bowie with his first smash U.S. singles hit, "Fame," which rose to number one on *Billboard* charts the week of September 20, 1975, and stayed there the following week. His single "Space Oddity," reissued in the U.K. that year, rose to the number one position on U.K. lists. Demonstrating his many-sided capabilities during that period, David also produced hit singles for other artists, such as "Walk on the Wild Side" for Lou Reed and "All the Young Dudes" for Mott the Hoople. (*See Mott the Hoople; Reed, Lou.*)

He had told reporters for some time that he wanted to emulate people such as Sinatra and Judy Garland, who could succeed on records, stage, and movies. He got his first chance to try his film wings in the science fiction *The Man Who Fell to Earth*, released in 1976. It was an eerie, thought-provoking venture with good acting by Bowie, but it was not a large-scale hit. When the film came out, David, then based in Los Angeles, was having severe emotional problems exacerbated by a drug habit. This was reflected in his least impressive album project, the 1976 RCA release *Station to Station*.

Looking back on that period, he said: "I was experimenting with my emotional life. I put myself through a test of absorbing every possible experience that I could while I was young, with no realization of what happens later, or that I was even going to be around later. It's the old adage: if I'd known I was going to live that long, I would have looked after myself better. I can't say that I regret any of it in any way. I've learned a lot from it."

In the mid-1970s in Los Angeles, he noted later: "I just went to pieces. I wasn't pulling anything together. So I went to Jamaica with my band and did a tour, half of which I can't remember. It was a fantasy world.

"Then I settled down in Berlin and started my recuperation period, which took me 2–3 years. And even today I sometimes get up and think, 'Well, I'm going to live this day as if it were the last day of my life.' Then about three o'clock in the afternoon, I think perhaps there is a future after all. But I don't have the kind of problems I used to have. I've learned to relax and be my present age and my present position. I feel comfortable in my midthirties. It doesn't seem such an alien place to be."

In Berlin, Bowie teamed with synthesizer whiz Brian Eno (*See Eno, Brian*) for *Low* (issued on RCA in 1977), the first of a series of electronically based avant garde albums. This had been preceded by another RCA release, the 1976 *Changesonebowie*). *Low* had a great number of instrumental offerings as did the next Bowie/Eno collaboration, *Heroes*, also issued in 1977. During that year, Bowie toured the U.S., not as a headliner, but as keyboards player behind rock vocalist Iggy Pop. (*See Pop, Iggy.*) After that tour, his new projects included work on *Just a Gigolo*, a film with Marlene Dietrich. Completed in 1978, it had only a few screenings and then disappeared into the film vaults.

After RCA issued a live concert album, the 1978 two-record *Stage*, Bowie crafted a trio of gems: *Lodger* in 1979, *Scary Monsters* in 1980, and *Changestwobowie* in late 1981. Those produced a number of chart singles, including "Ashes to Ashes" from *Scary Monsters*, which rose to number one on the U.K. charts in September 1980. Not allowing any grass to grow under his feet, while that was happening, Bowie was performing his first major stage role in pre-Broadway tryouts of *The Elephant Man*. The cast performances were well received —particularly Bowie's characterization of the terribly deformed hero, John Merrick—and opened the door for him to star on Broadway.

For all his accomplishments as a recording artist, Bowie in the early 1980s seemed to be making more headway as an actor than as a singer. His early 1980s film credits included highly praised roles in *The Hunger* and *Merry Christmas, Mr. Lawrence*. His album sales, though, paled besides artists such as the Cars and Billy Joel. Many of his best albums, like *Low*, *Heroes*, and *Scary Monsters*, still were far short of platinum or even gold sales levels. Thinking that a label change might reverse that situation, David left RCA for EMI America, signing a reported $10 million arrangement. His very first effort for EMI suggested it would prove profitable for both parties. His spring 1983 *Let's Dance* spawned Bowie's second number one *Billboard* hit in the title song, which reached that point the week of May 21. The album also became a best-seller, easily soaring past platinum levels and staying on the charts throughout 1984, eventually achieving worldwide sales of over four million copies. During 1983, Bowie embarked on one of his most audience-pleasing concert series, the "Serious Moonlight" tour, which drew standing-room–only crowds to places such as the Los Angeles Forum and New York's Madison Square Garden. In late May of the year, Bowie also headlined the huge US Festival concert in Glen Helen Regional Park near San Bernardino, California.

Bowie's second LP on EMI America, *Tonight*, came out in the fall of 1984 and was on the charts into 1985. The title song provided a charted single.

As Bowie himself agreed, however, *Tonight* was a step backward. He said the rather limp collection was a mistake. "I did a foolish thing," he commented, rushing out a follow-up at the record company's urging just to take advantage of the *Let's Dance* album's great success. He should have taken time to assemble and polish a better selection of material, he stated.

True to his word, he didn't come up with a new LP for several years. The end product, *Never Let Me Down* (1987, EMI), was a vast improvement over *Tonight*. All nine songs were Bowie originals, whereas on *Let's Dance* he wrote five and on *Tonight* only four.

He backed the album with the worldwide "Glass Spider" tour, a typical Bowie live spectacular. It employed a massive, translucent spider, 60 feet high by 64 feet wide hanging overhead. The complete stage set (made in duplicate to permit setting up the next auditorium on the tour in advance) weighed 360 tons and took four to five days to assemble. Cost of both sets was estimated to exceed $20 million. The show employed not only a five-piece band, but also a small dance troupe.

Bowie told John Pareles of *The New York Times* (August 2, 1987): "The idea was to concoct surrealist or minimalist stage pieces to accompany rock-and-roll songs. I wanted to bridge together some kind of symbolist theater and modern dance. Not jazz dance, certainly not MTV dance, but something more influenced by Pina Bausch and a Montreal group called Human Footsteps . . . I'm trying to stay on a fine line between what is acceptable in rock-and-roll and taking things out to the edge. I wanted to push the show as much as I could toward my indulgence of what I wanted to see onstage. But I also realized that in a stadium you have to keep some rock essence." (*See Queen.*)

BOY GEORGE: *See Culture Club.*

BREAD: *Vocal and instrumental group. James Griffin, born Memphis, Tennessee; David Gates, born Tulsa, Oklahoma, December 11, 1940; Mike Botts, born Sacramento, California; Robb Royer. Royer replaced in 1971 by Larry Knechtel, born Bell, California.*

As has happened more than a few times in modern music, Bread started out as a studio band, organized primarily to exploit the soft-rock compositions of its three founding members. The reaction to its first releases in 1970 was so good that the group had to add a fourth member and start making the rounds of the concert hall and club circuits.

The three original artists met as a result of their association with the group Pleasure Faire. Robb

Royer had come to the band after experience with small groups during his school years. He had started playing clarinet as a child, adding guitar and piano in his teens. However, he considered music a hobby, starting college as a theater arts major. But his talents as a musician led to a bid to join Pleasure Faire. While with the group, he met James Griffin when Griffin began writing material for it and later met David Gates, a studio musician in Hollywood.

Born and raised in Memphis, Tennessee, Griffin started on the piano while in grade school and took up guitar at 12. Initially he was primarily interested in the classics, but switched to rock by high school age. He also demonstrated an excellent singing voice, which eventually led to a contract as a solo artist from Warner/Reprise Records. In Hollywood, he turned out one album, *Summer Holiday,* that didn't succeed and then turned his attention to songwriting.

Gates grew up in a musical environment in his hometown of Tulsa. His father was a band director, his mother a piano teacher. David began taking lessons on violin and piano at an early age. While attending Will Rogers High School, he dated Leon Russell's sister. When he organized a group to play for local dances, Leon was a member. (*See Russell, Leon.*) By this time, David could play guitar and soon added experience on electric piano, organ, and drums.

After finishing high school, Gates moved to Hollywood to work as a session man and music arranger. One of his string arrangements was used in the Nitty Gritty Dirt Band's hit single, "Buy for Me the Rain." Soon after this, Gates became a member of Pleasure Faire. By the time he joined, Royer and Griffin were collaborating on songs both for the group and for use by other artists. Under the pseudonyms of Robb Wilson and Arthur James, they provided the lyrics to "For All We Know" (the theme for the movie *Lovers and Other Strangers*), winning the 1970 Academy of Motion Picture Arts and Sciences' Oscar for the best song of 1969.

When Pleasure Faire dissolved, Royer, Griffin, and Gates continued to get together to practice and to work on new material. In late 1969, they formed their own group under the name Bread and gained a contract from Elektra Records. They began taping original compositions for an album in February 1970. One of the songs written by Gates, "Make It with You," became a top singles hit that summer rising to number one on *Billboard* charts the week of August 22, 1970. The debut LP, *Bread,* also made the charts.

On the strength of this, offers for performances led to the addition of drummer Mike Botts for a series of appearances over the second half of 1970 and first three months of 1971 in 40 states. Botts had started playing drums when he was 11 and, at 12, lied about his age to the musicians' union so he could play professionally. An enthusiastic jazz fan, he worked with such greats as Wes Montgomery and Jimmy Smith while in his teens. Later, he switched to studio work with rock groups because it was more rewarding financially.

The group followed up its initial successes with more single and album hits. Singles included "It Don't Matter to Me" in 1970 and "Let Your Love Go" and "If" in 1971. Bread also placed the LPs *On the Waters* and *Manna* on the charts in late 1970 and in mid-1971, respectively.

During 1971, Royer was replaced by Larry Knechtel. By his midteens, Knechtel had taught himself piano, organ, guitar, and harmonica. He put these skills to use performing with a local band for church and private parties in Bell, California. Initially, he specialized in rhythm & blues, but by his late teens, he was essentially a rock musician.

He began working nightclubs at 18 and soon after played with various backup groups on concert tours. For five years, he was a member of the band that supported rock star Duane Eddy. (*See Eddy, Duane.*) When the "Shindig" TV rock show got underway, he joined its regular band. At the same time, he found an increasing amount of work as a studio musician, beginning with a number of jobs for Phil Spector. (*See Spector, Phil.*) In the second half of the '60s and into the early '70s, he was one of the top session men in the industry. Among the superhits he provided background accompaniment for were the Byrds' "Mr. Tambourine Man," Mason Williams' "Classical Gas," and Simon and Garfunkel's "Bridge over Troubled Water."

One of Knechtel's first recordings with Bread was the late 1971 hit single, "Baby, I'm-A Want You." The album of that name, the band's fourth LP, was released in January 1972. Both single and album won gold records. Later in the year, Elektra issued the group's fifth album, *Guitar Man,* which proved the band's weakest offering to the point even though it too went gold. Sensing that the band had passed its peak, the members agreed to split in 1973.

Gates and Griffin both opted for solo careers with David signing with Elektra and Griffin with Polydor. Gates debuted with the LP *First* in 1973 and followed with *Never Let Her Go* in 1975. Meanwhile Elektra issued the retrospective *The Best of Bread* (another gold album) in 1973 and *The Best of Bread, Volume 2* in 1974.

In 1976, the regrouped Bread quartet decided to try to regain their earlier position and recorded the LP *Lost without Your Love.* The title song made the *Billboard* top 10. However, overall album sales and

audience response to concerts made the bandsmen decide their original decision had been right and the group broke up again in 1978. Soon after, Gates had a hit single with the title number from the Neil Simon movie *The Goodbye Girl.* He also completed an LP of that title issued by Elektra in 1978 and began the 1980s with another solo album, *Falling in Love Again,* released by Elektra in 1980.

BROWN, JAMES: *Singer, band leader (THE FAMOUS FLAMES), songwriter, drummer, pianist. Born Pulaski, Tennessee, June 17, 1928.**

If someone asked a black teenager in the late 1950s or 1960s whom he would most like to emulate, the answer often would have been James Brown. To anyone outside the ghetto in those years, that would have indicated the great running back of the Cleveland Browns. But the James Brown referred to was not an athlete, but a singer, one of the most phenomenally successful vocalists of recent decades. As a rhythm & blues artist, Brown sold millions of records in the U.S. from the middle '50s to late '60s, yet remained virtually unknown to most white Americans. From the late '60s on, though, while maintaining his rapport with black fans, he achieved equally important status with other segments of the U.S. music audience.

It was the culmination of a life that fell into the Horatio Alger tradition, except that Brown had to overcome far more than poverty. His road to glory led through thickets of prejudice, temptations of crime and drugs, and several years of prison.

While he was still in his childhood, Brown's family moved to Augusta, Georgia. He spent most of his youth in Augusta, a youth marked by a struggle for survival that made him work as a shoeshine boy when he was still grade-school age. He ran with a tough crowd and was already known to local police by the time he reached his teens.

As Brown told Dinah Shore on her NBC-TV morning show in November 1971: "I was a juvenile delinquent. I was in and out of trouble. I tell kids it's not the end of things if they go to jail and to go on. My turning point was when I was confined. I wrote a letter to the parole board; I didn't use lawyers. I explained I was a kid and made mistakes, but wanted to change. And I did change!"

Brown had already done some singing and took music as the best way out of his problems. He started with gospel groups in the late 1940s and, while touring with them, learned to play drums and organ. Be-

---

*Some records indicate he was born in Tennessee, but Brown himself has said he was born in Macon, Georgia, in the '30s.

coming aware of the potential of rhythm & blues in the 1950s he went out on his own. His powerful, deep-throated singing voice caught on with the black patrons of the clubs and theaters of the R&B circuit and Brown began to gain a considerable following in ghetto areas. By the mid-1950s, word of the potential of Brown and his backup group, the Famous Flames, reached the ears of King Records executives. After catching his act, they signed him and released his first singles on the firm's Vocal Federal label.

Brown made some small inroads with his early recordings, then hit it big with his 1956 "Please, Please, Please," written by him in collaboration with John Terry. The record became a top-seller in the U.S. R&B field and also a hit in England. It gained him the first of dozens of million-sellers, though it went unnoticed by the disc jockeys who catered to the American mass market. In 1958, Brown gained his second million-seller with "Try Me," again a hit in the R&B field and in Europe.

By the end of the 1950s, Brown was considered king of R&B. Wherever he went in the U.S., he could fill major auditoriums with black fans, rather than having to settle for the bandbox clubs or rundown theaters where most black R&B artists performed. As the '50s gave way to the '60s, his dominance of the field grew even stronger. In the mid-1960s, he could fill a large concert hall all by himself, whereas the standard R&B troupe had to feature as many as a dozen name acts to do this. And his fee for a one-night concert was $12,500—huge by standards of that day.

The Brown touch was almost certain to give King Records a single or LP selling in the hundreds of thousands. In 1960, he had a major singles hit with "Think" on Federal. The following year, moved to the firm's King label, he scored with "Lost Someone." His singles hits in the mid-1960s included "Prisoner of Love" in 1963; "I Got You" and "Papa's Got a Brand New Bag" in 1965 (with both providing hit LPs of the same titles); and "Ain't That a Groove," "Don't Be a Drop Out," and "It's A Man's, Man's World" in 1966. In 1965, one of the rare Brown LPs issued on another label was a hit: *James Brown Plays James Brown Today and Yesterday* on Smash.

By 1966, Brown's fame had gone beyond the R&B boundaries. The breakthroughs scored by Berry Gordy's Motown Records and Jim Stewart's Stax-Volt helped propel Brown to the front in the mass market too. Brown already was a major star in England and Europe in the mid-1960s, playing to audiences every bit as enthusiastic overseas as in black sections of the U.S. From this point forward, he was a top drawing card for young white Americans and was eagerly sought for appearances on the major U.S. network TV variety shows.

Coming into the late 1960s, Brown showed no signs of slackening in the best-selling record department. In 1967, he had a top single, "Cold Sweat." In 1968, he was represented by "Lickin' Stick-Lickin' Stick (Part 1)," "I Got the Feelin'," and (reflecting the Black Consciousness movement) "Say It Loud, I'm Black and I'm Proud." He had one of his biggest years ever in 1969 with such hits as "Mother Popcorn," "Give It Up or Turn It Loose," "I Don't Want Nobody to Give Me Nothin'," and "Goodbye My Love." He was named number one male R&B vocalist by *Cash Box* and other music industry publications, an honor he had won from many of these publications quite a few times in the past.

By this time, Brown's recordings made their impact equally on the R&B and the pop charts. In the 1970s, his name could be found almost every month on either the top 100 singles or album charts, usually on both. His singles hits for 1970 included "Let A Man Come in and Do the Popcorn (Part 2)," "Brother Rapp," and "Super Bad (Parts 1 & 2)." In 1971, his string of singles best-sellers included "Get Up, I Feel Like Being a Sex Machine (Parts 1 & 2)," "Get Up, Get into It, Get Involved," "I Cried," "Escape-ism," "Hot Pants (Part 1)," and "Make It Funky." His LP hits in the early '70s included: *It's A Mother, Ain't It Funky, The Popcorn,* and *Sex Machine* in 1970; and *Super Bad, Hot Pants,* and *Sho' is Funky Down Here* in 1971.

As his career progressed, Brown devoted an increasing share of his time to helping the less fortunate, mostly in black communities, but in poor white areas as well. He spoke to young people in particular, urging them to better themselves and avoid the perils of crime and drugs. As he told an interviewer: "I tell them to get an education. I know from my experience that this is 75% of the thing you need to make your way in the world. And I don't talk down to them. I come from the ghetto and I still have my shoeshine box in my hand."

Though Brown's voice began to reflect the demands made on it over the many years of performing, he remained a favorite with black fans throughout the 1970s. During the decade, his record company, Polydor, continued to crank out new releases—some new recordings, some reissues or retrospective collections. These included *Soul Classics, Volume 1* and *There It Is* (1972), *Payback* (1973), *Everybody's Doin' the Hustle* (1975), *Get up offa That Thing* (1976), *Mutha's Nature* (1977), *Jam/1980s* and *Take a Look at Those Cakes* (1978), and *Original Disco Man* (1979).

At the start of the 1980s, some critics were beginning to write Brown off as something of a dinosaur.

He still had a record contract with Polydor, which issued such LPs as *People* and *Live/Hot on the One* in 1980, but his songwriting skills seemed to have grown fragile and he appeared unable to attract younger black fans. Even his stage routines seemed a bit weary compared to one of his pile-driving earlier shows capsuled in the *Live and Lowdown at the Apollo* set on the Solid Smoke label, released in 1980.

But Brown confounded his detractors by finding new verve and inspiration, fired in part by his finding support from young white fans who could see the roots of punk and new wave in Brown's repertoire. As he told reporters, not only was he "the Godfather of Soul," but he had in the '60s covered some of the themes and worn some of the hairdos popular with punk and new wave musicians in the 1980s. Many of those artists showed their respect for him by showing up at his concerts; Brown in turn reworked and updated the contents of his shows to reflect the music patterns of the decade. His concert material in the early and middle 1980s covered a range from ballads such as "Try Me" to up-tempo numbers "Papa's Got a Brand New Bag," "Say It Loud, I'm Black and I'm Proud," and his early '80s chart hit, "It's Too Funky in Here."

Even in his fifties, Brown continued to give onlookers a superhigh energy show. As he told Don Waller (*L.A. Weekly,* April 13–19, 1984): "What you should do is give people more than their money's worth. Make them tired 'cause that's what they came for. Anytime you can go out and work for an hour and make 10, 15, 40, 100,000 dollars as opposed to a man workin' 13 hours, 10 hours a day and makin' $75, you've been blessed. You owe those people something. And I wear uniforms so that you know you came to see a show—not to see somebody look like you look on the street. I'm not gonna look in the audience and see my uniforms. You're gonna have to look at the stage to catch the show 'cause nobody's gonna look like me in the audience. That's what it's about."

He also was proud that so much of his material still was available in record stores. "I have over 800 songs in my repertoire; 83 million-sellers. And so many other songs that sold 700-, 800-, 900,000. But some of the million-sellers were songs that sold eight, ten, fifteen million over a period of time. 'Please, Please, Please' was released in 1956—recorded in '55—and today you can get that song on a 45 or an album and that's unbelievable 'cause most songs have been deleted from the catalog."

For a while in the mid-1980s, Brown was without a record contract and, naturally, anything approaching a chart hit. But the ebullient artist continued to prepare new material and talk to label executives. To the surprise of many observers, Brown demonstrated he still could place new recordings on the hit lists. In 1986, he could point to his first top 10 chart hit in a dozen years, "Living in America" (on Scotti Bros./Epic from the "Rocky IV" soundtrack), an appropriate achievement for a man inaugurated as one of the first members of the new Rock'n'Roll Hall of Fame in Cleveland. His new-found success inspired Polydor to release the LP *In the Jungle Groove* in 1986, though its tracks were originally laid down from 1969 to 1971.

In late 1986, Brown was represented by an excellent new LP on Scotti Brothers/Epic (produced by Dan Hartman, who co-wrote, with Charlie Midnight, "Living in America") called *Gravity.* Songs from the album were important elements in Brown's concerts of 1987–88.

As he had enthused to Waller in 1984: "Let's not forget James Brown picked cotton. James Brown shined shoes. And yet James Brown is still active. Because James Brown worked all the way to the top or worked all the way to where I'm at. If it's considered the top, then I thank God. But I considered myself at the top a long time ago because I first started out tryin' to get a decent meal, a decent pair of shoes. So when I got to where I could do that, I thought I was on the top anyway."

BROWNE, JACKSON: *Songwriter, singer, pianist, guitarist. Born Heidelberg, Germany, October 9, 1948.*

It might be said that Jackson Browne was to the '70s as Bob Dylan was to the '60s. Not that they are alike in styles or songwriting approach; but if Dylan was the premier solo folk-rock artist of the '60s, Browne certainly could lay claim to that status for the following decade.

Browne was born in Germany, but moved to Los Angeles with his family when he was three. He studied several instruments at an early age and was a proficient pianist and guitarist by his late teens. By then, he had also demonstrated a budding talent for songwriting. In 1967, he went to New York City, where he worked at a number of local clubs through 1968. He picked up experience, but didn't make much headway in furthering his position in the music field.

In the late '60s, he headed back to the West Coast which became his home base from then on. He picked up some jobs as a sideman and session pianist in Los Angeles, but his reputation began to rise with his peers mainly because of his songwriting skills. He became friends with Linda Ronstadt, J.D. Souther, future Eagles' mainstay Glenn Frey, and other struggling young performers with a bent for blending folk and country elements with rock. (*See Eagles, The; Frey, Glenn; Ronstadt, Linda.*)

In fact, for a while, Frey and Souther joined Jackson in his frugal $60 a month apartment in L.A.'s Echo Park district as all of them waited for the big break. Frey and Brown worked on song material together; one creation—"Take It Easy"—was to prove highly important later on for the Eagles. Browne's version of the song was included in his *For Everyman* album. But Browne began to make progress as a songwriter in the late '60s and early '70s as more and more artists recorded his material, including Tom Rush, Linda Ronstadt, Johnny Rivers, the Byrds, and Brewer and Shipley.

During that period, he made several attempts to make his way as a solo artist, without notable success. However, in 1971, he finally struck paydirt when David Geffen signed him for his new label, Asylum Records. His debut LP, *Jackson Browne,* came out in October 1971 and gradually garnered considerable airplay across the country, particularly on FM stations. It made the charts in early 1972 and stayed on them for months, helping to spawn two hit singles, "Doctor My Eyes" and "Rock Me on the Water." Browne backed it up with a steady round of concerts that included tours with J.D. Souther and the Eagles in the fall.

After 1972, Jackson never looked back. Though his album output was relatively sparse in the '70s, every one contained a number of folk-rock gems, most completely written by him. Those songs plus other originals were often covered or introduced by other artists, among them Bonnie Raitt, Ronstadt, Joan Baez, Ian Matthews, Gregg Allman, and Warren Zevon. In his concert tours, Browne surrounded himself with excellent musicians, including noteworthy talents such as fiddler/pedal-steel player/guitarist David Lindley and lead guitarist Waddy Wachtel. Unlike other stars, Browne never disdained playing smaller venues. Much of his concert work was on the college circuit with ticket prices set within a typical student's budget.

His second LP, *For Everyman,* came out on Asylum in the fall of 1973; the single "Red Neck Friend" from it made regional charts. The album itself was on best-seller lists well into 1974. In the fall of 1974, he was represented by his third album, still one of his finest, *Late for the Sky,* which remained in upper chart levels into 1975.

Though Browne continued an intensive concert schedule, it was close to two years before he completed another LP. By the time that collection came out in late 1976, considerable anticipation had been built up among his now sizable following. Called *The Pretender,* the LP rose to the top five on the charts in December, having earned a gold-record award from the RIAA on November 14, 1976. His next release, *Running on Empty,* found even more

favor with the public. It turned up on the charts almost as soon as it was issued in late 1977, staying there into 1979, bringing a platinum-record award along the way.

During the 1970s, Browne remained a strong advocate of protecting the environment and saving endangered species, often giving fund-raising concerts for causes he believed in. At the end of the '70s, he joined forces with Graham Nash in urging a stop to the proliferation of nuclear power. They helped assemble a number of concerts in 1979 both to express that opposition and to collect money to fight nuclear energy. They were joined in 1979 by many rock and folk-rock artists in a series of concerts in New York's Madison Square Garden that provided material for a two-record *No Nukes* live album.

Browne's strong interest in antinuclear and other social causes may have caused him to reduce his emphasis on writing new singles candidates or touring. His album releases and concert tours were considerably more sporadic in the 1980s than in the previous decade. He began the decade with the 1980 Asylum album *Hold Out,* a reasonably good collection, though not up to his earlier standards. But it was certainly far better than his 1983 LP, *Lawyers in Love.* The latter was on the charts the last 19 weeks of 1983 and into 1984, earning gold-record certification, but it was one of the major disappointments of 1983. His 1986 collection on Elektra, *Lives in the Balance,* however, restored some of the luster to his writing credits and suggested he might have a brighter future in store for his still sizable following.

BRUFORD, BILL: *See King Crimson; Yes.*

BRUCE, JACK: *See Cream, The.*

BUCKINGHAM, LINDSEY: *See Fleetwood Mac.*

BUFFALO SPRINGFIELD: *Vocal and instrumental group. Members, as of 1967: Stephen Stills, born Dallas, Texas, January 3, 1945; Neil Young, born Toronto, Canada, November 12, 1945; Dewey Martin, born Chesterville, Ontario, Canada, September 30, 1942; Richie Furay, born Dayton, Ohio, May 9, 1944; Bruce Palmer, born Liverpool, Canada, circa 1947.*

The Buffalo Springfield has a massive reputation among pop music fans, which is surprising, since it remained together as a unit for only about a year. Members Steve Stills and Neil Young went on to great success as solo artists and with later groups. Yet the fame of the Springfield doesn't rest on this, but rather on their combined music, which is considered among the best ever turned out by a rock'n'roll aggregation.

Of course, in the ever-changing world of popular music, few groups have stayed together long. Partly because of the rigors of the road and partly because of the intense competition from countless other groups, intergroup rivalries develop or the lack of concerts or recording dates put an economic damper on the members. In most cases, the group (with a few changes in personnel over the years) that stays together for several years is the one with a chance for major recognition. There are a few exceptions, such as the Buffalo Springfield, based on some unusual blend of talents that makes the ensemble an almost overnight success.

The Springfield, also dubbed the "Herd," was formed in the spring of 1966 and gained notice among insiders so rapidly that it was featured in a Hollywood Bowl rock concert on July 25, 1966, before it ever had a record released. Its Bowl reception was so intense that Nick Vanoff (producer of ABC-TV's "Hollywood Palace") signed them immediately for six guest dates after seeing them there.

By the time of the Bowl show, the Springfield had signed with Atco Records, a subsidiary of Atlantic, though their first discs were still in the processing stage. The record world had heard of them because of a seven-city concert tour with the Byrds that spring followed by a long stay at the famed Whisky a Go Go on the Sunset Strip. After examining offers from 23 firms, the Herd went with Atco because lead performer Stephen Stills liked the work of Atco record producers Charles Greene and Brian Stone. Soon after the Bowl performance, the Herd had its first nationwide hit, "For What It's Worth," written by Stills.

The group became famous in a short period, but all of its members had put in considerable preparatory time before the Herd began. Stills, whose family lived in many parts of the South and, for a time, Central America, went to a wide assortment of schools. He entered the University of Florida in the early 1960s as a political science major, but found folk music more to his liking, and soon quit school for New York, where he polished up experience on a variety of instruments—drums, guitar, piano, tambourine. He joined a nine-member group called the Au Go Go Singers that included Richie Furay.

Furay, singer and rhythm guitarist, grew up in Ohio and entered Otterbein College in Westerville, Ohio. He formed a folk trio that won so much local attention that he left school for New York, finding work initially at a club called the Four Winds. Things went slowly for a while. Then he joined the Au Go Go group, which managed to cut one record, gain one TV appearance, and take one 1964 concert tour that wound up in Texas before breaking up. The tour went through Canada, where on one date in Winnipeg, the Au Go Go members played with a group called Neil Young and the Squires. After leaving the Au Go Go, Stills went west to Los Angeles, while Furay returned to New York. Both lived from hand to mouth for most of the next year and a half.

Young, meanwhile, left his group to work as a single for a time and then made a record in Detroit with a group called the Mynah Birds. Neil had been playing in groups since the ninth grade in public school, gaining incentive to learn guitar from Elvis Presley's hits. He left high school before graduating to concentrate on singing, playing guitar, and songwriting. After his wanderings took him to Detroit, he decided to head for California with another member of the Mynah Birds, Bruce Palmer, after the Mynah Birds' leader was drafted. Young arrived in Los Angeles in 1965, but had little success in his attempts to form a new group until he ran into Steve Stills again on Sunset Blvd. The two agreed to work together and, with Palmer on hand, Stills added a fourth member when Furay arrived on the coast to visit him.

The drummer the other four decided they needed was Dewey Martin, then playing with the MFO after a stint with the bluegrass-rock group, the Dillards. Martin had a heavy country orientation. Though born in Canada, he moved to Nashville, Tennessee, in the early 1960s. His drumming was good enough to gain him a place with the Grand Ole Opry. For the first half of the 1960s he supported many country music greats, including Carl Perkins, Roy Orbison and the late Patsy Cline. On a trip to Los Angeles in 1964 with Faron Young's group, he liked the climate and decided to move west. He played as a sideman at recording sessions for a time. Then he moved to Seattle, Washington, as lead vocalist and drummer for his own group, Sir Walter Raleigh and the Coupons. By the end of 1965, though, he was back in Los Angeles to stay.

The Herd practiced for several months in a remote L.A. location before trying for their first job. The five personalities merged into a single unit that combined excellent musicianship with the ability to compose everything from hard rock to folk music and country-rock.

The band signed with Atlantic Records in 1966, which released the group's recordings on its Atco label. The group's first single success was a Neil Young-penned number, "Nowadays Clancy Can't Even Sing." Released in August 1966, it made the top 10 in Los Angeles and was a regional but not a national hit. But the group gained a countrywide reputation with Steve Stills's composition "For What It's Worth," issued in December 1966 and up to number seven in *Billboard* in early 1967.

The latter song dealt with the Sunset Strip riots, which pitted young protesters against local law officers. Stills commented to Jeffrey C. Alexander of the *Los Angeles Times* ("The Buffalo Springfield Message," September 17, 1967): "When I write about something like [that], I'm separating myself from the whole thing. I'm an observer because I'm a songwriter and I'm here to spread the news like the minstrels of the 15th century.

"The news is that the straight world has been getting worse and worse since World War II. Those boys that won the world by fire were great, but now they're trying to do it again. Except they're going to lose this time 'cause the fire's too big."

Later in 1967, the group made some regional charts with the singles "Bluebird" and "Rock'n' Roll Woman," arguably among the best songs Stills has written. The band's albums on Atco comprised *Buffalo Springfield* (1966); *Buffalo Springfield Again* (1967); and *Last Time Around* (1968).

In 1967, at the height of their powers, the Springfield were being favorably compared to such landmark groups as the Beatles and Rolling Stones. Most observers expected still greater things to come when the group suddenly and irrevocably separated in mid-1967. The reason for the breakup was also one of the reasons for the Herd's greatness. It was composed of five strong-willed people, each an individualist and each very talented. The clash of ideas finally became too much for some of them, so first one, then another left. For a while, the Springfield continued with various replacement sidemen, but when all the original members had departed, it ceased to exist.

Atco repackaged some of the band's recording in later years. In 1969 the *Retrospective* LP was released. In 1976, a two-record anthology, *Buffalo Springfield*, was offered. That album included material from all three of the original LPs including the full nine-minute original version of "Bluebird," which had been edited down when included in *Buffalo Springfield Again*.

Stills and Young won further acclaim as solo artists and in Crosby, Stills, Nash & Young. Furay appeared in Poco and in the short-lived Souther-Hillman-Furay band organized by Asylum Records founder David Geffen. (*See Byrds, The; Crosby, Stills, Nash & Young; Loggins and Messina; Poco; Stills, Stephen; Young, Neil.*)

BURDON, ERIC: *Singer, songwriter, band leader. Born Newcastle-on-Tyne, England, April 5, 1941.*

Coming from the north of England, Eric Burdon's accent made him sound like someone who graduated from the factory to rock music, at least to Americans who heard him interviewed on TV or radio. Actually, unlike many members of the English pop groups of the 1960s, Burdon was attending college by the time he decided to earn his living as a singer.

As he told Sharon Lawrence of *The Los Angeles Times* in July 1970: "It's such a difficult thing for me to get across to people and make them understand that I got trapped in the music business. I was in college studying—the reason that I went to college in the first place was because I wanted to be a set designer or an art director. That was me ambition. And there was nowhere in England that I could be trained in that, so second best I took graphics and studied everything from photography to commercial art.

"During the period of being in college, I formed a group to entertain meself. When I left college, I couldn't get employment in a job to my satisfaction in a situation that excited me enough. And I couldn't break into television because it was a closed thing. Movies were a closed area too. So out of frustration to express myself, I kept on singing. Then I became popular and people wouldn't let me out of it because I'm a financial success to managers and agents."

Burdon was born and raised in Newcastle, a port city on Britain's east coast just below the Scottish border. He became interested in rock music when he was 12. A merchant seaman who lived below Eric's family brought home some American records, then unavailable in England, of such artists as Fats Domino and Bill Doggett. "I liked them better than anything I'd heard before and I began to wish I could play an instrument or sing. And I found I didn't have the talent to play an instrument, so I just kept on singing.

"I never looked on meself as a singer and I don't suppose I ever will. I'm really not a singer in the sense that the people I started out hero-worshiping were never singers either, people like Joe Turner. They were just blues shouters. You had to like them for their personality."

Burdon continued to sing as he progressed through early schooling and then college. In the early 1960s, as he noted, he turned music from a hobby to a profession, fronting a rock group in a Newcastle club for 30 shillings (about $4.16) a week per musician. Burdon and the group, called the Animals, asked the owner of the club to manage them. The latter laughed at the idea until one of England's best-known rock band leaders, Graham Bond, dropped by the club specifically to hear the group. He then turned most of his attention to capitalizing on the Animals' growing reputation. (*See Animals, The.*)

By 1963, the Animals were finding audience acceptance in other English cities and soon signed their first recording contract. In another year, they were among the top-rated rock groups in England and were ready for tours of the continent and the U.S. For the next half-decade, the Animals were ranked with the Beatles and Rolling Stones as one of the major attractions at rock concerts in most parts of the world.

In the late 1960s, the group cut down on its in-person appearances and finally disbanded. Burdon took time off to work on various projects, including a novel and plans for possible films on rock music. He moved to Los Angeles because he liked the climate and the recording studio capabilities and "because it's the center of the movie industry and movies are still a big dream of mine." In 1969, though, urged on by his manager, he agreed to find a new group to work with. This band, mainly recruited from an earlier one called Nite Shift, consisted of six black musicians from the U.S. and a Danish harmonica player.

He rehearsed the band for several months in the fall, then recorded new material, and started a series of tours of U.S. cities. They decided to name the band War. As Eric explained to Sharon Lawrence: "We were rapping one day about the ultimate exchange of egos between men and about what war is. So many people are going around saying peace these days and they don't mean it. War is such an anti-name. It's short and people won't forget it."

At the start of 1970, Burdon and War gained a hit single with "Spill the Wine" on MGM Records, the label on which the Animals has long been featured. This was followed by the highly successful LP, *Eric Burdon Declares War*, which stayed on the charts for a good part of 1970. During this time, War remained U.S.-based, not making an in-person appearance in England until the Isle of Wight festival in August 1970. In early 1971, the group was again represented on the charts with the LP *Black Man's Burdon*.

By 1972, however, the partnership between Burdon and War had come to an end and Burdon was out of the spotlight for the next few years. He later attributed that period of inaction, coupled with the release of several unauthorized LPs of outtakes and experimental tracks he'd made with War, as contributing to a loss of interest by critics and fans in his career. In the mid-1970s, he won a new recording contract from Capitol, which issued such LPs under the Eric Burdon Band banner as *Ring of Fire* (1974) and *Stop* (1975). Those albums, though, did nothing to rejuvenate his career.

During the second half of the 1970s, Burdon's forward progress was hampered by problems including legal entanglements with record firms and poorly planned concert efforts. In the early 1980s, however, he began to put the pieces back together and found

challenging work as an actor in a number of films and TV shows while slowly reestablishing himself as a valid rock vocalist. His concerts in small clubs in the early and middle 1980s proved he was still capable of considerable vitality and emotional power.

BURKE, SOLOMON: *Singer, songwriter. Born Philadelphia, Pennsylvania c. early 1940s.*

Blues music, though related to gospel material, generally is closer in tone and feeling to ragtime and jazz. Deeply religious Negro parents in the '40s and '50s often tried to shield their families from blues songs and singers, considering them to be sinful. As the strict fundamentalist outlook of many Negro religious denominations began to change with the rise of the Civil Rights movement, the taboos against the blues also began to die out. One result was a new mingling of traditional gospel with blues that resulted in the more sophisticated form of R&B known as soul.

A key figure in the transition is Solomon Burke, whose early roots were as deep in gospel as possible. From a religious family in South Philadelphia, Burke was taken to church almost as soon as he could walk. His parents were happy to find Solomon had a fine voice and saw to it that the members of the church were aware of it. When Solomon was nine, he made his debut as a soloist in church. Soon after, he showed an excellent speaking style and was giving sermons to the congregation.

By age 12, he had a broad reputation in the black community as "the wonder-boy preacher." Before his thirteenth birthday, he was leader of his own church, Solomon's Temple. He had his own religious program on a local radio station, combining his own gospel singing with his sermons. The wife of leading Philadelphia disc jockey Kae Williams tuned in on the program one day and told her husband about young Solomon's vocal prowess. Williams followed the lead and helped bring Burke to the attention of a record firm. Soon Solomon had a minor hit with the gospel song "Christmas Presents from Heaven," a song he wrote for his grandmother. He made three more records for the small firm, including one co-authored by former boxing champion Joe Louis, before signing with Atlantic Records in November 1960.

In early 1961, Atlantic brought out its first Burke single, "How Many Times." The disc made the charts, though not the top level. But the next release, a soulful, hardly religious ballad called "Just Out of Reach (of My Two Open Arms)," was a top 10 R&B hit and one of the best-sellers in the field for 1961.

From then on, Burke was one of the first-ranked stars both in the soul market and in the broader national pop market. From 1962 through 1964, he had such best-sellers as "Cry to Me," "Everybody Needs Somebody to Love," "Can't Nobody Love You," "If You Need Me," and "You're Good for Me." His popularity soared with both black and white fans. His contributions to pop music caused disc jockey Rockin' Robin of Baltimore station WEBB to designate him "King of Rock'n'Soul," an unofficial title seconded by many other record spinners.

Burke had a number of other singles hits on Atlantic, including "Got to Get You off My Mind" and the 1965 top 10 disc, "Tonight's the Night." He also was represented by a number of LPs, including *If You Need Me, Rock 'n' Soul, Solomon Burke's Greatest Hits,* and *The Best of Solomon Burke.* By the late '60s Burke was having trouble finding hits and he moved to Bell Records. An early result of the change was the 1969 top 10 hit of John Fogerty's composition, "Proud Mary." An LP by that title followed.

Throughout the '60s and '70s and into the early '80s, Burke returned many times to such mainstays of the soul circuit as the Apollo in Harlem, Chicago's Regal, Washington's Howard, and the Royal and Uptown Theaters. He also was the feature attraction at such nightclubs as the Baby Grand in New York, Sir John in Miami, Thunderbird in Los Angeles, Royal Peacock in Atlanta, and Pink Poodle in Indianapolis.

At the start of the 1970s, Solomon recorded for MGM, for whom he provided a number of r&b chart hits, including the album *Get Up & Do Something for Yourself* and the singles "Electronic Magnetism," "Love's Street and Fool's Road," and "We're Almost Home" during 1971–72. Later releases included the Chess LPs *Music to Make Love By* (1974) and *Back to My Roots* (1975), neither of which gave justice to his talents. At the end of the 1970s, Infinity Records released his LP *Sidewalks, Fences and Walls,* most of whose tracks showcased Burke at his best. In 1980, Charly Records in England issued the LP *From the Heart,* which was available as an import item in the U.S. Rounder Records put out *Soul Alive* (a two-disc concert set) in 1984 and *A Change Is Gonna Come* in 1986.

Burke's name in the 1980s was unfamiliar to most young soul or rock music fans in the U.S., but he still commanded great respect in England and Europe. Many British rock stars of the 1960s, including Mick Jagger, testified to the impact Burke's recordings had on their own creative development.

BURNETTE, DORSEY: *Singer, guitarist, songwriter. Born Memphis, Tennessee, 1933;* *died Woodland Hills, California, August 19, 1979.*

On October 12, 1979, a group of friends of Dorsey Burnette held a special benefit concert for his family at the Los Angeles Forum. Among those performing in honor of this gifted artist were Glen Campbell, Kris Kristofferson, Gary Busey, Delaney and Bonnie Bramlett, Johnny Paycheck, Roger Miller, and Tanya Tucker. The concert's advertisements called Burnette "the Father of Rock and Roll," which was a bit of an exaggeration, but there is no doubt that he contributed to the birth of that field just as he did over the years to progress in country and western music.

Memphis-born and bred, Dorsey's first love as a boy was country music. As he told Lee Rector of *Music City News* in 1975, as soon as he could drive a car and had some money in his pockets, "I used to drive all the way to Nashville every Saturday night to go to the Grand Ole Opry. I had been listening to it ever since I was just a little kid rolling around on the floor. My old man wouldn't miss that show for anything in the world."

Burnette and his brother Johnny (born Memphis, March 25, 1934) learned to play instruments at an early age and were playing for friends and in school events in their teens. In the early '50s, they had their own country band and played dances and clubs in Arkansas, Louisiana, and Mississippi. Ruggedly built, Dorsey considered trying for a career in boxing. "I went to St. Louis as a pro fighter," he told Rector, "but it got to where I would come home and there would be blood coming from somewhere. I remembered how I picked that guitar, so I said, 'It's time to learn to pick a little better.'"

Still, Dorsey wasn't certain he should concentrate on music. For six years, he worked to get his electrician's license. However, he found that he didn't enjoy crawling around in narrow passages in buildings "getting that fiberglass insulation down in your rear end where you can't scratch." But his electrical training did help when he and Johnny needed some money to tide them over between engagements. It provided living expenses, for instance, in the early '50s, when the brothers sought to score a breakthrough in New York. They finally got an audition for the "Ted Mack Amateur Hour" and won the show four straight times. "After that, we went on tour with the show playing banquets, Madison Square Garden, and for President Harry Truman."

In 1954, the Burnettes were in Memphis working at Crown Electric Company, where Elvis Presley first worked after getting out of high school. Presley was their friend during those years, as was another Crown employee, guitarist Paul Burlison. Burlison and the Burnettes formed the Burnette Trio, which played local clubs when the chance came along. During those times, as their friend, concert promoter Preston Pierce, recalled to Art Fein of *The Los Angeles Times*: "Elvis used to call Dorsey and Johnny the Dalton Gang, for all the trouble they'd get into." Not long before Elvis cut his first record, he did a guest spot in a Trio show.

The Burnettes began making singles of their own in the mid-1950s, though their efforts didn't come close to matching Elvis's blockbuster success. Two of their releases on Coral Records have become classics, though: "Tear It Up" and "Train Kept a-Rollin'." The first of those was revived by Britain's Yardbirds with great success in the mid-1960s and the latter was a major hit for the rock band Aerosmith in the late '70s. (*See Aerosmith; Yardbirds, The*.) Original versions have been reissued on *Johnny Burnette/The Rock 'n Roll Trio: Tear It Up* on Solid Smoke Records.

Becoming discouraged about chances of moving upward in the music field, the Burnettes moved to California in 1957. Back then, said Dorsey, "No one would listen to us in Memphis. We played a lot of times for our beer and passed the hats." But when they headed west, their fortunes changed for a while. They decided to stress their writing talents and in short order became associated with Ricky Nelson. (*See Nelson, Rick*.) Together or individually, they provided Rick with a series of smash hits: "Waitin' in School," "Just a Little Too Much," "Believe What You Say," and "It's Late."

At the start of the '60s, the brothers felt they were ready to return to the performing wars, this time as soloists. In 1960, Dorsey made the charts with "Hey Little One" and "Tall Oak Tree." (In 1968, his close friend Glen Campbell turned out a single of "Hey Little One" that went past platinum-record levels.) Before long, Johnny was in the winner's circle with hits such as "You're Sixteen" and "Dreamin'." However, on August 1, Johnny was killed in a boating accident, an event that left Dorsey emotionally scarred for years.

Dorsey's pop music efforts faltered in the mid-1960s and he began to concentrate on country-oriented songs, though initially without any marked impact on country charts.

For a while in the '60s, Dorsey had the house band at the Palomino Club in North Hollywood. One of his band members was a then-unknown named Johnny Paycheck. Among the artists Dorsey worked with or socialized with during the '60s and '70s were Roger Miller, Delaney and Bonnie Bramlett, and Glen Campbell.

Dorsey continued to develop new material and in the 1970s his ability as a singer and writer finally brought increasing attention from country fans. Between 1971 and 1977, he placed 14 songs on the national lists. During the first half of the '70s, chartmakers on Capitol Records included "In the Spring," "Darling Don't Come Back," "Let Another Good One Get Away," and "I Just Couldn't Let Her Walk Away." He also was respected for his gospel songs, one of the most recorded being "The Magnificent Sanctuary Band." He recorded two albums for Capitol, "but they really didn't go like I would have liked to see them go." To try to improve things in that department, he moved to Melodyland Records in 1975 and soon had one of his best-selling country singles, "Molly, I Ain't Getting Any Younger." He followed with three more charted singles over the next few years.

A comparatively young man, Dorsey seemed to be on the way to major acceptance as a country artist at the end of the 1970s. He had a lot of projects he was looking forward to in the summer of 1979; he had just signed a contract with Elektra/Asylum Records and his debut single on the label, "Here I Go Again," was finding favor with country fans. He also was discussing a new show in Las Vegas designed to showcase his own hits and those of his brother. At that juncture, he was felled by a heart attack in his Woodland Hills, California, home on August 19.

Tommy Thomas (owner of the Palomino Club where Dorsey had performed many times in the '60s and '70s and where he often came to cheer the acts of his many friends in country music) mourned Dorsey's passing. He told Art Fein: "Dorsey was a great artist. In many ways he was ahead of his time. But no matter what stage of his career he was at, we'd always book him into our club. The man had a lot of friends."

The Burnette name continued to appear on club and concert hall marquees in the 1980s thanks to Dorsey's son, Billy, and Johnny's heir, Rocky. Rocky began the decade with a rockabilly hit single, "Tired of Toein' the Line" and a 1980 LP on EMI, *Son of Rock & Roll*. Billy, who had two rather ineffective pop rock releases on Polydor in 1979, *Billy Burnette* and *Between Friends*, began to emphasize rockabilly in his 1980 label debut on Columbia, *Billy Burnette*, and the follow-up 1981 release, *Gimme You*.

BURNETTE, JOHNNY: *See Burnette, Dorsey.*

BUTLER, JERRY: *Singer, songwriter, record producer. Born Sunflower, Mississippi, December 8, 1939.*

From the late 1950s well into the 1970s, Jerry Butler maintained his position as one of the most successful performers and recording artists in the soul/R&B field. When those aspects of his career began to taper off, he still exerted considerable influence on other artists from his songwriting and record producing skills.

Jerry was born in a small town in Mississippi, but moved north to Chicago with his family in 1942 before his third birthday. His family was devout and took their children to church regularly. He emphasized to Bob Gibson of his public relations agency that because of the influences of his early years he had developed what he felt was "a universal sound which says to me that it doesn't have to be all brass, all strings, or all fuzz tones and wah wah pedals. If I feel like going into the studio and just adding hand-clapping, that's fine.

"There are folks that don't have musical instrument training that grew up on hand-clapping. I learned to sing a capella in a choir with nothing but voices, hands and feet stomping, but I would be very foolish to go through life thinking that I could just keep on singing a capella. So I really get bugged with self-styled critics that get off into the 'pure' blues or the pure R&B and they don't realize that the folks played it that way because they didn't have an alternative."

When Jerry was 12, he became a member of the choir of the Travelling Souls Spiritual Church. In the choir with him was a younger boy with an excellent voice, Curtis Mayfield. The two became friends and compared notes as both became involved in singing rhythm & blues material in the mid-1950s. (*See Mayfield, Curtis.*)

At first, they worked together, forming a gospel group called the Modern Jubelaires. Then they went separate ways as leaders of different groups and came back together again in 1957, when they organized a group called Jerry Butler and the Impressions. Picking up work in Chicago area clubs, they built a local following. This helped gain them a recording contract from Vee Jay Records. One of their first single releases, "For Your Precious Love" (co-written by Butler and two brothers named Brooks who then were with the Impressions) gained considerable airplay on R&B stations and became a top 10 hit in 1958. (*See Impressions, The.*) The song was first put out simply under the name of the Impressions, but the label was changed to read "Jerry Butler and the Impressions," paving the way for his solo career. He left the group, a move that almost ended the saga of the Impressions. It was an amicable parting, though, and later some of Butler's first hits were with Mayfield compositions: "Let It Be

Me" and his 1960 top 10 single, "He Will Break Your Heart."

In 1961, he had top 10 R&B hits with "Find Another Girl" and "I'm A-Telling You." In 1964, he had two R&B top 10 singles that also appeared on the pop charts: "Need to Belong" and "I Stand Accused." All were on Vee Jay.

In the mid-1960s, Vee Jay went out of business and Jerry moved over to Mercury. At first, he was more successful with albums than singles for them, attaining the R&B charts with *Soul* (April 1967) and *Mr. Dream Merchant* (February 1968). By this time, soul was "in" with the public at large, and such songs as "Never Give You Up," "Are You Happy," and "Western Union Man" worked their way high up on the general charts as well as R&B lists. Jerry now could pick and choose the spots for his in-person appearances, avoiding the back-breaking schedule of the early part of his career. He remained a top star on the R&B circuit, performing in the most prestigious theaters and clubs. He also played big name clubs everywhere from New York to Vegas and San Francisco.

From 1968 through the early 1970s, Jerry seemed to be leading a one-man assault on the best-seller lists. In 1969, he had two of the year's top-sellers, "Only the Strong Survive" and "Don't Let Love Hang You Up," and was ranked by most major industry trade publications in the top 20 among all singers and the top 10 in the soul category.

In 1970, he kept up his pace with the top 10 R&B single, "Where Are You Going" in the fall and two hit LPs, *You and Me* and *Special Memory*. In 1971, he did even better, beginning in the early part of the year with the hit LP, *Jerry Butler Sings Assorted Sounds by Assorted Friends and Relatives*. In May, he had a top 10 hit, one of the major R&B singles of the year, "If It's Real What I Feel." He followed it up in July with "How Did We Lose It Baby," in October with "Walk Easy My Son," and in December with a duet with Brenda Lee Eager, "Ain't Understanding Mellow." He had several chart-rated albums as well, including *Sagittarius Movement*. During the year, he teamed up with another Mercury artist, Gene Chandler, in a duo that won applause for a number of concert appearances and excellent recording efforts. At year end, Chandler and Butler were voted number two duo of the year by *Cash Box* and other trade publications.

In the early 1970s, Jerry was given the chance to do some film-related work. That included recording the soundtrack for the movie *Joe* and scoring the soundtrack for *Melinda*. He also appeared on the pilot taping for Don Cornelius's soon to be successful "Soul Train" TV program.

90

Butler moved to Motown Records in the mid-1970s, where his responsibilities included record production work with other artists besides making tracks for his own new releases. His own LPs during that period included *Love's on the Menu* (1976), *Suite for the Single Girl* (1977), *It All Comes Out in My Song* (1977), and, with Thelma Houston, *Thelma and Jerry* (1977). Among the artists who profited from his producing talents was Smokey Robinson. (*See Robinson, Smokey.*)

His Motown recordings were not of the caliber of his 1960s output, however, even though he placed a number of singles and LPs on the black music charts. In 1978, this spurred him to sign with the Philadelphia International label (owned by Kenny Gamble and Leon Huff, who had produced and written many of his late 1960s hits including "Only the Strong Survive," "Never Give You Up," "Lost," "What's the Use of Breaking Up," "Western Union Man," and "Moody Woman"). His debut on that label was the 1978 LP *Nothing Says I Love You.* He began the 1980s with the Philadelphia International album release *The Best Love I Ever Had.*

In 1985, Rhino Records issued a two record set titled *The Best of Jerry Butler, 1958–1969* (released on CD in 1987). Butler by then had become involved in politics, winning election to public office in Chicago, though continuing to do shows on a part time basis.

BUTTERFIELD, PAUL, PAUL BUTTERFIELD BLUES BAND; PAUL BUTTERFIELD AND BETTER DAYS: *Harmonica player, flutist, songwriter, band leader. Blues Band personnel as of 1971: Paul Butterfield, born Chicago, Illinois, December 17, 1942, died North Hollywood, California, May 4, 1987; Charles Dinwiddie, born Louisville, Kentucky, September 19, 1936; Roderick Hicks, born Detroit, Michigan, January 7, 1941; David Sanborn, born Tampa, Florida, July 30, 1945; Ralph Wash, born San Francisco, California, August 19, 1949; Steve Madaio, born Brooklyn, New York, July 18, 1948; Dennis Whitted, born Chicago, Illinois, July 1, 1942; Trevor Lawrence. Band broken up 1972. Better Days formed in 1973; original members: Billy Rich, Christopher Parker, Ronnie Barron, Amos Garrett, Geoff Muldaur.*

Paul Butterfield's series of blues bands never achieved many chart hits. Nonetheless, measured by the loyalty of his fans, Butterfield was an important influence on modern music. Some of his bands' alumni have gone on to fame in other groups or as soloists, while the amplified, rock-tinged arrangements of his blues numbers helped bring the blues new favor with American audiences.

Butterfield grew up in Chicago and studied classical flute in his youth. By the time he was high school age, he had concentrated on the harmonica. He began sitting in with blues artists at Chicago's South Side clubs when he was 16. Among the famous bluesmen who welcomed the young artist to their stages were Howlin' Wolf, Otis Rush, Magic Sam, and Little Walter. (*See Howlin' Wolf.*) Like Little Walter, Butterfield developed a style of playing a harmonica with a microphone cupped in his hands to provide amplification and by varying the position of harmonica and mike, different tonal effects.

Paul went on to the University of Chicago, where he became friends with a versatile musician named Elvin Bishop. (*See Bishop, Elvin.*) Butterfield, who by then had experience with local show bands (bands that play in nightclub lounges or as pit orchestras), joined Bishop in his spare time for harmonica duets. Bishop took up the guitar in 1960, becoming one of the most noted lead guitarists in the field as a member of the Butterfield Blues Band until mid-1968.

In the early 1960s, Bishop and Butterfield were the nucleus for Paul's first band. Its six members included a drummer, pianist, and two more guitarists. The group aroused considerable controversy among blues purists, because it used amplification and its material combined blues with elements of folk, rock, and jazz. Some critics referred to the group's music as "sound and soul."

The group became one of the best-known in Chicago. It found favor with young fans, despite the fact that, by the mid-1960s, the once flourishing blues field had declined sharply in popularity there. The group played to enthusiastic audiences for over a year at the Blue Flame and 1015 Club on Chicago's South Side, and then achieved similar success at a nightclub called Big John's on Wells Street. The reputation of the band reached record company executives even though Butterfield remained basically a Chicago artist at the time.

His first album, *Butterfield Blues Band* on Elektra, won warm praise from many critics. Syndicated columnist Ralph Gleason wrote: "What is interesting about [the LP] is that a young white Chicagoan can play the blues this well. It is as if a Negro sharecropper from Mississippi were suddenly to be expert in Gaelic song. What is of further interest is that this is the blues band which attracts all the attention when the originals on which it is patterned (Howlin' Wolf, Muddy Waters) go unrecognized by this audience."

In 1965, the group was invited to appear at the Newport Folk Festival in Newport, Rhode Island. To that point festival organizers had ruled out amplified instruments. However, they decided that Butterfield's music was so important that they would relax the rules in his case. The group, which then consisted of Butterfield, Bishop on second guitar, Jerome Arnold on electric bass, Billy Davenport on drums, Mark Naftalin on electric organ, and Mike Bloomfield on lead guitar, won one of the most resounding receptions of any of the acts and wound up backing Bob Dylan's controversial debut with electric guitar at the festival. Bloomfield, considered one of the best technicians on guitar in the country, was singled out for an ovation after some of his solo runs. (See *Bloomfield, Mike; Dylan, Bob.*)

Butterfield rearranged his band to include a brass section in 1967. The group then consisted of Butterfield, Bishop, Naftalin, Charles "Bugsy" Maugh on bass, Philip Wilson on drums, Charles Dinwiddie on tenor saxophone, Keith Johnson on trumpet, and Dave Sanborn (who won several jazz awards while studying classical music in college) on alto saxophone. The group earned generally favorable, though sometimes doubting reviews for the new arrangements worked up by Butterfield for such LPs as *The Resurrection of Pigboy Crabshaw* (1968) and *In My Own Dream* (fall 1968).

Typical of comments on *In My Own Dream* was the review by Jerrold Greenberg in *Rolling Stone* (September 14, 1968): "Butterfield has had a dream of a new music, rooted equally in the blues . . . in the technical virtuosity of jazz and in the amplified immediacy of rock: with this record that dream starts elbowing its way into reality. . . . I say starts because, while most of the cuts are excellent in varying degrees, some of them almost extraordinary in their musical togetherness, there are several that are impaired by hangovers from the band's (or individual musicians') previous incarnations."

Subsequent Butterfield LPs included *Keep on Moving* (September 1969), *Butterfield Live* (December 1970), and *East-West* (July 1971).

Continuing in pursuit of his dream, Butterfield presided over a group that changed considerably in personnel during the late 1960s. In 1968, Bishop left to form his own band and was replaced for a while by Buzzy Fieton (born New York City, 1949) who, in turn, was replaced by the time the 1970s started. In 1971, with an eight-man group that retained only Dinwiddie and Sanborn from the 1967 band, Butterfield maintained his reputation as one of the best, but most underrated band leaders in American pop music.

In 1972, in search of more creative and economic progress, Butterfield broke up his old group and formed a new one, Better Days. Original members of that band included Geoff Muldaur on vocals, Ronnie Barron on keyboards, Billy Rich on bass,

Christopher Parker on drums, and Amos Garrett on guitar. While Butterfield was assembling his new group, Elektra released the 1972 retrospective album, *Golden Butter/The Best of the Paul Butterfield Blues Band.*

By 1973, Paul had signed a recording contract for Better Days with Bearsville records (distributed by Warner/Reprise Records), where his band remained into the early 1980s with mixed results. His Bearsville releases included *It All Comes Back* and *Paul Butterfield/Better Days* in 1973, *Put It In Your Ear* in 1976, and *North/South* in 1981. The band's personnel changed from time to time during those years. They could draw respectable audiences to smaller halls throughout the 1970s, but never built up enough of a following for regular appearances in large venues.

At the start of the 1980s, though, Butterfield ran into difficulties that made his entertainment business disappointments seem insignificant. As he told Don Snowden (*Los Angeles Times,* June 26, 1986), he was felled by an attack of diverticulitis while working on new album material in Memphis, Tennessee. "To make a long story short, my intestines burst. . . . I ended up having four operations and you don't realize what it takes out of you energy-wise. You think you can come right back to work so I went back and herniated the scar tissue in my stomach. I had three hernias from playing the harmonica, so it was a vicious circle.

"Sure it occurred to me that I might not be able to play anymore, but I got that Irish ornery thing going and said, 'I'm going to make it through this,' and I did with a lot of help from God. I came through the wars."

The illness sidelined Paul for some four years. When he finally recovered, he ran into disagreements with his record company that resulted in his arranging his own financing for his next album. That collection remained on his hands for some 18 months while he tried to find a label to put it out. Butterfield's search finally won over executives of Amherst records in Buffalo, New York, who issued *The Legendary Paul Butterfield Rides Again,* in mid-1986.

To complete that and other projects, Paul moved from New York to the Los Angeles area in 1986. In May 1987, he was found dead in his apartment in North Hollywood.

BYRDS, THE: *Vocal and instrumental group. Original personnel, 1964: Jim McGuinn (McGuinn changed his first name to Roger in 1968), born Chicago, Illinois, July 13, 1942; Chris Hillman, born Los Angeles, California, December 4, 1942; Gene Clark, born Tipton, Missouri, November 17, 1941; Michael Clarke, born*

New York, New York, June 3, 1944; David Crosby, born Los Angeles, California, August 14, 1941. Gene Clark left in 1966. Crosby and Michael Clarke left in 1968. Crosby was replaced by Gram Parsons, born Winter Haven, Florida, 1946, died Joshua Tree, California, September 19, 1973. Clarke was replaced by Kevin Kelly, born California, 1945. By the end of 1968, group was reorganized to include McGuinn, Clarence White (died 1973), Gene Parsons, and John York. York replaced in 1969 by Skip Battin, born Galipolis, Ohio. Gene Parsons left in 1972, replaced by John Guerin. Group disbanded in 1973.

The two primal forces in the birth of folk-rock are considered to be the Byrds and Bob Dylan. Dylan may have been transitioning from pure folk to the new blend before the Byrds came into existence, but it was the treatment the newly formed Byrds gave a Dylan song, "Mr. Tambourine Man," that opened the door to a series of folk-rock superhits by both parties.

The catalyst in the birth of the Byrds was Californian Jim Dickson, a man in his early thirties who had been an artists & repertoire man with record companies for some years in the folk and jazz fields. He liked the Beatles, but thought there was room for a new kind of U.S. band that combined the melodic approach of the English group with elements of American folk and rock. During the summer of 1964 in Los Angeles, he helped bring together the original group: Jim McGuinn (lead guitar and vocals), Chris Hillman (bass guitar and vocals), Gene Clark (harmonica, tambourine and vocals), David Crosby (rhythm guitar and vocals), and Michael Clarke (drums). The group took the name Byrds because of McGuinn's belief that all music was related to the sounds and stresses of the age. In this case, he thought of the whining, persistent sound of jet engines, of his desire to write music that could soar, and fly. This pointed to birds, modified for greater audience impact to Byrds.

The members were in their early twenties, but all had some years' musical experience. McGuinn had traveled to many parts of the country in his boyhood, accompanying his parents on publicity tours for their best-selling book, *Parents Can't Win*. In his teens, he became hooked on music, learned guitar and began working as a folk singer. This led him to Greenwich Village in New York in the late '50s, where he worked in coffeehouses and made contact with many of the young stars of the folk boom. In the early '60s he wrote arrangements for many folk artists, including Judy Collins, was lead guitarist for Bobby Darin, and toured for two years with the Chad Mitchell Trio.

By mid-1964, David Crosby had some five years' experience under his belt as a singer-guitarist in folk clubs all over the U.S. Gene Clark, also a product of the folk field, had been a member of Randy Sparks' New Christy Minstrels. Chris Hillman brought along a background that included both folk and country roots. He had spent much of his youth in the cattle-raising country in northern California, where he worked for a while in his teens as a cowboy. He also organized his own country group, the Hillmen, with whom he sang and played bluegrass mandolin. (Their 1964 LP, *The Hillmen* on Together Records, was reissued in 1981 on Sugar Hill Records.) The only original member who varied from the folk pattern was jazz-based drummer Mike Clarke.

The group rehearsed for weeks in the World Pacific Studios in Hollywood before Dickson had them play for Columbia A&R man Terry Melcher (Doris Day's son). Also having a hand in the acceptance of the group was West Coast public relations director, Billy James, who later took part in their management. The label signed the Byrds in September 1964.

The band was preparing its first album when Bob Dylan flew into Los Angeles in early 1965. A close friend of Dickson's, he was interested in hearing the new group. He had supplied Dickson with "Mr. Tambourine Man," a song he had written and recorded on Columbia, but which had not yet been released. He listened to the band and expressed his approval. In March, the Byrds' single of the song came out, and by June 26, 1965 it was number one in the U.S. It was featured in the group's debut LP, *The Byrds* (released in August 1965), which quickly won a second gold record and which today is considered one of the all-time great rock releases.

The group made its public debut in March 1965 at Ciro's on the Sunset Strip for $30 a night per musician. The first night was a disaster. The equipment didn't work, the Byrds were nervous, and the audience wasn't very appreciative. The two-week engagement was a flop. However, with the success of "Mr. Tambourine Man" soon after, the group's confidence was restored. When the quintet played Ciro's again in April 1965, they were one of the sensations of the year. Every night, long lines of fans stretched around the block waiting to get in. Still another boost came in May when the Rolling Stones came to town for seven concerts and the Byrds played on each bill. As the year went by, the group steadily expanded its performing schedule and added to its following. Late in the year, the band toured throughout the U.S. and also had a successful concert series in England.

During the mid-1960s, the band's reputation soared, though more for its recording work than its concerts. Their stage appearances tended to be somewhat wooden compared to other top groups'. In the studio, though, they came into their own. The result was a string of best-selling releases, including such other singles hits from Dylan's pen as "All I Really Want to Do," "Spanish Harlem Incident," and "Chimes of Freedom." They also had hits by other writers (such as "Turn! Turn! Turn!," a biblical passage set to music by Pete Seeger) and boasted an increasing repertoire of originals by McGuinn and other band members.

Almost all the band's albums of the mid-1960s did well, including *Turn! Turn! Turn!* (February 1966), *Fifth Dimension* (September 1966), *Younger Than Yesterday* (April 1967), and *Greatest Hits* (October 1967). Its top 40 singles successes after "Turn! Turn! Turn!" (which rose to number one in the U.S. in late 1965) were: "Eight Miles High," "Mr. Spaceman" (1966); and "So You Want to be a Rock'n'Roll Star" and "My Back Pages" (1967).

By 1967, though, internal problems were negatively affecting their performance. McGuinn, who by 1967 was acknowledged band leader, told *Los Angeles Times* reporter Pete Johnson in April 1968 that the difficulties began in England.

"I got sick. I had like 103 something fever. And we were in the BBC studios doing some show and the doctor came in and said 'This guy shouldn't work; send him home to bed.' So I'm lying on a couch or something and everybody's going crazy. Nobody has any organization any more. Michael [Clarke] left; he just walked out. . . . Then the other three guys started fighting about whether Michael should be fired or not.

"And everybody quit right there and said, 'I quit. I'm going home,' you know. . . . Everybody was out for himself and running scared. The Africans have an expression 'Living with someone is like asking for a fight,' or something like that. A group is even worse. You're boxed in when you're traveling. It's hard pressure.

"Gene developed a tremendous fear of airplanes, this was maybe a year later. One day we were going to New York [from L.A.] to do a Murray the K special and Gene was on the airplane. I got there late, just as the thing was closing up. I always do. Gene was already freaked out and they were holding his arms. He got off and decided to quit the group."

The group went on as a foursome, but ran into more problems in late 1967 and early 1968, while making the LP *The Notorious Byrd Brothers*. In the middle of the project, Crosby and the others disagreed about the approach of the album. David left, later to become a founding member of Crosby, Stills, Nash & Young. Gene Clark came back to take Crosby's place for a while, but then left once more. (*See Crosby, Stills, Nash & Young.*)

Roger McGuinn (he changed his first name in 1968 as a result of membership in a religious group known as Subud) reorganized the band in early 1968, briefly adding Chris Hillman's cousin Kevin Kelly on drums. The fourth member was Gram Parsons, a guitarist with country roots who previously had been lead singer for the International Submarine Band. (*See Parsons, Gram.*)

The Byrds had previously shown great latitude in their approach to rock, starting with an emphasis on amplified folk-rock, proceeding to experimental combinations of Indian music and rock (some critics credited McGuinn with coining the descriptive phrase *raga-rock*) and then to arrangements using the Moog synthesizer. The addition of Gram Parsons signaled a new phase in the group's development: country-rock.

The Byrds went to Nashville to record their next LP, *Sweetheart of the Rodeo,* with fiddle, banjo, and pedal steel guitar accompaniment. The group was a little in advance of the times, however. The response to *Sweetheart* by record buyers was much weaker than for earlier releases. Still, the album had an impact on a number of young musicians who were to become factors in the country-rock surge of the 1970s.

Yet that foursome—McGuinn, Hillman, Gram Parsons, and Kelly—had advanced tremendously in stage presence over earlier versions. They seemed more relaxed, they conveyed a feeling of greater enjoyment of what they were doing, and they were tighter musically. However, the decline in record sales had its impact. Hillman and Gram Parsons left, soon started a new country-rock band, the Flying Burrito Brothers, which Michael Clarke later joined. McGuinn defied advisers who told him to forget the Byrds. He refused to give up, formed a new quartet with bluegrass picker Clarence White on lead guitar, Gene Parsons on drums, and John York on bass. The new aggregation seemed very promising, as indicated by its work on the March 1969 Columbia LP, *Dr. Byrds and Mr. Hyde.* During 1969, there was another change when York was replaced on bass by Clyde "Skip" Battin (formerly of Skip and Flip, who sang "It Was I" in 1959 and "Cherry Pie" in 1960). The feeling of a Byrds rejuvenation was further heightened by the group's music in the hit film *Easy Rider.* Also above average was the two-LP set *The Byrds (Untitled),* one live disc and one from studio sessions, issued by Columbia in September 1970. The album had advance sales orders for 100,000 copies and moved onto the best-seller lists for several months. Also making the charts was their next album, *Byrdmania* (released in August 1971).

The LP *Farther Along,* issued by Columbia in December 1971, was on the charts into 1972, but unfortunately didn't live up to its title. Also appearing on the album lists in late 1972 was the *Best of the Byrds, Greatest Hits Volume II*. During 1972, McGuinn broke up the current group, but during the winter of 1972–73, the five original members agreed to collaborate on a reunion album, *The Byrds*, on Asylum Records (distributed by Atlantic Records). Though it was on the charts for a time in 1973, it was an inferior effort. After the session, the members went their separate ways. (By then, the Byrds no longer were on the Columbia label, though the company did issue the LP *Preflyte*, essentially the original demo tape the group had made in its beginning phase.)

During the Byrds' active period, onetime members like Chris Hillman and David Crosby had gone on to other projects and the same held true for many alumni after the group broke up. McGuinn initiated a solo career with support from Columbia Records, which issued the mid '70s albums *Roger McGuinn* (1973); *Peace on You* (1974); *Roger McGuinn and Band* (1975); *Cardiff Rose* (1976); and *Thunderbyrd* (1977). Clarence White returned to his bluegrass roots with a new version of the Kentucky Colonels, a group he had performed with before joining the Byrds. That affiliation ended tragically with his death in a parking lot accident in mid-1973, following a 1973 Swedish reunion tour that formed the basis for the 1977 Rounder Records release, *The White Brothers (The New Kentucky Colonels)*. (The group's early sound was offered on other mid-1970s releases—*Livin' in the Past* on Takoma in 1975 and *The Kentucky Colonels* on Rounder in 1976). Another album by a band alumni during those years was Gene Parson's *Kindling* on Warner Brothers.

In the late 1970s, McGuinn got together with two other original Byrds members, Gene Clark and Chris Hillman, to form the McGuinn, Clark and Hillman group. Among Hillman's endeavors before that mini-reunion had been the Souther-Hillman-Furay Band, which had completed two disappointing LPs on Asylum, *The Souther-Hillman-Furay Band* (1974) and *Trouble in Paradise* (1975). Record output of McGuinn, Clark and Hillman comprised two Capitol LPs, *McGuinn, Clark and Hillman* (1979) and *City* (1980). Clark had decided to leave by the time the *City* recordings got underway and the remaining duo later recorded the 1980 Capitol LP *McGuinn and Hillman*.

Hillman, who had recorded two solo LPs before reuniting with McGuinn, the Asylum LPs *Slippin' Away* (1976) and *Clear Sailin'* (1977), returned to solo work in the early 1980s with the albums (on Sugar Hill) *Morning Sky* (1982) and *Desert Rose* (1984). In 1987 he was part of a new group whose debut LP, the *Desert Rose Band*, came out on the

MCA label. After parting from Hillman, McGuinn returned to solo work and was featured mainly in college or smaller venue concerts for the rest of the decade.

CAPTAIN & TENNILLE: *Vocal and instrumental duo. Daryl Dragon, born Los Angeles, California, August 27, 1942; Toni Tennille, born Montgomery, Alabama May 8, 1943.*

The undisputed top-selling single of 1975, "Love Will Keep Us Together," catapulted the husband-and-wife team of Daryl Dragon and Toni Tennille to stardom. The disc was certified gold by the Record Industry Association of America on July 1, 1975 and their debut album of the same title passed gold-record levels exactly a month later.

Each had a decade of classical training in piano. Daryl, son of symphony conductor Carmen Dragon, grew up in Los Angeles, while Toni moved to Los Angeles with her family in 1962. Daryl got his start in the record field in the early 1960s, when he and two brothers recorded an album for Capitol that received little attention. Soon after that venture, he met Toni, who by then was busy completing *Mother Earth,* a rock musical (written with Ron Thronson) for the South Coast Repertory Theatre. Later, when Daryl gained a job as keyboards player with the Beach Boys (*See Beach Boys, The*), he helped bring Toni in as the first female member of the group. His nickname, "the Captain," was coined by Beach Boy Mike Love based on the hat Daryl always wore on stage.

In the early 1970s, Daryl and Toni performed in small clubs. Failing to get a record contract, they pressed their own disc of Toni's composition, "The Way I Want to Touch You." The record did well enough to win a contract from A&M and actually was their first single that A&M issued. It didn't receive much airplay. Next came the 1975 Grammy-winning "Love Will Keep Us Together," written by Neil Sedaka. (*See Sedaka, Neil.*) A&M then re-released "The Way I Want to Touch You." The second time around, it too went gold. The duo followed up in 1976 with a new hit single version of Smokey Robinson's "Shop Around" and the LPs *Por Amor Vivremos* and *Song of Joy*. In mid-1976, the team was signed by ABC-TV to host a new variety show.

They made several more albums on the A&M label before the end of the 1970s and were represented on the charts with the LPs *The Captain and Tennille's Greatest Hits* and *Come in from the Rain*, both issued in 1977, and *Dream* (1978). However, buyer response was declining and this helped the team decide to sign with a new label, Casablanca Records, in 1979. The debut album, *Make Your Move*, came out in early 1980 and provided them with another hit single, "Do That to Me One More Time," which rose to number one on *Billboard* charts the week of February 16, 1980. They had several moderate singles hits on Casablanca in the early 1980s, before the death of their friend, Casablanca head Neil Bogart, ended their affiliation with the label.

In the mid-1980s, Toni began a solo career, with Daryl handling production chores on her new recordings. Her first LP, *More than You Know,* came out on Mirage Records in 1984 and opened a new career for her as a vocalist on tour with big bands. While she performed with bands and as a soloist in the mid-1980s, she and the Captain also continued to do their own shows in between. In early 1987, her second solo album, *Moonglow,* was released.

CAPTAIN BEEFHEART AND THE MAGIC BAND: *Vocal and instrumental group. Personnel as of 1971: Don Van Vliet, born Glendale, California, 1941; John French, born Mojave, California, 1949; Bill Harkleroad, born California, 1950; Mark Boston, born Lancaster, California 1949; Arthur Tripp, born New York, New York. French replaced by Orejon in 1982. Members in the mid-1980s included Richard Snyder, Jeff Morris Tepper, Gary Lucas, and Cliff R. Martinez.*

Remember the TV commercial in which a singer shatters a glass? Don Van Vliet, otherwise known as Captain Beefheart, can do that and more. With his astounding 4½-octave range, he can hit notes that can literally destroy rugged, costly recording equipment, as he proved during the 1965 session on his LP, *Safe as Milk.* Singing his composition "Electricity," he shattered the internal structure of a $1,200 Telefunken microphone. Engineers found that his vocal extremes on the song sometimes were beyond the capability of the tape recorders.

With his vocal ability plus his great talent as a lyricist, composer, and musician, Van Vliet has long been tremendously frustrating to many music-industry executives. He obviously has the potential of becoming a top star. However, because he insists on playing his own music his own way (music that often seems indescribably strange to most record buyers), he has mainly gained fame as an eccentric individual who believes in reincarnation, gives indications of extrasensory perception, and purveys a curious, involuted sort of logic in such publicly reported statements as "I'm not really here, I just stick around for my friends," "Everybody's colored or you wouldn't be able to see them," and "There are only 40 people in the world and five of them are hamburgers."

Van Vliet's odyssey began in Glendale, California, where he spent the first dozen years of his life. He showed signs of unusual ability at an early age. In grade school he was turning out pieces of sculpture that gained him a reputation with local artists. Before he was 12, he was featured on a TV show with Portuguese artist Augustonio Rodriguez in which Don sculptured objects from nature on the program. When he was offered an art scholarship in Europe at 13, his parents became alarmed that he might try to leave home and moved eastward into the desert towns of Mojave and then Lancaster.

In high school in Lancaster, he became friends with Frank Zappa, later leader of the Mothers of Invention. (*See Mothers of Invention; Zappa, Frank.*) Van Vliet recalled: "I'd begun to get interested in music about then. Mostly the blues singers—they sounded very human to me. I picked up a harmonica and learned how to play it, then turned on to the saxophone. I joined a group called the Blackouts. They ended up firing me because I was a little freakish for them. They were playing rhythm & blues and I was starting to experiment a little." What Van Vliet was becoming interested in was a blend of traditional blues with the progressive jazz of such artists as John Coltrane.

Van Vliet enrolled as an art major at Antelope Valley College, but soon gave it up in favor of music. He briefly discussed forming a band called the Soots with Zappa, but the two had different musical ideas. They also envisioned a movie, *Captain Beefheart Meets the Grunt People,* but nothing came of it. However, Van Vliet took his new pseudonym from the title and, in 1964, formed a group called the Magic Band, which gained considerable attention from its blues-rock sound performed at local teen dances. Word of this reached Los Angeles and the group was signed by A&M Records.

The initial single release, an updated version of Bo Diddley's famed "Diddy Wah Diddy," became a regional hit in Southern California. (*See Diddley, Bo.*) When Beefheart brought in recordings of such original compositions as "Electricity," "Zig Zag Wanderer," and "Frying Pan" for his first LP, A&M executives turned it down as being too bleak lyrically. (The words for "Frying Pan," for instance, include: "Go down town/You walk around/A man comes up, says he's gonna put you down/You try to succeed to fulfill your need/Then a car hits you and people watch you bleed.")

Hurt, Van Vliet retired to Lancaster for a year, then came back in 1965 to record the material turned down by A&M for another label, Kama Sutra (a subsidiary of Buddah Records). Released late in the year, *Safe as Milk* was not a best-seller, but it won considerable critical approval, particularly among avant garde rock reviewers in the U.S. and Europe. It also spurred interest in the Magic Band that led to a successful tour of Europe in early 1966, followed by engagements at the Whisky a Go Go in Los Angeles and Family Dog in San Francisco. The group was also scheduled to play Bill Graham's Fillmore and the Monterey Pop Festival in 1966–67, when the departure of the lead guitarist, a key element in Beefheart's complex arrangements and a musician always personally coached for long periods of time by Van Vliet, caused him to cancel what many thought would be the shows that would make him a top-ranked star.

Buddah wanted a second LP, but after Beefheart's producer signed a personal management contract with Van Vliet, further problems ensued. The producer, Robert Krasnow, reputedly gained production funds from two different firms, Buddah and MGM, when the sessions got underway in early 1968. While Van Vliet was touring Europe that summer, the album was released in altered form on Krasnow's own label, Blue Thumb. Despite the changes and Beefheart's anger over the situation, the LP, *Strictly Personal* is conceded to be an unusual one that some day may be considered a turning point in pop music. However, it scored few gains with the public.

The legal infighting that followed the album plus its poor sales once again put a damper on the band. Van Vliet retired to a hideaway, this time a small house shrouded by trees on a hilly area in the San Fernando Valley. He found a new manager after a while, reorganized his Magic Band, and responded to an offer from Frank Zappa to make a new album, free of all artistic restrictions, on Zappa's Straight Records. The sessions, which took much of 1969 and went into early 1970, led to *Trout Mask Replica*. Beefheart wrote the LP's 28 songs (boasting such titles as "Frownland," "Dachau Blues," and "Veteran's Day Poppy") in 8½ hours. Released in the spring of 1970, it was hailed by many rock publications as a major event. *Rolling Stone* called it "truly beyond comparison in the realm of contemporary music."

In early 1971, Van Vliet took his latest band on a coast-to-coast tour to highlight the songs from the album. The members all were given outlandish names that appealed to Van Vliet. Drummer John French, who wore a chimney sweep's cap, a mechanic's duster, and large sunglasses while playing, was called Drumbo. Raised in Mojave,

California, he had worked with the band for six years. Two other members born and reared in desert communities were guitarist Bill Harkleroad (Zoot Horn Rollo) and bass player Mark Boston (Rockette Morton). Rounding out the group was Arthur Tripp (Ed Marimba), a marimba player and drummer who was the only one not "trained" by Van Vliet. Tripp had studied for eight years at the Manhattan School of Music and played percussion with the Cincinnati Symphony before joining one of Zappa's Mothers of Invention assemblages.

The 1971 tour added a little to Beefheart's reputation in some locations. Often as not, the group's music seemed beyond the understanding of primarily teenage audiences. More than one local critic, though, stated he felt he had heard the music that would be hailed later in the decade.

There were indications that the forecast might come true in the next few years. The band's next Reprise album, *Lick My Decals Off, Baby* (1971), increased its status with "underground" music fans. Even more promising was the broader interest in *The Spotlight Kid* (1972). A hit in both the U.S. and Europe, the album helped launch a well-received English tour. Later in 1972, Beefheart had a second straight chart album, *Clear Spot*. Primary band members for that effort were Van Vliet, Zoot Horn Rollo, Rockette Morton, Ed Marimba, and new member Orejon (replacing Drumbo).

Reprise finally decided Van Vliet was a lot more avant garde than it could feel comfortable with and the group's contract wasn't renewed. Beefheart continued to concertize with different rosters of backing musicians, though after a while in the mid-1970s, he was able to get only limited exposure for his work. He continued to work on new material in his own way and gave no indication of compromising for commercial success.

In 1978, Warner Brothers gave him another recording opportunity, which led to the LP *Shiny Beast (Bat Chain Puller)*. As before, the album won critical acclaim but appealed only to a cult audience.

Appreciation of Beefheart's talents was growing apace in England and on the Continent, which helped win him a new contract from U.K.-based Virgin Records. First fruits was the 1980 LP, *Doc at the Radar Station*, which broke new creative ground for Beefheart and for other Van Vliet disciples for the 1980s. In the fall of 1982, Beefheart provided another fine Virgin album, *Ice Cream for Crew* (issued by Epic in the U.S.). Band members for the project included Gary Lucas on lead guitar and slide guitar; Jeff Morris Tepper on guitar and steel guitar; Cliff Martinez on drums and percussion; and Richard "Midnight Hatsize" Snyder on bass guitar.

CARA, IRENE: *Singer, keyboards player, songwriter, dancer, actress. Born Bronx, New York, March 1959.*

By the early 1980s, Irene Cara had established herself as a major force in many segments of the entertainment field, from singing and acting to songwriting. In her early twenties, she had the looks and emotional exuberance of a teenager, but was already a seasoned veteran whose career had begun at the age of five.

Becoming an entertainer had seemed the natural thing to do for both the child and her parents. As she told Jay Merritt of *Rolling Stone* (October 2, 1980): "I come from a family of performers. My father is a musician, so is my brother, and I have a great-aunt who plays five instruments. My mother always wanted to be in show business, but her parents discouraged her. So when I started performing for the mirror, she enrolled me in dancing, singing, and piano lessons. That's what's fortunate about my career. I have a ten-year jump on everybody. I didn't have to go to school, graduate, and then go, 'What am I going to do?' I knew from the beginning."

Her first public appearances came in 1966 on local New York Spanish-language radio and TV shows. In 1967, she debuted on Broadway, playing the role of an orphan in the Jack Cassidy–Shirley Jones musical *Maggie Flynn.* She also won a part in an ABC TV documentary, "Over 7."

In 1969, her credits included singing and dancing in a Madison Square Garden tribute to Duke Ellington. She opened the 1970s as a cast member of the Broadway musical *The Me Nobody Knows* and sang on the original cast LP issued by Atlantic Records. (The show, which won an Obie Award for Best Musical of 1970, ran for 587 performances before closing in November 1971.)

In early 1972, her mother, who served as her manager, got her a role on the educational TV series "The Electric Company." Irene was with the show for a year as a member of the Short Circus, a rock band that delivered grammar lessons in song. During 1972, she also appeared in the Broadway musical *Via Galactica* and co-hosted the NBC talk program "The Everything Show."

As the 1970s passed, Irene added to her performing credits by moving on to film roles. Her film debut came in the Columbia Pictures' 1975 *Aaron Loves Angela,* in which she played Angela. The next year, Warner Brothers' *Sparkle* gave her the chance to showcase her singing and dancing skills for movie audiences. In 1978, she was back in New York as an original cast member of the off-Broadway revue *Ain't Misbehavin'* based on the music of jazz great Fats Waller. The following year brought her biggest breakthrough: a featured role in episodes of the ABC miniseries blockbuster, "Roots: the Next Generation." She portrayed a youthful Bertha Palmer, the mother-to-be of *Roots* author Alex Haley.

Her critical acclaim opened still more casting doors, including one that finally made her a full-fledged star. She played a cult member in the CBS docudrama "The Guyana Tragedy: The Story of Jim Jones," which was first telecast in April 1980. While that was going on, film editors were putting finishing touches on a considerably brighter opus, the musical *Fame*—a movie that tempered its dynamic moments of electrified song and dance with insights into the disillusionment that awaited students from New York's High School of Performing Arts as they entered the real world. Irene's talents allowed her to run the gamut from passionate performer to saddened near–grown-up.

Irene's contributions to the soundtrack album included a driving rendition of the title song. The single reached the U.S. top 5 in mid-1980 and helped make the movie, released in June, one of the year's top box office hits. Later in the year "Out Here on My Own" (another track she had done for the soundtrack LP) made the top 20. Both songs were nominated for Best Original Song in the 1980 Oscar competition. *Fame* won the Oscar. Meanwhile, the soundtrack LP, issued on RSO Records in May 1980, was a chart hit into 1981 and exceeded RIAA platinum-record requirements.

Irene received many other nominations and some awards. She was a finalist in the Best New Female Artist and Best New Pop Artist categories for the 1980 Grammies and received a nomination in the foreign press (Hollywood-based) Golden Globe awards for Best Motion Picture Actress in a Musical. *Billboard* named her the Top New Singles Artist for 1980 and *Cash Box* voted her Most Promising Female Vocalist ~~and Top~~ New Female Vocalist.

Cara became even more familiar to movie and music fans in 1980–81 with a veritable avalanche of interviews and appearances in most major mediums. Her 1980 work included playing Dorothy in *The Wiz* at Milwaukee's Melody Top Theater; taking part in President Jimmy Carter's Command Performance benefit for the U.S. Olympics Committee at the Kennedy Center in Washington, D.C., in July; and, in August, being part of a tribute to Ray Charles' thirty-fifth anniversary in show business at the Dorothy Chandler Pavilion in Los Angeles, California. In 1981, she sang and danced in a Mitch Miller NBC-TV special and taped a pilot called "Irene" for a proposed NBC series about three girls seeking per-

98

sonal success in Manhattan. She also co-starred with George Segal in the movie *The Neighbor—Apt. 5A*.

On the recording front, Irene (who had originally signed as a solo artist for RSO Records) moved with former RSO president Al Khoury to his new label, Network Records (distributed by Elektra). First fruits of that was her debut solo LP, *Anyone Can See*, issued in the fall of 1981. The title song, released as a single, was on the U.S. charts for a time in late 1981 and early 1982.

The year 1982 was relatively quiet for Irene on the recording front, though she remained active on the concert scene and worked on new projects for coming years. This resulted in a banner record year for her in 1983. She already had demonstrated considerable competence as a songwriter by writing or cowriting many of the songs on her debut LP and now increased that reputation by collaborating on the *Flashdance* score (issued on the Casablanca/Polygram label). Her single of the movie theme, "Flashdance . . . What a Feelin'," was a top-selling disc of 1983. Gaining the U.S. top 10 was her single "Why Me?" on Geffen/Network, co-written by Irene, Giorgio Moroder, and Keith Forsey. At the end of 1983, she had another Geffen/Network single, "The Dream," on middle chart levels, and the song moved still higher in early 1984.

All of those achievements brought new Grammy and Oscar nominations. When the '83 awards were presented on February 26, 1984, Irene gained two of the coveted Grammies: one for Best Pop Vocal Performance Female for "Flashdance . . . What a Feelin'" and the other for contributing to the *Flashdance* score, voted the Best Album of an Original Score Written for a Motion Picture or a TV Special. (The award was made jointly to Irene and 15 other writers and composers—including Kim Carnes— who had worked on the score.) (*See Carnes, Kim.*) During '84 she had another singles hit, "Breakdance."

CARLISLE, BELINDA: *See Go-Gos.*

CARNES, KIM: *Singer, songwriter. Born Hollywood, California, c. 1947.*

Wear and tear on the vocal chords is a problem that almost every singer must face. The strain of performing often-demanding note patterns can by itself lead to irritated throat muscles, but the situation is frequently aggravated by the difficult environment of the club and concert circuit. This can result in damage that forces an artist to leave the profession. In a few rare cases, it adds a novel form to an artist's style that can bring unexpected rewards.

This was the case with singers Bonnie Tyler and Kim Carnes, whose voices took on husky shadings.

In Kim Carnes' case, she described her voice as "raspy," a condition partly caused, she quipped, by "a lifetime of too many late nights and far too many wine spritzers." In truth, the culprits were also smoke-filled concert venues and overuse, but the effect helped make her version of "Bette Davis Eyes" one of the notable pop songs of 1981.

Born and raised in Hollywood, California, Kim had stars in her eyes about show business from her childhood. Though her family made sure she took classical piano lessons, like most young people of the post–World War II decades, she favored pop and rock. In high school, she sang in school programs and with local bands and also ventured into songwriting.

After finishing high school, she made use of those skills in varied ways. She wrote and performed commercials and also made demonstration records of both her own original songs and material penned by other aspiring writers. By the late 1960s, she was working on occasion as an opening act for various touring performers. It didn't seem to further her singing career particularly, but it did bring her together with writer/performer Dave Ellingson, who soon became her husband and songwriting collaborator as well as career adviser. Quite a few demonstration tapes later, Kim and Dave finally gained the ear of producer Jimmy Bowen, who produced Kim's solo debut album, issued by Bell Records in the early 1970s. This alignment also led to a joint effort by all three on the score for the movie *Vanishing Point*.

Not much happened with Kim's Bell LP, although other artists were becoming interested in recording original numbers co-written by Kim and Dave. Kim continued to make demos of new material for presentation to record-company executives who might suggest that other singers record them. As sometimes happens, the demos brought new interest in Kim's vocal talents, this time from A&M Records. A contract with them led to two LPs, *Kim Carnes* (1975) and *Sailin'* (1976). In both, Kim performed her own songs as well as material from other top pop and rock writers.

A number of critics wrote favorable reviews and the albums were certainly well-crafted collections, but neither was a financial success. *Sailin'* did contain several numbers that were milestones in Carnes' work. The title track, which she co-wrote, and her rendition of Van Morrison's "Warm Love" still can be heard on radio programs in the U.S. and abroad. Another track, "Love Comes from Unexpected Places," co-written by Carnes and Ellingson, won the American Song Festival and the Tokyo Song Festival in 1977. Barbra Streisand included it in her 1977 Columbia LP, *Superman*.

Unhappy with her progress at A&M Records, Kim

and her husband sought to change record labels. She still had several commitments remaining on her recording contract, but A&M agreed to cancel that as long as Kim was willing to sign a long-term contract for her songwriting work with A&M Publishing. Once free to find a new record-company home, she signed with EMI's newly established EMI America subsidiary.

Her debut on EMI America, *St. Vincent's Court,* was released in 1979. Most of the songs were provided by Kim and Dave. The stylings reflected what she considered her primary influences, ranging from country-rock artists Glenn Frey (of the Eagles) and J.D. Souther (with whom she had worked in the past), to such urban pop/rock writers as Randy Newman and Tom Waits. Kim toured widely in support of the LP, as she did in succeeding years for her next EMI offerings, *Romance Dance* in 1980 (which provided the hit single "More Love" from the pen of Smokey Robinson; *see Robinson, Smokey)* and *Mistaken Identity* in 1981. The first two EMI LPs found a reasonable middle-of-the-road audience without becoming top hits, but began to build up a following for Kim's work. With *Mistaken Identity,* she finally moved from years of relative obscurity into the worldwide spotlight.

The prime mover for that was her single "Bette Davis Eyes." The song received seemingly nonstop airplay in the summer and fall of 1981 and moved to the number one position on the charts for nine weeks. As it happened, while the album contained a number of Carnes originals, "Bette Davis Eyes" was co-written by Jackie DeShannon and Donna Weiss. Like Kim's career, that song had not been an overnight success either. In response to some critics' comments that the timing was right for the feminist lyrics she said, "I read [those comments]. But the song was originally written by Jackie and Donna in 1974."

The song helped make *Mistaken Identity* one of the best-selling LPs of 1980–81 and a platinum-award winner for Kim and EMI. In the Grammy Awards for 1981, "Bette Davis Eyes" was named Record of the Year.

While Kim didn't match the dramatic success of that single in following years, she did place a steady series of LPs and singles on U.S. hit lists through the mid-1980s. Her album *Voyeur,* issued by EMI America in the fall of 1982, was on the charts into 1983, as was the single from the album, "Does It Make You Remember," co-written by Carnes and Ellingson. In 1983, Kim had several charted singles including "Invisible Hands." She also was one of the contributors to the score for the movie *Flashdance* and, with 15 other co-writer/composers (including Irene Cara), won a 1983 Grammy for Best Album of an Original Score Written for a Motion Picture or a TV Special. (*See Cara, Irene.*)

During 1984, she had four charted singles (one released on RCA, the rest on EMI America) and in 1985 she placed a new album and three singles on U.S. hit lists.

CARPENTERS, THE: *Vocal and instrumental duo. Both born New Haven, Connecticut. Richard Carpenter born October 15, 1945. Karen Carpenter born March 2, 1950; died Downey, California, February 4, 1983.*

The Carpenters became first-magnitude stars in 1970, but in spite of their youth, it was hardly an overnight success. The route to the series of gold-record awards that started in early 1970 took five years of persistence and musical experimentation.

As children, both Richard and Karen were influenced by their father's interest in the popular music of his generation. Carpenter Senior had a large record collection of Dixieland jazz, the big bands of the '30s and '40s, and such popular artists of the '40s and early '50s as Spike Jones, Liberace, and Les Paul and Mary Ford. Jazz was an early favorite for Richard, who started working out some of the material gleaned from records not very long after he started taking piano lessons at nine. When he was 16, he began studying classical piano at Yale and also branched out as a performer playing jazz piano in local clubs.

In the early 1960s, the family moved to Downey, California. Richard spent several years as a music major at the University of Southern California and California State University at Long Beach. In mid-1965, Richard decided to form his own group featuring his sister and a friend, Wes Jacobs, who played tuba and bass. His sister had joined the marching band in high school and had taken up the drums, encouraged by a boy in the band who had played them since age three. Thus the Carpenter trio had the unusual feature of a girl drummer.

In 1966, the trio entered the Hollywood Bowl Battle of the Bands. Hundreds of bands competed for the awards but the Carpenter Trio won the trophies, including the sweepstakes award. RCA executives at the show signed the group and the trio went into the studios for two records that were never released. The record company decided the trio's sound was too "soft" to make the pop charts, which were then dominated by hard rock groups. Despite this disappointment, the group performed at local Los Angeles clubs for a while, until Jacobs, who became a member of the Detroit Symphony, left to concentrate on the classics.

In 1967, Richard and Karen took some time out to regroup. The result was a new band called Spectrum.

Richard rounded the group out to six members by bringing in several Cal. State friends: Leslie Johnston, Danny Woodams, Gary Sims, and John Bettis. The group gained engagements at prestige nearby locations—Doug Weston's Troubadour, Disneyland, and even Los Angeles' main citadel of rock music in the late 1960s, the Whisky a Go Go. Their music had a rock beat, but with emphasis on a slower tempo and without hyperamplified, acid-type melodies. The effect on the hard rock fans at the Whisky was unusual. When Spectrum started playing, people on the dance floor stopped to listen to the music. The management was afraid this might lead to smaller audiences and terminated Spectrum's engagement.

The group disbanded soon after. Once more, Richard and Karen reexamined their plans. Karen started voice lessons with Cal. State Long Beach music teacher Frank Pooler. With Pooler's encouragement, Richard and Karen came up with a still softer rock approach based on a synthesis of their favorite pop artists—the Beatles, Beach Boys, Bee Gees, and Burt Bacharach. Using the garage recording studio of friend Joe Osborne, they experimented with multitrack recording of their vocals. For months in mid-1969, they took the final tapes from this work to record producers throughout Los Angeles. They received a steady series of turndowns until producer Jack Daugherty finally saw something in their work and took the tapes to Herb Alpert of A&M Records. Alpert seconded Daugherty's judgment and signed the Carpenters.

Their first LP, *Offering* (released November 15, 1969), scored some sales, but failed to make the charts. However, a single from the album, the Carpenters' version of the Beatles' "Ticket to Ride," moved onto the charts for many weeks in early 1970. Soon after, *Offering* was reissued under the title *Ticket to Ride* and sold considerably better, but still not in the million-dollar class. But the first LP plus appearances on network TV cleared the way for album number two, *Close to You*, released May 15, 1970. It and a single of the Burt Bacharach–penned title song both moved to number one on the charts. Later in the year, another single from the album, "We've Only Just Begun," also gained the number one spot for the group's third gold record of the year.

The Carpenters were recognized as major new stars of the year in all trade polls. They received awards from *Cash Box* and *New Trends* magazines and played to sellout audiences in concerts and clubs across the country. Their acceptance in the U.S. popular music market moved upward as 1971 came along. Their LP *Close to You* reached the multi-million–dollar platinum-record stage. Their album *We've Only Just Begun* moved into the top 10 for many weeks. Another single, "For All We Know," passed the million-copy mark in early 1971. By this time, they had achieved the status "instant gold" held by only a few pop artists. That is, their LP *The Carpenters,* released May 15, 1971, had amassed over a million dollars worth of orders before it came from the pressing plant.

During the summer of 1971, the Carpenters had their own variety show (also starring trumpeter Al Hirt) as a summer replacement on ABC-TV. That exposure didn't hurt their record sales, which continued to be among the most imposing in pop music from 1971 through the rest of the decade. Each new album showed up on the charts and many of their singles continued to rise into the top 20 and top 10 brackets. Their A&M album releases for those years included *A Song for You* (1972), *Now and Then* (1973), *Singles 1969–1973* (1973), *Horizon* (1975), *A Kind of Hush* (1976), *Passage* (1977), and *Christmas Portrait* (1978). Among their singles hits were two number-one successes, "Top of the World" (the weeks of December 1 and 7, 1973) and "Please Mr. Postman" (the week of January 25, 1975). Later in 1975, another single from the *Horizon* LP, "Only Yesterday," made the top 10. It proved to be the duo's last top 10 single. Richard Carpenter told Paul Grein of *Billboard* in 1981 that he attributed the post-*Horizon* slump to the great effort needed to finish the LP. "Around the time of *Horizon* we started to get tired. It took a long time to do that album and I was wearing out."

But an even more somber contributor to the duo's decline was Karen's undisclosed battle with the disease known as anorexia nervosa. It grew out of her efforts to keep her weight down, initially through dieting, later through self-starvation. Richard told Greg Barrios (*Los Angeles Times,* October 23, 1983): "When she got sick in Las Vegas in 1975, we knew something was seriously amiss. It turned out to be anorexia. My Lord, I remember she would come in between shows and just flop down. She was down to 80 pounds and she'd walk out on stage and her voice was absolutely marvelous. We were in awe at first. But then we had to cancel two tours the following year. It began to take its toll."

Karen continued to struggle against the disease, but wouldn't admit for some time that she had it. At the end of the 1970s, she began work on material for a solo album, but gave up the project before finishing it in favor of completing another LP with Richard. That album, *Made in America*, made the charts and also provided a top 20 single, "Touch Me When We're Dancing," in August 1981. It was their last top 20 entry.

Her illness got worse and she interrupted work on a new album with Richard to get professional help.

Richard told Barrios: "Near the end Karen was, I believe, finally aware she had anorexia nervosa and she wanted to fight it. She went back East for therapy. Obviously it didn't work and she was allowed to come back home. I guess they thought they had gotten her to lick it. And had she lived, she would have been on the road to recovery, but from so many years of abusing herself, her heart was now weakened."

Her insistence on working on new tracks for the forthcoming album put additional strain on her heart and likely contributed to her collapse at her parents' home in Downey, California, the morning of February 4, 1983. She was rushed to Downey Community Hospital, but the medical staff couldn't save her and she died of cardiac arrest. Later in the year, Richard completed the album they had been working on. Dedicated to her memory, *Voice of the Heart* was released by A&M in October 1983.

Shocked and saddened, Richard spent the next several years sorting things out for himself. For a while, he concentrated on preparing albums of previously recorded material with Karen, including the mid-1980s anthology *Yesterday Once More*. In 1985, he decided it was time to turn to a solo career for himself and began work on his first solo LP for A&M.

CARS, THE: *Vocal and instrumental group. Original members: Ric Ocasek, born Baltimore, Maryland, c. 1949; Ben Orr, born Cleveland, Ohio, c. 1950; Elliot Easton, born Brooklyn, New York, 1954; Greg Hawkes; David Robinson. Group disbanded in 1988.**

Blending no-nonsense midwestern rock with elements of the punk/new wave rhythms beginning to come to the fore in the eastern U.S. in the mid-1970s, the Cars became a major influence on pop music from then into the 1980s. Though some band members began to work on individual projects in the mid-1980s, the original bandsmen continued together as an unchanged unit on new Cars recordings a decade after the band made its initial mark on the rock scene.

The two band founders were Richard Otcasek (a transplant from the East Coast) and Benjamin Orzechowski (a native midwesterner). Otcasek, who later dropped the 't' in his name, grew up in Baltimore, son of a computer analyst of Polish extraction. Seeing Ric's excitement over Buddy Holly and the Crickets' "That'll Be the Day," his grandmother

gave him his first guitar when he was ten. He took lessons for three months, then got bored and put it aside.

He recalled: "When I was 16, my father got transferred to Cleveland and I finished high school there. I hadn't been doing that well in school but I hit the books and got my grades up to qualify for college." He spent some time at Bowling Green State University and Antioch College before giving up formal education in the late 1960s.

"When I left Antioch" he said, "I went to Columbus, Ohio. There's where I met Ben I think about a year later." By then, he had gotten interested in music again. He told Jon Pareles for a Cars cover story in *Rolling Stone* (January 25, 1979) that as soon as he decided he was through with college for good, he concentrated on learning guitar. Besides that, "I started immediately writing; I thought that was the thing to do. In fact, the first song I ever wrote, I copyrighted. After I started writing songs I figured it would be good to start a band. Sometimes I'd put together a band just to hear my songs. If a person couldn't play that well, there'd be fewer outside ideas to incorporate."

Like Ric, Ben Orr, as he called himself professionally, had become interested in rock music as a child, but he had consciously groomed himself for a career in the field very early. An initial influence was Elvis Presley, whose records he had mimed to entertain family friends as a boy. By his early teens, he had learned to play a variety of instruments—bass guitar, regular guitar, keyboards, percussion—and later dropped out of high school to earn a living as a session musician, songwriter, and lead singer/instrumentalist on the house band for the Cleveland TV rock show "Upbeat."

Ben hadn't set his sights much higher until he met Ric. Ocasek remembered: "Ben was in a band in Cleveland. I met him in Columbus. He came to a rehearsal of a band I had at the time. In fact, it probably was the first real band I ever had. He must have known somebody in the band. Anyway, he walked down while we were in rehearsal and introduced himself and later I went over to his place and we sang songs together. I thought he had such an amazing voice and I said: 'Why don't you join us?' So he did and mostly played keyboards and we got booked for college dates in Columbus and in Ann Arbor, Michigan, among others. We just happened to have the same agency as the Stooges and MC5 so we toured with them. It was sort of the end of their careers and the beginning of ours.

"What happened was we took off to New York City trying for the big time and stayed for two years. We played small clubs, sometimes rock and sometimes acoustic stuff. We moved back to the Midwest

---

*During 1987, Elektra issued the album *Door to Door*, which proved to be the group's swan song on the label. In January 1988, it was announced the group was disbanding.

after that, then I moved to Boston. It was a pretty good music scene there so I called Ben and said come out here. He did and we went through four bands—the last one was the Cars. One of them was just Ben and myself playing acoustic material. We played clubs all over New England, but never did cover songs, though we bluffed our way into some jobs by saying we did. Then we played our own songs. We got fired for doing that at times.''

One of the associations Ben and Ric had in the early 1970s was as part of a folk trio called Milkwood. That resulted in a 1972 LP *Milkwood,* on Paramount Records. While working on the project, they became friends with Greg Hawkes, whose talents included keyboards, saxophone, guitar, backing vocals, and arranging. Hawkes worked with them briefly in one of their bands, then left for better-paying gigs with Martin Mull's Fabulous Furniture and a country-rock group, Orphan. He kept in touch with Ben and Ric, sometimes doing demo work with them for other artists or writers.

In early 1976, Ben and Ric organized a band called Cap'n Swing. One of the musicians recruited for the band was left-handed lead guitarist and backing vocalist Elliot Easton, who had grown up on Long Island. His mother had majored in voice at Juilliard and loved to play classical and pop music at home, but his musical direction was firm after his first encounter with Elvis. After seeing Presley on Ed Sullivan's TV program in 1956, he said: "I ran into the bathroom and got in front of the little mirror on our credenza, stood there with my Mickey Mouse guitar, and started shaking my hips. That image stayed with me. . . . A few years later I had a little surf band that used to play on our back patio right behind the house in Massapequa, Long Island. It would be like three guys plugged into one amplifier and a set of drums, and all the kids in the neighborhood would sit around on the back fence or in the backyard and listen to us play all the surf hits.''

By his midteens, Elliot had a good electric guitar and had become adept at playing it. After finishing high school, he went to Boston. "What brought me to Boston was my decision to go to the Berklee School of Music to study theory and composition. I didn't like living in Long Island—there was nobody there to play with. I was into stuff when I was 15 or 16 that only people in their late twenties could play. Back then, I was listening to Robbie Robertson and John Hammond and Otis Rush. I learned a lot from Chicago blues.

"Something inside of me always had a different musical taste from others. In 1969, some people walked into a record shop and bought new records by English groups and copied some of their riffs. I used to go into budget record shops and buy old blues records or early Chuck Berry. When I was a kid, I always prided myself on being able to separate good music from bullshit music.

"I'm not one of the guitarists of my generation who copied people like Jimmy Page or Eric Clapton. I said to myself: 'Why listen to English kids a few years older than me and listen to their versions of Rush or Berry's playing when I can go to the source and make my own interpretations?' And not just them—I ran into old Les Paul recordings that blew my mind.

"But one thing I don't know much about is electronics. I know what my ear tells me. I play with the knobs and pedals to turn out what sounds good. I haven't invented anything. I'm just my own person. I can play to match all kinds of songs. Like I play certain softer chords for a song like 'Best Friend's Girl' and then go to a heavy lick in 'Night Spots' and it still sounds like me. At home I make what I call work tapes where I play with melodies and chord changes and throw them on cassettes for future use.''

After meeting Ric and Ben in Boston and becoming a member of Cap'n Swing, Easton had the pleasure of hearing some of the band's demo tapes begin to get played on a local station. After being lauded in Boston, the band went to New York to audition for major management companies. It was a disaster, Easton told Pareles. "We took it back to Boston with our tails between our legs. Ric made the decision that we were gonna get rid of people. When the smoke cleared, it was just Ric and Ben [and Easton], and we got Greg [Hawkes] back again.''

That quartet realized it needed a full-time drummer. After looking around, they chose David Robinson. Robinson had previously founded a group called the Modern Lovers, leaving it when it decided to do acoustic sets. He commented: "I could have stayed with the group if I'd wanted to play with towels over my drum set.'' After that, he worked with the Los Angeles band Pop!, Boston-based DMZ, and, finally, the Cars, in late 1976.

The new band debuted at a New Year's Eve 1976 date at Pease Air Force Base, New Hampshire. After that, now with a full-time manager, the group began to win over local fans in places such as the downtown Boston punk club the Rathskellar, usually referred to as the Rat. In March 1977, the band moved a step further when it got a last-minute chance to fill in as opening act at a Bob Seger concert. After that, more chances to open for major acts came along plus headline dates at other Boston clubs such as the Paradise. After the group's demo tape of "Just What I Needed'' became the top request number on Boston's WCOZ-FM and WCBN-FM, record companies came after them instead of the other way around. Before the year was out, the band was signed by Elektra/Asylum, which sent it to England to record its debut LP with top producer Roy Thomas Baker, who went on to produce the band's next three albums as well. The debut LP, *The Cars,* came out on E/A in May 1978. It won the group acclaim as best new group in almost every year-end poll, including the Grammy Awards.

Orr remained lead singer with Ocasek handling rhythm guitar with some lead-vocal opportunities. Though other bandsmen liked to write original songs, they deferred to Ocasek as the primary songwriter. Ocasek said: "I write lyrics pretty fast. I usually write five songs at a sitting in a three-day period. I might write five songs and then not do any more for a few weeks until I feel in the mood again, then do five more. If there's an album project coming up, I pick the ones I like. No matter what the song sounds like when I am writing it, I always finish it to see where it ends up. So it covers a lot of moods and directions."

Easton, who provided originals for his solo recordings, stressed that he felt Ocasek's music embodied what the Cars were all about. "With the band, I feel my main role is to be a player. I make my contribution to Ric's songs by the way I play. I write my parts and to me that's a very creative situation. It's writing in a sense. It's satisfying. It's a very satisfying band to play with because I can run the gamut of styles."

In June 1979, Elektra/Asylum released the band's second album, *Candy-O,* with all 11 tracks written by Ocasek. It proved a worthy effort. *Candy-O* was on the charts into 1980, earning platinum-record certification from the RIAA. With it all through that period was the debut LP, which was still on the charts into 1981—at multiplatinum levels. Also platinum by the end of 1980 was the third LP, *Panorama,* issued in August 1980.

By the time the Cars' fourth album, *Shake It Up,* came out in late 1981, the band was an acknowledged concert favorite internationally. A fine collection, the LP deservedly moved right into the U.S. top 10 soon after release and earned the band another platinum-record award from the RIAA in 1982.

After the concerts backing *Shake It Up* were over, the band members took time out to work on other projects. Ocasek wrote, produced, and recorded his first solo album, *Beatitude,* on Geffen Records (1982). He also helped produce recordings by other groups such as the Boston-based New Models and New York's Bad Brains. In addition, Ric prepared copy for a book titled *Pros and Cons.*

In mid-1983, Cars members began taking steps

*Article based partly on personal interviews with Irwin Stambler.

toward their next group album, *Heartbeat City* (issued by Elektra/Asylum in March 1984). The album made the *Billboard* lists right after release and still was in the top 20 at year-end. It was also gained platinum certification by the RIAA.

In February 1985, Elliot Easton's debut solo LP, *Change No Change,* came out on Elektra. That was just one of a number of things he did in between Cars recording and concert activities. From 1982 to 1984, his other efforts included guest appearances on an album by Peter Wolf (*see J. Geils Band*), a writing partnership with Jules Shear (whose album, *Watch Dog,* featured guitar work by Easton), and production work on an album by the Boston rock band Dawgs.

As of mid-1986, Cars fans were still eagerly awaiting a new album amid fears that band members might decide to go separate ways permanently. In the meantime, Elektra issued a *Greatest Hits* retrospective album in late 1985 that was at number 12 position on *Billboard* charts at year-end headed for the top 10 in early 1986.

CASH, JOHNNY: *Singer, guitarist, songwriter, band leader. Born Kingsland, Arkansas, February 26, 1932.*

When Johnny Cash reached his silver anniversary as a recording artist in 1979, he could look back on a career that had all the elements of a classic novel. He had reached the heights, then abruptly plunged to lows of self-destruction from which he was saved, in effect, by a woman's love and his own inherent toughness. He had figuratively been at the gates of Hell, but had defeated drug dependency and despair to become one of the most respected figures in country and popular music.

Some of the answers to the complex personality that made him an erratic comet across the horizons of American music lay in the poverty and daily fight for survival of his youth. The Ray Cash family was proud, but bent by years of sharecropping, tragedy, and near tragedy. Johnny almost died of starvation in infancy in Kingsland, Dyess County, Arkansas, a locale he called "just a wide place in the road." Life consisted of a dirt farmer's shack, five brothers and sisters, cotton patches to be hoed and weeded, and a fundamentalist Bible-oriented rearing by a determined mother and a work-wearied father. Young John was hauling water for a road gang when he was ten and pulling a nine-foot cotton sack when he was 12. Undertones of this background break through often in fragments of his songs and in his attitude toward life.

The family stayed together, but when Cash was in his early teens, sudden death claimed two of his brothers, leaving Johnny, Reba, Joann, and Tommy (another future country singer) to work the fields with their parents. During those years, Johnny already was showing signs of creative talent. He was writing songs by the time he was 12, trying to emulate country stars he heard on the radio. While attending high school, he sang on radio station KLCN in Blytheville, Arkansas.

He seemed reluctant to break away from home, though—until the Korean War. Johnny enlisted in the Air Force and was assigned to Germany, where he worked as a military cryptographer. Finding himself with a lot of time on his hands, he bought his first guitar; while he learned to play it, he wrote some new songs, including one of his future hits, "Folsom Prison Blues," inspired by the movie *Inside the Walls of Folsom Prison.* He recalled: "There wasn't much romance to the writing of 'Folsom Prison Blues.' I saw the movie, liked it, and wrote the song. That's all there was to that."

After his discharge in the mid-1950s, Johnny settled in Memphis, Tennessee, where he scratched for a living as an appliance salesman. He married his first wife, Vivian, who gave him four girls including future singer Rosanne Cash. In his spare time, he took a radio-announcing course as a gesture toward a more creative existence. In Memphis, he met Luther Perkins, who played an amplified guitar, and bass player Marshall Grant. They got together and practiced with the ultimate objective of auditioning for Sam Phillips of Sun Records. The first material they brought to the record company was turned down as being too "country," so they went back and worked to incorporate a little more rock flavor. Phillips at the time had cash flow problems, but as negotiations got underway with major labels for the sale of Elvis Presley's Sun Records contract, he could see better times ahead and was more receptive to new talent. An audition by Cash and his group finally brought a contract and the result of the first sessions of John and The Tennessee Two was the single "Hey Porter" (backed with "Cry Cry Cry"), released in June 1955 and a hit late in the year. These were followed with "Folsom Prison Blues" in 1956 and such hits as "So Doggone Lonesome," "There You Go," and "I Walk the Line"—all Cash originals. He also made the charts with his version of the Rouse Brothers' fiddle tune, "Orange Blossom Special."

Johnny by now was one of the most successful artists in Sun Records' short history. In 1957, he scored with such originals as "Train of Love" and "Next in Line" and a co-authored hit, "Home of the Blues." In 1958, Johnny had six country top 10 hits, including two number one–ranked songs, "Guess Things Happen That Way" and "Ballad of a Teenage Queen." The other four records included songs he wrote or co-wrote: "You're the Nearest Thing to Heaven," "What Do I Care," "All Over Again" and "The Ways of a Woman in Love."

By now his first manager, Bob Neal, had booked Cash and the Tennessee Two into personal appearances throughout the country and the money came easier. The band later became the Tennessee Three with the addition of drummer Bill Holland.

In 1958, Cash moved from Sun to the more affluent Columbia label, where his first release, his own song, "Don't Take Your Guns to Town," sold past the half-million mark and stayed in the number one spot on country charts for many weeks. His first Columbia LP, *Johnny Cash* (January 1959) scored an impressive 400,000 copies. Sun released more of his material and had another top 10 country single in 1959, "Luther Played the Boogie." Columbia hit pay dirt with "Frankie's Man Johnny" and "I Got Stripes."

The pressures of his growing success were beginning to tell on Cash, however. Adding to that was a feeling of depression when his friend Johnny Horton died in an auto accident in late 1960. Outwardly, as the '60s began, things seemed about as bright as could be. Cash was an established national favorite. He was featured on both regional country & western shows and major-network TV programs. He was able to fill large concert halls in all corners of the land. As the '60s went by, he also became a favorite with folk audiences, starring at major folk festivals and performing in folk clubs around the U.S. and Canada.

In his private life, however, things were far from serene. He had become increasingly dependent on amphetamines and barbiturates. He went on wild binges that made friends and associates despair for his future. Sometimes he failed to show up for concerts or, if he did show up, he was in poor form or pleaded laryngitis. The strain told on his marriage, resulting in a separation from his first wife by the mid-1960s. At the same time, he could do an about face and show the world a blaze of boundless energy and a driving desire to work almost around-the-clock on his career.

Those spurts of energy resulted in a continued outpouring of new compositions and recordings, including some of his most notable successes. His top 10 hits of the period included "Seasons of My Heart" (1960); "In the Jailhouse Now" (1962); number one–ranked "Ring of Fire" (1963); "Bad News," "It Aint Me Babe," "The Ballad of Ira Hayes," and number one–ranked "Understand Your Man" (a Cash original) (1964); "Orange Blossom Special" and "The Sons of Katie Elder" (1965); "Happy to Be with You" and "The One on the Right Is on the Left" (1966); and "Jackson" and "Guitar Pickin' Man" (1967). The last two were duets with June Carter (daughter of Mother Maybelle Carter of the original Carter Family), the lady who helped change the course of Johnny's life.

June had been a member of Johnny's troupe since the early '60s and performed with him in many memorable engagements, including the 1966 performance in Liverpool, England that shattered the attendance record set by no less a group than Liverpool's own Beatles. June and Johnny became close and marriage seemed in the air, but June asked him to take steps to cure himself of his drug habits. Johnny agreed and, at June's urging, got together with Dr. Nat Winston, former head of the Tennessee Department for Mental Health, for an extended period of treatment. These sessions, coupled with Johnny's renewed interest in his Christian roots, succeeded. Cash no longer found it necessary to require chemical crutches to keep going. His marriage to June in 1967 proved one of the happiest in the country-music fraternity. From then on, they were almost inseparable in a family show that also often featured June's sisters, Mother Maybelle, Carl Perkins, the Statler Brothers, the Tennessee Three, and a number of other excellent artists. (*See Perkins, Carl.*)

Johnny and June recorded such major hits of 1968 as "If I Were a Carpenter" and "Daddy Sang Bass." Johnny's TV appearances in 1967–68 won such fine response from critics and viewers that ABC gave him his own summer replacement series in 1969. The show was hailed by sophisticated urban reviewers as well as "downhome" observers and resulted in a regular-season version starting in January 1970.

The year 1969 was a halcyon one for Johnny. He was clean of drug problems, happily married, and recipient of all manner of awards. He received gold records for the LPs *Johnny Cash at Folsom Prison* and *Johnny Cash at San Quentin* plus the novelty single "A Boy Named Sue." In the Country Music Awards, he won in every category in which he was nominated: Entertainer of the Year, Male Vocalist of the Year, Best Group (with June), Best Album *(San Quentin)*, and Best Single ("A Boy Named Sue").

The TV show was renewed for the 1970–71 season and continued to be very popular, though its ratings declined somewhat. It might have gone on further, but it was caught in the "prime-time squeeze" caused by new Federal Communications Commission restrictions on network programming and was canceled. In November 1971 the Cashes fulfilled a long-time ambition by going to Israel to work on a film about Christianity and modern-day life in the Holy Land. Called *Gospel Road*, it originally was distributed by 20th Century Fox, but later was acquired by Reverend Billy Graham's World Wide Pictures of Burbank.

That was not the only movie credit of Johnny's career. He co-starred with Kirk Douglas in *A Gunfight* for Paramount Pictures, among others. TV acting credits included roles in "Columbo" opposite Peter Falk in March 1974 and (with June) in the 1978 CBS-TV movie *Thaddeus Rose and Eddie*. He hosted the mid-1970s ABC-TV special on railroad history, "Ridin' the Rail." In 1976, he filmed his first television Christmas special, a show that became an annual event for the rest of the decade.

Johnny continued to turn out a steady stream of singles and albums from 1969 through 1979, many of which made top country (and sometimes pop) chart levels. His singles included "See Ruby Fall" backed with "Blistered" (1969); "What is Truth," "Sunday Morning Comin' Down" and "Flesh and Blood" (1970); "Man in Black," "Singin' Vietnam Talking Blues," "Papa Was a Good Man," and "A Thing Called Love" (1971); "Kate," "If I Had a Hammer" (with June), "Oney," "Any Old Wind That Blows," and "The Loving Gift" (with June) (1972); "Children," "Praise the Lord and Pass the Soup" and "Allegheny" (with June) (1973); "Orleans Parish Prison," "Ragged Old Flag," "The Junkie and the Juicehead (Minus Me)," "Father and Daughter" (with Rosie Nix), and "The Lady Came from Baltimore" (1974); "One Piece at a Time" (1976); "After the Ball" (1977); "I Would Like to See You Again" and "It'll Be Her" (1978); and "There Ain't No Good Chain Gang" (with Waylon Jennings) (1979).

During his decades with Columbia, Johnny recorded dozens of albums, both secular and spiritual. Among his releases were *Ride This Train* and *There Was a Song!* (1960); *Johnny Cash Sound* (1962); *Blood, Sweat & Tears* and *Ring of Fire* (1963); *I Walk the Line* and *Bitter Tears* (1964); *Orange Blossom Special* and *True West* (1965); *Mean As Hell!*, *Everybody Loves a Nut*, and *Happiness Is You* (1966); *Carryin' On* and *Greatest Hits, Volume I* (1967); *Hello, I'm Johnny Cash*, *World of Johnny Cash*, *Jackson* (with June Carter), and *Walls of a Prison* (1970); *Johnny Cash Show, Man in Black, Greatest Hits, Volume 2*, and *Johnny Cash Sings Precious Memories (1971); Give My Love to Rose* (with June) and *America* (1972); *Any Old Wind That Blows, Johnny Cash and His Woman* (with June), *Sunday Mornin' Comin' Down*, and *Thing Called Love* (1973); *The Junkie and the Juicehead (Minus Me), Five Feet High and Rising*, and *Ragged Old Flag* (1974); *Look at Them Beans* (1975); *One Piece at a Time* and *Last Gunfighter Ballad* (1976); *The Rambler* (1977); *I Would Like to See You Again* (1978); and *Silver* (1979). Other early to mid-1970s LPs were *Johnny Cash's Children's Album, Ballads* of American Indians, Understand Your Man, and Strawberry Cake.

During the late '60s and '70s, Sun Records also issued LPs of Johnny's earlier work on that label: Get Rhythm, Living Legend, Johnny Cash—the Man, His World, His Music, Original Golden Hits, Volumes 1 and 2, Rough-Cut King of Country Music, Show Time, Singing Storyteller, Story Songs of the Trains and Rivers, and Sunday Down South (with Jerry Lee Lewis). Columbia's subsidiary Harmony Records provided such albums as Johnny Cash (1969) and Johnny Cash Songbook (1972).

Cash recorded many religious albums over the years. Among them were Hymns (1959), Hymns from the Heart (1962), Christmas: The Johnny Cash Family (1972), The Christmas Spirit, The Gospel Road (1973), The Holy Land, and The Holy Road. In 1979, he dedicated his two-LP A Believer Sings the Truth (on Cachet Records) to his mother, "who inspired me at the age of seventeen when she said: 'God's got his hand on you, son. Keep on singing.'"

Though a firm believer, Johnny wasn't obtrusive about his religious feelings, respecting the beliefs of others. He told writer Patrick Carr in 1978: "I don't impose myself on anybody in any way, including religion. When you're imposing, you're offending, I feel, although I am evangelical and I'll give the message to anyone that wants to hear it, or anybody that is willing to listen. But if they let me know they don't want to hear it . . . if I think they don't want to hear it, then I will not bring it up."

His approach was not necessarily that of formal religion. He told Carr that while "the churches are full . . . the slums and the ghettos are still full, and for the most part, the church and the needy haven't gotten together yet. And until more people in the church realize the real needs of the people, and go out rather than going in . . . I mean, to go into church is great, but to go out and put it all into action, that's where it's all at. And I haven't seen a lot of action."

Cash outlined his philosophy about life in his autobiographical Man in Black, published in 1975 by Zondervan.

Cash began his fourth decade as a Columbia Records artist with the 1980 album Rockabilly Blues. This was followed in 1981 with the releases Encore (Greatest Hits, Volume 4) and The Baron. Columbia, though, was becoming dissatisfied with Johnny's recording sales as the mid-1980s approached and in 1986 his contract wasn't renewed. In the spring of 1987, the retrospective collection, The CBS Years 1958–1986, was released. Among the tracks was a previously unreleased duet between Cash and superstar Bruce Springsteen of Bruce's composition, "Highway Patrolman."

CHAD AND JEREMY: *Vocal and instrumental duo. Both born England, circa mid-1940s; Chad Stuart, December 10; Jeremy Clyde, March 22.*

Projecting a softer sound than most pop stars of the mid-1960s, Chad and Jeremy met with surprising success for several years. From 1964 through 1966, their recordings were rarely absent from U.S. charts and their faces constantly graced TV screens.

Sons of affluent English families, the boys were well educated, progressing from exclusive preparatory schools to such institutions as Eton, Grenoble, and the Sorbonne. Though both were interested in popular music, they didn't seriously consider it as a full-time career until they met when studying acting at the Central School of Drama. By then, both had learned to play the guitar.

Their collaboration led to a recording contract. One of their first singles, "A Summer Song," was previewed on British TV's "Juke Box Jury" in 1964. Ringo Starr, one of the panelists, called it a "miss," but suggested it might do well in the U.S. His prediction proved accurate. Released on the World Artists label, it reached the top 20 in the States in '64. The duo, who moved to Hollywood, California, during the year, followed with the 1964 chart singles "Yesterday's Gone" and "Willow Weep for Me" and the 1965 World Artists successes "If I Love You," "What Do You Want with Me," and "From a Window." During 1965, the twosome signed with Columbia Records, making the best-seller lists that year with "I Don't Wanna Love You Baby" and "I Have Dreamed" and, in 1966, with "Distant Shores" and "You Are She."

Acting still held a strong attraction for Jeremy. In 1966, he left Chad to join the cast of the London stage musical The Passion Flower Motel. Chad wasn't happy about the break, but he was willing to reform the team when Jeremy completed his stage work.

In November 1967, with a number of critics praising their new album, Cabbages and Kings, the team again announced it was splitting up. Jeremy had once more accepted an acting assignment, this time with the national company of Black Comedy. While preparing for an engagement at the Carousel Theater in West Covina (a suburb of Los Angeles) in late November, Chad commented: "We've been trying to sink ourselves for years. The earlier split was painful. The difference between then and now is that I'm prepared for it. Musically I've never felt more articulate."

107

Jeremy, though, referring to what appears to have been the final breakup of the team, said: "And just now, I'm stale. I'm tired."

Besides *Cabbages and Kings,* the team's album output on Columbia included *Chad and Jeremy* (August 1965), *Don't Wanna Lose You* (December 1965), and *Distant Shores* (October 1966). Capitol Records issued the albums *Best of Chad and Jeremy* (May 1966) and *More of Chad and Jeremy* (July 1966).

Throughout the 1970s and into the 1980s the team was inactive and their recordings were out of print except for a 1980 Capitol LP *The Best of Chad and Jeremy.* In the mid-1980s, the duo got back together to take part in some of the revival shows of 1960s British rock and pop artists.

CHANDLER, GENE: *Singer, record producer, record-company executive. Born Chicago, Illinois, July 6, 1937.*

When the R&B boom of the 1960s is discussed, the two cities most often cited as its wellsprings of activity are Detroit (for the Motown sound) and Memphis. However, a close look at the picture indicates Chicago had far from a minor role in propelling R&B artists to the top ranks of all pop performers, providing such singers as Jerry Butler, Curtis Mayfield, the Impressions, and Gene Chandler. (*See Butler, Jerry; Impressions, The; and Mayfield, Curtis.*)

Chandler, whose real name is Eugene Dixon, was born and raised on Chicago's South Side. His background is somewhat unusual in that gospel singing had little effect on his development. Almost from the start, he was headed for a popular music career, beginning, as he recalls, "when I was about six, I guess. My mother used to take me around to the amateur shows and I'd sing, or try to."

Though neither of his parents were ever so inclined, he had his sights set on show business when he entered Englewood High School. He sang in school events and, at 15, helped form a group called the Gay Tones, for which he was lead singer. After graduating, he hung around local clubs, fraternized with other aspiring young musicians, and finally joined a group called the Dukays. The group was so much in demand that they sometimes hit two or even three South Side clubs in the same night—though the pay was not impressive.

In 1957, Gene decided to get his service obligations out of the way and enlisted in the Army. He was assigned to the 101st Airborne Division and stationed in Germany. There, he added to his experience by performing in Army Special Services shows.

Discharged in 1960, he returned to Chicago and rejoined the Dukays. This time they had a recording contract with Vee Jay Records. One of their releases featuring Gene, "The Girl Is a Devil," gained the charts in 1960. Success came relatively easy, Chandler points out. "I can't even talk about having to struggle when I was trying to get going. We never had to hustle to get a song to record or a recording contract. It was all like a hobby."

In 1961, Gene left the Dukays to try his luck as a solo artist. As he noted, things seemed to come easy to him. In November 1961, Vee Jay released his "Duke of Earl," one of the top singles of 1962, achieving number one on the U.S. rock and R&B charts and soaring to the top levels in Europe as well. ("Duke of Earl," co-written by Chandler, Bernice Williams, and Earl Edwards, became a number one single on *Billboard* charts the week of February 17, 1962 and stayed there for two more weeks. Chandler's single failed to reach top levels in the U.K., but a 1979 recording by the Darts made the English top 10.) The record sold well over a million copies and established Gene as a major performer. In late 1962, he made the charts with both the A and B sides of a singles release, "You Threw a Lucky Punch" and the Curtis Mayfield composition, "Rainbow." (The last named came out in a revised version by Gene a few years later.) For the next six years, Gene turned out one hit after another on the R&B lists, pop charts, or both.

In the mid-1960s, he moved to Constellation Records, formed by former Vee Jay president Ewart Abner, and placed nine singles on the charts. Those included "Just Be True" (1964) and "Rainbow '65" and "Nothing Can Stop Me" in 1965. In 1966, he made R&B charts with the single "I Fooled You This Time." With the Brunswick label in 1968, he made the charts with "From the Teacher to the Preacher," a duet with Barbara Acklin. Some of his other charted singles of the period, either on R&B or pop charts, were "Bless Our Love," "What Now," "Man's Temptation," "You Can't Hurt Me No More" and "The Girl Don't Care." Albums included *Gene Chandler* on Checker (April 1967) and *The Girl Don't Care* on Brunswick.

In 1968, Chandler decided the time had come to give up the wearing grind of one-nighters. He decided to restrict his appearances to a relative handful of major engagements and to spend more time in behind-the-scenes work, such as songwriting, record production, and developing new talent. He bought out a small record firm, Bamboo Records, moved it to Chicago, and established his own music publishing firm, Chand Music. He later added a new label, Mr. Chand Records. During the late '60s, he produced record sessions for many major R&B artists and worked on material for a new duo, Mel and Tim, producing their chart single "Backfield in Motion."

In early 1970, he signed a combined recording and distribution agreement with Mercury Records. One of his first Mercury singles, "Groovy Situation," won a gold record. His LP, *The Gene Chandler Situation*, also made the national charts during 1970, as did another single, "Simply Call It Love." In 1971, Mercury teamed him with Jerry Butler and the two gained recognition in national polls as the number two R&B duo of the year. Their album, *Gene Chandler and Jerry Butler*, was a chart hit on the pop and soul charts. Gene also placed the single "You're a Lady" high on the soul charts in the summer. As 1972 got underway, Gene was represented on the charts with the single "Yes I'm Ready (If I Don't Get to Go)."

Over the next few years, though, audience interest in Gene seemed to die out. For a while he was without a major–record-company contract.

A new pact with 20th Century Records sparked his career for a while in the late 1970s and early 1980s. Albums on the label included *Gene Chandler, Two Sides of Gene Chandler*, and *Get Down* (1978), *When You're Number One* (1979), *'80* (1980), and *Here's to Love* (1981). Also available in record stores was the British Charly label's 1980 reissue of some of Chandler's 1960s songs, *Just Be True*.

CHAPIN, HARRY: *Singer, guitarist, songwriter. Born New York, New York, December 7, 1942; died Long Island, New York, July 1981.*

A singer/guitarist/songwriter whose original compositions incorporated musical elements stretching from folk to jazz to rock, Harry Chapin not only was a troubadour of modern times but also a social reformer. Besides entertaining audiences all across the United States, he often persuaded them to contribute to humanistic causes ranging from world hunger to support for the performing arts. Describing his code to one interviewer, he said: "Our lives are to be used and thus to be lived as fully as possible. And truly it seems that we are never so alive as when we concern ourselves with other people."

He was born in New York's Greenwich Village, the son of a big-band drummer whose credits included stints with the Tommy Dorsey and Woody Herman bands. It was a closely knit family. Harry and his three brothers all drew inspiration from their father's musical interests. One of Harry's early musical pursuits was singing in the Brooklyn Heights Boys choir after the family moved to the Brooklyn Heights section of New York in the '50s. Among his acquaintances in the choir was Robert Lamm, later of Chicago rock group fame. (*See Chicago.*)

The first instrument Harry learned was trumpet; he later took up banjo and guitar. At 15, he organized a musical act with his brothers. The older one soon dropped music, but younger siblings Tom and Steve stayed with it and later were regulars in the band that accompanied Harry around the world. Their father, Jim, sometimes sat in with them when they were young; he too became a cast member of the Chapin troupe in the '70s, when he often opened one of Harry's programs with his own Dixieland jazz group.

Harry became enthused about the folk boom of the late '50s and '60s and played many of the folk hits of the day for his own pleasure or for friends while studying architecture at the Air Force Academy and then philosophy at Cornell University. In 1964, he decided he'd had enough of higher education and left school to join brothers Tom and Steve and his father in a group called the Chapin Brothers that worked in Greenwich Village spots. The group recorded an album, *Chapin Music*, on Rockland Records, but disbanded when Tom and Steve went back to school.

Meanwhile, Harry was also trying his hand in the film field, first working as a film packer, loading reels into crates, then moving into film editing. By the late '60s, he was making some of his own documentaries. Completed with associate Jim Jacobs, his documentary *Legendary Champions* won an Academy Award nomination for best documentary of 1969 and also received prizes at the New York and Atlanta film festivals. In the middle and late '60s, Harry also wrote original songs, mostly of the storytelling kind that was to become his trademark in the '70s.

In 1970, his family resurrected the Chapin Brothers and got a contract to cut an LP for Epic. Harry provided the songs, but didn't play in the group. Among the tracks on the LP were "Dog Town," "Greyhound," and "Any Old Kind of Day," which later were re-recorded by Harry and became important parts of his repertoire. Not too much happened with the 1970 group, but the following year, Harry got back into action, assembling a new band including brother Steve. Instead of looking for paying engagements with others, Harry hit on the idea of renting the Village Gate in New York for a summer run. Critics praised their work. Soon, not only local fans were coming to hear them, but record-company executives as well. In late 1971, this culminated in a contract with Elektra, which remained his label through the rest of the '70s.

In short order, he had a single and album that made the national charts. The single, a story song called "Taxi," drew on Harry's short-lived efforts to get a taxi driver's license in the mid-1960s. (The song itself deals with a chance meeting between two onetime lovers—the man now driving a taxi—whose paths and dreams have diverged sharply.) It received considerable airplay despite its unconventional length of six minutes. *Heads and Tales,* his debut LP containing the song, was released in early 1972. Harry continued to build up a following across the world during 1973 and 1974 with the albums *Sniper and Other Love Stories* and *Short Stories.*

The most played track from *Short Stories* was the hit single "W*O*L*D," a bittersweet view of the AM radio world through the eyes of an aging disc jockey.

His fourth album, *Verities and Balderdash,* proved even more exciting. One of its tracks, "Cat's in the Cradle," was a telling indictment of a father who was more concerned about becoming a success in business than helping his son grow up. Both single and album soared past gold-record levels and verified that Chapin was a bona fide star even though his balladeering approach to music didn't fit neatly into any particular cubbyhole. He essentially was a folk-singer, but in a completely modern idiom.

In the mid-1970s, without abandoning his steady recording pace (which included two LPs, *Portrait Gallery* and *Greatest Stories—Live*), Harry ventured into other entertainment areas. During 1974, he was working on a new musical, a multimedia concept show that opened on Broadway in 1975 under the title *The Night That Made America Famous.* The show was highly praised by reviewers and later was given two Tony nominations by New York theater critics. Two years later, this time across the country in Hollywood, a revue at the Improvisation Theatre based on his music and called *Chapin* achieved a seven-month run and later spawned similar productions elsewhere.

During the '70s, Chapin kept up a hectic touring schedule that averaged 200 concerts a year all over the United States and in many other nations. Besides his regular commercial shows, he constantly crammed in benefit appearances for the many causes and charities he believed in. In the mid-1970s, for instance, he organized a series of Concerts for Africa to help victims of the drought in sub-Sahara regions. In the summer of 1974, he gave three shows for that cause in the Astrodome in Houston, Los Angeles Forum, and Madison Square Garden that helped raise over $6 million in relief funds. In fact, of his 200 annual concerts, typically half were benefits.

Another continuing effort was his work to eradicate hunger throughout the globe. Chapin helped found the World Hunger Year, a campaign in which, besides giving many benefit concerts and enlisting other artists to do the same thing, he lobbied House and Senate members and the President of the United States to pass a resolution for a government commission on world hunger. At many of his concerts, he told the audience he would remain after the show as long as necessary to sign autographs and talk to peo-ple donating money to whatever charitable enterprise he was working on at the time.

Even with that hectic schedule, he still managed to write new songs and turn out new albums, though it must be said that sometimes the pace appeared to be reflected in some loss in creative results. After his 1976 LP, *On the Road to Kingdom Come,* he provided material for a two-album set released in August 1977, *Dance Band on the Titanic.* The theme running through its eleven songs was that the entertainment industry, to coin a phrase, was "on thin ice" and resembled the band on the sinking *Titanic.* However, the LP seemed far muddier and less interesting than his earlier releases. Harry was in better form for his next offering, *Living Room Suite,* issued in June 1978. Among the diverse groups providing backing vocals were the Persuasions, Dixie Hummingbirds, and Cowsills. Though he was still a favorite with concert audiences at the end of the 1970s, Chapin's recording efforts seemed to be bringing diminishing returns when he left Elektra to sign a new contract with Boardwalk Records. By the end of 1980, though, that part of his career was on the upswing with the success of his single "Sequel," in upper charts levels in December and his Boardwalk LP of the same title, on the charts from late 1980 well into 1981.

"Sequel," as the title indicates, was a follow up to his earlier hit "Taxi," in which the man and woman meet after ten years with their roles reversed—by then the one-time taxi driver is a success in the music field and the girl is divorced from her rich husband and working for a living. There turned out to be some irony in Chapin's comments to Paul Grein (*Los Angeles Times,* December 6, 1980): "My wife has been kidding me that in another ten years I've got to write a new song called 'Hearse' and finally haul 'em off."

Unfortunately, Chapin's own life was snuffed out in an automobile accident on New York's Long Island Expressway in July 1981.

Just before his passing, he had expressed his concern over political trends in the U.S. to Andrew Epstein of *The Los Angeles Times,* though at the same time indicating optimism that the younger generations would eventually improve things. (Chapin was somewhat apolitical himself; in the 1980 elections he had campaigned for five Republican and 19 Democratic Congressmen, basing his support on their stands in favor of action to alleviate world hunger.)

"Frankly," Chapin said, "there's more potential movement out of this generation than there was in the '60s. The real question is whether America is going to use Reagan as an excuse to forget about things it already knows it should stand up for. When David Stockman [Reagan's budget director] says to

America that there's no such thing as entitlement, it's giving us all an excuse to not feel guilty about [the poor] and just be selfish. And we know that's nonsense. Because we know that Nelson Rockefeller, when he was born, was entitled to $400 million and somebody else was entitled to brain damage because of malnutrition.

"The scary thing about the current political situation is that it is allowing people to have a political excuse to go to sleep."

Soon after Chapin's passing, there were indications others would rally to his causes. Benefits were planned to collect funds for them as well as to salute his memory. His manager, Ken Kragen, announced establishment of a Harry Chapin Memorial Fund "to keep his work going and try to accomplish some of the goals he set."

CHARLES, RAY: *Singer, pianist, songwriter, band leader, record-company executive. Born Albany, Georgia, September 23, 1930.*

"Soul is a way of life," Ray Charles once told a reporter, "but it is always the hard way." Ray should know, for he had a long, uphill fight to develop his talent and overcome the hindrances of racial prejudice and blindness. Despite those obstacles, he persevered and went on to become an acknowledged superstar, as gifted in capturing the essence of country & western songs as such other genres as R&B/soul, pop, rock, and jazz. And he also managed to remain singularly free from the bitterness and self-pity that might have accrued under the circumstances.

In general, Ray avoided social commentary about racial matters because, he once said: "My audiences have spent their hard-earned money to get a few minutes' entertainment. Everyone can see I'm black, so I guess I don't have to tell anyone about it."

But he didn't completely avoid the issue either. He took part in civil rights protests of the 1960s and recorded some pro–civil rights material, such as the 1970s LP *A Message from the People*. As he told Leonard Feather at the time, such a collection shouldn't have surprised anyone. "I was recording protest songs when it wasn't a popular thing to do. Back around 1961 I had one called 'Danger Zone' and there was another one called 'You're in for a Big Surprise.' Some of the words were: 'I call you mister, I shine your shoes/You go away laughin' while I sing the blues/You think I'm funny and you're so wise/But baby, you're in for a big surprise.' Now that was years before the black pride and black is beautiful songs came along, but it had the same sort of message."

He also recalled how his initial foray into country & western raised a few eyebrows. "But that first country & western album didn't indicate a change in direction any more than his new album *A Message from the People* does. These are all simply additional directions." Such efforts were significant not just for Ray, but for other artists. His success in country music, for instance, was a breakthrough of sorts against bigotry that made the path of the great black country singer Charlie Pride a little easier later on.

Color, of course, was a strange concept for Ray to grasp, for his world was one of sound after the onset of blindness. Born in Albany, Georgia, Ray Charles Robinson lost his sight at age six from what was later conjectured to have been glaucoma. As a child he moved with his family to Greenville, Florida. His father, a handyman, died when Ray was ten. On a neighbor's piano, he picked out tunes, becoming aware of boogie-woogie and other pop styles he would later prefer to the classical piano he was taught at St. Augustine's School for the Deaf and Blind in Orlando. At 15, he became an orphan. Leaving school, he soon found work with a country & western band in Jacksonville. In his late teens he wanted to try new musical directions and asked a friend to look at a map and tell him the furthest point away from Florida in the U.S. This led to his moving to Seattle, Washington, where he played piano at the Rockin' Chair club. Before long, Ray began seeking a record deal and got the chance to record the song "Confession Blues" for Los Angeles–based Swingtime Records. Unfortunately, the disc was made during a musician's strike and Ray was penalized by the union for strike breaking. Other musicians had gotten around the ban by using assumed names, but the still-naive Charles had used his own.

Eventually, Ray moved his home base to Los Angeles and signed with Atlantic Records. (According to David Ritz, who helped write Ray's autobiography *Brother Ray*, Charles made his first recording when he was 17 and already had recorded over 40 singles by the time he signed with Atlantic. Ray went on to record 34 albums with Atlantic, 24 with ABC, three with Tangerine and four with Crossover before joining the Columbia roster in 1983, according to Ritz's data.) He achieved his first R&B singles hit, "It Should've Been Me," on Atlantic in 1954, and his first national chart hit, "I Got a Woman," the following year. From then on, Ray was rarely out of the spotlight as a concert artist, TV performer, and recording artist. His name was constantly on the R&B and pop charts throughout the 1950s with such singles as "Blackjack," "Come Back," "Fool for You," "Greenbacks," "This Little Girl of Mine," "Drown in My Own Tears," "Hallelujah I Love Her So," "Lonely Avenue," "Mary Ann," "What Would I Do Without You," "Right Time," and "What'd I Say," all on Atlantic. Atlantic released many LPs of Ray's material during those years and continued to come out with albums of 1950s recordings in later decades. Among those still in print in the early 1980s were *The Great Ray Charles* (1957), *Soul Brother* (with Milt Jackson) (1959), *Genius of Ray Charles* (1960), *The Greatest Ray Charles* (1961), *Soul Meeting* (with Milt Jackson) (1962), *The Best of Ray Charles* (1971), and *Ray Charles Live* (1973). *A Twenty-fifth Anniversary in Show Business Salute to Ray Charles* (1973) is available as a Japanese import.

In 1960, Ray moved from Atlantic to ABC-Paramount and promptly had a hit single, "Sticks and Stones." Later in the year, he had his first number one national hit, a soul version of the pop classic "Georgia on My Mind," which was at the top of *Billboard*'s list the week of November 14, 1960. He followed with other hits, including "Them That's Got" and "Ruby." "Hit the Road Jack" hit number one on *Billboard*'s charts the weeks of October 9 and 16, 1961. He also made the charts with releases on ABC's jazz label, Impulse, scoring with "I've Got News for You" and the top 10 instrumental "One Mint Julep." In 1962, he made his initial move into country, turning out three singles on ABC-Paramount that made both country and pop charts: "You Don't Know Me," "You Are My Sunshine," and "I Can't Stop Loving You." The last of those became his all-time best-seller, rising to number one in *Billboard* the week of June 2, 1962 and staying there for four more weeks. It easily earned a gold-record award from the RIAA. From then on, country songs were a regular part of Ray's repertoire, with one or more often showing up on his albums throughout the 1970s and into the 1980s.

He continued to add to his list of charted singles throughout the 1960s and 1970s, though his pace slowed markedly after the 1960s. Among his top 10 hits on R&B and/or pop charts in the later 1960s were "Busted," "Don't Set Me Free," "No One," and "Take These Chains from My Heart" in 1963; "Crying Time," "Together Again," and "Let's Go Get Stoned" in 1966; and "Here We Go Again" in 1967. Among his ABC-Paramount LPs were *Live Concert, Together Again,* and *Cryin' Time* (1965); *Ray's Moods* (1966); *Man and His Soul* and *Listen* (1967); and, in the late '60s and early '70s, *I'm All Yours Baby* and *All Time Great Performances.* His best-selling albums on the label in the 1960s included two completely devoted to country-based material, *Modern Sounds in Country & Western Music, Volumes 1 and 2.*

Ray's activities from the late 1960s through the late 1980s included worldwide touring and such ventures as operating his own record operation and music publishing firm. His home base remained Los Angeles, but he was constantly on the road backed by his band and female vocal group, the Raylettes. He continued to be a featured guest on almost every TV music show of consequence during those years, including more than a few country music shows. In the latter category he was even a featured artist of an episode of the Public Broadcasting System's "Austin City Limits" in the early 1980s.

During the 1970s and 1980s, Ray continued to be a prolific recording artist, adding dozens of new titles to his discography over that time, not to mention reissues of earlier material. In the mid-1970s, he put out a series of albums on his own Crossover label (he also had other label names of his own, such as Tangerine) including *Come Live with Me* (1974) and *My Kind of Jazz, Part 3* and *Renaissance* (1975). Ray then returned to Atlantic with the 1977 LP *True to Life.* (That same year, King Records issued a collection of his early recordings, *Fourteen Hits/The Early Years.*) He followed with *Love and Peace* (1978), *Ain't It So* (1979), and *Brother Ray Is at It Again* (1980). In 1980, the retrospective *The Right Time,* available on Atlantic as a Japanese import, was issued. Ray's new alignment with Atlantic came to an end at the start of the 1980s, but in 1982 Atlantic issued a four-disc boxed set, *A Life in Music,* covering much of his recording career.

In 1983, Ray became a member of the CBS Records roster. One of his initial projects was a country album recorded in Nashville, Tennessee. This album, *Wish You Were Here Tonight,* he told Kip Kirby of *Billboard,* represented still another new direction in his song interpretations. The album, he said "encompasses traditional country and I've never really done that before. In the '60s, I did a lot of country songs, but I always made them sound contemporary. I'd add strings, give them a pop feel, so that way I got a lot of people into country for the first time." The public response to the LP was strong enough to justify a follow-up album in a similar vein, *Do I Ever Cross Your Mind* (April 1984).

Ray's enormous contributions to all facets of pop music and to the American heritage was recognized in 1986, when he was one of a number of distinguished Americans honored with a special Kennedy Center Award medallion presented by President Reagan. The president and the award recipients were guests of honor on a nationally televised program from the Kennedy Center in Washington, D.C. In the segment of the program dedicated to Ray, he was serenaded by the teenage choir from his old school, St. Augustine's, and by fellow blind superstar Stevie Wonder. (*See The Whispers.*)

CHEAP TRICK: *Vocal and instrumental group from Chicago, Illinois. Original members,* *mid-1970s: Rick Nielsen, born December 22; Robin Zander, born January 23; Tom Petersson, born May 9; Bun E. Carlos, born June 12. Petersson replaced by Jon Brant in 1982.*

With the powerful guitar playing and off-the-wall songwriting skills of Rick Nielsen plus the biting vocals of Robin Zander, coupled with excellent support from bass guitarist Tom Petersson and drummer Bun E. Carlos, Cheap Trick arguably was one of the finest rock bands the U.S. produced in the 1970s. The excellent musicianship coupled with Nielsen's wild stage antics and the odd appearance of the foursome helped make the band one of the more appealing live acts of the period. However, it was hard for the group to capture that excitement on records until its *Live at Budokan* set from a Japanese concert tour brought it commercial acceptance. Success, unfortunately, seemed to act as a deterrent and the band's new songs of the early 1980s fell short of the promise it had shown in the previous decade.

The band's origins go back to the high school environment of the early 1960s, where Nielsen and Petersson both cut their eyeteeth; and the midwest bar band circuit, where they joined forces in the mid-1960s. In those years, Nielsen played both guitar and keyboards, though he gave up keyboards for the most part once Cheap Trick came into existence.

By 1966, the two were in a band called Fuse. The band's first single (on the Smack label) was a version of "Hound Dog" backed with something titled "Cruising for Beaver." The group went on to record some additional singles for Epic Records, which led to sessions that resulted in a 1968 LP, *Fuse*, about which the less said the better.

About *Fuse*, Nielsen told Ira Robbins of *Trouser Press* (fall 1978): "The guys we were with were all rinky dinks; they're probably pumping gas now. Tom and I had the stick-to-it-iveness and positive thinking to know what we wanted to do, so we split the band and went off to hang out in England. We were big fans of the British bands; we always thought British bands were the coolest."

In England, Nielsen met Todd Rundgren at the Marquee Club. (*See Rundgren, Todd.*) Nielsen told Robbins: "It was 1969 and he had just quit the Nazz to go solo. When we got back [to the U.S.] I checked around and found the other guys from Nazz: Thom Mooney was in California and Stewkey was in Texas. The four of us had a band for four months; me on guitar, Tom on bass, Thom on drums, and Stewkey on keyboards and vocals." The group then appeared in a series of dates listed under any one of three band names—Nazz, Fuse, or a new name, Honey Boy Wiliams and the Manchurian Blues Band. Adding to the confusion was a release of a new Nazz album during those months based on outtakes from earlier LPs.

By 1970, the new band had folded and Rick and Tom went to Europe again for a while, performing in a group called the Sick Man of Europe. Again not much happened. A little while later, Stewkey called Rick and Tom by phone, asking them to meet him in Philadelphia to work on some demos that had the chance of bringing Stewkey a solo contract. Rick noted: "He [Stewkey] liked my songs, and I was brought in as a writer and guitarist. We did a demo, then another one. That's the origin of those bootleg Nazz tapes."

That project came to naught and Tom and Rick headed for Europe once more, this time for Germany, where there was a flourishing rock environment. They came across Bun E. Carlos and were impressed enough with his drum work to make plans for a new band. Carlos also came from the Midwest and had spent a number of years backing artists such as Chuck Berry, Freddy Cannon, Del Shannon, and the Shirelles on rock'n'roll revival tours. He also worked with relatively unknown new bands such as the 1967 group, the Pagans. He recalled recording a single with that band, which played Van Morrison–style material.

Rick and Tom had newly written or rewritten songs to play for the prospective new bandsman. Nielsen recalled: "The material was good and the ideas were good. We played the songs for Bun E. and he liked them, but we needed a singer. All of a sudden Robin appeared. He had been singing in Scotland or someplace."

In 1974, the quartet that was to become Cheap Trick headed back to the U.S. to try to win fame and fortune. For the next few years, the band worked out its somewhat frantic stage show, playing small clubs and bars around the U.S. To say the least, the content of a Cheap Trick show at the time was rather unpredictable, and might have surprised fans who saw their late 1970s show. Nielsen told Kristine McKenna of the *Los Angeles Times* (February 18, 1979): "No artist likes to admit it, but we have made certain concessions to commerciality—more in the live show than on record. When we used to play clubs, we were a lot more avant garde than we are now. We had a lot more freedom. Now we're forced to cater to the audience a little more and that's something we hope to break away from. I like to make audiences work, and we could be taking a lot more chances and still be progressing."

During the bar-circuit years, Cheap Trick continued to work up demo tapes and send them around to record-company officials. This finally paid off with a contract from Epic. The band's label debut, *Cheap Trick,* came out in 1976 with such tracks as

"Mandocello," "He's a Whore," "The Ballad of TV Violence," and "Daddy Should Have Stayed in High School."

The album cover showed that the quartet already had adopted its odd visual combination, blending the kooky looks of Nielsen (baseball cap, Cheap Trick bow tie, sweater top, jeans, white socks, and tennis shoes) and stock broker image of Carlos (tie and dress shirt), with the matinee idol features of Zander and Petersson. The contrasting visages, Nielsen emphasized, hadn't been preassembled like the Monkees. "I don't know how you'd plan a band like that—to say, 'Robin, you be good looking, me and Bun E. will be the kooky ones and so on.' You can plan a group like Kiss—the costumes and the show. But you can't plan the musicians' personalities or how they'll blend to make the music. And that's what matters—the music."

The debut LP won some attention, nurtured by the band's all-out tour schedule, mostly as opening act for better-known bands. The group's reputation was enhanced still more by its 1977 release, *In Color,* which included several songs that became concert staples: "Hello There," "Clock Strikes Ten," and "Come On Come On." The album was extolled as one of the year's best by many critics, and it did spend some time on the charts, but not enough to make it a best-seller. But the combination of two well-crafted rock albums and roof-shaking concerts helped create a core following of fans on which to build. The group kept the trend going with its third LP, the 1978 *Heaven Tonight,* whose contents included the track that would make the band a discjockey favorite, "Surrender."

The schedule for 1978 included a spring tour of Japan—an unexpected bonanza for the band's fortunes. To that point, the band's goal of gaining more than a relatively small share of the U.S. market had seemed an uphill battle. But the group literally took Japan by storm in its first visit there. Obviously familiar with the group's early LPs, fans snapped up tickets for the group's opening concert at the 12,000-seat Budokan Hall in Tokyo and did the same when a second show was added. After videotapes of those concerts and another at Osaka were shown on Japanese TV on July 4, 1978, the band was named by Japanese fans the "Number One International TV Act." A complete issue of Japan's *Music Life* magazine was devoted to the group, which is akin to having a monopoly of a single issue of *Rolling Stone* in the U.S. By the end of 1978, the band had won two Japanese gold records for sales of *In Color* and *Heaven Tonight.*

The two-disc *Cheap Trick Live at Budokan* initially was released only in Japan, where it quickly became a top-seller. After it became apparent that U.S. fans were buying import versions, Epic decided to release it in the U.S. as well, along with a new studio album, *Dream Police.*

The live album became a chart hit in the U.S. too, although it was often hard to hear the band over the audience. Nielsen told McKenna: "Live albums are often beefed up, and although it sounds phony, the Bodokan audience was for real. At Budokan everyone in the audience was singing—I was wondering what was happening at the time myself." Before the U.S. LP came out, a live cut from the Japanese concert of "I Want You to Want Me" (coupled with "California Man") was issued in the U.S. in November 1978.

That record was to finally prove that Cheap Trick could turn out hit singles, something that industry observers had faulted them for previously. In early 1979, Nielsen told a reporter: "We haven't had hit singles in the United States and a lot of people think we should be doing better—a lot of people think we shouldn't be doing anything at all—but I think we're doing fine. When Tom Petersson and I walk down the street, people know we're not Alice Cooper and Tom Petty, so we are known.

"I've got no sour grapes about our career. We've kept our credibility and built an audience on our own. It's a foundation that can't be pulled out from under us. If we make mistakes, it won't damage us the way it would someone who had skyrocketed to the top, and we're not trapped by a narrow style. We have a lot more flexibility than a group like Boston."

As 1979 progressed, it looked as though Nielsen's optimism was justified. *Live at Budokan* moved to upper U.S. chart levels, to be joined there later by the new studio album, *Dream Police.* Both were still on the charts in 1980. The band also earned its first gold-record single for "I Want You to Want Me." Also on the singles charts during 1979 were "Ain't That a Shame" (from *Live at Budokan*) and, from *Dream Police,* the title song and "Voices." All in all, Epic reported Cheap Trick had sold over two million singles and three million albums in 1979.

Commenting on *Dream Police,* Nielsen told McKenna: "We recorded the song 'Dream Police' for our first album but didn't use it. *Dream Police* is a theme album. All our albums have been theme albums, but none has been as clearly defined as this one. It's about the parts of yourself that you can't run away from, and music is part of that level of consciousness. Each song on the album is like a chapter in a book." Unfortunately, the album didn't seem as original musically as the earlier ones.

Coming off a banner year, the outlook seemed bright as the 1980s began. The band was represented by two new releases in 1980: a new studio collection, *All Shook Up,* and an Epic Nu-Disc mini-album, *Found All the Parts,* containing mainly material not included in earlier albums and one new live cut, "Day Tripper." Neither album added much to the band's stature. *All Shook Up* was on the charts briefly in late 1980 and early 1981, while *Found All the Parts* was only a modest success commercially.

There were hints of internal strains in the Cheap Trick organization. The next album, *One on One,* didn't come out until 1982. By then, Jon Brant had replaced Tom Petersson on bass guitar. The band demonstrated its usual excellent concert style even with the altered lineup, but the new albums fell short of earlier releases and failed to win over record buyers.

The band's ninth album on Epic Records, *Next Position Please,* came out during 1983. Produced by Todd Rundgren, the album featured some vintage Cheap Trick material, but still was only moderately successful. But the next LP, *Standing on the Edge,* issued in July 1985, showed improvement in both content and sales. Producer for that collection was Jack Douglas, whose credits included production work with Aerosmith and on the John Lennon/Yoko Ono LP *Double Fantasy.* The group's output in 1986 included the song "Mighty Wings" for the soundtrack of the hit movie *Top Gun* and its eleventh Epic LP, released in the fall.

CHECKER, CHUBBY: *Singer, dancer. Born South Carolina, October 3, 1941.*

Certainly one of the most sweeping dance fads in popular music history, the twist made Chubby Checker (born Ernest Evans) internationally famous. The impact of this rock-associated dance on the public consciousness was such that it still brought the name Chubby Checker to mind to many people in the late 1960s, 1970s, and even throughout the 1980s, long after his career had waned.

From 1960 to 1964, however, Chubby, who once had worked as a chicken-plucker, was one of the kingpins of the popular music field and a leader in the Philadelphia sound. He scored the odd feat of having the same single rise to number one on the charts on two widely separated occasions. When his single of "The Twist" was issued by Cameo-Parkway Records, it rose to number one on *Billboard* lists the week of September 19, 1960, and, like most pop discs, declined in sales the next year to the point that Cameo dropped it from its catalog. However, the song and the dance associated with it (after first finding favor with young fans) began to infiltrate the adult club scene. That popularity led to an invitation for Chubby to do the number on an "Ed Sullivan Show" on TV in October 1961. Cameo-Parkway then decided to reissue the single and it traveled up *Billboard* lists once more to reach the top spot the

weeks of January 13 and 20, 1962. "The Twist," it should be noted, wasn't originated by Checker, but by Hank Ballard (see Ballard, Hank).

At the height of his career, Checker was represented by many albums on the Cameo-Parkway label: *Twist, Twistin' round the World, Your Twist Party, Let's Twist Again, For Twisters Only, For Teen Twisters,* and *Don't Knock* (1961–62); *Limbo Party, Let's Limbo More, Chubby Checker's Biggest Hits, Beach Party,* and *Chubby Checker in Person* (1963); and *Folk Album* (1964). He had several more singles hits after "The Twist," including "Pony Time" (which rose to number one on the *Billboard* list the week of February 27, 1961, and stayed there two more weeks), "Let's Twist Again," "Slow Twistin'" (with Dee Dee Sharp) and "Twist It Up."

Chubby vanished from the record scene in the second half of the 1960s. His attempted comeback at the start of the 1970s gained some attention, but faded after a short time. He made another attempt in 1982 with a new album, *The Change Has Come.* He made a U.S. tour in support of it, but garnered little in the way of buyer interest. Still available in record stores in the early 1980s was his 1972 Abkco LP, *Chubby Checker's Greatest Hits.*

CHEECH AND CHONG: *Comedy duo. Tommy Chong, born Edmonton, Alberta, Canada, May 24; Cheech Marin, born Watts, Los Angeles, California, c. mid-1940s.*

The zany duo of Cheech and Chong, though they had some musical background, gained fame through offbeat humor that dealt with subjects germane to the 1970s rock culture—long hair, sex, acne, police, and dope. In the mid-1970s, they could well have billed themselves as the "kings of rock-comedy."

Cheech (Richard Marin) grew up in the Watts section of Los Angeles, son of a Mexican-American member of the L.A. police department. Chong (part Chinese) was the son of the owner of a topless night club. They met in their twenties, when Cheech, who had graduated from San Fernando Valley State College, fled to Canada to escape the draft.

By then Chong had been working with various rock groups for a number of years. He had played with a band called Bobby Taylor and the Vancouvers, which had been signed by Motown Records. After Cheech met Chong, they discussed forming a new group. As Chong told Chuck Thegze of the *Los Angeles Times:* "Originally, we thought we'd play as a rock group so we played a hall in Vancouver. But we started off with comedy and somehow never got around to playing."

The audience laughed and the team of Cheech and Chong was on its way. After doing clubs in Vancouver for a time, the duo moved on to Los Angeles, in the early '70s, playing small rock clubs before getting a shot at the Troubador. Lou Adler, head of Ode Records, heard them and signed them. Their debut LP, *Cheech and Chong*, made the best seller lists in midsummer 1971, remaining over a year to earn the team a gold-record award. Their second album, *Big Bambu*, released in mid-1972, was in the national top 10 in August and still a best-seller in mid-1973, bringing a second gold record in as many tries. In 1972–73, the duo became familiar to TV audiences, with guest appearances on talk and variety shows.

The team traced much of its efforts to the influences of the late Lenny Bruce and the comic group the Committee. As Chong told Thegze: "Lenny Bruce had a great influence on us. We would listen to his records over and over until we had worn out the grooves. His material was great, but most of all his sense of timing was perfect. We are trying to come close to what he achieved."

The Committee, "which we originally saw years ago, turned us on to new ways of thinking. They plugged us into ways of performing by creating little stories for the audience. We take simple truths about everyday life and blow them up into bulbous and funny presentations."

Most subsequent LPs rose to gold levels or better. They included the Warner Brothers releases *Los Cochinos* (which won the Grammy for best comedy album of 1973), *Cheech and Chong's Wedding Album* (1974), *Sleeping Beauty* (1976), and *Let's Make a Dope Deal* (1980). They achieved top 20 success with singles "Basketball Jones Featuring Tyrone Shoelaces" and "Earache My Eye Featuring Alice Bowie."

Starting in the late 1970s, the duo began to focus more on feature films than recording. Their film debut (the 1979 *Up in Smoke*) was followed by four more starring vehicles during the first half of the 1980s. After considerable success with the first movies, the duo had a major setback when their fifth movie, *The Corsican Brothers,* was a box-office flop. During that same period, though, they recouped some of their standing with a critically praised cameo segment of the Martin Scorsese film *After Hours.*

In 1985, Cheech and Chong signed a contract with MCA Records. For the new collection, they decided to combine comedy with rock music. Cheech noted: "One reason for doing this is the advent of videos and MTV. We've always been musicians, but now we can combine that with our comedy and filmmaking in a way that didn't exist before."

When the material for the LP, *Get Out of My Room,* was being assembled, the duo came up with the idea of using new lyrics to Bruce Springsteen's "Born in the U.S.A." to satirize the second-class citizenship of many Latino-Americans. This treatment, called "Born in East L.A.," was based on a true incident about an individual legally living in the U.S. who was shipped off to Tijuana, Mexico, when he couldn't prove his citizenship during an immigration raid.

Once the new lyrics were written, Cheech had to quickly gain Springsteen's approval. Bruce was on a tour of Europe and Cheech frantically called three hotels and even backstage at a Dublin concert, where he got hold of E Street saxophonist Clarence Clemons. "He reminded us that the first gig Bruce played professionally was as our opening act in York, Pennsylvania," he recalled for Craig Modderno of *USA Today*. "The promoter thought he was a folk act. He kicked Bruce offstage after two rock songs. Since we never got to see our opening act, we never saw Bruce. . . . Most of the time we weren't even there when we were onstage."

Cheech and Chong finally sent Bruce a cassette and personal letter. As Cheech told a *Los Angeles Times* reporter: "I told him in the letter that it was an extension of the feeling of his record, and if he had any sense of humor he would dig it. Obviously he did."

The result was a hit video and best-selling single of "Born in East L.A." in 1985, a gold LP containing the song, and eventually a feature film of the same name.

CHER: *Singer, songwriter, actress. Born El Centro, California, May 20, 1945.*

Throughout the middle and late 1960s, Cher was mainly known as part of the singing and songwriting team of Sonny and Cher. (*See Sonny and Cher*). In later years, after the breakup of her marriage to Sonny Bono, Cher gradually overshadowed him first as a hit recording artist in her own right and, in the 1980s, as an increasingly capable film actress.

Born to a mother with acting aspirations, Cherilyn Sarkisian was star-struck at an early age. She even practiced writing her autograph for the day when she would be a celebrity. In high school, she was active in plays and musical events and her mother saw to it that she also took acting lessons from Hollywood actor-teacher Jeff Corey.

In the early 1960s, Cher (full name Cherilyn La Pierre) became acquainted with Sonny Bono, who at the time was something of a jack-of-all trades for Phil Spector's West Coast record operations. Either she met Sonny while both were working as backing vocalists for Spector or he met her socially and brought her to Spector's attention (depending on which source is consulted). Their relationship evolved from a working partnership to a wedded team after they took their vows on October 27, 1964. Sonny had persuaded Spector to produce one single of Cher's, "Ringo I Love You," issued on the Annette label, with Cher known as Bonnie Jo Mason. Little happened with the disc and Sonny borrowed money to produce a single himself. At first, it was planned as a solo by Cher, but she had mike fright, so Sonny joined in to record "Baby Don't Go," a song he had penned.

Before much happened with that disc, Cher signed as a solo artist with Imperial Records, which soon issued her debut on the label, "Dream Baby." But Atlantic Records had become interested in Sonny and Cher as a duo and added them to its roster. It was a wise move. Their first single on the label, Sonny's composition "I Got You Babe," rose to number one on the *Billboard* chart the week of August 14, 1965, and stayed there for two more weeks. It was the start of a string of hit singles and albums as well as headline concerts worldwide for the twosome that lasted into the early 1970s.

As Sonny and Cher moved upward in the music field, Cher never completely gave up solo work. Her "Bang Bang (My Baby Shot Me Down)" was a major hit for Imperial in 1966 and in the late 1960s, she recorded a number of singles for Atlantic. In 1971, with the new "Sonny & Cher Comedy Hour" doing well on CBS-TV, interest in Cher's solo talents increased among recording officials. After signing with Kapp Records, she collaborated with producer Snuff Garrett on "Gypsys, Tramps and Thieves," which rose to number one on the *Billboard* singles list the week of November 6, 1971. Over the next few years, Cher had more hits, such as the top 10 "The Way of Love," the number one "Half Breed" (atop *Billboard* lists the weeks of October 6 and 13, 1973), and "Dark Lady" (number one in *Billboard* the week of March 23, 1974).

The "Sonny and Cher Show" still seemed to be a network TV staple, but the two had become increasingly alienated from each other. After they divorced, for a while they had separate TV programs. The split up had, in the end, been amicable, and they remained friends. Eventually, the two were brought back together to host their single TV program, but it failed to earn ratings equal to those achieved before, and it was phased out during 1977. The same year, Cher married musician Gregg Allman of Allman Brothers Band fame. The union was short-lived, but they did record an album together on Warner Brothers, *Two the Hard Way* (issued in the fall of 1977), which did little to further the career of either artist. (*See Allman Brothers Band.*)

During the 1970s, Cher could point to many solo albums on a variety of labels: *Cher* (1971) and *Cher, Vol. 2* (1972) on United Artists; *Cher's Greatest Hits* (1974) on MCA; *Stars* (1975), *I'd Rather Believe in You* (1976), and *Cherished* (1977) on Warner Brothers; and *Take Me Home* (1979) and *Prisoner* (1979) on Casablanca. While she placed a number of singles on the charts during the latter 1970s, she only scored one top 10 hit: the 1979 Casablanca disc "Take Me Home."

During 1980, Cher toured with the band Black Rose, insisting that she was just one of the members and not the featured artist. The group played small rock clubs across the U.S. and also served as opening act for Hall & Oates. (*See Hall & Oates.*) Cher and the group recorded the LP *Black Rose*, issued on Casablanca in 1980.

While not ignoring her singing career completely, in the latter 1970s Cher moved rapidly into the dramatic field. After demonstrating promising acting skill in films such as *Good Times* and *Charity*, she won critical praise from New York reviewers for her Broadway stage debut in *Come Back to the 5 and Dime, Jimmy Dean, Jimmy Dean*. After that, she had a major role in the movie *Silkwood*, an effort that won her an Oscar nomination for Best Supporting Actress. She took time off from her acting career for a contract with CBS Records, which started off with the 1982 LP *I Paralyze*. Her CBS releases made little impact, though, and in the mid-1980s she was without a recording agreement.

Harvard's Hasty Pudding Club voted her Woman of the Year for 1985, a distinction previously awarded to, among others, Katharine Hepburn, Jane Fonda, Meryl Streep, and Joan Rivers. Music aside, Cher's acting opportunities continued to mount. She showed herself to great advantage in the 1985 film *Mask* and the movie version of *Come Back to the 5 and Dime*. Cher's stature as an actress continued to grow in the second half of the '80s. Her 1986–87 film credits included *The Witches of Eastwick* and *Suspect*. Her role in the 1987 film *Moonstruck* won almost universal praise from the most respected critics and also earned her an Oscar in the Best Actress category in 1988. But she still hoped to maintain contact with the music field, as demonstrated by *Cher*, her debut album on the Geffen records label in November 1987. The first single, "I Found Someone," was a top 10 hit in early 1988, and the album went gold in 1988.

CHICAGO: *Vocal and instrumental group. Members in mid-1970s: Robert Lamm, born Brooklyn, New York, 1945; Peter Cetera, born Chicago, Illinois, September 13, 1944; James Pankow, born Chicago, Illinois, 1947; Daniel Seraphine, born Chicago, Illinois, 1948; Terry Kath, born Chicago, Illinois, 1946, died Woodland Hills, California, January 1978; Lee*

Loughnane, born Chicago, Illinois, 1946; Walt Parazaider, born Chicago, Illinois, 1948. Original group included Walt Perry, born Chicago, Illinois, 1945. Donnie Dacus replaced Kath in 1978, left in late 1970s. Bill Champlin added in early 1980s. Cetera left in 1986, replaced by Jason Scheff.

Chicago had to move to Los Angeles to prove that Chicago was evolving new directions for popular music in the '70s. Translated, this means the band Chicago gained top ranking in the U.S. music scene thanks to the record production and overall direction of James William Guercio. Guercio, a long-time friend of several band members and a former Chicagoan, was based in Los Angeles. Sure of the potential of the band, he moved them to the coast so they could take advantage of the considerably greater activity in the music field there.

The group's roots, though, were distinctly midwestern, with all but one of its seven members (as of the early '70s) Chicago-born and -raised. Oddly, the seventh, Robert Lamm, who spent his first 15 years in Brooklyn, New York, became unofficial group spokesman (though Chicago's members considered themselves of equal authority from the start, with no individual serving as leader). In October 1970, it was Lamm who told Harvey Siders of the difference between Chicago and a group with which they were often compared, Blood, Sweat & Tears. "Our roots are basically rock, but we can and do play jazz; Blood, Sweat & Tears is basically a jazz-rooted combo that can play a lot of rock."

In addition, as trombonist James Pankow (one of the group's original moving forces) pointed out, Chicago was founded in 1967, before BS&T came into being. "It just so happens that they came out with their album first. Besides, the instrumentation is not that similar. We have three horns in a seven-piece group; they have a nine-man band with a front line of five horns."

Besides Pankow and Lamm (singer, pianist, and writer of many group hits), the mid-'70s musical lineup included Terry Kath on guitar (plus banjo, accordion, bass, and drums), Peter Cetera on bass (plus steel guitar and songwriting), Walt Parazaider on woodwinds, Lee Loughnane on trumpet, and Daniel Seraphine on drums.

Though only in their early twenties when Chicago achieved success, all the members had considerable musical background. Only Kath and Cetera were completely self-taught; the others had substantial formal training with private teachers and/or in college.

Pankow, who played trombone in grammar and high school bands, went on to major in music at Quincy College in Illinois and later at Chicago's De-

Paul University. At Quincy, he became interested in jazz and formed his own quintet. While still in school, he played with such big bands as Bobby Christian's, Ted Weems', plus Bill Rosso's Chicago Jazz ensemble. At DePaul, he became more engrossed in rock and blues forms, writing many songs in these idioms. Also at DePaul, he met numerous young musicians (including Jim Guercio) who were to become involved in Chicago.

Among those who attended DePaul were Seraphine, Parazaider, and Loughnane. Loughnane had started trumpet lessons in the seventh grade and originally was mainly interested in the recordings of such old-time greats as Glenn Miller and Tommy Dorsey. In high school, he became attracted to rock, beginning his professional career with a group called Ross and the Majestics. After graduating, he took private lessons from John Nuzzo and spent two years at DePaul followed by a year at the Chicago Conservatory College. From school and from his outside activities in pop music, he met all the other future members of Chicago except Pete Cetera.

Parazaider, whose father played in Woody Herman's band, started clarinet and other reeds at 11 and the saxophone at 13. At 17, he enrolled in DePaul, majoring in classical clarinet. However, he became friends with Terry Kath, who turned his interest to rock music, inducing Walt to join him in auditioning for rock jobs. Born into a musical family, Kath learned a series of instruments only by sitting down by himself and playing them. In the early '60s, he joined a group called Jimmy and the Gentlemen, bringing in Parazaider as a member and concentrating on bass. He played bass only as a sideman for four years until joining Chicago.

Seraphine picked up drums at nine and started playing in rock groups at 12. Three years later, he met Kath and Parazaider at an audition for a group called the Executives. At DePaul, he studied percussion with Bob Tilles. Later, after leaving DePaul, he studied for some years with Chuck Flores, a former big band star.

Bob Lamm's early musical efforts began with his church choir in Brooklyn. He sang with groups at a number of concerts in the New York area. When he was 15, his family moved to Chicago, where he became a pianist with small high school groups. At 16, he formed his own rock band that played dances and clubs throughout the city. His musical engagements introduced him to some of the future Chicago artists and he met more while studying piano and composition at Roosevelt University. When the forerunner of Chicago, the Big Thing, began in the mid-1960s, Lamm was one of the six original bandsmen.

Peter Cetera first looked into music as a career in high school, when he learned to play bass guitar. He

served his apprenticeship with a series of school bands, playing small parties, weddings, and bar mitzvahs. He developed his vocal ability and also started writing original material that led to such Chicago recordings as "Where Do We Go from Here," "Low Down," and "What Else Can I Say." For the entire first half of the '60s, Pete played with the Exceptions, which was considered one of the best rock bands in the Chicago area. He left the group to join the Big Thing shortly before that band turned into Chicago Transit Authority.

The Big Thing got its name from the "Mafia types," to quote Lamm, who provided original direction for the band and who kept saying the group's music was "the big thing." Under this name, the band spent the mid-1960s playing seedy bars and small clubs all over the Midwest. As they gained experience and started looking for greater success, their mentor Guercio thought a name change might help and suggested Chicago Transit Authority. The band continued to play under the new name without particular improvement in its fortunes while Guercio moved to Los Angeles and built a reputation as one of the best young record producers in the music field.

In the late '60s, Guercio asked the group to move to Los Angeles, feeling there was more chance for them to gain attention there. He set them up in small frame houses in Hollywood to develop new material in a "creative community."

Just when the group seemed ready for a recording contract from Columbia, Blood, Sweat & Tears gained the national spotlight. Guercio was signed to produce the second BS&T LP while Chicago Transit Authority had yet to gain its first album. However, Columbia executives finally bowed to Guercio's arguments that the label had room for two bands that outwardly seemed similar. In late 1969, he completed work on the initial LP, the two-record *Chicago Transit Authority*, which moved onto the charts in early 1969 and was still there well into 1971, earning the group a gold record. The album also helped launch a hit single of 1969, Bob Lamm's ballad, "Does Anybody Really Know What Time It Is?"

Guercio and the group, which had shortened its name to Chicago by then, followed up with another smash LP, *Chicago*. On the charts for almost all of 1970, it was called the best album of 1970 by *Cash Box* and included two top 10 hits, Pankow's "Make Me Smile" and Lamm's "25 or 6 to 4." One of the unusual tracks is a six-movement rock composition by Pankow, "Ballet for a Girl in Buchannon."

The group's third LP, simply titled *Chicago III*, moved into the top 10 within weeks after its release in early 1971. It included a five-movement suite by Kath, "Hour in the Shower," plus "Travel Suite" (a six-number suite taking up the entire second side of the four-side set, with five parts by Lamm and one by Seraphine). Another complete series, "Elegy" on side 4, was mostly written by Pankow, but includes contributions by Guercio and Kendrew Lascelles.

In November 1971, the group had a best-selling single, "Questions 67 & 68"/"I'm a Man." About the same time, their fourth LP, *Chicago Live* at Carnegie Hall, a four-record album, was released and soon rose to the top 10 nationally.

Through the mid-1970s, the band continued to make the charts almost routinely with each new album: *Chicago IV—Live at Carnegie Hall* (1971), *Chicago V* (1972), *Chicago VI* (1973), *Chicago VII* (1974), *Chicago VIII* (1975), *Chicago IX—Greatest Hits* (1975), *Chicago X* (1976), and *Chicago XI* (1977). During those years, the band also had a string of top 10 singles including "Saturdays in the Park," "Just You 'n' Me," and their first number one hit (from *Chicago X*), "If You Leave Me Now," in top position on the *Billboard* list the weeks of October 23 and 30, 1976.

In January 1978, band members were shocked at the sudden death of key member Terry Kath. Kath had been examining a gun at a friend's house when he accidentally shot himself. The death cast a pall over the band for a time, but once the shock wore off, they decided to continue as a group. Seraphine said: "We definitely will continue because I'm sure Terry wouldn't want us to stop." After a series of auditions, vocalist/guitarist Donnie Dacus was chosen as Kath's replacement and he took part in recording the excellent 1978 LP *Hot Streets (Chicago XII)*.

But there seemed to be a delayed reaction to Kath's loss. The band's albums of the late 1970s and early 1980s fell off in quality and also in buyer interest. After issuing *Chicago XIII* (1979) and *Chicago XIV* (1980), Columbia unceremoniously dropped the band from its roster in 1980. (The label issued the retrospective *Greatest Hits, Volume 2* in 1981.) Lamm told Dennis Hunt of the *Los Angeles Times*: "That really hurt us. We figured some company would want us, considering our track record. We were tempted to say to hell with it and break up the band . . . [but] we were all so furious with Columbia. That kept us going. We wanted to show them they were wrong."

Their manager, Irving Azoff, finally saved the day by arranging for them to record new material on his Full Moon label with distribution by Warner Brothers. Among those taking part in the sessions was singer/keyboards player Bill Champlin (for many years head of a group called Sons of Champlin), who later became a full member of the band. The result was *Chicago 16* (Roman numerals now being considered passé for the new titles), which provided an amazing comeback. The LP became a best-seller, backed by very well received concerts across the U.S., and gained a series of charted singles including Peter Cetera and David Foster's composition "Hard to Say I'm Sorry" (number one on the *Billboard* chart the weeks of September 11 and 18, 1982).

The rejuvenated group continued to improve its image with rock fans. Its 1984 release, *Chicago 17,* provided four hit singles: "Stay the Night," "Hard Habit to Break," "You're the Inspiration," and "Along Comes a Woman." The LP's worldwide sales exceeded six million copies.

After finishing the tour in support of *Chicago 17,* Peter Cetera announced he was leaving to work on a solo career. His place was taken by bass guitarist/songwriter Jerry Scheff who helped record the next collection, *Chicago 18,* issued by Warner Brothers in September 1986. Cetera meanwhile did very well on his own, quickly achieving a number one single with "Glory of Love," the theme from the movie *The Karate Kid Part II.* The song appeared both on the sound-track album and Cetera's debut solo LP on Warner Brothers, *Solitude/Solitaire.* His next single, "The Next Time I Fall," a duet with gospel singer Amy Grant, by March 1987 had brought him a second gold record award and another number one placing on *Billboard* charts. Meanwhile, his old band started work in 1987 on the 19th LP, due for release in 1988.

CHI-LITES: *Vocal group from Chicago, Illinois. Members in 1960s: Marshall Thompson, born Chicago, Illinois, c. early 1950s; Creadal Jones; Eugene Record; Clarence Johnson; Robert Lester. In mid-1980s: Thompson, Record, Lester.*

Persistence and longevity are two words that can apply to the Chi-Lites, a group that, in essence, wandered in the wilderness of the small R&B/soul–club circuit throughout the 1960s before winning broad recognition in the 1970s. Despite personnel changes and record-label shifts, the group managed to renew itself a number of times and still remain a force in the soul/pop market in the 1980s.

In fact, many critics considered the group a pivotal one in the soul music annals for pioneering a new vitality in that art form in the 1970s as part of a style critic Vince Alessi called "neoclassical." That was based on a romantic yet melancholy sound that was at variance with the more macho flavor of the 1960s soul group stars such as the Temptations and the Spinners. (*See Temptations, The.*)

While the founder and the original driving force of the group was Chicagoan Marshall Thompson, the person who evolved the Chi-Lites style of the 1970s was lead singer/songwriter/producer Eugene Record. Commenting on the group's "unique persona" that evolved under Record's influence, onetime d.j. and sometime *Rolling Stone* critic Joe McEwen wrote: "The Chi-Lites' stark portrayal [in early 1970s recordings and concerts] was unlike that of even the Moments and Delfonics, two other groups who exercised melancholy with great effect. Record highlighted his thin tenor with the most plaintive production gimmicks: a forlorn harmonica on 'Oh Girl,' windstorms on 'Coldest Day of My Life.' While this type of pathos was occasionally overwrought, often it was quite dramatic and effective."

The group's roots were in Chicago, where Marshall Thompson first assembled a singing quintet called Marshall and the Hi-Lites in 1960. Thompson had begun working as a drummer and backup singer in his early teens, playing drums at the Regal Theater behind such soul/R&B notables as Major Lance, the Dells, and the Flamingos. He also had been in a vocal group called the Desideros with high school friend Creadel Jones, who became a charter member of the Hi-Lites. The new group took its early shape by absorbing three members of another group called the Chantours—Eugene Record, Clarence Johnson, and Robert "Squirrel" Lester.

As the Hi-Lites, the group managed to get a record arrangement with Chicago-based Mercury Records that led to the 1961 single "Pots and Pans." The single flopped, but the band got another chance with Brunswick Records, which released the LP *Half a Love* in 1961. By then, the group had changed its name after being threatened with legal action by another organization that called itself the Hi-Lites. Thompson later told an interviewer: "We figured if we added a 'C' to the front of our name, that'd give us an original name and identify us as coming from Chicago."

Now called Marshall and the Chi-Lites, the group made progress slowly as the 1960s went by. After the 1961 album proved a failure, the group managed to make some new recordings for the regional Daran and Ja-Wes labels in the mid-1960s. Some of those releases won popularity for the Chi-Lites on the Midwest "chitlin' circuit." On the strength of that, the group got a new contract from Mercury, which released two singles on its Blue Rock label. These made little headway. Undaunted, the members continued to seek new contacts and won an arrangement with Dakar Productions in 1967 that resulted in a contract with MCA Records. MCA, which then owned the Brunswick label, offered wider distribution to the group (which now called itself only the Chi-Lites) than its earlier labels. An early success was the single "Give It Away"—the group's first entry in *Billboard*'s Hot 100. Brunswick had similarly reasonably promising response to a 1969 album also called *Give It Away*.

Thompson told *Billboard*: "1969 was when we first made it. . . . We went and bought some new suits, went out on the road. All of a sudden, a record company was interested in us. Eugene was getting some big successes [writing songs that became hits for Brunswick vocalist Barbara Acklin]. Eugene was always a good writer. Some of the things we record now he wrote years ago when he was a nobody."

At the end of the 1960s and the start of the 1970s, Record's songs and his falsetto recordings of them made the Chi-Lite name a regular entrant on the low end of the hit charts. Those minor successes included "Let Me Be the Man My Daddy Was," "I Like Your Lovin' (Do You Like Mine?)," and "Are You My Woman? (Tell Me So)."

Marshall, Record, and cohorts still hungered for a really big hit that would go to the top levels of both soul and pop lists. He told a reporter: "We all figured that we needed to broaden our sound. Up until then we'd choose only ballads. Sweet things. There was a lot of unrest and injustice in the world and we all felt that artists couldn't ignore that situation and just sing about love. So Eugene wrote this uptempo number called '(For God's Sake) Give More Power to the People.' . . . We knew it'd be a big one."

It did indeed catch the mood of the times when dissatisfaction with Vietnam and the other policies of the Nixon administration were coming to a boil. The single made the top levels of the soul charts and the top 30 of the pop lists in the early summer of 1971. The Brunswick album of the same name, which contained other gems in addition to its title song, also made the charts. Before 1971 was over, the Chi-Lites had an even bigger singles hit, the ballad "Have You Seen Her," which went as high as number 3 on *Billboard* lists.

Though 1972 opened somewhat inauspiciously with only a minor hit single, "I Want to Pay You Back (for Loving Me)," it proved to be the year that made the group members international stars. The single "Oh Girl," a Record composition, was issued in the spring and moved steadily up the charts until it made number one in *Billboard* on May 27, earning the Chi-Lites a gold record. Also on the album lists during the year were the Brunswick releases *Lonely Man* and *Letter to Myself*.

Later recordings weren't quite up to the caliber of the 1972–73 period. Except for "Stoned out of My Mind," a top 30 pop hit in 1973, most of its singles made little progress on the pop charts, though they often did well on black music lists. The group continued to be represented by new Brunswick LPs: *The*

Chi-Lites and *Toby* (1974), and *Greatest Hits, Volume 2* (1976).

During 1976, the group suffered a major loss when Eugene Record left to try for a solo career at Warner Brothers. Marshall Thompson took over the reins, reformed the Chi-Lites, and produced a new album, *Happy Being Lonely*, issued in 1976 on the Mercury label. It was a surprisingly fine collection— equal in quality to some of the best of the Record era.

The group had one more release on Mercury (the 1977 album, *The Fantastic Chi-Lites*) before that association ended. The group signed a new agreement with 20th Century Fox Records, which issued several LPs, including *Heavenly Body* in 1980 and *Me and You* in 1981.

In the 1980s, Eugene Record returned to help produce and record new material for Chi-Sound and Private I Records. After signing with Private I in 1982, the group recorded a new album for that company's Larc Records. Issued in 1983, *Bottom's Up* was on R&B charts for a number of months. This was followed by the Record-produced LP, *Steppin' Out*, released by Private I in March 1984. It included the single "Stop What You're Doing," a chart hit in the spring of that year. By then, the group was a threesome of Thompson, Eugene Record, and Robert Lester.

CLAPTON, ERIC: *Guitarist, singer, band leader, songwriter. Born Ripley, England, March 30, 1945.*

As a member of Cream (*see Cream, The*), Eric Clapton (born Eric Patrick Clapp) made that trio one of the foremost groups of the 1960s, while also establishing himself as one of rock's finest guitarists. Decades later, he still held millions of fans in awe at his guitar prowess and many of those fans had not even been born when he first achieved prominence.

A bricklayer's son, for much of his childhood Eric was raised by his grandparents. Of those years, he told Paul Gambaccini of the BBC (as noted in Fred Bronson's *Billboard Book of Number One Hits*): "I was the one that used to get stones thrown at me because I was so thin and couldn't do physical training very well."

While attending Kingston Art School in his teens, he became enthralled by the early blues-rock and R&B of black American performers and began to imitate some of their chordings on his guitar. After working as a substitute bandsman for some early '60s British blues and blues-rock bands while earning eating money as a street musician, he became a member of the landmark Yardbirds (*see Yardbirds, The*) before helping form the Cream. After the

Cream broke up at the height of its fame, he became a member of another short-lived supergroup, Blind Faith, whose members included former Cream drummer Ginger Baker, Steve Winwood, and Rick Grech. (*See Winwood, Steve.*) The band gave a memorable concert before 100,000 fans in London's Hyde Park and completed one LP, *Blind Faith* (originally issued on Atco Records in 1969), which rose high on U.S. and U.K. charts. It then disbanded.

After that, Eric put together another ephemeral band, Derek and the Dominoes. He formed it on the U.S. West Coast, recruiting Jim Gordon, Bobby Whitlock, and Carl Radle. Some of them had worked the recording sessions (with Delaney Bramlett as producer) that provided Eric with his singles hit "After Midnight" that graced U.S. charts from late 1970 until early 1971.

The new foursome had begun working on material for an album, first released on Atco Records under the title *Layla,* when guitarist Duane Allman joined the session. (*See Allman Brothers, The.*) As Allman recalled: "I'd been a fan of Eric's a long time. Drove up from L.A. to San Francisco once, just to hear him play. So when Tom Dowd [the producer] mentioned that Eric was going to be cutting some stuff at the studios, I asked Tom to be sure and call me, so I could come down and watch.

"So I went down to listen and Eric knew me, man, greeted me like an old friend! The cat is really a prince—he said, 'Come on, you get to play this record'—so I did. We'd sit down and plan it out, work out our different parts, and try it one time. Then we'd say, 'Well, let's try some more of this in here, and some of that there.' Everybody contributed, just sorting it out, Memphis style. Most of it was cut live, not much overdubbing—and it was all done in ten days."

Allman's work on slide guitar and Clapton's usually brilliant instrumental line resulted in one of the classic recordings in rock history. The album made the best-seller lists soon after its release at the end of 1970 and rose into the top 20 in 1971. Allman, though technically a session man (he was asked to join the group for its tour, but agreed only to play a few dates because of commitments to the Allman Brothers band), was given full credit on the album cover. Some of the tracks were issued as singles, with "Layla" and "Bell Bottom Blues" making the charts in 1971.

For a few years after that project, Clapton largely withdrew from the music field. Those who wanted to hear him were restricted to buying his albums which included, in the early 1970s, such others on the Atco label as *On Tour* (1970) and *History of Eric Clapton* (1972). After Peter Townshend of the Who talked Eric into taking part in an all-star concert at Lon-

don's Rainbow Theatre in 1973, the crowd's enthusiasm for his playing inspired him to take up intensive recording and concertizing once more.

His first new album for RSO Records, *461 Ocean Boulevard,* issued in 1974, proved one of his most successful, if not necessarily his all-time best. It included a cover of Bob Marley's "I Shot the Sheriff," which became Eric's biggest 45 release yet, rising to number one on both U.K. and U.S. charts. It reached the top in *Billboard* the week of September 14, 1974. He followed this with a series of LPs on RSO during the 1970s that were maddeningly inconsistent in content and quality. These included *There's One in Every Crowd* (1975), *No Reason to Cry* (1976), *Slowhand* (1977), and *Backless* (1979). In 1977, Polydor also released some of his earlier material on *Eric Clapton.*

Eric continued to be a favorite on the concert circuit throughout the 1970s and 1980s. During that period, he continued as a solo artist backed by different combinations of musicians on his various tours. He opened the 1980s with the albums *Just One Night* (1980) and *Another Ticket* (1981), both on RSO.

Sensing that he needed outside help to craft albums that might bring him some new chart breakthroughs, Eric worked with a number of top-flight rock producer/artists in the mid-1980s. One of those was Ry Cooder, who helped shape Eric's 1983 LP *Money and Cigarettes.* Cooder's support seemed to encourage Eric to bring out new depths to his guitar work. He then made further progress in exploring new creative directions with Phil Collins. Collins produced his 1985 Warner Brothers LP *Behind the Sun* and, also, with Tom Dowd as co-producer, handled the reins on Eric's next Warner Brothers album, *August* (November 1986). Helping Eric on that LP were Collins (drums, percussion, and backing vocals), Greg Phillinganes (keyboard and backing vocals), and Nathan East (bass). Among the guest artists was Tina Turner, who recorded two duets with Eric: "Tearing Us Apart" and "Hold On." "Tearing Us Apart" was the initial single release from the LP. Also included in *August* was "It's in the Way That You Use It" (co-written by Clapton and Band alumnus Robbie Robertson), which appeared in the soundtrack of the Martin Scorsese film *The Color of Money* (starring Paul Newman), one of the box-office hits of 1986. (*See Band, The; Cooder, Ry; Genesis; Marley, Bob; Traffic; Turner, Ike and Tina; Turner, Tina.*)

DAVE CLARK FIVE, THE: *Vocal and instrumental group. Dave Clark, born Tottenham, London, England, November 15, 1942; Mike Smith, born Edmonton, London, England, December 6, 1943; Rick Huxley, born Dartford, England, Au-*

gust 5, 1942; Lenny Davidson, born Enfield, England, May 30, 1944; Denis Payton, born Walthamstow, London, England, August 11, 1943.

The Dave Clark Five rates as one of the major rock groups of the 1960s though it did not manage to maintain its impetus into the next decade. For a while, though, in the mid-1960s this English group competed with the Beatles and Rolling Stones for the top ratings in the pop field.

Clark, born and raised in the Tottenham section of London, knew most of the members of his group from childhood. In his early years, he was more interested in sports than music and, in his teens, was an excellent athlete in activities ranging from swimming and horseback riding to rugby, but he still found time to develop considerable skills as a drummer as well.

At the start of the 1960s, Clark had already worked some dates at local clubs and put together pickup groups for local dances, but his main interest still was rugby. His team did so well one year that it won a bid to an important tournament in Holland. However, the problem was finding travel expenses. Clark formed a five-man rock group from among his friends and acquaintances to play a series of concerts to help raise money for the team. The group included Mike Smith (lead vocals, organ, and piano), Rick Huxley (bass, harmonica, and guitar), Lenny Davidson (guitar), and Denis Payton (saxophone).

The group's music was so well received they decided to continue working together. One result was a long engagement at the Tottenham Ballroom. (The group's music became known as "the Tottenham Sound.") The music was aimed at entertainment rather than message. As Clark later told one reporter: "Records are for enjoyment; there's no message in our music; it's just for fun."

The group did not succeed overnight and Clark earned spare cash from a series of occupations after leaving Belmont Technical College. The first job was as a draftsman for a motorcycle company. Later he was a representative for a business transfer company, a film extra, and a stunt man.

Mike Smith, who co-wrote many of the group's hits with Clark, studied piano for ten years and also played rugby, in later years, on Clark's team. In his teens he worked for a time as pianist in a local pub. Huxley and Davidson were self-taught musicians who played with local groups before joining the Clark aggregation. Payton, who could play guitar and harp besides saxophone, started out aiming for a career as an electronics engineer, but gave it up when things seemed to be moving ahead for him in music.

The Dave Clark Five first hit the big time with "Glad All Over." The single sold over a million copies in England in 1964 and took over the number one spot on the charts from the Beatles. Similar success greeted its U.S. release by Epic Records. The following year, the group won gold-record awards in both countries for their LP of the same name. During 1964 and 1965, the band cemented its position with a series of engagements all over Europe and the U.S. In November 1965, they took part in a command performance for Queen Elizabeth.

In the mid-1960s, the Dave Clark Five consistently was represented on the top 40 at home and abroad. Singles hits included "Over and Over" which reached number one on U.S. *Billboard* charts the week of December 25, 1965; "Bits and Pieces"; "Do You Love Me"; "Come Home"; "Reelin' and Rockin';" "Catch Us If You Can"; "Try Too Hard"; "At the Scene"; and "You Got What It Takes." Albums included *The Dave Clark Five's Greatest Hits* (a gold record in 1966 in the U.S. market), *American Tour, Volume 1, Coast to Coast, Weekend in London, I Like it Like That, Try Too Hard, Satisfied with You,* and *5 x 5,* all on Epic in the U.S.

Starting with *Lucy* in 1965, Clark and his group were featured in several films. These included the U.S.-made *Get Yourself a College Girl* and *Having a Wild Weekend.* The *Wild Weekend* soundtrack achieved chart status in 1967.

Though still an attraction after 1967, the Dave Clark Five began to lose some of its vitality. Clark devoted time to other interests and none of the original members were eager to continue the breakneck grind of in-person concerts needed to keep their image constantly in front of new generations of teenagers. After the group disbanded, it was estimated that it had achieved total worldwide sales of over 50 million records. The group's official breakup was announced in 1970, but Clark and Mike Smith made several more recordings under the name Dave Clark and Friends until 1973. Afterward, Smith worked as a writer of ad jingles and a developer of radio promotions.

In the 1970s, though Clark occasionally took part in '60s revival projects, his main musical activities were behind the scenes, including songwriting. He also purchased the rights to tapes of the British TV pop music show "Ready, Steady, Go!" and marketed videos of some of these. As the decade went by, he considered new challenges including musical theater. The end result was the stage spectacular, *Time.* Clark commented in 1986: "The message of *Time* is simple and universal (based on a story in which Earth is judged by the rest of the universe). . . . I started work on the project in 1980 and I was warned on several occasions that I was setting my sights too high, yet nobody I approached turned me down and in fact all the artists showed a positive interest, not only in their own parts, but in the whole idea of the project.''

Clark persevered and the show opened in London in the spring of 1986 starring Cliff Richard in person and with Sir Laurence Olivier as a cast member in the form of a special three-dimensionally projected image. Almost all of the 27 original songs in *Time* were co-written by Clark, who also served as co-producer. British critics typically gave the show high marks. The *Music Week* reviewer, for instance, wrote: ''Clark's creation has taken the concept of stage theater into new realms. The sound, staging, and lighting effects are nothing short of stunning.'' In its first six months, *Time* was performed before more than 350,000 people.

In October 1986, a two-record set of songs from *Time* was issued, distributed in the U.S. by Capitol Records. Among the artists appearing on the album were (besides Richard) Julian Lennon, Freddie Mercury (of the rock group Queen), Ashford & Simpson, Dionne Warwick, Leo Sayer, Murray Head, and Stevie Wonder.

CLARK, DICK: *Disc jockey, record and TV executive, concert promoter. Born New York, November 30, 1929.*

During the mid-1950s, Alan Freed was the king of rock d.j.'s and New York was his base. (*See Freed, Alan.*) But as the payola scandals of the late 1950s bore down on him, the crown shifted southward to Philadelphia, where Dick Clark held forth on his ''American Bandstand.'' Though Clark also was investigated by Congress for possible illegal activities, he escaped unscathed and was a power in the pop music field throughout the '60s, '70s, and '80s.

Clark decided he wanted to be a disc jockey as early as age 13. In these years, there was no rock—R&B was still to be born and soul was unheard of—so his original taste in music ran to jazz, which remained a special enthusiasm when he got a job on the campus station at Syracuse University soon after entering as a business administration major. After finishing college at the start of the '50s, he worked on several stations in upstate New York before getting a job as a summer replacement on station WFIL in Philadelphia in 1952.

That year, the station's best known d.j. Bob Horn, teamed with another announcer, Lee Stewart, to do an afternoon show on WFIL-TV. The pair combined interviews with films of musicians of the period and discovered that high school girls in the audience liked to dance when the films were run. This concept evolved into a televised dance show with musicians who did not sing live on the show, but instead lip-synched (synchronized their lip movements to sound as their own voices were played). The lip-synch formula remained a standard of the show for most of its existence. Called ''Philadelphia Bandstand,'' the show became the most popular in the city and Bob Horn was a local celebrity. Clark stayed on the radio station, doing an afternoon show with Horn although he had nothing to do with ''Bandstand.''

In 1956, Horn, by then sole m.c. of ''Bandstand,'' got into trouble—first with a drunk-driving episode and then with a conviction on a payola charge. He was dropped from the show and well-groomed, clean-cut Dick Clark took over. Under Clark's direction, the show maintained its impetus. Soon after he became host, the station joined the ABC network. Clark persuaded ABC officials to send the show, which became known as ''American Bandstand,'' to network stations. Clark had already started introducing many new rock stars on ''Bandstand'' and, in 1958, he gained a new showcase when ABC initiated the ''Dick Clark Show'' on Saturday nights. While hosting that program in New York, Clark continued to run ''Bandstand'' from Philadelphia, helping to bring a steady procession of young local talent (such as Frankie Avalon, Fabian, and Danny and the Juniors) into the national spotlight.

Of course, Clark sought out talent from all parts of the nation. Among those featured on ''Bandstand'' in the late '50s were Chuck Berry, Fats Domino, Johnny Mathis, the Royal Teens, and Dion and the Belmonts. In 1957, the show presented the teenage team of Tom and Jerry, who lip-synched their chart single ''Hey Schoolgirl.'' Tom and Jerry later gained more lasting fame under their real names—Paul Simon and Art Garfunkel.

At the start of the '60s, Clark was a millionaire, but his empire was threatened by a subpoena to testify before a Congressional subcommittee investigating payola in the recording field. His testimony impressed the group; he was youthful looking, respectful, and obviously well educated. The records indicated Clark's widespread financial activities in various phases of the music field including interests in record companies and music publishers. They also showed he owned the copyrights of many of the hit songs of the day. However, he had done nothing illegal. He paid taxes on his earnings and he apparently took no money under the table to promote the material. Though some might carp over his business ethics, the House Committee could find no grounds for prosecution.

Clark returned to ''Bandstand,'' although the New York program was not retained in the '60s. ''Bandstand'' remained a fixture on ABC into the '70s, however Clark shifted his headquarters to Los Angeles. He expanded his organization in many other directions in the '60s, '70s, and '80s, with efforts ranging from production of a variety of TV programs to work on movies to consulting services concerning youth-oriented projects for major corporations.

In summer 1973, Clark demonstrated anew his rapport with audiences of all ages with his ABC-TV special on 20 years of rock. The program, which featured many stars who had long ago appeared on "American Bandstand," was in the top ranks in the Nielsen ratings. At the same time, the album *Dick Clark Presents 20 Years of Rock'n'Roll,* released on the Buddah label, reached gold-record levels by midsummer.

The pattern of Clark's activities remained the same into the mid-1980s. He was still at the helm when "American Bandstand" passed its thirtieth-year milestone in the '80s.

CLARK, PETULA: *Singer, actress. Born Epsom, Surrey, England, November 15, 1933.*

Though rock was considered a teenage phenomenon by many adults in the early '60s, a look at the roster of stars of the period showed many idols in their twenties and some well into their thirties. Most of those artists, of course, reached pop music fame while in their teens or early twenties, but in Petula Clark's case, full-scale rock success arrived when she was over 30.

Actually, she had been a show business success from her preteen years, though not in the mainstream of pop music. With her father's prodding, young "Pet" (Petula Sally Olwen Clark) was singing in school shows when she was seven. In 1941, her father, who was sure his daughter could be a star, arranged for a guest appearance on the BBC radio show, "It's All Yours." During rehearsal, an air raid began and the producer asked for someone to entertain to calm the other participants. Little Petula complied with "Mighty Like a Rose," a song the producer then had her do on the show.

Petula had her own BBC show, "Pet's Parlour," by 1943. In 1944, when she was 11, she signed a contract with J. Arthur Rank films and appeared in close to 30 movies over the next dozen years. The first of these was *A Medal for the General,* produced in 1944. Others included *I Know Where I'm Going* (1945), *Here Come the Huggetts* (1948), *Dance Hall,* and *White Corridors* (1950), *The Card* (1951), *Made in Heaven* (1952), *The Runaway Bus* (1953), *The Gay Dog* (1954), and *That Woman Opposite* (1957).

In 1951, she gained her first English record hit with "Gondolier." Her French company, Vogue Records, asked her to do a version in French and she gained a hit in France. She was wildly applauded at her first French performance at the Alhambra Theatre in Paris, but she had to read her French words from notes written in the palm of her hand. Soon, after intensive lessons, she became fluent in French.

Through the 1950s, her father retained a tight rein over her career and vetoed some of her ideas for combining more upbeat material with her mainly ballad repertoire. In 1959, she finally broke with him and moved to Paris. In 1960 at the Olympic Theatre in Paris, she introduced her new singing style, a rock format similar to the music coming to the surface in the teenage clubs of Liverpool. The French audience gave her a standing ovation, helping to launch a new phase of her career that made her one of the 1960s' most popular singers in France and led to the nickname "La Petulante Petula."

In the early 1960s, her swinging single, "Ya-ya Twist," was on European charts for months and won her the French Grand Prix National du Disque award. A number of her hit songs by this time were provided by songwriter Tony Hatch, who came up with "Downtown" for her in 1964. The song became a European hit and, after its release in the U.S. on Warner Brothers in late 1964 became a gold record in 1965.

"Downtown" reached number one on Billboard charts the week of January 23, 1965, and remained there a second week. In the voting for the 1964 Grammies the single won the award for Best Rock and Roll Recording. Her 1965 single, "I Know a Place," won a second Grammy for her in the Best Contemporary Rock and Roll Vocal Performance—Female category.

As the 1960s progressed, Petula made regular and successful tours of the U.S. She also made the hit charts with a series of other songs written by Hatch, including "Don't Sleep in the Subway, Darlin'," "I Couldn't Live Without Your Love," "A Sign of the Times," and "Round Every Corner." Other hits were "My Love" (number one the weeks of February 5 and 12, 1966) and "This Is My Song" (number three in 1967). In all, starting with "Downtown," she had 15 straight top 40 singles on U.S. charts.

In April 1968, Petula starred in her first special on NBC-TV. In one segment, she sang "On the Path to Glory" arm in arm with Harry Belafonte, a display the sponsor tried to have deleted from the show because of fears of offending racist viewers. However, Miss Clark refused to take the section out, and it was telecast with no visible harm to the viewing public. The reaction to the show was so favorable, in fact, that a second special, "Portrait of Petula," was shown in April 1969.

In the late 1960s, Petula resumed acting chores. She was featured in the 1968 film version of the

Broadway musical *Finian's Rainbow*. The following year, she was generally praised for her work in a remake of *Goodbye Mr. Chips*.

Some music critics of the 1960s wondered about Petula's ability to win followers in their teens and twenties. In response to this question by interviewer Alan Levy (*Good Housekeeping*, March 1969), she replied: "I never sought them out. The kids came to me. Because I'm reassuring. I'm on their wave length and they know I'm with them. I never try to be one of them or make a secret of my age and marriage." (Married to a Frenchman at the start of the 1960s, Petula has two daughters as of this writing.)

However, her recording career began to fade in the late 1960s. Warner Brothers phased out their affiliation after her last charted single with them ("Don't Give Up" in 1968). She signed with MGM Records, which released a number of singles and LPs in the early 1970s, but these had little impact with record buyers. Most of her activities from the mid-1970s on were centered in the U.K., where she had considerable TV exposure. In 1980, she starred in a restaging of the musical *The Sound of Music* in London. She continued to do some recording, including a disco remake of "Downtown" in 1976 that was featured by London dance club d.j.'s, plus some songs for Scotti Brothers, including the single "Natural Love" that made lower chart levels in the U.S. in 1982.

CLASH, THE: *Vocal and instrumental group from London, England. Original members, 1976: Joe Strummer, born England c. 1953; Mick Jones, born Brixton, England, c. 1955; Paul Simonon, born Brixton, England, c. 1955; Keith Levine, born England, mid-1950s. Levine left in mid-1976; Terry Chimes, born England, c. mid-1950s, added. Chimes replaced in late 1976 by Nicky Headon, born England, c. 1955. Headon left in early 1982 and was replaced by Chimes. Jones left in 1983. Group disbanded in 1986.*

As of the late 1980s, rock 'n' roll's domination of worldwide pop music for more than three decades seemed rooted in the art form's ability to renew itself through the emergence of challenging new artists, artists who are often energized by social upheavals. In the 1960s, performers such as Dylan, the Beatles, and Rolling Stones took over the mantle of Presley; the reggae movement exemplified by Bob Marley shook things up in the mid-1970s; and, in the late 1970s, England's punk movement gave birth to such landmark bands as the Clash.

That English group took the anger and frustration of the country's working class youth of the 1970s—given local voice by bands such as the Sex Pistols

(*See Sex Pistols, The*)—and gave it universal meaning, extending the U.K. complaints about lack of challenging work and hope for the future to symbolize worldwide problems of oppression and violence. Thus, unlike some British punk bands whose material had little relevance beyond U.K. borders, the Clash struck a chord that echoed in the minds of young people around the developed world.

Though the band's lyrics reflected working class concerns (albeit mixed with severe opposition to the nascent U.K. fascism and racism of the National Front, which was blue collar in origin), the members for the most part had middle class backgrounds. However, their early years weren't particularly happy. Two founding members, including lead guitarist Mick Jones, came from broken homes. Jones said: "I stayed with me gran and a lot of wicked aunts." Drummer Nicky Headon's father was a headmaster and his mother a teacher but home life didn't inspire contentment. He recalled: "I used to steal a lot and run with a gang." If he hadn't won a band position, he felt he eventually might have been a convict.

Founding members Joe Strummer and Mick Jones recounted the band's early stages in a record-company biographical note: "In May 1967 a drummer-less group began rehearsing in a small squat near Shepherds Bush Green in London. Paul Simonon was the bass player and he'd been playing for only six weeks. He was from the wilds of Brixton, his parents had split up and he'd lived mostly with his father before landing a free scholarship to a posh art school. Then a friend had said: 'Why don't you join my group?' The guy who said this was Mick Jones, the lead guitarist, also from Brixton. Mick's dad was a cab driver and Mick lived with his parents until they divorced when he was eight. His mum went to America and his dad left home so Mick went to live with his gran. When the Clash formed he was occasionally showing up at Hammersmith Art School. These two guys asked Joe Strummer to be the singer. At the time Joe was singing with a London pub band which he had formed in order to pass the time and pay the rent."

In Strummer's pre-Clash days, he had fronted a group called the 101ers, which featured 1950s-style rock, including a song called "Letsagetabitarockin'," an unlikely number for an artist who was to help write "White Riot," "London's Burning," and "Guns on the Roof." His early influences included such unusual artists as the avant garde American rocker Captain Beefheart. He told an interviewer: "When I was sixteen, Beefheart's *Trout Mask Replica* was the only record I listened to—for a year." (See *Captain Beefheart*.)

For the first few months, Jones and Strummer recalled, "Keith Levine, guitarist, was also a founding member, but he left the group early on saying he had some urgent business to take care of in North London. In August 1976, this group was refurbishing an abandoned warehouse in Camden Town. When it was finished, the rock began. Terry Chimes, a drummer, was enlisted and everyday the warehouse shook with the sound of hard practice. At this time there was nowhere to play. For example, the famous Marquee Club, supposed to be the home of rock 'n' roll, told the Clash: 'Sorry, mate. No punk rock in here.' So gigs were created by Bernie Rhodes, then manager. One day during a particularly nasty gig when the bottles and cans were coming down like rain, Terry Chimes quit after watching a wine bottle come over and smash into a million pieces on his high hat.''

Auditions then were held for a new drummer. "206 tried, 205 failed. Nick 'Topper' Headon outdrummed all comers and won the hot side. By this time, although the group had not noticed, they had caused a sizable reaction in the outside world. For example, CBS coughed up a load of money and signed them. They got to use CBS number 3 studios in London and they made an LP, *The Clash,* in three weekend sessions using their soundman as producer.''

After working as an opening act on a December punk/new wave U.K. tour that fell apart, the Clash organized their own "White Rock" tour in which they were accompanied by the Buzzcocks, the Slits, and Subway Sect. The tour got broad coverage in the English press and helped to catapult the debut LP into upper chart levels. It entered U.K. lists at number 12. Besides the album, CBS released a series of Clash singles in 1977, none of which received enough airplay to rise past number 28 on the charts.

With thoughts of penetrating the U.S. market in mind, the record company brought in Sandy Pearlman, of Blue Oyster Cult fame, to produce the next album. (See *Blue Oyster Cult.*) Most of the material was recorded in London with finishing touches made in the U.S. Before the LP came out, CBS had issued two more singles in the U.K.: "Clash City Rockers''/''Jail Guitar Doors'' (March 17, 1978) and "White Man in Hammersmith Palais''/''The Prisoner'' (June 16, 1978). While those weren't massive hits, the second LP, *Give 'Em Enough Rope,* opened at number two on U.K. charts after its release in November 1978. The LP also was released in the U.S. on the Epic label as plans were made for the band's first U.S. tour in early 1979.

Before that, the Clash went out on an English tour whose main result was a falling out with manager Bernie Rhodes, who left his post until a reunion in the 1980s. The North American tour started in February with dates in Canada, and major U.S. cities. Both critical response and fan support exceeded the group's wildest hopes. Though the group didn't come across as the greatest rock band of all time, its slashing instrumental attack and relentless driving energy marked it as far more than another punk/new wave organization depending more on shock value than content to win over audiences. The band's power-packed numbers, some giving evidence of the members' empathy for reggae, were exciting to listen to as rock music apart from the messages presented in the lyrics.

Headon told Jack Cocks of *Time* magazine (March 5, 1979): "We're nothing like the Sex Pistols. We don't set out to shock people through being sick onstage or through self-mutilation." Jones added: "I never was one for sticking a pin in me nose."

After experiencing one of the band's first U.S. shows, Cocks commented: "The Clash, though hardly elegant instrumentalists, makes far better crafted music than the Pistols ever did. The sheets of sound they let loose have the cumulative effect of mugging, but the songs, full of threat and challenge, never mean to menace. They are, rather, about anger and desperation, about violence as a condition more than a prescription."

The high-spirited arrangements and the multilayered meanings in the lyrics made the band much more understandable than other punk groups to non–U.K. fans. The debut LP did reasonably well in the U.S., but failed to become a gold record. One of the problems was the lack of airplay for album tracks. Pearlman commented: "The term *new wave* is a red flag for a lot of people in radio and record companies. I don't know why. If the record was by, say Tony and the Tuna Fish and they were known as the best new hard-rock band to come out of the Midwest since Ted Nugent, it would be getting all kinds of airplay."

Strummer told Bob Hilburn of the *Los Angeles Times* (February 3, 1979) that radio executives "just can't relate to it. It's the same as in 1954 when they started listening to rock and their mothers said, 'That's awful.' One day they grow up and become parents and it's them saying, 'Get that punk record out of the house.' They end up doing what they started out to destroy."

Undaunted, the group returned home and worked on a new album, the late 1979 CBS extended-play *The Cost of Living.* The album opened at 22 on U.K. charts and did well, helped by the success of a single from the previous album "Tommy Gun''/''One Two Crush on You," issued by CBS November 24, 1979. The track "I Fought the Law" (a cover of a 1966 Bobby Fuller Four hit) was the first single released in the U.S. and, considering earlier problems, got significant airplay. Before 1979 was over, CBS released the Clash single "London Calling"/"Armageddon Time."

During 1979, the band's reputation in the U.S. skyrocketed with release of *The Clash,* a two-disc set on Epic. This offered most of the songs from the band's debut U.K. album plus many of the singles issued afterward. Besides the 15 songs on the album, the release included a bonus single: "Gates of the West"/"Groovy Times." Headon played drums on most of the tracks, but the credits showed Tory Crimes (nom de plume of Terry Chimes) on drums for nine numbers. The collection was described by a *Rolling Stone* reviewer as "the definitive punk album," but it was more than that, with the songs, mostly written by Jones and Strummer, expanding rock horizons in subject matter and rhythmic patterns.

In 1980, the band was represented on U.S. charts by two Epic releases, the EP *Black Market Clash* and the excellent new studio album *London Calling.* At one time or another in 1980, both of those and the 1979 *The Clash* were on hit lists. Symbolic of the band's new-found U.S. prominence was their cover story in the April 17, 1980, *Rolling Stone,* which came out just after the band completed the first part of a standing-room–only concert series across the U.S.

In 1981, the band again had a hit with the three-disc CBS U.K./Epic album *Sandinista.* Before the next album appeared in the summer of 1982, Nicky Headon abruptly departed; his place for the summer tour of the U.S. was taken by original drummer Terry Chimes. That tour accompanied release of what was to become the band's biggest-selling album, *Combat Rock,* which went platinum. First singles from the album were "Know Your Rights" (the initial U.K. release) and "Should I Stay or Should I Go," issued in the early summer in the U.S. While both made the charts, it remained for "Rock the Casbah," the second U.S. single—accompanied by a humorous video—to make the top 10 in both countries. During 1982, besides their headline tour of the U.S., the Clash also were special guests on a series of U.S. stadium tours by the Who during September and October.

While the band was achieving the status of a supergroup, uneasy feelings were arising among the members that finally boiled over with the departure of Mick Jones in 1983. After the fact, Strummer told Hilburn in January 1984: "Mick was me best friend at one time. We were partners and I don't dispense with my partners easily . . . but he became indifferent. He didn't want to go into the studio or go on tour. He just wanted to go on holiday. He wasn't with us anymore."

Jones' departure had a corrosive effect on the band's creativity, it soon became evident. Mick came up smiling, assembling a new group called Big Audio Dynamite whose late 1985 Columbia Records debut (*This is Big Audio Dynamite*) went on to become a best-seller in 1986. The Clash, meanwhile, floundered, coming out in late 1985 with a new LP, *Cut the Crap,* that spent time on the charts, but never became a top-seller. It was not up to their earlier standards.

Strummer ruefully admitted that he was more to blame for the breakup than Jones. He told an interviewer from England's *New Musical Express* that part of the catalyst had been Bernie Rhodes's return as manager in 1983. "Mick and Bernie had never got on . . . and Bernie sort of coerced me into thinking that Mick was what was wrong with the scene. That wasn't hard because, as Mick will admit now . . . he was being pretty awkward. Plus my ego . . . was definitely telling me, go on, get rid of Jones."

Noting the two had made up and might write more songs together, Strummer said: "I did him wrong. I stabbed him in the back. Really it's through his good grace we got back together again in the future. We cover completely different areas so we're not interfering with each other's styles. That's a good thing, a rare thing, and in the last two years I've learned just how good and rare that is."

After disbanding the Clash in early 1986, Strummer embarked on a solo career. One of his projects was to write the song "Love Kills" for *Sid & Nancy,* a film about the tragedy enveloping Sid Vicious, Sex Pistols bass guitarist, who was accused of murdering his girlfriend Nancy Spurgen in 1978, but died before he could be brought to trial.

When Hilburn asked Joe whether the apparent demise of the Clash meant the end of his music career, Strummer gave an indignant no. He told Hilburn (*Los Angeles Times,* August 9, 1986): "Are you kidding? Have you ever thought what it would be like to be Joe Strummer driving a cab around London. To have people in the back go, 'He used to be Joe Strummer.' I've had a fair taste of hasbeeness and it's been deserved. The worst part is when people ask, 'Are you Joe Strummer?' and then they go, 'Oh, I used to be a fan of yours.'"

While mulling over future plans in 1987, Strummer, who contributed to the soundtrack for the film *Walker,* did some acting work and filled in as a rhythm guitarist for a U.S. tour by a band called the Pogues. All of those efforts, he told Richard Cromelin ("Strummer on Man, God, Law—and the Clash," *Los Angeles Times,* January 31, 1988), were only part of a holiday. "I just want to go back to rockin', but I'm uncertain as to what to actually do. The truth is, I never stopped thinking about rock'n'roll for a second that I'm on holiday." (*See Public Image Limited.*)

CLIFF, JIMMY: *Singer, guitarist, keyboards player, band leader, songwriter, actor. Born Somerton, Jamaica, c. 1949.*

A pioneer of reggae music and certainly a driving force in bringing it worldwide notice, Jimmy Cliff often seemed at cross-purposes in furthering his career interests. His albums and personal performances sometimes seemed maddeningly inconsistent. He would turn out a memorable LP and follow it with inferior, occasionally overproduced material. Just when it appeared that he would be on the verge of winning large-scale audience favor, he would change directions, even drop out of sight for years at a time. Despite all of that, he continued to resurface with new vigor, all the while building up a body of work that in its best elements ranks him as a major pop music influence.

In an interview with Michael Shore for CBS Records biographical material in 1982, Jimmy acknowledged he had not up to then balanced his artistic and commercial successes. The main reason was, he claimed: "I'm a spiritual musician. I've often done things that weren't necessarily best for my recording career, because my soul, my spirit demanded it. In 1972 (after his starring vehicle *The Harder They Come* attracted considerable film attention), Chris Blackwell told me he could make me one of the three or four biggest stars in the world. But at the time, my head just wasn't into it. Spiritual and cultural matters were much more important to me. I couldn't make music to satisfy myself or anyone else without first satisfying my soul, my spirit."

Thus, he took leave of show business and went to Africa for several years to study Islam. This led to his acceptance of the Muslim faith instead of Rastafarianism, the worship of the late Emperor Haile Selassie as godhead, which most reggae musicians espouse. He told *People* in a 1982 interview: "I realize the world is set up on publicity and propaganda and the wise thing for my career was to use it. But if I hadn't gone to Africa, I probably would have gone crazy. I don't regret it."

There is, of course, no doubting his sentiments. But at times in his career, he had willingly accepted record companies' "commercial" arrangements of his music aimed at cynically increasing "mass" audience interest. Some of those efforts, indeed, had been self-defeating.

He was born James Chambers in the hillside village of Somerton, 20 miles from Kingston, Jamaica. He changed his name to Cliff as a boy in the early '60s because it implied "heights" he aspired to. At its best, Jimmy's original songs reflected deep roots

in his environment. He told Shore his concentration on music began almost from birth. "As long as I can remember, I've never been into anything but singing and music. I was always singing in school. I wasn't what you'd call the brightest kid in school, but anything I put my mind to, I found I could do it. Yeah, just like 'You Can Get It If You Really Want.' The only things I was interested in at school were the arts, music, and acting. I acted in school plays and such. I sang in church too. It was the Pentecostal denomination and in that church there was no choir. The congregation was the choir. So I always enjoyed going and singing along and clapping. At first I'd just sing and bang a tambourine, then I started on guitar and piano."

In primary school, he began writing and performing original material. After completing primary school in 1961, he went to Kingston to attend technical school. "I left school after a year because I was writing a lot of songs and I wanted to start getting them recorded." Soon after, he made his first record, "Daisy Got Me Crazy," for a local studio. "It was never released and I got no money for it. All they offered me was a shilling for bus fare home, which I refused. I thought it was an insult that I should be paid for my work."

He persevered and finally had an island hit in 1962 with "Hurricane Hattie," issued on the new Beverly's Records label. He recalled: "Beverly's was a combination record store, restaurant, and ice cream parlor run by three Chinese-American brothers, the Kongs. I walked by one night and thought if I wrote a tune called 'Beverly' they might record it. So I did, and I went back a few nights later and played it for the three brothers. They all laughed, except for one of them who liked it and decided to record it and go into the record business. Previously they'd never made records, only sold them."

From 1962 to 1964, Jimmy provided the Kongs with a series of Jamaican hits in the pre-reggae ska style, including singles "Miss Jamaica," "My Lucky Day," and "Miss Universe." Cliff became a local star and Jamaican government officials decided to send him along with other ska artists on an American tour to promote the music and, hopefully, tourism. The tour organizer was Edward Seaga, who later became prime minister. The tour fell flat, but Cliff's sets (including one at the 1964 New York City World's Fair) brought recording offers from American and British labels. Cliff came to terms with Island Records (owned by Jamaican-born Chris Blackwell), and departed for England in 1964.

His stay in the U.K. from then to 1968 was a trying one. His Island recordings, including the LP *Hard Rock,* met with little economic success. He paid for room and board by working in small clubs or as a backup singer for British rock and pop artists. He told Shore: "They didn't really know Jamaican music over there at the time and there were no Jamaican musicians there, and what few there were were playing more of an American R&B sort of thing. So in my nightclub act I did two-thirds R&B and one-third ska, to bring the audiences along. That was fine, but I'd started as a recording artist and that's what I really wanted to concentrate on, and my recording career was going nowhere. At that time, the big thing was for a black singer to play with a white backup band."

Then came an unexpected breakthrough. He submitted his composition "Waterfall" to a song-festival contest in Brazil. He had decided to return to Jamaica, but detoured to Brazil to support his song. "I was only supposed to go there for ten days, but the reaction I got was so great and the people and the life-style so beautiful, I stayed for nearly a year."

The joy of this South American acclaim shone through his 1969 album *Wonderful World, Beautiful People,* issued in the U.K. on Island's Trojan Records label and distributed in the U.S. by A&M. The title track, done in the new reggae style, became an international hit and other tracks, such as "Many Rivers to Cross" and "Vietnam," also rose high on charts in the U.K., South America, and elsewhere. "Vietnam," a stinging antiwar number, did not sell well in the U.S., however. (Nine tracks by Cliff were included in the 1972 A&M LP *Reggae Spectacular.*)

Because the British music press condemned *Wonderful World* as too commercial, Jimmy next went to Muscle Shoals to record material for a soul/R&B collection released under the title *Another Cycle* at the start of the '70s. "I wanted to show what else I could do," he told Shore. "This time the English press loved it, but it didn't sell anything."

Then came another turning point, the chance for Jimmy to star in and write songs for the film *The Harder They Come.* It was a project of filmmaker Perry Henzell, who came to Chris Blackwell to suggest he enlist Cliff in the work. Blackwell told Carl Gayle of *Black Music* magazine that "Henzell really liked that picture of Jimmy on the jacket of *Wonderful World.* He really liked that image and felt he'd be the right image to play the character he wanted. So he asked me if Jimmy would do it and I asked him and he did it. And I feel that was the biggest boost for his career."

In the film, Jimmy plays a reggae artist named Ivan who comes to Kingston to seek stardom only to be thwarted by the machinations of the rich, powerful lords of the music establishment. In the end, he revolts, becomes a Robin Hood type of outlaw, and is shot down by the police. The soundtrack included excellent material by Jimmy and other major Jamaican reggae artists. His version of the title track became a reggae classic as did "You Can Get It If You Really Want" and "Many Rivers To Cross." Unfortunately, neither the soundtrack LP, issued on the Mango label in 1972, nor the film, were economically rewarding. The movie did gain a sizable cult following worldwide and still is shown at times in many places around the globe.

The lack of success of that project caused Cliff to leave Island and sign with EMI Records for U.K. distribution and Warner/Reprise for the U.S. His first work for the new association was the mainly disappointing *Unlimited,* issued on EMI and Reprise in 1973, though the LP did include some excellent tracks such as "Under the Moon, Sun and Stars" and "The Price of Peace." In 1974, his LP *Music Maker* also didn't come up to earlier standards. Other mid-1970s LPs were *Follow My Mind* (EMI in the U.K., Reprise in the U.S.), *Struggling Man* (Island), and *Jimmy Cliff* (Trojan).

Also in 1974, after two years of interest in Islam, Cliff made his first journey to Africa. "In Africa, I got the greatest satisfaction I've ever had as an artist. The acceptance and appreciation I received there, it made me feel so good. After all, the first song I'd ever written was 'Back to Africa,' right?" Since the mid-1970s, Cliff has performed in many places in Africa, including an integrated concert attended by 75,000 people in Soweto, South Africa, in 1980.

His first African visit seemed to reinvigorate his creativity. His tours of the U.S. and other nations were well received in the middle and late 1970s and he felt better satisfied with his new albums, which included the 1976 *Best of Jimmy Cliff/Live in Concert* (Reprise) and 1978 *Give Thanx* (Warner Brothers). Record sales, though, remained less than hoped for. In 1981, he put out two LPs on MCA: *I Am the Living* and *Give the People What They Want.*

In 1982, Jimmy found a new recording home, Columbia Records. His initial LP for the label, *Special,* was issued in June with Cliff's backup band providing a roster of top names in reggae for that period: Earl "Chinna" Smith and Rad "Dougie" Bryan on guitars; "Ranchy" McLean on bass; Ansell Collins on keyboards; Dean Frazier, "Nambo" Robinson, and David Madden on horns; and Mikey "Boo" Richards on drums. Many of them accompanied Cliff on his U.S. tour in support of the album. Over the next few years, Columbia issued three more LPs, the most successful being the 1985 *Cliff Hanger.* The album's release accompanied an upsurge of new interest in Cliff's music as a result of Bruce Springsteen's performance of his song "Trapped" on the *We Are the World* album. "Trapped" became one of the most played tracks on radio in the U.S. and around the world for 1985.

The new focus on Cliff's talents brought an offer for his first film role since *The Harder They Come*. Released in mid-1986, *Club Paradise* was a comedy featuring Cliff and Robin Williams as proprietors of a decrepit West Indies hotel. It boasted a duet between Jimmy and Elvis Costello.

CLINTON, GEORGE: *Singer, guitarist, songwriter, band leader (FUNKADELIC/PARLIAMENT, P-FUNK ALL STARS), record producer. Born Kannapolis, North Carolina, July 22, 1941.* George Clinton is a master of the style of rock/R&B known as funk. Commenting on Parliament, his group of the late 1970s, Clinton said: "A lot of folks feel our group and our songs are silly, ridiculous, and stupid. While they might expect me to get upset, I just laugh and consider even the negative things they say as highly complimentary—that's how stupid I am. As a matter of fact, I wrote a song for Funkadelic [Parliament offshoot] a few years ago called 'Super Stupid,' and I guess it applies even more today. People just have to realize that in the unlogical world we live in today, logic has gone completely out to lunch. I mean, I'm lunchin' too, but we're just eating at different counters."

For all the word play and wild musical touches in the material Clinton performed, wrote, or supervised, it was always eminently danceable and/or watchable. While people joked about his artistic efforts or, seeing him in public, gawked at his strange antics and dress (including during one period a two-inch–wide luminous purple mohawk haircut from which hung down rows of similarly colored cornrow braids), Clinton just winked knowingly and laughed all the way to the bank. For a while, he built up a veritable empire of funk whose products went out to many different labels from his own Detroit-based studio headquarters, but everything unraveled at once at the start of the l980s. Undaunted by economic misfortunes, Clinton bounced back to once more become a pop music force in the mid-1980s.

Clinton was the first of nine children born to poverty-ridden Julia Keaton in the small town of Kannapolis, fifty miles from Winston-Salem, North Carolina. As he told Michael Goldberg of *Rolling Stone* (June 23, 1983), she supported the family by cleaning and baby-sitting work. "It was very hard. Had to do a little bit of everything to make ends meet. It really put a strain on Mom."

George didn't consider music as a possible career until the family moved to Newark, New Jersey, in 1956. He heard Frankie Lymon and the Teenagers on a radio station and decided he could find a place in pop music too. For a while, he worked in a local barbershop by day and got together with friends for street-corner doo-wop singing in the evening. He told Goldberg he also earned some money for a time selling drugs. "Yeah, that was part of survival. Weed. But everything was survival there. And after dealin' with all the jive on the street, I thought the record business was just an ill-equipped similar version of the same thing. So I said, why the fuck should I settle for a Cadillac and three or four bitches when that same concept works better with them big bitches, the corporations."

It turned out to be easier saying it than doing it. Clinton and his friends formed a group called the Parliaments, which moved from street corners to the ghetto club circuit. Years went by and the group had little to show for its efforts but emotional scars from playing in smoky rooms for low pay and little respect from the recording industry. By the mid-1960s, Clinton had expanded Parliament into a ten-piece soul band that got the chance to make some discs for ABC. These had little impact on the market.

Things began to look somewhat better in 1967, when Clinton and his group had some success with the single "(I Just Want to) Testify," issued on the small, independent Revilot label. That disc came out, as it happened, right when the frustration of black Americans with their second-class status was boiling over. Clinton recalled for Paolo Hewitt of England's *Melody Maker* (January 8, 1983): "We'd just left Newark on the day of the riots, and we had a record out called 'I Just Want to Testify.' That was a hit and the chance to get out of Newark. . . . Newark was rioting all the time. We already had a riot scene so it was nothing big to Newark because people were getting frustrated in different parts of the town all the time.

"So when it happened, for us it was 'let's get out of town' because we got stopped by the police and National Guard and they took our brand new suits, stopping us to see if there were any drugs in the pockets. They knew we were in a group . . . 'hey we got the Temptations here!' Ha-ha-ha. . . . so we said 'fuck this' and we hit the road.

"By the time we got to Detroit—we was playing with Martha and the Vandellas, David Ruffin, a whole bunch of us—[the riots] started there. . . . Us having got out of town and having a hit record, we were just saying 'let's see what we can do to keep surviving until this thing blows over.' The group stuck together real tight then."

The trip to Detroit brought some Motown contacts that led to recording sessions, but nothing reached the market. Meanwhile, Revilot failed, and because of contractual entanglements, Clinton had to avoid using the name Parliament for a while. He got around that by taking the name Funkadelic and signing with another independent record label, Westbound.

The name Funkadelic is a merger of the words *funk* and *psychedelic*. Clinton's long-time friend, independent–record-company president Armen Boladian, told Michael Goldberg: "Psychedelic music was kind of starting at that time. George loved that music, but thought there should be some good old funk connected to it. That's where the Funkadelic came in."

Now that Clinton was seeing more of the recording/entertainment field up close, ideas of how to tap its potential began to come to him. In particular, he liked the concept of having a whole stable of different groups and artists. He told Hewitt he wanted to "Go multi and have a bunch of groups and have them on all different labels and don't matter which one has a hit, we'd just do it right."

It took a while for that concept to reach fruition. During that period, from the late 1960s into the early 1970s, Clinton was beginning to gain notice from R&B fans and fellow musicians for his concert showmanship and the toe-tapping rhythms later characterized as "R&B psychedelic music." In the early 1970s, record catalogues showed him with a Parliament album called *Osmium* on the Invictus label and a number of LPs under the Funkadelic logo (such as *Funkadelic, Free Your Mind,* and *Maggot Brain*) on the Westbound label.

The early 1970 stage shows in support of Clinton's albums were memorable both visually and musically, Boladian recalled: "It was wild onstage. One [member] would be dressed in an Arab costume, another would come out wearing a garment bag with the hangars sticking out of it, and another would have diapers on. If George didn't have his costume, he would take a sheet off the bed of his hotel, cut a hole in it, and pull it over his head and put some paint on his face and go out there. Of course, he had nothing on under the sheet. It would just freak everybody out."

His larger scheme began to take shape when James Brown's former bass guitarist William "Bootsy" Collins joined his entourage. Clinton told Hewitt: "Bootsy and his group came in and that was a whole different concept within itself. So what I did was record Bootsy by himself with another group, recorded Parliament (separately) which sounded like that but was a little more grown up. Bootsy was aimed more at kids—we called it silly serious—Parliament was a little older and Funkadelic was for a little older than that."

However, for live shows, Parliament and Funkadelic were one group (though with various backing artists, many of whom also were then recorded separately). The combined band typically was called P-Funk, which later was used for still more recordings.

After Bootsy, Clinton added: "We tried to make everyone pay their way, so we had background singers and we made them into a group called the Brides [a.k.a. The Brides of Funkenstein] and that one worked pretty good. They couldn't always be singing with us so we got The Parlettes and they did all right.

"So we just kept on going and then each individual member started getting contracts. Bernie Worrell was on Arista, Eddie Hazell was on WEA [Warner/Elektra/Asylum], Parliament on Casablanca, Funkadelic on WEA, Bootsy on WEA, Sweat Band was on Uncle Jam [Clinton's own label], Zapp was on Warner Brothers and Roger [Troutman of Zapp] was too."

Before all that activity began to flower in the mid-1970s, Clinton and Funkadelic turned out a total of eight albums on Westbound (including *Let's Take It to the Stage* and *Standing on the Verge*) prior to changing labels. In 1977, Westbound released a retrospective of the band's work, *Best of the Funkadelic Early Years*. By then, the group's albums (such as *Hardcore Jollies* in 1976, the sensational *One Nation under a Groove* in 1978, and *Uncle Jam Wants You* in 1979) came out on Warner Brothers.

At the same time Funkadelic was providing albums and a number of charted singles for Warner Brothers, Clinton was supervising a veritable stream of recorded material for Casablanca Records. Dave Marsh of *Rolling Stone* wrote: "Clinton has taken [Parliament and its various offshoots including Funkadelic, Bootsy's Rubber Band, and the Horny Horns] into a nether world of black rock & roll. Funkadelic and Bootsy are more outrageously entertaining—a good deal of their output is simply power rock with a dance beat—but Parliament has been used for Clinton's major statements: *The Clones of Dr. Funkenstein* suggests a rather unpleasant vision of the future, while *Funkentelechy vs. the Placebo Syndrome* is actually a prescriptive manifesto concerning the sad state of the Seventies music world."

The Casablanca Parliament output included the 1975 *Chocolate City,* whose spoken and sung tracks anticipated the rise of rap during the decade. It was followed by *The Clones of Dr. Funkenstein* and *Mothership Connection* in 1976; *Get Down and Boogie, Funkenstein vs. the Placebo Syndrome,* and *Up for the Down Stroke* in 1977; *Motor Booty Affair* in 1978; *Glory Hallastoopid* in 1979; and *Trombipulation* in 1980.

From 1975 to 1980, when not touring, Clinton was almost a whirling dervish as he tended his seemingly endless recording projects at his United Sound Studios in Detroit. Though he had a quiet retreat he sometimes repaired to with his wife, Stephanie, when he was at the studios directing some thirty musicians and dozens of support people, he often worked almost around the clock. It paid off in gold and platinum records for many of his projects, including platinum for Bootsy and Parliament releases.

But then everything went wrong at once at the start of the 1980s. He got into a contract wrangle with Warner Brothers that led to a $100 million breach-of-contract lawsuit. One result was Warner's refusal to continue to distribute new releases. Casablanca was sold to Polygram Records, which led to problems with the Parliament operation. Other projects (including his plans for a new label, Choza Negra, and expanded output on his Park Place and Uncle Jam labels) fell through. Overstretched financially, he no longer could meet the $150,000 a week payroll for his widespread recording and concert operations. Clinton suddenly was broke and found the doors to all major labels shut to him.

Armen Boladian told Michael Goldberg: "He hit rock bottom." In particular, he said, during that period, Clinton got hooked on freebase cocaine. Industry people and music critics opined that Clinton's career was finished.

But Clinton had been through hard times as far back as Newark—and he was inherently a survivor. Slowly he began to deal with his problems, both hard drugs and finances. In 1982, he was back working with the P-Funk All Stars on a single on which Bobby Womack, among others, performed. He also produced and mixed a single by Xavier and began assembling material for a solo album. By then, he had settled most of his outstanding debts and was able to gain a new contract with Capitol. His debut single on the label, "Loopzilla," came out in October 1982 and was followed soon after by the LP *Computer Games,* issued on November 5, 1982. Backing Clinton on the album were such long-time bandsmen as Bootsy, Bernie Worrell, Eddie Hazel, Junie Morrison, and the Horny Horns. The album showed up on the pop charts soon after release and remained into 1983. It also rose high on the black music lists. During 1983, another single from the LP, "Atomic Dog," became a best-seller.

Clinton continued to turn out new charted material under his own name. At the end of 1983, his single "Nubian Nut" was well inside the *Billboard* black music chart's top 20, where it stayed into early 1984. During 1984, he did well with a new solo LP, *You Shouldn't-Nuf Bit Fish.* By then, George was back in his multialbum project groove with a fine LP by the P-Funk All Stars, *Urban Dance Floor Guerrillas,* recorded on his Uncle Jam label and distributed by CBS.

In April 1986, Capitol issued the LP *R&B Skeletons in the Closet* (from which the initial single was the track "Do Fries Go with That Shake?"). This new LP was the fifty-sixth Clinton had produced either of his own work or that of other artists.

Discussing the album content, he indicated some bitterness about the compromises many black artists had to make to get crossover play on white-dominated radio or TV. He said: "This time we've done an album for all the R&B artists who crossed over and can't get black. In order to get that crossover appeal, they tell them to use less bass or don't say the word *funk* or something like that so they can get played on pop radio. Once you do that and sell all those records, you start gearing your music for that market. Before you know it, all the R&B you had in you is completely hidden."

For himself, he noted, though his stage show continued to draw exuberant crowds, his music was almost never included in the playlists of the 1980s. "I wouldn't say it's because I wouldn't compromise the Funk, but . . . I mean how can you Funk without heavy bass. I've always felt that music is music and our music does not only appeal to the Colored Purple People. Once they [other ethnic groups] hear it, they'll dance too."

CLOVERS, THE: *Vocal group, all born Washington, D.C., Delaware areas, early 1930s. Charlie White and John "Buddy" Bailey alternated as lead singers.*

Any history of rock'n'roll or rhythm & blues must rate the Clovers as one of the central groups in the evolution of both forms of popular music. It took a while for rock audiences to become familiar with them, because the gradual merger of R&B and country to form rock took most of the early 1950s to take hold. But the group was a dynamic force in R&B from the time its first disc was issued in 1950.

The five founding members of the Clovers grew up on the East Coast near the nation's capital. They were close friends during high school and started singing for parties and school events. By the end of the 1940s, they were working small clubs in the Washington area and building up a following among black residents of the region.

In 1950 at Washington's after-hours Rose Club, they came to the attention of the young Atlantic Records organization. Atlantic was already doing well in the blues field with Ruth Brown and was looking to expand its roster in this category. Company president Ahmet Ertegun liked the Clovers and signed them, the first black vocal group to join the company. Their first two Atlantic singles, ("Don't You Know I Love You" and "Fool, Fool, Fool") marked them as an act to watch, as both rose to number one on the R&B charts in 1951. They are considered classics by vintage R&B aficionados.

The following year was a peak one for the group.

The Clovers placed five songs in the R&B top 10: "Hey Miss Fannie," "I Played the Fool," "Middle of the Night," "One Mint Julep," and "Ting-A-Ling." The quintet performed at almost every major stop on the R&B round of theaters and clubs and occasionally was able to demonstrate its skills in clubs outside ghetto areas. The group continued to turn out hits—"Crawlin'" and "Good Lovin'" in 1953, plus "I Got My Eyes on You," "Little Mama," "Lovey Dovey," and "Your Cash Ain't Nothin' but Trash" in 1954. Some songs became best-sellers in the national market too. "Love, Love, Love" made the hit charts in 1956. This breakthrough boosted the group into the front ranks of rock acts of the period and gained them exposure in rock concerts and rock TV programs. More often than not, the race barrier caused the Clovers to lose out to white artists in terms of record success. For example, Bobby Vee gained considerably more mileage from his 1960 "Devil or Angel" than the Clovers did with their 1956 rendition. Similarly, Bobby Vinton's 1963 "Blue Velvet" far outsold the Clovers' December 1954 recording.

During the closing years of the '50s, the Clovers did better in the teenage market than in R&B. The group placed a number of releases on the general hit lists, including their 1959 classic United Artists novelty of "Love Potion Number 9" (a song that was still providing hit records for other performers in the late '60s and early '70s).

The group disbanded during the 1960s and for most of the decade was represented in the in-stock catalogues by a two-record album *The Clovers*, originally issued by Atlantic in November 1959. A number of the group's best singles were included in the History of Rhythm & Blues series Atlantic put out in the mid-1960s. In 1971, an upsurge of interest in the early days of rock caused Atlantic to compile albums of six of its 1950s acts, including *The Clovers: Their Greatest Recordings—The Early Years*.

COASTERS, THE: *Vocal group, all born early 1930s. Carl Gardner, born Texas; Billy Guy, born Hollywood, California; Cornelius Gunter, born Los Angeles, California; Adolph Jacobs, born Oakland, California.*

The first performers to make rock'n'roll a household phrase (to most parents, a rather unsavory phrase) were white graduates of country music. Once the door was opened, though, black artists began to move from R&B to their proper place in the mass market. A good many of the early black rock acts were vocal groups with sounds more imitative of the Ink Spots' ballads than the brassy rhythms of R&B. Nonetheless, such stars as the Coasters pro-vided a base for the eventual move of blues and R&B artists to major status.

The four original members of the group all met in Los Angeles' black ghetto, where most of them grew up. Singing in small clubs, they came under the direction of songwriting team Jerry Leiber and Mike Stoller, who helped them gain a contract from Spark Records in the early 1950s. At the time, Carl Gardner, Billy Guy, Adolph Jacobs and Cornelius Gunter (brother of Zola Taylor of the Platters; *See Platters, The*) collectively called themselves The Robins. They had some success under that name, gaining such rhythm & blues hits as "Cell Block Number 9" and "Smokey Joe's Cafe," songs written by Leiber and Stoller.

In 1955, the group took a new name—"Coasters," because they were from the West Coast—and consciously started performing the watered-down blues material that was beginning to make rock a candidate for popular music domination.

In 1956, they signed with Atlantic Records and soon had a major hit in both R&B and rock markets, "Down in Mexico." The record, which also rose high on the charts in England, sold over a million copies. This was enhanced by their even greater success in 1957 with a two-sided hit, "Searching" and "Young Blood." Both songs hit number one on the R&B charts and gained the top 10 on national charts as well. Indeed, the songs were aimed at the national market from the start by writers Leiber and Stoller (with an assist by Doc Pomus on "Young Blood").

For the balance of the '50s, the Coasters remained among the most important influences on popular music, though many of their major hits did not even show up in the top positions of the R&B charts, indicating the group's lack of acceptance by black fans. Two of the most notable recordings that followed this pattern were the 1958 R&B hit "Yakety Yak" (by Leiber and Stoller) and the 1959 success, "Charlie Brown."

Among the Coasters' other hits were "Poison Ivy" (R&B no. one in 1959), "Along Came Jones," "Framed," "Idol with the Golden Head," and "Shoppin' for Clothes." "That Is Rock and Roll" is often cited as the recording that best defines rock music, at least of the 1950s variety. The group also achieved good sales with its albums, though their main appeal was always to singles buyers.

Despite the group's phenomenal success in the late 1950s, it was unable to maintain its momentum into the 1960s and split up a short time after the new decade's start. By the mid-1960s, Atlantic had phased all the group's records out of its catalog. The group reassembled on occasion in the late 1960s and early 1970s to perform in the rock'n'roll revival concerts that came into vogue, and later in the 1970s, Leiber and Stoller produced material by a re-formed version of the group. Album credits in the 1970s included Atlantic's *The Coasters: Their Greatest Recordings—The Early Years* (issued in late 1971) and rather tepid remakes of group favorites on *Sixteen Greatest Hits* (produced by Leiber and Stoller for the Trip label).

In 1980, repackaged releases of early Coaster material on Atlantic were available as Japanese imports: *Wake Me, Shake Me* and *The Coasters*. With varying personnel, Gunter continued to keep the group on the concert circuit during the 1980s. In 1987, he was inducted into the Rock 'n' Roll Hall of Fame. In a press release for a Coasters appearance at the Winners Circle Lounge of the Sands Hotel in Las Vegas in early 1988, the claim was made that the group had sold 137 million records worldwide.

COCHRAN, EDDIE: *Singer, guitarist, songwriter. Born Albert Lea, Minnesota, October 3, 1938; died near London, England, April 17, 1960.*

In England, there is an Eddie Cochran Memorial Society; in the U.S., hardly anyone remembers his name. But he did have major impact on the rock field, particularly in Britain, and no one can say what he might have achieved had he not died tragically.

He was born and raised in the rural town of Albert Lea, Minnesota. The youngest of five children, he had a normal, happy midwestern upbringing. He attended school, played ball with his friends, and went hunting and fishing with his father. In grade school, he began listening to records on the radio and on the home phonograph. He was attracted to country western music for several reasons. One was the fact that a number of stations played country records; rural communities in all parts of the U.S. and Canada have long been close to such music. Equally important, his parents were country & western fans. They had grown up with it in Oklahoma City, which they left only because of the Dust Bowl of the early 1930s.

When Eddie was 12, he asked his parents to buy him an instrument so he could join the school orchestra. He considered the drum, trombone, and clarinet before finally settling on the guitar. The orchestra had no opening for a guitarist, but Eddie didn't care. Instead, he picked up a few chords from his older brother and rapidly taught himself to play. By the time his family moved to Bell Gardens, California, in 1953, he was an excellent guitarist.

After settling into life in a new town, he put together a group with two neighbors, picking up jobs playing for local parties, market openings, and the

like. By 1955, the band had broken up and Eddie was part of a duo with a namesake, Hank Cochran, who was no relation to him. They were playing local dates as the Cochran Brothers when Eddie met songwriter Jerry Capehart in a Bell Gardens music store. Capehart wanted a group to do demonstration records or tapes of his songs. This resulted in the Cochran Brothers first disc, "Tired and Sleepy." Issued on the Ekko label, it was a flop.

Not long after this, Eddie left Hank Cochran (who went on to become a country music star), dropped out of school, and moved to Nashville with Capehart. They aligned themselves with the American Music publishing firm and made test recordings of their own and other writers' songs. Eddie recorded his first solo record, "Skinny Jim." Released on American Music's Crest label, it had no more success than the previous single.

In early 1956, Capehart returned to Los Angeles and made the rounds of the major record companies with the demonstration records. Liberty board chairman Si Waronker liked Cochran's sound and signed him. His first single was a John D. Loudermilk song, "Sittin' in the Balcony," released in late 1956.

An important milestone for rock music occurred in 1956 with the release of the film *The Girl Can't Help It,* considered by many to be the ultimate 1950s rock movie. It had what Hollywood considered to be a big budget and "name" actors in lead roles. Cochran, Gene Vincent, and the Platters made cameo appearances. In one scene, a middle-aged mobster watches Cochran perform "Twenty-Flight Rock" on TV and decides if Eddie can be a star, anyone can. This inspires him to have his protégé (played by Jayne Mansfield) follow this route despite her foghornlike singing voice.

1957 started off more auspiciously for Eddie. "Sittin' in the Balcony" finally began to catch on with record buyers and reached the top 20 in the spring. However, the followup song, "Mean When I'm Mad," co-written by Capehart and Cochran, did poorly. That disappointment was tempered by the fact that Eddie had a major role in the film *Flaming Youth,* which starred Mamie Van Doren.

The year 1958 was a turning point. In March, Capehart and Cochran co-wrote "Summertime Blues." Released in May, it remained on the charts all summer long. Now considered a rock classic, it is still often played on radio shows during the summer months—either by Cochran or the Who. In the summer, the team wrote another song that became a classic, "C'mon Everybody." Released in late fall of 1958, it became a hit in the winter of 1959.

By late 1958, Cochran had gained a national reputation with teen rock fans. He was booked for one series of one-nighters after another. Eddie assembled a backup band for these that he named the Kelly Four: Connie "Guybo" Smith on bass (later replaced by Dave Shreiber), Gene Ridgio on drums, and a series of pickup musicians on piano and saxophone.

He also became friends with a number of his peers in the rock field, including Buddy Holly and Ritchie Valens. Strangely, he was originally supposed to be on the tour in early 1959 on which Holly, Valens, and J.P. Richardson (the Big Bopper) were killed in a plane crash. He had been taken off the program because of changes in booking plans, but sometimes indicated to friends his feeling that he was living on borrowed time. (See *Holly, Buddy; Richardson, J.P.; Valens; Ritchie.*)

During 1959, he continued to tour widely, appeared on a number of network TV shows, and turned out more records including "Three Steps to Heaven" and "Something Else." Together, "Something Else," "Summertime Blues," and "C'mon Everybody" embodied the feelings of American teenagers in the late '50s.

Eddie was on the threshold of becoming a superstar as the 1960s began. He already was as influential in Europe as Elvis Presley had been at a similar stage in his career. He was booked for a major European tour with such other luminaries as Gene Vincent and English star Billy Fury. (See *Vincent, Gene.*) Eddie reached Europe in February and worked his way from Italy to England. His shows in England in April were given a tumultuous welcome by fans and other musicians. Future Beatle George Harrison attended almost every performance and Georgie Fame gained a job as pianist in Eddie's backup band.

The tour came to an end in mid-April. Eddie was anxious to get back to California to rest and plan new work. On April 17, he, girlfriend Sharon Sheeley (who wrote some of Rick Nelson's hits), and Gene Vincent headed for the airport in a chauffeured limousine. On the way, a tire blew out, the chauffeur lost control, and the car rammed into a lamp post. Vincent and Sharon were hurt, but recovered. Cochran died within a few hours from multiple head injuries.

After 1960, Cochran's sadly short career became the stuff of legends. Over the years, some of his songs found their way into the repertoires of other artists; examples include Rod Stewart's version of "Cut Across Shorty," "Summertime Blues" by the Who, and the Stray Cats' performance of "Jeanie Jeanie Jeanie." Collections of Eddie's recordings continued to come out in the U.S. and abroad, including not only tracks released in his lifetime, but also some of the demonstration records he made for American Music Publishing and recordings by other

artists on which he performed as a session musician. Among the posthumous LP releases were *My Way* (Liberty, 1984); *Singing to My Baby* (Liberty 1968); *C'mon Everybody* (Sunset, 1970, British import); *The Legendary Masters Series, Volume 4: Eddie Cochran* (United Artists 1972—the two-disc definitive collection of Cochran material); *Cherished Memories* (Sunset, 1972, British import); *The Many Sides of Eddie Cochran* (Rockstar, 1979, British import); and *The Eddie Cochran Singles Album* (United Artists, 1979, British import)

COCKER, JOE: *Singer, drummer, songwriter, band leader. Born Sheffield, England, May 20, 1944.*

As noted elsewhere in this book, Continental Europe and England have harbored ardent blues fans for many decades. For a time, they were a relative minority of the music audience as they sought old 78 rpm records of American black artists of the past and welcomed any of the great blues singers to their shores with considerably more gusto than did white audiences in the U.S. When English teenage rock groups proliferated from the late 1950s on, they took up blues material as well, bringing blues-tinged music to the attention of the mass audience, first in Europe and then in the U.S.

Negro blues with English accents sometimes sounds odd to American ears in general and black music fans in particular. In the case of Joe Cocker, though, his versions of the blues strike a knowing chord in audiences of all creeds and colors in his home regions of Europe and abroad.

Born John Cocker, he grew up in the working class section of Sheffield, an industrial town in northern England. Central Tech, from where he graduated at 16, was basically a trade school. There, Cocker learned the rudiments of masonry, woodworking, and plumbing. For a while after graduating, he did little but hang around his home area or work a few music jobs at night until he finally found a job as a gas fitter. He installed and repaired gas lines during the day for most of his income and sang rock music more as a hobby than as a part-time job.

He had drifted into music at the start of his teens. "When we were kids, we were constantly bored. All there was to do was walk up and down the street. Then skiffle came along, Lonnie Donegan and that stuff. So when I was about 13, I bought a cheap drum-kit and began messing about with some kids who'd bought guitars.

"Eventually, when skiffle started to fade, only those who were strongest stayed with music. At this time, I was into Little Richard and Gene Vincent and the other rock and rollers, but I was especially attracted to the blues, which seemed to have a great honesty compared to all the bullshit English pop amounted to then. Then we started getting things like 'Twist with Muddy Waters' and I went off my blues-purist kick.''

In the late 1950s, Cocker added some, but not too much, of the blues feeling to the material played by his group, the Cavaliers. He varied this with effects borrowed from such rock artists as Buddy Holly and Chuck Berry. The performer who had the most effect on his musical future, though, was Ray Charles. After Cocker heard Charles' "What'd I Say," he bought Ray's *Yes Indeed!* LP and played it over and over.

By the fall of 1963, Cocker was playing with Vance Arnold and the Avengers. They signed their first record contract with a British company and turned out somewhat toned-down singles of the Beatles' "I'll Cry Instead" and Ray Charles' "Georgia on My Mind." By this time, Cocker was working solely as a musician. His group went on a brief English tour with the Rolling Stones and the Hollies. When they got back, they found they had lost their recording contract. They then toured American bases in France, playing blues-rock for the G.I.s. Cocker recalled: "We went down sensationally with the blacks and the white guys didn't want to know us.''

Cocker returned to England broke and discouraged and spent most of the mid-1960s working at odd jobs and drinking beer in local pubs. The Beatles' 1967 "Strawberry Fields Forever" and *Sergeant Pepper* LP made Cocker feel audiences might be ready for his style. He worked up new material with Sheffield musician-friend Chris Stainton (born March 3, 1943) and prepared a demonstration tape. The tape was presented to Procol Harum manager Denny Cordell, who was duly impressed. He set up a session for Cocker and Stainton in London, which resulted in a top 50 singles hit—Stainton's composition, "Marjorine." This was followed by some successful London engagements starring Cocker and a group of musicians called Joe Cocker's Big Blues Band.

Under Cordell's direction, Cocker recorded a slow, bluesy version of the Beatles' "With a Little Help from My Friends." The single rose to top spot in most European countries and made the charts (though not the highest levels) in the U.S. For most of 1968 and part of 1969, Cordell and Cocker spent hours in London recording studios working on an album that would feature the hit song as title track. The LP, released in the U.S. by A&M Records in the spring of 1969, eventually gained Cocker his first American gold record.

During the summer of 1969, Cocker made his first U.S. tour. His set at the Woodstock Festival in up-state New York was a showstopper. Critics and audiences both considered him one of the most promising newcomers to grace the scene. They talked favorably about his harsh, penetrating vocals and his weird body movements. He flung his arms about in strange, puppetlike motions and kicked his feet, as one observer suggested, somewhat like a singing Frankenstein.

Cocker noted: "I've always done me little theatricality bit of throwing me arms about with the music. Some people think it's a bit too much. Like when I was on 'Ed Sullivan,' they surrounded me with thousands of dancers to keep me hidden. But, you know, it's not contrived—why would anyone want to contrive a stage routine that turns so many people off?''

At the A&M studios in Los Angeles, Cordell and Cocker met Leon Russell, who was not yet famous. (*See Russell, Leon.*) Russell became close friends with them and later returned to England to help complete Cocker's second album. The album included two songs written specially for Cocker by members of the Beatles: George Harrison's "Something" and Paul McCartney's "She Came in through the Bathroom Window." Besides the work of Russell and other session men, the album featured Cocker's backup group for the 1969 tour, which included Stainton on piano, bass, and guitar; 26-year-old guitarist Henry McCullough; 21-year-old bassist Alan Spenner; and, on drums, Bruce Rolands, then in his late twenties. The LP, *Joe Cocker!*, was highly successful in all sections of Europe and the U.S. after its release in the fall of 1969.

In 1970, Cocker toured the U.S. with "Mad Dogs and Englishmen," a community band, assembled by Leon Russell, consisting of 42 men, women, and children. Besides Cocker, the show featured Russell's solo on such originals as "Hummingbird," Claudia (from Ike and Tina Turner's Ikettes) singing "Let It Be," and Rita Coolidge singing "Superstar." (*See Coolidge, Rita; Turner, Ike and Tina; Turner, Tina.*) The LP of material recorded live during the tour was released in 1970. In 1971, a full-length film of the tour, also titled *Mad Dogs and Englishmen* proved to be one of the year's best box-office attractions.

The "Mad Dogs" tour left him exhausted. That and other problems sidelined him until early 1972, when he finally had a new LP, *Joe Cocker,* out on A&M. The layoff apparently had proved traumatic for him. He seemed to lose some of his poise and hard-won self-confidence in the interim. In his stage appearances during the mid-1970s, he rarely came close to the soul-piercing dynamism that had set him apart from other vocalists. Instead of twisting, turning, and throwing his whole body into every phase, he tended to stay passively in one place. But more distressing was that, either because of the psychological factors or the physical abuse he'd subjected his body to during the hiatus, his voice lacked the drive and authority it had once had. During 1974, some of his concerts were so poorly done that much of the audience left before the show was over. In a few cases, he was unable to complete the gig.

Though it took time, Cocker finally began to pull himself together. This was reflected in 1974 with release of *I Can Stand a Little Pain*, his first representative album since *Mad Dogs*. One of the songs, "Put out the Light" by Daniel Moore, summed up some of Joe's feelings about the root of his troubles: "Somebody I trusted/Somebody I knew quite well/Somebody I loved/Put out the light/Turned day into night." That album provided him with a top 5 single, "You Are So Beautiful."

After that, his career moved forward, though hardly in a straight line. His stage presence improved, though he apparently never would recapture the inner fireworks that had made him such an imposing figure in years past. That remained a problem, since while he has written some original material, Joe basically is an interpreter of other people's writings.

His mid-1970s LPs on A&M, *Jamaica Say You Will* (1975) and *Stingray* (1976), seemed steps backward from his prior recordings. They also closed out his stay on A&M, which issued *Joe Cocker's Greatest Hits* in 1977. He moved to Asylum Records, which in 1978 issued *Luxury You Can Afford*—not a bad LP, but one that made little commercial headway.

In the early 1980s, Joe sang on several tracks for a Crusaders album that was nominated for a Grammy for best gospel record. During the February 1982 awards telecast, he sang "I'm So Glad I'm Standing Here" with them and his vocal work won a standing ovation. Since 1978, Cocker had been shut out from recording new songs, but Island Records finally gave him the chance to complete an album, *Sheffield Steel*, issued in 1982. It wasn't his best effort, but it was a step in the right direction. The same year he was invited to work with Jennifer Warnes on "Up Where We Belong" for the movie *An Officer and a Gentlemen*. Issued on Island as a single, it became a worldwide hit, moving to the top of the *Billboard* charts the week of November 6, 1982, and staying there a second week. It was nominated for a Grammy Award for Best Pop Performance by a Duo or Group and, after Joe and Jennifer sang it on the telecast the night of February 23, 1983, they found they also had been voted the trophy winners.

Joe signed with a new label, Capitol, in 1983, and recorded one of his better albums, *Civilized Man*, issued in 1984. His increasingly hectic schedule after

that included touring Europe with Huey Lewis and the News and Foreigner, writing and recording the song "We Stand Alone" for the movie *Wildcats*, and recording the Randy Newman song "You Can Leave Your Hat On" for the soundtrack of the movie *9 1/2 Weeks*. In April 1986, his second Capitol LP, *Cocker*, was released. In 1987, he had his recording of "Love Lives On" on the soundtrack of *Harry and the Hendersons* and, in October, a new LP on Capitol, *Unchain My Heart*.

COLE, NATALIE: *Singer, pianist, songwriter. Born Los Angeles, California, February 6, 1950.*

The name Cole, a great one in jazz and pop music annals, received new luster in the 1970s thanks to Natalie Cole, one of five children of the late superstar Nat "King" Cole. Yet Natalie achieved stardom not merely as Nat's daughter, but on her own terms, singing songs that spoke to the influences of her time and place.

She told Dale Adamson of the *Houston Chronicle* (November 5, 1978) that she recognized she was "an extension of my father. I don't think I'll ever be a separate entity. Everything I do revolves around the fact that he came first. And I'm his other half." But, she continued, there was a difference. "I'm doing all the things he'd never do. He was not a rock 'n' roll singer, but he turned me on to it. It was like he said, 'Here, you do it. I can't.' So he never put me down for listening to it. He turned my sister and me onto it.

"But he also turned us on to jazz. He said, 'This is where your roots are.' And we know this and we're really grateful for it. We haven't forgotten about it. We don't miss jazz because we're still using it, even though we don't [currently] do any jazz tunes. We somehow incorporate a jazz feel into a song."

With her background, Natalie hardly grew up in a black ghetto facing the traumas of poverty. She had a privileged childhood in Los Angeles' affluent Hancock Park section in a large home with a private swimming pool. The famous and near-famous, including such superstars as Harry Belafonte and Ella Fitzgerald, often visited during those years. One of her childhood memories is watching Belafonte in the pool and having him playfully reach out and pull her into the water.

Her first brief experiences with show business came at age six. Her father had her and her sister Carole join him on stage for one song; Natalie also sang on a Christmas record with him. In Natalie's preteen years, her mother, Maria (once a band vocalist), started her on the piano, but she was taught Bach and Beethoven rather than jazz and boogie. When she was 11, she and actress Barbara McNair sang and acted with Nat in *I'm With You,* a stage play at the Los Angeles Greek Theatre. At 12, she formed a combo with the children of well-known conductor/arrangers Carmen Dragon and Nelson Riddle. The trio of Natalie, Daryl Dragon, and Skip Riddle performed "just for fun," she replied. "I never planned on being a singer back then." (Daryl went on to become the Captain in the Captain and Tennille.) (*See Captain and Tennille, The.*)

In her teens, at several private schools, she didn't do anything to further a performing career. She was interested in the pop favorites of those years: Janis Joplin ("Janis taught me to hold back"), Jefferson Airplane, Sly Stone, the Beatles, and Stevie Wonder. But she didn't dream of joining them; at the time, she mulled over the possibility of studying medicine or psychology. She told Leonard Feather: "You know, people think it's only natural that Nat's daughter should be a singer. This may be true in terms of heredity, but not in terms of desire. It was like a hobby to me, and I had other things on my mind."

After her father died of cancer in 1965, she had a period of profound emotional distress. His illness already had had an impact on her. At the time, she was attending a private high school on the U.S. East Coast. After a close friend was expelled from school, she told Ben Fong-Torres of *Rolling Stone* (June 6, 1977), she went through what, in retrospect, was "a nervous breakdown. And then, after my father died, I went through an incident, and my mother sent me to a psychologist. . . . It was something wrong—it was illegal at the time . . . it still is. I just wanted to do it to see if I could get away with it. It was traumatic for my mom. It embarrassed her, and so she said, 'Go see a doctor.' He just told her I was normal. I was just going through a typical effect of my father having just died."

The incident didn't involve drugs, she stressed, since she didn't smoke her first joint until she was 18. "I was a late bloomer in everything."

She regained control of her emotions, finished high school, and enrolled at the University of Massachusetts in 1968. Some blacks on campus avoided her at first, suspecting she was a rich snob, but by her sophomore year, Natalie had gained acceptance and became involved in black activist causes. She returned west in mid-1970 to spend her junior year at the University of Southern California, but found it too bland and unexciting. The next summer, she was back at the University of Massachusetts. Once there, she met a friend who was singing with a group called Black Magic (with mostly white members). The friend had a strep throat and asked Natalie to fill in. Her debut performance was July 4, 1971. The band got a regular weekend engagement at a local club,

mainly because of the Cole name. It didn't bother her too much then, since she still felt music was a sideline.

After completing a degree in sociology in 1972, she found the idea of a singing career increasingly appealing. She began playing as a solo artist on the eastern club circuit. The clubs, she said, "hired me strictly for my name. Anyone who has gone through that knows it is an insult, but it was a step."

An important milestone came in early 1973, when she acquired a manager. Word of her potential had reached agent Kevin Hunter in Montreal, Canada. It took a few months, but Natalie finally decided Hunter could help her career. They began to change her musical emphasis from hotel ballroom material toward stylings with more appeal to younger audiences. Another step came in October 1974, when Hunter helped bring about meetings between Natalie and the Chicago production team of Chuck Jackson and Marvin Yancy. (Natalie became Mrs. Yancy a few years later.) They provided her with new material, including some strongly R&B based songs that became the basis for her mid-1970s breakthroughs.

Hunter began to look for a recording agreement. At Natalie's urging, he avoided Capitol Records (her father's company) because she was afraid they might typecast her and make her sing her father's type of arrangements. As it happened, the other majors all passed on the new singer and Capitol, the last on the list, officially signed her to a long-term contract on June 10, 1975.

The material for her debut LP already had been laid down by then with all songs written and produced by Jackson and Yancy. Called *Inseparable,* it was issued on July 7, 1975. Her debut single, "This Will Be," was prereleased on June 30. Backed by a series of excellent concerts and considerable airplay, the album soon made both R&B and general pop charts and went on to earn Natalie her first gold record. The title song and "This Will Be" both became hit singles.

For her second album, Natalie co-wrote two songs with Jackson and Yancy, "Sophisticated Lady" and "Not Like Mine." That LP, *Natalie,* came out in May 1976 and was certified gold by the RIAA in July. She also had a best-selling single in "Sophisticated Lady." She was acclaimed in concerts at home and abroad, including a 15-day tour of Japan where she was the top award winner in the Fifth Tokyo Music Festival International Contest.

By then, she already had received two other prestigious trophies during the telecast of the Grammy Awards on February 26, 1976. She was voted the Best New Artist of the Year and also won Best R&B Vocal Performance, Female, for "This Will Be." She was to win a third Grammy a year later (Best

R&B Vocal Performance, Female) for "Sophisticated Lady." Though not a winner, she was a finalist in the voting for Best Pop Vocal Performance, Female for *Natalie*.

She opened in 1977 with a charted single, "I've Got Love On My Mind," from her new album, *Unpredictable*, which included two songs she wrote herself. The album became her biggest hit to that point, rising to number one on soul charts and the top 10 in the pop lists. "I've Got Love On My Mind" made number one on soul lists and five on the pop charts, earning a gold record. During 1977, the RIAA certified the album platinum. Another hit single from the album was "Party Lights." At year-end, she was nominated for a Grammy in the Best R&B Vocal Performance category.

For part of 1977, Natalie was on tour while pregnant with her first child, Robert Adam Yancy. During November 1977, Capitol issued her fourth LP, *Thankful*, which also went on to be certified platinum. From it came her second gold single, "Our Love," and such other soul hits as "Be Thankful" (written by Cole) and "Annie Mae."

On April 27, 1978, Natalie hosted her first network TV special, "The Natalie Cole Special," on CBS. Joining her were Earth, Wind & Fire, Johnny Mathis, and Stephen Bishop. In June of that year, her first live LP, *Natalie . . . Live!*, came out on Capitol. It quickly made top levels of both soul and pop charts as did the first single from the LP, her version of the Beatles' "Lucy in the Sky with Diamonds." Among other honors that came her way that year was selection as Female Vocalist of the Year at the Eleventh Annual Image Awards.

As for her studio recordings, she told England's *Record Mirror* in early 1978, she usually did her own backup vocals, listed as the 'N' Sisters and the Colettes on the jacket. She said: "The Colettes sing the sweet backups and the 'N' Sisters the funky stuff. When I was a kid, my father gave me a tape recorder and I liked to use that kind of equipment after that.

"You can only record one voice at a time on a tape recorder. So now I have fun layering up all the backups. I do them all with a rough lead voice on top. When you sing back against yourself, I feel a kind of depth I don't get otherwise."

Natalie's career continued in high gear as the 1970s came to a close. She was a presenter at both the American Music Awards (where she had nominations for Best Female Artist and Best Soul Single for "Our Love") and the 1979 Grammy telecasts. She also taped a two-hour TV special for NBC, "Uptown—A Musical Comedy History of Harlem's Apollo Theater," which she co-hosted with Ben Vereen, Flip Wilson, and Lou Rawls. (*See Rawls, Lou.*) As part of her contribution she also gave a short monologue about her father, preceding a series of film clips of one of his Apollo performances.

In February 1979, she was given her own star on the Hollywood Walk of Fame and went from those ceremonies to appear on Johnny Carson's "Tonight Show." The next month, her sixth Capitol LP, *I Love You So*, was issued and quickly gained a sixth straight gold-record award for her. The initial single from the album, "Stand By," also was on the charts in the spring. Late in the year, she shared best-selling honors with another Capitol artist, Peabo Bryson, for their duet LP *We're the Best of Friends*. Hit singles from the LP were "Gimme Some Time" and "What You Won't Do for Love." During the early 1980s, the two showcased their talents in a series of memorable concerts across the U.S.

She opened the next decade with the album *Don't Look Back*. Released in May 1980, it contained more of her original contributions than past albums. She and Marvin Yancy wrote or co-wrote essentially all the material. She commented: "Though I've been writing lyrics for several years now, I'm now a lot less paranoid about putting my deepest feelings down on paper for the world to see, and Marvin and I have found we can write incredibly well together. He comes up with great music and it's just perfect."

The album made the charts for some months, but did not quite match earlier recordings in content. It fell short of the new beginnings Natalie had aimed for, and also failed to match previous releases commercially. For her September 1981 album, *Happy Love*, a new producer, George Tobin, was brought in. Sadly, it was the least rewarding album she had turned out, though her voice remained one of the most effective instruments in pop music.

By the early 1980s, Cole had to face up to the fact that she had an increasingly severe drug problem. On occasion, as she told Dennis Hunt of the *Los Angeles Times* in a 1987 interview, she had taken a 30-day "cure." But, she acknowledged, "That was a joke. After all the drugs I'd been doing, stopping for 30 days didn't mean a thing."

Finally, in November 1983, she turned her affairs over to her mother and entered a drug rehabilitation center in Minnesota. Though her marriage came apart and ended in divorce, her six-month stay at the Minnesota center did seem to work—she told Hunt she had been drug-free since then. She picked up her career with a recording contract with Modern Records that didn't work out well, but had better luck when she signed with EMI's Manhattan label. Her 1987 Manhattan LP, *Everlasting*, contained three hit singles, "Jump Start," "I Live For Your Love," and a remake of Bruce Springsteen's "Pink Cadillac."

COLLINS, PHIL: *See Genesis.*

COLLINS, WILLIAM "BOOTSY": *See Clinton, George.*

COODER, RY: *Guitarist, singer, banjoist, mandolinist, songwriter. Born Los Angeles, California, March 15, 1947.*

Restless and innovative, with almost unlimited musical curiosity, Ry Cooder always seemed to be exploring a different area of music with every new recording or concert series. One moment, he was playing avant garde rock; the next, roots blues; then country western, even jazz. For those who kept pace with him, he illuminated overlooked musical genres with striking results, but his refusal to be typecast tended to put off many members of the musical establishment. Though highly regarded by his musical peers (after his debut solo album came out in 1970, *Rolling Stone* called him "the finest, most precise bottleneck guitar player alive today, as well as the reviver of the lost art of blues mandolin"), his following remained a musical minority for most of his career.

Born and raised in Southern California, he received his first guitar at age three—a Sears Silvertone tenor four-string. After a while, he tried to play along with artists on his parents' folk records. "They bought me a Josh White album when I was eight. That was the first blues I ever heard. I learned all his runs, spent hours with him." His father bought the ten-year-old a six-string Martin guitar and tried to set up a series of lessons, but young Ry didn't like the teacher's instructions and dropped out.

Ry returned to self-teaching until, at 13, he became enthralled with some country-folk records that impelled him to find a teacher of Appalachian finger picking. This led him to what was the center of folk music in Los Angeles, the Ash Grove. As noted in his biographical material for Warner Brothers Records: "Whenever there was a pretty good player [at the Ash Grove], I'd sit in the front row and watch. If someone like [Reverend] Gary Davis was in town, I'd talk to him, go where he was staying, give him $5, and get him to play as much as he could while I watched. About a month later, I'd find that I'd start to remember how he did things.

"They used to have party nights at the Ash Grove, when people would get up out of the audience and play. And it seemed like when I was 16 I was good enough and somebody said 'Get up! Get up!' and

they pushed me on stage. I got up and was so scared I was petrified. I played and sweated and people laughed and clapped." He began to play more often at the club, which led to his forming a folk-blues act in 1963 with Jackie DeShannon. (*See Carnes, Kim.*) However, it proved a failure.

Meanwhile, Ry was expanding his musical skills, learning the banjo and the traditional bottleneck style of blues guitar playing whereby he used a three-inch neck from a bottle on his little finger to produce a ringing, sliding tone. To perfect his technique, Ry spent hours listening to records by Mississippi Delta blues bottleneck experts, playing them over and over until he was satisfied he had mastered every inflection.

"Sometime around 1964 or 1965, Taj Mahal showed up in Los Angeles. He was real raggedy and I was raggedy, so we got together and went to the Teenage Fair in Hollywood and sat in a booth for Martin Guitars and just played Delta blues. It was hard and it was good." The two started a rock group called the Rising Sons. The band was supposed to record an album for Columbia, but it was never completed. The band broke up and Taj and Cooder went separate ways.

Ry's next affiliation was with performer-songwriter Don Van Vliet, better known as Captain Beefheart. (*See Captain Beefheart.*) On the surface, it seemed an unlikely alliance—the Zappa-ish Beefheart and the folk-oriented Cooder. However, Cooder, always interested in new musical forms, proved an excellent session man for Beefheart's first LP. Ry even arranged its songs "I've Grown So Ugly" and "Rolling and Tumbling." From session work, including some with Paul Revere and the Raiders, he got an assignment in England working on the score for the film *Candy*. While there, he did some backing work for the Rolling Stones' *Let It Bleed* album, though only his mandolin playing on "Love in Vain" remained in the final product.

Back in the U.S., he did a number of other session jobs and, with the help of friends Van Dyke Parks and Lenny Waronker, finally gained a solo record contract from Warner/Reprise in 1969. The two of them co-produced that debut LP, *Ry Cooder*, which came out in October 1970 to well-deserved critical acclaim. In that collection, Ry demonstrated his superb fingerpicking skills on "Police Dog Blues." Also presented were songs such as "Alimony" and "How Can A Poor Man Stand Such Times and Live," a fiddle tune by country musician Blind Alfred Reed.

Cooder was paired with Captain Beefheart's Magic Band in a 1971 cross-country concert tour in support of their new albums. The concerts produced a lot of publicity, but not much buyer response to Cooder's LP. Things changed for the better in that regard with his second release, *Into the Purple Valley*, which made the pop charts in 1972. It was even more strongly received overseas, particularly in Holland, where it earned a gold-record award. Cooder played mandolin and bottleneck to good effect on such traditional numbers as "How Can You Keep on Moving" and "Billy the Kid." Other tracks included Leadbelly's "On a Monday" and a mid-1940s commentary, "F.D.R. in Trinidad."

Cooder continued to examine different aspects of American history in his 1973 album, *Boomer's Story*, with "Rally 'Round the Flag" and "President Kennedy." On "Maria Elena," he demonstrated his ability to play classical-style guitar. On his next LP, *Paradise and Lunch*, Cooder turned his hat around to emphasize gospel music. However, there were other kinds of music included, ranging from an upbeat "Ditty Wa Ditty" (with jazz pianist Earl "Fatha" Hines) to such ballads as "Tattler" (co-written by Cooder) and a folk-flavored version of Burt Bacharach's "Mexican Divorce."

In the mid-1970s, Cooder traveled to two widely separate areas to study and work with important, but little publicized instrumentalists. In one direction, he sought out Hawaiian slack-key guitar expert Gabby Pahinui to learn his techniques and do some jamming with him. Besides introducing slack-key stylings into his own work, Ry also arranged for Warner/Reprise to release an album by Pahinui in the United States. At other times, Ry went east to Rustin, Texas, to examine the accordion skills of Flaco Jimenez. As with Pahinui, Cooder not only spent time playing impromptu sessions with Flaco, he also took instructions on duplicating Jimenez's style on the accordion.

Both these influences were incorporated in Cooder's fifth Reprise album, *Chicken Skin Music*. Slack-key was emphasized on such tracks as "Yellow Roses," "Chloe," and "Always Lift Him Up" (in some cases by Pahinui, in others by Ry) and Jimenez provided accordion backing on such tracks as "Stand By Me" and "He'll Have to Go" (an old Jim Reeves country hit).

In 1977, Cooder put together a show featuring a merging of Tex-Mex and gospel sounds with instrumental backing provided by Jimenez and four other Tex-Mex musicians plus vocal support from three black gospel singers. The entourage, called the Chicken Skin Revue, played around the United States and Europe. Again, he found greater attention overseas (especially in Germany and Holland) than at home. The tour spawned his sixth LP, the live LP *Show Time*, recorded in San Francisco.

His next LP, released in May 1978, departed completely from all his earlier offerings. Called *Jazz*, it stressed some of the early jazz material from the '20s and early '30s with particular emphasis on the work of Bix Beiderbecke. Other material derived from the stylings of guitarist Joseph Spence, whom Cooder visited in his native Bahamas. In 1979, Ry explored other aspects of jazz and pop in *Bop till You Drop*, which Warner Brothers said was the first commercial album to be digitally recorded. It proved his most popular LP to that time, staying on the charts into 1980 and selling some 850,000 copies.

In the 1980s, Cooder continued to demonstrate his multifaceted talents as recording artist, record producer, and composer of motion picture scores. His album credits included *Borderline* in 1980, *Slide Area* in 1982 and performing work on such notable soundtrack albums as *Alamo Bay* and *Paris, Texas*, in 1985. From 1979 into the mid-1980s, he also wrote music for *The Long Riders*, *The Border*, *Southern Comfort*, *Streets of Fire*, *Crossroads*, and *Blue City*. For *The Long Riders*, he won the Los Angeles Film Critics award for best score of 1980.

Ry's first solo album since *Slide Area*, *Get Rhythm*, was released by Warner Brothers in October 1987. That was his eleventh solo LP on the label. Besides scoring commercials (which had been a lucrative area for him for many years), he found time in 1987 to produce a soul album by two of his longtime backup singers, Bobby King and Terry Evans, for Rounder Records. Turning his attention to a whole new genre—children's stories—Ry provided the music while comic Robin Williams narrated *Pecos Bill* (Windham Hill, 1988).

In the 1980s, his music continued to contain strong blues emphasis. Asked by a reporter whether the blues might be passé for new fans, he replied: "I think the blues still speaks to kids today. It's so old that it's new. It has a picturesque energy that represents such an alien, mysterious environment that I think kids will be fascinated by it, no matter how much they actually know about the blues. It's like *Star Wars*— everyone wants to go somewhere they haven't been before."

COOKE, SAM: *Singer, songwriter. Born Chicago, Illinois, January 22, 1935; died Los Angeles, California, December 11, 1964.*

Before a bizarre shooting incident in a Los Angeles motel ended his life, Sam Cooke rose to the top levels of popular music as a graduate of the gospel circuit and pioneer soul singer. His success encouraged the steady move of young black rhythm & blues performers into positions of dominance in the popular field.

One of seven children of the Reverend Charles Cooke, Sam began singing gospel songs as a small boy in Chicago. He was a featured artist in the choir until his teens, when he became active with gospel groups that performed in churches and auditoriums around the country. He worked with the Soul Stirrers in the mid-1950s and later was lead singer of the Pilgrim Travellers, a group that also included Lou Rawls for a time. (*See Rawls, Lou.*)

In the late 1950s, Sam turned to the popular field with his father's somewhat reluctant approval. His move to the secular area was sparked by record producer/songwriter Bumps Blackwell, who was impressed by the potential he heard in Cooke's voice. The two first tried to interest Cooke's gospel label, Specialty, in pop. Failing that, Sam won a contract from Keen Records. Cooke's third single on Keen, "You Send Me" (a song he had written), became one of the top hits worldwide in late 1957 and early 1958, selling over two million copies. It was Sam's only number one Billboard hit (December 2 and 9, 1957), but he placed 16 more in the top 20 through 1965.

Before he was signed by RCA Records, he had three more top 20 singles on Keen: "I'll Come Running Back to You" (1957), "For Sentimental Reasons" (1958), and "Wonderful World" (1960). His RCA hits spanned "Chain Gang" (1960); "Cupid" (1961); "Twistin' the Night Away," (1962); "Having a Party," "Bring It on Home to Me," and "Nothing Can Change This Love" (1962); "Send Me Some Lovin'," "Another Saturday Night," "Frankie and Johnny," and "Little Red Rooster" (1963); "Good News" and "Good Times" (1964); and the posthumous "Shake" (1965).

Strangely, despite his enormous recording success, Cooke's live appearances were primarily in small black clubs or theaters on the so-called "chitlin' circuit." His one-time manager, Allen Klein, told Robert Hilburn (*Los Angeles Times*, February 16, 1986), that it had been caused by the psychological impact of a disastrous performance at New York's Copacabana in 1958. "Sam was just destroyed at the Copa. He just was not prepared. He tried to go on with this 'white' act with a cane and a top hat, doing songs like 'Mona Lisa' and 'Hey There.' Remember, the only pop songs he had at the time were 'You Send Me' and 'For Sentimental Reasons.'"

Following that shock came trauma from the loss of a close friend and then his first wife in car accidents. "With this tragedy," Klein told Hilburn, "the rejection from the white clubs and financial frustrations with Keen Records, Sam just withdrew. That's why you'll find from '59 on, he just played Henry Wynn's chitlin' circuit with people like Jackie Wilson and James Brown. He continued to make records, but he often didn't even do most of those

songs on the shows. It was two different worlds."

Had he lived, that might have changed. For one thing, successful crossover artists from Motown widened opportunities for black artists with other racial groups. For another, a tour of England with Little Richard in 1962, where predominantly white audiences greeted him with enthusiasm, made him begin to savor the possibilities of winning similar acclaim back home. In fact, he made a successful return to the Copa that formed the basis for the RCA live LP, *At the Copa* (ironically issued the month he was killed). The exact details of how he died were still unclear decades after the event. At the time, it was reported that he was shot three times by the manager of the Hacienda Motel, Mrs. Bertha Franklin, when he allegedly was pursuing a woman friend who had taken refuge in the motel office with most of his clothes. The shooting later was ruled to have been done in self-defense by the coroner's jury. His family (a second wife and two children) didn't want additional publicity at the time. Klein later maintained that certain facts of the incident didn't come out because of a desire to avoid pain to the children.

After Sam's death, his name didn't disappear from the record catalogues. Many of his old recordings sold well and RCA added numerous new albums, some reissues of previously released material and some material that had not been issued. The posthumous credits included *Shake* (March 1965), *Best of Sam Cooke, Volume 2* (August 1965), *Try a Little Love* (December 1965), *Unforgettable Sam Cooke* (May 1966), the two-disc *This Is Sam Cooke* (September 1970), and, on RCA's Camden label, *Sam Cooke* (October 1970). Some of Cooke's early material was included on *Two Sides of Sam Cooke*, released in the early 1970s by Specialty Records. Other Specialty LPs available in the early 1970s included *Ain't That Good News* (originally issued in 1964), *The Gospel Soul of Sam Cooke, The Gospel Soul of Sam Cooke, Volume 2*, and *That's Heaven in Me*. He also was represented on Trip Records with *The Golden Sound of Sam Cooke* and *Sixteen Greatest Hits*.

As the 1970s went by, interest in Cooke died down, although new reissues came out occasionally, such as RCA's *You Send Me* in 1975. In the mid-1980s there was a revival of attention to his importance in the evolution of pop music with release of albums such as RCA's *Sam Cooke Live at the Harlem Square Club 1963* (1985) and *Sam Cooke: The Man and His Music* (February 1986). (*See Womack, Bobby.*)

COOLIDGE, RITA: *Singer, pianist, band leader. Born Nashville, Tennessee, 1944.*

With a background ranging from blues and R&B

to country music, Rita Coolidge was well adjusted to the complex musical scene of the early 1970s, which knew no artificial boundaries between one previously "specialized" category and another. Her vocal talent brought her up through the ranks of backup singers at recording sessions to the threshold of superstar ranks by 1971, a pinnacle she never quite achieved.

Rita's heritage included a mixture of Cherokee Indian and southern white blood. Her father was a Baptist minister and his children often sang in the church choir. All the children in the family were interested in music from their early years, following the country songs and, later, rhythm & blues in their home city of Nashville and, subsequently, in Memphis. By the time Rita was in her teens, Memphis had become a center of the rhythm & blues upsurge in the mass market paced by such artists of the Stax-Volt Record firm as Booker T and the M.G.s and Otis Redding. (*See Booker T and the M.G.s; Redding, Otis.*)

Rita and her sister Priscilla performed in shows in grade school and sang with small bands at high school dances. Priscilla started gaining professional work that brought her in contact with Booker T; they married and scored a number of chart albums. Rita learned much about R&B and rock from Booker T, who introduced her to both established and up-and-coming stars.

In the late 1960s, this led to a friendship with Delaney and Bonnie Bramlett, who were then on the Stax label. The Bramletts liked Rita's singing style and added her to their act for several national tours. She began to gain a first-rank reputation with other artists. Leon Russell even wrote his hit song "Delta Lady" as a tribute to Rita. (*See Cocker, Joe; and Russell, Leon.*)

In the famed Russell–Joe Cocker "Mad Dogs and Englishmen" act that toured the U.S. and Europe in 1970, Rita was a featured performer, receiving a standing ovation on many occasions for her delivery of the Delaney-Bramlett–Leon Russell composition "Superstar."

Before and after the "Mad Dogs" tour, she was in demand for major album work as a backup vocalist and, in some cases, as a pianist. Among the sessions she worked on were Eric Clapton's first solo album, Boz Scaggs' hit LP *Moments*, and Graham Nash's top-selling *Songs for Beginners*.

Late in 1970, Rita was signed by A&M Records as a vocalist. Her debut album, *Rita Coolidge*, was released in 1971. Testifying to the music field's regard for Rita is the list of superstars who sat in: Leon Russell, Steve Stills, Graham Nash, Clarence White of the Byrds, and Booker T. (*See Byrds, The; Clapton, Eric; Scaggs, Boz; Stills, Stephen.*)

During 1971 and 1972, Rita made the charts with two more A&M albums: *Nice Feelin'* and *The Lady's Not for Sale*. Her marriage to Kris Kristofferson began a new phase in her career as the two toured together and recorded a number of duets in the middle and late 1970s before they separated at the end of the decade. Rita and Kris won two Grammy Awards for Best Vocal Performance by a Duo, one in 1973 for "From the Bottle to the Bottom" and the other in 1975 for a remake of Clyde McPhatter's "Lover Please." (*See Kristofferson, Kris.*)

Rita's A&M album credits included *Fall into Spring* (1974), *It's Only Love* (1975), *Anytime Anywhere* (1977), *Love Me Again* (1978), *Satisfied* (1979), *Heartbreak Radio* (1981), and *Greatest Hits* (1981).

COOPER, ALICE: *Vocal and instrumental group; singer, songwriter, band leader. Band members, first half of 1970s: Alice Cooper, born Detroit, Michigan, February 4, 1948; Dennis Dunaway, born Cottage Grove, Oregon, December 9, 1948; Neal Smith, born Akron, Ohio, September 23, 1947; Glen Buxton, born Akron, Ohio, November 10, 1947; Michael Bruce. Group disbanded in 1975 with Alice Cooper continuing as solo performer.*

A group named after a man who initially performed in drag that tosses odd-looking toys around the proscenium and plays hyperamplified hard rock would by any standard be unusual. Until the early 1970s, even in the increasingly wide-open society of the young, such an organization would have been too bizarre for the public to accept. In fact, it was just this antipathy that at first slowed down Alice Cooper's progress toward the spotlight. The change in mores that allowed the group to come to the fore also led observers to conclude in surprise that the group, no matter what its personal proclivities, ranked with the best rock groups of the period.

Nonetheless, early onlookers were more occupied with the group's antics than its music. Dressed in multicolored unisex clothes, the man named Alice would do strange things as the set continued. He would grab a broom and prance around the stage like a witch; take a hammer and, after a mock war dance, splatter a watermelon all over the place; or untie a bag and let loose a live chicken or several pigeons. The rest of the band got into the act too, tearing up pillows and scattering feathers all over the audience or blowing up inflatable toys and throwing them at each other. The effect on the audience was unpredictable. Some enjoyed it; others sat there seemingly afraid and transfixed. Early in the group's career, more than a few audiences walked out en masse.

The organized chaos eventually served its purpose, garnering enough notoriety for the group to become a major attraction. This accomplished, they gradually cut back on the antics to emphasize music. And, as the charts showed in 1971, its music could stand on its own with record buyers. Critics had few unkind words to say about Alice Cooper by mid-1971. Reviewing their concert in the Long Beach auditorium, July 11, 1971, *Los Angeles Times* writer John Mendelsohn stated: "Each of the Coopers' songs was a more emphatic knockout than its predecessor. 'Sun Arise' and their two indisputably superb hit singles, 'Caught in a Dream' and 'Eighteen,' were utterly smashing musically. 'The Ballad of Dwight Fry,' the last half of which saw Alice singing in a straight-jacket, was a simply unforgettable theatrical spectacle."

The road to such encomiums began in Phoenix, where all the members of the group grew up. They all were from comfortable homes and were close friends in high school. All had creative interests in music and art and often got together to paint, play their instruments, and sing or just watch TV. The 16-year-old Cooper, a minister's son (real name Vincent Damon Furnier), was the prime mover. He told Mark Price (*The Fayetteville Times*, Arkansas, "People" section, December 16, 1986): "I had a choice of being the box boy at the local supermarket, working at the car wash, or joining a band. I discovered after the Beatles came along that girls loved the boys in the band, so a band it was." In 1965, the boys worked up an act with Alice Cooper on lead vocals and harmonica; Glen Buxton on lead guitar; Michael Bruce on guitar, piano, and organ; Dennis Dunaway on bass; and Neal Smith on percussion.

They were truly children of their age for, as Alice told a reporter from the *Berkeley Barb* in 1970, the main influence on the band was television. "We didn't have a blues influence. The music that affected us was the saucy theme songs, like on '77 Sunset Strip' and 'Bourbon Street Beat.' 'The Thin Man'—hip stuff, cool jazz. That was the kind of thing that was going on when we were watching TV. . . .

"Our conditioning has been television, our conditioning has been the space age, so that's the kind of music we're going to play. We're not going to play Delta blues. I couldn't care less about how many times his baby left him.

"We were upper middle class suburban brats that had anything we wanted. We never had a blues. The whole end is that we are what we are now—a living social criticism."

The group worked their way west in the late 1960s, finally settling down in the Los Angeles area. They found work at local clubs, leading up to an engagement at the Cheetah, where an audience's walkout caused a strangely reverse effect on the man who was to become their manager, Shep Gordon. "I knew I had to manage them after that. They exhibited the strongest negative force I'd ever seen." Gordon recognized their musical ability and accepted Cooper's method of using sexual aberrations to "break the conditioning of the audience. People feel threatened by the sexual thing."

Under Gordon's direction, things started to accelerate for the group. They were signed by Frank Zappa's Straight Records and began to gain engagements all over the U.S. The early response certainly remained strongly negative. In Michigan, a motorcycle gang tried to rush the stage, voicing threats to murder the band members.

Slowly the agitation quieted down. By late 1970, the group was starting to be accepted for its music rather than be rejected for its appearance. Tickets to Alice's concerts became increasingly difficult to obtain and people who attended them stayed to the last note. In early 1971, the group's records began to show up on the hit charts with regularity. (Distribution of the records was under the Warner Brothers label.) The album *Love It to Death* rose into the top 20 by summer. Their single "Eighteen" moved to the top 10 nationally in April as did the single "Caught in a Dream" in midsummer.

Late in 1971, Alice Cooper placed two new hits on the charts, the single "Under My Wheels" and the LP *Killer*. The band, which had begun as something of a novelty group, showed steady improvement with each new LP until it could lay claim to being one of the better rock bands on the concert circuit. Subsequent albums included *School's Out* in 1972 (whose title song became a hit single), *Billion Dollar Babies* (1973), and *Muscle of Love*. *Killer*, *School's Out*, and *Billion Dollar Babies* won gold records.

In 1975, during a period of acrimonious discussions between Cooper and his record company, he decided to break up the group, a move anticipated by Warner Brothers in 1974 with the retrospective LP *Alice Cooper's Greatest Hits*. He recalled for reporter Marc Shapiro of an Illinois magazine in September 1986, "I basically had a lot of problems with Warner Brothers. First they were afraid that theatrical heavy metal was drying up so they weren't as thrilled about promoting the band as they used to be. But they sure got excited when I told them I wanted to record solo albums under the name Alice Cooper. They wanted Alice Cooper to be a name and not just a person. At that point a bunch of lawyers with briefcases started getting into it."

Cooper then had his name legally changed to Alice Cooper and signed with Atlantic for a solo LP,

Welcome to My Nightmare, which spawned the hit single "Only Women Bleed." Hardly had that happened when he made up with Warner Brothers and rejoined the label. He continued to record new albums for the company over the next eight years, using session musicians rather than a full-time band. From time to time, he went back to the concert circuit with various rosters of performers. During those years, though, he tended to become a "personality," guesting on many interview shows and gracing TV screens as a game-show celebrity on such programs as "Hollywood Squares."

Cooper's solo albums on Warner Brothers were: *Alice Cooper Goes to Hell* (1976), *Lace and Whiskey* (1977), *The Alice Cooper Show* (1977), *From the Inside* (1978), *Flush the Fashion* (1980), *Special Force* (1981), and *Da-Da* (1983). After a hiatus of several years from recording, he signed with a new label, MCA, which issued his label debut album, *Constrictor*, in 1986, and followed with *Raise Your Fist and Yell*, issued in 1987. The latter album was backed with Cooper's most ambitious tour in years called "The Nightmare Returns." Backing him was a new band: Kane Roberts on lead guitar, Devlin 7 on guitar, Kip Winger III on bass, Paul Horowitz on keyboards and Ken Mary on drums.

COSTELLO, ELVIS: *Singer, guitarist, band leader (THE ATTRACTIONS), songwriter. Born London, England, 1955.*

He was arrayed in nondescript blue jeans and an old-style suit jacket, his head seeming a bit large for his slightly built body, affecting an odd pigeon-toed gait as he walked across the stage while tuning his electric guitar at a 1980s concert. All in all, Elvis Costello conveyed something less than the dynamic image of a true rock eminence. With his large horn-rimmed glasses, he looked like a bookworm who had accidentally stumbled on a musical instrument he didn't quite know how to handle. But once he started playing and became engrossed in his own special brand of song, you forgot first impressions and, as you tapped out the tempos with feet or hands, realized that surprising gifts can come in plain wrappings.

Costello typically projected a contradictory or elusive image. With his unassuming choice of clothes, close-cropped hair, and the employment of "Elvis" as an assumed first name, he could have passed as a throwback to the early 1950s. And his original compositions were much simpler in structure than most rock of the late 1970s and the 1980s. At the same time, the material had a modern sound; it didn't seem archaic at all. Outwardly, Costello seemed soft and mild-mannered, but when he talked about the music world, he was blunt and outspoken, mincing no words in his contempt of the field's shortcomings and his strong belief in his own talents. He conveyed a feeling of frustration and bitterness about the uphill fight required before he broke through, and peppered his speech with plenty of censorable epithets. But his songs, taken as a whole, presented the picture of a caring and sensitive artist—often reflecting anger and cynicism, but other times offering tenderness, insight, and humor—both gentle and sardonic.

His songs are a far cry from punk rock, yet he always was a revolutionary in his own way, inveighing in his lyrics not only against many of the evils and injustices of the world, but also on occasion against the increasing remoteness of modern rock from the average person. He told Allan Jones of *Melody Maker* in the late 1970s: "There's a lot of rock music that's become exclusive and it's of no use to anyone. Least of all me. Music has to get to people. In the heart, in the head, I don't care where, so long as it fucking gets them!"

His dictum was that good songs, in a rock context or otherwise, should have recognizable melodies and be relatively short. "I hate hard-rock bands. I hate anything with fucking extended solos or bands that are concerned with any kind of instrumental virtuosity. I can listen to maybe 15 seconds of someone like the Crusaders, say, before I get bored. I know how good they are because everyone keeps telling me how . . . marvelous they are, but I get bored."

Costello was born Declan Patrick McManus, the son of Ross McManus, a big band singer and solo performer. Costello spent his childhood in London, where most of his education was in Catholic schools, but after his father left the family, he moved to Liverpool with his mother for his last two years of secondary school, the English equivalent of U.S. high school.

He told Greil Marcus for a 1982 cover story in *Rolling Stone:* "I graduated from secondary school in 1973. It was the first year of 1 million unemployed in England in recent times—in Liverpool, anywhere up North, it was worse. I was very lucky to get a job. I had no ambition to go into further education; I just went out and got the first job I could get. I went along to be a chart corrector, tea boy, clerk—because I wasn't really qualified for anything. I got a job as a computer operator, which turned out to be comparatively well paid: about 20 pounds a week. I'd just put the tapes on the machines and feed cards in, line up printing machines—all the manual work the computer itself doesn't have arms to do.

"I had something of an ambition to be a professional musician. I was already playing guitar in high school—playing in folk clubs on my own. I was writing my own songs—dreadful songs, performing them more or less religiously. I didn't think the songs were worth recording—but the only way you get better is to play what you write. Then you have the humiliation of being crushed—if they're obviously insubstantial. If you don't put them over, you quickly learn from experience.''

Some of the early records he played at home, he recalled, were promotional discs sent to his father. As he became more interested in pop music in the early 1960s, he told Marcus, "I was into singles, whatever was on the radio—the Kings, the Who, Motown. It was exciting. . . . I was in the Beatles fan club when I was eleven.'' His tastes, by the late 1960s, had focused on soul artists such as Marvin Gaye and Otis Redding.

In the early 1970s, Costello was working as a computer operator during the day and picking up whatever work as a musician he could find in Liverpool clubs. His efforts brought him in contact with some established rock artists, including Nick Lowe, who later helped him make his first professional recordings. (*See Lowe, Nick.*) That 1974 meeting helped in Costello's decision to move to London during the year to be closer to the center of England's music industry.

In London, Costello earned most of his income from his computer job, while continuing his efforts to find his way in music. For a while, he had a small pub rock band, which he finally decided "trapped me in mediocrity." So he dropped the group and concentrated on whatever solo work he could find while writing and rewriting dozens of new songs.

That period coincided with the rise of punk rock in England, but Costello had little opportunity to observe the new punk performers in action. He told Marcus: "I was working—I didn't have the money to go down to the Roxy and see what the bands were doing: the Clash, the Pistols. I just read about them in *Melody Maker* and the *NME* the same as anyone else. Joe Public. I was living in the suburbs of London. I couldn't afford to go to clubs uptown. . . . I was married with a son. [He and that wife later separated.] I couldn't take the day off. I took enough time playing sick, taking sick time off of my job just to make [the debut album] *My Aim Is True.*''

In 1975, he began making demonstration tapes of his material, which he tried to bring to the attention of record-company officials. He received turndown after turndown until he finally placed a tape in the hands of Jake Riviera and Dave Robinson at West London–based Stiff Records in August 1976. (Robinson then managed rising rock star Graham Parker.) Both immediately felt Costello was a unique talent and signed him to the label.

He told *Melody Maker:* "There was no phenomenal advance. They bought me an amp and a tape recorder. . . . I don't want any charity. I want to be out gigging, I don't want anything for nothing. I'm not askin' anyone for their f——— charity.''

His experience prior to that hadn't made him a fan of the industry. He told Allan Jones: "Like, I went around for nearly a year with demo tapes before I came to Stiff, and it was always the same response. 'We can't hear the words.' 'It isn't commercial enough.' 'There aren't any singles.' Idiots. Those tapes were just voice and guitar memos. I didn't have enough money to do anything with a band. It was just a lack of imagination on the part of those people at the record companies. I felt as if I was bashing my head against a brick wall, those people just weren't prepared to listen to the songs.

"It's a terrible position to be in. You start thinking you're mad. You listen to the radio and you watch the TV and you hear a lot of f——— rubbish. You very rarely turn on the radio or TV and hear anything exciting, right? And, all the time, you know that you're capable of producing something infinitely better.

"But I never lost faith. I'm convinced in my own talent, yeah. Like I said, I wasn't going up to these people meekly and saying, 'Look, with your help and a bit of polishing up, and with all your expertise and knowledge of the world of music we might have a moderate success on our hands,' I was going in thinking, 'You're a bunch of f——— idiots who don't know what you're doing. I'm bringing you a lot of good songs, why don't you go ahead and f—— —— well record them.' They didn't seem to understand that kind of approach."

Nick Lowe was assigned as producer for Costello's first sessions. It was an exhilarating experience, Costello agreed, that inspired a flurry of songwriting activity on his part. Among the songs he wrote in 1977 were "Welcome to the Working Week,'' "Red Shoes,'' "Miracle Man,'' "Alison,'' "Sneaky Feeling,'' "Waiting for the End of the World,'' and "I'm Not Angry.'' "Less Than Zero,'' an impassioned indictment of the British fascist movement, became his first single release. He commented to Marcus: "They're [the fascists] really sick people. If there wasn't a danger that some people of limited intelligence would take them seriously, they'd be sad and you could feel sorry for them. But you can't.'' His other initial singles on Stiff included "Alison,'' which (like many of his songs) dealt with love and betrayal, and "Watching the Detectives.''

His debut album, *My Aim Is True* (the title coming from a line in "Alison'') came out in the summer of 1977 and quickly won attention from English critics, despite his label's limited resources at the time. Rumors of his ability began to filter across the Atlantic by late summer, but it was not until late in the year that an American label, Columbia, released the LP and Costello came over to make a few appearances in support of the disc as an opening act at various clubs. He had been backed on his album by an expatriate U.S. group called Clover, so he assembled a new backing trio called the Attractions for the U.S. dates. He earned the anger of some music writers for his insistence on avoiding interviews and keeping out of the limelight offstage, a stance that reflected his opposition to many of the conventional techniques of the music industry.

Some critics objected to his appropriation of the name Elvis, though later almost all agreed he was a worthy successor to the King of Rock. It wasn't his idea, though, he told *Rolling Stone*. "I hadn't picked the name' at all. Jake [Riviera] just picked it. It was just a marketing scheme. 'How are we going to separate you from Johnny This and Johnny That?' He said, 'We'll call you Elvis.' I thought he was completely out of his mind."

With the support of a major label (augmented, of course, by a continuing output of listenable and well-crafted original recordings), Costello's star began to rise. His second album, *This Year's Model* (1978), was as good or better than the debut LP and it proceeded to earn Costello his first gold-record certification from the RIAA. Before the year was out, he had another LP on the charts, *Armed Forces* (originally titled *Emotional Fascism),* his most impressive collection to that point. While those came out on Columbia, he and Riviera changed labels in the U.K., switching to Radar Records in the late 1970s. (In the early 1980s, they changed again to the F-Beat label in the U.K. while staying with Columbia Records in the U.S.)

The outlook seemed bright as the 1970s drew to a close, but Costello's reputation took a setback because of some alleged racial comments made in an argument between Elvis and Bonnie Bramlett plus several members of Stephen Stills' band after a 1979 concert in Columbus, Ohio. *(See Stills, Stephen.)* The Americans claimed no English artist could ever match the emotional depth of U.S. black performers and Costello silenced them with what sounded like a remark a Klansman would make. According to press reports, he called Ray Charles "a blind, ignorant nigger" and made similar disparaging remarks about James Brown, after which Bonnie Bramlett reportedly knocked him down, injuring her hand in the process. The story made headlines and brought profound apologies from Costello.

He told Robert Palmer of *The New York Times* (June 27, 1982): "Obviously, that was the most horrific incident of my whole career, and I've never been able to sit down in an unemotional atmosphere and say I'm very sorry. It was a drunken brawl, and I

wanted to say whatever would outrage those people the most, but that's no excuse. A lot of people were very angry, and rightfully so. Those words I used certainly don't represent my view of the world. I had always just assumed that people would recognize my allegiance to R&B, to black music, but it wasn't obvious enough. I suppose if you allow uncontrolled anger to run away with you, and if you make a career of contriving anger, up on stage, whether you're feeling anger or not, sooner or later you'll find yourself saying some things, using words you don't mean. It'll all come back at you. But I don't want to sound like I'm making excuses. There aren't any excuses for saying things like that.''

One result was the suspending of any U.S. tour efforts until 1981. He told Greil Marcus *(Rolling Stone,* September 1982), "The minute the story was published nationally, records were taken off playlists. About 120 death threats—or threats of violence of some kind. I had armed bodyguards for the last part of that tour.'' Elvis also noted to Palmer that the incident "colored everything I've done since. The next album I made after that, *Get Happy!* [issued in late 1979 on Columbia], I set out, subconsciously at least, to make a soul record. Not just in terms of style, but a record that was warmer, more emotional. And I think all the records I've made since then are more directly emotional, more personal. I've been trying to cut back on the clever wordplay and write songs with more heart.''

Get Happy!, though, was not up to the quality of his earlier albums. His 1980 album, *Taking Liberties,* was not composed of new material, but of songs (many well above average) previously issued as B sides on singles or issued only in the U.K. Both that album and *Get Happy!* were on U.S. charts for a number of months, but fell far short of best-seller status.

In 1981, Elvis was represented by two new albums, *Trust* and *Almost Blue* (a resurrection of vintage country songs). They were interesting, but not among his best efforts. Charted singles from them included "Clubland" and "Watch Your Step" from *Trust* and a remake of George Jones' "A Good Year for the Roses" from *Almost Blue*. By 1982, Elvis had completely recovered his balance as indicated by *Imperial Bedroom*. It met his original high standards and eventually brought another gold-record award from the RIAA.

By the mid-1980s, Costello had succeeded in accumulating a respectable, if not immense, corps of fans who valued his creative integrity and consistent efforts at musical experimentation—within the self-imposed limits of short, melodic song formats. His albums always made U.S. and U.K. charts, though not achieving sales levels threatening those attained by artists such as the Police or Michael Jackson. His releases during those years comprised *Punch the Clock* (1983), *Goodbye Cruel World* (1984), *Best of Elvis Costello and the Attractions* (1985), *King of America* (1986), and *Blood and Chocolate* (1986).

Costello once more raised media hackles during his 1986 tour in support of *Blood and Chocolate*, when he barred all press photographers from the concerts. It seemed like overkill since, as one public relations expert noted: ''Anyone with a $50 Brownie can take a photo from the eighth row.'' As might be expected, photos were obtained in spite of the prohibitions, although it might have been a publicity ploy in itself since it won Costello widespread news coverage.

The concert structure itself, though, was unique. In each city visited, it comprised a series of five shows in small venues, each one different from the other. Costello employed two different bands—the Attractions and the Confederates—and tried all kinds of vocal combinations—solos, duets, and more. He sang original compositions plus songs of other artists or writers he admired; at times, he asked the audience to suggest numbers.

It demonstrated he was still true to the philosophy he had expressed at the start of his recording career to Allan Jones. ''I don't want to be successful so that I can get a lot of money and retire to a house in the . . . country. I don't want any of that rock 'n' roll rubbish. I don't want to go cruising to Hollywood or hang out at all the star parties. I'm not interested in any of that. It's the arse end of rock and roll. I'm just interested in playing.''

In 1987, Costello ended a decade with Columbia Records and signed with a new label, Warner Brothers, which assigned T-Bone Burnett as producer on Elvis's label debut. Meanwhile, he was represented on record shelves with a collection of 1980s record session outtakes titled *Out of Our Idiot*, issued on the U.K. Demon Records label and available in the U.S. as an import.

CRAZY HORSE: *Vocal and instrumental group. Members in early 1980s: Billy Talbot, born New York, New York; Ralph Molina, born Puerto Rico; Frank Sampedro, born Welch, West Virginia.* *

An excellent California-based rock band, Crazy Horse might have become an independent force in pop music of the 1970s if not for a series of misfortunes and bad timing. In the early 1970s, this took the form of the loss of its early sparkplug, Danny

Whitten, to a drug overdose. Later, it was more a matter of being in the wrong place at the wrong time. For instance, several of its more promising album releases suffered from lack of promotion. Its 1979 debut RCA LP, for instance, came out when that organization was in the midst of a drastic management reshuffle. But if Crazy Horse didn't make its own special mark on rock 'n' roll, the band retains a major place in music history because of its long and close association with superstar Neil Young. (*See Buffalo Springield; Young, Neil.*)

The origins of the band go back to the early 1960s, when Billy Talbot came west from New York and formed a writing and singing partnership with the late Danny Whitten. Talbot recalled: ''Danny and I used to write the songs that we performed in a vocal group called Danny and the Memories. A cousin of Ralph's sang with us and he suggested Ralph come out from New York and join us. [Molina was born in Puerto Rico, but brought up in New York City. He didn't meet Talbot until he came to Los Angeles.] Then Danny started strumming a guitar and, after the Beatles hit big, the rest of us decided to play instruments too. Ralph played drums, I took the bass guitar.''

That group evolved into a band called the Rockets that recorded an album *The Rockets* on White Whale Records in the mid-1960s. Billy said: ''At the start we had three electric guitars, bass, drums, and electric violin. I'll bet you we were the first rock band with an electric violin. I know there was a jazz band that had one before—that's where we got the idea. John Handy had this electric violinist named Mike White. When we heard them, we flipped. Bobby Narkoff sat in then and he played on our 1979 RCA LP. We did rock 'n' roll songs where Narkoff was doing this falsetto effect on violin. We used the violin from blues to country and everything in between.

''We were friends with Neil [Young] for some time before Crazy Horse. One of Danny Whitten's girlfriends brought Neil up to the house one time when he was making the Buffalo Springfield album [issued in 1966]. We'd get together and talk and play music at times. After the Rockets LP came out, we'd been seeing each other for two to three years while he'd been working with the Springfield and we got together and listened to our album and he liked it. We were playing at the Whiskey on the Sunset Strip and he came to see us and jammed with our band.

''He was getting his solo career underway then. He showed us 'Cinnamon Girl' and several other things and asked us to work with him. We got together at the studio and helped record *Everybody Knows This Is Nowhere,* his second solo LP and later went on tour with him. Neil thought of the name Crazy Horse. We were discussing names, all of us

*Based on personal interviews of Crazy Horse by Irwin Stambler.

149

together. It was between Crazy Horse and War Babies at the end and you know which won."

The Rockets' career was closed out by the linkup with Young, though Talbot stressed they'd only thought of that as something peripheral at the start. "The Rockets was a good band. Its potential was incredible. We never meant to break up. Some of us just went to do some stuff with Neil. We meant to go back to the Rockets. It was just hard to get away from the new things that kept coming along. Neil always gave us this weird look when we said we have our own band, the Rockets."

But Talbot's and Molina's hopes for the Rockets were given a rude shock with the death of Whitten from a drug overdose at the beginning of the 1970s. With a roster that included such other stellar names as Nils Lofgren and Jack Nitzsche, Crazy Horse backed Young on such classic albums as *After the Gold Rush* (1970) and *Harvest* (1972). (*See Lofgren, Nils.*) Though becoming as attached to Crazy Horse as they had been to the Rockets, band members retained hopes of complementing their work with Neil with a separate identity. Indeed, with Neil's blessing and aid, Crazy Horse turned out several early 1970s LPs: *Loose* and *Crazy Horse* (1971) on Reprise and the 1972 Epic release, *At Crooked Lake*.

Bill commented: "We always thought of ourselves as equals in our band. The only reason Danny got the limelight was that he died." Whitten's death, though, cast a long shadow. It made it difficult to keep Crazy Horse going as something beyond a studio session band. Somehow the spark seemed to be missing. For a while, the group disbanded; then Frank Sampedro turned up and things started up again.

Frank said, "I was born in Welch, West Virginia, but moved to Detroit when I was two and lived there until I was 16. I started playing guitar in bands when I was eleven and was in them for years. That's how I got out of my neighborhood was the music. My folks didn't like my being in a band, though. I woke up one morning and found all my instruments were gone. I got angry, took whatever money I had, got on a bus and went to California. I didn't know anyone and I didn't have any instruments."

Somehow once in L.A., he earned enough through odd jobs to keep himself in food and clothing and enrolled in Hollywood High. He graduated and went on to take some college classes. While he did, he had nothing to do with the band business.

"Then I met Billy (Talbot) at a party," Frank said. "I knew this girl and one time I was at her place and Billy was there also. It was just a coincidence. When I met these guys at the party, they were all playing guitar, but I didn't have one and just listened and talked."

Billy recalled: "After Frank and I got talking he said he had rented this house in Mexico and how about going there for a bit. So we went and started playing guitar. Until then I didn't know he played guitar. But that's cool. We got together in Mexico and it went so well that when we got back I said he should come over to my house in Echo Park. He did and got to jam with a lot of our friends and as time went by he eventually took everybody down to his house in Mexico—Neil Young, Rusty Kershaw, Ralph. That's how we got to know him and to appreciate what a good person and fine musician he was."

Frank added, "So soon Billy, Ralph and I started playing together and playing new songs. We went through those changes without working with Neil. By the time we called him in we had enough material finished for a whole album of our own if we had a record contract.

"I remember Neil was in Nashville at the time doing some homegrown work that never came out. Then he came back and moved in for a week and played his stuff and ours. And ever since then we've been doing tours and albums with him."

Crazy Horse helped on Neil's *Tonight's the Night* and *Zuma* (both 1975), but then there was a gap in joint Young and Crazy Horse recording efforts, though they continued to tour together from time to time. The band was looking for the opportunity to record its growing backlog of original songs and finally got approval for a series of sessions from RCA in 1978. This resulted in the early 1979 release, *Crazy Moon,* which had some excellent material but received little promotional backing and made little impact on the charts.

However, the band also was involved in a new project with Neil that spawned his best-selling 1979 *Rust Never Sleeps*. The album's accompanying international Neil Young/Crazy Horse tour was one of the best of the year. Extensive film coverage of the tour served as the basis for a rock documentary issued in the early 1980s. Tapings selected from the tour provided the tracks for the LP *Live Rust* (Reprise, 1980). In the mid-1980s, the group continued to work on new projects with Young, such as the 1986 "garage band" tour.

Crazy Horse members bristled at suggestions their musical style was an echo of Neil's. Talbot said: "On our 1979 album Neil played guitar on five songs, but he is part of the Crazy Horse sound. When he plays with others he sounds different than when he works solo. Neil's 'Cinnamon Girl' doesn't sound right unless the four of us do it and we couldn't sing numbers of our own like 'Downhill' or 'She's Hot' without Neil. It's a band sound. That's the way we approach it.

"Y'know, when I was first singing in hallways as

a kid we tended to copy famous acts. But in our very first vocal group, we decided if we wanted to be original we just had to be ourselves and that's what we've done in anything I've been involved in. So if people say we sound like Neil Young, you could also say he sounds like us.''

With a broad grin, Frank said jestingly: "Yeah, he's copped our sound.''

CREAM, THE: *Vocal and instrumental trio. Eric Clapton, born Ripley, England, March 30, 1945; Jack Bruce, born Glasgow, Scotland, May 14, 1943; Ginger Baker, born Lewisham, England, August 19, 1940.*

In the second half of the 1960s, the Beatles remained phenomenally successful, but the most exciting group for avid rock fans was the Cream. The Beatles had the edge when it came to breaking new ground lyrically, but no one could approach the three members of the Cream from the standpoint of instrumental brilliance. As their name indicated, the members of the Cream felt they were superior musicians and few disagreed that in their respective specialties—Clapton on lead guitar, Bruce on bass, and Baker on drums—they were the best rock had to offer. (*See Clapton, Eric.*)

All of them had been playing professionally since their teens and all had been engrossed in the rhythm & blues revival in England in the late 1950s and early 1960s sparked by Alexis Korner and Cyril Davies. (*See Davies, Cyril; Korner, Alexis.*) Baker and Bruce both played in the famed Graham Bond Organization.

By the mid-1960s, Clapton, Baker, and Bruce had gained premier reputations for their work as sidemen. They decided in early 1966 to see what might happen if they worked together as a trio. By 1967, they were rated by most rock experts as the number one instrumental group in the world.

The Cream were signed to a recording contract almost as soon as they came into being, with Atlantic Records gaining U.S. distribution rights. Their recordings found immense demand, despite the lack of radio play because of the length of many of the selections. Word of their music spread rapidly among rock fans by word of mouth and by ecstatic reviews in the steadily expanding underground press in the U.S. and England. From 1967 through 1969, every album produced in the band's relatively short lifetime sold well over a million copies: *Disraeli Gears, Wheels of Fire, Best of Cream, Fresh Cream,* and *Goodbye.* The group also won a gold record for the single "Sunshine of Your Love."

Garbed in polka-dotted pants, fringed suede shirts, and neck chains, while flaunting long hair, they channeled equally flamboyant blues-based music at the audiences from banks of high-powered amplifiers. However, the amazing thing about their playing was that despite the electronic volume, the notes and drum solos were strikingly sharp and clear. Despite their garb, Cream was interested in musical performance, not dramatic movement.

Reviewing their concert at the Anaheim Civic Center in May 1968, Ian Whitcomb of the *Los Angeles Times* wrote: "There were no antics—no planned trouser-splitting, no undulation of the hips, no spitting . . . just great cataleptic hunks cut from the aged blues and pummeled out, slit up, reshaped, thoroughly examined by the violent guitars and drums.''

Though blues was at the heart of the group's repertoire, they used it as a takeoff point, as Clapton pointed out. "The Cream never really played that much blues. I think we aimed to start a revolution in musical thought. We set out to change the world, to upset people, and to shock them. At the start, we were going to play Elvis Presley numbers—but what happened was that we fell into doing these long instrumental pieces. Really the Cream was just an instrumental group''.

To some extent, the group combined elements of old time jazz with rock. In particular, they followed the approach of early jazz artists of starting off with a melody then having each instrumentalist take off from it. They called their style neocontrapuntal. Discussing it with a *Time* reporter in October 1967, Jack Bruce said: "We're all playing melody against each other.'' Clapton noted: "Our aim is to get so far away from the original line that you're playing something that's never been heard before.'' Clearly, much of their music was not written as much as improvised. However, all three members formally composed many of their numbers, including some of their hit recordings, apart from performances.

But at the peak of success, the Cream began to feel restless. They thought it was time to disband. Late in 1968, the group completed its final two concerts at home in London's Royal Albert Hall with 10,000 fans inside and thousands more turned away.

Jack Bruce told a reporter: "I was really depressed for two or three days afterward. It was quite moving; I just didn't expect it.'' However, this did not change anyone's mind about closing up shop. Clapton said the members felt they had expressed themselves as a group in music as much as they believed was possible. Basically, they wanted to take time to reorient themselves, hopefully to new and better patterns of music. "This business devours so much of your time. You don't know if you are doing the right thing or the wrong thing—or even who you are!''

The group never did reform although Baker and

Clapton performed together later in the briefly glorious group Blind Faith with Rich Grech on bass and Steve Winwood on vocals, organ, and guitar. (*See Winwood, Steve.*)

CREEDENCE CLEARWATER REVIVAL:

Vocal and instrumental group. Tom Fogerty, born Berkeley, California, November 9, 1941; John Fogerty, born Berkeley, California, May 28, 1945; Stu Cook, born Oakland, California, April 25, 1945; Doug Clifford, born Palo Alto, California, April 24, 1945. Tom Fogerty left the group in February 1971. Group broke up in 1972.

The synthesis of rock and country blues achieved by Creedence Clearwater Revival seemed so authentic that in the band's early days, a number of newspaper articles stated group members grew up in the bayou regions of Louisiana. However, the quartet was solely a product of the San Francisco Bay region and developed its unique sounds by listening to records of such Delta bluesmen as Howlin' Wolf and Muddy Waters, plus such early rock artists as Elvis Presley, Jerry Lee Lewis, Carl Perkins, and Chuck Berry.

The members of the group all met as boys in California schools, starting as a trio in junior high. The idea for the group was John Fogerty's, the other two original members being Stu Cook and Doug Clifford. It was not until the trio had been working for a while for school shows and local parties that John's brother Tom was added. John, of course, remained the major creative force in the band's success, overshadowing the writing skills of the others. His moving lead vocals were to Creedence what Jim Morrison's were to the Doors.

However, all of the bandsmen were talented musicians. By his mid-teens, John could play guitar, dobro, piano, organ, tenor saxophone, harmonica, drums, and several other instruments. He also had a good voice from the start of the group and contributed original compositions throughout the band's career. Similarly, Tom taught himself to play almost as many instruments as his brother, but his main instrument remained rhythm guitar.

The group paid its dues playing under a number of different names from 1959 through 1967. John Fogerty's drive and ambition kept the band going, despite long dry spells when work was scarce.

In 1967, after seeing a performer from a local record company, Fantasy, on TV, the group came and auditioned for the firm as the Golliwogs. They cut one record that made some inroads with the record buying public, but fell far short of hit status.

During the year, Fantasy was bought by one of its employees, Saul Zaentz. Looking over the firm's catalogue, he was impressed by the Golliwogs' recording. This resulted in discussions that led to the Golliwogs becoming Creedence Clearwater Revival in December 1967.

For the early part of 1968, Creedence spent many hours rehearsing material for its new recording sessions. In June, Fantasy released a debut LP, *Creedence Clearwater Revival*, and a single, based on an early rock hit by Dale Hawkins, "Suzy Q (Parts I and II)." The album earned a gold record by year-end and the single rose to number 22 on the charts.

Despite the good response to the group's first releases, their future was still in doubt. Many groups have only one or two successes in their entire careers. Creedence's second single, a remake of Screamin Jay Hawkins' "I Put A Spell on You," made the charts only briefly. Then came the group's second album, *Bayou Country*, and its single, "Proud Mary." In a short time, these discs were among the top hits throughout the world. With his writing of "Proud Mary," John Fogerty moved into the front rank of rock composers and lyricists. The song's words evinced the feel and mystique of the Mississippi ("Cleaned a lot of plates in Memphis/Pumped a lot of pain down in New Orleans/But I never saw the good side of the city/Till I hitched a ride on a riverboat queen."), a surprising tour-de-force for a writer who had never even been on the river.

From this time on, Creedence moved from triumph to triumph. The group followed the gold-record achievement of "Proud Mary" with three more double-sided gold-record hits: "Bad Moon Rising"/"Lodi," "Green River"/"Commotion," and "Down on the Corner"/"Fortunate Son," released, respectively, in April, July, and October 1969. In August, Creedence had another LP hit, *Green River,* which reached platinum-record levels. In November, their fourth LP, *Willie and the Poorboys,* had sales well over $1 million before the record reached dealers' shelves. The album marked an expansion of John Fogerty's themes from material with a Mississippi Delta flavor to social commentary on such topics as discord among Americans (particularly in the track "Effigy"), political/military pressures ("Fortunate Son"), and interdependence of people ("Don't Look Now"). Yet Creedence avoided cant and shock-value–only material. The lyric comments of Fogerty or other members of the group tended to be reasoned rather than emotional and there were few direct comments on sex or drugs. Unlike most rock stars, the Creedence quartet kept their private lives to themselves, living quietly with their families when off the road and avoiding lurid escapades.

Creedence started 1970 with another gold single, the autobiographical "Travelin' Band" backed with

"Who'll Stop the Rain" (which became the theme for a Nick Nolte film). In April, when its next gold disc, "Up around the Bend"/"Run through the Jungle" came out, the band was winning unprecedented acclaim from European audiences during its first tour of that area. Back home again, Creedence's fifth album, *Cosmo's Factory,* sold well over 3 million copies around the world. Accompanying the album on the charts was the single "Lookin' out My Back Door"/"Long as I Can See the Light," the band's sixth gold single.

By this time, group members not only kept up the performing end of their act, but also handled all its business affairs, including concert bookings. As John Fogerty told Robert Hilburn of the *Los Angeles Times:* "We decided to begin handling our own business affairs because we couldn't find anyone else who would give us the quality of service we wanted. . . . I was relying [on business associates] to know the right places for us to play and the right things for us to do for our career. But it didn't work. We'd ask them to make sure the sound systems were all right in the auditoriums that we were going to play and they'd tell us it had all been checked. But when we got to town, the sound was a mess.

"The business people are after the immediate dollar. They wanted to get us involved in television commercials, movies, anything that would mean money. But we are more interested in building a career." As Bill Graham told Hilburn, the switch was an enjoyable one. "This group is the best example of honest businessmen I've met in rock. They are very straightforward."

Creedence closed out 1970 with the release of another hit album, *Pendulum.* The band added many more awards to its trophy case, including *Billboard*'s ranking as Top Album Artists of the Year for 1970 and England's *New Musical Express* reader's poll nod as Top International Pop Group. The Record Industry Association of America also reported that the group ranked as the Top Gold Record Artists of 1970.

By the start of 1971, Creedence was beginning to run out of new worlds to conquer and, as often happens, a certain restlessness set in among the members. Even as the single "Have You Ever Seen the Rain"/"Hey Tonight," released in January 1971, moved toward the band's eighth gold-record award for singles, rumors persisted that changes were in order. In February, Tom Fogerty announced his departure from the group to work as a solo artist. The remaining trio, with John continuing to call most of the shots, stated it would carry on as before. The first single of the reorganized CCR, "Sweet Hitchhiker"/"Door to Door," was in the top 10 in midsummer.

But Doug Clifford and Stu Cook argued for the chance to write some of the new songs rather than have John remain almost sole songwriter. The trio arrangements didn't work out. John told Robert Hilburn of the *Los Angeles Times* (April 6, 1973): "The result was not the easier, more relaxed thing we all had hoped it would be. The end result was more uptight for all of us. I would get uptight because I couldn't have my way, then I'd feel guilty about having those kinds of feelings. The tension really reached a peak for me around [the LP] *Mardi Gras.* But it wasn't just rough on me. It was rough on us all. . . . We were all conscious things were getting more and more fragile. They were wondering what I was going to do . . . and I was wondering. I felt damned if I did, damned if I didn't. It ended up a three-way division. It wasn't just me leaving. We all felt the same way about it. We just had to admit it." The band announced its breakup in October 1972.

Moreover, John Fogerty was becoming increasingly bitter about recording arrangements with Fantasy. John refused to record any new material under the Creedence banner on Fantasy's terms. Years of heated legal wrangling and name calling ensued between the parties, some aspects of which were treated in the lyrics of songs Fogerty presented during his mid-1980s solo performing renaissance. (*See Fogerty, John.*)

Over Fogerty's objections, the record company continued to issue new collections, mainly of previously released tracks, throughout the 1970s and into the mid-1980s. These included *Mardi Gras* and *Creedence Gold* in 1972, *Live in Europe* and *More Creedence Gold* in 1973, *Chronicle* in 1976, *Creedence 1969* and *Creedence 1970* in 1978, and *Royal Albert Hall Concert* (later renamed *The Concert*) and *Creedence Country* in 1981.

CROSBY, DAVID: *See Byrds, The; Crosby, Stills, Nash & Young.*

CROSBY, STILLS, NASH & YOUNG: *Vocal and instrumental group. David Crosby, born Los Angeles, California, August 14, 1941; Stephen Stills, born Dallas, Texas, January 3, 1945; Graham Nash, born Blackpool, England, February 1, 1942; Neil Young, born Toronto, Canada, November 12, 1945.*

The names of Crosby, Nash, Stills, and Young, in various combinations—solo, duos, trios, or quartet—stood large on the pop music scene from the late '60s into the '80s. Their contributions included some of the finest folk-rock of the period and some of their original compositions fitted as well into the folk and country genres as into rock.

By the time the members came together in Los

Angeles at the end of the '60s, all had impressive credits behind them. David Crosby, of course, had been a founding member of the Byrds, with whom he remained from 1964 into 1968. Before that, he had been a singer-guitarist on the folk music circuit for five years. Steve Stills and Neil Young, who helped form the landmark Buffalo Springfield in the mid-1960s, first became acquainted when they were members of a folksong group called the Au Go Go singers in 1964.

Graham Nash, raised in Lancashire, England, already had a stage act called the Two Teens, which he performed with friend Allan Clarke in grammar school. At 15, they became the youngest artists to appear at a well-known English venue, the Manchester Cabaret Club. After several other group affiliations in the late '50s and early '60s, the two in 1963 founded vocal and instrumental group the Hollies that became one of England's top rock groups (and was still active in the '80s). With Nash as a main songwriter and lead singer, the group scored many major hits in the '60s. When he announced he had decided to leave the group in 1968, fans flocked to his last shows with the band.

By then, Nash already was rehearsing new material with the first CSNY alignment, Crosby, Stills & Nash. The origins of that threesome was described by Ellen Sander (*Hit Parader,* September 1969): "It all started one late summer afternoon in a picturesque house in Laurel Canyon [Los Angeles]. Crosby was preparing material for a solo album after having left the Byrds. Nash, still with the Hollies, was visiting, and Stills, after the breakup of Buffalo Springfield, had been sitting around and staring at the side of a mountain, trying to decide what to do next between playing sessions. Goofing around in the California living room, they all began to play and sing together. And they loved it immediately and they talked about making an album and, boy, it was going to be a hassle with each of them contracted to a different record company. Music biz wunderkind, David Geffen, a 26-year-old funky imp, was called in to move minds and signatures around to make it possible, no small feat, mind you, but he did it and then some."

The three went to England in the fall of 1968 to compose new songs and rehearse while Nash closed out his career with the Hollies. They then flew back to L.A. to record their debut LP, *Crosby, Stills & Nash* (Atlantic, spring 1969). The record, still one of the best in folk-rock annals, included Stills' 7-minute "Suite Judy Blue Eyes" to Judy Collins, "Helplessly Hoping," "49 Reasons," and "Bye Bye Baby"; David Crosby's lament for Sen. Robert Kennedy, "Long Time Coming"; Graham Nash's "Lady of the Island" and "Marrakesh Express";

and a postholocaust song by Crosby, Stills, and Paul Kantner of Jefferson Airplane, "Wooden Ships."

The LP spawned several hit singles and earned a gold record before 1969 was over. By the time the members were ready for a second album, Neil Young had joined the loosely organized operation. It was agreed from the beginning that the members could go or stay with the band as the spirit moved them. The first offering of CSN&Y, *Déjà Vu,* came out on Atlantic in the spring of 1970, matching the first LP almost song for song in quality, rising to number one on U.S. charts in May, and finding similar response all over Europe. Its top-10 single, "Woodstock," relived the joyous spirit of that summer 1969 festival. A year later, the quartet had another number one LP, the live *4 Way Street.*

However, the individuality of the four superstars was causing strains. By 1972, Neil Young had dropped out of the alliance to concentrate on solo work and, though efforts were made from time to time to get him to take part in reunion efforts, he kept on his own way. Stills, too, had his separate projects to work on during the mid-1970s, though he did return for trio work late in the decade. Besides *Déjà Vu* and *4 Way Street,* one other CSN&Y LP was a "best of" collection, *So Far.* It too went gold.

In the mid-1970s, Crosby and Nash worked together steadily as a duo. One of their albums, *Crosby-Nash,* came out on the old CSN&Y label, Atlantic, but most were on a new label affiliation, ABC. Their first ABC release, *Wind on the Water,* was one of the best folk-rock collections of 1975 and a top 10 hit in November '75. They followed with two more ABC LPs, *Whistling down the Wire* and *Crosby & Nash Live.*

Steve Stills returned to the fold briefly for the 1977 platinum-award-winning Atlantic LP, *CSN,* and accompanying concert tour. (Neil Young had been invited to take part, but reportedly backed out at the last minute.)

However, following that flurry, the group broke up once more with even Crosby and Nash giving up collaboration, at least for the last part of the '70s. Nash turned most of his attention to solo work (with his solo LPs coming out on Warner Brothers during 1979–80) and cooperation with Jackson Browne on environmentalist issues, including a concert series to raise funds to fight nuclear energy. One of those concerts formed the basis for a gold-award-winning two-record *No Nukes* on Elektra at the end of 1979.

For a while at the start of the 1980s, Crosby led the David Crosby Band, whose members included Carl Schwinderman on guitar, Tony Saunders on bass, and Jay David on drums. After a number of shows with that group, David reunited with Nash and Stills in 1982 and for much of the time from then through the mid-1980s, they continued to work together. During that period their record credits included the Atlantic LPs *Daylight Again* (1982) and *Allies* (1983). However, Crosby's continuing problems with substance abuse and related legal entanglements cast a shadow over the group. At one point, he was convicted in Dallas, Texas, for possession of cocaine and carrying a loaded gun. In early 1985, he served three months in jail for escaping from a New Jersey drug rehabilitation center.

Back on tour with Stills and Nash after that experience, he told Dennis Hunt (*Los Angeles Times*, June 30, 1985), "The guy would say, 'Hey there, rock star, mop that floor!' I'd say, 'Yes sir.' I don't look at myself as a rock star, but they did. You have a name and they have power over you for a while. They love that. To them, it's better than having control over an average prisoner. . . . I wouldn't give them any problems. That's suicide. That's what they want you to do. They try to bait you into reacting so they can stomp you."

The rules were that he couldn't write music or form a band. He told Hunt: "In my darkest hours in jail, thinking about playing music again helped me hang on. There were times when I'd just cry at night. I didn't know when I was getting out. But I'd hang on thinking about when I'd be free to play music again."

In 1985, with another possible jail term hanging over his head in Texas, he was encouraged by the support of his long-time musical associates and by the roars of approval from the large crowds that turned out for many of the Crosby, Stills & Nash shows all over the U.S.

Before 1985 was over, Crosby was back in prison in Texas to begin serving a five-year sentence for drugs and weapons convictions. Taking his good behavior into account, though, Texas authorities granted him a parole that resulted in his release in August 1986. By 1987, he was once more touring with Stills and Nash with a repertoire that included his composition "Compass." Written in prison, it described his joy at finding a revitalization of his songwriting skills that had dwindled during his years of drug abuse. (*See Browne, Jackson; Buffalo Springfield; Byrds, The; Crazy Horse; Hollies, The; Jefferson Airplane; Stills, Stephen; Young, Neil.*)

CROSS, CHRISTOPHER: *Singer, guitarist, songwriter. Born San Antonio, Texas, May 3, 1951.*

Musician/songwriter Christopher Cross won more laurels in pop music at the start of the 1980s than many artists achieve in a career. Still, his laid-back soft-rock style seemed to be going against the tide of new wave and heavy metal. In the mid-1980s, his efforts fell far short of his accomplishments in the first two years of the decade. But Cross had defiantly put things in perspective in a 1981 *Billboard* interview: "If it stops right now and my second album comes out and goes down the tubes and I'm forgotten, I can still be on my deathbed and say, 'I put out an album that went double platinum and I had a number one single and I was up for five Grammys. Now, what did you do?'"

For Cross, those attainments didn't come easy. It took half a decade of striving before he could get the ear of a record-company executive and even then there was considerable skepticism that Cross's country-tinged style could bring pop success. Even when he completed a debut LP that featured noted friends such as Don Henley of the Eagles, Nicolette Larsen, and ex-Doobie Brothers star Michael McDonald, there were moments when it seemed as though his label might not release the album.

The road to stardom began in San Antonio, Texas, a city associated more with country & western music than pop or rock. Cross, whose original name was Christopher Geppert, at least didn't have to cope with parental opposition. His father, who had played professionally at one time, welcomed his young son's interest in learning musical instruments. Cross's first efforts were on the drums, but in his teens he focused his attention on perfecting his guitar techniques, with some help from his father.

During his high school years, he played with local bands and went on to join a group that gained a small following in Austin, Texas. By the early 1970s, Christopher was writing steadily, although the Austin band mainly played cover versions of national hits by well-known bands or singers. They did occasionally include some of Cross's material, however.

Certain that his writing and singing had hit potential, Cross submitted a number of demo tapes to any record contacts he could find. Warner Brothers Records, his eventual label, was sent some in 1975, but nothing resulted from it. In 1978, Cross managed to obtain a live audition in Texas with a member of Warner Brothers' artists & repertoire department, Michael Ostin. Ostin was won over and recommended to the home office in Burbank, California, that they sign the young Texan.

The Burbank staff approved a contract and Cross went to California to begin working on his first album at the end of the 1970s. Cross had cultivated friendships with many talented people in the music field, which paid off both in the caliber of musicians who agreed to back his new recordings and in the increased interest in him by record-company officials.

Still, when the album was recorded and mixed, Warner Brothers held back from releasing it and

Christopher began to get nervous. It had been ready in time for release to catch the 1979 Christmas season, but it remained under wraps. Michael Omartian, the album's producer, told Paul Grein of *Billboard:* "Maybe we were intimidated by the press prediction of a new wave onslaught. Everybody got a little gun-shy and said, 'let's wait.' It turned out to be a wise decision. The album came out in January 1980 when nothing else was happening."

Soon after its release, the debut album, *Christopher Cross,* made the U.S. charts. The first hit was the initial single release from the LP, "Ride Like the Wind," which spent all of May in the number two slot in *Billboard.* The second single, Cross's composition "Sailing," did even better, rising to number one in *Billboard* the week of August 30, 1980. The last months of the year saw another original on the charts, "Never Be the Same," which stayed on the lists into early 1981.

Those 1980 offerings won an amazing array of honors for Cross. Not only was he nominated in five Grammy categories, he won all five: Record of the Year for "Sailing"; Album of the Year; Best New Artist; Song of the Year (a songwriter's award for "Sailing"); and Best Arrangement Accompanying Vocalist (presented to Cross and Michael Omartian for co-arranging work). Among his other 1980 rewards were four number one awards from *Billboard:* Single Artist, New Album Artist, New Male Single Artist, and New Male Album Artist.

His newly won reputation brought other opportunities. One of those was helping to write the theme song for a new movie starring comic actor Dudley Moore. He was asked to work on the number ("Arthur's Theme") by Burt Bacharach and Carole Bayer Sager. Bacharach told a *Billboard* reporter Chris had been their first choice for a collaborator. "We wanted him and what a logical move, too. Because the year before he'd won five Grammys, and it seemed like a good career move for him as well. Chris was in town, we had met him and we just said, 'Listen, you want to write this song with us?' It was pretty fast, because I basically wrote it in one or two nights with Carole and Christopher."

A fourth name, Peter Allen, appears on the credits for the song. Carole remembered a line from a song she and Allen had written some years back that seemed to fit the new project. After gaining Peter's approval, the line became an integral part of the movie composition, "Arthur's Theme (Best That You Can Do). (*See Bacharach, Burt.*)

The movie proved to be one of the funniest comedies of 1981 and a box office smash. The chemistry between record buyers, movie goers, and Christopher's single of the number (issued on Warner Brothers in the fall) also proved excellent. The disc spent most of October at number one on the *Billboard* lists, bringing Cross more gold and platinum RIAA awards. "Arthur's Theme," which remained on the charts into 1982, added still another feather to Cross's cap, bringing Christopher and his co-writers an Academy Award Oscar for best film song of 1981. Also on the charts for him in 1981 were two holdovers from 1980 ("Sailing" and "Never Be the Same") plus a new release, "Say You'll Be Mine."

However, disappointments were ahead. Cross didn't have a new album in 1982 and he only had one single on lower chart levels. The high hopes for his next album, *Another Page* (1983), proved ephemeral. The LP was not helped by tepid response to the initial single releases, "All Right" and "No Time for Talk." The third single (another Cross composition, "Think of Laura," issued in late 1983), turned things around a bit, helped in part by its choice as the theme music for an important character in the ABC-TV soap "General Hospital." The song rose into the U.S. top 10 in early 1984.

Though Cross had writing assignments and remained active on the concert circuit, his recording career seemed to falter in the mid-1980s. His late 1985 album on Warner Brothers, *Every Turn of the World,* spent only a little over a month on the charts.

CRUDUP, ARTHUR: *Singer, guitarist, songwriter. Born Forest, Mississippi, 1905.*

Play some of the recordings that Arthur "Big Boy" Crudup made in the 1940s, then play some of the early hits of Elvis Presley recorded a decade later. Hear the close resemblance of Crudup's guitar runs and vocal stylings on "Rock Me Mama" and "Mean Old Frisco Blues" to passages in the Sun label recordings that made Presley the most important figure in the rock revolution. Of course, this is not surprising. Any rock historian knows the influence of the black blues artist on Elvis; it was Crudup's composition "That's All Right" that gave Presley his first national hit. (*See Presley, Elvis.*)

For good reason, many experts call Crudup (pronounced *Croodup)* the father of rock 'n' roll. Actually, many other black soloists and groups performed music in the rock tradition even earlier, but none had the immediate, traceable effect that Crudup did on the early white rock pioneers.

Born in the small farm community of Forest, Mississippi, Crudup grew up in a poor family, working in the fields before his teens. Though Mississippi was the cradle of blues singing in the late 1800s and early 1900s, there is no evidence that Crudup did much more than occasionally listen to music by wandering minstrels until he was well into adulthood.

Until his thirties, his life was one of manual labor—farming, logging, construction work, working in a sawmill, driving a truck.

As he went through his twenties, he developed an interest in blues, sometimes singing songs he heard for his own entertainment. When he was 32, he finally got the urge to learn the guitar, copying the styles of some of the bluesmen who performed in his local area.

After playing small clubs around Forest, he moved to Silver City in the Mississippi Delta region. The Delta then was the base for many of the most famous names in the country blues tradition. Despite his formidable competition, Crudup showed enough ability to hold the attention of the audiences in the bars and nightclubs of the area.

Things were slowing down in the Delta, music-wise, though, as the '30s came to a close. Crudup heard things might be better in Chicago and headed there in 1941. Jobs proved hard to find in the blues field and Crudup earned a meager living performing on downtown street corners. Music publisher and talent scout Lester Melrose came by one day, liked Arthur's style, and arranged for an audition with RCA Victor. The result was a contract that led to the recording and release of over 80 record sides between 1941 and 1956.

The records were aimed at the ghetto market, but sometimes they could be found on juke boxes in truck stops or in bars in racially mixed communities. Thus, some of the early white rock artists had the chance to listen to Crudup and to incorporate his phrasings into their performing approaches.

Crudup first gained attention from black record buyers with his single, "If I Get Lucky," recorded on September 11, 1941, and released soon after. It was the first of many such singles hits during the '40s and early '50s, including "Mean Old Frisco Blues" in 1942; "Rock Me Mamma," "Cool Disposition," and "Keep Your Arms around Me" in 1944; "She's Gone" in 1945; "So Glad You're Mine" and "That's All Right (Mama)" in 1946; "Shout, Sister, Shout" in 1949; "My Baby Left Me" in 1950; "Mr. So and So" and "Keep on Drinkin'" in 1952; and "If You've Ever Been to Georgia" in 1954. Almost all of these were originals by Crudup, though many drew from earlier blues songs in the folk tradition of the Delta.

Because of the nature of the black entertainment field in Crudup's heyday, he never was able to translate his recording success into a major performing career. Even when his songs were in juke boxes in every black community across the U.S., he was only able to find work playing the seamier bars on the South Side of Chicago or small clubs back in Missis-

sippi and nearby states. Sometimes he had to work at odd jobs to tide him over between engagements. Though his records sold well in the blues field, it was a limited market and he made very little from them.

By the time young truck driver Elvis Presley first heard Crudup recordings, Arthur was in a declining phase of his career. Crudup had never changed his performing technique with the times and he was beginning to sound archaic to new black generations. In 1956, he cut his last recordings for Victor and faded from public view soon after. He could only find rare performing jobs in the late '50s and most of the '60s, working as a manual laborer in his home area and, in the mid-1960s, in Virginia.

The new interest in both the early blues and the roots of rock that grew in the '60s led to a revival of Crudup's reputation. His name figured prominently in a number of the books issued on blues history during the decade. In 1967, young blues historians sought him out in Virginia and helped launch a new career for him. During the late '60s and early '70s, he became a popular figure at small folk-blues clubs across the U.S. and was asked to perform at folk festivals. He was still playing only a small amount of the time and for a limited audience, but it seemed certain his name would grow in importance as time went by and rock's evolution was recognized as an important part of the American heritage.

In December 1971, RCA Victor took note of Crudup's new eminence by issuing *Arthur "Big Boy" Crudup—The Father of Rock and Roll* as part of its vintage series.

CRYSTALS, THE: *Vocal group from Brooklyn, New York. Original members, Barbara Alston, born 1944; Mary Thomas, born c. 1944; Dee Dee Kinnebrew, born c. 1944; LaLa Brooks, born c. 1945; Patricia Wright. For group's only number-one hit, roster comprised Darlene Love, Fanita James and Gracia Nitzsche.*

Of the groups hand-picked by Phil Spector in establishing his record empire of the early 1960s, none was more important to his success than the Crystals. The group gained four million selling singles (according to their record company's claims at the time) and several more that came close to that mark. Ironically, the biggest hit under the Crystals name was recorded by a replacement trio rather than the original members.

The group had its beginnings in a Brooklyn high school where Barbara Alston, Dee Dee Kinnebrew, Mary Thomas, Pat Wright, and LaLa Brooks were friends at the start of the 1960s. All were ardent rock fans and enjoyed singing the current hit songs. Thoughts of a professional career hadn't occurred to them until they met songwriter Larry Bates, who was interested in using them to perform the new numbers he was composing. (The quintet—later reduced to a foursome—took their name from Larry's daughter Crystal.)

They got the opportunity to audition for Phil Spector in 1961 and won a contract with his fledgling Philles Records. Their debut single came out in early 1962 and Bates's composition "There's No Other (Like My Baby)" (actually considered the B' side at first) made the Top 20. Soon after, Spector chose the Barry Mann (born Brooklyn, New York, April 3, 1958) and Cynthia Mann song "Uptown" for them and another Top 20 hit resulted, followed swiftly by a third single success, "He Hit Me (And It Felt Like a Kiss)."

While visiting Liberty Records to discuss some business matters with Snuff Garrett of that firm, he heard a demo of a song written by Gene Pitney, "He's a Rebel." Excited by the number, Phil decided he wanted to record it on Philles, though Liberty was planning to have Vikki Carr do it. Getting a copy of the demo from Pitney, an old friend, he headed to Los Angeles, where he could be more secretive about setting up recording sessions. He wanted to come out with a single before the Carr version, so time was of the essence. Since the original Crystals weren't in California, he brought in a backing group (then known as the Blossoms) whose members were Darlene Love, Fanita James, and Gracia Nitzsche. Released in the fall, their single of "He's a Rebel" became a chart buster, reaching number one on *Billboard* lists the week of November 3, 1962, and staying there for a second week.

In 1963, the original Crystals were back on the charts with a song whose title still sticks in people's memories when they think of the early days of rock, "Da Doo Ron Ron," co-written by Jeff Barry, Ellie Greenwich and Phil Spector. (*See Greenwich, Ellie.*) The single made the Top 10 as did another 1963 single, "Then He Kissed Me." Other singles numbers featured in their concerts were "He's Sure the Boy I Love" and "Wait til My Baby Gets Home." But by 1966, their popularity had run its course, abetted by Spector's switch in emphasis to other acts like Bob B. Soxx and the Blue Jeans and the Ronettes, and the group disbanded. In 1967, Philles reissued albums of Crystals material: *Greatest Hits, Twist Uptown*, and *He's a Rebel*.

CULTURE CLUB: *Vocal and instrumental group. Members, mid-1980s: Boy George, born Bexley, Eltham, England, June 14, 1961; Jon Moss, born near London, England, September 11, 1957; Roy Hay, born Corringham, Essex, En-*

gland, August 12, 1961; Michael Craig, born Hammersmith, England, February 15, 1960.

Fronted by the eccentric but talented Boy George, who flouted convention and typically appeared in drag with flamboyant, brightly colored attire, Culture Club in the 1980s became a worldwide flag bearer for England's "New Romantic" rock movement (which included such other groups as Duran Duran and Spandau Ballet). The group seemed on the way to more than passing prominence in rock until Boy George's problems with hard drugs threatened to bring a sad end to a very promising saga.

Boy George, whose real name was George Alan O'Dowd, was the third of six children born to a working class Irish Catholic family then living in a three-bedroom home in a rundown suburb of London. His father, Jeremiah, had been a soldier and boxer, but by the time George came into the world, was earning an indifferent living in the building trade. George recalled (as reported in Merle Ginsberg's biography, *Boy George*, Dell, 1984): "When we were young, my father was quite strict. He had a lot of problems. He didn't have any money, he left the army, and he had all these bloody kids real fast. He was a builder, and he really had a hard time at it for years."

During his childhood years, George resented the lack of privacy at home and found it hard to get along with his parents. He had a violent temper, which sometimes flared up when he felt his parents weren't treating him right. He later commented on that in his song "I'm Afraid of Me," his band's second single.

As he reached his teens, he had no direction in life, but began to find solace in pop music, particularly the glitter-rock dress-up style personified by artists such as Marc Bolan of T. Rex. (*See T. Rex.*) His own attire became increasingly bizarre. A girlfriend in 1975 got him to dye his hair orange and wear drainpipe pants. This triggered controversy with school administrators that led to his leaving when he was sixteen. Now on his own, he hung around London nightclubs and eventually drifted into working at stores that sold the exotic fashions favored by the London subculture that focused on combining unusual clothes with attendance at pop concerts. While working at a store called Shades in the Chelsea Antique market, he met artists such as Bob Marley, who aroused his interest in reggae rhythms.

Still, as the 1970s drew toward a close, he hadn't shown any interest in music as a profession. His bent, briefly in Birmingham in the north of England and then again in London, was to bring attention to himself for his unusual garb, which often included feminine dress. After a while, he began to earn money modelling clothes and then expanded his interest to include styling clothes and props for other models. During 1979, a friend helped bring George together with clothes designer Sue Clowes and the two opened their own shop, the Foundry, which became a center for the dress style that became part of the New Romantics movement. With its emphasis on fantasy-like apparel and softer, melodic rock, this movement stressed escapism rather than the concern with unemployment and other problems voiced in punk rock.

In 1980, O'Dowd finally began to like the idea of being in a band. Hearing that entrepreneur Malcolm McLaren (who earlier had helped form the Sex Pistols) was starting a new band, George asked if he could join. The new ensemble, a New Romantics-fashion group called Bow Wow Wow, had a 14-year-old girl singer named Annabella Lwin. Finding her hard to deal with, McLaren brought in O'Dowd briefly and then showed him the door. But a number of George's friends commented favorably on his singing and, though he went back to work on his fashion projects, he soon realized he liked the idea of performing.

He was still mulling over his options when a black musician named Mikey Craig approached him in a London club and said he'd like to be in a band with George as lead vocalist. Craig, a bass guitarist, had worked as a reggae session musician and with some local bands. George decided to go ahead with the band idea. Mikey brought in a mutual friend called Suede on guitar to form a trio called the Sex Gang Children. They soon realized they needed a drummer and O'Dowd remembered a friend had given him the number of someone called Jon Moss. Moss and George met in March 1981 and decided they could work well together.

Moss had considerably more experience in the field than the others. He had worked briefly with the Clash, had his own band called London, toured with the punk rock group the Stranglers, and been a member of the excellent group, the Damned. Disillusioned with music for a while, he took a two-year hiatus and was just getting back into performing when he heard from O'Dowd. Moss commented: "After I met him, I saw this great potential despite the fact that his original band was terrible."

In particular, he told George, Suede should go. He said, as Ginsberg related: "He's a great guy, but he isn't going anywhere—he's a three-chord wonder." George, who'd hung out with Suede long before the band was formed, said he couldn't fire a friend. Moss said: "Okay, I'll fire him then," and he did.

After auditioning replacements, it was decided

that another young guitar player, Roy Ernest Hay, should be added. Hay, who worked in an insurance firm and played music on the side, previously had been a member of his girlfriend's (later his wife) brother's band, Russian Bouquet. With Hay's addition, Moss told George he felt the band was complete. But he wanted a new name. After some brainstorming, the two of them came up with Culture Club.

In the fall of 1981, the band wangled some studio time from EMI records and taped two songs. EMI declined to sign them and the members decided they needed to spend more time rehearsing. In October, the band got the chance to play a date at a club called Crocs in Essex. George appeared in a clothing style he and Sue Clowes had worked out called the Foundry Look, which they described as a reaction against the New Romantics' dress. The London press focused more attention on the group's clothes than on its music. But all the publicity began to have an effect and the band got the chance to return to Crocs three months later. That show was attended by Virgin Records executive Danny Goodwin, who was impressed enough to get his company to back some new demos—which didn't prove good enough.

But EMI then provided support for more test numbers, including one titled "The Eyes of Medusa." EMI expressed interest after that, but the band tried the tapes out on Goodwin, who this time got the OK to sign Culture Club. In early 1982, Virgin issued two singles that flopped: "White Boy" and "I'm Afraid of Me." Boy George pressed Virgin to try one more single and provided a reggae-flavored number, "Do You Really Want to Hurt Me," that had an electric effect, rising to number one across Europe. The success of that and other recordings released soon afterward was buoyed by a series of concerts that inspired intensive press coverage focused on Boy George's transvestitism. Headlines such as "Is It a Her? A Him—or Neither" and "I Don't Care if People Think I'm a Girl Says Boy George" plus the *London Daily Express*'s calling George "the most outrageous character since Elton John and Liberace" made Culture Club instant celebrities. But critics also noted the band had promise and its lead vocalist was not without performing charisma.

By late 1982, the group had more U.K. chart successes: the singles "Time (Clock of the Heart)" and "I'll Tumble 4 Ya" and its debut LP, *Kissing to Be Clever*. It also had a U.S. label, Epic. U.S. reviewers generally were impressed. The *Los Angeles Times*' Robert Hilburn commented (March 13, 1983) that Boy George is "a clever songwriter, and he's got one of the sweetest, most soulful voices of any young singer in years. And his band has a great feel for mixing reggae, pop, and Latin rhythms into spicy dance numbers.''

Kissing to Be Clever made U.S. charts the second week in 1983 with a platinum-record certification from RIAA. Worldwide, the LP had sold over 3 million copies by year-end. The band's second album, *Colour by Numbers,* issued in the fall of 1983 by Virgin and Epic, picked up another platinum-record award. The first single from the album, "Church of the Poison Mind" (a top 10 hit in late 1983), also received wide coverage in music video format. The band's popularity was emphasized by a cover story on George and the group ("England Swings") in one of the November 1983 issues of *Rolling Stone.*

The second single from *Colour by Numbers,* "Karma Chameleon," rose to number one in England at the end of 1983 and in the U.S. on *Billboard* charts the week of February 4, 1984. It easily won gold-record certification. Commenting on the song to England's *Melody Maker* magazine, George said: "It was really an old tune that I had [written at school] which Roy [Hay] wouldn't work out, because he hated it so much. It was like 'Kumbaya'— y'know—and he wouldn't play it. I told him, 'It's a great song, you'll see.' It's one of those songs that you either love or hate immediately. It can really grow on you—it can kind of beat you to surrender.'' In the U.K. that record was followed by "Victims" (another hit single from the LP), which wasn't issued in the U.S.

In February 1984, Boy George was interviewed for the *Tonight Show* by guest host Joan Rivers, who sought insight into his sexual tendencies. She asked: "Which do you like, boys or girls?" to which he first responded: "You, darling!" "No, really," she pursued, and George replied: "Well, either one. . . . I don't really have time to think about that these days." One thing he could think about—and savor—was Culture Club's selection as Best New Band of 1983 in the Grammy Awards. Later in 1984, the band's third album, *Waking up with the House on Fire,* came out and was high on the charts into early 1985. But as the year went by, disturbing rumors began to circulate about George's drug problems. English papers carried stories about Culture Club's lead singer being sought for failure to answer charges of heroin possession. If he did not show up in court, it was stressed, he could face a jail term. His family, reports indicated, wanted him to comply with the requirements and go into rehabilitation to save his life.

George finally did appear in court in London (dressed in jeans and sport shirt) and pleaded guilty. He also acknowledged he needed help to try to solve his heroin addiction.

However, it remained to be seen whether this could be achieved and, equally important, whether Culture Club could survive the adverse publicity. Indeed, there were indications that some of the problems had affected the music. The band's fourth album, *From Luxury to Heartache* (April 1986), lacked freshness and repeated, rather than improved on, the kind of material presented earlier.

In 1987, the group left Epic and assigned worldwide distribution rights for new recordings to Virgin Records. In late summer of 1987, Epic issued a greatest hits package titled *This Time/The First Four Years.*

DANNY AND THE JUNIORS: *Vocal group, all born Philadelphia, Pennsylvania: Danny Rapp, born May 10, 1941, died Arizona, April 1983; Joe Terranova, January 30, 1941; Frank Maffei, November 1940; David White, September 1940.*

Though Danny and the Juniors placed several singles on the national charts in the late 1950s, the group had only one massive triumph. That one, though, was enough to give this group a niche in the history of rock 'n' roll. "At the Hop" still evokes a picture of what it was like to be a teenager when rock first became the collective voice of American youth.

The four members of the group began singing together in high school in Philadelphia. Danny Rapp handled the lead with Joe Terranova on baritone; Frank Maffei, second tenor; and Dave White, first tenor. The boys, then called the Juvenairs, began singing at school dances and private parties, then found work in local clubs. In 1957, one of the successful musical entrepreneurs of the day, Artie Singer, caught their act and took over direction of their careers. He also suggested the name change to Danny and the Juniors.

Singer wrote "At the Hop" with David White and songwriter John Medora. (The original version was "Do the Bop," but after disc jockey Dick Clark heard a demo, he suggested "At the Hop" would be a better title.) The song first was recorded on Singer's Singular Records and became a local hit. It then was taken over by ABC-Paramount, which handled national promotion. The song moved to number one on both the U.S. and European charts in 1958, reaching the pinnacle on *Billboard* lists for five weeks starting the week of January 6. Although the follow-up, "Rock and Roll Is Here to Stay," didn't make the top of the charts, decades later it remains an anthem of its genre. There were no subsequent hits.

One of the group, David White, turned up with a solo album in 1971: *Pastel, Paint, Pencil and Ink* for Bell Records, released under his real name, David White Tricker.

160

During the 1970s, Terranova and Maffei formed a new version of the group with Bill Carlucci as first tenor and took advantage of revived interest in early rock to gain engagements all over the U.S. and abroad into the 1980s. A sad note was the loss of Rapp, who killed himself in an Arizona motel in April 1983.

D'ARBY, TERENCE TRENT: *Singer, songwriter, band leader. Born New York, New York, March 15, 1962.*

There were more than the usual number of memorable moments in the Grammy Awards 1988 telecast, including an extended, sparkling performance by Michael Jackson. But one of the highlights that matched it in intensity was a turn by Terence Trent D'Arby, an artist who had already caused a stir in England, but was then mostly unknown in the U.S. Appropriately, D'Arby had named Jackson as one of his idols, crediting the Jackson 5 with awakening him to the opportunities in music outside the gospel realm, but he had also raised many eyebrows when he told British interviewers he considered himself the equal of Jackson (as well as Prince and the Beatles). In an interview with Denis Campbell of the *New Musical Express* he said, among other things, "I think I'm a genius."

Those were strong words for a performer in the first flush of discovery, although he was hardly a neophyte; at 26, he had been looking for his big break for quite a few years. But, as he later suggested to U.S. reporters, it was part of his career-launching strategy.

He told Robert Hilburn *(Los Angeles Times* Calendar, March 20, 1988), "You've got to realize that I said a lot of [outrageous] things in England. A lot of it was exaggerated to make a point. You have to hit people over the head to make them notice. I know how to play the game."

His pre-discovery years were summed up in England's *Q* magazine as follows: "Raised in a severe Pentecostal church family, son of a preacher man and a gospel-singing mother, [he] moved from Manhattan to Florida to Chicago and finally to New Jersey. [D'Arby] attended a school for gifted children, studied journalism, boxed [in the] Golden Gloves and joined the Army."

After going to Germany, supposedly with Elvis Presley's old regiment, he "went AWOL to sing with local bands, quit the Army, acquired a German manager and ended up in London where—tricked out in the finest of London street fashion and signed by CBS . . . he became the London rock scene's favorite adopted black American son since Jimi Hendrix."

He achieved that status despite such statements as one in which he suggested his debut U.K. album was better than the Beatles's *Sgt. Pepper's Lonely Hearts Club Band.* His widely reported self-praise kindled so much interest among record buyers that the LP entered English charts at number one.

The question of hype and possible exaggerations, both in his interview quotes and in his "official" bio, preceded his campaign to gain U.S. acceptance that started in late 1987. He was somewhat evasive when Hilburn sought more information about his earlier years. "Say anything you want about me. The only thing that really matters is what's in the music. Most of the things I read about people are snapshots anyway. You'd have to spend weeks with me to really understand me and you wouldn't have the space to print it anyway. So just take what you like from what you've heard."

At first it looked like his U.K. stardom might not wear well in his homeland. His self-penned debut single, "If You Let Me Stay," fell short of the Top 40. Still, even with his limited exposure, Grammy voters had been sufficiently impressed with the quality of his work to make him a finalist for Best New Artist of 1987. By the time he took the stage in New York City's Radio City Music Hall on March 2, 1988, his second single, "Wishing Well," was on the U.S. charts as was his debut album, *Introducing the Hardline According to Terence Trent D'Arby.*

His dynamic vocals and accompanying dance routine on the Grammy show obviously hit a responsive chord with U.S. TV viewers. Within two weeks the single was in the Top 20, eventually reaching number one, while the album was at number 23 in *Billboard* marked with a gold record award symbol.

D'Arby, as it happened, lost out for Best New Artist to Jody Watley amid predictions that the runnerup might have a far more momentous career than the winner.

DARIN, BOBBY: *Singer, songwriter, actor, music publisher, record-company executive. Born Bronx, New York, May 14, 1936; died Los Angeles, California, December 20, 1973.*

At the start of his career, Bobby Darin seemed the epitome of a callow, teenage idol. But he demonstrated the ability to mature and progress as a creative artist, steadily adding depth and understanding to his vocal work and eventually achieving a position of great respect from critics for his stage presence as both singer and actor. He was still at the height of his powers when a recurring heart condition felled him at age 37.

Raised in poverty in the Bronx, Darin (real name Walden Robert Cassoto) had more than his share of bad breaks. His father died before he was born and his mother passed away two months before he made his big recording breakthrough with "Mack the

Knife.'' (In her autobiography *Who's Sorry Now*, Connie Francis, with whom he had an ill-starred romance, states that Cassoto was an illegitimate child raised by his grandmother who told the child his real mother was his sister.) Darin got his diploma from Bronx High School of Science and then enrolled in Hunter College. However, he dropped out of college in the mid-1950s to try for a career in entertainment. (*See Francis, Connie*.)

Through a friendship with music publisher Don Kirshner, he was able to audition for Connie Francis's manager, George Scheck, who got him a contract with Decca Records, but the Decca alignment only resulted in four singles flops. Kirshner came to the rescue by getting Darin another chance, this time with Atlantic Records.

After missing with his first three singles on Atlantic's subsidiary, Atco, he hit in 1958 with the novelty song ''Splish-Splash'' (a song he co-wrote). The gold records he earned for that and three more singles the last years of the '50s reflected a rapid change in his style and choice of material. Two of those were ''Dream Lover'' and ''Queen of the Hop,'' but the next hit was his classic pop-rock version of ''Mack the Knife'' from the Bertolt Brecht–Kurt Weill musical *Threepenny Opera*. That song rose to number one on *Billboard* charts the week of October 5, 1959 and remained there for eight more weeks. The song was a track on his 1959 Atco LP, *That's All*. In fact, Darin had opposed issuing it as a single, but the record company did it anyway. Its success helped win him two Grammy Awards: Best New Artist of 1959 and Best Vocal Performance, Male.

The songs chosen by Darin from 1960 on had considerably greater melodic and lyric content than his earlier material. Though he gradually became a favorite of adult rather than high-school–age audiences, he still had enough impact on younger fans in the early 1960s to gain such hits as the folk-rock ''If I Were a Carpenter'' in 1962 and country ''You're the Reason I'm Living'' in 1963.

By 1963, Bobby had become active on the business side of the music field. He set up his own music publishing and recording firm, T.M. Music, Inc., with distribution handled by Capitol Records. Besides handling Bobby's compositions and recordings, the company had other artists on its roster, one of the early ones being Wayne Newton.

Darin retained a considerable following as a recording artist through the early 1970s, but he was primarily an album rather than a singles star. His output on Atco before his move to Capitol included *If I Were a Carpenter, In a Broadway Bag (Mame), Bobby Darin Sings Ray Charles,* and the August 1963 release *It's You or No One*. After signing with Capitol, he released such LPs as *You're the Reason*

I'm Living and *Bobby Darin* (1963), *Golden Folk Hits* and *Hello Dolly* (1964), *Venice Blue* (1965), and *Best of Bobby Darin* (1966). He left Capitol in 1966 to return to Atco, but soon after, shaken by the assassination of Robert Kennedy, he went into seclusion for a year at Big Sur before coming back in 1969 to release a new LP on his own label. Later, in the 1970s, he was on the Motown Records roster.

He also started gaining acting roles on TV and in the movies. One of his early roles, in the 1963 film *Captain Newman, M.D.*, earned him an Oscar nomination for best supporting actor. In February 1972, he was featured in a dramatic role on a Rod Serling ''Night Gallery'' episode. Bobby was given his own NBC-TV show during the summer of 1972 and was later signed for additional telecasts in 1973.

However, his history of heart problems, dating back to a siege of rheumatic fever in childhood, caught up with him. On December 11, 1973, he entered Cedars-Sinai Medical Center in Los Angeles, needing repairs to artificial heart valves that had been implanted previously. While on the operating table on December 20, he passed away.

As of the early 1980s, there still were several Darin LPs still in print. These included *The Bobby Darin Story* (originally issued by Atco in 1961), *Bobby Darin 1936–1973* (Motown, 1974), and *Darin at the Copa* (Bainbridge, 1981). At the start of 1986, Atco reissued *Two of a Kind*, a fine 1961 LP made by Bobby with the late Johnny Mercer.

DAVIES, CYRIL: *banjoist, harmonica player, band leader. Born England, 1932; died Eel Pie Island, England, January 7, 1964.*

Two names that occur frequently in the history of British rock 'n' roll are Alexis Korner and Cyril Davis. (*See Korner, Alexis*.) As individuals and, for some years, as collaborators, they laid the groundwork for England's blues-derived rock explosion, which was led by such young artists as the Beatles and Rolling Stones and which dominated the field for a decade, starting in the early 1960s. Davies, unfortunately, didn't live to see those developments take place.

Interested in jazz and blues in his teens, he played banjo with several jazz bands in the early 1950s and took part in the skiffle phase of British pop music in the late 1950s. (Many skiffle groups in the late 1950s based their music on the traditional music of American black blues greats, often going to great lengths to build replicas of the homemade guitars, banjos, and other instruments used when that kind of music was born.)

Toward the end of the skiffle craze, the emphasis shifted to urban blues, particularly rhythm & blues, and to less crude instruments. Davies, who was interested in the way such modern blues artists as Little Walter used microphones and other electronic aids in their harmonica playing, had a hand in these developments.

A turning point in the careers of both Davies and Korner occurred when the two started working together. They met during a skiffle session at the Houndhouse Pub on Wardour Street, London, in the mid-1950s. Soon after, they started a rhythm & blues club, the London Blues and Barrelhouse Club, in the Soho section. During those years, though, music was a part-time occupation for Davis. During the day he worked in a body and fender shop as a "panel beater" (English terminology for someone who fixes dents in car bodies).

Their music won the attention of many fellow musicians, but didn't draw enough patrons to keep the club going. After it closed, the two continued to put together groups to play blues material. When they won engagements, they often invited visiting blues performers from the U.S. to sit in with them, including Sonny Terry, Brownie McGhee, Memphis Slim, and Muddy Waters. There still was no great reaction among English fans, but word about Davies and Korner whetted interest among critics and rock buffs in the U.S.

Davies and Korner worked together as session men at times. They both backed Chris Barber's wife, Ottilie Patterson, for instance, on R&B sessions with which Barber ended his traditional jazz sets. This work encouraged them to take the then drastic step of using amplified instruments. These, of course, were used routinely in the U.S., but to English blues purists (as with folk fans when confronted with electric guitars in the States), they were rank heresy. The new arrangements performed by Davies and Korner were roundly condemned in the music sections of London papers. However, the music began to find favor with many teenage performers who spent every spare minute near the bandstand when Davies and Korner were playing. Among these fans were Mick Jagger, Keith Richards, Brian Jones, Eric Burdon, and dozens of others who were to become famous a few years later.

In early 1962, Korner and Davies decided to try again to run their own R&B club in a small pub in Ealing. They already had formed a band called Blues Incorporated in 1961, with Korner on lead guitar, Davies on harmonica, Dick Hextall Smith on tenor saxophone, and Charlie Watts on drums. (*See Rolling Stones, The.*) The group debuted on March 17, 1962. This time there was enough response that the band won the attention of the well-known Marquee Club. The band received weekly gigs at the Marquee.

Korner and Davies were besieged by young musicians and vocalists who wanted to join their group. This led to the addition of future superstar Jack Bruce on bass. When Charlie Watts left in early 1963, he was replaced by another unknown, Ginger Baker. The band moved to a new club, the Flamingo, and added a lead vocalist named Mick Jagger. Other talented performers sat in with the band whenever they could, including Long John Baldry, Zoot Money, and Paul Jones. (*See Baldry, Long John; Cream, The; Jagger, Mick.*)

The band had been at the Flamingo a few months when Davies and Korner decided to go separate ways. Korner remained as band leader while Davies became leader of a new group, the Cyril Davies All-Stars. The original lineup essentially was Screamin' Lord Sutch's Savages: Nicky Hopkins on piano; Bernie Watson, lead guitar; Ricky Fenton, bass; and Carlo Little on drums. Long John Baldry was his second vocalist. The group recorded a few sides for Pye Records, which issued two singles and an extended-play record. None of those was a best-seller, although "Country Line Special!" gained some attention. Later the All-Stars roster included Jimmy Page on guitar and Cliff Barton on bass, with Nicky Hopkins and Carlo Little as holdovers. (*See Led Zeppelin.*)

Many predicted greatness for the group, and their tremendous talent is evident in such recordings as "Someday Baby," "Steelin'," "L.A. Breakdown," "Down in the Boots," and "Piano Shuffle," all included in volume 3 of the *British Blues Archives* series (issued in the U.S. by RCA in 1971). Graduates of the All-Stars (including Jeff Beck, who performed with the group in its late stages) figured prominently in the most successful rock groups of the late 1960s and 1970s. (*See Beck, Jeff.*)

The promise of Davies group was never completely fulfilled, however. After being featured in the Marquee Club in 1963, Davies moved to a venue on Eel Pie Island on the Thames. During that engagement, he collapsed (from alcohol abuse) and died in January 1964, "robbed," as Jimmy Page sadly noted, "by an early death of the fruits of his labors."

DAVIS, MAC: *Singer, guitarist, songwriter. Born Lubbock, Texas, January 21, 1941.*

Though most of Mac Davis's reputation was made in pop music, there was no gainsaying his Texas roots. A good share of his popularity has always been with country fans and many of his recordings have shown up on country charts over the years.

Davis's upbringing in west Texas had many of the basic elements of a country background. He spent much of his time on his uncle's ranch and his early musical experience was derived to a great extent from the church. His first public singing efforts were in a church choir as a boy. He later sang in local choirs in high school. However, his teen years coincided with the rise of rock and he became increasingly interested in the music typified by Elvis, Jerry Lee Lewis, and Carl Perkins. By then, Davis was playing guitar and working with teen groups in his home area.

Later he moved to Atlanta, Georgia, where he worked days for the Georgia State Board of Probation and attended night classes at Georgia State University. His thoughts turned strongly to music, though, and he spent his spare time hanging around clubs or recording studios picking up contacts and trying to further his songwriting efforts. At the start of the '60s, he formed his own rock band and worked at college dances and private parties around Atlanta. In 1961, though, he gave that up because "I had this image of being in rock'n'roll at the age of 35, trying to make a buck."

Management, he decided, was the way to go. He found work as Atlanta district and regional manager for Vee-Jay Records, a position he held until 1965. He then moved to a wider-ranging job at Liberty: setting up local offices for the label throughout the South. (Liberty later became United Artists Records.) He did well enough for the company to bring him to Hollywood to head up its music publishing operation, Metric Music. It proved to be just what his career needed, since he had built up a backlog of original songs. Showing them to record-company executives and performers bore fruit in 1967–68, when two of his compositions made the charts: Lou Rawls's "You're Good to Me" and Glen Campbell's "Within My Memory." (*See Rawls, Lou.*)

Even more important, Davis's work caught the attention of his idol of his high school years, the King of rock himself, Elvis. Presley and his manager, Colonel Tom Parker, chose several Davis songs Elvis sang in 1968, including one that made upper chart levels, "A Little Less Conversation." Elvis next asked Mac to give him some new songs for his first recording session in many years in Tennessee. Among the material Davis turned over was a song about the deprivations of black life, "In the Ghetto." The song became a top 20 hit for Elvis in 1969 and, after Davis started his own singing career, a staple in Mac's repertoire. Davis and Presley teamed up on still more hits in 1969–70: "Memories" and "Don't Cry Daddy." (*See Presley, Elvis.*)

Presley wasn't the only artist prospering with Mac's songs (some published under such pseudonyms as Scott Davis (Scott is his son's name) and Mac Scott Davis). Hit releases of his material at the end of the '60s and in the early '70s included O.C. Smith's versions of "Friend, Lover, Woman, Wife"

and "Daddy's Little Man"; Bobby Goldsboro's single "Watching Scotty Grow" (written about Davis's son from his first, brief marriage); and Kenny Rogers and the First Edition's rock hit, "Something's Burning." Davis also prepared the music for the first Presley TV special and for two of Elvis's movies, and wrote five songs for the Glen Campbell film, *Norwood*.

At the start of the '70s, Davis decided to come out from behind the scenes and make his way as a soloist. He signed with Columbia Records. His label debut, *Mac Davis: Song Painter,* came out in mid-1971. That same year, he had two chart singles, both written by him: "Beginning to Feel the Pain" and "I Believe in Music." The latter did well in both pop and country markets. In 1972, he scored heavily with his gold single, "Baby, Don't Get Hooked on Me," number one on the *Billboard* charts the week of September 20, 1972. The album of the same title earned a platinum record. Other singles hits of the mid-1970s were "Stop and Smell the Roses" and "One Hell of a Woman." He also gained gold records for the LPs *Stop and Smell the Roses* (1974) and *All the Love in the World* (1975).

Most of his pop hits also did well on country lists. In fact, he was still placing songs on the country charts when his pop momentum seemed to be slowing down. Among his singles that made country lists in the mid-1970s were "Burning Thing' (co-written with M. James) and "I Still Love You (You Still Love Me)," both in 1975; "Forever Lovers," a top 20 hit in May 1976; and his composition "Picking up the Pieces of My Life" in the summer of 1977.

For a while in the early part of the '70s, he had his own TV variety show, which gave way to a series of specials on NBC. His 1977 Christmas special, "I Believe in Christmas," ranked sixth in the Nielsen ratings and his first of two 1978 specials in May of that year also did well with viewers. During the year, he signed a new contract with the network for two specials a year for the next three years, bringing his association with NBC to nine years, the longest association of that kind for any artist.

DEE, JOEY, AND THE STARLIGHTERS:
Vocal, instrumental, and dance group from New York–New Jersey area. Joey Dee, born Passaic, New Jersey, June 11, 1940; Carlton Latimor, born 1939; Willie Davis, born c. 1940; Larry Vernieri, born c. 1940; David Brigati, born c. 1940.

The Peppermint Lounge has been out of existence for many years, but for the first part of the 1960s, it was a beehive of activity on the New York entertainment scene. Many members of hit groups of the period met and set up new band arrangements there.

For some groups, such as Joey Dee's Starlighters, an engagement at the Lounge was the stepping stone to national fame.

Dee (real name Joseph DiNicala) grew up in an average home in New Jersey, one of a family of five girls and four boys. He became interested in pop music in high school and played saxophone and sometimes sang in school events. When he finished high school, he organized the Starlighters to play private parties and small clubs in his home area.

The group was well liked by local fans and this gave them encouragement to audition for jobs in larger clubs in New Jersey and New York City. At the start of the '60s, the band developed an act based on the teenage dances of the period that helped make it the regular band at the Peppermint Lounge in Manhattan. Besides Dee, the other members of the band were Carlton Latimor, organ, saxophone, and vocals; Willie Davis, drums and vocals; Larry Vernieri, saxophone and vocals; and David Brigati, saxophone and vocals. Vernieri and Brigati also developed the dance routines the group used in its act.

In 1961, newcomer Dee collaborated with veteran songwriter Henry Glover on a novelty song called the "Peppermint Twist." The number was featured at the Lounge and also was released as a single by Roulette Records. The disc became an international best-seller, gaining a gold-record award by late 1961.

The group's popularity as a purveyor of twist music rivalled that of Chubby Checker for a while and helped gain the band roles in such movies as *Hey Let's Twist* and *Two Tickets to Paris*.

The group continued to hold its place as a featured rock combo for the next few years, achieving a second million-selling single in 1962 with a version of the Isley Brothers' 1959 hit, "Shout." During 1962, Dee gained a Top 20 hit with the song "What Kind of Love Is This" from the *Two Tickets to Paris* soundtrack. The group also placed several albums on the charts, including *Joey Dee and the Starlighters* and *Doing the Twist at the Peppermint Lounge*.

In 1964, Dee opened his own night club in New York called The Starlighter. He organized a new backing band whose members were Felix Cavaliere on keyboards, David Brigati's brother Eddie on percussion, and Gene Cornish on guitar. That threesome later helped form the Young Rascals group. In 1965, Dee sold his club and went out on the concert circuit backed by a band whose members included the then unknown guitarist Jimi Hendrix.

Dee's prospects in music faded as the 1960s went by, but he later found a new outlet for his performing skills in rock and roll revival shows. In the late 1980s, he still was active in such shows organized by the Dick Clark organization. Backing him on keyboards by then was his son Joey Dee, Jr. (*See Rascals, The.*)

DEEP PURPLE: *Vocal and instrumental group. Original personnel (1968): Ritchie Blackmore, born Weston-super-Mare, England, April 14, 1945; Ian Paice, born Nottingham, England, June 29, 1948; Nicholas John Simper, born Norwood Green, Middlesex, England, 1946; Rod Evans, born England, 1945; Jon Lord, born Leicester, England, June 9, 1941. Simper and Evans replaced, respectively, in June 1969, by Roger Glover, born Brecon, South Wales, November 30, 1945; and Ian Gillan, born Hounslow, Middlesex, England, August 19, 1945. Glover left in mid-1973, followed soon after by Gillan. After Blackmore's departure, Tommy Bolin added (died 1975). Group disbanded in 1976; group reformed in 1985 with Blackmore, Gillan, Lord, Glover, and Paice.*

Just as some U.S. musicians, such as Jimi Hendrix, have had to go overseas to make their reputation, more than one English act has first gained fame in the States. One example is Deep Purple, whose first three hit singles went high on U.S. charts without even being released in the group's native England.

For a while, in fact, it seemed as though everything involving Deep Purple's progress took place away from home. The discussions that led to the start of the group took place between organist Jon Lord, drummer Ian Paice, and lead guitarist Ritchie Blackmore in Hamburg, Germany, in February 1968. All three had considerable experience as professional musicians by then. Blackmore had started studying classical guitar at 11 and, in his teens, switched to rock, becoming one of the most sought-after session men in England. Paice, though barely 20, had played drums with various groups beginning in the early 1960s. Lord studied classical music in his boyhood, later spent three years at drama school, and then went back to music as a sideman with a series of jazz and rock groups, the last of which before Deep Purple was the Artwoods.

To complete their new group, the three gained the services of vocalist Rod Evans and bassist Nick Simper. Both had worked with many well-known groups. Simper, in particular, had gained a reputation as one of England's top bassists. His route to Deep Purple began in 1963, when he gained his first professional job with Buddy Brothers and the Regents, after which he played in succession with Johnny Kidd and the Pirates, David Lord Sutch, Billie Davis, and the Flowerpot Men.

The group cut a single of Joe South's "Hush." Released in the U.S. on Tetragrammaton during the

165

summer of 1968, it moved into the top 5 on the charts. Soon after, their first LP, *Shades of Deep Purple,* also gained the best-seller lists. The following year, their reputation in America rose even higher with the release of hit singles "Kentucky Woman" and "River Deep, Mountain High" and the Tetragrammaton LPs *The Book of Taliesyn* and *Deep Purple.* Stateside critics were particularly enthusiastic about the 10½ minute version of "River Deep, Mountain High" on *Tailesyn,* a track built around the music used in the science fiction movie *2001.*

But none of their recordings had been issued in England as of mid-1969. As Blackmore told a reporter: "We got fed up with coming back from America to find everybody saying 'Deep Purple? Who? Never heard of them.' It was a bringdown. . . . We thought, right, we're going to stay in our country and get something going here."

One of the first steps the group's founders took was to reorganize the band. They decided the musical approach of Simper and Evans was different from theirs and, in July 1969, Ian Gillan took over as vocalist and Roger Glover as bassist. Gillan had performed with a number of groups both as vocalist and lyricist, the most recent before Deep Purple being Episode Six, which also had featured Glover. Glover had taken up guitar in his teens because of an interest in folk music and then spent two years at art school before deciding to work full time as a rock musician.

While the new group rehearsed during the summer of 1969, Jon Lord completed work on an ambitious work, a concerto for rock and symphony orchestra. Ian Gillan provided lyrics for the middle part of the three-part project. Classical conductor Dr. Malcolm Arnold was impressed with the work and agreed to conduct the concerto, which was presented in cooperation with the Royal Philharmonic Orchestra on September 24, 1969, at the Royal Albert Hall in London. It met with almost universal approval from both classical and rock reviewers. The performance was recorded live and later released in 1970 as an album, *Deep Purple and the Royal Philharmonic,* on Warner Brothers, the group's label until the early 1980s. When presented by Deep Purple at the Hollywood Bowl in Los Angeles on August 25, 1970, the work won a standing ovation as it had a year earlier in London. During the summer of 1970, Lord produced another work, "The Gemini Suite," presented by the British Broadcasting Corporation's South Bank Pops Orchestra and Deep Purple.

However, the main effort of Lord, Blackmore, and associates in late 1969 and the early 1970s was to improve their group's reputation with rock fans at home and abroad. Switching to Warner Brothers, they spent half a year working on their fifth album,

Deep Purple in Rock, an LP that finally was released both in England and the U.S. This became a major hit and firmly established the group as one of the major challengers to the Beatles' mantle in the 1970s.

Adding to the growing importance of the group members was Ian Gillan's selection to sing the part of Jesus Christ in the recorded version of the rock opera *Jesus Christ Superstar,* an album that became one of the greatest sellers in the U.S. In addition, Jon Lord completed his first film score for the American movie *The Last Rebel.*

In the fall of 1971, Deep Purple placed still another LP, *Fireball,* in the top rungs of English and U.S. charts. It followed in 1972 with its best LP of all, *Machine Head,* which included such memorable tracks as "Smoke on the Water," "Space Truckin'," and "Highway Star." Less impressive, but still best-sellers were the Warner Brothers LPs *Purple Passages* (1972), *Made in Japan* (1973), and *Who Do We Think We Are?* (1973,) the last named including one of the band's better-known tracks, "Woman from Tokyo."

The band began to fall apart in 1973 when Glover left, followed not long after by Ian Gillan. By 1975, Ritchie Blackmore also had gone. Jon Lord revamped the group with David Coverdale on lead vocals and U.S. musician Tommy Bolin on guitar, but both the group's sound and new songs didn't come up to earlier levels and it was broken up in 1976. Warner Brothers LPs of those years included *Stormbringer* (1974), *Come Taste the Band* (1975), and *Burn* and *Made in Europe* (1976). After that, the only legitimate releases into the early 1980s were retrospective such as the Warner Brothers set *When We Rock, We Rock, and When We Roll, We Roll* in 1978 and the 1980 *Deepest Purple.*

One reason for the band's demise in the mid-1970s, Glover told Mary Campbell of the Associated Press in 1985, was overwork. "We didn't stop working. In 1972, we did six tours of America and a tour of Japan and made and wrote an album. Everybody got tired of everybody. Ian Gillan was the first to say he was leaving. I decided to leave at the same time; I thought it would be easier on the others. They carried on a while with replacements. Then Ritchie Blackmore left 18 months later. They carried on with a replacement for him as well. The whole thing folded in 1976."

His departure, he said came after a concert in Osaka, Japan, on June 29, 1973. He told Campbell: "It was an emotional and traumatic experience. I didn't want to leave. I didn't want the way it was going. Being in a band like Deep Purple was like winning the pools. It was an incredible piece of luck to find yourself in such a monumental band. To have it turn sour on you was a trauma." (He told another reporter that when he left, it was at Blackmore's request.)

"It took me probably two years to get over being in that band. I couldn't go to a show—by anybody—without being uncomfortable. I felt wrong not being on the stage."

Glover eventually joined Rainbow, the band Blackmore formed after leaving Deep Purple. With that band, before Glover came aboard, Ritchie turned out three LPs, *Ritchie Blackmore's Rainbow* (Polydor, 1975), *Rainbow Rising* (Oyster, 1976), and *On Stage* (Polydor, 1977). Glover worked on the next LP, *Long Live Rock'n'Roll,* issued by Polydor in 1978 and such later Polydor releases as *Down to Earth* in 1979 and *Difficult to Care* in 1981.

The others from the 1973 alignment also ended up in different roles. Gillan opted for a solo career, recording such LPs as the *Ian Gillan Band* (Oyster, 1976), *Scarabus* (Island, 1978), and *Glory Road* (Virgin, 1980). Lord and Paice formed a new group, Whitesnake (joined by David Coverdale), whose LPs on Mirage Records included *Ready an' Willing* and *Live . . . in the Heart of the City* in 1980 and *Come an' Get It* in 1981.

For a while in the early 1980s, there was a band calling itself Deep Purple that played a number of concerts in the U.S. without any of the members of the group of the '60s and '70s on the roster. That attempt was short-lived, fortunately. Then in 1984, the five bandsmen from the group's glory days decided to bring the band back to life. Glover told Jerome Weeks (*Houston Post*, January 24, 1985): "It's actually a difficult question to answer" as to why the reunion. "But something happened that we'd not anticipated. Our music achieved a life of its own. [The group had four greatest hits repackagings released since its breakup.] There was this public pressure. I fought against it for six years. I thought I was looking backwards. It wasn't until last year when we started talking around a table and making music together that I began to accept the fact that we did have something to offer."

To everyone's surprise, the band really did. Its first new studio LP, *Perfect Strangers* (issued on Mercury Records in late 1984), and accompanying concert tour had the spark and freshness of its early 1970s work. The LP was in *Billboard*'s top 30 at year's-end and remained high on the charts in early 1985. For Deep Purple, at least, it looked like it really was possible to come home again. In 1988, Mercury released a two-LP set, *Nobody's Perfect*.

DEL VIKINGS: *Vocal group. Original personnel: Gus Bakus, born Southhampton, Long Island, New York; Kripp Johnson, born Cambridge, Maryland, mid-1930s; David Lerchey, born New Albany, Indiana, c. 1936; Clarence Quick, born Brooklyn, New York, mid-1930s; Norman Wright, born Philadelphia, Pennsylvania, c. 1938.*

One of the Del Vikings claims to fame was its having been one of the first integrated vocal groups in popular music—a sad commentary on the gap between America's principles and practices in the 1950s. When the three blacks and two whites quintet came into existence in 1955, few black artists were able to break out of the straitjacket of the specialized rhythm & blues market. The Del Vikings didn't have that problem, at least, since they were part of the general popular music scene from the time of their first record hits.

The group developed accidentally. The five members were all in the military when they met at a service club in the Greater Pittsburgh Airport in 1955. They started singing together and their voices blended so well that they decided to continue as a quintet. They soon were featured in shows at various bases and word of their ability began to reach upper echelons of the armed forces. In 1956, they were allowed to go to New York to take part in the regional Tops in Pops concert sponsored by the Air Force. Their success in that event led to a record contract from Dot Records and a single release, "Come Go with Me," that became one of the biggest hits of 1957. The record sold well over a million copies in the U.S. alone.

Most of the original group had almost as much background in athletics as singing. Lead singer Corinthian "Kripp" Johnson, for instance, won letters in basketball, football, soccer, and baseball at St. Clair High School in Cambridge, Maryland, where he also had musical exposure as a member of the glee club. Donald "Gus" Bakus played hockey for Canton High School in upstate New York. (He later graduated from Knox Memorial High School in Russell, New York.) David Lerchey was a member of his school's 1954 championship baseball team in New Albany, Indiana, and also lettered in basketball. Clarence Quick showed good form in the sprints while attending George Washington Vocational High School in New York. Norman Wright, who attended Northeast High School in Philadelphia, earned letters in fencing.

Except for Kripp Johnson, who briefly attended Morgan State College in Baltimore before enlisting in the Air Force, the others went into the service not long after they finished high school. Lerchey had a little more musical background than the others when the Del Vikings formed, having been a member of a quartet in high school as well as leading a group called the Chanters.

The group had one more top 10 hit ("Whispering Bells") for Dot in 1957, before signing with Mercury Records. On Mercury, they had the album *Record Session* and 1957 top 20 single "Cool Shake."

An album titled *Come Go with Me* was released on the Lunaverse label in the late 1950s. Distribution of the record was cut short by a lawsuit alleging the LP contained material owned by other record companies. As a result, this album is very rare and a collector's item.

There were numerous personnel changes in the group after the 1950s and some of the later alignments under the Del Vikings name had little relation to the original quintet.

DELFONICS: *Vocal and dancing group. William Hart, born Washington, D.C., January 17; Wilbert Hart, born Philadelphia, Pennsylvania, October 19; Randy Cain, born Philadelphia, Pennsylvania, May 2, c. 1946. Cain replaced in early 1971 by Major Harris, born Richmond, Virginia.*

The Delfonics rode the rising tide of soul music at just the right time in the late 1960s. The trio's high-pitched vocal blend caught the fancy of popular music followers, black and white, and made them a stellar attraction in rock concerts and on the theater and nightclub circuit.

It was the culmination of half a decade of effort and experience by the three founding members, the brothers William and Wilbert Hart and their boyhood friend, Randy Cain. William, the eldest of the three, was born in Washington, D.C., in the early 1940s, but moved to Philadelphia with his family at an early age. His brother Wilbert was born soon after and the brothers attended elementary and high school in that city. They were already interested in singing in their teens, as was their neighbor, Randy Cain.

The force toward a music career came from William, who was inspired by the recordings of Frankie Lymon and the Teenagers. At 14, William patterned his first group, the Veltones, after the Teenagers. *(See Teenagers, The.)* The group eventually included his kid brother Wilbert, Randy, and one or more other boys from their neighborhood. The group sang for local parties and dances and moved on to small clubs when the boys were older.

After they graduated from high school, Randy decided to go on to college. For two years, he did not work with the Harts, but concentrated on his studies at Lincoln University in Oxford, Pennsylvania. Meanwhile, the Harts kept on pecking away at the show business barriers. They performed with various groups, working dance routines into the act, around Philadelphia. In 1966, Cain decided to go back to singing and, with the Harts, rehearsed a new act under the name Delfonics. Cain's return brought them luck. A short time after he came back, the Delfonics achieved a regional hit, "He Don't Really Love You," on a small label. Like almost all of the group's hits, it was written by William Hart. The record helped bring them engagements in better clubs on the soul circuit, but they were still not in the major leagues. It took them two years to achieve another local hit, "He's Been Untrue."

Then Hart came up with "La La Means I Love You," based on the words his small son always repeated in the morning. The boys recorded it on the Philly Groove label, which was distributed nationally by Bell Records. It became a top 10 hit on the soul charts and also moved onto the national pop lists. Before long, the record was winning favor in Europe; the Delfonics were international celebrities.

The boys followed with a steady string of hit singles in 1968 and 1969: "You Get Yours and I'll Get Mine," "I'm Sorry," "Break Your Promise," and "Ready or Not, Here I Come." In late 1969 and early 1970, "Didn't I (Blow Your Mind This Time)" moved up the national charts until it rested at number one, a gold record. In the 1971 National Academy of Recording Arts and Sciences awards, "Didn't I" won the Grammy for top soul hit of 1970. As 1970 went by, the threesome's "sexy soul" style created such other singles hits as "Trying to Make a Fool Out of Me" and "When You Get Right down to It" and best-selling LPs *The Delfonics' Super Hits* and *The Delfonics.*

In early 1971, Cain left and his place was taken by Major Harris. Born and raised in Virginia, Harris moved to Philadelphia in 1969. He had a number of years of group work by then, including time with William Hart's early idols, the Teenagers. After breaking in as a professional with the Teenagers, Harris moved to the Jarmels, with whom he worked on a number of hits (including "A Little Bit of Soap"), then to the Impacts, the Nat Turner Rebellion, and finally the Delfonics.

DENVER, JOHN: *Singer, songwriter, guitar player, actor. Born Roswell, New Mexico, December 31, 1943.*

Throughout the 1970s, John Denver was one of the most popular musicians in the country. He wholesomely epitomized the era's folk-rock and country-rock phase as well as the general feeling of "getting back to the basics" and "living in the country." At the height of his popularity, his music was played on country stations as well as on middle-of-the-road channels and his fans were said to range in age from 3 to 99. As could be expected, tastes change, and John Denver was not represented often on the hit lists in the 1980s; however, a star of his magnitude could still command attention from a great many fans.

Born Henry John Deutschendorf, Jr., he was the son of an Air Force officer who was constantly being transferred to new locations. From Roswell, New Mexico, where he was born, the family moved to Tucson, to Oklahoma, to Japan, back to Oklahoma, and back to Tucson, where John's grandmother gave him an acoustic guitar and he started taking lessons. When the family moved again, to Montgomery, Alabama, ninth-grader John found that his guitar-playing ability attracted attention and soon people starting seeking out his friendship.

A year later, John's family moved again, this time to Fort Worth, Texas, but he no longer had to be the lonely new kid in school, a role he had played so many times before. He immediately started meeting people by singing in a church choir and by bringing his guitar to school. For a time, John's family stayed in Fort Worth, and John found himself being asked to perform with local rock bands and to play at school proms and parties.

After running away from home to California for a short while, Denver, frightened and confused, returned to Texas. He graduated from high school and enrolled at Texas Tech in Lubbock as an architecture major. But soon he found himself spending more time making music than studying. Folk music was in vogue in those early 1960s and he became an avid fan of folk-singers such as Joan Baez, Tom Paxton, Peter, Paul and Mary, and the Chad Mitchell Trio, singing their songs at local coffeehouses and college hootenannies.

Meanwhile, John's grades were slipping, which meant friction with his parents. At the semester break of his junior year, he dropped out of school, and, for the second time in his life, headed for California. This time he reached Los Angeles with more confidence than before. He got a job as a draftsman and spent all his spare time trying to break into the music business.

After a year of floundering, John got his first big break when he sang at Leadbetter's night club, a folk music center in West Los Angeles near the University of California at Los Angeles. The club's owner, Randy Sparks, who was also the founder of the New Christy Minstrels, told John that he liked his voice and that he wanted him to work as a regular performer at Leadbetter's.

John became a member of the Back Porch Majority, a Sparks-supervised group that acted as a sort of "farmclub" for the New Christy Minstrels. But soon the Back Porch Majority became a successful group in its own right, with Denver singing solos that were well received by the audience. However, he felt that the Back Porch Majority was a dead-end street, so he

auditioned for and won a job at a club called the Lumbermill in Phoenix.

Before he moved to Phoenix, John heard that Chad Mitchell was leaving his trio and was looking for a replacement. He sent a tape and was called for an interview in New York with the Trio's management. Around 300 other people were competing for the job, but Denver was selected. For nearly four years, he toured with the Trio (renamed "the Mitchell Trio" due to Chad's departure). During this time, he also developed as a successful songwriter.

John had done some songwriting before joining the Chad Mitchell Trio, but his efforts were sporadic and he often took eight or nine months to finish a song. One of those songs, "Leaving on a Jet Plane," he wrote in one evening in 1966, as he related in an interview in January 1971, "while holed up in a Washington, D.C., hotel room. You see, we [the Mitchell Trio] were always being invited to parties. I was never the type to play around on the road and time after time I'd be the only guy at these parties without a girl. This time I decided I'd had it with that. When the others left for the party, at eight, I got a pound of salami and a six-pack of beer and my guitar and locked myself in my room. When they came back about midnight, I had eaten the salami, drunk all the beer, and written 'Jet Plane.'"

The Mitchell Trio included "Leaving on a Jet Plane" in their stage act. Peter, Paul and Mary heard the song, liked it, and recorded it on their album *1700* in 1967. However, the song did not become a hit until 1969, when a girlfriend of a d.j. in Denver, Colorado, talked him into playing the song over and over again on the station. The song caught on and became one of the top hits of 1969.

Meanwhile, the Trio was going through changes and suffering from tensions between the various members. Joe Frazier left to go more deeply into rock music. Mike Kobluk eventually left the Trio in part because of personality clashes with Denver. John reorganized the group with new members David Boise and Mike Johnson. Chad Mitchell sued to remove his name from the group since none of the original members remained, but Denver pointed out that he had assumed $40,000 worth of debts from the old group, and that the suit would prevent him from continuing to pay it off. Mitchell dropped the suit; Denver paid off the debts and then changed the name of the group to Denver, Boise and Johnson.

In 1969, Mike Johnson decided to leave the group. At that point, John decided to disband the Denver, Boise and Johnson aggregation and to try his luck as a solo artist. He went to Aspen, Colorado, to perform at ski resorts. He was well received and was invited to perform at the Cellar Door in Washington, D.C.

During his run at the Cellar Door, he met Jerry Weintraub, a rising management expert then working out of New York. The two got along well and Weintraub took over management of Denver's career. He placed Denver as a guest artist on several shows, such as "Merv Griffin," and also got him a recording contract with RCA.

Denver's first album, *Rhymes and Reasons* (fall 1969), contained his version of "Leaving on a Jet Plane" as well as the title song, also an original Denver composition. (Most of the material, however, was written by other writers.) The album received good reviews but failed to hit the charts, as did his next two RCA albums: *Take Me to Tomorrow* and *Whose Garden Was This.* "Aspenglow" on the *Take Me to Tomorrow* LP was one of Denver's few original compositions in these years.

John co-wrote his first hit with Bill and Taffy Danoff, whom John ran into at the Cellar Door in Washington. The husband-and-wife song writing team, also performing under the name Fat City, were having trouble completing a song. Denver's act already featured one song they had written for him, "I Guess He'd Rather Be in Colorado," which he later recorded on his *Poems, Prayers and Promises* LP. They got together and finished the song, "Country Roads," before the night was over. Denver censored lyrics about naked ladies and a pink and purple farmhouse so the song could be played on the radio.

John recorded "Country Roads" for his upcoming album, *Poems, Prayers and Promises.* The single was released in early 1971 and climbed to the number fifty position on the charts, the highest a Denver single had ever reached. However, he and Weintraub were not satisfied with reaching number fifty. They pushed the song through performances on talk shows and by getting maximum radio coverage. The plan worked and the song moved up to the number two position. Before 1971 was over, Denver had his first two gold-record awards, one for the single "Country Roads" and the other for the album, *Poems, Prayers and Promises.*

Denver's next album, *Aerie* (released in November 1971), included "Eagle and the Hawk" (which he co-wrote with Mick Taylor for a TV special) and the original composition "Starwood in Aspen," in which Denver sang the praises of his new home in Colorado, where he settled permanently with his then-wife Anne in the early 1970s. The album was certified gold by the R.I.A.A. in January 1972.

John took some time off from doing concerts in the United States to do a series of telecasts for BBC II in England. The idea was to improve his performing ability in front of TV cameras. His increased skills in this area were evident when Denver returned to the United States. In 1972 and 1973, he appeared on numerous talk and variety shows. He also hosted *The Midnight Special,* a late-night 90-minute musical show on NBC, on which he not only sang some of his songs but also held discussions with other entertainers about the importance of getting young people to register to vote. Among Denver's other television endeavors was "Bighorn," his first prime-time special, which emphasized ecology.

John's sixth album, *Rocky Mountain High* (late 1972), was soon certified gold by the R.I.A.A. The title song was released as a single and soon climbed to the top of the charts. His next album, *Farewll Andromeda,* contained the hit single "I'd Rather Be a Cowboy" and was certified gold in September 1973.

Denver continued to use television to boost the sales of his records. In 1973, he wrote the score for the TV drama "Sunshine," one of the most highly acclaimed shows of that year. The score included his composition "Sunshine on My Shoulders" from the *Poems, Prayers and Promises* LP. The song was reissued on his next album, *John Denver's Greatest Hits,* which was certified gold within two weeks of its release in November 1973. "Sunshine on My Shoulders" received such enormous airplay that it was issued as a single in early 1974 and was certified gold by the R.I.A.A. not long afterward. It reached number one in *Billboard* the week of March 30.

In early 1974, Denver made some television appearances. He played a dramatic role on the TV series "McCloud" in February 1974. During that period, he served as guest host on "The Tonight Show," standing in for Johnny Carson. He continued to produce occasional television specials in the mid-1970s.

To coincide with a countrywide concert tour in the summer of 1974, RCA issued a new LP, *Back Home Again.* The album was certified gold within a week of its release. In addition, the Governor of Colorado, John Vanderhoof, declared the week of June 24–30 as "Welcome Back Home Again, John Denver Week" and proclaimed Denver the poet laureate of the state.

Meanwhile, *Back Home Again* went gold, as did its single, "Annie's Song." Another of its songs, "Sweet Surrender," was featured in a Disney movie, *The Bears and I.* Denver won his fourth gold-record award for a single for the song "Back Home Again" in January 1975.

1975 proved to be a year in which John Denver truly reached the heights of his profession and was generally agreed to be the number-one–selling record artist in the United States. Released in early 1975, *An Evening with John Denver* (a two-record set based on his 1974 concert tour) and the number one single "Thank God I'm a Country Boy" were certified gold by the R.I.A.A. Denver's *Windsong* LP, released in October 1975, had gone gold before the year was out. So did both sides of the single release from the album, "I'm Sorry" and "Calypso" (a song celebrating undersea explorer Jacques Cousteau). The combined "I'm Sorry/Calypso" disc reached number one on *Billboard* charts the week of September 27, 1975. Another single from that album, "Fly Away," also became a chart hit. His 1975 Christmas album, *Rocky Mountain Christmas,* was certified gold almost as soon as it was released. His earlier albums, *Back Home Again* and *John Denver's Greatest Hits* remained on the national hit lists throughout 1975, with the latter reaching a total volume of over 5 million units by December 1975, thereby becoming one of the biggest-selling albums in pop music history. Denver took the album title, *Windsong,* to be the name of his own record company formed during 1975. Among the acts signed to the label was a group called the Starland Vocal Band whose members included longtime friend Bill Danoff (born Springfield, Massachusetts, May 7, 1946) and Taffy Danoff (born Kathy Nivert, Washington, D.C., October 25, 1944). With Jon Carroll and Margot Chapman, they formed a quartet that earned a number one single, "Afternoon Delight," on Billboard charts the weeks of July 10 and 17, 1976.

Among the many kudos received by Denver in 1975, one of the greatest was undoubtedly being named Entertainer of the Year by the Country Music Association, perhaps the most prestigious award in all of country music. He accepted the award via closed-circuit satellite relay from Australia, where he was doing a concert tour.

After 1975, Denver's hit productivity declined somewhat. Still, the LP *Spirit* (1976) went platinum, while *John Denver* (1979) went gold. He continued to do TV specials, however, and he appeared in the box office smash movie *Oh, God!* with George Burns in 1977, receiving mostly positive reviews for his performance. As evidence of his continued popularity and respect as an all-around entertainer, he was asked by the record industry to serve as host of the annual televised Grammy Awards in 1979, and has hosted the event several times since. In the early summer of that year, his single "What's on Your Mind"/"Sweet Belinda" was on the country charts for two months. At year-end, his LP, *A Christmas Together* (with the Muppets), hit album lists, eventually going platinum. In 1980, his album *Autograph* was on both pop and country charts. His 1981 chartmakers included the country single "The Cowboy and the Lady" and the gold album *Some Days are Diamonds.*

Though essentially absent from the hit lists during the rest of the 1980s, Denver was constantly popping up in television specials and commercials and on interview shows. He traveled to Russia, where he performed to enthusiastic audiences. In addition, part of his home in Colorado became a center for ecological research. Denver increasingly became a sort of goodwill American musical ambassador to Communist countries. In December 1983, for example, he was invited to sing at a banquet for Chinese Premier Zhao Ziyang in New York City hosted by Mayor Edward Koch and that, in turn, led to an invitation to do a concert tour in China. In February 1984, he went to Sarajevo, Yugoslavia, to perform the theme song he wrote (at ABC-TV's behest) for the winter Olympics, "The Gold and Beyond." In March 1984, his 22nd album on RCA, *It's About Time,* was released. But his album sales were dwindling and his increasingly diverse interests, which included hosting his own Annual Celebrity Pro/Am Ski tournament in Colorado, and such charitable activities as an African trip to focus attention on the continent's food crisis and serving as a spokesman for a UNICEF fund raising drive, tended to dilute any emphasis on restoring his songwriting and recording luster. He did not abandon the recording field, though, ending his long alliance with RCA in 1984 and signing a new contract soon after with Geffen Records.

DEREK AND THE DOMINOS: *See Clapton, Eric; Cream, The.*

DERRINGER, RICK: *Singer, guitarist, songwriter, record producer, band leader (THE McCOYS, DERRINGER). Born Galena, Ohio, 1949.**

As of 1988, Rick Derringer only was in his mid-30s, but he could look back on a career spanning more than 20 years as a professional entertainer. When he was 16, his group, the McCoys, recorded one of the classic rock songs of all time, "Hang on, Sloopy." In later years, as performer, songwriter, and producer, he influenced the careers of many important pop artists.

He recalled: "I was born in Ohio just across the border from Indiana. My brother Randy played drums and I played guitar when I was nine. When I was in the eighth grade, my family moved 12 miles across the state line and we lived in a town called Fort Recovery. For some time, I'd been fascinated by the electric bass. In 1958, it seemed the instrument of the future. When I was 12 or 13 in Indiana, a neighbor named Dennis Kelly said he'd like to play it and if I'd show him how, he'd buy one. He got a

---

*Based partly on personal interview with Irwin Stambler.

brand new Fender bass with amp and I showed him a song from the Ventures LP *The McCoys*. He learned it and while he was playing it, we arrived in wonderland because we realized with him and me and Randy we had a band. We decided the Ventures song would be our theme song so we named ourselves the McCoys.''

After a short time, the boys decided they wanted a new name and switched to the title the Rick Z Combo (based on Rick and Randy's last name, Zehringer). As they began to find performing work in the Midwest in the early '60s, they came in contact with record promoters who thought the band had possibilities, but needed a different name. The band then became Rick and the Raiders and soon had its debut single, "You Know That I Love You," on Sonic Records.

The band personnel changed somewhat. It became a foursome with the addition of keyboard player Ronnie Brandon. When Dennis departed for college, his place was taken on bass by Randy Hobbs. The group was beginning to gain a following in the Midwest and had plenty of work at local dances and various clubs. During one club date in 1965, Rick and the Raiders opened for a trio called the Strangeloves that was on a New York label called Bang.

One of the founders of Bang was songwriter Burt Berns (born Bert Russell), whose output included a 1964 hit, "My Girl Sloopy," for the Vibrations, a R&B group. Berns thought it could become a rock hit too if he could find the right group to record. He asked the Strangeloves for help and they recommended Derringer's group. Rick and his friends went to New York accompanied by the Zehringers' parents to make the recording. Because Paul Revere and the Raiders had become nationally known, a name change was in order and on the suggestion of a producer who had seen the name "the McCoys" on a drum in a picture in the Zehringer family album, the old title was resurrected.

Before the single came out, the song title was changed to "Hang on, Sloopy" and Rick Zehringer became Rick Derringer. The name change, he said, came to him in a dream, inspired by a picture of a derringer gun on the Bang label.

"We were a typical rock'n'roll band. We didn't get paid much, but we didn't care. We were happy just playing music. The producers and engineers after they finished recording 'Hang on, Sloopy' jumped up and down and shouted 'Number one!' Being kids, we took it for granted people always did that. Later we learned that's not so and realized there are times people can really be blown away by a song.''

Disc jockeys and listeners were blown away as well. The single made the charts by late summer and moved swiftly upward until it nestled in the number one position in *Billboard* the week of October 2, 1965. Over the next few years, the McCoys became a headline attraction throughout the U.S. and Canada. Their succeeding record releases didn't outscore "Hang on, Sloopy," but the group had more than a half dozen other singles on Bang that made the charts. The group also was represented by a number of Bang LPs, including *Hang on, Sloopy* in 1965 and *You Make Me Feel So Good* in 1966. In 1968, the group left Bang for Mercury Records, which released the albums *Infinite McCoy* and *Human Ball* at the end of the decade.

However, the band's fortunes had taken a turn for the worse. At the start of the '70s, it was getting by through work as the house band at Steve Paul's Scene, a nightclub in New York's Times Square.

Looking for more challenging opportunities, Rick, Randy, and Randy Hobbs became the backing group for blues-rock star Johnny Winter. Winter brought them in because he wanted to emphasize mainstream rock rather than blues on his third LP for Columbia, the 1970 best-seller *Johnny Winter Band*. Afterwards, the McCoys alumni continued as part of Winter's touring show. Later, Rick became affiliated with the other Winter brother, Edgar, joining the Edgar Winter Group as lead guitarist and vocalist in October 1973. (*See Winter, Johnny and Edgar.*)

During 1974, Rick got the opportunity to record his first solo album for Blue Sky Records, a label formed by his old nightclub employer, Steve Paul. Those sessions provided tracks for the LP, *All-American Boy*, the source of another hit single, "Rock and Roll, Hoochie Koo," written by Rick. In 1975, Rick turned out an updated version of "Hang on, Sloopy" (which only barely made the *Billboard* top 100) and another album, *Spring Fever*.

Rick then assembled a new band for recordings and live concerts. He named it Derringer. It included Derringer and Danny Johnson on guitars, Kenny Aronson on bass, and Vinny Appice on drums. During the mid-1970s, the group became one of the better acts on the rock circuit. It started its recording career with a fine debut LP, *Derringer*, which featured such excellent tracks as "Sailor" and "Beyond the Universe." It followed with the albums *Sweet Evil* and *Derringer Live* in 1977, and *If I Weren't So Romantic, I'd Shoot You* in 1978. At the end of the decade, Rick returned his emphasis to solo recordings, turning out *Guitars and Women* (1979) and *Face to Face* (1980), both on Blue Sky.

In the 1980s, Derringer diversified his activities to include record production for other artists, writing material for the movies and how-to books, and creating videos. His soundtrack work in the mid-1980s included music for *Madame X, Bachelor Party,*

Splits, and *Where the Boys Are.* (One song he favored that was pulled from *Madame X,* he noted, was called "We Reserve the Right (to Rock)." "The producers took it out; they decided it was too heavy metal.")

Among his other projects, he noted, was a video called "I Play Guitar" and a guitar-technique book, *Rock Guitar Secrets.* "The book was issued by Columbia Pictures' publishing group and has sold over 40,000 copies so far. I also designed a guitar for B.C. Rich Guitars of Los Angeles which is the second-biggest-seller in their line. It's called the Stealth and it's an all hand-made guitar."

As a record producer, he worked with such performers as Johnny Dangerously and Weird Al Yankovic. With Weird Al, he helped produce several chart hit albums in the mid-1980s.

But he didn't ignore concert work in that decade. In the mid-1980s, his act comprised himself on lead guitar and vocals, Danny Kisselbach on bass, and Bernie Kenny on drums. It was, he said, "just a guitar-powered trio, but a good one."

He was satisfied with his performing achievements, he emphasized, even if he didn't have a long list of blockbuster singles to point to. "I have the rights to two songs every rock'n'roll band can play. I jammed with [heavy metal band] Triumph and came to Toronto where we were doing a show for multiple sclerosis. I said: 'Let's do "Hang on, Sloopy,"' and the audience went wild. So I said: 'Let's do another song' and sang 'Rock and Roll, Hoochie Koo,' which also broke everyone up. I said to the guitar player: 'It's your turn' and he said: "'Johnny B. Goode."' So I felt great to have two of my songs in that company."

What did he see in his future after 1985? He replied: "There's always the question—Mick Jagger gets it a lot—'How long are you going to be doing this? Will you be playing rock when you're 50?' Muddy Waters has been a great example of what's possible, where even in his sixties he could perform music that grandparents and young folks and everybody could like. I feel rock is going in the direction where it's not just for the young and I certainly want to be part of that."

DEVILLE, WILLY: *Singer, guitarist, band leader (MINK DEVILLE), songwriter, actor. Born New York, New York, c. 1950.* *

One of the bands to surface as the result of the mid-1970s New York–based new wave–punk ferment was Mink DeVille, whose central figure was tough-looking, plain-speaking Willy DeVille. In

---

*Based partly on personal interview with Irwin Stambler.

truth, the band didn't consider itself part of the punk genre, nor did its repertoire fit well into the new wave context, being essentially an evolution from '50s and '60s rock and R&B. But the new wave scene opened doors for Willy and his group, who became cult favorites both in the U.S. and in Europe.

Willy's musical tastes certainly were not consonant with the cerebral or dark-hued material of many rock bands of his time. He commented at one time: "I think rock'n'roll moves your tail and makes your heart go boom! boom! boom! Take 'Walkin' in the Rain' [the rock version]. How can you not get hit in the heart by that? It moves you emotionally. If it doesn't move you emotionally, I have no use for it. I think that's what rock is all about. I think that's what good art is all about. You feeling it inside—that's the magic.

"The idea that there was something wrong with caring, that came along in the late 1960s and in the '70s. I think that went against the whole idea of rock. Some artists got to think they were oracles. I can't pretend to be God. I'm human. I have these human emotions. But it got to be unhip to show you cared. If you're talking about rock'n'roll, then caring, letting your feelings show, was what it was all about. I found that in the music that gave birth to rock, black music by people like the Dominoes and the early Drifters, and that's why that plays a strong part in Mink DeVille's music."

In appearances during the late 1970s and the 1980s, Willy didn't look much like the romantic. Of medium height, lean and muscular with a gold earring in one lobe, flashing dark eyes and a slick prompadour hairdo, he gave the impression of someone who could handle himself in a fight. Indeed, he would have been a tough foe; he had a liberal education growing up in the lower part of Manhattan. Some of the seamy side of his early years showed up in his original compositions, but he always conveyed exuberance, a love of life, and love for his home city.

DeVille's formative years were those of a sensitive youngster who did not fit in with his family or peers. At 14, he recalled, he wandered around New York streets and often slept on roof tops. He told a reporter from the *Rocky Mountain Musical Express* (August 1977): "When I was 15, I left school. I didn't fit in with really anything [unless] it was real weird. Matter of fact, my nose was broken because I didn't fit in and I had two concussions because I didn't fit in. Most of my time was spent on MacDougal Street down in the Village. See I'm really kind of a teeny-bopper at heart and I hope I never lose that."

He enjoyed listening to street musicians and began

to do some performing himself to earn spare change.

Willy's restless nature propelled him to London in 1971 with the idea of forming his own band. Those plans fell through and, instead, he got work as a solo artist. He found club owners less than sympathetic to unknown Americans. "I can remember one club where the lady who did the booking gave me an especially hard time because I was American. Check this picture: this lady is standing there questioning my validity; meanwhile on her stage is this English guy singing 'Funky Broadway' with a Cockney accent!"

He soon gave up on London and went back to New York. Unhappy with the "'60s hangover" of the Big Apple rock establishment of the early 1970s, he fled to San Francisco, where he remained for a year and a half picking up whatever engagements he could find and ceaselessly trying out new combinations of backing musicians. "Cats were in and out of the band so fast that we had to stick to what was simple and what people knew. Which was blues. I mean, anybody who can play knows how to play 'Back Door Man,' right?"

He finally found two compatible sidemen, drummer T.R. Allen and bass guitarist Ruben Siguenza, whom he took back to New York with him in 1974. His timing was right. The punk–new wave activity was beginning to rejuvenate rock interest in the city and Willy eventually benefited from that. For a while, though, it was more of the hand-to-mouth existence he had known in England and the U.S. West Coast. The band accepted whatever club dates it could find, often performing for a handful of customers, and slowly won notice from some reviewers and fans. Things took a turn for the better when Louis X. Erlanger came on board as lead guitarist.

With his new band alignment, DeVille got some important dates at the Bowery-based CBGB's, the club that became the headquarters for the new wave movement of the middle and late '70s. CBGB's management had an open mind about pop music and weren't afraid to showcase performers with a wide divergence of styles from all-out punk bands such as the Ramones to more mainstream groups such as Mink DeVille. When CBGB's recorded a live LP (*Live at CBGB's*, issued in 1976) of some of its best-liked bands, Mink DeVille was represented on three tracks.

The exposure led to a record contract from Capitol Records. Veteran producer Jack Nitzsche, who had liked Willy's work when he heard him in San Francisco, went into the studio to fashion the debut LP, *Mink DeVille* (1977). The album, with ear-catching tracks "Spanish Stroll" and "Mixed Up Shook Up Girl," is generally agreed to have been one of the best debut collections by a new band of the mid-1970s. Of equal quality was the second Capitol release, *Return to Magenta* (1978).

Nitzsche produced *Magenta* and also was credited with co-writing some of the material with Willy. Asked about Jack, Willy agreed that Nitzsche was somewhat eccentric. "He is nuts. He's mad as a hatter. But I think he's very talented even though he seems like he hears things from other places."

At the end of the 1970s, Willy's love for art and many elements of French culture led to another move. He took up residence in Paris for a time, which led to the recording of his third Capitol LP in France. *Le Chat Bleu*, with its theme of living on the margins of Paris society, came out overseas in 1980 and later was brought out in the U.S. as an import. The album remains one of his most cohesive projects and has become a cult classic around the world.

Deville's record output and the vibrancy of Mink DeVille's live shows gained a loyal following into the 1980s, but not a huge one. DeVille was fighting the grip that formula programming had on radio, which tended to minimize the chance a new or little-known band had to win a mass audience.

He made the point in the late 1970s about *Magenta,* an excellent collection that most music fans probably never knew existed. "I feel we have pretty legitimate credentials. I mean this album is a good album. It deserves to be played.

"We're trying to play good stuff. We're not tryin' to make quick bucks and then thumb our nose at everyone. We're fightin' the battle of gettin' to those radio program directors. We say about our album: 'It's a record; it's a good record. Play the damn thing. Don't take the easy way out and play for the housewives!'"

At the start of the '80s, Willy switched labels, signing with Atlantic, which issued the LP *Coup de Grace* in 1981. Over the next half decade, a series of additional LPs came out, culminating with *Sportin' Life* (December 1985)—the first for which Willy didn't use all the members of his tour band. He told Duncan Strauss of the *Los Angeles Times* (April 9, 1986), that making the record had a rejuvenating effect on him. "What happened, I think, is the Mink DeVille band got so stylized that everything I laid down sounded like an old Mink DeVille song to me. I wanted something new and fresh and different. Which is what I finally got, but I had to bring in different [musicians]. . . . It showed me how restricted I was in a band format. So now I'm coming out on my own. I'm just going to be Willy Deville."

Before doing that, however, he took his tour band on the road in support of *Sportin' Life.* Prior to that, he had declared bankruptcy—apparently as much to cancel out an undesirable management agreement as to solve a growing debt problem. He commented,

"Mink DeVille had gathered debts up to about a half million dollars, but I failed because the contracts were in my name. I had to do it. Everybody loves Mink DeVille shows and everybody loved the band, but we were just hobbling along. And we couldn't just keep hobbling along."

Despite feeling a new freedom from such difficulties, he told Strauss: "This is going to be the last Mink DeVille tour and the last Mink DeVille record—except for a live one we did in Paris and Amsterdam during the last [1985] tour."

His program for the rest of 1986 included working on his first solo album, assisted by Mark Knopfler of Dire Straits, who handled production and lead guitar tracks. (*See Dire Straits.*) During the year, he made his movie debut in *Va Banque* by German director Deithard Kuester, and he began work on a book of vignettes of his early years in lower Manhattan.

The Knopfler–DeVille's project, *Miracle,* was released by A&M Records in late 1987. The LP included one of Willy's best original compositions in some time, "Heart and Soul." Knopfler also selected Willy's "Storybook Love" as the theme song for the movie *The Princess Bride* for which Mark provided the soundtrack material.

In general, Willy seemed to hew to his principles about life and rock. "Rock'n'roll originally was a thing that changed and it always should change. I mean any kind of good art should change. Like when Picasso put his first painting out, a six-year-old could understand it. But he kept evolving and showing that even if the meaning wasn't spelled out, you could feel what he was getting at. I think that's what rock is all about really."

Asked whether he considered himself a "passionate" man, he replied with a laugh: "You can ask my chick."

He then picked up the small tape recorder he often carried with him and flipped it on. The music that emerged was sung in French by Edith Piaf. Hardly rock'n'roll, but Willy likes what he likes. "Yeah, I like her a real lot. After all, she was singin' in the streets too."

DEVO: *Vocal and instrumental group. Members, all born Ohio: Jerry Casale, Bob Casale, Mark Mothersbaugh, Bob Mothersbaugh, Alan Myers.*

With a music and stage-show format designed to symbolize the dehumanizing effects of advanced technology, the group Devo—which, not incidentally, hailed from the midwestern industrial city of Akron, Ohio—cut an avant garde rock niche for itself in the late 1970s. The band's theme was hardly new—it had been dealt with by major films since the silent era and by more than a few rock artists—but Devo's robotlike style and strange stage antics gave some new twists to it, at least in the beginning. After the band first established its credentials as a "name" group, however, its members seemed increasingly locked into their original concept without showing the ability to expand creatively.

All the band members grew up in reasonably comfortable middle class families. In the early 1970s, Kent State University art students Jerry Casale and Mark Mothersbaugh became acquainted through their mutual interest in combining visual images and progressive electronic music. Jerry at the time could play rudimentary bass guitar and Mark wrote odd-sounding songs he performed on electronic keyboards. Their collaboration eventually evolved into a full-scale rock group with the addition of their brothers, Bob Casale and Bob Mothersbaugh, on guitars plus Alan Myers on drums. Mark Mothersbaugh handled most of the lead-vocal requirements.

During the mid-1970s, the band's blend of specially prepared back screen projections (which emphasized the concept of de-evolution from which the band's name derived) and its assumed stance of mechanical men began to find an audience, first in local Akron clubs and later in Ohio's largest city, Cleveland. Before long, the band was able to move on to such rock hubs as New York, where it was featured at CBGB's, and Los Angeles, where they drew capacity crowds to the Starwood. By 1977, the band had switched home base from the Midwest to Los Angeles as part of its campaign for national exposure.

Devo by then already had made one important convert—avant garde artist Iggy Pop, who included his version of the Devo song "Praying Hands" in his act. He also brought them to the attention of other artists in the forefront of new rock exploration, including David Bowie and Brain Eno. Eno later was to produce the group's debut album. (*See Bowie, David; Eno, Brian; Pop, Iggy.*)

The band's concerts spotlighted certain trademarks, such as a filmed or spoken query, "Are we not men?" to which the audience would respond "We are Devo!" plus a segment of the show in which Mark would don a babyish mask and sing certain songs as his alter ego Booji Boy.

Describing a mid-1970s Devo show at the Mabuhay Club in Berkeley, California, Michael Snyder reported in the *Berkeley Barb* (October 21–27, 1977): "Wearing identical yellow flight suits stenciled in front with a diagonal Devo, they jerked to their convulted, almost-reggae version of [the Rolling Stones] 'Satisfaction.' On 'Uncontrollable Urge' and 'Mongoloid,' Mark moved like a myopic jack rabbit suffering from muscular dystrophy. He broke keys on the mini-Moog during a pounding sonic blast. Trashing his bass in the air, Jerry scowled under strips of blue tape that crossed his face. Mark's brother seemed to be playing a guitar that wasn't much more than six strings and a two-by-four plank."

Other facets were noted by Richard Cromelin of the *Los Angeles Times* after a late 1977 concert. The show began with a short film produced by a Devo friend who made commercials in Minneapolis that outlined the "basic truths about de-evolution." As the concert progressed, Cromelin reported: "Motifs from the film materialize on stage. . . . Apes attack the crowd with ping-pong paddles; humanoid creatures packed into rubber body-bags hop blindly around the stage. Booji Boy, wearing a whiplash victim's neck brace, carries the weight during less theatrical moments. Looking like the young Clark Kent in the throes of a severe kryptonite attack, eyes popping and veins bulging, Booji Boy is the primary target of the audience's strange combination of fondness and antagonism."

Booji Boy also was the label name the band selected when it decided to market a single on its own. That disc, "Jocko Homo"/"Mongoloid," was placed in a scattering of record stores around the country, mostly in university towns, in the fall of 1977. The single sold around 10,00 copies, a good return for such a project. More important, it helped in the band's negotiations with major record companies that led to a contract with Warner Brothers Records in early 1978.

The band's debut album, *Q: Are We Not Men? A: We Are Devo* (fall 1978), naturally couldn't match the strange fascination of the live shows, but it still conveyed the essence of the band's message, most notably through the automaton ring to Mark Mothersbaugh's vocals. The lyrics by themselves tended to be rather muddy in meaning, but the LP still had the attraction of offering tracks that fans could pogo or dance to.

The band continued intensive touring throughout 1978 and 1979, including a swing through Japan in early summer of 1979 that drew large, if not capacity crowds to venues in Osaka, Nagoya, and Tokyo. The Tokyo show took place at Japan's best-known auditorium, Budokan. The latter concerts paid off in a good reception in that country for the fall 1979 LP, *Duty Now for the Future.*

That album did not advance the group's artistry beyond its debut release, though it was considerably more entertaining than album number three, *Freedom of Choice,* issued by Warner Brothers in mid-1980. Jerry Casale maintained in an interview with Jeff Spurrier of the *Long Angeles Times* (June 15, 1980) that the album represented broader insight into the state of the world as he and the other bandsmen saw it.

"*Freedom of Choice* has everything that is good about Devo in it. The songs do reflect the nature of living in a devolved world. I think we have the same subject matter, the same points of reference as the Clash. We are writing about the same things: schizoid pessimism and optimism in a world gone upside down where there is no real frontier left. The idea of what a human being is has been twisted inside out and the corporate state rules. If anything, the last four years have proved Devo's claims. Things are rapidly deteriorating."

In another interview reported in *Trouser Press,* he emphasized that Devo's outlook wasn't pessimistic or cynical, but simply an attempt to make listeners look at the world around them. "All we're doing is reporting the facts. . . . De-evolution is basically an extended joke that was as valid an explanation of anything as the Bible is, a mythology for people to believe in. We were just attacking the ideas that people have that they're at the center of the universe—that they're important, that they must be immortal, that there must be a Guide. The whole (what we think of as inverted) value system that precipitates every cultural/political form follows from it. . . .

"If there's anything important about history, it's that stupidity wins. We're paranoid for good reasons: hundreds of years when assholes take over, knowledge is lost and things go backward. We question the whole theory concerning progress, and the middle class idea of a 'better life.' . . . Devo deals with people who eat McDonald's hamburgers and wear Jordache jeans; that's our dilemma. I guess we're almost fed by the things we hate."

The problem was that the band had the zeal of reformers, but met difficulty in packaging the message to make it continuously satisfying. Or, to put it another way, the band's later albums put too much emphasis on preaching and less on finding intriguing new musical ways to say it.

The group did retain a following in the U.S. and abroad in the 1980s that encouraged Warner Brothers to issue new albums at a steady clip. Early '80s releases included the band's first in-concert LP, *Devo Live* (issued in extended-play format in 1981) and the studio productions *New Traditionalists* (1981) and *Oh No, It's Devo* (1982). In 1983, the group performed the title song on the soundtrack for the Dan Akyroyd comic film *Doctor Detroit.* In late 1984, Warner Brothers issued a new studio LP, *Shout,* which received subpar response in 1985 from critics and record buyers. A major disappointment, it indicated the group was rapidly losing claim to the reputation of one of rock's most innovative bands.

DIAMOND, NEIL: *Singer, guitarist, song-writer. Born Brooklyn, New York, January 24, 1941.*

One of the most versatile singers and composers of popular music from the mid-1960s on, Neil Diamond produced a seemingly endless string of hits in such varied veins as folk, folk-rock, gospel, and country-rock. The first two aren't too surprising, considering the growth of the urban folk movement in the late 1950s. The latter two areas, at first glance, seem a little unlikely for an artist born and raised in Brooklyn.

Diamond found an interest in music as soon as he could walk and talk. As a child, he loved to hum along with records on the radio. When he was 10, he performed on Brooklyn streets with a group of youngsters calling themselves the "Memphis Back-street Boys" for whatever change passersby would throw them. When he was 13, he ran away from home to the Midwest, forming a folk group, the Roadrunners, that worked the coffeehouse circuit.

He returned to Brooklyn, where he started writing songs at 15 and then made the rounds of the publishing houses to try to place them. For the next five years, he spent the required time in school, but devoted all his spare moments to writing, singing whenever he could gain engagements, and looking for a full-time job in the business. At 20, he was working as a song plugger for New York music firms, trying to get other peoples' records played by disc jockeys. Soon after, he was hired as a staff writer by Sunbeam Music to turn out songs, usually on order, for particular performers. In the mid-1960s, his byline appeared on many songs recorded by leading pop artists, including a number of the Monkees' hits. (*See Monkees; Nesmith, Michael.*)

During this period, though, Diamond began to move out on his own as a performer. He signed with Bang Records and, with the production skills of Ellie Geenwich, provided them with a series of hits: "Cherry, Cherry" and "Thank the Lord for the Nighttime" (1966) and "Kentucky Woman" and "Girl, You'll Be a Woman Soon" (1967). (*See Greenwich, Ellie.*)

He took a giant step to the top levels of popular music soon after he moved to a new record company, MCA's Uni subsidiary, at the close of the '60s. He scored gold singles in 1969 with compositions "Holy Holy" and "Sweet Caroline." LPs included *Velvet Gloves and Spit, Brother Love's Travelin' Salvation Show* and the gold *Touching You . . . Touching Me.*

Wrote Robert Hilburn of the *Los Angeles Times* in September 1970: "In both his writing and singing, Diamond has a high sense of drama. His songs are filled with sharp tempo changes that add to the impact of his powerful pure rock (as opposed to blues-rock or soul) voice and the unrelenting drum-guitar-bass beat. He is a particularly effective performer on stage. Though his comments between songs tend to wander, he has excellent projection when he is singing."

At the time of Hilburn's review, Diamond had five titles in the upper reaches of the charts. His gold single "Cracklin' Rosie" was in the top 5 nationally and his gold album *Gold* was in the top 10, both on Uni. Also on the charts under the Bang label were the single "Solitary Man" and the albums *Shilo* and gold-award-winning *Greatest Hits.* In December, Diamond had another top 10 single: "He Ain't Heavy, He's My Brother," which previously provided large sales when recorded by the Hollies. (*See Hollies, The.*)

In the spring and summer 1971, he provided Uni with two single hits: "I Am . . . I Said" and "Done Too Soon." In September, Bang dug out some previously recorded Diamond material to gain a singles hit with "I'm a Believer," Neil's own version of a composition he had originally written for the Monkees.

His gold LP *Tap Root Manuscript* on Uni demonstrated Diamond's continuing experiments with new approaches to popular music. The first side contained his hit single "Cracklin' Rosie" and several other rock songs. The reverse side was taken up entirely by a six-part composition, "The African Trilogy." The goal was to depict the three main stages in man's life (birth, maturity, and death) in rhythmic forms derived from gospel music and native African melodies. Not too many stations played the entire suite, but quite a few programmed sections of it, such as "Soolaimon" and "Childsong."

Material from his August 24, 1972 concert at the Greek Theatre in Los Angeles was used to compile the gold two-record LP, *Hot August Night.* Also in 1972, he made his mark on Broadway with a one-man show in the Winter Garden that ran for 21 performances.

The following year, he moved to a new record label, Columbia, which was still his recording company in the late 1980s. His debut on the label was the musical narrative soundtrack for the film *Jonathan Livingston Seagull,* which won him both Grammy and Golden Globe awards. He followed that with the 1974 album *Serenade.* The first single from that album, "Longfellow Serenade"/"Rosemary's Wine" became a top 5 hit. His next album, *Beautiful Noise* (June 1976) was produced by Robbie Robertson of the Band. Like *Seagull,* it earned platinum certification from the RIAA. (*See Band, The.*)

After a concert hiatus of several years, he took to the boards again in 1976, including another note-

177

worthy concert at the Los Angeles Greek Theatre. That served as the basis for a TV special and his second live album, the 1977 *Live at the Greek*. That album went platinum as did his remaining 1970s albums, *I'm Glad You're Here with Me Tonight* (1977) and *You Don't Bring Me Flowers* (1978). The title song of the latter, a duet with Barbra Streisand, rose to number one on *Billboard*'s charts the week of December 2, 1978 and stayed there the following week. (*See Streisand, Barbra*.)

At the end of the 1970s, Diamond's career was interrupted by a daunting health problem: discovery of a tumor on his spinal cord. He told Robert Hilburn (*Los Angeles Times*, April 17, 1983): "I had felt that something was wrong for a number of years. I was losing some of the feeling in my right leg, but it happened so gradually that I was able to convince myself that it wasn't anything serious." But when he fell on stage in San Francisco and "didn't have enough strength in either leg to get up, I knew then I had to get to a doctor."

Tests showed the presence of a tumor, which, though benign, was crushing his spinal cord. He had to cancel all engagements while the doctors rushed him into the operating room. "It was really a life-and-death situation. They didn't know how much damage had been done. . . . The night before the operation, I wrote all my 'last letters' to friends." The operation, fortunately, proved successful, though Diamond was confined to a wheelchair for a while and then had to use a cane until he regained full strength. As soon as he had recovered, he began work on his next new project: starring in a remake of the old Al Jolson film classic, *The Jazz Singer*. As he worked on the movie, he had another album on the charts, *September Morn*, issued by Columbia at the end of 1979. The film itself, which also featured Laurence Olivier, came out the end of 1980, but proved something less than one of the year's best. The soundtrack album, issued by Capitol Records, was more impressive, though, providing three top 10 singles: "Love on the Rocks," "America," and "Hello Again."

During the 1980s, Diamond continued his diverse and generally well received efforts as a recording artist and concert star. His new LPs on Columbia included *On the Way to the Sky* (November 1981); *12 Greatest Hits, Volume II* (May 1982); *Heartlight* (September 1982), which contained the top 5 single "Heartlight"; *Primitive* (1984); and *Headed for the Future* (1986). In May 1983, Columbia released the LP *Classics/The Early Years*, containing major hits from his Bang Records days. Besides a number of worldwide tours during those years, Diamond starred in his third TV special, "Neil Diamond . . .

Hello Again" on CBS on May 25, 1986. In October 1987, Columbia released a new live concert double album, *Hot August Night II*.

In February 1984, Diamond was inducted into the Songwriting Hall of Fame in ceremonies at New York's Waldorf Astoria Hotel.

DIDDLEY, BO: *Singer, guitarist, songwriter. Born McComb, Mississippi, December 20, 1928.*

By any yardstick, Bo Diddley ranks as one of the giants of rock'n'roll. He wrote and/or performed some of the standards of rock's gestation period, provided a level of musicianship that compared favorably with the jazz and blues masters of the period, and inspired many young musicians who later became vital forces in rock music.

With all this to his credit, it is sad that he seemed to run out of steam by the mid-1960s. Though he remained active and headlined many shows from the late 1960s into the 1980s, he usually seemed bored and lackadaisical to most observers. He could always cause excitement among young audiences with his offbeat electronic riffs and some of his intricate rhythmic patterns, but he created little in the way of new material, tending to just redo the songs that made him famous.

Part of this may result from the fact that, while he was only in his early forties at the end of the 1960s, he had been performing for over 30 years. He had taken up the guitar before he was 10 years old in Chicago, where he had moved with his family as a baby from his birthplace in Mississippi. He gave his first public performance when he was 10, playing for coins on a Chicago street corner with two other boys, one playing guitar and the second washboard.

He continued to play with friends in small groups at dances and parties during his teens and early twenties, but earned his living at unskilled jobs. He hung around clubs in the evening and spent some of his spare time teaching himself the guitar, but he seemed to be going no place fast as the '50s began. In 1951, though, things started looking up. He gained his first regular nightclub job, still using his real name of Elias McDaniel, at the 708 Club in Chicago. He played with a number of R&B groups in the midwest during the early 1950s and also did some solo work, emphasizing blues material.

In the mid-1950s, with rock'n'roll becoming a vital factor in the music field, he began to write songs in that vein. He came to the attention of the Chicago-based R&B label Chess and Checker. Elias McDaniel gained both his name and a recording career when he walked in off the street one day to audition for one of Chess Records' founders, Leonard Chess. Leonard liked his singing and, after signing

McDaniel, thought up the stage name Bo Diddley, "because it meant 'funny storyteller.'"

One of his first releases used Bo's new name as the takeoff for the lyric. "Bo Diddley" became one of the major hits of 1955 in both R&B and rock and established him as a major star. He added still more luster to his reputation that year with another top 10 single, "I'm a Man." His recordings were strongly plugged by the king of rock disc jockeys, Alan Freed, and Bo soon had a national following. (*See Freed, Alan.*)

Diddley remained an innovator and, as the 1950s went by, turned out such hits as "Mona" and, in 1959, the droll "Say Man." His appearances and recordings had a marked effect on many young English pop music aspirants as can be seen from their tributes to him in the mid-1960s. The Yardbirds, for example, gained a best-seller by reviving his "I'm a Man." The Rolling Stones did the same with "Mona." Eric Burdon and the Animals recorded "The Story of Bo Didley." (*See Animals, The; Burdon, Eric; Jagger, Mick; Rolling Stones, The; Yardbirds, The.*)

During the 1960s, he had no significant singles successes, though he remained an important album artist. Among the many LPs issued on the Checker label from 1959 through 1969 were *Go; Have Guitar, Will Travel; In the Spotlight; Bo Diddley Is a Gunslinger; Bo Diddley Is a Lover; Bo Diddley Is a Twister;* the two-disc *Bo Diddley; Bo Diddley and Company; Surfin'; Beach Party; Hey, Good Lookin'; The Great Guitars* (with Chuck Berry); and *500% More Man. (See Berry, Chuck.)*

When Richard Nader organized his "1950s Rock'n'Roll Revival Show" in 1969, Diddley was one of his acts and remained a regular in the show into the 1970s.

By the early 1970s, many of Diddley's earlier LPs were out of print. Among those still available were the 1962 album titled *Bo Diddley,* on Chess, and the 1967 Checker retrospective, *Sixteen All Time Greatest Hts.* His newer material on the Chess label included the 1971 *Got My Own Bag of Tricks, Another Dimension of Bo Diddley,* and *Where It All Began.* By the end of the decade, none of those was in the regular catalog either. During the 1980s, Diddley was represented on several reissues of recordings from previous decades, including *Bo Diddley/His Greatest Sides* (1983). In 1986, his 1959 LP *Go Bo Diddley* was released as part of the Original Chess Masters Series.

Diddley himself, finding new respect from younger fans in the 1980s, seemed to take heart and his live performances began to reflect some of the urgency of his '50s–early '60s work. In the mid-

1980s he was one of the first artists named to the Rock'n'Roll Hall of Fame in Cleveland.

DINNING, MARK: *Singer, guitarist. Born Grant City, Oklahoma, 1933, died c. 1985.*

The name Mark Dinning probably will ring no bells in the minds of most followers of popular music. However, his one great hit, "Teen Angel," will awake many memories for high school students of the early 1960s.

Dinning spent most of his early years in the Southwest. He had a musically oriented family that produced one of the top female singing groups of the '40s and '50s, the Dinning Sisters. Mark sang with his sisters at home as a boy and performed as a sideman with a number of groups in the '50s. Not too much happened for him career-wise until 1960, when he came up with the morbid tear-jerking ballad "Teen Angel." Released as a single on MGM Records, it sold well over a million copies. But he was never able to come up with a sequel that could capture public support. He had been inactive in the music field for many years when he died in the mid-1980s.

"Teen Angel' (written by the then married, later divorced team of Jean and Red Surrey) proved to have a life of its own. It was part of the soundtrack of the hit film *American Graffiti.* As of the late 1980s, it still was a staple item on the various oldies shows on radio stations across the U.S.

DIO, RONNIE JAMES: *See Black Sabbath.*

DION: *Singer, guitarist, songwriter, group leader (THE BELMONTS, STREETHEART BAND). Born Bronx, New York, July 18, 1939.*

There's no doubt that Dion ranks as a rock music survivor, one of the few luminaries of the 1950s who is still having an impact on the field at the end of the 1980s. In a career with many ups and downs, including a fight to overcome heroin addiction in the 1960s, he contributed many classic songs in rock and folk-rock veins to pop music's creative heritage.

Dion was born and raised as Dion DiMucci in the Bronx. As a high school student in the mid-'50s, he shared his peer group's enthusiasm for such rock pioneers as Elvis, Bill Haley, and the Coasters. He liked to sing and formed his own group, Dion and the Tamberlaines, that made one hit single, "The Chosen Few" (first on Mohawk, then on Jubilee) in 1957 and then broke up. Soon after, he emerged as lead singer of a new foursome, Dion and the Belmonts, whose other members were Fred Milano, Carlo Mastangelo, and Angelo D'Aleo. (The backing trio's name came from Belmont Avenue in the

Bronx.) In 1958, the group had hit singles "I Wonder Why" and "No One Knows" on Laurie.

In 1959, it made the top five with "A Teenager in Love." The next year was a good one as well, producing Dion and the Belmonts' all-time best-seller, a remake of the old pop hit "Where or When," plus "When You Wish Upon a Star" and "In the Still of the Night."

Dion was getting restless and by late 1960 had begun a solo career with the hit single "Lonely Teenager." He had several minor hits, such as "Little Miss Blue" in 1960 and "Havin' Fun" and "Kissin' Game" in 1961, hitting pay dirt with "Runaround Sue," a multimillion-seller and number one on the *Billboard* list, the weeks of October 23 and 30, 1961. His next release, "The Wanderer," also topped the million mark, rising to number two in the U.S. in 1962. The reverse side of that single, "The Majestic," also made the charts.

He had had a number of other chart-makers on Laurie in 1962–63 before accepting a bid from record-industry–giant Columbia to sign with them. Things started off well in the new alignment with a major hit, a remake of the Drifters' "Ruby Baby" in early 1963. Dion also made the pop lists with such 1963 releases as "This Little Girl," "Be Careful of Stones That You Throw," "Donna the Prima Donna," and "Drip Drop" (another Drifters' classic), and the 1964 remake of Chuck Berry's standard, "Johnny B. Goode." His LPs included, on Laurie, *Dion and the Belmonts* (1960), *Wish Upon a Star* (1960), *Alone, Runaround Sue,* and *Lovers Who Wander;* and, on Columbia, *Donna the Prima Donna* (1963).

But his career was beginning to slip in the mid-1960s. The impact of the Beatles and other British groups began to overwhelm the more simplistic "old-timey" U.S. rock of the previous decade. Dion continued to turn out new material, but his name rarely showed up on best-seller rosters. He severed connections with Columbia and later moved on to ABC without any noticeable improvement in his career. Meanwhile, Laurie released a number of albums, mainly retrospective ones, in October 1966: *Greatest Hits, Vol. 1; Greatest Hits, Vol. 2; 15 Million Sellers; Together, with the Belmonts;* and *Dion Sings to Sandy.* His initial LP on ABC, *Together, with the Belmonts* came out in March 1967.

In those years, Dion's tastes had begun to change. Already a fan of people such as Dylan and Joan Baez, he also took a close look at the blues in its various forms, listening to old 78 rpm discs of both urban and country blues artists. Originally only a singer, he had begun to learn guitar in the early '60s and, inspired by his new interest in folk and blues, he intensified his efforts to master the instrument. He

moved to Miami, Florida, in the mid-1960s, where his circle of friends included a number of writers in the modern folk tradition, such as Fred Neil. Besides adding the songs of some of those people to his repertoire, he spent a lot of time writing originals of his own in that vein.

In 1968, once more working with Laurie Records, he recorded a song by Dick Holler that gave vent to the emotional trauma resulting from the assassinations of American liberal leaders of the decade. That song, "Abraham, Martin and John," caught the feelings of the time and was certified gold by the Recording Industry Association of America on January 13, 1969. The single focused new attention on Dion, who was once more a featured artist on the concert circuit and on TV. Some of his original compositions also began to be recorded by other artists.

Disagreements over creative directions led to his leaving Laurie once more, this time for Warner Brothers. His first release on that label was the late 1969 *Sit Down, Old Friend,* a folk- and blues-oriented collection that included the song "Clean Up Your Own Back Yard," an antidrug composition that drew on his problems with addiction that went back to his teen years. He made several more albums on Warner Brothers in the early '70s, such as *You're Not Alone* and *Sanctuary,* generally receiving critical praise, but not much public support.

In 1972, the Belmonts put out their own engaging *Cigars, A Cappella, Candy* on Buddah, while Warner Brothers recorded Dion and the Belmonts' *Reunion: Live at Madison Square Garden* (later reissued by Rhino Records). The MSG concert represented the first "oldies" show on which Dion had agreed to appear.

Reissues of Dion's earlier recordings came out on Laurie and Columbia labels during the 1970s, including the Laurie albums *Sixteen Greatest of Dion and the Belmonts* (1971) and *Everything You Always Wanted to Hear by Dion and the Belmonts* (1973); and the Columbia LPs *Dion's Greatest Hits* (1973), *Ruby Baby* (1973), and *Donna the Prima Donna* (1979). For Dion himself, the 1970s proved a rather disappointing time. The 1976 Warner Brothers release *Streetheart,* intended to restore his luster, was a failure with record buyers. With an outstanding backing band (also called the Streethearts), he completed the excellent 1978 Lifesong LP *Return of the Wanderer,* which had little public impact, possibly because the record company gave it little promotional support. Several critics called it one of the overlooked gems of the year.

During the early 1980s, Dion's creative efforts were concentrated around his new-found Christian faith. He recorded a series of gospel albums, including the well-regarded 1985 release *Kingdom in the*

Streets. Another cycle of public nostalgia about the early days of rock'n'roll led him back to the pop music performing fold with a series of well-attended oldies concerts around the U.S. during 1987–88, and guest appearances at the Rock Hall of Fame concert in New York and on the 1988 Grammy Awards TV show.

DIRE STRAITS: *Vocal and instrumental group. Mark Knopfler, born Glasgow, Scotland; David Knopfler, born Glasgow, Scotland; John Illsley, born London, England; Pick Withers, born Leicester, England.*

Dire Straits has lived up to its name during several phases of its career. In its formative stage, the band fought an uphill battle to keep its subtle, blues-oriented rock afloat against the punk wave then receiving almost single-minded attention from the English music press. After overcoming great obstacles to become a worldwide success in 1979–80, the band's fortunes declined, only to revive sharply in the mid-1980s.

The dominant figure in Dire Straits's history was lead singer/guitarist/songwriter Mark Knopfler, and the group's fortunes waxed or waned with his achievements. Mark and brother David were sons of an architect who moved his family from Glasgow to Newcastle-on-Tyne when the boys were young. Growing up in Newcastle, the Knopflers didn't think of themelves as budding professional musicians. In fact, the high level of subtlety and erudition in Dire Straights songs may be traced to the original members' relatively extensive educational background. The Knopflers and Illsley all attended college; none was a music major. Illsley gained a degree in sociology while Mark majored in English literature, working while a student as a cub reporter. (His final story for the *Yorkshire Evening Post* dealt with the death of Jimi Hendrix.) Later, he spent a number of years teaching English literature, with his pop music interests essentially a sideline.

Illsley, who had opened a record shop after graduation from college, shared an apartment with David Knopfler. Illsley quickly became part of the band Mark and David were organizing in the mid-1970s.

Withers, whose credits were less academic, had taken up drums seriously in his early teens. In the mid-1960s, at age 17, he went to Germany on a forged passport to work with various minor club bands. In Rome, he did a three-year stint with the Primitives. He was working as a session drummer in the 1970s, based in Monmouth, England, when he was directed to the Knopflers' embryonic new band by mutual friend Brinsley Schwarz, a highly regarded English bandleader and producer who was impressed with the quality of Mark's compositions.

It had taken Mark a while to reach that point. He had become adept as a guitarist and interested in a musical career by the time he finished college, but an initial attempt as a performer had been discouraging. As he told Ken Emerson of *High Fidelity* magazine (June 1979): "Rock & roll and living in London cost me a lot in a lot of ways. It made me realize just how many guys there are who carry their dreams around with them all the time. It's quite a frustrating scene. I had a home-life bustup with me girl and I moved around with nothing definite, no bread."

He then took up a teaching job that assured a steady paycheck until an American vacation imbued him with a desire to take another try at full-time music work. He made the trip mostly by bus. "I felt very much alive. I liked the people and the food and the space and the energy, the optimism and the capacity for enjoyment and the desire to communicate and share in each other's happiness, the different ways of saying hello and goodbye. I liked the literature and the trashiness and the humor."

Some of those images found their way into later songs, though much of his material has been tinged with bitterness and cynicism rather than optimism. After one more year as a teacher, he made a final break with conventional employment and assembled Dire Straits in 1976–77. For many months, it seemed like he had made another wrong turn. With punk and new wave dominating the British club scene, jobs for the new band were few and far between. The group's effort to find a record company also was unrewarding. Their demonstration tapes were rejected by almost every label, large and small, in England.

Perhaps one difficulty, apart from the new wave dominance, was that many of Knopfler's melodies had a certain sameness about them and his vocals hardly could rank with stars such as Jagger or Robert Plant. Another possible deterrent was Knopfler's emphasis on minor keys, using the music as background for his insightful lyrics. (He indicated his choice of tone patterns derived in part from his love for the work of groups such as the Ventures and Shadows.) "The twang and the minor keys were a big deal for me when I was a kid. There was a kind of mystery to it that stayed with me. It's simple, evocative stuff."

Things finally took a turn for the better in 1978. An executive from Phonogram Records heard one of Dire Straits' demos, "Sultans of Swing" about a Dixieland jazz group, played by British d.j. Charlie Gillett. John Stainze signed the group and a single of "Sultans" became a hit, first in Holland, then in other nations around the world, and finally in the U.S. Warner Brothers signed for U.S. distribution and released the band's debut LP, *Dire Straits,* in late 1978. Backed by a far-ranging U.S. tour by the band, the album earned a gold record from the RIAA as did the follow-up, *Communique* (1979). The latter, however, did not contain a track as gripping as "Sultans," though the lyrics provided food for thought. At the end of 1979, *Billboard* named Dire Straits number one in its New LP Artists category.

The 1980 album, *Making Movies,* contained originals by Mark Knopfler that were of the quality achieved in the debut collection, notably "Tunnel of Love" and "Romeo and Juliet." The fact that there were no marked musical differences from the first two releases perhaps accounted for a decline in interest among record buyers. The LP made the charts but was not a major recipient of 1980 record honors. Warner Brothers continued to retain contract rights for the band's work in the 1980s, issuing the album *Love Over Gold* in mid-1982. It sold moderately well without spawning any major singles hits.

Knopfler gained more attention in the early 1980s for his recording work (and some touring) in conjunction with Bob Dylan projects than for his Dire Straits connection. (*See Dylan, Bob.*) For a time, it seemed as though Dire Straits history might essentially comprise one brief moment in the spotlight, though discussions with pop music fans suggested it continued to retain a sizable, if not massive core of faithful followers.

Then the pendulum took an upward swing once more. Knopfler gained attention for his contributions in the programs organized by Boomtown Rats leader Bob Geldof to help bring famine relief to Africa. Knopfler and Dire Straits played a set at the highly successful international Live Aid concert in the summer of 1985. (*See Boomtown Rats.*)

During that year, the band had major milestones of its own. One was the hit single "Money for Nothing" (the basis for one of the most effective music videos of the year), sung by Knopfler and Sting. (*See Sting.*) The other was the number one Warners album *Brothers in Arms,* which was triple platinum at year-end. The single was nominated for Record of the Year in the Grammy Awards and the LP won a nomination for Album of the Year.

DR. JOHN, THE NIGHT TRIPPER: *Singer, pianist, songwriter, guitarist, bassist, band leader, record producer. Born New Orleans, Louisiana, November 21, 1940.*

To say that Dr. John cut an unusual figure on stage when he appeared as the Night Tripper is an understatement. His spangled silver robes, ornate feathered headdress, and intricate necklaces brought to mind some of the characters in the jungle thrillers on TV's late, late show. His guise, though, did reflect the kind of music he often plays, which might be called voodoo rock. By the mid-1970s, he had discarded his exotic garb, but continued to be a respected exponent of New Orleans R&B and rock stylings the rest of that decade and throughout the 1980s.

Dr. John grew up in New Orleans under the more prosaic name of Malcolm John Rebennack, Jr., son of a professional model and an appliance-store owner. His mother's contacts resulted in young Mac's baby picture being featured as an "Ivory Soap baby" in company ads. Mac Sr. first worked with Emblem Appliances on Gentilly Boulevard and later operated Rebennack Appliances.

As his son recalled: "That was near Dillard University. He sold a lot of records. Classical to the students with music classes and some jazz, blues, and hillbilly records. He also had some sort of a deal with a juke box distributor. I'd get the old 78s when they were returned from the machines. I was a fanatic for Gene Autry, Hank Williams, and Roy Rogers. I remember liking 'race' records by Big Bill Broonzy and Memphis Minnie, too."

At the age of eight, Mac already knew far more about hillbilly and black music than his playmates. His interest deepened when illness confined him to home for a long time. He had already learned a little boogie-woogie piano from an aunt and, while recuperating, he started guitar lessons.

Back in school, Mac eventually joined school pop bands and became guitarist with a group called Leonard James and the Nighttrainers. "I played guitar with them, even though I started out knowing only one chord." Barely into his teens, he hung around Cosimo Matessa's recording studio, where he met many professional musicians. "I was really taught to play guitar by Walter 'Papoose' Nelson and Roy Montrell. They were the guitarists in Fats Domino's band. Al Johnson, who had a record called "Carnival Time," taught me some more piano, all kinds of boogie-woogie. I also learned piano by watching people like Huey Smith and Professor Longhair. James Booker showed me about the organ, how to use the stops and foot-pedals." (*See Domino, Fats.*)

At 15, Mac joined the musicians union and worked as head of his own group and as a sideman with others, such as the Paul Gayten group at the Brass Rail club. By 1956, Mac performed on his first recordings. On one, he backed Professor Longhair, whom he had met while playing guitar behind singer Roy Brown at Lincoln Beach, a black amusement park. The Longhair record, "Mardi Gras in New Orleans," notes Mac, "is still a hit. Every year at Mardi Gras, it's pulled out and all the radio stations play it." His first album work was on *Boppin' and Strollin' with Leonard James* on Decca. In 1957,

Mac recorded an instrumental album of his own, but it was never released.

In the late 1950s, Mac worked as producer and/or session man with Ace Records of Baton Rouge and Minit of New Orleans. When several black artists formed AFO (All For One) Records, Mac was the first white act signed. With Ronnie Baron, he cut material issued under the names Drits and Dravy and also did an album of organ instrumentals. "I was the label's answer to Jimmy Smith. They also had a mystical act named Prince Lala. He was the original version of what would later become Dr. John, the Night Tripper."

John had to take up bass for a while after being shot in a finger in a barroom brawl. "I played in a Dixieland band. I borrowed an upright bass from a guy in my band. But when I played it, my finger bled so much that the blood was ruinin' the guy's strings. So I switched to Fender bass. I introduced the instrument to the Dixieland world."

In the mid-1960s, Mac moved to Los Angeles, where he slowly became a top session man working for many pop producers, including Phil Spector. (See Spector, Phil.) In his spare time, he began developing an act based on voodoo ceremonies. "I'd been interested in the hoodoo ceremonies for quite a while in New Orleans. My sister worked in an antique store and had some books on the subject. And I'd go down into the 9th Ward to go to some of the church ceremonies. There's a place on Rampart Street called the Crackerjack Drug Store that deals in roots and incense. I'd go there to get some supplies. Though I hadn't done anything with them, I had written most of the songs on the first couple of [Los Angeles–recorded] albums before ever leaving New Orleans."

When the first Dr. John the Night Tripper album came out, its combination of soul and voodoo went over big with listeners to "underground" radio stations. On Atco, the album was called *Gris Gris* after certain objects used in voodoo ceremonies. However, John noted, "I didn't really use much of the real [voodoo] church music. What I tried to get was the feel of what was going on there."

His reputation increased at the start of the '70s both from more Atco releases and from his garish rock-concert appearances. Other performers, though, respected him for his musicianship rather than his showmanship. Thus, after his LP *Remedies* was released in 1970, his backing on the 1971 album *Sun, Moon & Herbs* included such famous English rock stars as Mick Jagger, Eric Clapton, and Ray Draper. The LP was on the best-seller lists during October and November of 1971. In April 1972, Dr. John made the singles charts with the African-flavored *Iko, Iko*. He continued with his voodoo-oriented material on the 1972 album, *Gumbo*. However, there was a change of pace in early 1973 when *In the Right Place* was issued. This album, one of the fastest-moving new releases on the hit charts in the spring, demonstrated Dr. John's background in blues and early rock. The title song provided Rebennack with a hit single.

During the same year, Dr. John was part of another project that had an album on the charts much of the year. The LP *Triumvirate* was recorded by a trio comprising Rebennack on keyboards, Mike Bloomfield on lead guitar, and John Paul Hammond on vocals, guitar, and harmonica. The group made additional recordings for Columbia Records, but the promise of the embryo supergroup never was realized. (*See Bloomfield, Michael.*)

As it turned out, *In the Right Place* was the high point of Dr. John's record output as a solo performer for Atco. By the mid-1970s he had left the label. He continued to be active as a solo performer through the 1980s while also working as a session artist and record producer. One of his high points of the mid-1970s was taking part in the farewell concert for the Band in San Francisco, California, on Thanksgiving night, 1976. His contributions were included in the documentary film of the concert, *The Last Waltz,* and the soundtrack LP of the same title. (*See Band, The.*)

In 1979, Rebennack put two albums out on the Horizon label: *City Lights* and *Tango Palace.* His 1980s output included *Dr. John Plays Mac Rebennack* on Clean Cuts Records in 1981. Other labels that repackaged his material included Trip (*Dr. John* and *Sixteen Greatest Hits),* Springboard (*Dr. John),* and Alligator (*Gris Gris* and *Gumbo).* Throughout the 1980s, he kept busy as a performer and sometime arranger/record producer. His credits during those years included the Clean Cuts LP *Brightest Smile in Town* and a role in the 1988 film *Candy Mountain.*

DOMINO, ANTOINE "FATS": *Singer, pianist, songwriter. Born New Orleans, Louisiana, February 26, 1928.*

When the Rock'n'Roll Hall of Fame was established in 1986, one of the first names proposed for entry was Fats Domino. It was certainly appropriate. Fats was writing and singing songs that became rock standards years before the phrase *rock'n'roll* came into the language. When Lew Chudd, head of Imperial Records of Los Angeles, signed the short, rotund $3-a-week pianist at the Hideaway Bar in New Orleans to his label in 1949, he was gaining a one-man hit parade. For a dozen years, Domino achieved the unparalleled feat of turning out one or more top 10 hits on the rhythm & blues or pop charts every year.

His influence on white and black rock artists of the 1950s and future decades was immeasurable.

Though self-taught, Domino mastered many forms of popular piano techniques, including blues, boogie-woogie, and ragtime. His own arrangements fused them into new building blocks for the R&B and rock genres in the '50s.

In the late 1940s, New Orleans band leader Dave Bartholomew hired Fats as his regular pianist. This job led to the Domino-Bartholomew songwriting duo, and to Fats's relationship with Imperial Records.

He started right off with a top 10 hit in the R&B field in 1950 with his first single, "The Fat Man." He followed with "Rockin' Chair" in 1951 and "How Long" and "Goin' Home" in 1952. "Goin' Home" moved to number one on the R&B charts, the first of many Domino records to achieve that lofty position on either R&B or pop lists. The year 1953 was a banner one, providing a bumper crop of top 10 hits: "Goin' to the River," "Please Don't Leave Me," "Rosemary," and "Something's Wrong." Even more important, Fats was increasingly popular with disc jockeys who spun records for the mass audience. His recordings were enjoyed by young music fans of all races and he became one of the first black artists to gain featured spots in pop music concerts.

Fats' output slowed a bit in 1954 with only one top 10 hit, "You Done Me Wrong." But he bounced back stronger than ever in 1955 with four best-sellers in pop and/or R&B categories, including the rock classic, "Ain't That a Shame," plus "All by Myself," "I Can't Go On," and "Poor Me." Pat Boone's cover version of "Ain't That a Shame" outsold Fats', though Fats shared author's royalties for Pat's sales with Dave Bartholomew. His 1956 discs included three number one songs, "Blueberry Hill," and the two-sided hit "I'm in Love Again"/"My Blue Heaven." His other five top 10 singles weren't far from number one: "Bo Weevil"/"Don't Blame It on Me," "Honey Chile," and "When My Dreamboat Comes Home"/"So Long."

In 1957, Fats made *Billboard*'s pop top 10 with "Blue Monday"/"What's the Reason I'm Not Pleasin' You?" "I'm Walkin'," and "Valley of Tears." He closed out the decade with such major successes as "Whole Lotta Lovin'" in 1958 (a hit for Alexis Korner's C.C.S. group in 1971), and "Be My Guest," "I Want to Walk You Home," and "I'm Ready" in 1959. He started the '60s with a number of best-sellers, including "Three Nights a Week" and "Walking to New Orleans" in 1960. "Let the Four Winds Blow" and "What a Price" in 1961 were his last *Billboard* top 20 pop singles.

Though Fats remained popular as a theater and nightclub attraction during the mid-1960s, he lost his magic touch in creating new material. People still bought his albums, though not at the rate of earlier years, and many of them remained in the Imperial catalogue after he left the label for ABC in 1963. Among these Imperial LPs were *This Is Fats* and *Fabulous Fats Domino* (1958); *12,000,000 Records* (1959), and *Here He Comes Again, Here Stands Fats, I Miss You So, Let's Dance, Lots of Dominos, Rock & Rollin', Super Million Record Hits, This Is Fats Domino*, and *Walking to New Orleans*.

On ABC Records, Fats was represented by such LPs as *Here Comes Fats Again* (1963), *Fats in the Fire!* and *Getaway* (1966). Mercury Records issued his LP *'65* in November 1965, and Sunset Records released such efforts as *Fats Domino* (1966), *Stomping* (1967), and, in the late '60s and early '70s, *Ain't That a Shame, Big Rock Sounds,* and *Trouble in Mind*. Liberty/United Artists, which bought out Imperial Records in the mid-1960s, released some of Fats' early material on such LPs as *Golden Greats, Volume 1, Superpak,* and *Fats Domino Swings*.

His method of capturing his musical thought involved tape recorders because Fats never learned to write music. "When I get an idea for a song, I sit down at that piano [in his special music room in his home] and sing it into the tape. Then I've got it so I can talk with Dave about it. Dave works on all my recordings and on my band arrangements and we're together a lot of the time."

In fact, his co-author Bartholomew was still helping coordinate Fats' concerts in the 1980s. Recalling the environment in which those songs came to be, Bartholomew told Robert Hilburn (*Los Angeles Times,* September 1, 1985): "The thing that made Fats' records so good was that people could identify with what he was saying. They were real songs. The best was 'Blue Monday.' That was a hell of a story . . . a real workingman's story, and that's where I come from—the working class of people. It was about the life I lived.

"Remember, I came up in a time when we didn't know anything about owning your own home or anything like that. All I ever wanted to do was get a little double house [duplex apartment] and maybe rent one side and get me a used car. I never dreamed I'd be able to buy a new car because it was such a rough life when I was coming up as a kid."

After the 1960s, Fats cut back sharply on his concert tours, preferring to spend more time in his palatial home in New Orleans with his wife and eight children. He became almost an institution in Las Vegas, regularly performing up to three months a year as a featured artist at the Flamingo Hotel. Though he went further afield a few times a year for an occasional concert, about his only other work in the 1970s was on the Lake Tahoe hotel circuit in Nevada.

During the 1970s, Fats was better known in England and Europe than at home, partly because his shyness, which made him want to avoid flashy promotional exposure, mitigated against the interview and TV performances that more outspoken performers typically gained. While U.S. releases of some new and many old recordings were available then and in the 1980s, many of his discs were overseas imports such as the six-volume U.K. set (United Artists), *The Fats Domino Story* (1977), covering his major recordings on the Imperial label from 1949 to 1962. Other 1970s LPs included *Fats Domino— Legendary Master Series* (United Artists, 1972), *Play It Again Fats* (U.A. 1973; available as British import), *Fats Domino Live at Montreux (Atlantic,* 1974; British import), and *Twenty Greatest Hits* (U.A. 1976; British import). Albums available as French imports for some years included *Rare Dominoes, Volume 1 and 2* (Imperial/U.A.), *The Best American Music* (ABC), *The Fabulous Mr. D* (Liberty), *Fats Domino in Concert* (Mercury), and, on Imperial, *Let's Dance with Domino, Let's Play Domino, Rock and Rollin' with Fats Domino, This is Fats Domino,* and *Cooking with Fats*. A Belgian import was titled *Rock and Rollin'* (Imperial) and a West German import was *Star Collection* (WEA). U.S. labels that issued Domino material included Evergreen (*Fats Domino, Volume 1 and 2*) and Pickwick (*My Blue Heaven* and the two-disc *Two Sensational Albums*).

Domino continued to keep a relatively low profile for much of the 1980s, but in 1985 he went on what was, for him, a fairly extensive tour. His limited live performance efforts were symbolized by his California appearances, first in Sacramento and later at the Los Angeles Universal Ampitheater in August 1985, which represented his first shows in that state in almost 20 years. (His Sacramento show at the Memorial Auditorium was taped for one of his rare TV program segments.) Those concerts showed him to still be a skilled artist able to thrill and delight audiences of all ages.

As of 1986, Domino had turned out more than three dozen top 40 singles with sales totals somewhere between 65 and 100 million records.

DOMINOES, THE: *Vocal group. Organized by Billy Ward, born Los Angeles, California, September 19, 1921.*

The roster of alumni of the Dominoes, like those of the Drifters and some other musical groups remaining in existence for many years, includes several of the most illustrious names in R&B and rock'n'roll of the '50s, '60s, and '70s: Clyde McPhatter, Clifton Chenier, and Jackie Wilson. The group itself went through dozens of changes over the years, except for its founder and constant member, Billy Ward. (*See Drifters, The; McPhatter, Clyde; Wilson, Jackie.*)

Ward's interest in music went back to childhood. He started piano and voice lessons when he was six and demonstrated skill as both artist and composer during his formative years. At 14, he won a national contest with a classically oriented composition titled "Dejection" and received an award from famous teacher and symphony conductor Walter Damrosch.

Billy's career directions changed somewhat as he entered adulthood, partly because of World War II. He entered the Army and gained officer's rank. He had athletic as well as musical skills and won notice as an excellent boxer. He was entered in the Golden Gloves and won in his division. During his service years, he gave boxing instructions and also staged camp shows to entertain the troops.

After his discharge, he moved east and became sports editor and columnist for Transradio Press. He also worked as a vocal coach at Carnegie Hall. By the late 1940s, he had his own New York studio on Broadway, a move that prompted him to start the Dominoes from among his students. The group started in small clubs and by the end of the decade was playing major centers on the R&B circuit.

An important turning point came in 1950 when a 17-year-old singer, Clyde McPhatter, joined as lead tenor. McPhatter's voice seemed to make things jell for the group, which soon became one of the best-regarded acts on the R&B circuit. In 1951, Billy Ward and the Dominoes made the R&B best-seller lists on the Federal label with three top 10 discs: "Do Something for Me," "I Am with You," and "60 Minute Man." The following year, "Have Mercy Baby" was in the number one position on R&B charts for several weeks.

The year 1953 was an even bigger one for the Dominoes, with such top 10 successes as "The Bells," "I'd Be Satisfied," and "Rags to Riches"; on Federal plus (on King) "These Foolish Things." During the year, Clyde McPhatter left to form his own group (the Drifters). His place was taken by an equally talented Detroit singer, Jackie Wilson. Wilson remained with the Dominoes during the mid-1950s, then going out as soloist to become one of the premier singers of the late 1950s and the following two decades.

Billy Ward always seemed able to come up with a new combination that could maintain the Dominoes' position as the '50s went by. The group of the middle and late part of the decade included Gene Mumford and Milton Merle, tenors; Milton Grayson, baritone; and Cliff Owens, bass. This is the group featured with Ward on the album *Billy Ward and the*

Dominoes. In 1957, the group recorded for Liberty and Ward took the lead vocal for a highly successful reworking of Hoagy Carmichael's classic, "Stardust." While his earlier hits were filled with earthy vitality, "Stardust" was poised and refined. The record was a top 10 hit on both the general and R&B charts and also was a major success in England. Total sales went well over a million for Ward's top-selling effort to date. The follow-up, "Deep Purple" (another reworked oldie), also hit the top 20.

The Dominoes remained an important stage attraction for much of the 1960s, though Ward wasn't able to come up with the best-selling discs of the previous decade. By that time, the group was playing not only traditional R&B theaters and clubs, but the prestige rooms of major cities in the U.S. and overseas.

By the 1970s, the group's days as a headliner were past, though it continud to be represented by occasional reissues of material from its glory days. These included several LPs issued by Gusto Records on the King label: *Billy Ward and the Dominoes' Fourteen Greatest Hits, The Dominoes Featuring Clyde McPhatter, Jackie Wilson with Billy Ward and the Dominoes,* and *Billy Ward and his Dominoes: 21 Original Greatest Hits.*

DOOBIE BROTHERS, THE: *Vocal and instrumental group. Original members, 1969: Tom Johnston, born Visalia, California; John Hartman, born Falls Church, Virginia, c. 1949; Greg Murphy. Murphy replaced by Dave Shogren, born San Francisco, California. Pat Simmons, born Aberdeen, Washington, added 1970. Shogren left October 1971 and was replaced by Tiran Porter, born Los Angeles, California, c. 1948. Michael Hossack added in late 1971, replaced in 1973 by Keith Knudsen, born Iowa. Jeff Baxter, born Washington, D.C., c. 1948, added late 1974. Michael McDonald, born St. Louis, Missouri, added in late 1975. Johnson left early 1977. Group disbanded in 1982, reunited in 1987.*

One of the most favored bands with middle-of-the-road rock fans of the 1970s was the Doobie Brothers. The Doobies, whose roster changed so much during its existence that one needed a scorecard to tell the players, never had any direct kinship to one another, but they did relate well to a large share of the rock audience of the decade.

The group began as a northern California trio whose original name was Pud. The catalyst was musician Skip Spence (a member at one time or another of Moby Grape and Jefferson Airplane). (*See Jefferson Airplane/Starship.*) Spence introduced singer/guitarist Tom Johnston to percussionist John Hartman. The two founders added Greg Murphy on bass

guitar. When Murphy demurred at the goals of the others at the end of 1969 his place was taken by Dave Shogren, an old friend of Tom's.

Johnston, who began on an old $12 guitar as a youngster in the early 1960s, started as a rhythm and blues performer in all-black clubs and later was working with country groups in the mid-1960s in Porterville, California. Late in the decade, he spent four years at San Jose State, majoring in graphic design and earning money for school partly from his music. On various occasions, his path crossed that of Shogren, who performed with various rock groups up and down the Pacific Coast.

Hartman was born into a military family. For his first 15 years, he lived on a number of military bases around the world. While his father was stationed in Guam, he got his first drum set. Later, after his family moved back to the U.S. and he finished high school in Virginia, he tried his hand as a professional drummer in local clubs. He wasn't making much progress when he met Skip Spence, who liked Hartman's style and urged him to move to the San Francisco Bay Area. While taking part in some jam sessions at Spence's house, Hartman met Johnston and the forerunner of the Doobies was born.

The trio (which sometimes added several other sidemen, but not on a permanent basis) remained known only to local fans until it expanded to a foursome with the addition of Patrick Simmons. Simmons had started playing guitar at the age of eight in Aberdeen, Washington, a pastime his parents long fought against. By the time they had moved to Los Gatos, California, where Pat attended high school, it seemed obvious that family objections wouldn't sway him from pop music. A singer and rhythm guitarist, he was primarily interested in bluegrass and folk music while a student at San Jose State. During college, he ran a small folk club, Acoustical Musicians, Inc., and performed in other local clubs. While sharing a bill at the Gaslighter Theatre, he so impressed the Doobies that they asked him to join them, which he did some months later. His recruitment was pivotal, since his songwriting abilities, alone or in combination with Tom Johnston, provided the material crucial to the band's future progress.

The group sent demonstration tapes to various record firms. Executives at Warner Brothers were duly impressed and signed the band. The group's first album, *The Doobie Brothers* (April 1971), was far from a best-seller, but it gained some favorable reviews and helped open the way for well-received appearances in many major rock centers during 1971 and 1972. Before 1971 was over, though, Shogren had left. His place was taken by guitarist/vocalist Tiran Porter. Porter, whose husky vocals became a trademark of the band, grew up in Los Angeles, where he played with several rock bands before heading north to join the Bay Area group Scratch. There he had encountered Simmons, who remembered Tiran when there was an opening with the Doobies. Soon after that, the group added Michael Hossack on drums. The new roster recorded the platinum album *Toulouse Street*, issued in March 1972. The source of such hit singles as "Listen to the Music" and "Jesus Is Just Alright," it established the band as one of the most promising new groups in rock. The band firmed that up with another platinum album, *The Captain and Me* (March 1973), which spawned the top 20 "China Grove" and top 10 "Long Train Runnin'." As the group got ready for a tour in support of the album, Hossack announced he'd had enough of the road. He was replaced by Keith Knudsen, who had been playing drums since 13 in his native midwest before coming to California from Wisconsin with a band called Mandelbaum. He had worked with a number of other acts, including Lee Michaels, prior to joining the Doobies.

Knudsen helped record the band's next platinum LP, *What Were Once Vices Now Are Habits* (February 1974). Culled from the LP was the gold single of Pat Simmons' composition "Black Water." At first, no one thought it had potential. It was issued as the B-side of a single that featured "Another Park, Another Sunday." Later, it began to catch on itself until on March 15, 1975, it became number one on all three industry-trade-publication lists.

Jeff "Skunk" Baxter had done some guitar work on that LP, which finally led to his becoming a full Doobies member in late 1974. Baxter, son of an advertising executive, was born in Washington, D.C., but spent many of his childhood years in Mexico City before being sent to Taft, a college preparatory school in Connecticut. He entered Boston University in 1967, but his interest in playing rock guitar induced him to leave and work with local bands, most notably Ultimate Spinach. When that group broke up, he moved to New York, where his contacts included Walter Becker and Donald Fagen, founders of Steely Dan. Their invitation later to join the band in California brought Baxter to the West Coast, where he eventually migrated to the Doobies. (*See Steely Dan.*)

His first full recording affiliation with his new band was *Stampede* (January 1975). Reflecting Baxter's interest, the gold LP had considerably more jazz/R&B influences than its predecessors, as evidenced in the hit of the Holland-Dozier-Holland song "Take Me in Your Arms."

During 1975, another new face graced the band's roster: pianist/vocalist/songwriter Michael McDonald, also a Steely Dan alumnus. As a writer and mu-

sician, McDonald added new dimensions to the band's material that set the tone for its last years as an active group. His contributions made the next album, *Takin' It to the Streets* (March 1976) one of the band's most consistently listenable collections. Among the charted singles from the platinum album were the title track and "It Keeps You Runnin'."

In 1976, based on public voting for CBS-TV's "Peoples Command Performance" program, the Doobies were voted the best rock group of the year. The show saluting their achievement was telecast in early 1977. In February 1977, Dinah Shore's syndicated TV show, "Dinah," devoted a full 90 minutes to the group. Among their activities given favorable comment by Dinah was their Doobie Brothers Christmas party for the Children's Hospital at Stanford, Palo Alto, California (an annual event since 1975).

The band lost the services of Tom Johnston in 1977 when he opted to try other creative avenues, but he still provided material for the gold LP *Livin' on the Fault Line* (July 1977). The band showed it could maintain a strong standing with fans even after the loss of one of its founders with continued capacity crowds attending its late 1970s concerts. By then, the band also had earned a platinum-record award for the restrospective *Best of the Doobies* (1976).

The 1978 album *Minute by Minute,* was dominated by songs co-written by McDonald with such associates as Pat Simmons and Kenny Loggins. (*See Loggins, Kenny; Loggins and Messina.*) One of the singles from the album, the Loggins–McDonald song "What a Fool Believes," featured a fine vocal by McDonald. The song rose to number one on the *Billboard* list the week of April 14, 1979. In the Grammy Award voting, the single won Record of the Year and Song of the Year, McDonald was named winner of the trophy for Best Arrangement Accompanying Vocalists, and the platinum LP, *Minute by Minute,* was voted the Best Pop Vocal Performance by a Duo, Group or Chorus.

But by the start of the 1980s, new opportunities arose for many of the band members. McDonald was working with Loggins on songs for other projects and thinking about possibilities of a solo career. Also, boredom with a long-running association began to take its toll. The platinum 1980 album, *One Step Closer,* wasn't as innovative as previous releases. The only new LP in 1981 was the gold *Best of the Doobies, Volume 2.* In early 1982, the group announced a farewell tour for later in the year and then disbanded. Part of the reason for the breakup was dissension among the members about creative choices. McDonald, though, told a *Los Angeles Times* reporter, "We were living on past laurels. The magic was gone."

After the 1982 "farewell" tour, group members began working on a variety of separate projects. Patrick Simmons completed a solo LP, *Arcade,* as did Michael McDonald with *If That's What It Takes.* A single from McDonald's LP, "I Keep Forgetting (Every Time You're Near)" reached number four in *Billboard* in October 1982. Two other alumni, Keith Knudsen and John McFee, later assembled a country rock group called Southern Pacific.

Some former Doobies earned some credits as record producers. McDonald, for one, produced albums for his wife, Amy Holland, and his sister, Maureen McDonald, while pursuing his own songwriting and performing activities.

In 1987, Knudsen spearheaded a brief reunion of the Doobies for a charity concert for the Vietnam Veterans Aid Foundation. For that, he recruited members from the 1982 roster as well as earlier groupings. The 1987 band included, besides Knudsen on drums, Tom Johnston and McDonald on lead vocals, Pat Simmons on vocals and guitar, Jeff Baxter and John McFee on guitars, Cornelius Bumpus on saxophone, John Hartman and Bobby LaKind on percussion, and two other drummers, Michael Hossack and Chet McCracken. The benefit concert was so well received by fans and critics alike that the reunion was continued for several more shows at West Coast venues.

DOORS, THE: *Vocal and instrumental group. Jim Morrison, born Melbourne, Florida, December 8, 1943, died Paris, France, July 3, 1971; John Densmore, born Los Angeles, California, December 1, 1945; Ray Manzarek, born Chicago, Illinois, February 12, 1935; Robby Krieger, born Los Angeles, California, January 8, 1946.**

Fronted by the Lizard King, surrounded by a virtual wall of sound that poured forth from 600- and 1000-watt amplifiers to engulf the audience in shock-wave patterns, Ray Manzarek, Robby Krieger, and John Densmore led what might be called a secluded stage existence for three triumphal years. Then their defenses crumbled. The raw, screaming vocals of Jim Morrison were silenced, first by an indecent-exposure charge, then by death.

As with many young rock bands, the Doors' saga started with rebellion against parental values, particularly in the case of Morrison, son of a Naval officer and the product of a family with a tradition of career service in the armed forces. For most of his youth, Morrison had a conventional American upbringing.

Born in Florida, he moved several times as his father was transferred to different bases. He graduated from George Washington High School in Alexandria, Virginia, in July 1961 and then entered St. Petersburg Junior College in Florida. He was already feeling uneasy about his life-style when he shifted to Florida State University in the fall of 1962. He dropped out in 1963 and then moved west in February 1964 to enter the UCLA theater arts department.

Morrison was a rock fan by the time he entered college; he also had more than one wild drinking bout to his credit. Poetry and philosophy both interested him at UCLA, particularly the writings of William Blake and Friedrich Nietzsche. In discussions with roommate Dennis Jakob, he anticipated his future band by creating an imaginary rock duo based on the literary works read in class. He and Jakob agreed a good name would be the Doors, derived from a phrase by William Blake: "There are things that are known and things that are unknown; in between the doors," and by the title of Aldous Huxley's book on mescaline experiments, *The Doors of Perception.*

In his art classes, Morrison met Ray Manzarek. Ray had been active in music since his childhood in Chicago, where he studied piano before he was 10. His first few years were devoted to the classics, but these did not interest him half as much as boogie-woogie, which he was introduced to at 12. Because he showed considerable talent, he continued classical work at the Chicago conservatory, but the more he played Bach or Tchaikovsky, the more spare time he spent in blues clubs on Chicago's South Side. He decided to seek his career outside music, majoring in economics at DePaul University in Chicago, going on to UCLA as a law student when his family moved west to Redondo Beach, California. A few weeks of law school were enough to convince Ray he wanted something more creative. He transferred to the film department.

By this time, Ray and his two brothers had developed their own blues-oriented group. They gained a regular weekend job at a bar in Santa Monica, not far from the UCLA campus, for which they each received $5 a night. They called themselves Rick and the Ravens, with Rick Manzarek on piano, Jim Manzarek on guitar, and Ray handling piano and doing the singing under the pseudonym Ray Daniels, "the bearded blues shouter."

In July 1965, Ray, then living in a hippie community in the beach town of Venice, encountered Morrison, whom he hadn't seen for some time. As Ray told writer Digby Diehl: "I had been friendly with Jim Morrison at UCLA and we had talked about rock'n'roll even then. . . . (When) I met him on the beach in Venice, he said he had been writing some

---

*Based partly on 1971–72 discussions between Bill Siddons and Irwin Stambler.

songs. So we sat on the beach and I asked him to sing some of them. He did, and the first thing he tried was 'Moonlight Drive.' When he sang those first lines—'Let's swim to the moon/Let's climb through the tide/Penetrate the evening/That the city sleeps to hide'—I said, 'That's it.' I'd never heard lyrics to a rock song like that before. We talked a while before we decided to get a group together and make a million dollars.''

One of their first additions was drummer John Densmore. Densmore, born and raised in West Los Angeles, started playing drums with a jazz group while attending University High School. He kept up his drum work while trying out many different majors, from literature to anthropology, in five local colleges, the last being UCLA, where he and Manzarek became acquainted while attending a UCLA chapter of the Maharishi Mahesh Yogi's transcendental meditation sect.

The fourth member of the Doors, guitarist Robby Krieger, also met Ray and John at the Third Street Meditation Center. Also a Southern Californian, he had learned guitar in his teens and later played in a jug band while going to the University of California at Santa Barbara. When he switched to UCLA as a physics and psychology major, he performed with several folk and blues groups.

Before Krieger came on the scene, the group rehearsed for a number of weeks and arranged to make demonstration tapes of six Morrison compositions at the World Pacific Jazz Studios in September 1965. The songs included ''Moonlight Drive,'' ''Summer's Almost Gone,'' ''End of the Night,'' and ''Break on Through.'' Instrumental support was provided by a woman bass player, Densmore, and Ray's brothers. However, the woman and the other two Manzareks didn't like Morrison's material and didn't work with the band after that.

When Krieger joined, the new foursome spent the next four or five months practicing. Seeking club work, they were rejected by many managers, but finally were hired at the London Fog on Sunset Strip for $5 each on weeknights and $10 on weekends. They remained there for four months, but the club became increasingly unhappy with them and finally gave them notice. The group auditioned for many jobs and were turned down. They thought they might have to disband, but on their last night, Ronnie Haran, talent booker for the Whisky A-Go-Go, heard them. She liked them and signed them as backup band at the club.

For months, the group was hardly noticed by people who came to hear the featured group. But as the Doors added more original compositions and Morrison began to develop his extroverted, screaming, sensual singing style, audiences started to take note

of them. The group not only experimented with new hard-rock styles, they also turned themselves on with almost every kind of drug except the very hard kinds, such as heroin. Though all but Morrison later abandoned drugs as a crutch, for a time they actually seemed to come up with better, more exciting music the more they got stoned.

In late 1966, Elektra promotion man Billy James, who had been instrumental in the rise of the Byrds, talked the founder of his company, Jac Holzman, into signing the group. Their first LP, *The Doors,* was released the next January and amply proved James' musical astuteness. Critics raved about Morrison's singing and about such tracks as ''Light My Fire,'' now a rock standard, written not by Morrison but by Robby Krieger, who also penned Doors classics ''Love Me Two Times'' and ''You're Lost, Little Girl.'' ''Light My Fire'' reached number one in *Billboard* the week of July 27, 1967, and stayed there two more weeks. The original six minutes plus version on the LP was cut sharply, over band members objections, for the single release. The song hadn't been written with single use in mind, Densmore was quoted as saying in the Doors biography by John Tobler and Andrew Doe. ''We always made an album as an album; we never reallly tried to make singles. We'd make the album, then we might think, OK, what might be commercial for AM play?''

Typical was the comment in *Disk Review:* ''The Doors laid down their style—hard rock with slippery, psychedelic overtones. Morrison got some of his lyrics from Nietzsche—he always said his main guide to his poetry is 'The Birth of Tragedy' from the 'Spirit of Music'—he combined Nietzsche with a little freshman psychology and a lot of very broad images (the sea, the sun, the earth, death) and came up with Morrison therapy: to become more real, to be a better person, cut your ties to the establishment past, swim in your emotions, suffer symbolic death and rebirth, rebirth as a new man, psychologically cleansed.''

They followed their gold debut album with such hit LPs as *Strange Days, Waiting for the Sun* (whose inside cover included Morrison's poem-lyrics to ''Celebration of the Lizard''), *Morrison Hotel/Hard Rock Case,* and *Soft Parade.* A single from *Strange Days,* ''Hello, I Love You,'' written by all the band members, brought the group its second (and last) number one *Bilboard* success. It sat atop the lists the weeks of August 3 and 10, 1968.

Everything seemed going the group's way, despite Morrison's controversial life style—his stage antics, reputation as a hard drinker and eccentric, and his lyrics that offended even some hardened rock fans because of lines that suggested he wanted to see his parents dead—until an April 1969 concert at the

Dinner Key Civic Audiorium in Miami. The concert itself didn't seem much different from any other frenzied activity of that sort that has taken place thousands of times in the U.S. since rock became king. But after the concert, when Morrison and the Doors had left Miami and were on an airplane heading for a short vacation, charges were made that Morrison had committed a flagrantly immoral act on stage. Newspaper columnist Alexandra Tacht wrote: "Morrison finally did it. He culminated his career as a sex symbol of the decade by dropping his pants in front of umpteen screaming teenies in Miami. Exit Morrison, who hopped the country and left in his wake 35,000 teens turning on a Decency Rally behind Jackie Gleason and Anita Bryant to show that Miami is really a straight town."

However, Morrison and the Doors constantly maintained the supposed incident never occurred as charged. As their manager, Bill Siddens, said in 1971: "We couldn't find anyone who saw the claimed exposure. The police had 150 photographs of the concert; none show any exposure. For me, it was always an absurd claim and in the end Jim was acquitted of such charges as lewd and lascivious behavior and drunkenness, and only a few minor counts remained. However, it affected the group's careers to a very large extent. It cost us at least a half million dollars—10 dates were cancelled immediately and we couldn't work for six months because we could never be sure when we might have to make a court appearance. It almost caused the group to break up. It really destroyed our morale. What we considered a minor incident turned into a tremendous problem."

By early 1970, the problem seemed to be clearing up. The group began recording and making in-person appearances once more. Morrison, however, had been taking stock of himself during the trying interim and was thinking about turning his atttention back to his first love, moviemaking. He did complete some films, such as *Feast of Friends,* which were never released and which were treated rather harshly by those critics who saw them. Morrison also was working on poetry, completing such books as *The Lords* and *The New Creation.* Both sold very well in hard cover when they were released by Simon and Schuster. (First printing was 5,000 copies for each.) Later they were issued in paperback.

The Morrison tribulation didn't affect the group's popularity with fans. At the start of the 1970s, they had two more gold LPs for Elektra, *L.A. Woman* and *The Doors' Greatest Hits.*

By late 1970, Morrison had become increasingly doubtful of his future as a singing star. He decided to go to France for an extended vacation to try to re-chart his life. He was not certain that he would drop

music. While he was gone, the other three Doors rehearsed new material on a regular weekly basis. They hoped Jim would work with them again, but those hopes were ended finally when Morrison was found dead in his bathtub of what was stated to be a respiratory illness and a heart attack in early July 1971.

The exact cause of his passing remained a mystery, however. Manzarek told a reporter for *Sound* magazine in 1973: "I don't know to this day how the man died and in fact I don't even know if he's dead. I never saw the body and nobody ever saw Jim Morrison's body. . . . It was a sealed coffin. So who knows, who knows how Jim died?"

The saga of the Doors seemed closed, but Manzarek, Densmore, and Krieger hoped otherwise. They felt the group was a musical tradition and doggedly returned to the rehearsal rooms, this time to work up material all their own. In late 1971, the results of this effort were demonstrated in the LP *Other Voices.* Obviously, it was a somewhat different sound and, in effect a different group, but it was a sound of promise. It suggested the Doors as a trio still could contribute to rock music. The album, indeed, did become a minor hit. But it soon became obvious this response was more in homage to past glories than endorsement of the band without Morrison. Unable to sustain forward momentum, the group essentially went out of existence by the mid-1970s, after which the members went off on various individual projects including solo recordings, formation of new groups, record session work, and record production for other artists. Manzarek, for instance, made two mid-1970s solo albums for Nite City Records and in 1983 collaborated with composer Philip Glass on an avant garde album, *Carmina Burana,* issued by A&M. Krieger assembled several different rock bands.

But that didn't mean that no new Doors projects developed. In 1978, for instance, one of the more interesting album releases was Elektra's *American Prayer,* a collection of poetry readings by Morrison that was blended electronically with new music recorded by the living members of the group. Doors music also was included in the soundtrack for Francis Ford Coppola's Vietnam War movie *Apocalypse Now.* And the group's catalog was expanded to include such 1970s–early 1980s Elektra LPs as *Weird Scenes Inside the Gold Mine* (1972), *Best of the Doors* (1973), and *The Doors' Greatest Hits* (1980).

In 1985, MCA Home Video released a videocassette (compiled and edited by Manzarek) titled *The Doors: Dance on Fire.* The video combined material from concert and in-studio films as well as some TV clips. In the summer of 1987, MCA issued a new videocassette containing color footage from a

1968 concert, *The Doors: Live at the Hollywood Bowl.* In the fall, Electra reissued the band's six studio albums on compact discs, digitally remastered from the original analog tapes.

DRAMATICS, THE: *Vocal and dance group from Detroit. Original members: Ron Banks, J. Reynolds, Lenny Mayes, Willie Ford, Larry Demps. Members in early 1980s: Banks, Mayes, Ford, and Craig Jones.*

At the end of the 1960s, it seemed that the explosion of top-flight soul/R&B performers from Detroit that fueled the Motown empire of that decade had run its course. The Dramatics then came along to show that the city still nurtured talented exponents of that art form. In the 1970s, when it sometimes seemed that racial segregation had returned to the pop music field, this vocal group proved it was possible to achieve crossover hits on both black and pop charts with music that reflected the classic roots of soul.

The original quintet began as a singing act in the early 1960s when their average age was 13. The Motown surge to prominence was gathering steam and many of the label's premier acts could be seen in concert in Detroit theaters and clubs. As Dramatics members recalled, they could see groups such as the Temptations, Four Tops, Spinners and Supremes all on the same bill for $2.50 a ticket. As young artists had done before them, the aspiring teenagers shaped their own act from what they saw or heard at such shows or from music on the radio. Before long, they moved from street corner harmony to engagements in small local halls or clubs. Lead singer Ron Banks commented: "It was worse than the Chitlin' Circuit. We were real young and the money was poor. But we'd all have good clothes, the girls would scream, and it was a lot of fun."

The group was good enough to get the chance to make some recordings for obscure Detroit labels, leading to a few small-scale regional hit singles. In 1966, the Dramatics' hopes rose when Motown executives gave serious attention to some of its demo recordings. However, Motown eventually turned down a contract. The group, while disappointed, refused to give up, particularly since the members had not polished any special skills other than music. Banks said: "We kept on pushing, rehearsing six days a week, eight hours a day. Sometimes we'd go to sleep together and wake up the next day singing."

For the next few years, the pattern was for them to continue polishing the act, including dance routines favored by most soul vocal groups, and pursue whatever performance opportunities came along. Whenever possible, the group made new demo tapes and tried to catch the attention of major labels. In 1969,

those efforts finally were rewarded with an agreement with Memphis, Tennessee–based Stax Records. The Dramatics members who began work on their debut recordings for the label comprised Banks as lead vocalist and first tenor, L.J. Reynolds as first and second tenor, Lenny Mayes as second tenor, Willie Ford as bass, and Larry Demps as baritone. Though Banks ranked as lead singer, the other four all could and did sing lead on many songs.

The group's first album on Stax didn't come out until 1972, but it made the Dramatics familiar to a wide range of fans. The record, *Whatcha See Is Whatcha Get,* made the top 20 R&B and pop charts. A single from the album, "In the Rain," became a major hit, rising to number one on soul charts in 1972 and gaining the top five on the general hit lists. The title track from the album also made both charts. Adding to the group's luster was the exposure it received as opening act on an eight-month national tour with the James Brown Revue. (*See Brown, James.*)

During 1972–73, the quintet earned words of praise from many quarters. Among others, the *Los Angeles Times* called them the "hottest new vocal group" in the field with "traces of gospel and R&B that provide a depth and fullness that keeps them well away from middle of the road."

The contract with Stax only covered a limited number of recordings so, despite the 1972 success the Dramatics went to Chess/Cadet Records for their next releases. The LPs issued on the Cadet label during 1973–75 included *Dramatically Yours* and *The Dramatics vs. the Dells.* During that period, the group had the top 10 R&B album *The Dramatic Jackpot* (also on the pop top 30) and the 1975 hit single "Me and Mrs. Jones." The group added to its performing credits with two national tours supporting singer Al Green and headline appearances in many U.S. and European cities. (*See Green, Al.*)

From Chess/Cadet, the Dramatics moved to ABC Records, remaining with that label and its eventual owner, MCA, until the early 1980s. One of the first releases on the new label was *Joy Ride* (1976). That album made the black music charts as did the 1976 single, "Be My Girl," which rose to number three on soul charts. The next year, the group made the lists with one of its best album efforts to that time, *Shake It Well.* Both the title track and "I Can't Get Over You" were top 10 soul hits. In 1978, the group made both soul and pop charts with its gold LP *Do What You Wanna Do.*

After ABC was acquired by MCA, the group recorded another series of albums that made U.S. charts, though not at the high levels of the earlier releases. These included *Anytime, Anyplace* (1979) and, in 1980, *The Dramatic Way* and *10½,* whose title refers to the fact that the members at that time had been recording together for almost eleven years. The group opened the 1980s with another top 10 single on black music charts, "Welcome Back Home." During the late 1970s, Stax had issued two LPs of their early material (*Whatcha See Is Whatcha Get* and *A Dramatic Experience*) on its Volt subsidiary.

In 1981, the group completed its stay with MCA and signed with Capitol. The roster, by then, had been reduced to a quartet: veteran members Banks, Mayes, and Ford plus a new vocalist, Craig Jones. For the debut collection on Capitol, Banks, who had increasingly become involved in all aspects of the group's activities, co-wrote six of the eight songs and also handled production. (In the late 1970s and early 1980s, he had become interested in outside production work as well, including supervision of recordings of two albums by the group Five Special with which his brother performed.)

The first Capitol LP, *New Dimensions,* came out in May 1982. First single from the album was "Live It Up" which appeared on black music charts soon after its release. Fantasy Records (which bought the post-1968 Stax catalog) put out *The Best of the Dramatics* (1986, CD only) and, in 1988, *The Dramatics Live* (previously unissued 1972–73 concert tapes)—both on the Stax logo.

DRIFTERS, THE: *Vocal group. Original personnel, 1953: Clyde McPhatter, born Durham, North Carolina, November 15, 1933; died 1972; Billy Pinkney, born Sumter, South Carolina, August 15, 1925; Andrew Thrasher, born Wetumpka, Alabama; Gerhart Thrasher, born Wetumpka, Alabama. By 1954, Andrew Thrasher was replaced by Charlie Hughes; Tommy Evans also added. Changes in 1955 included departure of McPhatter and addition of David Baugh, born Harlem, New York City, and Johnny Moore, born Selma, Alabama, 1934. Disbanded 1958. Reorganized group, 1959, comprised Ben E. King, Johnny Lee Williams; Elsberry Hobbs; Charlie Thomas; Reggie Kimber, born Henderson, North Carolina, September 28, 1938; King left in 1960; replaced by Rudy Lewis, who died 1963.*

The Drifters spanned almost two decades of rock and R&B. Listening to their dozens of best-selling recordings, the shift in style sounds so great that it seems like two completely different assemblages. Actually, this is what occurred, because Drifters personnel changed a great many times while it was on Atlantic Records' active roster, with a particularly sharp break and switch in direction occurring in 1959.

The group came into being in 1953, the brainchild of singer Clyde McPhatter. McPhatter already had

fame in the R&B field as the lead singer with Billy Ward's Dominoes. (*See Dominoes, The; McPhatter, Clyde.*) In 1953, he decided to go out on his own and formed his own group, including Andrew and Gerhart Thrasher and Bill Pinkney. The name Drifters was selected because all of the members "drifted" from one group to another, starting in their early years with gospel groups.

McPhatter aligned his new group with Atlantic Records in 1953 and promptly gained one of the year's best-sellers in R&B, "Money Honey." In 1954, they gained another number one single: "Honey Love." Over 30 years later, their doowop interpretation of Irving Berlin's "White Christmas" remains a classic.

The group had three top 10 R&B successes in 1955: "Adorable," "Steamboat," and "Whatcha Gonna Do." During the year, McPhatter was drafted into the Army. Before he left, the group consisted of McPhatter on lead; Tommy Evans, bass; Johnny Moore, first tenor; Gerhart Thrasher, second tenor; and Charlie Hughes, who replaced Andrew Thrasher early in the Drifters' career, baritone. By year-end, there were other changes and the lineup consisted of Pinkney, Thrasher, Hughes, Moore, and David Baughan.

Despite McPhatter's departure, the group made great strides in its development. It toured widely, working not only clubs in black areas, but with some of the integrated rock shows assembled by such people as disc jockey Alan Freed. (*See Freed, Alan.*) By 1956, the Drifters had moved out of the R&B straitjacket of the early '50s to take its place as a mass-audience group. Thus, its 1956 "Fools Fall in Love" made both the R&B and the general pop charts.

The group remained in the public spotlight during 1957 and 1958, touring as featured performers in several rock packages: "The Biggest Stars of 1957," "Biggest Stars of 1958," and "Dick Clark Caravan." During 1958, though, it became apparent the group was starting to lose its hold on the public. Record sales slowed to a trickle and none of the new releases made either national or R&B best-seller lists. One effort at change was the substitution of Bobby Hendricks as lead singer for a short time in 1958. Hendricks (born Columbus, Ohio, 1937) came to the Drifters from the Five Crowns. His addition had no affect on the group's popularity, though he later found success as a solo vocalist with "Itchy Twitchy Feeling."

Discouraged, the group broke up in 1958. However, its manager had a multiyear contract for appearances at New York's Apollo Theater. To meet these obligations, he persuaded Hendricks' old group, the Five Crowns, to become the Drifters in

1959. The Five Crowns comprised Ben E. King, lead; Charlie Thomas, tenor; Elsberry Hobbs, baritone; Johnny Lee Williams (who took over lead in 1960 when King left); and Reggie Kimber on guitar. (*See King, Ben E.*)

Atlantic assigned rock songwriters and record producers Jerry Leiber and Mike Stoller to work with the new group. The change proved very beneficial to the Drifters' image. The new Drifters' first release, "There Goes My Baby," sold well over a million copies. The popularity of the new Drifters among mass audiences quickly exceeded that of its predecessor namesake. The Drifters picked up two more gold-record awards in 1959 for "(If You Cry) True Love, True Love" and "Dance with Me." (The latter was written by the team of Mort Shuman and Doc Pomus, who then ranked with Leiber and Stoller as the best-known names in rock composing.)

The group's first release of 1960 was the top 10 hit, "This Magic Moment." In mid-year, the Drifters had one of its biggest successes to date with "Save the Last Dance for Me," a record that had a Spanish flavor in the arrangement. Ben E. King's lead vocal on this disc won such national acclaim that he left the group to work as a soloist, starting with a hit of a similar nature, the Phil Spector/Jerry Leiber composition, "Spanish Harlem."

The reorganized Drifters with Rudy Lewis completing the quintet continued to be an important influence on the pop music scene well into the 1960s. (Lewis died suddenly in 1963.) It got off on the right foot in late 1960 with the top 10 hit "Lonely Winds," followed with the 1961 top 10 hits "I Count the Tears," "Some Kind of Wonderful," and "Sweet for My Sweet"; "On Broadway" and "Up on the Roof" in 1962; "Under the Boardwalk" in 1964; and "At the Club" in 1965. An addition for the mid-1960s roster was Bill Fredericks. "Up on the Roof" and "Some Kind of Wonderful" came from the noted husband-wife songwriting team of Carole King and Gerry Goffin. (*See King, Carole.*)

Memories of the original Drifters were rekindled in 1972 with news stories reporting the death of Clyde McPhatter of a heart attack. By then, even the later versions of the group were largely inactive. In the mid-1970s, the act was revived for the oldies circuit, though that group didn't retain any of the bellwethers of yore. The mid-1970s Drifters did make some new recordings of old favorites, which were included in the 1975 British import LP (on WEA), *The Drifters 24 Original Hits*. Also still in the Atlantic catalog as of the early 1980s were the LPs *Drifters' Golden Hits* (1969) and *The Drifters—Their Greatest Recordings: The Early Years* (1971). Their continued impact on pop music is reflected in later recordings of their hits by Elvis Presley, Ry Cooder,

Mary McCaslin, Emmylou Harris, the Persuasions, and others. Dion did particularly well with top 10 versions of the Drifters' "Drip Drop" and "Ruby Baby." (*See Cooder, Ry; Dion; Presley, Elvis.*)

DURAN DURAN: *Vocal and instrumental group. Original members, 1978: Nick Rhodes, born Birmingham, England, June 8, 1962; John Taylor, born Birmingham, England, June 20, 1960; Simon Colley, born England; Steve Duffy, born England. Personnel 1980 to mid-1980s: Rhodes; John Taylor; Simon Le Bon, born Watford, Herts., England, October 27, 1968; Andy Taylor, born Newcastle-on-Tyne, England, February 16, 1961; Roger Taylor, born West Midlands, England, April 26, 1960.*

An article in the *London Daily Star* in the fall of 1982 proclaimed: "Twenty years ago, Beatlemania swept the country. Now, in 1982, another kind of pop hysteria is gripping the nation—Duran fever."

It was perhaps an exaggeration, but the similarities were there. The young, good-looking quintet, whose name came from a character in the 1968 Jane Fonda film *Barbarella*, became a target of attention for hordes of young, screaming female fans, first in England and, somewhat later, in the U.S. Like the Beatles, their initial material seemed lighthearted, easily listenable, and danceable, while their recordings sold in the millions. And, like the Beatles, the group indicated it had the creative talent to go beyond the faddish bubble-gum audience to reach young people in high school and college age brackets. Though it seemed unlikely that Duran Duran's popularity would ever quite match the Beatles', there is no doubt it ranks as one of the major rock stories of the '80s.

The group's music certainly wasn't a throwback to 1960s English rock. It unmistakably had the earmarks of its era with traces in its material ranging from punk and new wave through disco. In fact, it represented a synthesis of sorts of the techno-rock of Kraftwerk and David Bowie with disco. Talking to Parker Puterbaugh of *Rolling Stone*, Nick Rhodes said: "Because of our age, we didn't grow up with the Rolling Stones. We grew up with Roxy Music, David Bowie, Cockney Rebel, and Sparks." He told another reporter: "John and I had been working on the idea of crossing Chic [a disco group] and the Sex Pistols two and a half years before Duran Duran."

Rhodes and John Taylor were unemployed teens living with their families in the industrial city of Birmingham when they assembled the forerunner of Duran Duran in 1978. The group began as a foursome with Rhodes on synthesizer and rhythm box, John playing lead guitar, Simon Colley handling clarinet and bass, and Steve Duffy on vocals. The members got their start at the local Barbarella club—hence the band's name.

Before long, Colley and Duffy left, dissatisfied with the somewhat esoteric material then favored by Nick and John. The latter, after trying out a number of new vocalists, settled on Andy Wickett and also chose to add a drummer to the mix, recruiting Roger Taylor (like later member Andy Taylor, no relation to any other band Taylors). Roger had been a member of the punk Sex Organs. This band recorded some demo tapes, including the first version of what was to become the Duran Duran hit "Girls on Film." Soon after those recordings, Wickett left to be replaced on vocals by Jeff Thomas.

Rhodes and John Taylor meanwhile were influenced to change musical direction by hearing some of the new disco-style records from the U.S., such as the Chic material. One decision John made was to give up lead guitar in favor of his first love, bass. An ad placed in a music publication seeking a "Modern guitarist for Roxy/Bowie influenced band" led to a brief tour of duty for Londoner John Curtis, but he soon departed, as did vocalist Thomas.

Despite those events, the band's fortunes were soon due for an upturn. A Duran Duran demo tape impressed Paul and Michael Berrow, brothers who had just opened Rum Runners, a new disco club in Birmingham. The Berrows soon were managing the group and providing them with rehearsal space at the club. The band, of course, was now short several members. An ad in the trade publication *Melody Maker* for a "live-wire" guitarist resulted in Andy Taylor joining up as lead guitarist. Finding a vocalist was more difficult, but a bar girl at the club suggested they audition her boyfriend, Simon Le Bon, for the job.

Le Bon, who had tried a variety of activities from laundry man to work on an Israeli kibbutz, was taking art courses at the University of Birmingham at that point and not enjoying it too much. He showed up for the tryout wearing dark glasses and pink leopard-skin trousers with a batch of original lyrics and artwork in hand. Before the evening was over, he was a bonafide member. He not only became the lead vocalist but from then on was the group's chief lyricist.

The band released its first single, "Planet Earth," on its own label, Tritec, on February 2, 1981. This closely followed its first major tour as opening act for a Hazel O'Connor U.K. concert series that began in late 1980.

The band started out with a New Romantics image, part of the British "Blitz" movement at the start of the 1980s that was a reaction to the declining punk/new wave genre of the late 1970s. Bands identified with New Romantics wore carefully coiffed hair, exaggerated eye makeup, and fancy clothes, avoiding the unwashed, obscenity spouting, frantic style of typical punk groups. That could have been a fatal situation for Duran Duran, but the band quickly showed it was a good rock group above all.

The identification with the short-lived Blitz movement did help propel "Planet Earth" to number 12 on the U.K. charts. Distribution was handled by EMI Records, which had signed the group in late 1980 (with EMI's subsidiary, Capitol Records, picking up U.S. rights).On June 8, 1981, EMI issued the group's debut LP, *Duran Duran,* on its Harvest label. The LP achieved an impressive rise to number 2 on U.K. charts and the band supported it with tours of Europe and the U.S. The group scored another hit single on U.K. charts when "Girls on Film" rose to number five. A symbol of things to come was the group's emphasis on the visual medium with releases of music videos of both its 1981 hit singles. In 1981, the group had its first number one single when "Planet Earth" hit the top on Australian charts.

In early 1982, Duran Duran shot three new promo videos in Sri Lanka: "Hungry Like the Wolf," "Save a Prayer," and "Lonely in Your Nightmare." Later on, they went to another exotic locale to do two more: "Rio" and "Night Boat." Except for "Night Boat," all came out as tracks on the band's second LP, *Rio,* issued on May 4, 1982. The album reached number two on U.K. charts and went platinum in Australia, but it lingered only on lower charts levels in the U.S. The record didn't seem to be helped much by a summer U.S. tour during which the band headlined at 25 club dates and opened for Blondie in nine arena concerts. That tour, like the one the year before, proved a financial failure and, at the start of 1983, despite sales of 5 million records worldwide and star status in most of the developed world, it looked as though Duran Duran might join a long list of artists who couldn't win over the all-important U.S. mass audience.

But the band's intensive concert work and MTV came to the rescue. MTV began to air the group's videos and featured the group on its second annual New Year's Eve stereo simulcast from the Savoy in New York on December 31, 1982. The 60-minute set won approval from millions of young MTV fans. Constant playing by MTV of the "Hungry Like the Wolf" video finally helped a remixed version of the single move up U.S. charts and eventually propelled a remixed version of *Rio* to platinum levels in 1983. In April 1983, the band's debut LP was reissued in the U.S. by Capitol with the track "Is There Something I Should Know" added. During the year, it was represented with a gold-record award by the

RIAA. The band also had a top 10 single in the U.K. with "Rio," a disc that initially flopped in the U.S. market.

MTV appearances plus touring were credited by band members with its final breakthroughs in the U.S. in 1983, making it almost the first rock group to gain fame primarily from video exposure. It was the video field, Rhodes told Dennis Hunt of the *Los Angeles Times* (April 3, 1983) that brought radio airplay for new-generation English techno-rock groups. The catalyst, he noted, was Human League's "Don't You Want Me Baby?" "It was such a great single, no one could resist it. Suddenly the gate was opened for English bands (including Culture Club, ABC, Soft Cell, the Thompson Twins, and A Flock of Seagulls). Before Human League broke through, English [new-sound] bands had just about given up on America. But when they made it, that gave us all extra confidence."

The Blitz image also had to be overcome, he agreed. "We looked very strange to people here. We suffered from having that kind of image. We have always put music before image, but people here didn't know us well enough to know that. That flamboyant image made people suspicious of us. It put an air of doubt about us for a short time.

"We were naive about image. We thought it was fun at first. It wasn't until later that we realized it had done us damage. Now our image is much more natural. But we still wear some bright colors and different hair colors. For us that's toned down, but compared to a lot of bands it's still flamboyant."

After 1983, though, Duran Duran had clear sailing to worldwide superstardom, even in the U.S. The remixed version of "Hungry Like the Wolf," issued in December 1982 (the original version, backed with "Careless Memories" having been released the previous June) rose to number three on U.S. singles lists. A remix of "Rio," issued in March 1983, reached the number 3 spot. The single "Is There Something I Should Know?" became the group's first number one U.K. single in March 1983. Issued in the U.S. in May, it didn't do that well, but still hit upper chart levels. In March 1983, the group's first eleven videos were packaged in a video album distributed in the U.S. by Sony.

In November 1983, Capitol released the band's *Seven and the Ragged Tiger*. In advance of that LP, the first single, "Union of the Snake," was issued in October, quickly reaching the top 3 in the U.K. and top 10 in the U.S. The album shipped gold and was well over RIAA platinum-record levels at the end of 1984. During 1984, the band had three LPs and four singles on the hit lists. The singles included "The Reflex," "Union of the Snake," and "New Moon on Monday." The LPs, besides *Rio* and *Seven and the Ragged Tiger*, included the live LP *Arena*, issued in late 1984 and in the U.S. top five in December. The *Arena* LP remained a chart hit in 1985 and spawned three charted singles, the most successful being "The Wild Boys."

By the time *Arena* came out, it seemed possible that Duran Duran might have broken up. After completing the *Seven and the Ragged Tiger* tour in the spring of 1984, band members decided to go off on new projects. Rhodes, Le Bon, and Roger Taylor formed a group, Arcadia, while John Taylor and Andy Taylor became part of another superstar aggregation, Power Station. (For Power Station's debut LP, long-time rock star Robert Palmer handled studio vocals. On tour, lead singing chores were taken over by Michael Des Barres, previously lead singer for the group Chequered Past. On drums for live appearances was Tony Thompson, previously with Chic).

As Rhodes pointed out, John and Andy wanted to play "heavier rock" while he and Simon liked to try material "more experimental and abstract." Both groups recorded platinum-award-winning albums for Capitol: *The Power Station* (spring 1985) and Arcadia's *So Red the Rose* (late 1985). Arcadia also had the hit single "Election Day" in 1986.

The need for separate projects had become apparent when the Duran Duran members had recorded the theme song for the James Bond film *A View to a Kill*, a number that brought them a number one single on *Billboard* charts in 1986. Rhodes told Robert Hilburn (*Los Angeles Times*, December 7, 1986): "It was a hard record to make. We had just come off this tour. No one was delighted with the *Seven and the Ragged Tiger* album. There was a lot of tension in the studio. It was obvious that we were either going to take a break from Duran or make a dreadful Duran album."

In early 1986, Le Bon, Rhodes, and John Taylor felt they could cope emotionally with reviving Duran again and planned a new album. However, it turned out to be a trio effort because the members realized Andy Taylor preferred trying for a solo career and Roger Taylor had personal problems. In Roger's case, Rhodes told Hilburn: "His health wasn't that good. He started to get tense about everything. He finally realized that he wasn't well suited to this business. If he had stayed in it longer, he might have blown a fuse. So he left the music business. Now he's living in the countryside with his wife, who's pregnant. He's happy. He got out at the right time."

Issued by Capitol in late 1986, *Notorious* reflected a more mature style and feeling than earlier LPs. For the 1987 tour backing the album, the band replaced its missing Taylors with Warren Cuccurullo on guitar and Steve Ferrone on drums.

While the slimmed down Duran Duran threesome toured across the U.S. and in other nations during 1987, Andy Taylor was in the midst of launching his solo career. He had taken part in sessions for the group's *Notorious* LP, but announced his departure in 1986 after signing a contract with MCA Records. His 1986 efforts included writing and performing three songs on the soundtrack of the film *American Anthem*, as well as backing Robert Palmer on the singer's hit single "Addicted to Love" and Belinda Carlisle on her best seller, "Mad About You." His debut LP on MCA, *Thunder* (containing songs co-written by Taylor and former Sex Pistols member Steve Jones) was issued in the summer of 1987 and proved a first rate, high powered rock collection. Among the tracks was a song that became the theme of the Musical Majority's anti-drug campaign, "Don't Let Me Die Young."

DURY, IAN: *Singer, guitarist, songwriter, band leader (THE BLOCKHEADS). Born Harrow Weald, England, 1943.*

Almost 30 when he decided to give up his job as an art teacher to try for a full-time career in pop music, Ian Dury managed over the next decade to carve a niche for himself as one of Europe's best-regarded performers and songwriters. His achievements were all the more remarkable since he also had to overcome the handicap of permanent disabilities from the polio that ravaged his body as a child.

Born in Harrow Weald, England, and brought up in his mother's home area of Upminster, he was hospitalized with polio at seven and never recovered full use of his legs in addition to suffering a crippled arm. But he never lost his spirit. As he told an interviewer in the mid-1970s: "All this is irrelevant. I came to terms with it. You have to. I feel sorry for people who can't cope with the way you look. I was in hospital for 2½ years and the first thing you learn is that you don't moan. 'Cos you're alive. You keep yourself together 'cos the geezer in the next bed has been run over by a truck and is dying."

In his teens, Dury developed an interest in painting and at age 17 enrolled in the Walthamstow Art College. His responsibilities increased when he got married and had a family to support. When he finished at Walthamstow, he went on to become an art teacher at the Canterbury School of Art.

He had developed contacts in the music field by the time he was 27, when he and his wife, Betty, decided to move from their long-time Cockney environment in London to the country. He told a reporter from England's *Record Mirror* (January 1, 1979): "We 'ad a kid and not a load of money and if you 'aven't got much money in London, it's no fun for the kid. So we moved out to near Aylesbury an' got a vicarage for a fiver a week, with two acres of ground an' eight rooms. Well, cheap it was, but they slung us out after four years [in 1973]. That's where I started rockin'n'rollin'—rehearsing with Kilburn and the High Roads."

The Kilburn group evolved from a meeting between Dury and members of a band called the People Band, which included Davey Payne on tenor saxophone and percussionist Terry Day. Dury had been trying to make his way as a vocalist with little success when their paths crossed in 1968. In his singing efforts, he told *Sounds* magazine writer David Widgery: "Each time I tried to do it, it was with geezers who told me I was in another key. Leave it out, Ian,' they used to shout. In fact Chaz [his later musical director and songwriting collaborator Charles Jankel] only explained to me last week the rather unusual way I relate to a chord."

He felt he could overcome some of those problems working with the People Band so after a while he called its members. "I just phoned them all up and said you know what I'm like and I know what you're like so let's play some rock and roll. It was mostly Fats Domino, I think." The group renamed itself Kilburn and the High Roads and augmented the early 1970s rehearsals at Dury's with whatever performing work they could line up. At first, they mostly did covers of R&B or blues-rock material, but after a while, Dury's own lyrics were added.

It was around 1973 that Dury began to write song lyrics. He said, "Well, I 'ad done a little bit of delinquent poetry [in earlier years], but every time I looked at it I thought it was a bit of a wank-off, so I left it. I don't like poetry, personally. I just make things rhyme if I can, to keep me interested."

He favored rhyming couplets, often on off-the-wall subjects. And though he claimed to disdain poetry, the British musical press in the mid-1970s called him "the poet of punk." However, his recordings show he is not a punk artist. He probably qualified as new wave, but even that is arguable, since the original songs played by Dury and his group from the mid-1970s on (mostly with music by Jankel and lyrics by Dury) seemed to encompass all sorts of elements in its rock format—blues, funk, jazz, even reggae—with Dury's lyric comments generally tongue-in-cheek rather than reflecting the bitterness and anger present in punk compositions. He specializes in lyrics that usually are either irreverent or seemingly abstract.

With various personnel changes in the mid-1970s, the Kilburns were transposed into a new group named the Blockheads. In the late 1970s, Blockhead members included Davey Payne, Mickey Gallagher (keyboardist, born Fenham, England), John Turnbull (guitarist, born Walker, England), Norman Witt-Roy (born Bombay, India), Charlie Charles, Fred Rowe, and Kozmo Vinyl. During 1976, the new group began to make a name for itself in English clubs and helped Dury arrange his first major record pact with England's Stiff Records. The future was looking somewhat more promising for Dury, who recalled that in 1975, his income typically was only 25 pounds a week.

The band's debut on Stiff, *New Boots and Panties,* came out on September 18, 1977. It was an instant hit with English reviewers, which helped it gain the U.K. charts by the end of the year. It proved a breakthrough collection, still on the lists at the end of 1978 for its fifty-eighth straight week. By then, the album had been certified gold by the U.K. record-industry association. Meanwhile the Blockheads and Dury were on the way to ranking as one of England's top new live performance attractions with a wild, unpredictable show that made them seem something like the Spike Jones band of rock. A featured segment of the show was the hit single from the debut album, "Sex and Drugs and Rock and Roll."

During 1978, Stiff released the band's second LP, *Do It Yourself.* A worthy successor to the first LP, it quickly rose high on European charts. A U.S. version was released in 1978 and Dury and his band went on a 56-date U.S. tour to support it. Dury's heavy Cockney-based vocals seemed to put off U.S. audiences (though it didn't seem to bother fans in Europe, who flocked to many of his 1978–79 shows). While the U.S. tour didn't make him a household name in the States, it provided the inspiration for Dury's best-selling U.S. single of 1979, "Hit Me with Your Rhythm Stick."

John Turnbull told Andy Bone of the *Newcastle-on-Tyne Sunday Sun* (February 4, 1979): "It all started when we were touring America last year. We used to go around shouting these crazy chants. For instance we'd call out 'beefburgers' in a posh hotel. One of Ian's favorites was to go down the street shouting 'hit me, hit me' and waving his walking stick [the cane his polio required he always use] around in the air. I suppose it was inevitable he would end up writing a song about it." The single of that song made number one on the U.K. pop charts in January 1979. It was an unusual situation since the song had not been included in any LPs up to then.

After the release of *Do It Yourself,* Chaz Jankel left the organization and many of his duties were taken up by guitarist Wilko Johnson, who came to the Blockheads from the band Dr. Feelgood. His contributions to Dury's third album, *Laughter* (Stiff, 1980), made that disc the equal of the first two in innovative content. The album was well received in England and got high marks from U.S. reviewers though Dury's U.S. following remained essentially a cult one.

Dury continued to experiment with new formats as demonstrated by his next album, *Lord Upminster.* For that set of recordings, he was reunited with Jankel. The material they wrote or selected was presented in pulsating reggae stylings against a background of a flawless rhythm section by reggae greats Sly Dunbar and Robbie Shakespeare.

Though often grouped with the social-activist punk/new wave stylists such as the Clash and Sex Pistols, Dury maintained he was an entertainer, not a revolutionary. He told David Widgery of *Sounds* (December 16, 1978): "Well, I'm not a revolutionary. I believe in education, funnily enough. This is realistic. I'm an artisan. I learnt how to draw. I can impart that knowledge to other people. I hope one day I'll know enough about the craft of writing to impart that knowledge. As a painter I knew I wasn't doing it for the money. It was knowledge for the joy of it. And teaching it, however you want, is doubling it.

"Take it a stage further. If you've got yourself organized, you can have a student and be a student. Something has been trebled. I don't know what it is quite. It's an exchange of personal strength. If you die tomorrow, someone can sit on it. But it's got fuck all to do with posterity or heredity or inheritance or anything like that. It's now. I don't care if my so-called work dies the minute I die. I don't want to be Shakespeare. I just want do my gig."

DYLAN, BOB: *Songwriter, singer, guitarist, pianist, harmonica player, Born Duluth, Minnesota, May 24, 1941.*

From songs of social consciousness such as "The Times They Are A-Changin'" and "Blowin' in the Wind" to songs about his faith in Christianity (which he embraced and then renounced), Bob Dylan's music has sparked controversy and set trends. Refusing to be classified in any specific political or artistic posture, he has written about whatever strikes his fancy, restlessly probing one area of popular music, then moving on to another. His frequent shifts in musical style and subject matter have often outraged and confused his fans, yet he always managed to maintain favor with a large segment of the record-buying public.

Born Robert Allen Zimmerman, the legendary Bob Dylan grew up in the mining town of Hibbing, Minnesota. Although at one time he professed to have been a rebellious teenager, often running away from home, he later disavowed these stories. Actually, according to his mid-1980s interviews, he had a fairly normal childhood that did not change direction until his freshman year at the University of Minnesota. During his six months of college, Dylan did some singing at the campus coffeehouse and changed his name from Zimmerman to Dylan, taken from one of his favorite poets, Dylan Thomas. He also was influenced by folk songwriter Woody Guthrie and, in fact, when he left school, traveled to visit the dying Guthrie at Greystone Park Hospital, New Jersey. He managed to get to see Woody, and the two became friends.

Dylan remained in New York, trying to make his living in folk music as either a performer or songwriter. At one point he went to Hill & Range publishing to seek a $50 per week job as a staff writer, according to then company VP Grelun Landon. Landon recalled recommending to the firm's top executives that Dylan be hired, but the advice was rejected. A short time later, he was discovered by Columbia Records executive John Hammond, who heard him by accident during a rehearsal session of folk singer Carolyn Hester, for whom Bob played harmonica. Hammond set up Dylan's first recording sessions. His first album, *Bob Dylan,* was released in 1961 and was followed by other folk-oriented LPs, *Freewheelin' Bob Dylan* (1963) and *The Times They Are A-Changin'* (1964). The second and third remained on the best-seller lists for many weeks. (Columbia came close to missing the boat on those successes and later Dylan classics. Hammond recalled that company executives talked about dropping the artist after his debut LP, because they felt his style didn't fit the firm's roster).

At the same time, Bob was appearing at various coffeehouses in New York City. The critics raved about his work, and he soon became a focal point of the short-lived folk music boom of the early 1960s. The dozens of folkish songs he composed during this time that became all-time standards included "Masters of War," "Don't Think Twice, It's All Right," "Spanish Harlem Incident," and "Chimes of Freedom." Some of his songs helped propel other artists to stardom, as "Blowin' in the Wind" did for Peter, Paul and Mary and "Mr. Tambourine Man" did for the Byrds. (*See Byrds, The.*)

With the folk boom on the wane, Dylan's songs began to veer more toward a blend of folk and rock elements. He now employed wildly upbeat arrangements and intricate but hard-to-understand lyrics that sometimes seemed written more for the sound and imagery of the words. These albums—*Another Side of Bob Dylan* (1964), *Highway 61 Revisited* and *Bringing It All Back Home* (1965), *Blonde on Blonde* (1966), and *Bob Dylan's Greatest Hits* (1967)—had considerable influence on that period's rock renaissance. His first single to hit U.S. charts was "Sub-

terranean Homesick Blues," which made the lists in April 1965. Later in the year, he had a major hit, "Like a Rolling Stone," which reached number two. His other best-selling singles of the 1960s were "Positively 4th Street," "Rainy Day Women Nos. 12 & 35," "I Want You," "Just Like a Woman,"and "Lay Lady Lay."

In 1966, Dylan suffered a near-fatal motorcycle accident and spent several years recuperating, away from the public eye. When he resurfaced musically at the end of the decade, he had once again switched his musical style to a blend of country & western and rock'n'roll with lyrics emphasizing more basic, simple themes than his earlier songs. His best-selling Columbia albums, *Nashville Skyline* and *John Wesley Harding* helped spark the growing trend toward the merging of country, folk, and rock.

In the 1970s, Bob Dylan embraced many different themes and causes in his songs and tried several different musical styles. Although many critics felt his recordings in the early 1970s were not up to his earlier quality, his fans made up their own minds, propelling such albums as *Self-Portrait* and *New Morning* (1970) and *Greatest Hits, Volume 2* (1971) onto the best-seller lists.

If many people were concerned that Dylan had lost his sense of political concern, he demonstrated over and over again that this was not so. He expressed outrage over the death of George Jackson in San Quentin in his song "George Jackson." He also performed at a concert in support of the new nation of Bangladesh at Madison Square Garden in New York in 1971. This concert was organized by George Harrison and resulted in a three-LP album, *The Concert for Bangla Desh,* which featured a number of tracks by Dylan. (*See Beatles, The; Harrison, George.*) In 1975, he performed at a concert dedicated to freeing Rubin (Hurricane) Carter, an ex-boxer serving a life sentence for murder. Dylan felt he was falsely accused of this crime and wrote "Hurricane" specifically for the concert to free him.

All in all, however, the Bob Dylan of the 1970s was much more concerned with personal feelings and relationships than the Dylan of the 1960s. He expressed this himself in one song from his 1974 album, *Planet Waves:* "It's never been my duty/To remake the world at large/Nor is it my intention/To sound a battle charge."

The 1970s also witnessed Dylans' involvement in modes of communication other than music. His stream-of-consciousness–stylebook, *Tarantula,* appeared in print in 1970. In 1973, he published his own authorized text, *Writings and Drawings by Bob Dylan,* which contained lyrics to most of the songs he had written up through 1971 and also included album notes he had written and drawings he had made. In 1973 Dylan made his acting debut in the movie *Pat Garrett and Billy the Kid,* directed by Sam Peckinpah and also starring Kris Kristofferson. (*See Kristofferson, Kris.*) The soundtrack album, which included Dylan's "Knocking on Heaven's Door," was issued by Columbia. This actually marked Dylan's third movie effort. His first appearance had been in *Don't Look Back* (released in 1967), a documentary about a British tour with Joan Baez. A book of the dialogue from the film was a best-seller in the late 1960s. His second movie, *Eat the Document,* was actually intended as a TV special. Completed in the late 1960s, it was turned down by ABC (which sued for return of advances) as not professional enough.

For a brief period, his recordings appeared on the Asylum label. After his recording contract with Columbia expired in late 1973, he organized his own firm, Ashes and Sand, with distribution to be handled by Asylum Records. Plans for this new operation dovetailed with his decision to return to the concert stage after a long hiatus.

When Dylan announced that he would make a coast-to-coast tour in early 1974, a deluge of mail-order requests hit box offices across the nation. Bill Graham, producer of the concerts, estimated that 6 million orders came in, roughly ten times the 658,000 seats available. The lucky chosen who got seats went away happy. Dylan sang many of his old standards but also introduced new songs from his upcoming Asylum debut album, *Planet Waves.*

He was backed by the Band, a rock group he had discovered in Atlantic City, New Jersey, in the mid-1960s and that went on to become a highly regarded American musical aggregation in its own right in the late 1960s. (*See Band, The.*) The use of the Band, therefore, not only provided Dylan with fine backup musicianship but supplied further continuity with Dylan's past, for he had been backed by the Band on his last tour eight years earlier. The live album resulting from the 1974 tour, *Before the Flood* (Asylum Records), went gold.

In 1975, Dylan continued to build on the momentum he had gained the year before. He had meanwhile returned to the Columbia fold, which remained his label into the 1980s. As Robert Hilburn described his gold *Blood on the Tracks* LP: "The 10 songs . . . represent a variety of styles (acoustic, electronic, folk, blues, rock) and themes (tenderness, anger, sarcasm, humor, affection) that we've associated with Dylan's music over the years. The album's most arresting song—one that reflects the stinging intensity of 'Like a Rolling Stone'—is 'Idiot Wind.' Like so many of Dylan's songs, it contains a variety of crosscurrents and can be interpreted on several levels, but its most persistent theme is a sense of

being disappointed or betrayed. The song reflects the kind of direct, unguarded emotional outburst that is at the heart of much of Dylan's most interesting work."

Dylan also had a surprising best-selling album on Columbia in 1975, *The Basement Tapes*—surprising because the two-LP set had actually been recorded eight years earlier. The album set was the long-awaited legitimate, professionally prepared tracks made from bootleg magnetic tapes of Bob Dylan and the Band that had circulated many years before. Even though eight years had elapsed since the tapes were made, the songs stood the test of time so well that many fans and critics felt the LP was the most exciting rock release of the year. *The Basement Tapes* was ranked number one in the *Village Voice* 1975 Jazz & Pop Critics Poll, in which 38 music critics were allowed to divide 100 points among 10 1975 American-released LPs.

In the fall of 1975, Dylan embarked on the "Rolling Thunder Revue," an informal tour of some small New England cities, playing mostly in small (several hundred) to medium size (2,000-3,000 seats) auditoriums. Although Dylan was always the focal point and main attraction, the concerts featured a number of other excellent musicians, who stepped forward at various times in the concerts to do solo performances. Among the supporting cast of the "Rolling Thunder Revue" were Bobby Neuwirth, Roger McGuinn, Ramblin' Jack Elliott, guitarist Mick Ronson, Ronee Blakley, T-Bone Burnett, Rob Stoner, and violinist Scarlet Rivera. During this tour, Dylan introduced a few songs from his next album, *Desire,* which was released in January 1976.

Desire was received favorably by most music critics, further evidence that Dylan had indeed returned to the top of the rock heap. The album's songs could be seen as an overview of the major themes of Dylan's previous work, from social protest ("Hurricane"), to affection for the underdog ("Joey," about slain underworld figure Joey Gallo), to many different views about romance and man–woman relationships ("One More Cup of Coffee," "Oh, Sister," "Sara"). Dylan wrote all the music, but the lyrics to seven of the album's nine songs were co-written with Jacques Levy.

Dylan tried his hand at film-making once again in 1978 with *Renaldo and Clara,* which Dylan starred in, wrote, directed, and co-edited. Robert Hilburn, pop music critic for the *Los Angeles Times,* typified most critics' reaction to the movie when he wrote: "Bob Dylan will hopefully make a better film some day than *Renaldo and Clara,* but it's doubtful that rock's most acclaimed songwriter will ever make a more fascinating one. At once mocking and reinforcing his own almost mythical pop status, Dylan has crammed enough provocative symbolism into his nearly four-hour production to keep Dylan-cologists aflutter for years.''

The film featured Dylan as Renaldo, his ex-wife Sara as Clara, and Ronee Blakley and Ronnie Hawkins as Dylan's parents. (*See Hawkins, Ronnie.*) Joan Baez appeared as a reminder of the rumors about Dylan's long-ago romance with her. One of the film's scenes showed Dylan and poet Allen Ginsberg visiting the tombstone of novelist Jack Kerouac, affirming that one's art is all that will survive. In addition, a great deal of concert footage (47 songs) was included in the film.

His next record was *Street Legal* (1978) which sold well but seemed lightweight for Bob Dylan. His new songs incorporated Latin rock, reggae, and soul styles, the result being a more top-40 pop-oriented sound than usual. Dylan gave a week-long series of concerts at the Universal Amphitheater in Los Angeles in June 1978 before he embarked on a wide-ranging tour of Europe. He surprised his fans by playing totally new, almost unrecognizable versions of his old hits, such as a reggae-flavored rendition of "Don't Think Twice" and a soul-flavored version of "Just Like a Woman.''

The next year Dylan did another unexpected about-face. His new album, *Slow Train Coming,* reflected his conversion to Christianity. If anything could surprise Dylan's fans after all his previous changes in attitude and musical style, it was his new incarnation, for the Jewish-born rock poet had always seemed to be something of a cynic. However, as Gregory Reese and David Sperling pointed out in a column in *The News World:* "Dylan's exhortations are certainly at odds with the 'do your own thing' mentality of the '60s. But in a curious way, the album is true to Dylan's origins—in fact, this LP may be more pure Dylan than anything he's put out in a long time. Dylan has traditionally railed against hypocrisy, materialism, and corruption—the religious themes only serve to intensify the message.''

Whatever his fans thought of Dylan's conversion, many soon concurred that his new-found faith added power to his music. His voice seemed stretched by a new force. In addition, Dylan went beyond his own personal conversion and probed new aspects and applications of the morality implied in the embracing of Christianity. In "When You Gonna Wake Up,'' he expresses the idea that America is a great country, but warns that it must "strengthen the things that remain,'' "wake up'' to the corruption around it, and focus on a new set of values.

Not everyone received Dylan's conversion and gospel songs with pleasure, however. His 1979 concert tour was met with empty seats and, on some occasions, even boos. His 1980 album, *Saved,* continued in the gospel vein. By 1983, Dylan had renounced his conversion to Christianity and apparently returned to the Jewish faith, although this aspect of Dylan's life, like much of his private life, remains a mystery.

Dylan's twenty-fourth album, *Shot of Love,* was released by Columbia in August 1981. Some of its songs were included in the summer tour of Europe, a series of concerts played to standing-room-only crowds. In connection with these activities, he recorded a special, limited-edition promotional piece, *The Bob Dylan London Interview,* intended mainly for radio station use. (The world premiere broadcast of the interview was on station WNEW-FM in New York on July 27,1981.)

Dylan's next LP was *Infidels* (1983), produced by Mark Knopfler of Dire Straits. (*See Dire Straits.*) In this gold album, Dylan returned to the criticism of aspects of the state of the United States and the world that had marked his rise to fame in the 1960s, including "Neighborhood Bully" (saluting Israel's brave struggle for survival) and "Union Sundown" (lamenting the greed in American business). The summer of 1984 saw Dylan once again touring Europe before enthusiastic audiences. Then in 1985, at the invitation of Soviet poet Yevgeny Yevtushenko, Dylan traveled to the Soviet Union, where he performed in Moscow at a gathering of international poets. Yevtushenko introduced him as a "famous . . . singing poet.''

Earlier in 1985, Dylan had appeared with many of the most popular U.S. entertainers to sing "We Are the World'' to raise money to aid those starving in Africa. He also appeared in the Live Aid concert in Philadelphia for the same cause, and in September 1985 in the Farm Aid concert to assist failing farmers. (*See Geldof, Bob.*) He also released two albums, *Empire Burlesque* and *Biograph,* a five-record set including 21 selections not previously available on an album and 32 digitally remastered versions of previously released tracks. As he had done with his singles for *Infidels,* Dylan also did some music videos of his singles from *Empire Burlesque.*

In early 1986, in tribute to his lasting contribution to American music, ASCAP (American Society of Composers, Authors & Publishers) gave Dylan the Founders Award, an award to salute musicians whose songs changed the direction of American pop music.

Proving that he was still actively contributing to pop music, Dylan toured the U.S. in the summer of 1986 with Tom Petty and the Heartbreakers, singing old songs and new songs to delighted crowds. (*See Petty, Tom & the Heartbreakers*). He released another album, *Knocked Out Loaded,* that same summer.

In an interview in 1984, Dylan told Robert Hilburn of the *Los Angeles Times:* "When I started, I combined other people's styles unconsciously. . . . I crossed Sonny Terry with the Stanley Brothers with Roscoe Holcombe with Big Bill Broonzy with Woody Guthrie . . . all the stuff that was dear to me. Everybody else tried to do an exact replica of what they heard. I was doing it my own way because I wasn't as good technically as, say, Erik Darling or Tom Paley. So I had to take the songs and make them mine in a different way. It was the early folk music done in a rock way, which was the first kind of music I played. On the first album, I did 'Highway 51' like an Everly Brothers tune because that was the only way I could relate to that stuff."

Stating that he was glad that he had started his remarkable career in the 1960s, he said: "'Everything happened so quick in the '60s. There was just an electricity in the air. It's hard to explain—I mean, you didn't ever want to go to sleep because you didn't want to miss anything. It wasn't there in the '70s and it ain't there now.

"If you want to really be an artist and not just be successful, you'll go and find the electricity. It's somewhere."

In the second half of 1986, Dylan's schedule included work on a new film project called *Hearts of Fire,* in which he played the role of Billy Parker, a reclusive singer-songwriter who retires to a farm for a decade before a bittersweet return to the stage in an oldies concert. In the summer of 1987, Bob went back on tour, this time with the Grateful Dead band. In September he went to Israel for two concerts eagerly awaited by the nation's rock fans. He downplayed any symbolism, though, telling reporters it was just another part of his concert schedule. He jokingly told Hilburn (*Los Angeles Times,* Calendar, September 20, 1987), "I wish people here well, but it's not like this show is my biggest goal of the year or anything. My biggest goal of the year is getting back home alive."

In January 1988, after Bob was inducted into the Rock and Roll Hall of Fame in a ceremony at the Grand Ballroom of the New York Waldorf Astoria, he performed "Like a Rolling Stone" backed by a chorus of Mick Jagger, Bruce Springsteen and Supremes alumnus Mary Wilson and a band whose guitar roster included John Fogerty, George Harrison, Neil Young, Jeff Beck, and Les Paul.

E., SHEILA: *Singer, percussionist, songwriter, record producer. Born Oakland, California, December 12, 1959.*

With her movie-star looks, above-average singing voice, writing skills, and show-business family background, Sheila E. seemingly had most of the requisites for success. For all that, it took the backing of pop star Prince to finally open the record-company doors to her, but being Prince's protégé had its adverse effects as well. (*See Prince.*)

Sheila, born and raised in Oakland, was the daughter of professional percussionist Pete Escovedo (a Santana alumnus) and niece of another familiar name to followers of rock bands, Coke Escovedo, who also was a Santana sideman for a while and organized the group Azteca in the mid-1970s. She learned to play conga drums when she was five and soon after was performing on stage with Pete and Coke's group the Escovedo Brothers. At age 10, she began violin lessons and over the next five years developed a good enough touch with the instrument to be offered three musical scholarships.

She considered them, but she already was well on the way to making her mark in the entertainment field without additional schooling. In her midteens she joined her father in the group Azteca, playing congas and doing both lead and backing vocals in engagements in the U.S. and South America. While the group was playing clubs around San Francisco, jazz fusion keyboards player George Duke asked her to become part of his group. This led to a musical collaboration that lasted more than three years.

In the early 1980s, she returned to work with her father. They formed the duo Pete and Sheila and cut two albums under that name that unfortunately had little impact with record buyers. However, she didn't lack for other projects. Her vocal and instrumental skills brought plenty of opportunities for record-session work and chances to tour as a backing vocalist with many top name performers. Among those she recorded or toured with were Herbie Hancock, Spyro Gyra, Lionel Richie, Jeffrey Osborne, Diana Ross, Marvin Gaye, and Con Funk Shun.

While working with artists of that caliber was gratifying, it didn't bring her to center stage. At this point, her association with Prince proved the desired catalyst. He was lining up performers to work on the soundtrack for his 1984 film *Purple Rain* and approached Sheila to help out. Impressed with her vocal and writing abilities, he agreed to contribute to shaping up a solo album for her. Prince helped her get a recording contact with his label, Warner Brothers. The resulting solo album, *The Glamorous Life* (spring 1984), made the *Billboard* top 100 in midsummer, aided by Sheila's concert appearances with Prince. During much of that year, she worked with Prince on the "Purple Rain" tour, both as an opening act and a singer. The LP, helped by two chart singles (the title track and "The Ballad of St. Mark," both written by Sheila), earned her a gold-record certification from the RIAA.

During that time, she already was preparing for

her second album, as she stated in a record company bio. "I wrote the songs on the road and when we were ready to record, we'd go to a studio in whatever town we were playing that day and record until it was time for the show. After the gig we'd go back to the studio. Sometimes the sessions lasted from two in the morning until four the next afternoon when we'd have to get on a bus or a plane to go to the next concert. It was exhausting, but it was also one of the most exciting times in my life."

Hardly had the tour been completed when she was trying a new outlet for her talents as a featured actress in the film *Krush Groove*. Besides appearing in the movie, she authored two songs for the soundtrack: she wrote "Holly Rock" specially for the film, while "Love Bizarre"(co-written with Prince) was planned for inclusion on her second LP, *Romance 1600*.

Part of the inspiration for that project came from her response to the movie *Amadeus*. "I saw the clothes in the movie and went crazy. They set off a whole bunch of fantasies about old places and times—the kinds of fantasies I put into songs like 'Romance 1600' and 'Dear Michelangelo.' Those fantasies led to the look we shot for the cover. And it led to the title of the album about a romantic fantasy from a time hundreds of years ago. I wanted the video to look like an old French film. We even ended it with 'Fin.' I came up with names for the band as if they were the characters in a French historical fantasy—Dame Kelly, Sir Dancelot, The Earl of Grey, Sir Stephen, and Court Jester." If that seems a little like overkill, the album turned out to have a partyish flair that seemed to fit the mood of many younger fans.

The question remained as to whether Sheila had a following of her own or one essentially linked to Prince's fortunes. There was some indication that many of the people who attended concerts she headlined came in hope of also seeing Prince, their interest whetted by reports that he did, indeed, sometimes join the program, as happened during one of Sheila E.'s concerts in the L.A. area in March 1986.

In reviewing that event, Connie Johnson of the *Los Angeles Times* commented that while Sheila got her big break opening for Prince, she "inadvertently ended up in that role again . . . at the Universal Amphitheatre. . . . The show really began around 11 P.M. when Prince came on stage for an unannounced appearance with his new, expanded Revolution band. He took command of Sheila's recent hit, 'Love Bizarre,' exciting the crowd with a series of electrifying dance steps and a warm manner. . . . By the midpoint in the nearly 30-minute encore, Sheila E.'s band had been relegated to the wings."

At least such happenings didn't cause any second-album jinx for her. *Romance 1600,* issued in the fall of 1985, stayed on the *Billboard* charts well into 1986. Also on the charts much of that time was the single release, "Love Bizarre." In her case, perhaps the second album jinx had just been delayed a bit because her third LP, the early 1987 release *Sheila E.* (which sounded like a clone of her earlier LPs) met with buyer resistance.

It was Prince to the rescue. He asked her to join his new band as drummer for 1987 concerts, including shows in Amsterdam that were taped for a new concert film. Her drum work proved among the highlights of the movie *Sign O' the Times* when it was released in November 1987.

She stressed to Dennis Hunt of the *Los Angeles Times* (November 15, 1987) that it was her band debut. "I've never been in his band before. I've done some songs with him in some of his shows, but only as a guest."

She said her solo career hadn't ended. "I'm not giving up on my solo career. It's just on hold while I'm in this band. I'm working on new songs for my next album."

EAGLES, THE: *Vocal and instrumental group. Original personnel, 1971: Don Henley, born Gilmer, Texas, July 22, 1947; Glenn Frey, born Detroit, Michigan, November 6, 1948; Randy Meisner, born Scottsbluff, Nebraska, March 8, 1946; Bernie Leadon, born Minneapolis, Minnesota, July 19, 1947. Don Felder added early 1974, born Florida, 1948. Leadon replaced in 1976 by Joe Walsh, born Wichita, Kansas, November 20, 1947. Meisner replaced in 1979 by Timothy B. Schmit, born Sacramento, California. Group disbanded in 1982.*

From the mid-1970s to the start of the 1980s, the Eagles held sway as one of the great rock bands of the decade. But while rock was the group's forte, it blended elements of folk and country into many of its songs. While serving in some ways as heir to the mantle of such landmark country-rock bands as Poco and the Flying Burrito Brothers, the Eagles achieved a rapport with the mass audience far beyond those groups' and turned out consistently high-quality recordings throughout the '70s.

In fact, as Glenn Frey, who teamed with Don Henley as the primary writers for the band, pointed out, they learned from the problems of pioneer country-rock groups. He told Cameron Crowe of *Rolling Stone:* "We had it all planned. We'd watched bands like Poco and the Burrito Brothers lose their initial momentum. We were determined not to make the same mistakes. This was gonna be our best shot. Everybody had to look good, sing good, play good, and write good. We wanted it all. Peer respect. AM and FM success. Number one singles and albums, great music, and a lot of money.''

The Eagles evolved from the folk and country-rock movement that sprang up in Southern California in the late '60s and early '70s. None of the four founding members were native Californians, but all eventually settled in Los Angeles because of the musical environment. The closest to a native was Bernie Leadon, who was born in Minnesota, but moved to San Diego with his family at 10 and lived there until his father got a job in Gainesville, Florida, when Bernie was 17. An interest in folk music caused him to learn guitar and banjo before he reached his teens. Among the groups he played with in high school was the Scottsville Squirrel Barkers, headed by Chris Hillman, later of the Byrds, Burritos, and Desert Rose Band. Leadon played with local groups in Florida in the mid-1960s before heading back to Los Angeles in 1967, where he worked with a series of groups in the late '60s, beginning with one called Hearts & Flowers and followed by a stint with the bluegrass-rock pioneers the Dillards and then the Burritos.

Meisner's career began in his teens with local groups in the Midwest. Later, in Los Angeles, he was a founding member of Poco with Richie Furay and Jim Messina. Besides performing with Poco and Rick Nelson's Stone Canyon Band, he did session work from time to time, which brought him in contact with people such as Leadon and Linda Ronstadt. Though he played a lot of country-oriented material, he had less of an interest in it than other original Eagles. He told Crowe: ''No, I don't go along with everything they do. For example, I'm probably the only one who loves funky rock and roll, trashy music, and R&B. And I don't agree with some of our images either. But Don and Glenn have it covered. I guess I'm just very shy and nervous about putting myself on the line. They're used to doing that.''

Glenn Frey grew up in the more frenetic pace of urban Detroit. After dropping out of college, he moved to Los Angeles. Hanging out at the Troubadour club, he became acquainted with another habitue, Don Henley. Henley liked to play drums, but wasn't sure of his career direction while attending college in Linden, Texas. He finally heeded the advice of an English teacher that music suited him best and he headed for the big time of Los Angeles.

He had formed a band in high school called Shiloh and he took that nucleus along with him to California. The band made some inroads in the L.A. music club scene, but nothing dramatic. He had more hours to kill in the Troubadour than he cared to remember. Frey meanwhile was trying to use some of his songs as a wedge for a solo career and got the chance to play some for David Geffen, then manager of Joni Mitchell and Crosby, Stills, Nash, & Young and later president of Asylum Records. Geffen discouraged the solo approach and told Frey to join a band. Heeding this, Frey accepted a job with Linda Ronstadt. The band needed a drummer, which caused Frey to look up Henley. The two proved highly compatible. ''The first night of the Ronstadt tour,'' Frey recalled, ''we agreed to start our own band.''

The band, in effect, took shape around them. Ronstadt's manager, John Boylan, brought in Randy Meisner on bass guitar when Randy left Rick Nelson's group and also recruited Bernie Leadon on lead guitar. Much as the Band had gone on from being Bob Dylan's support group, the Eagles took shape and then left Ronstadt. As the Band has done with Dylan, the Eagles have appeared on joint concert bills with Linda over the years.

Henley points out that they didn't walk out on Ronstadt, but told manager Boylan of their goals. Both Boylan and Linda, while hating to lose them, he stressed, were sincere about not wanting to stand in their way.

Helped by a strong recommendation from Jackson Browne, the group got Geffen as their first manager. Geffen provided expense money so they could move to Aspen, Colorado, to rehearse, write songs, and polish their act in local clubs. Meanwhile, Geffen got Frey a release from Amos Records and lined up a recording contract with Asylum. In early 1972, he arranged for them to go to England to work on their debut LP under the direction of veteran producer Glyn Johns, who had supervised LPs by the Who, Rolling Stones, and Led Zeppelin. The first fruit of that was the hit single ''Take It Easy,'' written by Browne and Frey and issued in early summer. In July 1972, the first album, *The Eagles,* came out. Critical response was mostly positive, although some reviewers from eastern U.S. centers tended to shrug it off as lacking in social commentary. And even though only a cursory listen showed the group could play a diverse array of musical styles, some critics bracketed it as another typical country-rock band. But concert audiences were the final judge. It also was the source of two more charted singles: ''Peaceful Easy Feeling'' and Henley and Leadon's composition ''Witchy Woman.''

In 1973, the band went back into London's Olympia Studios to work on album two. It was an ambitious project, a concept album with all the songs tied into the theme of the rise and fall of the Doolin-Dalton gag of Wild West fame. Called *Desperado,* it came out in the spring of 1973 and was only moderately successful. The lukewarm reception to the LP stirred unease among some admirers, fearing the Eagles might go the way of Poco and the Burritos.

Adding to that were reports of internal dissension and, later, of arguments with Johns about the next LP.

In fact, after working with Johns on two songs, "You Never Cry Like a Lover" and "Best of My Love" in London, the Eagles decided to finish the album in L.A., returning in early 1974 to line up a new producer. Almost at the same time, the band switched from Geffen to Irving Azoff for management. But all ended well. With Bill Szymczyk moving in as producer, the resumed album work went smoothly. In the process, the band found a fifth member, Florida-born session guitarist Don Felder, one of the best slide guitarists in pop music. Said Frey: "He just blew us all away. It was just about the best guitar work we'd ever heard." When the album, *On the Border*, was released by Asylum on March 22, 1974, it was announced that Felder had become the Eagles fifth member. The album easily went past gold-record levels. Turnaway crowds thronged Eagles concerts and the "Best of My Love," became the band's first number one *Billboard* single the week of March 1, 1975, followed by "One of These Nights" on August 2, 1975.

Rumors persisted about internal problems as the months went by and no follow-up LP appeared. However, there was some exaggeration, Azoff told the author at the time. "There was a lot of give and take on the fourth album just as there is on the next one and the one before that. But I wouldn't call it fighting. It's sort of like the president can veto a bill. It's a matter of rounding out, of finishing off the rough edges. Obviously, success has mellowed them some. They feel an obligation to the music field to maintain quality. Even more than before, they all want to take their time. To us melodies, lyrics, and vocals all are really—and equally—important. And that's why we say the Eagles are the Beach Boys of the '70s."

The new album bore him out. *One of These Nights* is arguably one of the finest pop collections of the decade. Released June 10, 1975, it went well past platinum levels not long afterward. The initial single, "Lyin' Eyes" by Henley and Frey, was a top ten success hit and the LP produced such other singles successes as "Hollywood Waltz" (by Henley, Frey, and Bernie and Tom Leadon) and Meisner, Henley, and Frey's "Take It to the Limit."

By the end of 1975, though, Leadon indicated he had become tired of the touring grind and the pressures of band life and wanted out. His place was taken in early 1976 by Joe Walsh. Also managed by Azoff, Walsh was an excellent guitarist, singer, and songwriter, who had been a member of the James Gang and later a successful solo artist. His 1973 solo

LP, *The Smoker You Drink, the Player You Get* on Dunhill, had gone gold.

Perhaps feeling a bit nervous about the shift, Asylum released the retrospective LP *The Eagles: Their Greatest Hits* on February 17, 1976. However, once Walsh took hold, the Eagles soared even higher. It took a while for that to become apparent, but his contributions helped make the next release as good or better than *One of These Nights*. The new LP, *Hotel California* (1977) combined unique insights with first-rate musicianship on every track. Among the singles hits culled from it were gems such as the title song and "New Kid in Town," both number one in *Billboard* in '77. The LP was number one for eight weeks on the pop charts.

But another personnel shift was on the agenda. Randy Meisner departed during 1979 to seek a solo career. His place was taken by bass guitarist Timothy B. Schmit. He played with local bands in high school and while working on a degree in psychology at Sacramento State College. He opted for music, however, and became a long-time member of Poco prior to his Eagles affiliation.

The new lineup completed the next album in the fall of '79. Issued by Elektra/Asylum in October, *The Long Run* had many tracks up to previous Eagles standards, but several that fell short. But the public was happy to have new Eagles songs. The LP went platinum and provided three top 10 singles, "Heartache Tonight" in 1979, the title song, and "I Can't Tell You Why." The group had another platinum album in 1980: *Eagles Live*. "Heartache Tonight" was number one in *Billboard* the week of November 10, 1979.

But the two prime writing forces, Frey and Henley, were eager for new challenges. In the early 1980s, they began work on solo albums. With their decisions to concentrate on those efforts, the group was disbanded in 1982 with the formal announcement made by manager Azoff in May. Soon after that, Don Felder also embarked on a solo career with his debut album, *Airborne* (1983, Asylum). He admitted he would have preferred to stay with the Eagles, but with Frey and Henley both doing well on their own in the late 1980s, the chance of an eventual reunion seemed remote. (*See Browne, Jackson; Byrds, The; Frey, Glenn; Henley, Don; Loggins and Messina; Nelson, Rick; Poco; Ronstadt, Linda.*)

EARTH, WIND & FIRE: *Vocal and instrumental group. Personnel, mid-1970s: Maurice White, born Memphis, Tennessee, December 19, 1941; Verdine White, born Illinois, July 25, 1951; Philip Bailey, born Denver, Colorado, May 8, 1951; Larry Dunn, born Colorado, June 19, 1953; Albert McKay, born Louisiana, Febru-*

ary 2, 1948; Ralph Johnson, born California, July 4, 1951; Johnny Graham, born Kentucky, August 3, 1951; Andrew Woolfolk, born Texas, October 11, 1950; Fred White, born Illinois, January 13, 1955; Michael Harris, born Illinois, August 4, 1953; Louis Satterfield, born Mississippi, April 3, 1957; Donald Myrick, born Illinois, April 6, 1940. Reorganized group members, 1987-88: Bailey, Maurice White, Verdine White, Woolfolk, Sheldon Reynolds.

Earth, Wind & Fire certainly ranks as one of the most dynamic and original bands of the 1970s. In sheer size closer to a big band than a rock group, EW&F blended elements of almost every modern style from rock and soul to jazz and even, at times, country.

The band's origins lie in the Chicago ghetto, where founding member Maurice White moved with his family after spending his early years around Memphis. White, who sang with gospel groups as a child and was a drummer with a series of bands in Chicago in his teens, went on to attend Chicago Conservatory of Music. Later he was a member of the Ramsey Lewis Trio. In 1969, he formed his first version of EW&F, aided by his brother Verdine (whose fortes include vocals, bass, and percussion). This band had a limited amount of success in the early 1970s, turning out a single on Capitol and two albums for Warner Brothers Records.

Following the second album effort, Maurice and Verdine decided to completely revamp the group. The new incarnation was signed by Columbia Records in 1972. Its debut LP for the label, *Last Days and Time*, appeared briefly on the charts. Then came *Head to the Sky*, a disc that established EW&F as one of the truly heavy groups of the decade. Aided by well-received concert dates, the album was certified gold on November 11, 1973. EW&F followed with still another excellent album, *Open Our Eyes,* which went gold on May 14, 1974.

The band makeup never remained static. Coming into 1975, apart from the White brothers, only Philip Bailey (vocals, congas, percussion, and songwriting) remained from the 1972 band (*See Bailey, Philip.*) Maurice White handled vocals, kalimba, drums, songwriting, and production. Other members of the group as of 1976 were Larry Dunn, keyboards; Al McKay, guitars and percussion; Ralph Johnson, drums and percussion; Johnny Graham, guitars; Andrew Woolfolk, flute and tenor and soprano saxophone; Fred White, drums and percussion; Don Myrick, saxophones; Louis Satterfield, trombone; and Michael Harris, trumpet.

1975 proved a high point in EW&F's history, with release of the soundtrack LP *That's the Way of the World* from a film featuring EW&F as a rock'n'soul band. Maurice White, who had the main writing chores for that, stated, "It is a musical score in which each song is an event, relative to an experience we have lived." The LP won a platinum record and its single "Shining Star," a gold award. Late in the year, the platinum album *Gratitude* was released. In the Grammy Awards voting for 1975, the band won the trophy for Best R&B Vocal Performance by a Group for "Shining Star." That was the first of 16 Grammy nominations EW&F received between 1975 and 1983. During that period, besides the "Shining Star" award, the band earned first place votes for six of those nominations, including three in 1978: Best R&B Vocal Performance by a Group (*All'n'All* LP); Best R&B Instrumental Performance ("Runnin'"); and Best Arrangement for Accompanying Vocals (Maurice White—"Got to Get You Into My Life.")

The group followed in 1976 with the double-platinum album *Spirit,* from which the gold single "Getaway" was culled. In 1977, an equally impressive collection was released on Columbia, *All'n'All,* on which Verdine White and Larry Dunn served as assistant producers. The album, also a multiplatinum success, provided two top 10 singles: "Serpentine Fire" and "Fantasy."

The band backed *All'n'All* with one of the most visually striking shows of the decade. As Irwin Stambler reported in his syndicated column, "Pop, Rock & Soul": "Rockets shoot off with a shower of orange-yellow sparks and dense smoke. Two figures in ancient Egyptian garb stand poised with huge mallets before large dull-gold gongs. Nine tall gleaming cylinders materialize from above and slowly descend. As they near the floor, lights go on inside revealing nine stoic figures in flowing scarlet robes. The cylinders touch down, the gongs sound, and the nine doors open, and the figures move forward sedately—and suddenly erupt into a dervish-like dance.

"It's not a sequel to *Star Wars* or *Close Encounters of the Third Kind,* but the opening of another Earth, Wind & Fire concert. There is a not accidental resemblance to space adventures and fantasy, though, a theme carried through on the *[All'n'All]* album cover and reaffirmed at concert's end when the main band members retire into a shining pyramid which moves slowly skyward, then abruptly splits open into a series of slowly revolving triangular reflectors. And as the audience gasped to see emptiness within, a line of space-clad figures on the stage below removed mushroom shaped headgear to reveal leader Maurice White and his co-musicians alive and well.''

The question was, how could *EW&F* top that? The answer was, it never did. Not that the band and its creative associates couldn't brainstorm wilder concepts but it would have required coping with the soaring budgets needed to turn flights of fancy into reality. And besides, going for broke in special effects didn't seem necessary when the band's dance routines and musical expertise could stand on their own. So in the late '70s and early '80s, it was back to using more conventional gimmicks such as smoke bombs and laser beams, but still with some nuances, such as a finale featuring a mock war between good (in the form of a white-clad Maurice White) and evil as posed by a Darth Vader clone.

Subsequent releases on the hit charts included *The Best of Earth, Wind & Fire, Volume 1* (November 1978), *I Am* (May 1979), with two hit singles ("Boogie Wonderland," featuring a duet with the Emotions, and "After the Love Has Gone"); *Faces* (summer 1980); and *Raise!* (1981). The single "After the Love Is Gone" earned EW&F a Grammy Award for Best R&B Vocal Performance by a Group. For the 1981–82 tour in support of *I Am*, Al McKay's guitar slot was filled by Roland Bautista, who had been a band member in the early 1970s.

The band continued to work on new material in the early 1980s, although key members were becoming involved in side projects. Maurice White, for instance, set up his own American Recording Company in mid-1979 to handle production not only of EW&F numbers, but also work by such protégés as the Emotions and Deniece Williams, as well as the jazz group Weather Report. Among the early results of that operation were hit singles for the Emotions ("I Don't Want to Lose Your Love") and Deniece ("Free"). Earth, Wind & Fire projects at ARC included the early 1983 LP *Powerlight* (distributed by Columbia).

Powerlight earned a gold record award, but the next release, later in 1983, *Electric Universe,* fared poorly. After 11 straight albums had gone gold or platinum, *Electric Universe* was the first one not even able to reach gold record levels. It triggered a four year hiatus during which key members focused on individual projects. Maurice White attributed the situation to creative burnout and, as he told Paul Grein of the *Los Angeles Times* (December 6, 1987), "I needed to just sit back and find out who I was for a while. For 10 years, it was always a record or a tour. I never had any time of my own."

During the next four years, Bailey fashioned a very rewarding solo career. White, on the other hand, turned out a solo LP that made little inroad on the charts. White decided he needed a band environment to work most effectively, but when he talked about reviving EW&F with Bailey it was agreed Phi-

lip would, in effect, be co-leader. The 1987 group that recorded the LP *Touch the World* was of much smaller size than its predecessors with only five members as the core band.

Released in November 1987, the album spawned an initial single, "System of Survival," that made number one position on *Billboard*'s dance-club chart for three weeks and number one on the black singles charts. During that time, though, it only reached 63 on the pop lists. Bailey angrily told Grein the situation partly was due to unfair racial restrictions. "If you're black, you're labeled R&B. But if you're white and play R&B, you're pop. It's not what your music says at all.

"Before, [black and white] people's backgrounds were totally different. But now kids grow up listening to all kinds of stuff. The musicians coming up now have many different kinds of expression, but they're still labeled and marketed based on the color of their skin."

EASTON, SHEENA: *Singer. Born Bellshill, near Glasgow, Scotland, April 27, 1959.*

The diminutive Scottish singer Sheena Easton, with a strong, if not unique, voice for her petite 5-foot frame, surely did not lack confidence. Barely 20 years old, she displayed iron nerve and considerable resilience in making her first push for stardom in the full glare of ever-present TV cameras in an unusual year-long British Broadcasting Company (BBC) documentary program.

Sheena was one of six children born to a Scottish working class family. The family situation became far from comfortable after her father's death when she was 10. She enjoyed singing and, when she reached her teens, possessed what she felt was an above-average voice. Though not unaware of the punk/new wave movement that dominated English rock in the mid-1970s, she identified with more traditional pop vocalists. In particular, she credited listening to Barbra Streisand with inspiring a desire to make a career as a vocalist.

To get better training and also to earn a teaching credential that could serve as a backup in case her entertainment goals faltered, she attended the Royal Scottish Academy of Music and Drama. While there, she continued singing with local rock and pop groups, a sideline she had started when she was 17. Since she was determined to finish her school program, she was fortunate to have a job with the house band at a local hotel.

By the time Sheena graduated in June 1979, she already was making plans to further her performing career. To do that, she knew she had to move her base of operations from Scotland to a U.K. industry hub such as London. The open sesame proved to be an unusual alignment with the BBC. That government-supported TV operation had the idea of doing an entire year's program on a newcomer's efforts to shed anonymity and take initial steps toward music stardom.

Her acceptance for the show, which was to be called "The Big Time," hinged on her first getting a recording contract with a major label. BBC officials set up an audition for her with U.K. powerhouse EMI Records (owner of Capitol Records and EMI America in the U.S.), but with no guarantee that she would gain acceptance. The audition, filmed live as she demonstrated her singing ability to EMI Artists & Repertoire chief Brian Shepherd, could well have been her first and last session before TV cameras. BBC threatened to look for a replacement if she flunked. Shepherd later told reporters he had a "show-me" attitude before she sang and, in fact, expected to say no. But Sheena's poise and strong performance, he claimed, won him over and he agreed to sign her.

Filming of Sheena's novice year was scheduled to begin in the early 1980s, but she recorded some songs before then. EMI released her first single, "Modern Girl," in early 1980, but the song only rose to number 56 in the U.K. Her second release, originally called "Nine to Five," came out in the summer of 1980, this time coinciding with the debut program of "The Big Time." TV exposure proved to make the difference. The new single entered U.K. charts soon after the show was first screened, rising as high as number three. Its success ignited new interest among fans in "Modern Girl." At one point, both singles were in the U.K. top 10 at the same time, a feat that hadn't been achieved since Ruby Murray did it in 1956.

Sheena had beaten the odds and ridden the BBC-TV bandwagon to national fame. In the second half of 1980, her credits expanded to include an invitation to perform in front of England's Queen Mother in the Royal Variety Show and selection to sing the title song for the new James Bond film, *For Your Eyes Only*.

EMI now began to make plans to showcase their promising new artist before U.S. audiences. In February 1981, the company's American affiliate released the single of "Nine to Five," retitled "Morning Train (Nine to Five)" to avoid confusion with Dolly Parton's song "9 to 5." The company also issued her debut album, *Sheena Easton*, in the U.S.

Backed by Easton's appearance on TV talk and concert shows, the single showed up on U.S. hit lists in late winter and rose steadily upward. The week of May 1, 1981, it reached a higher pinnacle than it had achieved in the U.K., moving into the number one

position on the *Billboard* charts. It and the album both went gold. Before the year was out, Sheena had two more U.S. top 10 singles: "For Your Eyes Only" and "Modern Girl." In *Billboard*'s year-end review, she ranked as the seventh best-selling singles artist in the U.S. In the Grammy Award competition, she walked off with the trophy for Best New Artist of 1981.

Sheena's second album, *You Could Have Been with Me* (1881) was issued in the U.S. in late 1981 and was inside the top 100 at year-end. It remained on the charts into 1982, earning gold-record certification from the RIAA. During 1982, she had three singles on the U.S. hit lists, including the title song from her second album.

Her career took a temporary dip from late 1982 through early 1983 when her singles and albums fell well short of best-seller status. Her third LP, *Madness, Money and Music* (fall 1982) made only lower chart positions. However, Sheena quickly turned things around in 1983–84. Her singles included a top 10 hit of her own composition, "Telefone (Long Distance Love Affair)," a best-selling country duet with Kenny Rogers ("We've Got Tonight"), and the top 10 "Strut." Her fourth album, *Best Kept Secret* (fall 1983), was on the charts well into 1984. Her next album, *A Private Heaven* (fall 1984), earned gold-record certification by year-end.

During 1984, she also ventured into Spanish vocals, recording hit duets with Mexican singer Luis Miguel. One single, "Me Gustas Tal Como Eres," brought her a second Grammy for Best Mexican/American Performance. Besides successes in such unexpected categories as country and Latino music, she also was able to win over black music fans in the mid-1980s with the single "Sugar Walls." Co-produced by superstar Prince, "Sugar Walls" rose to number three on the black singles lists. (*See Prince.*) At the end of 1985, Sheena had the album *Do You* on the charts and the single "Do It for Love."

During 1987, Sheena joined several other pop/rock performers in making anti-drug videos presented on the MTV channel as part of the Rock Against Drugs campaign. She told a press conference, "I've never done drugs. The main asset I have is myself. Why would I want to blow it?"

Her 1987 credits included a guest appearance on the "Miami Vice" TV program and a duet with Prince, "You Got the Look," that earned a Grammy nomination. She also began work on an album for her new label, MCA, scheduled for release during 1988.

ECHO AND THE BUNNYMEN: *Vocal and instrumental group. Members as of late 1980s: Ian McCulloch, born Liverpool, England, May 5,*

1959; Will Sergeant, born Liverpool, April 12, 1958; Les Pattinson, born Ormskirt, England, April 18, 1958; Pete de Freitas, born Port of Spain, Trinidad, August 2, 1961.

The ferment in English pop music in the late 1970s and early 1980s, spawned in part by the economic hardships and bleak employment outlook facing young Britons, cast up a variety of rock offshoots that looked both ahead and, in some cases, back. Among the latter were the "new" school of heavy metal and a style called by some the "New Psychedelia" whose prime exponents included the Teardrop Explodes and Echo and the Bunnymen. Such groups tried with varying degrees of success to shape an avant garde form of rock that fused elements of '60s bands such as the Doors and Love with the jarring strains of punk.

The founding members of Echo and the Bunnymen all came from working class families sharply affected by the post–World War II slowdown in the British economy. Like many in their peer group, Ian McCulloch, Will Sergeant, and Les Pattinson reached their teens convinced that rock music could express the growing unhappiness and frustration of their generation while also offering them a way to move up in their own world. All were involved with embryonic punk/new wave bands in the mid-1970s with McCulloch for a time performing with a group formed by Liverpool songwriter/vocalist Julian Cope that evolved into the Teardrop Explodes. In 1978, McCulloch left to assemble a band of his own. It began as a three-member group with McCulloch handling vocals, guitar, and much of the songwriting plus Will Sergeant on lead guitar and Les Pattinson on bass guitar. For drums, they decided to employ a drum machine they dubbed Echo. The new band debuted at Eric's in Liverpool on November 15, 1978. It began attracting young fans to teen hangouts over the next few months, though its use of a drum machine was relatively restrictive. The band recorded two of its originals, "Pictures on My Wall" and "Read It in Books," which appeared on a single issued by the independent label, Zoo Records, in March 1979. One other track, "Monkeys," also was included in an album of underground Liverpool bands of the period, *Street to Street*. Those three numbers were the only ones issued by the three-piece group.

In October 1979, Echo was sent to the attic and a live drummer, Pete de Freitas, was added to form the quartet that was still intact as of 1988. The new alignment added power and broader dimensions to the band's sound, which helped it gain attention outside the Liverpool area as the 1980s began. Meanwhile, the group signed with Korova Records in November 1979. The group's first single on the label, "Rescue"/"Simple Stuff," was issued in April 1980 as a forerunner of its album debut, *Crocodiles*, which came out the following July.

Crocodiles established the group as one of the most promising newcomers on the rock scene in the early '80s and helped set the tone for U.K. rock of the decade. As reviewer Dave McCullough of England's *Sounds* magazine enthused, it demonstrated a major leap forward in sound and format for the group compared to its work of a year earlier.

"The sound is clear-cut crystal, big and echoey and packed with all sorts of unseen ghosts and demons. It perfectly tails off the Bunnymen's transition from limpalong drum-machine tots to colossal youth people, with a big fast music to match. . . . The [lead singer's] voice is poised but pained. The guitars are huge shafts of menacing light and shade. The drums provide a trampoline base and the synths are embellishing angst-filled extras that ebb and flow with mesmerizing syncopation."

The album made the top 20 on U.K. charts as the band backed it with its first U.K. club/college tour during July and August. They further enhanced their image on a fall swing featuring a specially designed "Apocalyptic" stage set. During those concerts, the band featured songs such as "The Puppet" and "Do It Clean," which came out as its second Korova single in October 1980.

In January 1981, the band performed at a "mystery" engagement at the Buxton Pavilion where attendees either followed special maps or took chartered buses to the location. Filmmaker Bill Butt recorded the event for release as a short. It was then agreed that the time seemed right for U.S. exposure and the band played its first dates in the country during March.

The next record was the live extended-play *Shine So Hard*, based on tapes made during the Buxton Pavilion show. The EP made the English top 40 a few weeks after its release in May 1981. The band's second LP, *Heaven up Here*, came out the following month and quickly moved into the U.K. top 10. Issued in the U.S. on Sire Records, the album was sought out by a respectable, if not overpowering number of fans. As 1981 went by, the band continued to add important credits, including the release of a single in July: "A Promise" from *Heaven up Here* (backed with "Broke My Neck"), which had been recorded some weeks before in Norway during a European tour. In August, the Buxton film, *Shine So Hard*, debuted in London along with another short film shot in Europe, *La Vie Lounge*.

During 1982, some of the Bunnymen took time out for other projects. Pete de Freitas, for instance, produced a single for the Wild Swans called "Revolutionary Spirit" and Will Sergeant recorded the soundtrack for the film *Grind* that remained unreleased through the mid-1980s. In the summer, the band became more active as its June single, "Back of Love," rose as high as number 12 on British charts. In July, the band headlined the second night of England's WOMAD Festival, the first of a series of festivals the band was featured in during mid-1982. The group closed out the year with a live performance in Liverpools' Sefton Park before an audience of over 20,000 as part of the BBC's Pop Carnival series and then began filming performances of six tracks of the planned third album in Liverpool and Iceland in December.

The first track from the new LP to be issued as a single was "The Cutter," a U.K. top 10 hit in early 1983. A 12-inch version of the song was backed with a live recording from the WOMAD Festival of the group's composition "All My Colours," played by the Bunnymen and an exciting African group, the Drummers of Burindi. The new LP, *Porcupine,* was issued in the U.K. in February and in the U.S. and Canada in March 1983. The album did better in England than in America, but tallies of its performance in the U.S. indicated McCulloch and associates were gaining respect. A few months later, another single from *Porcupine,* "Never Stop," provided a top 10 U.K. hit. During the group's summer tour of England, which included capacity performances at London's Royal Albert Hall, material for an hour-long documentary was shot during the concerts and in the group's home area in Liverpool for early 1984 exposure on English TV. In advance of the group's planned major North American tour in 1984, Sire Records released a mini-LP, *Echo and the Bunnymen* in the U.S. in October 1983. The album comprised five tracks of some of the band's best material: "Back of Love," "The Cutter," "Never Stop," "Rescue," and (recorded live at the Royal Albert Hall) "Do It Clean."

Its next album, *Ocean Rain,* was issued in May 1984. First single release from the LP was "The Killing Moon." The band's new recordings indicated much more polish and professionalism than the early releases, yet there also was a growing feeling that some of the sharp edge of its seminal work had worn off. Perhaps feeling the strain of maintaining its forward momentum, the band decided to take most of 1985 off. It was represented on the record rack by a retrospective collection of songs from the first four LPs *Songs to Sing and Learn,* and a new single, "Bring on the Dancing Horses." The latter, which was included in the repertoire for the group's spring 1986 tour of the U.S., perhaps symbolized the group's change in image.

Reviewing an April appearance at the Irvine Meadows Amphitheatre in Orange County, *Los An-geles Times* representative Craig Lee complained that "the Bunnymen may be making better-produced records and interesting videos, but the effusive prettiness of latter-day Bunny tunes like 'Bring on the Dancing Horses' sounded hollow and wan . . . while the video screen above the stage projected more colorful imagery than the [bandsmen] below it. Whatever happened to that tough, anxious Liverpool band that tried to capture the mysticism and intensity of peak-era Doors?"

Whether the group had lost its way remained a question. Audience reactions around the U.S. were as enthusiastic as the band could want. And, of course, critical favor often tends to diminish in direct ratio to a group's increasing popular success. The band's new sound was certainly less strident than its early years, which might simply reflect normal maturity and a band's need to reflect the changes of its own following.

In September 1986, the group began work on a new album with the first of a series of recording sessions that stretched over six months. In December some of the studio efforts were devoted to a remake of the Doors' "People Are Strange," produced by original Doors member Ray Manzarek, who also played on the recording. The number was the keynote song of Joel Shumacker's film, *Lost Boys,* released in 1987.

The new LP, *Echo and the Bunnymen,* was issued by Sire Records in July 1987 and was supported by an extensive tour during 1987–88 in company with the groups New Order and Gene Loves Jezebel. The band's first new album to come out in three years, it presented a winning combination of the band's early Doors-like moodiness with its less strident arrangements of 1983–84. The result was wider audience popularity and the band's best-selling album, a chart hit during 1987 and '88.

EDDY, DUANE: *Guitarist, songwriter, band leader. Born Corning, New York, April 26, 1938.*

Duane Eddy's success story might be said to hang on a single string—the lone bass string on a conventional six-string guitar. The unusual "twang" sound Eddy gained from using this for melody won him international acclaim, despite the fact that he had no singing voice and was too shy to ever give evidence of an imposing stage presence. (Although he overcame this shyness to some extent for some dramatic roles, he tended to just sit and keep his eyes focused on his guitar for in-person performances.)

Eddy was born in upstate New York, but spent most of his youth in Phoenix, Arizona, where he found an early affinity for the country & western music on that city's radio stations. His father played guitar and tried to interest his son in the instrument when the boy was five. Duane did nothing with it at the time and did little in the way of performing during elementary and high school. At 17, in 1954, he was given a recording by the great country music guitarist, Chet Atkins. He played the record over and over, and then decided to learn the instrument.

As his family was poor, Duane had no money for lessons or for buying more records. Instead, he started working, selling drinks and hot dogs in dance halls, and studying guitar styles in his spare moments. He devised his own method of playing in which he used the bass string for the melody instead of the other five strings, as is normally the case. In 1958, he felt confident enough of his ability to go into a Phoenix studio and cut two original compositions: "Rebel Rouser" and "Movin' and Groovin'." He gained a contract from Jamie Records, which issued his first single that year. "Rebel Rouser" became a top 10 hit. Subsequent hits with his backup group, the Rebels, included "Ramrod" and "Cannonball' (1958) and "Yep" and "Forty Miles of Bad Road" (1959).

"Because They're Young" one of the major hits of 1960, was the title song for the Dick Clark Columbia film in which Duane made his movie acting debut. In 1961, he had a hit with his single of the theme song from the TV series "Peter Gunn."

Eddy gained hits with gospel and country flavor as well as rock, reflecting his roots in those music forms. Among his successes were updated versions of such country songs as "A Satisfied Mind," the gospel "Peace in the Valley," and the Carter Family's classic "Wildwood Flower."

During the early '60s, Eddy's efforts included several film scores, including *Ring of Fire*, and TV acting spots, such as his small role in "Have Gun—Will Travel."

His album sales totaled many millions by the mid-1960s. His initial releases were on Jamie, which continued to issue previously recorded material long after Eddy signed with RCA in the early '60s. Among the Jamie LPs were *Especially for You, Have Twangy Guitar, Will Travel, The Twang's the 'Thang, $1,000,000.00 Worth of Twang* (1961), *Songs of Our Heritage* (1964), *Surfin' with Duwane Eddy, Girls! Girls! Girls, In Person,* and *$1,000,000.00 Worth of Twang, Volume 2* (1964). Among Eddy's RCA LPs were *Twangy Guitar—Silky Strings* (1962), *Dance with the Guitar Man* (1963), *Lonely Guitar* (1964), *Twangsville* (1965) and *Best of Duane Eddy* (1966). In 1966–67, several Eddy albums came out on Reprise, including *Biggest Twang of Them All* and *Roaring Twangies*.

For much of the late 1960s, Eddy remained in the background in U.S. popular music. He continued to perform on occasion, both in the U.S. and overseas, but no longer was represented on the hit list. The end of the decade and in the early '70s, he was featured in a number of rock'n'roll revival shows.

From the mid-1970s into the early 1980s, Eddy cut back on live appearances in the U.S., though (like numerous other early rockers) he remained a favorite overseas. He told a reporter: "I used to go over to England and work every couple of years and that satisfied me. I didn't have a big formal education so I educated myself through reading during those years." He did record some new material, including the single "Play Me Like You Play Your Guitar" which was a hit in Europe and Far East, but got little attention in the U.S. Albums in U.S. record stores during the 1970s included *Duane Eddy's 16 Greatest Hits* (Jamie, 1965), *The Vintage Years* (Sire), and *Pure Gold* (RCA, 1978). During that period, Eddy did some acting and record-production work and in between retired to his home in Zephyr Cove, Nevada.

In 1983, he returned to the U.S. concert circuit with some above-average shows backed by Don Randi on keyboards, Hal Blaine on drums and Steve Douglas (onetime member of the Rebels) on saxophone. He continued to perform periodically in small venues into the mid-1980s. In 1986, the British group Art of Noise made top chart levels with a remake of "Peter Gunn." Eddy joined them on stage at the Palace Theater in Hollywood that July for a performance of the song that had the crowd shouting for more. The single won a Grammy Award for Best Rock Instrumental performance.

During 1986, Duane signed a recording contract with Capitol Records, which issued his label debut, *Duane Eddy,* in the summer of 1987.

EDMUNDS, DAVE: *Singer, guitarist, songwriter, record producer. Born Wales, U.K., c. 1944.*

A long-time enthusiast about the seminal roots rock of the 1950s by such artists as Bill Haley, Elvis, and Jerry Lee Lewis, Dave Edmunds became a key force in reviving interest in early rock styles at home and abroad in the '70s and '80s. But while he typically concentrated on rockabilly material, he generated versions of both old and new songs that recalled the simpler days of rock without sounding dated.

Edmunds told Rob Patterson of *Lively Arts* (August 18, 1978): "Everyone in my age group became fascinated with that stuff. Back in the '50s, you know, I was only 13, I think, when it started—the early American rock scene. But it gripped me, got a hold of me somehow and I've been fascinated with it ever since. I think it's a good thing too. It's the whole roots of pop music."

Before that, as a boy growing up in Wales, he

hadn't been that much interested in pop music, but the impact of American rock inspired him to learn guitar and seek out like-minded school friends in the late 1950s. He recalled for an interviewer from *Modern Recording & Music:* "Nothing was making any sense until I heard my first rock'n'roll record and it all fit into place then. That disc was Jerry Lee Lewis's 'Whole Lotta Shakin' Going On' and the time was the summer of 1957." Later, he was equally knocked out by Little Richard's title song from the movie *The Girl Can't Help It.* "I just couldn't believe it, that sound, I'll never forget it."

During the 1960s, Edmunds paid his dues while gradually polishing his skills as musician and songwriter with a succession of bands and session work. In the late '60s, he gained some prominence as the mainspring of the U.K. power trio Love Sculpture. The group played a strange combination of high-voltage urban blues and rock versions of music by classical composers such as Bizet and Khatchaturian. In 1968, the band had a number one single in England of Khatchaturian's "Sabre Dance." It also made the charts in the U.S.

After the band broke up at the end of the 1960s, Edmunds retired to his own Rockfield Studios in Wales and for several years focused on making solo recordings of songs originally made famous by earlier rock artists. One result was his 1970 top 10 single reworking Smiley Lewis's 1955 hit, "I Hear You Knocking." The material laid down in the early 1970s provided the basis for his first solo album, the 1972 *Rockpile* on the Mamlish label. Songs from that period as well as the Love Sculpture phase later were packaged by EMI Records in the LP *Dave Edmunds and Love Sculpture—The Classic Tracks—1968/1972/One Up.* Besides producing his own recordings, Dave became increasingly involved in doing similar work for other artists. One such project in 1974 was production at Rockfield of what was to prove the last studio LP of the Brinsley Schwarz group, *New Favourites.* In the course of helping shape that album, Dave became friends with Brinsley member Nick Lowe, a friendship that evolved into close cooperation on songwriting, production, and performing activities. (*See Lowe, Nick.*)

In the summer of 1974, Edmunds went on tour with the Brinsleys and also worked with the Brinsleys (who called themselves the Electricians for the project) on two soundtrack numbers, "Let It Be You" and "A Shot of Rhythm and Blues," for David Bowie's *Ziggy Stardust* film. (*See Bowie, David.*) Lowe backed Edmunds on several tracks of Dave's second solo LP, *Subtle as a Flying Mallet,* recorded in late 1974 and issued on RCA Records in 1975. (The LP was phased out in 1976 and then reissued in 1978 by RCA.)

During 1976, Dave got approval to record a third solo work on Led Zeppelin's Swan Song label. The album, *Get It* (1977), included updated versions of early rock classics and a number of originals by Dave including several co-written with Lowe: "Here Comes the Weekend" and "Little Darlin'." Lowe also provided originals for the album, most notably "I Knew the Bride." For a 1977 tour as opening act for Bad Company, Edmunds and Lowe organized a quartet called Rockpile after Dave's 1972 disc. Besides Dave on vocals and guitar and Lowe on vocals and bass guitar, the band comprised Terry Williams on drums and Billy Bremmer on guitar. Because Bad Company had a sizable following, Rockpile tended to be overlooked by concert audiences, but the band obviously was one of the more resourceful and talented amalgams to come along that year.

By the time Rockpile returned to the U.S. for a 1978 tour, it was beginning to attract its own fans and already had become a favorite of critics from major media. The tour should have coincided with Dave's fourth solo effort, *Tracks on Wax 4,* on Swan Song, but the album wasn't available until the tour was over. With the album gaining some chart success during the summer, Rockpile contributed to a sold-out fall itinerary of a U.S. bill on which Van Morrison headlined.

Rockpile continued to be a respected, if not superstar band at the end of the '70s into the early '80s. It wasn't intended as an all-inclusive organization though, with both Lowe and Edmunds free to work on other projects as the opportunities arose. The Rockpile association brought rewards in unexpected ways, though. When the band took part in the Kampuchea Peoples Benefit Concert at London's Hammersmith Odeon in late 1979, Edmunds made the acquaintance of ex-Beatle Paul McCartney, which blossomed into some new projects in the 1980s. During 1979, Dave's fifth solo album and third for Swan Song, *Repeat when Necessary,* showed up on U.S. charts for several months.

Dave's final album on Swan Song, *Twangin',* was released in 1981. By 1982, he had switched to CBS Records, which issued his seventh solo compilation, *D.E. 7th,* during the year. The album was modestly successful as was the 1983 *Information* in which Edmunds experimented with styles other than his beloved rockabilly. As he told an interviewer: "I've decided that I've finally got my direction and it's just to do whatever the hell I want to do. And it doesn't have to sound like anything done previously, not in my case, I don't think."

Information provided Dave with his first single release to gain the U.S. top 40 in a dozen years, "Slipping Away" written by Jeff Lynne of Electric Light Orchestra. (*See Electric Light Orchestra.*)

During 1983, he kept up a drumbeat of outside work including helping prepare the soundtrack for the movie *Party Party,* backing Sting's solo recordings, and producing discs for George Thorogood, Stray Cats, and King Kurt (a new Stiff Records group). (*See Sting; Thorogood, George.*)

Attendance at the Everly Brothers' reunion concert at Royal Albert Hall in London in November 1983 generated enthusiasm for their work that remained high when Dave got the assignment to produce the Everlys' first studio album in 11 years. When the Mercury LP came out in late summer of 1984, it proved a gem. Reviewing *EB '84* in *Rolling Stone,* Kurt Loder enthused: "Dave Edmunds, the former Rockpile leader and long-time scholar of American pop styles, was the best possible choice to produce this record . . . [he] sees nothing quaint about the Everlys' sound and no reason to update it. Instead, he has brought the brothers back alive. It is a tribute to Edmunds' reverent but unmannered production approach." The album went on to have a multimonth position on U.S. charts from the fall of 1984 into early 1985. One of the best tracks on the album was the brothers' rendition of "Wings of a Nightingale," written specially for the album by Paul McCartney at Edmunds' request. (*See Everly Brothers, The; McCartney, Paul.*)

Meanwhile Dave played an important part in McCartney's movie project that led to Paul's fall 1984 LP, *Give My Regards to Broadstreet.* In early 1983, Dave had joined Paul's backup band for the film, which also included Ringo Starr, Linda McCartney, Chris Spedding, and Jodi Linscott. The group eventually provided three songs for the soundtrack album issued by Columbia in late 1984.

Dave also worked on another solo LP for Columbia, *Riff Raff* (September 1984). Jeff Lynne, who had worked with Dave on *Information,* took part in writing and some production work on five of the new album's tracks.

Edmunds continued a hectic pace as a record producer during 1985–86. His projects included Shakin' Stevens' LP *Lipstick Powder and Paint;* the Everly Brothers' album *Born Yesterday;* and the Fabulous Thunderbirds' *Tuff Enuff.* The last named earned a gold record and also was nominated in two 1986 Grammy Award categories. Edmunds also produced the Shakin' Stevens single "Merry Christmas Everyone" that was a number one hit in the U.K. For the Joan Jett/Michael J. Fox film *Light of Day* (released in 1987), Edmunds produced a new T-Birds track, "Twist It Off" and one by his own band, "Stay With Me Tonight" (a song he co-wrote).

In early 1987, Columbia Records released the first live concert album of Edmunds' career, *I Hear You Rockin',* which Edmunds backed with an extensive tour itinerary during the rest of the year.

ELECTRIC LIGHT ORCHESTRA, THE:
Vocal and instrumental group. Personnel in mid-1970s: Jeff Lynne, born Birmingham, England, December 30, 1947; Bev Bevan, born Birmingham, England, November 25, 1944; Richard Randy, born Birmingham, England, March 26, 1948; Kelly Groucutt, born Coseley, Staffordshire, England, September 8, 1945; Mik Kaminski, born Harrogate, Yorkshire, England, September 2, 1951; Hugh McDowell, born Hampstead, London, England, July 31, 1953; Melvyn Gale, born London, England, January 15, 1952.

If the Beatles had taken Sergeant Pepper on the road, they would have needed much the same lineup as the Electric Light Orchestra. Indeed, ELO leader Jeff Lynne said that Lennon and McCartney were the only major influences on his songwriting. The group became one of the most popular bands of the middle and late 1970s with U.S. fans, but never found the same success in its native England.

The ELO are the unlikely direct descendants of the Birmingham group, the Move, who combined violent onstage antics with melodic singles written by guitarist Roy Wood. The Move were reduced to two founding members in 1970, Wood and Bev Bevan, after internal strains had led to the departure of four other musicians. It was at this point that Lynne accepted an invitation to join. He'd been asked a year earlier, but had then declined because of the relative success of his own group, the Idle Race, which enjoyed a cult following, mainly on Britain's university campuses.

Though Lynne had received praise from reviewers for his songs, notably the enigmatic "Skeleton and the Roundabout," he was very much the junior partner in the Move. By that stage, Wood had already written seven hit singles for the band and even during Lynne's residency, two further U.K. hits for the Move were written by Wood, whose overall credits included "Night of Fear," "Flowers in the Rain," "Fire Brigade," "Blackberry Way," and "Brontosaurus."

But the first of several ironies occurred in 1972. The Move had a U.K. hit single with Wood's Jerry Lee Lewis pastiche, "California Man," but in the States, the record was turned over and Lynne's song, "Do Ya," became the A side. It was the Move's biggest hit in America and remained part of ELO's stage act.

A prime reason that Lynne joined the Move was his interest in Wood's pet musical project—the Electric Light Orchestra. In the words of a press release of the time, the band "would pick up where the Beatles left off with 'I Am the Walrus.'"

Three months after "California Man" peaked on U.K. charts, the Move had another hit, but this time under the name of ELO. It was possibly the world's smallest orchestra: Lynne on vocals and guitars, Bevan on drums and vocals, and Wood on vocals and various instruments. The song, "10538 Overture," was written by Lynne and taken from the first Electric Light Orchestra album, *The Electric Light Orchestra* (United Artists), whose sleeve featured the trio in Regency costume displaying hitherto unrevealed abilities to play violin, cello, and flute. For that recording they were augmented by Bill Hunt on horns and Steve Woolam on violin. Wood played all the other instruments in what reviewers called "a rough and rowdy style."

Not long after this, the original ELO split because they felt it was too confining for Wood and Lynne to work together. This reduced ELO to the duo of Bevan and Lynne, while Wood went off and had another half-dozen British hit singles with a new group, Wizzard, though again he had difficulty in exporting his success to the U.S.

Meawhile, Lynne and Bevan set about rebuilding the group, intending not only to continue recording, but to develop a good live act. In recruiting members for the new band, they sought not only the conventional rock instrument players, but such relatively unusual capabilities (for rock) as cello and violin work.

The first single by the new ELO was a version of Chuck Berry's "Roll over Beethoven" interspersed with fragments from famous classics. It seemed dangerously like a single-shot novelty, but through a string of hit singles in Britain and America and grueling tours in the U.S., the ELO surpassed the success of the Move.

"Roll over Beethoven" was featured in an eight-minute version on the band's second album, *ELO II*, issued on the Jet Records label. (U.S. distribution was handled by United Artists.) Jeff Lynne later said he found that rather boring, although at the time, long versions of songs seemed to be what was wanted. After that single gave the band identity with fans at home and abroad, the group expanded its reputation with terse versions of Lynne's compositions. The band's U.K. hits included "Showdown," "Ma Ma Belle," and "Evil Woman," the last named a number that became an ELO trademark.

One of the problems that dogged the band during its early live shows, Bevan recalled, related to proper blending of the conventional rock instruments with strings. He noted: "No one had really tried to combine strings with rock before, at least not in rock venues, and when we attempted it, we understood

why. The early tours sounded terrible. We just couldn't get a decent sound on the violin and cellos."

The ELO team kept looking at available equipment for the answer and finally were introduced to some U.S.-made Barcus-Berry electrical pickups. When those were installed on the string instruments, they could be directly amplified in the same way as an electric guitar. The result became obvious in mid-1970s concerts where violinist Mik Kaminski and cellists Melvyn Gale and Hugh McDowell sometimes roamed around the stage playing their instruments in all sorts of odd positions without any deterioration of sound quality.

The combination of new songs by Lynne and some of the others and improved concert sound helped build a sizable audience for ELO in the U.S. and, to a considerably lesser extent, in the U.K. Lynne stated he first became aware of the scale of the band's success when he found audiences singing along to numbers from the third album, *On the Third Day*, issued on Jet in 1973 (and distributed in the U.S. by United Artists). The group really hit full stride in 1974 with the LP *Eldorado*. It included Lynne's song, "Can't Get It out of My Head," and was also the first time he had augmented the group in the studio with a full orchestra, giving his songs a fuller sound. Though the album was gold in the U.S., the album was a relative failure in Britain.

The band's fifth album, *Face the Music* (1975), consolidated its American success, going up the charts twice. Two tracks were hit singles—"Evil Woman" and "Strange Magic"—with both also charting in Britain.

The band continued to place new albums on the charts during the second half of the 1970s, including *Ole ELO* and *A New World Record* (1976), *Out of the Blue* (1977), and *Discovery* (1979). From *A New World Record*, "Telephone Line" brought the band its first RIAA gold-record-single award. The LP sold over 5 million copies worldwide. In 1980, ELO and Olivia Newton-John won a platinum record for the MCA soundtrack to the film *Xanadu*. (*See Newton-John, Olivia.*)

With Lynne doing some solo recordings at the end of the 1970s and early 1980s and legal entanglements over U.S. distribution contracts impacting ELO's activities, the band seemed to lose considerable momentum. It provided new Jet albums in the early 1980s, such as *Time* (1981, with distribution by Columbia Records) and the mid-1983 *Secret Messages*.

In the mid-1980s, ELO took a back seat to Jeff Lynne's increasing production and non-ELO songwriting activities. His production work included album projects with Paul McCartney, Dave Edmunds,

213

and Tom Petty. During 1987 and the early part of 1988, besides assisting on a number of new tracks for Petty's next album, he also assisted Randy Newman on recordings for Randy's long-awaited new LP. Previously, Newman had voiced enthusiasm for ELO in the song "The Story of a Rock 'n' Roll Band," whose lyrics included the line "I Love that ELO."

EMERSON, LAKE AND PALMER; EMERSON, LAKE AND POWELL: *Vocal and instrumental group, all born England. Original band: Greg Lake, born Bournemouth, November 10, 1948; Keith Emerson, born Todmorden, Lancashire, November 1; Carl Palmer, born March 20, 1951. ELP disbanded in 1980. Reformed in 1984 with Cozy Powell replacing Palmer. In 1987, roster changed to Emerson; Palmer; and Robert Berry, born San Jose, California.*

From its birth at the start of the 1970s, Emerson, Lake and Palmer was generally considered a supergroup whose status was reflected for a number of years in close to unanimous critical praise. Yet that was not to last. In later years, some critics bandied around the joke: "How do you spell *pretentious?*" "Emerson, Lake and Palmer." But initially, its blend of high-decibel rock with classical undertones won wide acclaim.

After the group's first appearance in the Fillmore East in New York City in May 1971, *Cash Box* stated: "Emerson, Lake and Palmer have no faults." After attending the trio's Carnegie Hall concert during the same U.S. debut tour, Nancy Ehrlich of *Billboard* wrote: "Let's mention that Greg Lake is a fine singer and an excellent bass player and also very impressive on acoustic guitar. . . . Let's note also that Carl Palmer is the finest supportive drummer since Keith Moon [of the Who] . . . [but] it's still Emerson's show, which means it's enormous. Here is a man who has to keep running constantly to work off too much energy for one person to handle. It comes out in a constant rush of 32nd notes, played on two electric organs at once, plus Moog, plus piano, plus several obscure sound-producing devices."

Of course, praise from trade publications might be viewed askance, but those views were echoed by the people who really count, the rock fans who flocked to the group's early performances.

The three group members brought years of experience to ELP, even though all were still in their early or middle twenties. They started learning their instruments in their teens or preteens and performed with local rock groups from the time they were 12 or 13. Lake and Palmer were basically blues- and rock-oriented from the start, but Emerson began with classical piano lessons, as evidenced by the Béla Bartok strains in the group's debut LP, *Emerson, Lake & Palmer,* released on Cotillion (and distributed by Atlantic Records) in the U.S. in late 1970. As Emerson told Pete Senoff: "On the first album, there was a definitive Bartok influence and Bartok was a very percussive pianist. He treated the piano like a drum . . . like a drum melody."

In the late 1960s, each of the group members was with different well-regarded rock groups. Lake was one of the founders of King Crimson. (*See King Crimson.*) Palmer had been with the Crazy World of Arthur Brown before forming Atomic Rooster. Emerson had demonstrated superior musicianship as a member of the Nice. The Nice never achieved a breakthrough with American fans before it broke up in 1970, but was a sensation in England.

ELP began to take shape in San Francisco, California, in early 1970, Lake told Senoff. "Well, the first to get together were Keith and myself. It happened in San Francisco when Keith was playing the Fillmore with the Nice and I was there with King Crimson. At that time, we were both thinking of a musical change and got to thinking. Then we went back to England and eventually met up with Carl."

They signed with Island Records in England, which arranged for U.S. releases on Cotillion. Their debut LP, *Emerson, Lake and Palmer,* went gold, as did the follow-up *Tarkus* (issued in mid-1971) and its third LP (a rock version of Moussorgsky's "Pictures at an Exhibition," released in early 1972).

The Moussorgsky work became a central element in the band's live shows. Critics were amazed that a 45-minute set based on that classical composition could hold audience's attention. The trio emphasized the variety and content of the music; Emerson stressed that the instrumentation provided numerous different shadings. Palmer told one reporter: "It covers just about every style of playing. There's a 12-bar blues, there's light singing. . . . Everything imaginable can be gotten from it. It's just a glorious work."

The group continued to turn out challenging, though sometimes a little overblown, new albums throughout the mid-1970s. Its fourth LP, *Trilogy,* included the band's rock version of Aaron Copland's "Hoedown" and such originals as the title song and "Endless Enigma." In 1973, the band formed its own label, Manticore Records, with U.S. distribution rights contracted to Atlantic. The first LP under the new arrangement was *Brain Salad Surgery,* issued in late 1973. Tapes from 1973–74 concerts were used to prepare the band's first live album, the three-disc *Welcome Back My Friends* (August 1974).

During 1975 and 1976, the band took time off from touring while the members worked on various projects including the writing of new material and soul-searching about possible solo projects. But the trio slowly got around to a new ELP album program that led to the release of *Works, Volumes 1 and 2* on Atlantic in 1977. This included an "Original Piano Concerto No. 1" by Emerson (recorded with the London Philharmonic Orchestra), an Emerson arrangement of Copland's "Fanfare for the Common Man," a number of blues-based songs co-written by Lake and Peter Sinfield (including "C'est la Vie" and "Closer to Believing"), and some composing efforts by Palmer as well. The albums brought groans from reviewers, but (like all previous ELP albums), they went gold, while the worldwide concert tour, which required very complex instrumentation and accompanying amplification capabilities, still drew turnaway crowds.

The band continued to record new material, though it seemed to be laboring with late 1970s efforts *Love Beach* (1978) and *In Concert* (1979). Soon after release of *Best of Emerson, Lake and Palmer* in 1980, it was confirmed that the band had broken up. Thereafter, the three members worked on individual projects such as Greg Lake's 1981 solo LP on Chrysalis, *Greg Lake*. Keith Emerson's work included writing the musical score for the Universal film *Nighthawks* starring Sylvester Stallone and Billy Dee Williams. The soundtrack album was issued on Backstreet Records in February 1981.

In the summer of 1984, Emerson and Lake got back together to write some new material at Emerson's house (a 400-year-old Tudor structure where J.M. Barrie wrote *Peter Pan* at the turn of the century). Satisfied that they had found new creative wellsprings, they sought a new drummer and chose Cozy Powell, who had backed or been a member of groups such as Jeff Beck, Rainbow, and Whitesnake. (*See Beck, Jeff.*) The group's debut album, *Emerson, Lake and Powell,* was issued on Polydor Records the summer of 1985.

The Emerson, Lake and Powell LP featured very listenable progressive-rock tracks, but it failed to ignite record buyer interest in line with the peak years of Emerson, Lake and Palmer. The album did rise to number 23 in *Billboard,* but its stay on the lists was relatively short. Though the new band had considerable promise, economics held sway and another reorganization was begun. At first it was rumored the original ELP would reform, but in late summer of 1987, it was announced the band would comprise Emerson, Palmer and American-born bass guitarist/songwriter Robert Berry. The new trio signed with Geffen Records and its debut album on the label, *To the Power of Three,* was issued in January 1988.

ENGLISH BEAT, THE; *Vocal and instrumental group. Personnel in early 1980s: David Wakeling, born Birmingham, England, February 19, 1957; David Steele, born Isle of Wight, England, September 8, 1960; Andy Cox, born Birmingham, England, January 25, 1956; Everett Martin, born St. Kitts, West Indies, April 5, 1951; Ranking Roger, born Birmingham, England, February 21, 1961; Saxa, born Jamaica, West Indies, c. 1930.*

The large-scale immigration to England after World War II of former subjects of the fading Empire's one-time Caribbean possessions led to some social and creative upheavals. The blending of Caribbean soul/rock-influenced rhythms with the American rock variations of white British musicians led to interesting new sounds and reemergence in revised form of earlier pop strains. In the late 1970s and early 1980s, groups such as the English Beat spawned what some critics called the Ska Revival, ska having been a pulsating predecessor to Jamaican reggae. In truth, as the band's recordings demonstrate, its numbers might have ska flavor, but there also were obvious touches of reggae, soul, punk, and mainstream rock. Whatever the definition of the group's style, it was eminently danceable, often propelling concert goers onto their feet and, wherever possible, into the aisles to sway and move with the music.

The band's founding members—David Wakeling (vocals/guitar), David Steel (bass guitar), Andy Cox (guitar), and Everett Martin (drums)—claimed the industrial city of Birmingham as home base, although Martin didn't move there from his native St. Kitts until his early teens. Before joining the English Beat, he had kept afloat financially partly through routine jobs (including lemonade salesman and kettle maker) and partly through working nights with local bands. At one point, he did find relatively steady performing work as reggae drummer and percussionist in Joan Armatrading's group. (*See Armatrading, Joan.*)

Wakeling, who took up guitar in his teens, developing an unorthodox left-handed playing style patterned after the technique of Paul McCartney, left school and for a while kept music as more of a hobby than a livelihood. Among the jobs he essayed in the mid-1970s were fireman, bingo-caller, lifeguard, bricklayer and solar-panel maker. His solar-panel work took him to the Isle of Wight off the southern coast of England, where his path crossed that of Andy Cox.

Cox, who also began playing guitar during his

school years, performed with several nonprofessional bands in Birmingham before he gave up school at 16 and, like other future Beat bandsmen, picked up whatever day work he could to pay his room and board. He spent a while working as a bathroom cleaner at a police cadet school in between a series of factory jobs. His wanderings led him to a job in the same solar-panel shop as Wakeling where the two decided to pool their talents in hopes of organizing a viable music group.

One of the steps they took was to place an ad in the local paper for a bass guitarist. That attracted the attention of David Steele, born and raised on the Isle of Wight, who had early training on violin and classical guitar. He had just begun teaching himself bass the year before (1976), but felt confident enough about his newly acquired skills to leave school in 1977 to concentrate on pop music. The new trio of friends went to Birmingham to try to find performing work. Once there, Steele still had to find nonmusic employment, which took the form of menial work at a mental hospital. A staff nurse introduced him to drummer Martin, and the first alignment of the English Beat was set.

The quartet of Wakeling, Cox, Steele, and Martin began practicing together at the end of 1978 and gained their first engagement in a Birmingham club in March 1979. The group played a combination of original ska/reggae-based songs and cover versions of current reggae hits such as "My Boy Lollipop." Among the members of the punk rock group the Dum Dum Boys that headlined the bill on which the English Beat performed was a fine vocalist who called himself Ranking Roger. Roger, also born and bred in Birmingham, had previous to his punk rock activities been a dredlock-sporting rasta along the lines of Jamaica's reggae greats. He followed the fortunes of the English Beat and eventually joined as lead vocalist with some contributions as well on drums and percussion.

The band began to jell and found it easier to get full-time work. One series of gigs was as a supporting band for the Selecter. Through the members of that band, Wakeling and his co-workers met another ska group, the Specials, who had just started their own label, Two-Tone. Specials members were impressed with the English Beat and offered them the opportunity to make a single on the new label. For that recording, the band added a sixth member, saxophone player Saxa, who had been a part-time musician and sometime session player for much of the almost 30 years he had lived in England since immigrating from Jamaica in the early 1950s. Between band jobs, Saxa had earned money as a cobbler. His credits included occasional work with such reggae artists as Prince Buster and Desmond Dekker.

The group completed its first single for release on Two-Tone by the end of summer 1979. A ska version of the old Smokey Robinson hit, "Tears of a Clown," the disc was surprisingly successful for such a shoestring operation, making the U.K. top ten. The band then formed its own label, Go Feet, in the early 1980s, licensing Arista U.K. Records to handle distribution. The debut Go Feet single, "Hands Off . . . She's Mine"/"Twist and Crawl," was issued on February 14, 1980, and also became a top ten U.K. success. This was followed by a third single, "Mirror in the Bathroom," that was released in May and soon rose to number four on U.K. lists.

All of those songs plus many more originals and modernized versions of older numbers (such as Prince Buster's "Rough Rider" and a soul/reggae treatment of the Andy Williams hit "Can't Get Used to Losing You") were packaged on the band's debut LP *I Just Can't Stop It.* Soon after the album was issued by Arista in June, it made its way to number three on U.K. album charts. Sire Records obtained distribution rights for the U.S. and Canada, issuing the LP in July 1980 to generally good critical acceptance. *Rolling Stone* noted: "The English Beat is the only ska revival band whose melodies are as exhilarating as its beat—no mean feat in a movement that is defined by its rhythms. There are several reasons for this, but they boil down to a resolve to highlight melody over the beat wherever possible, and the wisdom to borrow from dub when grooving for its own sake. *I Just Can't Stop It* is everything a modern British pop album should be—relentlessly danceable, tuneful, and socially conscious, as well as soulful and swinging."

The band made its first U.S. tour in 1981 in support of its second album, *Wha'ppen,* issued in America by Sire. The band played mostly smaller venues as it worked to build a following in the all-important States. Progress in that direction was indicated by the performance of its third album, issued in the U.S. on the I.R.S. label. Soon after release in the last months of 1982, *Special Beat Service* was inside the top 100 and remained on *Billboard* charts well into 1983. The band's next album, *What Is Beat?* (also issued by I.R.S.), was on U.S. charts from the end of 1983 into the first part of 1984.

By the mid-1980s, the band had built up a solid, if not massive following in the U.S. and Canada to augment a sizable group of adherents at home. While the band wasn't in the superstar class with the ability to fill large arenas, it could comfortably sell out medium-sized halls in many parts of the U.S. and the world.

ENO, BRIAN: *Singer, instrumentalist (keyboards, synthesizers), songwriter, composer, record producer. Born East Anglia, England, 1948.*

While Brian Eno's name rarely appeared on the hit charts and he had few trophies from his solo albums to grace his mantelpiece, he had tremendous influence on pop music of the 1970s and 1980s as musician, writer, and producer for many landmark rock groups. With sometime collaborator David Bowie, he personified the experimental wing of England's avant garde movement that sought to revitalize the tired rock sounds of many of the 1970s headliners.

Eno, born and raised in England, spent much of his early years near one of the U.S. Air Force bases in Britain. This exposed him to the new style taking over pop music in the States, called rock'n'roll, almost from its swaddling phase. In the late 1950s and early 1960s, he recalled: "We used to get the new American records from the PX stores."

Still, while interested in music, he didn't think of making a career of it at the time, particularly since he did not try to learn an instrument in his early years. He liked to paint and draw, however, and moved from elementary grades into art school in Ipswich in the mid-1960s. There, he acquired a tape recorder and figured out novel ways to use it, including employing it as a tool for musical exploration. He began to get other recording devices and by the end of the 1960s had 30 different systems on hand.

During his years at Winchester School of Art (1966–69), he spent an increasing amount of time gaining experience with electronic music. When he became head of the Students Union, he used some of the budget to set up a lecture series featuring avant garde musicians. Among those he brought in—well known in their field but unfamiliar to most people outside it—were Cornelius Curlew, Christian Wolff, John Tilbury, and Norton Feldman. Eno made sure he made them more than passing acquaintances, managing after a while to work with some of them on ideas about advanced electronic works.

The capabilities of recording machines, he told Richard Williams of *Melody Maker*, caused him to realize "that there were certain areas of music you could enter without actually learning an instrument —which at my age I certainly wasn't about to do."

He earned a reputation as a promising new practitioner of such material, which led to an invitation from another young avant garde musician, Andy Mackay, for Brian to lecture on new music trends at the University of Reading. A few years later, when Andy was helping Bryan Ferry set up a group that eventually took the name Roxy Music, he bumped into Eno on a London subway train. That chance meeting led to an invitation for Eno to join the new band. (*See Roxy Music.*)

The band members all had the goal of achieving a new sound for rock. Eno's electronic wizardry played an important role in making that possible. One way he accomplished this was to manipulate the sounds of all the instruments with his synthesizers. He told Williams soon after Roxy Music's first album came out in England: "At the moment, I'm mostly interested in modifying the sound of the other instruments. You get a nice quality—the skill of the performer transformed by the electronics. Neither the player nor I know what each other is going to do—which means you get some nice accidents."

At the start of the 1970s, the band, both on records and in eerily challenging concerts, built up considerable backing among U.K. fans. The band presented a somewhat dissonant visual image, with some members using familiar stage attire and others affecting bizarre looks associated in later years with glamrock or some aspects of punk. Eno, with painted face, stripe-dyed hair and multicolored costumes, was of the latter segment. In England, the band quickly became a favorite of many top rock stars including David Bowie and Elton John.

By the time Roxy Music attempted to win over the American audience (its first album wasn't released in the U.S. until late 1972 on Warner Brothers), Eno had decided to go his own separate way. He signed with Island Records, which issued the LPs *Taking Tiger Mountain by Strategy* and *Here Come the Warm Jets* in 1973–74. Both albums offered innovative many-layered sound combinations that were intriguing to listen to, but not calculated to make top 40 programmers' mouths water. Most major print media hailed the albums, though the lion's share of record buyers couldn't have cared less.

Rolling Stone contributor Bart Testa typified some of the enthusiastic comments. "*Taking Tiger Mountain by Strategy* is the perfection of Eno's rock mannerisms, with guitars imitating machinery over a rhythm section of mesmerizing force and insistence. . . . *Here Come the Warm Jets* redefined the Roxy style as a fantastic vehicle for Eno's surreal unsentimental irony. The electronically altered guitars of Robert Fripp (of King Crimson) and Phil Manzanera (of Roxy Music) are devastating and Eno's vocals are a magical tour de force."

Robert Fripp, original motive force of the great English rock band King Crimson, was the first of a series of musical collaborators with Eno. In the mid-1970s, Fripp and Eno turned out several fine progressive rock albums such as *Discreet Music* and *Another Green World*. (*See Fripp, Robert; King Crimson.*)

From that time on, Eno seemed a veritable musical whirling dervish, adding to his credits with a stream of diverse albums on different labels while being equally prolific as a composer and a record producer of many new artists. He took great interest in the punk and new wave movements as both an ardent observer and a creative inspiration. From the mid-1970s to late 1980s, he was based in a variety of thriving new-music locales ranging from London in the punk-new wave gestation period to Berlin (where he worked on many projects with David Bowie) to New York. (*See Bowie, David.*)

His recorded output in the late 1970s included a series of joint efforts with Bowie, such as *Low* and *Heroes* (RCA, 1977). Besides such semicommercial packages, the two also recorded new experimental albums issued on small labels. Eno's other releases of those years included *Before and after Science* on Island Records and two almost Muzak-style albums: *Music for Films* (Polydor, 1978) and *Music for Airports* (Editions EG, 1979).

Eno had a hand in the careers of such new wave or post–new wave bands as the Talking Heads and Devo. His association with the Talking Heads began with the band's *More Songs about Buildings and Food* album and continued on later projects in the 1980s. His activities also included one-on-one efforts with David Byrne, unofficial leader of Talking Heads, including the 1981 album, released on Sire Records, *My Life in the Bush of Ghosts. (See Devo; Talking Heads.)*

Eno continued in effect to play both sides of the fence with some albums that were as different from "normal" pop music as imaginable at the time and other records with a much milder, accessible tone. Besides *Music for Airports* and *Music for Films*, he turned out others in a series he referred to as "environmental trance." As reviewer Kristine McKenna noted, the goal was to provide music "to effect subtle psychological shifts and, one assumes by its soothing tone, to promote a sense of well-being." Among such 1980 releases on the E.G. EGS label were *Ambient 2: The Plateux of Mirror* (a collaboration with composer-pianist Harold Budd) and *Fourth World, Volume 1: Possible Musics* (recorded with avant garde trumpeter Jon Hassell).

During the 1980s, Eno continued his multiplicity of projects with new and old co-workers, including more unusual recordings with David Bowie. He also provided soundtrack music for Al Reinhart's film on U.S. Apollo lunar missions that served as a major part of his late 1983 album on Editions EG ENO 5, *Apollo (Atmospheres & Soundtracks)*. He also steadily added to his producing credits during the decade, among others working with the Irish group U2. At the 1988 Grammy Awards, he watched from the audience as the band won the Grammies for Album of the Year for the LP *Joshua Tree* and for the Best Rock Vocal, Duo or Group for "The Joshua Tree." For production work on the album, Eno and Daniel Lanois were nominated for the Producer of the Year award. While they didn't win, they could enjoy the acclaim the Grammy voters gave the overall *Joshua Tree* project.

EURYTHMICS: *Vocal and instrumental duo. Dave Stewart, born Sunderland, England, c. early 1950s; Annie Lennox, born Aberdeen, Scotland, December 25, 1954.*

With his unkempt hair, generally scruffy appearance, and laid-back air, Dave Stewart and Annie Lennox (a slim, boyish-looking girl who could pass for a high-fashion model and possessed an absolutely electric persona on stage) outwardly seemed the prototypical odd couple—so much so that for a while after the Eurythmics attained star status, most reporters concentrated on Lennox's animated vocal stylings and relegated Stewart to a supposed backup role. But an analysis of their work disclosed soon enough that it was a true partnership and Stewart's contributions as writer, musical director, and instrumentalist almost perfectly complemented Annie's remarkable talents.

For a time, the two artists also had a romantic partnership, but this broke up before the birth of the Eurythmics. Stewart told Robert Hilburn of the *Los Angeles Times* (August 2, 1986): "Most couples get famous and then break up. But we broke up and then got famous. Our first reaction was that it was impossible—to break up and still make music together. But the experience made us stronger. We had this goal—and we were determined not to let anything get in its way."

Lennox commented to Hilburn: "I met Dave when I was about 22, 23. By the time the Eurythmics started, I was about 26, 27 and I think I needed to find myself. I had lived through a lot of other people and through Dave, and I wanted to sort of break away from that. But I knew creatively I didn't want to work with anybody else except Dave. So there was this strange tension—the pain of the breakup and the excitement of working together on the music. In some ways, that tension has never really gone away. There is always something that brings an edge to what we do."

Both Annie and Dave had considerable diversity in their lives before their paths crossed. As a boy growing up in the northern England town of Sunderland, Dave's first dreams were of sports stardom. He seemed athletically well coordinated in his preteen years and tried his hand at running, pole vaulting, soccer, and even skiing. But, he told a *Billboard* interviewer: "When I was 12, I broke my knee in a match and was in hospital for ages. I got so fidgety with nothing to do that someone brought me a guitar, which of course was near fatal."

He focused the next few years on learning as much as he could about playing guitar. But while he listened to pop music on the radio or records, he didn't attend his first rock concert until he was 15. (His primal influences, he said, were folk-rockers such as Dylan and American blues artists such as Robert Johnson and Mississippi John Hurt.) The first band he heard live was Amazing Blondel, which combined English folk music with rock. Dave was so carried away that he ran away from home, stowing away in the group's traveling van. His parents, after finding out about his whereabouts, reluctantly consented to his staying with the band as sometime roadie and backing guitarist.

After a while, he formed his own band, Longdancer, which was given a contract in the mid-1970s by Elton John's label, Rocket Records. (*See John, Elton.*) In pursuit of his musical goals, he spent a considerable amount of time on the road, driving to all sorts of engagements at small clubs throughout Europe. That phase of his career was brought up short by a car crash in Germany that caused, among other things, an injury to a lung. He returned to London for repair surgery on the lung and some rest and recuperation. While doing that, he began talking about new projects with another Sunderland musician, Peet Coombes. The two were having dinner in a London eating place when they struck up a conversation with their waitress, Annie Lennox.

Her route to the meeting, she recalled, began when she "was born at 11:20 P.M. Christmas night 1954 in the town of Aberdeen on the northeast coast of Scotland. My mother worked as a cook until I came along, then she stayed at home to look after me. My father was a boilermaker in the local shipyards. We lived in a big tenement house in Hutcheon Street, overlooking a textile mill. All the kids from the other tenements used to play outside in the streets together, or in the backyards. When I was three, I was given a toy piano on which I used to pick out simple tunes.

"At four I was accepted for the High School for girls. [High School as used here refers to the name of a school, not to the type of educational establishment known as a high school in the U.S.] I still have a photograph of my first day there, wearing a uniform several sizes too big. Anyhow, three years later they let me start piano lessons. I loved music and I used to sing in the local choir every Saturday morning. When I was 11, they asked if I would like to learn to play the flute. And at 17, I decided I was going to become a classical flute player. I practiced really hard and ultimately won a place at the Royal Academy of Music in London. Unfortunately, I never really fit in there so I spent the next three years looking for something better to do."

Her dissatisfaction with the demands of classical training led to "a desperate search for something that did have some meaning to me. I don't know why, but I started to sing and I realized my voice was good. Due to the influences of Stevie Wonder and other Tamla-Motown artists and other things—boys, dancing, clothes, dropping in, dropping out—I not only decided to sing, but also write my own songs."

She found occasional work as a vocalist, but for a while she earned most of her income as a waitress. She told *Billboard:* "The first words Dave said were, 'Will you marry me?' I thought he was a serious nutter. But from that night on, we were inseparable."

Annie took up residence with Dave. The two of them with Coombes formed a group called the Tourists in 1977. Over the next few years, the band had some successes and at times was on the verge of gaining more than local recognition. They signed with a label called Logo on which they had a top four single, a cover of "I Only Want to Be With You" that made a similar move for Dusty Springfield and the Bay City Rollers. The band made two LPs for Logo, but relations between band and label became severely strained over royalties, which boiled over into a lawsuit brought by the musicians. The group toured across the world, including the U.S., Europe, and the Far East, in pursuit of stardom, but finally disbanded during a visit to Bangkok, Thailand.

Not only did the band break up, so did the love affair between Annie and Dave. But soon after, they decided on a new working relationship based on friendship and a dual writing-performing scheme. The initial idea was that the two would form a creative nucleus augmented by different combinations of backing singers and musicians for concert and recording projects. The due got the green light to record material for an album called *In the Garden* on RCA U.K. (Though the Eurythmics later were signed to the RCA U.S. label, *In the Garden* wasn't available in the U.S. except as an import item.) Once the LP was complete, the duo lined up dates for U.K. concerts and set off in an old Volvo in late 1981 for a back-breaking schedule of appearances. It was a bitterly cold winter, one of the worst in recent U.K. history, and it proved an exhausting effort. Dave had a recurrence of his lung problems and Annie suffered a nervous breakdown.

They managed to recover by early 1982 and, with new songs written in the interim, set about making demo tapes in a studio set up in a London warehouse. The recordings were made on an eight-track system, Annie told *Billboard*. "We used so many different textures. It sounded so sophisticated, but often we had to wait for the timber factory downstairs to turn off their machinery before we could record the vocals."

The recordings proved the basis for the album *Sweet Dreams (Are Made of This)*, which helped win a contract for U.S. distribution from RCA. The album was issued in early 1983 and its progress was buoyed by the tremendous success of the single and video of the title song. The single reached the number one spot on the *Billboard* list the week of September 3, 1983. The album was certified gold by year-end. Right along with those breakthroughs, Annie and Dave and their backing musicians established themselves as major concert artists with fiery shows that blended music, dance, and spectacular lighting effects.

Experimenting with visual images was something Annie and Dave delighted in. One example was her use of male costumes as part of the 1984 video for "Who's That Girl," where she took both male and female parts, with the two images eventually coming together for an electronic kiss.

She continued the male masquerade during a sequence the Eurythmics staged for the February 28, 1984, Grammy Awards telecast. She told Hilburn: "The record company wanted us to make an appearance on the Grammy show because they thought it would be prestigious for us, but we were very reticent about it. We felt our stance was not in the bosom of the conventional music scene. We wouldn't have been comfortable simply going on and playing our latest hit song.

"So we wanted to find a way to present ourselves that would satisfy the record company and satisfy our own feelings. There had been a lot of talk about sexual ambiguity that year, so we decided this would be a perfect way to kind of put it back in their face . . . a way of saying: 'You want me to be a gender-bender? Here I am.'"

That guest spot, as it happened, simply added to the duo's mystique, which certainly was not displeasing to RCA. During a good part of 1984, the twosome worked on material for the soundtrack for the film *1984*, which starred Richard Burton and John Hurt. There was considerable controversy arising from the project since the film director substituted music by another writer for Eurythmic material at the last moment. A single from the forthcoming LP of their *1984* compositions titled "Sexcrime (Nineteen Eighty Four)" was banned by most American stations for so-called objectionable content.

Besides "Sweet Dreams," the Eurythmics were represented on the hit lists by several other songs during 1983–84: "Who's That Girl," "Love Is a

Stranger," "Right by Your Side," and "Here Comes the Rain Again." The duo's next regular studio album, *Be Yourself Tonight* (1985), was certified platinum by the RIAA. The first single (and video) from the LP, "Would I Lie to You?" was nominated in the Grammy voting for Best Rock Performance by a Duo or Group with Vocal. In late 1985, the Eurythmics teamed up with Aretha Franklin for a top 20 single, "Sisters Are Doin' It for Themselves." (*See Franklin, Aretha.*)

During the summer of 1986, the Eurythmics were represented on the LP charts with *Revenge*, showcasing many fine new songs co-written by Dave and Annie, such as "Thorn in My Side" and "When Tomorrow Comes." Once more, the duo backed its new recordings and videos with an exciting live show that drew SRO crowds throughout the U.S., Canada, and other parts of the world. Backing them for these concerts was a band made of Clem Burke (a one-time Blondie stalwart) on drums; Chucho Merchan, a Bogota, Colombia-born bass guitarist with many jazz credits; London-born session and backing musician Patrick Seymour on keyboards; and one-time Tom Petty harmonica and saxophone player Jimmy "Z" Zavala, a native of Sacramento, California.

In late 1987 the duo's seventh album was issued on RCA. Titled *Savage*, it featured Stewart on almost all the instrumentation and Lennox on all the vocals. More disco than rock, while it was an excellent record, it represented a look backward in style rather than forward.

EVERLY BROTHERS, THE: *Vocal and instrumental team. Both born Brownie, Kentucky: Don, February 1, 1937; Phil, January 19, 1939. Duo disbanded in 1973 and reformed in 1983.*

Taking their cue from their early idol, Elvis Presley, the Everly Brothers had an impact on pop music in the late '50s and early '60s almost as great as Elvis's. Their country-rock recordings of those years affected the styles of many rock stars of the 1960s, both in the U.S. and abroad. Among their fans of the late 1950s in England, for instance were future members of the Beatles and Animals. Their performances also had an impact on young folk and country-rock artists, which prompted Bob Dylan to say: "We owe those guys everything. They started it all." After the brothers parted company in mid-1973, their activities centered more and more on the straight country field rather than rock. This changed again after their performing reunion in 1983.

The boys had an impeccable country background. Their parents, Ike and Margaret Everly, were country artists well known to southern and midwestern audiences from the '30s into the '50s. The boys could sing many country standards at an early age and learned the rudiments of guitar as soon as they could hold an instrument. When Don was eight and Phil six, they made their first public appearance on radio station KMA in Shenandoah, Iowa. After that, the boys regularly joined their parents on performing tours each summer.

After their parents retired following the boys' graduation from high shool, the brothers decided to keep going on their own. They moved to Nashville, playing the local clubs and waiting for their first break. It was the mid-1950s, and traditional country music was reeling from the success of rockabilly artists such as Elvis and Jerry Lee Lewis. In 1957, the brothers got their first record contract. Looking for new material by making the rounds of music publishers, they met the songwriting team of Felice and Boudleaux Bryant at Acuff-Rose. The Bryants played them a new composition, "Bye Bye Love." The Everlys decided to record it, starting a close association with the Bryants that lasted many years and resulted in a series of hits, many of which have become standards and have since been recorded by many artists besides the Everlys in both the pop and country fields.

Sparked by the high-pitched, close harmonizing of traditional country music and bluegrass, "Bye Bye Love" rose to top levels on country and pop charts in 1957. The brothers soon provided Cadence Records with a number one *Billboard* hit, the Bryants' "Wake up Little Susie." They had another excellent year in 1958 with such hits as "All I Have to Do Is Dream," "Problems," "Bird Dog," and "Devoted to You" (all by the Bryants). 1959 brought the double-sided hit "Take a Message to Mary"/"Poor Jenny" and Don's composition "Till I Kissed You." "Cathy's Clown" (1960) marked a move to the newly formed Warner Brothers Records. Their names continued to appear regularly at the top of the hit lists at the start of the '60s, with some of the releases being material previously recorded on Cadence and some being brand-new tracks on Warner Brothers. Their top 20 hits on Cadence included, "Let It Be Me" and "When Will I Be Loved" (1960). On Warner Brothers, their successes spanned "So Sad" (1960), "Ebony Eyes," "Don't Blame Me," and "Walk Right Back" (1961), and "Crying in the Rain" and "That's Old Fashioned" (1962).

During those years, the duo also turned out a series of LPs. On Cadence, *The Everly Brothers* and *The Fabulous Style of the Everly Brothers* presented singles hits. *Songs Our Daddy Taught Us* (later reissued as *Folk Songs by the Everly Brothers*) showed the roots of their family's music in the timeless ballads of Appalachia and long-ago England.

Their early '60s albums on Warner Brothers included *It's Everly Time, Date with the Everly Brothers, Top Vocal Duet, Instant Party, Golden Hits,* and *Great Country Hits.* In the 1980s, Rhino Records rereleased all the Cadence albums.

The brothers moved to Los Angeles in the early '60s, but their career slowed down soon after, partly because Don enlisted in the Marine Corps. While he was away in the mid-1960s, the Everlys still were represented in the music field by Warner Brothers LPs *Rock'n'Soul, Gone, Gone, Gone,* and *Beat'n'Soul* (1965), *In Our Image* (1966), and *Hit Sound* and *The Everly Brothers Sing* (1967).

The brothers began working again in the late 1960s, hosting their own CBS-TV summer replacement series in 1970.

Their albums sold well enough for companies to keep issuing new ones, though sales did not approach gold-record levels anymore. Among their releases of the early '70s were *Everly Brothers Greatest Hits* on Epic Records, the live two-LP *Everly Brothers Show* on Warner Brothers, and *Chained to a Memory* (Harmony Records, 1970). Barnaby Records reissued their Cadence tracks on two two-disc sets, *The Everly Brothers' Original Greatest Hits* and *End of an Era.* In 1971, the Everlys' agreement with Warners ended and they signed with RCA. Their first RCA LP, *26,* was well received critically, but did not catch on with the public. The same held true for their *Stories We Could Tell* LP.

But the brothers retained a strong following as indicated by the fact that they still could fill medium-size concert halls and pop and country clubs all over the world. However, there were increasing strains on the team—differences of opinion on creative directions and rising unhappiness about continuing to follow a well-trodden path. This feeling was indicated, for example, in Don Everly's early '70s composition, "I'm Tired of Singing My Song in Las Vegas." Phil also showed a desire to go his own way by recording a solo album, *Star Spangled Springer,* on RCA in 1973.

The brothers announced they would give their final concert together at Knott's Berry Farm's John Wayne Theater in Buena Park, California, on Saturday, July 14, 1973. As Don said at the time: "It's over. I've quit. I've been wanting to quit for three years now and it is finally time to just do it. I'm tired of being an Everly Brother. I still like to sing 'Bye Bye Love' sometimes, but I don't want to spend my life doing it. I've got to find something else." Later, he added: "The Everly Brothers died 10 years ago."

Phil, who had stormed off stage during the first of three final shows that night, leaving Don to finish that set and the next two alone, noted in early 1974

1. ADAM & THE ANTS

**2. ANGUS YOUNG
OF AC/DC**

**3. DUANE ALLMAN
OF THE ALLMAN
BROTHERS BAND**

4. THE ANIMALS

5. RICK DANKO AND ROBBIE ROBERTSON OF THE BAND

**6. BRIAN WILSON
OF THE BEACH
BOYS**

7. THE BEACH BOYS

8. THE BEATLES DURING THE MAGICAL MYSTERY TOUR

9. THE BEE GEES

10. PAT BENATAR

11. CHUCK BERRY

12. DAVID BOWIE

13. JAMES BROWN

**14. JACKSON
BROWNE**

**15. BUFFALO SPRINGFIELD (*L. TO R.*): DEWEY MARTIN, RICHIE FURAY,
STEVEN STILLS, JIM FIELDER, NEIL YOUNG**

16. RAY CHARLES

17. ERIC CLAPTON

18. THE CLASH (*L. TO R.*): NICKY "TOPPER" HEADON, MICK JONES, JOE STRUMMER, PAUL SIMONON

19. THE COMMODORES— LIONEL RICHIE, *FRONT LEFT*

20. ALICE COOPER

21. ELVIS COSTELLO

22. CROSBY, STILLS, NASH & YOUNG

23. DEVO

24. NEIL DIAMOND

25. BO DIDDLEY

26. FATS DOMINO

27. THE DOORS

28. THE DRIFTERS

29. DURAN DURAN

30. BOB DYLAN

the decision to end the duo was his brother's, but it probably was inevitable. "It was simply a case of growing in different directions—musically, philosophically, politically—and add to that the normal, all-American brother-to-brother relationship, compound that by being together almost constantly for 15 years and you have a general idea of what went on. . . . There is some bitterness, yes. We do not see each other—but then you can't really say that we're on bad terms. That would seem to be a contradiction, but it's the only way to describe our relationship today."

Phil was the first to strike off on a new track. In early 1974, he inaugurated a syndicated rock program, "In Session," a combination talk-and-music program that he hosted. He also toured as a solo artist, playing many major country music clubs. In mid-1975, his composition, "When Will I Be Loved" provided a best-selling single for Linda Ronstadt. (See Ronstadt, Linda.) Other songs he wrote or co-wrote showed up on the charts now and then, including "Better than Now" (co-written with T. Slater) issued as a single by Dewayne Orender at the end of 1978. Phil continued to turn out new recordings of his own, including the 1979 Elektra LP Living Alone.

Don also continued doing stage shows and records, though with less intensity than Phil. Much of his activity took the form of behind-the-scenes work. As with Phil, he was represented on the hit charts from time to time with other artists' recordings of his songs. Among those were Connie Smith's "Till I Kissed You" and "So Sad (to Watch Good Love Go Bad)" in 1976 and a new version of the latter made by Steve Wariner in mid-1978. In 1976, Don had the single "Yesterday Just Passed My Way Again" (on Hickory Records) on the country charts for a number of months.

The brothers' parting in 1973 had been so bitter that for many years they would not even speak to each other. But as the old saw maintains, "Time heals all wounds," and in the spring of 1983, a reconciliation was effected. Soon after, they announced plans for a new series of concerts in the fall. As one of them told a reporter: "Once we got together, there was no way we couldn't start singing."

Their first concert together after all those years took place in September 1983 in London's Royal Albert Hall. They had chosen that venue, they said, partly from memories of a concert there with their father. Besides that, British fans never let their memories of the brothers grow dim. A two-disc set of the concert, The Everly Brothers Reunion Concert, was issued by Passport Records in early 1984. After their first series of shows in the U.K. and the U.S., the brothers began working on a new studio album, EB

'84 on Mercury, produced by English rockabilly revivalist Dave Edmunds, whose own music is heavily influenced by the Everlys. (See Edmunds, Dave.)

In July 1986, the reestablishment of the duo as a continuing act was recognized by a celebration in Shenandoah, Iowa. While the brothers hadn't been born there, they had lived there as children with their parents. The brothers' concert there was preceded by "The Everly Brothers Homecoming Parade" with floats and high school homecoming queens.

In mid-1986 the brothers had another new album released by Mercury/Polygram, Born Yesterday, also produced by Dave Edmunds. They also were among the first inductees into the newly established Rock and Roll Hall of Fame.

FABIAN: *Singer, actor. Born Philadelphia, Pennsylvania, February 6, 1943.*

The careers of Fabian and Frankie Avalon have a number of parallels. Both were born and raised in Philadelphia, were of Italian ancestry, became pop singers and later actors, and were turned into stars by the record executive–songwriting team of Bob Marcucci and Peter De Angelis. One major difference was vocal talent, which Avalon came by naturally and which Fabian was not blessed with.

As often happens in the entertainment field there are conflicting stories about how Fabian, whose real name was Fabian Forte, got started in show business. In one version he auditioned for Marcucci and De Angelis, who didn't care for his voice, but signed him because of his good looks; in another, Marcucci caught sight of Fabian near Forte's home and made that connection.

Fabian has maintained the second story is the factual one. He told Tony Kornhesier of *Newsday* (reprinted in the *Los Angeles Times*, January 3, 1973), the event occurred when the almost 15-year-old was sitting on the front steps of his home in South Philadelphia. "My father had just suffered a heart attack and was being taken out in an ambulance. Marcucci was walking by and we were introduced. He was intrigued by my name and he wondered if I'd be interested in the recording business."

He also told Dennis Hunt (*Los Angeles Times*, July 5, 1974), "At that time I was just hanging out on the corner with guys, playing three-card ante and stealing wine whenever we could. I was making a few dollars a week working in a drugstore and as a janitor's assistant at an insurance company. When I got the offer to record, I took it because I thought it might be exciting. Besides, my father was sick and the family needed money."

After Marcucci and De Angelis heard him sing, both agreed he was far from the greatest vocalist they'd heard. On the other hand, he was young, handsome, and offered the possibility of rapport with a teen audience. They decided to underwrite a year's vocal lessons for their new protégé.

They signed him for their Chancellor Records label and provided him with some of their compositions. The first releases went nowhere. In 1957, the partners financed a major publicity buildup and tour of theaters and auditoriums in major eastern cities. This time Fabian began to gain a following, resulting in his first hit singles, "I'm a Man," "Tiger," and "Turn Me Loose" in 1959. But he never again broke *Billboard*'s top 20.

Like Avalon, Fabian was sought out by movie studios. His first vehicle was *Hound Dog Man* in 1959. He moved up a notch after this in 1960, appearing with Bing Crosby in *High Time* and John Wayne in *North to Alaska*. In 1961, he showed up on the screen in the film *Love in a Goldfish Bowl*.

During the '60s, Fabian was occasionally signed for mostly small roles in films or on TV including a part in *Bus Stop* in which he played a psychopath. His recording career had ended by then and, by the end of the decade, his acting opportunities also had narrowed.

Fortunately for him, his performing career got a boost from the growing nostalgia craze for "the good old days." While not blazing any new trails creatively, he continued to be active singing his 1950s hits in rock revival shows of the '70s and '80s.

FACES, THE: *Vocal and instrumental group. All born England: Rod Stewart, born London, January 10, 1945; Ronnie Wood, born June 1, 1947; Ronnie Lane, born April 1, 1948; Ian Mc-Lagan, born May 12, 1946; Kenny Jones, born September 16, 1949. Original group (1966) included Steve Marriott, born January 30, 1947, who left in 1969. Rod Stewart added in late 1970.*

One of the problems of Faces was identity. For a long time, it was considered to be lead singer Steve Marriott's band. When he left, critics wrote the group off. Later, when Rod Stewart joined, people tended to consider Faces his backup group. However, as Stewart himself stressed and the group's recordings bear out, it is a band that played as a unit with a style uniquely its own.

The original group, called Small Faces, was founded by Ronnie Lane, then 18, and Steve Marriott. By then, Lane had several years of experience as a bass guitarist with English groups and had exhibited potential as a writer. The group was rounded out by Ian McLagan on piano and organ and Kenny Jones on drums. Jones had studied drums before joining Small Faces, but his first professional experience was with the group. After the first few engagements, he gained considerable favor with other rock drummers for his ability. McLagan, 20 when he joined, had played for a number of years with several groups, starting with the Boz People.

By 1967, with original songs written by Lane and Marriott, the band was building a reputation among English rock fans. It was signed by Immediate Records and placed a number of singles and LPs on the charts during 1967–68. The celebratory single "Itchycoo Park" also moved high on American charts. Almost as much attention was given to the round jacket cover of their hit LP, *Ogden's Nut Gone Flake*, as to the record itself.

At the end of the '60s, internal dissension between Marriott and other band members finally led to a parting of the ways. (Marriott became lead singer of Humble Pie.) The others looked for a replacement, doing some work as a group while also picking up money for living expenses as session men in London recording studios.

Their first important addition was Ronnie Wood, who agreed to join them in late 1969. Wood had performed as a bass guitarist with a succession of top groups of the '60s, including the Birds and Creation. When Jeff Beck formed the Jeff Beck Group, he brought Wood in as bassist. As is well known, the relationships among the band members were far from amicable at the time. Jealousies and internal wrangling grew, mainly because of Beck's insistence on ironclad control over every aspect of the band's performance.

Wood grew close to another band member, Rod Stewart. As Wood recalled: "We just had our own little island in the band. We helped each other keep our sanity. It was a pretty bad time."

The Jeff Beck Group, despite its problems, was recognized as one of the best in the business, but after particularly difficult times between leader and bandsmen, Beck fired Wood during their second U.S. tour. Wood returned to England and did session work. After being approached by Lane, Jones, and McLagan, he agreed to go with their band. He switched from bass to lead guitar and is now considered one of the best lead guitarists around.

As he told Robert Hilburn of the *Los Angeles Times* in December 1971: "The thing that appealed to me most about Faces was they always seemed to have a good time. I liked the music, too, but it was mainly their personality that seemed so right to me."

Stewart stayed with Beck for a time after Wood's departure, but finally he too quit. He decided to try to make it as a solo vocalist and his manager, Billy Gaff, gained him a contract with Mercury Records. When he was working on his first album, members of Small Faces came to help out as session men. Stewart's old friend Ronnie Wood was among them and he suggested Stewart would enjoy working as a member of the group, which by then had a recording contract with Warner Brothers.

Rod agreed. He and Gaff worked out an arrangement with the record firms allowing Stewart to perform as a solo artist on Mercury and a band member on Faces' Warner Brothers recordings. At that time, Faces probably was better known than Stewart, but during 1970–71, Rod placed one record after another on the hit charts.

At the same time, Small Faces was doing well with several singles on British charts in 1970 and two LPs on the U.S. best-selling lists: *Small Faces* and *Empty Rooms.*

During 1970, the group decided to change its name from Small Faces to just Faces. There was no loss of identity; if anything, the name change was a help in the rapid rise of the band to stardom in 1971 when its successes almost matched those of its famous member Stewart. Stewart remained a band member and disavowed any attempt to make it his personal group. As he told Hilburn: "The band is perfect for me. My voice has improved more the time I've spent with Faces than in all the other years combined. We're definitely one band. We're Faces."

Faces performances featured several of the members as lead singers and a repertoire that included original compositions by all its members. In 1971, their hit albums *Long Player* and *A Nod Is as Good as a Wink to a Blind Horse* underlined the variety of writing talent within the group.

Over the next few years, with Rod Stewart's star in the ascendant as a solo performer, Faces increasingly was thought of as Rod's backing group. The band retained a core of faithful fans who knew differently, but it wasn't able to expand that to a mass audience as Stewart had. It continued to have new LPs in its Warner Brothers catalog, such as the inferior *Ooh La La* and *Snakes and Ladders: The Best of Faces* (1976), but the lack of massive success, dissension over the relationship between the group and Stewart, and the lure of other opportunities for some of its members led to its disbanding before the end of the decade. Some people in the industry suggested that Stewart's solo success and the Faces' poor chart performance derived from Rod's keeping his best original compositions for his own use. It was denied by Ron Wood, who was quoted in the book *Rod Stewart* as stating: "Songs written with him were with the Faces in mind or Rod in mind. We never used to scheme and say, 'Oh, we'll save this one.'" The members may not have felt that way about Stewart's song decisions, but there were disagreements on creative directions that caused Ronnie Lane to leave in 1973. Later, Ronnie Wood became

a member of the Rolling Stones, while also turning out several solo albums. Ian McLagan signed with Mercury Records, for whom he completed such above-average LPs as *Troublemaker* (1979) and *Bump in the Night* (1981).

During the mid-1970s, Ronnie Lane showed signs of the crippling disease multiple sclerosis (MS). By the end of the decade, he had gotten to the point where it was difficult even to walk. He felt left out and depressed and avoided old friends for a while, but in the early 1980s, he decided he had to throw aside self-pity and go out in the world again. In the fall of 1983, Eric Clapton decided Lane's friends needed to give a memorable London concert as a benefit for Lane and also to inspire efforts to combat the disease. The show became an all-star event with such artists as Joe Cocker, Jeff Beck, and Jimmy Page taking part and Clapton delivering one of his most heated guitar performances. It was decided to extend the concert series beyond the U.K., which led to shows across the U.S. A prime goal was to raise money to establish a U.S. chapter of England's Action Research for Multiple Sclerosis (ARMS).

Lane, who continued to fight against his disease, told Robert Hilburn (*Los Angeles Times,* December 4, 1983): that this support had added to his determination to continue his struggle. "My spirit is back. It's not bullying me anymore. One of the terrible things was trying to figure out why this happened. Until then, my life had been so good. I had a good childhood, then there were the Small Faces, then the Faces, and all of a sudden it hits you. There must be a reason. So I just kind of made this [ARMS] campaign my reason. In a way, sharing this information [about MS] is a little bit like sharing music. It's a fantastic uplift and I hope it has some kind of positive effect, the way music does."

(*See Beck, Jeff; Clapton, Eric; Humble Pie; Rolling Stones, The; Stewart, Rod.*)

FAITHFULL, MARIANNE: *Singer, actress. Born England, c. 1946.*

Daughter of a baroness and blessed with the face of an angel (some observers said a fallen angel), Marianne Faithfull cut a striking figure on the rock scene of the mid-1960s. She placed a number of records on the hit charts of the period, though she achieved more notice for her outspoken views on sex and society than for her entertaining chores.

She was well educated in convent schools, but the sheltered atmosphere of those years probably contributed to her desire to kick over the traces when she got out into the world. Her career got underway as a result of a chance meeting with the manager of the Rolling Stones, Andrew Loog Oldham, at a party in

London. He was attracted by her long yellow hair, captivating smile, and sexually attractive figure. When he found she could also sing, he promptly signed her to a contract.

She was 18 when she gained her first hit single on London Records, "As Tears Go by." Soon after, she had another best seller, "Come and Stay with Me."

Her albums also sold well in the mid-1960s, including *Marianne Faithfull* (1965) and *Go Away from My World* and *Faithful Forever* (1966).

She was married briefly to art-gallery owner John Dunbar, but they were divorced and she became the steady girl friend of Rolling Stones lead singer Mick Jagger. The two were cofeatured in several movies in the late 1960s with Marianne gaining close attention for her usual garb of zippered leather jump suits. In addition to movies, she appeared in a number of stage presentations, including a Chekhov play. (*See Jagger, Mick; Rolling Stones, The*.)

Despite her escapades, most of the British public tended to look upon her antics with indulgence, partly a reflection of ingrained class distinctions. As Nik Cohn pointed out in his book *Rock from the Beginning:* "She might be shocking, but she did it in a nice accent; she wasn't vulgar with it. She could be coped with. Even in disgrace, she was a lady.

"She kept talking sex. For instance, she gave interviews that blue films should be legal and that sensitive actors would turn the sex act into something truly inspiring. What films? What actors? Umm, she said, 'me and Mick on a high bare rock.'"

By the end of the 1960s, Marianne's career as a rock singer had waned, though the buying public showed some interest in the London Records album issued at the start of the 1970s, *Marianne Faithfull's Greatest Hits*.

The outlook for an eventual comeback seemed dim indeed during most of the 1970s. Marianne's life was a jumble of life-defeating episodes—failed relationships, heroin addiction, and attempted suicides. But Faithfull turned out to have reserves of courage and perseverance. She finally fought back to overcome her problems, including drugs, and in 1979 completed a new album, *Broken English,* on Island Records. While her voice had lost much of its youthful sweetness, the emotion and insight she poured into the album tracks made it an amazing listening experience. It won widespread critical approval and did reasonably well with record buyers. In 1981 she followed up with another impressive collection on Island, *Dangerous Acquaintances*.

By the mid-1980s, she had established herself as an excellent concert performer and her level-headed comments on her past and present to interviewers

contrasted sharply with the jumbled image of her earlier years. As she told one interviewer: "My reputation is the biggest obstacle I've had to overcome in my life."

FERRY, BRYAN: *See Roxy Music.*

5TH DIMENSION: *Vocal group. Members, late 1960s, early 1970s: LaMonte McLemore, born St. Louis, Missouri, September 17; Marilyn McCoo, born Jersey City, New Jersey, September 30, 1943; Ron Townson, born St. Louis, Missouri, January 24; Florence LaRue, born Plainfield, New Jersey, February 4, 1944; Billy Davis, Jr., born St. Louis, Missouri, June 26, 1940. Trish Turner replaced Florence LaRue for part of 1970. During 1970s, most original members left group. Group continued performing through 1980s with varied personnel.*

One of the most successful singing groups of the late 1960s and early 1970s, the 5th Dimension achieved stardom, as might be expected, with a style that was different. The exact nature of this difference, though, aroused considerable controversy among "experts," some of whom derogatorily accused the group of singing "white," just as country music industry people had once played down Elvis Presley as a "white man who sang colored."

Ron Townson told *Los Angeles Times* critic Robert Hilburn (July 18, 1970): "I know that some people accuse us of singing 'white,' but it makes me laugh. It is based on ignorance. People sing styles. They don't sing colors. In the 5th Dimension, we sing like we feel. I don't think we sing 'white.' You have to recognize that each member of the group brought his own style with him. For instance, there was a lot of classical work in my background. LaMonte was into jazz. Billy was into gospel and rhythm & blues. The girls were into other areas of music. All these influences are reflected in the 5th Dimension."

The resulting sound, concluded Hilburn, "to various critics and fans, is something of a cross between (a) pop and jazz, (b) pop and rhythm & blues, or (c) a sort of 'champagne soul.'"

To record buyers, obviously, it didn't matter what the group's style consisted of. The mass audience only knew that they liked it.

The two founding members of the group, LaMonte McLemore and Marilyn McCoo, met when McLemore was a photographer for the Los Angeles–based black magazine, *Elegant,* and Marilyn was a fashion model. Both had performing experience before they became acquainted. McLemore was brought up in St. Louis, where he dabbled in photography and played baseball for his high school team. He thought about a baseball career, but changed his mind after enlisting in the Army. During his service years, he became a member of the Army Drum and Bugle Corps and played for many U.S.O. shows. When he left the service, he went back to photography, selling pictures to many major magazines, including *Harper's Bazaar, Life,* and *Ebony,* from his new home base in Los Angeles.

Marilyn McCoo, daughter of a physician, started singing almost as soon as she could talk. She kept it up through elementary and high school, debuting on Art Linkletter's "Talent Scouts," TV show at 15. At 19, by then living in Los Angeles with her family, she went on "Talent Scouts" again and won the "Miss Bronze Grand Talent Award" and "Miss Congeniality."

In the early 1960s, LaMonte and Marilyn got together with two other Los Angeles friends, Harry Elston (then an advertising salesman for *Elegant)* and Floyd Butler, to form a group called the Hi-Fis. In 1963, they sang at local clubs while taking lessons from a vocal coach. In 1964, they came to the attention of Ray Charles, who took them on tour with him in 1965. (*See Charles, Ray.*) He also produced a single by the group, "Lonesome Mood," a jazz-type song that gained some local attention. However, internal disagreements caused Butler and Elston to go their own way, eventually leading to their organizing the Friends of Distinction.

LaMonte and Marilyn sought to build a new group. One of their friends was Florence LaRue, who had received training as a youngster in singing, dancing, and violin, and who also won a "Miss Bronze Grand Talent Award" from Arthur Godfrey's show in her teens. In the 1960s, she graduated from Cal. State Los Angeles with a B.A. in elementary education. When she was approached to join the new group in early 1966, she initially said no, because she had started teaching school and enjoyed it. Finally, she agreed to try it for a while to see how it went.

About the same time, LaMonte recruited an old friend of his, Ron Townson, who at age six had started singing in choirs and gospel groups in his home town of St. Louis. His grandmother fostered his career by arranging for private voice and acting lessons as he grew up. In his teens, he toured with Dorothy Dandridge and Nat "King" Cole, joined the Wings over Jordan Gospel Singers for a while, and also played a small part in the film *Porgy and Bess.* He demonstrated his considerable skill as a classical artist by placing third in the Metropolitan Opera auditions held in St. Louis. After finishing high school, he worked his way through Lincoln University in Jefferson, Missouri, by conducting the

school and church choirs. After graduating, he organized his own 25-member gospel group, the Celestial Choir.

Billy Davis, Jr., the fifth member of the 5th Dimension, is a cousin of LaMonte's who started singing in gospel choirs at an early age. Later, he saved enough money from a succession of odd jobs to buy a cocktail lounge in St. Louis. He used the lounge as a base for experimenting with various musical groups, both his own and other local bands. From this, he evolved his own rock group, the Emeralds, that played small clubs and made a few records on a small label. Later, the group changed to gospel as the Saint Gospel Singers. Billy was looking for something with wider possibilities. When he was asked to join his cousin's new group, he immediately said yes. He later married Marilyn McCoo.

The members began rehearsing in early 1966 and took the name of the Versatiles. They auditioned for Marc Gordon, who previously had headed Motown's Los Angeles office, and he agreed to manage them. He brought them to the attention of singer Johnny Rivers, who liked them and arranged to record them on his new label, Soul City Records, which was distributed by Liberty Records. (*See Rivers, Johnny.*)

Their first release, "I'll Be Lovin' You Forever," gained some attention, but their second effort, "Go Where You Wanta Go" really took off, gaining major airplay on both R&B and pop stations. By then, the group had assumed the new name 5th Dimension as better reflecting the new, "psychedelic sound" it was trying to develop. By late 1966, it was working closely with songwriter Jimmy Webb through Webb's association with Rivers. This led to their recording Webb's "Up, Up and Away," a top 10 hit in mid-1967.

In 1968, the group scored major hit singles with Laura Nyro's "Stoned Soul Picnic" and "Sweet Blindness" and a gold-record award for its album *Stoned Soul Picnic.* At the 1968 Grammy Awards, Jimmy Webb's "Up, Up and Away" won five Grammys, four for the 5th Dimension, including Best Group Performance, and one for Webb for Song of the Year. (*See Nyro, Laura; Webb, Jimmy.*)

1969 brought two number one singles in *Billboard:* "Aquarius"/"Let the Sunshine In" from the rock musical *Hair* and Nyro's composition, "Wedding Bell Blues." The group's LP *The Age of Aquarius* was also a million-dollar success. Later best-selling singles on Bell Records included the gold "One Less Bell to Answer" (1970) and top 20 "Love's Lines, Angles and Rhymes" and "Never My Love" (1971).

All the group's albums of 1970–72 on both Soul City and Bell sold well. On Soul City, *The July 5th Album* and gold *Greatest Hits* were on the charts for much of 1970. The Bell LPs *Portrait, Greatest Hits on Earth,* and *Love's Lines, Angles and Rhymes* all went gold.

As the 1970s went by, the group's success tapered off. In 1972, it had its last *Billboard* top 10 singles: "If I Could Reach You" and the gold "(Last Night) I Didn't Get to Sleep at All." In 1975, pivotal members McCoo and Davis opted for separate performing careers. Their gold album *I Hope We Get to Love in Time* (ABC, 1976) included the number one single, "You Don't Have to Be a Star," number one on Billboard charts the week of January 8, 1977. The duo hosted their own summer variety show on CBS-TV in 1977, "The Marilyn McCoo and Billy Davis, Jr., Show." The two turned out more recordings over the next decade together or as soloists (Marilyn briefly had a contact with RCA) but failed to add new hits to their credits. They remained popular performers on the night club circuit and were often guests or presenters on TV variety or award shows. For a number of years in the 1980s, Marilyn was one of the hosts of the syndicated *Solid Gold* TV program.

But the name 5th Dimension didn't fade away. With various new members, it continued to be featured regularly on the club circuit through the 1980s, including many headline shows at Las Vegas hotels. In the mid-1980s, Rhino Records released the two-disc *The 5th Dimension Anthology (1967–1973).*

FLACK, ROBERTA: *Singer, pianist. Born Asheville, North Carolina, February 10, 1939.*

In a way, Roberta Flack paid more important dues than most popular music artists on the way to belated stardom. For the better part of a decade, she taught music to hundreds of schoolchildren, turning them on to the pleasure and excitement of many kinds of musical experience from classics to blues.

Raised in a lower middle class home in Arlington, Virginia, outside the nation's capital, she started learning the piano at an early age. She also developed an excellent voice. Her teachers in high school suggested she was potentially a first-rank classical singer. In her second year at Howard University in Washington as a music major, she recalls: "I realized I wasn't going to walk out of there and onto a concert stage."

Instead, she decided to aim for a career in teaching. After earning a master's in music education, she accepted a job teaching music, math, and English in a segregated black high school in Farmville, North Carolina, in the early '60s.

The work was far from easy, but she considers it one of the most important years in her life. As she told Jack Rosenthal of *The New York Times* (March 29, 1970): "All my life I'd been used to praise for my musical ability, but that didn't mean much down there. I had to work like hell, from 7 in the morning 'til 7 at night. I crammed so much music down their throats, you wouldn't believe it. I wanted to give them so much. They'd never sung four-part harmony before. Or heard of Bach chorales. And the kids loved it. They'd come to a rehearsal even after picking tobacco all day, when they couldn't even come to school."

After a year of this, she returned to Washington, where she worked in schools in several different sections of the city during the next six years. Toward the end of the '60s, she began to pick up singing jobs on the side. This led to an engagement at a local club run by Henry Taylor. Comedian Bill Cosby heard her there and was highly impressed. By 1969, she was at Henry Yaffe's Mr. Henry's Upstairs and had become one of the best-known popular singers in Washington.

Her repertoire ranged from ballads to soul to rock. As she told Rosenthal: "I've been told I sound like Nina Simone, Nancy Wilson, Odetta, Barbra Streisand, Dionne Warwick, even Mahalia Jackson. If everybody said I sounded like one person, I'd worry. But when they say I sound like them all, I know I've got my own style."

For a while, she remained known only in her hometown. Finally, she came to the attention of Atlantic Records executives, who signed her during 1969. Late in the year, her debut LP, *First Take,* was released. It remained on the charts into early 1970. When Bill Cosby heard one of her recordings, he recalled listening to her before. He signed her for his "Third Bill Cosby Special," nationally televised by NBC in April 1970. After she completed her two numbers, viewers across the country realized they had been in on the debut of a major new star.

In the late summer, her second album, *Chapter Two,* was released, and her third LP, *Quiet Fire* (November 1970) won gold-record awards.

During the summer of 1971, she teamed with Donny Hathaway on the hit single, "You've Got a Friend." The two also joined forces on a gold album, *Roberta Flack and Donny Hathaway,* issued by Atlantic in 1972. (*See Hathaway, Donny.*) That year proved a banner one for her, providing her with her first number one single, "The First Time Ever I Saw Your Face." Roberta actually had recorded the song (written by Scottish folk artist Ewan MacColl for his wife, Peggy Seeger) on her debut LP. The song stuck in actor Clint Eastwood's memory; while working on the film *Play Misty for Me,* he got permission to use it on the soundtrack. Movie audiences also fell in love with it and record stores' requests caused Atlantic to rush out a single of the number. The song won Roberta a Grammy for Record of the

Year. In the same voting, she won another Grammy, along with Donny Hathaway, for their duet "Where Is the Love," named the Best Pop Vocal Performance by a Duo, Group or Chorus.

Roberta started off 1973 in equally impressive fashion with another number one single, "Killing Me Softly With His Song," which rose to number one in *Billboard* the week of February 24, 1973 and stayed there four more weeks. The song also served as the title number for a gold LP. It won her another Grammy for Song of the Year and also gained her the trophy for Best Pop Vocal Performance, Female. It also won a songwriters award for its creators, Norman Gimbel and Charles Fox.

In 1974, she had her third number one single, "Feel Like Makin' Love," which made it to number one in *Billboard* the week of August 19, 1974. The album for which it served as title song didn't come out until 1975, its completion slowed by a falling out with her long-time record producer, Joel Dorn, which caused her to take over production in the late stages of the project. Her decision to also produce her next album coupled with a desire to find more outlets for her energy delayed her next LP for some two years. In the interim, she completed work on a doctorate in linguistics from the University of Massachusetts-Amherst, took acting and dancing lessons, and also ran a business of her own. She also was considered for the role of Bessie Smith in a film biography that never came to fruition.

Her next album, *Blue Lights in the Basement* came out in 1977 and spent time on the charts that year and the next. It somehow didn't have the intensity of earlier LPs, though it did provide a number two single, "The Closer I Get to You," in the spring of 1978. Atlantic also issued the LP *Roberta Flack* in 1978 and the retrospective *Best of Roberta Flack* in 1981.

Later activity included teaming up with Peabo Bryson for a number of duet recordings in the early 1980s and singing title tracks for such films as *If Ever I See You Again* and *Making Love*. (In the latter case, her number actually was titled "Feel Like Makin' Love.") In 1983, she and Bryson had a top 20 single, "Tonight I Celebrate My Love." In support of the LP that contained it, Roberta and Bryson set off on her most intensive concert tour in years, visiting most of the countries in the developed world.

FLEETWOOD MAC: *Vocal and instrumental group. Original personnel, 1967, all born England: Peter Green; Jeremy Spencer, born West Hartlepool, July 4, 1948; John McVie; Mick Fleetwood, born June 24. Danny Kirwan, born England, added in 1968. Peter Green replaced in 1970 by Christine (Perfect) McVie, born England, July 12, 1944. Jeremy Spencer replaced in mid-1971 by Bob Welch, born California, July 31, 1946. Welch left in late 1974. Reorganized band in 1975 comprised John McVie, Christine McVie, Fleetwood plus Lindsey Buckingham, born Palo Alto, California, October 3, 1947; Stevie Nicks, born Phoenix, Arizona, May 26, 1948. Tour band, 1987–88, comprised John McVie, Christine McVie, Nicks, Fleetwood, Rick Vito, Billy Burnette.**

There no doubt that one of the major success stories of the mid-1970s belonged to Fleetwood Mac. The band won massive public support as indicated by runaway sales totals for such albums as *Fleetwood Mac* and *Rumours* (Album of the Year in the 1977 Grammy Awards). At the same time, it steadily improved its musicianship, which earned it deserved respect as one of the best live-performance bands in rock in the late 1970s and early 1980s.

Its achievement underlines the fact that the whole can be greater than the sum of its parts. Bassist John McVie and drummer Mick Fleetwood, though good musicians, never ranked among the best in their instrumental specialties. Nor was Christine McVie number one on keyboards, though she is an above-average pianist and certainly one of the better female vocalists around. But their talents, combined with the excellent lead guitar work of Lindsey Buckingham and the superlative vocal contributions of Stevie Nicks, provided a distinctive sound that became increasingly exciting for millions of fans around the world from the mid-1970s on. It was, though, a middle-of-the-road sound, very different from the raw blues-rock format of the original Fleetwood Mac of the 1960s.

One of the strengths that John McVie and Fleetwood (whose last names formed the group's name since its inception in 1967) rendered was continuity and, in Fleetwood's case, a stabilizing influence. They managed to keep things together and moving forward despite major changes in personnel and musical direction from the late 1960s to the mid-1970s. The early jolts resulted from the departure first of Peter Green and later Jeremy Spencer, the two acknowledged stars of the original British foursome. In fact, the original focal point was Green, who preferred the unusual step of naming the band after its rhythm section. The reason, Fleetwood told Samuel Graham, was that "Pete was very preoccupied with not becoming a superstar guitarist, which he easily could have been. He wanted to downplay his own role."

---

*Welch quote from personal interview with Irwin Stambler.

Three of the original four members of the group (John McVie, Green, and Fleetwood) gained invaluable experience as sidemen in the band of the kingpin of the British blues revival, John Mayall. (*See Mayall, John.*) Lead guitarist Green (who also played harmonica and handled vocals), joined Mayall's Bluesbreakers in 1965 as replacement for the great Eric Clapton when Eric left to join Cream. In 1967, Green (by then idolized by British rock fans) got together with Jeremy Spencer to form a new band. Spencer, one of the smallest performers in rock (under 5 feet tall), had been playing guitar since his youth and was one of the best bottleneck-style guitarists in England.

They recruited McVie from the Bluesbreakers to play bass and Fleetwood to play drums. Fleetwood was not only a highly skilled drummer, but a great asset for in-person performances. As John Mendelsohn described him in the *Los Angeles Times* in August 1970: "With abdomen-length stringy hair and comic-strip features that are perpetually frozen into a gape of unspeakable horror, this gangling chap is certainly one of modern rock and roll's truly unforgettable characters."

The foursome rapidly built up an ardent following in England and gained the charts with its debut LP, *Peter Green's Fleetwood Mac,* issued on Blue Horizon in the U.K. (1968) and Epic in the U.S. Featuring two lead guitarists in Green (whose style has been compared to American bluesman B.B. King's) and Spencer (who played blues-rock along the lines of Elmore James), the LP won high praise from English reviewers.

During 1968, the group expanded to a quintet with the addition of Danny Kirwan. A third lead guitarist, vocalist, and (like Green and Spencer), a songwriter, he was featured on the second LP issued in the U.S., *English Rose,* released on Epic. (Before that, the band put out *Mr. Wonderful,* issued in Britain only on Blue Horizon in November 1968.) *English Rose* contained an impressive series of originals by band members: "Albatross" and "Black Magic Woman" by Green, "I've Lost My Baby" and "Evenin' Boogie" by Spencer, and "One Sunny Day" and "Something inside of Me" by Kirwan.

In 1969, the band had three of the best-selling singles of the year in England. Oddly, they came out on three different labels: "Albatross" on Blue Horizon, "Man of the World" on Immediate, and "Oh Well" on Reprise. (This reflected, first, the band's moving around to several different labels in its first phase and, second, some of the tensions both internally between group members and externally with record company management.) Album releases in 1969 were *The Pious Bird of Good Omen* (issued in England on Blue Horizon in March) and *Then Play On,*

issued in both England and the U.S. on Reprise in October.

Most observers expected 1970 to be Fleetwood Mac's premier year. However, before the year was half over, the group was shaken by the departure of Peter Green for a religious commune. The band didn't break up, but righted itself by bringing in the talented Christine McVie, John's wife, who had been a member of Chicken Shack before taking up a housewife's role for a while. On tour in California, however, another blow occurred. Jeremy Spencer became a member of a religious sect that required denial of all other ties. Bowing to the demands of the order, he quit the band. While all this turmoil ensued, the act was represented by several live or reissued LPs in 1970–71, including *Blues Jam in Chicago, Volumes 1 and 2* (issued on Blue Horizon in 1970), *Fleetwood Mac in Chicago* (Blue Horizon, 1970), and *Kiln House* (Reprise 1970).

For many months after Spencer's departure, the remaining members tried to keep the band going. It finally brought in the first non-Englishman, Bob Welch, in Spencer's place. Born and raised in California, Welch played much of the late 1960s with a show band in Las Vegas that backed such artists as James Brown, Aretha Franklin, and Fontella Bass. The band broke up in mid-1969 and Bob and two other members moved to Paris, France, from where they sallied forth to play engagements in many parts of Europe. A mutual friend recommended him to Fleetwood Mac. Almost effortlessly, the reorganized group took off from where it left off, winning renewed acclaim for the Reprise LPs *Future Games* (1971) and *Bare Trees* (1972). Reprise also put out the somewhat less effective *Penguin* and *Mystery to Me* (1973) and *Heroes Are Hard to Find* (1974). Reissues of those years included Epic's two-disc *Black Magic Woman* (a 1971 repackage of the first two U.S. LPs) and *Fleetwood Mac/English Rose* (1974). Sire also issued the retrospective *Vintage Years* in 1975.

During 1974, with the majority of members now calling Los Angeles home, new problems caused another reorganization. John, Mick, and Christine kept a stiff upper lip while riding out management difficulties that so depressed Welch that he resigned at the end of 1974. That turned out to be a blessing in disguise for the band (though Welch had contributed many fine songs to that phase of Mac's history, such as "Revelation," "Night Watch," and "Hypnotized") because it led to the introduction of the musical and songwriting artistry of two other Americans, Lindsey Buckingham and Stevie Nicks, who as a duo had released *Buckingham Nicks* on Polydor.

Welch himself agreed the change played a key role in the band's transition from a middle-level group to a supergroup. "I don't think the band would have had the success it had had I stayed with it. I felt they became successful for very apparent reasons. First of all, the music they were writing; I never wrote music that was as accessible and commercial as Stevie and Lindsey wrote. . . . The other reason is the stage show. When I was with the band, the stage show was never as dynamic or exciting as it is with Stevie and Lindsey with the band. And everybody else too. Those two people combined to make the package just that much more appealing."

The truth of that was demonstrated with the new alignment's first Reprise album, *Fleetwood Mac* (1975). It had such notable songs as "Over My Head" (the first single release) and "Say You Love Me." Stevie's composition "Rhiannon" not only emphasized her writing skills, but became a highlight of concerts where her vibrant, emotionally compelling renditions confirmed her as one of the first-rank female rock singers of the decade. Buckingham's contributions came into strong focus on the *Rumours* album (issued on Warner Brothers in 1977), where his "Second Hand News" and "Go Your Own Way" (two of a series of songs reflecting the emotional problems besetting the band's two couples then) were highlights, though no more so than Stevie's "Dreams" and Christine McVie's "Songbird" and "You Make Loving Fun." The tone of Christine's contributions was surprisingly positive, considering the breakup of her marriage to John. At the same time, Nicks and Buckingham had to cope with the end of their long relationship.

Facets of those situations were explored and interpreted with telling impact in *Rumours*. As John McVie said after accepting the Grammy for the LP in early 1978: "A lot of our personal lives came through on the disc. The theme, perhaps, was one of pain." Through their tears, the band members could smile about the tremendous commercial and critical impact of the album. It remained on the charts for several years. "Dreams" rose to number one on *Billboard* singles charts the week of June 18, 1977.

Some observers wondered whether history would repeat itself with another band reshuffling. This time, though, the group's five individuals decided to continue on a professional level even with the reminders of personal trauma. The result was the two-disc *Tusk* (Warner Brothers, 1979). Mick Fleetwood was asked whether the group was fazed at trying to top its *Rumours* album, which had sold over 20 million copies worldwide. He responded that they only concerned themselves with making *Tusk* as good as they could make it.

The album showed the band members weren't afraid to experiment with new directions. The tracks featured unusual rhythmic patterns, including African ones, a considerable change from the *Rumours* songs. Though not coming close to the phenomenal sales levels of *Rumours*, the LP won a platinum award, while the title song and "Sara" made the top 10 as well. The tour to promote the album provided material for the two-disc *Fleetwood Mac Live* (Warner Brothers, early 1981).

In the early 1980s, though the band recorded some new material and demonstrated continued success as a concert act, its members seemed increasingly interested in individual goals. Stevie Nicks and Lindsey Buckingham already were working on solo projects when the Fleetwood Mac LP *Mirage* came out on Warner Brothers in 1982. Buckingham's debut LP, *Law and Order*, came out on Elektra Records in November 1981 to be followed by other solo efforts later in the decade such as *Go Insane* on Elektra in 1984. By then he also had earned credentials as a record producer both for some of his own material and for other artists, including sessions for folk rock veteran John Stewart that resulted in the latter's first hit album in years, *Bombs Away Dream Babies*, from which the 1979 single success, "Gold," was taken. Mick Fleetwood made his solo debut in June 1981 with *The Visitor* on RCA Records. (For Nicks' solo projects, see *Nicks, Stevie*.)

Christine's solo debut with Warner Brothers, *Christine McVie*, came out in January 1984. While no one would say that Fleetwood Mac had finally finished its course, during the mid-1980s, the only new concerts were given by individual members such as Nicks and Christine McVie, both of whom achieved considerable success on their own.

Just about the time many fans were giving up hope for a Fleetwood Mac revival, the group surfaced with an exciting new album, *Tango in the Night*, released by Warner Brothers in April 1987. In a short time the album was in the Top 10 in the U.S. as well as Canada, Australia, England, and West Germany. Lindsey Buckingham was with the band for the album recording sessions, but when plans for the 1987–88 concert tour were announced, his name was conspicuously absent. Joining the remaining four Mac regulars were guitarists Rick Vito and Billy Burnette.

The indications were that Buckingham's work on *Tango* constituted his farewell efforts. He told Robert Hilburn of the *Los Angeles Times* (Calendar, June 14, 1987), "I would not have wanted to leave the group on the ambiguous note that *Mirage* sounded. There were lots of things left hanging out on limbs. . . , finances, emotions. I think there was also some pride at stake.

"This band has done some remarkable things and *Mirage* was no way to say goodbye. I think we had something to prove and we did it in the new album. So it now feels like the time."

FLEETWOODS, THE: *Vocal group. Gretchen Diane Christopher, born Olympia, Washington, February 29, 1940; Barbara Laine Ellis, born Olympia, Washington, February 20, 1940; Gary Robert Troxel, born Centralia, Washington, November 28, 1939.*

The Fleetwoods literally started at the top when its members were still in their teens and then slowly wound down. The group maintained its popularity for half a decade, but had a declining effect on the record buying public as the 1960s passed.

Gretchen Christopher, Barbara Ellis, and Gary Troxel all were born and raised in Washington. In their late teens, having met in school, they formed a trio to sing for local dances and parties, sometimes using well-known songs and sometimes doing their own compositions.

In 1958, they prepared demonstration records of one of their songs, "Come Softly to Me," and gained an audition with Dolton Records. Dolton recorded the number. The dreamy single moved to number one on the charts for four weeks beginning on April 13, 1959 and gained the trio its first gold record. In November 1959, they scored with another number one smash, "Mr. Blue," which sold over a million copies in the U.S. and also was a hit in England.

The Fleetwoods placed a number of songs on the hit charts in the early part of the next decade, but none reached the levels of their 1959 successes. They broke up in the second half of the '60s.

The group was represented by a number of albums and achieved total LP sales of several million. Their credits included, on Dolton, *Mr. Blue* (1959), *Deep in a Dream* (1961), *Goodies of Oldies* and *Greatest Hits* (1962), *Lovers by Night* (1963), and *Folk Rock* (1966), plus, on the Sunset Records label, *In a Mellow Mood* (1966).

The group broke up in 1966 and Gary took a job as a longshoreman, an occupation he still pursued in the late 1980s. In between, though, the trio reassembled on several occasions. In 1971 they reunited for four concerts at the New York Academy of Music that drew large audiences and encouraged them to add more concerts to their schedule through 1973. After separating again, they reformed the group in the mid-1980s for an appearance at the Bumbershoot Festival in Seattle, Washington. Meanwhile Gretchen helped edit a new album of newly discovered outtakes from their Dolton sessions. Liberty, which had bought out Dolton, released the LP, *Buried Treasures,* in the mid-1980s.

FLYING BURRITO BROTHERS, THE: *See Byrds, The; Parsons, Gram.*

FLO AND EDDIE: *See Mothers of Invention, The; Turtles, The.*

FOGERTY, JOHN: *Singer, pianist, guitarist, keyboards player, band leader (CREEDENCE CLEARWATER REVIVAL), songwriter. Born Berkeley, California, May 28, 1945.*

For a while, John Fogerty, who made Creedence Clearwater Revival one of the most popular bands in rock in the early 1970s, was setting more records in legal annals than in the studio. After he broke with the other members of Creedence over artistic direction in October 1972 and with their label, Fantasy, soon after, he became embroiled in legal battles that he said severely hampered his ability to continue his songwriting and performing career. During one nine-year stretch from the mid-1970s to mid-1980s, he did not have a new album in circulation. Under those circumstances, industry experts were astounded when Fogerty came back in the mid-1980s with new solo LPs as challenging and exciting as vintage Creedence offerings. (*See Creedence Clearwater Revival.*)

The pressures bred by Creedence's success were reflected by the decision of John's brother, Tom, to leave the band in February 1971 to pursue a solo career. The remaining members initially agreed to keep the band going as a trio, but in October 1972, the breakup of the trio was announced.

Fogerty then began a solo project in which he recorded all the instruments and vocals for a mythical band called the Blue Ridge Rangers. The material comprised country, R&B, and gospel classics that had inspired Creedence. It provided two hit singles in 1973: remakes of Hank Williams' country "Jambalaya" and Otis Williams and the Charms' doo-wop "Hearts of Stone." The exciting LP, *Blue Ridge Rangers,* issued on Fantasy in May 1973, was also a hit.

But before the year was out, John had become upset about many aspects of his affiliation with Fantasy. He felt the company hadn't supported his solo LP properly and had other objections about matters such as distribution and royalties. He wanted a release from his contract, but Fantasy had the rights for eight more albums from him. He refused to record new material and things remained at an impasse until David Geffen and Asylum Records worked out a reported $1 million deal with Fantasy allowing Fogerty to record on Asylum with Fantasy retaining overseas rights while Asylum had U.S. and Canadian rights. That did not void other legal battles, including one Fogerty and his old band mates eventually filed against their accounting firm, claiming it had not properly protected their investments.

John then went back into the studios and turned out an excellent new solo LP, *John Fogerty* (Asylum, 1975). Among its tracks were such notable songs as "Almost Saturday Night," "Rockin' all over the World," and "The Wall." However, the psychological trauma of continued legal skirmishing caught up with John and his efforts to assemble new material for a follow-up album were so far below his standards that Asylum cautioned against releasing them. Fogerty decided it would be best to wait until his legal problems were resolved before trying to pick up his career full-tilt again.

It turned out to be a long wait, a hiatus that took almost a decade. In early 1985, Robert Palmer asked him if it really had been necessary for Fogerty to maintain creative silence that long (*The New York Times*, January 16, 1985). Fogerty replied: "For a lot of that time, I was thwarted from doing what I wanted to do by legal and financial entanglements with Fantasy Records. During the early stage, I owed them so much product, it was going to take me something like 20 years to live up to it, and then much later, after I had freed myself from that, I was still tied to them financially. You can't be really creative in that sort of situation; the ability to do it just leaves you."

Thus, he said, he went back to working on developing the sound of his "mythical band" while "lawyers and accountants helped things drag on forever. It just didn't seem to be moving forward, and I had to do something to keep from going nuts. My mind didn't really get free from it until last year, when a trial went in our favor; that really kind of opened me up. The songs started to flow then, and I knew I was on the way."

(The lawsuit referred to had been filed in May 1978 against the Oakland accounting Firm of Edward J. Arnold Accountancy Corp., alleging the firm had failed to properly protect Creedence investments worth about $5 million. In the 1983 decision, the court awarded John $4.1 million with the other three band members awarded about $1.5 million each. However, the corporation still had the right to appeal the decision.)

In 1984, Fogerty began working up tracks for his comeback album, issued by Warner Brothers at the start of 1985. Called *Centerfield,* it proved a sensation with both critics and record buyers. Right off the bat, it provided a hit single, "The Old Man down the Road," while the LP itself became a number one chart hit. The album also included hard-driving rockers "Mr. Greed" and "Vanz Can't Danze," which seemed thinly veiled taunts against Saul Zaentz, head of Fantasy Records. By 1986, Zaentz had responded with a $142 million lawsuit claiming he had been slandered and libeled by *Centerfield* lyrics as well as by statements Fogerty had made in 1985 interviews. Fantasy also filed another suit claiming it was entitled to profits from the single "The Old Man Down the Road," asserting the song infringed on the copyright of a song Fogerty wrote for Creedence, "Run through the Jungle."

In September 1986, Fogerty had a second Warner Brothers album, *Eye of the Zombie.* With the collection, he felt he had enough new material to justify intensive live performances. The cheering crowds that greeted him around the country hungered for him to sing some of the Creedence classics, but he would not do it.

He told Palmer: "I just couldn't do these. I know those songs made a lot of people happy, and I'm very proud of that body of work, glad that people continue to like it. But with what happened to me, legally and financially, as a result of it . . . well, it just leaves me with a kind of bitter taste."

FOGHAT: *Vocal and instrumental group. Original members, early 1970s, all from England: Dave Peverett, born 1950; Rod Price, born c. late 1940s; Roger Earl, born 1949; Tony Stevens. Stevens replaced in 1975 by Nick Jameson, born England. Jameson replaced in 1976 by Craig MacGregor, born southern California.*

In the 1970s and 1980s, Foghat could lay claim to being one of the last of the blues-rock English bands that had been a dominant force in the country's pop music scene in the 1960s. That had both advantages and disadvantages. On the one hand, the band's energetic stage shows made it a favorite of the still large audience for blues-rock. Conversely, it was somewhat outside the mainstream of rock's developments of the post-1960s and was looked upon by most critics and some fans as something of a dinosaur.

Typical of many critics' evaluation was Terry Atkinson's (*Los Angeles Times*, April 1978) review of a Foghat concert at the Los Angeles Forum. Foghat's "music is typical of the blues-based hard-rock school in both its slashing energy and its mindlessness. The group's records are efficient exercises, but they don't bear close study. Their superficial sound is fun enough, but underneath lie derivative melodies and vacuous lyrics. In live performance, however, the band knows how to move an audience of hard-rock afficionados with throbbing beats and energetic delivery."

In defense of the group, lead singer Dave Peverett told another *Times* reporter, Dennis Hunt: "We don't mind being called a boogie band, because we do play that kind of music, but we do mind when people call us a boogie band and intend it as a negative comment. Most often that term does have negative connotations. People who think we're nothing but a boogie band probably haven't really listened to our recordings."

But he insisted that blues-rock/R&B rock was not necessarily limiting. "I guess you could say we're diverse within our area. We don't stray too far from blues-rock. We really like it and so we stick to it. . . . For instance, we would never get into something like classical rock."

All of the founding members had strong credentials from the '60s British blues-rock craze. Peverett became a fan of such U.S. artists as Chuck Berry and Little Richard when he was nine. Before long, he talked his father into getting him a guitar. He played with a number of school-based bands in his early teens before joining the Cross Ties Blues Band, where he met another performer of note, Chris Youlden. In the mid-1960s, after a brief stint with Les Questions, a group based in Switzerland, both joined Savoy Brown in 1967. Peverett, who took the nickname "Lonesome Dave," primarily played guitar in that blues-rock band, but he also did some vocalizing.

Tony Outeda, later manager of Foghat, recalled working for promoters of a U.S. tour of Savoy Brown and the group Family. "Originally we thought that Family was going to be the high point of the show, but it turned out to be Savoy Brown, and the high point of their show, the song that always brought the house down, was the song Dave sang, 'Louisiana Blues.' I knew then who the real star was."

Peverett met future Foghat members Tony Stevens and Roger Early in Savoy Brown. Stevens, like the others an alumnus of a number of English blues-rock groups, was bass guitarist in the late 1960s. Earl, who had joined the band in 1967, handled drums.

Earl got his first drum kit at 15 (when he also left school for good). He listed Little Richard, Chuck Berry, and Jerry Lee Lewis as among his early idols. He tried to work out drum patterns as a boy using a fork and knife. Later he took drum lessons for two years. For a while in the mid-1960s, he worked as a commercial artist by day and picked up performing jobs at night. At one point he auditioned for a job with Jimi Hendrix, but "froze." "The audition frightened me to death. I couldn't play a note. I had never heard anybody play guitar like that."

Earl, Peverett, and Stevens remained with Savoy Brown for several years, but at the end of 1970, Savoy Brown leader Kim Simmonds broke up the band in order to form a new one. The reason he did that, he told reporters, was a difference in opinion among band members about future directions.

Set adrift, Peverett, Earl, and Stevens put together their own band, taking the name Foghat after a cartoon character named Luther Foghat, and bringing in guitarist Rod Price to round out the quartet. Price, who was early impressed by such blues performers as Muddy Waters and Robert Johnson, eventually became adept at both electric and slide guitar. During the 1960s, he was a member of a number of English blues bands, including Shakey Vic's Big City Blues Band and Black Cat Bones. While with Shakey Vic, he became acquainted with Peverett. For a while at the end of the 1960s and into 1970, he had to work at nonmusic jobs to earn enough to live. He was working as a wine truck driver when he saw an ad in *Melody Maker* placed by the other founders of Foghat and, after auditioning, was welcomed aboard.

The new quartet eventually sought out Tony Outeda to manage them. He lined up a recording contract with U.S.-based Bearsville Records, a label founded by Albert Grossman (who had managed numerous U.S. folk-rock and rock stars of the 1960s and early 1970s, including Bob Dylan and Janis Joplin). Like many new bands, the group established its reputation in the early 1970s through intensive touring, mostly as an opening act for better-known bands. The band's first tour of the U.S. was a low-budget affair in which Outeda was, in effect, the band's roadie. Because of a delay in obtaining visas, the group couldn't legally play for pay for a while, so its first concert (in Oshkosh, Wisconsin) was for free. Peverett recalled: "We had been hidden away in rehearsals for a year and a half and had no idea of whether we were good or bad. When we got three encores, we figured we were good."

The band's debut LP, *Foghat (Rock & Roll)*, produced by roots-rock artist Dave Edmunds, came out on Bearsville in 1972. (*See Edmunds, Dave.*) It was followed by *Foghat* (1973) and *Energized* (1974). With strong tour and promotional support from Bearsville, that album (like those before and after distributed in the U.S. by Warner Brothers) brought the group its first gold-record-album award from the RIAA. *Rock and Roll Outlaws* (1974) also went past gold-record levels. *Fool for the City* (1975) went platinum.

During 1975, Tony Stevens left and was replaced on bass guitar by Nick Jameson, who had produced the *Fool for the City* and *Rock and Roll Outlaws* albums. Jameson decided he preferred working as a solo artist and was replaced on bass in 1976 by Craig MacGregor.

MacGregor, who had been playing cover songs in bar bands for 14 years before joining Foghat, was the son of a music teacher. Growing up in southern California, he had been influenced by R&B and surf and drag racing rock songs. His father first taught him to play cornet, but then switched Craig to piano lessons. After two years of that, he tried drums and then took up bass guitar in 1965. Among the many bands he had worked with, the one he left with least regret was Swan, his pre-Foghat affiliation. MacGregor's recording debut with his new band was on the 1976 Bearsville/Warner *Night Shift*, which brought still another gold-record certification for the group.

Later releases included its first concert LP, the platinum *Foghat Live* (1977) and the gold *Stone Blue* (1978). Then came *Boogie Motel* (1979), *Tight Shoes* (1980), and *Girls to Chat and Boys to Bounce* (1981). On many of those, Peverett, besides handling lead vocals, also provided original songs. On *Tight Shoes*, for instance, he supplied eight compositions, including "Stranger in My Home Town," "Full Time Lover," "Dead End Street," and "No Hard Feelings."

After the death in 1987 of Bearsville founder Grossman, Rhino Recorsd reissued the Foghat catalogue under a licensing agreement for the U.S. that covered the entire Bearsville label.

FOREIGNER: *Vocal and instrumental group. Original members: Mick Jones, born London, England, December 27, 1944; Ian McDonald, born London, England, June 25, 1946; Lou Gramm, born Rochester, New York, May 2, 1950; Al Greenwood, born New York, New York; Dennis Elliott, born London, England, August 18, 1950; Ed Gagliardi, born U.S. Gagliardi replaced in 1980 by Rick Wills, born England. Greenwood also left in 1980.*

When Foreigner became one of the success stories of 1977, many observers compared it with such other notable first-time-hit groups of the mid-1970s as Heart and Boston. However, what some overlooked was the fact that the others were, in fact, rock'n'roll novices whereas Foreigner's roster was comprised of veteran musicians with considerable experience with both previous groups and session work. Perhaps due to that, Foreigner was able to sustain its momentum in its follow-up efforts at a somewhat higher level than some more novice organizations.

Of course, as one of the band's founders, Mick Jones, emphasized, such comparisons were too glib anyway. "We're not trying to copy Boston," he told an interviewer in 1977, "and Atlantic Records wasn't looking for another Boston when they signed us last year. We're not really like them. We were looking for our sound and we found it. And it's not the Boston sound."

The band in its initial form was made of three English and three American musicians. That is a bit misleading, however. By the time Jones set about forming a new group, abetted mainly by fellow Englishman Ian McDonald, both had been living and working in the New York environment for several years. The third Englishman in the 1977 band, Dennis Elliott, also was in residence in New York City at the time. The insight this provided into the U.S. rock scene helped the new band gain a leg up with American fans before the band's success was extended back across the Atlantic.

Jones became a rock musician in his early teens, starting his professional career with Nero and the Gladiators. A tour of France with that band led to a new job as backing musician and songwriter for French pop star Johnny Halliday. After several years in France, he moved home base back to England, where he wrote and performed with American star Gary Wright, who previously had been a member of Spooky Tooth. Wright and Jones formed the band Wonderwheel and then were lured into a new Spooky Tooth alignment with which they stayed for 2½ years in the early 1970s.

It was a frustrating time, Jones told Dennis Hunt of the *Los Angeles Times* July 3, 1977. "That experience was ruined because there were lots of greedy people involved on the executive level. There was not a lot of consideration for the creative side of what we were doing." But the band had an important unexpected positive impact on his career when the members decided to settle in New York a short while before it broke up.

In New York, Jones first tried to pick up his career by joining the Leslie West band. This arrangement fell apart in early 1976. Jones told Hunt: "I was at a low point emotionally. I had lost a lot of faith in people and groups. I was confused and quite depressed at that time. My wife gave me a lot of strength and support which really helped to pull me through that period. Suddenly, almost overnight, I snapped out of it. Songs that were lurking about in my head came out of it and they were OK."

As he felt his creative juices flowing, Mick sought out other artists to help make some demo tapes. He first brought in keyboards player Al Greenwood, who had been with the group Storm and, when Jones approached him, was working with a Brooklyn-based band of his own. Jones then sought out Ian McDonald, whose credentials included membership in the first successful King Crimson band, a short association with U.K. artist Michael Giles in the early 1970s that led to the 1971 LP *McDonald and Giles,* and a move from England to the U.S. in the mid-1970s, where he concentrated on session playing and record production. (*See King Crimson.*)

Ian and Mick had first met in early 1976, when both were backing musicians for a solo project of one-time Stories bandsman Ian Lloyd. As Jones felt increasingly confident about his growing backlog of new songs, he remembered McDonald and contacted him.

At the time, Jones noted, he hadn't firmed up his plans in his own mind. "I didn't know what scale I was going to do it on—whether it was going to be a band with well-known names, just a name band, or whether to try and do something really quite original and use people that were unknown to a certain extent."

He wasn't certain at the start whether to assemble a permanent band. "It could have been just my doing a studio album, doing my songs in another setting apart from a group setting. It was only within the space of a few weeks that it became a group and I thought—I don't want to do a studio album with guest appearances and stuff like that."

Once the sessions began, the chemistry between Mick and Ian developed rapidly and both became excited about prospects for a touring band. Before long, they had a six-man group with the addition of a third U.K. musician, Dennis Elliott, and two more Americans, Lou Gramm and Ed Gagliardi. The group now consisted of Jones on lead guitar and vocals; McDonald on guitars, keyboards, horns, and vocals; Gramm on lead vocals; Greenwood on keyboards and synthesizer; Gagliardi on bass guitar; and Elliott on drums. Gramm had been with Black Sheep, which recorded two LPs during 1974–75; Elliott had played with many U.K. groups, going back to his first professional work with the Chevelles in 1966 and continuing through the Roy Young band, Brett Marvin and the Thunderbolts, and backing work for Ian Hunter that helped bring him to New York. Gagliardi had been with several U.S. groups.

Atlantic Records agreed to handle the band and Ian and Mick helped co-produce the first disc, *Foreigner* (1977). The album was certified gold by the RIAA in May and, as the year went by it had two top ten singles: "Feels Like the First Time" and "Cold as Ice." The LP eventually sold some 4 million copies worldwide.

The various media polls and critics' lists for 1977 brought a bonanza of awards. *Rolling Stone* readers voted the group number one Brand New Artists. *Circus* readers also tabbed it the number one Best New Group, as did *Creem*'s. The band was a finalist in the Grammy Awards' Best New Artist category. All three record-industry trade magazines listed the band at the number one spot in major classifications: *Billboard* in Pop New Artist (LPs and Singles combined), New Pop Albums Duos/Groups, New Pop Singles Duos/Group, and New Pop Album Artists; *Cash Box* in New Artists and New Group, both singles and albums; and *Record World* in New Male Group, pop albums and singles, Special Achievement—Album Category, and Top FM Pick.

By late 1977, the band was in the studio again working on its follow-up LP, *Double Vision,* with Ian, Mick, and Keith Olsen in charge of production. Mick was main songwriter with some contributions from McDonald and other bandsmen. Foreigner then embarked on its "Around the World in 42 Days" tour, which started off before 300,000 people at the California Jam II festival and continued on to Japan, Hong Kong, Australia, Greece, and Germany. After that, the band returned for final work on *Double Vision,* which was released on June 20, a week after the first single from the LP, "Hot Blooded," came out. The album was certified platinum by the RIAA within days of its release, accounting for over 5 million copies sold in the U.S. alone. The "Hot Blooded" single was certified gold in September 1978. Two months later, another single, the album's title song, won similar accreditation. Late in the year, the single "Blue Morning, Blue Day" was high on the charts, staying on them well into 1979.

In early 1979, the group had its first personnel change when Gagliardi was replaced on bass guitar by U.K.-born Rick Wills. Jones said at the time: "It was a tough decision. It was a group decision, too. He's not a bad bass player. We just wanted to go in a harder rock direction and we needed someone who could do that sort of thing better in the studio and on the stage. He was fine for what we had been doing, but he didn't fit into the new sound. It was a bad period for us. Getting a new bass player put us about two months behind schedule. . . . It was a matter of putting friendship aside for the good of the band. I like to think he's a friend."

Wills had performed with David Gilmour before Gilmour joined Pink Floyd and with Joker's Wild, Little Women (with Jerry Shirley of Humble Pie fame), and Plastic Penny (later known as Cochise). He backed Peter Frampton for 2½ years in the early 1970s before getting a spot with the Roxy Music tour band in 1975. He then replaced Ronnie Lane in Small Faces, contributing to two LPs and several major tours before leaving in late 1978. (*See Faces; Roxy Music.*) He had met Mick Jones in France in the late '60s and just happened to be in New York on a business trip in early 1979 when a friend informed him of Foreigner's need for a bass player. He borrowed a bass from friend Jerry Shirley, auditioned, and three weeks later, after he'd returned to England, he got a summons to fly back to New York right away.

He there joined the five others in recording material for the new album, *Head Games* (1979), a multi-platinum-seller that provided three hit singles during 1979–80: the title song, "Dirty White Boy," and "Women."

The band's fourth album, *Foreigner 4,* made number one on the *Billboard* charts on December 10, 1981. Two top 10 singles from the album were "Urgent" and the gold "Waiting for a Girl Like You."

The band's fifth LP on Atlantic, a retrospective *The Best of Foreigner* (also called *Foreigner Records*) (1982) eventually won another platinum-record award from the RIAA.

In 1985, it put out the gold album *Agent Provocateur* from which four chart hit singles were culled. The most successful of those was the initial single release, Mick Jones' composition "I Want to Know What Love Is." Released late in 1984, the disc made number one on *Billboard*'s list the week of February 2, 1985—Foreigner's first number one single, its best previous showings being the number two "Double Vision" in November 1978 and "Waiting for a Girl Like You" in November 1981).

Asked whether the success of the last named disc, also a ballad, had influenced the decision on the initial single from the 1985 album, Jones answered in the negative. He told Paul Grein of *Billboard,* such an interpretation by fans "was the one thing I was sort of dubious about—the fact that people might think we'd gone soft or something. I certainly want to retain the rock image. We just put this out because the song was so strong, and because it was coming out at Christmas and it had the right kind of mood."

Atlantic released the album *Inside Information* in late 1987. Paced by some excellent lead vocals by Gramm, it ranked with the best collections the group had turned out in its career. The album yielded "Say You Will," a top 10 hit in early 1988.

FOUR SEASONS, THE; FRANKIE VALLI AND THE FOUR SEASONS: *Vocal and instrumental group. Original members, mid-1960s: Frankie Valli, born Newark, New Jersey, May 3, 1937; Bob Gaudio, born Bronx, New York, November 17, 1942; Tommy de Vito, born Belleville, New Jersey, June 19, 1935; Nick Massi, born Newark, New Jersey, September 19, 1935. Massi replaced by Joe Long in late 1960s. Members, mid-1970s: Valli, Gerry Polci, John Paiva, Don Ciccone, Lee Shapiro.*

The Four Seasons rank as one of the most successful groups of the 1960s. They retained a strong following for almost the entire decade, as evidenced by their estimated total single sales from 1962–1970 of 50 million copies worldwide and 29 songs that made the best-seller charts. The latter included five singles that rose to number one on *Billboard* lists: "Sherry" (five weeks starting September 15, 1962), "Big Girls Don't Cry" (five weeks starting November 17, 1962), "Walk Like a Man" (March 2–16, 1963), "Rag Doll" (July 18 and 25, 1964), and "December 1963 (Oh What a Night)" (March 13 and 20, 1976). Valli made the top spot twice as a soloist with "My Eyes Adored You" (March 22, 1975) and "Grease" (August 26 and September 2, 1978).

All the original members were born and raised in the New York–New Jersey area. They each started performing with friends in their teens in the prerock era and moved into music as professionals in the early 1950s. Vocalist Frankie Valli (born Francis Castelluccio) had begun recording as a soloist in his teens before joining the Variatones, soon renamed the Four Lovers, which was the forerunner of the Four Seasons. (His first solo single was the 1953 disc "My Mother's Eyes" on which he used the name Frankie Valley). Other members of the original Four Lovers were Nick de Vito, Tommy de Vito (who sang baritone and played guitar) and Hank Majewski, who was replaced by Hugh Garrity, who later gave way to Nick Massi, who played bass and did much of the group's vocal arrangements.

The Four Lovers seemed to be going nowhere in particular at the start of the '60s when record producer Bob Crewe took an interest in them. He felt they had great potential, but needed a change in style and material. To achieve this, he helped bring Bob Gaudio in as a group member. Gaudio, a keyboards player and talented songwriter, had appeared with a number of rock groups, including the Royal Teens (who recorded the 1958 rock classic "Short Shorts"). Crewe also suggested a name change to the Four Seasons.

Soon after the reorganization, Gaudio provided the group with an original composition titled "Sherry." Recorded for Vee Jay, it earned the group its first gold record. The group followed up with another million-seller in 1962, "Big Girls Don't Cry," co-written by Gaudio and Crewe. Late in the year, the two wrote "Walk Like a Man," which was number one in March 1963 and gained gold-record status.

In 1964, they moved to a new record label, Philips, and continued their winning ways with the number one hit (July 1964), "Rag Doll," and the near-million-seller "Dawn Go Away." In 1966, they had four more top 10 singles: "Let's Hang On!", "Working My Way Back to You," "I've Got You under My Skin," and "Tell It to the Rain."

The group also became one of Philips Records' most successful LP acts, with each of their releases during the '60s selling 100,000 copies or better and several achieving gold-record levels. Among their credits on the label were *Born to Wander, Dawn Go Away,* and *Rag Doll* (1964); *4 Seasons Entertain You* (1965); *Gold Vault of Hits* and *Working My Way Back* (1966) and *Lookin' Back, Second Gold Vault of Hits,* and *New Gold Hits* (1967). In 1968, the group devoted much of their energy to the album *Genuine Imitation Life Gazette,* featuring complex packaging arrangement with an eight-page "newspaper" insert. The release received widespread publicity for its unusual format, but fell short of expectations as far as public response was concerned.

In May 1970, the LP *Half and Half* gained the lower levels of the best-seller lists, but the indications seemed clear that the group's popularity had declined with the record-buying public. However, they remained one of the best-received acts in club and college engagements, billed by that time as Frankie Valli and the Four Seasons. This name reflected Valli's success as a solo artist that gained him a number of chart hits, including his gold 1967 "Can't Take My Eyes off of You."

In 1970, the Four Seasons signed with a new label, Motown, where the group remained until 1973 with minimal results. The group's debut on the label, *Chameleon,* came out in 1972 on the MoWest label, but didn't get much promotional help because other projects occupied the attention of company executives. After the contract expired, Crewe, Gaudio, and Valli bought back one track that featured Valli, "My Eyes Adored You" (co-written by Crewe and Kenny Nolan). Issued several years later, in 1975, on the Private Stock label, the single brought Frankie his first number one hit on *Billboard* charts. The following year, Gaudio helped engineer a number one hit for the Four Seasons, this time on the Warner/Curb label. It was a song he co-wrote with Judy Parker (eventually Mrs. Gaudio) titled "December, 1963 (Oh What a Night)." It went on to become what group representatives said was its best-seller ever on a worldwide basis, even providing Valli and company with their first number one British chart hit. Except for Valli (and Gaudio, who played backing keyboards on the recording), the Four Seasons were completely different from the 1960s group. The group members were Gerry Polci on drums and co-lead vocals, Don Ciccone on bass, John Paiva on guitar, and Lee Shapiro on keyboards.

From an album standpoint, the 1970s weren't spectacular for the group. LPs included the *Four Seasons Story* on Private Stock and *Who Loves You* on Warner Brothers (both issued in 1975) and *Helicon* on Warner Brothers (1977). By the end of the decade, the group was without a recording contract although Valli had solo arrangements into the start of the 1980s. As a soloist, Frankie had a number hit in 1978 with his single on RSO Records of the theme song from the film *Grease*. The disc rose to number one in *Billboard* in late August 1978. Its success helped win new contracts, first from Warner Brothers and later from MCA. However, his releases on those labels, including *Frankie Valli Is the Word* (Warner Brothers, 1978), *The Very Best of Frankie Valli* (MCA, 1979), and *Heaven above Me* (MCA, 1981), were not successful.

Though Frankie was without a solo contract in 1982–83, he and the Four Seasons remained popular on the concert circuit thanks to nostalgia about 1960s music. He remained confident things would turn around on the record front as well. He told an interviewer in late 1983: "I don't get too upset over [slumps]. They're part of the business. I've been in this business long enough to expect them and to know how to deal with them."

Indeed, the group was back in the recording studios not long after to record a single with the Beach Boys, *East Meets West.*

In 1987, Rhino Records put out the four-disc *Frankie Valli and the 4 Seasons: 25th Anniversary Collection* with vintage tracks by the quartet and Valli's solos, plus a reissue of Philips' *The 4 Seasons' Christmas Album.*

FOUR TOPS, THE: *Vocal and dance group. All born Detroit, Michigan: Renaldo Benson, born 1947; Levi Stubbs, Abdul Fakir, Lawrence Payton, all born late 1930s.*

Much of the success of Berry Gordy, Jr.'s, Motown Records empire was based on his ability to find relatively new, untried talent, such as the Supremes, Smokey Robinson and the Miracles, and Martha Reeves. However, more than a few of the superstars on the roster by the late 1960s were people who had gained considerable show business experience without achieving recording breakthroughs. A prime example is the Four Tops, who spent almost a decade learning their trade before reaching stardom with Motown.

All of the group members were born and raised in Motown's home city of Detroit and all began singing at an early age, though they didn't come together as a group until several years after each finished high school. Two of them, Abdul Fakir and Lawrence Payton, were excellent athletes in high school and gave some thought to trying for sports careers at the time. Levi Stubbs, Jr., though, had no doubts about what he wanted to do after he won an amateur contest when he was 12.

The four of them had performed with various local groups before they got together in 1954 to form a quartet called the Four Aims. They auditioned for several talent agencies and finally were accepted by one that booked them into small clubs in such cities as Flint, Michigan, and Cleveland, Ohio, in the mid-1950s. In 1956, the boys thought bigger things would soon come their way after they signed their first recording contract with Chess Records. They changed their name to the Four Tops for their debut singles on the label, but few people remembered either their new name or any of the record titles during these years. The group moved to two more record firms in the late 1950s and early 1960s—Riverside and Columbia, but with little more success.

Finally, the boys decided to polish up their night club set, adding more dynamic dance routines and better vocal arrangements. As Payton describes their thinking at the time: "Some groups like the Traniers or Steve Gibson and the Red Caps have no hit records, but make it in clubs. We might have looked for another way to make a living, though, if we'd known how hard it would be to make it. It took us six or seven years to get started, and by that time we had blown our chances to get into anything else, so we had to stick with it."

By the end of the 1950s, they finally made progress. They toured much of the U.S. with the Larry Steele Revue, then gained a place with jazz great Billy Eckstine's Las Vegas show in the early 1960s. Eckstine gave them suggestions for improving their act that helped increase their reputation in the music industry.

In 1963, they signed with still young Motown Records. One of their first singles, "Baby I Need Your Loving," became one of the major hits of 1964 and the Four Tops were finally launched. They proved their staying power with "I Can't Help Myself" (number one in *Billboard* June 19 and 26, 1965) and "Reach Out, I'll Be There" (number one October 15 and 22, 1966). Top ten hits included "It's the Same Old Song" (1965), "Standing in the Shadows of Love" (1966), and "Bernadette" (1967).

One reason for their popularity, which continued unabated in the early 1970s, was their wide range of performing capabilities. They were able to switch from ballads to soul to rock and even to country and western with ease.

Their debut LPs, *The Four Tops* and *Second Album*, both released in 1966, made the best-seller lists. Motown followed with such LPs as *The Four Tops on Top* (1966), *Four Tops Live!*, *Four Tops on*

Broadway, Greatest Hits (1967); and *Reach Out* (1968).

In 1970, LPs *Soul Spin, Still Waters Run Deep*, and *Changing Times* made the charts, as did *Greatest Hits, Volume 2* in 1971. But only "Still Water (Love)" (1970) made the singles top 20 until 1972.

In 1971, the group left Motown and signed with Dunhill Records which later merged with ABC, which, in turn was taken over by MCA—which with its various successors remained their label for the rest of the decade.Their debut on Dunhill was the 1972 LP *Keeper of the Castle*, whose title track became a top 10 single, as did "Ain't No Woman." The group followed with the albums *Main Street People* (Dunhill, 1973), *Live and in Concert* (Dunhill, 1974, a year in which Motown also released the retrospective *Anthology*), *Night Lights Harmony* (ABC, 1975), *Catfish* (ABC, 1976), *The Show Must Go On* (ABC, 1977) and *At the Top* (MCA, 1978).

The quartet moved back to their old label, Motown, in the 1980s. They were represented by LPs of both new and old recordings on Motown, such as *Motown Super Star Series, Volume 14* (1981), *Reach Out* and *The Four Tops* (1982), and *Back Where I Belong* (1983). Casablanca released *Four Tops Tonight* in 1981. In 1986, Levi Stubbs scored a personal success as the singing voice of the man-eating plant in the movie musical *Little Shop of Horrors*.

During the summer of 1987, a retrospective of the group's career was presented on the first program on the HBO cable network series *Motown on Showtime*. The show, with Stevie Wonder as on-camera host, reviewed the group's history through interviews, archival film clips and recent performances taped in Detroit, including a medley with Aretha Franklin. Among the songs the Four Tops presented were "Reach Out (I'll Be There)," "Bernadette" and "It's the Same Old Song." The program, which also featured an overview of the Temptations, seemed an excellent candidate for future reruns as well as videocassette packaging.

FRAMPTON, PETER: *See Humble Pie.*

FRANCIS, CONNIE: *Singer. Born Newark, New Jersey, December 12, 1938.*

Connie Francis might be considered another example of the show business hex of too much too soon. In her late teens and early twenties she ranked as one of the top favorites of teenage fans, able to turn almost every record into gold sales material. Later on, when her star began to wane, she wasn't able to put the entertainment business behind her and go on to other pursuits.

Daughter of a roofing contractor with unfulfilled ambitions as a performer, Concetta Rosa Maria

238

Franconero was given an accordion by her father when she was only three years old. She also demonstrated promise as a singer. Her father saw to it that she sang at church events and secular gatherings. Later, he helped get her on Arthur Godfrey's "Talent Scouts." Godfrey suggested the child's name be shortened to Connie Francis.

In 1950, George Franconero took his daughter for an audition for the children's TV show "Startime." She recalled for *Billboard:* "We flagged down the producer of the show, George Scheck, who was hailing a taxi cab. My father said to him: 'Would you listen to my daughter sing?' He said: 'I'm up to here with singers, I can't use singers,' and that's when the accordion saved my life." Scheck was impressed by her ability to play the instrument and also sing so he signed her and later became her manager.

After four years on "Startime," she was becoming too old for a children's show. Her advisors began looking for a record contract. As a 16-year-old, she made a number of demos that were turned down by most major record firms until MGM finally signed her. Her debut single on the label was called "Freddy." Not much happened with it or a series of other releases. She was almost ready to give up and accept a scholarship to New York University when her father suggested she record an old song he admired, "Who's Sorry Now." The song became a hit in 1958 and Connie's career die was cast. Over the next five years she gained more gold records than most performers achieve over two or three times that period. While a number of her hits were hand-picked by her father from the pop standards of his generation, others came from the fledgling songwriting duo of Neil Sedaka and Howard Greenfield. (*See Sedaka, Neil.*) Her million-selling singles included (besides "Who's Sorry Now") "My Happiness," "Lipstick on Your Collar," and "Among My Souvenirs" (1959); "Mama"/"Teddy," "Everybody's Somebody's Fool"/"Jealous of You," "My Heart Has a Mind of Its Own," and "Many Tears Ago" (1960); "Together" and "Where the Boys Are" (1961); and "Don't Break the Heart That Loves You" (1962). "Everybody's Somebody's Fool," "My Heart Has a Mind of Its Own," and "Don't Break the Heart That Loves You" all hit number one in *Billboard.* She added many gold records for albums during those years as well.

"Where the Boys Are" was not only a hit song, but also the title of her first movie on MGM. She later appeared in such other MGM vehicles as *Follow the Boys, Looking for Love,* and *When the Boys Meet the Girls.* Neither the films nor her acting ranked as strong candidates for Oscar consideration.

From the mid-1960s into the early 1970s Connie's career tapered off from the hectic pace of earlier years. She continued to appear at major nightclubs, but avoided the lengthy one-night tours.

Her recording activities during that period mostly were centered on albums. Her most successful were *Italian Favorites* and *More Italian Favorites.* While she no longer turned out gold records, she retained a strong enough following that MGM felt it worthwhile to keep her on the roster.

On the night of November 8, 1974, she was hit by a shattering event that helped account for her later emotional problems. After appearing at the Westbury Music Fair in New York, she returned to her room at a nearby Howard Johnson's motel and was attacked by a rapist. The shock, she stated, caused her to lose her voice and, in fact, she was never able to regain more than a shadow of her earlier vocal powers. It took years for her to recover and she didn't make a major appearance until the fall of 1978, when she was featured on Dick Clark's "Live Wednesday" TV program. (The songs, as is not unusual on Clark's programs, were lipsynched to pretaped material.)

In March 1981, she had to cope with further tragedy, this time the murder of her brother in what some newspapers stated appeared to be gangland style killing. She dealt with the rape and her brother's death as well as unresolved feelings about her relationship with her domineering father in her autobiography, *Who's Sorry Now,* published in September 1984 by St. Martin's Press. (She stated when the book came out that while she began preparing it with two ghost writers, in the end she had dismissed them and written the final version by herself.) One example of her father's interference in her life, she reported, was his opposition to a budding romance between her and singer Bobby Darin. She recalled in one section of the book how her father, who did not consider Darin worthy of his daughter, ended the relationship by driving Bobby from a TV stage ("The Jackie Gleason Show") at the point of a gun. (*See Darin, Bobby.*)

In the mid-1980s, Connie was back on the concert circuit with a show that merged film clips of her glory days with vocals that included, besides her old hits, the moving song about a fallen singing star, "If I Never Sing Another Song." But the show had more low spots than high ones. Writing in the *Los Angeles Times* (October 28, 1985), Paul Grein commented that it "was a sad, unsettling affair. Her voice was almost painfully thin and the production values were frequently amateurish. . . . but few probably came expecting great art. Most were there just for the memories."

However, he added, "While the show lapsed into pathos, it didn't completely sink, thanks to Francis's plucky spirit and self-effacing sense of humor."

FRANKLIN, ARETHA: *Singer, pianist. Born Memphis, Tennessee, March 25, 1942.*

In 1960, when Aretha Franklin was 18, she already had been singing in public for six years. At that time, anyone trying to predict her future probably would have considered her a likely heir to the mantle of the great Mahalia Jackson. Aretha had almost literally been weaned on gospel singing as the daughter of one of the best-known ministers in Detroit, C. L. Franklin, pastor of the 4,500-member New Bethel Baptist Church. Beginning at 12, Aretha joined her father on his wide-ranging evangelical tours, with her strong, youthful voice lending emphasis to his fiery sermons.

Though brought up in a big house with wide lawns, Aretha had not escaped the sights and sounds of the nearby ghetto. She and her four brothers and sisters were only too aware of nearby streets' poverty and domination by pimps, hustlers, pushers and numbers men. Adding to the ingredients of blues and soul building up inside her were personal tragedies, the most important being her mother's leaving the family when Aretha was six, only to die a scant four years later.

As she noted on several occasions, she lived out her inner emotions in her singing. "If a song's about something I've experienced or that could've happened to me it's good. But if it's alien to me, I couldn't lend anything to it. Because that's what soul is all about."

Aretha was not unaware of the popular music scene. She enjoyed listening to soul singers and R&B performers such as Ray Charles and Sam Cooke. Realizing that many of the increasingly successful performers in the pop field had gospel backgrounds, she decided at 18 that she might emulate them. She went east encouraged by Major "Mule" Holly, bass player for pianist Teddy Wilson. She soon gained a manager in New York, Mrs. Jo King, and shortly afterward an audition for Columbia Records executive John Hammond. Hammond lost no time in signing her. For the first half of the '60s, her career didn't seem to be making much progress. Analyzing things in the mid-1960s, she realized that Columbia had changed her style and toned down her arrangements, both vocal and piano, because her record producers and other advisors thought her natural approach to music might be too raw for pop audiences.

She decided to change both her material and her label. In late 1966, she joined Atlantic. Soon after, she went to the recording studios in Muscle Shoals, Alabama (a place famous for the soul quality of its product) with Atlantic vice president Jerry Wexler producing. Their first singles, "I Ain't Never Loved a Man (the Way I Love You)," moved to the number one spot on the national hit charts in the spring of 1967. It and her album of the same title both achieved gold-record status.

It was the beginning of a string of gold records in 1967 including "Respect"/"Dr. Feelgood," "Baby, I Love You," and "Chain of Fools." Continuing her domination of the charts in 1968, Aretha had the gold singles "Since You've Been Gone," "Think," and "I Say a Little Prayer" plus the gold LP, *Lady Soul.*

The year 1968 was particularly sweet. Aretha appeared at standing-room-only concerts in all parts of the U.S. and was often featured on network TV. In addition, she made a triumphal tour of Europe where she was hailed as the successor to the great blues singer, Bessie Smith. Many awards came her way, including two Grammys from the National Academy of the Recording Arts and Sciences for her 1967 work and a 1968 selection from *Billboard* as the top vocalist of 1967.

The important factor in her success was the intensity the listener could feel in Aretha's performance. As *Time* analyzed it in a June 28, 1968, cover story, her "vocal technique is simple enough: a direct, natural style of delivery that ranges over a full four octaves, and the breath control to spin out long phrases that curl sinuously around the beat and dangle tantalizingly from blues notes. But what really accounts for her impact goes beyond technique; it is her fierce, gritty conviction. She flexes her rich, cutting voice like a whip; she lashes her listeners—in her words—'to the bone, for deepness.' 'Aretha's music makes you sweaty, gives you a chill, makes you want to stomp your feet,' says Bobby Taylor, leader of a soul group called Bobby and the Vancouvers. More simply, a 19-year old Chicago fan named Lorraine Williams explains, 'If Aretha Says It, then it's important.'"

In 1969, Aretha gained two more gold records for her single, "See Saw," and her album, *Aretha Now.* But she began to cut down on her activities. By the end of the year, it almost seemed as if she was in semiretirement. For the last months of 1969 and part of 1970, Aretha wrestled with problems that she said little about to outsiders. Some of her anguish reflected the scars of childhood, some the problems that pursued her in private life. There were differences with her husband, Ted White, who had taken over management of her career in the mid-1960s. Sometimes she poured out her feelings in song by returning briefly to her father's church to electrify the huge Sunday-night audiences with her religious solos. During this period, despite urgings of friends and her record company, she avoided new recording sessions.

In mid-1970, though, she seemed to overcome her

inner turmoil and entered the studios in Muscle Shoals for the first time in over a year. Songs from this session began to appear on the charts by the end of the year. "You're All I Need to Get By" stayed in the top 40 for much of spring 1971.

Her continued excellence was recognized by her Grammy in 1970 for Best R&B Vocal Performance, Female for the single "Don't Play That Song" after which she won in the same category in 1971 for her gold version of Simon and Garfunkel's "Bridge over Troubled Water." In 1972, she won two Grammies, one for Best R&B Vocal Performance, Female, for her Atlantic LP *Young, Gifted and Black,* the other for Best Soul Gospel Performance for her version of the hymn "Amazing Grace" (the title track of a gold-award-winning gospel LP issued by Atlantic in 1972). Also released that year was the Columbia repackage *All Time Greatest Hits.* The previous year Atlantic had issued *Aretha's Greatest Hits.* Other Atlantic LPs included *Aretha's Gold* (1969), *Spirit in the Dark* (1970), and the gold *Aretha Live at Fillmore West* (1971).

Aretha continued to win more Grammies for Best R&B Performance, Female: in 1973 for the Atlantic single "Master of Eyes," in 1974 for "Ain't Nothin' Like the Real Thing."

But Aretha seemed to hit a creative dry spell in the middle and late 1970s. Her Atlantic albums seemed like routine releases lacking the fire and verve of her previous recordings. Her output included *You* (1975), *Sparkle* (1976), the retrospective *Ten Years of Gold* and *Sweet Passion* (1977), and *Almighty Fire* (1978).

In the early 1980s, she moved to a new label, Arista. Whether it was the change of scenery or the challenge of working with a new production team, the move seemed to cause her work to perk up almost immediately. Her first two albums on the label, *Aretha* in 1980 and the 1981 *Love All the Hurt Away,* had far more emotional impact than her last Atlantic offerings. The new-found power was perhaps symbolized by her first victory in Grammy Awards voting in over half a decade, when she won the Best R&B Performance, Female, for the 1981 album track "Hold on, I'm Comin'." She proved this situation wasn't a temporary rejuvenation with a gold follow-up LP, the 1982 *Jump on It.* Next came *Get It Right* (1983) and the gold *Who's Zoomin' Who* (1985). She scored a singles hit with the latter's title song as well as the track "Freeway of Love" and joined the Eurythmics for a top 20 single in late 1985, "Sisters Are Doing It for Themselves."

For all her achievements—24 gold records and 14 Grammies as of mid-1986 and a continuing love affair with much of the music audience that had flocked to her concerts for decades, until 1986 she never had starred in her own TV special. This was remedied with the Showtime program "Aretha!" which first screened in July 1986.

The supervising producer for the show, Bonnie Burns, told Steve Schneider, *New York Times,* July 13, 1986: "Aretha had been approached for years about doing her own television special, but she declined all the offers. But now she thought the time was right and we gave her creative approval on all elements of the show—she picked the songs, the wardrobe, the musicians, and she wants to do it in Detroit, because that's her home base. . . . She wanted to define musically the last 25 years for her. First she does a chunk of old hits, then a chunk of newer stuff, and then a few songs that just meant something to her personally—like 'Love All the Hurt Away,' which she recorded as a duet with George Benson, although here she sings both parts herself. And then comes the big gospel numbers, because that's so much of her roots."

In late 1986 Arista issued the LP *Aretha,* which did well on both pop and black music charts in 1987. The album won the Grammy for Best R&B Vocal Performance, Female. During the 1988 Grammy Awards telecast, she also earned a trophy for a single recorded with George Michael, "I Knew You Were Waiting (for Me)," in the Best R&B Performance by a Duo or Group with Vocal category. Her 1987 output included the double album on Arista, *One Lord, One Faith, One Baptism;* issued late in the year, it comprised her first gospel collection in 15 years.

FREDDIE AND THE DREAMERS: *Vocal and Instrumental group, all born Manchester, England. Freddie Garrity, 1940; Roy Crewdson, May 29, 1941; Derek Quinn, May 24, 1942; Pete Birrell, May 9, 1941; Bernie Dwyer, September 11, 1940.*

A teenager in 1965 would remember "the Freddie." Introduced on U.S. TV shows by Freddie and the Dreamers, the Freddie became the dance craze of the younger set for a brief period. But within a year's time, the dance, a variation of the twist, became only a memory as did the group itself not too long after.

The scenario for this group is similar to dozens of other success stories of English rock bands of the period. The band members all came from working class families in an English industrial city—in this case, Manchester—and were swept up in the various phases of the rock revolution arriving in England from America during the 1950s.

Group organizer Freddie Garrity began his band career with a skiffle group called the Red Sox in the late 1950s. During this time and for a while at the start of the 1960s, most of his income came from working as an engineer and a milkman. In 1961, he formed his own band, recruiting its members from friends and acquaintances from his hometown of Manchester. They included Roy Crewdson on rhythm guitar, piano, and drums; Derek Quinn on lead guitar and harmonica; Pete Birrell on bass guitar, bass and accordion; and Bernie Dwyer on drums and piano. Freddie played some guitar and handled the lead vocals.

The group gained local attention by playing on the radio "Beat Show" in early 1961 and made its TV debut in October of that year on the BBC-TV program, "Let's Go." During 1962, the band gradually widened its audience in England, playing such clubs as the Dreamland in Margate and Leyton Baths. Late in the year, recording companies became interested in the band and Freddie signed with English Columbia.

In 1963, the group's first singles became best-sellers in England. "If You Gotta Make a Fool of Somebody," "You Were Made for Me," and "I'm Telling You Now" were all in the top 10. The last named was later issued in the U.S. by Tower Records and became number one on American charts in 1965, earning the group a gold record. During 1963, Freddie and the Dreamers played in many cities of England and Europe, including a lengthy stay at the Top Ten Club in Hamburg, then a center of rock music. At that time, the Dreamers was a headliner while another English group on the bill, the Beatles, was just beginning to gain a small German following. The year 1963 also provided the group with its film debut in *What a Crazy World.*

During 1964–65 Freddie and the Dreamers' first LP, *Freddie and the Dreamers,* chalked up advance sales of 200,000 before it arrived on the dealers' shelves, a new record for those days. By 1965, the group was invited to appear on the "Shindig" and "Hullabaloo" rock TV shows in the U.S. It was on these programs that "the Freddie" was introduced with a resultant clamor for tickets to the group's coast-to-coast tour of the country. Similar acclaim awaited the band in Europe, Australia, and New Zealand.

Following the success of the single, "I'm Telling You Now," in the U.S., the LP of the same name became a best-seller. The group remained popular and active for part of 1966, switching from Tower to Mercury for U.S. record distribution. Mercury was rewarded with chart status for the 1966 albums *Freddie and the Dreamers* and *Fun Lovin'.* Dissension among band members over future directions in 1966 brought reports the group would disband. However, the problems were papered over and the band did

perform on the night club circuit for a few more years. The band's final album was a children's collection in 1970, *Oliver in the Underworld.* In 1972, the band officially was broken up and Garrity and Birrell began new careers as hosts of a children's TV series, *The Little Big Time.* Garrity also demonstrated his ability as a pantomimist, a skill he showcased at various events in the 1980s.

Garrity organized a new Freddie and the Dreamers group (which had no other original members) in 1976 and took part in oldies concerts from time to time in later years.

FREED, ALAN: *Disc jockey, songwriter, music-industry executive. Born Johnstown, Pennsylvania, December 15, 1922; died Palm Springs, California, January 20, 1965.*

A colorful and controversial figure in the early days of rock, Alan Freed for a time rated as a kingmaker in the field because of the many listeners who followed his radio disc jockey shows in the New York area. Though claims that he was the main person responsible for the rise of rock are exorbitant, he certainly made many important contributions, not the least of which was the coining of the musical tag phrase *rock'n'roll.*

Freed first began to build a reputation for himself among black audiences in the Midwest when he became one of the top rhythm & blues disc jockeys. Raised in Cleveland, he started his rise to fame with a program on a Cleveland station in 1951. He not only played the latest R&B records, he also often sang along with them, keeping time by slamming his hand down on a telephone book near his microphone. Though he was white, he caught the spirit of the music and, before long, his name became known far beyond Cleveland's boundaries. These shows were presented in many other cities in the Midwest besides Cleveland.

His acquaintance with such black artists as Chuck Berry and Bo Diddley proved mutually profitable. (*See Berry, Chuck; Diddley, Bo.*) His close ties with R&B artists made it easier for him to field good shows and he also provided suggestions that helped some of them move up the ladder as R&B and rock became increasingly lucrative during the '50s.

The words *rock* and *roll,* not necessarily in that combination, often were used in the lyrics of R&B songs with a sexual connotation. In the early '50s, Freed decided *rock'n'roll* aptly described the new music popping up on stations all over the country. He began using it regularly in his broadcasts and later successfully filed a copyright application for the phrase.

When the new music began to gain national prominence, Freed was already considered one of its major spokesmen by the music industry. Thus, when station WINS in New York decided to feature rock in 1954, it signed Freed to be the pivotal d.j. in its new lineup. From then until the end of the decade, he was recognized as the most successful rock d.j. in the business. He also became increasingly prominent in assembling shows for the teenage circuit. In 1955, he played a key role in bringing R&B into the spotlight to gain some of the credit long denied one of the sources of rock. He accomplished this by bringing an interracial show of rock and R&B stars into the Brooklyn Paramount for Easter and Labor Day weekends. The audiences were so large and vociferously in favor of the new format that the color bar finally started to be laid aside in pop music.

Freed also was credited with co-writing several rock standards, most notably of Chuck Berry's "Maybelline." Berry wrote the song, but Freed helped put together lyrics that were in the new rock vein rather than traditional blues.

Freed's career was shattered by the "payola" hearings conducted by the House Subcommittee on Legislative Oversight, chaired by Rep. Oren Harris (D-Ark.) in 1960. He was indicted for accepting $30,000 from six record companies to plug their product on his program.

Some observers thought this would bring the rock craze to an end. However, they overlooked the fact that rock succeeded not because of machinations of the record industry, but because fans loved the music. In fact, one of the things that helped foster rock was the stranglehold of old-line songwriters and the so-called "big five" record firms on the field. In effect, the rules of ASCAP, and the closed-door policy of RCA, Columbia, etc., shut the industry doors to young writers and, to some extent, performers. The answer that evolved was for the outsiders to find a new kind of music and then get it in the back door by paying off radio announcers to play it.

This practice, though, was time-honored by then. Many of the hit songs of earlier eras got there by way of payola payments to band leaders, vocalists, and even lead musicians. Freed, however, was singled out for blame.

At any rate, the payola scandals did not ruin rock, but they caused Freed to lose most of his influence. His leading position as a rock broadcaster was taken over by Dick Clark. In January 1965 Freed died in Palm Springs, California. (*See Berry, Chuck; Clark, Dick; Moonglows, The; Rivers, Johnny.*)

In early 1978, Paramount Pictures released the movie *American Hot Wax* which dealt with a small segment of Freed's career. With Tim McIntyre playing the role of Freed, the film covered the week leading up to Alan's last big show before the payola probe ended his glory days, his "First Anniversary of Rock'n'Roll" concert at the Brooklyn Paramount in 1959.

FREY, GLENN: *Singer, guitarist, songwriter, record producer. Born Detroit, Michigan, November 6, 1948.*

When the Eagles broke up officially in 1980, many industry experts thought it would only be a temporary split. After all, the group was at the height of its fame with every new album virtually assured of selling well over platinum levels. It had over 50 million discs, had won countless critics' polls and awards, and ranked as one of the best live acts in rock. But the break proved to be final. The reason, as the band's long-time manager Irving Azoff said, was that its two creative mainstays, Glenn Frey and Don Henley, realized they didn't need the group anymore, that they could make great solo records. And that was, in fact, what happened in the 1980s. (*See Eagles, The; Henley, Don.*)

For Frey, the trail to stardom began in Detroit, Michigan, where he was born and raised. As soon as he was old enough to gain a certain amount of freedom from parental controls, he developed two main interests: girls and music. (In his early teens, he had been obsessed for a while with sports until he decided his relatively small size would prevent him from becoming a star athlete. This interest surfaced later with the organization of an Eagles softball team drawn from the band and its supporting group of roadies and office personnel.) He listened to rock and went to concerts at the city's Olympia Hall, including two performances by the Beatles. He recalled later that his dream about holding the spotlight as rock star did led him to take up the guitar.

Detroit then was the center of Motown's soul music empire, but other acts were coming along as well, such as the Bob Seger System. Frey learned which studio Seger recorded at and began to frequent it. As he told an interviewer, "Seger was cool. I was never in his band, but he liked me and let me come to some sessions when he was recording four-track. He let me play maracas, and on one song he let me play acoustic guitar." Frey also got the chance to sing backup vocals on one Seger hit, "Ramblin' Gamblin' Man," which came out on Capitol Records in 1968. (*See Seger, Bob.*)

Frey managed to find work as a guitarist with a number of Detroit groups, such as the Mushrooms, the Subterraneans, and the Four of Us. He liked performing not only for its own rewards, but also because it made him king of the hill with young groupies. His mother analyzed his drives somewhat differently, as Frey told Cameron Crowe of *Rolling Stone*. She said: "Glenn, your life revolves around groups of people. You can't relate that well to individuals. If your guitar had tits and an ass, you'd never date another girl."

Over his parents' objections, he finally dropped out of college and took off for Los Angeles. "The truth is I was gonna buy drugs in Mexico and see a girlfriend who moved [to Los Angeles] with her sister. My parents told me that if I was going to California, they weren't gonna give me a goddam dime. [But] they would send me five bucks, ten bucks in every letter. 'Buy yourself a breakfast and a pack of cigarettes'. . . .

"But anyway, the whole vibe of L.A. hit me right off. The first day I got to L.A. I saw David Crosby sitting on the steps of the Country Store in Laurel Canyon, wearing the same hat and green leather bat cape he had worn for *Turn! Turn! Turn!* To me, that was an omen. I immediately met J. D. Souther, who was going with my girlfriend's sister and we really hit it off. It was definitely me and him against whatever else was going on."

The friends formed a two-man band called Longbranch Pennywhistle that was good enough to get a contract from Amos Records. Amos issued their LP *Longbranch Pennywhistle* in 1971. For a while, Frey and Souther shared a low-rent apartment with another starving musician, Jackson Browne, with whom Glenn co-wrote a future hit, "Take It Easy." (*See Browne, Jackson.*)

A contract dispute with Amos that sidelined Souther and Frey led to the breakup of their duo. Frey, at loose ends, jumped at the chance to join a backing band for Linda Ronstadt, playing on her 1972 Capitol album, *Linda Ronstadt. (See Ronstadt, Linda.)*

In 1972, members of Ronstadt's band decided to go out on their own, as had occurred with Bob Dylan's 1960s support group, the Band. "Take It Easy" was the Eagles' debut single and, while not a top-seller, it did well enough to gain the band some industry notice. While Frey did not contribute much in the way of other originals to the first Eagles LP, he went on to establish himself, along with close associate Don Henley, as its main writers and, indeed, two of the premier songwriters in all of rock. Among the classic songs Frey co-wrote during the Eagles glory years were "Lyin' Eyes," "One of These Nights," "Desperado," "Heartache Tonight," "Take It to the Limit," "Life in the Fast Lane," "The Long Run," and "Hotel California."

After the Eagles disbanded in 1980, amid considerable rancor and soul-searching by various members, Glenn took some time off to gather his thoughts before establishing new career directions. He began working on new songs with non-Eagle collaborators, particularly a folk-rock performer-writer Jack Tempchin, who had written the Eagles' 1973 hit "Peaceful Easy Feeling." Before getting around to completing his debut solo album, he joined forces with veteran producer Jerry Wexler to co-produce an album by Texas singer Lou Ann Barton. Called *Old Enough*, that LP was issued by Asylum Records on February 5, 1982.

Frey's own album (co-produced by him, Allan Blazek, and Jim Ed Norman) was issued by Elektra/Asylum on May 28, 1982. Called *No Fun Aloud*, it included five songs co-written by Frey and Tempchin (like the title-track single) and went gold. The LP was preceded by a few days by the initial single, "I Found Somebody"/"She Can't Let Go," issued on May 24, 1982. The album was on the charts from soon after its release into 1983 and received gold record certification from the RIAA. The single was one of the year's pop hits, as was another single from the album, "The One You Love."

Irving Azoff's move from management to the presidency of MCA Records brought most of his former clients into that new fold, including Frey. One of the first fruits of the new association was Frey's single of the theme from the blockbuster Eddie Murphy movie, *Beverly Hills Cop*. That gold disc, "The Heat Is On," came out on MCA in late 1984.

For his debut album on MCA, Frey again co-produced with Allan Blazek. This time, he co-wrote all the songs. Jack Tempchin collaborated on all of them, with a third collaborator, Hawk Wolinski, on two numbers. Issued in late 1984, *The Allnighter* earned Glenn another gold-record award and spawned two chart hit singles. But his biggest solo hit was the number two "You Belong to the City," from the soundtrack *Miami Vice*. That achievement put Glenn in the top five grouping in *Billboard*'s 1985 year-end top Pop Singles Artists, Male, classification.

FRIPP, ROBERT: *Singer, guitarist, songwriter, band leader (KING CRIMSON), record producer. Born England, May 16, c. 1946.* *

A lot of the strands of English rock history, past and present, weave into the career of Robert Fripp. In his early rock efforts, he was a founding member of King Crimson, a seminal group of 1970s rock, whose roster initially included Greg Lake (later of Emerson, Lake and Palmer) and later enrolled Bill Bruford, onetime featured drummer with Yes. From the mid-1970s on, Fripp has worked with such stellar artists as Peter Gabriel, Daryl Hall, Brian Eno, and

---

*Based on a personal interview with Irwin Stambler.

David Bowie and had a hand in the development of the punk/new wave genre.

Of King Crimson, his primary interest from 1969 until he broke it up in 1974, he said: "The band ceased to exist in September 1974, which was when all English bands in that genre should have ceased to exist. But since the rock'n'roll dinosaur likes anything which has gone before, most of them kept on churning away, repeating what they did years before without going off in any new directions."

Because of the feeling that he was, in effect, "spinning his wheels," Fripp made a complete break with the field for a while. "From September '74 to August '77, I left the music industry completely and continued my education in a different area." Because of his reputation as one of rock's finest guitarists, offers to return kept coming to him, but he fought most of them off for almost three years. "The music field is a very seductive one that tends to appeal to the worst aspects of me and I don't trust myself. So I approached coming back into it very gingerly."

His first return to action took the form of playing lead guitar for Peter Gabriel. "I met him after seeing him in concert just before he left Genesis. It probably was a good idea he did so, because there was only Phil [Collins] and Peter in the band doing anything at all then and they were in completely different areas. At the same time, the kind of creative friction it gave them was gone and I didn't think what was then left of the group had much validity.

"He asked me to play on his first album [*Peter Gabriel*, issued on Atco in late 1977], which I really wasn't all that eager to do, but he gave me the reservation that if I didn't like it, I could leave. But once I was on the set and found I didn't like it, while I knew I could withdraw with honor, nevertheless I stayed there. It was a nasty situation for me and for the producer. In terms of what he wanted, I never should have been on that LP."

The project did bring Fripp back into the music field despite his misgivings. "Doing Peter Gabriel's first LP was like putting your toe into the bathwater to see if it's alright. I agreed to tour with him, but didn't want to use my name. So I went around with him as Dusty Rhodes. I learned something from that, which is that devoting all that energy to a touring band is pretty stupid."

Gabriel talked Fripp into taking over as producer of his second solo album, also titled *Peter Gabriel* (1978). Before he got around to that, Fripp took part in other projects including handling production of a solo album by Daryl Hall of Hall & Oates, *Sacred Songs,* that RCA took three years to release. That LP, he noted, "was really my first production work in the rock field. Whereas I contributed varying amounts of production to each of King Crimson's albums from 1969–74, I certainly wouldn't want to be called the producer of King Crimson. I did have some earlier credits, but they were in the jazz field. I guess you could say the first true production by Robert Fripp was Keith Typett's Centipede. He was a jazz star of '69 who formed a 50-piece band which consisted of virtually every good musician in London at the time. Later I produced a number of avant garde jazz albums before I withdrew from the field for a time."

Before the Hall project, though, he said he collaborated on an avant-garde rock album with Brian Eno, former Roxy Music keyboards artist. (The two previously had worked together on the 1974 British Island LP *No Pussyfooting,* which introduced a unique approach that *Rolling Stone* described as utilizing "a tape loop to layer guitar textures over Eno's electronic drones. That . . . later was scaled down to 'Frippertronics' in which the tape loop was provided by two tape decks in sequence and the additional electronics were abandoned.") The second collaboration had aspects that reinforced Fripp's antipathy to the rock establishment.

He recalled, "All the management people involved did all they could to stop us from working together and Island Records tried to keep from releasing the album, which became one of the most important in European avant garde pop music." Called *Evening Star,* it had an impact on many of the new albums made there in the late 1970s and early 1980s, including several releases by David Bowie and Iggy Pop. "Iggy and David continually whistled nearly all the melodies from *Evening Star."* Out of print in the late 1970s, *No Pussyfooting* and *Evening Star* were reissued on Editions EG label in 1981.

Among other things, Fripp played lead guitar on Bowie's album, *Heroes.* When plans were being made to record it, Fripp had moved his home base to New York. "I thought about going back to school there, but I'd agreed to do Daryl Hall's solo album and two weeks before I was due to work on it, I got a call from David Bowie and Eno. I'd known David since 1972. He actually met his wife at a King Crimson concert. They asked me to play guitar on the new album and I said I'd be glad to if they accepted the fact that I hadn't played lead for three years and didn't know how it would come out. I flew out on Friday night and did the lead parts on most of the pieces. I was in Berlin for three days working on that."

He then returned to New York to produce Hall's album, which Fripp thought was an excellent one, but which Hall & Oates' managers didn't want to release because it differed so much from Hall's previous work. That project finished, Fripp went on to produce the new Peter Gabriel LP. Recording sessions for that album began in Amsterdam, moved to London, and were completed in the Hit Factory in New York in early 1978 with mixing in the Trident Studios in London.

Fripp maintained: "Working with Peter is very difficult, because he has a definite view of himself and what he wants, coupled with a total inability to make a decision on what he wants, which makes it very hard on the producer." Obviously, Gabriel did know what he wanted in terms of who would handle the project since he called in Fripp rather than his previous producer.

Fripp didn't argue with that idea. "I don't think the first Peter Gabriel album has much to do with Peter Gabriel. But I think the second album has, by dint of years of suffering. It was one of the most exhausting things I've ever done, but I feel he got a very good LP which represented wherever he might be at the time."

Fripp kept his eyes open for promising new pop music trends. The onset of punk rock he thought very promising. "One of the things I did get a kick out of in 1978 was playing with Blondie at CBGB's. I like punk rock. It was something new, something I'd been waiting to hear for six years. It was very exciting. The most interesting thing was that a lot of the new artists had very limited technique so they had to work to create a vocabulary. I saw a lot of bands like Tuff Darts that really turned me on. I heard Brian Eno mixing one of the tapes from a new Talking Heads album and it was outstanding."

Though he had been in demand as a producer, Fripp had nagging doubts about whether artists should depend on an outsider for this work. "I'm not particularly in favor of using a producer, although for some artists a good producer is very useful provided he's sympathetic to the artists' needs. Whereas we artists and bands drove producers out of the business at the end of the '60s and in the early 1970s, now you have a very strong desire for them. That's because there are a lot of new artists without experience who demand producers because they think that's the way to guarantee hit records.

"I think there are two main approaches to producing. One way is to hire a successful, typically North American, producer to take care of the artists. It's very similar to the business approach to marketing any product. You take it and put it in a box and sell it without worrying too much about the product. There's perhaps a half dozen such producers with a given stamp and package approach, often without regard to the artist's feelings. It's geared to the profit motive and appeals to the lowest common denominator.

"The other approach is where you try to bring the artist out so he discovers new facets of himself, so he gets the chance to explore an area he wouldn't explore himself. It has the disadvantage that most artists are as egotistical as the producer and have a great tendency to waffle. Also, the producer is always trying to reinvent himself and edits out things he doesn't find useful. In that case, the recordings have a Hollywood polish, but lack the rough quality of the original that might be much more effective."

Naturally, Fripp favors course two. "For myself, I can't guarantee any hits, but I will promise to record what's played. I can't make a hit, but if the artist has hit material, I believe I will deliver it so it will achieve its full potential."

Apart from production chores for others, Fripp was producing new material of his own for the first of a series of solo albums. During 1978, he completed the tracks for a proposed LP he titled *The Last of the Great New York Heart Throbs*. Recalling unhappy experiences with Atlantic executives during his King Crimson days, he commented at the time: "I'm contractually free in America at present and I'm not sure who it will be [released] with other than it won't be with Atlantic. There are a number of demands I'll require of my record company now and some expressed willingness to go along with them."

Eventually he signed with Polygram Records which issued a number of solo LPs by Fripp. These included the excellent 1979 *Exposure* (on which Daryl Hall and Peter Gabriel, among others, provided solo parts) plus *God Save the Queen/Under Heavy Manners* (1980) and, in 1981, *Let the Power Fall* and *The League of Gentlemen* (1981). The last named did so poorly with both reviewers and record buyers that Fripp decided to assemble a new edition of King Crimson for the 1980s, which, by then, he hoped would be free of the creative baggage of his earlier band. The reformed group signed with Warner Brothers, which issued the albums *Discipline* in 1981 and *Beat* in 1982. Members were Fripp and Adrian Belew on guitars, Tony Levin on bass guitar, and King Crimson veteran Bill Bruford on drums.

In the 1980s, besides his new recording and concert work with King Crimson, Fripp kept active in other projects in the area of production and session work and continued to write much new material.

He never failed to be outspoken about the ills of the music industry. "When I was first getting into rock, I was stroppy and after I was involved more or less successfully for many years, I'm even stroppier because rock became more rigid. In one sense it's stupid of me to speak out against the industry icons because it will bring me under the kind of attack I really don't need or want. On the other hand, a lot of people out there need to be reassured they're not imagining things; the industry really is crazy as it exists.

"I think industry thinking, particularly [in the U.S.] is completely wrong. The role of the record firm, for instance, should be to make up its mind which music is worth selling and figure out the best way to sell it. The American approach is: 'This record sells, therefore it's good.'"

In the late 1980s, Fripp was in Claymont, West Virginia, holding Guitar Craft seminars through his American Society for Continuous Education (a group inspired by the writings of British philosopher J. G. Bennett). With his students, he did concert tours and released the LP *Robert Fripp & the League of Crafty Gentlemen* on the EG label.

(*See Bowie, David; Emerson, Lake and Palmer; Eno, Brian; Gabriel, Peter; Hall & Oates; King Crimson.*)

FUNKADELIC: *See Clinton, George.*

FUQUA, HARVEY: *See Moonglows, The.*

GABRIEL, PETER: *Singer, guitarist, keyboardist, harmonica player, songwriter. Born London, England, May 13, 1950.*

The English progressive rock band Genesis lived up to its name by giving birth to some of the most influential sole performers of the late 1970s and early 1980s. (*See Genesis.*) Among its alumni were Peter Gabriel, Steve Hackett, and Phil Collins. First to go out on his own was Gabriel, whose persona originally had given Genesis it upward impetus. He achieved stardom by eschewing the role-playing that marked his Genesis phase, concentrating instead on increasingly sophisticated social commentary in his new performing repertoire. Gabriel, who grew up in reasonably comfortable surroundings in the England of the 1950s and '60s, began learning various instruments, including piano, in his preteen years. His early inclination was toward folk music. In fact, at one point in the mid-1960s, he quit a job in a London travel agency to work as a street musician, or busker, performing songs such as the Kingston Trio's "Where Have All the Flowers Gone" at the Tottenham Court Road subway station.

The genesis of Genesis took form at Charterhouse School in London in 1966, when Gabriel formed a songwriters collective with friends Tony Banks, Michael Rutherford, and Anthony Phillips. The writing activities gradually evolved into a rock group, which became the basis for Genesis in 1969. With Gabriel as lead singer and a prime contributor of original words and music, the band began to win attention from London rock fans in 1970 when its debut LP, *Trespass,* came out on ABC Records. Over the next few years, buoyed by enthusiastically received concerts in the U.K. and the U.S., the band's albums reflected steady creative growth, though much of its popularity could then be traced in part to Gabriel's flamboyant stage presence.

In his live performances, Gabriel seemed more actor than vocalist. He affected heavy makeup, odd masks, and all manner of special costumes. For the song "Watchers of the Skies," for example, he wore a batwing-like garment; for "Dancing with the Moonlit Knight," he typically donned a "Britannia" outfit (a "cheap" Britannia format, as Tony Banks indicated, to represent the "degradation of the nation"). On "Willow Farms" (which dealt with a man who turned into a flower), Peter had a flower-like getup. Gabriel also used unusual hairdos, for example, having his head half shaven leaving a Mohawk-like sheaf of hair down the middle.

Other band members were appreciative of the visual impact he had on audiences, though uncomfortable that it tended to obscure the songs themselves. Tony Banks told Richard Cromelin of the *Los Angeles Times* in October 1974: "Unfortunately the publicity is angled very much around it, so the audience gets the wrong impression sometimes. They're all really overstatements of what the song's about just to try to get across the mood. We do a lot of lights and slides, but not to dominate the song, because we want to let people's reactions roam as much as possible."

Even as Banks made those statements, the situation was about to change. Gabriel had become increasingly restless with the restrictions of the Genesis format. After a 1974 tour, he decided to go it alone though he performed with the band into 1975.

As he told Robert Hilburn (*Los Angeles Times,* April 13, 1977): "The writing process with the band had become a little stale. We had fallen into habits. We weren't challenging or testing anything. As the band got more successful, it was increasingly difficult to encourage people to take a risk with something that might jeopardize their livelihood. I finally decided it was time for me to make a move. We were at a point where the real money was starting to come in for the first time. I was afraid that if I didn't leave, I might get used to the new way of living and would have found it hard to go because of the financial security."

He took all of 1975 off to expand his record-business contacts and work on new material. For a time, he toyed with the idea of remaining behind the scenes as a songwriter rather than returning to performing. His mood was further unsettled when Genesis' first post-Gabriel album, *A Trick of the Tail,* became a massive worldwide hit. Some people suggested his contributions to the band weren't as important as once thought. He noted: "When people became very enthusiastic about the new [post-Gabriel] albums, I felt a little bit like last year's performer who has been put away somewhere."

However, he was encouraged by U.S. musician friends to persevere and in 1976 got the go-ahead from Atco Records to start work on a solo LP. With Bob Ezrin as producer, the new collection took shape, including such Gabriel songs as "Solsbury Hill" (a country-flavored treatment of his breakup with Genesis), a high-powered rocker called "Modern Love," and a Randy Newmanish track "Here Comes the Flood." Reflecting his loss of confidence after Genesis' recent success, he began his concert tour in support of the well-received 1977 solo debut album, *Peter Gabriel*, in the U.S. instead of the U.K.

In keeping with his search for a new image, Gabriel played down the theatrics. Though he did make some minor adjustments for certain songs, he no longer sported a punk haircut and he came on stage without outlandish garb. In many of his concerts of the late 1970s and early 1980s, his dress comprised a black boiler suit with asymmetric white stripes down the side of one arm and one pant leg.

In early 1978, he began work on his second album, this time with former King Crimson leader Robert Fripp as producer. (*See Fripp, Robert.*) This LP, also called *Peter Gabriel*, came out on Atlantic in late 1978 and featured such notable tracks as "D.I.Y.," "On the Air," and "Home Sweet Home." In 1979, while touring in support of that LP, he began work on material for his next album, songs with such somber content that Atlantic demurred at releasing the new collection, claiming it would be commercial suicide.

As a result, Gabriel switched to a new label, Mercury, for U.S. distribution. Produced by Steve Lillywhite, the 1980 album (again titled *Peter Gabriel*) proved to be one of his most striking offerings yet and certainly not a commercial failure. Among its contents were "Games without Frontiers" (a top 5 hit in England), "Family Snapshot" (dealing with the motivations of an assassin), and "Biko" (homage to the South African black poet/activist murdered by that government's pro-apartheid regime). "Milgrams 37," as he explained to English reporter Lynn Hanna, was based "on the famous American experiment in which volunteers were split into 'teachers' and 'learners.' The teachers were told to assist the pupils by administering shocks in the form of electric shocks. It was discovered that 63% of the volunteers were prepared to administer charges of 450 volts, which would have severely damaged or exterminated the learner (unbeknownst

to the teachers, the learners were actors simulating pain.). . . . It shows just how far they'd go without questioning authority."

In the 1980s, Gabriel continued his approach of careful preparation of new material for each new album. Just as there was a two-year gap between his second and third studio LPs, there was a similar spread before his fourth release came out in 1982. This album, *Security (Peter Gabriel)* was on another label, this time Geffen Records. Among its tracks was "Shock the Monkey," which was a chart hit in both the U.K. and U.S.

In 1986, Gabriel released *So,* which was certified platinum by year's end and reached double platinum levels by early 1988. It yielded two hit singles: "Sledgehammer," a number one hit in the U.S. in July 1986, and "Big Time," a top 10 hit in 1987.

Though Gabriel had several nominations in the Grammy voting in 1986, he failed to win anything. However, he was a big winner in the 1987 American Video Awards, accepting the trophies for Best Pop Video and Best Male Performance ("Sledgehammer") at ceremonies in the Los Angeles Scottish Rite Auditorium. During the program, he was also inducted into the National Academy of Video Arts and Sciences Hall of Fame.

Gabriel joined Sting, U2 and other rock stars in a summer 1986 fund-raising concert series for the humanitarian Amnesty International organization. In a December 1987 press conference in Sao Paulo, Brazil, Gabriel and Sting announced they would perform as well in a 1988 tour called "Human Rights Now" to coincide with Amnesty's drive to collect public endorsements for the Universal Declaration of Human Rights. The objective was to present the endorsements to the United Nations on December 10, 1988, the 40th anniversary of that declaration.

GARFUNKEL, ART: *Singer, actor. Born Newark, New Jersey, November 5, 1941.*

Certainly one of the great folk/folk-rock duos of all time, Simon and Garfunkel set new standards for their art form in the 1960s before going separate ways at the start of the 1970s. Though Simon was more active following the split, Garfunkel also made his mark on the entertainment field as a solo recording artist and actor. (*See Simon and Garfunkel; Simon, Paul.*)

Young Art started to sing at the age of four after his father brought home one of the first wire recorders. "That got me into music more than anything else. Singing and being able to record it." His interest in music still remained strong when he became friendly with Paul Simon when both were in sixth grade in Queens, New York. (Though born in Newark, Art spent much of his youth in Queens.) Before long, the two were singing in school events—mostly popular songs of the day.

Their early attention from elementary school into their high school years went to the '40ish pop songs still dominating the field in the early '50s. "Then rhythm and blues . . . rock'n'roll came along." The two began developing material in those genres. "We practiced in the basement so much that we got professional sounding. We made demos in Manhattan and knocked on all the doors of the record companies with our hearts in our throats. Just a couple of kids."

Under the pseudonyms of Tom (Art) and Jerry (Paul), they actually did make an impact on the pop field in the mid-1950s. Their single "Hey School Girl" made lower chart levels in 1956. The duo appeared on Dick Clark's "American Bandstand" and in some of the multiartist shows playing eastern theaters.

The outlook looked promising, but Art decided not to take a chance on the vagaries of show business. "I left and went to college . . . . I was the kid who was going to find some way to make a decent living." He enrolled at Columbia University with a major in art history and minors in architecture and education, getting his B.A. in the early '60s.

But he didn't abandon singing. He turned out some solo singles and in 1962 rejoined Simon to sing at a fraternity house at Queens College, which Simon attended. That led to a decision to try to find more joint engagements. At the end of their sophomore year, they played Gerde's Folk City in Greenwich Village. A Columbia executive who heard the act offered them a contract. Those recording sessions provided the material for their debut LP, *Wednesday Morning, 3 A.M.* (1964).

The basic material for that was provided by Simon. As Garfunkel noted: "Up until then we sang and wrote rock and roll songs together . . . but suddenly one of us could write poetic folk songs. I really connected with that . . . so the rejoining, after several years, was on the basis of the two of us as singers and Paul as the songwriter. People always asked why I didn't write songs. It was because Paul was so good. It seemed foolish to go for equal time."

It took a while, and even another brief separation, but the debut album finally brought them national acclaim, primarily through the success of the song, "Sounds of Silence" in late 1965. Simon and Garfunkel rapidly became one of the most esteemed singing teams in the U.S. and the world. (For more details, see *Simon and Garfunkel*.) They still were at the peak of their careers when they both decided they wanted to try new creative directions.

For Garfunkel, one of his initial goals was acting. His work with director Mike Nichols on the soundtrack of *The Graduate* led to the chance for featured roles in the major films *Catch 22* and *Carnal Knowledge.*

Meanwhile, Columbia was urging him to record solo material. He finally got back into the studio in 1972 for his 1973 debut solo LP *Angel Clare.*

The gold album tended toward the sophisticated ballad side, but had folk elements as well. One of the tracks, "All I Know" (written for him by Jimmy Webb; *see Webb, Jimmy*) became a top ten hit.

He followed that with the 1975 platinum album *Breakaway*. Three of its songs made the hit charts: his update of the old pop ballad "I Only Have Eyes for You," the title track, and "My Little Town," a new song written by his old partner, Simon. The two recorded it together and it was included not only on *Breakaway* but also on a new Simon solo album. The two also made a rare joint appearance to sing the song on a "Saturday Night Live" telecast.

For his early 1978 third album, *Watermark,* most of the material was written by Jimmy Webb. Garfunkel handled production himself in the famous Muscle Shoals Studios in Muscle Shoals, Alabama. Discussing his approach, he stated: "In the past, I would have saved vocals for last. I would start with guitar and piano and build from there. This time I brought my voice down lower. I'm more a baritone tenor [as compared to the mainly high tenor stylings used on his previous two albums]. I wanted to stand there at the mike and sing the song."

To support the new album, Garfunkel agreed to do his first tour since the farewell concerts of Simon and Garfunkel in 1970. In 1979, he completed another album, *Fate for Breakfast,* issued by Columbia in April.

In August 1981, Art put out the Columbia LP *Scissors Cut,* which included a cameo vocal by Paul Simon. In September, the two reunited for a free open-air concert in Central Park attended by several hundred thousand people amid reports this might be a harbinger of a full scale reunion that would include a new Simon and Garfunkel LP. The concert was taped for telecasting on the HBO cable channel and also provided material for the 1982 double-album, *Simon and Garfunkel, The Concert in Central Park.*

The concert response encouraged the duo to do an international tour that was completed in the fall of 1983. The album project, though, fell through. The two began to record some new material for the LP, but Simon changed his mind and completely revamped the tracks, replacing Garfunkel's work with his own so that the final LP was a Paul Simon solo vehicle.

Garfunkel then resumed his own solo activities, which included a three-year effort to complete the album titled *The Animal's Christmas,* based on the Jimmy Webb cantata. Joining him on the recording was gospel star Amy Grant. Columbia issued the LP in October 1986 and Garfunkel moved on to record a new secular album, *Lefty,* issued by Columbia in March 1988.

GAYE, MARVIN: *Singer, pianist, drummer, songwriter, arranger. Born Washington, D.C., April 2, 1939; died Los Angeles, California, April 1, 1984.*

One of the finest artists of the 1960s through the early 1980s, Marvin Gaye had a somewhat erratic career path, with high points interspersed with lows in both his personal and creative spheres. Ironically, he had just made a strong comeback from one of the lows when his life was ended in a bizarre incident arising from an argument at home with his father.

Gaye's early years bore the almost universal stamp among black popular music stars' initial involvement with gospel singing. Born into a religious family (his father was a minister in Washington, D.C.), he sang his first solos in church at three. From then on, he was a regular performer during his father's services as a soloist and a member of the choir. At an early age, Marvin learned the piano and later added drums to his instrumental skills. In high school, he played in the orchestra and was often featured in school plays.

After graduating, he decided to concentrate on music and joined the vocal group the Moonglows, headed by Harvey Fuqua. (*See Moonglows, The.*) At the beginning of the 1960s, he decided to try his luck as a soloist. His timing was impeccable, because Berry Gordy, Jr., was in the process of changing the landscape of American pop music by bringing soul/R&B music into the musical mainstream. His seemingly unerring instinct for picking first-rank talents from the hordes of young, previously unknown black performers provided his own Motown Records with a tremendous roster. His choices, from the Supremes to Marvin Gaye, placed soul on a par with rock in the popular music world of the 1960s. Thus, once he discovered Marvin, Gaye's name, like other members of the 1960s Motown "family," could be found as often in the national top 10 as on the separate R&B hit charts. (*See Gordy, Berry, Jr.*)

The paths of Gaye and Gordy crossed when Marvin's travels as a singer took him to Detroit, where he and Gordy happened to attend the same party. In the course of the evening, Gaye sang informally and Gordy liked the sound enough to ask him to see him at his record company. The result was a contract for Marvin in 1962 that led to his first R&B hit, "Stubborn Kind of Fellow," on Motown's subsidiary, Tamla.

Gaye made Detroit home base and, as the 1960s unfolded, it became apparent his first mild hit was only the beginning. In 1963, he had two major singles, "Hitch Hike" and "Pride and Joy," the latter reaching number one on the R&B charts. The next year was even more impressive with "You Are a Wonderful One," "Try It Baby," and "Baby, Don't You Do It." He also teamed up with another Motown vocalist, Mary Wells, for a double-sided hit, "Once upon a Time"/"What's the Matter with You, Baby?" 1965 singles hits included "How Sweet It Is to Be Loved by You," "I'll Be Doggone," "One More Heartache," the number one R&B hit, "Ain't That Peculiar," and a best-selling album, *How Sweet It Is to Be Loved by You.*

Many of these songs—some composed and arranged by Gaye as well—began to show up on the national charts.

In 1966 and 1967, he had such single hits as "One More Heartache," "Take This Heart of Mine," "Little Darling (I Need You)," "You," and "Chained." In 1967, he found a new singing partner in Tammi Terrell, with whom he recorded such pop top 20 singles hits as "Ain't No Mountain High Enough," "Your Precious Love," and "If I Could Build My Whole World around You" (1967), and "Ain't Nothing Like the Real Thing" and "You're All I Need to Get By" (1968). Gaye and Terrell also turned out such hit LPs as *You're All I Need* and *United.*

Gaye's 1960s solo album credits included *The Soulful Mood of Marvin Gaye, Stubborn Kind of Fellow,* and *Marvin Gaye on Stage* (1962–63); *Marvin Gaye's Greatest Hits* and *When I'm Alone I Cry* (1964); *Hello Broadway, Tribute to Nat King Cole,* and *Moods of Marvin Gaye* (1966); and *Greatest Hits, Volume 2* and *In the Groove* (1968). *Marvin Gaye with Kim Weston* appeared in 1966.

Late in 1968 Tamla released Gaye's number one gold single, "I Heard It Through the Grapevine." In 1970, Gaye's LP *Super Hits* showed up on the national charts and, in 1971, his LP *What's Going On* moved into the top 10 in July as did his single, "Mercy, Mercy Me (the Ecology)."

Coming into the 1970s, Marvin already had had a share of brushes with the often-depressing realities of life. In a 1967 concert at Hampden-Sydney College in Virginia, Tammi Terrell collapsed into his arms while they were singing a duet. Suffering from what reportedly was a brain tumor, she wasn't able to work with him after that and she eventually died March 16, 1970. In the late 1960s and early 1970s, Marvin also had to cope with illness or problems of other friends in the music field and, as the first half of the 1970s went by, with increasing marital difficulties with his wife, Anna Gordy Gaye, a member of Berry Gordy's family.

Gaye's awareness that all was not sweetness and

light in his world was indicated in his excellent 1971 Tamla LP *What's Going On*. Songs such as "Mercy Mercy Me" and "Inner City Blues" commented on problems facing black ghetto dwellers. They and the title track all became top 10 singles. For that album and succeeding recordings, Gaye moved away from the line staff at Motown to record and produce his new material himself.

Having made his social statements, Gaye then moved in another direction—explicitly sexual material. In the liner notes for his next studio LP, for Tamla, *Let's Get It On* (1973), he maintained: "I can't see anything wrong with sex between consenting anybodies. I think we make far too much of it. After all, one's genitals are just one important part of the magnificent human body. I have no argument with the essential part they play in the reproduction of the species; however, the reproductive process has been assured by the pleasure both parties receive when they engage in it." He proceeded to emphasize those statements with sensual tracks such as the title number. Issued as a single, that struck an enthusiastic chord with record buyers, who made it the number one song on *Billboard* lists the weeks of September 8 and 15, 1973. During that year Gaye also found a new duet partner for a number of singles—Diana Ross. (*See Ross, Diana.*) It didn't prove as successful as his work with Tammi Terrell, though they did score two top 20 singles: "You're a Special Part of Me" and "My Mistake (Was to Love You)."

For the next few years, he added to his album credits mostly with retrospectives, such as the 1974 Motown collection *Marvin Gaye Anthology* and the 1976 Tamla release *Greatest Hits*. He also was on the charts in the mid-1970s with *Live* (Tamla, 1974) and *I Want You* (Tamla, 1976). *Marvin Gaye Live at the London Palladium* (Tamla, 1977) provided the last of his three *Billboard* number one singles hits, "Got to Give It Up, Part 1." Ironically, the song was not in the actual concert tapes. Motown had recorded the shows (triumphal sold-out events that comprised his first live concerts in England in ten years—a situation caused, not by lack of interest in him overseas, but by his fear of flying), with plans for a double LP. Album producer Art Stewart later found more material was needed to round out the set and asked Marvin to work up something to achieve that. Gaye complied and came up with a song he had written that originally was called "Dancing Lady" and later was titled "Got to Give It Up." Stewart told Gaye's biographer David Ritz for the book *Divided Soul:* "He had this riff that seemed very danceable. He was doing crazy things like banging on a half-filled grapefruit juice bottle for rhythm. Well, I kept stuff like that on the track. Also people talking in the studio—that loose feeling."

But it was not a happy period for Gaye. His rocky marriage with Anna ended in divorce in the mid-1970s. He gave vent to his emotions about that in the two-disc *Here My Dear* (Tamla, 1978). He waxed particularly bitter on the subject of alimony, part of a series of financial problems that hit him in the late 1970s. Difficulties with U.S. income taxes caused him to seek voluntary exile in Europe at the end of the 1970s and start of the 1980s, years in which he turned out little of importance as a recording artist. His 1981 Tamla album, *In Our Lifetime*, was interesting, but below his normal standards. During that year, when he severed relations with Motown, that label released a group of LPs repackaging earlier material: *Motown Super Star Series, Volume 15, A Tribute to the Great Nat King Cole, That Stubborn Kind of Fellow,* and *M.P.G.* (the initials standing for his original name, Marvin Pentz Gay, the "e" being added later).

By 1982, Marvin was considered a has-been by many observers. He had gone years without new songs able to match commercially or creatively those of his prime period. His long absence from the U.S. concert circuit didn't help, either. But Marvin had gained new self-confidence once he slashed his Motown ties and negotiated a lucrative new contract with Columbia Records. His platinum debut on the new label, *Midnight Love* (1982) produced the top 10 hit, "Sexual Healing." Most critics were euphoric. Dave Marsh wrote in *Rolling Stone* (January 20, 1983): "As a comeback album, Marvin Gaye's *Midnight Love* is remarkably arrogant: it simply picks up from 1973's *Let's Get It On* as if only ten minutes, and not a confusing ten years, had elapsed since Gaye hit his commercial peak. But make no mistake: this record, which has become the biggest crossover hit of the singer's career, is a comeback for Gaye, whose last couple of albums, despite their funkster defenders, committed the unpardonable sin of tedium. . . . *Midnight Love* is anything but boring. It has rhythmic tensions, melodic delicacy and erotic resilience of Gaye's greatest music."

In early 1983, Gaye set out on his first concert tour of the U.S. in some seven years. Cheering audiences all over the country demonstrated he had not lost his charisma as an in-person entertainer. In the voting for the 1982 Grammys, Gaye picked up two trophies, one for Best R&B Vocal Performance, Male, for the single "Sexual Healing," the other for Best R&B Instrumental Performance for the same song. (On the *Midnight Love* album, Gaye had recorded his own instrumental tracks for most of the songs.)

The world once more seemed to be Marvin's oyster, but this promising new phase of his career was cut shockingly short. The morning of April 2,

1984, newspaper headlines blared his death at the hands of his father. Los Angeles Police Department detectives told a *New York Times* reporter that the singer was at his father's home about 12:30 P.M. when the men "became involved in a verbal dispute that led to a physical altercation, pushing and shoving." Later, the *Times* was told, Gaye, Sr., got a pistol and fired several shots at his son. The singer was rushed to the California Hospital Medical Center, where he was pronounced dead at 1:01 P.M. (In the elder Gaye's trial evidence was presented indicating he was suffering from a brain tumor that caused irrational behavior.)

Marvin had not completed work on a second Columbia album at the time of his death. The label released two Marvin Gaye albums during 1985: *Dream of a Lifetime* and *Romantically Yours*, the latter an album mainly of pop standards. Both LPs were made up of unreleased material Gaye had recorded in previous years, but neither measured up to *Midnight Love* or his best music from his Motown years.

J. GEILS BAND: *Vocal and instrumental group. Members, 1969–1980s: Peter Wolf, born Bronx, New York, March 7, 1946; Jerome Geils, born New York, New York, February 20, 1946; Seth Justman, born Washington, D.C., January 27, 1951; Daniel Klein, born New York, New York, May 13, 1946; "Magic" Dick Salwitz, born New London, Connecticut, May 13, 1945; Stephan Jo Bladd, born Boston, Massachusetts, July 13, 1942. Wolf left group in 1984.*

A hard-working, highly professional blues-rock band, the J. Geils assemblage for a while was better known for the fact that lead singer Peter Wolf was the husband of actress Faye Dunaway than for its contributions to pop music. In its own low-key way (from a publicity standpoint, not its performing style, which almost always combined spontaneity with high-intensity musicianship), the band showed remarkable staying power. It still was a top attraction on the concert circuit and a producer of hit albums almost 20 years after its formation.

The group started as a bar band in Boston in 1964. Though an all-white group, it had been weaned on blues and R&B and its music reflected those black influences and to a lesser extent in later years echoes of British blues-rock bands such as the Rolling Stones. Geils, who developed a striking jazz-blues guitar style that placed him in a category with the best in rock, helped form the band and remained with it through a series of personnel changes in the 1960s. By the end of the decade, though, the band had shaken down to a six-man group, each of whom complemented the others in a performing chemistry that still worked over a decade later. The makeup

consisted of Geils on lead guitar, Peter Wolf on lead vocals, super harmonica player Magic Dick (perhaps the best harp player in rock), Seth Justman on keyboards (and also primary songwriter), Daniel Klein on bass, and Stephan Jo Bladd on percussion.

Atlantic records released its debut LP, *The J. Geils Band,* in 1970. The album featured driving boogie-style versions of John Lee Hooker's "Serve You Right to Suffer," Otis Rush's "Homework," and Smokey Robinson's drolly jaded "First I Look at the Purse." They followed that with a series of albums that in some cases were perhaps a little less exciting than The debut, but ranked among the better releases in the early 1970s: *The Morning After* and *Full House* (the group's first live LP) in 1972, *Bloodshot* in 1973, and *Nightmares and Other Tales from the Vinyl Jungle* in 1974. *Bloodshot* went gold.

The band stayed on the road almost constantly. Richard Cromelin of the *Los Angeles Times* noted, after attending one of the band's 1975 shows, that it proved "that boogie can be entertaining and that blues-rock doesn't have to be a mass of leaden clichés. The group's music is an insistent, hammering assault, depending largely on the superb precision and strength of the rhythm section. Yet for all its power, it retains a sparkling clarity (much of it due to Seth Justman's keyboard work) and a remarkable degree of taste and control at every level. It's clean, with a sheen (as singer Peter Wolf, whose rhyming raps sometimes sounded like the street/rock poetry of Patti Smith, might say), but avoids sterility; it's resolutely funky, but with a touch of the flashy and the fashionable."

In its approach to live shows, the band defied conventional music-industry logic, often going on the road even if it was between albums. This happened in early 1976, for instance. It had supported its previous LP, *Hotline,* issued by Atlantic in mid-1975, with a concert series and kept right on going even though its next release wasn't until the end of 1976.

Peter Wolf told interviewer Dennis Hunt: "We tour so often not so much because of the money, but because we simply love to play. I know that sounds weird because touring can be a grind, but for us the good things about touring outweigh the bad things."

Hunt noted that groups that tour without an album typically have at least singles to push, but this didn't hold true for the J. Geils group. Wolf commented: "We're an album band only, but not by choice. We put out singles, but they never get anywhere. I think one of the reasons is our image. People still think of us as a rowdy band that plays rowdy music. The problem is that program directors at the radio stations think this way too. They think our singles are too risque and raunchy for the radio. . . . Part of it's that we had a [single] record banned nationally in

1973 called 'Give It to Me.' That really boosted our rowdy image. There's always the possibility our singles don't make it because of their quality, but I doubt it.''

Being typecast as a blues band also didn't help, he claimed. "In fact, some people think we're called the J. Geils Blues Band. That's very wrong. We play blues, but we also play R&B, rock'n'roll, reggae, and so forth. I know some people think we're a blues band just because we have a harmonica player in the band. If we played nothing but Mozart, they'd still say the same thing. The blues image is a holdover from the 1960s when we were really heavily into the blues. We toured with people like John Lee Hooker and B. B. King and we played a lot of lowdown blues. But now we play everything.''

Wolf, who typically came on stage wearing a black sequined jacket and dark sunglasses, added a bit more to the band's mystique with his marriage to Dunaway, a union that splintered acrimoniously by the end of the 1970s. He told Hunt: "I have to move between two worlds, but I'm not really part of that whole movie world. My wife and I are not inseparable. She shows up at concerts when she can, but she doesn't travel everywhere with me. She can't. She has her own career and that takes a lot of time.

"Being the husband of a movie star is an image I have to contend with. I'm sure most people outside the music world don't know a damn thing about the band and only know me because of my wife. But this is one image that doesn't bother me.''

By the mid-1970s, the group had moved away from cover versions of other artists' material toward more original songs. On the *Bloodshot* album, for instance, seven of the songs were co-written by Wolf and Justman, including the high-energy, danceable "Southside Shuffle" and "Struttin' with My Baby" and fine rock ballads "Make up Your Mind" and "Start All over Again." The pattern of combining mainly new material with some driving remakes of top-flight blues, R&B, or blues-rock songs continued in the second half of the decade.

The band's albums customarily made the charts though few were massive sellers. After the two-disc live *Blow Your Face Out* (1976), the six band members handled their own production work for the first time on their next Atlantic LP, *Monkey Island* (1977).

In 1978, the band left Atlantic for a new contract with Capitol's recently established EMI-America label. Atlantic continued to release other albums after that, however, including the retrospective *The Best of the J. Geils Band* (1979), and *The Best of the J. Geils Band, Volume 2* (1981).

The group's debut album for EMI-America, *Sanctuary*, came out in 1978 and matched the best the

group had done before. *Love Stinks* (1980) hit gold, and *Freeze-Frame* (1981) proved to be their biggest hit yet, hitting platinum and yielding a top 10 hit in the title track and the droll number one single "Centerfold." The band also released a live album, *Showtime,* in 1982.

Wolf commented bitterly about the breakup of his marriage to Dunaway in some of the *Love Stinks* material. Several years later there was another separation, this time Wolf's departure from the J. Geils band in 1984. Wolf was in the middle of the recording sessions for the planned next LP when the split occurred. Band members decided to go on and finish the project without him.

Soon after the EMI-America LP, *You're Gettin' Even While I'm Gettin' Odd,* came out in late 1984, Seth Justman told Robert Palmer of *The New York Times* (October 31, 1984): "We wanted to make as strong a statement as we could, after this crazy year. I think that what happened was that when Peter left it brought the remaining five of us closer together because, without Peter, we were pretty much an unknown quantity. I wrote a lot of our songs, but I hadn't ever publicly sung lead before, and I was pretty scared. But it all worked out, because we could depend on each other. People haven't heard the album yet, but as far as we're concerned, it's already a success.''

Wolf went on to achieve considerable success as a solo performer. His debut LP on EMI America, *Lights Out,* released in the summer of 1984, was a dance rock hit. His follow-up album in 1987, *Come As You Are* (EMI America), seemed like an extension of his debut LP rather than a step forward creatively.

GELDOF, BOB: *See Boomtown Rats.*

GENESIS: *Vocal and instrumental group. Original members, mid-1960s, all born U.K., c. early 1950s: Peter Gabriel, born London, May 13, 1950; Tony Banks; Anthony Phillips; Mike Rutherford, born London, 1951. Members at start of 1970s: Gabriel, Banks, Phillips, Rutherford, John Mayhew. Phillips left in 1970, replaced briefly by Mike Barnard, then by Steve Hackett, born London, February 12, 1950. Mayhew replaced in 1970 by Phil Collins, born London, January 31, 1951. Gabriel left in 1975. Hackett left in 1977.*

Genesis might well have taken the name Phoenix in its unpredictable career as departures or changes in plans of key members often brought forecasts of its imminent demise. As one critic noted, one of the interesting things about coming to a Genesis concert was that you never knew who would be in it. Despite all that, the band as an entity survived those periodic shocks and seemed to bounce back even stronger to maintain its ranking as one of the best bands in rock into the late 1980s.

The group's roots went back to the formation of a songwriters collective by four students at England's Charterhouse School in 1966. Founding member Tony Banks told Jon Young of *Trouser Press* (March 1982): "Peter Gabriel and I used to play around with the piano at school. We did a lot of Otis Redding and Beatles songs; I'd play piano and he'd sing and play flute. We also wrote a couple of songs. At the same time we were close friends with Anthony Phillips, who knew Mike Rutherford. . . . Those two had done a bit more playing in groups and they were keen to make a tape. So Peter and I said: 'We'll help you do the tape, and maybe we could do one of our songs as well.' We did one of ours and five songs of theirs. The only track off the original tape that ended up on an album was called 'She Is Beautiful.' It later became 'The Serpent.'" (*See Gabriel, Peter.*)

They used the tape to gain the attention of English record producer, Jonathan King, whom they could approach because he was an alumnus of their school. Besides naming the band, he funded more taping sessions, which led to releases of a few singles and the band's 1969 debut album before the band members decided the chemistry wasn't right with King.

Banks told Young: "We had a single out called 'The Silent Sun' in 1968. . . . We needed a name for the band and King suggested Genesis. We thought it was quite nice. When we got to the [debut] album, we called ourselves Revelation [on the London label in the U.S.]; that's why the album is called *From Genesis to Revelation*. We were Genesis in England and Revelation [in America] 'cause there was another group called Genesis [in the U.S.] at the time."

At the end of the 1960s, the band finally decided to go full-speed ahead as a professional performance group. The makeup was Gabriel on lead vocals, Tony Banks on keyboards, Phillips on lead guitar, Rutherford on guitar and bass guitar, and another musician on drums. The group was still experimenting, trying to learn its craft, when its second album, *Trespass*, came out on Impulse in 1970. During that year, it continued to shake down its membership. Phillips developed too much stage fright and left. He was replaced on lead guitar by Mick Barnard, who didn't satisfy the others with his playing. By 1971, his place had been awarded to more experienced Steve Hackett. It also was decided that John Mayhew, the fourth drummer employed by the band, didn't fit in either. Auditions finally turned up Phil

Collins who took over as drummer and backup vocalist.

The new lineup was in place when the band's third LP came out, the 1971 Charisma release *Nursery Cryme*. Its song "The Musical Box" played a role in the evolution of Peter Gabriel's stage persona, which relied for much of his time with Genesis on the use of outlandish masks and unusual costumes and makeup. Banks recalled that at first, outside of flash pots, the group used no other stage props. "The masks in 'The Musical Box' came about [when] Peter put a fox's head on during that song just to get his picture on the front page of *Melody Maker*. There was no other justification for it."

Meanwhile the band was honing its style by consistent live performances and building its audience. Banks told Young, "We used to do support gigs, like opening for Mott the Hoople. We'd play to maybe 200 people, and pick up a certain number of people who would be interested. That is how we did it in England, just steady building; the smallest audience we played to was three people. We did a lot of very small gigs—10, 15, 20 people—in those early days. Even a group like us, who had no success with records or anything, could play 120, 130 gigs a year. And that's how it built up."

The band continued to have new albums out on Charisma, each demonstrating improvement in the members' writing and performing skills. These included *Foxtrot* (1972) with such progressive rock tracks as the over eight-minute-long "Stagnation" and a 10-minute version of "Musical Box"; *Genesis Live* and *Selling England by the Pound* (1973) on which Phil Collins sang some lead for the first time; and the *Lamb Lies down on Broadway* (1974).

By the time *Lamb* came out (released in the U.S. on the Atco label, while the band was represented in the U.K. and U.S. the same year by a reissue of some of its earlier material on the London LP *London Collector–In the Beginning*), Genesis no longer had to play as a warm-up act or for a mere handful of people. It could draw capacity crowds to large auditoriums at home and in the U.S. There was no doubt it was on the verge of supergroup status. But the pressures of getting there had proved wearing on most members. First to show it was Peter Gabriel, who left for a while during the recording of *Lamb*, finally returning for a long 1974–75 tour, before bidding goodbye completely in August 1975.

Critics prophesied it was all over for the band. One commented, losing Peter "was rather like Mick Jagger leaving the Rolling Stones. Just as Genesis was reaching the heights of the supergroups, it all seemed to fall to pieces."

Some thought Gabriel's leaving would remove the

main writing talents: hadn't he written most of the material for the band's best album, *Lamb Lies down on Broadway?* Phil Collins demurred. "It's true most of the lyrics were Peter's, but the lion's share of the music was written by the rest of us."

Still, it was a crisis. The band sought high and low for an equally charismatic replacement for Gabriel. No one seemed to fill the bill–then everyone thought of Collins. It proved a brilliant stroke. Though a different vocalist than Gabriel, Collins also proved a crowd pleaser. To give him more room to concentrate on singing, former Yes and King Crimson drummer Bill Bruford was brought in for the 1976 tour in support of the first post-Gabriel album, the platinum *A Trick of the Tail* (Atco, 1976). (*See King Crimson; Yes.*) For a time it was joined on the charts by another collection of reissues, the Buddah LP *The Best of Genesis.*

Discussing *A Trick of the Tail* with a *Los Angeles Times* reporter (April 25, 1976) Collins said: "The music on this album is softer and a bit more accessible. Some of our past songs were in bits and pieces and were not constructed as well as they could have been. I'm not putting down our old material, but I do think our new material is tougher, more concise, and less fragmented. These improvements have nothing to do with Peter leaving. They are just part of the evolution of our music."

The group followed up in 1977 with two more LPs (issued on Atco in the U.S.), *Wind and Wuthering* and a live set from the 1976 tour, *Seconds Out,* on which both Bruford and percussionist Chester Thompson (formerly with Weather Report and the Mothers of Invention) provided excellent support. Both albums sold adequately.

Hardly had fans become accustomed to the new alignment when lead guitarist Steve Hackett left in June 1977 to pursue a solo career. He already had turned out a solo album while still with Genesis, *Voyage of the Acolyte* (Chrysalis, October 1975). On his own, he put out *Please Don't Touch* on Charisma in April 1978 followed by *Spectral Mornings* in 1979 and *Defector* in 1980.

In some ways, Mike Rutherford later said, Hackett's departure was even more traumatic than Gabriel's, but the remaining members pulled themselves together and returned to the music wars as a trio, augmented by various sidemen. Rutherford told Young: "We thought of adding another guitarist [to the core group]." Collins added: "But then, when it comes down to it, you write within your capabilities." The band acknowledged the new state of affairs in the title of its gold 1978 album, *And Then There Were Three,* on Atlantic. Genesis obviously was still in business.

But as 1979 went by with no reports of new album or tour activity by the band, observers began wondering whether three might be a final number. When it became known that both Banks and Rutherford were working on solo albums and Collins had taken up residence in Canada, the heads shook even more. Confounding the naysayers, the three got together for the gold *Duke* (1980).

By 1981, Collins also was embarked on a solo career with his platinum debut LP, *Face Value* (Atlantic), from which the top 20 singles "I Missed Again" and "In the Air Tonight" were taken. His next solo LP, *Hello I Must Be Going,* issued by Atlantic in late 1982, also became a best-seller. The first single from the LP, a cover of the Supremes' "You Can't Hurry Love," reached number one on U.K. charts and the top 10 in the U.S. In 1984, he wrote and recorded the theme for the movie *Against All Odds.* The single, "Against All Odds (Take a Look at Me Now)" was number one in *Billboard* for three weeks, starting on April 21, 1984, and was nominated for an Oscar.

Phil also produced a solo album for Frida of Sweden's Abba and played drums on Robert Plant's *Pictures at an Exhibition* LP before starting work on his third LP, *No Jacket Required.* Atlantic issued it in early 1985 and it soon rose to number one on *Billboard* lists and provided a number one single, "One More Night" (written by Collins). Ironically, the single's time atop *Billboard,* March 20 and 27, 1985, coincided with the Academy Awards telecast, whose organizers had turned down a chance to have Collins sing "Against All Odds," apparently because they weren't aware of his star status in rock music.

But Phil didn't abandon his first love, taking a full part in the 1981 platinum Genesis album *Abacab* on Atlantic and all those completed thereafter through 1987. As the 1980s went by, all the three remaining Genesis members found plenty of other projects to fill their time. Besides writing new songs for their own recordings, they produced sessions by other artists and worked on movie soundtracks. In 1985, Mike Rutherford started a new band called Mike and the Mechanics, which had a hit album on Atlantic, *Mike and the Mechanics,* on the charts from late 1985 into 1986, and two top 10 singles: "Silent Running" and "All I Need Is a Miracle." Since singing wasn't Mike's forte, he brought in Paul Young (not the Young of mid-1980s solo fame, but an alumnus of the U.K. group Sad Cafe) and Paul Carrack (who embarked on a solo career in 1988) to handle vocals. The band was rounded out with Adrian Lee on keyboards and Peter Van Hooke on drums.

Genesis wasn't allowed to die, however. The 1983 Atlantic LP, *Genesis,* went platinum. The mid-1986 follow-up on Atlantic, *Invisible Touch,* was even more successful, staying in the *Billboard* Top 10 much of 1986 and going well past multi-platinum levels in 1987. Among the singles culled from the LP, which ranks as one of the band's best musically, was the 1986 top 5 disc "Throwing It All Away" and the 1987 success, "Land of Confusion." "Land of Confusion" won the band a 1987 Grammy Award for Best Concept Music Video.

GERRY & THE PACEMAKERS: *Vocal and instrumental group. Personnel (1964): Gerry Marsden, born Liverpool, England, September 24, 1942; Freddy Marsden, born Liverpool, England, October 21, 1940; Leslie Maguire, born Wallasey, Cheshire, England, December 27, 1941. Group disbanded in 1966.*

The first tidal wave of rock hits from England was given the generic title of the Liverpool or the Mersey Sound (the Mersey being the river that flows through Liverpool). This was an oversimplification, since many of the name groups, such as the Animals and Manfred Mann, didn't have the Mersey sound and certainly were not from Liverpool. However, the fact remains that many of the dominant names of the rock era of the early '60s were from Liverpool. The most notable, of course, were the Beatles. Others included Billy J. Kramer and the Dakotas, Freddie and the Dreamers, the Merseybeats, and Gerry and the Pacemakers.

Pioneer British rock artist Alexis Korner analyzes the Liverpool sound for Caroline Silver in this way: "There was a certain brashness about the Liverpool music which stamped it almost immediately—they played it the way they speak English, you know! You could definitely tell a Liverpool group. The Mersey Sound was basically a guitar sound: lead guitar, rhythm guitar, bass guitar, and drums was the basic Liverpool setup. What really caught on was not so much the Mersey Sound but guitars, purely and simply guitars, electric guitars."

One of the better young guitarists working in the area in the late 1950s was teenager Gerry Marsden. Gerry had become a follower of Elvis Presley and the other U.S. rock stars of the '50s and managed to get an old Spanish guitar in hopes of learning to play rock himself.

It took a little effort, because he came from a working class family where money was tight. However, he saved his pocket money for school until he could buy strings for the instrument. After he taught himself, he played with local skiffle groups, doing a mixture of rhythm & blues, jazz, and rock with a combination of guitars, odd-looking one-stringed instruments, and washboards.

Gerry continued this in his spare time in the late 1950s after leaving primary school. During the day, he earned a living at various jobs—from making tea chests for the Kardomah company to driving a truck for British Railways. At night he often played with amateur bands. As skiffle faded, Gerry joined the move toward music more closely aligned to American rock than old-time jazz traditions. He worked with some groups, formed some groups of his own, and started writing his own material. In the early '60s, he finally hit the right combination with a group called the Pacemakers.

Starting in the cellar rock clubs of Liverpool, the group gained a local following, then branched out to play other cities. By the time the Beatles moved to the top in 1962, Gerry's group was close behind in popularity in England. For the next four years, the band was one of the best known in England and also gained an impressive reputation with American fans. The group placed three top ten singles on U.S. hit charts: "Don't Let the Sun Catch You Crying" and "How Do You Do It?" (1964) and "Ferry Cross the Mersey" (1965) on Laurie Records. They also scored heavily with their LPs, including *Girl on a Swing, Second Album, Gerry & the Pacemakers, Don't Let the Sun Catch You Crying,* and *I'll Be There.* The group was featured in a movie of its own, *Ferry Cross the Mersey,* for which Gerry wrote nine songs.

By 1966, many of the Liverpool groups of the first half of the '60s were beginning to fade out as now rock patterns took over. The Pacemakers was not immune to this and finally disbanded during that year. Gerry fashioned a new career for a time as a solo performer. In July 1967, he was the leader of the British singing team entered in the Ninth European Song Cup Contest at Casino Knokke-le-Zoute on the Belgian seacoast. Later, he took part in a children's program, "Disney Wonderland," prepared by England's Rediffusion Television company. By the end of the '60s, though, Gerry had basically retired as an active recording artist. He devoted his time to producing and other behind-the-scenes work in the entertainment field.

GIBB, ANDY: *Singer, guitarist, songwriter. Born Manchester, England March 5, 1958; died Oxford, England, March 10, 1988.*

Andy Gibb was still a toddler when his brothers started on the road to show business prominence in the early 1960s in Australia. By the time he reached his teens, their group, the Bee Gees, was famous around the world. Rather than become another Bee

256

Gee, he took advantage of the opportunities that identification with the Gibb family offered to start a solo career that made him a teen idol for a while in the late 1970s and early 1980s. (*See Bee Gees, The.*)

Andy spent his earliest years in Australia, where his parents moved from their native England in 1958, but his brothers' burgeoning careers with the Bee Gees caused all the Gibbs to resettle in England by the end of the 1960s. Andy, considerably younger than his singing brothers, had to cope with the sometimes difficult responses of his own peer group to their celebrity status. As Andy told Dennis Hunt of the *Los Angeles Times* (September 4, 1977): "I never thought I was different from anybody else. I tried my hardest, but I never was accepted at school. I was marked as the Bee Gees' brother. The last school I went to was a modern public school that had a lot of children from poor homes. You can imagine what they felt like seeing me picked up at school everyday in a Rolls Royce. This set me apart and made them resent me. I was getting picked on all the time. I hated going to school so I just quit."

He was 13 at the time and his family moved from England to Spain, the idea being that he could enroll in a school there where he wouldn't have the same identity problem. But Andy had been learning to play a new guitar his brothers had given him and instead began performing in local bars, singing cover versions of hit songs. Bar owners were happy to oblige, he recalled, because he was willing to sing and play just for the experience rather than for a salary. The regulations in Europe being somewhat more lenient than in the U.S., he didn't have trouble with the authorities because of his age.

A little exposure to live audiences confirmed his desire to establish a singing career. He had no worries about dropping out of school, particularly since his brothers' formal education also had ended in their early teens and hadn't interfered with their becoming affluent and famous. Of course, that situation made it easier for him to pursue his own dreams. He noted in 1977: "I wouldn't have gotten as far as I have so quickly. I know how lucky I am to be part of this family."

For a few years, Andy continued the pattern of singing in small clubs for little or no pay. As he approached his mid-teens, he tried to figure out his career options. One possibility was to join his brothers' resurgent Bee Gees. (For a while in the early 1970s, internal strains had caused them to disband.) There were some discussions about it in 1973–74. "I was all ready to join even though I had some reservations about it," Andy commented. "It just didn't seem right somehow to be an instant success without doing anything to earn it. But it never happened. At that time they were touring so heavily that it was impossible to pin them down to get the whole thing together. So I just went back to doing what I was doing. Looking back on it, I'm glad I didn't become a Bee Gee."

(As it happened, when he did move into the pop-music limelight, many people thought he had been a member of the Bee Gees earlier in his odyssey. He emphasized this never had been the case.)

His brothers still encouraged him to pursue a solo career. They lent a hand in polishing his act and gave advice on songwriting when they had time. By 1976, Andy was ready for the next step, obtaining a recording contract. Not surprisingly, he signed with Robert Stigwood's RSO label, the same one his brothers recorded for.

His debut album, *Flowing Rivers,* came out in the summer of 1977. Brother Barry handled production and also was a backup vocalist for the collection, recorded at the Bee Gees' studios in Miami, Florida. All the songs, though, save one co-written with Barry, were written by Andy with a disco and ballad flavor with a trace of country-rock coming from a close association with members of the Eagles, who were recording a new album in the same studio complex.

Andy told Dennis Hunt: "Originally I had no intention of doing a country-rock album, but I was influenced by the Eagles' sessions just from having them nearby and hearing their songs all the time. That got me wrapped up in country-rock. Joe Walsh [of the Eagles] even came over and did lead guitar tracks on two songs. The whole structure of my session started to lean toward country-rock."

The combination proved right for the moment. It didn't take long for the platinum album and the debut single, "I Just Want to Be Your Everything," to bullet up the U.S. hit charts. Gibb's concert tour of the U.S. and numerous guest spots on nationally televised talk and variety shows helped make the single a number one hit in the U.S. in September 1977. Gibb's ingratiating manner and fresh good looks won over young fans even if his performing style was no threat to superstars such as Dylan or Neil Young. In March 1978, he scored a second number one single with "(Love Is) Thicker than Water," co-written by Andy and Barry Gibb.

In some of his interviews, Gibb demonstrated a maturity well beyond his years, a reflection of his family environment. The 19-year-old told Dennis Hunt: "I've had a lot of adventures and I've already traveled to most countries of the world. Sometimes I feel old because I've never mixed with kids my own age. I've always been around older people. I've always been accepted as an equal adult. My feelings and my outlook on life are adult because I've had so many adult experiences. What's funny is that now I feel old.''

The Gibb family remained close-knit and supporting in trying to maintain Andy's forward career momentum. This succeeded in keeping his name on the top segments of the pop charts worldwide into the early 1980s. His second album, *Shadow Dancing* (1978), also went platinum, providing another number one hit single, the title song. The next RSO LP, *After Dark* (1980), went gold and provided the top 10 single, "Desire." *Andy Gibb's Greatest Hits,* issued at the end of 1980, was on the charts well into 1981. In 1981, his top 10 single was "Time Is Time."

The financial problems that engulfed his record label, RSO, in the early 1980s seemed to have a strange parallel with Gibb's own growing personal problems. By 1981, he already had a severe drug abuse problem with cocaine, a situation that reportedly helped cause a breakup with his girl friend, actress Victoria Principal, in 1982. (He divorced his wife Kim, in 1978.) The separation may have induced even greater drug dependence during 1982–83. At the same time, Andy was having growing financial problems that eventually led to his filing for bankruptcy in September 1987. The legal papers stated he had over $1 million in debts and less than $50,000 in assets. His total earnings for 1986 were claimed to be $7,755.

The turmoil in his private life was reflected in his entertainment activities. His writing and recording efforts tapered off sharply after 1981. During 1981–82, he did serve as co-host on the syndicated TV program *Solid Gold,* but though the show continued after that, he was not rehired. He also made some appearances in stage productions in the early 1980s, including a role in the Gilbert and Sullivan operetta *The Pirates of Penzance.*

When the sudden announcement of his death in England came out in 1988, many observers felt it likely was the result of his drug problems. However, his family and friends emphatically stated Andy had kicked his habit after undergoing treatment in 1985 at the Betty Ford Center in Rancho Mirage, California, and also had straightened out his financial affairs. He had signed a new recording contract with Island Records and was making new career plans when he was rushed to the John Radcliffe Hospital in Oxford on March 7, 1988, complaining of stomach pains. He died there three days later. Afterward, medical officials reported it was not drugs, but the effects of a viral infection on his heart that ended his life.

GILMER, JIMMY, AND THE FIREBALLS:
Vocal and instrumental group. Jimmy Gilmer, *born Chicago, Illinois, 1939; Eric Budd; Stan Lark; George Tomsco.*

Another group that can arouse fond memories among those who were in high school or college in the early '60s, Jimmy Gilmer and the Fireballs had a moment at the top as ephemeral as youth itself. Their one great record, "Sugar Shack," still is a staple item on any show reviewing the history of rock.

Gilmer, whose lead vocal made that record a success, had been singing for a good many years by then, going back to his childhood in La Grange, Illinois. The time was the middle and late 1940s, long before rock came into vogue. The performers he admired were big band vocalists or country & western stars on such programs as "National Barn Dance" broadcast from his birthplace of Chicago.

In 1951, Jimmy's family moved to Amarillo, Texas. His interest in music intensified, particularly when he demonstrated considerable skill as a pianist. For four years, he studied piano at the Musical Arts Conservatory in Amarillo. He also learned guitar, inspired to some extent by the growing importance of Elvis Presley, Carl Perkins, and other teen favorites. In 1957, he formed his own rock band and worked at school dances, private parties, and other engagements. While Jimmy studied engineering at Amarillo College, music was a sideline that helped provide money for expenses.

His performing work took him to several states in the Southwest. While in Clovis, New Mexico, he was at the Norman Petty recording studios when he met the Fireballs. As Petty's house band, they had played the overdubbed backup on the posthumous Buddy Holly albums Petty produced. (*See Holly, Buddy.*) The group, consisting of Eric Budd, Stan Lark, and George Tomsceo, had been working the college and nightclub circuit in the southwest and was looking for another member who could sing and play rhythm guitar.

Petty eventually gained an audition of their material by Dot Records and release of their first singles in 1963. In May, "Sugar Shack" was issued, but didn't do much until the fall, when it rose to the number one position for 5 weeks beginning October 12, 1963. By mid-1964 it had sold well over a million copies in the U.S. alone and became a hit in other countries as well.

However, succeeding records did not duplicate the impact of "Sugar Shack," though "Daisy Petal Pickin'" did make the top 20 in 1964. A few years later the group left Dot and signed with Atco where, under the name the Fireballs, it made upper chart levels with a version of Tom Paxton's composition "Bottle of Wine." In the late 1960s, the group broke up, with the original Fireballs continuing to work together while Gilmer went his own way, eventually moving to Los Angeles in 1969 with plans to organize a new band.

Gilmer's West Coast sojourn didn't renew his career as an entertainer, but he moved to the business side of the industry, accepting a position with United Artists Music in Nashville, Tennessee. Later he became vice president of CBS Songs for the southern section of the U.S., where he was still employed in the late 1980s.

GO-GO's: *Vocal and instrumental group. Original members, mid-1970s, Jane Wiedlin, born California, c. 1958; Belinda Carlisle, born California, August 17, 1958; Margot Olaverra; Elissa Bello. Bello replaced in 1979 by Gina Schock, born Baltimore, Maryland, c. 1958. Charlotte Caffey, born California, added in 1978. Olaverra replaced early 1981 by Kathy Valentine, born Texas, c. 1959. Band broke up in 1985.*

Going against music industry prejudices against all-girl rock groups, the Go-Go's proved that such a band not only could sell a lot of records, but also could rock'n'roll with as much power and abandon as the best male artists. However, personality clashes and the chance for some members to carve out lucrative careers as solo performers contributed to the Go-Go's breakup in 1985.

The group evolved from the burgeoning punk/new wave movement in the Los Angeles area in the mid-1970s. Belinda Carlisle, who became lead vocalist for the band, was a onetime cheerleader at Newbury Park High School in Ventura County, just north of Los Angeles. On weekends she drove to Hollywood to watch punk-style bands at the Starwood Club. At one point she had the chance to join one called the Germs, but ironically she fell ill and had to rest up at home. Later she got a job as a night shift gas station attendant to earn money to get back to L.A. and try for a music career.

Her path soon crossed that of guitarist Jane Wiedlin, who briefly had worked with a punk group under the name Jane Drano. Wiedlin, while going to Taft High School in the San Fernando Valley community of Woodland Hills, became interested in rock because of hearing the Beatles records played by older siblings in her family. After finishing high school, though, she gave up hope of a music career and enrolled in Los Angeles Trade–Technical College to study fashion design.

She told a *Los Angeles Times* interviewer (March 7, 1982), "The ironic thing is that fashion got me back into music. Through fashion magazines I got interested in some of the punk things. I started going down to the Masque [the early Hollywood punk club] to check it out. Finally [some of us] decided to start our own band.

"I didn't worry about the fact we were girls and that we couldn't play. No one else seemed very good either at the time. The important thing was just to get involved. We started off writing some angry protest songs because that's what was in style. But I always liked pop and that's where we really belonged."

The original band, besides Carlisle and Wiedlin, included Margot Olaverra on bass and Elisso Bello on drums. In 1978, Charlotte Caffey was asked to join. Caffey, who attended Immaculate Heart High School in Los Angeles, had played guitar with several groups starting with Manuel and the Gardeners when she was 17. She went on to work with other bands, including drummer Don Bonebrake's group the Eyes. With replacement of Bello on drums in 1979 by Gina Schock, the band was starting to develop its own unique sound, attracting growing numbers of fans to local performances.

Schock, a Led Zeppelin aficionado, had worked with some groups in her hometown of Baltimore before moving to L.A. for greater recording opportunities. She told the *Los Angeles Times*, "When I first saw the band I didn't think they could play very well, but I thought they had a lot of potential." So did Ginger Canzoneri, an album cover graphics designer at CBS Records, who became their manager. She lined up bookings that started to win plaudits from rock reviewers as well as fans. In 1979, this helped bring an invitation from British ska groups Madness and the Specials for the Go-Go's to join them on a U.K. tour. While there, the group made a single, "We Got the Beat," on a one-disc deal with England's Stiff Records.

Back in Los Angeles, the group was spotlighted in a promotional concert at the Starwood set up by Canzoneri for U.S. record executives. No contract offers resulted, however, and, despite growing evidence that the band was a major local concert attraction, none were made that year or during 1980. In early 1981, while Margot Olaverra was out ill, her place was taken by bass guitarist Kathy Valentine. Born in Texas, Valentine had worked with many bands at home and in Los Angeles. Her previous alignment before the Go-Go's was with the Textones. The group members soon decided Valentine fitted in better with Go-Go's style than Olaverra, and Kathy became a permanent member.

Not long after, the reorganized quintet was signed by I.R.S. Records, a label associated with A&M Records. Their label debut LP, *Beauty and the Beat*, came out in the summer of 1981 and soon was high on *Billboard* charts, where it stayed into 1982, passing platinum award levels. A series of chart singles were culled from it, including the title song, "Our Lips Are Sealed," and "We Got the Beat." The LP was in the *Billboard* top 10 in early 1982, a position attained by their second album later in the year, *Vacation* (I.R.S.).

Outwardly everything looked wonderful for the band, but storm clouds were gathering. In early 1982, manager Canzoneri said she was getting tired of business matters and eventually quit. Later Irving Azoff, who had joined her as co-manager shortly before she departed, left his management firm to become president of MCA Records. Then emotional and health problems began to affect band members. In late 1982, Caffey found her left hand had developed a numbness she couldn't shake. After months of aggravation, it finally was diagnosed as Carpal Tunnel Syndrome, and a regimen of Vitamin B-6 tablets was prescribed as a cure.

Meanwhile, financial disagreements had surfaced with I.R.S. Wranglings over what the Go-Go's stated were $1 million in unpaid royalties led to a lengthy legal dispute that finally was settled out of court, but not without leaving bitter feelings among the participants.

In mid-1983 the band assembled in London, England, to begin plans for a new album, *Talk Show*.

While there, Schock found her health deteriorating. She felt worse after completing work on *Talk Show* in London during the winter of 1983–84. Back in Los Angeles, she went to her doctor for a checkup. While rehearsing for an upcoming tour in support of the new LP, she was informed the doctor urgently wanted to see her.

She told Robert Hilburn (*Los Angeles Times*, June 17, 1984): "I started crying right away because I knew there was something wrong. We all went over [to his office] together. He told me and I almost passed out. I couldn't even think. The rest of the girls got hysterical. It was a horrifying thing. I had a hole about the size of a golf ball in the vertical wall of the two top chambers of my heart." By the following Monday she was in the hospital awaiting surgery.

Fortunately, it was successful and the Go-Go's were back together and touring by mid-1984. *Talk Show* was on the charts on its way to gold record sales. It was a fine album, indicating steady creative progress, and it sold well even if it didn't approach the blockbuster levels of the debut LP.

But outside pressures and internal problems began to take too heavy a toll. In late 1984, Jane Wiedlin decided to leave for a solo career. In early 1985, she began work on her debut LP, *Jane Wiedlin*, issued by I.R.S. in late summer. By then, Belinda Carlisle had also resigned, leading to the official disbandment of the Go-Go's in May 1985.

Carlisle told Hilburn (Los Angeles Times, May 10, 1986) she also had thought about departing during 1984. "We were getting ready for a concert in Rio and it just didn't feel right. I remember it real clearly because I started to cry. It wasn't fun anymore. We were just sort of going through the motions, pretending to have all the fun on stage that we really did have in the beginning.

"I was so unhappy that I hated seeing new artists because I knew I couldn't be one of them. I couldn't [share their] freshness or excitement. I was sort of envious."

During the summer of 1985 she began working on her solo material, helped by Charlotte Caffey. Before completing the project, she decided to make important life-style changes, including going to a nutritionist for a healthier diet and joining Alcoholics Anonymous. She was encouraged to do that, she told Hilburn, by Caffey's earlier success in overcoming a substance abuse problem.

Her debut LP, *Belinda,* came out on I.R.S. in the middle of 1986 and was a chart hit, as was the single from the LP, "Mad About You." The latter was one of the biggest hits of 1986 and was included in MCA's *Mega Hits '86* LP, a fund-raising release for the T.J. Martell Foundation for Leukemia and Cancer Research. In mid-1987, her second solo album, *Heaven on Earth,* came out on a new label, MCA.

Gina Schock released *House of Schock* in 1988 on Capitol Records to start her solo career.

GORDY, BERRY, JR.: *Record-company executive, record producer, songwriter. Born Detroit, Michigan, November 28, 1929.*

Certainly one of the most important innovators of the 1960s, Berry Gordy, Jr., played a significant role in making soul an integral part of the total national mass market. Some progress had been made in this direction by the Chess brothers of Chess and Checker Records and the Erteguns of Atlantic Records, but it was the steady stream of hit records and superstars developed by Gordy from the Detroit headquarters of Motown Records that, in effect, obsoleted the time-honored approach of listing R&B and top 100 as separate markets.

Gordy was born and raised in the Lower East Side ghetto of Detroit. One of eight children, he learned how to make do with hand-me-downs and, in the rugged environment he grew up in, how to survive. In his teens, he already had developed a deep-seated desire to escape from the misery and squalor he saw around him, but was not sure of which of two routes to take. The obvious choices seemed to be sports and music. He was a good athlete and had learned to defend himself in fights with neighborhood opponents. He also enjoyed pop music and sometimes tried his hand at songwriting.

For a while, boxing seemed the most likely route to success. Gordy started in neighborhood gyms, got a manager, and turned professional as a featherweight. He won 10 of 14 fights, but decided that the ring game was a long, hard grind and, more important, the featherweight class was hardly the big-money end of the business.

Berry decided to settle down in Detroit and work at a regular job. He got a job on the Ford Motor Company assembly line as a chrome trimmer and, by the late 1950s, was earning $85 a week. But he kept working on songs and spent his spare time in night clubs listening to artists and discussing the music field with any industry people he could find.

Since his early twenties, he had started to try his luck as a songwriter. He went to New York and made the rounds of music publishers and record firms. There were plenty of turndowns, but in the middle 1950s, he did manage to place some songs. Some like "Reet Petite," "That is Why (I Love You So)" and "I'll Be Satisfied" became hits in the R&B field for Jackie Wilson. Gordy learned another fact of life—a hit song doesn't necessarily mean a gold mine for a songwriter. As he told one reporter: "I had problems getting money at the time that I needed it. I was broke even with the hit records in certain cases. When the companies paid me, it was three months later and I owed money out to the family."

From all of this, Gordy finally decided the only way to make it in the record business was to produce the records himself. He borrowed $700 from his family and set up a makeshift recording studio in an eight-room apartment in a run-down section of Grand Avenue. He called his new firm Motown Records (for Motor Town) and coined the name Tamla for his first label. He began to audition talent and, as luck would have it, he was in perfect position for this. Detroit in the late 1950s was a veritable treasure trove of young, eager, and gifted black singers, dancers, and musicians.

In 1959, one of these youngsters, 19-year-old Smokey Robinson, particularly impressed Gordy. Aided by other Detroit teenagers calling themselves the Miracles, Robinson demonstrated considerable skill as a performer. The act also presented their interesting original compositions for Gordy's approval. Gordy signed them and, within a year, had been amply rewarded with two major hits: "Shop Around" and "Way over There." With their profits, Gordy was able to add to the artist list. His judgment was unerring. During 1961 and 1962, he signed such promising newcomers as the Supremes, the Marvelettes, Martha and the Vandellas, the Temptations,

and Marvin Gaye. In the years that followed, he or his artist and repertoire men (who included the new renowned team of producer-songwriters Eddie Holland, Lamont Dozier, and Brian Holland) brought such others onto the roster as Stevie Wonder, the Four Tops, and Jr. Walker & the All Stars.

Enormous artistic and financial success greeted the company over the next decade. These results came from the blend of many talents, but underlying it all was Gordy's insistence on certain methods of working. Though by the early 1970s, Gordy had to depend increasingly on associates to conduct the day-to-day routine of what had become a major operation, for the most of the 1960s, he closely coordinated all the material turned out by his firm. One of his cardinal principles was to demand quality rather than quantity. He tried to insure this by insisting that he or his aides continually refine material developed in recording sessions, demanding that all or part be rerecorded until the product was up to what they considered were Motown standards.

As a result, for most of the 1960s, the number of singles issued by Motown (relative to company sales volume) was close to the lowest in the industry. However, the percentage of these that became hits was close to the highest. The success of Gordy's methods caused his company's output to be given a special designation, the "Motown Sound," by the music fraternity.

In addition to his approach in actual sessions, Gordy also established the goal of continuously upgrading the abilities of his artists. This was particularly important in the companion businesses to the record operation established by Gordy—booking, arranging special tours, and, starting in the late 1960s, preparation of TV specials featuring Motown artists. As Diana Ross, who moved from lead singer of the Supremes to solo stardom, noted: "Everyone with the [Motown] family has to go to class—a finishing school for beauty and charm, a choreography class, and a vocal class. Everyone goes, even if they don't have to sing or dance. They have to learn these different aspects of the business to improve their stage presence."

By the early 1970s, Motown and its associated activities was one of the top 10 in the record field. It had sales exceeding $10 million a year. Gordy, listed in *Who's Who in America* and winner of many awards for his outstanding creative and business abilities, was a legend in his own time.

The label lost many of its name stars in the 1970s and early 1980s, including Gladys Knight, Diana Ross, Marvin Gaye, Michael Jackson, and the Four Tops. But it was not a complete exodus and it still could point to such superstars as the Temptations and Stevie Wonder from its '60s roster and such newcomers to the label as the Commodores and Lionel Richie. Meanwhile, Gordy presided over his company's movements into other areas of entertainment, such as movies (one example being the hit *Lady Sings the Blues* starring Diana Ross as Billie Holiday), TV programs and even live theater.

As far as new recording artists for the label, Gordy told Robert Hilburn (*Los Angeles Times,* March 22, 1983): "We've developed and discovered every artist we've had. We never bought an artist who was already at the top. We took the kids off the street. If they're good enough, we advance them the money and work with them."

In March 1983, Gordy and Motown celebrated a milestone: 25 years under his guidance. Key part of the celebration was a twenty-fifth anniversary show at the Civic Auditorium in Pasadena, California, featuring past and present top stars with the label. Among those taking part in the tribute were Stevie Wonder, Diana Ross, Rick James, Smokey Robinson, Marvin Gaye, Richard Pryor, Michael Jackson, Lionel Richie, the Temptations, and the Four Tops. The show was taped for later telecasting as an NBC special and the music was recorded for future album release. Proceeds from the tickets, priced at from $500 to $25, were given to the National Association for Sickle Cell Disease.

Not all the past Motown headliners were in attendance, however, and some absentees suggested it reflected a less than harmonious relationship between Gordy and his artists. In his book on Motown history, *Where Did Our Love Go* (St. Martin's Press, 1985), Nelson George pointed to a quote interviewer Harry Weinger reported receiving from Gladys Knight: "We have felt for so long that one of the things that was really unfair about Motown was that the artists were really the backbone of the company and they got so mistreated over there. The least they could have done was said, 'We're going to do this tribute to Motown people, period. Including Mr. Gordy as the number one person.' I don't think you heard it (on the TV tape of the show). I might have missed it, but on the show they didn't say, 'And we thank all those acts here tonight, because in actuality if it weren't for them, there wouldn't be any Motown. Or Mr. Gordy, for that matter.' So we felt it was a little hypocritical to go and be part of that."

Gordy brushed aside criticism and suggestions that Motown had continued to lose momentum, telling Hilburn, "I'm as excited today as I was in the beginning. We've got new roads . . . the cable, the technology of the computer, digital recordings. We've got more movies to make and we've got several stage plays in the works."

But the optimism proved premature. In mid-1988, the company was sold to MCA Records and the investment company Boston Ventures for $61 million. It truly was the end of an era.

(*See Four Tops, The; Gaye, Marvin; Jackson, Michael; Jacksons, The; James, Rick; Knight, Gladys & the Pips; Martha and the Vandellas; Marvelettes, The; Moonglows, The; Richie, Lionel; Robinson, Smokey; Ross, Diana; Supremes, The; Temptations, The; Walker, Jr., & the All Stars; Wonder, Stevie.*)

GRAHAM, LARRY: *Singer, instrumentalist (guitarist, keyboardist, harmonica player, saxophonist, drummer), band leader (GRAHAM CENTRAL STATION), songwriter, record producer. Born Beaumont, Texas, August 14, 1946.*

When Sly and the Family Stone became a pop music force in the late 1960s with its special soul-rock sound, one of the most notable features of its arrangements was the strong and unique bass line. The thumping bass technique became a feature of the rock'n'roll groups that came to the fore in later decades, including the group that took over Sly Stone's mantle for a while in the 1970s, Graham Central Station. Appropriately, the founder and leader of that group was Larry Graham, the musician who also pioneered the new bass sound as a sideman with Stone's group. (*See Sly and the Family Stone.*)

Larry was the son of a talented musician, Ms. Dell Graham, who had a reputation for fine piano playing in Beaumont, Texas, where Larry was born. When he was two, his family pulled up stakes and headed for Oakland, California, where the opportunities for black artists reportedly were brighter. As Larry grew to maturity in that city, his mother made sure he was well schooled in the entertainment arts. When he was five, he started dancing lessons and when he was eight began taking piano lessons. An adept pupil, by his teen years he added skills on keyboards, guitar, harmonica, saxophone, and drums. Equally impressive were his vocal abilities, which eventually allowed him to demonstrate a 3½ octave range.

Larry did impromptu performing with his mother and friends during those early years, but he didn't go into full-time performing, he said, until his midteens. "My music career really started with my mom. We started out as the Dell Graham Trio, playing clubs around the San Francisco Bay Area. I was about 15 at the time, playing guitar and organ, with my mom on piano, and a drummer. One night we had a really important gig and the organ broke down. I went out at the last minute to rent another one, but all they had was a bass guitar. I've been playing bass ever since."

After a while, the drummer left and the group became the Dell Graham Duo. The mother-and-son act still found considerable work in local clubs playing mostly jazz standards such as "Time after Time" and "The Shadow of Your Smile." To compensate for lack of a drummer, Larry gradually evolved his unique style of bass work. "I used to thump and hit the strings to compensate for the lack of a drummer."

Word of the way his bass playing sounded began to circulate among other musicians in the San Francisco area. One of those who became interested in the mid-1960s was disc jockey Sylvester "Sly" Stone, who worked on Oakland soul station KSOL. Stone wanted to assemble his own band to play a mix of soul and rock. Any additional unusual musical angle he could integrate into such a band would make success that much more likely, Stone figured. After he watched a Dell Graham Duo show, he revealed his band plans to Larry and persuaded Graham to join. After rehearsals in Stone's garage, the new band went out on the soul/rock/jazz club network and in fairly short order had attracted enough interest to gain a record deal with CBS's subsidiary, Epic Records.

Graham helped record the band's debut album and the blockbuster single "Dance to the Music" that catapulted Sly and the Family Stone into top rock ranks. Over the next six years, Larry remained a valued band member for both recordings and concert tours that took him all over the world.

In the early 1970s, personal and other problems beset the band. Larry decided it was time to go out on his own and assemble a new group. The result was Graham Central Station, a group in which Larry combined his bass guitar shadings with other elements of R&B, jazz, soul, and rock to achieve a pulsating form of music that built on and expanded the scope of Sly Stone's concept. The group signed with Warner Brother Records in 1972 and released its debut album, *Graham Central Station,* in December 1973. Helped by a hit single, "Can You Handle It," the LP made the R&B and general pop charts. The band's debut coast-to-coast U.S. tour in 1974 had enthused onlookers dancing in the aisles at many stops.

The group's second album, *Release Yourself* (1974) also was a hit at home and abroad. From that collection, the single "Feel the Need" gained upper chart spots on both the R&B and pop compilations.

The band's third album, *Ain't No Bout-A-Doubt It,* came out on Warner's in July 1975 and was certified gold by the U.S. RIAA within months of its release. From it came another singles hit, "Your Love." After that, Larry settled down to write all the material for the next album, which he planned as a showcase for a sound he described as "progressive funk." *Mirror* (1976) was a good album, eminently danceable, but in truth it didn't sound much different

from the earlier releases. It made the charts, though its overall sales reflected growing competition from new, innovative funk and R&B-rock–oriented groups such as Earth, Wind & Fire and Parliament/Funkadelic.

Larry and his associates continued to provide new material for the record company's marketing mill and retained a sizable reputation for concert work. The new LPs included *Now Do U Wanna Dance* (1977), *My Radio Sure Sounds Good to Me* (May 1978), and *Star Walk* (June 1979). Graham wrote much of the material on those and also worked with other members and producers to try to add new features to the material. On *Now Do U Wanna Dance,* he used an electronic setup to provide what he believed was the world's first "talking" bass. On *My Radio Sure Sounds Good to Me,* he also employed some electronic effects to try to achieve a wilder, spacier feeling.

The basic dance qualities remained intact in all the albums, but the new effects seemed more in the nature of gimmickry than development of creative advances. Perhaps, too, Graham was becoming jaded with band routines. All of those factors helped move him toward a solo career. This direction already was evident on *My Radio Sure Sounds Good to Me,* where more focus than before was on Larry's lead vocal work. He took the format all the way along in the 1980 Warner Brothers album, *One in a Million You.* For that project, he was responsible for almost all aspects from writing the songs to performing them and producing the overall album. Most of the non-Graham touches came from Graham Central Station sidemen Wilton Rabb on guitar and Eric Daniels on keyboards. The album was a chart hit on black music lists. The title track, the first single from the collection, ranked as the sixth best-selling soul single of the year by *Billboard.*

Larry followed up with another solo album, *Just Be My Lady* (Warner Brothers, 1981). The title song, released as a single, was a top 10 soul hit during the year. Graham also had two other hit soul singles in 1981, "When We Get Married" and "Guess Who."

GRAHAM CENTRAL STATION: *See Graham, Larry.*

GRANDMASTER FLASH: *Disc jockey, composer, record producer, band leader (THE FURIOUS FIVE). Born Barbados, c. 1957.*

Whether or not Grandmaster Flash invented rap music—a combination of street talk with funky rhythm tracks—as he claims, there's no doubt he helped pioneer the art form into a major element of pop music in the 1980s. With his group The Furious

Five, he had the first singles breakthrough with "The Message" in 1982, a disc whose lyrics bluntly outlined the alienation felt by people living in the black ghetto.

Flash was born Joseph Saddler in Barbados, but moved to the Bronx in New York City at an early age and grew up there. He recalled getting his first enjoyment in music from listening to his father's record collection. Later, at his mother's insistence, he studied electronics, which provided him with new insights into music basics when he began to build up experience as a mobile disc jockey playing records for dances in New York parks and clubs in the 1970s. His electronic knowledge played a role in development of his unusual performance techniques.

He recalled: "Most disc jockeys at parties would simply play a record all the way to the end, but I was too fidgety to just wait for the end of the record. So rather than sit and wait, I would do something to enhance the music." From those experiments, he said, he evolved ways of mixing excerpts from different records to create new sound patterns. He employed methods called "break-mixing," "phasing," and "scratching"—techniques of varying sounds and rhythms by manipulating records while needles were in the grooves.

After a while, his reputation grew to the extent that he had to move from small venues to larger and larger clubs. By the end of the '70s, he already was receiving notice from pop music critics in New York. He took the next step of making recordings such as "Superrapping" and "We Rap More Mellow." His third release on the Sugarhill label, "Freedom," became a chart hit and was followed by another exciting disc, *The Adventures of Grandmaster Flash on the Wheels of Steel,* which featured his break-mixing and scratching techniques. His final singles on Sugarhill in the early 1980s ("White Lines," "New York, New York," and "The Message") established him as a new star on a nationwide level. At the end of 1982, major rock critics throughout the U.S. voted "The Message" single of the year.

By 1983, the Furious Five comprised main narrator Melle Mel (Melvin Glover), Kidd Creole (Danny Glover), Mr. Ness (Eddie Morris), Raheim (Guy Williams), and Cowboy (Keith Wiggins). During that year, however, dissension broke out among group members about creative directions and royalty payments. In late 1983, the band broke up into two factions, one composed of Flash, Raheim, and Kidd Creole against the other three, whose main spokesman was Melle Mel. Lawsuits were filed by Flash against Sugarhill claiming unpaid royalties and damages while the two groups also fought over the rights to the group name. The judge who heard the case ruled in early 1984 against a financial settlement with Flash and also stated that while Grandmaster Flash could continue to record under his own name, Melle Mel and Sugarhill (distributed in the mid-1980s by MCA Records) could also use the name Grandmaster. Thus, Sugarhill issued the 1984 single "Jesse" under the name Grandmaster Melle Mel.

Replying to questions about likely group-name confusion, Mel's attorney, Joe Zynczak, said to a reporter: "The identity of the group is in its voice and the voice has been Melle Mel's voice. So I think everyone will be able to tell them apart." The Mel lineups output after that included the single "Internationally Known" and performance of the title song for the rap-dance film *Beat Street.*

By 1985, Grandmaster Flash had signed with a new label, Elektra. His group, besides Kidd Creole and Raheim, added three new members: rapper Mr. Broadway, dancer Larry Love, and writer and bass player Lavon. The band's album debut on Elektra was *They Said It Couldn't Be Done* (1985). In Elektra press material Flash commented: "In the new album I tried to branch out as much as possible. There is uptempo material, rock, scratching, a ballad sung by Raheim, and intermixes of rapping and singing. One song, 'Sign of the Times,' continues the legacy of us being the cream of the crop for recording socially significant songs and videos. Frivolous rap is not as entertaining as it used to be. Now it is more important for rap artists to release socially significant songs because that is what the public wants to hear."

GRATEFUL DEAD, THE: *Vocal and instrumental group. Members, late 1960s to early 1970s: Jerry Garcia, born San Francisco, California, August 1, 1942; Robert Hall Weir, born San Francisco, California, October 16, 1947; Phil Lesh, born Berkeley, California, March 15, 1940; Bill Kreutzmann, Jr., born Palo Alto, California, May 7, 1946; Mickey Hart, born New York, New York, September 11, 1943; Ron "Pig Pen" McKernan, born San Bruno, California, September 8, 1946, died Corte Madera, California, March 1973. Added in early 1970s: Donna Godchaux, born August 22, 1947; Keith Godchaux, born July 19, 1948. Godchauxs left 1979, Brent Nydland added.*

The Grateful Dead is the band almost always bracketed with the Jefferson Airplane when the great era of San Francisco's rock'n'roll history is discussed. Unlike the Airplane (and its successors), for many years the Grateful Dead had no massive total of record sales to its credit because, as unorthodox as the Airplane was from a creative standpoint, its members always seemed more willing to play the record company and marketing game than the Dead.

Jon Pareles of *The New York Times* (July 26, 1987) pointed to one fetish of the band that made record industry executives cringe. "Where too many rock bands aim to re-create their records in concert, the Dead are known to warp and nudge and fiddle with their songs, risking mistakes while courting inspiration; they'll start a freeform jam with no idea what they'll end up playing. They're inconstant and unpredictable, unwilling to repeat themselves; they're a marketing expert's nightmare."

In its early years, the Dead seemed the equal of the best rock groups in concert, but it seemed unable or unwilling to transpose that sound onto discs. Later, oddly, its records sometimes began to seem more compelling than the concerts. But the band demonstrated the ability to survive. It continued to turn out new albums with relative regularity into the early 1980s (when a recording hiatus set the stage for hit releases late in the decade) and was still able to draw adoring crowds to its concerts year after year.

The lead guitarist of the group, Jerry Garcia—he of the black T-shirt, mustache and bushy beard (turned gray in the 1980s)—was born and raised in the Bay Area. He first became interested in rock as a teenager in the mid-1950s, but switched his interest to folk music after dropping out of school for a short stint in the Army, from which he was discharged as unfit for service. By the late 1950s, he was one of the more talented folk guitarists performing around San Francisco. Traditional country music attracted his attention for a while in the early 1960s. He did considerable research on the subject, along the way developing into one of the best bluegrass guitarists in the west. Later, he came back to playing country and folk with some of the separate groups he set up when not performing with the Dead.

During this period, Jerome John Garcia moved home base to Palo Alto, California, along with two close friends, Bob Hunter (who later wrote many songs for the Dead) and David Nelson (guitarist with the country-rock New Riders of the Purple Sage, with whom Garcia played pedal steel guitar in the early '70s).

Garcia's musical reputation attracted other young musicians to him, including Bob Weir and Ron McKernan. Weir, from an affluent San Francisco family, had been sent to a series of boarding schools in the area before he dropped out in his teens in favor of pop music. McKernan, son of a white rhythm & blues disc jockey, also quit high school before graduating. When he met Garcia in 1964, he was 17, "looked 15, and said I was 21." In 1964, Garcia, with Weir (who played rhythm guitar) and McKernan (on vocals, organ, and harmonica), formed Mother McCree's Uptown Jug Champions (some-times accompanied by Dave Parker, later the group's accountant and manager, on washboard)

The group had trouble finding work, but were offered equipment from a Palo Alto music store owner who played bass guitar, if they would switch to amplified rock. The three jug band originals agreed and sought more musicians. Jerry added long-time friend Philip Chapman Lesh. Lesh had been a child violinist who, after finishing his schooling, had gone into Stan Kenton–type jazz as a trumpeter and arranger. Lesh had no experience as a bassist, but Garcia told him he would play the instrument with the group and Lesh promptly learned it, soon taking over from the store owner. The fifth member was a teenage drummer, born William Kreutzmann, Jr., to a Palo Alto middle class family, but then known as Bill Sommers to match the name he carried on his fake ID card.

In July 1965, the new quintet, calling themselves the Warlocks, played their first date at a small club in Fremont, California. They performed conventional rock'n'roll initially, copying some of the groups then famous in the field, and gained fairly steady employment at a club in nearby Belmont. As 1965 went by, the group changed its style, playing with increasing intensity and with melodic innovations of its own. Highly amplified music was not fashionable at that time and place. As Garcia recalled: "People had to scream at each other and pretty soon we had driven out all the regular clientele."

The group, who had all dropped acid, were playing a type of music called psychedelic rock. Later in their careers, their combined efforts were described by one fan as "living thunder." The group left the Belmont club and began to play at La Honda, headquarters of one of the leading exponents of LSD, Ken Kesey. The group was the first of countless Bay Area rock bands to combine jam sessions at La Honda with drug taking, a technique that went on for several years during the height of the Haight-Ashbury hippie era under the collective name of the Acid Tests.

During this phase, the band's name changed to the Grateful Dead. Garcia and his associates felt they no longer were a rock band and needed a new title. According to one version of what happened, during a DMT smoking session at Lesh's house, Garcia opened the Oxford English Dictionary, saw the words Grateful Dead, and all accepted it on the spot.

In June 1966, the group moved to the Haight-Ashbury section of San Francisco, taking up quarters at 710 Ashbury. Before long, its reputation, which had already spread among the underground, took on major proportions. The group played some engagements at local clubs, but often as not they performed free at hippie gatherings. Their music was, if anything, even more highly amplified, but beneath the ear-splitting sound were intricately changing patterns that often ran the gamut in a single, long number from country and folk through Indian raga, hard rock, and other variations. The group played at the more or less informal series of rock concerts called the Trips Festival and were given ovations every time. In the summer of 1967, they played at the famous Monterey Pop Festival that brought fame to such artists as Janis Joplin and Jimi Hendrix. The Dead were also hailed as one of the best at the festival, but they were opposed to some of the propositions for wider exploitation of their music made by some of the music-industry executives who attended the event.

Meanwhile, the group had signed with Warner Brothers. Their first album, *The Grateful Dead* (1967), boasted psychedelic rock interpretations of old blues and blue grass standards. However, the album had been made amid constant dissension between the group and the record firm and did not have the excitement of their live performances. Warner Brothers tried to get around this on the second album by sending crews into the field to tape some of the Dead's in-person appearances. The resulting album, *Anthem of the Sun,* was pieced together from 18 live performances and four studio sessions, but again mistrust between the parties led to an uneven final product. Both LPs gained some attention, as did the 1967 single, ''Golden Road of Unlimited Devotion,'' but none were best-sellers.

After a tour of the Northwest in the fall of 1967 with Quicksilver Messenger Service and a group called Headlights, the Dead returned to San Francisco and set up their own operation in the Carousel Ballroom in San Francisco. The music drew great crowds of admirers, but the Dead were poor businessmen and finally lost their lease. Bill Graham, who had sought to gain both operating rights and management for the group, then acquired the lease and renamed the hall Fillmore West.

1968 saw not only this retreat, but the disintegration of the Haight-Ashbury hippie movement. The Dead had to move to separate houses in San Francisco and in Marin County. The group finally toured other sections of the U.S. and, while playing a New York engagement, acquired a sixth member, a private detective turned drum instructor named Mickey Hart. (At times, a friend of Jerry's named Tom Constanten had worked with the group as organist, playing on some of the tracks of the group's first four LPs. However, he never became a full-time member of the group.)

The group continued to grudgingly complete material for Warner Brothers. In 1969, their third album, *Aoxomoxoa* was released, followed by the concert *Live Dead.* In 1970, two more albums were issued, *Workingman's Dead* and *American Beauty.* Considerably more polished in content, reflecting, perhaps, some mellowing of the group's anarchistic tendencies toward the outside world, these LPs finally began to achieve sales in line with the historic impact the Dead have had on today's popular music, eventually going platinum.

In 1969, deeply in debt as usual, the group agreed to Bill Graham's offer to handle their bookings. A typical 1969 program by the Dead included such songs as ''Me and My Uncle,'' ''Everybody's Doing That Rag,'' ''King Bee,'' ''Lovelight,'' ''Dark Star,'' and ''St. Stephens.''

Ron McKernan was not in good health at the beginning of the '70s, so for insurance, the group added keyboards player Keith Godchaux, who had played piano in many East Bay clubs before joining the Dead during 1971. Also coming into the fold was his wife, Donna Jean, whose credits included singing with a vocal group, Southern Comfort, which had backed various R&B stars and Elvis Presley. The roster of the band essentially was set from the early 1970s into the 1980s.

The prime loss, of course, was McKernan, who was found dead in his Marin County apartment in March 1973. ''The cause of death apparently was from natural causes,'' the coroner stated. ''He had a history of liver disease.'' Band manager Jon McIntire said at the time: ''This was not a sensational rock'n'roll death. It was the death of a guy who was trying to get better.''

The group built up a strong following outside the U.S., aided by debut visits to England in 1970 and France in 1971 followed by a seven-nation tour in 1972 that served as the basis for the gold 1972 Warner Brothers triple-LP *Europe '72.* (Warner Brothers previously had released the live 1971 LP, *The Grateful Dead.*) After the Warner Brothers contract expired in 1973, the band put out a series of albums on its own Grateful Dead label for a number of years. Warner Brothers released several more albums, however, including previously unreleased tracks on *History of the Grateful Dead, Vol. 1 (Bear's Choice)* (1973), plus the retrospectives *Best of the Grateful Dead—Skeletons in the Closet* and *What a Long Strange Trip It's Been* (1978).

The band's first release on its own label, Grateful Dead Records, was the 1973 *Wake of the Flood.* This was followed by *The Grateful Dead from the Mars Hotel* (1974), *Blues for Allah* (1975) and *Steal Your Face* (1976). After a five-night standing-room—only concert at San Francisco's Winterland in 1974, a series filmed for a later documentary, the band took a two-year leave from live performances. During the hiatus, besides working on individual projects, band members helped shape the film, which was finally released under the title *The Grateful Dead* during the summer of 1977. It proved to be one of the better rock documentaries of the decade.

During the band's '75–'76 hiatus, Bob Weir formed a new band, Kingfish. That project didn't work out as hoped for and by 1977 he was touring again with the other Grateful Dead members. Of course, as Garcia always stressed, the band was a loose assemblage where no one objected to members going off on their own with other groups. He himself formed various sidebar projects including the stellar bluegrass-rock Old and in the Way and, in the early 1980s, the Jerry Garcia Band. Featuring Garcia on banjo, Vassar Clement on fiddle, David Grisman on mandolin, songwriter Peter Rowan on guitar, and John Kahn on bass, the live all-acoustic *Old and in the Way* album on Round (1975) was reissued on Sugar Hill Records in 1984 and later on CD by Rykodisc. Jerry recorded many solo LPs, including *Garcia* (Warner Brothers, 1972), *Garcia* (Round Records, 1974), *Reflections* (Round, 1976), *Cats under the Stars* (Arista, 1978), and *Run for the Roses* (Arista, 1982). He also joined organist Merl Saunders, bassist John Kahn, and drummer Bill Vitt for live shows at the Keystone Korner in San Francisco that formed the basis for the *Live at the Keystone* LP issued by Fantasy Records in 1973. In 1988, Fantasy put out *Keystone Encores, Vol. 1* and *Vol. 2* from those sessions. Other mid-1970s albums from the Dead family included *Keith and Donna*, Phil Lesh and Ned Lagin's *Sea Stones*, and Robert Hunter's *Tiger Rose* and *Tales of the Great Rum Runners,* all on the Dead's own label, Round Records. (Albums by the Dead as a group came out on Grateful Dead Records, while those by their splinter groups were on Round.)

The band signed with Arista Records in 1977, which was its record home through the 1980s. Among Grateful Dead LPs issued on that label were *Terrapin Station* (1977), *Shakedown Street* (1978), *The Grateful Dead Go to Heaven* (1980), and two live concert double albums in 1981, *Dead Reckoning* and *Dead Set.*

Though some critics complained increasingly that the band's concerts didn't blaze new trails and often seemed sloppy, the Grateful Dead continued to have rapport with large numbers of fans worldwide throughout the 1980s. Except for a period in the mid-1980s when Garcia was out of action due to severe, almost fatal, health problems, including a diabetic coma, the band continued to put in a lot of road work. Legions of ardent fans (Deadheads) would follow the band from city to city, attending every show the Dead gave. Through the early '80s, many of these cultists were aging hippies, but by 1987, a Dead revival was attracting neohippies in their teens and twenties, known to long-standing Deadheads as "little kids" regardless of their size.

Garcia actually didn't argue with critical evaluation. He told a *Los Angeles Times* reporter: "We're musicians, not performers. None of us is very good on stage. We don't think of ourselves as singers, either. That role has been forced on us. For me to get up there on stage to sing, I have to overcome this thing of feeling like a fool singing in front of a bunch of people."

But he also pointed out that people still seemed to enjoy the band's shows. "Our audience doesn't come to see showmanship and theatrics. They realize what we are and that we're not performers and that we're a group that's earnestly trying to accomplish something and we don't quite know what it is."

The band's concerts of 1987–88, which included a series of appearances with Bob Dylan in the summer of '87, showcased songs from *In the Dark,* the group's first new studio album for Arista since 1980. Though the band had given plenty of concerts in the interim, their dissatisfaction with their late '70s studio LPs for Arista had caused them to delay new studio work for an extended period. (Since, unlike most rock bands, they openly invited fans to tape concert numbers which, as noted, rarely sounded the same twice, it could be said there were many unofficial albums circulating in the 1980s). *In the Dark,* the band's 22nd official LP release, proved one of its best and also provided them with their first big hit single, "Touch of Gray."

GREEN, AL: *Singer, songwriter. Born Forrest City, Arkansas, April 13, 1946.*

Once considered heir to the mantle of James Brown as king of the soul singers, Al Green also was one of the most successful pop male vocalists of the 1970s. His striking popularity in the early 1970s was further proof of the acceptance by the mass audience of soul/R&B as a major art form in the popular sense. Yet at the height of his fame, Al moved sideways to rechannel his career into gospel singing.

When he was eight in his hometown of Forrest City, Arkansas, he heard a Sam Cooke record on the radio and resolved to become a singer. (Later influences, he states, included James Brown, Jackie Wilson, and Claude Jester of the gospel Swan Silvertones.) When he was nine, he and his four brothers organized a group that achieved a certain amount of attention on the gospel circuit for half a dozen years. Before Al reached his teens, his family had moved north to Grand Rapids, Michigan. While attending high school there, he decided to form his own pop group, Al Green and the Creations, which toured small soul clubs on the Chitlin' Circuit of the South and Midwest for the next three years. In the mid-1960s, he reorganized under the name of Al Green and the Soul Mates.

In 1967, he made his record debut: "Back Up Train" on the Hot Line label, which belonged to friend Palmer James. The song made the national soul charts in 1968. However, he held the spotlight for only a short time. The problem, Green said later, was that "I wasn't ready for a hit. I didn't have any material to follow it up with, so I went through all the disappointments and frustrations of being a one-record act."

In 1969, Green had returned to obscurity, playing small clubs in such places as Midland, Texas. In Midland, however, he met Willie Mitchell, bandleader, chief producer, and vice president of Hi Records of Memphis, Tennessee. Mitchell liked Green's singing and signed him for Hi. With encouragement from Mitchell, Al worked on some originals of his own as well as on arrangements of other writers' material.

From this came Green's first hit on his new label, "I Can't Get Next to You," a reworking of an old Temptations hit. It reached number one on the soul charts in early 1971. The response to this single helped propel the album containing it, *Al Green Gets Next to You*, onto the soul charts and then on the national charts as well, where it remained into the middle of 1972. In the fall of 1971 "Tired of Being Alone" reached top levels nationally, selling over a million copies.

Green then collaborated with Willie Mitchell and Al Jackson (formerly with Booker T and the M.G.'s) (*See Booker T. and the M.G.s*), on two more gold record singles: "Let's Stay Together" and "Look What You Done For Me." The first made number one in *Billboard* the week of February 12, 1972. Green's album *Let's Stay Together*, which included a well-received remake of the Bee Gees' "How Can You Mend a Broken Heart," also went gold.

In mid-1972, Green performed his fourth million-seller, "I'm Still in Love with You," also an original, and closed out the year with his fifth straight gold single, "You Ought to Be with Me." His 1972 LP, *I'm Still in Love with You*, won another gold award.

Discussing his writing efforts, Green said: "I can't write every day. I can only write when I feel there is something to write about, when something has happened. When I find something to write about, I find myself picking up the guitar, never knowing what to play. I just sit there and rock awhile. Finally something comes along."

In the mid-1970s, he was increasingly successful

as a crossover record star. He already had been named the Rock'n'Pop Star of 1972 by *Rolling Stone* and also picked awards as Best Pop and R&B Vocalist from *Billboard, Cash Box,* and *Record World.* In the American Music Award voting, he was the winner of the Top R&B Vocalist award for 1973 and was nominated for a 1973 Grammy for his single "Call Me" and for a 1975 award for his composition "L-O-V-E (Love)." His 1975 citations included being named Number One R&B Vocalist by *Cash Box,* Number One Male Best-Selling R&B Album Vocalist by *Record World,* and Number One Best-Selling Male Vocalist–R&B LPs by *Billboard.*

During those years, he continued to turn out often superior and always above-average albums on the Hi/London label. Those included *Call Me* and *Livin' for You* (1973), *Al Green Explores Your Mind* (1974), *Greatest Hits* and *Al Green Is Love* (1975), and *Full of Fire* and *Have a Good Time* (1976).

A reigning superstar, Green was having qualms about what he wanted out of life by then. One incident that had a tremendous impact occurred October 25, 1974, when an ex-girlfriend burst into his apartment while he was taking a shower, poured boiling grits on him, and then killed herself. He was hospitalized for weeks with second degree burns.

Some people considered this the tragedy that shifted his personal emphasis from the secular to the religious. He maintained otherwise. He told interviewer Geoffrey Himes (as quoted in the *Billboard Book of Number One Hits*): "I was born again in 1973. . . . It wasn't an incident that did it. No. People are silly when they write that. Nothing happened to bring me to Christ except coming into the knowledge of Christ and being transformed in mind and spirit on a particular morning. I'm a gospel singer now, and when it happened to me, I was singing rock'n'roll."

Nevertheless, it was after he recovered from his burns that he joined the ministry, purchased a church building in Memphis, Tennessee, and was ordained pastor of the Full Gospel Tabernacle.

He did not immediately give up pop music. He continued to tour and turn out new records in the second half of the '70s. His LPs included *The Belle Album* and *Greatest Hits, Volume 2* (1977) and *Truth'n'Time* and *Love Ritual* (1978).

In 1979, he fell from a stage in Cincinnati, hitting a steel instrument case and narrowly avoiding serious injury. He took that as a signal. "I spent a total of 15 days in the hospital. I realized that I was being disobedient to my calling. I was moving towards God, but I wasn't moving fast enough. The fall was God's way of saying I had to hurry up."

After that event, Green refused to sing any music

but gospel songs. His first gospel LP was the 1980 release on Myrrh, *The Lord Will Make a Way.* In 1981, Myrrh issued the LP *Higher Plane.* A reminder of his former greatness as a pop concert singer was *Tokyo . . . Live,* a 1981 release on the Cream label (available in the U.S. as a French import) taken from his wildly successful late '70s Japanese tour.

In 1982, Al joined forces with Patti LaBelle for the gospel-based musical *Your Arm's Too Short to Box With God,* which had a respectable run on Broadway in New York. (*See LaBelle, Patti.*) In the mid-1980s, he continued to draw large crowds to concerts across the U.S. and abroad, this time to hear him in gospel-only performances. His album output included the 1985 A&M LP, *He Is the Light.* In that project he was joined by old friend Willie Mitchell for the first time in three years to co-write most of the material.

Previously, as a pop artist, Al had been nominated for a number of Grammies, but never won one. As a gospel artist, he was a consistent winner. His trophies included the 1981 award for Best Soul Gospel Performance, Traditional, for the LP *The Lord Will Make a Way;* the same award in 1982 for the LP *Precious Lord* plus Best Soul Gospel Performance, Contemporary, for *Higher Plane;* in 1983, Best Soul Gospel Performance, Male, for the LP *I'll Rise Again;* and in 1984, Best Soul Gospel Performance by a Duo or Group for his duet with Shirley Caeser, "Sailin' on the Sea of Your Love" from her LP *Sailin'* on the Myrrh/Word label. His name didn't appear on Grammy lists in 1985, but in 1986 he again won the award for Best Soul Gospel Performance, Male, as he also did in 1987. His 1987 Grammy was for "Everything's Gonna Be Alright."

GREENWICH, ELLIE: *Singer, songwriter, record producer. Born Long Island, New York, 1940.*

Among the movers and shakers of '60s rock, Ellie Greenwich ranks with such giants as Phil Spector, Jeff Barry, Carole King, and Neil Diamond, all of whom she interacted with in one way or another during the decade. Her songs, still rock classics, reflect the tone of an exuberant, innocent period of U.S. adolescence before the somber overtones of Vietnam became the focus of growing frustration and uneasiness.

The staying power of the songs Ellie wrote or co-wrote (and occasionally performed) was indicated by the interest generated by a 1985 Broadway musical based on her material. Jack Kroll commented in *Newsweek* (April 22, 1985): "Underneath the glitz, *Leader of the Pack* is an endearingly unpretentious

show. It's the songs that count and the songs, for the most part, are terrific. Let's face it, man (and woman) does not live by Sondheim alone, and certainly not boy (and girl). Ellie Greenwich and Co. wrote their songs for and about kids, and they were true masters of scruffy teen poetry and heart-cracking teen anguish. These songs, written for immortal groups like the Ronettes, the Dixie Cups, the Crystals, the Shangri-Las and Bob B. Soxx and the Blue Jeans, are delivered with ferocious swingcerity by some real singers. Darlene Love, who originated many of the numbers for legendary record producer Phil Spector, is gorgeous and gifted, the Jessye Norman of girl-group rock. She finally gets to sing the classic 'River Deep, Mountain High,' which Greenwich wrote for her but which Spector gave to Tina Turner.''

The climax of the show, which had a book loosely based on the successful songwriting collaboration but failed marriage of Ellie and Jeff Barry, came when she appeared on stage in a cameo spot. For that moment in the spotlight, she accepted audience ovations for her rendition of "Da Doo Ron Ron."

Ellie's road to show-business fame began in a solid middle class environment in the Manhattan bedroom sector of Long Island. She reached her teens in the early 1950s just before Bill Haley and Elvis Presley were to revolutionize pop music. She wasn't oblivious to musical trends during her years at Levittown Memorial High School, but her biggest thrills came from school events and selection as a member of the cheerleading squad.

After high school graduation in the late 1950s, she enrolled in Long Island's Hofstra University with a major in education. During her college years, she was selected Spring Day Queen and named by her sorority as "Most Active" and "Most Beloved." She dabbled in singing at school affairs and songwriting, but when she graduated in 1962, she took a job as English teacher at General Douglas MacArthur High School. She spent only 3½ weeks at that task, coming to the realization that she was more interested in discussing top 40 music with her class than in concentrating on literary classics.

Soon after leaving there, she had a successful audition with the writing team of Mike Stoller and Jerry Lieber. Though she presented some vocal tapes, they brought her into their organization purely for her songwriting skills. Among the songs she turned out while working for them were "This Is It," recorded by Jay & the Americans, and "He's Got the Power" for the Exciters.

Ellie hadn't abandoned hopes for a singing career, though. During 1962, she became a "group" called the Raindrops. To do that, she recorded several different vocal tracks that were blended to form a synthetic group sound. The recording of "What a Guy" won some notice and "The Kind of Boy You Can't Forget" made the top 20. As a result, Ellie spent some time lip-synching Raindrops numbers on TV bandstand type shows. Besides her solo work, she was increasingly in demand to provide backing vocals on recordings of other artists. She also earned an increasing amount of money doing demonstration tapes as sales vehicles for other writers' songs. For a time, in fact, she was known as the "Demo Queen of New York."

As a result of her diverse music-industry activities, she got acquainted with Phil Spector. Soon she was an integral part of his booming record-production operations and one of Spector's most prolific writer of hit singles. For the Ronettes she penned such numbers as "Be My Baby" and "Baby I Love You" in 1963. She had a banner year in 1964, writing and producing such chart hits as "Chapel of Love" and "People Say" for the Dixie Cups, "Maybe I Know" for Lesley Gore, "I Wanna Love Him So Bad" for the Jelly Beans, "Goodnight Baby" for the Butterflys, and "Leader of the Pack" for the Shangri-Las.

In the mid-1960s, she collaborated on many songs with her husband Jeff Barry (born Brooklyn, New York, April 3, 1938). The twosome increasingly turned their efforts toward record production rather than writing. A major part of Ellie's 1965–67 activities revolved around the burgeoning career of singer-songwriter Neil Diamond. Ellie came in contact with Neil when she was asked to make a demo of some of his material at Associated Studios. Impressed with the content of the then unknown's offerings, she arranged to produce and publish his compositions through a company of her own called Talleyrand, Inc. The hit charts for the next few years featured a string of best-selling Neil Diamond singles that Ellie helped produce, including "Cherry, Cherry," "Thank the Lord for the Nighttime," "I Got the Feelin'," "Shilo," "Kentucky Woman," and "Solitary Man."

It seemed as though everything Ellie touched turned to gold, but her career took an abrupt downturn for a while in the late 1960s due to personal problems. These included incompatibilities that led to the breakup of her marriage to Jeff Barry and treatment for a substance-abuse problem. Her state of mind wasn't helped by the change in the rock environment triggered partly by the Beatles-led British invasion and partly by the Vietnam ferment that brought the girl-group era and the music it embodied to an end.

Greenwich was nothing if not resilient and she overcame those difficulties to find a new outlet for her energies in radio and TV commercials. She established a new firm, Pineywood Productions, to funnel her commercial material. In the early 1970s, she wrote advertising songs pushing Ford, Cheerios cereal, Prince Albert Tobacco, and United Milk. Besides writing the jingles, she also provided lead or backing vocals for Clairol, Helena Rubinstein, Coca-Cola, Beechnut, and Noxzema ads.

While such efforts were lucrative, they obviously weren't creatively satisfying. Ellie continued to seek chances to showcase her songwriting or vocal talents, a move helped by the post-Vietnam War nostalgia in the U.S. for the "good old days" of the '50s and early '60s. In 1973, she recorded her versions of many of her hit songs of the previous decade on *Let It Be Written, Let It Be Sung* on Verve Records. Most critics acclaimed it the best of the genre, surpassing many retrospective albums recorded by her 1960s contemporaries in the 1970–72 period. In fact, her vocals on "Maybe I Know," "Today I Met the Boy I'm Gonna Marry," "Chapel of Love," "Then He Kissed Me," and "Be My Baby" (on which she played accordion) presented new dimensions of the material compared to the original recordings of other artists.

The album wasn't the first such compilation she had done. In 1968, United Artists had released *Ellie Greenwich Composes, Produces and Sings*. The latter, however, paled in comparison to her 1973 collection.

From then on, Ellie's activities for the duration of the '70s and in the first years of the 1980s included live concerts of her original songs, though she continued her Pineywood commercial work. Besides advertising commercials, her writing included background music and theme songs for TV productions.

In the early 1980s, the steps leading to the 1985 Broadway show were set in motion. It was an unplanned series of events that culminated in that milestone. Initially, it took the form of a three-night revue at the Bottom Line in New York, where several singers belted out a program of Greenwich classics. The program gained such an enthusiastic audience response that it was brought back for an extended run. As momentum built, the principals decided to turn it into a full-scale musical, which opened on Broadway in the early spring of 1985.

Apart from *Newsweek* and a few other adherents, the majority of the theater reviewers condemned the show out of hand. The plot admittedly was weak, but the songs were well delivered and hardly anachronistic. Nostalgia plus word of mouth proved enough to overcome the naysayers and make the show a modest if not blockbuster success. The original cast album was issued by Elektra Records in May 1985.

(*See Crystals, The; Diamond, Neil; Ronettes, The; Shangri-Las; Soxx, Bob B., and the Blue Jeans; Spector, Phil; Turner, Ike and Tina; Turner, Tina.*)

GUESS WHO, THE: *Vocal and instrumental group. Personnel as of July 1970, all-born Winnipeg, Canada: Randy Bachman, 1946; Burton Cummings, December 31, 1947; Gerry Paterson, May 26, 1945; Michael James Kale, August 11, 1943. In August 1970 Bachman left; Kurt Winter and Greg Leskiw, both born Winnipeg, Canada, April 2, 1946 and August 5, 1947, respectively, added. Kale and Leskiw left in early 1970s. Leskiw replaced by Dom McDougall; Kale by Bill Wallace. Winter and McDougall left in June 1974. Don Troiano, born Canada, added. Group disbanded in 1976. Regrouped in 1977 with Kale, McDougall, David Inglis, Vance Masters. Disbanded again in early 1980s.*

An avid follower of popular music in the late 1960s would know the only similarity to the Guess Who and the Who is their names. To anyone else, it would sound a little like Costello trying to decipher Abbott's lineup in their "Who's on first" routine. One feature shared by both rock groups is their origins in the British Commonwealth, but the Who developed in Great Britain, while all members of the Guess Who grew up and continued to maintain their identity as Canadians.

The original members of the group and some subsequent replacements came from the Winnipeg area of Manitoba, the Canadian province bordering the states of North Dakota and Minnesota. Like most Canadians, they grew up with mixed feelings about the neighbor to the south. They were affected by music and other trends in the U.S., but even in their early years absorbed the resentments about the long shadow cast by the more powerful country.

The group coalesced around lead guitarist Randy Bachman in the mid-1960s. Bachman learned guitar in his high school years. While pursuing a degree from the Manitoba Institute of Technology, he played in various rock and country western bands. One of his heroes was country star, Chet Atkins, nicknamed "Mr. Guitar." Atkins' guitar runs can be detected in some of the arrangements on Guess Who recordings.

After finishing college in 1966, Bachman decided to move into the music field and lined up a four-man group from among those he had known or worked with in the Winnipeg area. One of the first he contacted was Burton Cummings, who had been collecting vintage rock records for years and who was interested in songwriting, as was Bachman. Cummings became lead singer and also provided instrumental support on the piano, organ, rhythm guitar, and harmonica.

Drummer Garry Peterson started banging away at a small Chinese drum when he was only a few days old. Part of his inspiration came from his father, who played percussion instruments. At the age of four, Garry first played drums in public and by the time he was grade school age was a child prodigy. He appeared on Canadian Broadcasting Corporation TV and radio programs and played with the Winnipeg Symphony for over a decade. The fourth member, bassist Michael James Kale, became interested in music during his school years. Blues and folk were his initial favorites. By his midteens, he was playing with local rock groups and had over a half dozen years experience before joining the Guess Who.

It didn't take too long for the group to gain a local reputation. By late 1966, they were considered one of the best rock bands in Winnipeg and, in 1967, gained a reputation throughout Canada with their own weekly TV show for CBC, "Where It's At." The show introduced many original songs by Bachman and/or Cummings. Bachman wrote the theme song and co-wrote, with Cummings, such songs as "And She's Mine," "Clock on the Wall," "Of a Dropping Pin" and "Laughing." All of these became available to Canadians on a Canadian label. Under this contract, 19 singles were issued during 1967 and 1968.

The group toured widely in those years, including a successful series in England and several U.S. engagements. The stumbling blocks to U.S. in-person shows caused some bitter comments from band members. Randy Bachman told reporters in New York that while American or English groups can gain a visa to perform in Canada in a few hours, a Canadian group had to wait 3 to 6 weeks for U.S. approval, a time period in which a record with chart promise could lose its momentum. All of this made the members determined to succeed without giving up their Canadian identity. Though many Canadians have become top attractions in the U.S., they noted, in most cases, they had to renounce their Canadian citizenship to do it.

Jim Kale stressed: "I wouldn't let someone take my Canadian citizenship from me for anything." At the same time, Garry Peterson had to admit frustration with the attitude of his own countrymen. "Canadians won't accept anything [in pop music] unless it has been accepted in the U.S."

They gained some notoriety in a Boston concert to promote their Canadian hit "Shakin' All Over" when they used a fog machine and smashed their instruments at the close, steps that aroused the audience to fever pitch and helped start a riot.

In late 1968, "These Eyes" became one of their most successful singles. Independent producer Jack Richardson of Nimbus 9 Productions in Toronto called this to the attention of RCA New York artists & repertoire man Don Burkheimer. The result was an RCA contract in January 1969, followed by U.S. release of the single on that label.

The record sold over a million copies as did the group's U.S. debut LP, *Wheatfield Soul*, featuring "These Eyes" and 10 more originals by Bachman and Cummings. The next album, *Canned Wheat*, (mid-1969), sold well and provided a gold two-sided single hit, "Laughing"/"Undun." Late in the year, another new single, "No Time," moved into the top 10. The U.S. putdown, "American Woman," ("American woman, stay away from me/American woman, mama let me be . . .") hit number one in 1970. It and the album for which it was title track both won gold-record awards.

But dissension about individual directions cropped up, resulting in a mutual agreement between Bachman and the others that he would leave as of July 1970. His goal was to branch out into more creative work in various areas of show business and initially to try going as a soloist.

In place of Bachman, the Guess Who added two fellow Canadians: Kurt "the Walrus" Winter and Greg Leskiw, both guitarists. Winter had gained some fame from his composition "Hand Me Down World" (a hit for the group he was then with, Brother). Leskiw, who is considered to closely resemble Neil Young, came to the Guess Who from the group Wild Rice. Those were the first of a number of changes that took place during the first part of the 1970s. Leskiw left in the early '70s and was replaced by Don McDougall. McDougall and Winter left in June 1974 and the lead guitar slot was taken over by Dom Troiano, formerly with the James Gang. By then, Kale had been replaced on bass guitar by Bill Wallace.

As those shifts went on, the band seemed to lose momentum. It continued to turn out new recordings and tour, but the quality of its material declined along with sales totals. During 1976, Cummings decided to break up the band. Its RCA LP catalog in the '70s included its last studio albums and a number of retrospectives issued during and after the band's existence. Those included *Best of the Guess Who* (1971), *Road Food* (1973), *Best of the Guess Who, Volume 2* (1973), *Rockin'* (1974), *The Way They Were* (1976), *No. 10* (1977), and *Greatest of the Guess Who* (1977).

In November 1977, Jim Kale and Don McDougall put together a new Guess Who for a one-shot studio session for Canadian Broadcasting Corporation radio. After that, they decided to try to revive the band's career with David Inglis on guitar and Vance Masters on drums. They did some touring and recorded the 1979 album *All This for a Song* on Hilltak Records with distribution by Atlantic. (Cummings, who had embarked on a solo career in the mid-1970s which got moving with the 1976 gold single, "Stand Tall," was not involved.) The new affiliation didn't work out as hoped for and the band broke up again in the early 1980s.

As for Guess Who's early leader, Randy Bachman, after leaving the band, he put out the solo LP *Axe* (RCA, 1970). He then formed Brave Belt with three fellow Winnipeg natives: his younger brother Robbie (born February 18, 1953) on drums; C.F. (Fred) Turner (born October 16, 1943) on vocals, lead guitar, bass, and pedal steel guitar; and Chad Allan (born c. 1944) on vocals and accordion. Songwriter Allan had played with Guess Who in its earliest years, leaving in 1965. Their LPs *Brave Belt* and *Brave Belt II* on Reprise enjoyed no great success. After Chad Allan departed, the band regrouped as Bachman-Turner Overdrive. Turner said the new name was sparked by the trucking magazine, *Overdrive*. They liked the idea of "power barreling along" at peak efficiency in creating what they called "heavy-duty rock."

Randy's brother Tim then joined on second lead guitar. Tim was replaced in early 1974 by Blair Thornton (born Vancouver, Canada, July 23, 1950).

On Mercury, they scored five gold albums: *Bachman-Turner Overdrive II* and *Not Fragile* (1974), *Four Wheel Drive* (1975), and *Head On* and *Best of B.T.O. (So Far)* (1976). The single "You Ain't Seen Nothing Yet" made number one in *Billboard* on November 9, 1974. In 1977, Randy left the band, regrouping it in 1984 with Turner and brother Tim.

HAGAR, SAMMY: *Singer, guitarist, band leader, songwriter, record producer. Born Monterey, California, October 15, 1947.* *

There are more than a few contradictions between the public and private faces of Sammy Hagar. On stage, thrashing out red-hot licks while he screams out raw-edged rock lyrics (and makes no-holds-barred comments between numbers), he seems the personification of the "cruisin' and boozin'" blue collar town he grew up in. Off-stage, he typically is relaxed and reflective, enjoying detailed discussions of favorite topics such as astronomy and the reality or nonreality of UFOs. Over the years, his favorite color was red and he usually performed in a bright

---

*Based partly on a personal interview with Irwin Stambler.

red jumpsuit. But it didn't symbolize leftish lean ings, but rather red as in red, white, and blue. In his 1980s concerts, before he left solo work to join the Van Halen band, he often waved the flag and, perhaps reflecting his blue collar roots, condemned musicians who took what he considered anti-American stances. (*See Van Halen.*)

Though he settled in the San Francisco Bay Area most of his adult years, he was raised in the industrial town of Fontana in San Bernardino County. "I grew up with a lot of guys who were good musicians. But it's hard to get away from a small town where there's absolutely nothing happening in music. Because of their environment, for instance, most of the people I knew were afraid to come to Los Angeles, even though it's close.

"Part of it is economic. For instance, my father worked for Kaiser Steel and the amount of money he earned didn't leave too much for kids. It takes a tank of gas to go to Los Angeles and if a guy's faced with the choice, he'll often figure he'd rather use the money to cruise around town on Saturday night and look for some action. If you live in a big city, on the other hand, you're more energized; you're exposed to more things. In a small town you fall into the regular pattern. It's easier after you finish high school to get a job and marry your hometown sweetheart.

"But I always wanted something different. Back when I was in grade school and my sisters were listening to Elvis, I dreamed of becoming a star. From the time I was 12 or 13, I was sure I was going to become a rock'n'roll star and no one could change me. I mean my mother tried hard, but she couldn't dissuade me."

Sammy's father, Hagar said, had been bantamweight champion in the mid-1940s under the name Bobby Burns. But a bad beating in a match against a heavier middleweight ended his career. He had hopes for Sammy or his other son to carry on the tradition and Hagar considered it, but decided that wasn't for him. "Dad hated my decision," he recalled. "I mean he lived for me to become a boxer."

Hagar senior didn't live to see his son's success in music. He was an alcoholic and, Hagar told Dick Richmond of the *St. Louis Post-Dispatch* (March 9, 1979): "He died in the gutter a few years ago. He never stopped being tough, fighting. He was a left-hander, broke his left hand nine times; his right one six times—on cops, Mexicans, blacks, hated everyone. He went from one menial job to the next and finally became a steelworker with Kaiser Steel. It was easy for him to be an alcoholic there. Most of those guys are pretty heavy drinkers. They understood and covered up for him.

"My father was around, but my mom raised us.

She and my big sister Bobbi. I didn't know we were poor. Everyone was about the same, and my mother kept us from being hungry. She'd go hungry. Maybe Bobbi did too, but I never did."

Though Sammy had fantasized about rock stardom, he didn't take serious steps in that direction until he was 16. It was then that he started trying to learn guitar. He has given different versions of where that guitar came from. He told one interviewer he stole it, another that his friend Ed Mattson's mother bought it for him. In any case, he and Mattson did form their own group (the Fabulous Castiles) to play for high school parties and then at seedy local bars. The Hagar-led band that evolved from that was called Skinny.

At the end of the 1960s, Hagar shifted his base of operations north to San Francisco. "What decided me was a trip I made there. I saw all these little bars all with people playing like 'til 4 A.M. They were all playing original songs too. L.A. at the time wasn't like that. You had to go to a place like Gazzari's and audition and if you got the job, they paid you $10 for the night. Any band up north could play its own material, but in L.A. you usually had to play the hits."

That bothered him, he said, because by then he was well into writing his own original material.

"Anyway, me and four other guys went to San Francisco and just started gigging. I mean we were starving. If a guy we knew had a one-room apartment, we just slept on the floor. But at least if we came into a club there wasn't a guy there asking to see our playlist." By the early 1970s, since Sammy was lead singer, any band he fronted became the Sammy Hagar Band.

While he began to get a local reputation, his career wasn't going anywhere in particular. He looked for greener pastures, which took the form of a job with a new band being formed in 1972 by Ronnie Montrose.

He said, "Ronnie Montrose had just left Edgar Winter and I had seen him. Some guys said the guitar player had just quit and Montrose was looking for a singer. I weaseled his number out of somebody and called him up. He invited me over. I had 'Bad Motor Scooter' and 'Make It Last' written at the time. I played them for him and sang a little bit and we jammed it up and he said: 'You got it.'"

After three years with Montrose, Sammy grew restless and decided to go solo in 1975. "I think fans came as much to see me as Ronnie. In fact, that's one reason after I left I never figured we'd work together again. We both had leaders' egos and a band just can't have two leaders.

"But it had a great influence on me. Before that, I knew nothing about the rock industry. Going out and playing before 60,000 people was an experience.

Everything I'd learned before was about being an artist, about playing guitar and singing better. With Montrose, I learned how to make records. I got the chance to work with a great guy like Ted Templeman on recordings. I also found out about what makes things tick. As far as I could see, Ronnie's record company [Warner Brothers] did zero for him. They never got behind us, pushed us. We never got any airplay at that time. I knew I had to get the right company support if I went out on my own."

Luck played a hand in that decision. After he left Montrose, he said: "I'd made a demo when I was working with Montrose and it caught the attention of a guy named Phil Charles who worked at station KSAN in San Francisco. The station played the demo a lot and he called John Carter of Capitol, who checked it out. Capitol was one of several companies that made offers after I decided to go solo." February 1976 saw the release of his debut album, *Nine on a Ten Scale*, on Capitol. (Nine is his favorite number.) Besides a number of originals by Sammy, the LP also contained his version of "Flamingos Fly," written for him by rock superstar Van Morrison. (*See Morrison, Van.*) The album was a good debut; the question was whether the follow-up would surpass it. The answer, when *Sammy Hagar* was issued in January 1977, seemed affirmative. It captured more of the excitement Sammy generated in his live shows and had tracks that became staples on his later concerts such as "Cruisin' and Boozin'," "Fillmore Shuffle" and "Red." ("Red" was later recorded by Bette Midler; *see Midler, Bette.*)

In placing Sammy Hagar on its recommended list, *Billboard* stated: "Thunderous rock featuring a lead singer who epitomizes the best of the emotionalism of the Daltrey-Plant school of tenor belters. The songs, mostly originals with a few well-chosen oldies, are performed with convincing abandon. Hagar has an overwhelming intensity."

The album made the pop charts, but Sammy was not yet an accepted star. He supported that album and the next one, *Musical Chairs* (Capitol, 1977), with saturation touring, headlining smaller venues and working as an opening act for better known groups such as Heart, Boston, and Thin Lizzy.

As opening act, Hagar and his band paid more dues. "One time we were opening for Thin Lizzy and Queen. It was on a West Coast swing by Queen where Thin Lizzy was second-billed. Someone in Queen got sick and we took their place. It was our home area, which Thin Lizzy didn't realize and when the local people put us on as closing act, Thin Lizzy people said: 'Hey, we've gotta headline!' The next night when we got there, we found they'd pulled all the plugs on our amplifiers and disconnected all the lighting. We wanted to fight them. We

never played with them since. Still, looking back I can see why it happened. Thin Lizzy did have a reason for sticking it to us and we've played with a few other bands that gave us a bad time for no reason."

Hagar and his group headlined enough small to medium-sized venues during 1977 and early 1978 to allow Capitol to set up tapes to get material for a live album. The backing band at the time comprised Gary Pihl on guitars, Bill Church on bass guitar, Alan Fitzgerald on keyboards, and Dennis Carmassi on drums. Most of these were Montrose alumni. (Fitzgerald went on to success in Night Ranger. *See Night Ranger.*) The first Hagar live album, *All Night Long*, was issued in July 1978 and was on the charts soon after.

By the end of 1978, things finally were coming together for Sammy. He retained a strong following in his San Francisco home area (who voted him Bay Area Musician of the Year in the first annual BAM magazine awards). He closed out the 1970s as concert headliner and also featured artist on three albums released by Capitol during 1979: *Street Machine*, *Danger Zone*, and *Harder, Faster*.

Hagar started the 1980s by changing record labels, leaving Capitol in favor of the new Geffen Records. Geffen, affiliated with Warner Brothers Records, issued his label debut, *Standing Hampton* in 1981, followed by *Three Lock Box* in 1982. The latter was the first in a while to match the quality of his initial Capitol albums. Both went gold. In mid-1984, Geffen issued his LP *Sammy Hagar*, earning Sammy a gold-record award from the RIAA. He also had another charted single, "I Can't Drive 55."

In late 1985, it was announced that Sammy had agreed to join the Van Halen band to take over lead vocal chores from David Lee Roth. This soon paid off for all concerned with the LP *5150*, which rose to number one on *Billboard* charts in April 1986. The first single release, "Why Can't This Be Love," was in the top 10 in April. In 1987, Hagar was focusing on his solo career again, starting with the single "Winner Take All" from the Columbia soundtrack album of the Sylvester Stallone film *Over the Top*. In mid-1987, Geffen issued his solo album *Sammy Hagar*, which was not, unfortunately, one of his better efforts.

Hagar felt that whatever success he achieved could be traced partly to his ability to evolve and change his creative approach over the years. His first concept of guitar playing, he recalled, had been inspired by Eric Clapton and his fellow bandsmen in Cream. "I also was heavily influenced by the Beatles and Stones and, of course, Elvis. I grew up with them. They influenced my life-style, not just my music. Since then my scope has gone off in all directions. For instance, now I really understand John

Fogerty. But when Creedence [Clearwater Revival] was happening, I said: 'These guys are terrible. My band's better than theirs.' I was a kid still and jealous of them. I know different now. But I hated other groups of that period. It was the same thing with the Doors. I hated them, now I love them. In fact, for a long time they were my favorite and I played their albums all the time.''

HALEY, BILL: *Singer, songwriter, guitarist, band leader (THE COMETS). Born Highland Park, Michigan, July 6, 1925; died Harlingen, Texas, February 9, 1981.*

When any history of early rock'n'roll is compiled, a few names stand out boldly: Presley, Jerry Lee Lewis, Chuck Berry, Bill Haley. In Haley's case, he was always linked with his famous band, the Comets, although not too much attention is focused on individuals in the band because the personnel changed many times during the decades that Haley kept his show going—though to the end, Bill sported his trademark spit curl in the center of his forehead.

It was Haley whose success laid the groundwork for the emergence of Elvis Presley and the other rock dynamos of the 1950s. He helped blaze new trails for rock music not only in the U.S., but in Europe too, where many fans now consider him the father of the rock revolution in England and on the Continent.

As Haley recalled for Robert Hilburn of the *Los Angeles Times* in April 1970: "We started out as a country-western group, then we added a touch of rhythm & blues. It wasn't something we planned, it just evolved. We got to where we weren't accepted as country-western or rhythm & blues. It was hard to get bookings for a while. We were something different, something new. We didn't call it that at the time, but we were playing rock'n'roll. We were lucky. We came along at a time in which nothing new was happening in the music field. The big band era had faded. We had an open market. It was easy to hit a home run.''

Haley was involved in country music from his earliest years, but he was not from the South. He was named William John Clifton Haley when he first drew breath in Highland Park, a suburb of Detroit, Michigan. All around him at home, the dominant music was country & western. His parents loved it and played both new and traditional country melodies, his father on the banjo or mandolin and his mother on piano or organ. Young Bill received his own guitar when he was still in grade school and could play well by the time he entered high school.

When he was 13, he started his professional career as a sideman with local country & western groups. Two years later, he organized his own band. After finishing high school, he traveled around the Midwest with his band. In 1951, his first record releases came out on Essex. They were country songs, though with a faster beat than most such songs. His first hits were "Rocket 88" and the prophetic "Rock the Joint.''

In 1952, the evolution to rhythm & blues began and Haley's single "Crazy, Man, Crazy" on Essex gained attention. As Haley and the Comets' new style began to catch on with teenage audiences, he moved to the more prominent Decca label and, in 1954, provided them with one of the major hits of the decade, "Shake, Rattle & Roll,'' a sanitized version of Big Joe Turner's top 10 R&B hit. (*See Turner, Joe.*) The Haley version became a bestseller in the U.S. and abroad, earning him a gold record for over a million copies sold.

Haley's star rose higher still in 1955 when "Rock around the Clock" became one of the biggest-selling singles the world over. The anthem of rock was number one on U.S. hit charts for eight weeks in a row, starting July 9, 1955, something few artists came close to in later decades. The song was still a staple item for Haley and for numerous other bands in the early '70s, by which time it had sold an estimated 16 million copies. During 1955, it was featured in the movie *Blackboard Jungle* and also was the theme for Haley's highly successful rock film, *Rock around the Clock.* In 1956, Haley added a third multimillion seller to his repertoire: "See You Later, Alligator.'' Besides these songs, Haley provided the Comets with many other audience-pleasing songs, including "Rock-a-Beatin' Boogie,'' "Razzle-Dazzle'' and "Skinny Minnie,'' though his only other *Billboard* top 10 hit was "Burn That Candle'' (1955).

As Elvis Presley and other solo vocalists became tremendous favorites, Haley and his comparatively subdued band slowly faded into the background in the United States. He retained his popularity overseas in the '60s, and managed to keep his group going during those years with a series of tours of Europe and Central and South America.

In the later 1960s, though, rock'n'roll revival shows, such as those produced by Richard Nader, renewed interest in the early greats. In one of the first ones in New York City in 1969, the audience gave Haley and the Comets an 8½-minute ovation after their set. Haley proved to be one of the pivotal attractions for successive shows in the early '70s. With both old-time rock fans and the new generation becoming interested in Haley's music, his engagement schedule began to fill up again in the U.S. His 1969 show at New York's Bitter End was recorded by Kama Sutra and released in 1970 under the title *Bill Haley's Scrapbook.* But by the mid-

1970s, he again lost attention from the U.S. audience, though he remained a star in England.

After Haley's passing in 1981, Ian Whitcomb noted Bill had never lost his position in the affections of English fans and suggested he would be mourned there more than at home. "Haley (and an assortment of Comets) continued to play to capacity crowds at major venues in Britain right up to the mid-1970s. I can remember rejoicing to his merry clickety-clack train rhythms at the Wembley Stadium in 1972. In fact, I wrote about how Haley had trundled us through a slew of rock-a-beating boogie hits, still calling the steps in that reassuring talk-sing voice, urging one and all to 'Rock the Joint,' 'Razzle-Dazzle,' and 'Rock through the Rye.' This last number always went down as a treat—reminding us that he was, in fact, half English, his mother having been born in Lancashire in the same town as Stan Laurel" (*Los Angeles Times*, February 14, 1981).

In the first part of the '70s, Haley was represented in record stores with a number of albums, including the 2-LP 1972 MCA release, *Golden Hits*. Other LPs in print at the time were *Greatest Hits* on MCA, *Rock and Roll Is Here to Stay* on Gusto, *Rockin'* on Coral and, on Crescendo, *Rock and Roll* and *Rock around the Country*.

Haley was not without personal problems, including alcohol addiction and increasingly severe emotional difficulties. Those things as well as income tax entanglements led to a sharp curtailment of his performing work after the mid-1970s, particularly in the U.S.

But long-time friends said some of the reports about his situation were exaggerated and that he was looking forward to renewed activity when in 1981 he died at his home, apparently of a heart attack. Jim Myers, who co-wrote "Rock around the Clock," told Robert Hilburn: "I talked to Bill last Saturday and he didn't sound well on the phone, but he didn't want to go to the hospital. He called me a couple of times a week during the last few months. It didn't involve business or anything. I just think he was a bit lonely.

"It's not true that he was retired, like a lot of the news stories said. He did a lengthy tour in South Africa last year [1980] and he appeared regularly overseas in recent years. He could pick up 25 grand a week whenever he wanted to. He was still huge in Europe and in South America. He had a nice house, a pool, and a 1981 El Dorado."

(Myers, under the pen name Jimmy DeKnight, wrote "Rock around the Clock" with songwriter Max Freedman. He always noted to interviewers it was written with Haley in mind. Haley at the time was on the Holiday Records label whose owner, Dave Miller, was at odds with Myers and forbade Haley to record it. Later, after Haley's contract with Miller ran out, he signed with Decca Records and recorded the song.)

Another associate, L.A. band manager Steve Brigati, added that Haley's tax problems had just been resolved. "I'd been trying to encourage him to work here again. He was the sweetest guy in the world. It didn't matter what problems he had offstage. Whenever he stepped behind the microphone, he'd always smile. Roy Brown predated him with rock. Elvis Presley was better looking. Chuck Berry was more creative. But Bill was the first guy who really got it all across."

In January 1986, Haley was one of 15 stars inducted into the new Rock'n'Roll Hall of Fame in Cleveland, Ohio.

HALL & OATES: *Vocal and instrumental duo, band leaders, songwriters, record producers. Daryl Hall, born Philadelphia, Pennsylvania, October 11, 1948. John Oates, born New York, New York, April 7, 1949.*

When Hall & Oates burst forth on the rock scene in the mid-1970s, their blend of rock, soul, and R&B was like a breath of fresh air. It was not an imitation of black idioms (though both are white musicians), but a unique melding that captured some of the essence of soul in a rock format. Critics hailed their band as one of rock's best. Yet, as is often the case when artists win mass audiences, some began complaining that the group was not experimenting enough with new-sounding material. But Hall & Oates' large group of admirers around the world were as happy with their new offerings of the 1980s as with their original songs of a decade and a half earlier.

The soul flavor in Hall & Oates' performances was legitimately earned, since both were engrossed in the Philly Sound movement of the late 1960s and early 1970s during their early years in music. In fact, both grew to adulthood in the area.

Oates was not a native Pennsylvanian. He was born in New York City, but his family moved to Philadelphia when he was four and he went through grade and high school there. His parents were rock'n'roll fans and never objected to his eventual choice of livelihood. In fact, he recalled his mother taking him to a concert by Bill Haley and the Comets in his preteen years. He started learning guitar when he was eight and later worked up a juvenile imitation of Elvis Presley.

Oates recalled in RCA interview notes: "When you got to junior high, you finally needed money. To take out girls, you need money. I never worked. I always knew it was music. I'd watch bands with my mouth open, chills running down my spine. I'd go to the Steel Pier in Atlantic City, New Jersey, to see Sam and Dave or U.S. Bonds and I'd go crazy. I always knew music was the way, the answer."

When he wasn't practicing guitar or playing with local groups, he spent time in rock hangouts. "I was a hoodlum, man. I changed my crew cut to a pompadour. Man, we'd walk into a dance and it was war—a music war. The guys would be wearing black trench coats, tab collars, pointy shoes. The girls would have teased hair with little pieces of scotch tape holding down the curls. There'd be people in a circle doing splits, dancing, grinding, pushing the girls into the coat racks. There were no bands, only records, and this was every Saturday night."

Meanwhile, Oates' eventual collaborator was following a somewhat different route in his early years. Hall grew up in Pottstown, about 40 miles west of Philadelphia. "It's sort of suburban now, but back then it was really country. I spent a lot of time alone. I had a lot of time to develop my fantasies. My parents were classical musicians and they gave me piano and voice lessons. But after the first time I heard rock'n'roll, it was all over."

Even in those early years he was enamored with soul-rock. The first record he bought was Ike and Tina Turner's "(I Think) It's Gonna Work out Fine." "I was running away to Philadelphia as soon as I could," he noted, which was during junior high and high school years in the early to middle 1960s. He was drawn to the young black doo-wop groups that sang on corners to draw change from passersby. He soon was performing with some of those under-the-streetlamp aggregations. In his teens he was leading a double life, musically. He couldn't bring himself to completely dash his parents' hopes for him, but he continued to further his pop career as well, moving from street corners to affiliation with professional artists. "It got to a point where I was singing with the Philadelphia Orchestra in the afternoon and then would sing backup for Smokey Robinson at the Uptown Theater later that night." He worked with other Motown stars as well. "I learned more from David Ruffin and Eddie Kendricks [then with the Temptations] than from anyone else."

At 17, Daryl already was doing keyboards session work at local recording studios and becoming acquainted with black talent that was to form the nucleus of the very successful Philly Sound of the late '60s and '70s. At 18, he was playing with local Jersey Shore bands and made his first recording as a sideman with a group called Kenny Gamble and the Romeos. Gamble soon was to become half of the management-production-writing team of Gamble and Huff (Leon Huff), who, with Thom Bell, opened the door to stardom for such artists as the Stylistics

and the Delfonics (whom Hall backed on keyboards during recording sessions at Philadelphia's Sigma Sound studios). In the 1970s, Gamble and Huff's Philadelphia International label was home for other greats, including Teddy Pendergrass.

When Hall met John Oates at a West Philadelphia "Cabaret Show and Dance" venue (the Adelphi Ballroom) in 1967, the two found common cause in love of the city's soul/R&B music. Initially, the main result was a desultory effort to write songs together. Their first performing collaboration was a disaster, Oates said. "It just sounded ridiculous. The song was bad and our voices sounded terrible together." Fortunately they remained friends and didn't abandon their writing work.

In the late 1960s, their interests took some strange side paths. Oates, who became a journalism major in college for a time, got into folk music. In fact, at one point during those years, he and Hall formed a folksong act. Hall became involved in a rock band called Gulliver, whose material leaned heavily toward Beatles-style melodies.

Hall told Robert Hilburn of the *Los Angeles Times* (July 10, 1977): "Philly has its own subculture. There were dozens of doo-wop groups, black street corner groups. When the Beatles came along in the '60s, I fought it. It sounded foreign to me. I don't just mean they were English. The whole sound and approach was foreign.

"We had a very narrow thing about what was cool and what wasn't in those days. I responded more initially to the Kinks and Yardbirds. Their music was more vital, less poppish. But I eventually got into Hendrix, the Velvet Underground, the Stones, and even the Beatles."

In fact, urged on by producer Tom Sellers and singer-songwriter Tim Moore, Hall agreed to work with the two of them in a group called Gulliver. (Occasionally Oates brought his guitar and vocal skills aboard as well.) "We were all guys who worked the sessions in Philly. The group was our form of recreation," he told Hilburn. "There was never any intention of going on the road. That's why I left it. I didn't want to stay in the studio all the time. So I decided to get together with John and try a live act." Before Gulliver disbanded, though, it did cut an album, *Gulliver*, issued by Elektra Records in the late '60s.

Hall & Oates' early performances in 1969 and the early 1970s were folk-oriented. They succeeded in gaining some recognition and by 1971 were opening for performers such as Harry Chapin. Hall recalled: "Some people thought [what we played] was folk because we used an acoustic guitar. There was that back-to-nature thing going and we probably were influenced by what the Band and Crosby, Stills &

Nash were doing, but we certainly weren't heavily into folk tradition or anything.'' That folk-rock feeling, however, carried into their debut LP on Atlantic Records, *Whole Oates* (October 1972).

For their second Atlantic album, which came out in 1973, the duo was beginning to retrace its steps toward its original Philadelphia roots. "For *Abandoned Luncheonette*," Hall said, "we tried to fuse progressive music with soul music." Toward that end, they added a rhythm section and introduced elements of advanced electronic arrangements using mellotrons, synthesizers, and other computer-based instruments. One track was the original "She's Gone," later to become a top 10 hit.

But "soft soul" or rock-soul wasn't really the direction either artist wanted to go. Hall said: "We didn't like the way people were starting to relate to us. It made us uncomfortable. So we decided to go to the other extreme. Urban rock music."

They lined up avant garde rock eminence Todd Rundgren to produce the next LP. (*See Rundgren, Todd.*) The result was the 1974 Atlantic album, *War Babies*, a work that shook up their original audience and heralded things to come. Daryl said: "It was cold, metallic, nihilistic. It was all our conflicts coming out. It was very naked music. We had uprooted ourselves, come to New York, and picked up all the madness around us."

Still lacking record-album success and having burned bridges with early fans of their mellow soul approach, Hall & Oates left Atlantic and signed with RCA Records. Their debut on the new label, *Daryl Hall and John Oates*, brought new appraisals, generally favorable, from critics. The track "Sara Smile," which has become one of their trademark songs, began to gather airplay, earning them their first gold-record award from the RIAA in 1976. Their U.S. and European tour in support of their first RCA album was something of a triumph. Reviewers, particularly in England, hailed their current band, which besides the duo comprised Todd Sharp on lead guitar, Steve Dees on bass guitar, David Kent on keyboards, and Edward Zyne on drums, as one of the best in rock.

The year 1976 was a watershed one for them. The success of their debut LP on RCA brought *Abandoned Luncheonette* into favor, earning it a gold record. "She's Gone" from that LP also showed up in the top 10. By year-end, their second RCA LP, *Bigger than the Both of Us*, was headed for gold-record status, as was the hit single from the LP, "Rich Girl" (which rose to number one in the U.S. the week of March 26, 1977). Honors that came their way included two NATRA Awards: one for "Sara Smile" as Best Song of the Year and the other naming them Best Duo of the Year. On the Rock Awards

show they were named Best New Group over such artists as Bruce Springsteen and Bob Seger.

With each new album and accompanying concert tour, Hall & Oates continued to build its status as a superstar act. While their singles didn't typically penetrate upper chart levels, their albums did quite well. Their releases on RCA in the second half of the 1970s included *Beauty on a Back Street* (1977), an excellent live album, *Livetime*, and *Along the Red Ledge* (1978), and *X-Static* (1979). The high-voltage tracks of *Red Ledge* included guest appearances by such rock notables as Robert Fripp (of King Crimson fame), Todd Rundgren, George Harrison from the Beatles, and Cheap Trick's Rick Nielsen.

Relating to that, Hall told Hilburn: "We were heavily influenced by black music, but our music is an assimilation of everything that is going on in the '70s. The groups I'm most into now are new rock bands like Television [a new wave band] and Cheap Trick.

"I think our music reflects part of the homogenizing of attitudes in America. The middle class is definitely the reigning class and everyone is allowed in it. Because of it you have a coming together of all these things. The perfect example is black pop, which never happened for Motown until now, and what's called blue-eyed soul. That's what the present [musical] experience is all about."

Along with their newer work, Hall & Oates had the sometimes unhappy experience of hearing many of their pre-RCA probing efforts come to light. In 1977, Atlantic issued another such collection (*No Goodbyes*) and Chelsea Records released *Past Times Behind*, which was essentially demo tapes from the 1960s.

Though the duo slacked off a little from its hectic late-1970s pace, they did enough to indicate they didn't intend to give up their hard-won laurels. In mid-year, John and Daryl earned their spurs as record producers when their platinum LP *Voices* came out. The LP provided a top 30 single, "How Does It Feel to Be Back" in September 1980, a top 12 cover of the Righteous Brother's classic, "You've Lost That Lovin' Feelin'" in November, and, in April 1981, a number one hit, "Kiss on My List." Also on the 1980 charts was the single "Wait for Me." Daryl's solo debut LP was issued by RCA in 1980. Titled *Sacred Songs* and produced by Robert Fripp, it actually had been recorded three years earlier, but RCA executives had considered it too radical at the time and shelved it until later Hall & Oates hits made it seem almost conventional. (*See Fripp, Robert.*)

The duo had a banner 1981-82. Joining *Voices* on the album charts was the gold *Private Eyes*, issued by RCA in the fall of 1981. It gave the team two number one singles: the title track and "I Can't Go for That (No Can Do)." Based on their production work on *Voices* and *Private Eyes*, *Record World* magazine named them the year's top record producers.

The momentum continued. The LP H_2O, issued in late 1982, earned an RIAA platinum-record award, while the single "Did It in a Minute" hit the top 10. The 1983 chart hit crop included the singles "Maneater" (number one the last two weeks of 1982 and the first two of 1983), "One on One," and "Family Man." A greatest hits set, *Rock 'n' Soul Part One*, was issued in 1983 and hit platinum, yielding two top 10 hits, "Say It Isn't So" and "Adult Education."

At the end of 1984, they had another platinum album, *Big Bam Boom*, which included the singles "Out of Touch" (number one the weeks of December 8 and 15, 1984) and "Method of Modern Love," which went top 10 in 1985.

Also that year, another live RCA release, *Hall & Oates Live at the Apollo*, earned a gold record. In all, the group's combined number of charted albums and singles in 1985 reached seven.

During the '80s, Hall & Oates received a number of Grammy Award nominations in varied categories without winning any as of 1987. A 1981 nomination for Best Pop Vocal Performance by a Duo or Group was for "Private Eyes." In the 1985 nominations, they were represented twice: Song of the Year for Paul Young's single of Hall's composition, "Everytime You Go Away," plus Best R&B Performance for a Duo or Group with Vocal for the single, "The Way You Do the Things You Do"/"My Girl" (featuring, besides Hall & Oates, R&B greats Eddie Kendrick and David Ruffin). The four also combined to sing it during the 1985 Grammy Awards TV show telecast February 25, 1986. (*See Kendrick, Eddie; Temptations, The.*)

Though the duo hadn't won any Grammies through 1987, they did receive other honors. For example, the songwriting organization BMI honored Hall for having two songs ("I Can't Go for That (No Can Do)" and "Kiss on My List") recorded by Hall & Oates that had been played over one million times each on the radio as of the mid-1980s.

Even before completing all the recordings due on their RCA contract, Hall & Oates signed a new agreement with Arista Records to go into effect after RCA commitments were over. One of the last RCA collections was the 1986 solo LP by Hall, *Three Hearts in the Happy Ending Machine*. With Oates, Hall soon began work on the debut album for Arista, *Ooh Yeah!*, released in May 1988. The first single, "Everything Your Heart Desires," quickly became a top 20 hit.

Hall credited his songs' lyrics for much of the long-term staying power of the duo's recordings. As he commented in a mid-1980s interview transcript released by the Howard Bloom Organization, "'Say It Isn't So' has the line 'We like to be the strangers at the party, two rebels in a shell.' That's what John and I are. We don't quite belong to the world of stardom. We're in it and we're out of it at the same time.

"A theme runs through my lyrics—taking charge of your own life. Becoming popular is not the main reason I make music. With my lyrics, I try to get people to think for themselves. I think it's important to outrage people, not for the sake of outrage, but to scatter their patterns, to make them think and feel. I've always wanted the freedom to run free, to outrage myself and everybody else."

HANCOCK, HERBIE: *Keyboardist, composer, band leader. Born Chicago, Illinois, April 12, 1940.*

A consummate keyboards player—both electric and acoustic—and superb composer, for much of his career Herbie Hancock was categorized as a jazz artist. By the '80s, though, he had demonstrated the ability to turn out superior work in almost every segment of popular music from rock and funk to jazz fusion, yet without losing his credentials with his peers as a first-rank jazz innovator.

In the '70s and '80s, he gained a reputation as one of the best performers and composers of electronically based material. This reflected his considerable skills in music-related areas of science and technology. He commented to jazz authority Leonard Feather (*Los Angeles Times*, May 29, 1983): "Ever since I was a kid, I had an interest in science. I used to go to these shops that had model airplanes and try to build the simple ones. I would take watches apart and try, without much success, to put them back together.

"When I went to Grinnell University, my first major was electrical engineering. I chose it because of my good grades in math and science. Donald Byrd, who heard me in Chicago and brought me to New York when I was 20, turned me on to electronic music and other types of twentieth-century classical music—Edgar Varese, John Cage, Elliott Carter.

"Then I heard Stockhausen's 'Song of Youth' in 1962 and fell in love with it. Around that time I met [drummer] Tony Williams, who was already into a lot of electronic music, and turned me on to some new sounds." (Williams was only 17 and Hancock 23 when they joined Miles Davis's quintet in 1963.)

As those lines suggest, long before Hancock focused on synthesizers and other elements of electronic music, he was building up background as an instrumentalist and music lover. Born and raised on the South Side of Chicago, he showed talent at an early age, starting to study piano at the age of seven. He became interested in the piano, he recalled, "because a friend of mine had one." He progressed so rapidly that when he was 11, he was performing the Mozart D Major Piano Concerto with the Chicago Symphony Orchestra.

Herbie continued his classical pursuits until he became enthralled with a jazz piece a fellow student performed in a high school talent show. "He was doing something I couldn't—he was improvising. I didn't know what he was playing, so I had to really find out what it was for myself."

He did that, he said, by closeting himself for hours with records by jazz artists such as Oscar Peterson and George Shearing. He wrote down every note of their solos and then tried the patterns out himself. "The first one I tried was Shearing's 'I Remember April.' It took me weeks. Then I got it down to days, then hours—and finally I found that I could recognize and write whole passages quickly, and away from the piano."

Still, he hadn't decided on a full-time musical career when he enrolled in Grinnell College in Iowa in 1956. His engineering courses were to prove very helpful later on, but his attention centered more and more on jazz. After a while he formed a 17-piece concert band for which he began doing arranging and composing. He then changed his major to music composition. After college, he went back to Chicago for whatever engagements were available, mostly pickup work with backing groups for touring jazz greats. Then came the turning point in the winter of 1960 when trumpeter Donald Byrd made Herbie his band's pianist.

After Herbie and Tony Williams became members of the famed Miles Davis jazz group in 1963, Hancock stayed with that master musician for 5½ years. Before Hancock left the band in 1968, he had performed in concerts throughout the world and also helped Davis record almost a dozen albums. Before then, however, thanks to Byrd, Hancock had made his own debut album, *Takin' Off* on Blue Note Records. That collection included a number of originals by him, including one later covered by dozens of artists, "Watermelon Man." Throughout his years with Davis, Herbie kept recording his own LPs for Blue Note, including *Maiden Voyage, Inventions and Dimensions, Empyrean Isles, Speak like a Child,* and *The Prisoner.*

Though Herbie had been a fan of electronic music for some time, he didn't begin working in that medium until Miles Davis, in effect, pushed him. He told Michael Zipkin of *BAM Magazine* (June 2, 1978): "It's funny, because I had always thought that the electric piano was kind of a toy, even though

I had never played one. One day I walked into the studio to do [the *Miles in the Sky* album] and there was no acoustic piano there—just this electric piano. So I said: 'Miles, what do you want me to play?' I couldn't imagine he wanted me to play that toy, right? So he said: 'I want you to play that.' So I went over to it, hit a chord, and it sounded so good! It blew my mind. It was rich and full with that round sound that's halfway between a guitar and vibes and a piano. I liked it right away and that wasn't even a good piano. In live performance, I still play acoustic, but I continued to use the electric in the studio."

Hancock played electric piano on his remaining LPs with Davis: *Miles in the Sky, Filles de Kilimanjaro* and *In a Silent Way.* Those Davis albums laid the groundwork for the jazz fusion genre that became a force in pop music in the 1970s. His work on those projects helped determine the shape of his future career. "With Miles I developed from kind of a generally all-round musician to finding a direction for myself. It was a great education."

By the late 1960s, Hancock was ready to strike out on his own full-time. He already was acknowledged as a major jazz and pop composer and had steady work backing other artists' record projects and turning out commercials. He also was asked to score his first film in 1969, Michelangelo Antonioni's *Blow Up.* Soon after, Bill Cosby asked Herbie to write the music for his TV special, "Hey, Hey, Hey, It's Fat Albert."

Herbie had formed a band of his own in November 1968, soon after leaving Davis, and signed a new recording contract with Warner Brothers. His debut on the label, *Fat Albert Rotunda* (1969), featured some of the material composed for the Cosby program. For that LP he essentially used studio musicians, but for his next album he was backed by his own group, which included Eddie Henderson on trumpet and flugelhorn; Bennie Maupin on alto flute, tenor sax, and bass clarinet; Julian Priester on trombones; Charles "Buster" Williams on bass; and Billy Hart on drums. The result was *Mwandishi,* voted one of the ten best recordings of 1971 by *Time* magazine. (During those years, Herbie also was voted number one jazz pianist a number of times in the *down beat* magazine reader's poll.) Among other things, *Mwandishi* included another of Hancock's best-known compositions, "Ostinato." The album featured intricate electronic rhythms by Hancock, as did his next Warners LP, *Crossings.*

After *Crossings,* Herbie moved to Columbia Records, which was still his record home in the late 1980s. His debut on that label, *Sextant,* was a good album, but not as unique as his next release, the 1973 *Headhunters.* That album ranged across genres from jazz fusion to electric funk. Though Herbie had played electric piano for some time, that album marked his recorded debut as a synthesizer artist. The album received platinum-record certification from the RIAA and spawned the hit pop-funk single "Chameleon."

Headhunters was still on the U.S. album charts during 1974 when it was joined on those lists by three other Hancock LPs: his new album, *Thrust*, a retrospective by Warner's called *Treasure Chest*, and his CBS soundtrack album for the film *Death Wish*. He followed those with a series of new albums in the late 1970s that kept fans guessing about what new creative avenues he would follow next: the mid-1970s *Man-child*, the 1977 *Sunlight* (in which he used the Vocoder voice synthesizer in his first recorded vocal work), and the 1979 disco-oriented *Feets Don't Fail Me Now*.

During those years, he continued to be a prominent feature on the festival and concert circuit. At the 1976 Newport Jazz Festival, he brought together almost the entire Miles Davis quintet of the '60s, except for Miles. The musicians were Ron Carter, Tony Williams, and Wayne Shorter, with Freddie Hubbard playing the parts Miles would have performed. With that group, the V.S.O.P. Quintet, Hancock later set out on an acclaimed round-the-world tour. In 1978, he got together with jazz fusion exponent Chick Corea for a worldwide acoustic tour.

Hancock didn't pause for breath in the 1980s, continuing his hectic schedule of recordings, concerts, composing, and TV appearances. His early 1980s albums included *Monster, Magic Window*, and *Lite Me Up!*, where he explored new worlds in funk, rock, and electronic music. He also recorded new pure jazz efforts with the V.S.O.P. Quintet, with Corea and Oscar Peterson, and with the Herbie Hancock Quartet (whose other members were Wynton Marsalis, Ron Carter, and Tony Williams).

In 1983, he joined electric bassist Bill Laswell and synthesizer player Michael Beinhorn in a loose-knit experimental electronic group, Material. One fruit of that collaboration was the album *Future Shock* on which Hancock played a bewildering array of instruments from electric piano to synthesizer to acoustic piano plus, on the track "Earth Beat," the Koto (a Japanese stringed instrument). The album became a major hit, staying on pop charts well into 1984. The track "Rockit" also was a best-seller. Among those contributing to "Rockit" was rap-master Grand Mixer D St. For that record, Herbie was awarded the Grammy for Best R&B Instrumental Performance for 1983.

Hancock came right back in 1984 with another best-selling album, *Sound System*, the Best R&B Instrumental Performance in that year's Grammy competition.

After his pop successes with *Future Shock* and *Sound System*, Hancock, having provided the score for the 1984 movie *A Soldier's Story*, took on the assignment to provide a jazz score for the movie *'Round Midnight*, which was to star saxophonist Dexter Gordon (and also have an acting part for Herbie). He followed *'Round Midnight* with the soundtrack material for Richard Pryor's film *Jo Jo Dancer, Your Life is Calling*.

He told Leonard Feather (*Los Angeles Times*, June 7, 1987), that he liked to separate his pop and jazz projects. "I have never minded moving back and forth. I suppose I could make a kind of jazz-based pop music, the way some musicians do, but I choose to keep the two separate. I pursue one objective, and when it reaches a logical conclusion, I pursue another. It's no big hassle for me to make the change; I don't even think about it."

His work on *'Round Midnight* earned him the Oscar for Best Original Score. He commented on the irony of the situation to Feather. "It's funny. After many years of waiting I got two Grammys and both of them were for R&B performances. . . . When I finally get a jazz award, it was [the Oscar] from the Motion Picture Academy."

During 1987 he toured Europe with a jazz trio (bassist Buster Williams and drummer Al Foster) and later did U.S. and Japanese concerts as part of a quartet (Michael Brecker on sax, Ron Carter on bass, and Tony Williams on drums). He also put the finishing touches on a new pop/R&B album for Columbia. His '87 work earned him a third Grammy (Best Instrumental Performance, "Call Sheet Blues," shared with Wayne Shorter, Ron Carter, and Billy Higgins).

HARRISON, GEORGE: *Singer, songwriter, guitarist, organist, sitarist, actor, record producer, record-company executive. Born Wavetree, Liverpool, England, February 25, 1943.*

After the Beatles' breakup, each of the members went on to pursue solo careers with varying degrees of success. The massive worldwide popularity of the group ensured that all of them could receive affectionate attention from sizeable numbers of fans for new projects even when those efforts lacked the freshness and excitement of the Beatles' golden era. Thus George Harrison initially added a number of gold records to his collection, though much of his output was not of the caliber of solo work by Paul McCartney and the late John Lennon.

Harrison was trying to establish his own persona even before the Fab Four split up. One of his first solo efforts was preparation of soundtrack music for the film *Wonderwall*. He began work on the project, which involved his composing, arranging, and recording the music, in January 1968 in Bombay, India. The album of the score, *Wonderwall*, was released on Apple Records on November 29, 1988, and was a chart hit, as was his next one, *Electronic Sound*, issued on the new Zapple label on May 2, 1969. Reflecting his interest in Indian religions, he produced the recordings by the Hare Krishna Temple "Hare Krishna Mantra" (issued in August 1969) and the second single, "Govinda," released the following March.

In May 1970, George began work on another album with Phil Spector handling producing chores. (*See Spector, Phil.*) Released in 1971, the resulting work, *All Things Must Pass*, earned his first gold record as a solo almost immediately. Its gold single, "My Sweet Lord," was number one for four weeks starting the week of December 26, 1970. The record was chosen as the year's best single in the *Melody Maker* British and International polls and also won George selection as Top Male Vocalist–Single in the *Record World* d.j. poll. During 1971, George also won a Grammy Award from the National Academy of Recording Arts and Sciences with the other Beatles for Best Original Score for Motion Picture or TV (*Let It Be*).

In 1971, Harrison helped organize the Bangla Desh relief concert held in New York's Madison Square Garden. The event was a landmark in rock history and the album of the concert, released in 1972 (with proceeds earmarked for Bangla Desh aid) went gold. Harrison's single, "Bangla Desh," was a chart hit in 1971 as was another single release, "What Is Life?"

Next came the single "Give Me Love (Give Me Peace)" and the album *Living in the Material World*, both issued during May 1973. Both hit number one and earned gold-record awards, the album receiving RIAA certification on June 1, 1973, two days after its release. The single reached number one on the *Billboard* list the week of June 20, 1973.

The public's enthusiasm was not shared by many critics. An example was the *Los Angeles Times'* Robert Hilburn, who wrote, (June 5, 1973): "Careful production, skillful musicianship and other elements of recording camouflage can give an ordinary song enough surface charm to make it pleasant in the light, casual world of pop music. . . . Flash, but not substance.

"For example, 'Give Me Love (Give Me Peace on Earth)' . . . is pleasant enough to soar . . . high onto the national sales charts, but hardly the level of work we'd expect from a major artist. 'Give me hope/Help me cope' indeed.

"The obvious question, then, is whether Harrison is a major artist. I have my doubts. *All Things Must Pass* was an acceptable, hugely commercial, but in-conclusive album. Despite its initial surface appeal, *Living in the Material World* is, for a variety of reasons, a discouraging one."

Undaunted, George went on to other projects, including movie work and plans to set up his own record label. The film on which he served as executive producer, *Little Malcolm*, won the Silver Bear Award at the Berlin Film Festival in June 1974. That same month, at a press conference in Paris, France, George announced formation of Dark Horse Records, to be distributed by A&M Records. (*Dark Horse* also was the title of his December 1974 Apple Records solo album.) In August 1974, *Little Malcolm* won a gold medal at the Atlanta, Georgia, Film Festival. The next month, the first Dark Horse LPs, both produced by him, were released: Indian sitar maestro Ravi Shankar's *Shankar Family and Friends* and Splinter's *The Place I Love*. On September 23, 1974, Harrison joined Ravi for a Shankar Festival at London's Royal Albert Hall followed by concerts in major European cities and an eagerly awaited U.S. tour the last months of the year featuring Harrison and Shankar.

During 1975, Harrison completed his last solo LP for Apple, *Extra Texture*, released in September and certified gold soon after. In 1976, he began work on his Dark Horse Records debut, *33⅓*, issued in November 1977, which brought him still another RIAA gold-record award. He scored hits with two singles from the album: "This Song" and "Crackerbox Palace." While Capitol issued the gold retrospective, *The Best of George Harrison* (1976), George took a hiatus from record making to concentrate on movie assignments. These included a role in the Beatles satire "All You Need Is Cash" (prepared for TV by Monty Python comedy act alumnus Eric Idle) and work as executive producer on the Monty Python film *Life of Brian*. While working on that comic opus in the fall of 1978, he collaborated with former Beatles press agent Derek Taylor on a book about his career, *I Me Mine*, published by Simon and Schuster, in the early 1980s.

His next solo album was *George Harrison* (February 1979) on Dark Horse with distribution now handled by Warner Brothers. The LP was far from a masterpiece, but there remained plenty of faithful fans out there and it was certified gold within a few months.

Harrison continued to turn out new LPs on his label, such as *Somewhere in England* (1981) and *Gone Troppo* (1982) without achieving any new creative breakthroughs. His 1981 tribute to John Lennon in the single "All Those Years Ago" was a poignant reminder for the music public of the Beatles' glory years and spent three weeks in the number two position on *Billboard* charts. His energies seemed to be increasingly focused on film production during the first half of the 1980s.

Though George spent much of the 1980s in behind-the-scenes work in the movie and recording industries, he did not intend to completely abandon his entertainer's role. He demonstrated this with his 1987 hit album, *Cloud Nine* (Dark Horse/Warner Brothers), his first LP in five years. Co-produced with Jeff Lynne (*see ELO*), it featured backing support from, among others, Ringo Starr, Eric Clapton, and Elton John. The tracks included a fond, serio-comic remembrance of years past, "When We Was Fab," and his first number one hit in 14 years, "Got My Mind Set on You."

HATHAWAY, DONNY: *Singer, pianist, organist, percussionist, composer-arranger, record producer. Born Chicago, Illinois, October 1, 1945; died New York, New York, January 13, 1979.*

With his diverse talents, Donny Hathaway had a major impact on pop music of the 1970s, both directly as an artist and behind the scenes as songwriter and producer.

Hathaway was born in Chicago, but was soon given into the hands of his grandmother, Martha Crumwell, who lived in the black ghetto of St. Louis. An established gospel singer, his grandmother taught the child religious songs almost as soon as he could talk. He was an apt pupil and learned so fast that he began singing when he was three, billed as "Donny Pitts, the Nation's Youngest Gospel Singer." He not only sang, but also accompanied himself on the ukelele.

He continued to perform as he grew up while also showing himself proficient in his school studies, gaining a fine arts scholarship to Howard University in Washington, D.C. His career thoughts at the time leaned toward either the ministry or teaching. He needed to earn some money, though, and, in 1964, found work as a member of the Ric Powell Trio that played clubs in the Washington area. This experience tended to focus his attention on pursuing a career in music.

As the decade went by, Hathaway expanded his activity in the entertainment field. He picked up work as an arranger and also did session work in studios on the East Coast. By the end of the '60s, he was recognized as one of the most promising new arrangers and record producers in the field. His credits as a producer eventually included records by Curtis Mayfield and the Impressions, Roberta Flack, Jerry Butler, the Staple Singers, Carla Thomas, and Woody Herman. (*See Butler, Jerry; Flack, Roberta; Impressions, The; Mayfield, Curtis; Thomas, Carla.*)

His name started to become familiar to the public at large after he signed a recording contract with Atlantic Records at the start of the '70s. His first album, *Everything Is Everything* (1970) on Atlantic's Atco subsidiary, did not cause too much of a stir at first. However, after his second Atco release, *Donny Hathaway*, won attention in spring of 1971, his first album gained new favor. His next album *Live* (1972) earned a gold-record award.

The year 1972 established Hathaway as a headliner as a concert and nightclub artist and recording star. His success extended to a series of duets with Roberta Flack, including the gold single "Where Is the Love." During the year, he was represented on the best-seller lists by six singles, five on Atco and one on Curtis Mayfield's Curtom label. In the *Billboard* survey of 1972, he was ranked as the ninth top album male vocalist in the U.S. and eleventh top LP soul artist.

In 1973, Atco issued his album *Extension of a Man*. After that, he seemed to have trouble completing material for a new album, though he remained under contract to Atlantic. As a songwriter, though, he continued to have a strong impact on both rock and R&B, with many artists profiting by singing his compositions.

In 1978, he and Roberta Flack got together on the gold single, "The Closer I Get to You," and then made plans for a joint album. They were in the early stages of that project when Roberta and his other friends and admirers got word that he had died from either jumping or falling from a fifteenth floor room in the Hotel Essex in New York City.

The police called it a suicide, but those who knew him disagreed. (The main police argument for suicide was the fact that his room was bolted from the inside.) He had no reason to want to die, they maintained. Not only was he working on the new LP with Roberta, he also was getting ready to make his fifth solo LP for Atlantic. He was still in great demand as a record producer, arranger, and conductor for dozens of artists.

His manager, David Franklin, pointed out he had been to dinner with Donny and Roberta the evening of Hathaway's death and he had been cheerful and wasn't using drugs or alcohol heavily. But whatever the course of events in Donny's last moments, nothing could bring him back.

Roberta completed the album they had started together and dedicated it to his memory. It included the two numbers they had recorded before his death. Those were included with minimal changes, she told reporter Steve Pond. "We really gave those songs special attention to make sure we weren't being disrespectful in any way. I rearranged them a little bit and, of course, we had to leave out the ad-libs that

Donny would have added. But I have no second thoughts about releasing them. It would have been selfish not to.''

The gold LP, *Roberta Flack Featuring Donny Hathaway*, was issued on Atlantic in early 1980. Looking back at their collaborations, she reminisced: ''I always thought he was a genius in a class with Stevie Wonder. At first I was in awe of him, but working with him was so easy; we finished [the first joint album] in three or four days.''

HAWKINS, RONNIE: *Singer, guitarist, band leader (THE HAWKS). Born Arkansas, c. 1937.*

Known as ''Mr. Dynamo'' to his fans (many of whom over the years have been Canadians), Ronnie Hawkins had a strong, if somewhat indirect, impact on folk and country-rock in the '60s and '70s. His own recordings often are classics of the genre, though known primarily to a cult following in the U.S., but some of the musicians he recruited for his backing groups went on to much wider fame, the most notable being the Band. (*See Band, The.*)

Born and raised in Arkansas, Hawkins was strongly influenced by gospel and country & western in his youth. However, like many others who reached their teens in the '50s, he was swept up in the early rock revolution spearheaded by Elvis and other rockabilly stars. He himself played a role in that development, working in the mid-1950s in local groups headed by such important artists as Carl Perkins and Conway Twitty. (*See Perkins, Carl.*) He wanted to make his own name known and formed his own rock group in Arkansas before he moved on to Memphis, Tennessee, where he was featured in a number of local clubs in the later 1950s.

Failing to make enough progress there, he took his band north of the border to Canada in mid-1958. (Band members included Will ''Pop'' Jones on piano, Jimmy Ray Paulman on guitar, and Levon Helm on drums.) He was impressed with the enthusiasm with which his then all-American group was greeted by young Canadians, though he didn't decide to remain there at that point in time. On the way home from Canada in April 1959, the band stopped in New York and auditioned for Roulette Records. This led to Ronnie's first major recording efforts, which provided such singles as ''Forty Days,'' ''One of These Days,'' and the top 10 R&B hit ''Mary Lou.'' All of those were on his early '60 debut LP, *Ronnie Hawkins and the Hawks.* The same band, plus James G. Evans on bass, was featured on Ronnie's next album, *Mr. Dynamo.*

The swing through Canada had made Ronnie eager to concentrate his live appearances there. When he decided to transfer his base of operations to that country, several of his musicians from the U.S.

stayed home. He took Levon Helm back with him and recruited the balance of his new band from Canadians. It was this group that, after some changes, became the forerunners of the Band. As the Hawks, they backed him on such early '60s Roulette releases as *Folk Ballads* and *Songs of Hank Williams*. The album titles emphasize the influences in Hawkins repertoire. Robbie Robertson of the Band, looking back at his early years with Hawkins, noted: ''There were only three kinds of rock then: rhythm & blues, corny white rock, and rockabilly. We played rockabilly.''

As the '60s went by, the sidemen who were to become the Band left one by one to try their luck in the U.S. Meanwhile, Hawkins simply added new musicians to maintain the supporting cast he needed. In 1965, while the five one-time Hawks were becoming acquainted with Dylan and other folk-rock stars, Ronnie continued to reign as one of Canada's most popular entertainers. He always seemed to have an unerring sense of a musician's potential. If the Band was the only group of ex-Hawks that became major stars, some of his other former associates showed great potential even if they missed the top bracket. A case in point is the Crowbars—a major contender for rock honors in the early '70s.

Though Ronnie had a number of hits in Canada, his releases rarely made much headway in the United States. He recorded for various labels in the '60s and '70s, including *Ronnie Hawkins* and *Hawk* on Phil Walden's Cotillion Records.

The success of the Band in the late '60s and early '70s sparked renewed interest in his abilities. Roulette reissued some of his early '60s material in 1970 on *Best of Ronnie Hawkins, with the Band.*

In November 1976, he was a guest at the final concert of his one-time support group, the Band, in San Francisco. He contributed to the album release of that last Band hurrah, *The Last Waltz*, and also could be seen in the excellent movie of the event, also titled *The Last Waltz*, issued in 1978. He also played the role of Bob Dylan's father in Dylan's 1978 film, *Renaldo and Clara*. His later 1970s LP credits included the British import *Rockin'* (Pye Records, 1977) and *Hawk* (United Artists, 1979).

HAYES, ISAAC: *Singer, pianist, saxophone player, organist, songwriter, record producer. Born Covington, Tennessee, August 20, 1942.*

It is perhaps an understatement to say that an Isaac Hayes concert of the 1970s was an extravaganza of sorts. Typically, he began singing off stage while his 40-piece band, the Isaac Hayes Movement, sent musical shockwaves through the audience. When he came out of the wings, accompanied by four bodyguards, he presented an exotic image—his shaven head and dark glasses giving him a monkish appearance that contrasted with his multicolored cape, leather shirt with fur cuffs, gleaming gold necklace, and black tights. A beautiful black girl then did a "dance of adoration" before removing his cape, after which he sat down to play some of the songs that made him a millionaire before he was 30—a fortune that unfortunately slipped through his fingers and that he was still trying to recoup in his forties.

Considering Hayes's early years, the pattern of his concerts could well have symbolized his ascent from mind-numbing poverty to musical godhead. Not only was he born on a sharecropper's farm about 40 miles north of Memphis, Tennessee, he never knew his parents, who died before he was old enough to walk. Luckier than some orphans, he at least had his grandparents to raise him. They saw to it that he attended church early in life, which gave him his first opportunity to sing in public—as a member of the choir at the age of five.

His schooling was sporadic as he had to help out in the field at an age when most boys didn't even clean up their rooms. His interest in music increased as he grew older, though, and he managed to teach himself to play piano and organ by his teens. He moved to Memphis soon after and worked at various jobs, such as gas station attendant and handyman, while he tried to further his musical career. Accompanying himself on the piano or the organ, he managed to work occasionally at small clubs, such as Curry's Tropicana and the Tiki Club. He also formed his own group, Sir Isaac and the Doo-dads, and gained several series of one-nighters on the rhythm & blues club circuit in the late 1950s. Some of the material he used were songs popular among R&B fans of the period, but he also tried his hand at writing his own songs.

At the start of the '60s, he had gained a reputation as an excellent musician among the Memphis music fraternity. When Stax-Volt Records came into being as the spearhead of the Memphis Sound in R&B, Hayes was one of the first regular session men on the firm's roster. From 1962 until Otis Redding's death in 1967, the same backup band played on practically every record Otis (and most of Stax-Volt's other artists) made. Hayes was the group's pianist, with the famed Booker T handling organ alongside him. (See *Booker T & the M.G.s; Redding, Otis.*)

Isaac's method of writing a melody, since he can't read or write music, is to take down tune and rhythm on tape recorders and have a professional arranger do the notation from the tapes. After several years with Stax-Volt, Hayes found a lyricist, David Porter, who perfectly complemented his writing style. Their songs soon won approval from the record firm's performers. A number of hits in the R&B field in the mid-1960s resulted. The Stax-Volt artists with whom Hayes and Porter worked most closely during the middle and late 1960s were Sam & Dave. Isaac and David provided most of the team's new material and also handled production of such best-sellers as "Soul Man," "Hold On, I'm Coming," and "You Don't Know Like I Know." (See *Sam and Dave.*)

Hayes's debut as a soloist was the upshot of overindulgence in liquor. Hayes and a Stax-Volt vice president had too much to drink at a 1976 party in Memphis and decided to leave and go back to the studios to capture some of Hayes's performing skills on tape. Even when everyone had sobered up the next day, the material sounded good so it was decided to go ahead and complete enough tracks for an album. The LP wasn't a chart hit, but it showed potential.

In early 1969, Hayes put together a number one album issued under the title *Hot Buttered Soul*. Subsequent top 20 LPs included *Isaac Hayes Movement* and . . . *To Be Continued* (1970) and *Black Moses* (1971). The soundtrack album for the movie *Shaft*, composed by Hayes, hit number one in 1971 as did the single "Theme from *Shaft*." "*Shaft*" won him an Oscar for movie song of the year and two Grammys: Best Instrumental Arrangement and Best Original Score Written for a Motion Picture.

In 1972, he had the best-selling LP *Black Moses* on Enterprise Records. In the Grammy voting for 1972, he won another trophy with *Black Moses*, voted the Best Pop Instrumental Performance by an Arranger, Composer, Orchestra and/or Choral Leader. During 1973, the RIAA certified two of Isaac's Stax-Volt albums as gold: *Live at the Sahara Tahoe* and *Joy.*

Other activities included more movie-related projects, including his acting debut in the film *Three Tough Guys* in 1973 and a starring role in *Truck Turner* in 1974. He also co-starred with Anthony Newley in the Canadian film *It Seemed a Good Idea at the Time*. He scored both *Three Tough Guys* and *Truck Turner* and was featured on their soundtrack albums. In 1975, he set up his own label, Hot Buttered Soul, under an agreement with ABC Records, with the label debut being *Chocolate Chip*. The album was certified gold, but it didn't do as well as his early '70s offerings. The same held true for the next LP, *Groove-A-Thon* (1975).

In 1976, he put out the solo LP, *Juicy Fruit*, and joined with Dionne Warwick in recording and concert projects. Their worldwide tour was named "A Man and a Woman" as was their 1977 album. (*See Warwick, Dionne.*) But 1976 proved to be disastrous for him financially. Though he had earned a lot of money, he hadn't paid much attention to what his advisors were doing with it and he suddenly found himself so deeply in debt that he had to declare bankruptcy. To make matters worse, his recording efforts were faltering, particularly in the singles category, where, after making the top 30 with "Joy—Pt. 1" in 1974, he couldn't get past lower chart levels with new releases throughout the mid-1970s.

But Hayes didn't lack for new things to do. He made his TV dramatic debut on a 1976 episode of James Garner's "Rockford Files" show and was on two more episodes the following year. He shifted to a new label in 1977, Polydor, which issued his label debut, *New Horizons*, that year. With his new label alignment, Hayes began to improve his status with record buyers and his late 1970s LPs and singles were more in line with what he had done in the earlier part of his career. His output on the label included *For the Sake of Love* (1978), *Don't Let Go* (1979), *Royal Rappins* (with Millie Jackson) and *Once Again* (1980), and *A Lifetime Thing* (1981). During those years, Stax issued some of his earlier material on the LPs *Hotbed* (1978), *The Isaac Hayes Movement* (1979), and *Enterprise—His Greatest Hits* (1980). After Fantasy Records bought the post-1968 Stax catalogue, it put out *The Best of Isaac Hayes, Volume 1* and *Volume 2* on compact disc only.

In the voting for the 1978 Grammies, Hayes was nominated in two categories: one as composer of the song "Deja Vu" (a hit single for Dionne Warwick), the other in the best male R&B category. His refound recording reputation was indicated by his gold single "Don't Let Go" and similar certification for the album that contained it. It looked as though things would go well for him in the 1980s as he made the charts with several singles, including the 1981 "I'm Gonna Make You Love Me," and had such other credits as a role in the film *Escape from New York* and host status in a new two-hour syndicated radio program, "Black Music Countdown Featuring Isaac Hayes."

But new problems, both business and personal, caught up with him and he dropped out of sight for almost five years. When he launched another comeback in 1986, he told Dennis Hunt (*Los Angeles Times*, October 11, 1986) that he had simply retired to his home in Atlanta after 1981, "sort of out of the way. I spent a year in London, too. I haven't been doing that much, just little odds and ends to survive and keep the bills paid. I couldn't really get into anything creative until those [problems] were cleaned up. Last year I was finally at a point where I could really concentrate on my work again."

His first new single, "Ike's Rap"/"Hey Girl" was an antidrug number. He told Hunt: "Back in the '60s I learned about drugs. I saw what it did to other entertainers. I've worked with musicians who were

addicted. We had them on methadone programs. I never wanted to fall into that trap."

HEART: *Vocal and instrumental group. Original members, all from Seattle, Washington: Ann Wilson, born c. 1950; Nancy Wilson, born c. 1954; Roger Fisher; Steve Fossen. Personnel, mid-1970s–early 1980s: Wilson sisters; Fisher; Fossen; Howard Leese, born Los Angeles, California; Michael Derosier. Fisher, Fossen, and Derosier replaced in early 1980s by Mark Andes, born Philadelphia, Pennsylvania c. 1947; and Denny Carmassi.*

The striking features of lead vocalist Ann Wilson—both vocally and physically—coupled with the songwriting talents of Ann and sister Nancy and a reasonably unique sound should have made Heart one of the creative stars of rock of the '70s and '80s. However, the group's output over those years was strangely erratic, varying from hard-rock classic originals to numbers that seemed pallid copies of other groups. Despite its inconsistencies, though, the group's still sizable number of notable rock singles, such as "Magic Man" and "Barracuda," marked it as one of the more important bands of the period.

While the band first came to prominence in Vancouver, Canada, the founding members' roots were south of the boarder in Seattle, Washington. The Wilson sisters, original lead guitarist Roger Fisher, and bass guitarist Steve Fossen called Seattle home through their preteen and teen years. The Wilsons both were music enthusiasts during high school. While Ann never had formal musical training, she did manage to learn to play guitar, flute, and trumpet before entering the Cornish School of Fine Arts in Seattle. Her initial career goal included art and writing; she was interested in writing poetry and looked forward to illustrating her own poetry books.

The siren call of pop music took her away from college before graduation. In the early 1970s, she performed in local Seattle clubs with a succession of bands. Her younger sister, Nancy, followed somewhat the same route. Like Ann, she was interested in folk music in high school and learned acoustic guitar to provide self-accompaniment on such songs. She also picked up flute which was to become an important element in Heart arrangements. She also went on to college with thoughts of trying her hand at short story writing and illustrating children's books. After two years in college, she left to become a full-time member of the new rock band being assembled by her sister and musician friends.

The other performers who helped form the original nucleus of Heart were Roger Fisher and Steve Fossen. The two worked together in diverse Seattle bands from their early teens. Of the two, Fossen had the more intense musical grounding, studying trumpet and guitar as a boy and later majoring in music at Shoreline Community College in Seattle. Like the Wilsons, Fossen left school when it looked as though success in the rock field might be within reach.

As it happened, the catalyst for that came from an odd corner. Ann became enamored with Fisher's brother, Mike, who was then living in Vancouver. She followed him there and quickly discovered that the Canadian city was a hotbed of innovative rock activity. When Roger Fisher, Fossen, and Nancy joined Ann there, they organized a new group to play local venues. For the next few years, with the usual coming and going of band members (Fossen, for instance, left for a while before returning to the fold), the band slowly coalesced into one of Vancouver's more accomplished organizations.

The group followed the usual route of preparing demo tapes in hopes of getting the all-important contract, but received a predictable number of rejections until 1975, when a small Vancouver label said yes. Nancy recalled for *Modern Recording & Music* magazine (December 1985): "Originally every major label turned us down. Then a little label up there called Mushroom—an affiliate of EMI—wanted to sign just Ann, and she said: 'No, I won't do it without my sister and the guitar player.'"

When the studio work on its debut LP got underway in 1975, Heart added Michael Derosier on percussion and Howard Leese on keyboards and guitar. Derosier, who began as a session contributor before becoming a regular member that August, had studied music through college and had received two music scholarships to help him along. Leese, who grew up in Los Angeles, where he studied music at Los Angeles City College, moved to Vancouver when he was 19 and soon was ranked as one of the top session musicians in the Seattle/Vancouver area.

He told *Modern Recording and Music*: "I was the hot session guitar player in the area. When they went in to record their first LP, the guitar player that was in the band at the time [Roger Fisher] was just a little slow in the studio and he wasn't getting the results everybody was looking for. They just hired me as a hired hand to play on some of the tracks. I ended up playing on all the cuts. When the songs that I did the big solos on, 'Magic Man' and 'Crazy on You,' became hits, they thought they better have me around. They asked me to join, but I originally said no."

The debut album, *Dreamboat Annie*, was released in Canada during 1975 and for a while looked like it might die aborning. Leese said: "We faced amazing odds on that first record because we made that record on a very small label in Vancouver. But we tried to get a deal with all the labels in the States and all the

major labels turned the record down. So we opened our own little American subsidiary of our label, Mushroom Records, and put it out ourselves and it sold 3½ million copies."

Not that the album or its three singles hits (the third was the title song) did poorly in Canada. It was a hit there before it made U.S. charts and won the group two Juno Awards from the Canadian Academy of Recording Arts and Science: one for Best Group of 1976 and one for Michael Flicker for Best Record Producer. But it was not until the fall of that year that it became a best-seller on U.S. lists, eventually going platinum, helped along by an intensive touring schedule in which Heart was opening act for such groups as the Beach Boys, Loggins and Messina, and Jefferson Starship. In all, Heart was on the road for 10 months of 1976 throughout Canada, the U.S., and Europe, playing some 150 concert dates.

The increased attention given the band related to some extent to its co-ed makeup. Ann Wilson told Dennis Hunt of the *Los Angeles Times* (November 14, 1976): "The fact that our group is led by women has certainly helped us. It has opened doors for us because there are so few female rockers that we're a novelty. People want to see women rockers. There are not enough of the kind of women rockers that people want to see."

The right image, she claimed, required walking a fine line. "When women rock singers try to be macho, I think it hurts them. That behavior appeals to a small group of people. Most men don't want to see a woman trying to be a man and women don't like it either. And too much femininity turns people off because it's so sweet and overdone that it seems phony. I think that image may have hurt us at first because the cover of *Dreamboat Annie* makes Nancy and me look like cute, pink, lacy girls. Naturally, people thought we sang that cute, pink, lacy music and didn't bother with the album. But that's not us. On stage we don't try to be like men and we don't go in for the heavy feminine bit either. We're sexy in an understated way. We're appealing, but not in a pornographic way."

By 1977, the band was appealing to major record labels, too. The band members opted for Portrait Records, one of the Columbia Records' subsidiaries. The move, as might be expected, triggered legal wrangling with Mushroom that perhaps contributed to the erratic course of the group's new material in the late 1970s.

The debut on Portrait, *Little Queen*, came out in 1977. It wasn't up to the standards set in the earlier LP, but did have some satisfying additions to Heart's repertoire, particularly "Barracuda." The album was a platinum-award recipient from the RIAA as was the next release, *Magazine* (1978) on Mush-

287

room, which represented the Canadian label's attempt to reap some monetary rewards from Heart's growing reputation. In its initial form, it included mainly old demos and some tapes of live early Vancouver performances. After legal hassles, Heart won the right to rework some of the material, but the revisions didn't prevent it from being arguably one of the worst releases by a name group during that year.

The band recovered ground with its platinum 1978 Portrait album, *Dog and Butterfly*. For its next album, *Bebe Le Strange*, Heart moved to one of CBS Records' labels, Epic, and the gold album was in the top 10 on U.S. charts soon after its release in February 1980.

Rolling Stone's reviewer commented: "The LP is a departure from Heart's previous albums. . . . Its sound is harder and more unpredictable. 'We ran guitar amps into tympanies, we used vacuum cleaner hoses and tiny amplifiers,' Ann [Wilson] says. 'We tried lots of weird stuff.'"

The album won much more acclaim from critics than earlier collections, though it fell short of the massive sales totals of its predecessors. Such numbers from the album as the title track, "Even It Up," "Rockin' Heaven Down," and "Raised on You," became crowd-pleasing parts of the band's live sets. The band's most consistent release quality-wise was the gold 1980 Epic *Greatest Hits/Live* LP, which, as the title indicates, excluded the considerable amount of average or below-par material in the first five LPs.

There were hints of internal strains in the group by the time *Private Audition*, its next studio album on Epic, came on in 1982. The band also seemed to be losing favor with the rock audience. With the end of Heart's contract with CBS approaching, the time was ripe for changes in makeup and label. Thus, in 1982, a new band lineup was announced comprising the Wilson Sisters and Howard Leese from the old band, plus newcomers Mark Andes on bass guitar and Denny Carmassi on drums. Both Andres and Carmassi had accrued years of experience as session musicians and members of different bands (Carmassi with groups such as Montrose and Gamma; Andes with, among others, Spirit, Jo Jo Gunne, and Firefall). The new group recorded one album for Epic, *Passionworks* (1983), and then moved over to Capital Records.

The band took its time preparing its debut material for Capitol. The Wilsons had been primary songwriters in years past, but considerable contributions for the new album came from Leese and Andes. The sisters also continued to try out some projects of their own. Nancy had shown acting talent and her credits as of the mid-1980s included the movies *Fast Times at Ridgemont High* and *The Wild Life*. Ann recorded the top 10 "Almost Paradise," a duet with Mike Reno of Loverboy for the soundtrack of the hit movie *Footloose*.

Some critics wondered whether Heart might have seen its day as a top rock band prior to its first release on Capitol. In truth, that album, called *Heart*, didn't represent a dramatic advance beyond the best of its work of the past decade, but it proved the group could command widespread respect from fans. Issued in the fall of 1985, the album—aided by typical mid-1980s well-crafted-videos—rose to number one on *Billboard* album charts on December 21, 1985 and passed RIAA platinum-record levels on the way to double-platinum totals by early 1986.

By the time the group's second Capitol album, *Bad Animals*, came out in mid-1987, *Heart* had passed the 5 million sales total worldwide. *Bad Animals*, which placed a greater emphasis on slow tempo rock ballads than their hard-rock dominated albums, was more interesting overall than earlier 1980s LPs. Soon after release it was past platinum and provided the single "Alone," number one in the U.S. for three weeks.

HELL, RICHARD: *Singer, guitarist, band leader (THE VOIDOIDS), songwriter. Born Lexington, Kentucky, c. late 1940s.*

Tremendously talented as a writer and performer, Richard Hell never translated that ability into widespread music audience recognition. This reflected in part his sometimes prickly personality and determination to follow his own creative instincts at all costs. While he remained essentially a cult figure, greatly respected by critics and musical peers but little noticed by the public at large, his influence on other artists who did achieve international stardom during the late 1970s and early 1980s was immense.

Hell spent his early years in Lexington, Kentucky, and the mid-1960s in Wilmington, Delaware, where his high school friends included another "outsider" named Tom Verlaine. (*See Verlaine, Tom.*) Hell was involved in various rock bands during that period, but his main interest lay in writing poetry. In the late 1960s, he moved to New York City's Greenwich Village, a move, he said, made "with the intentions of becoming a sexy drunken poet like Dylan Thomas." During those years, Verlaine and other acquaintances from Delaware also come to New York with vague ideas of starting new creative movements in poetry and pop music.

All of them, Hell included, worked at various, often menial jobs to keep body and soul together. Hell, who lived in a ghetto tenement, continued to write poetry and published a small poetry magazine for a while to which, among others, Tom Verlaine contributed.

Influenced to some extent by Verlaine, in the early

1970s he began to consider concentrating his energies on writing and performing avant garde rock music. He recalled: "Eventually I became completely fed up with the confining world of poets." The audience he wanted to reach, he decided, wasn't composed of the young people who like the kind of books he read ("Almost no one fell into that category," he noted), but the vast majority who were excited by the work of the Stones, Beatles, Dylan, and the newer rock stars.

In 1971, his first step in the direction came with the formation of a group called the Neon Boys, a trio with Tom Verlaine on vocals and lead guitar, Hell on bass guitar (which he bought for $65) and vocals, and mutual high school friend Bill Ficca on drums. The band didn't make much headway in the New York rock scene so before long the three members went separate ways with Verlaine and Hell trying to keep their careers going with occasional solo performances, coupled with the usual odd jobs to get spending money.

Some new contacts made by Verlaine in late 1973 opened the door for another attempt at band formation so Tom called Hell and Ficca back into the fold along with another lead guitarist, Richard Lloyd. The new band eventually adopted the name Television for its performing debut at New York's Townhouse Theater on March 2, 1974, followed by steady employment for a time at the 1970s New York focal point for new, young bands, CBGB's. There had been a vogue in the U.S. and the U.K. in the early 1970s for garishly dressed, often bisexual costuming for some bands, a phase given various names including glitter rock, but Television and Hell in particular took a different approach. Foreshadowing the punk rock movement, the band's members favored starker outfits. Hell typically wore tight, ripped clothing with short, spiky hair rather than the long locks of conventional rock musicians.

Though Verlaine became known as the writing mainspring of Television, in the band's early stages, Hell provided a number of notable songs, including "Love Comes in Spurts" and "Blank Generation," the latter becoming something of an anthem for the punk/new wave phenomenon in the U.S. in the middle and late 1970s. Both songs became part of the repertoires of Hell's later bands.

While Television was building a growing reputation with its Sunday night sets at CBGS's, Hell and Verlaine were increasingly at odds about the musical styles they felt the band should emphasize. During 1975, things came to a head with Hell leaving the band and former Blondie bass guitarist Fred Smith taking his place.

Richard let no grass grow under his feet. Enlisting the support of Jerry Nolan and Johnny Thunder (former members of the glamrock New York Dolls), he started a new group, the Heartbreakers. Among the numbers Hell supplied the band were "New Pleasure" and "The Plan," songs considered among the best of the punk/new wave ferment of the mid-1970s.

Hell and the Heartbreakers stayed together for about a year, winning some plaudits from fans and critics who saw their New York area club dates. Hell still didn't feel the band met his aesthetic standards and in 1976 he broke it up. Soon after, he began to assemble a new group, Richard Hell and The Voidoids.

One of his recruits was lead guitarist Robert Quine, who since has shown himself to be one of the most innovative rock instrumentalists in the field. Hell recalled: "Bob was a guy I'd known for years. We worked together in the packing department of this bookstore called Cinemabilia; it was a book store about movies. I used to go over to his house after work."

For drums he brought in Marc Bell. Hell noted: "Marc was a guy who was known by everybody in New York—he and Jerry Nolan were acknowledged as the rock'n'roll drummers in New York. He'd just left [the group] Wayne County and he came up to me at Max's [club] one night and said he'd heard I'd split from the Heartbreakers and asked if we should get together. I said yeah. So him and me and Bob started looking for another guitar player." They found him in the form of Ivan Julian to round out the quartet known as the Voidoids. They put together material for a debut album, an extended-play collection issued on the small Ork Records. That disc did very well as an underground recording and helped bring a contract from a larger company, Sire Records.

By the time the band's debut album on Sire came out in August 1977, Hell and his band had received considerable coverage in the music press, which touted them as a pioneering group. Hell was particularly lionized in the U.K., where his face was featured on the cover of *Sounds* magazine in mid-1977. The article about Hell and the Voidoids posed the question, "Are you ready for the future of American rock music?"

The debut album, *Blank Generation*, did indeed point the direction of American rock as exemplified by bands such as Talking Heads and the punk/jazz fusion of some 1980s groups. But Hell himself reaped little personal advantage from all that. Though *Blank Generation* was one of the best albums put out in late 1970s and remains a classic in innovative rock, it was not a great commercial success and Hell was never able to surpass it creatively. The band's live concerts of the late 1970s were spine-tingling, nerve-jarring events that deserved far better fan support than they received.

HENDRIX, JIMI: *Singer, guitarist, songwriter. Born Seattle, Washington, November 27, 1942; died London, England, September 18, 1970. Leader, JIMI HENDRIX EXPERIENCE, trio including Hendrix; Mitch Mitchell, born London, England, July 9, 1946; Noel Redding, born Folkestone, Kent, England, December 25, 1945.*

Experience, the name of Jimi Hendrix's famous rock trio, was also something Jimi crammed a lot of into his scant 27 years of life. Unfortunately, the experience ranged across the spectrum of drugs and robbed Jimi of the chance to be remembered even more for his remarkable musical ability rather than the wild physical acts of destruction that had helped gain him worldwide attention.

The son of a Seattle gardener, Jimi became interested in music as a youngster. During his early teens, he was particularly enthused about rhythm & blues, obtaining as many records as he could of such greats as Muddy Waters. Whenever he got the chance, he sat on his back porch with an old guitar and tried to play along with the individuals or groups in his record collection.

Jimi's desire to get out into the world didn't lead at first to the musical field. Instead, he enlisted as a paratrooper in the 101st Airborne Division at the end of the 1950s. His army career was cut short by a back injury suffered during a jump. After getting a medical discharge, he decided to go into the music field. By then, he was an accomplished guitarist and later was to develop into one of the best in the business, though this was overshadowed by the theatricality of his rock performance. Jimi started as a sideman with a small R&B group and, before long, was in demand to work with some of the best-known artists in the field. From 1961 to 1966, he toured widely with a series of R&B shows including (using the pseudonym Jimmy James) six months in New York as a member of James Brown's Famous Flames. (*See Brown, James.*)

In the late summer of 1966, Hendrix, who had mainly remained an instrumentalist, tried his hand at singing with a group working the Cafe Wha! in New York's Greenwich Village. One of the club's visitors was Charles "Chas" Chandler, then a member of Eric Burdon's Animals. (*See Animals, The.*) Chandler thought Hendrix was sensational and, on rehearing Jimi in September 1966, he met Jimi and talked him into moving to England, where Chandler thought he would be appreciated. With Chas's help, they auditioned musicians and chose Mitch Mitchell and Noel Redding to complete the new Hendrix group.

Mitchell had been started on acting and dancing lessons by his parents when he was three at London's Art Education School. At 10, he began to earn money working as a child actor in TV commercials. In his early teens, he developed considerable skill as a drummer and joined a group called the Coronets for a six-month tour of England. After this, he spent much time as a recording session drummer and a band performer on the English TV show "Ready, Steady Go." He then joined the Blue Flames of Georgie Fame for over a year before moving to the Hendrix Experience.

Redding already had a reputation as one of England's best guitar and bass players when he met Hendrix. He was interested in music long before his teens, but he didn't take up instrument training until then. At 13, he started on violin, then added banjo at 14 and guitar at 16 while also studying art at the Folkestone Art College. He was dropped from college for poor attendance and moved to London to find work in music. His guitar playing was excellent and he soon joined the Modern Jazz Group, staying with them for three months before moving to the Burnetts rock group. After 18 months with the latter band, he moved to Germany for a time where he gained considerable fame. He went back to England a year later to start his own group, the Loving Kind, which worked desultorily in the Folkestone area in 1965. The group broke up and Noel went to London to audition for the Animals. He missed out on that, but met Hendrix, who signed him after Redding stated he thought he could learn to play bass without major difficulty.

In late 1966, the Experience debuted at the Olympia in Paris and were an immediate hit. For the rest of the year and into 1967, the Experience broke attendance records at one European club after another, including the Tivoli in Stockholm, Sports Arena in Copenhagen, and Saville Theatre in London. A record contract followed and the group began a series of singles that gained top 10 rank in England: "Hey, Joe," "Purple Haze," and "The Wind Cries Mary."

Hendrix was now famous in England, but unknown in his native land. When the Monkees toured Europe in early 1967, they heard Jimi and liked him. (*See Monkees; Nesmith, Michael.*) He was asked to return with them as part of a U.S. series of engagements. Jimi's erotic stage actions, suggestive lyrics, and guitar-smashing antics won scant approval from young Monkees fans or adult authorities. Jeered and criticized, he was finally dropped from the tour before it ended.

Soon after, however, the Experience was invited to the 1967 Monterey Pop Festival. Here Jimi had an audience used to hyperamplified musicianship and not shy about raw language. The nerve-shattering sounds from the group's nine amplifiers and 18 speakers, topped by Jimi's dousing his guitar with lighter fluid and burning it, won a long, standing ovation. Newspapers, TV, and word of mouth quickly made Hendrix an American celebrity. As a result, his 1968 and 1969 American tours were standing-room–only affairs. Audiences went wild over his antics, such as those described in *Time* (April 25, 1968): "He hopped, twisted and rolled over sideways without missing a twang or a moan. He slung the guitar low over swiveling hips, or raised it to pick the strings with his teeth; he thrust it between his legs and did a bump and grind, crooning: 'Oh, baby, come on now, sockit to me.' . . . For a symbolic finish, he lifted the guitar and flung it against the amplifiers."

Platinum albums on Reprise included *Are You Experienced?*, *Electric Ladyland*, *Axis: Bold as Love* (1968) and *Smash Hits* (1969). Hendrix's songs were almost all originals. *Billboard* named him Artist of the Year for 1968.

The Experience split up in 1969, though Hendrix insisted it wasn't permanent, but just a chance for each member to develop individually. One of his goals was to try to change some of his musical directions. "I want to be respected in the music field," he said, later noting: "There are so many more things to do in music. Sometimes, no matter how badly you play, people come up to you and say: 'You were fantastic' and that really hurts, especially when you are trying to progress."

But Hendrix by this time had the problems of drug addiction riding him. Some indications appeared in Toronto, where he was arrested in 1969 for heroin possession. He denied he used hard drugs and claimed he had once used drugs, but had "outgrown" them. His personal problems did not interfere with continued experimenting in music, including concerts with other major rock artists such as Buddy Miles and Billy Cox. Their live album, *Band of Gypsys* (Capitol, 1970), won a gold record.

Jimi was ranked high on all pop music polls in 1969 and 1970, including being chosen by *Playboy* as its 1969 artist of the year. However, time was running out on Hendrix though his career seemed on the way to greater heights in mid-1970. In mid-September, he was discovered dead in his room in London from an overdose of drugs.

In his commemorative column on Jimi in the *Los Angeles Times* (October 4, 1970), Robert Hilburn concluded: "Hendrix's music was perfectly tied to the times. It was a troubled, violent, confused, searching music on the one hand, an assertive, demanding, triumphant, sensual music on the other. Though it was often lost beneath the theatrics,

Hendrix was a superb guitarist. His special attraction, however, was his masterful use of feedback. He got sounds out of the guitar that most people didn't imagine ever were there. His rise was timed just right. Stereo had just begun to become widespread and Hendrix's feedback electronics was perfect for stereo. Millions of young people could put headphones on and experience fully the Hendrix sound revolution."

The day after his death, Reprise released the gold album *Monterey International Pop Festival* with one side by the Jimi Hendrix Experience and the other by Otis Redding. (*See Redding, Otis.*) Ever since then, there have been numerous repackagings of his recorded material on a variety of labels. Some of the releases include not only numbers spotlighting Hendrix, but almost anything on which he played whether as a band leader or a sideman in other artists' recordings.

In the years immediately after his passing, a number of new LPs made top charts levels. Those included *The Cry of Love* (Reprise, issued March 6, 1971), which rose to number 3 on *Billboard* charts; *Rainbow Bridge* (Reprise, October 9, 1971); and *Hendrix in the West* (Reprise, March 4, 1972). All went gold.

Later Reprise releases included *War Heroes* (issued December 9, 1972), the soundtrack *Jimi Hendrix* (July 14, 1973), *Crash Landing* (March 22, 1975), *Midnight Lightning* (November 29, 1975), *The Essential Jimi Hendrix, Volume 1* (1978) and *Volume 2* (1979), and *Nine to the Universe* (1981). Releases of Hendrix material on other labels included, on Polydor, *Isle of Wight* (1971); on Barclay, *Loose Ends* (1973); on Maple, *Two Great Experiences/Together* (with Lonnie Youngblood, 1971); on T-Neck, *In the Beginning...* (with the Isley Brothers; *see Isley Brothers, The*); on United Artists, *World of Jimi Hendrix*; on Springboard, *Jimi Hendrix in Concert*; and on Trip, *Rare Hendrix* (1972), *Roots of Hendrix*, *Genius of Jimi Hendrix*, *Superpak*, *16 Greatest Hits*, and *Jimi Hendrix, Volumes 1* and *2*. In 1987, Rykodisc's CD *Live at Winterland* presented more of the October 1968 performances captured on the two-disc *Jimi Hendrix Concerts* (Reprise, 1982).

HENLEY, DON: *Singer, guitarist, percussionist, songwriter, record producer. Born Gilmer, Texas, July 22, 1947.*

The breakup of the superstar rock group the Eagles in 1980 proved a depressing experience for most of its members, including Don Henley, who with Glenn Frey provided most of its greatest hits. While Don wasn't happy about the situation, it proved a blessing in disguise, launching him on a solo career that brought considerable personal success by the mid-1980s. (*See Eagles, The; Frey, Glenn.*)

Henley's route to stardom began in the small Texas town of Gilmer. He spent his formative years there and in other small towns, such as Linden, Texas, population 200. He already was probing the music field in his teens, playing with various local bands until he eventually settled down with one group that evolved into a band called Shiloh. He was involved with the band while attending college; in fact, except for his music, he seemed out of place in Texas much as had another young Texan, Janis Joplin. He finally heeded a college English teacher's advice about a change of scene and moved his band activities to Southern California.

His parents may not have been enthusiastic about his following his muse, especially since his father was dying at the time, but they didn't oppose it. With the promise of as much help as they could provide, they sent him off with best wishes.

In Los Angeles, serving as percussionist and lead singer for Shiloh, Don could point to making some inroads on the local music scene, but nothing dramatic. The band did get a contract from the small Amos label, whose roster also included the duo Longbranch Pennywhistle (J.D. Souther and Glenn Frey). Without knowing they all were on the same label, Henley bumped into the other two in the bar at the small but important folk-rock club, the Troubadour, a hangout for many young musicians who were either underemployed or out of work. Souther and Frey were having contract problems with Amos that sidelined them, while Henley had time to kill between infrequent Shiloh gigs.

At first Frey and Souther ignored Henley. Frey recalled: "I thought Don was another fucked-up little punk." But eventually they became acquainted and found considerable rapport as musicians and songwriters. While a member of Linda Ronstadt's backing band at the end of the 1960s, Frey found that the group needed a drummer. (*See Ronstadt, Linda.*) Up to then, he and Henley had only talked sporadically, but realizing that Henley played drums, he sought him out at the Troubadour and asked if he'd like to try for the job. Henley was receptive, having just lost a key member of Shiloh, pedal steel man Al Perkins, to the Flying Burrito Brothers.

Frey and Henley got along so well together, Frey recalled, they began to think of bigger projects while rehearsing for an upcoming concert series with Linda. "On the first night of the Ronstadt tour, Don and I agreed to start our own band."

This evolved into the Eagles. Other members of the Ronstadt backup group, (bass guitarist Randy Meisner and lead guitarist Bernie Leadon) formed the other half of the original quartet. After getting underway at the start of the 1970s with Linda Ronstadt's blessing, the group went on to become one of the leading exponents of folk/county-rock from the mid-1970s until internal dissension resulted in the Eagles demise in 1980.

Henley indicated later he had not expected the band's problems to lead to a permanent rupture. He told Robert Hilburn of the *Los Angeles Times* in summer 1982 that he was "shocked and hurt" when it occurred. "It was a terrible year. The band broke up and I broke up with my girlfriend. I did a stupid thing and got into trouble with the law [an arrest for cocaine possession]. Then I met the girl I'm with now and we almost got killed in a plane crash. John Lennon got killed and that devastated me for a while."

By 1981, though, he had embarked on preparation for his first solo album under contract to Asylum Records. Working on its songs (several co-written with friend and top session guitarist Danny Kortchmar) took his mind of his earlier problems. By the time it was ready for release in mid-1982, Henley was feeling better about himself and his career. The album, *I Can't Stand Still*, went gold. At the end of 1982, the single "Dirty Laundry" from the LP, co-written with Kortchmar, was in the number four position on the *Billboard* charts.

In late 1984, his album *Building the Perfect Beast*, came out on Geffen Records (like Asylum, part of the WEA recording operation), earning platinum-record certification from the RIAA. Two singles from the album, "The Boys of Summer" and "All She Wants to Do Is Dance," made the *Billboard* top 10 in 1985.

HERMAN'S HERMITS: *See Noone, Peter.*

HOLLIES, THE: *Vocal and instrumental group, founding members: Graham Nash, born Blackpool, Lancashire, England, February 2, 1942; Allan Clarke, born Salford, Lancashire, England, April 5, 1942. Nash left in 1968; replaced by Terry Sylvester, born Liverpool, England, January 8, 1947. Personnel as of 1971: Clarke; Tony Hicks, born Nelson, Lancashire, December 16, 1945; Bobby Elliott, born Burnley, Lancashire, December 8, 1942; Bernie Calvert, born Burnley, Lancashire, September 16, 1942.*

The Hollies certainly would be considered one of the landmark groups in rock music even if they hadn't served as the proving ground for superstar Graham Nash. (*See Crosby, Stills, Nash & Young.*) The group never achieved the reputation in the U.S. it maintained in England and most other countries of the western world, but their music, directly through

Nash and indirectly through their impact on U.S. artists, certainly affected trends in America.

The two founders of the Hollies (Nash and singer-guitarist Allan Clarke) were close friends from childhood in their native Lancashire, England. In grammar school, their joint interest in music led them to develop a singing act called the Two Teens. They started working school functions and, at 15, became the youngest performers to appear at the well-known (in England) Manchester Cabaret Club. They completed school together and went on to the same engineering work in their home area. They kept up with their music by taking evening jobs as the Guytones, which they later expanded to a quartet called the Four Tones.

In the early 1960s, they combined with bass guitarist Don Rathbone and drummer Eric Haydock in a group called the Deltas. The group found favor locally for a time, then disbanded and reassembled in early 1963 under a new name, the Hollies. Nash and Clarke felt they needed an exceptional lead guitarist to provide the basis for a top-flight group. The artist they had in mind was Tony Hicks, considered one of the finest musicians in the Manchester area. Tony had a promising job as an electrical apprentice and was reluctant to give up steady work for the fragile chance of a music career. Nash and Clarke, who had managed to gain a London recording test, talked him into listening to a rehearsal prior to the trip. Hicks liked what he heard and finally agreed to take a leave of absence from his job, at least until the London visit was completed. The test was so well received by recording executives that Hicks agreed to become a full-time group member.

Soon after the Hollies got underway, Rathbone left and was replaced by Bobby Elliott, who came to the group from Shane Fenton and the Fentones. It took only a short time for Elliott to know he made the right move when the Hollies' first single, "Ain't That Just Like Me," made the English charts. The group rapidly gained star status later in the year with top 10 U.K. hits from their next two singles: "Searchin'" and "Stay." Similar success greeted their debut LP, *Stay with the Hollies* and their next single, "Just One Look." In June 1965, they scored their first number one single in Europe with "I'm Alive." In mid-1966, Eric Haydock left and was replaced by another Lancashire friend of the group, Bernie Calvert.

That year also witnessed the Hollies first *Billboard* top 10 hits in the U.S.: "Bus Stop" and "Stop Stop Stop" on Imperial. 1967 brought the top 20 LP *The Hollies Greatest Hits*. They hit the U.S. top 10 in 1967 with "Carrie-Anne" after switching labels to Epic.

The next change was a major one. Graham Nash announced in November 1968 that he was leaving the Hollies to concentrate on songwriting and performing in the U.S. A cheering, standing-room–only crowd greeted his farewell performance at the London Palladium on December 8, 1968. Nash was replaced the next month by the band's first non-Lancashireman: Liverpool-born singer-guitarist Terry Sylvester. Graham soon joined the supergroup Crosby, Stills & Nash.

Despite Graham's departure, the Hollies maintained their musical quality and hit-making consistency. In 1969, they had two top 10 LPs in the U.K., *Greatest Hits* and *The Hollies Sing Dylan*. They also had two best selling U.K. singles in 1969, "Sorry Susanne" and "He Ain't Heavy, He's My Brother." The last named became a top hit on *Billboard* charts in 1970. Later in the 1970s, the group earned gold record awards for the single "Long Cool Woman" (1972) and "The Air That I Breathe."

As of mid-1971, the Hollies had released 22 singles on the English Parlophone EMI label with all 22 making the English hit charts and 20 entering the top 10. Though some of their singles and LPs reached the U.S. charts too, few sold anywhere near the numbers reached elsewhere. The group never managed to gain the mass audience in the States, perhaps because of inadequate publicity or possibly because they were overshadowed by such "heavy" groups as the Beatles and Rolling Stones. Their U.S. LP releases were not handled by EMI's U.S. subsidiary, Capitol, but initially by Imperial, which issued *Hear the Hollies*, *Beat Group*, and *Bus Stop* in 1966. Epic Records offered the LPs *Evolution* (1967) and *Dear Eloise* (1968), and *He Ain't Heavy, He's My Brother*, which made upper levels of U.S. charts in 1970.

In the spring of 1971, the group returned to their home city of Manchester for their first concert there in three years to a warm welcome. One of the numbers played at The Free Trade Hall in that city was an Allan Clarke original, "Hey Willie," that gained the U.K. single charts soon after.

For the rest of the 1970s and into the 1980s, the pattern remained essentially the same for the group. It retained a strong following in England and Europe and a cult following in the U.S. Among the albums available to U.S. record buyers were such Epic releases as *Distant Light* (1972), *Romany* (1972), *Greatest Hits* (1973), *Crazy Steal* (1978), and *What Goes Around...* (1983).

HOLLY, BUDDY: *Singer, guitarist, violinist, songwriter, band leader (THE CRICKETS, BUDDY HOLLY BAND). Born Lubbock, Texas, September 7, 1936; died near Ames, Iowa, February 3, 1959. The Crickets comprised Holly;*

Jerry Allison, born Hillsboro, Texas, August 31, 1939; Niki Sullivan; Joe Mauldin. Backup group, early 1959: Tommy Allsup, Waylon Jennings, Charlie Bunch. In early 1960s, Crickets comprised Allison; Sonny Curtis, born Meadow, Texas, May 9, 1937; Glen Hardin, born Wellington, Texas, April 18, 1939; Jerry Naylor, born Stephenville, Texas, March 6, 1939.

In a life that lasted hardly more than 22 years, Buddy Holly gained the heights of popular music before he died in a plane crash. Like Elvis, he and his band, the Crickets, had a tremendous impact not only on American popular music, but the subsequent development of rock'n'roll in England. The styles of the Beatles, Rolling Stones, and many other British supergroups were partly derived from Holly's arrangements and methods of guitar playing. His story didn't end with his death. He became a part of popular legend, memorialized in such famous songs as Don McLean's 1971 hit "American Pie," which described Buddy's death as "the day the music died." (*See McLean, Don.*) Buddy's life story was the subject of a hit movie in the late 1970s and reissues of his recordings still were appearing in the 1980s.

Born Charles Hardin Holley (the "e" in Holley was accidentally dropped on his first record contract, a change he let stand), he was initially influenced by country music and began as a country artist in his early teens.

As the youngest of four children, he grew up in a conservative Baptist family. His parents encouraged musical ambitions in their children and Buddy began to play the violin and piano at four and took up the guitar when he was only seven. There were country records in his home, including some old 78 rpm discs of such early stars as Jimmie Rodgers (the Singing Brakeman) and the Carter Family. He also picked up pointers on current country trends by listening to local west Texas radio shows and sometimes the Grand Ole Opry from Nashville, Tennessee.

In the early 1950s, he started singing in country groups while attending high school. By 1954, he was gaining a local reputation as a country artist and was playing in small clubs in the Southwest. As rock swept over the country in the mid-1950s, Holly, like many other young country-bred performers, was attracted to the new style. Though he developed his own method of doing rock music, he was an early admirer of Elvis Presley and R&B stars Little Richard and Chuck Berry, whose hits he often rerecorded.

In 1956, Decca released several rough-edged rockabilly solo singles Holly recorded in their Nashville studios, but they failed to sell, so Decca dropped his contract. Holly and some Lubbock friends then formed a band, naming themselves "the Crickets" after considering calling themselves "the Beetles." (Years later, England's Fab Four would choose the name "Beatles" as a tribute to the Crickets.) Buddy handled guitar and vocals; Jerry Allison, drums; Niki Sullivan, guitar; and Joe Mauldin, bass guitar. They became the protégés of Clovis, New Mexico–based record producer Norman Petty (born Clovis, May 25, 1927; died 1985), who used his connections to get their song "That'll Be the Day" released on Decca's Brunswick subsidiary in 1957. A number one success in *Billboard*, it led to a contract for the Crickets on Brunswick and for Holly as a solo on another Decca subsidiary, Coral. "They kicked us out the front door so we went in the back door," Buddy remarked.

Subsequent Crickets hits included "Oh, Boy!" (top 10, 1957) and "Maybe Baby" and "Think It Over" (1958). Holly's solo "Peggy Sue" made *Billboard*'s top 10 in 1957. His lesser hits included "Early in the Morning" (1958, written by Bobby Darin and Woody Harris) and the posthumous "It Doesn't Matter Anymore" (1959, written by Paul Anka). (*See Anka, Paul; Darin, Bobby.*) "Peggy Sue" was originally titled "Cindy Lou," but Jerry Allison suggested substituting his girlfriend's name.

The Crickets' 1958 tour of England was one of the major pop music events in that country to that time. Many of the aspiring young rock and blues musicians in England took careful note of Holly's guitar style. Called the brush-and-broom style, it was a technique derived from country music groups in Holly's home area. His technique was described in *Golden Guitars* by Irwin Stambler and Grelun Landon (Four Winds Press, 1971). "He would hit the note, which was the 'broom,' and then 'brush' his fingers across the chord. For example, a guitarist might pluck the G string, or the D string, then strum the G chord. (This type of playing is also used in many Johnny Cash arrangements.) This technique of note and strums is much simpler than the fancy runs of an artist like Jimmie Rodgers. Holly's material combined a Jimmie Rodgers–Leadbelly blues feeling with heavy guitar sounds out front and a pronounced beat underneath."

Like most music stars, he maintained a hectic schedule of personal appearances that involved great amounts of travel from each one-night stand to the next. It was a wearing schedule that eventually cost him his life. Not long before his final, fatal tour, Holly had made a number of changes in his personal and music business life. For one thing, due to a feud with his mentor, Norman Petty, Holly and the Crickets became separate acts. Holly's role in the Crickets was taken over by an old Lubbock acquaintance, Earl Sinks, while Buddy set up a new backing band that eventually comprised Tommy Allsup on guitar, Charlie Bunch on drums, and future country star Waylon Jennings on bass guitar and backing vocals.

Buddy also had established New York as both recording and personal base. In the summer of 1958, he married Puerto Rican–born Marie Elena Santiago, whom he had met when she was working in his song publisher's office in New York. They took up living quarters in Greenwich Village, while he pursued his recording projects and studied acting. Among those projects were sessions backed by an orchestra led by Dick Jacobs, a far cry from his early rockabilly.

At the beginning of 1959, Holly and his backing group was booked for a Midwestern tour that also featured such best-selling artists as the Big Bopper (J.P. Richardson) and Ritchie Valens. (*See Richardson, J.P.; Valens, Ritchie.*) They traveled between concert sites by bus, so the musicians had to spend long, grueling hours going from one small town to another under cold, crowded conditions. In Clear Lake, Iowa, faced with another trying journey to a date in Fargo, North Dakota, Holly, Allsup, and Jennings decided to hire a light plane so they could reach Fargo early enough to get some rest and have their stage outfits cleaned, as described in the authoritative biography, *Remembering Buddy* by John Goldrosen and John Beecher (Penguin Books, 1987).

Before they got on the plane, the passenger list changed. The Big Bopper wasn't feeling well and talked Jennings into giving him his seat. Valens challenged Allsup to a coin toss for the other place. Valens won. Allsup and Jennings stayed on the bus. Piloted by 21-year-old Roger Peterson, the plane took off from the Mason City, Iowa, airport in a blinding snowstorm. It quickly crashed, killing all occupants.

Holly's popularity remained strong decades after his death, fueled by periodic posthumous releases of his recordings. Immediately after the crash, Coral rushed into print *The Buddy Holly story*, a gold-award-winning memorial album featuring his and the Crickets' major hits. Other Coral releases included *The Buddy Holly Story, Volume 2* (1960), the two-disc *Best of Buddy Holly* (1966), and *Buddy Holly's Greatest Hits* (1967). In 1962, Coral also reissued the 1957 LP *The Chirping Crickets* as *Buddy Holly and the Crickets. Reminiscing* (1963), *Showcase* (1964), and *Holly in the Hills* (1965) mainly presented unpolished yet interesting studio tracks and home tapes never released as singles (including standards of his favorite R&B and C&W artists). His pre-Crickets Nashville sessions appeared on *That'll Be the Day* (Decca, 1958), reissued as *The Great Buddy Holly* (Vocalion, 1967).

As owner of Decca, Coral and Brunswick, MCA continued to release Holly reissues in the 1970s and 1980s. The two-disc *Buddy Holly: A Rock & Roll Collection* (1972) was so clumsily assembled that it included a version of "Love's Made a Fool of You" the Crickets taped after Buddy left them. Originally released only in England, MCA's six-record *The Complete Buddy Holly* provided not only his professional recordings, but also interviews, tapes of a TV appearance on "The Ed Sullivan Show," and sessions Holly produced for Waylon Jennings and Lou Giordano. *20 Golden Greats* was released to coincide with the first screenings of the fictionalized Columbia Pictures film biography, *The Buddy Holly Story*, starring Gary Busey as Holly. The soundtrack album, which presented the film's stars (Busey, Don Stroud and Charles Martin) performing Holly's songs, was issued on American International Records, distributed by Epic Records.

In early 1983, MCA came out with *For the First Time Anywhere*, an impressive set of Holly recordings that had remained hidden in the vaults for almost 27 years. These songs had been issued on many LPs over the years, MCA noted, but never in the form Holly originally had made them. Norman Petty had reworked the tapes by overdubbing them with instrumental backing by another of his protégé acts, the Fireballs. (*See Gilmer, Jimmy and the Fireballs.*) For decades, MCA didn't realize the original unretouched tapes were still in existence. They proved a new revelation of the raw excitement and urgency of Holly performances.

In 1985, MCA issued a CD of what it stated were remastered versions from original Coral, Brunswick and Decca tapes of Buddy's 20 most famous songs, titled *The Legend*. In mid-1986, it was released in LP (2 discs) and cassette formats.

In the decades following Holly's death, rerecordings of his songs by the Beatles, John Lennon, Blind Faith, Rolling Stones, Grateful Dead, Nitty Gritty Dirt Band, and Waylon Jennings further attest to Buddy's influence. Linda Ronstadt had hits with Holly's "That'll Be the Day" and "It's So Easy," as did Peter and Gordon with his "True Love Ways."

HOLLYWOOD ARGYLES, THE: *Vocal and instrumental group from Southern California. Gary Paxton, Gary Webb, Bobby Rey, Ted Marsh, Deary Weaver, Ted Winters.*

The Hollywood Argyles had a brief moment in the sun in 1960 thanks to a hit single inspired by Neanderthal comic strip character Alley Oop and written by country singer-songwriter Dallas Frazier. The "group" actually started as one performer, singer Gary Paxton who, as Flip of Skip and Flip, had had earlier hits with "It Was I" and "Cherry Pie." Skip was Clyde "Skip" Battin who later joined the Byrds and Flying Burrito Brothers.

Young singer-songwriter Kim Fowley, whom Paxton met shortly after coming to Hollywood to further his music career, helped set up a recording session for Paxton with Lute Records that included "Alley Oop." (Kim Fowley told Mike Ochs he was working in a gas station when Frazier came in and showed him the song, which Fowley then took to Paxton.) They adopted the name Hollywood Argyles, as Fred Bronson noted in his *Billboard Book of Number One Records*, because Paxton thought an earlier record contract barred him from using his own name. Gary and Kim assembled a five-man backing group that helped record the *Alley Oop* LP and also toured with Paxton. Vocals were handled by Paxton, Bobby Rey, and Ted Winders with instrumental support from Deary Weaver on guitar and Gary Webb on drums. The Lute single of "Alley Oop" made number one in *Billboard* the week of July 11, 1960. A cover version by Dante and the Evergreens on Madison Records made the top 15. At the time, executives from both record firms claimed million copy worldwide sales for their respective discs.

The Argyles never had another major hit and broke up soon after "Alley Oop" faded from the charts. Paxton formed his own label, Garpax, and produced such hits as Bobby "Boris" Pickett's "Monster Mash."

HOOKER, JOHN LEE: *Guitarist, singer, songwriter. Born Clarksdale, Mississippi, August 22, 1917.*

A versatile, enduring artist, John Lee Hooker exerted an influence on many phases of popular music from the post–World War II years into the 1980s. His blues stylings over the years covered just about every facet from traditional country blues to rhythm and blues with excursions into rock'n'roll. His willingness to try such a wide variety of art forms has resulted in his being damned by some folk and blues purists as "uneven" and "opportunist," but Hooker has never paid much attention to such carping. Overall, while demonstrating an ability to survive in often difficult times, he carved out a justified reputation as one of America's greatest blues and folk-blues artists.

He spent his early years in the Mississippi Delta, a region that produced many of the legendary names in country blues. The first wave to gain recognition included Sonny Boy Williamson, Mississippi John Hurt, and Big Bill Broonzy. Those artists were sometimes looked upon as old-fashioned by the next generation, which encompassed such artists as Muddy Waters and Hooker. (*See Waters, Muddy.*)

Singing folk-blues was a living, everyday tradition in John Lee's home area. Few children had the chance for much schooling or to do much else but work in the fields or at odd jobs, so music was one of the few pleasures of life. Recalling his early years, Hooker told Jim and Amy O'Neal (*Living Blues*, Autumn 1979): "Well, I never did have a hard time 'cause my dad had a big farm down there. But I know it was rough. I didn't experience it 'cause I left there when I was 14, 'cause I was playin' music when I was 12 or 14. . . . I run off from my dad and I went to Memphis. I stayed around two months. I was workin' at a motion picture show, the New Daisy, and then goin' to school when I could. And when I couldn't, I didn't go, you know. And my dad followed me. He come and got me."

Hooker noted he always used the style of guitar playing he acquired as a boy, "percussive, with stomping chords slashed out, often laced with walking base lines." Though he knew many great players of the Delta slide guitar–style (guitar tuned to an open chord and fretted with a bottleneck or metal sleeve on one finger), he never mastered that approach. He told the O'Neals: "My style come from my stepfather, Will Moore. The style I'm playing now, that's what he was playing. . . . And nobody else plays that style. I got a style nobody else don't have."

At 17, John was on the road again, this time with no one in pursuit to take him home. First stop was Memphis. "Didn't nobody know me. Me and B. B. [King] and them, we just messed around there. But B. B. stayed there for a while. Me and B. B. and Bobby [Bland] we were playin' around Memphis, for house parties there. . . . We'd go over [to West Memphis] and party all night and mess around. And a lot of clubs, they wouldn't let me in—they usually wouldn't let us in 'cause we wasn't old enough." (*See Bland, Bobby "Blue"; King, B. B.*)

Hooker then settled in Cincinnati when he was about 18. He worked at various day jobs and performed his music wherever he could, for house parties or small clubs, often for little or no money. "I stayed there about three years, but I didn't get no break and I left there."

With the onset of World War II and the opening up of better paying jobs further north, Hooker became part of that black migration and settled in Detroit in 1943. The pattern was much the same as before. He worked for a time as a hospital attendant, then in an automotive plant, while singing and playing his music in bars and at parties. But eventually Detroit proved lucky for him, bringing him together with "Bernie Besman and Elmer Barber, this Jewish guy and this black cat. And this black cat, he had that record store there in Detroit—him and Bernie was really good friends. Bernie Besman had this big, big distributor.''

Barber heard Hooker play at a house party and was impressed. He approached John about making records. He arranged a meeting between Hooker and Besman for which John brought a tape of some songs. As Hooker told the O'Neals after hearing the tape, one of them said: "Man, I tell you, you got somethin' different, ain't nobody else got. I never heard a voice like that. Do you want to record?' I said, 'Yeah, but I've been jived so much, I don't know if y'all just puttin' me on.' They said, 'No, no, kid. We're not puttin' you on. You're really good. You written them songs on there?' I said, 'Yeah. You know, "Boogie Chillen," "Hobo Blues," "In the Mood."' ''

Hooker accepted and in a few weeks in late 1948 recorded his first single: "Boogie Chillen"/"Sally Mae." Originally made for the Sensation label, the disc was turned over to a larger company, Modern Records, for distribution. The record became a massive hit in the blues field in 1949. Soon Hooker decided to quit his day job and go on the road, aided by Besman, who was still a close friend decades later. He demonstrated he wasn't a one-hit artist by recording more songs that became favorites with blues fans around the country on Modern Records: "In the Mood for Love," "Hobo Blues," "Crawling King Snake."

During the 1950s, with stepped-up popular interest in both R&B and rock'n'roll, his name became increasingly well known both in the United States and abroad. Many of his old '50s records had dramatic impact on '60s English rock stars such as the Animals and Rolling Stones. Hooker ran into problems with Modern Records on matters of royalties, which triggered his working for many other labels under a variety of pseudonyms: Texas Slim and John Lee Cooker for King Records; Johnny Williams for Staff and Gotham, as well as John Lee for Gotham; Delta John for Regent; John Lee Booker for Chance, Gon, and Deluxe, plus Johnny Lee on some Deluxe releases; Birmingham Sam & His Magic Guitar for Savoy; the Boogie Man for Acorn; and Sir John Lee Hooker for Fortune. Though most of his output in the '50s was on singles, there were occasional albums, one of the best being *John Lee Hooker Sings the Blues* on King.

In 1955, he signed an executive recording contract with Chicago-based Vee Jay Records and remained on the roster until that company ran into financial problems in 1964. (After several years with Vee Jay, though, his name began to turn up on other labels, though some of those releases were reissues of older material.) Among the albums issued by Vee Jay were *Burnin'*, *I'm John Lee Hooker*, and *Travelin'* (1961); *The Folklore of John Lee Hooker* (1962); and *The Big Soul of John Lee Hooker* and *Best of John Lee Hooker* (1963). One of his most successful LPs came out on Riverside Records in 1969, at the height of the folk boom.

The folk movement of the late '50s and early '60s embraced country and folk blues artists so John Lee Hooker gained a new following that cut across racial lines. He was invited to perform at the 1960 Newport Folk Festival in Rhode Island and became an important figure on the coffeehouse/folk-club circuit. To fit the "folk image," he cut down on the amplification he used for his guitar playing or simply used an acoustic instrument.

Meanwhile, he was becoming known as an influence on English rock musicians. The Animals, for instance, recorded his song "Boom Boom" and other bands included some of his material in their repertoire. In 1965, he was enthusiastically received by English fans when he toured the country as part of a blues package. While there, he recorded an album with an English blues-rock group called the Groundhogs (*John Lee Hooker with John Mayall and the Groundhogs*, Cleve Records). (*See Mayall, John.*) English fans noted his ability as a harmonica player. At times he would put his guitar aside and play the mouth harp. However, by the '70s, he rarely played harmonica and almost no records are extant in which he plays that instrument.

From the start of the '60s on, Hooker became primarily an album artist rather than a singles performer. From then on, he almost always had a number of LPs in the active catalogue, as usual, on a bewildering list of labels. Many were repackages of earlier recordings, but there always were some new ones added. His early 1960s LPs included *Don't Turn Me from Your Door* (Atco), *John Lee Hooker* (Galaxy), and *Great Blues Album* (Fortune). Later in the decade, his new material included an LP with Muddy Waters Band with Otis Spann on piano. Album releases from the mid-1960s to the early 1970s included *Alone* (Specialty), *Big Band Blues* (Buddha), *Coast to Coast Blues Band* (United Artists), *Endless Boogie* (Tradition), *Simply the Truth* (ABC/Bluesway), and *That's Where It's At* (Stax).

In 1971, he toured with the blues-rock group Canned Heat in support of a double-disc LP set called *Hooker 'n' Heat*, an album that was on national charts for months.

In the 1970s, he was asked by Bonnie Raitt to join her in a number of concerts and in 1977 he was a featured artist in a "Tribute to the Blues" program at New York's Palladium, a show that also included Foghat, Paul Butterfield, Muddy Waters, Johnny Waters, and Honeyboy Edwards. A 1977 concert at the Keystone in Palo Alto, California, was recorded for a live album, *The Cream*, on Tomato Records. He was a longtime idol of the Rolling Stones and Mick Jagger covered one of his numbers in the '70 movie *Performance*. (*See Jagger, Mick; Rolling Stones, The*.)

In the summer of 1980, he appeared in the Blues Brothers movie that starred "Saturday Night Live" alumni John Belushi and Dan Ackroyd. The British Charly label released the LPs *This Is Hip* (1980) and *Everybody's Rockin'* (1981).

Through the late 1980s, Hooker remained active as a recording artist and in-person performer. His shows continued to reflect considerable fire and enthusiasm on his part, even though he was well into his sixties. Commenting on an engagement at the Music Machine in Los Angeles, Terry Atkinson of the *Los Angeles Times*, December 14, 1983, wrote: "Just the way John Lee Hooker looked at the Music Machine . . . was worth the price of admission. In black suit, black hat, black tie, and red shirt, the legendary blues singer gazed at . . . the crowd with an assured glare that would have sent shivers down Darth Vader's spine. . . . With exact images and the gutsiest of gut feeling [in his singing], John Lee Hooker showed that the blues and absolute cool can overcome a mere thing like time."

HOT TUNA: *See Jefferson Airplane.*

HOUSTON, WHITNEY: *Singer. Born New Jersey, September 1963.*

Without a doubt, one of the most impressive debuts of the mid-1980s was that of Whitney Houston, who captured the hearts of critics, fans, and disc jockeys with a combination of good looks, phenomenal poise for a new artist, and finely honed vocal skills. Her success in 1985-'86 underscored the unpredictability of pop music. While she was certainly at home with up-tempo R&B and disco, her strong point lay in ballads where her voice and style would not have been out of place among the singing stars of the 1940s and early '50s. The sensational response to her recordings and live performances by people of all age groups belied the belief among many record executives that only some new form of rock could win mass audience response in the '80s.

For Whitney, singing had been a way of life from her earliest years. Her mother was the gospel singer Cissy Houston and Whitney was performing in church concerts from an early age. Dionne Warwick was her cousin. (*See Warwick, Dionne*.) By her mid-teens it was obvious that she had inherited her mother's vocal talents and then some. But she was interested in secular as well as religious music, which inspired her to seek a show-business veteran to help direct her career. The man she eventually aligned with was Gene Harvey, with whom she completed a management pact in October 1981, a few weeks after her eighteenth birthday.

One reason why Whitney and her family selected Harvey was their faith that he would take a careful approach to developing her abilities. This, in fact, he did, insuring that Whitney had several years to take classes in acting and dancing while also pursuing the modeling career she had begun earlier in her teens and building up experience as a vocalist. Harvey told Robert Hilburn of the *Los Angeles Times* (June 8, 1986): "The most important thing was for Whitney to develop as an artist in an unhurried way. When she had just turned 18, two major labels wanted to sign her, but I felt it was too early. I didn't want her to have to deal with those kinds of pressures at that point."

Instead, he brought her along through relatively anonymous assignments that helped her gain familiarity with recording- and TV-industry techniques. Those jobs included background-vocal work in recording sessions and parts in commercials. In addition, Whitney continued to be part of the background vocal group in her mother's concerts as she had done for some time.

In early 1983, both Whitney and Harvey felt she was relaxed enough about solo opportunities to line up a record firm. They opted for Arista because of the feeling that company president Clive Davis would take the same slow but steady approach as her manager and also because of his reputation as an excellent selector of hit songs for his artists. Thus, while Whitney signed with Arista in April 1983, her debut on the label didn't appear until almost two years later.

In the interim, Davis showcased Whitney's singing ability in various ways to gain the interest of other members of the music industry. In 1983, she joined Davis as a guest on one of Merv Griffin's TV shows. Later she sang at a party for Jermaine Jackson during the Jackson's 1984 Victory Tour and also was featured at Arista's tenth-anniversary celebration.

During that time, Whitney and her advisers prepared for her first album by culling songs from many offered by eager songwriters. Plenty of studio time was allotted for her to perfect the ones finally agreed upon. The songs covered a range of styles from R&B/soul ballads to fast-paced danceable numbers.

In March 1985, her debut LP, *Whitney Houston,* at long last was completed and the first review copies sent to reviewers and disc jockeys.

Davis had worked out a careful approach to promoting the album based on a predetermined order of singles releases. The first issued, the R&B-flavored "You Give Good Love," was unabashedly aimed at the black audience. Davis told Hilburn: "We wanted to establish her in the black marketplace first. Otherwise you fall between cracks, where top 40 won't play you and R&B won't consider you their own. . . . We felt that 'You Give Good Love' would be at the very least a major black hit, though we didn't think it would cross over [to the pop market] as strongly as it did. When it did cross over with such velocity [rising to number 3 on U.S. singles charts] that gave us great encouragement."

The next target (adult-contemporary) was hit with the single "Saving All My Love for You," a disc that eventually rose to number one on U.S. charts in the fall of 1985. The third single, the disco-style "How Will I Know," was accompanied on release by a dynamic video that brought Whitney her first exposure on the MTV channel. That record also rose to number one. In 1986, Whitney gained a third number one hit from her album: "Greatest Love of All." That disc actually was a reissue. The song originally wasn't scheduled as an A side release but was merely the B side of "You Give Good Love." The airplay given to the B side persuaded Arista to make it a featured single. In fact, it became the biggest-seller of all the singles issued from the album.

Her debut album remained on *Billboard* lists for 78 weeks with multiplatinum sales. In spring 1986, it moved up to number one, where it remained for 14 weeks.

At the end of 1985, Whitney was ranked in the upper brackets of all pertinent *Billboard* lists. She was number five for Top Pop Album Artists, Female, and number three for Top Pop Singles Artists, Female. *Billboard* listed "You Give Good Love" as number two among the year's Top Black Singles. She also was ranked number three among Top Black Singles Artists and number five among Top Black Album Artists.

In the National Academy of Recording Arts and Sciences Grammy competition, she was among the five nominations for album of the year; "Saving All My Love for You" was nominated for Best Pop Vocal Performance, Female; and "You Give Good Love" won her a nomination for Best R&B Vocal Solo Performance, Female, and brought a nomination for songwriter LaLa for Best R&B Song. On the network telecast of the Grammy Awards show on February 25, 1986, "Saving All My Love for You" won Whitney her first trophy of what most experts

believed would be a series of Grammy successes for years to come.

These predictions seemed to be borne out with the success of her second Arista LP, *Whitney,* issued in mid-1987, from which the hit single "I Wanna Dance with Somebody" was taken. At the Grammy Awards telecast in March 1988, that single earned her a Grammy for Best Pop Vocal Performance, Female, and the album's producer, Narada Michael Walden, won the Grammy for Producer of the Year. Though *Whitney* didn't win the trophy for Album of the Year, it was one of the five finalists.

HOWLIN' WOLF: *Singer, guitarist, songwriter, disc jockey. Born West Point, Mississippi, June 10, 1910, died Hines, Illinois, January 10, 1976.*

The surly, guttural tones of country bluesman Howlin' Wolf have had a substantial effect on the evolution of popular music. Countless young, white English musicians took to his R&B recordings in the early 1960s and eagerly used them as the basis for their own performances. In particular, a then unknown singer named Mick Jagger sought all recordings he could find of Howlin' Wolf, as well as other black American blues artists, and distilled a style of his own from their phrasing and inflections. Other British rockers of the period also borrowed from Wolf's repertoire in varying degrees. Jagger's Rolling Stones and the others redirected the course of rock as the 1960s went by, eventually causing feedback that prompted American musicians to look back again to their homegrown blues roots.

In time, this led to belated fame for Howlin' Wolf, represented by a series of albums in the late 1960s and early 1970s that often made the best-seller lists. For most of his life, though, Howlin' Wolf was largely unknown in his own country except for brief moments of success with minority black R&B fans.

Like many country bluesmen, Howlin' Wolf (born Chester Burnett) grew up in southern farm country. His parents worked on a cotton plantation in Mississippi. At an early age, young Chester also was working in the fields rather than going to school. He learned some songs in his early years from the chants the field hands intoned to lighten their toil. Sometimes he hung around the small bars where blues musicians entertained black workmen on weekends.

Young Burnett was not that enthused about black blues material at the time, strange to say. Instead, his fancy was caught by the recordings of another Mississippian, white country blues singer, Jimmie Rodgers, (1897–1933) who now is revered as the father of modern country music. In a way, of course, Rodgers did not sound that foreign to a young black, since many of his songs were derived from Negro blues. (For more details on Jimmie Rodgers, see *Encyclopedia of Folk, Country & Western Music*.)

However, Burnett found that his voice wasn't suited to the blues yodeling that was a feature of Rodgers' style. As Arnold Shaw noted in *The World of Soul* (Cowles 1970), Chester turned to a blues shouting style, eventually settling on the pseudonym Howlin' Wolf from a series of nicknames that included "Bull Cow" and "Foot." "I just stuck to the Wolf. I could do no yodelin' so I turned to Howlin'."

In the 1920s and '30s, Howlin' Wolf sought out pointers on performing from well-known Delta bluesmen. In particular, he hung around Charley Patton in Cleveland, Mississippi. Patton's wife, Bertha Lee, recalled one time when "Charley worked with him all day before Chester Burnett would leave him alone." He also spent time studying the technique of the legendary Robert Johnson and Rice Miller. One of two bluesmen to call themselves Sonny Boy Williamson, Rice taught him to play the harmonica.

During the mid-1940s, he moved to West Memphis, Arkansas, then a center of blues activity and the place where performers such as Albert King and B. B. King would soon have major bands. (*See King; Albert; King; B. B.*) He worked on a plantation by day and performed with club groups at night, finally forming his own band in 1948. The band included two young harmonica players who were to become major names in R&B: James Cotton (born Tunica, Mississippi, 1925) and Little Junior Parker (born West Memphis, Arkansas, 1927; died Chicago, Illinois, November 18, 1971).

By the time Burnett formed the band, he had made his first recordings for Chess Records. This resulted from one of the many tours Leonard Chess, head of the then new Chicago R&B firm, made throughout the South looking for new talent. He was directed to Howlin' Wolf by other musicians in West Memphis and arranged to cut two sides. Assisting Wolf on those tracks, which included "Saddle My Pony," was James Cotton and pianist Ike Turner, since famous as half of the Ike and Tina Turner duo. (*See Turner, Ike; Turner, Ike and Tina.*)

Soon after this, Burnett became a disc jockey on station KWEM in West Memphis and built up a strong following among the black community. During those years, he made several records for Los Angeles–based RPM Records and for Crown Records.

In the early 1950s, Leonard Chess sought him out again and signed him to a contract. One of the early results was Howlin' Wolf's first hit: the 1951 "Moanin' at Midnight." Its success helped induce Burnett to move from Arkansas to Chicago, where he became a major attraction at such South Side

clubs as the Big Squeeze and in the better-known West Side nightspot, Sylvio's.

The move north brought some changes in Howlin' Wolf's performances, though he insisted to Arnold Shaw that these were minor. The changes were "not much, really, but of course I did have to step up the tempo. I used to play very slow, but I had to come up with the tempo of today. I didn't know my positions when I was playing those slow blues. But over the last few years [late 1960s] I went to the Chicago Music School and they taught me my positions."

During the 1950s, Howlin' Wolf recorded a number of songs for Chess that found a good-sized market by blues standards. Many of his releases made the charts without gaining the national top 10, including his "Sittin' on Top of the World" (1957) and his 1960s original composition, "Killing Ground." Both of these songs were among his many stylings that were later recorded by well-known rock groups such as the Grateful Dead, Rolling Stones, Cream, and Electric Flag.

Howlin' Wolf performed widely in clubs and at jazz and folk festivals of the 1960s, though for much of the decade he was inactive in the recording field. (an exception being his 1967 LP *More Real Blues*). But as the '60s went by, more and more young rock fans were attracted to his early discs. By the end of the 1960s, he was so well known that Chess urged him to work up new tracks. This resulted in the LP *Howlin' Wolf* released on Chess's Cadet subsidiary in 1969. In the early 1970s, Chess found a growing audience for such new albums as *Message to the Young* and *The London Howlin' Wolf Session,* featuring Eric Clapton, Steve Winwood, Bill Wyman, and Charlie Watts playing alongside their aging artistic forebear. (*See Clapton, Eric; Cream, The; Rolling Stones, The; Winwood, Steve.*)

Howlin' Wolf was in failing health when he began to record material for what was to be his last album, the 1973 Chess release *The Back Door Wolf*. He died before completing another album. The LP proved an excellent one that won highly favorable comments from reviewers on both sides of the Atlantic. Typical of those critiques were the words of *Rolling Stone*'s David Marsh: "Wolf's final album . . . is some kind of triumph. . . . The songs range over Wolf's life span from ancient Delta blues to Watergate and the Apollo moonshot program, and his easy mastery of such a broad set of songs, coupled with the spare, sympathetic backings he's given, make the album a minor Wolf masterpiece, and perhaps his finest memorial. To the end, a great one."

Many of his recordings were available on various labels in the 1970s, particularly in England, where respect for the blues far overshadowed the interest in the place of its birth. Among titles packaged in Britain and available in the U.S. as '70s imports were *The Legendary Sun Performers: Howlin' Wolf* on Charly (which presented material recorded in Memphis by Sam Phillips of Sun Records, who helped bring the artist to Chess Records attention), *The Real Folk Blues* (originally released by Chess in 1966), and *More Folk Blues* (originally issued by Chess in 1967). *Going Back Home* came out on Syndicate Chapter Records: Some of his early material was packaged on two Blues Ball releases: *Heart Like Railroad Steel: Rare and Unreleased Recordings, Volumes 1* and *2*. In 1977, Chess issued the LP *Change My Way.*

In the mid-1980s, the Chess catalog was sold to Sugarhill Records which in turn sold it to MCA Records along with masters of recordings by Wolf and other classic names on the company's roster.

New releases of Howlin' Wolf recordings continued to be issued in the 1980s, such as *Ridin' in the Moonlight* (Ace, import, 1982), *Howlin' Wolf: His Greatest Sides, Vol. 1* (Chess, 1983) and MCA reissues from the Chess catalog in the late 1980s.

HUMBLE PIE: *Vocal and instrumental group, all born England. Original members, 1968: Steve Marriott, born January 30, 1947; Jerry Shirley, born February 4, 1952; Greg Ridley, born October 23, 1947; Peter Frampton, born Beckenham, Kent, April 22, 1950. Frampton replaced in late 1971 by Dave Clempson, born September 5, 1949. Group disbanded in 1975. Reformed in 1980 with Marriott, Bobby Tench, Anthony Jones.*

When Steve Marriott left Small Faces in 1968, it was a near disaster for the group. (However, Small Faces reorganized and went on to stardom with Rod Stewart in the 1970s.) One of the finest rock lead vocalists in England at the time, Marriott was considered a prime candidate for eventual inclusion in any future British rock hall of fame. (*See Faces, The.*)

Small Faces' loss was Humble Pie's gain, although for a while there was doubt that Steve's new band would succeed. Like most of the prominent bands of the period, Humble Pie represented a recombination of artists from other organizations. In particular, it got its start because of the breakup of Peter Frampton's former band, the Herd.

It was late 1968 when Frampton and Marriott got together. As Steve recalled: "Peter and Jerry Shirley were looking to form a new band and were looking around for keyboard, bass, and guitar players. I told them that I would like to be part of the group and also that I could bring Greg Ridley [original bassist of Spooky Tooth] into the group." The matter was settled and the quartet moved into Marriott's cottage

in Essex to prepare their new material. They took their time about it, rehearsing for six months before they accepted a recording contract from England's Immediate Records in mid-1969.

Marriott, Frampton, and Ridley handled the vocals, with Shirley playing various instruments: drums, piano, organ, vibes, and guitar. Marriott also played an assortment: guitar, piano, organ, flute, harmonica, and drums. Ridley could play lead and rhythm guitar as well as bass. The group went into the studios during the summer of 1969 and completed their first single, "Natural Born Boogie" and material for two LPs: *Town and Country* and *As Safe as Yesterday.*

They received some encouragement from English fans, but made out poorly in the U.S., primarily because their music featured acoustic instruments rather than the hyperamplified electric ones American audiences had grown accustomed to. To make matters worse, when they returned home, they found that Immediate Records had gone out of business. There was some thought of disbanding, but they found a new manager, an American named Dee Anthony, who encouraged them to continue. Soon after he took over their direction, he won a contract from A&M Records of Los Angeles, California.

This time things went better. Their debut album on A&M, *Humble Pie*, was a modest success in 1970; their next, *Rock On*, did even better, becoming one of the best-sellers of 1971. The group's tour of the U.S. in early 1971 was a triumph, garnering rave reviews and standing ovations from large, enthusiastic audiences. A result of the tour was a gold album, *Performance: Rockin' the Fillmore*, issued in the fall of 1971.

Just after the *Fillmore* LP came out, Peter Frampton decided to leave in favor of a solo career. He signed with A&M Records, which released *Winds of Change* in 1972 followed in 1973 by *Frampton's Camel*, Camel being the name of his new backing band. He later had two platinum albums (*Frampton Comes Alive!* in 1976 and *I'm in You* in 1977) plus gold albums *Frampton* (1975) and *Where Should I Be* (1979).

Frampton's place in Humble Pie was taken by Dave "Clem" Clempson. Clempson had been one of the mainstays of Colosseum, which disbanded in 1971. Their next album effort *Smokin'*, went gold in 1972. That same year A&M released their two earlier albums on Immediate under the new title *Lost and Found*. In the spring of 1973, A&M issued the hit two-record set, *Eat It,* a combination of both studio and live tracks of material ranging from R&B to hard rock.

The band's next two A&M albums, *Thunderbox* (1974) and *Street Rats* (1975), seemed pale copies of earlier stylings. While the band didn't lack for a healthy rock following, Marriott sensed it was going downhill when he disbanded it the end of 1975.

Part of the problem, he told a reporter in the early 1980s, was sheer exhaustion. "I kept asking for time off, but I never got it. When my weight dropped to 94 pounds, I realized that I quite possibly was in the process of killing myself."

After some recuperation time, he sought to head a new version of Small Faces in 1977, but that only lasted until 1978. He recalled: "The British press called me an old man, said I ought to get out of the business. That hurt, mate."

But at the end of the decade, young English rock fans showed renewed interest in older bands and Marriott decided to assemble a new version of Humble Pie in 1980. Clempson and Ridley declined to rejoin, so he brought in Bobby Tench (a former Jeff Beck sideman) (*see Beck, Jeff*) on guitar and Anthony "Scotty" Jones on bass guitar. (Jones had been working in a band with one-time Humble Pie drummer Jerry Shirley.) The group signed with Atlantic Records, which issued the early 1980s albums of the revived band, *On to Victory* and *Go for the Throat*.

HUMPERDINCK, ENGELBERT: *Singer.* *Born Madras, India, May 3, 1936.*

There are many similarities between Engelbert Humperdinck and Tom Jones. Both are tall and broad-shouldered, possess powerful singing voices, were well represented on the hit lists in the late 1960s and early 1970s, and appeal mainly to "mature" female audiences rather than under-twenties. Additionally, both were originally piloted to superstar status by manager Gordon Mills. One prime difference, of course, is that Jones is a frenetic, upbeat performer, while Humperdinck is more sedate, emphasizing romantic ballads rather than fast-paced numbers.

Humperdinck was born Arnold George Dorsey in India, where his father was serving in the British army. He had little exposure to popular music until 1945, when his family moved to Leicester, England. In school he was particularly interested in science, which led to his taking engineering subjects in trade school in his teens. After leaving school at 16, he was an apprentice engineer for a while. He had a good voice and sang occasionally for pleasure. He found he could catch on with an audience after making his first solo appearance at 17. For a few years after this, he sang for small amounts of money at neighborhood pubs. He then went to London to try for better engagements, but had no major success.

He went into the British army for two years and, after his discharge in the mid-1950s, worked at various jobs, including some in engineering. He devoted most of his time, unsuccessfully, to his singing career. Sometimes he was so low in funds that he slept on the ground or on floors during tours of working-men's clubs. He came down with tuberculosis in 1959 and had to give up music for a time.

He was back at it again, working odd singing jobs and trying to place demonstration tapes with record firms in the early 1960s. He sometimes sought the advice of Gordon Mills, who was then gaining a reputation as a rising young songwriter, whom he had met when both were members of a vocal trio early in their careers. After Mills moved successfully into management in the mid-1960s with Tom Jones, he decided he could do as well for Dorsey. Dorsey made some new tapes, but the record companies turned them down. Mills then changed Dorsey's name to Humperdinck and made a new tape of an original Dorsey composition, "Stay," which eventually led to a Decca Records contract.

Not much happened with Engelbert's initial releases on Decca, but in 1966 he switched to Parrot, a label already reaping rewards from Tom Jones' recordings. Engelbert's single "Release Me" moved onto British charts in late 1966. (A 1950s country & western ballad, it had already been transformed into a soul hit by Esther Phillips in 1962.) The U.S. release in January 1967 won major airplay and a place high on the charts. Two more U.K. gold record singles followed, "There Goes My Everything" and "The Last Waltz." He rounded out 1967 with another remake of a country hit: "Am I That Easy to Forget."

The cycle continued with a steady series of chart recordings: "A Man without Love," "Les Bicyclettes de Belsize," "The Way It Used to Be," "I'm a Better Man," and "Winter World of Love" in 1968–69; "We Made It Happen" and "Sweetheart" in 1970. His first album, *Release Me*, earned a gold record in late 1967 as did the 1969 albums *A Man without Love* and *The Last Waltz,* 1970 *Engelbert Humperdinck* and *We Made It Happen,* and 1971 *Sweetheart* and *Another Place, Another Time. In Time* (1972) was considerably less successful. In the summer of 1973, he rebounded somewhat with a new album, *King of Hearts,* briefly on the charts.

From 1968 on, Humperdinck was an attraction of almost equal rank to Tom Jones on the easy-listening circuit. In December 1969, his first TV special was presented on ABC-TV in the U.S. and had good enough audience response that the network signed him for a January–June 1970 replacement series. The show didn't gain renewal, though he later was starred in specials prepared for syndication rather than network use.

Engelbert's career seemed to hit a plateau in the mid-1970s. He continued to be popular on the club circuit, including regular appearances at the Las Vegas Riviera under a multiple-year contract, but his recording efforts tended to fall flat.

In 1977, he decided he needed to make major changes. He signed with a new manager, Harold Davison, moved his family from England to the U.S., changed his appearance by shaving his trademark sideburns, and also signed with a new record label, Epic. Another change was a move from the Riviera in Las Vegas to a new contract with the MGM Grand guaranteeing him a reported $200,000 per performance.

All of this paid off with the success of his debut on Epic, *After the Lovin'* (1977). Both the LP and single of the title song were eventually certified platinum and gold, respectively, by the RIAA. Surprisingly, despite all his previous chart hits, that LP was the first of his releases to achieve platinum status.

The new stage show he unveiled in 1978 had new life and exuberance. It was acclaimed by critics in major cities across the U.S. and around the world. Among other tributes, the American Guild of Variety Artists gave him their award for Male Singing Star of the Year.

In April 1979, Epic issued his second album on the label, *This Moment in Time*. In the 1980s, though Humperdinck continued to record, turning out such material as the late 1986 *To You and Your Lover* (recorded in Nashville, Tennessee), he made little impact on the charts. He continued to be popular on the club circuit, including annual visits to Hilton Las Vegas Hotel, maintaining a schedule throughout the decade of some 200 performances a year. He also occasionally was a guest star on TV appearing in episodes of "Hotel" and "Love Boat." In late 1987, he had a new album, *Remember I Love You*, released in Germany and the Benelux countries, that was in upper chart levels in those nations in early 1988.

HYNDE, CHRISSIE, AND THE PRETEND-ERS: *Vocal and instrumental group. Original members, 1978: Chrissie Hynde, born Akron, Ohio, September 7, 1951; James Honeyman-Scott, born Hereford, England, 1957, died London, England, June 16, 1982; Martin Chambers, born Hereford, England; Pete Farndon, born Hereford, England, mid-1950s, died London, England, April 1983. Honeyman-Scott and Farndon replaced, 1983, by Rob McIntosh and Malcolm Foster, both born England.*

The blend of American-born lead singer Chrissie Hynde and three young musicians from Hereford, England, proved one of the most striking new rock bands of the late 1970s and early 1980s. But tragedy spawned by the effects of two key members' drug abuse tore the group apart in 1982–83. Somehow, Chrissie and remaining member Martin Chambers shook off the trauma of the deaths of half the band and came up with a reorganized quartet that retained the fire and emotion of the original lineup.

Of course, Chrissie was the key member, not only as one of the most exciting rock vocalists of the 1980s, but as a sensitive and insightful songwriter as well. Before helping to form the Pretenders, she had honed her performing and writing talents for well over a decade going back to her teen efforts in rock in her hometown of Akron, Ohio, in the middle to late 1960s.

Her music, she told Charles M. Young for an article in England's *Musician* magazine (March 1984), reflected influences from both 1960s and '70s rock and soul. "If I gave you all the albums I'd listened to for the past 15 years, it would be pretty damned obvious. It's very derivative, anything that a kid sitting in Akron, Ohio, with a transistor radio could pick up on.

"I saw Sam the Sham & the Pharaohs on stage. I saw Jackie Wilson. I saw the Yardbirds. I saw the Rolling Stones with Brian Jones. I saw Dennis Wilson throw his drumsticks in the air and storm off stage in disgust. I saw Mitch Ryder and the Detroit Wheels have a fistfight on stage. I was 14 and it freaked me out, so I stayed around for the second show and they had the same fistfight again and I realized they had faked the whole thing. How could I go wrong with influences like that?"

In her teenage efforts to become a professional artist, she tended to draw on the vocal styles of some of her favorites. She told Young, "Well, you have to learn how to sing, don't you? When I was sitting in Cleveland, starting to sing with a band, I'd go in the closet when everybody else left for their jobs and sing at the top of my lungs just to hear what the possibilities were. You can sit in an audience for years and imagine how you might sing, but you don't know until you try. One of the hard things to get over to a lot of people is learning to appreciate their own strong points. Like a girl with a weak chin always admires a girl with a big, boxy chin. You always admire what you don't have, but I sure didn't know what I had. The thing to do is just accept what you're best at. Don't try to do what you like in someone else unless it comes natural to you."

Chrissie, who also learned to play guitar, found her career wasn't progressing very much in the Akron environment. In her early twenties, lured by the reports of an exciting rock scene in England, she decided it was time to make a break and see what might go down in England. She moved there in 1973 and spent the next half-decade as a part-time performer, getting most of her income from other work, including several stints as a waitress and several years as a writer on pop music for the English trade paper *New Musical Express*. During those years she was making friends with many other young musicians, some of whom became founding members of punk/new wave bands such as the Sex Pistols, Clash, and Damned. Eventually her path crossed that of two young performers from Hereford: guitarist James Honeyman-Scott and bass player Pete Farndon.

In the spring of 1978, the three founded a new band that soon took the name of Chrissie Hynde and the Pretenders. Shortly after, they gained a record contract from Read Records, headed by Dave Hill, who became the band's manager. Their debut single on the label, "Stop Your Sobbing," produced by well-known rock artist Nick Lowe, became a top 40 entry on U.K. charts (*See Lowe, Nick.*) A short time after that milestone, the band expanded to a foursome with the addition of Martin Chambers on drums. Chambers, also from Hereford, recalled meeting James Honeyman-Scott in a local music store when Chambers went to buy drumsticks and found Honeyman-Scott behind the counter. Even in those years, James was experimenting with drugs, which eventually had a shattering impact on the band.

With their lineup now set, the group built on the momentum of its 1978 singles hit with dynamic concert appearances throughout the U.K. and more singles that became best-sellers in England: "Kid" and number one "Brass in Pocket."

Those songs were included in the band's debut LP, *Pretenders,* issued in January 1980 in England on Real Records and soon offered to U.S. record buyers on the Sire label. The album established the band as one of the finest rock prospects of the new decade. U.S. reviews were almost unanimously ecstatic. The *Rolling Stone* evaluation was typical, calling the LP one of the most brilliant debut releases in rock. "From the Motown pleading of 'Brass in Pocket' to the unrestrained joyousness of 'Mystery Achievement' to the lovely 'Stop Your Sobbing,' the album holds endless delights. All the ambivalences of love, lust, and hate are on display. There is no woman who loves rock who can't be thrilled by 'Precious,' when Chrissie wonders about getting pregnant against a background of killer rock'n'roll—this just hasn't happened before. The rest of the Pretenders are neither subservient to Hynde nor condescending to her; the Pretenders are a group and unlike certain other bands that make that claim, there is never any doubt about it."

The album, which opened in the number one spot

in the U.K. in early 1980, also earned a gold record from the RIAA in the U.S. along the way. The band demonstrated its skills in a series of concert tours throughout the U.S. and Europe. The repertoire included another hit single, "Talk of the Town," high on both U.S. and U.K. charts in April. In November, the band took up quarters in Paris to work on its second album, *Pretenders II,* released in August 1981. During 1981, the group also was represented by an LP appropriately titled *Extended Play.*

Its credits soon included another U.K. top 10 hit, the ballad "I Go to Sleep" (1982).

By the time the band returned home from a world tour, however, the seeds of destruction already had been sown. Behind-the-scenes difficulties surfaced June 14, when it was announced that Pete Farndon had been asked to leave. The situation unexpectedly became darker two days later when Honeyman-Scott was found dead of a drug overdose.

The problems with Farndon were largely due to the same cause, although a romantic fight between him and Chrissie also played a part. She told Paul Du Noyer of *New Musical Express* (November 26, 1983): "When Pete and I started the band we were very close—I mean boyfriend and girlfriend kind of close—and then when we stopped going out with each other, well, in that situation you usually don't want to see the person anymore, or you really don't want to work with them. But we had to carry on and work together, and that was right at the beginning of the band. So there was always this thing that wasn't quite right, y'know? Not really a rift, but a little bit of damage had been done, like a fissure had begun at an early stage.

"Really the best way of summing up the whole situation, I can sum it up in one word, *heroin.*

"And there's not really a lot you can say about heroin. End of story, really. As Pete got more and more into the drug habit, his playing suffered for it. There was always this tradition of musicians who could get pretty well stoned, but could still get together on stage to play. Now Pete wasn't like that, his playing suffered from it. He got sloppy and he drank a lot . . . so he was really a mess, and his playing got sloppier and sloppier.

"Now this infuriated Jim [Honeyman-Scott]. I can't tell you how adversely this affected Jim. Also we'd just been on an eight-months world tour, and we were on each other's fucking nerves, y'know? Everyone was on their nerve-ends, I mean. Martin punched a lamp at one point [injuring his hand] and we had to cancel the whole tour. And that's Martin, you see, this is the interesting point: Martin was always the buffer in the band."

Though other members knew Honeyman-Scott had a drug problem, it wasn't thought to be as severe as Farndon's. Hence his sudden death fell like a thunderclap. The night before, in fact, he had been thinking about ways to improve the band's stage show and had called guitarist friend Robbie McIntosh to see if McIntosh might be interested in such a job. Later in the year, Robbie did indeed join the group—as Honeyman-Scott's replacement. McIntosh's credits included performing with the Foster Brothers, Chris Thompson, and the Island and Night. The last-named band had a single called "Hot Summer Nights" that made the U.S. top 20.

Before turning to the painful task of rebuilding the Pretenders, Chrissie and Martin lined up two guest artists, guitarist Billy Bremmer and bassist Tony Butler, for a studio session to record some new material. Those sessions in July 1982 provided the single "Back on the Chain Gang" which reached the top 5 in the U.S. and later was included in the soundtrack of the Martin Scorcese film *King of Comedy* starring comedian Jerry Lewis.

Later in the summer, Chrissie, Martin, and manager Dave Hill started searching for compatible musicians for a reorganized band. (Some thought was given to recalling Farndon. It was perhaps fortunate that it was rejected, thus avoiding even more depression when Farndon was found dead in his bath in April 1983.) The first new addition was McIntosh, who helped direct attention to a friend of his, bass guitarist Malcolm Foster. McIntosh had worked with Malcolm in the Foster Brothers, a group organized by Malcolm's older brother.

Chrissie admitted it had been a particularly trying time for her not only because of the Honeyman-Scott tragedy, but also since she was expecting her first child (born mid-1983) from a liaison with Ray Davies of Kinks fame. (*See Kinks, The.*) Despite all that, she told Du Noyer, she had never given up on the Pretenders.

"No, there was never a point like that. I just didn't know. I mean, there was still Martin. And of course the obvious thing after Jim died was, well, if we got Pete back in, at least there's some of the band left. And I suggested that on a number of occasions to Dave [Hill] . . . and Martin, and everyone always said: 'No, we've made our decision, let's stick to it. If it was wrong, Jimmy's death won't make it right.'

"I mean, I was so bloody freaked out cos I was pregnant, for a start. I had to deal with that as well. Here I was pregnant, I'd just undergone the horrible trauma of firing someone, and then two days later the guitar player, y'know, goes to sleep and doesn't wake up again. And here I am getting bigger by the minute."

By December 1983, the new band had been settled upon and the group started getting musically acquainted in early 1984. With Chrissie and Chambers both working away intensively on new song candidates, the group spent most of the year rehearsing and then recording material for the next album.

She described the working methods for that LP to Charles Young of *Musician*. "I don't know how other people work, but we have a very straightforward, methodical, obvious way of working. We go in and out down the backing track. We'll do five or six if we have to, then we'll sit down and listen to them and decide that number four and number six are best because of the great drumfill on six. Then we'll do an edit. Then we mend anything that needs it. Then we'll put in the guitar solos. When there's enough for me to work with, I'll do the vocal. I might leave it to the very end, or I might do it early on so the rest of the band can work around it. Whatever's going on, everybody's gotta be there. You can't say: 'Well, I've done my bass line. See you next Thursday when we do the next track.' That would be unheard of in the Pretenders. If someone has a suggestion at any point, we want to hear it. That's why the album is very much a band product at the end."

On her songwriting method, she commented: "I'll just come in with the basic chords and the lyrics—not even that sometimes and say: 'More of this, more of that.' Okay, if it starts out with the bass: buh duh dum don. And then the drums: dah duh dah duh duh duh dah. And then the bass again: duh duh dump duh duh dum ding ding ching. Duh duh dah dum duh dah dah. Dodododododododunt. And then the guitar: dah duh duh day. Bass again: dunt dunt dunt, I don't know why we even bother to play the instruments. I'll just stand there like a loony and sing all the parts."

At the end of 1984, work on the new album was wrapped up and the first single, "Middle of the Road," issued. In January 1985, the LP, *Learning to Crawl,* was issued by Sire in the U.S. and went on to win a platinum award. The title, Chrissie noted, referred both to the fact that her child had reached the crawling stage and to the first steps taken by the group to reestablish itself. (That April, Chrissie had another daughter, this time with husband Jim Kerr of Simple Minds. *See Simple Minds.*) Both on the album and in the punishing worldwide tour to support it, the group proved it still had the characteristic sound people associated with the Pretenders.

The Pretenders released their fourth full-length album, *Get Close,* in late 1986. They enjoyed a top 10 hit with the first single from the LP, "Don't Get Me Wrong."

At times Chrissie expressed gratitude that she was a survivor able to keep going in music while also having the chance to see her children grow up. She told Young: "Maybe I'm more intelligent than people who do themselves in. Maybe they're not aware of death. Maybe they don't realize they could kill themselves by accident . . . I lost two of the closest people in my life. There were people I loved. But I do think about death all the time. Not like I'm afraid of her, but as a reality that we're here only so long. At least with cancer you have to prepare yourself. That's why I think it's damned sloppy to overdose on drugs by accident and go to sleep and not wake up again.''

In 1987 the Pretenders released *The Singles* (Sire), which is a collection of singles from 1979–86.

IAN, JANIS: *Singer, songwriter, guitarist, pianist. Born New York, New York, April 7, 1951.**

With her Orphan Annie-like mop of hair and slight figure, Janis Ian gave an impression of being very young indeed even in the early 1980s. This was increased by her 4-foot–10-inch height which made someone of average stature feel like a giant. And it is true that Janis is unusually shy for a performer. But in her creative persistence and the body of her excellent work she turned out, she stands tall.

Her association with music went back to her earliest years. "I started with classical music at two," she recalled with a shadow of a smile. "I lived in New Jersey until I was 13 and then my family moved to Manhattan. I started writing songs at 12. My early influences included Billie Holiday, Edith Piaf, and Odetta.''

For most of her childhood, her family was constantly on the move. During her first 15 years, she lived in 13 different places in New Jersey and New York, attending a variety of public schools before entering New York's High School of Music and Arts. Her musical efforts, she later noted, "were the only things that kept me going as long as I did without totally freaking out. School was always absurd . . . but then the whole fame thing was happening and I was going to a school where most of the teachers were frustrated musicians—they didn't like it.''

Janis had started singing for school events, then performing in small New York folk clubs. By that time she was well versed in piano and acoustic guitar. In 1966, her efforts led to a recording contract from Verve/Forecast, which soon found itself with a major—and controversial—hit composition, "Society's Child." Objections to the song were prompted by its story of a doomed love affair between a young white girl and a black boy. Compared to many of the popular hits of the late '60s and '70s, it seems in retrospect as mild as its folksong melody.

The success of the song made the 16-year-old a national celebrity. During most of 1967, Janis maintained a hectic schedule of concerts across the country. She achieved a chart hit with her debut LP on Verve, *Janis Ian* (January 1967), followed in January 1968 by the album *For All Seasons*.

But Janis wasn't particularly happy with her newfound attention. She gave her earnings away to friends and charitable causes and, after meeting a boy named Peter during the October 1967 peace march in Washington, D.C., decided to settle down with him in Philadelphia. She also gave up entertaining efforts. "I retired for a while. I just got very bored with performing, so I stopped doing it. It was basically the same thing night after night. I did the same songs, the same show. It becomes very predictable.''

But in the 1970s, the urge to create new material took hold again. The comeback began in 1970 and, after several ups and downs, brought her to new heights with the superb 1975 album *Between the Lines.* "I felt more mature, that I had more insight. I feel the songs are better now and I'm a better singer so the whole thing becomes more interesting. It isn't easy. It's hard work. The reasons I came back to the music field come down to this: I was writing songs that I liked and I wanted to record them.''

She signed with Capitol and her debut on that label, *Present Company,* came out in March 1971, accompanied by her first tour in a number of years. The response was mixed. Her performances were excellent, but her new songs fell short. Critic Richard Cromelin echoed many reviewers when he wrote in the *Los Angeles Times* (July 16, 1971): "Her most glaring defect is her writing. Her tunes are pretty, if forgettable, but her lyrics . . . lack both facility and depth.''

After several albums for Capitol, Janis signed a new contract in the mid-1970s with Columbia. Her first album on the label, *Stars,* had good spots, but nothing to bring her to creative prominence. Then came *Between the Lines,* a platinum album whose songs in some ways harked back to Janis's early glory years describing problems and relationships of young lovers, but the treatment showed a more reflective, less bitter approach. It included such gems as "When the Party's Over" (which recorded the singer's despair, tinged with hope, at the prospects of finding a loving companion) and the top 10 "At Seventeen," a song touching on the oft-felt feelings of inadequacy of a teenage girl. ("I learned the truth at 17/That love was meant for beauty queens . . . the pain of Valentines that never came.'')

The album and its related singles won a rash of nominations in the 1975 Grammy Awards. Discussing the TV program on which she sang "At Seven-

---

*Based partly on personal interview with Irwin Stambler.

306

teen'' and won two awards, including Best Pop Vocal Performance, Female, she noted, "That whole thing was great. I don't know if I'd like to perform again under that much pressure; it's pretty nerve-wracking. I wouldn't mind winning again. It's always nice to win.

"At that time, I figured since I'd been nominated for five Grammies I'd probably win something. Then when we won the engineering award [Best Engineered Song, Nonclassical to Brooks Arthur, Larry Alexander, and Russ Payne, engineers], I figured that was it. Winning another was frosting on the cake.''

Janis continued to turn out new albums on Columbia for the rest of the '70s. Most made the charts for a number of months, but none repeated the blockbuster success of *Between the Lines*.

There were fine things in all of them, but they lacked the consistency of the 1975 release. Still, all probably deserved better exposure than they received, particularly since Janis did not stand pat, but continued to experiment in subject matter and approach. In the 1977 album, *Miracle Row,* she introduced touches of Latin-style rhythms. "The *Miracle Row* influences essentially come from New York's Columbus Avenue. They're Puerto Rican rather than Latin. I thought it deserved a better reception—oh well, win some, lose some.'' In 1978, her album *Janis Ian* presented some of her best writing since *Between the Lines* and won a share of critical praise, though only moderate public support.

However, Janis wasn't able to sustain the promise of her 1978 material. Her 1979 Columbia LP, *Night Rains,* and the 1981 *Restless Eyes* didn't catch fire with record buyers.

After her contract with Epic expired in the early 1980s, Janis had trouble affiliating with another major label. Part of the problem, aside from her declining fortunes with record buyers, was the nature of some of her new material. Harking back to the outspoken approach of the early years of her career, she again started writing on topics many record company executives shied away from such as childhood incest, covered in her mid-eighties composition "Uncle Wonderful.'' Those taboos seemed somewhat ironic, considering the range of topics the majors accepted from rock groups covering other forms of sexual license, drug taking, and the like.

IDOL, BILLY: *Singer, guitarist, songwriter, band leader. Born London, England, November 30, 1955.**

With his short blond hair, arm tattoos, and typical leather-vest/bare-chest attire, Billy Idol seemed to

---

*Based partly on personal interview with Irwin Stambler.

personify the late '70s–early '80s punk rocker. In fact, in 1983, readers of *Creem* magazine voted him Punk of the Year. But as often happens in the entertainment field, surface appearances aren't necessarily the whole story. In person, he does not come across as a two-dimensional, uncaring poser, but as a rather thoughtful and musically serious individual with goals not much different from any creatively oriented person.

He commented, at a time when he was making his debut solo album: "I'm a rock'n'roller and I want to be good at it. They might type me as punk, but my music isn't really punk at all, yet it's got the attitude. Just like getting close to an audience and shouting in its face. Not that I'm actually screaming, but I like exciting, high-tension live performance. I wanna play live and I wanna get some of that live excitement into my recordings.''

In his early years, he could as easily have ended up under the influence of the more placid U.S. rock of the 1970s than the despairing, dead-end-future outlook of the British punk movement. Born William Broad, he recalled: "I was born in London, but I lived in the States a few years when I was a kid. My mom is Irish so she's got a lot of relatives around the U.S. I was only about 4–5, so I don't remember too much about the life or the music. I remember weird things like hurricanes. I liked peanut butter and carrot sandwiches then. I got me passion for bubble gum then.''

By the time Idol reached his formative years, home was back in England. He grew up in an essentially lower middle class setting just outside London where most of his friends went on to more or less conventional careers. "At first a lot of people I grew up with thought about a musician's life. One of the songs I wrote was about having a lot of friends who start out on the same road as you and want to do music and sacrifice things to do it. You turn around one day and they've all become accountants or bus drivers and you're the only one still doing it. Today I think I'm just the same as I've always been and they're different.

"Guess they thought I was stupid to really do it. But at least it's what I like. I think it's a shame. People give up their dreams. Really, it's a thing you just gotta do and not worry about.''

In his midteens, like many of his musical contemporaries, Idol left school to seek his fortunes as a rock performer. He gained a reputation with members of the club circuit in London as a high-powered singer. This evolved into the lead-vocals spot for the band Generation X that he formed with Tony James. He and James co-wrote most of the band's original material. The group gained some notice in 1977 with the single "Your Generation." A response to the

Who's "My Generation," it maintained that 1960s rock was passé and a new style was taking over. The song was included in the band's debut LP, *Generation X* (Chrysalis, 1978). But as an indication that one song does not a movement make, the album included another popular track, "Ready Steady Go," which sang the praises of the British rock program that showcased the talents of the soon-to-be-superstar English rock artists of the 1960s.

Besides singing, Idol also played guitar. However, he complained that he felt restricted by the Generation X formula. "Really, I've always believed you should write about what's affecting you now. Generation X kind of preferred a lot of anthem songs—things like 'Your Generation'; wild, wild, youth, and so on."

Perhaps some of Idol's qualms came from the less ecstatic reaction of fans and critics to Generation X's second album, *Valley of the Dolls,* (Chrysalis, 1979). And, of course, the rock scene was changing in England. Interest in punk rock was decreasing while movements such as New Romanticism and techno-rock came to the fore.

At any rate, in the early 1980s, he decided it was time to try to make it as a solo performer. He took up lodgings in New York and began to work on material for a debut album. He didn't rush it, he recalled, taking time to visit New York clubs and perform as a guest artist only on occasion.

"I do things step by step. I wouldn't want to jump into anything I wouldn't feel sure about. I want to get some soul into it. Not black soul—my own soul. With Gen X, the music didn't have soul in it. I didn't feel my character came out. Since I went solo, I've felt more honest because it is totally me. I'm sick of singing wild, wild things because they're soulless. I want to do things people can feel on their own. I want them to be able to dig it on their own, not as part of some organized multitude.

"I don't mind people ripping things up, but not for no purpose. I think about riots in London all because someone gave them an excuse to rip things up. I don't want to say things like that. Mindless violence isn't my thing."

His stay in New York impacted his songwriting outlook in a number of ways. "I've really got much more into the idea that people can dance to rock'n'roll. What I find annoying about [much of late 1970s] music is that you can't actually dance to it." It brought to mind a skit on British TV whose point was the impossibility of dancing to some of the punk/new wave music. "They used Generation X's 'King Rocker' to prove their point." He demonstrated his ability to provide danceable material with the song "Dancing with Myself," which gained considerable play at major New York discotheques.

That song and another that later made the singles charts, "Mony Mony," were included on his first solo collection, the mini-LP *Don't Stop*. However, that album didn't catch on with record buyers until after the album *Billy Idol,* (Chrysalis, 1982) became a worldwide top-seller. That collection included his "White Wedding," a song that went high on disco charts and then backed off to come back a year later as a top 40 number.

"White Wedding" demonstrated what he had meant by wanting to get specific feeling into his solo compositions. It told the story of a girl who has a "shotgun wedding" after becoming pregnant out of wedlock. Idol pointed out his more general theme. "The point of lines like 'There's nothing sure in this world' is that social institutions don't always lead to the kind of happiness they're supposed to. Following the rules won't give you absolute security." An odd theme for a danceable record? He replied: "Not every song can be 'I Want to Hold Your Hand.'"

By the end of 1983, he had three LPs on the U.S. charts, *Billy Idol, Don't Stop,* and his second full solo LP, the platinum *Rebel Yell*. He also had a top 10 single that year, "Eyes without a Face."

He attributed his solo achievements to his essentially mainstream rock abilities. "I've always been a real rock'n'roll singer. That's what I am. Since going solo, I brought my music back to basic. It's probably a little bit heavier than it was before. That means heavy like more meaningful, not like heavy metal."

He emphasized the hope that people would get from his work the pleasure he got from music and other artistic efforts. "For instance, I make my own T-shirts and I like to draw unusual shapes and things. When it comes out right, it's really amazing, like magic. It'd be kinda great if people felt like that about my music. I think that's the feeling you get off something you really like. If you could get that off my songs, it would be great. I felt one of the limitations of Gen X was that the group couldn't get into that. I mean you get two good tracks on an album—that's crummy. I don't wanna give an album of 10 songs and only two are good. I'd rather put out singles or extended play albums [EPs] if that's all you can do well. There's nothing wrong with an EP if everything is great on it. That's what I'm always trying for in the studio."

After the success of *Rebel Yell*, Billy demonstrated that his ideas about putting his art above simple commercialism weren't just talk by taking two years to develop material for his next album. During that time, he stayed away from the limelight, a situation that gave rise to rumors that he was sick, stoned out on drugs, or even dead.

When he resurfaced with his next group of recordings in the fall of 1986, he commented with amusement to Robert Hilburn of the *Los Angeles Times* (November 30, 1986): "Well, being dead has got to be the ultimate rumor. I've gone through a lot of [fast lane] things in my life, but never to the extent that people think.

"I guess the reason people started coming up with all those stories was that it's unusual for someone to drop out of sight after they've had a big hit. They expect you to rush back out with something else to keep the momentum going.

"But I didn't want to make the same record again. . . . *Outlaw Call* or whatever. I wanted to take time to sort things out . . . my music and in my personal life . . . and that took time."

Despite the hiatus, his fans didn't desert him. His 1986 album, *Whiplash Smile,* went platinum. The initial single release, "To Be a Lover," hit the top 10. Several other tracks including "Sweet Sixteen" received wide airplay. In 1987, he had another chart hit LP with the Chrysalis release *Vital Idol.* This album included "Mony Mony," which became Idol's first U.S. Number One hit.

IMPRESSIONS, THE: *Vocal and instrumental group. Curtis Mayfield, born Chicago, Illinois, June 3, 1942; Sam Gooden, born Chattanooga, Tennessee; Fred Cash, born Chattanooga, Tennessee. Mayfield replaced by Leroy Hutson in 1971.*

The Impressions, one of the most successful soul groups in the 1960s, always saw itself as a "message" group. The basic goal of a good percentage of the songs written by lead singer-guitarist Curtis Mayfield was to give black people pride in themselves and incentive to work to improve their lot. This sometimes overshadowed the fact that many of Curtis's compositions were aimed at inspiring people of all colors to make the world a better place to live in. (*See Mayfield, Curtis.*)

An example is Mayfield's 1970 "Mighty Mighty": "There really is no difference/If you're cut you're gonna bleed . . . And mighty, mighty/ Spade and Whitey/Your black and white power/Is gonna be a flower tower/And we who stand divided/ For now undecided/Give this some thought/In stupidness we've all been caught."

This song, like many performed by the group, has a gospel flavor, reflecting its members' earliest musical experiences. For Mayfield, this involved singing in the choir of the Traveling Soul Spiritualists Church where, at nine, he met 12-year-old Jerry Butler. The two became friends and later formed a gospel group called the Modern Jubilaires. In their teens, they each had different groups, but kept in

touch and eventually went back together to found the Impressions. (*See Butler, Jerry.*)

By the time that group was formed, Mayfield had become a competent guitarist. As he told Sue Clark: "I didn't really choose the guitar. I've found through most of my life . . . any instrument I happened to run into, I was able to get a few notes out of it. I started with the piano, and I found I was able to get a few beats out of the drums. And so it happens that my cousin had bought an old guitar, and he left it laying around the house, so it was just something else to do: So [at 14], it became a thing with me."

Fred Cash and Sam Gooden grew up in Chattanooga and came to Chicago in the mid-1950s to try for success as a vocal team, the Roosters. They met Jerry Butler, who liked their sound, and Jerry urged Curtis to join with them in setting up a new group. Curtis agreed in early 1957, and the group began singing wherever they could find work in the Chicago area. During the year, they met Eddie Thomas, who became their manager and who also came up with the name of the Impressions for them.

With Butler as lead singer, the group was called Jerry Butler and the Impressions. At the time, brothers Arthur and Richard Brooks rounded out the group. They auditioned and gained a recording contract from Vee Jay and, in 1958, on the Abner label, had a major hit, "For Your Precious Love," co-written by Butler and the Brooks brothers. Its success caused a rift between Butler and the others. Abner executives, without consulting any of the performers, changed the label credits to Jerry Butler and the Impressions. The Impressions objected and left, after which Butler embarked on a solo career that made him one of the most successful vocalists of the '60s.

The result dealt a severe blow to the Impressions. The group was not well known enough to continue on its own. For a while, it broke up with Gooden and Cash working at nonmusical jobs while Mayfield made his way as a songwriter and guitarist in Butler's band. Some of his material was important to Jerry Butler's rise to stardom, particularly such hits as "Let It Be Me" and "He Will Break Your Heart."

Curtis kept in touch with the other Impressions and finally reformed the group as a trio as the 1950s came to a close. For a while, the going was slow, but at the start of the '60s, buoyed by many new Mayfield compositions, the Impressions began to pick up momentum. In a short time, Curtis, Sam, and Fred became one of the hottest teams on the R&B stage circuit as well as leading recording artists.

By the start of the '60s, they had signed with ABC-Paramount, and they produced a steady stream of chart hits, beginning with "Gypsy Woman" in

1961. In 1963, Mayfield's "It's All Right" proved to be a top 10 pop hit as well as the group's first number one R&B recording. Things went even better in 1964, with such hits as "You Must Believe Me," "Keep on Pushin'," and "I'm So Proud." Other top 10 hits on the soul or pop lists during their stay with ABC included "People Get Ready" (later a hit for Aretha Franklin) and "Woman's Got Soul" in 1965, and "We're a Winner" in 1968. Also a top 10 hit was "Amen." Other songs that made the charts, though not the top 10, included such Mayfield songs as "I Loved and Lost," "Talkin' about You," "Jealous Man," and "Soulful Love."

The Impressions were second only to Ray Charles in album successes for ABC. Among their releases on that label were *Greatest Hits, The Impressions, Keep on Pushin', The Never-Ending Impressions, One by One, People Get Ready,* and *Ridin' High.*

When the ABC contract ran out in the late '60s and wasn't renewed, Mayfield and Thomas moved the Impressions to Mayfield's own record label, Curtom. Arrangements for distribution of Curtom products were made with Buddah Records. Within four weeks after the new firm was in operation, the Impressions had its first single on Curtom, "Fool for You," on the soul charts. Joining it was a single produced by Mayfield for the Five Stairsteps & Cubie, "Don't Change Your Love," the first outside group to join the label. (Mayfield and Thomas had helped start the Stairsteps on its way to fame years before when they produced some of the group's early hit records.) During 1969, the Impressions had two major hits on Curtom: "Choice of Colors" and "This Is My Country."

In the early '70s, Mayfield decided to work as a soloist, while continuing to supervise the career of the Impressions. His replacement was Leroy Hutson. The move worked out well at first for both parties. Curtis had such national hits as the single "If There's a Hell Down Below, We're All Gonna Go" and the LPs *Curtis, Curtis Live,* and *Roots.* The Impressions sold many copies of the single "Turn on to Me" and the hit LP of the same title.

The Impressions' R&B/Soul hits in 1970, besides the last named single, included "Amen 1970," "Check Out Your Mind," and "Say You Love Me" plus the LPs *Best of the Impressions* and *Young Mods, Forgotten Story.* In 1971, the group had the hit singles "Love Me" and "Ain't Got Time." ABC reissues of earlier material provided the charted LPs *Greatest Hits* and *16 Greatest Hits.* In 1972, the trio scored with the single "This Love's for Real" and the album *Times Have Changed.*

Without Mayfield as a regular member, the group seemed to lose its way creatively. It continued to record new material, first on Curtom, then on other labels, in the mid-1970s into the 1980s, but the emotional flame seemed to go out. Those releases included, on Curtom, *First Impressions* (1975) and *Loving Power* (1976); on Cotillion, *It's About Time* (1976); and on 20th Century, *Come to My Party* (1979) and *Fan the Fire* (1981). During the 1970s, the glory days of the group were recalled in such retrospectives as ABC's *The ABC Collection—Curtis Mayfield and the Impressions* and Sire Records 1976 set, *Vintage Years—The Impressions* featuring Jerry Butler and Curtis Mayfield.

The surviving singing group didn't make much progress with new hits in the late 1970s and the 1980s, but it could still awaken nostalgia with its performances of old successes on the concert circuit. In 1982, MCA issued a retrospective album, *The Impressions: Greatest Hits,* as part of its Collectibles Series. During 1983, Butler, Mayfield, Cash, and Gooden reunited for a concert tour.

IRON BUTTERFLY: *Vocal and instrumental group. Personnel as of 1969: Doug Ingle, born Omaha, Nebraska, September 9, 1946; Ron Bushy, born Washington, D.C., December 23, 1945; Lee Dorman, born St. Louis, Missouri, September 15, 1945; Erik Keith Braunn, born Boston, Massachusetts, August 11, 1950. Braunn left at the end of 1969; replaced by Mike Pinera, born Tampa, Florida, and Larry Reinhardt, born Florida. Group disbanded in 1971. Ingle, Bushy, Dorman, and Braunn regrouped in 1988.*

From late 1968 into the 1970s, the name Iron Butterfly was a household word to rock'n'roll fans. Unlike many group designations, this one was derived from a logical analysis of the musicians' goals.

Group leader Doug Ingle stated: "I wanted a name we could live up to. We wanted to be good. Good consists of being heavy, tight; together, not only musically, but as people. It also means being light, dynamic, versatile, and original. I added all those qualities together and it boiled down to heavy and pretty. At the time, insect names seemed to be the big thing, so we became Iron Butterfly."

This name was determined in San Diego, California, where Ingle had moved with his family from Colorado. Ingle's exposure to music began with his early years in the Rocky Mountain State. His family was poor and had an old piano, but no radio or record player. His father was the church organist and helped his son learn both piano and organ. Ingle played in school bands in San Diego before forming his own group at 16 to play at dances held at local Navy and Marine clubs. For almost five years, he worked with a succession of groups—his own or bands headed by others in his home area. Late in 1966, he gave serious thought to starting a new band that he could take to Los Angeles for a try at making the big time.

One of his first choices was drummer Ron Bushy, an East Coast native living in San Diego by the time he met Ingle. Bushy had started learning drums in the sixth grade when he built his own practice pad and drumsticks. He started college in San Diego aiming at a teaching career, but his spare-time work with local groups led to his forgetting about academia.

The Iron Butterfly began to audition in the Los Angeles area in the fall of 1966. Consisting of Ingle, Bushy, and three other San Diegans (bassist Jerry Penrod, vocalist Darryl DeLoach and guitarist Danny Weis), it won some fame among underground music fans by word of mouth. A single-night engagement at the Whisky-A-Go-Go was so well received that the management extended it to three weeks. At the start of 1967, the group moved to another Sunset Strip club, the Galaxy, where they were still going strong three months later when Atlantic Records signed them to a contract.

Released in January 1968, their debut album, *Heavy,* soon moved to number one on Los Angeles album charts. By then, however, internal dissension caused three of the group to quit, leaving only Ingle and Bushy. They first were directed to Erik Braunn and, about the same time, Bushy heard Lee Dorman playing with a group in a small Los Angeles club and asked him to join.

Born in Boston, but raised in California, Braunn showed talent on the violin at four and started vocal lessons while still in grade school. In his teens in the San Fernando Valley section of Los Angeles, he took guitar lessons and also gained the lead role in a little-theater production of *The Drunkard.*

The fourth member of the 1968 group, Lee Dorman, had only started to learn guitar in 1966, after moving to San Diego from the Monterey Bay area, where he had graduated from Carmel High School. Dorman's first instrument had been the accordion, on which he'd begun lessons at nine. Later, he added drums and piano before mastering bass and rhythm guitar.

With the impetus of the first album, the quartet began a national tour that took them into most major cities in the U.S. in April and May 1968. The wild reception of youthful rock fans underscored the fact that Iron Butterfly had superstar potential.

The group placed its first Atco single, "Possession" backed with "Unconscious Power," on the charts in 1968. Both songs were written by Ingle, and were played in the 1968 movie *Savage Seven* that also featured Cream. Ingle's 17-minute composition "In-A-Gadda-Da-Vida" (translation: In a Garden of Eden) became a feature of the group's act.

Released in shortened version as a single, it became a major hit; the LP *In-A-Gadda-Da-Vida* went gold. The group's third album, *Ball* (1969), also earned a gold record.

When Braunn departed in late 1969, he formed his own group, Flintwhistle, consisting of drummer Lenny Feigen as well as two of the original Iron Butterfly: Jerry Penrod and Darryl DeLoach. Ingle, Bushy, and Dorman were now complemented by two Florida-born singer-guitarists: Mike Pinera and Larry "Rhino" Reinhardt. Pinera had started playing in Tampa honky tonks at 15, and then toured with rhythm & blues bands. As a member of the Blues Image, he toured jointly with Iron Butterfly, sometimes jamming with it. After joining the Butterfly, he suggested that his long-time friend Reinhardt be added.

Reinhardt had played with a number of southern groups, including his own Tropical Trip Company and the Second Coming. When the invitation to join Iron Butterfly came, he was working as a session man at Phil Walden Studios in Macon, Georgia, and making plans to hitchhike to Los Angeles.

The revised group was featured on the 1970 LPs *Live* and *Metamorphosis.* Both the albums sold well, but not at as brisk a pace as *In-A-Gadda-Da-Vida.* There was evidence as 1971 began that they had lost some of their momentum. One indication was Iron Butterfly's change in booking arrangements from large auditoriums to smaller halls with seating capacities in the 3,000–5,000 range. As a result, the group decided to disband, each member going his separate way after completing their farewell tour on May 23, 1971.

After 17 years of anonymity, Ingle, Bushy, Dorman, and Braunn got together for a single reunion concert in Los Angeles. They had so much fun and met with so much interest that they reformed Iron Butterfly for a 50-city tour in 1988.

IRON MAIDEN: *Vocal and instrumental group from England. Members as of the mid-1980s: Steve Harris, born Leytonstone, East London, England, c. 1956; Dave Murray, born Hackney, England, c. 1957; Adrian Smith, born Hackney, England, c. 1956; Bruce Dickinson; Nicko McBrain.*

A major contender for heavy metal honors in the 1980s was Iron Maiden, a band that made its way to international stardom from the seamy working class pub scene of East London. By the mid-1980s, the group had gained a following that extended not only across the Atlantic and Pacific Oceans, but in Iron Curtain nations such as Poland, Hungary, and Yugoslavia. Considering the group's thundering musical style, it was surprising it was able to include concerts in those three Eastern European countries in its massive 1984–85 "World Slavery Tour."

The driving force behind Iron Maiden was bass guitarist Steve Harris, its organizer and primary songwriter. The first version of the band debuted in May 1976 in an East London pub called the Cart and Horses. Among the Harris songs that group performed that night was the one that became its name and theme, "Iron Maiden." During the next two years, Harris bustled around the local club circuit lining up engagements for his band, which went through a constant change in personnel. By the late 1970s, however, it began to gain some semblance of order with Paul Di'anno handling lead vocals and Dave Murray playing lead guitar. Di'anno, Murray, and Harris formed the core of the group that first brought Iron Maiden to the attention of a sizable number of heavy metal fans in the early 1980s. Handling drums for a time was Clive Burr (born Leytonstone, East London, England, c. 1958).

During the late '70s, the group became one of the most popular of its kind in East London. Club owners who paid the band 20 pounds a night to perform were assured the house almost always would be packed. As audiences requested recordings, Harris and his band decided to buy studio time for some demonstration tapes. At the end of 1978, they put together 200 pounds to rent the Spacewood Studios in Cambridge for two days. During that period they recorded sizzling versions of the Harris compositions "Iron Maiden," "Prowler," and "Strange World."

They managed to get the demos to one of London's best-known heavy metal disc jockeys, Neal Kay, then holding a regular "Heavy Metal Night" at the Bandwagon Soundhouse located on the side of the Prince of Wales pub at Kingsbury Circle, North London. Kay was impressed and played the group's material regularly at the Bandwagon. A few months into 1979, Iron Maiden ranked number one on the heavy metal chart Kay helped compile for *Sounds* magazine.

Another important milestone occurred later in the year, during July, when music industry executive Rod Smallwood (who had played an important role in the careers of Be Bop Delux, Judas Priest, and Mott the Hoople) was introduced to the band's demo tape by a friend at Rod's rugby club. He wanted to hear the group play on stage so he arranged for showcase appearances, one at the Windsor Castle in North London and the other at the Swan in Hammersmith. The group's fans followed them to both engagements (helped along by word-of-mouth urging from the bandsmen and their friends) and gave the sets rousing approval.

Smallwood agreed to take over booking activities and expanded the group's exposure to clubs throughout England. In time, he signaled their move toward the big time by getting them an engagement at the prestigious SoHo rock club, the Marquee. Smallwood made sure an artists & repertoire executive from EMI Records was present for the show. The band's powerhouse style and its magnetic effect on a capacity crowd of young fans was enough to get the EMI man to suggest that the label's director of A&R, Brian Shepard, catch the band's next gig at the Bandwagon Soundhouse. Shepard set the wheels in motion to add Iron Maiden to the EMI roster, resulting in final contract signing in December 1979. Soon after, Smallwood agreed to become the band's full-time manager.

Even while the group was beginning to work out material for its debut on EMI, the members decided to pay for pressing of the demo songs that had opened the door to major record alignment. They arranged for 6,000 copies, titling the album *The Soundhouse Tapes*. Within a short time, copies were sold out and Harris and the others declined to press any more.

The group's debut single, "Running Free," was issued by EMI on February 15, 1980. It brought a bid for them to play on the BBC "Tops of the Pops" show, which was usually lip-synched. Iron Maiden refused to follow that format and, after some weeks of discussions, finally became the first band to play live on the show since the Who in 1973.

When the debut album, *Iron Maiden,* came out in the early 1980s, it showed up at the number four position on the U.K. charts the first week of its release. Later in the year it was also doing well in the U.S. after its release there on EMI's U.S. affiliate, Capitol Records.

Helping to keep the group in heavy metal adherents' minds was its special symbol, a large skeletal head with bright, smoking eyes that typically formed the backdrop to its stage show. It was originally referred to as Eddie the Head, later shortened to Eddie. Eddie soon became a featured image on album covers, t-shirts, and the band's Christmas cards.

While its debut album still was finding new buyers in many parts of the world, the group completed its second LP, the 1981 *Killers*. Soon after the album came out, it was announced that Paul Di'anno was leaving the group. The piercing notes he sang in the band's roof-rocking exhibitions had destroyed his voice, according to the group's management. He was replaced on lead vocals by Bruce Dickinson, who previously had fronted the band Sampson.

In 1982, the LP *Number of the Beast* came out on EMI in the U.K. and Capitol's subsidiary, Harvest, in the U.S. and became a chart hit in both countries (platinum in the U.S.). Among its tracks was "Run for the Hills," a top 10 single in England. The band continued its approach of almost nonstop touring to back new releases. The 1982 series, the "Beast on the Road Tour," began in Dunstable in Northern England on February 25 and ended on December 18 in Niggata, Japan.

The band had made changes in other places besides lead vocals in the early 1980s, but the aggregation assembled for the platinum 1983 *Piece of Mind* on Capitol was still the lineup as of 1986. It comprised Dickinson on lead vocals, Dave Murray and Adrian Smith on lead and rhythm guitars, Steve Harris on bass guitar, and Nicko McBrain on drums. (McBrain replaced Clive Burr.)

In September 1984, EMI and Capitol released the album *Powerslave,* which featured a 15-minute rendition of Samuel Taylor Coleridge's poem "Rime of the Ancient Mariner." To back the album, the band embarked on its "World Slavery Tour" which, whether intentionally symbolic or not, began in Poland in August 1984 and went on to Hungary, Yugoslavia and 23 other countries, including Japan, Thailand, Singapore, New Zealand, Australia, and the U.S., finishing in Southern California on July 5, 1985. The LP earned a gold record in the U.S., U.K., and many of the other nations visited during the concert series. By the end of 1985, the band claimed a total of 46 gold and platinum awards internationally during the first half of the decade.

In late 1985, the group's sixth album on EMI/Capitol, *Live after Death,* was released. More successful was its gold 1986 album, *Somewhere in Time.*

ISLEY BROTHERS: *Vocal and instrumental group. All born Cincinnati, Ohio: O'Kelly Isley, December 25, 1937, died New Jersey, March 31, 1986; Rudolph Isley, April 1, 1939; Ronald Isley, May 21, 1941. Core group in 1970s included Ernie Isley, Marvin Isley, Chris Jasper.*

The Isleys seemed to have almost as many lives in their show-business careers as a cat. They started out as a hit on the black rhythm & blues circuit and later parlayed this into broad success as rock artists. When things slowed down for them in the U.S. teen market in the mid-1960s, they moved to England to become top stars there. Then in the late '60s, they reentered the U.S. pop music picture with new recordings on their own label and became as popular in the early '70s as they had been a decade earlier.

The three brothers who founded the group got started singing as children in their church choir in their hometown of Cincinnati. In the mid-1950s, they sang with gospel groups in the Midwest before turning to the burgeoning R&B field in the late 1950s. One of their best-liked songs was "Lonely Teardrops," and their spirited rendition of it one night at the Howard Theatre in Washington, D.C., proved to be a turning point in their career. In the band's version of the song, one of the Isleys sang the line, "You know you want to make me shout," with such emphasis on the word *shout* that the audience responded with cheers, handclapping, and shouting. An RCA executive, Howard Bloom, was present and decided a song using the word as its central theme might have hit potential.

His idea was accepted by the Isleys, who worked up the material. Soon after, RCA set up a recording session in which the brothers were backed by Joe Richardson on guitar, Professor Herman Stephens (organist in the boys' church in Cincinnati) on organ, and six session men. The resulting single, "Shout," earned the brothers a gold record in 1959. The LP of the same name, issued by RCA in January 1960, also became a chart hit.

Their follow-up singles on RCA didn't duplicate their earlier performance, and it seemed as though they might be a one-shot act, like so many other performers. They left RCA and signed with Wand Records. In 1961, they had another national best seller, "Twist and Shout," that was even bigger than their 1959 hit. Wand also gained a chart success with the follow-up LP, *Twist and Shout.*

Again the brothers lost ground. A switch from Wand to United Artists label did little to bring their ratings up. The 1964 United Artists LP *Twisting and Shouting* gained some attention, but by 1965, the Isleys again found it difficult to break into the U.S. hit lists. (On some of the group's recordings of the first part of the '60s, future superstar Jimi Hendrix was a session guitarist. The Isleys later issued some of Hendrix's early work on their T-Neck label. (*See Hendrix, Jimi*).

The group was signed by Tamla (part of the Motown Records family) and scored some success in the U.S. with their LPs *This Old Heart* (1966) and *Soul on the Rocks* (1968). By then, however, the group had moved its base to England, becoming one of the most popular in-person and recording acts there and on the Continent. Between 1966 and the end of 1968, they turned out such British top 10 successes as "This Old Heart of Mine" and "I Guess I'll Always Love You" on Tamla.

In 1969, the brothers decided the time was ripe for a new assault on the American market. They established their own recording firm, T-Neck Records, with Ronald as president, Rudolf as vice president, and O'Kelly as secretary-treasurer. (First distributor for T-Neck was Buddah Records.) Their first T-Neck single, "It's Your Thing," gained them a gold record. Like most of their hits, it was written by them.

This was the start of a steady series of hits by the Isleys, both singles and LPs, that kept their name on

R&B or pop charts from 1969 into the 1970s. In 1970, they had such singles hits as "Get into Something" and "If He Can, You Can." 1971 successes included the single releases "Warpath" and "Love the One You're With" and the LP *Givin' It Back*. Their other LPs on T-Neck in the early 1970s included *Brother Isley, In the Beginning* (with Jimi Hendrix), *It's Our Thing* and *Get into Something*. 1972 Isley Brothers singles hits included "Lay Lady Lay," "Work to Do," "Lay Away," "Pop That Thang" (the last two reaching the top 10 on the soul charts) and the best-selling album *Brother, Brother, Brother*.

During the early 1970s, the group expanded to include more family members—guitarist Ernie Isley, bass guitarist Marvin Isley, and cousin and keyboards player Chris Jasper. When the group switched distribution for T-Neck from Buddah to CBS in 1973, the expanded clan savored a gold single, "That Lady," drawn from the gold LP, *3 + 3*.

For the rest of the 1970s, the group continued to turn out one hit record after another. While the band didn't get the massive publicity exposure of many rock and soul headliners, its exciting live performances and the quality of most of its recordings retained a strong hold on a large segment of the pop audience. Almost all its '70s album releases and dozens of its singles achieved worldwide sales at the gold or platinum levels.

Its singles hits included "Highways of My Life," "Live It Up," "Midnight Sky," "Fight the Power" (gold in 1975), "Who Loves You Better," "Harvest for the World," "The Pride," "Take It to the Next Phase," "(It's a) Disco Night," and "Don't Say Goodnight, It's Time for Love"—all high flyers on black charts—and such crossover pop/soul hits as their versions of Seals and Crofts' "Summer Breeze" and James Taylor's "Don't Let Me Be Lonely Tonight." T-Neck/CBS LP successes included *Live It Up* (gold, 1974), *The Heat Is On* (gold, 1975), *Harvest for the World* (gold, 1976), *Forever Gold* (1977), *Go for Your Guns* (platinum, 1978), *Showdown* (platinum, 1978), *Timeless* (1978), and *Winner Takes All* (gold, 1979). Reissues of earlier material on other labels included *Rock around the Clock* (Camden, 1975), *The Best of the Isley Brothers* (Buddah, 1978), and *The Very Best of the Isley Brothers* (United Artists, 1975).

There was little change in the scenario for the Isleys in the 1980s. The group continued to tour widely and gain new RIAA gold and platinum awards to add to its already massive collection. It began the decade with the platinum 1980 LP *Go All the Way* and followed with *Inside You* in 1981 and gold *Between the Sheets* in 1983. The band's agreement with CBS ended shortly after that and it proceeded to split into two headline acts with the original three Isley Brothers signing a new arrangement with Warner Brothers while the younger artists stayed on the CBS roster under the name Isley/Jasper/Isley. By the end of 1985, both groups had hit albums on the black charts: Isley/Jasper/Isley with *Caravan of Love* at the number five position, and the Isley Brothers with *Masterpiece*, at number 19. The Isley Brothers' album contained still another hit single, "Colder Are My Nights."

The eldest of the three original Isleys, O'Kelly, died of a heart attack in his sleep in March of 1986. Ronald and Rudolph Isley recorded the 1987 album *Smooth Sailin'* as a duo.

In the early 1980s, Motown reissued some of the original Isleys' earlier material in the LPs *Superstar Series, Volume 6, Doin' Their Thing*, and *This Old Heart of Mine*.

JACKSON 5: *See Jacksons, The.*

JACKSON, JERMAINE: *See Jacksons, The.*

JACKSON, JOE: *Singer, pianist, vibraharpist, band leader, songwriter. Born Burton-upon-Trent, England, August 11, 1955.*

Chameleon-like Joe Jackson assumed a disparate variety of hues as his career unfolded. He could shout obscenities with the best of them as an apparently dedicated punk rocker. Coming on stage in suit and tie he could at times have passed for a down-at-the-heels businessman. Or he could be a sedate member of a classical orchestra or a cool keyboardist in a jazz group. Over the years, in fact, his original songs reflected all those influences and more, including reggae.

Jackson was born in Burton-upon-Trent, England, but essentially grew up in Portsmouth, where his family moved when he was a year old. Bothered by asthma, he was limited in physical activities, which turned him toward music in his childhood. He began violin lessons at 11 and taught himself piano. He said his original musical tastes were strongly influenced by such mid-1960s English groups as the Beatles and Rolling Stones. However, he also found classics to his liking, Beethoven in particular.

By the time he reached his teens, he already was making an effort to write original material, spending hours at the keyboard testing out different melodic combinations as he slowly worked out a playing technique. Sometimes he put words to some of his note patterns. Feeling the need to become more knowledgeable about the piano, he started formal lessons at 16. During that period, he also found work as a musician in local Portsmouth pubs. After a while, he formed a trio that played jazz in a Greek restaurant in Portsmouth.

In 1972, he was accepted by the Royal Academy of Music in London as a full-time student. He attended the Academy for three years, taking courses in piano, percussion, composition, and orchestration. To help meet expenses, he worked nights and weekends in a series of local pop bands that typically covered top 40 hits of the time. One such band, the Misty Set, used the ballad "Misty" as its theme. His performing credits during those years included dates at military bases, local pubs, discos, and a number of concerts with the National Youth Jazz Orchestra.

After graduating from the Academy in the mid-1970s, he formed a band called Arms and Legs with friend Mark Andrews. A contract with MAM Records resulted in two singles. However, management problems caused the band to break up in 1976. A disillusioned Jackson had to take a job at a London Playboy Club with a goal of saving enough money to record and possibly distribute his own album. Before he got that far, he was offered and accepted a more lucrative job as musical director for a popular cabaret act, "Coffee and Cream."

He still found time to write and tape his own material. To back him on most of the tracks, he recruited Gary Sanford on guitar, Graham Maby on bass, and Dave Houghton on drums. Though he was determined to press the proposed debut album himself as a last resort, he wasn't hesitant about passing the demo tapes around to record-company executives. One of the contacts he developed in the late 1970s was producer David Kershenbaum of A&M Records in England. Kershenbaum liked the demo and persuaded A&M to sign Jackson. The debut disc, *Look Sharp*, was released in early 1979 and its strong new wave elements helped make it a hit in England and gold in the U.S. A single from the album, Joe's composition "Is She Really Going Out with Him," made the top 20 in both England and the U.S. Joe's second A&M LP, *I'm the Man*, stayed on the charts from fall 1979 well into 1980, providing a top 5 U.K. single, "It's Different for Girls."

Joe had become a reggae devotee by the time he was ready for his next recording sessions. In 1980, with reggae artist Lincoln Thompson, he produced, recorded, and released a three-song EP, *Tilt*, featuring Jimmy Cliff's song "The Harder They Come." Reggae-flavored rock also dominated his next LP, *Beat Crazy* (A&M, 1980). Other highlights of 1980 included a guest appearance with reggae great Bob Marley at a London Crystal Palace concert and receipt of a prestigious Edison Award for *I'm the Man* from the Netherlands.

In early 1981, Joe was sidelined for a number of months by illness. While recuperating at home, he spent a lot of his time listening to jazz records by artists such as Cab Calloway and Louis Jordan. When he recovered, he put together a jazz group to play London venues. The music that evolved provided the basis for his 1981 A&M album, *Joe Jackson's Jumpin' Jive*. It wasn't a bad album but, while it might have satisfied Joe's artistic interests, it didn't represent any creative breakthroughs, either for him or for jazz. Possibly reflecting the typecasting syndrome of many critics, reviewers tended to suggest Joe's career had lost its way, perhaps permanently. A *Rolling Stone* critic commented: "He sidesteps the whole issue of working out his artistic problems by releasing a record of swing-era remakes. It's difficult to see where these faithful but soulless updatings of various '40s numbers will lead him." Joe soon showed the obits were premature. For the next phase of his career, he moved his home base from England to New York. He drew on his wanderings through the streets of his adopted home for a gold theme album, *Night and Day* (1982). The "night" side comprised a series of frenetic "sketches" of Manhattan after dark, while the "day" side had softer, more philosophical rock songs. It brought high praise from many who had criticized his previous two efforts. *Rolling Stone*, for instance, called it "an uncompromising success." It spawned several hit singles, such as "Steppin' Out," on top 10 lists in the U.S. and U.K. in 1982, and "Breaking Us in Two," a best-seller of 1983.

Even while on tour in the U.S. in late 1982, he found time to write the score for the movie *Mike's Murder*, starring Debra Winger. The soundtrack LP included Joe's first movie-related instrumental, "Moonlight."

That encouraged him to add several instrumental tracks to his next album, including "Loisaida," dedicated to Manhattan's Lower East Side. The album was recorded in an Old Masonic Lodge usually employed for classical sessions. Released in March 1984 by A&M, *Body and Soul* reflected growing insight and musical maturity in Jackson's compositions. But it was perhaps a bit more complex than his fans were used to and had much greater success with the critical community than with record buyers.

Jackson continued to turn his cap around and strive for new career opportunities. During January and February 1985, he worked on an assignment to compose a 20-minute score for full orchestra for the Japanese film *Shijin No le* (House of the Poet). He went to Japan for five weeks to help rehearse and supervise recording of the material by the Tokyo Symphony Orchestra. The film later was shown at the Expo '85 Science Exposition in Tsukuba, Japan. During the summer of 1985, his activities included co-producing an album developed by his guitarist,

Vinnie Zummo, and Zummo's wife Janice that was issued by A&M in February 1986 under the title *Modern Marriage*.

For his own musical efforts, he worked on material in 1985 and early 1986 sufficient for two new albums, of highly different content. The first, *Big World* (spring 1986) contained new rock songs, while the second, *Will Power* (1987), was an all instrumental collection.

He commented: "I'm planning to do a lot more of this kind of thing. I'm not just a singer, I'm first and foremost a writer. Because there's no one singing doesn't mean it's still not music."

In 1988 Joe Jackson released *Live 1980/86* (A&M), a two-disc set.

JACKSON, MICHAEL: *Singer, songwriter, actor. Born Gary, Indiana, August 29, 1958.*

When the five-member family group the Jacksons took its first steps toward stardom in 1963, five-year-old Michael was included mostly for the novelty effect of his youthful energy and dancing ability. As he outgrew the role of "baby" of the act (there were other Jacksons behind him who served in that capacity), he showed steady improvement in performing skills to the point that he became unofficial leader rather than a mere group member. In time, his achievements as a solo artist and songwriter overshadowed those of his brothers, even though the chemistry among them kept the Jacksons among the premier groups in rock and soul into the late-1980s. (*See Jacksons, The.*)

Even though the Jacksons became one of Motown's most successful recording groups and surely its mainstay during a troubled period in the early 1970s, company executives agreed it was worth giving Michael the chance to blossom as a solo singer. In late 1971, he proved it was a wise decision as his first solo single, "Got to Be There," made it to the top 5. In April 1972, he had an even bigger hit when his version of Bobby Day's 1958 hit "Rockin' Robin" rose to number two on *Billboard* lists. In July 1972, he had a top 20 success with the single "I Wanna Be with You" and topped all of those in the fall when his theme song from the movie *Ben* rose to number one in *Billboard* the week of October 14, 1972.

The music for *Ben* was written by film composer Walter Scharf with words by London lyricist Don Black. Scharf told a *Billboard* reporter: "I had just finished work on another film and was going away for a rest when the people at [the studio] sent me the script to *Ben* [where Ben is a rat befriended by a boy]. They needed a song to be used in the last few minutes of the film. The terms were so good that I just couldn't pass it up."

He called in Black to write the words and Black suggested they try to get Michael Jackson to sing it. Black told *Billboard:* "When Michael saw the song, he was anxious to do it. He's quite an animal lover—very sensitive you know. He enjoys anything that crawls or flies."

Besides his singles releases, Michael made the charts with a series of early 1970s Motown albums such as *Ben, Got To Be There,* and *One Day in Your Life*. All three of those were out of print the latter part of the 1970s, but were re-released by Motown in 1981 after Michael rose to superstar status with his work on another label, Epic. Besides those releases, Motown issued several retrospective albums such as *The Best of Michael Jackson* (1975) and *Motown Superstar Series, Volume 7* (1980).

For several years after the family group left Motown for Epic in 1975, Michael concentrated on helping advance its fortunes. The group, which had called itself the Jackson Five while with Motown, changed its name to the Jacksons to allow for changes and additions from the nine children in the family. Michael's last solo album for Motown, *Forever Michael,* came out just before the change to Epic took place and, as of 1988, that had been his last solo offering for Motown.

The Epic move did bring an arrangement for Michael to make new solo collections for the label, but he had become a little unsure of himself under new surroundings. Nonetheless, he was moving ahead in his songwriting efforts and decided he should look around for someone with good creative credentials in the industry to advise him on his next moves.

A longtime family was top-ranked musician and producer, Quincy Jones. (*See Jones, Quincy.*) In fact, Quincy had been involved in scoring the 1978 film *The Wiz* (starring Diana Ross) in which Michael had the major role of the Scarecrow (the old Ray Bolger role). Michael told England's *Melody Maker* in 1980: "It was the first time I fully wrote and produced my songs, and I was looking for somebody who would give me that freedom, plus somebody who's unlimited musically. Quincy calls me 'Smelly' and said: 'Well, Smelly, why don't you let me do it.' I said: 'That's a great deal!' It sounded phony, like I was trying to hint to that, but I wasn't. I didn't even think of that. But Quincy does jazz, he does movie scores, rock'n'roll, funk, pop—he's all colors and that's the kind of people I like to work with. I went over to his house just about every day, and we just put it together."

With Quincy handling production chores, Michael recorded the tracks for the 1979 *Off the Wall*, arguably one of the finest pop albums of the year and perhaps the decade. David Marsh who is usually not lavish in his praise, wrote in *Rolling Stone* that the LP was "a masterpiece of modern record making. Jackson's voice—adolescent breathiness crowding maturity—was the perfect vehicle for music that broke down stylistic and conceptual barriers with casual cool. *Off the Wall* features disco beat and rock guitar, soul intensity and good-time jive, a triumphant merger of the mechanical and the spiritual. It's hits ranged all over the map—the ballad 'She's out of My Life,' the dance-beat rockers 'Off the Wall' and 'Rock with You' . . . all made the airwaves much more invigorating in 1979 and 1980."

The album sold over 7 million copies worldwide, not disappearing from *Billboard* charts until 1984. Its first single, with words and music by Michael, was the number one "Don't Stop 'Til You Get Enough." (October 13, 1979).

Fred Bronson reported on Michael's discussion (with Dick Clark) of how he wrote in *The Billboard Book of Number One Hits*. The song was "written at home. I just came up with the melody. It's about the forces and the power of love. Walking around the house, I started singing it and kept singing it. I went into a 24-track studio we have at home. I told [younger brother] Randy what to play on the piano. I did percussion and piano, and when I played it for Quincy, he loved it."

Billboard noted the references to "the forces and the power of love" reflected his Jehovah's Witness religious belief inherited from his mother. He talked about that to *Newsweek* in 1983. "The thing that touches me is very special. It's a message I have to tell. I start crying, and the pain is wonderful. It's amazing. It's like God."

The single of "Don't Stop 'til You Get Enough" won Michael his first Grammy Award for Best R&B Vocal Performance, Male, in 1979. Before that was presented on the February 27, 1980 telecast, Michael had earned a second number one single on the *Billboard* charts—"Rock with You." He also had two other top 10 entrants from the album: "Off the Wall" and "She's out of My Life." This made him the first solo artist to have four top 10 singles on *Billboard* lists from the same album. At the end of 1980, *Billboard* named him number one in Soul LPs for the year for *Off the Wall* and the number one soul singles leader.

In 1982, Jackson began preparing for his next solo album. This time the plans called for him to co-produce the material with Quincy Jones. Not only did Michael write almost all the music and lyrics, he was intimately involved in every aspect of the work, including instrumental textures. For some tracks, he provided percussion and drum inputs; for instance, on "Billie Jean" he laid down the basic rhythm pattern on a drum machine. Besides doing solo vocal

work, he also collaborated with Paul McCartney on a duet track for the LP. (*See McCartney, Paul.*)

The duet, "The Girl Is Mine," was the first single issued from the album in late 1982. The platinum album, *Thriller,* came out the last week of 1982 and opened at number 11 on *Billboard* charts. That same week, "The Girl Is Mine" (written by Michael) was at number two on the magazine's singles list.

Those songs were just the tip of the iceberg for an album that was literally crammed with delights. There was no doubt that Jackson had done the near impossible by crafting a second solo album for Epic that was instrumentally and vocally quite different in content from its predecessor and that also was even better from an overall standpoint. When "Billie Jean" reached number one that March, *Thriller* also was at number one. As *Billboard* pointed out, that made Michael the first artist "in the history of *Billboard*'s charts to simultaneously top the singles and album charts in both pop and black categories. For good measure, *Thriller* was also number one on the dance/disco charts." *Thriller* was at number one on the pop lists at the end of 1983, a spot it had held for no fewer than 21 weeks of that year. Not only was it a smash at home, it also reached number one for the year in the U.K. and was a best-seller in many other nations.

Hardly had "Billie Jean" given up the top spot in 1983 when another single was poised to take over, Jackson's composition, "Beat It." Like the other singles, it was helped by a hit video played regularly on MTV and other outlets. The choreography Michael performed in these was acclaimed by such dance authorities as Bob Fosse, Gene Kelly, and Fred Astaire. Astaire was quoted in *Time* as stating: "He is a wonderful mover. He makes these moves up himself and it is just great to watch. I think he just feels that way when he is singing these songs. . . . Michael is a dedicated artist. He dreams, thinks of it all the time."

During 1983, Michael and Paul McCartney combined forces to write and record "Say, Say, Say" and "The Man" for Paul's album *Pipes of Peace.* When "Say, Say, Say" made number one in *Billboard,* still another single from *Thriller* was on the lists, "P.Y.T. (Pretty Young Thing)" (the sixth single from *Thriller* to reach the top 10, an achievement amazingly better than with *Off the Wall*).

Michael dominated the Grammy Awards voting for 1983 as no pop artist had before or since, picking up eight of the trophies (a number of them shared with Quincy Jones). The awards were for Record of the Year ("Beat It"); Album of the Year (*Thriller*); Best Pop Vocal Performance, Male (*Thriller* LP); Best Rock Vocal Performance, Male ("Beat It"); Best R&B Vocal Performance, Male ("Billie

Jean''); Best New Rhythm & Blues Song (songwriter's award for "Billie Jean"); Best Recording for Children (for narration and vocals on the LP *E.T., The Extra-Terrestrial*, produced by Quincy Jones); and Producer of the Year, nonclassical (Jackson and Jones). Michael was to earn another Grammy a year later for the Best Video Album of 1984, *Making Michael Jackson's Thriller*.

Coming into 1984, Michael concentrated on a new Jacksons project revolving around a new album (*Victory*, mid-1984) and one of the most ambitious concert plans in pop history. As a unique addition to the album, Michael got Mick Jagger to agree to do a duet. Talking about that number, "State of Shock," released as a single in 1984, Jagger told Robert Palmer of *The New York Times* (January 28, 1985) in response to Palmer's question about what it was like: "Quick. He had the two of us practice for two hours and then we recorded the vocals in two takes. When he sent the finished track to me later, I was kind of disappointed in the productions and the mix. But I think he's a really good singer." What about his dancing, Palmer asked. Jagger replied, "Well, yeah, but we didn't do too much dancing in the studio." (*See Jagger, Mick.*)

The six-month "Victory" tour set attendance records across the U.S. from July through early December of 1984 and generated considerable controversy about ticket prices and show length. But most of those who saw it agreed it was a memorable event and that Michael Jackson's singing and dancing alone were worth the price of admission.

Jackson took on other commitments in the mid-1980s besides recording and concert work, one of which almost ended his career. He had contracted to do TV commercials for Pepsi-Cola and during the taping, when he came down a long flight of stairs, a mishap with the lighting effects set his hair on fire. The blaze was put out and he was rushed to Brotman Memorial Hospital's Burn Clinic in Culver City, California, where the staff did yeoman work first in limiting the damage and later in healing the burns. In appreciation, Jackson later donated a large sum of money to support continued work of the facility.

During 1985–86, he turned his attention to a special three-dimensional video presentation to be featured in a new attraction at Disneyland and Disneyworld. The production, "Captain EO", was supervised by such movie luminaries as Francis Ford Coppola and George Lucas. The 10-minute special-effects show opened to great fanfare at both Disney theme parks in the fall of 1986. Also, in 1985, he and Lionel Richie wrote "We Are the World" as part of a campaign to aid the hungry. (*See Richie, Lionel.*)

From a performing standpoint, Michael Jackson

had broken through many of the artificial boundaries that still hampered black artists in the 1980s. Quincy Jones had pointed this out in a 1983 *Time* cover story on Michael after the release of *Thriller*. Jones commented: "He's taken us right up there where we belong. Black music had to play second fiddle for a long time, but its spirit is the whole motor of pop. Michael has connected with every soul in the world."

Michael's next solo album, *Bad*, was issued by Epic in September 1987. It was a good album creatively, but not as dazzling as *Thriller*. From a sales standpoint, it did well, staying in the *Billboard* top 10 for five weeks after its release and receiving RIAA certification for 3 million sales in its first two months. But it fell far short of *Thriller* saleswise. The first four singles from the album, "I Just Can't Stop Loving You" (with Siedah Garrett), "Bad," "The Way You Make Me Feel" and "The Man In the Mirror," all hit number one.

Jackson won a number of Grammy nominations, including one for *Bad* as Album of the Year. But on the awards telecast (March 2, 1988), Jackson was shut out except for selection of the album as best engineered. On the show itself, though, Michael won a deserved ovation for an electrifying nine minutes plus exhibition of dazzling dance and vocal routines. The following week, he was nominated for best single ("Bad"), best album (*Bad*) and best music video ("The Way You Make Me Feel") in the second annual Soul Train Music Awards.

In 1988 Jackson's autobiography *Moonwalk* was published by Doubleday.

JACKSONS, THE; JACKSON 5: *Vocal and instrumental group. All born Gary, Indiana. Original members: Sigmund Esco "Jackie" Jackson, born May 4, 1951; Toriano Adaryl "Tito" Jackson, born October 15, 1953; Jermaine Jackson, born September 11, 1954; Marlon David Jackson, born March 12, 1957; Michael Joe Jackson, born August 29, 1958. Steven Randall Jackson, born October 29, 1961, added in early 1976. Jermaine left the group in 1976, returned in 1984.*

The warnings against "over 30s" notwithstanding, good rock musicians didn't fade away as the field progressed, but simply joined new groups. Thus many of the popular favorites of the 1960s and early '70s were well past their teens. However, there always were dynamic youngsters coming along, such as the Jackson 5, probably the leaders of the youth movement in music at the start of the '70s.

The group came from Gary, Indiana, the family of nine children of Joe and Katherine Jackson.

Both parents were musically inclined. Joe, a crane operator, spent much of his leisure time playing guitar and writing songs while his wife had a good voice and enjoyed singing country & western and blues songs. Their children naturally were encouraged to take up music and all of them did to a greater or lesser extent.

Five of the six boys (the three girls being Maureen, LaToya, and Janet) began playing as a group for their own pleasure toward the end of the '60s. They included the oldest, Sigmund Esco "Jackie" Jackson (then in his late teens), and his four younger brothers: Toriano Adaryll "Tito" Jackson, Jermaine LaJaune Jackson, Marlon David Jackson, and Michael Joe Jackson. The youngest boy in the family, Randy, was too young to pitch in when the group was first formed, but was playing with it on occasion at the start of the 1970s, joining as a regular in 1976. Jackie and Michael handled lead vocals, though all the brothers sang, with Tito and Jermaine playing guitar and bass, respectively. Marlon, who showed dancing talent in his early years, helped work out the dance routines the group worked into its act, sometimes aided by Michael. (*See Jackson, Michael.*)

Though it made for a noisy house, their father enjoyed it. "It was fun. The kids liked it, and it was one way of keeping them home and not roaming the streets. The neighborhood we lived in offered a lot of ways to get into trouble."

Word about the family's talent got around the neighborhood and the group started playing for friends and then for school events. Before long, they had progressed to being one of Gary's featured groups. Among their fans was the city's mayor, Richard Hatcher, one of the first black mayors in the nation. He told Diana Ross of the group's ability when she was in Gary for a concert in 1969. The story goes she, in turn, brought the word back to Berry Gordy, Jr., president of Motown Records. Within a few weeks time, Motown had signed the quintet and the boys were busily recording their first tracks. (*See Gordy, Berry, Jr.; Ross, Diana.*)The boys soon had a single "I Want You Back," achieving number one position nationally in late January 1970.

For the next few years, the Jackson 5 was almost never absent from both single and album charts. The group's debut LP, *Diana Ross Presents the Jackson Five* was on the charts for over half a year. Their second album, *ABC,* was even more successful, moving into the top 10 a few weeks after its release in the spring and staying on charts for over a year. The Motown publicity department claimed the LP passed gold record sales

worldwide, though it didn't earn a R.I.A.A. award on U.S. sales alone. A similar situation took place with their third album, simply titled *Third Album* (fall 1970). As 1970 progressed, three more singles hit number one on *Billboard*'s pop lists: the title song from their album *ABC,* "The Love You Save," and "I'll Be There." At year-end, *Billboard* ranked the group number one in the singles category for the year and number one in album sales for a new group.

The Jackson 5 retained its touch in 1971, though Jackie was by then attending college and Michael had started to work as a solo artist. In February, they placed "Mama's Pearl" in the national top 10 singles list and followed with "Never Can Say Goodbye" (number two in May), and "Maybe Tomorrow" (top 20 in the late summer). "Sugar Daddy" (1972) proved the last top 10 single on Motown for the group until it hit with "Dancing Machine" in 1974.

The boys were featured in their own nationally televised show, one of the top-rated programs of the 1971–72 season. Their TV soundtrack from the show, *Goin' Back to Indiana,* hit the charts in October.

As 1972 started, the group's sixth album release on Motown, *Greatest Hits of the Jackson 5,* made the top 10 in February. During the year, the group's top 20 singles were "Corner of the Sky," "Little Bitty Pretty One," "Sugar Daddy," and "Lookin' through the Windows." The last of those also was the title track for a top 10 LP. In the spring of 1973, the group had another album, *Skywriter,* on the best-seller lists, but it didn't do as well as earlier LPs, nor indeed as Michael's debut solo album in 1972, *Got to Be There.* Jermaine also began his solo career with his Motown debut LP, *Jermaine,* a best-seller in 1972.

The group continued to perform as a unit on several worldwide tours into the mid-1970s even as some members spent time on separate projects. They gave several command performances before the English Royal Family including a Silver Jubilee concert for Queen Elizabeth at King's Hall in Glasgow, Scotland. They added more LP chart hits to their Motown catalog with the mid-1970s albums *Get It Together, Dancing Machine,* and *Moving Violation.*

But the Jacksons had become increasingly unhappy with their relationship with Motown. Their main objections, they said later, involved lack of creative control over their work. In particular, they wanted more leeway in choice of record producer and song selection. In the latter area, several Jacksons wanted more opportunity to record their own compositions. So when their obligations to Motown were completed, the group decided to change labels, announcing a new contract with Columbia Records' Epic subsidiary in March 1976. Actually, only four of the original Jackson 5 made the move. The fifth, Jermaine, stayed behind, a natural decision, since he married Berry Gordy's daughter, Hazel (which, ironically, made the Jacksons literally part of the Gordy family). The group remained a quintet, since youngest brother Randy by then was a full-fledged member, but the name was changed to the Jacksons.

The Jacksons' initial album, *The Jacksons,* (produced by the Philadelphia team of Kenny Gamble and Leon Huff) was an effective collection whose first single release, "Enjoy Yourself," made the national top 10 and earned a gold-record award on February 10, 1977. The album followed suit on April 5, 1977. Their next LP was *Goin' Places* (late 1977), an effort in which the Jacksons took on new responsibilities. They worked as co-producers with Gamble and Huff and also wrote two of the songs: "Do What You Want" and "Different Kind of Lady." The album was a well-crafted collection, but unfortunately, *Goin' Places* didn't.

The brothers turned that problem around on their next LP, *Destiny,* on which they served as sole producers and, with the exception of one track ("Blame It on the Boogie," on which writer E. Krohn collaborated with Michael and Marlon), they penned all the songs themselves. Issued in 1978, the LP proved the brothers hadn't lost their touch and deservedly went past platinum sales levels, providing the platinum single "Shake Your Body." The group followed with the multi-platinum album *Triumph* (1980). On that LP, Michael, Marlon, and Jackie shared lead vocals and Tito was featured in several extensive solo guitar passages.

The Jackson family was badly shaken in 1980 when Randy suffered severe injuries in a Los Angeles auto accident. At first, doctors thought both legs might have to be amputated and, after that was avoided, suggested he might never walk again. But Randy persevered and after intensive physical therapy, he was back on stage with the group for an extensive 1981 tour that grossed some $5.5 million in 36 cities across the U.S. The tour included a benefit concert that raised more than $100,000 for the Atlanta Children's Foundation. Before 1981 was over, the group had another hit LP for Epic: *The Jacksons Live!* with tracks recorded on the 1981 tour.

With almost all the members either involved in solo projects or considering them, many reporters suggested the 1981 tour might be the band's swan song. Indeed, Marlon fueled some of those predictions by noting the brothers could use a little sabbatical from years of concertizing, but at the same time he emphasized it was a grind they all were used to.

"Everyone thinks we started at the top [at the start of the '70s], but we traveled around for years before that—five brothers and two sisters—crammed into a Volkswagen van. We played around our home town of Gary, but we also went out to Kansas City and St. Louis and even to the Apollo Theater in New York. We'd get home at 5 in the morning a lot of times, then get up the next day and go to school. We're used to hard work."

At any rate, after that concert series, the spotlight over the next few years was mainly on the solo activities of Michael, Jermaine, and some of the Jackson sisters. Then word came out that the brothers were planning a brand new album to be released along with a massive tour featuring all six of the boys together again. By 1984, Jermaine's contract with Motown was up and he had decided to go to another label, a move that freed him to tour with the Jacksons once more. He explained: "I wanted to have the freedom to keep scouting talent [noting he and his wife had brought acts like DeBarge and Switch to Motown], but it was rough politically to keep doing it at Motown. So I decided to move to Arista. Berry Gordy let me go because he wanted me to be happy."

It was planned to have his debut on Arista, *Jermaine Jackson,* come out about the same time as the new Jacksons LP, *Victory.* By the time he left Motown, his solo LP on that label had included *My Name is Jermaine* (gold, 1976), *Feel the Fire* (1977), *Frontiers* (1978), *Jermaine* (1980), *Let's Get Serious* (1980), and *I Like Your Style* (1981). Motown also had repackaged many of the Jackson 5 recordings over the years, beginning with the *Jackson 5 Anthology* in 1976.

Plans for the 1984 "Victory" tour were headline items in newspapers and magazines across the U.S. for months before the tour got underway July 6, 1984 in Kansas City, Missouri. The concert series, which wound up with a group of six shows at Dodger Stadium in Los Angeles in November and early December, proved a Perils-of-Pauline situation for promoter Chuck Sullivan, whose main previous experience was as an executive of the New England Patriots football team. There were constant hassles among the participants' lawyers about financial responsibilities for tour costs (including unexpected batches of unsold tickets in some locales), while the logistics of handling the tremendous amount of equipment and people involved proved mind-boggling for someone not used to large-scale rock'n'roll projects. These logistics involved putting up, tearing down, and moving 365 tons of stage, lights, and other equipment for the show and also meeting a payroll for roadies and other support personnel of some 250 people. The weekly overhead was estimated at around $1 million. There also were problems in shifting concert sites and dates when it was found that some originally booked arenas weren't large enough for economically practical audience sizes. Some of the facilities on learning of cancellations naturally threatened lawsuits.

In the early stages, the Jacksons themselves had to cope with unexpected needs to vary their lineup when problems with Jackie's knees forced him to retire from the tour just as it got started. In spite of everything, the show ran its course before record numbers of people and with overall income estimated in the $75–80 million range. (Despite that, Sullivan maintained all the unanticipated extra expenses resulted in his incurring a loss of several million dollars.) The album *Victory* was certified platinum by the RIAA and provided a number of hit singles, including "Body" (written, produced, and sung by Marlon).

Once more when the tour was over, writers conjectured it might be the Jacksons' last. But Marlon, even as he announced plans for a film career, said the door wasn't closed. "We'll always be together as a group. That's where it all started. That's the mothership. Film is in my future, but music is in my blood."

Meanwhile, new solo albums continued to come out, including Jermaine's *Precious Moments* on Arista (1986) and Marlon's *Baby Tonight* on Capitol (1987).

JAGGER, MICK: *Singer, band leader, songwriter, actor, record producer. Born Dartford, Kent, England, July 26, 1943.*

Though Mick Jagger hit the headlines around the world so often during the first two decades of his association with the Rolling Stones that some people thought he had a separate individual career, in fact he did not attempt a solo record until the winter of 1984–85. With his debut album and singles releases in 1985, he served notice that he could, if he wanted, go it alone, though he emphasized he had no plans to desert his legendary group and, in fact, spent much of 1985 working with other Stones members on a new band album.

When asked by writer Lisa Robinson why after 20 years with the Rolling Stones he finally chose to do a solo LP, he responded that one reason was that the Stones' old U.S. record affiliate, Atlantic, wasn't much interested in it while the band's new label, CBS, was. Why was that the case, she pursued, to which he replied: "I don't know, they just weren't. Probably didn't think I could do it. But CBS was very interested, and they made that clear when they signed the contract; they wanted me to do at least two solo albums. And when you've got people who are very confident in that part of you, it makes you feel more confident."

The move, he told Christopher Connelly of *Rolling Stone* (February 14, 1985), had nothing to do with dissatisfaction with his Rolling Stones activities. "It wasn't from any great frustration. I was, you know, feeling in the mood for it, and I thought: 'Stop talking about the solo record you might do one day.' I didn't think about it too much, to be honest. I just went ahead and did it."

He stressed he discussed it with other Stones members as soon as he decided to start the project, but they could hardly protest too much since most had already done considerable solo work. Mick told Connelly: "They [the other members] know contractually that CBS had said, 'We want you to do this,' and I said, 'Well, do you mind if I take the time out?' For instance, Bill [Wyman] has done like four solo albums, and Ronnie [Wood] has done a lot of solo projects. [Wood's solo LPs after his becoming a member of the Stones included *Mahoney's Last Stand* (Atco, 1976), *Gimme Some Neck* (Columbia, 1979), and *1234* (Columbia, 1981).] And Keith [Richard], he's done, maybe not very many records, but he did the [New Barbarians] tour with Ronnie." The others, he said, said: "Do it, but do a good job of it."

Jagger lined up a roster of superstar musicians to back him. He told Connelly: "I started off with Sly [Dunbar] and Robbie [Shakespeare] [of the Wailers fame] and all the people I knew really. We had Jeff Beck, and we had Jan Hammer at the beginning, and I had Chuck Leavell and Eddie Martinez—he's a guitar player. So that was sort of the beginning, and then later on we had Michael Shrieve on one track. And on the ballad ['Hard Woman'] we had Tony Thompson—he was with [the disco group] Chic. Herbie Hancock did some overdubs. And Pete Townshend played acoustic guitar."

The platinum album, *She's the Boss*, came out in February 1985. It went platinum even though Jagger did not do an intensive live tour to support it.

The debut single release, "Just Another Night," made the *Billboard* top 10. The next single, "Lucky in Love"/"Running Out of Luck," was issued in both 7-inch and 12-inch versions. As a conventional single, "Lucky in Love" was high on the charts in early summer.

Jagger also marked the year with a memorable appearance on the Philadelphia segment of the Live Aid benefit for Africa project organized by Bob Geldof. (*See Boomtown Rats, The.*) To the delight of the huge live audience and hundreds of millions of TV viewers, he joined Tina Turner in a sizzling duet that was one of the highlights of the program.

In late October, Jagger was represented by a new computer-generated video for a revised version of the song "Hard Woman." This was a new arrangement of the song, not the track included on the album, in which the music portion featured, besides Jagger, such musicians as guitarists Rob Hyman on keyboards and Eric Bazilian, both from the Hooters; Will Lee of the David Letterman Show band on bass guitar; Peter Wood on keyboards; guitarist Rick DiFonzo; and drummer Anton Fig. The visual images were the first of their kind to be generated by a supercomputer using a process developed by Digital Productions called Digital Scene Simulation.

Of course, while *She's the Boss* was his first solo album, Mick had taken occasional flings at individual work in other areas, such as film acting. His roles included playing a rock singer in the 1970s film *Performance* and an outlaw in the movie *Ned Kelly*. He also worked in fits and starts on an autobiography, a project hobbled by dissatisfaction with his co-authors. That book reached first-draft stage in late 1984, but Jagger was unhappy with the results and fired his co-writer, John Ryle, deputy literary editor of the *Sunday Times of London*.

He still intended to complete the book, he told Connelly of *Rolling Stone,* but it had to go together properly. "I didn't really want to put out the book in the way that the first draft was. It was too flip.

"I didn't have any problem remembering [about my life]. I mean, you can't remember every detail. What's more difficult to put into perspective is life in the '70s. Much easier to put the '60s into perspective than the '70s.''

About his view of the '60s, he told Connelly: "Obviously it's a personal one. But also one of the society I found myself in when I was growing up. I was kind of a late grower-up. People didn't grow up at 15 then, they grew up when they were 20. The way that they changed, and the way that America changed, and your own personal experiences, and how that worked, and also the overview you've got now: what society was like and all those millions of examples of things that makes the mosaic up for the real picture."

He could sort out many of those factors now, he claimed, but one problem with the '70s, he commented, was that it's closer "and it was a time of retrenchment a little bit."

In the fall of 1987, Columbia issued Mick's second solo album *Primitive Cool,* an album that showed he could, indeed, provide an above-average LP without support from his famous band. In early 1988, Jagger generated tremendous enthusiasm with Japanese fans, who made tickets to his concerts there some of the hottest items of the entertainment year. (*See Faithfull, Marianne; Rolling Stones, The.*)

JAMES, ETTA: *Singer. Born Los Angeles, California, c. mid-1930s.*

A singer with great vitality and the ability to modify her style as musical trends changed, Etta James remained a favorite of rhythm & blues followers for decades. Among R&B female vocalists, only Dinah Washington and Ruth Brown had more top 10 hits than Etta over the period from the early 1950s to the early 1970s.

Like dozens of other soul stars, Etta was brought into the spotlight by Johnny Otis. (*See Otis, Johnny.*) As Johnny recounts the incident: "I was playing the Fillmore in San Francisco in the early 1950s. That was before it became a rock center; it was a ghetto theater then. We got there early and I went to my hotel room to rest. My manager called the room and said: 'There's a girl here who wants to sing for you.' I said: 'Tell her to see me at the theater.' She grabbed the phone and said: 'No! I want to sing for you now.' So I said come on up. She arrived with two little girls with her. After she sang a little, I was so impressed I called her mother and said I was taking Etta to Los Angeles with me. She stayed at my house and we wrote 'Roll with Me Henry' and it became a hit.''

That song was an answer to Hank Ballard's 1954 hit, "Work with Me, Annie," which has such lines as "Annie please don't cheat/Give me all my meat." (*See Ballard, Hank.*) Etta's song was slightly less off-color than "Annie." The opening verse ended: "Roll with me, Henry/You better roll it while the rollin' is on." The record was released by Modern Records (owned by the Bihari Brothers of Los Angeles, who recorded much of Otis's material over the years) under the title "Wallflower" and became a top 10 R&B hit in 1955. A milder cover version ("Dance with Me Henry" by white singer Georgia Gibbs) eventually gained the lion's share of the record sales.

During the mid-1950s, Etta became one of the most popular members of Johnny Otis's show. Her subsequent hits on the Modern Label included "Good Rockin' Daddy" and "Most of All."

In the late 1950s, though Etta remained popular with R&B fans as a performer, her recording success toned down considerably. At the start of the 1960s, however, she signed a contract with Chicago-based Chess Records and began a new and even more rewarding phase of her career. As a solo artist in 1960, she had such best-sellers on the R&B charts as "All I Could Do Was Cry" and "My Dearest Darling" on Chess and its Argo subsidiary. She also teamed with Harvey Fuqua, formerly of Harvey and the Moonglows, for the top duo of the year in soul. Their Chess single "If I Can't Have You" reached the top five on the soul charts and made the general charts as well. (*See Moonglows, The.*) With Argo, Etta demonstrated a style of singing somewhat different from her earlier efforts. It had considerably more gospel and blues content rather than the rough, strident inflections of old-time R&B.

During the first half of the '60s, Etta's name was rarely off the charts. In 1961, she had the top 10 hits "At Last" and "Trust in Me" and, in 1962, "Something's Got a Hold on Me" and "Stop the Wedding." In 1963, she had one of her greatest successes, "Pushover."

During the mid-1960s, Etta's career was plagued by drug addiction that sometimes sidelined her to her home in Los Angeles for long periods of time. She fought back and managed to keep going, despite occasional lapses, gaining such hits as "Tell Mama" (1968) and "Loser's Weepers" (1970), both on another Chess subsidiary, Cadet.

Etta had many Cadet albums that made the charts. Her LPs included *At Last* and *Second Time Around* (1961); *Etta James' Top Ten,* and *Etta James Sings for Lovers* (1963); *Etta James Rocks the House* (1964); *Queen of Soul* (1965); *Call My Name* (1967); and *Funk* (1970). One of her best (though flawed) collections came out in 1971. Called *Peaches,* the Chess LP of some of her early recordings demonstrated why the emotion she could pack into her husky, powerful voice made her one of the truly awesome performers in R&B. But as she also proved in concerts and on some of her other albums, she was far more than a rhythm & blues singer; she handled rock, pop, and even country & western with equally fine results.

But while *Peaches* chronicled her beginnings, renewed problems with drugs in the early 1970s threatened to write an early end to her career. Fortunately, she entered a drug rehabilitation center in late 1972 for a year and a half.

She then completed a new album on Chess, *Come a Little Closer* (1974), which unfortunately showed arrangements straining for commercial rather than creative success. Her last album for Chess, *Etta is Betta than Evah,* (1977), saw her focusing on raw R&B stylings, but again best-seller status eluded her. Still she remained a shining star to her musical peers, including Van Morrison (with whom she toured in the mid-1970s) and the jazz/R&B fans who gave her thunderous ovations for her sets at the Montreaux and Monterey Jazz Festivals of those years.

After completing her 1977 album for Chess, she was contractually free to seek a new alignment and she signed with Warner Brothers. With famed producer Jerry Wexler supervising, she completed one of her freshest post-'60s LPs, *Deep in the Night* (April 1978). Though critically applauded, the album wasn't a best-seller. Etta continued to play mostly small clubs and sing at special concerts in the late 1970s and early 1980s, but most music fans were hardly aware she was still active. Then in the mid-1980s, things began to pick up for her again with new opportunities in movies and TV.

She told reporter Don Waller in late 1985: "What's happening is that all the kids who grew up listening to me on their transistor radios in the '50s and '60s are now working for Steven Spielberg and network television and all that and they remember me from my records."

She said that with a smile, but it wasn't far from the truth. Among other things, the soundtrack for Spielberg's film hit *Back to the Future* included her vocal of "Wallflower." She also recorded "The Blues Don't Leave" for the film *Heartbreakers.* Another mid-1980s break was a bar scene in an episode of the TV series "Insiders" that focused on her singing.

Still, she wasn't the mass-audience favorite she should have been and she agreed her long bout with heroin was a factor. She told Waller she had been able to stay clean for over ten years. "I used to count how long I'd been off the stuff and now I don't. How did I do it? The judge sent me to a shrink 'cause I kept writing bad checks and I told him what was wrong. So they sent me to detox and helped me see that it was gonna be a matter of life or death, and I decided I wasn't gonna kill myself.

"That's why I don't care to associate with a lot of other entertainers. It's not the drugs, it's just that I've heard all that jive talk and ego games for too long. When I first started out, touring was fun— ridin' those old buses, eatin' sardines out of a can, white folks runnin' you out of town, and everybody talkin' about it for six months afterward."

JAMES, RICK: *Singer, guitarist, songwriter, record producer. Born Buffalo, New York, February 1, 1952.*

Rick James' earliest experience in pop music was as a rock performer and band leader, but he was never able to make much progress in rock. He attributed this in part to the categorization of performers that tended to exclude blacks from rock outlets. He finally focused on black music instead and proceeded to edge out long-established artists such as Bootsy Collins and George Clinton (mentor of Parliament-Funkadelic) for the unofficial title King of

Funk in the 1980s. The party music he crafted for the 1980s, though, proved able to cross over and win favor with white record buyers as well.

James, born and raised in upstate New York, was an ardent rock fan throughout his teens. His excellent instrumental skills gained him positions with a series of groups in the Buffalo area. Venturing north of the border during the mid-1960s, he formed his own band, the Mynah Birds, that for a time had as lead singer none other than Neil Young. (*See Buffalo, Springfield, The; Crosby, Stills, Nash & Young; Young, Neil.*) Later he moved from rock into the jazz field for a while, forming the band White Cane, which recorded an album for MGM Records.

Neither rock nor jazz proved very rewarding economically for Rick so in the early 1970s he opted for a staff writing job with Motown that promised a more reliable income. His work with Motown exposed him to a wide range of soloists and groups in the R&B, soul, and funk areas. Funk became increasingly appealing and he started to work out new songs he envisioned performing with a group of his own. As a Motown employee, he had access to record executives who listened to some of his demos and agreed to give him a chance to record.

His very first LP for the company, issued on its Gordy subsidiary, proved a bonanza for Rick and Motown. Released in 1978, the album *Come and Get It* became a best-seller on both black music and pop charts. Helping spark interest in the LP was the mushrooming disco use of the single "You and I" from the album. By 1979, the album was well past worldwide platinum levels with sales of over 2 million copies. With his group, the Stone City Band, he came on equally strong in 1979 with two listenable and danceable LPs: *Bustin' out of L Seven* (which spawned the hit single "Bustin' Out") and *Fire It Up. Fire It Up* stayed on soul charts into 1980 when Rick had another top 10 release on Gordy, *Garden of Love*. During 1980, he had four charted singles on soul lists: "Fool on the Street," "Love Gun," "Come into My Life," and "Big Time." Before the year was out, he had another album on the lists, *In 'n' Out*. James also worked as a producer for other artists such as Teena Marie. (*See Teena Marie.*)

His stage shows, exciting affairs where James dazzled onlookers with multicolored outfits and an aura of wild abandon in his performing gyrations, made him one of the best draws on the black music circuit. However, he cautioned Dennis Hunt of the *Los Angeles Times* (July 26, 1981) not to confuse show business with reality. "That's an image I created to go with the music, which is glitter funk. People think I'm into lunacy and craziness and wild parties, but I'm not. I'm basically a quiet, simple guy. I live on a ranch in upstate New York [near Buffalo] with my mother and my horses. I don't like being bothered by a lot of people."

Garden of Love, essentially a ballad collection, though certified gold, was nowhere near the commercial success of some of its predecessors so some industry observers thought James' career might be slowing down. He proved them wrong with his next release, the platinum *Street Songs* (1981). Reviewing the album in the *Los Angeles Times,* Connie Johnson commented: "*Street Songs* is James' strongest, most audacious album yet. It gives a perfunctory, surface glance at ghetto life, but what it lacks in insight it makes up for in sheer spirit. One of the most intriguing tracks is 'Mister Policeman,' since James rarely makes this kind of statement about society's ills. It's doubly intriguing in that one's first inclination is to dance to its rhythm-heavy song rather than concentrate on its lyrics about brutality in the name of law and order."

Besides his hit album, Rick had more hit singles on the charts in 1981: "Give It to Me Baby" and "Super Freak." Despite all that success, James still longed for a return to his old rock roots. He complained to Dennis Hunt: "There are too many barriers that keep blacks out of rock. It's hard to pinpoint them because they're very subtle and insidious. Let's face it. Rock is white music. The fans are mostly white. It's so tough for blacks to break into the white domain that most of us don't really bother.

"I know one problem. Rock stars are kids' heroes and I don't think a lot of white parents in Wyoming and Montana want pictures of black rock singers in their kids' bedrooms. It's too threatening. They'd rather see Andy Gibb up on those walls."

He said he had a stockpile of rock songs written in anticipation of eventually recording such an album, but it would have to wait until he stopped touring. "To go on the road you need a big core of fans," he told Hunt. "Now my fans are black and I have to give them what they want. If I recorded a rock album and went on tour, they wouldn't come and see me. I'd need the support of the white rock fans and I wouldn't get it right away. I don't want to get into rock now because I don't want to give up my black audience."

He also stressed he valued his reputation as a funk writer and artist. "The other funk [of people such as George Clinton and Bootsy Collins] is real silly. That's what has killed a lot of funk groups. . . . I don't like that Silly-Putty kind of music myself. I can't write anything that's babble. I write songs that have something meaningful to say. There's something in my songs, even the ones that are a little silly, that makes people think."

Perhaps unwilling to sacrifice his standing in funk, through the mid-1980s Rick didn't come out with his rock material, but continued as a best-selling soul/R&B artist. From 1982 through 1987, his albums were rarely absent from black music or pop charts and most eventually went gold or better.

He followed *Street Songs* with the LPs *The Boys Are Back* and *Throwin' Down*. The latter won a gold-record award. The gold album *Cold Blooded* (1983) made both black music and pop lists, spawning several chart singles including "Bring the Freak Out." Among his four charted singles were two that reached top positions on black music charts: "Standing on the Top" (recorded with the Temptations) and "Dance With Me." (*See Temptations, The.*) His 1984 hits included the LP *Reflections* and singles "You Turn Me On" and "17." His album *Glow* was among the top 50 black music releases of 1985. In 1986, Gordy Records issued his LP *The Flag*.

Rick continued to be outspoken about the plight of black artists in the context of the white-dominated entertainment establishment. Speaking to the press after he and Grace Jones had acted as presenters during one of the Grammy telecasts in the mid-1980s, Rick and Grace pointed out that their kind of videos were being frozen out of most coverage on MTV and other music video channels or programs. While the parties so accused denied the charge, the use of videos by black artists did appear to rise soon after James and Jones' statement was reported in the newspapers and on TV and radio news. (*See Jones, Grace.*)

JAMES, TOMMY; TOMMY JAMES AND THE SHONDELLS: *Singer, guitarist, songwriter, band leader. Born Dayton, Ohio, April 29, 1947. Shondell's personnel (1969): Ronnie Rosman, Mike Vale, Eddie Gray, Peter Lucia.*

An overdose of drugs—a not unusual story in popular music—felled Tommy James in 1970. It ended the story of Tommy James and the Shondells, one of the most consistently successful groups of the late 1960s, but not the career of James himself. Luckier than a number of other stars, Tommy managed to cheat death and come back as a solo performer.

James was in his early twenties when he collapsed on stage in Alabama in early 1970, but he had been performing professionally for a decade. He had become an ardent music fan well before his tenth birthday, starting with a gift from his mother of a phonograph and a pop single, "Sh-Boom." He asked for and got some more records, supplementing them with hours of listening to the stars of the new rock phenomenon on the radio. Young Tommy was only nine when he got his first guitar and it was not too much longer before he could play it well enough to perform at parties and school dances.

When he was 12, he formed a group that called itself the Shondells. They started playing for school dances, getting their first paying job for $11 at the local American Legion Post. For the next half-dozen years, James and the Shondells kept at it, taking whatever work they could find in their home area. The group occasionally cut records for small labels, including one called "Hanky Panky" in 1960. Released on the small Snap label, the single was sent to a number of disc jockeys in Midwestern cities, but little happened with it. Some of the other songs recorded in the group's early years came out on the Louisianne label as an LP titled *At the Saturday Hop*.

The group was still working bar dates at an average salary of $15 per musician per night when fate took a hand. A disc jockey at KDKA in Pittsburgh found a five-year-old copy of "Hanky Panky" in a pile of records, played it on his program, and found that the audience liked it. The record became the most requested single at the station. Record stores sought out Snap Records and flooded the firm with orders for 80,000 copies in Pittsburgh alone in 10 days. James and his group were tracked down and brought to Pittsburgh, where they played major clubs for $3,000 a performance. Roulette Records executives rushed out from New York to acquire the rights to "Hanky Panky" and to sign the group.

Within a few months, Roulette watched the single soar to number one nationally (July 16 and 23, 1966). The LP of the same title, released later in the year, also was a hit. James and the Shondells proved it was no fluke by placing more singles on hit lists for Roulette, four more in 1966 alone. Most of these, as well as the string of successive chart singles that totaled 26 by 1970 (14 that made the *Billboard* top 40), were co-written by James and his long-time friend, Bob King. Of their nine LPs released from 1966 to 1970 on Roulette, two were gold-record award winners and the rest sold well over the half-million–dollar mark each.

In 1967, the group had a national single hit, "I Think We're Alone Now," that many critics cited as the record that started the bubble-gum trend of the late '60s. In 1968, the group had a top 10 single, "Mony, Mony." In 1969, the group had its greatest year ever with top 10 hits "Crystal Blue Persuasion" and "Sweet Cherry Wine" while "Crimson and Clover" (co-written by James and band member Peter Lucia) was number one on *Billboard* charts the weeks of February 1 and 8, 1969, selling over 5½ million copies by 1971, according to Roulette Records. The Shondells in 1969 comprised Ronnie Rosman on organ, Mike Vale on bass, Eddie Gray on guitar, and Peter Lucia on drums.

Despite all the acclaim, Tommy James found life ever more difficult. He had started taking drugs well before 1970, and had gone on to harder and harder compounds in ever greater amounts. One reason for the habit was the steady grind of one-night stands. "After awhile," he recalled, "we were playing five nights a week without a break, not even making that much money, what with the expenses of touring, just going all the time. Sooner or later something had to give—me."

After he collapsed in Alabama, at least one doctor thought he might not recover. However, after some weeks in the hospital, Tommy moved to his upstate New York farm to recuperate. He disbanded the Shondells and tried to put the music business out of his mind for a while. "I just took off, doing nothing. Sleeping. Sitting and getting stronger. Not even writing for a while. Then I began to think about my future, where I was going and for what. One thing I knew. I wanted out of the image of Tommy James and the Shondells. I wasn't a teenager anymore. I had to grow."

By the end of 1970, James felt in sufficient control of himself to go back to work. With Bob King, he started writing new material and followed up with studio sessions that led to release of his first individual single, *Draggin' the Line*. Issued in the spring of 1971, it became a top 10 hit in July. His first solo LP, *Christian of the World*, was released soon after. On both records, he was supported by various groups of session musicians. For his concerts, which were planned to provide a less hectic schedule than before, the goal was to have a 10-man band that did not necessarily remain the same from performance to performance.

In the fall, James' second single, "I'm Comin' Home," showed up on the charts, indicating he could still command a strong following with his new approach to rock music. In 1972, he made the charts with still more Roulette Records singles: "Cat's Eye in the Window," "Celebration," "Love Song," "Nothing to Hide," and "Tell 'em Willie Boy's A-comin'." After that, though, his Roulette releases found less interest and he left the label during 1974. (While he still was on the label, Roulette issued an excellent anthology album, the 1971 *Best of Tommy James*.)

In the mid-1970s, he signed with Berkeley, California–based Fantasy Records, which issued a number of new singles and LPs that didn't further his career much. The LPs included *In Touch* (1976) and *Midnight Rider* (1977). At the end of the decade, he switched to another label, Millennium, which issued *Three Times in Love* (1980) and *Easy to Love* (1981). He showed he still could hold the attention of large numbers of music fans with several chart singles, leading off with the top 20 "Three Times in Love" (1980). In 1982, Joan Jett and the Black-

hearts released their version of Tommy's "Crimson and Clover," a single that made the *Billboard* top 10. (*See Jett, Joan.*)

JAN AND DEAN: *Vocal duo, songwriters. Jan Berry, born Los Angeles, California, April 2, 1941; Dean Torrence, born Los Angeles, California, March 10, 1940.*

In the 1950s, rock'n'roll moved to center stage mainly because of the influence of country-bred artists from the American South and Southwest. In the 1960s, the U.S. contribution to this music began to have a decidedly West Coast flavor, starting with the surfing music of the early 1960s and continuing with the folk-rock wave originating in San Francisco in the mid-'60s.

If the hippie pads of Haight-Ashbury were the breeding ground for folk-rock, then the sun-soaked sands of Southern California brought surfing music to the fore. Considerably more carefree than the often drug-related music that overwhelmed surf rock from 1965 on, the hits of such artists as Jan and Dean and the Beach Boys were concerned mainly with love, teenage hobbies (such as hot rods and motorcycles), and the pleasure of riding a towering Pacific Coast wave.

Both Jan Berry and Dean Torrence were born and raised in Southern California. They spent many boyhood hours on local beaches, but not to the extent that they ignored other things, such as school and music. They found a mutual interest in music while attending high school in the Los Angeles region. Influenced by the early rock of the mid-'50s, they sometimes joined together to sing songs gleaned from listening to the radio and records. Torrence, who had taken piano lessons as a child, provided the accompaniment.

By their mid-teens, Jan and Dean were collaborating on original compositions. They assembled recording equipment in Jan's garage and in 1958 made demonstration records such as "Jennie Lee" that later gained them some notice. Their work was halted temporarily when Dean, after finishing high school, spent six months in the Army. When he returned, though, they went back and prepared a series of demonstration tapes that won them a contract from Challenge Records.

Neither of them thought of music as a full-time career. While recording such songs as "Baby Talk," "There's a Girl," and "Heart and Soul" for Challenge, they continued their education. Jan majored in art and design at the University of Southern California, while Dean took premed courses at the University of California at Los Angeles. They managed to find time to perform nights and weekends in local clubs, sometimes traveling to engagements in outlying cities. Combining education and music became a little more difficult in 1961 when they left Challenge to sign with Liberty Records. Soon after the switch, they turned out a hit single, "Linda", and then began to gain a national reputation with a series of surfing songs. In 1963, they became one of the most successful teams of the year with a multimillion selling single, "Surf City," number one in *Billboard* July 20 and 27, 1963.

Increasing demands for in-person appearances caused Jan to concentrate on music without gaining his degree from USC. Dean dropped his medical plans, but did manage to gain his bachelor's degree in architecture.

Their LP output on Liberty included *Golden Hits* (1962); *Jan & Dean Take Linda Surfin'* and *Surf City* (1963); *Drag City, Dead Man's Curve, Little Old Lady,* and *Ride the Wild Surf* (1964); *Command Performance* and *Golden Hits, Vol. 2* (1965); and *Folk'n'Roll, Jan & Dean Meet Batman, Filet of Soul, Popsicle,* and *Golden Hits, Vol. 3* (1966). In 1967, they were also represented on the Sunset label with *Jan and Dean* and on Columbia Records with *Save for a Rainy Day*. United Artists issued a two-album retrospective of the duo's career, *Legendary Masters No. 3* (1974) and the two-disc *Gotta Take That One Last Ride* (1974). The team's glory days came to a close after Jan was injured in an auto accident the night of April 19, 1966. While driving along the Sunset Strip in Lost Angeles, he lost control of his car and ran into a parked truck. Taken to UCLA Medical Center in critical condition, he was in a coma for months. For a long time, he hovered near death, then spent years recovering from partial paralysis due to the mishap. At the start of the 1970s, he had managed to recover to a considerable extent, though he never was completely cured. Meanwhile Dean had gone on to achieve success on the business side of the music industry. He became head of Kittyhawk Graphics Los Angeles, which provided a large percentage of the album covers used for records produced in the western part of the U.S.

Jan surprised the doctors by recovering enough to ask Torrence to try to revive their act. Their first efforts in 1973 weren't too promising. They tried to give in-person performances where they lip-synched rather than sang their old hits. Once audiences realized what was going on, they strongly expressed their disfavor. Although Jan went on to record some new material in the mid-1970s, the act seemed permanently over. Dean concentrated on his business, though he did get together with a friend to outline a script for a film biography of the Jan and Dean story. For a long time nothing happened, but it finally was made into a movie for TV, *Dead Man's Curve,* presented on CBS in 1978.

The film revived interest in the duo and they were asked to tour with the Beach Boys. This time Jan and Dean were able to do their own singing without recorded help and audiences were on their side. During the late 1970s and through the late 1980s, Jan and Dean found doors open for concert work, mostly in smaller clubs or as part of rock revival shows. Dean was only willing to devote part of the year to such appearances, but Jan continued to work much of the remaining time as a solo performer. Their October 3, 1981 show at My Father's Place in Roslyn, Long Island, New York was taped for release on *One Summer Night/Live* on Rhino Records.

During the mid-1980s, Berry performed at two benefit concerts to help raise funds for programs developed by Disabilities Unlimited Inc., a firm that administers government funded rehabilitation facilities. One project the company brought to fruition in early 1987 was a new vocational center for brain-injured people in Downey, California, called the Jan Berry Center for the Brain-Injured.

JAY AND THE AMERICANS: *Vocal group, record producers. All born Brooklyn, New York; Jay Black, November 2; Kenny Vance, December 9; Sandy Yaguda, January 30; Marty Sanders, February 28.*

One of the relative handful of early '60s pop groups that stayed together from early in its career until over a decade later, Jay and the Americans showed stability in their performing successes as well.

All four members were born and raised in Brooklyn. One of them, Sandy Yaguda, completed work on his degree in business administration before joining the group. They came together in late 1961 to form the group called Jay and the Americans, with Jay Black handling lead vocal chores.

For several months, they worked clubs in and around New York while working on audition recordings in their free time. Their material was presented to United Artists Records early in 1962 and they signed soon after. Their first single, "She Cried," became a top 10 hit in the U.S. The LP of the same title also made the charts. They later had top 10 hits with "Come a Little Bit Closer" (1964) and "Cara Mia" (1965). Other well-received songs (some written by Marty Sanders) were "Only in America," "Let's Lock the Door (and Throw Away the Key)," "Think of the Good Times," "Sunday and Me," and "Livin' above Your Head." Accompanying their singles success in the mid-'60s were such United Artists LPs as *At the Cafe Wha?* (1963) *Come a Little Bit Closer,* and *Blockbusters,* and *Greatest Hits, Volume 1* (1965); *Sunday and Me* and *Livin' above Your Head* (1966); and *Try Some of This* and *Greatest Hits, Volume 2* (1967).

In the late '60s, the group members began to move strongly into the business end of the field. They established their own music publishing, artist management, TV and radio commercials, and record production organizations. In 1969, these were brought together into a single firm, JATA Enterprises, "JATA" being an acronym for Jay and the Americans.

One of the first record-production efforts of JATA was the group's single, "This Magic Moment" (a remake of the Drifters' 1960 hit). The record brought the group its greatest success to date, selling over a million copies for a gold-record award. Though not reaching gold status, the JATA-produced LP *Sands of Time* also made the charts in 1969 and sold several hundred thousand copies. The group opened the '70s with such hits as "Walkin' in the Rain," in the top 20 in January 1970, and the LP *Wax Museum* (spring 1970). The follow-up, *Wax Museum, Volume 2,* was far less successful as were other early '70s releases. By the mid-1970s, the group no longer was a factor in pop music.

JEFFERSON AIRPLANE; JEFFERSON STARSHIP; STARSHIP; KBC BAND: *Vocal and instrumental groups. Jefferson Airplane members (1966–71): Marty Balin, born Cincinnati, Ohio, January 30, 1943; Grace Slick, born Evanston, Illinois, October 30, 1939 (information in RCA bio material in the mid-1960s called out Chicago as place of birth on October 30, 1943); Paul Kantner, born San Francisco, California, March 12, 1942; Spencer Dryden, born New York, New York, April 7, 1943; Jack Casady, born Washington D.C., April 13, 1944; Jorma Kaukonen, born Washington, D.C., December 23, 1940. (Original female vocalist Signe Tory Anderson, born Seattle, Washington, 1941, replaced by Grace Slick in 1966. Original drummer Skip Spence, born Windsor, Ontario, Canada, replaced by Spencer Dryden in 1966.) Dryden replaced by Joey Covington in 1971. Covington replaced in 1972 by John Barbata, born upstate New York. Balin left in 1971. Papa John Creach, born Beaver Falls, Pennsylvania, May 18, 1917, added in 1971. David Freiberg, born Boston, Massachusetts, August 24, 1938, added in late 1972. Airplane disbanded by 1974, replaced by* Hot Tuna *(Kaukonen, Casady, Creach, Sammy Piazza, born Waco, Texas) and by* Jefferson Starship, *original members Kantner; Slick; Creach; Freiberg; Barbata; Pete Sears; Craig Chaquico,*

born c. 1955. Balin joined in 1975 and Creach left that year. Slick left in 1978, Balin in 1979. Balin replaced by Mickey Thomas, born c. 1950. Group in 1979 comprised Thomas, Kantner, Sears, Freiberg, Chaquico, Aynsley Dunbar. Slick returned in 1981. Dunbar left in 1982, replaced by Donny Baldwin. Kantner left in 1984, Freiberg in 1985. Band reorganized in 1985 as STARSHIP. *Members as of 1986 comprised Slick, Thomas, Sears, Chaquico, Baldwin. Kantner, Balin, and Casady formed KBC Band, mid-1980s.* *

Wild, unruly, and unpredictable as individuals, the original members of the Jefferson Airplane nevertheless were perfectly cohesive as a group. Thus, despite the usual behind-the-scenes bickering normal to most rock bands, Jefferson Airplane continued as a group for a surprisingly long time, providing some of the classic rock of the 1960s. The Airplane, like its name, flew high in many ways, providing an imaginative, but sometimes nerve-jarring acid-raga-blues-folk-rock sound that well represented the range of feelings about society felt by most of its peer group. The original members began to go different ways in the '70s, with some founding a new alignment, Jefferson Starship. In the mid-1980s, another offshoot, the Starship, though considered a dinosaur by many critics, developed surprising rapport with new generations of fans.

The original band had its roots in the rapidly evolving folk-rock music indigenous to San Francisco's Haight-Ashbury during its hippie period. The founder of the band, Marty Balin, was born in Ohio, but grew up in California, where he first exhibited talent as a performer in high school. In the early 1960s, he began his show business career as a singer and dancer in touring comedy shows. However, his interest was steadily drawn to the new folk sounds of Bob Dylan and the dynamic growth of rock music in the Bay Area. He began to learn guitar and harmonica and, in 1963, got his first job with a rock group. However, the music played by the band wasn't to his liking so he decided to start his own aggregation. His resolve strengthened when he met San Francisco–born Paul Kantner, a talented guitarist and five-string banjoist playing folk music in a local club. Kantner, who started playing guitar at 17, had completed three years of college before deciding to concentrate on music. Balin then contacted Signe Anderson (born in Seattle, but raised in

---

*Casady and Kaukonen quotes from personal interview with Irwin Stambler.

328

Portland, Oregon), with the idea that the addition of a woman would provide something different from the general run of rock groups appearing in the region. At the same time, Kantner brought in a friend, Jorma Kaukonen, whom he felt was the best lead guitarist available.

Kaukonen, the son of a member of the U.S. Foreign Service, had traveled widely with his family in his early years. By the early 1960s, he had moved to the Bay Area where he earned a degree in sociology from Santa Clara University. Kaukonen, heavily jazz- and blues-oriented, had picked up guitar in 1956 and played with various local groups ranging from folk to rock bands.

Jorma, in turn, recommended a former Washington, D.C., acquaintance, Jack Casady, as a first-rate bass guitarist. Casady, who had started guitar at 14, had taken lessons in classical music as well as playing jazz and blues during his teens with Washington-area bands. After receiving the invitation from Kaukonen, Casady promptly packed his bags and moved to the West Coast.

By early 1965, the group was performing both rock numbers by then famous artists and originals composed by Airplane members. During a mid-1965 engagement at a local folk-rock club called the Matrix, Balin met Spencer Dryden. Dryden, born in New York, had joined the migration westward to the Los Angeles area, where he finished high school and entered Valley Junior College and, later, Occidental College. He had begun playing drums and vibraharp at 10, playing in local groups when he was 15. By the time he met Balin, he had worked for IBM, been a music teacher and an actor, and had considerable credits as a jazz drummer, accompanying Charles Lloyd, Bobby Hutcherson, and Paul Bley. Balin eventually asked Dryden to replace Skip Spence, who joined Moby Grape.

With Dryden as regular drummer, the group sound coalesced, at first around soft rock featuring folk-type melodies. Several months later, when Bill Graham had his highly successful benefit concerts for the San Francisco Mime Troupe at the Fillmore Auditorium, the Airplane was one of the showstoppers. When Graham started his career as a rock impresario at the Fillmore in early 1966, the Airplane was one of the first featured bands to play there. (Graham became their manager and supervised some of their first steps to international renown.) As 1966 progressed, the group's fame spread throughout the world with articles in major news publications citing the Airplane as the most important element in the San Francisco Sound, a sound *Time* called "a cheerful synthesis of Beatles and blues, folk and country, liberally sprinkled with Indian raga."

For a while, major record companies had hung back from signing some of the increasingly heralded San Francisco groups because of the close interlocking of the music and many of the musicians with the hippie drug culture. However, as the Airplane's reputation grew, it couldn't be ignored and RCA Victor outbid several competitors. The first album, *Jefferson Airplane Takes Off*, did just that after its release in August 1966, moving onto the hit charts and staying there for many months.

The second LP, *Surrealistic Pillow,* released the following February, did even better and is today considered one of the most important rock albums of the decade. The album, which went gold, featured two tracks that became top 10 singles of 1967: "Somebody to Love" and "White Rabbit." A psychedelic reference to Lewis Carroll's *Alice in Wonderland,* "White Rabbit" was written by Grace Wing Slick, who had replaced Signe Anderson in late 1966. (Signe, who married soon after joining the group, had a baby in May 1966, came back to sing for a time, and then decided to retire to take care of family chores.) Grace Slick, now considered on a par with Janis Joplin as one of the greatest rock singers of all time, grew up in an upper middle class family in Chicago and worked as a model before choosing a show business career, coming to the Airplane from a group called the Great Society. Her pre-Airplane recordings of "White Rabbit" and "Somebody to Love" were repackaged on Columbia's two-disc 1971 *Grace Slick & the Great Society* (previously released as *Conspicuous Only in Its Absence* and *How It Was*). Slick's opera-influenced singing, classically-based composing, and scathing wit carried the Airplane to new heights, so much so that most people forgot there ever had been a lead female vocalist before her.

From the first Fillmore appearances on, the Airplane's career was one of almost nonstop success. Throughout the rest of the 1960s and into the 1970s, the group regularly sold gold-record quantities of its albums and singles. Some critics were unhappy with their third LP, the unfocused yet erratically brilliant *After Bathing at Baxter's* (1967). One reason may have been the change in the group's material from its early nonmessage songs, mainly concerned with love, to bitter, sharp-edged comments on man and modern society. However, fans bought the album, as they did such follow-up LPs in 1968 and 1969 as *Crown of Creation* (a gold album) and the live *Bless Its Pointed Little Head.* The gold *Volunteers* (1969) excellently captured the generation gap and political turmoil of the period. The Airplane continued to do well in the early 1970s with the retrospective *The Worst of the Jefferson Airplane* and science fiction buff Paul Kantner's own production, *Blows against the Empire,* the first LP attributed to the Jefferson Starship.

By the start of the 1970s, there were few places the group had not visited in and out of the U.S. The group was the first rock ensemble to be featured at the Monterey Jazz Festival and in 1967 was also the first to appear on NBC-TV's "Bell Telephone Hour." Typical of the praise of their work was Frank Kofsky's discussion of Jorma Kaukonen's handling of fuzz and feedback. After noting in *Jazz & Pop* (March 1968) the use of electronic guitar characteristics to hide a player's lack of talent, he concluded: "Happily, Jorma—who, if there is such a thing as the 'San Francisco Sound,' must get a large part of the credit for it—is never guilty of this sort of abuse. He employs feedback and fuzz to modify his sound, but only where it has the feeling of 'belonging,'—where that is, it appears called for and can be successfully integrated into the context.

"'Spare Change' (from the ubiquitous plea in the Haight last summer: 'Do you have any spare change?') is an excellent case in point. By judicious employment of feedback and fuzz, Jorma makes it sound as though there were several different solo voices on the track rather than a single one. . . . He is one of the few American rock guitarists who can be ranked as a peer of Cream's Eric Clapton."

In the early 1970s, there began to be some blurring of the edges of the Jefferson Airplane as a separate entity, as its members diluted their efforts by forming alternate groupings (such as bluesy Hot Tuna assembled by Casady and Kaukonen, Jefferson Starship, and the Grace Slick–Paul Kantner duo) or sitting in with other groups. In 1971, Balin left and vocalist/violinist Papa John Creach joined both the Airplane and Hot Tuna. Former Quicksilver Messenger Service star David Freiberg joined the group for the fall 1972 tour that took place just after release of the gold *Long John Silver* album. He also was represented on the live album, *30 Seconds over Winterland* (1973).

By then, the old Jefferson Airplane had fallen apart. Kaukonen and Casady had increasingly leaned toward making Hot Tuna their sole concern. Jorma recalled: "For a while we were working full-time with the Airplane, but the last tour was in 1971–72. After that Hot Tuna became an entity in itself." Casady added: "When we left, we said we'd do another concert tour, but the last one in late 1972 just didn't have the right feel. Although we were chastised for not going out on another tour in 1973, we felt the creativity of the old Airplane had stopped. Actually, Marty Balin was the first one to leave the Airplane to work by himself. His trouble was that he wasn't in tight with one or two musicians to form a band. With Jorma and myself it was different, because we had a lot in common and basically guitar and bass would work whether we had drums or not. And when we couldn't find a drummer to work with us, we worked as a duo."

After the Airplane's demise, its members' own label, Grunt, continued to issue the band's old material in new packages. These LPs (all handled by RCA Records) included *Early Flight* (1974) and *Flight Log (1966–1967)* in 1977. The latter included some tracks actually attributable to the new Jefferson Starship.

In 1974, Paul Kantner and Grace Slick put together the new band that took the name Jefferson Starship from the 1970 *Blows against the Empire* album. The group retained Creach and Freiberg from the old Airplane and added Pete Sears on bass guitar, keyboards, and vocals (skills complementing similar ones of Freiberg), teenaged Craig Chaquico on lead guitar, and John Barbata (formerly of the Turtles) on drums. (*See Turtles, The.*) The band's debut album was the gold 1974 Grunt/RCA *Dragonfly*. Marty Balin wasn't part of the new lineup then, but he sang lead on the track "Caroline," a song he co-wrote with Kantner, which also was one of the LPs best offerings. By 1975, he had returned to the group full-time, helping to make the gold album *Red Octopus*. That LP proved a solid combination of songs by him and Grace Slick, including his composition "Miracles" and Grace's "Play on Love" and "Fast Buck Freddie." "Miracles" was a top 10 hit, the first singles success in Jefferson Starship or Jefferson Airplane history.

The band toured widely in the mid-1970s and turned out platinum LPs *Spitfire* (1976) and *Earth* (1978). However, Slick was feeling the pressure of a continued hectic existence and she left the band in 1978, remaining on the sidelines until she overcame personal problems to return in 1981. By the time *Earth* was released, Creach had left to take up a solo jazz career. In 1979, Balin left and his place was taken by singer Mickey Thomas (an Elvin Bishop alumnus), who joined Kantner and the others to record the gold 1979 Grunt/RCA *Freedom at Point Zero,* an LP that was not one of the band's best efforts artistically. (*See Bishop, Elvin.*)

The reason for his 1979 departure, Balin said, was a renewal of internal dissension somewhat along the lines that caused his first split in 1971. He also complained to a reporter that he was being overworked by other members. "Not only did I write most of the songs, but I had to clean up everybody else's songs, rewriting and adding lyrics. I got tired of doing all that, especially when it was summer and I wanted to go to the beach and have a good time.'' He signed a solo contract with EMI Records, which issued his debut on the label, *Balin,* in early 1981. The LP provided a top 10 single, ''Hearts,'' and eventually earned Marty a gold-record award.

But the band, once again, managed to survive Balin's exit. Grace Slick returned to share lead vocal duties with Mickey Thomas in a group that also included Kantner, Sears, Freiberg, Chaquico, and veteran drummer Aynsley Dunbar. (*See Journey.*) The band turned out albums that regularly won RIAA gold-record certification, but fell short of the platinum levels expected for superstar groups.

The Jefferson Starship's 1980s LPs included *Modern Times* (1981), *Winds of Change* (1982), and *Nuclear Furniture* (1984). During those years, there were more roster changes. Dunbar left in 1982 and was replaced on drums by Donny Baldwin. In 1984, Paul Kantner stepped down and it was accepted that Jefferson Starship had joined the Airplane as ancient history.

There were hints that RCA executives were ready to write off any new versions. Mickey Thomas told Dennis Hunt (*Los Angeles Times,* March 16, 1986): ''RCA never came out and said we're getting old. But I'm sure they had thought and conversations about it.''

Critics didn't hide feeling the band was over the hill. Thomas told Hunt in 1986: ''We're still fighting that image. People think we're all 50 years old.'' By then, Grace Slick was well past 40, but he emphasized all the rest were ''only'' 31 to 37.

Slick and Thomas didn't want to give up and they resolved to organize a third incarnation. In 1985, with other veteran members Freiberg, Sears, Chaquico, and Baldwin, they began recording a new album. Before it was finished, Freiberg left, but in 1986, the other five were out on the road touring in support of the LP, cynically titled *Knee Deep in the Hoopla,* this time calling themselves Starship.

The new album's songs, Thomas stressed, went in a different direction. ''We had been doing too much of that heavy, message stuff, that heavy handed sci-fi stuff. We wanted to get our feet back on the ground.'' The message and sci-fi songs had, of course, been Kantner's contribution.

To everyone's surprise—and to most critics' dismay—the new material found tremendous favor with young fans. The LP became a platinum-seller and provided two number one singles: ''We Built This City (on Rock and Roll)'' and ''Sara.'' Record buyers at the time had another aggregation of Airplane alumni to consider, the KBC band, formed by Kantner, Balin, and Casady, whose debut LP, *KBC Band,* came out on Arista in 1986. In late 1987, the Starship followed *Knee Deep in Hoopla* with the album *No Protection.* The band was now pruned to Slick, Chaquico, Thomas, and Donny Johnson. By early 1988, that LP had gone platinum, but its sales lagged behind *Hoopla,* even though it included the number one hit ''Nothing's Gonna Stop Us Now.''

JEFFREYS, GARLAND: *Singer, guitarist, songwriter. Born Brooklyn, New York, c. mid-1940s.*

A brilliant songwriter and effective, if not overwhelming performer, Garland Jeffreys turned out some of the finest rock/pop recordings of the 1970s. His '70s albums, often heavy on social commentary, perhaps too heavy for many fans, remained as relevant in many ways in the 1980s as when they first appeared, while his early 1980s LPs also seemed likely to have lasting value beyond most material released in the decade. Nonetheless, as of the late 1980s, Jeffreys had not received the acclaim that had seemed his due, for reasons as hard to fathom as the nature of popular stardom itself.

Jeffreys grew up in a lower middle class section of Brooklyn; the Sheepshead Bay area near the beach locales of Brighton and Coney Island. He was of mixed ethnic background, which made his childhood considerably more traumatic than it should have been. His forebears included people of white, black, and Puerto Rican descent. When he was old enough to realize what was going on around him, he found it difficult to gain acceptance from other children in his community from any of those groups.

Living through that period, he often felt bitter and depressed, but later he felt that it had given him unique creative insights that had surfaced in his music. ''Much of the time I'm glad that I lived and experienced different worlds. It helps me understand people . . . feel what they go through just to stay alive.''

His early musical influences came from the pop and swing era of the 1940s and early 1950s: the Ink Spots, Ella Fitzgerald, Nat ''King'' Cole, Frank Sinatra, Ray Charles, and Charlie Parker. ''These were my mother's favorites and fortunately I had to listen to them too.'' He didn't pay too much attention to the rising tide of R&B and rock until the mid-1950s when he was in his early high school years and Frankie Lymon and the Teenagers became teen favorites. ''Frankie was my idol. He was my size, a little 13-year-old with a fantastic voice. I loved '50s rock'n'roll. It was part of my life.''

His interest in rock and pop continued at Syracuse University in upstate New York. He also had talent as a painter and took courses in art, literature, and language, studying in Florence, Italy, for a year in the early 1960s. He decided, however, that he preferred trying for a music career, which led him to seek out musicians such as Lou Reed, whom he had performed with in local New York bands. "I didn't give up my love for Leonardo and Vermeer, but I'd always wanted to sing and now was the time for me to rekindle that desire."

In 1966, he joined forces with Lou Reed, John Cale, and Eric Burdon of the Animals' renown to form a band that played small clubs in the New York area. (*See Animals, The; Burdon, Eric; Reed, Lou.*) Interested in concentrating more on his own original material, he left that group in 1967 to assemble his own backing group. This eventually evolved into the band Grinder's Switch, with which he recorded his first album (*Grinder's Switch*, Vanguard Records, 1969). It had little impact on the mass audience.

In 1970, he went out on his own as a solo performer, typically accompanying himself on acoustic guitar. "I started playing in all the New York City clubs, and I do mean all. From Gerde's Folk City and the Bitter End to Max's and the Castaways." Slowly he built up a following for his diverse repertoire which provided well-crafted lyrics to match music that had elements of folk, jazz, rock, Caribbean music, and other stylings.

He continued to pass demo tapes around to record executives and finally won a contract from Atlantic. His debut on the label, *Garland Jeffreys* (March 1973), won almost unanimous praise from reviewers. He was still on the Atlantic roster when he recorded the single "Wild in the Streets," a song that deserves ranking among the best compositions of the 1970s. However, when it came out on Atlantic, it failed miserably. Later Jeffreys bought the master for the single from Atlantic and included it on his debut LP on A&M Records. The song was given more promotional support by A&M and made the charts, giving indications for a while of becoming a major hit. While the A&M release never made the top 10, the single remains a classic and the song has proved rewarding for other rock artists who released cover versions.

Before joining A&M, though, Jeffreys had more frustration in a brief affiliation with the then new Arista label founded by former CBS Records executive Clive Davis. Jeffreys was the first artist signed by Arista, which soon issued the single "The Disco Kid," not one of Jeffreys' better efforts. "I was signed into a singles deal, which was a mistake. When they were not willing to produce an album, we were at an impasse. I have always known that I would have to pay a lot, be willing to sacrifice a lot to feel that I could legitimately call myself an artist. That is all I have ever wanted to be and I have

worked at it too many years to let any record company turn me into its current hype."

Garland left Arista and for a while did session work and whatever local engagements he could find to keep going until his next opportunity came along. This took the form of a multialbum contract with A&M signed in 1976. Its first result was *Ghost Writer* (1977), whose tracks included an updated version of "Wild in the Streets" and a song that expressed the feelings of many movie buffs, "35 Millimeter Dreams."

Critical praise was immense. Robert Hilburn in the *Los Angeles Times* wrote that the LP is like "a cross-town bus ride that allows glimpses of the confrontations, social unrest, joys, and disappointments of the city . . . a bold, striking work." John Rockwell of *The New York Times* praised the album's "haunting lyrics . . . and compelling musical twists." Overall, however, the album was nowhere near a best-seller. It might have been a reflection of the generally laid back and so-called "me" environment among teens and college-age individuals of that decade who didn't identify with an album specifically addressed to the "abused and battered children of the world." There was a similar situation of critical euphoria and mass-audience avoidance of his next albums on A&M: *One-Eyed Jack* (1978) and *American Boy and Girl* (1979), which was dedicated to the "new" 'city kids' whose lives are so miserable . . . they hardly have any meaning."

At the start of the 1980s, his contract with A&M having expired, Garland found a new record home with Epic Records. One of his first efforts for the label was the single "Matador." When initially issued in the U.S., the disc didn't find much more of an audience than his earlier material, but during 1980, "Matador" became a number one hit in West Germany, Belgium, and Switzerland (earning a gold-record award in Germany) and rose to number two in Austria. The record also was a top 20 hit in France, where it had first been released.

It was somewhat ironic that after fighting for attention at home for so long, Jeffreys' first major breakthrough came unexpectedly in another part of the globe. He made the most of it. "It started in Paris and spread all over. I had one of my greatest experiences as a performer in Rotterdam in the Netherlands, when I played to a thoroughly mixed audience . . . Africans, Jamaicans, Rastas [reflecting the reggae backbeat he used on many of his numbers], new wavers, punkers, old rockers, and new ones. A lot of different types of people responded to my songs."

"Matador" was included on his debut Epic album, *Escape Artist* (1981). The LP was a hit in Europe and also found more response from U.S.

listeners than earlier albums. During the year, Epic also issued a live album of Jeffreys' work, *Rock'n'Roll Adult*.

JETHRO TULL: *Vocal and instrumental group. Original members (1967): Ian Anderson, born Blackpool, England, August 10, 1947; Mick Abrahams, born Blackpool; Clive Bunker, born Blackpool; Glenn Cornick, born Barrow-in-Furness, Lancashire, England. Abrahams replaced in late 1968 by Martin Barre, born November 17. John Evans, born March 28, added in 1970. In 1971, Bunker replaced by Barriemore Barlow, born September 10; and Cornick replaced by Jeffrey Hammond-Hammond, born July 30. Mark Craney, Dave Pegg, and Eddie Jobson added in early 1980s. 1984 lineup: Anderson, Barre, Pegg, Peter Vettese. 1987 lineup: Anderson, Barre, Pegg.*

A group that features a progressive rock flutist playing his instrument in almost every conceivable position on stage—lying on the ground, standing on one foot, jumping up and down—is bound to shock value. Indeed, stories describing the redoubtable Ian Anderson as "a deranged flamingo," "mad-dog Fagin," or "demented dancing master" lured many rock fans to early Jethro Tull concerts just to see if the tales were true. However, a group usually must have something more than antics to gain acceptance as a supergroup, and Jethro Tull proved its merits with a string of sensationally successful recordings.

Home base for the original Jethro Tull was Blackpool, England, where Ian Anderson was born and grew up to complete grammar school and enter college as an art major. Anderson put his good voice to advantage initially in school shows and later in his teens as lead vocalist with blues-rock groups. In 1967, he formed his own group with three other friends from Blackpool: Mick Abrahams, who sang and played lead guitar, Glenn Cornick on bass guitar, and Clive Bunker on drums. They came up with the name Jethro Tull, one having no particular significance in relation to their music or background. (Tull invented a new kind of plow in the 1700s and wrote a book about it called *The New Horses Hoeing Husbandry*.)

Of their origins, Anderson told a record-company press agent: "We used to blow about home, in Blackpool, and then I came down to London. I'd never been away from home before. It was just like the yokel hitting the city with all his belongings in a knotted hankie at the end of a stick. I started out as a singer and, when the others were playing, I found I was just gazing round the lofty halls. I thought I'd like to be playing something and moving 'round too,

so I got hold of a flute and a harmonica and bluffed my way through."

The group found whatever work it could in small clubs in the London areas in early 1968 and, after some months had gone by, came to the attention of two young rock-band managers, Terry Ellis and Chris Wright. The two thought Jethro Tull was one of the most unique groups they'd heard and convinced Island Records of this almost as soon as they took over Tull's direction. By the start of the 1970s the group's U.K. label was Chrysalis; the band still was on that label at the end of the 1980s. The group went into the studios in mid-summer and cut its debut album, *This Was*, with nine of the ten songs original compositions by Anderson and other group members. The tenth song was "Serenade to a Cuckoo" by jazz saxophonist Roland Kirk.

Two weeks after its release, it was number five on the English LP charts. Later in the fall, one of Ian Anderson's compositions, "Reason for Waiting" was also a top 10 hit. Observing all of this, an executive of Hollywood-based Warner Brothers-Seven Arts Records, an Englishman home on vacation, obtained U.S. rights for the group's recordings. *This Was* was issued on the Reprise label in January 1969 and soon was as successful in the U.S. as in England.

There was a change in personnel during the year, with Martin Lancelot Barre replacing Mick Abrahams on lead guitar, but everyone agreed Barre was as good or better than his predecessor. The group's second LP, *Stand Up* (1969) earned the group a gold record in the U.S. The band also had two major top 10 singles in England: "Living in the Past" and "Sweet Dreams."

The group's third album, *Benefit* (1970) won another gold-record award. The group expanded to a quintet in 1970, adding pianist John Evans, a childhood friend of Anderson's, who left college just before he would have completed work for a degree in pharmacy.

In 1971, band turnovers left only Anderson from the original group as part of Jethro Tull. It was old home week for Ian, as two more old schoolmates from Blackpool joined up. Jeffrey Hammond-Hammond replaced Glenn Cornick on bass and Barrie Barlow took over percussion from Clive Bunker. Jeffrey was a logical choice, since a number of Anderson's songs had been about him: "A Song for Jeffrey," "Jeffrey Goes to Leicester Square," and "For Michael Collins, Jeffrey and Me."

Despite this new lineup, there was no loss in quality of new Jethro Tull material. The group's fourth LP, *Aqualung* (an expounding of Anderson and his wife Jennie's philosophy on religion), hit number one in the U.K. and the U.S. top 10 in 1971.

The title song, written by Jennie Anderson, was interpreted by Anderson in this way: "Take a person, one who is very lowly, right at the bottom like the tramp in the song. Well, there is still within such a man as much of God as there is in the Pope. I guess it's a song about spiritual equality, and that is what the rest of the songs are about too—spiritual equality, looking for God in man, any man."

The second side of the album presented Ian's statement on religion, a sort of rock-blues suite with five sections. The first, "My God," said Anderson, "is a blues for God, in the way of a lament. So many religions operate as a social service instead of a spiritual one. 'Hymn 43' is a blues for Jesus, about the glory seekers who use his name for a lot of unsavory things. 'Slipstream' is a song about dying. It doesn't mean it's the end of the world, but it hints at a life hereafter. 'Locomotive Breath' is another song about dying, but it's not so serious as 'Slipstream.' It's an analogy of the unending train journey of life. You can't stop, you've got to stagger on. But it's not that serious. All of the songs have an element of humor, and sometimes pure silliness." The side closes with a song with a meaning akin to its title, "Wind-up."

The band's fifth album, *Thick as a Brick* (1972), was even more successful than *Aqualung,* reaching the top of U.S. charts and exceeding $2 million in sales. (The group's albums were issued in England on the Chrysalis label and distributed in the U.S. by Warner/Reprise, an arrangement that remained in effect until the mid-1980s. Chrysalis then started a U.S. operation so that Tull recordings came out on that label worldwide.) *Living in the Past* (1972) and *Passion Play* (1973) also won gold-record awards. However, *Passion Play* was roundly criticized by reviewers, a situation that so depressed band members that they cancelled part of a summer–fall tour, despite capacity ticket sales in many concert sites.

Anderson's spirits revived after that, though, and he returned to the recording and concert circuit on a regular basis, perhaps realizing that while critics might no longer be on his side, millions of concert fans and record buyers were. His releases of the mid-1970s included *War Child* (1974), *Minstrel in the Gallery* (1975), and an album that capsuled the psychological problems of aging rockers, *Too Old to Rock'n'Roll, Too Young to Die* (1976). Also issued by Chrysalis in 1976 was the platinum *MU-The Best of Jethro Tull*. The band finished up the decade with a steady stream of additional albums: *Songs from the Wood* and *Repeat* (1977) and *Heavy Horses* and *Bursting Out* (1978).

The initial album of the 1980s, simply titled *A,* originally was planned as a solo album for Ian, but he liked the new band alignment used in the project, so he decided it should properly be a Jethro Tull effort. Among the members was Dave Pegg, a fine bass guitarist who previously had been a member of the folk-rock Fairport Convention. He later toured with the band in support of the album. Also making a strong statement in the recordings was keyboards player/electric violinist Eddie Johnson, who had been a member of Roxy Music. (*See Roxy Music.*) Mark Craney handled drums. The album not only was greeted with pleasure by Tull fans, but also won Anderson new respect from some of his former critical tormentors.

The pattern continued the same into the 1980s. The band toured regularly and was represented on the charts with albums *Broadsword and the Beast* (1982) and *Under Wraps* (1984). Band roster for *Under Wraps* comprised Anderson, Pegg, Barre, and Peter Vettese on keyboards. There were indications that the wear and tear of years of live performances were taking their toll on Anderson. During a late 1984 concert in Los Angeles at the Universal Ampitheatre, his voice was in such bad shape that he threatened to stop the show. He told his audience: "I've got a message for you people in the front row who are smoking marijuana. I've had a real problem with my voice and I'd appreciate it if you'd put that stuff out now. If you don't believe it, try me!"

It reflected, in part, his longtime antagonism to drugs. But it also reflected a loss in vocal range that suggested if he kept his band going, someone else would have to take over as lead singer.

By the time Chrysalis released the LP *The Crest of a Knave* in the fall of 1987, the group had been reduced to a trio: Anderson (still lead vocals and flute), Barre on guitar, and Pegg on bass guitar. The band's stature also seemed reduced by one of its poorest offerings yet. Anderson's vocals seemed tired and listless and the songs were bland and colorless.

JETT, JOAN: *Singer, guitarist, band leader (THE BLACKHEARTS), songwriter. Born Philadelphia, Pennsylvania, September 22, 1960.*

For a while it looked like the Joan Jett story could be summed up in the words "too much, too soon." At 15, she was the creative mainspring of the heralded all-girl rock band the Runaways, the focus of appreciative articles in major media from *Rolling Stone* to daily papers and teen magazines. A few years later, the music industry considered her a has-been, an undependable teenage alcoholic who might not last through her twenties.

But Joan was made of sterner stuff than many people suspected. She fought her internal demons and, with a combination of perseverance and just plain luck, overcame both her drug dependency and the related antisocial behavior to become one of the most exciting solo performers of the 1980s.

Joan was born in Pennsylvania but raised in a middle class environment in Los Angeles' San Fernando Valley (a region made famous in a somewhat deprecating manner by Frank Zappa's song "Valley Girl"). She was a rock fan from her early years and was experimenting with songwriting and band activities by her early teens. When she was 15 and still attending high school, she auditioned for and was accepted into the Runaways, a new group longtime rock performer/executive Kim Fowley was putting together. Other members included guitarist Lita Ford, singer Cherie Curry, and drummer Sandy West. Though Joan didn't found the group, she soon was considered its leader because she penned most of its original material. (*See Runaways, The.*)

Mercury issued its debut album, *The Runaways,* in 1976. That LP featured a gatefold cover, which was one thing that distinguished it from the album of the same title Mercury released in 1977. During 1976–77, the Runaways built up a cult following in the U.S., but became a favorite with Japanese audiences during a concert swing that helped make the single "Cherry Bomb" a top-seller in that country. The group was represented by a series of new LPs in 1977: *Queens of Noise* and *Waitin' for the Night* on Mercury and *Live in Japan* (issued overseas by Mercury-UK). Two albums appeared outside the U.S. on the Cherry Red label: *And Now . . . The Runaways* (1979) and *Flaming Schoolgirls* (1980).

Had the group been a male one or one with a female lead singer and male backing band, it might have succeeded, but rock audiences tended to treat all-girl bands as novelties. It was a situation that fortunately was to change in the '80s, helped certainly by the inroads the Runaways made on rock audiences' consciousness. As it was, the group was ahead of its time. Disappointing record sales and audience interest caused it to break up by the late 1970s.

Joan took it hard, which, along with her youth, made her reaction that much more unreasoning. She told Robert Hilburn of the *Los Angeles Times* (August 19, 1984): "When the band broke up, it was like my life was over. I had put so much of myself in that group and suddenly I was all alone. I began to think: 'Maybe everybody was right. Maybe the group was a joke.'"

She couldn't give up performing, though, despite her depression. She made her way to England, where she did some studio work with Steve Jones of the Sex Pistols. (*See Sex Pistols, The.*) Not much came from that, but good fortune was with her in another way. She became friends with aspiring music executive Kenny Laguna and his wife, Meryl. Laguna, who had been a sideman with bubble-gum groups such as the Ohio Express and 1910 Fruitgum Com-

pany, also had known the meaning of hard times when record companies shied away from him after the bubble-gum fad ran its course. He could sympathize with Joan's situation, but more importantly, could recognize her latent talent. He and his wife agreed to take over management of her career.

He told Hilburn: "When I first met her, Joanie was at the absolute bottom of the business. No record company wanted to touch her. She had a bad reputation. She would get really drunk and she was capable of total insanity. Besides, no one took a female rocker seriously."

Even Laguna initially took a condescending attitude, he recalled, but Joan straightened him out. The incident took place after he and Joan decided the only way out of her career impasse was to record a lot of new solo demonstration material. "I even laughed when she said she wanted to play guitar on her record. I said we'd bring in a man to do it. But she said: 'To hell with you, man—either I play my own guitar or I won't make the record.' I respected that. I could see that even with her problems, she was a strong-willed person. I had a feeling she'd pull herself out of it."

Laguna managed to place a debut solo album, *Joan Jett,* on the European Ariola label. Try as they might, they couldn't get a U.S. record company to issue the collection. Finally they decided to pay for pressing it themselves for U.S. distribution under the Blackheart label. The album sold enough copies and gained enough airplay for Kenny to get Neil Bogart, former head of Buddha Records when that was the prime bubble-gum label, to buy rights to *Joan Jett* for his new Boardwalk record firm. The album, retitled *Bad Reputation,* came out on Boardwalk in 1981 and went on to become one of the year's best-selling rock releases. (It also came out in slightly different versions in other places—on Boardwalk-Canada in 1981 and Liberation Records, Australia, in 1983.)

Laguna and Joan agreed that hard-driving, intense live appearances were vital to put the new material across. At first, though, it looked like Joan's personal problems might bring disaster. Her actions ruined a key TV guest spot he had set up for her on ABC's "20/20." She was standing talking to a member of the Blondie band when she was asked to say something for an ABC cameraman. Laguna told Hilburn: "So what does she do? She gives the camera the finger and shouts something like: 'Go to hell, ABC.' The TV people got so mad, they ended up splicing all shots of Joanie out of the show."

On another occasion, she fouled up a live broadcast from a New York club when she lost her voice just before going on stage. She consulted a doctor, who said the problem came from excessive drinking.

If she kept it up, he indicated, she might have to give up singing. This time the message sank in, she said later. She went on the wagon and as of 1988 still was clean, show-business observers concluded.

From then on, she earned a new reputation as one of rock's most dedicated and hardest-working performers. Her stage show became recognized as one of the top tickets on the major-arena circuit throughout the U.S. and abroad. In the early 1980s, she featured a combination of innovative versions of rock standards such as the Isley Brothers' "Shout," Sam the Sham's "Wooly Bully," and Gary Glitter's "Do You Wanna Touch Me" (all featured on the *Bad Reputation* LP) and originals such as "Let Me Go." By 1982, Joan was also featuring songs from the first studio album made for Boardwalk, the platinum 1981 *I Love Rock 'n' Roll*. That album, attributed to Joan Jett and the Blackhearts, also featured her new band, whose members included guitarist Ricky Byrd, bass guitarist Gary Ryan, and drummer Lee Crystal. Crystal came to the Blackhearts after working with such New York–based bands as Johnny Thunders, Sylvain Sylvain, and the Boyfriends, while Byrd had played with, among others, Rendezvous and Susan.

1982 singles included the top 10 "Crimson and Clover" (a remake of Tommy James and the Shondells' 1969 hit) and top 20 "Do You Wanna Touch Me (Oh Yeah)." With "I Love Rock 'n' Roll," Joan established herself as an important new force in rock, but the joy that came to Joan and Laguna when it rose to number one in *Billboard* the week of March 20, 1982, was badly tarnished by Neil Bogart's untimely death that same week.

Bogart's passing brought a new record alignment, this time with MCA. Joan and the Blackhearts' debut on Blackheart/MCA in 1983 was simply titled *Album*. With Joan and the band's improving reputation and the frenetic vocals she delivered in concert and on records, the album passed RIAA gold-record levels.

Her second Blackheart/MCA album, *Glorious Results of a Misspent Youth*, (1984) suggested the weakness of *Album* was a temporary aberration. Joan and her associates had not, as some feared, fallen into a formula approach to their music. In a glowing review, *Rolling Stone* (November 8, 1984) commented: "Miraculously, Jett and the Blackhearts breathe new life into the tired, old carcass of rock. They play it right down the middle: not light enough to be labeled pop, not heavy enough to be considered metal. The sound . . . is the snappiest Jett and company have ever been given. The guitars snarl, whine, and lash about on authentic rockers like 'Frustrated,' 'Talkin' 'bout My Baby,' and 'Push and Stomp.' When a lighter touch is called for, it's delivered, as in the surprisingly soft 'Hold Me' or the album's closing 'I Got No Answers.'"

The album stayed on the U.S. charts from late 1984 into 1985. (It was issued for the South American market on the Epic-Venezuela label under the title *I Need Someone*). One of the tracks recalled Joan's first love, The Runaways. It was a new version of "Cherry Bomb."

Jett told Hilburn, though, that while there were still fond memories of those days, she mainly was looking forward now, not backward. "I'm just so grateful I got a second chance and for the fact that I can do just what I want in life."

To his question about what a meeting between Joan and the old Runaways might produce, she replied: "I think they'd recognize each other. It's just that I think the Joan of '76 would say: 'Hi, you want a beer?' and the Joan of '84 would say: 'No, I've got a gig.'"

Jett co-starred with Michael J. Fox in the film "Light of Day" in 1987. Her performance of the title song, written by Bruce Springsteen and performed with the Blackhearts, was a top 40 hit.

In 1988 Jett and the Blackhearts released *Up Your Alley* (CBS).

JOEL, BILLY: *Singer, pianist, band leader, songwriter. Born Hicksville, Long Island, New York, May 9, 1949.*

A rock and pop superstar by the end of the 1970s, Billy Joel disdained the easy road to fame and fortune. An individualist, he ignored the advice sometimes given him by record-company executives in the early 1970s to imitate his first hits such as "Piano Man" or speed up his new record production for continued name identification, whether or not he liked the material being worked on. Nor did he change his song content to meet some critics' complaints that he was too personally aloof in his writings or not socially relevant. He maintained he would compose songs that fitted his feelings at the time and not make political comments in his music unless he had a strong emotional leaning about such messages. For a time in the mid-1970s, it seemed as though marching to his own drummer might prove disastrous to his career, but in the long run his approach proved eminently correct for him if not for other rock stars.

William Martin Joel was born into a family that was comfortable, but far from affluent, in the years just after World War II. His father, a German-born engineer then working at General Electric, was enthused about his young son's interest in a Mozart composition when Billy was four and started him on classical piano lessons. Those lessons continued for 10 years, but toward the end Billy was becoming more interested in the kinds of music that his Long Island peer group admired—rock'n'roll and early soul.

His interest in such music also began as a form of rebellion against his parents' classical tastes. He told Susan Elliott of *High Fidelity* (January 1978): "As I got older I realized that if you're going to be a concert pianist, then you've got to practice six hours a day and devote your whole life to it. You become a high-strung maniac. . . . It just seems to be so competitive. It doesn't seem to be a lot of fun. And I wanted to have fun." Besides, his father disapproved of pop. "It was almost forbidden—that's why I really got off on it."

Actually, Billy had started to push against those restrictions early on, playing some boogie-woogie when he was six or seven. His parents were having marital problems, which led to his father's going back to Europe in 1956, leaving his mother to struggle to meet the expenses of raising Billy and an older sister. That abandonment may have contributed to Billy's antisocial tendencies when he was in his teens.

In 1964, influenced by the British invasion spearheaded by the Beatles, the 14-year-old Joel joined his first group, the Echoes. The band played for parties and school events and Billy felt certain he could earn a living as a musician. Besides staying up into the early morning hours playing with his band, Billy spent many of his daytime hours doing anything but attending high school. "We were hitters, I mean I had a gang and that's what we did. They called us punks—we didn't call ourselves punks—we thought we were hoods. I was called a punk when I started because a real wise guy was a punk. I remember they called Elvis Presley a punk—and I thought the Young Rascals were punks!"

Though he didn't spend a lot of time in class, Joel usually managed somehow to get passing grades in school. Nonetheless, he was not allowed to graduate with his class in 1967 because of excessive absences.

Although his mother was upset, Bill didn't worry much because he was busily pursuing his pop music goals. For a while in the mid-1960s, the Echoes changed their name to the Lost Souls, without any marked improvement in their fortunes. In 1968, Billy and the band's bass player left to join the Hassles, a band that had a considerable local Long Island following. Billy helped record two late 1960s LPs with that band, *The Hassles* and *Hour of the Wolf*, issued by United Artists.

In the late 1960s, the band income wasn't enough to keep up with Billy's bills so he looked elsewhere for extra money. His activities included working as a painter at the Piping Rock Country Club in Locust Valley, New York, some factory jobs, writing crit-

icism for *Changes* magazine, and even recording a Bachmann pretzels commercial with Chubby Checker. (*See Checker, Chubby.*) Looking for better returns on his performing skills, Billy formed a duo, Attila, with ex-Hassles drummer Jon Small at the end of the decade. Their Epic album, *Attila* (1970) flopped.

By then, Billy had become increasingly involved in original songwriting. A demo of some of that material led to a contract with Family Productions in 1971 for a solo LP. That album, *Cold Spring Harbor,* came out in 1972 with Paramount Records handling distribution. Billy formed a band to try to back the LP and spent much of 1972 on the road. Lacking label promotional effort, not much happened as far as the LP was concerned, but one tour date at the Mar y Sol Rock Festival near San Juan, Puerto Rico, provided pivotal contacts.

Columbia Records executives at the festival were impressed by Joel's set. Later, those officials (including President Clive Davis) became even more interested when a tape of Billy's rendition of his song "Captain Jack" taken from a live broadcast on station WMMR-FM in Philadelphia was given considerable airplay on that outlet. However, Billy was not a free agent at the moment due to legal wrangling over his songs and even the 1972 tour proceeds. He told Susan Elliott: "I signed a lot of stupid papers. . . . I signed away my publishing and my copyrights."

He and his girl friend, Elizabeth (whom he later married and divorced), decided to move to Los Angeles and keep a low profile, taking an apartment in West Hollywood. For a time, he and Elizabeth were able to get by with income from being an opening act or playing piano bars. Under the pseudonym Billy Martin, he tickled the ivories for six months at a place called the Executive Cocktail Lounge. After he and Elizabeth moved to Malibu, he began to feel more relaxed and started writing new material.

Meanwhile, "Captain Jack" had become an underground hit in the East. Columbia, aware that Joel was getting free of his entanglements, sought him out and signed him in the late spring of 1973. Soon after, with producer Michael Stewart, engineer Ron Malo, arrangers Michael Omartian and Jimmie Haskell, and a group of top session musicians, Billy started recording his Columbia debut in Devonshire Sound studios in North Hollywood. On November 2, his first single on the label, "Piano Man," was released, a song that served as the title number for the LP issued a week later. Both single and album rose high on the charts, with the LP certified platinum by the RIAA.

His next LP, the gold *Streetlight Serenade,* came out on October 11, 1974. In November, the first single from the album, "The Entertainer," showed up on the charts. A number of honors came his way at year-end, including Best New Male Vocalist by *Cash Box,* Male Artist of the Year by *Music Retailer*'s New Faces poll, and Record of the Year for "Piano Man" by *Stereo Review.*

In 1975, Billy signed with James Guercio's management firm and went back to New York to prepare for the next album. Guercio started the project with more session performers, but Billy wasn't satisfied with the sound and began assembling his own group, starting with longtime associate Doug Stegmeyer on bass guitar and drummer Liberty DeVitto, a one-time member of Mitch Ryder's Detroit Wheels. Doug and Liberty once had worked together in the band Topper. They brought in guitarist Russell Javors from that group to work with Joel. With Richie Cannata added on tenor saxophone, Billy felt he had the band he needed. By the time he began work on the new album, he and Elizabeth, by then Mrs. Joel, had taken up residence again in New York. Billy underscored the move with the song "Say Goodbye to Hollywood," the lead track on the new LP.

Moving cross-country, he told Elliott, "was like leaving a whole school of production with the 10 million strings and the dive bomber effects. I just had the thought of the Ronettes with their beehive hairdos—'Say goodbah to Holleewoodd.''

It was, of course, a good-natured send-up of Phil Spector, one-time Ronettes mentor. Later, Ronnie Spector (one-time Ronettes star and former wife of Phil Spector) recorded the song, which, Billy commented, "was a gas. Wow—Ronnie Spector did my song with the E Street band. What more could you ask?" (See *Ronettes, The.*)

The new LP, *Turnstiles,* came out in May 1976. Along with "Say Goodbye to Hollywood," it included such notable tracks as "Summer, Highland Falls" and "New York State of Mind." The album and its accompanying singles did well, but were far from blockbusters and some critics thought Billy's career might have peaked. Columbia officials continued to argue with him about his approach to the commercial requirements of the field. They wanted him to record more than one album a year and to try to clone his only hit single up to then, "Piano Man."

Billy resisted. He told Dennis Hunt of the *Los Angeles Times* (February 20, 1977): "I've been on suspension a few times. They say I'm my own worst enemy. But I just can't see doing an album for the sake of having something on the market. I follow Randy Newman's philosophy—only put out a record when you have material you're satisfied with. If you force it, it's no good."

Nor would he redo "Piano Man" in another form. "I thought they were crazy to pick 'Piano Man' as a single in the first place. I could have done what amounted to 'Piano Man Two,' 'Three,' and 'Four.' But I wouldn't get into the formula routine. I'm not a singles artist anyway. I'm an album artist."

After finishing an extensive concert tour, he returned to the studios for a new collection under supervision of producer Phil Ramone. The multiplatinum result was *The Stranger,* (1977). The first single release, "Movin' Out (Anthony's Song)," seemed to bear out Billy's contention he wasn't a singles artist. But the next one, "Just the Way You Are," rocketed up the lists and stayed high on them for four months into 1978. In March, it became CBS Records' first single to be certified gold that year. At the same time, "Movin' Out" was reissued and became a top 20 entrant. In May, a third single, "Only the Good Die Young," was released and for a while Billy simultaneously had three singles on *Billboard*'s Hot 100. During the summer, he had still another top 20 singles from the album, "She's Always a Woman."

When the polls and awards for 1978 were completed, Billy had enough trophies and certificates to fill several mantelpieces. He won two Grammy awards, both for "Just the Way You Are" (Record of the Year and Song of the Year). For that song and "She's Always a Woman," he received ASCAP awards for Song of the Year and Artist of the Year. *Stereo Review* named *The Stranger* Record of the Year as did voters for Japan's Grand Prix award. Among other honors, Billy was named Best Male Vocalist in the Japan Radio Pop Disc awards.

He followed with an equally well regarded CBS LP, *52nd Street* (1979). By then, he had increased his working band with addition of a second guitarist, David Brown. The LP's first single, "My Life," rose to number three on *Billboard* lists while the album became Billy's first number one success, reaching that position during January in all three major U.S. trade magazines: *Billboard, Record World* and *Cash Box.* On January 23, the top 20 single, "Big Shot," was released.

By the end of 1979, *52nd Street* had sold millions of copies and *The Stranger* had gone past the 5 million mark. Among his many end-of-the-year honors were four number one awards from *Billboard:* Pop Album (*52nd Street*), Pop Album Artist, Male Pop Album Artist, and Male Pop Artist.

His 1980 platinum LP *Glass Houses* provided the number one single "It's Still Rock'n'Roll to Me." The live double-LP *Songs in the Attic* (1981) went platinum too, as did the 1982 *Nylon Curtain,* which contained his first overtly message-type songs, such as "Allentown" (about unemployment in the steel industry) and "Goodnight Saigon" (dealing with what he saw as injustices to the U.S. soldiers who had taken part in the Vietnam War).

Joel's new stance aroused some controversy—if not with the general public, among the critical establishment. Dave Marsh savaged the songs in his *Rolling Stone* review claiming "Allentown" was "defeatist" and calling "Goodnight Saigon" a "Vietnam song that refuses to take sides," material that "borders on obscenity." Robert Hilburn of the *Los Angeles Times,* on the other hand, hailed "Goodnight Saigon" as an important step in breaking the silence about Vietnam in the pop music of the '70s, "an 'American Pie'-ish look at the Vietnam experience that is as uncompromising a portrait as pop has given us in years."

Joel said he had been against the war to the extent of lying to his draft board to avoid service. But he felt veterans of the war shouldn't be treated as outcasts. He told Hilburn: "I'm trying to say that we should all face up to what happened in Vietnam and show more compassion to the people who served there. Whether it was right or wrong, they laid their asses on the line for us. And I think they got the royal shaft for it." "Goodnight Saigon" gained worldwide attention, reaching number one in Holland, where reviewers saw nothing weak about it. The paper *Het Parool* stated: "It takes guts to write a song like this."

In 1983, Billy turned his cap around with his platinum LP *An Innocent Man*. As fine an album as he'd done to that point, it explored different aspects of romance from making out to courting and marriage. In the top 10 at the same time were the singles "Uptown Girl" and "Tell Her About It" from the LP.

As Joel prepared to go on tour in early 1984 to help focus attention on *An Innocent Man*, his first concert video (the 80-minute *Billy Joel: Live from Long Island* based on the Nylon Curtain tour) was released. The video managed to capture some of the urgency of a typical high-energy live performance by Billy.

After the 1984 tour, Billy took a brief absence from working on a new album. For a while, he made the headlines more for his impending marriage to model Christie Brinkley than for his show business activities. The wedding in 1985 was a media event. He was represented on the charts in the second half of that year with a two-disc *Greatest Hits Volume I and II* issued in June.

In mid-1986, his first studio album in three years, *The Bridge,* was released on Columbia. Its songs ran the gamut from Broadway musical–flavored pieces to Billy's topical rock. Indicating he would be inter-

ested in turning his gaze on future Broadway-type projects, Billy told Stephen Holden of *The New York Times* (August 3, 1986): "I'm 37, and there's no point in pretending I'm a teenager anymore. That doesn't mean I don't love rock'n'roll, but I love other kinds of music [too]."

Describing his writing approach, he told Holden: "Some people write a hundred songs a year and choose what they like. I'm not one of them. When I'm doing an album, I only complete 10 or 11 songs. If I don't like something I've started, rather than continuing to work on it, I toss it into the trash can. There's no backlog of Billy Joel material. You'll never hear my basement tapes, because there are none. While I get ideas for songs all the time, I've found that the pressure to record has been the major motivation for me to finish anything. Once I get an idea, I write it down in a notebook. Six months later, when it has marinated, I'll look at it and probably think of something better. I enjoy catching up with myself like that. Then when I finally get into the studio, 80% of the actual recording process consists of cutting things out, changing, revising and editing.

"I write the tunes first and then the lyrics, which are dictated by the mood of the music. Though the two have to fit together, for me the language is really secondary. It's the strangest thing. I don't think about what I do. I like to be as nonthinking a writer as possible. It may take me a year to figure out why I wrote some of the songs I did, why I said some of the things I said, and what I really meant."

In mid-1987 Billy gave a series of concerts in the Soviet Union which provided the material for the late 1987 Columbia two-disc live set *Kohuept* (which translates to *Concert* in English).

JOHANSEN, DAVID: *Singer, guitarist, songwriter, record producer. Born Staten Island, New York, c. 1954.*

In the early 1970s, the New York Dolls was considered an oddity, an offshoot of conventional rock'n'roll that gained notoriety from its supposed offbeat behavior and from performing in drag rather than from its musical credentials. Though some critics praised it for innovation, few expected much to happen to its members after the group disbanded in 1974. For a while, there was little to change those opinions, but in 1978, former lead singer David Johansen surfaced as a promising new writer and solo performer.

Johansen was born and raised in the New York borough of Staten Island, which was not particularly known as a hotbed of rock'n'roll. He told Robert Hilburn of the *Los Angeles Times* (April 17, 1974) that his interest in music went back to his earliest years. "I come from a family with a lot of kids in it. My brothers and sisters were always playing rock'n'roll By the time I was four or so, I was singing things like 'Bye Bye Love' by the Everly Brothers. And I used to love 'I'm Walkin' by Fats Domino and Marty Robbins [song] about the big iron on your hip. I used to love the voice on that. I could just eat that record. I had this thing about records where I wanted to eat them. They sounded so good they reminded me of cream puffs or something. The first guy I really went crazy about, though, was Gary U.S. Bonds. He was my favorite."

When he was old enough to fend for himself, he told another interviewer, he became a "terror." To his family's dismay, he would run off with friends to hang out in Greenwich Village and Times Square without permission or letting anyone know he was going. In his midteens, he moved to Manhattan and became involved with other teens interested in breaking into the music scene. By the early 1970s, this evolved into the original version of the New York Dolls. "When we first started playing, we were in wild places. So we had to be more wild than the kids in the audience, which was good because they were really crazy . . . the whole dance floor was covered with these amazing maniacs. We were their band."

The performances that established the group's reputation were typically kicked off at midnight in the New York City Mercer Art Center. Marty Thau, who became their co-manager, recalled his first exposure to the group at Mercer in 1972. "Their brand of rock'n'roll was entertaining—their humor, their whole attitude, the complete disdain for any and all things. It didn't seem to be just a typical rock'n'roll group."

With word of the band's reception by youthful audiences making industry rounds, the way was opened for a recording contract with Mercury Records, which issued their 1973 debut LP, *New York Dolls*. Among the more favored tracks on the Todd Rundgren–produced LP were "Looking for a Kiss" and "Personality Crisis." (See *Rundgren, Todd*. The second album, *Too Much Too Soon* (whose title proved prophetic), was issued by Mercury in 1974. In retrospect, the LP is one of the more interesting rock releases of the first half of the 1970s, but the band's punk rock flavor was not yet in vogue and, despite a number of well-received concerts in many parts of the U.S., the record wasn't commercially successful. The album's failure was caused in part by personal problems of band members, some self-inflicted, that gave it a poor reputation with club owners and booking agents.

The group—whose members (besides JoHansen,

who capitalized the "H" in his name at the time) were Johnny Thunders (guitar), Sylvain Sylvain (guitar), Arthur Kane (bass guitar), and Jerry Nolan (drums)—was plagued to some extent by its glitter-rock image—6-inch platform shoes, lipstick, and heavy makeup—which might have won acceptance in England at the time, but was out of synch with U.S. tastes. Many rock fans confused the band's feminine-seeming attire with its sexual preferences. The band's attitude sometimes outraged club managers and booking agents, which restricted opportunities for concert exposure.

One example was the July 1974 cancellation of an engagement at the Roxy in Los Angeles because of alleged rudeness and failure to appear on time for scheduled shows. Johansen refuted it at the time, claiming it reflected management's inability to understand the band's outlook.

"We were not as late as [the Roxy manager] says we were. We behaved like we always do. We were not wild or rowdy. We were just having fun. . . . They were uptight about our audience. They think our fans are weird. They think we are weird. They just don't understand us. I'm really insulted. I've been insulted in hick towns before, but never in a big city like this one."

By 1975, the Dolls had broken up and little was heard in the national media about Johansen for the next few years. He had not abandoned hopes for a pop music career, however, and continued to search out contacts in the industry while working on new original material. In 1977, he got a new agreement with Blue Sky Records, a CBS label, and went into the studio to work on his debut solo LP with producer Richard Robinson. After the album, *David Johansen*, came out in 1978, Johansen projected a new image in concerts across the U.S. and in Europe in support of the record. Appearing as himself without makeup or unusual costumes, he clearly demonstrated he was an accomplished vocalist and increasingly insightful writer. It seemed obvious he was more than a cult figure, but rather an important new voice on the rock scene. Among the tracks from the new LP (on which he was supported in part by former Dolls associate Sylvain Sylvain) that became staples in his act were "Funky but Chic," "Frenchette," and "Lonely Tenement."

David's early love for R&B and soul music was reflected in his next album, *In Style* (Blue Sky, 1979). Soul, R&B, and reggae influences blended with rock on such tracks as "Melody" (a hit single), "Swaheto Woman," and "Flamingo Road." The album demonstrated his continued growth as writer and record artist and, Blue Sky reported, helped bring a welcome rise in copies sold as well.

The next album, *Here Comes the Night*, was not as consistent as its predecessor, though there were enough above-average tracks to maintain Johansen's growing reputation. Almost all the songs came from a new writing collaboration between Johansen and former Beach Boy bandsman Blondie Chaplin, including "You Fool You," "She Loves Strangers," "My Obsession," "Here Comes the Night," and "Rollin' Job." Chaplin also provided guitar and vocal backing. (See *Beach Boys, The*.)

Tongue in cheek, Johansen said when the album came out: "I dedicate this album to Willie the grocer who works next door to me, 'cause when we were rehearsing the songs for the new album in my apartment—we had two guitars, bass, piano and organ, a drum machine—he's the one who'd always say: 'Oh, I hear you're moving out!' I later realized there was this whole neighborhood conspiracy to get me outta there because of the racket we were making. I'd get notes hanging on my door saying: 'This facility was rented to you as living quarters, not as a rehearsal studio.' Finally we split to rehearse in a regular studio—but not before getting the songs down the way I wanted them."

Fortunately for his neighbors, Johansen's next album, the 1982 *Live It Up*, wasn't a compilation of newly prepared songs, but his first live LP. The album, whose contents included such concert showstoppers as Johansen's medley of songs made famous by England's '60s Animals group and an original titled "Build Me a Buttercup," was on U.S. charts a number of months during the year.

In the mid-1980s, Johansen became a fixture on the Manhattan entertainment scene with a popular lounge act he presented in local niteries under the pseudonym Buster Poindexter. He had no new solo albums at the time in March 1986, when Mercury reissued some of the earlier New York Dolls recording under the title *Night of the Living Dolls*.

By 1987, David had signed a recording contract for his alter ego with RCA which issued the LP *Buster Poindexter* in the fall to coincide with a cross-country tour in that guise by Johansen. Asked by Robert Palmer of *The New York Times* if that persona was "for real," Johansen responded: "There were all these songs, blues, R&B, and so forth, that I knew from my record collections. But they just wouldn't fit into one of my rock shows, so I started working with a couple of the guys from my band at this bar in my neighborhood, Tramps, doing these songs. And the whole thing just kind of took off from there."

The LP was on the *Billboard* charts during 1987–88, but was not a best-seller. In 1988, Johansen could be seen by moviegoers in the film *Candy Mountain*.

JOHN, ELTON: *Singer, pianist, songwriter. Born Pinner, Middlesex, England, March 25, 1947.**

Anyone who saw one of Elton John's fabulous debut U.S. concerts in the early 1970s had to feel a new superstar was in the making. In a way, he seemed a throwback to early rock star Jerry Lee Lewis—not in his singing style, which was much softer and based on a considerably better voice, but in his stage antics. Like Lewis, John embellished his act by kicking his piano bench away and jumping up and down, even while still pounding out rock rhythms on the keyboard. Of course, one thing Jerry Lee would never savor was the wild array of costumes Elton donned at different stages of his career, from a wild-haired punk guise to a flamboyant chicken.

In fact, for some critics, John's concert approach resulted in a belief that his career was affected by his gimmickry. He allegedly concentrated on his theatrics to the extent that his music suffered and, in late 1971, some observers suggested he might, in effect, paint himself into a corner. Over the next few years, he showed the naysayers were off-base as he turned out a series of superb albums that established him as a rock giant by the mid-1970s. Then, in the late 1970s, he hit a dry spell. Again, words of doubt appeared in the press. but he shook that off to return to the top ranks of writers and performers in the 1980s.

Of course, one thing that had helped steel his nerves against critical knocks had been the years of dues-paying he had put in before becoming an "overnight" sensation at the start of the '70s. Born Reginald Kenneth Dwight to a middle class English family, he proved a child prodigy on the piano. In 1958, at age 11, he was awarded a scholarship to the Royal Academy of Music.

However, once exposed to the new sounds of rhythm & blues and rock, his interest in classics waned and he spent hours listening to rock and blues artists on the phonograph and radio. He began to try his own hand at these forms on the piano, augmenting his skills by learning to play the organ. Still in his early teens, he took jobs as a pianist at small London pop-music clubs and also began to experiment with writing material of his own, ranging from slow, soulful folk-blues to rapid-paced rock and R&B.

In 1961, he started performing with another young English blues-rock fan, John Baldry. (*See Baldry, Long John*.) Soon Baldry assembled a band called

---

*Osborne quotes from personal interview with Irwin Stambler.

Bluesology with Elton (still known as Reg Dwight) as a charter member. Through the mid-1960s, Elton performed with the band, as one of the foremost blues-rock groups in England. In 1967, beginning to think about a solo career, Reg Dwight changed his name, combining the first name of Bluesology saxophone player Elton Dean with the given name of the band's leader.

Realizing his main writing forte was music rather than words, Elton placed an ad for a lyricist in a London paper. One of the responses came from 22-year-old Bernie Taupin (born Market Rasen, Lincolnshire, May 22, 1950), who had written poetry at school, but at the time was working as a laborer on local farms. Once the two got together, it proved a perfect match. For some eight years, it was hard for anyone to imagine a new Elton John composition not having words by Taupin. In March 1968, Elton's first single, "I've Been Loving You," was released in England. The following January, he had his first major success in the U.K. with the single "Lady Samantha." His 1969 U.K. output included the well-received album *Empty Sky* and the single "It's Me That You Need." On October 27, he wrote what in the next year became his first *Billboard* top 10 single, "Your Song."

In 1970, he formed a trio with Dee Murray on bass guitar and Nigel Olsson on drums. The new group made its performing debut on April 21 at the Roundhouse in London on a bill with Tyranosaurus Rex and the Pretty Things. By then, he already had developed a solo set that featured wildly unusual apparel with a repertoire that started with slow songs played in a relaxed piano style with a gradual buildup in energy, both in the intensity of the music and in his antics while playing it.

As his reputation grew at home, he found several U.S. record firms interested in him, with Universal Records (division of MCA) signing for American distribution. John's debut U.S. LP, *Elton John* (1970) on MCA's Uni subsidiary, went gold, as did his 1971 *Tumbleweed Connection, Friends* (the soundtrack from the film of that title), live *11-17-70*, and *Madman across the Water*.

In early 1972, he added guitarist Davey Johnstone to his band. Hits for the year included the gold Uni LP *Honky Chateau* with its top 10 singles "Rocket Man" and "Honky Cat." From the number one gold LP *Don't Shoot Me, I'm Only the Piano Player* (1973), "Crocodile Rock" rose to number one in *Billboard,* while "Daniel" peaked at two. In April, Elton formed his own record company, Rocket Records, with MCA handling distribution. In October, the two-disc *Goodbye Yellow Brick Road* reached number one in *Billboard.* Year-end honors included Male Singer of the Year from *Cash Box* and *Record*

World (awards he'd won the previous year as well) and Top Singles Artist of the Year from both of those and *Billboard* too.

1974 was another banner year. His gold MCA LPs *Caribou* and *Elton John's Greatest Hits* plus singles "Bennie and the Jets" and his remake of the Beatles' "Lucy in the Sky with Diamonds" all hit number one in *Billboard,* while "Don't Let the Sun Go Down on Me" and "The Bitch Is Back" made the top 10. Meanwhile, Elton was adding artists to his Rocket Records roster. His protégé Kiki Dee had a top 20 hit, "I've Got the Music in Me," while veteran singer/songwriter Neil Sedaka's "Laughter in the Rain" made number one in *Billboard.* *(See Sedaka, Neil.)* Industry sources estimated Elton's earnings for 1974 alone to be over $8 million.

In January 1975, his first British LP, *Empty Sky,* was finally released in the U.S., making the top 10. In March, he shone in his film debut as the Pinball Wizard in the Who's rock opera, *Tommy. (See Who, The.)* The gold MCA LP *Rock of the Westies* reached number one in *Billboard,* as did the singles "Philadelphia Freedom" and "Island Girl," while "Someone Saved My Life Tonight" peaked at number four. *Captain Fantastic and the Brown Dirt Cowboy* (originally packaged with a comic-book biography of Elton) scored the difficult feat of entering all three LP trade charts at number one. In July, he appeared on the cover of *Time* magazine. Elton was also honored with a star on Hollywood's Walk of Fame and on October 25–26, proved his spectacular popularity by filling the Los Angeles Dodgers' baseball stadium, drawing 110,000 people in all and knowing far more would have bought tickets if they'd been available. His shows were the first in that venue since the Beatles' in 1966. In December, all three trade magazines named him Top Male Record Seller.

At the start of 1976, acid-tongued clothes designer Mr. Blackwell included Elton on his "Worst Dressed Women of the Year" list. Elton could cry all the way to the bank as his live LP *Here and There* went gold and *Blue Movies* became his first platinum LP, while providing the top 10 single "Sorry Seems to Be the Hardest Word." He and Kiki Dee also made number one in *Billboard* with their duet single "Don't Go Breaking My Heart."

But 1976 brought a major realignment for Elton. His writing partnership with Bernie Taupin broke up, partly due to Bernie's desire to try to carve an individual career for himself. For a while Elton formed a new collaboration with lyricist Gary Osborne, who had co-authored "Amoureuse" on Kiki Dee's first LP on Rocket, *Loving & Free.*

Osborne recalled that the idea for the team evolved from social contacts. "For a while Elton and

I were just friends and hanging out together. Occasionally he'd say that with Bernie Taupin living in the U.S. and my writing partner Richard Kerr also over there, it was sort of logical for us to work together, since he's a music writer and I'm a lyricist. I tried to play it down as much as possible. I was obviously interested, but if it was going to happen, it would, and if I pushed it and it went sour, it could have ruined our friendship. That friendship was very important to my wife and myself because, though Elton's known as a loner, he's quite fun to be with and we had lots of good laughs with him.

"The way it happened is interesting. He hadn't written anything for a long time. He doesn't usually write between albums. So he's not an every-day or every-week type of writer. . . . But he's such a quick writer; I doubt if anybody writes faster than him.

"Anyway, he's a very competitive person and we played backgammon and pinball and other games. One of those we'd play was that we'd sit at the piano and sing a line each and gradually build up a ridiculous song. One day when we were doing this a proper song started to emerge and in about 20 minutes was finished. It was called 'Smile That Smile,' a song we sometimes have forgotten when people ask which was our first together, because it wasn't recorded. I think he was encouraged by the way that happened and without any conscious effort, he then played a melody he'd had kicking around for a while. I taped it and the next day wrote the lyric, which later became the first song on the new album A Single Man, 'Shine On Through.'

"Still, we hadn't thought of a formal collaboration. What happened was that a couple of months later Elton was recording a song he'd written with Bernie and decided to do another of Taupin's and our two new ones. I went along as a person he could bounce ideas off of. During one of the breaks, he wrote a little tune and very quickly I wrote a lyric to it and then another one in the next break and another one after that.''

This approach, Osborne noted, was different from the way Elton had usually worked with Taupin. Taupin always had written the lyrics first. "Before, Elton had always written tunes to the lyric and suddenly it was working another way."

But Osborne was aware it was a long shot. "Billboard pointed out that I had an uphill fight because people would compare one album written by me with 18 written by Bernie Taupin and, as a gamble, I figured the odds are 18–1 against me."

As it happened, Osborne's fears proved to be only too accurate. The problem was compounded by John's obvious unsettled feelings after the Taupin schism. It had been reflected by his limited new output in 1977: the single "Bite Your Lip," and two

fall albums, *Elton John's Greatest Hits, Volume II,* released October 1, and *Elton—It's a Little Bit Funny.* On November 3, 1977, Elton told a concert audience at Empire Pool, London, that he wasn't planning to do any more live shows after that. This was still the case in October 1978, when the Osborne–John collaboration was presented on the LP *A Single Man.* The album, while not another *Goodbye Yellow Brick Road,* was the equal of many of Elton's earlier collections, but critics tended to downgrade it due to Taupin's absence. Still, the album reached platinum sales levels. But when Elton's next MCA releases (*Victim of Love* in 1979 and gold *21 at 33* in 1980) fell far short of his best work, many suggested he had become another rock dinosaur.

Yet even as many people were writing Elton off, he was gaining new energy from challenging opportunities, including a series of concerts in the Soviet Union. In May 1979, he became the first rock star to send shivers of excitement through crowds in cities such as Leningrad and Moscow.

In September 1980, he announced he was leaving MCA and signing with a new label, Geffen. His Geffen debut, *The Fox* (1981), proved one of his best collections in some time. The following year, he seemed to have come back all the way with the gold *Jump Up* and its top 20 singles "Empty Garden" and "Blue Eyes." For his 1982 tour, Elton reassembled his band from his mid-1970s glory years: Davey Johnstone, Dee Murray, and Nigel Olsson.

1983 was memorable for his gold *Too Low for Zero* LP reuniting him with Bernie Taupin and for a lighter accomplishment as well. A lifetime soccer fan (and active player in his youth), he supported a team from Watford in the U.K. During 1983, he and the team visited China as guests of the Peking government.

In support of his excellent LP *Breaking Hearts* (gold, 1984), Elton went on a worldwide concert tour that broke attendance records in numerous places. At the close of the tour, he once more suggested that he might give up the road for good. He told a reporter in late summer: "The band and I have been on the road since the beginning of the year, and it has convinced me that I ought to move on." But two years later, with a costume writers suggested made him look like "a punk Amadeus," he was back at his old stand, thrilling large crowds with spectacular performances across the globe. Included in his program were his two recent top 10 hits, "I Guess That's Why They Call It the Blues" and "Sad Songs."

In 1986, Elton teamed up with Dionne Warwick, Stevie Wonder, and Gladys Knight on the gold single "That's What Friends Are For" (Arista). Attributed simply to "Dionne and Friends," it won a

Grammy for Best Pop Vocal Performance by a Duo, Group, or Chorus. (*See Knight, Gladys, & the Pips; Warwick, Dionne; Wonder, Stevie.*) Late in the year he had the LP *Leather Jacket* in record stores.

In 1987, back with MCA, he put out the two-disc *Live in Australia*, recorded with the Melbourne Symphony Orchestra. It included the surprise hit single, "Candle in the Wind," a fan's homage to Marilyn Monroe, which he first recorded on *Goodbye Yellow Brick Road* 14 years earlier, though no one had previously thought to make it a single.

JONES, GRACE *Singer, songwriter, actress. Born Jamaica, West Indies, c. 1953.*

With her extravagant, though often minimal costumes, piercing robot-like gaze, and straight-up crew-cut–like hairdo, Grace Jones established an image that was more striking than her vocal prowess. She was, in fact, an excellent actress who also sang, and her success as a disco star proved a stepping stone to a leading role in the 1985 James Bond thriller *A View to a Kill*.

Grace was born into a family that played an influential role in Jamaican politics for generations. Her clergyman father took most of the family to the United States when she was a child, but she was left with her grandparents for most of her preteen years. She attributed her kicking-over-the-traces approach to life to her early upbringing. She told Robert Hilburn of the *Los Angeles Times* (May 18, 1985): "As a little child I wasn't allowed to do anything because I was raised by my grandparents [in Jamaica] and they were very strict . . . no television, no radio, no movies, nothing. I wasn't even allowed to straighten my hair or wear open-toed shoes. They thought I was being too worldly.

"I didn't even have a sense of who I was except the daughter of this person and the niece of that one. Even when I moved to Syracuse [New York] to live with my parents when I was 13, I had to go by strict rules. I decided when I left home I was going to completely freak out and find out who I am. I've been searching ever since. The one thing I told myself: Never compromise."

In Syracuse, she spent her teens in a middle class environment. In college, she already was leaning toward an acting career, which perhaps added impetus to a crush she developed for her drama teacher. The relationship, brief though it was, led to her becoming a cast member in a musical written by the teacher. By that time, her brief college career had ended.

Once the play's run ended, she moved to New York City, where her unusual looks won her a place on the high fashion roster of the Wilhelmina Modeling Agency. She continued to seek out acting roles.

Her achievements included a role in the early '70s movie *Gordon's War*.

Her brother had taken up residence in Paris, France, and the restless Grace decided to join him there. She quickly picked up the threads of her modeling career and became one of the most sought-after faces and figures in Europe with occasional jet-set side trips for assignments in the U.S. Among the magazines that featured her on their covers in the first half of the 1970s were *Elle*, *Vogue*, and *Der Stern*. Not only was she handsome in face and figure, she also had become fluent in many languages, including French, Italian, Spanish, and, later, Japanese.

Since she enjoyed singing and dancing, she tried to break out of modeling into more creative endeavors. Her modeling success coupled with her unusual persona brought attention from news media and contacts that opened doors for recording opportunities. She soon had a contract with a French record company and was gaining recognition as a promising disco artist. Not only did she have hit singles such as "Pull Up to the Bumper," she also proved a stellar concert attraction.

She used her brash stage personality and outrageous special effects to good advantage. As she told Hilburn: "The more different you looked, the more attention people would pay to you. Being different comes to me naturally. Besides, I was different by the time I got to Syracuse. I had this funny accent and I was from Jamaica.

"I saw that people were fascinated by my [stark] aura. But that's just me. It's something that comes from my grandfather. He's 95 and I was in Jamaica for his birthday and people are afraid to approach him. He's got this independent, 'I-don't-need-you' attitude, and I'm like that too."

Becoming aware that it was important to record for a firm with good U.S. outlets, Grace soon moved from the French label to British-based Island Records, which issued her debut LP, *Portfolio*, in 1977. After testing out her new live act at the Les Mouches disco in France, Grace extended her performance back across the Atlantic with engagements that included the first concert presented at the famous New York disco, Studio 54. She soon had such hit disco singles to her credit as "I Need a Man," "That's the Trouble," and "Sorry," the last two written by Grace.

In the late 1970s and early 1980s, Grace was represented on a variety of hit charts with both albums and singles. At times her releases showed up at the same time on pop, black, and disco charts. Island albums of those years were *Fame* (1978), *Muse* (1979), *Warm Leatherette* (1980), *Nightclubbing* (1981), and *Living My Life* (1982). Among her charted singles were "Do or Die," "Nipple to the Bottle," and a remake of Edith Piaf's standard "La Vie en Rose." She was featured in a number of flamboyant videos in support of her releases, but as she and fellow disco star Rick James complained at a 1983 Grammy press conference that little airplay was given them due to what they felt was an anti-black attitude at many TV outlets. (*See James, Rick.*)

Grace had not abandoned her acting interests despite her growing following among pop-music fans. In 1984, she had her first major film credit in the Arnold Schwartzenegger vehicle *Conan the Barbarian*. Soon she was approached to do an even more demanding role as a hit woman in the 1985 James Bond release, *A View to Kill*. The movie was the same sort of camp-fantasy adventure odyssey as earlier Bond films, but many critics agreed that Grace had brought some new aspects to the formula.

By the time the movie came out in mid-1985, Grace had signed with a new record firm, Manhattan Records (an EMI subsidiary). Her debut album on Manhattan, *Slave to the Rhythm*, came out in late 1985 and was in upper charts positions on both black and pop charts in early 1986.

JONES, QUINCY: *Singer, trumpeter, pianist, songwriter, record producer, arranger, record company executive. Born Chicago, Illinois, March 14, 1933.*

For many record buyers, the name Quincy Jones became familiar when his albums moved onto the best-seller lists in the early 1970s. By then, Quincy was in his late thirties and he had already gained success in not one, but several aspects of music. Jazz fans and other musicians knew him as one of the finest instrumentalists and composers of the post–World War II decades. The movie industry hailed him as one of the most prolific and talented writers of film scores. Fellow performers in many areas of popular music had achieved hit records either because of some of Quincy's original songs or his skill as a record producer.

Quincy Delight Jones' apprenticeship was a long one, going back to his early teens. He was born in Chicago, but raised in Seattle, where he started learning trumpet before reaching high school. By the time he met another youngster, Ray Charles, in Seattle, in 1946, he had become as skillful on trumpet as musicians several times his age. Jones and Charles started their own band and spent several years playing for private parties, dances, and weddings in the Northwest. The two musicians gained from each other. Jones gained considerable grounding in arranging techniques from Ray. (*See Charles, Ray.*)

At 17, Quincy decided to increase his musical understanding by accepting a scholarship to the Berklee School of Music in Boston. Short on funds, he earned money to stay in school by playing in bands at local strip joints. The jazz world is relatively small and has an excellent grapevine. Word got around about his skills and jazz great Oscar Pettiford asked Jones to come to New York in mid-1949 to write two arrangements for an album.

"I got $17 an arrangement and I was thrilled," he recalled. "The city was kinda pretty then, and clean. Everyone was there, Tatum, Monk, Bird, Miles. I was only 17. I had to love it. The jazz cats had a kind of dignity that was lost later. They were still aristocratic drinkers, if you know what I mean."

In the early 1950s, Jones began to build his reputation as a premier musician and arranger-composer, starting as a sideman in Lionel Hampton's band. He played with several other major groups during the decade, including Dizzy Gillespie, with whom he went on the first U.S. Department of State–sponsored jazz tour of Europe. Quincy liked Europe and spent much of the '50s there. Among the jobs he held was musical director for the Parisian office of Barclay Records and composer for Harry Arnold's Swedish All Stars in Stockholm. While working at Barclay, he studied classical composition with famous French teacher Nadia Boulanger. For a long time, jazz has had a wider following in Europe than in America. Quincy became a celebrity with jazz fans there, winning awards in several countries as Best New Arranger and Composer.

Toward the end of the '50s, he returned to the U.S., accepting a job as vice president of Mercury Records, the first black artist to hold so high a job in a major record firm. During his seven years with Mercury, he produced many albums, often playing as a session man, and continued to arrange for many artists both on the Mercury roster and with other companies. Among those who often used his arrangements were Sammy Davis, Jr., Andy Williams, Sarah Vaughan, Frank Sinatra, and many major jazz artists. In 1963, he won his first Grammy: Best Instrumental Arrangement for "I Can't Stop Loving You" by Count Basie's Band.

Long interested in movie scores, he finally made inroads in this area with the music for *The Pawnbroker* (a nominee for an Academy Award for Best Picture of 1965). In the years that followed, he scored or wrote songs for several dozen pictures, including *Mirage, Walk Don't Run,* Sidney Poitier's *The Slender Thread,* Jose Ferrer's *Enter Laughing, Banning, In the Heat of the Night, In Cold Blood, A Dandy in Aspic, For Love of Ivy, MacKenna's Gold, Bob and Carol and Ted and Alice, John and Mary,* and *Cactus Flower.*

For most of these films, he wrote the theme song, which often became hit singles for major vocalists. Several Jones songs were nominated for Oscars, including the theme from *The Love of Ivy* and the song "The Eyes of Love" from *Banning* (with lyrics for both by Bob Russell). Jones also was an Oscar nominee for his score for *In Cold Blood*. Jones' credits also included a second-place award in the 1967 Brazil International Song Festival for "The World Goes On," whose lyrics were written by Alan and Marilyn Bergman.

Jones also gained experience with TV as songwriter and performer. He wrote the music for the "Ironsides" TV series theme, "Even When You Cry." He also provided music or appeared on the "Bill Cosby Show," "Ironsides," and such pilots as "European Eye," "The Pickle Brothers," and "Hey Landlord."

In 1969, a new phase of Jones' career began when he was signed as a recording artist by Herb Alpert's A&M Records. His initial LP, *Walking In Space* (1969) won a Grammy for Best Instrumental Jazz Performance, Large Group or Soloist with Large Group. His follow-up LP, *Gula Matari* (1970) made the charts. *Smackwater Jack* (1971) won a Grammy Award as Best Pop Instrumental Performance for 1971.

During 1971, Jones was honored by "Merv Griffin Presents a Tribute to Quincy Jones." Jones also arranged and conducted the music for that year's Academy Awards show.

Several releases on labels other than A&M made the charts in 1972. These were the soundtrack album *S* and single "Money Runner" on Reprise and the Mercury two-disc *Ndeda*. Throughout the summer of 1973, Jones' A&M album *You've Got It Bad, Girl* was a best-seller. Its remake of the Lovin' Spoonful's "Summer in the City" won him his fourth Grammy Award for Best Instrumental Arrangement of 1973.

Jones continued his multifaceted activities for the rest of the decade, though spending more time on behind-the-scenes projects such as arranging and record producing than on personal performances. His movie work included the score for the film version of the stage musical hit *The Wiz* (a film whose stars included Diana Ross and Michael Jackson). That work brought him another Grammy Award for Best Instrumental Arrangement of 1978 (shared with co-arranger Robert Freedmen) for the "Main Title (Overture Part I)" from *The Wiz Original Soundtrack* album on MCA Records.

It proved his last movie project for some years, partly because of friendships he formed during the job. He told famed jazz critic Leonard Feather (*Los Angeles Times*, March 6, 1983): "The best thing that

came out of *The Wiz* was that I met and worked with Michael Jackson, who made his screen debut in it, and he started talking to me about producing an album for him. I felt there was a side to his singing that hadn't been fully brought out, and we found it on the first album together, *Off the Wall*." (*See Jackson, Michael*.)

The 1979 Columbia LP sold over 5 million copies in the U.S. and another 2 million in other nations. Two singles pulled from the album, "Don't Stop 'til You Get Enough" (1979) and "Rock with You" (1980), made number one in *Billboard*. Two others, "Off the Wall" and "She's out of My Life" made the top 10. As producer, Quincy shared gold and platinum RIAA honors for those hits with Michael Jackson.

As always, Quincy wasn't a one-project person. He continued to work with many other top stars in the 1980s, including George Benson, a collaboration that won Quincy a 1980 Grammy for Best Instrumental Arrangement. That trophy was for "Dinorah, Dinorah" on Benson's Warner Brothers LP, *Give Me the Night* (an award Quincy shared with fellow arranger Jerry Hey). (*See Benson, George*.) His wide-ranging efforts won him no fewer than five Grammies in 1981 both for some of his own recordings and for his support efforts with other artists. Those included Best R&B Performance by a Duo or Group with Vocal for his A&M album *The Dude*; a production award for the Best Cast Show Album for *Lena Horne: the Lady and Her Music Live on Broadway*; Best Arrangement on an Instrumental Recording (with Johnny Mercer) for his track "Velas" on *The Dude*; Best Instrumental Arrangement Accompanying Vocals (with Jerry Hey) for his A&M track "Ai No Corrida"; and the most satisfying award—Producer of the Year.

In 1982, Quincy was back at work with Michael Jackson on a new solo album to follow *Off the Wall*, as well as planning or producing new releases by many other performers. And, as before, the hits kept right on coming for those people lucky enough to claim Quincy's professional attention. The Michael Jackson effort, *Thriller*, became one of the biggest hits, creatively and commercially, of the mid-1980s. Even as *Thriller* kept record-store cash registers busy in early 1983, the single "Baby, Come to Me," a duet by Patti Austin and James Ingram produced by Jones, sped up the singles charts to reach number one in *Billboard*. Not only did Quincy produce it, the single was released on his own record label, Qwest. (Other artists on Qwest at the time were Lena Horne and saxophone great Ernie Watts.) The single that pushed "Baby, Come to Me" out of number one was none other than Michael Jackson's "Billie Jean," a Quincy-produced track from *Thriller* as was the disc "Beat It," which took over number one. As if that wasn't enough, also on the charts during those months were two other Quincy-produced singles: Donna Summer's "The Woman in Me" and Michael Jackson's "The Girl Is Mine." (*See Summer, Donna.*)

In the 1983 Grammy Awards, Jones added to his hoard of trophies Record of the Year for "Beat It" (a production award shared with Michael Jackson); Album of the Year for *Thriller* (production award); Best Recording for Children for the MCA album *E.T. The Extra-Terrestrial*, performed by Michael Jackson and produced by Quincy; and a repeat as Producer of the Year (shared with Michael Jackson).

Jones' projects in 1984 included contributions to the music for the Olympic Summer Games in Los Angeles. This project brought still another Grammy for Best Arrangement on an Instrumental (shared with Jeremy Lubbock) for his track "Grace" (Gymnastics Theme) from the Columbia LP *Official Music of the XXIIIrd Olympiad in Los Angeles.*

In early 1985, Quincy became involved in another massive project, one that was to lead to the multistar recording of the USA for Africa single "We Are the World." Taking a cue from the Band Aid project organized in England by Bob Geldof to raise money to combat famine in Africa, Harry Belafonte and Ken Kragen evolved the idea of a similar recording effort by U.S. artists. Lionel Richie and Michael Jackson wrote "We Are the World" and the night of January 28, 1985, Quincy Jones supervised a who's who of pop, rock, and soul stars in taping the material. Among the many who took part, besides Richie and Jackson, were Belafonte, Bruce Springsteen, Stevie Wonder, Huey Lewis and the News, Dan Aykroyd, Ray Charles, Bob Dylan, Lindsey Buckingham, Diana Ross, Paul Simon, Al Jarreau, Cyndi Lauper, Jeffrey Osborne, Tina Turner, Stevie Wonder, the Pointer Sisters, Steve Perry, Smokey Robinson, Kenny Rogers, Dionne Warwick, Billy Joel, Waylon Jennings, Willie Nelson, Sheila E, Bob Geldof, Hall & Oates, James Ingram, and other members of the Jackson family.

The single rose to number one the week of April 13, 1985 and stayed there for three more weeks, earning millions of dollars for famine relief. Later it became the title song of a best-selling album that swelled the total still further. In the Grammy voting for the year, the single easily was victorious as Record of the Year and the LP was named Album of the Year.

JONES, RICKIE LEE: *Singer, songwriter, guitarist. Born Chicago, Illinois, November 8, 1954.*

A tough-talking, hard-drinking child of the streets, Rickie Lee Jones burst from obscurity in 1979 with her first album, which became one of the major successes of that year. That LP and her next one established her as potentially one of the more influential writers and performers in the rock/pop idiom. However, the very environment that nurtured her unique style proved a stumbling block to steady creative progress. Problems with alcohol as well as management difficulties sidelined her for a number of years in the early 1980s before she surfaced to try to resume her career in mid-decade.

Rickie Lee was born in Chicago in a neighborhood near the Chicago Cubs' ballpark, Wrigley Field. Some of her grandparents had been in vaudeville, but her parents earned a living, she jokingly said, "in the restaurant business," which meant that they had worked as a waiter and waitress. Her father did like to sing and, at one point, wrote a song called "The Moon Is Made of Gold," which Rickie Lee included in her stage performances of the late 1970s and early '80s.

It was not a tranquil upbringing. Her parents were often at odds with each other. During her childhood, they separated for a while and then got back together. The family, which included several other children, was uprooted a number of times as her parents drifted from one state to another, working at a series of relatively unsatisfying jobs. The environment helped make Rickie Lee more unhappy and rebellious than the typical teenager. Her formal schooling ended when she was expelled from high school in Olympia, Washington.

She already had started drinking and after that incident she went out on her own as a drifter and member of the seamier underclass of modern society. She found occasional work to pay the rent, but much of the time she simply hung out with friends and drank. As she later said: "I've been as far down as I can go and I made it out. So there's nothing to be afraid of anymore."

Her wanderings took her to many cities on the U.S. West Coast as the 1970s went by. Eventually she made her way to the Los Angeles area in the mid-1970s, where she settled for a time in the Venice section. Her income came primarily from work as a waitress in small bars and restaurants, but she had always liked to sing and increasingly the idea of going into show business crossed her mind. By 1978, she was finding occasional gigs, most of which she did for no pay. Sometimes she sang with local bands, including one called Spanish Logo she later used as the theme for one of her songs. In general, during that period, she said: "I performed in dives and little bars that pay about $10 per four sets. If I could get one, I'd use a jazz trio. If not, I'd go solo." The audience, she recalled, typically was "full of bikers, degenerates, drunken men, and toothless women."

Her friends and acquaintances included a mixture of down-and-outers and some creative types, like Tom Waits, who drew inspiration from living in the rough milieu of the urban jungle. (*See Waits, Tom.*) Among that group was a close friend named Chuck E., also a member of the Waits circle, about whom she later wrote, he was "king of the sidewalk, the most popular guy on Santa Monica Boulevard."

By the fall of 1978, a demonstration tape found its way to the desk of Warner Brothers artists & repertoire executive Len Waronker. He and fellow executive Russ Titlemen checked her out and soon signed her to the label. In short order, they had Ms. Jones in the studio recording her first album. That collection was issued in February 1979 under the title *Rickie Lee Jones.*

The songs she provided had subjects somewhat akin to the offbeat themes proffered by Tom Waits, sometimes described as '70s Beat ((though Waits always bristled at being compared to a movement of the '50s). There were elements of '50s pop, jazz, R&B, and rock in the melodies, as might be expected from a writer who listed among her favorite artists Van Morrison, Sarah Vaughan, Marvin Gaye, Laura Nyro, and Peggy Lee.

She acknowledged she wrote about things she knew about. She told Jeff Melvoin of *Time* magazine: "My writing is all from a particular neighborhood. I can pick any person on this street or the next and just be them."

She observed in biographical notes for Warner Brothers: "My songs are pretty eclectic. They're written on an acoustic guitar and some of them have an R&B feel. Others have a jazz base, and it's kind of young, it's kid, but it's really sensitive in a lot of ways . . . wait, I'll give it to you in colors: it's very dark reds and blacks and browns. That's much better.

"When people start comparing me to other singers and writers, I just ignore it. I've gotta laugh. My music is real personal. I think that's what—if anything—will make it noticed."

It certainly was noticed and in rapid order. The album soon became a favorite of reviewers and her cross-country tour that began in the spring of 1979 proved that she could win over a good share of the general public as well. Between songs she demonstrated the ability to use more off-color words than Joan Rivers (in her off-camera performances) and, despite a voice that wasn't particularly unique and a tendency to hit occasional sour notes on her guitar, she projected a charisma that enthralled the listeners.

Describing one of her shows that won over New York City fans, Jay Cocks wrote in *Time* (May 21,

1979): "The titles [of her original compositions] fix the tone and set the stage ("Easy Money," "Coolsville," "The Last Chance Texaco") while the songs spin out little narratives of hard luck and high spirits in the big town: 'There was a Joe/ Leanin' on the back door/A couple little kids with their eyes on a couple of bills/Their eyes was starin'/They was waitin'/To get their hands on some Easy Money.'

"Jones sings of such capers in a musky voice that slides across the lyrics, scatting between them and eliding words in vintage hipster style, as if English were a foreign language learned in a speed-speech course."

Rickie Lee Jones went past platinum levels. It was a hit in Europe and other countries as well. In Australia, it was number one on the album charts for five straight weeks. In the spring and summer, her single "Chuck E's in Love" made the top 5 in the U.S. The track "Company," among others, also got considerable airplay on AM and FM radio.

Her eagerly awaited second album came out in 1981 on Warner Brothers. Called *Pirates,* it was more uneven than the first LP, but overall had enough high points to make it one of the more interesting releases of the year and won Ricki Lee a gold-record award from the RIAA.

She completed another album, *The Magazine* (Warner Brothers, 1983), before her career came to a temporary halt. For a time, some columnists conjectured her problems might be too great for her to overcome. But in 1985, she returned to in-person performances seemingly no worse for wear and by 1986 was working on a new album for the Geffen label.

JONES, TOM: *Singer, drummer. Born Pontypridd, South Wales, June 7, 1940.*

Geographically speaking, Great Britain is so small it might be thought that a voice with a window-shattering intensity such as Tom Jones' would almost reach London from his home area in Wales. However, for a good many years, London was unaware of him and it was mainly a chance visit by Gordon Mills, later Jones' manager, that led to the discovery of the performer once touted as England's main challenger for Frank Sinatra's mantle.

Jones, born Thomas Jones Woodward, strayed very little from his home precincts for the first quarter-century of his life. Singing comes naturally to many Welshmen, as it did to Tom, who started in his church choir and later sang with the school choir at Treforrest Secondary Modern School. The strength of his voice was phenomenal, though not always appreciated by his teachers, who tried to tone him down because he could be heard over all other singers when the national anthem was sung.

Tom's formal schooling ended at 16, as it does for the majority of schoolboys in Britain. He married almost as soon as he left school and brought in money for his wife, Linda, from an assortment of jobs, including builder's laborer, glove cutter, and pub singer at night. He taught himself to play drums and worked with local groups for some years before forming one of his own. By 1963, he had gained a following who cheered his group, Tommy Scott and the Senators, at dates in local clubs. It was there that Gordon Mills, a fellow Welshman four years Tom's senior, happened upon him in 1964.

As Mills recalled: ''A friend persuaded me to go along and listen to this group because I had just left a singing trio myself to set up in songwriting and management. The first few bars were all I needed to hear—they convinced me that here was a voice which could make him the greatest singer in the world.'' Mills went backstage to compliment Jones and ended up as his manager. ''It's strange,'' Mills told Robert Hilburn of the *Los Angeles Times* (June 6, 1971), ''but Tom always had a feeling that some day, someone would come by the club and see him. He didn't take the traditional step of going to London to be discovered.''

After changing Tom's name to Tom Jones, reputedly because of the success of the movie of that name, Mills took him to London. Surprisingly, it was not an easy task. ''People gave me all kinds of excuses. They said he shouted and screamed. They said he moved like Presley. They said he was too old-fashioned.''

Mills and Jones persisted, though, gaining small club dates and finally gaining a recording contract in late 1964. The first single release was a flop and Jones told Mills he wanted to try a new song Mills had written, ''It's Not Unusual.'' At first, Mills said no, because he had promised it to a woman singer. But she turned it down and Jones' version became a major hit of 1965, reaching number one on the British charts and the *Billboard* top 10 in the U.S. His theme from the film *What's New Pussycat* hit the top 10 as well.

Jones now could find plenty of places he could sing. At first, he played teenage shows. Mills observed the audience and soon realized that ''he was too strong on stage, so aggressive that the kids were afraid of him. They would draw back from the stage. This is when I thought of trying him with a mature audience. I put him into the Cafe Royale and it was perfect. It was the first time I had seen mature women [in their 20s and above] get up on the stage. I could see they wanted someone to relate to just as the younger audience wanted to relate to rock stars.''

From then on, resplendent in a tuxedo—which he proceeded to divest himself of, in part, as he went through his emotional, hip-swiveling performance—Jones was a major in-person star. For a while, his recording career dipped, though, and few of his efforts turned up on hit charts in 1966 and 1967. Then Jones heard Jerry Lee Lewis's recording of the country hit, ''Green, Green Grass of Home'' and decided to do it himself. The recording, on Parrot (a subsidiary of London Records), moved to number one in England in 1968 in three weeks. Later it achieved *Billboard*'s top 20 in the U.S.

This started a virtual avalanche of successful singles and albums. During 1968, Jones followed up with such songs as ''Delilah'' and ''Help Yourself'' and in 1969 gained a U.K. gold record for ''Love Me Tonight'' and ''I'll Never Fall in Love Again.'' During 1969, he gained five gold-LP awards for *Help Yourself, Tom Jones Live!, Tom Jones Live in Las Vegas, Tom Jones, Fever Zone,* and *This is Tom Jones.* Continuing his string into the 1970s, Jones gained a gold record for *I (Who Have Nothing)* (1970) and *Tom Jones Sings She's a Lady* (1971), whose gold title track reached number two in *Billboard.* Later in 1971, his LP *Tom Jones Live at Caesar's Palace* made the U.S. charts.

Jones climaxed a series of guest appearances on major TV shows by hosting his own show in 1969. The show gained good ratings as a summer replacement and was brought back as a feature variety series in the fall.

During 1971, Jones appeared on American best-selling singles lists with such songs as ''Till,'' ''Can't Stop Loving You,'' ''Resurrection Shuffle,'' and ''Puppet Man.'' His top 10 hits in England during the year were ''She's a Lady'' and ''Lazybones.'' In 1972, he had the hit album *Close Up* and the single ''The Young New Mexican Puppeteer.'' In 1973 he was represented on the charts by the album *The Body and Soul of Tom Jones.* His other mid-1970s albums included *Memories Don't Leave Like People Do* on Parrot and the London anthology, *Tom Jones' Greatest Hits.*

After the mid-1970s, Jones' career turned into a pattern of annual visits to the hotel stages of Las Vegas and such medium-sized venues as the Greek Theatre in Los Angeles, where his devoted audience increasingly was made up of older fans, some of whom brought their families along. Jones seemed to have reached a plateau from which he had no desire to extend himself in any new creative directions. One result was that he tended to emphasize the successful songs of his earlier days rather than new challengers for either critical or chart acclaim. He left Parrot/London for a new U.S. label, Epic, in the late 1970s, turning out such LPs as *What a Night, Say You'll Stay until Tomorrow,* and *Tom Is Love.* In the early 1980s, he switched to Mercury Records, which issued his album debut, *Darlin'* in 1981.

During the 1980s, Jones' career essentially paralleled the pattern of the previous decade. He continued to record new material that sold moderately well around the world without making any major chart impact and he remained a good drawing card on the nightclub and theater circuit worldwide, including the usual trips to Las Vegas and annual performances at the London Palladium. In late 1987, the by then 47-year-old grandfather (whose marriage was still intact after 30 years), remained a favorite of many over-30 fans, particularly female adherents. (During 1986, a poll of its readers by *PM Magazine* resulted in Tom's being named Sexiest Male Singer.)

JOPLIN, JANIS: *Singer, lyricist. Born Port Arthur, Texas, January 19, 1943; died Hollywood, California, October 3, 1970.*

In her photographs or seen from the edge of the stage, Janis Joplin had the look of a sensitive, naive youngster. But close up, her features had a gaunt, haggard appearance of one considerably older. In truth, by the time she died from an overdose of drugs, she had packed more into her 27 years of life than most people do in three score and ten.

One thing was certain, Janis deserved enshrinement in the rock music hall of fame. But being there would not necessarily please her, for being a rebel in a rebellious generation, she tended to abhor formalism with a vengeance.

She was born into a reasonably comfortable family. Her father worked for the Texaco Canning Company in Port Arthur and her mother was registrar of a business college. The other children in the family grew up without posing much challenge to the familiar values of American society. But by the time she was 14, she already had begun to draw away from most of the people around her. In high school, her tastes in music seemed strange to her friends and neighbors. She liked folk music and blues, spending hours listening to records of such black artists as Leadbelly, Bessie Smith, and Odetta. In addition, she read a lot, concentrating on poetry and more intellectual books than appealed to the average Port Arthur teenager of her peer group.

At 17, she left home dressed in a white shirt and a pair of blue jeans. By this time, she realized her throaty, three-octave voice was a potential asset and she put it to use at first as a country & western singer in Houston, Texas. For the next few years, she hitched rides or scraped up money for bus fare to get away from Texas to the goal of most hippie-type children, California. She enrolled at some of the colleges on the West Coast, picked up various jobs as a folk singer, and, in between jobs, supported herself by drawing unemployment checks. In 1965 and early 1966, she sang at a number of folk clubs and bars in the San Francisco area where she made little money, but did impress a few friends in the music field with her vocal ability.

However, though she'd tried four colleges and wandered around many communes and other youth establishments of the region, things weren't going too well. As she said later, laconically: "Things got all messed up for me out there." She gave up the Coast scene and returned to Texas, where she had a job waiting as vocalist with a country & western band.

However Big Brother and the Holding Company (a relatively new group formed in 1965), was looking for a female vocalist to distinguish it from the hundreds of other promising combos in the San Francisco Bay Area. (*See Big Brother and the Holding Company.*) Chet Helm, a friend of the group, remembered Janis, sought her out, and brought her back to San Francisco. She joined the group in June 1966. Suddenly everything fell into place.

Janis hadn't done much rock singing, but now, with the group behind her, she found this kind of music released all the pent-up hatred, frustration, and dynamic energy inside her. Like a rock version of Edith Piaf, she didn't just sing her songs, she became a vibrating, explosive part of them. Her ability to transmit this tremendous energy to an audience became more and more apparent, reaching a climax in the famous appearance of Big Brother and the Holding Company at the Monterey Pop Festival in the summer of 1967. Janis stopped the show as she thundered her lyrics into the microphone like a blues shouter while simultaneously shaking her body in all directions and punctuating some of the notes by leaping into the air with the microphone clutched tensely in one hand and the other arm flung out wildly to the side.

In February 1968, the group made their first trip east to appear at the Anderson Theater on Second Avenue in New York. The *Village Voice* of February 22, 1968, said of the performance: "Although not beautiful in the usual sense, she sure projects. Janis is a sex symbol in an unlikely package. Her belting, grooving style combines Bessie Smith's soul with the finesse of Aretha Franklin covered all over with a James Brown drive. She jumps and runs and pounces, vibrating the audience with solid sound. The range of her earthy, dynamic voice seems almost without limits. At times, she seemed to be singing harmony with herself."

The in-person success of Big Brother quickly turned into the clink of gold for Columbia Records, which signed the group during this New York run. The first Columbia LP, *Cheap Thrills* (1968), exceeded $1 million in sales in a few months. (Actually, the first Big Brother LP, *Big Brother and the Holding Company* was issued earlier by Mainstream Records and reissued by Columbia in 1971.) Janis, though, so overshadowed the group that it was only a matter of time before she went her own way. During 1968, she organized her own backup group, taking only Sam Andrew of the original Big Brother assemblage with her. The other Big Brother members never hid their bitterness at the move, feeling, in part, that they had made Janis an international success, but smarting even more under her alleged remarks of putting down their instrumental ability. A second Big Brother LP, *Be a Brother* (1968), included some tracks with Janis, but she was given no special billing for them. Meanwhile, her first solo LP, the raspy-voiced *I Got Dem Ol' Kozmic Blues Again Mama!* (Columbia, 1969) went gold with its combination of vintage soul, rock, and compositions by the Bee Gees, Rodgers and Hart, and Joplin herself. In the fall of 1970, Janis came out to Hollywood to start work on a new album at Columbia's West Coast studios. Before the session was completed, Janis's body was discovered in the Landmark Hotel in Hollywood on Sunday, October 3, 1970. Fresh puncture marks on her arm seemed to tell the story, but the fact her death resulted from a heroin overdose was not confirmed for some time.

The session was released posthumously on the platinum *Pearl* (whose title came from her nickname).

Backing her was the five-member Full Tilt Boogie. (Sam Andrew was no longer a part of Janis' band.) A single from the LP, Janis's version of Kris Kristofferson's country composition, "Me and Bobby McGee," hit number one on *Billboard* for March 20 and 27, 1971. (*See Kristofferson, Kris.*)

In the years that followed, Janis's life became the stuff of legends, the subject of books and articles and, in 1980, a prime source for the script of the film *The Rose.* In the film, the character of the star-crossed rock vocalist played by Bette Midler was modeled on Janis (though the story-line is fictional). In the fall of 1973, Janis's former press agent from the Albert Grossman organization, Myra Friedman, authored the biography *Buried Alive,* published by William Morrow.

A major thesis of Myra's, she indicated in discussions with Robb Baker of *After Dark* magazine (November 1973), was that Janis really had been seeking someone to give direction to her life. As Friedman wrote in her book, "That is exactly the way Janis went through life, rippling lightning all the way, but depending on people to make her stop, as if she could neither read nor observe the signs herself."

Myra's analysis, Baker added, was that "It was a

control that she never really found, in her parents, in her friends, in the 'pretty young boys' and 'jive punks' and macho strongmen she kept chasing into bed, in her music business associates."

Friedman's summation from her association with Joplin was: "Janis was afflicted with emotional astigmatism. Each second was clear, but there was no focus. She was disordered, decentralized and diffused."

Those comments are open to discussion, but Janis's status as one of rock's most charismatic and influential performers is not. This holds true despite the fact it must be based on the limited amount of material left behind from her all-too-brief lifetime. Occasional compilations of her work continued to be issued from time to time, such as Columbia's early 1982 LP, *Farewell Song,* based mostly on material made in 1968 with the Big Brother group, and the 1985 Rhino LP, *Big Brother and the Holding Company Live* based on tapes of a 1966 concert. Some additional insight into her life and times came from the mid-1980s biography by David Marsh, published by St. Martin's Press.

Though the recorded work of Janis is relatively meager, it seems certain she will be remembered as long as people follow pop music. As a member of another group summed up: "Janis was really a very sweet person. She really lived for only one thing— her songs—and threw all of herself into it. The hard drinking, the drugs—those things were just fill-ins to keep away the threat of boredom for the times she wasn't performing." (*See Thornton, Big Mama; Womack, Bobby.*)

JOURNEY: *Vocal and instrumental group. Original members, (1973): Neal Schon, born San Mateo, California, 1954; Ross Valory, born California, 1949; George Tickner; Prairie Prince; Gregg Rolie, born California, 1947. Prince replaced in 1974 by Aynsley Dunbar, born England. Tickner left in early 1975. Steve Perry, born Hanford, California, added in 1978. Dunbar left in 1978, replaced by Steve Smith, born Boston, Massachusetts, 1954. Rolie left in 1980, replaced by Jonathan Cain. Core group reduced to Perry, Schon and Cain in mid-1980s.*

A middle-of-the- road band highly regarded by Midwestern music writers, but typically looked askance by the U.S. East and West Coast rock critic establishment, Journey got its share of snide press notices, but won love where it counted—from the fans. The band started with impeccable rock credentials, including instrumental stars from the Santana band and super drummer Aynsley Dunbar. (*See Jefferson Airplane; Mayall, John; Santana.*) However, it remained a cult favorite for years until changes in band makeup and style brought a toehold on the ladder of success in the late 1970s, an opening the band exploited for worldwide fame over the next half dozen years.

Original incentive for Journey's formation came from one-time drummer turned band executive Walter "Herbie" Herbert. After the first incarnation of Carlos Santana's group broke up in 1972, Herbert, who had been manager of Santana, suggested to former Santana guitarist Neal Schon and bass guitarist Ross Valory that they form a new band with rhythm guitarist George Tickner. (Tickner and Valory previously had been with the group Frumious Bandersnatch with which Herbert once had been associated.) Prairie Prince was added on drums and another Santana musician, Gregg Rolie, brought in as vocalist and keyboards player.

Rolie, who took over as primary writer in the band's early days, previously helped Carlos Santana form the Santana band in 1967 and had played all over the world with that group. Schon, only 20 when he joined Journey, had an awesome reputation as a guitarist before his midteens. At 16, he turned down a bid to join Eric Clapton in Derek and the Dominos. Before and after joining Santana, he backed many major artists as a session musician. Valory, a veteran Bay Area performer, had credentials that included, besides Santana and Frumious Bandersnatch, regular jamming with the Jerry Garcia—Mel Saunders group in San Francisco area clubs.

That first Journey quintet made its public debut on New Year's Eve, December 31, 1973, at Bill Graham's Winterland in San Francisco. Shortly after the turn of the year, Prairie Prince left to join the Tubes and English-born Aynsley Dunbar came aboard. Dunbar had backed or been a member of bands led by many notable artists, including John Mayall, Jeff Beck, Frank Zappa, Lou Reed, and David Bowie. His band work included his own group Retaliation, Zappa's Mothers of Invention, the Bonzo Dog Doo Dah Band, and, after Journey, the Jefferson Starship.

Talking of the rhythmic patterns of early Journey, Dunbar said: "We are working on times out of the four and three routine which gets very boring, and are into 20/8, 28/8, 5, 7, 10, and any other times that fit into a melodic run without falling into the old trap of stretching or shortening it into 4/4, but always keeping it rocking—which is my responsibility."

Herbert kept the band on the road almost constantly in 1974 as an opening act for all kinds of groups from Uriah Heep to Kiss to Weather Report while he fought to get a record contract. His persistence paid off with a pact from CBS that resulted in the debut LP, *Journey* (1975). Soon after its release, the grind of concert work caught up with Tickner, who left the band. The group's constant concert work in the mid-1970s was not without results. It did gain a following of sorts. But its emphasis on progressive-style instrumental numbers such as "Of a Lifetime" and "Kahoutek," Herbert and some group members decided, tended to limit its appeal. It took two more albums, *Look Into the Future* (1976) and *Next* (1977), plus thousands of road miles before a change in direction was agreed upon. Word was passed around that Journey was looking for a lead singer. The search brought in vocalist Steve Perry.

Perry's interest in music went back to his youth in the farming town of Lemoore in California's San Joaquin Valley, where he played drums in his high school band and sang in the choir. After a while, he adapted his drum and vocal talents to the needs of a series of rock bands, culminating in a promising group he assembled during the mid-1970s, Alien Project. Success seemed on the horizon in 1977 with a CBS recording contract in the offing when tragedy struck. Perry told Ruth Gershenzon of *BAM* magazine (June 27, 1980): "It was a fun band and . . . then the bass player unfortunately got killed in a car accident on the freeway in Los Angeles. On the Fourth of July weekend he was a statistic and on the seventh we were supposed to talk to Columbia about a contract."

Columbia executives contacted him and asked if he might now consider trying out for Journey. Perry sent a copy of the Alien Project demo tape to Herbert, who asked him to catch up with the band in Denver, Colorado. Perry did as requested and on his first day there he and Schon co-wrote two songs, "Patiently" and "Somethin' to Hide," that made the next album. That album, *Infinity* (1978), represented a changing of the guard. Perry co-wrote all but two songs and had a strong voice in the album's preparation. It signaled that vocals, rather than instrumentals, would be the focus of the band's style. From then on, Perry and Schon were the central songwriters, not Rolie.

As to his approach to lyrics, Perry told *BAM*: "I'm a simplistic lyricist. I'm into things that just say what you want to say (with emphasis on love themes). I don't want to make people get too deep with what I'm trying to say. But I do have some tunes where it takes a couple of times before you listen to it and kind of get what I mean. . . . Or maybe you never will."

The new combination worked. Backed, as usual, by a breakneck tour pace, *Infinity* went on to win platinum certification from the RIAA. For the first time, the band started to get sizable airplay for its singles and three made lower chart levels in 1978: "Wheel in the Sky," "Anytime," and "Lights." It was the newfound singles attention that helped give the momentum in album sales that was the key to success.

Before the next LP came out, Dunbar had been replaced by Steve Smith on drums, reflecting some internal disagreements. Perry told Patrick MacDonald of the *Seattle Times* (May 5, 1979): "The reason we changed is because we want to have the versatility to do anything we want. With Aynsley that was impossible. He definitely was one of those stylized drummers. He has a fantastic style, really strong, but I just feel the nature of the word *journey* is a movement situation. We had to change because [the album] *Evolution* could not have been done with Aynsley."

Smith, who grew up in Boston, Massachusetts, studied music at the Berklee College of Music there. Before coming to Journey, he appeared with Focus, Jean Luc Ponty, and Montrose. His first recording work with Journey was for the platinum *Evolution* (1979). Charted singles from it were "Just the Same Way" in 1979 and "Lovin', Touchin', Squeezin'" in late 1979 and early 1980. Also on the charts during the latter period was the LP *In the Beginning,* a CBS reissue of some of the band's earlier tracks.

In early 1980, Journey's next studio album, *Departure,* came out. The band's all-time best-seller, it remained on the lists into 1983, achieving multiplatinum sales totals of over 6 million copies. During 1980, Journey had four LPs on the lists at one time or another: *Infinity, Evolution, In the Beginning,* and *Departure.* It also was a good singles year with five releases making the charts: "Lovin', Touchin', Squeezin'" (held over from 1979), "Too Late," "Any Way You Want It," "Walks Like a Lady," and "Good Morning Girl"/"Stay A While."

After the *Departure* support tour was over, Gregg Rolie announced he was stepping down in favor of solo projects. His place was taken by Jonathan Cain, previously keyboards player with the Babys. In Cain, the band gained a talented songwriter as well as an instrumentalist.

Cain's first recorded work for Journey appeared on the platinum mid-1981 CBS LP *Escape.* (That album was preceded by the early 1981 platinum live LP, *Captured,* which still featured Rolie.) *Escape* included three top 10 singles: "Who's Crying Now," "Don't Stop Believin'," and "Open Arms."

The platinum 1983 LP, *Frontiers* provided the top 10 single "Separate Ways (Worlds Apart)." The National Gallup Poll year-end review showed Journey as the Most Popular Rock Band of 1983.

After the release of *Frontiers* and the accompanying tour, band members decided to take time off to work on various separate projects during 1984–85.

For Neal Schon, this involved a brief tour with Sammy Hagar under the name "HSAS" from which tracks for a live album were taken. (*See Hagar, Sammy.*) Jonathan Cain wrote a number of songs for other artists, handling production work for some of those recordings, which involved efforts with Loverboy and Australian vocalist Jimmy Barnes. (*See Loverboy.*)

Steve Smith completed a jazz album with his group Vital Information. This hiatus also offered Perry the chance for a platinum solo album, *Street Talk* (CBS, 1984). The collection provided four charted singles, including the top 5 hit "Oh Sherrie." (The other chart singles were "She's Mine," "Strung Out," and "Foolish Heart.") In 1985, he was one of many rock stars to help record the song "We Are the World" as part of the music industry's aid for Africa efforts. He also provided a track for the subsequent USA for Africa album, "If Only for the Moment Girl." Schon also contributed to the heavy metal musicians' project called Hear'N'Aid.

As a band, though, even while it was temporarily out of action, Journey was represented on singles charts or soundtrack albums in the mid-1980s with "After the Fall," "Send Her My Love," and the soundtrack songs "Ask the Lonely" from the film *Two of a Kind* and "Only the Young" from *Vision Quest.*

For a while, it seemed as though Journey as an entity might fade away, but in late 1985, three members of the band (Perry, Cain, and Schon) went into the studio to start another LP. Though Steve Smith played on three album cuts, by the start of 1986, it was acknowledged that he and Valory were gone. Cain maintained: "We all parted on a very good note. There weren't any hard feelings on anybody's part. Smitty basically wanted to get more into jazz. And Ross was just tired of the road and wanted a family life. Both of them will be replaced by session musicians for the world tour for our new album."

Co-produced by Perry and Jim Gaines, the April 1986 LP, *Raised on Radio,* was certified gold by year-end.

JUDAS PRIEST: *Vocal and instrumental group from Birmingham, England. Personnel in 1974, Rob Halford, K. K. Downing, Glenn Tipton, Ian Hill, Alan Moore. Moore replaced by Les Binks in 1977. Binks replaced by Dave Holland in 1979.** *

Swirling clouds of smoke envelop the stage as the crowd howls in anticipation. With wild rock guitar sounds pouring from the loudspeakers, a cheer goes

---

*Based partly on personal interviews with Irwin Stambler.

up as lead vocalist Rob Halford looms up from the manmade fog on a Harley motorcycle, clad in a black biker's jacket and shiny cap, briefly flicking a bull whip as he launches his slashing vocals through the haze-filled room. As the smoke floats away, other forms take shape—pinwheeling lead guitarist K. K. Downing and his two more stoic associates, Glenn Tipton and Ian Hill, whose high-pitched guitar attack is backed by the frantic drum tattoo of Dave Holland. It's a pace that rarely slackens throughout the evening as Judas Priest demonstrates its mastery of heavy metal rock.

This sort of imagery helped attract a steadily growing following when the band made its initial mark in the mid-1970s. But there has to be more than that for a band to maintain a worldwide audience for more than a decade. Tipton attributed this track record to the band's willingness to experiment and seek new directions. "Though we're known as heavy metal, we're always trying to update what we do. We don't go for the slow plodding approach of early '70s heavy metal. We have a new form of heavy metal, heavy metal for the '80s, which is faster and more exciting. I think more thought goes into what we do than for the typical heavy metal rock band. Every song has to mean something to us. When we do an album, every track has to count."

The band's roots were in the English industrial city of Birmingham, where the founding members were performing with various groups in their teens. The musicians who have remained the core of the band almost from the start got together in the early 1970s. Ian Hill recalled: "We had a group that split down the middle, leaving me and K.K. [Downing] looking for a drummer and a vocalist. We heard of Rob and the drummer in his band at the time, but we were interested more in him than the other guy. So we approached Rob and asked if he'd like to join and it's been like gold ever since."

Brushing a hand through his relatively short, sandy hair, Halford added: "Well, not exactly gold yet—more like platinum. Anyway, I knew I liked the band the very first time I saw it when I wasn't even a member. What they were playing was sort of vaguely blues. I guess you'd call it progressive rock."

That band already called itself Judas Priest and Hill noted the name predated his membership. "He means we don't know where 'Judas Priest' came from," Halford said with a laugh, "but it conjures up some kind of idea of what the music sounds like."

Downing commented: "Of course, the original [band] feeling came from blues, just sort of grew out of it. But not the kind of years-old blues the Rolling Stones did, like 'Little Red Rooster.' I think we've always been a rock group for today—but a basic rock band, not into punk or new wave."

Halford said: "I think we've reaffirmed the fact that rock'n'roll still turns on a lot of people. A lot of people, I think, were confused by the big media splurge on the Sex Pistols and other punk bands and thought that would be the way things would go. We felt from the beginning there would always be a place for straight-ahead rock and we haven't seen anything to change our minds."

After the band added Tipton and drummer Alan Moore and began to draw attention to itself around Birmingham, it gained its first major milestone in 1974 with a contract with Gull Records (part of Decca U.K.). The debut LP, *Rocka Rolla*, sold some copies but was hardly a blockbuster. In 1975, the band put on a hard-driving set at the Reading Festival in England that provided increased record buyer interest for material in the second Gull LP, *Sad Wings of Destiny* (1976). The album contained initial versions of two songs that later became hits for the band: "Victim of Changes" and "Epitaph." It showed up on lower chart levels in the U.K., Japan, and the U.S.

Before the year was out, the band had switched labels, signing with CBS Records worldwide. The new label helped finance the band's first major U.S. tour. Their first album for CBS was *Sin after Sin* (1977). A rather unusual number from the LP was a heavy metal version of Joan Baez' "Diamonds and Rust."

Sin after Sin did quite well sales-wise and set the stage for an even more successful release, *Stained Class* (1978). When the next studio album (*Hell Bent for Leather*) came out in February 1979, Judas Priest was in Tokyo, Japan, for five concert dates that were taped for the group's first live album, the two-disc *Unleashed in the East* issued the following September. Two singles from *Hell Bent for Leather* made the U.K. top 10 in 1979: "Take on the World" and "Evening Star." The latter became the first single from the band to crack the *Billboard* Hot 100.

Unleashed in the East proceeded to outsell all previous band albums, entering the top 50 on major U.S. album charts. Their next album, *British Steel*, issued in April 1980, did even better, going gold. The rock press began to take increased notice of the band. For the *Creem* magazine heavy metal issue in October 1980, Rob Halford was chosen for the cover photo. A *Rolling Stone* reviewer wrote that Judas Priest "define the heavy metal genre at the outset of the '80s." Other milestones of that year included another top 10 U.K. single ("Living after Midnight" from *British Steel*) and a debut video on the BBC of the song "Breaking the Law." From *Point of Entry* (March 1981), three songs were covered by videos:

"Heading out to the Highway," "Don't Go," and "Hot Rockin'."

The following year, another video, "You've Got Another Thing Comin'," played a role in the biggest commercial success the band had to date, the platinum LP *Screaming for Vengeance*.

The next album, *Defenders of the Faith* (gold, 1984), has become famous with heavy metal fans not only for songs like "Some Heads are Gonna Roll," but for the heavy metal monster (called "Metallion" by the band members) that graces the cover. The cover idea was theirs, they claimed, though its final form was worked out by illustrator Doug Johnson. The first video number based on the album, "Freewheel Burning," propelled the single to hit status in the U.K. before the complete album was released.

There was a somewhat longer gap than usual between *Defenders of the Faith* and the next release, the gold *Turbo* (1986), recorded in the Bahamas. A revamped stage presentation was developed for the ensuing tour, though KK told *Hit Parader* magazine this wouldn't affect the band's approach to its music. "We're very aware of what Judas Priest is and so are the fans. They wouldn't accept it if we started turning in a more commercial direction and we wouldn't be very happy either. We're very content with what we do and as long as the fans keep responding to it, we'll never change."

He had said previously: "Naturally I don't think anyone wants to be typecast. We're a rock band. There's lot of terms you can use—people like to come up with trendy names like heavy metal, but most bands don't fall into one classification that easy. Anyway, we like what we do."

Tipton added: "I think how you feel depends on the band you're into. I think what we do is very positive and I'm glad I get off on heavy metal. I think our music is exciting and aggressive. I think a lot of bands don't want to admit they're playing heavy metal because of the way critics write about it, y'know."

"Besides," Halford commented, "a change in music isn't necessarily a change in direction. It's the maturity thing. Never getting off the rails. I don't think we'll do anything sharply different, but each album is a little different. You can write a variety of material and still be in the heavy metal domain."

"Then there's the chemistry of different writers," Hill said. "Everybody in the band writes, though most of the songs are done by Ken, Glenn, and Rob."

All felt their sound was challenging and accessible, but not one-dimensional. "A lot of people think because a band is called heavy metal that its members are kinda thick and only can play a few chords," Halford said.

Tipton ventured: "We can play five."

Smiling, Halford added: "We can play five after a few drinks. Well, that sort of thinking is a hangover from rock's early days. People think we're semi-illiterates. But of course that isn't the case. We're not only interested in music, but the way the whole business works. You can't survive unless you know what you're doing and what's going on around you."

KANSAS: *Vocal and instrumental group. Members, early 1970s: Phil Ehart, born Kansas, 1951; Kerry Livgren, born Kansas, 1950; Dave Hope, born Kansas, c. 1951; Robby Steinhardt, born Michigan, c. 1951; Steve Walsh, born St. Joseph, Missouri, c. 1951; Rich Williams, born Kansas, c. 1951. Walsh replaced in 1982 by John Elefante, born Levittown, New York, c. 1958. Reorganized group, 1986, comprised Ehart, Williams, Walsh, Billy Greer, Steve Morse.*

Like many a group from their part of the U.S., Kansas started out as a bar band and sometime dance group on the Midwest college circuit before moving on to worldwide rock celebrity. Unlike most of their contemporaries from the region, Kansas had something of an identity problem. Its name caused country-rock fans to think it was their kind of band, which they quickly discovered was not the case. The band actually featured a mixture more closely related to British art-rock bands such as Yes and Genesis, but it took progressive rock fans a while to find that out.

Band co-founder Kerry Livgren pointed out to *Seventeen* magazine (January 1977): "Our band sounds the way it does because we grew up in a place—Topeka, Kansas—that had absolutely no musical tradition. We are a potpourri of every kind of music we ever heard. We've been called a classical rock band, told we're hard, heavy metal; that we sound like Marshall Tucker, like Yes, like Jethro Tull. Nobody can put their finger on us—except our fans. They always know."

Though violinist/lead vocalist Robby Steinhardt spent some of his early years in Michigan and Ohio with his adoptive parents before the family moved to Lawrence, Kansas, where his musicologist father joined the faculty of the University of Kansas, he regarded Kansas as his home state. Thus, most of the founding members essentially were native Kansans. Livgren said: "Our roots are so intertwined that it would be difficult to pick a replacement for any of us. Four of the guys were in junior high together and we all went to Topeka West High." That accounts in part for the fact that the band's roster remained intact for over a decade.

Except for Steinhardt, who was classically trained, the others became interested in performing rock in their teens. Their family backgrounds, for the most part, were middle class. Besides Steinhardt's professor father, other members' parents included a retired Air Force colonel, a judge, and, in Livgren's case, a white collar worker at Goodyear. Livgren told *Seventeen:* "My father was a weekend musician and he had a little more insight into it than most. He considered rock an occupation without security, which is pretty much true until you get to the level we're at. And even then the security's debatable. But his not wanting me to get into it made me want to do it all the more. My dad was a fanatic about my graduating from college. He never had the opportunity himself and thought it was the golden key that opened the magic door."

Livgren stuck with college while playing with local rock groups until a year before graduation. In 1970, he opted for starting his own band and trying for a musical career. He put together several versions of the band, including one named Kansas, and built up a reputation with local fans. "But it was a very meager living. The band paid the rent on a house in which we all lived, and everybody got $1 a day to build on."

Meanwhile his one-time high school friend Phil Ehart was following a different route toward the same goal. Ehart, after playing in various groups in Kansas, traveled to England in late 1971 to look for opportunities in the U.K. rock field. Finding his chances there slim, he returned home in early 1972, determined to assemble a new band. One of the first people he contacted was singer/keyboards player Steve Walsh, with whom he'd worked in previous bands. He found that Walsh was back in his hometown of St. Joseph, Missouri, working as a window washer. Ehart recalled: "I couldn't believe he was out of work. He was ready for anything."

Walsh said: "I got tired of climbing those 40-foot ladders. They were scaring the hell out of me. I'm a musician at heart anyway."

Ehart next sought out Steinhardt, who had shown some interest in rock in his later teens. Robby also said yes, being out of music altogether at the time. He told *People* magazine later: "I could probably have made it in classical music—but I never could take the six hours of practice a day. As a life-style it's much too disciplined and ascetic."

After he'd been with Kansas a while, he doubted he could return to classics anyway. "I've developed bad playing habits. I have to press an ear against the edge of the violin to hear myself [during rock concerts] and when I go running around onstage, it causes bad performing posture. I don't like earplugs—I need the intenseness and interaction of this kind of band."

"Then my phone rang," Ehart recalled. It was from another West Topeka High friend, Rich Williams, who reported he and Dave Hope just had left a successful show band that was touring the Midwest and were looking for a new association. "It took me a second to say: Hell yes!' Phil said.

Under the name White Clover, the band lined up dates in Midwest bars and clubs. That five-man band was made up of Steinhardt on violin, viola, Faucon lap cello, and vocals; Hope on bass guitar; Williams on electric and acoustic guitars; Walsh on lead vocals and keyboards; and Ehart on drums and percussion.

Though all band members could contribute to developing new material, Walsh was the primary songwriter. Ehart felt the band still needed another writer and kept his eyes and ears open. Hearing that Livgren's band wasn't doing too well, he asked Kerry to join. "I told him: 'Kerry, why don't you get rid of those wimps you're playing with and join us?' Prime psychology; hit a man when he's down." With Livgren's acquisition the band not only gained another keyboards player, guitarist, and vocalist, but also a new name. It was agreed to use Kerry's longtime favorite, Kansas. As of mid-1972, the new six-man group was on its way.

After spending the usual incubation period on the raunchy Midwest bar circuit, the band began to look around for a recording association. It sent a demonstration tape to promoter Don Kirshner, who was organizing a new label and was interested enough to start negotiations. Walsh told a reporter: "Their first offer wasn't very good. We put down a list of demands and figured we would never hear from this company again. But we heard from them two weeks later. We had to show them we weren't pushovers and we weren't hicks. Just because we're from Kansas, that don't mean we're green."

The band set to work recording its label debut in 1973, with most of the songs provided by Livgren and Walsh. "On our first album, we were pretty green," Livgren told Bob Weinstein of *Circus* (November 10, 1977). "We had never seen the inside of a [professional] recording studio. We had a kind of fresh innocent attitude."

The debut LP, *Kansas*, was issued on Kirshner Records (distributed by Columbia Records) in March 1974. Kirshner saw to it that the band got more exposure than in the past. That year, Ehart said: "We went from playing clubs and dumps to being an opening band in the large West Coast venues." This initiated a hectic touring schedule in the mid-1970s that encompassed an average of 250 performances a year, mostly as an opening act for well-known rock bands. Kansas's progress in acquiring its own audience was slow, though, and its debut LP and the following two releases, *Song for America* (1975) and *Masque* (1975), were only marginally successful.

All that changed with the release of the band's fourth LP, *Leftoverture* (October 1976). Aided by the group's first hit single ("Carry on Wayward Son," a Livgren composition), the album went platinum.

When band members returned to the studio to work on their next album in the summer of 1977, few still called Kansas home. Most had married and settled down in Atlanta, Georgia, while Steinhardt and his wife chose Tampa, Florida, as home base. The group also was looking to change its image a bit in its new album.

The goal, Livgren told *Circus*, was to "dispel the classical stigma the band has been saddled with. . . . When we first came out, we did some progressive music, or what was called 'progressive.' We had a violin, so immediately we were labeled. Maybe that is one aspect of the group, but it isn't anything that defines the total sound of the band. It's occasionally an element of the music, but it is not something we wanted to come to the forefront. Because of it, a lot of people had a preconceived idea of what Kansas was going to be like, before they even heard us. That's something we had to fight against. Maybe the classical label could fit one section of the song, but a second later, it may be more like Zeppelin."

Steinhardt was somewhat dubious about trying for what undoubtedly was meant to be a more commercial sound. He told Bob Weinstein: "For some people, money is not the key to success. Sometimes it's the other way around. Just the freedom to do albums is enough."

The next LP, *Point of Know Return*, undoubtedly was a more polished, musically somewhat simpler album than the earlier ones. Issued in September 1977, it went platinum and provided two top 10 singles: the title song (written by Walsh, Ehart, and Steinhardt) and "Dust in the Wind" (a Livgren composition). The band supported it with SRO shows across the U.S. and in other countries. But the audience was increasingly more concentrated in the mid-teens, which always poses the danger of future losses as fans move into adulthood.

Loss of momentum was, in fact, indicated by the less intense record-buying response to the group's first live release, the two-disc *Two for the Show* (Kirshner/CBS, 1978). The band's next two studio albums, *Monolith* (1979) and *Audio-Vision* (1980), went gold, but did not have anywhere near the staying power of *Leftoverture* and *Point of Know Return*.

There were indications of internal strains among group members in the early 1980s. This led to the first personnel change since the band had begun. Steve Walsh left because of disagreement with the group's creative direction in 1981 and was later replaced by New York–born singer/songwriter/keyboardist John Elefante. Ehart commented: "It's like any team. If it isn't clicking, then it should be changed. It isn't that we wanted Steve to leave. But after he did it, everybody said: 'He was right in making the move, and it was also right for us.' It added new blood, a new outlook, new material. The band feels new again."

This was not immediately apparent, however, though the next album, *Vinyl Confessions* (1982), showcased four songs by Elefante. The album suggested the group still was somewhat unsure of where it wanted to go and it spent a relatively short time on the charts. The same held true for the next release, *Drastic Measures* (1983).

The group and its advisors decided it was really time to go back to the drawing board and a drastically revamped lineup sought to repair Kansas' fortunes in the mid-1980s. The 1986 roster included three founding members (Phil Ehart, Rich Williams, and Steve Walsh) plus two newcomers to Kansas: bassist Billy Greer and guitarist Steve Morse. Greer had previously been with the band Streets while Morse had become well known to rock audiences for his work with the Dixie Dregs and as a solo album artist. *Guitar Player* magazine readers voted Morse Best Overall Guitarist for five consecutive years prior to his joining Kansas.

The revamped band signed with a new label, MCA, which issued the album, *Power*, in October 1986. First single from the LP was "All I Wanted," sung by Steve Walsh, who had rejoined the group after a five-year absence.

KATRINA AND THE WAVES: *Vocal and instrumental group. Katrina Leskanich, born Kansas, 1960; Kimberley Rew, born England; Vince De La Cruz, born Texas; Alex Cooper, born England.*

On the basis of its debut U.S. album of 1985, Katrina and the Waves had to be considered one of the most promising new groups of the 1980s. Though the future in rock music always is "iffy," the quality of its second Capitol Records release the following year suggested it had managed to withstand the feared "second-album jinx."

While half of its members could claim American citizenship, the band earned its musical spurs in Europe. Lead singer/guitarist Katrina Leskanich was the daughter of a U.S. Air Force officer whose assignments took him to many different places. The family remained in the U.S. until she was 10, when her father was sent to Europe. She spent the rest of her juvenile years overseas.

Like many youngsters of the period, she had some interest in music, but for a time sports seemed preferable. She told Dennis Hunt of the *Los Angeles Times* (April 13, 1986): "I was a good basketball player. I was the most valuable player on my team in Holland. I was on the softball team and the track team too."

She was, in fact, something of a tomboy. "I never had any boyfriends when I was in school. I couldn't be bothered with dresses and proms and stuff like that. You had to wear uncomfortable dresses and I didn't like that. Social functions like that just didn't interest me."

At 16, she changed direction and demonstrated sufficient skills to become a member of a rock band. Her parents, who wanted her to go back to the U.S. and attend the University of Kansas, were horrified. Her father, she recalled, was particularly upset and threw her out of the house, though they later let bygones be bygones when her career finally took off.

Her musical activities eventually took her to London, where the Waves took shape. The band, as it came together in 1981, comprised songwriter/ guitarist Kimberly Rew, bass guitarist Vince De La Cruz, and songwriter/drummer Alex Cooper. Rew and Cooper both were from England and had become acquainted while attending Cambridge University. Both had gained experience in local new wave groups in the late 1970s and the start of the '80s. Rew had served as lead guitarist and major songwriter for the well-regarded Soft Boys, whose 1980 LP, *Underwater Moonlight*, was hailed by *Trouser Press* as "one of the new wave's finest half dozen albums." His composition "Going Down to Liverpool" (included on the group's debut LP) provided the Bangles with a hit single in 1984. (*See Bangles, The.*) De La Cruz, originally from Texas, worked with English bands before joining Katrina and the Waves in 1981.

The group was hardly an overnight sensation. Initially it picked up intermittent income by playing for dances at military bases in England and gradually got some club exposure. For several years, Katrina told Hunt the band was "working ratty clubs in London for no money. No one cared about our music. It seemed like we might get a record deal by the time I was 40. I can't forget that. This is still a transition period. I don't want to get caught up in this glitter."

Rew's connections finally got them a contract from a Canadian record firm, which resulted in two albums during the 1982–84 period. Their sounds blended almost all aspects of pop and rock, reflecting influences from country, blues, new wave, and soul. The soul-like inflections of some of Katrina's vocals

made some people unfamiliar with the group think she might have black roots.

She traced that to the impact of Etta James music she heard in the early 1980s. That, in turn, made her seek out recordings of artists such as Aretha Franklin, Junior Walker, and Sam and Dave. She told Hunt: "For a long time I didn't listen to anything that wasn't black. Everything else seemed so tame. Before I got into black music, I was into the Eagles and Linda Ronstadt. After I got into black music, I melted down my Ronstadt records."

The success of "Going Down to Liverpool" by the Bangles in 1984 began to focus some record-industry attention on Rew and his cohorts. This led to a contract that year from Capitol Records. The gold debut LP, *Katrina and the Waves* (March 1985), featured mainly songs by Rew, including the hit single "Walking on Sunshine." De La Cruz also provided the originals "Do You Want Cryin'" and "Mexico." The album was given rave reviews by music magazines on both sides of the Atlantic. Recognition of the band's status came with its nomination as one of the five finalists for the Best New Artist in the 1985 Grammy Award voting.

The second LP, *Waves* (Capitol, early 1986) proved a worthy follow-up. For this album, Katrina demonstrated considerable potential as a songwriter, contributing five compositions in addition to Rew's new material. The album and the first single from it "Is That It?" quickly made their way onto U.S. and European charts, suggesting the group would not be a one-record sensation.

K.C. AND THE SUNSHINE BAND: *Vocal and instrumental group headed by Harry Wayne "K.C." Casey, born Hialeah, Florida, January 31, 1951; and Richard Finch, born Indianapolis, Indiana, January 25, 1954. Band members included Jerome Smith, born Hialeah, Florida, June 18; Robert Johnson, born Miami, Florida; Fermin Goytisolo, born Havana, Cuba, December 31, c. 1953.* *

In the 1970s, the two U.S. recording hubs for pop music, including soul/R&B-flavored entries, continued to be New York and Los Angeles, but for a time, their role was challenged by Miami, Florida, fueled by the disco success of K.C. and the Sunshine Band. Though an integrated group, the band was formed and headed by two white artists, Harry Wayne Casey, known as K.C., and Richard Finch, who derived a new disco sound by combining traditional soul and R&B with elements of junkanoo, a

---

*Based partly on a personal interview with Harry Casey by Irwin Stambler.

music style from the Bahamas. While the disco craze faded in the 1980s, Casey and Finch persevered and demonstrated the ability to turn out new recordings that still could command attention from a large segment of the pop audience.

Both K.C. and Finch were essentially native Floridians. Casey was born and grew up in Hialeah; Finch, though born in Indiana, was taken to that city by his family when he was one. He recalled being turned on by the Beatles. But as he grew a little older, he expanded his interest to other forms including soul and country & western. It was country & western material he began to work out on the bass guitar when he got his first instrument at 11. By 12, he was playing in a C&W band at the local Disabled Veterans Club. In high school, however, he focused on soul stylings, becoming a member of a mixed black and white group called Ball and Chain that performed together for five years, including working as a house band for 2½ years in a Miami Beach club, the Castaways.

During those years, Rick's curiosity also was aroused by the techniques used to make recordings. After a school friend introduced him to a soul artist named Clarence Reid, who recorded for a local label called T.K., Finch began hanging around the T.K. studios in his spare time and quickly learned the basics of recording. By his late teens, in fact, he was working as a part-time jack of many trades for T.K., ranging from packing records in the warehouse to occasional stints as a recording engineer. It wasn't too long before his path crossed that of Harry Casey.

As a child growing up in Hialeah, K.C. demonstrated an early interest in music and dramatics. His family believed in regular church-going and Harry's first instrumental efforts were inspired by listening to the organ in church. His parents saw that and he got keyboards lessons and he became good enough to serve as a replacement for the church organist at times.

But he was more than aware of secular music forms. "As I got a little older, I paid attention to all kinds of music—gospel, R&B, pop, classical. I didn't listen to anything intensively. I would listen off and on to different kinds of music. My family always was music-oriented. We often would gather around the piano on birthdays or other special occasions and sing and have a good time. I just grew up around music. I just decided early that was where I wanted to be. Whenever I could get some money together, I would go to the store and buy new records of whatever I was into at the time. In my neighborhood, only myself and one or two others bought more than one or two records at a time."

In his teens, though, his progress toward a career in music wasn't all that fast. "I was like in a group when I was 16 and in another when I was 18, then not in another one until we formed KC and the Sunshine Band." When he was 17, he scrounged together $500, mostly borrowed from friends, to cut a record on a fly-by-night label from Nashville. That disc, "If You're Ever in Miami"/"Emily, My Darling," he noted, deservedly never went further than the few hundred pressed as part of the deal.

After high school, he entered Miami-Dade Junior College for a time, earning money with part-time jobs, including one in a drugstore. From there, he moved on to a lower-level position with a Hialeah retail record outlet. His duties brought him in contact with Tone Distributors, which had the T.K. recording studio as a subsidiary. Casey, as Finch had done, hung around Tone/T.K. until company president Henry Stone allowed him to do such menial tasks as sweeping the floors and sorting records in the warehouse. While sorting discs in 1972, K.C. met Finch and a new team was born.

The two soon became close friends, experimenting with musical collaborations in the T.K. studio when no regular sessions were booked. Finch, who had developed considerable expertise in electronics, was more interested in the technical side, but K.C. made no secret of his desire to be a performer. "Everyone there knew I sang. I didn't try to hide it, but singers . . . singers are a dime a dozen . . . and a white singer who wanted to sing soul . . . well . . ."

A key turning point came in January 1973 at the wedding reception for Clarence Reid. The band chosen for the event was made up of musicians from the Bahamas who played junkanoo "a percussive blend of steel drums, cowbells, and whistle flutes." By then K.C. had improved his stature at T.K. to the point that he was interacting with other artists, including serving as personal secretary and booking agent for T.K. vocalist Timmy Thomas. After going with Thomas to a Washington, D.C., concert where Timmy opened for Rare Earth, he was impressed by the way the audience blew whistles during the show. It reminded him of junkanoo music. On the plane back to Florida, he outlined in his mind the basis of a song that was to become "Blow Your Whistle." After he and Finch finished writing it, they made their first studio recording, which came out on T.K. and made the R&B top 15 in 1973. With that under their belts, they came back with another single recorded with studio musicians, "Sound Your Funky Horn," which had similar success in 1974.

The duo continued to write and made demo tapes of other originals including one called "Rock Your Baby." Casey told interviewer Jim Marlowe: "One night we went into the studio to cut a whole finished track [of the song], but the vocals [were] way too high for me to sing. Now we already had a record released at the time ["Sound Your Funky Horn"] so we decided to give the song to someone else."

After Stone and T.K. A&R man Steve Alaimo heard the tape, they agreed it should be done and decided to give it to singer George McRae. The single came out in early summer and hit with both black and white record buyers. It sped up the charts to become number one on the *Billboard* pop lists the week of July 13, 1974, eventually selling an estimated 6.5 million copies worldwide.

Meanwhile, encouraged by their progress, T.K. officials were happy to approve increased activity by K.C. and Finch. For their new recordings, the duo brought in what was to become the core of the new Sunshine Band: lead guitarist Jerome Smith and drummer Robert Johnson. Also taking part, and later a longtime regular with the band, was conga player Fermin Goytisolo. The new group completed tracks for the Sunshine Band's debut LP *Do It Good*. The 1974 album had little impact in the U.S., but was a smash in Europe. The track "Queen of Clubs" became a top 10 single in England and Germany. Also a top 10 success overseas was the single "Sound Your Funky Horn."

To follow up on that popularity, plans were laid for a foreign concert in 1975. K.C. recalled: "We assembled a band for that and it was really hectic. We toured all over the U.K. and did 48 shows in 24 days. We were really well received and the disco scene in Europe was really incredible."

Although the Sunshine Band expanded to include 12 or more musicians and singers for various tours, the roster tended to vary from one series to the next, but K.C. pointed out the main recording team stayed constant. "There are changes in the band, but not in the central Sunshine Band group. The main core—four of us—me, Rick, Jerome Smith, and Robert Johnson—have stayed the same. The rest of the people are all interchangeable and don't play on the recordings. If we lose them, it's sad, but it doesn't affect our records. But if we lost one of the core four, that might affect our sound."

The next album, *KC and the Sunshine Band* (summer 1975), included the Casey/Finch composition "Get Down Tonight." Remembering the night he recorded its vocal, Casey told *Billboard:* "I couldn't believe it was such an incredible sound. I remember they must have played it back a hundred times and I couldn't believe it—it had that strange mystical feeling, a feeling I had never felt before."

His intuition was right. The single rose to number one on *Billboard* lists the week of August 30, 1975 (ironically, while the band was performing in Europe), followed a few months later by another number one *Billboard* hit, "That's the Way (I Like It)." The album became a multiplatinum-seller.

By the end of 1975, some observers were surprised at the sizable black audiences drawn to many Sunshine Band shows. K.C. commented to Richard Cromelin in *Phonograph Record* magazine (October 1975): "Sometimes I feel other people might think things about it, like 'What's the whitey doing up there?' But I've always wanted a black group behind me, because they're the only ones I felt can play the kind of music I love and the kind of music I feel. I was always rejected by white groups. My whole dream was to have a black group and that's what I have and I'm very happy with it. I don't think nothing about it. They can play the music I feel and the music I was brought up with and the music I like. I don't get rejected by them."

Finch said: "The groups I played in were all soul groups. I was always concentrating on soul music. I think people dig us because we are black and white . . . and because we're playing funky music."

There never was any doubt that it was danceable music. "In our shows," K.C. said, "we never put a time limit—we tried to play what we felt the crowd wanted to hear. It always seemed like we coulda played all night and we certainly didn't have to encourage people to dance. From the time we strike up, it's out of the seats by everyone until we leave. The fire marshal sometimes has said we got to have 'em in the seats. We'd say: 'You tell 'em!' Anyway they'd be safer standing up than in the seats."

Riding the crest of the disco boom, K.C. and his group could do no wrong for the balance of the '70s. In 1976, after picking up five Grammy Awards for the band's 1975 exploits, the group had another *Billboard* number one single, "(Shake, Shake, Shake) Shake Your Booty." The album *Part 3* also was a best-seller that year. In 1977, the group had number one single with "I'm Your Boogie Man," while "Keep It Comin' Love," reached number one on R&B charts and number two on the pop lists. The soundtrack (and soundtrack album) of the movie *Saturday Night Fever* also included the Finch/Casey recording of their "Boogie Shoes" composition.

By 1978, there was friction between K.C. and Rick and the T.K. organization, which they believed contributed to a lack of promotion for some of the group's new releases. The group's 1978 album on TK *Who Do Ya (Love)*, sold reasonably well, but didn't match the levels reached by earlier LPs.

But there were indications too that public tastes were changing and K.C. and his partner were anxious to probe new directions in writing. He noted in mid-1979: "On four LPs we used every chord there is practically. One way we haven't gone is slowing it down a bit for a more mellow approach. Some discos do play slow ballads—they don't like to keep the beat up all the time. We like to put on something for everybody. Not everybody goes to discos and we have to keep that in mind and remember those who just listen to radio. And of course if a song does well on radio, jukebox people go out and buy the record for their machines.''

This approach led to inclusion of some ballads in the next album *Do You Wanna Go Party* (which turned out to be the last recorded for T.K.). One of the first singles culled from the LP, ''Please Don't Go,'' moved upward at an unusually leisurely pace until five months later, it reached number one the week of January 5, 1980. During that year, T.K. issued a ''best-of'' collection, *KC and the Sunshine Band's Greatest Hits*. (The year before, that label issued an all instrumental LP, *Sound of Sunshine*, recorded by the band without K.C., but with Casey helping do the production.)

In the early 1980s, the Sunshine Band team and T.K. parted company, with the record firm filing for bankruptcy. K.C. and Finch then moved to Epic Records, which issued two albums under the Sunshine Band banner (*The Painter* in 1981 and *All in a Night's Work* in 1982) plus a solo effort by Casey, *Space Cadet*. None of those won much response from American fans, but the track ''Give It Up'' from *All in a Night's Work* was issued as a single by British Epic and provided K.C. with his first number one hit in England.

By then, he had much more serious things to contend with. While driving near his home in Hialeah, he was in a head-on crash with another vehicle. His injuries included a concussion and nerve damage that caused him to lose all feeling on one side of his body. For a time he was confined to a wheelchair and had to relearn how to walk. Two years later, though substantially better, he reported: ''I suffer through a lot of pain still, daily.''

But he had an indomitable spirit and by then had come back sufficiently to think about restoring his career. He had been shocked when Epic hadn't issued ''Give It Up'' in the U.S. after its overseas achievements. He negotiated an end to his contract and began his own company, Meca (Musical Entertainment Corporation of America). He issued ''Give It Up'' on the label in the U.S. and scored a top 20 hit in the spring of 1984.

This signified he could succeed even when disco had lost its bloom. As he related in Fred Bronson's *Billboard Book of Number One Hits:* ''I had always planned on having a long-range career, and never thought of being here today and gone tomorrow. I think dance or rhythm music never dies. I think a name [disco] died. A name that should never have been brought to the forefront anyway. Because the type of music that was being played in the clubs was actually rhythm & blues music and not disco and not

any other form. I had always been a little upset because the credit had not been given to rhythm & blues.''

KENDRICK, EDDIE (also Eddie Kendricks):
Singer, songwriter. Born Union Springs, Alabama, December 17, 1939.

Compared to many other vocal groups, the Temptations have had a fairly stable lineup over its long career. But there have been a few one-time members who went out to establish themselves as soloists, most notably Eddie Kendrick (whose falsetto stylings gave a spine-tingling edge to many Temptations hits of the 1960s) and another specialist in high-pitched harmonies, David Ruffin. (*See Temptations, The.*)

Kendrick spent his early years in Alabama, but moved to Detroit in his early twenties. (In his years with the Temptations, he spelled his last name Kendricks, but dropped the last letter in the 1970s.) As a member of the Temptations, he was able to convince long-time mentor, Motown record chief Berry Gordy, Jr., that he was ready for a solo career in the early 1970s. (*See Gordy, Berry, Jr.*) His 1971 debut LP, *All by Myself* on Motown's Tamla label, was a national pop hit and also made the soul top 10. He also had the hit single ''It's So Hard to Say Goodbye'' in 1971. In 1972, he placed the album *People—Hold On* on the charts and had singles hits ''Can I,'' ''Eddie's Love,'' and ''If You Let Me.'' He had an even better year in 1973 with the top 20 album *Eddie Kendricks* and disco-flavored number one single in *Billboard*, ''Keep on Truckin''' (November 10 and 17).

He continued to add to his reputation in the mid-1970s with a series of fine Tamla albums: *He's a Friend* and *Goin' Up in Smoke* (1976), *Slick* (1977), and *Eddie Kendricks at His Best* (1978).

In 1978, he switched labels, signing with Arista Records, which put out *Vintage '78* during the year and *Something More* in 1980. In the early '80s, though, his career seemed to lose steam and his releases no longer were certainties for top chart spots. Some of his earlier recordings showed up on Motown reissues, such as the 1981 *Superstar Series, Volume 19*.

Eddie and David Ruffin had been somewhat estranged from some of their old friends in the Temptations, but the wounds appeared to have healed in 1982, when they helped record the track ''Standing on the Top'' for a Temptations album.

Though Eddie continued active on the club circuit, his career seemed to be drifting for the next few years. But he gained new momentum helped by rock stars Hall & Oates, who had long admired Eddie and David Ruffin as two of the most important influences on modern rock and R&B. During 1985, Kendrick and Ruffin were featured with the Hall & Oates band during the Live Aid concert and they also helped make the gold *Hall & Oates Live at the Apollo* album (RCA, fall 1985). (*See Hall & Oates.*)

In the Grammy voting for the best of 1985, the single "The Way You Do the Things You Do"/ "My Girl," which showcased Hall & Oates, Ruffin, and Kendrick, was nominated in the Best R&B Performance by a Duo or Group with Vocal category. As part of the Grammy Awards telecast in early 1986, Kendrick and the others sang the song before a worldwide TV audience. That exposure provided the incentive for a new tour during 1985 and 1986, "The Eddie Kendrick and David Ruffin Revue." They also released an album on RCA in 1987, *Ruffin and Kendrick.*

KHAN, CHAKA: *Singer, songwriter. Born Great Lakes, Illinois, March 23, 1953.*

With one of the finest voices in pop music, Chaka Khan started out as a rhythm & blues stylist in her teens and steadily improved the scope and depth of her singing ability until she could handle with distinction almost any style from jazz to rock to soul. For much of her career, she was the backbone of the R&B/rock band Rufus, although increasingly in the 1980s she took her place as one of the new vocal eminences in modern jazz and soul.

Born in the Chicago suburb of Great Lakes in 1953, she was christened Yvette Marie Stevens. Her family lived for much of her childhood on an Air Force base in the Chicago area and she recalled growing up in an environment where jazz and R&B influences were strong. Even before her teens, she loved to tune in to Chicago jazz stations and sing along with the records. With other children in the family—her brother Mark and sister Yvone (who later took the stage name of Taka Boom)—there was considerable harmonizing by the time she was approaching high-school age.

She was beginning to think about a singing career in her early teens and made her professional debut at 15, in 1968. The secret of that achievement, she said, was persistence. "I went down and hung around the [Chicago] clubs until I found somebody who would let me sing." Her first band affiliation was with a group called Lyfe. That group, she noted, "played in any smoky bar that would let us." Lyfe broke up after a while and Chaka went on to sing with a number of other club bands, with names such as Baby Huey and the Babysitters.

In this process, she steadily built up contacts with other Chicago-area pop musicians, including members of the band American Breed, a seven-piece show band that played bubble-gum and soft rock and had a top 40 hit in the late 1960s, "Bend Me, Shake Me." Internal strains caused a shakeup at the end of the 1960s and keyboards player Kevin Murphy and vocalist Paulette McWilliams left to form a new alignment. Other former American Breed members (including Charles Colbert, Jimmy Stella, Al Siner, Dennis Belfield, and Ron Stockard) joined them in a band that first called itself Smoke. Finding that someone else already had the rights to that name, the group chose to call itself Ask Rufus, taking the name from a column in *Mechanics Illustrated.*

Though Murphy urged the band to abandon top 40 covers in favor of earthier, original material, the band resisted until a turndown of a demo tape by Epic Records caused a reassessment. When McWilliams left, Chaka was asked to take her place. Also joining the band was drummer Andre Fisher, who later became a top record producer. The group served an apprenticeship from 1970 through 1972 playing the club circuit not only in Chicago, but all over the Midwest.

The band still had difficulties in figuring how to go beyond the club grind when they enlisted the help of a one-time member of American Breed management, Bob Monaco, who had moved on to become a record producer on the ABC label. Monaco took over the reins and saw to it that the group made a professional-sounding demo tape. The band, whose name by then had been shortened to Rufus, went to Los Angeles to audition for ABC in 1973 and were signed to a multialbum contract.

In advance of the debut album, ABC issued the single "Whoever Is Thrilling You Is Killing Me." The disc got considerable airplay on black music stations and marked the band as an organization to watch, particularly supple-voiced female vocalist Chaka. The group's debut album, *Rufus* (1974), got some attention, but it was the second LP that established Chaka and Rufus as a major new force in pop music. The debut album had contained a song by Stevie Wonder, "Maybe Your Baby," that didn't have much impact, but while sitting through a session for the next LP, Stevie was inspired by Chaka's vocals to write a new song, "Tell Me Something Good." (*See Wonder, Stevie.*) Released as a single in mid-1974, it became a top 10 hit on both the pop and black music charts, earning the group its first gold-record award from the RIAA. The disc later went on to sell 3 million copies worldwide and win a Grammy award in the Best R&B Vocal Performance by a Duo, Group, or Chorus category. The 1974 album that contained it, *Rags to Rufus,* was certified gold by the RIAA. During 1974–75, ABC issued the top 20 singles "You Got the Love" (written by Ray Parker, Jr.) (*See Parker, Ray, Jr.*) and "Once You Get Started," with Chaka now getting star billing in the band. In 1975, the band had another gold album, *Rufasized*.

Chaka Khan's growing importance was recognized on the next album on ABC, the gold *Rufus Featuring Chaka Khan* (1976). Its track "Sweet Thing" made the top 5 in early 1976, earning the band and Chaka a second gold-record award for a single. Chaka and the band followed with an even more successful collection in 1977, *Ask Rufus*, which reached the top 10 on *Billboard* charts and earned platinum certification from the RIAA.

Meanwhile, Rufus was undergoing a number of changes. In 1973, Ron Stockard, Al Siner, and Dennis Belfield left and were replaced by Tony Maiden, Bobby Watson, and pianist Nate Morgan. Just after *Ask Rufus* was finished, Watson left and was replaced by David "Hawk" Wolinski. Thus Rufus as of 1978 comprised Kevin Murphy (born Minneapolis, Minnesota) on keyboards; Tony Maiden (born Los Angeles, California) on lead guitar; Bobby Watson (born Memphis, Tennessee) on bass guitar; David Wolinski (born Chicago, Illinois) on keyboards and synthesizer; and a 1978 addition, John Robinson (born Creston, Iowa), on drums.

During 1978, Chaka and Rufus went separate recording ways for the first time when she signed with Warner Brothers as a solo artist. Her 1978 gold debut *Chaka*, included one song co-written by her, "Some Love," plus the hit single "I'm Every Woman." Meanwhile, Rufus recorded its first album without Chaka, *Numbers* (ABC, 1979).

But Chaka and Rufus hadn't made a permanent break, and in 1980 they were back together for the gold album *Masterjam* on MCA Records (which had acquired the ABC record operation). It contained three hit singles: "Do You Love What You Feel," "I'm Dancing for Your Love," and "Any Love." Chaka's busy schedule for 1980 included such other projects as doing backing vocals for Ry Cooder's "Down in Hollywood" track on his *Bop 'Till You Drop* album, a session with Henry Gross that yielded the song "Better Now We're Friends," and a number of concerts both as a solo artist and with Rufus. (*See Cooder, Ry.*)

In 1981, Chaka had chart hits on her own and with Rufus. Rufus projects included the top 15 soul album *Camouflage* (which also made the pop charts) and top 10 soul single "Sharing the Love." She had two best-selling albums on the charts in 1981: *Naughty* (released in May 1980) and the gold *Wha Cha' Gonna Do for Me*. The first of those contained the charted singles "Clouds" and "Papillon (Hot Butterfly)." The second provided soul chart hit singles "Wha Cha' Gonna Do for Me," "We Can Work It Out," "Get Ready, Get Set," and "Any Old Sun-

day," all on Warner Brothers. Her 1981 activities included recording some material with keyboard artist Rick Wakeman (of Yes renown) and also doing the soundtrack for the Public Broadcasting System dramatic telecast *For Colored Girls Who've Considered Suicide When the Rainbow Ends*.

Rufus's second album on its own came out during 1981. Called *Party 'Til You're Broke*, the MCA release resulted in considerable coverage of some of its tracks by disco d.j.s.

In late 1982, Chaka's next solo album on Warner Brothers, *Chaka Khan*, was well into the *Billboard* top 100. The album stayed on both pop and black lists well into 1983. In late summer, she and Rufus had another well-merited hit with the album *Live Stompin' at the Savoy*. A top 10 single on the soul charts, "Ain't Nobody" (written by Hawk Wolinski), was culled from the album. In the Grammy Awards for 1983, Chaka won two trophies: one for Best R&B Vocal Performance Female, for the LP *Chaka Khan*, and one (shared with producer/arranger Arif Mardin) for the Best Vocal Arrangement for Two or More Voices for "Be Bop Melody."

Another fine vocal effort by Chaka was the platinum collection *I Feel for You* (Warner Brothers, fall 1984). The gold title song, written for her by Prince, rose to the top 3 on the pop singles charts and brought Chaka a 1984 Grammy for Best R&B Vocal Performance, Female. (*See Prince.*)

During 1985, Chaka was represented on the MCA label as a soloist for the first time. At year-end her MCA single "Own the Night" was moving up the charts. In mid-1986, Warner Brothers issued the album *Destiny*, which became a soul chart hit soon after.

KIHN, GREG: *Singer, guitarist, band leader (THE GREG KIHN BAND), songwriter. Born Baltimore, Maryland, c. mid-1950s.* *

The Greg Kihn Band from Berkeley, California, took a long time to make its way to the top. For most of the 1970s, it was one of the better-kept secrets in U.S. rock, though as much from choice as circumstance. During those years, in its home area around San Francisco, it was cock of the walk, winner of local polls for favorite rock group while, strangely, building up a growing following in Europe. But with the rather obscure Beserkley label as its record home, it had something less than saturation exposure for much of its career until distribution arrangements with the larger Elektra/Asylum organization brought broader exposure.

---

*Partly based on personal interview with Irwin Stambler.

Band founder Greg Kihn grew up in Baltimore, "within a few blocks of Memorial Stadium. I always was a fanatic [baseball] Orioles and [football] Colts fan." He learned to play guitar in his preteen years and, tongue-in-cheek, credited the impact on girls as the reason for joining rock bands in his high-school years. "It was rewarding when they'd say: 'Oooh, are you in the band?'" However, for much of his teen years he favored playing on the folk-music circuit.

In late 1974, he moved west to Berkeley, where he started out as a soloist playing guitar on the University of California campus, though he had in mind to eventually assemble a group. "I had always intended to form a band. Music has been my main interest since I first saw a rock'n'roll band onstage when I was growing up in Baltimore.

"My first appearances onstage in Berkeley were done as a solo playing acoustic guitar. Later [in 1975], I met bassist Steve Wright [born San Francisco] and we expanded to include Larry Lynch [drums, percussion, vocals; born Berkeley], and after that, in early 1976, Dave Carpender [lead guitar, vocals; born Oakland, California]. (The band grew to a five-piece in 1981 with the addition of keyboards player/backing vocalist Gary Phillips.)

During 1975, Greg gained the attention of the operators of Beserkley Records and cut several tracks for a compilation LP, *Beserkley Chartbusters Volume I*. In the fall of 1975, he completed tracks for his debut band album—*Greg Kihn* (1976)—accompanied by Steve, Larry, and, filling in on lead guitar, Robbie Dunbar from the band Earth Quake. In early 1976, the lead guitar post went to Carpender, whose first album work was on the band's second Beserkley release, the 1977 *Greg Kihn Again*. Those albums, along with the third release, *Next of Kihn* (1978), sold well, considering the lack of heavy promotion, though still far below commercial hit status. Meanwhile, the band was steadily increasing its rapport with Bay Area rock fans and, because Beserkley did have some overseas outlets, with many rock fanciers in the U.K. and on the Continent.

Unlike most pop musicians, Kihn and his associates weren't disturbed about the way things were working. "We've always been a consumer-oriented band. There's no hype ever been done about us, so every fan we get, we get honestly. In our early years and even now, a lot of our sales are word-of-mouth and kinda pyramid. Like someone comes to our concerts and tells others who tell others. I feel things are coming in logical sequence for us. We didn't have any overnight successes, but each of our albums typically did a little better than the last."

He talked fondly of his record company, something relatively rare in the music business. "I'm on a weird, eccentric, fiercely independent label. Beserkley is more like a mom-and-pop store trying to compete with a supermarket chain. When it started, the sales manager sold albums from the back of his VW. We do things on a low budget and try to substitute integrity. For instance, Beserkley has different distributors for us in every foreign country. We figure each country has its own personality, so we don't dictate how they should release our stuff. We send them the masters and they choose their own singles.

"It works well, I think. Each company knows the personality of its country. Taking our 1979 release, *With the Naked Eye*, as an example, you found the first single different in each place, though all came out with Beserkley's name on it. 'Moulin Rouge' was the single in Britain and France; in Germany, it was 'Roadrunner'; in Holland, they chose 'Rendezvous' and so on. In the U.S., the first single was 'Beside Myself.' As far as Europe was concerned, that approach meant we didn't become a one-song band, but got a spectrum of fans throughout the continent."

With that album, Beserkley concluded a distribution pact with Elektra/Asylum that brought the large company's greater marketing and publicity capabilities into play. The result was a strong rise in record sales and fan's interest. It also brought much greater airplay that continued for succeeding releases. The early 1980s albums *Glass House Rock* (1980), *Rockihnroll* (1981, the first LP with Gary Phillips on keyboards and backing vocals), *Kihntinued* (1982), and *Kihnspiracy* (1983) spent from weeks to months on U.S. and foreign charts and helped propel the band from a small-club act or opening act in larger halls to a bona fide headline group. In 1982 (when Greg Douglass took over from Dave Carpender on lead guitar), the band opened in large-size auditoriums across the U.S. for artists such as Journey and Rick Springfield. The following year, the band was able to get headline dates in many of the same places.

Kihn observed that he felt one advantage to a patient approach to building a reputation was learning how to shape a concert for different sizes and types of audiences. "We learned over the years progressing from playing small clubs to large festivals how to match what we play to the mood of the crowd. You have to take it from gig to gig and not have any preconceived notions. I don't write out our set list until just before the show and it's subject to change. I like to feel out the audience and see what they like.

"I do this thing we refer to as 'calling at the line.' You know, it's like in football when the quarterback goes up to the line and looks over the defense and calls out audibles. We've got about four different shows' worth of material and we can pick and choose what we play. We can do it because we started from ground zero. Since I put the band together, it's really changed very little and I like to keep it that way. If you've got a great infield you don't want to get rid of the second baseman or shortstop.

"We're not hidebound about music either. We play some new wave–sounding material, but we can do less frantic stuff. In our band, we go song by song and structure our style to the song's content and the way we feel it. Until the end of the '70s, I did most of the original songwriting—though we're not against doing our own covers of other songs—but now the other guys are writing some excellent songs and we're putting them in our repertoire."

This approach helped make the band a concert favorite with a growing number of fans in the 1980s. This included European concert-goers, a part of the world the band toured regularly after its first swing overseas in 1978. It took a while for that to pay off in large-scale respect, but that began to come in the mid-1980s. In 1983, the band had a hit single in France called "Jeopardy," drawn from its *Kihnspiracy* LP. The single brought a Golden Disc Award in that country for "Best New Artist."

The band continued to turn out new recordings at roughly a one album per year pace. It followed *Kihnspiracy* with the 1984 release *Kihntagious,* which spent much of the year on hit charts.

Meanwhile, Kihn relished his laid-back philosophy, one he had outlined to Teri Morris of *Bomp* magazine (March 1979) and continued to follow in the mid-1980s. "People ask us why we live in Berkeley. It's because nobody hassles us. . . . They tolerate us out here. Back East (or in L.A.) they would have hammered us into a mold by now, I think. We need the less frantic environment of San Francisco to just—I hate to use dopey phrases like this, but we need an environment to stretch out and do our thing without people descending on us and making it a scene.

"We relish paying the dues that we've paid and it's definitely Beserkley's fault we haven't made it [bigger], because it's a nowhere tiny label. . . . We may have been raped, but we were spared a lot of the indignities of the industry. We didn't have to tour constantly and we were allowed to develop. What we've come up with is our own, raw sound. . . . I think a major label would have gotten us into a groove too soon.

"Plus look, we're lazy guys. We live in Berkeley and we don't care. It takes us two years to do anything anyway. This just seems normal to me. Also there's no pressure to go out and do stuff you don't want to do. If you want to go to Europe go. . . .

"I'd hate to be in other bands' positions where they would have a humongous hit and worry about

following it. We had lots of time to think about it and realize its hangups. If your first record is a smash, it's almost like the kiss of death. Working our way ahead the way we did makes it easy for us to cope with success. But whether supersuccess happens or not, we believe we'll still have our core of fans when it's all over."

KING, ALBERT: *Guitarist, singer, songwriter. Born Indianola, Mississippi, c. 1924.*

Big Albert King, 6 feet, 4 inches and 250 pounds, became the darling of the young audiences at the Fillmore East and West in the late 1960s. His raucous, infectious renditions of songs based on the Mississippi Delta blues tradition had the fans marking time with hands and feet and shouting for more when each number ended. It had taken a while for Albert, but he had persevered through the lean years to become recognized as perhaps the greatest living country blues artist of them all. Though the passionate '60s interest in blues and blues rock tapered off in the 1970s, King still was able to sustain his performing career throughout that decade and the 1980s.

Albert's story was the usual one of black rural bluesmen. He grew up in poverty, his father dead and his mother hard-pressed to pay the bills. He had a smattering of schooling, but had to work as a field hand, chopping cotton and doing other chores, when he was only nine. He was aware of the blues before that, however. His birthplace was Indianola, Mississippi, a town replete with dozens of barn-like clubs where blacks sought respite from their cares on weekends. Indianola is also the home region of B.B. King. There is still controversy about whether or not B.B. and Albert are half-brothers; they decline to settle the matter. (*See King, B. B.*)

There also were many clubs with blues performers in Forest City, Arkansas (a town 75 miles from Memphis, Tennessee), where Albert's mother took the family when he was a child. As he told Phyl Gardner (*Sound of Soul,* Henry Regnery Co., 1969): "Like I was a little bitty boy when I used to listen to a blues singer called Dorothy Dailey (a man). Back in those days, now, Lonnie Johnson used to play the guitar and Mercer D. was a piano player then. He kept time with his feet; he played the bass with one hand, played the lead with the other, and sang and they would record him. If you listen to him, he really gets your attention because he's a man who really played from the heart, you know what I mean?"

King waited some years before he started playing music himself. In his early teens, he bought a guitar from another boy in Forest City for $1.25. He spent every spare hour he could for months on end learning to play the instrument. Once he had mastered it reasonably well, he played it for friends or for his own pleasure and occasionally for parties and in small clubs. For many years, though, it remained a sideline as he earned his living in other ways. When he was full grown, he found work in the construction field, eventually specializing as a bulldozer operator.

At the end of the 1940s, he settled in Little Rock, Arkansas, working on levee construction days and, in time, assembling his own band to perform in local clubs nights and weekends. He bought his first amplified guitar then and used it as he handled lead vocals for his band. The group, called the In the Groove Band, came into existence in the Arkansas city of Osceola. Slowly it built up a following. While King's group was overshadowed by better-known bands from nearby Memphis, it was considered the best homegrown organization. In the mid-1950s, King noted that things had improved to the point that he would get $14–15 for each weekend night he worked.

Things went along at this pace for the rest of the decade. In 1962, King moved north to try to improve his lot. He spent half a year as a service station attendant in South Bend, Indiana, and then moved to Gary, Indiana, just below Chicago. Soon after he got to Gary, he became acquainted with people at a small record firm called Parrot. He recorded a single, "Lonesome in the Night." The record didn't bring any money to King, but it received enough airplay to bring him recognition from Muddy Waters and other Chicago bluesmen.

In Gary, King became friends with singer-disc jockey Jimmy Reed. The two worked together in small Chicago clubs and also cut some discs for Vee Jay Records. These included a joint effort, "Baby You Don't Have to Go," and one King did with a group he led called the Dutones, "Shake a Tail Feather." They were local hits in the R&B market and received some attention in other parts of the country too. Reed later went on to fame as a solo artist.

By the mid-1960s, King had returned to Osceola briefly, then decided to make home base in Love Joy, Illinois, a St. Louis suburb across the river from the city. He assembled a new band from St. Louis-area musicians and won his greatest reception yet from audiences throughout the Southwest. His work in Memphis was well appreciated by Al Bell, an executive with the rising recording firm of Stax/Volt, the company responsible for the Memphis Sound of the 1960s. Bell signed King and the result was a steady string of top hits, including such singles as "Blues at Sunrise," "Let's Have a Natural Ball," "Ooh-ee, Baby" and "Travelin' to California." The recordings showed up initially on the soul charts, but by the late 1960s, King's releases were just as likely to gain the top 20 or top 50 on the pop charts.

Critics were hard-pressed to find enough praise for his ability. *New York Times* reviewer Albert Goldman called King's style "a fusion of the ancient Mississippi 'bottleneck' style (the fret finger sheathed with glass or metal tubing) and the sighing, swooning, 'psychedelic' sound of the Hawaiian steel guitar. King's blue note is so 'nasty,' so cruelly inciting, that after a quarter of an hour under its spell, one itches for a bottle to break and a face to cut."

Like B. B. King, Albert became a major album artist in the late 1960s and early 1970s. A major boost in that direction was his creative collaboration with Booker T and the MGs at Stax Records in the mid-1960s. (*See Booker T & The M.G.s.*) An early product of that was the fine album *Born under a Bad Sign* (1967) containing two cuts that became particularly associated with King, the title song (co-written by Booker T Jones and William Bell) and "Cross Cut Saw." Both became staple items in his concerts from the late '60s on. For about half a decade, into the early '70s, Albert placed a series of albums on the charts, such as *Live Wire: Blues Power, Albert King Does the King's Thing, Jammed Together, Lovejoy,* and *Years Gone By.*

A new generation of rock fans in the mid-1970s lost interest in some of rock's blues roots and King's career went into a decline for a while. He continued to perform, but mainly in small clubs. By then he had left Stax, though the label continued to reissue some of his material, such as the 1976 LP *The Pinch.* Meanwhile, he signed with a new label, Utopia, which issued *Albert* and *Truckload of Lovin'* (1976) and *Albert Live* (1977). In 1977, some of his Stax recordings were reissued on Atlantic Records' Atco subsidiary under the title *King of the Blues Guitar.* In the late 1970s, Berkeley-based Fantasy Records controlled his Stax catalog and reissued most of his albums from those years.

In the early 1980s, King's star began to rise again, powered by successes scored by new blues-rock performers such as Stevie Ray Vaughn who credited much of their guitar style to Albert's influence. Vaughn was cited by a writer in England's *New Musical Express* as "a young Texan who apparently believes that Albert King is God and the Lord should be praised regularly."

Asked about that by reporter Don Snowden of the *Los Angeles Times* in September 1983, King responded: "He's a good player. He's trying to play too much like me, but he'll never get it all. How's he gonna do it when I don't know how I'm doin' it?" By that he meant that some of his guitar work was essentially intuitive and some of the things he did at one time had slipped from his memory later on.

The new publicity helped bring new concert opportunities for King in the mid-1980s, both at home and abroad. Besides more chances to play rock clubs, he was featured in some of the blues festivals beginning to be organized in the U.S., such as the annual event in Long Beach, California. In 1983, he signed a new recording contract with Fantasy Records, which in midyear issued *San Francisco '83,* his first new LP in five years. A featured track on the album was titled "Floodin' in California." Fantasy later released *I'm in a Phone Booth, Baby* (1984) and (on compact disc only) *The Best of Albert King.* Using the Stax logo, in 1988 Fantasy reissued the triple-guitar *Jammed Together* teaming Albert with Steve Cropper and Pop Staples of the Staple Singers.

His career plans as of the mid-1980s, were modest, he told Snowden. "I never had the desire to be a millionaire. I never had the desire to be a big star. If I feel like playing a gig, I will. If I don't, I won't. Everybody needs money to live, but as long as I can make a decent living, I'll be all right."

KING, B.B.: *Guitarist, singer, songwriter. Born Ita Bena (near Indianola), Mississippi, September 16, 1925.*

It's lucky that B.B. King never worried all that much about personal schedules or he might not have attained his eventual eminence in blues and rock. Though considered one of the major interpreters of country blues, he really didn't focus full attention on that genre until he left his native "Delta blues" region. And he didn't gain recognition as a star until he was in his forties, and then as a favorite of young rock fans who generally didn't pay too much attention to artists of that advanced age.

B. B. was born on a cotton plantation near Indianola, Mississippi, in the heart of the Delta. Whether he and blues guitarist Albert King are half-brothers is an open question. (*See King, Albert.*) His parents separated when he was four and his mother took him to a hilly section of the state. Not that life was any easier then. As soon as young Riley B. King could do farm work, he was out doing chores, earning whatever he could to help out. There was plenty of blues being sung and performed in Negro ghetto areas of that area, but his mother, an ardent churchgoer, warned him against paying notice to it. She took him to church regularly, where he sometimes sang in the choir, and she saw to it that no profane blues material was played in their home.

It was a rugged life, but not unhappy. Unfortunately, young Riley's mother died when he was nine. To live at all, he had to work full-time for a tenant farmer, chopping and hoeing cotton. He got a little schooling in, but not much over the next six years. When he was 14, his father found him and took him back to Indianola. He still had to do farm work, but he was back within a family circle and could go to school somewhat more regularly. Equally important, he was directed toward the delights of the guitar. An uncle taught him some basic chords. Soon after, the then 15-year-old B.B. bought a guitar for $8. He rapidly gained mastery of the instrument and then formed his first group, a gospel quartet.

When World War II came along, he went into the Army, resulting in his first intensive exposure to the blues. In a black company, he found himself with many people who played and sang blues. He picked up songs and guitar techniques from some of them and had a reasonably large repertoire by the time he was discharged in the mid-1940s. However, back home he had to keep that interest secret. He sang no blues around his family but when he could he went off to sing on street corners, sometimes making more in a day than he made in a week as a farm laborer. He realized that music offered a possible escape from the drudgery of farm work.

In 1947, he hitchhiked to Memphis, Tennessee, where a cousin of his, the legendary blues artist Bukka White, lived. Bukka put him up and gave him pointers on both the blues and the music field. Eager to get ahead, King first got work as a freelance performer, singing commercials on black station WDIA. After a while, he developed contacts with club owners and found work under the name Riley King, the Blues Boy from Beale Street, which he soon changed to Blues Boy King and finally to its present form, B. B. King. This helped open the door to a job as a disc jockey in 1948, which, in turn, he employed to develop his recording career.

The recording executives B. B. met in the course of his d.j. work provided the entry to his first recording contract, in 1949, with RPM Records. One of his discs, *Three O'Clock Blues,* made the national R&B lists in 1950.

Throughout the 1950s, King was represented by singles or LPs on RPM or its subsidiary labels, Crown and Kent. Those sold well enough to satisfy the company, but never enough to gain any sizable royalties for King, a situation not helped any by the low 99 cent selling price of the records on drugstore racks. Among his many recordings were "Nany, You Lost Your Good Thing Now," "Five Long Years," "Every Day I Have the Blues," "Did You Ever Love a Woman," "Crying Won't Help You," and "You Upset Me Baby." To keep going, during the '50s and early '60s, B.B. played the Chitlin' Circuit of small clubs and rundown theaters in the ghettos of America.

He achieved what could be called a cult following in folk and rock fields, but not enough to make him a "name" artist. He didn't have the brash aggressiveness of Chuck Berry and Little Richard that let them fight the odds to cash in on the white-led rock boom. At the same time, his complex and polished blues style made folk purists damn him as "too commercial," a judgment later reversed in part, but which managed to keep him out of the folk resurgence of the late '50s and early '60s. His situation in the early '60s is well capsuled by a line from one of his songs: "I've been a good man, although I'm a poor man—understand?"

But the tide turned with the rise of the Beatles, Stones, and other British supergroups of the early and middle '60s who were weaned on roots blues and greatly admired blues artists of all kinds. They praised King's talents and occasionally included his material in their shows. Soon American musicians picked up on that. Mike Bloomfield was a particular fan of King's, copying some of B.B.'s techniques and spreading the word of King's superb guitar work to other musicians. (*See Bloomfield, Mike.*)

Even before that, King's star had started to rise at home. ABC-Paramount gave him a contract in 1961, but legal entanglements cropped up and he couldn't record for the label until 1963. From 1963 on, though, he was one of the company's most dependable artists, turning out one or more albums a year that came out on ABC or its subsidiary label, Bluesway. Close to two decades later, he still was on the ABC roster and moved with the label to MCA when MCA bought ABC in 1979. (Over the years, of course, some of his work came out on other labels, either as reissues bought from ABC or rereleases of earlier recordings.)

His '60s LPs included *Mr. Blues* (1963), *Live at the Regal* (1965), *Confessin' the Blues* (1966), *Blues Is King* (1967), *Lucille* and *Blues on Top of Blues* (1968), and *Live and Well* and *Completely Well* (1969). "Lucille," it might be noted, is B.B.'s name for his guitar.

As the '70s got underway, King was an established star. He began the decade in fine fashion with a gold single, "The Thrill Is Gone," from the LP *Live and Well*. In 1971, he had two hit albums, *Indianola Mississippi Seeds* and *Live at Cook County Jail*. By then, long overdue honors were starting to come his way. At the end of 1970, the *Guitar Player* magazine poll named him Top Blues Guitarist of the Year. He won the 1970 Grammy for Best R&B Vocal Performance, Male, for "The Thrill Is Gone."

In 1972, he had another premier year, placing nine singles and albums on the soul/R&B charts. Among those singles were "Ghetto Woman," "Ain't Nobody Home," and "I Got Some Help I Don't Need." His album hits included *B.B. King in London, Live at the Regal, Guess Who?,* and *L.A. Midnight.* In 1973, he had another hit R&B single, "To Know You Is to Love You." The late 1974 two-disc release of his duet work with his former valet, Bobby "Blue" Bland, *Together for the First Time, . . . Live,* earned a gold record. His album efforts won *Ebony* magazine's Music Awards for Best Blues Album two years in a row in 1975 and 1976. His late '70s albums included a series of collaborations with the Crusaders, starting with *Midnight Believer.* For the next one (*Take It Home,* 1979), the Crusaders, and Will Jennings wrote all the material. It was his first issued on MCA Records.

During 1979, the U.S. Department of State sanctioned a 22-concert trip to the Soviet Union, the first major tour of Russia by an American blues/blues-rock artist. He commented about it to Leonard Feather: "People are really not all that different, no matter where you go. I try to size up the crowd when I go onstage 'cause I'm always scared when I first step out there. After two or three numbers I can tell where to go for the rest of the program. Even when I was in the Soviet Union . . . I did the same thing I do at home. Just by noticing the way people moved their heads, I could tell the reaction, whether I had their attention, and how hard I was going to work to keep it. The audiences were all very polite; we had standing ovations every night."

In the 1980s, King continued on his way much as he had in the 1970s, touring widely each year through the U.S. and in other nations and recording new material on MCA, both conventional King stylings and some experimental efforts such as his first country-music–based album, *Love Me Tender* (1982).

His 1980s albums continued to be nominated for Grammies. His 1981 MCA LP, *There Must Be a Better World Somewhere,* won for the Best Ethnic or Traditional Recording. His 1983 *Blues'N'Jazz* album was voted the Best Traditional Blues Recording. In 1985, the track "My Guitar Sings the Blues" from his MCA LP *Six Silver Strings* was a nominee for Best Traditional Blues Recording.

KING, BEN E.: *Singer, songwriter. Born Henderson, North Carolina, September 28, 1938.*

The Drifters proved a stepping stone to stardom for a number of its lead singers, most notably Clyde McPhatter, Bobby Hendricks, and Ben E. King. In each case, the move was a rapid one, for none of these singers remained with the group for more than a year or two before going out as a soloist. (*See Drifters, The; McPhatter, Clyde.*)

King, like McPhatter was a North Carolinian. Born Benjamin Earl Nelson, he spent his first 11 years there before his family moved to New York. His father opened a luncheonette in Harlem and young Ben was pressed into service to do chores around the place. There are various versions about the way he was discovered but all agree it occurred in Ben's father's eating place. One account is that Lover Patterson, a member of the singing group the Five Crowns, came into the luncheonette one day in 1956, heard 18-year-old Ben singing for the diners, and recruited him. An alternate version is that a booking agent was looking for a singer to replace a group member and asked Ben if he knew of a good vocalist in the neighborhood, at which point Ben asked to try out himself.

At any rate, Ben joined the Five Crowns and toured the R&B circuit with them. At the time, the quintet included Bobby Hendricks (born Columbus, Ohio, 1937), who went on to be lead singer with the Drifters for part of 1958. The Five Crowns, as far as can be ascertained, made 11 records that were released between October 1952 and March 1958. King sang with the group on several of its late recordings.

But the Five Crowns were soon to have a new identity. In 1959, the manager of the Drifters, George Treadwell, found himself without a group. The quintet's record sales had gone downhill and it broke up. However, he had contracts for annual stage appearances for several years at Harlem's Apollo Theater; he solved the problem by bringing in the Five Crowns to take over, and renaming it the Drifters.

Atlantic Records liked the new group and assigned Jerry Leiber and Mike Stoller to produce a new series of recording sessions. The result was a new burst of public interest and a string of hits for the Drifters. (Actually, it might properly have been called the New Drifters.) One of the songs released in 1960, "Save the Last Dance for Me," featured King's lead vocal with a backing of Spanish guitars. The song did so well (reaching number one in *Billboard* the week of October 17, 1960), it was decided to see how King would do as a soloist. Leiber and Phil Spector developed "Spanish Harlem," a song that retained the Latin flavor of the previous Drifters' hit. (*See Spector, Phil.*) A top 10 hit on the Atco label in 1960, it established King as one of the most promising newcomers of the year in popular music.

King followed with an even more striking success, "Stand by Me," which was in the top 10 nationally in 1961 and rose to the number one position on the soul charts. In 1962, Ben added still another laurel to his crown with "I (Who Have Nothing)," a song that later was a million-seller for Tom Jones. (*See Jones, Tom.*) King had many other best-selling singles in the mid-1960s, including "Don't Play That Song," "Seven Letters," "Tears, Tears, Tears," and "What Is Soul?"

Many of his albums also made the best-seller lists. His credits on Atco included *Spanish Harlem* (1961), *Don't Play That Song* and *Ben E. King Sings for Soulful Lovers* (1962), *Ben E. King's Greatest Hits (1964), and Seven Letters* (1965).

Unfortunately, King began to lose his hold on his audience toward the end of the '60s. His record sales declined and he was unable to come up with new hits. It is a measure of his integrity that he left Atco of his own volition, without alibis, to try to develop new directions. He reviewed this painful decision in an interview with Charlie Gillett in 1970 that was published in Bill Millar's book, *The Drifters:*

"I didn't really want to leave Atlantic. But I find companies are like a husband and wife. Eventually you get to a point where there's really very little you can do for each other. Although you're married and you love each other dearly, but then there's still something else, and you have to, like sacrifice. And one has to leave. So I had to. I didn't so much want to, but I found out that if I would have stayed there, I would have accepted things out of friendship and I didn't want that. I didn't want a recording session because they felt, well, this is Benny and he's been here 11 years and we'll give him one.

"They're very great, very honest, very true people. You couldn't find better people to be with. They've stayed with an artist when he's been going down, down, down. . . . I said to myself, I'll give myself one more record . . . and if that don't happen, well . . . To keep myself from feeling that I'm sinking, I'll have to leave."

Fortunately, Ben's departure from Atlantic didn't prove permanent. After his efforts to continue his recording career away from that label for the first part of the 1970s, he was able to return to it in the mid-1970s and regained some of his old magic. His excellent *Supernatural* (Atco, 1975) made both black and pop LP charts. The title song also provided him with a hit single. His next album, *I Had a Love* (1976), proved a letdown, but he returned to form in 1977 when he collaborated with the Average White Band on the LP *Benny and Us. (See Average White Band.)* He kept on providing new recordings for the label into the 1980s: *Let Me Live in Your Life* (1978), *Music Trance* (1980), and *Street Tough* (1981). Some of his early material was available in the form of foreign imports in the early 1980s, examples being the Japanese collections *What is Soul* and *Stand by Me.*

From the mid-1970s to late 1980s, his performing career was in reasonably good shape with annual concert schedules that took him to many major cities at home and abroad. Among his credits was an appearance on the 1987 Grammy Awards telecast.

KING, CAROLE: *Singer, songwriter, pianist. Born Brooklyn, New York, February 9, 1942.*

Carole King had what amounted to two phenomenal careers in pop music embracing two different decades. In the '60s, her songwriting partnership with Gerry Goffin provided dozens of superhits in the R&B/soul/rock vein. In the '70s, as a writer and performer, she played a pivotal role in development of a softer, more reflective sound in pop music, a sound closer to folk music than the more strident compositions of her earlier years.

Carole Klein was born and raised in Brooklyn, New York, where jazz, swing bands, and the last stages of romantic ballads dominated pop music in her childhood. In her teens, she veered away from most of that, influenced by the new rock revolution represented by Bill Haley, Elvis Presley, and Fats Domino. As she progressed through high school, she delved a little deeper than her classmates into the roots of rock, finding a strong interest in the still submerged rhythm & blues stylings that were mainly restricted to the black population.

By the time she finished high school, though, R&B groups were beginning to show up regularly on the pop charts. She had started writing songs by then, some in the R&B format. (Neil Sedaka, in turn wrote his 1959 hit "Oh! Carol" to her.) After marrying young lyricist Gerry Goffin (born Queens, New York, February 11, 1939), she became part of a writing team that soon won the attention of New York publishers. Using the pen name Carole King, by the time she was 20 she and Gerry already had a reputation as songwriting greats of the future.

Their first massive success came with the Shirelles' "Will You Love Me Tomorrow" in 1961. Soon they had another top 10 hit with the Drifters' "Up on the Roof." Goffin and King compositions proved winners for an ever widening group of artists. "Locomotion" provided a number one hit for Little Eva (Eva Boyd, Carole and Gerry's babysitter) in 1962 and for Grand Funk Railroad in 1974. "Hi-De-Ho" became a major hit in 1970 for Blood, Sweat & Tears. Other successes included the Chiffons' "One Fine Day" (1963), the Drifters' "Some Kind of Wonderful" (1961) Bobby Vinton's and Tony Orlando's releases of "Half Way to Paradise" (1961 and 1968, respectively), Maxine Brown's "Oh No, Not My Baby" (1965), the Righteous Brothers' "Just Once in My Life" (1965), Gene Pitney's "Every Breath I Take," (1961), and Aretha Franklin's "A Natural Woman" (1967).

In the early '60s, Carole tried her hand at singing some of the Goffin-King songs. Several discs made the charts, the most successful being the 1962 "It Might as Well Rain until September" on Dimension records. However, Carole preferred to take time out to raise a family rather than pursue the pressure-laden route to pop stardom.

The Goffin-King writing partnership continued to be highly productive until they ran into problems with their marriage. The two finally divorced, after which Carole went into semiretirement to concentrate on looking after her two young daughters. In the second half of the '60s, that goal led her to move to the Los Angeles area. She kept on writing songs, though she didn't do much else in the music field for the first part of her stay in California. While she collaborated with various writers in the late '60s (including Toni Stern and musician Charles Larkey, who became her second husband), much of her new material was written alone.

In 1968, she formed a group called City with Larkey and Danny Kortchmar. Carole had known record-company owner Lou Adler since 1963 and he agreed to sign the group. His firm, Ode Records, issued City's LP, *Now That Everything's Been Said,* but it was a failure. However, Kortchmar introduced her to his friend James Taylor, who urged her to go on as a solo artist.

She finally agreed with that idea and was buoyed by a good reception to several West Coast concerts and the faith expressed in her by Adler. Her first album, *Writer: Carole King,* was issued at the start of the '70s and had a reasonably good if not sensational reception. But the next one provided the turning point. Titled *Tapestry,* it was released in early 1971 to coincide with a national tour in March and April on the same bill as James Taylor. So well were both album and tour received that by midyear, people were clamoring for her to headline rather than be a supporting act. The gold album provided a number one single in *Billboard,* "It's Too Late," plus her classics "I Feel the Earth Move," and "You've Got a Friend." In 1971, the last named also became a number one hit for Taylor and a top 30 hit for the team of Roberta Flack and Donny Hathaway.

Tapestry was a sensation, making its way to number one on *Billboard* charts during 1971. It was still on the charts in late 1976, having sold over 13½ million copies, the most ever sold by an LP up to then. In the Grammy Awards for 1971, Carole won no less than four trophies: Album of the Year, Best Pop Female Vocalist, Song of the Year (songwriter's award) for "You've Got a Friend," and Record of the Year for the single "It's Too Late." Before 1971 was over, Carole had added another gold-record award to her collection for her third Ode solo LP, *Carole King Music.*

As the '70s went along, while her sales were far less than the blockbuster levels of *Tapestry,* all her Ode collections reached gold-record status except the 1975 TV soundtrack LP, *Really Rosie.* Her LP *Rhymes & Reasons* gained the award on November 1, 1972, followed by *Fantasy* on June 26, 1973, *Wrap around Joy* on October 16, 1974 and *Thoroughbred* on March 25, 1976.

Always jealous of her privacy, Carole cut back on her live appearances sharply after the banner year of 1971. She did give concerts, but only at widely spaced intervals. In between, she stayed behind the scenes, spending as much time as she could with her family which, by the early '70s, included another daughter born to her and second husband Larkey. That approach probably tended to cut down on the potential sales totals of her new albums, but she never felt that was the overriding concern of her life. It was a theme she was to emphasize in her gold 1977 album, *Simple Things* whose title song (written by Carole and musician Rick Evers), said: "Simple things mean a lot to me."

The album represented a change in affiliation. In late 1976, she announced she had severed relations with Ode, though Ode stated it still had several LPs of her work to release. In December 1976, she signed with Capitol Records, which set up a new label, Avatar/Capitol, for *Simple Things.* Carole finished out the decade with two more LPs for Capitol, *Welcome Home* (1978) and *Touch the Sky* (1979). She began the '80s with the Capitol LP *Pearls,* which comprised her versions of Goffin-King songs that had been major hits for other artists.

By then she was living on her Robinson Bar Ranch near Stanley, Idaho, where she had moved in the late 1970s after her marriage to Larkey fell apart, followed by another brief marriage to Rick Evers. She liked being away from the hype and the pressures of Los Angeles, she stressed, and enjoyed trying to fit in as just another citizen. An example of that was her acceptance of a role as featured speaker at a convocation at Hemingway Elementary School in Ketchum, Idaho, in December 1982, where she told the gathering she was "a singer and a songwriter—also a notary public." A main theme of her speech was the need to carry on the fight for peace symbolized by artists such as the late John Lennon. She said: "Maybe if we believe, with the innocence of children, that peace is possible, we can make it happen. The light of love is there for all of us. Let it shine, and let it be."

For the most part, Carole continued to maintain a low profile in the 1980s, spending much of her time on her ranch and restricting much of her live concert work to shows for special causes. Among those were a series of appearances to raise money for Senator Gary Hart's 1984 presidential bid. During some of them, she acknowledged that she hadn't made much impact with record buyers after *Tapestry.* She opened a show at Los Angeles' Dorothy Chandler Pavilion with the comment: "So many people thought I died after *Tapestry.*" As it happened, though much of her performance focused on new songs she had written in the '80s, the ones that brought the most intensive audience response were from *Tapestry.* (Some of the new material had been included on her 1983 LP, *Speeding Time,* on Atlantic Records.)

In the mid-1980s, her career as a recording artist had, in effect, come full cycle as she got back together with her old associate, Lou Adler, who produced some of her new sessions. (*See Blood, Sweat & Tears; Drifters, The; Flack, Roberta; Franklin, Aretha; Hathaway, Donnie; Pitney, Gene; Righteous Brothers, The; Shirelles, The; Taylor, James; Vinton, Bobby.*)

KING, EVELYN "CHAMPAGNE": *Singer. Born Bronx, New York, July 1, 1960.*

From cleaning crew to singing star seems more fantasy than fact, but it happens from time to time in entertainment without special help from public relations experts' fertile imaginations. It happened to Kris Kristofferson in the country area and also is part of Evelyn "Champagne" King's story. Kristofferson, though, did that work in lieu of other occupations his Rhodes Scholar credentials would have brought him; Evelyn did it from necessity.

Unlike Kristofferson, whose family roots were white middle class with little show business background or interest, Evelyn was not without entertainment examples. Her uncle was actor/singer Avon Long, the original Sportin' Life in *Porgy and Bess;* her father, Erik, had been an R&B hopeful who spent a lot of time seeking opportunities at local black community clubs and theaters in the post–World War II period. From time to time, he did get some stand-in work with visiting vocal groups at the Apollo Theater. He also maintained that at one point, when the late Buddy Holly played the Harlem showcase, he taught the rock star some dance routines to go with his vocal and guitar work.

His daughter got inspiration for a performing career from her father, who brought her to the Apollo several times during her childhood. She spent much of her early years in the New York area but by her midteens, she was living in Philadelphia with her mother Johnniea. Though she had already demonstrated considerable vocal skill to her parents and friends, she hadn't made any great breakthroughs. Partly in hopes of making some contacts and also to help pay for life's necessities, her mother got jobs for herself and Evelyn on the cleaning crew at the Gamble and Huff recording studios in Philadelphia. At 16, Evelyn literally was cleaning bathrooms while her mother ran a vacuum cleaner in the offices.

The strategy paid off when Evelyn's potential was brought to the attention of a staffer on Gamble and Huff's Philadelphia International Record operation. Said individual, who called himself T. Life, was a writer, producer, and artist with the label who was impressed by young Evelyn's vocal efforts. "She had very big pipes for a kid," he said later.

Life took her under his wing, writing songs for her and coaching her in singing and recording techniques. They worked on initial tracks for a debut album which RCA Records agreed to support. The LP, Smooth Talk, came out in August 1977 and the first single, "Shame," in September.

Slowly at first, then with increasing momentum, both debut single and album caught on with the disco-going public. Evelyn's voice became a staple with dance-club d.j.s around the country and her recording also got good airplay, first on black and then on general-format stations. Her initial releases became best-sellers on the general charts, disco charts, and black lists. On June 30, 1978, the "Shame" single was credited with over a million copies sold for combined 7- and 12-inch versions. A week later, the standard single was certified gold by the RIAA. The album Smooth Talk also exceeded gold-record levels.

With the deserved success of her debut album, Evelyn appeared ready to become one of the best R&B vocalists on the music scene. However, she seemed to water down her styling in later albums, somehow losing some of the emotional edge of her early material. Her progress also was inhibited to some extent by a decline in the disco frenzy of the late 1970s to a significant but less dominant part of the music spectrum.

Through the mid-1980s, Evelyn remained a favorite with disco and soul adherents and she didn't lack for concert and TV performance opportunities. Her second album, Music Box (1979) went gold and provided a number of singles on disco charts, including "Let's Get Funky Tonight" at the end of 1980 and in early 1981.

Her first 1980s album, I'm in Love (RCA, 1981), was good, but not quite as dynamic as her debut, though its follow-up, Get Loose (1982), won a gold-record award. During 1982, she had three charted singles, including "Love Come Down," ranked as the fourth most successful black song in Billboard's year-end lists.

Evelyn's name continued to appear on either general pop or black music charts in the mid-1980s. Her RCA albums included Face to Face (1983) and A

Long Time Coming (1985). In late 1983 and early 1984, she had another hit single, "Action," which was one of four singles she placed on black music charts during 1984. At the end of 1985, she had the single "Your Personal Touch" moving toward the top 10 of disco/black music charts. The single was helped by being among the top 10 airplay favorites with black music d.j.s into early 1986.

KING CRIMSON: *Vocal and instrumental group. Original personnel (1969): Greg Lake, born Bournemouth, England, November 10, 1948; Michael Giles, born Bournemouth, England, 1942; Ian McDonald, born London, England, June 25, 1946; Robert Fripp, born England, c. 1946; Peter Sinfield, born England. In 1973, band comprised Fripp; David Cross, born Plymouth, England, late 1940s; John Wetton, born Derby, England, c. 1950; Bill Bruford, born England, May 17, c. 1950. Disbanded 1974, revived in 1981 with Fripp, Bruford, Tony Levin, Adrian Belew.*

The name King Crimson reflects the classical background of some of its founding members and the title of its debut album. But it has little to do with the group's sound, which has mainly been one of hard rock or, as one critic called their style, "organized anarchy."

Most of the original members of King Crimson grew up in Bournemouth and started playing professionally in their teens. By the time lead guitarist Robert Fripp and drummer Michael Giles got together in 1968 to begin assembling what was to be King Crimson, they had more than 18 years of total experience to their credit. (*See Fripp, Robert.*) Giles, the oldest of the group, started playing drums in 1954 and began performing with local groups soon after. He started with jazz and skiffle bands, shifting to rock in the '60s.

During the '60s, Giles played with a great many groups in England and on the Continent. He earned much of his income by working as a studio musician, especially after settling in London in the fall of 1967. His close associate in London was Robert Fripp, who had started playing guitar at 14. It remained a sideline as Fripp first left school to work in real estate at 16, then picked up his education again as an economics major in college. To defray college costs, he gained work with a resident hotel band in Bournemouth when he was 18 and remained with the band for three years, at which point he left Bournemouth for London and a fulltime career in music. There, he soon became involved in several projects with Giles, including an LP that flopped and a TV show called "Color Me Pop." An important influence on Fripp's approach to music was his longtime interest in recordings of such classical composers as Debussy, Ravel, and Bartok.

One of the first things Fripp did when he and Giles decided to form their new band in late 1968 was to go to Bournemouth to seek the cooperation of Greg Lake. Lake was a promising lead vocalist and a skilled guitarist, having started playing when he was 12. He began working with local groups soon after. His first engagement found him performing in a bingo hall between sessions. The band was paid from a collection plate passed among the audience. He left school at 15 to become a draftsman, continuing his music in his spare time. At 17, he gave up office work in favor of music and played with such groups as the Shame and the Gods. With the latter band, he switched to playing bass guitar.

After Lake agreed to join, Fripp and Giles sought a songwriting team, coming up with lyricist Peter Sinfield, and composer Ian McDonald. McDonald had the added advantage of ability as a vocalist, reed and woodwind player, vibraphonist, guitarist, pianist, and mellotron player. McDonald had taken an active interest in music at seven, when he was attracted to recordings of Louis Belson, Les Paul, and Earl Bostic. Later, he was influenced by such classical figures as Stravinsky and Richard Strauss. He started guitar at 11 and joined his first group at 13. At 16, after being asked to leave school, he enlisted in the Army as a bandsman. He served a five-year hitch, during which time he studied music theory, harmony and orchestration and learned to play many new instruments. His band experience ranged from classical orchestras and dance bands to leading a rock group in Gibraltar.

In 1967, he received his discharge and moved to London to try to break into the pop field. He met Sinfield there and the two agreed to collaborate on songs. Sinfield had been doing well as a computer chief operator after finishing school, but found the normal business routine too tame. He left to found the group Infinity, which he later called "the worst group in the world." The guitarist for Infinity was Ian McDonald and when the group broke up, Sinfield and McDonald remained together as a writing team. After they became members of King Crimson, Sinfield not only provided all the lyrics to their early songs, but also worked up a dazzling light show for the stage performances.

The group won relatively quick acceptance after it started club engagements in 1969. Its debut LP on Island Records, *In the Court of the Crimson King: An Observation by King Crimson,* was one of the best-sellers of the year in England. Introduced into the U.S. late in 1969 by Atlantic Records, it went gold.

Many observers forecast great things for the band,

if it remained together. However, by the start of the '70s, internal strains between the members were starting to surface. The group's second LP, *In the Wake of Poseidon,* (fall 1970), was a hit at home and in the U.S. The third King Crimson album, *Lizard,* (1971) also was on the charts, but did not meet with near as much consumer enthusiasm as the earlier efforts.

Greg Lake by then had left to found Emerson, Lake and Palmer. McDonald too departed, later helping to form Foreigner. (*See Emerson, Lake and Palmer; Foreigner.*) The band's lineup in 1973 comprised Fripp (guitar and mellotron), David Cross (violin, flute, and mellotron), John Wetton (bass guitar, viola, and vocals), and Bill Bruford (drums).

Cross had started playing violin at school in Plymouth and extended his musical studies at teachers training college in Exeter. "I'd been playing in a semipro rock band in the area as well as various orchestras and I took up the flute at college because music students had to study two instruments and I could never 'feel' the piano." In his final year in college, he joined a three-member folk-rock band, the Ring. After several other jobs as sideman or band leader, he joined King Crimson. "I started jamming with Robert. It is a long story, but revolves around the fact that our previous bands had been rehearsing in close proximity."

Wetton, originally from Derby, didn't turn to music until his family moved to Bournemouth in 1961. He joined his first group as a 12-year-old in 1962 and played with several local bands during school years. While attending Bournemouth College, he became acquainted with Fripp, though he didn't work with him after leaving the school. For some years he toured throughout England and the Continent with different soul bands and organ trios, then performing with the rock band Mogul Thrash. After that group disbanded, he spent some time in Southern California and then returned to England to perform with Family before joining King Crimson.

"I got into Crimson," he recalled, "after Robert and I bumped into each other in Wimbourne one afternoon—our paths have crossed roughly every six months for the past four years. This time we chatted and made some tentative plans for the future and the time for them turned out to be right this September [1972].

"I'm naturally left-handed, but I play right-handed. Robert's the same and I always felt it was the natural way, anyway, because it's the left hand that moves around a lot. I play very hard—in fact, I break a lot of strings, which is quite rare with other bass guitarists. And there's a flicking technique I use that just came naturally to me."

Joining the band in 1973 was Bill Bruford, considered one of the best rock drummers of the early 1970s. His move to King Crimson for a time left a gap in his previous star group, Yes. (*See Yes.*)

With this alignment, King Crimson turned out the LP *Lark's Tongue in Aspic* (on which Jamie Muir worked with the band on percussion), a fine collection that had much greater impact than the early 1970s albums. The band followed with an even more impressive tandem of 1974 LPs: *Starless* and *Bible Black* and *Red*. At that point, to the amazement of fans and critics alike, Fripp broke up the band. Fripp told Irwin Stambler in the mid-1970s: "The band ceased to exist in September 1974, which was when all English bands in that genre should have ceased to exist. But since the rock'n'roll dinosaur likes anything which has gone before, most of them are still churning away, repeating what they did years ago without going off in any new direction."

For the rest of the decade, Fripp occupied his time with other projects, though Atlantic did issue another King Crimson album, *USA*, in 1975. After a 1980 tour with a trio called the League of Gentlemen, Fripp became interested in leading his own band again and the result was another turnabout, the revival of King Crimson in 1981. The new version comprised Fripp and Bruford, with two other veteran artists, Tony Levin and Adrian Belew, rounding out the foursome.

Fripp acknowledged that having a new King Crimson seemed at odds with his statements of the 1970s. He told a reporter, "Rationally I knew that we couldn't call ourselves King Crimson. It was not a rational decision. It was simply the right one."

The new group signed with Warner Brothers, which issued the band's label debut, *Discipline*, in 1981, followed the next year by the album *Beat*. The records showed that Fripp did not intend to rest on past laurels. In keeping with his approach to pop music, the tracks presented considerable experimentation with stylings that were in tune with the 1980s. Through the mid-1980s, the band continued to tour across the U.S. and other parts of the world, mostly playing smaller venues. If the group didn't command the mass audience of the King Crimson of old, it gained considerable respect for its abilities from knowledgeable rock fans.

KINKS, THE: *Vocal and instrumental group. Personnel in mid-'60s: Raymond Douglas Davies, born Muswell Hill, London, England, June 21, 1944; David Davies, born Muswell Hill, London, England, February 3, 1947; Mick Avory, born Hampton Court, England, February 15, 1944; Peter Quaife, born Tavistock, Devonshire, England, December 27, 1943. Quaife replaced by Johnny Dalton in 1969. John Gosling* *added in April 1971. Dave Davies left 1973, returned 1975. Roster in 1988: Ray Davies, Dave Davies, Ian Gibbons, Jim Rodford, Bob Henrit.*

Though the Kinks exhibited creative abilities of a high order almost from their start in the early 1960s, they were long obscured, even in their native England, by the massive success of the Beatles and Rolling Stones. Persistence paid off, though, and they started to gain world attention as the 1960s came to a close. In the early 1970s, the group established itself as one of rock's finest and, almost 20 years later, despite many crises—personal, artistic and commercial—still remained a favorite with large numbers of fans around the world.

The founding members were the brothers Davies, Ray and Dave, both born and raised in London. The two started playing the guitar and writing original songs in their early teens, though music remained a spare-time occupation while they attended a London art school. In 1964, they decided to work full-time in music and dropped out of school to form the Kinks, with Dave on lead guitar and Ray on rhythm guitar and, occasionally, piano.

Joining them on drums was Mick Avory, who had started playing with small groups during the England skiffle craze of the late 1960s. He met the Davies brothers in a pub one night and agreed to go with their new group. Filling out the group was Peter Quaife on bass. (The group started as a quartet, adding a fifth member some years later.)

Before long they gained a recording contract and, for a while, things seemed to be looking up. During 1964–65, the group had a series of single hits in Britain and the U.S. ("You Really Got Me," "All Day and All of the Night" and "Who'll Be the Next in Line"), resulting in appearances on such TV shows as "Shindig" and "Hullaballoo." Later in the decade, the group had such notable singles as "Tired of Waiting for You," "Til the End of the Day," "Waterloo Sunset," and two well-crafted putdowns of conformity: "Dedicated Follower of Fashion" and "Well Respected Man."

The group had some success with their early Reprise LPs, such as *Kink Size* and *Kinda Kinks* (1965) and *Kinkdom* and *The Kinks' Greatest Hits* (1966). But their popularity waned despite the obvious improvement in their writings such as Ray's "Face to Face" (which dealt with the still prominent class distinctions in England) or in Dave's "Mindless Child of Motherhood," "Rats," and "Strangers."

"Face to Face" gained some sales in England and Continental Europe as a single, then as the title song of a January 1967 Reprise LP. The album did poorly in the U.S., as did the next two, *Kink Kontroversy* (1967) and *Something Special* (1968). During these years, the group was popular enough in Europe to insure good attendance in concerts in most cities there. However, the Kinks appeared at smaller halls and clubs, in general, playing to audiences of hundreds or thousands rather than 10, 20, or 30,000 as did the Stones, Cream, and Beatles.

For a little while, the Kinks almost disappeared from sight as far as most followers of rock were concerned. They resurfaced with a vengeance, though, in 1969, with the British presentation of the TV show "Arthur," featuring a score composed by Ray Davies and played by the group. The central figure in the song series was Arthur, a middle class, middle-aged English workman. It zeroed in on the many frustrations and problems of his segment of society and their effects on the next generation. In sequence, the LP covered such topics as England's past glory and tradition ("Victoria"), the restrictions of military service ("Yes Sir, No Sir"), the magnetism of England's World War II leader ("Mr. Churchill Says"), hopes for a new start by Arthur's children overseas ("Australia"), escapism ("Shangri-La"), and the generation gap ("Nothing to Say"). *Arthur* propelled the Kinks to top ranks among rock groups.

With Peter Quaife replaced on bass by Johnny Dalton in mid-1969, and Royal Academy of Music alumnus John Gosling joining on piano and organ in 1971, the group continued to add to its laurels in the early 1970s. Perhaps the first major hit to address transvestitism and homosexuality, Ray Davies' composition "Lola" was number one in England and in the top 10 in the U.S. in 1970. *Lola vs Powerman and the Moneygoround* was a best-seller at home and on the LP charts in the U.S. in early 1971.

By then, the group had attained considerable maturity, as indicated by its more deliberate approach to career decisions. In an interview with writer Tony Norman (*What's on in London,* August 6, 1971), for instance, Mick Avory explained: "We space things out now. We don't do any gigs unless we have a record on release. We don't do gigs in Europe just for the sake of it, we'd rather have something to promote. . . . There's also a bit of business to sort out—our recording contracts have run out. We'll probably re-sign with a leading company. We would like to have our own label, but that will come in a couple of years."

The group had come to realize that playing all the time was self-defeating. "We made mistakes when we were youngsters. We didn't care about the business side. We were just interested in being pop stars. Everything was new and exciting. But when you get a bit older and wiser, and maybe have a family, you've got responsibilities. You start to realize it's time to look after yourself."

The outcome was a contract with RCA Records. The band's first RCA release, *Muswell Hillbillies* (1971), immediately made the charts and was cited by critics of several major newspapers as their candidate for best album of the year. The group's excellent 1972 album, *Everybody's in Showbiz, Everybody's a Star,* included the hit single "Celluloid Heroes," a striking track that commented somberly on the transitory nature of fame. During the year, Warner Brothers issued a fine retrospective of the band's earlier work on that label, *Kink Kronickles.*

During 1973–74, Ray Davies put together a multiple-record rock-drama opus released on RCA as *Preservation, Act One* (1973) and *Preservation, Act Two* (1974) that proved pretentious. Coupled with Dave Davies' decision to leave the band for a while in 1973 (a move that seemed to weaken some of the band's live performances), the Kinks took a step backwards. But Ray brought the band back strongly the next year with a fine concept album on RCA, *Soap Opera,* whose 12 songs recounted the story of a flawed hero named Norman, who dreams of stardom as a rock singer without the talent or opportunities to make it happen. His wife finally tells him to abandon his "ridiculous fantasies" and accept the world as it really is. For the second album released on RCA in 1975, *Schoolboys in Disgrace,* Dave Davies had permanently returned on lead guitar.

In 1976, the band's association with RCA ended and that label released the retrospective album *Greatest Hits/Celluloid Heroes.* (In 1980, RCA issued another Kinks collection, *Second Time Around.*) The group signed with Arista. Its debut 1977 LP on the label, *Sleepwalker,* contained a number of impressive compositions by Ray Davies, particularly "Juke Box Music." The band followed with a series of fine albums on the label that helped bring new luster to its reputation: *Misfits* (1978), *Low Budget* (gold, 1979), a concert set, *One for the Road* (gold, 1980), and *Give the People What They Want* (gold, 1981). The group certainly didn't seem to worry about moving into a third decade of rock stardom. As Ray Davies told an interviewer: "Ever since we started, people have said the Kinks would never last. We survived the silly '60s, the sordid '70s and we're here in the hateful '80s."

The hit LP *Word of Mouth* (1984) proved the group's swan song on Arista. MCA became the band's fourth label since it first began to seek attention from U.S. fans in the 1960s. The first MCA collection, *Think Visual* (1986), was stated to be the band's twenty-fifth LP, including five "best-of" collections. The first single release was a Dave Davies composition. "Rock'n'Roll Cities."

Band makeup in 1986 included Ray Davies on vocals and guitar, Dave Davies on vocals and lead guitar, Ian Gibbons on keyboards, Jim Rodford on bass guitar, and Bob Henrit (formerly of the Zombies) on drums. Original drummer Mick Avory, who had been fired in 1984, joined in during the recording session for "Rock'n'Roll Cities."

Ray recalled for a reporter from *Rock Fever* magazine in early 1987 the circumstances of Avory's departure. "To actually go out for a drink with Mick and tell him he wasn't in the band anymore was one of the most horrible things I've ever had to do. He and Dave (Davies) were fighting a lot. Back when we started, they used to share a house together. But there's always been a really bad rivalry between them, and it got to the point, just before *Word of Mouth* where Dave said, 'I can't work with him anymore.'

"So I took Mick out for a drink—I didn't drive, so I picked him up at the station and we went by bicycles to the pub. We talked about it and said it was best that he left the group. . . . It was very hard, because Mick was my best friend in the band. And the ironic thing is that Mick ended up playing drums on 'Rock'n'Roll Cities,' which is Dave's song (and the first hit single written by him).

"Mick's still involved with us in a business sense, because we've still got our studios together; he looks after things, and pays me my wages."

That situation reflected some of the tensions that affected the band, the most severe of which over the years were personal and professional disagreements between the Davies brothers that often threatened to tear the Kinks apart. But, though each went off in different directions from time to time, they always resolved their problems and kept the band going.

The driving force remained Ray Davies, of course. The key to the group's longevity, he indicated, was that it continued to have a point of view about the world and where it was going. He told one interviewer: "I saw something in society I wanted to write about. I come from a London working class upbringing, but my success enabled me to be classless. I could observe things from a distance and write about them. I never considered myself a songwriter or a singer. We just liked to play simple R&B music. That was the essence of what we did . . . very simple." (*See Hynde, Chrissie, and the Pretenders; Zombies, The*)

KISS *Vocal and instrumental group. Original members, 1973: Gene Simmons, born New York, New York; Ace Frehley, born Bronx, New York, c. 1952; Paul Stanley, born New York, New York; Peter Criss, born New York, New York. Criss replaced in 1980 by Eric Carr, born Brooklyn, New York. Vinnie Vincent replaced Frehley in 1982. Mark St. John replaced Vincent in 1984. Bruce Kulick replaced St. John in 1985.**

---

*Based partly on personal interviews with Ace Frehley and Paul Stanley by Irwin Stambler.

Kiss never came close to being a classic rock band in the musical sense, but always put on unusual and flamboyant shows that delighted millions of mostly young rock fans around the world. Many critics wrote the group off as a passing fad, but its members proved to have the ability to recruit new ranks of wide-eyed youngsters as the previous teen followers moved on into the frustrations and restrictions of adult life.

Paul Stanley noted the band's urban roots. "We all grew up in New York and became interested in rock music in our teens. I was born in upper Manhattan and the other guys came from other New York boroughs."

Ace Frehley added: "When I hang around with buddies from the Bronx, that's when my accent comes out. I was born on the Grand Concourse. Before I earned my living from music, I did a lot of odd jobs. I think the turning point in my life came when I was 16 and saw the Who's first New York appearance. They were opening for Mitch Ryder and the Detroit Wheels and nobody knew who they were. They came out and did numbers like 'My Generation' and other great songs. That really inspired me and at that point in my life, I decided I'd rather get into music than anything else."

All of the original Kiss members were playing with local groups before they were out of their teens, but weren't having much impact until their new band got going. The stage was set for Kiss when Stanley and Gene Simmons got together in 1973. Stanley recalled for Gerald Rothberg of *Circus* magazine (March 31, 1982): "I had a group in upstate New York. Our guitar player got sick one weekend, and we had gigs that were booked. This was a half-original, half-top-forty band. I came into the city to get my old guitar player, Steve, to come upstate. In the meantime, he had started playing with Gene."

While at Steve's house, Stanley met Simmons, Steve noting that both wrote songs. Stanley and Simmons then performed some of their material for each other. Simmons recalled: "'Sunday Driver' is what I remember Paul played first. The first song I played for [Paul] was 'Seated Tonight.'"

The two decided they had a lot in common and soon set about forming a new band. They already had Simmons to handle bass guitar and Stanley on guitar, so they determined to find another guitar player and a drummer. An ad in *Rolling Stone* brought drummer Peter Criss into the fold while another insert in the *Village Voice* located Ace Frehley. From the start, the founders wanted to emphasize the theatrical side as well as the music, taking a cue from the great interest in New York in the rock'n'rouge image of the New York Dolls. Because the foursome didn't think they would look good in

376

drag, they decided to focus on the shock-rock approach of Alice Cooper. *(See Johansen, David; Cooper, Alice.)*

Stanley said: "What we wanted to do was play original material in an original setting. We liked the idea of emphasizing visual aspects. I was an art student—actually we all come from art backgrounds. If you look at rock in general, a lot of the biggest groups have come from art. Kiss really is about synchronizing music with a show. We really wanted to set the standard for what is the ultimate spectacle. We always try to incorporate show and effects into what we're doing. We try to have the show enhance the music because on stage we think that's what we're there for. We said since the beginning if you just want to hear music, there's no reason to come to a concert. You can sit at home and do very well with records or radio."

Frehley added: "In a nutshell, we always will pull surprises in concert. We always pull something out of the hat. Our costumes basically changed every time we went on tour. Because we wore high platform shoes for most of our tours didn't mean we'd always do that. If we can come up with special effects even more spectacular than fire breathing or spouting synthetic blood, we'll try to phase it into the show. But any effect we use has to have counterpoint in the songs we're doing with them."

The band started with ambitious goals, but it was able to move toward them in a surprisingly short time. Its early New York–area shows had enough color and energy to capture attention from both concert goers and record-company officials. By 1974, the band had its debut LP, *Kiss*, out on Casablanca Records followed by another LP, *Hotter than Hell*, the same year and the gold *Dressed to Kill* in 1975. Those releases included such notable originals as "Deuce," "Strutter," and "Nothin' to Lose," but to considerably less effect than in concert presentations.

The band's initial albums fell far short of capturing its impact in live performance. Of course, prior to music videos, there was no way to showcase the innovative lighting, bursts of flame, explosions, smoke patterns, rising and descending platforms for the bandsmen, and other features that set off frenzied screams from the audience. But the band's music had a thunderous presence on stage that didn't come through on its first LPs. This was remedied with the first live album, the gold *Alive* (Casablanca, 1975). An excellent concert mix, it included one of the band's best songs, "Rock and Roll All Nite."

Brought together with producer Bob Ezrin, the band then turned out its best studio album to that point, *Destroyer* (1976), a platinum concept album dealing with the symbolism of the band's stage persona. The album disclosed a band able to convey considerably more range and subtlety in its material than conventional heavy metal groups. Also on the charts during the year was a reissue of some of Kiss's early recordings, *Kiss—the Originals*.

During the next few years, the band continued to turn out new recordings at a breakneck pace, steadily adding to its collections of gold and platinum awards, though the LPs didn't match the superior quality of *Destroyer*. Casablanca albums included *Rock and Roll Over* (1976), *Love Gun* and *Alive II* (1977), *Double Platinum* (1978), and *Dynasty* (1979).

In 1978, in an unusual move for a major rock band, individual albums were released on Casablanca by all four members. The releases met with both deprecation and praise from reviewers. *Rolling Stone*'s David McGee commented: "These weren't great artistic achievements by any means, but did give fans an idea of what each musician brought to the band in terms of sensibility. There are plenty of surprises here. Frehley's is the hardest rocking and best of the four LPs, with the fine 'New York Groove,' which was a hit single. Criss' blue-eyed soul stylings have a certain gruff charm, but the material is so-so. Stanley's is the closest to the Kiss sound in all respects, but lacks the zip of Frehley's rock. Simmons' LP is a mellow, almost middle-of-the-road rock, heavily orchestrated in some instances, and only occasionally raunchy."

The release of solo LPs naturally brought rumors of the band's breakup. Before then, the group had toured heavily—as much as 10 months out of each year. That had played a role in Kiss's album success as had a savvy public relations campaign centered on the members' off-stage anonymity that came from the elaborate costume "disguises" worn on stage. Fans were kept wondering about what the musicians looked like under all the heavy cosmetic effects.

That did have the advantage of letting members circulate more freely in public than other rock stars. Still, Stanley noted: "We're recognized anyway, though not with the same frequency as other well-known performers. Usually we could walk the streets without getting mobbed."

Frehley said: "Some of our really devoted fans were able to figure out who we were out of makeup. It can be a little disturbing. I've been in restaurants where people knew who I was and it's hard to eat if people are looking at you. But really, we're grateful for what the public did for us, letting us realize many of our dreams."

By the end of the 1970s, Kiss had amassed a huge following outside the U.S. in the western Pacific and throughout Europe. In fact, at some periods of its career, Kiss did more overseas tours than U.S. appearances. When the band's popularity seemed to dip at home, it often could count on extensive support in other parts of the world.

Tours outside the U.S., Kiss members found, showed they could appeal to age levels other than the bubble-gum set. Stanley said: "The age level of our fans keeps changing both with time and place. In touring outside of the U.S., it was interesting that we drew different age groups in each country. In England, for instance, the average age at our concerts was in the mid-twenties. On the Continent, sometimes the average was younger or even a little older. And the level changes at different times. Sometimes longtime fans feel uncomfortable at our events as they get older. Of course, we always wanted to widen our audience as much as possible. We felt it shouldn't make anyone squeamish to have young people around them."

Frehley commented: "When we played the Forum in the early 1980s, we had a pretty wide range— from six into the late twenties. Parents came with the six-year-olds, and they seemed to enjoy the show very much. It's funny, a lot of times younger kids will have parents along and a lot of time we'd meet some of the parents and they'd tell us how they really had a lot of fun at the concert. I feel rock'n'roll transcends age if people let it."

Stanley said: "We've never made apologies for who likes us just as we never felt there was anything wrong with 'commercial.' Commercial is only bad when it's not you doing it. There's nothing wrong with finding the largest audience possible. We can be different things to different people. I don't think everybody who likes us likes the same things."

After the 1980 gold LP *Kiss Unmasked*, the band was reunited with Ezrin for a new project, the first with him since *Destroyer*. This was the concept album *Music from the Elder* (Casablanca, late 1981). The album did well with European fans with the single "I" from the LP high on overseas charts in early 1982. The LP featured Eric Carr on drums (also an experienced songwriter) in place of Peter Criss, who left the group in 1981.

On January 28, 1982, Kiss (less Frehley, who had come down with the flu) took over New York's Studio 54 club for a live satellite broadcast to Europe. The program was seen by an estimated 22 million viewers throughout Europe, including fans attending the annual San Remo Music Festival in Italy. That represented the first live remote telecast in the festival's 12-year history. During the telecast, the band was presented with the Golden Cat award for Most Important International Artists of the Year, voted them by the readers of Italy's major music magazine, *Sorrisi E Canzoni*.

Going into the mid-1980s, Kiss continued to place new recordings on the U.S. and foreign hit charts with regularity while demonstrating the ability to keep drawing new throngs of young fans to its live performances. In late 1982 and the first part of 1983, its Casablanca LP *Creatures of the Night* was in the *Billboard* Hot 100. In the fall of 1983, the LP *Lick It Up* hit the top 50. That album was on Mercury Records, which took over Casablanca acts after that label was acquired by their mutual parent company, Phonogram. The group also stopped wearing makeup at this point. In the last months of 1984 and early 1985, the LP *Animalize* made *Billboard* lists. *Animalize* was the band's best collection in years, helped in no small measure by the contributions of the group's new guitarist, Mark St. John. That LP was followed by another best-selling Mercury LP, *Asylum* (1985). In 1987 the group had another chart LP on Mercury, *Crazy Nights*.

The band certainly had staying power and had developed confidence in its concert and writing approach to maintain continuity. "The way we work on new material," Stanley said, "is that everybody goes off and writes and then brings back the song or songs to the band. As a rule, we don't write by jamming."

Frehley pointed out: "Sometimes we combined half of one song with half of another person's song to come up with something that's better than either one."

Stanley concluded: "There are some kinds of songs you probably can do better by getting together and jamming—like blues, for instance. We just like to have things a little more organized, particularly if we do a concept album like *The Elder*. In that case, for instance, we wrote a complete, detailed story before we ever wrote any songs for it. The songs we wrote amounted to episodes in the story."

KNIGHT, GLADYS & THE PIPS: *Vocal group, all from Atlanta, Georgia. Original personnel (late 1950s): Gladys Knight, born May 28, 1944; Merald Knight; Brenda Knight; William Guest; Elenor Guest. Brenda Knight and Elenor Guest left in 1960s, Edward Patten added.*

Birthday parties seemed to have a major impact on the career of Gladys Knight. Her first recording (an amateur family one) took place at a birthday party for her uncle, Alvin Woods. Later, the group that joined her on the road to stardom came into being at a party for her brother Merald, thanks to the incentive provided by Alvin Woods' son, James.

When her uncle made a tape of her voice, Gladys was only four years old. But she had already made her public debut when she sang her first gospel songs in front of the congregation at Mount Mariah Baptist Church in Atlanta. Her precociousness didn't surprise the parishioners; they knew she came from a musical family. Her father, Merald Knight, and her mother, Elizabeth, both had been members of the Wings over Jordan Choir and had often performed at church affairs in Atlanta.

Gladys's fame as a child vocalist rapidly spread to other Atlanta gospel groups. She was asked to sing at many churches and made her first tour through Florida and Alabama with the Morris Brown Choir before she became five.

When she was seven, her mother arranged for an audition for Ted Mack's amateur talent program on TV. She won first prize the first night she appeared. Later, she contended for the Grand Prize of $2,000 and was again the choice of the viewers.

Her victory led to many more offers of TV and in-person appearances and even contracts for commercials. She accepted many engagements, but her parents saw to it that the traveling wasn't overdone. Nonetheless, young Gladys added many more hours of experience as a solo artist before she turned 12.

She came from a large, closely knit family of brothers, sisters, aunts, uncles, and cousins. Birthday parties were always well attended. At one for her brother Merald toward the end of the 1950s, she recalled, everyone present was supposed "to get up and do something entertaining—a joke, a skit, singing, anything."

Gladys got together with Merald, their sister Brenda, and cousins William and Elenor Guest to sing as a quintet. They did such an excellent job that cousin James Woods urged them to continue as a professional group. His nickname was Pip, so the group called themselves the Pips. Woods took over as manager and soon launched them at a local amateur contest. Winning helped gain them a two-week engagement at a local nightclub. After this, they played other small clubs and then were signed to tour with R&B singing greats Sam Cooke and Jackie Wilson. (*See Cooke, Sam; Wilson, Jackie*.)

In the late '50s and early '60s, the act became popular on the R&B circuit, playing many of the major theaters and auditoriums across the North and South. The group won a recording contract from Vee Jay that resulted in a top 10 pop and number one R&B hit of 1961, "Every Beat of My Heart," a song Johnny Otis had written 10 years earlier with Jackie Wilson in mind. (*See Otis, Johnny*.) The worldwide sales total went over the million mark. The group followed in 1962 with another top 10 R&B hit on Fury Records, "Letter Full of Tears."

Through the middle of the decade, Gladys Knight & the Pips was well-known to rhythm & blues fans, but had little impact on the mass audience. This changed after the group was brought in as a guest act with one of Motown Records' touring reviews. They stayed with the tour and so impressed company executives that they were signed to a contract.

"I Heard It through the Grapevine" on Motown's subsidiary, Soul, made number two on *Billboard*'s pop charts in 1967. In 1968, they scored with "End of Our Road" and in 1969 turned out the single "The Nitty Gritty."

The group's throbbing singing style and polished dance routines brought widespread praise. In the spring of 1970, they had a best-selling single, "You Need Love Like I Do." "If I Were Your Woman" made *Billboard*'s top 10 pop chart in February 1971. In the summer of 1971, Gladys and the Pips had another candidate for record of the year in "I Don't Want to Do Wrong."

The group had Soul/Motown albums on the charts almost without pause from the start of 1970 into the middle of the decade. These included *Nitty Gritty* and *Greatest Hits* (1970), *If I Were Your Woman* (1971), *Standing Ovation* (1972), and *Neither One of Us* and *All I Need Is Time* (1973).

In 1972, the group had two singles hits: "Help Me Make It through the Night" (by country songwriter Kris Kristofferson) and "Make Me the Woman You Come Home To." "Neither One of Us (Wants to Be the First to Say Goodbye)" hit number two on *Billboard*'s pop lists, while "Daddy Could Swear, I Declare" made the top 20 during 1973. Later that year, the group switched to a new label, Buddah, for the top 40 LP *Imagination*. That album provided Gladys and the group with two gold singles: "Midnight Train to Georgia" (number one in 1973) and "I've Got to Use My Imagination." During 1974, Motown issued *Anthology,* a collection of the group's hits on that firm's label. During the 1974 Grammy Awards telecast, the group walked off with two trophies: one for Best Pop Vocal Performance by a Duo, Group, or Chorus (for the single "Neither One of Us" on Soul/Motown) and the other for Best R&B Vocal Performance by a Duo, Group, or Chorus (for "Midnight Train to Georgia" on Buddah).

During those years, it seemed like nothing could go wrong for the group. As a top favorite with the mass audience, it could place records on the charts with regularity and draw enthusiastic crowds to concerts around the world. On a personal level, Gladys Knight (whose first marriage had ended in divorce) began what appeared to be a well-founded new marriage to Barry Hankerson. The group turned out a series of albums on Buddah of varying quality that charted well, including *Claudine* and *I Feel a Song* in 1974, *Bless This House* and *Second Anniversary* in 1975, and *Gladys Knight and the Pips' Greatest Hits* and *Pipe Dreams* in 1976. (The title track to *Claudine* was a film theme written by Curtis Mayfield.)

But problems were on the horizon. The group's ability to place singles on the charts faltered, partly because the material didn't match the songs recorded in earlier years. Though Buddah kept releasing new albums in the second half of the 1970s—such as *Still Together* and *Love Is Always on Your Mind* in 1977 and *Miss Gladys Knight* in 1978—buyer interest dropped sharply. That, in turn, reduced the demand for concert work.

Other difficulties proliferated. In the late 1970s, Gladys's second marriage headed for the rocks—she and Barry Hankerson were divorced in 1981. A contributing factor was Hankerson's decision to become involved in group operations, including production of the movie *Pipe Dreams* (starring Gladys), an economic disaster. Gladys recalled in an early 1980s interview: "They kept running out of money in the movie and they kept coming to me to get them more money. I'm still paying for it today. I'm over $4 million in debt from that project."

As if that wasn't enough, the group became embroiled in a bitter battle with Buddah Records over royalty payments in the late 1970s. While the legal maneuverings continued, Gladys and the Pips were barred from performing together. That was the reason her 1978 LP on Buddah was a solo work. It was rumored the group had decided to split up. Gladys told Dennis Hunt of the *Los Angeles Times:* "Some people still don't realize that we legally couldn't record together. That separation was forced on us, and it was only temporary. We knew as soon as the suit was settled we'd be back working together."

Once that was accomplished in an out-of-court agreement in 1980, Gladys, brother Merald, and cousins William Guest and Ed Patten were reunited on a new concert tour. They signed a record contract with Columbia Records. Industry observers thought the label was foolish to sign a group that had seen its best days. Some joked the group should be called Gladys Knight and the Fossils.

Initially it seemed the detractors were right. The group's first two Columbia releases in the early 1980s, *About Love* and *Touch*, were not overly successful. But then in 1983 the group hit pay dirt with the gold album *Visions,* which showcased a more modern, sharp-edged sound and spawned a modest hit single, "Save the Overtime for Me." In the mid-1980s, the group continued to place releases on the charts. In 1986, Gladys joined Dionne Warwick, Stevie Wonder, and Elton John on the gold single "That's What Friends Are For" (attributed to "Dionne and Friends") on Arista. It won the Grammy for Best Pop Vocal Performance by a Duo, Group, or Chorus. *(See John, Elton; Warwick, Dionne; Wonder, Stevie.)*

In late 1987, the group released *All Our Love,* their first album on MCA Records. "Love Overboard" became a Top 20 pop hit in 1988, their first one since the late 1970's. *(See Kristofferson, Kris; Mayfield, Curtis.)*

KOOL & THE GANG: *Vocal and instrumental group from New Jersey. Original members, 1960s: Robert "Kool" Bell, born c. 1950; Robert "Spike" Mickens; Dennis "DT" Thomas; George Brown; Charles Smith; Ronald Bell. In late 1970s, group also included Earl Toon, Jr., and Kevin Bell. James "JT" Taylor added 1979, born Hackensack, New Jersey, c. 1954. Personnel, mid-1980s: James Taylor, Robert Bell, George Brown, Ronald Bell, Charles Smith, Dennis Thomas, Robert Mickens, Amir Bayyan, Clifford Adams, Michael Ray.*

In the 1970s and '80s, many groups with jazz roots broadened their audience either by taking the jazz fusion route (blending jazz with rock) or by overlaying jazz stylings with R&B and funk. (Neither course was approved by jazz purists, naturally.) Kool & the Gang took the latter approach to achieve stardom in the early '70s and, after a dry spell later in the decade, bounced back to even greater success in the '80s.

The band that evolved into Kool & the Gang originally was formed by bass guitarist Robert "Kool" Bell in 1964 when he was a 14-year-old fan of jazz great John Coltrane. Drawn from Bell's friends and associates in his New Jersey home area, the group began as essentially an instrumental jazz band, the Jazziacs, that worked its way into gigs in local clubs in the area during the mid-1960s. Band members at the time, besides Robert Bell, included his brother Ronald on tenor saxophone, Robert "Spike" Mickens on trumpet, Dennis "DT" Thomas on alto saxophone, George Brown on drums, and Charles Smith on lead guitar.

The band, Robert Bell told *Rolling Stone,* "used to play in jam sessions at a place called St. John's in Jersey City and Pharoah Sanders and Leon Thomas used to show up there." For the most part, the Jazziacs usually served as the opening act after which it would back up the headline jazz artist.

After a while, Bell and his fellow bandsmen began to moderate their jazz material with overlays of R&B and funk. Under various band names (including the Soul Town Band), the group attracted increasing attention from Jersey City black music fans. Bell recalled: "We had to learn to adjust our musical ideas. We had to make sure our jazz roots didn't overpower the funk."

In 1969, the band took the name Kool & the Gang

when it recorded its first material for De-Lite Records (an instrumental LP, *Kool & the Gang,* that made lower chart levels). It was a recording association still going strong almost 20 years later. The fact that its initial discs could make the charts seemed to bode well for the newly named group. It encouraged the record label to release a steady series of new singles and LPs and brought opportunities for the band to play important venues throughout the U.S.

After placing several more singles on lower black music chart levels, the group began to show strength with black and white fans with its third De-Lite album, *Wild and Peaceful* (fall of 1973). The gold album's first single, "Funky Stuff," made the pop top 30. In 1974, the band gained two gold top 10 singles from the collection: "Jungle Boogie" and "Hollywood Swinging." Over the next few years, the group added more chart singles and albums to its credit list. Among the De-Lite LPs of the period were *Open Sesame* (1976), *The Force* (1977), and *Kool and the Gang Spin Their Greatest Hits* (1978).

By 1978, though, the band was in trouble. Record sales went way down and concert dates from 1976 on had been decreasingly rewarding. The problem was the upsurge in disco music that for a time overshadowed the somewhat differently paced R&B/funk material. Although the band's early 1970s music certainly was danceable, it sounded dated to the disc jockeys in the growing number of disco clubs.

Bell and the others tried to adjust. He noted: "All of our early albums were very raw, relying on heavy rhythms and horn accents, instead of lush vocal arrangements. With the upswing of disco in the mid-'70s, we utilized strings and female vocals for a more orchestrated sound." The change didn't do much for the group's fortunes, though the band did supply tracks for two smash hit films of the late 1970s, providing "Open Sesame" for *Saturday Night Fever* and "Summer Madness" for the Sylvester Stallone epic, *Rocky.* But the band's 1978 disco-oriented album, *Everybody's Dancin'* was a disappointment.

In 1979, it seemed apparent more changes were in order. Bell commented: "Prior to 1979 we'd had two fairly slow years. We knew we needed another element. Basically, we'd been an instrumental band, so we added two vocalists, James 'JT' Taylor and Earl Toon. We also thought we needed an outside producer for the first time. Eumir Deodato was recording at the same studio, so we talked with him and he accepted. The timing was right."

Indeed it was. The new album, *Ladies Night* (De-Lite, late 1979), was a best-seller on both pop and R&B charts. The platinum LP provided two 1980 top 10 singles: the title track and "Too Hot." The

next Deodato-produced album, the platinum *Celebrate!* (1980), did even better. The title track rose to number one on the *Billboard* list the week of February 7, 1981. Besides earning a platinum record (a rare achievement for a single), the song "Celebrate!" became a staple for many special events. Among occasions when it was featured were the 1981 Super Bowl and after Walter F. Mondale won the Democratic presidential nomination in July 1984.

In 1981, the band was back on the LP charts with the platinum *Something Special.* It brought another top 10 single for the band, "Take My Heart." By this time, Toon had left and James Taylor reigned as sole lead vocalist. There also were some personnel changes from the late 1970s roster. The veterans still aboard, besides leader Robert Bell, included George Brown, Ronald Bell, Charles Smith, Dennis Thomas, and Robert Mickens. Newcomers were Amir Bayyan on keyboards, Clifford Adams on trombone, and Michael Ray on trumpet and fluegelhorn.

The group by the mid-1980s ranked as one of the top concert attractions in the world and it also received kudos from officials of New Jersey and New York (including New York's Governor Cuomo) for public service activities. Meanwhile, the band continued to turn out new worldwide hits, such as its platinum LP *In the Heart* (late 1983), whose single, "Joanna," rose to number two on U.K. and U.S. pop charts and number one on black music lists. The title song, released only in England in 1984, made the U.K. top 10.

The band topped that performance with its platinum LP, *Emergency,* issued by De-Lite (distributed by Polygram) in late 1984. During 1985, Kool & the Gang was the only group to have four top 40 singles from one album: "Emergency," "Misled," "Fresh," and "Cherish." All but "Emergency" made *Billboard*'s top 10 pop list. As of 1986, the band was credited with placing more singles in the top 40 than any other group of the 1980s.

Robert Bell savored those successes when he discussed the act's history with Robert Palmer of the *New York Times* in 1985. "We have gone through quite a few musical changes. We've been together now for 20 years, making records for 16, and our career has been up, down, up again. After our funky hits in the mid-'70s, we had a rough period. People thought the group had broken up. Disco was very big at the time and we couldn't sell records, which is ironic, because our music has been danceable since our first record."

A key part of the 1980s breakthroughs, he agreed, was the addition of James Taylor. "We had never had a real lead singer, and couldn't perform a lot of the tunes we wrote. J.T. has made a big difference.''

During 1987, the group added another gold LP, *Forever*, to its hit total as well as a top 10 single, "Victory.''

KOOPER, AL: *Guitarist, pianist, organist, songwriter, band leader, record producer, singer. Born Brooklyn, New York, February 5, 1944.* *

To those who follow rock closely, Al Kooper is regarded as one of the major figures in the field from the '60s into the '80s. His prematurely gray hair caused one writer to dub him the "gray eminence of rock.'' Besides being held in high esteem as an instrumentalist, for music-industry people he also built up an impeccable reputation as a songwriter and record producer. Even those music fans who are not overly familiar with his name often are aware of the groups he helped found, such as the Blues Project and Blood, Sweat & Tears.

Kooper became absorbed in music when he was just starting school. ''The first rock record I was really conscious of was 'Earth Angel.' My father used to take me out to eat at the diner and it was on the juke box. The first record I ever bought was one called 'The Closer You Are' on Whirling Disc Records. By 1958 I was playing professionally, so I've wasted little time until I was really into rock music. 1983 was my twenty-fifth in rock'n'roll.''

He began piano lessons at seven, switched to learning guitar at 12, and was performing professionally at 14. This commitment caused him to rebel at conventional schooling. A major irritant to his teachers, he had to shift to four different high schools during his teen years in Brooklyn.

His rock activities paid off from the start, though. His first group, the Royal Teens, were an early, but short-lived sensation of rock with their 1958 top 10 novelty, "Short Shorts'' (ABC-Paramount). When the '50s came to a close, the Royal Teens were only a memory and Kooper was kept busy as one of the most sought-after record session musicians in the business. From 1960 to 1962, Kooper earned a salary many times that of the average teenager by backing some of the most successful performers in popular music.

At 18, Al resumed fulltime education at the University of Bridgeport in Connecticut. After a year, he dropped out, returning to New York to get a job sweeping floors, manning the switchboard, and doing other chores at the Adelphi Recording Studios. He did some session work, but spent even more hours in 1963–64 writing songs with Bobby Brass

and Irwin Levine. Their output included "This Diamond Ring,'' a gold record hit for Gary Lewis and the Playboys that rose to number one in *Billboard* the week of February 20, 1965. Another success was Gene Pitney's "I Must Be Seeing Things.''

In early 1965, Kooper concentrated on learning to play the organ. Later in the year, he was asked to sit in on Bob Dylan's recording sessions that were to result in the classic album *Highway 61 Revisited*. Kooper asked Dylan's producer, Tom Wilson, for the chance to try out something on the organ and this provided the backing for Dylan's hit single from the record, "Like a Rolling Stone.'' Later, Kooper had even more influence on Dylan's *Blonde on Blonde* and *New Morning*.

Looking back at those days, he said: ''Dylan was always very undisciplined in the studio when I worked with him. When we were recording *Highway 61 Revisited*, that was what was great about it. It was pretty spontaneous. On *Blonde on Blonde*, I tried to make him more disciplined and if people like *Highway 61* better, I'm to blame. It was just that there was a chance to rehearse the musicians before we recorded *Blonde on Blonde*. I knew all the songs and rehearsed the band, whereas on *Highway 61* you can feel all that tension where people seem on the verge of playing the wrong note and sometimes do just that.''

Later Kooper and Dylan went different paths, but forgot old grievances in the early 1980s. Kooper felt he would like the chance to produce new Dylan recordings. ''I think he and I probably understood each other better than many others he worked with. So I think we could make a better record now [in the '80s] because of that understanding and because I know more about production now.''

The desire to work in public returned in the mid-'60s and Kooper helped form a new group, Blues Project, in 1965. That all-white group is credited with providing new directions for rock with its arrangements of urban blues material. Kooper performed with the group during most of its early existence—from 1965 to 1968—and can be heard on such Verve/Forecast LPs, as *Goin' Down Louisiana* (1966) and *Blues Project, Volume 2* and *Blues Project at Town Hall* (1967).

After that group's initial breakup, Kooper became a staff producer with Columbia Records and, almost simultaneously, laid the foundation for a new group, Blood, Sweat & Tears. He helped select the personnel with other founding members, several from Blues Project, and started out as a band member. He played on the group's first record, *Child Is Father to the Man*, hailed by most rock critics as a major milestone in development of jazz-rock . He had an important hand in selecting some of BS&T's initial

---

*Partly based on personal interview with Irwin Stambler.

successes. For instance, he recalled, "'You Made Me So Very Happy' was a black record that didn't make it and when Blood, Sweat & Tears did it, it became a top 10 hit. It was a single I had heard on Motown by Brenda Holliday."

This time, Al found being a group member too restricting and let BS&T go its own way to the top levels of popular music. In mid-1968, he focused more on solo projects and producing, starting with a combined effort with superstars Stephen Stills and Mike Bloomfield, *Super Session*. (Supporting the three stars on the album were Eddie Hoh on drums and Harvey Brooks on bass.) In 1969, he worked on another album with guitarist Bloomfield, *Live Adventures of Al Kooper and Mike Bloomfield*. Another result of Kooper's producing work of the late 1960s was the record debut of 15-year-old Shuggie Otis, son of R&B great Johnny Otis, on the album titled *Kooper Session*.

During this time, he also provided backup guitar for many classic albums, including Jimi Hendrix's *Electric Ladyland* and the Rolling Stones' *Let It Bleed*.

Kooper continued to turn out new solo albums from time to time in the '70s and '80s, including *You Never Know Who Your Friends Are; New York City, You're a Woman; Easy Does It; Unclaimed Freight;* and *Championship Wrestling,* all on Columbia. The albums weren't best-sellers, partly because of his difficulty in translating the driving energy of an in-person appearance onto a recording medium under the restrictions of a record or tape.

For example, his limitations as a singer were noted by Michael Sherman in reviewing Al's Los Angeles debut at the Bitter End in January 1971, but at the same time Sherman pointed out that Kooper's stage presence overcame them. "Although Al Kooper's singing voice is, at best, mediocre—he has a very limited range and often sings flat and off key—he manages to overcome this drawback— thanks to his superb musicianship, wonderful feel for a song's lyrics, and flawless phrasing. Interestingly enough, by the time Kooper finished three or four numbers (including his own compositions 'I Can't Quit Her' and 'Talkin' about My Baby') his vocal deficiencies become much less annoying and one was able to fully enjoy his overall style and presentation."

During the '70s, Kooper continued to add to his already extensive production credits and also tried out new music-business avenues. As he said in the 1980s: "I had my own record company then, Sounds of the South—Lynyrd Skynyrd was on that. I set up the company because it was something I hadn't done before. In fact, that's the trouble; I've achieved all my goals. That's why I like to work with new artists.

I enjoy helping others, 'cause I've had to do everything for myself."

In some ways, he noted, some of his disappointments as a producer stuck in his mind more than his successes. "One of the best albums I made, I think, was one with Ricky Nelson for Epic that was just never released. It would have been great for him. I got the best vocals out of him he ever did. We did it in 1978. I'm still real unhappy that nothing came of it.

"I like getting into different areas of production. It gives me a lot of leeway in terms of everything I'm capable of doing. It gets my creative juices flowing. Right now I think probably the Tubes' first LP was the best thing I've ever done. I think it contained at least two classic tracks, 'Whaddya Want from Life?' and 'White Punks on Dope.' I'm also proud of having produced the number two most requested song on FM stations, which is 'Firebird.'

"I never worked with Phil Spector, but I stole his producing techniques. He's a very strong influence on me as a producer. I have every album he ever did."

In the 1980s, based in Los Angeles, Kooper continued to be a whirling dervish, moving from one project to another with lightning speed, taking off for occasional tours with major artists and performing locally with various combinations of musicians.

During the early 1980s, Kooper went on tour with Dylan. He enthused: "It was wonderful. It rekindled our personal relationship, which was null and void for about eight years."

He also kept in touch with other former associates. "I still look back fondly on Blues Project. Actually, it's still alive in the memories of the members and could pop up again if an offer was made. I played with some of the Blues Project people in March 1981 in New York and it was exciting. Some of the group members, like Andy Kulberg, drop in regularly out here in L.A."

During the first part of the 1980s, he also performed with the band Sweet Magnolia. "It's really just a bunch of studio musicians who get off playing in clubs. It's a great band and I really enjoy playing with these people. We play all New Orleans–type material—like the Meters, Neville Brothers, Dr. John— it's real nice. I just love that kind of music. New Orleans music comes from the blues, but it's got its own drum beat, bass line, and overall kind of feel. It's great fun to play it and Sweet Magnolia is one of the best dance bands in L.A."

In late 1982, Columbia issued his first solo LP in six years, *Championship Wrestling*. Among the backing artists was vocalist Valerie Carter and former Doobie Brothers guitarist Jeff "Skunk" Baxter. During the mid and late 1980s, Baxter and Kooper often could be found jamming with other rock artists in L.A. clubs.

He noted that in the 1980s "I concentrate on guitar playing rather than piano. On the keyboards, as Rodgers and Hammerstein said, I've gone about as far as I can go, whereas I'm still getting better on guitar. It's more a hobby than a profession. I practice five hours a day when I'm not playing gigs."

He also kept up with his producing. "There are a lot of guys in the '80s trying to sound like the '60s and they'll come to me rather than somebody else for that. It's like a regression to make those kinds of records. Of course—I have a theory—it's all rock'n'roll. Every few years, they give it a new title like the San Francisco Sound or punk or new wave, but it's essentially all the same."

But he had pride in his producing skills. "I feel that I'm getting better in what I do in my area. I don't think I've peaked internally. I learn from every record I make and every concept I do. It's a good feeling that I've fulfilled almost all my goals. Most of all, I'm proud of doing it after 25 years and I hope I can do it another 25 because I don't know how to do anything else." (*See Bloomfield, Mike: Blues Project, The; Blood, Sweat & Tears; Dylan, Bob; Hendrix, Jimi; Lewis, Gary; Lynyrd Skynard; Nelson, Rick; Pitney, Gene; Rolling Stones, The; Stills, Stephen.*)

KORNER, ALEXIS: *Band leader, guitarist, pianist, singer, mandolinist, bouzouki player, songwriter, radio announcer. Born Paris, France, April 19, 1928; died U.K., 1985. Original Blues Incorporated group (1962) comprised Korner, Cyril Davies, Dick Hextall-Smith, Charlie Watts. Other early band members included Mick Jagger, Keith Scott, Hoogenboom, Ginger Baker.*

For years, most U.S. fans tended to ignore the close relationship between rock and rhythm & blues. To the British groups that took over leadership of rock in the 1960s, these two categories were always considered synonymous. The most famous of the '60s English groups—the Beatles, Rolling Stones, and Animals—started out calling themselves R&B bands. The man they credited to a large degree for laying the groundwork for the British rock boom, a man they respectfully called "the Guv'ner," was Alexis Korner.

Korner was born in France, the child of a cavalry officer in the Austrian army and a Greco-Turkish mother. During his early years, Alexis was shuttled among relatives in many places on the European continent while his father tried his hand at many business activities, including drilling for oil in Abyssinia. Korner's schooling took place in such diverse locations as France, Switzerland, North Africa, and England.

The family finally settled in England in the mid-1930s and his father took out English citizenship in 1938. Alexis was a difficult child. At last, his parents placed him in the Finchden Manor School for extremely disturbed boys with high IQs. While there, Alexis became interested in the guitar, to his father's dismay, and made his first instrument from plywood and a shaved-down table leg. His family was not opposed to classical music, only the popular variety; in fact, Alexis had begun learning classical piano, music theory, and harmony at an early age.

Alexis' father was looking forward to having his son join him in business eventually. However, the die was cast for young Korner in the '40s when he heard Jimmy Yancey's record "The Five O'Clock Blues." "I knew from the first time I heard it that that was what I wanted to play and ever since then that has been my major interest."

Korner's love for jazz increased as he went through his teens. This proved valuable background after he was drafted into the Army in 1946 and sent to Germany. There he ran the record library and arranged jazz broadcasts on the British Forces Network. He returned to England in 1947 and found work first as an artists & repertoire man with Melodisc Records, then a publicist with Decca Records, and a studio manager for the BBC.

On the side, he played in small amateur groups before getting his first professional job in 1949 with the Chris Barber Jazz Band. He began as a pianist, later also performing on guitar, three nights a week for five shillings per night.

In 1948, Korner formed his own band with trumpeter Dickie Hawdon. However, the group found the going rough because British audiences weren't prepared for the modern jazz the group played. In 1950, the band was dissolved and for much of the decade Alexis earned most of his living by working as a journalist and radio announcer. Those daytime activities provided the support he needed during the decade it took him to gain success in popular music.

Two years later, he returned to a Barber-led group, a new organization jointly run by Barber and a friend of Alexis's, Ken Colyer, who had just come back from playing jazz in New Orleans for a time. The band included three players of more up-to-date jazz: Colyer, Korner, and young Lonnie Donegan (whose major claim to fame with U.S. audiences was his 1961 novelty *"Does Your Chewing Gum Lose Its Flavor on the Bedpost Overnight"*). The interlocking groups made recordings together and as separate entities. In time, the old arguments about musical direction cropped up and Colyer and Korner left to play at a club on London's Greek Street.

In the mid-1950s, Korner became increasingly interested in blues. He met a young British blues harmonica player, Cyril Davies, and the two often played together at local clubs for the balance of the decade. They made an abortive attempt to run their own club, the Roundhouse, in London's Soho district in the late '50s. However, Korner's musical income came mostly from work as a session player at London recording studios. In 1961, both Korner and Davies were playing occasionally with Chris Barber's band at the Marquee Club, considered the top popular-music club in England. In addition, the sound of Korner's guitar and Davies' harmonica often could be heard at the growing number of rock-blues–oriented clubs.

Not only did Davies and Korner persevere in playing blues at the start of the '60s, they rounded up visiting American blues artists to sit in with them at local clubs whenever they could. Among those who performed with them at one time or another were Sonny Terry, Brownie McGhee, Memphis Slim, and Korner's particular favorite, Muddy Waters. The mass audience in England ignored them and jazz critics were generally no kinder. The ridicule from the reviewers increased when Korner and Davies introduced electric guitars into their group. However, more and more teenage musicians took notice of what Korner and Davies were doing. Small knots of then unknown youngsters clustered eagerly around the stage when Korner and Davies appeared; the names of those teenagers would now look like a who's who of rock.

In early 1962, Davies and Korner decided to open a rhythm & blues club at a small pub in the Ealing section of London. They recruited two other members, Dick Hextall-Smith on tenor sax and future Rolling Stone Charlie Watts on drums. The band debuted on March 17, 1962, and within a short time it was one of the most talked-about new groups in the city. The band soon moved to the Marquee, opening on May 3, 1962, performing on Thursday, the night off for the regular band. In a short time, however, they became far more popular than the regular act and became the featured attraction at the club. Young music fans and aspiring pop artists flocked to the Marquee from all over England. Many of them got the chance to perform a number or two with the group, including such now famous rock stars as Eric Burdon (founder of the Animals and War), Brian Jones and Keith Richards of the Rolling Stones, and Paul Jones, later lead singer of Manfred Mann.

The group continued to attract excellent young musicians and Korner and Davis demonstrated unerring judgment in selecting band additions. During the Marquee engagement, a magnificent bass player named Jack Bruce became a member. In early 1963,

when Watts left, his place was taken by fledgling drummer Ginger Baker. When the group moved to a club named the Flamingo, a lead vocalist named Mick Jagger took the spotlight. During this engagement, Davies and Korner split up with Cyril branching out as head of the Cyril Davies Blues Band, which showed great promise before Davies' untimely death. No sooner did Davies depart than Korner picked Graham Bond, another musician later to become famous.

For several years after this, Korner continued to be an important force on the European band scene, though he was never able to place any recordings on the top rungs of the charts. As of 1966, the Korner band was a quartet, consisting of Korner; Terry Cox on celeste, glockenspiel, vibraphone, and drums; John Renbourn on guitar, sitar, piano, and vocals; and Danny Thompson on string bass, cello, and trombone. This group of sidemen later created the shimmering folk-jazz-rock Pentangle and subsequent John Renbourn Group. By this time, of course, Korner alumni had revolutionized the pop-music scene in such groups as the Animals, Rolling Stones, Cream, Manfred Mann, Yardbirds, and Graham Bond Organization.

For some years in the mid-1960s, Korner gave up full-time performing to spend more time with his children. He did some concert work, but devoted his major energies to TV and radio as announcer, interviewer, and master of ceremonies. He was an interviewer on the BBC's "Today" radio program and had his own segment, "Korner's Corner," on the program "Roundabout." His TV activities included work as musical director on the shows "Gadzooks" and "Heartsong" and on the Rediffusion TV twice-a-week children's serial, "Five O'Clock Club." Alexis was also one of the most sought-after artists to do voice-over commercials.

In 1968, Alexis began to tire of such work. He began to work as a solo performer at universities and in small clubs and then joined forces with Victor Brox, who later was a member of Aynsley Dunbar's Retaliation. With Brox, Korner began to handle singing chores; previously, except on rare occasions, he restricted himself to instrumental work. This led to his first singing album, *New Generation of Blues,* backed by Danny Thompson, Terry Cox, and Ray Warleigh. As Korner stepped up his touring in 1968, he added such talented newcomers as Marsha Hunt and Robert Plant. Marsha later gained a starring role in *Hair* and Plant was drawn away to Led Zeppelin by Jimmy Page in the fall of the year.

Plant's place was taken by Andy Fraser, previously with John Mayall's Bluesbreakers. (Mayall credits his enthusiasm for Korner-Davies in the early 1960s with providing the incentive for his band activities.) When Fraser thought about forming a band of his own, Alexis encouraged him and played a part in the development of the group, Free.

In the spring of 1969, Alexis was asked to tour Denmark with that country's top rock/blues group, The Beefeaters. He shared vocal honors with the band's lead singer, 20-year-old Peter Thorup. Thorup and Korner got along so well they made plans for a band of their own. The new organization was called The New Church and included Alexis and Peter on vocals and guitars, Ray Warleigh on saxophone and flute, and Colin Hodgkinson on bass. The 1970 *New Church* LP was well received, though it failed to be a super hit. This situation finally changed for Korner when he and Thorup worked with a group called C.C.S. beginning in late 1970. The first single of Alexis's to make top levels of British charts was "Whole Lotta Love" in early 1971. This merited, but long-delayed achievement met with universal enthusiasm from British critics who had long since begun calling Korner "the grandfather of British rhythm & blues." C.C.S. followed with several more singles hits in the U.K. such as "Walking" and "Tap Turns on the Water" (1971), "Brother" (1972), and "Band Plays the Googie" in (1973). Even while enjoying C.C.S. successes, Korner continued to front his own band in England.

Korner always kept an eye open for interesting new projects. In 1972, he and Thorup made their first tour of the U.S. as an opening act for Humble Pie. They also worked with King Crimson and, with three of its members—Ian Wallace (drums), Mel Collins (saxophone), and Boz (bass)—they formed the band Snape that recorded one album, *Accidentally Borne in New Orleans*, issued in the U.S. on Warner Brothers. In 1975, Columbia released his *Get Off My Cloud*. Though not much happened with his U.S. discs, he continued to be an important figure in England and Continental Europe. He often was asked to give lectures on the evolution of the blues and other developments in modern pop music.

His 1985 death received considerable commentary in Europe, but little notice in the U.S., where only a small percentage of knowledgeable fans were aware of his great contributions to British blues and rock. (*See Animals, The; Burdon, Eric; Cream; Davies, Cyril; Jagger, Mick; Led Zeppelin; Mann, Manfred; Mayall, John; Rolling Stones, The; War; Yardbirds, The.*)

KRAFTWERK: *Vocal and electronic instrumental group from Dusseldorf, West Germany. Founding members: Ralf Hutter, born Germany, 1948; Florian Schneider, born Germany, c. late 1940s.*

When the future-rock or techno-rock format became a feature of the 1970s pop scene, the West German duo Kraftwerk could claim a large share of responsibility for the phenomenon. Reflecting the ceaseless surge of advanced technology, Kraftwerk's approach to its music was to emphasize machines rather than people.

In concert, in fact, Kraftwerk exhibited none of the instruments most onlookers associated with music, pop or otherwise. There were no guitars or pianos in evidence. As co-founder Ralf Hutter told Deane Zimmerman of *Hit Parade* magazine (August 1978), he and collaborator Florian Schneider felt synthesizer music was the next step after new wave. "It's happening everywhere. Already the guitar is like a relic of the Middle Ages. Why limit yourself to only six strings when you can play a synthesizer and get sound waves from 20 to 20,000."

He described Kraftwerk's approach to its concerts to a reporter from England's *Sounds* magazine. "Kraftwerk basically means 'power plant'; we plug our machines into the electrical system and create transformed energy. The Human Machine (*die Mensche Machine* in German—one of the group's nicknames for itself, another being *Klangchemiker* or sound chemists) means that we plug ourselves into the machines also. We play with our brains, our hands, our mouths, our feet and sometimes we use contact microphones which pick up the sounds of the clothes we are wearing or how much my beard is growing that day. We play the machines, but the machines also play us. This we do not deny like they do in conventional music. There the man is always considered superior to his machine, but this is not so. The machine should not do only slave work. We try to treat them as colleagues so they exchange energies with us."

Ralf and Florian's initial musical interests were certainly not particularly unusual. By the time they met at Dusseldorf Conservatory in 1968, both had studied classical music for some 10 years and had also experimented with other forms such as jazz and rock. (In those days, Ralf was studying piano and Florian the flute.) They soon discovered a common interest in going beyond traditional—and classical—instrumentation. As Hutter told *Sounds:* "We were trained on classical instruments and then we bought amplifiers and echo machines, but we found that normal instruments were too limited. From the very beginning we have thought of our music visually, creating films in our brains and transmitting them to the audience, but traditional instruments always make you think of the person playing them."

The duo began to implement its ideas by acquiring the initial electronic gear in the late 1960s. In 1968, that included a tape recorder, second-hand Fafisa, and some German-made amplifiers. Over the next few years, they saved all the money they could to increase their electronic hoard and in 1970 took the next major step by opening their own recording studio, which they named Kling Klang (in English, Ringing Tone). By the early 1970s, Kling Klang was outfitted with a wide variety of amplifiers, oscillators, sequencers, computer-storage synthesizers, rhythm machines, preprogrammed tapes, a machine that could be instructed to makes it own vocal sounds, and many other specially designed devices.

They felt they were, in effect, free to examine radically new musical directions because of the upheavals in twentieth century Germany. First, Hitler had dispersed the German artistic community of the pre-1930s; then World War II had shattered what was left, they asserted. They told a reporter from the *Rocky Mountain Musical Express,* as a result, "We have nothing to do with a past because we were stripped of everything. In this vacuum we were able to start something that is really new. All you had was space, and the after-the-war generation could do with it what they wanted. It is a most interesting cultural climate."

Ralf and Florian's experiments with sounds and sound machines evolved into their initial recordings for public release. Hutter concentrated on composing the duo's material while Florian provided the often minimal lyrics. Their first two albums, including one titled *Kraftwerk,* only were released in Germany on the Vertigo label. The third Vertigo LP, *Ralf and Florian,* was offered on the world market, but received negligible notice. In Germany, there were some respectable sales, the money from which was promptly plowed back into equipment funds for the studio.

After adding two more musicians to the group, percussionist Wolfgang Flur and violinist/guitarist Klaus Roeder (who served as electronic percussionists), a fourth album, *Autobahn,* was recorded on Mercury Records. One side, as the title indicates, essentially was a 22½–minute sound portrait of a drive along the German super highway. Released in the U.S. in 1975, the album rose to number five on *Billboard* charts. The title track was shortened and released as a single titled "Wir Farh'n Farh'n Auf der Autobahn." It became a chart hit and the exposure helped bring the earlier *Ralf & Florian* onto U.S. album charts.

Capitol Records then sought out and signed Kraftwerk to a multiyear contract. For the debut Capitol LP, *Radio Activity,* (March 1976), Roeder was replaced by percussionist Karl Bartos. That album exceeded the response of *Autobahn,* becoming a major hit in the U.S. and many other nations, reaching number one.

The robot-like appearance of the Kraftwerk foursome during its worldwide tour certainly seemed to match the founders' theme. It was a guise the band maintained for the balance of the 1970s. *Gallery* magazine, describing a fall 1978 New York concert noted: "They stand rigid, expressionless, self-controlled in their identical narrow-lapeled suits. Set off by short, clipped hairstyles, their faces (typically whiteface with lipstick) reveal a certain distance, even alienation, from their fellow human creatures. Like robots, they take the forms of men without betraying man's standard eccentricities. The 'image' is anti-image, the stance designed not to attract."

Their ideas began to rub off on other artists. In particular, more than a few disco hits by other performers of the 1970s reflected Kraftwerk influences. Giorgio Moroder, the German writer who helped propel Donna Summer to stardom, acknowledged Kraftwerk impact on numbers such as "I Feel Love." David Bowie became friends with the founders and used tracks from *Radio Activity* to introduce his concerts. He also based some of his stylings on his album *Low* on Kraftwerk-type arrangements.

Their next Capitol albums, *Trans-Europe Express* (1977) and *Man Machine* (1978), also spent time on album charts in Europe and the U.S. The first of those provided tracks that became longtime standbys in discos around the world, including the theme track and "Showroom Dummies." In the U.S., Capitol serviced discos with a 12-inch 45 rpm single of "Trans-Europe Express"/"Metal on Metal." Its 13½–minute running time kept the dancers whirling madly under the flashing, ever-changing lights of the world's discos. A disco single of "Showroom Dummies" also was issued. Those discs' popularity inspired voters in the 1977 Popular Music Disco poll to vote the band Best European Group, Male. The award show, held in New York City in September 1977, included footage from the band's *Trans-Europe Express* video, material also spotlighted in the nationally telecast version of the show that November. Schneider commented: "Kraftwerk hasn't discovered disco, disco has discovered Kraftwerk."

Another significant Kraftwerk-influenced recording came out during 1977, Meco Menardo's "Star Wars Theme," which rose to number one on *Billboard*'s singles charts. Meco told a reporter: "I've listened to *Trans-Europe Express* a lot and I really like it. I consider it one of the frontrunners in the field of electronic disco music."

Hutter and Schneider spent much of 1979 and 1980 back in Dusseldorf working on their next album. By then, they could afford to bring in outside experts to help in the work. Hutter commented: "Kling Klang is a laboratory where we do the work of scientists. We have ideas of sounds that have never been heard before and we work with engineers to produce them.'' Some of the patents they obtained covered systems of interest to other musicians and even some scientists.

But the new sounds of the '80s from Kraftwerk were not destined for Capitol. The group signed with Warner Brothers, which issued its debut on the label, *Computer World,* in late 1981.

KRAMER, BILLY J & THE DAKOTAS:
Vocal and instrumental group. Billy J. Kramer, born Bootle, Liverpool, England, August 19, 1943; Tony Mansfield, born Salford, England, May 28, 1943; Mike Maxfield, born Manchester, England, February 23, 1944; Robin Macdonald, born Nairn, Scotland, July 18, 1943; Raymond Jones, born Oldham, England, October 20, 1939. Group disbanded in 1966.

Brian Epstein is almost solely associated in the public mind with the Beatles, because he was their discoverer and the person generally credited with engineering their sensational rise to stardom. However, Epstein used his talent to promote the careers of a number of rock artists in the mid-1960s, some of whom, like Billy J Kramer & the Dakotas, achieved considerable status in pop music, if only for a short period of time compared to the Beatles.

Kramer, like Epstein and the Beatles, was a Liverpudlian. Under his real name of William Ashton, he grew up in a working class district of the city and attended the St. George of England Secondary Modern School.

In his midteens, he left school and found work as an engineering apprentice on British Railways. Musical activities were mostly a hobby. His performances as a rhythm guitarist with local groups, were generally for no pay. In 1962, he decided to move out as a lead vocalist, taking the name Billy J Kramer, and adding a backup group called the Coasters (who were no relation to the pioneer American rhythm & blues team of the same name).

Meanwhile, the careers of his future backup group followed similar patterns, except that the locale was Manchester. By the early 1960s, four young musicians had started a band called the Dakotas. They were Mike Maxfield on lead guitar, Robin Macdonald on rhythm guitar, Raymond Jones on bass, and Tony Mansfield on drums. All four came to the Dakotas after working with school friends in their early teens and with various skiffle or R&B groups around Manchester.

In February 1963, Brian Epstein auditioned Kramer and liked him. Epstein also had heard favorable comments about the Dakotas, but knew they were lacking a strong lead vocalist. He signed Kramer and combined him with the Manchester group. He then lined up their first major engagement in the Star Club in Hamburg, Germany, one of that country's most noted rock centers, a club that played an important part in the Beatles' early career. The excellent reception given the group by the Star Club audiences helped bring a contract for the band on EMI's Parlophone label, the label on which the Beatles too began their recording efforts.

Before 1963 was half over, Billy J and the Dakotas had an English hit single: ''Want to Know a Secret.'' By the end of the year, they had a million-seller for Parlophone, ''Bad to Me,'' a song that also made the top 10 in *Billboard* as a double-sided U.S. hit with ''Little Children'' on the Imperial label.

Besides singles hits, the group gained English and/or U.S. charts with a number of Imperial LPs; during 1964–65: *Billy J. Kramer and the Dakotas, I'll Keep You Satisfied,* and *Trains, Boats, Planes.* The group disbanded in 1966.

KRISTOFFERSON, KRIS: *Singer, songwriter, guitarist, actor. Born Brownsville, Texas, June 22, 1936.*

A multitalented individual, Kris Kristofferson could achieve brilliant results in varied entertainment fields when he concentrated on his work. The problem was that at times he seemed to spread himself too thin and that, combined with some of his personal problems, caused phases of his career—particularly in songwriting and concert work—to be distinctly erratic. But taken as a whole, he provided some of the finest original pop and country songs ever written.

The son of a two-star general, Kris moved to many places during his youth, a pattern that contributed to a somewhat disjointed feeling about life at times. Having spent some of his childhood in the South, he gained an affinity for country songs, though for a time he was more interested in pursuing a literary career than a musical one. He could play guitar quite well by the time he enrolled in Pomona College in Claremont, California. There he demonstrated considerable athletic ability, lettering in football and soccer, which helped him win a Rhodes Scholarship to Oxford University in England. The scholarship calls for both academic and athletic prowess and Kris was a fine student of literature, at one point winning the top four out of 20 prizes in the *Atlantic Monthly* collegiate short story contest. At Oxford, one of his major interests was the work of William Blake.

When he entered Oxford in the late '50s, his primary aim was to become a novelist. However, by the time he completed his work, he felt depressed about his abilities. When he returned to the United States at the start of the '60s, he had no real idea of what career to pursue. He had started to write songs, but was uncertain of their quality and soon took one way of dropping out: he enlisted in the U.S. Army. He became an officer, going through Ranger school, parachute jump school, and pilot training. He enjoyed flying and became an excellent pilot, specializing in helicopters.

However, in other ways, it was a destructive period for him. He told an interviewer in 1970: "For a time in the Army I quit writing. I nearly ended up destroying myself. I was drinking all the time, doing all kinds of reckless things. I totaled two cars and had four motorcycle accidents. But I had to write. I could no more not write than I could not breathe. It is a part of me." Unfortunately, a craving for alcohol also seemed to be a part of him and plagued his career a number of times in the future.

After leaving the service in 1965, he toyed with the idea of accepting an appointment to teach English literature at the U.S. Military Academy at West Point. But he had felt the pull of songwriting and decided to try to make the grade in Nashville. It was to prove a four-year, often desperate operation. He moved into a tenement and made the rounds of publishing houses, meeting with consistent turndowns. To stay alive and, by the end of the '60s, support a wife and two children as well, he took any positions he could find: a night janitor at Columbia Records Studios and day bartender at Nashville's Tally-Ho Tavern. Both had the advantage of providing contacts with the country-music industry, the Tavern being a hangout for many established and aspiring songwriters. At times during those years, he earned money by working as a laborer and by flying helicopters to offshore oil rigs in the Gulf States area. Eventually, the strain proved too great for his marriage and a separation ensued.

Some of his experiences were reflected in his hit songs of later years. His loves and hitchhiking days are recalled in "Me and Bobby McGee": "Busted flat in Baton Rouge/Headin' for the trains/Feelin' nearly faded as my jeans." The loneliness of the slum years appears in one of the songs from his 1972 hit LP, *The Silver Tongued Devil and I* where, in "To Beat the Devil," he sings of the days when "Failure had me locked on the wrong side of the door. No one stood beside me but the shadow on the floor."

In 1969, Kris's persistence finally paid off. A long-time admirer of Johnny Cash, he practically lived outside the studio where Cash's network TV show was being taped. He pestered anyone of note who came there to look at his material. Finally Roger Miller gave in and agreed to consider it. Roger decided to record "Bobby McGee," which became a country hit and encouraged cover releases by many other artists from pop, rock, and country genres.

Cash himself became a fan of Kristofferson's, featuring such songs as "Sunday Morning Comin' Down" on his show, referring to Kris as one of the new, great talents, and having Kris as a guest several times in 1969 and 1970. Johnny's single of "Sunday Morning" became a hit in 1969. Meanwhile, Janis Joplin decided to include her styling of "Bobby McGee" on her album, *Pearl*. Her posthumously released single of it became a number one hit in 1971.

By 1970, Kris was considered one of country music's most promising artists. He had signed with Monument Records in 1969, which in June 1970 released his debut LP, *Kristofferson* (later retitled *Me and Bobby McGee*). That year, too, many artists eagerly checked out his new songs to turn out covers. Many of them recorded his "Help Me Make It Through the Night," but it was Sammi Smith who had the number one country version (top 10 in pop). The Nashville Songwriter's Association recognized his achievements by voting him Songwriter of the Year in 1970. In 1971, he got his first Grammy Award when "Help Me Make It Through the Night," was voted Best Country Song.

During 1970, Kris worked on his first film score for Dennis Hopper's *The Last Movie*. On June 23, 1970, he made his first professional appearance as a performer at a big-name club, the Troubadour in Los Angeles. From the early '70s on, many of his shows also featured Rita Coolidge, later Mrs. Krisofferson. His concert work the first part of the '70s was excellent, but for a time in the mid-1970s, he seemed to become dispirited, partly due to an increasing preoccupation with movie acting. Late in the decade, starting with his tours of 1977, he seemed to find renewed interest in working in front of a live audience. Part of his problem, he told an interviewer in August 1977, had been the continued use of liquor as a crutch. He claimed his resurgence was due to cutting back on that: "It feels weird out there. I mean I have to get used to singing sober again. It's like singing in the daylight or something. But it's coming."

Kris' own single of "Bobby McGee" finally became a chart hit in September 1971, helped by the gold-record success of a new LP, *The Silver Tongued Devil and I*. Its single, "Loving Her Was Easier (Than Anything I'll Ever Do Again)" became a best-seller during that summer. In 1972, he gained a gold record for *The Silver Tongued Devil* and had two new albums on the charts, *Border Lord* and *Jesus Was a Capricorn* plus another chart single, "Josie." In 1973, he had a gold single, "Why Me, Lord."

There was a gap of almost two years before he had any new albums. In 1974, he was represented by

Spooky Lady's Nightmare and *Breakaway,* which contained some interesting material, but seemed to indicate a creative slowdown from his earlier work. Things picked up a bit with his 1975 LP, *Who's to Bless and Who's to Blame,* but regressed once more in 1976 with *Surreal Thing.* He continued to turn out LPs regularly as the decade went by, with most of the releases on Columbia (which bought his original label, Momument). However, very little of his new work in the second half of the decade measured up to what he had done in the first half. Among the albums were the soundtrack from his starring vehicle (with Barbra Streisand) *A Star Is Born* (1976); a "best-of" release, *Songs of Kristofferson* (1977); *Easter Island* (1978); and *Shake Hands with the Devil* (1979). *Easter Island* was the most disappointing of all, with little if any of the original work coming close to such earlier classics as "Bobby McGee," "The Pilgrim, Chapter 33." But the quality seemed to improve markedly in his 1979 LP, *Shake Hands with the Devil,* indicating better things might be in store in the '80s.

The slump in songwriting was perhaps traceable to his movie work. There he had proven himself one of the finest new actors to come along in the '70s. His initial major film breakthrough was as Billy in the 1973 *Pat Garrett and Billy the Kid,* co-starring Bob Dylan. From then on, a long series of movies featured his talents as both dramatic and comic actor: *Cisco Pike, Alice Doesn't Live Here Anymore, Bring Me the Head of Alfredo Garcia, Blume in Love, Vigilante Force, The Sailor Who Fell from Grace with the Sea, Semi-Tough* (co-starring Burt Reynolds and giving Kris some rein to use his athletic skills), *Convoy, A Star Is Born,* and, in 1979, *Heaven's Gate.* He won a number of awards for acting including Best Actor from the Foreign Press Association for *A Star Is Born.*

During the middle and late 1970s, Kris recorded many duets with wife Rita Coolidge, including such singles as "Rain"/"What 'Cha Gonna Do" (1974) and "Lover Please"/"Slow Down" and "Sweet Susannah"/"We Must Have Been out of Our Minds" (1975). Kris and Rita won two Grammy Awards for Best Vocal Performance by a Duo, the first in 1973 for "From the Bottle to the Bottom" and the second in 1975 for "Lover Please" (a remake of Clyde McPhatter's 1962 hit).

By the end of the '70s, his marriage to Rita Coolidge had gone sour and they were divorced. Late in 1979, Willie Nelson turned out an album of Kristofferson songs, and the two toured together during the 1979–80 winter concert season. During 1980, Columbia released the album *To the Bone,* which contained some of the final recordings Kristofferson recorded for that label.

In the 1980s, Kris continued to focus more on movie projects than on concerts, although for a time it seemed as though successful scripts eluded him. *Heaven's Gate* had been one of the costliest, most derided failures in modern film history, and it was followed by another box-office flop, *Rollover.* While Kristofferson in theory couldn't be blamed for the shortcomings of the story lines, the fact remained, as he told a reporter in the mid-1980s: "For three years there were no offers." Then he got the chance to join Willie Nelson in *Songwriter,* a 1984 satire on the country music industry that won both critical support and moderate economic rewards. For the movie, Kris wrote 11 new songs that worked well within the dramatic framework. His work in *Songwriter* brought contracts for work in three more mid-1980s films: *Flashpoint,* a movie version of Ernest Hemingway's *Across the River and through the Trees,* and *Trouble in Mind.* In 1987, Kris had a featured role in the controversial miniseries "Amerika" about a supposed takeover of the U.S. by the Russians. ABC-TV. (*See Cash, Johnny; Coolidge, Rita; Dylan, Bob; Joplin, Janis; Knight, Gladys, & the Pips; Streisand, Barbra.*)

Later, Kris's first new LP in six years, *Repossessed,* was released containing songs that took issue with Reagan administration policy in Latin America, something not calculated to endear him to some of the conservative country audiences he appeared before. He told Robert Hilburn of the *Los Angeles Times* (April 26, 1987): "I saw a clip of Muhammad Ali the other day, this clip of him speaking out and refusing to go over there. I wasn't really paying attention to all that at the time and I thought he was wrong to do that, just like most people in the country did.

"But I can see it clearer now. I admire him so much. He became a symbol for a lot of people back then and at great expense. I think people have a responsibility to speak out on things that they feel are wrong. But it's easier for me than for Muhammad. I don't have the same risk. They can't take my title away because I don't have one and they aren't catching me in my prime either.

"I haven't been on the charts for quite a while anyway, so it's not like I'm jeopardizing my commercial position. I feel that I have the luxury of being able to do what I am doing . . . to be able to address issues that I think are important." (*See Webb, Jimmy.*)

LABELLE, PATTI: *singer, songwriter, band leader. Born Philadelphia, Pennsylvania, May 24, 1944.*

The mid-1980s turned out to be comeback years for more than a few talented black female artists.

Aretha Franklin, for one, appeared more regularly on the charts, but even more dramatic rebounds were scored by Tina Turner and Patti LaBelle, both of whom became idols for tens of millions of music fans of all ages and ethnic backgrounds the world over. Turner had tasted those triumphs over a decade before, but for LaBelle it was a relatively new sensation, a response that exceeded even that for her mid-1970s best-seller, "Lady Marmalade."

She grew up in a relatively comfortable family environment in West Philadelphia, but she didn't have that happy a childhood as her parents divorced when she was 12. Looking back, she told Stephen Holden of *The New York Times* (February 23, 1986): "I was a strange, homely little bird with red hair that eventually changed color as I grew older. I was so shy that my mother offered to pay me to go out and play with other children, but I still wouldn't go. I used to stay inside the house and sing in front of the mirror. My favorite songs were 'I Loves You Porgy,' 'The Party's Over,' and 'My Funny Valentine.'"

She told another interviewer: "I started singing when I was about seven years old. Just started singing for myself around the house. When I got older, I started listening to Nina Simone, Dakota Staton, and Gloria Lynne. They were my favorite singers to listen to, but not to emulate or imitate. Other than listening to music, I just stayed in my room, playing with my animals and looking into the mirror. That was it. I had no other friends but the animals and the mirror.

"I had three sisters and one brother, but I didn't play very much with them either. I was a homely child, a very homely child, at least I thought I was, and I didn't like playing with people. I just thought animals and mirrors were safer. And today I'm finding out that in most cases this is still true."

In her teens, she did begin performing, particularly after she found that she lost her feelings of inferiority once she went on stage and started singing. When she was singing, she noted, it was as though someone else occupied her body "and that somebody wasn't afraid like my normal self was."

While still in her early teens, she became part of a group called the Ordettes whose members also included Cindy Birdsong, a future Supreme. (*See Supremes, The.*) When two girls left, the manager brought in Nona Hendryx (born Trenton, New Jersey, October 4, 1944) and Sarah Dash (born Trenton, New Jersey, August 18, 1945). A reformed trio, Patti LaBelle and the Bluebells soon emerged. The group signed with Newtown Records at the start of the '60s, actually taking its name from a subsidiary of that label, Bluebelle Records. Among the girls' singles for that label were "All or Nothing," "I Believe," and "Danny Boy." The high point of the

association was the (spring of 1962) top 20 hit "I Sold My Heart to the Junkman." (For the initial releases, the group called itself the Blue Belles, not changing to Patti LaBelle and the Bluebells until 1963.) None of the trio's other releases on Newtown reached the heights of "Junkman," though the 1963 single, "Down the Aisle," made the R&B top 40.

Its fortunes didn't improve much even though the group moved to Parkway and Atlantic Records during the late '60s. During those years, besides concert work and relatively unsuccessful recordings, the girls sang backup for a number of major performers including Jerry Butler and the Rolling Stones. In 1967, Vicki Wickham (then producer of the U.K. TV series "Top of the Pops") began working with the trio and helped revamp its style into a more rock-oriented format under the new group name LaBelle. Soon after, LaBelle was working as opening act for the Who during that band's debut tour of the U.S. Another milestone came in 1971, when Laura Nyro had the trio sing on her LP *It's Gonna Take a Miracle* and tour with her. (*See Nyro, Laura.*)

At the start of the '70s, the trio's recording fortunes took a turn for the better with a new pact with Warner Brothers. The trio's label debut, *LaBelle* (1971) was followed by the excellent *Moonshadow*, which spotlighted six songs written by Hendryx. The LPs won ecstatic reviews, but sales were less than phenomenal so the group moved on to RCA, which released the LP *Pressure Cookin'* and the debut label single, "Sunshine (Woke Me up This Morning)" in late 1973. By the next year, LaBelle had switched to Epic Records and good rewards came fairly rapidly. The group's first Epic album, *Nightbirds* (1974), became a top 10 the following year with the help of the number one single, "Lady Marmalade"(written by Bob Crewe and Kenny Nolan). The trio made the charts with the two follow-up Epic LPs *Phoenix* (1975) and *Chameleon* (1976), but those didn't have the creative consistency of *Nightbirds*. Meanwhile, when not touring with the group, Patti had a personal project at home—bringing up her son Zuri Kye, born to her and husband Armstead Edwards (later her manager) on July 17, 1973.

The group broke up in the middle of a concert tour in late 1976 when Nona Hendryx became emotionally upset and walked out. Patti told Quincy Troupe for an article in *Spin* magazine (April 1986), that it was a traumatic experience for her too. "It was painful, very, very painful. It was shrink time for me because it was like a marriage breaking up, and also I didn't know what I was going to do. I knew I had to sing, but I also knew that I had to sing by myself, which was very, very traumatic. I didn't think I could go out there by myself, because I wouldn't have anybody to blame if things went wrong. But I went on out, and the first time that I performed as a solo after the breakup, the people gave me a standing ovation. They accepted me. This was about a year and a half after the breakup, the summer of 1978, I think. But the year and a half before my solo debut had been hell. I went to a shrink for him to let me know that I was all right and that I shouldn't be afraid, that whatever I was feeling was natural, you know? And it was natural, and so I went out there and performed and saw that it was all right.''

Helping her regain her equilibrium was her husband. With her solo career in the offing, he resigned his position as an assistant school principal to devote full time to her performance management.

Her 1977 solo debut on Epic, *Patti LaBelle*, featured such excellent tracks as ''Since I Don't Have You,'' ''Dan Swit Me,'' and ''Joy to Have Your Love.'' This was followed by such collections as *Tasty* (1978), *It's Alright with Me* (1979), *Released* (1980), and the *Best of Patti LaBelle* (1981).

At the start of the 1980s, Patti's recording career seemed to be slowing down and she sought new outlets for her talents. One of these was in stage and TV work, beginning with a part in Stud Terkel's musical for PBS-TV, ''Working.'' She also was featured on two PBS special tributes: one to Duke Ellington, the other to centenarian jazz great Eubie Blake. She then agreed to tour in a revival of the stage play *Your Arms Too Short to Box with God*. After playing before enthusiastic audiences in other parts of the U.S., Patti and co-star Al Green opened with the show on Broadway in September 1982 and the vehicle remained a top ticket for many months after that. (*See Green, Al.*) Patti stayed with the show for post–New York engagements until it ended the tour in June 1983. In 1984, Patti made her film debut as a blues club singer in Norman Jewison's acclaimed version of Charles Fuller's Pulitzer Prize–winning play, *A Soldier's Story*.

Along with those credits came new vigor in her recording work as her name became almost a fixture on hit charts. Among her best-selling efforts of the mid-1980s were ''The Best Is Yet to Come'' (a duet with Grover Washington, Jr.); a duet with Bobby Womack (''Love Has Finally Come at Last''); and such solo releases as ''If Only You Knew,'' ''I'm in Love Again,'' ''New Attitude,'' and ''Stir It Up,'' the last two coming from the *Beverly Hills Cop* soundtrack. (*See Washington, Grover, Jr.; Womack, Bobby.*) In July 1985, she gave a show-stopping performance as part of the Live Aid worldwide telecast, appearing on the segment originating from Veteran's Stadium in Philadelphia.

The Live Aid set was just one of her many contributions to charitable causes. Among programs she had assisted in fund-raising efforts over the years were Big Sisters of America, One to One, The United Negro College Fund, and projects for such East Coast cities as Philadelphia, Baltimore, and New York. Her volunteer work won recognition several times from the NAACP, which awarded her the prestigious Image Award.

After many years with Epic (with releases that included the 1985 hit LP *Patti*), she left for a new alignment with MCA Records. Her best-selling first album on that label, *Winner in You* (1986), and number one single ''On My Own'' (a duet with former Doobie Brother Michael McDonald; *see Doobie Brothers, The*) helped bring belated recognition that she was, indeed, a superstar.

In 1987, she kept up a busy concert schedule that included a featured spot in the June R&B Superfest, a seven-hour event at the Rose Bowl in Pasadena that showcased, among others, Gladys Knight & the Pips, Frankie Beverly and Maze and the Whispers. During the year preparations were begun on her next MCA album project, due to be completed in 1988.

LAKE, GREG: *See Emerson, Lake and Palmer; King Crimson.*

LAUPER, CYNDI: *Singer, guitarist, songwriter. Born Queens, New York, June 20, 1953.*

With her orange-colored hair, baby-talk speaking voice, and asserted preference for wrestlers (such as self-proclaimed wrestling champion Hulk Hogan), Cyndi Lauper had no problem getting media exposure when her first solo recordings and videos flooded the airwaves in the mid-1980s. But her performances suggested she was not a latter-day female Tiny Tim who would gain a brief moment in the spotlight for eccentric appearance or behavior; rather, the vocal timbre and Midler-like extravagance indicated a talented and creative artist.

She demonstrated that versatility in many ways once she had taken initial strides toward stardom. An example was the time she unexpectedly came on stage at Los Angeles Greek Theater to sing a duet with concert headliner Patti LaBelle of Patti's trademark song, ''Lady Marmalade.'' Writing in the *Los Angeles Herald Examiner* (June 10, 1985), Todd Everett noted: ''Lauper came on and proceeded to demonstrate what a terrific vocalist she is. It takes more than nerve to share the stage with a performer as strong as LaBelle, particularly on her own turf, but Lauper acquitted herself more than adequately on 'Marmalade.'

''Even LaBelle, more than generous in her treatment of her guest, appeared both surprised and proud of the duet. Lauper then retreated to the side of the stage, becoming the fourth member of the backing vocal trio, the Sweeties, joining in on the doo-wahs and hand choreography and from all appearances having the time of her life.''

The sudden prominence Cyndi achieved in 1984–85 cloaked over a decade of dues-paying in small-time New York City singing and songwriting jobs before opportunity finally knocked.

Lauper's zany exuberance and quick wit seemed appropriate for a girl born and raised in New York City. Her family lived in Brooklyn before her birth and she recalled she was ''almost born in a taxicab on the way to Boulevard Hospital in Queens.'' Her parents were divorced when she was five, but she remembered growing up in a warm ethnic environment presided over by her Italian-American mother. As a child, she gave her first performances for old ladies in her neighborhood who rewarded her vocal efforts with small change. In high school, her creative interests broadened somewhat. ''I also painted and wrote poetry, but always sang and had a good memory for words and melodies.''

Her first pop-music influences came from the short-lived folk boom of the late 1950s and early 1960s. The music helped inspire her to learn to play guitar when she was 12. Around that time she also co-wrote some of her first original songs with her sister. Though she wasn't unaware of developments in rock'n'roll, folk-style material retained the strongest hold on her through high school.

She noted in 1983: ''I didn't get into a rock'n'roll band until after I'd gone to college for a year. That was also when I first discovered I had some harmonics in my voice. They're kind of like whistle notes, and you can hear them on my new album *[She's So Unusual]*.''

By the mid-1970s, Cyndi had given up the idea of finishing college in favor of concentrating on a vocal or songwriting career. In the early and middle 1970s, she polished her vocal ability with a number of groups around Manhattan. At first it was exciting, but after a while the restrictions of having to perform other artists' hits in small clubs or for local parties began to chafe.

The chance to extend her horizons came in 1977 when she met a kindred spirit in John Turi, an accomplished rock keyboards and saxophone player. From then through most of 1978, they collaborated on writing a series of original songs and assembled a co-ed band, Blue Angel, that began to win over audiences at new wave clubs in the New York area. Dave Marsh and John Swenson of *Rolling Stone* commented about Blue Angel: ''Rare delight from the New York, new wave, a group steeped in girl-group drama and the Spector aesthetic, with the talent to

put it across. . . . If you can imagine the Crystals with punk hair and Fender guitars, you've got the picture.''

A&R executives were impressed and Polydor Records signed the band in 1979. The debut LP, *Blue Angel* (1980), included originals by Lauper and Turi and some sizzling versions of old rock classics such as Gene Pitney's ''I'm Gonna Be Strong.'' The album was an excellent first effort and critics from major papers (such as *The New York Times*) as well as the rock underground clamored for more.

However, creative disagreements among band members and failure of record buyers' enthusiasm to match that of reviewers led to the group's breakup by 1982. In the spring of 1983, Cyndi determined to go it alone and signed a solo pact with Columbia Records' Portrait label. ''I decided to just go ahead and do it, though I hadn't written many new songs. I had broken my partnership with John Turi—and I didn't like the idea of just singing other people's songs. But for my debut album, producer Rick Chertoff and I selected songs that allowed me to keep my integrity and that meant something to me. And I wrote some too.''

The resultant collection included Lauper compositions ''Time after Time'' and ''I'll Kiss You'' plus specially arranged versions of other writers' material such as the Brains' ''Money Changes Everything'' and Prince's ''When You Were Mine.'' When the platinum *She's So Unusual* came out in 1983, it provided Cyndi with hits from both the writing and performing sides.

Her first success of 1984 was the album's single release, ''Girls Just Want to Have Fun,'' which rose to number two in *Billboard,* but the charts also resonated to such other singles as the number one ''Time after Time'' (co-written by Cyndi and Rob Hyman, number one on *Billboard* charts the week of June 9, 1984, number three ''She Bop,'' and number five ''All through the Night.'' At year-end, the single ''Money Changes Everything'' debuted on the charts on the way to a top 30 placing in 1985.

In *Billboard*'s awards at the end of 1984, Cyndi attained the number one rank in Top Album Artists—Female. In the Top Pop Singles Artists category, she ranked number two (with four chart hits) behind Lionel Richie. In the Grammy nominations, she won for Best New Artist.

Her follow-up album, *True Colors* (Portrait, fall 1986), was somewhat weaker than the previous LP, but still contained some excellent tracks. The album was a top five hit by year-end and the initial single (the title track) hit number one in *Billboard*.

During 1987, Cyndi worked on her debut movie, *Vibes,* in which she played the role of a beautician with psychic powers. Part of the movie was filmed on location in the South American country of Ecuador.

LED ZEPPELIN: *Vocal and instrumental group. Jimmy Page, born Middlesex, England, January 9, 1944; John Paul Jones, born London, England, January 31, 1946; John Bonham, born Birmingham, England, May 31, 1947, died U.K., 1979; Robert Plant, born Birmingham, England, August 26, 1947.*

More than one pop critic derogatorily referred to Led Zeppelin as the English equivalent of Grand Funk, despite the fact that the Zeppelin comprised musicians long bracketed with the top levels of English rock music. As was the case with the Flint, Michigan, trio, Led Zeppelin went its own way, pleasing no one but rock concert goers and record buyers. Led Zeppelin's sound, though more closely oriented to the blues than was Grand Funk's, still was even harder, more hyperamplified rock.

Founding father of the group was James Patrick Page, long a sought-after London session man and a member of one of the best-known English rock groups of the mid-1960s, the Yardbirds. (*See Yardbirds, The*.) Page grew up in a working class section of London, becoming a fan of the early wave of American hard rock artists while still a preteen. While attending a London art school in the late 1950s, he played the guitar with local groups on weekend dates and for occasional weeknight jobs.

His reputation grew with the many teenage musicians then thronging London and, as some became well known and were signed to recording contracts, offers for session work came to Page. By the mid-1960s, he was backing such acts as the Rolling Stones, the Kinks, and Donovan. Page also doubled as a producer, including supervision of Eric Clapton's 1965 session that led to the single "Witch Doctor" (backed with "Telephone Blues"), considered by some British music experts to be one of England's classic blues recordings. (*See Clapton, Eric*.)

In 1966, Page was asked to join the Yardbirds on five-minutes notice when bass player Paul Samwell Smith fell ill just before a show. He turned down the group's offer to join, but reversed himself later in the year when they asked him to go along on a U.S. tour. He played bass at the start, but switched to lead guitar when Jeff Beck was sidelined by illness. Later, when Beck returned, Page and Beck played joint lead. (*See Beck, Jeff*.)

Page remained with the Yardbirds until it dissolved in the summer of 1968. By then, he had decided to start his own group. He already had used Led Zeppelin as a name for some separate sessions while with the Yardbirds and retained it for his new band. He first discussed the idea with a friend of some years, John Paul Jones, who played bass, organ, and piano and was considered one of the best rock arrangers in England.

Jones, who started playing with rock groups in his early teens, had been a part of a highly regarded trio in the mid-1960s. The other two members, Jet Harris and Tony Meehan, formed the trio with Jones after leaving one of the top rock groups of the early 1960s, the Shadows. By 1966–68, Jones was concentrating on arranging and session work. His efforts including arranging Donovan's "Mellow Yellow," "Sunshine Superman," and several tracks on the *Hurdy Gurdy Man* album, as well as selections for the Rolling Stones' *Their Satanic Majesties Request*.

Jones and Page had worked together previous to the *Hurdy Gurdy* sessions. When Jones heard about Page's plans for Led Zeppelin during that album work, he asked if Jimmy could use a bass guitarist and received an immediate affirmative.

Page rounded out his quartet with two Birmingham-born artists: drummer John Bonham and lead vocalist, bassist, and harmonica player Robert Plant. Both Bonham and Plant started as teenage musicians with local Birmingham groups, playing with many different ones until both ended up in the blues-rock Band of Joy, which gained considerable notice in England in the mid-1960s. Plant had sung with Alexis Korner, considered the father of the English blues revival of the 1960s. (*See Korner, Alexis*.) A friend of Page's, singer-guitarist Terry Reid, liked Plant's style and recommended him to Page. Plant, in turn, brought Bonham along.

Plant's voice was well suited to blues shouting. Page recalled that it was so powerful "that when the speakers broke down during our first date in Sweden, you could still hear his voice at the back of the auditorium over the entire group."

The foursome assembled in a small rehearsal hall in late 1968 to see if they worked well together. In his biographical notes for Atlantic Records, Page wrote: "Four of us got together in this two-by-two room and started playing. Then we knew—we started laughing at each other. Maybe it was from relief, or maybe from the knowledge that we could groove together. But that was it. That was just how well it was going. . . . The statement of our first two weeks together is our album. We cut it in 15 hours, and between us wrote eight of the tracks."

The album, *Led Zeppelin, Volume 1,* (Atlantic, fall 1968), earned a gold record. Their first single "Good Times, Bad Times," was taken from the album. Released in March 1969, it also made U.S. charts. The group added more top 10 laurels in

1969–71 with a gold single, "Whole Lotta Love," and two more gold albums, *Led Zeppelin II* and *Led Zeppelin III*.

Among the tracks on *Led Zeppelin III* were "Gallows Pole" (a blazing adaptation of the folk song "Hangman"), "That's the Way," and "Tangerine." The last-named instrumental specialty was merged with new lyrics for Robert Plant to become the track "Stairway to Heaven" on the gold 1971 album on Atlantic, *Led Zeppelin IV (untitled)*. It wasn't the only notable number on an album that included "Black Dog" and "When the Levee Breaks," but it rapidly became the composition most associated with the band from then on.

From a recording standpoint, 1972 was quiet for the group. It did have "Black Dog" on the charts as well as another single, "Rock and Roll," but no new albums. In March 1973, the group's long-awaited gold *Houses of the Holy* LP was issued by Atlantic, providing such inspired tracks as "Dancing Days," "The Crunge," and "No Quarter."

In the mid-1970s, on the new Swan Song label (distributed by Atlantic) the group released such albums as *Physical Graffiti* (gold, 1975), *Presence* (platinum, 1976), and the platinum soundtrack LP for the Led Zeppelin concert film, *The Song Remains the Same* (1976). For a while, just before *Presence* was recorded, the group was prevented from touring by an auto accident that sidelined key member Robert Plant for many months. While he couldn't move around a stage due to leg injuries, he could sing and helped record the *Presence* collection, which included such tracks as "Royal Orleans," "Candy Store Rock," "Achilles Last Stand," and "Hots on for Nowhere."

There were rumors that the group had broken up, but by 1977 the group was touring again. However, after drummer John Bonham was found dead in a mansion owned by Jimmy Page in September 1980, the writing was on the wall. (A coroner's inquest concluded that Bonham had died from asphyxiation caused by his throwing up after drinking an estimated 40 shots of vodka in 12 hours). In December 1980, the remaining members confirmed the band had ceased to exist. The press was informed, "We wish it to be known that the loss of our dear friend and the deep respect we have for his family, together with the sense of individual harmony felt by ourselves and our manager, have led us to decide that we could not continue as we were."

The last studio album released by Swan Song was the 1979 platinum *In through the Out Door*. After the band's breakup, the label issued a final collection of earlier recordings, *Coda* (platinum, 1982). During the 1980s, the remaining alumni of the band worked on separate projects with Robert Plant concentrating on a solo career and Jimmy Page doing concert work with several all-star rock groups.

Plant's solo LPs included the gold *Pictures at Eleven* (Swan Song, 1982), platinum *The Principle of Moments* (Es Paranza, 1985). In 1984, Plant, Page, Jeff Beck, and Nile Rodgers hit *Billboard*'s top 10 as the Honeydrippers with a revival of Phil Phillips' 1959 "Sea of Love" and a platinum mini-LP, *Volume I,* on Es Paranza. In early 1988 Plant's fourth solo LP, *Now and Zen* (Es Paranza/Atlantic), was released and quickly passed gold record levels. As Plant began his tour in support of the album, news of another Zeppelin alumnus, Jimmy Page, hit the entertainment sections of newspapers. Page had signed with Geffen Records, the reports noted, and was working on a new solo LP for release in spring or summer of 1988. For his new concert tour, Page announced he was forming the Jimmy Page Band, whose members included Jason Bonham, son of John Bonham, on drums. In May 1988, Plant and Page re-formed Led Zeppelin to take part in the Atlantic Record 25th Anniversary Concert.

LEE, ALVIN: *Singer, guitarist. Born Nottingham, England, December 19, 1944.*

Since Alvin Lee hailed from Nottingham, originally made famous by the mythical bow string of Robin Hood, it seems appropriate that he became one of the more highly regarded guitarists in rock. After helping make the U.K. band Ten Years After a hit group in the late 1960s and early 1970s, he departed in favor of a solo career, a role he continued in the 1980s. (*See Ten Years After.*)

Lee, like many young Britons of the 1950s, became enamored with artists such as Elvis Presley and Jerry Lee Lewis. By the age of 13, he already was working out chords on a guitar and playing at local dances. The material he favored was blues-rock. Londoners first took notice of him when he played in a John Lee Hooker show in the prestigious Marquee Club. (*See Hooker, John Lee.*) When not working with one of a number of different bands during those years, he picked up extra income by doing recording session work.

Eventually he came across another musician from his home area, Leo Lyons, who played a variety of instruments including drums and bass guitar. In 1964, they formed an act called Britain's Largest Sounding Trio, which eventually evolved into the quartet Ten Years After. The band turned out a series of excellent rock albums (reflecting heavy jazz and blues influences) in the late 1960s and early 1970s that won over large numbers of fans first in England and later in the States. A major milestone in the progress of the band and of Lee's reputation came during a wondrous set at the legendary Woodstock Festival in upstate New York in 1969. Though Lee disliked being singled out, maintaining he was part of a band, not a show-off, his fiery playing was a highpoint of the concert for many fans and for the concert film, *Woodstock*.

Lee continued to tour and record with Ten Years After through the early 1970s, but by 1973 he was seeking new creative outlets. One example was his participation with American rock vocalist Mylon LeFevre in the LP, *Alvin Lee and Mylon LeFevre* (Columbia, 1973). They were backed by an all-star cast that included George Harrison, Steve Winwood, Ron Wood, and Mick Fleetwood.

By 1974, Lee had left Ten Years After and was pursuing a new course as a soloist. A series of concert dates in which he was backed by members of the soul group Kokomo provided material for his 1974 live two-disc *In Flight* (Columbia). That very impressive collection was followed by a disappointing studio LP, *Pump Iron* (Columbia, 1975).

During the mid-1970s and 1980s, Alvin's activities included solo concert work, session playing on new recordings of many of his rock-star friends, and new albums on several different labels: *Rocket Fuel* (RSO, 1978), *Alvin Lee* (Columbia, 1978), *Ride On* (RSO, 1979), and *Free Fall* (Atlantic, 1980).

LENNON, JOHN, AND ONO, YOKO:
Singers, songwriters, band leaders (PLASTIC ONO BAND, ELEPHANT'S MEMORY). John born Liverpool, England, October 9, 1940; died New York, New York, December 8, 1980. Yoko born Tokyo, Japan, February 18, 1933.

When Don McLean wrote the line "The day the music died," he was referring to the death of Buddy Holly, but it could apply as well to Black Monday, December 8, 1980, when a deranged young man, a complete stranger to John Lennon, shot and killed him. The senseless deed caused incalculable loss to the world in general and rock music in particular. In later years, Yoko Ono, his wife and longtime creative partner, sought to keep his memory bright while painfully trying to forge a new solo career for herself.

A little over a decade earlier, the couple had made happier headlines. One of the major stories of 1969 was the marriage of John Lennon of the Beatles and Yoko Ono, although it was something of an anticlimax, since the two had been living together for some time before the wedding. (The way had been cleared for the March 20, 1969 wedding on Gibraltar, when the divorce decree for John's first marriage to Cynthia Powell became final on Novem-

ber 8, 1968.) John and Yoko had already established close artistic rapport by then, as demonstrated by their first album collaboration, *Two Virgins* (Apple Records, November 1, 1968). The album was the first individual record release by a Beatle and heralded the impending breakup of the group.

The Lennons combined talents in a number of directions besides music, including dual art shows and such movie efforts as the TV documentary "Rape," which premiered in Vienna, Austria, on March 31, 1969. On May 2, 1969, their second LP, *Unfinished Music No. 2, Life with the Lions,* was released on the new Zapple label. Later in the month, in Montreal, Canada, the two conducted a "peace lie-in" in bed, with news photographers gathered around. During this time, the single "The Ballad of John and Yoko" was issued. They returned to England in June and soon after were in the recording studios with their Plastic Ono Band, whose first single ("Give Peace a Chance"/"Remember Love") was released on July 4. The band's next single, "Cold Turkey," issued on October 24, caused much controversy because of its drug-related theme. Because of that, it was not overly successful, but soon after that, the Lennons followed with *Wedding Album,* which was released on November 14, 1969.

On September 13, 1969, John and Yoko were back in Canada for a rock'n'roll revival concert. They appeared as the Plastic Ono Band, whose members for the occasion included Klaus Voorman, Eric Clapton, and Alan White. The fruit of this effort was the gold album *Live Peace in Toronto 1969* (released by Apple on December 12, 1969). Three days later, the Plastic Ono Band was featured at the Lyceum, Strand in London, its members then including besides Clapton, George Harrison, Billy Preston, Keith Moon, and Delaney and Bonnie Bramlett.

The next Plastic Ono Band release, the gold "Instant Karma" (1970), was the group's first top 10 single in *Billboard*. When performed on BBC-TV's "Tops of the Pops" on February 12 by John, Yoko, Klaus Voorman, and Alan White, it was the first live appearance by a Beatle on the show since 1965. During the year, two films featuring John premiered: the Beatles' *Let It Be* and John's first solo vehicle *How I Won the War*. In 1970, in honor of his wife, John legally changed his name to John Ono Lennon.

The Lennons' musical activities slackened somewhat in 1971, a year in which they took up residence in New York City while Yoko fought for custody of her eight-year-old daughter by a previous marriage. Nonetheless, work on two new albums went on during the year: *Imagine*, featuring John and the Plastic Ono Band, and *Some Time in New York City*, recorded by John, Yoko, and the Plastic Ono Band. *Imagine* which came out during 1971, went gold while its title track made *Billboard*'s top 10. Earlier in the year, Lennon gained another gold record for his album *John Lennon with the Plastic Ono Band*. Two Lennon/Ono Band singles were chart hits in 1971: the political "Power to the People" and "Mother" (one of John's songs stemming from unresolved feelings about his mother's death in a car accident during his youth).

The year 1972 was a traumatic one for the Lennons as they had to fight John's deportation case brought by the U.S. Immigration and Naturalization Service. The reason for the case, department officials stated, was Lennon's misdemeanor conviction on a marijuana-possession charge in England four years before, but Lennon supporters claimed it was government anger at the Lennons' sociopolitical views. Leading newspapers, including *The New York Times*, and liberal officeholders, such as New York's Mayor John Lindsay, rallied to the Lennons' cause. Many people in the rock field remained silent, though.

Phil Spector was among those music figures who abhorred industry neglect. "All John and Yoko want to do is live in New York City and the mayor has said they are welcome," he told Robert Hilburn of the *Los Angeles Times*. "Do we have to go through all that Chaplin bull again? Do we have to watch them kick Lennon out of the country the way they kicked Chaplin and then wait 25 years so we can invite him back, give him some kind of award, and say we are sorry? Or do we learn from what happened."

When *Some Time in New York City* was issued in 1972, its contents angered some U.S. conservatives. One of Yoko's songs, "Woman Is the Nigger of the World," a plea for women's equality, was a singles hit in 1972. John and Yoko didn't take part in the August 1971 Bangla Desh charity concert organized by George Harrison, but in August 1972, they set up their own concert to raise funds for facilities for retarded persons in New York. Backing John and/or Yoko (Yoko played the xylophone for some numbers) was Elephant's Memory, a group John had taken under his wing. The concert, though, was found to be artistically inferior to the Bangla Desh event.

Yoko's songwriting efforts increased as the 1970s went by. In December 1972, *Approximately Infinite Universe*, a double album totally composed by Yoko, was released. Produced by John and Yoko, it used the backup support of the Plastic Ono Band and Elephant's Memory. The album was not a popular success, however. Yoko gave several solo concerts in 1973, including a headline appearance at a show held in the San Diego Padres baseball stadium in San Diego, California.

John's troubles seemed to grow during 1973–74. Besides the continued hassles with U.S. immigration authorities, there were emotional problems with Yoko that caused a separation that later was repaired. His mood of depression was reflected in many of the songs on his next solo albums, *Mind Games* (1973) and *Walls and Bridges* (1974). (The fact that the cover art for *Mind Games* featured a large closeup of Yoko's face contrasted with a much smaller image of John reinforced the feelings of some Beatles fans that Yoko's "dominance" of Lennon caused the breakup of their beloved Fab Four. The antagonism of those fans in the early 1970s, who likely represented only a vocal minority of Beatles followers, still added to the problems of the relationship.)

Equally disheartening for John were critical comments that his writing and record production were not up to expected standards for him. For all that, both albums were chart hits, producing such best-selling singles as "Mind Games" and "#9 Dream," while "Whatever Gets You Through the Night" rose to number one in *Billboard* the week of November 16, 1974, his first such achievement as a solo performer and his first single to make the top 3 since "Imagine" several years earlier. He finished up that phase of his career with two 1975 Apple releases: *Rock'n'Roll* (Phil Spector production of old rock hits) and *Shaved Fish* (a collection of singles).

But life was changing again for John. He and Yoko had reunited and she was soon to have a baby, whom they named Sean. After Sean was born, to everyone's surprise, John gave up all his musical activities to stay close to his newborn son and his wife. Industry observers expected him to return to music momentarily, but the years went by with no sound from John. Finally, after five years out of the spotlight, John began to record new material in 1980 with Yoko.

During his first major interview in five years, Barbara Graustark of *Newsweek* (September 29, 1980) asked him if he went underground in 1975 because he was tired of making music or tired of the business itself. He replied: "It was a bit of both. I'd been under contract since I was 22 and I was always 'supposed to.' I was supposed to write a hundred songs by Friday, supposed to have a single out by Saturday, supposed to do this or that. I became an artist because I cherished freedom—I couldn't fit into a classroom or office. Freedom was the plus for all the minuses of being an oddball. But suddenly I was obliged to a record company, obliged to the media, obliged to the public. I wasn't free at all.

"I've withdrawn many times—part of me is a monk, and part a performing flea! The fear in the music business is that you don't exist if you're not at

Xenon. As I found out, life doesn't end when you stop subscribing to *Billboard*."

Why had he withdrawn for five years, she queried. He answered: "If you know your history, it took us a long time to have a live baby. And I wanted to give five solid years to Sean. I hadn't seen Julian [future rock star Julian Lennon, his son by his exwife, Cynthia] grow up at all, and now there's a 17-year-old man on the phone talkin' about motorbikes."

There also were suggestions the layoff had been in part an effort to establish his identity firmly as John Lennon, not Lennon, ex-Beatle. He told Robert Hilburn of the *Los Angeles Times* (October 14, 1980): "When I wrote 'The Dream Is Over' [in 1970], I was trying to say to the Beatles thing: 'Get off my back.' I was also trying to tell other people to stop looking at me because I wasn't going to do it for them anymore, because I didn't even know what the hell I was doing in my own life.

"What I realized during the five years I was away was that when I said th dream is over, I had made the physical break from the Beatles, but mentally there was still this big thing on my back about what people expected of me. It was like this invisible ghost. During the five years, it sort of went away.

"I finally started writing like I was even before the Beatles were the Beatles. I got rid of all that self-consciousness about telling myself: 'You can't do that. That song's not good enough. Remember, you're the guy who wrote 'A Day in the Life.' Try again!"

While vacationing in Bermuda in 1979, Lennon began writing again and felt he had gotten rid of many of his mental blocks. Yoko responded with new material of her own and they recorded a new album, *Double Fantasy,* that Geffen Records issued late in 1980. The collection thrilled listeners by suggesting Lennon might have new things to say to them in the 1980s, but hardly had the smiles appeared when tragedy struck.

On the evening of December 8, 1980, the Lennons were returning by limousine to their New York condominium in the Dakota building. As they drew up to the entrance, there was the usual crowd of fans eager to catch a glimpse of them. As John got out of the car, however, 25-year-old Mark David Chapman stepped up and pumped seven shots into John's body. Lennon was pronounced dead on arrival at the hospital.

Yoko Ono told Hilburn: "It was so sudden . . . so sudden. We had planned to go out to eat after leaving the recording studio but we decided to go straight home instead. We were walking to the entrance of the building when I heard the shot. I didn't realize at first that John had been hit. He kept walking. Then, he fell, and I saw the blood."

She emphasized: "This is not a time for hate or disillusionment. . . . The future is still ours to make. The '80s will blossom if only people accept peace and love in their hearts. It would just add to the tragedy if people turned away from the message in John's music."

Certainly over the short term, people moved more strongly toward his music. *Double Fantasy* was on the charts at John's death and it soon vaulted to number one, selling well past platinum levels. The single "(Just Like) Starting Over" moved to number one in *Billboard* the week of December 27, 1980. In the Grammy Awards, *Double Fantasy* was named Album of the Year for 1980. During 1981, five of John's older albums became chart hits again: *John Lennon and the Plastic Ono Band, Imagine, Shaved Fish, Mind Games,* and *Walls and Bridges.*

Some of Yoko's feeling about John's death played through her solo album *Season of Glass* (Geffen, 1981). By the time her next LP, *It's Alright,* came out on Polydor Records in late 1982, it seemed she had come to terms with the loss. As the 1980s went by, her support for charitable causes, her positive statements about her husband's life, and her increasingly insightful songwriting won admiration from critics and fans alike. In support of her fine album *Starpeace* (Polygram, 1985), she went on a worldwide tour that took her to major U.S. cities and across Europe, including the Communist Eastern Bloc. She urged huge crowds in cities in Hungary and Yugoslavia to help in the search for peace that she and John always had dreamt of.

Meanwhile, John was remembered regularly by fans who staged prayer vigils on the anniversary of his death. New albums continued to come out—repackagings of older releases or sometimes different recorded versions of his songs. These included the special rerelease by Capitol of *Imagine* in May 1986 and the LP *Menlove Ave.* in the fall of 1986. The latter (named for the street on which teenaged John lived with his Aunt Mimi and Uncle George), included a number of tracks originally made for *Walls and Bridges,* but without the horns and strings later added. As Lennon had first recorded the songs, they had much greater impact than the remixed versions. Also available for the first time in the mid-1980s was a video of Lennon's "One on One" benefit concert of 1972.

Through the late 1980s, Yoko continued to bring out all manner of previously unavailable material of John covering an impressive range of creative areas. In 1987, she issued a book of Lennon's unpublished prose and drawings, *Skywriting by Word of Mouth.* As had been the case since his death, she occasionally made his lithographs and other artworks available for gallery shows.

398

But all of that seemed dwarfed by the project she instituted in late 1987 when she provided the syndication firm of Westwood One with some 300 hours of previously unreleased tapes of John's performances and interviews. Westwood shaped these into a 52-week series called the "Lost Lennon Tapes" that began appearing on the radio in early 1988. Tape material covered a range from a 1960 rehearsal of the Quarry Men (sans drummer) to John's last studio sessions. The series included several dozen songs never heard before including "The Rikikesh Song," "Serve Yourself," "Tennessee," and "Life Begins at 40." Besides lengthy interview segments, the tapes also presented a group of personal productions called "mind movies." In original form, these were extended tapings he prepared for friends combining elements of music and comedy. (*See Beatles, The; Harrison, George; Lennon, Julian; McCartney, Paul; Nilsson, Harry; Spector, Phil; Starr, Ringo.*)

LENNON, JULIAN: *Singer, instrumentalist, songwriter. Born London, England, April 8, 1963.*

Déjà vu was a natural feeling for pop-music historians when young Julian Lennon hit the recording and concert fields in the mid-1980s. Both physically and vocally, he had an eerie resemblance to his father, the late John Lennon. Though not likely to achieve the level of artistry that John had attained in his Beatle and post-Beatle years, Julian demonstrated he was certainly an above-average writer and performer. (*See Beatles, The; Lennon, John, and Ono, Yoko.*)

As usually happens, he gained both advantages and disadvantages from his famous parent. The Lennon name certainly didn't do any harm in opening doors in the entertainment field. But it's not easy to be judged against the standards of a superstar whose tragically short life has assumed almost mythic proportions. And many critics and fans felt he was, in effect, taking bread out of the mouths of other, more deserving performers in his career efforts.

That was particularly noticeable in his own country, as he told Dennis Hunt of the *Los Angeles Times* (April 6, 1986): "In places like England, they think this was all handed to me on a silver platter. They say: Why is he bothering with this singing, he's got plenty of money in the bank?' But that's her [stepmother Yoko Ono's] money. I don't control it. They don't realize I worked hard to get where I am and to get what I have. But once some people get an idea in their heads, you can't pry it loose."

His parents, John and Cynthia Powell Lennon, were divorced while he was quite young. John Charles Julian Lennon wasn't estranged from his father, but the two didn't see much of each other for much of his childhood. Later, however, he told interviewers, they did become close and John did give his son some insights into music that later helped in his career. Unfortunately for Julian, his father was shot down on December 8, 1980, while the younger Lennon was only in his teens.

Julian did not let the emotional shock interfere with his private life after he began to become known in the mid-1980s. He told Hunt: "I have bodyguards on the road when I'm in situations I can't control, like at concerts, but otherwise I'm not constantly guarded. I live in a small apartment in London, not some big house with a lot of security. I don't like too much security. There's no freedom. I'm a person, not some precious diamond that needs guarding every second."

He also was fortunate that he was able to develop his writing and performing skills more or less out of the spotlight while growing to adulthood in London. His mother's household was not particularly affluent, he maintained, but neither was it a poverty environment. However, when he sought to expand his music-industry experience, he met with a good share of rejections until he gained his first major record-company contract in 1983.

His debut album, *Valotte* (Atlantic Records, 1984), caught many listeners by surprise. Some thought the tracks played on radio stations might have been old unreleased recordings of his father because of the vocal resemblance. Gradually, however, it became clear that a new Lennon was at hand as *Valotte* moved in the U.S. top 20 by year-end on its way to RIAA gold record status in 1985. The album, which featured many professionally crafted songs by Julian, spawned four charted singles in 1985, two of which, "Valotte" and "Too Late for Goodbyes," were best-sellers in the U.S., Australia, and Japan. In the voting for the 1985 Grammy Awards, Julian was one of the five finalists (losing out to another English act, Sade) for the Best New Artist honor.

The success of the first album and the Grammy nomination caused his record company to press him for a follow-up LP. In the midst of touring, taking care of TV and radio interviews, and other chores, he was asked to write the material for the new LP in a month's time. The project was so rushed, he said, that he had little time to repolish material or make sure the arrangements were in the proper key for his voice. Because of that, he said, it was a "very strained album." While he wasn't pleased with that, he was happy that he had managed to consciously achieve a sound he felt was his own and not his father's. The new album, *The Secret Value of Daydreaming*, was more up-tempo rock than the debut collection, which had a middle-of-the-road, "soft-rock" flavor.

Though there were a few harsh reviews, most critics commented positively on the second gold album and Julian seemed on the way to stardom, if not superstardom. Along the way, he knew he would always be fighting an uphill battle against outside jealousy and the inevitable rumors such as one to the effect that he and Yoko Ono avoided each other if at all possible.

He told Hunt: "I do have contact with her. I'll call her up and say: 'Do you want to have a cup of tea, do you want to go for a meal or a movie?' We keep in touch socially. It's all social too. But we don't talk business. We don't want to spoil things."

In early 1988, Lennon was back in the studio working on his next LP for Atlantic.

LETTERMEN, THE: *Vocal group. Personnel, 1970s and 1980s: Tony Butala, born Sharon, Pennsylvania, November 20, 1940; Jim Pike, born St. Louis, Missouri, November 6, 1936; Gary Pike, born Twin Falls, Idaho. Original trio member Bob Engemann, born Highland Park, Michigan, February 19, 1935, replaced by Gary Pike in mid-1960s.*

As groups such as the Lettermen have demonstrated, popular music is never monolithic—there is always room for talented performers in alternative styles to whatever is dominant at the moment. Thus, the Lettermen's basically romantic-ballad style of vocalizing found a wide audience despite rock'n'roll's preeminence in the 1960s. Moreover, their prime supporters were not oldsters, as indicated by their tremendous popularity on the college concert circuit.

The group's founding members (Tony Butala, Jim Pike, and Bob Engemann) met in California, though much of their early experience was gained in other parts of the country. Butala, who spent his childhood in Pennsylvania, got his start at the age of eight on a radio show. He continued to sing in local programs until his family moved to Los Angeles. There he was selected for the famous Mitchell Boys Choir with whom he sang for a number of years.

Jim Pike was born in St. Louis, Missouri, but soon moved west to Idaho with his family, where he attended public schools. He then entered Brigham Young University in Utah. When he left college, he formed a group called the Damons that performed with Stan Kenton's orchestra in Las Vegas, Nevada. When the group disbanded, Jim went to Los Angeles, where his family had moved, and started looking for another job in music.

He met Tony Butala and the two agreed on plans for a new singing act. They brought in Bob En-gemann, who also had considerable vocal experience, and started rehearsing. They sang in some local clubs and gained the attention of comedian George Burns, who engaged them to go with him on a 1961 tour. They were so well received that Burns' friendly rival Jack Benny signed them for one of his tours.

By then considered a rising young act, the Lettermen gained a contract from Capitol Records, for whom they were still providing best-sellers a decade later. Their first single, "The Way You Look Tonight" (1961), won a gold record for over a million copies sold. Their next two singles, "When I Fall in Love" and "Come Back, Silly Girl," also rode high on the charts.

They proved equally successful in the album field. Their debut LP, *A Song for Young Love,* moved into the top 10 nationally a short time after its release in February 1962, earning another gold record for the trio. The group placed many of their ensuing LPs of the early '60s on the charts, some in the top 40 or better. Among these were *Once upon a Time* and *Jim, Tony and Bob* (1962); *College Standards* and *In Concert* (1963); *A Lettermen Kind of Love, The Lettermen Look at Love,* and *She Cried* (1964); *You'll Never Walk Alone, Portrait of My Love,* and *The Hit Sounds of the Lettermen* (1965); *More Hit Sounds, A New Song for Young Love, Best of the Lettermen,* and *For Christmas This Year* (1966).

From the beginning, the group was a favorite with the nation's college students. By the end of 1971, the group had appeared at over 2,000 colleges and universities.

Before the '60s ended, the group had one change. Bob Engemann left to work as a soloist. Capitol released his debut album, *My Own Thing,* in 1970. The remaining members didn't have to look far for a replacement. Jim Pike's younger brother, Gary, was ready and had a voice as good as Jim's. Gary, born and raised in Twin Falls, Idaho, had moved to Los Angeles with his family at the start of the '60s. He was attending El Camino College when the lure of show business made him drop his studies.

The changeover had no effect on the trio's effectiveness. They continued to receive ovations at one concert after another and made the charts regularly with such LPs as *Spring!* (1967), *Goin' out of My Head* and *The Lettermen!* (both gold in 1968), and *Hurt So Bad* (gold, 1969).

The trio's 1970s releases on Capitol included *Traces/Memories* and *Reflections* (1970), *Feelings* and *Love Book* (1971), *Lettermen—Volume I* (1972), *Alive Again—Naturally* (1973), and *Lettermen Kind of Country* (1976). As of 1977, the group's album total exceeded 30 with 20 charted singles. During the '70s and '80s, the group continued as a concert attraction in clubs and concert halls around the world, singing their own hits as well as cover renditions of new successes for other rock and pop artists.

LEWIS, GARY: *Singer, band leader (THE PLAYBOYS). Born New York, New York, July 31, 1946. Playboys members: Dave Costell, Dave Walker, Al Ramsey.*

Rock lured many offspring from show-business families who might otherwise have first tried for acting careers. Among those who had at least a few years of stardom in the rock arena were Dean Martin's son, Dino (of Dino, Desi and Billy) and one of Jerry Lewis's heirs, Gary, who led the Playboys to the title "Most Promising Vocal Group of 1965" in trade-magazine evaluations by *Cash Box* and *Record World*. Lewis himself was chosen as Number One Male Vocalist of 1966 by *Cash Box*.

Gary grew up in a show-business atmosphere, of course, often traveling to distant cities or countries with his father, the famous comedian. He showed some interest in pop music in his early teens, and Jerry gave his son a set of drums as a birthday gift when Gary turned 14. Gary played them for a time, then dropped them in favor of just listening to major rock groups' records.

He spent his high-school years at the Black Foxe Military Academy in Hollywood. After graduating, he attended Los Angeles City College in the early 1960s, but at 19 left to enroll as a drama student at the Pasadena Playhouse. He began playing his drums again when he got home from school. Newly inspired, he lined up some friends from school and his neighborhood and formed a group to play for private parties. In August 1964, Gary and his group auditioned for Disneyland teenage dances and were soon regulars, playing every night the park was open.

Their success with young audiences caused Liberty artists & repertoire executive Snuff Garrett to sign them. Gary told reporters that Snuff heard them play at Disneyland one night and approached them to make some records. Garrett, as reported in Fred Bronson's *Billboard Book of Number One Hits*, remembered it a bit differently. He was induced to see the group by Jerry Lewis's piano player and conductor, he said, first at Disneyland, then while the band was rehearsing at the Paramount lot in Hollywood. "They weren't very good. They sounded like any other group I've ever heard. But then I got to thinking, if I could do a record with Gary and get Jerry to help me promote it, it might do well."

The song Garrett focused on was one rejected by Liberty star Bobby Vee, "This Diamond Ring." Released as a single, it did very well indeed, rising to number one on *Billboard* charts the week of February 20, 1965, and staying there a second week. (The song's writers were Al Kooper, Bobby Brass, and Irwin Levine.) (*See Kooper, Al; Vee, Bobby.*) During 1965 and 1966, it was followed by *Billboard* top 10 hits "Count Me In," "Save Your Heart for Me," "She's Just My Style," "Sure Gonna Miss Her," "Everybody Loves a Clown," and "Green Grass."

Many of those songs were included in hit LPs such as the debut *Gary Lewis and the Playboys* and *A Session* (1965); *Everybody Loves a Clown, She's Just My Style, with Gary Lewis and the Playboys, Gary Lewis Hits Again,* and *Golden Greats* (1966); and *Paint Me a Picture, New Directions,* and *Listen!* (1967). A number of Gary's LPs featured then-unknown Leon Russell as sideman, arranger, and/or songwriter. (*See Russell, Leon.*)

The 1967 releases came out after Gary had been drafted into the Army, an event he bitterly resented because it came at a time when his band had chalked up record sales exceeding 7.5 million and seemed solidly entrenched with their fans. The service offered him the option of forming a band to entertain troops, but he turned it down and spent part of his two-year tour of duty as a clerk/typist in Korea.

When he returned to civilian life at the end of 1968, he attempted to pick up where he had left off. While he began forming a new band, he enrolled in Chapman College as a theater and music major. There was some interest in the 1968 Liberty LP *More Golden Greats,* but Gary was unable to come up with a combination that could return him to star status.

After being out of the spotlight for many years, Gary surfaced again in the mid-1980s in a bid for new opportunities as a solo performer. As he told reporters in 1985, after breaking up the Playboys in 1971, he opened a music store called Gary's in the San Fernando Valley, where he gave guitar and drum lessons. He sold the store in the late 1970s and moved to Tulsa, Oklahoma, where he assembled a new band, Medicine. The name proved appropriate, he said, because he got hooked on downers for a time. "It was a terrible period," he acknowledged. "I admit it. I went to the doctor with a pain in my side one day and he said: 'Your eyes are yellow. You'd better go into the hospital right now.'"

By the mid-1980s, he said, all that was behind him. He was happily living in a small town in Ohio with his second wife and back on stage touring in '60s rock revival shows with acts such as the Turtles, Buckinghams, and Grass Roots. Meanwhile, Rhino Records advertised his *Greatest Hits!* reissue as "14 sides of classic '60s wimp rock."

LEWIS, HUEY, AND THE NEWS: *Vocal and instrumental group from San Francisco. Led by*

Huey Lewis, born Marin County, California. Original members, 1979–80: Sean Hopper, Johnny Colla, Mario Cipolina, Bill Gibson.

Though Huey Lewis grew up in the San Francisco Bay Area, his music had little in common with its acid rock of the 1960s or punk/new wave of the 1980s. In a sense, his approach might be described as "plain pipe rack" rock, a no-frills blue collar style that could be called the West Coast equivalent of the rock symbolized by Bob Seger in the Midwest and Bruce Springsteen in the East.

Lewis' music tastes in his teens leaned to the early roots-rock of Elvis Presley and Carl Perkins and the U.S. blues-rock tradition that still held a share of the audience in the 1960s despite the British Invasion. After graduating from high school, Huey hitchhiked around Europe for several years, earning support money as best he could.

Some of his income came from busking—playing his harmonica on street corners or in subway stations. "With my long hair, the harp seemed to fit the image. I didn't know how to play it at first, but I taught myself while waiting for rides beside European highways. I'd just imagine I was Paul Butterfield [of the Paul Butterfield Blues Band]. After a year of that, I was pretty good."

After getting the wanderlust out of his system, he returned home to the Bay Area, where he became part of a country-rock band, Clover, which slowly accumulated a local reputation in the mid-1970s. Later in the decade, the band moved to England, where it was able to find steady work on the pub-rock circuit and, later, session work in London. One of its opportunities was to back then unknown Elvis Costello on his 1977 debut LP, *My Aim Is True.* Other session work included supporting Phil Lynott of Thin Lizzy. It was a good learning experience, but Clover as a separate entity didn't seem to be going anywhere and finally broke up in 1979. (*See Costello, Elvis; Thin Lizzy.*)

In the spring of 1979, Huey was back in the Bay Area, unemployed and looking for a new affiliation. A new band evolved from a series of jam sessions at a local club called Uncle Charlie's. With another Clover alumnus, keyboards player Sean Hopper, Huey put together a band. Over the next few months, the membership grew to include guitarist Chris Hayes and three members of another Bay Area band, Soundhole: guitar and sax player Johnny Colla, drummer Bill Gibson, and bass guitarist Mario Cipollina (brother of John Cipollina who had been a featured member of the highly regarded 1960s acid-rock Quicksilver Messenger Service). With Huey handling lead vocals and occasional harp playing, the group took the name American Express.

Once the roster was firmed up, Lewis remem-

bered: "We were offered some free studio time after the word-of-mouth on the Monday night jams got out, so we cut this disco takeoff on 'Exodus,' called 'Exo-disco.' I sent that to this guy I knew from England, and the next thing I knew, we had a singles deal from Phonogram. We also recorded a demo of three original songs. The demo attracted a manager to us, Bob Brown, who also managed the Pablo Cruise band."

The band eventually signed a contract to do its first album for English-based Chrysalis Records. Chrysalis executives were wary of the American Express title, so the name was changed in January 1980 to Huey Lewis and the News. The band went into the studio in the spring of 1980 and recorded all the tracks for the new album in three weeks. The LP, *Huey Lewis and the News,* managed to make the charts briefly, but after a few weeks disappeared from sight with very disappointing sales. The album's plight wasn't helped by the videos that May of two of its tracks: "Some of My Lies Are True" and "Running with the Crowd."

Chrysalis remained confident that the band had the ability to eventually break through and gave the go-ahead for a second album. Unsatisfied with available producers, Huey and his associates decided to produce the new collection themselves. At the beginning of 1982, *Picture This* and its single "Do You Believe in Love" were released. Supported by a video shot in Los Angeles during February, the single made the U.S. top 10 and the LP went gold. the summer and fall. In July, another single was issued: "Workin' for a Livin'," written by band members. During the year, the group had another singles hit from *Picture This:* "Hope You Love Me Like You Say You Do," which hit the top 40.

For the first part of 1983, most of the band's energies were directed toward finishing its third LP for Chrysalis. Six originals by bandsmen were chosen: "The Heart of Rock'n'Roll," "Bad is Bad," "I Want a New Drug," "Finally Found a Home," "If This Is It," and "You Crack Me Up." The remaining tracks comprised an updated version of Hank Williams' "Honky Tonk Blues," a remake of the standard "Heart and Soul," and a song seeking solace for Vietnam veterans, "Walking on a Thin Line."

In advance of the album, a successful single and video of "Heart and Soul" were released. During the summer, the single rose to number eight on *Billboard* lists. The album, *Sports,* was issued in September and went onto the charts almost immediately. At the end of 1983, it was at number 33 and seemed to be slipping down the list, but buoyed by a new single ("I Want a New Drug") and enthusiasm generated by concerts throughout the U.S., it increased sales again in 1984, closing the year in the top 10. By the end of 1985, it had been on *Billboard* lists for 117 straight weeks and had sold over 8 million copies. During June 1984, the album stood at number one on U.S. charts and was a hit in many other nations as well.

In form and content, the album ranked as one of the best compilations to reach the popular-music rostrum in the mid-1980s. The consistency of the material was rewarded with almost wholesale success of its tracks as singles releases. During 1984, those credits extended to the top 6 "Heart of Rock and Roll" and "If This Is It" and top 20 "Walking on a Thin Line." The band's status was recognized by a cover story in a September issue of *Rolling Stone*. During that month, the band performed at the first annual MTV Awards at New York's Radio City Music Hall, where "The Heart of Rock and Roll" was nominated for Best Group Video.

The band began 1985 by being named the Favorite Video Group at the twelfth annual American Music Awards. During January, Huey and the band also helped record the "We Are the World" single and video on behalf of the USA for Africa hunger-relief program. In February, Huey and the News performed "Heart of Rock and Roll" on the Grammy Awards telecast; the song was one of the five finalists for Record of the Year. While the band missed out on that trophy, it did win five awards at the eighth annual Bay Area Music Awards in March.

The group also contributed "Power of Love" to the soundtrack for the hit film *Back to the Future*. The single of the song, released in June by Chrysalis, went to number one on *Billboard* charts and also charted high in many other countries. The video of the song won wide exposure too. Also receiving considerable airplay was "Back in Time," another song the band recorded for the soundtrack. In the movie, Huey also made a brief appearance playing a schoolteacher. Meanwhile, *Sports* continued to sell well around the world, earning a silver record in England and a gold record in Australia.

The group started off 1986 by winning awards for Favorite Single and Favorite Video in the thirteenth annual American Music Awards, both for "Power of Love." When the Grammy nominations for 1985 were announced, the band reached the finals in five categories: Record of the Year for "Power of Love"; Best Pop Performance by a Duo or Group with Vocal for "Power of Love"; Best Music Video, Long Form, for "Heart of Rock and Roll"; and as participants in the "We Are the World" recording, nominated both as Record of the Year and Best Music Video, Short Form. During the telecast in February (which involved performance work by Huey), the band picked up two trophies, one for its

long-form video, the other as part of the "We Are the World" Record of the Year group of recipients. That same month, the British Phonographic Industry honored the band with its International Artist of the Year Award.

In March 1986, "Power of Love" was an Academy Awards nominee for the Oscar in the Best Original Song from a Movie category. While losing out there, the band swept nine prizes in the ninth annual Bay Area Music Awards competition.

By then the group was polishing its final tapings for its fourth LP, which included six new originals, including "Stuck with You," "Naturally," "I Know What I Like," "Hip to Be Square," and the rockabilly-flavored "Whole Lotta Lovin'." Among songs from other writers was "Jacob's Ladder," the album's opening track, penned by talented singer/pianist Bruce Hornsby. Appropriately the August 1986 LP was titled *Fore!*, which could be taken to symbolize Huey's love for the game of golf. Hornsby, whom Huey helped to get a RCA recording contract that led to his debut album in mid-1986, related that he persuaded Huey to listen to some of his demo tapes during a round of golf the two played in the Bay Area. Huey in turn provided several songs for Hornsby's LP, which was on the U.S. charts in the fall of 1986 along with *Fore!*.

The first single from *Fore!*, "Stuck with You," hit number one in *Billboard*, as did "Jacob's Ladder," while "Hip to Be Square" made number three.

LEWIS, JERRY LEE: *Singer, pianist, songwriter. Born Ferriday, Louisiana, September 29, 1935.*

One evening in early 1979 at the Palomino Club in Los Angeles, the m.c. was singing the praise of the headliner, a relatively new female performer. He barely got out the words "I'm going to present one of the great country performers of the day" when Jerry Lee Lewis stood up in the audience and shouted "I'm the greatest." To the consternation of the host, he rushed on stage, sat down at the piano, and quickly worked the audience into frenzied excitement. It could never be said "the Killer" lacked confidence. And not without reason—in more than three decades as a performer, he cut a wide swath as a superstar, first in rock'n'roll, then in his original proving ground, country music.

Jerry Lee was born and raised in the small town of Ferriday, Louisiana, where gospel and country music were part of the environment. (Blues were sometimes considered off limits, but Jerry and his childhood friends—including his cousins, future country star Mickey Gilley and future evangelist Jimmy Swaggart—sometimes snuck into honky tonks to hear some of that music too.) He showed such an early aptitude for the piano that his father, Elmo, took the boy around to perform in small shows in neighboring towns, playing the keyboards from the back of a flatbed truck. As he grew older, Jerry Lee also performed in gospel meetings and church programs.

But his early love of the blues helped inspire an interest in the mid-1950s outburst of rockabilly. In 1956, he moved to Memphis and became a session pianist at Sun Records, backing rockabilly founders such as Carl Perkins and Billy Lee Riley. In the wake of selling Elvis Presley's contract to RCA, Sun was in the market for new talent and Jerry was quick to seize the opportunity. With his free-wheeling adaptations of Irving Berlin's "End of the Road" and Ray Price's country hit "Crazy Arms," Jerry Lee made his record debut in 1956 and soon was out on the road gaining rising attention in touring rock shows. Kicking the piano bench across the stage, waving the microphone with vigor as he played piano with the other hand, and jumping on top of the piano, he set off shock waves of enthusiasm among young onlookers.

In 1957, he hit his peak with the smash single "Great Balls of Fire," a worldwide hit which earned him his first gold record. Late in the year, he came out with the gold blockbuster, "Whole Lotta Shakin' Goin' On," an anthem of rock. During that period he placed other songs in top chart levels, including "Breathless" and "High School Confidential" (the title song of his first movie, which he sang from the back of a flatbed truck).

In 1958, though, his soaring fortunes plummeted abruptly when word came around that he had married his 13-year-old second cousin, Myra. (The marriage lasted 13 years.) That wasn't startling to many in the rural South, where early unions often occur. In fact, Jerry Lee had married the first of his two previous wives when he was only 14. But it shocked the rest of the nation and the world. The story broke amid a concert tour of England. The condemnation there was so great that concerts were canceled. The situation was only a little less bleak for him back home.

For the next half-dozen years, he fought to keep his career afloat. He had some minor successes on Sun during that period, including the singles "John Henry," "Carry Me Back to Old Virginny," and a remake of Ray Charles' "What'd I Say." He made another movie appearance in the 1960 *Young and Deadly*. But the Killer seemed relegated to a minor role in pop music from then on.

However, national morals were changing and the events of six years ago were ancient history to most fans. In 1964, with things at Sun in the doldrums,

Jerry Lee switched to Smash Records (a subsidiary of Mercury) and suddenly found his career rejuvenated. His first releases in March 1964 and January 1965 (both titled *Jerry Lee Lewis*) and *Rock Songs* in June 1965 all were aimed at rock fans. But the albums sold much better in the country field. Of course, country always was one of the elements in Lewis's stylings and by the mid-'60s, many youngsters in the South had adopted country-rock as part of their own culture. So without changing his approach too much, Jerry Lee set his cap in that direction and soon was doing quite well, thank you.

His new direction was indicated by the title of his January 1966 smash LP, *Country Songs*. After that album, his LPs did steadily better over the last half of the decade. He followed with such releases as *By Request* and *Return of Rock* (1967), *Soul My Way* (1968), and one of the best-selling country LPs of 1968, *Another Place, Another Time*. His singles sales also moved along nicely. The title song of the latter album moved high on the charts and he achieved another top 10 hit in 1968 with "What's Made Milwaukee Famous (Has Made a Loser Out of Me)." Other hit singles of the late '60s were "She Even Woke Me Up to Say Goodbye," "To Make Love Sweeter for You," and "She Still Comes Around (to Love What's Left of Me)."

Jerry Lee's in-person success moved right along with his recording achievements. He starred in such diverse places as plush Las Vegas hotels, college campuses, county fairs, and large auditoriums. In 1969 and into the early '70s, he was a prime drawing card in the rash of rock'n'roll revival shows. Another milestone occurred in 1968, when he starred in the role of Iago in "Catch My Soul," a rock version of Shakespeare's *Othello* presented at the Los Angeles Music Center.

In the 1970s, his albums kept coming out on several labels. When he still was on Smash in the late '60s, some of his earlier work was reissued by Sun. In 1970, Mercury Records absorbed its subsidiary, Smash. Among his Sun releases of the late '60s and early '70s were *Ole Tyme Country Music, Volume 1, 2 and 3; Monsters; Rockin' Rhythm & Blues; Taste of Country;* and *Original Golden Hits, Volumes 1, 2, and 3*. Sun's *Golden Cream of the Country* made the country top 10 in May 1970. Two Sun singles also brought him top 10 laurels in 1970: "One Minute past Eternity," and "I Can't Seem to Say Goodbye." At year-end, another Sun single, "Waiting for a Train" was high on the lists.

Smash LP releases of 1969 and the early '70s were *Together* (with Linda Gail Lewis, 1969), *Hall of Fame Hits, Volumes 1 and 2* (1969), *She Even Woke Me Up to Say Goodbye*, and *Best of Jerry Lee Lewis* (1970).

In the early 1970s, his material came out on Mercury Records, starting with his first releases on the label, *Live at the International, Las Vegas.* Also well received were such 1971 releases as *There Must Be More to Love than That, Touching Home,* and *Would You Take Another Chance on Me.* He also had a series of top 10 single country hits: "There Must Be More to Love than This," "Touching Home," "Would You Take Another Chance with Me"/"Me and Bobby McGee" (1971) and "Chantilly Lace"/"Think about It Darlin'" (1972). 1972–73 Mercury album hits included *The Killer Rocks On* and *The Session.* Among the singles he placed on the country charts were "Lonely Weekends," "Turn on Your Love Light," "When He Walks on You," and "Who's Gonna Play This Old Piano."

In the middle and late '70s, Jerry Lee continued to make the country charts with Mercury singles "Drinking Wine Spo-Dee-O-Dee," "Boogie Woogie Country Man" (1975), "Don't Boogie Woogie" (1976), "Let's Put It Back Together Again" (top 20, 1976), "Middle Age Crazy" (top 10, 1977), and "I'll Find It Where I Can" (top 15, 1978).

Besides a breakneck series of concert dates numbering in the hundreds each year, Jerry Lee still found time for other tasks including playing himself in *American Hot Wax* (1978), a film biography of rock impresario Alan Freed. (*See Freed, Alan.*)

Early in 1979, Jerry made another record company move, switching to Elektra. His March 1979 debut on the label, *Jerry Lee Lewis,* was recorded in Los Angeles, the first LP he had cut outside Nashville in some time. It offered a combination of rock and country songs, including a previously unrecorded Bob Dylan song, "Rita May," that Dylan had offered to Jerry.

He began the 1980s with two excellent new Elektra albums: *When Two Worlds Collide* and *Killer Country,* both released in 1980. In 1981, however, his career almost came to an abrupt end when he was hospitalized with an ulcerated stomach. The physicians told reporters it was a life-threatening illness, but Lewis recovered and by late 1982 was back on the concert trail again. Through the mid-1980s, despite various health and personal problems, Jerry Lee persevered and thrilled audiences with his musical antics. As reporter Kristine McKenna of the *Los Angeles Times* enthused, even at that stage of his career: "He still pulsates with arrogant leering life, and packs more sex and rhythm into a sideways glance than most bands can muster operating at full steam."

In the 1980s, Rhino Records issued the excellently annotated two-LP *Milestones,* featuring 1956–77 tracks, plus the CD *18 Original Sun Greatest Hits.*

Books concerning Jerry Lee included ex-wife Myra Lewis's *Great Balls of Fire* (Quill, 1982), Nick Tosches' *Hellfire* (Delacorte, 1982), Robert Palmer's *Jerry Lee Lewis Rocks* (Deliha, 1981), and Robert Cain's *Whole Lotta Shakin' Goin' On* (Dial, 1981).

As might be expected, when the new Rock'n'Roll Hall of Fame was organized in Cleveland, Ohio, in the mid-1980s, Jerry Lee was one of the first names proposed for entry and one of the first voted in.

During 1987, two extensive reissues of Jerry Lee's work became available. One of those was a 12-record boxed set of recordings Jerry made on Sun Records from 1956 to 1963, issued by England's Charly Records and distributed in the U.S. by Street Level Records, Gardena, California. The other was a series of three boxed sets with 10 albums per box issued by the German record firm Bear Family, covering material Lewis recorded on Mercury from 1963 to 1977. The series, collectively titled *Jerry Lee Lewis: The Killer,* was offered to U.S. record buyers by mail order from Down Home Music in El Cerrito, California.

LEWIS, RAMSEY: *Band leader (RAMSEY LEWIS TRIO), pianist, songwriter. Born Chicago, Illinois, May 27, 1935. Original Trio members: Red Holt, born Rosedale, Mississippi, May 16, 1932; El Dee Young, born Chicago, Illinois, January 7, 1936. Holt and Young left group in summer of 1966.*

One of the pop standards of the 1960s has to be "The In Crowd," the single that transformed the Ramsey Lewis Trio from a moderately successful jazz group to international stardom. As seems to happen more often than not when a jazz group makes it big, the reaction of hard-core jazz fans and critics was the usual accusation that Lewis had sold out.

Ramsey E. Lewis, Jr., grew up in Chicago, where Red Holt and El Dee Young were boyhood friends. (Holt was born in Mississippi, but moved north with his family at an early age.) All three showed musical ability in their youth, Ramsey on piano and as a singer. Young performed with R&B groups in the Midwest. However, when Lewis set about organizing his trio in 1956, Young agreed to join.

The trio began playing small clubs in the Chicago area, mostly jazz spots. Cadet Records (a subsidiary of Chess) released one of the trio's first LPs, *Gentlemen of Jazz,* in October 1958. The group became one of the label's more successful entries in the jazz category and provided several dozen albums in the Cadet catalogue through the 1960s.

As the '50s went by, the trio attracted attention beyond its home area, making its first New York date in 1959. Lewis, who wrote much of the group's material, continued to experiment with different types of compositions. In 1964, the group gained a chart hit with "Something You Got," whose success brought engagements in larger clubs and big-name hotels as well as appearances on network TV. This exposure increased even more in the summer of 1965, when the group's recording of "The In Crowd" became an international best-seller. The record sold over a million copies in the U.S., according to Cadet, and won a Grammy award from the National Academy of the Recording Arts and Sciences as the Best Small Group Jazz Record of 1965. The LP of the same title (Cadet, 1965) also was a top 10 hit. The group had another hit single in 1965 as well: "Hang on Sloopy." (*See Derringer, Rick.*)

The original trio broke up in the summer of 1966, when Young and Holt decided to form the Young-Holt Trio. Lewis continued to head the Ramsey Lewis Trio after this, using various combinations of sidemen, although the level of success in mass-audience terms in the 1970s was nowhere near that of the mid-1960s.

Among his Cadet LPs were *Hour* (1959); *Stretching Out* (1960); *Ramsey Lewis Trio In Chicago* and *More Music from the Soil* (1961); *Never on Sunday* (1962); *Bossa Nova, Pot Luck, Sound of Spring* and *Country Meets the Blues* (1963); *Barefoot Sunday Blues, Bach to the Blues,* and *At Bohemian Caverns* (1964); *You Better Believe Me* and *Choice* (1965); *Hang On!, Swingin',* and *Wade in the Water* (1966); *Goin' Latin, Movie Album,* and *Dancing in the Streets* (1967); *Up Pops* and *Maiden Voyage* (1968); *Mother Nature's Son* (1969); and *Another Voyage, Best of Ramsey Lewis, The Piano Player,* and *Them Changes* (1970). In the late 1960s, his backing group was composed of Cleveland Eaton on bass and Maurice White on drums. White left in 1970 to form his first Earth, Wind & Fire band, but he was to return to play an important role in Ramsey's career. (*See Earth, Wind & Fire.*)

In 1971, Ramsey joined Columbia Records, which was to remain his label into the 1980s, and turned out such albums as *Back to the Roots* (1971) and *Upendo Ni Pomojos* (1972). Ramsey recalled later: "The first three or four albums I did after joining Columbia were pretty close to what I had been doing all along. But in 1974, I was finishing up an album when Maurice [White] called to tell me he had a couple of tunes. We met in Chicago and recorded 'Hot Dawgitt,' which we all thought would be a monster. After recording it, we decided to experiment with another tune Maurice had. He had some of the guys from Earth, Wind & Fire with him so we used them on the record. After we got the music down, we figured why not add some vocals to it just to see what would happen. I had never put

vocals on any of my records, but I felt it would be a new, fresh approach for me, so Maurice and the guys sang. We didn't have a name for it, but we eventually came up with 'Sun Goddess' and the tune went on to become gold."

In 1975, Lewis was on the concert circuit backing that year's Columbia release, *Don't It Feel So Good,* this time with a quartet: Bernard Reed on bass, Morris Jennings on drums, Byron Gregory on guitar, and Derf Reklaw Raheem, who played flute as well as 20 different drums. That album did reasonably well, but not as well as *Love Notes,* a best-seller of the mid-1970s whose contents included original material from Stevie Wonder. (*See Wonder, Stevie.*)

The situation was similar to the scenario that provided "Sun Goddess," Ramsey noted. "Again, I had almost completed the record when I got a call from Stevie. He asked me what I was doing. I told him I was almost finished recording my next album and suggested he write a tune for me. He wrote 'Spring High' and the title tune, 'Love Notes,' which did very well."

In the late 1970s, Ramsey continued to experiment with new formats on his albums. Those included the 1977 *Tequila Mockingbird;* the 1978 *Legacy,* which was intended to blend jazz and classics and was premiered with the Kansas City Philharmonic; and the more pop-oriented 1979 release *Ramsey,* whose tracks included the "Aquarius"/"Let the Sun Shine In" medley from *Hair* and a contribution from composer James Mack (who had co-produced and provided original music for *Legacy*) called "Intermezzo," built around the "Don't Cry for Me Argentina" theme from the musical *Evita.*

The pattern remained the same in the next decade, which began with such releases as *Routes* (1980) and *Three Piece Suite* (1981). Besides recording projects, Ramsey continued to be active on the concert circuit with different band combinations that included a reunion series of shows in 1983 with original Trio members Holt and Young. Some of his earlier work for Chess Records was repackaged in 1987 by MCA (which had purchased the Chess catalog) and released as a two-disc set, *Greatest Hits of Ramsey Lewis,* as part of its Original Chess Masters Series.

LIGHTFOOT, GORDON: *Singer, songwriter, guitarist, pianist. Born Orilla, Canada, November 17, 1938.*

Starting as a folksinger/songwriter, Gordon Lightfoot never really abandoned his first love, though he often combined folk elements with rock to good effect during a long and eventful career. Even in the late 1980s, when the folk boom of the late '50s and

'60s was only a fleeting memory for most music observers, he commanded respect from a large segment of the music public embracing almost all age brackets.

Lightfoot was born in the small town of Orilla (mistakenly spelled in some of the early record-company biographical notes as Orillia), 80 miles north of Toronto. During his late teens, he spent summers playing in bands and driving trucks in northern Ontario. In 1958, after finishing high school, he went to Los Angeles to study piano and orchestration at a since-departed music school, Westlake College. For a time, he earned money at such behind-the-scenes jobs as arranging, copying music, and writing and producing commercial jingles.

"Then in 1960, I started to listen to some people like Pete Seeger and Bob Gibson. That's when I got interested in folk music and that's when I started to play guitar. Ian and Sylvia [a Canadian folksong team] were friends of mine from before and we used to hang out at the folk clubs and coffeehouses. I just started singing folk stuff. I used to get up on stage and play and sing like everybody else. Ian turned me on to the guitar because he was so adept with flat pick. The style of Bob Gibson also affected me a great deal.

"Actually, I'd written some songs before then, but they didn't have any kind of identity. I wrote 30 or 40 songs up until the time I started to write stuff that I could do on stage. Then the writing explosion started with Bob Dylan and Phil Ochs and Tom Paxton and everybody else who followed them and I started to get a point of view and that's when I started to improve." Gordon went back to eastern Canada in the early '60s and "sang in a lot of bars in and around Toronto."

In the early '60s, he began recording for a Canadian label, Chateau, and had a number of hits in his homeland. The first, "Remember Me," was followed by others on various local labels, including "I'm Not Saying," "Spin, Spin," "Go Go Round," "The Way I Feel," and "Black Day in July." But it was performances of his songs by others that focused attention on him south of the border.

His career moved faster after Ian Tyson of Ian and Sylvia brought his manager, Albert Grossman (then partners with John Court), to hear Lightfoot at Steele's Tavern in Toronto. Grossman became Lightfoot's manager and Court his record producer. Just as Grossman had previously boosted his then unknown protégé Bob Dylan by having another of his acts, Peter, Paul and Mary, record Dylan's compositions, he publicized Lightfoot by having the trio popularize his "For Lovin' Me" and "Early Morning Rain" (both of which Ian and Sylvia had already recorded for U.S. listeners). Grossman also landed him a contract with United Artists, which issued *Lightfoot* in 1966.

Over the next three years, UA followed with *The Way I Feel, Did She Mention My Name, Back Here on Earth,* and *Sunday Concert.* In 1969, he changed record companies, moving to Warner Brothers.

The move seemed to bring new vitality to his work. The debut album on Reprise, *Sit Down Young Stranger* (1970) went gold eventually. It was retitled *If You Could Read My Mind* when its song of that title became a top 10 hit. *Summer Side of Life* (1971) also gained the hit lists. A little later, UA repackaged his earlier work on *Classic Lightfoot.* In 1975, Warner Brothers released the platinum two-LP retrospective, *Gord's Gold,* featuring many of the memorable songs from his first decade as a U.S. recording artist. These included "Cotton Jenny," "If You Could Read My Mind," "Carefree Highway," "Candian Railroad Trilogy," and "The Last Time I Saw Her."

His career was then in excellent shape, but it must be said that it had slowed a bit not long before. For a time in the early 1970s, he appeared to lose some momentum. For instance, his two albums of 1972, *Don Quixote* and *Old Dan's Records,* while certainly above average in many ways, still seemed weaker than most of his previous work. Gordon returned to top form with the platinum 1974 album *Sundown,* which also provided him with a gold record for the title song (a number one hit in *Billboard*). In 1975, he was represented by the commendable album *Cold on the Shoulder.* The well-crafted *Summertime Dreams* (1976) went platinum. In 1978, the gold *Endless Wire* was released.

He began the next decade with his tenth release on Warner Brothers, *Dream Street Rose* (March 1980)—a good album, but not a major hit. The same held true for his 1983 *Salute.* Though he continued to tour steadily in the mid-1980s, Gordon sought different directions both in his musical efforts and career-wise. One step in a new direction was a debut acting role in the film *Harry Tracy* (starring Bruce Dern) for which he also wrote the theme song. In early 1984, he began studio work on a new album, starting with over 50 song "concepts" that finally were winnowed down to ten tracks for the album. That LP, *East of Midnight* (Warner Brothers, June 1986) had for its first single release "Anything for Love," co-written by Lightfoot and David Foster. The LP represented his twenty-third album.

LITTLE ANTHONY AND THE IMPERIALS: *Vocal group. All born Brooklyn, New York. Anthony Gourdine, January 8, 1941; Sam Strain, December 9, 1941; Ernest Wright, August 24, 1941; Clarence Collins, March 17, 1941.*

The success of white rock performers during the mid-1950s helped remove the "black-only" limitation on the originators of rock'n'roll. As a result, a steadily rising number of records by black singers from both the rock and R&B genres moved onto the national charts. One of the groups to take advantage of this was Little Anthony and the Imperials, who placed numerous singles in the top 40 in the late 1950s through 1965.

Unlike some of their white contemporaries, none of the Imperials had visions of college careers during their early years. Singing was a way out of their Brooklyn ghetto. They started doing songs for their friends and then made appearances at local school dances. They moved on to club dates in the mid-1950s. Then, as rock'n'roll became the bellwether of pop music, they won a recording contract that led to their hit single, "Tears on My Pillow" on End Records in 1958, a top 5 pop entry and number one on black music charts. A string of hit singles "It's Not the Same," "Better Use Your Head," "Shimmy, Shimmy, Ko-Ko-Bop," "I Miss You So," "Hurt So Bad," "I'm on the Outside Looking In," and "Take Me Back" followed.

At the start of the 1960s, the group broke up, with Little Anthony moving out as a single and the other three artists working as a trio as the Imperials. By this time, though, the old-line rhythm & blues in the music cycle had given way to the softer tones of the folk miniboom and the more restrained rock sounds of such English groups as the Beatles and Herman's Hermits. After two years apart, during which time neither segment made much headway in the hit-record arena, the act resumed as a foursome under its old name. This resulted in a little better schedule of dates in nightclubs and colleges and on the R&B circuit. While it did not return the group to its old star status, it did gain it a new hit single in 1965, "Going Out of My Head." In 1966, deciding that their appeal was to a somewhat more mature audience, they changed their name to Anthony and the Imperials, but then back to Little Anthony a few years later.

Toward the end of the 1960s, beginning in England and spreading back across the Atlantic to the U.S., there was a revival of interest in oldies rock, meaning the more simplistic styles of the 1950s. This reverse trend was helped by a number of syndicated radio shows reviewing the history of rock'n'roll. As a result, Little Anthony and the Imperials signed a new contract with Veep Records (a division of United Artists) and found it easier to gain star billing everywhere from Las Vegas lounge shows to Miami Beach's Eden Roc, San Juan Puerto Rico's Flamboyan Club, and in numerous college shows. One of their first singles for Veep, "Yester-day Is Gone" moved a respectable way up the R&B charts.

The group's albums in the years preceding the '70s included *Forever Yours* and *Greatest Hits* on Roulette, *Little Anthony* on Sunset Records, and *Little Anthony* and *We Are the Imperials* on End Records. *Out of Sight, Out of Mind* (United Artists) was a chart hit in 1970. The group's affiliation with United Artists brought several charted singles in the early 1970s, including the 1971 "Help Me Find a Way (to Say I Love You)."

Among the group's LPs still in record company catalogs during the first part of the '70s were *Out of Sight, Out of Mind* (UA); *We Are the Imperials* (End); *Forever Yours* (Roulette); and, on Songbird Records, *Daylight*. Some of those, such as *Daylight* and *We Are the Imperials*, showcased some of the group's early doo-wop stylings. Of those, in the 1980s only *Out of Sight, Out of Mind* remained in print.

The group's recording fortunes faded again in the mid-1970s as disco came to the fore. Sam Strain joined the O'Jays in the mid-1970s. (*See O'Jays, The.*) In the 1980s, renewed nostalgia about the good old days of rock kindled Little Anthony's hopes for new success. Reissues continued to appear on store shelves, such as the 1981 Liberty release, *Best of Little Anthony and the Imperials.*

LITTLE FEAT: *Vocal and instrumental group. Original members, early 1970s: Lowell George, born Hollywood, California, 1939, died Arlington, Virginia, June 29, 1979; Roy Estrada, born Santa Ana, California; Richard Hayward, born Ames, Iowa; Bill Payne, born Waco, Texas. Estrada replaced in 1972 by Kenny Gradney, born New Orleans, Louisiana. Paul Barrere, born California, and Sam Clayton, born New Orleans, Louisiana, added in 1972. Group disbanded in 1979, re-formed in 1988.*

One of the most versatile and talented rock bands, Little Feat gained most of its recognition outside home boundaries. Part of the reason for its relatively poor showing with the U.S. mass audience probably was the failure of most of its albums to capture the awesome concert presence of the group. For all that, the band's recordings still provided a very impressive body of work that added to the sadness of its disbanding in 1979 because of the untimely death of its longtime guiding light, Lowell George.

The band's origins went back to the end of the 1960s and the breakup of one edition of Frank Zappa's Mothers of Invention. Two alumni from that band, singer/lead guitarist Lowell George and bass guitarist Roy Estrada, set about forming a new band to keep them in spending money. Both had been in the business for a number of years. Lowell, a graduate of Hollywood High School, had been a session musician and later founded a number of his own bands (beginning with the Factory in 1965) before joining the Mothers. Estrada, who grew up in Santa Ana, California, had played with a number of bar bands before becoming one of the first members of the Mothers.

To round out the original foursome, they brought in keyboardist Bill Payne and demon drummer Richard "Ritchie" Hayward. Payne, born in Texas and raised in Santa Barbara, California, was musical director of a group called the Viscounts in the late 1960s and had become acquainted with George and Estrada when he was trying to find work with Zappa's band. Hayward, who spent his early years in Ames, Iowa, had moved to Los Angeles in the mid-1960s to improve his chances in pop music. He answered a music-trade-paper ad seeking a replacement drummer for the Factory and thus worked with George's band until it broke up. He moved on to the Fraternity of Man, which had one comic hit ("Don't Bogart Me," which appeared in the film *Easy Rider*), before rejoining Lowell in the new group.

The band didn't start out as Little Feat. Its first performances were under the name Country Zeke and the Freaks at a Los Angeles–area psychedelic club, Temple of the Rainbow. Band members soon realized that might typecast them as a country & western band so they sought another title. George recalled an incident during his Mothers of Invention days when drummer Jimmy Carl Black was kidding him about his "little feet." Changing the spelling a bit, à la the Beatles, he came up with Little Feat.

With Lowell as primary songwriter as well as lead vocalist, the new quartet assembled demos to win over record-company A&R men. George already had established his credentials as a promising writer with other artists. (The Byrds were friends and fans and recorded George's and Bill Payne's "Truck Stop Girl" on their 1970 album, *Untitled*). His band mates too were well regarded so it wasn't a tremendous surprise when Warner/Reprise signed them in the early 1970s. By November 1970, the band's Warner debut, *Little Feat,* was ready for release.

The album included several songs later considered Little Feat classics, including George's "Willin'," which became a high point of most of its live shows. Of course, the band continued to vary the way it played the song as could be verified by comparing live album cuts of "Willin'" of later years with the original recording. Another excellent track was a dual-guitar–paced "Forty-Four Blues/How Many Years" (with guitar luminary Ry Cooder joining

George during the session). Other unusual tracks were "Hamburger Moonlight" and "Snakes on Everything."

The debut LP was above average and the group backed it with audience-pleasing concerts, but the band really caught fire on its 1972 follow-up collection, *Sailin' Shoes,* an offering that reemphasized the band's dedication to down-and-dirty blues-rock. George demonstrated his capacity as one of rock's glowing new writing talents with such originals as the title song, "Cold Cold Cold," "Tripe Face Boogie," "Easy to Slip," and "Teenage Nervous Breakdown." The LP was hailed as a superb effort both in the U.S. and abroad, with no less an authority than Mick Jagger stating Little Feat was one of his favorites. After that, the band always was assured a warm welcome by large crowds at Britain's main venues, a respect duplicated among rock fans throughout Europe.

But it sometimes takes longer to catch on with the American mass audience. Before the album's fine points could be translated into U.S. stardom, internal strains caused a temporary shutdown of activities. Estrada departed to join Captain Beefheart's group while Lowell George concentrated on producing other artists' records.

By late 1972, though, Little Feat was being reborn, this time as a six-man group. George, Payne, and Hayward were joined by bass guitarist Kenny Gradney, guitarist/vocalist Paul Barrere, and percussionist/conga player Sam Clayton. Barrere, who grew up in the L.A. area, had been trying to establish his own band, Lead Enema, when the Little Feat job opened up. He proved a particularly important acquisition, not only for his first-rate guitar work as second lead and lead, but also for his songwriting skill. Clayton and Gradney were excellent musicians with considerable professional experience. Clayton had worked with the Soul Destroyers for a number of years, while Gradney's credits included backing people such as Jerry Lee Lewis, Hank Ballard and the Midnighters, and Arthur "Big Boy" Crudup. Kenny and Sam both had performed with Delaney and Bonnie before joining Little Feat.

The new group's first release was the 1973 *Dixie Chicken*, a scintillating LP that provided a number of the band's trademark songs. The title song, for instance, became a concert showstopper in the mid-1970s when Little Feat was augmented by the Tower of Power horn section. It served as the basis for a succession of style changes starting with a country-rock theme, easing into a Dixieland segment, a jazz-boogie phase, and back to the original rhythms. Another favorite that first surfaced on the album was George's "Fat Man in the Bathtub," which blended Latin and blues-rock elements. Other notable tracks were "Two Trains" and "On Your Way Down."

This was followed in 1974 by the gold Warner release *Feats Don't Fail Me Now,* which emphasized Bill Payne's writing and performing abilities on the blues-rock "Oh Atlanta" and title song. Barrere contributed an excellent original—the funky "Skin It Back"—in an album that showed Payne and Barrere edging out Lowell George for creative direction. The album, coupled with a memorable overseas concert tour, reinforced the band's European reputation and won it a rating from several important European critics as the best American rock band.

George's writing role continued to diminish with the next LP, *The Last Record Album* (1975). George did provide two excellent songs, "Down below the Borderline" and "Long Distance Love," but the balance of the collection essentially was written by Payne and Barrere and the arrangements tended to emphasize their instrumental work. Notable tracks were Barrere's composition "All That You Dream" and Payne's "Day or Night."

Lowell's diminished role in the group wasn't due to animosity among the members, but rather to his growing desire to pursue other performing avenues. He also felt freer to look in other directions with the increasing quality of the songs provided by his band mates.

After a hiatus of two years, the band's sixth Warner Brothers album, *Time Love a Hero,* was released in 1977. To a great extent that was Barrere's project. He had a hand in six of the nine songs (including the title track), being sole writer for two of those: "Hi Roller" and "Missin' You." The album was perhaps a notch or two less impressive than earlier LPs, but it still was a fine collection. Characteristically, it received a better reception outside the U.S.; while it made U.S. charts, it didn't make topmost rungs.

Many U.S. critics suggested one of the band's problems was that, good as the albums were, they didn't give the whole story. First and foremost, Little Feat was a premier concert band, one able to involve the crowd passionately in its constantly changing mixture of vocal and instrumental sounds. A possible answer, of course, was to try to capture the impact of audience dynamics with a live set. In 1978, this was tried with a two-disc live LP, *Waiting for Columbus.* The tracks gave some idea of audience response with the background roars of approval from concert goers in London and Maryland. It still wasn't the same as being intimately caught up in these emotions, but it was the next best thing. Significantly, the album earned gold-record certification from the RIAA in July 1979.

In 1978, George began work on his debut solo album *Thanks I'll Eat It Here* (Warner Brothers). Even as he worked on that project, Lowell found his interest in his beloved Little Feat rekindled and he began collaborating with the other five members on a new LP. In 1979, he divided his time between solo concerts in support of his new album and session work on the next Little Feat release. Unfortunately, his death occurred (ascribed to a heart attack) before the latter album was done. The other members completed the tracks and, when that LP, *Down on the Farm,* came out in 1979, announced Little Feat would be no more. The album showed how great a loss pop music had suffered by such stirring tracks written or co-written by Lowell as "Kokomo," "Six Feet of Snow," and "Be One Now."

As Payne pointed out, most of the album material, for which George was acting as producer, had been taped before Lowell died. "We had most of the vocals, which is really the only reason we were able to finish it."

Though the band broke up, Payne supervised one more recording project, a retrospective collection, *Hoy Hoy* (Warner Brothers, 1981). John Swenson commented in the *New Rolling Stone Record Guide,* Payne "assembled it with the attention to little details that brings out the project's underlying poignancy: bits of a George practice track, on which he was working out a song; demos from the band's early days; an amazing blues, 'Sweet China White,' that George mysteriously chose not to include on his solo album. *Hoy Hoy* also includes live tracks recorded during the height of the band's career."

Looking back in late 1979, Payne commented: "In a lot of ways, Little Feat was a band ahead of its time. I think the most fun I got out of it was playing all those different *kinds* of music. People would always say to us: 'This album sounds different from the last one,' and they were different. But there was a thread that went through it all, an ensemble sound, which is really what Little Feat was all about."

In 1988, he spearheaded re-formation of the band, which had a new LP on Warner Bros., *Let It Roll.* (*See Byrds, The; Captain Beefheart; Cooder, Ry; Mothers of Invention, The; Zappa, Frank.*)

LITTLE RICHARD: *Singer, pianist, songwriter, band leader. Born Macon, Georgia, December 25, 1935.*

For years, those in their teens or twenties in the 1950s might have wondered whatever happened to Little Richard. Then, suddenly, the most flamboyant pioneer of the early rock revolution was back, outrageous as ever, playing to enthusiastic audiences ranging in age from early teens to 40-plus. Just as people over 60 longed for the name bands of their youth, their sons and daughters yearned for the good old days when rock was in and message songs were a long way off. "I'm the real king of rock'n'roll. I was singing rock before anybody knew what rock was back when swing music was the big thing. People like Elvis Presley were the builders of rock'n'roll, but I was the architect," Richard Penniman maintained to Dennis Hunt of the *Los Angeles Times* in 1984.

Little Richard gained fame from songs, usually of his own composition, with often manic lyrics and a wild, driving rhythm. The first music he was exposed to as a child in Macon, Georgia, was far different in content. Like most of the popular black artists of recent decades, he was weaned on gospel music, singing in his church choir as a small boy. By his teens, Richard had begun to play the piano and also was taking note of rhythm & blues and boogie-woogie swing music popular with mass audiences of the era.

He began to experiment with these types of music, sometimes copying established artists and sometimes writing original material in the blues or boogie-woogie vein. On October 16, 1951, not yet turned 16, he made his first recordings in an Atlanta, Georgia, studio: "Get Rich Quick," "Why Did You Leave Me," "Every Hour," and "Thinkin' 'bout My Mother." The last two were written by Richard, one a boogie number, the second a slow, "moaning" urban blues song. On January 12, 1952, Richard recorded four more sides in the same studio: "Ain't Nothin' Happenin'," "Taxi Blues," "Please Have Mercy on Me," and "I Brought It All on Myself." These eight songs, reissued in 1970 on RCA Camden (*Every Hour with Little Richard*) reveal a strong, clear voice and lyrics that tell a definite story. Two reappeared in 1988 on Rhino Records' intriguing *Shut Up! A Collection of Rare Tracks, 1951–1964,* including 1953 blues numbers with Johnny Otis's Orchestra for Peacock Records plus later gospel and rock with Jimi Hendrix on guitar.

The early '50s were years of one-night stands, first with a medicine show, later as a soloist or a member of a group playing small black nightclubs in the South. By then, Richard was experimenting with his own version of rock, including such compositions as "Tutti Frutti," with a lyric that went "A wompbom-paloo bompalompbompbomp, tutti frutti." Black audiences didn't buy the new material, though. "It was funny," he later told one reporter, "I'd sing the songs I sing now in the clubs, but the black audiences just didn't respond. They wanted blues stuff like B.B. King sings. That's what they were used to. I'd sing 'Tutti Frutti' and nothing. Then someone

would get up and sing an old blues song and everyone would go wild."

With this experience, Richard avoided sending rock material to Specialty Records in 1954, when he made a bid for a recording contract. He sent a blues tape instead, but got no affirmative response until a year later. As he told Robert Hilburn of the *Los Angeles Times* in January 1970: "We met in New Orleans and I cut some blues songs. During a break in the session, someone heard me playing 'Tutti Frutti' on the piano and asked about the song. We ended up recording it and it sold 200,000 copies in a week and a half."

The record thrust Little Richard into the national spotlight, rising to number 17 on *Billboard* charts during February 1956. He proceeded to add to his luster with a steady string of chart singles from then through 1958. They included, in 1956, "Long Tall Sally," "Slippin' and Slidin'," "Rip It Up," and "Ready Teddy"; in 1957, "Lucille," "Jenny Jenny," and "Keep a Knockin'"; and in 1958, "Good Golly, Miss Molly," "Ooh! My Soul," and "Baby Face." He also sang the title track in *The Girl Can't Help It,* featuring numerous '50s rock and R&B notables. Such white performers as the Everly Brothers, Buddy Holly, and Pat Boone rerecorded his songs. His albums such as *Here's Little Richard* sold briskly in U.S. and foreign markets. Then, while still on top, he abruptly stopped performing. The incident that caused it was a flaming engine that developed during a flight to an overseas engagement. Richard swore he would enter the ministry if the plane made it to land. It did, and he returned to Alabama, where he earned a B.A. degree and was ordained as a minister in the Seventh Day Adventist Church.

In 1963, he returned to the music field, touring Europe with then relatively unknown groups the Beatles and Rolling Stones. "They knew more about my records than I know myelf. They knew all the notes, the screams, everything. I remember the Beatles getting $50 each some nights." During the mid-1960s, Richard mainly stayed on the sidelines, except for some little-noted recordings made first for Vee Jay and then Okeh.

In the late 1960s, however, supported particularly by many English artists who had grown up on rock of the 1950s, a movement to reemphasize rock's founders began. In 1967, Richard began the first of a series of triumphant tours of Europe. As the decade came to a close, the renewed interest in old-time rock spread back across the Atlantic to the U.S.

Richard happily told the story of his renewed fame. "The kids brought me back. They heard the Beatles talk about me, the Stones talk about me, Tom Jones talk about me. They wanted to hear for themselves. I get a chill when I see those young people applaud me; I'm grateful I'm back."

During the early 1970s, he signed a recording contract with Warner Brothers, which led to such releases as *King of Rock'n'Roll* (on the Reprise label), which was on the charts for a number of months, and *The Rill Thing*, whose tracks included his dynamic "Freedom Blues."

In 1975, he decided to give up the rock circuit again to concentrate once more on the ministry, a role he was still fulfilling a decade later. The death of his brother that year from drug abuse and the realization that he was subject to the same pressures in the rock field led to his decision. As he commented to Dennis Hunt: in late 1984: "I'm not going to lie. I was enjoying myself doing all that stuff. But some of those things kill you if you fool around with them long enough. Heroin, cocaine, and those other drugs, that's a one-way ticket to hell.

"I'm blessed to be alive. My brother and some friends had dropped dead. I thought I was next. I felt I was going to die. I cried and cried. I was so afraid." The answer, he concluded, was to forgo uncontrolled sex and drugs in favor of religion. "If I hadn't done that, I probably wouldn't be sitting here now. The Lord pointed the way. Praise the Lord."

When his biography, *The Life and Times of Little Richard: The Quasar of Rock* (written by Charles White, Harmony Books), came out in 1984, Little Richard not only was clean of drugs, but also was in superb physical shape. With his firm body and almost unlined skin, he could have passed for someone in his thirties. In interviews for the book, though, he hadn't pussyfooted, but had frankly discussed the wild times of his music days, which included not only drugs, but sexual orgies and, in his case, homosexuality.

He maintained to Hunt that homosexual behavior was a thing of the past. "I don't do that stuff anymore. But I don't have anything against gays. Jesus loves gay people. Jesus died for gay people too. I just can't be doing all that stuff I used to." He also noted he did not avoid calling drugs and other immoral practices as sins in his sermons.

While Little Richard's big hits of the '50s continued to bring in royalties for copyright owners decades later, he was in the position of odd man out. He had sold the rights for small amounts of money, he told interviewers in the 1980s, and had never seen a penny of the millions of dollars his material had earned later. Feeling cheated, in the mid-'80s he filed suit against those who controlled his music to try to gain some of the monetary rewards they had brought to others.

Richard had another brush with death in 1985 from which he recovered. The close call was the result of a serious automobile crash in Los Angeles. He had returned to L.A. for a few days while in the middle of recording tracks in London, England, for a new album, the first in a decade. (The LP, *Lifetime Friend*, finally came out on Warner Brothers at the end of 1986. It was religiously flavored, but, he emphasized, not a gospel album. It was a rock collection intended, he noted, to provide listeners with a "message in rhythm.")

His comments came in notes for a Warner Brothers bio in which he also commented. "It was a terrible experience. I was in the hospital for a month, very close to death. I was on the operating table for hours on end and now I'm full of plates and pins. I am the bionic man. But God saved me for a purpose. I was right at the doors of death and He said 'Hold it!' When I came back I tried to sing harder than I ever had before."

In full health again, in ensuing years he took part in such projects as fund raising to fight AIDS, acting in the 1986 film *Down and Out in Beverly Hills*, and making many guest appearances on television awards shows. From his home base in Riverside, California, he didn't abandon his work as an evangelist or gospel singer, but he also wasn't bashful about what he felt was his rightful place in pop music history.

He even startled the 1988 Grammy awards audience as he presented a trophy to Jody Watley by exclaiming: "I have never received nothing and I have been singing for years. I am the architect of rock'n'roll! I am the originator!" The National Academy of Recording Arts and Sciences, which had never given Richard a Grammy, responded by giving him a standing ovation.

LOFGREN, NILS: *Singer, pianist, guitarist, band leader, record producer, songwriter. Born Washington, D.C., c. 1950.*

Considered one of rock's instrumental prodigies in his teens in the late 1960s, Nils Lofgren hovered on the brink of stardom for over a decade and a half afterward. Part of the problem seemed to be that while his solo concerts were among the most stunning in rock, his albums typically didn't capture enough of that excitement to make them commercially hot items. Which didn't mean that he wasn't responsible for some of the finest, if overlooked, recordings in the field. While not what the industry salespeople would have called a superstar through the late 1980s, Nils had great influence on pop music as a songwriter, a musician whose moves were copied by many young artists, and a supporting player who contributed greatly to a succession of top names from Neil Young to Bruce Springsteen.

Of his early years, Nils once said: "I started playing classical accordion when I was about five years old and studied it for 10 years. Basically, that's the only kind of music I really liked until I was around 15 and the Beatles came out. The Beatles turned me on to rock'n'roll to begin with and then I quickly caught on to what I was missing—Little Richard, Elvis, Ray Charles, Stevie Wonder, old Motown, etc. When I first saw Jimi Hendrix, I had no idea what to expect. A friend I knew was playing guitar and said: 'Come on down and see this guy.' Hendrix was a beautiful man, and when he started playing I was blown away completely. At that moment I knew what I wanted to do and three or four weeks later I dropped out of school, ran away to New York and started trying to figure out what was going on in the music world.

"So Hendrix definitely was a major inspiration to me. I quit the accordion and started playing electric guitar and really got involved quickly with all the bands—the Stones, the Zombies, and the whole English '60s thing. Old Motown was a big inspiration too.

"After a few years I was in a local band. I worked my way up through the ranks playing in clubs, doing other people's songs. Then I started writing my own songs and I put the band Grim together. We were going to head out to L.A. and try to get a record deal. We were still pretty green, but we wanted to get out of Washington, D.C., and start finding out what was going on. Luckily I met Neil Young in Washington and after spending a few days with him, he really liked my songs and said he'd help me anyway he could. When I got to L.A., he was a big help."

Once Nils got to the West Coast in the late 1960s, Neil Young asked him to be backup pianist and lead guitarist on *After the Gold Rush*. A little later, after the death of Danny Whitten, he also worked with Young's favorite backing band, Crazy Horse, with whom he recorded the LP *Crazy Horse*. Later, Lofgren supported Young and Crazy Horse on another fine LP, *Tonight's the Night* (1975).

Lofgren still had plans for his own band and Neil helped open doors for Grin, which recorded four LPs over the 1971–74 period. The band, which had some material that may have influenced the mid-1970s punk movement in England, was a hard-driving quartet that undoubtedly was a little ahead of its time. At its peak, it was made up of Lofgren on lead vocals, guitar, and keyboards; Nils' brother Tom on guitar; Bob Gordon on bass guitar and vocals; and Bob Berberich on drums and vocals. The group's debut LP, *Grin,* came out on the Spindizzy/CBS label in 1971 and was followed by *1 + 1* and *All Out.* A&M released its last album, *Gone Crazy* in 1974. Epic later issued the retrospective album, *The Best of Nils Lofgren and Grin.*

In 1975, Nils made his first foray into solo work, signing with A&M for a series of albums that began with *Nils Lofgren,* on which Nils was backed by Wornell Jones on bass and Aynsley Dunbar on drums. More than a few critics named it to their list of 1975's 10 best. Included in it was a sparkling update of the Goffin-King rock classic "Goin' Back," plus such other fine offerings as "Back It Up," "I Don't Want to Know," and a tribute to the Rolling Stones' Keith Richards, "Keith Don't Go."

Lofgren seemed on the verge of achieving the success long predicted for him. Unfortunately, his next two albums were disappointing. Both *Cry Tough* (1976) and *I Came to Dance* (1977) were inferior to his solo debut. While his stage shows remained beyond compare, fans were more interested in spending their money to see him on stage than buying albums downgraded not only by critics, but word of mouth among rock aficionados. (There was interest, though, in the "official bootleg" album issued by A&M in 1975, *Back It Up!*)

Since Nils' primary strengths seemed to be concert performances, the logical step was to try to capture some of his live energy on the double-disc live album, *Night after Night* (A&M, 1977), but apparently Lofgren had dissipated his momentary hold on the rock audience. The album was not a best-seller and Nils, sick at heart, took a vacation from recording and touring for a while. In 1979, he came back with a new album on A&M that proved he was not finished as a creative artist. It included many excellent new songs, such as "Shine Silently," "A Fool Like You," and "Sail Away." Critics extolled the collection, but the gap between his 1975 hit LP and the new one seemed too wide for his following to bridge and its main impact wasn't on Nils' career but on other writers' and performers'.

In the early 1980s, Lofgren's contract with A&M ran out and he signed with Backstreet Records (distributed by MCA), putting out *Night Fades Away* (1981) and *Wonderland* (1983). The Backstreet albums didn't represent any major progress in terms of Nils' writing, though they again showcased his memorable instrumental abilities. During those years, Nils still could draw welcoming crowds to smaller venues and was also in demand as a session musician for top-flight artists.

In early 1984, Bruce Springsteen recruited Nils as the new lead guitarist for his E Street Band to take the place of Miami Steve Van Zandt, who had opted for a solo career. Springsteen's tremendous regard for Nils was indicated by the fact that Lofgren was the first newcomer to the band in 10 years. For 15 months, Nils was a key part of the Springsteen group on the tour supporting Bruce's multiplatinum album *Born in the U.S.A.*

Somehow, Nils managed to find time to sandwich in recording material for a new album for Columbia Records. He commented: "I've never made a record more efficiently than this one. I had just five weeks free in February and March between the U.S. and Australian/Japanese legs of Bruce's tour. And that's what it took to make it, working 20 hours a day at the Warehouse in Philadelphia. Why did I record there? Well, I've always had a warm spot in my heart for Philly. It's a great rock'n'roll town and has always been supportive of me. . . .

"Almost all the vocals were done live. I sang them with the band and those are the ones we wound up using, mostly second or third takes. Sometimes you'll hear I'm out of pitch, or I crack, but the emotion is there. It feels good, better than any other studio records I've put out, and comparable only to my live album, *Night after Night.*"

The new album, *Flip,* was issued in May 1985 and included some above-average songs, such as "Delivery Night" and "King of the Rock." Unfortunately, Lofgren's commitments to Springsteen's group delayed a tour backing his new album, which tended to dissipate its impact.

He got started on his U.S. and European live shows in the fall with Tom Lofgren on guitar, Wornell Jones on bass, Stuart Smith on keyboards, and 'Johnny B' Badanjek on drums. (Badanjek's credits included work with Mitch Ryder and the Detroit Wheels, Edgar Winter, Alice Cooper, and the Rockets.)

Nils hadn't lost any of his concert mystique. His performances almost all were spellbinding. Describing his appearance at the Coach House in Los Angeles for the *Los Angeles Times* (July 11, 1986), Duncan Strauss enthused about his format, which began with solo acoustic numbers and proceeded to pile-driving electric arrangements. "Operating without a rhythm section didn't prevent Lofgren from generating considerable power. . . . But (his) performance soared to an entirely different level during 'Delivery Night.' He picked up his electric guitar for the first time and reeled off a lyrical and riveting solo. Lofgren is such an accomplished player—a guitar hero in the best sense of the word—that for the rest of the night he drew applause by simply reaching for his guitar." (*See Crazy Horse; Petty, Tom, and the Heartbreakers; Springsteen, Bruce; Young, Neil.*)

LOGGINS, KENNY: *Singer, guitarist, songwriter. Born Everett, Washington, January 7, 1948.* *

When you've been part of as successful a team as Loggins and Messina (*see Loggins and Messina*), you aren't surprised when people shake their heads in doubt about the wisdom of sallying forth to try a solo career. Kenny Loggins, however, was certain he could do as well as a soloist as part of a team, emphasizing in the summer of 1977: "I love being on my own. It's been very exciting. It's very difficult to put the whole thing into words. Just the feeling of being responsible for your own fate and having the direction of your life in your own hands is the ultimate goal for an artist and I'm enjoying the hell out of it.

"I don't expect to do more work with Jim [Messina] at this time. But we keep in touch and we may help each other out now and then if it seems of value to do it. For instance, there may be a song he might be the right guitarist for or he may want me to help on one of his songs. But otherwise I don't see us reforming as a team."

At the time Kenny said that, his solo career was still on a touch-and-go basis. His debut album was finding a reasonable reception with record buyers, but it didn't seem quite as strong as some of the Loggins and Messina efforts. But Kenny persevered, turning out successively more impressive albums until, by the end of the '70s, the folk-music and soft-rock alumnus had retained most of the old Loggins and Messina following and added a sizable number of new enthusiasts as well.

He was born in Everett, Washington, but moved first to Seattle and then to Alhambra, California, with his family. In the seventh grade in Alhambra, he started to learn the guitar and was a proficient guitarist by the time he finished high school and entered college. His main musical preference then was folk music. As a sophomore in college, he joined a folk group. However, as time went by, he became more and more rock-oriented, although usually retaining elements of folk in both his performing style and songwriting approach.

As he said in the late '70s, though he hadn't considered himself a folk artist for many years, it still affected his approach to music. "I can't escape from my folk roots because it's a part of me. I remember when I showed [arranger] Bob James the material for my solo debut album and I'd sing and he'd write down notes and chords that totally were blowing my mind, he kept laughing as he did it. The reason, he

---

* Based in part on interviews with Irwin Stambler.

said, was that he couldn't write the musical phrases down the same way I did it because I used folk phrasing 'and that's unwritable.' His jazz roots interpreted what I was doing as folk while folkies would interpret it as rock."

In the late '60s, Kenny's main goal was to succeed in the rock field. He joined two rock groups during those years. One, Second Helping, recorded on Viva Records; the other, Gator Creek, did some tracks for Mercury. Neither band made any waves with the public at large. Kenny left Second Helping in 1969 to concentrate on writing and, hopefully, a solo effort.

Soon after, he got a writing contract with ABC Wingate Publishing. One of his compositions for that firm was the delightful "House at Pooh Corner," a hit for the Nitty Gritty Dirt Band. The song later became a staple of Loggins and Messina shows and still is often included in a Loggins concert.

In September 1971, Columbia Records executives were impressed sufficiently with his writings and performing potential to give him a contract. Jim Messina was assigned to produce Kenny's first solo effort, but as the sessions proceeded, Messina became involved in the performing as well as producing end. By the time the album was issued in early 1972, it bore the title *Kenny Loggins with Jim Messina Sittin' In*. The album became a major hit and also was the launching pad for one of the duo's most famous singles, "Danny's Song," which also was a top 10 hit for Anne Murray.

The tremendous acceptance of the Loggins and Messina team caused Kenny's solo career to recede into the background for a while as the group turned out a series of best-selling albums and singles in the mid-1970s and also became a headline concert act. However, by 1976, the group's popularity began to fade. Part of the reason was the lack of striking new songs for the duo's repertoire, perhaps reflecting a loss of enthusiasm on Kenny's part at being a team member rather than soloist. The slowdown in audience interest, whatever its cause, helped make Kenny and Jim decide to try new directions.

This time, Loggins was determined to go all out to make his solo ambitions pay off. Besides spending as much time as possible in writing and recording new material, he stressed performing before as many people as he could reach. "This is my shot and I'm taking it seriously. Part of my philosophy is giving 100% of your effort in the things that mean something to you creatively and that means going out and working in front of the public."

Part of his approach in the early phases of this campaign was to open for Fleetwood Mac shows. He was aware he could fill medium-size or small venues on his own as a headliner, but he took the approach that, in the long run, it would pay off more handsomely if he took second billing in order to showcase his talents to Fleetwood Mac's massive audiences. He noted in 1977: "I had to make a decision whether to be the headliner in 3,000–5,000 seat halls or opening for Fleetwood in 15,000–17,000–capacity auditoriums. I know I only have so much time to show people who I am and what I do. It made sense to do the Fleetwood thing and hopefully turn a lot more people onto my music."

The strategy worked. His solo debut, *Celebrate Me Home* (1977), didn't shoot up to the top of the charts. But it did stay in middle levels for a long time, selling steadily all the time, eventually going platinum. His rising prestige was reinforced with his second LP, the platinum *Nightwatch* (summer 1978). Something of a change in tone and content, it indicated that Kenny was not afraid to experiment with new musical and lyrical material. Though he was basically a solo, he was hardly working totally alone. He co-authored *Nightwatch*'s top 10 single "Whenever I Call You Friend" with Melissa Manchester and recorded it as a duet with Stevie Nicks of Fleetwood Mac. (*See Fleetwood Mac; Manchester, Melissa; Nicks, Stevie.*)

Discussing his approach to songwriting, he stated: "Essentially, it requires self-discipline. I find that creativity, inspiration will come into the room if I open the door. If I don't, if I don't work at it, it rarely arrives on its own. I wrote some things with the Bergmans [Alan and Marilyn Bergman, winners of several Academy Awards for movie songs] and Alan says songwriting is more perspiration than inspiration. I rather think at this point in my life it's more inspiration for me, but I feel there's always at least a small degree of perspiration.

"That's particularly true of my lyrics much of the time. Every once in a while I'll write a song and lyrics and music will be born almost simultaneously, but usually the music comes first and I wait until that moment comes when the lyrics fall into place. An example is my song 'Why Do People Lie?' from my 1977 solo album. I sat down four times after I wrote the music before the words came. I had a feeling about it; I felt I knew subconsciously what the theme would be, but it took several tries before it came. Then the fourth time I knew somehow the timing was right and the lines just came to me. I feel you're only a vehicle; the song writes itself. You have to wait for it to come out. It's wonderful, but it's scary too."

The 1980s for Loggins were marked by a steady broadening and deepening of his creative accomplishments before an audience covering an age spectrum from teens to middle years. He began with a banner year in 1980 with gold albums *Keep the Fire* and *Alive*. He had three singles high on the charts during the year: "This is It," "Keep the Fire," and "I'm Alright." On the Grammy Awards telecast, he and co-writer Michael McDonald (of Doobie Brothers acclaim) won for Song of the Year for the 1979 hit "What a Fool Believes." In the 1980 voting, he won a Grammy for Best Pop Vocal Performance, Male, for his single "This is It." (*See Doobie Brothers, The.*)

During 1982, he had another gold Columbia LP, *High Adventure*. Its single, "Heart to Heart," made *Billboard*'s top 20. In 1984, he hit number one with his single of the theme from the movie *Footloose*, co-written by him and screenwriter Dean Pitchford. The song also appeared on the platinum *Footloose* soundtrack album. Kenny followed this with the 1985 hit album, *Vox Humana*. In 1986, he again contributed soundtrack material to one of the movie blockbusters of the year, *Top Gun*. He had a top 10 single from the soundtrack with "Danger Zone" (co-written by Giorgio Moroder and Tom Whitlock) and also contributed the song "Playing with the Boys," which he wrote with Peter and Ina Wolf. (*See J. Geils Band, The*).

LOGGINS AND MESSINA: *Vocal and instrumental group. Kenny Loggins, born Everett, Washington, January 7, 1948; Jim Messina, born Maywood, California, December 5, 1947. Band personnel as of 1973: Al Hirth, Jon Clarke, Michael Omartian, Larry Sims. Disbanded 1976.*

Offering a mixture of old-timey rock, folk, and country-rock, Loggins and Messina became a favorite in the mid-1970s. Long after the group's dissolution, the original material, written primarily by the two principals, but sometimes by other band members or associates, was often recorded and re-recorded by other artists.

Loggins came to the band with a background in folk and rock (*see Loggins, Kenny*), while Messina's roots were in country and rock. Jim was born in California, but moved to Texas with his family when he was five. While living in the Lone Star State, he began to learn guitar. "Between the time I was five and 10, I watched a lot of musicians play on television. While watching, I learned to play their chords. I really knew at that time that I wanted to be a musician."

Most of the music he listened to was country & western, an influence evident in his work with Poco and Loggins and Messina. (In the first LP that the duo recorded, one of Messina's contributions was the song "Listen to a Country Song," co-written with Al Garth.) However, when Jim's family moved

back to live in the Los Angeles area ocean community of Manhattan Beach, 12-year-old Messina discovered rock. At 13, he joined his first rock group and played professionally while he completed high school in a new locale, Colton, California.

After graduation, he embarked on a career that mixed session work with learning to become a recording engineer. For several years, he engineered at various Los Angeles studios including Harmony Recorders, Audio Arts, Wally Heider, and Sunset Sound. In 1967, he was asked to join the legendary Buffalo Springfield, then already nearing the end of its mercurial, but brief career. One of his contributions with "the Herd" was to produce their last LP, *Last Time Around*. (*See Buffalo Springfield.*)

After the Springfield broke up, he joined forces with Richie Furay to found a new band, Poco, oriented toward blending country and rock. Messina performed with Poco for several years, leaving formally in 1971 when he decided to join forces with Kenny Loggins. (*See Poco.*)

The two really hadn't planned such an alignment. Loggins had signed with Columbia Records as a solo artist and Messina, who had continued to do a lot of production work with various artists besides his band commitments, was asked to produce the new LP. Once Loggins and Messina set to work, though, they hit if off well as musicians and each contributed original songs the other liked. As the sessions proceeded, they found themselves with a good band sound from such sidemen as horn players Al Hirth and Jon Clarke, keyboards player Michael Omartian, and bassist Larry Sims. A chance appearance at the Troubadour in Los Angeles in February 1972, resulting from the club's last-minute need to fill an opening-act gap, proved decisive. The audience loved the group's set and gave them an ovation that proved to equal the reception for the featured act. With the album becoming more and more a joint project between Loggins and Messina, they decided to keep things that way.

The first LP, *Kenny Loggins with Jim Messina Sittin' In* (1972), proved a hit, moving to top chart levels not once, but twice over a span from mid-1972 into 1973. The collection contained many songs that quickly became staple items in Loggins and Messina concerts: Loggins' "Danny's Song" and "House at Pooh Corner," Messina's "Peace of Mind," plus "Vahevala" (co-written by Kenny's brother Dan and Don Lottermoser).

The group's second LP, *Loggins and Messina* (late 1972), was an even greater success, going platinum. Its gold top 10 track "Your Mama Don't Dance" was nominated for a Grammy Award as Best Song of 1972. That same month, the team had another single high on the charts, "Thinking of

You," and followed that in the fall with another chart hit, "Ain't Gonna Change My Music." Between early 1973 and late 1974, Columbia released three more gold albums: *Full Sail,* the live *On Stage,* and *Mother Lode.* However, the duo seemed to be losing some of its creative fire. Its next albums, *So Fine* (summer of 1975) and gold *Native Son* (1976), had some interesting tracks, but overall didn't have the spark of earlier releases. Kenny Loggins also was becoming restless about resuming his solo career. The combination of factors led to the group's phasing out before the end of 1976. Columbia issued a greatest-hits album that year, *The Best of Friends.* Later it released another retrospective, *Finale.*

LONE JUSTICE: *Vocal and instrumental group. Members as of 1984: Maria McKee, born Los Angeles, California, 1964; Ryan Hedgecock, born Torrance, California, c. 1960; Marvin Etzioni, born Brooklyn, New York; Don Heffington. Tony Gilkyson added 1985, left 1986. Group reorganized mid-1986 with new band comprising McKee; Shayne Fontayne; Gregg Sutton; Rudy Richman; Bruce Brody.*

At his January 1984 concert in Los Angeles' Universal Ampitheater, a funny thing happened to Willie Nelson. The country superstar was upstaged by a little-known band called Lone Justice. The capacity audience of 6,000 knew it was in for something special from the moment it heard the youthful L.A. group's first number—harbinger of a fast-paced country-rock set spotlighting a throbbing tempo and the spine-tingling, evocative lead vocals of blonde Maria McKee. When the regular set ended, the crowd, all dyed-in-the-wool Nelson fans, roared for an encore, a rare tribute for an opening act. But all of them—and Nelson waiting in the wings—felt it could well be the historic first major appearance of a future super group.

Although the group had a strong instrumental base, its pièce de resistance, of course, was its amazingly poised young lead female singer. Though only 19 at the time, she had started to consider a singing career at 15, urged on by her brother Bryan, a rock musician who at one time had been with a well-regarded local group, Love. In 1980, she made her stage debut as a guest singer for a short-lived band of her brother's called the Bryan MacLean Band. The interest shown by record executive Peter Philbin after one of those shows helped convince her to continue in music, a course she hadn't thought about that much before.

Philbin, on the Columbia Records staff, recalled Maria had been a surprise add-on at the end of the band's set. He told Robert Hilburn of the *Los Angeles Times* (April 7, 1985): "She sang two songs . . . both R&B standards and I was mesmerized. She was only 16, but she had one of those rare voices that does not lay down on a record but jumps right out of the speakers at you." He expressed interest in her if she decided to become a regular member of a group.

When Philbin talked to her, she later told Hilburn: "I was thrilled because he was Bruce Springsteen's guy at Columbia and I was really into Springsteen. I saw Bruce at the Sports Arena—my first rock concert—and I was in shock.

"Up until then, I thought maybe I'd like to be an actress or try to do musical theater on Broadway. I was really involved in the theater department [in high school in Beverly Hills], but Bruce changed all that. . . . I just loved his energy on stage and the fact that he just seemed so happy with his job . . . and he made us all feel so happy.

"I knew I could sing—I had been in school musicals and I had sung in church. [Her devoutly religious Christian family had channeled her early interest toward such music because they felt much of rock'n'roll was morally offensive.] So I began thinking: Maybe I could write some songs some day and play the guitar.' "

Though her brother's band broke up before 1980 was over, word of her ability had reached other parts of the Los Angeles pop-music fraternity. While not agreeing to make any permanent alignment with bands that sought her out, she did make occasional guest appearances with progressive country bands such as Rank & File and Top Jimmy (the Blues Chimney). She still hadn't made her mind up on making the break to full-time performing status when she met guitarist Ryan Hedgecock.

Hedgecock had begun to learn guitar at 15, mostly as a hobby. After several years, he was motivated to do more with his music after a friend played some Grateful Dead records that had strong country and blues influences. He went on to form a rockabilly band that opened for Bryan MacLean one night, providing his first exposure to Maria McKee's talents. He was impressed, but thought she was much older than he was and unapproachable.

After continuing his apprenticeship with a variety of garage and basement groups, he helped form the rockabilly band Bedrock. Playing at a "mini-rockabilly" festival at Angelo's Drive-In in the summer of 1982, he had a chance meeting with Maria (not realizing at first that she was the singer he'd heard two years earlier). Soon they were developing an act of their own featuring updated versions of country songs made famous by such artists as Wanda Jackson, Rose Maddox, and Sparkle More. They managed to get some dates in local country nightclubs, where their performance was heard by a show-business–wise musician named Marvin Etzioni.

The Brooklyn-born Etzioni, who had grown up in California, was more rock- than country-oriented, but he was impressed by what he heard. He told Hilburn: "They were into this real country groove. It was very rough, but there was so much potential. There was this innocence about the whole thing. When I went to their rehearsal, it was just like it must have been walking in on Buddy Holly and the Crickets when they were just getting started. I thought I could help them in terms of song structure and by broadening the focus of their sound."

McKee at first shied away, but after a poorly conceived and ill-received show at Madame Wong's (a major pop club in Los Angeles), she and Ryan agreed they could use some outside assistance and called in Etzioni. Marvin, whose credits included playing bass guitar with the Model (a popular L.A. club band of the 1970s), pitched in to help arrange songs and produce demos including a five-song tape financed by Geffen Records A&R person Carole Childs. (She liked the tape, which included two Etzioni compositions, "Don't Toss Her Away" and "Workin' Late," that later made the debut album, but she couldn't overcome other executives' feelings that the group's sound was too country.) Etzioni also urged Maria and Ryan to write more original songs rather than cover older country and country-rock tunes.

Meanwhile, however, the band passed an important milestone with the acquisition of industry veteran Carlyne Majer as manager. Her interest had been whettted by hearing Maria do a guest duet with Rank & File's Tony Kinman of the Johnny Cash–June Carter hit, "Jackson," when that band was opening for country star John Anderson at L.A.'s Roxy nightclub in April 1983. Even before concluding an agreement with the group that July, Majer was seeking to raise record-industry interest.

Among those she contacted were Childs and her superiors at Geffen, who decided this time it was worth the gamble to sign the group, particularly since there was more rock flavor in its mid-1983 stylings. A major concession Majer required was that the band be brought along slowly rather than rushed into the recording studio. She said: "I think the industry is more responsible for the defeat of talent than just about anything. You'd be amazed at how few people realize the importance of nurturing young artists. Before we signed with Geffen, I went in and asked for at least a year to deliver an album and they were in full agreement. That's pretty rare."

This didn't mean she wanted to hide the band completely from view. After the recording contract was signed with Geffen on October 21, 1983, Majer decided to find a good spot where the group could move from its usual type of club date, where 250 to 300 people might attend, to a much larger venue. She knew Willie Nelson was due in L.A. the following January and decided to pitch her new band as opener. She could do that because she and Nelson were old friends. Even then, she recalled, he was somewhat suspicious before he finally agreed to accepting Lone Justice, a group he'd never heard of before.

The band that had the Nelson audience in an uproar in early 1984 comprised Maria on vocals and guitar, Ryan Hedgecock on lead guitar, Etzioni on bass guitar, and Don Heffington on drums. The excellent reception and the glowing critical mentions inspired band members to work hard to polish material for a debut album. Heffington came to Lone Justice after serving for a stint in Emmylou Harris's Hot Band.

In July 1984, everyone finally felt ready to start the album. With production handled by top-ranked producer Jimmy Iovine, the band spent the next half-year laying down tracks, including a never-before-recorded Tom Petty–Mike Campbell song, ("Ways to be Wicked"), a song by Bryan MacLean ("Don't Toss Us Away"), and a number of band originals that had been featured in their concerts, including "East of Eden," "Soap, Soup and Salvation," and "After the Flood." (*See Petty, Tom, and the Heartbreakers*.)

The album, *Lone Justice,* was released in March 1985 to generally favorable critical comment. Most West Coast critics hailed it, while East Coast writers tended to give grudging praise, admitting the band's great potential but suggesting the considerable rock content might be something of a sellout. John Rockwell of *The New York Times* (April 14, 1985) commented that one problem was his feeling Maria's lyrics weren't strong enough and the other was "that all this shopping around for idioms undercuts the sincerity and directness the band should project. Too much of this disc seems like posing—the assumption of dramatic characters and musical rhetoric extraneous to the band's true roots." But he also agreed: "Miss McKee's voice adapts itself handily to whatever idiom is involved, and the album coheres as an overall statement of tough-woman assertiveness." In support of the LP, the band (augmented by a fifth member, guitarist Tony Gilkyson), set off on an extensive cross-country concert tour as opening act for U2. (*See U2*.)

During 1986, McKee decided to emphasize a new, heavily rock-oriented style and the band was completely reorganized, with only Maria remaining from the previous Lone Justice lineup. Gilkyson went into the band X. (*See X*.) Joining Maria in the new band were Shayne Fontayne on lead guitar, Gregg Sutton on bass guitar, Bruce Brody on keyboards, and Rudy Richman on drums. In November 1986, Geffen released the second Lone Justice album, *Shelter,* a collection with little to remind a listener of the earlier country-rock underpinnings.

LOS LOBOS: *Vocal and instrumental group. Original members, all born Los Angeles, California, David Hidalgo, born c. 1954; Conrad Lozano, born c. 1952; Cesar Rosas, born c. 1954; Louie Perez, born c. 1953. Steve Berlin, born Philadelphia, Pennsylvania, c. 1957.*

East Los Angeles, for many decades the center of Mexican/American life in the City of the Angels, appeared ready to exert a strong impact on the still young rock field in the late 1950s with the emergence of a prospective superstar in teenaged Ritchie Valens. But after his tragic death in a plane crash in 1959, years passed without an artist or group from the area gaining widespread notice. Then, almost 30 years later, a film about his brief career, *La Bamba,* catapulted the band Los Lobos to national and international prominence, the first East L.A. rock act to achieve that since his passing.

The four founding members—Conrad Lozano (vocals, bass, guitarron), Cesar Rosas (lead vocals, guitars, bajo sexto, mandolin), David Hidalgo (lead vocals, guitars, accordion, lap steel, percussion), and Louie Perez (drums, guitar, quinto)—all grew up in East L.A. and still lived there in the late 1980s after Los Lobos had achieved star status. The four became close friends while attending Garfield High School in their home barrio and in the late 1960s became involved in the backyard party band activity that was the milieu of many Chicano teenage musicians. Their interest then was in Beatles-influenced rock, but in the early '70s Hidalgo, Perez, and another friend switched to an emphasis on learning Mexican folk material, particularly Nortenos music from northern Mexico. That became the basis for Los Lobos when it was formed in 1973. The band became a quartet of Hidalgo, Perez, Lozano, and Rosas.

The band played Mexican folk material using acoustic instruments. Rosas told Don Snowden *(Los Angeles Times,* December 18, 1982), "We got satisfaction from being able to play something that was real traditional, our own kind of roots. We were just doing it for the love of the music and would learn songs because they were really tough. They were a challenge to the max because all the cross-rhythms and different things are so difficult to play."

The group gained a sizable following in its own community, but the members were stymied in attempts to get gigs in other parts of the city. They tried to expand their audience by recording some of their folk songs on a self-distributed label, starting with the 1978 LP *Just Another Band from East L.A.* By the end of the '70s, however, the band had started to go to electric guitars along with formats that blended their Mexican roots music with everything from rock and blues to country music. The new repertoire brought increased exposure, including club appearances outside the barrio area. In 1981, band members had a chance meeting with Dave and Phil Alvin of the Blasters, who remembered the group from a program on which it played on Los Angeles Public Broadcasting Station KCET-TV. The Alvins asked the group to open for them at a Whisky-A-Go-Go show on L.A.'s Sunset Strip.

The Los Lobos set won audience approval and attracted attention from local pop music reviewers. One result was an opportunity to provide a Spanish version of the song "Devil with a Blue Dress On" for the soundtrack of the cult comedy film *Eating Raoul.* The performance also helped open doors to more engagements at L.A. area rock clubs that built up a growing fan following that crossed ethnic boundaries. The Whisky set also brought them in contact with saxaphonist/percussionist Steve Berlin, who then was with the Blasters. Berlin was attracted to the group's music and eventually became the fifth member in 1983.

Things soon began to move briskly for the group. They signed with Slash Records and Steve Berlin and T-Bone Burnett produced the Los Lobos label debut, an Extended Play album called *. . . And a Time to Dance.* The track "Anselma" won the Grammy Award for Best Mexican/American Performance of 1983. In the fall of 1984, the band's LP *How Will the Wolf Survive?,* also produced by Berlin and T-Bone Burnett, won raves from many critics, including those from *Time* and the *Los Angeles Times.* The album's quality also helped earn the group a tie for Best Band of the Year in the *Rolling Stone* critics poll. Sharing the honor with them was Bruce Springsteen and the E Street Band.

The group followed with another excellent album, *By the Light of the Moon,* issued by Slash/Warner Brothers (Warner Brothers handles distribution for Slash) in early 1987. By then, the group had another noteworthy credit, its work on the "All Around the World Track" on Paul Simon's 1986 smash LP *Graceland.*

But the real breakthrough was just over the horizon. After the film biography of Valens came out and became a hit with moviegoers, the soundtrack music by Los Lobos created a sensation. The album, *La Bamba,* became a best seller soon after its release in mid-1987 and Los Lobos' single of the title track reached number one in *Billboard* in August and stayed there for several weeks more. Soon after, a second Los Lobos single from the soundtrack, "Come on, Let's Go" (a staple of the band's act for a number of years) charted. Late in the year, the group had another single out, "One Time, One Night" (from *By the Light of the Moon*) which provided it with three discs on *Billboard*'s Hot 100 at the same time. (*See Valens, Ritchie.*)

LOVERBOY: *Vocal and instrumental group from Canada. Original members, 1980s: Paul Dean, born Windemere, Canada, c. 1957; Mike Reno, born Vancouver, Canada; Scott Smith; Doug Johnson; Matt Frenette.* *

In the second half of the 1970s, Vancouver, Canada, gained its place in the pop-music sun as an incubator of promising new rock groups, most notably Heart and Loverboy. Loverboy retained a warmer spot in the emotions of British Columbia fans, though, since Heart's members were from the States, while Loverboy's founders were Canadian-born and-bred. Those two bands retained close ties, though, as symbolized by the hit single "Almost Paradise" recorded by lead singers Ann Wilson of Heart and Mike Reno of Loverboy in 1984. (*See Heart.*)

The founding members of Loverboy—Paul Dean (the group's leader, lead guitarist, and main writer) and Reno—paid plenty of dues before their paths crossed in the late 1970s. Reno claimed: "I was born in the back of a Hillman. Been on the road since I was born. When I was two years old, I was going across Canada in a Hillman." Both were interested in music by their teen years. Dean said: "I woke up one day and said: 'Would I ever like to get a guitar.' I didn't know then that I would end up playing with 13 different bands before I finally hit with Loverboy on the fourteenth try."

Reno, who focused on singing once he joined forces with Paul, started as a drummer. "I bought my first set with money I made with a paper route in Victoria. They were called Made in England Earl Grey drums. I broke the head on my bass drum and couldn't find a replacement. So I reversed sides and painted red around the break and called the group the Bash Band."

Reno, like Dean, worked with a variety of bands in western Canada, typically enduring more frustration than success. In 1978, as a member of the band Moxy, he helped record the album *Under the Lights,* which was released in Canada to something less than overwhelming buyer response. Soon after, he was at loose ends employment-wise when he encountered Dean at a Calgary bar.

Reno told Philip Bashe of *Circus* (April 30, 1982):

---

*Based partly on personal interviews with Irwin Stambler.

"It was funny. We met each other when he was trying to molest the same girl as I was. We were both unemployed at the time, both looking for something better. But before we did anything, we wanted to get the right people involved."

Dean recalled: "The two of us got together in Calgary, though we both were from Vancouver. We'd been in various bands in those cities. Now we hope to say we're from North America. We jammed around a bit with Doug Johnson on keyboards, added a really perfect drummer in Matt Frenette and a bassist since replaced by Scott Smith, got our name and manager, and moved ahead."

The group rehearsed for many months before starting to play clubs in the Calgary area. Before long, band members knew it made sense to shift their locale to Vancouver, where there was a more dynamic rock-club environment. Once there, the group's high-decibel sound wooed sizable numbers of young rock fans and also brought a record contract with a Canadian label.

Loverboy's style reflected Reno and Dean's love for blues-rock and rhythm & blues. Mike said: "I like to sing 'real' and 'strong.' I sing from my heart. I've got kinda blues roots. I followed groups like Free and Journey because I like Steve Perry of Journey. For some of my vocal licks, I'll go blues even if it's heavy rock."

Dean, who sometimes characterized the band's music as Led Zeppelin meets the Cars, commented: "We wanted a distinctive direction. From the start I wanted a sound simultaneously new wave, funky, and heavy. That meant establishing a rhythm & blues bottom with good keyboards work and a powerhouse lead singer. We're a mainstream, straight-ahead band. We feel you should be able to dance to any of our songs. Our typical album hasn't any 2-4 or 7-4 shots. Our music always will have a beat to it so you can put the album on at a party and dance to it or play the whole album on FM and keep the listener interested."

For the band's debut LP, *Loverboy* (issued in Canada in July 1980), Dean wrote most of the material. He noted at the time: "I wrote 50% of the new album and Mike wrote 25% and our keyboards player wrote 25%. But the mix will vary from album to album—I think the next time I'll take 100% of the writing and get all the prestige."

Reno said: "Like most bands, we all throw things into the pot. When all is said and done, whatever tunes are the best, those will make the album. Then the key is to make sure the vocals capture the feel of the lyrics. Take 'The Kid Is Hot Tonight' [a song taking a poke at artists who try to copy successful formats rather than aiming for originality] on our first album—you need to put a sneer in it. We worked on it in the studio to get the right attitude. If we didn't get the attitude, people wouldn't pick up on it."

Canadian fans did, indeed, pick up on it and other songs in the debut LP, including the debut single, "Turn Me Loose." Helping to build momentum were some fortunate concert opportunities including a chance to open for Bob Seger. Dean recalled: "There was a cancellation and we filled it. We played before 27,000 at Toronto. But that wasn't our biggest audience of that period. We did a concert in Edmonton, Alberta, before 41,000. It was a free concert sponsored by the station CHED. After that, the kids made 'Turn Me Loose' number one in the CHED area. We worked with other bands, too, such as Prism and Cheap Trick."

All those things helped the album become a smash success in Canada. By early 1981, it had gone past double-platinum Canadian levels to sell over 170,000 copies. Reports of the group's phenomenal rapport with Canadian fans caused Columbia Records to add the band to its U.S. distribution list. The album was released in the U.S. in October 1980, but didn't make much headway until band members began to do interviews and concerts south of the border. In the spring of 1981, *Loverboy* and the single of "Turn Me Loose" began to make inroads on U.S. charts and the album was certified platinum. During 1981, the band had another best-selling single, "The Kid Is Hot Tonight," and also charted the single "Lady of the Eighties." In the 1981 Canadian Juno Awards (the equivalent of the U.S. Grammies), the band was named Most Promising New Act and Best Rock Band.

During 1981, the band made some headline appearances, but gained widespread exposure by opening for top-ranked bands such as Kansas, ZZ Top, and Journey. Constant touring before arena-size audiences across the U.S. paved the way for the band's next release, *Get Lucky* (Columbia, October 1981), a multiple-platinum seller, accounting for over 3 million copies as of mid-1986.

During 1982, the band continued its strategy of opening for better-known groups, including Foreigner and the Who, but increasingly it could call its own shots as a concert headliner. The Canadian shows included a major homecoming in Vancouver during which the mayor proclaimed May 21 "Loverboy Day." A month earlier, the band had scored a tremendous success in the Juno Awards, winning in six categories: Best Group, Best Album (the debut *Loverboy,*) Best Single ("Turn Me Loose"), Best Composer (Reno and Dean jointly), Best Producer (Dean and Bruce Fairburn jointly), and Best Engineering (Keith Stein and Bob Rock).

In 1982, the band had several singles from *Get*

Lucky on the charts, though none made *Billboard*'s top 20. These included "Working for the Weekend" and "When It's Over" and "Lucky Lady," all of which were backed by videos that received considerable play on the MTV channel as had the earlier one for "Turn Me Loose."

As 1982 went along, it was apparent Loverboy was moving toward star status, at least with fans, though many critics carped about the band's "middle-of-the-road" approach. Dean, happy with the way things were going in general, tried to keep things in perspective. He told Philip Bashe: "Luck had a lot to do with it; luck, timing, everything. It's insane; it doesn't take more than a couple of tunes to take you from being a bar band to a concert band. I have lots of albums in my collection that I think are great, but nobody's ever heard of them."

The band's next LP (*Keep It Up,* mid-1983) became multiple-platinum the following year. Its single "Hot Girls in Love" (widely shown in video form) made *Billboard*'s top 10. The band no longer had to play opening sets, but was able to fill the largest halls throughout the world.

In 1984, Mike Reno took a brief sabbatical to record a duet, "Almost Paradise," with Ann Wilson of Heart for the soundtrack of the film *Footloose.* Whereas almost all Loverboy's repertoire of the time was driving power-rock, in this duet, Reno showed he had an excellent rock ballad touch. The single, released on Columbia, became a top 10 hit—Reno's first.

Reno told a *Los Angeles Times* reporter that he liked doing a ballad, but had no plans to try for a solo career. He also noted: "We always concentrated on the fast rock stuff. We wanted to master that first. But [Loverboy] is starting to get into ballads."

He also stressed he and other band members didn't object to being tabbed as middle-of-the-road artists. "That's where we're at musically. We're commercial. That's a dirty word to some people, but not to us. We're middle-of-the-road and commercial. We're not trying to hide it. We don't really try to be middle-of-the-road. That's the way the songs turn out. That's probably because that's the way we are—the music reflects our personalities. As people, we're in the middle, that comfortable middle. Maybe a few albums down the road we'll change. . . . But it's hard to beat the middle. It'll certainly be tough to leave it. It's certainly been good to us."

And that proved to be so with the band's fourth U.S. LP, the platinum *Lovin' Every Minute of It* (summer 1985), with two singles, (the title song and "This Could Be the Night") entering *Billboard*'s top 10, breaking another barrier the band hadn't previously crossed.

421

Reno continued to be in good voice in 1985–86 concerts despite the high-voltage vocal demands. Pacing was a key, he emphasized. "I can do a pretty good number of dates in a row and feel O.K. The only thing that really gets a vocalist is climate change. If we go from L.A., say, a few hundred miles away where it starts to get dry, I can feel it."

Early voice training had helped Mike, but the others could have problems on backing singing, Dean added. "Mike's a trained vocalist and knows how to cope, but I sometimes have trouble with my voice. In a typical set, we may have 12 to 14 lead vocals and I do only two and feel the strain. You might say take it easier, but it's hard to hold back—that's what rock's all about."

For the 1986 movie success *Top Gun,* Loverboy provided the soundtrack song "Heaven in Your Eyes" (co-written by Dean, Reno, J. Dexter, and M. Moore). In August 1987, Columbia released the band's fifth LP on the label, *Wildfire,* whose songs were featured on the group's 1987–88 concert tour. First single release (which quickly charted) was "Notorious," co-written by Dean, Jon Bon Jovi, and Bon Jovi band guitarist Richie Zambora.

LOVIN' SPOONFUL, THE: *Vocal and instrumental group. Founded in 1965. John Sebastian, born New York, New York, March 17, 1944; Steve Boone, born New York, September 23; Joe Butler, born New York, September 16; Zalman Yanovsky, born Canada. Yanovsky replaced by Jerry Yester, born January 9. Disbanded in 1967.*

The Lovin' Spoonful existed for barely two years, but turned out as many rock hits in that time as most successful groups do in two or three times that life span. A replay of its recordings will bring a smile to the face of those fans who saw the act in the mid-1960s, an act filled with energy, wild humor, and music that was a curious blend of rock, roaring '20s ricky-tick, folk, blues, and in some cases, even downhome hoedown themes.

The two founding members, John Sebastian and Zalman Yanovsky, both came from families in which music was stressed. Sebastian, who grew up in New York's Greenwich Village, gained an early interest in the harmonica from his father, the famous classical harmonica player, John Sebastian, Sr. Sebastian and Yanovsky first came together in the early '60s as members of the Polkish Mugwumps, a short-lived New York group, rounded out by Cass Elliott and Denny Doherty, who later provided half of the Mamas and the Papas. (*See Mamas and the Papas, The.*)

After the Mugwumps broke up, Yanovsky stayed in New York, playing in various groups there while Sebastian moved to Marblehead, Massachusetts, to work as a sail maker and then went on to a folk-music–collecting tour of the South, spending a number of months with blues artist Lightnin' Hopkins. (*See Hopkins, Lightnin'.*) Sebastian met other bluesmen too, including Mississippi John Hurt. One of Hurt's songs had a line, "I love my baby by the lovin' spoonful," that was to become the name of Sebastian's rock group.

By the start of 1965, Sebastian was back in New York, looking for new directions in pop music. Early in the year, he got together with Yanovsky and they brought in Steve Boone and Joe Butler to form a new group. Sebastian handled lead vocals and also played harmonica, guitar, and autoharp. Yanovsky was lead guitarist and singer. (A particular forte of Zal's was comic or nonsense lyrics, such as the song "Bald Headed Lena.") Steve Boone played piano and bass guitar. Joe Butler, who had led a twist band for some years on Long Island, was on drums.

The group's first important appearance was at a New York–area club called the Nite Owl Cafe. It quickly gained a large following for its happy, wild antics and seemingly endless variety of rock melodies and rhythms that Sebastian tossed off with ease.

The group was signed by the relatively small Kama Sutra label and in 1965 was represented on *Billboard*'s top 10 by its first two singles: "Do You Believe in Magic?" and "You Didn't Have to Be So Nice."

The group had such major hits during the year 1966 as the number one "Summer in the City" plus "Daydream," "Rain on the Roof," "Nashville Cats," "Younger Girl," and "Did You Ever Have to Make Up Your Mind?" Other songs demonstrated innovations in rock compositions and arranging, such as "Groovin'," "Jugband Music," "Let the Boy Rock and Roll," "Lovin' You," "Big Noise from Speonk" (a takeoff on Butler's twist-band days in Speonk, Long Island), "Four Eyes" (Sebastian's wry comment on the disadvantages of wearing glasses), and "Bes' Friends."

During this period, Sebastian and the group provided soundtrack music for two major movies: *You're a Big Boy Now* and Woody Allen's comedy hit, *What's Up, Tiger Lily.* Among the songs Sebastian wrote for *You're a Big Boy Now* were "Lonely," "Darlin' Be Home Soon," and "Wash Her Away" (a burlesque of rock music written for a discotheque scene).

The group turned out a number of very successful LPs for Kama Sutra: *Do You Believe in Magic?* (1965), *Daydream* (1966), and *Hums of The Lovin' Spoonful* and the gold *Best of the Lovin' Spoonful* (1967). They also were represented on Elektra Records with *What's Shakin'* (1966).

Coming into 1967, the future seemed to hold tremendous financial and artistic success for the Spoonful. Things began well with a minor single, "Six O'Clock." Later in the year, there were other hits: "She Is Still a Mystery" and "Money." However, the steady grind of one-nighters across the U.S. and Europe was obviously beginning to catch up with the group by midyear. The breaking point came when members of the group were picked up on drug-possession charges. The Spoonful disbanded in late 1967.

One of the reasons for this, as Sebastian later indicated, was the chance the forced layoff gave him to think about the band's musical direction. His conclusion was: "It wasn't fun anymore. The band for about two years was really groovy. I guess what made it groovy was the chemistry of the people in the group. But after about two years, it began to get really muddied. We could have gone on cranking it along for a few more years and started to collect the enormous sums we were just beginning to get. Of course, breaking up wouldn't have been the best thing from a businessman's point of view. Lots of people were really brought down, but they were concerned with money rather than the music."

Of the four, Sebastian had the most subsequent success as a mellow, folkish solo act. His albums on Reprise sold adequately in the 1970s, while in 1976, he hit *Billboard*'s top 10 for one week with the single "Welcome Back" from the TV program "Welcome Back Kotter."

LOWE, NICK: *Singer, guitarist, songwriter, record producer. Born England, March 25, 1949.*

It's possible that had Nick Lowe not demonstrated abilities in so many areas of pop music, from record production to performing, that he might have made his mark as a superstar during the 1970s. As it was, he set a hectic pace for himself that crammed more into each year than many people in the field achieve in a career. If his own name didn't ring as familiarly with concert goers as it deserved, his production efforts helped bring fame to many other contemporaries, including such luminaries as Elvis Costello, Chrissie Hynde and the Pretenders, and Graham Parker.

His combined efforts as performer and producer in 1978, to take one of many notable years, led to a special award in the *London Daily Mirror*'s pop-music readers poll for Most Outstanding Contribution to Pop Music of the Year.

He acknowledged both the advantages and disadvantages of his multipronged endeavors that year in an interview with Bobby Abrams of *BOMP* magazine. "I think there's a lot of people who could do what I'm doing. I don't think that I'm particularly talented. What I have got which a lot of people don't is an eye for style and for people with style. I can recognize it. I don't even think that I have it, but I can certainly recognize people who have got it, which I think is a talent in itself. So, I'm just a jack of all trades and a master of none. I'm like a music fan and I'm in this position where I can do all of this. I have a very temporary attitude to the whole thing. I don't take it seriously and I don't think it will last forever. As soon as I stop thinking like that, I'll be bad. I don't want to go through all that pop star crap."

Lowe grew up under the influence of such '50s and '60s artists as Elvis Presley, the Beatles, and Rolling Stones. Like many of his generation, he dreamt of a music career by his early teens and learned enough guitar chords to team up with schoolmates in various loose band organizations. This coalesced into a longer-lasting arrangement when he accompanied school friend Brinsley Schwarz (a budding guitar expert) and keyboards player Bob Andrews into the group Kippington Lodge in 1965.

That band made some inroads into the English club circuit and was good enough to win nominal support from the Parlophone/EMI label. This led to the release of several singles in the second half of the '60s. In 1969, the band reorganized under the name Brinsley Schwarz, adding a fourth permanent member, drummer Billy Rankin. Lowe's importance was emphasized in the songwriting credits of the group's debut LP, the October 1970 *Brinsley Schwarz*—Nick wrote or co-wrote all the songs. On the next release, *Despite It All* (1971), which included his excellent "Country Girl," he penned all but one number.

The band's reputation picked up momentum with the addition of guitarist/songwriter Ian Gomm (later to establish himself as a solo artist and band leader). The Schwarz group is considered the central and most accomplished alignment in the British pub-rock movement of the early to middle 1970s. In 1972, the band was represented by two more LPs: *Silver Pistol* and *Nervous on the Road*. While Lowe wrote most of the material, Gomm and Andrews provided a number of entries. The group's recorded material of the next few years included the 1973 U.K. release on the United Artists label, *Please Don't Ever Change,* and the 1974 U.A. release, *The New Favorites of Brinsley Schwarz,* produced by Dave Edmunds (later to join Lowe in the group Rockpile) at his Rockfield Studios in Wales. Among the tracks on the LP was Lowe's composition "(What's So Funny 'bout) Peace, Love and Understanding," which Elvis Costello later recorded. During that year, Edmunds and the Schwarz group joined forces for an extensive concert tour. The band also worked with Edmunds on the 1974 soundtrack for David Bowie's *Ziggy Stardust* film, calling themselves Dave Edmunds and the Electricians. During 1974, Lowe played backup on Edmunds' RCA album *Subtle as a Flying Mallet*.

The Brinsley Schwarz era was coming to a close. It recorded its final single in March 1975 and disbanded, with Schwarz and Rankin joining Sean Tyla and Martin Belmont in another pub-rock band, Ducks Deluxe, while Lowe aligned himself with Jake Riviera under the name Modern Boys Productions. This team turned out a number of send-up type singles, including "Bay City Rollers We Love You," "Rollers Show," (both under the name Tartan Horde) and, as the Disco Bros., such singles as "Let's Go to the Disco"/"Everybody Dance."

Meanwhile, the band Brinsley Schwarz was gone but not forgotten. Its first two albums were reissued in the U.S. in a two-record set, *Brinsley Schwarz*, on Capitol Records in 1978. That same year, United Artists released *Fifteen Thoughts of Brinsley Schwarz* in the U.S.

Lowe's next main efforts were channeled into material for the newly formed Stiff Records (organized by Riviera and former Brinsley manager Dave Robinson). The first single on the label, which Nick wrote and co-produced with Riviera, was his "Heart of the City"/"So It Goes." Soon Stiff had signed a number of promising new acts, drawing on Nick's experience to help develop showcase recordings for many of them. On the 1977 *Bunch of Stiffs* sampler, besides his own "I Love My Label," Nick produced tracks by Wreckless Eric ("Whole Wide World"), Magic Michael, Stone's Masonry, and Elvis Costello ("Less Than Zero," the A side of his debut release). During that period, Nick wrote or co-wrote (with Dave Edmunds) a number of songs both he and Dave featured in recordings or concerts, including "Here Comes the Weekend," "Little Darlin'," "What Did I Do Last Night," and "I Knew the Bride."

Nick's debut album on Stiff, the EP *Bowi*, featured what were to become his trademark songs: "Marie Provost," "Shake That Rat," "Endless Sleep," and "Born a Woman." (The last two were also issued as a single.) In the spring of 1977, the newly formed Edmunds/Lowe quartet Rockpile played some of those numbers on its initial concert series. Lowe recordings also were presented during the year on other Stiff samplers: *Stiff Live Stiffs* and *Hits Greatest Stiffs*.

As if recording his own material and touring extensively weren't enough to occupy his time, Nick sandwiched in a breath-taking schedule of production work. 1976–78 production included work with the Damned, singles and the debut LP *Damned Damned Damned* (one of the seminal punk releases);

with Alberto y Los Trios Paranoias, a "snuff-rock" punk satirical EP; Graham Parker's debut LP, one track on his second album, his third LP, his *Live at Marble Arch* session, and the *Pink Parker* EP; Elvis Costello's first three LPs; Chrissie Hynde and the Pretenders' hit debut single "Stop Your Sobbin'"; and with Mickey Jupp, half the LP *Juppanese*.

From April 19 to June 7, 1978, Rockpile was featured on a U.S. tour that included Elvis Costello and the Attractions and Mink DeVille on the same bill. (The other members of Rockpile, besides Lowe and Edmunds, were Billy Bremmer and Terry Williams.) Later in the year, Rockpile was the backbone of the Edmunds' LP *Tracks on Wax 4* containing two Lowe originals ("Television" and "Heart of the City") and three Edmunds/Lowe collaborations ("Deborah," "What Looks Best on You," and "Never Been in Love").

During 1978, Lowe began to develop a solo career. His debut LP was titled *Jesus of Cool* in England, but came out in the U.S. on the Columbia label in March 1978 as *Pure Pop for Now People*. The album won enough attention to make lower U.S. chart levels. A similar performance was achieved by his second Columbia release, *Labour of Lust* (1979). After a gap of several years, Lowe surfaced again with his Columbia solo LPs, *Nick the Knife* (1982) and *The Abominable Showman* (1983).

In the 1980s, Lowe continued to divide his activities between production, some new songwriting efforts, and occasional touring on his own or as part of other groups. He also joined with another illustrious show business family by marrying Carlene Carter, member of the Carter Family of country music renown, stepdaughter of Johnny Cash, and a strong-voiced country-rock-pop singer in her own right.

Lowe continued to work on various projects with Dave Edmunds, though for a time in the mid-'80s, they were on the outs. Edmunds once told a reporter: "I don't need Nick Lowe. I'm sure I could walk onto a stage without him. I just want him to be there. It wouldn't be much fun without him. It wouldn't be as exciting. You just look around, and everyone's grooving. And I love it when Nick starts grooving. 'Cos I start grooving. Everyone starts grooving."

In 1984, Columbia issued Nick's fifth album, *Nick Lowe and His Cowboy Outfit*. The Cowboy Outfit band comprised Paul Carrack on keyboards, Martin Belmont on guitar, and Bobby Irwin on drums. The first single from the LP, "Half a Boy and Half a Man," was a top 10 hit in many European nations. In mid-1985, Nick and Cowboy Outfit had another LP in record stores, *The Rose of England*. In late 1985, the single "I Knew the Bride (When She Used to Rock'n'Roll)" from the LP was on U.S. hit lists.

During 1986, Lowe completed production work on a new Elvis Costello LP, *Blood and Chocolate,* and later played rhythm guitar on a number of Elvis's 1987 concerts. In March 1988, Columbia issued his seventh album on the label, *Pinker and Prouder Than Previous.* One track, "Lovers Jamboree," reunited him with Edmunds, who served as producer for the number.

(See Bowie, David; Cash, Johnny; Costello, Elvis; Edmunds, Dave; Hynde, Chrissie, and the Pretenders; Parker, Graham.)

LYMON, FRANKIE: *See Teenagers, The.*

LYNYRD SKYNYRD: *Vocal and instrumental group. Members (mid-1970s): Ronnie Van Zant, born Jacksonville, Florida, 1949, died near Mc-Comb, Mississippi, October 20, 1977; Allen Collins, born Jacksonville, Florida, c. 1949; Gary Rossington, born Jacksonville, Florida, c. 1949; Steve Gaines, born Florida, c. early 1950s, died near McComb, Mississippi, October 20, 1977; Artimus Pyle, born Spartanburg, South Carolina; Billy Powell, born Florida, c. early 1950s; Leon Wilkeson, born Florida, c. early 1950s. Group disbanded in late 1977, reorganized in 1987 with Rossington, Collins, Powell, Wilkerson, Pyle, Ed King, Randall Hall, Johnny Van Zant.*

It's possible to find all sorts of strange portents and symbols in the events leading up to the tragic plane crash in October 1977 that wrote "finis" to the Lynyrd Skynyrd band. The band had just released an album, *Street Survivors,* whose cover showed the seven musicians seemingly engulfed in flames (achieved by setting fire to an old set on the Universal Studios back lot). Some of the songs in the album reflected on what appeared to be self-destructive urges among many of the members from which they always previously managed to escape.

Even so, five of the seven bandsmen survived when an aging Convair 240 plowed into swampy ground near McComb, Mississippi. Unfortunately, the two who failed to come through were perhaps the key members of that group: lead singer/songwriter Ronnie Van Zant (whose younger brother, Donnie, starred in another successful band, .38 Special) and guitarist/songwriter Steve Gaines. Gaines' sister, Cassie (a singer with the band), also perished. Van Zant on several occasions commented on knowing success could be ephemeral, but his untimely passing occurred just when things seemed brightest for his band and when the mantle of number one country-blues-rock group in the South had shifted from the Allman Brothers to his boogie band from Jacksonville.

Van Zant was one of a trio of Jacksonville high schoolers who decided to form a band at a time when the Allmans, also Floridians, had been playing professionally for close to a half-decade. The other two were Gary Rossington and Allen Collins, who met in 1965, Gary recalled, when he was in eighth grade. A year later, they met Ronnie at a time when sports was the prime interest, not music. The three played Pop Warner baseball together and, Ronnie later recalled, he in particular dreamt of a sports career. "I went as far as playing [American] Legion ball. The next step would have been AA [minor league ball]. I played center field. I had the highest batting average in the league one year and a good arm—you've gotta have a good arm to play center field. Gary was good too, but he gave it all up when he got to like the Rolling Stones."

Gary's enthusiasm for rock music, he told interviewer John Swenson, came from seeing the Stones perform on the Ed Sullivan Show. Soon he was spending hours practicing guitars while urging Collins and Van Zant to join him in a band. "It happened slow at first. It took a long time to learn how. We were trying to learn from people, no lessons or anything, just watch. After about four years playin' at parties, playin' anywhere we could, we were makin' about $20 a week.

"We'd play anything on the radio, 'Satisfaction,' 'Day Tripper'—we were into Yardbirds, Blues Magoos. We used to play at clubs at night and go to school during the day. They called us a psychedelic band and it was hard for us to get work at dances because people wanted top 40."

During those years the three friends and whomever they got to play with them changed band names almost as fast as they changed socks. Their titles included the Noble Five, Wildcats, Sons of Satan, Pretty Ones, and One Per Cent. The last one stuck the longest before the band became Lynyrd Skynyrd. (Lynyrd Skynyrd was a takeoff on the name of their high school gym teacher, Leonard Skinner, who had them expelled from school for having long hair. Later on, when Skinner was working in real estate and the band was a success, everyone let bygones be bygones and Skinner introduced the group at one concert.)

In those early years, Gary reminisced to Swenson: "We used to practice after school until the cops would run us off every night, then on the weekends, early in the morning, all day, all night. Then every once in a while we'd play. Ronnie had a car and we'd load his car up about five times to run the equipment over there. Sometimes we'd do it all ourselves, get our parents to drop us off with our amps. All our parents helped us out. We were lucky enough; even though they gave us a hard time, they gave us a pull too, findin' places for us to practice, they'd sign for our amps and stuff.''

At the start of the 1970s, the band finally began to make some headway, partly through acquisition of an Atlanta-based manager, Alan Walden. At that time, under the name One Per Cent, it was a quintet comprising Van Zant on lead vocals, Collins and Rossington on guitars, Larry Junstrom on bass guitar, and Bob Burns on drums. By then, Van Zant and other band members were writing original songs, some of which were laid down on a rough demonstration tape that Walden asked his partners in Muscle Shoals Sound Productions in Muscle Shoals, Alabama, to consider as a basis for recording an album at Muscle Shoals Sound Studios.

Jimmy Johnson (a co-owner of the studio part of the organization along with Barry Beckett) was impressed. ''I like Ronnie's voice,'' he said, ''and I liked the guitars I heard on their demo tape. So I agreed to produce them without even meeting the band, just because I liked the demo. Ronnie had a very unique voice.''

The group signed with the production company and got ready to record an album in September 1971. Just before that, Burns announced he was leaving. The others frantically sought a replacement, finally choosing Rickey Medlow, a guitarist turned drummer.

Johnson said: ''We cut 'Freebird,' 'Preacher's Daughter,' and about one or two other things the first week. They made periodic visits back over the next six months, going back to Jacksonville to play clubs and one-nighters, anything that Alan could get for them.

''They were very inexperienced and insecure in the studio. In fact, the first time Skynyrd ever recorded [professionally] was in our studio. They didn't know much about recording at the time, so we basically taught them the ropes. They worked very hard and ended up writing 'Sweet Home Alabama' about their feelings from working in Muscle Shoals.''

After the first of those sessions, Junstrom moved to Miami with his parents and was replaced on bass by Greg Walker. Those early sessions resulted in 11 tracks that were submitted to almost every major label, with no takers. Undaunted, Johnson arranged for the band to record six more songs, including another due to become one of Lynyrd Skynyrd's best-liked number, ''Simple Man.''

Johnson remembered: ''I felt a big improvement the second time around. They had a new drummer [actually their old drummer, Bob Burns, who had returned] and a new bass player [Leon Wilkeson, who replaced Walker] and a batch of fresh songs. Musically they were getting better. The guitars—

Rossington and Collins—were really getting together, and the group was better acquainted with how to play in the studio. We cut what I considered better stuff on this next go-round.''

For various reasons, including misplaying of the tape by one potential label, the material fared little better. But the tracks were to resurface later when Lynyrd Skynyrd existed only on recordings.

The experience gained from those efforts and increased exposure in concerts outside the Jacksonville area, which helped give band members greater confidence in their future. One result of the broader touring was acquisition of a new guitarist, Ed King, whom band members came to know while opening for the band he was with, Strawberry Alarm Clock. With King on board, Lynyrd Skynyrd developed a unique style based on playing driving country-blues-rock with a three-guitar attack, an approach varied, Van Zant noted, only for a short period in 1975, when the band experimented with the use of two lead guitarists.

In 1973, after rock producer-performer Al Kooper agreed to handle the band through his Sounds of the South label, Lynyrd Skynyrd at long last gained a major label affiliation, MCA. (*See Kooper, Al.*) The band's debut on MCA, *Pronounced Leh-Nerd Skin-Nerd,* came out that year. Backed by extensive touring, mostly as an opening act, the gold album helped establish the band as a strong contender for southern blues-rock honors. This was given increased momentum by an equally exciting second MCA collection, the gold *Second Helping,* with the top 10 single ''Sweet Home Alabama.'' The band began to get widespread publicity both for its hard-driving rock performance and its off-stage hell-for-leather antics.

During those years, the band continued to change, though Van Zant, Collins, and Rossington remained at their posts. Burns left again and was replaced on drums by Artimus Pyle. The band became a seven-man group with the addition of Billy Powell on keyboards. Wilkeson continued as bass guitarist, though, until the band's flame was snuffed out in 1977.

Though increasingly popular as a headliner, the band seemed to slip a notch or two creatively. Its third LP on MCA, the gold 1975 *Nuthin' Fancy,* though it contained a rip-roaring track called ''Saturday Night Special,'' seemed much tamer than its two predecessors. The gold *Gimme Back My Bullets* (1976) was even weaker, perhaps reflecting the loss of Ed King, who left in 1975, pleading exhaustion from the band's frenetic tour schedule. His place was taken by Steve Gaines, brother of a woman backup singer, Cassie Gaines, who toured with the band. Once Gaines settled in, he proved to have not only good guitar skills, but first-rate songwriting talents that promised to give a new thrust to the group's future repertoire.

The band's first live album, the platinum double-disc *One More (for) from the Road* (1976), seemed to set the band back on track.

But then came a setback that could have ended the band's history in 1976. On Labor Day weekend, Rossington and Collins made headlines with separate car crashes. After the incident was over, it was agreed that the band needed to "grow up."

Ronnie Van Zant later told Cameron Crowe of the *Los Angeles Times* (October 24, 1976) that he was determined to bring hijinks to an end. The two friends were assessed heavy fines by other members. Van Zant said: "It's a terrible thing when you get behind the wheel and you're so drunk that you can't drive a car to begin with. Those boys will pay for it. Allen hit a parked Volkswagen and knocked it across an empty parking lot. That was just a fender bender compared to Gary.

"I can't tell you how mad I got at him for that. We're glad he's gonna make it, he's tremendously lucky to be alive . . . but it was his fault. He passed out at the wheel of his brand new Ford Torino, with his foot on the gas. He knocked down a telephone pole, split an oak tree, and did $7,000 worth of damage to a house. That's being just plain stupid. I told him that on his hospital bed." The accidents also cost the band a lucrative concert date with Aerosmith that weekend at Anaheim Stadium in Anaheim, California.

Some of those events came in for comment in the Collins-Van Zant song "Oooh That Smell," on the next LP: "Whiskey bottles and brand new cars . . . There's too much coke and too much smoke/Too much going on inside you." When the band members got to work on that next album in 1976, of course, there was no inkling of what was in store. The tracks of that LP reflected new-found exuberance and writing skills that built on the fine work in the first two MCA studio collections. Called *Street Survivors,* the LP was dynamic and up-tempo from the throbbing initial comments on groupies ("What's Your Name," written by Rossington and Van Zant) to the hard-rocking arrangement of Merle Haggard's "Honky Tonk Night Time Man." The impact of Steve Gaines is felt in such songs as the boogie-woogie rocker "I Know a Little" and his country-blues collaborations with Van Zant, "You Got That Right" and "I Never Dreamed." Gaines also contributed the one relatively slow track, the blues-rock "Aint No Good Life."

The platinum album undoubtedly would have been a best-seller even without the tragic events that ended Van Zant's and the Gaines' lives and made headlines throughout the U.S. and Europe. To some,

the shattering blow of the plane crash might have seemed symbolic of the band's reputed devil-may-care life-style. But there was evidence that the group was committed to a less destructive approach.

Van Zant had told Crowe in late 1976: "You know, the biggest change in myself that I've noticed is that for the first time I'm really thinking about the future. I'm 27 now and I've got a baby girl and I plan to stick around and watch her grow up. I also plan to collect for the last 10 years of self-abuse."

Though Collins and Rossington survived, they would not try to recreate the old band without Van Zant. They instead formed a new group, the Rossington-Collins Band that continued to record on MCA. (*See Rossington-Collins Band, The.*)

For its part, MCA continued to release albums of earlier material. The first of those, the platinum *Skynyrd's First . . . And Last* (1978), was drawn from the recordings Jimmy Johnson had labored over back in 1971–72. In 1979, MCA issued a two-disc retrospective of the band's hits, *Gold and Platinum,* which went gold and then platinum.

During the summer of 1987, almost a decade after the plane crash that had abruptly ended the band's career, plans were completed for a reorganized Lynyrd Sknyrd group to conduct a memorial concert tour starting with a September 6 appearance at Charlie Daniels' Volunteer Jam in Nashville, Tennessee. Lineup included original band alumni Collins, Rossington, Powell, Wilkerson, and Pyle plus Ed King on guitar and vocals (King had performed with some of the original band aggregations), Randall Hall on guitar and, on lead vocals, Ronnie Van Zant's brother Johnny. Coinciding with the group's re-emergence was the release by MCA of a new LP, *Legends. Legends* contained songs selected by current band members from MCA archives. All those featured Ronnie Van Zant's vocals and some spotlighted the late Steve Gaines. However, it was noted, all the tracks had been overdubbed and/or remixed.

MADONNA: *Singer, songwriter, actress, record producer. Born Bay City, Michigan, August 16, 1959.*

In the mid-1980s, it would almost have been easier to make an appointment to see President Reagan than to get a ticket to attend a concert by Madonna. In about as meteoric a rise as has occurred in pop music, the singer/actress went from a complete unknown to a fledgling superstar in little over a year. Her first concert tour in 1985 brought turnaway crowds to every performance. The available tickets for her three shows at the 6,250-seat Universal Ampitheatre in Los Angeles were gone in a matter of hours. An official of the computer ticket outlet,

Ticketmaster, commented: "The demand was unbelievable. We could've sold 100,000 tickets, if we had them."

Many cynical show business experts had thought her sensationally successful debut album and videos of 1984 might mark the peak of the young torch-voiced artist's career. But Madonna made believers out of them by turning out an even more favored follow-up in 1985. By 1986, she had quickly built on her musical breakthroughs to carve what looked like a major niche for herself in films as well.

It was indeed heady wine for a girl who grew up in the relatively sedate environment of Bay City, Michigan. Madonna Louise Veronica Ciccone was named after her mother and knew what it was like to be part of a crowd as part of a large family of five brothers and two sisters. Perhaps to draw attention to herself, she showed a flair for dramatics as a child. She was the subject of a super-8 movie a friend put together when she was in the eighth grade and proved eager to take part in school shows. She appeared in plays during her years at three Catholic schools. At home, she also took piano lessons and in her teens began ballet classes. She progressed well enough in ballet to gain a dance scholarship to the University of Michigan in the mid-1970s.

Her stay at the university was short. She left school for the bright lights of New York, arriving in 1978 with $35 in her pocket. She was able to get a tryout with the Alvin Ailey Dance Troupe and made the roster, but didn't stay long. She then moved over to a job as an assistant to Pearl Lange of the Martha Graham Dance group.

Her interest in dance, though, was giving way to greater fascination with the music field. She made contacts with members of the small groups trying to surface in the polyglot big-city entertainment environment. It was a kaleidoscope of shifting associations, occasional engagements in underground venues, and the chance for a newcomer such as Madonna to pick up experience as a singer, instrumentalist, and fledgling songwriter. It looked like she might make a breakthrough when an audition as a singer/dancer for French disco artist Patrick Hernandez led to a move to Paris.

That proved a false start and Madonna soon was back in New York, occupied again with a variety of music and dance activities that went largely unnoticed by the critics covering the entertainment scene. During those early 1980s, Madonna worked with various pickup bands when she could while spending her free hours writing songs and making occasional demonstration tapes. She made the rounds of small clubs where members of the music industry tended to hang out as she sought contacts that might further her career. This finally paid off when a four-track demo on which she sang some of her original compositions brought a contract from Sire Records, one of Warner Brothers' subsidiaries.

At 22, Madonna found herself in the recording studios under the aegis of a major company. Still, big labels release dozens of debut albums by unknowns every year, most of whom remain unknowns. Initially there was nothing to indicate her first collection, *Madonna* (July 1983), would do any better than countless other debuts. But disc jockeys started playing her tracks in disco clubs and soon after, some of the songs were added to the playlist of black music stations. Warner Brothers executives began to pay more attention to Madonna, and promoted her through high tech videos and carefully planned singles releases.

The album hit number one on the *Billboard* lists in 1984, rolling up sales to triple-platinum levels (3 million copies) by the end of 1985. During 1984, Madonna placed two singles in *Billboard*'s top 10: "Borderline" and "Lucky Star." *Billboard*'s 1984 year-end rankings placed her at number three in both the Top Pop Album Artists, Female, and Top Pop Singles Artists, Female, classifications.

Though she didn't tour in 1984, Madonna was hardly resting. She was occupied with the movies: a cameo role in *Vision Quest* and a starring role in the punk detective comedy *Desperately Seeking Susan*. She also was spending much of her time working on her second LP, the platinum, number one *Like a Virgin*. The first single release from the LP, the title song, rose to number one on the charts during December 1984.

The movie *Vision Quest* came out in early 1985 and, while the film fared poorly with audiences, the song Madonna performed in her brief appearance, "Crazy for You," proved a winner. At one point in April, Madonna had two singles in the top five: "Crazy for You" on Geffen Records and, from the *Like a Virgin* album, "Material Girl." Both songs rose to number one in the U.S. nationally or regionally at one time or another. Making matters more confusing for Warner record promoters was still another release from a third source, the single "In the Groove" from the film *Desperately Seeking Susan*. A video of that number, quickly snapped up for exhibition on MTV and other video outlets, then began competing for broadcast time with the one of "Material Girl."

Such a release schedule seemed at odds with normal record-industry planning. In fact, reports came out about "enormous arguments" between officials at the Warners record operation and executives of Warner Brothers Films, which had issued the movie *Vision Quest*. The film people insisted on the release timing of their single because they hoped the soundtrack LP would improve flagging box-office receipts.

While Eddie Rosenblatt, president of Warner Brothers' Geffen Records label, later acknowledged there had been a "major debate," he told Patrick Goldstein of the *Los Angeles Times:* "In retrospect, the concern may have been unwarranted. After all, the evidence points to the fact that there's plenty of room for both records."

Madonna, of course, had been an innocent bystander to the behind-the-scenes arguments. But her popularity had proven so great that she defied the normal odds to gain successes with a bewildering array of simultaneous projects. Not only did all her recordings do as well as anyone could hope for, but her work in *Desperately Seeking Susan* proved her considerable acting potential, including offbeat comedy.

She came in for what could have been, in decades past, publicity that might have proven a career stopper for other performers. This took the form of topless photos in *High Society* magazine. It turned out she had not been posing nude; the pictures were stills from a scene in *A Certain Sacrifice,* a movie she had made earlier in her career. Film producer Stephen Lewicki stated he had been contacted by the magazine for permission to publish the stills and he had refused because he didn't want the movie characterized as pornographic. The shots had been published in spite of that. He maintained that one of the film's themes was "the exorcism from society of predatory pornography."

Whatever the basic facts of the case, in the environment of the 1980s, music fans could care less. The incident was no more than a minor ripple in a triumphant 12 months. By the end of 1985, Madonna's second album had accounted for multiplatinum record sales of over 6 million copies. Besides "Like a Virgin," "Material Girl," "Crazy for You," and "In the Groove," she placed "Angel" and "Dress You Up" on top chart levels in the U.S. and around the world. In *Billboard's* year-end review, Madonna ranked number one in three major categories: Top Pop Album Artist, Female; Top Pop Singles Artist, Female; and Top Pop Artist (singles and LPs combined). In the 1985 Grammy Awards, she was nominated as a finalist for Best Pop Vocal Performance, Female, for the single "Crazy for You."

She made worldwide headlines for her marriage to volatile young movie idol Sean Penn on August 16, 1985, on a bluff overlooking the Pacific Ocean in Malibu, California. Soon after the wedding the two went to work as co-stars in *Shanghai Surprise,* a movie produced by ex-Beatle George Harrison for late 1986 release that proved a candidate for one of the poorest releases of the mid-1980s. Her third album, *True Blue* (July 1986), contained nine songs, all co-written by Madonna. The first single from the album, "Live to Tell," the theme from Sean Penn's 1986 film *At Close Range,* quickly rose to number one in *Billboard.* A second single from the album, "Papa Don't Preach," also hit number one.

Meanwhile the Penn/Madonna relationship made less romantic headlines, often focusing on brawls Penn was involved in about Madonna or other matters amid reports of their marriage's imminent breakup. In November 1987, for instance, it was disclosed she had had divorce papers served on Penn, but then it was reported they had reconciled. Earlier in that year, a new movie starring Madonna, *Who's That Girl,* was released, accompanied by a soundtrack album on Warner Brothers. The LP and the "Who's That Girl" concert tour proved far more satisfying than the film. In November 1987, Warner Brothers issued an album of extended versions of her danceable stylings, *You Can Dance,* that did well with record buyers well into 1988.

MAMAS AND THE PAPAS, THE: *Members (mid-1960s): John Phillips, born Parris Island, South Carolina, August 30, 1935; Dennis Doherty, born Halifax, Nova Scotia, Canada, November 19, 1941; Cass Elliott, born Baltimore, Maryland, September 19, 1941, died London, England, July 29, 1974; Michelle Gilliam Phillips, born Long Beach, California, June 4, 1945 (some '60s articles gave the date as April 6, 1944). Group broke up in the late 1960s, was reformed in 1982 with John Phillips; Doherty; Elaine "Spanky" McFarlane, born June 19; Mackenzie Phillips.*

For roughly three years in the mid-1960s, the Mamas and the Papas were one of the most successful and versatile groups in popular music. The combination of two men and two women was somewhat unusual for a period when 99% of all rock bands were 100% male. The group also bridged the musical spectrum from folk to rock, which wasn't surprising, because all of the members had begun their careers when the folk boom was threatening to displace rock. Besides having a direct impact on the field with songs of its own, the band's influence included helping to bring about the famous Monterey International Pop Festival of 1967, which helped showcase such coming stars as Janis Joplin, Jimi Hendrix, and the Jefferson Airplane. While the original group was no longer active in the 1970s, in the early 1980s a reorganized foursome brought new luster to the group's name.

The act's founder, John Edmund Andrew Phillips (son of a career officer in the Marines), had been active in folk music as early as 1957. His route to a music career was a somewhat disjointed one. He grew up in Virginia, where he attended a Catholic private school, Linton Hall, and displayed considerable athletic skill. By his midteens, he was well over 6 feet tall and won allstate honors in track and basketball. He alternated between dropping out (driving a Coca-Cola truck at one point) and attending college, spending time at various schools including the University of Virginia and George Washington University before winning an appointment to the U.S. Naval Academy. An intramural sports injury plus a growing interest in music caused him to finally quit school in favor of life in Greenwich Village, the Bohemian area of New York City, starting in 1957.

When he met Holly Michelle Gilliam in New York in 1962, he was a member of a promising folk trio, the Journeymen. Gilliam had attended Marshall High School in Long Beach, California, and came to New York to pursue a modeling career. After she married John in 1962, she switched her attention to music, sometimes appearing on the same show with her husband as a vocalist.

Cass Elliott (born Ellen Naomi Cohen) grew up amid comfortable surroundings in and around Washington, D.C. She took piano lessons in elementary school and later took up guitar because of her enjoyment of folk music. She sometimes sang at school functions at George Washington High School in Alexandria, Virginia, and Forest Park High School in Baltimore. Her parents had plans for her to attend one of the more important women's colleges in the area, but obese Cass, enamoured of show business, moved to New York in the early 1970s, where she gained considerable local attention as a member of a Greenwich Village folk group, the Big Three. Among the many Villageites who followed her performances with respect was John Phillips. Before Phillips asked Cass to join his new group, she won attention from rock fans for her driving vocals with the Mugwumps, which also included Dennis Doherty and future Lovin' Spoonful mainstays John Sebastian and Zal Yanovsky. (*See Lovin' Spoonful, The.*)

The last member of the Mamas and Papas, Dennis Gerard Stephen Doherty, grew up in Canada and became interested in a pop music career while attending St. Patrick's High in Halifax. By the time he made his first public appearance with a local Halifax group when he was 15, he had learned trombone, guitar, and bass. He recorded for Epic with the folkish Halifax Three before he made his way to New York to try to make it in the big time.

After the Journeymen disbanded in 1963, Phillips came up with the idea of a less folk-oriented group consisting of both men and women. He lined up Cass and Dennis to work with him and his wife and all

four went to a Caribbean Island for a while to rehearse their new act. When Phillips was satisfied with the group and some of the original compositions he had written for them, he moved his base of operations to Hollywood, California. There he settled upon producer Lou Adler as his manager and the result was the formation of a new record company, Dunhill.

In 1966, their first singles began to make the hit charts. "California Dreamin'" became one of the major hits of the year, though it took three months before it began to make its way to the top. "Monday, Monday," on the other hand, moved into the top 10 almost as soon as it was released, selling over 160,000 copies the first day it went on sale. For a time, the group's progress was threatened by a breakup between John and Michelle. She was replaced briefly during one of the group's well-attended tours, but the critics felt the new alignment was not as good. However, John and Michelle settled their marital differences for the time being and she rejoined the group.

With their well-crafted lyrics and gorgeous harmonies, the group consistently had both singles and albums on the charts during 1967 and 1968, though none of their singles sold in the millions during these periods. However, the act's first four albums moved into the top 10 with *If You Can Believe Your Eyes and Ears* and gold record awards won by *The Mamas and the Papas* (1966) and *The Mamas and the Papas Deliver* (1967).

As the 1960s came to a close, though, so did the saga of the Mamas and the Papas. The dissolution was not caused by their loss of popularity, but by the desire of some members to follow individual careers and the renewal of personal difficulties in John and Michelle's marriage, climaxed by a 1968 divorce.

After the quartet disbanded, reissues of their recordings continued to come out. Those included the Dunhill albums *The Mamas and the Papas: Sixteen of Their Greatest Hits (1969), A Gathering of Flowers* (1970), and *The Mamas and the Papas' Twenty Golden Hits* (1973). Some of the original group's recordings were used in film soundtracks of the 1970s and '80s.

Following the split, Cass occupied herself with losing some of her amazing weight, dueting with Dave Mason (*see Mason, Dave*), and building a moderately successful solo career. In 1974, she was found dead in a London hotel room, reportedly from choking on a ham sandwich.

John, who reputedly was a millionaire from his career with the Mamas and the Papas, settled in Malibu, California, to work on new compositions and develop ideas for possible movies. In collaboration with partner Lou Adler, he turned out some solo albums on Dunhill at the start of the '70s. As John told Joyce Haber of the *Los Angeles Times* in May 1970: "Groups are just about through. The individual composer and the singer is it. I think music will become much more gentle—again a mutation of rock and ballads and country & western, but more sophisticated, and jazz."

He also noted most of his songs are autobiographical, including one on his album released in early 1970 referring to his relationship with Michelle, who was planning to marry their mutual friend, Dennis Hopper, after her divorce decree became final. The lyrics went "Somewhere down the beach she's sleepin', sleepin' in the arms of an old friend." The marriage to Hopper was brief.

In the 1970s, John and exwife Michelle pursued various projects in the entertainment field. Besides his solo albums, none of which had much impact, John did a few acting jobs and at one point served as producer for Robert Altman's *Brewster McCloud*. Michelle's acting credits included a role in the film *Dillinger*. The biggest success in the 1970s was achieved by their daughter Mackenzie Phillips, who by the late 1970s had become a star in films and the TV sitcom "One Day at a Time." Mackenzie was named for John's longtime friend, Scott McKenzie, creator of the 1967 flower-power classic "San Francisco (Be Sure to Wear Some Flowers in Your Hair)."

Considering that songs such as "California Dreamin'" had talked of high spirits and good times, it was ironic, as John Phillips disclosed in talk-show interviews in the late 1970s and 1980s, that the lives of several of the original Mamas and Papas and their family members had been blighted by the scourge of drug abuse. He acknowledged that he had been an addict for years before finally overcoming his problem. He also expressed guilt about not preventing his daughter from becoming similarly hooked to the point that her acting career was almost destroyed. By the early 1980s, both had successfully completed treatment to hold their habit in abeyance, although both admitted it was a victory that never could be considered final.

In 1982, John felt the renewed interest in pop music of the '60s made the time ripe for a new version of his old group. For this he brought back Dennis Doherty and recruited his daughter to take Michelle's old role and as Cass Elliott's replacement, Elaine ("Spanky") McFarlane (lead singer of Spanky & Our Gang, whose Mercury recordings "Sunday Will Never Be the Same," "Lazy Day," and "Like to Get to Know You" made *Billboard*'s top 20 in 1967 and 1968). The group proved surprisingly effective on stage and, while not able to draw the massive crowds of yesteryear, still was popular on the smaller club circuit into the mid-1980s.

In 1986, the trials, tribulations, and successes of the group, as well as some less than cordial reminiscences of their personal relationship, were disclosed in autobiographies released by both John and Michelle. John's book, *Papa John*, was published by Doubleday, while Michelle's *California Dreamin'* bore the Warner Books imprint.

MANCHESTER, MELISSA: *Singer, pianist, harpsichordist, songwriter, actress, writer. Born Bronx, New York, February 15, 1951.*

The creators of the 1980 hit movie *Fame* could well have used Melissa Manchester as a role model. She attended Manhattan's High School of Music and Arts (acknowledged site of the film) and became one of its successful alumni. Appropriately, she later co-wrote and starred in an episode of the TV series based on the movie.

There was no lack of musical incentive during her childhood years, first in the Bronx and later in Manhattan's Upper West Side. Her father was a bassoonist with the Metropolitan Opera Orchestra and saw to it that his daughter was well schooled in piano. Though she became a star in pop music, she always maintained an interest in the classics, citing among her early influences Metropolitan Opera star Elizabeth Schwarzkopf along with Dusty Springfield, Aretha Franklin, and Elton John. "All kinds of music were important to me when I was growing up, not just rock'n'roll, although the energy of rock'n'roll has certainly been very influential."

In her teens in the late 1960s, she already was showing skill as a songwriter. While in high school, she gained some singing jobs and also was a staff writer for Chappell Music from the ages of 16 to 18.

After graduating from high school, she entered New York University School of the Arts. Among her courses was one on songwriting and record production taught by folk-rock superstar Paul Simon. Melissa was one of only nine people accepted for the course by Simon from over 100 applicants. (*See Simon, Paul.*)

At the end of the 1960s, she was spending more time on her performing career. She did a variety of things as a backup artist including singing and playing keyboards on the *National Lampoon Radio Dinner* album and the *Victory People's Chorus and Orchestra* LP. She also did vocals on many nationally televised commercials including ones for Pepsi Cola, McDonald's Hamburgers, and United Airlines. Providing more direct experience for a solo career was a position as part of Bette Midler's backing vocal group, the Harlettes, during the early '70s. (*See Midler, Bette.*)

In January 1973, Melissa felt she was ready to make a name for herself and quit the Harlettes. She already had prepared a nightclub act and assembled a group of original songs, co-written with Carole Bayer Sager, that had attracted attention from record executives in demo form. Her debut at the Paradise Room at Reno Sweeney's in Manhattan in January 1973 won accolades from many critics.

Her debut album, *Home to Myself,* was issued on Bell Records (which later became a part of Arista Records) during 1973. A pleasant album with listenable songs by Manchester and Sager, it heralded an important new voice in the middle-of-the-road or soft-rock format. As the 1970s went by, Melissa became a fixture on the concert circuit, slowly building up a large adult following and adding a wide range of credits for TV appearances.

Bell and then Arista issued a new album by Melissa every year from 1973 to the mid-1980s. Her 1970s output included: *Bright Eyes* (1974), *Melissa* (1975), *Better Days and Happy Endings* (1976), *Singin'* (1977), *Don't Cry Out Loud* (1978), and *Melissa Mancheser* (1979). Many of those made the charts, usually the lower levels (though *Melissa* went gold). Her charted singles during 1978–80 included "Don't Cry Out Loud," "Theme from *Ice Castles,*" "Pretty Girls," and "Fire in the Morning."

In the late 1970s, her songwriting helped other artists make the hit lists. A prime example was "Whenever I Call You Friend," co-written with Kenny Loggins and a best-selling single for him in 1978. (*See Loggins, Kenny.*)

Her 1980s Arista albums included the top 20 *Hey Ricky* (1982), with its *Billboard* top 10 single "You Should Hear How She Talks about You" winning a Grammy for Best Pop Vocal Performance, Female. During 1983, Melissa had three more singles on the charts and a new Arista LP, *Emergency.*

On April 2, 1984, she made her acting debut as a guest performer on the MGM/UA syndicated show, *Fame.* Her contributions included writing the script for the episode with her husband (Kevin DeRemer) and Christopher Beaumont. She played the role of a former singer turned teacher who went back to the Performing Arts High School as a substitute teacher when her confidence in her singing skills wavered. The script had her finding new resolve to return to entertaining. In the program, she performed two of her compositions: "Better Days" and "City Nights."

In 1985, she joined MCA Records which issued her label debut, *Mathematics,* in May.

MANGIONE, CHUCK: *Pianist, fluegelhorn player, band leader, composer/songwriter, rec-* *ord producer. Born Rochester, New York, November 29, 1940.* *

With his trademark little hat perched on his head and an exotic-seeming brass instrument, the fluegelhorn, in his hand, Chuck Mangione caught the fancy of millions of music lovers of all ages, many of whom placed him on a pedestal shared by their favorite rock artists. As a composer and musician, Mangione demonstrated the ability to hold his own in a wide range from pop to mainstream jazz.

Born Charles Frank Mangione in upstate New York, Chuck grew up in a loving, if initially nonmusical family. His father ran a grocery store and his mother was a housewife. Once he showed an interest in music, though, his parents were more than happy to let him begin music lessons at the age of eight. In 1950, after he made good grades on the Seashore Musical Aptitude Test, he was asked to play a band instrument in school and chose the trumpet. His choice, he said, came from seeing the movie *Young Man with a Horn.* "After about six months, my brother Gap would sit down at the piano and we'd play . . . just play anything . . . some blues or something. So I was into improvisation very early."

During the next few years, he bacame a jazz enthusiast. "I learned by listening. I had the chance to come into this world at a perfect time when big bands were still happening. Basie, Ellington, Ferguson—dozens of quartets and quintets—would come to Rochester as well as other cities across the country and they had this club circuit to work 50 weeks out of the year. They would stay in Rochester for two weeks, playing in clubs before intimate groups of 150–200 people. So I was exposed as a teenager to great artists like Gillespie, Miles Davis, and others."

His parents did all they could to help. Father Mangione would take Gap and Chuck regularly to hear concerts at the local Ridgecrest Inn. "And we would go hear somebody like Dizzy Gillespie. Father would walk up to them like he knew them all his life and he'd say: 'Hi, Dizzy! My name is Mr. Mangione, these are my kids. They play.' And before you'd know it, my father would be talking with the guy, and would invite them over for spaghetti and Italian wine, and we'd wind up having a jam session in the living room."

Gillespie became a particular friend who gave Chuck one of his unique upswept horns when the boy was 15. Chuck said later: "I regard him as my musical father."

During Chuck's senior year in high school he

*Based partly on a personal interview with Irwin Stambler.

formed the Jazz Brothers group with Gap, an act they kept going until 1964. Their first locally issued single, "Struttin' with Sandra," caught the ear of jazz great Cannonball Adderley, who asked to produce a series of sessions for Riverside Records. The group turned out three albums on the label: *Jazz Brothers, Hey, Baby,* and *Spring Fever.* While this was going on, Chuck was enrolled in Eastman School of Music from 1958 until he got his B.A. in 1963.

He learned such music basics as theory and arranging, which were invaluable for his later achievements. But he was unhappy at the exclusion of jazz from the curriculum. He noted that Eastman was "oriented to teaching students only about symphonic music—which is great music, of course—but then students would graduate and wait in line for someone to die. The graduates would meanwhile teach, and teach the same things they'd learned, and it all becomes a vicious cycle." Later he was influential in remedying that situation.

While attending Eastman, Chuck continued to work on many outside projects. In 1962, he completed his first solo album, *Recuerdo* on Jazzland Records, backed by Wynton Kelly, Sam Jones, Louis Hayes, and Joe Romano. In 1963, the course of his future was changed when he discovered the fluegelhorn.

"When I was a student at Eastman in 1963, one time Miles Davis and Gil Evans collaborated on some wonderful music in which Miles played the fluegelhorn. I fell in love with it right away. I loved the shape of the instrument and its sound—darker and mellower than the trumpet. But it's not a flexible instrument and you can't always use it."

For some years, Chuck tried to get around that by playing both trumpet and fluegelhorn, but then opted for the latter. "I waited until 1968 when I started my first quartet to give up the trumpet and use the fluegelhorn all the time. I don't play trumpet anymore. I think a lot of people who play both the trumpet and fluegelhorn don't play the fluegelhorn well because the two instruments are different. It takes a different kind of control and breath to play each well. A lot of people will pick up the fluegelhorn and get exhausted fast because they're putting too much air into it."

As Chuck's stay at Eastman neared completion, he wrote a piece called "Feel of a Vision" for his friend Lew Soloff to play at graduation. (Soloff later became a member of Blood, Sweat & Tears.) (*See Blood, Sweat and Tears.*) It represented his early experiments with blends of strings and swing. After graduation, he spent 1964 teaching music education in Rochester parochial schools.

In 1965, he decided to test the waters of the major music scene in New York City. He began by freelancing as a sideman with people such as Kai Winding and Maynard Ferguson, but then agreed to take a regular trumpet spot with Art Blakey and the Jazz Messengers, remaining with that premier jazz group until 1968, when he went back to Rochester to teach jazz education at the Hochstein School of Music and also serve as director of a jazz program at Eastman. He also wrote material for the rock group the Outsiders, whose 1966 *Billboard* top 10 single "Time Won't Let Me" was, unfortunately, its only major achievement.

In early 1969, Chuck had his new quartet playing in a Rochester singles bar, the Shakespeare. But he was writing music better fitted to large organizations, so later in 1969 he hired 50 musicians for a concert performance called Kaleidoscope. That was a financial failure, but it brought an invitation from Tom Iannoaccone, manager of the Rochester Philharmonic (and later Chuck's manager) for Chuck to direct that orchestra in some of his compositions. That May 9, 1970, concert, called "Friends and Love," drew a capacity crowd to the Eastman Theater and also was videotaped by the local educational TV station, WWXI.

The WWXI sound quality wasn't too good, but a backup 18-track tape gave Chuck the chance to press his own two-record set. The LP did well enough in upstate New York for Mercury Records to buy rights to it, signing Chuck to a four-year contract and reissuing the album, titled *Friends and Love,* in late 1970. It sold over 150,000 copies and won Chuck his first Grammy nomination (Best Instrumental, 1971) for the track "Hill Where the Lord Hides."

During 1971–72, Chuck's status nationally and internationally surged upward. 1971 activities included the benefit concert "Freddie's Walkin'" (referring to a young nephew with cerebral palsy whose condition improved greatly from treatment at the Rochester CP Nursery School); a second LP, *Together,* issued by Mercury in May, based on another concert with the Rochester Philharmonic (taped for TV presentation on PBS stations); and his first quartet LP, *The Chuck Mangione Quartet,* issued in August. In 1972, the quartet performed at the Montreaux International Jazz Festival in Switzerland, followed by a three-week stay at the top London jazz club, Ronnie Scott's. In August 1972, his second quartet album, *Alive,* was released.

Besides his fluegelhorn, one of the identifying symbols for Mangione was the odd little hat he always wore at his concerts and in his publicity photos. Its origins, he said, went back to 1965. "The first hat of that kind was a Christmas gift that year from two friends in Rochester who helped baptize my youngest daughter. I used it in the 'Friends and Love' project and a picture of that was used, so it became my symbol and sort of a good luck charm.''

The 1973 Mercury album *Land of Make Believe* was recorded live with the Hamilton Philharmonic at Toronto, Canada's Massey Hall. *The Chuck Mangione Quartet* (1974) received a Grammy nomination for Best Jazz Performance by a Group.

Mangione's jazz credentials were impeccable. The dean of jazz critics, Leonard Feather, wrote of a Los Angeles quartet appearance: "You find his quartet versions (of his compositions) fulfilling. . . . The reason, of course, is that so much of Mangione's music derives from his compositions and from the rich, flowing sound of his fluegelhorn. He may start a solo very simply, like a man speaking in a language whose alphabet has only seven letters, but after the first minute or so, a flurry of consonants will reveal his startling virtuosity and creativity.

"As a composer, too, Mangione knows the virtues of deceptive simplicity. The delightful 'Land of Make Believe' is grounded on two utterly basic seven-note phrases. It is not often that you walk out of a jazz club [Shelly Manne's Hole] with a melody ringing in your ears, but it can and does happen here.''

Mangione, whose stylings included not only jazz, but occasional folk-rock and soul-based material, by the mid-1970s was beginning to sense that he could expand his audience beyond the hard-core jazz fan. One approach to do this was to look for a record firm with broader distribution potential. This led to a new affiliation with A&M Records. "I met Jerry Moss [label co-owner] at the Half Note and we discussed my going with A&M. His response was: 'We'll decide on a budget, you'll go into the studio, you'll come out and hand us a tape and say: "This is my next album.' '' There was never any discussion of what I was going to do, or why I didn't tell them about it first, and then we'll see. It was just: 'Book the time, hire the people, do the job.' Beautiful.''

The result, *Chase the Clouds Away* (1975), was still finding favor with record buyers a decade later. Even while Chuck worked on that project, he was nominated for two more Grammies in the 1974 voting: one for Best Jazz Performance by a Big Band for the LP *Land of Make Believe*, the other for Best Arrangement Accompanying Vocalist for its title track (sung by Esther Satterfield). He had two more LPs to point to during 1975: a Mercury retrospective (*Encore: The Best of Chuck Mangione*) and his second A&M album, *Bellavia,* dedicated to his parents.

In early 1976, tracks from *Chase the Clouds Away* gained a worldwide audience as background music for the Olympic Games telecast. By then, the LP already had earned two Grammy nominations: one for Best Pop Instrumental Performance of 1975 and one for the title track, a finalist in the Best Instrumental Composition category. In October 1976, Chuck's third LP on A&M, *Main Squeeze,* was issued. Four months later, on February 19, 1977, Mangione finally won a Grammy: Best Instrumental Composition of 1976 for the track "Bellavia." In September 1977, Chuck began writing his first film score for Oscar Lewis's *Children of Sanchez.* The next month, his fourth A&M LP, *Feels So Good,* was issued, a breakthrough collection that cemented his standing as a headline pop as well as jazz favorite. The gold title track rose to number two on the singles charts by year-end. The LP passed the double-platinum milestone.

During 1979, two more two-disc A&M albums were issued: *Children of Sanchez* and *Live at Hollywood Bowl.* The *Sanchez* LP survived the film's debacle. "I think the movie died in the editing room. I saw five or six hours of uncut film which had some strong stuff in it, but that wasn't reflected in the end product, which only appeared in a few theaters and then disappeared. The amazing thing is the album—it sold 800,000 without the movie which, since it was a two-record set, was something like 1.6 million discs. The movie had Anthony Quinn and Delores Del Rio in it and if it had been a hit, who knows what might have been with the album.''

Chuck closed out the '70s with a literal hatful of honors. *Cash Box* magazine named him Composer/Arranger of the Decade and Top Charted Producer (for *Children of Sanchez*). *Billboard* named him Top Instrumentalist; *Record World* dubbed him Top Trumpet Artist (though, as noted, he didn't play trumpet); *Performance* magazine voted him Instrumentalist of the Year, Jazz Act of the Year, and Outstanding Jazz Artist; the *Playboy* Jazz Poll voted him Best Brass, Best Jazz Composer, and Best Jazz Group.

In the late 1970s, he got another important assignment—to write the theme for the 1980 Winter Olympics slated for Lake Placid, New York. "Roone Arledge of ABC came to one of my concerts and asked if I'd write the theme. I came up with 'Give It All You've Got,' which was played behind a lot of the events at the games and I also played live before a worldwide TV audience during the closing ceremonies.''

Chuck and his music were closely involved with the total event, whose highlight probably was the U.S. hockey team's amazing gold-medal win over the U.S.S.R. "It was one of the most exciting times of my life. I would have loved to watch the final hockey game, but I was doing interviews about 1½ miles away. Even then, I could hear the roar of the crowd at that game—it was unbelievable.'' The Olympics theme was included on *Fun and Games* LP (February 1980), a month when the *Live at the Hollywood Bowl* album earned his twelfth Grammy nomination: Best Pop Instrumental Performance. In the 1980 Grammy voting, *Fun and Games* was nominated in the Best Jazz Fusion Performance, Vocal or Instrumental category, and ''Give It All You've Got'' was a finalist for Best Instrumental Performance. In April 1981, his LP *Tarantella* came out on A&M. During the year, he also composed ''The Cannonball Run Theme'' for the Burt Reynolds movie. His contract with A&M expired during that year and he moved on to sign a worldwide arrangement with CBS Records, which issued his label debut, *Love Notes*, on June 17, 1982. In December 1982, he composed and recorded ''Chaia's Theme'' for the ''Larry King'' TV show.

Coming into the mid-1980s, besides his widespread concerts, recordings, and occasional TV work, he often was in demand to perform the National Anthem at major sporting events, including World Series and All-Star baseball games and major pro football contests. His Columbia albums included *Journey to a Rainbow* (issued in May 1983, when his 1975 LP, *Chase the Clouds Away*, finally reached gold status), *Disguise* (August 9, 1984), and *Save Tonight for Me* (April 3, 1986).

His many other projects included an acting role in the February 1984 ''Paradise Blues'' episode of ''Magnum PI,'' and composing the music for the play *Leonardo da Vinci*, written by Tony Award winner Joe Mantegna. Both those opportunities, he said, evolved from one evening's events at the La Sevre Restaurant in Los Angeles.

''I was at La Sevre on the Sunset Strip one night and the executive producer of 'Magnum P.I.' happened to be there. Whenever I go to La Sevre, I always bring my horn and sit in the same corner and if it's someone's birthday and the manager tells me, I go over and play 'Happy Birthday.' I played it for the 'Magnum' producer and said it would be nice if I could be on the show, and later I was called in to do it.

''He told actor Mike Tucci, who also was the executive producer of *Leonardo* and Tucci asked if I'd like to do something. Later he sent me the script and I wrote the music. Some of that—really two themes— you can find on my *Disguise* album on the 'Leonardo's Lady' track. Actors Equity did *Leonardo* in Los Angeles for a couple of weeks and it didn't really happen. I think Joe Mantegna wrote a strong script and it will hit one day.''

Looking back over his career, he said: ''I feel blessed we're an instrumental group and built up an audience that's been devoted to us for a very long

time so we don't come and go with each new record. Our audience isn't fickle. They like our music. They're there and have been supporting us since 1970. As for my work habits, I'm not ashamed to admit I've listened to very little music by others. My teenage daughters have music in the car, but I like to create my own music and not be a follower.''

That doesn't mean he wasn't aware of what went before. In fact, he decried the limited knowledge of pop and jazz history by many people. ''I still think one of the problems is that young musicians in order to look forward must also look back. When I was teaching at Eastman, young trumpet players would come in and if you asked them to name three great jazz trumpeters, they couldn't go beyond Doc Severinsen. It's shocking so many new artists have so little interest in their roots.''

In 1988, *Eyes of the Veiled Temptress* (Columbia) was released.

MANHATTAN TRANSFER *Vocal group headed by Tim Hauser, born New Jersey, c. 1940. Other members, Janis Siegel, Laurel Masse, Alan Paul. Cheryl Bentyne replaced Masse in 1979.*[*]

During the mid-1970s, many music-industry observers predicted that Manhattan Transfer, a vocal group whose material ran the gamut from '40s swing to pop and jazz fusion, would become one of America's most popular acts. The forecast came true in Europe, where the quartet were considered superstars before the 1970s were over. At home, Transfer members had to be satisfied with establishing themselves in a comfortable, if not mass-audience, niche as unique interpreters of many facets of America's pop-music heritage.

The Manhattan Transfer of the mid-1970s actually was a second incarnation of the organization. Tim Hauser had founded the original version in the late 1960s and later brought in guitarist Gene Pistilli as a co-leader. (Before reaching that point, Hauser had experimented with a variety of music styles, starting with a stint as a teenager in the 1950s with a rock group called the Criterions. During college, he performed with a folk group, The Troubadours Three. Afterward, during the 1960s, he did some work as a solo artist and record producer while earning most of his income in conventional pursuits.)

The concept of the Hauser/Pistilli band was to combine elements of swing, jazz, and rock. Capitol Records issued their LP *Jukin'* in 1971. However, conflict arose between Hauser and Pistilli, and Tim left. He recalled: ''[Gene] didn't agree with the di-

---

*Partly based on personal interview of Tim Hauser with Irwin Stambler.

rection I wanted to take toward emphasizing swinging jazz. I left in August 1971 and got a job as a construction worker to support myself. It was a strange situation for me because before the first Manhattan Transfer in June 1969, I'd been a marketing executive. Later that year, I began driving a cab, which was what I was doing when they disbanded in 1972 and I took the name back. I'm the only one left from the original Manhattan Transfer.''

The taxicab itself became a springboard for revival of the group. Money saved from fare earnings gave Hauser a nest egg toward demonstration-tape costs; the vehicle became a source of singing talent. ''I found Laurel Masse in my cab. We got talking and she got excited about the group and told me how to contact her when things got started. I got to know about our other girl vocalist, Janis Siegel, in a similar way. I met a drummer in my cab who was going to a party in a hotel and he invited me up to meet his friends. One of them was Janis, who was doing backup for singer Dianne Davidson. I told her about Manhattan Transfer and she loved the idea.''

The women and Hauser began demo work. In the fall, Tim felt he was ready to reform his group. A month later, he came in contact with singer/actor Alan Paul, who had been in the original cast of the rock musical *Grease*. The foursome was complete.

''We rehearsed in the basement of the Lamb's Club in New York. Alan was a [club] member because of being in *Grease*. We used an old piano that once belonged to Victor Herbert. We rehearsed for half a year and had six or seven tunes and a little choreography when we started performing in early 1973. We got good response from the start and we kept working and working and trying to perform wherever we could. We had our first gig at a bar called Dr. Generalities at 2nd and 73rd in New York City. But jobs weren't all that plentiful for a while. I was broke the worst in my life. I drove a cab just to pay the rent and eat. It was a matter of survival and the girls weren't too well off either.''

Things picked up in the summer with gigs, a concert in a large New York hotel and singing on a boat cruise up the Hudson ''before about 400 transvestites. Still, we turned down a lot of gigs. People said, 'You're nobodies. How can you turn those down?' But we only wanted ones that would create reverberations. By December '74, we were playing Reno Sweeney's.

''Up to the end of December, we'd been turned down by a lot of record companies. Then Ahmet Ertegun of Atlantic saw us and understood what we were doing right away and he signed us. We started cutting our first album in December '74 and January '75 and it was released in April '75.''

The LP, *Manhattan Transfer,* fared well with a number of critics, who found it an interesting change from the run-of-the-mill pop releases. The material reflected the basic concept on which Hauser founded the group. ''When we started out, our main idea was to do a kind of music no one else was doing at the time. It seemed in the pop culture, artists always are drawing on other elements than pop. Basically, when rock started in the '50s, it was drawing on R&B and country and, in the '60s, on folk music. I saw all those things going down, but never really saw early R&B and jazz. I said, it's such great music, why not do that and draw on other influences like cinematics and graphics. Of course, those weren't the only things we were into. I'd worked with Jim Croce as a folksinger; Janis was into country & western; Laurel was into rock; and Alan came from the theater. The whole key was to sing four-part harmony. Nobody was doing it then and nobody is now. When you do four-part harmony, you get into jazz because pop is based on triads and simple chords.''

The album did quite well for a debut effort in the U.S. and the group also began to build up a concert following with a stage act that stressed choreography, costuming, and a certain amount of play acting along with the music. Hauser said: ''In the spring of '75, we came to California to play the Roxy in L.A. Jack Good was putting together a Mary Tyler Moore show. When he saw us, he asked us to be in it. We played three weeks there and it was slow at first, then picked up. The same thing happened in San Francisco. We did well in Chicago with support from Hugh Hefner [of *Playboy*] and went back to New York where top execs of CBS-TV saw us at a special show at the Bottom Line in May and decided to give us a summer show. Later on, we went to Europe and created a lot of excitement.

''In London, where Laurel was educated because her father was over there in the marketing department of General Foods, the ovation after the first show was so great it made her break down and cry. . . . We did well in Stockholm and were on a TV program called 'Star Parade' in Germany. Just on the basis of that, we got a German Grammy as best new group of the year. We knew we had something there and by the time we went back to the U.S., the single 'Operator' became a hit and went to 21 on the charts.''

But things went downhill after that. The group's second LP, *Coming Out,* was a disaster in the U.S. market, which Hauser attributed partly to dissension between the group and its manager. One bone of contention was the steady diet of supper-club bookings. Hauser recalled: ''We broke attendance records in places like the Fairmont in San Francisco and the Empire Room of the Waldorf. It was good in some ways, but we only were attracting people who could afford it and not getting regular folks.''

There also were arguments about finances and other matters that eventually led to the law courts (a not unusual state of affairs in the music industry). Because of this air of acrimony, work on the second LP proceeded under a cloud. Highly successful producer Richard Perry, was in charge. "We were very friendly with him, but because of other problems, the album was made under very tense circumstances.'' It flopped in the U.S., but a good European response saved the day.

The group had a good summer tour there in 1976, although problems with management continued. In September, the previous manager quit and Brian Avnet took over. Hauser stressed: "He was a dedicated man and really believed in us. We were about $100,000 in debt then, so most of '77 we worked to get back on our feet.''

A 1977 European tour helped. "We went back in the spring and 'Chanson D'Amour' from the second album hit number one in Paris. We played an industry convention in front of recording executives from all over the world. One of the songs we sang is the French tune 'Je Voulais' and they threw roses to us on the stage. We sang in Paris and England and our records sold well in both places. A song from our first album, 'Tuxedo Junction,' hit twenty on their charts." The group came back home feeling with the right approach it could catch on in the U.S. as well.

For the third album, Hauser took over as producer. A major goal was to demonstrate that the group could handle diverse music stylings. For the LP, Hauser said: "Even where we used old tunes, we tried to showcase them in a very contemporary setting. We used very contemporary drum sounds. In our first album, we used a lot of big-band approaches to old tunes, but presented with electric piano with phaser, wah-wah guitars to replace muted trumpets, and drums played in popular fashion. We wanted to show it's not just nostalgia, but that songs from earlier decades could be updated to provide new insights.'' This didn't mean that Hauser and company meant to restrict themselves to the prerock era. On its third LP, for instance, one of the best tracks was a reworking of the Supremes' ''Where Did Our Love Go'' and the group constantly added new works both by its members and by other contemporary writers to its repertoire.

The third LP, *Pastiche* (Atlantic, 1978), did improve the Transfer's standing at home, though not enough to crack the top brackets of the hit charts. The next release, *Extensions,* improved on its prede-

cessor's showing and both albums demonstrated the group still retained an immense popularity overseas.

By the end of the 1970s, it seemed apparent that the worst was over for the group and it was on the way to accruing something more than a cult following at home and a growing reputation as an innovative and unique part of modern pop music. Indicative of this was the Transfer's 1980 single ''Birdland,'' a stunning arrangement by Janis Siegel of the tune originally crafted by the jazz fusion group Weather Report. The Transfer won its first Grammy for ''Birdland'' (Best Jazz Fusion Performance, Vocal or Instrumental).

In 1981, the group had two releases that made both pop and jazz charts: a new studio LP, *Mecca for Moderns,* plus the retrospective, *Best of the Manhattan Transfer.* A single from *Mecca for Moderns,* ''Boy from New York City,'' was a *Billboard* top 10 hit during 1981.

During the Grammy telecast for 1981, the group picked up two more awards: Best Pop Performance by a Duo or Group with Vocal for the ''Boy from New York City'' single and Best Jazz Vocal Performance, Duo or Group, for the album track ''Until I Met You/Corner Pocket.''

During 1981, the group recorded a version of the old pop/swing hit ''Route 66'' for the soundtrack for a Burt Reynolds film. The single made pop and jazz lists in 1982 and won still another Grammy for Best Jazz Vocal Performance by a Duo or Group.

The Transfer continued to prosper as a concert attraction and recording entity into the late 1980s. *Bodies and Souls* (Atlantic, 1983) made the jazz top 20. A track from the LP, ''Why Not,'' won a Grammy for Best Jazz Vocal Performance, Duo or Group. In 1984, the LP *Bop Doo-Wop* was on the charts. *Vocalese* (1985) brought a bonanza of eight Grammy nominations. These included one for Janis Siegel for Best Jazz Vocal Solo Performance, Female, for the track ''Sing Joy Spring''; one for the track ''Oh Yes, I Remember Clifford''; and another in the same category for Jon Hendricks and Bobby McFerrin, who were soloists on the Grammy-winning track ''Another Night in Tunisia.'' There were three nominations in the Best Jazz Vocal Performance, Duo or Group: to the entire group for the album *Vocalese,* to Manhattan Transfer and Jon Hendricks for the track ''Ray's Rockhouse,'' and to Manhattan Transfer and the Four Freshmen for the track ''To You.'' Also nominated for Best Jazz Instrumental Performance, Soloist, were Dizzy Gillespie for his work on *Vocalese*'s track ''Sing Joy Spring'' and James Moody for the ''Meet Benny Bailey'' track.

In early 1987, Atlantic issued a solo LP by Janis Siegel, *At Home.* Late in the year, a fine new collection by the entire Transfer, *Brasil,* was issued by the label.

MANILOW, BARRY: *Singer, pianist, songwriter, arranger, record producer. Born Brooklyn, New York, June 17, 1946.*

The worldwide impact of Barry Manilow provided dramatic evidence that pop music is not monolithic. His songs, typically love ballads, essentially are throwbacks to the big band era (one critic dubbed him the "king of schmaltz"), though with rock arrangements.

He told *New York Times* writer Betty Goodwin (December 1, 1985) it was something of a mystery to him how he had become "king of the middle-of-the-road." "To tell the truth, I'm not crazy about pop music. I never have been." The music he played for himself at home, he said, tended to be classical, rhythm & blues, and "very, very heavy rock'n'roll."

His musical stylings might have had roots in his childhood, when '40s and early '50s pop overlapped with early rock. He was born Barry Allen Pincus in Brooklyn's Williamsburg section. His last name actually was his father's mother's maiden name. Barry's father, Harold Kelliher, was of Irish descent. He changed his name to Pincus to avoid conflict with Barry's grandmother, who wouldn't have been pleased if she knew her daughter, Edna Manilow, was marrying out of the Jewish religion. As it happened, his father left the family when Barry was two years old (resuming acquaintance with his son after Barry became a star) and Edna changed his last name to Manilow when he was 13.

His mother wanted him to get some music education. Because she couldn't afford a piano, she bought him an accordion for his first instrument when he was seven. Later on, he did take up the piano and became reasonably competent on it in his teens. At the New York College of Music and Juilliard School, he also developed expertise in arranging and composing. During that phase, he earned room and board money by working in the CBS mailroom.

The CBS position, humble though it was, led to important contacts. One of them was a director whom Barry impressed enough that the man asked the 18-year-old to do some arranging for one of his productions. That experience brought other opportunities, including work as a vocal coach and the chance to provide the music for an off-Broadway show, *The Drunkard.* In 1967, at the age of 21, he became musical director for the WCBS-TV series "Callback!" That program won an Emmy Award during his tenure. After that, he worked as a conductor and arranger for Ed Sullivan Productions. Besides writing background music and original songs during those years, Barry also augmented his earnings by writing commercial jingles for such organizations as McDonald's, Pepsi Cola, and Kentucky Fried Chicken.

Besides all those activities, Barry also found time to add to his performance credentials. At the end of the 1960s, he and another performer developed a duo format that was featured at the Upstairs at the Downstairs nightclub in New York for two years.

A turning point in his career came in the spring of 1972. He was asked to fill in as house pianist in the showroom of the Continental Baths, one of a series of gay centers then springing up in the city. Typically, such places had nightclub rooms popular with heterosexual as well as gay pop-music fans. The featured singer he backed in one show series was a then unknown artist named Bette Midler. (*See Midler, Bette.*) The two complemented each other so well that Barry soon took over as her musical director, arranger, and pianist. Demo tapes they worked up helped get her a contract with Atlantic Records. Barry worked up the arrangements and co-produced her 1972 debut album, *The Divine Miss M.* After the LP earned a Grammy, Barry co-produced her second album, the 1973 *Bette Midler,* which was not quite as effective as its predecessor.

By then he had signed his own solo recording contract with Bell Records (later to become part of Arista) and wanted to give up his duties with Bette for that. She asked him to first serve as musical director for her debut major national tour. It also was agreed that he would open the second half of the show performing three of his own songs. That set gained enthusiastic audience response, which helped to erase some of his doubts about becoming a featured artist. He told Betty Goodwin he had never felt comfortable as a performer, but finally accepted that route as a new challenge. "If there's a choice, I usually take the one I'm going to learn from instead of the one that just has me coasting."

His debut album on Bell (now an Arista label release), *Barry Manilow,* came out in 1973. *Barry Manilow II* (1974) spawned his first top 10 single, "Mandy." From then on, each new Manilow album spent many months on the charts and all of them through the mid-1980s earned gold or platinum awards from the RIAA. Arista albums included *Tryin' to Get the Feelin'* (1975), *This One's for You* (1976), *Barry Manilow Live* (1977), *Even Now* (1978), *Barry Manilow's Greatest Hits* (two LPs, 1978), and *One Voice* (1979).

In the mid-1970s, Manilow had a valid claim to superstardom. During 1977, for instance, all five albums that had been issued since his solo career began were on the charts at the same time, something

438

only achieved before by Frank Sinatra and Johnny Mathis. *Barry Manilow Live,* recorded during his sold-out 1976–77 tour of 98 U.S. cities, moved to number one on the charts. In 1977, he sold 7 million albums in the U.S. alone and millions more overseas.

He also had no lack of singles hits in the 1974–78 period, scoring such chart successes as "It's a Miracle," "Could It Be Magic," "I Write the Songs," "Tryin' to Get the Feeling Again," "This One's for You," "Weekend in New England," "Looks Like We Made It," "Daybreak," and "Copacabana." His charted singles in 1979 included "Ships," "Ready to Take a Chance Again," and "Somewhere in the Night." During the second half of the 1970s, he always ranked in *Billboard*'s year-end lists for top albums and singles sales.

Manilow also proved a major draw on TV. His first network show, *The Barry Manilow Special* (March 2, 1977), drew an estimated audience of 37 million. In the TV Emmy Awards voting for 1977, the show was victorious in the Outstanding Musical/Comedy/Variety Special category. His next show, the *Second Barry Manilow Special* (which also featured Ray Charles; *see Charles, Ray*) was shown initially on ABC-TV on February 24, 1978 and later gained four Emmy nominations. During 1977, he presented a series of live concerts on Broadway that brought a special Tony Award from the New York Drama Critics.

Manilow starred in two more TV specials before deciding the format was becoming too formalized. The third one debuted on ABC on May 23, 1979. The fourth (May 1980) had Dionne Warwick as guest artist singing several songs from her 1979 Arista LP that Barry had produced. (*See Warwick, Dionne.*) On that LP, she recorded three Manilow compositions: "All the Time" (co-written with Mary Panzer), "Never Gonna Let You Get Away," and "In Your Eyes" (co-written with Bruce Sussman and Jack Feldman, longtime lyricists for Manilow music).

The 1980s got underway with Manilow's audience apparently as faithful as ever. His 1980 LP, *Barry,* went platinum and provided the *Billboard* top 10 single "I Made It through the Rain." LPs *If I Should Love Again* (1981) and *Here Comes the Night* (1982) went gold. In 1983, he scored a hit single with "Memory" from *Cats,* the new Broadway musical success of Andrew Lloyd Webber (composer of *Jesus Christ Superstar*). In 1983, he added another gold record with the LP *Greatest Hits, Volume II* and had the single "Read 'Em and Weep" which made the top 20 in early 1984.

Other highlights of 1981–83 included more TV exposure and record-setting concert tours in the U.S. and around the world. The cable-TV network Show-time taped two Manilow shows at the Pittsburgh Civic Arena in November 1981 for a concert special shown the following September; in England, it taped *Barry Manilow: The Concert at Blenheim Palace,* aired in May 1983. He began the U.K. phase of his 1981—82 "In the Round" world tour with five sold-out performances at London's Royal Albert Hall that brought such hectic response that the British *Daily Mail* called it "a fervor scarcely matched since the heyday of Presley and the Beatles." That paper and others in London ran the same headlines: "Manilow Mania." Material from the Albert Hall concerts was recorded for the Arista LP *Barry Live in Britain,* which debuted on British charts at number one on its release.

In late 1982, he was represented by a new EP featuring his version of Shakin' Stevens' rockabilly "Oh Julie." The four songs on the EP, he noted, "are all up-tempo rock'n'roll songs, or as rock'n'roll as I can get." Some of that was included in his 1982–83 "Around the World in 80 Dates" tour, which his management stated "established 95 sell-outs and set 30 house records for building attendance throughout the world." The tour concluded on October 6, 1983, with a charity concert in support of the Royal College of Music and the British Fund for World Jewish Relief at London's Royal Festival Hall. That was only one of his many charitable efforts, which included service during the '80s as National Chairman for Youth and Voluntarism for the U.S. United Way and contribution of his song "One Voice" as national theme for the United Way of America.

Indicating a desire to try new creative directions was his 1984 Arista album, *2:00 AM Paradise Cafe*— songs described as "saloon tunes" designed for jazz format. Among jazz greats taking part in the set were Sarah Vaughn and Mel Torme. Like all of his earlier releases, this too passed gold-record levels.

Paradise Cafe wound up Barry's contract with Arista. He signed with RCA Records, which issued his debut on the label, *Manilow,* in October 1985. During that year, he also persevered on another project, the TV movie *Copacabana,* based on the lyrics of his hit single of the same title. For this, he managed to gain the right to play the hero, Tony, a nightclub bartender with aspirations as an entertainer who is also involved in an ill-fated romance with a showgirl named Lola. CBS network executives worried about his lack of acting experience, but he stressed that he had taken a number of years of acting training and would have an acting coach, Nina Foch, helping him prepare for the program. When the show ran in December 1985, he proved capable enough if not an immediate threat for world's greatest actor.

In any event, indications in the mid-1980s were that he retained a strong grip on a very large audience, sometimes referred to as "adult contemporary" in the trade. Dick Clark, who produced *Copacabana*, commented: "There are forms of music that appeal to others than the very young. My seat-of-the-pants guess is that the audience is the 18-to-35-year-olds, mainly female."

Manilow gave his analysis of reasons for his relatively good staying power to the *New York Times'* Goodwin. "I think a good love song will never go out of style. And that's why some radio stations somewhere will always play one of my cuts, even though they may be sick of what I do. I think the people who have to worry are the trendy people, but I've never been trendy. I've always tried to write songs that will outlive me. As much as I hate elevator music, when I hear my stuff coming out of those tinny speakers, I know that I've accomplished something a lot of people haven't because that means my music is a part of the firmament of America. And that's what I've always wanted to accomplish."

It was generally understood in the record industry that Barry's move to RCA reflected a desire to get away from the pressure of working directly with Arista head Clive Davis. But after his RCA LP met relatively poor buyer response, he quickly went back to the Arista fold.

He told Paul Grein (*Los Angeles Times,* September 29, 1987, "You never miss the water till the well runs dry. . . . I missed [Clive's] guidance. I realized I needed that kind of input. I needed a bouncing wall; somebody from the record company to give me an opinion. I had none of that at RCA. They were going through internal changes at the time, and the people who signed me weren't there when I got there."

First fruit of his renewed Arista affiliation was the excellent album *Swing Street*, released in late 1987. The album theme was carried through to a new musical-variety special he prepared for CBS-TV, his first network special in eight years. Called *Barry Manilow: Big Fun on Swing Street*, it screened in March 1988. Besides many guests, the show also featured four new songs by Barry.

MANN, MANFRED: *Keyboardist, band leader (THE MANFREDS, CHAPTER THREE, THE EARTH BAND). Personnel of original group (THE MANFREDS), mid-1960s: Manfred Mann, born Johannesburg, South Africa, October 21, 1940; Mike Hugg, born Andover, Hantsfordshire, England, August 11, 1942; Paul Jones, born Portsmouth, England, February 24, 1942; Michael Vickers, born Southampton, England, April 18, 1941; Tom McGuinness, born Wimbledon, London, England, April 18, 1941. Jones replaced in late 1960s by Mike D'Abo. Manfreds disbanded in late 1969 after which Mann formed Chapter Three. Chapter Three replaced in 1972 by the Earth Band.*

Manfred Mann and the Manfreds ranked as one of the major rock groups of the mid-1960s, displaying a considerably higher level of musicianship than many top 40 bands of the decade. This was the natural result of the intensive training in theory and instrumental skills that was part of the background of the group's two pivotal members: Manfred Mann and Mike Hugg. Both were jazz artists of great talent who moved into the popular field as the line of least resistance. However, their interest in more complex music eventually led to the disbanding of the Manfreds while it was at the height of its fame. Mann, though, put together new rock groups that reestablished him as a star in the middle of the 1970s, though his successes diminished in the early 1980s.

While his bands won recognition for their musicianship, they were among the relatively rare well-known acts that depended more on cover records of other artists' songs for hits than on original compositions. Thus Mann gained considerable prominence in 1968 for a top 10 version of Bob Dylan's "The Mighty Quinn." In the 1970s, Mann's Earth Band earned chart success with Dylan's "Please Mrs. Henry," Randy Newman's "Living without You," John Prine's "Pretty Good," and Bruce Springsteen's "Blinded by the Light."

The route to those achievements for Manfred Mann began in the troubled land of South Africa, where he was born into an affluent family. He studied classical piano from childhood through teens, later adding the organ to his skills. As he grew up, he was attracted to jazz, initially the early styles such as Dixieland, and later progressive jazz. After attending college in his home country, he headed for England in 1961 to concentrate on a career in jazz. He played with a number of jazz groups in the London area, but interest in this kind of music was decidedly limited and so was Mann's income.

In 1962, he met Mike Hugg at a seaside holiday camp in England. He was delighted to find someone with a background much like his own as well as a similar musical outlook. They agreed to form their own modern jazz group and sent out word they were looking for additional group members. They found five more instrumentalists, mostly friends or acquaintances, and then sought a vocalist. Only one showed up for the audition: an Oxford undergraduate named Paul Jones. Jones had a good voice and had gained some experience, as a sideline to his school activities, singing under the pseudonym Thunder Odin.

Called the Mann-Hugg Blues Brothers, the group started playing jazz, but found engagements hard to come by. Finally, Mann and Hugg decided to change the group's style to rhythm & blues, at least to get living expenses. They developed an excellent rock-blues sound and were able to line up a considerable number of jobs along the south coast of England in the winter of 1962–63. By the spring of 1963, they were finding work in London clubs. In May, after listening to them at a club in London's southern district, an experienced group manager named Ken Pitt offered to handle them.

Pitt wanted two major changes: a name change and a reduction in size from eight members to four or five. After some head-shaking, Mann and Hugg agreed and by summer had reduced the group to themselves; Paul Jones, who played harmonica besides singing; Jack Bruce, who played bass guitar, trumpet, and sang; and Tom McGuinness on lead guitar. Mann concentrated on organ in most of the arrangements and Hugg played drums and vibraphone.

Under Pitt's direction, the group, now called Manfred Mann and the Manfreds, finally was established enough for a job at London's important Marquee Club. Pitt took demonstration records around to major record companies. As happened to the Beatles, Decca turned them down, but Electric and Musical Industries Ltd. (EMI) signed them.

Their first release, "Why Should We Not" (late 1963) was a dismal failure with the mass market. However, their next single, "Cock-a-Hoop," written by Paul Jones, won considerable airplay and a guest appearance on England's number one rock TV program, "Ready, Steady, Go." Stardom was hardly hampered by their third release, "54321," which was adopted as the theme song by "Ready, Steady, Go."

During 1964, they turned out a single called "Do Wah Diddy Diddy" on EMI that moved into the number one spot in England and, shortly after, repeated this success when released in the U.S. on the Ascot label. It reached number one in *Billboard* the week of October 17, 1964.

The group kept up a torrid pace during 1965 and 1966. The 1965 schedule included concerts in Czechoslovakia, the first such visit to an Iron Curtain country by a rock group. The group made the charts regularly in Europe and the U.S. with a series of LPs released in America on the Ascot and United Artists labels. Among those issued on Ascot were *Manfred Mann and the Manfreds, 5 Faces,* and *My Little Red Book* (1965) and *Mann Made* (1966). The United Artists LPs included *Pretty Flamingo* (1966) and *Greatest Hits* in (1967).

The group roster behind Mann and Hugg changed

from time to time. By the mid-1960s, Jack Bruce left to join Cream and was replaced by Michael Vickers. Paul Jones left after 1967 and was replaced on lead vocals by Mike D'Abo. From 1966 on, though, Mann and Hugg cut down on concert performances to leave more time for relaxation and composing. The group still made the hit charts regularly in the U.K. and U.S., gaining such singles hits as "Come Tomorrow" (Ascot, 1965), "Pretty Flamingo" (United Artists, 1966), "The Mighty Quinn" (Mercury, 1968), and, in its last year, 1969, "Fox on the Run" and "Ragamuffin Way" on Mercury.

In late 1969, the Manfreds were disbanded and replaced by a new aggregation, the Manfred Mann Chapter Three. The goal of this move was to give Mann and Hugg the chance to concentrate on new forms of pop, not necessarily jazz, but a blend of jazz, rock, blues, and other forms that appealed to the artists. It included Bernie Living on flute, Steve York on bass, and Craig Collinge on drums.

As Mann told an English interviewer at the time of the change: "I think you have to make fundamental decisions more than once in your life if you are going to achieve anything. Every musician makes one when he decides to give up being an insurance clerk or, in my case, giving up being the son of a successful printer in South Africa to come to the U.K. as a musician. . . . I felt this was the time for a fundamental change. Also, for the first time in years I'm interested in writing a few things, though I think of myself more as a musician than a writer."

In 1972, Mann had organized still another group, the Earth Band. In 1972, Polydor released *Mannfred Mann's Earth Band,* a chart hit both in England and the U.S., boosted by a fine version of Dylan's rarely heard "Please Mrs. Henry." The group also had the 1972 single hit "Living without You." In mid-1973, the group made the charts with the Polydor album *Get Your Rocks Off.* The title track, another Dylan number, received wide airplay. His crew's fascination with obscure Dylan songs also surfaced when Mann produced the cult classic *Lo & Behold: Words & Music by Boy Dylan* by Colson, Dean, McGuinness, Flint (McGuinness being Tom McGuinness of the Manfreds), released on Sire in the U.S. in 1972. During 1974, Polydor issued what was to prove the band's last collection for that label, *Solar Fire.* A retrospective, *The Best of Manfred Mann,* was released in 1974 by Janus Records.

In 1974, the Earth Band signed with Warner Brothers, which issued its label debut, *The Good Earth,* that year, followed by *Nightingales and Bombers* in 1975. The band, with Chris Hamlet-Thompson handling lead vocals, had a number one hit (February 19, 1977) in *Billboard* with its version of Springsteen's "Blinded by the Light," a track

31. JOE WALSH OF THE EAGLES

32. DON FELDER OF THE EAGLES

33. EARTH, WIND & FIRE

34. THE EURYTHMICS

35. FLEETWOOD MAC

36. JOHN FOGERTY

**37. ARETHA
FRANKLIN**

38. MARVIN GAYE

39. PETER GABRIEL

40. JERRY GARCIA OF THE GRATEFUL DEAD

41. HEART

42. JIMI HENDRIX

43. BUDDY HOLLY

**44. MICHAEL
JACKSON**

45. MICK JAGGER

46. JORMA KAUKONEN OF JEFFERSON AIRPLANE

47. BILLY JOEL

48. JANIS JOPLIN

49. JUDAS PRIEST

50. B.B. KING

51. KISS

52. PATTI LABELLE

53. JOHN LENNON AND YOKO ONO

54. LED ZEPPELIN

**55. LITTLE RICHARD
AND BILL HALEY**

**56. FRANKIE LYMON
AND THE
TEENAGERS**

57. LYNYRD SKYNYRD

58. MADONNA

**59. BOB MARLEY
AND THE WAILERS**

**60. PAUL
MCCARTNEY**

61. VAN MORRISON

62. MÖTLEY CRÜE

from the gold LP *The Roaring Silence* (1976). The band seemed to lose momentum after that and much of the material on its succeeding Warner Brothers albums of the late 1970s and early 1980s was of rather indifferent quality. (During that time, another collection of older recordings was released by Capitol Records, the 1977 *The Best of Manfred Mann*.) Members in the late 1970s included Chris Hamlet Thompson (vocals, guitar), Dave Flett (guitar), Pat King (bass), and Chris Slade (percussion). The post-1976 Earth Band Warners releases included *Watch* (1978), *Angel Station* (1979), and *Chance* (1980).

(*See Cream; Dylan, Bob; Newman, Randy; Springsteen, Bruce.*)

MARLEY, BOB: *Singer, guitarist, songwriter, band leader (THE WAILERS). Born Rhoden Hall, St. Ann, Jamaica, April 6, 1945; died Miami, Florida, May 11, 1981. The Wailers (1973): Carlton ("Carlie") Barrett, born Kingston, Jamaica, December 17, 1950 died Kingston, Jamaica, April 1987; Aston ("Family Man") Barrett, born Kingston, Jamaica, November 22, 1946; Neville ("Bunny") Livingston, born Kingston, Jamaica, April 10, 1947; Peter Tosh, born Church Lincoln, Westmorland, Jamaica, October 19, 1944 died Kingston, Jamaica, September 1987; Earl Wilber Force ("Wire") Lindo, born Kingston, Jamaica, January 7, 1953. The Wailers later comprised Aston Barrett, Carlton Barrett, Tyrone Downie, Alvin Patterson, Earl Smith, Donald Kinsey, Al Anderson.*

"Greeting in the name of his majesty, Emperor Hail-e-eye Selass-e-eye . . . Rastafar-I! Ever lovin' ever fearful, ever sure Selass-e-eye the First. . . . Yeh! . . . Yeh! . . . Rastafar-I ever lovin'."

Intoned from a concert stage by a slight, yet striking Jamaican with long, black corkscrew curls falling to his shoulders, these words signaled the typical beginning of a show by the king of reggae, Bob Marley, and his group the Wailers. Anyone fortunate enough to attend a live performance by Marley and his cohorts could not fail to experience the excitement generated by his style of reggae, that intriguing blend of rock, R&B, soul, and Jamaican folk rhythms. The difference between his roots reggae and the watered-down versions by non-Jamaican artists such as Eric Clapton (who had a 1973 hit with a cover of Marley's "I Shot the Sheriff") was like the difference between day and night. (*See Clapton, Eric.*) Though it took close to a decade before Bob was able to reach out successfully to the general U.S. and British audience, by the mid-1970s he was an acknowledged superstar whose memory remained even after his untimely death from cancer in 1981.

As Marley indicated in opening his shows, he was strongly dedicated to the Rastafarian religion, which was brought to Jamaica by the deported New York Harlem black nationalist leader Marcus Garvey (1887–1940). The pivotal figure of that belief is the late ruler of Ethiopia, Haile Selassie (whose family name was Ras Tafari), seen as the personification of God (Jah). Part of the teachings of Rastafarianism is that Selassie will one day return and lead his followers back to Africa (a theme touched on in Marley's 1977 hit, "Exodus: Movement of Jah People"). Bob's conversion to the religion as a young man in 1967 shocked his devoutly Christian mother and influenced both his songwriting and his general attitudes toward life.

The development of reggae, of course, is strongly (though not exclusively) related to Rastafarianism. But unlike some gospel singers in other religions, the writers of reggae never saw anything strange in adopting all topics to the pulsating rhythms of the music (rhythms, as one American drummer described them, based on "inside-out rock'n'roll with accents on the second two beats and you break your back just trying to keep it going"). If reggae sometimes sings praises of the Rastafarian religious beliefs, more often it reviews the ills, joys, and dreams of humanity, particularly from the vantage point of the downtrodden people trying to escape from the slums of Jamaican cities.

It was an environment all too familiar to Marley—the son of a white British army captain, who took no part in the boy's upbringing, and a Jamaican mother. Born in the northern part of the island, Robert Nesta Marley grew up in restricted circumstances where his mother worked for "t'irty shillings a week," barely enough to keep the family going. In 1961, while the 16-year-old Marley was learning the welding trade, he formed his first harmony group, which evolved into his first band, the Rudeboys, who became known as the Wailers as the '60s moved by. In 1964, he scored his first local hit with the song "Summer Down," which featured Bunny Livingston on lead vocal, backed by Marley, Peter Tosh, Junior Braithwaite, and Beverly Kelso. Most of that group left in 1966, but Marley, already a headliner, kept going with new alliances. (*See Tosh, Peter.*)

Marley was recognized as a rising talent in the highly competitive reggae world of Jamaica's capital of Kingston, but the financial rewards were meager. His group cut four albums in the late '60s and early '70s which were well below best-seller levels. In 1972, he was signed by another Jamaican, Chris Blackwell, founder of Island Records, which released his label debut, the superb *Catch a Fire*, shortly after. Marley's first U.S.-released LP, it received little attention from record buyers. It was followed by other brilliant collections such as *Burnin'* (containing Marley's version of his composition "I Shot the Sheriff") in 1973, *Natty Dread* (1975), and *Live* (1975). In 1974, two albums of pre-Island material, *African Herbsman* and *Rasta Revolution* on the Trojan label, became available in the U.S. as imports. By the time *Burnin'* came out, Peter Tosh and Bunny Livingston had left the group and Marley moved out from handling lead guitar to also taking over as primary vocalist. As future developments showed, the change proved rewarding for all three artists.

With the release of *Rastaman Vibrations* in 1976, Marley, already acclaimed in the U.K. and Europe as well as in the Caribbean, finally became a recognized star with U.S. fans. But even as Bob gained acceptance outside Jamaica, he found himself almost a man without a country. He had to spend much of the late 1970s away from his homeland after political turmoil (reflected in gang warfare) resulted in an attack on his life. Just before his group was to give a free government-sponsored concert in Kingston, seven men forced their way into Marley's home, injuring Bob and three others. It was conjectured that the raiders were partisans of the political party opposed to the government then in power. Marley was wounded in the arm, but escaped with his life. After that 1976 incident, though, he spent much of his time in other parts of the world, even when he wasn't touring.

Meanwhile, he continued to record spine-tingling new reggae on *Exodus* (1977), the two-disc live set *Babylon by Bus* and *Kaya* (1978), and *Uprising* (1980). Reissues of his earlier work continued to come out on other labels, such as *Birth of a Legend* and *Early Music,* both on Calla in 1977, and *Soul Sheakdown Party* on Ala in 1980.

Though other reggae artists gained followings in the U.S., none could match the successes achieved by Marley and his band. One of the reasons for his rapport with U.S. fans where few had even heard of most other reggae stars is indicated on *Babylon by Bus.* Other major reggae exponents such as Tosh and Bunny Wailer tended to turn out more somber, often almost atonal material. Marley, on the other hand, always maintained a lighter touch. In fact, in mid-1970s concerts, he changed the arrangements of songs such as "Rat Race" and "Rebel Music" to make them more accessible. But this didn't mean he sugar-coated his message. In "Rat Race," the music was compellingly danceable, but the words retained their sting. ("Oh, it's a disgrace to see the human race/In a rat race/You got the horse race/You got the dog race/You got the human race.")

Marley's subjects covered a range of sociological topics from light-hearted love songs ("Is This Love," "Stir It Up," "Little Darlin'") to the optimistic overview ("Positive Vibrations") to the political warnings of "No More Trouble." ("Until the philosophy/Which holds one race superior and another inferior/Is finally and permanently abandoned/Well everywhere is war.") And though some reggae activists complained about the bright tone of the music in such songs it seems likely that the words struck home even more effectively due to the light mood. Certainly this is the case in "Concrete Jungle" (one of the best musical indictments of recent times about the terrible plight of many inner cities) where the singer cries out: "A light must somehow be found/Instead of a concrete jungle" while making the point that "No chains on my feet/ But I am not free/I am down here in captivity."

Still advancing creatively and at the height of his writing and performing powers as indicated by his excellent 1980 Island release *Uprising* (which ironically included the dramatic track "Wake Up and Live"), Marley was struck down by cancer. After his death in 1981, though, he left the magnificent legacy of his record catalog and family survivors, including his wife Rita (who performed in his backing group the I-Threes for many years) and a talented son to keep his traditions alive.

In the years after Bob's passing, indeed, there was a profusion of Marley/Wailer relations and/or alumni on the concert circuit or in recording studios. At the same time, albums of earlier Bob Marley material, some previously unreleased, came out. In 1982, a substandard posthumous collection *Chances Are,* was released on Atlantic/Cotillion. In 1983, though, Island issued the well prepared LP *Confrontations* offering only songs never before released or previously unreleased in the U.S. In 1986, Bunny Wailer coordinated a new double album, *Together Again,* which provided tracks made by the Wailers and Marley in the 1960s and new recordings by Bunny, Peter Tosh, Junior Braithwaite, and Constantine Walker. Braithwaite, who had moved to Chicago in 1965, had been lead singer of the first Wailers band in 1963, whose other members were Marley, Tosh, Bunny, and Beverly Kelso. Walker had replaced Marley as lead singer for the year 1966 and later toured with Tosh.

Bunny, who had gone into seclusion on a rural Jamaican farm in 1975, returned to action as a solo performer in 1980 and had such U.S. releases on Shanachie Records in the 1980s as *Roots Radics Rockers Reggae* (1983) and *Marketplace* (1986).

The group that bore the Wailers title during the last years of Bob's life had major problems for a number of years thereafter because, they stated, six months after Bob's death they had signed an exclusive recording contract with Rita Marley that included a clause in which they agreed to relinquish control of the Wailers name. The legal and financial problems involved kept that group, which included the Barrett brothers, Al Anderson and Junior Marvin, from doing any extensive touring until early 1987 after they had filed an $8 million lawsuit against the Marley estate alleging they had signed the earlier contract without legal counsel and hadn't understood its provisions. The suit also demanded an audit of royalty payments made to the estate after Marley's death.

Hardly had the group gotten its new career underway when drummer Carlton Barrett was shot to death in April 1987, apparently due to a lover's quarrel. By summer bassist Aston Barrett had revamped the band by adding Cornell Marshall on drums, former Third World member Irvin Jarrett on percussion, and Martin Batista on keyboards.

Still, it appeared that the true torchbearers of the Marley legacy would be his own family. The early 1980s European success of the LP *Legends,* presenting a group of Marley's old hits, encouraged Rita to organize the first of a series of worldwide tours featuring members of the old Wailers, the I-Threes and son David "Ziggy" Marley, as well as other Marley children.

Before Bob's death he had been able to hear the promise of his youngsters in 1980 when they recorded a song he'd written for them, "Children Playing on the Street." The children took the group name The Melody Makers, which they used five years later for their debut album on EMI-America, *Play the Game Right.* Nine of the LP's ten songs were written by Ziggy and were of high enough quality to warrant a Grammy nomination in the 1985 reggae category.

The Melody Makers first U.S. tour occurred in 1986. The group was made up of Ziggy (born 1968), his 14-year-old brother Stevie, and sisters Sharon, 22, and Cedalla, 19. He told Don Snowden (*Los Angeles Times,* July 19, 1986), "We're just trying to make our own style and to also make new trends. We can't be keeping the same thing. We have to keep adding on."

In early 1987, at the sixth annual Bob Marley Day concert in Santa Monica, California, Ziggy had progressed to being one of the stars of the show. His charismatic performance suggested he had the ability to lead reggae to new creative heights. He didn't feel any pressure from that, he told Steve Hochman (*Los Angeles Times,* February 10, 1987). "It feel good and so that why I do it." But he also indicated he hoped reggae would find many new leaders. "Even my father say reggae can't die. It's not only one man to carry on. It's many people. I just want to play reggae music and give my message."

MARLEY, ZIGGY: *See Marley, Bob.*

MARTHA AND THE VANDELLAS: *Vocal group. Original members (1963): Martha Reeves, born Detroit, Michigan, July 18, 1941; Betty Kelly, born September 16, 1944; Rosalind Ashford, born September 2, 1943. Group disbanded in 1970, reformed in 1971 with Reeves, Lois Reeves, and Sandra Tilley.*

It stands to reason that a talented person working for a music company would have a good chance at being discovered. This doesn't always follow, but it did in Martha Reeves' case, although she did not have a singing career in mind when she started working for Motown Records.

She joined the company as a secretary a few years after finishing high school in Detroit. Initially she performed the usual tasks of answering the phone for her boss, typing letters, and filing. Because she had a good voice, she was given an added responsibility of singing song lyrics into a tape recorder. The tape would then be turned over to an artist to study the words for an upcoming recording session. (Most of the material prepared in this way was for background vocalists for one of the firm's "name" performers.)

Then a backup singer fell ill when a recording date was scheduled and a Motown executive decided to let Martha take the woman's place. She did so well that the session producer suggested teaming her with two other supporting singers, Betty Kelly and Rosalind Ashford, to provide a regular trio for future session needs. Soon after, the girls sang behind Marvin Gaye on his 1962 hit, "Stubborn Kind of Fellow." During 1962 and early 1963, they worked with Gaye on more songs, as well as with several other major vocalists. (*See Gaye, Marvin.*)

In 1963, Motown executives agreed that the trio had potential as a featured act with Martha as the lead singer. They were signed to the label and their second single release, "Come and Get These Memories" (on Motown's subsidiary, Gordy), was a top 10 R&B hit soon after. Later in the year, their "Heat Wave" soared to number one on R&B charts and number four on *Billboard*'s pop charts. The record also became a top 10 hit in England, providing combined U.S./overseas sales of well over a million copies. Also achieving considerable sales totals in 1963–64 were the LPs *Come and Get These Memories* and *Heat Wave.*

From 1963 through 1967, Martha and the Vandellas ranked with the most important stars on the various Motown labels, turning out a string of singles that made the hit charts, including one top 10 hit on *Billboard*'s pop charts: "Quicksand" in 1963, "Dancing in the Street" in 1964, "Nowhere to

Run'' in 1965, "I'm Ready for Love" in 1966, and "Jimmy Mack" in 1968. Successful LPs included *Dance Party, Watchout,* and the top 10 1966 disc *Greatest Hits.*

Starting in 1968, though the trio remained an important in-person act, it hit a dry spell as far as new record hits were concerned. At the start of the '70s, Martha decided to break up the group and stop touring for a while. In early 1971, though, she returned to the musical wars accompanied by two new vocalists: her sister Lois Reeves and Sandra Tilley. "Bless You" was in the top 20s on both the R&B charts and *Billboard* pop charts. Also a R&B chart hit in 1971 was the single "I Gotta Let You Go." In 1972, the group placed the singles "In and Out of My Life" and "Tear It on Down" and the album *Black Magic* on the R&B charts.

In the mid-1970s, Martha broke up the group again in favor of a solo career. She moved to other labels, first Arista Records, which issued the LP *The Rest of My Life* in 1977, and then Fantasy, where her LPs included *We Meet Again* (1978) and *Gotta Keep Moving* (1980). As of the early 1980s, though, none of her solo albums captured the emotional fervor of the old Vandellas offerings. That was easily observed by comparing her individual recordings with such Motown retrospectives as *Anthology* (1974) and *Super Star Series, Volume 11* (1981).

MARVELETTES, THE: *Vocal group from Detroit, Michigan, all born c. 1945. Original group: Gladys Horton; Katherine Anderson; Georgeanna Tillman, died January 6, 1980; Juanita Cowart; Wanda Young. Cowart and Tillman left by mid-1960s. Horton replaced by Anne Bogan in 1968.*

The rapid rise of Motown Records in the early 1960s was fueled by a seemingly inexhaustible supply of exceedingly talented Detroit youngsters. First there was Smokey Robinson and his Miracles, followed in rapid succession by such Motor City high school products as the amazing Supremes and, almost simultaneously, the Marvelettes.

The latter group, which was reduced to a trio by the mid-1960s, started as a quintet of teenage girls at Inkster High School. All five had been singing since childhood in church choirs or school events before forming their group at the start of the '60s. Berry Gordy, Jr., whose fledgling record firm had gotten underway in Detroit just about the time the girls started at Inkster, began to keep an eye on musical developments in local high schools, sometimes catching school shows himself and usually having at least one contact at a school who could keep him abreast of any promising newcomers. Berry generally didn't like to sign people until they were in line

to complete their schooling—he told the Supremes to come back after they graduated, for example—but he did try to be ready to welcome new talent at the proper time. (*See Gordy, Berry, Jr.*)

So it was that he found out about the Marvelettes when they performed in a talent show in their senior year at Inkster High School in early 1961. The group, whose original members were Gladys Horton, Katherine Anderson, Georgeanna Tillman, Juanita Cowart, and Georgia Dobbins, called itself the Casinyets (derived from the words "can't sing yet"). They finished fourth in the competition. Only the first three groups were guaranteed an audition with Motown, but the girls' teacher, Mrs. Sharpley, thought they were good enough that the school principal should ask Motown to listen to them too.

At the audition they sang cover songs of material performed by other artists. Motown officials liked them, but suggested they bring in some original numbers. Georgia Dobbins then got the song "Please Mr. Postman" from songwriter friend William Garrett; the girls' rendition of it finally won them a contract. (Ironically, Georgia had to leave to take care of her ill mother and was replaced by Wanda Young, but she still ended up sharing writing credits on "Please Mr. Postman" with Garrett, Brian Holland, and Robert Bateman.)

As was his practice, Motown head Berry Gordy didn't rush them into a studio, but had vocal coaches rehearse them at length. Before they turned out any recordings, he also changed their name to the Marvelettes. One of the first songs they recorded was "Please Mr. Postman." It rose to number one on the *Billboard* pop singles list the week of December 11, 1961. In 1962, the group turned out two more best-sellers, "Playboy" and "Beechwood 4-5789."

The group remained one of the most successful in the business as the decade went by. Their major successes on R&B or pop charts over the period were "As Long As I Know His Name" (1964), "Too Many Fish in the Sea" (1965), "Don't Mess with Bill" (1966), "The Hunter Gets Captured by the Game" (1967), "My Baby Must Be a Magician" (1968), and "That's How Heartaches Are Made" (1969).

The girls placed most of their LPs on the best-seller charts as well, including *Playboy* (1963), *The Marvelous Marvelettes* (1964), *Greatest Hits* (1966), and *Marvelettes* (1967).

Reduced to a trio in the mid-1960s, the group continued to be a major concert attraction. Juanita Cowart was first to leave, followed by Georgeanna Tillman. Gladys Horton then left to start a family and her place was taken in 1968 by Anne Bogan. The group began the 1970s with such LPs as *In Full Bloom* and *Return of the Marvelettes.* During the early 1970s, however, other members decided in favor of domestic duties and the group broke up. Most of its hits were repackaged in the 1975 Motown retrospective *Marvelettes Anthology*.

Georgeanna died after a lengthy illness on January 6, 1980. In the mid-1980s, Gladys indicated an interest in reviving the Marvelettes, but Katherine and Wanda resisted, stating they preferred staying at home.

MASON, DAVE: *Singer, guitarist, songwriter, band leader. Born Worcester, England, May 10, 1946.*

It took a while for British rock guitarist and songwriter Dave Mason to "happen." Greatly admired by other musicians, Mason always seemed on the verge of greatness in the second half of the 1960s without quite breaking through. His first attempt at songwriting, "Hole in My Shoe," proved to be the number that started Traffic on the way to supergroup status, but by then Mason was no longer a member. His eminently professional guitar playing helped make the "Delaney and Bonnie Bramlett's and Friends" tour of Europe a stepping stone to the Bramletts' stardom, but most of the attention went to fellow "sideman" Eric Clapton.

At the start of the 1970s, however, Mason went out as a soloist and his recordings and stage appearances initially won unvarnished praise from all quarters, though by the early 1980s he seemed to have lost much of his creative drive.

Born and raised in the English Midlands, Mason became interested in rock at an early age. He learned to play guitar in his teens and began performing with local groups. He acquired excellent technique in a fairly short time and was considered one of the best musicians in Birmingham, England, by the mid-1960s. Working with him at the time was drummer Jim Capaldi. In 1967, the two met rock prodigy Stevie Winwood in Birmingham. Winwood had just left the Spencer Davis Group and was interested in starting one of his own.

The three formed what was to become Traffic. However, there was dissension from the start about the arrangements and music selection. Winwood and Mason could not agree on things and Mason left before the album was released. The two respected each other's abilities, but could not merge their personalities when they worked together. (Most music columnists put the blame more on Winwood than on Mason.) As Winwood later told a reporter: "Dave expresses himself in a different way than we do, not altogether through 'music' as through 'songs.' He wasn't so much into moods as sounds."

The debut album (*Traffic*, United Artists, 1968) was an international hit and brought the group acclaim as one of the best of the decade. Much of the LP's flavor was due to Mason's contributions and, recognizing this, the group attempted to reconcile differences when the second LP was in preparation. Mason returned, briefly, in 1968 to do some tours and complete the second album which, like the first, was stated by its record company to have achieved gold record levels. Just before the group was scheduled to start its third album, the old frictions flared again and Mason left for good.

For a time, in fact, Traffic dissolved, and Capaldi got together with Mason to form a quartet that included Chris Wood and Wynder K. Frog. The group lasted only a short time. As Mason told Richard Williams of *Melody Maker:* "I got hung up very quickly with that band, because it wasn't handled right. I wanted to get it together in the States rather than [England], but the general feeling wasn't that good, anyway."

The group folded and Mason stayed in London for a while, without finding any worthwhile new venture. Finally he thought of going to the U.S. to find an agent and a recording contract. "I already knew Gram Parsons and Cass Elliott," he told Williams, "so I went to Los Angeles. I'd met Delaney and Bonnie through Gram two years earlier [in 1967] when they were playing little clubs in L.A. and I'd established a good relationship with them." Once in Los Angeles, Mason joined the Bramletts' troupe, performing on their live 1970 Atco LP *Delaney & Bonnie & Friends on Tour with Eric Clapton.*"

After returning to Los Angeles from the European leg of the tour, Dave went into (Sunset Sound Studio and Elektra Records' studio) with a contract from a new record company, Blue Thumb. For three months he polished up earlier songs, wrote new ones, and set down tracks for his first solo effort. Accompanying him were Delaney & Bonnie, Jim Capaldi, Rita Coolidge, and Leon Russell. The gold album, *Alone Together* (1970), won high marks from reviewers, who agreed his new compositions in the LP (such as "Feelin' Alright" and "Only You Know and I Know") were on a par with his previous rock "standards," such songs as "Can't Stop Worrying," "Look at You Look at Me" and "Shouldn't Have Took More than You Gave."

During the summer of 1970, he flew to LA and he and Cass Elliott (formerly of the Mamas and the Papas) began working on an act that debuted at Los Angeles' Hollywood Bowl in September. Most reviewers were not impressed with their combined efforts, and both went their own ways in 1971. Reviews of their LP, *Dave Mason and Cass Elliott* were mostly favorable, but the tenor was that the album added more luster to Mason's reputation than to Cass's.

He spent much of 1971 working on his second solo LP, released under the title *Headkeeper* in early 1972 and a chart hit later in the year. During the summer of 1973 his Blue Thumb album *Dave Mason Is Alive* made the best-seller lists, though by that time Mason had moved to another label, Columbia. His first Columbia release, *It's Like You Never Left*, appeared on the charts in mid-November 1973 and remained on them into 1974. This was followed by the gold *Dave Mason* (1974) with a fine rendition of Bob Dylan's "All along the Watchtower" and the old Sam Cooke hit, "Bring It on Home to Me." (Also issued during 1974 was the Blue Thumb LP *The Best of Dave Mason*.)

His 1975–76 releases included the two-disc album *Certified Live* and the studio LP *Split Coconut*, both on Columbia, and *Dave Mason at His Very Best* on ABC. His fifth album on Columbia (*Let It Go, Let It Flow*, 1977), which he co-produced with Ron Nevison, found him at the peak of his popularity with rock fans. Cuts such as "We Just Disagree," "So High," "Mystic Traveler," and "Let It Go" got a great amount of airplay, which helped push the disc to worldwide platinum sales levels.

In truth, however, the album didn't seem to mark any major advance over Dave's earlier albums. Nor were his next two Columbia releases, *Mariposa de Oro* (1978) and his first release of the '80s, *Old Crest on a New Wave*, strikingly different. They were, of course, eminently professional in their musicianship. Certainly many tracks were as good or better than most new releases of the period, but Mason seemed to have reached a plateau in his writing and performing skills.

For several years in the mid-1980s, Mason maintained a very low profile vis-a-vis the entertainment field. He commented for an MCA Records bio release in 1987, "Music stopped being fun. I didn't even pick up a guitar for a year. I stopped writing. I had my bouts with drugs and alcohol like many of us, and I really needed to get away to see what I wanted in life."

The phase ended when executives of the small Voyager label sought him out in his hideaway in Lake Tahoe and offered a new recording contract which led to the late 1987 LP release (distributed by MCA Records), *Two hearts*.

(*See* Clapton, Eric; Coolidge, Rita; Mamas and the Papas, The; Parsons, Gram; Traffic; Winwood, Steve.)

MATTHEWS, IAN: *See Southern Comforts.*

MAYALL, JOHN: *Singer, guitarist, organist, harmonica player, record producer, songwriter, band leader (THE BLUESBREAKERS). Born* Manchester, England, November 29, 1934. (*See footnote * for partial listing of band personnel 1963–75.*)

Tall, gangling John Mayall could always be counted on to defy existing musical tradition. He formed his first major band at 30 at a time when a pop musician over 20 was considered ancient. He played blues-rock and jazz-rock in his own relatively subdued way when hyperamplification was the rage. He continually experimented, varying groups and musical content no matter how commercially successful a particular pattern seemed to be. Despite a lack of best-sellers for most of his career, he persevered and outlasted many of the big-name stars of the moment.

After graduating from art school, where he majored in graphic design, in the early 1950s, he spent many years in the advertising field and won a reputation as one of Manchester, England's best typography and graphic design experts. (He later put this experience to work in preparing the artwork for several of his album covers.) He also worked as a window dresser.

During the 1950s, Mayall was caught up in the skiffle craze then sweeping England, a movement that helped solidify his interest in traditional blues. He performed with small groups in Manchester for a while, moving to London at the start of the 1960s to

---

Partial Listing of Mayall Bands Personnel
1963—guitar: Bernie Watson; bass guitar: John McVie; drums: Peter Ward. 1964—guitar: Roger Dean; bass guitar: John McVie; drums: Hughie Flint. 1965—guitar: Eric Clapton; bass guitar: John McVie and Jack Bruce; drums: Hughie Flint. 1966—guitar: Eric Clapton (six months), Peter Green; bass guitar: John McVie; drums: Hughie Flint (six months), Aynsley Dunbar. 1967—guitar: Peter Green (six months), Mick Taylor; bass guitar: John McVie (nine months), Paul Williams; drums: Mick Fleetwood (six months), Keef Hartley; saxophones: Dick Heckstall-Smith. Chris Mercer. 1968—guitar: Mick Taylor; bass guitar: Andy Fraser (three months), Tony Reeves (three months), Steve Thompson; drums: Keef Hartley (three months), Jon Hiseman (three months), Colin Allen; saxophones: Dick Heckstall-Smith, Chris Mercer; trumpet: Henry Lowther. 1969—guitar: Mick Taylor (six months), Jon Mark; bass guitar: Steve Thompson; drums: Colin Allen; saxophones: Johnny Almond. 1970—guitar: Jon Mark (six months), Harvey Mandel; bass guitar: Steve Thompson (three months), Larry Taylor; drums: none; saxophone: Johnny Almond (six months); violin: Sugarcane Harris. 1971—guitar: Harvey Mandel to Jimmy McCulloch to Freddy Robinson; bass guitar: Larry Taylor; drums: Paul Labos to Keef Hartley to Ron Selico; violin: Sugarcane Harris; saxophones: Clifford Solomon; trumpet: Blue Mitchell. 1972— guitar: Freddy Robinson; string bass: Victor Gaskin; drums: Keef Hartley; horns: Blue Mitchell (trumpet), Clifford Solomon (saxophone), Fred Clark (saxophone). 1973—guitar: Freddy Robinson; string bass: Victor Gaskin; drums: Keef Hartley; horns: Blue Mitchell (trumpet), Red Holloway (saxophone and flute). 1974-75—Larry Taylor (bass); Sugarcane Harris (violin); Dee McKinnie (vocals).

447

work as a sideman with some of the blues-rock groups flourishing as an aftermath of skiffle. He started his own band in 1964 and soon won approval from most of the English rock stars as one of the most innovative band leaders around. In particular, Mayall from the start was a superb judge of young performers. Because so many Bluesbreakers alumni went on to international fame, John was given the nickname "grandfather of British rock."

His 1965–66 band featured two of the most impressive talents in rock history: lead guitarist Eric Clapton and bassist Jack Bruce. The recordings made by the group, which strangely never became hits, are now considered classics of rock. Clapton and Bruce later influenced an entire generation of young guitarists when they left Mayall to join Ginger Baker in Cream. (*See Clapton, Eric; Cream.*)

Personnel changes never seemed to worry Mayall. In fact, on at least one occasion, he dissolved a group to give a musician a chance to join another internationally successful band. One reason probably was Mayall's faith in his judgment. If one skilled sideman left, he always seemed able to find another expert to take his place. Thus his band rosters through the early 1970s look like a who's who of rock: besides Clapton and Bruce, there were such artists as Aynsley Dunbar (*see Jefferson Airplane; Journey*); Peter Greene (*see Fleetwood Mac*); Mick Taylor, lead guitarist during mid-1967–mid-1969, who took Brian Jones' place with the Rolling Stones (*see Rolling Stones, The*); and many others.

Despite the great competence of Mayall's bands, it took most of the 1960s before his hard core of avid followers were complemented by the mass audience. He gained some success in England in the mid-1960s, after signing with London Records, with such 1967 LPs as *Blues* and *Hard Road,* but he was hardly a threat to top 10 groups. Slowly, however, rock fans became aware of his musical contributions and, by the end of the '60s, Mayall was receiving the attention he deserved.

His tours of the U.S., which started in the late 1960s, made him decide to buy a house in the Los Angeles area, where he spent half of each year from then on. Fans were impressed with his 1969–70 group that included John Thompson on bass and versatile Johnny Almond (born 1946), who could play a dozen instruments, including saxophone, flute, vibraharp, organ, and guitar. This group, as was to be expected, was unorthodox. It was a jazz-blues band, but it had no drummer. The introduction of jazz elements into a pop format was daring, considering the tastes of most rock fans.

By this time, Mayall was recognized for his new and old work. In 1969, he played the Newport Jazz Festival and his final LP for London, *Looking Back* (reviewing his material and group makeup during 1964–67) was a top 20 U.K. hit, while his new label, Polydor, released the gold LP *Turning Point,* recorded live at the Fillmore East.

In the early 1970s, some of Mayall's albums seemed to be assembled more for quantity than quality. London Records reached into its vaults to release *Diary of a Band* (1970) and *John Mayall in Europe, with the Bluesbreakers* and *John Mayall through the Years* (1971). Ampex Records reissued an album of his early work with Eric Clapton, while Polydor issued *Empty Rooms, Memories, USA Union,* the two-disc *Back to the Roots, Jazz-Blues Fusion, Moving On,* and *10 Years Are Gone.* London kept on repackaging his older material on *Down the Line* (1973) *A Banquet in Blues* (1976), and *Primal Solos* (1978).

Through it all, Mayall continued to go his own way, playing what Leonard Feather called his "blues without bedlam." John showed his independence in the lyrics he wrote for many of his songs, which avoided the stereotyped response of many rock artists to police brutality, drugs, and other problems. Thus in "The Laws Must Change" on his first Polydor LP, he wrote: "You're screaming at policemen, but they are only doing a gig." He expanded on his intent at one point to Feather. "I meant that it's not the law enforcers we should worry about—after all, they're only the hirelings—but rather the laws themselves. In the same song, I hinted at [late comedian] Lenny Bruce's much more extended discussions and theories along these lines, about not throwing rocks at cops, but getting the knots of laws untied."

In 1975, he switched to a new label, ABC, which released *New Year, New Band, New Company* and, later in 1975, *Notice to Appear.* He followed with such ABC albums as *A Hard Core Package* (1977) and *Last of the British Blues* (1979). By the end of the decade, Mayall had left ABC and his new material, such as the albums *The Bottom Line* and *No More Interviews,* came out on DJM Records.

MAYFIELD, CURTIS: *Singer, guitarist, songwriter, record producer. Born Chicago, Illinois, June 3, 1942.*

The lead singer and driving force behind the Impressions, one of the most important groups in the history of soul, Curtis Mayfield brought his own name into the spotlight in 1971. Though still providing material and encouragement for his old group, he went his own way as a soloist in 1969 and in the early 1970s established himself as a first-rank individual performer. Later in the decade, he cut back on his performing activities to concentrate more on producing records for other artists and writing film scores. As he noted in the mid-1970s, "I'm too busy to tour."

Curtis was involved in music even before his teens. "I was always writing when I was 10, 11, 12 years old, I guess. I suppose a lot of it had to do with my mother and grandmother. I used to write church songs, too. I used to write gospel and sing in a gospel group and actually, the only difference later was that instead of putting the word *God* in it, I would just leave that open for the individual to take in. As a matter of fact, 'Keep On Pushin' was a gospel song and I changed some of the lyrics. Instead of saying, 'God gave me my strength,' I'd say, 'I've got my strength and it don't make no sense not to keep on pushin'.'"

At 14, Curtis was part of a group called the Alphatones when his family left his neighborhood for a new location on Chicago's North Side. His new neighbor was Jerry Butler, a few years older and part of a gospel group of his own. The two became friends and, after a while, became part of a pop group called the Roosters that evolved into the first version of the Impressions. It was that quintet that achieved the classic R&B hit "For Your Precious Love" in 1958. The record company had decided to change the group's name to Jerry Butler and the Impressions and the internal dissension that caused resulted in the group's falling apart. (*See Butler, Jerry; Impressions, The.*)

Curtis noted: "It created somewhat hard feelings among fellows that were all striving equally and trying to make it." Soon after, Butler departed in favor of a solo career and the others, Curtis said, "went back and starved a little bit."

Butler, however, asked Curtis to continue touring with him as his guitar player. Mayfield stayed on for two years, saving his money in hopes of reforming the Impressions. While with Butler, he wrote a song that became a 1960 *Billboard* top 10 hit for Jerry, "He Will Break Your Heart." By the start of the '60s, Curtis had enough funds to bring the other Impressions to New York (with Fred Cash replacing Butler), where in 1961 they recorded his composition "Gypsy Woman." A top 20 pop hit on ABC-Paramount, it encouraged the reactivated group to think it could go forward from there. They achieved many more R&B and pop hits during the decade before Mayfield felt it was time for him to find new creative opportunities.

With the Impressions, Mayfield had established a reputation as a thoughtful lyricist on the problems of race in particular and the nation in general. As he told one reporter: "We're complimented that people look on us as spokesmen, but we think we're just singing what all the brothers feel." Though he could express anger (as in his 1970 hit, "If There's a Hell Down Below, We're All Gonna Go)", in general his was a soft, high-pitched voice of moderation. He stressed that his two main messages, faith and inspiration, stemmed from his childhood and particularly reflected the deep religious faith of his grandmother.

His approach continued to find favor with R&B audiences with his emergence as a soloist. *Billboard*'s 1971 year-end assessment found Curtis to have the second-best album sales in the soul field. Even more impressive was his standing in the overall male vocal field—ranking eighth in the *Billboard* review for his first album on his own (*Curtis,* issued in the fall of 1970), his two-LP *Curtis Mayfield Live* (a mixture of previous hits and new compositions, such as "Hell Down Below," "Mighty Mighty," "We're a Winner," "Stare and Stare," "Stone Junkie," and "I Plan to Stay a Believer") and *Roots*. All three came out on his own record label, Curtom. He started off 1972 with another hit single, "Get Down."

1972 was a banner year for him, particularly due to his score for the movie *Superfly*. His *Superfly* soundtrack album went gold as did his singles "Freddie's Dead" and the theme from the movie. Mayfield was thought likely to win an Oscar for his work, but the Academy of Motion Picture Arts and Sciences ruled the music out because the words were not sung in the picture. Mayfield had two other charted singles during the year: "We Got to Have Peace" and "Beautiful Brother of Mine." *Back to the World* (1973) earned him another gold-album award.

He continued to add to his film credits in 1974–75 by providing scores for *Claudine* and *Let's Do It Again*. *Claudine*'s material was recorded by Gladys Knight & the Pips. (*See Knight, Gladys & the Pips.*) Mayfield's work on *Claudine* won nominations for a Golden Globe Award from the Hollywood Foreign Press Association and for an Oscar. The Staple Singers' single of "Let's Do It Again" hit number one on *Billboard*'s pop singles list (December 27, 1975).

Meanwhile, Curtis placed more solo albums on the charts, including *Sweet Exorcist* (1974). *America Today* (1975) was released under a new Curtom distribution arrangement with Warner Brothers Records. In 1976, he scored the film *Sparkle* and also completed work on another solo LP, *Give, Get, Take and Have*. The following year he was represented by the soundtrack album of the film *Short Eyes* and his seventh solo set, *Never Say You Can't Survive*. Not only did he write the score for *Short Eyes*, he also was featured in an acting role. His late 1970s work included the score for the Sidney Poitier–Bill Cosby film *A Piece of the Action* and production of Aretha Franklin's 1978 album, *Almighty Fire*. (*See Franklin, Aretha*.) Also issued that year was his own LP, *Do It All Night*.

In 1979, he signed a new record agreement with RSO Records, putting out *Heartbeat* and the 1980 LP *Something to Believe In*. He was represented on the Brunswick label starting with the album *Love Is the Place* in 1981.

Curtis continued to record and make occasional concert tours throughout the 1980s, but had no singles or album successes to match the high points of earlier decades. In 1983 he was reunited with Butler, Cash and Gooden for a concert tour.

MAZE FEATURING FRANKIE BEVERLY:
Vocal and instrumental group led by Frankie Beverly, born Philadelphia, Pennsylvania, c. late 1940s. Members (mid-1970s) Ronald "Roame" Lowry, McKinley "Bug" Williams, Sam Porter, Robin Duhe, Joe Provost, Wayne Thomas (later called Wuane Thomas). Provost replaced by Ahaguna G. Sun in fall 1977. Sun left in early 1980s. Thomas left in early 1970s. Personnel as of 1983–84: Beverly, Duhe, Porter, Lowry, Williams, Ron Smith, Billy Johnson, Philip Woo. Smith, Johnson, and Woo left by end of 1984, replaced by Wuane Thomas and Wayne "Ziggy" Linsey.

With the many-faceted Frankie Beverly as band leader, lead vocalist, primary songwriter, producer, arranger, and sometime rhythm guitarist, the band Maze quietly became a power in the soul-rock genre from the mid-1970s on. It was obvious that Beverly was the force behind the group's success, but in the band's excellent concerts, its ensemble playing demonstrated that the whole definitely was greater than the sum of its parts. And it was those concerts that initially propelled its early albums to high positions on both black and pop charts while the band's record company was still trying to determine how or whether it could properly promote its new act.

Though there were occasional rumors about Beverly's leaving the band or internal dissension because of members' unhappiness with his dominance, all parties denied such problems. Maze told an interviewer from England's *Blues and Soul* magazine (April 16–29, 1985): "I look at it this way. There really isn't anything that I can't do from within Maze. I have all the room I need as a singer, as a writer, and as a producer. Therefore, I have no desire to do anything without them. . . . And the guys know that too. So, regardless of what they hear or what they read, they know the situation and they know they have no need to worry.

"Look, Maze is something I have built and devoted most of my life to. Why would I want to destroy that? I certainly don't have an ego need for something like that and I am in no way held back by being a part of Maze."

Beverly began his path to Maze in Philadelphia, where he was born and raised. As with many black artists, his first public performing was in his church choir. In his teens, he switched his interest to secular music, singing with several local doo-wop groups before forming his own band, the Blenders, when he was 17. After that, he joined the Butlers, who had such small-scale regional hits on local labels as "She Tried to Kiss Me" and "The Sun's Message." One, "I Want to Feel I'm Wanted" (a Beverly original), resurfaced many years later on the 1985 Maze LP *Can't Stop the Love*. He pointed out that the song "was written while I was in Philadelphia. I was pretty young when I wrote that song. It was one of the first two or three songs I put out. I can't even remember the label . . . maybe it was Cameo Parkway. That was 20 years ago. . . . But I was too young then to interpret the song the way I do now."

From the Butlers, Beverly went on to form Raw Soul, the direct antecedent of Maze. The group recorded two singles on RCA ("Color Blind" and "While I'm Alone") and worked as opening act for such artists as Kool & the Gang, Mandrill, and Isaac Hayes. It was good experience, but there was no sudden surge of popularity for the embryo group.

In 1972, Beverly and his associates agreed to go cross-country to establish a new base in San Francisco. He told Dick Richmond of the *St. Louis Post Dispatch* (March 16, 1978): "We moved to San Francisco because from '68 to '72 people like Sly Stone and Santana were happening there. They were like us, self-contained. I think we're the first instrumentally self-contained black group to come out of Philadelphia. The rest were singing groups backed by studio musicians.

"I really identify with Sly's group a lot. We have the same kind of thing. Black groups are often like families. When Sly broke his up, I think it hurt him."

There was no immediate bonanza on the other side of the rainbow for Raw Soul. Beverly told Richmond: "We didn't have any bread and we were out in the street. We survived playing small dates in rock clubs and the like, a night here, a night there. It took about eight months to find out who would hang on and who would leave. Since then we've added people, but Ronald Lowry [vocals, congas], McKinley Williams [vocals, percussion], and Sam Porter [keyboards] have been with me for about 10 years.

"What made it rougher was that we were playing

all original music. We never played top 40 music. We finally became a house band for a San Francisco club called the Scene. That's where Marvin Gaye's lady found us. Actually it was her sister who saw us and she brought Marvin's lady in.''

That contact proved a crucial first step. Beverly took tapes of the band down to Gaye in Los Angeles and Marvin was impressed enough to give the band a hand. Some of his plans for a close collaboration never materialized, but Beverly and his band did get to perform at many of Gaye's concerts. (*See Gaye, Marvin.*)

Gaye also recommended the band change its name, saying Raw Soul didn't fit the mellower, sultry sound of the group. Maze told Connie Johnson of *Black Stars* magazine (October 1978): "We started to call ourselves San Francisco. Then we threw around names like Karma, Charisma, Caravan. All the K and C sounds! It took us about a week to figure on Maze. The A-Mazing Maze!"

During the mid-1970s, the band gradually shook down to the seven-man combination that brought the first important successes. Robin Duhe joined as bass guitarist in 1973. In 1975, Joe Provost took over drum chores and the next year Wayne Thomas became lead guitarist. Those three, along with Beverly, Lowry, Porter, and Williams, recorded the demonstration tapes that won a contract from a major label, Capitol Records.

Actually, getting signed by Capitol was a stroke of good fortune the band hadn't envisioned. Beverly told Johnson: "We were aiming for a good independent label, and there are a million of them out there. We thought we'd at least be in the realm of possibility if we sent our tapes to them!

"Well, it turned out that wasn't true at all, 'cause we sent a tape to Capitol's New York office and they fell in love with it. It was like a dream come true. We recorded that first album and I listened to it night and day. I only got to the point where I could accept it after half a million . . . bought it and said it's okay."

The debut LP, *Maze Featuring Frankie Beverly*, was issued in January 1977 and amazed Capitol by surpassing gold-record levels by July. Beverly recalled for Johnson: "Capitol was kinda caught off guard when that happened. They thought we might catch on with the people by the time we released our third album, so they didn't really promote the first one like they should have."

Capitol itself was frank about it, issuing a press release that stated Maze's success "didn't result from a massive advertising and press campaign, but because the band toured extensively during the summer of '77. . . . In every city they played, immediate sales response followed their stunning concert performance.''

As it happened, not only did the debut album reach gold sales levels, but so did the next four albums: *Golden Time of Day* (1978), *Inspiration* (1979), and *Joy and Pain* and the band's first live LP, *Live in New Orleans* (both 1980). On those albums, Ahaguna G. Sun replaced Joe Provost on drums.

The group proved popular with buyers of singles as well as albums. The debut LP provided three songs that did well on soul and pop charts: "While I'm Alone," "Lady of Magic," and "Time Is on My Side." The last of those also became a top disco hit with the result that Maze was named "Most Promising Disco Group" in the 1977 Popular Music Disco Awards show in New York City. Charted singles from the second album were "Travelin' Man," "Workin' Together," "I Wish You Well," and the title song, "Golden Time of Day." From the next two studio albums, the group could point to such charted releases as "Feel That You're Feelin'," "Southern Girl," and "The Look in Your Eyes." The *Live in New Orleans* album, which also included some studio tracks, provided four top 30 singles including the top 10 hit "Running Away."

While Beverly and Maze became a top-rated act on the soul/funk concert circuit, it didn't break through to anything approaching superstardom in the U.S. That was partly due to the disdain the American critical "establishment" in influential publications such as *Rolling Stone* and *Village Voice* gave the group's offerings. But just as a change of scene from Philadelphia to San Francisco helped vitalize the band's career, a first visit to England in 1982 brought paeans of praise from the British press. As a critic for the London paper *The Guardian* wrote (April 25, 1985) in light of a by now annually triumphant overseas tour: "Maze . . . are truly a phenomenon in West London. With their first appearance at the Hammersmith Odeon in 1982, Maze seemingly crystallized a unique bond with the London soul audience which has grown apace. This time around they have sold out six nights at the Odeon without so much as a single concert booking outside London, engendering something of the excitement of the return of the conquering heroes."

Adrian Thrills in the May 1985 *New Musical Express* enthused: "Without resorting to hollow showmanship, gold lamé gimmickry, cosmic pretense, cabaret schmaltz, or coke-brained bravado, Maze delivered the finest R&B/soul that these white socks 'n' loafers have ever shuffled to."

The rapport Maze established with English fans helped place its 1983 Capitol album, *We Are One*, on U.K. charts. But the album didn't fall flat at home, reaching the top 25 on U.S. pop charts and spawning a top five R&B chart single: "Love Is the Key."

Recognition of his new status overseas came with his 1985 album *Can't Stop the Love*, which was released in the U.K. before being issued in the U.S. The album stayed on black album charts in the U.S. from the spring well into 1986 and earned another RIAA gold-record award.

The group makeup—which had comprised Beverly, Duhe, Porter, Lowry, Williams, and newcomers Ron Smith, Billy Johnson, and keyboard star Philip Woo for a while in the mid-1980s—changed again with the latter three musicians' departure in 1984 and the return of Wuane Thomas on lead guitar and addition of Wayne "Ziggy" Linsey on keyboards and synthesizers.

With Thomas's return, Maze was almost the same as it had been for most of its history. The reintroduction of Thomas bore out Beverly's point that many black groups are something like a family. He told *Blues and Soul:* "In Wuane's case, he never really left. He felt a calling—a religious calling—that he wanted to pursue and now that he has done that, he is able to realize again that playing with Maze is not a counter to that. So, in his case, it's like a homecoming."

MCCARTNEY, PAUL: *Singer, bass guitarist, keyboards player, band leader (WINGS), songwriter, record producer, record-company executive. Born Liverpool, England, June 18, 1942. Original Wings personnel (1971): Linda McCartney, born Scarsdale, New York, September 24, 1942; Denny Laine, born on a boat off England's Jersey coast, October 29, 1944; Henry McCullough, born Scotland; Denny Seiwell, born United States. Last Wings version (1979) comprised Paul, Linda, Laine, Laurence Juber, Steve Holly.*

Though the Beatles' breakup was officially announced during 1971, the four members of that legendary group had all started doing individual projects some time before. Hardly had the marriage between Paul and the former Linda Eastman been celebrated on March 12, 1969, than the two had begun work on Paul's first solo album. On April 10, 1970, a week before release of *McCartney* on Apple, Paul announced he had no further plans to record with the Beatles.

The album was the start of a literally gold-studded new career phase for McCartney, though one marked by considerably less enthusiasm from critics than he enjoyed in his Beatle days. *McCartney*, despite reviewer's cavils, was an unequivocal hit, earning a gold record. Paul and Linda's next effort, *Ram* (1971), also earned a gold record, as did its single "Uncle Albert/Admiral Halsey" (number one in the U.S. the week of September 4, 1971). During 1971,

Paul also won the National Academy of Recording Arts and Sciences award for Best Original Score Written for a Motion Picture or TV Special for the film *Let It Be.*

During the summer of 1971, Paul and Linda decided it was time to form a new band. The first member selected was Denny Seiwell. A top session drummer in New York, he had helped out on *Ram*. Next to join was Denny Laine (second guitar, bass guitar, vocals), who had worked with the Moody Blues and later had his own band, Balls. Laine was collecting and arranging material for a solo album, but dropped that project when McCartney's offer came along. With Linda playing electric piano and mellotron and aiding on vocals, the new group, Wings, released its debut LP, *Wings Wild Life*, in December 1971. The gold album included seven McCartney songs, most having a reggae flavor. In January 1972, Wings was rounded out with the addition of Henry McCullough on lead guitar. McCullough previously played with Joe Cocker's Grease Band.

One of the first projects Paul thought up for Wings was a two-week concert tour of England, his first public appearance as a performer in six years. It was highly unusual. The group loaded their equipment on a van and set up dates on the fly, coming into various cities unannounced and uninvited. First stop was Nottingham. As one of Wings' advance men recalled: "We went into Nottingham University's students union at about 5:00 and fixed it up for lunchtime next day. Nottingham was the best because they were so enthusiastic. No hassles. No one quite expected or believed it. Ian and I went down there at half-past eight the next morning with the gear. We threw up a few posters and put the word out on the tannoy." The tour continued before delighted audiences in York, Hull, Newcastle, Lancaster, Leeds, Sheffield, Manchester, Birmingham, and Swansea. The results elated McCartney, who noted that "Performing hasn't changed any since last I went out. It's just a different band and different material. It could never change. Performing is performing. It's still just you singing a song."

For the rest of 1972, the McCartney efforts were directed toward a new album and work on a TV special for 1973. The 1972 album, *Red Rose Speedway*, included the McCartney composition "My Love," which rose to number one in the U.S. the week of June 2, 1973. (Earlier that year the single "Hi Hi Hi" made *Billboard*'s top 10.) The album fell far short of some of McCartney's material in his Beatles days, but record buyers propelled it to number two in the U.S. in June (number one at the time being George Harrison's *Living in the Material World*). Both the album and "My Love" easily reached gold-record levels. A more interesting Wings single, from a creative standpoint, was the title number for the James Bond film *Live and Let Die*. Released on Apple, it rose to number one in August 1973 on some trade charts though it peaked at number two in *Billboard*.

In January 1974, McCartney and Wings had another top 10 hit with the single "Helen Wheels," which was eventually included on the 1974 LP, *Band on the Run*, though not originally planned for that project. The McCartneys had decided to record the basic material for *Band on the Run* in Lagos, Nigeria, but oddly, when they got to the plane to take them there, they found they had been deserted by Henry McCullough and Denny Seiwell. Paul, Linda, and Denny Laine finally had to go by themselves. As Paul told Vic Garbarini of *Musician* magazine: "So we ended up just the three of us in Lagos and I played a lot of stuff myself. I played the drums myself, the bass myself, a lot of guitar with Denny, did a lot of the vocals myself. I took a lot of control on that album. So it was almost a solo album. Almost."

It proved Paul's best post-Beatles album to that point. The first single from it, "Jet," made the *Billboard* top 10 and was followed by the even more successful title song which reached number one in the U.S. the week of June 8, 1974. Also a chart single from the album was "Nineteen Hundred and Eighty Five." (As with most Wings songs, McCartney wrote both words and music for all three.)

The departure of two key Wings members caused some critics to write premature obits for the group, but the temporary hiatus for part of 1974 proved only to be a breathing space. Scottish-born guitarist Jimmy McCulloch (formerly with such British bands as Thunderclap Newman, John Mayall, and Stone the Crows) joined up and soon found himself in Nashville, Tennessee, where a number of country-tinged rock tracks were laid down. Two of those songs were issued as a single on November 11, 1974: "Junior's Farm"/"Sally G." Neither song appeared on an album, maintaining an approach the McCartneys and Laine followed a number of times since the first Wings single in 1971, "Another Day"/"Oh Woman, Oh Why." In 1972, for instance, such nonalbum singles appeared as "Give Ireland Back to the Irish," "Mary Had a Little Lamb," and "Hi Hi Hi." One of the most unusual of that series of singles-only releases was "Mull of Kintyre" (1977). McCartney's paean to Scotland, it was number one on English charts for 10 straight weeks—McCartney's best-selling U.K. single ever—but was hardly noticed in the U.S.

After the Nashville stint, the group moved on to New Orleans to lay down tracks for a new album.

Lacking a drummer with the departure of English-born Geoff Britton, Paul asked arranger Tony Dorsey for suggestions and was directed to Joe English (born Rochester, New York). Those sessions resulted in the hit 1975 album *Venus and Mars*, whose release was preceded by the first single from the LP, "Listen to What the Man Said," number one in *Billboard* the week of July 19, 1975.

The new Wings alignment remained stable through the fall of 1977, when McCulloch and English stepped down. In between, though, the two took part in such notable events as Wings' first world tour in September 1975 and the landmark "Wings over America" visit during the first half of 1976 (Paul McCartney's first concerts in the U.S. in 10 years). The tour coincided with the March 23, 1976, release of the platinum LP *Wings at the Speed of Sound* and, later, another number one single, "Silly Love Songs" (at the top of the *Billboard* list for five weeks starting May 27, 1976). Tapes of the concerts provided the material for the three-record live *Wings over America* (Capitol, 1977). Recorded in order of presentation, the LP is an object lesson in the proper way of pacing a concert.

Wings' albums all came out with only the band name on them, rather than Paul McCartney and Wings. He always emphasized he wanted to be known as just one of the band members. He told a reporter: "It was never Paul McCartney and the Beatles, Paul McCartney and the Quarrymen, or Paul McCartney and the Moondogs."

In 1977, the group began work on the album *London Town*—the final release on Capitol for a while. Before that project was finished, McCulloch and English had gone. Their places eventually were taken by guitarist Laurence Juber and drummer Steve Holly. However, the final touches on *London Town* were handled by the McCartneys and Laine. The album wasn't the best in the Wings saga, but it provided more chart hits, including Paul's "With a Little Luck," which hit number one in *Billboard* the week of May 20, 1978 and stayed there a second week.

By 1979, Paul had signed with Columbia Records. His first single on the label, "Goodnight Tonight," was a top five hit in May 1979. His 1979 debut LP on Columbia, *Back to the Egg*, was platinum. It wasn't one of Paul's more memorable collections overall, but his spirits were buoyed at year-end when the new edition of the *Guinness Book of Records* called him one of the most successful pop songwriters of all time. *Guinness* noted that between 1962 and 1978, he had written 43 songs that sold over a million copies. His output included 43 gold records with the Beatles, 17 with Wings, and one with Billy Preston. He added another song to the total when his single "Coming Up (Live at Glasgow)" rose to number one in *Billboard* for three weeks starting June 28, 1980.

By then, the handwriting seemed on the wall for Wings. The band was officially disbanded in April 1981, though it had really been out of action for some months before. (Its last recorded material was included in the *Concerts for the People of Kampuchea* album issued by Atlantic in April 1981.)

Meanwhile, Paul turned out new solo albums for Columbia: *McCartney 2* (1980), *Tug of War* on which Denny Laine assisted (1982), and *Pipes of Peace* (1983). In this new phase of his career, Paul began to experiment on projects with other superstars. In early 1982, he got together with Stevie Wonder to work on a new composition that presented a strong argument for racial amity. Called "Ebony and Ivory," the single hit number one on *Billboard* lists for seven weeks as of May 15, 1982. The following year, he co-wrote "Say Say Say" with Michael Jackson—number one in the U.S. for six weeks starting December 10, 1983. That duet and another ("The Man") were included in Paul's *Pipes of Peace* LP, while their duet "The Girl Is Mine" was included in Jackson's superhit album *Thriller*.

Turning his cap in still another direction, in 1984 Paul became involved in acting and doing the soundtrack for the movie *Give My Regards to Broadstreet*, his first feature film since *Let It Be*. The film was a box-office dud, but Paul had a top 10 singles hits from the score, "No More Lonely Nights," which reached number six in *Billboard* during December 1984.

After the failure of that project, Paul licked his wounds for a while and then began a new creative partnership, a songwriting collaboration with Eric Stewart, who had been a primary writer for the 10 cc band. He also went back to his old label, Capitol, which released the fruits of the new effort on the mid-1986, LP, *Press to Play*. The album did promise a resurgence in McCartney's creative achievements, though it also indicated Paul still had a ways to go.

McCartney surprised the press by giving freely of himself for interviews and also not avoiding the subject of the Beatles, a topic he had avoided since the breakup. He told Robert Hilburn of the *Los Angeles Times* that he had come to terms with the public's longing for the good old days of the Beatles. "It must be a little like Charlie Chaplin never escaping the Little Tramp figure. The whole thing is kinda inevitable, I guess. People just want to talk about the Beatles. But you know what is funny now? I want to talk about them too.

"Some people say: 'Don't talk too much about the

Beatles . . . talk about your new album.' But I don't mind. I think what happened for a while . . . the reason I didn't want to talk about the Beatles . . . is that we all felt like we'd just gone through a divorce and it was painful to keep on discussing it."

In December 1987, Capitol issued the greatest hits LP *All the Best* whose 17 tracks included all Paul's number one *Billboard* hits from the 1971 duet with Linda McCartney, "Uncle Albert/Admiral Halsey" to the 1983 disc with Michael Jackson, "Say, Say, Say." Also in the LP was "Goodnight Tonight," previously available as a single only.

In January 1988, Paul's failure to appear with Ringo and George Harrison at the Rock and Roll Hall of Fame induction dinner at New York's Waldorf Astoria sparked some adverse comments from some critics and honoree Mike Love of the Beach Boys. In a press statement issued just before the event began, Paul was quoted as saying, "I was keen to go to [the dinner] and pick up my award, but after 20 years the Beatles still have some business differences which I hoped would have been settled by now. Unfortunately they haven't been, so I would feel like a complete hypocrite waving and smiling [with the other Beatles] at a fake reunion."

Later in the year, Harrison appeared on a British TV program and said he and Paul were not at odds. In fact, he stated the two had discussed getting together with Ringo to "write a tune and play together." But, he stressed, if this came about it wouldn't be a Beatles reunion. "There's just three guys named George, Paul and Ringo who may sing a song together." (*See Beatles, The; Harrison, George; Jackson, Michael; Lennon, John, and Ono, Yoko; Moody Blues, The; Peter and Gordon; Perkins, Carl; Starr, Ringo; Wonder, Stevie.*)

MCCOYS, THE: *See Derringer, Rick.*

MCDANIELS, GENE: *Singer, saxophonist, band leader. Born Kansas City, Kansas, February 12, 1935.*

One of the best-known pop singers of the early 1960s, Gene McDaniels still rings a bell with many music fans even though he had no subsequent hit recordings. His performances left a deep impression on many audiences, partly because he had spent a good many years as a sideman and band leader before he became a teen favorite.

Eugene B. "Gene" McDaniels spent his earliest years in Kansas City. In the 1940s, though, his minister father moved the family first to Lincoln and then to Omaha, Nebraska, where he took over a new pulpit (and eventually became a bishop in the Church of God and Christ). Gene sang with the choir in his father's church and learned to play the saxophone before he reached his teens. In junior high, 11-year-old Gene formed a gospel quartet, the Echoes of Joy, which later changed its name to the Echoes and then the Sultans. For several years the group performed on the gospel circuit, but gradually began to add secular music to its repertoire.

In bio notes for Liberty Records in the early 1960s, McDaniels recalled, "I had the group for nine years, but after my first year in high school we went into folk tunes and popular music. Though I sing baritone now, in those days I was a lyric tenor. And whenever the group was not working, I worked alone as a single."

McDaniels still found time for other things during his high school years. He did well in his studies and also was a good athlete and a starter on the basketball team at Omaha Technical High. He also tried out for football, but a knee injury during his first practice session ended that career attempt.

After finishing high school, Gene earned his living from music, but used some of his income to defray tuition costs at several schools. During the first half of the '50s, he attended the University of Omaha and University of Nebraska and took music theory at the Omaha Conservatory of Music.

By the mid-1950s, his repertoire was aimed mostly at the popular market. He auditioned for a number of record companies without success until Liberty finally gave him a contract late in the decade. This paid off with a number of regional singles hits, such as "In Times Like These" and "The Green Door." In 1961, he had his biggest year ever with two *Billboard* top 10 hits: "Tower of Strength" and "100 Pounds of Clay." The latter sold well over a million copies when totals from the U.S., Canada, and Europe were combined.

McDaniels continued to be popular into the mid-1960s, but faded from top ranks after that. By the late '60s, only two of his many albums were still on the Liberty active list: *Gene McDaniels* from the early '60s and *Golden Greats,* a 1967 reissue of earlier material. Renewed interest in pop oldies that started in the early 1970s didn't bring him new hits, but it did open up new opportunities on the concert circuit. Throughout the 1970s and '80s, his songs of the '60s continued to receive air play on the many oldies radio programs that sprang up around the U.S. during those years.

MEDLEY, BILL: *See Righteous Brothers, The.*

MCLEAN, DON: *Singer, guitarist, banjoist, songwriter. Born New Rochelle, New York, October 2, 1945.*

A runaway pop best-seller of 1972 was Don McLean's epic "American Pie." Had there been a separate folk chart, it would have reached the top there as well, since the song represented an amalgam of folk and rock, an enigmatic nine-minute portrait of the musical and social currents of the late '50s and '60s. The starting point was the passing of rock star Buddy Holly in 1959 ("I was a lonely teenage bouncin' buck/With a pink carnation and a pickup truck/But I knew I was out of luck/The day the music died."), presented as a symbol of the sorrows and occasional joys of the next 10 years. (*See Holly, Buddy.*)

"American Pie" proved a mixed blessing for McLean. It catapulted him to national prominence, but it also set a pinnacle so high that he couldn't seem to reach it again in later years. He turned out some interesting work, mainly in a folk vein, but wherever he went, "American Pie" tended to overshadow his new offerings.

McLean, whose family was in the U.S. from colonial days, was born and raised in the New York City suburb of New Rochelle. His idol was Buddy Holly. "He was the person that made me learn the guitar. I loved the way he played and thought for a while that I might dig playing rock'n'roll, but by the time I was 18, I was deeply into folk music."

In high school, he tended to be a loner, looking askance at schoolmates who "were afraid to strike out on their own and do what they really felt like doing." This attitude affected his approach to music. For a time as a teenager, he played in school groups, but decided to restrict himself to solo work at 15 because "I didn't like the problems of working with other musicians" or "being saddled with a lot of equipment."

He completed his precollege studies at Iona Prep School (a Catholic institution connected with Iona College in New Rochelle) and enrolled at Villanova University. He only stayed six months, the urge to make his way as a musician becoming too strong to deny. He began playing in coffeehouses and small clubs in upstate New York and then moved on to work larger cities, performing in such New York night spots as the Bitter End and Gaslight. During his travels, he became friends with such folk luminaries as Lee Hays of the Weavers and bluesmen Josh White, Brownie McGhee, and Sonny Terry.

For several years after leaving Villanova, he also took night courses at Iona College, concentrating on philosophy and theology. "I took all kinds of stuff I knew I would never be exposed to again because I planned to be in music for the rest of my life. I knew I was going to make a living at music for the simple reason that I couldn't stand to wear a suit or do a day job."

In the mid-1960s, while continuing to play folk clubs all over the Northeast and Midwest, often hitchhiking from one town to the next, he found renewed interest in rock caused by the emergency of the Beatles. "I became a Stones freak for a time and I also dig [soul man] James Brown—his band is fine."

In 1966, he began performing summers at the Cafe Lena in Saratoga Springs, New York, a folk art center run by Lena Spencer. The association proved particularly valuable two years later when the New York State Council on the Arts asked Lena to recommend someone to give free concerts in a special program. He recalled: "It was the summer of 1968 and I was broke. Lena got me a job with the state, figuring I'd make a good bureaucrat. I had to play in 50 river communities (billed as the Hudson River Troubadour), three a day a month or more while the state paid me $200 a week. Man, they got their money's worth. I sang about 40 songs a day, sometimes 60. That's cheaper than the juke box."

Those efforts, plus Don's activities on behalf of restoring the Hudson's ecology, brought him in contact with Pete Seeger. Seeger contacted him to join in the 1969 cruise of the sloop *Clearwater,* a voyage from South Bristol, Maine, to New York City, undertaken by a group of folksingers to enlist public support against industrial pollution of the rivers. The project resulted in a National Educational TV special, "The Sloop at Nyack." Besides performing on that show, Don also edited a book about the voyage, *Songs and Sketches of the First Clearwater Crew.* Seeger, meanwhile, had become one of McLean's major enthusiasts, calling Don "the finest singer and songwriter I have met since Bob Dylan." Following the *Clearwater* activity, Don became a familiar figure at many folk concerts, appearing with people such as Arlo Guthrie, Janis Ian, Josh White, Lee Hayes, and Seeger.

But he was finding favor with the broad spectrum of pop artists as well. At the start of the '70s, he shared bills with Blood, Sweat & Tears, Laura Nyro, Dionne Warwick, and the Nitty Gritty Dirt Band. He had built up a repertoire of original songs besides continuing to try his hand at prose and poetry. He also was interested in films, working in 1971 with Bob Elfstrum, who helped prepare the Academy Award–nominated *Other Voices,* a movie in which 25 of Don's original songs were used.

But while many well-known entertainers thought highly of Don's growing body of songs, he was consistently frustrated in his efforts to land a record company. He approached 27 different firms with tapes of what was to be his debut LP, *Tapestry,* and was turned down by all of them. Finally, the small Mediarts put it out in 1970 with very little fanfare and very little notice from the public.

McLean toured the country's coffeehouses in support of *Tapestry.* The tour didn't help sales much, but during his travels, he began slowly assembling "American Pie," finishing it in early 1971. By then, United Artists was interested in him and gave him the go-ahead to work on a new album. The song debuted long before the LP came out, being presented on station WPLJ-FM in New York the day Bill Graham closed his Fillmore East rock theater.

The single and album both reached number one in February 1972. McLean was the rage of pop music all over the world. Soon the attention given his work caused a second song from *American Pie* ("Vincent," an ode to painter Vincent Van Gogh) to become an international hit. (Later, when the Van Gogh Museum opened in Amsterdam, the song was played at the inaugural ceremonies and still is played at the entrance area.)

McLean soon became unhappy about the whirlwind success of "American Pie." It had, he believed, caused people to overlook the messages in such other compositions as "Three Flights Up," "And I Love You So," and "Tapestry." He also felt most people had missed what he considered the song's main theme "which isn't nostalgia, but that commercialism is the death of inspiration. If only one person can relate to it on that level, I'll be satisfied."

Much of his bitterness colored his next album, *Don McLean,* as reflected in the strident tone of songs such as "The Pride Parade" and "Narcissisma." The LP did provide him with another hit single, though, the fast-moving "Dreidel." That song's words in places were far from optimistic: "My world is a constant confusion/My mind is prepared to attack/My past a persuasive illusion/I'm watchin' the future—it's black."

For close to a year, McLean's state of mind prevented him from writing any new material. He also sharply curtailed his concert work. However, a friend from Cafe Lena days, bluegrass mandolinist Frank Wakefield, helped restore McLean's interest in music. The result was the album *Playin' Favorites,* which contained no originals but various folk, country, and bluegrass songs that appealed to Wakefield and McLean. Well-received tours of Europe and Australia added to Don's rebound and he finally set to work on his next LP, the 1974 *Homeless Brother,* whose title track sang the praises of the American hobo.

But though Don was writing again, he had lost the attention of much of the audience. His record sales declined and his association with UA came to an end. For two years, little was heard from him, but in 1976, he signed with Clive Davis's new label, Arista. Late in the year he appeared in clubs across the U.S. in his first concerts since 1974. Among his material were "Echo" and "Color TV Blues," new songs included in his first Arista release, *Prime Time* (1977), a collection not up to his earlier standards. It was obvious he continued to bear some of the scars from his earlier brush with being atop the musical pedestal. At one concert, he became angered at the way record-industry people talked to each other during his performance and angrily suggested it was a waste of time playing for them. Emphasizing that point, he did not return for an encore, thus leaving out the awaited presentation of his gem—and personal bane—"American Pie."

At the end of the 1970s, Don signed with a new label, Millenium (distributed by RCA), which issued *Chain Lightning* in 1979. That album received some attention from record buyers and his next collection on the label, *Believers,* did even better, spending several months on the charts in late 1981 and early 1982. During 1981, McLean had his first singles hit since the mid-1970s when his version of Roy Orbison's "Crying" made *Billboard*'s top five. (*See Orbison, Roy.*)

McLean's recording fortunes declined again after "Crying," but he retained a core of fans who assured him the opportunity to remain active as a solo concert artist in small clubs or on college campuses for the rest of the decade. Though in most cases he appeared on stage as a one-man act, he sometimes worked with other groups ranging from bluegrass bands to the Israel Philharmonic Orchestra. For some appearances in the late 1980s he handled lead vocals for Buddy Holly's old band, the Crickets. He and the Crickets played some of Holly's songs on a segment of the 1988 Grammy Awards Telecast from Radio City Music Hall in New York.

MCPHATTER, CLYDE: *Singer, songwriter, band leader. Born Durham, North Carolina, November 15, 1932; died New York, New York, June 13, 1972.*

One of the giants of early rock and R&B, Clyde McPhatter is sometimes slighted by rock historians who refer to him mainly as the founder of the Drifters. Actually, he spent only two of his more than 20 years as a performer with the group, gaining many of his hits as a solo artist. His efforts went a long way toward achieving the virtual merging of R&B and the general field of pop music that occurred in the '50s and '60s.

Son of a Baptist minister, Clyde Lensey McPhatter started as a gospel singer in his childhood, going into the R&B field during his teens after moving to Teaneck, New Jersey at age 12. In 1950, at 17, he became lead tenor of one of the most popular groups of those years, Billy Ward and the Dominoes. (*See Dominoes, The.*) The group turned out many hits on

King Records and its Federal subsidiary, including "Do Something for Me" and "I Am with You" (1951), the R&B number-one "Have Mercy, Baby" (1952), and "The Bells" (1953). With his high pitch and urgent tone, Clyde brought the fervor and excitement of traditional black gospel singing to the sensual lyrics of the new R&B.

In 1953, McPhatter (Ward claimed he fired Clyde) left the Dominoes and formed his own group, the Drifters. Another rising star, Jackie Wilson, replaced him in the Dominoes. (*See Drifters, The; Wilson, Jackie.*) Atlantic Records founder Ahmet Ertegun rushed to sign the group, while urging McPhatter to change his name since it sounded too country & western. Clyde insisted on keeping his name. Under McPhatter's direction, the group fast became one of the most acclaimed in R&B and later one of the pioneering combinations in rock'n'roll with such classics as "Money Honey" and "Honey Love." Even then, he was turning out solo records for Atlantic, including such 1954 top 10 hits as "Lucille" and "Such a Night."

McPhatter was drafted into the army in 1954. When he received his discharge in 1956, he did not go back to the Drifters, but concentrated on working as a soloist on Atlantic. He proved he hadn't lost his touch with such R&B ballad hits as "Seven Days" and "Treasure of Love." His songs gained acceptance among white audiences as well. During 1957, he continued to place songs on both pop and R&B charts, including "Just to Hold My Hand," "Long Lonely Nights," and "Without Love." In 1958, he achieved his greatest success with the Brook Benton–Johnny Williams composition "A Lover's Question." The song gained the number one spot on both the U.S. R&B charts (top 10 on *Billboard*'s pop lists) and the British hits lists, selling over a million copies in the U.S. alone.

Moving to Mercury Records, Clyde started off with a number of singles that made the charts, including top 10 hits "Ta-Ta" (1960) and "Lover Please" (1962). A series of Mercury LPs sold well in the early '60s, including *Greatest Hits* (1963) and *Songs of the Big City* and *Live at the Apollo* (1964). As the last title indicates, he was a headliner during much of the 1960s in shows that played such major R&B theaters as Harlem's famous Apollo and Washington, D.C.'s Howard.

But as the 1960s went by, McPhatter could no longer find the key to the mass audience. He left Mercury in the mid-1960s, signing with MGM and Bell Records, but garnered no further hits. McPhatter's long battle with alcoholism hampered his career and may have contributed to his death in June 1972, which was reported to be due to a heart attack suffered while visiting friends in Manhattan.

In the 1980s, he had no solo LPs in print in the United States, though Atlantic's *The Drifters: Their Early Recordings* showcased his group work, as did *The Dominoes* and *The Dominoes Featuring Clyde McPhatter* (including songs with teenaged Little Esther Phillips), repackaged on the King label by Gusto Records. (*See Phillips, Esther.*) Import solo albums included *Treasure of Love* on Atlantic's Japanese subsidiary and, from England, *Bip Bam* on Edsel, *Rock and Cry* and *Have Mercy Baby* on Charley, and *Clyde McPhatter with Billy Ward and His Dominoes* on Sing.

Rerecordings of Clyde's classics by Elvis Presley, Tom Jones, Jonathan Richman, Rita Coolidge, Ry Cooder, and Ray Charles attest to his influence.

MELLENCAMP, JOHN COUGAR: *Singer, guitarist, band leader (THE ZONE), songwriter. Born Seymour, Indiana, October 7, 1951.*

Midwestern fans have tended to favor no-nonsense, straightforward mainstream rock (as against heavy metal or new wave) as performed by artists such as Bob Seger and John Cougar Mellencamp. Sometimes called the midwestern Bruce Springsteen, Mellencamp demonstrated a far less romantic outlook in his song lyrics than Bruce or, for that matter, Seger, and his biting, often bitterly cynical comments turned off some critics, though not his rapidly growing ranks of admirers not only in the Midwest, but all over the world.

John grew up in the working class town of Seymour, Indiana, not far from the industrial city of Bloomington. Though his father had brought the family into a middle class environment, John noted their roots were rural. He told a reporter from *Billboard*: "We were farmers, basically, of Dutch stock. My grandfather was a carpenter, never got past the third grade, could barely speak English. My dad became a vice president of an electrical company—one of those self-made guys. I'm the runt of the litter [referring to his short, stocky shape]; everybody else has big muscles."

Like many a rock musician, Mellencamp was a rebellious, outspoken teenager. He had some athletic ability and made his high school football team, but was thrown out for violating smoking rules. He also didn't take to any of his peers trying to order him around. He had a quick temper that, he recalled, often led to fights with other teens. "You had to fight," he claimed. "Your dignity depended on it."

Rock'n'roll became a strong influence during those years. He listened to records and radio programs and also ventured into playing guitar with school friends and some early attempts at songwriting. His carefree phase came to an abrupt stop when

his girlfriend, a relatively mature 23 to his 18, informed him she was pregnant; the two eloped and moved in with her parents in Louisville, Kentucky.

She got a job with the local phone company, but John demurred at 9 to 5 work since he was determined to carve out a career in music. To his in-laws' dismay, he was underfoot all the time, often just drinking, smoking, or listening to records with occasional time out for songwriting. After 18 months, they gave him an ultimatum: work or leave. He told *Rolling Stone:* "It was 1971 and I refused to get a job." He took off and sought work with local bar bands in the Midwest, living from hand to mouth for the next few years.

After a while, he felt ready to try for bigger things. He recorded a demo tape of some of his songs and headed to New York to seek recording contracts. In 1975, he finally caught the ear of David Bowie's manager, Tony DeVries, who liked the tape enough to actively pursue a recording contract for his new client. He won approval from MCA executives and Mellencamp's debut came out under the title *Chestnut Street Incident.* When Mellencamp saw his first copy, he was upset to find that someone had given him the pseudonym of Johnny Cougar.

He told writer Martin Torgoff: "So I get the record finally—my first record—and it says Johnny Cougar on it! Nobody ever called me 'Johnny' in my whole life, ever—and that's the name people in the Midwest know me by now because of that record. It's a ridiculous name, but I'm stuck with it. It doesn't bother me that much anymore. I just laugh about it now."

From 1976 to 1978, Mellencamp's subsequent album output included *Kid Inside* (issued by MCA in the U.S.) and *Biography* (released only in Europe). Little happened with his MCA material and he was dropped from the label, which later licensed his two U.S. LPs to Rhino Records for reissue. He, in turn, left DeVries' organization and moved under the wing of Billy Gaff, at the time the manager of Rod Stewart. Gaff soon arranged for Mellencamp to record an album for Gaff's label, Riva. John worked on that for the first part of 1979 and rehearsed his band, the Zone, for live performances in support of the LP the latter part of the year. The band comprised Larry Crane and Mike Wanchic on dual lead guitars, a bass guitar player called Ferd, and a pianist only known as "Doc."

The band began to play small clubs and work as an opening act before the first Riva LP, title *John* (rather than Johnny) *Cougar,* came out in the fall of 1979. With Cougar in top singing form and the band giving compelling backing, the group won praise in newspaper columns around the country. Some of their musical associates thought the group sounded too good. Thus, during October 1979, Cougar and company were dismissed as opening act for a Kiss tour because they tended to upstage the better-known band.

Many reviews compared John to Seger and Springsteen, but he took it in stride. He said: "That's OK. Where would the Rolling Stones be if they didn't start out sounding like Bo Diddley?"

Though disco and new wave were the musical buzzwords in 1979, Mellencamp had no apologies for his somewhat "conservative" approach to rock. He told Jo-Ann Wong of the *Deseret News* that with punk or new wave, "You can't tell by listening who's who. With disco there's nothing personal. I'm not into fads. They cost too much money. I can't afford to go out and buy a disco shirt, shoes, and pants or go to discos every night. Same for new wave. I can't go out and buy a leather jacket.

"I'm into natural, honest people on a one-to-one basis. . . . I'm influenced by all singer-songwriters from the '60s. I don't understand synthesizers. We bought a $6,000 Yamaha for Doc and it turns out we don't like it. It's been out of the case one time."

Enough fans agreed with him to allow his Riva debut to do reasonably well, even if it fell far short of gold-record sales. Songs such as "A Little Night Dancin'," "Small Paradise," "Sugar Marie," "Great Mid-west," and "I Need a Lover," suggested that an important new force had appeared in pop music for the 1980s. With "I Need a Lover," John had his first singles hit, peaking at 28 in *Billboard* in December 1979.

The second Riva release, *Nothing Matters and What If It Did* (1980), met with about the same response as his debut on the label. It did produce two moderate hit singles: "This Time" (which reached 27 in *Billboard* that December) and "Ain't Even Done with the Night" (number 17 the next May). Meanwhile, Mellencamp continued to slowly increase his following with headline appearances in small clubs and as an opening act for other performers.

In late 1981 and early 1982, Mellencamp put the finishing touches on his third album on Riva (which was by then part of the Mercury Records organization). It was to provide the breakthrough he had been seeking for almost a decade. Called *American Fool,* the album remained number one in *Billboard* for nine straight weeks in summer 1982, earning John his first platinum-record certification. Its success pulled the previous LP, *Nothin' Matters and What If It Did,* onto the hit lists in late 1982.

Helping propel *American Fool* to the heights were several hit singles, the first being "Hurts So Good."

He recalled a friend had been with him at his home in Bloomington and suggested that "a great idea for a song" was based on the phrase "It hurts so good!" Right after that, John went to take a shower and "the song came to me so fast that I grabbed a piece of soap and wrote it on the glass of the shower door. That's what I call a good, clean song." The single made a clean break to the top, faltering just shy of number one at the second position in *Billboard* the week of August 7, 1982. It stayed at number two for four weeks while another single, "Jack and Diane," entered the top 10, giving Mellencamp the rare accomplishment of having two discs in the top 10 simultaneously. "Jack and Diane" did even better than "Hurts So Good," ranking number one for four weeks starting October 2. In the Grammy Awards for 1982, "Hurts So Good" won the trophy for Best Rock Vocal Performance, Male.

John commented to Christopher Connelly of *Rolling Stone:* "I had no idea 'Jack and Diane' would be like it was. A lot of people think that chorus ['Life goes on/Long after the thrill of living is gone'] is negative, but I don't. I think it makes people feel good to hear somebody else say: 'Hey . . . you can deal with it.'"

During 1982, Mellencamp demonstrated he was not without compassion for others by giving a free concert in Fort Wayne, Indiana, for 20,000 high schoolers who had worked for eight days in March to pile up sandbags and save the city from flooding. He said: "These kids don't have money to go to concerts or have much of a good time. The point of this free show was to help them have a little fun." Later in the 1980s, he contributed his services to benefits intended to help impoverished Midwestern farmers.

As Mellencamp began working on his next LP, he was determined to restore his full original name to his album listing. Though the label argued it might confuse his audience, he persevered and the platinum fall 1983 release, *Uh-Huh,* bore his full name on the cover. Its top 10 *Billboard* singles included "Pink Houses" and "Crumblin' Down." At the end of 1984, *Billboard* ranked him in its top 10 of Pop Album Artists—Male.

His 1985 album proved his biggest success to date. Called *Scarecrow,* by year-end, it was number three in the U.S. Easily exceeding triple-platinum levels, it provided two top 10 1985 singles, "Small Town" and "Lonely Ol' Night" (like most Mellencamp singles, written by him). In the 1985 Grammy competition, *Scarecrow* was one of the finalists in the Best Rock Vocal Performance, Male, category. In 1986, *Scarecrow*'s track "R.O.C.K. in the U.S.A." hit number one in *Billboard.*

During the summer of 1987, PolyGram released a

new LP by John, *The Lonesome Jubilee,* which by early 1988 had sold over 2 million copies. The material obviously wasn't aimed at teenagers, though Mellencamp still drew sizable numbers from that age bracket to his concerts. The song "The Real Life," for example, had for its hero a 40-year-old who still had no sense of purpose about his life.

Mellencamp told Robert Hilburn (*Los Angeles Times,* February 26, 1988), "Every song on the album came out of table talking. Anybody who know me knows you can come over just about any night of the week and there will be four or five people sitting around the kitchen table, drinking coffee, smoking cigarettes and talking about all sorts of things.

"Take 'The Real Life.' It was just another night at the table. Jackson Jackson is a real person, though that's not his name. He said to me one night, 'I'm 40-something years old and divorced and, hell, I haven't done one thing with my life that I really wanted to do when I was young and strong and a worldshaker.' But when I asked him what it was he wanted to do now, he looked at me and said, 'I don't know.'

"I think that is a very common thing among people who aren't very directed and I don't think 98 percent of the world is very directed."

MELVIN, HAROLD AND THE BLUE NOTES: *Vocal and dance group. Personnel (early 1970s): Harold Melvin, Bernard Wilson, Lawrence Brown, Lloyd Parks, Theodore Pendergrass. Pendergrass left in 1976, replaced by David Ebo.*

One of the most successful soul groups of the early 1970s, Harold Melvin and the Blue Notes rarely were off the best-seller lists during the first part of the decade. To a great extent, this was due to Teddy Pendergrass, who had become the group's lead vocalist during those years. However, the group had been around a long time before that. In fact, its origins on the U.S. East Coast went back to the second half of the '50s, when Harold Melvin helped organize his first vocal and dance aggregation. For a while after Pendergrass left, though, there was some doubt about the Blue Notes' survival, but Melvin managed to hold the reins of his group and keep it going into the 1980s, though it never regained the prominence of the Pendergrass years. (*See Pendergrass, Teddy.*)

Members of the 1950s group, besides lead singer Melvin, included Bernard Wilson and Lawrence Brown. Melvin was a self-taught pianist who arranged most of the group's music over the years. He also helped with the choreography, though the person mainly responsible for the Blue Notes' routines was Wilson. Indeed, many other groups (including

the O'Jays, Brenda and the Tabulations, and the Delfonics) sought his advice on choreography. The third original member, Larry Brown, handled the vocal range from bass to first tenor.

For well over a decade, the group kept going by playing club and concert dates, first on the Chitlin' Circuit and gradually in more important clubs and theaters. It turned out a number of recordings for R&B labels without scoring any major breakthroughs until the end of the 1960s. The catalyst for the newfound success was a merger Melvin effected with another Philadelphia-area R&B/soul group, the Cadillacs. The combination brought along the Cadillacs' backing band, whose members included drummer Teddy Pendergrass. The need for another Blue Notes reorganization during a 1970s tour of the French West Indies gave Pendergrass the chance to become a key member in the singing group.

In a short time, Pendergrass became the focal point of Blue Notes concerts and his presence helped bring a contract from Philadelphia International Records, the label owned by the great writing and production team of Kenneth Gamble and Leon Huff. The Blue Notes swiftly became one of the top recording and concert groups in the R&B/soul field, achieving such major singles hits as "I Miss You," "If You Don't Know Me by Now," "Yesterday I Had the Blues," "Won't You Let Me into Your World," "This Time Will Be Different," "Never Gonna Leave You," and "Go Away." *I Miss You, Black and Blue,* and *Harold Melvin and the Blue Notes* were hit albums in the early 1970s.

Group members at the time included Melvin, Wilson, Brown, Lloyd Parks, and Pendergrass.

Mid-1970s LPs included *To Be True, Wake Up Everybody* (both gold), and *Collector's Item.* But Pendergrass had become increasingly unhappy with his position in the group. Feeling he was the mainspring in its new popularity, he wanted to have lead billing, but Melvin balked. In 1976, Teddy walked out and for a while there were two competing groups, with some members going with Teddy as the Blue Notes featuring Teddy Pendergrass and the others remaining with Melvin. Finally, Teddy opted for a solo career with Philadelphia International as his record label while Melvin moved over to ABC Records.

In the late 1970s and into the 1980s, Harold Melvin and the Blue Notes turned out a number of albums for ABC and later for ABC's new owner, MCA. These included *Reaching for the World* and *Now Is the Time* (1977) and *All Things Happen in Time* (1981). Also available in record stores in the early 1980s was *Blue Album* on Source.

The group had no new hits to add to its earlier successes in the mid and late 1980s, but it still could draw enthusiastic audiences to its shows in small R&B clubs across the U.S. Catching one of those performers at the Total Experience in Los Angeles in late 1987, critic Connie Johnson of the *Los Angeles Times* (October 27, 1987) observed, its set "proved that the group still can cut it . . . while it now lacks a star player with [Teddy Pendergrass's] polish and charisma, the group is still the equal of many soul/pop hitmakers."

MEN AT WORK: *Vocal and instrumental group from Melbourne, Australia. Members (early 1980s): Colin Hay, Greg Ham, Ron Strykert, John Rees, Jerry Speiser. Group reduced to Hay, Ham, and Strykert in early 1985. Strykert left in summer 1985, Ham in September 1985. Fall 1985 lineup, comprised Hay, Chad Whackerman, Jeremy Alsop, James Black, Colin Bayley.*

During the early and middle 1980s, it looked as though the Australian middle-of-the-road rock group Men at Work might challenge U.S. and U.K. groups for worldwide dominance. Critics in the U.S. in particular hailed the "fresh sound" of the newcomers from Melbourne, although there was a strong Police-style flavor in many of its recordings. By the mid-1980s, though, overwork in support of the band's initial blockbuster hits might have taken its toll as everyone but original lead singer Colin Hay left the group for other opportunities.

The original personnel, all Australian-born, first gained performing experience in Melbourne beer joints and nightclubs in the late 1970s before coming together to form Men at Work in 1979. The band makeup at the time comprised lead singer and primary songwriter Colin Hay, Greg Ham on woodwinds and keyboards, lead guitarist Ron Strykert, bass guitarist John Rees, and drummer Jerry Speiser. The band picked up engagements at local bars before settling in to a long run at the Cricketers Arms Hotel pub. Talking about the enthusiastic crowds that soon came to hear them, Hay told a writer from Australia's *RAM* magazine: "They were looking for a warm and meaningful experience they could share with someone." Ham added: "A meaningful, drunken experience. Cheap drinks and no money at the door!"

The group's growing popularity with Melbourne fans finally elicited interest from a CBS-Australia talent scout. He arranged for them to make a demonstration record of a band original, "Who Can It Be Now?" with hopes of getting the U.S. home office interested. For a time, that ploy didn't work, but the song gained Australia's top five in summer 1981. Later in the year, the band's "Down Under" rose to number one in Australia and New Zealand. Both sin-

gles earned gold-awards from the Australian recording industry.

With those milestones behind them, the band was virtually assured that its debut album, *Business as Usual,* would be a hit, as indeed it was, reaching number one on both Australian and New Zealand charts in the spring of 1982 with multiplatinum sales levels for those regions. By then, CBS Records in the U.S. was convinced it had a potential worldwide success on its hands and *Business as Usual* was issued in America that April. Soon after, "Who Can It Be Now?" was given double-barreled exposure with an excellent music video and a well-publicized 45 rpm disc. The releases gathered momentum slowly, but by the fall everything began to fall into place as both hit number one in *Billboard.*

Band members kept things in perspective, though. In somewhat prophetic vein, John Rees told Christie Eliezer of *Record Magazine* just before a 1983 tour: "We're lucky to have got to the States when people were searching for something new. I don't deny that we play well and have some good songs, but timing had a lot to do with it. I don't know how long the Men will go on together, but our biggest contribution has been to open the door for those Australian bands which are far more original and musically better than we are. In the States the Men are considered new wave, but in Australia we're seen to be a very good mainstream pop band and nothing more."

Despite that diffidence, record buyers took the band's debut LP to heart in the U.S. and the U.K., where it was also number one. By the end of 1985, Columbia reported worldwide sales totals of over 15 million copies.

The band reaped a mantelpiece full of awards for its 1982 work. Those included a Juno Award in Canada for Best New Band and a similar accolade in the 1982 U.S. Grammy Awards. In accepting the latter trophy, Hay commented: "We are the Men and we'll be back again." In Sydney, Australia, in early 1983, the band also had the satisfaction of receiving the Outstanding Achievement prize in that country's Countdown Awards, the equivalent of the Grammies. The announcement was made via closed-circuit TV to the Sydney Capitol Theatre by Prime Minister Robert Hawke speaking from his official residence.

The unexpectedly long tenure of *Business as Usual* on the charts (15 weeks at *Billboard*'s number one) had the adverse effect of delaying release of the group's second album in the U.S. and Britain until many months after its completion. There also was an impact on the schedule for singles releases. Greg Ham told Eliezer: "There's not much to say, except to hope that people will see it *[Cargo]* as an album in its own right. See, in Australia, we released 'Dr.

Heckyll and Mr. Jive' which was a hit, then 'Overkill,' so the continuity continued, whereas the rest of the world didn't get 'Jive' or 'Be Good Johnny' as singles. Right after 'Down Under,' they're getting 'Overkill.' I must admit it was a bit reassuring that it came onto the American charts at number 28, so at least the [new album] has some sort of chance.''

By year-end, *Cargo* was multiplatinum according to the RIAA, with both it and its predecessor on the charts simultaneously. But the second album seemed a bit weaker than the debut release and that, coupled with the fatigue from several years of constant activity, seemed to have taken its toll. Little was heard about new material from the group in 1984. Apparently differences about direction cropped up among group members.

When work got underway in the spring of 1985 at Melbourne's Fast Forward Studios on the long overdue third LP, the band was reduced to a trio of Hay, Ham, and Strykert with studio musicians filling out the vacated spots. By the time the new album, *Two Hearts,* was ready for release in late summer, the only founding member left was Hay. In announcing Ham's departure that September, it was stated his decision was based on a desire to avoid touring for a while and to work in other areas such as scoring films.

For the planned fall concerts, which included three November dates in the people's Republic of China and a tour of Japan, a new lineup was assembled to back Hay: James Black, formerly with the Mondo Rock group, and Colin Bayley, ex–Mi-Sex, on guitars, keyboards, and vocals; top-rated Australian bass guitarist Jeremy Alsop; and Chad Whackerman. Later in the '80s, Hay became a solo act.

METERS, THE: *Vocal and instrumental group. Members (mid-1970s): Art Neville, Leo Nocentelli, George Porter, Jr., Joseph Modeliste, Cyril Neville.*

Among pop musicians from soul/R&B stars to giants of rock, the Meters' brand of New Orleans funk was legendary before the group gained major–record-company representation in the 1970s. During the 1960s, its members—separately and collectively—ranked among the best-regarded session men in the music industry. As an independent band, the Meters never achieved the status with the public at large that its musical peers thought it deserved, but its body of work had an important influence on R&B and rock in the 1970s and '80s.

The four founding members of the band—singer-pianist Art Neville, guitarist Leo Nocentelli, bassist George Porter, and drummer Zig Modeliste—came to adulthood in the New Orleans area in the 1950s and, by the early 1960s, had established themselves individually as among the best studio artists in that

city. From playing various recording dates with one another, the foursome gradually gravitated toward informal jam sessions together and occasional outside engagements under the name Art Neville and the Neville Sound. By the mid-1960s, the band was finding steady work at local clubs.

Allen Toussaint, one of the most successful performers and record-industry executives to come from New Orleans, heard the band play at the Ivanho Club on Bourbon Street and decided to sign them for his Sansu Enterprises. Toussaint was interested in them both as a recording band on its own and as a backing group for his own songs and for other artists on his roster.

Toussaint suggested the group find a new name, which resulted in the choice of the Meters. In the late 1960s, while continuing to back recording work by others, the band was represented on a series of releases on the small Josie label. Among its singles in the late '60s were ''Ease Back,'' ''Look-Ka Py Py,'' ''Chicken Street,'' ''Stretch Your Rubber Band,'' and ''Message from Meters.'' ''Sophisticated Cissy'' was a hit far beyond New Orleans confines in 1969. Some of the material was included in the Josie albums *The Meters, Look-Ka Py Py,* and *Struttin'.*

During 1971, Toussaint helped the group get a new recording contract with Los Angeles–based Reprise Records. Their 1972 debut on that label, *Cabbage Alley,* was produced by Toussaint and Marshall Sehorn. Among the cuts that expanded the band's reputation with R&B and rock artists were the title track, the reggae-tinged ''Soul Island,'' and a funky version of Neil Young's composition ''Birds.''

The 1972 album, while not a blockbuster with record buyers, did well enough to insure Reprise support for a follow-up LP, *Rejuvenation* (1974). Its track ''Hey Pocky A-Way'' made upper R&B chart levels. Another cut, ''Love Is for Me,'' earned a double-gold award in South Africa.

In the late 1960s and first part of the 1970s, the Meters usually was in the top ten year-end grouping of R&B bands in *Billboard* and *Record World.* It was even rated number one by both publications two years in a row.

Meanwhile, the Meters' name was appearing on credits for albums by many top names—during the first half of the 1970s, Patti LaBelle, Paul McCartney, King Biscuit Boy, Toussaint, Robert Palmer, and another New Orleans local-boy-makes-good, Dr. John the Night Tripper (aka Mac Rebennack). The band provided backing for Dr. John's worldwide 1973 singles hit ''Right Place, Wrong Time.''

In 1975, the band expanded to a five-man group with the addition of Art Neville's brother Cyril on vocals and percussion. Cyril took part in recording the 1975 album *Fire on the Bayou.* During the year, two other LPs of earlier Meters' recordings were issued by other labels: *The Best of the Meters* on Virgo and *Cissy Strut* on Island.

During that year, Mick Jagger of the Rolling Stones asked the band to open for their eagerly awaited summer tour of the U.S. The Meters also were featured in the Monterey Jazz Festivals' blues segment in September 1975.

On the fourth Reprise album by the group, *Trick Bag* (1976), tracks such as "Disco Is the Thing Today" suggested that the band was pushing for commercial success rather than trying to refine its own special style. The album did have more of an impact with record buyers than earlier LPs, but it reflected a loss of creative momentum.

The bottom line as the band approached its next album appeared to be that it retained a cult following, but was failing the commercial litmus test most record firms apply to artists. To try to turn things around, a new producer, David Rubinson, took over the reins from Allen Toussaint, though the album, *New Directions,* still featured a Toussaint song, "I'm Gone." Creatively, the new album again showcased a cohesive, ultraprofessional band, but one that still had not gone beyond the classic performances on its earlier discs.

Joe McEwen, record-company executive and sometimes contributor to various publications, commented in the *Rolling Stone Record Guide:* "The Meters' early style (represented on *Cissy Strut*) was revolutionary. As a quartet, the New Orleans–based group developed a bare-boned, quirky brand of funk that leaned heavily on clipped rhythms and syncopated accents. The languid, off-center groove of songs like 'Sophisticated Cissy' proved to be the forerunner of '70s funk."

The lack of progress either creatively or in recording success caused band members to go different ways in 1978. The Nevilles formed an all-family band, a quartet with brothers Aaron and Charles, whose debut LP, *The Neville Brothers,* was issued by Capitol Records in late 1978. The album did indicate the creative juices were flowing better as did the even more impressive collection, *Fiyo on the Bayou,* self-produced by the Nevilles, which came out on A&M in 1981. In 1984, Black Top released *Neville-ization.* The 1987 Rhino Records' two-disc *Treacherous: A History of the Neville Brothers, 1955–1985* ranged from Art and Aaron's solo ventures to their work with the Wild Tchoupitoulas.

MICHAEL, GEORGE: *See Wham!*

MIDLER, BETTE: *Singer, songwriter, actress. Born Paterson, New Jersey, December 1, 1945.*

"Bette Midler, she's a great broad," Tom Waits told Irwin Stambler as he leaned back against a grimy motel wall in a broken-down chair. "She's a real sweetheart, real down to earth. Saddest mouth in town. She sings a version of 'La Vie en Rose' that just breaks your heart, man! She puts her hands out to the audience and the sparks fly; she's like Marilyn Monroe singing to the troops." That tribute from one "original" to another, delivered during the mid-1970s, when the two collaborated on several projects, reflected the view of many of her show business peers.

Another observer commented: "She moves like her muscles are made of rubber. She moves like a gay Charlie Chaplin. Her voice turns from silky soft to pile-driving intenseness in an instant." Dubbed "the Divine Miss M" after she burst on the entertainment scene in the early 1970s, this chameleon-like artist seemed like a brassy throwback to bawdy humorist Sophie Tucker one moment, soul sister to Aretha Franklin the next, or a clone of vocalists Janis Joplin, Barbra Streisand, and Carole King rolled into one a moment later.

Named after movie star Bette Davis by her film-buff mother, she harbored dreams of becoming a great actress even as a youngster in Hawaii. Her father, a house painter, moved his family from Paterson, New Jersey, to Oahu because, as Bette said, he had "an incredible spirit of adventure." Her hopes didn't seem likely to be realized as she went through high school (where she was class president) and on to the University of Hawaii while working at an assortment of part-time jobs that included sorting pineapple slices in a food plant and working as a secretary.

She kept looking for opportunities in the theater, though, and finally gained a job as an extra in the film *Hawaii* in 1965. She quit college after a year to go to Los Angeles with the movie's firm, where she received $300 a week and $70 per diem, but film success was still years away. After six months in L.A., she had managed to save enough money to finance a trip to New York. Settled into the run-down Broadway Central Hotel, she felt exhilarated. "I wanted to go on the stage," she said later. "I wanted to be a great dramatic actress. I really felt I was finally home."

She met other young theater hopefuls, tried out for various shows and gained some small roles. In 1966, she auditioned for the national company of *Fiddler on the Roof,* but ended up in the chorus of the New York cast. She remained with the hit musical for three years, working her way from the chorus into the part of the eldest daughter of Tevya, the show's central figure. Later, she gained a role in the rock musical *Salvation.*

Before she left *Fiddler,* Bette had decided she would try for a career as a singer rather than as an actress. The catalyst, she recalled in 1972, was Aretha Franklin's tribute to Dinah Washington. "It was mind-blowing. She was singing but she was talking. I had not heard that combination before of music and language all at once and I just freaked out. The very next day I said: 'I bet I could do that too.'"

She began collecting material and practiced with friends who could accompany her. She found occasional jobs in small Greenwich Village spots, getting what turned out to be her big break in 1970 on a tip from Bob Elston, a teacher at the Herbert Berghof studio where she took acting lessons. He told her of a friend who was starting the policy of providing entertainment at a place called Continental Baths, a Turkish bath catering to a homosexual clientele. After Bette landed the singing job, word of her phenomenal ability drew an increasing number of rapt gays clad only in loin cloths or towels. The grapevine passed word about her to the TV field and Karen Prettyman, talent coordinator for David Frost sought her out, followed closely by members of Johnny Carson's staff who lined her up for the "Tonight Show." The appearances and bids for nightclub work were prompted more by the shock value of her homosexual club gig than expected talent. Once she got the chance to reach a wider audience, however, the depth of her ability became apparent. David Frost signed her for five more shows after her first one and just about every talk show sought to feature her.

She honed her act in 1972 with performances in leading clubs across the nation. By year-end, she had rocketed from almost complete unknown to one of the best-known pop vocalists. This was amply demonstrated on New Year's Eve when capacity crowds greeted both her performances at New York's Philharmonic Hall in Lincoln Center. Reviewing the show in the *New York Times* (January 14, 1973), Chris Chase enthused: "Bette pushes her hair back, poses like early Rita Hayworth. She imitates Laura Nyro—speaking, not singing. She welcomes the front rows. Though she wouldn't do her act in front of her father . . . there's nothing off-putting about it; her raffishness seems to come from a deep well of merriment, she has a gaiety and sweetness one seldom finds in a comic, man or woman.

"And there's nothing she can't sing. Rock. Blues. Songs from the '40s, the '50s, the '60s, songs which once belonged to the Shangri-Las, the Dixie Cups, The Andrews Sisters."

Record and tape buyers' reaction to her vocal prowess was also affirmative after Atlantic released *The Divine Miss M* in late 1972. Within a month after its release, it had sold over 100,000 copies. It included such fine tracks as her version of John Prine's "Hello in There" and a top 10 remake of the Andrews Sisters' "Boogie Woogie Bugle Boy." Other chartmakers were "Do You Wanna Dance" (a previous hit for Bobby Freeman and the Beach Boys) and Frank Sinatra's standby, "Strangers in the Night." During that period, she scored a Broadway success in her show *Clams on the Half Shell*, but her succeeding LPs, *Bette Midler* (1973) and *Songs for the New Depression* (1976) didn't match the quality of her debut release.

The important thing for her, though, was her growing name identification with the general public, which finally opened the doors to the movie industry for her. During the summer of 1976, announcement was made that she had signed a multimillion-dollar contract with Columbia Pictures calling for her to make four films over the following seven years. As it happened, her movie debut came in a 20th Century Fox project, *The Rose,* whose producer-writer Marvin Worth first had conferred with Columbia and then later dealt with 20th Century after Columbia bowed out of the film. The new vehicle seemed a natural for Bette—she would have the starring role of a tragic Janis Joplin–like rock star involved in a love-hate relationship with her manager (a role assigned to Alan Bates). Filming began in 1978. (*See Joplin, Janis.*)

Before then, she placed 1977 Atlantic LPs *Live at Last* and *Broken Blossoms* on the charts. In anticipation of her new film venture, *Broken Blossoms* was much more rock-oriented than her earlier releases. She said at the time: "I always identified with the great rock'n'roll figures of the '60s, the Janises, Jaggers, Morrisons. I came from that. I was growing up then. But it's not what the audience that came up with me really wanted from me. Not just that."

When *The Rose* was released in late 1979, Bette was coming off a disappointing reception by record buyers of her Atlantic studio album *Thighs and Whispers.* But the new film gave a tremendous impetus to her career. Her performance as the self-destructive singer known as the Rose was stunning and made the film an audience favorite. The title song of the soundtrack album was a gold top 10 hit and the LP sold in platinum numbers. Bette received on Oscar nomination for her performance in the movie and the single of "The Rose" won the Grammy for Best Pop Vocal Performance, Female, of 1980.

In early summer of 1980, Bette was busy signing autographs for her book, *A View from a Broad,* an appropriately comic description of her four-month European tour of 1978. Later in the year, she was represented on top chart levels with her Atlantic soundtrack LP for *Divine Madness* (a concert film).

By the mid-1980s, though, music increasingly took a back seat to her film projects as she established herself as a first-rank screen comedienne.

During 1986, she won accolades for her work with Richard Dreyfuss in *Down and Out in Beverly Hills* and with Danny DeVito and Judge Reinhold in *Ruthless People*. In 1987, she added still another hit to her film credits with *Outrageous Fortune*. (Between films she managed to complete a comedy album for Atlantic, *Mud Will be Flung Tonight*). In 1988 she co-starred with Lily Tomlin in the film *Big Business*.

She appeared on the cable channel HBO in 1988 as the offbeat hostess (sporting a thick mock-Italian accent) of a show called *Mondo Beyondo* that featured performance acts like Bill Irwin and the Kipper Kids.

MILLER, STEVE: *Singer, guitarist, band leader (STEVE MILLER BAND). Born Milwaukee, Wisconsin, October 5, 1943.*

"My scene's from Texas, that's where I grew up . . . Texas and then Chicago, where I spent some time learning Chicago blues and by the time I got to San Francisco I realized I had picked up a whole lot of Chicago blues. . . . I've gone through a lot of changes, man. I'd like to think I've been growing."

That in a nutshell, in Steve Miller's words, is his career—roughly a decade and a half of dues-paying that brought him into the top echelons of rock performers at the start of the 1970s. It also underlines his preoccupation with the blues, which, like most rock artists of the electronic age, he modernized with hyperamplified arrangements and rock chord progressions. Miller defined the results of this process as "hot rod blues."

Though born in Wisconsin, he moved to the Southwest with his family as a small child. Just approaching his teens when rock'n'roll first laid claim to the popular music market, he immediately fell under the sway of such pioneers as Presley and Chuck Berry. Bill Doggett's work particularly appealed to him. As he told an interviewer, he was entranced by Doggett's guitar player "and I don't even know the guy's name."

He learned to play rock guitar by listening to Doggett's 1956 instrumental hit "Honky Tonk." At 12, he formed his first group, the Marksmen Combo, including Boz Scaggs on guitar. (*See Scaggs, Boz.*) The only song they really could play well was "Honky Tonk." During his high school years, he fronted a band called the Ardelles that featured four singers. The group played school events, small clubs, and dances in Texas and nearby states. After high school he enrolled in the University of Wisconsin at Madison as did Boz Scaggs. The two of them organized a group called the Fabulous Night Trains that did quite well on the Midwest college pop music circuit. Once finished with his UW studies, he tem-

porarily dropped show business in favor of going to Denmark to attend the University of Copenhagen. He studied literature for a year, but decided this wasn't his calling and returned to the U.S., settling in Chicago in 1964. His literary courses, though, probably played some part in his later success as a pop songwriter.

In Chicago in the early and middle 1960s, he hung around blues clubs and recording studios, picking up knowhow on the techniques of the great bluesmen working in the city at the time. He was a sideman with some groups before forming his own band with Barry Goldberg in the mid-1960s. Hearing of the burgeoning hippie-rock culture in San Francisco, he decided to move there in 1966.

Soon after reaching the Bay Area, he formed the Steve Miller Blues Band. The group built up a reputation with local fans from performances at rock festivals and in clubs and auditoriums, including the then newly opened Fillmore club of Bill Graham. The group backed Chuck Berry at the Fillmore in an act taped by Mercury Records and released under the title *Chuck Berry at the Fillmore Auditorium* in November 1967. During August 1967, the Steve Miller Blues Band joined many other young rock performers at the legendary Monterey Pop Festival that led to the publicizing of such newcomers as Janis Joplin and Jimi Hendrix. Miller's group didn't get the national coverage that Janis, Jimi, and some others did, but when it was mentioned, it was with great enthusiasm. One reviewer described his impression of the group's music as feeling like "huge sheets of steel violently shaken."

The band signed with Capitol soon after Monterey. Its debut LP, *Children of the Future* (early 1968), gained generally favorable comment. The second album, *Sailor* (fall 1968), was greeted with both artistic and financial success. The album gained the top 20 on the charts by the end of the year and also spawned a hit single, "Living in the USA." The band backed up its recording work with several nationwide tours using the new name, Steve Miller Band.

By the end of the decade, Miller had replaced his supporting musicians a number of times, but there was no lowering in quality in the group's performances in person or on record. The band continued to flirt with supergroup status, though it still had not gained the breakthrough expected for it by the early 1970s.

The band continued to make the LP charts with *Brave New World* and *Your Saving Grace* in 1969. Midway through 1970, the band was represented by its most successful album to date, *Number 5,* which made the top 20 soon after its release. *Rock Love* (fall 1971) was on the best-seller lists for several months. The other group members at that time were Ross Vallory on bass guitar and Jack King on drums.

During 1972–73, a reorganized version of the band held forth consisting of Miller, Jack King, Gerald Johnson (formerly with the Sweet Inspiration) on bass, and Dickie Thompson on organ. The group went on a phenomenally successful six-nation European tour in early 1972. During most of the tour, Miller was in pain from an injury received in a car accident in Rochester, New York, in January. Finally diagnosed in March as a broken neck, the injury (coupled with hepatitis) sidelined him for half of 1972. Despite the physical problems, it was a good year for Miller, providing him with two hit albums: *Recall the Beginning . . . A Journey to Eden* and the gold *Anthology*. Miller's ninth album, *The Joker* (1973), proved to be a milestone in his career. In mid-January 1974, the title-track single took over first position on the *Cash Box, Record World*, and *Billboard* surveys. The gold album also made number one on the charts.

Miller told a reporter from *Guitar Player* that he had consciously crafted "The Joker" for top 40 formats, although he was mainly thinking about getting it on the charts rather than scoring a major triumph. "I said: 'Okay, it's got to be 2½ minutes long, and it's got to play on top 40 radio, and it's got to follow a soul-disco symphony.' I always wanted to make singles. I like singles. . . . So I just started taking that 2½ minute thing and started looking for sounds that record well. It's like a game, like a crossword puzzle. And as long as you've got some tunes that've got feeling and soul and substance to them, there you go.''

Still, Miller soon found that success doesn't necessarily bring happiness. Business problems and a falling out with his girlfriend so embittered him that he broke up his band and moved to a farm in Medford, Oregon, where he holed up until early 1976, when he felt ready to return to action in the music field. He enlisted bass guitarist Lonnie Turner and drummer Gary Mallaber to get together with him for his album *Fly Like an Eagle* (May 1976). The layoff had proved beneficial. The platinum LP was his best to that point and provided three top 10 singles: "Take the Money and Run," "Rock'n Me," and the title song. "Rock'n Me," reached number one in *Billboard* the week of November 6, 1976. The title song reached number two the following March. Besides writing most of the material himself, Steve also served as producer. At the same time the material for *Eagle* was recorded, Miller also laid down the tracks for another album, the platinum *Book of Dreams* (1977). Those two LPs ranked as some of the finest rock issued in the late 1970s. Like its predecessor, *Book of Dreams* yielded three Top 10 singles

(though no number one hit): "Jet Airliner," "Jungle Love," and "Swingtown." Band members besides Turner and Mallaber, were Norton Buffalo, on harmonica, David Denny and Greg Douglas on guitars and Byron Allred on keyboards.

Having shown he remained a top rock creative force, Miller again retired to his Oregon hideaway during 1978, a year he was represented on the charts by the platinum retrospective *Steve Miller Band's Greatest Hits 1974–78. This time he kept a low profile for four years. In 1981, he came out of hibernation again with his eleventh Capitol album, the gold Circle of Love* (thirteenth including greatest hits LPs). This collection seemed much weaker than his earlier material and some critics thought Miller's long hiatus might have proved fatal to his career. Undaunted, he returned the next year with the platinum LP *Abracadabra*, co-produced with Gary Mallaber. It didn't win much approval from critics, but record buyers made the title track number one on *Billboard* for two weeks starting September 4, 1982. Most of the songs on the LP were co-written by Steve with the other band members, but "Abracadabra" was solely written by him.

He attributed the album's success, though, to a team effort. As reported by Fred Bronson in *The Billboard Book of Number One Hits*, Steve said the LP was "basically a creative explosion of the drummer, Gary Mallaber, and the two new members of the band, guitarists Kenny Lewis and John Massaro.''

The next album, *Italian X-Rays* (late 1984) was on the charts into 1985, but seemed a letdown from the previous release and received considerably less fan support. In October 1986, Capitol issued the LP *Living in the 20th Century*. Steve's backing band on the 1986–87 tour comprised Lewis, Buffalo, Allred and Mallaber.

MINK DEVILLE: *See DeVille, Willy.*

MIRACLES, THE: *See Robinson, Smokey.*

MITCHELL, JONI: *Singer, songwriter, guitarist, pianist, artist. Born Fort McLeod, Alberta, Canada, November 7, 1943.*

During her concert tour of early 1974, Joni Mitchell changed one of the verses to her classic folk composition "Both Sides Now" to "But now old friends are acting strange/They shake their heads, they say I've changed . . . And I have!" Indeed, at the time, Ms. Mitchell was shedding her image of a shy, soft-spoken contemporary folk artist to a dynamic rock image. After that, she continued to change, moving more and more toward jazz until, by the end of the '70s, her music ranked among the more interesting experiments in avant garde jazz. Whatever genre she worked in, she made important and lasting contributions. Even as some jazz enthusiasts welcomed her to their ranks, folk performers still covered some of her earlier writings and aspiring rock performers often drew musical insight from some of her up-tempo recordings.

Born in Fort McLeod, she grew up in Saskatoon, Saskatchewan, daughter of a schoolteacher mother and a former Royal Canadian Air Force officer turned grocery-store manager father. She found an early interest in art and, without benefit of lessons, became a fairly capable painter. In her late teens, she enrolled in the Alberta College of Art in Calgary with the thought of making a career in commercial art. She took along a baritone ukelele just for the fun of it and, after learning a few chords, started singing folk songs during leisure moments. When friends urged her to go further with her musical talent, she found work at a local coffeehouse called the Depression. Music became more and more engrossing and her interest in commercial art faded. The same wasn't true for painting, which remained a major love. Later on, she did many excellent original pieces of art for use on her album covers.

She started to go wider afield to perform. On a train trip to the Mariposa Folk Festival in Toronto, she wrote her first song, "Day after Day." Once in eastern Canada, she became enthused about the folk scene and decided to stay. At 19, she lived in Toronto, wrote more contemporary-folk–style songs, and built a reputation with folk fans and other young performers in the city. She also met and married Chuck Mitchell. Up to then, she had been known as Roberta Joan Anderson, but she soon combined her married name with a modification of her middle one to gain her stage name. It was as Joni Mitchell that she began to perform in coffeehouses in Detroit, where she and her husband moved in mid-1966. They divorced soon after, but Joni Mitchell she remained. Meanwhile, the impact of her performance and the quality of her original material continued to improve.

As a Detroit critic enthused in 1967: "She is a beautiful woman. Her voice and her acoustic guitar are free, pure instruments in themselves; there is additional beauty in the way she uses them to convey such a full range of emotions. But if she knew only three chords, her performance would be justified by her songs alone. As a songwriter, she plays Yang to Bob Dylan's Yin, equaling him in richness and profusion of imagery and surpassing him in conciseness and direction."

Soon after that, Joni packed her belongings and moved to New York. There she quickly made important contacts such as David Geffen (the record-company executive who helped advise her on industry operations), Elliott Robert (who became her manager), and David Crosby, who encouraged her musical efforts. Word of her talents spread among her musical peers. Soon Judy Collins, Buffy Sainte-Marie, Tom Rush, and Dave Van Ronk were including her songs in their acts and telling audiences of her strengths as a performer. Before long, her debut album on Reprise, *Song to a Seagull,* was released and, during 1968–69 she had her first song hit, "Clouds." Joni's single did reasonably well, but the major success was for Judy Collins' version (retitled "Both Sides Now").

By 1968, Joni had moved to a home in Laurel Canyon above Los Angeles, where she still spent much of her time when not on the road throughout the '70s. Besides that, after she became an acknowledged star, she also built a retreat for herself near Vancouver, British Columbia.

During the years she recorded for Reprise, she continued to be identified with contemporary folk music or, to some extent, with soft-rock. Among the standards she wrote or had recorded success with during that period were "The Circle Game," "The Same Situation," and "Ladies of the Canyon."

Her second album on Reprise, *Clouds* (which featured Joni's self-portrait on the cover), came out in 1969 and was a chart hit. Her third, *Ladies of the Canyon* (1970), went platinum. The track "Woodstock" captured the euphoria and idealism of the 1969 festival and was an early intimation of some of the new directions Joni's writing would take in the '70s. She closed out her album efforts on Reprise on a high watermark with *Blue,* certainly one of the best albums of 1971 and arguably one of the best LPs of the decade. Many of its 10 songs underscored her ability to work several themes into a single song. An example is "All I Want": "Alive, alive, I want to get up and jive/I want to wreck my stockings in some juke box dive," but ends in her suggesting those are only daydreams to supplement the more restrained yearning for love. The quality remained high in every song, whether slow or fast, and such tracks as "My Old Man," "Little Green," "This Flight Tonight," "Carey," "River," and "The Last Time I Saw Richard" remain favorites of her long-time adherents.

Her move away from folk stylings was abundantly evident in *Blue,* though there still was a strong contemporary-folk feeling to the overall collection. Some of the songs in that collection she had written on the piano, which she had only begun to play during preparation of *Ladies of the Canyon.* After completing *Blue,* she realized she was feeling increasingly uptight about the inroads of her career on her private life. She decided to take time out to re-evaluate things and for the next year and a half stayed away from concerts, spending time in travel and visiting with friends.

However, she didn't give up writing and recording. She moved from Reprise to Asylum Records (newly founded by David Geffen), which later was merged with Elektra. On her first LP on that label, *For the Roses* (November 1972), backing her was rock-jazz artist Tom Scott, who helped put together the "band sound" stressed in the collection. Its country-flavored "You Turn Me On, I'm a Radio" became a hit single, Joni's biggest to that point, and the album earned Joni a gold record.

Though Joni was stressing more rock and jazz in her music by the time her next LP, *Court and Spark,* came out in January 1974, it didn't diminish her appeal. She held on to most of her earlier fans and added a host of new ones. Proof was the success, both critical and commercial, of the gold LP, which also spawned three hit singles: "Raised on Robbery," "Help Me," and "Free Man in Paris" (a song about Geffen).

In early 1974, she went on her first major tour in a long while, accompanied by Tom Scott and the L.A. Express. Her new rock image was met by shrieks of joy, thunderous applause, and dancing in the aisles wherever the show played. Unlike earlier tours, when mellow acts such as Jackson Browne opened for her, Scott and his band began with a hard-driving electric set. The results of that combination were captured in the gold double-disc live *Miles of Aisles* (November 1974). Her updated treatment of an earlier favorite, "Big Yellow Taxi," brought her another hit single.

She diverged from rock to avant garde jazz the next time out with the November 1975 LP, *The Hissing of Summer Lawns.* The lyrics, as often held true in the '70s, were richly poetic and multilayered, accompanied by complex, usually minor key melodies. Discussing the material in the liner notes, she cryptically wrote: "The whole unfolded like a mystery. It is not my intention to unravel that mystery for anyone, but rather to offer some additional clues."

Jazz continued to preoccupy her to a greater and greater extent as the late '70s went by. In November 1976, bassist Jaco Pastorius of Weather Report fame was one of those who contributed to her *Hejira* album. He was joined in session work on the next effort, *Don Juan's Reckless Daughter* (Asylum/ Elektra, December 1977) by such artists as Wayne Shorter, John Guerin, Chaka Khan, and Airto. Her next project particularly excited her since it was to be a joint effort with jazz great Charlie Mingus. Mingus, however, died January 5, 1979, before the project could be completed. Issued that summer, the LP was dedicated to Mingus and included some impressive paintings of him by Joni on the cover.

Mingus spent months on the charts during 1979. The following year, Joni had a hit with another jazz-based Asylum album, *Shadows and Light,* a live set recorded in Santa Barbara, California, with backing from such jazz fusion performers as Pastorius, Pat Metheny, and Michael Brecker with backing vocals from an a capella R&B group, the Persuasions. The tracks included a revision of Frankie Lymon and the Teenagers' 1956 "Why Do Fools Fall in Love." Many observers were surprised that Joni could bring a large segment of her folk-pop fans along with her into the jazz domain as shown by the continued chart status of her new releases.

During the 1980s, Joni moved away from jazz, blending elements of other types of pop music into her new compositions and recordings. In her first album release on the Geffen label, *Wild Things Run Fast* (1982), she lyrically explored the problems of aging. Her work of the mid-1980s included the socially and politically pessimistic Geffen albums *Dog Eat Dog* (1985) and *Chalk Mark in a Rainstorm* (1988).

MONKEES, THE: *Acting, vocal, and instrumental group. Mickey Dolenz, born Los Angeles, California, March 8, 1945; David Jones, born Manchester, England, December 30, 1946; Peter Tork, born Washington, D.C., February 13, 1944; Mike Nesmith, born Houston, Texas, December 30, 1942. Group disbanded in 1969, Dolenz, Jones, and Tork regrouped in mid-1980s.*

The Monkees, like several acts since then (the Partridge Family, the Archies), basically were a manufactured group. In most cases, a new rock group results from the interplay of musicians and their associates. In this case, Columbia Pictures producers came up with the idea for a TV comedy program based on a rock band and then auditioned some 500 young applicants in the fall of 1965 to find four performers that met predetermined requirements.

The emphasis was not on musical talent, but on a group having what the producers felt was the right combination of personalities for the projected scripts. As a result the rejected applicants included such talent as Stephen Stills and Danny Hutton—not to mention cult leader and mass-murder–mastermind Charles Manson. (*See Stills, Stephen.*) As it happened, two of those selected, Mike Nesmith and Peter Tork, had some experience as guitarists. The other two Monkees had little instrumental background, but could sing and were experienced young actors. This created controversy for a time when the success of the show was used as a vehicle to make sales of Monkees records reach some of the highest levels of the late 1960s.

Mickey Dolenz grew up in a show business family. His father, George, starred in many movies, and Mickey became a child star at 10 as the central character of the TV series "Circus Boy." (His stage name for the show was Mickey Braddock.) In his early teens, he appeared in a number of TV shows, including "Mr. Novak," "Peyton Place," and "Playhouse 90." He also did a little work with guitar, but did not begin to learn the drums until he was chosen for the Monkees.

David Jones, son of an English railway engineer, became interested in amateur plays in grade school. At 15, he appeared in a British Broadcasting Corporation show about juvenile delinquents. After a while, he almost forsook show business for horse racing because his small stature and horsemanship seemed ideal for a jockey. His short-lived racing career paid off in acquaintanceship with several London theatrical executives. One of them arranged for Davy to audition for the Artful Dodger in the Lionel Bart musical *Oliver.* He was acclaimed as one of the stars of the hit show and later also starred in *Pickwick,* another musical version of a Charles Dickens novel. His stage presence, plus the fact that he'd been featured singing rock songs on a number of network TV shows, led to his winning the Monkees role, though he could play only a tambourine.

Peter Tork spent most of his early years in Connecticut, where his family moved soon after his birth. After starting on the ukelele while in elementary school, he learned guitar and five-string banjo and developed a broad folk-song repertoire. He enrolled twice in college, initially at Carleton College in Minnesota, majoring in English. However, he did not do well academically and dropped out. In the early 1960s, he moved to New York's Greenwich Village, where he became a member of folk group the Phoenix Singers. After this, he moved to California and, reading an ad about the audition for the Monkees, tried out and made the group.

The fourth member, Mike Nesmith, came to the group with the most musical experience. *(See Nesmith, Mike.)* He also had tried his hand at composing and eventually wrote some of the group's hit material.

First screened in September 1966, the NBC-TV show was at the top of the TV ratings for the better part of three years. In all, 56 episodes of the half-hour program were made.

The show was on TV only a short time when the first Monkees records moved onto the hit charts. However, this was a galling step to Mike Nesmith in particular, because he discovered that the group was supposed only to sing, with the instrumental backing provided by topflight studio musicians in Los Angeles. This did result in gold records for such 1966 singles as "Last Train to Clarksville" and "I'm a Believer" and the LP *The Monkees.*

The problem facing the group was that its record firm, Colgems, didn't want to tell the public that the TV group did only the vocals. This made things very embarrassing, as Nesmith recalled, when the group began to make personal-appearance tours. By then, they could play reasonably well on stage, but couldn't reproduce some of the excellent sounds of their initial recordings.

The group argued among themselves about what to do, but Nesmith finally told a New York press conference in 1967: "There comes a time when you have to draw the line as a man. We're being passed off as something we aren't. We all play instruments, but we didn't on any of our records [to then]. Furthermore, our company doesn't want us to and won't let us."

Screen Gems called a meeting in Beverly Hills about the matter after the story ran in *Look* magazine. There was heated argument about Nesmith's demand that the group be allowed to play for its own recordings from then on. Company executives reminded him he could be legally suspended according to his contract, in reply to which, Nesmith later told a reporter: "I rammed my fist through a door. I told the man who said that: 'That could have been your face,' and walked out. We did the instrumental work on the next album."

Despite the worried brows of management, the Monkees' own productions did as well as the earlier releases. The group won gold records for three more LPs—*Monkees Headquarters* in 1967 and *Pisces, Aquarius, Capricorn and Jones, Ltd.* and *The Birds, the Bees and the Monkees* in 1968. The group also made million-selling singles as "A Little Bit Me, Little Bit You," "Pleasant Valley Sunday," and "Daydream Believer" (1967) and "Valleri" (1968). (Some of these releases, such as "Valleri," were from the pre-Monkees instrumental days.)

The group toured worldwide during 1967 and 1968, finding exuberant audiences awaiting them. During one visit to London, Dolenz brought the others' attention to a promising American musician, Jimi Hendrix. Dolenz invited Hendrix to return to the States to work with them on the continuation of the tour. At that time, though, the Monkees' American audiences weren't attuned to the hyperamplified rock played by Hendrix. In some places they booed Hendrix, saving their applause for the Monkees. *(See Hendrix, Jimi.)*

In 1968, Tork left, but the other three continued as a group into 1969 and were still rated among the most popular groups in the nation for the year. By then the show had run its course on TV, the ratings dropped, and the remaining threesome went their separate ways.

In the early 1970s, Tork was teaching guitar and French in Venice, California, while Dolenz and Jones pursued acting careers and Nesmith continued solo songwriting and recording efforts. In 1975–76, Dolenz and Jones returned to Monkee-dom by forming a group called Dolenz, Jones, Boyce and Hart (the others being Tommy Boyce and Bobby Hart, who had written a number of Monkees hits, including "Last Train to Clarksville" and "Valleri"). Legal restrictions at the time kept them from calling themselves the Monkees, but the foursome assembled a stage act called Great Golden Hits of the Monkees Show.

That project had only minimal impact on the mass audience and the Monkees lay dormant until the mid-1980s, when reruns of the old Monkees show on TV created new interest in the group. This time Tork joined with Dolenz and Jones to attempt a Monkees revival. Nesmith, who always had been vocal in his dislike of the whole Monkees concept, declined to rejoin. The threesome embarked on a reunion tour during 1986–87 that surprisingly won general support from many critics and drew respectable crowds. The group completed its first new album in 18 years, *Pool It!*, which was released in the summer of 1987 on Rhino. Later, Rhino, which already had been putting their original recordings back in print, released a two-disc set, *20th Anniversary Concert Tour 1986*, in early 1988.

All of that activity inspired an attempt by TV entrepreneurs to initiate a new syndicated TV program called the *New Monkees*. The new quartet, Marty Ross, Larry Saltis, Jared Chandler, and Dino Kovas, taped a series of shows during 1987 that failed to recapture the flavor of the 1960s episodes.

MOODY BLUES: *Vocal and instrumental group, all born England. Personnel (mid-1960s): Mike Pinder, born Birmingham, December 12, 1942; Graeme Edge, born Rochester, Staffordshire, March 30, 1942; Ray Thomas, born Stourport-on-Severn, December 29, 1942; Clint Warwick, born Birmingham, June 25, 1949; Denny Laine, born on a boat off the Jersey Coast, October 29, 1944. Laine replaced by Justin Hayward and Warwick by John Lodge in late 1960s. Pinder replaced by Patrick Moraz in 1977.*

The Moody Blues were recognized as an excellent pop group in the early 1960s and did, indeed, have some best-selling recordings at that time. However, for most of the decade, the band was overshadowed by groups like the Beatles and Rolling Stones. But perseverance paid—the Moody Blues didn't fold in the face of this awesome competition, but continued as an active group, despite some personnel changes, until, from 1969 into the 1970s, it had some of the most sensationally successful recordings in record-industry history.

All of the original members of the band became active in rock or R&B groups in their early teens. In several cases, they were with groups whose paths crossed those of the Beatles before the Fab Four become international stars. Harmonica player Ray Thomas, for instance, played with the group El Riot and the Rebels at some of the rock clubs where the Beatles were on the bill; El Riot later even shared a TV stage with them. Mike Pinder was lead singer and instrumentalist (electric piano, organ, guitar, bass) with the Crew Cats, who were well received in Hamburg and Hanover, Germany, while the Beatles were having their early success there.

Home base for most of the original Moodies was Birmingham, where Denny Laine (born Brian Hines) was lead singer/guitarist for the Diplomats in the early 1960s. Laine won a large following in that city for his work and the Diplomats were considered the best group in town until they disbanded. Drummer Graeme Edge was born and raised in Birmingham as was bass guitarist Clint Warwick (born Clinton Eccles). Warwick was rated one of the best bass players in the area for his work with the Rainbows.

In 1964, Laine decided to form his own group and soon had gained an associate in Mike Pinder. Thomas, Warwick, and Edge were then recruited. The vocals of Laine and Pinder and the quintet's driving R&B sound quickly caught the fancy of Birmingham teenagers. (Laine, besides vocals and guitar, also demonstrated talent on such instruments as ukelele, piano, drums, and harmonica.) It took only a few months for word to reach London about the long lines of people waiting to get in and hear the Moodies in Birmingham.

The group started at the top, debuting in London in the number one rock club, the Marquee.

They were signed in a short time by British Decca. Their first single, "Lose Your Money," was no blockbuster, but did gain a respectable sales total. Their second, "Go Now," hit number one in England for two weeks in 1964 and the top 10 in the U.S. in 1965. The record's worldwide sales went well over a million copies.

The Moodies were consistent in placing albums such as *Go Now: The Moody Blues #1* (issued on London in 1965) on the charts as well as a number of singles, but for a time their efforts seemed to lose momentum compared to their earlier offerings. However, beginning with the gold 1968 LP *Days of Future Passed* (released on Decca's Deran subsidiary), the Moodies again scaled the heights with a series of hits. *Days of Future Passed* dropped off the charts for a time and then reappeared on them in 1971, dropping off finally in 1973. Other gold LPs included *In Search of the Lost Chord* (1968) and *Threshold of a Dream* (1969). The Moodies formed their own label, Threshold (distributed by Decca), for the gold *To Our Children's Children's Children* (1969) and *A Question of Balance* (1970).

The group's recording output began to slow down in 1971, but *Every Good Boy Deserves Favour* won a gold record, and the band had a hit single, "The Story in Your Eyes." The next album, *Seventh Sojourn* (1972), reached number one in the U.S. in December, by which time it was certified gold. 1972 was a good singles year as well with "Isn't Life Strange" and gold "Nights in White Satin."

Writing enthusiastically about the Moodies' early 1974 concert at the Los Angeles Forum, Dennis Hunt of the *Los Angeles Times* cited the large number of teenagers in attendance as proof of their continued rapport with a range of age groups. The audience responded resoundingly to the group's original compositions, he reported, "which . . . are enigmatic, highly rhythmic rhapsodies. It is eerie, spacy music that creates an atmosphere of edginess and desolation. What is unique about them is their reverence for melody. Their songs are among the most melodic in all of rock. . . . The lyrics of Moody Blues songs are exceptionally well written."

By 1974, though, the members had become weary of touring and the restrictions of band work. Several had hopes of solo careers. The closing of that phase was signaled by the restrospective *This Is the Moody Blues* (Threshold, 1974).

After several years of soloing, the main alumni found that the whole actually was greater than its parts. The group reformed and began work on a new album. Before that came out, London Records issued the 1977 two-disc live set with unreleased studio tracks, *Moody Blues Caught Live Plus Five.* In 1978, the new album, *Octave,* came out on London. Its release was backed by a wide-ranging concert tour demonstrating that the band retained a large following, but the album turned out to be rather pedestrian. By 1978, veteran member Mike Pinder had stepped down in favor of a fine new keyboardist, Patrick Moraz.

In the 1980s, the band continued active with some changes in personnel along the way. Their output on the Threshold label included *Long Distance Voyager* in 1981, *The Present* in 1983, and *The Other Side of Life* (1986), which provided a top 10 single "Your

Wildest Dreams." At that point, the lineup comprised Hayward, Thomas, Edge, Lodge, and Moraz.

MOONGLOWS, THE: *Vocal group from Louisville, Kentucky. Original members (1951): Bobby Lester, born Louisville, c. early 1930s; Harvey Fuqua, born Louisville, c. early 1930s; Prentiss Graves; Alexander Graves; Buddy Johnson.*

An important group in the history of both R&B and rock, the Moonglows probably are better known in the latter field than the former, and then as Harvey and the Moonglows. Actually, during their R&B days, they were billed either as just the Moonglows or as Bobby Lester and the Moonglows, since Lester was the original organizer of the group.

Lester already had picked up a following on some parts of the R&B circuit in early 1951 when he decided to form his own quartet. By then, he had worked with several well-known vocal groups. He lined up his hometown friend Harvey Fuqua first, then adding Alexander "Pete" Graves and Prentiss Barnes for the vocal foursome. Also recruited was guitarist Buddy Johnson. Fuqua had no professional experience, but he had sung in school shows and church choirs. In addition, he came from a family with some tradition in show business. His uncle, Charley Fuqua, was one of the original Ink Spots.

During 1952, they came to the attention of Cleveland disc jockey Alan Freed, who later had such a great hand in the rise of rock. Freed helped place them with the Champagne Record Company of Cleveland, which released their first single, "I Just Can't Tell No Lie" in 1953. Before much could happen with the disc, the company went out of business and Freed took the Moonglows to Chance Records of Chicago. Their first release on Chance (December 1953) was "Baby Please" backed with "Whistle My Love," cowritten by Freed and Fuqua. In 1954, two other Freed–Fuqua compositions—"Rockin' Daddy" and "Secret Love"—became minor R&B hits. But that December, before Chance could capitalize on the Moonglows' growing national popularity, it closed down.

This time the group went to one of the most important R&B-oriented record firms, Chess. Their first Chess single, "Sincerely," was a top 20 hit nationally on the R&B lists and also made inroads on the popular market, though the gold version was a cover by the McGuire Sisters. The Moonglows followed with a second hit on its second disc for Chess, "Most of All." The group had another best-seller in 1955 with "In My Diary" and achieved good response with such other recordings as "Foolish Me," "Slow Down," and "Starlite."

In 1955, the Moonglows was featured in many of the concerts organized by Alan Freed and took part in the film *Rock, Rock, Rock*. 1956 hits included "We Go Together" and "Over and Over Again." During those years, Chess's Checker subsidiary released a number of recordings of the group, billed as Bobby Lester and the Moonglows. In 1957, "Don't Say Goodbye" and "Please Send Me Someone to Love" made the charts, but internal strains led to Harvey taking over as lead singer. In 1958, the group's biggest hit ever, the million-seller "Ten Commandments of Love," was released under the name Harvey and the Moonglows. Despite its success, though, the group broke up and most of the members went separate ways.

Harvey remained with Chess and recorded a number of songs, including such late 1950s releases as "I Want Somebody," "Blue Skies," and "The First Time." He also teamed with Etta James on two single releases: "If I Can't Have You"/"My Heart Cries" and "Spoonful"/"It's a Crying Shame." In 1960, in association with Berry Gordy, Jr., Harvey formed two of his own labels: Harvey Records and Tri Phi Records. One of his first releases on Tri Phi was a major hit, "That's What Girls Are Made For." On the record, Harvey was backed by a group called the Spinners that later had many hits for Gordy's Motown Records. (The Spinners evolved from the group that backed Harvey on his Chess solo discs. At that time, Marvin Gaye was a member, but he left by the time the Tri Phi records were made.) Harvey also made several discs on the Harvey label, backed by the Quails, but none were major successes.

By the mid-1960s, Harvey, who married a sister of Berry Gordy, gave up singing to handle record producing and other administrative chores for Motown. His producing credits for Motown are impressive, including singles "Yester-Me, Yester-You, Yesterday" by Stevie Wonder, "Someday We'll Be Together" by Diana Ross and the Supremes, "What Does It Take to Win Your Love" by Jr. Walker & the All Stars, and "My Whole World Ended" by Marvin Gaye and Tammi Terrell. In the early 1970s, he set up his own independent producing and talent firm. One of his first contracts—with RCA—involved a talent package of four different working acts who could perform separately or as part of a fifth group called New Birth. The acts included eight musicians known as the Nite-Lighters, four female vocalists called the Mint Juleps, four male singers called the New Sound, and solo singer Alan Frye.

Bobby Lester, who similarly went his way as a soloist for a while, also moved into production in the 1960s. One of the original group, Alexander Graves, formed a new Moonglows quartet in 1964 that included Doc Greene, George Thorpe, and Bearle Easton. The quartet made several discs for Lana Records, Times Square Records, and Crimson Records, none of which had any great impact on the public.

The Moonglows were featured on a number of LPs, some released after the group had dissolved. Their album credits included *Rock, Rock, Rock, The Best of Bobby Lester and the Moonglows*, and *Look, It's the Moonglows* on Chess and *Collectors Showcase—The Moonglows* on Constellation. *The Flamingos Meet the Moonglows on the Dusty Road of Hits* on Vee Jay was still available in the 1980s. (*See Freed, Alan; Gaye, Marvin; Gordy, Berry, Jr.; James, Etta; Ross, Diana; Supremes, The; Walker, Jr., & the All Stars; Wonder, Stevie.*)

MORRISON, VAN: *Singer, songwriter, band leader, saxophonist, bassist, guitarist, drummer, harmonica player. Born Belfast, Northern Ireland, August 31, 1945.*

Many stars seem to take up music almost in rebellion against their parents. Not so with Van Morrison, who credits his parents with giving him a feeling for blues and jazz from his early years.

He heard many examples of such music—plus opera—both from his parents' records and from his mother's singing. As he grew up, his musical tastes expanded to include the new strains of rock and R&B beginning to influence the British isles in the late 1950s. He also gained some affinity for American country music. Hank Williams affected his approach to music, as did bluesmen John Lee Hooker, Leadbelly, Muddy Waters, and Sonny Boy Williamson.

Morrison began to learn saxophone (initially soprano sax) and guitar in his school years. At 15, he quit school to concentrate on music. He learned tenor sax the following year and joined a rock group called the Monarchs with whom he toured Europe. While appearing in Germany, a movie director became interested in his instrumental skill and signed him to play the part of a jazz musician in a German movie.

After completing his film role, Morrison returned to Belfast, where he opened a spot called the R&B Club. He formed his own group, Them, and played his own club before taking off on a tour of England in 1965. British record producer Bert Berns heard the group during the tour and offered to produce recordings of some of their material. Two singles hit both British and U.S. charts: "Here Comes the Night" and "Gloria" on Parrot. "Gloria" was written by Morrison, who sang lead on both recordings.

In 1966, Morrison was asked to tour Europe with

a number of pioneer rock and blues stars, including Bo Diddley and Little Walter. Morrison took the opportunity to closely study Little Walter's harmonica technique, spending many hours off the stage listening to him demonstrate his methods.

After completing the tour, Morrison took Them to the U.S. in May 1966 to play the West Coast. The band was the featured attraction on the bill at Los Angeles' Whiskey-A-Go Go that included a then unknown group called the Doors, who later revamped his "Gloria." (*See Doors, The*).

When Van returned to Europe in the summer, he was exhausted from the steady grind of one-nighters or short engagements. In August, he temporarily stopped being an active entertainer and went home to Belfast. He took it easy, spending most of his time writing songs and thinking about what he wanted to do next. In March 1967, he signed a new recording contract. One of his first efforts, "Brown-Eyed Girl," became a top 10 hit in England and in the U.S. on the Bang label.

Toward the end of the 1960s, Warner Brothers Records signed as the U.S. distributor of Morrison's recordings. Things were slow for a while, but as the 1960s came to a close, he began to catch on with U.S. disc jockeys and their mass audience. His *Astral Weeks* LP moved on the charts in 1968–69 and *Moondance,* completed in mid-1968, went platinum, remaining on the charts 90 weeks into the summer of 1970. The single "Come Running" was a chartmaker in 1970.

His popularity continued to grow as evidenced by his top 20 singles "Domino" (1970), "Blue Money," "Call me Up in Dreamland," and Wild Night" (1971). In early 1971, his third Warners LP, *His Band & the Street Choir,* appeared on the hit lists and remained there through most of the first half of the year. Later in the year, he had another charted album, *Tupelo Honey* (which continued to sell copies after leaving the charts until it finally reached gold-record status in December 1977). In 1972, he provided Warner Brothers with the chart album *Saint Dominic's Preview* and the singles "Jackie Wilson Said" (in part a tribute to his R&B forebear) and "Redwood Trees." During that year, the restrospective album, *Them—Featuring Van Morrison,* released on Britain's Parrot label, was a hit. Also in 1972, some of his earlier material, (including his original recording of "Brown-Eyed Girl") was released by Bang Records on *T.B. Sheets.* In August 1973, his Warner Brothers album *Hard Nose the Highway* showed up on the charts and remained on them through year-end.

Despite the fact that his albums and singles made the charts and his following worldwide numbered in the millions, and despite the creative excellence of most of his music, Morrison as of the early 1970s had not become the superstar many had expected him to be. Winning a huge U.S. following remained a key for such success and Morrison found this difficult to do even though he called the U.S. home from the late 1960s on. He alluded to some of his disappointments in the songs of his fine 1974 LP *Veedon Fleece.* It was a year in which Warners released another excellent collection, the live two-LP *It's Too Late to Stop Now.* The relatively tepid response to those—except from critics—caused Morrison to give up recordings and touring for a while.

Though he dropped out of circulation for three years, he continued to be among the most highly regarded artists in the field with both critics and his fellow musicians, many of whom urged him to return to action. Significantly, he was one those featured in the farewell concert of the Band in San Francisco on Thanksgiving Night 1976. (*See Band, The.*) The warm reception given him by the audience perhaps influenced him to begin working on new material. The following year, Warner Brothers was able to release a new LP, *A Period of Transition,* that fully met Morrison's standards.

Commenting on one of Van's shows, Philip Elwood wrote in the *San Francisco Examiner* (October 6, 1978): "Hearing Morrison is hearing contemporary vernacular pop music at its best—always has been. Morrison is an enigmatic character—millions of fans consider him among the most powerful and creative personalities in the world of rock—or jazz-rock, folk-rock, soul-rock, what have you. [But] other millions have never heard of him. The latter I find hard to believe, since Morrison, if nothing else, is a superb composer and has a keen ear for harmonies at all levels, vocal or instrumental."

By the late 1970s, though, Morrison seemed to have come to terms with his position in the pop music spectrum and was willing to accept the respect of those who valued his contributions to the field. He continued to maintain that respect with a steady output of top-flight albums on Warner Brothers. These included *Wavelength* (1978), *Into the Music* (1979), *Common One* (1981), *Beautiful Vision* (1982), and *Inarticulate Speech of the Heart* (1983). Switching to Mercury, he put out *A Sense of Wonder* (1984), *Live at the Grand Opera House Belfast* (1985), *No Guru, No Method, No Teacher* (1986), and *Poetic Champions Compose* (1987).

MOTELS, THE: *Vocal and instrumental group. Members (1979): Martha Davis, born Berkeley, California, January 19, 1951; Jeff Jourard, born 1955; Marty Jourard; Michael Goodroe; Brian Glascock. Jourard replaced in 1980 by Tim McGovern. McGovern replaced in 1982 by Guy*

Perry. Scott Thurston added in 1983. Davis began solo career in 1987.

Until the 1970s, in the pop music world, Los Angeles essentially was a place where artists from other states moved to remain in close touch with important entertainment-industry executives and the many recording studios from which came a steady flow of new, often sensationally successful albums. In the mid-1970s, L.A. suddenly became a talent incubator of its own, with a growing number of home-grown, dynamic young bands—the Pop, the Dogs, and the Motels, for example—making the rafters ring at small clubs and bars all over the city. As Los Angeles–based recording officials gradually became aware of this wealth of potential starring acts under their very noses, they began to sign many of them. One group gaining particular attention at the end of the decade was the Motels, a band with a steaming punk/new wave style whose centerpiece was charismatic, dark-haired vocalist Martha Davis.

Along with Exene of X, Pauline Black of the Selecters, and Chrissie Hynde of the Pretenders, Davis was part of a growing roster of pulse-quickening female rock singers coming to the fore after the mid-1970s. The reason for this, Davis told Robert Hilburn of the *Los Angeles Times* (June 1980), was that "People are finally accepting us. And because people are accepting it, you have all these women who have been closet cases for years finally getting the freedom to come out.

"I don't know Chrissie, but I have met Lene Lovich and we're all in the same boat. We haven't spent the last five years in the supermarket. We've been in bands getting ready. And there are a lot more women on the way. Every time I go to a rehearsal hall, there's a new band with a girl singer. The door is now open."

For Martha, the thought of going through such a door didn't enter her mind for most of her preadult years. She grew up in Berkeley, California, daughter of a University of California administrator and a former kindergarten teacher. Her mother, she told *People* magazine (September 20, 1982), "was a complete bohemian nut who loved art, music, and philosophy," while her father was "basically conservative." Davis attributed her mother's suicide when Martha was 19 (by which time her parents were divorced) to her suppression of her own interests to meet the restrictions of her husband.

Martha began ballet and guitar lessons at eight. She played "mostly Negro spirituals. When I was 11, I was hooked on musicals. Between Igor Stravinsky and musicals, I was set." But romantic involvement, not music, was her primary concern as she approached her teens. She told *People:* "I wore short black skirts, little spiked heels and teased my hair up. I was a wimp studying the art of juvenile delinquency."

She told Michael Goldberg of the *San Francisco Examiner/Chronicle* (August 19, 1979) how at 12, she fell in love with a boy she termed "a hardcore juvenile delinquent." She became pregnant two years later with the first of two girls. The two got married and moved to Florida, where her new husband was sent as an armed-services recruit.

She told Goldberg: "My husband joined the Air Force. I had my other kid in Florida. Then he went off to Vietnam. And being an Air Force wife was a real dreary fate. I thought: 'Davis, what are you doing here?' So I wrote him a 'Dear John' letter. I was scared to tell him to his face (he was due back on leave) 'cause he'd beat me up. So that was the end of that."

For some years after that, she faced the grind of trying to get by with few resources, often on welfare in Florida and then California. "There's been a bunch of [desperate] days. Living on my own and raising two kids. We lived on watermelon for three weeks straight in Florida. We've been thrown out of houses by irate roommates. [In] the house we live in now [mid-1979, in Encino, California], the guy downstairs was trying to kill his mom 'cause he was on Angel Dust. I had a bunch of people arrested 'cause they were on Angel Dust and the police came and said: 'You best move out to and take your kids within two days or they're gonna come back and kill you.'"

By her late teens, she had returned to Berkeley with her children, where she dabbled in painting for a while before drifting into music. She told Goldberg she went to a rock show and the combination of the rhythms and the bandsmen turned her on. "I came of age. I went and saw a band. I think it was actually a physical attraction. One of the members of the band gave me the eye."

She became friends with other local musicians and finally got the courage to try to work with some of them. This led to membership in the Warfield Foxes in the early 1970s. At her first live show, she told Hilburn: "I was so nervous I was on the verge of complete collapse. But I just transformed once I got on stage. I was suddenly crawling around on my knees. I don't know what made me act like that. It was like I was possessed or speaking in tongues. Afterwards I thought: 'Wow, what was all that about?'"

With that band and another, Angel of Mercy, Davis improved her stage presence and gained notice from local fans. But she soon realized there wasn't much further advancement in pop music in Berkeley.

In the mid-1970s, she and another musician, Dean Chamberlain, moved to Los Angeles to be closer to the recording industry's movers and shakers.

They soon found that most of the top-ranked rock nightclubs were shuttered or offered few opportunities for unknown bands. But there were other aspiring bands coming along with whom Martha and her associate soon connected. She and Dean formed a forerunner of the Motels and sought ways to reach the rock audience they were sure was out there. One novel approach was the Radio Free Hollywood Concert, a 1975 performance they organized with two other avant garde bands, the Pop and the Dogs. An exciting offering, it gained publicity from local rock writers.

By 1976, that version of the Motels had become a key element in the reviving local rock underground. The band had regular engagements in clubs and small theaters all over the Los Angeles area. Just when things seemed going in the right direction, internal disagreements about creative directions or personal hangups among band members caused the group to break up. Chamberlain, for instance, left and went on to be a featured member of highly regarded Code Blue.

Davis was determined to reform the Motels. But it took a lot of trial and error until a new regular roster evolved in late 1978. This was a quintet with Martha on lead vocals and rhythm guitar; the Jourard brothers—self-proclaimed "R&B bop-sax fanatic" Marty on keyboards, sax, and vocals plus Jeff on lead guitar; Michael Goodroe, with early credentials in country and jazz bands, on bass guitar; and English-born Brian Glascock on drums.

There had been rising industry interest in the earlier Motels, particularly because of Martha Davis's electrifying stage presence. When word filtered out that the new band had an even tighter sound, recording executives perked up their ears. When a series of shows at Madame Wong's club in January 1979 had enthusiastic onlookers screaming for more, Capitol Records A&R men were convinced the time was right. They signed the band, a penstroke ahead of several other eager talent scouts. Not the least cause for optimism was the fact that Davis not only was a superb rock vocalist, but also had developed into a fine songwriter who explored areas of human conflict and love with poetic intensity not usually achieved in rock songs of the period.

Shortly after the signing, the band began working on its debut album. Among the tracks laid down were two Davis songs that were showstoppers in its 1979 concerts: "Celia" and "Total Control." "Celia" related a rejected lover's threat to gain revenge on his former girlfriend not by murdering her, but by messing up her "pretty face." The other song's lyrics dealt with a love-obsessed individual's willingness to sell his soul for total control over the object of that love.

The debut LP, *The Motels* (September 1979), showcased not only Martha's searing vocals, but also a band that was no routine backup group. Its instrumental and vocal support added depth and emotional impact to each number. This was particularly true in live shows; one of the group's problems in its early albums was the difficulty record producers had in capturing the Motels' concert exuberance on tape or vinyl. Commenting on the band's style, Jeff Jourard told a reporter: "Our stuff is dreamlike, sketchy. It's more suggestive than specific. Like when you half remember something. You remember the feeling, but don't remember exactly what happened. We play a sort of fusion of R&B, rock, and reggae . . . muted rhythm & blues."

The first album sold a respectable 150,000 copies—not a bad showing, but far short of what the record industry regarded as commercial success. (The album did earn a gold record in Australia in 1980.)

By the time the band was ready to start on its second album, Jeff Jourard had left to form his own band after expressing dissatisfaction with the band's creative trends. Taking his place was guitarist Tim McGovern (then and for the next year, Davis's love interest), who had been with the Pop. The group proceeded to complete tracks for the album *Careful* (June 1980). The numbers included five written by Martha, two by Tim, and three by Marty Jourard and Michael Goodroe. The reception for the album was about the same as for the first—critical praise and moderate sales.

Some record companies might have called it quits, but Capitol maintained its support. The band also did its part by a continuous series of live shows that kept its name in front of rock fans. Davis told Dave Zimmer of *BAM* magazine: "We've always been a nice-guy band, hard-working, like a 110 percent band, always on time, never too crazy. And that registers on a record company's roster as a big plus."

But a big disappointment was just ahead. Capitol didn't like the radically new direction it detected in tracks planned for the third album. The tapes featured unusual guitar solos by McGovern and some challenging rhythm/percussion concepts. Davis recalled: "They never said: 'Do the album over.' They just said: 'Guys, we knew you were gonna take a giant step, but we didn't know how big. We'll put the record out if you want us to, but we don't think it's the kind of record that's gonna get our sales staff hoppin'.'"

McGovern was hopping mad. In addition, the romance between him and Martha had cooled down. The upshot finally was that he left the group for another band, Burning Sensations. He had no regrets about his contributions, he told Bob Hilburn. "I feel I helped establish the group as a creditable musical entity and I'm proud of what we did on [the first version of] the new album. It's a shame that people won't hear it. The album may have needed a more 'obvious' single, but I sometimes wonder about that kind of thinking. Anyway, it's all in the past."

Part of the basis for their romantic breakup, Davis told *People,* could be traced to band problems. "He [McGovern] began demanding the power. I'm not territorial at all until its taken away from me and then I get into a protective-bitch attitude."

Once more, the band regrouped and also agreed to rework its proposed third album. With new producer Val Garay (who had supervised preparation of Kim Carnes' superhit "Bette Davis Eyes"), the band recorded the LP *One Four All* (April 1982). This time, the commercial chemistry was right. Helped by the band's first top 10 single, "Only the Lonely," the LP went gold.

The band followed *One Four All* with gold *Little Robbers* (fall 1983). The single "Suddenly Last Summer" was a top 10 hit in the fall and was still on the lists after 17 weeks at the start of 1984. The Motels now included another member, guitarist/horn player Scott Thurston.

Davis, whose reputation as a songwriter continued to grow, told Zimmer of *BAM:* "I always try to stay armed with pen and paper. 'Suddenly Last Summer' was written on cocktail napkins at Le Cafe on Ventura Blvd. [in Encino]. I was just sittin' there having a glass of wine when Whoops! Here it comes, get out the pen and start writing stuff down. I basically spew and edit. And it's getting to the point where me and them, me and the songs, have a great relationship going. I just have a mental picture of what my songs are about and, even with my limited vocabulary and limited education, which stopped at the ninth grade, I can always come up with some words."

She told him she sometimes liked to play with word arrangement. For *One Four All,* for instance, she wrote "Take the L out of lover and it's over" and on *Little Robbers* came up with the wordplay title "Isle of You."

In 1985, the band's next LP, *Shock,* came out, an album that continued a trend toward slicker production values rather than musical content. Behind the scenes, there was considerable unhappiness among band members, who objected to producer Val Garay's use of studio musicians as replacements for regular sidemen for some sessions, an approach that had been initiated with the 1982 *All Four One* LP.

In 1987, when work got underway on what was to become Martha Davis's debut solo album on Capitol, the group was disbanded. She told Chris Willman (*Los Angeles Times,* December 17, 1987), *Policy* had begun as "a Motels album all year long, until we were two weeks into the studio. I had pins made up that said 'Motels Rule '87.' I was totally into it.

"But by then I was doing all the arrangements, doing everything. It's too hard to point a finger or say specifically what happened in a situation like that. Maybe it was just time. It's so hard to talk about because, basically, I love all those guys a lot and we had the best eight years that any band could have."

Initially, at least, it didn't seem a change for the better. *Policy,* issued in October 1987, didn't dent *Billboard*'s Top 100 and the first single, "Don't Tell Me the Time," peaked at 80.

MOTHERS OF INVENTION, THE: *Vocal and instrumental group founded in 1964 by Frank Zappa. (See Zappa, Frank.) Personnel (late 1960s): Jimmy Carl Black, Bunk Gardner, Art Tripp, Ian Underwood, Don Preston. Group makeup as of 1971–72: Ian Underwood; Howard Kaylan, born New York, New York, June 22, 1947; Mark Volman, born Los Angeles, California, April 19, 1947; Jim Pons; Aynsley Dunbar, born England; Don Preston.*

"You say you're aware of the 'overall shape' of the group's output so far?"

"I say we're not only aware of it, we control it. It is an intentional design."

"You think this makes the Mothers better than some other group?"

"It makes the Mothers different, certainly. We do not claim that control of conceptual continuity automatically insures superiority on any level. The reason for explaining this process is to simply let you know it exists and to give you . . . some criteria by which to rationally judge what we do. It is not fair to our group . . . to review detailed aspects of our work without considering the placement of a detail in a larger structure."

"Listen, nobody puts together a pop group, simultaneously planning years of absurdly complicated events, lives out those events, then writes about it in a press kit, and expects somebody to believe it"

"The basic blueprints were executed in 1962–63. Preliminary experimentation in early and mid-1964. Construction of *project/object* began in late 1964. Work is still in progress."

"We wonder you guys never had a hit single."

"I'm sure you realize that total control is neither possible nor desirable. (It takes the fun out of it.) The *project/object* contains plans and nonplans also precisely calculated *event-structures* designed to accommodate the mechanics of fate and all bonus statistical improbabilities attendant thereto. . . . What we sound like is more than what we sound like. We are part of the *project/object*. The *project/object* . . . incorporates any available visual medium, consciousness of all participants (including audience), all perceptual deficiencies, God (as energy), THE BIG NOTE (as universal basic building material), and other things. We make a special art in an environment hostile to dreamers."

"I still don't get it. . . . Art? What art? *Rolling Stone* and all other groovy important publications have convinced me that you guys are nothing more than a bunch of tone-deaf perverts, faking it on the fringe of the real rock'n'roll world. . . . All you guys do is play comedy music. . . . So I should believe all this crap about a conceptual program spanning decades?"

"Yes."

"Why don't you guys just play rock'n'roll like everybody else?"

"Sometimes we do play rock'n'roll like everybody else (sort of). Our basic stylistic determinant is Rock, only sometimes it gets extrapolated into curious realms."

"You probably get into that 'classical rock' . . . real intellectual with ugly chords and the beat's no good."

"Any association we might have with 'serious music' has to be considered from a Rock viewpoint because most of us are strictly Rock musicians. There is also the element of humor to consider."

"I would like to bring to your attention at this time one of the basic tenets of our group philosophy: It is in spite of all evidence to the contrary, theoretically possible to be 'heavy' and still have a sense of humor. . . . And another precept which guides our work: Somebody in that audience out there knows what we're doing and that person is getting off on it beyond his/her wildest comprehensions."

This exchange between an imaginary interviewer and Frank Zappa, written by Zappa as part of the promotional material for his 1972 movie *200 Motels,* probably is as good a summation of his band creation, the Mothers of Invention, as can be found. There obviously had to be some method in the chaotic history of the group, for it remained an important factor in the rock field in the early '70s, close to a decade after its debut in 1964—and without a hit single.

The personnel changed many times during this period. Even Zappa himself performed only occasionally with the band in the 1970s, though he retained control over its activities. The incarnation of the group in 1971–72 included Ian Underwood on woodwinds and keyboards; Howard Kaylan and Mark Volman, vocals and visual effects; Jim Pons, vocals and bass guitar; Aynsley Dunbar, percussion; and Don Preston, keyboards and synthesizer. (Three of this group—Kaylan, Volman, and Pons—previously were members of the Turtles. Kaylan and Volman later continued their social satire as Flo and Eddie.)

The group was an object of controversy from its earliest performances on the West Coast. Some audience members were bored or offended by the weird antics. Others finally gave up on the ear-splitting sounds given out by the powerful amplifiers. However, for all those who scoffed, there were several times as many who considered the Mothers' music the wave of the future.

The group was signed by MGM/Verve in 1966 and was first represented on albums with *Freak Out!* (August 1966). Its reception was good enough for MGM/Verve to bring out *Absolutely Free* (1967), *Lumpy Gravy, We're Only in It for the Money* (1968), *Cruising with Ruben & the Jets,* and *Uncle Meat.*

In 1969, Zappa completed a new recording agreement with Reprise. One of the first fruits of this was *Hot Rats,* a 1969 LP featuring Zappa with the Mothers providing backup. In 1970 and 1971, six more LPs were released, the early ones on Reprise, the later ones on Zappa's own label, Bizarre/Straight Records (distributed by Reprise as of 1972). These were *Burnt Weeny Sandwich, Mothermania, Weasels Ripped My Flesh, Chunga's Revenge, Mothers/Fillmore June 1971,* and *200 Motels.*

200 Motels provided part of the score for the movie of the same title produced by Zappa in late 1972. It included excerpts from a tremendous backlog of film he took during Mothers tours going back to the mid-1960s. (Zappa also compiled a large amount of live tapes of the group's concerts, enough, he said, to turn out 10 or 12 albums beyond those released through 1973.)

Zappa continued to release new recordings of the Mothers' music through the mid-1970s with the band's makeup, as usual, being subject to regular change. Those releases included *Over-Nite Sensation* (1973), the live *The Roxy and Elsewhere* (1974), *One Size Fits All* (1974), and *Bongo Fury* (a 1975 collaboration with Captain Beefheart). All of those were issued on Zappa's Discreet label.

By the late '70s, Frank seemed to have lost interest in the Mothers as a separate entity and focused instead on a solo career backed by sidemen hired for specific tours or album sessions. In the 1980s, Zappa licensed his Mothers catalogue to Rykodisc for release on compact discs.

(*See Captain Beefheart, Jefferson Airplane; Turtles, The.*)

MOTLEY CRUE: *Vocal and instrumental group. Members, (mid-1980s): Vince Neil, born Hollywood, California, February 8, 1961; Mick Mars, born Terre Haute, Indiana, c. 1957; Nikki Sixx, born Seattle, Washington, c. 1961; Tommy Lee, born Athens, Greece, c. 1963.*

A 1980s version of Kiss, though with more heavy metal in its music, Motley Crue stressed visual attire that included heavy makeup (not to the extent that the bandsmen would go unrecognized off stage), harlequin-bright costumes, and such other accoutrements as studded armbands and belts and chains. Band members affected disdain for rules of society—at least in interviews—until the group's lead singer, Vince Neil, was involved in a drunk-driving incident that cost one person's life and almost led to a jail term. Afterwards, though not abandoning the group's all-out–attack concert approach and generally defiant attitude, the members were contrite about actions that could endanger the lives and well-being of others.

Even before that, band members had denied that their music and stance were destroying the fabric of society, however. Nikki Sixx said, in 1983: "We are militant. When we perform, it's like going into battle. But our messages are mostly positive. Instead of killing, we take prisoners. We do entertainment. The kids see us and get their aggressions out. They go to school during the day and get subdued. Then at night, with us, they get crazy. It's their hour. The reason for Motley Crue is excitement. We're energy and good songwriting. It's not just music and not just a look. We're both."

The band's roots were in Southern California, though only one member—Neil—was born and raised there. By his early teens, more interested in rock'n'roll than schooling, he was suspended from several Hollywood-area high schools. He said: "Rock'n'roll is in my blood. This is always what I wanted to do. I couldn't punch a time clock, work 9 to 5."

Nikki Sixx shared that desire to drop out of conventional society. Sixx started playing rock guitar in his teens in Seattle. He wasn't shy about admitting that he stole his first guitar. "I was a rowdy kid. The only person I listened to was me." Eager to move up in the music world, he sold his guitars to get bus fare to Los Angeles when he was 17 in 1978. There, he

hung around local clubs such as the Whisky-A-Go-Go, Roxy, and Starwood. He worked with several groups that had little impact and broke up. For a while, he also was in a street gang called the Gladiators, engaging in occasional rumbles that caused brief periods in jail.

At the start of the 1980s, Sixx was playing bass guitar with a group called London when he decided to form a more promising group of his own. In February 1981, he took the first step in that direction by joining forces with drummer and vocalist Tommy Lee, who just had left Suite 19. Lee, born in Greece, moved to the Los Angeles area with his family when he was four. He was still in high school, performing with local bands in his off time, when he met Sixx.

Their next move was to find a lead guitarist. They found their man after seeing Mick Mars' ad in a local paper: "Loud, rude, aggressive guitarist available." Mars, the oldest member of the group, spent his first eight years in Indiana before his family shifted locale to Southern California. With Mars' addition, the band still lacked a lead singer, but Mars solved that soon after when he saw Vince Neil perform with the group Rock Candy. He sought Neil out and sold him on the potential of the new band. Mick recalled: "We looked at each other, and our hair was the same and it turned out our musical tastes were the same. We knew we could click."

Vince agreed to audition for the older members, but he didn't show up so the association almost didn't come about. He was persuaded to try out again. This time the prospective bandsmen decided the chemistry was right with that lineup.

From the start, their goal was to offer no-holds–barred high-decibel "shock rock." Mars called it "a cross between hard-ass rock'n'roll and borderline heavy metal."

Sixx emphasized: "We wanted to be the loudest and grossest band in the history of rock. We'd do anything to get attention." The quartet intended to appeal to fans roughly in their age group—teens and early twenties. He told Andy Secher of *Hit Parader* (December 1983): "We're appealing to a generation of kids who are too young to have ever seen Alice Cooper in his prime. Maybe they're too young to even have seen Kiss. They want a band they can relate to. . . . We're not gonna go out there and play 20-minute songs. Our attention span isn't that long. We like to keep everything about three or four minutes long—about the same time between commercials on TV."

The group's act caught on locally in a surprisingly short time. Within four months of its formation, Motley Crue had a strong toehold in the local L.A. club circuit. In June 1981, the group itself pressed a thousand copies of its debut single: "Stick to Your

Guns''/''The Toast of the Town.'' The response was enough to gamble on self-producing an album, *Too Fast for Love* (1982), on its own label, Leathur Records.

Sixx told Secher: ''That first album was really nothing more than our demo tapes. We went in and just laid down the set that we were playing in the clubs. We released it on our own.'' The album did surprisingly well in Los Angeles area outlets, selling more than 20,000 copies in a short period of time, enticing a major label, Elektra/Asylum, to sign the group and do some rework on the album before issuing it nationwide. The new version, remixed by Roy Thomas Baker, was put out by Elektra in August 1982 along with a promotional 12-inch single containing ''Live Wire'' and ''Take Me to the Top'' backed with ''Merry-Go Round.'' The band's debut music video, based on ''Live Wire,'' also came out during the summer of 1982.

The follow-up LP, *Shout at the Devil* (Electra, September 1983), went platinum. Elektra supported the best-selling collection with a series of single releases (primarily featuring songs written by Nikki Sixx) spanning ''Piece of Your Action'' (January 1984) to ''Helter Skelter''/''Red Hot'' (November 1984).

During most of 1984, the band was constantly on the road, performing across the U.S. and Canada and all over Europe. People in some of the communities they were scheduled to visit raised alarms about their persona and music. Some objectors claimed that *Shout at the Devil* had demonic references. Sixx told Secher: ''This album has absolutely nothing to do with the devil. We're about as anti-Satan as you can get. We're trying to say that the devil is any authority that tells you what you can do and what you can say. It can be your parents, it can be your teachers, or it can be your boss. We're saying shout at that fucker—don't let 'em get you down. That's our philosophy. It's got absolutely nothing to do with the devil—believe me.''

At the end of 1984, the band collected kudos from many sources. *Hit Parader*'s monthly reader's poll showed Motley Crue at number one with heavy metal fans, ahead of Van Halen. In *Circus* magazine's annual reader's poll (published in February 1985), *Shout at the Devil* was named top album of 1984. *Circus* readers also voted Nikki best bassist, Vince best vocalist, and Tommy best drummer. Only Mars wasn't first—he finished second to Eddie Van Halen in the best guitarist classification.

But in the middle of what seemed like a halcyon period for the band, it's private macho stance caught up with it. Vince Neil was involved in a fatal accident that, the newspapers reported, was triggered by his excessive drinking. After legal maneuvering,

Vince remained a free man, promising he would do what he could to warn others of the dangerous consequences of drinking and driving. One form this took was a warning in the liner notes of the band's next album, the platinum 1985 *Theatre of Pain:* ''To all Crue fans; If and/or when you drink, don't take the wheel. Live and learn so we can all fuckin' rock our asses off together for a long time to come. [signed] The Crue. We Love You!''

Vince commented: ''We're not here to represent sobriety, but the danger of drinking and driving. We don't want to see anyone hurt. If we can save one person, the message will be well worth it. Kids don't think an accident could happen to them, but it can. We want them to be aware so that when they leave our concert or a party, the message will stick in the back of their minds and they'll think about it and have someone else drive them home. Our eyes have been opened about drinking and driving.''

For a while after the incident, there were rumors that the band would break up. But by June 1985, its new LP was out and the band was once more on the concert trail. *Theatre of Pain* was on the charts right after Elektra issued it and by the end of 1985 it had been certified platinum. It continued to stay on lists well into 1986. First single (and video) from the LP was a remake of Brownsville Station's 1973–74 hit ''Smokin' in the Boys Room'' backed with ''Use It or Lose It.''

In the fall of 1987, the LP *Girls Girls Girls* was issued. It included an anti-drug song, ''Dancing on Glass.'' But as Sixx told a press briefing, he didn't include alcohol in that category. ''I'm not going to put myself above anybody or preach to anybody. I don't do drugs, but I do drink like a fish.''

Questions arose about the possibility that marriage might change the band's rebel stance. (Tommy Lee by then had married TV star Heather Locklear and Sixx had announced plans to tie the knot with singer-actress Vanity). Sixx remonstrated, ''You don't have to be a bachelor to have fun. If I'm married, I won't be dead.''

MOTT THE HOOPLE: *Vocal and instrumental group. Members (early 1970s): Ian Hunter, born Shrewsbury, Shropshire, England, June 3, 1946; Verden Allen, born Hereford, England; Mick Ralphs, born Hereford, England, March 31, 1948; Overend Watts, born Birmingham, England, May 13, 1949; Terry Buffin, born Ross-on-Wye, England, October 24, 1950. Group disbanded in 1976.*

In a way, the oddly named Mott the Hoople gained more attention after it went out of existence than during its seven-year pursuit of fame and fortune, only to become something of a cult favorite.

The band demonstrated considerable instrumental technique and creativity when it debuted in 1969, but took a long time to generate attention either at home or in the U.S. Things did pick up for it for a few years starting in 1972, but it couldn't sustain the momentum and disbanded in 1976.

The band's origins were in the verdant, hilly section of Hereford, England, where its four original members—lead guitarist Mick Ralphs, bassist "Overend" Watts, organist Verden Allen, and drummer Terry Buffin—grew up. All were playing in rock groups in their early teens, though not together. Their paths began crossing in 1966 as their various bands played on the same bills, and they had a casual acquaintanceships for the next three years. In early 1969, though, they decided to form a new band and made some demonstration tapes that Mick Ralphs took to London to try for a recording contract.

He played the tapes for Guy Stevens of Island Records. The tapes were deemed only average and Stevens wasn't too interested in the band, but he liked some of the songs. A major flaw in the band's style, he felt, was the lack of a lead singer. This was soon rectified by the addition of singer-pianist-composer Ian Hunter. Hunter, who spent his formative years in Shrewsbury, was then a Londoner, earning a living from songwriting and preparing demonstration records for other writers. Hunter provided Mott the Hoople not only with a vocalist, but with a source of new material.

Stevens, becoming increasingly enthused about the band, supervised their debut LP, *Mott the Hoople*, released in England in fall 1969 and in the U.S. (on Atlantic Records) in early 1970. Its country-rock flavor intrigued British reviewers because few English groups played such music at the time. U.S. critics, used to such material from American bands, were more sanguine. Some noted its similarity to some of Dylan's work, particularly *Blonde on Blonde* (a point several English reviewers made as well).

As Ian Hunter, who wrote much of its material, told a reporter: "It just came out that way by accident. We use organ and piano, which must make the sound similar for a start, and the studios we cut the album in had a lot to do with the vocals sounding like Dylan." Mick Ralphs added: "Mind you, we were never really influenced by anyone—there weren't many bands to go and hear in Hereford, and in fact, there wasn't much to do except play our own music."

As 1970 went by, the group gained new adherents at home with its second album, *Mad Shadows*. But it followed that in 1971 with *Wildfire,* a flop both at home and in the U.S. It bounced back from that with the excellent, hard-driving rock set, *Brain Capers* (Atlantic, 1972). The setbacks of those early '70s almost caused the group to disband, but it rallied to sign a new contract for U.S. distribution with Columbia Records. Davie Bowie (*See Bowie, David*) was selected as producer for the band's debut on the label, resulting in *All the Young Dudes,* which was on U.S. charts part of 1972 and into 1973. That album provided the band with two hit singles: the title song and "Sweet Jane." The excellent album, *Mott,* stayed on the charts from summer 1973 into 1974.

At that point, it looked as though the band might become one of the major success stories of the '70s. But then the members hit a severe creative dry spell that brought forth a series of below-par collections starting with *The Hoople* (an album hurt by the departure of Mick Ralphs) in 1974 and such later Columbia LPs as *Drive On* (1975) and *Shouting and Pointing* (1976). (Columbia also issued the album *Mott the Hoople Live* in 1974.) Seeing the handwriting on the wall, the remaining members of the band decided to go separate ways in 1976. During that year, Columbia issued the retrospective *Mott the Hoople's Greatest Hits.*

NAZZ: *See Rundgren, Todd.*

NELSON, RICK: *Singer, guitarist, songwriter, band leader (STONE CANYON BAND). Born Teaneck, New Jersey, May 8, 1940; died near DeKalb, Texas, December 31, 1985.*

A youthful idol on TV and records in the 1950s and early '60s, Rick Nelson had to work out new career directions when his parents' long-running "Ozzie and Harriet" show finally phased out in the mid-1960s. The choice he made in 1967 (when he debuted in a station KOBS country-music show at the Shrine Auditorium in Los Angeles) was to perform country/country-rock material. It was no easy task to overcome the opposition of country purists to what they regarded as Johnny-come-latelies from the pop field, but at the end of the '70s, Rick could point to some successes and a growing amount of respect over the years for his abilities.

Eric Hilliard Nelson's show business career began as a child actor on the Nelson family program. It wasn't until he was 16 that he essayed a move into singing and recording. His first release was Fats Domino's song "I'm Walkin'," which Rick cut to impress a girl he wanted to date. It turned out to be a smash hit, selling over a million copies in two weeks on Verve. From 1957 through 1964, he remained one of the top stars in rock, placing a string of singles (and albums) on the charts while rolling up overall sales of an estimated 35 million records. His *Billboard* top 10 successes included "A Teenager's Romance," on Verve and, on Imperial, "Be-Bop Baby," "Stood Up," "Believe What You Say," "I Got a Feeling," and "Lonesome Town," plus two-sided smashes "Never Be Anyone Else But You,"/"It's Late," and "Just a Little Too Much," "Sweeter Than You."/"Hello Mary Lou" (1961) was written by Gene Pitney. "Poor Little Fool" hit *Billboard*'s number one in 1958, as did "Travelin' Man" in 1961, selling over 5 million copies worldwide. (Most of these were available in the 1980s on *Greatest Hits* on Rhino Records.)

Some of those songs, such as "Hello Mary Lou" and "Poor Little Fool" reflected Rick's interest in country music. As he told an interviewer in the mid-1960s: "I've liked country music for as long as I can remember. I've always been a big fan of guys like Johnny Cash and Jim Reeves. Most of my early records were at least part country."

In 1963, Rick signed with Decca and for a while turned out LPs more in the vein of Frank Sinatra or Johnny Mathis, including *For You* and *The Very Thought of You* (1964), *Spotlight on Rick* and *Best Always* (1965), and *Love and Kisses* and *Bright Lights and Country Music* (1966). None did particularly well, nor was Rick himself enthralled with his change in style. He also felt certain, if his audience didn't notice it, that he was maturing as a musician and singer. He worked hard to improve his skills and his peers generally agreed he had made progress.

He told Shaun Considine of *The New York Times* (January 23, 1972): "Sure, in the beginning I used to fake it on the guitar. I was too scared to play, and anyhow, no one could hear you with everyone screaming. But in time I learned to play and enjoy it. Also I had guys like Joe Osborne in my band and later Glen Campbell and James Burton on guitar. [Burton later backed Elvis Presley.] We had some fantastic musicians' musicians at that time." When he could, Rick picked up tips on how to improve his guitar work from some of those people.

The idea of combining his love for country music with a break with his past musical efforts finally bore fruit in 1967 as Rick assembled his first country band and turned out the LP *Country Fever*. Before 1967 was over, he had his first mild country hit, "You Just Can't Quit," which reached number one in Los Angeles and several other major cities. Nelson gained favorable reviews for a series of concerts across the U.S. in which he was backed by a band that included Burton on guitar, Junior Nichols on drums, Lynn Russell on bass, Bob Warford on banjo, bluegrass maestro Clarence White on rhythm guitar (*see Byrds, The*), and Glenn D. Hardin on pi-ano. Rick concluded he had found his musical niche and, from that time on, he never looked back.

In 1968, his second country release, *Another Side of Rick,* came out and was followed in 1969 by the live folk-country-rock *In Concert,* which spawned the single, "She Belongs to Me" (his first *Billboard* pop top 40 hit in over five years). Written by Bob Dylan, it seemed an appropriate tribute to an artist whose work had greatly influenced Nelson's new style. His third studio country LP was *Rudy the Fifth* (1969).

Meanwhile in the late '60s, Rick had started to work with the fist Stone Canyon Band lineup: Allen Kemp, Randy Meisner (later a founding member of the Eagles (*see Eagles, The*), Pat Shanahan, and Tom Brumley. When he and the band started working together, he told Considine: "We improvised and experimented and listened to other people's work, people like Randy Newman and Tim Hardin. Then one day I heard *Nashville Skyline,* by Bob Dylan, and I knew where I wanted to go. I listened to that album for days. The songs were so simple, yet cryptic at times. I wanted to sing songs like that and, if possible, also write like that. So for a year and a half that's all I did. We'd rehearse during the day and I'd write at night."

A rock nostalgia concert at New York's Madison Square Garden in October 1971 laid the groundwork for Rick's most notable success of the decade. He wanted to sing his new material, but the audience continued to scream for old pop songs. The frustration this aroused in him led him to write "Garden Party." In 1972, it gained Rick his first top 10 hit since 1964 and also provided the title number for a hit album on Decca. Looking back he said: "I really didn't want to do the show. I'm not into that whole rock'n'roll revival concept, but I had never played Madison Square Garden and the idea of playing there before 22,000 people sounded interesting." His feelings translated into lyrics that went: "When I got to the Garden Party/They all knew my name/But no one recognized me/I didn't look the same."

Rick placed a number of songs on the charts as the '70s went by, though none equalled the success of "Garden Party." However, he retained a strong following and continued to add to it with regular tours of campus auditoriums and progressive country venues. In the late 1970s, he signed with Epic Records, which released the disappointing album *Intakes* in 1977. Part of the problem, as producer Al Kooper pointed out, was a difference of opinion about creative direction between the artist and label executives. Though Epic released another album in 1981, *Four You,* Rick had left the label two years before for a new affiliation with Capitol Records.

The first fruits of Rick's work with Capitol was the 1981 LP *Playing to Win*, a distinct improvement over his first Epic release. Though not a massive seller, it did well enough for Capitol to give the go-ahead for work on a follow-up album.

Meanwhile, as Rick had been doing over the years since founding his Stone Canyon Band, he kept up a busy in-person schedule. It was in the middle of one such tour en route to a New Year's Eve 1985 date in Dallas in a chartered DC-3 that Rick was killed when the plane caught fire in midair and exploded upon landing near DeKalb, Texas. The pilot and co-pilot survived, but Nelson and his group died.

There were newspaper reports about drugs being found in the bodies. John Beland, who had played guitar with Rick for several years at the end of the '70s, later told a reporter from the *San Francisco Chronicle:* "There were drugs. It's a national problem and it touched Rick. But it was nothing that got in the way of a performance. It was never anything that got in the way of his personality or the way he dealt with people. He would never freebase."

After the tragedy, CBS released *Memphis Sessions* drawn from tapes Nelson had made in 1979 that hadn't been released. Beland was indignant about the way the material had later been prepared in Nashville, maintaining it had been butchered in re-mixing and was likely put out purely for financial reasons. He told the reporter: "The album released by CBS after his death was totally ruined. That album is not the Memphis Sessions. Only one track is like the original.

"What CBS did on that album was exactly what Rick hated about Nashville. CBS wasn't even aware of the tapes until I called them. They took those tracks after the artist died and overdubbed them." The released version, he noted, ended up as a country album. "When we cut *Memphis,* we wanted a rockabilly album, not a country album." (*See Domino, Fats; Eagles, The; Kooper, Al; Pitney, Gene; Poco.*)

NESMITH, MIKE: *Singer, guitarist, songwriter, band member (THE MONKEES), band leader (FIRST NATIONAL BAND, SECOND NATIONAL BAND). Born Houston, Texas, December 30, 1942.*

As a writer and musician, Mike Nesmith made a number of contributions to the folk and country fields. Some of his songs became hits for other artists over the years and several of his country-flavored solo rock albums rank among the underrated gems of the '70s. For all that, he remained best known for his part in the Monkees' TV show of the mid-1960s, a part of his career about which he always had decidedly mixed feelings. (*See Monkees, The.*)

His first musical love was the blues, a by-product of his early environment. He was born in Houston, but spent most of his youth in Farmer's Branch, just outside Dallas, where his family had inherited some property that turned out to be in the black ghetto. Recalling those years to Todd Everett (*Phonograph Record,* December 1970), he said: "Most of my friends were black, my first girl friend was black. I'm surprised that I didn't marry a black girl. I was married by a black preacher.

"Music didn't really mean anything to me until I was 20. It was just something I'd hear in the back of a bar while I was shooting illegal pool. The kind of music I was exposed to? Well, I remember when B.B. King had something like six hits in a row. They were hits to me because they were what got played a lot on the juke boxes. People like Ray Sharpe, Jimmy Reed. . . . Hell, they lived right there."

Mike learned to play guitar in the early 1960s and eventually gravitated to Los Angeles, where he was performing in small folk clubs when he successfully auditioned for The Monkees in the fall of 1965. He remained with the group until it broke up in mid-1969.

Nesmith wasn't particularly sad about that. Though the work had been lucrative, he hadn't held on to much of the money and, in addition, it had been creatively stifling. He wanted to concentrate on improving his image as a writer and musician. He signed with RCA for whom he recorded a number of LPs over the next few years: *Magnetic South* and *Loose Salute* in 1970; *Nevada Fighter* and *Tantamount to Reason* in 1971; *And the Hits Just Keep on Comin'* in 1972.

In the middle and late 1970s, Nesmith concentrated on songwriting, providing hit singles for various pop and country performers. After leaving RCA, Nesmith recorded many albums on his own Pacific Arts label: *Pretty Much Your Standard Ranch Stash* (1973), *The Prison* (1975), *Compilation* and *From a Radio Engine to the Photon Wing* (1977), *Wichita Train Whistle Songs* and *Live at the Palais* (1978), and *Infinite Rider on the Big Dogma* (1979).

By the end of the '70s he was increasingly engrossed in the production of video films. One of those, *Michael Nesmith in Elephant Parts,* won the Grammy Award for video of the year in 1981. In the mid-1980s, there was renewed interest in the Monkees when old episodes were placed in TV syndication. Nesmith, however, still had no desire to relive those days and declined to tour with the other members of that group.

NEVILLE BROTHERS, THE: *See Meters, The.*

NEW YORK DOLLS, THE: *See Johansen, David.*

NEWMAN, RANDY: *Songwriter, singer, pianist. Born Los Angeles, California, November 28, 1943.*

In the early 1970s, the three "N's"—Nilsson, Nyro, and Newman—were given credit for adding more subtle, melodic material to rock and pop music in general than had been heard since the Beatles' heyday. The three turned out songs with less obviously biting comment than "message" or acid-rock material, songs that often were closer in feeling to the slow popular ballads of the 1950s. But there was far more complexity and insight in their lyrics than in most of the old Tin Pan Alley standards. The name sometimes given to the output of these writers and performers was "salon rock." It was a demanding occupation, though, which perhaps accounts for the fact that in the middle and late 1980s, only one of the three—Randy Newman—retained the creative spark needed for a flourishing career.

Of the three, Newman had by far the most training in music theory. His family relationships included uncles Lionel and Alfred Newman, orchestra leader–composers and long-time writers of movie scores. Though Randy was born in Los Angeles, for the first few years of his life, his family wandered through the South, residing, in turn, in New Orleans, Louisiana; Jackson, Mississippi; and Mobile, Alabama. By the time he was seven, however, the Newmans were firmly entrenched in Los Angeles and little Randy was taking his first piano lessons, which he continued after entering University High on L.A.'s west side.

Randy capsuled those years and, indeed, his life, in 1983 as follows: "I was born in '43 in Los Angeles and went to public school. I went to UCLA as a music major, but didn't graduate. I started writing songs when I was 16 and as a staff writer [for Metric Music], earning $50 a month, did some stuff for people like the Fleetwoods and Gene McDaniels. One of my songs was covered by the O'Jays. My first album was released in 1968. I'm married and have three boys, ages 14, 11, and 4. The oldest one is into hardcore punk music."

In other biographical notes for Warner Brothers Records, he maintained, perhaps facetiously: "I really never wanted to do anything. Really I never have. My decisions have always been made for me. Much easier that way."

Thus, he maintained, it was at his family's suggestion that he went to college and gained basic grounding in music theory.

After leaving school, Randy spent several years doing relatively little. His song output was not immense, though indeed he never had been or would be a prolific writer. He spent a great deal of time daydreaming, did some arranging on order for record firms, and, in 1967, got married. The next year his wife, Roswitha, gave birth to their first son, Amos. His Warner Brothers album debut, *Randy Newman,* was issued in 1968. The company wasn't quite sure how to handle his unorthodox blend of music and lyrics, which partly contributed to the album's poor sales.

But other pop and rock artists recognized Randy's unique talents. His compositions were increasingly sought out by other performers. Nilsson, who became a close friend during the late 1960s, included several Newman songs in his early singing act and even recorded an entire album of Randy's material, *Nilsson Sings Newman* (RCA, 1970). Meanwhile, such other artists as Peggy Lee, Judy Collins, and the rock group Three Dog Night scored major successes with Newman's songs. Collins gained a chart single with his "I Think It's Going to Rain Today," originally included in her 1967 LP *In My Life.* (Folksinger Dave Van Ronk and Joni Mitchell later a featured the song in their concerts. In 1969–70, Newman was in the national spotlight as a result of two top 10 hits: "Love Story" by Peggy Lee and "Mama Told Me Not to Come" (number one for Three Dog Night in mid-July 1970) and later recorded by soul man Wilson Pickett, a track on his second album *Twelve Songs* (Reprise, 1970), on which he was backed by guitarist Ry Cooder. As the 1960s drew to a close, he had already begun to win concert engagements, typically in college auditoriums. His stoop-shouldered, somewhat near-sighted appearance and his rather limited voice contrasted sharply with the blond-haired, exuberant, outgoing impression of Nilsson, who often played the same circuit. In truth, though, both shared a desire to limit their personal exposure and concentrate on creative endeavors.

As noted in *Time* (July 13, 1970): "One of the many ironies about Newman is that, although he sings in a raspy, soul-based blues style, his chief concern as a lyricist is Middle America. In 'Love Story,' . . . Newman sums up middle-age with painful accuracy: 'Some nights we'll go out dancin'/If I am not too tired/And some nights we'll sit romancin'/Watchin' the late show by the fire.' In 'So Long, Dad,' he captures the turned around relationship of a grown son and his father: 'Come and see me, papa, when you can/There'll always be a place for my ol' man/Just drop by when it's convenient to do/Be sure and call before you do.' ''

Because of Randy's slow writing pace, his label issued the album *Randy Newman Live* in 1971. The album did better than the first two with buyers, indicating that the audience was beginning to catch on to Newman's talents. His third studio album, *Sail Away* (1972) soon was on the charts. With sharply honed satire, Newman commented on such disparate subjects as the slave trade (in the title song), the pollution of Ohio's Cuyahoga River (which caused some stretches to literally blaze) in "Burn On," and the nuclear age in "Political Science" (with the refrain "Let's drop the big one").

Again, there was a lapse of two years before his eagerly awaited next album came out. Called *Good Old Boys,* it covered such topics as white racist attitudes in the South in "Rednecks," Faulkner-like scenes in "A Wedding in Cherokee County," and revered political demagogue Huey P. Long in "Kingfish." More than a few critics commented, though, that the comic nuances could be too subtle, making some songs sound like apologies for racist acts.

Once more Randy's growing phalanx of supporters had to wait a long time before the next collection: *Little Criminals* (1977). Randy's best-selling release to that point, it featured such tracks as "Sigmund Freud's Impersonation of Albert Einstein in America" and "Short People." Though actually an argument against disparaging people because of their physical attributes, "Short People" was angrily misinterpreted by some as only a diatribe against individuals of diminutive stature. The controversy, if anything, caused more people to buy the album to see what the fuss was all about. The LP, Warner Brothers reported sold over 750,000 copies while "Short People" hit 1.5 million worldwide.

As Newman commented some years later to Robert Hilburn of the *Los Angeles Times,* he never could see himself writing about simplistic topics; placing that demand on himself was one reason he found it very hard to come up with new compositions. "I just don't write 'I love you, you love me' songs. They all have such a strange adversity to them that when I'm done, I can't imagine that I'll ever write another one.

"All this experience and knowledge and it never gets any easier. Sometimes I wish I was a vice president at one of these big record companies, with an office, a secretary, and people to talk to. Now that would be fun."

His creative juices did seem to flag on his 1979 album, *Born Again,* which made the charts, but seemed far less innovative than his previous offerings. It might have been getting ready to complete the score for the movie *Ragtime* that threw him off a

bit. Actually, he had been working on score material earlier (the "Sigmund Freud–Albert Einstein" song had originally been written for the film version of the best-selling book by E.L. Doctorow), but other people involved in the project kept running into roadblocks about moving it into production. When the movie finally came out in late 1981, Newman's soundtrack work proved to be a highly professional effort and the album might have done very well if the film had become a box office smash.

After another gap of several years, Randy released a new studio album, *Trouble in Paradise,* at the start of 1983. In a way it seemed like a geographic concept album with tracks such as "I Love L.A.," "Christmas in Capetown," and "Miami." He commented: "I've never been to Capetown and I don't imagine I ever will. I wrote the song because I love the idea of a hot weather Christmas and I'd seen Capetown in some surfing movies. Everyone loves California." As for Miami: "I've only been there once, but it made a very strong impression on me. It doesn't really seem like a part of America. It's kind of exciting and decadent." Concerning "I Love L.A.": "I've always defended Los Angeles all over the world. People always attack it on such a simplistic level. Of course, unless they're idiots, the Chamber of Commerce isn't going to use this as the city's theme song." Ironically, it became something of an unofficial anthem of Los Angeles. The single won wide airplay in 1983 and again in 1984 when it seemed to embody the spirit of Southern California during the euphoric times of the Summer Olympiad.

Though not possessed of a great voice nor unusual piano skills, Newman in concert was an extremely effective performer, thanks in part to his impeccable phrasing and the manner in which he seemed to embody the various characters he employed as "spokespersons" for his usually brilliant lyrics, lyrics that might seem simple on the surface but offer considerable thematic complexity in their varied blends of humor, irony, and satire. Taken at face value, some of his words can be interpreted as meanspirited, but Newman always stressed that was not his intent.

He told Lynn Van Matre of the *Chicago Tribune* (May 7, 1978), "I would never write a song just to make fun of someone or something. At least I hope I wouldn't. Even the songs I've written that some people might see as making fun, I've never considered nasty. What I'm making fun of is people's callousness and insensitivity, and often that callousness is exaggerated to the point where it's funny. I mean, as in [the song] 'Yellow Man' (which could be considered as humor derived from Asian stereotypes) that guy is an idiotic bigot. A pinhead. See, that's one thing that makes me a little different from a lot of other singers—I'm willing to act the part of an idiot in my songs.''

He stated he felt his other contributions to pop songwriting included ''Some multilevel lyrics that aren't always what they seem to be. The idea of writing a third person song, songs that are not about yourself but are about characters, songs in which the writer and singer become another characer.'' (*See Cooder, Ry; Fleetwoods, The; McDaniels, Gene; Nilsson; Nyro, Laura; O'Jays, The; Pickett, Wilson; Three Dog Night.*)

NEWTON-JOHN, OLIVIA: *Singer, actress, songwriter. Born Cambridge, England, September 26, 1947.*

There was grumbling among country-music die-hards when Olivia Newton-John was named Country Music Female Vocalist of the Year for 1974. It didn't seem right, they suggested, for an artist from overseas who had primarily been known in England as a pop-ballad and rock vocalist to suddenly gain such honors in her initial foray into the U.S. market. But many country-music people brushed that aside, noting that the U.S. audience had, in effect, validated Ms. Newton-John's credentials by buying her recordings in large numbers. Had she wanted to debate the matter, Olivia could have pointed out that the roots of country music lay in the centuries-old folk music of the British Isles and many a U.S. country star was descended from immigrants from her father's home region, Wales.

It was, in fact, folk music that first interested Olivia as a girl growing up in Australia. She was of English birth, having first seen the light of day in Cambridge, but her father, a college professor, had moved the family to Australia when Olivia was five to take an administrative post at a university. (Intellectual and scientific pursuits bulked large in Olivia's family. Her grandfather was Nobel Laureate German physicist Max Born.) When Olivia was in her late teens, she began to move away from folk toward the pop idiom.

Victory in a talent contest in Australia gained her a trip to England in the late '60s. In the early '70s, she became one of the more successful young pop singers in Britain. As her reputation grew there, she naturally started thinking about the more affluent U.S. market, a move matched by growing interest in her by American record firms. MCA Records offered a contract and Olivia began working on her initial recordings for the label in 1973. One of the first fruits was the gold single ''Let Me Be There.'' The song proved acceptable to both pop and country listeners. It made the country top 10 from year-end into 1974.

Olivia proved it was no fluke with an even greater country hit, the gold ''If You Love me (Let Me Know),'' which became number one on country lists in the spring of 1974. She showed her versatility by earning another gold record in the fall of 1974, this time for a number one pop single, ''I Honestly Love You.'' Meanwhile, she also stormed the country album charts during 1974 with the gold *Let Me Be There* and *If You Love Me*.

With that kind of success, it's not surprising Olivia gained four Country Music Association Award nominations for 1974: Entertainer of the Year, Album of the Year, Single of the Year, and Female Vocalist of the Year. She came in number one in the last named category.

She continued to be an almost perennial resident on the country charts throughout the 1970s. In 1975, her singles hits included ''Have You Never Been Mellow,'' ''Please Mr. Please,'' and ''Something Better to Do.'' (The *Have You Never Been Mellow* LP also hit number one on *Billboard*'s pop list.) In 1976, she came up with the number one country single ''Come on Over'' in May and the top 10 ''Don't Stop Believin''' in late summer. LPs *Clearly Love* (1975) and *Come on Over* (1976) went gold. Still going strong in 1977, she turned out the top 10 album *Making a Good Thing Better*, whose title track also rose high on the singles charts.

In 1978, Olivia stressed rock rather than country, starring opposite John Travolta in the film *Grease* and having a featured part in its gold soundtrack album, which also spawned her hit single ''You're the One That I Love.'' On the surface, it might have seemed she was turning strongly away from the country field, particularly when her next solo album, *Totally Hot,* was issued in late 1978. However, a closer listen to the album's contents showed that, despite its title, it still had several country-oriented numbers, such as ''Dancin' Round and Round'' and ''Borrowed Time,'' the latter an original composition by Olivia.

After *Grease,* Olivia signed to do the movie *Xanadu* in 1979. Besides appearing in the film, she worked on the soundtrack album with the Electric Light Orchestra. (*See E.L.O.*) The film, released in 1980, was a flop, but the album went platinum. Besides getting a hit album, MCA Records also could point to chart singles from it, most notably Olivia's ''Magic,'' a number one pop hit in *Billboard* late in 1980. Commenting on the film's failure, Olivia told a reporter: ''There were lots of problems on the film. The script was weak to begin with and there were rewrites going on every day. I suppose I should have spoken up more, but I hate to make waves. One thing I did learn from that film was not to say yes to anything unless the script is good.''

Her first solo album of the '80s was the platinum *Physical* (MCA, fall 1981). The title song rose to number one on *Billboard*'s singles list the week of December 18, 1981 and stayed there for nine more weeks. At the end of 1982, *Billboard* named "Physical" its number one single of the year.

Olivia supported the album with a wide-ranging tour, her first in five years. For many of the concerts, she was joined on stage by John Travolta. The series comprised a stunning success in which Olivia demonstrated more stage presence than at any previous time in her career. Near the end of the tour in late 1982, she told an interviewer: "I'm just more confident now. I can relax more and be myself on the stage. I was always rigid. I was afraid to try new things, but I think I've gone through a lot of changes in the last few years."

Part of her problems had gone back to her growing-up years in Australia, she noted. "Where I came from, it wasn't considered proper for a woman to be considered ambitious. It had this sinister ring, as if you were someone who was trying to claw your way to the top. So I denied to myself for a long time that I had ambition. I'm more comfortable with that now because I realize my drive isn't improper. I'm just out to improve myself."

Besides touring in 1982, Olivia had her fourth TV special, "Olivia Newton-John: Let's Get Physical." Singles "Make a Move on Me" and "Heart Attack" made *Billboard*'s pop top 10. Late in the year, MCA issued *Olivia's Greatest Hits, Volume 2*, which stayed on the LP charts into 1984, earning multiplatinum sales. Her projects during that period included a new film with John Travolta, *Two of a Kind,* which unfortunately was another cinematic dud, though the soundtrack LP went platinum. The film score also brought her another top 10 single in early 1984, "Twist of Fate." During late 1985 and early 1986, she had another album on the charts, *Soul Kiss.*

NICKS, STEVIE: *Singer, songwriter. Born Phoenix, Arizona, May 26, 1948.*

With her eerily piercing vocals and seductive whirling on stage, Stevie Nicks was a vital contributor to the awesome success of the middle to late 1970s version of Fleetwood Mac. Her insightful songwriting also helped make the group one of the biggest concert attractions as well as challenger for the mantle of top record-selling group of the decade. In Fleetwood, though, each of the five members seemed to blend in as an integral part of the entire musical fabric, so some wondered whether Stevie would be as effective as a soloist as she had been with the band. In the 1980s, she did go out on her own (though not shutting the door on future appearances with a revived Fleetwood Mac) and showed she was able to be a star in her own right. (*See Fleetwood Mac.*)

She was born in Phoenix, but spent much of her growing-up years in other places. Her father was an executive who made a number of job shifts that called for his family to relocate. Among the companies he worked for were Greyhound and Armour Meat. By the time she was in her teens the family was settled in the San Francisco area at a time when the Beatles were generating a new rock era with the "British Invasion," and the U.S. response was taking form with the birth of the psychedelic rock movement centered on the Bay Area.

Stevie was swept up in the rock panorama in her early teens. She began writing songs at 16. In her late teens, she became lead vocalist for a band called Fritz, whose members included talented young bass guitarist Lindsey Buckingham. Unable to make much progress beyond being a regional favorite, the band eventually broke up and Lindsey and Stevie, who had developed a close affection for each other, moved to Los Angeles in hopes of furthering their musical careers.

After several years of getting by with whatever assignments they could scrounge up through either session work or sidebar nonmusic jobs, they finally got the chance to record their own album, *Buckingham Nicks* (Polydor, 1973). The album, which showed only occasional flashes of the vocal and guitar work the two would achieve with Fleetwood, received minimal attention from reviewers and record buyers. But it did prove the accidental catalyst that changed their lives.

In November 1974, drummer Mick Fleetwood, one of the co-founders of Fleetwood Mac, got into a conversation with a friend while shopping in a Los Angeles supermarket. The band was suffering another of the reorganizations that seemed to hit it every few years; Fleetwood, somewhat at loose ends, had the time to search for a better recording studio. It was suggested that he examine the Sound City Studios in nearby Van Nuys. When he got there, studio engineers used a tape of the Buckingham Nicks album to demonstrate the facility's capabilities. Stevie, who was in a nearby room, grew curious about why her album was being played. She came in and met Fleetwood. Apparently this all made an impression because a few weeks later, Mick got in touch with Stevie and Lindsey and asked them to audition for his band.

The result was a five-member group that turned out some of the most striking rock of the 1970s. Starting with *Fleetwood Mac* (Warner Brothers, 1975), the group sold hundreds of millions of LPs with releases that included *Rumours* (1977), *Tusk*

486

(1979), and *Fleetwood Mac Live* (1980). Top 10 singles were often written by Stevie. The biggest-selling Fleetwood Mac single was of her "Dreams" (number one in *Billboard* the week of June 18, 1977, and also number one on singles charts around the world).

Still, those achievements exacted a price. In 1977, all the band members had personal disappointments. In Stevie's case, it was Lindsey Buckingham's decision to break up their eight-year love affair. Some of the pain showed through in many of the tracks the members wrote for the superhit album *Rumours*.

Though the band somehow reconciled those differences enough to record and tour together for several more years, there were indications that Stevie remained troubled by it all. She even commented to an interviewer from *People* magazine (November 26, 1979) that perhaps she should get out of the entertaining bind.

Noting she had moved from a fancy mansion above Sunset Boulevard to a modest beachfront apartment, she said: "I'm 31. I won't always be in a rock band and I don't want to come out of this absolutely helpless. Some people thrive on being a rock star. I hate it. I don't like being waited on all the time, people following me around saying: 'Let me do this, let me do that.'"

She had by then made a move somewhat away from her band activities, signing with former boyfriend Paul Fishkin, who owned a label called Modern Records, to play one of the roles and record the soundtrack of a film titled *Rhiannon*. The story was based on her composition "Rhiannon," a 1976 top 10 single with Fleetwood Mac.

She also tried her hand at other forms of writing. One 1979–80 project was to seek support for making an animated film of a children's story she'd written. She told Jim Jerome of *People:* "It's a love story about a goldfish and a ladybug. A friend told me it would be the *Doctor Zhivago* of children's films."

But the association with Modern Records soon moved into the forefront. In late 1980, Stevie began recording songs for a solo album on the label. It seemed a good time since Fleetwood Mac's operations were winding down. Released in the summer of 1981, the platinum album, *Bella Donna*, still was on *Billboard*'s Hot 200 more than 2½ years later, a performance in line with Fleetwood Mac LPs. Top 10 singles for the album included "Leather and Lace" (a duet with Don Henley of the Eagles) and "Stop Draggin' My Heart Around" (written by Tom Petty and his teammate Mike Campell). (*See Eagles, The; Henley, Don; Petty, Tom, and the Heartbreakers.*)

Stevie's second solo album, *The Wild Heart*, was released on Modern (with distribution by Atlantic Records) in mid-1983. Singles hits from the platinum album included "Stand Back" in 1983 and "Nightbird" (co-written by Stevie and Sandy Stewart) in top chart positions in late 1983 and early 1984. Stevie took things easier in 1984 before going to work on her next LP, the platinum *Rock a Little* (1985) with the top 10 1986 single "Talk to Me."

Between *Rock a Little* and the start of a reunion album project with Fleetwood Mac, she spent a month at the Betty Ford Center in Palm Springs, California, for treatment of a chemical dependency. She attributed her problem to the pressures of almost nonstop recording and touring for years on end.

She told Robert Hilburn (*Los Angeles Times,* June 14, 1987), "I figured that if I wanted to continue going like an absolute maniac . . . that it would eventually hurt my music. I had planned to do it for a long time, but I wanted to wait until I'd have a break from touring and recording.

"I didn't feel I was strong enough to do Betty Ford in the middle of a tour because anybody in the world will tell you that if you are going to do something that serious you shouldn't be stupid and turn around and go right back on stage in front of 75,000 people where you are going to be terribly nervous and probably want to go back to whatever it was you gave up."

When the new Fleetwood Mac LP, *Tango in the Night,* came out in the spring of 1987, it contained her composition "Welcome to the Room . . . Sara," which reflected on her treatment experiences.

NIGHT RANGER: *Vocal and instrumental group from San Francisco. Members (mid-1980s): Jack Blades, Kelly Keagy, Brad Gillis, Alan "Fitz" Fitzgerald, Jeff Watson.*

Admired by both heavy metal and mainstream rock followers, Night Ranger could lay claim to the best of two worlds. It was perhaps that dual image that brought it a considerably larger audience than a typical U.S. heavy metal group.

Three of the band's five regulars of the 1980s had been involved in its early incarnations in the 1970s. This trio—Jack Blades, Brad Gillis, and Kelly Keagy—all were involved in the shifting patterns of multiple startup groups in their high school years in California. Gillis, in particular, had experience as a member of Ozzy Osbourne's backing band before joining forces with the others in the mid-1970s. (*See Osbourne, John "Ozzy."*) The band that Blades and Gillis formed at the time (1976–77) was the funk-rock Rubicon. It built up a local following in the San Francisco Bay area and made two LPs for 20th Century Fox that got little attention. Kevin Keagy joined just before the band folded in 1979.

But the three friends got back together soon after in a new group, Stereo, that didn't make much commercial headway either. Blades told a reporter from *BAM* magazine (February 24, 1984): "The three of us put Stereo together with a couple of other guys. We covered all the bases. We played pseudo–new wave funk-rock-jazz. We had a good time, but it was really strange because everybody was trying to turn us into this new wave band. They would look us over and say things like: 'I know this great barber.'"

Keagy added: "And also, we played way too loud for the places where we were booked."

At the beginning of the 1980s, that group folded, but within a short time a new band had started that rapidly evolved into Night Ranger. As in the earlier bands, Night Ranger from the start placed major emphasis on the songwriting skills of Blades and Keagy, who also could each handle lead vocals. Instrumentally, Blades' work on bass guitar and Keagy's drumming were blended with the double lead guitar work of Gillis and Jeff Watson, who previously had performed with his own band, and keyboardist Alan "Fitz" Fitzgerald, who came to Night Ranger with credits that included work with the Ronnie Montrose and Sammy Hagar groups. (*See Hagar, Sammy.*)

The double lead guitars became a hallmark of the group's style. Gillis told Suzanne Stefanac of *BAM:* "I play a '62 Stratocaster and Jeff plays a '56 Les Paul. He plays fast picking, I play tasty vibrator bar. The song pretty much determines who is going to play a solo. If it's a fast-burning tune, Jeff usually picks up on it. If it's something that needs a little taste and fancy footwork, I take it. When it comes to the end of a song and we don't know who's going to take it, then we take it together, like a harmony."

All of this contributed to a sound Gillis called "metal power pop '80s concert rock," which might be described, he told Stefanac, as "stainless steel, because we're more polished than regular heavy metal."

The band developed its act in local clubs and soon won the support of San Francisco's rock promoter par excellence, Bill Graham. Graham got them engagements as opening acts for such groups as the Doobie Brothers, Santana, and Judas Priest. The band's diverse musical background allowed it to mesh well with groups that covered a range from blues-rock to high-voltage heavy metal.

Naturally, Blades, Keagy, and company began making demonstration tapes to win the all-important recording contract. Most record-company executives were decidedly unimpressed. Blades recalled: "Every record company in America but one turned us down twice." The exception was Boardwalk Records, founded by Neil Bogart, one-time bubble-gum–music king when he headed Buddah Records. The band had gained an adherent in record-industry executive Bruce Bird, who urged that Boardwalk sign them when he became a vice president of that company in 1981. The band soon was in the studios working on is debut, *Dawn Patrol* (1982).

Boardwalk and the band's new manager, Bruce Cohn (who also managed the Doobies) saw to it that the group had plenty of concert dates, almost all as an opening act, to support the album. The album, mostly hard-driving heavy metal tracks but with a leavening of rock ballads, slowly made its way into listener consciousness, helped by airplay of the single "Don't Tell Me You Love Me" and screening of well-designed videos on MTV. The LP made the charts for a while in 1982–early 1983.

The outlook was bright, but it clouded a bit when Neil Bogart died suddenly and Boardwalk closed its doors. Bruce Bird responded by founding a new label, Camel, signing Night Ranger as his first act. The group's track record looked good enough to MCA Records executives for them to make Camel and Night Ranger part of its operation. Later, MCA acquired the rights to *Dawn Patrol,* which it reissued late in 1983. Riding on the growing popularity of the band, it became a platinum hit the second time around.

The band's platinum debut on MCA, *Midnight Madness* (October 1983), had a less frenetic tone than the debut LP, which incurred the wrath of some heavy metal commentators, but didn't seem to retard fans' rising interest in the quintet. It also brought forth three singles hits: a *Billboard* top 5 success ("Sister Christian") the top 15 "When You Close Your Eyes," and the top 40 "(You Can Still) Rock in America." When the album completed a year on the *Billboard* list, a party in the band's honor at San Francisco's Hard Rock Cafe on November 9, 1984, was attended by a strange amalgam that included other rock stars and California state Assembly Speaker Willie Brown, Jr., who presented the group with a Proclamation from the Assembly honoring their achievement.

Commenting on why a band spurned by the record industry a few years back had become so successful, band members attributed it to its musical variety. Keagy told Rob Andrews of *Hit Parader:* "We've always tried to keep a balance between the type of music we do. Somewhere along the way we got tagged as a heavy metal band. I don't know how true that is. I'll accept the term *melodic metal,* if there is such a thing. But I think we're just a rock and roll band with a wider scope than a lot of other groups."

Blades told another reporter: "We don't try to be AC/DC or Iron Maiden, but we can't be like Air Supply or Crosby, Stills & Nash either. From the beginning, we've been branded as every sort of band, but I consider what we do to be rock.''

He maintained to Tom Lanaham of *BAM* that he and his band mates also had a goal of matching intelligent lyrics to music that was not frozen in one form. He gave Keagy's composition ''Sister Christian'' as an example of a number that was carefully polished over a period of time before it became the softer-hued singles hit. ''It's easy to string a series of guitar licks together and sing some lyric lines over it, but it's a practice we never got into. Our songs shine through because we develop a good tune first. Then we embellish it until it feels comfortable.''

The group's third album, *7 Wishes* (1985), went multiplatinum. Its first single, Blades' composition ''Sentimental Street'' (with Keagy on lead vocal), was a top 10 hit in the summer. By fall 1985, a second single from the album, ''Four in the Morning,'' was in the top 20.

In a typical concert, Night Ranger was big on patriotism, à la Sammy Hagar. Typically, Blades drew rousing cheers when he shouted at show's end: ''There's no place like the U.S.A.'' In most of its concerts, the closing number was ''(You Can Still) Rock in America,'' replete with a huge American flag and, in 1985–86, with a picture of the Statue of Liberty flashed on the back screen.

That stance did not prevent band members from taking issue with Washington-based attempts to establish ''moral'' boundaries for pop music. While claiming to be a conservative Republican and conservative songwriter, in an interview with Jonathan Takiff of the *Philadelphia Daily News* (November 8, 1985), Blades said he opposed the record-rating system proposed by the Parents Music Resource Center. ''I think it's morally wrong for the government to get involved in any kind of censorship. I think what really got this crusade going was not the lyrics themselves, but the recognition that rock music is a strong force in society, that music can literally move mountains. It really came home this summer, when Live Aid and Farm Aid raised millions upon millions of dollars, and raised consciousness levels—in the process embarrassing the government for lagging behind. So some power that be decided to put rock in its place. . . .

''My main concern as an artist is in being able to write and develop songs without any restraints. When you're into a creative flow, it's a real drag to have to stop and look at your lyric and think: 'Uh oh, will they be reading something into this that I didn't mean, or get unduly upset by something I do mean?'

''And besides, any effort to tame rock'n'roll has to fail. Rock has always been rebellious, offensive to the establishment. That's half its reason for being.''

In 1987 the band was back on the road supporting a new album, *Big Life.*

NILSSON: *Singer, songwriter, pianist, guitarist. Born Brooklyn, New York, June 15, 1941.*

In 1967, Harry Edward Nelson III often could be found having a sandwich or coffee at Revell's Coffee Shop near the RCA Victor building in Hollywood, California. During working hours, he could sometimes be discovered hanging around RCA's fourth floor public relations office, where he went mainly to escape from his closetlike office elsewhere on the floor. Tall (6 feet, 2 inches), clean-shaven, blond and blue-eyed, usually wearing sports clothes and a sweater, he gave the impression of an all-American boy of Scandinavian ancestry.

In conversation, he handled himself well on a range of subjects from computer theory to philosophy to music. The picture one gained was of someone quite intelligent with strong self-control, a quick sense of satire, and, particularly, an underlying toughness of the kind needed to succeed in show business. While RCA hadn't provided this young unknown with lavish office space, it had signed him to an exclusive $75,000 contract (non-recoupable advance against royalties). The reason became obvious, within a year, with the release of his first RCA album, *Pandemonium Shadow Show.*

The LP focused critical attention on Nilsson, almost all of it highly favorable. Typical was Pete Johnson of the *Los Angeles Times,* who enthused: ''His voice has a three-octave range, his imagination a somewhat wider one. He is a vocal chameleon, but, unlike some singers whose lack of limitations robs them of identity, each voice shares a personality common to every [Nilsson] voice. Nilsson is easily identifiable whether he is shouting the dramatic lyrics of '10 Little Indians' or musing tenderly in 'Sleep Late My Lady Friend,' or screaming in 'River Deep, Mountain High.' . . .

''His phrasing is perfect, but there is more. He embellishes many of his songs with bits of scat singing, sometimes noodling through an octave or two, sometimes imitating an instrument, sometimes doing things for which there is no adequate description. His voice doubles and triples and quadruples in harmony and counterpoint. All the singing voices on the album are his, even on the Beatles' 'She's Leaving Home,' with its lattice-work of complex harmony. He can be a one-man group.''

The Beatles' reaction to Nilsson matched Johnson's. Derek Taylor, just moved from Los Angeles to London to join the Beatles' Apple Records, gave them copies of the LP. He called Nilsson long-distance and then put John Lennon on the phone. Lennon, who had spent 36 hours listening to the album, said to Nilsson: "It's John . . . John Lennon. Just wanted to tell you that your album is great! You're great!" Later, Beatles manager Brian Epstein tried unsuccessfully to lure Nilsson onto Apple.

Despite all this, the LP sold poorly. However, cuts from the album provided songs for other artists: "Ten Little Indians" for the Yardbirds, "Without You" for Herb Alpert. ("Cuddly Toy" had been recorded by the Monkees before the album came out.) But the exposure paid off later. *Aerial Ballet,* released in late 1968, had a good run on the charts the next year. Its track "One" became a top 10 hit for Three Dog Night. Harry finally was on his way.

Much of Nilsson's songwriting is autobiographical. "1941" on his first album refers to his year of birth in the Bushwick section of Brooklyn; other material obliquely mentions his father's separation from the family in Nilsson's early years. His mother took him (then called Harry Nelson) and his sister to Southern California in 1958. There, Nilsson attended St. John Vianney's Parochial School in Los Angeles, where he won letters in baseball and basketball.

After graduating, he spent half a decade trying to find his niche. He worked at several odd jobs, including theater usher, before settling down to work in a San Fernando Valley bank. By the mid-1960s he was a supervisor in the computer-processing department with 32 people working for him. However, he had slowly grown fonder of music, expanding his ability to play piano and guitar and beginning to compose. Working the night shift at the computer center, he had his days free to make the rounds of music publishing and recording firms.

For a while, nothing encouraging resulted. But his persistence paid off when dynamic producer Phil Spector selected three of his songs: two for the Ronettes and one for the Modern Folk Quartet. Harry made several singles and the 1967 LP *Spotlight on Nilsson* for Tower Records. Meanwhile, he was earning side income from singing radio commercials. In 1967, RCA simplified things by signing him to a long-term writing-performing contract. By 1968, Harry had resigned from the bank and was devoting full time to creative work, including fitful efforts at novel writing.

Nilsson's second RCA album brought him success with the mass audience. In particular, his version of "Everybody's Talkin'" became a top 10 hit. Ironically it was the only one of the LPs 13 cuts not written by him (rather, by Fred Neil), except for "Little Cowboy," a song his mother made up and sang to him when he was a child. Adding to the irony was the fact that the song became the theme of the hit movie *Midnight Cowboy,* edging out Nilsson's own candidate, "I Guess the Lord Must Be in New York City"—a hit for Nilsson in 1970, a year in which he also made singles charts with "Waiting."

"Waiting" was one of 13 he performed on his third RCA LP, *Harry* (1969). The selections demonstrated his interest in lyric inventiveness, as reflected in such diverse titles as "Nobody Cares about the Railroads Anymore," "The Puppy Song," and Randy Newman's "Simon Smith and the Amazing Dancing Bear."

Nilsson's talent and versatility resulted in many offers from various segments of show business. He was retained to do the score for Otto Preminger's comedy *Skiddo* in 1968. Preminger even gave him a cameo role in the movie, which starred Jackie Gleason. The film, as it turned out, received far less praise than the score. In 1969, Nilsson also provided the background score for the TV series "The Courtship of Eddie's Father."

Nilsson's record sales might have been higher if he had been more interested in performing. He was featured on a number of TV shows in the late 1960s; however, except for the special programs that interested him, he preferred to spend his time writing and composing.

Early 1970s included *Nilsson Sings Newman* (a 1970 tribute LP to fellow songwriter Randy Newman), plans for Broadway musicals, and the script and music for a 90-minute animated TV special, "The Point." Shown in early 1971, the program generally was considered by TV critics to have been an excellent achievement. Nilsson's own album of the score for the program (RCA, April 1971) made the charts.

Other Nilsson chart successes in 1971 included the single "Me and My Arrow" and the LPs *Aerial Pandemonium Ballet* and gold *Nilsson Schmilsson.* One of *Schmilsson*'s singles, "Without You" (written by Pete Ham and Tom Evans of Badfinger), proved his biggest singles hit ever, staying as number one in *Billboard* for four weeks starting February 19, 1972. In August 1972, Nilsson had another top 10 single, "Coconut." Other chartmakers that year were the singles "Jump into the Fire" and "Space Man" and gold album *Son of Schmilsson.* Nilsson's next album, *A Little Touch of Schmilsson in the Night* (1973), also made the charts.

Nilsson's relationship with Beatles alumni had become quite close, particularly with Lennon and Ringo Starr. Lennon, who called Nilsson his favorite American singer, produced Harry's 1974 RCA LP *Pussy Cats.* Ringo also worked with him on the score and soundtrack album for the 1974 movie *Son of Dracula.*

After 1974, Nilsson's recorded output seemed to

enter a decline. Such LPs as . . . *That's the Way It Is* (1976) and *Knnilsson* (1977) were pale shadows of his earlier collections. For some reason, Nilsson had run out of emotional energy for his music and increasingly seemed to seek excuses to get out of doing new work. In the late 1970s, RCA ended its association with him with such albums as *Nilsson/Greatest Hits* and *The World's Greatest Lover*.

In the 1980s, Nilsson essentially retired from creative work to pursue business interests, particularly in the movie field. In the late 1980s, he owned a film distribution company in Studio City, California.

(*See Alpert, Herb; Lennon, John; Monkees, The; Newman, Randy; Ronettes, The; Spector, Phil; Starr, Ringo; Three Dog Night; Yardbirds, The.*)

NOONE, PETER: *Singer, guitarist, actor, band leader (HERMAN'S HERMITS), songwriter. Born Liverpool, England, November 5, 1947. (Birthplace also has been given as Manchester.)*

In the late 1960s, some American music fans wondered what had happened to Herman's Hermits, a dynamic force in rock during the mid-1960s. The group actually was still in existence, performing around Europe. Its founder and leader, Peter Noone, who used the professional name Herman when working with the group, was devoting more and more time to solo work under his real name and this led to the group's disbanding in mid-1971 after completing its last contracted live engagement. In the decade and a half that followed, Noone never approached the success of the Hermits days, though he kept quite busy in a variety of enterprises.

Noone, who began his career as a child star on television series, became increasingly interested in pop music as he reached his teens. In the early '60s, he was part of a Manchester band called the Cyclones. That band became the Heartbeats with Noone as lead singer. Record producer Mickie Most, who had seen Peter on TV, thought he looked like John F. Kennedy and said so when he approached the group about making recordings, but the other bandsmen disagreed. They thought he looked like a character named Sherman in the TV cartoon program "The Bullwinkle Show." But they got the spelling confused, hence the Herman designation.

In August 1964 the group reorganized and became Herman's Hermits. Only bass guitarist Karl Green (born England, July 31, 1947) stayed in the new band. To complete the roster, Derek Leckenby (born England, May 14, 1943) and Keith Hopwood (born England, October 26, 1946) were added on guitar and Barry Whitwam (born England, July 21, 1946) on drums. With Mickie Most handling production (often with session musicians other than the Hermits providing instrumental backing), the band turned out a series of singles that hit, first in the U.K., then in the U.S.

In late 1964, the single "Can't You Hear My Heart Beat" came out and provided the group with its first sizeable chart hit in early 1965. It was followed on the charts by a remake of the Rays' 1957 hit "Silhouettes." The band topped both of those with "Mrs. Brown, You've Got a Lovely Daughter," which reached number one in Billboard the week of May 1, 1965 and remained there two more weeks. The week of August 7, 1965 the group had its second (and last) number one single, "I'm Henry VIII, I Am." Before the year was out, though, the band issued two more discs that made the top 10, "Just a Little Bit Better" and "A Must to Avoid." While the group never had as phenomenal a year as 1965, when it had seven songs on the charts (including its version of Sam Cooke's 1960 "Wonderful World"), all top 10 hits that year or in early 1966, it still often had singles in the U.S. top 40 through 1968. In mid-1965, the band went to Los Angeles to work on the film *Where the Boys Meet the Girls*.

Its album output included *Herman's Hermits* and *Herman's Hermits on Tour* (1965); *The Best of Herman's Hermits, Volume 1, Hold Out,* and *Both Sides* (1966); *There's a Kind of Hush, Blaze,* and *The Best of Herman's Hermits, Volume 2* (1967); and *Best of Herman's Hermits, Volume 3* (1968).

Then the band went into semieclipse until it broke up. Noone pointed out when that occurred: "Not many people are aware that we have not released a new album in four years because we could not mutually agree on material, but with only myself to worry about, I can broaden my repertoire.

"But I'm not ashamed of my past career as Herman. On the contrary, I am extremely proud of our recording achievement. Twenty-two hit singles and world sales of 40 million records is nothing to be embarrassed about. I've felt for some time that we have realized our potential as Herman's Hermits. I now need the freedom and broader scope of an individual."

Noone's outside activities in the early 1970s included several records with the Hermits using his own name. On April 30, 1971, his first solo single as Peter Noone was released on the Rak label. Written by David Bowie (*see Bowie, David*), it was titled "Oh You Pretty Things" and soon gained the U.K. top 20. After that, however, his solo recording career went down hill. Taking it all in good grace, he and his wife moved to France later in the '70s and Peter concentrated on songwriting, turning out tunes that were recorded by many performers including soul star Deniece Williams.

In the late 1970s, Noone moved again, this time to New York City, where he opened a clothing boutique and sought to renew his performing career. Early in the 1980s, he played for a while with a promising new wave band, the Tremblers. The band put on a good show, but couldn't build up a large enough following to keep going. He also acted in an unreleased film, *We're All Crazy Now*, with Joan Jett. (*See Jett, Joan; Runaways, The.*) In 1982, Peter put out a solo album *One of the Glory Boys*, on Johnston, a small label operated by Bruce Johnston of the Beach Boys. He still kept his eyes open for stage roles, which brought the opportunity for a stint playing Frederic in a 1982 revival of Gilbert and Sullivan's *The Pirates of Penzance* in London.

NUGENT, TED: *Singer, guitarist, band leader, songwriter. Born Detroit, Michigan, December 13, 1948.*

Known variously as the ''noble savage,'' ''madman of rock,'' and ''wild man of feedback rock'' for his uninhibited onstage antics and blunt offstage demeanor, Ted Nugent created a unique persona that made him a superstar in the mid-1970s. For all that, in his personal life, he demonstrated qualities far different from what rock's opponents ascribe to such artists—a decision once past his teens to stay clear of alcohol and drugs, a deep love for his children (his late 1970s divorce seemed to have an adverse impact on his career in the 1980s), and a close relationship with his own family.

Though his language on stage often could put a truck driver to shame and he had no compunction against focusing on sex and wild living in some of his songs, his mother, Marian Nugent, told a reporter from the *Chicago Reader* it didn't reflect his worth as a person. Noting that he grew up in a normal middle class household where there was mutual respect between the members, she noted: ''Ted told me years ago: 'Mom, I love you. When I'm talkin' [on stage], I'm talkin' to the kids.' [Going to his shows] I'm used to it. It doesn't bother me. He has to relate to his audience.'' As far as his being a wild man or a mad man, she said: ''Oh, it's all a gimmick, really. Anyone who has ever met Ted said he is the most wonderful person in the world. And he really is. He has a very vivid imagination and a lot of talent to think up all the things he does.''

Nugent, who spent his first 16 years in Detroit, began to teach himself guitar at age eight, inspired by the first wave of the new rock revolution in the mid-1950s. Only a few years later, he was in his first rock band, the Royal Highboys. Then, when only thirteen, he helped organize the Lourds, which earned a local following before he had to bid the group goodbye at the end of 1964. Though he later

became enamoured of country living—most notably hunting and taking four-wheel–drive vehicles down back roads—in those years, he was strictly an urban boy who was quite unhappy about his family's decision to move to Chicago. He told Fred Schruers in an interview for *Rolling Stone* (March 8, 1979): ''I am a citified motherfucker. I am jack concrete git-down. I have my master's degree in concrete jungleism. I was born and raised in Detroit—well, the outskirts, Redford Township—then we moved to Chicago in 1965. I was smokin' in Detroit; the Lourds were just kickin' ass. We opened a sold-out show in Cobo Hall with the Supremes and the Beau Brummels. We were the cat's ass, we were rockin' sons of bitches. I was totally bummed out at havin' to move.

''We moved into a little house in the suburbs of northwest Chicago, a little town called Hoffman Estates. I started lookin' for a band the day we got there. . . . I wanted to prove to my parents what I had in mind was good, proper, and right. I would go to high school—a Catholic boy's school—and I would wear my hair and clothes in the way they wanted me to, but I said: 'When I graduate, look out, 'cause I am gone. And I'm gonna make it'''.

He recalled that his father demanded that the children—Ted, his older brother Jeff, and younger brother and sister John and Kathy—toe the line in their conduct, the foods they ate, and so on. ''Sure we were on a budget,'' he told Schruers. ''But that's insipid. He was in the phone company and then he had a salesman's business, traveled a lot. I'm sure he did all these things because he loved us and he was out there in our best interest. He was from the old school of discipline for discipline's sake, which I disagree with totally. He was a staff sergeant at the age of 19 in the army, and he maintained that approach throughout our lives.''

The band Nugent helped assemble once he was in Chicago was the Amboy Dukes. True to his word, once Ted graduated from school, he left home and went on the road with the band, the start of over a decade of almost constant touring (typically over 200 live shows a year) with upwards of 50 different musicians at one point or another before he finally made it big in the mid-1970s. While he did some partying and enjoyed female acquaintances along the way, much of his spare time was spent in writing ideas for new songs in a series of battered black and white school-type notebooks.

He told Schruers: ''From 1963 through 1973, I was overwhelmed by, and a victim of, rock'n'roll. Day, night, rock'n'roll—gigs, amps, cars, jammin', jammin', jammin', writing, new strings, new speakers, new musicians, rehearsals, auditions, tours, pussy, new songs, louder amps, more pussy. All the things that are essential to rock'n'roll.

"And then, in 1970, I got married [to Sandra Jezowski]. That was a major thing in my life. Another person that I would give vast consideration to prior to any decision of mine. Though that person, my wife, knew who she was marrying and what I was already deep, deep into." For much of the 1970s, during which a boy and a girl were born, it was a happy relationship, but eventually the inevitable pressures of touring and stardom proved too much for the marriage.

Before the two met in 1969, Ted had gained a foretaste of musical success with the Amboy Dukes. The group's debut LP, *Amboy Dukes* (1967), was followed by *Journey to the Center of the Mind* and *Migration* (1968). Those releases on Mainstream provided the regional hit single "Baby Don't Go" and the 1968 top 20 national hit "Journey to the Center of the Mind." (On the last named, Nugent wrote the music and a band member the lyrics.) With those achievements, the band moved up a notch in label reputation with two LPs on Polydor: *Marriage on the Rocks/Rock Bottom* (1969) and *Survival of the Fittest* (1970).

The Polydor releases didn't do much with record buyers and Nugent spent a while reorganizing the band. Now known as Ted Nugent and the Amboy Dukes, the group continued to work the Midwest rock circuit and completed two LPs, *Call of the Wild* and *Tooth, Fang and Claw,* on the Discreet label in 1973. The band often seemed on the verge of success, but lack of record-company backing and internal problems got in the way.

There were times, he told Billy Altman of *Creem* (May 1978), when he felt depressed about the outlook. "Well, in the early 1970s, I was discouraged. But where other people get discouraged and hang their heads and say 'Gosh darnit,' I just got pissed. I was being ripped off—financially and pride-wise—and I would not take it. At times I'd succumb to band members' suggestions, let them change songs, and then, when I heard the final product, God! I'd want to cook up this incredible dish with my own ingredients and take a bit out of it and goddamn it, that's not what I wanted to cook and now I don't like it. And I'd tell guys to get out of the band—if you don't like my ideas, then get the flyin' fuck outta here. I'll be damned if I have my music reduced to trivia and wimpo pussy rock."

In 1975, he decided to go solo. He would call the shots and band members would be there to back him, not to be a separate group. He was able to convince Epic Records of his solo potential and the label issued his solo debut LP, *Ted Nugent,* in 1975. The individual tracks didn't fit the singles format favored by top 40 radio so the answer, Nugent and Epic agreed, was live performances. In 1976, Ted took off on his first full-scale coast-to-coast tour of the U.S. During the year, he gave over 250 concerts and his high-decibel guitar work and ear-piercing vocals, delivered as he ran, jumped, and occasionally slid on his knees across the stage, punctuated by energetic leaps—sometimes from atop the drum stand or one of the large high-voltage amplifiers—whipped the audience into a frenzy. By the tour's end, he had established himself not as an opening act, but a bona fide headliner. His first solo album eventually went platinum, and his second Epic release, *Free for All,* issued while the 1976 concerts were in full swing, followed suit.

In 1977, Ted was represented by his most effective albums yet, *Cat Scratch Fever* and *Double Live Gonzo* (both platinum). He backed those with more cross-U.S. and overseas concerts that drew standing-room–only crowds to rock citadels worldwide. *Cat Scratch Fever* gave him his first top 10 single—the title song. The second LP capsuled his best numbers in his live shows, including "Stranglehold," "Motor City Madness," "Baby Please Don't Go," and "Cat Scratch Fever," plus two new songs: "Yank Me, Crank Me" and "Gonzo."

The *Gonzo* LP, while it did convey some of the atmosphere of a Nugent live appearance, still wasn't the same as being there. He commented: "Aggression is a natural reaction to hard-on rock'n'roll. Lightweights don't get that kind of response. When I'm on stage and I'm right, I literally demand a reaction from an audience. If they ain't foaming at the mouth after 10 minutes, then I've screwed up."

Asked by Scott Cohen of *Circus* magazine (March 16, 1978), about what he saw as the difference between studio and live recordings, Ted responded: "Well, when I walk in the studio, I'm doing me, they're Ted Nugent compositions. There's an inescapable relationship between the studio and the stage, however removed they are. There's no way anyone will ever capture a live performance on record because you just don't have all the elements. You don't have the face-to-face, body-to-body, flesh-to-flesh, volume-to-skull; but seeing how my entire inspiration comes from the stage and the intensity thereon, I secure that whole desire for that intensity in the studio and that's where these songs come from. Now, the studio offers an element of extended creativity that is not available to me on stage, unique to the studio where I can overdub and I really get immense satisfaction out of that."

During his 1976–77 tours, Ted was backed by a trio composed of guitarist/vocalist Derek St. Holmes (born U.S., c. 1953), bass guitarist Rob Grange (born U.S., c. 1952) and drummer Cliff Davies (born London, England). Holmes and Grange left by tour's-end and their places were taken by Charlie

Huhn and John Sauter, who stayed with Nugent to the start of the 1980s. By then, Ted had completed three more LPs for Epic: *Weekend Warriors* (1978, platinum), *State of Shock* (1979, gold), and *Scream Dream* (1980, gold).

For his worldwide 1981 tour backing the live *Intensities in Ten Cities* LP, Ted brought in a completely new backing band, a five-piece group instead of the three-musician lineup he previously favored. The quintet, a Michigan-based group that had called itself the D.C. Hawks, was made up of a three-brother lead-guitar section—Kurt, Rick, and Verne Wagoner—plus Mike Gardner on bass and Mark Gerhardt on drums.

In the 1980s, Nugent retained a strong concert following, but his albums were not the best-sellers of yesteryear. *Intensities* and the follow-up 1981 retrospective, *Great Gonzos: The Best of Ted Nugent,* made the charts for some weeks, but failed to reach top positions. As the 1980s progressed, Ted gained more attention for appearances on talk-shows and as a racing driver in celebrity events than for his musical exploits.

Nugent's efforts to introduce new life into his music career in the second half of the 1980s were less than encouraging. His albums *Penetrator* (1986) and *If You Can't Lick 'Em . . . Lick 'Em* (1988) did not sound much different from his 1970s offerings. No longer able to draw capacity crowds to large arenas, he performed mainly in small- to medium-size venues.

NYRO, LAURA: *Singer, songwriter, pianist. Born Bronx, New York, October 18, 1947.*

A shy, soft-spoken, highly capable artist, Laura Nyro had an almost across-the-board impact on pop music of the late '60s and early 1970s with original songs that combined often poetic lyrics with musical elements ranging from urban folk (somewhat in the Dylan tradition) to jazz and soul. The appeal her songs had to artists of all genres could be seen from the names of those who recorded them: Peter, Paul and Mary, Three Dog Night, 5th Dimension, Blood, Sweat and Tears, Mongo Santamaria, Frank Sinatra, Linda Ronstadt, and Aretha Franklin.

Music was a part of her life from her earliest years on College Avenue in the Bronx. Her father, a jazz trumpeter, spent many hours practicing at home. Young Laura Nigro was intrigued by his playing and by other music she heard on the radio and on records. When she was eight, she wrote her first songs. She attended Manhattan's prestigious High School of Music and Art depicted in the film *Fame*. Always independent, though not always articulating herself well, she was often trying to her teachers, but they had to admit her considerable creative potential.

In her teens, she experimented with both song-writing and drugs. On a harrowing LSD trip, for nine hours she imagined a stream of half-men, half-rat monsters were coming into her room to destroy her. She later referred to that incident as a turning point in her life when she gained confidence in her ability to succeed. Later she stopped using LSD.

Her interests musically at the time ranged from Bob Dylan to jazz great John Coltrane. She began singing in local clubs in her late teens and impressed more than a few people in the music field with her promise. When she was 18, she went cross-country to San Francisco, where for two months she performed at the hungry i nightclub (long a proving ground for new folk stars).

Back in New York, Verve/Folkways Records released her first album, *More than a New Discovery,* in 1966. Rights to the LP later were purchased by her next record label, Columbia, which reissued it in January 1973 under the title *The First Songs*. By 1967, so many people in the pop and folk audience were interested in her that she was asked to take part in the Monterey Pop Festival. It proved to be a disaster. Her low-key, introspective music seemed out of place against the high-powered acid rock of Jimi Hendrix and Janis Joplin. She was hooted off the stage.

However, it proved only a temporary setback. People in other segments of music began to appreciate the subtleties of her work and the expert craftsmanship that made her songs adaptable to different musical arrangements. Six months after Monterey, Nyro-penned songs started to show up on the hit lists. The 5th Dimensions' versions of her "Stoned Soul Picnic" rose to number three in *Billboard* and number one on other industry charts and "Sweet Blindness," to the top 20 in 1968. By the time "Stoned Soul Picnic" moved to the top of the charts, Laura had completed her first album for Columbia, *Eli and the Thirteenth Confession* (March 1968). Its songs revolved around the central theme of a young girl's path from childhood to maturity. An example was the song "Emmie": "Emily/You're the natural snow/the unstudied sea . . . and I swear you were born a weaver's love/Born for the loom's desire." In "The Confessions," she wrote, "Love is surely gospel."

That album wasn't an immediate smash, but by word of mouth it's excellence was relayed among fans. Though some termed Laura's frequent jumps in volume and tempo mere gimmickry, eventually the LP was on the charts for many months. Her next album, one of her best, *New York Tendaberry* (August 1969), almost immediately was on the charts. It included such fine tracks as "Save the Country" and "Time and Love." This was followed by *Christmas and the Beads of Sweat* (November 1970). Her only album of nonoriginal material, *Gonna Take a Miracle* (R&B oldies recorded with the soul/R&B group LaBelle), came out in November 1971.

During the late '60s and early '70s, other artists continued to do well with covers of her songs. In late 1969, Three Dog Night won a gold record for their recording of "Eli's Coming." In 1970, the 5th Dimension had a million-seller in "Wedding Bell Blues" as did Blood, Sweat and Tears with "And When I Die." In 1971, Barbra Streisand scored a major success with Laura's "Stoney End."

But after *Gonna Take a Miracle*, though Laura made some concert appearances, nothing new took shape in the recording studios. Finally, in 1972, she retired completely from the music field and for a long time nothing much was heard from her. She got married, severed all ties with industry people, and moved to a small town in New England. Later, discussing the reasons for that sudden and complete break, she told Michael Watts of England's *Melody Maker:* "It just got to the point where people who met you had preconceived notions. And your phone rings 20 times a day. It's really nice to get away to a place where you can say 'Now wait a minute' and throw the phone out the window. I think it's good to get away from this horrible business when you begin to feel like a commodity. There are many other things in life."

For some three years, she remained in artistic seclusion, but eventually she got the incentive to take up writing and performing again. For one thing, she felt a new maturity in her approach to the art; for another, her marriage ended in divorce after three years. In late 1975, she made Columbia executives happy by agreeing to go into the studios and work on a new LP. That collection, *Smile* (February 1976), proved to be a coherent, well-written, and well-sung group of songs that matched many of her finest efforts of the past. Though most were new songs, including "Midnight Blue" (which provided a hit for Melissa Manchester), a major track was "I Am the Blues," a song she had performed in 1971 on a British TV special. In support of the album, Laura made a coast-to-coast tour of the U.S. in early summer that showed her to be at the peak of her form as an entertainer.

That four-month tour with a full band provided the material for the live album, *Season of Lights,* stressing versions of older songs. In June 1978, over two years after *Smile,* she was represented on Columbia by *Nested,* an album of new songs. Six years later, she returned to the recording scene with *Mother's Spiritual,* inspired by her own motherhood. In mid-1988 she toured for the first time in 10 years, presenting some new songs intended for a 1989 LP.

(*See 5th Dimension; LaBelle, Patti; Manchester, Melissa; Streisand, Barbra; Three Dog Night.*)

OINGO BOINGO: *Vocal and instrumental group from Los Angeles, California. Members (early 1980s): Danny Elfman, born near Amarillo, Texas, May 29, 1955; Kerry Katch; Rich Gibbs; Steve Bartek; Dale Turner, born Minnesota; Johnny Hernandez; Sam Phipps; Leon Schneiderman. Katch and Gibbs replaced in 1985 by John Avila and Mike Bacich. Bacich left in 1986.*

For a long time, Oingo Boingo was one of the best-kept entertainment secrets except on the U.S. West Coast, where the band had tremendous "underground" popularity. One of the band's problems was its leader and primary writer Danny Elfman's penchant for constant experimentation in musical styles—ranging over such diverse influences in its early 1980s LPs as Balinese polyrhythms, West African melodies, and R&B-tinged horn-paced songs—that made it hard to categorize.

Another aspect of its music that brought constant critical putdowns was the lack of relevance in much of Elfman's words. Oingo Boingo lyrics often were obscure or seemed like mindless backdrops to dance arrangements, something particularly heinous for some reviewers of the time. Elfman commented: "The press hated us. We were L.A.'s most despised band. Both our image and our attitude conflicted with their image of what 'relevant rock'n'roll' was supposed to look and sound like. However, we got so we liked the bad reviews."

The son of an air force officer, Elfman was born in Texas, but later moved to California. Initially he didn't see himself as a professional singer, though he was interested in the rock of the 1960s and early 1970s. For a while, he traveled outside the country, including an extended stay in Africa. While some of Oingo Boingo's early songs took aim at American institutions—"Capitalism" made sarcastic comments on the U.S. economy—he generally endorsed democratic values.

He told Lawrence Henry of *Music Connection:* "I'm not a doomist. My attitude is always to be critical of what's around you, but not ever to forget how lucky we are. I've traveled around the world. I left thinking I was a revolutionary. I came back real right-wing patriotic. Since then, I've kind of mellowed in between. It affected me permanently and totally."

He also stressed to writer John Blenn: "We're not antiestablishment, we're just into doing our own thing. . . . We've just tried to create as much freedom as we could for ourselves. You can't be antiestablishment and be on a label. Sure I poke fun at society, but I don't want to be pigeonholed. Lyrically, I've never been one for metaphors. I just say what I feel. When you think about everything, nothing is wonderful.''

In a way, Elfman and his associates backed into the music field. In the mid-1970s, Elfman and some of his friends organized a stage act that combined satire, humor, and wild visual techniques (masks, odd props, and so on) under the name of the Mystic Knights of the Oingo Boingo. Virtually unnoticed by the media, the troupe won a following among college-age and young-adult groups and soon could draw capacity audiences to nightclubs throughout the Los Angeles area. Gradually the show incorporated musical elements until it evolved at the end of the 1970s into a band with the shortened name of Oingo Boingo.

The new band alignment came together officially in 1979 and managed to gain a record agreement before the year was out. As Marc Shapiro, writing for the *Santa Ana [California] Register*, noted: "The prevailing feeling when Oingo Boingo signed its first recording contract was: 'Why them?' The group had dumped its Mystic Knight of the Oingo Boingo monicker and then traded stream-of-consciousness hip-comedy schtick for live music and lyrics. A new wave attitude was apparent, but a lot of people continued to question the seriousness of the band's venture.''

The group's initial release, *Oingo Boingo* (an extended-play album on the IRS label), brought fierce negative appraisals from local critics. Among the charges was that the main reason for the new stress on music was to pander to teenage tastes for commercial ends. Stung by press barbs, Elfman got back at reviewers with the scathing lyrics of the 1981 song "Imposter" (whose primary targets reportedly were the music writers of the *Los Angeles Times*).

Elfman indignantly denied he had slanted his early writing specifically for the teenage level. "On the contrary," he told Henry, "when we started up, one of the reasons it was hard to get signed was because they said our music was too complex for a young audience to understand, rhythmically, melodically, and lyrically. And as the kids out here discovered us on their own, we were surprised. We had almost begun to believe what they had been telling us. But we came out with our first EP and it was with the kids that we caught on.''

The band had a modest local hit with the EP, which encouraged A&M Records to sign them to a multiyear contract. The debut on that label, *Only a Lad* (1981), contained "Imposter.''

A&M issued two more Oingo Boingo albums, *Nothing to Fear* and *Good for Your Soul,* from 1982 to 1984. Both contained tracks that received extensive dance-club play (supported by videos that appeared on MTV and other music video outlets), notably "Private Life" on *Nothing to Fear* and "Wake Up, It's 1984" on *Good for Your Soul.* The albums achieved modest sales and, backed by constant nationwide touring, helped slowly to add to the group's audience across the U.S. The band had a rather unorthodox size for a rock group, numbering eight members including Elfman on lead vocals. One reason for the large total was the group's emphasis on horn-driven arrangements. The other seven musicians as of 1983–84 were Kerry Katch on bass guitar; Rich Gibbs on keyboards; Steve Bartek, lead guitar (and co-arranger with Elfman); Dale Turner on trumpet and trombone; Sam "Sluggo" Phipps, tenor sax and reeds; Leon Schneiderman, baritone sax; and Johnny "Vatos" Hernandez on drums. In 1985, Katch and Gibbs were replaced by bass guitarist/vocalist John Avila and keyboardist Mike Bacich.

During the mid-1980s, the group became popular with movie executives as a soundtrack contributor. It placed numbers on such soundtracks as *Last American Virgin, Fast Times at Ridgemont High,* and *Bachelor Party.* The year 1985 was particularly productive for Elfman and his band. The group was represented on the *Beverly Hills Cop* soundtrack with the song "Gratitude" and also had the theme number for the film *Weird Science.* The single of "Weird Science" became the band's first top 40 success, aided by a widely telecast video. Elfman, besides working on those projects, wrote and supervised recording of the score for the comic film *Pee-wee's Big Adventure* plus music for the TV series "Amazing Stories.''

Meanwhile, the band's reputation increased markedly with disc jockeys and fans. Was this primarily because of the soundtrack work? Elfman told Blenn: "Gee, I don't really know if it's the key. A soundtrack song is really a very different thing. Its fate is directly tied to the success of the movie. We really haven't done anything on a major hit, but I guess it's helped.''

As to why Elfman and the band were offered so much film work, he said: "I think that Oingo's music is good for the audience for those films; the people will relate to it. They were youthful, energetic films and so was the music, so I guess it succeeded in that aspect.''

The fact that Oingo took a hiatus from touring

in 1984 and Elfman recorded his first solo album, *SoLo* (including "Gratitude"), issued in 1985, caused rumors that the band had broken up. But this was quickly disproved by a late 1985 album *Dead Man's Party*, on a new label, MCA. The band's move to critical "respectability" was indicated by favorable comments from most critics. The *Los Angeles Times* reviewer commented on the alternately "mature and morbid concerns of the manic band's . . . release [which] is actually a goofy wake in which Elfman largely deals (in various degrees of seriousness) with the art of becoming aware of one's mortality. . . .The horn-driven, hyperpercussive sound of one of L.A.'s most distinctive and talented bands had been smoothed out a bit, though it's only a tad less frantic."

Elfman agreed the new LP was more melodic than earlier albums and had less obvious ethnic influences. He told Lawrence Henry: "We already established ourselves with the ability to play pounding, driving rhythms, eighth notes as fast as anybody. We feel like the first two albums got plenty of that out. There hasn't been a conscious effort—'Okay, we're going to be more melodic now'—but I think it's more a direction that songs have been taking.

"In my own writing, I've been going back to my roots more. I know that sounds funny, because you don't hear any ethnic stuff on the album. The only music I've actually studied is African and Indonesian music. The root of that music, to me, is a certain kind of melody. When I think of the year that I spent in West Africa, what I think of is not the big tribal, driving stuff. Most of the music I heard in Africa was played by small ensembles, sometimes just two or three, or even one person with a stringed instrument singing beautiful, strange little patterns. I started doing that more on the solo album, where melodies were in my head from a decade ago."

Before returning to the recording studio with his band, Danny completed work on the score for the 1986 hit comedy that starred Rodney Dangerfield, *Back to School*.

In 1987, the new Oingo Boingo LP was in record stores. For that album, *Boi-ngo*, except for Bacich, the lineup remained the same as for the previous album. In 1988 MCA put out *Oingo Alive* and A&M issued the LP *Skeletons in the Closet*.

O'JAYS: *Vocal and dance group from Canton, Ohio. Original members: Eddie Levert, born 1941; Walter Williams, born c. 1942; William Powell, born c. 1941, died May 26, 1977; Bill Isles, born early 1940; Bobby Massey, born early 1940s. Isles left in 1965, Massey in early 1972. Powell retired from active touring in 1976 and was replaced by Sammy Strain, born Brooklyn, New York, December 9, 1941.**

Anyone trying to think of a group that personified the flavor and excitement of R&B at its finest wouldn't have to look much further than the O'Jays. This vocal and choreographic act consistently provided some of the most memorable records in the field from the early 1970s on. Good as those discs were, they still couldn't convey the power and soul-stirring impact of the group in concert. In the mid-1980s, though the group had been in existence for more years than many of its latest admirers had been on this earth, it continued to generate a feeling of freshness and innovation that many artists lose after only a few years of touring.

As of 1988, two members of the group have been going through their intricate stage gyrations for three decades. Eddie Levert and Walter Williams harken back to the original team, a quintet called the Triumphs that assembled at McKinley High School in Canton, Ohio, in 1957, later becoming the Mascots and finally the O'Jays.

Levert said proudly: "The biggest thing as a group is to be big this long. When we started, Walt was 15 and I was 16 and we weren't sure we could get along together. We were in different groups and we'd told each other we'd never sing in the same group. But luckily we changed our minds."

"What's our sustaining power?" Walt asked himself. "It has to be we enjoy what we're doing and enjoy doing it together. Eddie and I have been together for years while group members and music patterns changed. Of course, it's also a business and to keep it up around that number one spot, you have to stay humble and make sure you don't take things for granted."

The other original members of the group were William Powell, Bobby Massey, and Bill Isles. Isles left in 1965 when the group was just starting to make inroads in the pop field. Massey departed in early 1972—poor timing for him, because that was the year the O'Jays made its first big move toward its golden era. But friendship remained, Levert said. "We were into a few things in the music field with Bobby after he left. Bill lived in L.A. and when we were there we got together to talk over old times and Walt and him would go fishing together."

Powell remained a key member of the group until illness forced him to step down in January 1976. He continued to record with Levert and Williams until death claimed him in 1977. After a lengthy search, his place was taken by Sammy Strain, who proved an excellent fit. Before taking Powell's place, Strain

---

*Based partly on personal interview with Irwin Stambler.

spent some years with other R&B acts, most notably Little Anthony and the Imperials. (*See Little Anthony and the Imperials.*) Though he'd been around a while, as had Walt and Eddie, the R&B audience hasn't considered age a negative factor. Like country listeners, R&B fans typically remain staunchly loyal to favorites as long as the performer maintains artistic resilience.

Levert said after Strain's addition in 1976 that experience had been his hole card. "He was recommended by our choreographer. At first we were going for a young guy who needed a break. But the choreographer advised us that a more experienced guy would be better. A younger guy would need a lot of time to break in and build up poise and confidence. It only took Sammy three weeks to learn the routines well enough to do them adequately."

The realignment helped preserve the O'Jays' tradition of achievement that got underway in the late 1950s. The original members (who in 1961 changed their name to the Mascots when they recorded several singles for King Records) received a lot of advice and backing in the early '60s from Cleveland disc jockey Eddie O'Jay and they repaid the compliment. "He taught us about the business and how to be gentlemen," Levert recalled. "He was the one who got us set up in the right direction. So we changed our name in his honor."

As with so many soul/R&B artists, the right direction proved to require considerable sweat and perseverance. The early O'Jays spent a good many years playing for slim purses in rundown theaters and ghetto clubs of the Chittlin' Circuit. It wasn't until 1963 that things took a turn for the better with a contract from Imperial Records. This resulted in a hit single, "Lonely Drifter," and several other mid-1960s charted singles such as "Comin' Through," "Lipstick Traces," and "I'll Be Sweeter Tomorrow." The group's debut album on Imperial, *Comin' Through,* was released in November 1965. The group also was represented on another label, Minit Records, with the 1967 *Soul Sounds.*

But the most important milestone occurred in 1968, when the O'Jays entered what amounted to a creative partnership with the songwriter-production team of Kenny Gamble and Leon Huff. Though O'Jays members had written some good songs for themselves over the years, the material that transformed them into international superstars was provided by Gamble and Huff. Early fruits in the late 1960s and early 1970s included such charted singles on Neptune Records as "One Night Affairs," "Deeper in Love," and "Looky Looky (Look at My Girl)."

(Though O'Jays members often had original song ideas, Levert pointed out they were hampered by the inability to read music. "We know what we want to say, but we can't write it down. We just hum and hope. When we were growing up and going to school, we all wanted to be stars, but forgot the basic musical needs that make it easier. But we seem to get along alright.")

Things really went into high gear in 1972 after Gamble and Huff set up a new record firm, Philadelphia International. Almost immediately, they provided the O'Jays with their first massive hit song, "Back Stabbers." The single sold over a million copies in 1972–73. Similar success accrued for the debut Philadelphia International album, *Back Stabbers* (1972). The group soon had more hit singles including "992 Arguments" (1972) and, in 1973, "Love Train" (number one on *Billboard* pop charts the week of March 24) and "Time to Get Down." The 1973 album *The O'Jays in Philadelphia* also was a best-seller.

The group kept right on making both soul and pop singles and album charts as the decade slipped by. Gold albums included *Ship Ahoy* (1973), *Live in London* (1974), and *Survival* (1975). *Family Reunion* (1975) went platinum. Among their better-known singles were "Let Me Make Love to You," "Put Your Hands Together," "Give the People What They Want," and "I Love Music." A rousing version of "For the Love of Money" typically ended the group's concerts of the mid-1970s.

As long as Walter Powell could continue to make recordings, he remained the third member of the trio. Thus, he helped complete the gold 1976 album *Message in the Music,* while Sammy Strain did not sing on the album though he handled concert chores. After Powell died, Strain assumed the recording role as well.

The group continued to turn out quality albums in the second half of the 1970s, but with more emphasis on disco than straight soul/R&B. Albums included *Travelin' at the Speed of Thought* (1977, gold) and, in the same year, the retrospective *O'Jays Collectors Items. So Full of Love* (1978) and *Identify Yourself* (1979) went platinum. The group also was well represented on singles lists with numbers such as "Cry Together" and the gold "Use Ta Be My Girl."

The O'Jays' act and their recording style in the late 1970s was somewhat slicker than in its earlier years, but the members insisted they remained true to their roots. Walt Williams commented: "We've been willing to modify material a bit in the past for crossovers to the general pop market, but we've found it's better to play it straight. We don't want whites to convert us. For instance, when we played the Waldorf Astoria Hotel in New York a while back, suggestions were made that we should be more like a Las Vegas act. But we realized the people who want to see us want to see us black. What happened that time was that we had the people in the Waldorf getting up in their seats and bumping.''

But that didn't mean the band wasn't willing to evolve within its own musical genre. It tried to keep up with trends in the black music field and was able to overcome a dry spell in its recording success in the early 1980s with a mid-1980s comeback.

The band opened the decade with the moderately rewarding album *The Year 2000* (1980) on TSOP Records. (Also available in record stores at the time was *The O'Jays* on Up Front Records, a repackaging of pre–Philadelphia International recordings.) After that, though the group remained a highly regarded concert attraction, its albums and singles had little impact on top levels of either black music or pop lists for several years.

In mid-1985, the O'Jays came up with a sparkling new LP, *Love Fever* on Philadelphia International, that made both black and pop charts. Robert Palmer commented in *The New York Times* (September 11, 1985): ''[The album] finds the familiar Philadelphia sound and modern synthesizer-funk and rap stylings co-existing and enriching each other. The O'Jays themselves haven't changed. Their rich, sumptuously textured vocal blends and Eddie Levert's lead vocals are the sort of thing that don't go out of date. It is context—the songs, the rhythm, the arrangements and instrumentation—that is crucial for a group like this. *Love Fever* successfully places the O'Jays in a contemporary context while retaining the group sound that is at least partially responsible for their longevity.''

Contributing to the updated mix was multitalented musician, writer, and producer Reggie Griffin, who brought his previous experience with rap groups such as Gardenmaster Flash to bear on the backing tracks. With his own recording engineer, self-titled Shameek the Mix, at the control panel, he handled all the instruments on some tracks to provide an unusual and striking blend of sounds with the O'Jays' R&B harmonies.

ONO, YOKO: *See Lennon, John, and Ono, Yoko.*

ORBISON, ROY: *Singer, guitarist, songwriter. Born Vernon, Texas, April 23, 1936, died December 6, 1988 in Hendersonville, Tennessee.*

Along with Elvis, Jerry Lee Lewis, and the Everly Brothers, a country-bred artist considered highly influential in the worldwide rise of rock'n'roll was Roy Orbison, a man with whom the Beatles felt privileged to tour in 1963. Despite his tremendous achievements, by the time Elvis introduced Roy to the audience at the ''Great One's'' last Las Vegas show in 1977 as ''the greatest singer in the world,''

it had been over a dozen years since his last major hit. A major reason for Orbison's decline had been a series of tragedies in the middle and late '60s that might have shattered weaker people completely. But Roy hung in there while cover versions of some of his earlier songs brought hits for '70s artists (including Linda Ronstadt's number one country hit of his ''Blue Bayou''). In 1979, he began still another comeback attempt, starting with a new LP on Elektra, that eventually led to his first Grammy Award in the early 1980s. Later in the decade he was one of the first inductees into the newly established Rock and Roll Hall of Fame.

As might be expected of a boy growing up in Texas, his early influences were almost all country- and gospel-based. His father started teaching him how to play guitar when the boy was six and he was well versed in the instrument by the time he reached his teens. While attending high school, he was leader of his own country group, the Wink Westerners, and had his own radio show on station KVWC in Vernon, Texas. When he was 16, he represented Texas at the International Lions Convention in Chicago, singing and accompanying himself on guitar.

At North Texas State College, he met another young artist with show-business ambitions, Pat Boone. Boone encouraged him to keep up with his music and Roy responded by organizing a new band that soon backed him on a 1955 TV show presented on a Midland, Texas, station. His TV work and engagements at various venues with his group brought him in contact with many of the new rock-oriented country artists, including Jerry Lee Lewis, Elvis, and Johnny Cash. It was Cash who proved the main catalyst, suggesting that Roy make a demo tape of some of his material and take it to Sam Phillips, head of Sun Records in Memphis (the pioneer label in early rockabilly). It was a move that determined Roy's main musical direction from then on, pushing him into the rockabilly fold even though his main interests tended toward mainstream country.

As he told an interviewer: ''I sent Phillips 'Oooby Dooby' because that was the kind of material Sun was releasing at the time. But I was really more interested in ballads. I hadn't felt comfortable doing rhythm & blues or rock. I got into [rock] by accident. We were working a dance one New Year's Eve and someone asked for 'Shake, Rattle and Roll.' I planned to do it at midnight, but started too soon so we had to keep doing it over and over. By the time midnight came, I was used to it and began to incorporate some rock numbers into our list of songs.''

Actually, he almost struck out with Sun. After Phillips heard over the phone that Roy was recommended by Cash, the record executive snapped ''Johnny Cash doesn't run my business'' and hung up. But he eventually heard the tape and the resultant single became a major hit of 1956. (Credence Clearwater Revival later recorded it as well.)

After touring all over the U.S. with such artists as Cash, Lewis, and Carl Perkins, Roy responded to an invitation from Wesley Rose of Acuff-Rose music publishers to become a staff songwriter and departed from Sun in 1957. One of his first efforts was "Claudette," named after his wife, which was recorded by the Everly Brothers and was a chart hit. Jerry Lee Lewis also made the charts with Roy's "Down the Line" (redone decades later by the Blasters under its original title, "Go, Go, Go"). Buddy Holly too used some of Orbison's material in his repertoire.

Rose, who had also taken over as Roy's personal manager, arranged for a new recording contract with Fred Foster's Monument Records in 1959. The next year, Roy's "Only the Lonely," sold over 2 million copies. This was followed by a stream of best-sellers, most originals by Roy, a few from other writers. Among his *Billboard* top 10 pop singles were "Running Scared" and "Cryin'" (backed with "Candy Man") in 1961, "Dream Baby" (1962), "In Dreams," and "Mean Woman Blues" backed with "Blue Bayou" (1963), and in 1964, "It's Over" and "Oh, Pretty Woman" (one of the most successful singles of the '60s, selling over 7 million copies worldwide). In all, Orbison placed 27 straight records on the charts the first part of the '60s. One of the first rockabilly stars to use string sections, he often turned out lush country-pop rather than the raw, unleashed rock of Lewis and Presley.

He became a major international star in 1963, contracting to tour Britain with a rock group that at the time had much slimmer credentials than he did, the Beatles. It brought a close rapport between all of them and it also involved an accidental event that reshaped Roy's image. After his plane trip to England, he left his regular glasses in his seat and so had to wear his prescription "shades." Everyone liked the effect and from then on his combination of dark hair, dark glasses, and black suit became a personal trademark. After co-headlining with the Beatles, he returned to Europe in the mid-1960s for other tours with top groups, including several series with the Rolling Stones. He established a rapport with European fans that remained strong for decades. In the '70s when he was only vaguely remembered by many U.S. fans, he always could play before capacity houses overseas.

In 1965, after a half-decade of unparalleled success with Monument, he switched to MGM Records. His reasons were that "MGM offered access to motion pictures and television as well as records. It also provided financial security and that meant I would

have all the time I needed to create." Soon after joining MGM, he made his first film, *Fastest Guitar Alive*. He also scored a mild hit with "Ride Away," but the sales fell far short of blockbusters such as "Oh, Pretty Woman."

Still, he had had dry spells before and there seemed no reason why he wouldn't be making top chart levels again in due time. At that point, fate struck a devastating blow. His wife Claudette was killed as a result of a motorcycle accident. Stunned and disorganized, he sought escape in an ever more intensive concert schedule. As he told Robert Hilburn of the *Los Angeles Times:* "All I was doing was surviving. I was trying to work my way out of the turmoil. It takes time to get back on your feet. I just wasn't up to the demands of recording.

"I've got nothing against a performer who only sings, but it really puts a strain on someone who write the songs, arranges them, and also sings. That's what I had been used to doing. For a while, I just couldn't put it together."

In 1967, it seemed as though Orbison had ridden out the storm. He began to find it easier to write again. Plans for new recordings began. Then tragedy hit with redoubled force. A fire at his Nashville home killed two of his three children. After weeks of grief, he gave up writing in favor of the old concert-grind palliative.

Although he remained under contract to MGM, not much happened from a recording standpoint even when he was in the mood to work, mainly because the company was going through continuous upheavals in executive personnel. When Mike Curb took over at the start of the '70s, one of his first moves was to get Roy, whom he admired greatly, back in the studios. This resulted in some early '70s albums and a few singles, but Roy's long absence from the record field in the U.S. seemed to have dissipated interest in him at home.

Still popular elsewhere, though, Roy brought his live act to other parts of the world and was rarely in evidence in the U.S. for much of the '70s. He did appear in concert with Johnny Cash in 1973 and made a few other special engagements, but that was about it. As he noted: "I tended to fulfill commitments around the world, then come home and rest." He didn't lack for engagements. He made many tours of Europe and Australia in the '70s. Typical of his schedule was the period in 1974 when he worked foreign venues seven months straight with only nine days off, including dates in Crete, Greece, and Taiwan. He did some recordings for Mercury in the mid-1970s after leaving MGM, but without any notable results. He did have some recording achievements during the decade, though, earning a gold record in Australia for a single release in 1974 and demonstrating his popularity with English fans when a reissue of some of his earlier material, *The Very Best of Roy Orbison,* rose to number one in 1976.

Late in the decade, though, he and his work started to resurface at home. Linda Ronstadt scored a striking success with his "Blue Bayou," while his "Oh, Pretty Woman" became the theme for a series of TV commercials. He himself tried out the water in 1977 with a minitour of California venues. The results were positive. Almost all the shows were sold out and were critically acclaimed. His stature with fellow artists was indicated by the Eagles, Jefferson Starship, Tubes, and Boz Scaggs' appearance in the audience at his Los Angeles date.

To add new impetus, he signed a recording contract with a new label, Elektra, during 1978. His debut on the label, *Laminar Flow* (May 1979), contained three new songs by him: two ballads and the fast-paced rocker "Movin'."

Among his albums over the years were such Monument collections as *Greatest Hits* (1962), *In Dreams* (1964), *Early Orbison* and *More Greatest Hits* (1964–65), *Orbisongs* (1965), and *Very Best of Roy Orbison* (1966). MGM LPs included *There Is Only One* (1965), *Orbison Way* and *Classic Roy Orbison* (1966), *Roy Orbison Sings Don Gibson* (1967), *Great Songs, Hank Williams the Roy Orbison Way,* and *Roy Orbison Sings.* Sun reissued some of his earliest recordings *Original Sound.* In the 1980s, the two-disc *All-Time Greatest Hits of Roy Orbison* (Monument) and two-disc *In Dreams* (Virgin) kept his classics in print.

Though Roy kept active in the 1980s as a performer and writer, his main rewards came from successes achieved by other artists with some of his classic compositions. Those credits included top 10 hits scored by Don McLean with "Crying" and Van Halen with "(Oh) Pretty Woman." During 1980, he recorded a duet with Emmylou Harris, "That Lovin' You Feelin' Again," for the soundtrack of the film *Roadie* on Warner Brothers Records. When the Grammy Award winners were announced on February 25, 1981, he and Emmylou won trophies for Best Country Performance by a Duo or Group with Vocal. That was the first Grammy Roy had ever received, an ironic situation considering his tremendous contributions to the rock and country fields over the decades.

In late 1986, officials of the Rock and Roll Hall of Fame announced that Roy would be one of the new inductees. At the ceremonies, held in New York's Waldorf Astoria in January 1987, he was introduced by Bruce Springsteen who said, in part, "Some rock'n'roll reinforces friendships and community. Roy's ballads were always best when you were alone in the dark." The songs, he continued, "addressed the underside of pop romance—they were scary.

"When I went in to the studio to make (the album) *Born to Run,* I wanted to write words like Bob Dylan that sounded like Phil Spector, but with singing like Roy Orbison. But nobody sings like Roy Orbison."

Later in the year a *Salute to Roy Orbison* program was taped in the Cocoanut Grove in Los Angeles for presentation as a Cinemax cable TV special. Paying respect to Orbison, who performed many of his hits on the program, were many of the superstars of both English and U.S. rock music, including Bruce Springsteen, Elvis Costello, and Tom Waits. The time also seemed ripe for the revival of Roy's recording career. Soon after the Hall of Fame induction he signed a new contract with British-based Virgin Records and he began work with producer T-Bone Burnett on tracks for a 1988 album release. In 1988, Rhino Records' CD *For the Lonely: 18 Greatest Hits* and two-LP *For the Lonely: A Roy Orbison Anthology, 1956–1965* combined his Sun and Monument sessions. (*See Blasters, The; Creedence Clearwater Revival; Everly Brothers, The; Holly, Buddy; McLean, Don; Pitney, Gene; Ronstadt, Linda; Van Halen.*)

ORIOLES, THE: *Vocal group from Baltimore, Maryland: Sonny Til, died 1981; George Nelson, died late 1960s; Alexander Sharp, died c. 1959; Johnny Reed. Guitar accompanist, Tommy Gaither, died 1950.*

Talent is obviously a vital requirement for most musicians and singers, but achieving stardom calls for music with public appeal. In many instances, in fact, it has been the songwriter who opened the door to success for a vocalist or group by using them to demonstrate a composition.

This was an important part of the emergence of the Orioles, a pivotal group in the early history of rhythm & blues. The group original members all were raised in Baltimore and achieved some local fame in the mid-1940s as the Vibranaires (also given as Vibra Naires). The group members had been performing since their early teens, but music was mainly a sideline. Lead singer Sonny Til (born Earlington Tilghman) drove a truck for Western Electric; second lead George Nelson was a maitre d' at a nightclub. The other two singers—tenor Alexander Sharp and bass Johnny Reed—had various nonmusical jobs.

In the late '40s, a Baltimore saleslady-songwriter, Deborah Chessler, heard them and approached them to help demonstrate her new song, "It's Too Soon to Know." They agreed, later changing their names to the Orioles after the bird usually associated with Baltimore teams.

Deborah, who acted as their manager and booker,

took them to New York and got them on to the "Arthur Godfrey Talent Scouts" show in early 1948. They sang "Barbara Lee," but lost. Godfrey liked them, however, and added them to his regular program, which led to favorable response to their vocals of "Barbara Lee" and such other songs as "I May Be Wrong" and "It's Too Soon to Know."

Deborah also was auditioning the group for record executives. She gained the attention of exbandleader Jerry Blaine, who headed a label called It's a Natural. The first single release was "Barbara Lee"/"It's Too Soon to Know" in August 1948. "It's Too Soon to Know" made the R&B top 10 later in the year. (In 1958, it joined the ranks of R&B classics watered down into pop hits by Pat Boone.) After this, Blaine changed his label's name to Jubilee Records, for which the Orioles recorded most of their subsequent hits. Among their top 10 R&B best-sellers for Jubilee were "What Are You Doing New Years?" and "Forgive and Forget" (1950) and "Baby, Please Don't Go" (1952).

As one of the most popular new groups in R&B, the Orioles toured throughout the country, playing the top theaters and clubs in the black sections of U.S. cities. On occasion, it also was featured in important entertainment centers outside the ghetto areas. One tour in late 1950 ended in tragedy when an auto crash took the life of Tommy Gaither and severely injured George Nelson and Johnny Reed. Sonny and Alex carried on by handling the next show in Washington, D.C., as a duo. Some time later, George and Johnny returned, taking part in a show that featured Duke Ellington in Philadelphia. The group paid tribute to Gaither on "I Miss You So," its next single release after the accident. Gaither's place was taken by Ralph Williams. The group remained stable for several years until Nelson left in 1953 to be replaced by Gregory Carol, who previously sang with the Four Buddies. Carol's 1953 debut on Orioles recordings was the number one R&B hit "Crying in the Chapel" (a song resurrected by Elvis in 1965). About this time, a sixth member, pianist Charlie Hayes, was added. The six-member group made several recordings before disbanding in 1954.

In later years, several groups made appearances and/or recordings using the Orioles' name. Sonny Til joined a group called the Regals soon after the original Orioles broke up. (Other members of the Regals were Albert Russell, Paul Griffin, Billy Adams, and Jerry Rodriguez.) This group made a number of sides for Vee Jay that were issued under the Orioles' name. Til organized another Orioles quartet in 1962, with Delton McCall singing tenor, Billy Taylor singing baritone, and Gerald Gregory handling bass. That assemblage made several discs for Charlie Parker Records.

In the early 1970s, RCA Records had a group under contract called the Orioles, comprising Clarence Young, Bobby Thomas, and Louis Robinson.

George Nelson died of asthma around 1959 and Alexander Sharp passed away from a heart attack in the late 1960s. Til died in 1981. Yet their music lives on. In 1983, Murray Hill Records released *The Best of the Orioles, Volumes 1* and *2* plus a five-disc boxed set, *For Collectors Only: The Orioles* including hits as well as previously unreleased tracks.

OSBOURNE, JOHN "OZZY": *Singer, harmonica player, songwriter. Born Birmingham, England, December 3, 1946.*

After making his initial heavy metal reputation as lead singer for England's Black Sabbath, Ozzy Osbourne won a following as a solo performer. His admirers, mostly teenagers, were attracted to him apparently more for his outrageous stage behavior—both actual and perhaps mythical—than the musical content of his songs. Despite, or perhaps because of, a series of lurid controversies about his song subjects and their influence on young fans, he became for a while one of the biggest concert draws and album sellers in 1980s rock.

Osbourne, who grew up in a working class section of Birmingham, England, performed with the usual variety of hopeful—if not particularly talented—rock bands in that area in the mid-1960s before joining with three other local musicians, Tony Iommi, Terry "Geezer" Butler, and Bill Ward to form a band called Earth at the end of the 1960s. In late 1969, the group changed its name to Black Sabbath and went on to become one of the first stars in the heavy metal spectrum. (*See Black Sabbath.*)

In the late 1970s, Osbourne decided the time was ripe for a new career phase and he quit the band to go solo. At the start of the 1980s, he was given a contract by Jet Records, a CBS subsidiary, which issued his debut LP, the platinum *Blizzard of Oz,* in March 1981. His second solo LP, *Diary of a Madman* (October 1981), also went platinum. Recorded live at the Ritz in New York, his third LP, *Speak of the Devil* (1982), went gold. All three of his albums were on the charts simultaneously in December 1982. In early 1984 he had another album, *Bark at the Moon* (Jet/Epic) on the charts.

For the stage shows, Osbourne wore garish costumes and makeup, typically being demonic in appearance. Stories circulated about his supposed antisocial actions in live performances. One particularly abhorrent tale was to the effect that on stage he bit the head off a live creature, variously said to have been either a dove or a bat. Osbourne never publicly acknowledged or denied it and it has never been definitely shown that the event ever took place. Industry observers tend to believe it was a promotional gimmick to build up Osbourne's antiestablishment image. But it was one of the things that drew fire from outside critics, including more than a few clergymen who felt he provided a satanic role model for young people.

One of the things that brought Ozzy's name into the headlines was a lawsuit filed against him in Los Angeles Superior Court in October 1984 by the parents of a 19-year-old boy who killed himself, allegedly after listening to Osbourne's song "Suicide Solution."

Accompanied by attorney Howard Weitzman in a January 1985 press conference, Ozzy expressed sorrow over the boy's death, but disclaimed responsibility. Weitzman told reporters that the recording actually was an antisuicide song about a one-time singer with AC/DC and friend of Ozzy's who died because of acute alcoholism. (See AC/DC.)

He maintained that his client was "a family man with a wife and three children who understands parents' concerns" and not someone who would write material deliberately intended to cause harm to individuals. He also drew analogies with other events and music, such as the suicide scene in Shakespeare's Romeo and Juliet or the claimed impact of the Beatles' "Helter Skelter" on the Manson Family's Tate–La Bianca murders as an argument that punishing Osbourne for his writings would amount to an attack on artistic freedom. He said: "Next thing, songs will have to be monitored and approved before [performers] can go on stage."

Osbourne used the conference not only to claim innocence in causing a death, but to point to the emphasis in his new album (The Ultimate Sin, issued on the CBS Associated label that month) on the dangers of nuclear war. The LP, he stated, contained nine songs decrying the potential horrors of nuclear war.

He said that despite the lawsuit, though, he had no intention of changing his performing style. "I'm not going to start singing Barry Manilow songs." In December 1986, L.A. Superior Court Judge John L. Cole dismissed the suit, stating, in part, "We have to look very closely at the First Amendment and the chilling effect that would be had if these words (in the song lyrics) were held to be accountable." The plaintiff's attorney stated he intended to appeal the dismissal ruling.

However, Ozzy's career did seem to suffer a downturn in the mid-1980s, but it was far from certain that adverse headlines had anything to do with it. In part, it probably reflected the typical fickleness

of teen audiences. But another factor was the March 1982 death under odd circumstances of Ozzy's backing-band guitarist, Randy Rhoads (formerly of Quiet Riot; see Quiet Riot). Rhoads was killed in the crash of a small airplane that just before the accident had been buzzing the place the group was staying in, apparently as a prank. Rhoads' loss was a serious one, not only because he was a good friend of Osbourne's, but also because he was one of the group's primary writers whose efforts had played a considerable role in Ozzy's success.

Posthumously, Rhoads helped Ozzy gain new career momentum. In the spring of 1987, the album Tribute was released, based on tapes of the 1982 tour in which Rhoads backed Osbourne. The album featured Rhoads on the cover with the comments "The Legend Live" and "He Would Have Been the Greatest." The album spent weeks in the top 10 in Billboard. Osbourne emphasized these were the last cuts he had of Rhoads performances.

During 1987, he entered the Betty Ford Center in Palm Springs, California, to try to overcome an alcohol problem, but left early because he said he didn't like to have to make his bed every morning. This did not mean, his management company said, that he wasn't making progress in fighting the addiction. In early 1988 he began work on a new studio album scheduled for release in the fall. Titles of some of the songs stated to be definite for the final cut suggested he wasn't turning mellow: "Demon Alcohol," "Blood Bath in Paradise," and "Fire in the Sky."

OSMONDS, THE: *Vocal and instrumental group, all born Ogden, Utah. Alan Osmond born June 22, 1949; Wayne, August 28, 1951; Merrill, April 30, 1953; Jay, March 2, 1955; Donny, December 9, 1957; Marie, born October 13, 1959.*

The number 13 proved far from unlucky for the Osmonds. In 1971, their thirteenth year as performers, the family group had its greatest year ever, earning nine gold-record awards (including those for the five-brother quintet plus several won by Donny as a solo artist). This total exceeded even the single-year collection of gold records attained by the Beatles at their peak. The Osmonds hardly seemed likely to have their recordings compete with the Beatles' on long-term standards, but for the first half of the '70s, the group maintained a stronghold on a large segment of the music audience. After that, the popularity of the male side of the family faded, but in the mid-1980s, sister Marie carried on the performing tradition with considerable success.

Home for the Osmond family was Ogden, Utah, where the first eight of its nine children were born. Because eldest brothers Virl (born 1945) and

Tommy (born 1947) were deaf since early childhood, their parents considered having no more children, but after Alan turned out to have sound hearing, they decided it would be all right to produce a large brood in keeping with their Mormon faith. During the Osmonds' heyday, Virl and Tommy handled the group's business affairs. The youngest sibling, Jimmy (born Canoga Park, California, April 16, 1963), gained a reputation outside the U.S. in Japan. Known affectionately as Jimmy-Boy, he earned three gold records there amid the family's peak years.

The Osmonds' saga began in Ogden in 1959, when four of the boys—Alan, Wayne, Merrill, and Jay—sang in church and, in their home, rehearsed barbershop songs. Recalling those early days, their mother Olive told an interviewer: "The [Mormon] church encourages talent, beginning with such things as singing, sports, and speeches when the children are small. That's how the four boys got started singing together."

Tracing their musical evolution in 1971, Alan said: "We started out in the barbershop vein, with a four-part, square-block chord harmony, but now we've broadened. We haven't lost our harmony, which seems to be coming back, like Crosby, Stills, Nash & Young. We like what's going on today, and we're performing it. And we can get this close harmony, too. You might say that we've been in a music school, learning structures of chords, harmony, techniques, and now we're loose with all this in the background."

In 1962, the Osmond quartet had gained a reputation for their religious singing and were asked to go on a tour of church wards in the western states. The tour brought them to Anaheim and they decided to visit Disneyland. They walked around the "Magic Kingdom" dressed in identical clothes as they did in their church performances. They stopped to listen to a barbershop quartet. Seeing the Osmonds' outfits, the group asked if they'd like to sing. The boys did and were so well received by the crowd that they came to the attention of Disneyland talent scouts. As a result, the Osmonds began their professional career in the amusement park.

During one performance, they were heard by Andy Williams' father. He suggested that Andy audition the brothers for his forthcoming TV show. Their combination of youth and middle-of-the-road repertoire appealed to Williams and the show's producers, so the Osmonds were signed. They became a featured act on the show until it went off the air after several years. In the mid-1960s, expanded to a quintet with the addition of little brother Donny, the group moved to the "Jerry Lewis Show." In the late '60s, when Williams started a new program on NBC-TV, the Osmonds were back with him on a semiregular basis, remaining on the show until 1970.

During the 1960s, the brothers spent much of their spare time learning to play musical instruments. As of the early '70s, the five group members could handle a combined total of 28 instruments. In their act, each one concentrated on the instrument that he felt most comfortable with: Donny on electric organ, Alan on piano and guitar, Wayne on guitar and saxophone, Merrill on bass guitar, and Jay on drums. Stylistically, they evolved from barbershop to ballads to bubble-gum rock and, by 1972, were showing an ability to perform some music that could find favor with midteen and college-level fans as well.

The group recorded on Andy Williams' label, Barnaby, and MCA's Uni subsidiary before signing with MGM Records at the start of the 1970s. Suddenly they caught fire in the disc field. Their MGM debut, *The Osmonds* (early 1971), was certified gold by the RIAA. For five weeks starting February 13, the quintet was in *Billboard*'s number one spot nationally with the platinum single "One Bad Apple." Meanwhile, Donny's gold single debut, "Sweet and Innocent," scored top 10 success and aptly described his and his siblings' musical style and marketing image throughout their heyday. For four weeks starting September 11, he had a solo number one success with "Go Away Little Girl" (a previous hit for Steve Lawrence in 1963 and the Happenings in 1966). The quintet's hit singles included "Double Lovin'" and the gold "Yo-Yo."

The Osmonds followed their debut LP with the gold albums *Homemade* (1971) and *Phase III* (1972) with *Phase III* containing six songs written by the brothers. Donny's debut effort, *The Donny Osmond Album,* and the follow-up, *To You with Love, Donny* (both 1971) went gold. The group and Donny continued to add to their best-selling totals in 1972 with more singles and albums: the gold albums *Crazy Horses* and *Live* and the singles "Down by the Lazy River" (gold) and "Hold Her Tight." Donny scored with gold albums *Portrait of Donny* and *Too Young.* His hit singles "Puppy Love," "Why," and "Too Young," were oldies from Paul Anka, Frankie Avalon, and Nat "King" Cole, respectively. Jimmy Osmond also chipped in with the charted album *Killer Joe* and the single "Long-Haired Lover from Liverpool."

Donny started off 1973 with another hit album, *Alone Together,* and the single "The Twelfth of Never" (a remake of a Johnny Mathis hit). In the summer, the quintet placed the album *The Plan* and single "Goin' Home" on the best seller lists. Another solo effort by Donny, "A Million to

One"/"Young Love," was a two-sided hit during the same period. In the fall, the quintet shared the hit single "Let Me In."

In 1974, sister Marie began to make her mark as a pop performer, appearing in concerts with the group and also recording duets with Donny such as the LP *I'm Leaving It All up to You*. She already had made the charts the year before with her country-flavored solo LP, *Paper Roses*. The various combinations of the clan Osmond continued to release a barrage of new MGM/Kolob LPs in the mid-1970s, though with declining sales. Those releases included the Osmonds' *Around the World Live in Concert* (1976), Marie's *Who's Sorry Now* (1975), and Donny and Marie's *Make the World Go Away*. Kolob was the family's private label within the MGM network.

During 1976, Donny and Marie signed for their own TV variety series on ABC-TV, a show that gained high enough ratings to last for three seasons. The rest of the Osmonds naturally took part in the proceedings. Over that time period, more LPs came out, this time on the Polygram label, which owned MGM. Those included Donny's albums *Disco Train* (1976) and *Donald Clark Osmond* (1977); Donny and Marie's *New Season* (1976), *Winning Combination* (1978), and *Goin' Coconuts* (1978); Marie's *This Is the Way That I Feel* (1977); and The Osmonds' *Osmonds' Christmas Album* and *Brainstorm* (1976) and *Osmonds' Greatest Hits* (1977). The group's *Steppin' Out* appeared on Polygam's Mercury label in 1978.

By the time the TV series had ended at the end of the '70s, the group had pretty much lost its mass-audience rapport. In 1980, the announcement was made that the Osmond Brothers group had disbanded. However, in 1982, some of the brothers, but not Donny, reformed to take aim at the country-music audience. Donny's activities in the 1980s focused more on production and direction. His directing work included supervising a TV special for jazz/pop star Grover Washington, Jr. (*See Washington, Grover, Jr.*) Marie, after a brief marriage that produced a child she took time out to raise, began a new solo performing career in the mid-1980s.

OTIS, JOHNNY: *Singer, band leader, songwriter, drummer, record producer, record-company executive. Born Vallejo, California, December 28, 1921.* *

In the early 1970s, Johnny Otis could look back more than a quarter of a century as a band leader and pivotal figure in the rise of both rhythm & blues and

rock'n'roll. At the time, his Johnny Otis Show continued to be an exciting, crowd-pleasing venture, as vital in the '70s as it had been for decades before. More than that, it amounted to a living history of pop music after 1950, featuring such pioneers as bluesman Eddie "Cleanhead" Vinson and Big Joe Turner (who had recorded the first R&B success of "Shake, Rattle and Roll" in 1954 before the Bill Haley cover that scored with the white audience) and such newcomers as Johnny's son, the brilliant guitarist Shuggie Otis. But Johnny tired of the touring grind for a while and, during the '70s, disbanded his show in favor of a career as a minister. In the mid-1980s, he came out of retirement with a new version of his band and stage act.

Though in actual fact not a black person, Otis always identified with the black community once he fell in love with the music developed by black artists. The son of Greek immigrants, he was born and grew up in Vallejo, California, and was still calling that state home over 65 years later. He did not become interested in music until he was through with high school in 1939. "I saw Count Basie at the [San Francisco] World's Fair and wanted to be a drummer after I saw Jo Jones." Johnny got himself a set of drums and taught himself to play them. He had a natural talent for percussion instruments and could play with the best jazz drummers before he was 20.

"As a teenager in Berkeley, I played with Count Otis Matthews and his West Oakland House Rockers. We played boogie-woogie and barrelhouse blues. It was one of the great experiences of my life. Count Otis had moved to California from the South and played sensational barrelhouse piano. We used to play in small clubs and gyms in black areas and often got paid off in wine."

Johnny played with a number of bands in different parts of the West during the early 1940s. He worked in Reno, Nevada, in a group that included bassist Robert Johnson, Count Otis, on piano, and "a fellow named Brussard on trumpet." Later he joined George Morrison's band in Denver, Colorado, switched to the Lloyd Hunter group, and, in 1943, formed the Otis Love Band with Preston Love to work in the Barrelhouse in Omaha, Nebraska. "While I was there, first Nat Cole, then Jimmy Witherspoon came through and told me Harlan Leonard needed a drummer in Los Angeles at the Club Alabam. I went back there, played with Leonard a while, then gigged around L.A. with Jack McVey and Bandu Ali (who was the man who discovered Ella Fitzgerald).

In 1945, Johnny got the chance to form his first big band as the house group at the Club Alabam. "In October '46, we went on the road. The first engage-

*Otis quotes from personal interview with Irwin Stambler.

505

ment was 10 weeks in the Pershing Hotel in Chicago. Then we began to play a lot of black theaters and landed the annual Ink Spots tour and played all over the country. Late in 1947, we were back in L.A. and things had changed. Big bands had had it; even Basie and Ellington were in trouble.

"So I broke the group down in 1947 to what today would be called an R&B combo. All the members had big band experience. We still kept the trombone, trumpet, and two saxes. All of us really wanted to stay in the big band field, but we had to go to the blues to survive. So we were very blues, but the horns still played riffs with the seventh on top. Soon I found I liked it and I think this was how R&B was born. What you had was a small big band playing blues and that sound became R&B.

"In 1948, we opened the Barrel House in Watts. I believe this was the first night club to feature R&B entertainment exclusively. Between 1948 and 1950, I found Little Esther Phillips, Mel Walker, Lady Dee Williams, Redd Lite, Pete Lewis, and the Robins and formed the first Johnny Otis Show. We called it the Johnny Otis Rhythm & Blues Caravan. While we were at the Barrel House, Ralph Bass heard us and sent for the head of Savoy Records and we began to record for them. We had made some discs for Excelsior and Modern—Little Esther first recorded for Modern—but we started getting hits on Savoy."

Thus Otis dominated the R&B charts in 1950 as few artists or band leaders have since. The Otis group's single of "Double Crossin' Blues" was number one for several weeks. He had two best-sellers with Mel Walker ("Dreamin' Blues" and "Rockin' Blues") and one with Little Esther ("Far Away Places"). He also combined with Little Esther and Walker on two more top 10 hits: "Deceivin' Blues" and "Wedding Blues." Johnny kept up his string in 1951, turning out such top 10 singles with Mel Walker as "All Night Long," "Mambo Boogie," and "Gee, Baby" plus "Sunset to Dawn" in 1952.

"All of our hits made us a big attraction on the road and I traveled steadily throughout the first part of the '50s. In 1951, I discovered Little Willie John, Hank Ballard and the Midnighters, and Jackie Wilson." Otis recommended them to several record firms including King, but King only signed Ballard at the time. "I was so impressed with Jackie Wilson, I wrote a song for him called 'Every Beat of My Heart,' but nothing happened with it. Others recorded it and 10 years later, Gladys Knight had a hit record." During 1953–54, Johnny added still another new legendary performer to his show, Big Mama Thornton, the first popularizer of "Hound Dog." Then-unknown Little Richard also sang with the band.

In 1955, Johnny gave up his traveling show in favor of working as a disc jockey. "It may sound corny, but I quit traveling because of my kids. I was in New York on Christmas and I called home. My little daughter got on and said: 'Daddy, why aren't you home like other daddies?' I decided I should give up the rat race. So when I got back to L.A., I said: 'I'll be a disc jockey. They don't need hit records; they play other people's hits.' So I put my finger in the phone book and hit KFOX. I called the station manager and told him what I wanted. He said: 'Is this Johnny Otis, the Duke Ellington of Watts?' and soon I had my own show."

The Otis show became one of the most popular in Southern California and led to a TV show that did well for several years in the late 1950s. As a sideline, Johnny promoted dances and concerts for various acts and worked some dates with his own group. He also kept writing music and, in 1958, had one of the smash hits of the rock era, "Willie and the Hand Jive."

"In 1957, I made a record for Capitol, 'Ma, He's Makin' Eyes at Me,' that my partner, Hal Zeiger, and I thought would be a hit in the U.S. But it bombed here and was a hit in England. Hal went over to set a tour in England and came back and told me about the skiffle craze. He told me there was no dancing, so the kids did a thing called the hand jive and he thought I should write a song about it. So I wrote 'Willie and the Hand Jive' with the idea of scoring a hit in England. Instead it was a smash in the U.S."

In the early '60s, Johnny's career was set back by the sudden emergence of the English rock groups. "Around that time, the bottom fell out of R&B. With the Beatles taking over the audience, many people in R&B couldn't even get a job. So I went into politics as deputy for [state] Senator Mervyn Dymally." (Otis met Dymally in 1946 at New York's Apollo and the two became close friends.)

Throughout the mid-1960s, Otis had little contact with the music field as a performer. Toward the end of the decade, though, the emergence of soul made R&B a thriving field again. "I was talking to Frank Zappa and he suggested I contact the Bihari brothers. [The Biharis, Joe and Jules, were pioneer producers of R&B records as owners of Modern Records in Los Angeles] I talked to Saul and he said come on down and use his studio." By then, Johnny was playing small clubs in the area in a little band that featured his son Shuggie and Delmar "Mighty Mouth" Evans. "So Shuggie and I came into the studio and we made a single that was a rhythm & blues hit. In 1969, we got a contract with Columbia Records and soon had our show going full-blast again." As of 1972, the major members of the show included, besides Shuggie and Johnny, Big Jim Wynn, the Otisettes, Margie Evans, Big Daddy Rucker, Eddie "Cleanhead" Vinson (alternating with Big Joe Turner, who was ailing in 1972), the Mighty Flea on trombone, Jitterbug Webb on guitar, and Clifford Solomon on saxophone.

By the mid-1970s, Johnny had become more interested in religion than pop music and he broke up his tour group in favor of preaching the gospel. In the mid-1980s, however, his pop-music pursuits revived, helped in part by growing nostalgia among fans for earlier rock and R&B material. He organized a new 12-piece band whose members included Shuggie and once more delighted audiences across the U.S., including attendees at the "R&B Reunion" segment of the tenth annual Watts Towers Music and Arts Festival in Los Angeles in July, 1986.

Johnny Otis! Johnny Otis (Hawksound, 1984) showed his '80s work. Arista's two-disc *The Original Johnny Otis Show* resurrected 1945–51 sessions including Jimmy Rushing, Esther Phillips, and the Ravens. (*See Ballard, Hank; Knight, Gladys, & the Pips; Little Richard; Phillips, Esther; Ravens, The; Thornton, Big Mama; Turner, Joe; Wilson, Jackie.*)

PAGE, JIMMY: *See Led Zeppelin.*

P-FUNK ALL STARS: *See Clinton, George.*

PARKER, GRAHAM: *Singer, guitarist, band leader (THE RUMOUR, THE SHOT), songwriter, record producer. Born London, England, 1951.*

A compelling performer and talented writer, Graham Parker burst upon the world rock stage in 1976 with two albums that without question rank as among the finest of the decade. Bracketed with such luminaries as Bruce Springsteen and Van Morrison in critical praise of the middle to late 1970s, he never received the mass-audience response in the U.S. that seemed his due. In other parts of the world, he was recognized as one of the major influences on rock'n'roll from the mid-1970s on.

Parker, from an English working class environment, saw music as a way out of dead-end occupations from his early teens. The group that first fired his enthusiasm for rock was the Rolling Stones of the mid-1960s when he was just past his thirteenth birthday. He told Robert Hilburn of the *Los Angeles Times:* "Music was always the main thing. You went to school and did this or that, but the real thing was what was on the charts."

U.S. black-spawned music—roots blues and R&B—was an obvious base on which the Stones and other British blues-rock groups built their styles, and young Parker also became enamoured of the form. He learned to play guitar and formed a group called the Black Rockers, which later became the Deep Cut Three, to play songs culled from recordings by R&B artists on the Stax-Volt, Chess and, to a lesser extent, Motown labels. There were, of course, far more unknown, unheralded bands than opportunities for performing dates or record contracts. Most fell by the wayside, including Parker's early combinations.

He followed the path of most of his defeated contemporaries, taking any kind of work to earn food and shelter money while hoping for a break that might change things. Parker's jobs included breeding animals for scientific experiments, working in a bakery, washing windows, and, finally, in the early 1970s, pumping gas in a service station in Surrey, England.

He kept his eyes open for occasional night or weekend gigs, from time to time working up demonstration tapes of some of his original songs. He sent one of those to the Hope and Anchor pub, thinking members of some of the rock bands that played the venue might hear it. Somehow it was brought to the attention of Dave Robinson, who ran a recording studio in the Hope and Anchor building. The music impressed Robinson, whose contacts included a variety of members of London's rock musical fraternity. He contacted Parker and arranged for him to get together with a new band in the process of formation by experienced performers from recently defunct top-level groups such as Brinsley Schwarz, Ducks Deluxe, and Boutempts. When the original demo numbers were redone with Parker fronting the group (which by then called itself the Rumour), the gritty, driving energy was sufficient to make disc jockeys on Radio London's "Honky Tonk" show program them.

The exposure soon earned Parker and the Rumour a recording contract from the U.K. branch of U.S.-based Mercury Records. With Nick Lowe producing, the debut LP took shape during 1975. (*See Lowe, Nick.*) The Rumour comprised Brinsley Schwarz and Martin Belmont on guitars, Bob Andrews on keyboards, Andrew Bodnar on bass guitar, and Steve Goulding on drums. The debut LP, *Howlin' Wind* (early 1976), offered such high-energy tracks as "Nothin's Gonna Pull Us Apart," "Back to Schooldays," "Gypsy Blood," and "White Honey" that marked it as something special. Right on its heels came an equally exquisite collection, *Heat Treatment* whose title track later was featured in the film *Between the Lines.*

Those two albums had undeniable R&B roots, but blended all manner of other elements from Van Morrison's melodic, mainstream touches to hints of the almost-at-hand punk rebellion. Dave Marsh and

John Swenson of *Rolling Stone* commented: "These are tough, passionate, and hungry albums in which Parker refuses to accept anybody's vision of himself except his own. What these two albums share with punk is the frightening implications that the culture around him is collapsing, that there is nothing to hold on to." Also issued in 1976 was a four-song EP (originally pressed on pink vinyl and thus called *The Pink Parker*) featuring "Hold Back the Night."

At the end of 1976, Parker could look back on overwhelming approval—from critics. *Crawdaddy* called *Howlin' Wind* "rock'n'roll of classic stature." *Rolling Stone* gave Parker and Rumour its Red Suspender Award for the best new band of the year. In the *Village Voice*'s annual critics poll, the debut albums were ranked two and four in the top 10 nationally. The band also had begun to build a following, at least on a cult level, at home and abroad.

Parker's problem was how to go beyond such already thunderous achievements. His eagerly awaited third Mercury LP, *Stick to Me* (1977), was an excellent collection that might have made a breakthrough to best-seller status with more intensive promotional support from the record company, but it was not as consistently letter-perfect as the previous releases. Critics did not hesitate to express reservations and the chorus of disappointment was even louder with the 1978 double-disc live *Parkerilla*. The 1977 and 1978 releases were certainly not bad albums—they still ranked among the top creative efforts of the late 1970s—but from the rock establishment's standpoint, they should have preceded instead of followed the 1976 classics.

Parker did not take too kindly to the situation, as he told Michael Watts of England's *Melody Maker* (March 17, 1979). On one level, he accepted it as part of the "cycle of discovery/acclaim/rejection/re-assessment; the contrary opinions the business so enjoys.

"The thing is that you never expect it yourself, you never think it'll happen to you. But as soon as I read the first knocking reviews it became clear that I was in for it. And you prepare for it. Hope you can laugh at it. . . . It'll happen to other people after me. . . . It had something to do with the fact that I didn't immediately become a fucking superstar or something. I can imagine people thinking: 'Oh we made a bit of a mistake here. Let's kick the little bugger in the teeth.' I got the feeling a bit from some of the reviews. I thought that was just sad."

By then, Parker had bitterly ended his association with Mercury, accusing the label of sabotaging things through inadequate promotional backing, and signed with Arista. He fought back at his critics on several fronts in his 1979 debut on Arista, *Squeezing Out Sparks,* an LP as good if not better than his 1976

release. Its songs such as "Protection" and "No One Hurts You" had lines that could be interpreted as criticism for critics. In his wide-ranging U.S. and European tour in support of the new LP, he usually included the song "Mercury Poisoning," an obvious slap at his former label. As with his earlier releases, though, he couldn't penetrate the rigidly enclosed AM-radio format with either album or single releases. His following did increase, but essentially by word of mouth. At year-end, the *Village Voice* poll showed *Squeezing Out Sparks* to be an overwhelming choice for best album of 1979.

His 1980 Arista release, *The Up Escalator,* was also a fine collection. Its subject matter covered a wide range, from a paean against complacency in "Stupefaction" to the pangs of desire in "Love without Greed" and "Endless Night" (which commented on opportunities lost and independence wasted to no good end). Singing backing vocals on "Endless Night" was none other than Bruce Springsteen.

Before his next Arista album, the 1982 *Another Grey Area,* Parker and the Rumour separated company. The split came from the band's continued desire to try to establish an identity of its own. (The group had three releases through the early 1980s: *Max* on Mercury in 1977, *Frogs, Sprouts, Clogs and Krauts* on Arista in 1979, and *Purity of Essence* on Stiff in 1980.) Parker said: "When the backing band thinks their own records are more important than yours, it's time to split." For *Another Grey Area,* he completed all the tracks with the help of session musicians, as was the case for his 1983 compilation on Arista, *The Real McCaw.* Both those albums seemed more polished, but also less hard-edged and gritty than "classic" Parker.

In 1984, Parker left Arista and signed with Elektra Records. For his next album, he worked as co-producer with William Wittman (who had served as associate producer and engineer of Cyndi Lauper's massively successful *She's So Unusual*). Graham noted: "I was credited as co-producer on *Another Grey Area,* but this one was the real thing. Although I didn't know a decibel from an egg, I knew I wanted more of the attack of *Squeezing Out Sparks* than I'd had in my last few records."

When the Elektra LP, *Steady Nerves,* came out in March 1985, he asserted: "It should dispel any suspicion that I've mellowed out. It attacks in a way my last few albums haven't . . . but people will have to listen and make up their own minds."

For that LP he went back to an association with Brinsley Schwarz, though not with the old Rumour. He now had a new backing group called the Shot made up of Schwarz on lead guitar and, from his previous album's session musicians, George Small on keyboards, Michael Braun on drums, and Kevin Jenkins on bass guitar. Looking ahead to his 1985 tour, he said: "When you say, 'Graham Parker and the Shot,' it's got some rhythm."

In 1987, Parker signed with RCA Records, which issued his label debut, *The Mona Lisa's Sister,* in April 1988. The LP, co-produced by Parker and Brinsley Schwarz, proved to be an excellent, exciting collection on a par with his best offerings of the 1970s.

Some of those 1970s albums had joined the ranks of rock classics. In its August 11, 1987 issue, *Rolling Stone* included *Howlin' Wind* and *Squeezing Out Sparks* in its top 100 list of the best rock releases over the previous 20 years. It stated the latter was "as exhilarating, driving and downright fearsome as anything else to come from the late seventies."

PARKER, RAY, JR.: *Singer, guitarist, clarinetist, band leader (RAYDIO), record producer, songwriter. Born Detroit, Michigan, May 1, 1954.*

One of the music industry's highly regarded backing musicians and record-session artists in the first part of the 1970s, Ray Parker, Jr., blossomed into a major star by the end of the decade. First as the central figure in the fine, funky, horn-based band Raydio, then as a solo performer, he proved to have the kind of talent that easily transcended the sometimes artificial ethnic boundaries set up by the music-business establishment.

Born and raised in the heartland of soul and R&B music, Ray demonstrated musical skills at an early age. When he was just entering elementary school at the start of the 1960s, he learned to play the clarinet. In the next few years, he also proved adept at other instruments, including keyboards; at 12, he began guitar. When he reached his teens, he already ranked as something of a prodigy with local entertainment people and the opportunities arose for him to earn handsome sums as a professional bandsman.

By the start of the 1970s, he already had gained considerable experience backing some of the top names in the black music pantheon. He was a regular member of the house band at the 20 Grand Club in Detroit, which backed such luminaries as Gladys Knight & the Pips, Stevie Wonder, the Temptations, and the Spinners. The Spinners thought enough of Ray to have him back them on some of their tour dates. Besides in-person performances, in the late 1960s and early 1970s Ray was kept busy with studio work including many sessions backing artists under contract to the Hot Wax or Invictus labels owned by the famed writing/production team of Eddie and Brian Holland and Lamont Dozier. Quite a few of the recordings Parker worked on made the charts, including a number one hit single by the Honey Cone, "Want Ads," in June 1971. Though Ray hadn't written any hit songs himself at the time, he already was sharpening his skills in that department.

In 1972, a major milestone in his career took place when he accepted an offer from Stevie Wonder to become part of his tour group. Besides traveling throughout the world with Stevie, Ray helped record two of Wonder's award-winning albums, *Talking Book* (1972) and *Innervisions* (1973). (*See Wonder, Stevie.*)

The association with Wonder prompted Ray to move from the Midwest to the Los Angeles area, one of the most important recording-industry centers in the world. For a while in the mid-1970s, Ray's activities were pretty much what they had been before—extensive session playing and backup instrumental and vocal work in L.A. concerts or on tour dates with top performers. He was, though, becoming known as a promising songwriter. A growing list of artists were doing his material in their recordings or shows. Some of those singles made lower chart levels and, in late 1974, he was responsible for a top 20 hit recorded by Rufus and Chaka Khan, "You Got the Love." (*See Khan, Chaka.*)

In the mid-1970s, Ray felt he was ready for the spotlight and became the central figure in a band recruited from Detroit-area musicians. Called Raydio, the group signed with Arista Records in 1977 and released its gold debut LP, *Raydio,* in 1978. During that year, the band had a gold top 10 pop single—a soul-rock rework of the old nursery rhyme "Jack and Jill." Over the next few years, Ray Parker and Raydio turned out a string of hit albums and singles. The LPs included *Rock On* (1979), *Two Places at the Same Time* (1980, gold), and *A Woman Needs Love* (1981, gold). The group's top 10 soul hits in 1980 comprised "Can't Keep from Cryin'," "Two Places at the Same Time," and "For Those Who Like to Groove." In 1981, they hit with "A Woman Needs Love," "That Old Song," and "It's Your Night."

In 1982, Parker shifted direction a bit to take center stage as a solo artist. From then into the mid-1980s, most of his albums and many of his singles were crossovers reaching top sections of both the pop and the black-music charts. In 1982, he had two hit albums: *Greatest Hits* (which included most of his best-selling work with Raydio) and gold *The Other Woman.* The title song of the LP became a *Billboard* top 10 pop single. During the year he made the charts with the single "Let Me Go" and at year-end was represented by "Bad Boy," which rose into the top 10 on soul lists in 1983.

In 1983, Ray added to his accomplishments with several chart singles including the pop top 20 hit "I Still Can't Get Over Loving You." His third solo LP on Arista, *Woman Out of Control,* also made *Billboard* charts. Meanwhile, Ray was at work on another project that was to link his name with one of the most successful films of the decade, *Ghostbusters.*

With the help of his management, he was looking for the chance to take on some movie projects in the mid-1980s, but hadn't been offered or come across anything inspiring. Discussing the situation with Dick Clark on a Mutual Broadcasting program, he recalled: "Then at the last minute, here comes *Ghostbusters.* They showed me the film and said: 'We have about 60 songs for this already, but we don't like any of them. Can you come up with one?'"

Ray said he'd try and started work on a candidate right away. Within two days he had written and made a demo tape of the number. He told Craig Modderno of *USA Today:* "It's hard to write a song where your main objective is to use the word *ghostbusters!* In order for that to work I had to have something before it and after it. That's when I came up with the line, 'Who you gonna call?' I wanted to make a simple, easy song people could sing along with and not have to think about."

The film's producers decided almost immediately that he had hit the mark. It was a perfect setup to have the song and movie help each other. To back the single, which was to be released by Arista, a special video was prepared featuring not only Parker, but the film's stars, Bill Murray and Dan Aykroyd, with cameo contributions from well-known comedians and rock stars.

Everything fell into place—a music-industry supersuccess story. The film was one of the biggest-grossing comedy fantasies in movie history and the theme song was a hit both in video form and as a single. The 1984 single rose to the number one in *Billboard* the week of August 11, achieving multi-platinum sales. In the Academy Award nominations, "Ghostbusters" was selected as a finalist for best film song of the year and won a Grammy for Ray for Best Pop Instrumental Performance.

At the end of 1984, Ray had more recordings moving up the charts: the album *Chartbusters* and the single "Jamie." Both stayed on the lists into 1985. At the end of 1985, Ray had another LP on the charts, *Sex and the Single Man.*

Ray switched to a new label, Geffen, for his next album, *After Dark* (September 1987). The album credits included some illustrious names: among those contributing backing vocals were Natalie Cole and Philip Bailey.

PARLIAMENT: *See Clinton, George.*

PARSONS, GRAM: *Singer, songwriter, guitarist, band leader. Born Winter Haven, Florida, November 5, 1946; died Joshua Tree, California, September 19, 1973.*

Immensely talented, dedicated, but haunted by personal demons that cut his life distressingly short, Gram Parsons never achieved the stardom that seemed his creative due. But he left a legacy of original songs and influence on others that went a long way toward ultimately reaching his objective of uniting all segments of the pop music audience under the country-rock banner. As he said in the late '60s: "We want the rock fans at the Whiskey and the truck drivers at the Palomino to get together and talk to each other and understand each other."

Had he lived, he might have accomplished much of that. But his musical heirs, including the Eagles and Emmylou Harris, went a long way toward bringing Parsons' dreams to pass.

He was born Ingram Cecil Conner, son of a cattle and citrus farm heiress and country singer "Coon Dog" Conner, who worked on his mother's father's land. After Connor died in 1959, Gram's mother married Robert Ellis Parsons and Cecil became Gram Parsons. He showed musical talent at an early age, beginning piano lessons when he was only three. Growing up in the South, he loved country, gospel, blues, and rockabilly. At 13, he decided to learn guitar "because Elvis played one. . . . I can remember when Elvis first came down to town as second billing with Jimmie Dickens on the Grand Ole Opry Show. He was only about 18 then, and they had it in the local high school gym and everybody came."

It didn't take Gram long to become proficient enough as a guitarist to be a key performer in a teen band called the Pacers. "We played Everly Brothers and attempted Ray Charles. That lasted for six months. At 14, I joined a band called the Legends—for six months—this time playing Everly Brothers and Chuck Berry. We worked all through Florida, did lots of club and TV work. This was about 1960–61." From 1963 to 1965, he was in a folk quartet, the Shilos.

Intellectually as well as musically gifted, he was accepted at Harvard University in 1965. He attended that prestigious institution briefly. "Acid was the major reason I dropped out—I had taken so much of it. Remember, I was interested in psychedelic trips, so I checked into them on my own and dropped out of Harvard."

He never had dropped out of music, so he formed a new quartet, the International Submarine Band, while still in Cambridge, Massachusetts. He changed home base for the group to New York for a time in hopes of moving into the musical big time, then shifted again to Los Angeles. He did manage to record an LP *Safe at Home,* for Lee Hazlewood's LHI label there, but that proved a commercial flop and the final alignment of the Submarine Band (which he reorganized several times) broke up. The LP (reissued on Rhino Records in 1985) gave insight into Parsons' continued love for country, blues, rock, and folk, including songs from Merle Haggard, Johnny Cash, and Arthur "Big Boy" Crudup.

His next move was to the Byrds in 1968, where he had artistic kinship with country-oriented bassist/mandolinist Chris Hillman. The two helped persuade leader Roger McGuinn to go to Nashville to make the country-rock LP *Sweetheart of the Rodeo* with songs by Haggard, the Louvin Brothers, and Dylan plus two Parsons originals: "Hickory Wind" and "One Hundred Years from Now." A haunting country song, "Hickory Wind" was presented with great impact by Emmylou Harris on her 1979 album, *Blue Kentucky Girl.* Its lyrics express the disparate rural and city influences tugging at Parsons: "It's a hard way to find out that trouble is real/In a faraway city with a faraway feel/But it makes me feel better/Each time it begins/Calling me home, hickory wind."

But the Byrds' plans to play in segregated South Africa sat poorly with Gram. In 1969, he and Hillman left the Byrds to form their own band, the landmark country-rock Flying Burrito Brothers with bassist Chris Ethridge and pedal steel guitar maestro "Sneeky" Pete Kleinow. Byrds drummer Michael Clarke signed up subsequently, as did guitar, banjo, and dobro player Bernie Leadon, who later joined the original Eagles. The band's first LP, *The Gilded Palace of Sin* (A&M, 1969), included the gripping Parsons–Hillman composition "Sin City." The April 1970 follow-up, *Burrito Deluxe,* continued Gram's fusion of life-in-the-fast-lane rock with country gospel. It closed with a Mick Jagger–Keith Richard composition, "Wild Horses," reportedly written to Parsons (and not to Maryanne Faithfull, as many listeners had assumed), which the Stones themselves had not yet released. Bob Dylan, among other major rock stars, called the group a favorite of his. Despite the band's great promise, it was a few years ahead of its time. The idea of combining country and rock was still anathema to most rock and country fans.

Still, things might have gone better if Gram hadn't been sidelined by a motorcycle accident in early 1970. After he recovered, he returned to the Burritos for a short time, but his musical ideas had changed somewhat during his layoff and he left to concentrate on solo work. His initial solo efforts came to naught

in 1970 and he went to France for a while, partly at the behest of Rolling Stones members. Discussions of a solo LP by him on their own new label proved inconclusive.

Going back to Los Angeles, Parsons spent much of 1972 writing new material primarily in the country vein. This time he had record-company interest leading to release of his flawed but promising solo debut, *GP* (Warner Brothers) with stunning vocal accompaniment by his newfound protégé, future country star Emmylou Harris. Warners approved a follow-up that was to come out in 1973 under the title *Grievous Angel,* but by the time it appeared, Parsons was dead.

His passing resulted from the problem he long had fought with varying degrees of success—drugs. On September 19, 1973, he was found unconscious on the floor of his room at Joshua Tree Inn. He was rushed to the Yucca Valley High Desert Hospital, but died soon after arrival. A strange incident took place in ensuing days. His road crew stole his coffin from the airport where it was awaiting transport back to his home area and burned it near the Joshua Tree Monument—as he had told them he would want done.

After his passing, he attained cult-hero status for his musical ideas, his cracking but soulful vocals, and his brilliant writings—laced with the sin and salvation of his southern Protestant roots—that eerily forebode his end. In 1974, A&M put out a two-disc Burrito retrospective, *Close Up the Honky Tonks,* including "Wild Horses" and tracks from a never-released LP of rock oldies. *Sleepless Nights* (A&M, 1976) dug further into the vaults of tracks rejected for earlier albums. In 1979, Sierra Briar Records put out a lovingly annotated *The Early Years, 1963–1965,* recordings with the Shilos. Far more exciting was *Gram Parsons and the Fallen Angels—Live 1973* (Sierra, 1982), which captured his rough-edged genius in a Garden City, New York, radio broadcast on WLIR-FM.

Numerous Emmylou Harris albums have included songs by her mentor, Parsons, while her exquisite composition "Boulder to Birmingham" was written to him. Perhaps his biggest tribute was Harris's moving concept album *Ballad of Sally Rose* (Warner Brothers, 1985). Autobiography masked as fiction, it went from the singer's discovery of a young musician, his awakening her to the roots of country music, their love and breakup, her desolation over his self-destruction, and her vow to keep his music alive.

As she told a reporter: "Gram was a real pioneer. He cut straight through the middle with no compromise. He was never afraid to write from the heart, and perhaps that's why he was never really accepted. It's like the light was too strong and bright and people just had to turn away. They couldn't look at the light because it was all too painful. It could rip you up. Not many people can take music that real.

"If there's one thing in my life I really want to do, it's get Gram's music out in the open where it should be. A lot of people who would've appreciated him never got to hear him. . . . I feel like I've glided in at a time when people are beginning to listen to country music. But what I'm trying to get them to realize is that they should look a little behind me to all that was going on before with Gram and the Burritos."

(*See Byrds, The; Eagles, The; Rolling Stones, The.*)

PEACHES AND HERB: *Vocal duo. Original members: Francine Hurd, born Washington, D.C., c. 1947; Herb Feemster, born Washington, D.C., c. 1943. Group disbanded in early 1970s, revived in mid-1970s with Linda Greene as "Peaches."*

One of the most popular singing duets in popular music at the end of the 1960s, Peaches and Herb were nicknamed "the Sweethearts of Soul." The act, which actually employed several female singers as Peaches, consistently ranked among the top three or four soul duos according to industry-trade-magazine ratings of the period. When the act's fortunes declined sharply at the start of the '70s, Herb left the music field for a time, but with a new Peaches, achieved a comeback at the end of the decade.

Though the two original members were born and raised in the nation's capital, they didn't join forces until both were on the roster of the same recording company. Peaches, whose real name was Francine Hurd, received her nickname as a child, she said, because of her pleasant disposition. She already was singing with neighborhood groups in elementary school. In high school, she was the lead singer of a group called the Keytones. In her teens, she sang with a number of groups until she formed one of her own, the Darlettes, with two other Washington girls. In the mid-1960s, the group auditioned for Date Records and, upon signing, changed their name to the Sweet Things.

Already performing on the label as a soloist was Herb Fame (born Herb Feemster). Herb had started singing in church choirs at seven and performed with a number of neighborhood groups during his school years. After graduating from high school, he went to work in a large Washington record store. One of the customers was Dave Kapralik, a producer for Date. The two got into a conversation that led to Fame's asking for an audition.

After Fame signed with Date, Kapralik helped line up appearances on the soul circuit for him. Later, when the Sweet Things joined the tour package, Kapralik got the idea of combining the talents of Peaches and Herb. Their first single, "Let's Fall in Love" (1967), did well enough to prove his judgment was sound. The duo followed with a *Billboard* pop top 10 hit, "Close Your Eyes," and also placed their first album, *Let's Fall in Love,* on the charts in 1967. In mid-1967, their second LP, *For Your Love,* met with excellent response.

During 1967, Francine gave up touring and her place for live performances was taken by other vocalists. She did continue to record new material with Herb, including the top 10 R&B 1969 single "When He Touches Me." The *Cash Box* year-end assessment for 1969 ranked the act number two in the U.S. among soul duos. Other late 1960s hits included "For Your Love" and the number one R&B hit, "Love Is Strange" (a remake of Mickey and Sylvia's 1957 classic).

At the start of the 1970s, though, Herb Fame became depressed about what appeared to be a lessening of interest in the act among R&B and pop fans. He told an Associated Press reporter: "One day we were off work and I was riding down the street in Washington. I went in and took the exam for the Police Department. When they told me I had the job, I just quit Peaches and Herb and went to work for the city July 20, 1970. But I missed singing. That's why I'm back [in the late '70s]. In 1976 I started thinking Peaches and Herb could come back."

Though Herb Fame stepped down in 1970, Peaches and Herb as an act didn't fade out right away. The group was on the charts in 1970 with the single "It's Just a Game, Love" on Date Records and, in 1971, on a new label, Columbia, with "The Sound of Silence." And a new Peaches and Herb duo continued to perform widely in the early 1970s. By the mid-1970s, though, the group's name was out of circulation.

When Herb decided to reform the act in 1976, another Washingtonian, Linda Greene, was brought in as his partner. The act signed with MCA Records. Their first LP, produced by Van McCoy, was a flop. But their next effort, *2 Hot* (produced by Freddie Perren for Polydor Records), proved a turning point. The first single, the gold disco number "Shake Your Groove Thing," was a top 5 hit in March 1979. The next Polydor disc, the platinum ballad "Reunited" (written by Perren and Dino Fekaris), stayed at number one in *Billboard* for four weeks starting May 5, 1979.

The group followed with more charted singles and albums that year and in the early 1980s including the

LPs *Twice the Fire* (Polydor, 1979, gold), *Worth the Wait* (Polydor, 1980), and *Saying Something* (Polydor, 1981).

PENDERGRASS, TEDDY: *Singer, drummer, songwriter. Born Philadelphia, Pennsylvania, March 26, 1950.*

At the start of the 1980s, Teddy Pendergrass seemed on top of the world—an acknowledged superstar who turned out one million-selling record after another and who could pack adoring crowds into the largest arenas throughout much of the developed world. He had it all—fame, fortune, fast cars, palatial homes. Then in an instant in 1982, it all seemed a mirage when the car he was driving went out of control and was wrecked. Severely injured, Teddy was in danger of losing his life. He pulled through, but was paralyzed from the waist down and confined to a wheelchair. No longer would he stride across concert stages with pantherlike grace as his seductive, soulful voice whipped female onlookers into a romantic frenzy. Some of his friends feared Teddy's postaccident depression not only might end his career but could even make him suicidal. But he was built of sterner stuff. His voice had not been damaged and he came back to the entertainment field in the mid-1980s and also became a strong advocate of increased public concern and support for the disabled.

At the time of his accident, Pendergrass was barely 30 years old, but he had been involved in show business for most of his life and, as lead singer of Harold Melvin and the Blue Notes, a budding star since 1970. (*See Melvin, Harold, and the Blue Notes.*)

Teddy claimed he had shown promise as a singer when he was only two in his hometown of Philadelphia when his mother brought his talents to the attention of members of her church. Long before high-school age, he was singing gospel music in Philadelphia churches and was an ordained minister at 10. In public school, he sang with the citywide McIntyre Elementary School Choir and later in the All-City Stetson Junior High School Choir. He taught himself to play the drums before he was 13 and reverted to that instrument after a local record producer's promises to make stars of Teddy and his teenage pop vocal group turned out to be fool's gold. (Teddy recalled his first professional appearance as a secular performer came when he was 15.)

In his late teens, Teddy wasn't even working as a singer. Instead, he was a drummer with a backing band for a Philadelphia vocal group called the Cadillacs. That group and another called Harold Melvin and the Blue Notes were among the better-known acts in Philadelphia R&B/soul activities. The Blue Notes were the more established group. When Melvin, as a result of a reorganization in the late 1960s, approached the Cadillacs to fill out his group, the merger was agreed upon with the Cadillacs' band taken into the fold to provide instrumental support.

In 1970, when the revamped Blue Notes broke up again during a tour of the French West Indies, Melvin—increasingly aware of Teddy's vocal potential—asked Pendergrass to move into the front row. Teddy agreed. The result was a new vocal blend that won a recording contract in the early 1970s from Kenneth Gamble and Leon Huff's Philadelphia International label.

The first Blue Notes single release on which Teddy was spotlighted, ''I Miss You,'' made some R&B writers sit up and take notice. Tony Cummings of *Black Music* commented: ''The key to the record's massive chart success was Teddy Pendergrass' lead—jagged, hoarse, apparently on the verge of breakdown, but somehow always winning his struggle to articulate his sorrow. More chillingly desperate a sound has yet to be heard.''

The combination of Pendergrass's powerful lead vocals and Gamble and Huff's production and songwriting know-how soon made the Blue Notes national celebrities with a string of hits that included ''Bad Luck,'' ''Wake Up Everybody,'' and ''The Love I Lost.'' In the *Rolling Stone Record Guide*, such recordings were called ''among the greatest disco-soul records of the middle '70s, with hot tracks and really ferocious vocal attack.''

However, Teddy and Harold Melvin were not getting along well. According to news stories of the time, the split between the two revolved around Teddy's desire for more recognition as the driving force of the Blue Notes, a change that Melvin resisted. In 1976, they finally went separate ways. As has happened with other headline groups in the music industry, the dispute led for a time to two competing groups both claiming the Blue Notes' mantle. Since some of the members went with Teddy and some with Harold after the breakup, for a short while R&B fans found themselves trying to figure which was which between the Blue Notes featuring Teddy Pendergrass as opposed to Harold Melvin and the Blue Notes. But this was solved when Teddy decided to give up group singing and try for a solo career. He signed a new contract with Philadelphia International while Melvin and company moved over to ABC Records.

Teddy actually dropped out of sight for most of 1976 before moving into the solo phase in early 1977. Part of the reason, he admitted to a reporter, was legal problems. But he claimed there was another factor. "I wanted to take time to create an air of mystery. I wanted people to wonder what I was doing. I wanted them to be eager for the first album and the first tour. I wasn't worried about people forgetting me. People wouldn't forget me!"

Plenty of performers have taken that approach and found out just how easy it is for the public to forget. In Teddy's case, though, his talent wouldn't be denied. His platinum debut album, *Teddy Pendergrass* (spring 1977), spanned a series of excellent singles, such as "I Don't Love You Anymore," "You Can't Hide from Yourself," and "The More I Get, the More I Want." Though his wide-ranging series of concerts exhibited some rough edges in style and the shows suffered from some shortcomings in pacing, there was no doubt about Teddy's hypnotic effect on his audiences.

In the last years of the 1970s, Teddy consolidated his status as a giant of soul music. His next three solo albums—*Life Is A Song Worth Singing* (1978), *Teddy* (1979), and his in-concert *Teddy Live (Coast to Coast)* (1980)—all went gold or platinum. Among his singles hits of that period were "Close the Door" (gold, 1978) and "Two Hearts" (a 1981 duet with Stephanie Mills). Typical of the enthusiasm he generated among leading critics was the *New York Times* evaluation that declared Teddy "the most important pop and soul shouter since the Four Tops' Levi Stubbs."

He also could point to a growing list of honors, including Grammy nominations in 1977 and 1978, an American Music Award for best R&B performer of 1978, and selection by *Billboard* for the Pop Album New Artist Award for 1977. He also was presented with awards for his performing achievements and charitable contributions from the NAACP, *Ebony* magazine, and the Afro-American Historical and Cultural Museum. In the Disco Awards presentation ceremony at the Hollywood Palladium, he was named the Best Male Performer for 1979.

But he kept his eye on other challenges during that period. In early 1979, he agreed to star in a proposed movie about another soul supertalent, *The Otis Redding Story*.

In the early 1980s, Teddy had no trouble maintaining his momentum as a best-selling record artist, though his releases were somewhat slicker and more pop-oriented than his 1970s material. His fifth release on Philadelphia International, *TP* (summer 1980), went platinum. His chart singles during 1980 included "Turn off the Lights," "Come Go with Me," "Shout and Scream," "It's You I Love," and "Can't We Try." His late summer 1981 album, *It's Time for Love*, won gold recognition. His best-selling 1981 singles were "Love TKO" and "I Can't Live without Your Love." Though he didn't win a

Grammy in 1981, he again was one of the final five nominees in one of the categories.

Among his other projects during those years were a role in the movie *Soup for One* and merchandising projects (including a line of designer jeans) through his company Teddy Bear Productions.

There didn't seem to be a cloud on the horizon for Teddy in the early '80s. He still lived in Philadelphia, but in a setting far removed from the ghetto of his childhood. He told a reporter he had no apologies for living in style. "I love luxurious things. Why not? Why should I feel guilty about having luxuries and digging luxury. I've worked hard to be able to afford the good life. I'm having a ball. The way I see it, it's all uphill from here."

A minor car accident in early 1981 caused a few anxious moments among his fans, but he shrugged it off and soon was in the midst of another demanding tour, including a debut swing through Europe. That series began in May with three standing-room–only shows in London, where he was joined at the end of the final concert in a memorable duet with Stevie Wonder.

No too long after that, the near-fatal March 18, 1982 accident that restricted him to a wheelchair made questions about "suggestive movements" moot. But Teddy still had his voice. After months of physical therapy and emotional recuperation, he was ready to record and perform again. Making a break with the past, he left Philadelphia International and signed with Elektra/Asylum in 1983. After completing recording sessions for his label debut, he commented: "I think I've had a test. Everything is brighter to me now. I think I'm here for a reason, and that is to continue to bring forth good feelings in my music. If one must judge how I'm doing, let me talk to them through my new recordings."

The gold album, *Love Language* (May 1984) was his ninth solo LP overall and his first new studio album since *It's Time for Love*. (His old label, Philadelphia International, issued two albums based on outtakes from earlier recording sessions: *This One's For You* 1982 and *Heaven Only Knows* in 1983.) His next Elektra/Asylum album, *Workin' It Back* (late 1985), was well received by black record buyers, but had only a brief stay on the general pop hit lists. After a two-year gap, Teddy had a new LP on Elektra, *Joy,* issued in April 1988.

PENGUINS, THE: *Vocal group. Curtis Williams, born 1935; Dexter Tisby, born 1936; Cleveland Duncan, born July 23, 1935; Bruce Tate, born 1935.*

One of many groups that had major hits in the early days of rock and were unable to come up with a second one, the Penguins nonetheless are important in pop music history. Based in Los Angeles, the quartet built up a following among black R&B fans in the early 1950s before recording "Earth Angel" (a song written by Jesse Belvin, who in 1959 won fame for himself by singing "Guess Who"). Released on the independent Dootone label, the song became a major R&B hit in 1954 for the group. However, the lion's share of record royalties later accrued to a white group, the Crew Cuts, who covered the song for Mercury Records as they had done a little earlier with "Sh-Boom," a song first recorded by the black group the Chords. (Some experts single out "Sh-Boom" as the first true rock hit, since it preceded Bill Haley's first million-seller.)

In the mid-1950s, the Penguins were managed by songwriter Buck Ram, who ironically gained them a contract in 1956 with Mercury. Added almost as an aside was a second group managed by Ram, the Platters, who went on to fame and fortune, while the Penguins hit a dry spell and eventually broke up. (*See Platters, The.*)

PERKINS, CARL: *Singer, songwriter, guitarist, band leader. Born Tiptonville, Tennessee, April 9, 1932.*
Born the same year as his long-time close friend, Johnny Cash, Carl Perkins had a career that tended to parallel Cash's over the years. Both started as country performers, picked up on rock, became nationally known in that field in the mid-1950s, and then moved back into the country market in the '60s and '70s. Both also fought hard battles against drugs and other dangerous habits—and won out. But in terms of commercial success, there's no doubt that Cash had a considerable edge over the years.

Which isn't to downplay Perkins' considerable contributions to both rockabilly and country music. Along with Elvis, Jerry Lee Lewis, and Roy Orbison, he was part of the wave of young country-bred artists on the tiny Memphis, Tennessee-based Sun label who helped propel rock to its dominant status. His biggest milestone, of course, was his record of his composition "Blue Suede Shoes," done at Sam Phillips's Sun Studios on December 19, 1955. Early the next year, it topped charts in pop, country, and R&B.

One of the earliest anthems of teenaged identity, the song was inspired by a boy at a dance where Carl was playing. Poor but proud of his blue suede shoes, the youth wouldn't let anyone step too near them. At 3 in the morning after the dance, Carl got out of bed in his subsidized housing project and dashed off the song on a potato sack since there was no writing paper in the house.

Carl was to receive a gold record for it on the "Perry Como Show." Toward the end of March 1956, he left a concert in Norfolk, Virginia, to go to New York for the event. Early the next morning, though, he was almost killed in a car accident outside of Wilmington, Delaware. He stayed in bed for the better part of a year recuperating, during which time Elvis's version of "Blue Suede Shoes" eclipsed Carl's. Presley sent a note to Carl after his "Ed Sullivan Show" debut suggesting Perkins might have been the superstar if the accident hadn't occurred.

Though Carl had some minor rock hits in the late '50s, such as "Your True Love" on Sun and "Pink Pedal Pushers" and "Pointed Toe Shoes" on Columbia, his career languished after the accident. The frustration and despair led Perkins to do things that impaired his health including bouts of heavy drinking. At one point in 1963, he had about decided to quit show business when his wife persuaded him to take an offer to tour England with Chuck Berry. While there, the Beatles gave a party in his honor and later indicated their esteem for him by recording three of his classics: "Honey Don't," "Everybody's Trying to Be My Baby," and "Matchbox" (a rural blues standard popularized decades earlier by Blind Lemon Jefferson).

Still, back home for a while things went from bad to worse as far as Carl's outlook was concerned. Then, in the mid-1960s, as did Johnny Cash, Carl got his thinking straightened out and rebuilt his life and career. In 1965, Cash asked Carl to join him for a two-day concert appearance in the South. "We got there and John had me come up and do a couple of songs. That two-day tour lasted 10 years. That's how long I played with John." On Cash's network TV show from 1969–71, Perkins not only did backing work but generally had a solo spot during each program.

The TV exposure brought a new recording contract from Columbia that led to several LPs, including *Greatest Hits* and *On Top* (1969) and *Boppin' the Blues* (1970). Concentrating on the country field, Carl had several songs on the charts in the early 1970s, such as "Me without You" in 1971 and "Cotton Top" and "High on Love" in 1972.

In 1976, Carl left the Cash tour to organize a new band of his own. Continuing the country music tradition of family bands, it featured his sons Stan on drums and Greg on bass guitar. They were still part of the tour group when Perkins' debut album on a new label, Jet Records, came out in the fall of 1978. Called *Ol' Blue Suede's Back*, it included country-rock versions of several Perkins songs, including the title track, plus other artists' familiar early-rock numbers such as "Maybellene," "Whole Lotta Shakin' Goin' On," "Rock around the Clock," and the Arthur Crudup song that started Elvis on the road to superstardom, "That's All Right, Mama." In the 1980s, record companies specializing in reissues kept his early rockabilly classics in print on *Original Sun Greatest Hits* (Rhino) and several discs on England's Charly label. Less well-known Perkins compositions were found on albums by Emmylou Harris and the late Patsy Cline.

Charly, which had bought rights to all of Sun's tapes, released the first commercial version of a fabulous 1956 jam session at Sun's studios in Memphis called the *Million Dollar Quartet*. (Previously that material only was extant in bootleg tapes). It was called *Million Dollar Quartet* because it was believed it involved Elvis Presley, Jerry Lee Lewis, Johnny Cash, and Perkins, but later it was determined that Cash left before the session began. Sam Phillips had turned on his tape machine to record the music just for his own pleasure, but the tape was misplaced and didn't surface again until some time later.

After listening to the new version, Carl Perkins said he thought the session had lasted much longer. Later on, Charly archivists found additional session tapes, and in early 1988 the label issued a new two-disc set, *The Complete Million Dollar Session*.

Carl and sons were still touring in the late 1980s. For a while, he toyed with the idea of retiring, but in the mid-1980s put that thought aside as he gained new respect, particularly in England, as one of the founding fathers of rock. His career was buoyed by an acclaimed special show for cable TV during those years and his nomination as one of the first artists for the new Rock'n'Roll Hall of Fame.

Carl told Don Waller (*Los Angeles Times,* September 5, 1986), "I was all set to go off the road and spend the rest of my time huntin' and fishin'. I've got a house on the lake here [Jackson, Tennessee] that I've managed to buy with my songwriting royalties over the years.

"But I wanted to do just one television special 'cause I'd never had one of my own and I thought it would be sorta like a farewell gesture. So I got out my video machine and made little videos of myself and sent 'em to all the biggest dudes I'd met in all my years in the music business. I told 'em what I was plannin' and said if you'd like to be a part of it, please sign the postcard enclosed.

"I'll never forget walkin' into my lawyer's office, pullin' them postcards from out of my coat and seein' the look on his face. George Harrison, Dave Edmunds, Ringo Starr, the Stray Cats. All of 'em. Signed up and ready to go.

"And I'll tell you, when we went over to England to do that show, it was one of—if not the—highlight of this ol' rockabilly's musical career. To be up there playin' with those guys, really workin', seein' the

sweat drip down their noses, made me feel highly honored."

Instead of retiring, the event inspired him to stay on the concert circuit in the late 1980s backed by his Imarocker band, whose members were sons Stan and Greg and saxophone player Ace Cannon.

PETER AND GORDON: *Vocal and instrumental duo. Peter Asher, born London, England, June 22, 1944; Gordon Waller, born Braemar, Scotland, June 4, 1945.*

In the mid-1960s, Peter and Gordon were one of the most successful pop music teams in the world. In the long run, though, one of them, Peter Asher, probably has had far more impact on the music field from his activities as a record-industry executive, talent manager, and record producer.

Both boys came from well-to-do families and were sent to distinguished private schools. In their early teens, they met while studying at the Westminster School for Boys in London. Like many of the English academies, Westminster is a boarding school where the students live on campus in dormitories. In general, the rules are strict and students are not expected to be away from the campus during school sessions without permission.

Peter and Gordon became close friends and soon shared a growing interest in the folk and rock of the early '60s. The boys got themselves guitars and learned to play them. Whenever they found time, they worked up their own arrangements of some of the hit songs they heard on the radio or bought for their record collection. They won the approval of their classmates and soon were regularly asked to perform at school concerts. After a while, they felt they were good enough to try to work in some of the small London clubs. Because curfew in the Westminster dormitory was 9 PM, the boys had to sneak out over a 12-foot, spike-topped wall. They managed it for quite some time, though, and auditioned successfully for a series of jobs at coffeehouses and nightclubs.

In their late teens, the boys left school to concentrate on music. They taped a number of demonstration records and made the rounds of record companies. In late 1963, this finally paid off with a contract. Soon after, the boys recorded a song specially written for them by Paul McCartney of the Beatles, who was then courting Peter's sister, Jane Asher. Released in 1964, "A World without Love" became a top 10 English hit. Issued in the U.S. on Capitol, it made number one in *Billboard* the week of June 27.

Their style found favor with music fans of all ages, consisting as it did of ballad-type material superimposed on a soft-rock beat.

The team followed its first hit with a series of successes during 1965–67, such as "Knight in Rusty Armour," "Lady Godiva," "True Love Ways" (an oldie from Buddy Holly), "If I Were You," "I Told You So," "To Know You Is to Love You," "I Go to Pieces" (written by Del Shannon), "Don't Pity Me," "I Don't Want to See You Again," "Love Me Baby," "If You Wish," and "Woman." Most of these served as the centerpieces for equally high-selling LPs, including *World without Love* (1964), *Peter and Gordon* and *True Love Ways* (1965), *Best of Peter and Gordon,* and *History of Nashville* (1966), and *Lady Godiva, Knight in Rusty Armour,* and *In London for Tea* (1967).

In the late '60s, the team broke up. Peter accepted a bid from the Beatles to become managing director of their new Apple record firm. Among the newcomers he signed was a young North Carolinian named James Taylor. Taylor's first record on Apple didn't do too well when first issued, but Peter had great faith in the American's potential. He took over as Taylor's manager and soon lined up the recording contract with Reprise Records that started Taylor toward superstar status. Asher moved his headquarters to Los Angeles and, by the early 1970s, headed one of the major agencies for pop music talent in the U.S. Starting in the mid-1970s, Asher played a key part in Linda Ronstadt's rise to superstar status in his dual role of manager and record producer. His production work with Linda included her first number one LP and single (*Heart Like a Wheel* with its single "You're No Good") in 1974. He performed similar chores for a series of her best-selling LPs into the '80s. (*See Beatles, The; McCartney, Paul; Ronstadt, Linda; Shannon, Del; Taylor, James.*)

PETTY, TOM, AND THE HEARTBREAKERS: *Vocal and instrumental group headed by Tom Petty, born Gainesville, October 20, 1953. Original band members, all from Florida: Mike Campbell, Benmont Tench, Ron Blair, Stan Lynch. Blair replaced in 1982 by Howard Epstein, born Milwaukee, Wisconsin.*

For a long time, Florida's main claim to fame in rock annals was as the late 1960s proving ground for the Allman Brothers Band. In the early 1970s, it could point to the exploits of the ill-fated Lynyrd Skynyrd, but in the mid-1970s it was represented by a new band, Tom Petty and the Heartbreakers, that promised to rank with the best rock groups of all time.

Unlike the Allmans (who were born in Nashville, though they grew up in Daytona Beach), band leader Petty is a native Floridian, born and raised in Gainesville. However, as his albums and concerts quickly demonstrated, he was not in the Southern–bar-band,

raunch'n'roll tradition of either the Allmans or Lynyrd Skynyrd. Though all kinds of influences can be detected in Petty's work, his music essentially is in direct line of descent from the rock mainstream, a modern evolution of the contributions of people such as Presley, the Beatles, Rolling Stones, and Dylan. It incorporated some of the free-wheeling instrumental elements associated with new wave, which led some critics to lump the band with others in that genre. But Petty never was new wave, let alone a punk rocker. He varied stylings and tempos to suit his needs, while the lyrics he wrote or selected for the band avoided the cynicism or self-interest adapted by many punk/new wave writers.

Petty's love for rock went back to his childhood. When he was 11, an uncle working on the set of Elvis Presley's movie *Follow That Dream* took him along to watch the shooting. Caught up in the excitement, Tom became enthralled with the Elvis mystique, listening to Presley's records hour after hour and consciously copying his idol's dress and hair styles.

Rock became an obsession with Tom, who taught himself his first guitar chords from a Beatles songbook. He put together his first band at 13 and at 15 already was playing dates away from his hometown. His initial public exposure, he recalled, was the result of an act of false bravado. He told a girl at school he wanted to impress that he had assembled a band that already could play many hit numbers. She quickly asked him to perform at a school dance the following week and he said yes while knowing his so-called band knew hardly any songs.

He told an interviewer: "We hadn't played anywhere except in our garage, but I didn't want to lose face. I got the guys together and worked at five or six Rolling Stones songs. When the kids wanted to hear more, we just went to the same songs again. We didn't know anything else."

A disc jockey heard them play and told band members he could line up University of Florida gigs at $100 per show. The band was on its way. "We played the next day at a dance. I've been working at rock'n'roll ever since. I was on the road by the time I was 15. I eventually got thrown out of school. They even sent me to a shrink. He asked why I wanted to play rock'n'roll rather than go to school. I said it was more fun."

By the late 1960s, Petty's band, the Mudcrutches, had a considerable local reputation. The Allmans' surfacing as national recording stars in the early 1970s inspired the group to make a demo tape, pile into a VW van (with little or no folding money), and drive cross-country to Los Angeles in 1973. After a number of turndowns, the band was signed by Denny Cordell's Shelter Records (then the label of

517

Leon Russell and Joe Cocker). The recording sessions went poorly, though, and the group broke up. Cordell still had faith in Petty and got him together with some L.A. studio musicians for another try, but it still fell short of what Tom had in mind.

Petty refused to become discouraged. He told Robert Hilburn of the *Los Angeles Times* (June 28, 1981): "I think it must have been total preoccupation with music that kept me going during those times when nothing seemed to be happening. But you could also take great comfort in small steps. I was thrilled the first time we went to California. It didn't matter that we were still struggling. I had made it out of Gainesville. Nobody in my family had done that. It was real hard in the beginning to think I'd ever make it out of town either or that I'd have enough money to pay the rent, much less own my own house."

After deciding against working with a studio group, Tom began auditioning musicians for a new backing band. A number of performers who either had been in the Mudcrutches or known Tom and the band in Gainesville also were in L.A. by then, but Petty didn't think of contacting them. When the audition call went out, keyboardist Benmont Tench sought Petty out. Tench's original intention was to enlist Tom's help in preparing some demo tapes another label had asked him to submit. When the group got together, Petty found he was working with friends and acquaintances from back home. It soon occurred to him that he now had the band he was looking for. Tench forgot about his own demos and agreed to join the new band, which became the Heartbreakers. Besides Petty on lead vocals, guitars, and keyboards and Tench on piano and organ, the group comprised Mike Campbell on lead guitar, Ron Blair on bass guitar and cello, and Stan Lynch on drums and, occasionally, keyboards. While Petty took over as primary songwriter, all the members— particularly Campbell—contributed.

Its debut LP, *Tom Petty and the Heartbreakers*, came out in late 1976 on Shelter with ABC Records handling distribution. Promotion was slight, though. As of early 1977, few fans even knew the LP was available, much less the first singles: "American Girl" and "Breakdown."

But notice was being taken elsewhere. Reviewers for the British magazine *Sounds* heard the album and, based on reports from their American correspondents, cited the Heartbreakers as the Best New American Band. Then Nils Lofgren asked the group to join him as opening act for a 1977 U.K. tour. The band was so well received by English audiences that it was given the opportunity to headline its own tour. As a result, the debut album made the U.K. top 20.

This gave Petty more bargaining power to insist on better future support from ABC.

Meanwhile, he was beginning to win acclaim back home. As the band served the usual apprenticeship there as opening act for other bands (including Blondie and Be Bop Deluxe), its tightly packaged set proved it was a first-rate band, not the creation of the recording studio's engineer's console.

Now Petty had momentum building. ABC reissued "Breakdown," which became a hit, and the album also made it into the *Billboard* top 40. The album was just beginning to move up the charts when it was joined by the band's second album, *You're Gonna Get It*. Before long, growing ranks of concert goers were cheering renditions of "American Girl," "Breakdown," and "Anything That's Rock'n'Roll" from the debut album and "Listen to Her Heart," "Magnolia," "Restless" and "(My) Baby's a Rock'n'Roller" from the second LP. By the end of 1978, both albums had been certified gold by the RIAA.

Then ABC Records was purchased by MCA Records and Petty's career became embroiled in controversy. ABC had not only distributed Shelter Records, but had other contractual ties with that firm. MCA claimed that made Petty one of its artists, but Tom strongly disagreed. He stated: "I am not a piece of meat to be bought and sold at a supermarket cash register." He stressed an artist should have an emotional as well as a business tie to the company he recorded for. He also pointed out that there was a clause in his ABC contract stating that label couldn't sell the contract without his approval. With the agreement of band members, Petty decided to fight and the matter headed for the courts. During the summer of 1979, before the case was settled, Petty and the Heartbreakers took off on a concert series called the "lawsuit tour" to help bolster their finances.

As that storm arose, the band was recording material for its next LP, the platinum 1979 *Damn the Torpedoes*. Petty chose to pay for the sessions himself and the tapes were moved from one location to another to keep them from falling into the hands of MCA. At last, Tom ran out of money and had to file for bankruptcy. Eventually a compromise was reached in court where MCA agreed to let the group work for a new label, Backstreet.

Damn the Torpedoes eventually sold over 3 million copies in the U.S. alone. Petty also was ahead of his time in seeing the potential of music videos. The MTV channel wasn't in existence in 1979 when he prepared videos of two songs from *Damn the Torpedoes*: "Refugee" and "Here Comes My Girl."

When his next collection, *Hard Promises*, was

ready for release in 1981, MCA stated it would charge $9.98 for it instead of its normal $8.98. Petty again demanded a change, saying it wasn't fair to his fans to raise the price after they had helped make him and his band top record sellers. He told Patrick Goldstein of the *Los Angeles Times* (February 1, 1981): "For once in my life I'd like to make a record without a legal battle. It's just not fair to the kids who buy records. It all comes down to greed—MCA doesn't need a new [office] tower. And if we don't take a stand, one of these days records are going to be $20."

Petty won out and the multiplatinum album came out at $8.98. MCA supported the record by financing four music videos of its songs. The band also buoyed fans' interest with another intensive international tour. It brought on the usual mixed blessings of a tour: exhilaration at audiences' enthusiasm coupled with fatigue and sometimes depression from the pressures involved.

Tom told Hilburn: "Sometimes I feel like I'm just stepping back on the same carousel when I go on the road. You jump up, grab a horse, and go round and round. By the time we stopped touring last year [1980], we had been out for nine months and we were all a little nuts. We needed to get away from it for a while."

Guitarist Campbell commented: "I always like it the first couple of weeks, but it can get to you after that. These four walls get real old. If you're not going to chase women or do a bunch of drugs, there's not a lot left on the list. . . .

"Another hard thing about touring is coming off stage, where there is all this energy and adrenalin, and rushing back to the hotel and the silence. Going from one extreme to the other is real disconcerting. We tried drugs for a while.

"I find it hard to believe people can do cocaine all the time and continue in this business. It starts to mess with the music and with personal relationships. It can get you a little paranoid. You think you have played great because you have all this energy on stage. But you listen to the tapes after the shows and find you were playing everything twice as fast as you should have been."

In late 1982, the band's fifth LP, the platinum *Long after Dark,* came out. The first single from the album, "You Got Lucky," also was a *Billboard* top 20 hit in late 1982 and early 1983. Just before *Long after Dark* was recorded, Ron Blair had left and his place was taken by Howie Epstein.

Once the supporting tour for that album was over, Tom Petty decided to take a sabbatical for a while. He had not been happy with the LP's material (though to others it seemed a fine collection) and

wanted to take some time out to regain some creative perspective. As a result, no new Heartbreakers albums came out for three years.

In the interim, band members occupied themselves with many other projects, either together or separately. Their work could be found on mid-1980s albums by Bob Dylan, the Eurythmics, Stevie Nicks, 1960s star Del Shannon, Lone Justice, the Blasters, Rosanne Cash, Rank and File, the Ramones, Ry Cooder, T-Bone Burnett, and John Hiatt. Campbell added steadily to his songwriting credits. With Petty, he co-wrote "Ways to Be Wicked" for Lone Justice's debut LP and Stevie Nicks' hit "Stop Draggin' My Heart Around." With Eagle alumnus Don Henley, he co-wrote Henley's top 10 single "The Boys of Summer." During that period, Stan Lynch toured with T-Bone Burnett, while Howie Epstein backed John Hiatt in a number of concerts.

In 1984, the Heartbreakers rejoined Petty to record the platinum album *Southern Accents.* In it, the group broke new ground musically and thematically. Petty had not specialized in regional-style rock, but he never denied his Southern roots. In the new album, he made a knowledgeable and loving statement about his roots.

The LP actually was scheduled for fall 1984 release, but an odd incident delayed it until 1985. During final mixing of the tapes, Petty became frustrated with some of the material and rammed his hand against a wall, breaking it. There were anxious moments when he thought it might interfere with his instrumental abilities. He told Mikal Gilmore of the *Los Angeles Herald Examiner* (April 27, 1985): "Since I write on piano or guitar, it would have changed the whole feel of what I do. It would also have made a big difference with the band, because we work around the rhythm guitar a lot. So we just had to wait out the operation for the first five or six weeks, because I always took the attitude that I would play again. It seemed a little drastic to accept [not playing], you know." By summer, fortunately, he had recovered complete use of his hand.

The new album involved new creative alignments—Dave Stewart of the Eurythmics, for instance, co-wrote some material with Petty, but the package reflected Tom's observations on the South. When he took a close look at his home region, he told Gilmore: "There are subtle things that start to tear at you. I'd seen these people I'd grown up around, and one way or the other they were struggling with that idea of what's called the 'Southern tradition'—that conflict between old ways and new ideals. Some wouldn't accept the old tradition, but some would. The ones that did, for the most part, looked like their lives were totally lost. They'd given up all their dreams and bought a trailer and accepted that as the limits of their life. Then there were the ones that just refused to live by those restrictions. To me they seemed more hopeful, though a few still don't know exactly how to break out of it. Every time they do, there's a little bit of guilt, like they're breaking from a family tradition, so you see this real strong mix of emotions."

In September 1985, Petty and the Heartbreakers took time out from the concert trail to perform in Willie Nelson's Farm Aid benefit. There they became friends with Bob Dylan. One result was that Campbell, Tench, and Epstein took part in the recording sessions for Dylan's new LP, *Empire Building*. The other was that Dylan and Petty agreed to look for ways to work together in the future.

By the end of 1985, the video of *Southern Accents'* single "Don't Come Around Here No More" won the MTV Award for Best Special Effects and the Grand Prix for Best Video Clip at the Montreaux Golden Rose Television Festival in Europe. Late in 1985, the band had its first live album out (now on MCA, since it management had changed to comprise people for whom Petty had a closer affinity). Called *Pack up the Plantation,* it was high on the charts into 1986.

The Petty band and Dylan toured together in 1986. Featuring joint numbers by the headliners as well as separate sets for each, the tour began in the Far East. The Australia appearances provided material for a Home Box Office one-hour TV special of Petty and the Heartbreakers that also was released as a long-form video cassette through CBS/Fox Video Music.

The Petty/Dylan concert schedule included a one-month break in the spring of 1986 when Dylan had booked studio time for a new album. Dylan wasn't ready when the time arrived, as the Heartbreakers decided to use it themselves. The result was the 1987 MCA release *Let Me Up (I've Had Enough),* arguably one of the year's gems, filled from the opening bars to the closing track with passionate, free flowing, high octane music. Among the tracks was "Jammin' Me," co-written by Petty, Dylan, and Mike Campbell, which Petty stated in bio material for MCA that he and Dylan "wrote sitting around the table reading the newspaper, with just a guitar. We'd just kind of read a line out loud and every one that we liked we'd write down. There were times then I would start a line and Bob would finish."

That relaxed tone extended throughout the album. Petty told Jon Pareles (*The New York Times,* April 20, 1987), "It was after-hours stuff. We were trying to write songs, basically, and we'd arrange them into sets as if we were playing at a bar—five 45-minute sets a night. . . . The real magic of rock music is that

it sounds so free, which is why most good bands sound better when they're warming up. We almost had to trick ourselves to get that feeling on tape."

(See Dylan, Bob; Eagles, The; Eurythmics, The; Henley, Don; Lofgren, Nils; Lone Justice; Nicks, Stevie; Shannon, Del.)

PHILLIPS, ESTHER: *Singer. Born Galveston, Texas, December 23, 1935; died Carson, California, August 7, 1984.*

The debt of rock'n'roll to rhythm & blues has been acknowledged many times by the most important innovators in rock. Thus, the Beatles paid tribute to one of the early greats of R&B, Little Esther Phillips, when they featured her on their November 1965 BBC-TV show. Esther was well known to many British fans, who were deeply interested in the blues in the 1950s when it was all but ignored by most Americans. In 1965, though, Esther had finally become nationally famous in the U.S. in the second and most successful phase of her career.

Among the many R&B artists discovered by bandleader Johnny Otis, none displayed more talent and artistry than Little Esther Phillips. She had great influence on many aspects of pop music from the '50s on, a fact recognized by many of her peers. In 1973, when both she and Aretha Franklin were nominated for Best R&B Vocal Performance, Female, and Aretha was named the victor, Aretha gave the trophy to Esther, saying Phillips was the rightful winner. Unfortunately, like many of her friends and associates, she could not resist the temptation of ever-present drugs, and addiction problems helped shorten her life and probably prevented her from rising to even more notable performing heights.

Born Esther Mae Jones, she sang in church as a child, but was so excited by Dinah Washington's jazz and blues that she would save her milk money to play Dinah's songs on the juke box on her way home from school. Before her teens, her family moved from Texas to Los Angeles. In 1949, at 13, she entered a local talent show and walked off with first prize. In the audience was band leader Johnny Otis. Recognizing her great ability, he asked her to join his group.

Through 1951, she toured with Otis as his vocalist, billed as Little Esther. She was featured as a soloist, with Otis, or with other members of his band on numerous R&B hits on the Savoy label. In 1950, her best-selling efforts included "Double Crossin' Blues" with the Robins, "Far Away Places" with Otis, and "Cupid Boogie," "Deceivin' Blues," and "Wedding Blues" with Mel Walker. Deciding to work as a solo, she signed with Federal Records in 1951, scoring a major R&B success the next year with "Ring-A-Ding-Doo." Federal tracks with Billy

Ward's Dominoes included the droll, risqué "The Deacon Moves In." But as she traveled the grueling Chitlin' Circuit, the ravages of the road, hard drugs, and drink took their toll. Seriously ill, she retired from show business for much of the 1950s, settling in Houston, Texas.

At the start of the '60s, having overcome her problems, she resumed her career with the newly formed Lenox Records. Too old to call herself "Little Esther," she chose a new name after noticing a Phillips 66 gasoline billboard. In 1962, she rose to international stardom with the best-selling single of her career, an R&B version of the country standard "Release Me" (which Engelbert Humperdinck revised yet again into a pop hit in 1967). When Lenox went bankrupt, Alantic bought her contract, reissuing her Lenox LP *Release Me* under the new title *The Country Side of Esther Phillips* along with such new albums as *Esther* and *Burnin'* plus the 1965 hit single "And I Love Him." In 1966, she was featured at the Newport Jazz Festival, returning there and to other festivals later in the decade.

The next decade began auspiciously for her with many prestigious appearances in 1970, including the Monterey Jazz Festival in California and Quaker City Jazz Festival in Philadelphia. During the year, her Atlantic album *Burnin'* made jazz and soul charts. Her single "Set Me Free" also was on soul lists in 1970.

Switching from Atlantic to the Kudu label, Esther enjoyed 1972 hit singles "Baby, I'm for Real," "Home Is Where the Hatred Is," and "I Never Found a Man (to Love Me Like You Do)" and the album *From a Whisper to a Scream* (a Grammy nominee). The album *Alone Again (Naturally)* (1972) also made the charts.

Into the 1980s, Esther continued to be one of the most highly respected artists in the blues and jazz-rock categories with her musical peers and critics, but she was mostly overlooked by the pop audience at large. Her albums included, on Atlantic, *Confessin' the Blues* (1975); on Kudu, *Black-Eyed Blues* (1973) and *Capricorn Princess* (1976); on Power, *Little Esther Phillips* (1975); and on Mercury, *You've Come a Long Way Baby* (1977), *All About Esther Phillips* (1978), *Here's Esther . . . Are You Ready* (1979), and *A Good Black Is Hard to Crack* (1981).

Two days before she was to give a scheduled show at the Los Angeles Wilshire Ebell Theatre, heart and liver ailments caught up with her. She was rushed to UCLA-Harbor Medical Center in Carson, California, where she died on August 7, 1984. Yet she lives on through her recordings. That year, Savoy Jazz put out the two-LP *Little Esther Phillips: The Complete Savoy Recordings,* 1949–59 sessions including her work with Johnny Otis. The next year, England's Charly Records reissued 1951–53 Federal tracks on *Bad Baad Girl.* Named after her 1951 single "I'm a Bad Bad Girl," it was a sad epitaph for a troubled singer who had done so much over so many years for soul and R&B. (*See Dominoes, The; Humperdinck, Engelbert; Otis, Johnny; Washington, Dinah.*)

PICKETT, WILSON: *Singer, songwriter. Born Prattville, Alabama, March 18, 1941.*

The story of Wilson Pickett, not unexpectedly, is similar to dozens of other R&B greats of the 1960s and '70s: early years in the rural South, a move to the industrial North with his family, gospel training, and finally stardom in rhythm & blues.

In Pickett's case, the hometown was Prattville in central Alabama, near Montgomery, where he completed grade school and part of high school. He started singing in church at an early age and continued on to join small-town gospel groups before his family left for Detroit, Michigan, in the mid-1950s. Motor City offered plenty of opportunity for good gospel performers at the time and teenaged Pickett sang with a series of groups from 1955 to 1959.

In 1959, Willie Schofield of the Falcons (one of the better-known R&B acts for "You're So Fine") heard Pickett sing. He convinced his teammates that Wilson would be an important addition to the group (which also included Eddie Floyd—who had the solo hit "Knock on Wood" in 1966—and Joe Stubbs, brother of Levi Stubbs of the Four Tops). Pickett joined and in a short time was contributing original songs. He wrote dozens that the Falcons incorporated in their act, including "I Found a Love" that became a chart hit for the group in 1962 on the LuPine label.

Pickett became known in the Detroit-area music industry. In 1963, Wilbur Golden, head of Correctone Records, arranged an audition for Wilson with former R&B star Lloyd Price, who was then head of a small R&B label, Double LL Records. (*See Price, Lloyd.*) Price liked Pickett's style and signed him. Soon after, Double LL, issued Wilson's first solo single: his own composition, "If You Need Me." The song became a hit on the R&B charts (and later was recorded by Tom Jones, the Rolling Stones, Bill Doggett, and Solomon Burke) as did another from Wilson's pen, "It's Too Late" (also 1963).

The following year, Pickettt's contract was purchased by the major national label Atlantic. With the distribution gained from this arrangement, Pickett greatly increased his airplay across the U.S. In 1965, his "In the Midnight Hour" moved to number one on the R&B charts and was a major pop hit as well, establishing Pickett as a star to rank with James Brown, Otis Redding, and Marvin Gaye.

His single hits of the 1960s included "Don't Fight It" (1965); "Mustang Sally" plus two number one R&B hits ("634-5789" and "Land of a Thousand Dances") in 1966; and "Funky Broadway" in 1967. Coming into the 1970s, Pickett took advantage of the gradual merging of R&B with rock and other pop music forms to score even more impressive successes. His 1970 pop top 30 single "Sugar, Sugar" was followed by "Engine Number 9" which moved into *Billboard*'s top 15 in November 1970. In 1971, "Don't Let the Green Grass Fool You" and "Don't Knock My Love, Part 1" went gold.

Pickett's albums of the 1960s included *Great Hits* on the Wand label and, on Atlantic, *In the Midnight Hour, The Exciting Wilson Pickett, The Best of Wilson Pickett, Wicked Pickett, The Sound of Wilson Pickett,* and *Great Hits. In Philadelphia* (1970) and *The Best of Wilson Pickett, Volume 2* (1971) also did well.

In 1972, he made the pop and/or soul charts with the singles "Fire and Water," "Funk Factory," and Randy Newman's droll composition "Mama Told Me Not to Come" and the album *Don't Knock My Love.* The following year, he switched labels to RCA for moderate-hit LPs *Mr. Magic Man* and *Miz Lena's Boy* in 1973. That sales decline reflected Wilson's difficulties in adapting his 1970s material to the changing demands of the pop audience, who no longer sought soul stylings of the '60s. Other RCA albums such as *Join Me and Let's Be Free* (1977) also made little dent on the top chart levels. Nor did the album issued on his own label, Wicked Records, and the excellent 1978 collection on Big Tree Records, *A Funky Situation.* For fans of his early vocal stylings, for a time in the late 1970s record stores made available such albums as *The Sound of Wilson Pickett,* a collection of Atlantic hits reissued in Japan, and *Wickedness,* an album released on the Trip label that presented material he had originally recorded on the Double LL label before signing with Atlantic.

In the 1980s, as had been true in the '70s, Pickett continued to be active on the concert circuit, playing mostly smaller clubs and concert halls around the U.S. and abroad. Though he didn't command the following of his glory days, it wasn't through loss of power. As Don Waller commented after attending a 1982 concert at the Los Angeles Country Club venue: "His magnificent torn-and-frayed voice hasn't deteriorated one bit. . . . On the dance tunes, Pickett's hard-edged vocals and trademarked white-hot scream cut through the tough, choppy rhythms like a new saw."

In the late 1970s and early 1980s, Pickett recorded new material for another major label, EMI Records, including *I Want You* (1979) and *The Right Track* (1981). (*See Burke, Solomon; Jones, Tom; Newman, Randy; Price, Lloyd; Rolling Stones, The.*)

PINK FLOYD: *Vocal and instrumental group. Original personnel (1964): Syd Barrett, born England; Roger Waters, born Cambridge, England, September 6, mid-1940s; Nicky Mason, born London, England, January 27, mid-1940s; Rick Wright, born London, England, January 28, mid-1940s. In 1968, Barrett replaced by David Gilmour, born Cambridge, England, March 6, mid-1940s. Waters left in 1983.*

During its first years of existence, Pink Floyd established itself as one of the more controversial groups in rock. It was hailed immediately by many critics as a band that would help set the tone for the pop music of the 1970s, while others termed its compositions formless and boring. By the mid-1970s, though, few could argue that it was not one of the more innovative bands in rock, willing to take chances as it experimented with new sound techniques and musical concepts. For many, it remained a love-hate relationship—it was hard for rock fans to be neutral about Pink Floyd's blend of rock, progressive jazz, country, blues, and electronic music.

The band can be said to have gone through two main phases. The first, from 1964 to 1968, was sparked by the group's original lead guitarist, Syd Barrett. A gifted songwriter, he helped found the first foursome, whose other members were Roger Waters on bass guitar, Richard "Rick" Wright on keyboards, and Nicky Mason on drums.

The member probably most responsible for the group's sound of the late '60s and later years, composer and lead singer Roger Waters, grew up in the university town of Cambridge, England, where one of his school friends was David Gilmour. Gilmour, who could play excellent lead guitar in his teens, decided to go out on his own after finishing the English equivalent of high school in the early '60s. After working for a time as a male model, he went to Paris, where he formed a rock group and toured Europe for several years. Meanwhile, Waters headed for London to study architecture at the Regent Street Polytechnic, where he met the other members of the future Pink Floyd.

In college, Waters maintained interests in music and electronics as sidelines. His fascination with unusual electronic effects was shared by fellow student Rick Wright, who was studying both architecture and music. Wright had learned to play piano, harmonium, harpsichord, and cello before coming to Regent Street Polytechnic and had developed an interest in electronic compositions, especially those written by Stockhausen. Many of these interests were shared by another architecture major, Nicky

Mason, an excellent tympanist. An acquaintance who shared their interests was eccentric but brilliant Syd Barrett, who became the catalyst for a new band.

In 1964, Barrett, Waters, Wright, and Mason formed Pink Floyd, starting by playing some of their original material, mostly provided by Barrett, for classmates, then at small gatherings in the London area. Their melange of hyperamplified sound, intricate light patterns, and almost concert-length renditions (some songs lasted 20 or more minutes) gradually brought them a large following within the burgeoning London rock underground.

Its first LP, *Pink Floyd*, was issued on the Tower Records label in September 1967. By then, as Richard Cromelin wrote in biographical notes for Capitol/Harvest Records: "The rather wiggy Barrett had developed into the creator of a style as strong and distinctive as anything that was being turned out by his fellow British rockers. Starting with a melodic aptitude that gave birth to some tunes that were as simple, as endearing, and as rich in that evocative but elusive 'British feel' as [exemplified] by the music of Ray Davies, he combined equal portions of English psychedelic fairy-tale rock, electric free-form amorphous rock, and his own mad-gleam-in-the-eye humor to come up with a product whose point of origin could as easily be the bowels of an insane asylum as a recording studio. Barrett-vintage Pink Floyd music is unavoidably insane, swimming in that glorious ecstatic madness that is undeniably, disturbingly real."

Drug experiments, particularly with LSD, sidelined Barrett in 1968. He was hospitalized for a time, though he turned out solo albums in succeeding years. His place was taken by Gilmour, whose songwriting talents were strongly supplemented by original work by Waters and Wright, some of which was presented on the second Tower album, *A Saucer Full of Secrets* (July 1968).

Impressed with the group's talents, avant garde filmmakers began asking Pink Floyd to write scores for new movies. This resulted in much praised material for Peter Whitehead's *Let's All Make Love in London* and Paul Jones' *The Committee*. The *More* soundtrack (Tower, 1969) included the hit "Cymbelline." During 1969, the group worked on a new album, *Ummagumma* on Harvest (dubbed "the underground event of the year" by England's *Music Business Weekly*), and on Italian film director Michaelangelo Antonioni's *Zabriskie Point*.

The group continued to work both on new material and on electronic systems to go with it, culminating in 1969 with the band's 360-degree stereo system. The aim of this effort, Waters said, was "to throw away the old format of the pop show standing on a square stage at one end of a rectangular room and running through a series of numbers. Our idea is to put the sound all around with ourselves in the middle. Then the performance becomes more theatrical. And it needs special material—it can include melodrama, literary things, musical things, or lights."

During 1970, Harvest released *Atom Heart Mother,* with a six-section tone poem making up the entire first side. The reverse side's "If" and "Alan's Psychedelic Breakfast" demonstrated that the group members could write and perform rock of highly melodic content.

The accompanying tour introduced the band's 360-degree stereo system to U.S. audiences in arrangements that included a 10-piece orchestra and 20-member choir. The effect was notable, most critics agreed. The *Los Angeles Free Press* reviewer wrote, with an air of astonishment: "The great thing about Pink Floyd is that they can make the freaks sit down and listen. It was not an easy thing to do; it was obvious that a lot of the 3,700 people were there to trip. . . . When the sound from the multitrack 360-degree sound system started moving around the room, the people were forced into submission to be able to appreciate the effect. From then on, it was an honest concert with the audience in their seats LISTENING."

Harvest Records' retrospective *Relics* (July 1971) was followed by a new album, *Meddle,* which had a song format on one side and the electronic composition "Echoes" on the other. In June 1972, Harvest issued *Obscured by Clouds,* an album featuring music from the movie *The Valley.* Arguably a rock masterpiece, *Dark Side of the Moon* (1973) became an all-time best-seller, remaining on the *Billboard* charts into 1988 for over 700 consecutive weeks on the lists. The CD of *Dark Side,* issued in August 1984 went gold in the fall of 1987.

In the mid-1970s, the group switched record labels, signing with Columbia for platinum albums *Wish You Were Here* (1975), *Animals* (1977), and *The Wall* (1979). In support of the *Animals* album, the band devised an elaborate stage show that included huge inflated figures for presentation in outdoor stadiums such as the California Angels' baseball park in Anaheim. Typically, crowds of 50,000 or more jammed in to see the shows. Another ambitious effort was *The Wall,* a concept group of songs used in a dramatic stage offering that told a complete story. In the concerts, the problems of society expressed in the songs led to the construction of a wall on stage that later was torn down as the climactic event of the show. The two-disc album provided the group's first *Billboard* number one single "Another Brick in the Wall, Part 2." In the early 1980s, the film *The Wall* was released.

But by then, members of Pink Floyd were becoming increasingly restless with group restrictions. Some were already turning out solo albums such as the solo debut *David Gilmour* (Columbia, 1978). Soon after Columbia issued the band's *A Collection of Great Dance Songs* in 1981, it was announced that Rick Wright was leaving. The remaining threesome indicated they still could provide fresh musical insights with the LP *The Final Cut* (1983), though critical reaction was quite mixed. The LP did go platinum, but by previous Pink Floyd sales standards it represented something of a comedown.

After *The Final Cut* was completed, Waters departed to begin a solo career. His first LP, *The Pros and Cons of Hitchhiking* (1984) on Columbia, established his credentials as a star in his own right. He followed that with *RADIO K.A.O.S.* (June 1987). Meanwhile, Gilmour and Mason had decided to revive Pink Floyd and started work on a new album on a boat in English waters that had been turned into a floating studio. When work on the new LP was a little over half finished, Wright agreed to rejoin.

When the new Pink Floyd collection, *A Momentary Lapse of Reason,* came out in late summer of 1987 (and soon went platinum), it brought anguished complaints from Waters, who maintained the others didn't have the right to the Pink Floyd name and took legal action to try to prove it. At Waters' concerts, T-shirts were on sale with the logo "Which One's Pink?" The other three seemed to have the last laugh; where Pink Floyd typically drew capacity crowds to 1987–88 concerts in major U.S. cities, this was not always true for Waters' shows. Gilmour, who had taken over Waters' mantle as chief Pink Floyd composer, wasn't bashful in making barbed retorts to Waters' statements to the press. Among other things, he said the group was a lot happier and its recording sessions and concerts no longer drudgery now that "that person" was gone.

PITNEY, GENE: *Singer, songwriter, guitarist, pianist. Born Hartford, Connecticut, February 17, 1941.*

In a varied career that spanned roughly a decade of stardom, Gene Pitney did well in several areas of music: rock, pop, and country & western. He provided hit songs for many artists, but his own recording successes were gained with other writers' compositions.

Gene was born into a reasonably comfortable environment in Hartford, Connecticut. He had a normal upbringing, studied piano and drums, and took a year of guitar lessons in his teens. His main interest was songwriting, though, and he had already placed songs with New York music publishers by the time he finished Rockville High School and went on to the University of Connecticut. He dropped out before gaining his degree, although he took courses at Ward's Electronic School with the thought of possibly working in that field. Understanding electronics came in handy when he started developing equipment for some of his multivoice recordings.

By the start of the '60s, Gene had become known to the music industry as a promising songwriter. A number of rock stars of the '50s recorded his material, including Ricky Nelson, Tommy Edwards, and Roy Orbison. Becoming dissatisfied with songwriting alone, Pitney started work on his own renditions, turning out the single "I Wanna Love My Life Away" on which he did seven separate voice tracks. He then mixed down the tapes to create his first hit on Musicor Records in 1961, followed by another success, "Town without Pity."

The top songwriting duo of Bacharach and David teamed with Pitney for film-title-song hits "24 Hours from Tulsa" (1962) and "The Man Who Shot Liberty Valance" (1963). Gene also scored a hit with their "Only Love Can Break a Heart." The Bacharach-David movie songs often were for westerns, which fitted in well with Musicor's main focus—country & western. One result was Pitney's move toward songs aimed at the country market.

During the mid-1960s, Gene did well in country, pop, and folk. "Looking through the Eyes of Love" (1965), written by the well-known team of Barry Mann and Cynthia Weil, sold a million copies worldwide for him.

Until the late 1960s, Pitney was one of the top album performers for Musicor with *Only Love Can Break a Heart* (early '60s); *Gene Pitney Sings Just for You, Many Sides of Gene Pitney,* and *World-Wide Winners* (1963); *Gene Pitney Meets the Fair Young Ladies of Folkland,* and *Gene Pitney's Big 16* (1964); and *Gene Pitney Show, Being Together, More Big 16, Volumes 2 and 3, Espanol, Famous Country Duets, I Must Be Seeing Things, It Hurts to Be in Love, Gene Italiano, It's Country Time Again* (with George Jones), *Looking through the Eyes of Love,* and *Nessuno Mi Puo Guidicare* (all 1966).

During the late '60s, Pitney had several hit singles in the U.S., such as "Heartbreaker," but he no longer commanded a mass audience. However, he maintained his high level of popularity with English fans. In the late '60s and early '70s, he had a number of hit singles and albums on the English charts that didn't make it in America. In late 1968, for instance, he made the English top 40 with the single "Yours Until Tomorrow" and, in the fall of 1970, was represented by "Shady Lady."

Soon after that, Pitney gave up his entertainment efforts. Little was heard of him for several years until he resurfaced in 1975 with an album on Bronze

Records, *Pitney '75*. This was followed by another long stretch of inactivity punctuated by occasional rumors that Gene was working on another comeback collection.

During the 1970s, Pitney had a number of albums still available in record stores of his earlier material, though almost all were out of print by the 1980s. These included the Musicor LPs *This Is Gene Pitney (Singing the Platters' Golden Platters)*, originally issued in 1969, *A Golden Hour of Gene Pitney* (1972), and *Double Gold: the Best of Gene Pitney;* Trip Records' *Sixteen Greatest Hits;* Springboard Records' *Gene Pitney;* and Hallmark Records' *A Town Without Pity* and *Greatest Hits, Volume 1*. In the 1980s, Rhino Records put out the two-disc *Anthology 1961– 1968*. (*See Bacharach, Burt; Nelson, Rick; Orbison, Roy.*)

PLANT, ROBERT: *See Led Zeppelin.*

PLATTERS, THE: *Vocal group. Original members: Tony Williams, born Roselle, New Jersey, April 5, 1928; David Lynch, born St. Louis, Missouri; Paul Robi, born New Orleans, Louisiana; Herbert Reed, born Kansas City, Missouri. Zola Taylor added in 1955.*

In many ways, the smooth vocal blend of the Platters was closer to the Ink Spots than to rock'n'roll. But the group proved that the popular music of past eras could still hold the attention of the rock generation if performed in arrangements updated to provide the rhythmic patterns of the day. Ironically, as rock and the Platters simultaneously moved to the forefront of pop music, the Platters shifted back toward soothing crooning, successfully swimming against the tide.

One reason for the predominance of 1940s-type material in the group's repertoire was the control exercised by its manager, Buck Ram. Ram, a successful songwriter for many years, discovered the original Platters, using them initially to make demonstration records of his own compositions. Ram secured the quartet and another of his acts, the Penguins (*see Penguins, The*), contracts with Mercury Records, which used a realigned Platters' redone rendition of Ram's song "Only You" as the act's first release on the label.

All of the original members of the group were born outside California. However, they came to Los Angeles, on their own or with their families. Founded by Herbert Reed in 1953, the group recorded on the Federal label, but the going was slow. In 1954, the boys were working as parking lot attendants when they met Ram. Within a short time after their second version of "Only You," they were performing in rock concerts, on TV, and in major nightclubs all over the world.

The success of "Only You," which reached number one on the R&B charts in 1955 and the top 10 on national lists, gained them a long-term contract from Mercury. For their next recording session, Zola Taylor (a sister of Cornell Gunter of the Coasters) was added to the original foursome of Tony Williams, David Lynch, Paul Robi, and Herbert Reed. (*See Coasters, The*). The first single of the new group was an even bigger hit than "Only You." Called "The Great Pretender," it moved to the number one spot on both R&B and general popular lists in the U.S. and Europe. Decades later, the gold record remains one of the classics of modern popular music.

Through the late 1950s, the Platters remained one of the premier teams in pop music. In 1956, they enjoyed top 10 hits "It Isn't Right" and "The Magic Touch" and hit number one with the dramatic gold "My Prayer" (an updated version of 1939 hit). In 1958, the group revived two more oldies for gold number one hits: "Twilight Time" (co-written by Buck Ram and Al and Morty Nevins in 1944) and Jerome Kern's "Smoke Gets in Your Eyes" (composed for the 1933 musical, *Roberta*). The group closed out the '50s with another top 10 disc, "Enchanted."

One of the reasons for the group's decline in popularity in the 1960s was a headline-making incident of August 10, 1959. The four men in the group were arrested in a Cincinnati hotel room for using drugs and soliciting prostitutes. The negative publicity caused many radio station programmers to refuse to play Platters recordings and many of the group's concert dates were canceled. The group, which had achieved three number one singles on *Billboard* lists during the second half of the '50s, never approached that pinnacle thereafter.

Fred Bronson in *The Billboard Book of Number One Hits* cited comments by Ron Grevatt of *Billboard* (August 17, 1959) on the seeming unfairness of the situation. "The story . . . is a good illustration of the kind of pressure any performer . . . is constantly under to avoid those human failings in which many people—stars and the common man—become involved. . . . It has already been noted that had the four Platters been four itinerant businessmen and had an issue of race not been involved, the matter would not have become a subject of scrutiny. . . . Is it fair to let this grievous incident become the source of permanent damage to the career of the Platters?"

The four were let off by the judge with a reprimand, but fair or not, the Platters never regained the heights of the late 1950s though the group continued to be a popular concert act. Contributing to the group's decline—perhaps even more so than the morals arrests—was Tony Williams' 1960 decision to leave the group for a career as a soloist. His place was taken by Los Angeles native Sonny Turner, a fine singer, but one lacking the emotional depths Williams provided. Other changes in the early 1960s included replacement of Robi and Zola Taylor by New Yorkers Nate Nelson and Sandra Dawn.

Into the 1960s, the Platters continued to be represented on record-store racks with a steady series of Mercury albums. These included *The Platters, Remember When,* and *The Flying Platters* from the 1950s. In the 1960s, Mercury released *Encore of Golden Hits* and *Reflections* (1960); *More Encore of Golden Hits; Encore of Broadway Hits* (1962); *All Time Movie Hits, Latino,* and *Moonlight Memories* (1963); *Golden Hits of the Groups* and *10th Anniversary Album* (1964); *New Soul Campus Style* (1965); and *I Love You 1000 Times* (1966). In the early 1970s, Musicor reissued some of the group's early material in the LP *Only You.* Another Musicor '70s repackage was the album *Double Gold Platters.* Also available during the decade were such reissues as Trip Records' *Sixteen Greatest Hits* and, on Federal Records, *Nineteen Hits* from its pre-Mercury period. In the 1980s, Rhino put out the two-disc *Anthology* of their Mercury sessions.

The group having the official Platters title (handled by Ram, who held copyright title to the name) continued to be active on the concert circuit into the 1980s. In the early 1970s, the group was featured in a number of Richard Nader's rock'n'roll revival shows. Pseudo Platters groups continued to spring up from time to time, which kept Ram busy filing suits to prevent unauthorized use of the name.

POCO: *Vocal and instrumental group. Personnel (mid-1971): Richie Furay, born Dayton, Ohio, May 9, 1944; Jim Messina, born Harlingen, Texas, October 30, 1947; Rusty Young, born Long Beach, California, February 23, 1946; George Grantham, born Oklahoma, November 20, 1947; Timothy B. Schmit, born Sacramento, California. Messina replaced in 1971 by Paul Cotton, born February 26, 1943. Furay left in 1973, Schmit in late 1970s.*

The reason why the Buffalo Springfield is considered one of the landmark groups in rock music is evident from the later careers of that relatively short-lived aggregation. Steve Stills and Neil Young became superstars as solo artists and as members of Crosby, Stills, Nash & Young. Two other onetime members of the "Herd," Richie Furay and Jim Messina, formed the nucleus of Poco, one of the more important rock bands of the early 1970s. While it never quite realized its full potential, Poco had a major influence on the country-rock of the '70s and '80s.

Furay, who was rhythm guitarist, vocalist, and contributor of original songs to the Buffalo Springfield, started to learn guitar at eight. During his college years, he moved from folk to rock because of his friendship with Steve Stills. While with the Herd, he became acquainted with Jim Messina, who took over as bassist with the group during its last seven months of existence in 1968.

Messina grew up in a country-music–oriented family. His father, a country musician, started Jim on guitar at an early age. At 13, Jim started playing in local bands in Colton, California, where his family had taken up residence. After high school, he worked as a producer with a small record company before moving on to employment as an engineer and producer in Hollywood recording studios. He supervised recordings of many major groups, including the Buffalo Springfield. After joining that group, he not only performed with them, but also produced their last album, *Last Time Around.*

Soon after this, he and Furay decided to found their own group, called Pogo at first. They added Rusty Young on pedal steel guitar, George Grantham on drums, and Tim (Timothy Bruce) Schmit on bass. All of the members were vocalists and all had originally proved themselves as songwriters.

Young, though born in California, spent most of his youth in Colorado. At 14, he became the only male musician in an otherwise all-girl band. He dropped out of the University of Colorado after a year, to join a Denver group called Boenzye Creque. When it disbanded, he went to work as a studio musician in Los Angeles. One of the sessions was for the Springfield's last LP, on which he provided support for the song "Kind Woman." This led to an invitation from Furay and Messina to join their new band. He brought in George Grantham, born and raised in Oklahoma, from Boenzye Creque.

The fifth member of the band, Tim Schmit, played with small bands while working for a degree in psychology at Sacramento State College. After coming within a few units of his bachelor's degree, he decided he was more interested in pursuing a career in music. He moved to Los Angeles just before Pogo was organized, auditioned, and was accepted as the final member of the original quintet. (The band name soon was changed from Pogo to Poco to avoid legal problems with copyright owners of the cartoon of that name.)

The group rehearsed for much of the summer and fall of 1968 before its first public appearance that November at the Troubadour in Los Angeles. Its sound was oriented toward country-rock, though its repertoire ranged from blues and blues-rock to experimental contrapuntal-type harmonies. The press was almost wholly positive toward the new group. Pete Johnson of the *Los Angeles Times*, wrote: "Poco . . . is one of the tightest groups I have seen, a coordination which obviously stems from endless practice and good feelings within the combo. . . . The band seems the natural heir to the originality, diversity, and togetherness which marked the beginnings of the Byrds and the Buffalo Springfield, Southern California's two best folk-rooted rock groups so far."

The band's acceptance with disc jockeys and fans started off reasonably well in 1969 with its debut LP. *Picking up the Pieces* on Epic Records sold over 100,000 copies and appeared briefly on the charts. The group's second album, *Deliverin'* (1970), stayed on the charts from March into July. Similarly, the album *Poco* was on the charts for the entire summer. Two singles made the charts in 1970–71: "You Better Think Twice" and "C'mon."

In 1971, Jim Messina left to form a new band, Loggins and Messina, a first indication of some doubts about band direction among original members. His place was taken by Paul Cotton, who performed on the group's 1972 hit single "Railway Days." During that period, the band had a mild hit with its fourth Epic LP, *From the Inside* (late 1971). The band's June 1972 album, *A Good Feelin' to Know,* spent considerably more time on the charts, but still fell short of mass success.

After working on the 1973 album *Crazy Eyes,* Richie Furay left in favor of a solo career and Asylum Records head David Geffen's brief brainchild, the Souther, Hillman, Furay Band including J.D. Souther and former Byrd and Flying Burrito Brother Chris Hillman.

Poco then kept its core membership down to four. Without both of its founding members, the band seemed at a loss creatively, as exemplified by one of its weakest offerings to that time, the 1974 release *Seven.* But it seemed to bounce back later that year with its eighth album, *Cantamos.*

Still, neither the remaining members nor Epic were satisfied with the band's progress. It always had seemed on the verge of supergroup status in the early 1970s, but never achieved the hoped-for mass-audience approval. The band did build up a loyal following, but not enough to make the project economically attractive. One result was the band's departure from Epic in the mid-1970s. Epic, realizing the band still had many fans, continued to release earlier recordings on such LPs as *The Very Best of Poco* (1975), *Live* (1976), and *Ride the Country* (1979).

In 1975, the band signed with ABC Records, which issued its label debut, *Head over Heels,* in that year. The album suggested the group might be on the way to a fresh, exciting start. Unfortunately, the new creative surge proved temporary and such succeeding LPs as *Rose of Cimarron* (1976) and *Indian Summer* (1977) were disappointing. The departure of Timothy Schmit, who had become a central figure in the band, for a role in the Eagles, seemed the final blow. The band did manage to make the singles charts with "Crazy Love" and "Heart of the Night" from its 1978 album *Legend,* but that appeared to be a last hoorah. After Poco's early 1980 *Under the Gun* on MCA (which had acquired ABC Records), the band's history, for all intents and purposes, was a closed book.

(*See Buffalo Springfield; Byrds, The; Crosby, Stills, Nash & Young; Eagles, The; Loggins and Messina; Stills, Stephen.*)

POINDEXTER, BUSTER: *See Johansen, David.*

POINTER SISTERS, THE: *Vocal group, all born Oakland, California. Ruth, born c. 1946; Anita, c. 1948; Bonnie, c. 1953; June, c. 1954.*

Taking a page from Ray Charles' book, this group made its mark across the music spectrum from soul to country. At first glance, the Pointer Sisters might not be thought of as country artists; they are associated in most peoples' minds with jazz, pop, or R&B stylings. But the sisters made their mark in country as well, both as singers and as songwriters, a fact borne out by their nominations in country categories in both Grammy and Country Music Association competition in the mid-1970s.

The girls, along with their two older brothers, began their musical careers as members of the choir of the West Oakland Church of God, where both their parents, Elton and Sarah Elizabeth Pointer were ministers. As Ruth Pointer, oldest of the sisters, noted in biographical data for Planet Records in 1978: "Our parents naturally, as ministers, wanted to protect us from the bad lives people had led in the blues and jazz worlds. We weren't allowed to go to the movies or hear music other than gospel and TV soundtracks. [Later, as the girls made their way successfully in the music world, their parents came around to being firm supporters.] In the beginning we had no one to imitate. We'd never heard of the Andrews Sisters or nostalgia. We started 'scatting' stuff.'' The situation, as they had no preconceived notions, later made all kinds of music seem interesting to them, including country. "We're a very country family," Ruth noted.

The changing world helped make the elder Pointers relax their restrictions as the girls came of age. The three older girls became enthused at the idea of a singing career and sought work in the field while earning money in clerical jobs. Their initial attempts in 1969 met with no success, but a friendship with producer David Robinson finally led to session work as backup singers for the San Francisco group Cold Blood's album *Sisyphus*. This was followed by more assignments, first with the Elvin Bishop Group and then with artists such as Dave Mason (who took them along on a European tour) and Taj Mahal. Finally, they got their initial record contract in the early '70s with Atlantic, which classified them as straight R&B singers. Two singles were released, which the Pointers noted "were heard only in our living room."

Robinson got them signed to ABC/Blue Thumb Records in 1973. That May, a sensational debut (including younger sister June) at Doug Weston's Troubadour in Los Angeles led to appearances on major TV shows, including Helen Reddy's, Johnny Carson's and "The Midnight Special." In September, the quartet was featured at the Monterey Jazz Festival. Their debut album on ABC, *The Pointer Sisters* (including Willie Dixon's old Chicago blues song "Wang Wang Doodle," Allan Toussaint's "Yes We Can Can," the sisters' originals "Sugar" and "Jada"), was certified gold by the RIAA on February 7, 1974.

Their second album, *That's A Plenty,* continued the momentum, receiving a gold-record award on July 25, 1974, only a short while after its release. The girls' country inclinations were emphasized during 1974 by the original song "Fairytale," a Grammy winner for Best Country Vocal Performance by a Duo or Group. Its authors, Anita and Bonnie, also were nominated for the songwriter's award, Best Country Song of 1974. The following year, the Pointers had another country-flavored song on the charts, "Live Your Life Before You Die," a nominee for the 1975 Grammy for Best Country Vocal Performance by a Duo or Group. The Sisters, of course, continued to find favor for other types of songs, such as the *Billboard* top 20 pop hit, "How Long (Betcha Got a Chick on the Side)," a song from their 1976 album, *Steppin'* (their fourth LP on ABC/Blue Thumb, having been preceded by *Live at the Opera House*).

Meanwhile, despite audience approval, the Sisters were unhappy. As June recalled: "We didn't read contracts in those days and we lived on the road and came home broke. But we enjoyed singing so much we just kept on." They also chafed at the typecasting of their record firm, which wanted to stress nostalgic songs with Swing-Era feel, such as "Salt Peanuts" and "That's a Plenty." June stressed: "We weren't growing as singers. We didn't really know what our voices could do."

The women were represented on two more ABC albums in the mid-1970s: *The Best of the Pointer Sisters* and, in 1977, *Having a Party*. After the latter, which completed their contract agreement with ABC, the group broke up for a while. In 1978, though, three of the girls (Ruth, June, and Anita) returned to action, joining a new label, Planet Records, which issued their debut LP, *Energy,* in November.

During 1979, the trio had two major singles hits, "Fire" and "Happiness" from *Energy,* their third gold record LP. "Fire" also was their first gold single. In 1980, the next Planet album, *Special Things,* spawned their second gold single, "He's So Shy."

[Meanwhile, Bonnie had launched her own solo career, signing with Motown Records. Her late 1979 debut LP, *Bonnie Pointer* was the source of two hit singles: "Heaven Must Have Sent You" (1979) and "I Can't Help Myself" (1980).]

In mid-1981, Planet issued its fourth album by Ruth, June, and Anita, the gold *Black & White*. The first single "Slow Hand," went gold, and by late September, the second single, "What a Surprise," was on the charts. It was an auspicious month for the girls in another way: at the conclusion of *Billboard* magazine's Talent Forum in New York's Savoy Hotel, the trio was named R&B Group of the Year.

The trio followed up with one hit after another in the mid-1980s. In 1982, the LP *So Excited* was a best-seller and provided such hit singles as the title track and "American Music." Break Out (Planet, 1983) went platinum and provided top 10 singles (on black, disco and/or pop charts) "I Need You" in 1983 and "Jump (For My Love)" and "Automatic" in 1984. This resulted in two Grammy Awards. "Jump" won for Best Pop Performance by a Duo or Group with Vocal. "Automatic," which was arranged by the Pointers, was voted the Best Vocal Arrangement for Two or More Voices.

In 1985, the trio moved to RCA Records. Their platinum album debut on the label, *Contact,* provided the singles hits "Dare Me" and "Freedom." In early 1988, the group's second RCA LP, *Serious Slammin',* came out and soon charted, though it didn't seem as consistently fresh and exciting as some of the Pointers' earlier collections.

POISON: *Vocal and instrumental group. Members: Bret Michaels, born Harrisburg, Pennsylvania; C.C. DeVille, born Brooklyn, New York; Rikki Rockett; Bobby Dall.*

A fledgling band of the mid-1980s that had earmarks of eventual stardom, Poison embraced such garb as lipstick, bouffant hairdos, and quasi-feminine attire—reminiscent of such early 1970s groups as the New York Dolls and the initial Be Bop Deluxe—when it took central stage on the Los Angeles rock scene. The all-male band's music belied its costuming, however, falling somewhere between the mainstream rock of Tom Petty and the heavy metal of Van Halen. The group's appearance still gained attention as part of the "glam-rock" subgroup, but such preening no longer was considered outrageous by many rock fans as it had been for the Dolls a decade before.

Or at least this was true in major urban areas such as New York and Los Angeles. As Rikki Rockett told Roy Trokin of *BAM* magazine: "We didn't just decide to put together a glam-band. I wanted to be in a band that's glamorous. We're not the New York Dolls, even though there's a lot of that influence. We're not underground. We're trying to strike a middle ground. Back there [in Pennsylvania] we were freaks for what we were doing. Here, we're art."

The founding members of Poison were all from the eastern part of the U.S. The initial staging ground was Harrisburg, Pennsylvania, hometown of lead singer Bret Michaels. After performing with the usual array of teen amateur combinations, he eventually joined forces with drummer Rikki Rockett and bass guitarist Bobby Dall to form the nucleus of a local band. With C.C. DeVille eventually rounding out the group on lead guitar in mid-1983, the quartet—then called Paris—became reasonably successful on the Harrisburg-area bar circuit.

As with thousands of aspiring groups, it didn't take long for the group's members to realize that to proceed from occasional bar gigs or party engagements it had to move on to one of the music-industry centers. Michaels joked: "We figured that if we were going to have no money, no food and have to sleep in the streets, at least we could pick a warm climate."

After moving to Los Angeles in 1984, the group slowly began to break into the local music field. Its good-natured, but intense, stage presence coupled with constant self-promotion made it one of the biggest attractions on the local club circuit.

Achieving that took hard work that had little to do with stage shows and practice sessions. Michaels told Duncan Strauss of the *Los Angeles Times:* "You've got to promote in order to get people there. You've got to go out and distribute flyers plugging the shows. After a show [by other rock groups] like Loverboy at the Los Angeles Forum, I'll be passing out flyers and saying 'Come out and see us.' They'll crumble 'em up and throw 'em in my face. But I'll give out a thousand flyers and a hundred people will show up because of it—which is a hundred people that have never seen us before."

What those people see, he pointed out to Trokin,

wasn't necessarily all they got. "We've got a very open-door policy. You don't have to look like Poison to enjoy Poison. We strive as much with our personalities as we do with our look. The music's always got to be the most important factor. Just because I wear makeup doesn't mean I can't sing."

Rockett added: "We just want to give people the freedom to dress and do what they want at the show. We want a wide-ranging audience. Come to one of our shows and you'll see skinheads, punks, new wavesters, moms and dads, Springsteen types, metal kids, glam people. You can learn from each other. When everybody in the band likes the same thing, you preclude the chance for something different to emerge from the combination of personalities. I can appreciate Elton John for his melodies and Motorhead for their power. I mean, what did Elvis Presley do? He put together country and rhythm & blues. I'm not saying we can change the world, but maybe we can, just a little bit."

In truth, Poison's initial material didn't seem geared for changing the world. For the most part, it was macho-oriented man-chases-girl lyrically. But in some songs, the group showed it could make insightful comments on boy–girl relationships.

More to the point, the group demonstrated it could play hard-driving rock that inspired the audience to sing, dance, and generally enjoy itself. This rapport helped attract notice from rock entrepreneurs and eventually led to an association with rock promoter Kim Fowley.

Fowley, who had been influential in the rise of a number of L.A.-based groups (including the all-girl band the Runaways; *see Jett, Joan; Runaways, The*) suggested that the band record for an independent label. But the members had their own ideas of what they wanted to do and instead said they would keep on building up their local audience while pushing for a contract with a major label.

In early 1986, this paid off when Capitol Records decided to add the band to its roster. The agreement provided for the band to use its own label name, Enigma, in conjunction with Capitol. During the early spring, the group went into the Music Grinder Studios in L.A. and in a mere 12 days laid down all the tracks for its debut LP, *Look What the Cat Dragged In.* Buoyed by extensive video exposure on MTV and a concert tour with Ratt, the album soon was high on *Billboard* charts, spending weeks in the top 10 during the summer. In early 1988, the group was named Best New Heavy Metal Band in *Performance* magazine and placed second in the *Rolling Stone* readers poll in the Best New American Band category.

But the group was accruing less favorable press coverage. In late 1987, Geffen Records publicity director Bryn Bridenthal brought suit against band members Dall and Michael for repeatedly dousing her with ice-cold buckets of champagne in a party after a Motley Crue concert. A few months later, news stories told of a $45.5 million breach of contract lawsuit filed against the group by its management executives, alleging unruly actions by the musicians imperiled management investment of time and energy.

Some reviewers made no secret of hopes that Poison would prove a one-hit album phenomenon. But the band's second Capitol LP, *Open Up and Say Ahh*, debuted on *Billboard* at 43 in May 1988 and moved rapidly upward after that.

POLICE, THE: *Vocal and instrumental group. members (late 1970s and 1980s): Sting, born Wallsend, England, October 2, 1952; Andy Summers, born Bournemouth, England, January 31, 1943; Stewart Copeland, born United States, July 16, 1952.*

In the midst of the punk/new wave foment, the Police emerged to demonstrate that new variants of the less frenetic, melodic rock recalling the Beatles era could win over large numbers of rock adherents. Though usually considered an English group because of the origin of its primary writer and singer Sting (born Gordon Sumner), a major contributor to its success was American-born Stewart Copeland, who gave the band its name and who brought in his talent-agent brother, Miles, to bring the band's effort to commercial fruition.

Product of a working class family, Sting attended Warwick College as a candidate for teaching credentials. He was leading his own jazz group, Last Exit, at a pub in Newcastle, England, when he caught the eye of two other young musicians, Stewart Copeland and Henri Padovani, who were in the process of forming a rock band of their own. Copeland at the time was unhappy with the status of the group he was drumming for, Curved Air. Guitarist Padovani also was looking for a band format more in line with the type of music he liked to play.

They wanted to enlist a third member in the embryo band, but didn't have anyone particularly in mind when they sat through a Last Exit set. The jazz combo was decidedly unimpressive, but the audience liked it because of Sting, Copeland told Barney Cohen, author of the biography *Sting, Every Breath He Takes* (Berkley Publishing, 1984). "But they went down a storm," Copeland said, "Just because of Sting. Sting had then what he has now. This fantastic presence. It was really pretty obvious that he had this enormous potential."

The two engaged Sting in urgent conversation after the set. Sumner wasn't overly enthusiastic at first. He loved jazz and looked on rock as an occasional sideline to earn spare money. But he finally agreed to work with the others after a compromise approach was made for the new band. "Where we arrived," he told Cohen, "wasn't in the rock vein, which Stewart had been in, or in the jazz vein, but something totally different, which was punk. This actually appealed to me greatly because it had energy. And it wasn't far removed [from jazz great] Ornette Coleman. Although I knew that serious music people thought it was terrible, it did have what good music should have, which is excitement, whereas all this heavy rock stuff had gotten so turgid, so pompous and arrogant, that it didn't have any life left in it at all."

The trio began practicing with Copeland originally taking most lead vocals besides his drum chores and providing most of the new songs. Sting handled vocals and bass guitar while also doing some writing. Padovani did backup vocals and played lead guitar. In the summer of 1976, Copeland borrowed the money to record and press the band's first single, "Fall Out." Because it was one of the first punk-style discs, Copeland recalled, it eventually sold an estimated 10,000 copies. Copeland also gave the band its name, intending it as an ironic comment on his father, an important official in the U.S.

Copeland's brother, Miles, agreed to manage the band, arranging it to be an opening act for Cherry Vanilla, another act he was showcasing in England. During one 1977 show, Henri Padovani established close rapport with the leader of the band Electric Chairs and soon left for what he thought were greener pastures. Sting and Copeland simply turned around and brought in veteran lead guitarist Andy Summers, whose playing had impressed them during club dates in Paris. Summers, nine years their senior, had worked with many rock bands over the years as well as compiling extensive session credits.

The new alignment provided much better chemistry than the old one, particularly for Sting, who began to provide interesting new compositions that gradually set the tone of the band. Miles Copeland's imagination also caught fire and he moved to set up a German tour for the Police with electronic music artist Eberhart Schoener to produce money to help finance the group's first album. Work on that began at the Surrey Sound Studios in London in January 1978 and continued at intervals for most of that year. At one session, Sting brought in a ballad he'd been working on for some time, "Roxanne."

It was hardly punk rock, but the others liked it. Copeland, who had become enthused about the reggae so prevalent on the London music scene because of the city's large West Indian population, suggested combining the "Roxanne" melody line with a reggae beat. Miles loved the tape and quickly got A&M Records' London office to release it as a single in England. The record made its expenses and more besides, but wasn't a smash hit at the time.

To help defray costs, Miles lined up commercial gigs. During a job for Wrigley's gum, the director suggested the trio would have more impact if they bleached their hair. After that, the group continued to touch up its hair for live concerts.

Later in 1978, the group completed another A&M single, "Can't Stand Losing You," which performed in about the same fashion as "Roxanne." The income from that single was applied to the band's first U.S. tour in the fall of the year. Though the band played a number of cities and the famed New York new wave club CBGB's, there were few listeners and no sensational critical reviews. But the Police did begin to get attention from disc jockeys on some U.S. college stations.

The band's debut album, *Outlandos D'Amour,* completed by late 1978, was released by A&M in England initially and later in the U.S. One of the cuts was "Roxanne." The album began to win converts for the group among critics on both sides of the Atlantic. After attending a New York date at the Bottom Line, John Rockwell of *The New York Times* wrote (April 5, 1979): "In a curious way, what Sting does recalls Pete Townshend of the Who at his most experimental, although the results don't sound like that band. In other words, the Police take basic elements from the vocabulary of popular music and construct from them elaborate structures. Yet the original elements are always clear . . . eliciting the emotional response of its roots. In this case, the elements come from English new-wave rock, reggae, and the sparer, more structural kinds of progressive rock.

"In addition, Sting's voice . . . is high and plaintive and he and the other two Police are visually appealing. If the Police don't sound like the Who, they don't sound like the Talking Heads either. But no other rock band in recent memory has been able to combine intellectuality, progressivism, and visceral excitement so well."

Despite such seeming breakthroughs, for a time things looked bleak. Because the BBC banned the initial singles releases, including "Roxanne," for various reasons, record sales in England were negligible. And A&M had problems breaking into the airplay format on U.S. stations. However, when an A&M U.S. executive decided to include "Roxanne" on the sampler album *No Wave,* the song caught on. By year-end, the group had a hit single in "Roxanne," while its debut LP had made both English and U.S. charts. A&M executives felt they had a hit group on their hands and now were willing to provide much more support for promotion and concert tours.

The band's second album, *Regatta De Blanc* (late 1979), provided such favorites as "Message in a Bottle" and "Walking on the Moon." In the Grammy voting for 1980, the band gained the first in a series of awards for Best Rock Instrumental Performance for the title track.

Then came a letdown with album three, *Zenyatta Mondatta* (late 1980). Record-company officials were beginning to let band members feel some of the pressures of the commercial world. Copeland, as Cohen stated, remembered: "There was a lot of depression in the studio. There were record-company executives hanging around the studio and stuff . . . making us aware by their presence that we had to deliver an important piece of product. We could actually feel the pressure." The LP did go platinum, but it suggested the band might be past its peak. Yet it still had good material. "Don't Stand So Close to Me" earned a 1981 Grammy for Best Rock Performance by a Duo or Group with Vocal, while "Behind My Camel" was named Best Rock Instrumental Performance.

The band showed it still had plenty in reserve creatively on the platinum LP *Ghost in the Machine* (late 1981) with the hit single and video "Every Little Thing She Does Is Magic."

To gain a more serene setting for the next LP, the trio decided to work on the island of Montserrat in the Caribbean. Though Sting remained the main writer, all three members contributed songs, and their arrangements often were collaborations. Talking about the making of the *Ghost* LP, Copeland told Jim Green of *Trouser Press:* "Whoever wrote the song will show the others the chords. In my case, I don't know the names of 'em so I just play 'em. Andy looks at my fingers and says: 'You moron, that can't be done' or 'Why have you done that?' and everybody figures out whatever they can. In Montserrat, Andy was in the studio, Sting in the mixing room playing through the board, and I was in the dining room in the next building. We all have our cans [headphones] on; while they get the chords, I fiddle with the rhythms. Then we run through it once. Usually somebody plays too many times around the chords or something that's not right and we do it again. If that isn't it either, we do it once more. If we haven't got it then, it starts to get lost. Usually we have it though; 'One World (Not Three)' was right the very first time, for instance."

Summers pointed out he helped provide some of the musical sophistication of Police arrangements. He thinks of his guitar playing as a continuous solo, "only a bit more orchestral—a harmonic support and shaping of the songs. We are a reggae-based band, but I write harmonically on top of that, as influenced by [classical composers] Messiaen, Bartok, Schoenberg, and Takemitsu, as well as jazz. It's a more wide-ranging role than most lead guitarists have played in the past."

During 1982, Sting and the others went separate ways for a while to work on various personal projects. Though some pop bands might find it impossible to overcome a year's lack of exposure on the concert circuit or on hit charts, the Police had no difficulty in continuing to hold a preferred position with fans and critics as proven by the platinum sales of its 1983 release, *Synchronicity*, one of the band's best. The pièce de résistance was the rock ballad from Sting, "Every Breath You Take," a best-seller in both single and video form. That song, Sting told Cohen, "nearly wrote itself. I woke up in the middle of the night in Jamaica and went straight to the piano and the chords and song just came out within 10 minutes. Wrote the song. Went back to bed. It's a way of saying there's still something meaningful and useful in the old way of doing a rock and roll ballad."

Released in mid-1983, that album was still in the top five on U.S. charts at year-end. In fact, it helped pull all the band's albums up or back onto the lists. At the end of 1983, all five albums were on the *Billboard* charts, with all except the first two well past platinum sales levels and those two over RIAA gold-record levels. In the 1983 Grammy voting, the band won two more trophies: Best Pop Vocal Performance by a Duo or Group with Vocal for the single "Every Breath You Take" and Best Rock performance by a Duo or Group with Vocal for the *Synchronicity* album.

The group also proved how extensive its early 1980s following had become by drawing 70,000 people to concerts in New York's Shea stadium.

After the tremendous success of *Synchronicity*, the Police again took a sabbatical while Sting pursued a variety of solo projects and the others made plans for their own solo work. (In 1987, Stewart Copeland's solo album *The Equalizer and Other Cliff Hangers* was released by I.R.S.) However, Police fans continued to hope this was only temporary; when the group reformed for three benefit concerts for Amnesty International in the summer of 1986 a full reunion album and tour was anticipated.

But Sting rejected such ideas. He told Robert Hilburn (*Los Angeles Times*, October 11, 1987): "To me the Amnesty tours were definitely the Police's way of saying good-bye. There had been constant offers to get back together and the longer we stayed away the bigger the offers became. But I just wasn't interested. We had done it.

"We achieved what a band sets out to do; we had played Shea Stadium and sold millions of records. To do it again would just be boring and repetitious."

Why had he approved the Amnesty shows? "I felt it would be nice to say good-bye properly and the Amnesty shows meant we could say good-bye in a good cause. It allowed us to feel good about bowing out as compared to just cashing our chips in and saying let's make as much money as we can. I have too much respect for what the band did to sell it like that." (*See Sting.*)

POP, IGGY: *Singer, songwriter. IGGY POP AND THE STOOGES: vocal and instrumental group. Personnel (late 1960s): Iggy Pop, born Ann Arbor, Michigan, 1947; Ron Asheton; Scott Asheton; Dave Alexander. First group disbanded in 1971. Reorganized group (1972): Iggy Pop, Asheton brothers, James Williamson. After mid-1970s, Pop continued career as a solo performer.*

Avid rock fans found it hard to be neutral about Iggy Pop and the Stooges. Some thought this pioneer of shock-rock represented the wave of the future while others believed the group's wild antics led up just another dead-end street. By the 1980s, it was apparent that both Iggy and his original band had been major influences in the evolution of punk and its offshoots. Iggy himself in the 1980s, however, was essentially a cult favorite rather than a star.

Stooges founding member Iggy Pop (born James Osterberg) grew up in Ann Arbor, Michigan. His first love was drums. The rootless feeling of his later work with the Stooges can be traced to his early years. As he told David Walley (*Jazz & Pop*, January 1970), he was "a very unhappy person, a very self-conscious person, a very schizoid person when I was young. I had a full fantasy life at all times, and then when I was about 18 and I was really loony at the time, I got into a series of tremendous car accidents, unbelievable ones, where everybody else got killed and I never got scratched, and that was the first time in my life I ever felt anything like it—it was like drugs [though Iggy stated he didn't smoke dope until he started playing music]—such power and such timelessness."

In the mid-1960s, he worked with a number of bands in Michigan and Chicago, Illinois, one called the Iguanas, another a blues band called the Prime Movers. For a time he played with blues artist Sam Lay on Chicago's South Side. As he told Walley: "I started in Chicago and ended up in Chicago with one of the black soul bands. Like Johnnie Young and Pete Wallingford and all those guys, you know, good musicians but a little too old to keep their minds together. Like children, complete children, playing—the most fantastic things that ever happened, because it's just like playing with a bunch of 10-year-olds who've got knives and guns and things."

In 1968, he decided to form his own band and gathered three friends who had little band experience—an approach that seemed to fit his nihilist view of music. Iggy was vocalist. His backing trio consisted of Ron Asheton on lead guitar, Scott Asheton on drums, and Dave Alexander on bass. While Iggy went through a series of contortions and performed such antics as throwing himself from the stage to be passed along supported by the hands of the audience—singing all the while—the band put down a series of primitive sound patterns notable mainly for tremendous volume and only occasional chord changes. At first, the group met with little audience approval, but gradually they became regarded as a symbol of the times and were celebrities with many Midwestern fans.

This helped win a recording contract with Elektra, leading to two albums: *The Stooges* (mid-1969) and *Funhouse* (1970, produced by John Cale of Velvet Underground fame). (*See Velvet Underground, The*.) This helped win more adherents, but no star status. In 1971, the ground disbanded and little was heard from Iggy for nearly a year.

He turned up in London late in 1972 and soon announced he had a new band, which comprised Scott Asheton, Ron Asheton (on bass instead of lead guitar), and James Williamson, who had played rhythm guitar with the group just before it broke up in 1971. The group gained considerable attention from English fans and U.K. avant garde musicians. *Raw Power* (Columbia Records, early 1973) made top chart levels back in the U.S. The LP, on which Iggy described himself as a "runaway child of the nuclear A-bomb," proved a high point of the careers of both Iggy and the band and ranked as one of the seminal albums of the decade.

But Iggy couldn't improve on it in succeeding releases and by mid-decade he had opted for a solo career. He signed with RCA Records and turned out a series of albums on which David Bowie served as producer and backup instrumentalist. These included *The Idiot* and *Lust for Life* (1977) and *TV Eye-1977 Live* (1978). During those years, Pop presented a series of dynamic concerts across the U.S. and abroad, where Bowie stayed in the background as part of the backing band. (*See Bowie, David*.)

At the end of the 1970s, Iggy moved to a new label, Arista, which issued *New Values* (1979), *Soldier* (1980), and *Party* (1981).

In the mid-1980s, Iggy left Arista for A&M Records. His work on the label included the first-rate *Blah Blah Blah*, whose sound benefited strongly from the blues rock guitar work of one-time Sex

Pistols member Steve Jones. (Jones also co-wrote a number of the songs on the LP.) In the spring of 1988, A&M issued his new album *Instinct*. He continued to draw devoted fans to concerts around the world in the 1980s, touring with such acts as the Gang of Four. Typically, he taunted his fans between numbers, on one occasion shouting at a crowd in Los Angeles that they were "overfed white kids with nice complexions. Do you fools have any brains?"—words that onlookers simply accepted as part of the Pop mystique. (Offstage, Iggy shed his image of what one critic referred to as "an out-of-control, hyperactive 12-year-old" and was typically quiet and studious. One of his prime interests, for instance, was reading and analyzing the works of Medieval English author Geoffrey Chaucer.)

PRESLEY, ELVIS ARON: *Singer, guitarist, actor. Born Tupelo, Mississippi, January 8, 1935; died Memphis, Tennessee, August 16, 1977.*

When Elvis Presley died at the age of 42, the news shocked the world. Two days after he was found dead, his embalmed body, displayed in a casket in the foyer of his Graceland mansion in Memphis, Tennessee, drew thousands of mourners who stood patiently in long lines for the chance to get a last glimpse of the revered rock star. So many people lined up to see the body, in spite of sweltering heat, that dozens fainted from heat exhaustion. In the years that followed, throngs of fans made regular pilgrimages to Graceland to honor his memory.

Over a decade after his death, other performers were still doing big business as Elvis impersonators while a stream of new books and articles continued to keep alive the controversy about Presley's life and early death, admittedly from a heart attack induced by a drug overdose. He was, even after his death, the one and only king of rock'n'roll and a country music superstar as well. A featured exhibit at the Country Music Hall of Fame in Nashville was his gold Cadillac, with Presley's first gold records embedded in its walls.

Some material on his career was even entered into the *Congressional Record*. A calculator would be in order to count the several hundred millions of recordings (both genuine copies and perhaps nearly as many counterfeit discs and tapes), T-shirts, and other franchised products purchased worldwide. There were also over 30 motion pictures. Even at the end of the 1980s, the image of Presley seemed ever present, which begs the question, "What sort of man was this?"

There was the singer, the performer-actor, and the individual. In the 1980s, the individual seemed to draw the most interest from a public yet to be sated in its compulsion to gain insight into what made

Presley tick. Despite all the writings, that part of him remained an enigma. Perhaps publicist and author Bob Levinson summed it up best when he said, tongue in cheek, he was considering writing a book titled *I Never Knew Elvis.*

During the 1980s, a growing amount of analysis was devoted to Presley's voice and singing dynamics. Most overlooked was his ability as an actor. Elvis performed to an audience at all times, whether it was a solitary person or thousands of people. He played roles that said: "Notice me! Like me!" long before he went before Hollywood cameras, whether it was his all-black school outfits and sideburns days at Humes High School in Memphis or later, as he bought new cars by the six-pack to give away to friends. The roles were myriad and possibly a defense mechanism to keep others away from his personal self—a speculation at best, but one that helps explain the bafflement not only of the authors of the many posthumous books about him, but also of his associates going back to his pre–"Memphis Mafia" days. The man who understood this was his brilliant and canny manager, Colonel Thomas A. Parker, whose wavelengths are unique unto themselves; Elvis and the Colonel seemed to ride the same carrier band in their very special relationship.

Elvis was born in Tupelo, Mississippi, to Gladys and Vernon Presley. His twin brother Jesse was stillborn. It was during the Depression and both parents worked at whatever jobs were available. Elvis was brought up as part of a tight family unit—the three of them together—a bedrock that held even as some parts of his life crumbled around him later. He was influenced by country and gospel music, naturally, and by so-called race and middle-of-the-road pop songs. The traditional template for modern artists, the guitar, was a family gift that he came to cherish more than the hoped-for bicycle. His parents chose the guitar over the bicycle for their one remaining child because he couldn't get hurt with a guitar. The move from Tupelo to Memphis happened when he was 13 years old.

Elvis's quick ear, remarked upon by musicians throughout his career, was augmented by a quick eye that seized upon detail sometimes more than the overall picture. Aside from his high school days—he never quite left them—he held jobs that included working as an usher in a movie theater. He seized upon some of the things he saw in the films as cues for actions in social and other situations—a finishing school away from home and regular school.

Elvis's recording career began in 1953, when he entered Memphis-based Sun Studios to make an acetate recording of two pop ballads as a birthday present for his mother. Sun staffer Marion Keisker brought him to the attention of owner Sam Phillips,

who eventually set up formal taping sessions for his Sun Records, which also put out blues records. In addition, Phillips produced blues discs by Memphis-based artists such as B.B. King and Tuff Green for Bullet Records of Nashville. Bullet's principal, Jim Bullet, helped arrange financing and limited distribution for Sun, later selling his interest back to Phillips for $1,200. Though only in his twenties, Phillips was also involved with a radio station, WHER, and other projects. After adding Elvis to Sun's roster, he helped arrange for local disc jockey and booking agent Bob Neal to manage Presley and his band (Scotty Moore on guitar and Bill Black on stand-up bass).

Raw and untamed, Presley's 1954–55 tracks for Sun were the most exciting he ever recorded. His first release typified his rockabilly fusion of blues and hillbilly: bluesman Arthur "Big Boy" Crudup's "That's All Right (Mama)" backed with bluegrass founder Bill Monroe's "Blue Moon of Kentucky." Some Memphis disc jockeys refused to play a record with a "black" song on one side and a "white" song on the other, but local listeners' response to the polite young truck driver's debut disc was instant and overwhelming. Four more Sun singles followed, including a steamy remake of Roy Brown's 1947 R&B classic "Good Rockin' Tonight" and a haunting interpretation of bluesman Junior Parker's 1953 Sun hit "Mystery Train."

But Elvis wasn't Sun's only promising young artist. Besides, the label had money problems. Among other shortcomings, Sun product only was distributed in seven or eight states rather than nationally. When the opportunity came to sell Presley's contract to a major label, Phillips took it. Though Columbia and the newly formed ABC Records turned him down for various reasons, RCA bought Elvis for $35,000—an outrageous sum then. The money presented to Sun was used principally to pay of pressing debts (in both meanings of the word), especially to a record-manufacturing plant in Atlanta. This move gave Phillips the leverage needed to work other talent, including Johnny Cash and Carl Perkins. Also a catalyst in Presley's move to RCA was Colonel Parker, with whom Elvis signed for career management in mid-1955. (Still with one foot in the country field, Elvis was billed for some concerts booked by Parker as the "hillbilly cat.") Besides the RCA agreement, two music firms—Elvis Presley Music, Inc. (BMI) and Gladys Music, Inc. (ASCAP)—were formed with the New York publishing firm Hill & Range Songs, Inc. Under the arrangement, including a $5,000 advance, Elvis and Hill & Range each controlled 50% of the stock.

Much has been made of the assumption that Elvis was signed only as a songwriter to his own firms but, in fact, he was a co-owner and it was only logical that whatever talents he might develop as a writer be assigned to his own companies. (In fact, almost all of Presley's songs over the years were written by others.) As always, he checked out the essence of all business deals negotiated by the Colonel, some of which he turned down, while for others he pressed for more favorable terms. The latter were rarities because Parker was very thorough in what often were precedent-setting arrangements later followed by others in the industry.

The Colonel studiously stayed away from the Presley personal life and Elvis's private investments, unless asked to advise either directly or by a surreptitious call from a concerned Vernon. The same applied to Elvis's performances, whether on stage, in the studio, or in movies. Even for Elvis's initial appearances on the Dorsey Brothers' network TV show, the Colonel remained in Madison, Tennessee, while Elvis, Scotty, and Bill were squired about by a talent agent from the William Morris Agency and a publishing-firm representative. It worked well until Elvis became such a celebrity that he lost the freedom to move about and the Colonel organized a well-knit team to handle the star's safekeeping and his concert demands.

It was on guest appearances on several Dorsey shows and a "Milton Berle Show" that Presley performed his first national hit, "Heartbreak Hotel" (number one in *Billboard* for eight weeks starting April 21, 1956). The week of July 28, 1956, Elvis had "I Want You, I need You, I Love You" atop the charts, followed in short order by "Don't Be Cruel"/"Hound Dog" (number one for 11 weeks starting August 18) and "Love Me Tender" (number one for five weeks starting November 3). The Presley musical revolution had begun.

He added more *Billboard* number one hits to his collection in 1957: "Too Much" (three weeks starting February 9), "All Shook Up" (April 13 and seven weeks after), "(Let Me Be Your) Teddy Bear" (seven weeks starting July 8), and "Jailhouse Rock"/"Treat Me Nice" (seven weeks starting October 21). He began 1958 with "Don't"/"I Beg of You" atop the charts for five weeks beginning February 10. But on March 24, his career was interrupted when he was inducted into the U.S. Army. During his two-year hitch (much of it in Germany), he only did one recording session for RCA, but that provided the hit "A Big Hunk of Love," number one in *Billboard* the weeks of August 10 and 17, 1959. (In July 1958, he also reached the top of the charts with the single "Hard Headed Woman," recorded before his induction but released after it.)

When Presley's army phase ended on March 1, 1960, he quickly returned to action both to record and to renew his film career that had begun with *Love Me Tender* and *Jailhouse Rock*. On April 25, 1960, his single "Stuck on You" hit *Billboard*'s number one for four weeks. Later in the year, he starred in his fifth movie, *G.I. Blues* (a Paramount release that included footage shot in Germany while Elvis was still in uniform). Before 1960 was over, his "It's Now or Never" made number one in *Billboard* for five weeks starting August 15 and "Are You Lonesome Tonight" for six weeks starting November 28. March 10 and 17, 1961, he had his next number one success, "Surrender." In April 1962, he had another number one single, "Good Luck Charm." That proved to be his last chart-topper for many years, a situation that reflected both the decline in the excitement of his music as it moved toward the middle of the road and his shift in career emphasis for most of the 1960s to movies rather than concert work. For four years after his 1965 "Crying in the Chapel" (a remake of the Orioles' 1953 R&B hit), he didn't even break the top 10.

The Hollywood years seemed like an answer to Presley's youthful fantasies. The fascination for film had been there since his days as a theater usher in Memphis and, for a long time, the chance to act in movies made him feel the same as a youngster let loose in a candy store. He tasted the off-screen delights of Hollywood with a bigger-than-life appetite and shared them with his friends. At one time, he had 39 people on his own payroll, including those working in Graceland and his nearby Mississippi ranch. It was a substantial overhead that was whittled away only to rise again and again. He remained confident that the money machine would be greased well by his manager, who continued to come up with solutions to keep cash rolling in.

During the '60s, recording-contract requirements with RCA were met mainly by soundtrack material from mediocre movies, augmented by a rare recording session. It was a period when he was kept before a worldwide public by the Colonel's ingenuity and a dedicated staff.

By the late 1960s, most observers considered Elvis a has-been from a recording and concert standpoint. But his May 1, 1967, marriage to Priscilla Ann Beaulieu triggered a change in attitude and gave him a fresher outlook that made him more amenable to venture from his by then stifling Hollywood existence. Presley finally began to tire of his film chores and welcomed suggestions to renew his musical career. The decision to make the now-classic December 3, 1968, Singer TV special for NBC, followed a few months after the birth of his daughter, Lisa Marie, on February 1, 1968. The change in approach—as positive as the death of his mother in 1958 had been negative for him—and the reassuring success of the TV special opened his mind again to new challenges that the astute Colonel quickly channeled into the Las Vegas International Hotel opening on July 26, 1969, his first live appearance in eight years. The decision to tour had been made even before that show and the concerts proved all-out, exciting entertainment for an adoring America. By then, even recording sessions had recaptured his attention as evidenced by "U.S. Male" and "Guitar Man" (1968) and 1969's "In the Ghetto," "Don't Cry Daddy," and "Suspicious Minds" (number one in *Billboard* the week of November 1). Playing a strong role in many of the new releases was RCA-named producer Felton Jarvis.

More successes followed on both the recording and concert fronts, the latter including the Madison Square Garden Show in 1972—his first in that tough town—that won critical accolades including one dubbing him "prince of the heavens." Another milestone was the live concert telecast worldwide from Hawaii in January 1973 with all proceeds from ticket sales donated to charity and with the album *Aloha from Hawaii via Satellite* going instant platinum in the new quadraphonic format.

Meanwhile he placed new songs on the singles chart such as the 1970 "Kentucky Rain," "The Wonder of You"/"Mama Liked the Roses," and "You Don't Have to Say You Love Me." In 1971, he hit with "I Really Don't Want to Know"/"There Goes My Everything," "Where Did She Go, Lord"/"Rags to Riches," "I'm Leavin'," and "Life,"/"Only Believe." His 1972 chart makers were "Until It's Time for You to Go," "Separate Ways," and "It's a Matter of Time"/"Burning Love." In 1973 he scored with "Steamroller Blues"/"Fool" and "Raised on Rock"/"For Ole Times' Sake. "Hits in subsequent years included "Moody Blue" and "(I'm So) Hurt."

Throughout his active career, Elvis turned out dozens of studio, live, and film soundtrack albums, most making pop and/or country charts for a harvest of gold and platinum awards. A sampling includes *Elvis Presley* and *Elvis* (mid-1950s); *Elvis' Golden Records* and *King Creole* (1958); *A Date with Elvis* and *For LP Fans Only* (1959); *Elvis' Golden Records Volume 2* and *Elvis Is Back!* (1960); *Something for Everybody* and *His Hand in Mine* (1961); *Pot Luck with Elvis* (1962); *Girls! Girls! Girls!, It Happened at the World's Fair*, and *Elvis' Golden Records Volume 3* (1963); *Roustabout* (1964); *Elvis for Everyone* (1965); *Spinout* (1966); *How Great Thou Art* (1967); *From Elvis in Memphis* (1969); *That's the Way It Is, Almost in Love, Let's Be Friends, Worldwide 50 Gold Award Hits, From Memphis to Vegas: Elvis in Person at the International Hotel Las Vegas, Nevada*, and *Elvis Back in*

Memphis (1970); *Elvis Country, Love Letters from Elvis, The Other Sides—50 Gold Award Hits Volume 2*, and *You'll Never Walk Alone* (1971); *Elvis as Recorded Live at Madison Square Garden, Elvis Sings Burning Love and Hits from His Movies*, and *He Touched Me* (1972); *Raised on Rock/For Ole Times Sake* (1973); *Elvis: A Legendary Performer Volume 1* and *Elvis Recorded Live on Stage in Memphis* (1974); *Elvis Today* (1975); and *A Legendary Performer Volume 2* and (resurrecting his earliest efforts) *The Sun Sessions* (1976).

In the mid-1970s, Elvis's comeback was accomplished fact and it seemed to outsiders his life couldn't be better—but it was an illusion. His divorce from Priscilla in 1972 had taken its traumatic toll and there were violent swings and excesses in both mood and appetite. He had proved it all, but what was it, what did it prove? There were more recording sessions (which, in most cases, he tried to avoid) and more appearance dates—Las Vegas and Lake Tahoe contracts where aborted shows became more common. He also was increasingly concerned over the health of his father, Vernon, who, aside from daughter Lisa, was the last strong link to the private Elvis.

His remarkable constitution was taking a beating past the fail-safe point. His once quick energy and infectious sense of humor ebbed despite the efforts of close associates to turn things around. Hints of drug dependence circulated among his peer group and the industry as he secluded himself within Graceland or his Palm Springs home. A habit acquired years before, starting with "bennies" (an upper commonly used by country artists in those days in order to stay awake when driving to the next show date a hundred or more miles away) led to mid-1960s drug experimentation common to the Hollywood colony. Elvis always pushed the limit in everything.

His death in August 1977 shocked and saddened fans the world over who equated him with their own fantasies, a massive transference. Here was a man who loved his mother and father, served his country willingly, and embodied the young and restless spirit for all age groups. He was an American original who dispensed his gifts freely to all kinds of people, both in performing and in a personal way.

When Elvis died, he had a new album, *Moody Blue*, moving up the pop charts, as well as the chart single "Way Down." As soon as word got out about the music public's tragic loss, there was a literal rush on record stores as fans snapped up all his available recordings. RCA was soon releasing both old packages as well as new combinations of previously recorded material assembled by Joan Deary. Still, for over a year, record stores had trouble keeping his recordings in stock. By the end of 1977, half a dozen of his LPs were high on the charts. During 1978, his hit LPs included *Legendary Performer Volume 2* and *Elvis Sings for Children and Grownups Too.* In 1979, there were best-selling LPs *Legendary Performer Volume 3, Our Memories of Elvis, Our Memories of Elvis Volume 2* and *Elvis: A Canadian Tribute.* In 1980, RCA put out an eight-LP boxed set *Elvis Aaron Presley,* and in early 1981, the LP *Guitar Man* (whose selections, RCA announced, had been reengineered to reduce background sounds). The title track hit number one single on country lists in March. As the decade went by, still more albums and singles posthumously made the hit lists. The charted LPs included *The Elvis Medley* (1982) and *A Golden Celebration* and *Rocker* (both 1984). New discoveries of material from the early part of his career also continued to surface during the 1980s, such as *Elvis: The First Live Recordings* (Music Works/Jem Records, 1984) and Charly Records of England's releases of cuts from Elvis's legendary Sun jam sessions with Jerry Lee Lewis and Carl Perkins, the *Million Dollar Quartet* (mid-1980s) and *The Complete Million Dollar Session* (1988).

It was a situation where, in death, Elvis continued to share his largesse (especially to RCA Records, whose fortunes soared for many years). There were specials (e.g., *Elvis: One Night With You* and *Elvis Presley's Graceland,* both on HBO, 1985; *Elvis and Me* (1988), dramatization of Priscilla Presley's account of their marriage.) Among the more sincere memorials was a chapel dedicated two years after his death by the Elvis Presley Memorial Foundation in his hometown of Tupelo and, of course, the Gold Cadillac display in Nashville visited by over 500,000 people annually.

The day of his funeral in Memphis, his producer, Felton Jarvis (for whom Elvis earlier had arranged a life-saving kidney transplant), met Sam Phillips at the crypt. Returning from the graveside service in a limousine with another long-time Elvis associate, Grelun Landon, Jarvis said in his soft Southern drawl, "You know, Grelun, it's the first time I met Sam and it feels right that his first and last producers should finally gather here."*

(*See Crudup, Arthur; Orioles, The; Perkins, Carl; Price, Lloyd.*)

---

*Entry by Grelun Landon, who co-authored *The Encyclopedia of Folk, Country & Western Music* with Irwin Stambler, worked closely with Presley throughout most of the artist's career. Initial contact came in 1955 when Landon was a vice president of Hill & Range Songs and helped set up Presley's first publishing companies. Later, as a publicist with RCA, Landon was involved with Presley and Colonel Parker on career developments right up to Elvis's death.

PRETENDERS, THE: *See Hynde, Chrissie, and the Pretenders.*

PRICE, LLOYD: *Singer, trumpeter, band leader, songwriter, record-company executive. Born New Orleans, Louisiana, March 9, 1933.*

Longevity as a star performer would seem a state of grace more common among soul singers than rock artists. Such a continuing rapport with the primarily black audience for soul is demonstrated in the career of Lloyd Price, who remained a favorite with those fans for decades.

He was born and raised in New Orleans, where members of his family had long been known for their musical ability. As a child, he started singing in church choirs. In high school, he took up the trumpet and was considered one of the best musicians for his age in his neighborhood. The time was the late '40s, when dance bands were still the rage. Lloyd formed a five-piece group that played for school dances and in local clubs. At the start of the '50s, he lined up a regular job for his group on a local radio station.

He wrote original material for his band and also supplied station-break jingles. This led him to write a tune that he later expanded into the song "Lawdy Miss Clawdy." The song came to the attention of Specialty Records, which signed him to a contract. Released in 1952, it became one of the top R&B hits of the year. Elvis Presley recorded it early in his career and was still singing it in concert decades later. 1952 singles "Oooh, Oooh, Oooh" and "Ain't It a Shame" also moved into the top 10 on the R&B charts.

His recording career hit a temporary snag when he was drafted into the armed forces. While in the service, he formed a new band with which he toured bases in the Far East, including Korea and Japan. After his discharge in the mid-1950s, he resumed his pop music career by forming a new nine-piece band. He signed with ABC-Paramount Records and soon provided a new hit, "Just Because," in 1957. In 1958, he collaborated with Harold Logan on a rhythm & blues version of the old folk ballad, "Stack-O-Lee," retitled "Stagger Lee." Price's single of the song gained the national pop charts and also moved to number one on the R&B lists. (Over a decade later, in 1969, Tommy Roe made a top 10 hit of the song.)

In 1959, Lloyd had an even greater track record. He provided four of the top hits of the year (again songs co-written with Logan): "I'm Gonna Get Married," "Personality," "Come into My Heart," and "Where Were You (on Our Wedding Day)?" The first two made *Billboard*'s pop top 10, each accounting for a reported million copies sold in the U.S.

In 1960, Price maintained his 1959 pace with such top 10 R&B hits as "Lady Luck," "Question," and "Won't Cha Come Home." As the '60s progressed, Price remained a star as an in-person performer, though his new releases no longer attained the top rungs of either the pop or R&B charts. He had his own record label, Double LL, and played a part in the development of other artists, mostly notably Wilson Pickett, who started his professional recording career on Double LL in 1963.

During the late '50s and in the 1960s, Price was represented on several dozen LPs. Among the ABC-Paramount releases were *Cookin', Exciting Lloyd Price, The Fantastic Lloyd Price, Lloyd Price Sings the Million Sellers, Mr. Personality, Mr. Personality Sings the Blues,* and *Mr. Personality's 15 Hits.* During the 1970s, his recordings were available on reissue LPs such as *Sixteen Greatest Hits* on Trip, *Original Hits* on Sonet (an import collection), and, on ABC, *Sixteen Greatest Hits* and the 20-song *The ABC Collection* (1976). In 1986, Specialty (which, unlike countless other small labels of the '50s, had never been bought out by a larger record company) resurrected Lloyd's early material on *Personality Plus* and *Walkin' the Track,* while keeping Lloyd's decades-old *His Greatest Recordings* in print. Import albums available in the '80s included *Lawdy Miss Clawdy* on Ace and *Mr. Personality Revisited* on Charly.

(*See Pickett, Wilson; Presley, Elvis.*)

PRINCE: *Singer, instrumentalist (guitar, keyboards, percussion, drums, and other instruments), band leader (THE REVOLUTION), songwriter, arranger, record producer. Born South Minneapolis, Minnesota, June 7, 1959.*

Many of the tracks on Prince's albums would bring not just an x-rating, but a whole alphabet full of adverse letters from those who would like to censor pop recordings. There seemed almost no taboo or any other subject—religious hypocracies, kinky sex, politics—that Prince would not write or sing about in blunt, descriptive terms. For a while, the shock value of his repertoire tended to obscure the fact that he was an amazingly multitalented artist who could play almost any instrument a band might use, and write unique music that could be sensitive, sensual, funky, soulful, blast-furnace rock, or blends of all of those. He was, in truth, a wunderkind who had all the skills of music professionals with decades of experience when he was still in his teens. In fact, when he produced his debut album for Warner Brothers Records he was only 19—the youngest person ever to produce an album for the label.

His parents, John and Nattie Nelson, both had strong musical interests. His father headed a swing dance band; his mother for a time was vocalist for the group. (Prince took his stage name from his father's professional name, Roger Prince.) Prince became fascinated by music, he said, when he was five, though he didn't try to do much musically until he was seven and began picking out on the family piano themes he heard on TV programs. He told Tim Carr of the *Minneapolis Tribune* (April 30, 1978): "Around the time I was eight, I had a pretty good idea what the piano was all about. I had one piano lesson and two guitar lessons when I was a kid. I was a poor student because when a teacher would be trying to teach me how to play junky stuff, I would start playing my own songs. I'd usually get ridiculed for it, but I ended up doing my own thing. I can't read music. It hasn't gotten in the way yet. Maybe it will later, but I doubt it."

His parents separated before he reached his teens, which was troubling in some ways, but he also told a reporter he felt freer to experiment with different instruments and types of music after his father left. By the time he was 12 and in the seventh grade at Bryant Junior High School, he already was adept at many different instruments and was part of his first band. Before long, with school friend and bass player Andre Cymone (born c. 1960), he headed a group called Champagne that played local events. Though much of the band's material consisted of covers of hits of the day, the group also played some originals by Prince and Cymone. The band held together for about five years before Prince decided it was time to move on to more challenging activities.

After his father left, his mother eventually found a new companion whom Prince found it hard to relate to. He sought to solve his problems by living elsewhere. He told a *Billboard* reporter: "I ran away for the first time because of problems with my stepfather. I went to live with my real father, but that didn't last too long because he's as stubborn as I am. I lived with my aunt for a while. I was constantly running from family to family."

Finally his friendship with Andre Cymone offered the best avenue of escape. Cymone's mother agreed to let Prince fix up living quarters for himself in her basement. He later used it as a refuge after he finished his high school days at 16 and decided to assemble a lot of new material for an eventual solo demonstration tape. He told Barbara Braustark of *Musician* magazine that he holed up there for weeks on end, typically writing two or three new songs a day, some sexually explicit. He told her they were "sexual fantasies. . . . All fantasies. Because I didn't have anything around me . . . there were no people. No anything. When I started writing, I cut myself off from relationships with women."

He already had made some demo tapes with

Champagne at Moon Sound in south Minneapolis. When the studio operator, Chris Moon, wanted to get backing for a demo tape of some of his own material, he remembered Prince as a good pianist and asked him to do the keyboard track. As Moon told Tim Carr, Prince asked if Moon also wanted some bass. Moon said yes, but he didn't want to pay a bass player, whereupon Prince volunteered to lay down bass tracks and followed with drums, lead guitar, and backing vocals. Moon played the tape for his friend and manager Owen Husney, who was amazed to learn the background music wasn't a band, but one individual—a 17-year-old at that.

This helped set up a chain of circumstances where Prince was able to trade his support work as musician and writer for studio time. Doing everything himself, including acting as his own producer, he assembled a demo tape that he took to New York to try for a record contract. The tape was good enough for two companies to propose to sign him. But he didn't like the terms, he told friends in Minneapolis. ''I didn't take either one of them because they wouldn't let me produce myself. They had a lot of strange ideas . . . tubas and cellos and such. I know I'd have to do it myself if it was going to come out right.''

He returned to the Minneapolis studio and cut another demo of three songs, which he submitted to Warner Brothers. Label executives were so amazed at the quality of the recordings and the promise of the songs they agreed to Prince's terms and gave him an allowance of $100,000 to produce his debut album. As it happened, he went far past that figure, but the songs he was recording seemed so promising he wasn't challenged. In 1978, Warner Brothers issued the debut LP, *Prince-For-You,* and soon determined they had a potential star performer on their hands. The album was well received by many important critics and soon spawned a chart single, ''Soft and Wet.''

The label agreed to help fund concert efforts by Prince to support his recordings. He went back to Minnesota and formed a tour band made up of Andre Cymone on bass guitar, Des Dickerson (born c.1959) on guitar, Gail Chapman on keyboards (later replaced by Lisa Coleman, born c.1962), Matt Fink (born c. 1960) on keyboards, and Bobby Lee (born c. 1958) on drums. Prince commented for a Warner Brothers bio: ''There's a lot of undiscovered talent in Minneapolis. I chose these guys because they were all fresh, new, and unknown.''

By the end of the tour, Prince had begun to establish a core following. His next album, *Prince* (1979, gold) expanded it to more than a cult audience. Again he did almost everything himself, writing all nine songs and doing all production work with help only from an engineer. Its gold single ''I Wanna Be Your Lover'' won considerable disco exposure. Also a hit from the album was ''Why You Wanna Treat Me So Bad.''

On some songs, *Prince* was far more suggestive than his debut release, but the content paled besides the songs on his third LP, *Dirty Mind* (1980). Living up to its title, the album probed such subjects as incest, lesbianism, and oral sex. Apart from the lyrics, the rhythms and melodic content of the album represented pop music at its most vibrant and dazzling. It was followed by an equally brash and often off-color album, the 1981 *Controversy.*

While *Dirty Mind* and *Controversy* had chart action, they had less buyer impact, at least at the time, than earlier releases. But the pendulum swung more positively for Prince when his next album, the platinum *1999* (Warner Brothers, late 1982), remained on *Billboard*'s top 100 110 straight weeks. The album provided Prince with three chart singles, including a sizzling rocker that potential censors couldn't fault, ''Little Red Corvette.'' By the end of 1983, Prince was established as one of the most promising new lights on the pop rock (and soul) scene, able to bring tens of thousands of fans to a fever pitch at live concerts.

Except for singles from *1999,* little new was heard on the recording front in 1983 from Prince. But he was laying the groundwork for a combined assault on a wide variety of segments of the entertainment field in 1984. This was based on an independent movie production by his music management firm of Cavallo-Ruffalo-Fargnoli (with financing by Warner Brothers' movie division) that was to blend concert footage with the story of Prince's rise from painful obscurity to stardom. Prince, intimately involved in the project, made sure much of it was filmed in Minneapolis with many parts played by hometown friends from the black community. Besides acting and singing in the film, titled *Purple Rain,* Prince also assembled the movie soundtrack to be released in album form in conjunction with the film.

The *Purple Rain* LP—released (June 1984), a month before the movie opening—proved an eye-opener. Against competition from the likes of Michael Jackson and Bruce Springsteen, it more than held its own, selling 1.5 million copies its first week on store shelves. Warner Brothers, which had only modest expectations for the film, suddenly realized it had a major product on its hands. The film drew raves from almost everyone who saw it.

An example of the euphoria in the reviewing community came from Mikal Gilmore of the *Los Angeles Herald Examiner,* who called it ''the best rock film ever.'' It was not just a concert movie, but a probing drama blending rock with insights into the human condition. In some sense, he wrote, it bore comparison with Orson Welles' film classic *Citizen Kane*. "This isn't to say that it's exactly a masterpiece, but that like Welles' tale of innocence lost, it is a story about overcoming or falling prey to the prime forces that face us all. Prince's screen character, referred to simply as 'the Kid,' is like Welles' Kane, not a particularly likeable celebrity. At the Minneapolis club (where along with Morris Day and the Time he holds court as a cool iconoclast in a self-made, biracial punk-funk nighttime community) the Kid is an arrogant prodigy who callously insults the creative leanings of the female members of his band, disregards the well-meaning advice of the club's no-nonsense manager, and lets loose with a nonstop display of self-satisfying, oblique music that is gradually costing him the fealty of his band and audience.

"At home, though, the kid is altogether different; a frightened, hurting child shattered by the nightmarish violent reality of a battered mother and alcoholic father. . . .

"If this sounds a bit more heavyweight than one might expect from a film by and about a black punk sex star . . . I can only say *Purple Rain* is an uncommonly aspiring, constantly surprising movie. . . . I felt I was finally seeing a rock artist live up to the cinematic ideal that so many of us dreamed about (for rock superstars like Elvis and Mick Jagger) namely, that such artists might make a film as exciting, meaningful, involving, and uplifting as their best work."

Both film and soundtrack album became major events of the year. The album (his first showcasing not only Prince, but a true backing band) rose to number one in *Billboard* within a month of its release, staying there 21 straight weeks on its way to becoming one of the biggest-sellers ever. It also was a treasure trove of hit singles: the title song, "I Would Die 4u," and two number one songs—"When Doves Cry" (for five weeks starting July 7, 1984) and "Let's Go Crazy" (for two weeks starting September 19, 1984). At year-end, *Billboard* tabbed "When Doves Cry" the number-one–selling disc in both the black and pop singles categories.

The response to the *Purple Rain* LP reinvigorated sales of earlier releases so that at the end of 1984, *Dirty Mind, Controversy,* and *1999* all still were on the charts. *1999*, of course, long ago had soared past platinum levels, while the other two received gold-record certifications.

For the concert tour supporting film and album, Prince assembled a revised band lineup called the Revolution. The group retained veteran players Lisa Coleman, Bobby Z, and Matt Fink and replaced Des Dickerson on guitar (who had formed a new band that appeared in the film) with Wendy Melvoin (born

Los Angeles, California, c. 1964) and added Brown Mark from Minneapolis on bass. For the tour, another new Prince protégé, Sheila E, was signed as opening act with Sheila also doing backing vocals with the Revolution. (*See E, Sheila.*) The international tour was as sensationally well received as the film and LP. In Washington, D.C. alone, 100,000 tickets were sold. Overall, the tour drew almost 2 million ticket buyers.

When the tour was over, Prince announced he was retiring from live performances for a while. But few expected that situation would last very long. Meanwhile he was represented on the charts with singles from *Purple Rain* and a new LP, the platinum *Around the World in a Day*.

While the tour was still in progress, Prince picked up three Grammies: Best Rock Performance by a Duo and Group for the LP *Purple Rain;* Best New R&B Song (a songwriter's award) for "I Feel for You" and Best Album or Original Score written for a Motion Picture or TV Special for *Purple Rain,* with trophies going to Prince, John L. Nelson, Lisa, and Wendy. Prince picked up honors in other polls as well, earning several American Music Awards and also an Oscar in the movie-industry Academy Awards for Best Original Song Score.

One of the things Price did in his later 1985 "retirement" was work on a new movie. In early 1986, a soundtrack LP *Parade Music from the Motion Picture Under the Cherry Moon* was released on his own Paisley Park label (which was handled by Warner Brothers). It wasn't a bad album—for someone else, it probably would have ranked as a high point—but despite platinum sales, it wasn't quite as strong as *Purple Rain* or *1999*. On the positive side, many of the best tracks did not use offbeat sexual subjects simply for provocativeness, which suggested a certain maturing in taste.

When the movie came out in mid-1986, it demonstrated the difficulty of any artist trying to surpass a generally acknowledged gem. Compared to *Purple Rain,* it seemed forced and far more disoriented in shape and content.

But even as disappointment mounted about *Cherry Moon,* Prince was demonstrating he had not lost his personal magnetism and sense of pacing as a stage performer. The route he took in coming out of hibernation was to do a series of sneak warm-up concerts in early summer in L.A. and San Francisco theaters. With an expanded Revolution band, he had no trouble bringing things to an emotional boil for the fans who somehow got word of the shows at relatively small locales such as the Wiltern in L.A. and Warfield Theatre in San Francisco. The warm-up shows set things up for another triumphal series of concerts later in the year.

1988 saw the arrival of another Prince concert film, *Sign o' the Times,* which had been preceded by a two-disc soundtrack LP in 1987 that provided two top 5 singles, the title track and "U Got the Look." The album was named the best LP of 1987 in the annual Village Voice critics poll. It had been reported that another album with the working title "Black Album" would be issued in 1987, but the rumors proved false. Some said it was so raunchy that Warner Brothers wasn't willing to put it out, though others reported that Prince himself made the decision. Some of the albums were produced in England, then destroyed, but by then someone had taped the contents so that bootlegs became available in early 1988. In May 1988, a new studio album, *Lovesexy,* came out and its content quickly brought announcements from some radio stations that their disc jockeys would be barred from playing it. Some record stores also stated they wouldn't stock it because of the nude picture of Prince used on the cover. The LP, however, won critics' praise and sailed past platinum sales levels.

PROCOL HARUM: *Vocal and instrumental group. Personnel (1967), all from London, England: Gary Brooker, born May 29, 1949; Robin Trower (replaced Ray Royer), born March 9, 1945; Matthew Fisher, born 1946; Barry Wilson (replaced Bobby Harrison), born March 18, 1947; Keith Reid, born October 19, mid-1940s; David Knights, born June 28, 1945. Fisher and Knights left in mid-1969, Chris Copping, born England, added. Trower left in July 1971 and was replaced by David Ball, born England, March 30. Alan Cartwright, born North London, England, was added at the same time. Ball left in July 1972 and was replaced by Mick Brabham, born England.*

Apart from its music—some of the most intelligent rock of the second half of the '60s and early '70s—Procol Harum's other claim to uniqueness was the inclusion of a nonperforming lyricist, Keith Reid, as a regular group member. In fact, it was a meeting between Reid and lead vocalist Gary Brooker that led to the organization of the band.

Both Brooker and Reid were Londoners, though their early upbringing differed considerably in material comforts. Reid was brought up in one of the seamier slums of that sprawling city while Brooker had the relative luxury of an average, middle class home. Gary's musician father was able to afford piano lessons for his son, who moved on to study classical music composition in his early teens. His teacher had no objection to Gary looking into more popular musical forms, so Gary worked on boogie-woogie and then jazz in addition to classics.

In Brooker's midteens, he started playing with a London group called the Paramounts, whose other members originally included Robin Trower, Chris Copping, and a drummer called Mick who was later replaced by Barry "B.J." Wilson. The group made a demonstration tape called "Poison Ivy" that won a contract from Parlophone Records, but its five singles made for the label between October 1963 and September 1965 had little success. After a while, Brooker grew unhappy with the band's progress and thought about trying new directions. By then he was composing original music, but he wasn't good with lyrics. Then, in September 1966, a mutual friend introduced him to Keith Reid, reputedly with the terse comment: "This is Keith. He writes words. This is Gary. He doesn't write words."

Keith, who had been working at relatively uninteresting jobs, had started writing lyrics in 1966. A number of friends thought he would do well in music if he could find a writing partner. When Reid met Brooker, he was able to hand him a portfolio of lyrics that proved tremendously exciting to Gary. Gary wrote music to many of them, then sought out a friend well known in the English recording industry, Guy Stevens, whose background included producing and songwriting credits and work as a disc jockey and as a top executive with Island Records. Stevens supervised studio sessions to make demos of four songs. He took them to Island without success, but the tapes found favor with Denny Cordell (later manager of Joe Cocker and then acclaimed for work in the group the Move). When Cordell agreed to produce the new material, it was decided to line up a band.

Gary and Keith ran a small classified ad in *Melody Maker* and placed handwritten notices on bulletin boards in union halls and other places frequented by musicians looking for work. In a short time they had assembled Ray Royer on lead guitar, Matthew Fisher on organ, David Knights on bass, and Bobby Harrison on drums. By early 1967, the group had a contract from Deram Records (a subsidiary of Decca). Its first single featured a rerecording of one of the demo songs, "A Whiter Shade of Pale," a spring best-seller.

But even as "A Whiter Shade of Pale" climbed the hit charts to eventual worldwide sales of 4 million copies and offers for engagements flooded in, the group was breaking apart. There were disagreements between group and manager; internal arguments had been simmering for several months among the bandsmen. Drummer Harrison, for instance, brooded over the fact that he had been shunted aside during the recording sessions in favor of a more seasoned session man, Johnny Eyden. In June, manager Jonathan Weston announced that the group had broken up. "The strain has been too much. It has all been too sudden."

Nothing more was heard for several months. Then in the fall, the band came to life once more as another single on Deram, "Homburg," moved onto the charts and the band's debut album, *Procol Harum*, was issued on EMI's Regal Zonophone label in August. The group had reorganized, with Robin Trower replacing Royer on lead guitar, B.J. Wilson taking Harrison's place on drums, and Tony Secunda taking over as manager. The new alignment worked out well, with no changes in bandsmen until mid-1969 (although Secunda gave way to Ronnie Lyons as manager).

The backgrounds of the four now working with Brooker were similar—childhood in working class sections of London, interest in rock music in pre- and early teens, and a start in the field playing with school friends. Trower, for instance, had left school early, performing with rock groups as a sideline while earning his living as an asbestos sprayer, laborer, window cleaner, and manager of a coffee bar and club.

B.J. Wilson also had earned his living mainly at nonmusical jobs. As he exclaimed when a reporter asked if he had any reputation as a performer when he joined Procol Harum: "Was I unknown? Man, until I joined the Procol Harum, my biggest engagement was with the Marakesh corn exchange."

Of the four, only Fisher had much in the way of musical education, having studied the classics at the Guildhall School of Music on a full scholarship. Later he wrote the score for the avant garde movie *Separation*. Before joining Procol, his credits included playing organ in Screaming Lord Sutch's backup band.

For a time, the band looked as though it might be a flash in the pan. By the spring of 1969, none of its efforts had come close to the acceptance of "A Whiter Shade of Pale." The group had turned out two more albums: *Shine on Brightly* (the second and last album produced by Cordell) and *A Salty Dog* (produced by Matthew Fisher). Both came out in the U.K. on Regal Zonophone, the first in November 1968 and the second in April 1969. Issued in the U.S. on A&M Records, *Salty Dog* was a 1970 hit. But for a time, despite critical approval of the new material, the band remained largely overlooked in the U.K. and hardly better known in the U.S.

However, the lack of public reaction started to change with a new U.S. tour starting in New York's Fillmore East in March 1969. The previous October, Procol Harum had appeared there as the bottom act on the bill. In March, it was the headline act and won considerable applause for Matthew Fisher's composition, "A Salty Dog," which was surprising,

since the ballad is slow and dirge-like (completely different from the folk song of the same title) though with an underlying rock beat. The group went on to receive excellent reviews for other appearances, the most notable being the joint performance with a symphony orchestra of "Salty Dog" and "In Held Twas in I" at the Stratford Shakespeare Festival in Ontario, Canada.

Soon after this performance, however, Fisher, not realizing the band had turned an important corner, became discouraged and quit. Knights also departed to become manager of the band Legend. Onetime Paramounts sideman Chris Copping, who had completed most of the work necessary for a Ph.D. in chemistry, was persuaded to join as a combination bass guitarist and organist—thus reducing the group to a foursome.

Home, the first album for the new quartet, was issued on Regal Zonophone in England and A&M in the U.S. in August 1970. A first-rate effort for such tracks as "Whiskey Train" and "Whaling Stories," the album was reasonably successful, making the U.S. charts, but not quite rising to gold-record level. The band then switched to Chrysalis Records in England, for whom its first effort, *Broken Barricades* (August 1971), did about as well as *Home*. A fine album, it highlighted the guitar ability of Trower. The respect that generated for him among fans and critics helped him decide to leave Procol, after a particularly disastrous tour of Italy, to join a new group, Jude, in July 1971. (*See Trower, Robin.*)

Another ad in *Melody Maker* and a series of auditions resulted in the addition of lead guitarist David Ball from Birmingham, England. Coinciding with this change was a decision to go back to a five-man lineup with Copping concentrating on organ. The new fifth member was bassist Alan Cartwright, a friend of B.J. Wilson.

In November 1971, Procol accepted an offer to go to Canada for a performance with the Edmonton Symphony Orchestra. The concert was recorded and released in the summer of 1972 by Chrysalis and A&M. The gold album, *Procol Harum Live in Concert with the Edmonton Symphony Orchestra and the De Camera Singers*, became one of the record events of the year. Public response was so favorable that the group had to drop work on a new album (*Grand Hotel*) for a hastily arranged U.S. tour. No sooner had the tour ended in July than Dave Ball decided to leave to work as a soloist. His place was taken by Mick Grabham, who had an excellent reputation for his work as lead guitarist several years earlier with the group Cochise. Grabham meshed well with the band, as was soon demonstrated during a European tour with orchestra and choir and a fall swing through the U.S.

Back at full strength, the band completed *Grand Hotel* by late January 1973. It was released by Chrysalis in March, with U.S. distribution shifting to Warner Brothers, which remained Procol's U.S. label the rest of the decade. The LP showed up on U.S. charts almost immediately and stayed on them through the summer.

Considering that the band's history started with a massive singles hit, it was surprising that it had so few singles successes to its credit for many years thereafter. In 1972, Procol had its first large-scale hit since "Homburg" with "Conquistador," but its primary record achievement remained in the album area. Rising interest in its earlier material was shown during 1972–73 by record buyers' response to retrospectives such as the double album *A Whiter Shade of Pale/A Salty Dog* on MFP Records and *Shine on Brightly/Home* on Fly Records. During 1973, A&M Records released *The Best of Procol Harum*.

During the middle and late 1970s, the band continued to be a favorite with large numbers of concert fans in Europe and the U.S. though that interest seemed to reach a plateau after the middle part of the decade. Its albums continued to contain challenging new material, mainly provided by the Reid-Brooker team, though augmented in later releases by songs written by others. The band's output on Chrysalis/Warner Brothers included *Exotic Birds and Fruits* (1974), *Procol's Ninth* (based on a sequence excluding "best of" albums) in 1975, and *Something Magic* (1977). After *Procol's Ninth*, Cartwright left and his place was taken by keyboards player Pete Solley, who had previously worked with such U.K. rock bands as Chris Farlowe and Fox.

PSYCHEDELIC FURS : *Vocal and instrumental group from England. Members (late 1970s): Richard Butler, born Horseley, Surrey, England; Tim Butler, born Horseley, Surrey, England; Roger Morris; Duncan Kilburn; John Ashton; Vince Ely. Roster in 1982: Richard Butler, Tim Butler, Ashton, Phil Calvert. Calvert left in 1983.*

When the Psychedelic Furs made their appearance on the rock scene in the late 1970s, music writers wondered whether the name symbolized an interest in an updated form of the LSD-influenced genre of the 1960s or was intended as an ironic comment on that format. A *Rolling Stone* reviewer, for example, opted for the latter explanation, while Robert Palmer of *The New York Times* concluded (October 27, 1982): "The Furs are a psychedelic band, but a 1980s psychedelic band, influenced by Johnny Rotten [of the Sex Pistols] as well as by such 1960s psychedelia as the Beatles' album *Revolver*."

Such esoteric considerations didn't faze potential fans. Those who attended the band's concerts were on their feet even before the first note sounded (often because the band played under "festival seating" conditions where everyone congregated on a seatless dance floor) and were in constant motion as soon as the Furs' swirling, glass-shattering music hit the amplifiers. The band's offerings (paced by lead singer Richard Butler's sandpaper-edged vocals and the drone-style two-guitar rhythms), while they reflected considerable innovation and intelligent writing skills, were among the most danceable of the postpunk period.

The group's evolution was spurred by two brothers from Surrey: Richard and Tim Butler. Both were rock aficionados from their early years and progressed from amateur bands to the club scene during the first part of the '70s. By the time they assembled the first version of the Psychedelic Furs in the mid-1970s, Richard had demonstrated considerable potential as a writer to go along with his driving vocal skills. The initial group that started performing in small English venues in January 1977 included Richard Butler on lead vocals, Tim Butler on bass guitar, Roger "Dog" Morris on lead guitar, and Duncan Kilburn on saxophone. Those four remained the core of the band through the rest of the year and into 1978 while a variety of drummers came and went. This finally was resolved when Vince Ely became the regular member on the traps.

The band was gaining recognition from English rock adherents during 1977 and '78, initially featuring a single lead guitarist. During a club date in September 1978, another highly regarded guitar player, John Ashton, asked to sit in. The chemistry proved good enough for him to become the band's sixth member and its co-lead guitarist with Morris.

By then, record-company executives were becoming interested in the group, spurred on by demonstration tapes making the office rounds. In September 1979, the Furs finally signed with a major label, CBS. Its debut album, *The Psychedelic Furs* (1980), proved promising. Such tracks as "We Love You" (the initial singles release), "Sister Europe," "Imitation of Christ," and "India" helped win considerable critical acclaim and some numbers received wide exposure in discotheques.

A *Rolling Stone* reviewer, for instance, enthused: "On their audacious debut album, the Psychedelic Furs seemed to have the musical makings of a postpunk fave rave. Its relentless, throbbing beat, crush of droning guitars, and wry saxophone asides quickly made the band dance-club favorites, but what made the group stand out from the pack was singer Richard Butler, whose gritty voice and semi-melodic delivery had a distinct Johnny Rotten charm to them."

The album was reasonably successful in the U.K.,

but did not entice enough U.S. record buyers to make the top 100 lists. The same situation held true for the next release, *Talk Talk Talk* (CBS, May 1981), including the British hit single "Pretty in Pink." The album was creatively above average, though taking a somewhat different direction in content, which Richard Butler described as "a wall of melody as opposed to the first album's wall of sound." Some of the songs dealt with the failed expectations of the 1960s, including emphasis on love and understanding. Butler explained to the English trade magazine *Melody Maker* in May 1981: "It's not saying love is a thing you shouldn't believe in. All it says is you shouldn't believe in the word *love* to mean what you're told it does, you should work it out for yourself."

Melody Maker commented: "If there's living refutation of the current popular myth that rock'n'roll is dead, it must be the Psychedelic Furs. Richard Butler parodies Jagger's grossest camp and Lydon's sharp-tongued spleen with the double-standards of a disillusioned fan. So in love with the rebel image, so sick of its inevitable acquiescence, he confronts his confusion with a bitter, boasting bid to simultaneously emulate and cruelly deflate the best of past pop's irritative potential."

Behind the scenes, though, there were some disagreements over future musical directions that surfaced just before the band got ready to record its third album. Richard Butler had in mind a new approach with songs more accessible than in the first two LPs. Duncan and Morris were unsatisfied with their career outlook and decided to leave for other projects. Of the six-man band that made the first two albums, only the Butlers, Ashton, and Vince Ely remained to complete the new project and Ely left just after the new tracks were finished.

The new album, *Forever Now* (September 1982), proved a good match in style and content with the first two releases. The Butler-penned songs, if anything, were catchier and easier to recall than earlier efforts. Soon after its release, *Forever Now* appeared on upper U.K. chart levels and penetrated the *Billboard* top 100—a first for the Furs. The single "Love My Way," backed with "I Don't Want to Be Your Shadow," proved the band's most successful U.K. release to that point.

The band that audiences came to see and hear at concerts in the U.S., U.K., and other nations in fall 1982 and the first part of 1983 was now a foursome: the Butlers, Ashton and, on drums, Phil Calvert, who came to the Furs after working with the highly regarded band Birthday Party. For the U.S. shows, their sound was augmented by three other musicians: Ed Buller on keyboards, Gary Windo on saxophone, and Anne Sheldon on cello. After the tour, Calvert

left, reducing the core group to the Butlers and Ashton.

The trio worked with *Flashdance* producer Keith Forsey on new material that included the hit LP *Mirror Moves* (1984). During 1985, Richard Butler helped compile an album of Kurt Weill songs (*Lost in the Stars*, A&M, 1985) sung by many pop stars including Lou Reed, Sting, Marianne Faithfull, and Todd Rundgren. Butler sang Weill's "Alabama Song" for the LP.

During 1985, the Furs' 1981 song "Pretty in Pink" served as the basis for a John Hughes movie of the same title starring Molly Ringwald. Band members re-recorded the song for release as a single in the U.S. to coincide with the film's opening on February 28, 1986. The single made the *Billboard* top 40 and the soundtrack album on A&M went platinum. After concerts in Spain and Italy in early 1986, the band went to Switzerland to finish tracks for the group's fifth LP, *Midnight to Midnight*, (Columbia, October 1986). Issued in late 1986, the LP became the band's biggest-selling and highest-charting disc up to then earning a RIAA gold record award in 1987. It also provided the band's highest-charting single, "Heartbreak Beat."

PUBLIC IMAGE LTD. *Vocal and instrumental group. Original band members (late 1970s): John Lydon, born London, England, 1958; Keith Levene; Jah Wobble; Jeanette Lee; Dave Crowe.*

While it wasn't the first and certainly not the last to play such music, the Sex Pistols' brief, tumultuous existence came to epitomize the spirit of punk rock. When the band's driving force, who called himself Johnny Rotten in his Sex Pistol days, put together his new band, Public Image Ltd., he reassumed his real name, John Lydon, to symbolize new, hopefully less traumatic, beginnings.

As Lydon told an interviewer for a record-company biography in 1984: "I'm sure the public's perception of me is that I'm a narrow-minded, ignorant git. You see, that's what the name of the [present] group is all about: Public Image Limited. Nobody knows who I really am; I'm really very shy. I've made a collection of everything that's written about me for the past 10 years, and it's full of contradictions. And only about 10% of it is true. But that's all right; I've never really cared about the truth. The press are going to write about what they want, aren't they? It's always going to be bigger than the truth and slightly warped."

As he indicated to reporters during Public Image Ltd. tours of the late 1970s and early 1980s, he felt the message of the Sex Pistols and his new band was valid and unchanged—a cry against the restrictions young people had to face and the hypocrisy of many parts of modern society. But he hoped audiences would get off on the music more and spend less time venting anger or despair by pelting band members with spit, bottles, or other debris.

Born into a struggling Irish Catholic family in northern London, Lydon rebelled against accepted conventions from childhood, impelled in part by the difficult family circumstances he grew up in. As early as seven, he recalled, he began to fight against what he felt were the overly rigid doctrines of the church. "I practiced real hard to learn to sing off key so they wouldn't put me in the choir and make me wear those silly dresses."

Like many of his contemporaries, he found solace in the new forms of pop music swirling all around England. In the late 1960s, his favorites were soul and the reggae favored by London's growing ranks of West Indians. He didn't find it easy to pursue his interests, though, considering his parents' strained financial picture. "It's very hard to listen to reggae in England," he said, "when you're freezing cold and there's no heat."

In his teens, he began to consider a career in rock'n'roll as a way out of the deepening unemployment problems that faced working class youth. He frequented underground clubs and performed with various teen musicians. His father didn't like this trend and finally ordered John to leave home when the boy was 15. "My father was always on me about getting my hair cut. So one day I went out, chopped it off and dyed it green. That's the day he threw me out. I was expecting it, and I was ready for it."

Lydon, who was by then experimenting with his own song compositions, knew he could get by staying with friends and gaining money from odd day jobs and occasional performing dates. He was a part of a ferment that was to lead to many landmark groups of the late '70s and the 1980s, such as the Clash, with whom he played at one time in its early stages. (See Clash, The.)

In late 1975, he helped form the Sex Pistols, a four-man band whose angry lyrics were spat out against a backdrop of furiously paced rock. The group, Lydon said, stood for "anarchy in music," offering blunt words that dealt "with common problems like guilt and hate." (See Sex Pistols, The.)

What listeners or the press made of that, he said, was their own business. "I just revolutionized my own life. . . . It was never my intention to hurt anyone. Still isn't. . . . It's all a beginning, isn't it? To build something new you first have to reject the old. 'Out of the rubble' and all of that."

One thing many people don't understand, he maintained, is that "It's okay to do what you want to do—I'm a great example of that—but you have to be able to accept the responsibility and consequences of your actions. People don't see that. All these kids just take up a label or a movement and follow what someone else does. That's never been what I was trying to say. The 'punk' label was created by a British journalist called Caroline Coon. I had nothing to do with it. I'm offended by any kind of label; it implies imitation, and that's the antithesis of everything I stand for."

The Sex Pistols created considerable turmoil in both rock music and the teen music environment during its roughly two-year history. However, it fell apart partly because of American audiences' lack of empathy with the U.K.'s economic situation and partly due to self-destructive impulses of some members, including the bizarre death of bandsman Sid Vicious.

Lydon began to pick up the pieces soon after that incident, determined to make a fresh start with a new band. He brought together other veterans of the mid-1970s rock scene including bass guitarist Jah Wobble, Clash alumnus Keith Levene, and such others as Jeanette Lee and Dave Crowe.

One performer who stayed longest with the group was drummer Martin Atkins. Atkins, born in the Newcastle area of England in 1959, saw an ad for a drummer Lydon placed in *Melody Maker*. Atkins auditioned for the band and was asked to join, but family problems required him to return home for a while. He finally joined in 1979 and was on drums for Public Image Ltd.'s first U.S. tour that year.

In the interim, the band's debut album, *Public Image Ltd.*, came out in England on Virgin Records in 1978. The LP won praise in England, but only appeared in the U.S. as an import disc. It suggested, though, that Lydon still was trying to get his bearings after the Sex Pistols' denouement. The next album, *Metal Box* (issued on Virgin in the U.K. in 1979 and, in shorter form, on Island Records in the U.S. the same year), was one of the year's best rock releases and a top 20 entry in U.K. charts.

The collection came out in the U.S. under the title *Second Edition*. As Dave Marsh pointed out in the *New Rolling Stone Record Guide*, it indicated a difference in packaging from the U.K. version. "*Metal Box* is a flat metal box, sort of like a film can, which holds three 12-inch 45 rpm discs that have an incredible sonic impact—this may be the hottest mastered record in history. It is certainly one of the most exciting, hypnotic, and danceable, building wave after wave of postdisco synthesizer, percussion, and guitar washes, over which Lydon's chanting, taunting, blistering, pestering, pleading, and cowering voice hovers like a muse, a demon, and a whispering child."

The drawback to *Metal Box* in its original form was price—it retailed in the range of $25 to $50 a copy. Today, of course, it's a collectors' item. *Second Edition*, on the other hand, came out at the normal LP price.

That album, however, seemed to represent the high point of the band's career from a creative standpoint. The next release, the live *Paris au Printemps* (Virgin, 1980), didn't match *Metal Box* in quality, although Martin Atkins' recorded debut with the group was a good one. One of the problems was the internal conflicts and incidents affecting band makeup. Before *Paris au Printemps* was released, for instance, Jah Wobble was fired, reportedly for appropriating some leftover tapes from PiL sessions for use on his own solo album. The band lineup changed considerably, with only Atkins still on board from the 1970s roster as of the mid-1980s, and he spent part of his time with a band of his own, Brian Brain.

Despite the ups and downs, Lydon persevered with the band in the 1980s with a number of new albums and tours of the U.K., Continental Europe, the U.S., and elsewhere. American album releases included *Flowers of Romance* (Warner Brothers, 1981) and *This Is What You Want . . . This Is What You Get* (Elektra, 1984).

Though the albums weren't chartbusters, Lydon was satisfied with what he had accomplished. "I'm achieving exactly what I set out to do—without definitions or labels and without anyone pressuring me to conform, which is something I won't do. That's what it's all about. If you tell me to do something—even if it was my own idea—I'll do the opposite. Every time. It's creative anarchy."

PiL's late 1987 album, *Happy?*, and the accompanying concert tour suggested that Lydon, like many early punk protagonists, had decided it was better to join the rock establishment than fight it. Certainly the music was far different in tone than earlier Lydon offerings.

Mainstream critics like Robert Palmer expressed mixed emotions about the apparent transition. Palmer wrote (*The New York Times*, October 18, 1987), "Mr. Lydon has embraced the craftsmanship and professionalism he once scorned. PiL's *Happy?* finds him leading a quartet that includes former members of Magazine, Siouxsie and the Banshees, Shriekback and Rip Rig and Panic. But it is squarely in the rock tradition. The songs are riff-based and conventionally structured, more reminiscent of heavy metal than the early PiL's *Metal Box*. And Mr. Lydon is singing them like a musician, hitting the notes and holding them, rather than letting bite and frenzy fracture and distort his pitches as he did with the Sex Pistols and the early PiL.

"Mr. Lydon used to enjoy arguing that rock is dead; now he is playing the rock game, and playing it by the rules. [The album] was evidently mixed with commercial radio play in mind. It's more agressive than, say, Mick Jagger's latest solo album, but not so different in essentials. No matter how well it succeeds on its own terms, fans of the Sex Pistols, and especially of early PiL, are bound to be disappointed."

QUATRO, SUZI: *Singer, guitarist, band leader, songwriter, actress. Born Detroit, Michigan, June 3, 1950.*

A trailblazer, in a way, Suzi Quatro was one of the first performers to prove that a woman could handle hard-driving rock'n'roll as both solo vocalist and rock guitarist. She helped open the door for stars such as Joan Jett and Pat Benatar, though she had to leave her native U.S. and go to England to achieve it.

Her interest in pop music—particularly the recognition that could come from performing before a live audience—began in childhood, she told Robert Hilburn of the *Los Angeles Times* (May 19, 1974): "When I was a kid, I was never ever in with the popular crowd of girls. I was always cast out. I don't know why. I even used to offer sweets if I could hang around with them for a day. Maybe I was too tomboyish for them or something.

"But it made me lonely and I used to turn to singing. I can remember many, many times just walking down the street singing crazy stuff like 'Me and My Shadow.' I'm not trying to do the violin/sympathy bit, but maybe that's what I'm all about today.

"In my own mind, I probably made myself into some kind of orphan . . . if you're lonely you feel like an orphan even if you have a big family. You sort of cast yourself out all on your own. Maybe that's why I love show business so much. All of that applause is a bit of love that I need."

As she moved into her teens, her desire for outside recognition led to fantasies about a stage career. She told Hilburn: "I remember going to a Beatles concert in Detroit when I was 14 or so and I heard this incredible noise from the crowd. I couldn't believe how great the screams sounded to me. I said to myself: 'Someday I'll be up there.'"

Not long after, she started putting that idea into operation. One June night she was dissatisfied with a rock group playing at a local Detroit club. She voiced her disapproval to the club owner, who told her something like: "Oh yeah! Well, if you're so good, why don't you form your own band."

She told Hilburn: "Well, I've always picked up on things like that. I've always been something of a smartass. So I got all my friends together and we started a band. Everyone sort of chose an instrument and I was left with the bass [guitar]. I had taken some classical piano lessons as a child and had played drums in the school band, but I didn't know anything about the bass. I remember it was as big as I was, but I learned to play it and we went back to the club and did an audition."

Suzi was still a teenager at the time, but she got a fake ID indicating she was over 18 so she could work in places serving liquor. The audition with the Detroit club owner earned her and her friends their first gig, although not all of them tried to persevere in the rough rock-band environment.

For the next half-dozen years, Suzi pursued her goal with a succession of groups, all composed of female musicians. Among the groups she worked with or headed were the Pleasure Seekers and the Cradle. She assembled the Cradle with some of her sisters as members. She wasn't a superfeminist about it, she told interviewers. In fact, she would have preferred to have added male members to those groups, but it was difficult to persuade her other band people to accept that. When she would bring up a male musician's name as a replacement, she said, the others would protest that it would ruin the all-girl image. "I was never into that," she said. "I just wanted to be a rock'n'roller. I just wanted to entertain. That was always my goal."

By 1971, Suzi was beginning to doubt her capacity to move out of Midwestern obscurity. She ran into British record producer Mickey Most, who suggested that she might find more opportunities in England. After mulling it over, she finally took his advice and, by 1972, had settled down in London. She did session work and made demo tapes as part of the campaign to become accepted on the U.K. rock circuit. It was slow going for a while, but she finally gained the ear of U.K. songwriting-production team Nicky Chinn and Mike Chapman, who decided she could give some of their new songs the right exposure.

Chinn and Chapman helped her assemble a new, all-male band to record songs they selected. Once the band was in working order, Suzi also started co-writing original numbers with guitarist Len Tuckey. Many of the numbers on her debut U.S. album, released on Bell Records in 1974, were Quatro/Tuckey collaborations. The new alignment soon brought rewards in the form of a string of hit singles in the U.K. and Europe. The first, Chinn and Chapman's "Can the Can," achieved sales totals of over 3 million copies. Other overseas chartmakers included "48 Crash" and "I Wanna Be Your Man." During the mid-1970s, Quatro gained star status not only in the U.K., but in many other countries outside the U.S. She even starred in her own TV specials in East Germany, New Zealand, and Australia.

Achieving major recognition in her own country proved harder. She won attention as an opening act for Alice Cooper on a U.S. tour in 1975, but without hits in the U.S. to match her U.K. laurels, there was no impetus for headline status. Critical evaluation in the U.S. was mixed. A number of established writers, including those at the *Los Angeles Times*, acclaimed her the equal of any male rocker, but others, such as *Rolling Stone* reviewers, suggested she was only a novelty whose hits were "mindless variations" of a formula developed by Chinn and Chapman.

Some of the adverse reactions came in response to many rock writers' disdain for TV sitcoms. She stirred their wrath by becoming the resident rock singer on a number of "Happy Days" episodes. Her first appearance as Leather Tuscadero came in a two-hour episode called "Fonzie—Rock Entrepreneur." It went over well with viewers if not rock critics and resulted in the role being expanded to several later programs.

But her TV roles probably increased her potential as a rock performer. She gained a new U.S. recording agreement with RSO Records, which issued her label debut *If You Knew Suzi* in 1978. From that were culled several hit singles, including "If You Can't Give Me Love" and top 5 "Stumblin' In" (her initial gold record in the States).

September 1979 brought her second RSO album, *Suzi . . . and Other Four Letter Words*. Its first single release was "I've Never Been in Love." Also featured were two new Chinn-Chapman numbers: "Four Letter Words" and "She's in Love with You," as well as tracks penned by Suzi and Tuckey. That album didn't match the success of its predecessor, partly because RSO had encountered financial problems that limited the support it could give the new material.

In 1980, Suzi moved to a new company, Dreamland. Her label debut, *Rock Hard* (fall 1980), and title track appeared on upper charts levels in a number of countries outside the U.S. by year-end.

QUEEN: *Vocal and instrumental group. Freddie Mercury, born Zanzibar, September 5, 1946; Brian May, born England, July 19, 1947; John Deacon, born Leicester, England, August 19, 1951; Roger Taylor, born Norfolk, England, July 26, 1949.*

"No synthesizers" was the proud boast of England's Queen for its formative musical approach as spelled out on the jacket sleeves of its early albums. Though it disdained such electronic props during its first decade of existence, it found no problem in gaining success on both sides of the Atlantic by blending many instrumental and vocal patterns into a distinctive style. Though its creative juices seemed to flow less freely in the 1980s, it still retained a healthy following among rock fans, particularly for its innovative efforts of the early and middle 1970s.

Queen evolved out of Smile, a group formed in 1968 by Brian May (guitarist) and drummer Roger Taylor (Meddows-Taylor on Queen's first LP) while they were at London University. With singer Roger Staffell, they released a single in the U.S. that flopped, which resulted soon after in the band's breakup.

At the same time, though, Taylor was running an antique clothes stall in a London market with Mercury, whose idea it was to form a new band—to be called Queen—with Taylor and May. In 1971, the group added bassist John Deacon to complete the lineup that remained intact over a decade and a half later.

With Mercury on lead vocals, the group was allowed to make a demo tape free in exchange for testing a London studio's acoustics. The result was contracts with EMI for the U.K. and the rest of Europe and Elektra Records for the rest of the world.

The debut album, *Queen*, appeared in July 1973 and "Keep Yourself Alive" was released as a single. A U.K. tour followed with Queen opening for Mott the Hoople. Noting Mercury's shrill lead vocals and May's flamboyant guitar style, reviewers suggested the group drew inspiration from Led Zeppelin, but also put great emphasis on harmonies in vocals and guitars. Particularly noteworthy was May's unusual playing style in which he loosened the guitar strings to get a curious purring quality.

A second album, *Queen II* (1974), and a single, "Seven Seas of Rhye," made the charts in Britain. A tour as headliners followed and the group rapidly moved toward becoming a mass-audience favorite in Europe, especially after their third album, *Sheer Heart Attack* (released later that year).The single "Killer Queen," which eschewed the heavy rock sound, was a hit in Britain and other parts of the world, and so was the follow-up, "Now I'm Here."

From the gold 1975 *A Night at the Opera* LP, "Bohemian Rhapsody" broke commercial rules to become one of the biggest hit singles released in Britain. Nine weeks at number one was the longest stay at the top for a single in the U.K. since Tom Jones' 1966 "Green, Green Grass of Home." "Bohemian Rhapsody" was noteworthy for Mercury's elaborate vocal arrangements and the fact that its playing time was over five minutes.

Critics duly noted the educational background of the key band members as contributing considerably to the more complex nature of the group's original material. Deacon, for instance, had earned a degree

in electronics, Taylor in biology, and May in astronomy.

The group continued to add to its laurels in the middle and late '70s. Gold and platinum albums included *A Day at the Races* and *News of the World* (1977), *Jazz* (1978), and the two-disc *Queen Killer Live* (1979). In early 1978, the band had a spectacular singles success with "We Are the Champions" backed with "We Will Rock You." Not only was "We Are the Champions" played for many major athletic contests in Britain and the U.S., it was also used in a variety of other environments, including political meetings.

At the end of 1979, Elektra released the single "Crazy Little Thing Called Love," a Freddie Mercury composition. On February 23, 1980, it became number one, the first Queen single to hit *Billboard*'s number one, staying there for three more weeks.

Actually, it almost wasn't given that opportunity. Initially issued in the U.K. (a number two hit there), Elektra resisted doing anything special with it in America. As Mercury told Fred Bronson (*The Billboard Book of Number One Hits*): "We all felt it was a hit, except Elektra, which didn't want to release it." Recalling its origins, he noted, "We arranged the song at band rehearsals [after he had written it while taking a bath at the Munich Hilton] . . . with me trying to play rhythm guitar. Everyone loved it so we recorded it. The . . . finished version sounded like the bathtub version. It's not typical of my work but that's because nothing is typical of my work."

In October 1980, the band scored its second number one U. S. hit with Deacon's composition "Another One Bites the Dust," one of Queen's few numbers not written by Mercury. Impetus for issuing the single, Queen noted, came from Michael Jackson, a friend of Mercury's, who saw the track's hit potential. (*See Jackson, Michael.*)

After the banner year of 1980 (including the platinum LP *The Game*, issued in America on Elektra), the band's fortunes seemed to decline, though not precipitously. From then through the mid-1980s, Queen wasn't able to place another single in the top 10, though it made the top 20, 30, or 50 on several occasions. The theme number the band wrote and recorded for the 1981 Dino De Laurentis film *Flash Gordon* made the top 50 and a collaboration with David Bowie, "Under Pressure," made the top 30 in 1981. (*See Bowie, David.*) In June 1982, "Body Language" just missed top 10 status, petering out at number 11. Meanwhile, the Elektra retrospective *Queen's Greatest Hits* (1981) went platinum while *Hot Space* (1982) went gold.

In 1983, the group tried to improve its fortunes by leaving Elektra in favor of Capitol Records for

American distribution. The band's debut single on Capitol, "Radio Ga-Ga," made the top 20 in April, but couldn't move past number 16 in *Billboard*. Its 1984 LP, *The Works*, did reach gold levels.

Perhaps one reason for the band's loss of momentum in the mid-1980s was diffusion of members' energy into solo projects such as Brian May's 1983 single "Star Fleet" and Roger Taylor's 1981 Elektra album *Fun in Space*. Freddie Mercury provided a track for Giorgio Moroder's soundtrack assemblage for the film *Metropolis* and recorded the solo album *Mr. Bad Guy* from which the single "I Was Born to Love You" was taken.

Though all the members complained they needed some time off for rest and relaxation, they agreed to take part in the summer 1985 Live Aid concert to help victims of starvation in Africa. In comments for a 1986 Capitol promotion brochure, Deacon stated, "Live Aid turned our whole world upside down. Before it we'd promised ourselves a good long rest. But the band was rejuvenated by that wonderful day; it breathed new life into us. Now we're bursting with enthusiasm and ideas. There's so much we want to do, it's hard to find the right order."

The group recorded a new album, *A Kind of Magic*, that won high praise in Europe (but much less respect in the U.S.) and entered English charts at number one (June 1986). The title song within weeks was at number three on the English publication *Music Week*'s charts.

?QUESTION MARK AND THE MYSTERIANS: *Vocal and instrumental group from Mexico. Bobby Balderrama, born 1950; Frank Rodriguez, born 1951; Frank Lugo, born 1947; Eddie Serrati, born 1947; ?Question Mark, born 1945.*

With a lead singer known only by the pseudonym ?Question Mark, the Mysterians moved briefly into the spotlight in 1966 with the number one single "96 Tears." The group placed a few other songs on the charts during 1966–67, but was not able to maintain its new following and disbanded.

The founding members of the band were born in Mexico, but by the mid-1960s were established in the Detroit area. A great deal of rock'n'roll activity was taking place in clubs and auditoriums in the Saginaw Valley area a short distance north of Detroit. ?Question Mark and the Mysterians became a favorite of local teenagers. The group comprised ?Question Mark (real name Rudy Martinez) on vocals, Bobby Balderrama (20 years later with Joe "King" Carrasco's Crowns) on lead guitar, Frank Rodriguez on organ, Frank Lugo on bass, and Eddie Serrati on drums. The original band had two other members,

Robert Martinez and Larry Borjas, who were away in the U.S. armed forces when the band scored its successes.

The group wrote most of its material including "96 Tears." The organ-heavy number became a great crowd pleaser at the Mt. Holly dance hall in the Saginaw Valley in 1966. Word of the song reached small record firms in Flint and resulted in a single that became the number one request on local station WTAC. This situation was repeated a short time after on Detroit's CKLW and the record soon was given national distribution on the Cameo label, selling over a million copies.

The song was featured on the group's debut LP, which made the charts during 1966. The album included such other compositions by the group as "I Need Somebody" (their only other single to break *Billboard*'s top 40), "You're Telling Me Lies," "Ten O'Clock," "Set Aside," "Don't Tease Me," and "8-Teen." "I Need Somebody" and "8-Teen" were issued as follow-up singles to "96 Tears," but fared poorly with record buyers. In 1971, though, Alice Cooper had a chart hit with "8-Teen," retitled "Eighteen."

The band fell apart soon after, but "96 Tears" became a classic, thanks in part to the keyboard styling and overall garage sound that anticipated the rise of punk and new wave in the 1970s. Available as a Japanese import in the late 1970s and early 1980s was a reissue on the London label of the LP *96 Tears*.

A new recording of "96 Tears" by Garland Jeffreys made the *Billboard* Hot 100 in 1981. While not anywhere near a top 40 hit, it encouraged Martinez to form a new Mysterians band for tour dates.

QUIET RIOT: *Vocal and instrumental group from Los Angeles. Members (mid-1980s): Kevin DuBrow; Frankie Banali; Rudy Sarzo; Carlos Cavazo. DuBrow left early 1987, replaced by Paul Shortino. Sarzo replaced by Chuck Wright, 1987; Wright left early 1988 replaced by Sean McNabb.*

Although new wave and Springsteen-style rock received the most attention in the 1980s, heavy metal was, to say the least, alive and well. In the 1980s, U.S. competition against its many U.K. and Australian exponents increasingly seemed to come from California, which spawned such aggressively successful groups as Mötley Crüe, Night Ranger, and Quiet Riot.

Central figure of Quiet Riot from its inception until 1987 was lead vocalist Kevin DuBrow. DuBrow, who grew up in the Los Angeles area, was listening to rock from his childhood and singing with amateur groups in his high school years. Among the people he was associated with was guitarist Randy Rhoads, son of a prominent Southern California industrial company executive. In 1975, DuBrow and Rhoads formed the first version of Quiet Riot.

DuBrow and Rhoads made the requisite demonstration tapes usually needed to win a recording contract. At the time, though, heavy metal was not one of the "in" forms with the U.S. artists and repertoire executives and Quiet Riot received a steady series of turndowns. However, the tapes found their way to representatives of the Japanese-based CBS/Sony label. The resultant contract provided the basis for two LPs released in Japan: *Quiet Riot* (1977) and *Quiet Riot II* (1978). A single from the 1978 LP, "Slick Black Cadillac," became an overseas hit, selling over 100,000 copies in Japan and also getting airplay on Los Angeles rock station KROQ.

Still, that wasn't enough to keep the operation going. DuBrow and Rhoads decided to break up the group in 1980. DuBrow asserted: "We were frustrated at not being acknowledged by American record companies." Without that recognition, of course, the band didn't have the support needed to become more than a regional success. Rhoads went on to become lead guitarist and major songwriter for Ozzy Osbourne in a career cut short by his death in a light plane crash in March 1982. (*See Osbourne, John "Ozzy."*)

For a while, DuBrow performed locally in Los Angeles with another group he formed, but didn't make much progress. In 1982, with the outlook in the U.S. improving for heavy metal, particularly with new record-company interest, DuBrow decided to reincarnate Quiet Riot. One of the first recruits was bass guitarist Rudy Sarzo, a former member of the '70s Quiet Riot who had toured afterward with Ozzy Osbourne and backed him on his *Speak of the Devil* album. Guitarist Carlos Cavazo, who had played in the L.A. group Snow, and drummer Frankie Banali (an experienced bandsman and session player whose credits included work on Billy Idol's single "Mony, Mony") rounded out the foursome. (*See Idol, Billy.*)

This time the demo tapes accomplished their purpose. The band won a contract from Pasha Records, a label distributed by CBS. The debut collection *Metal Health* was released in the spring of 1983. At last Quiet Riot had the backing for saturation touring of the U.S. in support of the LP. The program also included plans for singles releases in coordination with MTV-aimed videos. The band went on the road for a total of 205 shows in 1983—including openings for established groups AC/DC, Loverboy, ZZ Top, Black Sabbath, and the Scorpions—playing before an estimated 2.5 million people. All this helped *Metal Health* become the first heavy metal debut LP to hit number one in *Billboard*. By the end of 1984, it had exceeded platinum levels several times over, achieving sales of more than 4.5 million copies. Besides U.S. success, *Metal Health* went triple-platinum in Canada and also was a hit in England, Australia, Japan, and Mexico.

Several singles from the album made the charts, including the band's version of U.K. rock band Slade's song, "Cum on Feel the Noize," which rose to number five in the U.S. The band reached the top without the threatening physical appearance usually adopted by heavy metal purveyors. DuBrow commented: "People think heavy metal music is all leather and studs, but I think it's in the vibe of the music. The old Quiet Riot sometimes had to work at being outrageous with wild clothes and stuff, but in this band we can just be what we are and people will remember us because there's so much insanity going on among the four of us."

The group was ranked as one of the best new bands of 1983 in a number of polls. Besides that, Carlos Cavazo was runner-up to Stevie Ray Vaughan in *Guitar Player* magazine's reader's poll for Best New Talent.

The band now had the challenging task of equalling or bettering its debut. DuBrow said: "People said that our first album brought the anthem back to hard rock. It did, but not intentionally. This time, though, we really went for anthems, and you can tell from the song titles: 'Party All Night,' 'Stomp Your Hands Clap Your Feet,' 'We Were Born to Rock.'" Also included was another cover of a Slade song, "Mama Weer All Crazee Now."

DuBrow acknowledged the recordings were made with commercial possibilities uppermost in mind. "In a way, we're making music for the same reasons we were back when we played clubs. But we're not the same guys anymore; we're an arena rock band now, and we have our sights set on sticking with the big time."

The second album, *Condition Critical* (mid-1984), went platinum, but it didn't have the dramatic acceptance of the previous one. At year-end, the band ranked in the top 20 in *Billboard*'s Top Album Artists category. The group also was represented on singles charts with three songs during the year, including the top 40 entry "Bang Your Head."

A major upheaval in band organization took place before the group's new LP, *QR III*, came out (1987). Early in 1987, DuBrow left, stating he intended to pursue a solo career and other projects including production of an album (tentatively titled *Boys Will Be Boys*) for the band Juliet. His lead vocal chores were

550

taken over by Paul Shortino. During 1987, Chuck Wright took over from Sarzo on bass; by early 1988, Wright also had left.

RAINBOW: *See Deep Purple.*

RAMONES: *Vocal and instrumental group from Forest Hills, New York. Original members, 1974: Joey Ramone; Dee Dee Ramone; Johnny Ramone; Tommy Erdelyi. Erdelyi replaced in 1978 by Marc Bell (Marky Ramone). Marc replaced in 1983 by Richie Beau (Richie Ramone). Beau left 1987, Marc Bell returned.*

The raw intensity of the Ramones' no frills, high-powered rock songs was an important catalyst for the U.S. punk movement and also had an impact (exactly how much is open to question) on the English punk scene of the mid-1970s. The leather-jacketed group from a middle-class section of New York's Nassau County won great critical acclaim at the time, but the punk movement's excesses also brought on many adverse reactions. The failure of England's Sex Pistols in their American efforts seemed to put a crimp in mass audience acceptance of the Ramones. But the band persevered and continued to influence the rock field in the 1980s.

The original quartet first gained attention on the New York rock scene in August 1974 when its simple, searing sonic attack brought rousing approval from audiences in CBGB in the Manhattan Bowery district. (The band roster had Joey on lead vocals; Johnny on lead guitar; Dee Dee on bass and vocals; and Tommy on drums.) Some people later suggested the band took its name from recording expert Phil Ramone, but the band asserted it came from the Beatles' use of pseudonyms during one career phase, when Paul McCartney had called himself Paul Ramone. Over the years the band makeup changed from time to time, but the concept of using Ramone as everybody's last name continued. Thus the group originally was Johnny, Joey, Dee Dee, and Tommy Ramone; later, Tommy left; to be replaced by Marky Ramone, and so on.

The group evolved from one called Dusk, which already had an album on Kama Sutra. After the CBGB breakthrough, the Ramones became one of the best-known nonrecorded bands in the New York area from 1974–76, playing CBGB many times as well as other rock clubs in and around New York. In late 1975, Sire Records signed them. A dozen years later, Sire still was the group's label (distributed by Warner Brothers).

Quoted in a 1988 press bio, Joey Ramone explained the band's musical origins: "We decided to start our own group because we were bored with everything we heard in the early '70s; there was nothing to listen to anymore. Everything was tenth generation Elton John or overproduced or just junk. Everything was long jams, long guitar solos. We missed hearing songs that were short and exciting . . . and good! We wanted to bring the energy back to rock & roll."

But as he noted, the band did have heroes—Gene Vincent, Eddie Cochran, the Beatles, the Beach Boys, the Kinks, MC5, the Stooges, Alice Cooper, and Slade. The band members had rather rudimentary musical skills, though. He observed, "We just couldn't figure them [the aforementioned groups] out, so we decided to write our own, and we had to make them basic enough so we could play them."

When their debut LP, *Ramones,* came out in early 1976, the sound was far from polished and the lead singer sang off key more than once, but the overall effect was vibrant and fresh, a return to some of the roots of early rock and a protest against the increasing blandness of then current rock recordings. The band's 1976 concerts included a summer visit to London venues where some members of the English punk-style bands were in the audience.

The band followed with a series of albums that remain among the best rock discs of the 1970s: *Ramones Leave Home* (early 1977), from which the chart single "Sheena Is a Punk Rocker" was taken; *Rocket to Russia* (late 1977); and *Road to Ruin* (1978). Tommy (Ramone) Erdelyi co-produced all three, the first two with Tony Bongiovi and the third with Ed Stasium. By the time *Road to Ruin* was in preparation, Erdelyi had given up performing work in favor of producing and his place was taken by Marc Bell, formerly of the Voidoids.

Not all the band's late '70s projects were notable. One misstep was its participation in the cardboard cutout movie, *Rock'n'Roll High School.* (The group wrote and performed the title song, which was included on the soundtrack LP issued by Sire in mid-'79.) During the group's stay in Southern California to work on the film it became acquainted with famed record executive and writer Phil Spector, who produced the Ramones' next album, *End of the Century* (1980).

It was not an auspicious start for the Ramones in the new decade. *End of the Century* diverged little from the group's 1970s releases and *Pleasant Dreams* (1981) was even less effective. David Marsh, for one, wrote (*New Rolling Stone Record Guide,* Random House/Rolling Stone Press, 1983) that *Pleasant Dreams* was a "dead-end, a faint-hearted reiteration of what made the Ramones initially intriguing. The problem with amatuerism, it seems, is that you can't make a career out of it.''

But the band continued to be a good attraction throughout the 1980s, mostly in small- to medium-size venues at home, though the band retained a sizable following overseas. Its early material was still excitingly performed and it did come up with provocative new themes from time to time on topics ranging from the KKK to some of President Reagan's actions. After *Subterranean Jungle* came out in early 1983, there were worries about the group's future when health problems sidelined Joey and Johnny that summer and Marky left. But Joey and Johnny returned, and with Richie Beau taking over on drums went back into the studio to complete *Too Tough to Die* (late 1984), for which Erdelyi (with Ed Stasium) handled production chores for the first time since 1978.

Albums like *Animal Boy* (1986) and *Halfway to Sanity* (1987) had their share of Ramones cynicism. One mid-1986 singles release was "Bonzo Goes to Bitburg" (a reference to President Reagan's visit to a German cemetery containing graves of members of Hitler's SS) which was a hit in Europe. (For U.S. release, some record execs wanted to water the title down to "My Brain is Hanging Down.")

In mid-1988, a two-disc retrospective of the band's most successful and most notorious songs was released under the title *Ramonesmania*. By then Richie had departed and Marky once more held forth on drums.

RARE EARTH: *Vocal and instrumental group, all born 1940s. Personnel (early 1970s): Pete Rivera, born Detroit, Michigan; John Persh, born Detroit, Michigan; Gil Bridges, born Detroit, Michigan; Mark Olson; Ray Monette; Ed Guzman.*

Because Rare Earth's hits invariably turned up on both the general pop lists and the soul charts and their record label was Motown, many people assumed they were a black group. This was not the case, although Rare Earth's combination of hard rock, funky blues, and soul seemed authentic enough to many black fans.

One explanation for the group's sound was the fact that its founding members—John Persh, Pete Rivera, and Gil Bridges—grew up in Detroit at a time when the Motown sound was in full bloom. Soul music was to be heard in clubs and theaters all over the city, performed by an almost unending stream of exuberant, talented black artists. From their early teens, Persh, Rivera, and Bridges were attracted to this music and they spent many hours listening to soul groups before branching out as professional musicians.

The three attended elementary and high school together and started rehearsing as a trio in their mid-teens, with Persh on bass and trombone, Bridges on saxophone and flute, Rivera on drums, and all three singing. At 16, at the close of the 1950s, they started playing for parties, dances, or "whatever paid." Under the name of the Sunliners, they worked in and around Detroit in small clubs and on the campus circuit for most of the 1960s.

In 1969, they reorganized and added several members, changed the group name to Rare Earth, and gained a contract from Motown. Their first album, *Get Ready*, was released on the Rare Earth label (a division of Motown) in the fall of 1969. With strong promotional support by Motown, it made the top 20 nationally in May 1970. It was even more successful in the soul field, making the top 5 in April. The title track made *Billboard*'s pop top 10. Both the album and the single exceeded gold record totals worldwide according to Motown.

The group's second LP, *Ecology* (summer 1970), moved even more rapidly than the first one, hitting the top 10 in October and achieving gold-record status by the end of 1971. By the time the group's third LP, *One World*, was released in the fall of 1971, there were three new faces in the band. Ed Guzman (percussion) joined Rare Earth in September 1971 and Mark Olson (organ and piano) and Ray Monette (guitar) became band members in early 1971. The second and third hit albums resulted in three more singles hits for the group: "I Know I'm Losing You," "Born to Wander," and "I Just Want to Celebrate." These songs, like most tracks on the group's albums, were composed by band members.

The group started 1972 in good style with both a single ("Hey Big Brother") and an album (the two-LP *Rare Earth in Concert*) moving up the best-seller lists. Later in the year, the group hit with singles "Good Time Sally" and a remake of Ray Charles' "What'd I Say" plus the album *Willie Remembers*.

The group's forward momentum continued into the mid-1970s, but then its ability to make the hit lists declined sharply. It turned out new albums on the Prodigal label, such as *Rare Earth* (1977) and *Band Together* (1978). In 1981, Motown issued a compilation of the group's hits on the Rare Earth label titled *Super Star Series, Volume 16*.

RASCALS, THE: *Vocal and instrumental group. Original members: Felix Cavaliere, born Pelham, New York, November 29, 1943; Dino Danelli, born New York, New York, July 23, c. 1945; Eddie Brigati, born New York, October 22, 1946; Gene Cornish, born Ottawa, Canada, May 14, 1945. Reorganized group (1971) included Cavaliere; Danelli; Buzzy Feiten, Born New*

"Blue-eyed soul brother" and "the groups' group" were just two of the unofficial titles collected by the Rascals in the second half of the '60s. By any standard, the band must rank as one of the United States' most striking contributions to both rock and soul music.

The three founding members—Felix Cavaliere, Dino Danelli, and Eddie Brigati—all had grown up in and around New York and had considerable experience as sidemen before founding the Rascals, then called the Young Rascals, in early 1965. Cavaliere began classical piano lessons as a boy. However, when he started listening to such R&B greats as Ray Charles and Otis Redding, he knew this was the kind of music he had to play.

By the time he started frequenting the soul clubs of Harlem in his teens, he had learned many R&B standards on both piano and organ. In high school, he was the only white member of a soul group from Pelham called the Stereos. He left the group and attended Syracuse University in upstate New York. However, whenever he could, he returned to New York and spent time at such clubs as the Peppermint Lounge and Metropole.

Dino Danelli learned drums before his teens and started playing professionally at 15. His first interest was jazz rather than R&B. He found a job in his midteens with Lionel Hampton and later moved on to work with a band on Bourbon Street in New Orleans. As he recalled, that job was a turning point. "The roots are all still there in the South. You listen and learn playing with funky New Orleans cats. New Orleans taught me a lot and changed the direction I was going musically, from jazz to R&B." Dino returned to New York and found work as a sideman and session performer in the R&B field. By the time he met Felix, he was supporting R&B artists such as Little Willie John.

Felix and Dino became acquainted at the Metropole. A short time before this, Dino had met Eddie Brigati, a young singer who sat in with R&B groups when he could, while Danelli was playing with a band in a New Jersey club. After meeting, Felix and Dino went to work in Las Vegas for a time in 1964 as part of a backup group for singer Sandy Scott. After that job, Felix joined Joey Dee's Starlighters at New York's Peppermint Lounge. This group included Eddie Brigati, who had added tambourine playing to his talents, and a guitarist from Canada named Gene Cornish. (*See Dee, Joey, and the Starlighters.*)

As these three and Dino spent spare time together, the idea for beginning their own group took hold.

During the winter of 1964–65, they sequestered themselves in Felix's house and worked out a repertoire of 25 songs, many with music by Felix and lyrics by Eddie, who jointly wrote many of the group's later hits. In February 1965, the band opened in a small roadhouse in New Jersey, the Choo Choo, and later in the year became the regular band at the Barge, a floating nightclub in Westhampton, Long Island. After Sid Bernstein, the promoter who brought the Beatles to America, heard them, he became their manager.

Soon after, the (Young) Rascals signed with Atlantic and provided a hit single in their early effort, "I Ain't Gonna Eat My Heart Out Anymore." They followed with successes, "Good Lovin'" (number one in 1966), "You Better Run," and "I've Been Lonely Too Long." Their debut albums, *The Young Rascals* (1966) and *Collections* (1967) went gold.

The group usually featured Brigati as lead vocalist but in some instances, as on the 1967 gold "Groovin'," Cavaliere's performance caused some critics to compare his vocal ability with Ray Charles'. The LP *Groovin'* also went gold, as did the 1968 retrospective *Time/Peace: The Rascals Greatest Hits,* both of whose covers were painted by Danelli. *Once upon a Dream* made *Billboard*'s LP top 10 in 1968.

The Rascals appeared regularly on the charts in the late 1960s. Singles hits from 1967–69 included "A Girl Like You," "How Can I Be Sure," "It's Wonderful," and "A Ray of Hope." The 1968 singles "A Beautiful Morning" and "People Got to Be Free" and 1969 two-disc LP *Freedom Suite* won gold records. The group entered 1970 with a chart album, *See.*

But at the start of the '70s, there were internal strains among the members and little chart action for the band's recordings. In 1971, the group moved from Atlantic to Columbia and also changed personnel. Cavaliere and Danelli remained as the central figures, but three new performers were added: Buzzy Feiten, Robert Popwell, and Ann Sutton. (A sixth performer, vocalist Molly Holt, worked with them in their first Columbia sessions.)

Feiten—a lead guitarist, pianist, singer, bassist and songwriter—had been working with instruments since his youth. In 1969, he joined the Paul Butterfield Blues Band as the replacement for Mike Bloomfield and, in 1970, he did considerable session work, including Bob Dylan's *New Morning* LP.

Popwell, born and raised in Florida, started learning drums in grade school. At 17, he took up the bass guitar and became a much sought after studio guitarist, backing Livingston Taylor, Dylan, Eddie Floyd, Tim Hardin, and Aretha Franklin. He also could be heard on two of the LPs by Swamp Dogg.

Ann Sutton began voice lessons for opera while attending high school in western Pennsylvania. She majored in music at the University of Pittsburgh, but also sang with soul groups around the city. By 1965, she was living in Philadelphia and performing with soul and jazz groups, including the Joe Bel Castro Trio, which won the Notre Dame Jazz Festival award that year. Later, she was a member of Jimmy Belmont and Groov-U and Mika before joining the new Rascals in 1971.

The new group's debut album, *Peaceful World*, was on the hit lists in the summer of 1971. The next, *Island of Real* (spring 1972), also made the charts for a time. However, it was obvious that the audience for the band had diminished, and it broke up during the year. Danelli later joined Cornish in the group Bulldog that had a charted debut album, *Bulldog*, on Decca in 1972 and a Hot 100 *Billboard* single "No."

Later in the 1970s, Bulldog was reorganized and the name changed to Fotomaker. In 1976, Eddie Brigati and his brother David recorded the LP *Brigati* for Elektra, which unfortunately was eminently forgettable. At the start of the 1980s Cavaliere made the charts once more with a top 40 single, "Only a Lonely Heart Sees." In 1982, Danelli joined a group headed by Steve Van Zandt called Little Steven's Disciples of Soul.

In 1988, Rhino Records licensed a number of the Rascals' most popular LPs for reissue and also put out *Searching for Ecstasy: The Rest of the Rascals, 1969–1972* (tracks from their less successful and therefore hard-to-find *See, Search and Nearness, Peaceful World*, and *The Island of Real* LPs). During 1988 Daneli, Cavaliere and Cornish reunited for a national tour.

RATT: *Vocal and instrumental group from San Diego, California. Members (mid-1980s): Stephen Pearcy; Robbin Crosby; Warren De Martini, born 1963; Juan Croucier; Bobby Blotzer.**

Drag racing's loss might be heavy metal's gain. If not for a motorcycle accident in his early teens, Ratt founder Steven Pearcy might have gone on to glory on the quarter-mile strips instead of fronting one of the more promising new bands of the mid-1980s.

Pearcy's dreams of challenging people such as Don Garlits or Shirley Muldowney for top fuel honors went back to his preteen years. In fact, he once had a goal of becoming the youngest professional wheelman on the drag-racing circuit. Growing up in San Diego, he wasn't that far away from the championship tracks in the Los Angeles area. He began to

make contacts in the field before he reached high school age.

Things seemed promising for him in that direction in the early 1970s. "At 14, I toured with a twin-engine gas dragster team called the Gashouse Gang. I poured the bleach [on the start-up track area] to heat the tires to give them more grip. All I wanted to do in life was race. At 15, I was waiting to get a driver's license so I could start driving the fuel cars. One of the guys was going to lend me his $100,000 dragster so I could take the test."

Those hopes had to be put aside when he collided with a car while driving his motorcycle. Both his legs were broken so badly he had to spend a year in a hospital. Though he finally was on the road to recovery, he was warned by his doctors it would be dangerous for him to try to return to racing.

Fortunately, while his bones were mending, he found a new outlet for his energies. A friend gave him a guitar and he overcame the boredom of lying in bed by learning to play. In 1978, another friend took him to see a concert by Van Halen at the Los Angeles Starwood, one of that band's early steps on the road to stardom. Impressed, Pearcy decided he wanted to become involved in that kind of rock'n'roll. He spent an increasing amount of time attending rock concerts in L.A. clubs, seeking opportunities to play with local musicians. He told himself: "This is easy. I'm going to do this" and soon was performing with bands in San Diego. After a few years of this, he moved to L.A. and took steps to form his own band.

He first enlisted two musically inclined friends from San Diego: singer/guitarist Warren De Martini and Robbin Crosby, who was also adept on guitar and vocals. Pearcy decided to downplay his own guitar work in favor of handling lead vocals. The band evolved into a quintet paced by the twin-guitar interplay of De Martini and Crosby.

Crosby recalled that he, De Martini, and Pearcy had been close friends since childhood and were somewhat antisocial during that period. The trio, Crosby said, tended to be "troublemakers." De Martini added: "Stephen Pearcy and I both grew up angry. Our anger grew into initiative to do something. Stephen is very proud. He's been bashed around a couple of times in his life and he's not going to be bashed around anymore. Anger can work for you or against you. It worked for us. Our songs come out dark because of it. But anger is what gives us our fire."

Crosby's involvement in rock, he commented, preceded Pearcy's. "When I was about twelve, I got interested in rock guitar. My friends in school were listening to the Monkees, but I had older sisters who were into the Yardbirds and Jimi Hendrix and that

*Based partly on Robbin Crosby personal interview with Irwin Stambler.

turned me on and later seeing the film *Woodstock* got me even more excited. I had a paper route and saved money to buy myself a $35 guitar and taught myself to play. My sister taught me a few chords she knew and I added to it by listening to records.''

Playing with local groups, he began to write original material. ''One of the things that made me move to L.A. was that nobody in San Diego was interested in hearing original music. Warren, Steven and I all migrated to L.A. in different bands and then decided to join forces and make the ultimate rock'n'roll band. Originally in L.A. we had a different drummer and bass player but that was only for a little while. We found Bobby [Bobby Blotzer, drummer/percussionist] and he knew Juan Croucier from playing in other bands. That led to the true original Ratt lineup in late 1981.

''After I got together with Steven and Warren we all lived together in a converted garage we called Rat Mansion West. After a while we had the whole band and our road crew living there getting our meals from cans and sleeping on the floor. We were seven guys in a studio with practically no furniture and Marshalls [Marshall amplifiers] and instruments stacked against the walls.''

The group rehearsed, wrote new songs, and petitioned club owners for a chance to perform. This finally brought an ok to open for the English heavy metal group Saxon at the Whisky on the Sunset Strip. That helped open other doors on the local club circuit and the band began to attract enough of a reputation to earn headline dates at some venues.

Croucier commented: ''It was dog-eat-dog. We would play gigs where we would go to get paid at the end of the night and the club owner would hand us $13. But we did those gigs to get the exposure, to get the name happening around L.A. until we felt we had gotten as successful as we could without releasing an album.''

Crosby recalled, ''The band initially called itself Mickey Rat after a character in a comic book. But the cartoon writer objected, so we just changed it to Ratt. We thought about changing it too, but once we got a big following that didn't make sense. We couldn't see using a name with the words 'formerly Ratt' in parentheses.''

During 1982 and early 1983, the group made some demo tapes they used to try to gain a record contract. When no executives bit, the band gambled on pressing its own extended-play disc, which cost around $3,000, on their own label, Time Coast Records. Local rock station KMET played some of the tracks, but even that failed to gain the ear of major-label A&R people. Ratt and its managers went one step further, somehow putting together enough money to lease the Beverly Theater on Wilshire Bou-

levard in Beverly Hills for a showcase performance in July 1983. Friends and record-company bigwigs were asked to attend—the friends to give audible support and the executives in hopes of future financial backing. The ploy worked. Atlantic Records president Doug Morris came to the concert and concluded Ratt should be on his label.

Crosby stated, ''Our first Atlantic album came out in February 1984 and it took until summer to catch on. Since we thought of our garage home as a cellar, naturally our album title was *Out of the Cellar*. We worked hard to break it, played a gig almost every night for most of the year, and it was a terrific pleasure when it finally caught on. The fact it eventually went multi-platinum exceeded our wildest dreams.''

As part of its almost non-stop concertizing, the band opened for a number of top draws including Ozzy Osbourne, Night Ranger, Billy Squier and ZZ Top, as well as working in tandem with another new Atlantic act, Twisted Sister. During 1984, the band played 205 concerts, traveling over 72,000 miles, and winning the allegiance of what a trade magazine called ''1,537,534 screaming rodents.'' In early 1985, the band drew capacity crowds to a series of performances in Japan.

''The first single from the LP,'' Crosby observed, ''was 'Round and Round'; it eventually got to number 10 in *Billboard*. The video had Uncle Milty—Milton Berle—on it. He's our manager's uncle and we thought it would be fun to have him get dressed up in drag and do a video with us. At the time it was one of the first videos to use a star of another type, but now it's commonplace.''

The single was one of the better heavy metal style releases of the year. *Rolling Stone*'s critic wrote: '' 'Round and Round' may rework an old theme (Romeo and Juliet), but the unorthodox song structure, neat production twists, and driven twin-guitar attack make this teen vignette—'Out on the streets/That's where we meet'—feel desperate and right. 'Round and Round' will . . . belong on a 1984 version of [the compilation album] *Nuggets*.''

By July 1985, when Ratt's next album, the platinum *Invasion of Your Privacy*, came out, the band was a ''name'' group. After its apprenticeship of playing small venues or opening for other bands, it now could headline major shows and had the chance to appear before huge crowds including 80,000 at the Oakland Coliseum and 75,000 in a British show. Did the band have difficulty in shaping its set for larger crowds? Crosby said, ''We always saw ourselves as an arena band even when we were performing in small clubs like the L.A. Troubadour. We sort of pretended it was the L.A. Forum. We just wanted the opportunity to get out on a big stage and let 'er rip, so it wasn't a big problem when we got there.''

The group's 1986 release, *Dancing on the Cover,* also was a best seller, making it three hits in three tries. By early 1988, the band was back in the studio at work on a new LP, tentatively titled *Reach for the Sky,* intended for fall release. As for band directions, Crosby commented, "I think basically our goals always have been to keep doing what we're doing, hopefully always evolving and getting better with time and writing things we enjoy playing. We never say let's write a hit single, something we'd record even though we hated it. We have been fortunate to do what we like and find out that other people accept us for what we do. A lot of people get lucky and put out one record that hits and that's it. We've been fortunate to have three platinum albums in a row. It really gives us a feeling of support; like your gang is still on your side."

As Pearcy put it, "Ratt is an even better lifestyle than drag racing! We're finally out of the cellar and into your living room. Ratt cannot be exterminated."

RAVENS, THE: *Vocal group. Original personnel (1945), all from New York, New York: Warren Suttles, Jimmy Ricks, Leonard Puzey, Ollie Jones. Jones replaced by Maithe Marshall in 1945.*

A striking feature of a number of R&B vocal groups, and later a feature in some major rock acts of the mid-1950s, was the use of a bass lead. The group that probably had most to do with this development was the Ravens, a quartet that reached its peak in the years before R&B moved from the ghetto wings to center stage in pop music.

The two founding members were bass Jimmy Ricks and baritone Warren "Birdland" Suttles. The two were aspiring singers who often discussed plans for careers while waiting on tables at clubs in New York's Harlem in 1945. Having decided to organize a quartet, they found two other members, second tenor Leonard Puzey and first tenor Ollie Jones, through inquiries at the Evans Booking Agency. After some engagements in small New York clubs, the group was signed by Ben Bart of Universal Attractions and Hub Records. Bart lined up a series of jobs for them in RKO and Loew's theaters and in such clubs as the Baby Grand and Club 845. He also arranged for their first Hub recordings, including Ollie Jones' composition "Lullaby" and such other numbers as "Honey," "Out of a Dream," "My Sugar Is so Refined," "Bye Bye Baby Blues," and "Once and for All."

Before the end of 1945, the group had switched to King Records and suffered its first change in personnel. Jones left, and Ricks replaced him with Maithe Marshall, who was then working as a bartender in New York. Marshall added an unusual falsetto voice. A little while after Marshall joined, the group came up with its distinctive bass-lead style.

As Jack Sharbori noted in his comprehensive biography of the Ravens in the March 1972 *Record Exchanger* magazine, this approach was achieved by accident. The group was booked at Harlem's famed Apollo Theater on a benefit program that featured such stars as Nat Cole and Stan Kenton. Part way through the Ravens' offering of "My Sugar Is so Refined," Ricks nervously came on too strong with his bass voice. The resulting wild applause from the audience was repeated when the group performed "Old Man River" as a follow-up with similar bass styling.

The Ravens' 1946 recording of this old favorite was one of the greatest hits ever achieved by an R&B group, selling in excess of 2 million copies nationwide on the National label. The group stayed with National for the balance of the '40s, providing such other hits as "Write Me a Letter," "It's Too Soon to Know," and "Deep Purple" plus the 1950 R&B top 10 success "I Don't Have to Ride No More."

During the late 1940s, both Warren Suttles and Maithe Marshall left the group for varying amounts of time. Their places were taken by a number of other singers. Suttles gave way to Joe Medlin for a short time in 1947 and to Bubba Ritchie later in the decade. Marshall's place was taken for a time in 1948 by Richie Cannon. Ricks (who had rights to the group name) and Puzey remained regulars throughout those years. Puzey, in addition to his singing, worked out dance routines for the group to perform while vocalizing. In 1950, Suttles again left for a time, giving way to Louis Heyward, who sang lead on the 1950 National hit "Count Every Star."

The group left National at the start of the '50s and, in different combinations of singers, recorded for Columbia, Okeh, Mercury, Jubilee, and Argo from 1951 to 1953. For a short time, Ricks joined Benny Goodman as a solo vocalist, touring Europe with the Goodman band, while Tommy Evans handled bass for the Ravens. By 1951, he was back with the group, but soon after, Puzey and Marshall left. Puzey was replaced by Jimmy Stewart. Taking over on falsetto for Marshall was the talented Joe Van Loan from Philadelphia, Pennsylvania, who previously had sung with the Canaanites.

Though the quality of the Ravens' arrangements on the Columbia and Okeh sessions was excellent, not much happened with the relatively few singles released. The group reorganized, with Louis Frazier taking Suttles' spot briefly until Warren returned once more and turned out a series of hits for Mercury: "Out in the Cold Again," "Come a Little Bit

Closer," and the 1952 R&B top 10 "Rock Me All Night Long." By the time the group moved to Jubilee Records in 1954, Suttles had left for good and Frazier had returned. The Ravens provided Jubilee with R&B best-sellers "On Chapel Hill" and "Green Eyes." Soon after the group left Jubilee in the mid-1950s, Frazier died.

The final metamorphosis of the group took place in the mid-1950s, when the quartet was reorganized by Joe Van Loan to include David Bowers on bass and Joe's two brothers, Paul and James Van Loan, handling the parts once taken by Puzey and Ricks. The group signed with Argo, having some success with "Kneel and Pray," "A Simple Prayer," and "Here Is My Heart."

By the mid-1950s, this alignment also had disbanded with its members going several different directions, as was the case with other Ravens alumni. Ricks, for example, continued as a featured soloist for decades, while Marshall performed with such other groups as the Hi-Hatters, Marshall Brothers, Buccaneers, and Orville Brooks' Ink Spots.

Joe Van Loan eventually joined the Du-Droppers, a group that, in the early 1950s, had achieved several major R&B hits, such as "I Found Out" and "I Wanna Know." With Van Loan in that group were Bob Kornegay, J.C. Gineyard, and Willie Ray.

In 1978, many of the Ravens best recordings, spotlighting its important contributions to the rise of doo-wop in the '50s, were reissued on Savoy Records' Two-LP *The Greatest Group of All* and later on Savoy Jazz's *Old Man River* and *Rarities*.

RAWLS, LOU: *Singer, actor, record producer. Born Chicago, Illinois, December 11, 1935.*

"Grandma died when I was 14, but her guidance up to that point kept me straight," Lou Rawls told Leonard Feather in April 1969 in a *Los Angeles Times* interview. "It wasn't just that she said: 'You should be a singer.' It was a religious thing. I sang with the church choir from the time I was seven. She told me I had to go to church every Sunday come rain or shine.

"I'm thankful now, because when I go back to Chicago, the guys I grew up with are all mailmen, bus or cab drivers, policemen—or in jail, or junkies, or dead. So I was never supposed to make it, because I had nine strokes against me, but she did it. In the evening, when the street lights come on, there'd be no Lou Rawls around—she kept me off that street."

Actually, Lou was raised by his mother and grandmother. But because his mother had to work to support the family—his father left when Lou was a small child—his grandmother was the one who directed him toward what was to become his life's

work. Like so many black artists, he progressed from singing in church choirs to performing professionally with a gospel group. He started with local gospel organizations in his teens, then going west to join the Los Angeles–based Pilgrim Travellers in the mid-1950s. The group lived up to its name, appearing in churches and gospel programs in ghetto theaters throughout the U.S. In 1956, when the Travellers played Chicago, Lou received a notice from his draft board and did his traveling for the next two years in an Army uniform. He didn't take the easy route, though, volunteering for the paratroopers once he had been inducted.

In 1958, Lou received his honorable discharge and rejoined the Pilgrim Travellers, which then included Sam Cooke. (*See Cooke, Sam.*) It was almost a fatal step. In November, while going from one date to another, Cooke and Rawls' car was in an accident. Cooke wasn't badly hurt, but Lou was in a coma for five days due to a brain concussion. "They went and pronounced me dead, but I got back on my feet and went on the road again—had a complete loss of memory, didn't know what happened."

In 1959, the group broke up in Los Angeles and Rawls began a succession of obscure jobs on the Chitlin' Circuit. He sang the blues in small clubs in ghetto areas—sometimes for barely enough to pay living expenses. At times, it looked as though he might break out of this hand-to-mouth pattern. He auditioned for acting jobs and gained a part as a gun bearer for Efrem Zimbalist in the TV show "77 Sunset Strip." Late in 1959, he won attention from critics for his singing in the "Dick Clark Show" at the Hollywood Bowl. However, neither event led to anything else and Rawls was happy to work at all in the early 1960s, even at $10 a night at a minor Hollywood club called Pandora's Box.

He was only a stone's throw from the headquarters of Capitol Records, but it was not until 1961 that he was signed by them and 1962 when they issued his first single, "Love Is A-Hurtin'"/"Memory Lane" and his first LP, *Stormy Monday*. The LP *Black and Blue* followed later that year.

The breakthrough from small-time performer in black clubs to superstar occurred when Lou came up with the idea of combining an introductory monolog with some of his blues songs. In almost poetic fashion, he recreated the mood of poverty, despair, and occasional joy and elation of the world black people knew in the U.S. Such numbers as "World of Trouble," "Dead End Street Monologue," and "Tobacco Road" caught on with his ghetto audiences and, in recorded form, gained the attention of white fans too. This regard continued to build as Capitol released each new Rawls LP, starting with *Tobacco Road* (1964), *Nobody but Lou* and *Lou Rawls and*

Strings (1965), and, in May 1966, *Lou Rawls Live.* 1966 was a good year for Lou, with two more LPs (*Pilgrim Travellers* and *Soulin'*) gaining the charts. *Soulin'* also was gold, though not until 1969.

From that time on, Lou was an established music-industry great. While he was on the label, Capitol regularly released three or four LPs annually, plus a steady flow of singles. His credits from 1967 through the early 1970s included LPs *Carryin' On; Too Much; That's Lou; Merry Christmas HO! HO! HO!; You're Good for Me; Central Park Musical Festival; The Best of Lou Rawls; The Way It Was, The Way It Is; Close-Up; Your Good Thing; You've Made Me So Very Happy;* and *Bring It on Home.*

In 1968, he hosted his own TV special, "Soul," on NBC and also played a dramatic role in an episode on the "Big Valley" TV show. He also signed for his first film role, playing a member of a pop group led by Jordan Christopher in *Angel, Angel Down We Go.* In the summer of 1969, he was the star of his own TV show, heading up Lou Rawls and the Golddiggers' summer replacement for Dean Martin on NBC.

In the late 1960s, Rawls could begin to invest his growing income in many things, such as Crossroads of the World office buildings in Hollywood; Sherman Oaks Travel Service; his own music publishing company and artist management firm; a record firm called Dead End Productions aimed, he stated, "at helping young kids from ghetto areas particularly in getting started in show business, provided they finish their education"; and a TV-movie production company, Cross Roads Productions.

He also devoted a sizable amount of his personal efforts to inspire those on the low rungs of the economic ladder to move up in the world. He did this by visiting schools, playgrounds, and other community centers to sing and then talk to children, encouraging them to continue their schooling and have confidence in their own abilities.

In 1971, after 10 years and 28 albums, Lou switched from Capitol to MGM. His debut single on the label, "A Natural Man," was a top 10 soul hit. The album of the same name was on best-seller lists through early 1972. He also was in the movie *Believe in Me.* In 1972, his hit recordings were the album *Silk and Soul* and the singles "Walk on In" and "His Song Shall Be Sung."

Disagreements with MGM about creative directions led to a decision to leave the label. As Rawls told Dennis Hunt, executives wanted him to concentrate on MOR (middle-of-the-road) material. "Imagine me singing bubble gum. The Osmonds were really doing well for MGM then and MGM figured I could do well singing that same kind of music. No way, baby. I started my career singing jazz and blues

and I got to be a respected entertainer. I wasn't going to stoop to being a bubble gum machine."

Rawls moved to Bell Records for a while and then approached Kenny Gamble and Leon Huff of Philadelphia International Records to add him to their roster. This quickly paid dividends in the form of another top 10 hit, "You'll Never Find Another Love Like Mine," number two on pop lists in the summer of 1976. His debut LP on the label, *All Things in Time,* which contained the hit single, went platinum. Other 1976 albums were *Naturally* on Polygram Records and a Capitol retrospective, *The Best from Lou Rawls.*

From then into the 1980s, Rawls turned out a series of often striking albums on Philadelphia International: *Unmistakably Lou* (1977 Grammy winner for Best R&B Vocal Performance, Male), *When You Hear Lou, You've Heard It All* (1978), *Let Me Be Good to You* and *Sit Down and Talk to Me* (1979), and *Shades of Blue* (1980).

Throughout the 1980s, Lou continued to be a featured entertainer on the concert circuit and on TV. On the March 1987 telecast of the Oscar Awards, he and Melba Moore performed the best-song nominee from the film *Top Gun,* "Take My Breath Away." When the award envelope was opened, it proved to be the Oscar winner.

Lou's TV activities in the 1980s included initiating and serving as host and co-producer of the Black Gold Awards Show and hosting an annual telethon for the United Negro College Fund called the Lou Rawls Parade of Stars. From 1981, when he began hosting the telethon, through 1987, the program raised over $100 million. In March 1988, he was given an award for his efforts by the Los Angeles County Board of Supervisors. Rawls' comments echoed the words he had used in an early 1980 press conference, "I never got a college education but I sure know the value of one." His 1970s singles releases included the enormously successful gold single "You'll Never Find (Another Love Like Mine)," which was nominated for a Grammy. In the 1980s, he had a number of albums on the Epic label such as *Love All Your Blues Away* (1986).

REBENNACK, MAC: *See Dr. John, The Night Tripper.*

REDDING, OTIS: *Singer, songwriter. Born Macon, Georgia, September 9, 1941; died near Madison, Wisconsin, December 10, 1967.*

For a few years, it seemed as though Otis Redding had been born under a lucky star. He reached maturity at a time when the mass market in music seemed prepared for the rise of black rhythm & blues artists. Had he been born a decade earlier, he would have labored in relative obscurity in ghetto clubs, despite the widespread success of rock. For, though the early wave of rock artists built their stylings on black rhythm & blues, national stardom went mostly to white artists, primarily from the country field.

But Redding came along in the early 1960s, when R&B artists were starting to make inroads into the top 40, a trend that became even stronger as the decade went by and the subtler, less strident patterns of soul became important. Basically, soul was much more blues and gospel-oriented than the R&B of earlier days. By the mid-1960s, if James Brown was considered the king of R&B, Otis Redding generally was hailed as the monarch of soul. Unfortunately, just as Redding's career was beginning to gain major momentum, his life ended in a tragic accident.

Redding was one of many R&B/soul artists born in or near Macon, Georgia; others included Little Richard and Ray Charles. He first sang in his church choir and later did vocalizing in school. However, Otis was shy. Though he dreamed of a professional singing career, he didn't see it happening until a chance trip brought him to Memphis, Tennessee. It was a journey he took not as a performer, but as a chauffeur for a Macon, Georgia, group headed by Johnny Jenkins. The band traveled from Macon to Memphis because Jim Stewart had agreed to audition it.

Stewart headed Stax Records, a rapidly growing R&B-oriented company that was only two years old at the time. As more and more records bearing the Stax imprint became hits, the type of music featured on them became the national standard for the "Memphis sound." Stewart—aided initially by the talents of Memphis disc jockey Rufus Thomas and his daughter Carla—was constantly on the lookout for new talent. But some of his greatest discoveries, such as Redding, came out of the blue—as well as out of the blues.

Thus, the winner in the Johnny Jenkins audition saga was the band's driver. The story, related by Stewart to reporter Van Gordon Sauter (*Chicago Daily News,* March 2, 1968), went as follows: "'He was a shy old country boy,' Stewart said. 'He never said a word. They would say: "Otis, go get us lunch," or something like that.' After the band recorded, someone suggested that Otis be given a chance to sing. 'He did one of those "Hey, heh, baby" things,' Stewart said. 'It was just like Little Richard. I told them the world didn't need another Little Richard. Then someone suggested he do a slow one. He did "These Arms of Mine." No one flipped over it.'"

But Stewart did decide to record "These Arms of Mine." The single became first a local hit and then a national success in the R&B field. Stewart hastened to sign Otis to a long-term contract and assigned one of his most promising young staff members, Steve Cropper of Booker T and the M.G.s, to work with the newcomer. He also came up with a new label, Volt Records, for Redding's releases.

Each new disc verified that Stewart had a winner. The records found favor with black record buyers in increasing numbers. This, in turn, led to concert engagements for Otis in major theaters and auditoriums instead of rundown clubs. In 1965, Redding hit full stride with R&B fans with "Mr. Pitiful," "I've Been Loving You Too Long," and his own composition "Respect" (which helped propel Aretha Franklin to stardom). His records still attracted mainly black fans in the U.S., but they became widely successful with the mass audience in Europe.

Redding toured England and a number of countries on the Continent in 1966 and '67, drawing capacity audiences wherever he went. His overseas record sales in those years for such singles as "Satisfaction" and "Try a Little Tenderness" equaled or bettered his U.S. totals. France rated him one of the world's top singers in its polls for 1966 and 1967. Several British publications named him the Top Male Singer of 1967 in the U.K.

By the mid-1960s, Redding was on the verge of crossing over from R&B-only status to superstar ranking. His recordings, distributed by Atlantic Records, were starting to sell to young fans in white areas of the U.S. as well as in the traditional R&B/soul market. His 1967 Monterey Pop Festival performance in California became one side of an LP on Reprise (Jimi Hendrix's set forming the other side).

His advisors were sure as 1967 progressed that the late 1960s would see Redding develop as strong a national following as fellow soul singer Ray Charles. Then a plane crash ended those expectations. Traveling to an engagement in the Midwest in December 1967, Redding was drowned in an icy lake near Madison, Wisconsin, when a private twin-engine Beechcraft hit the water in heavy fog. The crash also claimed the lives of four members of Redding's troupe: 19-year-old Ron Caldwell and 18-year-olds Jimmy King, Phalin Jones, and Carl Cunningham, all of Memphis. One musician, Ben Cauley, age 20, was the only survivor. He heard Caldwell and Cunningham call for help, but they went under before he could get to them.

Soon after Redding died, he achieved the major hit that had been expected—a relaxed, soft-soul ballad, "Dock of the Bay," recorded 2½ weeks before his death. Issued in January 1968, the disc had chalked up sales of 4 million by the end of May.

Jerry Wexler of Atlantic Records commented in 1968: "It's his epitaph, and it proves that a singer can do his own thing and still be commercially successful. Otis is tremendously responsible for the fact that . . . the white audience now digs soul the way the black does.''

In the years after Redding's death, many of his Atlantic/Atco LPs were available, but some only as imports. The selection included *Pain in My Heart* (1965); *Otis Redding Live in Europe* and *Otis Blue* (1966); *King & Queen* (featuring his duets with Carla Thomas) and *History of Otis Redding* (1967); *The Dock of the Bay, The Immortal Otis Redding,* and *In Person at the Whisky Au Go Go* (1968); *The Best of Otis Redding* (1972); and *Otis Recorded Live* (1982). Among Volt collections available as import items in the 1970s were *Dictionary of Soul* and *The Soul Album.* Atlantic/Atco reissues that had been phased out of the catalog by the 1980s included *The Great Otis Redding Sings Soul Ballads, Otis,* and *Otis Redding Sings Soul.* But the four-disc *Otis Redding Story* (1987) preserved his memory well. (*See Booker T and the M.G.s; Franklin, Aretha; Hendrix, Jimi; Thomas, Carla.*)

REDDY, HELEN: *Singer, songwriter. Born Melbourne, Australia, October 25, 1942.*

During the 1970s, Australia contributed more than its share of luminaries to the U.S. pop music scene, not the least of whom was vocalist/songwriter Helen Reddy. Among her contributions was the composition and recording of what came to be considered the women's lib anthem, ''I Am Woman.''

Born to show business parents, Helen first performed professionally at the age of four at the Tivoli Theatre in Perth, Australia. She toured with her parents for much of her childhood, but later was sent to boarding school for her education, an experience she found distinctly depressing. She had a good voice and enjoyed singing, a combination that led to her leaving school at 15 to find work with a road show that toured small towns and remote regions of Australia. The show was an excellent proving ground. Helen had parts in skits or plays in addition to singing, sometimes wearing three costumes, one on top of the other, for quick changes from one role to the next.

After a number of years, she gained work in larger towns and finally became one of the better-known entertainers in her country. She eventually was given her own show, ''Helen Reddy Sings,'' on the Australian Broadcasting Commission. She was backed by a 22-piece orchestra on the twice-weekly broadcasts of 15 minutes each.

Feeling increasingly like a big fish in a little pond, Helen turned her sights toward the U.S. In 1966, she won the Australian ''Bandstand International'' contest sponsored by Philips-Mercury Records. That re-

sulted, supposedly, in a trip to New York, but she found she had to put up a fight to actually obtain it. The record company did little for her once she reached the U.S., but she met and married talent agent Jeff Wald, who became her manager. (They divorced years later.) The Walds moved to Chicago in 1967 and Los Angeles in 1968, but show business doors did not open wide for her until the early 1970s.

By early 1971, the Walds had settled in the Hollywood Hills above Los Angeles and Helen had begun recording for Capitol Records. She made the charts with her version of ''I Don't Know How to Love Him,'' a song from the hit rock musical *Jesus Christ Superstar.* In May 1971, Capitol featured it as the title track for Helen's debut album, which also included her composition ''I Am Woman.'' The song did not catch on right away, but after she sang it during appearances on TV and in concert and it began to receive recognition from women's lib groups, it eventually became a hit single. Before that single came out, Capitol had issued such other 1971 Reddy discs as the singles ''Crazy Love'' and ''No Sad Song'' and the LP *Helen Reddy.*

''I Am Woman,'' issued in May 1972, finally rose to number one in *Billboard* the week of December 9, 1972. It became the title song for Helen's third album, issued in November 1972 and certified gold 1973.

Despite her success as a recording artist, Helen still found some critics questioning her rapport with live audiences. For instance, Dennis Hunt of the *Los Angeles Times* wrote (April 9, 1973): ''There is an iciness about Helen Reddy that creates a formidable gulf between her and an audience. . . . Throughout most of her cheerless hour of songs, she received just sparing applause. . . . But her performance had some merit because, technically, she is a superb singer.''

A happier occasion for Helen was the 1973 Grammy Awards telecast on which she sang ''I Am Woman,'' a nominee for Best Song of 1972. Later in the show, she accepted the Grammy for that category. Soon she was adding to her following with her own summer show on NBC-TV. Her relaxed and ingratiating performance on the series gave the lie to previous complaints about her inability to establish audience rapport. One result of this exposure was a new spurt in recording success. *Long Hard Climb* (1973) went gold. Its single ''Delta Dawn'' rose to number one in *Billboard* the week of September 15, 1973, and also brought her a gold record. Her earlier LPs *I Don't Know How to Love Him* and *I Am Woman* returned to the hit lists in September to give her three chart albums at the same time.

In November, the Music Operators of America named her Artist of the Year on Jukeboxes. That season, she had another top 10 single, ''Leave Me

Alone.'' In 1974, she had gold albums *Love Song for Jeffrey* and *Free and Easy* and hit singles "Keep on Singing," "You and Me against the World," and "Angie Baby" (number one in *Billboard* the week of December 28, 1974). She followed in 1975 with such singles as "Emotion," "Bluebird," and the top 10 "Ain't No Way to Treat a Lady" plus gold LPs *No Way to Treat a Lady* and *Helen Reddy's Greatest Hits*. Her credits in 1975 included a role in the film *Airport '75* and, starting July 18, a stint as the regular host of NBC-TV's "The Midnight Special."

In the second half of the 1970s, though she continued to be a featured guest on many TV variety programs and to be represented by a number of new recordings, her following diminished considerably. She wasn't able to place another song in the top 10, though some releases did make lower chart levels. Her album output on Capitol comprised *Music, Music* (gold, 1976), *Ear Candy* and the soundtrack album from the film *Pete's Dragon* (1977), and *We'll Sing in the Sunshine* (1978). 1976–79 singles included "I Can't Hear You No More" and "Gladiola" (1976), "You're My World" (1977), and a remake of Gale Garnett's 1964 hit "We'll Sing in the Sunshine." Capitol albums included the 1978 *Live in London* (taped at the London Palladium), *Take What You Find* (1979), and *Reddy* (1980).

During 1979, she left Capitol for MCA Records to put out two LPs: *Play Me Out* (April 1981) and *Imagination* (1983). Neither did well with record buyers and by the mid-1980s, Helen had no major-label affiliation. She told a *Billboard* reporter she had lost some of her enthusiasm for the field. "I certainly don't have the interest in music I once had. I'll always sing, but I would like that to become a smaller part of my life."

One of her nonmusic projects in the mid-1980s was authoring a book about the history of Australia. She also sought stage roles in musical theater.

REED, LOU: *Singer, guitarist, songwriter. Born New York, New York, March 2, 1944.*

In 1972, Lou Reed achieved major notice as a rock performer. He seemed to fit right into the outrageous "new rock" of the early 1970s as exemplified by Roxy Music, Gary Glitter, and David Bowie. Bowie, in fact, produced *Transformer*, the album that brought Reed into the worldwide spotlight. The only irony was that, to Reed, the "new rock" was hardly new; he had been performing in that vein for most of the 1960s and had caused some East Coast reporters to nickname him the "King Freak of New York." Apart from his role playing, though, few could deny his great potential as a performer and a writer, though many critics condemned his concentration on decadence and decay and some took umbrage at his abrasive personality. Despite bouts of self-doubt and self-destructive tendencies, Reed persevered to remain a star throughout the '70s and '80s.

Born Louis Firbank, Reed grew up on Long Island, New York. Fanatically interested in rock'n'roll almost from childhood, he had learned the guitar by his teens and made his first record when he was 14. As he described his early career: "I played in Long Island hoodlum bands where there were fights. . . . Attended many schools—always led bands, i.e., Pasha and the Prophets; L.A. and the Eldorados; the Jades, originally called the Shades, we appeared on stage in sunglasses and sequins. People thought we weren't very cool; now it's O.K. . . . Expelled from R.O.T.C. for threatening to shoot officer . . . worked as songwriter and met rejection."

One of the reasons his favorite songs were turned down by the record company that had put him on its payroll in the mid-1960s was his subject matter. Reed preferred bluntly honest lyrics about such normally taboo subjects at that time as transvestitism, drugs, and death. For a time, he went along with requests that he write songs to order on conventional early-'60s themes, but eventually he could no longer stomach lyrics about hot rods and surfing. After meeting another disenchanted rock artist, John Cale, he decided to organize a new rock band to play his kind of material. The result was the Velvet Underground, which combined forces with avant garde artist Andy Warhol to achieve a measure of fame, mostly in the New York area, during the second half of the '60s.

The nature of Reed's songs effectively kept the Velvets' MGM records off the airwaves. This contributed to their eventual disbanding at the start of the '70s. Still, as critic Paul Nelson wrote: "Had Reed accomplished nothing else, his work with the Velvet Underground would still have assured him a place in anyone's rock and roll pantheon."

During 1971, Reed was little in evidence in the pop music field, but in 1972 he signed a new contract with RCA Records. For all but a few months of 1972, he made London, England, home base. There he worked on two albums—one produced by Richard Robinson, the second by David Bowie. The first, titled *Lou Reed,* was issued by RCA in June 1972 and attracted some attention, but the blockbuster proved to be the Bowie-supervised album, *Transformer* with the top 10 single "Walk on the Wild Side."

This time, Reed found a wide following among rock fans throughout the U.S. and Europe, reflecting changing mores from the Velvet Underground era. For a while, his stage act was built along the same lines as Bowie's. But he emphasized he did not have to copy anyone. As he told a reporter from *Disc* magazine: "I'm NOT going in the same direction as David. He's into the mime thing and that's not me at all. I know I have a good hard-rock act. I just wanted to try something more—to push it right over the edge. I wanted to try that heavy eye makeup and dance about a bit. . . . Anyway, I've done it all now and stopped it. I don't wear the makeup any more."

In the fall of 1973, RCA released *Berlin,* one of Reed's finest albums. As the title indicated, it drew some of its inspiration from the German city's divided status, physically and psychologically. Critical comments ranged from "disgustingly brilliant" to "*Sergeant Pepper* of the '70s." Many listeners found the contents more than a little depressing. Reed himself told interviewer Steven Gaines *(Sunday News,* January 6, 1974): "I can't listen to it any more. It makes me too taut and nervous. And it brings back too many bad trips. Does it matter that it's laying those bad trips on other people? If people don't like *Berlin,* it's because it's too real. It's not like a TV program where all the bad things that happen to people are tolerable. Life isn't that way, and neither is the album."

Gaines noted: "I asked him if he was happy, and he laughed: 'Happy? What does that mean?' Well, does he have what he wanted out of life at least? He pointed to a pretty blonde. " 'That's peace of mind,' he told me, and stared back down at his drink."

As it turned out, *Berlin* didn't do as well with record buyers as the next album, *Rock'n'Roll Animal* (1974). A live set recorded at the Academy of Music in New York, it became his best-selling release to that date. Material from that concert was also used for *Lou Reed Live* (1975), a follow-up to the studio album *Sally Can't Dance.* Other RCA albums issued during 1975–76 were *Metal Music Machine* (a two-disc set of experimental electronic material) and *Coney Island Baby* (stressing doo-wop stylings in such songs as "She's My Best Friend," "Kicks," and "The Gift"). After Reed departed RCA in favor of Arista Records, RCA issued the 1977 retrospective *Walk on the Wild Side: The Best of Lou Reed.*

Lou's debut on his new label was the 1977 *Rock and Roll Heart,* followed by *Street Hassle* (1978). Record buyers didn't make either LP a best-seller. The pattern remained roughly the same for Lou's association with Arista into the 1980s. His releases on the label included *Take No Prisoners—Lou Reed Live* (1978), *The Bells* (1979), and *Growing Up in Public* and the excellent retrospective, *Rock'n'Roll Diary, 1967–1980* (on the charts from late 1980 into early 1981).

By 1982, Reed had returned to RCA Records, which issued *Blue Mask* (1982), *Legendary Hearts*

(1983), and *New Sensations* (1984), and *Mistrial* (1986).

As part of the Tribute to New York theme of the 1988 Grammy Awards telecast, Reed performed "Walk on the Wild Side." It also was announced in early 1988 that he had signed a new recording contract with Sire Records with planned release of his label debut later in the year.

Reed's 1980s albums indicated a revitalization of his creative and performing skills. While some of his late 1970s LPs seemed flawed and inconsistent, it was difficult to find anything to quibble about in the newer collections. This rejuvenation was attributed to two main factors: a happy marriage in which, he told some interviewers, his wife was his best critic, and his close association with guitarist and Reed band member Robert Quine. (The other mid-1980s bandsmen were Fernando Saunders on bass and Fred Maher on drums.)

Of his working relationship with Quine, Reed told Robert Palmer at one point (*The New York Times,* October 17, 1984), "Sometimes we talk about the traditions our music comes from. The other day, I told Quine, 'You know, there are just these few basic chords in rock and roll, and I've spent all these years trying to strum those chords *right,* in a really good traditional way, but souped up a bit.' The challenge isn't really the chords, though; it's how far you can take the music with your voice, your imagination and your emotions. And talking about that reminded me all over again that I love this music very, very intensely. From the day I first heard it on the radio, it changed my life. And you know, I can go back and play a record that thrilled me 20 years ago, and I find that its power over me hasn't diminished by one notch."

REO SPEEDWAGON: *Vocal and instrumental group from Illinois. Members (mid-1980s): Kevin Cronin, born Evanston, Illinois, c. 1953; Gary Richrath, born Peoria, Illinois, 1952; Neil Doughty; Alan Gratzer; Bruce Hall.** *

REO Speedwagon was a band that for years didn't get much respect from critics. But through ceaseless performing, it honed its act to the satisfaction of a large segment of the rock audience. After a long apprenticeship, it moved from opening act to headline band in the late 1970s, scoring a blockbuster hit with its 1981 album *Hi Infidelity* only to fail dismally with its follow-up. Written off by industry observers, including many critics only too eager to bid farewell to a group they had predicted wouldn't go very far,

---

*Based partly on personal interview with Gary Richrath by Irwin Stambler.

REO regrouped and returned to prominence in the mid-1980s.

The origins of the band lay in the bar circuit around the University of Illinois town of Champaign. Among the founding members were pianist Neil Doughty and drummer Alan Gratzer. The usual personnel shifts in a new group led to the addition of another key member, lead guitarist and songwriter Gary Richrath.

Richrath recalled that while growing up in Peoria: "I started playing guitar when I was 15 or 16. The thing I remember most was that I didn't like learning other people's songs. So I just sat around with the guitar my uncle gave me and just made up music. I still don't like playing other people's material unless it's something the other people in our band come up with."

By his late teens, Gary was playing with a band in his home area when the 1970 invitation to join REO came. "At the time, Irving Azoff [later manager of the Eagles and Jackson Browne before becoming president of MCA Records] managed REO and called the manager of my band and said this group in Champaign needed a guitarist. I was in Peoria and I agreed to go to Champaign because it was like a music mecca then. Dan Fogelberg came out of there. The biggest reason a lot of music was happening was because it was a college town and there were a lot of bars where bands could play. Also, the people who went to the bars then wanted original bands, not copy bands. So that helped us to develop ourselves as songwriters. But that's changed since then. We played there in the early 1980s and the clubs now make house bands play top 40."

When Gary joined, the band already had its name. He noted: "Neil thought it up while he was going to college there. REO Speedwagon was the first fire truck built somewhere around 1918–20 by Ransom E. Olds, who was like a renegade against GM and other big companies. So the symbolism seemed good and it also was a nice catchy name for a rock band. We also stuck with the name because when it was put on a marquee with other band names, those capital letters stood out."

Gary quickly was accepted as a core member by Doughty and Gratzer to the extent that he got the task of looking for a new lead singer in 1971. Before then, the band already had recorded its debut album, *REO Speedwagon* (Epic, 1971). That project, for which Richrath provided much of the original material, left a somewhat bitter taste in his mouth. He said: "A producer came out to see us in Peoria and said: 'Let's make an album.' So we did and he shopped around and sold it. On the one hand it was great, but on the other it was costly. For 10 years, half of my artist's royalties and half my songwriting

royalties went down—I forgot to look at the fine print. He said: 'Hey boys, sign this and I'll make you famous.' I have no gripes with our label—Epic's been great to us over the years though for a while I think we were the biggest local band on the label. Our goal at the time was to be the biggest band in Champaign, Illinois. And when we hit there, we said: 'Let's be the biggest band in the Midwest' and now we say: 'We're going for the cosmos.'"

After finishing the first album, the band realized it needed a new lead singer, which led to the discovery of Kevin Cronin. Gary recalled: "I 'found' him in Chicago. What I was looking for was a singer with a good melodic voice. I was very much into Elton John and very much into a rock band, but I liked the kind of sound Elton had."

Raised in the Chicago area, Cronin had tried his hand at singing during his high school years and also had done some writing. But in 1971, he started an organization called the Musicians Referral Service, whose goal was to match up performers with bands. Richrath called the service anonymously and hesitated to disclose the band name since the group still had a lead singer who hadn't been told he was being let go. Cronin finally got Richrath to give him this information and then asked Gary to come to his apartment in Chicago and meet the new candidate. Cronin then sang an Elton John song and gave Richrath a demo tape, which won him the job within the next week. The band soon found it had gained not only a new vocalist, but a promising songwriter as well.

Kevin found his new role was no picnic. He told Don McLeese of the *Chicago Sun Times:* "We've worked hard. We played every single little bar, every single little town, every single high school in Illinois, Wisconsin, and Michigan. . . . We went out there and worked and beat the bushes, playing for everybody we could play for."

Cronin's first album project with the group was *REO II* (1972), which in time became the band's first LP to be certified gold by the RIAA. While he was working on the next album in 1973, he had a falling out with Gary about the album's content and walked out. He told a *Billboard* interviewer: "The most basic reason [for the break] was immaturity. I was 20; Gary was 21. . . . After the second album, Gary and I were having trouble with just what direction the band should go. The fact that we broke up was a blessing in disguise. There is creative tension there, but we learned that without creative tension, there is nothing. We learned to deal with it."

The third album, *Ridin' the Storm Out,* went gold, thanks particularly to the loyal Midwestern fans the band had laboriously accumulated. But the next albums suggested something important had been lost when Cronin left. Neither *Lost in a Dream* (1974), *This Time We Mean It* (1975), nor *REO* (1976) approached the previous two in buyer appeal.

Cronin, meanwhile, was making little progress in his attempts to have a solo career. In 1976, he indicated to REO he was available and the others welcomed him back. Soon after, bass guitarist Bruce Hall joined and the band roster that was to remain unchanged a decade later was complete. Critics still tended to look down their noses at the band, but it had become a concert favorite. Band members decided they should try to capitalize on their live appeal.

Richrath noted: "Into the mid-1970s, our band didn't produce itself. We would get a budget and a time span of two months to do a record and two to mix it. There always were people between us and the LP saying: 'This is the REO sound.' But we'd go on tour and fans would say: 'We love your live concerts, but not your albums.' So we said we'll solve that by doing a live album. The producer only will mix it, so what can go wrong with that. So the producer would go home at midnight after doing mixes and I'd listen to what he'd done and find it still didn't sound right. So I began to do mixing myself and I came to Kevin one night and played both tapes and said: 'Which one do you like?' He picked the one I did. So we fired the producer and this led to our putting down on tape what we wanted.

"That gave us our best-selling album up to then, *You Get What You Play For* [1977, platinum]. In 1977, we had the first single that was a near hit, 'Roll with the Changes.'" (That song had been written on a paper bag by Cronin in the early 1970s when the band was driving cross-country to move its home base from Illinois to Los Angeles.)

Still, Gary didn't think it might have been better if the band had taken over production earlier. "Now I look back, we were just a bunch of dumb kids in a band. I'm strongly behind the way our label handled it. If we'd tried to take over earlier, we'd probably have fallen on our face. It took a long time to have enough knowledge to say we wanted to produce ourselves and know how to go about it."

The band followed the live LP with another platinum-seller, *You Can Tune a Piano, But You Can't Tuna Fish* (1978). *9 Lives* (1979), which demonstrated better craftsmanship than the 1978 album, but did not sell as well (it did pass gold record levels by 1980, though), caused some nay-sayers to suggest the band finally might be on the downhill slide. However, as *Creem* magazine noted: "Out in the flatlands of America . . . REO Speedwagon is one of the most popular and best-loved of all American bands." And that regard shone through again in 1980 when *Hi Infidelity,* arguably its best collection

ever to that time, became a runaway best-seller. (Earlier that year, the band was on the charts with a gold "best-of" LP, *A Decade of Rock and Roll 1970–1980.*) During 1981, the LP stayed at number one in *Billboard* for many months and helped sell a worldwide album and singles total of an estimated 18 million copies through mid-1982.

Before *Hi Infidelity,* as Alan Gratzer noted, the band had sold over 6 million albums without having a hit single, but that all changed with the new LP. The first single from the album, "Keep on Loving You," reached number one in *Billboard* the week of March 21, 1981. The second single, Gary Richrath's "Take It on the Run," reached the top five and a third single, "In Your Letter," made the top 20.

Recalling how "Take It on the Run" came to be, Richrath said: "When I wrote that, I woke up one night, half asleep, and sat down in front of the TV. There was a soap opera on it. I was just sitting there strumming a guitar thinking: 'God, these guys' relationships are worse than mine.' I just sat there and sang vocals about the effects of gossip and relationships breaking up, which was what was on the tube and all that was similar to what was going on in my life."

In fact, both he and Cronin emphasized that much of the emotional impact in *Hi Infidelity* came from personal problems both were encountering as the album came together.

But the tremendous high of that album was followed by an almost disastrous low with the 1982 follow-up, *Good Trouble.* Everyone, including band members, agreed it was the worst overall collection it had been involved with.

Good Trouble, Richrath said, just was done in too much of a hurry. "When *Hi Infidelity* happened, we had been used to taking two months to make an album and for financial reasons then had to go on the road to make money. So before *Hi Infidelity,* our album output was on a yearly cycle. After that hit, we came right in from one of our most exhausting tours and went right into the studio to do another album. After that came out, it still sold a lot of copies, but nowhere near *Hi Infidelity* and we also know it wasn't as good creatively. So we sat back and said we're not going to do another LP like that."

Kevin Cronin pointed out some of the difficulties arose from trying to cope with the heady experience of being acclaimed a superstar band. He told a *Los Angeles Times* interviewer (April 10, 1985): "We had worked so hard for so many years to get on top. Our lives were supposed to be fulfilled, I thought things would change, like magic—I thought the whole world would be a great place to be. But it wasn't. Being on top didn't solve anything, it just created new problems. It was a big letdown . . . very depressing. It took me a while to put success into sensible perspective.

"People build you up and you start believing all the press releases and the stories. You can't take it all too seriously. You start to think you're Superman. Your ego gets distorted, your world gets pushed out of shape. But then you crash and come back down to earth. That hurts.

"You always see stories where celebrities are saying it's bad to take fame and success too seriously, that it's dumb to believe all the hype. I never understood what they meant. But after I went through it and did it wrong, I finally understood exactly what they were talking about."

After returning home in April 1983 from the *Good Trouble* tour, Richrath remembered, the band decided to take time off. "We didn't want another half-baked, confused batch of songs. So we just took six months off for relaxation and then started work on new songs. We wanted to get back to the roots. We took a warehouse outside Los Angeles and called it the Clubhouse and we were the ultimate garage band. We took six months just rehearsing like we were starting out. Instead of coming in and working on songs, we came in and just started playing. It was a great atmosphere for getting away from business pressures and just living out our lives again. I'd look forward to just going down and playing with the guys."

Cronin stressed it was agreed the band would go on to the next album only when it felt ready. "If we needed five years, we would have taken five years."

It didn't take that long, but it still was almost three years to the next release. Slowly in that interval, the band had resharpened its writing and ensemble skills. The results were evident in the new release, *Wheels Are Turning* (Epic, spring 1985), which quickly entered the U.S. top 10. Its first single, "Can't Fight This Feeling," rose to number one in *Billboard* for three weeks starting March 9, 1985. As the band's 1985–86 concert series demonstrated, REO had lost none of its popularity with its fans. Its comeback was complete.

Cronin told John Milward of *USA Today:* "The greatest thing about having another number one record is that it finally puts to rest the notion that we were a one-hit wonder." To Michael Goldberg of *Rolling Stone* he stated: "A lot of people did think we were washed up," but he emphasized band members never believed that.

For a period after the *Good Trouble* tour, while Gary and the others took it easy at home, Cronin went to Hawaii to settle down and work on new material. While he came up with completely new songs, "Can't Fight This Feeling" actually evolved from something he had worked on, but not finished 10

years before. The song, he told Dick Clark on "The National Music Survey," is about "that moment in time where . . . it gets too painful to be where you are and you know you have to change . . . but change is hard [but still] you overcome that fear of change."

As the roster for the 1987 LP, *Life As We Know It,* showed, the band makeup hadn't changed for over a decade. Richrath said: "One of the reasons I believe the band has been together for so long is that we all really like working together. The chemistry between Kevin and me just works. That's all. There's always temptations to go off. People ask if we're going to go off and do solos, but we enjoy what we're doing and we're a good team."

REPLACEMENTS, THE: *Vocal and instrumental group from Minneapolis, Minnesota. Members: Paul Westerberg, born 1959; Tommy Stinson; Bob Stinson; Chris Mars.*

In the mid-1980s, the Replacements were on the verge of supergroup status, a position it achieved the hard way. Typically, a band from outside the centers of music-industry activity, no matter how much promise it shows, has to move to one of those centers to reach the top. Defying that logic, the Replacements (like Hüsker Dü and the Violent Femmes) insisted on keeping its home base in Minneapolis, Minnesota, in the U.S. Midwest even after it moved from a small regional record company to an affiliate of the major Warner Communications organization. And, as of the mid-1980s, the band seemed on the way to success despite its stubborn resistance to the music business's unofficial "rules of the game."

Actually, in its early stages, the band's biggest hurdle seemed to be a self-destructive urge. It gained a reputation as a hard-drinking group of renegades who often arrived onstage so inebriated they could hardly play their instruments. In fact, according to releases from its first record label, Twin/Tone, the group arrived for its first professional engagement in Minneapolis in 1980 in such bad shape it couldn't even begin the show. Managers of the club stated they would see that the band, which then called itself the Impediments, would never get another gig in town. To get around that, the band changed its name to the Replacements. Eventually, band members realized they had a choice between falling victim to drug abuse or reforming their life-styles enough to permit them to try for the gold ring of rock success.

Lead singer Paul Westerberg recalled that the members all were attracted to rock'n'roll in their early 1970s preteen years in the Minneapolis area. His early idols included English stars Rod Stewart and the Faces. He told Robert Hilburn of the *Los Angeles Times* (January 6, 1986): "I liked the fact that it was exciting and entertaining and that they seemed to be having so much fun.''

This impelled him to learn to play guitar and to get together with other friends in impromptu jam sessions in his high school years in the mid-1970s. ''We were all in the same boat,'' he told Hilburn. ''We had older brothers or sisters and we were still sort of under their wing so we felt we should like their kind of music. That meant we ended up playing a lot of like Allman Brothers–type stuff.''

His musical ideas changed after a friend brought a Sex Pistols album to his house. ''The record put an end to all the other crap we were doing. The important thing wasn't just the music they were playing, but the fact that the record made you feel that anybody could be in a band. [Johnny Rotten's] voice was unlike anything I had ever heard. It wasn't a singer singing. It was the kid down the block who couldn't sing his way out of a paper bag and didn't give a damn.

''The Sex Pistols record didn't make me think I wanted to do the same thing they were doing as much as it told me I could do something. But you tend right off the bat to imitate that for a while.''

With that incentive, Paul began to think more seriously about band work. Various associations in the late 1970s eventually shook down into the foursome of friends that became the Replacements in the early 1980s: Westerberg on lead vocals and guitar; Bob Stinson on vocals and guitar; his brother, Tommy Stinson, on bass guitar and vocals; and Chris Mars on drums. Despite its inauspicious debut (or non-debut) in 1980, the quartet managed to have enough sober moments to win a respectable following among local rock fans. The band, which combined covers of hit numbers of well-known artists with a certain amount of original material, was able to align itself with Twin/Tone Records, which released its label debut, *Sorry Ma, Forgot to Bring in the Trash,* in 1981. This was followed by *The Replacements Stink* (1982) and *Hootennany* (1983).

By 1983, the band was beginning to win the attention of rock critics outside the upper Midwest. Listeners to their albums were impressed by the high-intensity sound and the often innovative and unusual guitar work. And there were new stories circulating about the band's love of beer and whiskey that made their live shows, to say the least, rather unpredictable.

Part of that, Westerberg later claimed, was a lingering self-consciousness. ''One of the reasons we used to drink so much is that it was scary going up on stage. That's one of the things 'Swingin' Party' is about on the [1985 album, *Tim*] . . . how it is a little frightening to put yourself on display all the time.

The funny thing is people think you must have all this confidence to get up on stage.

''I get very nervous, especially before going on stage. The temptation to have a drink is very great. But I keep telling myself [in 1986] that I was going out there to have fun playing rock'n'roll and not going to let anything interfere with that . . . and it really was much more fun [without heavy drinking], a real thrill, like it hadn't been for years.''

It took another year or two of experience after early 1983 and a calamitous, chaotic alcohol/drug influenced concert at the Hollywood Palace in April 1985 before the band tried to change its ways, however. By the April 1985 show, the group had scored a record breakthrough by leaving Twin/Tone (which released the band's last album prepared for the label, *Let It Be,* in 1984) for Sire Records. With Sire, the Replacements enjoyed the worldwide distribution of Warner Communications as well as promotional support for important concerts all over the U.S. More episodes like the Palace show could jeopardize that, Westerberg and his band mates understood. Subsequent performances suggested they had gotten the message.

Paul told Hilburn in early 1986: ''I think the idea of the rowdy, barroom band has run its course pretty well. It's not like we are trying to shed that image because that was us. We are just trying to leave room to grow in other areas. Besides, the drinking and falling about all the time got old. We needed new challenges.''

During mid-1985, the Replacements recorded its debut Sire LP, *Tim.* (The title had no particular meaning, band members stressed, just like they'd chosen *Let It Be* for the previous LP because they happened to hear a Beatles song on the radio at the time.) The album (including such notable original compositions as ''Bastards of Young,'' ''Swingin' Party,'' and the poignant ''Here Comes a Regular'') demonstrated slicker production values than earlier releases, but the band didn't sacrifice its basic, hard-edged style. It certainly ranked as one of the better rock releases of the year and many critics included it in their top 10 selections at year-end. The consensus of *Los Angeles Times* reviewers, in fact, was that it was the best rock album of the year.

The band supported *Tim* with a cross-country concert series notable for its lack of drink-related incidents. Westerberg told Hilburn he was happy about the new maturity. ''The funny thing is if you go on stage drunk or stoned, you can't really enjoy the show. You sort of kid yourself that you are having a good time. Drinking does make the boring things in the day pass much more easily, but it gets in the way of performing. It's fun to look clearly at the people and see how they're reacting to your music.''

When the band's second Sire/Warner Brothers LP, *Pleased to Meet Me,* came out in mid-1987, the jury was still out on whether the band could keep its rebellious renegade spirit intact or would knuckle under to music business restrictions intended to home in on commercial success. The band's ambivalence was indicated by the cover art, which showed a hand extending from a frayed jean jacket sleeve meeting one whose fingers sparkled with diamond rings.

REVERE, PAUL, AND THE RAIDERS; PAUL REVERE AND THE RAIDERS STARRING MARK LINDSAY; THE RAIDERS:

Vocal and instrumental group. Paul Revere, born Boise, Idaho, 1942 (birthplace also has been given as Caldwell, Idaho); Mark Lindsay, born Eugene, Oregon, March 9, 1942. Sidemen (late 1960s) included Freddy Weller, born Georgia, September 9, 1947; Joe Correrro, Jr., born Greenwood, Mississippi, November 19, 1946; Charlie Coe, born Idaho, November 19, mid-1940s.

One of the main products of Idaho has been Paul Revere. Not the Revolutionary War hero—though his name and colonial style of dress provided important bits of showmanship for his latter-day namesake—but the rock idol. Among many young people of the 1960s and early '70s, the modern Paul Revere became at least as well known as the original. He surely became much wealthier before the band faded into obscurity in the mid-1970s.

The western Revere was born and raised in Idaho, where he found his first work in his teens as a barber. Later, showing considerable business sense for his age, Paul became owner of a drive-in restaurant in his home base of Caldwell. He had learned to play piano and organ in his boyhood, and he supplemented his income by leading a small pop group at local clubs. In the early '60s, an important addition to the band came in the form of a delivery boy, Mark Lindsay, who met Revere while delivering bread to Paul's drive-in and who went home and learned the saxophone because Revere said he could join the band if he could play an instrument.

Paul began to look for more outlets for his group's musical talents. The band recorded a number of singles, the most successful being "Like Long Hair," released on the Gardena label in April 1961. In November 1962, he gained an engagement in Portland, Oregon, billed as Paul Revere and the Raiders. (Previously it had been known as Paul Revere and the Nightriders.) By then, Lindsay was handling lead vocals as well as saxophone. Also an original member was a former nightclub owner, Michael Smith.

Two months later, Revere met one of the better-known disc jockeys in the Northwest, Roger Hart. The two began collaborating on promoting dances featuring the Raiders. In the spring of 1963, Hart paid for a recording session to make demonstration tapes of the band. The tapes were sent to several record companies. Columbia responded with a contract, reputedly the first the label inked with a rock band. Columbia issued the Raiders' single "Louie, Louie" in June 1963. The record became a regional hit, but was beaten out for national honors by the Kingsmen's version, which since has become a classic. In September of that year, Hart took over as the group's official manager.

During 1964, the group became one of the hottest attractions in the Northwest. Its lineup for much of this period didn't include Lindsay, who parted company with the group for a while.

In January 1965, Philip Volk joined as bass guitarist and, soon after, the base for the Raiders shifted to Los Angeles, where Mark Lindsay rejoined. In early 1965, the reorganized group gained its first hit single, "Steppin' Out," which also helped focus Dick Clark's attention on the band. He was preparing a show called "Where the Action Is" for ABC-TV and chose the band to be regulars on the program after the show was accepted by the network in April. Within a short time, the performers' dynamic rock beat and their Revolutionary War–style outfits—complete with high boots, lace cuffs, frilled shirt fronts, and George Washington-like hairdos—entered the consciousness of the nation's teenagers. At year-end, the band had the hit single "Just Like Me," which reached number 11 in 1966, followed with the top 5 hit "Kicks."

The band made the single and LP charts regularly into the early 1970s. Many of the band's songs were written by Lindsay, including "Oh! To Be a Man," "Louie, Go Home," "Undecided Man," "Steppin' Out," and "Melody for an Unknown Girl." Hit singles included "Hungry," "The Great Airplane Strike," and "Good Thing" in 1966; "Ups and Downs," "Him or Me—What's It Gonna Be," "I Had a Dream," and "Peace of Mind" in 1967; "Too Much Talk," "Don't Take It So Hard," and "Cinderella Sunshine" in 1968; and "Mr. Sun, Mr. Moon," "Let Me," and "We Gotta Get Together" in 1969.

The major impetus for the group's rise to international favor was an appearance at the Columbia Records Convention in July 1965. Company executives decided to mount a major promotional effort, beginning with a national tour in the fall. One result was the first substantial album hit, *Just Like Us* (March 1966). The group followed with such other 1966 hit

LPs as *Midnight Ride* and a release of pre-Columbia material, *In the Beginning,* by Jerden Records.

In April 1966, lead guitarist Jim Valley replaced Drake Levin, who had been with the group for some time. Apart from Revere and Lindsay, turnover among Raiders in the 1960s and early 1970s was considerable—something like 30 different musicians.

The year 1967 was even more successful for the group than 1966. During the first four months, it had four LPs on the hit charts simultaneously, including *Spirit of '67* (issued in January). Later in the year, the Raiders had chartmakers *Greatest Hits* and *Revolution.* The group's debut appearance on the "Ed Sullivan Show" in April also was the debut for a new Raider, Freddy Weller, who left his work as a sideman for Billy Joe Royal to replace Jim Valley on lead guitar. (Weller went on to success as co-author of "Dizzy" with Tommy Roe and then as a solo country star.) Also with the group by then was Charley Coe, an old friend of Mark's and Paul's from Idaho. Coe, an early band member, had left for three years to major in music at Boise College before returning to handle guitar (as well as some piano, violin, and saxophone) for the band. Rounding out the quintet as of 1967–68 was drummer Joe Correrro, Jr., who had attended high school with Bobbie Gentry in his hometown of Greenwood, Mississippi.

Signifying Mark Lindsay's importance to the group as lead vocalist, the name of the band was changed in the mid-1960s to Paul Revere and the Raiders starring Mark Lindsay. The somewhat unwieldy designation indicated, as well, a division of responsibility between Revere and Lindsay. Revere concentrated on business matters while Lindsay handled the music end—production, arrangements, songwriting, and song selection. In 1968, the equal status of the two was underlined by their work as co-hosts of the ABC-TV show "Happening '68." Late in the year, the Raiders had a hit with the LP *Something Happening.*

In 1969, Lindsay decided to try his hand as a solo artist while maintaining his ties with the band. His first Columbia single, "Arizona," issued in late 1969, was a gold top 10 hit in early 1970. He followed with the hit LP *Arizona* later in the year. He also had such chart singles that year as "Silver Bird" and "And the Grass Won't Pay No Mind." His 1971 chart singles included "Been Too Long on the Road" and "Problem Child."

In 1971, with Lindsay handling production, the band added several hits to its total. Most noteworthy was the gold "Indian Reservation," featuring Freddy Weller on lead vocal, which rose to number one in *Billboard* the week of July 24, 1971. That was

the Raiders' only number one single as well as its last top 20 success. The LP of the same title also was a chart hit. In September, the Raiders' single "Birds of a Feather" made the charts.

During 1972, both Lindsay and the Raiders frequently made the charts, but the releases peaked at lower levels than previously. Among those discs were Lindsay's album *You've Got a Friend* and singles "Something Big" and "Are You Old Enough." The Raiders' chartmakers were *All Time Greatest Hits* and singles "Country Wine," "Song Seller," and "Powder Blue Mercedes Queen." Over the next few years, the recording fortunes of both Lindsay and the Raiders declined steadily to the point that they were dropped from the Columbia roster. Revere kept the band going with varying rosters over the rest of the 1970s and '80s. In the late 1980s, trading mostly on nostalgia, the band played dates in small clubs and venues including occasional appearances in Las Vegas hotel lounges.

RICH, CHARLIE: *Singer, pianist, songwriter. Born Colt, Arkansas, December 14, 1932.*
The struggle for success in the music world is so brutal that among many industry people it breeds indifference to the fate of other aspirants. So it is a great tribute to Charlie Rich that his belated rise to stardom in 1973 was almost universally welcomed by those in his field. His renown was finally achieved primarily as a country performer, but his talent was such that he could easily have made it in rock'n'roll, blues, or jazz.

As a child growing up on a small cotton plantation near Colt, Arkansas, Charlie was exposed to many types of music. He heard white gospel music at the Baptist church he and his parents faithfully attended; he heard blues from the black field hands who worked on the plantation; and he heard country on the radio listening to the Grand Old Opry. Piano was the instrument he studied as a child. Enamoured of Stan Kenton and devoted to jazz, he played the tenor saxophone in his high school band.

After one year at the University of Arkansas, he joined the Air Force during the Korean War. In Enid, Oklahoma, where he was stationed, Charlie was playing in a jazz band and performing with a small combo in town when he married his high school sweetheart, Margaret Ann, the group's vocalist.

Rich tried farming for a year after his discharge for added financial security (as his wife was soon to have their third child). Then he returned to his music, with the encouragement of his wife. Charlie became a regular performer in Memphis piano bars, while he and Margaret Ann wrote songs, sometimes together, sometimes individually. Margaret Ann, without telling Charlie, brought a tape of the songs to Bill Justis, artist & repertoire executive for Sun Records of Memphis. Justis liked them, but he felt that they weren't commercial enough. He signed Rich as a session musician and told him to keep writing songs.

Charlie started out at Sun backing performers such as Johnny Cash and Roy Orbison. He also wrote songs recorded by a number of other artists, including Cash's "The Ways of a Woman in Love" and "I Just Thought You'd Like to Know," and Lewis' "Break-up." (*See Cash, Johnny; Lewis, Jerry Lee; Orbison, Roy.*) At the end of the 1960s, Sun started issuing some of Rich's own recordings. The third release, "Lonely Weekends," was on the national charts in 1960. Unfortunately, none of his follow-up records caught on, in large part because of insufficient support from Sun Records.

Rich switched to RCA Records and had a minor hit, "Big Boss Man." A few years later, he switched to Mercury Records' Smash subsidiary and had a smash rock hit, "Mohair Sam" (1965), but once more he failed to produce any follow-up hits. Again he returned to a life of engagements in small bars and clubs, mostly in the Midwest. His fall from the heights of success hit him very hard, and he reputedly turned to pills and liquor to try to boost his confidence. He moved to Hi Records in the mid-1960s without any noticeable improvement in outlook and finally joined Epic, a subsidiary of Columbia Records, in 1968.

Charlie's move to Epic proved to be the turning point in his career. He was teamed with producer Billy Sherrill, a dynamic partnership. Sherrill believed in Rich's talent and worked hard to win him the attention he deserved. Some of their earliest collaborations became regional hits, but none made the upper levels of the charts. Those that made the lower rungs on the hit charts included the 1970 album *Big Boss Man* and singles "July 12, 1939," "Nice'n'Easy," and "Life's Little Ups and Downs" in 1970; "A Woman Left Lonely" in 1971; and "A Part of Your Life" in 1972. "Life's Little Ups and Downs," one of Charlie's favorites, was one of a number of songs written by his wife, Margaret Ann. For the most part, however, Rich's early years with Epic were disappointing and frustrating.

Finally, in 1972, Charlie achieved the breakthrough he needed. "I Take It on Home" (written by Kenny O'Dell) entered the country music top 20. It and another O'Dell composition that Charlie recorded, "Behind Closed Doors," impressed Bill Williams, a public relations executive who had just joined Epic's Nashville office. Williams gave Rich a great deal of publicity and arranged for him to make numerous personal appearances. His efforts paid off. "Behind Closed Doors" went gold, climbing to the number one position on the country charts and pop top 10 in 1973.

Rich's follow-up, "The Most Beautiful Girl," did even better, selling more than 2 million copies to achieve platinum status. In 1973, he received many awards, including a Grammy as Best Country Male Vocalist and the Country Music Association's awards for Male Vocalist of the Year, Single of the Year, and Album of the Year for *Behind Closed Doors.* After nearly 20 years in the business, Charlie had finally achieved the success many people had felt he deserved all along. Some of his earlier recordings were released by RCA in 1973 on *Tomorrow Night*, which did very well, ensuring that Rich's earlier output would not be forgotten.

The year 1974 was also extremely successful for Charlie Rich. That year, "the silver fox," as Rich came to be called because of his prematurely gray hair, was honored as Entertainer of the Year by the Country Music Association, probably the most coveted award in country music. His hit singles were "There Won't Be Anymore," "A Very Special Love Song," and "I Love My Friend" (number one on country charts in October).

His 1975 successes on Epic were "My Elusive Dreams," "Everytime You Touch Me," and "All Over Me." In 1976, his hits were "Road Song" and "Since I Fell for You." 1977 Epic releases included the number one country disc "Rollin' with the Flow." In 1978, he had a hit single on United Artists, "I Still Believe in Love," and, on Epic, the top 10 "Beautiful Woman" and, in September, the number one country duet with Janie Fricke of his composition "On My Knees."

As Charlie closed out the 1970s, his name often appeared on pop and country charts with both new and old releases. His 1979 charted singles were "The Fool Strikes Again," "Life Goes On," and "I Lost My Head" on UA, "Spanish Eyes" on Epic, and "I Wake You Up When I Get Home" on Elektra. He had, by then, severed his relationship with Epic and signed with Elektra. 1980 hit singles were "You're Gonna Love Yourself in the Morning" on UA, "Even a Fool Would Let Go" on Epic, and "A Man Doesn't Know What a Woman Goes Through" on Elektra.

Charlie Rich's voice remained one of the most distinctive and easily identifiable in pop and country music. His performing style was a successful combination of all the musical influences in his life: gospel, blues, rock, country, and jazz. Perhaps, as wife Margaret Ann suggested, the fact that he was so difficult to typecast was one reason success eluded him for so long. Nevertheless, the blending of all those musical elements with Charlie's deep, expressive voice led to the formation of a sound of major importance in the progression of pop and country music.

RICHARD, CLIFF: *Singer, actor, guitarist. Born Lucknow, India, October 14, 1940.*

Whatever reputation Cliff Richard had gained in the U.S. as of the early 1970s was primarily based on his appearances in English movies. Strangely, few among the U.S. pop music audience were aware of his success in England and many other countries of the world that put him in a category with such all-time stars as Bing Crosby, Frank Sinatra, and the Beatles.

Richard was born Harry Roger Webb. His father, a catering employee, kept his family in India until 1948, when they returned to England, settling in Cheshunt, Hertfordshire. Cliff gained a reputation at school for his athletic ability, particularly as a rugby player. He left school in his teens to work as a credit control clerk in the factory where his father was employed. It was the mid-1950s and Cliff, like many English youngsters, was interested in an offshoot of blues called skiffle.

He formed his own band and gained bookings in towns in the London area. After quitting his job to work full-time at furthering his music career, he managed to gain an audition with London music executive Carroll Levis in the summer of 1958. Levis, in turn, introduced him to the band leader and recording artist Norrie Paramour. Cliff put together a backup group (then called the Drifters and later made famous as the Shadows) and made a demonstration record. *(See Shadows, The.)* Paramour liked the disc and arranged for an audition with EMI Records (the number one recording firm in England). EMI signed Richard. His first recordings, issued late that year, sold well enough to mark him as a major artist. "Living Doll" (one of his biggest hits) made *Billboard*'s top 30 in 1959 on ABC-Paramount in the U.S.

From 1959 on, Richard's name was rarely absent from the singles or album charts in England. In 1969, for instance, he marked the start of his second decade as a recording artist with such top 10 singles as "Good Times," "Big Ship," and "Throw Down a Line" and his hit LP *Best of Cliff*. In 1970, he turned out one of the best-selling single hits of the year, "Goodbye Sam, Hello Samantha," as well as another hit, "I Ain't Got the Time Anymore." 1971 singles successes included "Sunny Honey Girl," "Silvery Rain," and "Flying Machine." When "Goodbye Sam, Hello Samantha" was released in May 1970, it was the fiftieth single of his career, all

of which had gained the British hit charts and many of which were top 10 successes.

In the early 1960s, Richard made his film debut in a small role in *Serious Charge*. He then was cast as the central figure (pop singer Bongo Herbert) in the movie *Expresso Bongo*. This film made a stir in England and in the U.S., gaining him considerable critical attention among reviewers in both countries. He was then starred in a series of musicals: *The Young Ones, Summer Holiday, Wonderful Life*, and *Finders Keepers*. Late in the '60s, he essayed a dramatic role in the movie *Two a Penny* and, in 1969, completed work on a documentary filmed in Israel.

In 1970, he was featured in concerts behind the Iron Curtain in Czechoslovakia and Rumania and on several German TV shows aired from Berlin. He also lectured on Christian living to young audiences in Durban, South Africa, where he went at the invitation of the Bishop of Natal. This reflected his deep interest in religion and his work with the English Christian youth group known as the Crusaders. In August 1970, he combined a reading of the life of Christ taken from the New English Bible with four specially written songs in the album . . . *About the Man*.

In addition to all his other activities in 1970, a typical year in Richard's professional life, he made his first acting appearance in live drama as the young son in *Five Finger Exercise*, presented at the New Theatre, Bromley.

Besides collecting gold- and silver-record awards, Richard often was named as one of England's major music stars in trade-magazine polls. In the *New Musical Express* poll, he was voted number one in one or more categories every year from 1959 through 1970.

In the first part of the 1970s, Richard continued to retain a strong following in the U.K. while still receiving relatively little attention from U.S. fans. For instance, he had three British hit singles in 1972 ("Jesus," "Living in Harmony," and "Sing a Song of Freedom"), none of which appeared on U.S. lists.

In the mid-1970s, he was signed to Elton John's Rocket Records, which enhanced his U.S. career. First evidence of that was his 1976 single "I'm Nearly Famous," which rose high on U.S. charts and opened up new opportunities for Cliff to headline shows throughout the U.S. the rest of the decade. His album credits for those years included *I'm Nearly Famous* (1976), and *Every Face Tells a Story* and *Green Light* (1978), and *We Don't Talk Anymore* (1979). All of those spent some time on U.K. or U.S. charts or both.

Soon after the release of *I'm Nearly Famous*, Richard got the chance to give a series of 20 concerts in the Soviet Union. All of those sold out and the demand from Moscow and Leningrad fans was so great that tickets brought up to ten times their face value on the black market. He received rave notices in Russian papers, including comments in *Sovetskaya Kultura* to the effect that "Even those to whom his performing was unfamiliar could not fail to give credit to Cliff Richard's talent and mastery."

Cliff began the 1980s with the album *I'm No Hero* (EMI-America) in the *Billboard* top 100 the last quarter of 1980 and some weeks in early 1981. The album also yielded two top 20 hits, "Dreaming" and "A Little In Love." Although he continued to appear from time to time in U.S. venues later in the decade, his recording rapport with U.S. fans tapered off after the early '80s.

RICHARDSON, J.P. (THE BIG BOPPER):

Singer, songwriter, disc jockey. Born Sabine Pass, Texas, October 24, 1930; died Mason City, Iowa, February 3, 1959.

The plane crash that killed rock star Buddy Holly in early 1959 ironically helped perpetuate his name by raising him to a cult idol. The memorial album issued by Coral Records soon after the tragedy was one of the major successes of the early 1960s and subsequent posthumous releases also were eagerly snapped up by record buyers. But the other two stars who perished with him, Ritchie Valens and J.P. Richardson, were almost forgotten once the headlines had faded. Valens was brought back into the spotlight three decades later by the film biography *La Bamba*, but even then, the Big Bopper remained little more than a footnote in pop music history.

Holly, of course, was a great talent, but it is possible that Richardson and Valens would have made major contributions to the music field had they lived—not necessarily as a performer in the Bopper's case, but as a writer.

Jiles P. Richardson, born and raised in a small town in east Texas, was interested in music in his boyhood. The main influence, as might be expected, was country & western. He played with small groups in the region and started writing original songs in his teens. Along the way, he became one of the top d.j.s in the region. Like Buddy Holly, who also was from Texas, Richardson shifted to rockabilly in the mid-1950s, following the footsteps of such other young innovators in the country field as Jerry Lee Lewis and Elvis Presley.

He had built up a following among teenagers in his home area when Mercury Records executive Shelby Singleton swung through the region looking for new talent for the label. Singleton also was country-oriented and was particularly interested in rock-abilly artists. He signed a number of east Texas performers, including Richardson, Johnny Preston, and Bruce Channel.

Under the nickname "the Big Bopper," Richardson became one of the more promising newcomers to the Mercury roster in the late 1950s. His droll versions of his own compositions "Big Bopper's Wedding" and "Chantilly Lace" became hits in 1958. "Chantilly Lace" was in the U.S. top 10 for five weeks and was a major hit overseas as well. The Bopper also wrote—and provided war whoops—on Preston's first hit, "Running Bear."

The Big Bopper became a featured attraction on the rock circuit, traveling the country with various rock packages. In early 1959, he was going through the midwest in a grueling tour that also featured Buddy Holly and Ritchie Valens. (Richardson and Holly were old friends from Texas and had appeared together a number of times in the past.)

Ironically, Richardson was not supposed to be on the plane that carried Holly to his death. Two members of Holly's band were scheduled to go with Buddy on the flight while other cast members, including Richardson, were to travel to the next gig in Fargo, North Dakota by bus. However, Richardson had the flu and didn't think he could rest very well with his big frame in a small seat on a long overland trip. He asked Holly's sideman—future country star Waylon Jennings—to change places as a favor.

There were no posthumous hits for the Bopper and his records were unavailable in later years. However, his compositions were recorded by different artists from time to time. In 1972, Jerry Lee Lewis gained a major hit with a new version of "Chantilly Lace." (*See Holly, Buddy; Lewis, Jerry Lee; Valens, Ritchie.*)

RICHIE, LIONEL:
Singer, pianist, saxophonist, songwriter, record producer. Born Tuskegee, Alabama, June 20, 1949.

In a relatively low-key way, Lionel Richie became a dominating force in pop music of the 1980s. He didn't wear odd costumes, play ear-pounding funk or rock, or draw attention to himself through outrageous behavior. He simply wrote well-crafted, compelling music—typically ballads—that struck an emotional chord with millions of listeners from all walks of life whether performed by him or by other artists. His feat of having at least one number one song written by him (though sometimes recorded by others) every year from 1977 through 1985 bettered the achievements of such great pop writers as Stevie Wonder and Paul McCartney.

He didn't grow up in a deprived ghetto family having to worry about where the next meal might come from. Nor did it enter his mind as a child that he wasn't college material. In fact, he grew up in a house owned by his grandparents right across the street from Tuskegee Institute. His grandfather had worked in the business office of the college when its founder, Booker T. Washington, was still alive. His grandmother, a music teacher, was an accomplished classical pianist. His parents also were hardly school dropouts. His father retired from the Army with the rank of captain to work as a systems analyst for that service; his mother, a teacher, in time became a school principal in Joliet, Illinois.

It was an environment conducive to education and a broad musical exposure that was to help Richie cross a variety of boundaries in what became his chosen field. He told Stephen Holden of *Rolling Stone* (October 15, 1981): "Being a country-pop-R&B crossover person was not something I consciously planned. I think my upbringing had a lot to do with it. I grew up . . . on the Tuskegee college campus. Because it was the South, it was hard not to hear country music. At the same time, all you heard at campus parties were the Temptations and the Supremes. And my grandmother, whose house we grew up in, was a piano instructor who played Bach and Beethoven all day. There's a little of that in my songs too."

For all that, when his grandmother tried to teach him to play the piano, he strongly resisted and she gave up after a short time. He thought it was "sissy" to learn the instrument. He also said there was friction between them at the time because he kept wanting to make up songs rather than pay attention to the lessons. In any case, he proved to have a natural ear for piano and was able to teach himself to play in later years from watching or listening to others. He also credited his Uncle Bertram, who played in a big-band horn section, with influencing him. Bertram gave him his first saxophone, an instrument that accidentally affected his career when he reached college.

In high school—initially in Tuskegee followed by a two-year stint in Joliet, Illinois—Lionel, while interested in music, didn't focus on it as a possible life work. He enjoyed sports and for a time considered going into the ministry. Eventually, though, he enrolled in Tuskegee as an accounting and economics major. Though he often told interviewers that in those years he was "too small to play football, too short to play basketball, and too slow to run track," in fact he got into college on a tennis scholarship.

In his freshman year at Tuskegee, he was recruited by another student for a group. The other boy had merely observed Richie walking across campus carrying a saxophone case, though Lionel didn't really know how to play it very well. He told an interviewer: "On campus I ran into a guy named Thomas McClary who wanted me to join a group. He could play guitar and figured a group would be a good way to meet girls. We soon were six little guys sitting in my grandmother's house talking about taking over the world. We wanted to be bigger than the Beatles."

The group entered a talent contest as the Mighty Mystics. Their efforts came to the attention of the Jays, then considered the best Tuskegee group. Most of its members were seniors and graduating, but some Jays were staying to do graduate work and they asked the Mighty Mystics to merge into a re-organized Jays. Besides McClary and Richie, among those in the new group were trumpeter William King and keyboards player Milan Williams. To keep peace among the new members, a new name was to be chosen. They agreed to choose one by pointing to words in a dictionary at random. King's finger landed on *commodore* so the group became the Commodores.

In a relatively short time, the Commodores developed into a highly cohesive singing and instrumental group. Word of their ability spread to other towns in Alabama and during summer vacation in 1968 the band became a favorite with soul/R&B audiences in Montgomery. Group members felt they were ready for bigger things and planned to pound on some doors in New York City. Lionel's parents were dubious about the project, but finally withdrew their objections. The Commodores weren't completely on their own. McClary had an aunt in New York with whom the group could stay. One of the contacts they made was Benny Ashburn, a public relations man with some marketing experience. After hearing them at McClary's aunt's house, he agreed to represent them and soon got them a booking at Smalls Paradise in Harlem and later at a more important downtown club, the Cheetah. It was the start of a close relationship that continued until Ashburn's death in the mid-1980s.

When summer vacation was over, the boys went back to classes in Tuskegee, while Ashburn went about building up their reputation in the music field. For the next summer, Benny lined up dates that included concerts in Europe. There were some changes in personnel during that period until the founding members still with the group at the start of the 1970s were Richie, McClary, King, and Williams. When bass guitarist Ronald LaPread and drummer Walter Orange were added, the lineup that was to make the group world-famous was in place.

Demo tapes that Ashburn used to increase industry awareness of the act's promise finally paid off in an audition with Suzanne de Passe, who was looking for a group to open for a Jackson Five tour in 1971. The Commodores got the nod. The pairing was so satisfactory that the group spent two more years working with the Jacksons. (These opportunities led to Lionel's having to abandon a full-time college career, but he plugged away when he got the chance until he earned his degree in 1974.) Despite the exposure this provided, the Commodores didn't make any progress on the recording front until children of Motown head Berry Gordy, Jr., saw them perform at a Jackson Five concert at the Hollywood Bowl and touted them to their father. He followed up and signed them in early 1974. From the group's first four tracks cut for Motown, the instrumental "Machine Gun" rose to number 22 in *Billboard* in July and became the title song on their 1974 debut LP. With increasingly important contributions from Richie, the group became an important part of the Motown roster in the middle and late '70s.

Mid-1970s albums included *Caught in the Act* and *Movin' On* (1975), *Hot on the Tracks* (1976), and *Commodores* and *Commodores Live* (1977). The group earned its first major singles success in April 1976 when "Sweet Love" made the top 5 in *Billboard*. Over the next year and a half, the group added still more top 10 discs: "Just to Be Close to You," "Easy," and "Brick House." Those releases brought three Grammy nominations for 1977: "Easy" for Best R&B Song and Best R&B Performance by a Duo or Group and "Brick House" for Best R&B Song.

The week of August 12, 1978, the group achieved its first number one single—Lionel's composition "Three Times a Lady." The LP *Natural High* went platinum. Singles and the album brought three 1978 Grammy nominations but no wins. However, "Three Times a Lady" was named Most Popular Single in the American Music Awards and (based on a Gallup Poll) Best Song in the People's Choice Awards.

The Commodores continued strong with the retrospective album *Greatest Hits* (1978), top 10 LP *Midnight Magic* (1979), and platinum *Heroes* (1980) and *In the Pocket* (1981). In October 1979, the group scored a top five singles hit with Richie's "Sail On" and then placed its flip side, "Still," at number one the week of November 17. In the early 1980s, the Commodores were named Favorite Soul Group in the American Music Awards and "Still" received the People's Choice Award for Best Song.

By then, however, pressure was building for Lionel to go out on his own. Contributing to that was major performers' interest in doing material written by someone so obviously becoming one of the best new pop songwriters in the world. A turning point came in 1980, Richie recalled. "One day Kenny Rogers called and wanted me to write and produce a song for him. I knew of him, but I'd never met him.

I got on a plane and flew to meet him in Las Vegas and ended up doing 'Lady.' My life changed all of a sudden."

Rogers' single of "Lady" went to number one in the U.S. for six weeks starting November 15, 1980. Rogers' next album, produced by Lionel, accumulated worldwide sales of over 5 million copies. "Lady" brought Lionel his first two Grammy nominations for Song of the Year and Record of the Year and won a People's Choice Award as Best Song.

During 1980, Richie also got the assignment to help prepare the theme music for the film *Endless Love*. Also eventually contributing to the soundtrack music were Thomas McClary of the Commodores and Jonathan Tunick. Producer Franco Zefferelli originally wanted an instrumental theme; then, after hearing what Richie had in mind, he asked for lyrics. Finally, he also came up with the idea of having a female artist, such as Diana Ross, record the song. Because Diana had a hectic concert schedule and Lionel was working on both Kenny Rogers and Commodores record projects, a carefully timed meeting in Reno, Nevada, had to be arranged to fit both artists' itineraries. Each had to finish previous projects to meet there in the wee hours of the morning.

Richie still was working on the song. He told Dick Clark during a Mutual Broadcasting special (as reported by Fred Bronson in his *Billboard Book of Number One Hits):* "The lady did not have any lyrics prior to the session. She just had the melody. I said: 'I'll bring the lyrics with me.' At 3:30 in the morning we started singing. At five o'clock in the morning we had 'Endless Love' down on tape."

The single hit number one in *Billboard* for nine weeks starting August 15, 1981—the biggest-selling single of Diana Ross's career, Motown's biggest-selling single ever, and the biggest-selling duet single of all time. While "Endless Love" was making its mark, Richie gained another first by becoming the first person in *Billboard* singles history to make its top 10 as a composer, producer, and performer of three different records, the other hits being Kenny Rogers' version of Lionel's "I Don't Need You" and the Commodores' "Lady You Bring Me Up." "Endless Love" won an Academy Award nomination and five Grammy nominations with a sixth Grammy nomination going to the Commodores for "Lady You Bring Me Up." None of those won a trophy, however.

1982 was even brighter. The week of November 27, Lionel had another number one single on Motown: his composition and recording "Truly." In the voting for the 1982 Grammies, "Truly" won for Best Pop Male Vocal Performance. "Endless Love" also won in the American Music Award's Best Soul

Single Category. "Truly" and the platinum LP it came from, *Lionel Richie,* signaled Richie's emergence as an individual performer. It had been a rough decision, he said, but in a group meeting with the Commodores late in 1981, he finally had told them he couldn't find time to keep touring with the group while also meeting the growing number of challenging commitments he was being offered.

By 1983, he was busily involved in projects that would cement his new standing as a superstar. For four weeks starting November 12, 1983, his single "All Night Long (All Night)" was number one in *Billboard.* His second solo LP, *Can't Slow Down,* proved an even better collection than his debut LP. In late December, the Motown album was number one in the U.S. Richie's worldwide popularity caused David Wolper (producer of the opening and closing ceremonies at the 1984 Summer Olympic Games in Los Angeles) to ask Lionel to take part in one of those spectaculars. As a result, a highlight of the globally televised closing celebration at the Los Angeles Coliseum in August 1984 was Lionel's center-stage performance (surrounded by 200 break dancers) of a special version of "All Night Long" with a new verse in praise of the world's athletes.

Richie's first two solo albums still were on *Billboard* charts at the end of 1984. *Can't Slow Down,* in fact, was still in the top 10. Total worldwide sales of both as of early 1986 was estimated to be over 20 million copies. Eight singles were drawn from those two LPs, all of which made the top 10, with three rising to number one (the third, "Hello," the week of May 12, 1984). The five other best-sellers were "You Are," "My Love," "Running with the Night," "Stuck on You," and "Penny Lover." In the Grammy Award voting for 1984, Lionel won trophies for Album of the Year for *Can't Slow Down* and Producer of the Year. He also had two other nominations for "Hello": Song of the Year and Best Pop Vocal, Male. In 1984, the American Society of Composers, Authors and Publishers (ASCAP) named him Writer of the Year (an honor he won again the next year). In the *People* magazine Readers Poll, he was voted the country's favorite male singer (an achievement repeated in 1986). One of his most coveted honors of 1985 was Tuskegee Institute's Honorary Doctor of Music degree. In the American Music Awards presentations during 1985, he won in five categories: Best Pop/Rock Video Single ("Hello"), Best Pop/Rock Video Artist, Best Black Male Vocalist, Best Black Male Video ("Hello"), and Best Black Male Video Artist.

In the spring of 1985, Lionel joined 39 other American music luminaries in what was to become one of the most heartfelt moments in pop music history. Taking a cue from the late 1984 Band Aid project organized by Bob Geldof, many U.S. industry people joined together to help starving people in Africa and in the U.S. After Harry Belafonte suggested the project, many of the best talents in pop rallied to the cause. Richie collaborated with Michael Jackson on writing the theme song. The single, "We Are the World," was broadcast simultaneously on some 5,000 stations around the world on April 5, 1985. Eight days later, it was number one in the U.S., where it remained for a month. The Columbia single and the album of the same title (both produced by Quincy Jones) raised tens of millions of dollars for charitable causes.

Besides that project, Richie had plenty of other activities reaching fruition in 1985, including music for two major motion pictures: *White Nights* and *The Color Purple.* The song for *White Knights* ("Say You, Say Me") reached number one in the U.S. in early 1986. High on album charts in early 1986 was his third solo LP for Motown, *Say You, Say Me.* His rendition of his song "Miss Celie's Blues" from *The Color Purple* came out in 1986 on the Quest label (distributed by Warner Brothers).

One of the featured songs in his live shows naturally was "Say You, Say Me." He stressed that it was intended to be more than a movie theme. "You think I'm talking about a boy and a girl. But there's something else whispering to you under the surface. 'Say You, Say Me' could be about a romance, about white and black, American and Russian, Baryshnikov and Hines. It's about the awakening of the inner person to stand and be strong. . . . The line 'behind the lines of doubt' applies to what we go through falling in and out of love or discovering a loved one. Yet it also deals with capitalism and communism and human rights, the complete spectrum of barriers. Why isn't the world the way it should be? Why can't people get along? Why can't we love each other? These are the questions it touches."

Richie maintained his rapport with record buyers in late 1986 with another best-selling album, *Dancing on the Ceiling.* The RIAA certified it gold, platinum, double platinum, and triple platinum simultaneously. (*See Gordy, Berry, Jr.; Jackson, Michael; Jacksons, The; Jones, Quincy; Ross, Diana.*)

RIGHTEOUS BROTHERS: *Vocal duo. Bill Medley, born Santa Ana, California, September 19, 1940; Bobby Hatfield, born Beaver Dam, Wisconsin, August 10, 1940. Team dissolved in January, 1968, with Medley going out as soloist and Hatfield retaining Righteous Brothers title. Various reunions were short-lived.*

For much of the 1960s, the singing team of Bill Medley and Bobby Hatfield was one of the most successful in popular music. Their versions of rock and rhythm & blues material resulted in sales of millions of records between 1962 and 1968 and many of their records were still in record-company catalogues long afterward. None of their later activities could match that.

Their early upbringing and steps into music were similar, but took place in widely separated parts of the country. Despite their professional group name, they were not brothers or even relations and had not known each other before 1962. Another paradox is Medley's speaking voice, which sounds like a southern drawl, but developed in Southern California, where he was born and raised. Though their vocal efforts had considerable gospel and blues tinges, both artists came from middle class white environments. Their singing was sometimes described as "blue-eyed soul"—the title of one of their albums.

William Thomas Medley had little in the way of formal music education in his youth. At various times, he fitfully took some lessons at his parent's request—three on the saxophone, three on trumpet, and two on piano—but each time, he objected strongly and gave them up. He had a good voice from his early years, though, and sang in church choirs from his preteens to the halfway mark in his high school career. He didn't get interested in popular music until his last year in high school in Santa Ana. Then he formed a small band with several friends and played school dances and coffeehouses in his home area for several years.

Meanwhile, Hatfield was growing up in nearby Anaheim, where his family moved from Wisconsin when Bobby was a child. Bobby had many career options open up for him while he attended Anaheim High School. Popular and active in the student body, he co-ordinated school talent shows and gave evidence of executive potential. He put his excellent singing voice to good advantage part way through his school career by founding a rock group, the Variations. He also was one of the best all-round athletes in school, starring on several teams and receiving a baseball tryout offer from the Los Angeles Dodgers in 1958.

He still had not made his mind up which way to go when he entered Fullerton Junior College. His spare-time performing activities began to gain more attention, though, and by the early '60s, he had decided to concentrate on the music field. In 1962, he met Bill Medley at a small club in California. The two hit it off and decided to work up an act. Their 1963 debut album, *Righteous Brothers*, was followed by *Blue Eyed Soul, This Is New*, and *Best of the Righteous Brothers*, all on Moonglow Records. Their career really took off when the best-known record producer of the day, Phil Spector, began personally

supervising their sessions. (*See Spector, Phil.*) In 1965, two of the most important singles of the year were theirs: "You've Lost That Lovin' Feelin'" and "Unchained Melody" (a remake of Les Baxter, Al Hibbler, and Roy Hamilton's 1955 hit) on Spector's Philles label. Sales were excellent for Philles albums *You've Lost That Lovin' Feelin'* and *Just Once in My Life* (1965) and *Back to Back* (1966).

During 1966 and 1967, they continued their record efforts on the Verve label, writing much of their own material. The single "Soul and Inspiration" went over the million-copy mark in 1966. LPs included *Go Ahead and Cry* and *Soul and Inspiration* (1966) and *Sayin' Somethin', Greatest Hits*, and *Souled Out* (1967).

By mid-1967, Medley was concerned about his future in music. He felt the format of the Righteous Brothers was restricting creative growth for both team members. At the end of the year, he decided to terminate his work with Hatfield and try to make it as a songwriter and solo performer. Hatfield, in turn, was satisfied with the act as it was and decided to continue it with a new partner.

In February 1968, two weeks after the split was announced, Medley was signed as a replacement act for Sarah Vaughan at the Cocoanut Grove in Los Angeles. The reviewers were highly complimentary as were those in the Bay Area where Medley appeared with Jack Benny at the Circle Star Theater in San Carlos in March.

After 1968, Hatfield and Medley remained active as performers and writers with occasional attempts at reviving their old partnership. After the breakup, both remained on the MGM roster for a while. As a soloist, Medley had some success with singles "Brown-Eyed Woman" and "Peace, Brother, Peace" at the end of the '60s. He also recorded several albums—including *Someone Is Standing Outside, Nobody Knows*, and *Gone*—none of which had any impact on the record-buying public. In announcing a move to A&M Records in 1971, Medley admitted his problems. "After leaving the Brothers, I floundered a bit. I had always been billed as part of an act and I really had no separate identity. I played nightclubs to keep alive in the business and I tried to produce myself. It turned out to be difficult, because things were rushed."

Meanwhile, Hatfield formed a new Righteous Brothers with Jimmy Walker, previously a member of the Knickerbockers (best known for "Lies" in 1966). That alignment didn't work out well either.

On a February 1974 broadcast of the "Sonny and Cher Comedy Hour," the host and hostess proudly announced that two of their guests, their long-time friends Medley and Hatfield, were reforming the original Righteous Brothers. Ironically, the announcement coincided almost exactly with the off-camera news of the impending divorce proceedings of Sonny and Cher. (*See Cher; Sonny and Cher.*)

During that year, the Brothers made *Billboard*'s top 10 once more with the single "Rock and Roll Heaven" on Haven Records. However, they couldn't sustain that success on later recordings and, after performing together for a while, went separate ways once more. In the 1980s, they tried to regain some of the old glory on several occasions, including some TV exposure on the twentieth anniversary show of Dick Clark's "American Bandstand" and their own thirtieth anniversary celebration in 1983.

In 1987, Medley teamed with Jennifer Warnes to record "(I've Had) The Time of My Life" for the soundtrack of the film *Dirty Dancing*. The song was included in the RCA soundtrack album and also achieved a number one placing in *Billboard* as a single. In the Grammy Awards voting it won for Best Pop Performance by a Duo or Group with Vocal. The single's success renewed interest in the Righteous Brothers who gained many concert dates across the U.S. in 1988.

RIVERS, JOHNNY: *Singer, guitarist, songwriter, record producer, record- and music-publishing–company executive. Born New York, New York, November 7, 1942.*

In the 1960s, the center of activity in popular music moved westward from New York to Nashville, Tennessee, and California. During that period, Johnny Rivers traveled in a similar direction, playing an important role, both behind the scene and in the stage spotlight, in making California a new power in the music industry.

Rivers was born John Ramistella in New York, son of John and Nancy Ramistella, but moved to Baton Rouge, Louisiana, when he was three. His father, a house painter, just managed to keep his family fed and clothed. As Rivers recalled: "We weren't poor, we were double poor." Johnny got an old guitar when he was eight and started to learn to play, influenced by such varied music styles of the region as country and blues. Later, he also became proficient on the mandolin. He started playing in local groups in his early teens. From 14 on, he saved his money to finance summer trips to New York and Nashville to try for work in recording studios and with bands.

During one New York trip in the late 1950s, he met Alan Freed—the disc jockey often credited with coining the phrase *rock'n'roll*—who changed Johnny's last name to Rivers and got him his first recording contract with Gone Records. After graduating from high school in 1959, Rivers moved to

Nashville, where he became friends with another unknown, Roger Miller. The two earned meager livings by making demonstration records for other writers while also trying to place their own songs with major artists. Rivers finally was signed as a staff writer for the New York rock-country-gospel music-publishing firm of Hill & Range. In 1969, he left New York for Los Angeles, where Johnny did occasional performing jobs, but mainly worked as a record producer. He continued songwriting and one song, "I'll Make Believe," made the flip side of a major Ricky Nelson hit of the early 1960s.

In 1963, he spent his free time at a small club called Gazzari's. One night, the regular band left and Johnny was asked to stand in. He called a friend, drummer Eddie Rubin, and the two filled out the three days of the band's engagement. The audience liked it so much that Rivers was held over. From there, he gained an engagement at the Condor in San Francisco and returned to an offer to headline the show at a new club, the Whisky-A-Go-Go, just opening its doors on the Sunset Strip.

With Rivers as a star attraction, the Whisky quickly became one of the best-known discotheques in the world. In years to come, it showcased almost every important rock group in the U.S. and England, as well as providing the place where many new artists first gained notice. Rivers signed with Imperial Records and his first album, *Johnny Rivers Live at the Whisky-A-Go-Go*, became one of the best-sellers of 1964. The album's single "Memphis" (a Chuck Berry standard) hit number two in *Billboard*.

During the rest of the 1960s, Johnny's name was rarely absent from the hit lists. His chart singles during the decade were "Maybelline" and "Mountain of Love" (remakes of Chuck Berry and Harold Dorman hits, respectively), "Midnight Special," "Cupid," "Where Have All the Flowers Gone," "Under Your Spell Again," and the top 10 "Seventh Son," in 1965; "Secret Agent Man" (number three in the U.S.), "Muddy Water," and "Poor Side of Town" (co-written by Rivers and Lou Adler and number one in *Billboard* the week of November 12, 1966) in 1966; "Baby, I Need Your Lovin'" (a number three success), "The Tracks of My Tears," and "Summer Rain" in 1967; "Look to Your Soul" and "Right Relations" in 1968; and "These Are Not My People," "Muddy River," and "One Woman" in 1969. He often created hits with mainstream interpretations of blues, folk, or soul standards from the likes of Leadbelly, the Kingston Trio, and the Miracles.

As part of his contract-renewal arrangement with Imperial Records in 1966, Rivers established his own record label, Soul City.

Besides *Live at the Whisky*, Rivers had two albums that sold in the hundreds of thousands: *Realization* and *Changes*. His other LPs included *Go Johnny, Sensational Johnny Rivers,* and *Here We Go Again* (1964); *In Action* and *Meanwhile Back at the Whisky-A-Go-Go* (1965); *. . . And I Know You Wanna Dance* (1966); and *Whisky-A-Go-Go* (1967).

In 1966, Rivers became acquainted with another young writer, Jimmy Webb. They recorded each other's songs and Rivers then helped Webb's career get underway by buying out his contract with another firm. About the same time, Rivers also was asked by Marc Gordon, manager of a new group called the Versailles, to listen to their performance. He liked them and signed them to his label. He didn't care for their name and also felt they needed to develop their own vocal sound rather than copy the Motown Sound as they were doing. He renamed them the 5th Dimension and produced and played guitar on their first record. After they won some success with their early releases, Rivers gave them one of Jimmy Webb's compositions, "Up, Up and Away," to record, a move that started the group on the way to stardom on his Soul City label. (*See Fifth Dimension.*)

By the end of the 1960s, Rivers was once more heavily involved in producing as he had been at the start of the decade. In addition to his record firm (which was distributed by then by Liberty Records, which had bought out Imperial and which later became United Artists, which eventually was absorbed by EMI), Rivers also headed his own music-publishing company, Johnny Rivers Music. In the fall of 1970, he recorded a number of songs published by his own firm on his hit album *Slim Slo Slider*. Other 1970 hit chart records included the album *Touch of Gold* and the singles "Fire and Rain/Friends," "Into the Mystic," and "One Woman." In 1971, after Liberty became part of United Artists, he turned out the charted album *Home Grown* as well as hit singles "Sea Cruise" (a 1959 Frankie Ford hit) and "Think His Name" (with guru Ram Das). Johnny's 1972 releases included the excellent album *L.A. Reggae* with its rollicking gold single "Rockin' Pneumonia and the Boogie Woogie Flu" (a 1957 Huey "Piano" Smith hit).

Subsequent United Artists LPs included *Blue Suede Shoes* (1973) and *Wild Night* (1976). After leaving United Artists, he also put out *Road* (Atlantic, 1974) and *New Lovers and Old Friends* (Epic, 1975) plus, on his own Soul City label, *Outside Help*. In 1977, he scored a top 10 single with Jack Tempchin's composition "Swayin' to the Music (Slow Dancer)" on Big Tree Records.

Johnny wasn't able to hit top chart spots in the late 1970s or 1980s, but his many earlier hits stood him in good stead with fans. Throughout the 1980s, he kept active as a performer, headlining shows in clubs and theaters around the U.S. and abroad.

One of those dates at the Beverly Theatre in early 1984 marked the 20th anniversary of his appearance as the first act at the original Whisky-A-Go-Go on the Sunset Strip. While it had been a long time since his name had been on the hits lists, he told Steve Pond (*Los Angeles Times,* January 21, 1984): "I had a hard time finding a home for my music [in the late 1970s]. If we could have kept our original label together I think I would have continued my string of hits right into the '80s. Neil Diamond was able to do it, and I remember Neil when he used to hang out at our office on Sunset." (*See Berry, Chuck; 5th Dimension; Freed, Alan; Nelson, Rick; Webb, Jimmy; Wilson, Al.*)

ROBINSON, SMOKEY; SMOKEY ROBINSON AND THE MIRACLES: *Respectively, group leader and vocal and instrumental group. Smokey Robinson, singer, record-company executive, songwriter, producer, born Detroit. Michigan, February 19, 1940. Original Miracles, all born Detroit, Michigan: Robinson; Ronnie White, April 5, 1939; Bobby Rogers, February 19, 1940; Warren Moore, November 19, 1939; and Marv Tamplin. Robinson replaced by Billy Griffin in 1972. Don Griffin added in 1977.*

The success story of Berry Gordy's Motown Records often is related to the careers of such stars as Diana Ross and the Supremes, Marvin Gaye, and the Temptations. As anyone familiar with the history of the organization is aware, the initial base for Gordy's dynamic rise was provided by Smokey Robinson and his group. Just as Robinson helped make Motown great in many ways, Gordy was the guiding hand behind the Miracles' breakthrough to superstardom.

All of the group were born and raised in the Motor City. William "Smokey" Robinson demonstrated singing talent at Detroit's Dwyer Elementary School before going on to Northern High. At 13, he formed the Miracles, adding school friends Ronnie White, Bobby Rogers, and Pete Moore on vocals plus guitarist Marv Tamplin. They started entertaining at school functions and local dances soon after, though they weren't at all definite about plans for lifetime careers in music. Robinson, for example, was an outstanding athlete in football and basketball while Rogers and White both thought they would become engineers.

As they progressed through high school, the group became more engrossed in music and the greater opportunities they felt it held for them. By their late teens, they were still together and performing in nightclubs in their home city. Much of their material by then was based on original writings by Robinson alone or in collaboration with other group members. (During those years, the group also included a girl vocalist, Claudette Rogers, who became Mrs. Robinson. In later years, she did not appear with the group, although she sometimes sat in for recording sessions.) They made demonstration tapes of some songs and tried to gain a recording contract.

In 1958, this led to a meeting between 18-year-old Robinson and part-time record producer Berry Gordy, Jr. Gordy was working at Ford Motor Company to earn a living while trying to break into the record business on a full-time basis. In Robinson's notes for his Motown biography, he recalled the first meeting: "Berry heard our group at a talent audition, and he hired me to do the background for some of his independent productions. He liked one of my songs, 'Mama Done Told Me,' so he put it on the flip side of our first record. Then he listened to the other song I had written; I had composed over a hundred by that time. Berry tore each one apart and showed me what was wrong with them. Then he told me how to develop a basic plot and stick to it. He explained how every song should be a complete story. Berry Gordy has been the greatest thing that ever happened to me."

It worked both ways, because one of the Miracles' early discs, "Get a Job" on End Records, became a top R&B seller and helped provide the impetus for Gordy to form Motown Records. In 1959, Gordy established the Tamla label with Robinson and the Miracles as the first featured act. Their version of Smokey's composition "Shop Around" rose to number one on the R&B charts and number 3 on pop lists in early 1961, earning a gold record, and Motown went on steadily from there to become one of the top recording firms in the industry.

Robinson was an important associate of Gordy in the burgeoning firm, helping with arrangements for its growing list of young artists on the label and providing new material for some of them. An example was the 1965 hit "My Girl," written for the Temptations by Robinson and Ronnie White. Other Robinson-Miracles collaborations were their own hits, "I'll be Doggone," "Ain't That Peculiar," and "Going to a Go-Go." Robinson was named a vice-president of Motown early in his association with Gordy, a post he still held in the 1980s.

The group followed up "Shop Around" with a series of singles that made the R&B charts and, in many cases, turned up on the national top 100 as well. In the first half of the 1960s, these included "You've Really Got a Hold on Me," "Ain't It

Baby," "Brokenhearted," "Everybody Gotta Pay Some Dues," "What's So Good about Good-bye," "I'll Try Something New," "A Love She Can Count On," "Mickey's Monkey," "I Gotta Dance to Keep from Crying," "The Man in You," "I Like It Like That," "That's What Love Is Made Of," and "Come On and Do the Jerk."

The group's middle and late 1960s chart singles included "Ooo Baby Baby," "The Tracks of My Tears," "My Girl Has Gone," and "Going to a Go-Go" (1965); "Whole Lot of Shakin' in My Heart" and "I'm the One You Need" (1966); "The Love I Saw in You Is Just a Mirage," "More Love," and the top 5 "I Second That Emotion" (1967); "If You Can Wait," "Yester Love," and "Special Occasion" (1968); and "Baby, Baby Don't Cry" (top 10), "Doggone Right," "Here I Go Again," "Abraham, Martin and John," and "Point It Out" (1969). During this period, Robinson and his group also did well on the albums *Hi! We're the Miracles, Cookin' with the Miracles, I'll Try Something New, Christmas with the Miracles, The Fabulous Miracles, The Miracles Live on Stage,* and *The Miracles Doing Mickey's Monkey.* Other LPs were *Miracles Going to a Go-Go* and *The Miracles Greatest Hits from the Beginning* (1965), *Away We a Go-Go* and *Make It Happen* (1966), and *The Miracles Greatest Hits, Volume 2* and *Special Occasion* (1968).

As the *Los Angeles Times* vividly described (August 8, 1967): "The group, which consisted of Robinson and his three-man vocal group, appeared in black patent leather shoes, white suits, red ties with white polka dots, and matching pocket handkerchiefs. Robinson stood at one microphone while the other Miracles danced and sang around two mikes on his right. The three always moved in unison, part modern dance, part ballet, sometimes shing-a-ling and boogaloo. Fingers snapping together, twirling in a tight triangle formation, they act out the lyrics Smokey belts out. When Robinson sang: 'I may not be the one you want, but I'm the one you need,' 20 swaying girls in the front row began screaming."

Robinson and the Miracles visual appeal made them highly desirable for such early 1970s TV shows as Tom Jones' and Flip Wilson's. In 1971, they were stars of their own special that also highlighted other Motown superstars.

In 1970, the group turned out its most successful single to that date, "Tears of a Clown" (co-written by Robinson, Stevie Wonder, and Henry Cosby). It spent two weeks at number one in *Billboard* starting December 12, 1970. The LP of the same title was a best-seller in 1971. Other albums on the charts in the early 1970s were *Four in Blue, Pocketful of Miracles, Time Out for the Miracles,* and *Whatlovehas-joinedtogether* (1970), *One Dozen Roses* (1971), and

Flying High Together (1972). Charted singles were "Darling Dear" in (1970), "Crazy about the La La La," "I Don't Blame You at All," and "Satisfaction" (1971); and "We've Come Too Far to End It Now" (1972).

In early 1972, Robinson announced he was going to leave the Miracles. (His place as lead singer was taken over by Billy Griffin.) His reason was that he wanted to cut down on touring to spend more time with his family and concentrate on songwriting and record production as well as tasks associated with his position as executive vice president of Motown. In the summer of 1973, though, his high-pitched voice—which ranged from high tenor all the way to soprano—was presented on his debut solo LP, *Smokey.*

Meanwhile, the Miracles' new albums often made upper charts levels. Their first without Smokey, *Renaissance* (Tamla, 1973), was followed by *Do It Baby* (1974), *Don't Cha Love It* and *City of Angels* (1975), *Power of Music* (1976), and *The Miracles Greatest Hits* (1977). The group placed a number of singles on upper chart levels, such as "Do It Baby" (1974) and "Love Machine Part 1" (number one in *Billboard* the week of March 6, 1976). The group left Motown for Columbia in 1977 with Billy Griffin's brother Don added to make the group a quintet. The group's success didn't extend to the new label as such releases as *Love Crazy* and *The Miracles* were disappointments.

For a long time, Robinson's solo career had less success than the efforts of his old group. Though he placed a number of singles on the charts in the middle and late 1970s, none penetrated the top 20. Into the 1980s, he continued to record quality solo albums on Tamla that paid for themselves without becoming best-sellers. These included *A Quiet Storm* (1974), *Smokey's Family Robinson* (1975), *Deep in My Soul* and *Big Time* (1977), *Love Breeze* and *Smokin'* (1978), *Where There's Smoke* (1979), and *Warm Thoughts* (1980). *Where There's Smoke* included a top 5 pop hit, "Cruisin'." In 1981, he was also honored on Motown's superstar reissue series with the LP *Motown Superstar, Volume 18.*

He continued to be active as record producer, Motown executive, and songwriter through the 1980s. Many artists made the charts with his compositions, including Kim Carnes with his song "More Love." When he offered some new tunes to her producer, George Tobin, at the end of the '70s, Tobin noted he wasn't producing Kim's material any more and suggested Smokey record the songs himself. The result was Robinson's biggest hit since his solo career began, the 1981 single "Being With You." The single and the album of the same name both were certified gold.

Robinson continued to demonstrate his great performing skills from time to time in 1980s tours. He also guested on a number of TV shows during those years. A memorable occasion was Motown's twenty-fifth anniversary telecast the night of May 16, 1983, when he was reunited with the Miracles for a dramatic set.

Smokey continued to record new material for Tamla throughout the 1980s with some chart success, primarily on black music lists. Among releases that charted were the singles "Tell Me Tomorrow" (1982), "I've Made Love to You a Thousand Times" (1983), and "Just to See Her" and "One Heartbeat" (1987) and the album *Yes, It's You Lady* (1982). He won a 1987 Grammy Award in the Best R&B Vocal Performance, Male, for "Just to See Her."

(*See Carnes, Kim; Gordy, Berry, Jr.; Temptations, The; Wells, Mary; Wonder, Stevie.*)

ROE, TOMMY: *Singer, band leader, songwriter. Born Atlanta, Georgia, May 9, 1942.*

The rising importance of Atlanta, Georgia, in the rock world was exemplified by the careers of Tommy Roe, Billy Joe Royal, and Joe South. All became major stars in the '60s (though their careers later lagged). Their paths often crossed, though Roe's route to fame was a circuitous one—through England.

Born and raised in Atlanta, Tommy attended elementary school and Brown High School there. At 16, he formed a group called the Satins, supplying it with a number of original compositions, including one titled "Sheila." In 1960, he cut a record of the song on Judd Records, but nothing happened.

In the early 1960s, he passed demonstration tapes around to major record firms and finally was signed by ABC-Paramount in 1962. One of his first singles was his old favorite "Sheila." This time it went gold, partly because of the increased promotion provided by a major label. Perhaps since it was so similar to the late Buddy Holly's "Peggy Sue," it was particularly well received in England, a Holly stronghold.

His follow-up records did poorly in the U.S., but sold well in Britain. Taking the hint, Roe moved to England and there became a top attraction as an in-person performer and recording artist during the mid-1960s. His ABC albums of those years were issued both in the U.S. and England, but were more successful overseas. They included his debut album, *Tommy Roe* (January 1963) plus *Something for Everybody* (1963), *Sweet Pea* (1966), and *Phantasy* (1967). His gold single of "Sweet Pea" also was one of the top-selling singles in England in 1966.

In the late 1960s, Roe returned to the U.S., where

he appeared on Dick Clark's new ABC-TV rock show, "Where the Action Is." This exposure opened up new opportunities with American fans and his recordings of those years found increasing favor with Stateside audiences. That culminated in a series of hits for him in 1969. His new releases came out on ABC, which had bought out its subsidiary Dunhill. With producer Steve Barri, he recorded three tracks, one of which was "Dizzy," a song he co-wrote with Freddy Weller, one of Paul Revere and the Raiders. Roe thought "Dizzy" was the best of those, Barri argued it was the worst. The first two turned out to be flops, but when "Dizzy" came out in early 1969, it rapidly shot up to number one on *Billboard* for four weeks, starting March 15. The disc was certified gold in March by the RIAA (which also awarded gold records for "Sheila" and "Sweet Pea" the same month). Later in the year he had the top 30 single "Heather Honey."

He continued his streak with the gold "Jam Up, Jelly Tight," issued in late 1969 and in the top 10 in January 1970. "Pearl" hit the charts in the summer. He was also represented on the 1970 album charts with the retrospective *Twelve in a Roe*. But things started to slow down in late 1970. His single "We Can Make Music" was a hit, but didn't quite make the top 40 and his LP of the same title didn't do as well as its immediate predecessors. In late 1971, he had better luck with a remake of the folk standard "Stagger Lee," which reached number 25 nationally in October. During the year, his album *We Can Make Music* also made the charts. In the early '70s, the ABC catalogue included two more retrospective albums: *Beginnings* and *Tommy Roe's 16 Greatest Hits*. In 1972, he moved to MGM Records and had one charted single for the year, "Mean Little Woman."

Things weren't going well with his writing any more than with his recording work. In part, he told a reporter from *Los Angeles* magazine in 1979, it came from a creative letdown after he hit the heights with "Dizzy." "All artists want to outdo themselves, but how did I top 'Dizzy,' which sold 6 million records. . . . I lived in a beautiful Malibu beach house, the ultimate in the California dream, but in my mind it was foggy every day. I needed a cleansing, so I went home to Georgia, back to the people who knew me when I wasn't anybody."

For much of the '70s, he stayed in his home region, doing local shows and expanding his backlog of compositions, which numbered more than 200 by then. He made a first attempt to revive his career with a recording pact with Monument Records that resulted in the albums *Energy* (1976) and *Full Bloom* (1977). Neither was successful. In 1979, he once more tried for a comeback, returning to California to sing with Warner/Curb Records. After the single "Dreamin' Again" proved a failure, he went back to Georgia again. During the 1980s, the wave of nostalgia about '60s rock and pop gave some spark to his performing career and he was able to extend his in-person appearances outside his home region again.

ROLLING STONES, THE: *Vocal and instrumental group, all born England. Brian Jones, born Cheltenham, February 26, 1942, died London, July 2, 1969; Charles Watts, born London, June 2, 1941; Bill Wyman, born Lewisham, London, October 24, 1941; Keith Richard, born Dartford, Kent, December 18, 1943; Mick Jagger, born Dartford, Kent, July 26, 1943.* Jones replaced by Mick Taylor, born Hertfordshire, January 17, 1948. Tayor left in December 1974, replaced in 1976 by Ron Wood, born Hillington, Middlesex, June 1, 1947. Richard changed the spelling of his name back to the original Richards in the mid-1980s.*

When the Rolling Stones were linked with the tragedy of Altamont, it seemed to many observers to be in character. From the start, the group seemed to cultivate an image almost diametrically opposite from its competition for the title of English supergroup of the 1960s, the Beatles. Rightly or wrongly, the general media associated the Beatles with an aura of boyish lightheartedness, while the Stones—"their satanic majesties" in one album title— were seen as reflecting the darker, surlier side of human nature.

To some extent, the Stones' reputation was part of a calculated publicity plot, one of the ways to break through the Beatles' near-stranglehold on public attention in the mid-1960s. However, some of the disparity between the two groups is based on a difference in musical roots. The Beatles took their lead originally from the rock movement of Presley, Holly, and the Everlys, whose rock format is essentially a watered-down version of the blues. The Rolling Stones evolved from the British skiffle craze, which received its incentive from the more brutal, seamier tone of rhythm & blues, music reflecting the bitterness and indignities of American ghetto life along with the exuberance blacks still managed to express despite their troubles.

The Stones did not represent the Liverpool or Mersey Sound often associated with English rock of the early '60s; all the members grew up in or near London in working or lower middle class homes.

---

*Some bios have given both Jones and Jagger's years of birth as 1944.

They all were attracted by the blues played by the countless skiffle groups in England in the second half of the 1950s, though it was beginning to phase out by the time most of the embryo Stones became active as performers in the late '50s and early '60s. For some it was more of a hobby than a prospective career. Vocalist Mick Jagger, for example, was attending London School of Economics with a view toward a job in business when he began singing with the blues group headed by Alexis Korner in 1961.

Korner acted as a midwife in the birth of many famous rock groups, but never more directly (if unintentionally) than with the Stones. Jagger was doing some of the vocals and Charlie Watts played drums in the Blues Incorporated band assembled by Korner and harmonica player Cyril Davies. Rounding out the regular lineup in 1961 were saxophonist Dick Hexstall-Smith, pianist Dave Stevens, and bassist Jack Bruce (later of Cream). Many other young English artists came to listen to the group or to play with it either for specific engagements or on a more or less regular basis. Among them were singers Eric Burdon and Paul Jones, and guitarists Long John Baldry, Keith Richard, and Brian Jones.

In March 1962, Blues Incorporated was offered its first radio broadcast by the British Broadcasting Company, an event that led indirectly to the birth of the Stones. As Korner recalled: "As we were still quite a small name, the BBC wouldn't pay for an extra singer. And as it happened, Mick wasn't really bothered if he did the broadcast or not. So for that particular evening, it was decided that Mick should team up with Keith Richard, Brian Jones, and Long John Baldry and 'deputize' for us that evening at the Marquee. That was the first gig for the Rolling Stones.''

Jagger (born Michael Phillip Jagger), Richard (born Keith Richards) and Jones (born Lewis Brian Hopkins-Jones) enjoyed working together so much that they decided to form a group, adding Charlie Watts and guitarist Bill Wyman. They got their name from a line in a Muddy Waters blues song. In 1963, they began to build an audience in England, though it was rough working in the increasingly long shadow of the Beatles. The Beatles rapidly dominated both the English and American markets to the extent that the Rolling Stones made hardly any inroads among U.S. rock fans. However, their heavily blues-oriented repertoire caught on in England and they placed a series of singles on the hit lists, including "Tell Me," "Time Is on My Side," "Not Fade Away" (B-side for the Crickets' 1957 "Oh! Boy"), "It's All Over Now," "Heart of Stone," "The Last Time," and "Play with Fire." The Stones' version of Willie Dixon's blues standard "Little Red Rooster" made number one, but was never released in the U.S. because of its blatantly sexual lyrics—a reflection of the Stones' no-holds-barred approach to music. The group flouted convention almost from the start, with little starry-eyed sweetness in Jagger's snarling, whiplike vocals and little effort by any of the members to hide their partying and wild lifestyle. Writing about them in the *Los Angeles Times* in May 1971, English rock writer Geoffrey Cannon reflected the view of many pop music followers: "The Stones are perverted, outrageous, violent, repulsive, ugly, tasteless, incoherent. A travesty. That's what's good about them."

This perversity that gained them such nicknames as "Satan's jesters" set up the counterpoint to other groups that made the Stones seem enticingly different. However, this alone would not have been enough. The group also provided excitement with Mick's shattering singing and insistently violent instrumental backing. In addition, the Stones added new life to traditional blues and showcased one hit composition after another, most written by the team of Jagger and Keith Richard.

The group's debut albums, *England's Newest Hit Makers: The Rolling Stones* and *12x5*, were released in the U.S. on London Records in middle and late 1964 and fell well short of gold record sales. Their third LP, *The Rolling Stones, Now!* (May 1965) did better, but their fourth offering, *Out of Our Heads*, hit number one in late 1965 as did its raunchy track "(I Can't Get No) Satisfaction"—a rock classic. The follow-up single, "Get off My Cloud," also made *Billboard*'s top slot.

The Stones strengthened their rising recording stature with concerts all over the world that left platoons of young fans—occupying every available space in the major auditoriums and concert halls—emotionally drained at the end of each performance. Their albums were surefire hits before they even reached dealers' shelves and most of them sold more than enough for gold-record awards in the U.S. alone. In 1966, they made the top 10 gold LPs with *December's Children (and Everybody's), Big Hits (High Tide and Green Grass), Aftermath* (with such new Jagger-Richard compositions as "Paint It Black," "Lady Jane," "Going Home," and two banes of feminism—"Stupid Girl" and "Under My Thumb"), and *Got Live If You Want It!*

Continuing their Midas touch, the Stones kept turning out hit records, even though as of 1967, they announced their retirement from the grind of constant touring. In 1967, they put out *Between the Buttons, Flowers,* and *Their Satanic Majesties Request,* whose experimental electronic effects won rebukes from some critics, but the usual million-dollar outpouring from record buyers. During 1967, the group had a gold single, "Ruby Tuesday," a feat they repeated in 1969 with the raw country-blues-rock "Honky Tonk Woman." The group rounded out the '60s with three more gold LPs: the exquisite Mississippi Delta blues–laced *Beggar's Banquet,* the retrospective *Through the Past Darkly,* and *Let It Bleed.*

But serious events were on the rise. In the early days many fans considered Brian Jones to be the star of the group rather than Jagger. Rivalry within the band and disagreements over policy led to his departure in mid-1969. Soon afterwards, he drowned in his swimming pool. His place was taken by young Mick Taylor, who had served as lead guitarist for the Gods before John Mayall tapped him to replace Eric Clapton in Mayall's blues band. Commenting on Taylor's move, Led Zeppelin lead guitarist Jimmy Page philosophized: "Mick Taylor is an extremely fortunate man, kind of like a fellow who wins the sweepstakes. All of a sudden he is worth $1,000,000. No, maybe more. But he is a nice fellow."

After three years' absence from the American concert scene, the Stones finally returned in late October 1969. The tour was a triumph, but its denouement was harrowing tragedy at Altamont.

The itinerary began at the Forum in Inglewood, California. The 18,000-plus–capacity auditorium was packed to the rafters twice in one frantic eight-hour span stretching from the evening of October 26 to the early morning hours of October 27. Writing in *Rock* magazine (December 8, 1969), Allen Rinde described the Stones' appearance following such preceding acts as Terry Reid, B.B. King, and Ike and Tina Turner: "The aisles start filling up, despite attempts to keep everybody back. And out comes Jagger, in studded black pants, with a silver-studded belt and black full-sleeve jersey, an Uncle Sam red, white, and blue hat, and a gray and black scarf hanging down between his legs, looking like a clown prince of darkness. An angelic devil, smiling sweetly and bouncing on stage, Jagger's eyes make a quick sweep of the crowd, and the Stones are off and running with 'Jumping Jack Flash.'

"Elvis does the bump and grind, but Jagger is into sex theatre. . . . As I sat there, part of my mind was thinking of a word to describe the way Jagger moves around the stage. Strut, prance, bounce, duck-walk, away-we-go. They all came to mind and they all fit, for he does it all. Even Jagger's eyes were involved, reaching skyward in innocence, darting right and left."

The Stones went on to an even more frantic reception at Madison Square Garden in New York, then on to Miami. Joining them in New York was a film crew directed by brothers Albert and David Maysles

and Charlotte Zwerin, who had gained a contract to do a movie about the tour. They took endless footage of the regular engagement and then accompanied the group for an unscheduled concert the Stones decided to give in the San Francisco area. The idea, the band members told the press, was to do a free concert to thank the U.S. rock public for its support.

The site selected was a dusty auto-racing track, the Altamont Raceway, in an outlying section of Alameda County on the other side of the bay from San Francisco. The date was December 6, 1969. The end results were unexpected, to say the least, though they provided one of the most terrifying moments ever presented in a documentary film.

Leonard J. Berry of the *Los Angeles Times* described what happened in his review of the resulting movie, *Gimme Shelter* (December 27, 1970): "Murder was done. Sometime about 8 in the evening of that ragged, drug-ridden day, after this reporter and his party had departed from the host of 300,000 because it was impossible to sit peacefully or hear the music, Mick Jagger sang 'Under My Thumb' while right before the stage, several members of the fabled Hell's Angels motorcycle gang stomped and stabbed a boy to death.

"And one of the dozen or so cameramen engaged by the Maysles for the day happened to have aimed his lens at one of the many scuffles involving the Angels and unknowingly captured the killing.

"*Gimme Shelter,* the resultant 90-minute feature culled from more than 60 hours of exposed stock, is a murder story with a brittle, violent soundtrack provided by the Rolling Stones with Ike and Tina Turner, the Flying Burrito Brothers, and the Jefferson Airplane in counterpoint."

Echoes of Altamont have haunted the Stones' image since then, of course, but could not dim their luster as a supergroup. Late in 1970, their LP *Get Yer Ya-Ya's Out* easily earned a gold record. Taken from live recordings of their 1969 Madison Square Garden concerts, the LP included "Jumping Jack Flash," "Stray Cat Blues," "Midnight Rambler," "Sympathy for the Devil," "Street Fighting Man," and Chuck Berry's "Carol" and "Little Queenie."

In 1971, the Stones severed their ties with London Records and established their own firm, Rolling Stones Records, with U.S. distribution by Atlantic Records. There was no softening of their message, as evidenced by such tracks on the gold *Sticky Fingers* LP as "Sister Morphine." As the *Time* reviewer wrote (May 17, 1971): "Rarely had rock music invoked such an invitation to hell. An electric guitar quivers menacingly, like a poised cobra. Off in the distance somewhere, the piano groans a low, dark, mournful chord. Jagger, sounding like John Lennon baring his soul, speaks from a hospital bed of the mind: 'Oh, can't you see I am fadin' fast/And this shot will be my last.'"

In 1971, the Stones also had two chart singles: "Brown Sugar" and "Wild Horses." At the start of 1972, London Records issued the gold retrospective album, *Hot Rocks, 1964–71*, followed by the gold *More Hot Rocks (Big Hits and Fazed Cookies)* in 1972. The raw-flavored two-disc *Exile on Main Street* (1972, Rolling Stones Records) also went gold while providing two hit singles: "Happy" and "Tumbling Dice." In 1973, the London single "You Can't Always Get What You Want" (first released in 1969) made the charts. That fall, the Rolling Stones Records release *Goat's Head Soup* (one of the band's weakest efforts, which caused some critics to suggest the Stones might have begun to show signs of age), still went gold and rose to number one in Billboard in November—as did its single "Angie" the week of October 20, 1973.

In 1974, the band had the gold LP *It's Only Rock'n'Roll* and made the hit list in '75 with the gold LP *Made in the Shade*. The album, containing earlier recorded cuts, still seemed below band standards despite its sales. During 1974, Mick Taylor cited "musical differences" as a reason for quitting the band. Rumors that Faces guitarist Ron Wood would succeed him were rife, particularly when Wood joined the band in Munich to help record some tracks for the platinum 1976 album *Black & Blue*. The rumors became stronger when Wood joined the band for its summer 1975 tour of the U.S. However, both parties denied the merger. Wood said he still was a member of Faces and he also was represented by his second solo album that summer, *New Look* (a follow-up to his September 1974 *I've Got My Own Album to Do*). But when *Black & Blue* came out in April 1976, Wood's face was on the cover and it was acknowledged that he had become a full-fledged Stones member.

With *Black & Blue*, the band had recovered considerably from the deficiencies of *Made in the Shade*. The upward momentum was reflected in the next two LPs, the in-concert *Love You Live* (1977, gold) and the fine 1978 collection, *Some Girls*, whose sales totaled over 5 million copies. Its single, "Miss You," reached number one in *Billboard* the week of August 5, 1978. But the album's success was preceded by more than a few negative headlines.

For one, Mick Jagger's divorce from Bianca Jagger was a gossip item and Keith Richard gained the front pages when he was arrested by Canadian authorities in Toronto for possession of cocaine and heroin. While the band went on for other commitments, he remained behind in Toronto, out on bail but unable to leave. The Stones meanwhile were in Paris making the final recordings for *Some Girls*. Tapes of those sessions were flown to Toronto,

where Richard recorded his parts of the arrangements. When his case finally came to trial in October, he persuaded the judge he was on the way to recovery and was released after agreeing to headline a benefit concert for the blind.

In 1979, Richard was once more on the road with the band. The massive crowds throughout the world showed that fans didn't consider the band the dinosaur many critics had called it. He soon was back in the studio with the group recording tracks for *Emotional Rescue* (1980, platinum). The title track rose to number three on *Billboard* singles charts during September. In late 1981, the band put out another platinum album, *Tattoo You*, with its number two single "Start Me Up." During 1981, a London reissue of the *Hot Rocks 1964–71* album was on the charts for a number of months.

Stones members continued to take part in various outside projects in the 1980s. Bill Wyman, who had turned out two solo albums in the '70s, worked on the soundtrack for the Ryan O'Neal movie *Green Ice* and made lower U.K. chart levels with his disc "(Si Si) Je Suis un Rock Star." He also assembled a series of photographs with legendary artist Marc Chagall. Some of the other members of the band worked on production or other support work of material prepared by various performers. In 1985 Jagger came out with his debut solo album, *She's the Boss*, on Columbia.

Since the last Rolling Stones album was the late 1983 platinum *Undercover*, by the time Jagger's solo came out, nearly three years had passed without a new Stones LP. Some observers wondered if the band had broken up. But this was disproved in 1986 when the group had a hit video and single of "Harlem Shuffle" followed by *Dirty Work*, the platinum album containing the song.

(*See Animals, The; Baldry, Long John; Burdon, Eric; Cream; Davies, Cyril; Faces, The; Faithfull, Marianne; Jagger, Mick; Korner, Alexis; Meters, The; Parsons, Gram; Procol Harum; Tosh, Peter; Trower, Robin; Turner, Ike and Tina; Turner, Tina; Waters, Muddy.*)

RONETTES, THE: *Vocal group from New York, New York. Veronica "Ronnie" Bennett, born August 10, 1943; Estelle Bennett, born July 22, 1944; Nedra Talley, born January 17, 1946.*

Phil Spector became the "tycoon of teen" at 21 because of his ability to spot unknown acts that could be groomed to become teenage favorites. One of the discoveries that helped earn him his reputation was the Ronettes.

Born and raised in New York, the girls were all related: sisters Veronica and Estelle Bennett and their cousin Nedra Talley. In high school, they started singing together as a trio in their spare time. The year was 1959 and rock music dominated the charts, though some experts thought it was beginning to fade.

The following year, rock got a new boost when Hank Ballard started the twist dance craze and Chubby Checker made it a national mania. Twist clubs sprang up in major cities at the start of the '60s, providing opportunities for acts that could sing and perform the many variations of the dance. The girls worked up an act that won them engagements in some of these clubs. By 1963, they were featured vocalists in the Peppermint Lounge chain, performing in both its New York and Miami Beach, Florida, branches.

Spector, who had started his Philles Records firm in 1962, heard them at one of the Peppermint Lounges and signed them to a recording contract. With Ellie Greenwich and Jeff Barry, he co-wrote a song for them called "Be My Baby"—a gold single in 1963.

Under Spector's direction, the trio had several more hits in the mid-1960s, though none came close to "Be My Baby" in popularity. "Walking in the Rain" (not a remake of Johnnie Ray's 1956 pop favorite, but a Spector-Mann-Weil original) sold over 240,000 copies in the U.S. in 1964. Other chart-makers were "Baby, I Love You" (late 1963–early 1964), "(The Best Part of) Breakin' Up" and "Do I Love You" (1964), "Born to Be Together" and "Is This What I Get for Loving You" (1965), and "I Can Hear Music" (1966).

By the late 1960s, the original Ronettes had ceased to be in action as an entity. Ronnie and Spector were married in 1968 and divorced in 1974. In subsequent decades, the trio's recordings were included in several movie soundtracks and continued to be played on oldies radio programs.

(*See Greenwich, Ellie; Spector, Phil.*)

RONSTADT, LINDA: *Singer, songwriter. Born Tucson, Arizona, July 15, 1946.*

One of the most popular female singers since the early 1970s has been Linda Ronstadt. She has kept her star shining bright all this time by following her heart in what she sings and by not being afraid to try new material and new styles while still remaining true to her roots. In the 1970s, she did a lot to popularize country-rock, but in the 1980s, she daringly ventured away from this sound and performed in an opera and operetta and also did three albums of nostalgic, 1950s-type ballads, managing to maintain old fans while gaining new ones.

Linda grew up in Tucson, Arizona, where her pre-teen idols were Hank Williams and Elvis Presley. She liked rock music but also listened to country and

Mexican music. After a year at the University of Arizona, Linda left for California to pursue a career as a singer.

With two friends, Bob Kimmel and Ken Edwards, Linda formed the Stone Poneys. They made three albums for Capitol and had a top 20 rock hit in 1967 with "Different Drum." (Written by Michael Nesmith of the Monkees, it was one of numerous songs in her early repertoire she got from records by the folk-bluegrass Greenbriar Boys.) However, the group broke up about that time and Ronstadt started off in her own direction.

Her first solo album, *Hand Sown, Home Grown,* evidenced a shift from the soft-rock sound of the Stone Poneys to a stronger country emphasis. The album was a good one, featuring such songs as "Silver Threads and Golden Needles," which was to become a favorite with audiences through the late 1970s, and country standards such as John D. Loudermilk's "Break My Mind" and Ivy J. Bryant's "The Only Mama That'll Walk the Line." However, she had no chart hits from the album. Her second solo LP, *Silk Purse* (1970), continued in the country vein. The album was on the pop charts for a few months, while its top 30 single, "Long, Long Time," won Ronstadt her first Grammy nomination.

For her third album, *Linda Ronstadt,* she assembled a new band, which included Glenn Frey and Don Henley. They later went on to form their own influential country-rock group band, the Eagles. In 1973, Ronstadt left Capitol for Asylum Records and released the shallow but successful album *Don't Cry Now.*

The turning point in Linda's career came in 1974, when she signed Peter Asher (formerly of Peter and Gordon) as her manager as well as her record producer. From that time on, all of Linda's albums were gold or better. She still owed Capitol an album under her previous contract so she and Asher decided to get it out of the way. Ronstadt and Asher's first collaboration, the platinum *Heart Like a Wheel* (Capitol, 1974), reached number one on the LP charts. Its remakes of "You're No Good" (a 1963 R&B hit by Betty Everett) and the Everly Brothers' "When Will I Be Loved" also made number one and top 10 respectively. Its tearful version of Hank Williams' "I Can't Help It" won her the Grammy Award for Best Female Country Vocal in 1975. In addition, *Don't Cry Now* returned to the charts to become Linda's second gold record.

Ronstadt's second album produced by Peter Asher (the platinum *Prisoner in Disguise,* Asylum, 1975) was a bit more rock-oriented than some of her previous albums. The big hit single was "Heat Wave" (a remake of Martha and the Vandellas' 1963 soul hit). There were also country-influenced cuts such as

Dolly Parton's "I Will Always Love You" plus Neil Young's "Love Is a Rose" (a hit on the country charts).

1976 witnessed a continuation of Linda's previous successes. *Hasten Down the Wind* included, for the first time, two songs that she had written herself: "Lo Siento Mi Vida" (co-written with bassist and former Stone Poney Kenny Edwards as well as Linda's father) and "Try Me Again" (co-written with sideman Andrew Gold). Other cuts were "That'll Be the Day" (a Buddy Holly classic, which added fuel to the growing Buddy Holly revival craze) and Willie Nelson's composition "Crazy" (a 1961 hit for the late Patsy Cline). Both became pop as well as country hits. The album achieved platinum status and won for Linda a Grammy for Best Female Pop Vocal Performance. That year, the *Playboy* Poll named her the Top Female Singer in both pop and country categories.

Ronstadt's next album, *Simple Dreams* (August 1977), contained five major hits. Two were smash rock hits, "Tumbling Dice" from the Rolling Stones and "It's So Easy" from Buddy Holly. Its three country hits were Roy Orbison's "Blue Bayou" (which won a Grammy Award for Best Single), "Poor, Poor Pitiful Me," and the traditional folk ballad "I Never Will Marry" (recorded with Dolly Parton). Linda was once again named Top Female Singer in both pop and country divisions in the *Playboy* poll. *Simple Dreams* sold 3.5 million copies in less than a year in the United States alone. Ronstadt continued to receive a great deal of media attention, appearing on the covers of *Time, Rolling Stone,* and *People* magazines.

September 1978 saw the release of Linda's platinum *Living in the U.S.A.* Its opening cut, "Back in the USA," written by Chuck Berry, made the upper echelons of the country and rock charts. In 1980, she reflected the growing punk and new wave movements on the platinum *Mad Love* with its top 10 single "Hurt So Bad."

After this, Ronstadt took a hiatus from rock and appeared in a Joseph Papp production of Gilbert & Sullivan's operetta, *The Pirates of Penzance,* in New York City. The production was a big hit and Ronstadt's voice adapted itself well to the operetta.

In the meantime, her *Greatest Hits, Volume 2* (Asylum, late 1980) was certified gold by year-end. The next album with new material, *Get Closer* (fall 1982), also went gold.

Ronstadt's next move was a surprise—an entire album of ballads from the 1920s through 1950s, backed with rich orchestrations by arranger-conductor Nelson Riddle. The resulting album, *What's New,* surprised everyone by going platinum, attracting young audiences as well as older ones. *What's New* was followed by a similar Riddle-backed LP, *Lush Life* (1984), featuring a few up-tempo numbers along with the ballads. A third LP in the genre, *For Sentimental Reasons,* appeared in 1986. Asylum released a three-record set of the Ronstadt–Nelson Riddle LPs under the title *Round Midnight.*

Ronstadt returned to the New York opera scene in 1984 as Mimi in Puccini's *La Boheme.* Her performance was given mixed reviews. She had done operatic training prior to taking on the role, but some critics felt that her voice, though certainly beautiful, had not been trained early enough to adapt to the rigors of opera.

Linda continued to do concerts of her pop-rock-country material. She even performed at a mariachi festival at Los Angeles' Universal Studios in September 1986, which was natural for her as her father, a Mexican-German, often listened to and sang *rancheras,* the songs sung to mariachi music. Her *Canciones de mi Padre* (1987) preserved these songs on disc.

In 1987 came the album *Trio* (Warner Brothers)—the long-awaited and second attempt at a collaboration between Linda Ronstadt, Dolly Parton, and Emmylou Harris on an idea they had been germinating for ten years. The album was mostly country and folk songs, and the blend of the three voices, a lovely experience. *Trio* won a Grammy for Best Country Performance by a Duo or Group with Vocal. At the same ceremony, "Somewhere Out There" (written by James Horner, Barry Mann, and Cynthia Weil and recorded in a duet by Ronstadt and James Ingram) was named 1987 Song of the Year.

By all accounts, Linda Ronstadt is a superstar. She had her first hit at the age of 21; and 20 years later, was still going strong. Her voice has a natural quality, although the voice is operatic and nearly flawless. That natural quality reflects her personality. She seems to be a person without pretenses, which, along with her lovely voice, has endeared her to her fans. This charm has always helped her career. Girls and women could identify with her giggling stage manner and her songs about failed romance. Men found her pretty and sexy in addition to enjoying her voice.

Ronstadt also carried her honesty into the songs she chose to record. As she told Robert Hilburn of the *Los Angeles Times* in December 1974: "Though the melody has to match up with what I can do, the lyrics are the main thing. I look for something that feels like it is about me. Just like a songwriter will write a song that is about some feeling he just went through, I can't really sing a song that doesn't express my feelings in some way." This attitude, perhaps more than anything else, accounted for her numerous appearances at the top of the hit charts.

Nearly a decade later, she told Dennis Hunt of the *Los Angeles Times* that it was her fascination with the phrasing on the ballad-type songs that led her to record *What's New*. "I thought if I learned that immaculate phrasing, it would make me a better rock'n'roll singer . . . but those songs just seduced me. I just had to record them. It was total obsession. I can't really explain how it happened, but after a while, I thought I'd just die if I didn't record them. I knew the obsession would eat away at me until I did something about it." This type of obsession and the drive to see it through, her beautiful voice, and her willingness to change and take risks, are the reasons why Linda Ronstadt could remain popular 20 years after her start in the fickle rock industry. (Entry by Alice Seidman.)

(*See* Berry, Chuck; Eagles, The; Frey, Glenn; Henley, Don; Holly, Buddy; Nesmith, Mike; Orbison, Roy; Peter and Gordon; Zevon, Warren.)

ROSS, DIANA: *Singer, actress. Born Detroit, Michigan, March 26, 1944.*

For pop music fans of the 1960s, it was difficult to envision the Supremes without Diana Ross or vice versa after her decision to leave the group was officially announced in January 1970. For a while, it seemed as though both parties would survive the separation in excellent shape as the reorganized trio scored several new hits, but in time it became apparent that Diana's departure sounded the death knell for the group that had brought her from an unknown Detroit teenager to superstar. On her own, however, Diana forged a new saga that retained its luster into the late 1980s.

During the transition year of 1970, record buyers were offered tempting new releases by Diana and the Supremes made before the split plus later solo recordings by Ms. Ross. Hits by Diana and the Supremes included the single "Someday We'll Be Together" and the albums *Cream of the Crop, Let the Sunshine In, Greatest Hits, Volume 3* and the top 10 *Farewell*. Also hits were albums that combined the talents of Diana and the Supremes and the Temptations: *On Broadway* and *Together,* as well as the singles hits "We'll Be Together" and "The Weight." Midyear, Diana's solo debut LP, *Diana Ross,* came out on Motown and was on the charts into 1971. For the album, the writing team of Ashford & Simpson wrote and produced "Reach Out and Touch (Somebody's Hand)," which was Diana's debut solo single in April, 1970. The song only made it to number 20 on *Billboard* lists, but became a standard concert centerpiece for Ross. Ashford and Simpson also came up with a new version of their "Ain't No Mountain High Enough" (a 1967 hit for Marvin Gaye and Tammi Terrell) tailored to Ross's

style. The song rose to number one in *Billboard* for three weeks starting September 19, 1970. Also a charted single for Diana during the year was "Everything Is Everything."

In 1971, Diana achieved excellent Nielsen ratings for her TV special and her TV soundtrack album was on the general charts as well the soul top 10. She also made top chart levels with the singles "Surrender," "I'm Still Waiting," "Reach Out, I'll Be There," and "Remember Me," but much of her time was spent preparing for her debut movie role as Billie Holiday, the fabled and troubled jazz vocalist. When the film *Lady Sings the Blues* was released in 1972, Diana's acting performance was acclaimed as one of the year's best and won her an Oscar nomination. (In the voting, she lost out to Liza Minnelli's work in *Cabaret.*) The Motown soundtrack album made number one on the charts. A single from that album, "Good Morning Heartache," made the top 40 in early 1973, but Diana easily outpaced that with a new studio disc, "Touch Me in the Morning" (number one in *Billboard* the week of August 18, 1973). The album in which it served as title song made number five in *Billboard*. In early 1974, another Ross single, "Last Time I Saw Him," was a chart hit.

In 1975, Diana had a featured role in another Motown-sponsored film, *Mahogany*. She played a fashion designer turned model who had to cope with the impact of fame on her personal relationships. The soundtrack album (featuring Marvin Gaye) was a hit in 1975 and 1976, while the single "Theme from *Mahogany* (Do You Know Where You're Going To)" brought her another number one success in *Billboard* the week of January 24, 1976. A controversy arose when the Oscar nominating committee initially passed over the song, but later included it among the candidates, though it eventually lost out to Keith Carradine's "I'm Easy" from the film *Nashville*.

During 1976, Diana had two more albums on the charts: *Diana Ross* and *Diana Ross' Greatest Hits*. Initial single from the former, the ballad "I Thought It Took a Little Time (But Today I Fell in Love)," made the charts, but wasn't making much progress when it was observed that another track, the disco-flavored "Love Hangover," was getting considerable airplay. Released as a single, it made number one in *Billboard* for two weeks starting May 29, 1976.

That proved to be Diana's last number one success for the balance of the decade. She continued to turn out new albums and singles for Motown, but the quality level varied considerably from one release to the next. Late 1970s LPs included *An Evening with Diana Ross* and *Baby It's Me* (1977), *Ross* (1978), and *The Boss* (1979, gold). In mid-1980, one of her more consistently excellent collections, *Diana,* reached number two in *Billboard.* The platinum LP proved to be the best-selling LP of her solo career up to then. The first single from the album, "Upside Down," spent four weeks at number one in *Billboard* starting September 6, 1980. It was followed by two more top 10 hits: "I'm Coming Out" and "It's My Turn." Those accomplishments allowed her to leave Motown on a high note, a decision she made because of a desire to exercise more direct control of her career. After she left, Motown issued such 1981 albums of her work as *To Love Again* and *All the Great Hits.* But Motown also had another important farewell gift from Diana; she combined forces with Lionel Richie to record the theme song for the film *Endless Love*—number one in *Billboard* for nine weeks starting August 15, 1981.

By then, Diana had signed a new contract with RCA. Her LP debut on the label, *Why Do Fools Fall in Love* (1981), went platinum. She followed with such other charted (and typically gold) RCA albums as *Silk Electric* (1982), *Swept Away* (1984), *Eaten Alive* (1985), and *Red Hot Rhythm and Blues* (mid-1987). Soon after the '87 LP's release, Diana left RCA and joined the roster of EMI London.

(*See Ashford & Simpson; Gordy, Berry, Jr.; Moonglows, The; Richie, Lionel; Supremes, The; Temptations, The.*)

ROSSINGTON COLLINS BAND: *Vocal and instrumental group. Members (early 1980s): Dale Krantz, born Indiana; others, all born Jacksonville, Florida: Gary Rossington, c. 1949; Allen Collins, c. 1949; Billy Powell, c. early 1950s; Leon Wilkeson, c. early 1950s; Barry Harwood, Derek Hess.*

A tragic plane crash snuffed out the lives of Lynyrd Skynyrd's lead vocalist/primary songwriter Ronnie Van Zant, guitarist Steve Gaines, and backup singer Cassie Gaines in September 1977, but was survived by most band members, including Gary Rossington and Allen Collins, who had taken part in the Skynyrd odyssey with Van Zant from the time all three were in junior high school in Jacksonville, Florida.

It would not have been inappropriate for them to try to pick up the pieces and retain the Lynyrd Skynyrd name and repertoire. But both felt that would have been demeaning to the memory of Ronnie, whom they regarded as the heart and soul of the old group. Once they recovered from their plane-crash injuries, they chose to assemble a new band, not only in name, but to some extent in the type of music it would perform. Rossington and Collins did not

simply want to cover the old hits of Lynyrd Skynyrd, but desired to develop new material that could be identified with the new organization.

The nucleus of the band remained from the old one: Rossington on lead, rhythm, and slide guitars; Collins on lead and rhythm guitars; Bill Powell on keyboards; and Leon Wilkeson on bass guitar. The last two musicians, though not founding members of Lynyrd Skynyrd, were from Jacksonville and had joined the group just before it made its 1973 debut album on MCA, *Pronounced Leh-Nerd Skin-Nerd,* and had been represented on the eight gold LPs (according to MCA, which states seven of those also went platinum) issued between then and 1979. As for Rossington and Collins, they had worked with Van Zant in a series of groups: the Wild Cats, the Nobel 5, the One Per Cent, the Pretty Ones, and Lynyrd Skynyrd.

Rossington commented: "Actually, it was always the same band; we just kept changing the name."

To round out the Rossington Collins Band, other recruits in 1979 were Barry Harwood (lead, rhythm, and slide guitars and vocals), Derek Hess (drums), and Dale Krantz (lead vocals). Hess, like almost all the members, was Jacksonville-born and -raised. He had started playing piano at six and was inspired by Ringo Starr of the Beatles to switch to drums at 13. Later, he joined Jacksonville friend Barry Harwood in two local bands: Running Easy and Family Portrait. Harwood, the child of musicians, went in a reverse direction from Hess, starting out on drums at six and switching to guitar at 12. Later, besides playing in local bands, he also did considerable session work, supporting Joe South, Melanie, Lobo, and Lynyrd Skynyrd.

Dale Krantz in a way symbolized the aim of the band organizers to avoid being Skynyrd clones. The small, vivacious performer gave the band a female lead singer whereas Skynyrd had been an all-male group with female backup singers. Krantz, born and raised in Indiana, had started singing as a child in the church choir her father directed. After earning a bachelor's degree in music education from Indiana University, she moved to Los Angeles, where she did some concert and recording work with Leon Russell. In 1977, she joined .38 Special (the group headed by Ronnie Van Zant's brother Donnie) as a backup singer, which caused her to settle in Jacksonville.

As part of the Jacksonville music scene, she became acquainted with all the Skynyrd alumni. Their appreciation of her vocal talents led to the invitation to join Rossington Collins. Dale recalled that when they queried her for the job in 1979, "I thought they meant background vocals. I was flustered, but thrilled, when they said: 'No, no, we want you to be up front . . . just get out there and do what you were meant to do—sing your ass off, lady!' ''

With Rossington and Collins handling production, the new group finished its debut LP in early 1980. Many industry observers suspected that despite protestations to the contrary, the album would simply be warmed-over Skynyrd-style southern boogie. It did have some of Skynyrd's blues-rock flavor, but *Anytime, Anyplace, Anywhere* (MCA, mid-1980) had interesting touches of its own. As noted in the *New Rolling Stone Record Guide*, the band "is hardly a Skynyrd Mark II . . . any comparisons would have to be tempered by the obvious differences between RCB singer Dale Krantz and the late Ronnie Van Zant. Krantz's voice, lighter and more flexible than Van Zant's, opens up new territory for RCB that was inaccessible to Skynyrd, although at the cost of hardcore boogie credibility.''

The band emphasized its new direction in a cross-country concert tour in which it did not use any Skynyrd material until the encore—"Free Bird," dedicated to Van Zant, with Krantz going offstage so that the spotlight was on former Skynyrd performers. Overall, audiences and critics accentuated the positive. *US* magazine noted the untimely demise of Skynyrd "tore a hole in the hearts of many music fans. Luckily the South has a way of rising again. The Rossington Collins Band . . . is cause for celebration. Birth follows death. The mourning is over.''

The LP was certified gold by the end of 1980. The band's second MCA release was on the hit lists the last three months of 1981 and in early 1982. *This Is the Way* was a tighter collection than the debut LP, but seemed to find less favor with record buyers, suggesting that Skynyrd's audience was finding it increasingly difficult to come to terms with a group that obviously was going to play Southern rock its own way and not in the accepted patterns of the earlier band.

During 1982, the Rossington Collins group disbanded. After the breakup, the leaders went their separate ways. MCA released the Allen Collins Band's *Here, There & Back* in 1983. Three years later, Atlantic Records put out *Return to the Scene of the Crime* by the band Rossington, featuring Gary, his wife Dale Krantz-Rossington, and Derek Hess from Rossington-Collins plus Jay Johnson on guitar, Gary Ross on keyboards and synthesizer, Tim Lindsay on bass, and Ronnie Eades on sax.

Neither the new Rossington group nor Collins' band seemed able to recapture the magic of the old Lynyrd Skynyrd. In 1987, both of them got together again to help organize a reunion Lynyrd Skynyrd group with other alumni for a series of memorial concerts.

(*See Lynyrd Skynyrd; Russell, Leon.*)

ROTH, DAVID LEE: *See Van Halen.*

ROXY MUSIC: *Vocal and instrumental group. Founding members (1971): Bryan Ferry, born Washington, County Durham, England, and Brian Eno, born East Anglia, England, 1948. Personnel in mid-1970s comprised Ferry; Andy Mackay, born July 23; Phil Manzanera, born Colombia, South America, January 31; Edwin Jobson, born Billingham, Cleveland, England, April 28; Paul Thompson, born Newcastle upon Tyne, England, May 13. Group disbanded in 1976, reformed by Ferry in 1979. 1980 lineup: Ferry, Manzanera, Mackay.*

With an intellectual approach molded by its art-school origin, Roxy Music was an instant success in Europe in the early '70s. But it took four years and a disco single, "Love Is the Drug," for the group to break through in America. At times, the group's activities were overshadowed by the solo efforts of its central figure, Bryan Ferry.

The group was founded in 1971 by vocalist Ferry and keyboards player Brian Eno. (*See Eno, Brian.*) Before getting together with Eno, Ferry had spent three years as a student at the University of Newcastle upon Tyne, studying painting and singing in a campus soul group, Gas Board. Looking back over his career, he told Kristine McKenna of the *Los Angeles Times* in 1982: "I see myself as a sophisticated modern blues singer. Jazz is the music that first excited me. The first LP I ever got was by Charlie Parker, and I played it so much I can remember every solo on it to this day. My main influences were black American artists, and yet I'm very white and very English. These are the two polarities I work within, and I think interesting things happen when I manage to make them meet.''

Instead of working its way up through club and college gigs, Roxy made its debut at Britain's largest ever rock show, the Lincoln Festival, shortly after its first album, *Roxy Music*, had been released by Island Records in June 1972. (U.S. release was on Atco.)

Part of the appeal was certainly Roxy's appearance—a curious amalgam of science-fiction costumes and '50s hairstyles. Brian Eno in particular attracted a cult following, even though the group's songs were mainly Ferry's. Synthesizer whiz Eno, though, left in 1973, following a difference of opinion with Ferry over creative directions. He was replaced on keyboards by Edwin Jobson, who also played violin and later was part of Jethro Tull. (*See Jethro Tull.*)

The group's first single, "Virginia Plain," reached number four on the British charts following appearances supporting Alice Cooper and David

Bowie. The band was voted 1972's brightest hope by readers of the four major British rock music papers.

Roxy Music made its first American tour in the fall of 1972, but despite favorable reviews, failed to make much impact, having been promoted as a would-be rival to Alice Cooper. Back in Britain, though, Roxy's second album, *For Your Pleasure,* went to number three on the charts in March 1973 with the second single, "Pyjamarama," a hit a month earlier. By the summer of 1973, the group had chart records in several European countries.

In November 1973, the group's third album, *Stranded,* went to number one in the U.K. At this time, Roxy faced competition from Ferry himself, who in October released his first solo album, *These Foolish Things,* showcasing his versions of others' songs. His rendition of Dylan's "A Hard Rain's Gonna Fall" was a British hit, as was the Roxy single "Streetlife."

A second American tour followed in 1974 with Roxy as headliner. *Stranded* (on Atco) climbed the American charts. Lester Bangs wrote in *Creem* magazine: "Once you let them work their venal magic on your inner ear canals, you'll know why I'm frothing." That same month, Ferry released his second solo album, *Another Time Another Place*, on the Atlantic label in the U.S. His solo single of the old standard "Smoke Gets in Your Eyes" was a British hit. Saxophonist Andy Mackay also released a solo album, *In Search of Eddie Riff.*

A fourth Roxy Music album, *Country Life,* went high on the British charts in October 1974 and a fifth, *Siren,* was number one by the end of 1975. The single from it, "Love Is the Drug," was also number one in England and the band's first single to make *Billboard*'s top 30 in the U.S.

Having reached this peak, the group decided to disband for a year. Ferry had a hit single with "Let's Stick Together" and he also revived the EP. His extended-play release was among the British top 10 singles in August. Its songs included the Everly Brothers' "Price of Love" and the Beatles' "It's Only Love." *Let's Stick Together* was the title of his 1976 album issued in the U.S. by Atlantic Records.

Other group members also worked on solo projects during that period. Guitarist Phil Manzanera released two albums: the solo *Diamond Head* plus *Mainstream* featuring Quiet Sun, a band he'd worked with before Roxy was formed. Jobson moved to America, where he joined Frank Zappa's group. (*See Zappa, Frank.*)

The most successful project was Mackay's *Rock Follies,* named after a spring of 1976 British TV serial that followed the fortunes of a female rock group. Mackay wrote the music for the serial and an album of his songs reached number one in the U.K.

During 1976, a live album, *Viva! Roxy Music,* made the charts, after which it was confirmed that the band had officially broken up. In 1977, Atlantic released a *Greatest Hits* retrospective in the U.S. Meanwhile, Ferry continued his solo career with the 1977 LP *In Your Mind.* His 1978 *The Bride Stripped Bare* was recorded with U.S. session musicians. While the albums, like his earlier solo efforts, had many fine offerings, they failed to find the hoped-for response from the American public.

In 1979, Ferry reformed Roxy and focused his attention on the band rather than his solo career into the 1980s. The first release of the reorganized band was the excellent 1979 *Manifesto.* In 1980, Atco issued *Flesh and Blood,* the band's biggest commercial success with American record buyers. In the summer of 1982, *Avalon* (nominally the last Roxy Music LP) rose to number one on U.K. LP charts, though it was less successful in the U.S. after being issued by Atco in July. The trend of good sales response in England and relatively weak response from U.S. fans continued into the mid-1980s for such releases as the four-song live EP *The High Road* (EG/Warner Brothers) in 1983 and the Ferry solo album *Boys and Girls.* This was so despite considerable critical praise from U.S. reviewers. Part of the reason for that may have been the lack of U.S. concert exposure.

Ferry's reluctance to tour, he told McKenna, reflected in part his feeling that "Commercial success is fairly important to me but that's not my main motivation in life, and I think life would become really miserable if it did become too important. . . . The novelty of touring has worn off, and I'd prefer to just go back into the studio. I find touring destructive because you quickly reach the point of complete mental and physical exhaustion. Plus, even though we filled medium-size halls everywhere we went on our last tour, we couldn't really fill big places and that's the only way you can make any money. It gets depressing working really hard then being told: 'Well, you only lost $50,000 on this tour.' I've always thought video could accomplish what touring accomplishes and for years I've been asking why we can't just send out a video of the album.''

With the release of his excellent album *Bête Noire* in late 1987, Ferry gave no indication he intended to make any sudden change in his limited concert scheduling. Critics again responded positively, often commenting on the lasting influence of earlier recordings. Robert Palmer (*The New York Times,* November 29, 1987) lauded *Boys and Girls* and *Avalon* as well as *Bête Noire,* commenting, "Thematically, *Boys and Girls* was a meditation on Mr. Ferry's customary concerns—love, obsession, civilization and its discontents. Musically, it carried his preoccupa-

589

tions with sonic intensity to extremes; some of the arrangements featured what sounded like two complete rhythm sections, playing in elaborate counterpoint. As usual, the complexities were so subtle that they were inaudible to the casual listener. But the more one unravels the music's densely woven textures, the more detail is revealed. *Boys and Girls,* which seemed like a letdown after the indelible lyricism of *Avalon,* has held up very well.''

RUNAWAYS, THE: *Vocal and instrumental group. Members (1976–79): Lita Ford, born London, England, c. 1959; Joan Jett, born Philadelphia, Pennsylvania, September 22, 1960; Jackie Fox, born Southern California, c. 1960; Cherie Currie, born Southern California, c. 1960; Sandy West, born Southern California, c. 1958.*

The all-girl group the Runaways had a brief vogue at home and abroad in the late 1970s, but never quite broke through to mass success. The band had a major impact on the rock field, however, opening the door to stardom for such high-intensity girl bands as the Go-Gos and Bangles and serving as the proving ground for Joan Jett, who went on to become a superstar of the 1980s. (*See Jett, Joan.*)

The guiding light in formation of the group was Kim Fowley, one-time rock performer and later head of his own music-publishing and talent organization. The band evolved from Kim's chance meeting with Kari Krome at a Los Angeles party in 1975. Kim, who found one way to keep in touch with teen music interests was to talk to teens, got into a conversation with 13-year-old Kari and found she liked to write song lyrics. After she related a few samples, he decided to sign her as a writer with his publishing company.

After working for the firm for a short time, she suggested that Kim consider forming a teenage girl band to perform the kind of material she was writing. When Fowley expressed interest, she brought in friend Joan Jett to audition. Joan demonstrated considerable promise on guitar, a skill she had picked up from listening to records at teen clubs and on the radio. Fowley then put out an audition call that brought in many more hopefuls, from which 19-year-old bass guitarist/vocalist Micki Steele and 15-year-old drummer Sandy West were culled. The band began practicing as a trio of Joan, Micki, and Sandy, but Steele, who was deemed too old for the concept anyway, left after a short time to be replaced briefly by a girl named Peggy, who also quickly departed to be replaced by Jackie Fox. The band meanwhile expanded to a quintet with addition of guitarist Lita Ford and sultry vocalist Cherie Currie.

Of the group that then comprised the Runaways,

most had grown up in either Los Angeles' San Fernando Valley or nearby Orange County. Lita Ford, though born in London, had moved to America with her parents in 1962 and lived in California from the age of nine. At the time she joined the band, she had been playing guitar for nine years, performing with local school groups before moving into the Runaways.

Jackie Fox dreamed of becoming an actress in her early teens, but progressed to becoming an expert surfer. Music also interested her. She already was a good guitarist when she tried out for the Runaways. Since the band needed a bass guitarist, she agreed to switch to that with the group.

Sandy West had learned music theory while still in grade school. ''My family was classically oriented, my music teacher was jazz crazy, but I always retained my rock'n'roll vision.'' When she was nine in 1967, she took up drums and by her teens was an impassioned performer in high school groups.

Currie, who came to the band's organizers' attention because of friendship with other members, had no professional experience prior to the Runaways, but had been sharpening her singing ability in school shows and singing along with hit records on the radio at home. She insisted she had first started singing when she was two. ''I've always loved music and singing. I've always wanted to be onstage. Being in front of an audience is exciting and fulfilling.''

Fowley, who thought of the band as a vehicle for some of his own compositions, at first had the group concentrate on those numbers along with covers of songs originally performed by successful rock bands of the past. Before long, however, it became apparent that songs crafted by Kari Krome and other band members, Joan Jett in particular, were as good or better, than anything prescribed by Fowley and his associates. Among the numbers that inspired audience enthusiasm in the band's early concerts were ''Cherry Bomb'' (Currie's frequent opening number) and Jett's guitar and vocal work on ''Me and You,'' ''Blackmail,'' and ''California Paradise.''

Word about the group's style soon flashed around the record industry. After attending a rehearsal, Mercury Records executive Denny Rosencrantz signed the group on the spot. The band's debut album, *The Runaways,* produced by Fowley, came out in May 1976. The same album, with a different jacket design, was re-issued by Mercury the following year. With an album to its credit and its reputation enhanced by steady performances in the L.A. area and other parts of the country, the band became a favorite with a sizable, but still minor part of the pop audience during 1976–77. Included in those concerts were a series in Japan that helped make the single ''Cherry Bomb'' a hit in that country.

But the band's power base remained Los Angeles. Discussing a set at the Whisky in January 1977, Robert Hilburn of the *Los Angeles Times* enthused: "On stage the Runaways play with authority and spirit—more of either than any other girl band. Currie, especially, has gained in confidence since the group's appearance last summer at the Shrine. But the other Runaways contribute to a fully creditable instrumental sound. The sound is a cross between Suzi Quatro and Chinn-Chapman produced records. But the stance is an original and personable one."

One of the band's problems remained fighting prejudice against female rock groups. As Joan Jett told Hilburn: "Sure a lot of people come to see us because we're girls. They're curious. They want to see if we can really play rock'n'roll. We show them that we can. That's the important thing. We're serious about our music." But the band proved to be ahead of its time. While it made adherents of many concert goers who had previously only been curious, it couldn't gain acceptance from the mass audience. While it did have some success with its recordings, the overall effect wasn't enough to keep the band going beyond the late 1970s.

It did have a number of additional albums to its credit before disbanding in the late 1970s. In 1977, Mercury issued *Queens of Noise* (featuring Joan Jett on lead vocals on many tracks) and the first live album, *Live in Japan*, the latter issued outside the U.S. by Mercury-U.K. Two other releases following those both came out overseas on the Cherry Red label: *And Now . . . The Runaways* (1979) and *Flaming Schoolgirls* (1980), while in America, years after their breakup, Rhino Records released their final sessions on *Little Lost Girls*. Kim Fowley tried to rekindle the band's spirit with a new group called the Runaways, which released the album *Young and Fast* on Allegiance Records in 1985, but no one from the previous Runaways was involved.

RUN–D.M.C.: *Performance (rap) group from Queens, New York. Members, all born c. 1965: Joseph Simmons, Daryll McDaniels, Jay Mizell.*

Though begun by performers from impoverished ghetto areas of New York City, by the 1980s, rap music had attracted young artists from all economic levels, including middle-class–spawned stars such as Run–D.M.C. and LL Cool J. In fact, some of those performers—Run–D.M.C. in particular—became the biggest attractions in rap of the mid-1980s as rap moved beyond the black market to the larger worldwide pop audience.

The two artists who became the rap part of Run–D.M.C. were Joseph Simmons (Run) and Daryll McDaniels (D.M.C.). Both were raised in comfortable surroundings in the New York borough of Queens. Simmons, in fact, told Robert Hilburn of the *Los Angeles Times* that their upbringing gave them a desire to emphasize positive things for their fans. "Some of my [fans in big cities] haven't been around anything positive because of some of the areas they live in and their parents don't have anything positive to offer them. I come from the middle class and I'm fortunate to have good parents who did set a good example. I knew by the time I was 10 what was good and what was bad and I always try to be on the good side."

Both Simmons and McDaniels were involved in the rap movement in their teens. At 13, Simmons already was supporting rap star Kurtis Blow, appearing in concerts with the Commodores billed as the "son of Kurtis Blow." Despite that, he went on to study sociology at St. John's. All three future members of Run–D.M.C. grew up in the same neighborhood and, while Run and D.M.C. were gaining rap experience, Jason Mizell earned money as a teenager by working as a club disc jockey. Eventually the three got together to form the new act with Mizell taking the pseudonym Jam Master Jay.

In the early 1980s, they cut initial sides for Profile Records, which had become a major factor in disco-rap-dance recordings in the New York area. Their single "It's Like That (and That's the Way It Is)" became a top 10 hit on black music charts in 1982, followed by six more chart singles. All those numbers were included on the group's debut LP, *Run-D.M.C.* (spring 1983). The LP made the charts as did the single "Rock Box," which sold 200,000 copies in mid-1984.

Meanwhile, the group added to its audience through touring and TV exposure on shows such as "Soul Train," "Graffiti Rock," and "Entertainment Tonight." During 1984, the group toured 29 U.S. cities as part of a show called the Fresh Festival showcasing such other New York rap groups as Kurtis Blow, Whodini, and Newcleus. The show combined both rap and dance sets with the rappers and disc jockeys performing on one stage while breakdance groups, such as the Magnificent Force, did their thing in another part of the auditorium.

In early 1985, Profile issued the group's next LP, *King of Rock*. The hit album reinforced the growing belief that Run–D.M.C. was indeed becoming the leading exponent of rap. The group added to that sentiment with a sparkling new (and soon gold) album, *Raising Hell* (Profile, May 1986). Among the tracks was a hard-rock/rap collaboration, a reissue of the rock number "Walk This Way" performed by Run–D.M.C. members with Steven Tyler and Joe Perry of the Aerosmith rock band. (*See Aerosmith.*) The album shipped gold (a very unusual happening for independent labels) and eventually went platinum.

Everything looked rosy for the group as it conducted its summer 1986 tour before huge crowds across the U.S. But an August 17, 1986, show at the Long Beach Arena in California was disrupted by a vicious dislay of gang violence that caused considerable adverse publicity and cancellation of several dates, including a planned appearance at the Los Angeles-sponsored Street Festival in September.

However, fans across the country as well as Run–D.M.C. members argued forcefully that the gang situation was an aberration caused by local conditions. Certainly it didn't reflect the outlook expressed in Run–D.M.C. lyrics. Despite the LP title *Raising Hell*, the tracks' narratives urged listeners to avoid drugs and violence and emphasized the importance of education. Simmons told Hilburn: "I help people so much with my messages. Kids come up to me all the time and tell me things like 'I used to not go to school, but I do now because I know that's what you want me to do.' That makes me so happy."

Mizell added: "Even if the guys who are deeply into [gangs] don't want to listen to our message, the kids who were looking up to them will get the message because they look up to us more and they won't follow in their [gang] footsteps."

Later concerts in 1986 and 1987 went by without incident and it seemed as if the band could put the Long Beach incident behind it and concentrate on future creative plans.

Besides concert work in 1986, the group began work on an action-adventure movie starring its members called *Tougher Than Leather*. The plan was to release the film in conjunction with a new album, but a series of lawsuits between Run and Profile Records threw a monkey wrench into the schedule. Though the film was finished in 1987, it was put on hold pending settlement of the legal battles.

Opening gun in the court maneuvers was filing of a $6.8 million lawsuit against Profile and its publishing company, Protoons, by Run's management firm, Rush Productions, charging nonpayment of royalties and publishing incomes. Profile entered a $2 million countersuit in August against Rush (owned by Joseph Simmons's brother Russell), accusing Russell of trying to move the group to a different label and also failing to meet contract requirements for delivery of a new album by October 1, 1986. While this went on, Run–D.M.C. was on a worldwide tour with another rap group, the Beastie Boys (who threatened Run's position in the rap world with the four-million-selling 1987 LP *Licensed to Ill*).

In late 1987 and early 1988, the group polished tracks for a new album, including one called "Papa Crazy," that reportedly was one of its best efforts

yet. However, only a few fortunate reviewers had been able to hear the tape by early 1988 since the legal tangles stood in the way of any new release. The album *Tougher Than Leather* was finally released in the spring of 1988, and group members expressed optimism that the movie would be out before the end of the year.

RUNDGREN, TODD: *Singer, guitarist, band leader (RUNT, UTOPIA), songwriter, record producer. Born Philadelphia, Pennsylvania, June 22, 1948.*

A multifaceted artist, Todd Rundgren had great impact on the popular music field before he was 21 and promised to have an even greater effect as a performer, writer, and producer in later years.

Born and raised in Philadelphia, Rundgren learned to play guitar by his early teens. His first professional experience in the late 1960s was with a little-noticed Philadelphia-area band, Woody's Truckstop. By the end of the decade, he had become the central figure in the Nazz, which gained a substantial following among East Coast teens partly as a result of a promotion campaign backed by the band's record label, SGC. One result was a hit single, "Hello, It's Me," that made the national charts during late 1969 and early 1970.

In 1970, Rundgren decided the Nazz was too limiting for his tastes. He left and got an agreement to do an album for the Warner Brothers/Reprise organization. His first effort was a virtuoso one in which he not only wrote original material, but also handled seven backup tracks (six different guitars plus drums), did all the singing, and also served as his own sound engineer. The resulting LP, *Runt*, won the attention of reviewers around the U.S. It wasn't a million-seller, but it did reach well over 100,000 copies sold and established Rundgren as an important new face on the music scene.

Within the industry, Rundgren's technical skill in preparing *Runt* won a series of requests for him to help engineer and produce sessions of other artists. One of his first clients was the top-rated Capitol group, the Band. Jesse Winchester, American Dream, Paul Butterfield, and Halfnelson (later known as Sparks) on the Ampex and Bearsville labels also used his production talents.

Rundgren managed to fit this work into his schedule while still exercising his skills as a writer and performer with his backup band, Runt. In early 1971, he made *Billboard*'s top 20 with the single "We Got to Get You a Woman." Later in 1971, he placed his second LP, *Ballad*, on the charts. Another chart single on Ampex during this period was "A Long Way to Go." When Ampex went out of the record business, its associate, Albert Grossman, took artists Jesse Winchester and Rundgren and set up Bearsville Records (distributed by Warner Brothers), for whom Todd turned out the late 1971 hit single "Be Nice to Me."

His third album, *Something/Anything?* (1972), was by far his most successful album, going gold. Continuing his production work, he supervised preparation of the 1972 Badfinger hit album *Straight Up*. He had two charted singles during that year: "Couldn't I Just Tell You" and "I Saw the Light." In 1973, he scored a major hit with a remake of the Nazz's "Hello, It's Me" and his Bearsville LP *A Wizard, a True Star* made the charts for a time. Its fine tracks included "I Don't Know What to Feel," "International Feel," and "Just One Victory."

Bearsville releases of 1974 included *Todd* and *Todd Rundgren's Utopia*. The last named unveiled a new band approach that Rundgren called a "band–life-style concept." In its original form, Utopia had three keyboards players, but by the end of the 1970s, all those tasks were consolidated with one musician, Roger Powell. The other band members as of 1979 were Kasim Sulton on bass guitar and John Willie Wilcox on drums. With his new band, Todd continued to tour steadily into the early 1980s and put out Bearsville releases *Initiation* and *Another Live* (1975), *Faithful* (1976), and *Oops! Wrong Planet* (1977), *Hermit of Mink Hollow* and the two-disc live *Back to the Bars* (1978), *Adventures in Utopia* (1979), and *The Ever Popular Tortured Artist Effect* (1984). Rundgren also sometimes toured as a solo artist without Utopia and continued to experiment with new formats, including special video concepts. He added to his producing credits by work with such artists as Hall & Oates, Patti Smith, the New York Dolls, Rick Derringer, Grand Funk Railroad, and the Tubes, while also serving as a session musician and/or engineer on recordings by Bette Midler, Foghat, and Johnny Winter.

In the 1980s, Rundgren continued all of his various pursuits, concentrating as a performer in mid-decade more as a soloist than a band leader. In a typical solo show, he accompanied himself on guitar or piano or made use of taped instrumental and backup vocals. Describing one such concert in Los Angeles, Kristine McKenna wrote in the *Los Angeles Times*: "Rundgren presented a one-man variety show that included excerpts from his video biography, a rambling comedy monologue, a medley of '60s tunes, a piano instrumental, an audience participation segment, and a selection of his greatest hits. It was an intimate, fairly modest show in contrast with the lavish stagings Rundgren has toyed with in the past, and the most striking thing about it was what a truly fine vocalist Rundgren is. His sing-ing is usually overshadowed by his reputation as an eccentric pop genius."

After Bearsville's founder Albert Grossman died in 1986, Rhino Records licensed their entire Rundgren and Utopia catalogue for reissue.

RUSH: *Vocal and instrumental group from Toronto, Canada. Members, all born Canada: Geddy Lee, born July 29, 1953; Alex Lifeson, born August 27, 1953; Neil Peart, born September 12, 1952.*

The no-nonsense power-rock Rush from its earliest days disdained the trappings adopted by many high-decibel supergroups. Yes, the band might come on stage behind a dry-ice smoke screen and there naturally was a dazzling light show in large venues, but essentially Rush simply belted out its mostly original music. There were no motorcycles, bull whips, or unusual attire in evidence, just three solid performers whose up-tempo renditions typically kept crowds in a happy uproar, dancing in place or shouting approval of the thoughts expressed in drummer Neil Peart's incisive lyrics.

Unlike many rock musicians, Rush members did not pursue wild offstage activities that would get their names in gossip columns. In fact, the threesome guarded their private lives rather closely, shied away from most interviews, and even avoided publicity pictures if they could. Geddy Lee told Dennis Hunt of the *Los Angeles Times* (February 2, 1986): "We haven't really tried to build any kind of image. We're not these wild, exciting people anyway. We don't do the kinds of things people want to read about. We're not going to generate great gossip. We're more concerned about invasions of our privacy. Privacy is too valuable for us to sacrifice it to build a public image."

Fortunately for Rush, its public was willing to take it on its own terms. Lee noted: "We've done well without [a special image]. People come to see our shows. They buy our records. I'm glad we don't have to count on a gaudy public image. We'd be in bad shape." He certainly wasn't exaggerating. For over a decade, as of 1988, Rush usually could fill the largest arenas all over the industrialized, noncommunist world. Most of its albums had gone gold, platinum, or better, resulting in total sales exceeding 20 million at the time.

The three musicians that became collectively known as Rush formed that lineup in the fall of 1974. Lee was on lead vocals, keyboards, and bass guitar, Lifeson on guitar, and Peart on drums. However, for a half-dozen previous years, Lee and Lifeson had played the Ontario bar and school-dance circuit with someone else handling drums. Peart paid his dues in similar fashion, starting with high school groups and progressing to part-time professional gigs while he worked at various day jobs to keep body and soul together.

He told a reporter in 1981 that it took perseverance and willingness to play night after night in all types of clubs, arenas, and school gyms to finally break through. "It was like banging your head against the wall until someone tells you to shut up. One time I was selling farm equipment during the days and playing at night."

Actually, Peart did not join the band until after it recorded its first album. Lee, Lifeson, the pre-Peart drummer, and their advisors decided in 1973 that the best way out of the club/bar one-nighter grind was to record their own album and use that to try to gain more industry attention. The band laid down the initial tracks in one eight-hour period; overdubbing and remixing took another few months. The album was rejected by established record companies, so the band and its managers set up their own label, Moon Records, and issued it themselves in early 1974.

Review copies placed with some U.S. stations in the Midwest managed to catch the attention of a few disc jockeys. When listeners responded positively to Rush's material, it provided an opening for a contract with the important U.S. booking agency American Talent International, which also sent a copy of the album to Mercury Records. Mercury signed the group and in August 1974 issued the LP, *Rush*. The door to success was ajar.

As the group prepared for its first tour of the U.S., problems arose that led to the departure of the band's drummer. Six days before the four-month tour started, Neil Peart came aboard. Peart then took part in recording sessions for the second LP, *Fly by Night* (Mercury, January 1975). The album quickly became a hit in Canada. Its momentum in the U.S. was helped by another lengthy four-month tour in which Rush opened for Aerosmith and Kiss. *Fly by Night* easily passed gold-record levels in Canada and was joined on Canadian gold record lists in the fall by the album *Caress of Steel* (Mercury, July 1975). At year-end, in the Juno Awards (Canada's equivalent of the Grammies), Rush was voted Most Promising New Group.

Some of the band's brash, driving concert persona was captured in the 1976 *All the World's a Stage*. The band was experimenting with its instrumental interaction and its songwriting efforts to try to advance creatively, as initially evidenced by the 1976 concept album *2112*. One side was a science-fiction suite of songs describing life on another planet where native beings' existence was controlled by high technology devices. It reflected a theme that recurred in many Rush songs, the importance of individual free-

dom. Both 1976 albums eventually earned RIAA platinum-record awards.

A steady progression of new albums into the early 1980s all sold at least a million copies worldwide: *Farewell to Kings* (1977), *Hemisphere* (1978), *Permanent Waves* (1980), and *Moving Pictures* and *Exit . . . Stage Left* (1981). The group had its first top singles hit in 1980 when "Spirit of the Radio" from *Permanent Waves* made upper levels of charts in the U.S., Canada, and elsewhere. Another charted single from that album was "Jacob's Ladder."

While the band's intensive touring demonstrated year after year that it had become a favorite of a large segment of the rock audience, its reputation among rock critics was decidedly mixed. As Peart told Mike Glynn of the *Los Angeles Times* (May 24, 1981): "It's a healthy polarity. We're the type of band people either love or hate and we can live with that."

Among those who loved them were voters in the English music paper *Melody Maker*'s 1980 annual poll, who voted the band into the top 10 in an imposing number of categories: Lifeson, number six for Best Guitarist; Peart, number three for Best Drummer; Geddy Lee, number three for Best Bass Player; Rush, number five for Band of the Year, number four for Best Live Act, number five for Best Single ("Spirit of Radio"), and number four for Best Album (*Permanent Waves*); number five for all three members for Best Composers; and number eight for Best Producers for the band and Terry Brown (who produced or co-produced the first ten Rush LPs).

Band members didn't disagree with conclusions by most critics that *Signals* (1982) represented a step backward in content (even though it sold over 1.4 million copies).

Indeed, there had been problems as Lee told Dennis Hunt. "Neil wasn't happy then but neither [were] the rest of us. We were burned out on tour and not playing too well and not caring about it—that's the worst. You just go on stage and do another show, but you're not all there. It's too much an automatic pilot."

The group's reassessment included the decision to change producers. Peter Henderson was brought in to coordinate the next album, *Grace under Pressure* (1984). Though platinum, it was still below Rush's personal standards. Lee commented: "We thought we had good songs, but we didn't have enough. We didn't achieve what we started out to. What happened is that we got caught up in making it and weren't looking at it objectively enough. A few songs could have been taken farther. The whole thing was convoluted and confused. It could have been a whole lot better."

Again, the band evaluated the situation. Henderson was replaced by Peter Collins and a conscious effort was made by all parties to polish and repolish all the material. The result was *Power Windows* (Mercury, late 1985). The various songs and their interpretations indicated that the band was, indeed, back on course. The concert tour in support of the platinum album also reflected a fresher approach than in the 1982–84 period. All of that suggested that Rush, if it so desired, could remain a rock favorite for many years more.

RUSSELL, LEON: *Singer, band leader, pianist, trumpeter, guitarist, songwriter. Born Lawton, Oklahoma, April 2, 1942.*

It surprised some people when Leon Russell, rock superstar, began turning out country-oriented albums in the 1970s, starting with *Hank Wilson's Back, Vol. 1* in late 1973. It shouldn't have, considering Leon's exposure to folk and country material in his Oklahoma childhood and his early association with pioneers of the rockabilly era.

Still, his first training wasn't in any pop format, but in classical music. His musical studies began when he was three in his hometown of Lawton where his father worked as a clerk for the Texas Company. Both his parents played the piano and started him on the instrument as soon as he seemed old enough to learn. He continued those studies until he entered high school at 13, then quit. "I didn't really have the hands for classical stuff, and my teachers discouraged me from making up my own music."

He turned to the trumpet with a goal of becoming a pop musician. At 14, he formed a band and lied about his age to get a job in a Texas nightclub. He worked many concerts and dances in Oklahoma during 1956–57, including sessions with Jerry Lee Lewis as well as with Ronnie Hawkins and the Hawks. (One of Ronnie's later Hawks aggregations went on to fame as the Band.) Looking for broader horizons, in 1958, teenaged Leon moved to Los Angeles, where "I'd borrow a friend's ID to get a job, then I'd return the card and work until I was stopped by the police for being underage and out after curfew."

By the early '60s, his talents on piano, trumpet, and other instruments he'd learned to play along the way earned him a glowing reputation in the music industry. He became one of the most sought after session musicians in Los Angeles. One of the first producers to seek him out was Phil Spector, who employed Leon's talents on the 1963 LP *Ronnie and the Ronettes* and on tracks by Bob B. Soxx and the Blue Jeans. During the mid-1960s, he was particularly active with Gary Lewis and the Playboys, serving as sideman, arranger, and sometimes songwriter on 14 of Gary's albums. Among his other credits of

those years were working on Herb Alpert's 1965 success, *Whipped Cream and Other Delights,* handling piano on the Byrds' classic 1965 single "Mr. Tambourine Man," and doing session work for Frank Sinatra, Ike and Tina Turner, the Righteous Brothers, Paul Revere and the Raiders, and others.

One of his early solo efforts was the 1965 single "Everybody's Talking 'Bout the Young," on Dot Records. It didn't make much headway. Another single, released in 1966 by A&M Records, didn't please many people, nor has it pleased Leon since, who would just as soon forget about it. In 1967, Russell dropped much of his outside work to concentrate on building his own studio, though he still did some touring and session work with friends, including Delaney & Bonnie (Delaney, like Russell, being a former Shindog from the network TV show "Shindig").

But Leon was eager to strike out on his own in the late 1960s. As one step toward that end, he teamed up with another young musician, Marc Benno. Calling themselves Asylum Choir, they made some tapes that earned them a contract from Smash Records in 1968, which led to release of their debut LP, *Asylum Choir,* in 1969. The LP got good reviews, but didn't win much public attention. Meanwhile, through Delaney & Bonnie, Leon had become acquainted with blues-rock singer Joe Cocker and his manager Denny Cordell. Cordell asked Russell to work on Cocker's second LP and, impressed with Russell's skills, took him back to England to work up material for a solo LP. The collaboration resulted in the two's formation of a new label, Shelter Records, to handle Russell's product. The first album—originally titled *Can A Blue Man Sing the Whites* and later changed to *Leon Russell*—came out in early 1970 and remained on the hit lists a respectable number of months. As the year went by, Russell bolstered his growing reputation by touring with Joe Cocker in the famous "Mad Dogs and Englishmen" series.

Russell's activities continued at a frantic pace in 1970–71 with session work on LPs by the Rolling Stones, Glen Campbell, Rita Coolidge (for whom he wrote "Delta Lady"), Delaney & Bonnie, and Dave Mason. He also took part in the landmark Concert for Bangladesh in New York's Madison Square Garden. All of that contributed to the gold sales level of his next release on Shelter, *Leon Russell and the Shelter People* (1971).

Similar fortune awaited successive releases such as *Carney* (which spawned his major hit "Tight Rope") in 1972 and the 1973 three-record concert set *Leon Live.*

By the end of 1973, when *Hank Wilson's Back* came out, Leon was one of the brightest stars in pop music. This LP was a change of pace, including his treatment of such folk and country standards as "Battle of New Orleans," "Am I That Easy to Forget," and "She Thinks I Still Care." It was a fine offering, but it puzzled some reviewers and fans and gained only a fair response from record buyers. But one cut," "Rollin' in My Sweet Baby's Arms," rose high on country lists, indicating Leon could find a following in the genre.

In 1974, Leon moved in still another direction musically with the LP *Stop All That Jazz*, which met with only lukewarm response. The same year, he backed a singer named Mary McCreary (formerly of Sly and the Family Stone) on her LP *Jezebel* on Shelter. It was a harbinger of things to come—two years later she became Mrs. Leon Russell. In 1975, Leon proved he still had drawing power with the pop audience by turning out the gold LP *Will o' the Wisp*. At the time, Leon's relationship with Shelter Records was tenuous and he soon left to form a new company, Paradise Records, with distribution through Warner Brothers Records.

His first release on the new label, appropriately, was *Wedding Album*, a duet with Mary Russell in celebration of their marriage. In 1977, the duo followed up with *Make Love to the Music* and, in 1979, Leon backed Mary on her solo collection *Heart of Fire*. From 1975 through 1977, Leon did some session work in addition to his work with Mary, but didn't complete any solo releases. He finally broke that silence with *Americana* (Paradise, 1978), one of the weakest LPs he'd ever done.

Increasingly from the mid-1970s on, Leon had been including country-oriented material in his recordings. In 1979, he stressed that side of his musical interests more than ever before and it seemed to act as a catalyst in restoring his standing in pop music in general. In late 1978 and early 1979, he teamed up with a long-time friend, country giant Willie Nelson, for a series of concerts that since have become almost legendary with music buffs. In 1979, *One for the Road,* a two-record set taken from those appearances, was issued on Columbia. Presenting superb versions of all manner of songs from pop standards of the '40s and '50s to classic country and folk tunes, the album was named Best Album of the Year by the Country Music Association. During the same period, a new collection of Leon's, *Life and Love,* came out on Paradise. As consistently strong in music and performance as *Americana* had been weak, the album presented both sides of Leon—fine country and country-rock tracks plus blues-rockers that harked back to his work of the early '70s. By the end of 1979, Leon could point to a banner year that included a gold-record award for *One for the Road* and the rise of the single "Heartbreak Hotel" to number one on country charts. (*See Alpert, Herb;*

Byrds, The; Cocker, Joe; Coolidge, Rita; Hawkins, Ronnie; Lewis, Gary; Mason, Dave; Revere, Paul, and the Raiders; Ronettes, The; Rossington Collins Band, The; Sinatra, Frank; Sly and the Family Stone; Soxx, Bob B., and the Blue Jeans; Spector, Phil; Turner, Ike and Tina.)

SADE: *Singer, songwriter, band leader (SADE). Born Nigeria, c. 1960.*

The elegant, vocally sophisticated jazz-pop singer-songwriter Sade (pronounced *sar-DAY*) challenged more raucous performers Madonna and Cyndi Lauper for best-new-female-performer accolades of the mid-1980s. In her own quiet way, she accrued an audience of rapt admirers that probably equaled her contemporaries' followings in numbers if not in applause volume at concerts.

It was a satisfying odyssey for an artist whose roots were in the African nation of Nigeria. Daughter of an African father and an English mother, she was born Helen Folasade Adu in a village 50 miles from the Nigerian capital of Lagos. (The name Sade is a diminutive of her middle name.) Her life might have developed quite differently had her parents not separated when she was four. Her mother returned to England, where Sade grew up in London's North End.

In her teens, Sade demonstrated a fine singing voice that inspired her to think about finding work as a performer. She had balanced school and a series of part-time jobs (ranging from waitress to bicycle messenger) with efforts to find a niche in the music field. Her idols at the time, drawn from the jazz and soul fields, included Billie Holiday, Marvin Gaye, Al Green, and Nina Simone.

For a while, it seemed as though she might concentrate instead on fashion design—her major at St. Martin's College in London—and she won attention in the field. At the start of the 1980s, she created her own line of menswear that was exhibited in New York City in conjunction with the first U.S. appearance of the Spandau Ballet rock group. (*See Spandau Ballet.*)

However, the opportunity to front the jazz-funk group Pride settled the matter. As it happened, though some people in London thought highly of the group, it made little progress toward gaining a recording contract and broke up after a few years. The exposure, however, had established Sade among music-industry insiders as a rising star, which smoothed the way to organization of her own band in early 1984. This time the results were more positive. The new group was signed by CBS Records worldwide, which issued her debut album, *Diamond Life,* on the Epic label in the U.K. later in the year. Featuring many originals co-written by Sade, the album was in the top 10 late in the year.

In January 1985, *Diamond Life* was released in the U.S. by CBS on its Portrait label. By mid-May, it had passed platinum-record levels representing over a million copies sold. Two top 10 singles were culled from it, "Smooth Operator" and "Hang on to Your Love," which moved into the top position on both the dance and black singles charts.

Sade and her backing band (whose primary members were guitarist/saxophonist Stuart Matthewman, keyboards player Andrew Hale, and bass guitarist Paul Denman) followed their debut album with the equally attractive, if not startlingly different, platinum album *Promise* (Portrait, November 1985). Again, Sade co-wrote all the songs and also co-produced one track, "Maureen," with overall record producer Robin Millar. The first single (and also initial video) from the album, "Sweetest Taboo," stayed on U.S. pop charts from late 1985 into early 1986.

Her live performance drew high praise from many influential critics. Stephen Holden of *The New York Times* wrote: "Stunningly photogenic, Sade possesses a dusky, haunting pop-jazz alto whose blasé sensuality perfectly matches her sleek appearance."

Not everyone was enthralled, though. Richard Cromelin of the *Los Angeles Times* (December 21, 1985) acknowledged that "With its overtones of glamour and its sultry samba beat, this music has a certain appeal, and Adu writes some interestingly downbeat and bittersweet lyrics. . . . [But] Versatility is not their forte, and when they tried to fire up their lukewarm pop they just tended to get showy. Adu isn't really a jazz singer, and she didn't do enough improvising and stretching to make things exciting."

The general consensus, though, was in Sade's favor as a potential major star of the future. She was named New Artist of the Year by the British Phonographic Institute and was nominated for a U.S. Grammy in the Best New Artist category. When the winners were announced on the worldwide telecast on February 25, 1986, Sade was the one presented with the New Artist trophy.

Sade was slow in releasing her follow-up album, *Stronger Than Pride,* which came out in May 1988, more than two years after her previous LP.

SAM AND DAVE: *Vocal duo, band leaders. Samuel David Moore, born Miami, Florida; Dave Prater, born Oscilla, Georgia, c. 1938; died near Sycamore, Georgia, April 9, 1988.*

Rapid movement, let-it-all-hang-out emotion, pulsating rhythms—all of these are hallmarks of soul music. The team of Sam and Dave had these capabilities and then some, making even such ener-

getic performers as Otis Redding and Wilson Pickett seem almost tame by comparison.

As anyone who observed the Sam and Dave show in action knew, these two artists well deserved their nickname "double dynamite." A *Time* reporter wrote in October 1968: "Of all the R&B cats, nobody steams up the place like Sam and Dave. . . . Weaving and dancing [while singing], they gyrate through enough acrobatics to wear out more than 100 costumes a year."

Sam and Dave enjoyed their moments in the spotlight, because it had taken well over a decade to get there. They grew up in different parts of the South, but their early years were much the same. Both started singing in church choirs in their early years and were touring with gospel groups in their teens. At the start of the '60s, both had decided there was more future in pop music than gospel and had gone out as soloists, playing the small theaters and rundown clubs of the R&B ghetto circuit.

The two met in the early '60s and decided to form a duo. For several years, they spent much of their performing time in clubs around their home base, Miami, Florida. By 1965, they had added a backup group that included the brass section common to R&B acts. Their following in Miami came to the attention of record executives and Stax Records soon signed them. In 1965, their first big hit single, "You Don't Know Like I Know," earned them nominations as most promising male vocal duo of the year from several music-industry publications.

In 1966, they proved they had arrived with a series of hits: "Said I Wasn't Going to Tell Nobody," "You Got Me Hummin'," "When Something Is Wrong with My Baby," and one of the major R&B successes of the year, "Hold On, I'm Coming" (the title song for the number one ranked (R&B) 1966 LP). Record production for Sam and Dave was placed in the capable hands of such Stax staff members as Isaac Hayes, who wrote many of their hits.

The year 1967 brought their best-selling Stax single and LP to that point, both titled "Soul Man." Both exceeded gold records sales and gained number one positions on both U.S. and European charts during the year. (The single reached number one on some industry charts, though it peaked at number 2 in *Billboard).* The duo added to their laurels in 1968 with the pop top 10 single "I Thank You." Starting in 1969, they were on Atlantic Records, which issued the retrospective album *The Best of Sam and Dave* that year.

In the early 1970s, except for the 1970–71 single "Don't Pull Your Love," the duo's impact on pop and soul music all but disappeared. A prime reason, as Sam Moore related in the early 1980s, was drugs. Moore told reporters he became so dependent on drugs that nothing else mattered in the world. During one phase of his dependency, he spent most of his time lying in a "shooting-gallery" establishment, hardly knowing whether it was day or night or anything else about the outside world. From time to time, he managed to shake off his habit long enough to return to action with Dave. An example was the 1981 series of shows presented mostly in third-rate clubs across the U.S. The duo seemed able to recapture some of the spirit of their '60s hits but, as Sam told a reporter a few years later, it was all a blur. "I was high," he admitted.

Finally, shortly after that, Sam managed to find the inner strength to defeat his addiction and by the mid-1980s could tell interviewers he was completely clean. Meanwhile, Dave had formed a new team that also called itself Sam and Dave, but the other half of the duo was not Sam Moore, but Sam Daniels. During 1985, Sam Moore brought suit against Atlantic Records for releasing an album and single by the new team, both titled "The Sam and Dave Medley" (on the Stars on 45 label). The group also toured, calling itself the All New Sam & Dave Revue.

In his lawsuit, Moore maintained that neither Atlantic nor his old partner had a legal right to substitute someone else for him under the Sam and Dave descriptor. His manager, Joyce McRae, told Patrick Goldstein of the *Los Angeles Times:* "The whole situation is outrageous. Atlantic's attitude has been 'catch us if you can.' They've practically challenged us to continue taking them to court, figuring it would just run up another big legal bill for us. They're just flaunting their power as a major record company—they'd never pull this stuff if we were a powerful record company, instead of just one solitary black artist."

Meanwhile, Moore set about charting a new career for himself as a solo artist in the mid-1980s. In a series of concerts in clubs and theaters around the U.S., he could still call on his remarkable vocal powers to fine effect, though the prime question remained whether he could find songs to match his singing talents.

During those years, a number of reissues of earlier Sam and Dave material remained in print. These LPs included *Sweet and Funky Gold* (Gusto Records, 1978), a German import of *Sam & Dave* (Roulette), and 1980 Japanese reissues of such Atlantic albums as *Double Dynamite, Soul Man,* and *Hold On I'm Comin.'*

Yet problems continued to plague Dave. On March 5, 1988, in his home base of Paterson, New Jersey, he was fined and sentenced to three years of probation for selling crack to an undercover policewoman the previous summer. A month later, en route to visit his mother in Georgia, he ran his car off the highway, hit a tree, and died. (*See Hayes, Isaac.*)

In May 1988, Sam teamed with Dan Aykroyd to perform some of the Sam and Dave hits, including "Soul Man," at the fortieth anniversary of Atlantic Records concert at New York's Madison Square Garden.

SAM THE SHAM AND THE PHARAOHS:

Vocal and instrumental group, led by Domingo Samudio, born Dallas, Texas, c. 1937. Group members (1965): David Martin, Ray Stinnet, Jerry Patterson, Butch Gibson.

In the music field, a novelty act can often achieve meteoric success but, unless it demonstrates considerable latitude in its musical skills, this is usually short-lived. Thus, Sam the Sham and the Pharaohs sold millions of records of its lively, nonsense songs during the mid-1960s, but was out of existence by the end of the decade.

The band's founder, Sam (born Domingo Samudio), showed vocal talent in his high school years in Dallas, but a career in music seemed remote to him at the time. He enlisted in the navy for four years during the late '50s and early '60s. After his discharge, he returned to Texas and worked in the construction field for a while until he had enough money to enroll in Arlington State College. While in college, he spent much of his spare time learning to play the organ and singing with local pop groups.

He left school to join a friend's band in Louisiana. The group later became a favorite among Memphis nightclub attendees, but disbanded when Sam's friend left in 1963.

Sam decided to form a new group with David Martin, bass guitarist with the old band. Initially, it was a quartet, with lead guitarist Ray Stinnet and drummer Jerry Patterson rounding out the group. In 1965, saxophone player Butch Gibson joined the band.

The group started playing small clubs in border-state cities. Domingo developed the new group name by taking part of his last name and combining it with a word from the rhythm & blues jargon, *sham.* Shamming refers to the gyrations of a vocalist—shuffling his feet, twisting his hips, and so on—while singing. The band made some demonstration records of their upbeat material, much of it written by Sam, and gained a contract from the small Penn Record firm. The group's first release on Penn, "Haunted House" (May 1964), gained some airplay and follow-up singles helped bring the group to the attention of executives of larger record firms.

In 1965, an arrangement for distribution was completed with MGM Records. Sam's composition "Wooly Bully," reputedly referring to a pet cat, was released that spring. It made the group national celebrities, gaining the number two spot nationally in June. Classic party rock, it scored combined sales in the U.S. and Europe of over 3 million copies. The group gained engagements in major cities all over the world and its garish, pseudo-Arab costumes became familiar sights to TV viewers from the band's appearances on the "Ed Sullivan Show" and other network programs.

The band maintained its popularity through 1966, placing a series of recordings on the hit charts, including the 1966 million-seller, "Li'l Red Riding Hood." It also gained the charts with several of its MGM albums, which included *Sam the Sham and the Pharaohs* and *Sam the Sham* (1965), *On Tour* (1966), and *Li'l Red Riding Hood.* The band continued to hold a sizable audience in 1967, though its popularity was starting to wane. MGM issued several more LPs, including *The Best of Sam the Sham and the Pharaohs* and *The Sam the Sham Revue* (1967), before the group split up. In the 1980s, Rhino Records' *Pharaotization: The Best of Sam the Sham & the Pharaohs* put some of their songs back in circulation.

In the early 1970s, Samudio worked as a solo performer and also moved into record production. In 1970, Atlantic Records released his solo album, *Sam, Hard and Heavy.* Samudio won a Grammy Award from the National Academy of Recording Arts and Sciences for his liner notes for the LP.

Sam left the music field to work in the offshore oil fields. In the late 1980s, he was preaching on the streets of Memphis.

SANTANA: *Vocal and instrumental group. Original members, then called Santana Blues Band (1966): Carlos Santana, born Autlan, Jalisco, Mexico, July 20, 1947; David Brown, born Houston, Texas, February 15, 1947; Gregg Rolie. By late '60s, other members were Jose Areas, born Leon, Nicaragua, June 25, 1946; Michael Shrieve; Michael Carabello. Members (1973): Brown; Santana; Shrieve; Areas; Richard Kermode; Tom Coster, born Detroit, Michigan, August 21, 1941; Armando Peraza, born Havana, Cuba, June 20, 1924; Doug Rodriguez; Doug Rauch. Neal Schon, born San Mateo, California, 1954, joined in 1971, left by 1973. Roster (1974): Santana; Brown; Areas; Coster; Peraza; Jules Broussard, born Marksville, Louisiana, March 27, 1937; Leon "Ndugu" Chancler, born Shreveport, Louisiana, July 1, 1932; Leon Patillo, born San Francisco, California, January 1, 1947. Personnel (1977): Santana, Coster, Areas (absent from group 1976), Pablo Tellez, Raul Rekow, Graham Lear.*

Some of the most original rock sounds produced in the late 1960s and early '70s were by Santana, a group that became famous before it even had a single recording. Its fusion of Latin American, African, and basic blues rhythms had the sprawling multitude at the famous 1969 Woodstock Festival screaming for more; Santana's set became one of the most gripping parts of the documentary film *Woodstock.*

The group had been playing together for three years, mostly in the San Francisco area, by the time it appeared at Woodstock. It evolved from bull sessions and occasional jamming between guitarist Carlos Santana, bass guitarist David Brown, and pianist-organist Gregg Rolie. They corralled two more musicians and gave themselves the name Santana Blues Band. (At first, Santana never considered himself actual leader, regarding the group as a team effort. His name was chosen because the musicians union required that each group have a designated leader.)

The group began playing small rock clubs in San Francisco's Mission District, center of the city's Spanish-speaking population. Their torrid instrumentals, offset now and then by mostly low-keyed group vocals, caught the fancy of the district's young people. Word of the band's abilities began to seep out to Haight-Ashbury and other rock centers of the San Francisco Bay Area during '67 and '68. Helping to spread the word about Santana's accomplishments was their manager, Stan Marcus, a local barber.

As Michael Carrabello, drummer, conga player, tambourine player, and vocalist, told a *Time* reporter (September 21, 1970): "Stan sold his clothes for us. He went out and cut hair while we all stayed home and played music. He really pushed us into it." (Carabello did not join the group as a regular until early 1969.)

At the start of 1969, the group reorganized around a nucleus of Santana, Rolie, and Brown, adding Carabello, Jose Chepito Areas (congas, percussion, vocals, and timbales), and drummer Michael Shrieve—the combination that stopped the show at Woodstock that summer.

Until that time, Santana had still not signed a record contract, though a number of companies offered them one. Soon after Woodstock, Santana finally signed with Columbia. Their first album, *Santana* (November 1969), climbed to number one on some industry trade press charts and went platinum. The group's first single, "Jingo," a top 40 hit, was popular on FM underground radio and on juke boxes in Spanish Harlem.

Critical reception was good across the board for their next albums: *Abraxas* (November 1970, platinum) and *Santana Three* (January 1972, gold). The group placed several singles in the top 20 national charts during 1970–71 as well: "Black Magic

Woman, "Evil Ways," "Everybody's Everything," and "Oye Como Va." The group was one of the top attractions on the concert circuit of the early 1970s, ranking fourth in the *Cash Box* poll for Top Vocal Group of 1971.

During 1972 and '73, the makeup of the band changed several times. Rolie and guitarist Neal Schon departed and soon formed Journey. *(See Journey.)* Carlos Santana increasingly went his own way to perform as a co-star with other major names in pop music. He also expanded his personal stylings from Latin rock to blues-rock and jazz fusion, particularly in his work with such artists as Buddy Miles and Mahavishnu John McLaughlin. His band's albums continued to do well, with both 1972 releases, *Santana (Now)* and the platinum *Caravanserai,* making top chart levels. *Welcome* (late 1973) earned a gold record. The band's only chart single during this period was "No One to Depend On" in 1972.

The band members for the *Welcome* album included Tom Coster (who joined the group in 1972) on piano and Yamaha organ; Richard Kermode on piano, mellotron, and Hammond organ; Carlos Santana on acoustic and electric guitar and percussion; Armando Peraza on congas and bongos; Doug Rodriguez on rhythm guitar; Doug Rauch on bass guitar; and Michael Shrieve on drums. Handling some of the vocals were Leon Thomas and Wendy Haas.

Carlos Santana appeared in a number of concerts with Buddy Miles in 1972 and the Columbia album *Carlos Santana and Buddy Miles Live* went platinum. During 1973, Carlos joined with Mahavishnu John McLaughlin on the gold album *Love, Devotion, Surrender.* Another collaboration led to the album *Illuminations* by Devadip Carlos Santana and Turiya Alice Coltrane during that period.

Band LPs during the mid-1970s included, in 1974, *Santana's Greatest Hits* and *Borboletta; Amigos* in 1976; and, in 1977, *Festival* and the excellent *Moonflower,* whose tracks included the hit single "She's Not Here." The 1977 roster, besides Santana, included Coster on keyboards, Pablo Tellez on bass and percussion, Raul Rekow on congas and bongos, Chepito Areas on timbales, and Graham Lear on drums. By the time the next album, *Inner Secrets,* came out in 1978, the band members changed again. Devadip Carlos Santana, Lear, and Rekow remained, with newcomers Chris Rhyne on keyboards, Pete Escovedo on timbales, David Margen on bass, and Chris Solberg on rhythm guitar. Returning to the fold again was percussionist Armando Peraza.

During the late 1970s, the various Santana groupings achieved a number of firsts. In 1976, Santana was featured on the initial BBC TV-radio simulcast,

taped at the Royal Albert Hall in London. In 1976, Japanese critics named *Amigos* Album of the Year. In 1977, CBS awarded the group its first Crystal Globe Award signifying the sale of 5 million record units in Europe alone. In 1977, the single of the Zombies' 1964 hit "She's Not There" brought the band its first top 30 *Billboard* hit in five years.

In 1979, the band placed another album, *Marathon,* on the charts. Band members by then included Santana, Lear, Rekow, Peraza, Margen, and Solberg plus new vocalist Alexander J. Ligertwood (born Glasgow, Scotland) and Alan Pasqua on keyboards.

As he had in the 1970s, Carlos worked on both solo projects and new Santana band records and concerts. The band roster, though, changed almost yearly while Santana remained as the unifying force. The group continued to turn out new albums on Columbia such as *Zebop* (1981) and *Shango* (1982).

His 1980 solo or special projects included the LPs *Havana Moon* (1983) in which he was backed on most tracks by Booker T. Jones and The Fabulous Thunderbirds and the *Silver Dreams–Golden Reality* album inspired by his long time spiritual mentor Sri Chinmoy. He also scored the 1986 film *La Bamba,* the biography of the earlier Chicano star Ritchie Valens. *(See Valens, Ritchie).*

The 1987 LP *Freedom* reunited him with Buddy Miles with backing from such veteran Santana bandsmen as Coster, Lear, Peraza, Rekow and Orestes Vilato. Other members who had been regulars at one time or another were bassist Alfonso Johnson and keyboardist Chester Thompson. For the worldwide tour in support of the LP that began in the spring, Gregg Rolie also returned to the fold. (In 1988, Columbia issued a three-disc retrospective.)

Both his band efforts and solo albums usually spent a respectable amount of time on the charts. He and his band maintained a rigorous worldwide touring schedule. If many critics had become tired of the band, throngs of fans who attended the concerts seemed to bear faithful allegiance to the group. In truth, the live performances, which included some of Santana's rather bland Latin rock styles, but mainly focused on his hard driving jazz fusion/rock offerings usually were considerably more exhilarating than some of the 1980s records.

SCAGGS, BOZ: *Singer, instrumentalist (guitar, keyboards), band leader, songwriter, record producer. Born Ohio, June 8, 1944.*

An artist who had an enormous impact on rock and pop music from the late 1960s into the early 1980s, Boz Scaggs provided a body of material encompassing elements from soul/R&B and rock to folk music that included many tracks now considered classics. While he became largely inactive as a writer and performer in the 1980s, his work influenced many pop artists of the decade.

Born William Royce Scaggs in Ohio, he spent his boyhood in Dallas, Texas, where he acquired the nickname Boxley, which evolved into Boz. In 1959, he earned a scholarship to St. Marks, a private high school in Dallas, where his path crossed that of Steve Miller. Miller, who later also went on to become a major rock star, already was interested in playing pop music and his enthusiasm made Scaggs a convert. Boz bought his first guitar and became a member of Miller's teenage band the Marksmen.

In 1962, at the University of Wisconsin at Madison, Scaggs and Miller organized a new group—often billed as the Ardells or Knightrains—to play for student affairs and area club dates.

Scaggs, however, was spending most of his time on music rather than studies and he flunked out of school in 1963. He went back to Texas, settling in Austin, where he attended night school briefly before opting for full-time performing at fraternity parties, bars, and R&B joints with a band called the Wigs. He soon became restless again and in 1964 moved to London, England, with two other musicians. Already interested in soul and R&B, he gained new perspectives on the blending of British pop music with American roots music by frequenting blues-revival clubs whose young English artists included Eric Clapton, Eric Burdon (who gained fame as lead singer of the Animals), and John Mayall's Bluesbreakers.

By the following year, Boz was on his way through Europe on what he referred to later as "the bum scene." To pay his way, he worked as an itinerant musician, playing for spare change on street corners or occasionally in small clubs. During 1965, he decided to stay put in Stockholm, Sweden, for a while. There his blues and folk stylings attracted a core of fans. His first album (for Polydor International) was released in 1965 in Sweden.

He might have gone on to become an expatriate star, but in 1967 Steve Miller summoned him to San Francisco to join a new band Steve was in the process of forming. Scaggs made his way to the Bay Area at the end of that summer and took up a position as rhythm guitarist in the first of a series of Steve Miller Bands. Boz contributed to the group as both sideman and writer. (One of his compositions was "Dime-a-Dance Romance.") During 1968, he took part in sessions for two Miller LPs on Capitol: *Children of the Future* (recorded in London) and *Sailor.* Though Scaggs went out on his own again in the fall of 1968, the experience was important, he recalled. "When I was with the Miller band, it was the first opportunity I'd had to develop my own

songs in a studio. To a great extent, Steve did his songs by himself and I did my songs by myself."

After leaving Miller, Boz continued to write new songs and also put together bands of his own to play night spots in the Bay Area. A neighbor of his was Jann Wenner, who achieved fame and fortune in the 1970s as editor and publisher of *Rolling Stone.* That contact and a 1969 trip to Georgia that brought him together with Atlanta management people Alan and Phil Walden eventually led to work on a new album at the Muscle Shoals Recording Studio in Alabama with Wenner as co-producer. For the LP, issued on Atlantic Records under the title *Boz Scaggs,* he was backed by Muscle Shoals session men. One was Duane Allman, co-founder of the Allman Brothers Band, whose slide guitar work highlighted the 12-minute cut "Loan Me a Dime." *(See Allman Brothers, The.)*

That album won some critical attention, but little else at the time. In 1970, Boz was back in San Francisco fronting his own band once more. Many of the musicians remained with him throughout the early 1970s, a period during which constant performing slowly began to build up a steady following for him in many parts of California. Among the members were horn players Mel Martin and Pat O'Hara and, in the guitars/percussion section, George Rains, David Brown, Joachim Young, and Doug Simril.

By late 1970, word of Scaggs' talents had reached major–record-company executives; the successful suitors were from Columbia, which signed him before year-end. His LP *Moments* (February 1971) provided a top 40 single, "We Were Always Sweethearts." Later in the year, he went to London to record a new group of songs which was the basis for *Boz Scaggs and Band* (November 1971). The featured singles release from that LP was "Runnin' Blue."

After starting work on new material with his band, he cut those sessions short and went back to Muscle Shoals, where he taped new blues-rock numbers backed by the Muscle Shoals studio musicians. The August 1972 album *My Time* contained two particularly notable tracks: "Dinah Flo" (the featured single) and a fast-paced rocker, "Full-Lock Slide Power."

For his next effort, Scaggs began working with veteran Motown record producer Johnny Bristol, whose major successes included Gladys Knight, Junior Walker, and the Supremes. Scaggs credited Bristol with helping him achieve the synthesis of rock and soul vocal phrasing that opened the door to international stardom. The album, *Slow Dancer,* was somewhat uneven compared to his later collections, but such tracks as "You Make It So Hard" and the title song were among his best work to date. On initial release in February 1974, *Slow Dancer* made the lower rungs of the hit charts. After Boz hit the jackpot two years later with *Silk Degrees*, it was re-released in November 1976 and became a best-seller.

Though Boz depended on studio musicians for his 1972–74 albums, he kept up the touring grind with his own group. As of 1974, its members comprised Les Dudek on lead guitar, Gene Santini on bass guitar, Joachim Young on keyboards, and Rick Schlosser on drums. His association with Dudek proved to be the accidental stimulus for Scaggs' rise to prominence in the mid-1970s.

It started when Boz agreed to produce the debut solo album of the guitar whiz from Macon, Georgia, Dudek *(Les Dudek,* Columbia, 1976). For that Boz commuted from his home in San Fancisco to a Los Angeles studio. There he became impressed with the unexplored abilities of young session musicians such as David Paich, Jeff Porcaro, and David Hungate (future founders of Toto; *see Toto).* He also met fellow producer Joe Wissert, whose work with Earth, Wind & Fire and Australian vocalist Helen Reddy gave him an interesting mixture of experience in R&B and pop styles. Scaggs decided to have Wissert produce his next Columbia album with studio musicians he'd met during the Dudek project. This combination led to the album *Silk Degrees,* which included such songs as "Lido Shuffle" and "Lowdown."

To back the LP after its release in February 1976, Columbia and Scaggs lined up a massive cross-country tour. Up to that point, Scaggs had been a favorite among fellow musicians, with many major critics and a nucleus of faithful fans valuing his searing rock/R&B/soul vocal skills and his excellent song crafting, but he remained a reasonably well kept secret from most listeners. With *Silk Degrees,* all that soon changed. The first single release, a remake of "It's Over," was a modest chart hit, but the next, "Lowdown," went gold. It first moved up R&B and disco charts and then crossed over to the pop lists. By the end of 1976, *Silk Degrees* had sold over 2 million copies; before it left the charts over two years later, the total had exceeded 5 million. In Grammy voting for 1976 awards, Boz was given five nominations including Album of the Year and Best Pop Vocal Performance. At the awards ceremony, he received the Grammy for Best R&B Song for "Lowdown."

The momentum continued to build in 1977. The single "Lido Shuffle" hit number 11 in *Billboard.* Meanwhile, many artists covered the song "We're All Alone" from *Silk Degrees,* with Rita Coolidge's version going gold. *(See Coolidge, Rita.)* Capitalizing on Scaggs' popularity, Atlantic Records reissued

Boz Scaggs during the year and reaped profitable rewards.

Scaggs found a new writing partner in '77 for the platinum LP *Down Two Then Left* (Columbia, November 1977), which Wissert produced. With his own band, Scaggs spent most of 1978 touring across the U.S. and also making his first appearances with the group in Europe, Australia, and Japan. While that went on, key backing musicians for *Silk Degrees* formed a new band, Toto, that became a worldwide favorite in the late '70s.

Now at the height of his fame, Boz backed off and, while he did a number of concerts, he did far fewer than in previous years and didn't attempt to complete a new LP in 1978 or 1979. He felt he had to in effect recharge his batteries, as had been the case before in the two-year lag between *Slow Dancer* and *Silk Degrees.* As he said to reporter Sean Mitchell: "After I left Steve Miller and made those first three albums for Columbia, I was working 365 days a year. After *Slow Dancer* I had to sit back for a while and find out what I wanted to do."

In 1979, Boz slowly prepared material for a new album, *Middle Man* (Columbia, March 1980). Though it went platinum and was interesting in some ways, it lacked the creative flair of earlier LPs. But Boz had not limited his work to the album. Two of his songs from the soundtrack of the movie *Urban Cowboy* ("Jojo" and "Look What You've Done to Me") made *Billboard*'s singles top 20. Also on the charts in 1980 was a retrospective LP, *Hits!* His 1981 single "Miss Sun" made the top 20 as well.

After a seven-year absence from the recording scene, Boz returned with *Other Roads* (spring 1988, Columbia) accompanied by Jeff Porcaro, Steve Luckather, and David Paich from his *Silk Degrees* days.

SEALS AND CROFTS: *Vocal and instrumental duo. Jim Seals, born Sidney, Texas, October 17, 1941; Dash Crofts, born Cisco, Texas, August 14, 1940.*

Both born and raised in small southeastern Texas towns, both involved in music from an early age, Jim Seals and Dash Crofts had enough in common to bring them together and to keep them making music together for over two decades. Their association brought them through various musical stages at various times, from rock to jazz to folk-rock and back to rock. Eventually they added another unifying factor to their relationship; both of them converted to the Baha'i faith, a change that affected not only their lives, but their music as well.

Listening to their music, one might think folk and rock were their major influences, but country music and the classics were the early influences on Seals and Crofts. Jim Seals had been exposed to country music since his infancy; his grandfather had his own country music group which frequently got together for local hoedowns. One of his earliest memories came from when he was four. The fiddle player from his grandfather's group came to Seals' house. When little Jimmy heard him play, he became so excited that his grandfather ordered him a fiddle from the Sears catalogue. When the fiddle finally arrived, however, Jimmy became frustrated that he couldn't master it immediately and put it under the bed to gather dust for a year. Then one night he had a dream that he could play. When he got up, he took out his fiddle and found that he could play a little bit. By age nine, he played so well that he won the Texas state fiddle championship. By that time, he had also started picking out chords on his father's guitar.

Growing up in Texas, Dash Crofts could not avoid hearing country music, but it was in the classics that he first got his training. He started picking out tunes on the household piano when he was five. His mother recognized his talent and encouraged him to study the classics, which she loved. Dash worked diligently on the piano until he was nine, when he decided he would rather play ball. But after several years, his interest in music revived, this time as a result of listening to late-night broadcasts of rhythm & blues from a Memphis radio station. He decided to concentrate on drums instead of piano.

By the time Crofts met Seals in the local junior high school, Jim had amassed many hours of experience playing with country bands. He also had learned a new instrument, the tenor saxophone. The time was the mid-1950s and rock'n'roll was on the rise, so the two merged forces as part of a high school rock band.

Out of high school, Seals and Crofts moved to California in 1958. There they became part of the Champs, that year turning out one of the all-time rock instrumental successes, "Tequila," which sold an estimated 6 million copies on Challenge Records. For the next seven years, the Champs played all over the world, though its star had set by the time it broke up in 1965.

After this, Crofts went back to Texas, while Seals remained in California, writing music and doing recording sessions. A year later, he began playing sax and rhythm guitar with guitarist Louie Shelton and bass player Joseph Bogan. The group needed a drummer, so Jim called Dash in Texas, and within a few days the group was complete. In the year that followed, the four musicians met Marcia Day, who was to become their manager, and they all took up residence in a three-story gray house known as Marcia's Place on Hollywood Boulevard in Los Angeles.

Marcia had a profound influence on the lives of all four men. She introduced them to the Baha'i faith, which most of them adopted, and she also introduced them to her five daughters. Three of the daughters joined with the men to form a group, the Dawnbreakers. In the act's two years together, Dash, Louie, and Joe, respectively, married Billie Lee Day, Donnie Day, and Lana Day. Not long afterward, Seals married Ruby Jean Anderson, another resident of Marcia's Place.

The Dawnbreakers' short existence was in part because of the religious conversion. They decided to take time to study the Baha'i sacred writing and to pray and meditate. During this time, Jim and Dash began to experiment with new vocal harmonies. Dash found a new challenge in learning to play the mandolin and Jim virtually abandoned the saxophone for the guitar. As a result, the duo started developing musical forms very different from their previous efforts. In addition, Louie Shelton pursued his interest in production (he went on to produce Seals and Crofts' LPs starting with *Year of Sunday*, released in November 1971) and Joe Bogan mastered the technology of record engineering.

The duo of Seals and Crofts made their first professional appearance in 1969 at a small club in Riverside, California, filling in for a headline act that had taken ill. The next two years were lean and difficult, although their first two albums for the TA label, *Seals and Crofts* and *Down Home,* won some critical notice. Nevertheless, they continued to perform at various nightclubs and attracted a faithful underground following.

Soon it became clear that Seals and Crofts were headed for success. Their first Warner Brothers release, *Year of Sunday,* appeared on the hit charts at the end of 1971. *Summer Breeze* (August 1972) did even better, reaching *Billboard*'s number 7 position and achieving a gold-record award in early 1973. The album and the single of the same name continued to sell enough copies to reach for platinum sales levels. Their next album, *Diamond Girl,* was greeted with critical acclaim and went platinum.

Seals and Crofts consistently turned out hit singles and albums in the next few years. LPs *Unborn Child* (February 1974), *I'll Play For You* (1975), and *Get Closer* (1976) went gold as did their "Get Closer." *Seals and Crofts Greatest Hits* (October 1975) went platinum. In 1977, they released their first soundtrack album for the movie *One on One.* They also scored an animated film for Hanna-Barbera that was produced by the newly formed Day Five Productions. They also released several more studio albums in the late 1970s and early 1980s, such as *Sudan Village* (1976), *Takin' It Easy* (1978), and *Longest Road* (1980), but none cracked *Billboard*'s top 40.

Warner Brothers also reissued their two albums for TA on the two-disc *Seals & Crofts I and II.*

Following their religious conversion, many of Seals and Crofts' songs reflected their religious beliefs, often expressing a feeling or an inspiration gained from studying the Baha'i sacred texts. Their music changed due to their newfound faith, becoming much softer, more folk- than rock-oriented. Their new sound, however, was rather difficult to classify, for it reflected the diverse elements of their musical background: a new blend of jazz, country, rock, folk, and, at times, classical music as well.

Their immense commercial success enabled them to move from Marcia's Place to their own community in the Los Angeles suburb of San Fernando, where they not only lived but also produced their albums.

In concert, Seals and Crofts did not try to preach or to impose their faith on the crowds. Their live performances often featured bluegrass and country solos on mandolin, fiddle, and guitar by Dash and Jim as well as their usual fare. On the road, they were prone to playing pranks. In Boston, they fashioned UFOs out of plastic cleaning bags, drinking straws, and birthday candles. When the lit candles were placed in the straw framefork, the bags filled with hot air and began to float. The UFOs caused an uproar around Boston that night; many people called radio stations and the police. As Crofts told Shel Kagan of *Circus Magazine:* "They called out the air force, and one lady said on a radio talk show that she saw the windows on the things and little people inside. We've got the clippings to prove it, too."

SEDAKA, NEIL: *Singer, songwriter. Born Brooklyn, New York, March 13, 1939.*

When Neil Sedaka reappeared on the hit charts in the early 1970s, it put to rest the question of whatever happened to him. Actually, as music-industry people knew, Sedaka had really never been away after his first starring years as a singer ended a decade earlier. He had continued to be a force behind the scenes as a songwriter—just as he was while becoming a top singer.

Sedaka's interest in music went back to his childhood in Brooklyn. His family had musical roots. Both parents were trained pianists; his grandmother had been a concert pianist under the tutelage of famous conductor Walter Damrosch, founder of what is now the Julliard School of Music. Neil took piano lessons while he attended elementary school, but, like most youngsters, followed popular music with far greater interest than classics.

He spent many hours listening to pop records by the time he was attending Lincoln High School and picking out melodies on the piano. Having no feel

for lyrics, at 14 he enlisted the aid of schoolmate Howard Greenfield. It was the start of a collaboration that lasted into the 1970s—by which time Sedaka and Greenfield had written over 500 songs together, a good percentage of which proved to be hits.

For a while, Sedaka was only able to present these compositions at school events and gatherings of friends. In his midteens, though, he started to make the rounds of music publishers and record firms in New York. Eventually, Neil and Greenfield became associated with Aldon Publishing Company, a firm jointly owned by Don Kirshner and Al Nevins (a member of popular vocal trio the Three Suns). Kirshner tried to push their material to new star Connie Francis. As Francis said in her autobiography, *Who's Sorry Now* (St. Martin's, 1984), she initially found their songs well written but too intelligent to be commercial. In a last-ditch effort, they offered her "Stupid Cupid," though Sedaka thought it wasn't classy enough for her. It became a smash hit for Connie in 1958. They later provided her with "Fallin'," "Frankie," and "Where the Boys Are."

But Nevins and Kirshner also felt that Sedaka had a future as a vocalist. They produced a demonstration record that quickly won the approval of RCA executive Steve Sholes. Sholes signed Neil to a contract and Neil promptly turned out a 1958 hit single, "The Diary" backed with "No Vacancy." The next year, he enjoyed hits "I Go Ape" and "Oh! Carol" (written to future songwriting whiz Carole King).

Sedaka fast became a star on the pop circuit. Among his *Billboard* top 10 singles were "Calendar Girl" in 1961 and "Happy Birthday, Sweet Sixteen" and "Breaking Up Is Hard to Do" in 1962. Successful albums included *Little Devil and His Other Hits* (1961) and *Neil Sedaka Sings His Greatest Hits* (1963).

By the end of 1963, Sedaka had cooled off as a performer. Styles in music had changed, other artists moved to the fore, and Neil's record sales declined sharply. By the mid-1960s, many younger fans didn't know who he was. However, Sedaka was able to analyze musical trends and, with Greenfield, still turned out songs that brought enormous sales for other artists. For most of the second half of the decade, their output usually accounted for at least one or two songs on the charts each month. Their touch continued into the '70s. Among the hits from their pens were the 5th Dimension's "Working on a Groovy Thing," Tom Jones' "Puppet Man," Davy Jones' "Rainy Jane," and "(Is This the Way to) Amarillo" for Tony Christie.

In late 1971, Sedaka was again singing for the man who helped discover him, Don Kirshner. Neil's first LP on Kirshner Records, *Emergence,* was released that September. Along with this, Sedaka undertook his first extended in-person tour in years, starting with an engagement at New York's Bitter End in mid-October. However, none of this made for much improvement in his career during the early 1970s. That lack of progress, in fact, caused the breakup of his longtime writing partnership with Howard Greenfield. Among their final joint efforts was "Our Last Song Together."

After that, Kirshner put him in touch with a new writing partner, Phil Cody. The two wrote a number of new songs, some of which Sedaka unveiled during a tour of England. "Solitaire" in particular won thunderous applause and led to Sedaka's recording the album *Solitaire*, which did well in the U.K. in the mid-1970s, but had much less impact at home. He followed up with another U.K.-recorded collection, *The Tra-La Days Are Over*, backed by the group Hotlegs (later renamed 10 cc). That LP wasn't released in the U.S. at all.

Before leaving London, Phil and Neil wrote several new tunes, including "Laughter in the Rain." When Sedaka got the chance to cut a new album for Elton John's record label, Rocket, that song was included along with some tracks recorded in Los Angeles and some from the *Tra-La* LP. The album appeared in late 1974 under the title *Sedaka's Back*. And indeed he was. Released as a single, "Laughter in the Rain" rose to number one in *Billboard* the week of February 1, 1975. It was followed with other chart singles from the album during the year: "The Immigrant" (dedicated to John Lennon, who was having problems in gaining approval for continued residence in the U.S.) and "That's Where the Music Takes Me."

To Neil's surprise, his next major single was "Bad Blood," which wasn't from *Sedaka's Back*, but from the LP *Overnight Success*, a disc released only in the U.K. It proved a welcome surprise, because "Bad Blood" rose to number one in *Billboard* for three weeks starting October 11, 1975. Right away, a revised version of *Overnight Success* titled *The Hungry Years* was released in the U.S. by Rocket and went gold. With Neil's newfound stardom, RCA Records started reissuing some of his earlier material for that label, including *Breaking Up Is Hard to Do* (on RCA's Camden label in 1975), *Oh Carol* and *Neil Sedaka Sings His Greatest Hits* (1975), *Pure Gold* (1976), and *Sedaka: The Fifties and Sixties* and *The Many Sides of Neil Sedaka* (1977).

Neil followed "Bad Blood" with a new version of his 1962 hit "Breaking Up Is Hard to Do," which made the top 10. According to Fred Bronson, this was the only number one single to later be re-recorded by the same artist and become a top 10 success the second time. Since Rocket Records had

operating problems around that time, Neil soon was in the market for a new label, signing with Elektra. Rocket in the interim had gained two charted albums with *Sedaka's Steppin' Out* (1976) and *Neil Sedaka's Greatest Hits* (1977).

Neil's Elektra debut *(Song, 1977)* was followed with such LPs as *All You Need Is the Music* in 1978, *In the Pocket* in 1980, and *Neil Sedaka* in 1981. He placed several Elektra singles on the charts, the most successful being a 1980 duet with his daughter Dara, "Should've Never Let You Go." In 1983, Neil left Elektra for MCA/Curb. Soon after, he and Dara made the charts with the single "Your Precious Love," a remake of a 1967 Marvin Gaye–Tammi Terrell hit. *(See 5th Dimension; Francis, Connie; John, Elton; Jones, Tom; King, Carole.)*

SEGER, BOB: *Singer, guitarist, band leader (The Silver Bullet Band), songwriter, record producer. Born Detroit, Michigan, May 6, 1945.**

If Horatio Alger were a rock writer, Bob Seger might have been one of his subjects. Adversity reared its head when Bob was 12 and his father left. His mother kept things going for a while, but by the time Seger was in his senior year in high school in Ann Arbor, Michigan, in 1963, he had to work in his spare time to help the family's fragile finances. When he decided to make music his career, he had to persist through endless frustrations and setbacks to finally hit paydirt in his thirties—which is almost considered retirement age for rock artists still aspiring to stardom. Through it all, Seger maintained a proper balance, not boasting or swaggering when his star at last was in the ascendant and continuing to live modestly on the outskirts of Detroit even when albums *Night Moves* and *Stranger in Town* established him as a belated superstar.

In storybook fashion, Seger's breakthrough occurred just when he was beginning to resign himself to more modest goals. Years as the hottest rock act in Detroit had brought some opportunities to record for major labels from 1969 to 1975, but lack of promotion had left him a prophet only in his hometown. Just past 30 in early 1975, he told Bill Gray of the *Detroit News:* "I'll always be in the music business. I love it too much to do anything else. If the day comes when nobody wants to hear me play, I'll probably become a disc jockey."

His second album on a new Capitol Records contract, a two-record concert set with his new Silver Bullet Band called *Live Bullet*, had just come out, but Seger had been through the wringer too many times before to be overly optimistic. "Right now I'm

*Alto Reed quotes from personal interview with Irwin Stambler.

605

numbed," he told Gray. "I used to be a basket case every time we turned out an album. Now I'm just numb."

But *Live Bullet* proved the shot heard round the music world. The tight, joyful musicianship of the five-piece band (Drew Abbott, lead guitar; Robyn Robbins, keyboards; Charlie Allen Martin, drums; Alto Reed, saxophone; and Chris Campbell, bass) and Seger's gravel-edged renditions of his primarily R&B-based rock compositions or arrangements (he credits James Brown with being a major influence) demonstrated what his fanatic Detroit fans had known for years. Seger was an original—a talented creator of music that was both dynamic in the old rock'n'roll tradition and emotionally moving in the way it assessed the world of average people. That his first top 40 album (a platinum album at that) was live seemed proper, for good as his recordings were, his concerts were better, providing the added dimensions of thousands of people whom Seger set into motion—cheering, hand-clapping, singing, and dancing in place—as few other artists could.

Bob followed up that achievement with the collection that established him once and for all as a force to be reckoned with in modern rock—the album *Night Moves*, with the autobiographical title song fondly recalling a romance from his junior year in high school in 1962: "We weren't searching for some pie in the sky summit/We were just young and restless and bored/ . . . And we'd steal away every chance we could/ . . . Working on our night moves/Trying to lose the awkward teenage blues."

That effort won him a nomination for Best New Male Vocalist of 1976 from the Rock Music Awards. It also won a belly laugh when he heard about it—a "new vocalist" whose first record (an original composition, "East Side Story") had appeared in 1966. It took many dates in sleazy bars and as opening act in local concerts and many changes in band makeup before Bob went much beyond that position in music.

His interest in pop music was nurtured by his father before Bob's parents separated. He recalled to Timothy White for record-company biographical notes: "When I was a kid, my father, Stewart Seger, earned a living as a medic for the Ford Motor Company and led a band in his spare time. He had started to become a doctor when he was younger and I think he had three to four years of medical school, but never quite finished. He was a poor litle rich kid, since his mother was a wealthy descendant of the Scottish Stuart royal clan, but the money he'd inherited was largely gone by the time I was born."

At an early age, Bob was influenced by his father's musical interests. "We always had a piano in the house, because besides his 13-piece orchestra, my father also sang bass in a barbershop quartet and he'd sometimes practice at home. My father also kept a bunch of instruments that he played handy: guitar, sax, banjo, ukelele, and clarinet. My dad wanted me to take clarinet and I did, from fourth to sixth grade. I didn't like it at all, but I still know my scales.

"Up until I was 10, we were okay—we were middle class. But after that [when his father moved to California] we were very poor. After my dad left, my brother George started supporting the family. He got a job at 14 and he's worked ever since. The low point was when I was a junior in high school; we were living in one room with one bed and a hotplate. Whew, boy, that was rough." Then his brother got more money, his mother got work as a housekeeper, and things got better.

By then, Bob was deeply into the early stages of his music career. He had started with a trio called the Decibels when he was 14 and finally reached some sort of plateau in the late 1960s when his foursome, the Bob Seger System, built up a following around the Detroit area and won a contract from Capitol Records in 1967 on the strength of his local singles hit, "Ramblin' Gamblin' Man," issued by Capitol in September 1968. That rave-up single rose as high as 17 on *Billboard* lists, but while the album of that title, issued in December 1968, made the charts, it didn't go beyond the lower positions. This was followed by three more albums *(Noah* in September 1969, *Mongrel* in August 1970—both by the Bob Seger System—and *Brand New Morning* in October 1971) and a number of singles ("Ivory" in April 1969, "Lucifer" in February 1970, and "Lookin' Back" in September 1971), none of which did exceptionally well.

Discouraged, Bob broke up his group and started work on a college degree. But he couldn't stay away from music and he soon was touring with the band Teegarden and VanWinkle. He also set up arrangements for albums on his own label, Palladium, to be distributed on Warner Brothers' Reprise label. Three more albums resulted: *Back in '72* (January 1973), *Smokin' O.P.'s* (August 1972), and *Seven* (March 1974). (The last two were reissued by Capitol in December 1977.) But the results were disappointing, even though he had some success with singles "If I Were a Carpenter" (April 1972) and "Get Out of Denver" (July 1974). Someone with less tenacity might have changed professions, but Seger was a survivor whose move back to Capitol in 1975 brought the long-deferred rewards.

His debut on Capitol the second time around was the LP *Beautiful Loser* (March 1975). The album had some chart action, as did the singles "Katmandu'' (issued in July) and Tina Turner's composition "Nutbush City Limits" (1975).

This set the stage for *Live Bullet* (April 1976). With live versions of his best songs up to then, it slowly worked its way up the charts, eventually winning platinum certification from the RIAA. It was followed by the even more successful *Night Moves* (November 1976) with such singles hits as the title track (issued in November 1976), "Main Street" (April 1977), and "Rock and Roll Never Forgets" (June 1977).

Bob's years of struggle made him realize one rose (or even two) doesn't make a summer. So he continued a back-breaking round of tours both at home and abroad into the early 1980s to solidify and maintain his standing with a broad-based audience, annually doing 250–265 shows. He also took great pains in preparing his releases, both in selecting songs by others and in writing new ones.

Long-time band member Alto Reed, who did occasional songwriting for other groups, stressed that Seger remained the Silver Bullet Band's primary writer. "And he prefers to write alone. With Bob I did no writing. He's a solo writer. But don't get me wrong. I love playing with the band. Bob always has selected great musicians and it's always been a family from the people in the office to Bob and Punch [band promoter Eddie "Punch" Andrews]."

Seger's efforts continued to pay off in a string of platinum albums: *Stranger in Town* (April 1978), *Against the Wind* (February 1980), the live two-disc *Nine Tonight* (September 1981), *The Distance* (December 1982), and *Like a Rock* (1986). Those albums spawned a series of charted singles, many of which made *Billboard*'s top 10. *Stranger in Town*, for instance, yielded "Still the Same," "Hollywood Nights," and "We've Got Tonight." Other charted singles were "Old Time Rock & Roll" (in March 1979), "Fire Lake" (February 1980), "Against the Wind" (May 1980), "You'll Accomp'ny Me" (July 1980), "Horizontal Bop" (November 1980), "Tryin' to Live My Life without You" (a top 5 track from *Nine Tonight*), "Feel Like a Number" (November 1981), "Shame on the Moon" (a number two hit from *The Distance*), "Even Now" (March 1983), and "Roll Me Away" (May 1983).

After *The Distance* came out, there was a three-year period when relatively little was heard from Seger. No new albums appeared and his fans waited in vain for major new concert tours. He did, though, have two singles hits derived from the soundtracks of the movies *Risky Business* and *Teachers*. In the first case, where star Tom Cruise mimed Seger's 1979 hit "Old Time Rock & Roll," a Capitol reissue of the single in September 1983 made new chart inroads.

The 1984 single "Understanding" from *Teachers* also made the top 20.

The reasons for the lag between his 1982 album and the March 1986 *Like a Rock*, Seger indicated, lay both in his private life and in creative challenges. The personal setback was outlined to Jack Curry of *USA Today* (spring 1986): "Well, I ended an 11-year relationship in 1983. That put me in different territory for a while, and it wasn't a real happy place to be."

That didn't help the difficulties he encountered in working up new material for his next LP. He told Robert Hilburn of the *Los Angeles Times* (March 1986): "I never planned to take this long to make the record, but I wanted to produce it myself and it took me months just to learn how everything worked in the studio. It was an experiment and the whole thing got out of hand. There was nobody to 'say no' to me and I ended up recording 25 songs in four different cities."

But for fans, it was worth the wait. When the album finally came out, it proved to be vintage Seger and arguably one of the year's best in rock—his seventh straight platinum LP. His supporting group had changed somewhat from earlier times, although Alto Reed and Chris Campbell were still aboard. Seger enthused: "I'm pleased with the exciting new musicians who are part of *Like a Rock* because they've made their own contributions to my life in the last few years, particularly keyboard man Craig Frost, who's been with me since *The Distance*, lead guitarist Rick Vito, who did some excellent work with Jackson Browne, and drummer John Robinson, who's played with Quincy Jones and Chaka Khan."

The first single from the new LP, "American Storm," a top 20 hit, offered Seger's strong antidrug sentiments. He told Hilburn: "I knew some people would think the song was about America . . . [but] I'm talking about drugs. The whole thing was getting to be so depressing around the time I wrote the song, which was nearly three years ago now.

"The reason I called it 'American Storm' is that it isn't just a U.S. problem. Before I started researching the subject, I assumed that people in places like Colombia were supporting [the drug traffic] because it is bringing so much money down there, but most of the people in those countries are against it, too, because it is corrupting their whole way of life and their governments."

He told Hilburn he had never gotten heavily involved in drugs, but people "important to me have. Drugs are destroying so many people and I thought I ought to stand up and be counted. If they want to call me square, they can."

He also told reporters that by the time he and his band were ready for a new tour in the late summer of

1986, he planned to get rid of his addiction to smoking. He told Curry he felt this would let him hit certain high notes that once had come easily and now proved elusive when he sang. "I think there are three or four more notes up there I can get if I stop."

He looked forward to getting back on stage, he noted, particularly since he felt confident that the old industry maxim "once you are beyond *Teen* magazine in rock, you are history" no longer applied. "But things have changed," he told Hilburn. "The rock audience has grown up, too, and the important thing—just as I said in 'Rock and Roll Never Forgets'—is whether you can relate to the passion and innocence that is rock'n'roll."

Alto Reed echoed those sentiments. "I feel rock'n'roll will always prevail. It's participatory and some of the greatest moments I've had came when, in the heat of excitement, the band and audience merge into one unit. It just so happens that you're playing the instrument, but the fans out there are playing right with you. That exchange of electricity is enormous. You can play o.k. without audience feedback, but you can't duplicate the effect when everyone out there is really giving their enthusiasm back to you. And Bob Seger really knows how to pace a concert so that situation comes about."

Seger told Timothy White he still felt he had something to give back to fans of all age groups. "You know, somebody asked me the other day what it's like to be beginning a third decade in rock'n'roll. The chance to play rock'n'roll as an adult feels like a privilege to me. I look at guys like Jagger and Springsteen to James Brown and Chuck Berry, and I figure they're damn nice company to be in."

SEX PISTOLS, THE: *Vocal and instrumental group, all born England. Members (1977–78): Johnny Rotten; Sid Vicious, born 1958, died New York, New York, February 2, 1979; Steve Jones; Paul Cook.*

While the Sex Pistols wasn't the first punk band, for a time in the mid-1970s, it essentially personified the genre. Its rise to prominence—or notoriety— was meteoric, but echoes of its brief, sordid, and tragic saga remain in rock annals to the present day.

All the eventual members of the group were performing with various teenage groups in the early 1970s, a period of intense frustration among working class youth in England. Under the name Sex Pistols, the quartet that featured the rasping vocals of John Lydon (who took the pseudonym Johnny Rotten) began to gain notice from fans at small clubs around London in 1975. The group managed to increase its following despite attempts by the authorities in England to restrict radio and TV coverage of its material, which contained stinging tirades against the

established order as well as choice use of all kinds of obscenities.

The original group, besides Lydon/Rotten, included Steve Jones on guitar, Glen Matlock on bass, and Paul Cook on drums. Matlock later was replaced by Sid Vicious. The band was first signed by England's EMI Records, but after release of the single "Anarchy in the U.K." EMI dropped them. Even though the record was widely banned in England, it still made the U.K. top 10.

In the U.S., word of the group began to filter back to mainstream and underground rock publications. Some observers, in the absence of available Sex Pistols recordings, voiced suspicions that this might be another case of the time-honored hype used to make headliners of previously obscure and often meagerly talented performers.

In England, the band's growing appeal resulted in release of some of the group's songs on a local label. The debut album, *Never Mind the Bollocks, Here's the Sex Pistols,* came out in 1977 on Virgin and quickly rose to number one on English charts. This was a remarkable achievement, since the band was effectively banned from playing any of the major venues in its home country and an almost total radio and TV blackout was maintained. When the album gained U.S. sales as an import, Warner Brothers decided to take over distribution. The Warner Brothers package was released in the fall of 1977 and arrangements were initiated for the band to tour the U.S. in 1978.

The album proved a revelation. True, the band didn't hesitate to use obscenities normally excluded from even the raunchiest previous rock releases, but there wasn't the use of them for shock value alone. More to the point, the band conveyed a surging, relentless energy that is the essence of punk rock and combined this with a statement on the world around it. The problem was that this world essentially reflected the problems besetting a segment of British society, problems rather far afield from what average American teenagers or music fans in their early twenties could identify with.

The Sex Pistols used their nerve-frazzling instrumental pyrotechnics and incensed, snarling vocals to etch a picture of despair and disillusionment that gripped a sizable portion of England's younger generation. For example, in "Anarchy in the U.K.," Rotten hoarsely spat out "Don't know what I want/But I know how to get it. . . . Anarchy in the U.K. is coming sometime." "God Save the Queen" went: "God save the Queen/The Fascist regime/That made you a moron. . . . She ain't a human bein'/There ain't no future in England's scene. . . . No future! No future! . . . For you!"

To kick off the band's U.S. tour, manager Malcolm McLaren arranged for an appearance on NBC's-TV "Saturday Night Live" on December 17, 1977. The tour itself got underway in early 1978 and had the band crisscrossing the country for much of the year. There was plenty of media coverage, although airplay on rock stations was limited. The band drew sizable crowds into relatively small concert sites, but it gained essentially a cult following rather than the mass audience. The question had always been whether the Sex Pistols could find rapport with U.S. listeners who were relatively contented and unpoliticized. The answer seemed to be no, at least for that time and place.

The group was unable to repeat its English successes on an equivalent scale. Although its key members seemed to become infatuated with American life and established temporary residences in the country, the band itself broke up by the fall of 1978. In 1979, Virgin released the album *The Great Rock'n'Roll Swindle.*

For a while, the band members were lost to view as far as the media were concerned. Later, though, Rotten (*see Public Image Limited*) went on under his real name to form more successful groups, and the others eventually carved out new niches for themselves as well. For a while Cook and Jones worked together in a band called The Professionals. Jones for a time after that played lead guitar for the Checquered Past, whose members included Blondie alumni Nigel Harrison and Clem Burke, before going on to a successful career as a solo artist.

But first, Sid Vicious (born John Simon Ritchie) made bizarre headlines. On October 12, 1978, he was arrested by New York police, charged with the stabbing murder of girlfriend Nancy Spungen. Although Sid didn't recall killing her, it might have been intended as a murder-suicide. Ten days after her death, he tried to kill himself, reportedly after screaming: "I want to die. I want to join Nancy! I didn't keep my part of the bargain."

After being released on bail (pending trial) on February 1, 1979, he was found dead of a drug overdose the next day in the Greenwich Village apartment of a friend. The tragedy formed the basis for the director Alex Cox's fascinating 1986 film *Sid and Nancy.*

Due to their cult status, new records of old tapes kept surfacing, such as Skyclad Records' *We Have Cum for Your Children (Wanted: The Goodman Tapes)* from Glenn Matlock's period as bassist, and, in 1988, *Better Live than Dead* and *The Mini-Album* on Restless Records. (*See Thin Lizzy.*)

Looking back at the Sex Pistols period in 1987 in a comment for an MCA press release, Jones suggested there was more theatricality than conviction in the band's supposed anti-social stance. "We weren't ex-

actly serious. It was a laugh. I wanted to meet girls. It's neat to think we started so much, but I was never really into that punk stuff. I just wanted to get laid and get drunk. I was really a football hooligan. I went to matches and bashed people. Punk was the perfect way to do what I wanted to do—cause trouble—and get paid for it."

But he observed, he paid himself in other ways. After the Sex Pistols disbanded, he extended his drug experience into addiction. "I was bored after all that excitement. Somebody came round my house with some (heroin) and that was it. For years."

In the early 1980s, he moved to Los Angeles where he tried detoxication treatments. "Gettin' off dope wasn't so hard. Stayin' straight is much harder. I couldn't find nuthin' to keep me straight. I had a lonely hole inside me, and I didn't know how to fill it."

With the help of some friends, he was able to kick heroin in the mid-1980s and resume his career. He got together with Duran Duran guitarist Andy Taylor to write and record some songs for the movie *American Anthem* and later he provided the song "Pleasure and Pain" for *Sid and Nancy* and with "With You or Without You" for *Something Wild.* He also provided material for veteran American punk rocker Iggy Pop and backed him on tour (*See Pop, Iggy*) and co-produced all the tracks for Andy Taylor's debut solo album.

He then proceeded to complete his debut solo LP, *Mercy,* released by MCA in May 1987. Reflecting his changing attitudes since the Sex Pistol days, he also became active in anti-drug campaigns, including an MTV/Rock Against Drugs spot.

SHADOWS, THE: *Vocal and instrumental group. Original members (1958): Hank Marvin, born Newcastle, England, October 28, 1941; Bruce Welch, born Bognor Regis, England, November 2, 1941; Tony Meehan, born London, England, March 2, 1942; Jet Harris. Meehan and Harris later replaced by Brian Bennett, born London, England, Feburary 9, 1940; John Rostill, born Birmingham, England, June 16, 1942.*

The origin of one of the most successful English pop groups of the 1960s, the Shadows, goes back to April 1958, when two teenaged schoolmates from Newcastle—Hank Marvin and Bruce Welch—began playing skiffle in a London coffee bar. Marvin began playing banjo at 15 and took up guitar when his father gave him one in 1957. Born in Bognor Regis, Welch was taken to Newcastle by his parents when he was six months old. He also learned to play guitar and the two friends started a group called the Railroaders in school.

Deciding to try for bigger things, they auditioned

and gained their coffee bar job at the Two I's in Soho. However, the pay was slight and the outlook doubtful. Marvin recalled: "We used to get to bed very late and about four in the afternoon, when we got up, we would have a slice of bread. For two weeks when things were really bad, our diet was a roll and a cup of Oxo for lunch and an apple for tea."

As Bruce noted: "Often we felt like packing up and going home. But we didn't want to return as failures as somehow we were certain things would get better. After all, they couldn't have got any worse."

Things did pick up in the early summer when they met another young performer, singer-guitarist Cliff Richard. *(See Richard, Cliff.)* Richard wanted a backing group and combined the talents of Marvin and Welch with two others, Jet Harris and Tony Meehan. The group took the name of the Drifters and, led by Richard, played at a number of small clubs in the London area. In the late summer, Richard and his group paid six pounds (about $15) for a demonstration record that eventually led to a recording contract with EMI.

The group backed Richard on a series of English hits and then began to be featured on its own. Its debut single was "Feelin' Fine" (1959). In 1960, now known as the Shadows, the group gained major recognition with the million-seller "Apache" and won the *New Musical Express* poll as the top British instrumental group for the year.

Writing many of their songs through most of the 1960s, the Shadows were rarely absent from the English hit charts. In 1961, they gained the number one spots in three different categories during the year with "Kon Tiki" in singles, the extended-play disc *The Shadows to the Fore,* and the LP *The Shadows.* Hit singles spanned "F.B.I.," "The Frightened City," "Wonderful Land," "Atlantis," "Shindig," "I Met a Girl," "A Place in the Sun," and "The Dreams I Dream." LPs included *Out of the Shadows, The Shadows Greatest Hits, Dance with the Shadows, The Sound of the Shadows, More Hits!,* and *Shadow Music.*

The group continued to work with Richard on stage, in TV, and in a series of movies (some hits) such as *Expresso Bongo, The Young Ones, Summer Holiday,* and *Finders Keepers.* Group members wrote the score for the last of these and also scored and performed in their own summer 1964 film, the satirical half-hour *Rhythm & Greens.* They also wrote the music for a series of pantomime shows at London's Palladium including *Aladdin* (1964) and *Babes in the Wood* and *Cinderella* (1965).

By the mid-1960s, the Shadows consisted of Marvin and Welch complemented by John Henry Rostill on bass guitar and Brian Bennett on drums. Bennett had first taken up the violin in school in London before eventually concentrating on percussion. For a while, he studied art and, after leaving school, worked as a printer until going into music full time.

In mid-1968, just after Richard and the Shadows celebrated its tenth anniversary, Bennett announced his decision to leave the group. In the fall, Rostill departed and the Shadows was officially dissolved. For a while, Rostill toured regularly with Tom Jones and also wrote a number of songs recorded by such other performers as Engelbert Humperdinck and the Family Dogg. *(See Humperdinck, Engelbert; Jones, Tom.)* In 1971, he recorded several singles, the first of which, "Funny Old World," was issued by EMI in June.

After the group's breakup, Marvin and Welch continued to work with Richard and, beginning in 1969, concentrated on a close-harmony vocal group with guitarist-singer John Farrar, whom they had met during a tour of Australia in February 1968. This was a departure from the Shadows' approach, which had emphasized instrumental work with vocals mainly added for variety. During 1970, the three wrote a series of new songs for their debut LP, *Marvin, Welch and Farrar,* released by Capitol on February 5, 1971. The trio made their live debut as part of the Cliff Richard show that toured Europe in the spring.

SHA NA NA: *Vocal, dance, and instrumental group. Members (1970s): Scott Powell, Johnny Contardo, Frederick Dennis Greene, Don York, Rich Joffe, Elliot Cahn, Chris Donald, Bruce Clarke, Screamin' Scott Simon, John Baumann, Lonnie Baker, Jocko Marcellino.*

One of the more original acts on the rock circuit, Sha Na Na blended vocal harmonies, dance routines, and instrumental arrangements to both recall and satirize the hits of the middle and late 1950s. As one reviewer analyzed the 12-man group: "They appear with slicked back DA haircuts, gold lamé suits, undershirts, and dirty jeans. They carry packs of cigarettes in their rolled-up summer shirt sleeves. That gleam in their eye is perhaps more than stage presence. The name of Sha Na Na's game may be satire, but like all good satire it is played seriously, and sometimes even the actors can't tell if they're kidding or not."

The group, formed in the New York area with performers from many parts of the country, came into being at the end of the 1960s. Its renditions of such rock oldies as "Teen Angel," "Duke of Earl," "Great Balls of Fire," and "Jailhouse Rock" were presented on a number of nationwide TV shows in the late 1960s and early '70s. In 1969, Sha Na Na was a showstopper at the legendary Woodstock Festival. In 1972, the group was also featured in Bill Graham's movie *Fillmore*.

Buddah Records released the LP *Sha Na Na* in 1971. The sound was good, but (as with subsequent Buddah albums) it couldn't convey the satire of the group, which was essentially visual in nature. Part of the album was recorded during a live performance at New York's Columbia University, one of many college appearances Sha Na Na made both in the U.S. and in many other countries. LPs still in print in the early 1980s were *Best of Sha Na Na* (1976) and *Sha Na Na Is Here to Stay* (1977).

In 1976, the group gained a network TV contract for a series of variety programs (which included provisions for a guest star each week and comic skits typically involving Sha Na Na members with the guest). For several years, the group made new TV shows, which continued to be screened in syndication in the 1980s.

The instrumental section of the group in the early and middle 1970s comprised Elliot Cahn on guitar; Chris Donald, lead guitar; Bruce Clarke, bass; Screamin' Scott Simon, piano and bass; John Baumann, piano; Lonnie Baker, saxophone; and Jocko Marcellino, drums.

The group members varied over the years, though many of the original members continued to perform as part of the group into the late 1980s.

One original member who went on to success as a solo performer was lead guitarist Henry Gross, whose albums included his A&M debut *Henry Gross* (1973) plus *Plug Me into Something* (A&M, 1975), *Release* (Lifesong, 1976), *Show Me to the Stage* (Lifesong, 1977), *Love Is the Stuff* (Lifesong, 1978), and *What's in a Name* (Capitol, 1981). Singing falsetto like a Beach Boy, Henry hit number 6 in *Billboard* in 1976 with the enigmatic ballad "Shannon" (Lifesong), which was actually an elegy to Beach Boy Carl Wilson's deceased Irish setter.

SHANGRI-LAS, THE: *Vocal group, all born New York, c. 1947. Mary Ann Ganser; Margie Ganser, died 1980s; Betty Weiss; Mary Weiss, born 1948.*

Providing another saga in the rock Cinderella department was the rapid rise to stardom of the teenage vocal group the Shangri-Las in the mid-1960s. Their career also reflected the other side of the coin—the very brief tenure of most groups at the rarefied heights of pop music, although the Shangri-Las continued to be active in '60s revival shows through the '70s and '80s.

All of the girls grew up in New York and started following pop music before their teens. The quartet consisted of two sets of sisters: twins Mary Ann and Margie Ganser plus Betty and Mary Weiss. They all were attending Jackson High School in Queens, New York, when they began getting together to sing songs they heard on the radio or played on their home phonographs. The time was early 1964, and all of them were 16 or 17 years old.

They won the ear of record-industry executive George Morton, who took them into a studio and made a demonstration record that gained the support of Artie Ripp of Kama Sutra Productions. Morton then worked with writers Jeff Barry and Ellie Greenwich on the arrangement for the girls' mid-1964 debut single, "Remember (Walkin' in the Sand)" on Red Bird Records. *(See Greenwich, Ellie.)* It stayed in the number one position for five consecutive weeks on some trade-press lists (though it didn't go that high in *Billboard*). It also became a hit in Europe, resulting in estimated total sales of over a million copies.

Later in the year, the girls achieved another bestseller with the Barry/Greenwich/George Morton melodramatic, motorcycle-oriented composition "Leader of the Pack" (a later success for Twisted Sister; *see Twisted Sister*). Greenwich recalled making the disc in Fred Bronson's *Billboard Book of Number One Hits:* "We even had one of the guys in the studio, an [engineer] named Joey Veneri, [bring in] his motorcycle, which we put into an echo chamber in the hall and miked it. We actually used his stepping on the gas to get the motor going."

Jeff remembered the problems in calming the young girls down enough to do the recording properly. Sixteen-year-old Mary Weiss, for instance, had mike fright. "I was sitting across the mike from her, kind of mouthing the words with her and letting her feel free to let it out emotionally. She was crying; you can hear it on the record."

The disc rose to number one on all trade lists, reaching that position in *Billboard* the week of November 28, 1964. Total worldwide sales easily topped a million. The disc became a classic played regularly on radio oldies programs throughout the '70s and '80s. The girls placed a number of other songs on the charts in the mid-1960s, though none achieved the levels of their 1964 successes. These included "Maybe" (the Chantels' 1958 hit) and "Give Him a Great Big Kiss" (late 1964–early 1965) and "Out in the Streets," "Give Us Your Blessings," and "Right Now and Not Later." The tear-jerking "I Can Never Go Home Anymore" reached number six in *Billboard* in 1965. "Long Live Our Love," "He Cried," and "Past, Present and Future" appeared in 1966.

By the end of the '60s, however, their record sales had all but disappeared. Though they had turned out several albums that sold well, the only one still in record store catalogues in the late 1960s was *The Shangri-Las Golden Hits* (Mercury, February 1967). Morton, meanwhile, went on to produce such classics as teenaged Janis Ian's "Society's Child" and Vanilla Fudge's "You Keep Me Hanging On."

Growing interest in earlier groups brought about by the pop and rock revival shows in the early 1970s brought opportunities for the act to gain considerable concert exposure, though never to the point that their recording career gained new life. For many of the shows in the '70s, the group appeared as a trio because one or another member wouldn't take part for various personal reasons. In the 1980s, a trio format could not be avoided since Marge Ganser had died of a drug overdose.

In the late 1980s, their tracks were available on *Leader of the Pack, Shangri-Las—65!*, and *Teen Anguish Vol. 2—Their Greatest Hits* on England's Charly label.

SHANNON, DEL: *Singer, guitarist, songwriter, record producer. Born Coopersville, Michigan, December 30, 1939.*

A major name in pop music in the early 1960s, Del Shannon was out of the spotlight a decade later. However, he was still an important force in the music field, with his name showing up as producer on many hits of the early '70s. He remained a star in the U.K. in later years and became active again as a U.S. recording artist in the 1980s.

Shannon's childhood in Michigan was not very different from the average American boy's of the 1940s and '50s. Born Charles Westover, he did not become deeply interested in music until his early teens. At 14, he started to learn guitar and soon was performing in school shows. After graduating from high school, he took up entertaining as a career, singing and playing guitar at dances and small clubs in the Grand Rapids area. Though he picked up work here and there, there were long dry spells when he had nothing to do but stay home and rehearse.

In the early 1960s, one of his performances was monitored by a disc jockey from local station WHRV. The d.j. liked Del's style and arranged for an audition in Detroit with Bigtop Records. Company executives followed with New York recording sessions with Del singing mostly original compositions. The result was the gold single "Runaway," which Shannon co-wrote with Max Crook (number one in *Billboard* for four weeks starting April 24, 1961). Del followed with other hits in the next few years, including "Hats Off to Larry" and "Little Town Flirt" on Bigtop and "Keep Searchin'" on Amy.

In the mid-1960s, he was signed by Liberty Records, which issued albums including *The Further Adventures of Charles Westover* and, in 1966, *My Bag* and *Total Commitment*. In November 1967, Dot Records released *The Best of Del Shannon*. In the late 1960s, Shannon signed with Dunhill Records and made several records without making any mark on the mass audience.

By the early 1970s, Shannon had switched most of his attention to the production area as head of his own independent company. His first ventures into the production area came in the late 1960s when he set up an organization with Brian Hyland. (Hyland also had been a teen favorite in the early 1960s, scoring a million-seller in 1960 with his novelty single "Itsy Bitsy Teenie Weenie Yellow Polka Dot Bikini" on Leader Records.)

Still, he didn't give up live performances or recordings completely. He was particularly popular with British audiences, who welcomed him back with enthusiasm during 1970s tours. Among his albums were the retrospective *Tenth Anniversary Album* (Sunbeam, 1971), *Del Shannon Live in England* (United Artists, 1973), and *The Vintage Years* (Sire, 1975).

At the start of the 1980s, Shannon, on the advice of friends, got together with rising rock star Tom Petty to work on a comeback album. To their surprise, he expressed doubts about it, noting he didn't know about Petty's credentials. He told a reporter: "I'd heard of Tom Petty; I just hadn't heard him. When I wasn't hot, I avoided anyone who was hot."

Once he'd heard Petty in concert, he agreed it would be great to have Petty serve as producer and sometime session man. The result was the 1981 Elektra release *Drop Down and Get Me*. A single from the album, a remake of Phil Phillips' 1958 "Sea of Love," provided Del with his first hit in 16 years. His concert series in support of the album proved an eye-opener for critics and fans alike across the U.S. Shannon looked and sounded in top form. His falsetto vocals still packed the punch they had provided in the 1960s and audiences typically shouted for one encore after another. His program included his major '60s hits that he wrote plus "I Go to Pieces" (the 1965 hit he wrote for Peter and Gordon), his version of the Beatles' "From Me to You" (a hit for him in 1963), and various new songs, some from the album and others, like the impressive "Cheap Love," not yet recorded.

During the rest of the 1980s, Shannon remained active as a performer, without giving up his various behind-the-scenes operations. In 1984, he signed a contract with Warner Brothers, going to Nashville, Tennessee to record the tracks for his debut on that label. Meanwhile, his bygone classics reappeared on Rhino Records' *Runaway Hits. (See Peter and Gordon; Petty, Tom.)*

SHIRELLES, THE: *Vocal group, all born New Jersey, c. late 1930s. Original members: Addie Harris, born June 22, died Atlanta, Georgia, June 10, 1982; Shirley Owens, born January 10; Doris Kenner, born August 2; Beverly Lee, born August 3. Owens left the group in 1975.*

One of the best female singing groups in the early days of rock, the Shirelles were stars from 1958 to 1963. Their career also led to the founding of Scepter Records, a firm that had an impact on the careers of a number of major pop artists of the '60s, including Dionne Warwick and B.J. Thomas.

The four members of the group grew up in New Jersey, attended high school together in the city of Passaic, and sang together in school shows and at parties. Deciding to expand their horizons, they entered a talent show in late 1957 and made such an impression on music-industry people present that they soon gained a contract from Decca Records. In 1958, they gained their first hit single, "I Met Him on Sunday."

Their manager, Florence Greenberg (mother of one of their schoolmates), was not overly happy with the financial returns from the group's Decca ties. When their contract was up in 1960, she started Scepter Records with the Shirelles as the first artists. The move paid off almost immediately with two best-selling singles: "Dedicated to the One I Love" (a previous hit for the Five Royales and later hit for the Mamas and the Papas) and "Tonight's the Night." Both gained the top of the hit charts in the U.S. and England for combined U.S. and foreign sales of well over a million copies each.

In 1961, the young songwriting team of Carole King and Gerry Goffin wrote a hit song for the Shirelles, "Will You Love Me Tomorrow." *(See King, Carole.)* This too went over the million mark in combined worldwide sales. The King-Goffin team provided the girls with a number of other hits, although none hit the levels of "Will You Love Me Tomorrow." In 1962, the Shirelles had their all time best-selling single, the gold "Soldier Boy."

The Shirelles were represented by several albums on Scepter in the mid-1960s: *Tonight's the Night, Baby, It's You, Greatest Hits Volume 1,* and *Greatest Hits Volume 2.* But the group only was able to add one more *Billboard* top 10 single to its credits in the mid-1960s: "Foolish Little Girl" in 1963. After the girls brought a lawsuit against Scepter for trust-fund money due them when they reached age 21, their recording efforts were curtailed for a while. Settlement of the suit in 1967 led to recording of some new material for Scepter, but no new hits resulted.

In 1968, Doris retired from the Shirelles for a while and the group continued as a trio known as Shirley and the Shirelles. The trio recorded first for Bell Records and then RCA, but again failed to click with record buyers. Meanwhile, they were featured in some of Richard Nader's Rock'n'Roll Revival Shows.

Shirley left the group in 1975, initially billing herself as Shirley of the Shirelles. Under terms of a 1961 contract signed by all the women, no member was to have individual rights to the group name. After legal action, Shirley changed that to the description "former lead singer of the Shirelles."

After Shirley's departure, Doris (by then Mrs. Doris Jackson) agreed to return and the reformed trio remained active on the concert circuit into the early 1980s. While the trio was in Atlanta, Georgia, for a concert in June 1982, Addie "Micki" Harris suffered a severe heart attack that took her life. With that loss, it was acknowledged that the group's brightest days were long behind it.

Among albums available in the 1970s or 1980s were the United Artists package *The Very Best of the Shirelles* (a British import), *The Shirelles Sing Their Very Best;* on Springboard, *The Shirelles* (Everest, 1981), and Rhino's two-disc *Anthology (1959–1967).*

SIMON AND GARFUNKEL: *Vocal and instrumental duo. Paul Simon, born Newark, New Jersey, November 5, 1942; Art Garfunkel, born Queens, New York, October 13, 1942.*

Simon and Garfunkel were sometimes described as urban folk singers, folk-rock artists, or soft-rock musicians. Their music, of course, was closer to folk than rock, but whatever its style, it reflected one main color—gold—the color of an almost unbroken series of phenomenally successful recordings.

Considering their relatively meager output compared to other pop stars', their total sales of singles and records by the time they broke up in the early '70s came to a surprising 20 million plus. Painstaking craftsmen, both often polished and repolished their material for months before presenting a new song, usually an original composition by Simon. (Garfunkel contributed to some songs, but almost all the duo's material, both words and music, was written by Simon.) Thus, they rarely recorded more than one album in a single year. Their only singles release in 1969, for example, was "The Boxer," a song included in their sole LP of 1970, *Bridge over Troubled Water.*

During their 1960s heyday, the duo could have reaped considerably higher income from even a small increase in concert dates. However, they kept their in-person appearances to a relative minimum while Garfunkel pursued graduate school studies.

When they did give a concert, it was certain to be a sellout within hours after tickets went on sale.

In a way, popular music can be thankful for any of the fruits of their labors, because they came very close to breaking up after high school because of an apparent lack of success.

The two were friends from childhood, having first met as cast members of a sixth-grade presentation of *Alice in Wonderland* at Public School 164 in Forest Hills, Queens. Art appeared as the Cheshire Cat while Paul acted the part of White Rabbit. As their friendship flourished, a mutual interest in pop music led to their collaboration on their first song, "The Girl for Me," in 1955. Two years later, they had a song on the hit charts, "Hey Schoolgirl" on the Big Records label. Then calling themselves Tom and Jerry, the duo appeared in 1957 on Dick Clark's "American Bandstand." However, after the next two singles went nowhere, the boys went to college, doing some music-business efforts on their own during the early '60s while spending most of their time hitting the books.

Both boys favored pseudonyms. Under the name Art Garr, Garfunkel recorded some material for Warwick Records. Paul's efforts included recording the 1962 single "Motorcycle" as leader of Tico and the Triumphs and, in 1963, the single "The Lone Teen Ranger" as Jerry Landis. He also used the name Landis for the writing credit on the song "Red Rubber Ball," a hit for the Cyrkle in 1966. As Paul Kane, he also wrote and recorded the song "Carlos Dominguez."

But Art and Paul kept in touch and in 1964 they reformed their partnership, working up some new demo material while performing in coffeehouses in the Greenwich Village folk-music circuit. One of the demos won the duo a contract from Columbia Records. The sessions for their label debut, *Wednesday Morning, 3 A.M.*, brought Simon back from England, where he had moved for a while in 1964. When the album failed to catch fire, Paul went back to England while Art decided to continue graduate school at Columbia University. However, a Boston radio station's decision to give considerable airplay to one of the LP's tracks, "The Sounds of Silence," caused Columbia executives to add some electric instrumentation and issue the song as a single in late 1965. The week of January 1, 1966, it rose to number one in *Billboard* and other trade-press charts.

Simon, still in England, had completed a solo LP, *The Paul Simon Songbook*, and was finding work as a record producer when he was informed of his sudden success back home. He soon returned to the U.S. to work with Garfunkel in earnest on the concert and recording fronts. Before the year was out, they had two more top 10 singles ("Homeward Bound" and "I Am a Rock"), while "Sounds of Silence" went on to become the second best-selling single of 1966, eventually achieving worldwide totals of over 2 million copies. From then on, just about every single they released made the top 30 or better, including "The Dangling Conversation," "A Hazy Shade of Winter," "At the Zoo," and "Fakin' It." In 1968, the duo had its best-selling single ever with "Mrs. Robinson," the theme song for one of the most popular films of the year, *The Graduate*. "Mrs. Robinson" rose to number one in *Billboard* for two weeks starting June 1, 1968, and won the team two Grammy Awards: Record of the Year and Best Contemporary-Pop Performance, Vocal, Duo, or Group.

Simon and Garfunkel fared even better wth albums than with singles. They were awarded gold records by the RIAA for at least one LP every year from 1967 through 1970: *Parsley, Sage, Rosemary and Thyme* and *Sounds of Silence* (1967), *Bookends* (1968), *Wednesday Morning 3 A.M.* (1969), and *Bridge over Troubled Water* (1970). *Bridge over Troubled Water* was one of the most acclaimed records of 1970, winning five Grammy Awards as well as many other honors at home and abroad.

At the start of the 1970s, Simon and Garfunkel appeared increasingly to have divergent career objectives. Garfunkel had become very much interested in acting and was featured in a number of major films, including a critically hailed performance in the 1971 hit *Carnal Knowledge*. Simon wanted to expand his writing opportunities. After the breakup was announced, Simon began work on his platinum debut solo album on Columbia, *Paul Simon* (January 1972). Later in the year, Columbia issued the platinum retrospective *Simon and Garfunkel's Greatest Hits*.

The two artists had little to do with one another for a decade (except for an appearance on NBC's *Saturday Night Live*), but finally mended fences and were welcomed back as a team by a half-million excited fans at a free concert in New York's Central Park during the summer of 1981. The show was taped for later TV coverage and Warner Brothers released the platinum album *The Concert in Central Park* in 1982. The duo went on to perform before throngs of people at home and abroad during 1982–83 and even indicated they would collaborate on a new album. But after Simon decided that the LP—which had started as a solo project—should return to solo status, the two completed concert commitments and went separate ways again. *(See Garfunkel, Art; Simon, Paul.)*

SIMON, PAUL: *Singer, songwriter, guitarist, actor, record producer. Born Newark, New Jersey, November 5, 1942.*

The team of Simon and Garfunkel indisputably was one of the premier acts of the 1960s. Despite the fact that the group's songs primarily were in what might be called a contemporary folk vein with any rock touches essentially secondary, the team vied with the best of the rock bands for mass-audience attention and respect. Thus, it was not surprising that there were many cries of alarm when the team broke up soon after its wondrously fine song and album, *Bridge over Troubled Water,* came out in 1970. Fortunately, both Simon and Garfunkel proved as capable of sustaining individual careers as in working in harness.

There were some harsh words said when the split occurred, particularly by Simon who indicated in a *Rolling Stone* interview that one reason he hastened the event was the feeling that he was the main creative force in the partnership. Another contributing factor, though, was Garfunkel's increasing desire to further his acting activities. But perhaps the primary reason was simply that the two had been together too long, having formed their initial association as teenagers in Long Island. As Tom and Jerry, they had their first taste of success in 1957 with the minor rock hit "Hey Schoolgirl." After an interval, they came back in the 1960s to place hit after hit on U.S. and international pop lists.

It's not surprising that all the pressures involved finally caused a coolness between the two friends. By 1973, though, with his solo career well established, Simon could take a more well rounded view of the matter. He told Robert Hilburn of the *Los Angeles Times* (May 27, 1973): "Some people thought it was unnecessary to say some of those things. But that's how I felt. I do think there is no question that I was angry when I said that, but I don't think I exaggerated too much.

"What I didn't do that I should have done was to say how good Artie is. I said what I thought he didn't do, but I didn't say, for instance: 'Here's a guy who had one of the finest voices in popular music, who has a very intelligent mind, who was enthusiastic about his work . . . and who offered very useful ideas.' I didn't emphasize his legitimate strengths.

"I wasn't feeling very friendly toward him [then]. The anger was a reflection of the tensions we had gone through during the making of *Bridge.* We both said: 'This is ridiculous. If it is this hard to make an album, this should be the last album.' It was very tense."

That album, of course, and its title song, were the main stories of the 1970 Grammy Awards, but soon after, the word came out that the duo was going separate ways. There were both excited anticipation and worries as Paul prepared his solo debut on Colum-

bia. But fears quickly were put to rest when *Paul Simon* came out in February 1972. The album was one of the year's finest with Paul reaffirming his skill as one of the great lyricists and melodists of his era. The LP easily earned a platinum record and provided several singles hits including the enigmatic "Me and Julio down by the Schoolyard," which made the top 10 on some trade press lists.

His next album, *There Goes Rhymin' Simon* (spring 1973), proved even better, providing a series of memorable songs including the gospel-rock "Loves Me Like a Rock," "Was a Sunny Day," and the unusual "Take Me to the Mardi Gras," which blended Dixieland and reggae. The album's themes ranged from a relaxed evaluation of memory's tricks when it comes to romance ("Kodachrome") to a solemn assessment of the U.S. in the early '70s ("American Tune"). His lyrics, as always, verged on the poetic. "Kodachrome" started: "If you took all the girls I knew/When I was single/And brought them all together/For one night/I know they'd never match/My sweet imagination/Everything looks worse/In black and white." "American Tune" said: "We came on the ship/They call the Mayflower/We come on the ship that sailed the moon/We come in the age's most uncertain hour/And sing an American tune."

In the spring of 1973, Paul made his first concert tour of the U.S. since his rift with Garfunkel. He felt he couldn't fill huge auditoriums on his own, so he stuck to smaller venues of 3,000–5,000 seats or less. It was a case of too much humility. Tickets were snapped up almost as soon as they went on sale and there probably were enough disappointed fans to fill any hall Simon and Garfunkel had played in years past. One product of the tour was the gold live album *Live Rhymin'.*

Because of Paul's perfectionist attitude about his work, there was almost a two-year wait before fans could buy a new studio LP. When it arrived in the fall of 1975, it proved another gem. *Still Crazy after All These Years* offered a letter-perfect collection of Simon songs, including such hits as the title track and the equally potent "50 Ways to Leave Your Lover." The gold LP reached number one in *Billboard* for three weeks starting February 7, 1976.

It also gained Simon two Grammies: Album of the Year and Best Pop Vocal Performance, Male. In accepting one of them in person, Paul joked about the fact that the main reason he won was the absence of new releases from Stevie Wonder, saying, "I want to thank Stevie Wonder for not having a new album out this year."

With those two victories, he could point to a total of nine Grammies won over his career, the others going back to his days with Garfunkel. Of that total, five were for various aspects of *Bridge over Troubled Water* (1970) and two were for the 1968 single "Mrs. Robinson."

As Simon had noted earlier to Robert Hilburn, he sometimes was plagued with self-doubts about his ability to create viable new material. "I'm neurotically driven. It has always been that way. What happens is I finish one thing and start to take a vacation. I lay off for a while and then I get panicky. . . . I say to myself: 'Oh my God, I'm not doing anything. I can't write anymore. It's over.' All that kind of thing. . . . Then I laugh and tell myself: 'Don't be silly. This is exactly what happens every time you finish an album. So, of course, you write again.'

"And so I continue to take it easy for a while. I don't write for a while longer and then I say: 'Hey, this is no kidding. You're really not writing now.' And somewhere along the line, I really believe I'm not going to write again and I get panicky and start to write. I don't want to think that I peaked in my twenties. There is so much more time ahead."

In the late '70s, disputes arose between Simon and Columbia Records that caused a long delay in the next phase of his career. After a long legal wrangle, Simon ended his association with Columbia and, in 1979, signed with Warner Brothers. In the interim, Columbia had issued a retrospective album of his '70s solo work, *Greatest Hits, Etc.*

His Warner Brothers album debut in 1980 was the soundtrack from *One-Trick Pony*, a film Simon scored as well as starred in. The record was far more successful than the film. A single from the gold LP, "Late in the Evening," provided Paul with a top 10 hit.

In 1981, Paul reunited with Art Garfunkel for a free summer concert in New York's Central Park that drew an estimated 500,000 fans. This inspired them to schedule a series of shows overseas (not for free) that also were dramatic successes. The concerts drew some 130,000 people in Paris, France, and 75,000 each in London, Tokyo, and Sidney, Australia. In early 1982, a concert film of the Central Park engagement was telecast on the pay-TV Home Box Office cable operation.

All of that made the team agree to a wide-ranging U.S. tour in 1983 in places such as Dodger Stadium in Los Angeles and Jack Murphy Stadium in San Diego that could accommodate crowds of tens of thousands. They also announced they would work together on a new album, tentatively titled *Think Too Much*, which Paul originally had started as a solo project. Later, however, Paul decided to eliminate new Garfunkel material and return to the solo concept. A spokesperson for Warner Brothers said: "Paul simply felt the material he wrote is so close to his own life that it had to be his own. Art was hoping to be on the album, but I'm sure there will be other projects that they will work on together. They are still friends."

When the revised LP, now called *Hearts and Bones*, came out in October 1983, the duo was completing concert commitments in Europe that followed the U.S. appearances. The album was in the top 40 by year end, but didn't go gold. Among Simon's other high points of 1983 was his much-publicized marriage to actress Carrie Fisher of *Star Wars* fame.

Paul's next major project was the album *Graceland*, recorded with many black music stars of apartheid-torn South Africa. The album proved one of Paul's most impressive projects. The blend of his songwriting skills with strains of such South African musicians as the a cappela Zulu male choir and Ladysmith Black Mambazo had both a creative and social impact on listeners. When the platinum LP first came out in 1986, Simon was criticized widely for violating the anti-apartheid boycott of South Africa by recording there, but he claimed he was helping blacks and coloreds there through the attention *Graceland* brought them. It also demonstrated the tremendous talent to be tapped among the oppressed black majority in South Africa while providing spine-tingling American-African rhythms. It was named Album of the Year in the 1986 Grammy voting. During 1986, Simon and many black performers struck a symbolic blow against apartheid with a concert in Zimbabwe, Africa, that drew a massive, integrated audience of black and white fans, including many whites who crossed into Zimbabwe from South Africa to attend the show.

The title track from *Graceland* (which referred to Elvis Presley's Memphis mansion) was voted the Record of the Year in the 1987 Grammy poll. One of the high points of the Grammy Awards telecast in March 1988 was an appearance by the Ladysmith Black Mambazo group, which won the Best Traditional Folk Recording Grammy for its version of "Shaka Zulu." *(See Garfunkel, Art; Simon and Garfunkel; Snow, Phoebe.)*

SIMPLE MINDS: *Vocal and instrumental group from Scotland. Members (mid-1980s): Jim Kerr, Charles Burchill, Michael MacNeil, Mel Gaynor, John Giblin.*

Rock'n'roll's detractors often pointed to certain groups that appeared to promote promiscuity, violence, drugs, and even demonism. Such analyses always conveniently overlooked the many positive contributions of rock artists that included outspoken support for world peace and elimination of dangerous pollution from the environment, and, increasingly in the mid-1980s, benefit concerts to fight hunger in Africa and the U.S., attract funds to help debt-ridden American farmers, and support efforts by Amnesty International to free political and other unjustly held prisoners around the world. Among the international rock groups that took part in many of those efforts was Scotland's Simple Minds.

The founding members of the group, which included lead singer Jim Kerr, became active in England's rock scene in the mid-1970s when punk and avant garde groups held center stage. Though the members came from working class, relatively depressed environments, they didn't reflect the pessimism of the Sex Pistols in their music, though they didn't avoid taking note of negative aspects of U.K. life for unemployed or underemployed youth of the period. The band seemed to take its early cue from the electronically based rhythms of artists such as Roxy Music and Brian Eno. Indeed, Kerr's vocal style had echoes of Roxy Music's lead singer, Bryan Ferry.

The band started to build a U.K. following in the late 1970s, which helped it win a contract from British-based Zoom Records. Its initial albums on that label—the debut *Life in a Day* (1978), *Real to Real Cacophony* (1979), and *Empires and Dance*—found favor with record buyers first in the U.K. and, more and more in the early 1980s, with Continental European fans. The group added to its following in the late 1970s and early 1980s by opening for well-known performers, including Genesis alumnus Peter Gabriel. A number of appearances with Gabriel were made in 1981 when Simple Minds albums came out on new labels—*Themes for Great Cities* on Stiff Records and a limited-edition double album, *Sons and Fascination/Sister Feelings Call* on Virgin (later issued as separate albums). With Virgin, the band had a number of singles that made U.K. charts, such as the late 1983 top 20 "Waterfront."

None of those U.K. releases were directly issued in the U.S. at the time, but were brought in as British imports. As usually happens under those conditions, the band, while establishing itself with English and Continental fans, was largely unknown in the States. To help remedy that, the group's manager sought a U.S. record-company affiliation, signing in 1982 with A&M. The group's first two releases on A&M—*New Gold Dream* (1982) and *Sparkle in the Rain* (1983)—did somewhat better with the U.S. audience though they still weren't major chart hits.

Meanwhile, Kerr gained some headlines on a purely personal level when he married rock vocalist Chrissie Hynde in 1984. Their first child, a girl, was born in April 1985. Hynde, lead singer of the Pretenders, previously had a daughter by Ray Davies of the Kinks rock group. *(See Hynde, Chrissie.)*

For the third LP planned for U.S. release on A&M, the band decided to come to the U.S. for recording sessions, shifting production responsibility from U.K.'s Steve Lillywhite to the U.S. team of Jimmy Iovine and Bob Clearmountain. The group, previously a quartet, expanded to a five-member band by the time work started on the new project in early 1985. The quintet was composed of Kerr on lead vocals, Charles Burchill on lead guitar, Michael "Mick" MacNeil on keyboards, Mel Gaynor on drums, and new member John Giblin on bass guitar. Giblin had become friends with the others when Simple Minds opened for Peter Gabriel at a time when Giblin was in Gabriel's backing band.

Kerr stressed that while all the members were from Scotland: "Simple Minds have always considered themselves an international band willing to consider creative advantages in other parts of the world." He and the others, he said, began noticing "the vibrancy of American recordings versus British and the others you hear on British radio. I think that's what sparked us to look for American producers. Of course, Jimmy Iovine and Bob Clearmountain are two of the best America has to offer."

He noted that Iovine had changed the way band members approached songwriting, an effect he credited them with sharpening the structure of songs for the new LP. "Before now, we generally wrote songs from the standpoint of melody first, lyrics later. Charlie and Mick would go into the studio and jam until they came up with a melody, I'd absorb the feel and write the words later. This time, I considered the whole style and makeup of the song from the beginning. That resulted in more formal song structures and tighter, more tangible arrangements instead of our usual atmospheric approach. I think 'Alive and Kicking' and 'Oh Jungleland' [from the 1985 album] are especially good examples of that."

Ironically, before the new U.S.-recorded album came out, the band had its first big U.S. top 10 hit: "Don't You (Forget about Me)," a song written by others (Keith Forsey and Steve Schiff) for the soundtrack of the highly successful movie *The Breakfast Club.* Kerr and his associates later called it an "inane" song.

But that was all part of a year in which everything seemed to come together for the band. The group became increasingly popular in the U.S., helped by headline appearances in major U.S. cities and considerable praise for its support for humanist causes. The Simple Minds band took part in the massive July 1985 Live Aid concert/TV project organized by Bob Geldof to help starving Africans. Being committed to recording and concert work in the States, the quintet took part in the Philadelphia part of the show rather than the U.K. segment.

Simple Minds' U.S. presence did not go without

sharp adverse comments from the British music press. Kerr insisted the group hadn't "sold out." He told Chris Willman for a *Los Angeles Times* interview (April 13, 1986): "That doesn't hold up, that 'American album' stink. It's absolutely ridiculous. So you make a record with Americans because you happen to think that the best engineer in the world is American. That doesn't mean that you've made a sort of American concept album. It is a much more international album. The songs on there are actually inspired by a couple of Lebanese friends of ours.

"You can sit and debate until the cows come home about which album had the best melodies and which had the most sensitivity and which had the best atmosphere, but this is our best balanced album, I think."

The album, *Once Upon a Time* (October 1985), certainly had the right balance for U.S. fans, going gold and moving into the top 10 in the spring of 1986. Its single "Alive and Kicking" was number three on U.S. charts at year-end. The album did not avoid difficult topics, including songs such as "Oh Jungleland" and "Ghost Dancing" that dealt with the troubles in Ireland and warned of the growing bitterness and frustration among large numbers of young people in Glasgow, Scotland. But its songs, while bearing witness to world problems, also sought to energize listeners to take steps against those ills.

It was, Kerr said, part of a continuing commitment to the ideals underlining musical projects such as Live Aid and the anti-apartheid *Sun City* release. He told Willman: "I think it's interesting to see how many people walk on and do Live Aid and nothing else—the token gesture of conscientiousness. For the past few years, especially on the last album, Simple Minds has been connected through our songs with ideals—maybe they're naive ones—of love, peace, and freedom. And how long can you just go on singing about it and not really taking it that next step up."

The next step, for the band, was to continue support for worthy causes on a regular basis. Thus, the proceeds of a number of 1986 Simple Minds concerts were donated to Amnesty International. That June, the band joined with such other artists as U2, Sting, and the Police in a series of special U.S. shows for the Amnesty organization.

He told Willman he saw such efforts, as well as the songs and actions of American stars such as Bruce Springsteen, as major breakthroughs for rock and humankind. "See, I love the idea of rock music in the pure sense as a communication, as in passing on, as in learning, as in folk music. We're so used to the way it's been sold and caricatured as trivia—and

it's right to trivialize it—but thinking people seem to be doing well now."

Public acceptance of Springsteen's efforts, he said, proved that the adage "good guys finish last" didn't have to be true. "All these Halloween bands in their whole heavy-metal, 'Rocky Horror' pantomime thing are a total farce. I don't believe that rock'n'roll's the devil's music."

In 1987, the group had another album on the charts, *Live in the City of Light* (2 LPs, A&M). In June 1988, the band continued its fight for good causes by taking part in the London Freedomfest concert (telecast worldwide) in honor of the seventieth birthday of the imprisoned South African black leader Nelson Mandela.

SINATRA, FRANK: *Singer, actor, record-company executive. Born Hoboken, New Jersey, December 12, 1915.*

In 1942, Tommy Dorsey and his orchestra played a record-shattering engagement at New York's Paramount Theatre. Eager crowds, largely made up of high school students, stood patiently in block-long lines waiting to get in. The Dorsey organization was a major attraction in those days of the big band, but the audiences came to see its young, lean vocalist, Frank Sinatra. When Sinatra (a band member since the start of the decade) would start a song, girls sighed in unison and some swooned in the aisles (though some of the swooners reportedly were publicity plants). The sighing and swooning (which anticipated the wild screams that later met Elvis and early Beatles concerts) were fads that lasted only a short time, but Sinatra went on to become one of the greatest all-around entertainers in show business, still a legendary performer 4½ decades later.

Frank was an only child. His father, Anthony Sinatra, was a fireman in Hoboken, New Jersey. His mother, Dolly, often sang at social functions. At A.J. Demarest High School in Hoboken, Frank helped organize the glee club and sang with the band. In 1933, he got a job on a delivery truck of the *New Jersey Observer*. He moved up to work as a copy boy, then as a cub sports writer. One evening in 1936, he took his fiancée, Nancy Barbato, to hear Bing Crosby sing in Jersey City. The concert inspired him to quit the paper and try for a singing career.

He started vocalizing with local bands. Then, with three instrumentalists, he formed the Hoboken Four, which won first prize on "The Major Bowes Original Amateur Hour" in 1937. By 1939, he was singing on 18 radio shows a week in New York and Hoboken, but for no pay. The owner of the Rustic Cabin night spot in Teaneck, New Jersey, heard a show and hired Frank as singer and head waiter at

$15 per week. Band leader Harry James heard Sinatra there and signed him to a two-year contract at $75 a week. Soon after, Tommy Dorsey was driving from one engagement to another in the Midwest. Turning on the radio, he heard a James record and was so impressed with the vocalist—Sinatra—that he determined to try to sign him. Later, a reluctant James let Sinatra out of his contract and Frank signed with Dorsey at the then princely sum of $250 per week.

With Dorsey, Frank made many hit records. One of the earliest, "I'll Never Smile Again," showed up as the number one song on the first industry chart published in *Billboard* the week of July 20, 1940. Other best-sellers with Dorsey included "Oh Look at Me Now," "Violets for Your Furs," "Night and Day," and "This Love of Mine." He also developed his special vocal delivery by analyzing Dorsey's trombone phrasing. In late 1943, Sinatra left Dorsey to go out on his own. From 1943 to 1945, he was a regular on the top-ranked radio program "The Hit Parade." In 1943, he appeared in *Higher and Higher,* the first of a long series of film projects. Others during the decade were *Anchors Aweigh* (1945), *Till the Clouds Roll By* (1947), and, in 1949, *The Kissing Bandit* and *On the Town.* Through the rest of the '40s and for three decades thereafter, his great array of recordings sold millions of copies.

The one exception was the early 1950s when several factors (including physical problems and romantic entanglements) combined to force his popularity to a low ebb. His record sales fell off, offers of movie roles stopped, and his throat began hemorrhaging. Frank fought his way back the hard way by taking a screen test for the dramatic role of Maggio in the 1953 blockbuster movie *From Here to Eternity.* To get the role, he agreed to work for a minimum salary. The performance won him an Academy Award. That achievement, plus renewed confidence (buoyed by restored vocal health) was the turning point for a string of successes in many areas of entertainment that led to his becoming one of the most powerful and wealthiest performers in the world.

He put on the highly successful "Frank Sinatra Show" on ABC-TV during 1957–58. In later years, he made more specials and also guested on other artists' shows. Major record hits of the late '50s and early '60s included "Learnin' the Blues," "Love and Marriage," "Hey! Jealous Lover," "All the Way," and "Witchcraft" on Capitol and "Pocketful of Miracles" on Reprise. He continued to add to his screen credits with such vehicles (many produced by him) as *The Man with the Golden Arm* and *The Tender Trap* (1955), *Johnny Concho* and *High Society* (1956), *The Joker Is Wild* and *The Pride and the Passion* (1957), *Can Can* and *Oceans 11* (1960), and *Come Blow Your Horn* (1962).

Throughout the middle and late 1960s, despite the dominance of rock, Sinatra held his own as entertainer and recording artist. He made the charts with many releases, particularly albums. His gold LPs on Reprise (the company he helped found) included *Sinatra's Sinatra* in 1963; *September of My Years* in 1965; *Strangers in the Night, A Man and His Music,* and *Sinatra at the Sands* in 1966; *That's Life* in 1967; and *Cycles* and *My Way* in 1969. Hit singles in the second half of the '60s included "Strangers in the Night" (number one in *Billboard* the week of July 2, 1966), "Something Stupid" (a duet with his daughter Nancy that made number one for four weeks starting April 15, 1967) and "Cycles" in 1969.

For five years, starting in 1965, Sinatra did an annual one-hour TV special. Basically one-man shows in which Frank offered his versions of old and new songs and ribbed his own career, they won high marks from almost all TV reviewers. Commenting on Frank's 1969 offering titled "Sinatra," *Los Angeles Times* critic Cecil Smith wrote: "The Face is eroded by the years . . . and there's sometimes a rasp and a scratch in the voice, but no one sells a song like Francis Albert Sinatra and tonight's one-man special . . . is proof positive."

Apart from Las Vegas engagements, Sinatra kept his personal appearances in the late '60s and early '70s to a minimum, apart from occasional charity shows. In early 1971, he announced his retirement from show business. A special farewell tribute was arranged for him, featuring many of the biggest names in show business, for presentation during the summer at the Los Angeles Music Center. The proceeds of the sellout event went to charity.

Few observers thought Frank could stand the limitations of retirement indefinitely. They were right. By mid-1973, he was making plans for a comeback. In the fall, he resumed his career with a standing-room–only engagement in Las Vegas and a TV special, "Ol' Blue Eyes Is Back." The 1973 Reprise album of the same title went gold. From then on, Sinatra said no more about retirement and continued with various personal appearances and new recordings for the rest of the '70s and, except when sidelined by illness, in the 1980s.

Reprise albums included *Watertown* (1970), *Sinatra and Company* (1971), *Frank Sinatra's Greatest Hits, Volume 2* (1972), and *Some Nice Things I've Missed* and *The Main Event* (1974). None made *Billboard*'s top 40, nor did any of his singles of the '70s. But in 1980 he reached number 32 in *Billboard* with "Theme from *New York, New York,*" which provided him with a new signature song. He began the

1980s with the impressive three-disc *Trilogy: Past, Present and Future*, prepared by three different arrangers who impacted his singing stylings (Billy May, Don Costa, and Gordon Jenkins) and *She Shot Me Down* (1981). *L.A. is My Lady* (1984) aroused controversy about Sinatra's attempt to gain a more modern feeling. It was recorded for Quincy Jones' Qwest label with the Quincy Jones Orchestra providing backing instrumentals. *(See Jones, Quincy.)*

Though once known as a liberal democrat, Sinatra's stance seemed to atrophy in later years. An example was a 1981 concert appearance with Liza Minnelli at the lavish Sun City resort in the so-called "homeland" of Bophuthatswana in South Africa for which, according to news reports, both artists accepted "huge" fees. Performances by artists in Sun City were condemned by opponents of apartheid as contributing to the continuation of that oppressive system.

During the 1970s and '80s, Frank renewed his film career from time to time, though things seemed up in the air after the failure of the early 1980s movie *First Deadly Sin*. In 1983, he did agree to make a cameo appearance in the movie *Cannonball I*, which starred such long-time close friends as Sammy Davis, Jr., Shirley MacLaine, Dean Martin, and Burt Reynolds.

In late 1987, plans were unveiled for a reunion "Rat Pack" tour in 1988 by Frank, Dean Martin, and Sammy Davis, Jr. Early in the tour Martin was hospitalized and had to drop out, but the dates were completed with Liza Minnelli as Martin's replacement.

SLY AND THE FAMILY STONE: *Vocal and instrumental group. Members (late 1960s and early 1970s): Sly Stone, born Dallas, Texas, March 15, 1944; Freddie Stone, born Dallas, Texas, June 5, 1946; Cynthia Robinson, born Sacramento, California, January 12, 1946; Larry Graham, Jr., born Beaumont, Texas, August 14, 1946; Greg Errico, born San Francisco, California, September 1, 1946; Rosie Stone, born Vallejo, California, March 21, 1945; Jerry Martini, born Colorado, October 1, 1943. Graham left in early 1970s, replaced by Rusty Allen. Errico replaced by Andy Newmark. Pat Rizzo added in early 1970s. Band makeup changed widely during the rest of '70s and in the '80s, except for Sly Stone.*

The West Coast sound of acid rock provided by such groups as the Jefferson Airplane and Grateful Dead drew attention to the San Francisco Bay Area in the mid-1960s. Late in the decade, a new sound, compounded of some of the elements of that music plus a strong input of black "roots" music—hard-

driving rhythm & blues and funk—came to life in the city by the Golden Gate under the guiding hand of a dynamic individual named Sylvester Stewart, professionally known as Sly Stone. The group organized by Sly, described by writer Charles Wright as "rock's elegant gypsies," took the rock circuit by storm, stopping the show everywhere from Woodstock to the Isle of Wight at the end of the '60s and in the early '70s. Unfortunately, Sly Stone squandered his wealth—both creative and material—in later years, to a great extent due to hard drugs. Despite his many artistic achievements that profoundly influenced pop music of the 1970s and '80s, *Jet* magazine reported in 1976 that he was broke. During the 1980s, his struggles with drugs made many sad headlines.

To form what has been called "psychedelic rock'n'roll," Stone in his productive years drew on a diversified background in music going back to his first childhood appearance at age four in a gospel family group in Texas. He was joined after a few years by younger brother Freddie "Pyhotee" Stone, who, like Sly, began learning guitar from their father at an early age. Sly later also mastered keyboards playing. The Stewart family moved to the San Francisco area in the 1950s, where the children continued their deep interest in music, both gospel and popular, through high school and into college. Sly took trumpet, music theory, and composition for three years at Vallejo Junior College, while Freddie studied theory for several years at San Francisco City College.

Sly had fashioned a career for himself in the music business by the time he took up his college studies. During the mid-1960s, he had succeeded in a range of tasks—disc jockey, songwriter, record producer, and group leader. In his teens, he not only gained a position with rhythm & blues station KSOL in San Francisco, but was generally considered the top R&B commentator by the time he moved over to station KDIA. He also produced most of the recordings made on Autumn Records in those years by such artists as the Beau Brummels, the Mojo Men, and Bobby Freeman. A number of the groups featured such Stone compositions as "Mojo Man" and "The Swim."

In early 1966, Sly formed his own group, the Stoners, which included a talented female trumpet player, Cynthia "Ecco" Robinson, who had learned music from her mother, a concert pianist, and who later took up bass and saxophone as a member of the Sacramento High School marching band. Sly, who also attended Sacramento High for a while, was impressed with Cynthia's work and later asked her to join his new group. Sly dissolved the Stoners in the fall of 1966 because he didn't like its sound, but he retained Cynthia when he organized his new band in early 1967.

Sly's new aggregation included future solo star Larry Graham on bass, Jerry Martini on sax, and Greg "Hand Feet" Errico on drums.

Graham, like the Stewarts, was born in Texas, but grew up in California, where he graduated from Hayward High School and attended Chabot College for a year and a half. For four years before joining Stone, he performed with his mother on the night club circuit. Larry also supported many well-known artists at one time or another, including John Lee Hooker, Jimmy Reed, the Drifters, and Jackie Wilson. *(See Graham, Larry.)*

Errico and Martini were friends of Sly's who heard of his plans to form a new group in casual conversations at the radio station where Sly worked. Errico had started drums at an early age while Martini took up a range of instruments during his years at Balboa High School and as a music major at San Francisco City College. When he heard about Stone's group, Martini already had experience playing sax, accordion, piano, and clarinet with local bands.

Rosie Stone later came to the group before completing her studies at Vallejo Junior College. From her teens, though, she had performed professionally, working on shows with such stars as the Coasters, Jimmy Reed, and Bo Diddley and guesting on many TV and radio shows aired from Chicago in the mid-1960s. She brought ability as a vocalist, electric piano player, organist, and harmonica player to the Stone band.

The new act gained attention locally during 1967. Epic Records, a Columbia subsidiary, put out its debut album, *A Whole New Thing*, late in the year. The 1968 hit "Dance to the Music" served as the title song for the second LP.

Once Sly and the Family Stone made its first dent in the charts, it continued to add laurels with almost every new release. In 1969 and 1970, they had three more *Billboard* top 10 singles: "Hot Fun in the Summertime" and the gold "Everyday People" and "Thank You (Falettinme Be Mice Elf Agin)." "I Want to Take You Higher" became an anthem for young people. Two platinum albums demonstrated great staying power on the charts. *Stand*, issued in early 1969, was still on the charts over 80 weeks later in 1970. *Sly and the Family Stone's Greatest Hits* (fall 1970) was still in the top 100 in mid-1971.

The 1971 single "Family Affair" won a gold record, as did the powerful (and bitter) Epic album *There's a Riot Goin' On*. It was followed by such Epic LPs as *Fresh* (1973, gold), *Small Talk* (1974, gold), *High on You* (1975), and *Hear Ya Missed Me, Well I'm Back* (1976).

Going into the mid-1970s, the band continued to command a large following, although the pressures of stardom seemed to affect Sly. He became increasingly unpredictable, often showing up late for concerts and, in some cases, failing to appear at all. Behind the scenes, his friends were aware that much of the problem related to drug dependency. The group's record output was not as great as in the past, although it had charted singles "Runnin' Away" and "Smilin'" in 1972 and "Frisky" and the gold "If You Want Me to Stay" in 1973.

The band roster continued to change. In the early 1970s, Larry Graham left to form Graham Central Station. He was replaced on bass by Rusty Allen. Andy Newmark took over from Greg Errico on drums and Pat Rizzo was added on saxophone. However, Sly Stone's personal difficulties made it increasingly hard for him to keep a regular group together. For a time after 1976, he was essentially out of the music business.

After a few years, Sly pulled himself together to try to revive his career. He signed a contract with Warner Brothers, resulting in the October 1979 album *Back on the Right Track*. For that project, he reassembled as many of the original band members as possible. He noted: "Of course, I've always used my brothers and sisters, that's never changed." He also maintained that this first recording work in three years "has the authenticity that comes from clear thought, musical ability, and family Stone cooperation." (Meanwhile, Epic put out the 1979 album *Ten Years Too Soon,* overdubbing new instrumental tracks on some of Stone's old tapes. Epic also released the retrospective LP *Anthology* in 1981.)

However, Stone's attempts to put his career in shape again foundered in the 1980s on his old addiction problems. Things seemed to be looking up in 1982 when Sly and his band started a nationwide tour, but not long afterward he checked into the Lee Health Center in Fort Myers, Florida, for a drug-rehabilitation program. As part of his treatment, as announced in May 1984, he was allowed to make some special appearances on a nationwide tour of Bobby Womack's. *(See Womack, Bobby.)* But his efforts to shake his habit didn't work and in the later 1980s he was picked up by police in several states for drug possession. In April 1987, news stories reported that Stone, after having spent two months in jail in Los Angeles for having rock cocaine, was in court fighting extradition to Florida on other drug charges. *(See Trower, Robin.)*

SMITH, PATTI: *Singer, songwriter, poet, band leader. Born Chicago, Illinois, December 31, 1946.*

"She shocked me the first time I saw her. Real old-fashioned shock, the whole bit—dropped jaw, stunned brain. . . . This 27-year-old skinny punk who hammered out dirty poetry and sang surreal folk songs. Who never smiled. Who was tough, sullen, bad, didn't give a damn. . . . [Sang] a song in praise of cocaine—the rhythm was an itch, speed itself. . . . I felt both ravaged and exhilarated." That's the effect Patti Smith had on Amy Gross of *Mademoiselle* and many other eastern rock fans in the early 1970s. For a time, it looked as though she might remain a local cult idol, but her mid-1970s releases on Arista Records brought her to the brink of worldwide stardom, a position she decided to pull back from in the early 1980s, then resumed late in the decade.

Born in Chicago, Patti grew up in southern New Jersey, the area that also could claim Bruce Springsteen as one of its own. An ungainly child, still she had a strong belief in herself, despite her blue collar family's scarcity of resources and her own lack of special physical attributes. As she told a reporter: "When I was a kid, I had an absolute swagger about the future. . . . I wasn't born to be a spectator." Her interest in rock'n'roll she said began in her preteen years when she first heard Little Richard's "The Girl Can't Help It."

Her affinity for rock continued unabated through her teens, but it was not something she considered central to her future. Through an abortive stay at Glassboro College in New Jersey, followed by a relationship with artist Robert Mapplethorpe in Brooklyn in 1967 to a sojourn in Paris in 1969, her career thoughts focused on art and poetry. But as the '70s got underway, she became enthusiastic about the idea of combining rock and poetry. Soon she joined forces with guitarist/rock writer Lenny Kaye for a series of poetry-rock presentations in St. Mark's Church-in-Bouwerie in New York City. It inspired the beginning of a cult following in New York, a process buoyed by the first publication of some of her poems in *Creem* magazine in September 1971.

Some of her rock favorites provided themes for both songs and poems. The death of Doors lead singer Jim Morrison in Paris caused nightmares in which she dreamed of him imprisoned in stone with wings of stone. Later, the feelings poured forth in the pleading "Break It Up," one of the high points of her LP *Horses.*

Career progress from her early work with Kaye was hardly spectacular. The association gradually expanded to comprise a four-man backing band with the addition of pianist Richard Sohl, guitarist Ivan Kral and, finally, drummer Jay Dee Daugherty. But in the absence of recordings, the group was largely unknown outside the New York area.

It wasn't that the members didn't try to attract attention to the growing body of original songs provided mainly by Patti. But record executives routinely said "No!" Some of that disinterest probably was due to Patti's initial impression. Never a beauty, she looked more like a member of the Rolling Stones than a purveyor of female romantic or sexual fantasies. Not that those were her prime goals, but male executives tended to want artists to fit preconceived pigeonholes. But she had an inner spirit that somehow transformed her on stage to the point that—despite her sticklike figure and odd, waiflike face—she could seem increasingly attractive, even sexy. Finally, Clive Davis's new label Arista (which he formed after leaving his post as head of Columbia Records), decided to gamble on her potential. Davis himself believed recordings of her cutting, flexible voice combined with the multilevel rhythmic offerings of the band signaled the arrival of a major new talent.

Produced by John Cale (formerly of the Velvet Underground), her 1975 debut disc, *Horses,* was not just an album, but an event, one of the most promising releases by a newcomer in the mid-1970s. Tracks such as "Break It Up," "Land," and her remake of Van Morrison's "Gloria" lingered hauntingly in the listener's memory. But her 1976 album, *Radio Ethiopia,* proved a letdown and after that, little was heard of her for the next year and a half. But she came roaring back in 1978 with another superb album, *Easter.* Among its tracks was a song she had co-written with Bruce Springsteen—"Because the Night," her first and only top 20 hit as of the mid-1980s. Backing her on the album and on the supporting concert tour were most of her former band associates (Kaye, Kral, and Daugherty) plus a new keyboards player, Bruce Brady.

On tour in support of *Easter,* Patti noted that the extended delay between *Radio Ethiopia* and *Easter* resulted from a year-long battle to overcome injuries suffered when she fell off a stage in Florida. But the time off, she told interviewers, gave her the chance to come to terms with the demands of stardom.

She told Robert Hilburn of the *Los Angeles Times* (April 2, 1978): "I've had a chance to think about myself and my music over the last year. Until now, I've always been intimidated. I've admired Jagger and Morrison and all those other rock stars so much that I never felt like I've really belonged on the stage. But I'm comfortable up there now. We just did a show in Ann Arbor and I noticed a change. I don't feel like a gawky kid looking up at legends any more. I feel equal to anyone in rock'n'roll."

Easter sold many more copies than her previous LPs and was highly praised by critics. Patti followed in 1979 with another fine album, *Wave,* that only suffered by comparison to such masterpieces as *Horses* and *Easter*.

Still, it seemed that for someone of her creative talents, the best was yet to come. But she startled the music field at the start of the 1980s by retiring from active participation in favor of domestic duties. Her growing number of adherents hoped she would come back later in the decade and realize her full musical potential. These hopes were realized in mid-1988 when Arista issued *Dream of Life. (See Springsteen, Bruce; Velvet Underground, The; Verlaine, Tom.)*

SNOW, PHOEBE: *Singer, songwriter, guitarist. Born New York, New York, July 17, 1952.*

A gifted artist with a superb voice, Phoebe Snow also demonstrated remarkable versatility, being comfortable with almost every form of pop music from folk to rock to jazz. She was highly regarded by her musical peers and many knowledgeable music buffs without ever quite earning the massive public support her skills seemed to warrant. One stumbling block was establishing rapport with concert audiences; somehow many of her live shows fell short of the magnificent effects she typically achieved on records.

Born Phoebe Laub in New York, she moved to Teaneck, New Jersey, with her family when she was three. Teaneck, of course, was just across the river from New York, and her mother was a close friend of many of the artists who pioneered the short-lived folk music boom in the late 1950s and early '60s. Among the performers Phoebe was acquainted with from her childhood years, directly or through friends' reminiscences, were Woody Guthrie, Cisco Houston, Leadbelly, and Pete Seeger. She recalled hearing her first blues song from Pete Seeger—his version of a Leadbelly tune. "I remember thinking it was very sexy music, thinking 'This is real earthy stuff.' . . . I couldn't believe it. I was embarrassed by it. I thought: 'This is too raw.'"

In her teens, she became much more understanding about blues and hard-edged folk. One of her early favorites was Big Bill Broonzy's "Key to the Highway," which she learned from a record of her father's. At the time she was learning to play guitar from Eric Schoenberg, whom she asked to teach her other blues numbers. Soon she was picking up songs by Mississippi John Hurt, Sonny Terry, and Brownie McGhee. "I had a love affair for several years with the folk blues. I used to go to the Folklore Center when Israel Young was there and buy out all the Yazoo Records. I even met [Yazoo founder] Nick Perls."

Those folk influences were tempered by her interest in the rock and pop material on such TV shows as Dick Clark's "American Bandstand" and the

"Make Believe Ballroom." Later she auditioned for a friend's jug band. The leader, named Charlie, turned her down because he said she was too good for his band, but he took her under his wing, introducing her to other types of blues and jazz recordings while also urging her to try for a performing career.

At first, the idea of getting up in front of an audience seemed too scary. She had thought about that, but couldn't see herself being a solo performer at first. She noted later how she had thought: "How could anybody ever have the nerve to get up there and do that in front of all those people. That fascinated me." She paid particular attention to Judy Garland. "I was into the incredible mesmerizing effect she had on the audience; people would swoon at the sight of her. That intrigued me immensely."

After a while, however, she was ready to try out her singing talents in local clubs as well as work up some original songs of her own. In 1972, during hoot night at the Bitter End in New York, she got up on stage and sang Jesse Fuller's "San Francisco Bay Blues," accompanying herself on guitar. A guitar string broke, but she calmly borrowed one from a friend and kept on going. An executive from Shelter Records was in the audience and was impressed by both her singing ability and stage presence. Soon after, Dino Airali saw to it that Phoebe was signed to Shelter, which gave her a new last name: Snow.

Her record debut took two years to come out. One of its songs, her composition "Poetry Man," was to become the number most often associated with her. Produced by Airali and Phil Ramone, the track became the first hit from the late 1974 gold album, *Phoebe Snow*. Later, she won attention from a duet she performed with Paul Simon on "Gone at Last," issued as a single by Columbia Records in July 1975. *(See Simon, Paul.)*

During 1974, Phoebe became dissatisfied with Shelter and wanted to get out of her contract. After legal maneuvering that sometimes took ugly turns (as when Shelter claimed it and not she owned the stage name Phoebe Snow), she finally won her freedom to pursue new directions and promptly signed with Columbia Records, which issued the gold LP *Second Childhood* in January 1976. But new problems were at hand. The previous December 12, she had given birth to a daughter, Valerie, who later was found to have severe medical problems. As she sadly commented later: "Coming to grips with the fact that my daughter was not going to be a normal child was the most incredibly exhausting, emotionally difficult thing that I'd ever been through in my life. . . . It still is."

Her music, though, did provide a form of escape. She continued to turn out new albums that probed many areas of pop music, often with considerable brilliance. In 1976, she had a second Columbia album, *It Looks Like Snow*, featuring such originals by her as "Autobiography (Shine, Shine, Shine)" and "My Faith Is Blind" plus songs by such other writers as the Beatles, Sammy Cahn, and the Temptations. Her versions of Cahn's "Teach Me Tonight" and the Temptations' "Shaky Ground" were issued as singles in that year.

Her late 1970s albums including *Never Letting Go* (1977) and *Against the Grain* (1978). Among the tracks of note in the first of those was a stunning update of Barbara Acklin's 1968 hit "Love Makes a Woman," issued as a single along with Phoebe's "Elektra" and a fine rendition of Paul Simon's "Something So Right." Phoebe also demonstrated her way with a fast-moving oldie by a steam-heated version of "Garden of Joy Blues" (originally performed by Clifford Hayes and the Dixieland Jug Blowers in 1927). *Against the Grain* included an inspired offering of Paul McCartney's "Every Night."

While Phoebe's Columbia albums won glowing critical notices, they didn't hit the top chart levels record companies desire. By the start of the 1980s, her association with Columbia came to an end, after which the label released the 1981 retrospective *Best of Phoebe Snow*. She moved to a new company, Mirage, which in 1981 issued her label debut, *Rock Away*, her most consistently rock-oriented album to that time, with backing provided by Billy Joel's band.

SONNY AND CHER: *Vocal duo, songwriters, actors. Sonny Bono, born Detroit, Michigan, February 12, 1935; Cher Bono, born Cherilyn Sarkisian, El Centro, California, May 20, 1946.*

Until their marriage foundered in the mid-1970s, Sonny and Cher could claim to be one of the relatively few husband-and-wife teams in rock music. As a duo, they became one of the most successful acts of the 1960s and early 1970s, proving their versatility by fashioning a second career as top-flight adult artists after first attaining stardom with teenagers.

Both began preparing for show business careers in their early years. In Cher's case, performing was a family tradition. Her mother was an actress in Hollywood and started grooming her daughter for the stage as young Cherilyn grew into a comely young lady. *(See Cher.)*

Sonny was born Salvatore Phillip Bono in Detroit, Michigan, but moved to Inglewood, California, with his family in his teens. A singing career had appealed to him from childhood. He recalled writing his first song while working as a stockboy in a grocery store as a teenager. By 1957, he had gotten on the staff of Specialty Records in Los Angeles as a

writer and producer. By the time his path crossed Cher's, he had moved into a job with rising rock impresario Phil Spector, serving as a jack-of-all-trades with duties that included handling West Coast promotion and hiring musicians and backup singers for Spector's artists' recording sessions. He met Cher in a coffee shop next to radio station KFWB in the early 1960s, and soon began trying to promote her career. At first, his efforts focused on getting her backing vocal work for Spector, which included sessions by the Ronettes, Righteous Brothers, and Crystals. Later, he suggested to Spector that he take Cher under his wing. One failed single ("Ringo, I Love You" on the Annette label) caused Phil to lose interest and Sonny decided to record a new disc on his own. When Cher began to record the song ("Baby Don't Go"), she got mike fright and asked Sonny to sing with her, the first time they worked as a team.

As husband and wife (which they became soon after starting working together), they recorded a single for Vault Records under the names Caesar and Cleo, but it flopped. In 1964, they signed a contract with Atlantic Records' Atco subsidiary, this time using their real names. For a time, more success resulted from Sonny's songwriting efforts than from their vocal efforts, either as a team or as individual vocalists. His song "Needles and Pins" (co-written with Jack Nitzsche) provided a 1964 hit for the Searchers; other groups scored in 1964 and 1965 with Sonny's "The Boy Next Door" and "Dream Baby."

In 1965, however, Atco released the Sonny and Cher single "I Got You Babe," backed with "It's Gonna Rain," both written by him. After fighting off Atco's efforts to push "It's Gonna Rain," the duo had the pleasure of watching "I Got You Babe" rise to number one in *Billboard* for three weeks starting August 14. They gained attention not only for their singing, but for their unusual clothes, which they designed themselves, featuring such items as bobcat fur jackets and slacks with multicolored striped patterns. They further added to their popularity in 1965 with a gold debut album on Atco, *Look at Us*, and top 10 single "Baby Don't Go" on Reprise. The magnitude of their success was shown by their income. In 1964, they had total earnings of under $10,000. For the following year, the figure was estimated to be $2 million.

Throughout the mid-1960s, their singles successes included "But You're Mine," "What Now My Love," and "Little Man." Album hits included *Baby Don't Go* on Reprise and *In Case You're in Love, The Wondrous World of Sonny & Cher, and The Best of Sonny & Cher* on Atco.

In 1967, they began to change their image from a

teen-oriented team to a sophisticated adult act. As Sonny told a reporter in September 1967 while discussing his and Cher's appearance on Jerry Lewis's TV show: "Adults have to enjoy us too, and it can be done without our going over on their side. Of course, now the extreme hippies think we're squares, but the squares think we're hippies." Sonny and Cher pointed to their relatively conservative clothes style for the program as indicating one phase of their image change. Those outfits consisted of Cher's bright blue cord bell-bottom slacks, pink paisley collarless shirt, and double strand of colored beads alongside Sonny's cerise wool slacks and colorful shirt with a brocade design and off-the-shoulder buttons.

On the Lewis show and other late 1960s programs, the Bonos came out strongly against drugs. At that time, Sonny wrote a musical, *The Beat Goes On,* aimed at combating hard-drug use. Another example of their increased interest in social comment was their song "You'd Better Sit Down, Kids," in which a father explains to his children that he and their mother are separating.

During the late '60s, their names disappeared from the top rungs of the hit charts. Starting in the early 1970s, though, they developed a new act that first increased their stature as supper-club artists. The *Los Angeles Times* critic said of Sonny: "He has developed a nice sense of comedy timing, but should speak up for the edification of the over-40 set."

During 1970 and 1971, their TV and concert appearances won them a new following from all age groups. In mid-1971, they hosted a summer replacement TV show. They also became forces to reckon with again in the record world with a series of successful releases on Kapp Records. These included number one and top 10 hit singles for Cher and the gold album *Sonny & Cher Live.*

As one result of this renewed success, Sonny and Cher were signed to do their own TV series in 1972. The "Sonny and Cher Show," which took over the Monday-night time slot of the "Carol Burnett Show" on CBS-TV in January, soon was highly popular. The exposure gave a push to the duo's recording efforts, which in 1972 included another top 10 single ("A Cowboy's Work Is Never Done") and the album *All I Ever Need is You.* Also on the charts during the year were an Atco album *(The Two of Us),* a United Artists two-disc set of their early hits, and a Kapp single ("When You Say Love"). Cher's 1972 Kapp hits included the album *Foxy Lady* and the single "Don't Hide Your Love." In 1973, Cher's album *Bittersweet White Light* was on the charts and she had another gold single, "Half Breed," both on MCA, which had absorbed Kapp.

Contracted for the full 1972–73 season, the "Sonny and Cher Show" started strong, then faltered in the ratings, and faced possible cancellation. CBS decided to keep the show for the 1973–74 season, but moved it to a midweek position. The shift did the trick, and the hour—which relied equally on the comic and vocal skills of the duo—regularly placed in the top 20 in the Nielsen ratings.

But in February 1974, it was revealed that in private life, all was far from well with the successful performing duo. Soon after, it was announced the duo had moved to dissolve their marriage of 11 years. The "Sonny and Cher Show" was cancelled. They continued their TV careers with two separate programs, "The Sonny Comedy Hour" on ABC and "Cher" on CBS. Neither did well and the twosome was brought back together for another Sonny and Cher series. That effort also failed and went off the air for the last time in August 1977. After that, Cher went on to success as a solo vocalist and award-winning actress while Sonny went back to primarily behind-the-scenes work in the entertainment field. He also tried his hand at nonmusical projects, including operation of his own restaurant, Bono's, in Los Angeles in the mid-1980s, as well as another bistro in Palm Springs.

In early 1988, Sonny was back in the spotlight with a role in John Waters' film *Hairspray* and, as a registered Republican, with his election as mayor of Palm Springs, California (the day after Cher won her Oscar for *Moonstruck). (See Cher; Crystals, The; Righteous Brothers, The; Ronettes, The; Spector, Phil; Toto.)*

SOUTH, JOE: *Singer, guitarist, songwriter, record producer, disc jockey. Born Atlanta, Georgia, February 28, 1942.*

The interaction of country music with rhythm & blues to form rock'n'roll has been well documented by now. In the late 1960s, there was something of a reverse trend, the effects of modern country music on rock, leading to a school of performers and performances with less emphasis on the rhythmic aspects of rock and more on melody and lyrics. A major source of these new sounds of the late 1960s and early 1970s was Atlanta, Georgia, which has nurtured such talents as Ray Stevens, Billy Joe Royal, Tommy Roe, and Joe South.

South grew up amid comfortable, but far from lavish, surroundings. His parents, who married young, worked hard to pay the relatively low rent in the housing project where they lived. Neither had finished high school, but both had a natural flair for music, particularly country music, long a part of southern family tradition. His father played guitar. Joe began picking out notes on it at age eight.

As South recalled, though money was scarce,

"there was always a record player around the house and one of my earliest memories is standing on the woodpile out back with my father's guitar, visualizing an audience. Music was always around. I never wanted to be anything but a musician."

When Joe was 11, his father bought him his own guitar. A year later, the precocious young musician walked into country music station WGST in Atlanta and told d.j. Bill Lowery he wanted to be on the radio. Lowery noted: "I admired his courage so much that I put him on the air every Saturday morning at 6 A.M. He'd just come in every week with his guitar, stand in front of the microphone, and start singing. Once in a while, he'd bring in a little song he'd written and I began to realize that there was something special about this boy—something called talent."

At 15, Joe was asked to join a band led by Pete Drake, later one of the best-known steel guitarists in country music. "We played down on 42 Highway, Atlanta's Strip, at the bloody buckets and dives where the rednecks went to get drunk."

During those years, Joe built his own station in his home and broadcast over a 1½-mile radius. He also worked for a time as a country d.j. After high school, he went on to Southern Tech to study electronics and communications. However, he had become the lead performer on the Saturday-night country show "Georgia Jubilee" and he quit school for a performing career.

In the early 1960s, Lowery had set up his own music-publishing and recording firm, NRC, in Atlanta. Joe gained two regional hits for Lowery with "I'm Snowed" and "Purple People Eater Meets the Witch Doctor." However, Joe had become depressed at his lack of progress and his moods irked others in the field. He could no longer find work locally and he settled for odd jobs, including running pressing equipment in a record-producing plant.

In the mid-1960s, though, his skill on guitar got him jobs as a sideman for record sessions. In Nashville and Muscle Shoals, Alabama, he backed one name artist after another, including Fats Domino, Eddy Arnold, Bob Dylan, Marty Robbins, and Aretha Franklin. Columbia even paid his way to New York to back Simon and Garfunkel on their hit LP *Sounds of Silence*.

In 1966, South settled down in Atlanta. Welcomed by Lowery, he wrote and produced a series of hits for other artists including Billy Joe Royal's "Down in the Boondocks" and "Hush" and the Tam's "Be Young, Be Foolish, Be Happy" and "Untie Me." South finally decided, in 1968, that he could do better for himself by recording his own material. He gained a Capitol contract late in the year and recorded a series of songs. A single from the session, "Birds of a Feather," became a regional hit. The LP from the work, *Introspect* (late 1968), won more acclaim from fellow musicians than from fans, but it did get onto the charts. Other performers quickly covered some of Joe's originals in the album, particularly "Games People Play," which became a gold hit for Joe himself in 1969.

It was not until *Introspect* was reissued under the title *Games People Play* in 1969 that Capitol stated it too passed gold record sales levels. The National Academy of Recording Arts and Sciences awarded Joe two Grammies for "Games People Play": 1969 Song of the Year and Best Contemporary Song.

In 1970 and 1971, South contributed many more songs to the popular music repertoire. His composition "I Never Promised You a Rose Garden" as sung by country vocalist Lynn Anderson was number one on country charts (and top 10 on pop lists) for several weeks in 1970. (South's own single of the song was backed with "Mirror of Your Mind.") His single "Walk a Mile in My Shoes," a plea for tolerance and understanding among all people, made *Billboard*'s pop top 20. It also was featured by many major artists, including Harry Belafonte and Lena Horne on their joint 1970 network TV show. Meanwhile, his Capitol LPs included *Don't It Make You Wanta Go Home, Joe Smith's Greatest Hits,* and *So the Seeds Are Growing.*

By the mid-1970s, South apparently had tired of the pressures of the music field and essentially retired from recording and touring. At the start of the 1980s, his only album still in print was the 1970 Capitol release *Joe South's Greatest Hits.*

SOUTHERN COMFORT: *Vocal and instrumental group. Originally backup band for Ian Matthews, born London, England, 1946. Members (early 1970s): Gordon Huntley, born Newbury, England, c. 1930; Carl Barnwell, born California; Mark Griffiths, born Northampton, England; Andy Leigh, born Manchester, England; Ray Duffy, born Glasgow, Scotland.*

Southern Comfort is the name of a blended whiskey that gained a certain popularity during World War II and of two unrelated rock groups. The U.S. namesake was short-lived, but the English band became one of the stellar rock organizations of the early 1970s.

The British group was organized in 1969 by Ian Matthews (born Ian McDonald), who adopted his middle name for his stage last name to avoid confusion with Ian McDonald of King Crimson. Ian first achieved a reputation as a lead singer and guitarist with the folk-rock Fairport Convention, becoming the first founding member to quit the group. His next band, Matthews Southern Comfort, backed him on concert tours of England and the Continent and on a series of recordings released on Decca in both England and the U.S.

After a major reorganization, only steel guitarist Gordon Huntley remained from the original band. Huntley represented almost a father figure; his first professional performance was at the Dudley Hippodrome in 1947, in which he played both the ukelele and double bass. During the 1950s and '60s, he performed with many groups—including jazz, skiffle, Hawaiian, and rock bands—and was generally acknowledged to have become the best steel guitarist in England.

The reorganized Southern Comfort included Carl Barnwell on rhythm guitar, Mark Griffiths on lead guitar, Andy Leigh on bass, and Ray Duffy on drums. Each had a considerable performing background, though none was nearly as extensive as Huntley's.

The paths of a number of band members had crossed before they got together in Southern Comfort. Leigh had met Matthews in Pyramid in 1968 and then went on to the Electric String Band and Gary Farr's Spooky Tooth while Matthews was working with Fairport Convention. Duffy came to Southern Comfort from the Gaylords, which later won fame under the name Marmalade. The only non-Englishman was Carl Barnwell, who was born and raised in California.

The new group worked with Matthews on the LPs *Second Spring* (1969) and *Later That Same Year* (1970), with its hit version of Joni Mitchell's euphoric composition "Woodstock." *(See Mitchell, Joni.)* The band also made the singles charts with "Mare, Take Me Home."

Early in 1971, it was announced that Matthews was going to go out as a solo artist and Southern Comfort would work separately. The band signed with EMI's Harvest subsidiary and put out *Frog City* that May. Its title number was Mark Griffiths' composition "Return to Frog City." The album also featured six originals by Barnwell, one of which, "(The Dreadful Ballad of) Willie Hurricane," was released as a single during the spring of 1971.

Southern Comfort disbanded in 1971, but its recording of "Woodstock" became a classic in later years, being played often on rock oldies programs and included on several collections of British all-time favorites. Meanwhile, singer/writer Matthews' solo career prospered for a while. On the Vertigo label, he made U.S. charts with the single "Da Doo Ron Ron" (a 1963 hit for the Crystals and a 1977 hit for Shaun Cassidy as well) and put out albums *If You Saw thro' My Eyes* (1970) and *Tigers Will Survive* (1971). In 1972, he was performing with the quartet Plainsong, whose Elektra LP *Plainsong* was in part a

concept album revolving around aviatrix Amelia Earhart. Later solo albums in the U.S. included, on Elektra, *Valley Hi* (1973) and *Some Days You Eat the Bear . . . & Some Days the Bear Eats You* (1974); on Columbia, *Go for Broke* (1976); on Mushroom, *Stealin' Home* (1978) and *Siamese Friends* (1980); and on RSO, *Spot of Interference* (1980). His late 1978 single "Shake It" on Mushroom made *Billboard*'s top 20.

After years of behind-the-scenes work as an artists & repertoire man (his main accomplishment being bringing Canadian art-song singer/writer Jane Siberry to U.S. audiences via Windham Hill's subsidiary Open Air), Ian put out *Walking a Changing Line* (Windham Hill, 1988), an entire album of songs written by Jules Shear with new age instrumentation.

SOUTHSIDE JOHNNY AND THE ASBURY JUKES: *Vocal and instrumental group headed by Johnny Lyon, born Neptune Park, New Jersey, 1948. Band members (early 1980s): William Rush, Joel Gramolini, Kevin Cavanaugh, Gene Boccia, Stephen Becker, Walter Gazda, Mike Spangler, Joseph Spann, Edward Manion, Richard "La Bamba" Rosenberg.*

Hailing from the Asbury Park region of New Jersey, Southside Johnny Lyon's career often interacted with that of the artist who, in effect, put Asbury Park on the pop music map, Bruce Springsteen. *(See Springsteen, Bruce.)* Lyon suffered to some extent from the inevitable direct comparisons. While his and Springsteen's musical tastes were similar— R&B and blues-flavored rock—Lyon couldn't come close to matching his friend's writing ability. In his own way, though, he ranked as one of the best vocalists in his vein in the 1970s and 1980s.

Johnny grew up in a home where music was constantly played on radio or records. His family liked blues and R&B, rather than pop or the early rock of white artists. As Johnny grew up, he shared that enthusiasm. He recalled later: "You grow up listening to people like Billie Holiday, Jimmy Rushing, and Wynonie Harris and you're hearing music in which people are trying to express something. It's music made to move people emotionally. You grow up with that kind of stuff and it gets into you and you know it's always going to be with you.

"I suppose that if I had grown up in a Hit Parade house, I would have latched onto white pop. But I was drawn to music that recognized the darker side of life. It's not that I had anything against, for instance, the Beach Boys, but, for me, the Stones, Yardbirds, and Animals struck a more familiar, compelling chord."

Lyon was trying out his voice, singing along with records and later with school friends in his early teens. He also taught himself the harmonica, playing it at one point during talent nights at the local Upstage Club. It wasn't until he was 16, though, that he joined his first group, the Sonny Kenn Blues Band. It was not a long association and for much of the decade Lyon worked with dozens of bands that assembled, broke up, and reformed with new members. It was a period of searching for many young musicians in the area, including Springsteen and Miami Steve Van Zandt (born Boston, Massachusetts, November 22, 1950). Lyon said: "Bands changed and broke up so often because of boredom, lack of jobs, but mostly because there was a desire to experiment and try something new. At 16 or 17, you were in a band to have fun, make a little money, and pick up chicks. . . . We weren't looking for anything permanent. We used to put a band together every week."

Because Johnny and many of his friends in the field hated the idea of playing cover versions of hit recordings, their road was even harder than other Jersey "bar bands." During one period of his early career, he, Van Zandt, and two other musicians shared a three-room apartment in a seamy neighborhood. They just managed to scrape together enough money to pay the rent from their weekly salaries of about $15 each.

At the time, Bruce Springsteen was just another struggling performer working whatever dates he could find at local bars or private parties. His path sometimes crossed that of Van Zandt and Lyon, which led, in the early 1970s, to the three combining talents in the short-lived group Dr. Zoom and the Sonic Boom. During rehearsals with that band, Lyon got his nickname. "At the time, I was basically known for playing Chicago blues and since the South Side of Chicago was where it all happened, the name sort of popped up and stuck."

After Dr. Zoom broke up, Lyon and Van Zandt tried for a while to work as a duo. Set up in early 1973, under the name Southside Johnny and the Kid, the acoustic-blues twosome found a little work, but not enough to justify continuing on. The two friends decided to go separate ways for a while.

After playing with several bar bands, Johnny joined the Blackberry Booze Band in October 1974. In December, the BBB was signed as house band at a club called the Stone Pony. By then, Lyons had become the central performer and he gradually changed the group's roster to suit his tastes. With steady work at hand, Johnny was able to induce Miami Steve to return in early 1975 as co-leader. In June 1975, they changed the group's name to Southside Johnny and the Asbury Jukes. In July, however, Van Zandt was asked to join Bruce Springsteen's new E Street Band. Since Bruce had a recording contract and a good national tour lined up, Van Zandt agreed to go as lead guitarist.

Steve kept in touch with Lyon and, when the E Street tour was over, he returned to New Jersey to lay plans for a demonstration record by Lyon's group. The band started recording the material in February 1976 and finished it five weeks later. The tracks included two previously unrecorded compositions by Springsteen that Bruce had provided for the sessions. The tape brought a contract from Epic Records, which released the band's debut LP, *I Don't Want to Go Home,* later in the year. One particularly impressive track was the group's version of Springsteen's "The Fever." Overall, it was an excellent first album and deservedly won considerable critical praise across the U.S.

In support of the LP, the band set out on a grueling tour that was to set the pattern for the rest of the decade. For instance, the band gave 240 or more shows a year at home and abroad in 1977, 1978, and the early 1980s. The roster as of 1976–77 included Johnny on lead vocals and mouth harp, Kevin Cavanaugh on keyboards, Alan Berger on bass guitar, Billy Rush on lead guitar, and Stephen Becker on drums, with different combinations of horn players brought in for various gigs. Besides its touring activities during 1976, late that year the group made an appearance in the movie *Between the Lines.*

The material for the second album mainly comprised original songs written by Van Zandt or by Van Zandt and Springsteen. *This Time It's for Real* (1977) was a good follow-up collection, though perhaps a trifle less exciting than the first. That was remedied by the 1978 LP *Hearts of Stone*'s excellent renditions of songs such as Springsteen's title track and "Talk to Me" plus first-rate Van Zandt offerings "Take It Inside" and "This Time Baby's Gone for Good."

The album had the earmarks of Johnny's first commercial hit, but then disaster struck. Near the end of a performance in late 1978 at a club in Sacramento, California, Johnny slipped on stage, suffering severe hand injuries that forced cancellation of engagements for over two months. The mishap contributed to the lack of promotion for the new album and its failure prompted Epic to drop the band. Depressed, Lyon considered giving up performing, but a change in management in February 1979 helped bring a new agreement with Mercury Records soon after.

Johnny's debut on the new label, *The Jukes,* came out in 1979 as did another Epic LP *(Havin' a Party with Southside Johnny and the Asbury Jukes,* a retrospective drawn from the three previous Epic LPs).

With his arm recovered, Lyon resumed his hectic touring schedule, initially supporting his debut on

Mercury and then the second Mercury album, *Love Is a Sacrifice* (1980). On those albums, Johnny took more of a hand in writing phases, co-writing two cuts on the latter album. Also handling many of the writing chores was guitarist Rush, who co-wrote some material on *Love Is a Sacrifice* and wrote most of the songs on *The Jukes*.

The band meanwhile was working to enhance its stage persona with good effect. Describing a concert in *Rolling Stone* (August 7, 1980): Steve Pond wrote: "The Jukes have always been a great bar band, but in the past few years they've also become a great concert band. Lyon, a fine R&B singer on record, is a whirling dervish onstage, bouncing off equipment and spinning off in unexpected directions like an off-kilter gyroscope. He was in peak form at these performances; even the delightfully choreographed frenzy of porcine trombonist Richard 'La Bamba' Rosenberg couldn't upstage him."

Some of the flavor of such shows was captured on the next Mercury/Polygram release, *Reach Up and Touch the Sky—Southside Johnny and the Asbury Jukes Live!* The 1981 two-disc set ranged from Jukes performances of Springsteen and Van Zandt classics to exuberant renditions of songs originally made famous by people such as Sam Cooke.

By the early 1980s, the band had incorporated a stable horn section to improve continuity in concert and recording projects. The makeup then included (besides Lyon, Rush, Cavanaugh, Rosenberg, and Becker) John Gramolini on rhythm guitar, Gene Boccia (in place of Alan Berger) on bass, Walter "Rick" Gazda on trumpet, Mike Spangler on trumpet, Joseph Spann on tenor saxophone, and Edward Manion on baritone saxophone.

In mid-1988, Johnny was working on an album for Cypress Records. Meanwhile, his former teammate Van Zandt—dressed like a cross between a gypsy fortune teller and a biker—was carving out a niche for himself apart from Johnny and Springsteen via blazing rock with lyrics on U.S. involvement in the Third World and the need for everyday people to take charge of the situations around them. Alongside EMI America LPs *Men without Women* (1982) and *Voice of America* (1984) plus *Freedom—No Compromise* (Manhattan, 1987), Little Steven's largest accomplishment was spearheading the all-star *Sun City* LP (Manhattan, 1986), a fundraising and public-awareness effort by Artists United against Apartheid to aid downtrodden black and coloured South Africans. In June 1988, he took part in the Freedomfest concert in London, an anti-apartheid event honoring jailed black South African leader Nelson Mandela's 70th birthday.

SOXX, BOB B., AND THE BLUE JEANS:
Vocal group: Darlene Love, Fanita James, Bobby Sheen.

Phil Spector's phenomenal ability to produce recordings with appeal to young music fans made him the boy wonder of the early 1960s. Among the hand-picked artists he propelled to stardom during the period was the humorously named Bob B. Soxx and the Blue Jeans.

The trio Spector assembled as the original Bob B. Soxx group included future solo singer Darlene Love, Fanita James (her teammate in the Blossoms), and male vocalist Bobby Sheen. All had been singing in public since their early teens and had done some session work on other Spector projects. As was his practice, Spector took a lot of time and care in selecting and recording material for the trio and gave maximum emphasis to promoting the releases. Within a short time after the group completed its first recording sessions, they hit *Billboard*'s top 10 with their 1962 version of the Walt Disney song "Zip-A-Dee-Doo-Dah" from the movie *Song of the South*.

The song served as the title number for the group's debut album on Spector's Philles label. The LP included a mixture of standard pop songs from the past and Spector originals. Some of the tracks were "The White Cliffs of Dover," "This Land Is Your Land," "Dr. Kaplan's Office," "Let the Good Times Roll," "I Shook the World," and "Everything's Gonna Be Allright." The studio musicians on the LP give one clue to reasons for Spector's success. The names include many then-unknowns who would later leave their mark in various phases of popular music: Glen Campbell and Billy Strange on guitar and pianists Al Delory, Nino Tempo, and Leon Russell.

Bob B. Soxx and the Blue Jeans broke *Billboard*'s top 40 once more, with "Why Do Lovers Break Each Other's Hearts" in spring 1963. But Spector had other ideas for Darlene. He had already used her as lead singer on the Crystals' number one *Billboard* hit "He's a Rebel" in 1962. Later in 1963, he produced her top 40 hits "(Today I Met) The Boy I'm Going to Marry" and "Wait til My Bobby Gets Home." (*See Crystals, The; Russell, Leon; Spector, Phil.*)

SPANDAU BALLET: *Vocal and instrumental group from London, England. Members (all born U.K.): Tony Hadley; Gary Kemp; Martin Kemp; Steve Norman; John Keeble.*

Catching the disco wave near its crest, England's Spandau Ballet became a European favorite with its brand of somewhat watered-down American soul-rock. Perhaps on the principle that distance lends enchantment, the group also was able to win more than a few North American fans, with its extended-play dance remixes of some of its songs (among the first such discs to be offered to the U.S. market by a white English group) even getting considerable airplay on black radio stations.

The band's members grew up in working class sections of London and found mutual interest in avant garde fashion and funky rhythms. After the usual trial and error efforts during their formative years, the founding members of Spandau Ballet formed their new association in the late 1970s. The roster comprised Tony Hadley on lead vocals; Gary Kemp, who became the primary songwriter, on guitar and backing vocals; Gary's brother Martin on bass guitar; Steve Norman on saxophone and percussion; and John Keeble on drums and percussion.

After working on their new act, the quintet made their live performance debut in November 1979 at a private rehearsal hall before an invited audience of graphic artists, writers, disc jockeys, musicians, and fashion designers. It was the starting point for appearances at a number of clubs in London's SoHo area, such as Blitz, Billy's, Hell, and St. Moritz, where the audience typically wore unusual clothes while dancing to music that ranged from Bowie/ Roxy Music/Eno avant garde rock to soul/funk. Spandau Ballet in the early 1980s also featured attire that changed with its song content—for instance, tartans to accompany the song "To Cut a Long Story Short," tribal garb for "Musclebound," and zoot suits when "Chant No. 1" was popular.

The band's debut LP, *Journeys to Glory* (Chrysalis, 1981), was a hit throughout Europe. Three tracks received wide play in dance clubs: "To Cut a Long Story Short," "Musclebound," and "The Freeze." Remixed extended dance versions of all three also were issued. The album made the top five and was certified gold in England. Though the band didn't attempt a major U.S. tour at the time, it did win some media attention with its American debut at New York City's Underground club, providing musical support for a fashion show by a group of London clothes designers called Axiom.

Among the numbers the band readied for its next album was Gary Kemp's composition "Chant No. 1 (I Don't Need This Pressure On)." For the recording sessions, Spandau brought in a black London horn section, Beggars & Co., to help provide a funk-rock hybrid sound. That sound and Beggars & Co. backup were retained for all the songs on one side of the second album, *Diamond* (Chrysalis, 1982). The second half of *Diamond* had a softer emphasis, presenting ballads backed by oriental instruments such as chengs and tablas. The album did well in Europe, but not much happened in the U.S., although "Chant No. 1" got a fair amount of airplay.

For its third Chrysalis album, Spandau took up quarters in the Bahamas in the fall of 1982 to work up material at the Compass Point Studios. The result was *True* (1983), which not only became a hit overseas, but provided the band's first U.S. success, entering *Billboard*'s top five. Critics remained ambivalent, though *Rolling Stone* commented: "Guitarist/songwriter Gary Kemp's best numbers either churn with an effervescing emotiveness or rise to a plain, sexy simmer."

Songs "Lifeline" and "Communication" became dance-club hits in Europe. The title song and "Gold" as well as the LP itself brought the band top five successes across the world.

In 1984, the band's fourth LP, *Parade,* entered the charts in the U.K. at number two on the way to English gold-record status. It also did well in Continental Europe, reaching number one in Holland and moving high on the charts elsewhere. In the U.S., however, it failed to repeat the achievements of *True,* despite the large crowds that welcomed the band's live shows in support of the new collection.

During 1984–85, the band demonstrated its great popularity by drawing massive crowds that sold out U.K. and European venues within a few hours after tickets went on sale. For the group's appearance at Rome's Palasport, two chain-link fences and phalanxes of police were required to control crowds of frustrated concert goers who could not get tickets.

The band also did S.R.O. business in the U.S. Richard Cromelin of the *Los Angeles Times* was hardly a Spandau fanatic. He queried: "Why Spandau's shrill-sounding, starchy imitations of soul music and second-hand Roxy Music should command any real loyalty is a tough question."

The American phase of the tour proved costly to the band. During a May concert in Los Angeles, Steve Norman tore a ligament in one leg when he jumped off a riser during one of the wilder moments of the show. His leg was put in a brace and the rest of the tour had to be cancelled, including dates at Rome's Palasport involving some 75,000 fans and a series at Madrid's Casa di Campo that would have drawn 120,000.

The band decided to extend its hiatus from live performances to include time for completing writing and recording a new album for 1986 release. For that, the band members moved headquarters temporarily to Dublin, Ireland, the second half of 1985 and early 1986. In the interim, Chrysalis released an album of singles issued from 1980–1984 *(The Singles Collection,* 1985). Before 1986 was over, the group had a new album out on Epic, *Through the Barricades.*

SPANIELS, THE: *Vocal group. Members (mid-1950s), all born late 1930s: James "Pooky" Hudson, Gerald Gregory, Donald Porter, Carl Rainge, James Cochran.*

Street singing proved to be the route to success for a number of groups in both R&B and rock. In the Spaniels' case, it also was the incentive for the founding of a record company that played a leading role in the evolution of pop music for over a decade.

The original Spaniels came into being in the ghetto of Gary, Indiana. Five teenage boys together worked up some songs to perform on street corners for whatever change passersby would give them. Local disc jockey Vivian Carter heard them and decided they had a future as a professional group. Carter took over their management and arranged for a recording session with the goal of releasing their material on Vee Jay, the label she founded with her husband, James Bracken. ("Vee" stood for Vivian; "Jay" for James.) Its first single, the Spaniels' "Baby, It's You," was a regional hit and then broke out to become a nationwide R&B top 10 hit in 1953, establishing the Spaniels as a well-known group and Vee Jay as a record firm to watch. (Later, Vee Jay's roster included such dynamic newcomers as Jerry Butler, Jimmy Reed, Wade Flemons, the Pips, and the Four Seasons.)

The Spaniels followed "Baby, It's You" with another top 10 R&B hit in late 1953, "The Bells Ring Out." Their biggest hit, "Goodnight, Sweetheart, Goodnight," moved into the R&B top 10 in early spring 1954 and also hit the lower rungs of the national lists, though the white McGuire Sisters' cover version chalked up many of the song's sales.

In the mid-'50s, the group went through several personnel changes until only two of the original quintet were left: James "Pooky" Hudson on bass and Gerald Gregory, also a bass. Complementing them were Donald Porter, Carl Rainge, and James "Dimples" Cochran. This group was featured on the LP *Goodnight, It's Time to Go,* which was still in print three decades later. Its tracks comprised a good sample of the Spaniels' repertoire: "Baby, It's You," "The Bells Ring Out," "Please Don't Tease," "This Is a Lovely Way to Spend an Evening," "Do You Really," "You Gave Me Peace of Mind," "I Need Your Kisses," "Let's Make Up," "Play It Cool," "Painted Pictures," "Housecleaning," and "Do Wah."

The group failed to maintain its momentum into the late 1950s and had faded from the scene by the start of the '60s.

Interest in the group revived during the 1970s and '80s, particularly in England, where many fans looked back fondly on the great doo-wop groups of the '50s and '60s. During the 1970s, the LP *The*

Spaniels on Lost Nite Records was available in record stores. In 1981, Charly Records in the U.K. released the excellent retrospective *Great Googley Moo!*. Solid Smoke released *16 Soulful Serenades* in 1984. All three LPs included the Spaniels' 1954 classic "Goodnight, Sweetheart, Goodnight." In 1986, Charly put out still more vintage Spaniels tracks on *Stormy Weather*.

SPECTOR, PHIL: *Record-company executive, producer, guitarist, songwriter. Born Bronx, New York, December 26, 1940.*

In California, where he made his headquarters in the late 1960s, Phil Spector seemed as inaccessible as Howard Hughes, living as he did on a huge estate behind high walls with locked gates. Nonetheless, he did sally forth from time to time and, when he did, he still often produced hit records, though by that time he did not work with relative unknowns as he had early in his career, but with superstars the likes of the Beatles.

In effect, though only approaching 30 at that time, Spector was in semiretirement. It was another interesting phenomenon of the music world created by rock'n'roll, an artist-entrepreneur who became "the First Tycoon of Teen" (as Tom Wolfe described him in his book, *The Kandy Kolored Tangerine Flake Streamline Baby*). Indeed, Spector achieved a net worth of over $1 million at 21 years of age from writing, producing, and manufacturing rock records.

Spector spent his early years in the Bronx, New York, but was taken to Los Angeles, California, at nine by his mother after his father died. Strangely, his father's passing later played an important part in Spector's rise. Phil attended public schools in Los Angeles and started to learn guitar while a student at Fairfax High School. At 16, he began to play with jazz groups in local coffeehouses. Rock was beginning to take over pop music and Spector soon began playing that instead.

Unlike some jazz artists, Spector didn't change because of financial rewards, but because he liked the music. As Wolfe quoted him in his book, Spector said (c. 1964): "I get a little angry when people say it's bad music. This music has a spontaneity that doesn't exist in any other kind of music and it's what is here now. It's unfair to classify it as rock'n'roll and condemn it. It has limited chord changes, and people are always saying the words are banal and why doesn't anybody write lyrics like Cole Porter anymore, but we don't have any president like Lincoln anymore, either. . . . Actually, it's more like the blues. It's pop blues. I feel it's very American. It's very today. It's what people respond to today."

In 1958, Phil wrote his first hit, the ballad "To Know Him Is to Love Him," inspired by the epitaph his mother had had inscribed on his father's tombstone ("to know him was to love him"). Spector recorded it on Los Angeles-based Dore Records with his trio, the Teddy Bears, including his schoolmates Annette Bard (born Kleinbard, Los Angeles, 1941) and Marshall Lieb (born Los Angeles, 1938). It made number one in *Billboard* and sold over 2½ million copies in the U.S. and Europe combined. But the record promoters managed to walk off with $17,000 of the $20,000 due Spector for the disc. The angry Teddy Bears moved to Imperial Records to make several singles that never broke the top 40. More importantly, the exploitation convinced Phil that he needed to control his music's production and distribution to be certain of a proper return for his efforts. This later led him to establish his highly successful Philles label.

After high school, Phil entered the University of California at Los Angeles, but did not have enough money for his college expenses. He worked for a while as a court reporter, but then moved to New York, intending to work as an interpreter at the U.N., using the French his mother had taught him.

Once in New York, though, he became involved in the music field again. He played with some small groups and went back to writing songs. "Spanish Harlem" (co-written with Jerry Leiber), became a major hit in 1961 for Ben E. King (and in 1971 for Aretha Franklin). His reputation had grown to the point that he was named an artists & repertoire man for Atlantic Records, which was then almost solely a rhythm & blues firm. He stayed with Atlantic for a while, but then branched out as an independent record producer. Among the major artists he worked with were Elvis Presley and Connie Francis.

In 1961, Spector formed his own record company with two partners. But this didn't work out well, so he bought them out the following year. In October 1962, his new label, Philles Records, was officially underway. Much as Berry Gordy did in developing the Motown Records empire, he followed a policy of quality, at least from his standpoint, rather than quantity. Spector waited until he had written a song he felt would succeed, then he carefully selected the artist, recorded as many takes of the song as he felt necessary to gain the effect he wanted, and, finally, concentrated promotion on the specific song rather than spreading the effort among a dozen or more titles.

This rapidly paid off with a top 10 single, "He's a Rebel," recorded by the Crystals. He followed this with another *Billboard* top 10 hit in mid-1963, "Be My Baby" by the Ronettes, featuring his future wife, Ronnie Bennett. From then until the mid-1960s, he was almost continuously represented on the singles charts by such songs as "Da Do Ron

Ron," "Then He Kissed Me," "Uptown," and "He's Sure the Boy I Love" by the Crystals; "Zip-a-Dee-Doo-Dah" by Bob B. Soxx and the Blue Jeans; "Wait Til' My Bobby Gets Home" by Darlene Love; and the song that made the Righteous Brothers national favorites, "You've Lost That Lovin' Feelin'." His name was legendary not only in the U.S. by that time, but in England as well. In the mid-1960s, up-and-coming English supergroups such as the Beatles and Rolling Stones were already seeking him out for material and for production insights.

For a time in the late 1960s, Spector faded from general view. He sold his record interests and moved from his penthouse suite overlooking New York's East River to a secluded estate in the Los Angeles area. Some show business observers wondered if he were ill or had other problems. Apparently, though, his goal was to get away from the spotlight until things quieted down and he was not plagued by favor seekers wherever he went. Whatever the reason, as the 1960s drew to a close, Spector once more became active, initially with a group called the Checkmates and then with some of his old friends from England's top rock ranks, such as the Beatles.

In 1971, he handled production of what promised to be the most talked about record of 1971–72, the three-LP *Concert for Bangla Desh*. Spector donated his time free for the project, as did its prime mover, George Harrison, and the other performers. The goal was to provide a large amount of money from concert, record, and film royalties to help alleviate suffering of the Bengali refugees in India.

Later in the decade, Phil helped to produce some of John Lennon's material (such as the 1974 roots rock album *Rock'n'Roll*) and in 1977 produced Leonard Cohen's LP *Death of a Ladies' Man*. He also produced the Ramones' *End of the Century* LP (Sire, 1980). Compilation albums of records he produced for various artists during his glory years included *Phil Spector's Greatest Hits* on Spector and *A Christmas Gift for You* on Philles. The Beatles' Apple Records reissued the holiday LP as *Phil Spector's Christmas Album*. In the 1980s, it was reissued once again under its original title by Rhino Records, which also put out *Phil Spector: The Early Productions (1958–1961)*, 12 pre-Philles tracks including the Teddy Bears, the Paris Sisters, and Gene Pitney. *(See Cher; Crystals, The; Francis, Connie; Franklin, Aretha; Harrison, George; King, Ben E.; Lennon, John; McCartney, Paul; Nilsson; Pitney, Gene; Presley, Elvis; Righteous Brothers, The; Ronettes, The; Russell, Leon; Sonny and Cher; Soxx, Bob B., and the Blue Jeans; Turner, Ike and Tina.)*

SPENCER DAVIS GROUP: *See Winwood, Steve.*

SPRINGFIELD, RICK: *Singer, guitarist, songwriter, actor. Born Sydney, Australia, August 23, 1949.**

With his dashing good looks and resonant speaking voice, Rick Springfield seemed on the way to becoming a matinee idol during his role as Dr. Noah Drake on the TV series "General Hospital." But when he had the opportunity to choose between acting and pop music, his first love won out.

As he noted in 1981, when he had a lead role on the TV series and a hit album on the charts: "I keep being asked whether I'll keep doing both acting and music. I'd never give up music because I love to do it and I also love to act. I certainly have time to keep 'em both happening now, but it depends on which one takes off first as to how much energy I devote to one or the other." The answer came rapidly. Starting in 1981, Rick placed a string of albums and singles on best-seller lists and also built up a following of younger rock fans who flocked to his concerts across the U.S.

Springfield grew up in a middle class Australian family. "I got into music listening to it on the radio and it seemed the most effective form of rebellion against my parents. I used to make guitars out of wood and they finally gave in and bought me a fairly good one. That was the start of a long painful process of trying to be able to do what I wanted to do, which included getting into rock bands along the way.

"I had my first band in high school called the Jordan Boys, which came from the name of a town we used to play in a lot—Jordanville. The other members had been in jail for things like armed robbery. They were 25 and I was 16. One time we were parked near a milk bar and they ran into it and held it up. I stayed out in the car. Lucky we didn't get caught or it might have started me on the wrong foot."

Rick went on to work with other Australian musicians, eventually joining the band Zoot, which became the top group in his homeland. Another member of Zoot was Beeb Birtles, later a founding member of the Little River Band. "I was with Zoot about three years," Rick said. "Then the band split up and I worked as a solo artist for a while. I got a record deal with an Australian label and had a hit single, 'Speak to the Sky.' That record got me my first record deal in the U.S. I came here in 1972 and signed with Capitol.

---

*Based partly on personal interview with Irwin Stambler.

"Actually I'd always wanted to come to the U.S. When I was in Australia, I had no real conception of America. The U.S. was like the capital of your golden dreams. I knew I was going to get over here and it was just a matter of how. By 1972, I'd reached the point at home where I'd achieved pretty much what I wanted to do. I'd been in the top band and then had done well as a solo."

Capitol had the idea of making him into a teen idol along the lines of David Cassidy when it released his label debut, *Beginnings,* in 1972. It broke *Billboard*'s top 40 and provided the top 20 single "Speak to the Sky." Rick moved to Columbia Records, which had similar marketing ideas for him, but the 1973 album *Comic Book Heroes* (which Columbia reissued in 1982 after Springfield finally became a star) flopped. Rick was depressed at the time, but in retrospect, he later told Dennis Hunt of the *Los Angeles Times,* it probably was a blessing in disguise. "Even then it hurt my credibility to be considered the next David Cassidy. When you're a teen idol, people never take you seriously. If I had made it as a teen idol, it would have been nice in the short run, but not in the long run. It probably would be all over for me now. Then you're just an ex-teen idol. In this business that's like having the plague."

After Columbia showed him the door, legal problems with his management group put his music career on the shelf for two years. While waiting for things to clear up, Rick concentrated on writing original material for his hoped-for next album. He finally got the chance to record the songs for Chelsea Records. However, soon after the LP, *Wait for the Night,* came out in 1976, the company went bankrupt and Rick's music career came to a standstill again. It made him consider trying some other form of entertainment career.

"I got into acting because I had nothing better to do. I couldn't record. I could have kept on playing in the club circuit, but it was really difficult to do at the time. I was pretty much tied up."

He had no intention of going back to Australia. He had settled in Glendale, California, where he bought his own home and commuted to acting classes and, after a while, to work in TV. "After I hired an agent, he began getting me guest roles in a variety of shows including 'Battlestar Galactica,' 'The Rockford Files,' 'The Six-Million Dollar Man,' and 'Wonder Woman.' I did about 10 to 12 episodic shows. It was the business of cutting my teeth and building an acting presence, but I never stopped writing songs because I knew I was going to be recording again sooner or later."

In 1979, he had enough new demo tapes to seek a new record arrangement, which finally fell into place with RCA in 1980. While he was working on material for the first RCA collection, a casting director who once had talked to him about a possible spot in a TV pilot asked him to audition for a role on "General Hospital." He got the job and decided to sign up for a year of shows since there was no way of knowing how his new record would do. As it happened, he began the new TV appearance on March 25, 1981, soon after the album, *Working Class Dog,* came out. The album not only went platinum, but also spawned the number one single "Jessie's Girl" and *Billboard* top 10 "I've Done Everything for You."

His sudden recording prominence caused the TV executives in charge of "General Hospital" to consider having him sing on the show. Springfield gave an emphatic no. He told Hunt that he said: "Forget it. My character wouldn't sing. He's a doctor. His father was a doctor. His grandfather was a doctor. This guy wouldn't have the time or the inclination to get into rock'n'roll. He's not the type. It wouldn't be believable.

"Look, I'm concerned about my credibility. For me to sing on 'General Hospital' would smack of sellout. It would look like I'd do anything to sell records. I want to be accepted in the music community. Could they take a singing doctor seriously?"

By the end of 1981, Rick had initial momentum toward rock stardom, but he still had to beat the so-called follow-up barrier. He sailed through it without difficulty, however. His second LP on RCA, *Success Hasn't Spoiled Me Yet* (late 1982), achieved multi-platinum sales. During 1982, Rick placed six singles on the charts (including the top 10 "Don't Talk to Strangers") and was ranked number seven on *Billboard*'s year-end list of top pop male singles artists.

Into the mid-1980s, Rick added to his recording credits. In 1983 he put out another platinum LP, *Living in Oz.* Among the four singles he placed on the charts that year were best-sellers "Affair of the Heart" and "Souls." In 1984, he was represented on U.S. album lists with the Mercury/Polygram LP *Beautiful Feelings* (a compilation of some of his pre-RCA recordings) and the platinum RCA soundtrack album *Hard to Hold.* During 1984, he had six singles on the charts (five on RCA and one on Mercury). In 1985, his charted singles numbered three.

With his recording goals more or less achieved, Rick's possible future activities included continuation of the script-writing exercises he had done earlier. He had, for instance, done a treatment for a comedy pilot some years before and had thought about likely film scripts.

"My first writing was stories. In fact, I used to be an insatiable reader, mainly humor and science fiction. I wrote those kinds of stories when I was still at school. I used to go into second-hand bookstores and

buy one book and hide another batch under it. I didn't have money to buy more than one book then.

"At the time I was obsessed with books. I had to have them and I didn't have the money. I'd gladly pay them back today if I had the chance. I used to stay home from school to read. I hated school, absolutely hated it. One of the happiest days in my life was when I realized I'd finished with school, that I wasn't going back the next year."

Some of his earlier feelings were since resolved, he pointed out, including the generation gap. "I have gone back to see my parents, though I didn't want to spend too much time back there. They used to be resentful about how I went about things, but afterward they had a lot of pride in me."

Though no one would confuse Bruce Springsteen's music with Springfield's, the name similarity has caused a few gaffes, leading Rick to write the song "Bruce." "The only Springsteen comparison I've had is my name. I like Springsteen a lot so I wouldn't take offense at such a comparison. I get a lot of people who call me Bruce, but I don't suspect he'd get anyone calling him Rick."

SPRINGSTEEN, BRUCE: *Singer, songwriter, guitarist, band leader (THE E STREET BAND). Born Freehold, New Jersey, September 23, 1949.*

Unlike many artists who become popular and stick to a set format, Bruce Springsteen hasn't been afraid to change. Thus, he has not only become more popular, but also increasingly influential. In 1975, the blue collar rocker burst onto the national scene with the album *Born to Run.* He wrote street dramas laden with images and characters from his native New Jersey shore. As he matured as an artist Springsteen began gradually to shift his attention to America. His songs in the 1984 album *Born in the U.S.A.* are stark; their characters struggle against a landscape of decaying cities and shuttered factories. His fans have stayed faithful throughout. To them, Springsteen remains "the Boss."

Even in such venues as the Los Angeles Coliseum, in front of 80,000 people most of whom could only see him via gigantic video screens, he has the ability to touch each individual with his energy. He runs from one end of the stage to the other, jumping atop speakers while wielding his guitar. Or he clowns around on stage with long-time friend and saxophonist Clarence "Nick" Clemons. He'll select a pretty woman from the audience to share a dance. And it is not uncommon for fans to do the singing for him on songs such as "Hungry Heart."

In short, his concerts are a celebration. Because of Springsteen's power on stage, it's fitting that in 1986 he released *Bruce Springsteen & the E Street Band Live/1975–1985,* a five-disc retrospective capturing the essence of his live performances plus the evolution of an artist—from his performances in clubs such as Los Angeles' Roxy to progressively larger arenas, from his early introspective and heavily textured anthems to his stark dramatic monologues about despair and futility. No artist during that period has had a larger impact on the American rock scene.

Indeed, in 1984 his influence had become so great that President Reagan and Walter Mondale each claimed that Springsteen shared their views of an America filled with hope and prosperity. Springsteen was forced to disassociate himself from both presidential candidates, becoming openly critical of "blind faith" in anything, according to *Los Angeles Times* columnist Robert Hilburn. "Here's a song about blind faith," Springsteen said, introducing "Reason to Believe." "That is always a dangerous thing, whether it's in your girlfriend . . . or if it's in your government."

Since 1980, Springsteen has become a powerful spokesman for America's dispossessed. In that year, he turned to Woody Guthrie's "This Land Is Your Land," sung in minor tones to reflect his view that something is amiss in the land. He reminds his audiences of the importance of commitment to their local communities as a way of bettering the world.

"Life is a struggle," Springsteen explained to Hilburn in 1980. "That's basically what the songs are about. It's the fight every one goes through every day. . . . I'm a romantic. To me, the idea of a romantic is someone who sees the reality, lives the reality every day, but knows about the possibilities too. You can't lose sight of the dreams."

Indeed, Springsteen's career began with dreams set against the backdrop of a working class family. His father, Douglas, held jobs as a bus driver and factory worker. Bruce attended elementary and high school in his hometown, Freehold, New Jersey, a place offering few role models. "It's like I come from an area where there was not a lot of success," he told Hilburn in 1978. "I didn't know anyone who made a record before me. I didn't know anybody who had done anything. It was like climbing the mountain or something."

In the late 1950s, he was attracted to rock by Elvis Presley. As he later told a reporter: "Anybody who sees Elvis Presley and doesn't want to be like Elvis Presley has got to have something wrong with him." (And indeed, one night in 1976 when he was performing in Memphis, Springsteen hopped the gate of Elvis' Graceland mansion in an attempt to see the rock legend, only to be turned away by a guard.) When he was nine, Bruce got a guitar, but his fingers couldn't handle it and he gave up. At 14, he tried once again; this time he stuck with the instrument.

Once he could play reasonably well, he organized the first of a series of bands that worked high school parties and small Jersey clubs in Asbury Park. It was there that he met such musicians as Southside Johnny Lyons of the Asbury Jukes. He formed a hard-rock group called Steel Mill. Later he started a soul group under his own name that had 10 members and incorporated the brass section sound that Springsteen continued to stress in his smaller bands of the '70s.

Two members of that band—keyboard artist David Sancious and saxophonist Clarence Clemons—remained with Bruce when he formed the E Street Band. Other early members of the E Steet band, most of whom he met in his Asbury Park days, were: Danny Federici, organ; Roy Bittan, piano; Garry Tallent, bass; Max Weinberg, drums; and Steve Van Zandt, guitar. Sancious left the band in 1974, signing a recording contract with Epic, and Van Zandt left the band in 1983 to begin a solo career. Van Zandt was replaced by Nils Lofgren in 1984. Patty Scialfa joined the band in 1988 as a background vocalist-guitarist on the "Tunnel of Love Express" tour.

Bruce briefly attended Ocean County Community College, but left when he got the chance to play at Bill Graham's Fillmore West. That experience didn't open any doors, so he returned to New York and worked whenever he could at clubs around the city. A meeting with two management executives, Mike Appel and Jim Cretecos, finally led to an audition with John Hammond of Columbia Records. Hammond was impressed with Springsteen's original street dramas such as "It's Hard to Be a Saint in the City," which evoked insistent images ("The sages of the subway sit just like the living dead/As the tracks clack out the rhythm/Their eyes fixed straight ahead.")

Appel became Bruce's first manager, a relationship that eventually ended in a legal dispute. According to Dave Marsh, who wrote *Born to Run: The Bruce Springsteen Story* (Dell, 1979), the arrangements with Appel were not favorable to Bruce: "Prolific Bruce may have been. Shrewd he was not. He signed a long-term management contract only a few days later, on an automobile hood in the unlighted parking lot of a bar."

That contract with Columbia was signed in 1972, and Bruce's debut album, *Greetings from Asbury Park, N.J.*, was released in January 1973. Many reviewers didn't even give the disc passing notice, but a few found it extremely powerful. It was not a commercial success, selling about 25,000 copies initially, according to Marsh. Hammond and his associates urged him to complete a second LP: *The*

Wild, the Innocent, and the E Street Shuffle (November 1973).

At first, the record-buying public also stayed away from this record, in part because the songs did not lend themselves to widespread radio airplay. But this time, almost all the critics paid attention. *Rolling Stone* selected the album as one of the best of 1973. Jon Landau, who became Springsteen's manager/record producer in 1977, wrote the most often-quoted Springsteen review after viewing Springsteen in a 1974 concert: "I saw my rock and roll past flash before my eyes. . . . I saw rock and roll's future and its name is Bruce Springsteen."

The critical acclaim paid off in the short term. By August 1974, sales of *E Street Shuffle* were approaching 100,000, according to Marsh.

But it was another year before Landau's prophecy came true. Part of the problem seemed to be Springsteen's low profile; he liked playing the small East Coast clubs where he had become a celebrity but shied away from coast-to-coast touring. Springsteen also suffered from inertia in creating new material, accounting for a long gap between albums. It took much prodding from admirers such as Landau (a contributing editor to *Rolling Stone*) before Bruce capitulated and wrote enough songs for album three. When *Born to Run,* which was co-produced by Landau, was released in August 1975, it was hailed in most quarters as a landmark in rock. The LP was aided by Springsteen's first national tour and, on October 8, 1975, brought him his first gold-record award. Accompanying it on its chart journey were the two earlier albums, which also went gold.

Springsteen became a national celebrity. His face graced the covers of both *Time* and *Newsweek* in the same week. In the pictures, he seemed a throwback to an earlier rock era with his black leather motorcycle jacket, t-shirt, and jeans. But his music, almost all agreed, had not been heard before. It was a blend of many things in pop from R&B and swing to hard-driving rock, but, as often happens, the sum of the parts added up to something considerably removed from any individual element.

In his first three albums, Springsteen focused on New Jersey plus his youth, independence, and coming of age. Many were dazzled by such songs as "Blinded by the Light," and "Growin' Up" on *Greetings.* "Rosalita" and "4th of July, Asbury Park (Sandy)" continued his focus on specific involvements in his second album, which had an adventurous and heavily-textured sound.

In "Born to Run," Springsteen wrote of escaping along Highway 9 from small-town life (perhaps a foreshadowing of artistic changes to come): "Baby this town rips the bones from your back/It's a death trap, it's a suicide rap/We gotta get out while we're young/'Cause tramps like us, baby we were born to run."

But despite the critical and popular acclaim of *Born to Run,* Springsteen did not release another album until 1978's *Darkness on the Edge of Town.* The three-year hiatus was in part caused by legal entanglements. In 1976, Springsteen and Appel had a series of disagreements over the management deal, royalties, and the rights to his songs, according to Marsh. The two sued one another in July of that year, and one ruling restrained Landau from producing any of Springsteen's albums. A settlement was not reached until May 1977. But Springsteen was also attempting to deal with his newfound stardom. Early in his career, Springsteen had said: "There's no way we'd ever play in one of those barns." But in 1978, he switched from playing clubs such as New York's Bottom Line (where he kicked off the '75 tour in support of *Born to Run)* to such "barns" as the Nassau Coliseum and the 18,000-seat Los Angeles Forum. It took him a while, though, to learn how to project his personality to all parts of huge arenas, for the timing and musicianship needed to be a bit different from the techniques used on the club circuit.

In *Darkness,* Springsteen also began to change his focus. He had fulfilled his dream of becoming a rock star and now had to deal with its realities. As Irwin Stambler wrote in his "Pop, Rock & Soul" column: "It is a work that diverges sharply from what has gone before. For the most part, it talks of the problems and frustrations of a real, recognizable world rather than the special surroundings of Bruce's youth in New Jersey."

Though *Darkness* reached the top 5, it did not receive the acclaim of *Born to Run.* Nevertheless, such songs as the title track, "The Promised Land," and "Badlands" all became Springsteen concert standards.

It was clearly a time of transition for Bruce. "I felt like I had lost a certain control of myself," he told Hilburn in 1980. "There was all the publicity and all the backlash. I felt the thing I wanted most in life—my music—being swept away and didn't know if I could do anything about it."

In 1980, Springsteen released *The River,* a two-album set recapturing the artistic energy of his first three albums. His reputation as a performer also improved sharply in 1980, when he showed he not only could sell out arenas night after night, but also could electrify the largest crowds. He displayed tremendous endurance, with shows often lasting more than four hours. He told Hilburn: "I don't count on my tomorrows. . . . If you do that, you begin to plan too much and begin rationing yourself. . . . If you start rationing, you're living life bit by bit when you can live it all at once."

The River was more accessible and commercially successful than *Darkness*. "The Boss" received more widespread radio airplay with such spirited songs as "Hungry Heart" and "Out on the Street." But his work also included dramatic songs such as the title track, written from the perspective of a young man whose dreams and aspirations are cut down when his girlfriend becomes pregnant and they are forced to get married. "Independence Day" paints a bittersweet image of a decaying hometown seen through the eyes of a man who is leaving his family. ("Now the rooms are all empty down at Frankie's joint/And the highway she's deserted clear down to Breaker's Point.")

Such concerns about recession and decay could in retrospect be seen as leading directly into Springsteen's next album, *Nebraska* (1982). The album seemed like such a departure from his earlier work that it caught many by surprise. It received critical acclaim, but did not do as well with record buyers as previous releases. Still, it sold more than 750,000 copies.

The album is a collection of stories about drifters and criminals. Springsteen recorded it at home on a four-track cassette recorder, accompanying himself on guitar and harmonica. The acoustic, rough-cut quality reminds one of Woody Guthrie singing "Pretty Boy Floyd."

The title track was based on the true story of Charles Starkweather, who went on a killing spree in Nebraska in 1958 and was executed the next year. Springsteen ended speaking in the matter-of-fact voice of the murderer: "They wanted to know why I did what I did/Well sir I guess there's just a meanness in this world."

In tracks such as "Johnny 99," "State Trooper," and "Open All Night," Springsteen depicted the desperation of individuals, many of whom were isolated and trapped by circumstance. The bare-bones album represented a risk for Springsteen, especially after his success with *The River*. Hilburn wrote in 1982 that Springsteen was deliberately moving toward a "harsher sociopolitical stance. . . . Rather than continue to mix these thoughts into the otherwise celebrative mood of his albums and shows, Springsteen obviously wanted to focus on them so that the message couldn't be ignored."

But he changed gears again in his next, and most successful album. In *Born In the U.S.A.* (1984), Springsteen returned to the E Street Band but retained the themes of *Nebraska*. He reportedly culled the 12 songs from more than 60 tracks recorded during an 18-month period.

Many critics hailed *Born in the U.S.A.* as another landmark. As Stephen Holden of *The New York Times* wrote: "[Springsteen] forged a dense, metallic sound that embraces more mechanical rhythms and textures, but without severing Mr. Springsteen's ties with Chuck Berry, Motown, rockabilly, and other traditional rock and roll idioms. . . . [It] is a sad and serious album about the end of the American dream—of economic hope and security, and of community—for a dwindling segment of our society."

On the album cover, Springsteen posed in blue jeans and t-shirt in front of what looked like an American flag. The image was taken by many, including Reagan, as emblematic of Springsteen's patriotism. But for his fans, the album's upbeat sound could not mask the disillusionment in his lyrics. The album began with the title track, a song about a downtrodden Vietnam vet: "Born down in a dead man's town/The first kick I took was when I hit the ground/You end up like a dog that's been beat too much/Till you spend half your life just covering up."

Songs such as "My Hometown" and "Reason to Believe" depicted the decay of the towns and the determination of many to escape, as well as the blind faith some seem to need to survive. Even the catchy single "Dancing in the Dark" portayed the loneliness of a man who "could use just a little help."

The album sold more than 11 million copies worldwide. The posters of Springsteen in front of the American flag could be seen in stores worldwide as he embarked on an international tour in 1984. At many stops, Springsteen urged fans to contribute to local food banks. For example, in an Oakland concert, Springsteen introduced "My Hometown" by asking people to "help the Berkeley Emergency Food Project . . . to feed people—people who have been cut down by the injustices in our social system and by the economic policies of the current administration."

Springsteen continued to show his commitment to combating hunger by playing a key role in the 1985 "We Are the World" album and video. His distinctive voice was easily recognizable on the song, which raised millions of dollars for relief of the famine in Ethiopia. (Former lead guitarist Steve Van Zandt became involved in another African cause later that year by spearheading the *Sun City* record and video protesting South Africa's policy of apartheid.)

"The Boss" was now being called things like "rock's popular populist" as critics compared him to Guthrie, Dylan, and Presley. Many fans, including rock critic Robert Hilburn, began to make pilgrimages to New Jersey to discover Springsteen's roots. But others also began wondering if Bruce's immense popularity would lead to a backlash. Most critics discounted the notion. But in the *Los Angeles Times* article "Tellin' Off the Boss," Kristine McKenna criticized Springsteen's "pedestrian thematic vocabulary. There's some serious Stone Age thinking going on in Bruce's songs, which basically begin and end with girls."

Amid the hoopla, Springsteen found time to break many hearts in May 1985 by marrying actress and model Julianne Phillips. That too was well covered by the media. In fact, according to Dave Marsh, who wrote *Glory Days: Bruce Springsteen in the 1980s* (Pantheon, 1987), the media even intruded upon the ceremony. "The guy looked at me at the end of that wedding scene (which included photographers shooting from helicopters) and said: 'I do not believe or comprehend the world that I live in. Put that at the top of the chapter,'" Marsh told *USA Today*.

In 1986, the publicity died down a bit until the release of the five-LP live set in November. Despite the $25 price tag, record buyers besieged the stores, which received advance orders of more than 1.5 million copies. As Stephen Holden of *The New York Times* put it: "At the very least, it is a record of how one singer and his band have helped to sustain and put their personal stamp on a rock tradition that electronic keyboard technology has steadily eroded over the last decade. More important, the album is the pop-record equivalent of an epic American novel, its story told in the ungrammatical, rough-hewn vocabulary of rock."

The *Live* set was the end of an era. He told Edna Gundersen *(USA Today,* March 15, 1988): "We played it in my room. We all sat there and listened to it. And I said, 'Well, 10 years, there it is. When you have those little babies and they want to know what you did these past 10 years, you play them this record.' I think it's something to be proud of. After that, I said, 'Well, time for a new adventure.'"

That adventure was *Tunnel of Love* (October 1987), which represented a change in direction. Songs such as the title track, "One Step Up," and "Brilliant Disguise" focused on the dashed hopes and desires in modern romance. The album was perhaps more autobiographical than most had thought at first, since in 1988 rumors began circulating that Springsteen and Julianne Phillips had separated.

The album was certified double-platinum and earned Springsteen the distinction of being the only artist in the past 10 years to chart four No. 1 LPs in *Billboard*.

In February 1988, Springsteen embarked on the "Tunnel of Love Express" tour, a carefully crafted show that represented a shift from his previous, more spontaneous concerts. "It felt like the time to break with the past a little bit," he said.

But in *Tunnel of Love,* he remained committed to

fighting against living in a world of mirrors and illusions, he told Bill Barol *(Newsweek,* November 2, 1987), "People deserve better. They deserve the truth. They deserve honesty. The best music, you can seek some shelter in it momentarily, but it's essentially there to provide you something to face the world with." *(See Lofgren, Nils; Smith, Patti; Southside Johnny and the Asbury Jukes.)* (Entry by Lyndon Stambler.)

SQUEEZE: *Vocal and instrumental group. Original members (1975) all born United Kingdom: Chris Difford, born August 31; Glenn Tilbrook, born November 4; Gilson Lavis; Jools Holland; Harry Kakoulli. Kakoulli left in 1979, replaced by John Bentley. Holland replaced by Paul Carrack in 1980. Carrack left in 1981. Group disbanded in 1982, reformed in 1985 with Difford, Tilbrook, Lavis, Holland, and Keith Wilkinson.*

Based on the excellent writing skills of Glenn Tilbrook and Chris Difford, Squeeze was one of the more unique quintets to evolve from the England's new wave genre of the late 1970s. Indeed, some reviewers went so far as to call the Tilbrook/Difford writing team the Gilbert and Sullivan, Lieber and Stoller, or Lennon and McCartney of the 1980s—comparisons that the Squeeze co-founders were not particularly happy with. The best of their material (which one reviewer described as "musical sketches" at times approaching a "working class comedy of manners") suggested new directions for rock, but perhaps were a bit too complex for the tastes of 1980s audiences.

Commenting on a Squeze concert of 1981, Robert Hilburn of the *Los Angeles Times* wrote: "The cumulative effect of the inventive melodies and colorful imagery was reminiscent of the inventive melodies and rich tapestries associated with the best British bands of the '60s—bands like the Kinks and the Who. If Squeeze had arrived during that time, it would have been in the forefront of the British invasion. In these blander, more regimented times, however, it faces an uphill climb."

During the first phase of Squeeze's existence, it seemed on the verge of such a breakthrough in the U.S. several times, most notably after placing several singles high on U.S. charts in 1982. But Difford and Tilbrook's belief in creative experimentation and a refusal to comply with the formula approach dictated by the rock-radio establishment of those years ruled out compromises just for the sake of money alone.

Tilbrook told Hilburn: "You don't measure a band only by sales. You want to be successful, but on your own terms. I know a lot of people do try only for the hits. But I think it's important to write for your own satisfaction, so you can feel you've achieved something. Otherwise, rock'n'roll is just like 'Bowling for Dollars,' isn't it?''

Difford said: ''We're quite aware of the way [top 40 format] radio works and the problems in breaking a band like ours. We've been listening to the radio for four or five years here and it hasn't changed much. The only difference from the time we first came here is that they're playing REO Speedwagon instead of 'Baker Street.' If you look at the sales charts, you also see that heavy metal is dominating things. That worries me. I always thought of heavy metal as just a pair of dirty old jeans. I don't think it teaches or inspires the audience much. But I am hopeful.''

Difford and Tilbrook began writing together in the early 1970s and had a sizable backlog of original numbers when they got together with three others to found Squeeze (originally called U.K. Squeeze) in 1975. The group consisted of Difford and Tilbrook on guitars and vocals, Harry Kakoulli on bass guitar, Jools Holland on keyboards, and Gilson Lavis on drums. In 1976, the group had its first record on the market, a three-song extended-play disc on the Fun City label. The EP paved the way for a contract with the larger A&M Records, which provided a potentially important entry to the key U.S. market. The band's first A&M album, *U.K. Squeeze* (produced by veteran rock artist John Cale), provided a top 10 hit in England, ''Take Me I'm Yours.'' Issued in the U.S. during May 1978, the album won praise from critics, but had little impact on the listening public. Their next two releases—*Cool for Cats* (March 1979) and *Argy Bargy* (March 1980)—demonstrated the band's ability to probe many aspects of modern society and were even more highly lauded by critics but scored minimal inroads with record buyers.

Key problem was lack of U.S. airplay. Hilburn pointed out: ''The answer lies partially in Squeeze's image and style, neither of which fits conveniently into rock's most commercial slots these days. The music is too challenging at times for the mainstream pop-rock that radio favors, yet too melodic for the hard core elements of new wave.''

The band did gain favor with English fans and also was popular with many peer musicians, including Elvis Costello, with whom the group played a number of concerts in the U.S. in 1981. Among tracks English adherents praised on *Cool for Cats* were ''Up the Junction'' and ''Slap and Tickle,'' while ''Pulling Mussels (from the Shell)'' and ''If I Didn't Love You'' from *Argy Bargy* became Squeeze concert staples. Meanwhile, the band was undergoing personnel changes. Kakoulli left after the *Cool for Cats* period and was replaced on bass by John Bentley. Following *Argy Bargy*, Holland was replaced on keyboards by former Ace bandsman Paul Carrack. Carrack sang the lead vocal on the song ''Tempted'' from the May 1981 album *East Side Story* that was a hit in England and also made U.S. charts, but in the fall of that year, he too departed.

The next LP, *Sweets for a Stranger* (April 1982), spawned the first major U.S. singles hit ''Black Coffee in Bed,'' another Difford/Tilbrook collaboration. At long last, it seemed the band was on its way to commercial acceptance in America. To the surprise of a growing number of appreciative fans, the group broke up with the terse announcement ''Squeeze has decided that the band as a horse has run its course, and the jockeys are considering new mounts.''

Tilbrook told the English trade magazine *Melody Maker* soon after that he and Difford just had become too unhappy with the restrictions of an organized group, particularly one with five strong-willed and often competitive individuals. ''The dissatisfaction we were feeling manifested itself in two direct ways. The last record Squeeze made contained some tracks that were really good, but as a whole album it didn't stand up to the other ones. And secondly, the enthusiasm slipped out of the live shows.''

Lavis, the other remaining original member, added: ''It's such a claustrophobic atmosphere to be in a band with five strong individuals. We couldn't stop things going out of balance, because we weren't aware enough to see it coming.''

With no new studio albums on the horizon, A&M issued a retrospective of sorts in November 1982, *Singles—45's and Under.*

For the next few years, Difford and Tilbrook pursued a variety of creative avenues, including a duo album, *Difford & Tilbrook* (A&M, 1984), and performing at home and overseas with a newly assembled band. While they kept in touch and occasionally played with former Squeeze associates, as of 1984 they still maintained Squeeze was a thing of the past.

Tilbrook told Kristine McKenna of the *Los Angeles Times* in July 1984: ''It's inevitable that this [new duo] will be reviewed as a Squeeze album, particularly in America, which is slower to adapt to change than England is. It goes without saying that the band is not something I'd still like to be involved with. We'd done our best work, were on a downhill roll, and a creative malaise had settled on the group.

''The new record is more emotional and mature than music we've previously made, and the production is much more elaborate. We backed ourselves into a corner with Squeeze in that we were determined to be able to play everything live properly to the point that we restricted ourselves in the studio and didn't fully develop certain songs. With this record, we gave the songs full breathing space in the studio, partly because we simply had more time to spend on it.''

Besides the new album, the two put together a stage show in England, ''Labeled with Love,'' based on their songs past and present. The two friends also wrote and produced a record for rap artist Grandmaster Flash. Tilbrook spent some time as a disc jockey at a London club.

But it proved easier to talk about Squeeze in past tense than to avoid waxing nostalgic about it. In January 1985, four of the original members—Difford, Tilbrook, Lavis, and Holland—plus Keith Wilkinson, bass guitarist with the 1983–84 Difford/Tilbrook backing band, got together to do a charity performance at a pub in Catford, England. The set went so well, both for the musicians and the audience, that the band was inspired to try a new Squeeze incarnation. Holland commented that while the Squeeze alumni had enjoyed the long sabbaticals from the band: ''We decided each of us on our own aren't nearly as good as we are together.''

With a nod of approval from A&M Records, the band went back into the studio to record new tracks for the album *Cosi Fan Tutti Frutti*, released in August 1985. As the title indicated, the album combined such seemingly divergent influences as Mozart and Little Richard. The new compilation, Carol Clerk of *Melody Maker* stated, ''fulfills [Squeeze's] intentions to widen their scope, fatten and dramatize their sound, and compound the impact with an 'extreme' production.''

In 1987, the band made U.S. charts with a new album, *Babylon and On* (A&M), from which its first U.S. top 40 single, ''Hourglass,'' was culled.

STARR, RINGO: *Drummer, singer, songwriter, record-company executive, record producer, actor. Born Dingle, Liverpool, England, July 7, 1940.*

Long before the official announcement of the Beatles' disbandment in 1970, Ringo Starr (born Richard Starkey) was working on his own projects. In December 1967, he was in Rome for a cameo role as a Mexican gardener in the film *Candy*, starring Richard Burton and Marlon Brando. (The film premiered on February 20, 1969.) During most of 1969, Ringo worked on the film *The Magic Christian*, in which he co-starred with Peter Sellers.

On October 27, 1969, he started work on his first solo album, *Sentimental Journey*, released on April 3, 1970 by Apple Records with distribution by Capitol. In January 1970, he and wife Maureen (the former Maureen Cox, born England, August 4, 1946, whom he married on February 11, 1965) flew to Los Angeles for the *Magic Christian* premier. While there, he taped an appearance on Rowan and Martin's TV comedy show, ''Laugh-In.'' On June 22, he flew to Nashville to work on his country album, *Beaucoups of Blues,* produced by steel guitarist Pete Drake.

During 1971, Ringo took part in the famed charity concert for Bangla Desh held in New York's Madison Square Garden. During the year, he achieved his first solo gold record for the single ''It Don't Come Easy,'' written by him and George Harrison. A song he wrote alone, ''Back Off Boogaloo,'' was a top 10 hit in 1972. In October 1973, Apple put out the gold LP *Ringo,* on which he was assisted musically at various times by all three other ex-Beatles (although they did not perform as a foursome on any of the tracks). Also working as sidemen or backing vocalists were such notables as the Band, Nilsson, Marc Bolan, Merry Clayton, Martha Reeves, and Billy Preston. It spawned two number one singles: ''Photograph'' (co-written by Ringo and George Harrison), number one in *Billboard* the week of November 24, 1973, and ''You're Sixteen'' (a 1960 Johnny Burnette hit written by Richard and Robert Sherman), at the top the week of January 26, 1974.

Mid-1970s hit singles included ''Oh My My,'' the two-sided success ''No No Song''/''Snookeroo,'' and a remake of the Platters' 1955 ''Only You.'' He also added to his acting credentials with a well-regarded role in *That'll Be the Day* (a smash in England and a flop in America). By the time of its filming, he had separated from his first wife and his acquaintanceship with actress Barbara Bach led to her becoming his second.

Ringo's last LPs for Apple were *Goodnight Vienna* (1974, gold) and the retrospective *Blast from Your Past* (1975). The demise of the Beatles' record label in the mid-1970s caused him to find other recording homes. But Starr's albums after Apple seemed to lose some of their drive and focus compared to earlier solo collections. Atlantic albums *Ringo's Rotogravure* (1976) and *Ringo the 4th* (1977) provided no major singles hits and made only weak showings on the charts. The same held true for such later releases as *Bad Boy* (Portrait, 1977) and *Stop and Smell the Roses* (Boardwalk, 1981). His mid-1980s RCA album *Old Wave* was issued in Canada and only available in the U.S. as an import.

In his low-key way, Ringo continued to keep active with writing and occasional guest appearances in the 1980s. He was always willing to lend his talents to help people he admired on recording sessions or special programs, such as Carl Perkins' cable-TV special (with backing from many English rock stars) that helped bring new luster to Carl's career in 1985.

(See Beatles, The; Harrison, George; Lennon, John; McCartney, Paul; Nilsson; Perkins, Carl.)

STEELEYE SPAN: *Vocal and instrumental group from England. Original members (1969): Tim Hart, Maddy Prior, Ashley Hutchings, Gay Woods, Terry Woods. Gay and Terry Woods replaced in 1971 by Martin Carthy and Peter Knight. Hutchings and Carthy replaced in 1972 by Bob Johnson and Rick Kemp. Nigel Pegrum added in 1974. Group disbanded in late 1970s. Regrouped in 1980s with Prior, Knight, Johnson, Kemp, and Pegrum.*

Over the lifetime of many rock bands, so many personnel changes take place you might quip you can't tell the players without a scorecard. This certainly was true for the excellent folk-rock Steeleye Span during its first decade. Though the group's style changed with its shift in members and record producers from early offerings that tended to be folk music with rock flavoring to an eventual folk-tinged rock approach, there was continuity provided by founding members Tim Hart and Maddy Prior—the only original performers to remain with the band throughout its first incarnation.

Like the other original members, Hart and Prior emerged from the British folk scene of the 1960s. As a duo, they were major draws on the folk-club circuit late in the decade before helping form Steeleye Span.

Guitarist/dulcimer player Hart actually started out as a rock adherent in the Beatles-Rolling Stones era. His first group experience came during his teens when he and some school friends started a rock band called the Ratfinks. But when he met a promising folk singer named Donovan at a St. Albans pub, he changed his musical goal.

He told a reporter from England's *Melody Maker* magazine in 1973: "I started singing folk at the Cock. I'd already started getting fed up with the group and Don [Donovan] was a big influence on me. Together with records by people like Dylan, of course, and Jesse Fuller and Peter, Paul and Mary, which were flying about that time.

"We used to have great times at the Cock, although it wasn't a proper pub, just a bar where all the folk freaks used to gather, most of them underage. It's remarkable how many well-known singers got started there."

Among the talented, if unknown performers who showed up there was clarion-voiced Maddy Prior, who soon found common musical ground with Hart. Prior had made her stage debut at the age of eight with the Blackpool Opera. Her career didn't burgeon then or in her teens, though she continued to sing various kinds of pop music when she got the chance.

She had some interest in early rock and the kinds of folk songs Joan Baez and Judy Collins recorded in the early 1960s, but didn't develop a particularly individual style at the time.

For some years, she was better known among folk artists as a rare female roadie rather than as a singer. For a while she chauffeured American folk duo Sandy and Jeanie Darlington around the U.K. and later helped do concert setup chores for blind American blues singer Reverend Gary Davis.

But she desired to be on stage rather than behind it. Her chance finally came in the late 1960s through her association with Hart. Initially they performed songs drawn from American pop folk of the '60s, but gradually they incorporated more and more upgraded versions of traditional British airs such as "Maid That's Deep in Love" and "Prince Charlie Stuart."

While appearing at the Loughborough Folk Festival in 1969, Tim and Maddy got into conversation with another highly regarded musician, Ashley Hutchings. A little while before, Hutchings had started rehearsing a new band whose other members were drawn from the disbanded folk act Sweeney's Men. The latter were Terry Woods (later of the Pogues) and his wife Gay, Johnny Moynihan, and Andy Irvine. Shortly before the festival, Moynihan and Irvine quit and Hutchings was looking for replacements. He asked Tim and Maddy to join and they agreed, provided that they still could continue fitting in their duo gigs.

The new quintet took its name from the hero of a folk song that English composer Percy Grainger had collected from a certain Joseph Taylor. After rehearsing for some months, the band got a go-ahead to record a debut album. That collection, *Hark the Village Wait* (RCA, 1970), came out in England only. The group had hardly finished the project when Gay and Terry Woods left before the band had played in concerts. In fact, the first version of Steeleye Span never did make any public appearances.

The band regrouped by adding harsh-voiced veteran English folksinger and instrumentalist Martin Carthy and fiddle player Peter Knight. Knight, whose eventual tenure with the band was second only to Maddy's, came from a musical family. His father, a dance band member who played guitar and mandolin, taught the latter instrument to Peter when the boy was eight. Initially grounded in the classics, he was accepted in the Royal Academy of Music in his teens, but left because he saw little chance for a rewarding career.

Instead, he got a job selling musical instruments, which inspired him to make a collection of instruments on his own. He spent some of his spare time listening to folk artists at local clubs, but didn't consider a folk career until a friend played him a record by Irish fiddler Michael Coleman. "I thought that if I could achieve anything like that sort of lilt and could understand the feel of the music, then that was what I wanted. [I began] listening to people like Coleman and Bobby Casey and Jimmy Power as well as a lot of flute players. That was my first introduction to any form of folk music, but at that time it wasn't specifically English folk music that I liked."

He and guitarist Bob Johnson began to appear in folk clubs. The money from music was minimal, but Knight loved performing. He quit his job and gained living expenses by selling instruments from his collection.

In 1971, he told *Melody Maker:* "I'd been going a year without work when Tyger Hutchings phoned me up one day and asked me to join Steeleye. Apparently Martin Carthy had been to see some gigs that Bob and I had done, but whether that had anything to do with it or not I don't know. I'd also done a BBC gig with Maddy.

"I was shocked to find out how many professional musicians knew me just on the strength of those gigs I'd done with Bob."

In 1971, the new band put out two albums: *Please to See the King* (on Big Tree in the U.S.) and *Ten Man Mop or Mr. Reservoir Butler Rides Again* (issued in England only on Pegasus). Tracks by Steeleye also were included in a Charisma sampler titled *Individually and Collectively.* Those releases and audience reaction to a number of concerts by the new group brought attention not only in Europe, but in the U.S. as well. The band, which had no drummer for several years, used bass guitar or percussion instruments to provide a strong rhythm base.

Though the outlook looked promising, there were disagreements about direction and Hutchings left, complaining that the band focused too much on Irish rather than British folk tradition. Carthy also decided the format was too constraining and took leave. (He and Hutchings then played in the Albion County Band. Carthy later put out such fascinating traditional folk LPs as *Crown of Horn* and *Because It's There,* released in the U.S. on Rounder.) Their places were taken by Knight's former partner, Bob Johnson, and bass guitarist Rick Kemp (who eventually married Prior and then separated from her). Both had extensive experience as session musicians as well as rock bandsmen.

Johnson originally liked the trumpet, but when he asked for one at 13, his father said it was too noisy an instrument, so Bob began learning harmonica. He told *Melody Maker:* "I was very hung up on Larry Adler, but I wasn't really getting anywhere when I passed a second-hand shop and I saw a battered guitar in the window. It was totally unplayable, of course, but it was my fourteenth birthday, so I got it.

I just loved the feel of it round my neck, standing in front of the TV when '65 Special' was on and miming. I really had delusions of grandeur. I really wanted to be a pop star."

In the next few years, he got a decent guitar and learned to play well enough to join a band in the town of Tooting named Earl Sheridan and the Houseshakers. After Earl left, the band continued on as the Pack. Afterwards, Johnson said: "We got picked up by this singer called Paul Raven, who is now known as Gary Glitter, and we backed him as Paul Raven and the Pack for about two years, but we never made any money."

Discouraged, Johnson took a regular job for a while, but Raven's brother helped him get session work as part of the house band at Immediate Records. He was asked to join a folk-oriented band, Thane Russell, which piqued his interest in traditional music. He liked the songs' content, but felt they could use more of a current feel. "Then I started working with Peter and what was nice about that was he had this classical feel and I had all these pop influences. Then Fairports [Fairport Convention] and Steeleye happened and I was really jealous because this was what I'd thought of many years before."

Naturally, he jumped at the chance to join Steeleye. Once aboard, he imparted more electric instrumentation to the band's arrangements.

Kemp's introduction to pop music went back to the skiffle (blues-based period) in England. In his teens, his group won the all-England skiffle contest at a club called the Cafe de Paris. He told *Melody Maker:* "Larry Parnes offered me a contract, but I was only 13 and my old man wouldn't hear of it. He thought I was going to be an airline pilot or a brain surgeon or something."

He continued to play guitar in his later teens when his family moved to Hull. There, he got his first professional job with a group called the Aces as bass guitarist. "After a while I really fell in love with the bass because I was at the bottom of it all instead of being out in front and that appealed to me."

After that band broke up, he got a job in a music store, where he was befriended by songwriter/band organizer Mike Chapman. He did some backup on two of Chapman's albums and then toured the U.S. with him. Back in England, Kemp did more session work, where he met the producer of early Steeleye recordings, Sandy Roberton. When Hutchings left, Roberton brought Kemp into the band.

The first two albums with the new roster, *Below the Salt* (1972) and *Parcel of Rogues* (1973) on Chrysalis Records, were thought by some to have added too much electric influence. The albums, however, still were impressive for unusual material (such as the Latin hymn "Gaudete" and numerous tales of bewitchings, human transfigurations, and struggles for eighteenth century pretender to the British throne, Bonnie Prince Charlie Stuart) and Maddy Prior's bell-like soprano on tracks such as "One Misty Moisty Morning" on *Parcel of Rogues*. The band by then had a healthy, if not massive following in the U.S., which enthusiastically performed an in-place dance called jigging to Steeleye Span music in rock clubs across the country. Also unique to Steeleye's live shows was a recreation of a medieval mummers play.

For the group's 1974 Chrysalis release, *Now We Are Six*, the group finally added a drummer—Nigel Pegrum. With this sixth member, Steeleye also had shaken down to a stable grouping that did not change until the group disbanded (except for the return of Martin Carthy, accompanied by his friend John Kirkpatrick on concertina, in its final days).

This sextet turned out what some consider the band's best trio of albums: *Now We Are Six* and, in 1976, *Commoner's Crown* and *All Around My Hat*. Some novel additions were a saxophone solo by David Bowie on the hardly folk Phil Spector composition "To Know Him Is to Love Him" on *Now We Are Six* and Peter Sellers' ukelele playing on *Commoner's Crown's* "New York Girls" track.

Though the group continued to concertize and record new material after the mid-1970s, the quality didn't match the previous releases. Chrysalis albums of that period included *Rocket Cottage* (1976), *Storm Force Ten* (1977), and *Live At Last* (1978). In 1977, Chrysalis issued a two-disc retrospective, *The Steeleye Span Story—Original Masters*.

Late in the 1970s, Steeleye disbanded. Prior tried for a solo career, but her contemporary LPs *Woman in the Wings* and *Changing Winds* were never released in the U.S., nor was the Maddy Prior Band's *Hooked on Winning*. Carthy and Kirkpatrick returned to traditional folk music in Brass Monkey and the Albion County Band. Shanachie Records licensed most of Steeleye's albums for reissue in the U.S., along with Prior and Hart's sterling 1971 *Summer Solstice* and Prior and June Tabor's rich (and hardly silly) 1976 *Silly Sisters* duets.

In 1981, the act reassembled informally for a few dates. Prior, Knight, Kemp, Johnson, and Pegrum formally regrouped in 1983. (Hart by then had gone into music management. Carthy and Kirkpatrick continued their other projects.) The reunion LP, *Back in Line* (Shanachie, 1986), combined ancient folk balladry with their own compositions, including several about Scotland's legendary fourteenth-century King Robert the Bruce.

STEELY DAN: *Vocal and instrumental duo or group. Members (middle to late 1970s): Donald Fagen, born New York, New York, c. late 1940s; Walter Becker, born New York, New York, c. late 1940s.*

Anyone wanting proof that the rock field is far from homogeneous need look no further than Steely Dan. This group, for most of its history essentially a duo of writer/performers Walter Becker and Donald Fagen, rarely toured and produced recordings usually far more intricate in melodies and lyrics than typical mainstream rock bands, yet it retained the favor of millions of record buyers around the world throughout much of the 1970s.

In fact, the Dan's reputation was partly based on its irreverence for accepted rock practices and also a certain mystique rooted in the duo's reclusiveness. People buying the band's latest album never knew exactly what would be found either musically or in the roster of musicians. Actually, there was no one Steely Dan band; the central duo added various bandsmen for recordings or concerts to provide whatever they felt was needed to interpret its latest compositions.

Though Fagen and Becker called Los Angeles home from the early '70s on, they were born and raised on the U.S. East Coast. When people got the chance to ask what their newest music was about (which wasn't often, because the twosome hated to give interviews), they suggested the place to look for answers was the Big Apple. Fagen told one reporter: "Our heart is still in 2nd Avenue and that's what we like to write about." That certainly was an exaggeration and, anyway, Fagen and Becker liked to play hide-and-seek about the definitions and wellsprings of their music. Still, there was no doubt that it was urban in nature and intellectual in conception. Frank Zappa, referring to its often dark lyric content, called it "downer surrealism."

Compared to mainstream rock, Steely Dan's material was distinctly offbeat, though Fagen and Becker had the ability to write simpler, more accessible songs if they wanted to, an example being their 1974 top 10 hit "Rikki Don't Lose That Number."

The duo's main objective, however, always was to explore new pathways in rock and other forms of pop music. They essentially agreed on that in the beginning when they first met as students at Bard College in upstate New York in the mid-1960s. At the time, they shared an affinity for jazz and avant garde writers such as William Burroughs. The name Steely Dan derives from a pornographic reference in Burroughs book *Naked Lunch*. During their college years, singer-keyboardist Fagen and guitarist Becker, besides collaborating on original songs, also worked together in various bands, which they continued to do after finishing college at the start of the 1970s. One group they worked with had future comedian Chevy Chase on drums. They also were part of a group headed by guitarist Denny Dias, which they helped break up when they constantly found fault with other members. During that period, their initial record was the soundtrack for a short-lived underground film, *You Gotta Walk It Like You Talk It (Or You'll Lose That Beat)* (available in the late 1980s on Visa Records).

During 1970–71, the duo tried to storm the New York music scene with their often difficult-to-understand material. There was almost unanimous disinterest among record and music-publishing executives. An exception was producer Gary Katz, who was impressed enough that when he found a position with ABC/Dunhill in Los Angeles, California, he invited the duo to move west and audition for the label.

Katz, too, initially had doubts. Recalling that episode for Richard Cromelin of the *Los Angeles Times* (June 29, 1975), Becker said: "We had a lot of tunes in minor keys, very sinister sounding, and we had to play them for people who had record companies or publishing companies and stuff, and they got depressed, and slightly hostile, and withdrew immediately. They'd leave, or make some kind of excuse and turn off the tape recorder and they never wanted to see us again. All except Gary Katz—''

Fagen demurred: "No, he ran out of the office the first time too.''

To which Katz replied: "No, no, no. The first time was in the studio, and I didn't run. It was really strange to hear. The music was a little more bizarre than it is now. . . . You were doing 'Let George Do It or No Deal' and 'Brain Tap Shuffle.' I was really intrigued, but I mean it didn't hit me at all. They kept playing it for me and saying: 'Listen, just keep listening.' And one day I got it.''

After joining ABC/Dunhill, Katz first brought the duo in as staff writers, then eased them onto the company recording roster. For the debut album, Katz, Fagen, and Becker put together a band with guitarist Jeff Baxter (later of the Doobie Brothers; *see Doobie Brothers, The), drummer Jim Hodder, guitarist Denny Dias, and lead singer David Palmer. The album, *Can't Buy a Thrill* (1972), and the follow-up, *Countdown to Ecstasy* (1973), featured more upbeat and more simply structured songs than later Steely Dan collections. Strong airplay created such hit singles as "Do It Again" and "Reeling in the Years." Supported by some excellent concert work, the two albums went gold, but the second album's increasing emphasis on the more unusual aspects of Becker and Fagen's style caused some backlash.

Undaunted, the twosome went still further in their preferred directions for album three, *Pretzel Logic* (1974). Just before the album came out, Becker and Fagen predicted it might diminish their already restive audience. Fagen told a reporter: "At concerts there's always a lot of younger kinds, so I guess they come to hear 'Do It Again' and 'Reelin' in the Years,' and then there's a smattering of people who seem to appreciate the irony of the lyrics and so forth, and the generally bizarre musical arrangements we come up with. It's mainly a cult-type atmosphere among a very few people who appreciate what we're trying to do. But we're definitely cold at the moment, I would say.

"We've more or less abandoned hope of being one of the big, important rock'n'roll groups, simply because our music is somehow a little too cheesy at times and turns off rock intelligentsia for the most part, and at other times it's too bizarre to be appreciated by anybody. But we're hoping that we're going to make some kind of miracle sweep and just worm our way into the hearts of America.''

And that's exactly what happened. While the band lost many of its teenage followers with *Pretzel Logic*, it suddenly found great favor with college-level and younger-adult segments of the population at home and abroad. In what was to become an increasingly rare emphasis on touring, the duo and assorted backing musicians put on one of the best concert series of that year. The album easily passed gold-record levels and one of its less esoteric tracks, "Rikki Don't Lose That Number," broke *Billboard*'s top 10.

Over the next few years, Fagen and Becker essentially remained studio musicians, shaping a series of gold or platinum albums that gratified most critics and large numbers of record purchasers: *Katy Lied* (1975), *The Royal Scam* (1976), and *Aja* (1977), plus the restrospective *Greatest Hits* (1978). With *Aja* (pronounced *Asia),* the duo hit a creative peak that apparently drained their writing energies for future joint efforts.

Like all their mid-1970s work, *Aja* required a number of hearings for the listener to absorb the full impact of the intricate tonal patterns and multi-layered lyrics. An example was the track "Home at Last," whose words at first hearing simply discussed the return of a wanderer. But closer examination indicated a synthesis, to engrossing fast-paced blues-rock themes, of the final movements of Homer's "Odyssey." The title song was a good indication of Becker and Fagen's musical tastes—a medium-tempo number in a minor key featuring a lengthy instrumental combining blues, jazz, and rock. The music might be called be-bop rock in that, like be-bop, it was an attempt to introduce more complex, totally different elements into a more familiar framework, in this case rock rather than jazz. Lead vocals, as in all mid-1970s Steely Dan records, were by Fagen, with Becker handling lead or backup guitar.

In March 1978, *Aja* became Steely Dan's first LP to receive its gold certification by the RIAA. Culled from *Aja* was ''Peg,'' top 10 on some trade press lists, and another charted single, ''Deacon Blues.'' During that period, Becker and Fagen also wrote and recorded the title song for the Universal film *FM*.

The recorded output of Steely Dan after *Aja* was meager and inferior to its previous work. The final studio album (issued by MCA, which had bought ABC) was the platinum *Gaucho* (1980), after which Steely Dan apparently ceased to exist as an entity. The album provided a top 10 single in 1981, ''Hey Nineteen.''

It was announced in 1980 that the duo had signed with Warner Brothers Records, but as of the mid-1980s, no collaborative work appeared under the Steely Dan name, though both Becker and Fagen did complete some solo efforts. Becker's credits included record production work, such as a 1988 LP by the group China Crisis. Among Fagen's efforts was the LP *The Nightfly* (1982, Warner Brothers), and the score to the 1988 film *Bright Lights, Big City. (See Toto.)*

STEPPENWOLF: *Vocal and instrumental group. Members (early 1970): John Kay, born Tilsit, East Germany, April 12, 1944; Nick St. Nicholas, born Germany, September 28, 1943; Goldy McJohn, born U.S., May 2, 1945; Jerry Edmonton, born Canada, October 24, 1946; Larry Byrom, born U.S., December 27, 1948. Nicholas replaced in mid-1970 by George Biondo, born Brooklyn, New York, September 3, 1945. Group disbanded in 1972.*

The European background, at least in part, of Steppenwolf was indicated by the group's name, taken from the central figure of a novel by German author Herman Hesse. It reflected the fact that group founder and lead singer John Kay (born Joachim Krauledat) was German by birth. He escaped from East to West Germany under gunfire from communist police in 1958. By the time he started Steppenwolf, though, he had long since left Europe and was, in fact, a resident of Los Angeles.

For most of the 1960s, Kay lived in Canada, where he completed his schooling, with emphasis on music. In 1967, he moved to California and, soon after, organized Steppenwolf. The new group was formed partly from his previous one, Sparrow (organized in Toronto, Canada), whose hard-rock/blues approach won approval from fellow musicians, but little public attention. Among those in his early band

were a Canadian friend, son of a nightclub owner, drummer/guitarist/pianist Jerry Edmonton; lead guitarist Michael Monarch; bassist John Russell Morgan; and organist Goldy McJohn, who had studied classical piano for a number of years. (Rushton Moreve was the original bassist, but he was replaced by Morgan after a short time.)

Though the hyperamplification and intricate arrangements used in Sparrow were toned down a little, Steppenwolf still emphasized Negro blues roots. The group's repertoire included traditional blues numbers with new lyrics and rock rhythm patterns as well as originals with blues feeling by Kay and other group members.

Its debut LP, *Steppenwolf,* and such singles as ''Sookie, Sookie'' and ''Born to Be Wild'' in 1968 appeared on Dunhill. Hailed by many critics as the greatest motorcycle song ever written, ''Born to Be Wild'' along with Steppenwolf's ''The Pusher'' were in the soundtrack of the classic 1969 hippie biker film, *Easy Rider,* starring Peter Fonda, Dennis Hopper, and Jack Nicholson.

From the start, the group was unabashedly political. Kay, who at one point ran for a city council seat, summed up his approach by saying: ''We are centralizing our thoughts and direction of our generation through music. We are a reflection of what is happening today. We could be called the 'thinking man's rebel with a cause.''' Referring to the riots at the 1968 Democratic National Convention in Chicago, he said: ''Democracy died there; but it's not buried yet. We must save this country because it is the best one in the world. I don't feel Steppenwolf is a platform from which to preach, and I'm not setting us up as the all-knowing spokesmen; but only the masses can make the changes that are needed, and the kids across the country look to us and ask how they can do it. We must not have generations of hate and prejudice.''

Whether younger fans understood the Steppenwolf message is a moot question. But they did like the group's style and, from 1968 on, the group became one of the foremost rock organizations in the U.S. and Europe.

As usually happens, changes in personnel took place along the way. By late 1969, Monarch and Morgan had left. Their places were taken by German-born bassist Nick St. Nicholas and lead guitarist Larry Byrom, whose experience included several years with such groups as the Hard Times and T.I.M.E. Besides lead guitar, Byrom also played bass, trumpet, drums, piano, mandolin, trombone, banjo, saxophone, and clarinet. In mid-1970, when Nicholas left, Byrom recommended former T.I.M.E. associate George Biondo as new bassist.

From 1969 through 1971, there was hardly a week

when one or more Steppenwolf albums were not on the national charts. Almost all of these earned gold records for over $1 million in sales. The list included *Steppenwolf* and *Steppenwolf the Second* (1968), *At Your Birthday Party* and *Monster* (1969), *Steppenwolf 7* and *Steppenwolf Live* (1970), and the retrospective *Steppenwolf Gold* (1971). The group also gained over a million sales for its 1968 singles "Born to Be Wild" and "Magic Carpet Ride." Other hit singles were "It's Never Too Late," "Rock Me," "Move Over," "Hey Lawdy Mama," and "Monster."

On February 14, 1972, the formal end of the group was announced in a press conference at the Holiday Inn in Hollywood. The reason, said Kay, was that: "We were locked into an image and a style of music and there simply was nothing new for us to look forward to. By retiring Steppenwolf, each of us can now move creatively into other areas, restore most of the challenge and excitement we felt leave as the group grew in popularity and became trapped by its own success." His sentiments were echoed by the other two early group members present at the meeting, Jerry Edmonton and Goldy McJohn.

Summing up the statistical history of the group to that point, it was reported that the band accounted for over $40 million in single and LP sales for ABC/Dunhill. Eight of the band's nine albums exceeded the million-dollar sales mark. In limited personal appearances, Steppenwolf played to more than 2 million people over its four-year span to gross over $7 million in ticket sales. The band had appeared in every state in the U.S. and every province in Canada.

Following the group's dissolution, Edmonton and McJohn formed a new band while Kay went out as a solo artist. Kay's spring debut LP on ABC/Dunhill, *Unsung Songs and Little Known Heroes,* appeared on the hit charts in late April. Kay also had the single "I'm Movin' On" in 1972 and in 1973 he placed the album *My Sporting Life* on best-seller lists. During 1973, Dunhill issued the retrospective *Steppenwolf's 16 Greatest Hits.*

Kay's solo career began to lose momentum in the mid-1970s and he decided to revive Steppenwolf. The new alignment signed with Epic Records, which issued such LPs as *Hour of the Wolf* and *Reborn to Be Wild.*

Steppenwolf albums still in print in the early 1980s included *Hour of the Wolf* and such Dunhill collections as *Steppenwolf, Steppenwolf the Second, Steppenwolf Live, Steppenwolf 7, Steppenwolf Gold,* and *16 Greatest Hits,* but under the logo of Dunhill's new owner, MCA.

STEVENS, CAT: *Singer, pianist, guitarist, songwriter. Born London, England, July 21, 1948.*

The first name Cat Stevens assumed for his professional music career might have referred to his very different lives as a popular musician. Born Steven Georgiou, he first rose to stardom as a clean-shaven, handsome teenage idol. Then, after a pause punctuated by illness and depression, he returned to achieve new fame as a shaggy-haired, bearded singer and writer of songs with considerable depth and meaning. In 1977, he made another sharp change, converting to Islam, changing his name to Yusaf Islam, and giving up his pop recording and concertizing career altogether.

Though born in the heart of London, he was reared in a home with cultural origins far removed from the tenements and bustle of that great city as his Greek parents introduced their son to the music of their native land at an early age. Though aware of the different sounds he heard on the radio or friends' phonographs during his school years, he enjoyed the folk songs his parents sang in Greek and the wild dance melodies played at Greek gatherings.

By the time he was in high school, though, he had turned more and more to the music of his peers, rock'n'roll. His vocal style and good looks, coupled with his increasing skill as an instrumentalist and songwriter, gained him a growing circle of followers in small London clubs. Soon word of him reached some of the major artist managers and one sought him out and signed him. Within a short time, the youth's first demonstration records won a multiyear contract from British Decca.

In short order, Stevens became a favorite of teenage music fans. His singles of such original compositions as "Mathew and Son," "I Love My Dog," "Here Comes My Baby," and "First Cut Is the Deepest" showed up on British top 20 lists. His songs also were in demand for other performers, who found them a good passport to gold records.

Stevens, though, became more and more unhappy with the way things were going. He found his early songs too shallow and started writing in a different vein, but his managers and record-company executives fought his use of the new material. The frustrations that resulted didn't do young Stevens much good, adding to a mood in which he worked too hard and neglected such things as getting enough rest or leisure. By the late summer of 1968, he had contracted a cold that he couldn't seem to shake. Finally, he was too run down to go on and had to enter a hospital.

As he recalled: "I was too hung up on what I was doing to worry about my health, and I just let it get to a head, and it got to the stage where another four weeks in the state I was in and I would have copped it. I went into hospital in September 1968, and stayed three months. My lungs were really screwed up, really a mess.''

This enforced confinement saved Stevens' life and also gave him time, as he convalesced, to think about the future. He read a lot, listened to a variety of records and, when he left the hospital, decided to drop out of music for a while until he knew what course he wanted to follow.

He was sure the old routine was no good. "The whole process I went through, being with a big anonymous company like Decca who are very into the top 20 thing, very pop-conscious, was bad. There are a lot of heavy pressures in that kind of setup, all in a very fickle direction. In fact, no direction at all apart from making large figures on paper.

"Then there were the heavy agency figures who really didn't know me. Like the minute I said I wanted to develop, that the stuff I was doing wasn't really me or what I wanted to do, that didn't interest them. What did interest them was how much I was getting that night and making sure they got half the bread before. That's all they were worried about. And I just wanted a complete break from that because it just wasn't the way I wanted to go. It was the way I had hoped it would go from the beginning, but it just didn't work out that way.''

For all of 1969 and early 1970, Stevens lived on income from earlier work and tried different approaches to writing the songs he knew he had inside him. Finally, in the spring of 1970, he came up with a series of compositions that pleased him. This time he went into the studio and, aided only by a few musicians—Alun Davies on guitar, Harvey Burns on percussion, and Peter Gabriel on flute *(see Gabriel, Peter)*—instead of a mass of session players, did the songs more or less as a live performance. The material came out under the title *Mone Bone Jakon*. Released in the U.S. by A&M Records, the LP became one of the critically hailed efforts of 1970. Besides the title song, it included "I Think I See the Light," "Lady D'Arbaville," "Katmandu," "Time," "Fill My Eyes," and "Lilywhite."

Stevens' newfound popularity was underscored with his next LP, the gold *Tea for the Tillerman* (winter 1971). Audiences flocked as readily to hear Stevens in concert with his new material as the teenagers of the mid-1960s had done for his earlier musical incarnation.

In Los Angeles in June 1971, Stevens did his own public-broadcasting-network TV show along the informal lines pioneered by Leon Russell and Johnny Otis. Funded by A&M, local NET station KCET brought Stevens into its Hollywood studio and just allowed him to play his own concert before a few dozen people invited to the show, which was under the direction of Allen Muir and produced by Alan Baker. As Robert Hilburn wrote in the *Los Angeles Times* (June 8, 1971): "In Stevens, Baker and Muir most certainly have a musician worthy of attention . . . an exceptional singer and artist whose highly distinctive voice has the rare ability to combine the strength, fragility, and sometimes mystery of his highly personal compositions." The program featured such songs as "Moonshadow," "On the Road to Find Out," "Where Do the Children Play," "Wild World," "Miles from Nowhere," "Longer Boats," "Father and Son," and "Hard-Headed Woman."

Stevens' third LP for A&M, *Teaser and the Firecat* (late 1971), quickly made the top 10 and earned a gold record. (Press releases on Stevens at the time also stated *Mona Bone Jakon* had reached gold record levels, but the RIAA did not certificate it as a gold LP). Its singles "Peace Train" and "Morning Has Broken" made *Billboard*'s top 10. A year later, he had another gold record, *Catch Bull at Four*. (During 1972, Deram Records issued an album of earlier material, *Very Young and Very Early Songs.*) In 1973, he won his fourth gold record with *Foreigner,* an album that received a markedly cooler critical reception than its predecessors. Singles hits during 1972–73 included "Sitting" and "The Hurt."

Cat's albums in the later '70s were not as striking as his early '70s work. His new studio albums of that period, all gold, were *Buddah and the Chocolate Box* in 1974, *Numbers* in 1975, and *Izitso* in 1977. A&M also issued the excellent retrospective *Cat Stevens' Greatest Hits* in 1975.

In 1977, he became a convert to Islam, adopted the new name Yusaf Islam, and decided to make no more records as Cat Stevens. (In 1978, A&M did issue another album of his material, *Back to Earth.*) Little was heard of him in the media until the July 19, 1984, issue of the weekly gossip magazine *Globe.* Writer Len Stone, among other things, alleged that the singer had become a disciple of Iran's Ayatollah Khomeini, was living in Iran, and was studying to become an ayatollah.

Some weeks later, Islam/Stevens filed suit in the U.S. District Court in Chicago claiming $5 million in damages for what were claimed to be false statements in the article. Discussing the matter with United Press International, Islam said he was not living in Iran, but resided with his wife and three daughters in London, where he helped manage an Islamic school. He had never visited Iran, he maintained.

As far as following Ayatollah Khomeini, he told a

press conference: "When I converted to Islam, I devoted myself to God and not to any human being. The Koran changed my life and, after reading it, I knew I had to either follow it completely or continue my ways of making music."

He also said he was not ruling out doing some work in music in future years. He noted that music is not strictly forbidden in his religion and the time might come when he would be inspired to write and record music promoting the message of Islam.

STEVENS, SHAKIN': *Singer, songwriter. Born Wales, U.K., c. 1950.*

The first wave of American rock'n'roll—the blend of country music and rhythm & blues created by artists such as Elvis Presley, Jerry Lee Lewis, and Carl Perkins—swept over the world in the middle and late 1950s, but then was superseded in the U.S. by blander forms of rock. While the early style essentially faded out in the U.S., it found a life of its own overseas, particularly in England—so much so that even in the 1980s, U.K. performers such as Shakin' Stevens could vie with new wave or punk practitioners for star status, and American rockabilly groups who rarely got beyond small clubs at home could draw capacity crowds to large auditoriums in Great Britain.

Stevens maintained that he was a true rock'n' roller according to England's definition of the term. "I love the music [Americans] call rockabilly, but I wouldn't want to be known as a rockabilly artist. I'm an artist that goes right across the board, from Elvis Presley to [punk rocker] Johnny Rotten. In England, people like Carl Perkins are rock'n'roll artists, and rockabilly artists were people like Warren Smith. It's the same music, but you use different terms over here. The sad thing about it is that Americans have forgotten about it."

Stevens heard the early sounds of rock in his childhood. "When I was in school in Wales, there were a lot of records of this sort being played. I guess I was around 10 years old when I picked up on it. I didn't try to imitate anyone in particular. I was listening to Joe Turner, Louie Jordan, Conway Twitty, and people like that. Then I left school at 15 and formed a band. It was really a gang of kids who got together. This was around the time when Americans were trying to sound like English bands such as the Beatles and Stones.

"I guess I'm a purist, but not a 1950s purist," he said in 1980. "I'm a 1980s purist. The Eddie Cochrans, Gene Vincents, Presleys, and Buddy Hollys are all dead and I guess you need somebody to carry on, which you don't have in America, or in England, where I'm the only one who's doing it successfully." His last statement might be open to argu-

ment, but there was no doubt of his achievements with European fans in the 1970s and '80s.

After the typical trial-and-error process of an aspiring artist, Stevens made the contacts needed to begin moving from obscurity to center stage. At the end of the 1960s, the almost-20-year-old singer gained his first major record contract and completed tracks for the LP *Legend,* released on Parlophone in the 1970s. It and the other recordings he made during the decade were available in the U.S. only as British imports. Over the next half-dozen years, Stevens slowly built up rapport with a large segment of English concert goers and record buyers with an engaging stage show and a series of albums on various labels such as *I'm No D.J.* (CBS U.K., 1971), *Rockin' and Shakin'* (Contour, 1972), and *Shakin' Stevens and the Sunsets* (Philips U.K., 1974).

After the death of Elvis Presley, Stevens' career took a giant step forward when he played the part of his idol in a hit show, *Elvis,* in London's West End. Stevens could do a credible representation of Presley's vocal style, though over the years he did not try to be a clone on most of his offerings. With the momentum provided by his work in a hit show, Stevens' singles and albums established a consistent presence on hit charts all over Europe. His output in the late 1970s through 1980 included such charted albums as *Shakin' Stevens* on the Track label in 1978, *The Legend* on EMI in 1979, *At the Rockhouse* on Magnum Force in 1980, and his first releases on U.K. Epic in 1980, the Epic/NuDisk four-song EP *Take One.* The latter included his first single to pierce the U.K. top 20, "Hot Dog," a rockabilly remake of a U.S. country song by Buck Owens and D. Dedman. During that period, he also made the charts with singles such as "This Ole House" (a 1954 pop hit for Rosemary Clooney written by Stuart Hamblen), "Marie Marie" (written by Dave Alvin of the U.S. rockabilly group the Blasters), and "You Drive Me Crazy." *(See Blasters, The.)*

For his debut U.S. release on Epic in 1980, *Get Shakin',* songs were selected from several of his late 1970s LPs, including "Hot Dog," "Marie Marie," and "Hey Mae" (another derivative from U.S. country music, written by Cajun fiddler Doug Kershaw and his brother Rusty). That album also offered three songs penned by Stevens: "Baby You're a Child," "Make It Right Tonight," and "Let Me Show You How."

At the start of the 1980s, Shaky (as he was called by many U.K. followers) began his own weekly TV show, "Let's Rock." The series was successful in the U.K. and parts of Europe but had minimal impact on the U.S. market though it was telecast over 86 stations in 1980–81.

While Stevens was welcomed by the relatively

648

small—but growing—rockabilly audience in the U.S. in the 1980s, his main impact continued to be in Europe, where he remained a major star during the decade. New album releases in the English top 40, often in the top 10, spanned *Shaky* in 1981, *Give Me Your Heart Tonight* in 1982, *The Bop Won't Stop* in 1983, and *Shakin' Stevens Greatest Hits* in 1984. Among his hit singles during those years on Epic U.K. were "Cry Just a Little Bit" (1983) and "Merry Christmas Everyone," which was number two on U.K. charts in mid-December 1985.

STEWART, ROD: *Singer, guitarist, banjoist, songwriter. Born Highgate, London, January 10, 1945.*

In 1971, Rod Stewart came into his own. His solo albums were hailed by almost all popular music critics as among the finest of the year, both in content—with some of the best songs being original compositions by Rod—and in the quality of Rod's vocals. In the British *Melody Maker* poll, Rod was named top British male singer of the year, a confirmation of his high ranking the year before with American rock fans. An overnight success, some casual observers of the music field thought. Actually, it climaxed almost a decade of work by the prime challenger for the blues mantle previously worn by Joe Cocker.

Early bios indicated that Rod was born in Scotland and taken to London soon after by his Scottish parents. Later it was stated that his birthplace actually was Highgate, London. Roderick David Stewart, the fifth child in the family, started to pay attention to pop and rock music before he entered the English equivalent of high school. He learned to play guitar and five-string banjo in his early teens, but for a while it seemed as though his future might lie in sports rather than music.

He proved particularly adept at soccer. At the William Grimshaw Secondary Modern School in Hornsey, he was a star player and also captained the team. Later he also was a standout performer on the Middlesex Schoolboys Team. At 16, he signed a professional contract with the Brentwood Football Club, but he finally gave that up in favor of music. At first, he showed interest in folk music, but he also was impressed by the many British groups playing blues-related songs, such as the Alexis Korner Blues Incorporated and the Cyril Davies Band. He also became increasingly interested in American soul singers.

As he said in 1970: "The British blues scene has been the greatest single influence on my career as a performer. I've been especially influenced by the songs of the late Sam Cooke and I love to listen to Richie Havens. I also dig anything by the team of Holland-Dozier." (Holland-Dozier-Holland was one

of the most successful writing-producing teams for Motown Records in the 1960s.)

At 17, he hitchhiked around Europe to expand his horizons both musically and socially. Soon after he got back to the U.K., he got his first music job as a harmonica player with the R&B-oriented Jimmy Powell's Five Dimensions. Rod sometimes augmented his income by street singing for whatever passersby would pay him.

Another young fan of the blues, Long John Baldry, happened by one time and was impressed. Baldry recalled: "I had heard Rod before, playing harmonica, but never singing. But I discovered him, at Twickenham railway station, waiting for a train. Roddy was sitting on the platform, singing the blues. He rather impressed me, so I asked him how he'd fancy a gig. So Rod joined my band as a vocalist." Starting in 1964, Rod was an important member of Baldry's Hoochie Coochie Men. While working with that group, he had his first featured single released on the Decca label: "Good Morning Little Schoolgirl" (a Mississippi Fred McDowell and Big Joe Williams blues classic) backed with the pop standard "I'm Gonna Move to the Outskirts of Town." After a time, Baldry broke up the Hoochie Coochie Men and Rod moved over to the Soul Agents. But before long, Baldry was assembling a new band, Steampacket, which Stewart hastened to join. While with that group, he recorded some new sides for Columbia Records, but nothing much happened with them. But his singing and writing were slowly earning him the respect of many fans in the U.K. and U.S. In Steampacket, he shared equal billing with Baldry, keyboards player Brian Auger, and singer Julie Driscoll. Still, that group wasn't meeting Baldry's hope in terms of widespread public acceptance and he disbanded it during 1967. Rod worked briefly with Shotgun Express and then got his biggest break when he was asked to join Jeff Beck's new rock band as lead singer.

Beck, already the holder of a major reputation in England, took his new band to the U.S. in May 1968 for a six-week tour. The results were sensational, particularly for Stewart as his vocals won standing ovations. By the end of the tour, Rod was well known to many U.S. rock fans, though still only lightly regarded at home.

Stewart's talents showed to good advantage on the Beck group's highly successful debut album, *Truth*. Stewart sang the title song (which made the U.S. singles charts) and with Beck co-wrote two major hits on the album: "Rock My Plimsoul" and "Let Me Love You." Executives of Mercury Records were so enthusiastic about Stewart's work that they signed him as a solo artist in 1969. This was the start of Stewart's joint efforts as a soloist and a group member, because his Mercury contract did not interfere with his continuing as a vocalist with Beck. His contributions included work on that group's next album, *Beck-Ola*.

After the Beck group broke up in 1969, Stewart continued his dual activities—recording solo material for Mercury (for its subsidiary Vertigo in Britain) while also touring and recording with Faces (originally Small Faces), which included another Beck alumnus, Ron Wood. In Faces, Wood played guitar (rather than bass guitar as he'd done with Beck) with Stewart, Ronnie Lane, Kenny Jones, and Ian McLagan on such successful LPs as *Long Player* and *The First Step*, which were issued in the U.S. on the Warner Brothers label.

Stewart's first solo album, *The Rod Stewart Album* (Mercury, fall 1969), was followed a year later by the hit LP *Gasoline Alley*. An even greater reception was awarded his next LP, *Every Picture Tells a Story*, which quickly gained over $1 million in sales and was number one in *Billboard*. The single "Maggie May"/"Reason to Believe" rose to number one in *Billboard* for five weeks starting October 2, 1971. This time Rod was honored in the U.K. with a number one ranking for his album even before he attained the equivalent success overseas.

In 1972, Rod earned another gold record for his album *Never a Dull Moment*. He also put out the hit singles "Angel," "Handbags and Gladrags," and "You Wear It Well." His 1973 successes included the retrospective album *Sing It Again Rod* and the singles "Oh No, Not My Baby" and a remake of Sam Cooke's 1962 hit "Twistin' the Night Away." In early 1974, the joint Stewart-Faces album *Coast to Coast Overture & Beginners* was on the hit lists.

Although Stewart continued as part of the Faces into 1975, he steadily increased his individual importance, overshadowing the contributions of the other group members. Writing in *The New York Times* of November 28, 1971, Don Heckman observed after attending a Faces concert at Madison Square Garden: "The support [the Faces] provides the lead singer is only minimally effective. But Stewart doesn't need much help. He has the almost hypnotically appealing stage presence of a Mick Jagger; one watches his strutting, cock-of-the-walk antics even while he isn't singing. And his voice—slightly hoarse-sounding, but ringing with a crackling masculine authority—is an unmistakably original expression."

Rod next made the album charts with *Smiler* (Mercury, 1974) and the gold *Atlantic Crossing* (his 1975 debut on a new U.S. label, Warner Brothers), which provided him with a major U.K. hit single, "Sailing." Before 1975 was over, Rod had announced his departure from the Faces. His first solo album after

that event was the platinum *A Night on the Town* (Warner Brothers, 1976). Its notable originals by Rod included "The Killing of Georgie" about the death of a homosexual friend and "Tonight's the Night," one of his best-selling singles worldwide.

In August 1976, Rod announced the makeup of a new backing band: New York City–born Carmine Appice on drums, John Jarvis (born Pasadena, California, c. 1955) on keyboards, guitarist Gary Grainger (born in the Kilburn district of North London), guitarist Billy Peek (born St. Louis, Missouri), guitarist Jim Cregan (born Somerset, U.K.), and bassist Phil Chen (born Kingston, Jamaica). That group backed Rod on his platinum 1977 album *Foot Loose & Fancy Free* with hit singles "You're in My Heart (The Final Acclaim)" and "Hot Legs." During 1977 Mercury issued the LPs *Best of Rod Stewart, Volume I* and *Volume II*.

Stewart closed out the '70s with another platinum album, *Blondes Have More Fun* (1978), on which his backing group included Appice and keyboardist Nicky Hopkins. In 1979, Warners issued the LP *Greatest Hits, Volume I*.

With the success of *Blondes Have More Fun*, Stewart seemed to be more interested in establishing himself as a sex symbol, somewhat to the detriment of his creative efforts. But there could be no doubt about his continued charisma as a rock vocalist and his albums, though now considerably more racy than thoughtful in content, rarely failed to make uppermost chart levels through the mid-1980s. Those included *Foolish Behaviour* (late 1980, platinum), *Tonight I'm Yours* (late 1981, platinum), *Absolutely Live* (late 1982), and the multiplatinum *Camouflage* (mid-1984). However, his 1983 release, *Body Wishes*, sold only some 300,000 copies.

Stewart continued to tour intensively for most of the 1980s and from time to time was featured in his own TV specials, such as the 1984 concert taped for presentation on Cinemax that November 27. He raised some eyebrows when an agreement was made with Sony Tape to sponsor a tour series. Record officials looked askance at an agreement with a blank tape maker, considering the losses in album sales unauthorized taping caused. His manager, Billy Gaff, told a reporter: "It's a simple matter of economics. There's just not enough money to go around. In 1979, our tour costs were $1.3 million. The expenses on this tour have almost doubled, while ticket prices have stayed virtually the same. . . . Anyway, we're not endorsing the product, we're merely lending our name to it. [Besides] lots of people buy both—an album for the home and blank tape so they can hear music in their cars. It's really unfair to blame the sad state of the industry on blank tape."

The relatively poor showing of *Body Wishes*

caused some music-industry observers to wonder if Stewart's day might be coming to an end. However, Stewart told a *Los Angeles Times* reporter in late 1984 (by which time he could point to a new hit LP, *Camouflage*) that the career obits were premature. "I don't feel old. I'm 39. I don't think I'm getting too old for this. The body is in good shape, the bones don't creak. I'm not ready for the rocking chair just yet. My face hasn't gone to pot, has it? Not too many lines, huh?

"I'll know when it's time to quit. When being on stage is embarrassing. I put a great deal of myself in a show. When I can't do that or it gets to be superficial, then it's time to quit. When it feels wrong and awkward, when I feel like some old guy, then it's time to quit. I hope my instincts will tell me when I don't have it anymore. Then maybe I can stay home and drink and chase women and do all the other evil things I supposedly do."

In 1988, Rod had another new studio LP, *Out of Order*, his first such project since 1986. He shared production chores with bassist Bernard Edwards and guitarist Andy Taylor, who also backed him on the album. *(See Baldry, Long John; Beck, Jeff; Davies, Cyril; Faces, The; Korner, Alexis.)*

STILLS, STEPHEN: *Singer, guitarist, pianist, drummer, tambourine player, songwriter, band leader. Born Dallas, Texas, January 3, 1945.*

One of the most important influences on pop music from 1966 through the mid-1970s, Stephen Stills was long known mainly to music-industry insiders because he submerged his individuality within rock groups. By the late 1960s, he was ready to stand on his own, which he did with a vengeance as he moved beyond Crosby, Stills, Nash & Young as a solo artist.

The Stills family was almost constantly on the move during Steve's youth. His parents' work took them to many cities throughout the South and, during one period, to Central America. They resided longest in New Orleans, Louisiana, which Steve called home because "at least I can remember the names of some of the streets there."

Steve was interested in music from his early years. By his teens, he had tried a variety of instruments ranging from drums to tambourine. He started working at both musical and nonmusical jobs at 15, his first occupation being stable boy at a racetrack. At the University of Florida he majored in political science, but spent much of his time as a folk singer at local clubs and dropped out to move to New York, where the folk boom of the early 1960s was concentrated.

He played and sang with a number of groups during 1963–64. Deciding to devote most of his time to playing guitar rather than the other instruments he had toyed with, he joined the Au Go Go Singers and toured much of the East Coast and Canada, making a number of friends among fellow musicians who he later used in forming his next group.

Tiring of this and becoming increasingly interested in folk-rock, he moved to Los Angeles in early 1965. There, he found work as a session musician, played with local groups, and auditioned for various performing jobs. One of these auditions, which he did not win, was for the TV group to be known as the Monkees.

In 1966, he formed his own group, Buffalo Springfield, calling on such then undiscovered musicians as Neil Young and Richie Furay. Almost as soon as they were assembled, the band was off on a seven-city tour with the Byrds and, almost overnight, was one of the most acclaimed rock groups in the country. Buffalo Springfield was only in operation for a little over a year, but its singles and albums became classics.

After the group disbanded in late 1967, Stills retired to work on new songs, play occasional solo concerts, and sit in as a sideman on numerous major recording sessions. He also put out the gold album *Super Session* (Columbia, 1968) with two other artists considered among the best rock had to offer: Mike Bloomfield and Al Kooper. The record had some great moments, but in general was not up to the capabilities of the three artists.

In mid-1968, he teamed up with Graham Nash (formerly of the Hollies) and ex-Byrd David Crosby after the three jammed together and enjoyed the results. Hailed by critics as one of the musical events of the year, their lush country-rock *Crosby, Stills & Nash* (Atlantic, Spring 1969) won a gold record as did the single of Stills' composition "Suite Judy Blue Eyes" (written to Judy Collins). From the start, it was agreed that each member, including Neil Young when he joined in mid-1969, would be free to work either with the band or separately. In the group arrangements, Stills alternated with Young as lead vocalist and lead guitarist.

Thus, each of the four artists was working on material for his own solo recordings while also touring with CSN&Y. To concentrate on his original compositions and arrangements, Stills moved from California to the 350-year-old country home outside London he purchased from another superstar, the Beatles' Ringo Starr. He commuted from there to engagements in many parts of the world and also to Atlantic Records' studios in the U.S.

His top 10 debut LP for Atlantic, *Stephen Stills* (winter 1970), had a prerelease sale of over $1 million. His single "Love the One Your With" moved into the top 20 in February 1971. That June, his top

10 LP *Stephen Stills II* was released. Other hit singles were "Change Partners," "Marianne," and "Sit Yourself Down" during 1971 and, in 1972, "It Doesn't Matter."

During 1972, Stills toured widely with a new backup group, Manassas, whose members included former Byrd and Flying Burrito Brother Chris Hillman. These concerts were greeted by large audiences, though the band did not arouse much enthusiasm in critics. The new alignment's first album, *Manassas* (Atlantic, 1972), earned a gold record and provided the singles success "Rock'n'Roll Crazies." In 1973, Stills and Manassas' album *Down the Road* and single "Isn't It about Time" made the charts.

In 1975, Stills signed as a solo artist with Columbia Records, after which his old label, Atlantic, issued such albums as *Steven Stills Live* (1975) and *Still Stills* (1976). His debut LP on Columbia was the relatively undistinguished *Stephen Stills* (1975), followed in 1976 by *Illegal Stills*.

In 1976, plans were made for Stills to tour during the summer with Neil Young. Unfortunately, throat problems sidelined Young so Stills had to carry out the commitments by himself. The two were represented on record racks that year, though, with a new LP on Reprise, *Long May You Run.*

During the late 1970s and in the 1980s, Stills continued to tour and record as a solo artist while occasionally renewing ties with old associates David Crosby and Graham Nash. Reunion efforts included a 1977 concert series (providing the Atlantic release *CSN)* and several 1980s revivals. Atlantic albums of Crosby, Stills, & Nash included *Replay* (1980) and *Daylight Again* (1982). In 1988 the threesome united again to work on a new album for Atlantic. CSN also was one of the acts taking part in the May 1988 concert at New York Madison Square Garden to celebrate the fortieth anniversary of the label. *(See Bloomfield, Mike; Buffalo Springfield; Byrds, The; Hollies, The; Kooper, Al; Monkees, The; Poco; Young, Neil.)*

STING: *Singer, guitarist, keyboardist, band leader, record producer, songwriter. Born Wallsend, England, October 2, 1952.**

No doubt one of the most charismatic rock stars of the 1980s was Sting, whose soft-rock stylings—limned by the reggae touches of his group, the Police—helped sell tens of millions of records and a healthy volume of music videos. *(See Police, The.)* Ironically, rock had not been his first love. In fact, were it not for the blandishments of the other founding members of the Police, he might have remained a relatively little known jazz musician. His success in rock, however, gave him the clout to combine jazz and rock as the lead singer and songwriter of an all-star jazz group of the mid-1980s.

Born Gordon Sumner, he was the first of four children in the family of milkman Earnest Sumner and his wife, Audry, a hairdresser. But after a while, the family's working class circumstances improved. His father progressed to manager of the dairy and, eventually, owner. By the time Gordon was in his early teens, the family was comfortably middle class.

Sting's mother, besides being a hairdresser, was a classically trained pianist. She gave her son lessons and he developed into a promising young keyboardist, good enough to earn a scholarship for advanced training. However, young Gordon turned it down because by then he preferred to play guitar. He had been fooling around with that instrument since age nine, when he came across an old one an uncle had left in the house. Sting taught himself guitar at the start by listening to records of major '60s rock groups such as the Beatles and Rolling Stones. But when he was 14, he discovered jazz. Listening to jazz records and working out jazz progressions on guitar became his main musical preoccupation.

Sumner was not only a good student while attending St. Cuthbert Catholic School, but a promising athlete too, showing talent in track and soccer. He won the 100-meter spring championship for the Northern Counties and was entered in the event for the entire U.K. He finished third in the nationals and immediately gave up track. He told author Barney Cohen of *Sting: Every Breath He Takes* (Berkley Books, 1984): "You're either the best or you're not. I realized when I came in third that there were two people in my age group that were better than I was. And there was no possibility of my beating them. So I just stopped running."

As graduation neared, he was accepted at prestigious Warwick College. Before finishing even a year there, however, he decided the restrictions of college life didn't please him and he dropped out. He took various day jobs, including ditch digger and file clerk with the Inland Revenue Service (the British counterpart to the IRS). He also spent nights and weekends seeking opportunities to play with jazz and Dixieland groups in the coal port of Newcastle. He told Cohen: "Leaving Wallsend for Newcastle was like running away to Pittsburgh."

When he was 17, he got a bit more adventuresome. He applied for his seaman's card and signed on with Princess Cruises as electric bass guitar player with the Ronnie Pierson Trio. Soon after that, still not sure what he wanted to do with his life, Sumner enrolled in a teachers training college. He

---

*Some sources give 1951 as year of birth.

decided to stick it out this time, completing the three-year course and graduating with his teaching certificate. He then accepted a position with St. Catherine's Convent School in Newcastle as an English instructor and soccer coach.

He kept up his jazz interests and, while still working as a teacher, formed the group Last Exit, which played clubs, dances, and parties, usually wearing formal tuxedos. By then, he also had a girl friend, actress Frances Tomelty. Despite his musical efforts, he seemed to be moving along a typical middle class path, following in his father's footsteps.

He told Cohen: "So here I was with a girlfriend and a job. You can become middle class so easily, and wear a white shirt—have a garden around your house, a car, a nice wife. Then I realized what a shallow ambition it was. . . . You could become an assistant headmaster in 10 years, maybe a headmaster 10 years after that. A fine life, but not for me. I decided to become a teenager at the age of 25."

He quit his job and began hanging around local teen and nightclub spots when he wasn't working with his band. Still, outside of deciding to concentrate on a music career, Sting's plans were somewhat nebulous. At this point, luck took a hand when two professional rock musicians saw a Last Exit show. The two (drummer Stewart Copeland and guitarist Henri Padovani) wanted to form a trio and, after seeing Sting's audience rapport, decided he was the logical third member.

At first, Sting resisted their suggestion. He told Cohen: "Look. I played Dixieland, mainstream, be-bop, free-form, even some progressive jazz. It was totally outside rock'n'roll. I wasn't interested in rock'n'roll. I found the rock music of the time abhorrent. It was all Led Zeppelin and Deep Purple. I hated it."

Finally, however, he agreed to join the others in a band that would try to come up with new material blending elements of rock and jazz. The Police was born. After about a year and a half of trial and error, it came up with a reggae-influenced style that gave it its own unique sound. From 1978 through 1983, the band produced a series of brilliant albums, supported by innovative music videos and increasingly intriguing concepts that made it one of the most influential rock bands for that period.

Despite the tremendous success of the Police, Sting had energy to spare for other projects. Besides providing the *Brimstone and Treacle* soundtrack in 1982, he also did cover versions of the songs "Tutti Frutti" and "Need Your Love So Bad" for the soundtrack on the 1982 movie *Party, Party*. He also was represented on the 1982 soundtrack LP for *The Secret Policeman's Other Ball*, taped at an Amnesty International benefit concert.

After the Police completed its enormously successful worldwide tour in support of the album *Synchronicity* in early 1984, the members agreed to go separate ways, at least for a while. Sting's activities over the next few years included an increasing amount of acting work, a continued emphasis on songwriting, and further interest in good causes such as the Band Aid aggregation's 1984 single "Do They Know It's Christmas?" to raise funds to help starving people in Africa.

He also provided support for albums by other artists. In 1985, he contributed to Phil Collins' LP *No Jacket Required,* Dire Straits' *Brothers in Arms* (for which he co-wrote the hit track "Money for Nothing"), and Miles Davis's *You're Under Arrest,* while preparing for his first solo album. His goal was to cover styles from reggae-rock to different forms of jazz. To achieve that, in January 1985 he gave an open invitation to American jazz artists to join him in a workshop in New York to see what might develop in terms of an interesting jazz association.

"When I put out the call, big names walked through the door, people I looked on as demigods. They wanted to play with me, to play my material. I was thrilled and excited."

Out of those sessions, a foursome evolved to work with him on the new project: saxophonist Bradford Marsalis, bass player Darryl Jones, keyboardist Kenny Kirkland, and drummer Omar Hakim. Sting stressed: "My interest is to break down the rigid barriers between music types. There has to be cross-pollination, so I deliberately used musicians from a different genre on this record. What we ended up with is not a jazz record at all, nor is it easily classifiable as rock'n'roll. It doesn't have a label, because labels are destructive."

Sting helped produce the record with Pete Smith on the island of Barbados in the Caribbean. When the completed collection, *Dream of the Blue Turtles,* was released in June 1985, Sting said: "This record is more difficult than most I've worked with. I'd like it to be a big hit—although I wouldn't regard it as a failure if it wasn't."

Sting had his wish as it went platinum. Creatively, from any standpoint, it ranked as one of the year's best. It was nominated for a Grammy for Album of the Year, but lost out to the *We Are the World* benefit LP. However, Sting shared the 1985 Grammy for Song of the Year with Mark Knopfler of Dire Straights for "Money for Nothing."

During 1985, Sting won praise from many movie reviewers for his starring role in the film *Bring on the Night*. Acting was an area in which he had gradually been acquiring professional polish for a half-dozen years going back to his role of Ace Face in the Who's *Quadrophenia*. *(See Who, The.)* His movie credits after that included *Radio On* (1980), Martin Taylor in *Brimstone and Treacle* (1982), *The Great Rock'n'Roll Swindle* (1983), Feyd Rautha in the science fiction *Dune* (1984), and Dr. Frenkenstain in *The Bride* (with Jennifer Beals) and Mick in *Plenty* (with Meryl Streep) in 1985 He also appeared in "Artemis '81" for the BBC in 1981.

Sting continued to retain rapt enthusiasm among rock fans as shown by the ovations given his performances in the six-city Amnesty International tour of the U.S. in the summer of 1986. On the first three dates he performed solo, but, to everyone's delight, Copeland and Andy Summers came out to reform the Police for the last three concerts of the benefit series.

Sting's philosophy about his songwriting appeared in an interview bio for the *Dream of the Blue Turtles* album. "I've been lucky in the past that I've always written music that by accident seemed to fit into what people wanted to hear. It does me good to excavate my feelings. I certainly don't have to dig very deep. I exist in a state of almost perpetual hysteria. I'm moved very easily by a chord progression or a painting. At its best, [pop music] is subversive . . . capable of subtle interpretations of relationships and problems. Instead of beating people over the head with an idea, I think it's better to get people comfortable. . . . Then you start beating them with the message. If we're going to save the world, we have to do it from the inside. Save yourself first, be happy, and then you can save the world."

While not ignoring his rock material, as a solo performer Sting continued to focus more on his earlier jazz and funk interests. Among the musicians who backed him on his 1985–86 non-Amnesty concerts were such jazz stars as saxophonist Branford Marsalis, keyboardist Kenny Kirkland, and vocalist Dolette McDonald. All three were back on tour with him during 1987–88, accompanied by five other musicians with excellent jazz credentials. The numbers performed in the shows included songs from Sting's 1987 A&M album, *Nothing Like the Sun*.

Among the highlights of his 1987 efforts was an appearance in a charitable concert in London along with such other stars as Tina Turner and Elton John. This event was captured on a video titled "The Prince's Trust All-Star Rock Concert" that won the 1987 Grammy for Best Performance Music Video. During 1987, Sting also began work on the film *Stormy Monday*, released in 1988. Late in 1987, Sting announced he would again appear in several 1988 concerts in behalf of Amnesty International. In June 1988, he was one of the artists taking part in the Freedomfest concert, designed both to make an anti-apartheid statement while also celebrating the seventieth birthday of South African black leader Nelson Mandela.

STOOGES, THE: *See Pop, Iggy.*

STREISAND, BARBRA: *Singer, actress, songwriter, movie producer, movie director. Born Brooklyn, New York, April 24, 1942.*

In the early 1960s, people in and out of show business were predicting a brilliant career for Barbara Joan Streisand (who later changed the spelling of her first name to Barbra). Decades later, if anything, she had proven the earlier forecasts to be major underestimations. She had become a superstar and accomplished performer not in one field, but in a variety of media from records to movies to TV. She not only starred in the 1983 movie *Yentl*, but also handled the chores of producer, director, and script writer.

Part of the inspiration for *Yentl* were her thoughts about the father she had hardly known. He had died when she was 15 months old, leaving his wife and three children, as she said, not "poor poor, [but] we didn't have anything." Still, her mother managed to keep the family together and Barbra didn't have an unhappy childhood.

She said that her first deep interest in an entertaining career came when she was 14 (by then attending Erasmus Hall High School in Brooklyn) and saw the Broadway drama *The Diary of Anne Frank*. Within a few years, she was trying to find an opening into show business in between working such jobs as theater usher and switchboard operator. As quoted by Fred Bronson in the *Billboard Book of Number One Hits,* she remembered her mother looking askance at her dreams. "I was certain I'd be famous one day. When I'd tell my mother about it, she would say: 'How can you be famous? You're too skinny.'" Her mother wanted her to master secretarial skills, but Barbra demurred. "I knew I had talent and I was afraid that if I learned how to type, I'd become a secretary."

Her first big break came at 18, having graduated from Erasmus, when she won a talent contest at a Greenwich Village club. It brought a two-week engagement at the Bonsoir, which worked out so well she was held over another nine weeks. She parlayed that experience into a singing job at the more prestigious Blue Angel, where her act was caught by Broadway impresario David Merrick. He offered her the role of Miss Marmelstein in the musical *I Can Get It for You Wholesale.* With that 1962 opportunity, her career was ready to blossom. The exposure helped her get a recording contract from Columbia Records. Her label debut, *The Barbra Streisand Album* (1963), became one of the year's best-sellers as did her 1963 follow-up, *The Second Album*. Both went gold, as did her early 1964 release, *The Third Album*.

Her career proceeded to the heights with her starring role in the 1964 musical *Funny Girl*, based on the life of comedienne/singer Fanny Brice. The show brought accolades from critics and theater goers in New York and later in London. The original cast album was a best-seller and her single of the song "People" from the score was her first chart single—a top 5 hit.

She soon translated her skills into stardom in another medium, TV. From 1965 into the early 1970s she was featured in several top-rated TV specials of her own, including one based on a concert taped live in New York City's Central Park. The show, free to those who could squeeze into the open-air concert area, took place in July 1967 before an audience estimated at 150,000 people. Her first special, "My Name is Barbra" (1965), won five Emmy Awards. Other programs were "Color Me Barbra" in 1966, "The Belle of 14th Street" in 1967, "A Happening in Central Park" in 1968, and "Barbra Streisand . . . And Other Musical Instruments" in 1973.

In the mid-1960s, she also continued the pace set by her first three Columbia solo LPs with four more gold albums, to bring her total to seven gold awards in a row by the end of 1966. Those four were *People* and *My Name is Barbra* in 1965 and *Color Me Barbra* and *My Name is Barbra, Two,* in 1966. It was a torrid pace, too torrid to maintain, and for the last years of the 1960s, while her albums sold well, only the *Funny Girl* soundtrack went gold. Almost all of them made the charts, though, including *Je M'Appelle Barbra* (late 1966), *Simply Streisand* (late 1967), and *What about Today?* (1969). As she diversified in the kinds of songs she recorded and built up new followings with expanding movie work, her recording career also came back to peak form. Every new album from 1971 into the late 1980s make the top 20 of the industry charts or better.

She made her movie debut in 1968, reprising her role in the stage version of *Funny Girl*. Movie critics found her portrayal as charming as had theater reviewers and the movie became a worldwide hit. Her performance won her an Oscar Award. The soundtrack album, which also featured her co-star, Omar Sharif, was released by Columbia in September 1968.

She followed *Funny Girl* with her first straight acting role in *The Owl and the Pussycat,* a well-regarded comedy co-starring George Segal that was released in late 1970. In her third film, the 1971 musical *Hello Dolly,* she essayed the role originally played by Carol Channing on Broadway. It too won almost unanimous rave reviews for Barbra's performance.

Barbra had shown her in-person abilities during the 1960s, with engagements at a number of prestige nightclubs. Her busy schedule tended to keep club and concert appearances to a minimum. A notable exception was her debut in Las Vegas at the start of the 1970s, an appearance that was known as a "top ticket" among show business people in that city. Already a legend, Barbra played to turn-away crowds every night and was given standing ovations most of the time. Strangely, she was unable to unwind at the start of the run, falling prey to the pressures of living up to critical expectations of her. However, critics who commented on this and who went back to see later performances changed their doubts to praise.

Nonetheless, as time went on, Barbra became increasingly inclined to avoid any more public exposure than necessary. She refused to go on any new concert tours. In the late 1980s, her myriads of fans still waited in vain for announcement of such in-person appearances.

Coming into the 1970s, Barbra began adding more contemporary, semirock arrangements and songs by such young writers as Nilsson, Laura Nyro, and Randy Newman to her repertoire. Though some reviewers grumbled about this—older ones felt she should have maintained her straight ballad approach, and younger ones sometimes suggested she should write her own new material—many music fans, young and old, responded favorably. The result was a new string of gold singles such as "Stoney End" (by Laura Nyro) in late 1970 and early 1971. The song was her first million-selling single and also the title song for a 1971 gold album. Late in 1971, she made the best-seller lists again with the LP *Barbra Joan Streisand.* (Proof that plenty of record buyers still liked her older stylings came when her 1970 LP, *Barbra Streisand's Greatest Hits,* went platinum.)

During 1972, she made the singles charts with "Mother," "Sing a Song"/"Make Your Own Kind of Music," and "Sweet Inspirations"/"Where You Lead." Her album *Live in Concert at the Forum* (late 1972) won another platinum award.

Barbra's major success of 1973–74 was her film *The Way We Were,* co-starring Robert Redford. It won six 1973 Academy Award nominations including Best Actress for Streisand and Best Song for the theme. Barbra's gold single "The Way We Were" hit number one in *Billboard* for three weeks starting Feburary 2, 1974, while the soundtrack LP on Columbia went platinum.

Barbra's hit albums over the next few years were *Butterfly* (1974), *Lazy Afternoon* (1975), and, in 1976, *Classical Barbra* and the soundtrack from the film *A Star Is Born,* co-starring Barbra and Kris Kristofferson. The film's song "Love Theme from *A Star Is Born* (Evergreen)" (co-written by Barbra and

Paul Williams), rose to number one in *Billboard* for three weeks starting March 5, 1977, and won Barbra and Paul an Oscar for the best original movie song of 1977 plus a Grammy for Song of the Year (in a tie with Joe Brooks' "You Light Up My Life"). For Barbra, it also netted a Grammy for Best Pop Vocal Performance, Female.

Barbra's platinum albums of the late 1970s, some not quite up to her earlier standards, included *Streisand Superman* in 1977; *Songbird* and *Barbra Streisand's Greatest Hits, Volume 2* in 1978; and *Wet* in 1979. Her duet with Neil Diamond, "You Don't Bring Me Flowers," rose to number one in *Billboard* the week of December 2, 1978, and won two Grammy nominations (Record of the Year and Best Pop Vocal Duo). Barbra scored another number one single with a duet—"No More Tears (Enough is Enough)" with Donna Summer—the weeks of November 24 and December 1, 1979.

Ms. Streisand started the 1980s with one of her best collections in some time, *Guilty*. The title track (sung with Barry Gibb of the Bee Gees) won a Grammy for Best Pop Performance by a Duo or Group with Vocal in 1980, while "What Kind of Fool" made *Billboard*'s top 10. Barry and Robin Gibb provided Barbra with *Guilty*'s song "Woman in Love"—number one in *Billboard* the weeks of October 25 and November 2. Her late 1981 LP *Memories* slowly earned a platinum award by the end of 1983.

Meanwhile, Barbra devoted most of her creative energies to the movie *Yentl*, based on a story by Yiddish writer Isaac Bashevis Singer (though in interviews after the film came out, he expressed considerable dissatisfaction with the changes in the story line for the movie). The movie proved one of the hits of 1983 and the soundtrack album went platinum. After that, Barbra had still more platinum albums to point to, such as *Emotions* (late 1984) and the late 1985 *The Broadway Album*, a collection of songs from Broadway musicals. That LP earned the 1986 Grammy Award for Best Pop Vocal Performance, Female.

In 1987, Barbra had a new album in print, *One Voice*. A private concert she gave to raise money for Democratic political candidates formed the basis for a 1988 program on cable TV. During 1987, she completed composing the score for her new starring vehicle, *Nuts*. The film, which she also produced, premiered in November, and a recording of the score was issued by Columbia in late December 1987. *(See Bee Gees, The; Diamond, Neil; Kristofferson, Kris; Manilow, Barry; Nyro, Laura; Summer, Donna.)*

STYLISTICS, THE: *Vocal group from Philadelphia, Pennsylvania, headed by Russell Thompkins.*

One of many rhythm & blues groups to feature falsetto lead singing, the Stylistics vied with the Delfonics and Eddie Kendricks for top ranking in that genre in the early 1970s. As long as Thom Bell and Linda Creed handled most of the songwriting and production chores, Russell Thompkins and his backing group prospered, but after switching to other alliances in the mid-1970s, their rapport with concert goers and record buyers seemed to decline.

The group first gained notice with hits on the Avco Embassy label. (By the mid-1970s, that company left the field and both old and subsequent releases came out on producer Hugo & Luigi's label, H&L.) In 1971, it made R&B charts with such Thom Bell–produced singles as "You're a Big Girl Now," "You Are Everything," and "Stop, Look, Listen (to Your Heart)." Gold singles included "I'm Stone in Love with You" (1972), "Break Up to Make Up" (1973), and "You Make Me Feel Brand New" (1974). "Rockin' Roll Baby" (1973) and "Let's Put It All Together" (1974) made *Billboard*'s top 20. The group's debut album, *The Stylistics* (1971), went gold, as did *Round 2* (1972) and *Let's Put It All Together* (1974).

Though still a featured act in the mid-1970s, the Stylistics didn't repeat its resounding achievements of early in the decade. Still, most of its LPs made the charts at some level, including *Heavy* (1974) and *The Best of the Stylistics, Thank You Baby,* and *You Are Beautiful* (1975), all on Avco. *Once upon a Juke Box* and *The Fabulous Stylistics* (both 1976) and *Wonder Woman* came out on the H&L label. In 1976, the group signed with Mercury, which issued such albums as *In Fashion* in 1978 and *Love Spell* in 1979. The group then moved to Philly International, turning out *Hurry Up This Way Again* in 1980. TSOP put out *Closer than Close* in 1981. In the late 1980s, Amherst Records (which had bought the Avco catalogue) had in print *All-Time Classics, The Stylistics Greatest Love Hits,* and *The Best of the Stylistics Volume 1* and *Volume 2.*

STYX: *Vocal and instrumental group. Members (early 1970): Dennis DeYoung, born Chicago, Illinois, February 18, 1947; James Young, born Chicago, Illinois, November 14, c. late 1940s; Chuck Panozzo and John Panozzo, both born Chicago, Illinois, September 20, c. late 1940s; John Curulewski, born Chicago, Illinois. Curulewski replaced in 1975 by Tommy Shaw, born Alabama, September 11, 1952.*

At the height of its fame in the early 1980s, Styx included three happily married members, one of whom (lead vocalist and primary writer Dennis DeYoung) typically took his wife and two children on tour. Styx material often dealt sensitively with problems affecting the U.S. Obviously, the quintet didn't have the image normally associated with a rock band. This perhaps accounted in part for the hostility shown Styx by some segments of the print media and for the relatively low level of newspaper and magazine coverage. Despite that, for a time the group was one of the favorites of the worldwide mass audience.

Discussing the group's somewhat conservative Midwestern outlook and avoidance of controversy, Chuck Panozzo, one of the twin Panozzo brothers in the band, told Steve Pond of the *Los Angeles Times* (February 22, 1981): "Boring isn't it. No wonder we don't get any good press." James "JY" Young, guitarist-vocalist, added: "People tell us not to act too conservative. It's always: 'Don't do that. You'll lose credibility.'" That included the band's decision to make commercials in favor of solar energy, but Young maintained: "We've got tremendous power to influence some people, and we've got to use that to say what we believe in.

"I'd hate to make it sound like we're totally political, like we're forming a new political party based on the idea [of the 1981 *Paradise Theater]* album. But we do have to speak up, to tell people that it's irresponsible to have the current American idea that I'm owed something because I exist in this space on the globe."

All the original band members grew up in Chicago. The Panozzo twins and DeYoung lived in the same South Side neighborhood. All were experimenting with rock and R&B as teenagers. Before becoming a rock fan, DeYoung had taken accordion lessons in his preteen years, and at first continued on the instrument when he joined the Panozzos in a pop-oriented trio. Both twins had taken drum lessons from an uncle (a professional orchestra performer), but when it was decided to form a group, Chuck switched to guitar. Recalling the first trio, he commented: "It was just like kids getting together to play sandlot baseball. It was sandlot music."

After a while, DeYoung abandoned the accordion in favor of keyoards and other high schoolers were added to form a group that played for school dances and local events. But music remained mainly a sideline until the key participants finished their college careers. The band was known for a time as TW4 and it was this group that James Young joined as lead guitarist after leaving a rival group. Bass guitarist Chuck Panozzo recalled: "He was the best guitarist we had ever heard." At the start of the 1970s, with the band on the verge of winning its first record contract, John Curulewski provided the other half of the band's twin–lead-guitar format.

DeYoung and some of the others were writing original songs by then, though (as is usually the case) they had to stress cover versions of hit songs by others to keep working. DeYoung noted: "When we were appearing locally, audiences only cared about the easily recognizable music of already successful artists. The real test was to perform original material and have it accepted."

Naturally, the key to winning attention for new songs was to have records on the market. After following the usual route of sending demo tapes wherever possible and trying to get record-firm executives to attend band gigs, the group finally got a contract from small, Chicago-based Wooden Nickel Records in 1970. Along with the recording agreement came selection of a new name: Styx.

The band's debut album, *Styx I* (1971), fell far short of becoming even a local favorite. While the follow-up, *Styx II,* showed considerable musical improvement, it too was largely ignored by reviewers and disc jockeys, even though it did have one of DeYoung's best compositions to that point, "Lady." The band was beginning to build up some sort of following, however, through tours of Midwest venues such as Chicago's Aragon Ballroom and various college campuses. The Wooden Nickel releases, including a single of "Lady," were handled by RCA Records, but the association didn't bring any large-scale breakthroughs.

The band continued to turn out new material, presented on the Wooden Nickel/RCA LPs *The Serpent Is Rising* (1973) and *Man of Miracles* (1974). In late 1974, the two-year-old single "Lady" caught the attention of the music director of Chicago station WLS, who began playing it regularly, eventually propelling it to top 10 status, which wasn't enough, however, to do much for the fourth Wooden Nickel album. "Lady," however, was the breakthrough that finally convinced the band it could find a path to success.

Said DeYoung: "It was summertime when I wrote 'Lady.' I was sitting in my garage playing a tune on my little Wurlitzer and searching for a subject that meant something to me. Since love is the common denominator of my life, I tried to capture the relationship of two people and how they can work together."

Now that "Lady" provided a calling card, the band decided to change managers and work out an agreement to void the Wooden Nickel contract. After talking to different record-company executives, the band signed with A&M, which issued its debut on the label, *Equinox,* on November 11, 1975. That album, which spawned the hit "Lorelei" and such other notable DeYoung songs as "Suite Madame Blue," did much better than earlier LPs, though the band still was far from a household name. John Curulewski decided to go on to other things after the intensive album-support tour was over and his place was taken by singer-guitarist-songwriter Tommy Shaw. Shaw's experience included work with a group that backed R&B artists in Montgomery, Alabama, and membership in Chicago-based MS Funk.

Shaw's addition completed the alignment that remained together for the rest of Styx's activities into the mid-1980s. The first album the reorganized quintet completed for A&M, *Crystal Ball,* was released on September 24, 1976. The response was more promising than for the first A&M offering and band members eagerly began writing and practicing songs for the next collection whenever there was opportunity between concerts. The result was *The Grand Illusion,* released July 7, 1977, which included songs that were to become concert staples for Styx: DeYoung's "Come Sail Away" (a top 10 single in 1977–78), Shaw's "Fooling Yourself," and Young's "Miss America." The LP eventually passed triple-platinum levels. (Canada, which took Styx to its bosom before it became a superstar combination at home, also accounted for a gold-record award for *Equinox.)*

With Styx becoming well known, Wooden Nickel sought to recover more of its investment in the band with a reissue of some of Styx's earlier tracks in the 1977 *Best of Styx.* Some of that Wooden Nickel catalogue also came out in the late 1970s on the RCA LP *Lady.*

By the time of LPs *Pieces of Eight* (issued September 17, 1979) and *Cornerstone* (1979), Styx had become a headline group able to sell out the largest halls throughout the U.S. as well as Canada and much of Europe. A gold single from *Cornerstone* was DeYoung's song "Babe." The band's next LP, *Paradise Theater,* shipped gold on January 6, 1981, later reaching platinum sales totals.

From *The Grand Illusion* on, DeYoung and the other band songwriters demonstrated interest in presenting songs with more thoughtful content about youthful romance or teenage frustrations. Taking *The Grand Illusion* as an example, DeYoung told Steve Pond: "The print media, ads, radio, television all foster an illusion. But what kind of mentality really believes that if you put on a certain pair of jeans, you'll score every night? I bought the illusion too—I figured if I had lots of fans, I'd be different from everyone else.

"The idea was there on the next two albums, too. On *Pieces of Eight* I was saying: 'Don't cash your freedoms in for gold,' because by then the money was really rolling in and I saw it happening to me. And on *Cornerstone* I wrote about a guy who grew up before Vietnam, who was confused. People thought I was writing about a rock star, but I was talking about America when I sang: 'I was so cool back in '65.'"

He agreed fans didn't pick up on some references to begin with. "Not initially. And it's partly our fault for being so ambiguous. But if they don't necessarily pick up on the lyrics, if they're attracted by other things, we still want to put those lyrics there so they can get them if they want. We do want the fans to understand our lyrics. Desperately we want them to understand."

Reaction to *Paradise Theater* marked the high point of the Styx saga. A week after A&M released it, the album took over *Record World*'s number one FM-play position from Bruce Springsteen's *The River.* The album also rose to number one in *Billboard* and placed several singles on the charts including DeYoung's "The Best of Times."

The band continued its string of multiplatinum albums with *Kilroy Was Here,* issued February 22, 1983. Its two top 10 singles (both written by DeYoung) were "Mr. Roboto" and "Don't Let It End." The band's extensive tour in support of the album included three New Orleans concerts taped by Westwood One for its Superstar Concert series broadcast nationally during the summer over 350 U.S. radio stations.

Though the band retained a very large following in the mid-1980s, its members had become restless with the restrictions of group work. It was decided to let Styx as such lie fallow for a while after the 1983 concerts. Several bandsmen then began working on solo recordings. One of the first to surface was DeYoung's debut album *Desert Moon* (A&M, 1985). The title track was the subject of a top-ranked video given considerable exposure on the MTV channel and a top 10 single in *Billboard.* Shaw was represented by two solo LPs on A&M during 1984–85: *What If* and *Girls with Guns,* while James Young completed his own solo album on another label.

In July 1986, the members of Styx got together once more to discuss a new album project, but nothing was finalized. In the spring of 1988, Tommy Shaw stated new discussions might result in a new LP later in the year.

SUMMER, DONNA: *Singer, songwriter, actress. Born Boston, Massachusetts, December 31, 1948.*

With an excellent musical-comedy–quality voice and the ability to inject moods ranging from gospel-like sweetness to searing passion into her songs, Donna Summer carved a niche for herself as a first-rank artist starting in the mid-1970s. Initially feted as the Queen of Disco by many critics, she proved herself able to handle a range of material over the years from straight-ahead rock to soul and gospel.

Born LaDonna Gaines, she was raised in the Boston area, one of seven children of a butcher father and a schoolteacher mother. Her first experience in music was in her church choir. By the time she entered high school, her tastes began to sway between religious songs and rock'n'roll. Her favorites included gospel great Mahalia Jackson and rock superstars of the period. She recalled she often cut school (once having a pile of several hundred truancy slips in her dresser) to listen to records and perform with a local rock band.

After dropping out of high school two months prior to graduation, she worked for a while as a file clerk before returning to the entertainment field full-time in the German production of the rock musical *Hair* in 1968. Europe was her home base for the next eight years.

She moved on to sing and act in other European musicals and became a regular performer with the Vienna Folk Opera. Along the way, she married Austrian actor Helmut Sommer. The two parted when Donna hit paydirt as a disco singer, but she kept a slightly changed version of her married name as her stage name.

The Munich-based writing/record production team of Giorgio Moroder and Pete Bellote saw her vocal skills as the growing '70s disco market in Europe and the U.S. The first fruit of the new collaboration was her steam-heated single of the Moroder-Bellote song "Love to Love You Baby." The song gained notice in Europe, but really took off after it was released in the U.S. on Casablanca Records & Tapes. The song made number one on some U.S. charts and in many other nations in 1975 and also served as the title track for Donna's gold debut LP that year.

She followed up swiftly in 1976 with two more gold albums for Casablanca: *A Love Trilogy* and *Four Seasons of Love*. Two more gold singles came from them: "I Feel Love" from *A Love Trilogy* and the sensational "Last Dance" from *Four Seasons of Love*. Donna showed her excellent stage presence in extensive touring during those years, captivating audiences of all age levels and ethnic origins.

The audiences for disco and rock, however, to a large degree remained separate, with rock bands' antidisco statements often bringing huge roars of applause from their fans. That situation suggested that new waves of former teenagers might not maintain the rage for disco that swept the 20–30-year age bracket in the later '70s. Donna, in fact, worried about being typecast. She told *Newsweek* (April 2, 1979) that she knew she had to avoid being known as a one-style artist. "People bagged me as incapable of singing anything but 'Love to Love You Baby,' but I was totally aware I had more going for me."

One thing she had was the ability to write her own songs as well as giving life to other writers' creations. With her future albums, she consciously tried to include more varied as well as more original material. Her next LP, *I Remember Yesterday* (1977, gold), had an essentially all-disco format on one side and a combination of songs from pop and rock to soul on the other including her gold single of Jimmy Webb's pop classic "MacArthur Park" that made number one in *Billboard* in November 1978.

She followed by co-authoring her 1977 concept album *Once upon a Time,* a disco-style "mini-opera." As Donna pointed out to reporters, the theme was a Cinderella story of the kinds of girls who, as the lyrics stated, "live in a land of dreams unreal/ Hiding from reality. . . . Trapped within their world." She told *Newsweek:* "It was mostly autobiographical." It maintained her string of gold-LP successes and provided the gold single "Heaven Knows."

Donna continued to experiment with varied material in her 1978 concerts. Besides disco, pop, and soul, she included more blues and mainstream rock in her repertoire. The concerts provided the renditions for her first live album, the platinum two-record *Live and More* (1978) (number one that November).

1978 proved a milestone in her career in other ways. She made her first featured film appearance in *Thank God Its Friday*. While her acting was hardly Academy-Award–nomination caliber (as opposed to her singing), most critics felt she did reasonably well in her role as an aspiring singer determined to gain the attention of disco d.j. Ray Vitte. Among the songs she performed was a movie version of Paul Jabara's composition "Last Dance." It subsequently won an Oscar for best movie song of 1978 and a Grammy for Best R&B Vocal Performance, Female. Among her other trophies of that period were three from the American Music Awards (Favorite Female Vocalist–Disco, Favorite LP–Disco for *Live and More,* and Favorite Single–Disco for "Last Dance") and acclamation as Number One Disco Artist from *Billboard*.

Her 1979 number one double album *Bad Girls,* which was to be her last LP on Casablanca, shipped platinum according to the record company and on the way to triple-platinum sales levels in the early 1980s. The material ranged from high-octane disco and rock to slow-paced blues-disco or pop songs. Its singles "Hot Stuff" and the title track went platinum and made number one in *Billboard*. Its gold "Dim All the Lights" hit number two. Besides contributions from longtime associate Moroder, the album contained several songs co-written by Donna and the rock trio Brooklyn Dreams, whose debut LP she helped produce.

In early 1979, Donna joined other top performers in the 90-minute special "A Gift of Song—The Music for UNICEF Concert" telecast on NBC-TV from the United Nations General Assembly. (Others taking part included Elton John, Kris Kristofferson, Olivia Newton-John, Rod Stewart, ABBA, the Bee Gees, John Denver, and Earth, Wind & Fire.) In *Billboard*'s year-end rankings, she was named number one singles artist in the U.S. and the number two album performer.

Artistic controversy and other problems had arisen between Donna and Casablanca, which resulted in her move to a new label, Geffen Records, as of 1980. She was, in fact, the first artist signed by David Geffen's new organization (an affiliate of Warner Brothers Records), a record firm that soon claimed many stars of equal luster. Her 1980 debut for Geffen, *The Wanderer* (produced by old friends Moroder and Bellotte), passed gold-record levels. In the first part of 1980, Casablanca issued the two-disc *On the Radio*. Primarily a "best-of" compilation, it included her number one "Enough Is Enough" duet with Barbra Streisand, a track that also appeared in a new Streisand album. *(See Streisand, Barbra.)*

Another 1980 milestone was her first TV special, aired January 27 on ABC. The program capsuled her career from her church-choir beginnings to her status as artist, writer, and family head. Song sequences included clips from a Hollywood Bowl concert in 1979 attended by a crowd of 17,000. A choreographed "Bad Girls" sequence featured Donna, Twiggy, character actress Pat Ast, and TV star Debralee Scott.

In the show, as in her concerts and new albums, Donna included religious songs. Her decision in her private life to "go back to singing in church" reflected a feeling that she needed such an outlet to gain inner peace. One impetus, she told *Newsweek*, had been the long struggle with her original label to expand her scope beyond disco. She had become depressed, she recalled, "stuck doing something that had been choking me to death for three years."

As it happened, in the first half of the 1980s, with disco in decline, Donna received more attention for some of her gospel songs included on her '80s albums than her secular material. Thus, in the 1983 Grammy Awards, she won for Best Inspirational Performance for "He's a Rebel," a track from *She Works Hard for the Money* on Mercury/Polygram. The following year, she won the same award for "Forgive Me" from her 1984 Geffen/Warner Brothers album *Cats Without Claws*. Pop top 10 singles of the period were "Love Is in Control (Finger on the Trigger)" (from the 1982 Geffen LP *Donna Summer*

produced by Quincy Jones; *see Jones, Quincy)* and the disco-style "She Works Hard for the Money" (Mercury, 1984).

In September 1987, her fourth Geffen LP, *All Systems Go*, was released. The album reunited her with Harold Faltermeyer, a member of the German production team that had helped launch her career. In interview notes for Geffen, she recalled, "I've known Harold for more than 20 years. He was one of the first people I met when I initially came to Munich. There's a club there called the Tambourine, and Harold used to play there when he was 16 and I was 18. They used to have Sunday jam sessions, and Harold was playing the organ one day while I was singing, and that's how we met. Then we started jamming together in the studio and subsequently we started to work with Giorgio Moroder. We did the *Bad Girls* together, and the rest is history."

SUPREMES, THE: *Vocal group. Original members (1960): Diana Ross, born Detroit, Michigan, March 26, 1944; Florence Ballard, born Detroit, Michigan, June 30, 1943; died Detroit, Michigan, February 21, 1976; Mary Wilson, born Greenville, Mississippi, March 6, 1944; Barbara Martin. Martin left late 1961. Ballard left in 1967, replaced by Cindy Birdsong, born Camden, New Jersey, December 15, circa 1943. In 1970, Ross was replaced by Jean Terrell, born Texas, November 26, after which the group took the name the New Supremes for a while. Birdsong left in early 1970s for a year and was replaced for that period by Lynda Laurence. Terrell left in 1973, replaced by Scherrie Payne. Birdsong left again in mid-1970s, replaced by Susaye Greene. Group disbanded in 1977.*

The elimination of the color bar that kept rhythm & blues artists from gaining national prominence in pop music began with the success of rock in the mid-1950s and finally reached a crescendo in the 1960s. A major reason for the newfound strength of R&B and its kindred form, soul, was the Motown or Detroit Sound of Berry Gordy's Motown Records. Though many Gordy stars helped bring those changes about, a primary factor in the transition was the Supremes, the dynamic vocal threesome who had tremendous impact on hit lists worldwide from 1964 to the end of the decade.

The Supremes' saga included more than its share of ironies. Though known as a threesome in its glory days, it began with Motown as a quartet. And the group that evolved into the Supremes, the Primettes, initially didn't include the performer who became its pivotal figure, Diana Ross. In the early days, she wasn't even considered lead vocalist; that role initially was held by the original founder, Florence Ballard.

The women who made the Supremes a national favorite all originally lived near each other in Detroit's black ghetto, an environment, they recalled, that featured the three R's: rats, roaches, and R&B music. Despite physical proximity, some eventual Supremes didn't get to know each other until they were group members. The story began with a 15-year-old resident of the Brewster-Douglass housing project, Florence Ballard. In 1959, she began to sing in shows featuring a male group called the Primes, whose members included Eddie Kendricks and Paul Williams, later with the Temptations. Later, Florence added friend Mary Wilson and two others, Barbara Martin and Betty Travis, to form the Primettes. Soon after, pressured by her mother to concentrate on school work, Travis decided to leave. According to Nelson George in his book *Where Did Our Love Go: The Rise and Fall of the Motown Sound* (St. Martin's, 1985), Kendricks brought in Travis's replacement, another girl from the Brewster-Douglass complex, Diane Ross (who later changed her first name to Diana). However, Fred Bronson in *The Billboard Book of Number One Hits* (Billboard Publications, 1985) cited Williams as claimant for that role.

In 1960, the group won first prize at the Detroit/Windsor Freedom Festival talent contest, which Ross used to get an audition with Berry Gordy and his associates at Motown. The Motown executives said the girls were too young and should finish high school first. But after doing some recording for another label, Lupine, while also continuing to work with the Primes, the Primettes got another chance with Motown after the label signed the Primes.

Gordy finally agreed to sign the quartet of high school girls in late 1960s. Their first records for the company were made as the Primettes. On December 15, 1960, they recorded the song "I Want a Guy," which Gordy decided would be a good singles candidate on the Tamla label. Before using it, he suggested a name change and Ballard came up with the Supremes. It still wasn't certain who would be the lead artist. Both Florence and Mary felt they were as well qualified for it as Diana. In fact, Ballard was lead vocalist on the Supremes' second single, "Buttered Popcorn." However, Berry Gordy favored Ross, perhaps because she had a more outgoing, assertive personality than the others. He groomed the girls carefully for what he hoped would be eventual success, though for a while not too much happened with their releases, which, starting with their third single, "Your Heart Belongs to Me" (which just edged into *Billboard*'s top 100), came out on Motown rather than the Tamla label. In late 1961, Bar-

bara Martin left to get married. From then on, the Supremes was a trio.

After less than spectacular years in 1962 and 1963, the group finally hit its stride during the summer of 1964. A song provided by the writing team of Brian Holland, Lamont Dozier, and Eddie Holland, "Where Did Our Love Go," became the catalyst, rising to number one in Billboard for two weeks starting August 22. It was the first of many smash hits the Holland-Dozier-Holland team provided the team. There were, in fact, two more number one hits from their pens before 1964 was over: "Baby Love" for four weeks starting October 31 and "Come See about Me" the weeks of December 19 and 26.

From then on, the group had records in the top 10—often in the number one spot—each year for the rest of the decade. In 1965, their number one hits were "Stop! In the Name of Love" in March, "Back in My Arms Again" in June, and "I Hear a Symphony" in November. In 1966, their hits included "Love Is Like an Itching in My Heart," "My World Is Empty Without You," "You Can't Hurry Love" (number one in September), and "You Keep Me Hanging' On" (number one in November). During 1964-65 the Supremes had the unprecedented achievement of placing five successive songs on the number one spot on the national charts. Besides singles, the Supremes also had many albums that sold in gold or platinum volumes.

They maintained a hot pace in 1967 with such top 10 hits as "Reflections," "Love Is Here and Now You're Gone" (number one in March), and "The Happening" (number one in May). But by then, Florence Ballard was no longer a member. She had become increasingly unhappy about losing her lead role in the group and felt that she was, in effect, being pushed out of something she had been instrumental in forming. She left abruptly in the middle of an engagement at the Flamingo Hotel in Las Vegas and her place was taken by Cindy Birdsong (a former teammate of Patti LaBelle's). Ballard was flown to Detroit and admitted to Ford Hospital, suffering from exhaustion. This was officially given as the reason for her replacement, but later both she and outside observers maintained that she had been dismissed from the group before leaving Vegas. Ballard grew increasingly embittered as the years went by and eventually became involved in legal disputes with Motown. Before that, in February 1968, she had signed a solo contract with ABC Records, which issued the singles "It Doesn't Matter How I Say It" and "Love Ain't Love." After those failed to go anywhere, Ballard's career slid downhill to the point that she and her three children were receiving government aid in the mid-1970s. Her health also declined, reputedly in part due to an alcohol problem. After complaining of numbness in her arms and legs

63. THE O'JAYS

64. OZZY OSBOURNE BAND (*L. TO R.*): BOB DAISLEY, LEE KERSLAKE, OSBOURNE, THE LATE RANDY RHOADS

66. TEDDY PENDERGRASS

65. CARL PERKINS

67. TOM PETTY & THE HEARTBREAKERS

68. PINK FLOYD—DAVE GILMOUR, ROGER WATERS, NICK MASON, RICK WRIGHT

69. THE POLICE

70 & 71. ELVIS PRESLEY

**72. THE
PRETENDERS**

73. OTIS REDDING

74. SMOKEY ROBINSON AND THE MIRACLES

75. THE ROLLING STONES IN '69

**76. LINDA
RONSTADT**

77. SEX PISTOLS

78. ART GARFUNKEL AND PAUL SIMON—CONCERT IN (NEW YORK) CENTRAL PARK, SEPTEMBER 19, 1981

79. PATTI SMITH

**80. BRUCE
SPRINGSTEEN**

81. BRUCE SPRINGSTEEN AND THE E STREET BAND

82. ROD STEWART

83. TALKING HEADS

84. THE TEMPTATIONS

85. IKE AND TINA TURNER

86. U2

87. RITCHIE VALENS

88. VAN HALEN

89. MUDDY WATERS

90. THE WHISPERS

91. THE WHO

92. NEIL YOUNG

93. FRANK ZAPPA AND ONE VERSION OF THE MOTHERS OF INVENTION

on February 21, 1976, she was taken to Mt. Carmel Hospital, where she died of cardiac arrest the next day.

About that time, rumors began to circulate that Diana Ross was interested in striking out as a solo performer. The rumors persisted in 1968, even after the group name was changed to Diana Ross and the Supremes. In fact, Mary Wilson later said that as soon as it was announced that change would take place, she was sure Diana would be leaving. During the year, no further changes were made in the trio and the hits continued to come, including "I'm Gonna Make You Love Me" (a duet with the Temptations), "Love Child" (introduced on the "Ed Sullivan Show" and number one in *Billboard* for two weeks starting November 30), and "Some Things You Never Get Used To." That fall, the trio's first TV special, "Diana Ross & the Supremes," was shown on NBC. In late 1968, the Supremes released four albums in two months, including the soundtrack LP (T.C.B.) from a joint NBC special with the Temptations. In December 1969, the two acts teamed up again for another NBC special resulting in the album *On Broadway*.

The top 10 lists of 1969 showed the Supremes' "I'm Livin' in Shame" and "Someday We'll Be Together" (number one the week of December 27). The suggestions of Diana's departure grew even stronger when she was featured by herself on Dinah Shore's April special "Like Hep" on NBC-TV. However, no substantiation came along until December 1969, when it was officially announced that she would leave the group in January 1970. On December 21, 1969, Diana Ross and the Supremes made their final TV appearance on the "Ed Sullivan Show," followed by farewell stage shows in Las Vegas during the holiday season.

In early 1970, the group reformed with Jean Terrell, sister of boxer Ernie Terrell, taking Diana's place. At first, the indications for the group's survival seemed positive. It placed a series of songs on the charts in 1970 and 1971, including "Stoned Love" and "Everybody Has the Right to Love." The Supremes teamed up with the Four Tops for TV appearances, hit albums *The Magnificent 7* (1970) and *The Return of the Magnificent 7* (1971), and singles "River Deep/Mountain High" and "You Gotta Have Love in Your Hearts." (Somewhat confusing during those years was the fact that some releases of the old group came out along with ones of the new trio.) Supremes albums on the charts in 1970 included *Right On* and *New Ways But Love Stays*.

A July evaluation of the New Supremes by *Los Angeles Times* critic Leroy Robinson was favorable: "The Supremes gave not the slightest indication of missing Diana Ross, or that in their reorganization they are riding any other crest but the one set aside for superstars." By the mid-1970s, that evaluation proved to be overly optimistic.

In 1972, the Supremes hit the charts with singles "Automatically Sunshine," "I Guess I'll Miss the Man," "Your Wonderful, Sweet, Sweet Love," and "Floy Joy" plus albums *Supremes* and (with the Four Tops) *Dynamite*. But it was apparent that the public didn't take to the group as it had before Ross left. Though the trio had respectable sales totals for its initial early '70s releases, they didn't come close to the heyday of the late '60s and, even worse, the response was declining as the group continued to encounter changes in membership.

For one, Cindy Birdsong left for a year in the early 1970s and was replaced by Lynda Laurence. Terrell left in 1973 and was replaced by Scherrie Payne (sister of vocalist Freda Payne). Cindy returned for a time, but then left again and was replaced by Susaye Greene. Of the original members, only Mary Wilson persevered.

That revolving-door situation impacted the group's performance. For one thing, from the end of 1973, there were no new albums until *The Supremes* came out in the summer of 1975. Wilson told a reporter: "These personnel changes haven't helped our situation at all. The main reason we haven't had an album out in so long is because of these personnel changes. Motown was waiting to see whether we were stable before they let us record another album."

The 1975 alignment stayed together for two more years, but the trio finally went separate ways in 1977. Little more was heard of the once renowned act until Ross, Birdsong, and Wilson reunited briefly as part of the Motown twenty-fifth anniversary tribute in 1983. Wilson presented far from idyllic reminiscences about the glory days of the group in her book *Dreamgirl: My Life as a Supreme* (St. Martin's Press, 1986). Meanwhile, she continued to be involved in legal wrangles over her right to use the group's name in the billing for her stage act. She won one battle in 1985 when a federal judge decided she could use the name Supremes in promoting her show. But in June 1988, the 9th Circuit Court of Appeals overturned the lower court ruling, stating the name belonged to Motown. Motown lawyer Alan Dowling said the company had told her earlier she could use a billing like Mary Wilson of the Supremes, but would not approve the wording Mary Wilson and the Supremes.

In late 1987, the Supremes were among the artists selected for entry into the Rock and Roll Hall of Fame. In the induction ceremony at the New York Waldorf Astoria in January 1988, presenter Little Richard brought the house down with his comment,

"I love them so much because they remind me of myself—they dress like me."

(See Gordy, Berry, Jr.; Kendrick, Eddie; LaBelle, Patti; Ross, Diana; Temptations, The.)

T. REX: *Vocal and instrumental duo. Original members (1967): Marc Bolan, born England, September 30, 1947, died England, September 16, 1977); Steve Took, born England. Took replaced by Mickey Finn in 1969. In 1970s, band essentially became Bolan with various backing musicians.*

Though the basic membership of T. Rex was two people (sometimes augmented by other musicians), the sound usually was the equivalent of a whole band.

The founding members were Marc Bolan, who handled guitar and vocals as well as writing most of the group's material (and poetry as well), and Steve Peregrine Took, second vocal and percussion. The twosome had a small, but devoted following for the better part of two years, a following that rapidly expanded at home and abroad a short time after Took left and Mickey Finn replaced him.

Born Marc Feld, Bolan grew up in London and became interested in rock in the mid-1950s while still a preteen. "The first record that I had was 'The Ballad of Davy Crockett' by Bill Hayes. Remember that I played that all the time until my dad came home one day and said: 'I've got this new Bill Hayes record for you,' and I thought, great! I looked at the cover and there was this guy jumping around with a guitar. I said: 'But Dad, this isn't Bill Hayes, this is Bill Haley.' It was a real downer. But I played it—'Rock around the Clock,' 'See You Later Alligator'—and I thought: 'Wow! What's this?' Bill Hayes got thrown out the window."

Marc's interest in rock provided incentive for him to learn the guitar. Before he became a musical entertainer, though, he was a child star for a time in the late 1950s. A professional musician in the mid-1960s, he toured as a solo artist or with the group John's Children until early 1967. At that point, he joined forces with Steve Took to form Tyrannosaurus Rex.

Took and Bolan gained some fame playing small clubs in several English cities, with most attention coming from flower children and the underground press. At the outset, the group had a strong folk flavoring, with Bolan favoring acoustic guitar. By 1969, though, he was using an amplified instrument. The trend to amplification and a harder rock sound was strengthened when Finn became the other half of the band.

Finn, who played a number of instruments, had both music and art for hobbies in his teens. His trav-

els in the mid-1960s took him to avant garde centers in England and Continental Europe, including a stay in Amsterdam with the band Haphash and the Coloured Coat. In 1967, he received considerable publicity for his paintings in the Beatles' original Apple Shop and Granny Takes a Trip.

Soon after Finn and Bolan joined forces, they had a hit album, *Bead of Stars* (released in England by Regal Zonophone and in the U.S. by Blue Thumb Records). In late 1969, an earlier LP, *Unicorn*, was a hit. In 1970, the band had a number one single in England, "Hot Love." In October 1970, after the band's name was abbreviated to T. Rex, it made both English and U.S. charts with the single "Ride a White Swan." In summer 1971, the single "Get It On" made number one in England.

In late 1970 the duo switched U.S. record affiliation to Reprise Records, which issued hit LPs *T. Rex* and *Electric Warrior*, but its main support continued to come from English fans. In 1972, for instance, it made American hit lists with the top 10 single "Bang a Gong" and the albums *A Beginning* (an A&M release of early Tyrannosaurus Rex material that earned a gold record in 1973) and *The Slider*. The band's English credits, on the other hand, included albums *Bolan the Boogie* on Fly, *Best of T. Rex* on Flyback (number one on English lists in 1971 and remaining on them into 1972), and the Fly double album *Prophets, Seers & Sages/My People Were Fair*. The group's singles in England included "Jeepster" on Fly Records, "Children of the Revolution" and "Telegram Sam" on the T. Rex label, "Debora" backed with "One Inch Rock" on Magni Fly Echo, and "Metal Guru" and "The Slider" on EMI.

In 1973, T. Rex was represented on English charts by singles "Groover," "Solid Gold Easy Action," and "20th Century Boy" (all on EMI) and on LP charts by Cube Records' reissue of the early albums *A Beard of Stars* and *Unicorn*. The new release *Tanx* on EMI in England and Reprise in the U.S. was the only one to make the charts in both countries that year.

In the mid-1970s, still a cult rather than a mass favorite in the U.S., Bolan and his band found their U.K. following diminishing as well. Still, considering his great guitar and writing talents, no one was counting out a possible comeback. Those expectations were dashed, however, when Marc was killed in the crash of a car driven by his second wife, American singer Gloria Jones.

In the fall of 1985, many of Bolan's most memorable recordings were reissued on the Warner Brothers retrospective *T Rexstasy: The Best of T. Rex, 1970–73*.

TALKING HEADS: *Vocal and instrumental group. Members (mid-1970s–late-1980s): David Byrne, born Scotland, May 14, 1952; Martina Weymouth, born U.S., November 22 c. 1951; Chris Frantz, born U.S., May 9, c. 1951; Jerry Harrison, born U.S., February 21, c. 1953.*

As Talking Heads became a force on the pop scene of the mid-1970s, it generally was considered a standard bearer of the post–punk/new wave genre. Its early recordings typically employed the frenzied rhythmic intensity that had been the hallmark of punk bands such as the Ramones and Sex Pistols. But it offered interesting diversity in melodic content while commenting on the world around it with subtlety and satire rather than the often violent lashing out of the punk movement. As its career progressed, group members refused to be typecast, individually and collectively experimenting with new music formats as well as probing other creative avenues such as film and prose.

The driving force behind the group was primary writer, lead singer, and multi-instrumentalist David Byrne. He was born in Scotland, but grew up in Baltimore. He already had experience as a rock bandsman in his teens before enrolling at the prestigious Rhode Island School of Design (RISD) in the early 1970s. He soon found common musical ground with another art major, Chris Frantz, and the two started the Artistics (a.k.a. the Autistics) at RISD in 1974, with Frantz handling drums and percussion. Soon after, another RISD student, bass guitarist Martina Weymouth (daughter of an admiral) joined the group. Byrne recalled: "We were all working in the visual and conceptual arts there. We became disenchanted, actually bored, with the contemporary art scene. So we decided that pop music would be the most fun, accessible way of communicating."

As they got more into their music, the trio decided to leave Rhode Island and move to New York, where there seemed to be a growing audience for new, experimental rock bands. During 1975 and 1976, the group built up its experience while also making contact with other aspiring new groups playing at small clubs all over the New York area. Like other young musicians of the period, they sought opportunities at CBGB's, the punk/new wave mecca in the Bowery. Before long, they were appearing regularly on bills with such avant garde bands as the Ramones, Television, and Blondie.

The band began to get noticed by rock fans and also the New York press. A *New York Times* reviewer wrote that the band members "have a sound with no previous precedent on the underground circuit or in music itself."

The group, still a trio, by then was calling itself the Talking Heads, deriving the title from TV close-up interview shots of individuals talking in which only the person's head appears on the screen. Band members naturally punctuated their stay in New York with occasional taping sessions of demo material for an eventual record contract. In January 1977, Seymour Stein, the president of Sire Records (then an independent label distributed by ABC Records and later a part of the Warner Brothers organization), announced signing of the group. He stated the debut single, "Love Goes to a Building on Fire"/"New Feeling," would be issued the following February 4 with work on a debut album to begin later in the month. While that work was in progress, the trio expanded to a quartet with the addition of guitarist/keyboards player Jerry Harrison. Harrison, who had been a graduate student at Harvard University, previously had been a member of Jonathan Richman's humorous garage-rock Modern Lovers.

The group's debut LP, *Talking Heads '77*, was released in August to ecstatic reviews in the U.S. and abroad. The album sold a respectable 100,000-plus copies and the band backed it with excellent live appearances. After seeing them in action, a reporter for England's *Record Mirror* commented: "After all these years, someone can still take the five basic components of rock—a singer, a song, guitar, bass, and drums—and come up with something totally fresh."

The group's academic background contributed to its stress on what might be called "literate rock," combining unusual, often psychoanalytic lyrics with well-crafted, usually hard-driving melody and rhythm. As Irwin Stambler noted in his column "Pop, Rock and Soul": "The most important thing about the band is that the foursome plays good, exciting, infectious rock music, music that makes you want to wave your hands, move your feet, forget your troubles. And the group doesn't water that down by bombarding you with self-pitying feeling or audience deprecation. There's no insistence that you spit at your neighbor or throw bottles at the stage to get your kicks. Which isn't to say that the band wants to convey the idea all's right with the world. Talking Heads likes to mix it up, poking incisive fun at today's complex environment in places, giving new rhythmic dimensions to classic pop songs in others."

Chris Frantz told a *Newsweek* reporter (August 21, 1978): "When we started, it was mostly in reaction to what was happening. We were anti-showbiz, anti-arrogant, anti-glitter and anti-overprofessionalism."

Harrison added: "We don't look that different from the audience. We'd like them to feel they can take a stab at something different—the way we have."

Byrne commented: "I'm not sure whether we

have an effect, but we are trying to encourage people to take control of their lives." But as he pointed out in later interviews, he didn't want to overintellectualize things either. The group believed in encouraging the high spirits and pure entertainment value of good rock, while sometimes interjecting elements to make people think a bit. That aspect of the band's approach, he suggested, embodied recognition that college students and people in their twenties and thirties in general follow rock as do teenagers. There's no reason for rock bands to play down to audiences, he noted, nor is there anything wrong with giving listeners food for thought as well as enjoyment.

The band did just that with their second album, *More Songs about Buildings and Food,* produced in collaboration with avant garde keyboardist and producer Brian Eno. *(See Eno, Brian.)* John Rockwell of *The New York Times* named it his choice for the best album of 1978 and *People* magazine listed it in its year's top 10. While most of the songs were originals written by Byrne, the hit single from the LP was a high-intensity cover version of an old Al Green hit, "Take Me to the River."

Compared to the first two albums, the band's third, *Fear of Music* (Sire August 1979), seemed somewhat inconsistent, though it went gold and still offered many above-average tracks including "Air" and "Life during Wartime" (a favorite with dance d.j.'s).

Produced by Eno, the follow-up LP, *Remain in Light* (October 1980), demonstrated experimentation not only with unusual electronic effects, but with blending of new wave elements with funk and African-style rhythms. The latter influences were evident in the single "Crosseyed and Painless," issued in a 12-inch version in advance of the LP.

As the 1980s began, band members started projects outside their Talking Heads commitments. David Byrne joined Eno for a collaboration that led to the LP *My Life in the Bush of Ghosts* (Sire/Warner Brothers, 1981). A striking, evocative album that highlighted a variety of percussion and trancelike vocal effects, it was a creative success if not a candidate for a gold or platinum award. Band members, besides Byrne and Eno, included several expert percussionists and bassist Basta Jones.

While Byrne was engaged in that effort, husband and wife Chris Frantz and Tina Weymouth were recording material as part of the Tom Tom Club. The gold 1981 debut LP on Sire/Warner Brothers, *Tom Tom Club,* emphasized fast, danceable numbers such as "Wordy Rappinghood."

Individual projects and a sabbatical by Tina and Chris to have their first child resulted in almost a three-year gap before Talking Heads' next album, *Speaking in Tongues* (Sire/Warner Brothers, summer 1983, gold). Tina recalled: "Our son Robin was born in the Bahamas just as we were completing the final mixes of *Speaking in Tongues.* When Robin was four months old, we began recording Tom Tom Club's second album, *Close to the Bone* [1983]. In the summer of 1983, we began six weeks of rehearsals for the Talking Heads tour that was eventually to be filmed in Los Angeles by Jonathan Demme as *Stop Making Sense.* That tour was primarily in the U.S., but in early 1984 we also played Australia and New Zealand.

"After that we lay fallow for a few months, trying to think of what to do next without trying to one-up ourselves with a still bigger and more expensive production. Chris and I were writing and enjoying Robin while Jerry worked on his music and David worked on songs and script for a film to be called *True Stories.* He also wrote song sketches which became the completed material for Talking Heads' next album, *Little Creatures* [July 1985, platinum]. Chris and I then did a New England club tour and played at Rock in Rio as the rhythm section for the B-52's." *(See B-52's, The.)*

The concert film, *Stop Making Sense* (publicly released in October 1984), proved one of the better examples of that genre. The film began with only Byrne on stage singing the searing "Psycho Killer" and then gradually brought the other Talking Heads musicians and backing performers on stage until it built up to a climactic number featuring all of the artists. In pacing and attention to detail, it provided insight into the underpinnings of a rock concert and good showcasing of the band's approach to its music. The soundtrack album, issued in August 1984, went gold.

Before moving on to their next album, band members accumulated still more experience in other work. Between *Speaking in Tongues* and *Little Creatures,* Byrne said: "I've been working on *The Knee Play* collaboration with [playwright] Robert Wilson, acting in *Survival Guide,* and co-writing a script. I also wrote the music for 'Alive from Off-Center' [a series of avant garde TV shows for the Public Broadcasting System that emphasized dance and performance art] and did two short performance presentations at the Public Theater and the Kitchen in New York City."

Harrison said: "Since [filming *Stop Making Sense]* I've worked on its promotion and on my own record. I also did a single, '5 Minutes,' on Sleeping Bag Records."

In fall 1985, Byrne went to Dallas, Texas, to direct and perform in his film *True Stories.* The feature-length movie's goal, Michael Ruhlman noted in *The New York Times (New Film Celebrates the Ordinary,* December 1, 1985), "will not be a concert documentary about Talking Heads, nor will it mimic Talking Heads' videos. Instead, it will attempt to achieve a complex texture in which image, rhythm, and gesture become as much a language as words.''

All the instrumentals for the soundtrack were done by Talking Heads, who also sang nine songs in the background. Although characters in the film sang some of the numbers, only Talking Heads material was on the 1986 soundtrack album. The movie, also released in 1986, tended to confuse movie critics, who generally expressed strong reservations about it.

During the 1980s, Talking Heads often expanded its numbers for concerts or recordings, adding as many as six musicians in 1980–81, for instance, for its *Remain in Light* LP. Tina Weymouth emphasized, though: "We always record the basic tracks live as a four-piece first for that special feeling. It's also true that we've always asked other performers to play or sing for an overdub when we needed something that was appropriate to a song and that they could do instinctively . . . something we wouldn't have thought to do ourselves. For instance, when we needed a distinctive black gospel sound, although we could play the instruments authentically, we needed Nona Hendryx to add her background vocals. But I think their role has been exaggerated because people see them playing parts live that we might have done in the studio ourselves. The exceptions are Alex Weir, who played rhythm guitar on quite a few songs on *Speaking in Tongues,* and Steve Scales, who had played percussion on nearly every song on that album and *Little Creatures."*

Band members expressed pride in their contributions to pop music. Harrison said: "I think we stand for a certain kind of honesty of expression which has been an influence on both other musicians and our audience. In a strictly musical sense, we have been able to incorporate modern instruments, interesting polyrhythms, etc., without becoming a slave to them.''

Byrne claimed: "We proved that it's possible to do something without compromise and sell it in the marketplace with everything else . . . and make a living at it. That's an inspiration to many people.''

When Bernardo Bertolucci's movie *The Last Emperor* came out in 1987, it featured a score co-written by Byrne, Ryuichi Sakamoto, and Cong Su. That won the three composers Oscars for Best Original Score, one of nine Oscars the film garnered (including Best Picture) in dominating the Academy Awards.

With all the individual activities of Byrne and the other Talking Heads members, which included Jerry Harrison's excellent solo LP *Casual Gods* in early 1988, observers wondered how the group managed to find time for another band LP, *Naked,* also re-

leased in early 1988. Harrison commented to Patrick Goldstein of the *Los Angeles Times* (March 15, 1988), "I think the fact that we've made room for everyone's solo identities has a lot to do with why we've survived. Groups have an interesting psychological makeup. When you're in a band for a long time, you have a tendency to fall into certain roles . . . but as I've had the chance to assume other roles, either on my albums or as a producer [with production work in the late '80s including material by the BoDeans and Semi-Twang], I've gained lots of appreciation for the demands and dilemmas of those other duties.''

Naked proved to be one of the best albums of the year. As usual, the band sought out new directions instrumentally and in lyric content. This time, they emphasized Afro-French influences with the tracks recorded in Paris with backing musicians from the U.S., Africa, England, Ireland, and the Caribbean. Afro-French rhythms, as Jon Pareles noted *(The New York Times,* March 20, 1988), included soukous from Zaire and Cameroon, mbalax from Senegal and zouk from the French Antilles.

Talking Heads members stressed innovative performance techniques of their own. Chris Frantz told Pareles, "I changed to jazz drumsticks and played a lot with brushes and I got some little piccolo snare drums. I visited Trinidad, where I saw carnival, and I bought a lot of records, and tried to study up on things that were basically not rock and roll.''

With *Naked* in the record stores, Byrne decided against a concert tour for the time being. He had plenty of other projects to pursue including work on the score of a movie planned for German production called *The Forest* and an updating of the Babylonian epic of Gilgamesh to the Industrial Revolution. The Gilgamesh project included a film, which Byrne was to direct, and a theatrical version, on which he collaborated with Robert Wilson. Chris and Tina, the remaining members of Talking Heads, whose production chores included an album by Ziggy Marley and the Melody Makers, spent the first part of 1988 completing work on a new Tom Tom Club album.

TAUPIN, BERNIE: *See John, Elton.*

TAVARES: *Vocal and dance group. Members (all brothers, born New Bedford, Massachusetts): Ralph Vierra Tavares, born c. 1947; Arthur Tavares, born c. 1948; Antone Tavares, born c. 1960; Feliciano Tavares, born c. 1951; Perry Lee Tavares, born c. 1953.* *

A family singing group from New England, Tavares became one of the top-ranked funky soul groups

---

*Based partly on personal interview with Irwin Stambler.

of the 1970s. With harmonies reflecting a bit of the group's Portuguese-speaking heritage, Tavares achieved considerable crossover success among diverse ethnic groups in the U.S. and also earned a following among European pop and disco fans.

The brothers were part of a large family of 10 children who spent childhood years in such New England cities as New Bedford and Boston, Massachusetts, and Providence, Rhode Island. The brothers were harmonizing from the time they were knee high, often joining their father in song. They sang on street corners, too. Among their early experiences was being arrested for doing so in Providence.

Ralph Tavares, who often served as group spokesman, pointed out that in its formative years: "We sang songs from the Cape Verde Islands. Our grandparents came from there. Those are Portuguese possessions 350 miles off the coast of Africa. The language is a dialect of Portuguese. Anyway, that's what we started singing with our father. We did it because we didn't know any other kind of music."

However, it didn't take long for them to become aware of major directions in U.S. pop music. Their older brother John (who wasn't in the group) was instrumental in that. Ralph said: "John turned us on to the harmonies of groups like the Flamingos, Cadillacs, and Penguins. By the early 1960s, several of us were developing our own harmonies. Later on, we were influenced by groups like the Temptations and the O'Jays. But we developed our own style. It's one thing to be influenced by people, but that doesn't mean you won't be original."

The vocal blend that eventually evolved employed Feliciano "Butch" Tavares on counter tenor, Antone "Chubby" Tavares on first tenor, Ralph Tavares on second tenor, Perry Lee "Tiny" Tavares on baritone, and Arthur "Pooch" Tavares on bass. Arthur stressed: "Depending on the song, any one of us will sing lead. But no matter which one of us does that, our fans say they always recognize the Tavares sound."

Perry Lee noted: "Not only was it John's idea for us to form an R&B-type group, he gave us our first name, the Del Rios [in 1964]. Later in the '60s, we changed our name to Chubby and the Turnpikes and then to the Turnpikes."

Meanwhile, under direction of manager Brian Panella, who discovered them in Rhode Island in the early 1960s and still managed them in the 1980s, the group was slowly getting established. After becoming known among soul/R&B fans in New England, the group looked further afield. Feliciano said: "We traveled a whole lot before we made any records. We performed around the states and in places like Puerto Rico and Nassau. In 1971, we made a trip to Italy with [dancer/singer] Lola Falana. That's where

we got our present name. The people there couldn't pronounce Turnpikes, so we changed to our family name. It was the smartest thing we ever did."

"We really went over well in Italy," Ralph added. "We did everything: show tunes, pop, R&B, even some songs in Italian." It was a harbinger of things to come later in the decade when Tavares records often made the top 10 throughout Europe.

The key to that, of course, was obtaining a record contract, something Panella finally managed to set up with Capitol Records in 1973. Ralph recalled: "We beat on doors for nine years before we got that contract. We used to go to New York and take different floors of an office building, knocking on doors to see if people were looking for groups. Most would say: 'No!' When somebody would say: 'Yeah, let me hear you,' guys would be running all through the building trying to find the rest of the group. We would audition right there, but they would always say we were too modern. We'd go home disappointed, but we'd still keep on singing."

The brothers' debut album, *Check It Out* (January 1974), made the R&B top 20 and also showed up on the pop lists. Released as a single, the title song made the top 5 on black music charts. Soon Tavares had another charted LP, *Hard Core Poetry* (Capitol, August 1974).

The group's momentum held up during the mid-1970s with albums *In the City* (August 1975), *Sky-High!* (May 1976), *Love Storm* (April 1977), and the retrospective *The Best of Tavares* (September 1977). Among the singles hits were "It Only Takes a Minute" (a number one soul success in 1975) and gold "Heaven Must Be Missing an Angel" (a 1976 top 10 hit in England, number 2 in Holland, number 3 in Belgium, and number 13 in Ireland as well). In support of the 1976 recordings, Tavares made an extensive tour of Europe.

In the late 1970s, Tavares, like other R&B/soul vocal teams, could feel the pressure from the disco boom. As Panella observed, a challenge was posed not only by disco, but by the increasingly preset top 40 programming. "The station's playlist had a lot to do with the problem. A combination of an increase in records released and a decrease in the playlist made the competition fierce."

Tavares took stock of its position and decided it could qualify as a disco-type team by calling attention to its longtime repertoire. Feliciano pointed out: "We had been turning out disco-style numbers as part of our regular releases. A song like 'Don't Take Away the Music' was very danceable, but no one called it a disco number."

Ralph said: "We just did fast songs—still do. We never did a study on it. One of the good things about disco is that it's generally simple and simplicity is the way to go to involve people. If you get too complicated, you lose the audience, just like jazz did a few decades ago. But that didn't mean we were suddenly going to change our style. We figured if we just kept doing what comes naturally creatively and our record company highlighted how it related to the new trends, we would hold our own.''

As it happened, a fortunate association with another brother group, the Australian/U.K. Bee Gees, solved the disco question. After Tavares opened for the Bee Gees at New York's Madison Square Garden in early 1978, the Bee Gees' Gibb brothers were inspired to write a song, ''More than a Woman,'' to fit Tavares' style. The Tavares version became part of the soundtrack for the blockbuster film *Saturday Night Fever*, and the multiplatinum album was later named Album of the Year in the Grammy Awards voting. The song also was included on Tavares' own 1978 hit LP, *Future Bound*.

The group closed out the decade with the LP *Madame Butterfly* (January 1979) in the soul/R&B top 15. During the year, the group had two top 10 soul singles: ''Never Had a Love Like This Before'' and ''Bad Times.''

1980 brought two new albums: *Supercharged* (February) and *Love Uprising* (November). Both showed up on the charts, but their content seemed somewhat less exciting than earlier offerings'. The title song from *Love Uprising* was a 1980–81 top 20 hit in the soul field.

After the 1981 LP *Loveline*, the group's Capitol contract had run out and Tavares moved over to RCA Records. The group's RCA debut LP, *New Directions* (late 1982), spent some time on pop and soul charts. Its single ''A Penny for Your Thoughts'' made the pop top 30 in early 1983. Over the next few years, the group placed several singles on the black music charts for RCA, including the late 1983 ''Words and Music.'' However, Tavares, while still retaining a strong following on the live-performance circuit, couldn't match its 1970s recording achievements. By the mid-1980s, the RCA pact expired and wasn't renewed.

Tavares members had recognized for many years that pop music popularity can wax and wane and wax again, as can be the case for creativity. Feliciano had noted: ''The important thing is never say die. There are talented people like Peaches and Herb and Gene Chandler who didn't do well for years and then suddenly came back. Persistence is the name in this business; you never can predict how the audience will react from one moment to the next.''

TAYLOR, JAMES: *Singer, songwriter, guitarist, cellist. Born Boston, Massachusetts, March 12, 1948.*

A child of his times, James Taylor initially expressed the alienation and restlessness that beset those who came of age during the years of the Vietnam War. Later, his music conveyed the more relaxed atmosphere combined with the desire to come to terms with life that ensued in the U.S. and Western society in general once the agony of Vietnam was over. However, while finding favor with his peer group, because of the strong country-folk elements in his writings, he also bridged the generation gap to appeal to members of all age groups.

When he became a superstar in the early 1970s, he was only in his early twenties, but in his brief lifetime to that point, he had packed experiences ranging from exultation to despair. In this sense, his background was similar in part to some of the black blues artists. Unlike most of them, his scars were self-inflicted. He was born into a loving and affluent family, his early years were sheltered and—in what was probably a major element in the problems he and his three brothers and sister encountered—few of his wishes were denied.

He was born in Boston's Massachusetts General Hospital, where his father, from an old, affluent Southern family, was completing work on his medical degree. His mother, daughter of a Massachusetts fisherman and boat builder, was trained as a lyric soprano, but gave up the idea of a career in favor of raising a family. She allowed her children to start lessons on various instruments, but did not pressure them to continue when they resisted formal instruction.

As James grew up, he moved between two beautiful locales. During most of the year, the family lived in a 28-room house near the campus of the University of North Carolina in Chapel Hill, where his father was a member of the medical faculty and eventually dean of the medical school. Summers were spent in another large house near the white beaches of Martha's Vineyard off the coast of Massachusetts.

The family enjoyed music, and James heard both his father and mother singing at family get-togethers as he went through public school and then the expensive Milton Academy near Boston. One of his close friends on Martha's Vineyard was musically oriented Danny Kortchmar (born Kootch). When Taylor was 15, he and Danny won a local hootenanny contest with Danny playing harmonica and Taylor guitar and both alternating on vocals. But each soon turned his attention from folk to rock.

James found his time at private school trying. He was not sure of his goals and missed his family and friends. At 16, he felt he had to get away and left school for a term to return to North Carolina and join his older brother Alex in a rock band, the Fabulous

Corsairs. He then returned to Milton, but at 17 found himself increasingly despondent. When he began to have suicidal urges, he signed himself into a mental institution, McLean Hospital in Belmont, Massachusetts.

During a nine-month stay there during 1965, he managed to improve his emotional outlook, though he still had stretches of sadness. He completed work for a high school degree before leaving for New York, where he reestablished contact with Danny Kootch, who was forming a new band, the Flying Machine, which enjoyed a number of low-paying engagements in the New York area. Taylor, who played guitar and sang, also wrote original compositions for the band, some of which—"Knocking round the Zoo," "Night Owl," and "Rainy Day Man"—appeared on his debut LP a year later.

Living in a small apartment, mostly on money from his parents, 18-year-old Taylor provided a haven for many alienated people. After a while, he began to join some of them in experimenting with drugs. He tried increasingly stronger stuff and soon became hooked on heroin, something he commented on his song "Fire and Rain": "Won't you look down on me, Jesus/You've got to help me make a stand/You've just got to see me through another day."

Realizing he had escaped one trap just to fall into another, he decided to leave New York and try to kick the drug habit. He went to London in 1968 and rented studio time to make tapes of his material. He took them to the Beatles' Apple Records and managed to get them auditioned by producer Peter Asher (originally of the Peter and Gordon vocal duet and later producer of Linda Ronstadt's big hits of the '70s). Asher liked them, as did Beatle Paul McCartney, and the debut LP *James Taylor* came out in midyear. The promising LP didn't sell well, though one of the tracks, the folk-flavored "Carolina on My Mind," later became a hit.

Taylor returned to the U.S. in December 1968 and spent another brief period in a mental hospital, Austin Riggs, in Stockbridge, Massachusetts. By mid-1969, he felt well enough to go back to work. Peter Asher had become his manager and, with Apple in legal difficulties, he gained Taylor a new contract with Warner Brothers and produced Taylor's label debut, *Sweet Baby James* (spring 1970). With strong promotion help from Warners, this LP slowly sold more than 2 million copies. It also brought the Apple album eventually new attention, so the debut too went gold. In late 1970, Taylor also had a top single, "Fire and Rain."

Now a national celebrity, Taylor performed to turn-away crowds in 27 cities across the U.S. in March and April 1971. Joining him for the show were such fine musicians as Danny Kootch and Jo Mama, drummer Russ Kunkel, bassist Lee Sklar and singer/pianist Carole King. Besides adding to Taylor's reputation, the tour was instrumental in Carole King's emergence as a major pop star in her own right.

Spring 1971 brought his second Warner Brothers album, *Mud Slide Slim and the Blue Horizon.* A fine collection, it also was platinum. Its version of Carole King's composition song "You've Got a Friend," reached number one in July. Meanwhile, material from his early days with Kootch *(James Taylor & the Original Flying Machine* on Euphoria) was a hit in early 1971.

Much of the original material in *Mud Slide Slim* described the emotional problems that went along with sudden success. Those new pressures caused self-doubts reflected in his work. His next LP, *One Man Dog,* though it was a gold top 10 hit in 1972 and spawned two chart singles ("Don't Let Me Be Lonely Tonight" and "Long Ago Far Away,"), was not up to the level of earlier collections. Nor was his next album, *Walking Man* (1974), much of an improvement.

Fortunately, this phase soon went by, thanks mainly to a milestone in his private life, his relationship with singer-songwriter Carly Simon (born New York, New York, June 25, 1945). When the two married in 1972, it was a major social highlight. More important, Taylor evidenced a new self-confidence and emotional maturity. In redoing many of his best-regarded numbers for Warner Brothers' 1976 *James Taylor's Greatest Hits,* he demonstrated new depth and shading in his vocal treatment of such numbers as "Carolina on My Mind" and "Something in the Way She Moves." The gold 1975 album *Gorilla* proved to be his best work since the early '70s both as a performer and as a writer. Meanwhile, he and his wife joined forces on entertaining new material, such as their duet on the gold 1974 single "Mockingbird" (a remake of Inez Foxx's 1963 hit) from Carly's gold Elektra LP *Hotcakes.*

There also was change in his stage presence. In the early part of his career, he often seemed shy and ill at ease on stage. From the mid-1970s on, he became a much more relaxed performer, achieving closer rapport with audiences and projecting considerably more effective stylings.

After his gold 1976 LP *In the Pocket,* he moved to Columbia Records, which issued his well-balanced platinum LP *JT* in midsummer 1977. One of its high spots was Taylor's version of Jimmy Jones' 1960 R&B hit "Handy Man," which provided him with a top 10 single. Subsequent Columbia LPs *Flag* (1979) and *Dad Loves His Work* (spring 1981) went gold.

By the early 1980s, the Taylor/Simon marriage had fallen apart and in 1982 Carly filed for divorce. Taylor seemed to have come to terms with it, however, and his numerous concerts of the mid-1980s reflected a feeling of quiet self-confidence without any recurrence of the emotional problems that had plagued his early years. His records continued to find an audience, as was indicated by the response to his late 1985 Columbia LP *That's Why I'm Here.*

After spending much of 1987 touring and working on his next album, Taylor ended the year by taking part in three special benefit performances. On December 4, he performed (along with such other stars as Elton John, Robin Williams, Belinda Carlisle and the Miami Sound Machine) at the Prince's Trust Concert at the London Palladium. On December 10, he went to Washington, D.C., to take part in the Amnesty International celebration of International Human Rights Day. Three days later he joined such luminaries as Bruce Springsteen, Paul Simon, and Billy Joel in a New York Madison Square Garden concert to raise funds for medical relief for homeless children.

His new album, the decidedly low-key, easy listening collection called *Never Say Die,* came out in January 1988. Before embarking on a tour backing the LP, Taylor made guest appearances on "Saturday Night Live" and "The Tonight Show." Columbia Records stated that all of his earlier four LPs on the label had been certified gold by the RIAA, adding to his pre-Columbia totals of six gold and three platinum albums.

(See Beatles, The; King, Carole; Peter and Gordon.)

TEDDY BEARS, THE: *See Spector, Phil.*

TEENA MARIE: *Singer, guitarist, songwriter, record producer. Born Santa Monica, California, 1957.*

It has been said that music knows no boundaries, but it's also a truism that few nonblack performers have been able to handle such music as rhythm & blues and soul with the feeling and intensity of its ethnic originators. But Teena Marie is one of the exceptions, a white Californian whose dynamic singing voice and rhythmic sense made her a force to reckon with in the R&B, funk, soul, jazz, and, yes, pop of the 1980s.

Born Mary Christine Brockert in the relatively affluent beach city of Santa Monica, Teena Marie spent most of her childhood and teen years in nearby Venice, a somewhat earthier area whose ethnic makeup included sections largely populated by blacks and Hispanics along with a leavening of avant garde poets, painters, and musicians. As a child during the 1960s, she was a fan of the Beatles and Rolling Stones, but also enjoyed black performers such as Sarah Vaughan and Marvin Gaye. All the members of her family were musically inclined. She had a brother who loved rock'n'roll, sisters who preferred Motown's soul greats of the 1960s, and parents who opted for the musical theater of Cole Porter and Rodgers and Hammerstein.

Teena made her professional debut at age eight. A good student, she got above-average grades in high school, but still found time for her musical activities. At 13, she formed her first band and throughout her teens she added to her performing experience on the Los Angeles club circuit. She naturally hoped for a chance to move up in the field and recorded various demo tapes she sought to get heard by record-company artists & repertoire executives.

Surprisingly, despite her vocal accomplishments, she wasn't able to find a recording home with any major label while she was pursuing her studies at Venice High School. With the possibilities of a music career still insubstantial, she went on to enroll at a local college. She didn't give up seeking an opening, though. During her first year in college in the late 1970s, she was finally signed by Motown Records to record on its subsidiary Gordy.

At Motown, Rick James, the unofficial king of funk, took her under his wing and helped organize recording sessions for her label debut during late 1978 and early 1979. *(See James, Rick.)* Besides handling production, Rick also wrote most of the material for the project. That LP, *Wild and Peaceful* (1979), showcased an artst who obviously was a diamond in the rough. While there were some inconsistencies in her treatment of the various numbers, overall it was an excellent first effort. The album provided two charted singles: "I'm Just a Sucker for Your Love" and "Deja Vu." Teena's impact on the music world was even greater thanks to her soon-demonstrated audience rapport in live performances.

A quick study, she rapidly picked up the basics of studio work as evidenced by a first-rate follow-up album, *Lady T* (1980). The record company culled two more hit singles from that album: "Behind the Groove" and "Can It Be Love."

Teena quickly took more and more control of her career directions. For her third album, she wrote most of the songs, arranged a considerable part of the rhythm and vocal tracks, and also co-produced the collection, *Irons in the Fire* (September 1980). Even more impressive than *Lady T,* it made the soul charts almost immediately. Its singles hits included "Young Love" and "I Need Your Lovin'," the latter her first top 10 success on the soul charts. The album sold over 500,000 copies and earned Teena a gold-record award from the RIAA.

In June 1981, Gordy issued her album *It Must Be Magic*, another gem that a *Rolling Stone* reviewer called "superb thinking man's dance music. Ordinary lyrical concerns are made extraordinary by Teena's idiosyncratic imagery and wordplay. Your booty and your brain are equally motivated." Teena herself commented once: "My songs are a reflection of my life as an English major and my life in the streets." Charted singles from the album included "Portuguese Love" and "Square Biz" (a song that did well on pop charts as well and was named one of the year's best in a reader's poll conducted by *New York Rocker* magazine).

After that album and the backing concert tour, Teena's association with Motown came to an end. This time there were plenty of suitors for her services from other labels. The winner proved to be Epic Records. Her Epic debut, *Robbery* (September 1983), was in the top 25 on black charts at year-end and also starting to move up on the general pop list. The title track provided Teena with another hit single.

For her next album, the gold *Starchild* (1984), Teena was involved in almost every facet. She wrote six of its nine songs and co-wrote the other three. She also supervised much of the arranging and was overall producer. Its tracks included the well-received "My Dear Mr. Gaye" and "Out on a Limb," while "Lovergirl" reached the top 10 on *Billboard*'s pop charts and made Teena a 1985 Grammy finalist for Best R&B Vocal Solo Performance, Female.

The next album too was produced by Teena, who wrote five songs herself and collaborated on the other three. Among the backing musicians were some of the best-known names in jazz, rock, and funk: Stevie Ray Vaughan, Bootsy Collins, Bradford Marsalis, Stanley Clarke, Paulinho daCosta, and Nathan East. The album, *Emerald City*, reflected Teena's efforts to expand her musical horizons a bit, though without betraying her R&B heritage. She pointed out: "'Shangri La' has a strong Italian flavor to it and 'You So Heavy' [featuring Vaughan on guitar] shows off my rock and Beatles influences." Besides those, she noted, "Sunny Skies" (with solos by Marsalis and Clarke) was a fortyish jazz ballad and "Battacuda Suite" was intended to have a strong Brazilian flavor, as she noted, "built around eight percussion instruments." The July 1986 album quickly made both pop and black charts as did the single "Lips to Find You." Her fourth Epic LP was *Naked to the World* (March 1988).

TEENAGERS, THE: *Vocal group from New York City. Members: Frankie Lymon, born Washington Heights, New York, September 30, 1942,* *died Harlem, New York, February 28, 1968; Sherman Garnes, born June 8, 1940, died February 26, 1977; Joe Negroni, born c. September 9, 1940, died September 5, 1978; Herman Santiago, born February 18, 1941; Jimmy Merchant, born February 10, 1940.*

The saga of the Teenagers might be called a Cinderella story without a happy ending. The group's lead singer was an idol of countless youngsters when he was just into his teens, but a has-been and a drug addict before he was 26.

The group came together on the street corners of Harlem in the mid-1950s. The five members had been school friends for a number of years. The development of the quintet was sparked by high-voiced young Frankie Lymon when he was not yet past the age of 13. Besides Lymon as lead singer, Negroni sang baritone, Garnes bass, Santiago first tenor, and Merchant second tenor. The group rehearsed where it could, sometimes in the members' homes, but often in a junk-filled backyard or on the roof of an old tenement. In 1955, they sang on city pavements and were rewarded with coins from passersby.

They were overheard by Richard Barrett, leader of a group called the Valentines, who recorded for Gee Records. Barrett brought the Teenagers to the offices of Gee, where company heads George Goldner and Joe Kilsky were just as enthusiastic. The executives raved about the Teenagers' song "Why Do Fools Fall in Love" and found it hard to believe that young Lymon had written it. Kilsky asked: "You got any sheet music for it?" Lymon replied: "Nope, we don't know anything about written-down music."

Gee rushed the boys into the studio the next day to record the song without a written arrangement and with backing supplied by Jimmy Wright's band. Released January 10, 1956, it became a true blockbuster, staying in the top 10 in the U.S. for 16 straight weeks, during part of which time it was number one on some lists. The disc also reached top chart levels in England and had estimated worldwide sales of over 2 million records. Despite cover versions by white pop singers Gale Storm and the Diamonds, the Teenagers' sales were more than enough to pass nominal gold record levels. The Teenagers suddenly were international stars.

During 1956, they took part in Alan Freed's movie *Rock, Rock, Rock*, introducing two new songs: "I'm Not a Juvenile Delinquent" and "Baby, Baby." Both appeared on the group's debut LP on Gee, *Why Do Fools Fall in Love?* The album included four other songs that made the charts during 1956: "I Promise to Remember," "I Want You to Be My Girl," "I'm Not a Know-It-All," and "Who Can Explain?"

By the start of 1957, Lymon had left the group to

try to make it as a soloist, but once he went through puberty and his voice changed, he lost his appeal. The group remained around for several years, but never approached its early success. Lymon got hooked on drugs and his career took a nosedive during 1957–58. He was only 17 and a has-been when he found the inner strength to kick his habit. He tried a comeback, but failed and, at 18, was taking hard drugs again. Once more he was encouraged to try to break away, this time by a girlfriend, and he managed to do it for a year. However, the romance faded and, after going into the Army, Lymon resumed his old habit.

After discharge, Lymon returned home to New York, strung out on drugs and unable to hold a steady job. In late February 1968, he was found dead of a heroin overdose on the floor of his grandmother's apartment. Though he had earned hundreds of thousands of dollars as a boy, he was penniless when he died.

TEMPTATIONS, THE: *Vocal group. Original members (early 1960s): Otis Williams, born Texarkana, Texas, October 31, 1941; Melvin Franklin, born Montgomery, Alabama, October 12, 1942; Paul Williams, born Birmingham, Alabama, July 2, 1939, died August 17, 1973; Eddie Kendricks, born Birmingham, Alabama, December 17, 1939; David Ruffin, born Meridian, Mississippi, January 18, 1941. Ruffin left in 1968, replaced by Dennis Edwards, born Birmingham, Alabama, February 3, 1943. Kendricks left in 1971, replaced by Damon Harris. Paul Williams replaced by Richard Street. Harris replaced by Glenn Leonard, in turn replaced in early 1980s by Ron Tyson. Edwards replaced in 1985 by Ali-Ollie Woodson, born Detroit, Michigan. Edwards rejoined in late 1987.*

During the 1960s, one of the brightest jewels in the crown of Motown Records was the Temptations, a vocal and dance group that helped make the Motown Sound a favorite with millions throughout the world. With various changes in personnel, the group remained a top act for close to three decades, though its recordings of the '70s and '80s typically didn't rank with its classic hits of the '60s.

The early experience of the artists who eventually formed the Temptations followed a familiar pattern for the black superstars of the 1950s and '60s. Most had considerable experience with gospel music from their earliest years. Though all the founding members and most later additions were born in the South, most had gravitated to the Detroit area by the late 1950s.

As is often the case in the entertainment field, particularly for multiple-member acts, there are varying versions of the way the members came together and finally evolved into the Temptations quintet. It's generally agreed that Eddie Kendricks and Paul Williams were friends in Birmingham, Alabama, who decided to go North in the mid-1950s to try to find fame and fortune in the music field. They had enough money to get to Cleveland, Ohio, where they could stay with relatives. There, while performing with a group called the Cavaliers (whose other members were Cal Osborne and Willy Waller), they were heard by Milton Jenkins, a sometime booking agent, who suggested Kendricks and Williams could further their careers better by moving to Detroit. He offered to let them stay at his place while he tried to help them get properly connected.

Already in Detroit was a young singer named Otis Williams (born Otis Miles) who, depending on which source you refer to, either was taken to Detroit as a baby or moved there with his family as a nine-year-old. As he grew up, Williams organized doo-wop vocal groups that evolved into the Distants. According to the version given by Nelson George in *Where Did Our Love Go: The Rise and Fall of the Motown Sound* (St. Martin's, 1985), after bass singer Arthur Walton left the Distants, Williams heard another bass vocalist, 15-year-old Melvin Franklin, working with a street group and got him to replace Walton. However, other bio material from the 1960s stated the two had become friends soon after Franklin's family moved north from Alabama and were close acquaintances throughout their teens.

According to Fred Bronson in his *Billboard Book of Number One Hits*, Williams evolved the Distants over several years, starting with groups named the Elegants (not the Elegants who sang "Little Star") and the Questions. The members in the late '50s, he noted, were Otis Williams, Franklin, Richard Street, Elbridge Bryant, and Albert Harrell. After Street and Harrell left, in that version, Milton Jenkins (who supposedly was manager of both the Distants and a group called the Elgins, whose members included Kendricks and Paul Williams) suggested that the two groups merge to form a new quintet.

Nelson George, on the other hand, stated that Jenkins was not involved with those artists in the late 1950s and that the new alignment arose from the fact that by 1958, Kendricks, the two Williams, Elbridge Bryant, and Franklin were hanging out together in Detroit. They had become friends after their paths crossed many times on the Detroit performing circuit. At one point, he noted, Kendricks stated that his group called the Primes took part in one of the doo-wop competitions that were a feature of that scene, taking first place over Otis Williams and the Distants. Whatever the exact facts are, it's certain that during 1959, Otis, Paul Williams, Bryant, Kendricks, and Franklin joined forces as the Primes quintet and gained a growing following among local fans. Their prestige also had a hand in the organization of a "sister" group called the Primettes, which evolved into the Supremes.

As the Primes, the group was signed to Berry Gordy's Motown organization in 1960 and initially cut some sides on the firm's subsidiary Miracle. After a short time, the group was shifted to the new Gordy designation. And the group soon had a new name, the Temptations, coined by Otis Williams. During that time, group members decided that Bryant was more interested in being a ladies man than concentrating on making the quintet a success, so he exited and was replaced by David Ruffin, whose gospel style seemed to fit the group's harmonies. This gave the group three lead singers: Ruffin, Kendricks (who sang lead and high tenor), and Paul Williams, who at first was the main lead vocalist and baritone. Otis Williams handled baritone and second tenor, while Mel Franklin sang bass.

For several years, it seemed that the group couldn't find the formula for recording success. The Temptations placed singles on the charts, but couldn't seem to penetrate highest levels on either soul or pop lists. The group served as opening act for Smokey Robinson and the Miracles at a number of concerts. During one tour, both groups were on the bill at the Apollo in Harlem when Temptations members went to a New York recording studio while Smokey recorded the rhythm track for a new song of his, "My Girl." It was intended for the Miracles, but Temptations members talked him into letting them record it. That song, co-written by Ronald White, proved the turning point for the group, reaching number one on both *Billboard*'s pop list (the week of March 6, 1965) and R&B/soul list. This was followed by four straight hit singles (all written by Robinson): "It's Growing," "Since I Lost My Baby," and "My Baby" in 1965, and "Get Ready" in 1966.

The group paralleled its recording achievement with a stage show that ranked among the best in the field. The Temptations drew capacity crowds to concerts throughout the U.S. and abroad and were considered, with the Supremes, the main breadwinners for the Motown organization. Ruffin, however, had become increasingly unhappy with his position as one of five equal members and made no secret of his desire to pursue a solo career. In the summer of 1968, he made the break. His place was taken by Dennis Edwards, who originally signed with Motown as a soloist, but was asked first to fill in for the lead singer of the Contours and then was briefly considered by the label as head of a group he had formed earlier, the Firebirds. Finally, Motown executives decided the best solution would be to have him take Ruffin's place with the Temptations.

The reorganized quintet, if anything, increased its popularity with Edwards as a member. The first single on which he was featured, "Cloud Nine," made the top 10 in early 1969. The group followed with hit singles "Runaway Child, Running Wild," "Don't Let the Joneses Get You Down," "I Can't Get Next to You" (number one in *Billboard* the weeks of October 18 and 25, 1969), and, with the Supremes, "I'm Gonna Make You Love Me."

The group's well-blended, spirited vocals plus their intricate rock/R&B dance styles had made them a favorite with concert and TV audiences in all segments of pop music before Ruffin left and this rapport continued unabated for the reorganized group. In 1969, they co-starred with the Supremes on two NBC-TV specials taped for LPs: "T.C.B." and "Diana Ross and the Supremes and the Temptations on Broadway."

During those years, they did not lag in album sales. Almost all the group's LPs sold well and several went past the million-dollar mark. Among those releases were *The Temptations Meet Smokey, Temptin' Temptations,* and the number one R&B hit LP *Getting Ready* (1966); *Live* and *Greatest Hits, Volume 1* (1967); *The Temptations Wish It Would Rain* and *In a Mellow Mood* (1968); and *T.C.B., Live at the Copa, Cloud Nine,* and *Puzzle People* (1969).

The 1970s began with promise equal to that of the late 1960s. In 1970, the single "Ungena Za Ulimwengu" (Unite the World) moved into the soul top 20, and "Ball of Confusion" reached number three nationally in June. "Just My Imagination (Running Away with Me)" reached number one in *Billboard* the weeks of April 3 and 10, 1971. Other 1971 hit singles were "It's Summer" and the top 10 soul success "Superstar (Remember How You Got Where You Are)." 1970 album hits included *Psychedelic Shock* (top 10), *Live at London's Talk of the Town,* and *Greatest Hits, Volume 2.* The 1971 LP release *Sky's the Limit* hit *Billboard*'s pop top 20.

But by the time its track "Just My Imagination" reached number one, with Kendricks on lead vocal, Eddie had decided to leave the group in favor of a solo career. Meanwhile, Paul Williams' career was winding down due to marital problems, financial difficulties, and alcohol-related physical ailments. His mounting worries finally led him to commit suicide on August 17, 1973. Damon Harris took over Kendricks' tenor role. Eventually, Williams' place was taken by Richard Street.

At least for a while, the group's changes didn't affect its popularity. In 1972, it had two top 10 soul albums: *All Directions* and *Solid Rock,* whose track

"Papa Was a Rollin' Stone" reached number one in *Billboard* the week of December 2, 1972. Other successes were "Funky Music Sho' Nuff Turns Me On"/"Mother Nature" and the top 10 soul single "Take a Look Around." In 1973, the group was represented on album charts with the retrospective *Anthology* (soul top 10) and *Masterpiece* (pop top 10) and the singles "Hey Girl (I Like Your Style)" and "Plastic Man" in the soul top 10 plus "Masterpiece" in the pop top 10. The album *1990* moved onto the national sales charts in December 1973 and was in the top 20 by February 1974.

But the Temptations long stay at the very top began to slip. After "Masterpiece," the group couldn't achieve another top 10 hit the rest of the decade. There also were more roster changes during those years. In 1975, Harris was replaced by Glenn Leonard. The following year, Edwards opted for a solo career and was replaced by Louis Price. The group's 1975 album, *A Song for You,* was one of its weakest on Gordy and did much less saleswise than previous releases. In 1976, the group issued *The Temptations Do the Temptations,* a rare collection where group members wrote all the material, but that failed to yield any singles hits.

To try to restore its fortunes, the group left Gordy for Atlantic Records, turning out LPs *Hear to Tempt You* (1977) and *Bare Back* (1978), neither of which had much impact. Gordy reissued some of the group's finest efforts in 1979 on *The Temptations Sing Smokey* and in 1980 welcomed the group back with the album *Power*. The title song (co-written by Berry Gordy to celebrate the Temptations' return home) made the charts, though not the pop top 40. In 1981, the group had the chart album *Temptations* on Gordy. The group was still a major drawing card as it showed in a series of tours throughout the 1980s. One of the more memorable series took place in the fall of 1982. Called the "Reunion Tour," it featured the regular group (then comprising Otis Williams, Franklin, Glenn Leonard, Richard Street, and Dennis Edwards) accompanied by its two noted alumni: Kendricks and Ruffin. Among the new numbers in the act was the hard-driving funk hit of 1982, "Standing on the Top."

The Temptations, Kendricks, and Ruffin all took part in the 1983 NBC-TV special celebrating Motown's twenty-fifth anniversary and contributed songs to the album of the event. Afterwards, the Temptations took off on a cross-country tour with the Four Tops with the quintet's members during those concerts comprising Williams, Franklin, Edwards, Street, and Ron Tyson.

During the 1980s, Leonard was replaced by Ron Tyson and Edwards by Ali-Ollie Woodson. The group's 1986 work included the chart single "Lady Soul" and a video for their recording of the title track to the film *A Fine Mess*. The quintet also taped a program telecast on the cable-TV Showtime channel in the summer. The same year, a two disc retrospective of the group's recordings came out *(The Temptations 25th Anniversary,* Motown). In 1987 Motown issued the album *Together Again*. A sad page was added to the Temptations' history in April 1988, when former lead singer David Ruffin was jailed in Detroit on cocaine possession charges after he could not post $150 in cash for a $1500 bond. Charged with intent to distribute a small amount of the drug, he faced a possible 20-year prison sentence, but fortunately for him the next month he was found guilty only of drug use and ordered to undergo substance abuse treatment. *(See Gordy, Berry, Jr.; Kendrick, Eddie; Robinson, Smokey; Ross, Diana; Supremes, The.)*

TEN YEARS AFTER: *Vocal and instrumental group. Ric Lee, born Cannock Staffs, England, October 20, 1945; Alvin Lee, born Nottingham, England, December 19, 1944; Chick Churchill, born Mold, Flintshire, England, January 2, 1949; Leo Lyons, born Standbridge, Bedfordshire, England, November 30, 1944.*

The group name Ten Years After referred to the fact that it originated roughly a decade after rock became the dominant form of pop music. It also symbolized the fact that the founders of the group initially were interested in playing "primitive" rock similar to the way it had been done in the mid-1950s. As time went by, the name seemed prophetic—in the early 1970s, the band's makeup remained the same as it had been in 1967 with a good chance that it might celebrate its tenth anniversary still intact, an unusual achievement in a field where overnight changes are the rule.

The two original members, Alvin Lee and Leo Lyons, came from Nottingham (a town mainly famous as Robin Hood's supposed locale). Both were immediately caught up in the early rock craze of the mid-1950s. Alvin learned to play guitar and started performing for local dances at 13. Lyons (who eventually played drums, bass, double bass, and guitar) took a little longer, not becoming a performer until he was 15. By the early 1960s, both were in heavily blues-oriented organizations. Lee first gained attention when he took part in a John Lee Hooker show at London's Marquee Club, while Lyons' first important appearance was at a Windsor Jazz Festival in the early '60s. During those years, both gained considerable work as studio musicians for record sessions.

The two became acquainted on the rock circuit

and, in 1964, with Lyons handling drums, formed their own trio, called Britain's Largest Sounding Trio. Playing a mixture of old-time rock and jazz, for several years, they spent much of their time in Continental Europe, particularly in Hamburg, Germany, where the Beatles had tasted early popularity.

In 1967, Lee and Lyons reorganized their band, adding another Lee—Ric, no relation to Alvin—and Chick Churchill. While drumming at the Windsor Jazz Festival, Ric came to the attention of Lyons, who later sought him out for Ten Years After. Churchill, youngest of the group, learned piano and organ from the age of five and continued it as a hobby through most of his school years. In 1966, he turned professional and was good enough to find work in London clubs soon after.

After playing around London for a while in 1967, the group signed with London Records and put out the successful debut album *Ten Years After* on its Deram subsidiary. LPs *SSSH* (1969) and, in 1970, *Cricklewood Green* and *Watt* all broke *Billboard*'s top 30.

The group's hyperamplified sound, wild leaping antics, and long drum solos created one of the countless high spots at the Woodstock Festival in 1969. The highly successful movie of the festival devoted 10 minutes to the group's set.

In 1971, though the quartet took three months out early in the year to relax and renew its creative energies, it still remained as a unit. The next goal was to change direction toward more electronic-style music. As Alvin Lee noted: "We're getting into abstract sound, not exactly avant garde stuff, but we're getting something together. Why abstract sound? Obviously it's a new thing and all that . . . or new to me. The grass is greener."

It remained to be seen how the public would react to their new arrangements on *A Space in Time,* released on a new label, Columbia, in mid-1971.

The verdict seemed to be favorable as *A Space in Time* earned a platinum record. The next Columbia LP, *Rock & Roll Music to the World* (1972), was also on U.S. and British charts. A Deram album of earlier material, *Alvin Lee & Company,* was also a best-seller in 1972. During 1973, the band had the hit Columbia album *Recorded Live.* The band placed several singles on the hit lists in the early 1970s: "I'd Love to Change the World" in 1971, "Baby, Won't You Let Me Rock & Roll You" in 1972, and "Choo Choo Mama" in 1973.

By 1973, Alvin Lee was becoming restless about his band restrictions. By the time the 1974 Columbia LP, *Positive Vibrations,* came out, he was firmly committed to a solo career. *(See Lee, Alvin.)* After his departure, the group kept on going for a while, but without him it no longer packed the same musi-

cal punch. During the mid-1970s, two retrospective albums appeared: *Goin' Home: Their Greatest Hits* (Deram, 1975) and *The Classic Performances of Ten Years After* (Columbia, 1976). Also available for a time was the London release, *London Collector: Ten Years After.*

TEX, JOE: *Singer, songwriter. Born Rotgers, Texas, August 8, 1933; died August 13, 1982.*

One of the most talented of the young blues singers of the post–World War II decades, Joe Tex was compared by some observers to such greats as Sam Cooke and Big Joe Turner. For a time, though, it seemed as though he would find more success as a songwriter than as a performer. Later on, he gave up many of his entertainment projects to further his adopted Muslim religion.

He was born Joseph Arrington, Jr., into a poverty-ridden sharecropper family in Rotgers, Texas. Most of his formative years were spent in Baytown, Texas. He had his first singing experience in church and by the time he was in high school in Baytown, he was performing with local gospel groups. Later he also sang popular music at local functions on weekends. After finishing high school in 1955, he decided the most likely route to escape poverty and also help his family was to become a professional entertainer.

He told Dennis Hunt *(Los Angeles Times,* June 17, 1977): "I came to show business because I wanted to build homes for my grandmother and my mother. Our source of making money was picking cotton and I couldn't see cotton-picking money being enough for what I wanted to do. My mother and grandmother had sacrificed a lot for us. I had seen them go without food and clothes so we could have what we wanted. I had to do something for them after all they had done for us."

Soon after deciding on a musical career, he won an amateur contest in Baytown. The prize was a two-week trip to New York. Once in the Big Apple, he found his way to Harlem, where he entered the weekly amateur show at the famed Apollo Theater. He took first place and audience response was so good that he was hired for a four-week engagement. Now officially a professional, he worked small clubs and theaters around the country for a number of years, spending much of his spare time writing songs that he placed with other artists. Among those who liked his material were James Brown and Jerry Butler. *(See Brown, James; Butler, Jerry.)* In 1961, James Brown's single of Tex's song "Baby You're Right" became a best-seller. That same year, Tex got his first recording contract, though he didn't hit paydirt as a soloist until several years later.

He did make lower R&B chart levels with some

releases in the early 1960s before he finally hit in 1964 with the top 10 pop single "Hold on to What You've Got" on Dial Records. Finally, his first dreams of helping his family came true, although almost a decade later. He told Hunt: "My first royalty check was $40,000. I cashed that in a bank in Nashville, put the cash in a briefcase, and drove to Texas. Then I bought the houses for my mother and grandmother. At that time their living conditions were just terrible. When I finally fulfilled my 10-year-old dream, I was so relieved that I went out and had me a little cry."

In early 1965, Parrot Records issued the album *Best of Joe Tex* and Checker released the LP *Hold On* in July 1965. By then, Atlantic Records had agreed to distribute material recorded by Tex on the Dial label. Before 1965 was over, Joe had such successes as "You've Got What It Takes" and "I Want To (Do Everything for You)," a number one hit on the R&B charts. In 1966, he had three soul chart singles, "S.Y.S.L.J.F.M. (The Letter Song)," "The Love You Save (May Be Your Own)," and "I Believe I'm Gonna Make It." Other 1965–66 Dial/Atlantic singles included "A Woman (Can Change a Man)," "Papa Was, Too," "A Sweet Woman Like You," "You Better Get It," and "I've Got to Do a Little Bit Better." 1966 was a momentous year for Joe in other ways. He converted to the Muslim religion because, he said: "It gives me a spiritual fulfillment Christianity doesn't." For some years, while he devoted more time to what he felt was his Muslim ministry, he continued with his career in music much as before.

In 1967, some of his releases not only made upper black chart levels, but also appeared on the pop charts: "Show Me," "Woman Like That, Yeah," "A Woman's Hands," and the gold pop top 10 "Skinny Legs and All." 1968 chart makers were "Men Are Gettin' Scarce," "I'll Never Do You Wrong," "Keep the One You've Got," and "You Need Me Baby." In 1969, he connected with "That's Your Baby," "Buying a Book," and "That's the Way."

As for albums, in 1965 he made the soul list with *Hold What You've Got* on Atlantic. Other LPs of the late 1960s included *The New Boss, The Love You Save, I've Got to Do a Little Bit Better, Soul Country,* and *From the Boots Came the Rapper.* Pickwick Records put out *Turn Back the Hands.*

After a slow year with no major hits in 1970, Tex made the soul charts in 1971 with the single "Give the Baby Anything the Baby Wants." The following year he made the pop charts with "You Said a Bad Word" and had one of his biggest successes with the gold pop top 5 "I Gotcha" (backed with "A

Mother's Prayer"). The album of the same title made *Billboard*'s pop top 20. Right after that pinnacle, Joe put his music aside in favor of concentrating on his Muslim ministry. (However, his recordings were still released after that, such as the 1973 chart single "Woman Stealer.")

He stepped away from pop music, he told Hunt, because the Muslim leader Elijah Muhammad, also known as the Messenger, asked him to. "I asked him what I could do to show my appreciation for what Islam had done for me. He said I could go on a speaking tour and tell people about what Islam had done for me.

"The Messenger said leaving while my record was on top was necessary because people listen to you when you're on top and later on they couldn't say I left the business because I wasn't selling any records. He said it would be meaningful for people to see that I gave up so much just to go around and make speeches about what I found in Islam." Under the new name Yusuf Hazziez, he did just that for the next 2½ years.

After Elijah Muhammad died in 1975 and his son Wallace D. Muhammad took on the religious mantle, the situation changed. Tex commented: "The honorable Wallace D. Muhammad didn't want me to continue with the work I was doing. He told me what I was doing was a phase of his father's program and he would be moving into a whole new thing. Let me say this: If he had wanted me to continue I'd still be doing the work I was doing."

Tex was not averse to resuming his music efforts because he wanted to earn money to insure a bright future for his wife and children. He signed with Epic Records in 1976 (after briefly recording for Mercury after his years with Atlantic) and his next LP, *Bumps and Bruises,* became a hit, providing the gold novelty single "Ain't Gonna Bump No More (With No Big Fat Woman)." He followed with another above-average collection, *Rub Down* (Epic, 1978). Meanwhile, he could point to 1977 Power Pak retrospective, *Another Woman's Man,* comprising singles he had recorded for Mercury.

In the late 1970s and early 1980s, Joe again found much solace away from the pop field. He continued active in Muslim affairs and also worked his own farm in Texas. Also a major interest was the Houston Oilers football team. Still a young man, he suffered a massive heart attack three days after his forty-ninth birthday in 1982 and passed away soon after. In late 1985, Atlantic issued *The Best of Joe Tex,* which presented him at the top of his vocal and songwriting form. In 1988, Rhino Records reissued 1964–72 tracks on *I Believe I'm Gonna Make It: The Best of Joe Tex.*

THEM. *See Morrison, Van.*

THIN LIZZY: *Vocal and instrumental group. Original members: Philip Lynott, born Dublin, Ireland, c. 1951, died January 4, 1986; Brian Downey, born Dublin, Ireland; Eric Bell, born Ireland. Reorganized group, 1974, comprised Lynott; Brian Robertson, born Scotland; Scott Gorham, born Los Angeles, California. Downey left briefly, returned by 1975. Gary Moore joined in late 1970s, replaced by Midge Ure in 1979.*

For its size, Ireland has produced more than its share of excellent rock musicians and groups, among them Van Morrison, U2, and the Boomtown Rats, not to mention Thin Lizzy—a talented but unpredictable organization whose central figure was a brash black musician-poet from Dublin named Phil Lynott. Thin Lizzy seemed several times on the verge of greatness, but its members' often turbulent interactions seemed to interfere with any consistent creative progress. In spite of that, the band had considerable impact on U.K. rock trends in the 1970s and '80s.

The two founding members, Lynott and drummer Brian Downey, both grew up in working class areas of Dublin, Lynott in the Crumlin area. Discussing his background with Dennis Hunt of the *Los Angeles Times,* Phil said: "Me mother is Irish and me father is from Rio. I haven't seen him since I was 4. He's a real lover. He loved them and left them. I think that's the only thing I learned from him.

"Being a black in Dublin wasn't a problem. The Irish never showed me any prejudice. Besides, I'm a big lad and I'd deck anybody who said anything nasty to me. When I moved to London in 1972, I finally saw that being black meant there are a lot of restrictions on you. On the whole, blacks aren't treated that well in London."

As a teenager, Lynott showed promise as a poet and, in fact, was well received when he read some of his verses before groups of recognized Irish poets. In the mid-1970s, he had several books of his lyrics published. Some reviewers considered them poetic rather than musical offerings.

He also was interested in rock'n'roll as a teenager, showing skill as a bass guitarist as well as a vocalist by his late teens. He performed with a number of youthful bands at the end of the 1960s, including one called the Black Eagles where he worked with Downey. The two soon considered starting a band of their own. The prime requisite was to find a good lead guitarist, something they felt they'd found when they met instrumentalist Eric Bell. Bell, at the time, was playing pop cover songs with a local show band and was only too happy to move on to a new hard-rock–oriented band. Under the name Thin Lizzy, they began to play the bar and club circuit in Ireland

in 1971. The trio's wild, aggressive sound and Lynott's charismatic stage presence helped make the group a local favorite, but it was obvious that forward progress for the new band was limited in Dublin.

The group moved to London in 1972 to be closer to important music-industry home offices, though it returned to play Irish venues during the decade. The band's debut album, *Thin Lizzy,* came out on British London in 1972 and that company released a second LP, *Shades of a Blue Orphanage,* in early 1973. Both did considerably better in Ireland than in England since the band's core fans at the time were from its home turf. Irish adherents, in fact, helped get the band named Ireland's number one band in both 1972 and 1973 and the second album was runner-up for best LP of the year in that country.

During 1973, the group had a top 10 hit in the U.K.—a folk-rock version of a traditional Irish song, "Whiskey in the Jar"—but that disc actually had a reverse impact on the group's career. It temporarily brought new fans who favored that genre, but confused followers who had liked the band's hard-rock image. When the band's third LP, *Vagabonds of the Western World,* came out on British London in late 1973, it was a decidedly hard-edged collection that offended "Whiskey" fans and pleased earlier followers.

During a 1973 New Year's Eve show, Eric Bell collapsed on stage and later decided he wouldn't stay with the band. Finding a replacement proved difficult. Three separate guitarists took his place, but the band sound didn't please Lynott or Downey. Downey, in fact, finally quit for a while because of his frustration with developments. Lynott and band managers persevered and finally produced an acceptable blend with two guitarists: Scotland-born Brian Robertson and American Scott Gorham. With that accomplished, Lynott was able to lure Downey back into the fold.

He told Hunt: "I hired two guitarists because if one decides to leave, I'll still have another one. Besides, we can do a lot more with four musicians than three. Two guitarists augment the sound and make the music far more interesting. That change was the turning point for the band. That's when our career really started to take off."

In 1974, the first LP for the new Thin Lizzy combo, *Night Life,* came out on Polygram in Europe and Mercury in the U.S. It was well received in the U.K. and had some impact on U.S. record buyers. Encouraged by U.S. reactions, the group made a short debut tour of the country that provided Lynott with fuel for many of the songs on the next LP, *Fighting* (1975), which included heated versions of the band's concert staples "Rosalie" and "Suicide." It was a moderate hit in the U.K. and helped win over more U.S. fans, though not enough to make it an American best-seller.

But the stage was set for a commercial breakthrough, which took the form of the 1976 Phonogram/Mercury release *Jailbreak*. Helped by the single "The Boys Are Back in Town," which made the top 10 in both the U.S. and the U.K., *Jailbreak* rose high on album charts in both countries, going gold in the U.S. To take advantage of this surge in the band's popularity, the label released another new album, *Johnny the Fox*, later in the year. Though it, too, was a hit, it failed to match *Jailbreak*'s success. In addition, an ambitious tour of the U.S. was planned in conjunction with *Jailbreak*, but after a good start it had to be cancelled when Lynott came down with hepatitis.

By 1977, Lynott had recovered his health and the band's management team arranged a hectic schedule to back a new album, *Bad Reputation*, on Phonogram/Mercury. Commenting on his approach to rock, Lynott told Dennis Hunt: "The aggression is what I really love. I'm sure I'd be locked up for doing something horrible if I didn't have this rock outlet. It quiets my aggression and it does the same thing for the kids. They get off on the aggression. We have a lot of violent songs. We show that violence can be put to a good use. At the end of one of our shows, the kids are as tired as we are because they use up a lot of energy screaming and shouting. We're not enticing kids to be violent, we're working it out of them."

During the mid-1970s, some of the British teens' unhappiness due to bleak economic prospects brought support for the punk/new wave movement in British rock. Lynott was one of the early supporters of what he called emerging–third-generation rock. Besides spotlighting some of the new groups in shows Thin Lizzy headlined, he also formed a spare-time band, Greedy Basstards, that played avant garde rock. Its members included Gary Moore of Colosseum on lead guitar, Gary Holton of the Heavy Metal Kids on vocals, and Jimmy Bain (previously with Ritchie Blackmore's Rainbow) on bass guitar. From that band, Moore was recruited to join Thin Lizzy on concert tours.

Perhaps Gary was brought in as insurance against increasing disagreements between Brian Robertson and other band members. After things reached fever pitch, Robertson announced he was leaving to work on a solo album. Moore took over Brian's lead guitar work for 1977 American shows. By the time recording was in progress on the band's 1977 album *Bad Reputation*, though, the breach was healed and Robertson did some overdubbing on several tracks. By 1978, he was again part of the group for concerts.

After Phonogram/Mercury issued *Bad Reputation*, the band signed with Warner Brothers. Its debut on Warners, the moderately successful 1978 concert LP *Live and Dangerous*, included most of the group's best-known material such as "The Boys Are Back in Town" and a cover of Bob Seger's "Rosalie."

The group's first studio album for Warner Brothers was the 1979 *Black Rose—A Rock Legend*. But controversy continued to plague the band. At the start of a U.S. tour during July, band manager Chris O'Connell fired Gary Moore for unnamed reasons and guitarist Midge Ure was hastily called in from London to take Moore's place. Ure had been featured in the British band Slik and had formed a short-lived group called the Rich Kids with ex–Sex Pistol Glen Matlock. *(See Sex Pistols, The.)* A long-time friend of Lynott's, he had co-written the song "Get Out of Here" on the *Black Rose* album. It was a temporary arrangement, though, because Ure had already agreed to join the band Ultravox in 1980.

In the early 1980s, the band continued to rank as a good live act, though its recordings didn't indicate much progress beyond the 1976 pinnacle. Among the Warner releases were *Chinatown* (1980) and *Renegade* (1982). There were considerable uncertainties about the band's outlook in the mid-1980s, but a possible comeback was ruled out by the death of Lynott in early 1986.

THIRD WORLD: *Vocal and instrumental group, all born Jamaica, West Indies. Founding members (1983): Michael Cooper, born January 14, 1955, and Stephen Coore, born April 6, 1959. Members (mid-1970s): Cooper; Coore; Milton Hamilton; Richard Daley, born July 4, 1953; William Stewart, born February 15, 1956; Irwin Jarrett, born c. 1952. Hamilton replaced in 1979 by William Clarke, born February 6. Members (late 1980s): Cooper, Coore, Clarke, Daley, Stewart.*

One of the most commercially successful reggae bands, Third World helped expand the music beyond its relatively small native and expatriate West Indian base, but at a price. At times, the band's "progressive-reggae" blend of Jamaican folk music, rock, R&B, and funk compared favorably with the best of the art form, but much of its "crossover-reggae" material lacked the cutting edge of the work of artists such as Bob Marley and the Wailers and Burning Spear.

Though Stephen "Cat" Coore and Michael "Ibo" Cooper were in their teens when they founded the band, both had considerable earlier training. Coore (who played lead guitar, bass, harmonica, cello, and percussion and also helped write original material) received early encouragement and instruction from his mother, Rita Coore, one of Jamaica's most respected music teachers. He also studied at the Foster Davis School of Music and began working as a session musician in his early teens. In the early 1970s, he formed a band called the Alley Cats, whose members included Michael Cooper. Coore's nickname "Cat" derived from that group.

Cooper (keyboards, percussion, vocals, songwriting) completed classical piano studies at the Royal School of Music in 1969. The next year, he formed his first band, the Rhythms. After that group broke up, he performed with such other bands as William Stewart's the Dynamic Visions and the Alley Cats before he and Coore formed Third World in 1973.

Among the other early members of the band were lead singer Milton Hamilton; drummer Cornell Marshall; Irwin "Carrot" Jarrett on congas, drums, and percussion; and Richard "Richieboo" (later "Richie") Daley on bass guitar, guitar, percussion, and vocals. Jarrett had performed as a drummer with the Jamaican National Dance Theatre and the Inner Circle as well as working as a TV director and producer for several years before joining the band. Daley taught himself to play guitars and percussion as a youth. His first public performances were with the Astronauts, whose credits included backing the Slickers on the reggae classic "Johnny Too Bad." Before joining Third World, he was a member of such groups as the Hell's Angels and Tomorrow's Children.

William Stewart, who took over drumming chores from Cornell Marshall soon after Third World completed its first LP in 1975, had known the band's founders for a long time. He had formed the Dynamic Visions when he was 13 and still in school. He then joined the Inner Circle. At 18, he joined Byron Lee & The Dragonaires, for several years traveling with that group for concerts in the U.S., Canada, the U.K. and Mexico.

William ("Rugs" or "Bunny") Clarke took over lead vocal assignment from Milton Hamilton in the late 1970s (and also contributed rhythm guitar skills). His previous credits included session and vocal work with a number of local Jamaican bands and some performances as a solo singer.

When the group began as a six-member organization in 1973, it worked in small clubs, primarily around Jamaica's capital city of Kingston. Sensing that the opportunities to stand out from the teeming reggae-band scene would be greater outside the home island, the group moved to England and gained a recording contract in a relatively short time from British-based Island Records, one of the leading purveyors of the reggae sound worldwide. 1975 proved a watershed year for Third World. Its debut

LP, *Third World,* appeared and the band attracted critical observation as the opening act for the July 1975 U.K. tour by Bob Marley and the Wailers.

Third World continued a hectic touring pace for the rest of the 1970s. Superstar acts with which it appeared included the Jackson Five and Stevie Wonder. A close association with Stevie was to pay off handsomely in the 1980s. *(See Wonder, Stevie.)*

The group's second Island LP, *96 Degrees in the Shade,* reflected growing political concerns in the band's material. (The title track dealt with the hanging execution of Jamaican freedom fighter Paul Bogle in 1865.) Despite the band's name, as leader Cooper recalled, it had not emphasized political themes at the start. "In the beginning, it looked like a political statement, but we considered ourselves political innocents. Over time we have gone through a period of growth. What we were searching for came, and we have become one with the name we took. It is as if we knew intuitively what we were to become."

Later Island releases included *Journey to Addis* (1978), *The Story's Been Told* and the live *Prisoner in the Street* (1979), and *Arise in Harmony* (1980). *Journey to Addis* contained "Now That We've Found Love," the group's first sizable crossover hit. *Prisoner in the Street* offered songs from the band's film of that name. In 1980, the band cracked the British top 10 for the first time with the single "Hooked on Love." (The year before, it had made lower levels with "Talk to Me" from *The Story's Been Told.)*

Now on the threshold of commercial success, the band moved from Island to a larger, American-based company, Columbia, which released their label debut, *Rock the World,* in 1981, followed by *You've Got the Power* in 1982 and in 1983, *All the Way Strong* (whose hit single "Lagos Jump" was inspired by concert appearances in Africa). The combination of high-powered record-company publicity and continued concert and, by then, video exposure helped place the albums on U.S. charts for respectable periods of time. During this period, band members also were working on several writing projects with Stevie Wonder, which led to the hit single and video "Try Jah Love." The group had not only become a major international success, but had earned respect at home as shown by its prominent place among the groups taking part in the Reggae Sunsplash Festival in Kingston, Jamaica, every August.

In the late 1970s and early 1980s, the band received many honors around the world. These included the German Black Music Award and the Urban Contemporary Music Award for Best Reggae Act, selection by the French Disc Jockeys Association as Best Presenters of Reggae Music, and nomination of *Prisoner in the Street* as one of the best films shown at the 1980 French Film Festival. In 1982, Third World was nominated for a Grammy for its participation in the film *Tribute* in honor of the late Bob Marley. *(See Marley, Bob.)*

Columbia released the band's next album, *Sense of Purpose,* in 1985. During that year, Cooper co-produced and the group took part in an all-star benefit recording for Ethiopian famine relief called *Land of Africa* (RAS Records). Besides Third World, other artists heard on the recording were Rita Marley, Gregory Isaacs, Mutabaraka, and members from the groups Steel Pulse, the I-Threes, and Aswad. In mid-1987, Third World's fifth Columbia LP, *Hold on to My Love,* was released.

.38 SPECIAL: *Vocal and instrumental group. Members (mid-1980s): Donnie Van Zant, born Florida, June 11, 1952; Don Barnes, born December 3; Jeff Carlisi, born July 15; Larry Junstrom, born June 2; Jack Grodin, born October 3; Steve Brookins, born June 2.*

It seemed appropriate that .38 Special became one of the best exponents of southern rock'n'roll in the 1980s. The band had been in its formative stages when the headline group Lynyrd Skynyrd was destroyed in a tragic plane crash that killed its central figure, Ronnie Van Zant, older brother of .38 Special lead vocalist Donnie Van Zant. The torch had, in effect, been passed on to Donnie and, while it took a few years, by the 1980s, .38 Special could lay honest claim to the mantle of Ronnie's band. *(See Lynyrd Skynyrd.)*

Donnie, like Ronnie, grew up in Florida and was an avid fan of southern rock (sometimes called raunch'n'roll). By his midteens, he already had performed with a number of school groups and by 1968 had formed his own band, Standard Production. When his parents gave him a 1938 Buick Special on his sixteenth birthday, he promptly converted it into an equipment van for his group.

In 1969, he joined forces with guitarist Jeff Carlisi and bass guitarist Ken Lyons in a trio they named Sweet Rooster, playing for parties and any other gigs they could line up. After Carlisi finished high school, he studied architecture at Georgia Tech. His place was taken by singer/guitarist/songwriter Don Barnes. The band, whose roster for a time included Steve Brookins on drums, didn't make enough inroads to keep going. By the early 1970s, Sweet Rooster quietly disappeared as an entity.

But its ex-members remained active in the southern rock environment as much as possible, while earning money from routine daytime jobs. Van Zant worked as a railroad brakeman for a while and

Barnes took odd jobs including chicken delivery-man. Lyons labored as a house painter.

Meanwhile, Barnes and Donnie continued to collaborate on original songs while performing singly or together in a series of bands that formed, broke up, and reformed with new combinations of musicians.

In 1974, they decided it was time to assemble a new band, encouraged in part by the growing success of Donnie's brother's band, Lynyrd Skynyrd. It figured that the older Van Zant might open doors for such a band with his important music-industry contacts. The Barnes/Van Zant team lined up part-time computer programmer Jack Grodin on drums, at the suggestion of Lyons, who had joined as bass guitarist. It was decided to go to a two-drum format. The second drummer brought aboard was Brookins who, after leaving Sweet Rooster, had worked as a truck driver. Since Jeff Carlisi was again interested in band work, he was asked to join to complete the six-man group.

From 1975 to mid-1976, .38 Special paid its dues with a steady grind of mostly one-nighters across the South and Midwest. The group's musical style was gradually improving, helped in part by continued contact with the Skynyrd group, with whom .38 Special members often jammed during free moments between dates or on occasional joint appearances. When Peter Rudge of the New York talent firm Premier Talent Agency heard the band's material in 1976, he agreed it was ready for bigger things and took over as manager. During that year, he arranged for .38 Special to open southern shows for such acts as Peter Frampton, Kiss, Foghat, and the Winter Brothers. More to the point, he won a contract with A&M Records, which assigned Dan Hartman of Edgar Winter's White Trash to produce the debut LP, *.38 Special* (1977), a reasonably good first album, but far from challenging for best of the year. Its sales, while modest, were enough to convince A&M the band had a future. *(See Winter, Johnny and Edgar.)*

When Ken Lyons left the group in 1977, his place on bass guitar was taken by another longtime friend of .38 Special members, Larry Junstrom, who had done session work on one track for the debut LP. (Years before, he had been part of Ronnie Van Zant's One Per Cent, a forerunner of Lynyrd Skynyrd.) After Junstrom's addition, the band makeup remained the same through the mid-1980s.

The band continued to hone its skills through intensive touring, mostly as an opening act but with some solo dates in small venues. On the second album, *Special Delivery* (1978), was "Take Me Back," Ronnie's tribute to his late brother. The band's following continued to grow steadily, if not spectacularly, as indicated by rising sales of new albums, such as the 1979 *Rockin' into the Night.*

In 1981, the band came into its own with its best album to that time, the platinum, supercharged *Wild-Eyed Southern Boys* (with 1981 hit singles "Hold On Loosely" and "Fantasy Girl"), followed by the platinum *Special Forces* (1982), with the top 10 single "Caught Up in You."

In preparation for its next album *(Tour de Force,* late 1983, platinum), the band went on location near Calgary, Alberta, Canada, to shoot its first video, using three cinematographers, fire and special effects experts, and 60 wild horses. The song chosen for it, "If I'd Been the One," rose to *Billboard*'s top 20 as did the LP's second single and video, "Back Where You Belong." In 1987, it had another A&M album, *Flashback,* on the charts.

THOMAS, CARLA: *Singer, songwriter. Born Memphis, Tennessee, December 21, 1942.*

Thomas is an illustrious name in the saga of the Memphis Sound. The first two outstanding performers to grace the roster of Jim Stewart's new R&B record company on McLemore Street at the start of the 1960s were Rufus Thomas and his teenage daughter, Carla. *(See Thomas, Rufus.)* Their discs were the first building blocks in the Stax-Volt organization, the major competitor of Motown for soul supremacy in the '60s.

Carla grew up in an environment where music and the recording industry were everyday topics of conversation. She became acquainted with many of the best-known blues and R&B artists of the 1950s who gravitated to Rufus, since he was a singer as well as a disc jockey on a Memphis station.

In the summer of 1960, Rufus Thomas brought his daughter along when he auditioned for Jim Stewart. The 17-year-old girl had considerable poise and vocal ability even then and Stewart was quite agreeable to their cutting a duet. "Cause I Love You" became a local hit on Stewart's Satellite label, achieving a relatively respectable sale for a debut disc of 20,000 copies. Then Carla came up with her own composition, "Gee Whiz (Look at His Eyes)." Satellite (which later became Stax) arranged for national distribution through Atlantic Records. The song entered the top 10 on both the R&B and pop charts, selling well over a half-million copies.

Young, vivacious, and good looking, Carla quickly became a featured artist on the national level. She had the advantage of starting her career when the color line had largely disappeared between R&B and rock.

Later hits included "I'll Bring It Home to You" in 1962 and "B-A-B-Y" in 1966. Her LPs, most on Stax except for her first one *(Gee Whiz,* Atlantic,

August 1961), included *Comfort Me, Carla,* and *Queen Alone.* 1967 duets with Otis Redding included "Knock on Wood" and the humorous "Tramp" plus the LP *King & Queen* (Stax, 1967). *(See Redding, Otis.)*

Toward the end of the '60s, Carla was criticized by some reviewers for her change in style from earthier R&B material to more sophisticated soul vocals. Her record sales declined markedly. From 1971 through 1973, her only chart single was the 1972 "You Got a Cushion to Fall On." Her album releases of those years included *Best of Carla Thomas* on Atlantic and *Love Means* on Stax. (Some of her tracks later resurfaced on Rufus and Carla's *Chronicle: Their Greatest Stax Hits* (1979) and *Stax Soul Sisters* (1988), released on the Stax logo by Fantasy, which had rights to Stax's post-1968 catalogue.)

For the rest of the '70s and into the 1980s, though Carla still appeared on the concert circuit, her days as a best-selling recording artist seemed behind her.

THOMAS, RUFUS: *Singer, disc jockey. Born Memphis, Tennessee, c. 1917.*

The success of Stax/Volt Records in the 1960s was a prime factor in making the Memphis Sound a household word among soul fans. Rufus Thomas, in turn, was a vital element in the Memphis firm's rise to a position of influence in the music business.

Thomas had begun shaping rhythm & blues trends in Memphis long before Stax founder Jim Stewart came into the picture. Born and raised in the area, Rufus sang in church choirs in his youth, growing interested in the blues in his teens. In the 1930s, Rufus tap danced in the Rabbit Foot Minstrels' traveling tent show. He later worked in a textile factory by day and m.c.'d talent shows by night. In the 1950s, he became one of the top disc jockeys on WDIA (a station beamed at the black community) with a program of both top R&B artists and such traditional blues artists as Howlin' Wolf and B.B. King. His musical choices had an impact, after a while, far beyond the black audience. For example, white artists Steve Cropper and Don Nix, who played in several of the top soul groups in Memphis in the 1960s, credited their interest in that kind of music to Thomas's show. Cropper, who produced the great recordings of Otis Redding and was an original member of Booker T & the M.G.s, recalled his excitement as a teenager at hearing Thomas play records of Chuck Berry, the Five Royales, Ray Charles, Bo Diddley, and the Platters.

Thomas was singing in R&B shows at the same time he worked as a d.j. In the 1950's, he put out a few records on Star Talent, Chess, and Meteor. Appeared on Sam Phillips' Memphis-based Sun Records, the company that issued Elvis Presley's first discs the next year. Not too much happened to the recordings and Thomas went back to concentrating on his other activities for a while.

But Rufus kept his eyes open for opportunities in the record field. He was quick to check the new record firm established in the old Capitol Theater in 1960 by sometime accountant and country fiddler Jim Stewart. Stewart and his sister, Mrs. Estelle Axton, rented the theater because it met their needs as a recording studio. As he later noted, neither he nor his sister were familiar with R&B. "We just happened to move into a colored neighborhood." On the other hand, local musicians were equally confused. Because of the theater's name, Stewart recalled, "For a while they thought we were Capitol Records."

The die was cast when soul artists began to come to audition. Among the first were Rufus and his 17-year-old daughter Carla. (See Thomas, Carla.) They sang a duet titled "Cause I Love You." Stewart and his sister liked it and released it on their label at that time, Satellite. A local hit, it sold about 20,000 records. Soon after, Carla provided them with their first national success, "Gee Whiz."

As time went by, Rufus continued to record for what had become Stax Records. In 1963, his single "Walking the Dog" was a top 10 hit on both the R&B and general charts and Thomas was established as a star. From that time on, he was a featured attraction on both the soul and the prestige nightclub circuit.

Thomas placed many singles on the soul/R&B charts in the years after 1963. As he entered the 1970s, he became even more successful, beginning with his novelty "Do the Funky Chicken," which made the soul top 10 in January 1970. He had one of his biggest years ever in 1971 with such hit singles as "Do the Push & Pull (Part 1)" (number one on the R&B charts in February), "The World Is Round" (a hit in May), "Breakdown, Part 1" (soul top 10 in October), and "Do the Funky Penguin" (which reached the top 10 in January 1972).

Among his Stax albums were *Walking the Dog* (1964), *Funky Chicken (1970), and Rufus Thomas Live Doin' the Push & Pull at P.J.s* (1971).

Thomas's recording career faded in the mid-1970s, coinciding with a drastic decline in the fortunes of Stax/Volt Records. He did have material out on other labels later on, such as the 1977 albums on Avi Records, *If There Were No Music* and *I Ain't Gettin' Older, I'm Gettin' Better,* without causing much of a stir among record buyers. In 1979, Fantasy Records (which had taken over Stax/Volt's post-1968 catalogue) put out *Chronicle: Their Greatest Stax Hits* featuring Rufus and Carla on the Stax logo. In 1980, Gusto Records issued *Rufus*

Thomas featuring remakes of some of his old Stax hits, while Rufus, calling himself "the world's oldest teenager," continued on the concert circuit well into the decade.

THOMPSON TWINS, THE: *Vocal and instrumental group. Members (1982–85): Tom Bailey, born England, January 8, 1956; Alannah Currie, born Auckland, New Zealand, September 28, 1957; Joe Leeway, born Islington, London, England, c. 1955.*

In rock, there often is no relation between a band's name and any particular member. The Thompson Twins, in fact, took its name from a pair of U.K. cartoon detectives in Herge's "Adventures of TinTin." But the name soon became identified with a rollicking young group of English-based musicians whose blend of rock, African rhythms, Caribbean reggae, and American funk provided some entertaining and eminently danceable music in the 1980s.

The band got started in Sheffield, England, in 1977 as a four-piece group and expanded to seven by the end of the decade. That band won a sizable following in the U.K. by the early 1980s, but it remained for a nucleus of three 1980s members to win over the mass audience in the U.S.: founding member Tom Bailey (lead vocals, keyboards, guitar, arranging, record production), Alannah Currie (vocals, saxophone, percussion), and Joe Leeway (backing vocals, synthesizer). All three contributed to the band's original songs of the 1980s, though Currie wrote all the lyrics.

Bailey, son of a medical practitioner, was brought up in an affluent family. Introduced to the piano as a small boy, he later studied classical piano, a background he expanded on in college, where he also took courses in classical guitar and clarinet. After finishing his college work, he taught music for a time before his sideline interest in pop music became an all-absorbing passion. After helping assemble the first version of the Thompson Twins, he continued to be the mainstay of the band after all the other original members had departed.

Joe Leeway, whose mother was Irish and father was Nigerian, was brought up by foster parents in Dartford, Kent. An excellent student, he finished the English equivalent of high school and went on to study drama and English in college, taking part in many school shows. After leaving college, in the early 1970s, he sought an acting career, working in confrontational troupes in small, unheralded theater companies. He did other work on the side to earn money, including serving as a roadie for pop bands in the mid-1970s. It was in that capacity that he met the Thompson Twins members. During one show, he surprised them by jumping on stage and playing congas. His position evolved into full band membership after a while. Gradually he added other skills, including synthesizer and emulator playing and music writing. He also gradually took over as the designer and organizer of the stage show's special effects.

The third member of the mid-1980s triumvirate, Alannah Currie, was a relative latecomer to the band. Born and raised in New Zealand, for her first 20 years she didn't give much thought to making a career in music. Starting in her midteens, she held such jobs as factory worker, tobacco picker, and radio journalist before moving to England in 1979. New contacts and a different environment channeled her efforts toward the pop field and led to her joining the Thompson Twins in 1980. Initially she played an amateurish brand of saxophone, after a while shifting her main energies to percussion and vocals. With her orange hair and exuberant movements, she became a focal point of attention during Thompson Twins stage shows. She also contributed in other ways, such as designing unusual attire for the band, helping create ideas for band music videos, and providing such odd ideas as having the road crew play toy saxophones on some numbers.

In the late 1970s and the start of the 1980s, the band became increasingly well known to English fans as a seven-member group. In 1979, the band gained a U.K. record contract, resulting in the debut LP *Set* in 1980, followed by *A Product of Participation* in 1981. Along with the LPs, the record company issued three singles from those collections: "Animal Laugh," "Make Believe," and "In the Time of Love." The last named was included in the second album, which was issued in the U.S. as a British import by Arista Records. Both the album and the track did well enough with American fans for Arista to decide to release future albums in the U.S. upon initial release. The single "In the Name of Love" became a number one dance hit in the U.S.

Bailey noted its inclusion on the album was pure chance. "We were short a track for the second U.K. album and some of the Twins came up with 'In the Name of Love.' That track stood out so much, it made us think very hard about the kind of music we were playing." The song served as the title track for Arista's first official U.S. release, which combined recordings from the band's two U.K. LPs. Even as that LP showed up in American record stores in 1982, the band had undergone a major reorganization with four of the seven members departing.

The remaining three (Tom, Alannah, and Joe) went to the Bahamas with producer Alex Sadkin to record a new album at Compass Studios. The emphasis now was on infectious dance-oriented rhythms similar in tone to "In the Name of Love." The new LP, issued by Arista in the U.S. as *Side Kicks* and in the U.K. as *Quick Step and Side Kicks,* was an instant success in England, appearing at number two on U.K. charts a week after release. It made inroads on U.S. lists, though not as strongly as in Britain. The group backed the album with an extensive 1983 tour of the U.S. and Europe and placed a series of singles high on European charts:—"Love on Your Side," "Lies," and "We Are Detective."

In mid-1983, the band returned to the Bahamas with Sadkin for the next set of recordings. "Hold Me Now," issued as a single in late 1983 in advance of the album, earned a gold record in England. After being introduced to U.S. audiences during the band's live set on MTV's special New Year's Eve 1983 telecast, the song made *Billboard*'s top 10. The LP containing it, *Into the Gap* (1984), became the second-biggest-selling album in the U.K. for the year and went platinum in the U.S. During 1984, besides "Hold Me Now," the group placed three other singles on U.S. charts.

In late 1984, the band took up residence in Paris to work on a new album with Tom Bailey taking over as producer. The pressures of supervising the LP while touching other important bases for the band caught up with Bailey in early 1985. During a hectic promotional effort in London, he collapsed and was ordered by his medical advisors to take several months off for a complete rest, which he did in the Bahamas. By June, he felt strong enough to resume work on the album. This time, the sessions were planned for New York. While preparing the new tracks, the band was on hiatus from live shows, but made an exception for Bob Geldof's Live Aid (for Africa) spectacular from the U.K. and the U.S. The Thompson Twins did their bit in Philadelphia, playing "Hold Me Now" and the Lennon-McCartney composition "Revolution," which was being recorded in the Twins' style for the new album. Supporting the band on those numbers were guitarists Nile Rodgers (co-producer with Bailey of the new LP) and Steve Stevens of Billy Idol's backing group.

The gold 1985 album *Here's to Future Days* included the antiheroin song "Don't Mess with Doctor Dream," and spawned two *Billboard* top 10 singles: "Lay Your Hands on Me" (1985) and "King for a Day" (1986).

Though the band seemed poised to become a stable favorite of U.S. fans, problems still threatened to derail it. After rebounding from the temporary loss of Bailey, the group narrowed to a twosome with the exit of Joe Leeway in 1986. In 1987, Arista released a new album, *Close to the Bone.*

THORNTON, BIG MAMA: *Singer, drummer, harmonica player, songwriter. Born Montgomery, Alabama, December 11, 1926; died Los Angeles, California, July 25, 1984.*

Literally and figuratively, Willie Mae "Big Mama" Thornton cut a huge figure in the history of rhythm & blues and its later pop offshoots. Her booming voice, sometimes 200-pound frame, and exuberant stage manner had audiences stomping their feet and shouting encouragement in R&B theaters from coast to coast from the early 1950s on. In later years, she won attention from white audiences the world over as well. Her early recording career, though she didn't plan it that way, helped assure the future popularity of Elvis Presley, who sold millions of records of his 1956 version of "Hound Dog," a song first released by her four years earlier for the R&B market.

One of a minister's seven children, she began singing at an early age in Montgomery, Alabama, and was playing in small clubs in the west years later when she came to the attention of band leader Johnny Otis. Otis, a supreme judge of talent, added her to his touring show, which already included such famous names as Little Esther and Mel Walker. By the time the show reached the Apollo Theater in New York on her first circuit with the band, she already had people in other cities discussing her talent, and she knew a success at the Apollo would really give her career momentum.

She told columnist Ralph Gleason that she got her nickname after her initial Apollo performance. "They put me on first. I wasn't out there to put no one off stage. I was out there to get known and I did! I didn't have no record and I was singing the Dominoes' hit, 'Have Mercy Baby.' They had to put the curtain down. Little Esther never got on that first show. That's when they put my name in lights and Mr. Schiffman, the manager, came backstage to Johnny Otis, who packaged the show. Poking me in the arms with his finger—it was sore for a week. 'You got to put her on to close the show!'" It was decided, indeed, the "Big Mama" would have that coveted spot.

"I traveled with Johnny Otis," she continued. "But I went even further on my own after I recorded 'Hound Dog.'" Her chance to do the song came after she signed a contract with Peacock-Duke Records of Houston, Texas. One of her first numbers for Peacock, it was written by two young New Yorkers, Jerry Lieber and Mike Stoller (with some contributions by Johnny Otis) and recorded in Los Angeles in August 1952.

As she told Gleason: "They were just a couple of kids then and they had this song written on a paper bag. So I started to sing the words and join in some

of my own. All that talkin' and hollerin'—that's my own. That song sold over 2 million copies. I never got what I should have. I got one check for $500 and I never seen another." Another side she recorded in that session was "They Call Me Big Mama."

During the mid-1950s, Big Mama was a featured attraction in the R&B field, placing several discs on the charts. By 1957, though, interest in her had waned, and Peacock-Duke did not renew her contract. For several years, she kept active in the music field by playing drums and harmonica with small bands in the San Francisco Bay Area. Among the songs she sometimes sang was her composition "Ball and Chain," which Janis Joplin later featured in her act.

As the folk boom, with its emphasis on blues, developed in the late 1950s, Big Mama became better known to white fans. Her career picked up again after a well-received appearance at the 1964 Monterey Jazz Festival in California. She performed in leading folk clubs all over the country and was invited to major folk and blues festivals throughout the world.

In late 1964, she made a new recording of "Hound Dog" for Fontana Records in Europe during a tour of the Continent. In October 1966, Chris Strachwitz's Berkeley, California–based Arhoolie Records put out *Big Mama Thornton in Europe* followed by *Big Mama Thornton with the Chicago Blues Band* (Arhoolie, July 1967), with backing from blues greats Muddy Waters, James Cotton, and Otis Spann. *Ball and Chain* (Arhoolie, 1968) featured separate tracks by Big Mama, Larry Williams, and Lightning Hopkins. In the early 1970s, still touring theaters and clubs across the country, Big Mama could point to two more albums: *Saved* on Pentagram Records and *She's Back* on the Backbeat label. In 1975, Vanguard Records released LPs *Sassy Mama!* and *Jail*. Recorded live in two penitentiaries, *Jail* included such Thornton classics as "Hound Dog," "Ball and Chain," and Willie Dixon's "Little Red Rooster."

She continued to play the big jazz festivals into the 1980s. As time went on, an increasing number of festivals were devoted solely to the blues. At the 1983 Newport Jazz Festival, which actually was held in New York, she joined such blues greats as Muddy Waters, B.B. King, and Eddie "Cleanhead" Vinson in one session that provided material for the Buddah album *The Blues—A Real Summit Meeting*.

Though Big Mama died of a heart attack in a Los Angeles boarding house in 1984, her Arhoolie albums, *Jail*, and *Quit Snoopin' 'round My Door* (a British import on Ace) remained in print years later so listeners could still discover a classic blues shouter. *(See Big Brother and the Holding Com-*

pany; Joplin, Janis; King, B.B.; Otis, Johnny; Phillips, Esther; Presley, Elvis; Waters, Muddy.)

THOROGOOD, GEORGE: *Singer, guitarist, band leader (THE DESTROYERS), songwriter. Born Baton Rouge, Louisiana, 1951.*

George Thorogood was nothing if not his own man. He violated many accepted music-industry canons for success in the 1970s and '80s and still became a worldwide star. Through the sheer exuberance of his performance, he attracted millions of fans—many of whom would normally have favored heavy metal or new wave—with his supposedly dated rockabilly and rhythm & blues material. He sold hundreds of thousands of albums on a small label, Rounder, that could afford only minuscule promotion budgets compared to major labels. And he didn't hesitate to arrange his concert schedule around the season of his beloved Wilmington, Delaware, baseball league.

Thorogood was born in Baton Rouge, Louisiana, but spent almost all his formative years in Wilmington. He fell in love with roots music of people such as Chuck Berry (he recalled the first album he owned was Berry's *Golden Decade*), Bo Diddley, John Lee Hooker, Elmore James, and Johnny Cash before he reached high school age. However, he was more interested in baseball and movies than attending high school in Wilmington, which perhaps accounted for his claim that he was voted "least likely to succeed" by his classmates.

In fact, after finishing school, music was a sideline. He earned money through various odd jobs while focusing his main attention on playing as much baseball as possible (hardball, not softball). He asked Charles Young of *Rolling Stone* in 1979: "Why do you play softball. I'm too young to play softball! They don't allow bunting or stealing. That's all I can do, man."

In fact, he told Greg Linder of the *Twin Cities Reader* that baseball provided the impetus for his music career (though it should be stressed that his reminiscences about the event were not always consistent). The time, he said, was the fall of 1973 when he and friends were talking about the shortcomings of the Delaware Destroyers of the Roberto Clemente league, for whom Thorogood played second and third base in the '70s and early '80s.

"Basically, the idea was that we had a baseball team and we didn't have enough money for uniforms. So we said: 'Let's put this band together and play at parties, pick up a little bread, and get some bad uniforms.'"

The original band, named Destroyers after the ballclub, comprised George on lead vocals and guitar, his then roommate Ron Smith on bass guitar,

and longtime friend Jeff Simon on drums. The repertoire was, of course, Thorogood's beloved R&B and rockabilly, which he typically performed with the slide guitar style he had evolved over the years by listening to artists such as Elmore James and Hound Dog Taylor.

He told a reporter from *Cash Box* (January 20, 1979): "I didn't choose the type of music I play. It chose me. I just listened to the songs that I liked and tried to figure them out. The tunes I play are the ones I grew up with and will always feel comfortable playing. So when people call our music a revival of sorts, it's really nothing to me. My whole life, no matter what I did or where I went, I was always something different."

The "temporary" band they assembled in 1973 proved to be different too. As word of its ability spread, it won gigs in local clubs, with each performance usually attracting more curious people who were caught up in the excitement generated by Thorogood's ceaseless movement and energy. Though the band was becoming successful, Ron Smith decided he didn't want to devote more and more time to the music. He stepped down and another of George's boyhood friends, Billy Blough, took over on bass. (The band remained essentially a trio for the rest of the decade, although Smith sometimes returned to work with the group.)

Still, Thorogood didn't permit the band or the potential for pop stardom to become all-consuming. He enjoyed performing, but didn't let it interfere with the baseball schedule. Thorogood told *Cash Box*: "Very few people understand our attitude. I don't want to be a big rock star. Playing clubs is just fine the way it is. When I get home, I just do the things I always do—go bowling, watch TV. I'm just glad to be doing something I like.

"Guys come up to me and say: 'George, I know 100 guitar players who are better than you and I know 50 people who can sing better than you. But I don't know anybody I'd rather go see play.' You just can't beat that feeling. You can be out of tune or you can play the wrong note, but if you can put a smile on someone's face . . . getting up there and really pleasing people, well, that's something good. Then I figure we're successful."

The band continued to play clubs in the Wilmington-Baltimore-Washington area for four years, steadily adding to its local following while remaining unknown elsewhere. Record-company scouts sought them out, but Thorogood didn't want to become part of a big organization at the time. He finally opted for small, Massachusetts-based Rounder Records (primarily a folk and bluegrass label), which issued his debut, *George Thorogood and the Destroyers*, in 1977. When the LP came out, the band had an engagement at a local club at $35 for the night.

That situation was to change before very long, helped by an unexpected breakthrough on the West Coast. The Destroyers went there to play a series of benefits for the California Homemakers Association, mainly to extend the band's recognition. San Francisco station KSAN became enamored of the group and gave it intensive airplay, publicity that brought an extra month of performing dates in the area. Buoyed by favorable reviews, the album went on to sell over 100,000 copies and paved the way for even greater success for the gold follow-up, *Move It on Over* (1978).

In selecting *Move It on Over* (issued in Canada on the Attic label) as his choice for best album of 1978, Peter Goddard of the *Toronto Star* wrote: "This album proves that rock isn't a question of big budgets, months of studio time, high-priced session players, and lots of bloated hype surrounding it. It also proves that it's not necessary to be part of any particular style or ism, and that success is not necessarily equated with the number of people who've turned out to hear you."

Meanwhile, reports of the band's exciting concerts continued to circulate, making the group one of the top new attractions in 1978. The group's renditions of classics such as Bo Diddley's "Ride On, Josephine," John Lee Hooker's "One Bourbon, One Scotch, One Beer," Chuck Berry's "It Wasn't Me" and "Johnny B. Goode," and Elmore James' "The Sky Is Crying" won over cynical reviewers as well as hordes of satisfied concert goers.

Steven J. Hoffman, writing about a December 1978 show in *Unicorn Times,* reported: "On stage, Thorogood comes to play, loud and long, and he is a natural showman. The insistent flailing of his slide guitar, the infectious beat of his boogie riffs, and his hearty gravelly voice knock audiences out night after night. People shout, stomp their feet, call out for more—and Thorogood grins, because that's what his music is about. Off stage, Thorogood would rather shoot the breeze about baseball than analyze his music. 'It's crazy,' he complains. 'Interviewers hear what I play, like Chuck Berry and John Lee Hooker and Elmore James—and then they ask me who my musical influences are.' "

Some critics took aim at Thorogood's admittedly limited vocal range or voiced the standard reservations about a white musician taking off on black music. But far more veteran rock writers accepted Thorogood's art on its own terms. Fred Schruers of *Rolling Stone* commented: "This wasn't a white boy doing roots music; this was simply a free spirit taking his favorites and blowing the place out with them." In *Rolling Stone*'s look back at the year

1978, Thorogood and the Destroyers placed second on its list for the best new band behind the Cars. Thorogood quipped that he challenged the Cars to competition on neutral ground.

Thorogood's preoccupation with athletics helped him fight off habits that could threaten his coordination. He found it easy to say no to drugs, though he didn't take a holier-than-thou attitude. He told *Rolling Stone:* "A lot of people don't like liver and peas. It's the same thing with me and drugs. It's not something I get involved with. Some people have been trying to say I'm the upstanding young man of rock'n'roll on some moral crusade. That's a lot of crap. I've taken out some shortstops in my time, argued with umpires, kicked the ball out of the catcher's gloves, all of it."

Thorogood continued his practice of keeping the summer open for baseball—thus abandoning one period the music industry considered optimum for large-scale touring—while going on the road in what he considered the off-season. Though his reputation was reaching the point where he was a candidate to fill large arenas, he still preferred to play small to medium-size venues where he could have closer rapport with his audience. Nor did he rush to record new material to take advantage of his growing popularity.

In 1979, he was represented on record racks with an album of early demonstration tapes issued on MCA under the title *Better than the Rest.* While the album was not without its high points, it certainly was nowhere near as good as his Rounder releases. Thorogood even took MCA to court to try to halt production of the LP. In 1980, Rounder's *More George Thorogood and the Destroyers* made the charts. Nick Lowe and Dave Edmunds, who also liked to include roots rock in their records, pressed in vain for the chance to produce a Thorogood album.

In the early 1980s, George grew too popular for Rounder to handle, so he switched to EMI-America (a U.S. arm of England's major EMI label), though Rounder co-founder and vice president Ken Irwin still helped produce his 1982 EMI debut LP, *Bad to the Bone.* In 1985, George had two more EMI-America albums on the hit lists: *Live* and the more successful (and appropriately named) gold *Maverick.* By this time, Thorogood was beginning to turn out a number of original songs to supplement his catalogue of R&B and rockabilly classics.

Thorogood might have become a much wealthier individual and also received broader acclaim as a superstar had he gone in for more extensive concertizing and public-relations exposure, but his philosophy was that he played his music because he enjoyed it. Typically he would tell the audience: "To us, life is spelled *F-U-N.*"

Born to Be Bad (EMI/Manhattan, 1988) continued his format of oldies and George's original compositions.

THREE DOG NIGHT: *Vocal and instrumental group. Danny Hutton, born Buncrana, Ireland, September 10, 1942; Chuck Negron, born Bronx, New York, June 8, 1942; Cory Wells, born Buffalo, New York, Feburary 5, 1942; Mike Allsup, born Modesto, California, March 8; Jim Greenspoon, born Los Angeles, California, February 7; Joe Schermie, born Madison, Wisconsin, February 12; Floyd Sneed, born Calgary, Alberta, Canada, November 22.*

Indisputably one of the most popular acts of the late '60s and early '70s, Three Dog Night was far from a favorite with critics. Though not damned as stridently by reviewers as another mass audience idol, Grand Funk Railroad, Three Dog Night nonetheless was often described in the media as "not innovative" or "too mechanical" in its arrangements. It could be said that the group members cried all the way to the bank, except that they did, indeed, feel their contributions to rock music had been unjustly maligned.

Their history was somewhat unusual. They gained gold records for all six of their initial albums and for seven of their 21 top 40 singles. Other groups with varying degrees of talent could say almost as much, but few could point to so many song successes that helped build national reputations for so many other composer-performers. Among those vaulted from relative obscurity to acclaim by Three Dog Night renditions of their songs were Nilsson, Laura Nyro, Randy Newman, Elton John and Bernie Taupin, and Hoyt Axton.

Core of the group was its three lead singers: Cory Wells, Danny Hutton, and Chuck Negron. Wells and Negron, though white, both grew up near black neighborhoods and became interested in rhythm & blues in their youth. As Wells recalled: "When most kids were listening to rock'n'roll, I was listening to Bobby 'Blue' Bland and Ray Charles." In 1964, he formed a group called the Enemies, which gained a recording contract from MGM Records. At MGM, he later met Danny Hutton, who was assigned to work as the Enemies producer. Hutton, though born in Ireland, was raised in the U.S. He started working in music at 18, initially as a producer, but later as a solo vocalist as well. In 1965, he wrote, produced, and recorded a hit single for Hollywood-based Hanna-Barbera Records, "Roses and Rainbows." A little bit after this, he signed with MGM, providing that label with a hit single, "Big, Bright Eyes."

The Enemies broke up in the mid-1960s and Cory worked for a time as a sideman in a house band at the Whisky-A-Go-Go. In 1967, he formed the Cory Wells Blues Band, which fared poorly and disbanded by the end of the year. At this point, Wells and Hutton got together to form a new group, a step encouraged by executives of Dunhill Records.

Their first addition was a third lead singer, Chuck Negron. Born in New York's northernmost borough, the Bronx, Negron started singing blues songs before he was in high school. At 13, he auditoned at Harlem's Apollo Theater's weekly talent show. He became a regular in the Wednesday night show at the Apollo when he was 14, going on to sing at a number of clubs in black ghetto areas. In the mid-1960s, he was signed by Columbia Records, but little came of that and his career remained pretty much in limbo until he joined the new Hutton-Wells organization.

Though the band's goal was to emphasize vocals, plans involved a good instrumental support group. The four musicians rounding out Three Dog Night when it began in 1968 were lead guitarist Mike Allsup, organist Jim Greenspoon, bassist Joe Schermie, and drummer Floyd Sneed. All had considerable experience as sidemen, band leaders, or session men. Raised in California, Allsup had been singing gospel songs since he was three and had played guitar with a number of groups starting in high school. Greenspoon, son of silent screen star Mary O'Brian, started piano lessons in grade school, graduated to playing with Sunset Strip house bands at 14, and went on to develop a group called the East Side Kids that was one of Denver, Colorado's favorites in the mid-1960s.

Schermie was born in Wisconsin and raised in Arizona, where he followed the familiar pattern of becoming involved in rock groups in his teens. Sneed, raised in Calgary, Canada, learned drums while in school, but kept it as a sideline for a while after graduation, earning a living working for Consolidated Mining and Smelting of Canada. In the mid-1960s, he decided to stick to music, moving to Vancouver to play with the group Heat Wave, with which he later traveled to Hawaii and Los Angeles. A year after Heat Wave disbanded, he joined Three Dog Night.

From the start, it was a seven-man act, though its name focused on the number three for the multi-lead-vocalist concept. The actual derivation of the name was from colloquial Australian, referring to the use of a dog to keep a person warm at night in the "outback," a "one-dog night" being only slightly cold, a "two-dog night" being colder still, and a "three-dog night" referring to a very icy evening.

Dunhill prepared the way carefully for its new group, with a nationwide series of press conferences and considerable promotion. The group's initial single, "Nobody," gained a healthy sales volume. The next release, a remake of Otis Redding's "Try a Little Tenderness," while it didn't sell a million copies, did stay in *Billboard*'s top 40 for four weeks in 1969. Their next 1969 effort, "One," hit number one on the charts, going gold and refocusing national attention on talented songwriter-vocalist Nilsson. The group's 1969 debut LP, *Three Dog Night—One*, also went gold. Its popular track "Lady Samantha" was composed by the then-unknown team of Elton John and Bernie Taupin. The group followed up with a string of massive hit singles and LPs in 1969 and 1970. In 1969, their top 10 singles were "Easy to Be Hard" from the rock musical *Hair* plus Laura Nyro's "Eli's Coming." 1969 LPs *Suitable for Framing* and *Captured Live at the Forum* eventually won gold awards.

The group's hit recordings sold at a fast clip in the first part of the 1970s. In 1970, the band hit *Billboard*'s number one July 11 and 18 and sold well over a million copies of its version of Randy Newman's droll "Mama Told Me (Not to Come)." The next year, its gold interpretation of Hoyt Axton's exuberant composition "Joy to the World" did the same for six weeks starting April 17. The string of gold albums continued with *It Ain't Easy* and *Naturally* in 1970 and *Golden Bisquits* and *Harmony* in 1971. The group earned subsequent gold awards for LPs *Seven Separate Fools* (mid-1972) and *Recorded Live in Concert—Around the World* and *Cyan* (1973).

The group had many more singles hits in the early 1970s. 1971 chartmakers included "Liar," "One Man Band," and the gold "An Old Fashioned Love Song." 1972 best-sellers were "The Family of Man," the top 10 "Never Been to Spain" written by Axton, and the multimillion-seller "Black and White" (number one in *Billboard* the week of September 16). In 1973, the group made the charts with "Let Me Serenade You" and the gold "Shambala." In 1974, the group had a gold top 5 hit with a cover of Leo Sayer's "The Show Must Go On" and in 1975 made the top 40 with "Til the World Ends"—its last single to make *Billboard* charts.

The band seemed to be suffering a popularity loss for its new recordings in the mid-1970s. Still, it remained a successful concert attraction, drawing large crowds worldwide who wanted to hear the many hits the group had scored over the years. Several new albums appeared on ABC Records, which took over Dunhill in the mid-1970s, such as *American Pastime* (1976), but they did not match the achievements of previous albums. An album that did do well was the gold 1974 Dunhill retrospective, *Joy to the World—Their Greatest Hits*.

In 1982, MCA, into which ABC and Dunhill have been merged, released the retrospective *The Best of Three Dog Night*. As of 1988, that album and *Joy to the World—Greatest Hits* still were available on MCA in disc and cassette form while *Three Dog Night, Suitable for Framing* and *It Ain't Easy* were offered on CDs.

While the group undoubtedly could have remained a staple item on the concert circuit for many years, the founders grew tired of the format and wanted to direct their energies to other projects. By the end of the '70s, Three Dog Night had disbanded, though with the new interest in pop music of the '60s and '70s with young '80s fans, the group did eventually agree to take part in revival shows. *(See John, Elton; Newman, Randy; Nilsson; Nyro, Laura.)*

TOM TOM CLUB: *See Talking Heads.*

TOOTS & THE MAYTALS: *Vocal and instrumental group headed by Fred "Toots" Hibbert, born Jamaica, c. early 1940s.*

Though the late Bob Marley and his group, the Wailers, probably have come to symbolize reggae music, in truth equal honors should go to singer/songwriter Fred "Toots" Hibbert and his band, the Maytals. Not only was Hibbert a pioneer in the evolution of reggae, all the evidence indicates he gave it its name with his 1968 song, "Do the Reggae."

Like other artists of the Jamaican pop music explosion that began in the 1960s, Hibbert came from the impoverished underclass of that Caribbean island. He made his way to the Trenchtown area of the island in the first part of the 1960s and became part of the wave of young singers and instrumentalists experimenting with variations of U.S. blues and rock blended with West Indies folk music. By the mid-1960s, his style already was evolving toward the music that became known as reggae and he had become one of the more popular performers around Jamaica's capital of Kingston.

At the same time, Bob Marley, Bunny Livingston (also known as Bunny Wailer), Peter Tosh, and others were coming to the fore and contributing to Jamaican music's development. By the end of the 1960s, all of them, along with Toots and his band, had adopted a recognizable format, based on a certain "inside-out" drum beat that was generally classified as reggae.

Though both Marley and Hibbert became Rastafarians (members of a home-grown religion based on deification of the late Ethiopian Emperor Haile Selassie), Marley tended to focus on religion in his material whereas Toots leaned more toward secular topics. In other ways as well the two artists seemed to symbolize two poles of reggae. For many Rastafarians, their adopted religion also was part of a general expression of dissatisfaction with the situation in Jamaica, where much of the black population suffered severe poverty and police oppression. In Marley's lyrics, as in the words sung by many reggae artists, there was great concentration on sociological and political aspects as reflected in titles such as "Revolution" and "Get Up, Stand Up." Toots and the Maytals, on the other hand, were more oriented toward reggae as entertainment and a more optimistic view of the future.

Not that Hibbert and his group didn't sing of the poverty and exploitation of their environment, but they also typically looked beyond it to a better world based on love and mutual understanding. This is reflected in the upbeat sound of songs such as "Funky Kingston," the title track of their initial U.S. release on Island Records in 1975. The comparison can be carried over to the differing sounds of the Maytals and the Wailers. The Maytals' music was more a blend of traditional Jamaican patterns with rock and soul, while the Wailers, though maintaining the reggae rhythm, pursued a hard-edged, predominantly blues-rock sound.

Defining reggae as he saw it to *New York Times* writer Stephen Davis in the mid-1970s, Toots said: "Reggae means comin' from d'people, you know. Everyday ting, like from the ghetto. Majority beat. Regular beat that people use like food down there. We put music to it, make a dance out of it. I would say that reggae means comin' from the roots, ghetto music. Means poverty, suffering, and, in the end, maybe union with God if you do it right."

Toots and his group, typically composed of two backing musicians, had released many songs in Jamaica and in the West Indian–populated sectors of London, England, before he gained any U.S. exposure. Some of his pre–mid-1970s recordings (including "Funky Kingston" and a reggae version of the rock classic "Louie, Louie") were included in *This Is Reggae Music,* a reggae sampler issued by Island Records in England in 1974. The LP, mainly intended to gain the attention of critics and music writers for the new music, was not released for public sale in the States.

In the early 1970s, word of reggae's vitality spread slowly beyond the limited Caribbean island audience. Toots and his group found club dates in European cities. Interest also rose in the U.S. and Canada. Toots's recording fortunes improved in the mid-1970s as some of his LPs, such as *From the Roots* (Trojan, 1973), appeared as import items in U.S. record stores. In 1975, Island Records in the U.S. released his *Funky Kingston* album (including such Jamaican hits as the title song, "Time Tough," "Pressure Drop," and "Pride and Pomp"), which served as the basis for a major tour of U.S. cities.

Both on records and in person, Toots showed himself to be a superlative pop singer. Some critics preferred Marley's strident antiestablishment pose, but Toots came in for much well-deserved acclaim. David Marsh and Russell Gersten echoed the views of many reviewers when they stated in the *New Rolling Stone Record Guide:* "Toots Hibbert, unquestionably one of the greatest vocalists to appear in popular music in the past decade . . . is a sort of a sweet Antilles version of Otis Redding—he occasionally sings Redding's material in concert and the effect is startling."

While only Bob Marley and the Wailers could be said to have attracted a mass worldwide audience before his untimely death, Toots & the Maytals managed to build up a following outside Jamaica that, while small by pop standards, still numbered in the millions. From the mid-1970s on, he could count on enough support from fans for regular tours of North America. From the mid-1970s through the late 1980s, the group drew full houses at small and medium-size clubs and theaters in major cities around the world.

Meanwhile, Toots & the Maytals' album credits mounted steadily. They included *Reggae Got Soul* (Island, 1976), *Pass the Pipe* (Mango, 1979), the retrospective *The Best of Toots & The Maytals* (Trojan, 1979), and *Just Like That* and the in-concert *Toots Live* (Mango, 1980). *(See Marley, Bob; Tosh, Peter.)*

TOSH, PETER: *Singer, guitarist, keyboardist, band leader, songwriter. Born Church Lincoln, Westmorland, Jamaica, October 19, 1944; died Kingston, Jamaica, September 11, 1987.*

One of reggae's founding giants, Peter Tosh was overshadowed for many years by Bob Marley outside the bastions of the art form in Jamaica and the West Indian ghettos of England. In those locales, however, he was always considered on an equal footing with Marley and even a more important influence. Some of Marley's best-known recordings, after all, were of songs written by Tosh. On many of those, of course, Tosh himself could be heard, since for a decade, those two Jamaicans and a third artist, Bunny Livingston (also known as Bunny Wailer), were the heart of reggae's landmark group, the Wailers.

During Peter's childhood in the western part of Jamaica, he was interested in the pop music he heard on broken-down record players or echoing from radios. Reggae had not been born yet, but those who would give it life were picking up influences from such varied sources as West Indian folk music, gospel, and American rhythm & blues and rock. Even before his teens, Tosh was experimenting with instruments. His first love was the Hawaiian guitar, after which he began to try his hand at the organ and, at 12, the piano. At 15, he learned to play guitar and determined that a career in music might be the only route from the poverty-stricken environment afflicting most black islanders.

The center of an essentially youth-based music movement was in the Jamaican capital of Kingston, where Tosh gravitated in his midteens. In the ghetto area called Trenchtown, where teens were as likely to become petty crooks as musicians, Tosh made his new home and became acquainted with other aspiring artists such as Marley and Livingston, who had moved to Trenchtown from other parts of the country. In the mid-1960s, they started the band that gained fame as the Wailers. Because Peter was from the west, Bob from the middle, and Bunny from eastern Jamaica, they were referred to as "the three wise men" of music by Jamaican reporters.

Drawing on a combination of West Indian and mainly American black styles and the new Rastafarian religious movement (based on worship of Ethiopian King Haile Selassie as a celestial figure), Jamaican performers experimented with exciting new musical forms. After passing through variations ska, bluebeat, and rocksteady, the genre known as reggae evolved. Among the major innovators of this homegrown musical revolution—a format that sprang not from a large culture like the U.S. or U.K., but from a small, economically depressed island—were the Wailers.

Although there were hundreds of groups and solo artists coming to the fore in reggae in the late 1960s and early 1970s, until the original Wailers broke up in 1974, it was regarded as "the" reggae band. In its glory years, Marley, Livingston, and Tosh were considered equal partners in writing, arranging, and performing their material. The group made a number of recordings on small local labels before getting wider exposure on Island Records in the 1970s. Some of its most notable discs employed songs written by Tosh, including "Get Up, Stand Up," "One Foundation," "Stop That Train," and "400 Years."

For a number of reasons, including conflicting career goals of the three main artists and hopes by each to gain more attention outside the relatively small West Indian community, the original Wailers association ended in 1974. For a while, Tosh kept his activities close to home, writing and producing new records for release in Jamaica. His songs continued to protest the inequalities and indignities faced by the black population of Jamaica and by blacks everywhere. Tosh's anger reached out to many of the oppressed after an unprovoked beating by Jamaican police in early 1975 caused him to write and record

"Mark of the Beast," a song quickly banned from airplay on the island.

A similar initial fate befell his next single, "Legalize It," which argued for free use of marijuana. For Rastafarians, this was considered a religious matter, since marijuana (also called, among other things, ganja) was thought to be part of the way to commune with God. Rastafarians, however, opposed the use of alcohol and other drugs as well as meat consumption.

Meanwhile, Tosh had become one of the top concert draws in Jamaica and interest in his music was growing outside the country. This gave incentive for him to record his first solo LP, *Legalize It* (Columbia, 1976). In London, he told a reporter from *Melody Maker:* "Reggae is only what you hear and think is reggae. Most people don't know what the word means. The word *reggae* means king's music, and that means it is highly sophisticated and should be highly appreciated. But it is black kings and that is why they keep a good man down, because it is getting to the people; it is relating to the people and the voice of the people is the voice of the almighty. It is dangerous to keep back anything that is relating to the voice of the people, very dangerous, mon."

In 1977, Tosh completed his second solo album for Columbia, *Equal Rights*. As the title song put it: "I don't want no peace, I want equal rights and justice." Other tracks continued the theme of struggle against oppression and the need for all blacks to look to Africa as a common homeland. Peter's other compositions for the collection included "Apartheid," "Jah Guide," "African," "Downpressor Man," and "Stepping Razor."

Despite the message of the lyrics, the album spoke to all people through its joyful, infectious melodies and complex, but highly listenable rhythms. The *Village Voice* reviewer commented: "In this mix, melody merges with rhythm, harmony with polyrhythm, each instrument fulfilling both functions." The album was undoubtedly Tosh's most impressive to that time and one of the classic reggae collections ever released. But while critics enthused over it in the U.S. and Europe, it had minimal chart impact. Tosh did have a small, dedicated following of several million outside his homeland, but not enough for him to rival Bob Marley as a popular favorite.

In the late 1970s, Tosh moved to Rolling Stones Records, becoming the first artist on the label other than the Stones. The Rolling Stones, like many English rock stars, were passionate reggae fans and welcomed the chance to sign Tosh to their label (distributed by Atco Records in the U.S.). Peter's label debut *(Bush Doctor,* 1978) included a Tosh–Mick Jagger duet on a Temptations song, "Don't Look Back." Though it indicated an effort to water down his roots-reggae approach for more commercial impact, overall, it was still a fine collection, only a shade less powerful than earlier albums. The second and last Rolling Stones LP (*Mystic Man*, 1979) was considerably weaker in content and style.

However, the worldwide tour Tosh undertook to help promote *Mystic Man* proved a sensation. Backed by his excellent band, Words, Sound and Power, he proved he could excite crowds of all sizes and ethnic makeup.

As one reviewer described Tosh's stage work: "He is an explosive performer. His voice, honey-toned, soulful, and exquisitely restrained, is a beguiling and accomplished instrument. . . . [He] roams the stage with the grace and agility of a panther, often stopping in midstage for a martial arts routine that looks like his own blend of T'ai Chi and Kung Fu."

The band also epitomized the finest in reggae. Besides Tosh on rhythm guitar, its members included Sly Dunbar on drums and Robbie Shakespeare on bass, a still legendary reggae rhythm section, Mikey "Mao" Chung on keyboards and guitar, Robbie Lyn and Keith Sterling on guitars and percussion, and Darryl Thompson (the only American member) on guitar. As an onlooker commented, when Tosh and the band went into his new song "Jah Seh No," in which he demanded that the walls in Babylon be torn down, corruption rooted out, and "the captives set free": "There is not a person on the site that doesn't buy his ideas, at least speculatively, at least for the moment."

It was a tour with other rewards as well. On August 23, for instance, Brooklyn's Deputy Borough President Ed Townsend presented Tosh with a proclamation of freedom of the borough. It also was declared "Peter Tosh Day" in Brooklyn.

That and other shows across the world made it seem like Peter Tosh year in reggae. Indeed, his *Mystic Man* album did outsell *Bush Doctor* (his most successful commercially up to then). But it still fell far short of top ten status in the major U.S. and U.K. markets.

Those results plus perhaps Tosh's desire to return to greater artistic freedom led to another label shift in the early 1980s. He moved to EMI Records, which issued his label debut, *Wanted Dead or Alive*, in 1981. A gem of a collection, it demonstrated that Tosh remained committed to his goals of innovating and renewing the sources of reggae.

Tosh continued to tour and record excellent new material over the next half dozen years, including *Captured Live* in 1985 (nominated for a Grammy for Best Reggae Album) and his fine 1987 collection *No Nuclear War*. The latter won the Grammy for Best Reggae Album of 1987, but the award had to be pre-sented posthumously to his 20-year-old son Andrew Tosh in the spring of 1988, because Peter's life had been snuffed out the previous September by an apparent robbery at his home in Kingston in which two others were killed and four seriously wounded.

Many Jamaicans wondered whether robbery had been the prime motive, since Tosh had gained many enemies for his outspoken criticism of social ills in his country and corruption in government and business. However, the authorities, after arresting one person who was charged with murder (with two suspects still reported at large), stated the evidence did not support any cloak and dagger theories.

In 1988, Andrew took his father's place as lead singer for Peter's Word, Sound and Power band. The tour included a "Tribute to Peter Tosh" performance at the Starlight Ampitheater in Burbank, California, with proceeds earmarked for a proposed museum near Peter Tosh's grave, the Freedom College in Tanzania and the magazine *Music Times*, a Los Angeles reggae-oriented publication.

Andrew told Don Snowden *(Los Angeles Times*, April 7, 1988), "There are people watching me towards what I got out of it [his father's death]. They see I'm serious and strong, so they may want to keep a bullet behind my head. I got to keep watching.

"It feels good that Peter will receive a Grammy for his good works. It's nice to know they're still respecting him. I'm sorry he's not here to come forward and receive it, so I'll receive it and do my work." *(See Marley, Bob; Rolling Stones, The; Toots & the Maytals.)*

TOTO: *Vocal and instrumental group. Original members (1976): David Paich, born California, c. 1950; Jeff Porcaro, born Hartford, Connecticut, c. 1953; David Hungate, born Texas, early 1950s; Steve Porcaro, born Connecticut, c. 1955; Steve Luthaker, born California, c. 1957; Bobby Kimball, born Vinton, Louisiana. Hungate replaced in early 1980s by Mike Porcaro. Kimball left in 1984, replaced by Fergie Fredericksen, born Wyoming, Michigan. Fredericksen replaced in 1986 by Joseph Williams, born Santa Monica, California.*

Galloping nepotism might have been a reasonable description of the making of the rock group Toto. The founding members came from families with considerable success and contacts in the pop field, and the pattern continued with several of the later additions. Still, the group became one of the most commercially successful if not creatively unique bands from the end of the 1970s to the end of the 1980s.

The mainstays of the group, David Paich and the Porcaro brothers, were encouraged to take an interest in pop music from their early years by show business parents—in David's case, the noted Hollywood arranger/conductor Marty Paich, and the Porcaro boys by well-known jazz percussionist Joe Porcaro. David started piano lessons as a child and became a reasonably capable keyboards player by his teens. The Porcaro brothers, who spent their early years on the East Coast before their father moved the family to California, might all have become drummers under their father's tutelage, but fortunately for the future makeup of Toto, only Jeff followed that course and even he was more interested in other instruments for a while.

In fact, Jeff at first wasn't sure he wanted to make music a career. "I just did music for fun. I took lessons for a while, but stopped because they were boring." When he entered high school, he envisioned becoming an artist, but found that he could earn money by being in a band. "I didn't think in high school I'd be any kind of great drummer. I wanted to play guitar because I was a [Jimi] Hendrix freak."

Michael Porcaro (who eventually replaced Toto's original bass guitarist, David Hungate) said: "My father thought I was going to be the drummer. All of us used to line up at his practice set, play for 10 minutes, and say: 'Dig me, dad!' but after we moved to California, I started studying string bass. Even in junior high school, I got work playing bass at weddings and bar mitzvahs. Soon my dad bought me an electric bass. I never intended it, but one day I thought to myself: 'I guess I'm a bass player.'"

Steve, youngest of the Porcaro brothers, started piano at five, but stressed: "As a kid, I spent more time playing baseball than I should have. Music wasn't forced on me. It was often a struggle for my father [to accept his sons' musical activities], and my parents would have been very happy if we'd gotten jobs as plumbers."

The Paich and Porcaro families became friendly after Marty and Joe worked together on Glen Campbell's TV program. The boys soon found common pop music interests, although David was three years ahead of Jeff at Grant High School in the San Fernando Valley, where both were students. The two organized the band Rural Still Life and tried to follow in the stylistic footsteps of Jimi Hendrix. Among its members over the next few years, besides more Porcaros, were high school friends David Hungate and Steve Luthaker.

Unlike the others, Hungate was a relative latecomer to the San Fernando Valley, having moved there from Texas as a teenager. Singer/guitarist Luthaker was born and bred in the Valley. "Nobody else in my family has any musical talent whatever. I'm a freak!" Eventually, he and the youngest Por-

caro, Steve, inherited Rural Still Life after first Paich and then Jeff Porcaro graduated.

As the future members of Toto finished their high school years, some opted to try for immediate musical careers while others went on to more formal education. But as time passed, one after the other all became working musicians, amassing extensive credentials as session players, band sidemen, prospective songwriters and, in Paich's case, a highly regarded arranger as well.

Among the earlier achievers was bassist Hungate, who backed recording activities of Leo Sayer, Barbra Streisand, and the Pointer Sisters. He helped Jeff Porcaro get a start in the field by pointing him to a stint as drummer with then-married Sonny and Cher. Jeff stayed with the Bonos until 1973, when he became part of Steely Dan, playing on the *Katy Lied* album. David Paich, meanwhile, made his mark in the early and middle 1970s co-writing and arranging material for Boz Scaggs' superb 1976 album *Silk Degrees* and arranging songs for the Doobie Brothers. Paich was joined on mid-1970s Boz Scaggs tours by Steve Porcaro, who also played with other luminaries of the period including Leo Sayer and Gary Wright. Luthaker was no slouch in this department either, playing guitar behind Hall & Oates and Alice Cooper, writing original songs, and performing on a mid-1970s LP by Valerie Carter.

While laying down backing tracks for *Silk Degrees* in 1976, Paich and Jeff Porcaro agreed the time seemed right for them to organize a band of their own. They lined up Hungate, Steve Porcaro, Luthaker, and Mike Porcaro, though Mike didn't end up in the initial recording group at the time. Needing a lead singer, they approached Bobby Kimball, who had performed with several New Orleans–area groups before coming to Los Angeles to join S.S. Fools. He had gotten to know Paich and Jeff Porcaro during a demo session they produced.

While some band members said the group name was derived from Kimball's original last name (Toteaux), on other occasions different Totoites maintained the name came from Dorothy's dog in *The Wizard of Oz*.

The group's first LP, *Toto* (Columbia, September 1977), was preceded by a gold debut single, "Hold the Line." The top 5 single helped the LP go platinum. Two other singles from the album were issued ("I'll Supply the Love" and "Georgy Porgy"), but neither even broke *Billboard*'s top 40.

The band did well enough its first time out, though, to receive a Grammy nomination for Best New Artist. For a while, it didn't seem as though the band had much pull as a singles group. Until 1982, no more Toto singles showed up on the top 20. In truth, Columbia didn't seem too interested in releasing them. Only one single, "99," was issued from the band's second LP, *Hydra* (1979), which, while not as successful as the debut LP, still managed to earn a gold-record award. After a gap of two years, Toto came up with its third album, *Turn Back* (1981), from which "Goodbye Eleanor" was released as a single. That LP was a commercial disappointment, and it seemed as though the band might prove another asterisk on the rock-success ledger.

Then came *Toto IV* in March 1982—a platinum treasure trove of hit singles, beginning with "Rosanna" (number 2 in *Billboard* for five summer weeks). After "Make Believe" made the top 30 later in the summer, the single "Africa" was issued in October and began an odyssey that resulted in its reaching the pinnacle 14 weeks later, nestling at number 1 in *Billboard* the week of February 5, 1983. Other charted singles from *Toto IV* were "I Won't Hold You Back" and "Waiting for Your Love."

In the 1982 Grammy Awards, Toto waxed triumphant, receiving a bonanza of six trophies. *Toto IV* was named Album of the Year and Best Engineered Recording. "Rosanna" won for Record of the Year and Best Vocal Arrangement. Toto members were voted Producer of the Year. Paich, Jeff Pocaro, and Jerry Hey won for Best Instrumental Arrangement Accompanying Vocals for "Rosanna." Besides all that, Steve Luthaker shared honors for another project, winning the Grammy for Best Rhythm & Blues Song with Jay Graydon and Bill Champlin for "Turn Your Love Around" (a hit for George Benson).

For Toto members, those victories were solace for strident attacks on their achievements by a number of critics. Dave Marsh of *Rolling Stone* was particularly vitriolic: "This conglomeration of L.A. session musicians made a hit out of a debut album that is all chops and no brains. Formula pop songs, singing that wouldn't go over in a Holiday Inn cocktail lounge." Other critics made comments in a similar vein.

Jeff Porcaro responded in an interview for *BAM* magazine: "These [critics] are dimwitted idiots and I dare any publication to include a list of the writer's credentials beside the interview or review. Is he a musician? What is his background and what gives him the right to say this?"

Certainly it seemed as though the band members' peers did not lack respect for their abilities. Other rock stars welcomed having Toto artists back them on important projects. Michael Jackson enlisted several Totoites to play on his *Thriller* LP (one of the blockbusters of the 1980s, and the Grammy front-runner in the 1983 awards that *Toto IV* had been in 1982). After the 1983 voting, Jeff Porcaro, Steve Porcaro, and Steve Luthaker won award certificates for performing behind Jackson on the single "Beat

It," named Record of the Year. Steve Porcaro was recognized for his arranging and vocal work on *Thriller,* voted album of the Year. Paich and Steve Luthaker also contributed arranging on that album.

Before Toto could begin work on its next album, it had to look for a new vocalist, since Kimball had left to try for a solo career. Replacing him was Fergie Fredericksen, a Midwestern singer/songwriter who previously was with the Chicago-area Trillion and the New Orleans rock band LeRoux. Besides Fergie, the lineup now comprised Luthaker on guitars and vocals, Paich on keyboards and vocals, Jeff Porcaro on drums and percussion, Mike Porcaro on bass guitar, and Steve Porcaro on keyboards.

Before the reorganized Toto moved on to its next album, its members had several other challenging projects. One was the score for the science fiction film *Dune,* for which David Paich and his father, Marty, collaborated on arranging. Toto members also composed the instrumental theme "Moodido" ("The Match") for the boxing program at the 1984 Los Angeles Summer Olympics. The song was included on the Columbia LP *The Official Music of the XXIIIrd Olympiad Los Angeles, 1984.*

Its next LP, *Isolation* (fall 1984), fell far short of the sales totals of *Toto IV,* despite well-attended concerts throughout 1985 that began with visits to Australia, Japan, and Europe and ended with a cross-country tour of the U.S. The first single and video from the album, "Stranger in Town" (written by Paich and Jeff Porcaro), was in *Billboard*'s top 30 at year-end.

In 1986, Toto had another change in vocalists with John Williams replacing Fredericksen. With that addition, another famous family was represented in band ranks. Williams' father was noted composer/conductor John Williams (leader of the Boston Symphony Orchestra); his mother was the late actress Barbara Ruick. Brought up in Encino in the San Fernando Valley, he had put out a solo LP on MCA Records and done three years as a backup singer for pop star Jeffrey Osborne. Williams' first spotlight with Toto was on the group's sixth album, *Fahrenheit* (Columbia, August 1986), from which a hit single, "I'll Be Over You," was taken. That roster remained intact for the next LP *(The Seventh One,* Columbia, 1988), the group's first digitally recorded collection. *(See Benson, George; Doobie Brothers, The; Hall & Oates; Jackson, Michael; Scaggs, Boz; Sonny and Cher; Steely Dan.)*

TOWNSHEND, PETER: *See Who, The.*

TRAFFIC: *Vocal and instrumental group. Original members (1967): Steve Winwood, born Great Barr, near Birmingham, England, May 12, 1948;*

Jim Capaldi, born Evesham, Worcestershire, England, August 24, 1944; Chris Wood, born Harbourne, Birmingham, England, June 24, 1944; Dave Mason, born Worcester, England, May 10, 1946. Mason left in 1967. Rick Grech, born Bordeaux, France, November 1945, added in 1970, left in late 1971. Members (1973): Wood; Capaldi; Winwood; Reebop Kwaku Baah, born Africa, February 13; Barry Beckett; Roger Hawkins; David Hood. Members (late 1974): Wood; Capaldi; Winwood; Rosko Gee, born Jamaica.

Any group with an artist rated as highly in the entire popular music field as pianist-guitarist Steve Winwood, had to be paid attention to. In the case of Traffic, as of the early 1970s, the entire group's musicianship made it a legitimate claimant to the supergroup label. Unfortunately, by the mid-1970s, it seemed to lose its collective enthusiasm and before the end of the decade was only a fond memory for its many rock fans.

Winwood was already hailed as a superstar at 18, the year before Traffic was formed. He grew up in a family where music was emphasized. His older brother Muff and he both started piano lessons in their early years. Steve also took up guitar not very long afterwards. By the time he was in the English equivalent of high school, he was highly proficient on both instruments and was also writing some of his own material.

At 15, he attended a music college for a year to learn music theory and notation. Before he finished this year, he was playing with his brother's jazz band. After a short time, the brothers joined with a young music teacher named Spencer Davis to form the Spencer Davis Group, one of the most highly regarded acts by their peers. By the end of 1964, their fellow musicians were referring to them as a group's group and many critics called Winwood a musical genius.

After several years with Davis, Winwood decided he was tired of the group's sound and wanted to start in new directions. This resulted in his joining with three other young, talented pop musicians—Jim Capaldi, Chris Wood, and Dave Mason—in early 1967 to go into semiseclusion to prepare new arrangements. The four retired to a small cottage in the rural area of Berkshire Downs, where they spent six months writing new material and rehearsing for many hours a day.

Chris Wood had taken piano lessons for a short time when he was five. He didn't take to being taught and went on to work out his style by himself as he grew up. Before his teens, he added flute to his repertoire. After finishing high school, he studied painting at art college. During this period, he taught himself the tenor saxophone and later added alto and soprano sax to his accomplishments, as well as the oboe and certain percussion instruments. By the mid-1960s, he had decided to concentrate on music instead of art. Among his friends within the music fraternity were the Winwoods, which led to his agreement to help found Traffic.

Capaldi's family was even more directly involved in music than those of other Traffic members. His father, a music teacher, had once been on the stage; his mother had been a professional singer. He started piano at six and formed a group with three friends when he was high school age. Despite this background, he took up engineering as a career in his teens, working as an apprentice while forming a second group as a sideline. With this group, Capaldi learned to play drums and gained a reputation as one of the most promising young rock percussionists. His ability as a lyricist made him a much-needed addition to Traffic.

Replying to queries from British reporters during the group's half year in Berkshire Downs, Capaldi noted: "We're not really leading a hermit-like existence out there. We just use the place to rehearse and to work. We don't like the rush of London or the noise. We can wake up when we want to. Most important, though, is the fact that we can make as much musical noise as we want without having some raving idiot coming to the door to complain. If we want total isolation, we can just pull out the telephone plug."

The upshot of this work was the British number one single "Paper Sun" in the summer of 1967, followed by the million-seller "Hole in My Shoe." In November, the title song for the movie *Here We Go 'Round the Mulberry Bush* (a film using much background music written by Traffic) was issued. Island Records issued the group's first album, *Mr. Fantasy,* in December. Mason left at the end of 1967. The remaining trio continued Traffic's growing impact on rock in 1968. Successive releases showed great flexibility in style, with arrangements ranging from soft rock to highly amplified semihard rock, to blues, jazz, and folk.

Inroads on the U.S. scene commenced in 1968, when United Artists released LPs *Mr. Fantasy* and its gold sales sequel (according to U.A.), *Traffic,* followed by *Last Exit* (1969) and the retrospective *Best of Traffic* (1970). The gold fifth album, *John Barleycorn Must Die* (inspired by a medieval folk tale), proved the most successful to that point.

During 1970, Traffic expanded to a foursome again with the addition of Rick Grech, a former member of Family, Blind Faith, and Ginger Baker's Air Force. The next year, it added African percussionist Reebop Kwaku Baah, who played on the album *Welcome to the Canteen* (fall 1971). The act also provided United Artists with the hit single "Gimme Some Lovin'—Part I" in 1971. Starting with the gold *Low Spark of High Heeled Boys* (December 1971), Traffic discs were on Island in the U.S. as well as in Britain, with American distribution by Capitol. In 1972, the band had the hit single "Rock & Roll Show" and gold LP *Shootout at the Fantasy Factory*. The live *On the Road* followed in October 1973. Besides Winwood, Wood, Capaldi, and Kwaku Baah, members during 1973 and early 1974 included U.S. session musician Barry Beckett (keyboards), David Hood (bass), and Roger Hawkins (drums). By late 1974, the group was back to a quartet (Winwood, Capaldi, Wood, and Jamaican-born bass guitarist Rosko Gee), which prepared the 1974 album *When the Eagle Flies,* issued in the U.S. on Asylum Records. After the mid-1970s, group members seemed to lose interest in Traffic as an entity. Meanwhile, some of the band's best work was repackaged by United Artists in the 1975 albums *Heavy Traffic* and *More Heavy Traffic. (See Clapton, Eric; Mason, Dave; Winwood, Steve.)*

TRAMMPS, THE: *Vocal group from Philadelphia. Members (mid-1970s): Earl Young, Jimmy Ellis, Robert Upchurch, Harold Wade, Stanley Wade.*

The Trammps were pioneers in the evolution of the danceable soul/R&B format that became disco in the 1970s. Their biggest hit, "Disco Inferno," which served as an 11-minute backdrop to one of John Travolta's dance sequences in *Saturday Night Fever,* was a factor in the movie's impact on worldwide movie goers in the late 1970s. Yet the group often presented inept live performances that suggested its dynamic sound was more the result of recording engineers than inherent performing skills.

The upward movement of groups such as the Trammps, Bluenotes, and Delfonics symbolized a tilt in the soul/R&B genre during the 1960s from the Motown/Stax axis to the East Coast, specifically the Philadelphia area. Original members, including founding singers tenor Earl Young and bass Jimmy Ellis, grew up in the urban ghettos of Philadelphia where R&B and doo-wop were the main vocal formats in the late 1950s. Young noted: "Most of the guys were raised on street corners and doin' all kinds of crazy things and bein' chased away by the man . . . hearing: 'All you'll ever be is tramps.'"

Like many of their compatriots, future members of the Trammps realized music, in the form of street singing, was a way to pick up badly needed spare change and might even offer a way out of the poverty that engulfed many of their friends and relatives. By the mid-1960s, Young and Ellis had moved on to professional singing in a group called the Volcanoes,

which had an R&B hit single, "Storm Warning," on a small label in 1965.

By the end of the 1960s, the group evolved into the Trammps. In the early 1970s, it began to win notice beyond the Philadelphia area with singles on Buddah Records that typically were updated covers of old pop songs, such as "Zing Went the Strings of My Heart" (a hit in mid-1972). The group's vocal blend had elements of 1950s R&B artists such as the Coasters, combined with a grittier, more up-tempo rhythmic base. An example of a single of that period that incorporated the frantic pace associated with disco was "60 Minute Man."

Switching to Golden Fleece Records, its charted, if not best-selling, singles included "Love Epidemic" and "Where Do We Go from Here" in 1974.

During the first half of the 1970s, the group had more success with its singles than its albums such as *The Trammps* on Golden Fleece and *The Legendary Zing Album* (Buddah, 1975). Moving to Atlantic Records, for a while its fortunes took a giant step for the better. From its 1976 label debut *Where the Happy People Go* (a favored collection with disco disc jockeys), the title song became a singles hit. The Trammps, after a decade of effort, finally won major recognition. In *Billboard*'s year-end review, the act was named Disco Group of the Year.

But the best was yet to come. The early 1977 Atlantic LP *Disco Inferno* caught the fancy of disco fans not only in the U.S. but all over the world and went gold. The title track reached top levels on black and pop (dance/disco) charts both in an extended-play disco version and as a conventional 45 rpm single. In many ways, that song came to symbolize the disco craze that swept much of the western world in the mid-1970s. In late 1977, the LP *Trammps III* (Atlantic, late 1977) exceeded gold record sales worldwide according to Atlantic.

Next came the blockbuster movie *Saturday Night Fever* starring John Travolta as a fanatical disco dancer. The Trammps' "Disco Inferno" was a prominent part of the platinum soundtrack album (RSO Records, 1978), which also included the Bee Gees, Tavares, Kool & the Gang, David Shire, KC and the Sunshine Band, MFSB, Walter Murphy, and Ralph McDonald. The LP won the Grammy for Album of the Year with the Trammps among the artists given trophies.

During the mid-1970s, the group was accorded headliner status on the soul/disco concert circuit. As is typically the case with a soul/R&B vocal group, the Trammps' shows incorporated instrumental backing from a sizable supporting band usually comprising eight musicians. Besides the three-part harmony of Young, Ellis, and Upchurch, supplemental vocals were provided by the Wade brothers, Harold and Stanley. Though eastern critics often enthused about the performances, some of the live concerts outside the group's home area tended to be uneven and ragged with attempts at comedy that detracted rather than added to the overall impact.

After Atlantic's retrospective *The Best of the Trammps*, the band's next regular release was *The Whole World's Dancing* (May 1979). Though Stevie Wonder contributed a harmonica solo on one number, "Soul Bones," the album didn't represent any major advance byond the group's previous Atlantic LPs.

In the early 1980s, while disco had not disappeared, its importance had diminished considerably. That situation, coupled with the Trammps' difficulties in coming up with innovative new material, caused the group's career to taper off sharply. At the start of the new decade, Trammps fans welcomed songs "Hooked for Life" and "Soul-Searchin' Time," but Atlantic albums *Mixin' It Up* and *Slipping Out* made little dent in either the black or the pop lists.

TRIUMPH: *Vocal and instrumental group. Members, all born Toronto, Canada: Rik Emmett, Mike Levine, Gil Moore.* *

In the 1970s, Canada seemed to have a climate conducive to the birth of power trios to export to the world. While not always respected by critics, such groups as the Stampeders, Rush, and Triumph won allegiance from millions of rock fans and had unusual longevity. Triumph, for instance, went into its second decade in the mid-1980s still an important element on the concert circuit and still boasting all three founding members.

As anyone attending a Triumph concert could affirm, the group didn't stint on amplification or lavish special effects, but its style wasn't easily assignable to specific rock categories. As Rik Emmett put it: "Triumph is not strictly heavy rock or precious metal or weird combination. We're simply a rock band. I think the image of Triumph as heavy rock came about because of our extravagant stage production, the hydraulic lighting trusses and lasers we use in the live show, but that's only one side of it."

Mike Levine commented to Steve Pond of the *Los Angeles Times* (March 3, 1985): "Sometimes stories lump us in with Judas Priest and Iron Maiden, and sometimes they compare us to Journey and Foreigner. I think we're sort of in a middle ground. We

play a lot of heavy music, but we also play melodic stuff. We're not studs in leather and we're not pretty harmonies all the time either, so it's hard to say where we fit in."

The band origins were in the bar circuit of Toronto, Canada, hometown of all three musicians. Drummer Gil Moore and bass guitarist Mike Levine had been in a series of groups in the first part of the 1970s that hadn't gone anywhere. The two came together in the summer of 1975 determined to form a new group with brighter prospects. Levine recalled: "Gil and I got together through a mutual admiration society and went out looking for a lead guitarist. From the start we knew we were gonna be a three-piece band, knew we'd play rock'n'roll, and wanted the band to be visual and entertaining and that's all we knew to start with. As we played and grew, we became confident we could accomplish all those things.

"Anyway, we had heard from friends that Rik Emmett was a top guitarist. We went out looking for him and found him. We saw him play and he knocked us out so we got him to jam with us and it worked. That's when we started—in late 1975."

The group's Canadian concert debut was at Simcoe High School in Toronto on September 19, 1975. After that, the trio steadily expanded its activities to larger venues in its home area, using any spare change that could be accumulated to add smoke, special lighting, and other effects. Levine stressed: "We've never been able to play clubs, partly because we've always wanted a good stage show and partly because we don't want to play where people drink. We want to be the focal point rather than a secondary attraction.

"We always wanted to do more than just get up on stage and play. In our original concept, we thought that a concert is like theater. That's how we look at it. People pay their money and want to have a good time. So we put on a rock show, not a James Taylor show. Otherwise why shouldn't a fan stay at home and listen to the stereo. We use visuals to stress a point. As soon as someone comes up to me after a show and says: 'I hate flash pots' or 'I hate strobe lights or laser beams,' then we'll stop using it, 'cause they're the people that support us, not the critics."

He also emphasized the band tried to vary the kind of songs it played for maximum audience impact. "Gil and I learned about the importance of pacing from our early rhythm & blues band days. Even as a rock band it's stupid to stay up there for one-and-a-half hours and play everything at the same speed and same chords. We wanted to have good pacing and be respected as musicians. Once an audience respects that, we feel they're going to be fans evermore."

---

*Partly based on personal interview with Mike Levine by Irwin Stambler.

The approach seemed to work. Within a fairly short time after its inception, Triumph was performing in front of sizable crowds in many parts of Canada. It was also getting some notice south of the border, where it played its first concert in San Antonio, Texas, on February 18, 1977. (However, it didn't embark on its first full-scale U.S. tour until November 14, 1978 at the Stanley Theatre in Pittsburgh, Pennsylvania.)

After recording for a Canadian label, the group scored significant breakthrough in 1978, when it signed with RCA Records for U.S. and overseas distribution. To many, mating a power trio with a relatively conservative label seemed a mistake. Levine recalled: "Nobody believed RCA could do it for us. People came to us and said: 'How can you go with RCA? You must be crazy!' We said: 'Wait and see,' and they did do a great job for us."

RCA provided good promotional support, backed extensive tours for the band, and helped finance the outlays for special equipment for the persistent touring that remained a hallmark of the group's approach. From the late 1970s into the mid-1980s, Triumph typically did over 200 concerts a year. Its 1984–85 world tour drew over 1 million attendees and 85 percent of the shows sold out in 10–15,000-seat halls.

This plan of operations helped place the band's RCA debut *Rock'n'Roll Machine* (1978) on U.S. charts for some months. The next U.S. release, *Just a Game*, did better, selling steadily at a rate of several thousand a week until it edged past gold levels several years after release. Those LPs found equally fertile ground in Canada and Europe, earning several gold and platinum awards. *Performance* magazine readers recognized the group's visual experimentation by voting it "Innovators of the Year" for 1979.

During those early years, Levine said, the band constantly strove to upgrade the show. "For a long time, almost every nickel we made we plowed back into the show, that's our working capital. We typically carry 15 or more guys in our crew, of which the most important are the lighting and sound specialists. We don't know how many tons of stuff we usually take with us on a couple of tractor trailers and a straight truck. We still try to come up with new ideas. We tell the lighting and effects guys what we'd like and they take that and tell us what they need to do it. If they can't do what we want, they come to us and say: 'Hey, we can't do this, but we can do this.'"

The group began the 1980s with the moderately successful album *Progressions of Power*, followed by gold LPs *Allied Force* (1981) and *Never Surrender* (1983).

By 1984, the band's contract with RCA was up.

Neither party was overly satisfied with the relationship. That fall, it was announced that the band had signed a long-term contract with MCA Records. The band's debut on MCA, *Thunder Seven* (November 1984), went gold. The band, on leaving RCA, had successfully negotiated for rights to its material on that label and Mike Levine remastered the five RCA albums for reissue on MCA.

In 1985, the band celebrated its tenth anniversary with the live album *Stages* (including two studio tracks: "Empty Inside" and "Mind Games) in *Billboard*'s top 10. Material for the LP mainly was recorded during the 1984–85 "Worldwide Thunder Seven" tour.

In March 1986, the group began recording its fall studio album, *The Sport of Kings,* which was completed later in the band's own Metalworks studio in Toronto. First single from the album was "Somebody's Out There," written by Emmett, who also did the vocals. (Besides his writing and vocal skills, Emmett was winning increasing recognition for his instrumental work. In *Guitar Player* magazine's year-end poll for 1985, Emmett placed third in the best rock guitarist category.) That album also included an R&B-style ballad, "Just One Night," co-written by Neil Schon (of Santana and Journey fame), Eric Martin, and Tony Fanucci. *(See Journey; Santana.)* But on most of the band's albums, the majority of material was written by Emmett and/or Moore. Levine commented: "Rik and Gil write most of our material, but I often have my input anyway, though I sometimes come up with the odd thing we can use."

The band's next LP, *Surveillance,* was released by MCA in November 1987. During 1987, Emmett again placed high in *Guitar Player*'s readers poll and also was invited by the magazine to write and record an instrumental piece to be used on a flexi-disc insert also featuring other top guitarists from around the world. Emmett also received the Toronto Musician's Award for Guitar Player of the Year.

Unlike some groups, Triumph as of the late 1980s had never changed in membership or size. Levine noted: "We like the trio format and never thought much about expanding. But if we expanded, it would have to be a quintet. We run Triumph as a democracy where majority rules. If we went to four, we could have a standoff."

TROWER, ROBIN: *Guitarist, songwriter, band leader (JUDE, ROBIN TROWER BAND). Born London, England, March 9, 1945.*

The death of guitar great Jimi Hendrix inspired Procol Harum lead guitarist Robin Trower to write his first song, "Song for a Dreamer." With lyrics by

Keith Reid, it was one of the best tracks on the band's 1971 album, *Broken Barricades*. The album title proved symbolic, for the response to it and Trower's composition helped give him the self-confidence to leave Procol in search of a solo career. It was a wise decision as Robin went on to become a star in his own right during the 1970s, building up a following still devoted to him in the '80s.

As a youngster in a working class section of London, Robin was impelled toward a music career by the new sounds reaching English shores from the U.S. in the early days of rock and rhythm & blues. As he said later: "Elvis Presley first turned me onto music and guitar playing [before then he had favored learning to play trumpet] by being the first one to do something musically great and since then I've been influenced the last 20 years by black music. Someone like Muddy Waters creates a standard in music, even more than just a style, which after you hear it, you have to just try and achieve."

His teenage band, the Paramounts, formed in 1962, originally included Gary Brooker, Chris Copping, and a drummer named Mick who later was replaced by Barry "B.J." Wilson. As Robin recalled: "Our first kick was when the [Rolling] Stones heard us; they dug our music, which was somewhat similar to their own, and they introduced us to their gig circuit, which they were in the process of leaving to do cinema tours and things like that. In fact, the Stones were about the only people who helped us . . . everyone else we came into contact with was out to rob us, but they even got us on the bill of some of their package shows."

The Paramounts, though they made some recordings, never had much impact on the rock scene until the group evolved into Procol Harum in the mid-1960s. *(See Procol Harum.)* As they gained large-scale popularity on both sides of the Atlantic, Trower's excellent guitar work won particular attention.

After leaving Procol, Robin first formed the band Jude in the autumn of 1971. Its members included Frankie Miller on guitar and vocals, Clive Bunker (previously with Jethro Tull) on drums, and Jimmy Dewar (born Scotland) on bass guitar. Dewar came to the group from the band Stone the Crows. Within a short time, Trower decided the band wasn't what he had in mind and he broke it up. With Dewar, whom Robin found had a good lead-vocal ability, he organized a trio with West Indies–born drummer Reg Isidore.

The new group's debut album, *Twice Removed from Yesterday* (Chrysalis, 1973), quickly found favor with critics and fans in England and the U.S. The follow-up albums, if anything, exceeded the debut LP in quality. *Bridge of Sighs* (1974), *For Earth Below* (1975), and *Long Misty Days* (1976) were certified gold by the RIAA. Before work began on *For Earth Below*, Isidore left and was replaced by Bill Lordan, whose credits included four years with Gypsy and one with Sly and the Family Stone.

Desiring a purer version of the R&B styling he admired, Trower next collaborated with black American producer Don Davis on albums *In City Dreams* (1977, gold) and *Caravan to Midnight* (1978). "Those two albums with Don weren't rock'n'roll, but I didn't realize it at the time when I was making them. I was just doing what I thought felt good. I've never said to myself: 'Oh, the punters like this so I'd better give it to them.' "

His love for R&B was unabated, he stressed. "The reason that early R&B retained such potent appeal was that it was totally devoid of equivocating. The words and the music struck a resounding common note the first time around."

For those who wanted to compare the R&B directions of the Davis-produced tracks with earlier Trower material, Chrysalis provided the basis with its 1976 LP *Robin Trower Live!* Robin's next release was *Victims of the Fury*, the first for which he handled co-production chores. The latter, unfortunately, was weaker than his previous efforts.

In the late '70s and early 1980s, Robin joined forces with legendary Cream bass guitarist Jack Bruce for a number of studio sessions. The first fruits of that work were the hit 1981 album *BLT*, with Trower handling all production responsibilities and the title standing for Bruce, Lordan, and Trower, and *Truce*. On *Truce*, Reg Isidore returned to handle drums.

Later in the 1980s, Robin organized a new group, this time featuring dual drummers: Alan Clark and Bobby Clouter (both Londoners). The other members were James Dewar, back to take over on vocals and bass, and another bass guitarist as well, David Bronze. The new assemblage's first album was *Back It Up* (Chrysalis, July 1983).

In the mid-1980s, he left Chrysalis and he issued his next album, *Passion*, independently. The album sold considerably better than his last Chrysalis releases and helped win him a new contract with a major record firm, Atlantic, which issued his debut on the label, *Take What You Need*, in 1988. His band by then comprised Bronze, Davey Pattison on vocals, and Pete Thompson on drums. *(See Jethro Tull; Sly and the Family Stone.)*

TURNER, IKE AND TINA: *Vocal and instrumental duo. Ike Turner, guitarist, pianist, band leader, singer, record producer, born Clarksdale, Mississippi, November 5, c. 1933; Tina*

Turner, singer, dancer, songwriter, born Nutbush, Tennessee, November 26, 1939. *

In its headline days, it was hard to find a show that exemplified the roots of rock'n'roll better than the Ike and Tina Turner Revue. Entwined in the numbers played by Ike's band, the Kings of Rhythm, or sung and danced by the female trio, the Ikettes (who backed Tina's sinuous, suggestive vocals), were the sounds of the ghetto, the raucousness of low-down blues, the plaintiveness of country blues, and the hope for the future of gospel. All of this was recognized by British audiences in the mid-1960s, which finally helped reflect back to the Turners' homeland the importance of their art form. The husband-and-wife team became superstars until marital tensions and, according to Tina, Ike's problems with alcohol and drugs caused her to break away in the mid-1970s and become a solo success.

Ike and Tina's overdue recognition in the U.S. in the late 1960s ironically came at a time when many black radicals were condemning old-style R&B with its wild dancing and blaring brass as a form of Uncle Tomism. However, black audiences still joined the growing number of white fans in applauding these major music innovators.

In providing background for his Capitol Records biography in 1971, Ike recalled how he had first gotten interested in music in his hometown of Clarksdale, Mississippi, when he was six. "I played an old piano in a church lady's house. She would let me play if I would cut wood for her in return. At that time, I didn't really know what a piano was. All I knew was that when I pushed down on the keys, it made a sound that I liked. After picking out a few notes to 'Blues in the Night' and other tunes that were popular at the time, I started to beg my mother to buy me my own. When school was out that year, I came home with my report card full of good grades. I walked in the house and there it was . . . a new piano, and she said it was all mine. This was the real beginning of my career."

Ike rapidly taught himself to play the piano. After completing high school, he organized a band called the Kings of Rhythm. He got local dates and gradually expanded to playing small clubs in other towns and cities. At the start of the 1950s, he gained his group a recording session in Memphis, where it cut "Rocket 88." The song became a hit, but, as Ike noted: "It was a big financial score, but some dude at the record company beat me, and I only got $40 for writing, producing, and recording it. Well, I took

the Kings on the road doing shows with Howlin' Wolf, B.B. King, and people like that."

In the mid-1950s, Ike's band became a regular attraction at a club in St. Louis. It was there he met young Annie Mae Bullock. Annie, now Tina Turner, grew up as a member of a large family in the Knoxville, Tennessee area. After performing with local gospel groups, she moved to St. Louis with a sister in the mid-1950s, partly with the idea of trying to make her way as a vocalist.

As she recalled: "I was going to nightclubs with my sister. Ike was working at one that we used to go to all the time. Well, I used to ask him to let me sing. He'd say OK, but never call me to the stage. One night he was playing organ and the drummer put a microphone in front of my sister for her to sing. She said no, so I took the microphone and started singing. Ike was shocked! When he finished the tune, he called me on stage. I did several numbers with them that night. Later I joined the group."

That was in 1956. Ike and Tina married in 1958 and Tina sang with the group much of the time. In 1959, they got their first big break somewhat by accident. Ike wrote a song called "Fool in Love," but the singer who was supposed to record it didn't show up for the session. Tina filled in and the single, on Sue Records, became a major R&B hit of 1960.

From then on, the show was revamped to spotlight Tina. Ike added a female vocal group, usually a trio, to back her and worked out arrangements and routines himself. The revue became one of the best liked on the R&B circuit. In 1961, Ike and Tina were represented on R&B charts with three hits: "It's Gonna Work Out," "I Pity the Fool," and "I Idolize You." In 1962, there were singles successes "Poor Fool" and "Tra La La La." Some of their material began to receive airplay in England, paving the way for the 1966 number one hit "River Deep, Mountain High." A classic example of producer Phil Spector's wall-of-sound technique, it made them one of the most famous groups there.

For a while, English acclaim had little effect on their American career. They still played the R&B circuit, occasionally in major concert halls, but more often in small clubs. Nor did their records have much impact outside the R&B market. The Turners were considered to have great potential by the industry and they were signed by various labels. Warner Brothers, for instance, issued the LP *Ike and Tina Turner*. In 1965, Ike and Tina joined Liberty, an association fruitful for both parties over the years.

Toward the end of the '60s, things began to change. The Turners were asked to accompany the Rolling Stones, one of many major English groups who admired them, on an American tour. They were approached for major Las Vegas venues and began

---

*Some sources give Ike's year of birth as 1931 and Tina's as 1938.

to be guests on major TV shows. A typical concert ranged from Ike's soul compositions to Sly Stone's "I Want to Take You Higher," the Rolling Stone's "Honky Tonk Woman," and the Beatles' "With a Little Help from My Friends." The Kings of Rhythm, as of this period, numbered eight (including Ike), featuring trombone, trumpet, two saxophones, two guitars, drums and organ.

Affirming that Ike and Tina had arrived was their growing list of hits. In 1970, they were represented on singles lists with "Bold Soul Sister" and "The Hunter" on Blue Thumb Records, "Come Together" on Minit, and "I Want to Take You Higher" on Liberty. Album hits were *Come Together* and *In Person* on Minit, and *River Deep Mountain High* on A&M. During 1971, they earned a gold record for their single of Credence Clearwater Revival's "Proud Mary" on Liberty and also had the best-selling Liberty album *Workin' Together*. After the label designation was changed from Liberty to the parent company's name, United Artists, Ike and Tina made the lists for UA with the single "Ooh Poo Pah Doo" and albums *Nuff Said* and *What You Hear Is What You Get/Live at Carnegie Hall*.

1972 best-sellers included singles "I'm Yours (Use Me Any Way You Wanna)" and "Up in Heah" and the album *Feel Good*. In 1973, they hit with singles "Early One Morning" and "Nutbush City Limits" and albums *World of Ike and Tina Turner* and *Nutbush City Limits*. Also available in 1973 was a British import LP, *The Soul of Ike and Tina Turner* on Kent.

Outwardly all was fine, but in their private lives, Ike and Tina were not getting along. In the mid-1970s, Tina decided she'd had enough and abruptly left the group in the middle of a tour. In 1976, she won a divorce from Ike and eventually went on to her very successful solo career. Ike, on the other hand, seemed unable to pick up the threads of his life and in later years made newspaper headlines more often for drug problems than for entertainment achievements. His problems continued to haunt him throughout the 1980s. In March 1988 he was placed on five years' probation and fined $500 in Pasadena, California, Superior Court after he pled guilty to possession of cocaine for sale and two additional felonies in connection with a 1985 arrest.

Reminders of happier days came in the form of the retrospective LP *The Best of Ike and Tina Turner* (EMI America, 1987). *(See Creedence Clearwater Revival; Rolling Stones, The; Spector, Phil; Turner, Tina.)*

TURNER, JOE: *Singer, songwriter. Born Kansas City, Missouri, May 18, 1911; died Englewood, California, November 24, 1985.*

Typically a rock star is thought of as someone in his teens or not too far past them. Big Joe Turner, an early pioneer of what became known as rock, didn't come anywhere near such a definition. He was past 40 when his name began to appear on R&B and national charts. At 300 pounds and 6 feet, 2 inches in height, he certainly didn't look like a callow teenager. Yet he was still going strong in concert in his seventies.

Joseph Vernon Turner spent the greater part of his first 30 years in the jazz and blues mecca of Kansas City. His first exposure to music came from hearing gospel singing in church as a child. Later, though, he became aware of another, rawer, yet more realistic type of music, the kind itinerant blues singers performed in the streets.

As he told Leslie Gourse *(Los Angeles Times, March 14, 1982)*: "I learned from two street singers with a harp [harmonica] and guitar. I used to follow them around. Then I earned 50 cents a day leading a blind man around with his guitar, singing with him, when I was 13. And I listened to some records, folk blues and pop songs—so long ago I don't remember which ones anymore. I didn't get my first singing job until I was 21. Until then I sold papers, and I had a horse and wagon and sold junk."

By the late 1930s, he was considered one of the best blues shouters by those black audiences who heard his performances. He sang in seedy bars and ghetto theaters in the Midwest as the Depression made money scarce in every segment of the population, but scarcest in the black community. Thus, Turner had to augment his income from performing by a series of odd jobs. The day of gala, nationwide tours for blues artists was still far off. Nonetheless, his reputation extended far beyond his local area. Not only was he known as a top-flight singer, but other artists already were becoming interested in his songs, such as his 1930s "Cherry Red." (Among his many compositions later covered by other artists were "Hold 'Em Pete," "Piney Brown," and "Lucille.")

As far as is known, there are no recordings extant of Turner's early 1930s style. By 1938, when he made his first commercial recordings, he was an exponent of boogie-woogie, demonstrating considerable skill as a pianist. Gaining recognition from both black and white fans, Big Joe appeared in the legendary 1938 "Spirituals to Swing" concert at Carnegie Hall in New York and in 1941 even played with Duke Ellington.

However, as boogie-woogie began to go out of style (along with the big bands that had helped bring it popularity), Turner sought something else to do in music. Executives of the then-young Atlantic Records saw possibilities of grooming Turner as a rhythm & blues singer and signed him in 1951 when he was 40. Company co-founder Ahmet Ertegun provided the lyrics for ''Chains of Love'' (a song by Van Walls) and had Turner record it. The ballad sold steadily for several years in the U.S. and England, finally passing gold levels in 1954.

For the next five years, Turner was rarely absent from the highest levels of the R&B charts and also turned up on the pop charts. In 1952, he had a top 10 R&B hit with ''Sweet Sixteen'' and scored again in 1953 with ''Honey Hush.'' In 1954, he was the first to succeed with still another rock classic, ''Shake, Rattle and Roll'' (later a massive hit for Bill Haley), and with Elmore James also turned out the top 10 R&B hit ''TV Mama'' (revised years later by Johnny Winter). By then, billed as ''boss of the blues,'' he was a welcome sight to R&B audiences throughout the country. His baritone voice seemed to make a theater pulsate with energy. In 1955, he hit with ''Flip, Flop & Fly.'' In 1956, radio stations all over the U.S. were playing his updated version of an old Negro blues song, ''Corinna Corinna.''

After this, although his pop recording successes were few, Turner continued to captivate audiences, especially jazz fans, at major festivals and clubs all over the world for the rest of his life.

Through the years, his dozens of albums covered styles from roots blues to jazz and rock. Among his Atlantic albums were *Joe Turner, Rockin' the Blues* (1958), *Big Joe is Here* (1959), *Big Joe Rides Again* (1960), *Boss of the Blues*, and *Best of Joe Turner* (1963). Savoy Records put out *Joe Turner and the Blues* and *Careless Love*. In late 1971, as part of its rock'n'roll revival series, Atlantic issued most of Turner's hits of the '50s in the *Joe Turner His Greatest Recordings* LP.

Even as the Atlantic reissue appeared, Turner was still winning new followers as a featured member of the Johnny Otis Show into the mid-1970s. *(See Otis, Johnny.)* He then went back to performing mostly as a soloist.

During the 1970s, a variety of labels issued his albums, most of which were no longer in print in the 1980s. These included the United Artists collections *Joe Turner Turns on the Blues, Still Boss of the Blues,* and *The Soul of Big Joe;* MCA's *Early Big Joe;* Black and Blue Records' *Texas Style;* Big Town Records' *Really the Blues;* and Spivey Records' *Big Joe Turner.*

In the 1980s, Big Joe continued strong despite his years, touring, putting out *Blues Train* (Muse, 1983) with the younger-generation Roomful of Blues assemblage, and appearing in *The Last of the Blue Devils* (a 1980 documentary film on long-ago Kansas City jazz). He died of kidney failure near his Los Angeles home in 1985. Still, the spectrum of his mu-

sic remained available on *Jumpin' the Blues* with Pete Johnson's Orchestra (Arhoolie, 1962), . . . *And the Blues'll Make You Happy Too* (Savoy), and numerous 1970s–80s albums on Pablo, including *In the Evening, Things That I Used to Do, Every Day I Have the Blues, Midnight Special, The Bosses* (with Count Basie), and *Kansas City Shout* (with Basie and Eddie ''Cleanhead'' Vinson). As for two-disc reissues, *Have No Fear, Big Joe Turner Is Here* (Arista, 1977) provided 1945–47 tracks, while *Rhythm & Blues Years* (Atlantic, 1986) contained 1951–59 sessions.

TURNER, TINA: *Singer, dancer, songwriter. Born Nutbush Borough, Tennessee, November 26, c. 1939.*

The saga of Tina Turner, if it were presented as a fictional book or film, might strain the audience's credulity. Who would believe that a girl who chopped cotton as a child would go on to attract the attention of a successful band leader and form one of the top pop music teams in the world, or that they might part company, leaving her penniless? Who would then believe that she would stage a comeback to become an even bigger star on her own? But to think she could achieve that when almost 50 years old in the youth-dominated pop/rock field—in the process, becoming both a sex symbol and vocal superstar for fans in the teen and college age brackets—that does seem unlikely. Except, of course, it's all true.

Born Anna Mae Bullock in the borough of Nutbush near Memphis, Tennessee, she brought her birthplace worldwide fame in 1973 with her composition ''Nutbush City Limits.'' Recalling her childhood, she told David Thomas for an article in *The Face* (January 1984): ''There are still three stores in the town and a gin house. There's a church house, but only for the white people, and an outhouse which basically is for the poor people. In all the local communities, the white people own the land and the black people work the crops. It's on Highway 19—just a single track with a yellow line down the middle. . . .

''Every day you went to the fields, whether you were doing the corn or just the regular cultivating or picking cotton. My daddy was the caretaker on the plantation. People worked for him and he answered to the boss. But I actually worked in the fields.''

Her talents as dancer and singer showed through even at a young age. Before she was in her teens, she performed with trombone player Bootsie Whitelaw at local dances and picnics. Then her family moved to Riplea, another small town near Memphis. In her early teens, her parents separated and she moved to St. Louis, Missouri, with her mother and sister.

There she caught the ear and eye of established R&B band leader Ike Turner. Still in her teens, she joined him initially as a band vocalist and later, in 1958, as Mrs. Turner. *(See Turner, Ike and Tina.)*.

Their collaborative efforts as performers and writers made the Ike and Tina Revue a major act on both the R&B circuit and the general pop-rock club/concert network. Their breakthrough to crossover from the black market to the mostly white pop-rock realm was helped by the respect given them by rock artists, particularly the English bands of the 1960s. After the Rolling Stones hired Ike and Tina as opening act on their 1969 tour, a close rapport built up between Tina and many British stars that played an important part in her comeback in the 1980s.

Tina remained a mainstay of the Ike and Tina Revue from 1958 until the mid-1970s. But, as she maintained in her 1985 autobiography, *I, Tina*, co-written by Kurt Loder (Morrow, 1986), after a while the marriage steadily deteriorated. Ike, she wrote, not only became more distant, but also increasingly abusive to her both verbally and physically. Finally, she couldn't stand it anymore and walked out on Ike in the middle of a tour in Dallas in 1975. (Ike at the time was in a drunken stupor, she stated.) She only had a charge card and no money, but managed to get help from actress Ann-Margret, with whom she had become friends while filming the Who's rock opera, *Tommy*. For six months, she remained hidden in Ann-Margret's home in Los Angeles because she didn't want Ike, who was searching for her, to find her.

Eventually she got a divorce and set about trying to put her life back together again. It wasn't easy, in part because her sudden departure from the show had angered promoters and booking agents, who lost money when they had to cancel prearranged appearances. Ike and Tina's personal problems were not their concern; they felt Tina had walked out on obligations to them, so for a time many important doors were closed to her.

She still could find work in smaller clubs in the U.S. and her ties overseas remained strong. Into the early 1980s, she concentrated on building up her solo career, typically touring nine months each year and often appearing six days a week. She wasn't out of favor with European promoters, fortunately. Her fortunes at home were helped after a while by her English friends. At the start of the 1980s, Rod Stewart put her on his tour bill and in 1982 she was featured on the blockbuster Rolling Stones U.S. tour. Not only were she and her backing group asked to open for the Stones, Mick Jagger had her come back to do a sizzling duet with him of the Stones' classic "Honky Tonk Women." The two reprised that as one of the show-stopping moments on the July 1985 Live Aid Concert, telecast to a worldwide audience in the hundreds of millions.

Though her professional career had been revived, record-company executives looked askance at her potential, considering her something of a has-been. Once more, her British friends came to the rescue. She was urged and helped in reviving her recording career by both veteran performers and new young artists such as the English group Heaven 17.

She gave David Thomas a 1982 example of moral backing from U.K. stars. "I don't like to know when anyone [special] is in the house because when I do, it gets to me—I forget a line or something. . . . Roger [manager Roger Davies] was nervous and he was pacing around and saying: 'Darling is everything alright?' So I knew something was going on. After the show he said: 'Guess who's here—Keith Richard and David Bowie.' I just started screaming and pictures were taken and it looked like we were having a party, but there was no one in the room except us.

"Afterwards, we all got together and Keith played the piano and we pulled out some songs and Ronnie Wood came by and played guitar. Keith kept saying: 'I'll find you a hit—we've got thousands of tracks we've never used. Do you want to come over to Paris tomorrow—we'll cut some tracks?' I said: 'Keith, we're in the middle of a tour,' but he just went: 'Come on over anyway—no one will mind.'"

But it was relative newcomers, members of Heaven 17, who proved the initial catalyst. They asked her to come to London in 1982 and do a track on their new LP. The song, the Temptations' 1970 hit "Ball of Confusion," was produced by group members Greg Walsh and Martyn Ware. This helped set the wheels in motion for Tina to get a contract from Capitol Records. She asked Walsh and Ware to produce her new version of soul/gospel artist Al Green's composition "Let's Stay Together." It became a top 10 hit in the U.K. in October 1983, chalking up sales of over 250,000 to earn Tina a U.K. Silver Disc Award. Issued in both 7- and 12-inch versions in the U.S., the record reached the R&B top 5 and became a favorite with disco d.j.'s.

Capitol decided this called for a strong push to complete material for a full album. Tina suddenly was engulfed in a whirlwind effort involving eight different songwriters and four producers (including Mark Knopfler of Dire Straits) that provided the new tracks in only two weeks time. The multiplatinum album, *Private Dancer* (May 1984), took the pop world by storm. Backed by videos and concerts that showcased Ms. Turner's phenomenal energy as a hip-shaking, high-stepping dancer and iron-lunged singer with a chorus-line figure, the album spun off hit singles right and left (such as the U.S. pop top 10 title track and "Better Be Good to Me"), while rising quickly to the top of pop charts around the world. The second single from the LP, "What's Love Got to Do with It," made number one in *Billboard* for three weeks starting September 1—almost exactly 24 years after she and Ike had their first charted single, "A Fool in Love." The song's writers, Terry Britten and Graham Lyle, took home the Grammy Award for Song of the Year in a competition dominated by Tina's recording efforts.

She recalled for *Billboard* that when Britten (brought in as a producer by her manager) played her the demo of that song, she almost turned it down, saying she hated the way it sounded on the tape. "He told me that when a song is given to an artist, it's changed for the artist. He said for me he needed too make it a bit rougher, a bit more sharp around the edges. All of a sudden, just sitting there with him in the studio, the song became mine."

In the Grammy Awards for 1984, Tina earned three trophies: Record of the Year and Best Pop Vocal Performance, Female, for the single "What's Love Got to Do with It" plus Best Rock Vocal Performance, Female, for the single "Better Be Good to Me." She also won two American Music Awards and several number one awards from *Billboard*.

During 1984, her career took another turn when she was asked to play a major role in Australian director George Miller's "Mad Max" film series. As Aunt Entity (founder of a post–atomic war wild-west–type city called Bartertown), Tina won high praise for her work in *Mad Max Beyond Thunderdome* (starring Mel Gibson as Mad Max). She also performed two songs in the film that were included on the soundtrack album (Capitol, mid-1985). One, "We Don't Need Another Hero (Thunderdome)" made number two in *Billboard*, while "One of the Living" broke the top 20 in 1985.

But Tina had plenty of other projects to keep her going without worrying about the film's progress. In February 1985, she was one of the 40 top artists who recorded the single "We Are the World" to raise funds to fight hunger in Africa. She also contributed a track, "Total Control," to the *We Are the World* album. On the road around the world, she filmed a live special (with guest artists David Bowie and Bryan Adams) for presentation on the HBO network.

In the Grammy voting for 1985, she was a finalist for Best Pop Vocal Performance, Female, for the single "We Don't Need Another Hero" and for Best Rock Vocal Solo Performance, Female, for the single "One of the Living." The last named earned a Grammy.

Her second solo album, *Break Every Rule* (Capitol, September 1986), was slicker and more consciously oriented toward commercial success than the earlier one, but it still presented an artist at the top of her form. It received mixed reviews from the media, but record buyers brought it platinum status. Its first single, "Typical Male," hit number two in *Billboard*. Another track from the album, "Back Where You Started," won the 1986 Grammy for Best Rock Vocal Performance, Female.

Her "Break Every Rule" tour, which began in late November 1986 with a TV special taped in London, spanned 25 countries and 145 cities in 5 continents before winding up in Osaka, Japan, on March 27, 1988. The Osaka concert, the last of 220 on the tour, included an appearance by Mick Jagger who performed a duet of "Honky Tonk Women" with Tina. Earlier in the week, she had dropped in on his show and sang "Brown Sugar" and "It's Only Rock'n'Roll" with him. After the Osaka performance, Tina insisted she would do no more live concert tours.

The tour served as the basis for the 1988 two-disc set, *Tina Live in Europe!* Earlier she had received a Grammy for her part in "The Prince's Trust All-Star Rock Concert" (along with Elton John, Sting and others), which was voted the Best Performance Music Video of 1987.

In lieu of solo concertizing after 1988, Tina stated she planned to concentrate more on an acting career. She also planned to act as consultant on the autobiographical film of her life planned by Disney, which had purchased rights to *I, Tina*. (See Bowie, David; Dire Straits; Green, Al; Jagger, Mick; Rolling Stones, The; Spector, Phil; Stewart, Rod; Who, The.)

TURTLES, THE: *Vocal and instrumental group. Original members (1965): Howard Kaylan, born New York, New York, June 22, 1947; Mark Volman, born Los Angeles, California, April 19, 1947; Chuck Portz, born March 28, 1945; Al Nichol; Don Murray. Murray left in 1966, replaced by John Barbata, born upstate New York. Portz left in 1967, eventually replaced by Jim Pons. Barbata replaced by John Seiter in 1969. Group disbanded in 1970.* *

In its several incarnations, the Turtles managed to stay among the most successful rock groups in the U.S. throughout the second half of the 1960s. It began basically as a "message"-oriented folk-rock band in the mid-1960s, but changed its style to achieve success. It evolved toward a style reminiscent of some of the early years of rock. In its last years, before it broke up at the start of the 1970s, the band emphasized melody and more singable, noncontroversial lyrics.

---

*Chuck Portz quotes from personal interview with Irwin Stambler.

Four of its founding five—Chuck Portz, Howard Kaylan (born Howard Kaplan), Al Nichol, and Mark Volman—were school friends who began singing and playing guitar together toward the end of their high school years in southern Los Angeles. They continued to perform for parties and dances after they went on to local Los Angeles universities. The fifth member, drummer Don Murray, came from nearby Inglewood High School.

The group began performing as the Crossfires in 1964–65. After an engagement at the local Rendezvous Ballroom, the group got an audition with disc jockey and club owner Reb Foster in early 1965.

As Chuck Portz recalled: "We played for Reb Foster at his Rebellaire Club in Manhattan Beach [one of a number of beach cities below Santa Monica, California]. He hired us to perform there weekends. We'd been playing together for several years, so I didn't get too excited. It was just another place I had to go to on the weekend."

Foster liked them and took over management of the group. He arranged for a recording contract with a new company, White Whale, formed by two former distributors for Liberty Records: Lee Laseff and Ted Fagan. The quintet, which changed its name from Crossfires to Turtles for its debut album, was the first on the firm's roster. In the summer of 1965, the Turtles' version of Bob Dylan's "It Ain't Me, Babe" made *Billboard*'s top 10. Singles "Let Me Be" and the raga-rock "Grim Reaper of Rock" and LP *It Ain't Me, Babe* also made the charts in 1965–66.

After "Grim Reaper of Love," Don Murray left and was replaced on drums by John Barbata (a veteran of several years with other rock groups and later member of Jefferson Starship). Best selling albums of 1966–67 included *You Baby, The Turtles Present the Battle of the Bands,* and *Happy Together* (whose platinum title song—by far the Turtles' biggest single—rose to number one in March 1967). The group followed with top 10 singles "She'd Rather Be with Me" in 1967 and "Elenore" in 1968. Just after "Elenore" was released, Chuck Portz left. He stressed: "I was just tired from the constant demands of touring—living out of a suitcase, always on a train or plane or in a car, never calling your soul your own." He left the music field altogether, returning to UCLA for a while and later working for the Sea World aquarium complex in San Mateo, California. His place was taken by a musician named Taylor, who left and was replaced at the end of the 1960s by former bass player of the Leaves, Jim Pons.

Alongside their 1969 top 10 single "You Showed Me" their late '60s–early '70s album credits included *Wooden Head, Turtle Soup* (produced by Ray Davies of the Kinks), *Golden Hits* (gold), and *More Golden Hits*. The lineup during 1969 and early 1970 was Kaylan and Volman on vocals, Nichol on lead guitar, Pons on bass, and Jim Seiter (previously with Spanky and Our Gang) on percussion.

In 1970, the group made its final tour and disbanded, primarily due to financial disputes with White Whale that ended up in bitter legal battles. Volman and Kaylan joined Frank Zappa's Mothers of Invention.

Afer a few years with Zappa, Kaylan and Volman started a new act, the Phlorescent Leech & Eddie, which first surfaced with a 1972 debut album on Reprise, *The Phlorescent Leech & Eddie,* followed by a well-received tour with Alice Cooper. Their band included Jim Pons on bass, Aynsley Dunbar on drums, and Gary Rowles on guitar. The act's name evolved into Flo and Eddie. In March 1973, Reprise issued *Flo & Eddie,* which unfortunately was not a success with record buyers though it contained many fine tracks.

As Flo and Eddie, Volman and Kaylan continued a variety of activities, from concerts with different groups of backing musicians to writing work that in the mid-1970s included a "Blind Date" column in *Phonogram* magazine, fictional satire for *Creem,* and even a lovelorn column for the *L.A. Free Press.* For a while, they hosted a popular two-hour radio show on KMET-FM in L.A. called "Flo & Eddie by the Fireside," which combined playing parts of old records with typically humorous interviews with rock and pop stars.

In the mid-1970s, the duo signed with Columbia Records, which issued *Moving Targets* (1974) and *Illegal, Immoral and Fattening* (1976). In 1981, Epiphany Records released *Rock Steady with Flo and Eddie.* Sire Records put out the *Turtles' Greatest Hits* in 1974 with liner notes by Flo & Eddie themselves.

In the 1980s, Rhino Records' extensive Turtles/Flo and Eddie reissue series included original albums, material from a final Turtles album that was never completed, the turtle-shaped EP *Turtlesized,* and the three-disc *The History of Flo & Eddie and the Turtles.* (See *Jefferson Airplane, The; Kinks, The; Mothers of Invention, The; Zappa, Frank.*)

TWISTED SISTER: *Vocal and instrumental group from Long Island, New York. Members (mid-1980s): Dee Snider, Jay Jay French, Eddie Ojeda, Mark Mendoza, A.J. Pera.*

With his elongated features framed by long, stringy hair, Twisted Sister's lead singer and primary songwriter Dee Snider certainly wasn't just another pretty face. But cover-boy looks never have been a prerequisite for rock'n'roll. In fact, Snider's unique appearance helped him to stand out from other guests when he went on the talk-show circuit in the mid-1980s to help publicize his hard-rock band. While that approach tended to keep the other four members of the band in the background, it succeeded in establishing Twisted Sister as a candidate for star status in the competitive world of heavy metal.

Group members, who all picked up experience with diverse high-intensity bands in the New York area in their formative years, came together to form the new band in the late 1970s. With Snider as the central figure, the group slowly increased its stature on the pup/club circuit along the upper eastern seaboard, though there were plenty of lean times before their fortunes took a turn for the better in the 1980s. The group typically used a combination of new songs with revised versions of older rock classics such as the Shangri-Las' gruesome 1964 hit "Leader of the Pack." *(See Shangri-Las, The.)* Their high-decibel treatment of that song was one of the tracks packaged on a 1978 demonstration tape passed around to major labels with high hopes, but—unfortunately—no positive results.

Thwarted in that effort, in 1979 the band released its first single independently, featuring the original song "I'll Never Grow Up Now." The group continued to play anyplace it could line up dates, a move that helped bring it to the attention of European fans in the early 1980s. During that period, Twisted Sister finally got a record deal, but from a U.K. label, Secret Records. That led to release of such LPs as *Ruff Cuts* (with "Leader of the Pack" among its tracks) and the October 1982 *Under the Blade.*

The respect the group was receiving from critics and fans overseas finally opened doors in the States. In late 1982, the band was signed by New York-based Atlantic Records and set to work on its debut album and video for the label. Videos, in particular, proved the stepping stone to success. As Snider later said: "Video is ultraimportant. I think it's as important as the music. I've always said that Twisted Sister is a musical and a visual band. Video was a godsend because it enabled us to show both aspects simultaneously." Besides his riveting performance on those new playthings of the 1980s, Snider also proved adept at using TV in general to get across the image of the group to a broad audience.

The debut video, "You Can't Stop Rock'n'Roll" (April 1983), piqued TV viewers' curiosity about the album of the same title, which wasn't issued until June. Featuring Snider on vocals, Jay Jay French and Eddie "Fingers" Ojeda on dual lead guitars, Mark "the Animal" Mendoza on bass guitar, and A.J. Pera on drums, the album wasn't a best-seller, but it wasn't a failure either, and Snider's willingness to talk at length to interviewers for all types of media paid off in wide exposure for the band.

Snider later said that approach was important to get the ball rolling, but maintained that this would give way to greater recognition of the talents and contributions of the others. "It's kind of like football, where the quarterback is the main guy and seems to be the most important man on the team. In the beginning, everybody talks about the quarterback, but after a while, once they become aware of him, they tend to focus on the other players. It's the same thing in the movies—you can't have a good film without a strong supporting cast, as well as the leading actors. Last year, everybody met me, so to speak. This time, they'll still see me, but at the same time I want them to realize that this is a band that's been together for a long time. And that it wouldn't go on as Twisted Siser without these other people."

The band's second Atlantic LP *(Stay Hungry,* June 1984) was followed in July by the first single and video from the album, "We're Not Gonna Take It." Powered by strong play on MTV and other video outlets, consistent touring, and plenty of Dee Snider TV interviews, the album was platinum in the U.S., New Zealand, Australia, and Sweden and even went quintuple platinum in Canada. Its momentum was aided by two more single/video releases: "I Wanna Rock" (September 1984) and "The Price" (February 1985).

But Snider recognized the psychological problems of trying to match the group's first blockbuster LP. "I saw the writing on the wall and, when *Stay Hungry* started breaking big, I realized that it was going to be a hard act to follow. So, while we were on tour I was always making notes, thinking of ideas and directions.

"I think that one of the biggest problems I discovered with success is that you start doubting and questioning yourself and the things you believed in all along. With *Stay Hungry,* it was a case of: 'You made it, you proved it, you had what it takes, you had the right ideas, and everything you believed in was correct.' Then all of a sudden, you start to question those same things that got you where you are, which is sort of ridiculous. And I had to keep fighting back those feelings and say to myself: 'Go with what you know.' But even so, I was much more critical about the music for the new album than ever before. I must have written 100 songs for the album and 90 of them weren't used."

For those that finally were selected, Jay Jay French noted, there was an effort to try to vary the content somewhat. "I don't see why metal bands should be restricted to three-chord bashing. The fact of the mattter is that, within the context of the new album we do have four or five absolutely wild, no-nonsense metal songs that are just the best that Dee has ever written. But along with them, he has fully expanded his creativity and the band has pushed ahead. And that's important for us. The fans know and expect that the three or four songs that might get played on the radio aren't necessarily the heaviest on the album. But at the same time, I think that the fans are more open to different styles of music these days.''

Before that album came out, Atlantic reissued Secret Records' 1982 album, *Under the Blade,* in June 1985 in a remixed version with the song "I'll Never Grow Up Now" added. It spent some time on the charts, but wasn't a major success. The band's third Atlantic LP, *Come Out and Play* (November 1985), was on the charts by year-end. Its first single and video was familiar to Twisted Sister followers: "Leader of the Pack."

To further support the new project, Atlantic issued a long-form video of *Come Out and Play* in January 1986. A long-form *Stay Hungry* video also was on dealers' shelves, issued under the Embassy aegis in the U.S. and Virgin label in other countries. In 1987, Atlantic issued a new studio LP, *Love Is for Suckers.*

UB40: *Vocal and instrumental group from England. Members (1985): James Brown, Ali Campbell, Robin Campbell, Earl Falconer, Michael Virtue, Astro, Ruby Turner, Mo Birch, Josh Fifer, Brian Travers, James Graham, Norman Hassan.*

UB40's brand of ska/reggae rock gained the band acceptance on its own terms even though the group's approach violated accepted music-industry "wisdom." A reggae band from outside Jamaica, the knowledgeable people said, could never really sound "authentic" even if everyone in it were black. UB40, formed by English musicians, was multiracial in makeup and, in addition, its main front men were white. Yet even though the group avoided such typical reggae subjects as the Rastafarian religion and symbolism of *ganja* (marijuana), its music had the true feel of reggae. Though the subject matter was linked to people and events confronting U.K. citizens, the sense of protest and idealism was in the spirit of reggae artists such as Bob Marley and Burning Spear.

The band moved into public view in England at the end of the 1970s as part of a musical ferment that spawned the punk/new wave movement and a simultaneous upsurge of interest in West Indies–type artists. Typically, many of the U.K. bands that played ska and/or reggae material were larger than conventional rock bands because such groups used sizable brass sections to provide an R&B kind of base to arrangements. Many bands slimmed down as the ska revival faded, but UB40 was still a stage-filling oper-

ation in the mid-1970s when it had from 8 to 12 musicians on its regular roster.

The band opened the 1980s with a best-selling album on British charts, *Signing Off* on Graduate Records. The single "Signing Off" also was a 1980 hit in the U.K. Over the next few years, the group became a major concert attraction in Europe and its name was rarely absent from the hit charts in those places. In 1981, it made the album charts on the Deptford Fun City label with *Present Arms* and *Present Arms in Dub.* In 1982, it had the hit album *UB44* on Deptford and was on the charts in 1983 with *The Singles Album,* a compilation of 1979–80 Deptford material. Among the band's song targets were British Prime Minister Margaret Thatcher (savaged in the song "Madame Medusa"), the dangers of nuclear war in "The Earth Dies Screaming," and the high U.K. unemployment rate, particularly among young people, in "One in Ten."

While the band scored one hit after another at home, through 1983 its recordings only were available to American record buyers as import items. The reluctance of U.S. firms to sign the group reflected pessimism that there was enough of an audience for any but a few Jamaican reggae bands to make such a venture profitable. Finally, A&M Records decided it was worth the gamble and signed the band for U.S. distribution. In the fall of 1983, the band's label debut, *Labor of Love,* came out in the U.S. A&M officials were pleasantly surprised to find that American fans could pick up on UB40's offerings, as the LP reached RIAA gold levels in 1984. The band roster then comprised Ali and Robin Campbell (vocals, guitar); James Brown (drums); Earl Falconer (bass); Norman Hassan (percussion, trombone); Brian Travers (saxophones); Michael Virtue (keyboards); Astro (trumpet, vocals).

The next LP, *Geffrey Morgan,* entered *Billboard* charts in November 1984 and remained on them into 1985. It was followed by *Little Baggariddim* (A&M/Virgin, summer 1985), which was on U.S. LP lists into early 1986. Popularity back home was evidenced by its late 1985 U.K. top 20 single (written by band members) "Don't Break My Heart" on Deptford/Virgin.

In the late summer of 1986, the group had another album doing well on U.S. and U.K. charts—*Rat in the Kitchen.* With principal lead singer and guitar player Ali Campbell and lead guitarist Robin Campbell the focus of attention, the band backed that LP with a cross-country U.S. tour. Shows included reggae versions of classic rock songs such as Sonny and Cher's "I Got You Babe" and Neil Diamond's "Red Red Wine" plus band originals "If It Happens Again," "Don't Break My Heart," and "All I Want to Do."

After seeing the group's L.A. show, Chris Willman commented in the *Los Angeles Times* (September 18, 1986): "Longtime reggae champions tend to agree that it's something of a miracle that any reggae band has made it big among teens here. But while some think UB40's success speaks well for the open-mindedness of the young . . . crowd that had adopted tthe group as its own, others are suspicious. A band whose two most visible frontmen are white, now playing for a predominantly white and trendy audience, must have sold reggae out somehow. . . .

"It may be true that UB40 wouldn't enjoy its current level of popularity if its principal lead singer wasn't an adorable gum-chewing blond [Ali Campbell], but it would be a mistake to try to equate this band's success with Pat Boone singing Little Richard and Fats Domino safe for the world three decades ago.

"The band's current show and latest album find UB40 sticking to the real thing, holding to that familiar beat and topical themes while resisting what must be a strong commercial temptation to smooth out some of the style's rough rhythmic edges."

The group was one of many Western bands to take advantage of relaxed prohibitions against pop acts by Soviet authorities in the mid and late 1980s. Some of its performances in the Soviet Union were captured for the album *Live in Moscow* (A&M 1987).

URIAH HEEP: *Vocal and instrumental group, all born England. Members (late 1971): Ken Hensley, born August 24, 1945; Dave Byron, born Epping, Essex, January 29, 1947; Mick Box, born Walthamstow, June 8, 1947; Mark Clarke, born Liverpool, July 25, 1950; Lee Kerslake. Gary Thain replaced Clarke in 1972 and was replaced by John Wetton in 1974. Byron left in 1976, replaced by John Lawton. Wetton replaced by Trevor Bolder in mid-1970s.*

One of the more promising new rock groups to be formed in England at the start of the 1970s, Uriah Heep demonstrated its potential by effecting an almost complete change in style from its first album to its second. The former's title, *Very 'Eavy, Very 'Umble*, was, of course, Dickensian and also denoted the fact the group used a relatively simple, bass-loaded "heavy" style. *Salisbury*, issued later in 1970, was more sophisticated, with considerable latitude for individual solos. The 16-minute title track was backed by a 26-piece brass and woodwind orchestra.

Though the band started out with simple group arrangements, the musicians brought considerably varied backgrounds into the organization. All founding members had played with several groups that had gained some degree of success with English audiences.

Singer Dave Byron and lead guitarist Mick Box, the two organizers, had been performing since their youth. Byron started at the age of eight. "Variety shows, social club events, holiday camps—I've done the lot." He didn't learn an instrument, but already had a number of compositions to his credit by his midteens. At 17, he joined the Stalkers, where he became close friends with Box, working with Mick on arrangements and new songs.

Box started playing guitar at 14 and soon was part of a backup group for two female vocalists. He joined the Stalkers in his midteens and stayed with them for a few years. He was inactive for a while after leaving the band, then worked with Byron in forming the group Spice. Before it broke up at the end of the 1960s, it added bassist Paul Newton, a move causing the dissolution of Paul's previous group, the Gods, and eventually leading to the association of the Gods' co-founder (organist-slide guitarist Ken Hensley) with Uriah Heep. (Hensley's co-worker in the original Gods organization was Mick Taylor, who went on to international fame as the 1969 replacement for Brian Jones in the Rolling Stones.)

Hensley's route to Uriah Heep began in his very early teens when he became guitarist for Kit and the Saracens in Stevenage, England. From there, he went on to a seven-man soul band, the Jimmy Brown Sound, before starting the Gods. After the Gods folded, he joined a band formed by Cliff Bennett that made its debut album under the name Toe Fat. He quit soon after the album was made when Paul Newton suggested he join the newly formed Uriah Heep in February 1970.

Byron and Box were now ready to go with their new band as soon as they settled on a drummer. After several people tried for the job, they finally stayed with Keith Baker, who had gained an excellent reputation for his work with several bands in the Birmingham, England, area.

With Gerry Bron assuming management, Uriah Heep was underway in early 1970, starting with engagements in smaller clubs and soon blossoming out to perform in some of the major rock centers in England.

The group's first LP, *Very 'Eavy, Very 'Umble*, on Vertigo, was released in the U.S. on the Mercury label, which then handled Vertigo's U.S. distribution. It became a best-seller in England in mid-1970 and made the U.S. charts too. The band continued to increase its popularity in England and Europe with highly acclaimed concerts in one city after another.

The LP *Salisbury* was a European and U.S. hit in 1971. During the year, Uriah Heep underwent several changes in membership. First to go was drummer Keith Baker, who was replaced by Lee Kerslake (who also handled vocals). Lee had played with Toe Fat and the National Head Band before moving to Uriah Heep. Late in the year, Mark Clarke took over briefly as bass guitarist. Clarke began playing with the Downbeats in the late 1960s and then moved to Portugal as a member of the country's top rock band, the Pops. He went back to Liverpool to enter the group St. James Infirmary, joining Colosseum in August 1970. When it broke up in November 1971, Mark signed up with Heep.

Uriah Heep ended up 1971 with their third successful LP, *Look at Yourself*. Manager Bron established a new label for it, Bronze, though Mercury continued to release Heep's LPs in the U.S.

In 1972, the group put out the singles success "Easy Living" and gold albums *Demons & Wizards* and *The Magician's Birthday*. Also gold were 1973s LPs *Uriah Heep Live* and *Sweet Freedom*, their first Bronze album to come out on Warner Brothers in the U.S. Later Warners LPs included *Wonderworld* in 1974, *Return to Fantasy* in 1975, *High and Mighty* in 1976, *Firefly* in 1977, and *Innocent Victim* in 1978. Only *Wonderworld* broke *Billboard*'s top 40. In 1976, Mercury issued the retrospective *Best of Uriah Heep*. The group's late '70s album, *Fallen Angel*, was released on Chrysalis. The band lineup as of 1977 comprised John Lawton (previously with Lucifer's Friend) on lead vocals, Hensley on guitar and vocals, Trevor Bolder on bass, Box on lead guitar, and Kerslake on drums.

In the 1980s, the band kept turning out new albums, most of which achieved modest sales. On *Equator* (Columbia, 1985), it comprised Box, Kerslake, Bolder, and, on keyboards and vocals, John Sinclair. Throughout the decade, the band maintained rapport with a core group of fans around the world, marking it as one of the longest-lived rock groups of the post-1970 years.

U2: *Vocal and instrumental group from Ireland. Members: Paul "Bono" Hewson, born 1960; Dave "The Edge" Evans, born 1961; Adam Clayton, born 1960; Larry Mullen, born 1962.*

For its size, the Republic of Ireland has spawned more than its share of popular rock bands compared to much more populous nations. The center of rock activity naturally was in the country's main city, Dublin, whose offspring included one of the most promising new bands of the 1980s, U2. At the start of the decade, some critics went so far as to call the band "the future of rock."

At the time, the members tried to shrug off the predictions of greatness. As lead vocalist Bono Vox (born Paul Hewson) told Jim Green of *Trouser Press*

(March 1982): "We may well be the future of rock, but so what? When I go back to Dublin, to my girlfriend it's more of a distraction that I'm in a band than any big deal—and my old man still shouts at me for not doing the dishes before I go to bed."

All the members were in their midteens when drummer Larry Mullen in 1976 pinned a note on the message board at Dublin's Mount Temple School asking for volunteers to form a rock band. From the responses, he eventually assembled Hewson on lead vocals and guitar; Dave "The Edge" Evans on lead guitar, piano, and vocals; and Adam Clayton on bass guitar.

Hewson recalled for Green: "When we started out, I was the guitar player, along with The Edge—except I couldn't play the guitar. I still can't [though he does do some backing playing]. I was such a lousy guitar player that one day they broke it to me that maybe I should sing instead. I had tried before, but I had no voice at all. I remember the day I found I could sing. I said: 'Oh, that's how you do it.'"

From the start, the goal was to play what its members considered down-to-earth rock rather than emulate "bands in satin trousers who take the money and run." Rock, they maintained, should be "about sweat, about the real world."

When the group began playing for school events and local venues in Dublin in the mid-1970s, the punk movement was in fashion. Hewson stressed: "We weren't a punk band. We were loud and aggressive, so people said: 'Yeah, a punk band,' but we called ourselves U2 to take ourselves out of the usual category of the Sex Pistols, the Clash, even Led Zeppelin—so that people'd hear the name and say: 'What sort of a band would that be, then?'"

For a while, the band performed in an abandoned tin-roofed parking lot in the middle of Dublin and its hard-driving style brought growing numbers of teens to hear them. Word about this helped bring an opening with CBS Records's Irish office and local release of a three-track EP, *U2—3*, late in 1979. The disc became an Irish hit and extended the band's following throughout the Republic. In early 1980, readers of the Irish rock magazine *Hot Press* voted the group number one in five categories.

During that period, the group made its London debut with December 1979 dates in such clubs as the Hope and Anchor and the Rock Garden. For one show, only nine people turned up. In one better-attended performance, band members took note of the way the audience was segmented among different cultists, such as punks, skins, and mods. Hewson commented: "We looked down from the stage and saw all these strange little cliques. . . . All these people in the so-called City of Freedom, y'know, the Permissive Society, trapped in little boxes. It was so sad. And we told them that. We said: 'We're from Dublin and we don't want to become part of your set of boxes, sorry and everything, but that's the way it is.' "

The group then used that as the theme for its single "11 O'Clock Tick Tock," an argument against conformity. By then, U2 had been signed by a new label, Island, which wanted to promote them beyond the confines of Ireland. That single was the band's first U.K. release on the label. The May 1980 disc did well in Ireland as did the follow-up, "A Day without Me," though they weren't U.K. hits. Its October 1980 debut LP, *Boy* (produced by Steve Lillywhite and recorded at Dublin's Windmill Lande Studios), proved one of the most enticing first LPs of the year. Accompanying its release was a new single, "I Will Follow."

The band backed the LP with its first tour of Europe after which, in November 1980, it played its first American concerts in East Coast cities. The band retained its Irish following, though, as shown by its collecting a record of nine firsts in the *Hot Press* readers poll. During July, the band had its first major U.K. singles hit with "Fire."

The band's second album, *October*, came out that month in 1981 and opened at number 11 on U.K. charts. Its song "Gloria" gave U2 its second U.K. hit single.

Those who saw the band's concerts over an extended period of time typically were impressed with how the group tended to broaden and expand the depth and texture of specific songs. Hewson noted to Jim Green: "Live, the songs evolve; they're still evolving. In Dublin, there's a record with an early version of 'Twilight' on the B side. It's a demon version we cut in five minutes literally—and the lyrics are totally different. If you put the two together, they fit; one is the start and one is the finish. I switch lyrics, the band changes things—we go for a bigger, rawer sound."

For his part, he commented: "I'm more interested in creating an atmosphere, an environment, than I am in telling a story, like 'Johnny meets Mary,' etc. Because things take a while to come out of me, they also take a while to sink in. Part of the reason U2 sounds much better a year later than the first time you heard it is that it takes ages before you get a feel for what's happening."

What was happening in 1982 and 1983 was that the band was well on the way to becoming an accepted supergroup worldwide. In March 1982, the band had its third straight U.K. hit single, "A Celebration." Its third LP, *War*, was released worldwide in February 1983 (with U.S. distribution handled by Atco Records). Before that, the single "New Year's Day," issued in December 1982, had become a

U.K. hit and later was the first single from *War* issued in the U.S.

War proved the band's major breakthrough with U.S. fans. Though its previous albums hadn't even broken *Billboard*'s top 40, *War* went platinum, as did *Under a Blood Red Sky* (1983, live) and *The Unforgettable Fire* (late 1984). "(Pride) In the Name of Love" (late 1984) became U2's first single to make *Billboard*'s top 40.

The band's fortunes continued to improve in the late 1980s. In 1987 it had the multi-platinum hit album *The Joshua Tree* and two back-to-back number one singles, "With or Without You" and "I Still Haven't Found What I'm Looking For." Its 1987 concert tour, according to *Pollstar*, a newsletter on concert itineraries and grosses, rolled up the biggest total gross of the year—a tasty $35 million. *Joshua Tree* won the Grammy for Album of the Year and also earned U2 the British industry award for top international group) and the album's title song also got the Grammy for Best Rock Performance by a Duo or Group with Vocal for 1987.

In 1988, U2 fans could find a biography of the band in book stores (*Unforgettable Fire* by Eamon Dunphy, Warner Books). The band continued to appear for what it felt were good causes in 1988, taking part in the London Freedomfest concert against South Africa's apartheid system. In the fall of '88, Island issued a superb new two-disc soundtrack LP, *Rattle and Hum*, from the performance film of the same name.

VALENS, RITCHIE: *Singer, guitarist, songwriter. Born Pacoima, California, May 13, 1942; died Mason City, Iowa, February 3, 1959.*

The first Chicano rock star, Ritchie Valens might well have been one of the important artists of the 1960s had he lived. But he died almost before he had a chance to get started on his career.

He was born Richard Valenzuela in Pacoima at the far end of Los Angeles' San Fernando Valley. At 17, he gained an audition with Del-Fi Records in Los Angeles and was signed by that firm. Soon after, one of his first singles, his composition "Come On, Let's Go," gained considerable airplay in the western states, providing Ritchie with a regional hit and a small reputation among teenage fans in other sections of the U.S. Shortly after this, Ritchie wrote and recorded the top 10 "Donna" (a song for his girlfriend). Its flip side, "La Bamba" (an adaptation of a Latino folk dance), was also a success.

In early 1959, his engagement calendar called for an extensive tour with several other rock stars, including Buddy Holly and the Big Bopper (J.P. Richardson). In Clear Lake, Iowa, Holly and his sidemen—tired of traveling in a cold, crowded bus—chartered a small plane to get them to their next gig in Fargo, North Dakota. The Bopper talked Holly's bassist (future country star Waylon Jennings) out of his seat. As John Goldrosen and John Beecher relate in *Remembering Buddy* (Penguin, 1987), Valens had never flown in a small craft and eagerly pestered Holly's guitarist, Tommy Allsup, for his seat. Allsup flipped Valens' new half-dollar. Ritchie called heads and won. The plane crashed almost immediately after takeoff in the snowy night. All aboard—Holly, the Bopper, Valens, and crew—were killed. It was, as Don McLean sang years later in "American Pie," "the day the music died."

Using the original Del-Fi logo, in the 1980s, Rhino Records reissued Valens' entire recorded output on *Ritchie Valens, Ritchie*, and *Ritchie Valens in Concert at Pacoima Jr. High* and in a three-disc boxed set, *The History of Ritchie Valens*. Yet to many, he remained little more than a footnote in the tragedy of Buddy Holly's death. That changed in 1987, when Valens' memory too was restored in Columbia Pictures' entertaining film biography *La Bamba*, written and directed by Chicano Luis Valdez and starring Lou Diamond Phillips as Ritchie. Latino artists Los Lobos and Carlos Santana provided music for the film on the man who moved their people's ethnic music into the rock mainstream. The soundtrack LP on Slash Records included Brian Setzer as Eddie Cochran and Marshall Crenshaw as Buddy Holly. (*See Holly, Buddy; Los Lobos; McLean, Don; Richardson, J.P.; Santana.*)

VALLI, FRANKIE: *See Four Seasons, The.*

VAN HALEN: *Vocal and instrumental group. Original members: David Lee Roth, born Bloomington, Indiana, October 10, 1955; Eddie Van Halen, born Amsterdam, The Netherlands, January 26, 1957; Alex Van Halen, born Amsterdam, The Netherlands, May 8, 1955; Michael Anthony, born Chicago, Illinois, June 20, 1955. Roth left in 1985, replaced by Sammy Hagar.*

Though none of its founding members actually was born in California, Van Halen seemed to personify the hard-edged sound of Los Angeles rock in the late 1970s. Long before the group gained international acclaim, its unique potential seemed obvious to many local observers. As Irwin Stambler predicted in his "Pop, Rock & Soul" column in early 1978: "Van Halen . . . has all the earmarks of a major group of the future. Their just released debut album has all the high intensity of roots rock combined with a polish that matches that of groups with years of recording experience."

That musical savvy did not accrue overnight. While all four members of the 1978 group were only in their early twenties, they had been performing together for almost five years and had been active with amateur bands for several years before.

The Van Halen brothers, who were born in Holland, had been given classical piano lessons by their parents as children. After the family moved to Pasadena, California, in 1968, however, the boys quickly were turned on to rock American style and started to play appropriate instruments. At first, Eddie tried his hand at drums and Alex played guitar, but by the time they began assembling combinations with Pasadena High School friends, Alex had become the drummer and Eddie was developing the skills that would make him one of the most vibrant, pace-setting guitarists in rock.

Like the Van Halens, David Lee Roth and Michael Anthony were born outside California—in their cases, in the U.S. Midwest—but were taken to the Los Angeles area as children. In their teens, both joined friends in high school rock bands—bass guitarist Anthony at Arcadia High School and lead vocalist Roth at Pasadena's Muir High School. Their paths crossed and recrossed as their groups performed for local parties and dances. After a while, the four came together to form a new band, originally called Mammoth. As the group moved into the professional music sphere, they had to change the name because another band already had claims on it. Thus, the band renamed itself Van Halen.

Recalling those early days for Robert Hilburn of the *Los Angeles Times* (July 11, 1978), Roth said: "We were all local yokels from around Pasadena. . . . We were all playing in local bands—not really bands, just teenage stuff. They were the kind of groups that'd change members every two weeks. But I wanted to get serious about it. I wanted to be in a real band, make records, travel, and do all that stuff. The Van Halens were always around. We were archrivals so it was only natural that we should eventually get together."

The new foursome cut its eyeteeth in 1974, beginning years of hard work on rock's back roads before Los Angeles disc jockey Rodney "the Killer B" Bingenheimer caught their act one night and helped start them on the road to superstardom.

By then the band had evolved its special style from hundreds of dates in small or obscure clubs and bars. Roth told Hilburn in 1978: "We used to do shows everywhere [around Southern California]. We played in Glendora at Louie's Night Gallery, which was the size of this table. It was so small we used to tape my wallet to Alex's snare drum to keep it from being too loud. . . .

"We played the Rock Corporation in Van Nuys and did five shows a night of hard rock, no slow stuff. We played Gazzari's on the Strip, the Smokestack in Redondo Beach. We'd work five nights a week, seven nights a week, 23 nights a week . . . But we always felt we were moving ahead. From the minute we started, we felt we could make it. We thought: 'We're cool now and we're going to be cooler.' That's why we never even bothered to take a demo tape around to record companies. We figured if we were really good, people would tell other people about us and someone from the record companies would finally pick up on what we were doing.''

One path the group took to attract an audience was to gamble on sponsoring its own show at Pasadena Civic Auditorium in 1976. At the time, the group had none of the conventional trappings of an upwardly mobile band—no manager, agent, or record contract. Band members paid for flyers which friends helped pass around at major rock concerts and local high school campuses. Over a period of months and with a number of band-financed concerts in Pasadena and later in Orange County, Van Halen developed a small, but enthusiastic following. That, in turn, helped bring engagements at more prestigious clubs in the area. Once Bingenheimer took up their cause, record-company executives grew curious about the still underground group.

Bingenheimer helped them line up performances at clubs in Los Angeles proper that then were major showcases for rising rock performers. During a show at the Starwood, Warner Brothers executives Mo Ostin and Ted Templeman were overwhelmed by the band's intensity and the audience's rousing approval. With new demo tapes in hand that had been financed by Gene Simmons of Kiss, the Warner Brothers officials gained company approval to sign the band. Roth commented: ''We always knew we'd be discovered, but when it happened it was right out of the movies.''

The debut LP, *Van Halen* (November 1977), was accompanied by a single, ''You Really Got Me,'' which got unexpectedly heavy airplay and buyer response. Aided by that, the album also made the charts worldwide, eventually going triple platinum.

The question remained, of course, whether the band could sustain its recording momentum. Would the second LP represent a step forward? Would it add to the band's repertoire of audio delights? When *Van Halen II* came out in 1979, the answer was a definite yes, although the multiplatinum album was not 100% top-drawer.

The performance throughout was excellent. David Lee Roth delivered colorful and commanding vocals and Eddie Van Halen's lead guitar work was striking and innovative. Nor was there any complaint about the way Anthony and Alex Van Halen blended their instrumental talents into the whole. The only shortcoming was that such side-one tracks as ''Somebody

Get Me a Doctor'' and ''Gotta Love Again'' lacked substance as compositions compared to the previous album's numbers.

But those discrepancies were more than offset by a majority of new and exciting offerings, such as the fast rocker ''Dance the Night Away.'' The album's second side was first-rate from the torrid rocker ''Light Up the Sky'' to the musically and lyrically intense ''D.O.A.'' (usually an acronym for *dead on arrival* but here subtly changed to *dead or alive*) and short acoustic solo ''Spanish Fly.''

Billboard's review of 1979 rock showed the band to be in the top 5 for album artists of the year; top 10 for overall pop group, overall male artists, and live performances; and holder of two of the top 3 top box-office–draw concerts. In *Guitar Player* magazine's reader's poll for 1979, Eddie Van Halen was voted best rock guitarist.

The band started off the 1980s with the platinum albums *Women and Children First* (1980), *Fair Warning* (1981) and *Diver Down* (spring 1982), all—like their predecessors—produced by Ted Templeman.

The early 1984 platinum LP *1984 (MCMLXXXIV)* included the gold number one ''Jump,'' Van Halen's first top 10 single, which exceeded the success of such other well-received singles as ''Panama'' (1984) and the 1982 ''(Oh) Pretty Woman'' (a cover of Roy Orbison's 1964 classic).

In *Musician* magazine, Roth said that ''Jump'' actually had been written two years earlier by Eddie Van Halen and sat around until Roth finally wrote the lyrics. Roth noted: ''Man, there's so much music, so many snippets of good riffs and bad riffs—who knows what is getting thrown out after awhile?

''Eddie wrote this thing on synthesizer. I really hadn't heard it for a long time, then he laid it down one night in the studio they have at Ed's house. I went in the next day and heard it and it just killed me. It was perfect. And I played it for the people at Warner Brothers, just the track, there wasn't a song. And everybody at Warners flipped out and we went in and cut the track the same way, almost identical.''

He told *Musician* how he wrote the lyrics for that song as well as the others on *1984* in the back of a 1951 lowrider. ''I'd call up Larry the roadie; he'd show up after lunch, we'd hop in the car and go driving off through the Hollywood Hills, up the Coast highway, through the San Fernando Valley. I'd sit in back and write the words for whatever music I had on the cassette. Every hour and a half or so, I'd lean over the front seat and say: 'Lar, what do you think of this?' He's probably the most responsible for how it came out.''

Following the dictum of quitting while you're ahead, after ''Jump'''s phenomenal success, Roth left the group to go solo. It didn't take him long to demonstrate his appeal apart from Van Halen with 1985 singles hits "California Girls" (a top 10 cover of the Beach Boys' standard) and the oldies medley "Just a Gigolo"/"I Ain't Got Nobody." The top 20 "Yankee Rose" (mid-1986) was one of several hit solo videos for Roth. Warner Brothers LPs *Crazy from the Heat* (1985) and *Eat 'Em and Smile* (1986) went platinum.

Meanwhile, Van Halen reorganized with longtime rock star Sammy Hagar taking over Roth's spot beside the other three original members. The new alignment's debut LP, *5150* (Warner Brothers, early 1986), was inferior to previous releases on some tracks, but still caught fire on such numbers as "Good Enough," "Inside," and "Get Up." But *5150* did not moulder on record dealer racks, reaching number one in *Billboard* in April and going platinum, with the first single, "Why Can't This Be Love," making the top 10 the same month.

The band's next album, *OU812*, came out in late May 1988 and was at number one in *Billboard* within a week. On Memorial Day weekend, Van Halen began the "Monsters of Rock" tour joined by three other head-banging groups, Dokken, Scorpion, and Metallica. (*See Hagar, Sammy; Kiss.*)

VAN ZANDT, STEVE: *See Southside Johnny and the Asbury Jukes; Springsteen, Bruce.*

VANDROSS, LUTHER: *Singer, songwriter, arranger, record producer. Born New York, New York, April 20, 1951.*

For years, Luther Vandross was one of the best-kept secrets in popular music. Few people outside the industry knew his name, but millions heard his remarkably sensual voice on countless commercials (many of which he helped write as well) and on backing vocals for recordings and live performances of other artists such as Chic and Bette Midler. During the 1970s, he also gained status in the record field as a sensitive and innovative record producer in the soul and pop fields. In the 1980s, however, he came out of the shadows to establish himself with the general public as one of the finest interpreters of his own and other writers' songs.

He was interested in pop and soul music as a child growing up in the Alfred E. Smith Housing Project in lower Manhattan. His family, for the most part, was musically inclined and his mother saw that he began piano lessons when he was only three years old. He told David Hinckley of the *Los Angeles Daily News* (November 7, 1982): "Her influence was incredible, but subliminal. My brother would get a bicycle for Christmas; I would get Aretha [Franklin] records." Also an influence on his development was his sister, who sang in vocal groups in her teens.

He recalled standing in front of the mirror at home in his early teens singing the soul hit "My Girl" and imitating Temptations dance steps. He also demonstrated a phenomenally good musical ear. For instance, he could identify vocal traits of backup singers on recordings. "I heard Aretha's 'Ain't No Way' and I immediately thought those were the same backup voices as on Wilson Pickett's 'Mustang Sally.' It seemed obvious to me: the same tonality." The singers were indeed the same—the Sweet Inspirations. This ability proved very helpful in his future arranging and producing activities.

He dabbled in music during his high school years, but didn't think of it as an occupation at the time. He went on to college in the late 1960s, but decided after a while that music interested him more. He was already writing original songs and figured that his voice would help get him work as a backing singer at recording sessions. From time to time, he made efforts to break out of that lucrative, but restrictive area, helping form or joining a number of groups in the '70s such as Luther, Bionic Boogie, and Change. Some of those made promising recordings, but failed to generate enough momentum for Vandross to drop his other commitments.

A milestone came in 1974, when his growing contacts in the music industry brought an invitation to watch David Bowie cut some tracks for his *Young Americans* album. During a break in the work, Bowie happened to overhear Luther telling a friend about changes he thought could be made to achieve more impact. Liking what he heard, Bowie brought Vandross in to do all the vocal arrangements for the album and also had his newfound associate write an original number for him. Later Bowie introduced Vandross to Bette Midler, who was equally impressed. Besides doing arranging work for her, Vandross joined her on tour, singing backing vocals on songs such as "Married Men" and charming the audience with solo spots featuring "Hot Butterfly," "The Glow of Love," and "Searching."

In the late 1970s, he also worked with up-and-coming soul/disco groups such as Chic. He made important contributions in his backing work on Chic's first hit, "Dance, Dance, Dance (Yowsah, Yowsah, Yowsah)." During those years, besides session and concert backing activities, Vandross was in great demand as a writer and singer of commercial jingles. His anonymous voice focused many a TV viewer's attention on all manner of products from foods to auto accessories.

Vandross indicated to reporters in the late 1980s that he felt his solo career might have come about faster if it hadn't been for the roadblocks facing many black artists in the 1970s. He told Hinckley: "It was definitely easier to cross over [from black-music audiences to white] in the '60s. They don't allow black artists to do it now—which is a big irony, because so much of rock and pop was influenced by R&B. When a record like [Aretha Franklin's] *Jump to It* can't cross over, there's something rotten in the state of Denmark.''

He attributed this partly to the rise of '70s disco, which had for many people in the industry become a catchall for black performers. "I can't knock disco, but it's not the be-all and end-all of black music. Artistically, it's just dead wrong to say all black singers sound alike. It's like saying Michelangelo and Peter Max are the same because they're both artists. If you've got to put people in categories, at least make categories where there's some mobility."

The last situation seemed to arrive in he early 1980s when disco, while still strong, lost some of its importance. Significantly, Vandross got his first solo opportunity with a major label when Columbia signed him for its subsidiary Epic in 1980. Almost 30, he didn't intend to let this chance get away; one thing he insisted on was that he write and/or arrange all the material for the LP and also handle production. When his debut album came out in the summer of 1981, it was quickly apparent that he had hit the mark. The collection proved that whatever problems existed for other black artists in achieving cross-overs, it was no difficulty for him. The gold LP, *Never Too Much*, made both black and general pop charts. The title song (its first Epic single) also was a hit on soul and pop lists, reaching number one on all the trade-press R&B charts.

Reviewers of all colors and pop persuasions waxed ecstatic about both the album and Vandross' singing talent. Brian Chin in New York's *SoHo News* (October 6, 1981) stated that Luther's work on the LP was "minutely detailed, like carefully constructed essays, on the first single, 'Never Too Much,' and on 'Sugar and Spice' and 'She's a Super Lady.' In each, he delivers a blizzard of descriptions, actions, motivations, all with thoughtful precision. His magnificent, complex revival of Dionne Warwick's 'A House Is Not a Home' makes the point best: it's not any vocal over effort that makes him such a persuasive singer, but his intelligence and tact. Sure, he'll develop the personality cult that Teddy [Pendergrass] or Peabo [Bryson] did, and he'll thrill all the women with his amazing vocal range, but he's also likely to prove himself a stylist equal to Nat 'King' Cole or Frank Sinatra."

As is usual for a new kid on the block, Vandross started out as an opening act for groups such as Frankie Beverly and Maze, but his sets often over-shadowed the headliners'. Stephen Holden of *The New York Times* commented (November 16, 1981): "Mr. Vandross combined the light-hearted theatrics of an old-time band leader with one of the most impressive pop-soul baritones this listener has heard in a while. . . . The highlight of his set was an extended version of the Dionne Warwick ballad, 'A House Is Not a Home,' which showed off the pure beauty of his voice—a creamy baritone with echoes of Lou Rawls's suaveness, but sweeter and more fluent in its phrasing."

The runaway success of the debut album didn't lure Vandross away from his interest in producing recordings for other artists. He welcomed the chance to work on his boyhood idol Aretha Franklin's gold *Jump to It* (Atlantic, 1982), which became her best received release since the mid-1970s (though not a big crossover success). He also worked with Dionne Warwick on mid-1980s recordings as well as with another soul superstar, Teddy Pendergrass.

His solo career was not hindered in the least by those projects. His second album, *Forever, For Always, For Love* (fall 1982, multiplatinum), was on both black and pop charts. During 1982, Luther had four singles on *Billboard* soul charts, including "Bad Boy"/"Having a Party," and in 1983 was represented by three more soul singles hits.

Playing to ethnically mixed crowds, his shows typically went beyond straightforward presentations of songs to segments that amounted to capsule dramas. It reflected his desire to probe other entertainment avenues to try to broaden audience involvement. His recording popularity continued to sustain itself with platinum Epic LP, *Busy Body* (late 1983) and *The Night I Fell in Love* (early 1985). During 1985, Vandross had three charted soul singles, including "Till My Baby Comes Home," which also reached number 29 on the pop charts.

In late 1986, his new Epic LP *Give Me a Reason* rose to number one on the *Billboard* soul list. The album went gold, as had all his previous Epic LPs, and also finished the year inside the pop top 20, the highest position ever for him on *Billboard*'s pop lists. In late 1986 and in 1987, several singles from the album made the soul charts. (*See Bowie, David; Franklin, Aretha; Midler, Bette; Pendergrass, Teddy; Warwick, Dionne*.)

VAUGHAN, STEVIE RAY: *Singer, guitarist, songwriter, record producer, band leader (TRIPLE THREAT, DOUBLE TROUBLE). Born Dallas, Texas, c. 1955.*

During the 1960s and '70s, the Texas bar and small nightclub circuit was the staging ground for many blues/R&B-rock stars such as Doug Sahm and the Winter Brothers (Johnny and Edgar). The tradition remained alive in the 1980s as demonstrated by guitar whiz Stevie Ray Vaughan's meteoric rise from obscurity to international fame. As *People* magazine noted in 1984: "For a kid who failed music theory in high school, the past two years have been a wild ride from local legend to stardom, from sleeping on club floors to playing Carnegie Hall. If Stevie's dizzy from this sudden height, it ain't showin'."

For Stevie, the die was cast from his childhood in Dallas. His older brother Jimmie, who went on to gain a measure of success with the Fabulous Thunderbirds, was a blues-rock fanatic and active in amateur bands with his friends while Stevie was in elementary school. Before Stevie was eight, he already was being taught guitar chords by Jimmie and had his music appetite whetted by listening to his brother's collection of blues discs. At age eight, Stevie had mastered guitar playing well enough to be accepted as a member of bands organized by older boys. He had more performing credits when he approached teen years than most musicians could point to by their middle or late teens.

From adolescence through high school years, Stevie paid little attention to class work, focusing his energies on performing professionally with Dallas-area bands. Among the groups that welcomed his phenomenal guitar licks from the late 1960s through the early 1970s were the Chantones, Blackbird, and Night Crawlers. When the chance came for somewhat more interesting band work outside the Dallas region at the start of the '70s, Stevie dropped out of high school in his senior year and moved to Austin, Texas, which was still the place he called home in the late-1980s.

In 1975, he joined Austin-based blues/R&B group the Cobras, whose reputation as one of the most exciting local blues bands grew steadily, sparked to considerable degree by the intricate string work of its young lead guitarist. Feeling more confident about his audience rapport, Stevie left the Cobras in 1977 to form his own R&B revue, Triple Threat. Though there were rough periods when engagements and performance money was hard to come by, Stevie kept things going until 1981, when he disbanded the group with a view toward incorporating blues and R&B themes into a more hard-driving rock format.

The vehicle he chose for that was a "power-trio" concept somewhat in the tradition of that "little ol' band from Texas," ZZ Top. For his new act, Stevie Ray brought in bass guitarist Tommy Shannon and drummer Chris Layton. The backing twosome was given the name Double Trouble after a song in blues singer Otis Rush's repertoire. (Rush had made some of his best recordings on a label called Cobra, incidentally). In the trio's early period, it wasn't easy finding work or financial support, but slowly the group began to pick up a following in Texas among blues-rock fans, to a considerable extent by word of mouth.

As the band's musical peers sang their praises, chances arose for Stevie and Double Trouble to perform in small clubs and as opening act in places outside Texas. This exposure finally brought an opportunity for the trio to go overseas to Switzerland in mid-1982 for the annual Montreaux Festival. They proceeded to take full advantage of what festival organizers had seen as a relatively minor role in the event. It truly was a rags to riches story. As James McBride wrote in *People*, Vaughan came "roaring into the 1982 Montreaux festival with a '59 Stratocaster at his hip and two flame-throwing sidekicks he called Double Trouble. He had no record contract, no name, but he reduced the stage to a pile of smoking cinders and, afterward, everyone wanted to know who he was."

Montreaux typically lures famous musical personalities and a good share of record-industry executives, which augured well for the trio's future. One of the first to respond was David Bowie, who, after seeing the group's virtuoso performance, asked Stevie Ray to handle lead guitar on his next album, *Let's Dance* (spring 1983), Bowie's debut on a new label (EMI-America) and one of the biggest hits in his career. Meanwhile, the Montreaux showcase had brought other offers for Stevie and his cohorts, including a suggestion by Jackson Browne that the trio record an album at his studio in Los Angeles. Negotiations also got underway with Columbia for a contract, an agreement urged on the company by Columbia record producer and fabled discoverer of new talent, John Hammond.

Ranging from updated versions of roots blues to high-powered blues-rock, the debut, *Texas Flood* (early 1983), was produced by Hammond and released on Columbia's subsidiary Epic. It broke *Billboard*'s top 40 and eventually went gold. At the end of 1983, Stevie Ray made himself felt via a number of awards and readers' polls. Grammy voters provided two nominations: Best Rock Instrumental (for the song "Rude Mood") and Best Traditional Blues Recording. While Stevie didn't win the Grammies, he and Double Trouble did take number one honors in three categories of *Guitar Player* magazine's readers poll. *Texas Flood* was named Best Blues Album and Stevie headed the lists for Best New Talent and Best Electric Blues Guitarist.

For the second album, *Couldn't Stand the Weather* (summer 1984), Stevie and his associates brought to bear other influences, including jazz and mainstream rock on a new version of Jimi Hendrix's "Voodoo Chile" and jazz-flavored "Stang's

Swang.'' It broke the top 20, went platinum, and brought the group a third Grammy nomination.

Stevie and Double Trouble won their first Grammy trophies in early 1985. This wasn't for their Epic album, but for a track on Atlantic Records' *Blues Explosion*, voted Best Traditional Blues Recording of 1984. Besides Stevie's group, that album featured John Hammond, Jr. (son of the CBS executive), Sugar Blue, Koko Taylor & the Blues Machine, Luther ''Guitar Junior'' Johnson, and J.B. Hutto & the New Hawks.

Increasingly, Vaughan was providing original songs to complement his group's versions of blues and R&B numbers written by others. The August 1985 LP, *Soul to Soul* (gold), included his ''Empty Arms,'' ''Life without You,'' and ''Ain't Gone 'n' Give Up on Love.'' By this time, he had revamped Double Trouble to include new member Reese Wynands on keyboards. In voting for the 1985 Grammy Awards, Stevie and Double Trouble were Best Rock Instrumental Performance finalists for the track ''Say What!'' from *Soul to Soul*.

Vaughan in the mid-1980s established credentials as a record producer as well as a performer. Besides producing all the tracks for his second and third albums, he supervised work by other artists, including a comeback collection by blues-rocker Lonnie Mack, *Strike Like Lightning* (Alligator, 1985). When not working with his own band, Stevie liked to sit in with many legendary blues artists. Among those he played with in the mid-1980s were Big Mama Thornton, Albert Collins, B.B. King, Bobby ''Blue'' Bland, Johnny Copeland, and Albert King. (*See Bland, Bobby ''Blue''; Bowie, David; Browne, Jackson; King, Albert; Thornton, Big Mama.*).

VEE, BOBBY: *Singer, guitarist, songwriter. Born Fargo, North Dakota, April 30, 1943.*

There are a number of similarities in the careers of Bobby Vee and Bobby Vinton. Both were born in April, both became teenage idols at about the same time and toured together at the start of their careers, both sang pop ballads rather than rock, and both managed to remain active and reasonably successful performers long after the majority of their contemporaries of the early '60s had been relegated to the sidelines.

Vee, born Robert Thomas Velline, grew up in Fargo, North Dakota. His father, a chef by profession and avid amateur musician, played piano and violin in his spare time. Both of Bobby's older brothers, Sidney, Jr., and Bill, became accomplished guitarists in the mid-1950s and were members of a 15-piece band that performed at local events in the Fargo area. When Bobby was 15, he persuaded his

brother Sid to teach him guitar. With Sid's help, he also learned lyrics to many pop songs of the day.

According to his early bios, the turning point in his career came as a result of the tragic death of Buddy Holly on February 3, 1959, in a plane crash while on the way to an engagement in Fargo. (Some doubts about what happened in Fargo have since been expressed.) According to the story, after Holly died, the Vellines' band was asked to fill in for Buddy's troupe. The group members bought new sweaters and called themselves the Shadows. Since Bobby was the only one who knew a lot of song lyrics, he was appointed lead singer. The Vellines built on that experience to get a recording date in Minneapolis, Minnesota, where Bobby sang ''Susie Baby.'' That disc did well enough for the brothers to revise and record the Clovers' 1956 hit ''Devil or Angel,'' making *Billboard*'s top 10 in 1960 on Liberty Records. Producer Snuff Garrett had arranged for Bobby to record ''Devil or Angel'' in Norman Petty's studio in Clovis, New Mexico, where many of Buddy Holly's classic recordings had been made.

Vee followed that with another top 10 hit, ''Rubber Ball.'' He scored his biggest hit ever with ''Take Good Care of My Baby,'' which reached number one in *Billboard* for three weeks starting September 18, 1961. ''Run to Him'' (1961) and ''The Night Has a Thousand Eyes'' (1962) hit the top 10, while ''Please Don't Ask about Barbara,'' ''Sharing You,'' and ''Punish Her'' (1962) and ''Charms'' (1963) made the top 20. Hit albums included *Bobby Vee* (1961), *Bobby Vee's Golden Greats* (1962), and *The Night Has a Thousand Eyes* (1963). About the same time he made his film debut in 20th Century Fox's *Swingin' Along*.

Though things slowed down in the mid-1960s, Vee still was able to hit the charts with many songs, though none reached the top 20 until 1967's ''Come Back When You Grow Up'' (top 10, gold). During 1969, he made the charts with ''Someone to Love Me,'' and in late 1970 had a minor hit with ''Sweet Sweetheart.''

Vee's consistency as a pop singer was indicated by the longevity of his ties with Liberty Records. Many of his LPs sold steadily, often years after their original release. Among the titles that stayed in the Liberty catalogue into the early '70s were *30 Big Hits of the '60s* (1964), *Bobby Vee Live!* (1965), *30 Big Hits of the '60s Volume 2, Golden Greats Volume 2*, and *Look at Me Girl* (1966), and *A Forever Kind of Love* and *Come Back When You Grow Up* (1967).

Bobby continued to record sporadically during the 1970s. One album, *Nothin' Like a Sunny Day* (United Artists, 1972), was released under his real name, Robert Thomas Velline, and included an updated version of "Take Good Care of My Baby." Though no longer a mass-audience star from the 1970s on, Vee kept busy with dates on the nightclub circuit and some appearances in rock-revival shows. Among his albums in the late 1970s, all out of print by the 1980s, were *Bobby Vee's Golden Greats* (by then on United Artists) and Sunset Records' *Tribute to Buddy Holly* (1978), available in the U.S. as a British import. *(See Holly, Buddy.)*

VELVET UNDERGROUND, THE: *Vocal and instrumental group. Members (1968): Lou Reed, born New York, New York, March 2, 1944; Maureen Tucker; John Cale, born Garnant, South Wales, 1942; Sterling Morrison. Cale replaced by Doug Yule in 1969.*

An unusual group, hated by many critics, idolized by others, the Velvet Underground became one of the most talked about groups in New York in the late 1960s. Though it became legendary, the group never gained mass attention in the course of its existence.

Focal point of the band was lead singer/rhythm guitarist/songwriter Lou Reed, who since went on to stardom as a solo performer. Reed formed the group in the mid-1960s after meeting John Cale who, like Reed, had performed with many local rock groups in the New York area. The band's name was taken from the title of a pornographic paperback Reed had seen. In addition to Cale (who handled vocals, electric viola, organ, and bass), the band included Sterling Morrison (vocals, guitar, bass) and one of the few female performers on the rock scene, percussionist Maureen Tucker.

The band began working in small New York clubs. Appearing at a sleazy night spot in Greenwich Village, the Cafe Bizarre, it was overheard by poet Gerard Malanga, a friend of avant garde artist and filmmaker Andy Warhol. Knowing Warhol was looking for a rock group for a multimedia show called "The Exploding Plastic Inevitable," Malanga brought Andy to hear it, ironically, on the night the band was fired.

Warhol combined the group with the vocal and histrionic effects of German-born Nico, an actress in his movies. The show opened in Manhattan during 1966 under the title Nico and the Velvet Underground. It then toured the U.S. and Canada, drawing a mixed response from critics. Some enthused about the combination of wild visual effects and mostly original music, while others echoed the Los Angeles magazine reviewer who said the "screeching rock'n'roll reminded viewers of nothing so much as Berlin in the decadent '30s."

A major objection of some critics was the subject matter of Reed's songs. "Heroin" and "I'm Waiting for the Man" dealt with smack, "Run, Run, Run" with cocaine, and "Venus in Furs" with sadomasochism. Other topics covered by Reed then and in later songs extended across the full gamut normally avoided in "polite" company including lesbianism, male homosexuality, and transvestitism.

As might be expected, all of this militated against heavy radio exposure for the group's debut album, *The Velvet Underground & Nico* (Verve, 1967). As Reed later told a reporter from the *New Musical Express* (October 14, 1972): "Our references were up front—I laid it out on the line with those songs. No one has come out with statements *that strong*. That album was five years ahead of its time—if it was to be released now it would get the recognition it deserved then."

The group remained together for several years after leaving Warhol's aegis. Reed continued to supply the band with controversial material, including "Sister Ray" (which dealt with a transvestite heroin dealer) on *White Light/White Heat* (Verve, December 1967) and a series of songs (on *The Velvet Undergound*, MGM, March 1969) about Candy, a girl who "wants to know what others talk of so discreetly" and whose adventures take her on a tour, with a junkie boy friend, through the underground culture. Also noteworthy was the long number "Rain," which often went on for tens of minutes during club performances of late 1968 and 1969. The original lineup from 1966 remained intact until 1969, when organ chores were taken over by Doug Yule after John Cale signed a solo artist contract with Elektra Records and later went on to produce LPs for such artists as Patti Smith and Iggy Pop.

Loaded (Cotillion, 1970) was the group's last studio album. Issued after the band broke up were *The Velvet Underground Live at Max's Kansas City* (Cotillion, 1972), the two-disc *1969 (Velvet Underground Live)* (Mercury, 1974), *V.U.* (Verve, 1984), and *Another View* (Verve, 1986).

After the Velvets disbanded, Reed went into seclusion for a while, reemerging in 1972 as a star in his own right. In mid-1972, Doug Yule tried to revive the group without Reed, but as one reviewer noted, it was like a gin tonic without the gin.

In the mid-1980s some of the previous members assembled a new version of the Velvet Underground. Ironically, hardly had that been announced when Andy Warhol died at 58 on February 22, 1987, of complications from surgery. *(See Pop, Iggy; Reed, Lou; Smith, Patti.)*

VENTURES, THE: *Vocal and instrumental group. Original members (1961): Bob Bogle, born Portland, Oregon, January 16, 1937; Don Wilson, born Tacoma, Washington, February 10, 1937; Nokie Edwards, born Washington, May 9,*

1939; Howie Johnston, born Washington. Johnston replaced in 1962 by Mel Taylor, born New York, New York; Nokie Edwards by Jerry McGee in 1967. Johnny Durrill, born Houston, Texas, added in 1968. Members in late 1980s were McGee, Wilson, Bogle and Taylor.

The Ventures had few sudden, fantastic, highs in their career, but neither did they have frustrating lows. Consistency was the hallmark of one of the best rock instrumental groups of the 1960s and one of very few rock bands that could celebrate a tenth anniversary. When this event occurred in 1971, the band could point to an almost unbroken string of albums that sold several hundred thousand copies each. It was a pace that slowed down considerably during the mid-1970s. However, the band, with various rosters, continued active on the concert circuit through the late 1980s.

The group might have called itself the Hod Carriers, because the two founding members—still with the group in the late '80s—had held such jobs at one time. Bob Bogle's route to the Ventures began in Portland, Oregon, where he grew up with three brothers and a sister. In his early years, he was the only one not interested in learning an instrument, while others took up clarinet, piano, guitar, and flute. In Bob's early teens, though, he started teaching himself guitar after his older brother, Dennis, gave him his before he left for the air force.

Bob could play reasonably well by the time he quit school at 16 and found work as a hod carrier (a person bringing wet cement to bricklayers). Eventually he worked his way up to apprentice bricklayer and then head of his own crew in Seattle, Washington.

Don Wilson was born in nearby Tacoma, Washington, where he learned piano at an early age. He later took trombone lessons. He played with army bands after enlisting in the service upon graduation from high school. While stationed in Germany as a member of the 39th Regimental Band, he also played stand-up bass in a dance band on the side. After a friend in need of cash sold him an old guitar, it became Don's favorite and he looked forward to becoming a professional guitarist following his discharge. Band jobs were hard to find, though, so he became a hod carrier, a starting point to a promotion and a transfer to Seattle, where he went to work for Bogle in 1958.

The two became friends and, when Don spotted a guitar in Bogle's car, he suggested they practice together. By then, they had been transferred to Pullman, Washington, where they practiced in the recreation room of their hotel, drawing favorable comments from onlookers. Thus encouraged, they sought and found work in local clubs during 1959. After a short time, they added Nokie Edwards on

lead guitar and Howie Johnston on drums. The year was 1960 and the Ventures were underway. With the help of Don's mother, Josie, the foursome paid for studio sessions to make demonstration tapes. They sent their song "Walk Don't Run" to major record firms and, when nothing happened, Mrs. Wilson put it out on her own label, Blue Horizon. Featuring a wild blend of driving guitars and insistent drum patterns, it became a regional hit. Bob Reisdorf of Dolton Records then offered to handle national distribution using a tie-in with Liberty Records. "Walk Don't Run," issued in November 1960 on Dolton, reached number two in *Billboard* and Dolton became the Ventures' regular label. They followed with a rock version of "Perfidia" that hit number 15.

Their output on Dolton was so great it seemed as though they would quickly wear out their welcome. However, both the artists and Liberty were happy with the growing ranks of Ventures fans' seemingly insatiable desire for their recordings. All of their albums of 1961–62 sold over 100,000 copies; these included *The Ventures, Another Smash, The Colorful Ventures, Twist with the Ventures* (repackaged as *Dance!*); *The Ventures Twist Party,* Volume 2 (repackaged as *Dance! Volume 2*); *Mashed Potatoes and Gravy* (repackaged as *The Ventures Beach Party*); and *Going to the Ventures Dance Party.*

By the start of 1963, the group had its first personnel change, with Mel Taylor taking over from Howie Johnston on drums after an auto accident caused Howie's doctors to advise him getting away from the strain of touring. In 1967, Jerry McGee became lead guitarist in place of Nokie Edwards. After these changes, there were no other variations in the group's lineup into the 1970s, except for the expansion to a five-man band when pianist Johnny Durrill joined in 1968.

The changes had no effect on the group's phenomenal rapport with record buyers. The albums kept moving off the production line and people kept buying them. In 1963, they had such hits as *Telstar/The Lonely Bull, Surfing, I Walk the Line* and *Let's Go.* 1964 successes included *The Fabulous Ventures* and *Walk Don't Run, Volume 2.* There was no let up in the mid-60s with *The Ventures Knock Me Out, The Ventures on Stage, The Ventures a-Go Go, Christmas with the Ventures* (1965); *Batman Theme, Runnin' Strong* (on Sunset Records), *Where the Action Is, Go with the Ventures,* and *Wild Things* (1966); and in 1967, *Guitar Freakout, The Guitar Genius of the Ventures, Super Psychedelics* (on Sunset Records) and *Golden Greats by the Ventures* (on Liberty Records).

Not only were their recordings popular with the general public, they had great impact on other artists. Among those who listened excitedly to the act's steadily evolving musical styles were such later stars as Jerry Garcia (lead guitarist of the Grateful Dead) and Jorma Kaukonen (a moving force behind the Jefferson Airplane). Some of the rhythmic patterns of Quicksilver Messenger Service's 1970 album, *Happy Trails*, can be traced to Ventures recordings of the early '60s. Future professional and amateur musicians alike taught themselves to play guitar from the Ventures' series of training albums in the mid-1960s.

As the '60s drew to a close, though the Ventures did not tour as much as in their early years, they still were innovators and stars. Their albums of the late '60s and early '70s demonstrated new approaches to the use of fuzztone and other electronic techniques in guitar playing, while their musical scope covered such diverse combinations as blues, bossa nova, and calypso.

In 1969, they were right up among the top groups with a top 10 single and gold album based on the theme from the TV show "Hawaii Five-O." Lesser LP hits included *Swamp Rock* (1969) and *Tenth Anniversary Album* (1970). In 1971, the group was represented by its forty-first LP, *New Testament*, and could claim a total of over 20 million copies sold for the previous 40 albums. (*New Testament* appeared on Liberty Records' new parent company, United Artists.)

In 1972, the Ventures made the charts with the albums *Joy: The Ventures Play the Classics* and *Theme from Shaft* and in 1973 had the middle-of-the-road chart single "Skylab." Mid-1970s albums included *TV Themes, The Ventures Play the Country Classics*, and *The Very Best of the Ventures*. After that period, the group no longer had a major-label affiliation, though its name often could be seen as featured act on the club and theater circuit in the late 1970s and throughout the 1980s. The band did gain a little more attention from new generations of pop fans in the early 1980s when it recorded a single, "Surfin' and Spyin'," with the all-girl rock group the Go-Gos. (*See Go-Gos*). The song was written by the Go-Gos. In 1985, the group (comprising founding members Wilson and Bogle and later additions Taylor and McGee) teamed up with L.A. heavy metal lead guitarist Paul Warren for an updated version of "Wipe Out," but no record firm was willing to release it.

The band was not without its supporters in the industry. In 1986, *Guitar Player* named it "the quintessential '60s guitar band" and called its first LP "the album that launched a thousand bands," selecting it as one of the 20 essential rock records. At the end of the 1980s, the group still played an average of 150 concerts a year. As of the end of 1987, the band stated it had sold over 85 million records worldwide, including 40 million in Japan, where it was still considered a superstar group.

VERLAINE, TOM: *Singer, guitarist, band leader, record producer, songwriter. Born Wilmington, Delaware, December 1949.*

As a musical innovator and inspired performer, Tom Verlaine was a major influence on the direction of rock'n'roll in the U.S. and U.K. in the 1970s and 1980s. But it didn't take the form of blockbuster hits or standing-room–only concerts in huge arenas. Instead, it was the result of imaginative and challenging original songs and recordings that fueled the budding punk/new wave movement. More than a few of the new bands who made the charts in the U.S. and England in the 1980s had stylistic elements traceable to earlier Verlaine work.

It wasn't that Verlaine opposed success as such, but his fierce creative independence would not let him compromise his work. He told an interviewer from England's *Sounds* magazine (September 8, 1984): "I'm not a career-minded person," but also indicated he wouldn't have objected to more support from his record companies. "It's not a question of avoiding the limelight so much as what's made available to you. If I was promoted properly, I'd have a larger following, but promotion is something I've never had [though considerable critical attention was paid to his group Television, of course]. Virgin Records did a bit for the [1982] album *Words from the Front*, but only in London. Besides, everybody at the company was telling me that I could forget having a hit with a record that had guitars on it that year because it was the height of the synth [synthesizers] pop boom."

In Verlaine's childhood in Delaware, he wasn't paying much attention to pop music or guitars. His family saw to it that he took classical piano lessons at seven and he recalled sometimes daydreaming while listening to symphonic renditions. Later he became interested in modern jazz and tried to develop such material on the saxophone.

Not until his teens did he pay much attention to rock'n'roll. The first rock record that made him sit up and take notice, he said, was the Rolling Stones' "19th Nervous Breakdown," though he was more interested in poetry than music at the time. Somewhat of an introvert, the shy, gangling youngster was not a top scholar either. His high school class voted him "most unknown."

Once he got out of high school, he gravitated north to New York's East Village in August 1968. He soon found other rootless and restless teens and young adults who had vague interests in literary pursuits, alternative life-styles, and avant garde pop music. Verlaine worked at various jobs, including clerking at the Strand Book Store, while experimenting in his leisure time with poetry writing and occasional informal music sessions with friends.

In 1971, he formed his first band, The Neon Boys, with two Village friends. Verlaine handled guitar and vocals, Richard Hell did bass guitar and vocals, and Billy Ficca (born February 1949) played drums. Ficca was a high school friend with whom Verlaine had played music in 1967. The group only stayed together for a short time before the members each decided to go separate ways with Ficca heading to Boston to play with several blues bands.

Verlaine, who had become steadily more intrigued with guitar playing and original songwriting, remained active in New York as a soloist, giving occasional electric-guitar performances at local venues or in friends' apartments. During an October 1973 show, another young musician in the audience, Richard Lloyd (born October 1951), was impelled to seek out Verlaine in hopes of forming a new band. Lloyd recalled: "As soon as Tom started playing, I knew something in his approach was correct, and I knew I could augment it."

Verlaine brought Hell and Ficca (who returned from Boston) into the new band, which now featured Tom and Lloyd on dual lead guitars. The band members tossed around possible names and finaly settled on Television. "We selected it," Lloyd said, "because it's something that's in every home in America. It's so obtrusive it's unobtrusive."

The band debuted at New York's Townhouse Theater on March 2, 1974. Soon after, Verlaine persuaded the owner of CBGB's in the Bowery, the center of the city's burgeoning new rock revival, to let Television perform regularly on Sunday nights. Within a short time of that showcase opportunity, the band members' peer group was spreading the word that a phenomenally talented combination had appeared. Among those voicing their praises was poetess and soon-to-become rock star Patti Smith, who wrote: "Tom plays guitar like a thousand bluebirds screaming." During 1974, Smith's single, "Hey Joe," came out with Tom providing backup guitar.

The band expanded to a quintet in 1975 with the addition of Fred Smith on bass guitar. Smith (who moved from the band Blondie to Television and in the 1980s joined cowpunk Kristi Rose's Midnight Walkers) had been a fan of Verlaine's band almost from the first time he heard it perform. He liked the challenge of the Television format, he told an interviewer. "In some bands a bassist can relax back in the pocket with the drums, but Tom likes the bass to be melodic, so I have to fit notes into some unusual places."

The band felt its mix was right for a move into recordings and started off with a single they pressed themselves, "Little Johnny Jewel" (issued August 19 on Ork Records, named after group manager Terry Ork). The band naturally tried to get record-company executives interested in them through sending out the usual demo tapes and excellent reviews Television performances were getting from local critics. It turned out to be a slow process. Not until early 1976 did Elektra express some interest, which finally resulted in a contract that July. Its debut album, *Marquee Moon*, was issued the following February. Surely one of the finest debut albums of the mid-1970s, it ranks as one of the best releases of the decade.

Though the band developed a strong cult following at home, its greatest impact was in England. After touring the U.S. as opening act for Peter Gabriel in early 1977, the band went on to England in May where it was wildly applauded at a series of standing-room–only concerts. The album did well with English record buyers and at year-end, *Sounds* called *Marquee Moon* the album of the year while *Melody Maker* voted Television the most promising new act (international).

For the band's follow-up album, *Adventure* (early 1978), Verlaine wrote words and music to all of the songs except "Days," which he co-wrote with Richard Lloyd. The new LP was on a par with the first album and, as in that case, its reception was greater in the U.K. than in the U.S. Within a week after its release, *Adventure* was in the top 10 in England.

But while the outlook still seemed bright for the band, internal and external problems arose to blight its future. Before any plans could be made for a third album, the group broke up and Verlaine began to concentrate instead on a solo career. His first offering, *Tom Verlaine* (Elektra, 1979), indicated he could achieve as much creatively on his own as submerged in a group. His searing, cascading guitar lines compared favorably with some of the best rock guitarists', including Neil Young and the Grateful Dead's Jerry Garcia.

The album was warmly welcomed by most critics, as was his next, the superb *Dreamtime* (Warner Brothers, 1981). Though Verlaine did tour in support of those solo works, publicity was not particularly evident and neither album was a hit. His next albums, *Words from the Front* (1982) and *Cover* (fall 1984), were issued on Warner Bros. in the U.S. and Virgin in the U.K. Both received generally glowing comments from reviewers in the U.S. and England, particular *Cover*, which seemed likely to be bracketed with *Marquee Moon* as among Verlaine's finest contributions to rock.

Allan Jones, for instance, wrote (*Melody Maker*,

September 1, 1984) that *Cover*'s "best tracks . . . whisk you into their orbit even before you've realized how profoundly you've been seduced by the richness and dexterity of their arrangements and the persuasive passion of their keen emotional bias. There's a frankness about this LP . . . an openness, a vulnerability that's attractively exposed, touchingly expressed."

A *New Musical Express* reporter noted a quality of introspection about much of Tom's solo guitar work. Tom replied, "That's true. Have you ever seen film of Coltrane? That was very much an inside sort of situation, not standing back and playing at things . . . the feel of the whole thing became more and more essential.

"Everyone I've ever admired has had good technique. Even Dylan's folk guitar and the way he strummed on it in those early records. The sound of the strum! He was no half-assed player. Simple, but intricate. Stole it off Ramblin' Jack Elliott though.

"I would say this completely seriously. Once a year I'll go back and listen to the last record I made and it seems to me, when I hear my records back, that there's a real obsession with sex! The rhythm content and everything seems to be unconsciously fascinated with sex. All the guitars seem to have a certain amount of pleasure involved. When you listen to the guitar breaks, instead of the usual melodic purpose there's a release of tension."

When Verlaine was giving those interviews, he was living in England, where he had taken up at least temporary residence in 1984. Still, he wasn't planning to make a clean break. He told the *NME*: "There's a time when New York becomes destructive to your work. I could see myself living in Europe . . . but the only thing about Europe is, America still has an incredible wild element that you don't find here. I don't know what Europe's done with it. Maybe England buried it with its empire. I'd like to check out the Mediterranean. Robert Graves threw everything up and went to live there. A certain part of that appeals to me, living somewhere fairly rural."

Tom was still spending much of his time in England (where he ranked as a superstar) when his next album, *Flash Light*, came out in 1987 on the British label Fontana. The LP rightfully was compared with some of the best of the Television years. His guitar patterns were more striking and powerful than anything he'd done on his earlier solo albums and the original songs were among the best he had written. (*See Blondie; Hell, Richard; Smith, Patti.*)

VINCENT, GENE: *Singer, guitarist, songwriter. Born Norfolk, Virginia, February 11,* *1935; died Newhall, California, October 12, 1971.*

Gene Vincent's career paralleled those of many of the first wave of performers who made rock the mainstay of pop music. He rose to fame in a very short time from almost complete obscurity, was a national teen idol for a few years, and then faded from prominence almost as rapidly as he had gained it. Or at least, so it seemed to American observers, because Vincent did retain a considerable following overseas.

Born Vincent Eugene Craddock, he spent his youth in southern, navy-oriented Norfolk, Virginia. His first musical interest was country music and this helped direct his attention to the guitar, which he learned to play in his teens. When the Korean War came along, Vincent lied about his age, enlisted in the navy, and found a ready audience among his shipmates, singing country songs to his own guitar accompaniment. His military career ended abruptly, though, when he was severely injured in the Korean theater.

The exact way he was hurt is something he never fully cleared up. He variously said he stepped on a mine or he was shot in the leg, presumably while ashore on leave. Whatever the circumstances, Vincent lost a leg and was sent home to Norfolk to recuperate and get used to a new artificial limb. He had a good voice, actually better than most of the major stars of the mid-1950s, and his mother suggested that a recording career might be the answer to his problem of earning a living.

Seeking its own counterpart to RCA's new star, Elvis, Capitol Records sponsored a talent search. Contestants had to come to Capitol in California. Gene won the prize (a contract) and cinched his career with a song he wrote en route on the train, "Be-Bop-a-Lula." Years later, he told a reporter: "Me and Don Graves were looking at this bloody comic book. It was called *Little Lulu* and I said: 'Hell, man, it's bebopaLulu.' And he said: 'Yeah, man, swinging.' And we wrote the song. Just like that. And some man came to hear it and he bought the song for $25. Right. Twenty-five dollars! And I recorded it and told all my friends that I was going to get a Cadillac, because all rock'n'roll singers had Cadillacs."

Gene's 1956 record debut reached number seven in *Billboard* and went gold. Its sound was so similar to Elvis's that when Gladys Presley first heard "Be-Bop-a-Lula" on the radio, she congratulated her son on his new hit. Actually, according to some reports, Capitol intended it to be the B side to Gene's panting "Woman Love." Though it's mild compared to rock fare of the '80s, back then most radio stations considered "Woman Love" too suggestive for airplay.

720

It even netted Gene a $10,000 fine for public lewdness and obscenity in Virginia. But Gene was on his way anyhow.

Backed by his four-man Blue Caps (who got their name and trademark from President Eisenhower's blue golf cap), black-leather–clad Gene's "Lotta Lovin'" made the top 20 the next year. "Race with the Devil" and "Bluejean Bop" (1956) and "Dance to the Bop" (1957) also were popular. Albums such as *Gene Vincent Rocks! And the Blue Caps Roll* and *Bluejean Bop!* showed the range of interests and influences on the founding fathers of rock: lean, mean rockabilly alongside country, folk, and even schmaltzy pop ballads.

In the late 1950s, Vincent's success waned in the U.S. though he remained popular in Europe. Near London on a 1960 tour, he was riding with friend and fellow rockabilly star Eddie Cochran and Eddie's girlfriend (songwriter Sharon Sheely). Their chauffeured car rammed a lamppost at a high speed. Cochran was thrown from the vehicle and killed. Vincent survived, but his injuries sidelined him for many months.

After recovering, he made London his home base for the 1960s, earning a modest income from appearances in England and on the Continent. As the decade progressed, he enjoyed English youths' resurging interest in early rock stars typified by Ian Dury's song "Sweet Gene Vincent." In 1969, he signed with Dandelion Records, owned by his friend, English disc jockey John Peel. Since Gene's Capitol contract had expired, Elektra Records agreed to handle U.S. distribution. The LP, *I'm Back and I'm Proud*, was recorded at Elektra's Los Angeles studio in mid-1969, with arrangements by Skip Battin of the Byrds.

On his way back from the sessions, Vincent stopped in Toronto, Canada, to take part in a rock'n'roll revival show that featured such other 1950s greats as Little Richard, Bo Diddley, and Jerry Lee Lewis as well as Eric Clapton, John Lennon, and the Plastic Ono Band. This was so well received that similar shows were presented in many parts of the U.S. in the early 1970s. Vincent performed at a number of these in 1970 and early 1971.

In late 1969, Capitol released an album of Vincent's early work, *Gene Vincent's Greatest!* The following year, the Dandelion/Elektra album and *Gene Vincent* (Kama Sutra) were issued, but none made the hit charts.

Gene's comeback dreams were not to come true. He was living in California in the fall of 1971 when he fell ill and had to be taken to the Inter-Valley Community Hospital in Newhall, suffering from internal hemorrhaging due to a bleeding ulcer worsened by his drinking. Shortly after entering the hospital, he died at age 36 on October 12, 1971.

In the years after his death, there was no lack of reissues of his recordings along with a few numbers that only became available posthumously. Many were only available in the U.S. as import items. They included the 1972 Starline album *Pioneers of Rock* and an eight-volume series of LPs, all titled *The Gene Vincent Story*, released on French Capitol in 1973. In 1974, U.S. Capitol issued *The Bop That Just Won't Stop (1956)*, and later released the 1977 LP *Gene Vincent's Greatest*. Releases on French Capitol included *Gene Vincent and the Bluecaps* (1976) and *Rock'n'Roll Legend* (1977). In 1979, British Capitol put out *Gene Vincent's Greatest, Volume 2*. Other 1970s import items were *Crazy Beat* (French Capitol) and *Rhythm in Blue* on the Canadian Blue Cap label. In England, Charly Records released a ten-disc boxed set, *Gene Vincent: The Capitol Years '56-'63*.

In 1980, four previously unreleased songs by Vincent appeared on the Rollin' Rock label along with a track by his daughter, Melody Jean, and covers of his songs by various other artists on *Forever Gene Vincent*. Record-company head Ronny Weiser told Jim Dawson for a *Los Angeles Times* article that he had made it his business to know Vincent in the artist's declining years because of his great love for his music. Originally from Italy, he said, he had tried to find Vincent for years in the '60s before discovering the singer lived a few blocks from him in 1969 when Weiser had taken up residence in West Hollywood. Vincent was in failing health, he recalled. "I began visiting him several times a week. Gene was a very kind, low-key guy. He was surprised there were still Gene Vincent fans. I knew he was going to die soon, so I asked him to record a few songs and give me the right to release them whenever I formed my label." Gene then sang four songs, accompanying himself on guitar, into Weiser's Sony recorder. For almost a decade, the tapes languished in storage. When Weiser issued them on *Forever Gene Vincent*, he commented: "The time seems right now. Two years ago, nobody cared about rockabilly or Gene Vincent, so the songs would've been wasted." (*See Byrds, The; Cochran, Eddie; Dury, Ian; X.*).

VINTON, BOBBY: *Singer, trumpet player, saxophonist, band leader, songwriter. Born Cannonsburg, Pennsylvania, April 16, 1935.*

Not many teen idols at the start of the 1960s were still active performers decades later, but Bobby Vinton was an exception. As he grew older, he had the ability to suit his style to adult audiences, becoming a star on the prestige nightclub circuit. However, for many years he also was able to come up with material that appealed to younger fans, with the result that he often was represented on best-seller charts during the second half of the '60s and early 1970s.

As a boy growing up in Cannonsburg, Pennsylvania, not far from Pittsburgh, he had a great desire to emulate his father, a big band leader. As he said in the early 1960s: "I always wanted a big band with a young sound for young people. I was sure that the kids of my generation wanted a full swinging group which would play even rock'n'roll with a solid beat and rich voicing."

He formed his first band in high school and later, while attending Duquesne University, formed a new one for university affairs and teenage dances around Pittsburgh. In the army during the late 1950s, he played trumpet in a military band. After being discharged, he formed another band that got the chance to perform on an NBC variety program. He gained the attention of Pittsburgh disc jockey Dick Lawrence, who made some demos of Vinton's vocals. The tapes eventually were submitted to CBS, which signed Vinton to its subsidiary Epic, but more to stay on Lawrence's good side than because of faith in Vinton's potential.

Bobby managed to fight that disinterest long enough to record "Roses Are Red (My Love)." A surprise hit, it rose to number one in *Billboard* for four weeks starting July 14, 1962. CBS executives could no longer deny that they had a potential star on their hands, as Vinton soon verified with more hits in 1963, such as the two-sided success "Trouble Is My Middle Name"/"Let's Kiss and Make Up" and a remake of the Clovers' 1955 "Blue Velvet" (number one in *Billboard* for three weeks starting September 21). He began the following year with another smash, a rehash of Vaughn Monroe's "There I've Said It Again," number one in *Billboard* for four weeks starting January 4. Several more hits in following months were climaxed by his fourth number one success, "Mr. Lonely" (co-written by Vinton and Gene Allen), on top the week of December 12. The future looked rosy indeed for Bobby, but the onslaught of rock supergroups from England in what was dubbed the British invasion cut sharply into his ranks of followers.

Not that Bobby did that badly for the rest of the decade. He continued to place singles on the charts (though none made it to number one) and he did quite well with Epic albums *Mr. Lonely, Lonely Nights,* and *Drive-In Movie* (1965); *Satin Pillows, Live at the Copa,* and *More Bobby Vinton* (1966); *Newest Hits* (1967); and *Please Love Me Forever* (1968), the latter bearing the title of a top 10 single in 1967.

In 1968, the singles "Halfway to Paradise" and "Just as Much as Ever" broke *Billboard*'s top 30,

and the gold "I Love How You Love Me" entered the top 10 in December. 1970 hits included singles "No Arms Can Ever Hold You," "My Elusive Dreams," and "Why Don't They Understand" plus albums *My Elusive Dreams* and *Greatest Hits of Love.*

In 1971, Bobby's career seemed to plateau. He only placed one single on the charts, the middle-of-the-road "I'll Make You My Baby." Things improved some the next year with the charted singles "Every Day of My Life" and "Sealed with a Kiss," both title songs of hit LPs. He also made the charts with the album *All-Time Greatest Hits.* In 1973, he made the general hit lists with the single "But I Do" and the easy-listening charts with "Hurt."

Still, from Epic's standpoint, Bobby no longer could command the huge following he once had and, in 1974, the two parted company. Soon after, he gained a pact with ABC Records and promptly had the gold, top 10 single "Melody of Love," a song he had written whose lyrics included some lines in Polish, his family's ancestral language. That success helped Vinton get backing for a syndicated TV series, "The Bobby Vinton Show," which aired from 1975 to 1978.

During the 1980s, Bobby kept busy as a performing artist, sometimes taking part in oldies concerts, other times headlining shows in Las Vegas as well as smaller venues around the U.S.

WAITS, TOM: *Singer, songwriter, pianist, actor. Born Southern California, December 7, 1949.**

A wondrously gifted lyricist and music writer, Tom Waits had considerable influence in the entertainment field beyond his recording and concert work. His music contributed to the careers of singers as diverse as Bette Midler and Crystal Gayle and enhanced several striking films of the 1980s. From a record-industry viewpoint, he was considered a cult favorite since he probably numbered his audience in the millions worldwide instead of the tens or hundreds of millions. One element of his work that perhaps limited his following was its diversity—jazz, blues, R&B, and rock. Besides that, more than a few folk-music fans claimed him as one of their own because his blend of music and multilayered lyrics provided vignettes of many odd corners of modern life in the folk tradition.

Waits himself seemed to be living the kind of Damon Runyonesque existence on the seamy underside of American culture he described in many of his songs. In the late 1970s, when Waits' star was strongly on the rise, he still resided in a run-down

---

*Based partly on an interview with Irwin Stambler.

motel in a seedy section of Santa Monica Boulevard in Los Angeles and greeted callers in a room littered with empty beer cans and wine bottles and butt-filled ashtrays scattered over such oddities as an old stove, an ancient-looking upright piano, and a slightly askew, aged card table.

As he talked to this writer in 1978, he flicked ashes from his cigarette on a pile of books near one elbow, appearing to reflect more kindly on the recent past than the apparently bright future ahead. (That year his activities included releasing his hit album, *Foreign Affairs*; writing special songs for Diane Keaton; and providing three songs for the score of Sylvester Stallone's movie *Paradise Alley* in which Waits acted as well.) Said Tom: "I've got a lot of miles under my belt. Played a lot of dives and a lot of small clubs. I'm still playing beer joints—just played one called the Choo Choo Room. I still keep a low profile. I still keep one foot in the streets."

He indicated with a wave of his hand that it was the back alleys, the flophouses he'd slept in (and where he still holed up at times on the road) that enriched his creativity and provided the themes for many of his songs.

He compared most of his songs to mini-short stories. "I don't think I'd write stories for books or magazines. If I'd write a short story, I'd put in an album. 'Potter's Field' [a song on *Foreign Affairs*] is like a short story for me. Anything I write isn't valid for me unless I can perform it on stage or use it in an album."

California was always home. "I grew up in East Whittier. My father, Jesse Frank Waits, was named after the James Brothers and he grew up in LaVerne, California."

He noted that, while he liked to show off a bit as a teenager, he never thought of going into show business at the time. "I used to take regular jobs. I never really looked at the world of entertainment as a thing I could parlay into money. You don't really find it; it finds you. I had a lot of different jobs before moving over. It takes a great deal of courage to get up on stage. It's really an unnatural act."

After dropping out of school and working at everything from driving delivery trucks to selling vacuum cleaners, Tom got a job as a doorman at a club in San Diego in the late '60s. "I started working at the door taking tickets. I saw a variety of acts—string bands, country & western, comedians, miscellaneous performers. I liked it. I made eight bucks a night and lived next door." Almost without his knowing it, he became interested in music. One time while visiting his parents, he came across an old piano of his mother's in the garage and started to teach himself to play. Soon he had a small repertoire. "I played a couple of Ray Charles songs. I used to do

an Elvis Presley impersonation. I did some folk songs and I was also sort of toying with writing."

After a while, he felt confident enough to drive up to Los Angeles and try out on the amateur shows called Hoot Nights at the Troubadour nightclub. One of those visits in 1969 resulted in his acquiring long-time manager, Herb Cohen. The two met at the bar and Cohen suggested they work together. With Waits' typical tongue-in-cheek recall, he noted: "We met and he asked to borrow a dollar. Actually, he told me he just needed it until his brother straightened out. . . . His brother is a hunchback."

The alliance worked out, but it took a lot of persistence and hard work on both sides. Once Cohen started getting engagements for Waits, he toured constantly, which he still did at the start of the '80s. "I usually hit about 50 cities per tour. At one time I might have stayed in a joint for a while, but these days generally I do all one nighters so I can play in more cities."

As Tom's following slowly began to build in the early '70s, he gained a recording contract from Asylum. His 1971 debut album, *Closing Time*, was followed by *The Heart of Saturday Night* (1974) and *Nighthawks at the Diner* (1975). Though Waits had started playing low-down bars, by the mid-1970s he was a major attraction on college campuses. However, Waits stressed he felt good about the fact that his audience wasn't restricted to academia. "I'm not limited to the college scene. It's not just young people that listen to me. I get letters from waitresses, truck drivers, fry cooks, people from all different walks of life."

The offbeat nature of much of his material caused some critics to refer to him as a musical evocation of the beat generation of the 1950s. In truth, his music, while having some of the flavor of the beat movement, went off in many other directions. He himself disliked being so typecast. "I didn't even have a driver's license back in the '50s. I think some of the books written by beat writers represent an important event in the content of American literature. But I'm not nostalgic. I wouldn't want to live in the '50s. I mean I've read a lot of those cats. But, y'know, I'm not a throwback. I don't live in a vault. I try to stay abreast of current affairs."

Certainly, by the latter half of the 1970s, Waits had proven his ability to stay abreast of the musical tastes of his growing audience. His 1977 LP *Small Change*, 1978 *Foreign Affairs* and *Blue Valentine* were among the more interesting releases of those years and did well on the charts. Even before *Foreign Affairs* came out, its song "I Never Talk to Strangers" had appeared on Bette Midler's LP *Broken Blossom*.

His parents, he stressed, were well satisfied. "My

dad teaches a language course in downtown L.A. now. He supports what I do. Thinks I'm a chip off the old block. He's proud of me." He indicated his mother was a little dubious about his career direction in the past, but things such as the mid-1970s Public Broadcasting TV special on him had brought her around. "I was in *Vogue* magazine a while back. A little shot of me in a club in New York. It said I was 'up and coming.' My mother liked that."

Tom began the 1980s with another excellent and unusual album on Elektra/Asylum, *Heart Attack and Vine*. Soon after he was working on the Oscar-nominated score for a Francis Ford Coppola movie, *One from the Heart*. The soundtrack album, issued on Columbia Records, featured both Waits and country singer Crystal Gayle. More than a few critics commented that Gayle's versions of Waits' songs added new dimensions to her singing. In 1983, Waits signed with a new label, Island Records, which issued *Swordfishtrombones* in September. Meanwhile Waits had worked on material for another Coppola film, *Rumble Fish* (1983). He once more demonstrated his acting skills with a role in the movie. In 1985, he had another record on store shelves, *Rain Dogs*, followed by the 1987 *Frank's Wild Years*. Perhaps his biggest triumph of 1987 was the role of a Depression Era derelict in director Hector Babenco's film version of William Kennedy's novel, *Ironweed*. In 1988 he completed a concert film, *Big Time*. (*See Jones, Rickie Lee; Midler, Bette.*)

WAKEMAN, RICK: *See Yes.*

WALKER, JR., & THE ALL STARS: *Vocal and instrumental group. Jr. Walker, born South Bend, Indiana, c. 1942; Vic Thomas; Willie Woods; James Graves, born Cleveland, Ohio.*

In the mid-1960s, the joint was jumpin' any time Jr. Walker & the All Stars played such major R&B houses as Harlem's Apollo, Chicago's Regal, the Howard in Washington, D.C., or the Uptown in Philadelphia. As the decade came to a close, Walker broke through on the national level, placing his releases of the late '60s and early '70s on the general pop best-seller lists, sometimes without even gaining the top 20 in the soul field.

Born Autry DeWalt, Jr., he showed talent on the piano at nine and made even faster progress on the tenor saxophone a few years later. He started performing with high school groups in his teens, by which time he had decided to try for a career in music.

After finishing school, Walker worked as a sideman with several Midwestern acts, steadily gaining the respect of his fellow musicians for his ability. In 1962, he started his own group and, after several years of experience playing in small clubs and theaters in various parts of the country, he gained a recording contract with Berry Gordy's Motown organization. The Walker band, which included Willie Woods on guitar, Vic Thomas on organ, and James Graves on drums, was assigned to Motown's subsidiary Soul Records.

It took only a short time for the group to catch on with R&B fans. In 1965, it had four top hits: "Cleo's Back," "Do the Boomerang," "Shake & Fingerpop," and "Shotgun." "Shotgun" moved to number one on the soul charts and number four on *Billboard*'s pop list. 1966 brought pop top 20 singles "How Sweet It Is (to Be Loved by You)" and "(I'm a) Road Runner" plus successful LPs *Soul Session, Shotgun,* and *Road Runners*.

In 1967, Walker had the top 10 soul hit, "Pucker Up, Buttercup." In 1969, "What Does It Take" broke the pop top 10 and "These Eyes" made the top 20. On "These Eyes," Walker made his debut as a singer on records, previously having only presented himself as an instrumentalist. Lesser hits were "Do You See My Love (for You Growing)" (1970) and "Take Me Girl" and "Way Back Home" (1971).

His albums almost all made the national charts, including *What Does It Take to Win Your Love?* (late 1969), *Jr. Walker & the All Stars Live* (1970), *A Gasss* (fall 1970), *Rainbow Funk* (early 1971), *Moody Jr.* (early 1972), and *Peace and Understanding Is Hard to Find* (1973).

The group began the '70s with a pop singles hit, "Do You See My Love (for You Growing)" (1970). Also on pop or soul singles lists that year were "Gotta Hold On to This Feeling" and "Those Eyes." In 1971, it placed the singles "Way Back Home," "Take Me Girl, I'm Ready," "Holly Holy," and "Carry Your Own Load" on hit rosters. Soul chartmakers in 1972 included "Walk in the Night" (top 10) and "Groove Thing" and, in 1973, "Gimme That Beat."

But the group's popularity began to slip soon after, caused in part by a switch in public interest from strident R&B toward softer ballad stylings. After Motown released the retrospective *Anthology* LP in 1974, the company made little effort to record new material by Walker and his group for almost two years. However, dance clubs' mid-1970s resurgence to the disco beat inspired a revival in the band's fortunes. Albums *Hot Shot, Whopper Bopper Show Stopper* (1976), and *Smooth* (1978) on the Soul label and *Back Street Boogie* brought Walker back on the charts.

Though the band continued to tour in the 1980s, reduced emphasis on disco among young adults again relegated it to smaller venues. In 1981, the band's greatest hits, including its most memorable number, "Shotgun," were reissued in the Motown retrospective *Superstar Series, Volume 5*. Walker and the All Stars were included in the Motown twenty-fifth anniversary show in 1983, but the band only was allowed a brief role in a medley with Mary Wells and Martha Reeves. (*See Gordy, Berry, Jr.; Moonglows, The.*)

WAR: *Vocal and instrumental group. Papa Dee, born Wilmington, Delaware, July 18, 1931; Harold Brown, born Long Beach, California, March 17, 1946; B.B. Dickerson, born Torrance, California, August 3, 1949; Lonnie Jordan, born San Diego, California, November 21, 1948; Charles Miller, born Olathe, Kansas, June 2, 1939; Lee Oskar, born Copenhagen, Denmark, March 24, 1946; Howard Scott, born San Pedro, California, March 15, 1946. Dickerson replaced in 1979 by Luther Rabb.*

An American football star and an English rock singer are rather unusual catalysts in the success story of an essentially black, California-bred band. Nonetheless, these were the elements that helped make War a top group of the 1970s.

The band's roots were around Long Beach, California, where four of its members spent all or part of their boyhood. Harold Brown was born and raised in Long Beach; B.B. Dickerson (born Morris DeWayne Dickerson) was raised in Harbor City, California; Leroy "Lonnie" Jordan grew up in Compton, a city near Long Beach; and Howard Scott was born and raised in San Pedro, bordering on Long Beach.

All were playing instruments and/or vocalizing at early ages. Brown started on piano, switched to violin from fourth to seventh grade, and finally zeroed in on drums and percussion before entering high school. Dickerson began teaching himself guitar when a cousin from Texas gave him an old guitar and amplifier; he then switched to bass guitar. Jordan first played percussion on an oatmeal box, but switched to piano as a sideline to singing in the church choir, taking lessons from the church pianist. Scott started on trumpet in elementary school, became discouraged when he was discharged from the school band, but later took up bass guitar.

During elementary and high school years, these four boys were close friends and often performed together, first for friends and later at various small clubs in the area. In the mid-1960s, they formed the Creators, achieving a local reputation and gaining a recording agreement with the small Dorey Records label. Their first single, "Burn, Baby Burn," came out just before the eruption of the riots in Los Angeles' Watts ghetto. Before the group broke up, it made a few more singles for Dorey, including "Lonely Feeling" and "That's What Love Will Do." One reason for the disbandment was the induction of lead guitarist Howard Scott into the army for 18 months. (He was discharged in 1968.) Soon after, B.B. Dickerson accepted a bid to play with a group in Hawaii.

Meanwhile, the three other future members of War were building up experience in various ways. After moving to Long Beach with his family at an early age, Charles Miller seemed headed for a football career until sidelined by injuries in junior college. He then switched his main attention to music. He had started lessons as a boy on piano and woodwinds and later added guitar to his capabilities. In his teens, he performed with jazz and blues groups and was a member of such organizations as the Debonaires, Brenton Wood, Senor Soul, and the Afro Blues Quintet plus 1 before joining Brown, Jordan, Dickerson, and Scott in Nite Shift, the backup band for football superstar David Deacon Jones of the Los Angeles Rams.

Papa Dee (born Thomas Sylvester Allen) did not reach California until he was 36. Born and raised in Wilmington, Delaware, he played in the Howard High School band's trumpet section with Clifford Brown, considered one of the best jazz trumpeters of post–World War II decades. (Later Dee played in Brown's band.) He had a good voice and took operatic vocal lessons for a while, but dropped this in favor of learning the conga drums after finishing school. He became a first-rate percussionist and found work with many jazz groups in the '50s and '60s, including Herbie Mann, Clifford Brown, and Dizzy Gillespie. He moved to the Los Angeles area in 1967, where some friends converted him into a rock enthusiast. He became acquainted with some of the members of Nite Shift and later joined them when War was organized.

The only white member of War, Lee Oskar started to learn the harmonica when he was six years old in Copenhagen, Denmark. He was already a local celebrity as a harp player in his midteens. In 1964, he left Denmark to play with various groups throughout Europe, ending up in England in the mid-1960s. There he was recruited to work as a studio musician for Capitol Records in Hollywood. Once there, things didn't work out too well for him at the studio, but he did find work after a while with Hugh Masakela's group.

He became close friends with former Animals lead singer Eric Burdon and they decided to form their own group. While they were in the middle of discussing this, music-industry executive Jerry Goldstein suggested that they see Nite Shift, then appearing with Deacon Jones at a local L.A. club. Eric and Oskar went along with Goldstein and agreed it made sense to use Nite Shift as the nucleus for the new group. The result was the act called Eric Burdon and War.

The group debuted in 1969 at Mother Lizards in San Bernardino. During late 1969 and in 1970, their LPs and singles with Burdon on MGM scored a number of hits. (*See Animals, The; Burdon, Eric.*)

In 1971, War began to go out as a separate act. It signed with United Artists and its debut LP, *War*, was on the charts during June and July. Later in the summer, War had a hit single, "All Day Music," the title song for its gold second LP. The band clearly didn't suffer from Burdon's departure. Indeed, it seemed to gain new cohesiveness and creative progress. Despite Eric's leaving, Oskar remained a key member into the 1980s, though he also turned out solo LPs such as *Lee Oskar* (United Artists, 1976) and *Before the Rain* (Elektra, 1978).

During 1971, the group even enjoyed a soul hit, "The Lonely Feeling." 1972 was an all-gold year for the band, which won gold awards for "Slippin' into Darkness" and "The World Is a Ghetto" (the title track of a gold album). Three major singles hits—"Cisco Kid," "Gypsy Man," and "Me and Baby Brother"—highlighted War's 1973 efforts, while the gold album *Deliver the World* made *Billboard*'s top 10. *War Live* (early 1974, gold) included the fast-paced "Ballero." *Why Can't We Be Friends?* (1975, gold) provided two top 10 singles: "Low Rider" and the gold title track.

U.A.'s lack of promotion of the platinum 1976 *War's Greatest Hits* suggested that both parties were ready for a parting of the ways. The band switched to MCA, but its label debut, *Galaxy* (1977), didn't come up to its earlier standards even if it went gold. (Also issued during 1976–77 were LPs *Love Is All Around* on ABC, a repackage of some Eric Burdon and War recordings, and the gold *Platinum Jazz* on United Artists' jazz subsidiary, Blue Note.) In 1978, U.A. put out the LP *Youngblood* (recorded before War left the label). In 1979, the band got back on the track at MCA with the hit LP *Music Band*. Dickerson then left to try for a solo career and was replaced on bass by Luther Rabb.

The band started the 1980s with *Music Band 2* (MCA). The album was Rabb's first recording work with War as a regular and also included its first female backup singer, Tween Smith.

WARD, BILLY: *See Dominoes, The.*

WARWICK(E), DIONNE: *Singer, pianist, songwriter. Born East Orange, New Jersey, December 12, 1940.*

The decades of the '60s and '70s were dominated by rock, but some of the most consistent successes for many of those years were scored by the combination of Dionne Warwick's vocal ability and Burt Bacharach and Hal David's songs. (In the 1970s Dionne spelled her last name Warwicke for several years.) Unlike many pop stars of the day, Dionne had excellent vocal range and voice quality and, while many of her hits were basically ballads or show tunes, she could make exciting recordings of blues, R&B, or disco. In the mid-1970s, misunderstandings between Dionne and the Bacharach/David team caused her career to flounder for a time, but she soon showed she could find successful new directions and material to maintain her ranking as a top pop vocalist in the 1980s.

Born Marie Dionne Warrick, she started singing at six as a member of the choir of the New Hope Baptist Church in Newark. Her family had a tradition of gospel singing and saw to it that she had vocal training through most of her youth. Her parents also were involved in the music business by the time she reached her teens. Her mother managed a gospel group, the Drinkard Singers, for whom Dionne was pianist for a time. Her father became promotion director for gospel records with the Chess label. As a music education major at the Hartt College of music in Hartford, Connecticut, in the early 1960s, she earned some money to help pay tuition in a gospel trio, the Gospelaires, whose other members were her sister Dee Dee and cousin Cissy Houston (later mother of Whitney Houston).

Through work as a backing singer she became acquainted with Burt Bacharach. This, in turn, brought her a contract with Scepter Records. In 1962, Scepter released her single of Bacharach and David's "Don't Make Me Over." The song became a big hit in 1963 and Dionne left college to devote all her time to her career. Her first large-scale tour was in France, where she stayed for much of 1963 and was given the ecstatic support of almost all the music reviewers. During a long engagement in Paris, she won the nickname of "Paris's Black Pearl." In the French magazine *Arts*, critic Jean Monteaux wrote: "The play of this voice makes you think of an eel, of a storm, of a cradle, a knot of seaweed, a dagger. It is not so much a voice as an organ. You could write fugues for Warwicke's voice."

After this, Dionne regularly recorded material written for her by Bacharach and David. Among her hits of the mid-1960s were "Walk on By," "Anyone Who Had a Heart," "You'll Never Get to Heaven," "Are You There," "I Just Don't Know What to Do with Myself," "Trains and Boats and Planes," "Message to Michael," "Alfie," and the gold "I Say a Little Prayer." Her Scepter albums of the early and middle 1960s included: *Presenting Dionne Warwick; Anyone Who Has a Heart; Make Way for Dionne Warwick; The Sensitive Sound of Dionne Warwick; Dionne Warwick in Paris;* and *Dionne Warwick on Stage and in the Movies.*

In 1968–69 she hit full stride with major single and LP hits. Her singles included "Do You Know the Way to San Jose," "Valley of the Dolls," "There's Always Something There to Remind Me," and "You've Lost That Lovin' Feeling'." Making the 1968 LP charts were *Dionne in the Valley of the Dolls, Windows of the World, Dionne Warwick's Golden Hits Part 1,* and *Promises, Promises.*

In the early 1970s, Dionne's career proceeded along much the same path as in the late 1960s. She continued to play to capacity houses in concert halls, clubs, and auditoriums throughout the world, to provide soundtrack vocals for a number of movies, and to be featured on TV variety and talk shows. 1970 hit singles included "Let Me Go to Him," "The Green Grass Starts to Grow," "Make It Easy on Yourself," and (from Bacharach's score for the hit musical *Promises, Promises*) "I'll Never Fall in Love Again." Her charted LPs were *Golden Hits Volume 2, Soulful,* and *I'll Never Fall in Love Again* in 1970 and in 1971, *Very Dionne,* the soundtrack album from the movie *Love Machine,* and gold *The Dionne Warwicke Story.*

Dionne left Scepter in 1971 and signed with Warner Brothers Records. The move seemed promising at first. Her first albums on that label, *Dionne* and *From Within,* both made the charts in 1972, though they didn't have the impact of her best Scepter releases. 1973 singles "If We Only Have Love" and "Just Being Myself" (title song of an album) reached lower chart levels. Her later albums on Warner's included *Then Came You* and *Track of the Cat* (1975) and *Love at First Sight* (1977). There were many good things in all her Warner Brothers releases, but neither albums nor singles won large-scale support from record buyers.

Her only major success during her five years with Warner Brothers came on the Atlantic label, part of the same corporate organization. Ironically, it turned out to be her biggest-selling single ever. The recording came about from her concert work with the five-man vocal group the Spinners, whom she asked to open her show during a five-week summer tour in 1974. Thom Bell (producer for Spinners recordings for Atlantic) thought a combination of the group with Dionne made a lot of sense. Warners approved the project and the result was the single "Then Came You," number one in *Billboard* the week of October 26, 1974—her only number one single until 1986.

In the mid-1970s, creative antagonisms between Dionne and the Bacharach/David team finally built to the point that they separated as both friends and collaborators. Looking back in 1986, Bacharach told *Los Angeles Times* writer Paul Green: "There was a 10-year period when we not only hadn't been in the studio, but we weren't even speaking more than 'hello.' When Hal David and I started to come apart, we weren't able to be there in the studio for Dionne. So she sued us and Hal sued me and I sued Hal. It was all very messy. It's great to leave all that stuff behind you, to clean out that excess baggage." Finally, in 1986, he noted, the rift between him and Dionne had been repaired.

The discordant elements affecting her behind-the-scenes life probably played a role in the decline of her recording fortunes in the mid-1970s. Somehow she couldn't seem to find the right match of material and vocal stylings to regain the public approval she once had enjoyed. When she moved to Arista Records at the end of the 1970s and was given the chance to work with Barry Manilow, suddenly things began to come up roses once more. With Manilow providing some of the new material and supervising production of the recordings, Dionne's career took on new luster. Her 1979 debut on Arista, *Dionne,* went platinum and provided her with a gold, top 5 single, "I'll Never Love This Way Again."

She came into the 1980s with newfound energy and self-confidence that translated into increasing favor with record buyers and concert goers. Auguring good things for her in the new decade was the Grammy voting for 1979. Dionne won two trophies: Best Pop Vocal Performance, Female for the single "I'll Never Love This Way Again" and Best R&B Vocal Performance, Female, for "Deja Vu" from *Dionne.*

Among her successful Arista LPs were *No Night So Long* in 1980, *Hot Live and Otherwise* in 1981, *Heartbreaker* in 1982, and *How Many Times Can We Say Goodbye* in 1983. Among the tracks on *Friends* (late 1985, gold) was "That's What Friends Are For," performed by "Dionne and Friends," said friends including Gladys Knight, Stevie Wonder, and Elton John. The gold single of the song was number one in *Billboard* for four weeks starting January 18, 1986, and won two Grammies: Best Pop Performance by a Duo or Group with Vocal and, for writers Burt Bacharach and Carole Bayer Sager, Song of the Year.

Among the projects Dionne took part in during the mid-1980s was the USA for Africa effort that resulted in the smash worldwide hit single "We Are the World." Dionne was one of 45 stars who recorded the song, whose proceeds were earmarked to alleviate hunger in Africa. She also contributed to the best-selling album of the same title. During her 1986 joint tour with Johnny Mathis, her rendition of

"We Are the World" was one of the highlights of concerts even without the presence of the 44 other singers who had recorded the original version. Also in 1986, she launched her own perfume line, called Dionne. Her 1987 credits included a part in the film *Rent-a-Cop* (with Burt Reynolds and Liza Minnelli) and a new Arista album, *Reservations for Two*. In July 1988 she was featured soloist on a PBS telecast of *Evening at Pops* with the Boston Pops Orchestra. (*See Bacharach, Burt; Houston, Whitney; Manilow, Barry; Vandross, Luther.*)

WASHINGTON, DINAH: *Singer. Born Tuscaloosa, Alabama, August 29, 1924; died Detroit, Michigan, December 14, 1963.*

Dinah Washington was known as Queen of the Blues and a look at R&B history shows this was no idle boast. She dominated the ranks of female blues singers of the 1950s by a wide margin and was on the way to challenging for '60s honors when her life was cut short. At the end of the 1960s, though she had been dead over half a decade, her total of top 10 hits still exceeded any other female R&B singers' to that time for the post–World War II years.

Born Ruth Jones, she moved to Chicago, Illinois, at three. She began singing in her church choir at an early age and was one of the lead vocalists by her teens. In her late teens, she moved up to the position of choir director.

Like many youths of the period, she followed the big bands and sang popular ballads of the day for her friends and for high school audiences. Word of her vocal talent got around, resulting in her joining Lionel Hampton's band in 1943. She toured widely with him in the mid-1940s and then started fashioning a career as a solo vocalist late in the decade.

Within a short period of time, she had become one of the most popular singers of the day with rhythm & blues fans. Her experience as a band vocalist also gained her a following among devotees of the swing era. Thus, she was a star on the R&B circuit and also was featured in the top nightclubs all over the country. In terms of record sales, though, she did better in the R&B market than the general pop field.

In 1950, she opened a new decade with one top 10 R&B hit after another. Her Mercury singles hits included "I Only Know," "I Wanna Be Loved," "I'll Never Be Free," "It Isn't Fair," and "Time Out for Tears." During the next five years, she did not have as sensational a year as 1950, but she gained at least one top 10 R&B success each 12-month period. Hits included "I Won't Cry Anymore (1951); "New Blowtop Blues," "Trouble in Mind," and "Wheel of Fortune" (1952). ("Wheel of Fortune" was a best-seller in the pop field in Kay Starr's version.) "Fat Daddy" and "TV Is the

Thing" (1953); "I Don't Hurt Anymore" and "Teach Me Tonight" (1954); and "That's All I Want from You" (1955).

Though she continued to be a star attraction in clubs and theaters, she hit a period of doldrums as far as records were concerned, snapping out of it in 1959 with the pop top 10 "What a Difference a Day Makes" and top 20 "Unforgettable." In 1960, she had one of her best years ever, teaming with Brook Benton (born Lugoff, South Carolina, September 19, 1931; died Queens, New York, April 9, 1988) to form one of the best duos of the period on rollicking *Billboard* pop top 10 singles "Baby (You've Got What It Takes)" (gold) and "A Rockin' Good Way" (number one on R&B charts). Dinah's bluesy "This Bitter Earth" also gained number one on the R&B charts during the year.

While playing in England, she performed in the movie *Jazz on a Summer's Day*.

Dinah had two more pop top 40 singles before her death: "September in the Rain (1961) and, moving from Mercury to Roulette Records, "Where Are You" (1962). New Mercury packagings of her vocals came out, such as *Dinah Washington Sings Fats Waller* (1964), *Queen and Quincy* with Quincy Jones (1965), and *Discovered* (1967).

Her earlier Mercury catalogue included *Best in Blues* (1957), *Dinah Washington Sings Bessie Smith* (1958), *What a Difference a Day Makes* (1959), *Unforgettable* (1960), *For Lonely Lovers* and *September in the Rain* (1961), and the two-LP autobiographical *This Is My Story* (1963). Mercury's jazz subsidiary EmArcy had *Dinah Jams*, and *After Hours with Miss "D"*, while its budget line, Wing, put out *Late, Late Show* (1963). Roulette Records' large catalogue of Dinah's LPs included *Back to the Blues, Best of Dinah Washington, Dinah '62, Dinah '63, Dinah Washington, Drinking Again, In Love, In Tribute, Strangers on Earth, World of Dinah Washington*, and *Dinah Washington Years*. Grand Award put out *Blues* and Pickwick Records had *I Don't Hurt Anymore*.

As described in the excellent liner notes to *Wise Woman Blues: Dinah Washington: Rare & Earthy* (Rosetta Records, 1984), Detroit Lions halfback Dick Lane (at least her seventh husband) found her on the bedroom floor, dead from an overdose of diet pills, on December 14, 1963. Decades later, her fans still sought Mercury reissues such as the 1943–54 tracks on *A Slick Chick (on the Mellow Side): The Rhythm & Blues Years* (two discs, 1983) plus older albums retitled *The Fats Waller Songbook* (1984) and *The Bessie Smith Songbook* (1986). (*See Jones, Quincy; Phillips, Esther.*)

WASHINGTON, GROVER, JR.: *Saxophonist, keyboardist, band leader (LOCKSMITH), record producer, composer. Born Buffalo, New York, December 12, 1943.*

Despite rock's continued domination of pop music in the 1970s and '80s, its hegemony was far from complete. Pop charts disclosed a wide range of styles, including material offered by many artists whose roots were in jazz, such as George Benson and the saxophonist extraordinaire Grover Washington, Jr. Though jazz purists looked askance, those performers added nuances to their material that allowed them to extend their impact beyond the relatively limited jazz audiences to reach the public at large.

For Washington, music almost was a way of life from his early childhood. He recalled in 1982: "My mother used to sing in church choirs in Buffalo and my father used to play saxophone and has an extensive collection of jazz 78s. Now my brother Michael is the organist for a gospel group in Buffalo called the Varsons—they're in the process of completing their second LP. My brother Darryl is a drummer who's played with the likes of Angela Bofill, Gato Barbieri, Charles Earland, Groove Holmes, Jimmy Owens, and myself, just to name a few. We came out of the ghetto, but despite that fact, and despite Buffalo's cold winter climate, the city had a warm creative atmosphere, as far as I was concerned.

"My father bought me a saxophone when I was 10 years old. After I started playing, I'd sneak into clubs and see guys like Jack McDuff, Harold Vick, and Charles Lloyd. My professional life began at the age of 12. I played a lot of R&B when I was with a singing group and I also played with a blues band— even funkier than the blues; we called it 'gutbucket.' We played in key every night. It was a perfect training ground. I'd play in a club until three o'clock in the morning, then be at school at quarter to eight."

But music wasn't his only interest at the time. "In the afternoon, I'd stay outdoors as long as I could. I'd play basketball all afternoon, get my clothes dirty, and did I get my ass beat! I was always into everything that involved movement, whether I was riding a bike, playing marbles, handball, whatever."

In fact, as a teenager he dreamt of making a career in basketball. But he reluctantly realized that was an impossible dream when he stopped growing at 5 feet, 8½ inches. Later, when he lived in Philadelphia and was a musical celebrity, he sublimated his sports passion by playing the national anthem before Philadelphia 76ers basketball games or Philadelphia Eagles football events.

His parents saw to it that he got a good grounding in the classics as well as jazz. His classical studies,

he pointed out, proved very valuable for his composing and saxophone style. Among other rewards was the ability to sight-read music.

A good student, he finished high school at 16. Almost as soon as he graduated, he was off on his own as a member of the Four Clefs, a group formed with some friends. The act made Ohio its home base and picked up performing dates wherever it could all over the U.S. "When I left home I found myself playing piano one night, saxophone one night, bass one night. And I was behind everything from singing groups to snake charmers. I did just about everything but play in a burlesque house."

In his late teens, he was drafted into the army and sent to radio school at Fort Dix, New Jersey. There he won a spot in the 19th Army Band, an affiliation that kept him in the States rather than overseas in Vietnam. It also allowed him to build up his outside performing credits. "I did a little moonlighting in New York and Philadelphia, playing all kinds of music. I became friends with Billy Cobham and got to know a lot of important New York musicians."

After his discharge from the army, he decided to make Philadelphia his home, a choice reinforced a little while later when he met and married his wife Christine. Needing a steady salary, he took a job with a record wholesaler and added to his income via a series of engagements with jazz groups in the Philadelphia–New York area. Besides club work, he also was in demand as a session musician for other artists' recordings.

In the later 1960s, he got a steady position in organist Charles Earland's band. In 1970, he backed Earland on the LP *Living Black!* on Prestige Records. His contributions were impressive enough for other artists to ask him to record with them, which led to credits on Joe Jones' *No Way* (Prestige) and several albums with Johnny Hammond Smith. One of those, *Breakout* on Kudu, became one of the best-selling jazz releases of 1970–71.

Hammond Smith's producer, Creed Taylor, was pleasantly amazed by Washington's saxophone work and took steps to let Grover front his own recording group. In 1971, his debut LP, *Inner City Blues,* earned excellent reviews for Grover's sax passages and the overall content. The album did well enough, in fact, to permit Washington to resign his record-distributor work and assemble his own band for live jazz-club dates.

Each successive Kudu album—*All the King's Horses* (1972), *Soul Box* (1973), and *Mister Magic* (1974)—brought growing critical recognition and increased sales. *Mister Magic* caught fire with record buyers, moving to number one on jazz charts and eventually selling in the neighborhood of a million copies, according to Kudu. With its success, he qualified as a headliner in large concert venues rather than only the small–jazz-club circuit.

Besides starring on his own recordings, from then on he also often worked with other major artists, contributing instrumental backing to such people as Bob James, Randy Weston., Eric Gale, and Dave Grusin. His solo albums included *Feels So Good* in 1975, *A Secret Place* in 1976, and *Live at the Bijou* in 1977. His record company stated all of those achieved gold or better sales levels worldwide. During 1975 and 1976, he won the NAACP Image Award as Jazz Artist of the Year. In 1976, he placed first in three *Ebony* Music Award categories: Best Album for *Mister Magic*, Best Alto, and Best Tenor Sax Player. In 1977, he won the Golden Mike Award. In 1978, England's *Blues and Soul* magazine named him Top Instrumentalist of the Year, while the city of Philadelphia gave him a Citation of Merit for Community Service (the first of many such plaudits his adopted hometown gave him in the '70s and '80s).

By the late 1970s, Grover was dissatisfied with the support Kudu Records was giving him. He told an interviewer that *Live at the Bijou* became a hit mainly through his own efforts. "It's sort of surprising with the fact that we didn't have any record-company support, but the band got out there and worked just as hard as I did and we promoted the album by ourselves." Those efforts helped make the album a platinum-seller in 1978.

Part of it, of course, was Washington's instrumental eminence. As critic Welch D. Everman commented in *The Drummer* (March 21, 1978): "There is no doubt that Washington is one of the most talented reed players in jazz today. Whether he is playing soprano, alto, or tenor saxophone, his sound is broad and open, crackling and bright; his intonation never falters, even on high-pitched wails, and even in his fastest and most complex passages each note is so pure and precise that it seems to linger in the air long after the actual sound is gone. Washington does not use tricks or gimmicks to impress his audience; he builds excitement through sheer virtuosity, through a complete command of his instruments. In short, he never seems to make a mistake."

After the 1977 album, Grover sought record labels that promised wider distribution and promotion capabilities. His first move was to Motown for a series of albums starting with *Reed Seed* (1978). He also signed with Elektra/Asylum to do albums with more of a popular market flavor.

He maintained in an interview with Bill Douglas of the Columbia, South Carolina, publication *Gamecock* that he had no inhibitions about trying styles different from "classical" jazz forms. "I don't like categories. I like to keep it as low-key as possible.

We try to communicate with our audience by playing the widest spectrum of music possible, not playing down to our audience, but trying to play what they want to hear and play what we want to play, and play something that they can think on. It's starting to work because the audiences are getting much hipper."

When people defined jazz in certain ways, he indicated, it caused undue restrictions on it. "I feel jazz never really went away," he told Douglas. "The audience sort of grew away from it looking for their own kinds of things they wanted to get into. I think things go around in cycles of maybe 5 or 10 years. When jazz came back around, it sounded different because [where] 10, 15 years ago, the jazz purists said: 'I can't use rock in a jazz tune,' now you can do anything and everything and it's not considered compromising the music any because the audience finally realizes that everybody has something to say and they try to use all the implements to say that."

Grover started to emphasize some of those new directions in his Elektra/Asylum debut, *Paradise* (March 1979). The album, which included two tracks written by him ("Shana" and "Tell Me about It Now") and one he co-wrote with Richard Stecker ("The Answer in Your Eyes"), was moderately successful. Grover produced *Paradise* himself as he did the follow-up, *Winelight* (fall 1980). A platinum blockbuster, *Winelight* stayed on *Billboard*'s pop list for 102 weeks, was number one on jazz charts for 31 weeks, and made the top 5 on R&B lists. Its single "Just the Two of Us," featuring Bill Withers on vocals, rose to number two on the pop charts.

Grover won two Grammy Awards for 1981: Best Jazz Fusion Performance, Vocal or Instrumental, for *Winelight* and Best R&B Song for the Withers single.

During 1980–81, Washington was represented on album charts by two more Motown releases, *Baddest* (1980) and *Anthology* in 1981. Grover's activities during those years included production responsibilities for a promising new Philadelphia jazz trio called Pieces of a Dream, whose debut album, *Pieces of a Dream* (Elektra/Asylum, September 1981), did well on U.S. jazz and R&B charts.

Grover's third Elektra/Asylum album, *Come Morning* (October 1981), showed up at number one on the jazz lists, his ninth album to do so, and also made the pop top 30. In early 1982, he was appointed Goodwill Ambassador for the state of Pennsylvania's three-hundredth birthday and also was awarded a Freedom Road Medallion in a ceremony held in the rotunda of the U.S. Capitol. Later, he produced Pieces of a Dream's second album, *We Are One*. On July 16, his native city of Buffalo welcomed him with a Grover Washington, Jr., Day coinciding with a concert there. Another 1982 milestone was the release of his first video, *Grover Washington Jr. in Concert,* filmed at Philadelphia's Shubert Theater in June 1981.

His next Elektra/Asylum album, *The Best Is Yet to Come* (fall 1982), included three more Washington compositions: "More than Meets the Eye," "I'll Be with You," and "Cassie's Theme" (a song written for the TV series "Cassie & Co.").

In the mid-1980s, he continued to be a popular performer with concert audiences, though his pop-music touch seemed to cool somewhat with his new releases such as *Inside Moves* (Elektra/Asylum, fall 1984).

Washington did not lack for new projects as a composer, instrumentalist, or producer. One of his goals in the mid-1980s was to try his hand at film scores. But he always kept his proficiency on the instrument that had brought him fame with constant practice. "To play correctly, I had to have the right posture and play long tones for hours without even moving my fingers. I had to get my body into the right habits, not just pushing air out, but trying to put shadings and colorings in each note. Then I worked the scales up and down, inside out, working them every which way in order to be heard distinctly, no matter how fast or slow. The main thing is not to play a tune just to be playing it, but to be really saying something."

In the late 1980s, Grover signed with Columbia Records, which released his label debut, *A House Full of Love*, in 1987, and followed with *Strawberry Moon* the next year. (*See Withers, Bill.*)

WATERS, MUDDY: *Singer, guitarist, harmonica player, band leader, songwriter. Born Rolling Fork, Mississippi, April 4, 1915; died Chicago, Illinois, April 30, 1983.*

A legendary figure of post–World War II music, Muddy Waters had a dramatic influence on almost every phase of pop. As a performer, writer, preserver of traditional black music, and pioneer electric guitarist, he contributed to developments in blues, R&B, folk, country, and rock. One of his most famous songs, "Rollin' Stone," inspired the names of the English rock group, a song by Bob Dylan, and a leading rock magazine.

Born McKinley Morganfield, Muddy was heir to the great black Delta Blues tradition, though it took a number of years until he became seriously involved in the music. In rural Mississippi where he grew up, poverty was the normal state of affairs and music—gospel and blues—a way of dealing with it. After his mother died when little McKinley was three, his father, Ollie Morganfield, sent him to his grandmoth-

er's house in Clarksdale, Mississippi. At an early age, McKinley was working as a field hand.

Clarksdale being a hotbed of blues singing, Muddy heard many blues renditions by local people, both while they worked and at evening get-togethers. During those years he got what became his stage name. His grandmother "used to say I'd sneak out and play in the mud when I was little so she started calling me Muddy. The kids added Waters; it was a 'sling' [slang] name and it just stuck."

There are some contradictions about when he first learned guitar and earned money in music. Though he always noted that he sang at local events fairly early in life, his early biographies indicated that he really didn't stress it or learn guitar until he was 22. But later he stated that he was playing harmonica at 13, earning 50 cents a night plus food, which later escalated to $18 a night working with several sidemen in the 1930s. He recalled starting to learn guitar at 17, rather than 22, basing much of his bottleneck style on the playing of such bluesmen as Eddie "Son" House and Robert Johnson.

Word of this Mississippi farm hand's ability was circulating among academic folk-music collectors. In 1941, folklorist Alan Lomax traveled to Mississippi to record Muddy for the Library of Congress Archive of American Folk Song. Initially, with associate John Work, Lomax recorded "I Be's Troubled" and "Country Blues." Later, several more sides were recorded. Those 1941–42 tracks were still available in the late 1980s on *Down on Stovall's Plantation* on Testament Records.

In 1941, eager to break away from the drudgery of farm labor, Muddy joined the Silas Green tent show as an accompanist for blues singers. That work was short-lived, but it inspired Muddy to look for new opportunities to make a career in music. The turning point came in 1943, when he asked the Stovall plantation overseer to raise his pay from 22½ cents to 25 cents an hour. The overseer refused, so Muddy headed for Chicago, where he soon had a job in a paper mill. For the next few years, he held several other regular jobs while trying to make his way as a performer in the evenings. He met a number of other artists then working in the city, including Big Bill Broonzy, and his name began to be mentioned when recording executives were in the market for new blues artists. In 1946, he recorded three sides for Columbia that were never issued. In 1947, things finally fell into place when he signed with Chicago-based Aristocrat Records. His debut single paired "Gypsy Woman" with "Little Anna Mae." Soon after, he provided the label with two big hits: "I Feel Like Going Home" and "I Can't Be Satisfied." For the balance of the '40s, he slowly increased his stature in the industry with his own recordings and as a sideman for other artists.

After another short, unsuccessful fling with Columbia Records in the late 1940s, he returned to Aristocrat, which by then had been absorbed by Chess Records. Muddy formed his own band in 1950 and soon became one of the label's bread-and-butter artists as well as a featured attraction on the R&B circuit. In 1951, he had R&B top 10 hits "Louisiana Blues" and "Long Distance Call," following those with "She Moves Me" (1952) and "Mad Love" (1953). 1954 was a vintage year as he presented "Rollin' Stone" (also known as "Catfish Blues") and such R&B top 10 singles as "I'm Ready," "I'm Your Hoochie Coochie Man," and "Just Make Love to Me." In 1955, he made R&B hit lists with another Waters standard, "Mannish Boy," and later in the decade added such other noteworthy hits as "Close to You" and "Got My Mojo Workin'."

His career hit a new high in 1958 when he made a triumphal tour of England, where his concerts had a strong impact on many aspiring young musicians who were to become the cutting edge for the British rock surge of the '60s. The universality of his work was apparent in the way artists and audiences from such varied fields as folk, jazz and rock all venerated his music. From the late '50s into the 1980s, he and his band were favorites at major festivals all over the world. Among the major events to which he returned again and again were the Monterey Jazz Festival, Newport Folk Festival, and Newport Jazz Festival in both its Rhode Island home of the '60s and its New York locale in the '70s.

Over the decades, Muddy made many dozens of albums on a variety of labels. Interestingly, in the latter 1970s, his albums were marketed by Columbia Records, finally bringing him success in an alignment that had only resulted in false starts early in his career. Among his Chess LPs were *Best of Muddy Waters* (1958), *Muddy Waters Sings Big Bill Broonzy* (1959), *Muddy Waters at Newport 1960* (1961), *Folk Singer* (1964), *Real Folk Blues* (1966), *Brass and the Blues* and *More Real Folk Blues*, (1967), and (on Chess's subsidiary Cadet) *After the Rain* (1969). *They Call Me Muddy Waters* (1971) and *The London Muddy Waters Sessions* (1972) won him Grammies for Best Ethnic or Traditional Recording. Accompanying him on the 1972 tracks and *London Revisited* (1974) were British stars Stevie Winwood and Rick Grech and Ireland's Rory Gallagher. Other Chess albums in his catalogue as of the mid-1970s included *Live at Mr. Kelly's, Can't Get No Grindin', Electric Mud, Fathers and Sons* (with Otis Spann, Mike Bloomfield, Paul Butterfield, and Buddy Miles), and *McKinley Morganfield a/k/a Muddy Waters*. He contributed several songs to *The

Blues: A Real Summit Meeting, Buddah's 1975 LP of the New York Newport Jazz Festival. *Mud in Your Ear* (1973) and, with Luther Johnson, *Chicken Shack* (1974) appeared on Muse Records.

Though Muddy was in his sixties in the second half of the '70s, his career seemed to generate new momentum rather than slow down. Throughout those years, he maintained a breakneck schedule that might have sent much younger artists to the sidelines suffering from exhaustion, keeping up a worldwide tour schedule of 35 to 40 weeks a year.

Nor did his recording work suffer. He signed with Columbia Records' subsidiary Blue Sky in the mid-1970s for a series of new albums (with blues-rocker Johnny Winter as producer) that explored new facets of the man and his music. The first LP, *Hard Again* (1977), showed Muddy at the top of his form backed by a band comprising Winter, James Cotton, Charles Calmese, and long-time Waters sidemen "Pinetop" Perkins, Bob Margolin, and Willie "Big Eyes" Smith. The equally impressive follow-up, *I'm Ready* (1978), reunited him with some of his '50s sidemen: harmonica player Big Walter Horton and guitarist Jimmy Rogers. In 1979, material recorded during his 1977 and 1978 national tours was issued on *Muddy "Mississippi" Waters Live*. It and *I'm Ready* scored Grammies for Best Ethnic or Traditional Recording.

There were many other highlights of Muddy's illustrious career that took place in the '70s. In 1971, he and his group were the subject of an award-winning one-hour documentary presented by the National Educational network. It gave insight into Muddy's skills and philosophy with the story of a typical live program (at a Chicago blues club) beginning with rehearsals and continuing through the set.

In November 1977, Muddy was a guest of honor at the farewell concert of the folk-rock Band in San Francisco, where he shared the stage with such other legendary artists as Bob Dylan, Dr. John, and Van Morrison. His performance of "Mannish Boy" was an important part of the concert album, *The Last Waltz* (Warner Brothers, 1978) and director Martin Scorcese's film of the event.

On August 9, 1978, he was one of the artists to perform at the annual White House staff picnic in Washington, D.C. His 40-minute set included "Hoochie Coochie Man," "I Got My Mojo Working" and "The Blues Had a Baby and They Called It Rock and Roll" to several ovations from more than 700 guests. Commenting on Muddy's musical stature, President Jimmy Carter told the gathering: "As you know, Muddy Waters is one of the great performers of all time. He's won more awards than I could name. His music is well known around the world, comes from a good part of the country, and represents accurately the background and history of the American people."

In the 1980s, dozens of Muddy's albums were available in reissued form and he also completed some new material before his death. He remained active on the concert circuit during the 1980s, despite failing health, continuing to delight audiences almost up to his passing in April 1983.

In a tribute to Waters' work, in 1988, blues-rockers Z.Z. Top gave Clarksdale, Mississippi's Blues Museum a white electric guitar fashioned from a cypress log from Muddy's childhood cabin. (*See Berry, Chuck; Bloomfield, Mike; Butterfield, Paul; Rolling Stones, The; Winter, John and Edgar; Winwood, Steve; Z.Z. Top.*)

WEBB, JIMMY: *Songwriter, singer, pianist, organist, record producer. Born Elk City, Oklahoma, August 15, 1946.*

When Jimmy Webb became one of the nation's most successful songwriters before his twenty-first birthday, many critics tried to analyze the kind of music he was writing. Some called it soft rock, others considered it to be in the romantic ballad tradition of earlier days of pop music. Webb himself was not sure what form it took, but had a vague feeling it wasn't gaining him the image he desired with his own generation—at least from the way his songs were performed by others. But one point was beyond controversy—Webb's songs obviously appealed to someone out there, to so many, in fact, that Jimmy was a millionaire at a time when most young people are trying to get their careers underway.

All this caused him inner turmoil that would have been beyond the comprehension of the younger Jimmy Webb of Oklahoma, the choir-accompanist son of a Baptist minister. Jimmy spent most of his early years in rural Oklahoma, learned to play the organ and piano while he was grade school age, and helped his father at services. He took an interest in popular music as well as hymns and started writing original songs from time to time at 13. In his teens, the Webbs moved to Texas and later to California, where Jimmy entered San Bernardino Valley College as a music major in 1966.

However, Jimmy found college harder than he had anticipated. When his mother died during his second semester, he quit school. He moved to Hollywood to try to make his way in the recording field. Jimmy had little money and, for a while, had to sleep on the floor in a blanket in his small, unfurnished apartment. He made the rounds of recording studios, finally gaining a job in one at $50 a week.

He began to make friends in the industry, one being singer and record executive Johnny Rivers. Rivers liked Webb's material and included some in his sessions. In one song, "By The Time I Get to Phoenix," Webb sadly recalled a broken love affair with a San Bernardino coed. Released as part of Rivers' early 1967 album *Changes*, the song got little attention at the time. Rivers teamed Jimmy up with the 5th Dimension, a group starting out on Johnny's new record label, Soul City. The act made Webb's "Up, Up and Away" the title track on its (and Soul City's) debut LP in mid-1967. Jimmy's "The Worst That Could Happen" was on its next.

The second song did little, but the first became one of the top hits of 1967, selling close to a million copies and winning both the group and Webb a total of five Grammy awards. Later, taken over by TWA as a theme song for an ad campaign, the song paved the way for another Webb enterprise, a company that made TV commercials for such firms as Hamm's Beer, Doritos, and Chevrolet.

Meanwhile, Glen Campbell released his own version of "Phoenix" in the fall of 1967. It won more Grammies for 1968. The success of reincarnated versions of Webb originals continued in 1969 when the Brooklyn Bridge achieved a gold single with "The Worst That Could Happen."

Webb's star was rapidly ascending. He was asked to write and, in some cases, produce, material for many major artists, among them Frank Sinatra and Barbra Streisand. For actor Richard Harris, Webb provided enough material for two albums, including the song "MacArthur Park" that made *A Tramp Shining* a top 10 LP in 1968. A somewhat enigmatic song having to do in part with a cake left in the rain, it gained major sales via cover records by a number of performers (including a number one hit for Donna Summer in 1978). Webb also provided Campbell with "Paper Cup" and the gold "Wichita Lineman" in 1968 and the gold "Galveston" in 1969.

In 1969, Webb was wealthy and sought after for many projects, including film scores and in-person appearances, working on movies *How Sweet It Is* and *Tell Them Willie Boy Is Here*. He also tried to compose what he called classically styled works intended for performance by rock groups and for orchestras with electronic elements. Another project was a partly autobiographical Broadway musical, *His Own Dark City*, aimed at a target date of 1971.

Despite these activities, Webb was dissatisfied. As he told Robert Hilburn of the *Los Angeles Times* (April 27, 1971): "By the time I was 21, I had accomplished all the goals I had set up for myself for a lifetime. That's destructive in a way. You have all this energy left and you don't know exactly what to do with it. You find yourself sitting down and saying: 'Well, that's fine for today; now, what am I going to do tomorrow?' From what I've seen of this business, there is a tendency for songwriters, once they have become successful, to stick to a formula. They drift along in the formula that established them, playing the same kind of songs until they die, I suppose. Maybe I'll learn in my lifetime that it has to be that way, but I hope it isn't true.

"I decided that I want to keep writing, that I wanted to evolve. I wanted to break out of the formula. I wanted to improve as a writer and to interpret the songs myself rather than just keep producing records and writing songs for other artists."

Starting in early 1970 in earnest, Webb recorded his songs himself, striking out on a series of tours of concert halls and clubs across the country. Music critics' reactions were on the negative side. Commenting on what he felt were Webb's poor program organization and thin voice, Leonard Feather wrote (*Los Angeles Times*, February 24, 1970): "Webb's theory that a writer can sing his own works better than everyone else, even if he is not a real singer, was destroyed."

Jimmy persisted, though, with concert appearances for the rest of 1970 and early 1971. He also completed an album of his own, *Words and Music* (Reprise), featuring material more rock-oriented than his earlier work. His stage presence did seem to improve and his 1971 tour gained him new attention from younger fans, but two years later it was apparent this phase of his career wasn't moving ahead. His songwriting skills were still working for others, though, as shown by Art Garfunkel's gold single "All I Know."

To try to further his recording status, Jimmy signed a new agreement with Asylum Records, which resulted in the 1974 album *Land's End* and the single "Crying in My Life." Though the discs were above average, they fell mostly on deaf ears among music fans as was true for later endeavors such as the 1977 Atlantic album *El Mirage*. At the same time, interest in his songs seemed to wane among other artists as well as the record-buying public.

From the mid-1970s into the early 1980s, Jimmy's star was in eclipse. However, he took it philosophically and, happily married by the early 1980s, didn't fret about lost glories. He told Nancy Miles of the *Los Angeles Times* in late 1983: "You can't be on top forever. The world changes around you. I woke up one day in 1977 and realized it had been 10 years since my heyday. It gets to be other people's turns and it doesn't matter how good your work still is. You have your time, then you go off. I decided I had to readjust myself to what it was possible for me to accomplish. If you're lucky, you've created new resources that you can use when opportunity knocks again."

At the time he said that, he already had new projects underway. He had completed a Christmas cantata called "The Animals' Christmas," which Art Garfunkel performed that December at St. John's Cathedral in New York. In 1986, Columbia issued a record of it featuring Garfunkel and gospel star Amy Grant. In the mid-1980s, he also did movie soundtracks including the score for *Hanoi Hilton* (1987). Meanwhile, he could smile about new recordings of his songs, such as Waylon Jennings, Kris Kristofferson, Willie Nelson, and Johnny Cash's hit "The Highwayman." Introduced on one of his solo albums of a decade earlier with little success at the time, it won Webb a Grammy for Best Country Song of 1986.

In early 1988, after a 10-year absence, Webb made his return to live performances with engagements in New York and Los Angeles. His songwriting star was rising once more, with some of his tunes prominently included on new releases by Amy Grant, Glen Campbell, Toto, Patti Austin, and Joan Baez. He also was completing work on a new musical called *The Children's Crusade* and collaborating with science-fiction writer Ray Bradbury on a musical version of the latter's *Dandelion Wine*. (*See Cash, Johnny; 5th Dimension, The; Kristofferson, Kris; Rivers, Johnny; Sinatra, Frank; Streisand, Barbra; Summer, Donna.*)

WELLS, MARY: *Singer, songwriter. Born Detroit, Michigan, May 13, 1943.*

A beehive of gospel and R&B activity in the decades right after World War II, Detroit supplied a seemingly inexhaustible supply of great singers and instrumentalists. Not the least of these young artists was Mary Esther Wells, who was as important as the Supremes and the Miracles in the early development of the Motown empire.

Born and raised in the Motor City, she had a strong, clear voice as a child and began singing in public at ten. She performed in the choir at church and also in high school events. By her midteens, she was singing at local dances and trying her hand at writing songs. Berry Gordy's new Motown Records was just beginning to become a factor in the R&B field when she turned 18.

Hearing of the firm's regular auditions for new talent, she tried out and was accepted. In 1961, she gave notice of her potential when her composition "Bye Bye Baby" became a top 10 R&B single.

Company vice president Smokey Robinson worked closely with her as record producer and songwriter, providing her with 1962 hits "The One Who Really Loves You" and pop top 10 entries "You Beat Me to the Punch" (number one on the R&B charts) and million-selling "Two Lovers."

Minor 1963 hits included the two-sided success

"Laughing Boy"/"Two Wrongs Don't Make a Right" and "You Lost the Sweetest Boy."

1964 was a big year for Mary. She became the first Motown artist to travel to England, where she toured with the Beatles, backed in her portion of the show by the Earl Van Dyke band. "My Guy" (written by Smokey Robinson) rose to the top of the U.S. R&B and pop lists (reaching *Billboard*'s number one in pop for two weeks starting May 16) and even the British lists. Motown teamed her with another rising star, Marvin Gaye, on the double-sided pop top 20 hits "What's the Matter with You Baby"/"Once upon a Time."

After Mary reached her twenty-first birthday in May 1964, she began to look for what she hoped would be greener pastures with a label other than Motown. Taking the advice of her then husband Herman Griffin, she accepted a lucrative offer from 20th Century Fox, maintaining her existing contract with Motown was invalid because she had signed it as a minor. The result, as might be expected, was a legal battle with Motown.

The move to 20th Century, however, proved nonproductive. She then had some top 10 R&B hits on Atco: "Set My Soul on Fire" and, in 1966, "Dear Lover," but she was not as popular with record buyers as in her earlier years. Recording for the Jubilee label, she made the R&B charts with singles "Dig the Way I Feel" (1969) and "Give a Man the World" (1970).

Her album credits on Motown, some of which still were in print in the 1980s, included *Bye Bye Baby, I Don't Want to Take a Chance* (1961); *The One Who Really Loves You, Two Lovers and Other Great Hits, Mary Wells Live on Stage* in 1962; *Together* (with Marvin Gaye) in 1963; *Greatest Hits* and *Mary Wells Sings My Guy* in 1964; and *Vintage Stock* (1967). On other labels during the '60s she had such albums as *Love Songs to the Beatles* on 20th Century Fox, *Two Sides of Mary Wells* on Atco, and *Ooh!* on Movietown (1966).

In the 1970s, Mary recorded for Reprise and Epic (such as the LP *In and Out of Love*) without any marked success. For part of the decade, she collaborated with new husband Cecil Womack on new projects, but they divorced in 1977. In the early 1980s, she discussed a possible return to Motown but nothing came of that. Later in the decade, she completed a new collection of tracks (mainly remakes of her '60s hits) for Allegiance Records. *(See Gaye, Marvin; Gordy, Berry, Jr.; Robinson, Smokey.)*

WHAM!: *Vocal and instrumental duo. George Michael, born Watford, England, June 26, 1963; Andrew Ridgeley, born Watford, England, January 26, 1963. Michael began solo career, '85.*

While teenage performers achieved stardom many times in the rock milieu of the late 1950s and the 1960s (and just as often disappeared from sight soon after), from the 1970s on, most successful artists had to put in a lot more dues. But there were exceptions, such as England's Wham!, a duo that moved from the dole to star status in the early 1980s.

The two grew up in Watford, just over the border from North London, and met as adolescents in the late 1960s. They became close friends and eventually started a musical collaboration in the late 1970s when they were "shoulder to shoulder at Bushy Meads Comprehensive School." George (real name Georgios Panayiotou) recalled: "We spent most of the time round at Andrew's house mucking about on instruments and writing songs." Their first strong interest was disco as they listened intently to import discs of U.S. artists Chic and Sylvester. But when ska, reggae, and other West Indian music took hold in England, they moved in that direction as members of ska group the Executives.

George told a reporter: "Ska had that energy. That's what we've always listened to, the stuff that's got the energy at the moment."

For a while, Andrew went off to college while George remained in the sixth form, but they kept working away at their music to the point that their grades suffered dramatically. George told Lynn Hanna of England's *New Musical Express* (November 27, 1982): "I think we both stayed on at school so we'd have an excuse to stay at home and wouldn't have to go out to work, being lazy. We both knew that all we wanted to be was pop stars."

Deciding finally that grades were not worth the effort, both left school and went on unemployment relief while they continued composing new material and making demos to send record company executives. Though their parents went along with this for a while, they finally became restless about their offsprings' lack of steady income.

George told *NME:* "You're surrounded by people who are trying hard and failing dismally, and you've got to convince your parents that you're not one of those people. They don't realize the difference between a hit song and a bad song, they just think it's totally a matter of luck. I always told them, obviously it's a matter of luck, but it's not all luck. If you write good songs for long enough, someone's going to want to make money out of them."

The boys' optimism proved sound in a relatively short time. Their song "Enjoy What You Do (Wham Rap)," whose angry lyrics addressed adult apathy about teenage fears for the future, won a contract from Innervision (a small subsidiary of CBS U.K.), with an advance of 500 pounds, part of which was used for making a studio demo on which George sang lead and played bass guitar, Andrew played guitar, and other backing was provided by musician acquaintances.

Their record debut—a 12-inch dance single with "Enjoy What You Do (Wham Rap)" on one side and an instrumental version of "Wham Rap" on the other—won some attention, mainly in England rather than the U.S. Their next release, "Young Guns (Go for It)" (1982), provided the breakthrough. Pointing out the problems of early marriages, it rang a bell with teen and near-teen audiences in England, becoming a best-seller in early 1983. By summer, they had another singles hit with "Bad Boys."

Their debut LP, *Fantastic* (mid-1983), premiered in the number one position in Britain. The Innervision single "Club Fantastic Megamix" was on U.K. upper chart levels for some months late in 1983.

By 1984, Wham! was a major act in England, but the boys hadn't earned their spurs on the other side of the Atlantic. All that quickly changed as 1984 went by. A succession of releases accompanied by videos that earned massive play on MTV as well as noncable outlets made Wham! one of U.S. Columbia Records' most valuable acts. From the triple-platinum album *Make It Big*, the single "Wake Me Up before You Go-Go" reached number one in *Billboard* in November as did "Careless Whisper" the next February and "Everything She Wants" in May. "Freedom" later peaked at number three.

From the platinum LP *Music from the Edge of Heaven* (1986) came top 10 singles "I'm Your Man," "The Edge of Heaven," and Michael's solo "A Different Corner."

Another milestone for Michael was participation in the May 19, 1985, NBC-TV special celebrating the fiftieth anniversary of Harlem's famed Apollo Theater. George sang one number with Stevie Wonder and, with Smokey Robinson, dueted on Wham!'s hit "Careless Whisper."

By then, George and Andrew had agreed to split up. Michael increasingly had become the dominant component of Wham! (on *Music From the Edge of Heaven*, which was released after the band broke up, he not only wrote and produced most of the songs, but also played most of the instruments as well). In bio notes for Columbia Records, he stated, "Going solo gives me a totally open approach to songwriting. I can explore any territory."

Wham! gave a farewell concert at London's Wembley Stadium in June 1985 before 80,000 fans, after which Michael embarked on his solo career. The first fruit of that to reach the public was a 1986 duet with Aretha Franklin, "I Knew You Were Waiting (For Me)," which rose to number one on charts in the U.S. and abroad and earned a Grammy nomination for Best R&B Vocal Performance by a Duo or Group. From mid-1985 through mid-1987, he worked on his debut Columbia solo LP, *Faith*, for which he wrote all the songs and also served as producer.

The first single, the controversial "I Want Your Sex," came out during the summer of 1987 and made number one on *Billboard* charts, despite being banned from airplay on 30 percent of U.S. radio stations. (The song also was part of the *Beverly Hills Cop II* soundtrack). That was followed with the title song from the new album, which was number one on Billboard charts for four straight weeks in late 1987. The LP *Faith* was released on November 2, 1987; the multi-platinum album made number one in *Billboard* and made similar inroads on charts around the world. The next single from the LP, "Father Figure," came out in early 1988 and also rose to number one. In the voting for the British Phonographic Industry BPI award, the U.K. equivalent of the U.S. Grammy, Michael was named the Best British Male Artist of the Year (1987).

WHISPERS, THE: *Vocal and dance group. Members (late-1980s): Nicholas Caldwell, born Loma Linda, California, April 5, 1944; Leaveil Degree, born New Orleans, Louisiana, July 31, 1948; Marcus Hutson, born St. Louis, Missouri, January 8, 1943; Wallace "Scotty" Scott, born Fort Worth, Texas, September 23, 1943; Walter Scott, born Fort Worth, Texas, September 23, 1943.*

Combining precision dancing with five-part harmony, the Whispers offered one of the most polished soul/R&B shows on the concert and nightclub circuit in the 1970s and 1980s. Highly professional performances reflected decades of experience by a group that had recorded only one change in personnel since its teenage beginnings in a Los Angeles high school. It was fortunate that the members had that persistence, because after years of failures or near misses in the all-important record area, the Whispers moved up to star rank in the late 1970s and '80s.

Except for Nicholas Caldwell, a native Californian, the other founding members were born in other parts of the U.S. and came to the Los Angeles area with their families at early ages. The two who initiated the group in their teens were twin brothers, Wallace ("Scotty") and Walter Scott. They got encouragement as boys from relatives. Walter recalled: "We had an uncle we would always listen to. He taught us a lot about harmonizing. That's where we learned that kind of singing."

Noting that the group's repertoire typically ranged from new material to songs from decades earlier,

Scotty pointed out: "When we first started together we did a lot of vaudeville tunes like 'Me and My Shadow' and that's where I think we learned to tap dance." In fact, he reported the brothers debuted on stage at the age of five singing "Me and My Shadow."

From that time forward, the Scotts dreamed of careers in music. Fortunately their voices, smooth and clear in childhood, became effective tenors after they passed through the awkward teen years. They spent spare time working on singing skills over the years while their family moved from Hawthorne, California, to Nevada, and back to south central Los Angeles. As the Scott Brothers, they already had considerable show business credits before the Whispers came into being. In their midteens in high school, they teamed up with three other friends to form the first incarnation of the Whispers.

One of those friends, Nicholas Caldwell, began singing with choral groups in junior high school and soon sought opportunities to expand his performing activities. His first professional work was for Sly Stone, who was then working as a disc jockey in San Francisco, prior to forming Sly and the Family Stone. From his early years, Caldwell showed considerable aptitude as a dancer, which he later applied in developing the Whispers' choreography. Marcus Hutson had less performing experience in his childhood, though he paid close attention to jazz, pop, and R&B during those years. It wasn't until he became close friends with the Scotts and other original Whispers, he said, that he thought of making music his career.

The original quintet at the start of the 1960s comprised Caldwell on tenor; Hutson, baritone; the Scott brothers, lead vocals and tenors; and Gordy Harmon, first tenor. Hutson said: "At first we were really singing as just a hobby, but after we got out of school, we decided to quit our jobs and really go all the way."

At the start, the Scotts said, the group patterned itself after such '50s jazz vocal stylists as the Hi-Los and Four Freshmen. As Motown and Stax/Volt soul/R&B penetrated the mass market, its elements began to blend into the group's vocal arrangements.

The road ahead turned out to be long and bumpy. The group subsisted by engagements at small clubs and local dances and parties. Often it didn't seem as though the performers could stay together, but the Scotts' optimism about the future won out each time depression threatened to set in. By the late 1960s, the Whispers had built up a following among soul/R&B fans and were gaining respect from fellow artists. In fact, Wallace Scott began to earn a reputation as a songwriter. In the '60s and '70s, many name artists recorded some of his work. Both Isaac Hayes and Ray Charles sang "Your Love Is So Doggone Good," and Aretha Franklin did "I Can't See Myself Leaving."

But even by the early 1970s, as Walter remembered: "There would be times when we would share a hotel room together while we were on the road—all nine of us, including our musicians."

When Gordy Harmon left in 1973, his place was taken by Leaveil Degree, completing the lineup that was still the same in 1988. Degree said that a vocal coach's enthusiasm over his singing ability during junior high school helped direct him toward music. During his high school years, he sang with many street-corner harmony groups. "There must've been 20 of them—they always broke up after three months or so." Later he sang for a time with Barbara Love's Friends of Distinction before leaving music for a while to work in other fields. But he had made contacts, including a friendship with Wallace Scott, that brought some show business assignments. After Harmon left, Scott asked Degree to become the Whispers' new first tenor.

With the new alignment, the group's fortunes slowly took a turn for the better. Its popularity on the concert circuit and opportunities for recordings both increased. Its first single, "It Only Hurts for a Little While," appeared in 1964 on Dore. Not much happened with that, with some subsequent singles, or with the late 1960s debut album, *Planets of Life* (Soul Clock). The group then signed with Chicago-based Chess. On its subsidiary Janus, the Whispers began to show up on soul charts, albeit at low levels. (Those minor successes were combined on the mid-1970s Janus album *The Whispers' Greatest Hits.*)

After 1976, however, when the group signed with Soul Train Records (a new black-owned label that soon became Solar Records, with Solar standing for Sounds of Los Angeles Records), its record efforts picked up speed. The debut on Soul Train, *One for the Money* (1976), was followed by *Open Up Your Love* (1977). *Headlights* (1978) proved the turning point. Distributed for Solar by RCA, the album achieved a respectable sales volume and provided the near-gold single "Olivia (Lost and Turned Out)." Describing the LP's contents, Caldwell said: "It's a good mixture of club things, jazz things, and ballads. A good way to describe it would be to say it's 'funk jazz.' Contemporary soul would be another."

The next Solar release, *Whisper in Your Ear* (1979, platinum), demonstrated the group finally had arrived. The first single, "A Song for Donny" (dedicated to soul great Donny Hathaway, who had recently died, with parts of the single's proceeds promised to the Donny Hathaway Scholarship Fund), soon was on soul charts. The second single, a revision of Sonny and Cher's "And the Beat Goes On," proved a crossover hit, moving high on both pop and R&B charts to earn the group its first gold record. Another 1979 Solar release was the Christmas LP, *Happy Holidays to You*, followed by *Imagination* (1980), *This Kind of Lovin'* (1981), and *Best of The Whispers* (1982). All of these passed gold-record sales levels, according to Solar.

During 1981 the group had three soul chart singles, "This Kind of Lovin'," "I Can Make it Better," and "It's a Love Thing." Late in the year, Solar moved its distribution arrangement from RCA to Elektra/ Asylum. The first Whispers LP handled by Elektra/Asylum was *Love Is Where You Find It* (December 1981, gold), which produced two 1982 charted soul singles: "In the Raw" and "Emergency." *Love for Love* (Solar/Elektra, March 1983) was on album charts for many months.

In the 1980s, the Whispers became a member of the soul elite. Featured in Solar All Stars programs that drew capacity crowds across the nation, the group also was well received abroad, including debut appearances in Africa. In Nigeria, it performed with singer Carrie Lucas. Members of the group also demonstrated skills as record producers. Among artists whose records they helped assemble in the '80s were Carrie Lucas, Leroy Hudson, Grady Wilkins, Collage, and Sheila Escovedo.

The 1985 hit LP *So Good* added three more charted soul singles to the Whispers' list of honors. In the late 1980s, with Solar now handling its own record distribution, the Whispers made soul charts once more with the album *Just Gets Better With Time* (1987). *(See Charles, Ray; Franklin, Aretha; Hathaway, Donny; Hayes, Isaac; Sly and the Family Stone.)*

WHO, THE: *Vocal and instrumental group, all born England (London area). Peter Townshend, born Chiswick, May 19, 1945; John Entwistle, born Chiswick, October 9, 1946; Roger Daltrey, born Hammersmith, March 1, 1944; Keith Moon, born Wembley, August 23, 1947; died London, September 7, 1978. Moon replaced in 1979 by Kenny Jones, born England, September 16, 1949. John Bundrick added in 1979.*

"On a rainy night in late 1964, a group called the Who made their first appearance at the Marquee Club, Wardour Street, in the West End of London. Keith Moon literally attacked his drums, breaking several drumsticks in the process and ending the performance with his clothes stuck to him and his jaw sagging from exhaustion. Roger Daltrey, shouting until he was hoarse, dripping with sweat, smashed his microphone into the floor. Pete Townshend . . . rammed the neck of his guitar into its amplifier until the guitar split in two. John Entwistle, the bass guitarist, stood a discreet distance apart, dressed in black, quite still." Thus opened the saga of one of the wildest, most innovative groups to come out of England after the Beatles, in the words of Gary Herman, author of *The Who* (November Books, Ltd., London, 1971, p. 7).

It was not quite instant fame, but it was a start. All four were born and raised in London, three of them (Townshend, Daltrey, and Entwistle) in middle class Shepherd's Bush. Entwistle and Townshend were school friends and began playing in a Dixieland group at 13, John on trumpet and Peter on banjo. They drifted apart for a while, but then worked in a new group two years later after Peter learned guitar. (Initially, Townshend was a rhythm guitarist, later transitioning to lead.) The new group didn't do much and Entwistle was lured away to play bass guitar with another friend, Roger Daltrey in the Detours. They soon decided that their rhythm guitarist wasn't good enough. (As Entwistle noted, the individual knew only three chords.) Townshend, then in art school, agreed to take over. The group added Colin Dawson on vocals and Doug Sanden on drums and, in a short time, was one of the better-known groups playing small clubs around London in 1963.

Late that year, management of the group was taken over by Pete Meaden and Helmut Gordon. They gained the band its first record contract and changed its name to the High Numbers. The result, the single "I'm the Face"/"Zoot Suit" (both written by Meaden), made little headway on Fontana Records. Meanwhile, Gordon and Meaden had decided the group should replace Sanden on drums because, at 35, he seemed too old for its audience. The band auditioned several drummers before meeting Keith Moon during an engagement at the Oldfield Hotel in Greenford. Moon, previously with a surfer beat band, the Beachcombers, agreed to join and the makeup of the future Who was complete.

The High Numbers was doing well with mod fans in mid-1964, but still lacked direction. At this point, two young film directors, Kit Lambert and Chris Stamp, entered the picture. Lambert and Stamp made movies of pop groups and were on the lookout for new subjects. One night, Lambert heard the High Numbers perform in the Railway Tavern in north London. He was impressed and attended the next evening's concert at the Watford Trade Hall. As he later told reporter John Heilpern of *The Observer:* "The excitement I felt wasn't coming from the group. I couldn't get near enough. It was coming from the people blocking my way." The crowd empathized with the band because its music was perfectly suited to the mod emotions, music derived from the soul sounds of Berry Gordy's Motown products and James Brown.

Four days later, Lambert and Stamp took over management of the group. They chose a name for the band (by then down to a quartet), the Who, that had been used by the group earlier in its career. Lambert noted: "It was a gimmick name—journalists could write articles called 'The Why of the Who' and people had to go through a boring ritual of question and answer. 'Have you heard the Who?' 'The Who?' 'The Who.' It was an invitation to corniness and we were in a corny world."

For three months, the new organization made little headway. Then Lambert and Stamp gained the Marquee date. Despite intensive advertising and promotion, the first performance was poorly attended. However, the club management felt the group generated excitement and kept it on. Billed as Maximum R&B, the Who began to capture attention in the press for its violent stage antics, self-indulgence, and alleged antisocial attitude. People began coming to hear it and the group remained at the Marquee for 16 weeks.

The group was turned down by EMI Records (the Beatles' label) in October 1964. Lambert and Stamp then arranged for U.S. independent producer Shel Talmy to supervise a demonstration record, "I Can't Explain." Talmy, in turn, interested American Decca in the act. After the U.S. firm signed the Who, it induced English Decca (which had earlier turned down the Beatles) to handle it in Europe. "I Can't Explain" was released January 15, 1965, with little Decca support, but Lambert and Stamp did their own plugging until the record caught on, especially after an appearance on England's top rock TV show, "Ready, Steady, Go." The record went into the top 10 after the Who had the lucky opportunity to replace another group on the BBC's "Tops of the Pops."

However, the contract with Decca was such that the band made no meaningful profit on the record. The group turned out several more singles while wrangling with Decca for more support. During these discussions, Lambert, Stamp, and the Who became so angered at one point that they signed to do some sides for another company, including the single "Substitute," which reached number three in England in 1966. This maneuver, plus the success of other Decca releases, induced Decca to meet the Who's demands, one of which was a Decca-sponsored tour of the U.S.

The group's 1965–66 campaign for English stardom received a strong push from the fall 1965 hit single "Anyway, Anyhow, Anywhere" (written by Townshend and Daltry and released on Decca's Brunswick label), followed with the even bigger

"My Generation," an anthem of the '60s generation gap.

At concerts, enthusiastic English youngsters screamed approval when Townshend (nicknamed "the Birdman") leaped in the air with his guitar and, sooner or later, smashed it to pieces. They loved Keith Moon's destructive antics. The tumult made it impossible to hear the band's music. To do this required buying its records, which people all over Europe did in ever larger numbers from 1966 on. The group's 1966 output included singles and extended-play discs "The Kids Are Alright," "A Legal Matter," "Ready, Steady, Who" (recorded live on "Ready, Steady, Go"), "I'm a Boy," and "Happy Jack." Townshend, the group's main writer, turned out such hit songs as "Pictures of Lily" and "I Can See for Miles" in 1967 and "Call Me Lightning" and "Magic Bus" in 1968. The others did some writing, of course, such as Moon and Entwistle's 1966 collaboration "In the City" and Entwistle's "I've Been Away," "Boris the Spider," and "Whiskey Man."

Album successes included *My Generation* in 1965, *A Quick One* (released in the U.S. as *Happy Jack*) in 1966, *The Who Sell Out* in 1967, and, in 1968, *Direct Hits* and *Magic Bus—The Who on Tour*. *Happy Jack*'s track "A Quick One While He's Away" reflected Townshend's growing dramatic interests via a tale of a wife who takes her pleasure with a truck driver while her husband's gone, confesses her escapade, and is forgiven.

During 1968, the group took a vacation from touring while Townshend worked on his classic rock opera *Tommy,* the moving yet macabre tale of a blind child traumatized by his elders who grows up to become a pinball champ and then messiah. It was originally intended for performance on TV in 1968, but was judged too controversial to air. Issued as a two-disc album in Britain late that year and in the U.S. the next spring, *Tommy* became a worldwide hit and the Who's first U.S. gold record. Live performances in such places as the London Coliseum in 1969 and New York's Metropolitan Opera House in 1970 were triumphs. In the early 1970s, *Tommy* was presented by troupes in major cities across the world. The brilliant 1975 film version starred Daltrey as Tommy, Ann-Margret as his mother, Tina Turner as the Acid Queen, and Elton John as the Pinball Wizard.

A string of gold Decca LPs followed: *Live at Leeds* (1970) and *Who's Next* and *Meaty Beaty Big and Bouncy* (1971). In the early '70s, Who members began putting out solo albums as well, starting with Entwistle's *Smash Your Head against the Wall* (Decca, 1971). Setting up their own label, Track (with distribution by Decca), they released Townshend's *Who Came First* (1972), Daltrey's *Daltrey*

(1973), and Entwistle's grotesque *Whistle Rhymes* and *Rigor Mortis Sets In* (1973) plus, with his band Entwistle's Ox, *Mad Dog* (1975). Back on MCA (Decca's new name), Townshend had the superb *Rough Mix* (1977) and Daltrey turned out *Ride a Rock Horse* (1975) and *One of the Boys* (1977).

The brief early 1970s gap in album output as a group was also due to Townshend's developing another long concept work. That Track album, *Quadrophenia* (the tale of a 1960 London Mod, Jimmy, whose personality facets were modeled after the various Who), was finally released in late 1973 and almost immediately made the U.S. top 10. The gold album wasn't as accessible as earlier ones, though it tended to grow on the listener with repeated playing.

During those years and, indeed, throughout the group's history, it was primarily successful with record buyers on the album level, though songs such as "My Generation" and the revision of Eddie Cochran's "Summertime Blues" remained classics on rock radio. While the Who never had a number one U.S. single it did break *Billboard*'s top 20 with "I Can See for Miles" (1967), "Pinball Wizard" (1969), "See Me, Feel Me" (1970), "We Won't Get Fooled Again" (1971), "Join Together" (1972), "Squeeze Box" (1976), "Who Are You" (1978), and (after leaving MCA for Warner Brothers) "You Better You Bet" (1981).

The group followed *Quadrophenia* with two more excellent gold albums: 1974's *Odds and Sods* (previously unreleased 1964–72 tapes) and (back on MCA instead of Track) *The Who by Numbers* (1975). In the latter, Townshend's compositions dealt with whether a rock artist can continue to be relevant as he grows older and, by extension, addressed the subject of aging in general. Among its tracks were "However Much I Booze," "How Many Friends," and "In a Hand or a Face."

After that LP and concerts supporting it, there was a period of almost three years when little was heard about the group, spurring rumors it had broken up. But the group came back with the fine platinum *Who Are You* in 1978. Before the year was out, however, the music world was shocked at the death of Keith Moon from a drug overdose. Moon's style of drumming and manic clowning were poignantly recaptured in June 1979 with the release of the documentary film *The Kids Are Alright* along with a platinum soundtrack album on MCA. Later in the year, the movie *Quadrophenia* was accompanied by a new soundtrack album on Polydor with such tracks not in the 1973 album as "Four Faces" and "Get Out and Stay Out" plus the rarely heard "Zoot Suit" from the group's days as the High Numbers.

Moon's passing once more revived predictions that the Who would disband, but by 1979 his place had been taken by Kenny Jones, former drummer with the Faces. Also added was keyboardist John "Rabbit" Bundrick. The Who with Jones started a 1979–80 concert series that showed the band still to be a formidable array. In fact, Townshend told a reporter: "It's amazing in a way how things have turned out. Keith died at a time when the Who really were finished. . . . We were at the end of an era because we [had] learned to enjoy ourselves. Up to that point, we were about something else. We were about struggle and we stopped struggling."

For all that, the first album by the revamped Who, *Face Dances* (Warner Brothers, 1981), didn't seem as vital as the collections from the Moon era, though it still went platinum. In 1981, the group was on the charts with the MCA "best-of" LP *Hooligans*. In 1982, it was announced that the band would make what was likely to be its final tour in support of the next Warner Brothers album, the gold *It's Hard*. Band representatives hedged a bit, saying while once the tour was over the band would make a definite break from the road, it didn't mean the group wouldn't record together (it owed Warner Brothers more albums, for one thing) and perhaps finance more films such as *Quadrophenia*.

The group started its farewell tour at the Capital Center in Maryland, just outside Washington, D.C., on September 23, 1982, in a concert series that included the Clash at some locations. It proved to be triumphant and emotionally charged as the band still seemed at the height of its powers.

Before the tour, Townshend commented to *Rolling Stone*: "I don't see the Who going on for very much longer. I think that with this next album and tour we're really gonna throw ourselves into it 100 percent. And then we're gonna stop. I'm pretty sure of that. It's not because we want to stop, but because we've come to the point . . . where the tension is just too much.

"I like the richness of what I do in other areas. That's become almost as important to me as being in a band. And I think when you get to that point, you have to think very seriously about what it is you're doing it for."

The band continued on the concert circuit into 1983 with European appearances. It also made a brief reunion in mid-1985 for the Live Aid (for African famine relief) concert. After that, into the late '80s, Townshend's forecast held true. The group's albums continued to appear, though, such as MCA's *Who's Last* (late 1984) and another retrospective, *Who's Missing* (1985). Solo LPs of the '80s included Daltrey's *Parting Should Be Painless* (1984) and *Under a Raging Moon* (1985) on Atlantic, plus Entwistle's *Too Late the Hero* (Atco, 1981) with Joe Walsh and Joe Vitale. On Atco, Townshend released

Empty Glass (1980), *Chinese Eyes* (1982), *Scoop* (two discs, 1983), *White City: A Novel* (1985), *Pete Townshend's Deep End Live!* (1986), and *Another Scoop* (two discs, 1987).

While Townshend didn't seem eager to revive the band in the late 1980s, other members were more agreeable to the idea. Roger Daltrey, in particular, was outspoken. While promoting his new solo album in mid-1987 *(Can't Wait to See the Movie,* Atlantic), he told Dennis Hunt *(Los Angeles Times,* July 26, 1987), "I didn't want it to end. I understand the pressure on Pete, because he's the songwriter. But it was the height of stupidity to build up a name for over 20 years and then throw that name in the dust heap.

"We needed to stop what we were doing and take a break. Pete needed a rest from the Who. But we didn't have to end it. If Pete wanted to [reform the group] tomorrow, I'd say yes so fast you wouldn't believe it." Finally the Who members agreed to start work on a new LP in early '89. *(See Clash, The; Cochran, Eddie; Faces, The; John, Elton; Sting; Turner, Tina.)*

WILLIAMS, MAURICE: *Singer, songwriter, group leader (THE ZODIACS). Born Lancaster, South Carolina, April 26, 1938.*

Over his long career, Maurice Williams wrote hundreds of songs and recorded quite a few as a soloist or part of a vocal group. Not too many were major hits, but among those that caught on were several of the most important standards in R&B and rock history.

Williams began singing as a boy at the local church in Lancaster, South Carolina. He had a good voice and did not lose it when he reached his teens. In Barr High School, he began to concentrate on popular music, organizing a quartet that included three other boys from Lancaster: Henry Gasten, Willie Bennet, and Charles Thomas. The four took the name of the Charms and decided music would be their careers after they won first prize in a Lancaster talent show in the early 1950s.

The boys sang current R&B hits, standard blues, and original songs Williams was beginning to write. By the mid-1950s, they had moved their base of operations to Nashville, Tennessee, and gained a contract with Excello Records. Perhaps to avoid confusion with Otis Williams and the Charms (noted for the 1954 doo-wop hit "Hearts of Stone), the group changed its name to the Gladiolas and, after a while, to the Excellos.

The Gladiolas' 1957 record of Williams' composition "Little Darlin'" received little response, but when the White Diamonds recorded it on a major national label, Mercury, and it received massive pro-motion, it won the Diamonds a gold record for their singing and Williams one for his songwriting.

Still, it didn't seem as though the Gladiolas would ever have a best-seller of their own. In 1960, Williams came up with a new song, "Stay." As the Zodiacs, the group recorded it on the Herald label. It moved into the top 10 on the R&B charts and made number one on *Billboard's* pop list the week of November 21. Total sales went well over the million mark.

The group remained active with some changes in personnel for much of the 1960s. However, despite minor hits "Come Along," "Come and Get It," "Running Around," and "We're Lovers," the Zodiacs weren't able to repeat their 1960 success and eventually broke up. Still, some of Williams' songs became hits for other artists, such as Jackson Browne's parody of "Stay" in 1978.

In 1988, Williams' tracks were available on *Barefootin'* (Brylen, 1982), *Maurice Williams and the Zodiacs* (Relic), and *The Best of Maurice Williams & the Zodiacs* (Collectables).

WILSON, AL: *Singer, drummer. Born Meridian, Mississippi, June 19, c. mid-1930s.*

Al Wilson became a celebrated artist toward the end of 1973 and in early 1974 with his single "Show and Tell" and album of the same title. But he had been around the music field a long time before that.

Born and raised in Meridian, Mississippi, he started singing in his church choir as a boy. "Our preacher never had any formal music training, but when he laid down a beat and established the root bass, it was a thrill. No singer could miss." After high school, Al began singing with a small group on the R&B circuit up and down the Mississippi River. He then toured the southern states for four years with Johnny "Legs" Harris and the Statesmen.

After a stint in the navy, he moved to Los Angeles at the end of the '50s, where he worked a series of odd jobs, eventually ending up in the town of San Bernardino in the Jewels, which soon changed its name to the Rollers. As the Rollers, it had some mild success with the 1961 single "The Continental Walk."

Wilson left the Rollers the next year and kept in touch with the music field over the next few years mainly by working as a drummer. He kept his eyes open for good contacts and in time managed to get support from Marc Gordon, manager of the 5th Dimension. Gordon brought Wilson to the attention of Johnny Rivers (for whose Soul City label the 5th Dimension recorded). Al was signed by Rivers soon after. In 1968, Wilson's Soul City single "The Snake" made the top 30. However, subsequent releases on the label fell far short of that.

After Marc Gordon began his own record firm, first called Carousel and later Rocky Road Records, Wilson was given a new opportunity to record. The gold single "Show and Tell," issued in October 1973, made number one in *Billboard* the week of January 19, 1974. Later in the year, Wilson provided Rocky Road with a top 30 single, "La La Peace Song."

Without a big hit from Wilson in 1975 nor any contributions from other label artists, Rocky Road shut down. Al moved to Playboy Records for a time where he had the 1976 pop top 30 single, "I've Got a Feeling (We'll Be Seeing Each Other Again)" and a chart LP in which the song was the title track. *(See Rivers, Johnny.)*

WILSON, JACKIE: *Singer. Born Detroit, Michigan, June 9, 1934; died Mount Holly, New Jersey, January 20, 1984.*

The best-seller charts for 1958 list the single "Lonely Teardrops," but give no indication of the importance of the song's success to two of Detroit's best-known sons. The record was the first step to national stardom for singer Jackie Wilson. At the same time, it was a building block in the career of writer Berry Gordy, Jr., who was to begin laying the foundation for his Motown Records empire the next year.

Wilson, a few years younger than Berry, had a childhood much like Gordy's. Raised in the ghetto, he learned to defend himself at a young age. Like Gordy, Jackie tried his hand at boxing. In his case, the first results were promising. He gained entry into the Golden Gloves at the start of the 1950s, saying he was 18 instead of 16. He then proceeded to win his division. However, when his mother found out, she made him give it up; the boxing world might have lost a future champion, but the music public gained a top-flight vocalist.

After graduating from Highland Park High School, he built up a following singing in local clubs. Along with Levi Stubbs (later of the Four Tops), he sang with the Royals, who later evolved into Hank Ballard and the Midnighters (after changing their name to avoid confusion with the Five Royales). In 1953, when Billy Ward, organizer of the famed Dominoes R&B group, was looking for a lead singer to replace Clyde McPhatter, he settled on Wilson. Wilson stayed with the Dominoes for over four years, finally deciding to go out as a solo artist in late 1957.

Detroit publisher Nat Tarnpol became Jackie's manager and soon gained his new protégé a contract with Brunswick Records. It was a good combination; in the 1970s, Jackie was still one of Brunswick's most successful artists. In 1957, Wilson had some success with the song "Reet Petite," co-authored by Berry Gordy. Gordy also co-wrote Jackie's next four hits: "To Be Loved" and the pop top 10 "Lonely Teardrops" (1958) and "That's Why (I Love You So)" and "I'll Be Satisfied" (1959). From other writers, "You Better Know It" (1959) and "Talk That Talk" (1960) also broke *Billboard*'s pop top 40.

1960 was his biggest year ever. Two singles reached number one on the R&B charts and also moved high on the general charts: "Doggin' Around" (a million-seller whose flip side, "Night," also was a hit) and "A Woman, a Lover, a Friend." "Alone at Last" broke the pop top 10; its flip side, "Am I the Man," made number 32.

Later *Billboard* pop top 10 singles were "My Empty Arms (1961), "Baby Workout" (1963), and "(Your Love Keeps Lifting Me) Higher and Higher" (1967). "Please Tell Me Why" and "I'm Comin' on Back to You" (1961) and "Whispers (Gettin' Louder)" (1966) made the top 20.

Brunswick albums included *He's So Fine, Lonely Teardrops* (1959); *My Golden Favorites, Jackie Sings the Blues,* and *A Woman, a Lover, A Friend* (1960); *You Ain't Heard Nothin' Yet* and *Jackie Wilson By Special Request* (1961); *Body & Soul* and *Jackie Wilson At the Copa* (1962); *Jackie Wilson Sings the World's Greatest Melodies, Baby Workout,* and *Shake a Hand* (1963); *My Golden Favorites Volume 2* and *Somethin' Else* (1964); *Soul Theme* and *Spotlight on Jackie Wilson* (1965); *Soul Galore* (1966); *Whispers* and *Higher and Higher* (1967); *It's All a Part of Love* and *You Got Me Walking* (1971); *Jackie Wilson's Greatest Hits* and *Beautiful Day* (1972); and *Nowstalgia* (1974).

Although Jackie never broke *Billboard*'s pop top 40 after 1968, his subsequent soul hits spanned "Helpless" and "Let This Be a Letter to My Baby" in 1970; "Love Is a Funny Thing" and "This Love Is Real" in 1971; "The Girl Turned Me On," "Love Is Funny That Way," and "You Got Me Walking" in 1972; and "Because of You" and "Send a Little Song" in 1973. His total that made the national pop charts for his overall career was 54. He remained widely popular as a concert artist into the mid-1970s.

As Don Waller fondly recalled in his *Los Angeles Time* requiem (January 29, 1984): "A Golden Gloves champ at 16, Wilson knocked out audiences uptown (at the Apollo) and downtown (at the Copacabana) alike with his dazzling footwork and incredible stamina. Contemporaries remember him doing a back-flip, tearing off his jacket, and coming up twirling it around his head all in one fluid motion—just in time to sing the next line, of course. There's precious little live footage of Wilson in existence, although rumors of home movies featuring 'Mr. Excitement' in action have whetted collectors' appetites for years.''

It was while Jackie was in action that his career suffered its final flame-out. Performing at the Latin Casino in Cherry Hill, New Jersey, in 1975, he suffered a heart attack that made him, for most of the following years, a hospitalized vegetable, lying in bed in a semicoma with occasional rousings that caused his family momentary hopes of a rejuvenation. It was not to be; he finally died on January 20,1984, in a hospital in Mount Holly, New Jersey.

Among the numerous reissues of his soaring, dramatic vocals were *Jackie Wilson with Billy Ward and the Dominoes* (Gusto, 1977), *The Jackie Wilson Story* (Epic, 1984, two LPs), and *Reet Petite—The Best of Jackie Wilson* (Columbia, 1987). The more obscure tracks on Rhino Records' *Thru the Years* (1987) included duets with Linda Hopkins and Lavern Baker. *(See Ballard, Hank; Dominoes, The; Four Tops, The; Gordy, Berry, Jr.; McPhatter, Clyde; Morrison, Van.)*

WINTER, JOHNNY AND EDGAR: *Singers, guitarists, band leaders, songwriters. Both born Beaumont, Texas. Johnny born February 3, 1944, Edgar, born December 28, 1946, also played saxophone, keyboards, and drums.*

For generations, Texas has been a fertile ground for grass-roots music—the searing blues of Mance Lipscomb, the rockabilly of Buddy Holly, the poetic folk balladry of Townes Van Zandt, the fiery rock of Joe Ely. Blues-rock too has thrived in Texas, as shown by Johnny and Edgar Winter in the '70s and, a decade later, by Stevie Ray Vaughan, who clearly reflected the Winters' influence.

Johnny and his younger brother Edgar grew up in Beaumont. Their family always encouraged music. Their father played saxophone and banjo and sang in church choirs from his youth. Their mother often played the piano for family songfests. The boys learned several instruments in their early years and, under the title It and Them, were playing local clubs in their teens. In their late teens, they adopted the group name Johnny Winter and the Black Plague.

The blues were the boys' passion, though they followed trends in rock and were aware of the local impact of country music. After graduating from high school, Johnny enrolled in Lamar Technical College as a business major. He couldn't get his mind off music, though. Almost every weekend, he hitchhiked to Louisiana to play in small clubs. After one semester, he decided to forget school and become a musician.

One of his first decisions was to head north to the blues mecca of Chicago. He watched such blues

greats as Muddy Waters perform in clubs. He found out where aspiring newcomers to the blues field hung out and sat in with them. His talent with harmonica and guitar impressed his contemporaries. Among the young musicians with whom Winter played for a few weeks in 1962 were Mike Bloomfield and Barry Goldberg.

Johnny didn't feel comfortable away from the Southwest at the time and headed back to Texas. During the next six years, he performed as a soloist and with several rock and blues bands in southern roadside bars, small clubs, and campus concerts. For most of that time, he was part of a gypsy-like group of musicians, wives, and friends who traveled the Atlanta-Birmingham-Pensacola circuit. Many who heard him raved about his blues vocals and guitar runs, but most of the nation was unaware of his existence. In 1968, though, *Rolling Stone* sent out the word. Reviewing pop trends in Texas, Larry Sepulvado wrote that Winter was ''a hundred-and-thirty-pound cross-eyed albino with long fleecy hair, playing some of the gutsiest, fluid blues guitar you have ever heard.''

The article caused East Coast club owner Steve Paul to fly to Houston to hear Winter and, as fast as he could, sign the Texan for his nightspot, Paul's Scene. It was a smart move. Before long, lines formed every night in front of the club. In December 1968, Winter was booked into New York's rock center, Fillmore East. He didn't go on until 2 A.M. But after none other than Mike Bloomfield introduced him, he kept the crowd spellbound—when it wasn't screaming for encores—for a full hour.

His debut LP, *Johnny Winter* (Columbia, 1969), cemented his reputation across the country with his variations on such vintage blues songs as ''Good Morning Little School Girl'' and ''Mean Mistreater.'' For his next album—*Second Winter* (January 1970), recorded in Nashville, Tennessee—Johnny assembled a group including his brother Edgar on piano, organ, harpsichord and alto sax; ''Uncle'' John Turner on percussion; and Tommy Shannon on bass. The material spanned Winter's own compositions and songs by Dylan, Percy Mayfield, and Little Richard. Lester Bangs of *Rolling Stone* called it ''an unrelenting floodtide of throbbing, burning sounds, a work of folk art which captures the tradition of blues and rock from the prehistoric Delta bottleneck sundown moans to the white-hot metal pyrotechnics of today and tomorrow.''

Backing him on his third LP, *Johnny Winter and* (October, 1970), were Rick Derringer on second guitar, Randy Hobbs on bass, and Randy Z on drums. (With brother Edgar, the others also formed Edgar Winter's White Trash, which debuted on Columbia's subsidiary Epic in July 1970 with the LP *Entrance.*) The new threesome came to Winter from the McCoys of "Hang on Sloopy" fame and provided the experience Johnny wanted for an album that was deeply into rock rather than the blues. Derringer and friends continued as part of Johnny Winter's personal appearance band. While playing in New Orleans, the drummer departed and Winter recruited Bobby Caldwell (born 1950) to take over percussion chores.

By 1971, Winter had settled in the Woodstock region of New York. *Johnny Winter Live* (April 1971) made the best-seller lists. His recording credits of the early 1970s included material on several other labels, primarily reissues of pre-Columbia work. Buddah issued *First Winter*. Janus Records included an album on tape, *Almost Blues*, and the LP *Early Times* in its catalogue. GRT tapes also issued cassette and cartridge albums of *The Johnny Winter Story*.

That story during those years was not a good one. Johnny had developed a severe addiction to heroin that threatened both his career and life. During 1971–72, he agreed to seek help to cure his habit. While he was sidelined, Edgar's career on Epic Records flourished. His second LP with White Trash titled, naturally, *Edgar Winter's White Trash* (June 1971), made the charts. *Roadwork* (1972) went gold. *They Only Come Out at Night* (also 1972) went platinum. 1972 hit singles "I Can't Turn You Loose" and "Keep on Playing that Rock'n'Roll" were followed in 1973 by "Frankenstein" (number one, gold) and "Free Ride" (top 20) from *They Only Come Out at Night*. By then, however, White Trash had disbanded to be succeeded in 1972 by the Edgar Winter Group, which consisted originally of Dan Hartman on vocals, Ronnie Montrose and Boz Scaggs on guitars, and Chuck Ruff on drums. Montrose later was replaced by Jerry Weems. In 1973, Rick Derringer joined as lead guitarist and vocalist.

In 1973, Johnny returned to action, free from his addiction—hopefully forever. His resurfacing was celebrated by the top 30 Columbia album *Still Alive and Well*. In early 1974, *Saints and Sinners* made the album charts. Columbia then moved him to its subsidiary Blue Sky for *John Dawson Winter III* (1974), *Captured Live* (1976), *Nothin' But the Blues* (1977), and *White Hot and Blue* (1978). *Together* (1976) teamed him with brother Edgar.

In the mid-1970s, Johnny began working as a producer for Blue Sky. One of the artists assigned to him was his idol, the great Muddy Waters, for whom he produced the impressive *Hard Again* (1977), while also serving as a sideman in the backing band, and Grammy-winning *I'm Ready* (1978). He re-

mained a friend and associate of Muddy's until the latter's death in April 1983.

Meanwhile, Edgar's band stayed active through concerts and records during the middle and late '70s. Albums included *Shock Treatment* (Epic, 1974, gold) and, on Blue Sky, *Jasmine Nightdreams* and *The Edgar Winter Group with Rick Derringer* (1975), *Recycled* (1977), *The Edgar Winter Album* (1979), and *Standing on the Rock* (1981). *Edgar Winter Anthology* (Back-Trac, 1985) resurrected his '70s work.

In the 1980s, the brothers' days of mass popularity seemed over. Johnny, who began the decade with the Blue Sky album *Raisin' Cain*, became more involved in producing than entertaining in the '80s. Then, moving over to one of Chicago's small blues labels, Alligator, he put out the scorching *Guitar Slinger* (1984), *Serious Business* (1985), and *3rd Degree* (1986). *(See Bloomfield, Mike; Derringer, Rick; Scaggs, Boz; .38 Special; Waters, Muddy.)*

WINWOOD, STEVE: *Singer, guitarist, keyboards player, harmonica player, songwriter. Born Birmingham, England, May 12, 1948.*

With his choirboy voice and instrumental flamboyance, particularly on keyboards, Stevie Winwood was a rock wunderkind in his teens and seemingly a has-been by his mid-twenties. After several years out of the spotlight in the mid-1970s, though, he came back to become a reigning star of the 1980s.

By the time he joined his first major band—the Spencer Davis Group in the early 1960s—though only 15, he already was considered to be a star of the future by many in the English music field. He had started playing piano as a child and had developed into an excellent guitarist in his early teens. After a year at music college learning to read and write music, he played with a jazz band organized by his brother Muff.

In 1963, the Winwoods met a young teacher named Spencer Davis (born Wales, July 17, c. early 1940s), who played rhythm guitar, had performed as instrumentalist and vocalist with several rock bands in England, and also had done some session work. Davis proposed starting a new band and Muff, who played bass guitar, and Steve agreed to join. Steve was to handle keyboards, including organ, as well as lead guitar and lead vocals, plus filling in on harmonica from time to time. English-born Pete York was added on drums.

Much of the material that audiences applauded was written by Steve, such as "Trampolines," "Waltz for Lumumba," and (co-written with Muff and Davis) "Gimme Some Lovin'." Among the numbers composed by the entire band were "This Hammer" and "Goodbye Stevie."

In the mid-1960s, Island Records turned out a number of British singles and albums that were issued in the U.S. by United Artists. Among the LPs were *The Spencer Davis Group, Gimme Some Lovin'* (with such notable songs as "Keep on Running," "I'm a Man," and the title track), and after the band broke up, *The Best of the Spencer Davis Group.*

In late 1966, Winwood decided to leave and at the start of 1967 retired to a cottage in Berkshire Downs with Jim Capaldi, Chris Wood, and Dave Mason to form Traffic, which gained worldwide fame in the late 1960s and early 1970s.

However, despite its enormous success, Steve remained restless, taking leave of the group at times for supergroup projects such as Powerhouse (whose members included Eric Clapton and Rick Grech) and Blind Faith (Winwood, Clapton, Grech, and former Cream drummer Ginger Baker). The searing *Blind Faith* LP (Atco, 1969) went gold. Some of Steve's songs with those bands ("Cross Roads" with Powerhouse and "Sea of Joy" with Blind Faith) were included in the May 1971 U.A. "documentary" LP *Winwood,* covering his career to that point. (Both Winwood and Island Records strenuously objected to the U.A. release at the time.)

After the Blind Faith project failed, Steve returned to Traffic until he quit the band in the early 1970s and faded from view for some years. He outlined the chain of events to Kristine McKenna *(Los Angeles Times,* January 1, 1983): "Contrary to popular rumor, I didn't drop out of the music business after I came off the road in 1973. I continued to work on projects, but most of them were fairly unsuccessful, so I was sort of forced into a low-profile existence. In ways, the mid-1970s were a bad time for me, but an important time as well.

"I got very sick with peritonitis in 1973 and came close to losing my life. Being forced off the road by my illness and the commercial failures I subsequently had, the life of a touring rock star was taken from me and I came to realize how false that life is. After being on the road so many years—since I was a kid, actually—I found myself unable to do mundane things and cope with parts of life that most people do cope with. So I made a conscious effort to get to know people who had nothing to do with the music business, and a whole richness of life opened up to me. There are people who manage to tour and lead a full life, but I was one who couldn't."

Steve made moves to revive his career with his 1977 solo album, *Steve Winwood,* on Island. Such fine tracks as "Hold On," "Let Me Make Something in Your Life," and "Vacant Chair" signaled he had not lost his touch as a writer or interpreter.

The even more impressive *Arc of a Diver* (1980, gold) provided Steve's first *Billboard* top 40 single as a solo, the number seven "While You See a Chance."

Talking Back to the Night (1982) didn't match the success of *Arc of a Diver.* The album was, he said, more consciously upbeat than previous recordings. One of its themes, he told McKenna, was the need for people to realize how good life could be free from drug use. "I wanted to address the rumors of my being a junkie. I certainly would never want to make a preachy antidrug record, but I did want to make it understood how I felt about the subject. There've always been rumors of my having a drug habit, maybe because of some of the people I've associated with, or perhaps I appeared like a druggie when I was touring and I was ill. But it's simply not true, and it's not something I want associated with my work."

He carried his more optimistic outlook into his next album, *Back in the High Life,* (fall 1986, multi-platinum). Its single "Higher Love" was number one in *Billboard* the week of August 30 and won Steve Grammies for Pop Vocal Performance, Male and Record of the Year. *Chronicles* (Island, 1987) provided a retrospective of his work.

Winwood switched to the Virgin label for his 1988 LP *Winwood.* The album featured the number one single "Roll With It," which many critics compared to the music from his Spencer Davis days twenty years before. *(See Clapton, Eric; Traffic; Waters, Muddy.)*

WITHERS, BILL: *Singer, guitarist, song-writer. Born Slab Fork, West Virginia, July 4, 1938.*

From any angle, Bill Withers' success story seems more like fiction than fact. He might be compared to football's George Blanda, because, like Blanda, he gained fame at an age when such opportunities would have seemed long past. Then again, he could be considered a male Cinderella, going from rags to riches "overnight" (but actually after considerable dues-paying).

Show business was the farthest thing from Withers' mind as a boy from a black family growing up in the small West Virginia mining town of Slab Fork. His father died when he was a child and his mother had to work hard to support the family. On many occasions, she put young Bill in a movie theater to occupy him because she didn't have enough money for a babysitter. Part of the time, his grandmother helped raise him, as he later recounted in his song "Grandma's Hands."

Bill kept up his school work, though, and finished high school in the mid-1950s. He worked at various jobs, first near home, then in California, where he labored as a mechanic in the mid-1960s. At first, he had no particular desires apart from his normal working life, but slowly he found himself propelled toward writing rhythm & blues songs. In 1967, he moved to Los Angeles to try to find a publisher for his material.

He landed a job in an aerospace factory and started making demonstration records on the side. As he told Leonard Feather of the *Los Angeles Times* (October 1971): "I spent $2,500 on the records. By my standards it was quite an investment—my wages usually hovered around $3.50 an hour. But if you live frugally, you can save. I never spent a lot on night life and wasn't hung up on liquor or anything. In fact, I always considered myself to be living pretty good."

The demonstration records didn't win any friends for Withers when he started taking them around the Hollywood offices of record firms in the late 1960s. He had almost given up on show business when he took a new job producing toilet seats for Boeing 747 jet transports. By this time he had taught himself to play guitar, which helped when he got his first major break in the spring of 1970. The head of a small record firm, Sussex, thought Withers' recordings showed promise and introduced him to Booker T. Jones, leader of the famous Booker T. & the MGs. Jones encouraged Withers to continue and Bill used the guitar to help compose ten new songs.

The material was recorded with Booker T. in charge of production in the second half of 1970. Jones himself played in the backup group and also brought along the great Stephen Stills on lead-guitar. The single "Ain't No Sunshine" (backed "Harlem") and album *Just as I Am* were released by Sussex (with distribution by Buddah Records) in February 1971. Ironically, Withers was laid off from his aerospace job the same month.

However, as spring went by, the single picked up radio play, first in Los Angeles, then all over the country. Meanwhile, Withers got additional writing assignments, including the lyrics for J.J. Johnson's song "Better Days" for Bill Cosby's movie *Man and Boy*. Withers also was called on to sing the song for the soundtrack.

On June 26, 1971, a little over a week before Bill's thirty-third birthday, he made his debut as a professional singer in a Los Angeles club. This was followed with a series of appearances in other cities and TV exposure. "Ain't No Sunshine" moved into *Billboard*'s top pop 10, earning a gold record in September. Later in the year, he had another hit single, "Grandma's Hands."

Now a celebrity, Withers tried to retain his perspective. As he told Feather: "I enjoy the applause and recognition and the money—but at the same time I realize that the making of music is an absolute luxury. Anyone who can get paid for it—and overpaid, as all of us are, ought to acknowledge that. . . . When I was repairing airplanes, that was a vital gig, because you can lose a lot of lives if that job isn't done properly. Even when I was working on the bathroom seats, this was at least constructive. I challenge anybody: I won't sing for a month and you don't go to the bathroom for a month and let's see . . . who comes off with less misery."

When the 1971 Grammy winners were announced, Bill picked up a trophy for "Ain't No Sunshine": Best R&B Song. In 1972, he received gold records for the Sussex album *Still Bill* and singles "Use Me" and "Lean on Me." In 1973, he put out his Sussex LP of his 1972 *Live at Carnegie Hall* and had chart singles "Friend of Mine," "Kissing My Love," and "Let Us Love." Next came the album *+ Justments* (Sussex 1974).

Soon after that, however, he became embroiled in a legal dispute with Sussex Records that had a negative impact on his career. He told Dennis Hunt of the *Los Angeles Times* in 1975: "I have to compose before I record and I have a very hard time being creative when I'm worried about business problems. . . . In order to write, you have to be vulnerable and open. I haven't been vulnerable often in the past few years. The part of my mind I write with has been closed off a lot of the time. If you're paranoid, you don't write much because all you can think about is what's making you paranoid."

It seemed as though his troubles might recede after he signed with Columbia, which, in turn, bought his old masters from Sussex. However, his output on that label lacked the emotional content and uniqueness of his previous offerings. His singles typically made lower chart levels or didn't show up on them at all. An exception was "Lovely Day" (top 30, 1978). Columbia albums included *Making Music* (1975), *Naked and Warm* (1976), *Menagerie* (1977, gold), *'Bout Love* (1978), and *The Best of Bill Withers* (1980).

Things took a turn for the better in the 1980s. During 1981, "Just the Two of Us" (a single recorded with instrumentalist Grover Washington, Jr.) went gold and rose to number two on *Billboard*'s pop charts. "Turn Your Love Around" won the Grammy for Best R&B Song for 1981.

Withers kept active during the 1980s as a performer and writer. Some of his songs, both old and new, provided hits for other artists. He even won a 1987 Grammy for Best R&B Song (shared with co-writer Reggie Calloway) after Club Nouveau resurrected his 1972 hit "Lean on Me." *(See Booker T. & the M.G.s; Washington, Grover, Jr.)*

WOMACK, BOBBY: *Singer, guitarist, record producer, songwriter. Born Cleveland, Ohio, March 4, 1944.*

A prolific songwriter and compelling singer and instrumentalist (who even devised his own left-handed guitar style), Bobby Womack had an important influence on many artists, black and white. Though he never quite received his due at home, fans in Europe considered him a superstar and he was held in highest regard by his musical peers on both sides of the ocean. While the quality of his enormous amount of recorded material was inconsistent, overall he provided a body of work ranking among the finest in modern pop music.

One of five sons of a steel worker, he got his first exposure to music in church. He and his brothers formed a gospel group in his preteen years. As the Womack Brothers, it had plenty of engagements on the gospel circuit, performing in churches and auditoriums around the Midwest and other parts of the U.S., often sharing bills with such other noted singers as the Five Blind Boys and the Caravans. Appearances with the Soul Stirrers brought young Bobby in contact with its leader, Sam Cooke, who was just beginning to branch out into secular music. Impressed with Womack's guitar skills, Cooke offered the 16-year-old a spot with his backing band in 1960, so Bobby left school. Taking an interest in the entire Womack clan, Cooke suggested they change their group name to the Valentinos. Under that title, the brothers had a hit single, "Lookin' for a Love" (later a best-seller for the J. Geils Band). During the mid-1960s, Bobby and the Valentinos often toured with the James Brown show. (An odd footnote to Womack's relationship to Sam Cooke was the fact that some months after Cooke was shot to death by a Los Angeles motel manager in 1964, Bobby married Sam's widow.)

Soon after Bobby left Cooke's band in 1963, he wrote and recorded "It's All Over Now." The song came to the attention of England's Rolling Stones, whose version of it brought them their second U.S. singles hit in 1964. It led to a close friendship between Bobby and the Stones that paid important dividends for him in the 1980s.

Bobby ended his work with the Valentinos in the mid-1960s to pursue other goals, including initial steps toward a solo career. He made Memphis his home base in the middle and late 1960s, where he exercised his skills as songwriter, session musician, and record producer. Among the artists he backed during those years were King Curtis, Ray Charles, Joe Tex, Aretha Franklin, and Dusty Springfield. He became closely involved with soul star Wilson Pickett, handling production of many of Wilson's recordings and co-authoring "Midnight Mover."

In the late 1960s and early 1970s, Bobby contributed material to many other major stars in both the soul and rock categories, including Marvin Gaye, Jackie Wilson, and Janis Joplin, all of whom he knew well. Janis's memorable "Trust Me" was a Womack composition. Among others who benefited from Womack songs were Leon Russell, Vickie Sue Robinson, Ron Wood, and Sly Stone. He also wrote George Benson's "Breezin'."

By the end of the 1960s, Bobby began to make headway himself as a solo performer, primarily with the black audience in the U.S., but also across ethnic boundaries in Europe. His chart singles in the late 1960s and early 1970s included "Woman's Gotta Have It," "Daylight," "You're Welcome, Stop on By," "Check It Out," "That's the Way I Feel About Cha," and "Across 110th Street." "Harry Hippie" (1973) and a remake of "Lookin' for a Love" (1974) went gold on United Artists, which also issued such LPs as *Communication* (1971), *Understanding* (1972), *Facts of Life* (1973), *Lookin' for a Love Again* and *Greatest Hits* (1974), *I Don't Know What the World Is Comin' To* (1975), and *Bobby Womack Goes C&W* and *Safety Zone* (1976).

In 1976, Bobby moved to a new label, Columbia. During his brief stay there, he turned out two self-produced LPs: *Home Is Where the Heart Is* (1976) and *Pieces* (1977). He wound up the decade with Arista, which issued *Roads of Life* in 1979. Throughout the '70s, he remained active on the concert circuit, maintaining a faithful following that was mainly female. Somewhat tongue in cheek, he told Connie Johnson *(Los Angeles Times* November 26, 1985) that his core groups were "church ladies, mostly. The sisters who wear the hats with the plastic fruit on 'em. I toured for a while with Millie Jackson and I had to stop because she was cursing and carrying on and offending all the church sisters I attract. They were walking out during her act! I draw the ladies who aren't into all that—the same ones who don't listen to Prince."

Bobby's career was flagging at the start of the 1980s, but he signed with a new label, Beverly Glen Music, turning out a new album, *The Poet* (fall 1981), which not only became a hit with the black audience, but added some new fans from other segments of U.S. society. It rose into the top 10 on black lists and top 30 on *Billboard*'s pop chart. His single "If You Think You're Lonely" made the black top 20 in early 1982.

Just when things seemed to be looking up again for Bobby, unexpected tragedy intervened. His brother was shot to death by a girlfriend (whose jealousy reportedly was unfounded). Depressed, Bobby gave up touring and working on new records for close to two years. (It was not the first problem to hinder his advancement, of course. At other times he had battled drug addiction.) But in 1984 he was back in action with *The Poet II* on the soul LP charts (MCA stated in 1987 that *The Poet* and *Poet II* together had sold over three million copies worldwide) as well as a duet single with Patti Labelle, "Love Has Finally Come at Last." The LP *Someday We'll All Be Free* followed in 1985. In 1984 the retrospective *Bobby Womack and The Valentinos* (Chess, 1964-66 sessions) was released. But the happiness at new successes was diluted by problems with the label that led to messy court wrangles between Bobby and Beverly Glen.

Once more Bobby bounced back, this time with the excellent summer 1985 *So Many Rivers* on MCA, arguably one of his finest collections ever and one that brought some of the most positive responses in his career from white record buyers in the U.S. It also made the black top 10 lists. Its debut single, "I Wish He Didn't Trust Me So Much," was a top 5 soul hit in late summer and was followed by another soul hit that fall, "Let Me Kiss It Where It Hurts." *So Many Rivers* was an even greater success in the U.K. Many U.K. critics named the album the number one release in 1985. (Even before that album came out, Bobby had received four awards in the annual poll conducted by Britain's *Blues & Soul* magazine. In the voting, announced in June 1985, Bobby was named Best Male Vocalist, Best Songwriter, and Best Live Performer, while *Poet II* was voted Best Album of 1984.)

During 1984–85, Bobby had a number of other rewarding projects among his new credits, including a collaboration with jazz artist Milton Felder on the chart single "(No Matter How High I Get) I'll Still Be Looking Up to You"; a soul chart single, "Strange and Funny," co-written with his sister-in-law Linda Womack and his brother Cecil; and even a presence on country & western charts in the form of John Anderson's version of his song "It's All Over Now."

One of the reasons that *So Many Rivers* had more crossover success than earlier albums was a concerted push by the Rolling Stones to increase their friend's media exposure. For instance, all the group members except Mick Jagger told MTV they'd come in with Bobby if that video channel would promise to interview him.

Womack told Connie Johnson: "MTV won't play my videos, but they said they'd interview me if I could get one of the Stones to appear with me. They gave me the rights to the interview and I liked being in that position. It was: 'Yeah, yeah, just make sure you keep the camera on me.' I know MTV doesn't give a damn about Bobby Womack. The music industry has always been more racist than the artists themselves."

Ron Wood of the Stones was a particularly enthusiastic supporter, noting he believed he owned more Bobby Womack records than Bobby did. In a joint interview with England's *Record* magazine, Womack noted: "They're tryin' to cross us over! You know what's funny? We'll be riding in a cab and if it's a white guy, he'll say: 'That's got to be Ron Wood.' So Ronnie'll say: 'Yeah, and this is Bobby Womack!' And the cabbie'll say [unimpressed]: 'Yeah . . . but Ronnie, what's goin' on?'"

Wood added: "When it's a black cab driver, the guy says: 'I ain't even gonna turn around. I know that's Bobby Womack's voice.' And Bobby'll say: 'Yeah, and this is Ronnie Wood of the Rolling Stones!' To which the driver replies: 'That's what I said, Womack's voice!'"

Bobby emphasized that he liked to expand his audience, but not at the sacrifice of his creative principles. He told *Blues & Soul* (October 1985): "You know, another of the big problems today is that blacks no longer want to be soul singers anymore. Have you noticed how they all want to be crossover artists these days? Me? I'm not ashamed. People like Otis [Redding], Sam [Cooke], and James Brown have laid down a tradition and I'm proud to say that I want to continue in that tradition. I want to be one of the true survivors."

Commenting on his approach to songwriting, he told the interviewer: "In my music, I have already tried to tell the truth. I've never been afraid to do so because the truth never dies. It lives on beyond the person. Look, I'm not ashamed to tell you that I was hooked on drugs. Everybody around me always used to tell me not to talk about it but . . . it's the truth. But . . . we made a complete turnaround and I'm proud of that. Man, I'll tell you—I'm just glad to even be here today to talk to you about it. It could easily have been me up there on the night shift with Marvin Gaye."

He sang of his lost friends on *So Many River*'s track "Only Survivor," naming people such as Janis Joplin, Jimi Hendrix, Otis Redding, Marvin Gaye, Jackie Wilson, and Sam Cooke. He told Steve Morse of the *Boston Globe* (October 18, 1985): "Sometimes I think I remember more people who are in the graveyard than are living. It's a fast business, and it's tough to see how so many get taken out so quickly by overchasing the dollar."

Reminiscing about a few of the lost friends to Morse, he said about Hendrix: "I met him before he ever made it. In 1960 he played guitar for Gorgeous George, who is now my personal valet. . . . Everybody stayed away from Hendrix because they thought he was a beatnik. He played the guitar with his teeth, and he'd eat half a sandwich one day and the other half the next. And I don't know if he ever took a bath. But after he made it, George met him walking down Broadway one day, and Hendrix handed him $3,000. It was his way of saying thanks.''

Of Marvin Gaye, he commented: "Marvin was a very sensitive person. He had so many leeches on him, and they drained him so that he was just paying the bills to catch up. He had a lonely life.''

And finally, Janis Joplin: "She called me one night really drunk, and asked about suicide. She really scared me, but I've been told every time she got drunk she said that just to get sympathy. And the next morning she was dead. And now they say that Bobby Womack was the last person to ever talk to her.''

Womack, however, had persevered and his career was on the upswing in the mid-1980s. During 1985, when he wasn't touring in support of his album, he spent time contributing to the Rolling Stones' LP *Dirty Work,* singing a duet with Mick Jagger on the 1986 top 10 "Harlem Shuffle," the album's first video and single. In 1986 MCA released his new LP, *Womagic* followed in November 1987 by *The Last Soul Man. (See Benson, George; Brown, James; Charles, Ray; Cooke, Sam; Franklin, Aretha; Gaye, Marvin; J. Geils Band, The; Hendrix, Jimi; Joplin, Janis; LaBelle, Patti; Pickett, Wilson; Rolling Stones, The; Sly and the Family Stone; Tex, Joe; Wilson, Jackie.)*

WONDER, STEVIE: *Singer, harmonica player, organist, pianist, drummer, songwriter, arranger, record producer. Born Saginaw, Michigan, May 13, 1950.*

Steveland Morris's stage name, Stevie Wonder, proved particularly apt. He was indeed a boy wonder, already a polished performer on a variety of instruments at 12, when he was brought to the attention of Berry Gordy, Jr., head of Motown Records. Signed to Gordy's Tamla label, he became a star almost with the release of his first record in 1963. More important, he did not burn out, as sometimes occurs with child prodigies, but continually improved his performing skills as he grew to manhood so that his impact on pop music in the '70s and '80s was profound.

Born blind, it was only natural that one of his boyhood idols was the equally afflicted Ray Charles. (In tribute to Ray, young Stevie's second album in 1963 was called *Tribute to Uncle Ray.)* Soon after he was born, his family moved to Detroit, where Stevie spent most of his youth. At five, he started playing the piano and harmonica.

One of Stevie's neighbors and friends in the early 1960s was Gerald White, brother of Ronnie White of Smokey Robinson's Miracles. After hearing young Stevie play the harmonica and sing, he had Brian Holland (talent scout and artists & repertoire man of Tamla) audition the boy. Holland was impressed, as was Berry Gordy later on, and Stevie was signed to an exclusive contract.

Stevie's first record, "I Call It Pretty Music" (early 1963), gained some attention. Follow-ups "Water Boy" and "Contract on Love" did progressively better. That August, his single "Fingertips—Part 2" and debut LP, *The 12 Year Old Genius* both hit number one on *Billboard*'s pop lists.

Outstanding singles during 1964–65 included "Workout, Stevie, Workout," "Castles in the Sand," "Hey Harmonica Man," "Sad Boy," "Kiss Me Baby," and "High Heel Sneakers." In 1966, he had a number one R&B hit and top 10 pop hit with Bob Dylan's composition "Blowing in the Wind" as well as such other successes as "Nothing's Too Good for My Baby," "With a Child's Heart," and pop top 10 "Uptight" and "A Place in the Sun." LPs during these years included *The Jazz Soul of Little Stevie Wonder, With a Song in My Heart, Stevie at the Beach, Fingertips,* and *Up-tight: Everything's Alright.* He also had parts in the low-budget beach movies *Bikini Beach* and *Muscle Beach Party.*

Stevie's schooling included a special teacher when he was on the road and classes at the Michigan School for the Blind in Lansing, Michigan, when he was at home. He studied music theory via braille books and songsheets.

Late '60s pop top 10 singles included "I Was Made to Love Her" (1967), "Shoo-Be-Doo-Be-Doo-Da-Day" and "For Once in My Life" (1968), and "My Cherie Amour" and "Yester-Me, Yester-You, Yesterday" (1969). Ironically, despite his debut LP's popularity, none of his others—such as *Down to Earth* (1967), *I Was Made to Love Her, Someday at Christmas, Stevie Wonder's Greatest Hits,* and 1969's *My Cherie Amour* and *Eivets Rednow* (his name spelled backwards)—even broke *Billboard*'s pop top 20 for almost a decade as he widened their focus to cover soul, rock, and slower-paced ballads.

Wonder continued his personal growth as the 1970s began. He spent some time at the University of Southern California expanding his knowledge of music theory and composition. He also demonstrated some talent for comedy in sketches on Flip Wilson's NBC-TV show. In addition, he showed considerable promise as a record producer, working with a Motown group called the Spinners on the V.I.P. label. Under his direction, they recorded such hits as "It's a Shame" (1970) and "We'll Have It Made" (winter 1971).

In addition, Wonder continued to charm audiences in many cities and was represented with a single or LP on the national charts for most of 1970 and '71. "Signed, Sealed, Delivered, I'm Yours" and "Heaven Help Us All" (1970) and "If You Really Love Me" (1971) were pop top 10 singles. "We Can Work It Out" and "Never Dreamed You'd Leave in Summer" also did well in 1971. LPs included *Stevie Wonder Live* and *Signed Sealed & Delivered* in 1970 and *Where I'm Coming From* in 1971.

On the singles charts in 1972 were "Keep on Running" and "Superwoman (Where Were You When I Needed You)." He began 1973 with a number one single—his classic composition "Superstition." On top of *Billboard* charts the week of January 27, it was his first number one single since "Fingertips—Part 2" in August 1963 (back before he wrote almost all his songs himself). On May 19, he had another number one single, "You Are the Sunshine of My Life." Other hits that year were "Higher Ground" and "Living for the City." In 1972, he released the albums *Greatest Hits Volume 2, Music of My Mind, Where I'm Comin' From,* and (returning him to the LP pop top 10) *Talking Book.* The top 10 *Innervisions* continued his success in 1973.

Stevie's importance to pop music was underscored at the 1973 Grammy Awards by his dominating as Best Pop Vocal Performance, Male ("You Are the Sunshine of My Life"), Best R&B Vocal Performance, Male ("Superstition"), Best R&B Song (a writer's award for "Superstition"), and Album of the Year *(Innervisions)*. It was a pattern that continued through the mid-1970s. In accepting a Grammy in a later year when Stevie was between albums, Paul Simon quipped that he gave thanks to Stevie for not having a record for him to compete with that year. Yet the year brought problems as well. He was sidelined for much of 1973 with injuries from a near-fatal auto accident on August 6 in North Carolina.

In 1974, Stevie enjoyed hit singles "Living for the City" (a holdover from 1973), "Don't You Worry 'bout a Thing," and "You Haven't Done Nothin'" (on top of *Billboard* lists the week of November 2). In the Grammy voting, he walked off with five awards including trophies as both producer and artist of the Album of the Year (the number one *Fullfillingness' First Finale)* plus Best Pop Vocal Performance, Male, for that LP; Best R&B Vocal Performance, Male, for its track "Boogie On Reggae Woman"; and the writing award for Best R&B Song ("Living for the City").

In August 1975, with Stevie's Motown contract up for renewal, he quieted rumors about another star leaving the label by signing a new agreement report-

edly providing for a guarantee of $13 million over the next seven years. That out of the way, he went back to work on material for his next Tamla album, the two-disc *Songs in the Key of Life,* which scored the rare feat of debuting at number one in *Billboard* in October 1976. Its first single, "I Wish," rose to number one the week of January 22, 1977. Almost predictably, Stevie was the big winner in the 1976 Grammy Awards, earning two trophies as producer and artist of Album of the Year *(Songs in the Key of Life);* one for Producer of the Year; one for Best Pop Vocal Performance, Male, for the LP; and one for Best R&B Vocal Performance, Male, for the track "I Wish."

From then into the 1980s, his every release was considered an event by critics and record buyers alike. Rarely disappointing with subpar material, his LPs were thought-provoking best-sellers each time out, including *Looking Back* (1977), *Journey through the Secret Life of Plants* (1979), *Hotter than July* (1980, platinum), and the 1972–82 gold retrospective *Stevie Wonder's Original Musiquarium I* (1982). As for singles, "Sir Duke" was number one in *Billboard* for three weeks starting May 21, 1977. "Send One Your Love" made the pop top 10 in 1979.

Increasingly over the years, Stevie came out against injustice and for policies that would increase understanding among peoples of the world. One of his major projects was lobbying the U.S. government to declare January 15—the birthday of Rev. Martin Luther King, Jr.—a national holiday. He paid tribute to the occasion on *Hotter than July*'s track "Happy Birthday." In the mid-1980s, he was able to smile about the final passage of legislation for the King holiday. He told Robert Hilburn of the *Los Angeles Times* in the early 1980s, "I think it's ridiculous that it's taking so long. Here was a man who stood for the unification of all people . . . a man who saw how this country was capable of being the spearheading force to move the rest of the world in that direction. [The holiday] wouldn't be a day of significance just for black people, but for all people."

He also contributed his services to programs against nuclear weapons and war such as the 1982 Peace Sunday concert at the Rose Bowl, which also featured Jackson Browne, Stevie Nicks, Linda Ronstadt, and Gil Scott-Heron.

He told Hilburn that he drew inspiration for some of his songs of the '70s and '80s from Marvin Gaye's concept album *What's Going On.* "I loved that album. I still do. I think it will always be current because we will always have those problems until we [as a society] come to grips with them. I think it's really important for people, especially those immediately responsible, to be honest about the way things are. Look at religion. We say God is colorless, but everything we do tends to draw a distinction. Religion is still a very racial thing . . . black churches and white churches. How can people in South Africa talk to the Creator and then hate someone? It just doesn't make sense.''

During that period, Stevie joined Paul McCartney in a duet on Paul's composition urging racial harmony. Called ''Ebony and Ivory,'' it reached number one in *Billboard* for seven weeks starting May 15, 1982.

Stevie's next major project was to write the score for Gene Wilder's movie *The Woman in Red*. The mid-1984 soundtrack LP went platinum. Its track ''I Just Called to Say I Love You'' (number one in *Billboard* for three weeks as of October 13) provided him with his first number one single ever in England, an Oscar for Best Original Song, and a Golden Globe from the Hollywood Foreign Press Association. The film's ''Love Light in Flight'' hit the top 20 in early 1985.

In 1984, Stevie added another cause to his list when he wrote the song ''Don't Drive Drunk'' in behalf of the nationwide organization Mothers against Drunk Driving (MADD). He told reporters: ''I tried to put [the message] in a way where people will like the melody and dance to it. You can't just tell people not to drink—it's part of the American fiber.'' But, he emphasized: ''They [MADD] have a right to be mad. Not only mothers, but all people. We all are angry.''

In early 1985, Stevie was one of the 45 artists who recorded the USA for Africa single ''We Are the World'' (number one in the U.S. for a month starting the week of April 13). During the year, he also completed work on his first new studio LP in four years, *In Square Circle* (top 10, platinum). The first two singles from the album, ''Part Time Lover'' and ''Go Home,'' made the top 10. The *In Square Circle* LP won him a Grammy for Best R&B Vocal Performance, Male, of 1985.

In August 1987, Wonder gave a benefit concert for Retinosa Pigmentosa International at the Dorothy Chandler Pavilion in Los Angeles that raised $1.5 million to help the organization combat that degenerative eye disease. The group stated the money would be used as part of the funding for a new research and care facility to be called Wonderland. At a backstage press conference, Stevie said the cause meant a lot to him since his private teacher during his elementary school days had suffered from the ailment.

Late in the year Motown issued his new *Characters* LP in several formats including a 10-song album and CD and cassette collection that included two extra tracks. Originally, the record company stated, it had been planned as a two-disc set. The songs not used on *Characters* likely would come out on a future album. Another possibility, Motown noted, was that all the songs for the *Characters* sessions might form the basis for a future feature-length film. *(See Gordy, Berry, Jr.; McCartney, Paul; Moonglows, The; Parker, Ray, Jr.; Robinson, Smokey; Third World.)*

X: *Vocal and instrumental group. Members (1978–85): Exene Cervenka, born Chicago, Illinois, February 1, 1956; John Doe, born Decatur, Illinois, February 25, 1954; D.J. Bonebrake, born Burbank, California, December 8, 1955; Billy Zoom, born Illinois, February 20, late 1940s. Zoom replaced in 1985 by Dave Alvin, born Downey, California. Tony Gilkyson added in 1986.**

Partly inspired by the punk/new wave movement in England, the Southern California rock scene in the mid-1970s experienced one of the sudden upsurges of talented underground bands that marks the genre's history. Small clubs sprang up all over the Los Angeles area—often in dilapidated surroundings—where innovative young musicians experimented with all manner of new rock offshoots. Clubs and bands came and went with dizzying speed, but a few groups, such as the Motels and X, proved to have staying power and the ability to reach audiences beyond the local scene. Creatively, if not commercially, X ranked as one of the most influential new bands of the 1980s.

Three of the four founding members were born in Illinois, but had moved around considerably before finding their respective ways to Los Angeles in the 1970s. John Doe, bass guitarist and, with lead singer Exene Cervenka, primary songwriter, recalled: ''I was born in Decatur, Illinois, but as a kid I moved all around America from Decatur to Knoxville to Madison to Baltimore. In Baltimore, I started playing bass in a bunch of bar bands. There was no place to go, musically speaking, in Baltimore and I wanted a big change, so I came to L.A. on Halloween in 1976.''

Lead guitarist Billy Zoom (a name, like Doe's, that is a pseudonym) was in love with music from his earliest years. ''I've been playing music all my life. My musician father [who played at one time with the great jazz guitarist Django Reinhardt] started teaching me before I could walk and my mother played all kinds of different music while I was growing up. After high school I played with black R&B bands

---

*Based partly on personal interviews with Exene Cervenka and D.J. Bonebrake by Irwin Stambler.

around the country. I played guitar and sax in Gene Vincent's last group, and before X, fronted my own rockabilly band. We cut several sides for Rollin' Rock Records.''

In the fall of 1977, both Zoom and Doe were at loose ends musically. Each placed an ad seeking a new band alignment in a throwaway local classified paper, the *Recycler*. And each saw the other's ad. Zoom remembered: ''I went down and picked up a copy the morning it came out. While walking back to my car, I saw John's ad and circled it. When I got home there was a message for me next to the phone: 'John Doe called.''''

The two got together and talked about a new band. They practiced together on rock standards they both knew and liked. During one session, Doe brought over his girlfriend (and future wife), Exene Cervenka. She became enthused enough about the new project to think about singing with the group, though she hadn't considered working as a vocalist before.

Exene noted: ''I was born in Chicago, but I grew up in a small town in Illinois. It was a really little town. It had no movie theater, for instance. We moved to Florida when I was 15 and I lived there for five years. I was living in Tallahassee writing poetry when this friend said he was going to California, did I want a ride? When I got to Los Angeles, I just kept on writing.''

In L.A. she made contact with other people interested in the arts and soon found out about places where poets could read their material. During a poetry workshop in the Venice section of Los Angeles, John Doe heard her read her work and went up afterward to introduce himself. He said: ''She was wearing dark lipstick and read this poem about Lois Lane. [''Lois Lane is a redhead/A neat slick chick/In a blue-eyed suit''] We went out that night, got drunk, and became a couple.''

After spending some time at the new band's rehearsals, Exene reworked her poem ''I'm Coming Over'' into a song to demonstrate her singing ability to Zoom and Doe. She not only became lead singer, but her first name suggested the name of the band.

During that initial phase at the end of 1977, Mick Basher was the band drummer, but in early 1978, he was replaced by Don ''D.J.'' Bonebrake. Both the original X members and Bonebrake had performed at a basement Hollywood club called the Masque, which for a while was the center of the L.A. punk movement. Reviewing that club's brief history, Robert Hilburn wrote in the *Los Angeles Times* (June 12, 1980): ''Everything about the Masque was perfect for the new wave scene. Housed in the basement of a Hollywood porno theater, the club's only entrance was through a garbage-strewn alley that ran between Cherokee and Las Palmas streets. The inside of the club was stark: a series of cavernous rooms with naked bulbs hanging from the ceiling and exposed piping. The Masque looked like something Hollywood would design for a nightmare scene. Little wonder that the Masque ran afoul of building and safety codes. Opened in July of 1977, it was closed in January of 1978 for lack of a fire-exit.''

Doe and Exene watched Bonebrake play with his group, the Eyes, and became excited about his percussion skills. In particular they liked his powerful use of a marching snare. After the set they persuaded him to join their group. He made his debut with X at the Elks Lodge Hall on February 18, 1978, for a while playing with both X and the Eyes.

Bonebrake was the only native Californian in the group. ''I was born in Burbank, California, and started drumming in marching bands when I was 12. From there I learned how to play marimbas, vibes, tympani—all the percussion instruments. I played in everything from stage bands and classical percussion ensembles to jazz trios. I went to junior college for a while. I never graduated. I went there for fun to take music courses and play in a big band. I've always liked to play as many things in music as possible. At one time I was in eight groups: Dixieland, three orchestras, percussion ensembles, and two rock bands. Guess you could say I like to spread myself thin.''

During 1978 and 1979, X played gig after gig in new wave clubs, as it evolved its own special style that combined the high-speed instrumental rhythms of new wave with all manner of influences from Appalachian folk music to rockabilly to blues. The lyrics typically provided by John and Exene reflected their strong interest in avant garde poetry. Exene maintained: ''I think there's always been poetry in rock and the music styles it evolved from. I think if you look at an artist like Big Joe Turner who's been around for years, his music is really poetic and that's the kind of stuff we love. 'Shake, Rattle and Roll' is really poetry. I think heavy metal bands play bad poetry and we think ours is like good poetry or word painting.''

In shaping the originals that she and John wrote for the band in the late 1970s, Exene said: ''We write the words, the basic melody and then the band works on it and makes changes.''

Bonebrake told an interviewer from *Musician* magazine (June 1982): ''When John and Exene bring in a new song, they usually have the chords, which Billy will occasionally elaborate on or change. But the words and structure are there, although we'll sometimes restructure a song. It's pretty basic, really. We play the song over and over and I just play along. Sometimes I'll get a specific idea I'll work from. On 'We're Desperate,' for instance, I wanted a rhythm that combined the Ramones and Captain Beefheart.''

By late 1978, the group had established a considerable following among young local fans and felt it was ready to expand its audience beyond city limits. It already had completed its first single release, "Adult Books"/"We're Desperate" on the Dangerhouse label. In November, the group piled its gear into a car and drove cross-country to New York to try to match its skills with the New York punk/ new wave groups. *New York Times* critic, Robert Christgau, who later became a strong supporter of X, saw them at the time. Exene recalled: "He thought us boring, humorless, and not worth looking at.''

Back in L.A., the band's manager, Jay Jenkins, took new demo tapes to major labels in early 1979, but got a complete turndown. The independent label Slash had expressed interest before and when the big firms said no, the band signed with it. Ray Manzarek of Doors fame had seen X play at the Whisky on the Sunset Strip and had been so impressed he asked to serve as producer. Under his direction, the debut LP, *Los Angeles* (1980), took shape. It sold over 80,000 copies, a major achievement for an independent-label LP. The 1980 single from the album, "White Girl"/"Your Phone's off the Hook (But You're Not)," was a concert favorite. The title track had been in the band's repertoire for some time. An early studio version of the song had appeared on *Yes L.A.* (Dangerhouse Records, 1979), a sampler of such punk bands as the Bags, the Germs, the Alley Cats, Black Randy, and Bonebrake's old group, the Eyes. X's live numbers "We're Desperate," "Beyond and Back," and "Johny Hit and Run Paulene" were on the soundtrack LP (Slash, 1980) of Penelope Spheeris's documentary film about L.A. punk, *The Decline . . . of Western Civilization.* "Beyond and Back" was also on the 1981 A&M soundtrack LP for *Urgh! A Music War,* a performance film showcasing 27 bands.

Los Angeles was one of the most distinctive rock albums of 1980 and deservedly topped many critics' lists of the year's best. The band even improved on it with a superb second LP, *Wild Gift* (Slash, summer 1981). At year-end, critics from both *The New York Times* and *Los Angeles Times* selected it as album of the year. By then, major labels were coming after X. The band signed an eight-album contract with Elektra Records, which made Slash officials cry disloyalty. But members stressed they had contributed to Slash's exchequer and had gone about as far as they could with a small label. The band's 1982 debut on Elektra, *Under the Big Black Sun,* proved to be a fine collection, if not quite on a par creatively with *Wild Gift.* While not a blockbuster hit, it easily outsold the earlier Slash releases. The Elektra affiliation

opened the door to much greater promotional support, including three music videos issued in 1982: "The Hungry Wolf," "Motel Room in My Bed," and "Because I Do." Elektra singles from the album included the 7-inch disc "Blue Spark"/"Dancing with Tears in My Eyes" and the 12-inch "Blue Spark" backed with "The Hungry Wolf" and "How I Learned My Lesson."

While the band was making progress as a concert act and recording group, its members continued to pursue outside projects. Bonebrake and Zoom sometimes backed other bands during recording sessions while Doe and Cervenka still wrote and performed poetry. In 1982, *Adulterers Anonymous,* a book of verse by Exene and Lydia Lunch, came out on Grove Press. The May 1983 issue of the small L.A.-based literary magazine *Rattler* included Exene's poem "Peas Beans" and Doe's "Stockton."

The band's second album on Ekektra, *More Fun in the New World* (fall 1983), was consciously crafted toward making commercial inroads, but Exene stressed she felt rather uncomfortable going that route. "It sold the most and did the most on radio, but we still have to be true to ourselves. I don't think the next one may be as successful commercially, but it will get a lot of love and care."

Bonebrake added: "For the album after *More Fun in the New World* we take aim at people who are pretending to be cool and they might take offense. But I really liked the last LP myself even if we did design it so it would be more commercial."

X always had country elements in its music. Between concerts in 1984, John and Exene worked with Henry Rollins of Black Flag, Dave Alvin of the Blasters, and bassist Jonny Ray Bartel in a down-home folk and country band they called the Knitters (whose name was a tribute to 1950s folk quartet the Weavers). X's old label, Slash, put out the Knitters' *Poor Little Critter on the Road* (spring 1985). While Doe and Cervenka indulged their country leanings in 1984, they showed another side of their art with a heavy metal–like remake of the Troggs' 1966 hit "Wild Thing." Said Exene: "It's not really a metal song, or a punk song, or anything. We just wanted to cut a record with a lot of power and feeling."

In 1985, a full-length movie about the band, *The Unheard Music,* was released by Skouras Pictures. The film had been assembled in bits and pieces by independent producers Christopher Blakely and Everett Greaton over a five-year period. Bonebrake commented: "They just came and said they wanted to do a movie about us around the middle of 1980."

Exene added: "It must have been 1980 because 'White Girl' was on the radio. I didn't think it would take this long, because I didn't think it was ever actually coming out."

The film blended dramatic sequences (some fictional) with filmed interviews and performance shots. It was better than most films about rock bands, but it didn't get extensive support and faded from view in a short time, though it may well surface to better effect in the future. In a sense, it symbolized what generally was a down year for the band. Its 1985 album, *Ain't Love Grand,* for the most part, didn't measure up to its earlier releases. Billy Zoom left the act and, before year-end, Exene and John had agreed to get a divorce.

But in 1986, the bitterness had passed between the two and they were ready to collaborate on new material and a new band roster. Bonebrake remained on drums and percussion and Zoom's spot on lead guitar was taken by Blasters alumnus Dave Alvin. For the first time, the band expanded to five pieces with the addition of former Lone Justice guitarist Tony Gilkyson. That fall, the new X sharpened its act in local clubs in shows that demonstrated it had lost none of its timing and dynamic audience rapport.

Exene indicated that, while she would continue to do other things such as poetry readings (as on her *Twin Sisters* LP with Wanda Coleman on Rhino Records) and acting (including a part in an episode of "The Twilight Zone" on TV and the role of TV evangelist in director Beth B's 1987 film *Salvation),* she expected that X would be the main band focus. "Now that Dave Alvin is playing with us, we probably won't do as much Knitters. When Billy was in the band, there was a stricter kind of guideline on what we could do in X. With Doe, on the other hand, we can play anything we want so we don't need the Knitters to let off steam."

Alvin took part in recording sessions for the band's next album *(See How We Are,* Elektra), but by the time it was released in mid-1987 he had left to concentrate on a solo career. However, it was the writing and singing of Exene and Doe that made the LP the band's best collection since the early 1980s. The band's record company followed up in 1988 with a new concert album, *X Live at the Whisky-A-Go-Go on the Fabulous Sunset Strip.*

In the annual *L.A. Weekly* magazine readers' poll, X was named best band of 1987, *See How We Are* best major-label release, Exene tied for best female performer with Johnette Napolitano of the Concrete Blonde group, and Doe was voted best singer/songwriter and male performer.

Exene and Bonebrake pointed to the liberating influence of the mid-1970s punk scene for X and many other new bands. Bonebrake stressed the need to differentiate between American and English punk. "When punk got attention in England a lot of people tried to imitate English punk here and that just didn't get off the ground."

Exene said: "There were two roads to that—one funky American music and the other political, which was the English way. Some people were just doing English-style material because it was in fashion. But the music scene in L.A. didn't worry about that. One of the things that happened in the mid-1970s was that those involved in the punk thing began to find out what music had gone before. That's one thing the punk movement really did was bring about revival of interest in older music like rockabilly and blues. That freed us to make use of some of that to form new directions for rock and pop. I don't know why that happened—perhaps just the desire among musicians and fans for something different." *(See Black Flag; Blasters, The; Doors, The; Lone Justice; Vincent, Gene.)*

XTC: *Vocal and instrumental group. Original members (1976): Andy Partridge, born Malta; others all born U.K.: Barry Andrews, Colin Moulding, Terry Chambers. Andrews replaced by Dave Gregory in 1979. Chambers left in 1982.*

A group that provided melodically challenging and high-vitality postpunk rock, XTC might be bracketed with Talking Heads as a thinking person's band, though the two groups' styles weren't directly comparable. XTC gained enormous popularity in the U.K. in the late 1970s and early 1980s, but remained essentially a cult favorite in the U.S. during those years.

The group's members mostly grew up in working class areas of Swindon, England, where all forsook formal education in their teens in favor of essaying pop music careers. Andy Partridge, born on the Mediterranean island of Malta, was taken to England by his family at an early age and stayed in school until age 15. After that, he worked as a "teaboy" (English equivalent of a U.S. "gofer") at a newspaper and then took art classes at a local technical college while teaching himself to play guitar at home in his off hours. About the same time, Colin Moulding, who lived on the same block as Partridge, was learning bass guitar while bringing in spare change as a milkman's assistant, day laborer, and council worker. Their drummer acquaintance Terry Chambers had been thrown out of school at 15 for an incident in which he overimbibed hard cider. Like others of his age group, he dreamed of music success as he worked at a series of jobs including builder's merchant and lithographic printer.

Those three played with many different bands, sometimes together, sometimes separately, including Star Park, the Helium Kids, Skyscraper, and Snakes, before getting together to found XTC in

1976. The group started as a foursome with Barry Andrews joining as keyboards player. By early 1977, they had built up a substantial following in the Swindon area. Encouraged by that reception, as well as favorable comments from local writers about the band's combination of humor and incisive comment on the depressing teen-employment environment, Partridge and friends felt the time was ripe to move to London, where the punk movement was in full flower.

In mid-1977, the group signed with Virgin Records, which issued its debut single, "3 DEP," in October, followed by five more singles through 1979 including "Making Plans for Nigel," a top 20 U.K. hit in late 1979. In 1978, Virgin released the band's first two British albums: *White Music* and *Go 2*. Both made the English top 30.

The band supported its records with almost nonstop touring, initially in the U.K., but later in Japan, Australia, New Zealand, Venezuela, Continental Europe, and eventually the U.S. The band's debut in the States came on New Year's Eve 1978 on a bill that included the Talking Heads. The audience reaction was good enough to bring proposals for a dozen more appearances in early 1979. It also spurred the record company to make plans for a more ambitious tour later in the year to coincide with the band's first LP to be released in the U.S., *Drums & Wires*. Before that took place, XTC had to reorganize a bit back in Swindon when Andrews decided to leave. His place was taken by Dave Gregory, who had played keyboards on occasion with the band in the past. His previous credentials included working as a guitarist/keyboardist with Dean Gabber and his Gabberdines.

The new alignment still won praise from British critics. Writing in *New Musical Express,* Paul Morley enthused that XTC continued to excel at "making multilayered music of wit and elegance . . . music that demands new adjectives." John Orme of *Melody Maker* called *Drums & Wires* a very impressive album in which "with a mix of complexity, contrast, fluency, and humour, XTC has broken cover and broken ground."

Partridge stated in record company bio notes: "I came into music about the time of psychedelia and it was magic. It was sort of R&B plus magic—which is really what we do. . . . I like lumps and spike bits and music that makes you think 'Oh! Gosh! What's that?' XTC have always made people say 'Gosh' and for all the right reasons."

The *Drums & Wires* album, backed by a number of live appearances in the U.S., made a respectabe number of stateside fans aware of the band. Its excellent follow-up, *Black Sea* (1980), moved into the top 50 region.

However, by late 1981, there were signs of burnout among band members that caused a hiatus in live performances. Partridge, for one, had developed a strong antipathy to crowds of all kinds. The band's newest LP, *English Settlement,* was released both in the U.K. and in the U.S., but while it did well at home, it didn't expand the audience acquired with *Black Sea,* perhaps because of the dearth of concert support. In late 1982, Terry Chambers, disgruntled with the lack of activity, left the group for new pastures in Australia. Partridge, Moulding, and Gregory decided to carry on as a threesome.

During 1983, they began work on another studio album, one that emphasized acoustic instruments. *Mummer* (fall 1983) was released on a new U.S. label, Geffen Records. The album did not spend much time on the charts in either Britain or the States, suggesting some confusion among fans about its softer tone compared to the previous album's.

In 1984, band members returned to the hard-blues approach of its salad days for the next studio compilation. Partridge stated: "With our new album I wanted to crank it up again, to let the music have a more boisterous feel. The lyrics of *Mummer* had a very small horizon about the size of my back garden. The new album *(The Big Express)* is a harder record that has us looking out at the world again."

The album, released by Geffen in the U.S. in October 1984, was an interesting one, but again did not catch fire with record buyers beyond the band's hardcore following. (In 1985, the group's psychedelic alter ego, the Dukes of Stratosphear, completed the LP *25 O'Clock,* issued only in England.) Geffen executives expressed confidence that the band's importance would eventually be realized by a larger number of rock fans as the label issued the new LP *Skylarking* in 1986.

Despite the group's problems in winning large-scale respect outside England, optimism had always been part of Partridge's outlook. He expressed that to Kristine McKenna *(Los Angeles Times,* April 4, 1982): "Pop music is full of lots of fun and carnage—the microphone bending, shirt-slashed-to-the-waist stuff. We don't deal with that, not only because we're not particularly handsome, shirt-slashed-to-the-waist types, but because we have different goals. Music can't change the culture, but I do believe it can reflect hope. Perhaps it's naive of me, but that's something I want to do."

YARDBIRDS, THE: *Vocal and instrumental group. Original members (1964): Keith Relf, born Richmond, Surrey, England, March 22, 1944, died May 14, 1976; Chris Dreja, born Surbiton, Surrey, England, November 11, 1944; Jim McCarty, born Liverpool, England, July 25,*

1944; Paul Samwell-Smith, born England, May 8, c. 1944; Eric Clapton, born Ripley, England, March 30, 1945. Clapton replaced in mid-1965 by Jeff Beck, born Surrey, England, June 24, 1944. Samwell-Smith left in 1966, replaced by Jimmy Page, born Middlesex, England, January 9, 1944.

As 1960s rock groups went, the Yardbirds remained in existence as a unit for about the average time, three years approximately. During that short period, they gained a reputation as one of the most influential bands in rock history, an assessment that remained true decades later. Any discussion of rock groups of the '60s had to include their name in the same breath as the Beatles or Stones and many of their recordings continue to be heard regularly on rock stations the world over up to the present day.

The group coalesced in 1963 when the five original members got together amid the constant ebb and flow of young rock performers around London during that period. All were just reaching the end of their teens and had considerable experience—full- or part-time—in British rhythm & blues–oriented bands. It started out with two already heralded artists: lead vocalist Keith Relf (also one of the best harmonica players of the period) and the great lead guitarist Eric "Slowhand" Clapton.

Chris Dreja had taken up guitar in his early teens and by 1963 was considered one of the top rhythm guitarists in the London area. Rounding out the group were bass guitarist, harpsichordist, and songwriter Paul "Sam" Samwell-Smith and drummer Jim McCarty. McCarty had played drums as a hobby during his school years and had seemingly been on his way to a career in the stock market as a statistician. However, after two years of regular office hours, complete with the pin-stripe office "uniform," he decided the chancier, but freer, existence of pop music was more appealing.

After playing small clubs around London, it replaced the Rolling Stones as house band at the Crawdaddy Club in mid-1965. By then Eric Clapton had decided to move on, soon joining John Mayall's Bluesbreakers and then Cream. His replacement was another formidable guitar talent, Jeff Beck. Before Eric departed, though, he recorded a number of singles and albums with the Yardbirds, some of which didn't become hits until later on. Among them were Epic singles "I Wish You Would" (1964) and "For Your Love" (1965). Marquee Club tapes appeared on British Columbia's 1964 *Five Live Yardbirds* (which wasn't released in the U.S. until 1988). *Sonny Boy Williamson and the Yardbirds* (Mercury, 1965) reflected the band's roots in American blues.

During the summer of 1965, the group's recordings finally started getting enough airplay to focus

widespread attention on it. The single "For Your Love" was the first disc to extend the band's audience to other parts of the world, even behind the Iron Curtain in Czechoslovakia.

The Crawdaddy Club exposure helped ease the band into its first cross-country U.S. tour in the fall of 1965. That visit included a guest appearance on the network rock show "Hullaballoo." Late in the year the band also appeared with the Beatles in a concert in Paris.

By late 1965, the group was one of the featured bands on the weekly "Zowie One" program originating at the New Brighton Tower ballroom outside Liverpool and broadcast over the offshore "pirate" rock station, Radio Caroline. Groups performed for no fee in return for receiving promotional plugs over the radio. In a typical Yardbirds segment of the show, material ranged from high-pitched, fast-paced numbers featuring blues-shouting songs by Relf and explosive guitar runs by Beck to Samwell-Smith's "Still I'm Sad," based on a Gregorian chant.

In 1965 and 1966, the group hit the U.S. and U.K. charts regularly with such singles as "Still I'm Sad," "Shapes of Things," "I Wish You Would," "Heart Full of Soul," and "Over Under Sideways Down." Epic LPs included *For Your Love, Over Under Sideways, Down*, and *Having a Rave Up with the Yardbirds*. (*Rave up* means partying it up and here refers to a musical set in which the playing increases steadily in tempo until audience interest is brought to an emotional peak and maintained.)

Internal tensions were manifest in the departure of Samwell-Smith in mid-1966. He was replaced by the highly capable bass player and lead guitarist James Patrick (Jimmy) Page, later a founder of Led Zeppelin. Page had begun playing guitar at 15 and also had studied painting. For well over a year before joining the group he had been one of the most sought-after session musicians in London. Page also had writing credits to match Samwell-Smith's as well as other Yardbirds' and had co-written over 20 songs with Jackie DeShannon.

The group maintained its star status after this change, playing to standing-room–only audiences in the U.S. and Europe in the second half of 1966 and in 1967. Yet the band scored no U.S. top 40 singles in 1967. Its Epic LPs were *Little Games* and *The Yardbirds' Greatest Hits* (its one album to break *Billboard*'s top 40 despite the act's popularity and importance). By the end of 1967, the members had either grown tired of touring or encountered strong differences among themselves concerning musical directions. The Yardbirds dissolved soon after, with alumni going on to important roles in new bands. The Jeff Beck Group soon was winning accolades. Relf and McCarty formed the folk duet Together and then Renaissance. In 1976, Relf died from an electric shock. Dreja moved on to photography. Page tried to keep a semblance of the band going as the New Yardbirds, which evolved into Led Zeppelin.

Yardbirds reissues appeared on various labels: *Eric Clapton and the Yardbirds with Sonny Boy Williamson* (Mercury, 1970), *Yardbirds Favorites* (Epic, 1977), *Eric Clapton and the Yardbirds* and *Shapes of Things* (Springboard), and *The Best of British Rock: The Yardbirds* (two discs, Pair, 1987). Britain's Charly released a two-LP compilation and seven-disc boxed set, both titled *Shapes of Things*. In 1988, Rhino Records finally put out *Five Live Yardbirds* in the U.S., while Polydor's boxed set *Crossroads* spanning Clapton's career even unearthed early Yardbirds demo tapes.

Dave Marsh commented in *Rolling Stone:* "The Yardbirds helped introduce almost every significant technical innovation in the rock of their period: feedback, modal playing, fuzztone, etc. Their influence can't be overestimated. Cream, Led Zeppelin, and heavy metal in general would have been inconceivable without them." *(See Beck, Jeff; Burnette, Dorsey; Clapton, Eric; Cream; Led Zeppelin; Mayall, John; Nilsson.)*

YES: *Vocal and instrumental group. Original members (December 1968), all born England: Jon Anderson, born October 25, 1944; Peter Banks; Bill Bruford, born May 17, c. 1950; Chris Squire, born March 4, 1948; Tony Kaye. Banks replaced in 1969 by Steve Howe, born London, April 8, 1947. Kaye replaced in summer of 1971 by Rick Wakeman, born London, May 18, 1949. Bruford replaced in 1972 by Alan White, born Pelton, County Durham, June 14, 1949; Wakeman replaced in 1974 by Patrick Moraz, born Morges, Switzerland, June 24, 1948. Wakeman returned in 1976. At end of 1970s, Wakeman and Anderson replaced by Geoff Downes and Trevor Horn. Anderson returned in mid-1980s and with Chris Squire headed a reorganized band including Trevor Rabin, White, and Kaye.*

"In England somebody said: 'Yes play music, and the things they play together are things people don't normally play together.' Like we play two things together at once which are harmonically right. We've got a bass player [Chris Squire] who often plays a kind of top line lead, and a drummer [Bill Bruford] who is very rarely content to just play a straight beat. He usually figures in with the whole rhythm of the song and the bass player a lot and Rick [Wakeman, keyboards] and I have a fairly easy job of just using our imaginations and overlaying the right kinds of expresssions on top of it all."—Steve Howe, *Guitar Player* interview, April 1973.

As the Howe quote indicated, Yes was a unique rock group, one not afraid to innovate and draw its inspiration across the gamut of music from classical to rock. One result was a gap of several years between the band's founding by Jon Anderson in December 1968 to its acceptance as a major force in pop music in the early 1970s.

Anderson, who had been singing with rock groups for some time, started Yes after returning to London from a job in Germany. He lined up Bill Bruford on drums, Chris Squire on bass, Peter Banks on guitar, and Tony Kaye on organ. The band did not receive much attention until it got the chance to substitute at the last minute for Sly and the Family Stone at a major London night spot. Its first two Atlantic albums, *Yes* (issued October 15, 1969) and *Time and a Word* (November 2, 1970), caused little stir.

Just after the second album was completed, Banks left and was replaced by Steve Howe. Howe, who had started playing guitar at 12 in the 1950s, already was considered a first-rate artist for his work with such groups as Tomorrow and Bodast. Anderson's compositions for the third LP, *The Yes Album* (March 19, 1971), which reflected a steady improvement in technique, coupled with development of the band's overall style led to a blend that soon made critics sit up and take notice. The album went gold. Its single "Your Move" reached *Billboard*'s top 40.

In midsummer, just before the group's debut U.S. tour, Kaye left and was replaced on keyboards by Rick Wakeman, formerly with Strawbs. *Fragile* (January 4, 1972, top 10, gold) provided the hit single "Roundabout."

On September 13, 1972, the fifth album, *Close to the Edge* (top 10, gold), won the most enthusiastic praise to date. But Bill Bruford departed to join King Crimson. Taking over on drums was Alan White, whose credits included the Plastic Ono Band, Balls, and Joe Cocker's backup group (Chris Stainton's All Stars). On the 1973 triple-disc live *Yessongs,* issued May 4, 1973 (which marked up gold sales levels before it reached dealers' shelves), Bruford is heard on three tracks and White on the rest.

After the group completed its next studio set, the ambitious but overindulgent *Tales from Topographic Oceans* (January 9, 1973), Rick Wakeman left to concentrate on solo work, moving rock beyond its usual confines for A&M Records. *The Six Wives of Henry VIII* (1973, gold) provided instrumental portraits of the infamous sixteenth-century monarch's spouses. *Journey to the Centre of the Earth* (1974, gold) was recorded with the London Symphony Orchestra. *The Myths and Legends of King Arthur and the Knights of the Round Table* featured the English Chamber Choir.

Wakeman's place was taken by Patrick Moraz,

a fine keyboardist, but one who somehow never seemed to mesh properly with the Yes format. The one album on which he performed, *Relayer* (released December 5, 1974), was the band's weakest disc, though it too went gold. Followed as it was by a spate of solo releases by all five members (including Moraz), it inspired predictions from critics that the band's demise might be at hand if, in fact, it hadn't taken place already. This feeling was heightened by the lack of any new Yes releases in 1975 other than the collection of earlier material in the LP *Yesterdays*, issued February 27.

Luckily the scenario had a happier denouement, primarily due to Wakeman's decision to return to the fold in 1976. As Steve Howe told a reporter: "We had just seemed to take up things where they'd been before just as though Rick never left. He fits in smoothly where it just didn't work out with Patrick. Patrick wasn't doing anything wrong. We just weren't jelling."

It never had been any secret that one reason Wakeman left was his dissatisfaction with the pretentiousness of *Tales from Topographic Oceans*. Significantly, the most noticeable aspect of the next two Yes albums, *Going for the One* (July 12, 1977, gold) and *Tormato* (September 26, 1978, platinum), was a retreat from long, almost symphonic-length numbers in favor of relatively concise songs. Wakeman told a reporter he hadn't intended to rejoin the band, particularly since his solo albums were doing well. But he did agree to do session work on *Going for the One* and was impressed. "The music I sat in on was my kind of Yes music. I rejoined because they were back to playing the kind of music they should be playing."

However, his enthusiasm only lasted a few years. By the end of the 1970s, he again decided he was losing his way creatively and departed. This time founding member Anderson also left. Their places were taken by Geoff Downes and Trevor Horn and the band kept on going, but it seemed as though the essential saga of Yes was a thing of the past. This view was reinforced by such weak early 1980s Atlantic releases as *Drama* (August 2, 1980) and *Yesshows* (December 1, 1980). The retrospective *Classic Yes* was issued December 4, 1981.

In the mid-1980s, another turnaround took place as Anderson came back to head up a revamped version of the band, whose members included Chris Squire, Alan White, Tony Kaye, and new guitarist Trevor Rabin. In early 1984, the band suddenly seemed in vogue once more thanks to a platinum LP, *90125* (Atco, November 11, 1983), with a number one single, "Owner of a Lonely Heart," atop *Billboard* for two weeks starting January 21, 1984. The song not only hit on top 40 stations, but also was played regularly on black-music programs. As Chris Squire commented to a *Los Angeles Times* reporter: "Well, that's a phenomenon for you. The '70s white English progressive-rock group crosses over to black radio. Who would have thought it would come to that."

On November 8, 1985, the band put out another charted LP, *90125—The Solos*. Next out (September 25, 1987) was a new studio LP, *Big Generator. (See King Crimson.)*

YOUNG, JESSE COLIN: *See Youngbloods, The.*

YOUNG, NEIL: *Singer, guitarist, songwriter. Born Toronto, Canada, November 12, 1945.*

A variety of influences shaped Neil Young's evolution into one of the foremost folk-rock writers and practitioners of the late 1960s and throughout the 1970s. His musical interests first were stirred by the initial wave of rock stars from south of the Canadian border. Later he briefly became a part of the folk movement before combining those forms into folk-rock and later country-rock.

Though born in Toronto, Neil spent much of his early years further west in Winnipeg. He became interested in rock when Canadian radio began to broadcast the mid-1950s recordings of people such as Bill Haley and Elvis Presley. In his teens, he made his first serious efforts to become a musician, first teaching himself to play on Arthur Godfrey–style ukelele and later progressing to acoustic guitar. In the early 1960s, he worked the coffeehouse circuit with various groups and then organized his own folk-rock band, Neil Young and the Squires, which became a local favorite in Winnipeg.

Looking for more career opportunities, he gave up band work and moved to Los Angeles in 1966, intending to concentrate on writing and solo vocalizing. There, he renewed acquaintances with Steve Stills and Richie Furay, whom he had met previously on the folk circuit. They persuaded him to join their new group, Buffalo Springfield. It was an excellent match. Neil's fine guitar work and original songs played a key part in making the band one of the all-time great folk-rock combinations, even though it remained intact for less than two years. Among the classic Springfield songs Neil provided were "On the Way Home," "Broken Arrow," "Expecting to Fly," "Mr. Soul," and "I Am a Child."

After the band broke up in 1968, Young again wanted to strike out as a solo performer, but was sidetracked to some extent by the arguments of Crosby, Stills, and Nash in favor of his joining their superstar assemblage. He accepted only because they stressed it would be a loose alignment with each member free to pursue his individual music goals if he so desired. However, before he joined them in mid-1969, he had already released his debut solo LP *Neil Young* (Reprise, January 1969), and moved on to a second one, *Everybody Knows This Is Nowhere* (May 1969). For that collection, he brought in a new backup band, Crazy Horse, whom he had first heard at the Whisky-A-Go-Go on Los Angeles' Sunset Strip. The group originally comprised Danny Whitten on guitar, Billy Talbot on bass guitar, and Ralph Molina on drums. He expanded it to a quartet for a time by adding producer/arranger/songwriter/instrumentalist Jack Nitzsche. The album went platinum and Neil's solo reputation was assured.

Even as he began working in CSN&Y, he was thinking about his next solo effort. He only remained a regular member of that now legendary band into the early 1970s, but helped turn out two classic albums for Atlantic: *Déjà Vu* (1970) and *Four Way Street* (1971), both gold and number one in *Billboard*.

In between those two, Reprise released his third solo effort, *After the Goldrush* (August 1970, platinum), arguably one of the all-time great folk-rock LPs for such songs as "Southern Man," "Tell Me Why," "Only Love Can Break Your Heart," "Don't Let It Bring You Down," and "I Believe in You." The album was certainly rock'n'roll, but with the subtle flavor of folk music and lyrics tinged with poetry.

Young's next solo LP didn't come out until February 1972, but it too was a platinum blockbuster. Called *Harvest*, it contained such hits as "Old Man," "War Song," and, most notable of all, Neil's gold, number one rock standard, "Heart of Gold." In addition to his other projects, in the early 1970s, Neil wrote, directed, and took part in the unsuccessful film *Journey through the Past*, whose charted soundtrack album came out in November 1972. *Time Fades Away* (October 1973) won another gold record. However, as a whole it didn't measure up to the previous few albums and some critics wondered whether Neil might have written himself out.

As the decade went by, though, Young proved those fears were groundless with a body of material that often matched his best work of the early 1970s. His LP *On the Beach* (1974, gold) was much better than *Time Fades Away* and his two 1975 releases, *Tonight's the Night* and *Zuma* (issued, respectively, in June and November) reflected considerably more despair and disillusionment than his earlier work. *Tonight's the Night,* for instance, was a concept album that explored his feelings about the drug-overdose deaths of Crazy Horse's Danny Whitten and another friend from the CSN&Y band, Bruce Berry.

In the mid-1970s, he returned briefly to recording and concert work with Steve Stills, which resulted in the LP *Long May You Run* (Reprise, September 1976, gold). After that, he only did solo work (usually with Crazy Horse, by then a threesome of Talbot, Molino, and, on guitar and keyboards, Frank Sampedro), starting with *American Stars 'n Bars* (June 1977, gold). In October 1977, Reprise issued one of the period's best retrospective collections of a major pop artist, the three-record *Decade*. In September, another gold solo LP, *Comes a Time,* came out. In support of his platinum June 1979 LP, *Rust Never Sleeps*, Neil and Crazy Horse embarked on a coast-to-coast U.S. concert tour, his first in several years. The concerts were among the best of the late 1970s. The LP based on those shows, *Live Rust* (1980), went gold.

In the 1980s, Young demonstrated a considerably more conservative outlook than in previous decades. From *Hawks & Doves* (Reprise, late 1980), the track "Union Man" was called not just conservative, but reactionary, by many critics. Neither it nor its follow-up, *Re-Ac-Tor* (1981) sold as well as earlier LPs.

Whereas his 1982 shows involved a great many musicians, for Neil's next project, he whittled the cast down to one—himself. The 1983 performances were an outgrowth of his first LP for Geffen Records, *Trans* (1983), based on the concept of the computer/electronics age. In his live concerts (perhaps an overstatement), the backing vocals and music came from various electronic devices: synthesizers, taped tracks of other instruments, and videos. He used the videos at times to sing duets with images of himself on the large stage screens. The next year, he was back touring with a five-piece band and demonstrating his less strident political leanings, emphasizing patriotism via lyrics such as "I'm proud to be livin' in the U.S.A."

He marked another change in direction the following year with his Nashville-recorded *Old Ways,* featuring duets with country superstars Waylon Jennings and Willie Nelson. Absent from the album's songs were protest numbers such as the early '70s "Southern Man," a severe indictment of anti-black sentiments. In 1986, though, he reassumed his rock'n'roll mantle with a hard-driving LP with Crazy Horse, *Landing on Water.*

Sampedro and Molina of Crazy Horse were among the musicians who performed on Neil's next album, *This Note's for You* (Reprise, April 1988), along with another longtime Young associate, saxophonist Ben Keith. However, the main backing group was what Reprise described as "a full complement R&B band" called the Blue Notes. *(See Buffalo Springfield; Crazy Horse; Crosby, Stills, Nash & Young; Poco; Stills, Stephen.)*

YOUNG, PAUL: *Singer, guitarist, bandleader (THE ROYAL FAMILY), songwriter. Born Luton, England, January 17, 1956.*

European appreciation of American black music, which often exceeded or anticipated interest among fans in the music's U.S. homeland, had both good and bad aspects. On the one hand, it focused attention on important creative areas and provided a place where black jazz, soul, and/or R&B artists could maintain their careers. On the other hand, it often spawned inferior imitations. But there always were exceptions, Paul Young being a case in point. His stylings of soul with hard-driving rock offered new approaches to the general rock genre.

A *New York Times* critic wrote (August 7, 1985): "Of the many white soul singers to emerge from the British pop scene in the last five years, no one captures the intense kinetic energy of a '60s soul revue with more brio than Paul Young. In concert, the 29-year-old singer's urgently soulful delivery is accentuated by such acrobatics as sliding on his knees to the center of the stage, leaping from the rafters, and alternately making love to the mike stand and tossing it high over his head."

Young, born and raised in the working class area of Luton, England, near London, was interested in pop music from his early years. In the mid-1960s, his first big influences were Stax/Volt artists—such as Rufus and Carla Thomas and Otis Redding—rather than Motown stars. However, he didn't ignore rock either. He sometimes picked out both types of melodies on the keyboards when he started taking piano lessons at 14. He also experimented on bass guitar with local bands in his midteens. His idol in his early years in pop music wasn't a soul singer, he said, but British rocker Paul Rodgers, driving force behind bands such as Free, Bad Company, and the Firm. Ironically, when Young had a major singles hit on British charts in 1985, it did considerably better than Rodgers' current release with the Firm.

At 16, he left school to work days as an apprentice at the Vauxhall auto plant where his father worked. By night, Paul paid his dues with a series of obscure groups before becoming lead singer of Streetband in the mid-1970s. That was a hard-driving new wave band and Young had to not only tone down his soul inclinations but consciously try to sound "more like an English rocker." He recalled for Sheila Rogers of *US* magazine (September 9, 1985): "It was rock music and it was very loud, but well played. The group had a lot of potential, but it never really came out in any way."

But Streetband did achieve some success. The single "Toast" made English charts in 1977 and its two albums gained mild interest. But it wasn't enough to keep going on and the group disbanded in the late '70s. Young then joined Q-Tips, an eight-piece, soul-oriented band. Typical of its material was a cover version of Smokey Robinson's "Tracks of My Tears." The band gained a cult following in England, but wasn't able to get beyond it. Young told *US:* "One social set would say to another: 'They've got a great show.' We sort of lived off that for three years."

The band broke up during 1981, but Young had begun to gain a reputation as a potential star singer. Muff Winwood, head of artists & repertoire at CBS Records in England, had become convinced that Young was worth pursuing. In December 1981, he signed Paul to a solo contract. Young said later: "They didn't know what I was going to do. I think they were expecting Huey Lewis and the News or something."

He and Ian Kewley (another former Q-Tips member) co-wrote several songs (such as "Broken Man") that showed up on the LP *No Parlez* (early 1983). Though Young also penned numbers for his next album that suggested an impressive writing potential, he downplayed that part of his talent. He told Merle Ginsburg of *Rolling Stone* (September 12, 1985): "My top enjoyment in life is singing on a stage. Second to that comes singing in the studio. But I dislike writing. It's really laborious and boring, and it takes such a long time. I've never found my ideal situation to write in. When I do, maybe I'll write some great songs."

Buoyed by his hit single of a relatively obscure Marvin Gaye number, "Wherever I Lay My Hat" (which rose to number one on British charts in May), *No Parlez* hit top chart levels almost everywhere but the U.S. One of his problems was the difficulty U.S. top 40 radio had in fitting his unique blend of rock and soul into their preordained formats.

Despite back-breaking touring in 1983 in the U.S. in addition to dates in other countries, *No Parlez* remained stuck on lower U.S. chart levels. An intensive 1984 U.S. series was planned to change that, but only a few weeks into it he encountered voice problems that eventually cost him the six top notes in his vocal range. He persevered in meeting concert dates, winning over more fans, but not achieving overnight stardom.

Frustrated, but still hopeful, he went back into the studio to work on *The Secret of Association*, which entered U.K. charts at number one after its release in early 1985. As for that title, he told a reporter: "There's no real meaning to it. We just jumbled some words from an advertisement in the *Sunday Times*. It was an ad for a secretary. I thought it sounded like a good title and would make people think about the album."

In April, he was represented on U.K. charts with a

hit single of a song written by Daryl Hall of Hall & Oates, "Everytime You Go Away," which, oddly, wasn't on the British version of *Secret of Association*, though it was on the U.S. release.

Determined to win over U.S. audiences, CBS decided to give Paul a new, bubble-gum–type image in a video of "Everytime You Go Away." The video unabashedly aimed at the teenage female audience, particularly younger teens. It was another irony in the career of an artist who said, at one point: "My strategy for [longevity] is to go for an older audience to develop a following with a few good records and take that crowd with me. I'm not worried about teenagers."

The video worked. Young soon became the darling of younger fans and his mid-1985 U.S. tour became a triumph. Philosophically he told *Rolling Stone:* "I think it's OK that I'm getting this sort of a following. I guess I do flirt with the audience a bit. Every good performer does. The sex-symbol marketing is a little bit conscious. You have to present yourself as being appealing in some way. I can't really do it. I need someone to point it out to me: 'Do this, do that.'"

The single, backed with "This Means Anything," hit number one on U.S. charts in July 1985. The album went gold in the U.S. after going platinum in England. Another single, "I'm Gonna Tear Your Playhouse Down," made the U.S. top 15 that fall.

In the Grammy Awards voting for 1985, the increased attention generated by a second U.S. hit single helped win "Everytime You Go Away" a nomination for Song of the Year.

While happy with his apparent move toward stardom, Young pointed to his work in Bob Geldof's heroic Aid for Africa programs. In December 1984, he played on the *Band Aid* album and, in July 1985, at the internationally televised U.S./U.K. Live Aid concert.

YOUNGBLOODS, THE: *Original members (1965): Jerry Corbitt; Jesse Colin Young, born New York, New York, November 22, 1941; Banana, born Cambridge, Massachusetts, 1946; Joe Bauer, born Memphis, Tennessee, September 26, 1941, died c. 1985. Corbitt left in 1969. Michael Kane joined c. 1970. Group disbanded in 1972.*

In a way, the Youngbloods represented some of the changes in rock in the 1960s compared to the previous decade. Many of the "name" groups of the 1950s were made up of teenagers who learned a few chord patterns and began playing at dances almost immediately. The Youngbloods, on the other hand, were in their twenties when they joined forces in the mid-1960s and rehearsed for almost a year before trying for any major engagements.

The group took its name from the lead singer Jesse Colin Young (born Perry Miller), a New York City native raised in Bucks County, Pennsylvania. From an affluent family, Young attended exclusive Phillips Andover Academy in New England, going on to Ohio State University and, in the early 1960s, New York University. His original goal was to become a writer, though he was interested in folk music and learned to play bass guitar. His excellent singing voice made him a natural for folk ballads and, in 1963, he left school to concentrate on music. As with many of his contemporaries, he played the coffeehouse circuit from New York to Boston, making just enough money to keep body and soul together. He created his new name, Jesse Colin Young, from his fascination with the Wild West of Jesse James and Cole Younger and with the racing world of Grand Prix driver Colin Chapman.

In his travels, he made friends with pianist-composer Bobby Scott, who brought him to the attention of major record companies and produced two albums by Young: *Soul of a City Boy* on Capitol and *Youngblood* on Mercury. Neither made any major mark on the record market, but the second LP eventually provided a name for the successful rock group.

The origins of the Youngbloods can be traced to Cambridge, Massachusetts, where Young got the idea for a group after meeting guitarist Jerry Corbitt while both were appearing in that college town in 1965. Jazz drummer Joe Bauer recalled that he joined up because he needed the work, though it took him quite a few months to overcome his jazzman's instinctive aversion to rock.

Bauer had started playing drums at 14. He taught himself to play by emulating some of his idols on jazz records. As he moved through his high school years, he played with local bands—mostly country-oriented, though some with jazz repertoires—in beer joints around Memphis or at school dances. After high school, he toured the Southeast with small show bands for a few years.

When he was 21, he moved to San Francisco, where a brother lived, to try to move up in the music world. However, band jobs were scarce and he earned a living delivering samples door to door. In the early 1960s, he moved to New York, where he managed to find work with a summer band. When this ended, he again worked at any available jobs, starting as a clerk in a camera store, then settling down for a year as night watchman in a Brooklyn chocolate factory while working for a light moving operation in the daytime. He made the rounds of union hiring halls and talked to band leaders, but, until he went to Cambridge in 1965, made little headway.

Soon after Corbitt, Young, and Bauer started their group, they returned to New York. Two weeks later, New Englander Lowell Levinger (who took the name Banana) came to them and displayed considerable skill on guitar. He was quickly accepted as the fourth member of the group. Originally, he had seemed on the way to becoming a classical pianist, but at 13, he gave up piano and took up bluegrass banjo and guitar. During high school, he played and sang as leader of a series of groups; the first was named Banana and His Bunch, Old Time Music with Appeal, and the last was the Trolls. At Boston University, he studied acting for a while until he heard about the Youngbloods in 1965 and joined them.

The group spent most of 1966 working on their material in hours of rehearsal. Occasionally they played local clubs and gradually built up rapport with underground music fans. As word about them spread, several record firms offered contracts and the group finally settled on RCA Victor. Late in 1966, they recorded enough material for an album and several singles. Produced by Felix Pappalardi, their first LP, *The Youngbloods* (February 1967), gained some attention in the East and their single, ''Grizzly Bear,'' became a regional hit in the East and Midwest.

The group made its first cross-country tour in 1967, including an engagement at San Francisco's Avalon Ballroom. While there, they stayed on a farm in Marin County owned by Joe's brother, an environment they found to their liking. They returned to New York to record a second album, *Earth Music* (November 1967), packed up, and moved home base to Inverness in the San Francisco Bay area, where they still were living 20 years later. Most of the time they played in San Francisco clubs and continued to do so as a three-man group after Jerry Corbitt left in 1969 to try his hand at producing records and, eventually, to work as a solo performer for Capitol Records.

In 1969, they finally gained a national reputation and gold record with the rerelease of their 1967 single ''Get Together,'' written by folk-rock composer-performer Dino Valente of Quicksilver Messenger Service. Its ''Come on people now/smile on your brother/everybody get together and love one another right now'' became anthem for those interested in human rights and dignity.

The group's output—never very large, partly because of their insistence on long periods of playing and replaying each number in the recording studios—usully was augmented by two new albums in 1969–70: *Elephant Mountain* and *Get Together*.

RCA also released a recap LP, *The Best of the Youngbloods.*

At the end of 1970, the contract with RCA expired and they established their own label, Raccoon Records, distributed by Warner Brothers. In 1971, they made the charts with their first Raccoon release, *Rock Festival,* and with two RCA LPs of earlier material: *Ride the Wind* and *Sunlight. Good and Dusty* (1972) continued their charming fusion of mellow folk-rock, hippie idealism, and country, blues, and rock oldies. The group then disbanded. Jesse went out as a solo, breaking *Billboard*'s top 40 with Warners LPs *Together* (1972) and—named for his daughter—*A Song for Julie* (1973). With decreasing creative impact, he put out *Light Shine* (1974), *Songbird* (1975), *On the Road* (1976), and *Love on the Wing* (1977) for Warner Brothers and *American Dreams* (1978) and *The Perfect Stranger* (1982) for Elektra. In 1974, Capitol reissued his exquisite *Soul of a City Boy.*

After *The Perfect Stranger* bombed, Jesse disappeared from the big-time music world for a while, though he still worked for environmental, American Indian, and other causes. Following a brief Youngbloods reunion in 1985, Jesse produced his solo LP *The Highway Is for Heroes* (Cypress, 1987) for $25,000 in his home studio. True to the spirit of his old days, it mixed vintage rock with his own songs of social concern and a love of the open road.

ZAPPA, FRANK: *Singer, guitarist, composer, actor, movie producer. Born Baltimore, Maryland, December 21, 1940.*

A genius of electronic avant garde music, a musical charlatan and impostor, a massive put-on—will the real Frank Zappa please stand up? It probably will be a while before Frank Zappa's importance to popular music is fully evaluated—whether he is to rock what Mahler and Schoenberg were to the classics or whether his efforts just constituted a long-lived novelty. Whatever rock historians conclude, they could hardly consider Zappa boring or noncontroversial.

Zappa grew up in a middle class, not necessarily conventional family. His father had various positions at one time or another: barber, data-reduction clerk, metallurgist, high school math teacher, and history professor. His mother was a librarian for a while, but mainly devoted her time to raising her family after Frank (the eldest of three sons and a daughter) was born.

By the time Frank was in his teens, the family was living in the desert area of Southern California east of Los Angeles. He graduated from Antelope Valley High School in Lancaster in June 1958, already exhibiting an interest in R&B and rock and an attitude some teachers and acquaintances considered zany. (He noted: "I graduated with about 20 units less than what was required, simply because they were in a hurry to be rid of me.") He spent one semester in Chaffey Junior College in Alto Loma, California, and then dropped out of formal schooling.

His autobiographical notes summarized his early musical training: "My formal musical education consists of one special harmony course which I was allowed to take during my senior year in high school (I got to go over to the Antelope Valley Junior College campus and sit in Mr. Russell's room), another harmony course (with required keyboard practice) at Chaffey J.C., taught by Miss Holly, and a composition course at Pomona College which I would sneak into and audit. . . . I have played band and orchestra percussion in school ensembles. . . . The rest of my musical training comes from listening to records and playing in assorted little bands in beer joints and cocktail lounges, mostly in small towns. I also spent a lot of time in the library."

His "little-band" work began around Lancaster, where his path crossed those of other young progressive rock fans in the early 1960s. Among his friends was Don Van Vliet, with whom Zappa planned to make a film titled *Captain Beefheart Meets the Grunt People*. The movie fell through (although it signified Zappa's continuing interest in cinema that culminated in *200 Motels* in the early '70s), but Van Vliet took the name Captain Beefheart for his own.

In late 1964, Zappa formed the group that brought him to national prominence (or notoriety), the Mothers of Invention, a vehicle for his ideas of total band–audience involvement, with music forming only part of a stage package including satire, grotesque comedy, and anything else that seemed to strike band members' fancy during a performance. As *Life* magazine noted in a special article on Zappa and "The New Rock": "On stage there is the possibility that anything can happen. Dolls are mutilated. A gas mask is displayed. A bag of vegetables is unpacked and examined. There are spaced intervals of 'honks' and suddenly the Mothers perform 'Dead Air.' They stop, sit down, and ignore the audience. Zappa might get a shoeshine from Motorhead, the percussionist. They keep this going for as long as it takes the audience to become unsettled, uncomfortable, and angry. Then Zappa calmly approaches the mike and says: 'It brings out the hostilities in you, doesn't it?'"

Strange though the Mothers performance was, it found rapid acceptance by young rock fans of the late 1960s and early 1970s. Though some adults who happened into Mothers sessions despaired at the ear-shattering hyperamplification and the dizzying sensation of the light show, the group won numerous ovations.

Its recordings also found enough buyers to bring joy to the hearts of the first firm that signed them, Verve Records. At the end of the 1960s, Zappa established his own record firm, Bizarre-Straight, as well as a music-publishing company, movie-production organization, and other enterprises. Through 1972, Mothers and Zappa releases on MGM/Verve and Bizarre-Straight totaled some 14 albums, including the nine-disc anthology *The Story of the Mothers* (three triple-disc sets issued in early 1972). Zappa continued to turn his attention to an ever wider spectrum of creative activity as the 1970s began. After filming his group's engagements for years, he worked on a movie based on a typical Mothers tour. He also took part in Zubin Mehta's special program for the Los Angeles Philharmonic, "20th Century Music: How It Was, How It Is." Zappa's part represented an effort to combine rock and symphonic material. Though some relished it, *Los Angeles Times* classical music critic Martin Bernheimer commented (June 7, 1970): "Frank Zappa's sprawling 'Excerpts from *200 Motels*' shirked the much publicized problem of how to fuse rock with 'classical' music and concentrated instead on lots of half-digested, 50-year-old clichés. Fun, perhaps, but hardly the most controversial musical event since the world premiere of Stravinsky's 'Rites of Spring.'"

The full scope of Zappa's movie score wasn't felt until *200 Motels* was released in late 1971, playing to substantial audiences in most major U.S. cities. To some reviewers, all it meant was more confusion. Popular music critics generally thought Zappa's vehicle a great success. The overall consensus was that those who were Zappa fans would adore the movie, while others might just as well stay home and listen to records.

Zappa's album output with various Mothers of Invention rosters during the first part of the 1970s included Bizarre releases *Mothers Live at the Fillmore East—June 1971* (1971) and *Just Another Band from L.A. (1972)* and, on Reprise, *The Grand Wazoo* (1973). On his own Discreet label, he and his band were represented by *Over-Nite Sensation* (1973, gold), *The Roxy and Elsewhere* and *One Size Fits All* (1974), and a collaboration with Captain Beefheart, *Bongo Fury* (1975).

Legal problems in the mid-1970s forced Zappa to make what amounted to a new career start. The Mothers became a thing of the past and he concentrated on building up his solo career. *Studio Tan* appeared in 1978 and *Sleep Dirt* and *Orchestral Favorites* in 1979, all three released by Warner Brothers. In 1980, his material began to come out on his new label, Zappa. *Joe's Garage, Act I* and *Joe's Ga-*

rage, Acts II and III (both 1980) took satirical aim at such targets as Scientology ("A Token of My Extreme"), groupies ("Crew Slut"), and sexual mores ("Catholic Girls"). He continued his irreverent commentaries in later 1980s albums on his own Barking Pumpkin label: *Tinseltown Rebellion, You Are What You Is* (two discs, 1981), *Shut Up 'n' Play Yer Guitar* (1981), *Shut Up 'n' Play Yer Guitar Some More* (1981), *Return of the Son of Shut Up 'n' Play Yer Guitar.*

In 1982, Frank collaborated with his daughter, Moon Unit, on a best-selling single, "Valley Girls," a takeoff on the slang phrases popular with teenage girls in the San Fernando Valley of Los Angeles. In early 1983, Frank went to court to fight plans for a film tentatively titled *Valley Girls,* claiming that the production company involved was diluting its trademark and posing unfair competition. A few months later, Zappa was back on the concert circuit to support his thirty-first album, *The Man from Utopia. Them or Us* (two discs, 1984) and *Frank Zappa Meets the Mothers of Prevention* (1985) followed on Barking Pumpkin. *Jazz from Hell* (1986) won a 1987 Grammy for Best Rock Instrumental Performance (Orchestra, Group, or Soloist).

During the mid-1980s, when not recording new albums or doing in-person shows, Zappa made the news for his determined opposition to various groups that sought to censor rock lyrics or force record companies to provide album covers with warnings about so-called suggestive or obscene material. Besides taking part in panel discussions, Zappa testified before Congressional committees about his beliefs in freedom of speech.

In the late 1980s, Zappa licensed his solo and Mothers catalogues to Rykodisc for release on CDs. In 1988, besides the two-disc *Guitar,* Barking Pumpkin put out the two-LP *You Can't Do That on Stage Anymore, Vol. 1* to inaugurate a 12-disc collection of previously unreleased material spanning his entire career. *(See Captain Beefheart; Cooper, Alice; Little Feat; Men at Work; Mothers of Invention, The; Turtles, The.)*

ZEVON, WARREN: *Singer, songwriter, guitarist, pianist, record producer. Born Chicago, Illinois, January 24, 1947.*

For a while in the 1970s, the Los Angeles area was a hotbed of a form of rock'n'roll that might have been called the California folk-rock movement. It was a genre whose members included luminaries Jackson Browne, Linda Ronstadt, J.D. Souther, and the Eagles. Warren Zevon was associated with that scene, but not really of it. His melodies had some of the flavor of the kinds of songs Browne or the Eagles wrote, yet it was more raucous in tone and featured lyrics that dealt more forcefully with the darker side of life—violence, deceit, and death—than those of his musical compatriots.

One reviewer called him the Sam Peckinpah (the movie director) of rock. Charlie McCollum of the *Washington Star* (March 9, 1978) commented: "Both [Zevon and Peckinpah] have a feeling of the internal workings of a violent society; both find beauty in the strangest of places, like death. Peckinpah lacks Zevon's intuitive homor, so what listeners get on [an album such as] *Excitable Boy* [where the subject of the title song is a 'boy' who rapes and murders his girlfriend, yet gets off with only a 10-year sentence] is a cross between Peckinpah and Randy Newman—a combination born of some other world."

It took considerably more time for Warren's career to blossom than for most successful rock artists'. He was nearing 30 before he began to take the steps that won him recognition from his fellow musicians, critics, and, to a lesser extent the general public. Though he was almost totally immersed in music from an early age, it took a lot of soul searching and some breaks before he decided to try for a solo career rather than remain in a supporting role.

Zevon was born in Chicago, but the family moved to California when he was young and he spent most of his formative years there. His father was a Russian immigrant whose family name originally was Livotovsky before Warren's grandfather changed it to Zevon. Zevon senior was a professional gambler, a profession that tended to keep the family moving from one place to another. Talking about him to Judith Sims of the *Washington Post* (February 27, 1978), Warren said, "[he] looks like George Burns. Well, not exactly like George Burns."

As for those early years, he told her: "We always had enough to eat, but it was definitely . . . up and down. Friends tell me I should write a screenplay about it." Apparently his relationship to his parents was somewhat strained. He indicated he had not remained close to his father and, as of the mid-1970s, didn't stay in touch with his mother, who was divorced from his father when he was in his teens.

He learned to play piano as a child, concentrating on the classics, which remained his prime musical interest into his teens in the early 1960s. His desire to continue in that vein was strengthened briefly when a high school music teacher introduced him to the great composer Igor Stravinsky. But as family tensions intensified, he rebelled, turning his sights toward pop music and also becoming something of a delinquent, though "I never was a big-time hood."

Once his parents separated, the 16-year-old Warren headed for New York City in a Corvette (which his father had won in a card game) with a guitar in the back seat. He was inspired by reports of the folk ferment in New York and had dreams of emulating a rising young singer/writer named Bob Dylan. However, things didn't work out and he headed back west, this time to San Francisco.

In the Bay Area, he told Sue Reilly of *People* magazine (May 2, 1978): he formed a "preppy" band "that tried to sound like the Beatles and looked like Yale. We finally broke up because of dramatic lack of potential." For a while after that, he remained in the region, picking up performing gigs and also becoming involved in the drug scene in Berkeley. But the psychedelic music and flower-power phase dominant in that locale in the mid-1960s faded and Zevon betook himself south once more to Los Angeles.

Back in Southern California, he teamed up with another artist to form a duo called Lyme and Cybelle. Their single "Follow Me" received airplay and something more than negligible sales. But it didn't do quite well enough to insure any major record-industry support. After that, Warren remained active in the music field in a variety of ways: performing as a record session pianist and guitarist ("I learned to play frustrated banjo-style guitar from listening to folk music. I still play that way."), writing original songs, and even doing some commercials, including a few for Ernest and Julio Gallo wine. He also did live shows as a backing musician for other artists.

While he paid those dues, he also made friends with many aspiring musicians and songwriters in the same boat he was in. Among them was Jackson Browne. The two first met in 1968 and remained close friends and occasional writing collaborators from then on.

Despite setbacks, Warren had no plans for seeking another work outlet. He told Robert Hilburn of the *Los Angeles Times* (August 8, 1976): "There were times when I was very frustrated, points at which I was writing bad songs and resenting the fact they weren't regarded as good ones. But I never considered doing anything else. Besides, I felt I was making progress. It may have been slow, but each new song was a step closer to what I wanted to do."

Some of his songs were finding interested ears, though. He got the chance to record an album for Imperial Records, *Wanted Dead or Alive* (1970). It was a flop—deservedly, Zevon said some years later.

Then the Everly Brothers asked him to serve as musical director and instrumentalist for their backing band. He chose the band members, including guitarist Waddy Wachtel (an important contributor to many of Warren's solo recordings of the mid-1970s). He worked with the brothers for two years and then with each alternately after they broke up their partnership.

Warren told Hilburn: "There were some great nights. A lot of gooseflesh, a lot of pride. We may have played the songs 1,000 times before, but they're good songs and Phil and Don—no matter how they felt offstage—would always go out and perform with passion. If anything, I learned that when you go out on stage, you give your all even if you have been doing it for 15 years and are sick of giving your all."

He was inspired from what he called the emotional feeling he got from the Everlys to write a song called "Frank and Jesse James," later featured on his 1976 solo album. He found time to write other songs that found favor with his California folk-rock friends. Among them were "Hasten Down the Wind," "Poor Poor Pitiful Me," and "Mohammed's Radio," which Linda Ronstadt eventually recorded and included in many concerts.

The Everly Brothers' breakup forced Warren to try to take stock of what he wanted from his career and his life. He was getting old for a rock performer and hadn't made any major impact on his chosen field. In 1974, he decided to drop his other projects and take a sabbatical in Spain, playing the piano and singing in a small club in the tourist town of Sitges while spending his spare time relaxing, writing, and pondering his future. In 1975, he was in the midst of negotiating a recording agreement with a European company when he got a message from Jackson Browne urging him to come back to L.A. Browne had suggested to Asylum executives that they assemble a solo LP of Zevon songs. Warren assented, though he took time off on the way back to stop in London, England, and arrange Phil Everly's solo album *Mystic Line* (Pye, 1975).

Back in the States, with Browne acting as producer, Zevon completed the new collection, *Warren Zevon* (May 1976), a stunning offering that his peers acknowledged as a potential classic. Despite that and Zevon's pulsating live performances, the LP was not a major commercial success. But it received enough buyer support and critical praise that the record company gave the green light for a follow-up.

Zevon, though, was not to be rushed. He took a lot of time writing and polishing the songs for the next album and, where he had written both words and music to all the tracks on his Asylum debut, he brought in Browne and others to help on the next candidates. As on its predecessor, he got heartwarming support from his musical friends. Among those helping to lay down the new tracks were Browne, Linda Ronstadt, Waddy Wachtel and other members of Ronstadt's band (the Section, which often backed Browne and James Taylor), and Fleetwood Mac.

The gold *Excitable Boy* (early 1978), if not quite as consistently unique as the earlier LP, still had sterling moments, such as the comically eerie hit single "Werewolves of London."

Though Zevon by the end of the 1970s was a concert headliner, he had trouble maintaining his creative momentum. *Bad Luck Streak in Dancing School* (1980, top 20) had some excellent tracks, but there were relatively uninspired ones as well. It was also far less successful commercially than its predecessor, though more popular than its follow-ups.

Meanwhile, Asylum's gold soundtrack LP for the 1980 hit film *Urban Cowboy* included a song by Warren. His first live album, *Stand in the Fire,* was also issued by Asylum in 1980. A fine compilation, it caught much of the fervor and excellent musicianship that made Zevon shows among rock's best in the early 1980s. Besides presenting driving versions of Zevon's previous best writing, the album showcased some new songs that demonstrated his creative well had not yet run dry. Zevon followed with more studio albums as the 1980s moved along, such as *The Envoy* (1982).

In the mid-1980s, Warren's career slowed down. Whether due to writer's block or a desire for a more low-key existence, Zevon had little new to match his classic work of the mid-1970s. He maintained a devoted but small following and performed mainly in smaller clubs and concert sites. A long silence record-wise ended with *Sentimental Hygiene* (Virgin, 1987).

He had told Hilburn in the mid-1970s that he always tried to keep things in perspective. "I think in songs that are supposed to have a wry or humorous twist, I'm trying to remind myself not to take myself seriously. I would not presume to tell my friends or colleagues what kind of attitudes they should take, but I find it very important to remind myself not to take myself seriously. So that may be the basis for humor in my songs."

He didn't want to be considered a cynic or one who had no sense of social responsibility, however. "But it has been stressed to the point where certain writers seem to see me as a comedian or something . . . a kind of extreme satirist, which I don't see at all. I'm very much not a cynic. I think, actually, that I'm quite idealistic. I think caring is, perhaps, the most positive force in life. I've always felt there is something redeeming about every experience, something affirmative, and it's that quality I hope people would see in my work, not that I'm an 'expert satirist' or a 'dissector of L.A. culture,' but someone who looks at life good-naturedly and has the ability to see the human side of things." *(See Browne, Jackson; Everly Brothers, The; Ronstadt, Linda.)*

ZODIACS, THE: *See Williams, Maurice.*

ZOMBIES, THE: *Vocal and instrumental group, all born England. Colin Blunstone, born Hatfield, Hertfordshire, June 24, 1945; Paul Atkinson, born Cuffley, Hertfordshire, March 19, 1946; Rodney Argent, born St. Albans, Hertfordshire, June 14, 1945; Hugh Grundy, born Winchester, March 6, 1945; Chris Taylor White, born Barnet, Hertfordshire, March 7, 1943.*

The Zombies might be said to have been saved by the bell. One of England's more successful rock bands in the mid-1960s, it came within an eyelash of leaving the music field in favor of more conventional occupations, but a newspaper contest made the difference.

The three founding members (Paul Atkinson, Rodney Argent, and Hugh Grundy) organized as a trio while attending St. Albans School in their home county of Hertfordshire, just north of London. All were learning instruments by their teens, with Paul gaining experience on guitar, Hugh on drums, and Rodney on piano, organ, harmonica, clarinet, and violin.

In 1963, the group became a quintet and took the name of Zombies with the addition of Colin Blunstone (lead vocals and guitar) and Chris Taylor White (bass, double bass, and guitar). All the members were finished with the English equivalent of high school by then and were trying to decide on careers. They enjoyed music, but it was hard to find steady work in the field; mostly it continued to be a sideline.

At this point, the boys thought seriously about breaking up the group. Rod and Paul had been accepted at a university, Chris was ready to attend teacher's college, and the other two already had regular jobs, Colin as an insurance broker and Hugh as a bank employee.

One last opportunity arose: a paper called the *Evening News* had a rock-band contest, the Heart Beat Competition. The group decided to enter and won first prize. This encouraged them to continue working together. They made demonstration tapes, including Argent's composition "She's Not There." Sent around to recording firms in London, the tapes won them a contract from British Decca in 1964.

One of their first releases, "She's Not There," became a hit in England and, soon after, moved to the top 10 on U.S. charts on the Parrot label, as did "Tell Her No" in 1965. Two decades later, Rhino Records brought out *The Zombies Live on the BBC (1965–1967)*.

In 1969, they came up with their biggest success to that time, "Time of the Season" on Decca in England and Date in the U.S. Though it never got into the British top 20, it rose to the U.S. top 10 and went gold. This time, however, the bell rang too late to save the group. By the time "Time of the Season" rose high on the charts, the Zombies had disbanded.

Lead singer Colin Blunstone retired from music for a time before coming back as a solo artist in 1971. As he recalled in late 1971: "We just could not afford to go on. At the time no one was really interested in us, although *Odyssey and Oracle* [the group's last LP, issued in 1969 with "Time of the Season" one of the tracks], is probably the only material by the Zombies I'd still play to people. When the last track was recorded, the band was within two weeks of breaking up. As it happened, when it was successful in America, the Zombies were irrevocably split.

"When the Zombies broke up, I went straight back into an insurance office. It was difficult to readjust at the start, but it was a regular living and besides, there was nothing else I could do."

Blunstone couldn't stay away from music, however, and at the start of the 1970s, he recorded "She's Not There" under the pseudonym Neil Macarthur. After the song made the charts, Blunstone picked up engagements on stage and TV and put out Epic LPs *One Year* (1971), *Ennismore,* and *Journey* (1973) under his own name. Under a mid-1970s pact with Elton John's Rocket Records, he turned out some above-average albums, but he again was unable to build a firm following.

Rod Argent had somewhat more success after the Zombies. He founded a new band, Argent, whose other members were Russell Ballard (born Waltham Cross, England, October 31, 1947); Jim Rodford (born St. Albans, England, July 7, 1945) and Robert Henrit (born Broxbourne, U.K., May 2, 1946). Argent handled keyboards, Ballard lead guitar and piano, and Rodford bass guitar. Henrit (who later joined the Kinks) was on drums.

The group's first two U.S. releases on Epic—*Argent* (1970) and *Ring of Hands* (1971)—were good but didn't win much buyer support. *All Together Now* (1972) made number 23 in *Billboard* thanks to the top 10 single "Hold Your Head Up."

However, the group couldn't match the earlier albums in quality with *In Deep* (1973) and *Nexus* and the live *Encore* (1974). Ballard's departure during 1974 seemed to have a depressing effect on the band's creative spirit. After making little headway with 1975 LPs *Circus* (Epic) and *Counterpoints* (United Artists), the group disbanded in 1976. That year, Epic closed its book on the band with the retrospective *The Argent Anthology. (See Kinks, The.)*

ZZ TOP: *Vocal and instrumental group. All born Texas, 1949: Billy Gibbons, Houston; Dusty Hill, Dallas; Frank Beard, Frankston.*

Psychedelic blues-rock was almost a musical way of life in Houston, Dallas, and other Texas cities for a while. Countless bands played variations of that kind of music in small clubs and local concerts month in and month out. Most never become well known beyond the Texas borders, but every now and then a name such as Johnny Winter or ZZ Top broke out to achieve enormous national and international fame.

In 1970, when Winter's band was just starting to gain momentum, ZZ Top was in its seminal stages. The three members of what now is popularly known as "that little ol' band from Texas" all had worked with local groups before forming their new trio in 1969. Singer-guitarist Billy Gibbons had been lead guitarist in Houston-based Moving Sidewalks. Frank Beard (drummer-percussionist with many Houston bands) had become friends with vocalist-bass guitarist Dusty Hill while both were part of Dallas-based American Blues.

All three came to love blues in their teens, though from slightly different vantage points. Gibbons' father was a pianist and part-time conductor of the Houston Philharmonic. The family's maid, Stella Matthews, first introduced him to black music. Hill, from a pop-oriented family, said his mother was a "Kate Smith–type" big band singer. He liked pop and boogie-woogie from his childhood. After he began to play guitar, he often snuck into black blues clubs. Beard was more interested in athletics in his early teens, playing quarterback in high school, but took up performing with school rock groups because, he said, it offered more opportunities to meet girls than his football pursuits.

After the three joined together in ZZ Top, they began on the usual round of performances at Texas bars and small clubs. But its sound attracted more than the usual notice and the trio's management soon got them a contract with London Records. The trio's debut, *ZZ Top's First Album* (January 1971), helped build a local following which expanded to other parts of the country when the second LP, *Rio Grande Mud,* came out in March 1972.

Then came the gold *Tres Hombres* (July 1973) with the hit single "La Grange." *Fandango* (1975) quickly went gold too and provided the hit single "Tush."

Tejas (1976) was backed with a multimedia concert show that became one of the largest-grossing live tours of the decade. The band's driving blues-rock was presented in a setting that included, among other things, longhorn steers, buzzards, and rattlesnakes. Although *Tejas* went gold and spawned the hit single "Arrested for Driving While Blind," neither the band nor its manager, Bill Ham, were happy with the promotional help given them by London, which was running into financial problems at the time. After coming off the road in 1976, it was decided the band would retire from action for a while, during which time Ham would seek an agreement for a label change.

As Hill told Daisann McLane of *Rolling Stone* in 1980: "We all agreed not to play anywhere [during that period]. We didn't know if jamming together, or sitting in with somebody else, would affect the negotiations, so we just didn't do it."

The threesome went on vacations to places such as Mexico, the Caribbean, New York, and Paris. Gibbons commented: "It got nerve-wracking toward the end." Hill added: "A lot of people said to me: 'You guys are nuts.' We were taking a gamble. Sometimes you win and sometimes you lose. I'm a gambling man."

In this case, the dice were in the trio's favor. Ham was able to disentangle them from the London contract and gain a new deal with Warner Brothers, which bought the band's catalogue from London (including the 1977 LP *The Best of ZZ Top)* and re-issued all those discs on the Warners label. The band's debut album on Warner Brothers, *Deguello* (1978), was an international success.

Coming into the 1980s, the band had regained its position as a top-ranked aggregation. *El Loco* (1981) earned gold-record certification from the RIAA as had *Deguello*. *Eliminator* (March 1983) was still on the *Billboard* lists at the end of 1985, having spent 141 weeks in that august company. By then, the LP had sold over 5 million copies in the U.S. alone while also reaching platinum levels in Australia and England, double-platinum in Ireland, and septuple-platinum in Canada. World sales at the end of 1985 topped 8 million copies. It also brought renewed interest in all the band's previous releases, helping *Deguello* win a platinum award five years after its initial release. Chart singles spawned by the upsurge included "Gimme All Your Lovin'," "Sharp Dressed Man," "TV Dinners," and "Legs."

In October 1985, Warner Brothers issued the band's tenth LP, *Afterburner*. It made number four in *Billboard,* going platinum and providing the top 10 single "Sleeping Boy." *(See Waters, Muddy.)*

Appendix A

Recording Industry Association of America, Inc.

Gold and Platinum Record Awards

The Recording Industry Association of America (RIAA) program for gold-record album and single awards began in 1958 and platinum-record awards were instituted on January 1, 1976.

From 1958 until January 1, 1975, the requirement for a gold-album certification was a minimum of $1 million in manufacturer's dollar volume (wholesale price) based on 33⅓ percent of the list price of each LP and/or tape sold. Since 1975, album certification has been based on a minimum sale of 500,000 units with a multirecord or tape package counting as one unit. Since late 1983, sales of compact discs also have been combined with LP and/or tape sales. In addition, manufacturer's dollar volume must be at least $1 million based on 33⅓ percent of the list price of each unit sold.

For a gold-single certification, a minimum sale of one million copies is required with disco/dance-music records (12-inch 33s or 45s with one selection per side) counted as two units. Sales of 12-inch singles may be combined with counterpart 7-inch discs if the repertoire on both sides is identical as to artist and title.

Platinum-album awards are based on a minimum sale of one million units (LPs, tapes, and/or CDs) with manufacturer's dollar volume of at least $2 million based on 33⅓ percent of list price for each unit sold. A platinum-single award calls for a minimum sale of two million copies. For both albums and singles, all other gold-record stipulations also apply.

In the following listings, (S) after a title indicates that the record is a single. Twelve-inch singles are noted as (S, 12-inch).

GOLD-RECORD AWARDS

1958

3-14	Catch a Falling Star (S) (RCA Victor)—Perry Como
7-8	Oklahoma (Capitol)—Gordon MacRae
7-8	He's Got the Whole World in His Hands (S) (Capitol)—Laurie London
8-11	Hard Headed Woman (S) (RCA Victor)—Elvis Presley
8-18	Patricia (S) (RCA Victor)—Perez Prado

1959

1-21	Tom Dooley (S) (Capitol)—Kingston Trio
2-20	Hymns (Capitol)—Tennessee Ernie Ford
6-1	Johnny's Greatest Hits (Columbia)—Johnny Mathis
11-16	Music Man (Capitol)—original cast
11-16	Sing along with Mitch (Columbia)—Mitch Miller
12-18	South Pacific (RCA Victor)—Rodgers & Hammerstein
12-31	Peter Gunn (RCA Victor)—Henry Mancini

1960

1-19	Student Prince (RCA Victor)—Mario Lanza
2-17	60 Years of Music America Loves Best (RCA Victor)—Various artists
2-17	Elvis (RCA Victor)—Elvis Presley
2-12	Pat's Great Hits (Dot)—Pat Boone
4-18	Kingston Trio at Large (Capitol)—Kingston Trio
4-18	Kingston Trio (Capitol)—Kingston Trio
4-21	More Sing along with Mitch (Columbia)—Mitch Miller
4-21	Heavenly (Columbia)—Johnny Mathis
5-5	Warm (Columbia)—Johnny Mathis
10-24	Love Is the Thing (Capitol)—Nat "King" Cole
10-24	Here We Go Again (Capitol)—Kingston Trio
10-24	From the Hungry i (Capitol)—Kingston Trio
12-7	Sound of Music (Columbia)—original cast
12-7	Merry Christmas (Columbia)—Johnny Mathis
12-7	Christmas Sing along with Mitch (Columbia)—Mitch Miller
12-7	Still More! Sing along with Mitch (Columbia)—Mitch Miller

1961

2-14 Calcutta (S) (Dot)—Lawrence Welk
3-16 Calcutta (Dot)—Lawrence Welk
6-22 Come Dance with Me! (Capitol)—Frank Sinatra
6-22 Sold Out (Capitol)—Kingston Trio
6-28 Glenn Miller Story (RCA Victor)—Glenn Miller Orchestra
9-18 Christmas Carols (London)—Mantovani
9-18 Theatre Land (London)—Mantovani
9-18 Film Encores Volume 1 (London)—Mantovani
9-18 Gems Forever (London)—Mantovani
9-18 Strauss Waltzes (London)—Mantovani
10-10 Spirituals (Capitol)—Tennessee Ernie Ford
10-16 Belafonte at Carnegie Hall (RCA Victor) —Harry Belafonte
10-17 Elvis' Golden Records (RCA Victor)— Elvis Presley
11-22 Tchaikovsky Concert (RCA Victor)—Van Cliburn
12-7 Encore of Golden Hits (Mercury)—Platters
12-14 Big Bad John (S) (Columbia)—Jimmy Dean
12-21 Blue Hawaii (RCA Victor)—Elvis Presley

1962

1-9 The Lion Sleeps Tonight (S) (RCA Victor) —Tokens
1-12 Holiday Sing along with Mitch (Columbia) —Mitch Miller
1-12 Party Sing along with Mitch (Columbia)— Mitch Miller
1-12 More Johnny's Greatest Hits (Columbia)— Johnny Mathis
1-12 West Side Story (Columbia)—original cast
2-9 Camelot (Columbia)—original cast
2-9 Flower Drum Song (Columbia)—original cast
2-16 Theme from A Summer Place (Dot)—Billy Vaughn
2-16 Blue Hawaii (Dot)—Billy Vaughn
2-16 Sail along Silv'ry Moon (Dot)—Billy Vaughn
3-1 Button Down Mind of Bob Newhart (Warner Bros.)—Bob Newhart
3-7 Memories Sing along with Mitch (Columbia)—Mitch Miller
3-7 Sentimental Sing along with Mitch (Columbia)—Mitch Miller
3-8 Saturday Night Sing along with Mitch (Columbia)—Mitch Miller

3-12 Star Carol (Capitol)—Tennessee Ernie Ford
3-22 Nearer the Cross (Capitol)—Tennessee Ernie Ford
3-20 Can't Help Falling in Love (S) (RCA Victor)—Elvis Presley
6-21 Frank Sinatra Sings for Only the Lonely (Capitol)—Frank Sinatra
6-21 Nice 'n' Easy (Capitol)—Frank Sinatra
6-21 Songs for Swingin' Lovers (Capitol)— Frank Sinatra
6-27 String Along (Capitol)—Kingston Trio
6-27 Music, Martinis, and Memories (Capitol)—Jackie Gleason
6-27 Music for Lovers Only (Capitol)—Jackie Gleason
6-27 Judy at Carnegie Hall (Capitol)—Judy Garland
7-6 Happy Times Sing along with Mitch (Columbia)—Mitch Miller
7-19 'S Marvelous (Columbia)—Ray Conniff
7-19 I Can't Stop Loving You (S) (ABC-Paramount)—Ray Charles
7-19 Modern Sounds in Country & Western Music (ABC-Paramount)—Ray Charles
7-20 Memories Are Made of This (Columbia)— Ray Conniff
7-20 Concert in Rhythm (Columbia)—Ray Conniff
8-13 Roses Are Red (S) (Epic)—Bobby Vinton
8-31 Theme from A Summer Place (S) (Columbia)—Percy Faith
10-30 Breakfast at Tiffany's (RCA Victor)— Henry Mancini
11-7 This Is Sinatra (Capitol)—Frank Sinatra
12-4 Bouquet (Columbia)—Percy Faith Strings
12-4 So Much in Love (Columbia)—Ray Conniff
12-4 Faithfully (Columbia)—Johnny Mathis
12-4 Swing Softly (Columbia)—Johnny Mathis
12-4 Open Fire, Two Guitars (Columbia)— Johnny Mathis
12-10 Peter, Paul and Mary (Warner Bros.)—Peter, Paul and Mary
12-10 My Son, the Folk Singer (Warner Bros.)— Allan Sherman
12-18 The First Family (Cadence)—Vaughn Meader

1963

1-7 West Side Story (Columbia)—soundtrack
1-7 Glorious Sound of Christmas (Columbia)—Eugene Ormandy, Philadelphia Orchestra

2-5 1812 Overture—Tchaikovsky (Mercury)—Antal Dorati and the Minneapolis Symphony

2-26 Hey Paula (S) (Mercury)—Paul and Paula

3-12 Exodus (RCA Victor)—soundtrack

3-12 Calypso (RCA Victor)—Harry Belafonte

3-12 G.I. Blues (RCA Victor)—Elvis Presley

3-12 Season's Greetings from Perry Como (RCA Victor)—Perry Como

3-22 Viva (Columbia)—Percy Faith

3-27 The Music Man (Warner Bros.)—soundtrack

4-19 Time Out (Columbia)—Dave Brubeck Quartet

7-11 I Left My Heart in San Francisco (Columbia)—Tony Bennett

8-13 Elvis' Christmas Album (RCA Victor)—Elvis Presley

8-13 Girls, Girls, Girls (RCA Victor)—Elvis Presley

8-13 Belafonte Returns to Carnegie Hall (RCA Victor)—Harry Belafonte

8-13 Belafonte (RCA Victor)—Harry Belafonte

8-23 Jump-Up-Calypso (RCA Victor)—Harry Belafonte

8-27 Moving (Warner Bros.)—Peter, Paul and Mary

9-3 Exodus (London)—Mantovani

9-19 Days of Wine & Roses (Columbia)—Andy Williams

10-14 Moon River and Other Great Movie Themes (Columbia)—Andy Williams

10-21 Handel's Messiah (Columbia)—Eugene Ormandy, Philadelphia Orchestra

10-21 Christmas with Conniff (Columbia)—Ray Conniff

10-21 The Lord's Prayer (Columbia)—Mormon Tabernacle Choir

10-21 Porgy and Bess (Columbia)—soundtrack

11-6 Folk Song Sing along with Mitch (Columbia)—Mitch Miller

11-13 In the Wind (Warner Bros.)—Peter, Paul and Mary

11-29 Sugar Shack (S) (Dot)—Jimmy Gilmer and the Fireballs

12-17 Singing Nun (Philips/Mercury)—Soeur Sourire

1964

1-8 My Fair Lady (Columbia)—original cast

1-15 John Fitzgerald Kennedy: A Memorial Album (Premier)

1-15 Carousel (Capitol)—soundtrack

1-15 The King and I (Capitol)—soundtrack

1-15 Ramblin' Rose (Capitol)—Nat "King" Cole

2-3 Meet the Beatles! (Capitol)—Beatles

2-3 I Want to Hold Your Hand (S) (Capitol)—Beatles

3-31 Can't Buy Me Love (S) (Capitol)—Beatles

4-4 Honey in the Horn (RCA Victor)—Al Hirt

4-13 The Beatles' Second Album (Capitol)—Beatles

5-12 The Second Barbra Streisand Album (Columbia)—Barbra Streisand

6-2 Hello, Dolly! (RCA Victor)—original cast

8-10 Hello, Dolly! (Kapp)—Louis Armstrong

8-17 The Wonderful World of Andy Williams (Columbia)—Andy Williams

8-19 Everybody Loves Somebody (S) (Reprise)—Dean Martin

8-19 Christmas Hymns and Carols (RCA Victor)—Robert Shaw

8-19 Victory at Sea, Volume I (RCA Victor)—Robert Russell Bennett

8-24 Rag Doll (S) (Philips)—Four Seasons

8-24 Something New (Capitol)—Beatles

8-25 A Hard Day's Night (S) (Capitol)—Beatles

9-4 The Best of the Kingston Trio (Capitol)—Kingston Trio

9-4 Unforgettable (Capitol)—Nat "King" Cole

9-21 Funny Girl (Capitol)—original cast

10-16 Ramblin' (Columbia)—New Christy Minstrels

10-16 The Barbra Streisand Album (Columbia)—Barbra Streisand

10-30 Oh, Pretty Woman (S) (Monument)—Roy Orbison

11-2 Johnny Horton's Greatest Hits (Columbia)—Johnny Horton

12-16 Cotton Candy (RCA Victor)—Al Hirt

12-18 The Andy Williams Christmas Album (Columbia)—Andy Williams

12-18 Call Me Irresponsible (Columbia)—Andy Williams

12-31 I Feel Fine (S) (Capitol)—Beatles

12-31 Beatles '65 (Capitol)—Beatles

12-31 The Beatles' Story (Capitol)—Beatles

12-31 Mary Poppins (Vista)—soundtrack

1965

1-21 Glad All Over (Epic)—Dave Clark Five

1-21 Peter, Paul and Mary in Concert (Warner Bros.)—Peter, Paul and Mary

1-29 Everybody Loves Somebody (Reprise)—Dean Martin

771

2-11 Wonderland of Golden Hits (Columbia)—Andre Kostelanetz

2-11 The Third Album (Columbia)—Barbra Streisand

2-11 Ring of Fire (Columbia)—Johnny Cash

2-18 Beach Boys in Concert (Capitol)—Beach Boys

2-18 All Summer Long (Capitol)—Beach Boys

2-20 Sugar Lips (RCA Victor)—Al Hirt

3-1 Downtown (S) (Warner Bros.)—Petula Clark

3-23 People (Columbia)—Barbra Streisand

3-30 The Sound of Music (RCA Victor)—soundtrack

4-26 Trini Lopez at PJ's (Warner Bros.)—Trini Lopez

5-19 King of the Road (S) (Smash)—Roger Miller

6-16 Getz/Gilberto (Verve)—Stan Getz

6-16 Mrs. Brown, You've Got a Lovely Daughter (S) (MGM)—Herman's Hermits

7-1 Beatles VI (Capitol)—Beatles

7-19 (I Can't Get No) Satisfaction (S) (London)—Rolling Stones

7-30 Dear Heart (Columbia)—Andy Williams

8-5 Woolly Bully (S) (MGM)—Sam the Sham and the Pharaohs

8-23 Help! (Capitol)—Beatles

8-31 I'm Henry VIII, I Am (S) (MGM)—Herman's Hermits

8-31 Introducing Herman's Hermits (MGM)—Herman's Hermits

8-31 Herman's Hermits on Tour (MGM)—Herman's Hermits

9-1 More Encore of Golden Hits (Mercury)—Platters

9-1 Return of Roger Miller (Smash)—Roger Miller

9-2 Help! (S) (Capitol)—Beatles

9-16 Eight Days a Week (S) (Capitol)—Beatles

9-17 I Got You, Babe (S) (Atco)—Sonny and Cher

9-17 Great Songs from My Fair Lady (Columbia)—Andy Williams

9-21 Gunfire Ballads & Trail Songs (Columbia)—Marty Robbins

9-30 Look at Us (Atco)—Sonny and Cher

10-1 The Beach Boys Today (Capitol)—Beach Boys

10-5 The Pink Panther (RCA Victor)—Henry Mancini

10-12 Out of Our Heads (London)—Rolling Stones

10-20 Yesterday (S) (Capitol)—Beatles

10-28 Fiddler on the Roof (RCA Victor)—original cast

11-15 Surfer Girl (Capitol)—Beach Boys

11-15 Surfin' USA (Capitol)—Beach Boys

11-15 Sinatra's Sinatra (Reprise)—Frank Sinatra

12-2 My Name Is Barbra (Columbia)—Barbra Streisand

12-2 The Door Is Still Open to My Heart (Warner Bros.)—Dean Martin

12-7 A Lover's Concerto (S) (Dynavoice)—Toys

12-15 Going Places (A&M)—Herb Alpert & the Tijuana Brass

12-15 Whipped Cream and Other Delights (A&M)—Herb Alpert & the Tijuana Brass

12-24 Rubber Soul (Capitol)—Beatles

1966

1-4 My Name is Barbra, Two (Columbia)—Barbra Streisand

1-6 We Can Work It Out (S) (Capitol)—Beatles

1-11 The Best of Herman's Hermits (MGM)—Herman's Hermits

1-15 December's Children (London)—Rolling Stones

1-29 Joan Baez (Vanguard)—Joan Baez

1-29 Joan Baez, Vol. 2 (Vanguard)—Joan Baez

1-29 Joan Baez in Concert (Vanguard)—Joan Baez

2-6 September of My Years (Reprise)—Frank Sinatra

2-6 A Man & His Music (Reprise)—Frank Sinatra

2-7 Summer Days (Capitol)—Beach Boys

2-11 Golden Hits (Smash)—Roger Miller

2-14 Sounds of Silence (S) (Columbia)—Simon and Garfunkel

2-17 Ballad of the Green Berets (S) (RCA Victor)—Sgt. Barry Sadler

2-25 These Boots Are Made for Walkin' (S) (Reprise)—Nancy Sinatra

3-3 Lightnin' Strikes (S) (MGM)—Lou Christie

3-24 Roy Orbison's Greatest Hits (Monument)—Roy Orbison

4-1 Nowhere Man (S) (Capitol)—Beatles

4-5 Living Language Spanish (Young People's)

4-5 Living Language French (Young People's)

4-20 Color Me Barbra (Columbia)—Barbra Streisand

4-25 I'm the One Who Loves You (Reprise)—Dean Martin

4-27 Big Hits (High Tide and Green Grass) (London)—Rolling Stones

5-4 Oliver (RCA Victor)—original cast

5-9 Soul and Inspiration (S) (Verve)—Righteous Brothers

5-9 South of the Border (A&M)—Herb Alpert & the Tijuana Brass

5-9 The Lonely Bull (A&M)—Herb Alpert & the Tijuana Brass.

5-9 What Now My Love (A&M)—Herb Alpert & the Tijuana Brass

5-9 Herb Alpert's Tijuana Brass Vol. 2 (A&M)—Herb Alpert & the Tijuana Brass

5-12 My World (RCA Victor)—Eddy Arnold

5-16 South Pacific (Columbia)—original cast

6-10 California Dreamin' (S) (Dunhill/ABC)—Mamas and the Papas

6-10 Monday, Monday (S) (Dunhill/ABC)—Mamas and the Papas.

6-10 If You Can Believe Your Eyes and Ears (Dunhill/ABC)—Mamas and the Papas

7-8 "Yesterday" . . . and Today (Capitol)—Beatles

7-14 Paperback Writer (S) (Capitol)—Beatles

7-15 When a Man Loves a Woman (S) (Atlantic)—Percy Sledge

7-20 The Best of Jim Reeves (RCA Victor)—Jim Reeves

7-28 The Best of the Animals (MGM)—Animals

8-4 Dang Me (Smash)—Roger Miller

8-4 Gold Vault of Hits (Philips)—Four Seasons

8-9 Aftermath (London)—Rolling Stones

8-11 Li'l Red Riding Hood (S) (MGM)—Sam the Sham and the Pharaohs

8-11 Dr. Zhivago (MGM)—soundtrack

8-16 Think Ethnic (Mercury)—Smothers Brothers

8-16 Strangers in the Night (Reprise)—Frank Sinatra

8-22 Revolver (Capitol)—Beatles

8-24 Hanky Panky (S) (Roulette)—Tommy James and the Shondells

8-24 The Dave Clark Five's Greatest Hits (Epic)—Dave Clark Five

9-12 Yellow Submarine (S) (Capitol)—Beatles

9-19 Summer in the City (S) (Kama Sutra)—Lovin' Spoonful

9-20 Somewhere My Love (Columbia)—Ray Conniff

9-27 The Shadow of Your Smile (Columbia)—Andy Williams

10-4 Sunny (S) (Philips)—Bobby Hebb

10-11 The Best of Al Hirt (RCA Victor)—Al Hirt

10-14 I Started Out as a Child (Warner Bros.)—Bill Cosby

10-14 Wonderfulness (Warner Bros.)—Bill Cosby

10-14 Why Is There Air? (Warner Bros.)—Bill Cosby

10-14 Bill Cosby Is a Very Funny Fellow Right! (Warner Bros.)—Bill Cosby

10-18 Cherish (S) (Valiant)—Association

10-27 Jeanette MacDonald & Nelson Eddy Favorites (RCA Victor)—Jeanette MacDonald and Nelson Eddy

10-27 Perry Como Sings Merry Christmas Music (RCA Camden)—Perry Como

10-27 Last Train to Clarksville (S) (Colgems)—Monkees

10-27 The Monkees (Colgems)—Monkees

11-1 Elvis Presley (RCA Victor)—Elvis Presley

11-1 Elvis' Gold Records, Vol. 2 (RCA Victor)—Elvis Presley

11-1 Elvis' Golden Records, Vol. 3 (RCA Victor)—Elvis Presley

11-7 Dean Martin Sings Again (Reprise)—Dean Martin

11-7 Boots (Reprise)—Nancy Sinatra

11-11 96 Tears (S) (Cameo)—? (Question Mark) & the Mysterians

11-28 Soul and Inspiration (Verve)—Righteous Brothers

11-28 I'm a Believer (S) (Colgems)—Monkees

11-28 Winchester Cathedral (S) (Fontana)—New Vaudeville Band

12-1 The Mamas & the Papas (Dunhill)—Mamas and the Papas

12-12 Bobby Vinton's Greatest Hits (Epic)—Bobby Vinton

12-20 Battle of New Orleans (S) (Columbia)—Johnny Horton

12-21 Good Vibrations (S) (Capitol)—Beach Boys

12-21 Little Deuce Coupe (Capitol)—Beach Boys

12-21 Shut Down—Vol. 2 (Capitol)—Beach Boys

12-21 Winchester Cathedral (Fontana)—New Vaudeville Band

12-30 Spanish Eyes (Capitol)—Al Martino

1967

1-6 Just Like Us (Columbia)—Paul Revere and the Raiders

1-6 More of the Monkees (Colgems)—Monkees

1-12 Snoopy vs the Red Baron (S) (Laurie)—Royal Guardsmen

1-19 Mellow Yellow (S) (Epic)—Donovan

773

1-19 S.R.O. (A&M)—Herb Alpert & the Tijuana Brass

1-19 Got Live If You Want It (London)—Rolling Stones

1-20 Till (Kapp)—Roger Williams

1-20 Songs of the Fabulous Fifties, Part 1 (Kapp)—Roger Williams

1-20 Songs of the Fabulous Fifties, Part 2 (Kapp)—Roger Williams

1-20 Roger Williams' Greatest Hits (Kapp)—Roger Williams

2-7 Yakety Sax (Monument)—Boots Randolph

2-7 That's Life (Reprise)—Frank Sinatra

2-16 Lou Rawls Live! (Capitol)—Lou Rawls

2-22 The Two Sides of the Smothers Brothers (Mercury)—Smothers Brothers

2-24 Between the Buttons (London)—Rolling Stones

3-8 A Little Bit Me, a Little Bit You (Colgems)—Monkees

3-20 Midnight Ride (Columbia)—Paul Revere and the Raiders

3-20 Penny Lane (S) (Capitol)—Beatles

4-3 Sugartown (S) (Reprise)—Nancy Sinatra

4-7 Thoroughly Modern Millie (Decca)—soundtrack

4-10 The Best of Mancini (RCA Victor)—Henry Mancini

4-10 An Evening with Belafonte (RCA Victor)—Harry Belafonte

4-12 Best of the Beach Boys (Capitol)—Beach Boys

4-14 There's a Kind of Hush (All over the World) (S) (MGM)—Herman's Hermits

4-17 Winchester Cathedral (Dot)—Lawrence Welk

4-17 Spirit of '67 (Columbia)—Paul Revere and the Raiders

4-19 Somethin' Stupid (S) (Reprise)—Frank and Nancy Sinatra

4-20 The Mamas & the Papas Deliver (Dunhill)—Mamas and the Papas

4-24 Born Free (Kapp)—Roger Williams

4-28 This Diamond Ring (S) (Liberty)—Gary Lewis

5-1 Ruby Tuesday (S) (London)—Rolling Stones

5-4 Happy Together (S) (White Whale)—Turtles

5-14 Mame (Columbia)—original cast

5-19 Headquarters (Colgems)—Monkees

5-19 My Cup Runneth Over (RCA Victor)—Ed Ames

6-1 Respect (S) (Atlantic)—Aretha Franklin

6-1 Green Onions (S) (Stax)—Booker T & the M.G.s

6-1 Stranger on the Shore (S) (Atco)—Mr. Acker Bilk

6-1 Stranger on the Shore (Atco)—Mr. Acker Bilk

6-13 I Never Loved a Man the Way I Love You (Atlantic)—Aretha Franklin

6-13 I Never Loved a Man the Way I Love You (S) (Atlantic)—Aretha Franklin

6-13 Groovin' (S) (Atlantic)—Young Rascals

6-15 Sergeant Pepper's Lonely Hearts Club Band (Capitol)—Beatles

6-23 Sweet Soul Music (S) (Atco)—Arthur Conley

6-28 Man of La Mancha (Kapp)—original cast

6-30 Revenge (Warner)—Bill Cosby

7-6 Parsley, Sage, Rosemary & Thyme (Columbia)—Simon and Garfunkel

7-6 Born Free (Columbia)—Andy Williams

7-7 The Best of the Lovin' Spoonful (Kama Sutra)—Lovin' Spoonful

7-14 Themes for Young Lovers (Columbia)—Percy Faith and His Orchestra

7-14 I Walk the Line (Columbia)—Johnny Cash

7-14 Pleasant Valley Sunday (S) (Colgems)—Monkees

7-14 Windy (S) (Warner Bros.)—Association

7-24 Surrealistic Pillow (RCA Victor)—Jefferson Airplane

7-26 Little Bit o' Soul (S) (Laurie)—Music Explosion

8-14 Georgy Girl (S) (Capitol)—Seekers

8-16 Flowers (London)—Rolling Stones

8-22 A Man and a Woman (United Artists)—soundtrack

8-24 Ebb Tide (Decca)—Earl Grant

8-24 Blue Midnight (Decca)—Bert Kaempfert

8-25 Sounds Like (A&M)—Herb Alpert & the Tijuana Brass

8-25 Sergio Mendes & Brasil '66 (A&M)—Sergio Mendes & Brasil '66

8-25 Sounds of Silence (Columbia)—Simon and Garfunkel

8-25 Paul Revere and the Raiders Greatest Hits (Columbia)—Paul Revere and the Raiders

8-25 Blonde on Blonde (Columbia)—Bob Dylan

8-25 Highway 61 Revisited (Columbia)—Bob Dylan

8-25 Bringing It All Back Home (Columbia)—Bob Dylan

9-5 Baby, I Love You (S) (Atlantic)—Aretha Franklin

9-11 Ode to Billie Joe (S) (Capitol)—Bobbie Gentry

774

9-11 All You Need Is Love (S) (Capitol)—Beatles

9-11 The Doors (Elektra)—Doors

9-11 Light My Fire (S) (Elektra)—Doors

9-13 Can't Take My Eyes off You (S) (Philips)—Frankie Valli

9-13 2nd Vault of Golden Hits (Philips)—Four Seasons

9-25 The Letter (S) (Mala)—Box Tops

10-9 Ode to Billie Joe (Capitol)—Bobbie Gentry

10-16 Come Back When You Grow Up (S) (Capitol)—Bobby Vee & the Strangers

10-17 Tony Bennett's Greatest Hits Volume III (Columbia)—Tony Bennett

11-2 To Sir with Love (S) (Epic)—Lulu

11-2 Pisces, Aquarius, Capricorn and Jones Ltd. (Colgems)—Monkees

11-22 Daydream Believer (S) (Colgems)—Monkees

11-22 Soul Man (S) (Stax)—Sam and Dave

11-27 Sinatra at The Sands (Reprise)—Frank Sinatra

11-27 Along Comes the Association (Warner Bros.)—Association

11-27 Never My Love (S) (Warner Bros.)—Association

12-6 Their Satanic Majesties Request (London)—Rolling Stones

12-6 Release Me (Parrot)—Engelbert Humperdinck

12-8 Herb Alpert's Ninth (A&M)—Herb Albert & the Tijuana Brass

12-15 Magical Mystery Tour (Capitol)—Beatles

12-15 Hello Goodbye (S) (Capitol)—Beatles

12-15 Merry Christmas to All (Columbia)—Ray Conniff

12-19 Incense & Peppermints (S) (UI)—Strawberry Alarm Clock

12-19 The Rain, the Park & Other Things (S) (MGM)—Cowsills

12-21 The Button-Down Mind Strikes Back (Warner Bros.)—Bob Newhart

12-28 Insight Out (Warner Bros.)—Association

1968

1-5 Jim Nabors Sings (Columbia)—Jim Nabors

1-5 Bob Dylan's Greatest Hits (Columbia)—Bob Dylan

1-10 Chain of Fools (S) (Atlantic)—Aretha Franklin

1-12 Strange Days (Elektra)—Doors

1-26 Skinny Legs & All (S) (Dial)—Joe Tex

1-31 Judy in Disguise with Glasses (S) (Paula)—John Fred & the Playboys

1-31 Bend Me, Shape Me (S) (Acta)—American Breed

2-2 Dream with Dean (Reprise)—Dean Martin

2-7 Guantanamera (A&M)—Sandpipers

2-8 Woman, Woman (S) (Columbia)—Union Gap

2-9 Farewell to the First Golden Era (Dunhill)—Mamas and the Papas

2-14 Green Tambourine (S) (Buddah)—Lemon Pipers

2-15 I Say a Little Prayer (S) (Scepter)—Dionne Warwick

2-16 How Great Thou Art (RCA Victor)—Elvis Presley

2-26 Valleri (S) (Colgems)—Monkees

2-26 Distant Drums (RCA Victor)—Jim Reeves

2-27 Love Is Blue (S) (Philips)—Paul Mauriat

2-27 Blooming Hits (Philips)—Paul Mauriat & Orchestra

3-5 Simon Says (S) (Buddah)—1910 Fruitgum Co.

3-6 Best of Buck Owens (Capitol)—Buck Owens

3-11 (Sittin' on) The Dock of the Bay (S) (Volt)—Otis Redding

3-13 Doctor Dolittle (20th Century-Fox)—soundtrack

3-13 The Byrds Greatest Hits (Columbia)—Byrds

3-19 Welcome to My World (Reprise)—Dean Martin

3-19 Houston (Reprise)—Dean Martin

3-19 Are You Experienced (Reprise)—Jimi Hendrix

3-19 John Wesley Harding (Columbia)—Bob Dylan

3-27 The Graduate (Columbia)—soundtrack

3-28 The Best of Eddy Arnold (RCA Victor)—Eddy Arnold

3-28 The Great Caruso (RCA Victor)—Mario Lanza

4-1 Since You've Been Gone (S) (Atlantic)—Aretha Franklin

4-4 Honey (S) (United Artists)—Bobby Goldsboro

4-5 Young Girl (S) (Columbia)—Union Gap

4-6 Modern Sounds in Country & Western Music, Vol 2. (ABC)—Ray Charles

4-6 Greatest Hits (ABC)—Ray Charles

4-8 Lady Madonna (S) (Capitol)—Beatles

4-9 Loving You (RCA Victor)—Elvis Presley

4-12 Turtles' Greatest Hits (White Whale)—Turtles

4-17 The Birds, the Bees & the Monkees (Colgems)—Monkees

4-17 Gigi (MGM)—soundtrack

4-18 Bookends (Columbia)—Simon and Garfunkel

5-2 Somewhere There's a Someone (Reprise)—Dean Martin

5-2 Cry Like a Baby (S) (Mala)—Box Tops

5-8 Persuasive Percussion (Command)—Enoch Light

5-8 Songs I Sing on the Jackie Gleason Show (ABC)—Frank Fontaine

5-14 Love, Andy (Columbia)—Andy Williams

5-14 Cowboys to Girls (S) (Gamble)—Intruders

5-17 Doris Day's Greatest Hits (Columbia)—Doris Day

5-22 Disraeli Gears (Atco)—Cream

5-22 Tighten Up (S) (Atlantic)—Archie Bell & the Drells

5-23 Merry Christmas (Columbia)—Andy Williams

6-10 Mrs. Robinson (S) (Columbia)—Simon and Garfunkel

6-17 Yummy, Yummy, Yummy (S) (Buddah)—Ohio Express

6-28 Beautiful Morning (S) (Atlantic)—Rascals

7-2 Glenn Miller & His Orchestra (RCA Victor)—Glenn Miller

7-12 To Russell, My Brother, Whom I Slept With (Warner Bros.)—Bill Cosby

7-18 Grazing in the Grass (S) (UI)—Hugh Masekela

7-18 Lady Willpower (S) (Columbia)—Gary Puckett & the Union Gap

7-19 The Beat of the Brass (A&M)—Herb Alpert & the Tijuana Brass

7-19 This Guy's in Love with You (S) (A&M)—Herb Alpert

7-22 Think (S) (Atlantic)—Aretha Franklin

7-22 Wheels of Fire (Atco)—Cream

7-22 Groovin' (Atlantic)—Rascals

7-23 Vanilla Fudge (Atco)—Vanilla Fudge

7-29 The Horse (S) (Phil.–L.A. Soul)—Cliff Nobles & Co.

7-29 Collections (Atlantic)—Rascals

7-30 Somewhere My Love (Kapp)—Roger Williams

8-6 Waiting for the Sun (Elektra)—Doors

8-14 The Good, the Bad and the Ugly (United Artists)—soundtrack

8-16 A Man and His Soul (ABC)—Ray Charles

8-23 Lady Soul (Atlantic)—Aretha Franklin

8-23 People Got to Be Free (S) (Atlantic)—Rascals

8-26 Harper Valley P.T.A. (S) (Plantation)—Jeannie C. Riley

8-28 Hello, I Love You (S) (Elektra)—Doors

9-4 Look Around (A&M)—Sergio Mendes & Brasil '66

9-4 The Young Rascals (Atlantic)—Rascals

9-4 Time Peace—The Rascals' Greatest Hits (Atlantic)—Rascals

9-13 Slip Away (S) (Atlantic)—Clarence Carter

9-13 Hey Jude (S) (Apple)—Beatles

9-17 Camelot (Warner Bros.)—soundtrack

9-17 Stoned Soul Picnic (S) (Soul City)—5th Dimension

9-19 Born to Be Wild (S) (Dunhill)—Steppenwolf

9-20 1, 2, 3, Red Light (S) (Buddah)—1910 Fruitgum Co.

9-24 Turn Around, Look at Me (S) (Reprise)—Vogues

9-26 Sunshine of Your Love (S) (Atco)—Cream

10-4 Feliciano (RCA Victor)—Jose Feliciano

10-10 Axis: Bold as Love (Reprise)—Jimi Hendrix

10-11 I Say a Little Prayer (S) (Atlantic)—Aretha Franklin

10-15 Cheap Thrills (Columbia)—Janis Joplin with Big Brother and the Holding Company

10-17 By the Time I Get to Phoenix (Capitol)—Glen Campbell

10-17 Gentle on My Mind (Capitol)—Glen Campbell

10-30 My Love Forgive Me (Columbia)—Robert Goulet

10-30 Johnny Cash at Folsom Prison (Columbia)—Johnny Cash

11-1 Honey (Columbia)—Andy Williams

11-1 Little Green Apples (S) (Columbia)—O.C. Smith

11-13 At the Purple Onion (Mercury)—Smothers Brothers

11-15 Who's Making Love (S) (Stax)—Johnnie Taylor

11-18 Wichita Lineman (Capitol)—Glen Campbell

11-18 Electric Ladyland (Reprise)—Jimi Hendrix

11-20 Those Were the Days (S) (Apple)—Mary Hopkin

11-25 The Kinks Greatest Hits! (Reprise)—Kinks

11-27 Honey (United Artists)—Bobby Goldsboro

11-27 Dean Martin Christmas Album (Reprise)—Dean Martin

11-27 Steppenwolf (Dunhill)—Steppenwolf

12-3 Girl Watcher (S) (ABC)—O'Kaysions

12-3 Midnight Confession (S) (Dunhill)—Grass Roots

12-3 Fire (S) (Atlantic)—Crazy World of Arthur Brown

12-3 Aretha Now (Atlantic)—Aretha Franklin

12-3 In-A-Gadda-Da-Vida (Atco)—Iron Butterfly

12-3 Fresh Cream (Atco)—Cream

12-4 The Time Has Come (Columbia)—Chambers Brothers

12-5 Walt Disney Presents *The Jungle Book* (Disneyland)—soundtrack

12-6 The Beatles (Apple)—Beatles

12-16 The Christmas Album (A&M)—Herb Alpert & the Tijuana Brass

12-19 I Love How You Love Me (S) (Epic)—Bobby Vinton

12-19 Over You (S) (Columbia)—Union Gap

12-20 Harper Valley P.T.A. (Plantation)—Jeannie C. Riley

12-23 Funny Girl (Columbia)—soundtrack

12-23 Beggars Banquet (London)—Rolling Stones

12-30 The Sea (Warner Bros.)—San Sebastian Strings

1969

1-2 Walt Disney Presents *The Story of Mary Poppins* (Disneyland)—Storyteller LP

1-7 Chewy, Chewy (S) (Buddah)—Ohio Express

1-10 Hey Little One (Capitol)—Glen Campbell

1-13 Abraham, Martin and John (S) (Laurie)—Dion

1-13 See Saw (S) (Atlantic)—Aretha Franklin

1-17 The Christmas Song (Capitol)—Nat "King" Cole

1-17 The Lettermen!!! . . . & "Live" (Capitol)—Lettermen

1-20 Soulful Strut (S) (Brunswick)—Young Holt Limited

1-20 Wildflowers (Elektra)—Judy Collins

1-22 Wichita Lineman (S) (Capitol)—Glen Campbell

1-27 Album 1700 (Warner Bros.)—Peter, Paul and Mary

1-29 Gentry/Campbell (Capitol)—Bobbie Gentry and Glen Campbell

2-3 Dean Martin's Greatest Hits, Volume 1 (Reprise)—Dean Martin

2-5 Yellow Submarine (Apple)—Beatles

2-12 Steppenwolf the Second (Dunhill)—Steppenwolf

2-13 Touch Me (S) (Elektra)—Doors

2-13 Everyday People (S) (Epic)—Sly and the Family Stone

2-17 Who Will Answer? (RCA)—Ed Ames

2-18 Boots with Strings (Monument)—Boots Randolph

2-19 The Worst That Can Happen (S) (Buddah)—Brooklyn Bridge

2-24 Dionne Warwick's Greatest Hits (Scepter)—Dionne Warwick

2-24 Can I Change My Mind (S) (Dakar)—Tyrone Davis

2-24 Hooked on a Feeling (S) (Scepter)—B.J. Thomas

2-24 Too Weak to Fight (S) (Atlantic)—Clarence Carter

2-27 Stormy (S) (Imperial)—Classics IV

2-27 A Man without Love (Parrot)—Engelbert Humperdinck

2-27 The Last Waltz (Parrot)—Engelbert Humperdinck

3-3 The Association's Greatest Hits (Warner Bros.)—Association

3-4 Build Me Up Buttercup (S) (Uni)—Foundations

3-4 Wednesday Morning 3 A.M. (Columbia)—Simon and Garfunkel

3-4 Wonderland by Night (Decca)—Bert Kaempfert

3-4 Bert Kaempfert's Greatest Hits (Decca)—Bert Kaempfert

3-7 Dizzy (S) (ABC)—Tommy Roe

3-10 Drummer Boy (20th Century-Fox)—Harry Simeone

3-21 200 MPH (Warner Bros.)—Bill Cosby

3-25 Hair (RCA)—original cast

3-25 It Must Be Him (Columbia)—Ray Conniff

3-25 Young Girl (Columbia)—Union Gap

3-25 Magic Carpet Ride (S) (Dunhill)—Steppenwolf

3-25 Sheila (S) (ABC)—Tommy Roe

3-25 Sweet Pea (S) (ABC)—Tommy Roe

3-31 Indian Giver (S) (Buddah)—1910 Fruitgum Company

4-9 His Hand in Mine (RCA)—Elvis Presley

4-9 It's Your Thing (S) (T-Neck)—Isley Brothers

4-10 Blood, Sweat & Tears (Columbia)—Blood, Sweat and Tears

4-11 Time of the Season (S) (Date)—Zombies

4-16 Galveston (Capitol)—Glen Campbell

4-21 Freedom Suite (Atlantic)—Rascals

4-21 Goodbye (Atco)—Cream

4-22 Donovan's Greatest Hits (Epic)—Donovan

4-24 Hair (S) (MGM)—Cowsills

10-7 Little Woman (S) (Metromedia)—Bobby Sherman

10-7 Get Together (S) (RCA)—Youngbloods

10-8 Who Knows Where the Time Goes (Elektra)—Judy Collins

10-10 Jean (S) (CGC)—Oliver

10-10 Golden Instrumentals (Dot)—Billy Vaughn & Orchestra

10-14 Galveston (S) (Capitol)—Glen Campbell

10-14 Baby, I Love You (S) (Steed)—Andy Kim

10-14 Jimi Hendrix, Smash Hits (Reprise)—Jimi Hendrix

10-27 Abbey Road (Apple)—Beatles

10-27 Something (S) (Apple)—Beatles

10-27 Tom Jones—Live in Las Vegas (Parrot)—Tom Jones

10-28 Laughing (S) (RCA)—Guess Who

10-28 Suspicious Minds (S) (RCA)—Elvis Presley

11-10 Rudolph, the Red-Nosed Reindeer (S) (Columbia)—Gene Autry

11-10 Best of Cream (Atco)—Cream

11-10 Best of the Bee Gees (Atco)—Bee Gees

11-10 Led Zeppelin II (Atlantic)—Led Zeppelin

11-24 Green, Green Grass of Home (Parrot)—Tom Jones

11-24 Let It Bleed (London)—Rolling Stones

11-26 The Band (Capitol)—Band

12-2 Santana (Columbia)—Santana

12-2 The Child Is Father to the Man (Columbia)—Blood, Sweat and Tears

12-3 Kozmic Blues Again Mama! (Columbia)—Janis Joplin

12-4 I Got Dem Oll to Stand! (Epic)—Sly and the Family Stone

12-5 Wedding Bell Blues (S) (Soul City)—5th Dimension

12-8 Na Na Hey Hey Kiss Him Goodbye (S) (Fontana)—Steam

12-11 Take a Letter, Maria (S) (Atco)—R.B. Greaves

12-12 Suitable for Framing (Dunhill)—Three Dog Night

12-12 Cycles (Reprise)—Frank Sinatra

12-12 Hot Buttered Soul (Enterprise)—Isaac Hayes

12-12 Going in Circles (S) (RCA)—Friends of Distinction

12-12 From Vegas to Memphis (RCA)—Elvis Presley

12-12 Smile a Little Smile for Me (S) (Congress)—Flying Machine

12-17 Chicago Transit Authority (Columbia)—Chicago Transit Authority

12-23 Raindrops Keep Falling on My Head (S) (Scepter)—B.J. Thomas

12-23 Back Field in Motion (S) (Bamboo)—Mel & Tim

12-24 Buddy Holly Story (Coral)—Buddy Holly & the Crickets

12-24 Honey (Columbia)—Ray Conniff

12-30 Leaving on a Jet Plane (S) (Warner Bros.)—Peter, Paul and Mary

12-30 That'll Be the Day (S) (Coral)—Buddy Holly & the Crickets

12-31 Holly Holy (S) (Uni)—Neil Diamond

1970

1-14 Engelbert (Parrot)—Engelbert Humperdinck

1-14 Engelbert Humperdinck (Parrot)—Engelbert Humperdinck

1-14 And When I Die (S) (Columbia)—Blood, Sweat and Tears

1-16 Captured Live at the Forum (Dunhill)—Three Dog Night

1-19 Easy Rider (Dunhill)—soundtrack

1-19 Jam Up, Jelly Tight (S) (ABC)—Tommy Roe

1-19 The Best of Charley Pride (RCA)—Charley Pride

1-20 La La La (If I Had You) (S) (Metromedia)—Bobby Sherman

1-21 Don't Cry, Daddy (S) (RCA)—Elvis Presley

1-21 Volunteers (RCA)—Jefferson Airplane

1-23 Crown of Creation (RCA)—Jefferson Airplane

1-28 Venus (S) (Colossus)—Shocking Blue

1-28 From Elvis in Memphis (RCA)—Elvis Presley

1-29 Hello, I'm Johnny Cash (Columbia)—Johnny Cash

1-29 See What Tomorrow Brings (Warner Bros.)—Peter, Paul and Mary

1-29 Jingle Jangle (S) (Kirshner)—Archies

2-9 Alive Alive-O! (RCA)—Jose Feliciano

2-9 Bridge over Troubled Water (Columbia)—Simon and Garfunkel

2-9 Thank You (Falettinme Be Mice Elf Agin) (S) (Epic)—Sly and the Family Stone

2-10 Bobby Sherman (Metromedia)—Bobby Sherman

2-18 Without Love (S) (Parrot)—Tom Jones

2-18 Mantovani's Golden Hits (London)—Mantovani

2-19 Try a Little Kindness (Capitol)—Glen Campbell

2-19 Get Together (Columbia)—Andy Williams

2-23 Morrison Hotel (Elektra)—Doors

2-27 Bridge over Troubled Water (S) (Columbia)—Simon and Garfunkel

3-2 Goin' out of My Head (Capitol)—Lettermen

3-6 Hey Jude (Apple)—Beatles

3-12 My Way (Reprise)—Frank Sinatra

3-17 The Plastic Ono Band—Live Peace in Toronto (Apple)—Plastic Ono Band

3-17 Hey There Lonely Girl (S) (ABC)—Eddie Holman

3-17 Let It Be (S) (Apple)—Beatles

3-18 Didn't I (Blow Your Mind This Time) (S) (Philly Groove)—Delfonics

3-18 Monster (Dunhill)—Steppinwolf

3-18 Rainy Night in Georgia (S) Cotillion)—Brook Benton

3-20 Feliciano/10 to 23 (RCA)—Jose Feliciano

3-25 Déjà Vu (Atlantic)—Crosby, Stills, Nash & Young

3-26 Up Up and Away (Soul City)—5th Dimension

3-26 Warm (A&M)—Herb Alpert & the Tijuana Brass

3-27 The Rapper (S) (Kama Sutra)—Jaggerz

4-1 A Gift from a Flower to a Garden (Epic)—Donovan

4-2 Easy Come, Easy Go (S) (Metromedia)—Bobby Sherman

4-13 Don't Come Home a Drinkin' (with Lovin' on Your Mind) (Decca)—Loretta Lynn

4-13 Whole Lotta Love (S) (Atlantic)—Led Zeppelin

4-13 Chicago (Columbia)—Chicago

4-13 Arizona (S) (Columbia)—Mark Lindsay

4-16 Tammy's Greatest Hits (Epic)—Tammy Wynette

4-17 Claudine (A&M)—Claudine Longet

4-17 Joe Cocker (A&M)—Joe Cocker

4-20 Love Grows (Where My Rosemary Goes) (S) (Bell)—Edison Lighthouse

4-23 Spirit in the Sky (S) (Reprise)—Norman Greenbaum

4-24 Tom (Parrot)—Tom Jones

4-30 A Song Will Rise (Warner Bros.)—Peter, Paul and Mary

4-30 McCartney (Apple)—Paul McCartney

5-4 House of the Rising Sun (S) (Parrot)—Frijid Pink

5-4 Midnight Cowboy (United Artists)—soundtrack

5-4 Turn Back the Hands of Time (S) (Dakar)—Tyrone Davis

5-11 Give Me Just a Little More Time (S) (Invictus)—Chairmen of the Board

5-19 The Ventures Play Telstar, The Lonely Bull and Others (Dolton)—Ventures

5-19 Golden Greats (Liberty)—Ventures

5-22 The 5th Dimension—Greatest Hits (Soul City)—5th Dimension

5-22 Butch Cassidy & the Sundance Kid (A&M)—Burt Bacharach

5-22 American Woman (RCA)—Guess Who

5-22 American Woman (S) (RCA)—Guess Who

5-22 Woodstock (Cotillion)—various artists

5-26 Let It Be (Apple)—Beatles

6-3 Band of Gypsys (Capitol)—Jimi Hendrix

6-5 Love on a Two-Way Street (S) (Stang)—Moments

6-5 Hurt So Bad (Capitol)—Lettermen

6-12 Cecilia (S) (Columbia)—Simon and Garfunkel

6-22 Self Portrait (Columbia)—Bob Dylan

6-22 Which Way You Goin', Billy (S) (London)—Poppy Family

6-26 Everything Is Beautiful (S) (Barnaby)—Ray Stevens

7-6 Grand Funk (Capitol)—Grand Funk Railroad

7-8 Here Comes Bobby (Metromedia)—Bobby Sherman

7-8 Blood, Sweat and Tears 3 (Columbia)—Blood, Sweat and Tears

7-8 Hitchin' a Ride (S) (Page One)—Vanity Fair

7-14 Mama Told Me (Not to Come) (S) (Dunhill)—Three Dog Night

7-14 Live Steppenwolf (Dunhill)—Steppenwolf

7-14 Golden Grass (Dunhill)—Grass Roots

7-14 It Ain't Easy (Dunhill)—Three Dog Night

7-22 Raindrops Keep Fallin' on My Head (Scepter)—B.J. Thomas

7-22 To Our Children's Children's Children (Threshold)—Moody Blues

7-22 Band of Gold (S) (Invictus)—Freda Payne

7-22 The Devil Made Me Buy This Dress (Little David)—Flip Wilson

7-24 Absolutely Live (Elektra)—Doors

8-4 Ride Captain Ride (S) (Atco)—Blues Image

8-6 Live at Leeds (Decca)—Who

8-6 Here Where There Is Love (Scepter)—Dionne Warwick

8-6 Valley of the Dolls (Scepter)—Dionne Warwick

8-6 Make It with You (S) (Elektra)—Bread

8-11 O-O-H Child (S) (Buddah)—Stairsteps

8-12 (They Long to Be) Close to You (S) (A&M)—Carpenters

8-12 Closer to Home (S) (Capitol)—Grand Funk Railroad

12-16 The Partridge Family Album (Bell)—Partridge Family

12-17 All Things Must Pass (Apple)—George Harrison

12-18 Pendulum (Fantasy)—Creedence Clearwater Revival

12-18 The Freewheelin' Boy Dylan (Columbia)—Bob Dylan

12-18 We Made It Happen (Parrot)—Engelbert Humperdinck

12-21 John Barleycorn Must Die (United Artists)—Traffic

12-21 Jesus Christ Superstar (Decca)—various artists

12-21 In My Life (Elektra)—Judy Collins

12-23 Ladies of the Canyon (Reprise)—Joni Mitchell

12-23 Dean Martin's Greatest Hits, Vol. II (Reprise)—Dean Martin

12-23 Portrait (Bell)—5th Dimension

1971

1-4 Groove Me (S) (Chimneyville)—King Floyd

1-6 Gypsy Woman (S) (Uni)—Brian Hyland

1-15 I Who Have Nothing (Parrot)—Tom Jones

1-18 Taproot Manuscript (Uni)—Neil Diamond

1-28 Plastic Ono Band (Apple)—John Lennon

2-1 Love Story (Paramount)—soundtrack

2-3 Rose Garden (S) (Columbia)—Lynn Anderson

2-4 One Bad Apple (S) (MGM)—Osmonds

2-4 Chicago III (Columbia)—Chicago

2-12 The Worst of Jefferson Airplane (RCA)—Jefferson Airplane

2-17 Elton John (Uni)—Elton John

2-23 On Stage, February 1970 (RCA)—Elvis Presley

2-23 Charley Pride's 10th Album (RCA)—Charley Pride

2-23 Just Plain Charley (RCA)—Charley Pride

2-23 Charley Pride in Person (RCA)—Charley Pride

2-24 Pearl (Columbia)—Janis Joplin

3-3 For the Good Times (Columbia)—Ray Price

3-10 Precious, Precious (S) (Atlantic)—Jackie Moore

3-11 Doesn't Somebody Want to be Wanted (S) (Bell)—Partridge Family

3-11 The Fightin' Side of Me (Capitol)—Merle Haggard & the Strangers

3-17 Have You Ever Seen the Rain (S) (Fantasy)—Creedence Clearwater Revival

3-17 Gary Puckett & the Union Gap's Greatest Hits (Columbia)—Gary Puckett & the Union Gap

3-22 Don't Let the Green Grass Fool You (S) (Atlantic)—Wilson Pickett

3-22 Tumbleweed Connection (Uni)—Elton John

3-22 Love Story (Columbia)—Andy Williams

3-25 Rose Garden (Columbia)—Lynn Anderson

3-25 Up to Date (Bell)—Partridge Family

3-25 She's a Lady (S) (Parrot)—Tom Jones

3-29 Amos Moses (S) (RCA)—Jerry Reed

3-30 Lonely Days (S) (Atco)—Bee Gees

4-1 The Cry of Love (Reprise)—Jimi Hendrix

4-1 Woodstock II (Cotillion)—various artists

4-6 Friends (Paramount)—Elton John

4-6 Whales & Nightingales (Elektra)—Judy Collins

4-8 If I Could Only Remember My Name (Atlantic)—David Crosby

4-9 Joy to the World (S) (ABC/Dunhill)—Three Dog Night

4-9 Naturally (ABC/Dunhill)—Three Dog Night

4-12 Golden Bisquits (ABC/Dunhill)—Three Dog Night

4-12 Steppenwolf 7 (ABC/Dunhill)—Steppenwolf

4-12 Steppenwolf Gold (ABC/Dunhill)—Steppenwolf

4-12 Greatest Hits (A&M)—Herb Alpert & the Tijuana Brass

4-12 For All We Know (S) (A&M)—Carpenters

4-12 Four-Way Street (Atlantic)—Crosby, Stills, Nash & Young

4-15 The Battle Hymn of Lt. Calley (S) (Plantation)—Terry Nelson

4-26 Help Me Make It through the Night (S) (Mega)—Sammi Smith

4-28 Stoney End (Columbia)—Barbra Streisand

4-30 Survival (Capitol)—Grand Funk Railroad

4-30 Mud Slide Slim & the Blue Horizon (Warner Bros.)—James Taylor

5-3 Put Your Hand in the Hand (S) (Kama Sutra)—Ocean

5-4 Greatest Hits (Columbia)—Barbra Streisand

5-6 Proud Mary (S) (Liberty)—Ike and Tina Turner

5-7 Paranoid (Warner Bros.)—Black Sabbath

5-11 Sticky Fingers (Rolling Stones)—Rolling Stones

5-12 Tea for the Tillerman (A&M)—Cat Stevens

5-13 Bridge over Troubled Water (S) (Atlantic)—Aretha Franklin

783

11-16 Led Zeppelin (Atlantic)—Led Zeppelin
11-17 Yo-Yo (S) (MGM)—Osmonds
11-19 Gypsys, Tramps and Thieves (S) (Kapp)—Cher
11-29 E Pluribus Funk (Capitol)—Grand Funk Railroad
11-29 Easy Loving (S) (Capitol)—Freddie Hart
11-30 Family Affair (S) (Epic)—Sly and the Family Stone
11-30 Trapped by a Thing Called Love (S) (Westbound)—Denise LaSalle
12-6 Barbra Joan Streisand (Columbia)—Barbra Streisand
12-9 Rainbow Bridge (Reprise)—Jimi Hendrix
12-9 Scorpio (S) (Sussex)—Dennis Coffey and the Detroit Guitar Band
12-9 A Space in Time (Columbia)—Ten Years After
12-9 Carole King Music (Ode)—Carole King
12-13 Candles in the Rain (Buddah)—Melanie
12-13 All in the Family (Atlantic)—original cast
12-13 Rock Steady (S) (Atlantic)—Aretha Franklin
12-13 The Donny Osmond Album (MGM)—Donny Osmond
12-16 Cherish (S) (Bell)—David Cassidy
12-16 Brand New Key (S) (Neighborhood)—Melanie
12-16 Live (Bell)—5th Dimension
12-19 An Old-Fashioned Love Song (S) (ABC/Dunhill)—Three Dog Night
12-23 The World of Johnny Cash (Columbia)—Johnny Cash
12-23 Dionne Warwicke Story—Decade of Gold (Scepter)—Dionne Warwicke
12-30 Clean Up Woman (S) (Alston)—Betty Wright

1972

1-3 You Are Everything (S) (Avco)—Stylistics
1-3 American Pie (S) (United Artists)—Don McLean
1-3 American Pie (United Artists)—Don McLean
1-3 Bob Dylan's Greatest Hits, Vol. II (Columbia)—Bob Dylan
1-4 The Concert for Bangla Desh (Apple)—George Harrison & Friends
1-5 Aerie (RCA)—John Denver
1-6 Drowning in the Sea of Love (S) (Spring)—Joe Simon
1-6 Let's Stay Together (S) (Hi)—Al Green
1-7 Baby, I'm A-want You (S) (Elektra)—Bread

1-12 She's a Lady (Parrott)—Tom Jones
1-13 Wildlife (Apple)—Wings
1-17 Meaty Beaty Big and Bouncy (Decca)—Who
1-17 Sunshine (S) (Capricorn)—Jonathan Edwards
1-17 Stones (Uni)—Neil Diamond
1-18 Loretta Lynn's Greatest Hits (Decca)—Loretta Lynn
1-20 Homemade (MGM)—Osmonds
1-20 Hot Rocks (London)—Rolling Stones
1-26 To You with Love (MGM)—Donny Osmond
1-27 I'd Like to Teach the World to Sing (S) (Elektra)—New Seekers
1-28 Killer (Warner Bros.)—Alice Cooper
1-31 Blessed Are (Vanguard)—Joan Baez
1-31 Any Day Now (Vanguard)—Joan Baez
2-3 Leon Russell and the Shelter People (Shelter)—Leon Russell
2-4 A Nod Is as Good as a Wink . . . to a Blind Horse (Warner Bros.)—Faces
2-7 Low Spark of High-Heeled Boys (Island)—Traffic
2-15 Charley Pride Sings Heart Songs (RCA)—Charley Pride
2-18 Harvest (Warner/Reprise)—Neil Young
2-19 Madman across the Water (Uni)—Elton John
2-21 Precious & Few (S) (Carousel)—Climax
2-23 Rockin' the Fillmore (A&M)—Humble Pie
2-29 Hurting Each Other (S) (A&M)—Carpenters
3-1 Paul Simon (Columbia)—Paul Simon
3-3 Nilsson Schmilsson (RCA)—Nilsson
3-3 Without You (S) (RCA)—Nilsson
3-4 Day after Day (S) (Apple)—Badfinger
3-8 Kiss an Angel Good Mornin' (S) (RCA)—Charley Pride
3-9 Baby, I'm A-want You (Elektra)—Bread
3-10 America (Warner Bros.)—America
3-10 Fragile (Atlantic)—Yes
3-15 The Lion Sleeps Tonight (S) (Atlantic)—Robert John
3-22 I Gotcha (S) (Dial)—Joe Tex
3-22 Jungle Fever (S) (Polydor)—Chakachas
3-24 Puppy Love (S) (MGM)—Donny Osmond
3-24 A Horse with No Name (S) (Warner Bros.)—America
3-24 Down by the Lazy River (S) (MGM)—Osmonds
3-31 Tom Jones Live at Caesar's Palace (Parrot)—Tom Jones
3-31 Another Time, Another Place (Parrot)—Engelbert Humperdinck

785

12-18 Homecoming (Warner Bros.)—America

12-18 Nights in White Satin (S) (Deram)—Moody Blues

12-18 I Am Woman (S) (Capitol)—Helen Reddy

12-20 Summer of '42 (Columbia)—Peter Nero

12-21 An Anthology (Capricorn)—Duane Allman

12-21 Manna (Elektra)—Bread

12-21 On the Waters (Elektra)—Bread

12-22 For the Roses (Asylum)—Joni Mitchell

12-23 Hot August Night (MCA)—Neil Diamond

12-30 Portrait of Donny (MGM)—Donny Osmond

12-30 The Osmonds "Live" (MGM)—Osmonds

12-30 Son of Schmilsson (RCA)—Nilsson

12-30 Rocky Mountain High (RCA)—John Denver

1973

1-4 Long John Silver (Grunt)—Jefferson Airplane

1-4 Funny Face (S) (Dot)—Donna Fargo

1-8 You're So Vain (S) (Elektra)—Carly Simon

1-9 It Never Rains in Southern California (S) (Mums)—Albert Hammond

1-17 More Hot Rocks (Big Hits & Fazed Cookies) (London)—Rolling Stones

1-18 Super Fly (S) (Curtom)—Curtis Mayfield

1-22 The Magician's Birthday (Mercury)—Uriah Heep

1-24 Crazy Horses (MGM)—Osmonds

1-24 Too Young (MGM)—Donny Osmond

1-26 Creedence Gold (Fantasy)—Creedence Clearwater Revival

1-29 Rockin' Pneumonia and the Boogie Woogie Flu (S) (United Artists)—Johnny Rivers

1-29 The Happiest Girl in the Whole U.S.A. (Dot)—Donna Fargo

2-2 Loggins and Messina (Columbia)—Loggins and Messina

2-5 Crocodile Rock (S) (MCA)—Elton John

2-9 Love Jones (S) (20th Century)—Brighter Side of Darkness

2-9 Love Train (S) (Philadelphia International)—O'Jays

2-9 360 Degrees of Billy Paul (Philadelphia International)—Billy Paul

2-12 Don't Shoot Me, I'm Only the Piano Player (MCA)—Elton John

2-13 Worldwide 50 Gold Award Hits (RCA)—Elvis Presley

2-13 Elvis—Aloha from Hawaii via Satellite (RCA)—Elvis Presley

2-13 Live Concert at the Forum (Columbia)—Barbra Streisand

2-13 Could It Be I'm Falling in Love (S) (Atlantic)—Spinners

2-14 Harry Hippie (S) (United Artists)—Bobby Womack and Peace

2-16 The Stylistics (Avco)—Stylistics

2-22 Killing Me Softly with His Song (S) (Atlantic)—Roberta Flack

3-2 The World Is a Ghetto (S) (United Artists)—War

3-6 Cisco Kid (S) (United Artists)—War

3-6 Around the World with Three Dog Night (ABC/Dunhill)—Three Dog Night

3-7 I Am Woman (Capitol)—Helen Reddy

3-7 Shoot-Out at the Fantasy Factory (Island)—Traffic

3-7 Your Mama Don't Dance (S) (Columbia)—Loggins and Messina

3-7 Dueling Banjos (S) (Warner Bros.)—Eric Weissberg

3-7 Dueling Banjos (Warner Bros.)—soundtrack from *Deliverance* as performed by Eric Weissberg and Steve Mandel

3-7 Baby, Don't Get Hooked on Me (Columbia)—Mac Davis

3-7 Wattstax—The Living Word (Stax)—various artists

3-15 Last Song (S) (Capitol)—Edward Bear

3-22 Clair (S) (MAM)—Gilbert O'Sullivan

3-23 In Concert (RSO)—Derek and the Dominos

3-27 Billion Dollar Babies (Warner Bros.)—Alice Cooper

3-27 Kenny Rogers & the First Edition, Greatest Hits (Warner/Reprise)—Kenny Rogers & the First Edition

4-2 Ain't No Woman (S) (ABC/Dunhill)—Four Tops

4-2 The Night the Lights Went out in Georgia (S) (Bell)—Vicki Lawrence

4-2 Tie a Yellow Ribbon round the Old Oak Tree (S) (Bell)—Dawn

4-4 The Cover of *Rolling Stone* (S) (Columbia)—Dr. Hook & the Medicine Show

4-6 Break Up to Make Up (S) (Avco)—Stylistics

4-10 Houses of the Holy (Atlantic)—Led Zeppelin

4-10 The Best of Bread (Elektra)—Bread

4-11 Who Do We Think We Are! (Warner Bros.)—Deep Purple

4-13 The Beatles 1962–1966 (Apple)—Beatles

4-13 The Beatles 1966–1970 (Apple)—Beatles

4-17 The Dark Side of the Moon (Harvest)—Pink Floyd

4-23 Call Me (Come Back Home) (S) (Hi)—Al Green

4-25 The Divine Miss M (Atlantic)—Bette Midler

4-25 Little Willy (S) (Bell)—Sweet

4-30 They Only Come out at Night (Epic)—Edgar Winter Group

5-8 Back Stabbers (Philadelphia International)—O'Jays

5-11 Sittin' In (Columbia)—Loggins and Messina

5-14 Funky Worm (S) (Westbound)—Ohio Players

5-17 Yessongs (Atlantic)—Yes

5-17 The Yes Album (Atlantic)—Yes

5-17 Sing (S) (A&M)—Carpenters

5-21 Pillow Talk (S) (Vibration)—Sylvia

5-23 Leaving Me (S) (Wand)—Independents

5-25 Red Rose Speedway (Apple)—Paul McCartney & Wings

5-25 William E. McEuen Presents "Will the Circle Be Unbroken" (United Artists)—Nitty Gritty Dirt Band

5-31 Can't Buy a Thrill (ABC/Dunhill)—Steely Dan

5-31 Made in Japan (Warner Bros.)—Deep Purple

6-1 Living in the Material World (Apple)—George Harrison

6-6 Curtis (Curtom)—Curtis Mayfield

6-6 Back to the World (Curtom)—Curtis Mayfield

6-6 I'm Gonna Love You Just a Little More, Baby (S) (20th Century)—Barry White

6-7 Now and Then (A&M)—Carpenters

6-13 Class Clown (Little David)—George Carlin

6-14 The Sensational Charley Pride (RCA)—Charley Pride

6-14 From Me to You (RCA)—Charley Pride

6-14 The Country Way (RCA)—Charley Pride

6-14 Round 2 (Avco)—Stylistics

6-15 There Goes Rhymin' Simon (Columbia)—Paul Simon

6-19 Frankenstein (S) (Epic)—Edgar Winter Group

6-21 Moving Waves (Sire)—Focus

6-25 Diamond Girl (Warner Bros.)—Seals & Crofts

6-26 Fantasy (Ode)—Carole King

6-26 Will It Go round in Circles (S) (A&M)—Billy Preston

6-26 Leon Live (Shelter)—Leon Russell

6-28 Elvis—That's the Way It Is (RCA)—Elvis Presley

7-3 Live at the Sahara Tahoe (Stax)—Isaac Hayes

7-3 Playground in My Mind (S) (Epic)—Clint Holmes

7-3 The Captain and Me (Warner Bros.)—Doobie Brothers

7-5 Drift Away (S) (Decca)—Dobie Gray

7-6 My Love (S) (Apple)—Paul McCartney & Wings

7-12 Call Me (London)—Al Green

7-13 One of a Kind (Love Affair) (S) (Atlantic)—Spinners

7-13 Spinners (Atlantic)—Spinners

7-18 Chicago VI (Columbia)—Chicago

7-19 Natural High (S) (London)—Bloodstone

7-20 Dick Clark: 20 Years of Rock 'N' Roll (Buddah)—various artists

7-23 Doin' It to Death (S) (People)—Fred Wesley & the JB's

7-24 Shambala (S) (ABC/Dunhill)—Three Dog Night

7-24 Bad Bad Leroy Brown (S) (ABC/Dunhill)—Jim Croce

7-27 A Passion Play (Chrysalis)—Jethro Tull

7-30 Give Your Baby a Standing Ovation (S) (Cadet)—Dells

8-1 Foreigner (A&M)—Cat Stevens

8-13 Yesterday Once More (S) (A&M)—Carpenters

8-14 The Morning After (S) (20th Century)—Maureen McGovern

8-17 Cabaret (ABC/Dunhill)—soundtrack

8-17 Fresh (Epic)—Sly and the Family Stone

8-21 We're an American Band (Capitol)—Grand Funk Railroad

8-21 Brothers and Sisters (Capricorn)—Allman Brothers Band

8-21 Tolouse Street (Warner Bros.)—Doobie Brothers

8-22 Brother Louie (S) (Kama Sutra)—Stories

8-27 Killing Me Softly with His Song (Atlantic)—Roberta Flack

8-27 Farewell Andromeda (RCA)—John Denver

8-28 Monster Mash (S) (Parrot)—Bobby Pickett

8-28 Here I Am (Come & Take Me) (S) (Hi)—Al Green

8-28 Smoke on the Water (S) (Warner Bros.)—Deep Purple

8-30 Delta Dawn (S) (Capitol)—Helen Reddy

8-31 Live and Let Die (S) (Apple)—Paul McCartney & Wings

9-4 Behind Closed Doors (S) (Epic)—Charlie Rich

9-5 Jesus Christ Superstar (MCA)—soundtrack

9-5 Anticipation (Elektra)—Carly Simon

9-11 Deliver the Word (United Artists)—War

9-12 If You Want Me to Stay (S) (Epic)—Sly and the Family Stone

9-14 Bloodshot (Atlantic)—J. Geils Band

9-14 Twelfth of Never (S) (Kolob)—Donny Osmond

9-14 My Best to You (Kolob)—Donny Osmond

9-17 Love Devotion Surrender (Columbia)—Carlos Santana and Mahavishnu John McLaughlin

9-18 Get Down (S) (MAM)—Gilbert O'Sullivan

9-19 Long Hard Climb (Capitol)—Helen Reddy

9-25 Beginnings (Atco)—Allman Brothers Band

9-25 Goat's Head Soup (Rolling Stones)—Rolling Stones

9-26 Focus 3 (Sire)—Focus

10-2 That Lady (S) (T-Neck)—Isley Brothers

10-2 Los Cochinos (Ode)—Cheech and Chong

10-9 We're an American Band (S) (Capitol)—Grand Funk Railroad

10-9 Loves Me Like a Rock (S) (Columbia)—Paul Simon

10-9 Say, Has Anybody Seen My Sweet Gypsy Rose (S) (Bell)—Dawn

10-12 Half-Breed (S) (MCA)—Cher

10-12 Goodbye Yellow Brick Road (MCA)—Elton John

10-12 Cyan (ABC/Dunhill)—Three Dog Night

10-12 Sing It Again, Rod (Mercury)—Rod Stewart

10-12 Uriah Heep Live (Mercury)—Uriah Heep

10-18 Midnight Train to Georgia (S) (Buddah)—Gladys Knight & the Pips

10-23 I Believe in You (You Believe in Me) (S) (Stax)—Johnny Taylor

10-24 Angel Clare (Columbia)—Arthur Garfunkel

10-29 Quadrophenia (MCA)—Who

10-29 Meddle (Harvest)—Pink Floyd

10-30 Johathan Livingston Seagull (Columbia)—Neil Diamond/soundtrack

11-1 The Golden Age of Rock 'N' Roll (Kama Sutra)—Sha Na Na

11-2 Life and Times (ABC)—Jim Croce

11-2 The Smoker You Drink, The Player You Get (ABC/Dunhill)—Joe Walsh

11-5 Imagination (Buddah)—Gladys Knight & the Pips

11-6 I've Got So Much to Give (20th Century)—Barry White

11-6 Heartbeat—It's a Lovebeat (S) (20th Century)—DeFranco Family featuring Tony DeFranco

11-8 Head to the Sky (Columbia)—Earth, Wind & Fire

11-8 Why Me (S) (Monument)—Kris Kristofferson

11-8 Ringo (Apple)—Ringo Starr

11-9 The Silver Tongued Devil and I (Monument)—Kris Kristofferson

11-9 3 + 3 (T-Neck)—Isley Brothers

11-15 Angie (S) (Rolling Stones)—Rolling Stones

11-26 You Don't Mess Around with Jim (ABC/Dunhill)—Jim Croce

11-27 Behind Closed Doors (Epic)—Charlie Rich

11-28 Joy (Stax)—Isaac Hayes

11-29 Welcome (Columbia)—Santana

11-29 Jesus Was a Capricorn (Monument)—Kris Kristofferson

11-30 Mind Games (Apple)—John Lennon

12-6 I Got a Name (ABC/Dunhill)—Jim Croce

12-6 The Joker (Capitol)—Steve Miller Band

12-7 Paper Roses (S) (Kolob)—Marie Osmond

12-7 Muscle of Love (Warner Bros.)—Alice Cooper

12-7 Full Sail (Columbia)—Loggins and Messina

12-7 Time Fades Away (Warner/Reprise)—Neil Young

12-7 Band on the Run (Apple)—Paul McCartney & Wings

12-10 The Most Beautiful Girl (S) (Epic)—Charlie Rich

12-11 John Denver's Greatest Hits (RCA)—John Denver

12-11 The Singles 1969–1973 (A&M)—Carpenters

12-11 Top of the World (S) (A&M)—Carpenters

12-12 Brain Salad Surgery (Manticore)—Emerson, Lake and Palmer

12-12 Bette Midler (Atlantic)—Bette Midler

12-17 Show and Tell (S) (Rocky Road)—Al Wilson

12-18 Space Race (S) (A&M)—Billy Preston

12-19 If You're Ready (S) (Stax)—Staple Singers

12-21 Snowbird (Capitol)—Anne Murray

12-21 Dylan (Columbia)—Dylan

12-21 American Graffiti (MCA)—soundtrack

12-28 The Love I Lost (S) (Philadelphia International)—Harold Melvin and the Blue Notes

12-28   Photograph (S) (Apple)—Ringo Starr

1974

1-2   Just You and Me (S) (Columbia)—Chicago

1-3   Time in a Bottle (S) (ABC)—Jim Croce

1-4   Goodbye Yellow Brick Road (S) (MCA)—Elton John

1-8   Americans (S) (Westbound)—Byron MacGregor

1-8   Leave Me Alone (Ruby Red Dress) (S) (Capitol)—Helen Reddy

1-8   The Early Beatles (Apple)—Beatles

1-11   The Joker (S) (Capitol)—Steve Miller Band

1-15   Smokin' in the Boys Room (S) (Big Tree)—Brownsville Station

1-15   The Lord's Prayer (Columbia)—Jim Nabors

1-21   Ship Ahoy (Philadelphia International)—O'Jays

1-22   Livin' for You (Hi)—Al Green

1-22   Eagles (Asylum)—Eagles

1-22   Colors of the Day (Elektra)—Judy Collins

1-22   Hot Cakes (Elektra)—Carly Simon

1-22   Planet Waves (Asylum)—Bob Dylan

1-28   Johnny Winter Live (Columbia)—Johnny Winter

1-30   I Have Got to Use My Imagination (S) (Buddah)—Gladys Knight & the Pips

1-31   You're Sixteen (S) (Apple)—Ringo Starr

2-6   The Way We Were (S) (Columbia)—Barbra Streisand

2-7   The Pointer Sisters (Blue Thumb)—Pointer Sisters

2-7   Alone Together (Blue Thumb)—Dave Mason

2-7   Never, Never Gonna Give Ya Up (S) (20th Century)—Barry White

2-7   Stone Gon' (20th Century)—Barry White

2-7   Love's Theme (S) (20th Century)—Love Unlimited Orchestra

2-7   Under the Influence of Love Unlimited (20th Century)—Love Unlimited

2-8   Live—Full House (Atlantic)—J. Geils Band

2-8   Tales from Topographic Oceans (Atlantic)—Yes

2-8   Let Me Be There (S) (MCA)—Olivia Newton-John

2-14   Seasons in the Sun (S) (Bell)—Terry Jacks

2-20   Until You Come Back to Me (S) (Atlantic)—Aretha Franklin

2-21   Jungle Boogie (S) (De-Lite)—Kool & the Gang

2-26   The Way We Were (Columbia)—Barbra Streisand

2-27   Court and Spark (Asylum)—Joni Mitchell

2-28   Ummagumma (Harvest)—Pink Floyd

3-4   Half Breed (MCA)—Cher

3-5   Sweet Freedom (Warner Bros.)—Uriah Heep

3-5   Laid Back (Capricorn)—Greg Allman

3-6   Spiders and Snakes (S) (MGM)—Jim Stafford

3-12   Unborn Child (Warner Bros.)—Seals & Crofts

3-13   War Live (United Artists)—War

3-18   The Payback (Polydor)—James Brown

3-18   Chicago VII (Columbia)—Chicago

3-20   Burn (Warner Bros.)—Deep Purple

3-20   Sabbath, Bloody Sabbath (Warner Bros.)—Black Sabbath

3-22   Dark Lady (S) (MCA)—Cher

3-26   Rock On (S) (Columbia)—David Essex

3-26   Tubular Bells (Virgin)—Mike Oldfield

3-28   Hooked on a Feeling (S) (EMI)—Blue Swede

3-28   Sunshine on My Shoulder (S) (RCA)—John Denver

3-29   Shinin' On (Capitol)—Grand Funk Railroad

4-1   TSOP (S) (Philadelphia International)—MFSB

4-2   What Were Once Vices Are Now Habits (Warner Bros.)—Doobie Brothers

4-8   The Lord's Prayer (S) (A&M)—Sister Janet Mead

4-8   Lookin' for a Love (S) (United Artists)—Bobby Womack

4-8   Buddha and the Chocolate Box (A&M)—Cat Stevens

4-8   Bennie and the Jets (S) (MCA)—Elton John

4-15   The Best Thing That Ever Happened to Me (S) (Buddah)—Gladys Knight & the Pips

4-16   Love Is the Message (Philadelphia International)—MFSB

4-17   Hard Labor (Dunhill)—Three Dog Night

4-18   The Payback (S) (Polydor)—James Brown

4-19   The Sting (MCA)—soundtrack

4-22   Very Special Love Songs (Epic)—Charlie Rich

4-22   Come and Get Your Love (S) (Columbia)—Redbone

4-23   Head Hunters (Columbia)—Herbie Hancock

4-24   The Streak (S) (Barnaby)—Ray Stevens

4-24	The Loco-Motion (S) (Capitol)—Grand Funk Railroad
4-29	Rhapsody in White (20th Century)—Love Unlimited Orchestra
4-30	The Best of the Best of Merle Haggard (Capitol)—Merle Haggard
5-9	Bachman-Turner Overdrive II (Mercury)—Bachman-Turner Overdrive
5-10	Just Don't Want to Be Lonely (S) (RCA)—Main Ingredient
5-10	Wild and Peaceful (De-Lite)—Kool & the Gang
5-13	Maria Muldaur (Reprise)—Maria Muldaur
5-14	Mockingbird (S) (Elektra)—Carly Simon and James Taylor
5-14	Open Our Eyes (Columbia)—Earth, Wind & Fire
5-14	Pretzel Logic (ABC)—Steely Dan
5-14	The Show Must Go On (S) (Dunhill)—Three Dog Night
5-17	The Way We Were (Columbia)—soundtrack
5-21	Mighty Love (Atlantic)—Spinners
5-22	You Make Me Feel Brand New (S) (Avco)—Stylistics
5-23	Tres Hombres (London)—ZZ Top
5-31	Be Thankful for What You Got (S) (Roxbury)—William DeVaughn
5-31	Sundown (Reprise)—Gordon Lightfoot
5-31	It's Been a Long Time (RCA)—New Birth
6-4	Band on the Run (S) (Apple)—Paul McCartney & Wings
6-5	On the Border (Asylum)—Eagles
6-5	Billy Don't Be a Hero (S) (Dunhill)—Bo Donaldson and the Heywoods
6-6	Love Song for Jeffrey (Capitol)—Helen Reddy
6-7	Claudine—motion picture soundtrack (Buddah)—Gladys Knight & the Pips
6-7	The Entertainer (S) (MCA)—soundtrack from *The Sting*
6-11	Live Rhymin' (Columbia)—Paul Simon
6-12	Ziggy Stardust (RCA)—David Bowie
6-12	For The Love of Money (S) (Philadelphia International)—O'Jays
6-18	On Stage (Columbia)—Loggins and Messina
6-18	Sundown (S) (Reprise)—Gordon Lightfoot
6-21	Hollywood Swinging (S) (De-Lite)—Kool & the Gang
6-24	Back Home Again (RCA)—John Deacon
6-24	Rock the Boat (S) (RCA)—Hues Corporation
6-28	Skin Tight (Mercury)—Ohio Players
7-5	Caribou (MCA)—Elton John
7-8	The Great Gatsby (Paramount)—soundtrack
7-8	Before the Flood (Asylum)—Bob Dylan and the Band
7-11	Workingman's Dead (Warner Bros.)—Grateful Dead
7-11	American Beauty (Warner Bros.)—Grateful Dead
7-15	On and On (S) (Buddah)—Gladys Knight & the Pips
7-18	Shock Treatment (Epic)—Edgar Winter Group
7-25	That's a Plenty (Blue Thumb)—Pointer Sisters
7-26	Annie's Song (S) (RCA)—John Denver
7-26	Diamond Dogs (RCA)—David Bowie
7-26	If You Love Me (Let Me Know) (S) (MCA)—Olivia Newton-John
8-8	Feel Like Makin' Love (S) (Atlantic)—Roberta Flack
8-8	461 Ocean Boulevard (RSO)—Eric Clapton
8-9	Tell Me Something Good (S) (ABC)—Rufus
8-9	The Night Chicago Died (S) (Mercury)—Paper Lace
8-12	Let's Put It All Together (Avco)—Stylistics
8-14	(You're) Having My Baby (S) (United Artists)—Paul Anka
8-14	Endless Summer (Capitol)—Beach Boys
8-16	Sideshow (S) (Atco)—Blue Magic
8-22	The Air That I Breathe (S) (Epic)—Hollies
8-23	Not Fragile (Mercury)—Bachman-Turner Overdrive
9-4	Journey to the Centre of the Earth (A&M)—Rick Wakeman
9-5	Rags to Rufus (ABC)—Rufus
9-6	Don't Let the Sun Go Down on Me (S) (MCA)—Elton John
9-9	If You Love Me, Let Me Know (MCA)—Olivia Newton-John
9-9	His 12 Greatest Hits (MCA)—Neil Diamond
9-10	Bridge of Sighs (Chrysalis)—Robin Trower
9-11	Can't Get Enough of Your Love, Babe (S) (20th Century)—Barry White
9-19	Can't Get Enough (20th Century)—Barry White
9-19	So Far (Atlantic)—Crosby, Stills, Nash & Young
9-19	I Shot the Sheriff (S) (RSO)—Eric Clapton
9-19	Welcome Back, My Friends, to the Show That Never Ends (Manticore)—Emerson, Lake and Palmer
9-19	Bad Company (Swan Song)—Bad Company

9-20 I'm Leaving It (All) up to You (S) (MGM)—Donny and Marie Osmond

9-20 Moontan (MCA)—Golden Earring

9-20 Second Helping (MCA)—Lynyrd Skynyrd

9-23 Desperado (Asylum)—Eagles

9-23 The Souther, Hillman, Furay Band (Asylum)—Souther, Hillman, Furay Band

9-23 Stop and Smell the Roses (Columbia)—Mac Davis

9-23 On the Beach (Reprise)—Neil Young

10-3 Santana's Greatest Hits (Columbia)—Santana

10-3 Rock Me Gently (S) (Capitol)—Andy Kim

10-4 The Beach Boys in Concert (Reprise)—Beach Boys

10-8 Then Came You (S) (Atlantic)—Dionne Warwicke and the Spinners

10-8 Black Oak Arkansas (Atco)—Black Oak Arkansas

10-9 I Honestly Love You (S) (MCA)—Olivia Newton-John

10-9 Body Heat (A&M)—Quincy Jones

10-9 Cheech and Chong's Wedding Album (Ode)—Cheech and Chong

10-11 Bachman-Turner Overdrive (Mercury)—Bachman-Turner Overdrive

10-14 Let Me Be There (MCA)—Olivia Newton-John

10-15 Alice Cooper's Greatest Hits (Warner Bros.)—Alice Cooper

10-16 Nothing from Nothing (S) (A&M)—Billy Preston

10-16 Wrap around Joy (Ode)—Carole King

10-22 Photographs and Memories, His Greatest Hits (ABC)—Jim Croce

10-22 Walls and Bridges (Apple)—John Lennon

10-23 There Won't Be Anymore (RCA)—Charlie Rich

10-25 Skin Tight (S) (Mercury)—Ohio Players

10-30 Serenade (Columbia)—Neil Diamond

10-30 Holiday (Warner Bros.)—America

10-31 It's Only Rock n' Roll (Rolling Stones)—Rolling Stones

11-4 Live It Up (T-Neck)—Isley Brothers

11-5 When the Eagle Flies (Island)—Traffic

11-7 David Live (RCA)—David Bowie

11-8 Small Talk (Epic)—Sly and the Family Stone

11-8 War Child (Chrysalis)—Jethro Tull

11-8 Greatest Hits (MCA)—Elton John

11-12 I Feel a Song (Buddah)—Gladys Knight & the Pips

11-20 Anka (United Artists)—Paul Anka

11-25 Do It ('til You're Satisfied) (S) (Scepter)—B.T. Express

11-25 Mother Lode (Columbia)—Loggins and Messina

11-27 Miles of Aisles (Asylum)—Joni Mitchell

11-27 I Don't Know How to Love Him (Capitol)—Helen Reddy

11-27 Kung Fu Fighting (S) (20th Century)—Carl Douglas

12-2 I Can Help (S) (Monument)—Billy Swan

12-2 This Is the Moody Blues (Threshold)—Moody Blues

12-5 Here's Johnny . . . Magic Moments from The Tonight Show (Casablanca)—various artists

12-5 My Melody of Love (S) (ABC)—Bobby Vinton

12-9 Odds and Sods (MCA)—Who

12-9 Goodnight Vienna (Apple)—Ringo Starr

12-9 When Will I See You Again (S) (Philadelphia International)—Three Degrees

12-13 You Ain't Seen Nothing Yet (S) (Mercury)—Bachman-Turner Overdrive

12-13 Fire (Mercury)—Ohio Players

12-16 Dark Horse (Apple)—George Harrison

12-17 Verities and Balderdash (Elektra)—Harry Chapin

12-18 Me and Bobby McGee (Monument)—Kris Kristofferson

12-18 Roadwork (Epic)—Edgar Winter's White Trash

12-18 New and Improved (Atlantic)—Spinners

12-18 Relayer (Atlantic)—Yes

12-18 You're the First, the Last, My Everything (S) (20th Century)—Barry White

12-18 Free and Easy (Capitol)—Helen Reddy

12-18 All the Girls in the World Beware!!! (Capitol)—Grand Funk Railroad

12-18 Pronounced Leh-nerd Skin-nerd (MCA)—Lynyrd Skynyrd

12-24 Late for the Sky (Asylum)—Jackson Browne

12-24 The Best of Bread: Vol. II (Elektra)—Bread

12-27 Rufusized (ABC)—Rufus

12-31 Cat's in the Cradle (S) (Elektra)—Harry Chapin

1975

1-3 Back Home Again (S) (RCA)—John Denver

1-6 Butterfly (Columbia)—Barbra Streisand

1-8 Elvis—A Legendary Performer, Vol. I (RCA)—Elvis Presley

1-9 Did You Think to Pray (RCA)—Charley Pride

792

1-9 (Country) Charley Pride (RCA)—Charley Pride

1-9 Stormbringer (Warner Bros.)—Deep Purple

1-10 Al Green Explores Your Mind (Hi)—Al Green

1-13 Angie Baby (S) (Capitol)—Helen Reddy

1-14 Average White Band (Atlantic)—Average White Band

1-14 Joy to the World—Their Greatest Hits (ABC/Dunhill)—Three Dog Night

1-14 So What (ABC/Dunhill)—Joe Walsh

1-20 Caught Up (Spring)—Millie Jackson

1-22 Sha-La-La (Make Me Happy) (S) (Hi)— Al Green

1-23 Fire (S) (Mercury)—Ohio Players

1-29 Lucy in the Sky with Diamonds (S) (MCA)—Elton John

1-31 Mandy (S) (Bell)—Barry Manilow

1-31 Heart Like a Wheel (Capitol)—Linda Ronstadt

1-31 Dawn's New Ragtime Follies (Bell)— Dawn

2-11 Please Mr. Postman (S) (A&M)—Carpenters

2-12 Blood on the Tracks (Columbia)—Bob Dylan

2-19 An Evening with John Denver (RCA)— John Denver

2-19 Dragon Fly (Grunt)—Jefferson Starship

2-21 I'm Leaving It All up to You (MGM)— Marie and Donny Osmond

2-26 Have You Never Been Mellow (MCA)— Olivia Newton-John

2-26 Something/Anything? (Bearsville)—Todd Rundgren

2-26 Energized (Bearsville)—Foghat

2-28 Together for the First Time (ABC/Dunhill)—Bobby Bland and B.B. King

3-5 Have You Never Been Mellow (S) (MCA)—Olivia Newton-John

3-6 Pick up the Pieces (S) (Atlantic)—Average White Band

3-6 Physical Graffiti (Swan Song)—Led Zeppelin

3-6 Do It ('Til You're Satisfied) (Scepter)— B.T. Express

3-6 A Touch of Gold Volume II (Imperial)— Johnny Rivers

3-6 Johnny Rivers' Golden Hits (Imperial)— Johnny Rivers

3-18 Tommy, Original Soundtrack Recording (Polydor)—various artists

3-21 Perfect Angel (Epic)—Minnie Riperton

3-25 Lady Marmalade (S) (Epic)—Labelle

3-31 Chicago VIII (Columbia)—Chicago

4-1 Tuneweaving (Bell)—Tony Orlando & Dawn

4-1 My Eyes Adored You (S) (Private Stock)—Frankie Valli

4-8 Lovin' You (S) (Epic)—Minnie Riperton

4-8 White Gold (20th Century)—Love Unlimited Orchestra

4-8 Just Another Way to Say I Love You (20th Century)—Barry White

4-9 That's the Way of the World (Columbia)— Earth, Wind & Fire

4-9 Phoebe Snow (MCA)—Phoebe Snow

4-14 Black Water (S) (Warner Bros.)—Doobie Brothers

4-18 Get Your Wings (Columbia)—Aerosmith

4-23 Philadelphia Freedom (S) (MCA)—Elton John Band

4-30 Spirit of America (Capitol)—Beach Boys

5-1 Eldorado (United Artists)—Electric Light Orchestra

5-1 Styx II (Wooden Nickel)—Styx

5-5 Chevy Van (S) (GRC)—Sammy Johns

5-6 Nightbirds (Epic)—LaBelle

5-8 Straight Shooter (Swan Song)—Bad Company

5-12 Katy Lied (ABC)—Steely Dan

5-12 Sun Goddess (Columbia)—Ramsey Lewis

5-21 Captain Fantastic and the Brown Dirt Cowboy (MCA)—Elton John

5-22 Before the Next Teardrop Falls (S) (ABC/Dot)—Freddy Fender

5-23 (Hey Won't You Play) Another Somebody Done Somebody Wrong Song (S) (ABC)—B.J. Thomas

5-27 Four Wheel Drive (Mercury)—Bachman-Turner Overdrive

5-28 Stampede (Warner Bros.)—Doobie Brothers

5-30 Welcome to My Nightmare (Atlantic)— Alice Cooper

6-2 Venus & Mars (Capitol)—Wings

6-9 He Don't Love You (Like I Love You) (S) (Elektra)—Tony Orlando & Dawn

6-12 Survival (Philadelphia International)— O'Jays

6-12 Janis Joplin's Greatest Hits (Columbia)— Janis Joplin

6-12 Hearts (Warner Bros.)—America

6-17 Horizon (A&M)—Carpenters

6-19 Shining Star (S) (Columbia)—Earth, Wind & Fire

6-19 Live in London (Philadelphia International)—O'Jays

6-25 Love Won't Let Me Wait (Atlantic)—Major Harris

6-26	Thank God I'm A Country Boy (S) (RCA)—John Denver		9-11	Aerosmith (Columbia)—Aerosmith
6-26	The Hustle (S) (Avco)—Van McCoy and the Soul City Symphony		9-11	Fight the Power Part I. (S) (T-Neck)—Isley Bros.

6-26 Thank God I'm A Country Boy (S) (RCA)—John Denver
6-26 The Hustle (S) (Avco)—Van McCoy and the Soul City Symphony
6-27 Fandango (London)—ZZ Top
6-27 Nuthin' Fancy (MCA)—Lynyrd Skynyrd
6-30 One of These Nights (Asylum)—Eagles
6-30 The Heat Is On (T-Neck)—Isley Brothers Featuring Fight the Power
6-30 To Be True (Philadelphia International)—Harold Melvin and the Blue Notes Featuring Theodore Pendergrass
7-1 Love Will Keep Us Together (S) (A&M)—Captain & Tennille
7-2 Young Americans (RCA)—David Bowie
7-15 Chocolate Chip (ABC)—Isaac Hayes
7-18 Barry Manilow II (Bell)—Barry Manilow
7-21 Wildfire (S) (Epic)—Michael Murphey
7-24 Cut the Cake (Atlantic)—Average White Band
7-25 Why Can't We Be Friends? (United Artists)—War
7-30 Fire on the Mountain (Kama Sutra)—Charlie Daniels Band
8-1 Love Will Keep Us Together (A&M)—Captain & Tennille
8-4 Express (S) (Scepter)—B.T. Express
8-7 Made in the Shade (Rolling Stone)—Rolling Stones
8-11 Toys in the Attic (Columbia)—Aerosmith
8-13 Magic (S) (Capitol)—Pilot
8-14 The Marshall Tucker Band (Capricorn)—Marshall Tucker Band
8-15 Cat Stevens Greatest Hits (A&M)—Cat Stevens
8-15 Honey (Mercury)—Ohio Players
8-18 Light of Worlds (De-Lite)—Kool & the Gang
8-19 Why Can't We Be Friends? (S) (United Artists)—War
8-21 Jive Talkin' (S) (RSO)—Bee Gees
8-22 Red Octopus (Grunt)—Jefferson Starship
8-25 Don't Cry Now (Asylum)—Linda Ronstadt
8-29 Before the Next Teardrop Falls (ABC/Dot)—Freddy Fender
9-5 Listen to What the Man Said (S) (Capitol)—Paul McCartney & Wings
9-5 Rhinestone Cowboy (S) (Capitol)—Glen Campbell
9-8 Funny Lady (Original Soundtrack Recording) (Arista)—Barbra Streisand and James Caan
9-10 Someone Saved My Life Tonight (S) (MCA) —Elton John

9-11 Aerosmith (Columbia)—Aerosmith
9-11 Fight the Power Part I. (S) (T-Neck)—Isley Bros.
9-11 Between the Lines (Columbia)—Janis Ian
9-12 Gorilla (Warner Bros.)—James Taylor
9-12 Fallin' in Love (S) (Playboy)—Hamilton, Joe Frank & Reynolds
9-16 Please Mister Please (S) (MCA)—Olivia Newton-John
9-17 Wish You Were Here (Columbia)—Pink Floyd
9-18 Wasted Days and Wasted Nights (S) (ABC/Dot)—Freddy Fender
9-18 Pick of the Litter (Atlantic)—Spinners
9-19 Windsong (RCA)—John Denver
9-19 Mr. Jaws (S) (Private Stock)—Dickie Goodman
9-24 Tony Orlando & Dawn's Greatest Hits (Arista)—Tony Orlando & Dawn
9-29 Clearly Love (MCA)—Olivia Newton-John
9-29 I'll Play for You (Warner Bros.)—Seals & Crofts
9-29 Is It Something I Said? (Warner/Reprise)—Richard Pryor
10-6 Win, Lose or Draw (Capricorn)—Allman Brothers Band
10-8 Prisoner in Disguise (Asylum)—Linda Ronstadt
10-8 For Everyman (Asylum)—Jackson Browne
10-8 Blow by Blow (Epic)—Jeff Beck
10-8 Born to Run (Columbia)—Bruce Springsteen
10-15 Ain't No 'Bout-A-Doubt It (Warner Bros.)—Graham Central Station
10-17 Fame (S) (RCA)—David Bowie
10-20 Full Moon (A&M)—Kris Kristofferson and Rita Coolidge
10-20 The Six Wives of Henry VIII (A&M)—Rick Wakeman
10-21 Rock of the Westies (MCA)—Elton John
10-24 Rocky Mountain Christmas (RCA)—John Denver
11-6 Raunch 'n Roll (Atco)—Black Oak Arkansas
11-7 Where We All Belong (Capricorn)—Marshall Tucker Band
11-7 Wind on the Water (ABC Records/Atlantic Tape)—David Crosby and Graham Nash
11-11 Foghat (Bearsville)—Foghat
11-11 Extra Texture (Apple)—George Harrison
11-11 Sedaka's Back (Rocket)—Neil Sedaka
11-11 Diamonds and Rust (A&M)—Joan Baez
11-11 Piano Man (Columbia)—Billy Joel
11-13 Feelings (S) (RCA)—Morris Albert

11-13 Minstrel in the Gallery (Chrysalis)—Jethro Tull

11-14 They Just Can't Stop It (Games People Play) (S) (Atlantic)—Spinners

11-17 Still Crazy after All These Years (Columbia)—Paul Simon

11-17 Do It Anyway You Wanna (S) (Philadelphia International)—Peoples Choice

11-17 Blue Sky—Night Thunder (Epic)—Michael Murphey

11-18 Chicago IX—Chicago's Greatest Hits (Columbia)—Chicago

11-18 I'm Sorry (S) (RCA)—John Denver

11-18 Sheer Heart Attack (Elektra)—Queen

11-19 Judith (Elektra)—Judy Collins

11-24 Let's Do It Again (S) (Curtom)—Staple Singers

11-25 Bad Blood (S) (Rocket)—Neil Sedaka

12-1 History—America's Greatest Hits (Warner Bros.)—America

12-2 Fly, Robin Fly (S) (RCA/Midland International)—Silver Convention

12-3 Helen Reddy's Greatest Hits (Capitol)—Helen Reddy

12-4 Alive! (Casablanca)—Kiss

12-4 Island Girl (S) (MCA)—Elton John

12-4 The Hissing of Summer Lawns (Asylum)—Joni Mitchell

12-5 Seals & Crofts Greatest Hits (Warner Bros.)—Seals & Crofts

12-5 Fleetwood Mac (Warner/Reprise)—Fleetwood Mac

12-5 Breakaway (Columbia)—Art Garfunkel

12-5 Gratitude (Columbia)—Earth, Wind & Fire

12-5 Family Reunion (Epic)—O'Jays

12-10 Save Me (RCA/Midland International)—Silver Convention

12-10 The Who by Numbers (MCA)—Who

12-16 Saturday Night (S) (Arista)—Bay City Rollers

12-17 The Way I Want to Touch You (S) (A&M)—Captain & Tennille

12-18 The Best of Carly Simon (Elektra)—Carly Simon

12-18 The Hungry Years (Rocket)—Neil Sedaka

12-19 Atlantic Crossing (Warner Bros.)—Rod Stewart

12-19 Convoy (S) (MGM)—C.W. McCall

12-23 Head On (Mercury)—Bachman-Turner Overdrive

12-23 Main Course (RSO)—Bee Gees

12-30 Trying to Get the Feeling (Arista)—Barry Manilow

12-31 Rhinestone Cowboy (Capitol)—Glen Campbell

12-31 Bay City Rollers (Arista)—Bay City Rollers

1976

1-5 Love Rollercoaster (S) (Mercury)—Ohio Players

1-6 High on the Hog (Atco)—Black Oak Arkansas

1-6 I Write the Songs (S) (Arista)—Barry Manilow

1-12 I Love Music (S) (Philadelphia International)—O'Jays

1-12 Wake Up Everybody (Philadelphia International)—Harold Melvin and the Blue Notes

1-13 You Sexy Thing (S) (Big Tree)—Hot Chocolate

1-14 Rufus—Featuring Chaka Kahn (ABC)—Rufus Featuring Chaka Kahn

1-14 Desire (Columbia)—Bob Dylan

1-15 Numbers (A&M)—Cat Stevens

1-15 Mona Bone Jakon (A&M)—Cat Stevens

1-19 Love to Love You Baby (Oasis)—Donna Summer

1-19 No Way to Treat a Lady (Capitol)—Helen Reddy

1-21 A Christmas Album (Columbia)—Barbra Streisand

1-23 Face the Music (United Artists)—Electric Light Orchestra

1-28 Proud Mary (Fantasy)—Creedence Clearwater Revival

1-29 Black Bear Road (MGM)—C.W. McCall

2-4 Searchin' for a Rainbow (Capricorn)—Marshall Tucker Band

2-10 Base Trees (Warner/Reprise)—Fleetwood Mac

2-10 Run with the Pack (Swan Song)—Bad Company

2-11 Inseparable (Capitol)—Natalie Cole

2-11 Theme from S.W.A.T. (S) (ABC)—Rhythm Heritage

2-23 Fox on the Run (S) (Capitol)—Sweet

2-24 Their Greatest Hits 1971–1975 (Elektra)—Eagles

2-25 M.U.—The Best of Jethro Tull (Chrysalis)—Jethro Tull

2-26 Station to Station (RCA)—David Bowie

2-27 Sing a Song (S) (Columbia)—Earth, Wind & Fire

2-27 Frampton Comes Alive! (A&M)—Peter Frampton

3-2 Sweet Thing (S) (ABC)—Rufus Featuring Chaka Khan

8-13   Shop Around (S) (A&M)—Captain & Tennille
8-17   Spirit (RCA)—John Denver
8-17   Don't Go Breaking My Heart (S) (Rocket)—Elton John and Kiki Dee
8-17   This One's for You (Arista)—Barry Manilow
8-19   Native Sons (Columbia)—Loggins and Messina
8-19   You'll Never Find Another Love Like Mine (S) (Philadelphia International)—Lou Rawls
8-23   All Things in Time (Philadelphia International)—Lou Rawls
8-23   Play That Funky Music (S) (Epic)—Wild Cherry
8-24   War's Greatest Hits (United Artists)—War
8-25   Get Closer (Warner Bros.)—Seals & Crofts
8-30   Hasten Down the Wind (Asylum)—Linda Ronstadt
9-1   15 Big Ones (Reprise)—Beach Boys
9-8   Dreamboat Annie (Mushroom)—Heart
9-8   A Fifth of Beethoven (S) (Private Stock)—Walter Murphy and the Big Apple Band
9-8   Wild Cherry (Epic)—Wild Cherry
9-13   Frampton (A&M)—Peter Frampton
9-14   Wired (Epic)—Jeff Beck
9-14   Summer (S) (United Artists)—War
9-15   Royal Scam (ABC)—Steely Dan
9-15   You Should Be Dancing (S) (RSO)–Bee Gees
9-21   Best of BTO (So Far) (Mercury)—Bachman-Turner Overdrive
9-21   Children of the World (RSO)—Bee Gees
9-22   Hard Rain (Columbia)—Bob Dylan
9-22   Heaven Must Be Missing an Angel (S) (Capitol)—Tavares
9-28   More, More, More (S) (Buddah)—Andrea True Connection
10-5   Abandoned Luncheonette (Atlantic)—Hall & Oates
10-6   Disco Duck (S) (RSO)—Rick Dees & His Cast of Idiots
10-7   Spirit (Columbia)—Earth, Wind & Fire
10-7   The Manhattans (Columbia)—Manhattans
10-7   Dave Mason (Columbia)—Dave Mason
10-12 I'd Really Love to See You Tonight (S) (Big Tree)—England Dan and John Ford Coley
10-12 Happiness Is Being with the Spinners (Atlantic)—Spinners
10-19 Whistling Down the Wire (ABC)—David Crosby and Graham Nash
10-19 The Clones of Dr. Funkenstein (Casablanca)—Parliament

10-19 Tear the Roof off the Sucker (S) (Casablanca)—Parliament
10-19 In the Pocket (Warner Bros.)—James Taylor
10-20 Devil Woman (S) (Rocket)—Cliff Richard
10-20 A Night on the Town (Warner Bros.)—Rod Stewart
10-21 Message in the Music (Philadelphia International)—O'Jays
10-22 Barry Manilow I (Arista)—Barry Manilow
10-25 A New World Record (United Artists)—Electric Light Orchestra
10-25 Let 'Em In (S) (Capitol)—Paul McCartney & Wings
10-26 Agents of Fortune (Columbia)—Blue Oyster Cult
10-26 If You Leave Me Now (S) (Columbia)—Chicago
10-26 Boston (Epic)—Boston
10-26 Summertime Dream (Reprise)—Gordon Lightfoot
10-26 One More (for) from the Road (MCA)—Lynyrd Skynyrd
10-26 A Fifth of Beethoven (Private Stock)—Walter Murphy and the Big Apple Band
10-28 Free to Be . . . You and Me (Bell)—Marlo Thomas & Friends
10-29 Getaway (S) (Columbia)—Earth, Wind & Fire
10-29 Blue Moves (Rocket)—Elton John
10-29 Lowdown (S) (Columbia)—Boz Scaggs
10-29 For Earth Below (Chrysalis)—Robin Trower
11-3   Firefall (Atlantic)—Firefall
11-3   The Song Remains the Same (Swan Song)—Led Zeppelin
11-4   Bigger than Both of Us (RCA)—Hall & Oates
11-9   Mystery to Me (Reprise)—Fleetwood Mac
11-9   Rock and Roll Outlaws (Bearsville)—Foghat
11-9   Over-nite Sensation (Discreet)—Mothers of Invention
11-11 Rock and Roll Over (Casablanca)—Kiss
11-11 Free for All (Epic)—Ted Nugent
11-11 Four Seasons of Love (Oasis)—Donna Summer
11-12 Brass Construction II (United Artists)—Brass Construction
11-15 Times of Your Life (United Artists)—Paul Anka
11-15 The Pretender (Asylum)—Jackson Browne
11-16 Jackson Browne (Asylum)—Jackson Browne
11-16 Teddy Bear (S) (Gusto)—Red Sovine

11-17 Ol' Blue Eyes Is Back (Reprise)—Frank Sinatra

11-19 Moondance (Warner Bros.)—Van Morrison

11-23 Alice Cooper Goes to Hell (Warner Bros.)—Alice Cooper

11-23 Best of the Doobies (Warner Bros.)—Doobie Brothers

11-24 And I Love You So (RCA)—Perry Como

11-30 You Don't Have to Be a Star (S) (ABC)—Marilyn McCoo and Billy Davis, Jr.

11-30 Tonight's the Night (Gonna Be Alright (S) (Warner Bros.)—Rod Stewart

12-1 Nights Are Forever (Big Tree)—England Dan and John Ford Coley

12-7 Bicentennial Nigger (Warner Bros.)—Richard Pryor

12-8 Muskrat Love (S) (A&M)—The Captain & Tennille

12-8 Don't Stop Believin' (MCA)—Olivia Newton-John

12-8 Greatest Hits (Asylum)—Linda Ronstadt

12-8 The Rubberband Man (S) (Atlantic)—Spinners

12-10 Best of the Beach Boys, Volume 2 (Capitol)—Beach Boys

12-10 That Christmas Feeling (Capitol)—Glen Campbell

12-13 Hotel California (Asylum)—Eagles

12-13 Wings over America (Capitol)—Paul McCartney & Wings

12-13 Long Misty Days (Chrysalis)—Robin Trower

12-14 Dr. Buzzard's Original Savannah Band (RCA)—Dr. Buzzard's Savannah Band

12-14 Daryl Hall and John Oates (RCA)—Hall & Oates

12-21 Car Wash (MCA)—Rose Royce (soundtrack)

12-21 Car Wash (S) MCA—Rose Royce

12-22 Live Bullet (Capitol)—Bob Seger & the Silver Bullet Band

12-22 James Taylor's Greatest Hits (Warner Bros.)—James Taylor

12-23 Hejira (Asylum)—Joni Mitchell

12-23 Donny & Marie Featuring Songs from Their TV Show (Polydor)—Donny and Marie Osmond

12-23 A Star Is Born (Columbia)—Barbra Streisand and Kris Kristofferson

12-27 Occupation: Foole (Little David)—George Carlin

12-28 You Make Me Feel Like Dancing (S) (Warner Bros.)—Leo Sayer

12-29 Love So Right (S) (RSO)—Bee Gees

12-29 A Day at the Races (Elektra)—Queen

12-29 The Best of Leon Russell (Shelter)—Leon Russell

12-30 ABBA's Greatest Hits (Atlantic)—ABBA

1977

1-3 Hot Line (S) (Capitol)—Sylvers

1-4 After the Lovin' (Columbia)—Engelbert Humperdinck

1-5 Beth (Casablanca)—Kiss

1-12 Long May You Run (Warner/Reprise)—Stills & Young Band

1-14 Year of the Cat (Janus/GRT)—Al Stewart

1-18 I'll Be Good to You (S) (A&M)—Brothers Johnson

1-18 Nadia's Theme ("The Young & the Restless") (S) (A&M)—Barry DeVorzon and Perry Botkin, Jr.

1-18 Tejas (London)—ZZ Top

1-19 Thirty-Three & 1/3 (Dark Horse /Warner)—George Harrison

1-20 Ohio Players Gold (Mercury/Phonogram)—Ohio Players

1-21 Stand Tall (S) (Portrait/CBS)—Burton Cummings

1-25 Sorry Seems to Be the Hardest Word (S) (MCA)—Elton John

1-25 Leftoverture (Kirshner/Columbia)—Kansas

1-25 Night Moves (Capitol)—Bob Seger & the Silver Bullet Band

1-26 Flowers (Columbia)—Emotions

1-27 Ask Rufus (ABC)—Rufus featuring Chaka Khan

1-31 You Are My Starship (Buddah)—Norman Connors

2-8 Night Shift (Bearsville/Warner)—Foghat

2-10 Enjoy Yourself (S) (Epic/CBS)—Jacksons

2-10 Torn between Two Lovers (S) (Ariola America/Capitol)—Mary MacGregor

2-12 Animals (Columbia)—Pink Floyd

2-15 After the Lovin' (S) (Epic/CBS)—Engelbert Humperdinck

2-15 Rumours (Warner Bros.)—Fleetwood Mac

2-15 The Best of George Harrison (Capitol)—George Harrison

2-15 Songs from the Wood (Chrysalis)—Jethro Tull

2-17 Lost without Your Love (Elektra)—Bread

2-17 Southern Comfort (Blue Thumb/ABC)—Crusaders

2-17 I Hope We Get to Love in Time (A&M)—Marilyn McCoo & Billy Davis, Jr.

2-23 . . . Roots (A&M)—Quincy Jones

2-28 Dressed to Kill (Casablanca)—Kiss

799

6-28 Undercover Angel (S) (Atlantic)—Alan O'Day
6-28 CSN (Atlantic)—Crosby, Stills & Nash
6-30 Love Gun (Casablanca)—Kiss
7-5 J.T. (Columbia)—James Taylor
7-5 Unmistakably Lou (Philadelphia International)—Lou Rawls
7-7 Gonna Fly Now (Theme from *Rocky)* (S) (United Artists)—Bill Conti
7-8 Beethoven: The 9 Symphonies (Polydor/Deutsche Grammophon)—Berlin Philharmonic Orchestra/Karajan
7-11 Angel in Your Arms (S) (Big Tree/Atlantic)—Hot
7-11 Cat Scratch Fever (Epic/CBS)—Ted Nugent
7-12 Rejoice (Columbia)—Emotions
7-12 Travelin' at the Speed of Thought (Columbia)—O'Jays
7-13 Even in the Quietest Moments . . . (A&M)—Supertramp
7-13 I Remember Yesterday (Casablanca)—Donna Summer
7-15 On Your Feet or on Your Knees (Columbia)—Blue Oyster Cult
7-18 Star Wars (20th Century)—soundtrack
7-19 Da Doo Ron Ron (S) (Warner Bros.)—Shaun Cassidy
7-26 Alleluia—Praise Gathering for Believers (Benson/Impact)—various artists
7-28 The Floaters (ABC)—Floaters
8-1 Are You Ready for the Country (RCA)—Waylon Jennings
8-1 Maze Featuring Frankie Beverly (Capitol)—Maze
8-2 Best of My Love (S) (Columbia)—Emotions
8-2 Going for the One (Atlantic)—Yes
8-2 Crime of the Century (A&M)—Supertramp
8-9 I Just Want to Be Your Everything (S) (RSO/Polydor)—Andy Gibb
8-9 Nether Lands (Full Moon/Epic)—Dan Fogelberg
8-9 You Get What You Play For (Epic/CBS)—REO Speedwagon
8-9 Shaun Cassidy (Warner Bros.)—Shaun Cassidy
8-10 Travelin' Man (S) (Imperial/United Artists)—Ricky Nelson
8-10 Kenny Rogers (United Artists)—Kenny Rogers
8-10 Platinum Jazz (Blue Note/United Artists)—War
8-16 A New Life (Warner Bros.)—Marshall Tucker Band

8-17 Do You Wanna Make Love (S) (20th Century)—Peter McCann
8-17 It's a Game (Arista)—Bay City Rollers
8-18 Anytime . . . Anywhere (A&M)—Rita Coolidge
8-25 Float On (S) (ABC)—Floaters
8-25 A Place in the Sun (A&M)—Pablo Cruise
8-25 Equinox (A&M)—Styx
8-30 (Your Love Has Lifted Me) Higher and Higher (S) (A&M)—Rita Coolidge
9-6 Ozark Mountain Daredevils (A&M)—Ozark Mountain Daredevils
9-7 Looks Like We Made It (S) (Arista)—Barry Manilow
9-8 The King Is Gone (S) (GRT)—Ronnie McDowell
9-12 Way Down (S) (RCA)—Elvis Presley
9-12 Pure Gold (RCA)—Elvis Presley
9-14 Dreams (S) (Warner Bros.)—Fleetwood Mac
9-14 Livin' on the Fault Line (Warner Bros.)—Doobie Brothers
9-16 I Robot (Arista)—Alan Parsons Project
9-16 Chicago XI (Columbia)—Chicago
9-16 Beauty on a Back Street (RCA)—Hall & Oates
9-19 Simple Dreams (Elektra/Asylum)—Linda Ronstadt
9-20 Celebrate Me Home (Columbia)—Kenny Loggins
9-20 The Outlaws (Arista)—Outlaws
9-20 Barry White Sings for Someone You Love (20th Century)—Barry White
9-23 Telephone Line (S) (Jet/United Artists)—Electric Light Orchestra
9-23 Simple Things (Capitol)—Carole King
9-28 *Star Wars* Theme/Cantina Band (Millenium)—Meco
9-28 Star Wars and Other Galactic Funk (Millenium)—Meco
9-30 Elton John's Greatest Hits, Volume II (MCA)—Elton John
9-30 Welcome to My World (RCA)—Elvis Presley
10-3 Luna Sea (Atlantic)—Firefall
10-4 That's Rock'n'Roll (Warner Bros.)—Shaun Cassidy
10-4 Love You Live (Rolling Stones/Atlantic)—Rolling Stones
10-4 Aja (ABC)—Steely Dan
10-4 In Full Bloom (Whitfield/Warner)—Rose Royce
10-5 Southern Nights (Capitol)—Glen Campbell
10-7 From Elvis Presley Boulevard, Memphis, Tennessee (RCA)—Elvis Presley

800

10-10   Too Hot to Handle (Epic/CBS)—Heat-wave

10-11   Point of Know Return (Kirshner/CBS)—Kansas

10-11   Foghat Live (Bearsville/Warner)—Foghat

10-11   American Stars 'n' Bars (Warner Bros.)—Neil Young

10-17   Boogie Nights (S) (Epic/CBS)—Heat-wave

10-18   It's Ecstasy When You Lay Down Next to Me (S) (20th Century)—Barry White

10-19   Strawberry Letter 23 (S) (A&M)—Brothers Johnson

10-19   You Light Up My Life (S) (Warner Bros.)—Debby Boone

10-19   The Grand Illusion (A&M)—Styx

10-20   Jailbreak (Mercury/Phonogram)—Thin Lizzy

10-21   Greatest Hits (MCA)—Olivia Newton-John

10-24   Love Songs (Capitol)—Beatles

10-25   Elvis—A Legendary Performer, Volume II (RCA)—Elvis Presley

10-25   The Johnny Cash Portrait/His Greatest Hits, Volume II (Columbia)—Johnny Cash

10-25   You Light Up My Life (Warner Bros.)—Debby Boone

10-26   Telephone Man (S) (GRT)—Meri Wilson

10-26   Rock & Roll Love Letter (Arista)—Bay City Rollers

10-27   Eric Carmen (Arista)—Eric Carmen

10-27   Street Survivors (MCA)—Lynyrd Skynyrd

11-1   You Light Up My Life (Arista)—soundtrack

11-1   Captured Angel (Full Moon/Epic)—Dan Fogelberg

11-4   Let It Flow (Columbia)—Dave Mason

11-4   Elvis Sings the Wonderful World of Christmas (RCA)—Elvis Presley

11-4   Anthology (Capitol)—Steve Miller Band

11-9   Nobody Does It Better (S) (Elektra)—Carly Simon

11-9   I Feel Love (S) (Casablanca)—Donna Summer

11-9   Something to Love (A&M)—L.T.D.

11-14   Don't It Make My Brown Eyes Blue (S) (United Artists)—Crystal Gayle

11-22   Foot Loose & Fancy Free (Warner Bros.)—Rod Stewart

11-29   Swayin' to the Music (S) (Big Tree/Atlantic)—Johnny Rivers

12-5   The Story of *Star Wars* (20th Century)—original cast with narration by Roscoe Lee Browne

12-7   Bay City Rollers/Greatest Hits (Arista)—Bay City Rollers

12-9   Draw the Line (Columbia)—Aerosmith

12-9   French Kiss (Capitol)—Bob Welch

12-9   Once upon a Time (Casablanca)—Donna Summer

12-9   Friends & Strangers (Blue Note/United Artists)—Ronnie Laws

12-12   Heaven on the 7th Floor (S) (RSO/Polydor)—Paul Nicholas

12-13   Greatest Hits (A&M)—Captain & Tennille

12-13   Tupelo Honey (Warner Bros.)—Van Morrison

12-15   Daytime Friends (United Artists)—Kenny Rogers

12-16   How Deep Is Your Love (S) (RSO/Polydor)—Bee Gees

12-16   Viva Terlingua (MCA)—Jerry Jeff Walker

12-16   Masque (Kirshner/Columbia)—Kansas

12-16   A Chorus Line (Columbia)—original cast

12-19   Feelin' Bitchy (Spring/Polydor)—Millie Jackson

12-20   Thankful (Capitol)—Natalie Cole

12-22   (Everytime I Turn Around) Back in Love Again (S) (A&M)—L.T.D.

12-27   Here You Come Again (RCA)—Dolly Parton

12-28   Action (Fantasy)—Blackbyrds

12-28   Running on Empty (Elektra/Asylum)—Jackson Browne

12-30   Works, Volume II (Atlantic)—Emerson, Lake and Palmer

12-30   Best of ZZ Top (London)—ZZ Top

1978

1-1   Bee Gees Gold, Volume 1 (RSO/Polydor)—Bee Gees

1-5   Brass Construction III (United Artists)—Brass Construction

1-9   Close Encounters of the Third Kind (Arista)—soundtrack

1-9   Diamantina Cocktail (Harvest/Capitol)—Little River Band

1-10   Funkentelechy vs. the Placebo Syndrome (Casablanca)—Parliament

1-12   New Season (Polydor)—Donny and Marie Osmond

1-12   Baby Come Back (S) (RSO/Polydor)—Player

1-13   My Way (S) (RCA)—Elvis Presley

1-13   Waylon Live (RCA)—Waylon Jennings

1-17   Hey Deanie (S) (Warner Bros.)—Shaun Cassidy

1-18   Reach for It (Epic/Columbia)—George Duke

1-19   Spectres (Columbia)—Blue Oyster Cult

1-23 Blue Bayou (S) (Asylum)—Linda Ronstadt

1-24 Short People (S) (Warner Bros.)—Randy Newman

1-24 Little Criminals (Warner Bros.)—Randy Newman

1-25 We Are the Champions (S) (Elektra)—Queen

1-26 Slowhand (RSO/Polydor)—Eric Clapton

1-26 Stayin' Alive (S) (RSO/Polydor)—Bee Gees

1-31 Leif Garrett (Atlantic)—Leif Garrett

2-1 Here You Come Again (S) (RCA)—Dolly Parton

2-2 We're All Alone (S) (A&M)—Rita Coolidge

2-3 Waylon & Willie (RCA)—Waylon Jennings and Willie Nelson

2-8 You're in My Heart (S) (Warner Bros.)—Rod Stewart

2-9 Emotion (S) (Private Stock)—Samantha Sang

2-10 It Was Almost Like a Song (RCA)—Ronnie Milsap

2-13 Don Juan's Reckless Daughter (Asylum)—Joni Mitchell

2-14 Double Live Gonzo (Epic/CBS)—Ted Nugent

2-14 When You Hear Lou, You've Heard It All (Philadelphia International/CBS)—Lou Rawls

2-15 Even Now (Arista)—Barry Manilow

2-15 Ten Years of Gold (United Artists)—Kenny Rogers

2-16 Love Is Thicker than Water (S) (RSO/Polydor)—Andy Gibb

2-16 Dance, Dance, Dance (S) (Atlantic)—Chic

2-24 Street Player (ABC)—Rufus

2-27 Blue Lights in the Basement (Atlantic)—Roberta Flack

2-27 Night Fever (S) (RSO/Polydor)—Bee Gees

2-28 Sometimes When We Touch (S) (20th Century)—Dan Hill

2-28 A Weekend in L.A. (Warner Bros.)—George Benson

2-28 Earth (Grunt/RCA)—Jefferson Starship

3-2 Watermark (Columbia)—Art Garfunkel

3-2 Countdown to Ecstasy (ABC)—Steely Dan

3-6 Just the Way You Are (S) (Columbia)—Billy Joel

3-8 Bootsy? Player of the Year (Warner Bros.)—Bootsy's Rubber Band

3-10 The Album (Atlantic)—ABBA

3-10 It Feels So Good (Columbia)—Manhattans

3-10 Golden Time of Day (Capitol)—Maze

3-17 Always and Forever (S) (Epic/CBS)—Heatwave

3-17 Longer Fuse (20th Century)—Dan Hill

3-20 London Town (Capitol)—Paul McCartney & Wings

3-27 Feels So Good (A&M)—Chuck Mangione

3-28 Emotion (Private Stock)—Samantha Sang

3-29 Chic (Atlantic)—Chic

4-4 Carole King . . . Her Greatest Hits (Ode/CBS)—Carole King

4-5 Son of a Son of a Sailor (ABC)—Jimmy Buffett

4-6 Our Love (S) (Capitol)—Natalie Cole

4-6 Can't Smile without You (S) (Arista)—Barry Manilow

4-10 Central Heating (Epic/Columbia)—Heatwave

4-10 Showdown (T-Neck/Columbia)—Isley Brothers

4-11 Champagne Jam (Polydor)—Atlanta Rhythm Section

4-12 You're the One That I Want (S) (RSO/Polydor)—John Travolta and Olivia Newton-John

4-17 Lay Down Sally (S) (RSO/Polydor)—Eric Clapton

4-17 Excitable Boy (Asylum)—Warren Zevon

4-18 Heavy Horses (Chrysalis)—Jethro Tull

4-20 Flash Light (S) (Casablanca)—Parliament

4-24 Player (RSO/Polydor)—Player

4-24 FM (MCA)—soundtrack

4-25 Endless Wire (Warner Bros.)—Gordon Lightfoot

4-26 Jack and Jill (S) (Arista)—Raydio

5-1 Rock'n'Roll Animal (RCA)—Lou Reed

5-1 The Closer I Get to You (S) (Atlantic)—Roberta Flack and Donny Hathaway

5-2 If I Can't Have You (S) (RSO/Polydor)—Yvonne Elliman

5-2 Too Much, Too Little, Too Late (S) (Columbia)—Johnny Mathis and Deniece Williams

5-2 Together Forever (Capricorn)—Marshall Tucker Band

5-2 Grease (RSO/Polydor)—soundtrack

5-2 You Light up My Life (Columbia)—Johnny Mathis

5-2 So Full of Love (Philadelphia International/CBS)—O'Jays

5-3 Infinity (Columbia)—Journey

5-5 The Sound in Your Mind (Columbia)—Willie Nelson

5-7 Flying High on Your Love (Mercury/Polydor)—Bar-Kays

5-10 Secrets (Mercury/Polydor)—Con Funk Shun

5-15 Boys in the Trees (Elektra)—Carly Simon

5-16 Thank God It's Friday (Casablanca)—soundtrack

5-16 Warmer Communications (Atlantic)—Average White Band

5-16 Double Platinum (Casablanca)—Kiss

5-18 Menagerie (Columbia)—Bill Withers

5-19 Shadow Dancing (S) (RSO/Polydor)—Andy Gibb

5-22 Bat out of Hell (Epic/Cleveland International)—Meat Loaf

5-24 Van Halen (Warner Bros.)—Van Halen

5-25 The Best of Rod Stewart (Mercury/Polydor)—Rod Stewart

5-26 City to City (United Artists)—Gerry Rafferty

5-30 Shadow Dancing (RSO/Polydor)—Andy Gibb

5-30 Stranger in Town (Capitol)—Bob Seger & the Silver Bullet Band

5-31 And Then There Were Three (Atlantic)—Genesis

5-31 Songbird (Columbia)—Barbra Streisand

5-31 Disco Inferno (Atlantic)—Trammps

5-31 But Seriously, Folks (Asylum)—Joe Walsh

6-2 Magazine (Mushroom)—Heart

6-7 Greatest Stories—Live (Elektra)—Harry Chapin

6-8 Don't Let Me Be Misunderstood (Casablanca)—Santa Esmeralda starring Leroy Gomez

6-12 The Best of Dolly Parton (RCA)—Dolly Parton

6-12 Some Girls (Rolling Stones/Atlantic)—Rolling Stones

6-16 Life Is a Song Worth Singing (Philadelphia International/CBS)—Teddy Pendergrass

6-16 Use ta Be My Girl (S) (Philadelphia International/CBS)—O'Jays

6-16 It's a Heartache (S) (RCA)—Bonnie Tyler

6-16 Darkness on the Edge of Town (Columbia)—Bruce Springsteen

6-19 Octave (London)—Moody Blues

6-20 Double Vision (Atlantic)—Foreigner

6-21 Send It (Warner Bros.)—Ashford & Simpson

6-21 Love Me Again (A&M)—Rita Coolidge

6-21 Worlds Away (A&M)—Pablo Cruise

6-21 Stone Blue (Bearsville/Warner Bros.)—Foghat

6-21 Sounds . . . and Stuff Like That (A&M)—Quincy Jones

6-21 Togetherness (A&M)—L.T.D.

6-26 You Can Tune a Piano, But You Can't Tuna Fish (Epic/CBS)—REO Speedwagon

6-27 Street Legal (Columbia)—Bob Dylan

6-27 It's a Heartache (RCA)—Bonnie Tyler

7-6 Eddie Money (Columbia)—Eddie Money

7-7 You're Gonna Get It (Shelter/ABC)—Tom Petty & the Heartbreakers

7-14 Dust in the Wind (S) (Kirshner/CBS)—Kansas

7-17 The Groove Line (S) (Epic/CBS)—Heatwave

7-18 Baker Street (S) (United Artists)—Gerry Rafferty

7-19 Last Dance (S) (Casablanca)—Donna Summer

7-19 Natalie Live (Capitol)—Natalie Cole

7-19 Sgt. Pepper's Lonely Hearts Club Band (RSO/Polydor)—soundtrack

7-20 Two out of Three Ain't Bad (S) (Epic/Cleveland International)—Meat Loaf

7-20 Stardust (Columbia)—Willie Nelson

7-20 That's What Friends Are For (Columbia)—Johnny Mathis and Deniece Williams

7-24 Pyramid (Arista)—Alan Parsons Project

7-26 Miss You (S) (Rolling Stones/Atlantic)—Rolling Stones

7-27 Elite Hotel (Warner/Reprise)—Emmylou Harris

7-27 Grease (S) (RSO/Polydor)—Frankie Valli

8-1 Blam (A&M)—Brothers Johnson

8-2 Under Wraps (Warner Bros.)—Shaun Cassidy

8-2 A Taste of Honey (Capitol)—A Taste of Honey

8-4 Macho Man (Casablanca)—Village People

8-8 Take a Chance on Me (S) (Atlantic)—ABBA

8-8 Boogie Oogie Oogie (S) (Capitol)—A Taste of Honey

8-11 Shame (S) (RCA)—Evelyn "Champagne" King

8-15 An Everlasting Love (S) (RSO/Polydor)—Andy Gibb

8-16 Heartbreaker (RCA)—Dolly Parton

8-17 Reaching for the Sky (Capitol)—Peabo Bryson

8-22 Natural High (Motown)—Commodores

8-22 Come Get It (Motown)—Rick James

8-23 King Tut (S) (Warner Bros.)—Steve Martin

8-24 Who Are You (MCA)—Who

8-25 Don't Look Back (Epic/CBS)—Boston

8-25 Loveshine (Mercury/Polydor)—Con Funk Shun

8-28 Get It Out 'Cha System (Spring /Polydor)—Millie Jackson

8-29 Sleeper Catcher (Harvest/Capitol)—Little River Band

8-31 Hopelessly Devoted to You (S) (RSO/Polydor)—Olivia Newton-John

8-31 Summer Night (S) (RSO/Polydor)—John Travolta, Olivia Newton-John and cast of *Grease*

9-6 Smooth Talk (RCA)—Evelyn "Champagne" King

9-7 Copacabana (S) (Arista)—Barry Manilow

9-8 Skynyrd's First and . . . Last (MCA)—Lynyrd Skynyrd

9-10 Emotional Rescue (Rolling Stones)—Rolling Stones

9-11 Do What You Wanna Do (ABC)—Dramatics

9-12 Hot Blooded (S) (Atlantic)—Foreigner

9-14 Got to Get You into My Life (S) (ARC/Columbia)—Earth, Wind & Fire

9-14 Sunbeam (Columbia/ARC)—Emotions

9-14 Nightwatch (Columbia)—Kenny Loggins

9-14 Mariposa de Oro (Columbia)—Dave Mason

9-14 Live and More (Casablanca)—Donna Summer

9-15 When I Dream (United Artists)—Crystal Gayle

9-15 Love or Something Like It (United Artists)—Kenny Rogers

9-18 Village People (Casablanca)—Village People

9-19 Flat as a Pancake (A&M)—Head East

9-20 Rose Royce Strikes Again (Whitfield/Warner Bros.)—Rose Royce

9-22 Raydio (Arista)—Raydio

9-22 Living in the USA (Asylum)—Linda Ronstadt

9-26 I've Always Been Crazy (RCA)—Waylon Jennings

9-27 Dog and Butterfly (Portrait/CBS)—Heart

9-29 Hot Child in the City (S) (Chrysalis)—Nick Gilder

9-29 Twin Sons of Different Mothers (Full Moon/Epic/CBS)—Dan Fogelberg and Tim Weisberg

9-29 Bursting Out (Chrysalis)—Jethro Tull

9-29 The Wiz (MCA)—soundtrack

10-2 Kiss—Peter Criss (Casablanca)—Peter Criss

10-2 Kiss—Ace Frehley (Casablanca)—Ace Frehley

10-2 Kiss—Gene Simmons (Casablanca)—Gene Simmons

10-2 Kiss—Paul Stanley (Casablanca)—Paul Stanley

10-4 Kiss You All Over (S) (Warner/Curb)—Exile

10-4 One Nation under a Groove (Warner Bros.)—Funkadelic

10-5 Sunburn (Capitol)—Sun

10-10 Is It Still Good to Ya (Warner Bros.)—Ashford & Simpson

10-10 Hot Streets (Columbia)—Chicago

10-10 Images (ABC/Blue Thumb)—Crusaders

10-10 Mixed Emotions (Warner/Curb)—Exile

10-10 Children of Sanchez (A&M)—Chuck Mangione

10-10 Pieces of Eight (A&M)—Styx

10-10 Tormato (Atlantic)—Yes

10-12 Let's Keep It That Way (Capitol)—Anne Murray

10-13 Only One Love in My Life (RCA)—Ronnie Milsap

10-13 Cruisin' (Casablanca)—Village People

10-16 The Cars (Elektra)—Cars

10-17 Elan (Atlantic)—Firefall

10-17 Danger Zone (RSO/Polydor)—Player

10-23 52nd Street (Columbia)—Billy Joel

10-24 A Single Man (MCA)—Elton John

10-25 Close the Door (S) (Philadelphia International/CBS)—Teddy Pendergrass

10-25 Along the Red Ledge (RCA)—Hall & Oates

10-25 Time Passages (Arista)—Al Stewart

10-26 You Needed Me (S) (Capitol)—Anne Murray

10-26 MacArthur Park (S) (Casablanca)—Donna Summer

10-26 What Ever Happened to Benny Santini (United Artists)—Chris Rea

10-27 Inner Secrets (Columbia)—Santana

10-30 Macho Man (S) (Casablanca)—Village People

10-30 Weekend Warriors (Epic/CBS)—Ted Nugent

10-30 Marshall Tucker Band's Greatest Hits (Capricorn)—Marshall Tucker Band

10-31 Live Bootleg (Columbia)—Aerosmith

11-1 A Wild and Crazy Guy (Warner Bros.)—Steve Martin

11-6 Goin' Coconuts (Polydor)—Donny and Marie Osmond

11-7 Brother to Brother (A&M)—Gino Vanelli

11-8 Feel the Need (Scotti Bros./Atlantic)—Leif Garrett

11-9 Magnet and Steel (S) (Columbia)—Walter Egan

804

11-9 Songs of Kristofferson (Columbia)—Kris Kristofferson

11-10 You Had to Be There (ABC)—Jimmy Buffett

11-10 Crystal Ball (A&M)—Styx

11-13 Double Vision (S) (Atlantic)—Foreigner

11-13 A Retrospective (Capitol)—Linda Ronstadt

11-14 Backless (RSO/Polydor)—Eric Clapton

11-14 Chaka (Warner Bros./Tattoo)—Chaka Khan

11-15 Le Freak (S) (Atlantic)—Chic

11-15 Totally Hot (MCA)—Olivia Newton-John

11-16 Two for the Show (Kirshner/CBS)—Kansas

11-16 Barbra Streisand's Greatest Hits, Volume II (Columbia)—Barbra Streisand

11-16 You Don't Bring Me Flowers (S) (Columbia)—Barbra Streisand and Neil Diamond

11-20 In the Night-Time (Arista/Buddah)—Michael Henderson

11-21 One Nation under a Groove (S) (Warner Bros.)—Funkadelic

11-21 Sesame Street Fever (Sesame Street)—The Muppets and Robin Gibb

11-21 Greetings from Asbury Park, New Jersey (Columbia)—Bruce Springsteen

11-21 Comes a Time (Warner/Reprise)—Neil Young

11-22 Too Much Heaven (S) (RSO/Polydor)—Bee Gees

11-27 Greatest Hits (Arista)—Barry Manilow

11-27 The Steve Miller Band's Greatest Hits 1974–78 (Capitol)—Steve Miller Band

11-28 C'Est Chic (Atlantic)—Chic

11-28 Jazz (Elektra)—Queen

11-30 The Gambler (United Artists)—Kenny Rogers

12-6 Wings Greatest (Capitol)—Wings

12-7 Bish (ABC)—Stephen Bishop

12-7 You Don't Bring Me Flowers (Columbia)—Neil Diamond

12-7 The Best of Earth, Wind & Fire, Volume I (ARC/Columbia)—Earth, Wind & Fire

12-7 Steely Dan's Greatest Hits (ABC)—Steely Dan

12-12 Toto (Columbia)—Toto

12-13 Motor-Booty Affair (Casablanca)—Parliament

12-13 Blondes Have More Fun (Warner Bros.)—Rod Stewart

12-14 Hemispheres (Mercury)—Rush

12-14 Tanya Tucker's Greatest Hits (Columbia)—Tanya Tucker

12-18 I Love the Night Life (S) (Polydor)—Alicia Bridges

12-18 Y.M.C.A. (S) (Casablanca)—Village People

12-18 Take This Job and Shove It (Epic/CBS)—Johnny Paycheck

12-18 A Legendary Performer—Elvis, Volume 3 (RCA)—Elvis Presley

12-19 Entertainers . . . on and off the Record (Mercury)—Statler Brothers

12-22 Briefcase Full of Blues (Atlantic)—Blues Brothers

12-22 Barry White, the Man (20th Century)—Barry White

12-26 Sharing the Night Together (S) (Capitol)—Dr. Hook

12-27 Minute by Minute (Warner Bros.)—Doobie Brothers

12-29 The Last Farewell and Other Hits (RCA)—Roger Whittaker

1979

1-3 (Our Love) Don't Throw It All Away (S) (RSO/Polydor)—Andy Gibb

1-16 Heaven Tonight (CBS)—Cheap Trick

1-16 My Life (S) (Columbia)—Billy Joel

1-16 Got to Be Real (S) (Columbia)—Cheryl Lynn

1-16 Spark of Love (ABC)—Lenny Williams

1-19 John Denver (RCA)—John Denver

1-19 10th Anniversary of Golden Piano Hits (United Artists/Liberty)—Ferrante & Teicher

1-23 Life for the Taking (Columbia)—Eddie Money

1-25 Love Beach (Atlantic)—Emerson, Lake and Palmer

1-23 September (S) (Columbia)—Earth, Wind & Fire

1-23 Instant Replay (S) (Blue Sky/CBS)—Dan Hartman

1-30 Do Ya Think I'm Sexy (S) (Warner Bros.)—Rod Stewart

1-30 Spirits Having Flown (RSO)—Bee Gees

2-2 Every 1's a Winner (S) (Infinity)—Hot Chocolate

2-5 Tragedy (S) (RSO)—Bee Gees

2-5 Fire (Elektra)—Pointer Sisters

2-5 Love Tracks (Polydor)—Gloria Gaynor

2-5 New Kind of Feeling (Capitol)—Anne Murray

2-6 Sanctuary (EMI/Capitol)—J. Geils Band

2-9 Gold (Grunt/RCA)—Jefferson Starship

2-12 I Will Survive (S) (Polydor)—Gloria Gaynor

2-12 A Little More Love (S) (MCA)—Olivia Newton-John

6-19 Bad Girls (S) (Casablanca)—Donna Summer

6-19 Annie (Columbia)—original cast

6-26 Good Times (S) (Atlantic)—Chic

6-26 Communique (Warner Bros.)—Dire Straits

6-26 The Kids Are Alright (MCA)—Who (soundtrack)

6-27 Best of Nat King Cole (Capitol)—Nat "King" Cole

6-28 Million Mile Reflections (Epic)—Charlie Daniels Band

6-28 Molly Hatchet (Epic)—Molly Hatchet

7-2 Classics (United Artists)—Kenny Rogers and Dotty West

7-3 Where I Should Be (A&M)—Peter Frampton

7-11 Get the Knack (Capitol)—Knack

7-12 Music Band (MCA)—War

7-13 Waiting for Columbus (Warner Bros.)—Little Feat

7-20 You Take My Breath Away (S) (Columbia)—Rex Smith

7-20 Hot Property (Epic)—Heatwave

7-24 Candy-O (Elektra)—Cars

7-24 Queen Live Killers (Elektra)—Queen

7-31 Makin' It (S) (RSO)—David Naughton

7-31 Just When I Needed You Most (S) (Bearsville/Warner Bros.)—Randy Vanwarmer

8-1 Reality . . . What a Concept (Casablanca)—Robin Williams

8-2 One for the Road (Columbia)—Willie Nelson and Leon Russell

8-6 She Believes in Me (S) (United Artists)—Kenny Rogers

8-9 Decade (Reprise)—Neil Young

8-l0 Bustin' Loose (Source)—Chuck Brown & the Soul Searchers

8-13 I Want You to Want Me (S) (Epic)—Cheap Trick

8-13 In Color (Epic)—Cheap Trick

8-13 Rock-On (Arista)—Raydio

8-16 My Sharona (S) (Capitol)—Knack

8-16 I Was Made for Lovin' You (S) (Casablanca)—Kiss

8-16 Street Life (MCA)—Crusaders

8-16 McFadden & Whitehead (Philadelphia International)—McFadden & Whitehead

8-17 Mama Can't Buy You Love (S) (MCA)—Elton John

8-21 The Devil Went Down to Georgia (S) (Epic)—Charlie Daniels Band

8-21 What Cha Gonna Do with My Lovin'? (20th Century)—Stephanie Mills

8-21 A Night at Studio 54 (Casablanca)—various artists

8-22 When You're in Love with a Beautiful Woman (S) (Capitol)—Dr. Hook

8-23 Candy (Mercury)—Con Funk Shun

8-28 Rust Never Sleeps (Reprise)—Neil Young

8-30 You're Gonna Make Me Love Somebody Else (S) (Philadelphia International)—Jones Girls

8-30 Main Event (S) (Columbia)—Barbra Streisand

9-11 Sad Eyes (S) (Capitol)—Robert John

9-11 Pleasure & Pain (Capitol)—Dr. Hook

9-11 Look Sharp (A&M)—Joe Jackson

9-12 The Main Event (CBS)—soundtrack

9-14 Bring It Back Alive (Arista)—Outlaws

9-18 Lead Me On (S) (RCA)—Maxine Nightingale

9-19 Morning Dance (Infinity)—Spyro Gyra

9-23 Dionne (Arista)—Dionne Warwick

9-25 Rise (S) (A&M)—Herb Alpert

10-16 Ronnie Milsap Live (RCA)—Ronnie Milsap

10-19 I'll Never Love This Way Again (S) (Arista)—Dionne Warwick

10-23 Joy of Christmas (CBS)—Mormon Tabernacle Choir

10-30 Devotion (A&M)—L.T.D.

11-13 Born to Be Alive (S) (CBS)—Patrick Hernandez

11-13 Great Balls of Fire (RCA)—Dolly Parton

11-14 Voulez-Vous (Atlantic)—ABBA

11-19 After the Love Has Gone (S) (CBS)—Earth, Wind & Fire

11-19 Adventures of Panama Red (CBS)—New Riders of the Purple Sage

11-20 Don't Bring Me Down (S) (Jet/CBS)—Electric Light Orchestra

11-20 First under the Wire (Capitol)—Little River Band

11-29 Don't Stop Till You Get Enough (S) (CBS)—Michael Jackson

12-4 Secret Omen (Casablanca)—Cameo

12-5 Pop Muzik (S) (Sire/Warner Bros.)—M

12-5 Nine Lives (Epic)—REO Speedwagon

12-6 Highway to Hell (Atlantic)—AC/DC

12-6 The Muppet Movie (Atlantic)—soundtrack

12-10 Ladies Night (S) (Phonogram)—Kool & the Gang

12-10 Chicago XIII (CBS)—Chicago

12-10 Off the Wall (CBS)—Michael Jackson

12-11 Dim All the Lights (S) (Casablanca)—Donna Summer

12-11 Stay Free (Warner Bros.)—Ashford & Simpson

12-26 Slow Train Coming (CBS)—Bob Dylan
12-26 Home Free (CBS)—Dan Fogelberg
12-26 Give Me Your Love for Christmas (CBS)—Johnny Mathis
12-26 Identify Yourself (Philadelphia International)—O'Jays
12-27 Volcano (MCA)—Jimmy Buffett

1980

1-7 Escape (The Pina Colada Song) (S) (MCA)—Rupert Holmes
1-7 Head Games (Atlantic)—Foreigner
1-7 Low Budget (Arista)—Kinks
1-7 In Through the Out Door (Atlantic)—Led Zeppelin
1-10 Miss the Mississippi (Columbia)—Crystal Gayle
1-10 Flirtin' with Disaster (Epic)—Molly Hatchet
1-16 Kenny (United Artists)—Kenny Rogers
1-21 Don't Let Go (Polydor)—Isaac Hayes
1-21 Ladies Night (Phonogram)—Kool & the Gang
1-22 Comedy Is Not Pretty (Warner Bros.)—Steve Martin
1-22 Uncle Jam Wants You (Warner Bros.)—Funkadelic
1-23 Strikes (Atco)—Blackfoot
1-25 Live & Sleazy (Casablanca)—Village People
1-28 Babe (S) (A&M)—Styx
1-29 One Voice (Arista)—Barry Manilow
2-1 Heartache Tonight (S) (Asylum)—Eagles
2-1 Eat to the Beat (Chrysalis)—Blondie
2-1 A Christmas Together (RCA)—John Denver and the Muppets
2-1 The Long Run (Asylum)—Eagles
2-1 Stormwatch (Chrysalis)—Jethro Tull
2-5 Rise (A&M)—Herb Alpert
2-5 Cornerstone (A&M)—Styx
2-6 Dream Police (Epic)—Cheap Trick
2-6 Keep the Fire (Columbia)—Kenny Loggins
2-7 Second Time Around (S) (Solar)—Shalamar
2-7 We Sold Our Soul for Rock 'n' Roll (Warner Bros.)—Black Sabbath
2-7 I'll Always Love You (Capitol)—Anne Murray
2-7 Twice the Fire (Polydor)—Peaches and Herb
2-11 Do That to Me One More Time (S) (Casablanca)—Captain & Tennille

2-11 No More Tears (Enough Is Enough) (S) (Columbia)—Barbra Streisand
2-11 No More Tears (Enough Is Enough) (S, 12-inch) (Casablanca)—Donna Summer
2-11 Eve (Arista)—Alan Parsons Project
2-12 Tusk (Warner Bros.)—Fleetwood Mac
2-14 Rock with You (S) (Epic)—Michael Jackson
2-15 Injoy (Mercury)—Bar-Kays
2-21 Prince (Warner Bros.)—Prince
2-21 On the Radio, Volumes I & II (Casablanca)—Donna Summer
2-22 Wet (Columbia)—Barbra Streisand
2-25 Damn the Torpedoes (MCA)—Tom Petty & the Heartbreakers
2-26 Bee Gees' Greatest Hits (RSO)—Bee Gees
2-26 Rod Stewart's Greatest Hits, Volume I & II (Warner Bros.)—Rod Stewart
3-3 What Goes Around (RCA)—Waylon Jennings
3-5 Deguello (Warner Bros.)—ZZ Top
3-6 Willie Nelson Sings Kristofferson (Columbia)—Willie Nelson
3-6 Hydra (Columbia)—Toto
3-7 Coward of the Country (S) (United Artists)—Kenny Rogers
3-7 Classic Crystal (United Artists)—Crystal Gayle
3-10 Freedom at Point Zero (Grunt)—Jefferson Starship
3-11 On the Radio (S) (Casablanca)—Donna Summer
3-11 Gloryhallastoopid (Casablanca)—Parliament
3-11 Masterjam (MCA)—Rufus and Chaka
3-11 Live Rust (Warner Bros.)—Neil Young and Crazy Horse
3-13 Night in the Ruts (Columbia)—Aerosmith
3-13 September Morn (Columbia)—Neil Diamond
3-13 ELO's Greatest Hits (Jet)—Electric Light Orchestra
3-13 The Wall (Columbia)—Pink Floyd
3-13 Phoenix (Full Moon/Epic)—Dan Fogelberg
3-13 Teddy Live! Coast to Coast (Philadelphia International)—Teddy Pendergrass
3-14 Skeletons from the Closet (Warner Bros.)—Grateful Dead
3-14 Richard Pryor's Greatest Hits (Warner Bros.)—Richard Pryor
3-17 Permanent Wave (Mercury)—Rush
3-18 I Wanna Be Your Lover (S) (Warner Bros.)—Prince
3-18 And the Beat Goes On (S) (Solar)—Whispers

3-18 The Whispers (Solar)—Whispers

3-21 Yes, I'm Ready (S) (Casablanca)—Teri De Sario and KC

3-21 Y'All Come Back Saloon (MCA)—Oak Ridge Boys

3-24 Another Brick in the Wall (Part II) (S) (Columbia)—Pink Floyd

3-25 In the Heat of the Night (Chrysalis)—Pat Benatar

3-25 Gold and Platinum (MCA)—Lynyrd Skynyrd

4-2 Ray, Goodman & Brown (Polydor)—Ray, Goodman & Brown

4-7 Call Me (S) (Chrysalis)—Blondie

4-7 Big Fun (Solar)—Shalamar

4-8 American Gigolo (Polydor)—soundtrack

4-10 Workin' My Way Back to You (S) (Atlantic)—Spinners

4-10 The Rose (Atlantic)—Bette Midler (soundtrack)

4-11 Mickey Mouse Disco (Disneyland)—Mickey Mouse

4-14 . . . But the Little Girls Understand (Capitol)—Knack

4-21 Gap Band II (Mercury)—Gap Band

4-22 Love Stinks (EMI/America)—J. Geils Band

4-23 Greatest Hits, Volume 2 (Atlantic)—ABBA

4-29 Fun and Games (A&M)—Chuck Mangione

4-29 Light Up the Night (A&M)—Brothers Johnson

4-29 Against the Wind (Capitol)—Bob Seger & the Silver Bullet Band

5-5 Bebe Le Strange (Epic)—Heart

5-5 Glass Houses (Columbia)—Billy Joel

5-5 Departure (Columbia)—Journey

5-6 Christopher Cross (Warner Bros.)—Christopher Cross

5-7 Chapter Two (Atlantic)—Roberta Flack

5-7 After Dark (RSO)—Andy Gibb

5-12 Crazy Little Thing Called Love (S) (Elektra)—Queen

5-12 Mad Love (Asylum)—Linda Ronstadt

5-13 Special Lady (S) (Polydor)—Ray, Goodman & Brown

5-20 The Sinatra Christmas Album (Capitol)—Frank Sinatra

5-23 Funky Town (S) (Casablanca)—Lipps, Inc.

5-27 Partners in Crime (Infinity)—Rupert Holmes

5-27 Mouth to Mouth (Casablanca)—Lipps, Inc.

5-28 Turnstiles (Columbia)—Billy Joel

5-28 Ridin' the Storm Out (Epic)—REO Speedwagon

5-28 Gideon (United Artists)—Kenny Rogers

5-29 Women and Children First (Warner Bros.)—Van Halen

6-2 Pretenders (Warner Bros.)—Pretenders

6-4 Roberta Flack Featuring Donny Hathaway (Atlantic)—Roberta Flack and Donny Hathaway

6-4 Go All the Way (T-Neck)—Isley Brothers

6-4 Middle Man (Columbia)—Boz Scaggs

6-6 Straight Ahead (Columbia)—Larry Gatlin

6-20 Take Your Time (Do It Right) (S) (Tabu)—SOS Band

6-20 Song for America (Kirshner)—Kansas

6-20 Sweet Sensation (20th Century)—Stephanie Mills

6-23 Just One Night (RSO)—Eric Clapton

6-23 Star Wars—The Empire Strikes Back (RSO)—soundtrack

6-25 The Rose (S) (Atlantic)—Bette Midler

6-25 Spirit of Love (Mercury)—Con Funk Shun

7-2 Two Places at the Same Time (Arista)—Ray Parker, Jr. and Raydio

7-3 Some Enchanted Evening (Columbia)—Blue Oyster Cult

7-3 Electric Horseman (Columbia)—various artists (soundtrack)

7-10 Sexy Eyes (S) (Capitol)—Dr. Hook

7-10 After Midnight (CBS)—Manhattans

7-14 Urban Cowboy (Asylum)—various artists (soundtrack)

7-14 Best of Roger Whittaker (RCA)—Roger Whittaker

7-15 I'm Alive (S) (MCA)—Electric Light Orchestra

7-15 Magic (S) (MCA)—Olivia Newton-John

7-17 Cameosis (Chocolate City)—Cameo

7-17 The Boss (Motown)—Diana Ross

7-18 Shining Star (S) (Columbia)—Manhattans

7-18 Move It on Over (Rounder)—George Thorogood & the Destroyers

7-21 Coming Up (S) (Columbia)—Paul McCartney

7-21 Duke (Atlantic)—Genesis

7-23 It's Still Rock 'n' Roll to Me (S) (Columbia)—Billy Joel

7-23 Scream Dream (Epic)—Ted Nugent

7-25 McCartney II (Columbia)—Paul McCartney

7-30 Unmasked (Casablanca)—Kiss

8-5 Make Your Move (Casablanca)—Captain & Tennille

8-11 Hot Box (Spring)—Fatback Band

8-11 S.O.S. (Tabu)—S.O.S. Band

8-11 Empty Glass (Atco)—Pete Townshend

809

8-12 Little Jeannie (S) (MCA)—Elton John
8-19 The Breaks (S) (Phonogram)—Kurtis Blow
8-19 Fame (RSO)—various artists (soundtrack)
8-19 Anytime, Anyplace, Anywhere (MCA)—Rossington Collins Band
8-19 Xanadu (MCA)—Olivia Newton-John and Electric Light Orchestra (soundtrack)
8-22 Music Man (RCA)—Waylon Jennings
8-29 The Oak Ridge Boys Have Arrived (MCA)—Oak Ridge Boys
9-10 The Blues Brothers (Atlantic)—Blues Brothers (soundtrack)
9-15 Weird Scenes inside the Gold Mine (Elektra)—Doors
9-15 No Nukes (Asylum)—various artists
9-15 The Game (Elektra)—Queen
9-16 Give Me the Night (Warner Bros.)—George Benson
9-16 One in a Million You (Warner Bros.)—Larry Graham
9-22 21 at 33 (MCA)—Elton John
9-24 One in a Million You (S) (Warner Bros.)—Larry Graham
9-29 Full Moon (Epic)—Charlie Daniels Band
9-29 TP (Philadelphia International)—Teddy Pendergrass
10-1 Another One Bites the Dust (S) (Elektra)—Queen
10-7 Best of Don Williams Volume II (MCA)—Don Williams
10-10 All Out of Love (S) (Arista)—Air Supply
10-10 Together (MCA)—Oak Ridge Boys
10-13 Back in Black (Atlantic)—AC/DC
10-14 Let There Be Rock (Atco)—AC/DC
10-14 If You Want Blood You've Got It (Atlantic)—AC/DC
10-14 Chipmunk Punk (Pickwick International)—Chipmunks
10-14 One Trick Pony (Warner Bros.)—Paul Simon
10-15 Panorama (Elektra)—Cars
10-15 Honeysuckle Rose (Columbia)—Willie Nelson & Family (soundtrack)
10-21 Crimes of Passion (Chrysalis)—Pat Benatar
10-23 The Glow of Love (RFC/Warner Bros.)—Change
10-24 Horizon (Elektra)—Eddie Rabbitt
10-24 The Best of Eddie Rabbitt (Elektra)—Eddie Rabbitt
10-24 Sweet Forgiveness (Warner Bros.)—Bonnie Raitt
11-7 Woman in Love (S) (Columbia)—Barbra Streisand
11-7 Beatin' the Odds (Epic)—Molly Hatchet

11-10 Greatest Hits (Capitol)—Anne Murray
11-14 Alive (Columbia)—Kenny Loggins
11-18 Lookin' for Love (S) (Asylum)—Johnny Lee
11-18 The B-52's (Warner Bros.)—B-52's
11-18 One Step Closer (Warner Bros.)—Doobie Brothers
11-18 Zapp (Warner Bros.)—Zapp
11-19 Suite for Flute & Jazz Piano (CBS Masterworks)—Claude Bolling and Jean-Pierre Rampal
11-21 Freedom of Choice (Warner Bros.)—Devo
11-25 He's So Shy (S) (Elektra)—Pointer Sisters
11-25 Lady (S) (Liberty)—Kenny Rogers
12-2 Greatest Hits (Capitol)—Kenny Rogers
12-2 The Wanderer (S) (Warner Bros.)—Donna Summer
12-2 I Believe in You (MCA)—Don Williams
12-5 Jessie (S) (Warner Bros.)—Carly Simon
12-5 Linda Ronstadt's Greatest Hits, Volume II (Asylum)—Linda Ronstadt
12-8 One for the Road (Arista)—Kinks
12-9 Theme from "The Dukes of Hazzard" (S) (RCA)—Waylon Jennings
12-10 Triumph (Epic)—Jacksons
12-10 Paris (A&M)—Supertramp
12-12 Whip It (S) (Warner Bros.)—Devo
12-12 Audio Visions (Kirshner)—Kansas
12-12 Zenyatta Mondatta (A&M)—Police
12-12 The River (Columbia)—Bruce Springsteen
12-12 The Wanderer (Geffen)—Donna Summer
12-16 Celebrate (Phonogram)—Kool & the Gang
12-22 Conquistador (Columbia)—Maynard Ferguson
12-22 Touchdown (Columbia)—Bob James
12-22 Streetlife Serenade (Columbia)—Billy Joel
12-24 (Just Like) Starting Over (S) (Geffen/Warner Bros.)—John Lennon
12-24 More than I Can Say (S) (Warner Bros.)—Leo Sayer
12-30 All Shook Up (Epic)—Cheap Trick
12-30 Greatest Hits (Elektra)—Doors
12-30 Feelings (Columbia)—Johnny Mathis

1981

1-6 Heaven and Hell (Warner Bros.)—Black Sabbath
1-6 Joy and Pain (Capitol)—Maze Featuring Frankie Beverly
1-7 Live (Asylum)—Eagles
1-7 Faces (ARC/Columbia)—Earth, Wind & Fire
1-10 Double Fantasy (Geffen)—John Lennon and Yoko Ono

810

811

6-16 Bette Davis Eyes (S) (EMI/America)—Kim Carnes

6-16 Mistaken Identity (EMI/America)—Kim Carnes

6-16 Elvira (S) (MCA)—Oak Ridge Boys

6-16 The Dude (A&M)—Quincy Jones

6-19 Double Dutch Bus (S, 12-inch) (WMOT)—Frankie Smith

6-19 Heavy Weather (Columbia)—Weather Report

6-22 Zebop! (Columbia)—Santana

6-26 The Originals (Mercury)—Statler Brothers

6-29 Where Do You Go When You Dream (Capitol)—Anne Murray

7-1 What Cha' Gonna Do for Me (Warner Bros.)—Chaka Khan

7-2 Powerage (Atlantic)—AC/DC

7-2 Stars On 45 (S) (Radio)—Stars On

7-2 Stars On Long Play (Radio)—Stars On

7-7 Being with You (S) (Tamla)—Smokey Robinson

7-7 Street Songs (Gordy)—Rick James

7-7 Being with You (Tamla)—Smokey Robinson

7-7 Fair Warning (Warner Bros.)—Van Halen

7-14 My Home's in Alabama (RCA)—Alabama

7-14 Hard Promises (Backstreet)—Tom Petty & the Heartbreakers

7-16 Modern Times (Grunt)—Jefferson Starship

7-17 Sukiyaki (S) (Capitol)—A Taste of Honey

7-20 The One That You Love (Arista)—Air Supply

7-20 Ghost Riders (Arista)—Outlaws

7-21 Long Distance Voyager (Threshold)—Moody Blues

7-23 Fancy Free (MCA)—Oak Ridge Boys

7-23 Don't Say No (Capitol)—Billy Squier

7-31 Blizzard of Ozz (Jet)—Ozzy Osbourne

8-4 Working Class Dog (RCA)—Rick Springfield

8-4 Jessie's Girl (S) (RCA)—Rick Springfield

8-6 Knights of the Sound Table (Chocolate City)—Cameo

8-6 It Must Be Magic (Gordy)—Teena Marie

8-11 Theme from "Greatest American Hero" (S) (Elektra)—Joey Scarbury

8-12 The One That You Love (S) (Arista)—Air Supply

8-13 Juice (Capitol)—Juice Newton

8-13 R.E.O./T.W.O. (Epic)—REO Speedwagon

8-18 Blows against the Empire (Grunt)—Jefferson Starship

8-21 Endless Love (S) (Motown)—Diana Ross and Lionel Richie

8-21 In the Pocket (Motown)—Commodores

8-28 Urban Chipmunk (RCA)—Chipmunks

8-28 Share Your Love (Liberty)—Kenny Rogers

9-2 Queen of Hearts (S) (Capitol)—Juice Newton

9-2 Slowhand (S) (Planet)—Pointer Sisters

9-3 Let's Get Serious (Motown)—Jermaine Jackson

9-4 My Aim Is True (Columbia)—Elvis Costello

9-4 Saddle Tramp (Epic)—Charlie Daniels Band

9-8 Endless Love (Mercury)—soundtrack

9-9 Greatest Hits (Columbia)—Larry Gatlin

9-10 Precious Time (Chrysalis)—Pat Benatar

9-14 Evita—Premiere American Recording (MCA)—original cast

9-15 Leather & Lace (RCA)—Waylon Jennings and Jessi Colter

9-15 Stephanie (20th Century)—Stephanie Mills

9-16 Black & White (Planet)—Pointer Sisters

9-18 I Am What I Am (Epic)—George Jones

9-18 4 (Atlantic)—Foreigner

9-18 Escape (Columbia)—Journey

9-18 Heavy Metal (Full Moon)—soundtrack

9-22 Double Dutch Bus (S) (WMOT)—Frankie Smith

9-30 Pirates (Warner Bros.)—Rickie Lee Jones

10-5 Time (Jet)—Electric Light Orchestra

10-5 Step by Step (Elektra)—Eddie Rabbitt

10-6 She's a Bad Mama Jama (S) (20th Century)—Carl Carlton

10-7 Bella Donna (Modern)—Stevie Nicks

10-9 Evangeline (Warner Bros.)—Emmylou Harris

10-12 Sheena Easton (EMI/America)—Sheena Easton

10-15 Live in New Orleans (Capitol)—Maze Featuring Frankie Beverly

10-19 Koo Koo (Chrysalis)—Debbie Harry

10-21 Wild Planet (Warner Bros.)—B-52's

10-21 Trilogy (Reprise)—Frank Sinatra

10-22 Harder . . . Faster (Capitol)—April Wine

10-22 El Loco (Warner Bros.)—ZZ Top

10-28 Breakin' Away (Warner Bros.)—Al Jarreau

10-29 Rainbow (MCA)—Neil Diamond

10-29 Greatest Hits, Volume II (MCA)—Loretta Lynn

10-29 Greatest Hits, Volume I (Decca)—Conway Twitty

10-29 Lead Me On (Decca)—Conway Twitty and Loretta Lynn

10-30 Tattoo You (Rolling Stones)—Rolling Stones

11-2 Whiskey Bent & Hell Bound (Curb)—Hank Williams, Jr.

11-3 The Innocent Age (Full Moon)—Dan Fogelberg

11-3 Willie Nelson's Greatest Hits (& Some That Will Be) (Columbia)—Willie Nelson

11-4 Private Eyes (RCA)—Hall & Oates

11-4 Nine Tonight (Capitol)—Bob Seger & the Silver Bullet Band

11-18 Time Exposure (Capitol)—Little River Band

11-20 The Many Facets of Roger (Warner Bros.)—Roger

11-24 If I Should Love Again (Arista)—Barry Manilow

12-3 Physical (S) (MCA)—Olivia Newton-John

12-3 Something Special (De-Lite)—Kool & the Gang

12-8 Songs in the Attic (Columbia)—Billy Joel

12-8 There's No Gettin' Over Me (RCA)—Ronnie Milsap

12-8 Never Too Much (Epic)—Luther Vandross

12-11 Abacab (Atlantic)—Genesis

12-15 Private Eyes (S) (RCA)—Hall & Oates

12-15 Beauty and the Beat (I.R.S.)—Go-Gos

12-15 O Holy Night (London)—Luciano Pavarotti

12-15 Ghost in the Machine (A&M)—Police

12-16 Upside Down (S) (Motown)—Diana Ross

12-16 Physical (MCA)—Olivia Newton-John

12-23 Christmas Tyme (Epic)—Engelbert Humperdinck

12-23 It's Time for Love (Philadelphia International)—Teddy Pendergrass

12-30 Some Days Are Diamonds (RCA)—John Denver

12-30 Raise! (ARC/Columbia)—Earth, Wind & Fire

12-30 Freeze-Frame (EMI/America)—J. Geils Band

12-30 Get Lucky (Columbia)—Loverboy

12-30 Circle of Love (Capitol)—Steve Miller Band

12-30 Greatest Hits (Elektra)—Queen

1982

1-4 Diary of a Madman (Jet)—Ozzy Osbourne

1-5 Christmas (Liberty)—Kenny Rogers

1-5 Exit . . . Stage Left (Mercury)—Rush

1-7 Arthur's Theme (The Best You Can Do) (S) (Warner Bros.)—Christopher Cross

1-7 I Can't Go for That (No Can Do) (S) (RCA)—Hall & Oates

1-7 Hooked on Classics (RCA)—Royal Philharmonic Orchestra

1-7 Tonight I'm Yours (Warner Bros.)—Rod Stewart

1-11 Coal Miner's Daughter (MCA)—soundtrack

1-12 Let's Groove (S) (ARC/Columbia)—Earth, Wind & Fire

1-12 On the Way to the Sky (Columbia)—Neil Diamond

1-14 The George Benson Collection (Warner Bros.)—George Benson

1-14 Controversy (Warner Bros.)—Prince

1-17 The Best of the Doobies, Volume 2 (Warner Bros.)—Doobie Brothers

1-20 Waiting for a Girl Like You (S) (Atlantic)—Foreigner

1-20 For Those about to Rock, We Salute You (Atlantic)—AC/DC

1-20 Shake It Up (Elektra)—Cars

1-20 The Fox and the Hound (Disneyland)—soundtrack

1-22 Why Do Fools Fall in Love (RCA)—Diana Ross

1-25 Centerfold (S) (EMI/America)—J. Geils Band

1-27 Give the People What They Want (Arista)—Kinks

1-29 A Collection of Great Dance Songs (Columbia)—Pink Floyd

1-29 Memories (Columbia)—Barbra Streisand

2-5 Quarterflash (Geffen)—Quarterflash

2-9 Best of Blondie (Chrysalis)—Blondie

2-18 The Time (Warner Bros.)—Time

2-22 I Get Around (S) (Capitol)—Beach Boys

2-22 Live (MCA)—Barbara Mandrell

3-1 Chariots of Fire (Polydor/Polygram)—Vangelis (soundtrack)

3-2 Chronicle (Fantasy)—Creedence Clearwater Revival

3-3 Nightcruising (Mercury)—Bar-Kays

3-4 Skyy Line (Salsoul)—Skyy

3-8 Perhaps Love (Command)—Placido Domingo and John Denver

3-15 Great White North (Mercury)—Bob & Doug McKenzie

3-22 Pac-Man Fever (S) (Columbia)—Buckner & Garcia

4-6 The Beach Boys Christmas Album (Capitol)—Beach Boys

4-6 Bobbie Sue (MCA)—Oak Ridge Boys

4-12 I Love Rock 'n' Roll (S) (Boardwalk)—Joan Jett & the Blackhearts

4-12 I Love Rock 'n' Roll (Boardwalk)—Joan Jett & the Blackhearts

4-13 The Pressure Is On (Elektra)—Hank Williams, Jr.

4-26 Pac-Man Fever (Columbia)—Buckner & Garcia

4-29 Always on My Mind (Columbia)—Willie Nelson

4-29 Mountain Music (RCA)—Alabama

5-11 Star Wars (S) (Buena Vista)—various artists

5-11 Success Hasn't Spoiled Me Yet (RCA)—Rick Springfield

5-12 Lookin' for Love (Full Moon)—Johnny Lee

5-12 The Concert in Central Park (Warner Bros.)—Simon and Garfunkel

5-14 This Time (Warner Bros.)—Al Jarreau

5-14 Aldo Nova (Portrait)—Aldo Nova

5-24 One on One (Columbia)—Bob James and Earl Klugh

5-25 We Got the Beat (S) (I.R.S.)—Go Go's

5-26 The Empire Strikes Back (S) (Buena Vista)—various artists

5-26 Reel Music (Capitol)—Beatles

5-26 Tom Tom Club (Sire)—Tom Tom Club

6-2 Asia (Geffen)—Asia

6-7 Ebony and Ivory (S) (Columbia)—Paul McCartney and Stevie Wonder

6-9 Freeze-Frame (S) (EMI/America)—J. Geils Band

6-10 The Other Woman (Arista)—Ray Parker, Jr.

6-16 Friends (Solar)—Shalamar

6-22 Jazzercise (MCA)—Judi Sheppard Missett

6-24 Blackout (Mercury)—Scorpions

6-29 Tug of War (Columbia)—Paul McCartney

6-30 Toto IV (Columbia)—Toto

6-30 Allied Forces (RCA)—Triumph

6-30 Diver Down (Warner Bros.)—Van Halen

7-2 Special Forces (A&M)—.38 Special

7-6 American Fool (Riva)—John Cougar

7-9 Annie (Columbia)—soundtrack

7-9 Stevie Wonder's Original Musiquarium (Tamla)—Stevie Wonder

7-12 Hot Space (Elektra)—Queen

7-12 Reach (Elektra)—Richard Simmons

7-14 Dare (Virgin)—Human League

7-16 Alligator Woman (Chocolate City)—Cameo

7-16 Quiet Lies (Capitol)—Juice Newton

7-19 Keep It Live (Motown)—Dazz Band

7-19 Throwin' Down (Gordy)—Rick James

7-21 Gap Band IV (Polydor/Polygram)—Gap Band

7-23 British Steel (Columbia)—Judas Priest

7-26 Don't You Want Me (S) (Virgin)—Human League

7-26 Eye of the Tiger (S) (Scotti Bros.)—Survivor

7-27 Now and Forever (Arista)—Air Supply

7-27 Hooked on Swing (RCA)—Les Elgart and the Manhattan Swing Orchestra

8-9 Abracadabra (Capitol)—Steve Miller Band

8-9 Eye of the Tiger (Scotti Bros.)—Survivor

8-16 Rocky III (Liberty)—soundtrack

8-23 Abracadabra (S) (Capitol)—Steve Miller Band

8-25 Mirage (Warner Bros.)—Fleetwood Mac

8-27 Daylight Again (Atlantic)—Crosby, Stills & Nash

8-27 Pictures at Eleven (Swan Song)—Robert Plant

8-30 Love Will Turn You Around (Liberty)—Kenny Rogers

8-31 Chicago 16 (Full Moon)—Chicago

9-15 Hard to Say I'm Sorry (S) (Full Moon)—Chicago

9-16 Planet Rock (S) (Tommy Boy)—A. Bambatta & Soul Sonic Force

9-21 Jane Fonda's Workout Record (Columbia)—Jane Fonda

9-21 Eye in the Sky (Arista)—Alan Parsons Project

9-21 Good Trouble (Epic)—REO Speedwagon

9-21 Emotions in Motion (Capitol)—Billy Squier

9-21 Donna Summer (Geffen)—Donna Summer

9-21 Zapp II (Warner Bros.)—Zapp

9-29 Chase the Clouds Away (A&M)—Chuck Mangione

9-29 Hooked On Classics II (RCA)—Royal Philharmonic Orchestra

10-4 Three Sides Live (Atlantic)—Genesis

10-4 Vacation (I.R.S.)—Go-Go's

10-8 Hurts So Good (S) (Riva)—John Cougar

10-13 If That's What It Takes (Warner Bros.)—Michael McDonald

10-13 All Four One (Capitol)—Motels

10-19 Neil Diamond's Greatest Hits, Volume II (Columbia)—Neil Diamond

10-20 Christmas Card (Mercury)—Statler Brothers

10-22 Business as Usual (Columbia)—Men at Work

10-25 Christmas Wishes (Capitol)—Anne Murray

10-26 E.T.—The Extra-Terrestrial (MCA)—soundtrack

10-29 Jack and Diane (S) (Riva)—John Cougar

10-29 Screaming for Vengeance (Columbia)—Judas Priest

11-3 What Time Is It? (Warner Bros.)—Time
11-3 It's Hard (Warner Bros.)—Who
11-5 Built for Speed (EMI/America)—Stray Cats
11-8 Combat Rock (Epic)—Clash
11-9 Love Is Where You Find It (Solar)—Whispers
11-10 As One (De-Lite)—Kool & the Gang
11-10 Signals (Mercury)—Rush
11-15 Olivia's Greatest Hits, Volume II (MCA)—Olivia Newton-John
11-17 Night and Day (A&M)—Joe Jackson
11-19 Fire of Unknown Origin (Columbia)—Blue Oyster Cult
11-19 Perry Como Christmas Album (RCA)—Perry Como
11-19 Windows (Epic)—Charlie Daniels Band
11-19 No Control (Columbia)—Eddie Money
11-22 Jump Up (Geffen)—Elton John
11-22 High Adventure (Columbia)—Kenny Loggins
11-22 Pretty Paper (Columbia)—Willie Nelson
11-23 Get Closer (Asylum)—Linda Ronstadt
11-29 Heartlight (Columbia)—Neil Diamond
11-29 The Nylon Curtain (Columbia)—Billy Joel
11-29 Forever, for Always, for Love (Epic)—Luther Vandross
11-30 Heaven's Just a Sin Away (Churchill)—Kendalls
12-2 Astral Sounds/A Natural High (Dr. Mark Presents)—Dr. Mark Beshara
12-2 A Flock of Seagulls (Jive)—A Flock of Seagulls
12-8 No Fun Aloud (Asylum)—Glen Frey
12-8 I Can't Stand Still (Asylum)—Don Henley
12-9 Truly (S) (Motown)—Lionel Richie
12-9 Lionel Richie (Motown)—Lionel Richie
12-14 H2O (RCA)—Hall & Oates
12-14 The Nightfly (Warner Bros.)—Donald Fagan
12-14 Get Loose (RCA)—Evelyn "Champagne" King
12-14 A Very Mancini Christmas (RCA)—Henry Mancini
12-14 Silk Electric (RCA)—Diana Ross
12-16 Sexual Healing (S) (Columbia)—Marvin Gaye
12-17 High 'n' Dry (Mercury)—Def Leppard
12-19 Nebraska (Columbia)—Bruce Springsteen
12-21 Mickey (S) (Chrysalis)—Toni Basil
12-21 Nobody (S) (RCA)—Sylvia
12-27 Greatest Hits (Full Moon/Epic)—Dan Fogelberg
12-27 Christmas (MCA)—Oak Ridge Boys
12-28 All Time Greatest Hits (Columbia)—Ray Price

12-28 All Time Greatest Hits (Columbia)—Marty Robbins
12-30 Midnight Love (Columbia)—Marvin Gaye

1983

1-4 Long after Dark (Backstreet)—Tom Petty & the Heartbreakers
1-5 Famous Last Words (A&M)—Supertramp
1-6 Seven Year Ache (Columbia)—Rosanne Cash
1-7 Gloria (S) (Atlantic)—Laura Branigan
1-7 Eagles Greatest Hits Volume II (Asylum)—Eagles
1-11 Showtime (EMI/America)—J. Geils Band
1-11 1999 (Warner Bros.)—Prince
1-13 The Girl Is Mine (S) (Epic)—Michael Jackson and Paul McCartney
1-14 Maneater (S) (RCA)—Hall & Oates
1-17 Here Comes the Night (Arista)—Barry Manilow
1-18 Still Life (Rolling Stones)—Rolling Stones
1-20 Spring Session M (Capitol)—Missing Persons
1-24 Speak of the Devil (Jet)—Ozzy Osbourne
1-28 Standing Hampton (Geffen)—Sammy Hagar
1-31 Thriller (Epic)—Michael Jackson
2-1 Jump to It (Arista)—Aretha Franklin
2-7 Hello, I Must Be Going (Atlantic)—Phil Collins
2-7 Records (Atlantic)—Foreigner
2-7 Coda (Swan Song)—Led Zeppelin
2-11 The Distance (Capitol)—Bob Seger & the Silver Bullet Band
2-15 Just Sylvia (RCA)—Sylvia
2-23 The Fox and the Hound (S) (Disneyland)—various artists
2-23 Peter Pan (S) (Disneyland)—various artists
2-23 Bambi (S) (Disneyland)—various artists
2-23 Cinderella (S) (Disneyland)—various artists
2-25 Down Under (S) (Columbia)—Men at Work
3-1 Rio (Capitol)—Duran Duran
3-1 Baby Come to Me (S) (Qwest)—Patty Austin and James Ingram
3-7 Word of Mouth (Chrysalis)—Toni Basil
3-7 Get Nervous (Chrysalis)—Pat Benatar
3-7 Waitin' for the Sun to Shine (Epic)—Ricky Skaggs
3-14 Friend or Foe (Epic)—Adam Ant
3-15 All the Great Hits (Motown)—Diana Ross
3-21 Pyromania (Mercury)—Def Leppard

816

9-30 Flight Log 1966–1976 (Grunt)—Jefferson Airplane

9-30 Never Surrender (RCA)—Triumph

10-3 Total Eclipse of the Heart (S) (Columbia)—Bonnie Tyler

10-3 An Innocent Man (Columbia)—Billy Joel

10-3 San Antonio Rose (Columbia)—Willie Nelson and Ray Price

10-3 Highways & Heartaches (Epic)—Ricky Skaggs

10-3 Faster than the Speed of Night (Columbia)—Bonnie Tyer

10-4 Sweet Dreams (Are Made of This) (S) (RCA)—Eurythmics

10-4 The Number of the Beast (Capitol)—Iron Maiden

10-5 Children's Favorites II (Disneyland)—various artists

10-7 Rhythm of Youth (MCA)—Men without Hats

10-11 Alpha (Geffen)—Asia

10-11 Julio (Columbia)—Julio Iglesias

10-12 Air Supply Greatest Hits (Arista)—Air Supply

10-17 No Parking on the Dance Floor (Solar)—Midnight Star

10-17 The Principle of Moments (Atlantic)—Robert Plant

10-18 Islands in the Stream (S) (RCA)—Kenny Rogers with Dolly Parton

10-19 Little River Band Greatest Hits (Capitol)—Little River Band

10-19 Rant 'n' Rave with the Stray Cats (EMI/America)—Stray Cats

10-31 Dolly Parton's Greatest Hits (RCA)—Dolly Parton

10-31 Eyes That See in the Dark (RCA)—Kenny Rogers

11-7 Greatest Hits (Columbia)—David Allan Coe

11-8 Puttin' on the Ritz (S) (RCA)—Taco

11-8 Lawyers in Love (Asylum)—Jackson Browne

11-8 Sweet Dreams (Are Made of This) (RCA)—Eurythmics

11-8 Crash Landing (Reprise)—Jimi Hendrix

11-14 20 Golden Greats (MCA)—Buddy Holly & the Crickets

11-16 More Songs about Buildings and Food (Sire)—Talking Heads

11-17 What's New (Asylum)—Linda Ronstadt

11-18 On Through the Night (Mercury)—Def Leppard

11-21 Age to Age (Myrrh)—Amy Grant

11-22 Live from Earth (Chrysalis)—Pat Benatar

12-7 Seasons of the Heart (RCA)—John Denver

12-8 The Very Best of Conway Twitty (MCA)—Conway Twitty

12-9 Gap Band V—Jammin' (Mercury)—Gap Band

12-12 Say Say Say (S) (Columbia)—Paul McCartney and Michael Jackson

12-12 Cum on Feel the Noise (S) (Pasha)—Quiet Riot

12-12 All Night Long (S) (Motown)—Lionel Richie

12-12 Cold Blooded (Gordy)—Rick James

12-12 Can't Slow Down (Motown)—Lionel Richie

12-12 The Big Chill (Motown)—soundtrack

12-16 Making Love out of Nothing at All (S) (Arista)—Air Supply

12-16 Uh-Huh (Riva)—John Cougar Mellencamp

12-19 Colour by Numbers (Virgin)—Culture Club

12-19 Genesis (Atlantic)—Genesis

12-20 Rock 'N' Soul, Part I (RCA)—Hall & Oates

12-21 Little Robbers (Capitol)—Motels

12-21 20 Greatest Hits (Liberty)—Kenny Rogers

12-22 Lick It Up (Mercury)—Kiss

12-23 Family Tradition (Elektra)—Hank Williams, Jr.

12-27 Stay with Me Tonight (A&M)—Jeffrey Osborne

1984

1-4 Greatest Hits Volume II (Arista)—Barry Manilow

1-4 Undercover (Rolling Stones)—Rolling Stones

1-9 Pipes of Peace (Columbia)—Paul McCartney

1-9 Eddie Murphy: Comedian (Columbia)—Eddie Murphy

1-9 Eddie Murphy (Columbia)—Eddie Murphy

1-9 Without a Song (Columbia)—Willie Nelson

1-9 Yentl (Columbia)—Barbra Streisand (soundtrack)

1-12 Shout at the Devil (Elektra)—Motley Crue

1-16 Seven and the Ragged Tiger (Capitol)—Duran Duran

1-16 Uptown Girl (S) (Columbia)—Billy Joel

1-16 Two of a Kind (MCA)—Olivia Newton-John and John Travolta (soundtrack)

1-16 On the Rise (Tabu)—S.O.S. Band

1-17 A Chipmunk Christmas (RCA)—Chipmunks

8-21	Camouflage (Warner Bros.)—Rod Stewart
8-21	Hank Williams Jr.'s Greatest Hits (Curb)—Hank Williams, Jr.
8-28	Stay Hungry (Atlantic)—Twisted Sister
8-29	Purple Rain (Warner Bros.)—Prince & the Revolution (soundtrack)
8-31	State of Shock (S) (Epic)—Jacksons
8-31	Victory (Epic)—Jacksons
8-31	Eddie & the Cruisers (Steed)—soundtrack
9-4	No Brakes (EMI/America)—John Waite
9-12	Pleasure Victim (Geffen)—Berlin
9-12	Chicago 17 (Full Moon)—Chicago
9-12	Breaking Hearts (Geffen)—Elton John
9-12	Holy Diver (Warner Bros.)—Dio
9-12	The Last in Line (Warner Bros.)—Dio
9-17	Love Language (Asylum)—Teddy Pendergrass
9-17	Condition Critical (Pasha)—Quiet Riot
9-17	The Warrior (Columbia)—Scandal
9-18	Ice Cream Castle (Warner Bros.)—Time
9-27	Too Fast for Love (Elektra)—Motley Crue
10-1	You Could Have Been with Me (EMI/America)—Sheena Easton
10-1	Signs of Life (Capitol)—Billy Squier
10-4	20 Greatest Hits (Capitol)—Beatles
10-5	Primitive (Columbia)—Neil Diamond
10-5	Don't Cheat in Our Home Town (Epic)—Ricky Skaggs
10-22	Phantoms (MCA)—Fixx
10-22	1100 Bel Air Place (Columbia)—Julio Iglesias
10-24	Suddenly (Jive)—Billy Ocean
10-31	Caribbean Queen (S) (Jive)—Billy Ocean
11-5	Swept Away (RCA)—Diana Ross
11-7	Let's Go Crazy (S) (Warner Bros.)—Prince
11-7	Powerslave (Capitol)—Iron Maiden
11-8	I Just Called to Say I Love You (S) (Motown)—Stevie Wonder
11-8	The Woman in Red (Motown)—soundtrack
11-8	Sam Harris (Motown)—Sam Harris
11-8	Bullfrogs and Butterflies (Birdwing)—Candle
11-13	VOA (Geffen)—Sammy Hagar
11-16	Right or Wrong (MCA)—George Strait
11-21	Tonight (EMI/America)—David Bowie
11-21	A Private Heaven (EMI/America)—Sheena Easton
11-21	Oak Ridge Boys Greatest Hits 2 (MCA)—Oak Ridge Boys
11-21	Teachers (Capitol)—soundtrack
11-30	I Feel for You (S) (Warner Bros.)—Chaka Khan
12-3	Big Bam Boom (RCA)—Hall & Oates
12-3	It's Your Night (Qwest)—James Ingram

12-3	The Blitz (Arista)—Krokus
12-3	Animalize (Mercury)—Kiss
12-3	What about Me (RCA)—Kenny Rogers
12-3	Once upon a Christmas (RCA)—Kenny Rogers and Dolly Parton
12-3	The Unforgettable Fire (Island)—U2
12-5	Purple Rain (S) (Warner Bros.)—Prince & the Revolution
12-5	New Edition (MCA)—New Edition
12-12	December (Windham Hill)—George Winston
12-13	Volume I (Atlantic)—Honeydrippers
12-13	I Feel for You (Warner Bros.)—Chaka Khan
12-17	Run–D.M.C. (Profile)—Run–D.M.C.
12-18	City of New Orleans (Columbia)—Willie Nelson
12-18	Emotion (Columbia)—Barbra Streisand
12-18	Wake Me Up before You Go-Go (S) (Columbia)—Wham!
12-19	Do They Know It's Christmas? (S) (Columbia)—Band Aid
12-20	Don't Stop (A&M)—Jeffrey Osborne
12-26	Give My Regards to Broad Street (Columbia)—Paul McCartney
12-26	Make It Big (Columbia)—Wham!
12-28	Waking Up with the House on Fire (Virgin)—Culture Club
12-28	Disney's Christmas Favorites (Disneyland)—various artists

1985

1-4	Cool It Now (S) (MCA)—New Edition
1-9	Tropico (Chrysalis)—Pat Benatar
1-9	Valotte (Atlantic)—Julian Lennon
1-10	Like a Virgin (S) (Sire)—Madonna
1-10	Arena (Capitol)—Duran Duran
1-10	The Glamorous Life (Warner Bros.)—Sheila E
1-10	Major Moves (Warner Bros.)—Hank Williams, Jr.
1-11	Nuclear Furniture (Grunt)—Jefferson Starship
1-14	2:00 A.M. Paradise Cafe (Arista)—Barry Manilow
1-15	Perfect Strangers (Mercury)—Deep Purple
1-15	Mormon Tabernacle Choir Sings Christmas Carols (CBS)—Mormon Tabernacle Choir
1-15	Joy to the World (CBS)—Mormon Tabernacle Choir
1-17	Planetary Invasion (Elektra)—Midnight Star
1-17	Lush Life (Elektra)—Linda Ronstadt
1-23	Like a Virgin (Sire)—Madonna
1-24	Escape (Jive)—Whodini

1-29 Building the Perfect Beast (Geffen)—Don Henley

1-29 Men of Steel (Warner Bros.)—Hank Williams, Jr.

2-5 Reckless (A&M)—Bryan Adams

2-11 Agent Provocateur (Atlantic)—Foreigner

2-11 Beverly Hills Cop (MCA)—soundtrack

2-15 You've Got a Good Love Comin' (MCA)—Lee Greenwood

2-28 Isolation (Columbia)—Toto

3-1 Emergency (De-Lite)—Kool & the Gang

3-1 Stop Making Sense (Sire)—Talking Heads

3-4 Welcome to the Pleasuredome (Island)—Frankie Goes to Hollywood

3-7 Solid (Capitol)—Ashford & Simpson

3-11 Easy Lover (S) (Columbia)—Philip Bailey & Phil Collins

3-11 Chinese Wall (Columbia)—Philip Bailey

3-11 Careless Whisper (S) (Columbia)—Wham!

3-11 Wheels Are Turnin' (Epic)—REO Speedwagon

3-12 Centerfield (Warner Bros.)—John Fogerty

3-15 A Little Good News (Capitol)—Anne Murray

3-25 I Want to Know What Love Is (Atlantic)—Foreigner

4-1 We Are the World (S) (Columbia)—USA for Africa

4-1 We Are the World (Columbia)—USA for Africa

4-1 40 Hour Week (RCA)—Alabama

4-1 Sign in Please (RCA)—Autograph

4-1 Starchild (Epic)—Teena Marie

4-2 Crazy from the Heat (Warner Bros.)—David Lee Roth

4-2 Autumn (Windham Hill)—George Winston

4-4 Why Not Me (RCA)—Judds

4-8 Does Fort Worth Ever Cross Your Mind (MCA)—George Strait

4-9 Vision Quest (Geffen)—soundtrack

4-11 The Firm (Atlantic)—Firm

4-18 No Jacket Required (Atlantic)—Phil Collins

5-2 Straight Ahead (Myrrh)—Amy Grant

5-6 Fat Boys (Sutra)—Fat Boys

5-6 She's the Boss (Columbia)—Mick Jagger

5-6 Diamond Life (Portrait)—Sade

5-8 Nightshift (Motown)—Commodores

5-8 Rhythm of the Night (Motown)—De Barge

5-11 Vital Signs (Scotti Bros.)—Survivor

5-16 Songs from the Big Chair (Mercury)—Tears for Fears

5-19 All the Great Hits (Motown)—Commodores

5-21 The Power Station (Capitol)—Power Station

5-21 The Night I Fell in Love (Epic)—Luther Vandross

5-24 Southern Accents (MCA)—Tom Petty & the Heartbreakers

5-31 Rowdy (Curb)—Hank Williams, Jr.

6-3 King of Rock (Profile)—Run–D.M.C.

6-5 Catching the Sun (MCA)—Spyro Gyra

6-11 Can't Stop the Love (Capitol)—Maze featuring Frankie Beverly

6-11 Heart over Mind (Capitol)—Anne Murray

6-11 The Breakfast Club (A&M)—soundtrack

6-13 Tao (RCA)—Rick Springfield

6-17 Dream into Action (Elektra)—Howard Jones

6-20 Only Four You (Motown)—Mary Jane Girls

6-20 More Songs from *The Big Chill* (Motown)—soundtrack

6-24 Whitney Houston (Arista)—Whitney Houston

6-25 More than Wonderful (IPT)—Sandi Patti

7-2 Around the World in a Day (Paisley Park)—Prince & the Revolution

7-11 Be Yourself Tonight (RCA)—Eurythmics

7-16 Crazy for You (S) (Geffen)—Madonna

7-18 Shaker 'n' Stirred (Es Paranza)—Robert Plant

7-22 The Hobbit (S) (Disneyland)—various artists

7-22 Mother Goose Rhymes (S) (Disneyland)—various artists

7-22 The Wizard of Oz (S) (Disneyland)—various artists

7-22 Winnie the Pooh & the Blustery Day (S) (Disneyland)—various artists

7-22 Brer Rabbit & the Tar Baby (S) (Disneyland)—various artists

7-22 7 Wishes (MCA)—Night Ranger

7-22 Best of Disney Volume II (Disneyland)—various artists

7-23 Brothers in Arms (Warner Bros.)—Dire Straits

7-23 Rock Me Tonight (Capitol)—Freddie Jackson

7-29 Air Supply (Arista)—Air Supply

7-30 Angel/Into the Groove (S, 12-inch) (Sire)—Madonna

7-31 Greatest Hits (MCA)—Patsy Cline

7-31 Invasion of Your Privacy (Atlantic)—Ratt

8-1 Vanity 6 (Warner Bros.)—Vanity 6

8-5 Maverick (EMI/America)—George Thorogood & the Destroyers

820

8-6 The Allnighter (MCA)—Glenn Frey

8-7 Bad to the Bone (EMI/America)—George Thorogood & the Destroyers

8-8 Ghostbusters (Arista)—Ray Parker, Jr.

8-13 Tooth and Nail (Elektra)—Dokken

8-13 The Secret of Association (Columbia)—Paul Young

8-19 Fly on the Wall (Atlantic)—AC/DC

8-19 World Wide Live (Mercury)—Scorpions

8-20 Little Creatures (Sire)—Talking Heads

8-21 Boy in the Box (EMI/America)—Corey Hart

8-21 Heart (Capitol)—Heart

8-22 Theatre of Pain (Elektra)—Motley Crue

8-26 Who's Zoomin' Who? (Arista)—Aretha Franklin

8-28 The Dream of the Blue Turtles (A&M)—Sting

8-29 Jesse Johnson's Revue (A&M)—Jesse Johnson's Revue

9-3 Contact (RCA)—Pointer Sisters

9-5 Unguarded (Myrrh)—Amy Grant

9-6 Back to the Future (MCA)—soundtrack

9-11 Two Hearts (Columbia)—Men at Work

9-11 Voices Carry (Epic)—Til Tuesday

9-17 Remain in Light (Sire)—Talking Heads

9-17 Fear of Music (Sire)—Talking Heads

9-18 Branigan 2 (Atlantic)—Laura Branigan

10-2 Greatest Hits Volume 2 (RCA)—Ronnie Milsap

10-2 Ready for the World (MCA)—Ready for the World

10-8 7800 Degrees Fahrenheit (Mercury)—Bon Jovi

10-12 Hunting High and Low (Mercury)—ABBA

10-16 Picture This (Chrysalis)—Huey Lewis & the News

10-18 Nervous Night (Columbia)—Hooters

10-18 Greatest Hits Volume I & Volume II (Columbia)—Billy Joel

10-24 Scarecrow (Rival)—John Cougar Mellencamp

10-29 Live at the Apollo with David Ruffin and Eddie Kendricks (RCA)—Hall & Oates

10-29 St. Elmo's Fire (Atlantic)—soundtrack

10-29 Five-O (Warner Bros.)—Hank Williams, Jr.

11-1 A Decade of Hits (Epic)—Charlie Daniels Band

11-1 Lovin' Every Minute of It (Columbia)—Loverboy

11-7 Greatest Hits (MCA)—Lee Greenwood

11-11 Single Life (ATS)—Cameo

11-13 20/20 (Warner Bros.)—George Benson

11-13 Asylum (Mercury)—Kiss

11-13 In Square Circle (Motown)—Stevie Wonder

11-15 Alabama Christmas (RCA)—Alabama

11-15 Sacred Heart (Warner Bros.)—Dio

11-15 Knee Deep in the Hoopla (Grunt)—Starship

11-22 Music from the TV Series "Miami Vice" (MCA)—soundtrack

11-22 George Strait's Greatest Hits (MCA)—George Strait

11-25 A Christmas Album (Myrrh)—Amy Grant

11-25 Meeting in the Ladies Room (MCA)—Klymaxx

11-26 Welcome to the Real World (RCA)—Mr. Mister

11-26 Here's to Future Days (Arista)—Thompson Twins

12-3 Color of Success (Warner Bros.)—Morris Day

12-3 Give It Up (Warner Bros.)—Bonnie Raitt

12-3 Cats (Geffen)—original Broadway cast

12-5 Heart of the Matter (RCA)—Kenny Rogers

12-10 Winter into Spring (Windham Hill)—George Winston

12-11 The Pachelbel Canon (RCA)—Paillard Chamber/Maurice Amore

12-18 Power Windows (Mercury)—Rush

12-18 Live after Death (Capitol)—Iron Maiden

12-23 Party All the Time (S) (Columbia)—Eddie Murphy

12-23 How Could It Be (Columbia)—Eddie Murphy

12-23 That's Why I'm Here (Columbia)—James Taylor

12-23 Couldn't Stand the Weather (Epic)—Stevie Ray Vaughan & Double Trouble

12-30 Do You (EMI/America)—Sheena Easton

1986

1-3 All for Love (MCA)—New Edition

1-6 Afterburner (Warner Bros.)—ZZ Top

1-9 The Fat Boys Are Back (Sutra)—Fat Boys

1-13 Rocky IV (Scotti Bros.)—soundtrack

1-13 The Broadway Album (Columbia)—Barbra Streisand

1-15 That's What Friends Are For (S) (Arista)—Dionne Warwick & Friends

1-16 The Cars Greatest Hits (Elektra)—Cars

1-21 Rock a Little (Modern)—Stevie Nicks

1-21 Say You, Say Me (S) (Motown)—Lionel Richie

1-21 Anthology (Motown)—Diana Ross and the Supremes

8-4 Rapture (Elektra)—Anita Baker

8-7 Invisible Touch (Atlantic)—Genesis

8-11 Emotional (A&M)—Jeffrey Osborne

8-11 White Winds (CBS)—Andreas Vollenweider

8-18 Ruthless People (Epic)—soundtrack

8-19 Who Made Who (Atlantic)—AC/DC

8-25 Headlines (Solar)—Midnight Star

8-28 The Monkees Greatest Hits (Arista)—Monkees

8-28 Then & Now . . . The Best of the Monkees (Arista)—Monkees

8-29 Music from the Edge of Heaven (Columbia)—Wham!

9-8 True Blue (Sire)—Madonna

9-8 Back in the High Life (Island)—Steve Winwood

9-9 Eat 'em and Smile (Warner Bros.)—David Lee Roth

9-11 El DeBarge (Gordy)—El DeBarge

9-18 The Jets (MCA)—Jets

9-18 #7 (MCA)—George Strait

9-23 Revenge (RCA)—Eurythmics

10-1 True Confessions (London)—Bananarama

10-1 Night Songs (Mercury)—Cinderella

10-2 Poolside (Atlantic)—Nu Shooz

10-8 The Bridge (Columbia)—Billy Joel

10-8 Lisa Lisa & Cult Jam with Full Force (Columbia)—Lisa Lisa & Cult Jam with Full Force

10-10 The Bellamy Brothers Greatest Hits (MCA)—Bellamy Brothers

10-10 Storms of Life (Warner Bros.)—Randy Travis

10-10 Upstairs at Eric's (Sire)—Yaz

10-13 The Best of Bill Cosby (Warner Bros.)—Bill Cosby

10-13 Pieces of the Sky (Reprise)—Emmylou Harris

10-13 That Nigger's Crazy (Reprise)—Richard Pryor

10-15 Slippery When Wet (Mercury)—Bon Jovi

10-16 Dancing on the Ceiling (Motown)—Lionel Richie

10-29 Word Up (Atlanta Artists)—Cameo

10-29 Graceland (Warner Bros.)—Paul Simon

11-4 Mast of Puppets (Asylum)—Metallica

11-6 John Conlee's Greatest Hits (MCA)—John Conlee

11-6 Inside Out (MCA)—Lee Greenwood

11-6 Break Every Rule (Capitol)—Tina Turner

11-10 Heartbeat (Epic)—Don Johnson

11-12 The Way It Is (RCA)—Bruce Hornsby & the Range

11-12 True Colors (Portrait)—Cyndi Lauper

11-18 Solitude/Solitaire (Warner Bros.)—Peter Cetera

11-18 Eye of the Tiger (Warner Bros.)—John Fogerty

11-18 Somewhere in Time (Capitol)—Iron Maiden

11-18 True Stories (Sire)—Talking Heads

11-21 Full Sail (Columbia)—Loggins and Messina

11-24 Belinda (I.R.S.)—Belinda Carlisle

11-25 Third Stage (MCA)—Boston

11-25 Dancing Undercover (Atlantic)—Ratt

12-1 Chicago 18 (Full Moon)—Chicago

12-4 Fore! (Chrysalis)—Huey Lewis & the News

12-4 16 Greatest Hits (MCA)—Steppenwolf

12-5 Avalon (Warner Bros.)—Roxy Music

12-8 Can't Hold Back (Columbia)—Eddie Money

12-8 For Sentimental Reasons (Elektra)—Linda Ronstadt

12-8 Give Me the Reason (Epic)—Luther Vandross

12-10 Stand by Me (Atlantic)—soundtrack

12-15 Some Great Reward (Sire)—Depeche Mode

12-16 Aretha (Arista)—Aretha Franklin

12-16 Just Like the First Time (Capitol)—Freddie Jackson

12-16 The Troublemaker (Columbia)—Willie Nelson

12-18 Hymns Just for You (Impact)—Sandi Patti

12-22 Get Close (Sire)—Pretenders

12-22 Live (EMI/America)—George Thorogood & the Destroyers

12-22 Montana Cafe (Warner Bros.)—Hank Williams, Jr.

12-29 Fields of Fire (EMI/America)—Corey Hart

1987

1-6 The Touch (RCA)—Alabama

1-6 Double Vision (Warner Bros.)—Bob James and David Sanborn

1-12 Forever (Mercury)—Kool & the Gang

1-13 Whiplash Smile (Chrysalis)—Billy Idol

1-13 Every Breath You Take the Singles (A&M)—Police

1-20 Notorious (Capitol)—Duran Duran

1-20 First Offense (Capitol)—Corey Hart

1-20 Killers (Capitol)—Iron Maiden

1-21 Guitars, Cadillacs, Etc., Etc. (Reprise)—Dwight Yoakam

1-23 Whoever's in New England (Elektra)—Reba McEntire

824

8-11 Life as We Know It (Epic)—R.E.O. Speedwagon
8-11 Beverly Hills Cop II (MCA)—soundtrack
8-11 One Voice (Columbia)—Barbra Streisand
8-11 Soul to Soul (Epic)—Stevie Ray Vaughan
8-11 Hank Live (Warner Bros.)—Hank Williams, Jr.
8-19 Coming Around Again (Arista)—Carly Simon
8-24 Kiss Me, Kiss Me, Kiss Me (Elektra)—Cure
8-28 If I Were Your Woman (MCA)—Stephanie Mills
9-1 The Art of Tea (Reprise)—Michael Franks
9-2 The Manilow Collection/Twenty Classic Hits (Arista)—Barry Manilow
9-4 In the Dark (Arista)—Grateful Dead
9-4 Shakedown Street (Arista)—Grateful Dead
9-4 Terrapin Station (Arista)—Grateful Dead
9-8 One Heartbeat (Motown)—Smokey Robinson
9-15 Sammy Hagar (Geffen)—Sammy Hagar
9-15 La Bamba (Slash/Warner Bros.)—soundtrack
9-15 Mechanical Resonance (Geffen)—Tesla
9-15 Born to Boogie (Curb)—Hank Williams, Jr.
9-21 10 from 6 (Atlantic)—Bad Company
9-23 Something to Talk About (Capitol)—Anne Murray
9-28 One Way Home (Columbia)—Hooters
9-28 I Just Can't Stop Loving You (S) (Epic)—Michael Jackson
9-28 Bangin' (Columbia)—Outfield
9-29 Who's That Girl (Sire)—Madonna (soundtrack)
9-30 The Lost Boys (Atlantic)—soundtrack
10-7 Hysteria (Mercury)—Def Leppard
10-7 Best of Manhattan Transfer (Atlantic)—Manhattan Transfer
10-7 Manhattan Transfer (Atlantic)—Manhattan Transfer
10-12 Once Bitten (Capitol)—Great White
10-14 The Big Life (MCA)—Night Ranger
10-15 The Big Throwdown (Atlantic)—Levert
10-20 Hearsay (Tabu)—Alexander O'Neil
10-21 Door to Door (Elektra)—Cars
10-21 Hillbilly Deluxe (Reprise)—Dwight Yoakam
10-22 The Lonesome Jubilee (Mercury)—John Cougar Mellencamp
10-22 Dirty Dancing (RCA)—soundtrack
11-2 Document (I.R.S.)—R.E.M.
11-5 Ride the Lightning (Elektra)—Metallica
11-5 No Protection (RCA)—Starship

11-9 Bad (Epic)—Michael Jackson
11-9 Wildside (Columbia)—Loverboy
11-9 A Momentary Lapse of Reason (Columbia)—Pink Floyd
11-9 Hold Your Fire (Mercury)—Rush
11-10 Permanent Vacation (Geffen)—Aerosmith
11-11 Richard Marx (EMI/America)—Richard Marx
11-16 Greatest Hits Volume II (MCA)—George Strait
11-16 Tiffany (MCA)—Tiffany
11-17 Vital Idol (Chrysalis)—Billy Idol
11-17 Crazy Nights (Mercury)—Kiss
11-23 Actually (EMI/America)—Pet Shop Boys
12-2 Never Mind the Bollocks Here's the Sex Pistols (Warner Bros.)—Sex Pistols
12-2 Violent Femmes (Slash)—Violent Femmes
12-4 Paid in Full (Broadway)—Eric B. and Rakim
12-4 Somewhere in Time (MCA)—soundtrack
12-7 Heaven on Earth (MCA)—Belinda Carlisle
12-8 Garage Days Re-revisited (Elektra)—Metallica
12-8 Big Generator (Atco)—Yes
12-9 Greatest Hits (MCA)—Reba McEntire
12-15 Nothing Like the Sun (A&M)—Sting
12-15 A Very Special Christmas (A&M)—various artists
12-17 Out of the Blue (Atlantic)—Debbie Gibson
12-17 A Winter's Solstice (Windham Hill)—various artists
12-22 Kick (Atlantic)—Inxs
12-22 Magic (MCA)—Jets
12-31 Tunnel of Love (Columbia)—Bruce Springsteen

1988

1-5 Elton John Live in Australia (MCA)—Elton John
1-8 California Raisins (PRI)—California Raisins
1-8 Hot, Cool & Vicious (Next Plateau)—Salt-N-Pepa
1-8 Characters (Motown)—Stevie Wonder
1-12 Cloud Nine (Dark Horse)—George Harrison
1-12 Chronicles (Island)—Steve Winwood
1-14 Back for the Attack (Elektra)—Dokken
1-14 A Change of Heart (Warner Bros.)—David Sanborn

825

826

6-28	Open Up and Say . . . Ahh (Capitol)—Poison	9-28	The Hits (Epic)—R.E.O. Speedwagon
6-28	In Effect Mode (Warner Bros.)—Al B. Sure!	9-30	Supersonic—The Album (Ruthless)—J.J. Fad
6-30	Ooh Yeah! (Arista)—Hall & Oates	10-5	Greatest Hits (RCA)—Judds
6-30	Conscious Party (Virgin)—Ziggy Marley & the Melody Makers	10-12	Wide Awake in Dreamland (Chrysalis)—Pat Benatar
7-6	Scenes from the Southside (RCA)—Bruce Hornsby & the Range	10-21	Robbie Robertson (Geffen)—Robbie Robertson

6-28 Open Up and Say . . . Ahh (Capitol)—
Poison

6-28 In Effect Mode (Warner Bros.)—Al B.
Sure!

6-30 Ooh Yeah! (Arista)—Hall & Oates

6-30 Conscious Party (Virgin)—Ziggy Marley
& the Melody Makers

7-6 Scenes from the Southside (RCA)—Bruce
Hornsby & the Range

7-7 In My Tribe (Elektra)—10,000 Maniacs

7-12 Colors (Warner Bros.)—soundtrack

7-13 Diesel and Dust (Columbia)—Midnight
Oil

7-18 Lap of Luxury (Epic)—Cheap Trick

7-18 Ram It Down (Columbia)—Judas Priest

7-18 Even Worse (Scotti Bros.)—Weird Al
Yankovic

7-19 Tougher than Leather (Profile)—Run–
D.M.C.

7-26 OU812 (Warner Bros.)—Van Halen

8-5 Stronger than Pride (Epic)—Sade

8-9 Out of Order (Warner Bros.)—Rod Stewart

8-11 Alabama Live (RCA)—Alabama

8-17 Roll with It (Virgin)—Steve Winwood

8-19 I'm the Man (Island)—Anthrax

8-19 Samantha Fox (Jive)—Samantha Fox

8-19 Reg Strikes Back (MCA)—Elton John

8-19 Heart Break (MCA)—New Edition

8-23 19 (Reprise)—Chicago

8-23 Outrider (Geffen)—Jimmy Page

8-23 Joy (Elektra)—Teddy Pendergrass

8-23 Wild Streak (Warner Bros.)—Hank Williams, Jr.

8-24 Coming Back Hard Again (Tin Pan Apple/Polydor)—Fat Boys

8-24 Heavy Nova (EMI)—Robert Palmer

8-31 Simple Pleasures (EMI)—Bobby McFerrin

9-6 Don't Be Cruel (MCA)—Bobby Brown

9-9 Just Us (RCA)—Alabama

9-9 Long Cold Winter (Mercury)—Cinderella

9-13 Old 8 × 10 (Warner Bros.)—Randy Travis

9-15 In God We Trust (Enigma)—Stryper

9-20 Don't Let Love Slip Away (Capitol)—
Freddie Jackson

9-26 It Takes a Nation of Millions to Hold Us
Back (Def Jam/Columbia)—Public Enemy

9-27 Follow the Leader (Uni)—Eric B. &
Rakim

9-27 Small World (Chrysalis)—Huey Lewis and
the News

9-27 Cocktail (Elektra)—soundtrack

9-28 Up Your Alley (CBS)—Joan Jett & the
Blackhearts

9-28 The Hits (Epic)—R.E.O. Speedwagon

9-30 Supersonic—The Album (Ruthless)—J.J.
Fad

10-5 Greatest Hits (RCA)—Judds

10-12 Wide Awake in Dreamland (Chrysalis)—
Pat Benatar

10-21 Robbie Robertson (Geffen)—Robbie Robertson

10-26 Don't Be Afraid of the Dark (Mercury)—
Robert Cray Band

10-26 1988 Summer Olympics Album (Arista)—
Various Artists

10-31 And Justice for All (Elektra)—Metallica

11-9 Strictly Business (FRS)—EPMD

11-10 Time and Tide (Epic)—Basia

11-10 Out of This World (Epic)—Europe

11-16 New Jersey (Mercury)—Bon Jovi

11-18 Guy (MCA)—Guy

11-21 All That Jazz (A&M)—Breathe

11-21 Hangin' Tough (Columbia)–New Kids on
the Block

11-22 Power (Sire)—Ice-T

11-28 Peace Sells . . . But Who's Buying (Capitol)—Megadeth

11-28 Move Somethin' (Lucky)—The 2 Live
Crew

11-29 It Takes Two (PRF)—Rob Base & D.J. E-
Z Rock

11-29 Silhouette (Arista)—Kenny G

11-29 Conway Twitty's Greatest Hits, Volume II
(MCA)—Conway Twitty

11-29 Number Ones (MCA)—Conway Twitty

11-29 The Very Best of Conway Twitty & Loretta
Lynn (MCA)—Conway Twitty and Loretta
Lynn

11-29 We Only Make Believe (MCA)—Conway
Twitty and Loretta Lynn

11-30 A Fresh Aire Christmas (AMG)—Mannheim Steamroller

12-1 Rock the House (Jive)—DJ Jazzy Jeff &
Fresh Prince

12-1 A Salt with a Deadly Pepa (NXP)—Salt-
N-Pepa

12-2 Loving Proof (Columbia)—Ricky Van
Shelton

12-5 Lovesexy (Warner Bros.)—Prince

12-6 Wild, Wild West (Atlantic)—Escape Club

12-6 Information Society (TMB)—Information
Society

12-6 Rattle and Hum (Island)—U2

12-7 Disney's Children's Favorites, Volume III
(Disney)—Various Artists

12-12 Giving You the Best That I Got (Elektra)—
Anita Baker

12-13 Reba (MCA)—Reba McEntire

12-14 The Gift Goes On (Word)—Sandi Patti

12-19 Machismo (ATS)—Cameo

12-19 No Rest for the Wicked (CBS)—Ozzy Osbourne

12-19 Any Love (Epic)—Luther Vandross

12-20 Shooting Rubberbands at the Stars (Geffen)—Edie Brickell & New Bohemians

12-20 Big Thing (Capitol)—Duran Duran

12-21 Britny Fox (Columbia)—Britny Fox

12-21 Everything (Columbia)—Bangles

12-21 This Woman (RCA)—K.T. Oslin

12-21 Till I Loved You (Columbia)—Barbra Steisand

12-22 Introspective (EMI America)—Pet Shop Boys

12-22 Lead Me On (Myrrh)—Amy Grant

1989

1-4 Don't Worry Be Happy (S) (EMI America)—Bobby McFerrin

1-4 Traveling Wilburys (Warner Bros.)—Traveling Wilburys

1-4 Buenos Noches from a Lonely Room (RPS)—Dwight Yoakam

1-5 Imagine (Capitol)—Soundtrack (John Lennon)

1-10 Kokomo (S) (Elektra)—Beach Boys

1-10 My Prerogative (MCA)—Bobby Brown

1-10 A Groovy Kind of Love (S) (Atlantic)—Phil Collins

1-10 American Dream (Atlantic)—Crosby, Stills, Nash & Young

1-10 Wild, Wild West (S) (Atlantic)—Escape Club

1-10 Green (Warner Bros.)—R.E.M.

1-10 Reach for the Sky (Atlantic)—Ratt

1-10 Buster (Atlantic)—Soundtrack

1-10 Wild Thing (S) (Broadway)—Tone Loc

1-10 Desire (S) (Island)—U2

1-17 Up Where We Belong (S) (Island)—Joe Cocker & Jennifer Warnes

1-17 Beast from the East (Elektra)—Dokken

1-17 Relax (S) (Island)—Frankie Goes to Hollywood

1-17 Only in My Dreams (S) (Atlantic)—Debbie Gibson

1-17 Shake Your Love (S) (Atlantic)—Debbie Gibson

1-17 Supersonic (S) (ATco)—J.J. Fad

1-17 Addicted to Love (S) (Island)—Robert Palmer

1-18 Look Away (Come in from the Night) (S) (RPS)—Chicago

1-18 What's on Your Mind (Pure Energy) (S) (TMB)—Information Society

1-18 Karyn White (Warner Bros.)—Karyn White

1-19 Don't Be Cruel (S) (MCA)—Bobby Brown

1-20 Hold an Old Friend's Hand (MCA)—Tiffany

1-23 Greatest Hits (Columbia)—Journey

1-23 Delicate Sound of Thunder (Columbia)—Pink Floyd

1-23 Baby I Love Your Way (S) (Epic)—Will to Power

1-25 Red Red Wine (S) (A&M)—UB40

1-26 Every Rose Has Its Thorn (S) (Capitol)—Poison

1-27 Winger (Atlantic)—Winger

1-30 Love Is a Battlefield (S) (Chrysalis)—Pat Benatar

1-30 I Want a New Drug (S) (Chrysalis)—Huey Lewis & the News

1-30 Power of Love (S) (Chrysalis)—Huey Lewis & The News

2-1 The Innocents (Sire)—Erasure

2-1 Greatest Hits (Warner Bros.)—Fleetwood Mac

2-1 Smashes, Thrashes & Hits (Mercury)—Kiss

2-6 At This Moment (S) (Capital)—Billy Vera & the Beaters

2-6 Vixen (EMI America)—Vixen

2-8 Straight Up (S) (Virgin)—Paula Abdul

2-8 State of Euphoria (Island)—Anthrax

2-13 I'll Always Love You (S) (Arista)—Dayne Taylor

2-14 Forever Your Girl (Virgin)—Paula Abdul

2-14 Off the Wall (S) (Epic)—Michael Jackson

2-14 She's Out of My Life (S) (Epic)—Michael Jackson

2-14 Greatest Hits Volume III 1979–1987 (Geffen)—Elton John

2-14 Let It Roll (Warner Bros.)—Little Feat

2-14 Vivid (Epic)—Living Colour

2-15 Eazy-Duz-It (PRI)—Eazy-E

2-16 The Best Years of Our Lives (Columbia)—Neil Diamond

2-17 It Takes Two (S) (PRO)—Rob Base & D.J. E-Z Rock

2-17 Surfing with the Alien (Rebel)—Joe Satriani

2-21 Swass (NAS)—Sir Mix-A-Lot

2-23 Girl You Know It's True (Arista)–Milli Vanilli

2-24 Never Gonna Give You Up (S) (RCA)—Rick Astley

2-24 Parents Just Don't Understand (S) (RCA)—DJ Jazzy Jeff & Fresh Prince

2-24 I Wanna Have Some Fun (S) (RCA)—Samantha Fox

2-24 I Wanna Have Some Fun (RCA)—Samantha Fox

2-24 (I've Had) The Time of My Life (S) (RCA)—Bill Medley & Jennifer Warnes

2-24 Nothing's Gonna Stop Us Now (S) (RCA)—Starship

2-24 We Built This City (S) (RCA)—Starship

3-1 G 'N R Lies (Geffen)—Guns 'N Roses

3-1 Kylie (Geffen)—Kylie Minogue

3-9 Lost in Your Eyes (S) (Atlantic)—Debbie Gibson

3-9 Catch Me (I'm Falling) (S) (Virgin)—Pretty Poison

3-9 A Show of Hands (Mercury)—Rush

3-9 The Way You Love Me (S) (Warner Bros.)—Karyn White

3-14 Les Miserables (Geffen)—Original Cast

3-15 When I'm With You (S) (Capitol)—Sheriff

3-16 Electric Youth (Atlantic)—Debbie Gibson

3-16 Casanova (S) (Atlantic)—Levert

3-16 Living Years (Atlantic)—Mike & the Mechanics

3-21 Just Coolin' (Atlantic)—Levert

3-21 Beaches (Soundtrack)(Atlantic)—Bette Midler

3-28 The Right Stuff (WNG)—Vanessa Williams

3-29 Biograph (Columbia)—Bob Dylan

3-29 Melissa Ethridge (Island)—Melissa Ethridge

3-29 You Got It (The Right Stuff) (S) (Columbia)—New Kids on the Block

3-29 Mystery Girl (Virgin)—Roy Orbison

3-29 Skid Row (Atlantic)—Skid Row

4-4 Southern Star (RCA)—Alabama

4-4 The Look (S) (EMI America)—Roxette

4-6 Watermark (Geffen)—Enya

4-7 Messages from the Boys (Motown)—The Boys

4-7 Deep Breakfast (MWT)—Ray Lynch

4-11 Lovelife (Geffen)—Berlin

4-11 The Great Radio Controversy (Geffen)—Tesla

4-11 Hank Williams, Jr.'s Greatest Hits (Warner Bros.)—Hank Williams, Jr.

4-12 Retrospect (Atco)—Buffalo Springfield

4-13 Straight Outta Compton (PRI)—N.W.A.

4-14 Operation Monocrime (EMI America)—Queensryche

4-17 Eternal Flame (S) (Columbia)—Bangles

4-17 Walk Like an Egyptian (S) (Columbia)—Bangles

4-17 Let's Get It Started (Capitol)—M.C. Hammer

4-17 She Bop (S) (Portrait)—Cyndi Lauper

4-17 Time After Time (S) (Portrait)—Cyndi Lauper

4-17 Can't Fight This Feeling (S) (Epic)—R.E.O. Speedwagon

4-17 Take It on the Run (S) (Epic)—R.E.O. Speedwagon

4-17 Beautiful Loser (Capitol)—Bob Seger

4-17 Great Adventures of Slick Rick (Columbia)—Slick Rick

4-18 Bulletboys (Warner Bros.)—Bulletboys

4-18 She Drives Me Crazy (S) (I.R.S.)—Fine Young Cannibals

4-18 2 Hype (SBL)—Kid 'N Play

4-18 Superwoman (S) (Warner Bros.)—Karyn White

4-20 The Lover In Me (MCA)—Sheena Easton

4-21 The Raw & the Cooked (I.R.S.)—Fine Young Cannibals

4-24 Flashback (A&M)—.38 Special

4-28 Beyond the Blue Neon (MCA)—George Strait

5-2 Girl You Know It's True (Arista)—Milli Vanilli

5-9 Cherish (S) (Delite)—Kool & the Gang

5-9 Get Down (S) (Delite)—Kool & the Gang

5-9 Joanna (S) (Delite)—Kool & the Gang

5-9 Too Hot (S) (Delite)—Kool & the Gang

5-9 Shout (S) (Mercury)—Tears for Fears

5-9 Funky Cold Medina (S) (DEL)—Tone Loc

5-9 Loc'ed After Dark (DEL)—Tone Loc

5-11 101 Dalmations (S) (Disney)—Various Artists

5-11 Mickey's Christmas Carol (S) (Disney)—Various Artists

5-16 Like a Prayer (S) (Sire)—Madonna

5-16 Kill 'Em All (Elektra)—Metallica

5-16 Life Is . . . Too Short (RCA)—Too Short

5-23 Like a Prayer (Sire)—Madonna

5-23 Singable Songs for the Very Young (SHU)—Raffi

5-24 Forever Your Girl (S) (Virgin)—Paula Abdul

5-24 Electric Youth (S) (Atlantic)—Debbie Gibson

5-24 Wind Beneath My Wings (S) (Atlantic)—Bette Midler

5-26 Larger Than Life (MCA)—Jody Watley

5-30 3 Feet High and Rising (TMB)—De La Soul

6-1 After All (S) (Geffen)—Cher & Peter Cetera

6-2 Look Sharp! (EMI America)—Roxette

6-9 River of Time (RCA)—The Judds

6-13 Sonic Temple (Sire)—The Cult

6-13 Twice Shy (Capitol)—Great White

829

830

8-30 Anderson Bruford Wakeman Howe (Arista)—Anderson Bruford Wakeman Howe

8-30 After the Snow (Sire)—Modern English

9-6 Love (Sire)—The Cult

9-6 The End of the Innocence (Geffen)—Don Henley

9-11 Anything for You (S) (Epic)—Gloria Estefan & Miami Sound Machine

9-11 Bad Boy (S) (Epic)—Gloria Estefan & Miami Sound Machine

9-11 Conga (S) (Epic)—Gloria Estefan & Miami Sound Machine

9-11 Cuts Both Ways (S) (Epic)—Gloria Estefan & Miami Sound Machine

9-11 Don't Wanna Lose You (S) (Epic)—Gloria Estefan & Miami Sound Machine

9-11 Indigo Girls (Epic)—Indigo Girls

9-11 Anniversary—Ten Years of Hits (Epic)—George Jones

9-11 New Kids on the Block (Columbia)—New Kids on the Block

9-11 Greatest Hits Volume II (Epic)—Johnny Paycheck

9-11 Shower Me With Your Love (S) (Columbia)—Surface

9-13 Heart of Stone (Geffen)—Cher

9-13 Girl I'm Gonna Miss You (S) (Arista)—Milli Vanilli

9-13 18 and Life (S) (Atlantic)—Skid Row

9-18 I Like It (S) (Broadway)—Dino

9-18 Take It to the Limit (Columbia)—Wilie Nelson

9-18 Heaven (S) (Columbia)—Warrant

9-18 Bust a Move (S) (DEL)—M.C. Young

9-20 If I Could Turn Back Time (S) (Geffen)—Cher

9-22 Paul's Boutique (Capitol)—Beastie Boys

9-22 No One Can Do It Better (Atlantic)—The D.O.C.

9-24 Killin' Time (RCA)—Clint Black

9-24 Christmas Time with The Judds (RCA)—The Judds

9-25 By All Means Necessary (Jive)—Boogie Down Productions

9-25 Ghetto Music: the Blueprint of Hip Hop (Jive)—Boogie Down Productions

9-27 As Nasty As They Wanna Be (Lky)—The 2 Live Crew

10-5 24/7 (Broadway)—Dino

10-5 Money for Nothing (Warner Bros.)—Dire Straits

10-13 Don't Make Me Over (S) (NXP)—Sybil

10-16 Unfinished Business (FRS)—EPMD

10-18 Heaven (Capitol)—BeBe and CeCe Winans

10-19 Tender Lover (Solar)—Baby Face

10-19 Eat It (S) (Scotti Bros.)—"Weird Al" Yankovic

10-20 12 × 5 (ABK)—The Rolling Stones

10-20 The Rolling Stones (ABK)—The Rolling Stones

10-20 Back to Life (S) (Virgin)—Soul II Soul

10-27 Steel Wheels (Columbia)—The Rolling Stones

10-30 Sleeping with the Past (MCA)—Elton John

11-2 Blow My Fuse (Atlantic)—Kix

11-2 Dr. Feelgood (S) (Elektra)—Motley Crue

11-2 Dr. Feelgood (Elektra)—Motley Crue

11-3 Bad English (Epic)—Bad English

11-3 Trash (Epic)—Alice Cooper

11-3 Miss You Much (S) (A&M)—Janet Jackson

11-8 Blame It on the Rain (S) (Arista)—Milli Vanilli

PLATINUM-RECORD AWARDS

1976

2-24 Eagles—Their Greatest Hits 1971–1975 (Asylum)—Eagles

3-4 Desire (Columbia)—Bob Dylan

4-8 Frampton Comes Alive! (A&M)—Peter Frampton

4-12 Presence (Swan Song)—Led Zeppelin

4-22 Disco Lady (S) (Columbia)—Johnnie Taylor

5-3 Wings at the Speed of Sound (Capitol)—Paul McCartney & Wings

6-14 Rock 'N' Roll Music (Capitol)—Beatles

6-23 Black and Blue (Rolling Stones)—Rolling Stones

7-9 Rocks (Columbia)—Aerosmith

8-10 Breezin' (Warner Bros.)—George Benson

8-23 Kiss and Say Goodbye (S) (Columbia)—Manhattans

9-13 Look Out for #1 (A&M)—Brothers Johnson

9-14 Chicago X (Columbia)—Chicago

9-20 Mothership Connection (Casablanca)—Parliament

9-20 Beautiful Noise (Columbia)—Neil Diamond

9-22 Silk Degrees (Columbia)—Boz Scaggs

9-23 Song of Joy (A&M)—Captain & Tennille

9-27 Fly Like an Eagle (Capitol)—Steve Miller Band

9-18 Spitfire (Grunt)—Jefferson Starship

10-6 Spirit (RCA)—John Denver

10-13 Spirit (Columbia)—Earth, Wind & Fire
10-15 Play That Funky Music (S) (Epic)—Wild Cherry
10-28 Hasten Down the Wind (Asylum)—Linda Ronstadt
11-5 Dreamboat Annie (Mushroom)—Heart
11-11 Destroyer (Casablanca)—Kiss
11-15 The Song Remains the Same (Swan Song)—Led Zeppelin
11-22 Boston (Epic)—Boston
11-23 A Night on the Town (Warner Bros.)—Rod Stewart
11-24 The Outlaws (RCA)—The Outlaws (Waylon Jennings, Willie Nelson, Jessi Colter, and Tompall Glaser)
12-1 Run with the Pack (Swan Song)—Bad Company
12-6 A New World Record (United Artists)—Electric Light Orchestra
12-9 Blue Moves (Rocket)—Elton John
12-10 Brass Construction (United Artists)—Brass Construction
12-13 Disco Duck (S) (RSO)—Rick Dees & His Cast of Idiots
12-15 Hotel California (Asylum)—Eagles
12-17 Wild Cherry (Epic)—Wild Cherry
12-20 Wings over America (Capitol)—Paul McCartney & Wings
12-22 Best of the Doobies (Warner Bros.)—Doobie Brothers
12-23 Children of the World (RSO)—Bee Gees
12-30 Soul Searching (Atlantic)—Average White Band
12-30 One More (for) from the Road (MCA)—Lynyrd Skynyrd

1977

1-5 Rock & Roll Over (Casablanca)—Kiss
1-6 Greatest Hits (United Artists)—War
1-6 This One's for You (Arista)—Barry Manilow
1-19 Greatest Hits (Elektra/Asylum)—Linda Ronstadt
1-21 A Star Is Born (Columbia)—Barbra Streisand and Kris Kristofferson
1-25 All Things in Time (Philadelphia International)—Lou Rawls
2-22 Car Wash (S) (MCA)—Rose Royce
3-9 Rumours (Warner Bros.)—Fleetwood Mac
3-10 Animals (Columbia)—Pink Floyd
3-15 Leftoverture (Kirshner/Columbia)—Kansas
3-24 Year of the Cat (Janus/GRT)—Al Stewart
3-25 Night Moves (Capitol)—Bob Seger & the Silver Bullet Band

4-12 The Pretender (Elektra/Asylum)—Jackson Browne
4-13 Ask Rufus (ABC)—Rufus Featuring Chaka Khan
5-23 After the Lovin' (Epic/CBS)—Engelbert Humperdinck
6-2 Go for Your Guns (T-Neck/Columbia)—Isley Brothers
6-10 Book of Dreams (Capitol)—Steve Miller Band
6-13 I'm in You (A&M)—Peter Frampton
6-16 Barry Manilow Live (Arista)—Barry Manilow
6-22 Rocky (United Artists)—soundtrack
6-30 Love Gun (Casablanca)—Kiss
7-5 Love at the Greek (Columbia)—Neil Diamond
8-2 Little Queen (Portrait/Columbia)—Heart
8-2 Right on Time (A&M)—Brothers Johnson
8-9 Superman (Columbia)—Barbra Streisand
8-11 Foreigner (Atlantic)—Foreigner
8-12 Unpredictable (Capitol)—Natalie Cole
8-12 The Beatles at the Hollywood Bowl (Capitol)—Beatles
8-17 Star Wars (20th Century)—soundtrack
8-18 CSN (Atlantic)—Crosby, Stills & Nash
9-1 Rejoice (Columbia)—Emotions
8-1 J.T. (Columbia)—James Taylor
9-12 Moody Blue (RCA)—Elvis Presley
9-19 Endless Flight (Warner Bros.)—Leo Sayer
9-20 Shaun Cassidy (Warner Bros.)—Shaun Cassidy
9-27 Cat Scratch Fever (Epic/CBS)—Ted Nugent
9-27 Free for All (Epic/CBS)—Ted Nugent
11-22 You Light Up My Life (S) (Warner Bros.)—Debby Boone
12-14 Changes in Latitudes, Changes in Attitudes (ABC)—Jimmy Buffett
12-15 Greatest Hits (MCA)—Olivia Newton-John
12-16 Live Bullet (Capitol)—Bob Seger & the Silver Bullet Band
12-20 Foghat Live (Bearsville/Warner)—Foghat
12-20 Foot Loose & Fancy Free (Warner Bros.)—Rod Stewart
12-22 Boogie Nights (S) (Epic/CBS)—Heatwave
12-22 Too Hot to Handle (Epic/CBS)—Heatwave
12-22 The Grand Illusion (A&M)—Styx
12-27 Aja (ABC)—Steely Dan
12-28 News of the World (Elektra)—Queen

1978

1-3 Saturday Night Fever (RSO/Polydor)—Bee Gees

1-18 The Stranger (Columbia)—Billy Joel

2-1 Greatest Hits, Etc. (Columbia)—Paul Simon

2-15 We Must Believe in Magic (United Artists)—Crystal Gayle

2-22 Even Now (Arista)—Barry Manilow

3-13 Stayin' Alive (S) (RSO/Polydor)—Bee Gees

3-14 Slowhand (RSO/Polydor)—Eric Clapton

3-30 London Town (Capitol)—Paul McCartney & Wings

4-11 Waylon & Willie (RCA)—Waylon Jennings and Willie Nelson

4-21 Emotion (S) (Private Stock)—Samantha Sang

4-25 We Are the Champions (S) (Elektra)—Queen

4-28 Here You Come Again (RCA)—Dolly Parton

5-1 French Kiss (Capitol)—Bob Welch

5-2 Night Fever (S) (RSO/Polydor)—Bee Gees

5-3 Weekend in L.A. (Warner Bros.)—George Benson

5-3 Showdown (T-Neck/CBS)—Isley Brothers

5-3 M.U.—The Best of Jethro Tull (Chrysalis)—Jethro Tull

5-4 Earth (Grunt/RCA)—Jefferson Starship

5-4 Funkentelechy vs. the Placebo Syndrome (Casablanca)—Parliament

5-9 Grease (RSO/Polydor)—soundtrack

5-9 Let's Get Small (Warner Bros.)—Steve Martin

5-10 Son of a Son of a Sailor (ABC)—Jimmy Buffett

5-10 FM (MCA)—soundtrack

5-12 I Want to Live (RCA)—John Denver

5-16 Double Platinum (Casablanca)—Kiss

5-18 Feels So Good (A&M)—Chuck Mangione

5-23 Carolina Dreams (Capricorn)—Marshall Tucker Band

5-30 Stranger in Town (Capitol)—Bob Seger & the Silver Bullet Band

5-31 So Full of Love (Philadelphia International)—O'Jays

6-2 Magazine (Mushroom)—Heart

6-8 *Star Wars* Theme/Cantina Band (S) (Millenium)—Meco

6-8 Star Wars and Other Galactic Funk (Millenium)—Meco

6-8 Thank God It's Friday (Casablanca)—soundtrack

6-17 Shadow Dancing (RSO/Polydor)—Andy Gibb

6-20 City to City (United Artists)—Gerry Rafferty

6-21 Thankful (Capitol)—Natalie Cole

6-21 Central Heating (Epic/CBS)—Heatwave

6-21 Teddy Pendergrass (Philadelphia International/CBS)—Teddy Pendergrass

6-22 Double Vision (Atlantic)—Foreigner

6-22 Some Girls (Rolling Stones/Atlantic)—Rolling Stones

6-27 Darkness on the Edge of Town (Columbia)—Bruce Springsteen

7-6 You Light Up My Life (Columbia)—Johnny Mathis

7-12 Shadow Dancing (S) (RSO/Polydor)—Andy Gibb

7-17 Agents of Fortune (Columbia)—Blue Oyster Cult

7-18 You're the One That I Want (S) (RSO/Polydor)—John Travolta and Olivia Newton-John

7-19 Sgt. Pepper's Lonely Hearts Club Band (RSO/Polydor)—soundtrack

7-20 Greatest Hits (Atlantic)—ABBA

7-20 Double Live Gonzo (Epic/CBS)—Ted Nugent

7-20 Ten Years of Gold (United Artists)—Kenny Rogers

7-27 Takin' It to the Streets (Warner Bros.)—Doobie Brothers

8-4 Flowing Rivers (RSO/Polydor)—Andy Gibb

8-7 Boys in the Trees (Elektra)—Carly Simon

8-7 But Seriously, Folks (Asylum)—Joe Walsh

8-8 The Album (Atlantic)—ABBA

8-22 Natural High (Motown)—Commodores

8-25 Don't Look Back (Epic/CBS)—Boston

8-25 Running on Empty (Asylum)—Jackson Browne

8-25 Bat out of Hell (Epic/Cleveland International)—Meat Loaf

8-25 Life Is a Song Worth Singing (Philadelphia International/CBS)—Teddy Pendergrass

8-25 Songbird (Columbia)—Barbra Streisand

9-19 Worlds Away (A&M)—Pablo Cruise

9-19 Blam (A&M)—Brothers Johnson

9-19 Togetherness (A&M)—L.T.D.

9-20 Who Are You (MCA)—Who

9-22 Living in the USA (Asylum)—Linda Ronstadt

9-26 Champagne Jam (Polydor)—Atlanta Rhythm Section

10-2 Kiss—Ace Frehley (Casablanca)—Ace Frehley

10-2 Kiss—Peter Criss (Casablanca)—Peter Criss

10-2 Kiss—Gene Simmons (Casablanca)—Gene Simmons

10-2 Kiss—Paul Stanley (Casablanca)—Paul Stanley

10-4 A Taste of Honey (Capitol)—A Taste of Honey

10-10 Boogie Oogie Oogie (S) (Capitol)—A Taste of Honey

10-10 Under Wraps (Warner/Curb)—Shaun Cassidy

10-10 Infinity (Columbia)—Journey

10-10 Pieces of Eight (A&M)—Styx

10-10 Van Halen (Warner Bros.)—Van Halen

10-13 Nightwatch (Columbia)—Kenny Loggins

10-17 Grease (S) (RSO/Polydor)—Frankie Valli

10-19 Live and More (Casablanca)—Donna Summer

10-23 52nd Street (Columbia)—Billy Joel

10-25 I Robot (Arista)—Alan Parsons Project

10-27 Hot Streets (Columbia)—Chicago

10-27 Dog and Butterfly (Portrait/CBS)—Heart

11-10 Sounds . . . And Stuff Like That (A&M)—Quincy Jones

11-10 Skynyrd's First and . . . Last (MCA)—Lynyrd Skynyrd

11-14 Backless (RSO/Polydor)—Eric Clapton

11-15 A Single Man (MCA)—Elton John

11-16 Weekend Warriors (Epic/CBS)—Ted Nugent

11-16 Barbra Streisand's Greatest Hits, Volume II (Columbia)—Barbra Streisand

11-21 A Wild and Crazy Guy (Warner Bros.)—Steve Martin

11-27 Greatest Hits (Arista)—Barry Manilow

11-27 The Steve Miller Band's Greatest Hits 1974–78 (Capitol)—Steve Miller Band

11-18 Jazz (Elektra)—Queen

12-5 Totally Hot (MCA)—Olivia Newton-John

12-6 Wings Greatest (Capitol)—Wings

12-7 Le Freak (S) (Atlantic)—Chic

12-7 You Don't Bring Me Flowers (Columbia)—Neil Diamond

12-7 The Best of Earth, Wind & Fire—Volume I (ARC/Columbia)—Earth, Wind & Fire

12-7 Steely Dan's Greatest Hits (ABC)—Steely Dan

12-12 Twin Sons of Different Mothers (Full Moon/Epic/CBS)—Dan Fogelberg and Tim Weisberg

12-13 Cruisin' (Casablanca)—Village People

12-14 You Get What You Play For (Epic/CBS)—REO Speedwagon

12-19 One Nation under a Groove (Warner Bros.)—Funkadelic

12-19 Let's Keep It That Way (Capitol)—Anne Murray

12-22 Barry White, the Man (20th Century)—Barry White

12-26 Live Bootleg (Columbia)—Aerosmith

12-26 Stardust (Columbia)—Willie Nelson

12-26 Macho Man (Casablanca)—Village People

12-27 The Cars (Elektra)—Cars

12-27 C'Est Chic (Atlantic)—Chic

12-27 Blondes Have More Fun (Warner Bros.)—Rod Stewart

1979

1-4 Hot Child in the City (S) (Chrysalis)—Nick Gilder

1-5 Briefcase Full of Blues (Atlantic)—Blues Brothers

1-10 Elan (Atlantic)—Firefall

1-18 Brother to Brother (A&M)—Gino Vanelli

1-23 Toto (Columbia)—Toto

1-25 Y.M.C.A. (S) (Casablanca)—Village People

1-26 Octave (London)—Moody Blues

1-30 Spirits Having Flown (RSO)—Bee Gees

2-9 Too Much Heaven (S) (RSO)—Bee Gees

2-21 Do Ya Think I'm Sexy (S) (Warner Bros.)—Rod Stewart

2-27 The Gambler (United Artists)—Kenny Rogers

3-6 Minute by Minute (Warner Bros.)—Doobie Brothers

3-14 Two for the Show (Kirshner/CBS)—Kansas

3-16 Time Passages (Arista)—Al Stewart

3-27 Dire Straits (Warner Bros.)—Dire Straits

3-27 Love Tracks (Polydor)—Gloria Gaynor

3-28 2 Hot (Polydor)—Peaches and Herb

4-4 Go West (Casablanca)—Village People

4-16 I Will Survive (S) (Polydor)—Gloria Gaynor

4-26 Desolation Angels (Swan Song)—Bad Company

5-3 Bad Girls (Casablanca)—Donna Summer

5-8 Destiny (Epic)—Jacksons

5-8 Breakfast in America (A&M)—Supertramp

5-8 Van Halen II (Warner Bros.)—Van Halen

5-9 Sleeper Catcher (Harvest)—Little River Band

5-11 Reunited (S) (Polydor)—Peaches and Herb

5-14 Tragedy (S) (RSO)—Bee Gees

5-22 Live at Budokan (Epic)—Cheap Trick

5-23 We Are Family (Atlantic)—Sister Sledge

6-6 Parallel Lines (Chrysalis)—Blondie

6-7 I Am (Columbia/ARC)—Earth, Wind & Fire

6-11 Shake Your Body (S) (Epic)—Jacksons

6-18	Back to the Egg (CBS)—Wings
6-19	Discovery (Jet/CBS)—Electric Light Orchestra
7-10	Dynasty (Casablanca)—Kiss
7-27	Ain't No Stoppin' Me Now (S) (Philadelphia International)—McFadden & Whitehead
7-27	Teddy (Philadelphia International)—Teddy Pendergrass
8-1	Knock on Wood (S) (Ariola America)—Amii Stewart
8-1	Hot Stuff (S) (Casablanca)—Donna Summer
8-3	Get the Knack (Capitol)—Knack
8-6	Candy-O (Elektra)—Cars
8-7	Rickie Lee Jones (Warner Bros.)—Rickie Lee Jones
8-16	Million Mile Reflection (Epic)—Charlie Daniels Band
9-4	Bad Girls (S) (Casablanca)—Donna Summer
9-7	Greatest Hits (RCA)—Waylon Jennings
10-5	The Kids Are Alright (MCA)—Who (soundtrack)
10-19	Disco Nights (Arista)—G.Q.
10-19	Evolution (CBS)—Journey
11-13	Eddie Money (CBS)—Eddie Money
11-20	First under the Wire (Capitol)—Little River Band
12-6	Risque (Atlantic)—Chic
12-10	Off the Wall (CBS)—Michael Jackson
12-26	Nether Lands (Full Moon/Epic)—Dan Fogelberg
12-26	Identify Yourself (Philadelphia International)—O'Jays

1980

1-7	Head Games (Atlantic)—Foreigner
1-7	In through the Out Door (Atlantic)—Led Zeppelin
1-16	Kenny (United Artists)—Kenny Rogers
1-21	Ladies Night (Phonogram)—Kool & the Gang
1-28	One Voice (Arista)—Barry Manilow
2-1	A Christmas Together (RCA)—John Denver and the Muppets
2-1	The Long Run (Asylum)—Eagles
2-5	Rise (A&M)—Herb Alpert
2-5	Cornerstone (A&M)—Styx
2-6	Dream Police (Epic)—Cheap Trick
2-7	Summertime Dream (Reprise)—Gordon Lightfoot
2-7	Rust Never Sleeps (Warner Bros.)—Neil Young
2-12	Tusk (Warner Bros.)—Fleetwood Mac

2-15	Prince (Warner Bros.)—Prince
2-21	On the Radio, Volumes I & II (Casablanca)—Donna Summer
2-22	Flirtin' with Disaster (Epic)—Molly Hatchet
2-22	Wet (Columbia)—Barbra Streisand
2-26	Bee Gees Greatest (RSO)—Bee Gees
2-26	Rod Stewart's Greatest Hits (Warner Bros.)—Rod Stewart
2-27	Damn the Torpedoes (MCA)—Tom Petty & the Heartbreakers
3-6	Willie and Family Live (Columbia)—Willie Nelson
3-11	Dionne (Arista)—Dionne Warwick
3-13	Phoenix (Full 1 Moon/Epic)—Dan Fogelberg
3-13	The Wall (Columbia)—Pink Floyd
3-18	Highway to Hell (Atlantic)—AC/DC
3-28	The Whispers (Solar)—Whispers
4-18	Gold and Platinum (MCA)—Lynyrd Skynyrd
4-19	A Place in the Sun (A&M)—Pablo Cruise
4-29	Against the Wind (Capitol)—Bob Seger & the Silver Bullet Band
5-5	Glass Houses (Columbia)—Billy Joel
5-9	September Morn (Columbia)—Neil Diamond
5-9	Slow Train Coming (Columbia)—Bob Dylan
5-12	Mad Love (Asylum)—Linda Ronstadt
5-28	Gideon (United Artists)—Kenny Rogers
5-30	Mickey Mouse Disco (Disneyland)—Mickey Mouse
6-2	Women and Children First (Warner Bros.)—Van Halen
6-4	Go All the Way (T-Neck)—Isley Brothers
6-11	The Rose (Atlantic)—Bette Midler (soundtrack)
7-3	Departure (Columbia)—Journey
7-10	Eat to the Beat (Chrysalis)—Blondie
7-17	Funkytown (S) (Casablanca)—Lipps, Inc.
7-24	Urban Cowboy (Asylum)—various artists (soundtrack)
8-19	Christopher Cross (Warner Bros.)—Christopher Cross
8-19	Xanadu (MCA)—Olivia Newton-John and Electric Light Orchestra (soundtrack)
9-10	Emotional Rescue (Rolling Stones)—Rolling Stones
9-15	Hold Out (Elektra)—Jackson Browne
9-25	Light Up the Night (A&M)—Brothers Johnson
9-29	Take Your Time (Do It Right) (S) (Tabu)—S.O.S.
10-1	The Game (Elektra)—Queen
10-13	Back in Black (Atlantic)—AC/DC
10-14	Give Me the Night (Warner Bros.)—George Benson

10-15 Panorama (Elektra)—Cars
10-15 ELO's Greatest Hits (Jet)—Electric Light Orchestra
10-30 Crimes of Passion (Chrysalis)—Pat Benatar
11-7 Full Moon (Epic)—Charlie Daniels Band
11-7 You Can Tune a Piano, But You Can't Tuna Fish (Epic)—REO Speedwagon
11-12 Honeysuckle Rose (Columbia)—Willie Nelson & Family (soundtrack)
11-12 TP (Philadelphia International)—Teddy Pendergrass
11-18 One Step Closer (Warner Bros.)—Doobie Brothers
11-19 Guilty (Columbia)—Barbra Streisand
11-25 Another One Bites the Dust (S) (Elektra)—Queen
11-26 Greatest Hits (Capitol)—Anne Murray
12-2 Greatest Hits (United Artists)—Kenny Rogers
12-8 In the Heat of the Night (Chrysalis)—Pat Benatar
12-10 Triumph (Epic)—Jacksons
12-12 The River (Columbia)—Bruce Springsteen
12-22 Annie (Columbia)—original cast
12-22 Celebrate Me Home (Columbia)—Kenny Loggins
12-30 Molly Hatchet (Epic)—Molly Hatchet

1981
1-7 Live (Asylum)—Eagles
1-10 Double Fantasy (Geffen)—John Lennon and Yoko Ono
1-12 Lost in Love (Arista)—Air Supply
1-14 The Jazz Singer (Capitol)—Neil Diamond (soundtrack)
1-22 Gaucho (MCA)—Steely Dan
1-26 Autoamerican (Chrysalis)—Blondie
2-2 Hi Infidelity (Epic)—REO Speedwagon
2-3 Heroes (Motown)—Commodores
2-3 Diana (Motown)—Diana Ross
2-3 Hotter than July (Tamla)—Stevie Wonder
2-4 Barry (Arista)—Barry Manilow
2-6 Middle Man (Columbia)—Boz Scaggs
2-23 Horizon (Elektra)—Eddie Rabbitt
2-25 Celebrate (De-Lite)—Kool & the Gang
2-25 2112 (Mercury)—Rush
2-27 Zenyatta Mondatta (A&M)—Police
3-4 All the World's a Stage (Mercury)—Rush
3-4 Foolish Behaviour (Warner Bros.)—Rod Stewart
3-19 Celebration (S) (De-Lite)—Kool & the Gang
3-19 Paradise Theater (A&M)—Styx
4-23 Gap Band III (Mercury)—Gap Band

4-27 Moving Pictures (Mercury)—Rush
5-6 Winelight (Elektra)—Grover Washington, Jr.
6-3 Dirty Deeds Done Dirt Cheap (Atlantic)—AC/DC
6-5 John Denver's Greatest Hits, Volume II (RCA)—John Denver
6-26 Arc of a Diver (Island)—Steve Winwood
7-7 Street Songs (Gordy)—Rick James
7-14 Greatest Hits (RCA)—Ronnie Milsap
7-16 Mistaken Identity (EMI/America)—Kim Carnes
7-29 Fancy Free (MCA)—Oak Ridge Boys
8-10 Hard Promises (Backstreet)—Tom Petty & the Heartbreakers
8-12 The Turn of a Friendly Card (Arista)—Alan Parsons Project
8-13 Somewhere over the Rainbow (Columbia)—Willie Nelson
8-18 Long Distance Voyager (Threshold)—Moody Blues
8-28 Share Your Love (Liberty)—Kenny Rogers
9-10 Precious Time (Chrysalis)—Pat Benatar
9-15 Feels So Right (RCA)—Alabama
9-15 Changesonebowie (RCA)—David Bowie
9-15 Fame (RSO)—soundtrack
9-18 Greatest Hits (Elektra)—Doors
9-18 4 (Atlantic)—Foreigner
9-18 Escape (Columbia)—Journey
9-18 Don't Say No (Capitol)—Billy Squier
9-18 Face Dances (Warner Bros.)—Who
10-7 The One That You Love (Arista)—Air Supply
10-7 Bella Donna (Modern)—Stevie Nicks
10-16 Endless Love (S) (Motown)—Diana Ross and Lionel Richie
10-30 Tattoo You (Rolling Stones)—Rolling Stones
11-4 Nine Tonight (Capitol)—Bob Seger & the Silver Bullet Band
11-10 The Innocent Age (Full Moon)—Dan Fogelberg
11-18 Fair Warning (Warner Bros.)—Van Halen
12-2 Working Class Dog (RCA)—Rick Springfield
12-13 Raise! (ARC/Columbia)—Earth, Wind & Fire
12-15 Ghost in the Machine (A&M)—Police
12-16 In the Pocket (Motown)—Commodores
12-16 Physical (MCA)—Olivia Newton-John
12-22 Private Eyes (RCA)—Hall & Oates
12-23 Captured (Columbia)—Journey
12-28 Something Special (De-Lite)—Kool & the Gang
12-30 Songs in the Attic (Columbia)—Billy Joel

| 12-30 | Best of Friends (Columbia)—Loggins and Messina |
| 12-30 | Greatest Hits (Elektra)—Queen |

1982

1-5	Physical (S) (MCA)—Olivia Newton-John
1-5	Juice (Capitol)—Juice Newton
1-5	Christmas (Liberty)—Kenny Rogers
1-7	Hooked on Classics (RCA)—Royal Philharmonic Orchestra
1-11	Freeze-Frame (EMI/America)—J. Geils Band
1-12	On the Way to the Sky (Columbia)—Neil Diamond
1-20	For Those about to Rock, We Salute You (Atlantic)—AC/DC
1-20	Shake It Up (Elektra)—Cars
1-22	Voices (RCA)—Hall & Oates
1-22	Why Do Fools Fall in Love (RCA)—Diana Ross
1-28	Tonight I'm Yours (Warner Bros.)—Rod Stewart
1-29	Memories (Columbia)—Barbra Streisand
2-8	Loverboy (Columbia)—Loverboy
2-24	The Dude (A&M)—Quincy Jones
2-24	Wild Eyed Southern Boys (A&M)—.38 Special
3-2	Beauty and the Beat (I.R.S.)—Go-Go's
3-8	Elvira (S) (MCA)—Oak Ridge Boys
3-12	Get Lucky (Columbia)—Loverboy
4-8	Chariots of Fire (Polydor)—Vangelis (soundtrack)
4-12	I Love Rock 'n' Roll (Boardwalk)—Joan Jett & the Blackhearts
4-16	The Oak Ridge Boys Greatest Hits (MCA)—Oak Ridge Boys
4-29	Mountain Music (RCA)—Alabama
5-3	Abacab (Atlantic)—Genesis
5-10	Diary of a Madman (Jet)—Ozzy Osbourne
5-11	When I Dream (Liberty)—Crystal Gayle
5-11	Success Hasn't Spoiled Me Yet (RCA)—Rick Springfield
6-2	Asia (Geffen)—Asia
6-15	Always on My Mind (Columbia)—Willie Nelson
6-15	Willie Nelson's Greatest Hits (& Some That Will Be) (Columbia)—Willie Nelson
6-18	Blizzard of Ozz (Jet)—Ozzy Osbourne
6-29	Tug of War (Columbia)—Paul McCartney
6-29	Quarterflash (Geffen)—Quarterflash
6-30	My Home's in Alabama (RCA)—Alabama
6-30	Diver Down (Warner Bros.)—Van Halen
7-9	Annie (Columbia)—soundtrack
7-12	Reach (Elektra)—Richard Simmons

8-11	Pretenders (Sire)—Pretenders
8-23	Eye of the Tiger (S) (Scotti Bros.)—Survivor
8-25	Mirage (Warner Bros.)—Fleetwood Mac
8-26	American Fool (Riva)—John Cougar
9-20	I Love Rock 'n' Roll (S) (Boardwalk)—Joan Jett & the Blackhearts
9-21	The Nature of the Beast (Capitol)—April Wine
9-21	Eye of the Tiger (Scotti Bros.)—Survivor
10-1	Breakin' Away (Warner Bros.)—Al Jarreau
10-1	Good Trouble (Epic)—REO Speedwagon
10-26	Emotions in Motion (Capitol)—Billy Squier
11-10	Signals (Mercury)—Rush
11-16	Abracadabra (Capitol)—Steve Miller Band
11-22	Business as Usual (Columbia)—Men at Work
11-29	Olivia's Greatest Hits Volume II (MCA)—Olivia Newton-John
12-1	Built for Speed (EMI/America)—Stray Cats
12-7	The Nylon Curtain (Columbia)—Billy Joel
12-9	Lionel Richie (Motown)—Lionel Richie
12-14	16 (Full Moon)—Chicago
12-16	Heartlight (Columbia)—Neil Diamond
12-16	H2O (RCA)—Hall & Oates
12-17	Gap Band IV (Polygram)—Gap Band
12-30	Midnight Love (Columbia)—Marvin Gaye
12-30	Toto IV (Columbia)—Toto

1983

1-7	Daylight Again (Atlantic)—Crosby, Stills & Nash
1-10	Combat Rock (Epic)—Clash
1-14	Welcome to My World (RCA)—Elvis Presley
1-24	Jane Fonda's Workout Record (Columbia)—Jane Fonda
1-31	Thriller (Epic)—Michael Jackson
2-1	Now and Forever (Arista)—Air Supply
2-4	Eye in the Sky (Arista)—Alan Parsons Project
2-4	Special Forces (A&M)—.38 Special
2-7	Coda (Swan Song)—Led Zeppelin
2-11	The Distance (Capitol)—Bob Seger & the Silver Bullet Band
3-7	Mickey (S) (Chrysalis)—Toni Basil
3-7	Get Nervous (Chrysalis)—Pat Benatar
3-7	Forever, For Always, For Love (Epic)—Luther Vandross
4-4	Frontiers (Columbia)—Journey
4-11	Pyromania (Mercury)—Def Leppard

4-18 Screaming for Vengeance (Columbia)—
Judas Priest

4-26 Rio (Capitol)—Duran Duran

4-29 Kilroy Was Here (A&M)—Styx

5-3 The Closer You Get (RCA)—Alabama

5-17 1999 (Warner Bros.)—Prince

5-23 The Final Cut (Columbia)—Pink Floyd

6-17 Flashdance (Casablanca)—soundtrack

6-20 Cargo (Columbia)—Men at Work

6-27 Let's Dance (EMI/America)—David
Bowie

7-18 Greatest Hits (Full Moon/Epic)—Dan
Fogelberg

8-12 Keep It Up (Columbia)—Loverboy

8-17 Cuts Like a Knife (A&M)—Bryan Adams

8-30 Synchronicity (A&M)—Police

8-30 Staying Alive (RSO)—soundtrack

9-12 The Wild Heart (Modern)—Stevie Nicks

9-14 Eliminator (Warner Bros.)—ZZ Top

9-30 Living In Oz (RCA)—Rick Springfield

10-3 An Innocent Man (Columbia)—Billy Joel

10-11 Alpha (Geffen)—Asia

10-11 Mental Health (Pasha)—Quiet Riot

10-12 Air Supply Greatest Hits (Arista)—Air
Supply

10-31 Eyes That See in the Dark (RCA)—Kenny
Rogers

11-7 Kissing to Be Clever (Virgin)—Culture
Club

11-7 Faster than the Speed of Night (Columbia)—Bonnie Tyler

11-18 High 'n' Dry (Mercury)—Def Leppard

12-7 Islands in the Stream (S) (RCA)—Kenny
Rogers and Dolly Parton

12-9 Live from Earth (Chrysalis)—Pat Benatar

12-12 Can't Slow Down (Motown—Lionel
Richie

12-14 No Parking on the Dance Floor (Solar)—
Midnight Star

12-14 What's New (Asylum)—Linda Ronstadt

12-16 Uh-Huh (Riva)—John Cougar Mellencamp

12-16 Genesis (Atlantic)—Genesis

12-19 Colour by Numbers (Virgin)—Culture
Club

12-20 Rock 'N' Soul, Part I (RCA)—Hall &
Oates

12-21 20 Greatest Hits (Liberty)—Kenny Rogers

12-29 I Am What I Am (Epic)—George Jones

1984

1-4 Undercover (Rolling Stones)—Rolling
Stones

1-5 Reach the Beach (MCA)—Fixx

1-9 Yentl (Columbia)—Barbra Streisand
(soundtrack)

1-12 The Principle of Moments (Atlantic)—
Robert Plant

1-16 Seven and the Ragged Tiger (Capitol)—
Duran Duran

1-16 Two of a Kind (MCA)—Olivia Newton-
John and John Travolta (soundtrack)

1-17 90125 (Atlantic)—Yes

2-7 Shout at the Devil (Elektra)—Motley Crue

2-17 Pipes of Peace (Columbia)—Paul Mc-
Cartney

2-29 Sports (Chrysalis)—Huey Lewis & the
News

3-8 Blackout (Mercury)—Scorpions

3-12 1984 (Warner Bros.)—Van Halen

3-29 The Big Chill (Motown)—soundtrack

4-2 Roll On (RCA)—Alabama

4-2 Footloose (Columbia)—soundtrack

4-18 Learning to Crawl (Sire)—Pretenders

4-30 Love at First Sting (Mercury)—Scorpions

5-7 She's So Unusual (Portrait)—Cyndi
Lauper

5-11 Deguello (Warner Bros.)—ZZ Top

5-17 Heartbeat City (Elektra)—Cars

5-21 Tour De Force (A&M)—.38 Special

6-19 Midnight Madness (MCA)—Night Ranger

6-20 Rebel Yell (Chrysalis)—Billy Idol

6-26 Grace under Pressure (Mercury)—Rush

7-10 Hard to Hold (RCA)—Rick Springfield

7-13 Street Talk (Columbia)—Steve Perry

7-27 Breakin' (Polydor)—soundtrack

8-6 Out of the Cellar (Atlantic)—Ratt

8-7 Poncho & Lefty (Columbia)—Merle Haggard and Willie Nelson

8-7 Born in the U.S.A. (Columbia)—Bruce
Springsteen

8-14 Madonna (Sire)—Madonna

8-15 Outlandos D'Amour (A&M)—Police

8-17 Julio (Columbia)—Julio Iglesias

8-21 Private Dancer (Capitol)—Tina Turner

8-21 Hank Williams Jr.'s Greatest Hits
(Curb)—Hank Williams, Jr.

8-21 When Doves Cry (S) (Warner Bros.)—
Prince

8-23 Ghostbusters (Arista)—soundtrack

8-29 Purple Rain (Warner Bros.)—Prince & the
Revolution (soundtrack)

8-31 Victory (Epic)—Jacksons

9-17 Condition Critical (Pasha)—Quiet Riot

10-1 Signs of Life (Jive)—Billy Squier

10-2 Into the Gap (Arista)—Thompson Twins

10-3 Stay Hungry (Atlantic)—Twisted Sister

10-4 Touch (RCA)—Eurythmics

10-4 Break Out (Planet)—Pointer Sisters

10-5 12 Greatest Hits Volume II (Columbia)—Neil Diamond

10-5 Eddie & the Cruisers (Scotti Bros.)—soundtrack

10-17 Chicago 17 (Full Moon)—Chicago

10-22 1100 Bel Air Place (Columbia)—Julio Iglesias

11-8 The Woman in Red (Motown)—soundtrack

11-21 Tonight (EMI/America)—David Bowie

11-21 Star Wars (Disneyland)—various artists

12-3 Big Bam Boom (RCA)—Hall & Oates

12-3 What about Me (RCA)—Kenny Rogers

12-3 Once upon a Christmas (RCA)—Kenny Rogers and Dolly Parton

12-12 Animalize (Mercury)—Kiss

12-13 Volume I (Atlantic)—Honeydrippers

12-18 I Feel for You (Warner Bros.)—Chaka Khan

12-18 Emotion (Columbia)—Barbra Streisand

12-28 Waking Up with the House on Fire (Epic)—Culture Club

12-28 Make It Big (Columbia)—Wham!

1985

1-2 Suddenly (Jive)—Billy Ocean

1-2 Busy Body (Epic)—Luther Vandross

1-4 Duran Duran (Capitol)—Duran Duran

1-9 Tropico (Chrysalis)—Pat Benatar

1-10 Arena (Capitol)—Duran Duran

1-10 Ice Cream Castle (Warner Bros.)—Time

1-11 Controversy (Warner Bros.)—Prince

1-17 New Edition (MCA)—New Edition

1-17 Lush Life (Elektra)—Linda Ronstadt

1-21 Hooked on Swing (RCA)—Larry Elgart

1-23 Like a Virgin (Sire)—Madonna

2-5 Reckless (A&M)—Bryan Adams

2-7 The Unforgettable Fire (Island)—U2

2-11 Agent Provocateur (Atlantic)—Foreigner

2-25 War (Island)—U2

3-11 Wheels Are Turnin' (Epic)—REO Speedwagon

3-12 Centerfield (Warner Bros.)—John Fogerty

3-13 Hello, I Must Be Going! (Atlantic)—Phil Collins

3-13 Valotte (Atlantic)—Julian Lennon

3-15 A Private Heaven (EMI/America)—Sheena Easton

3-22 Theatre of Pain (Elektra)—Motley Crue

4-1 We Are the World (Columbia)—USA for Africa

4-1 Beverly Hills Cop (MCA)—soundtrack

4-1 40 Hour Week (RCA)—Alabama

4-9 Perfect Strangers (Mercury)—Deep Purple

4-9 Building the Perfect Beast (Geffen)—Don Henley

4-16 Comedian (Columbia)—Eddie Murphy

4-16 Warrior (Columbia)—Scandal Featuring Patty Smyth

4-18 No Jacket Required (Atlantic)—Phil Collins

5-6 Diamond Life (Portrait)—Sade

5-21 The Night I Fell in Love (Epic)—Luther Vandross

6-11 Crazy from the Heat (Warner Bros.)—Van Halen

6-24 Age to Age (Myrrh)—Amy Grant

6-24 She's the Boss (Columbia)—Mick Jagger

6-24 Vital Signs (Scotti Bros.)—Survivor

6-25 Songs from the Big Chair (Mercury)—Tears for Fears

7-2 Around the World in a Day (Paisley Park)—Prince and the Revolution

7-12 Emergency (De-Lite)—Kool & the Gang

7-16 Vision Quest (Geffen)—soundtrack

7-18 Under a Blood Red Sky (Island)—U2

7-31 Invasion of Your Privacy (Atlantic)—Ratt

8-8 The Power Station (Capitol)—Power Station

8-13 Brothers in Arms (Warner Bros.)—Dire Straits

8-26 Whitney Houston (Arista)—Whitney Houston

8-28 The Dream of the Blue Turtles (A&M)—Sting

9-3 Contact (RCA)—Pointer Sisters

9-13 Be Yourself Tonight (RCA)—Eurythmics

9-18 Face Value (Atlantic)—Phil Collins

9-20 Southern Nights (MCA)—Tom Petty & the Heartbreakers

9-26 Rock Me Tonight (Capitol)—Freddie Jackson

9-30 Heart (Capitol)—Heart

10-10 O Holy Night (London)—Luciano Pavarotti

10-18 Greatest Hits Volume I and II (Columbia)—Billy Joel

10-24 Scarecrow (Riva)—John Cougar Mellencamp

11-1 Keep the Fire (Columbia)—Kenny Loggins

11-1 Lovin' Every Minute of It (Columbia)—Loverboy

11-13 Little Creatures (Sire)—Talking Heads

11-13 In Square Circle (Motown)—Stevie Wonder

11-15 Alabama Christmas (RCA)—Alabama

11-15 7 Wishes (MCA)—Night Ranger

11-19 VOA (Geffen)—Sammy Hagar

839

10-13 I Started Out as a Child (Warner Bros.)—Bill Cosby

10-13 The Best of Bill Cosby (Warner Bros.)—Bill Cosby

10-13 Wonderfulness (Warner Bros.)—Bill Cosby

10-13 Machine Head (Warner Bros.)—Deep Purple

10-13 Made in Japan (Warner Bros.)—Deep Purple

10-13 The Captain and Me (Warner Bros.)—Doobie Brothers

10-13 Toulouse Street (Warner Bros.)—Doobie Brothers

10-13 What Were Once Vices Are Now Habits (Warner Bros.)—Doobie Brothers

10-13 Fleetwood Mac (Reprise)—Fleetwood Mac

10-13 Fool for the City (Bearsville)—Foghat

10-13 American Beauty (Warner Bros.)—Grateful Dead

10-13 Workingman's Dead (Warner Bros.)—Grateful Dead

10-13 Alice's Restaurant (Reprise)—Arlo Guthrie

10-13 Are You Experienced? (Reprise)—Jimi Hendrix

10-13 Axis: Bold as Love (Reprise)—Jimi Hendrix

10-13 Electric Ladyland (Reprise)—Jimi Hendrix

10-13 Smash Hits (Reprise)—Jimi Hendrix

10-13 Gord's Gold (Reprise)—Gordon Lightfoot

10-13 Sundown (Reprise)—Gordon Lightfoot

10-13 Blue (Reprise)—Joni Mitchell

10-13 Ladies of the Canyon (Reprise)—Joni Mitchell

10-13 Montrose (Warner Bros.)—Montrose

10-13 Moondance (Warner Bros.)—Van Morrison

10-13 Peter, Paul and Mary (Warner Bros.)—Peter, Paul and Mary

10-13 The Best of Peter, Paul and Mary: (Ten) Years Together (Warner Bros.)—Peter, Paul and Mary

10-13 Is It Something I Said? (Reprise)—Richard Pryor

10-13 Seals & Crofts' Greatest Hits (Warner Bros.)—Seals & Crofts

10-13 Frank Sinatra's Greatest Hits (Reprise)—Frank Sinatra

10-13 Camelot (Warner Bros.)—soundtrack

10-13 Mud Slide Slim & the Blue Horizon (Warner Bros.)—James Taylor

10-13 Sweet Baby James (Warner Bros.)—James Taylor

10-13 Disney's Children's Favorites Volume II (Disneyland)—various artists

10-13 The Dream Weaver (Warner Bros.)—Gary Wright

10-13 After the Gold Rush (Reprise)—Neil Young

10-13 Everybody Knows This Is Nowhere (Reprise)—Neil Young

10-13 Harvest (Reprise)—Neil Young

10-15 Slippery When Wet (Mercury)—Bon Jovi

10-16 Dancing on the Ceiling (Motown)—Lionel Richie

10-24 Rapture (Elektra)—Anita Baker

11-6 Piece of Mind (Capitol)—Iron Maiden

11-6 Break Every Rule (Capitol)—Tina Turner

11-21 Aerosmith (Columbia)—Aerosmith

11-21 Get Your Wings (Columbia)—Aerosmith

11-21 Toys in the Attic (Columbia)—Aerosmith

11-21 Rose Garden (Columbia)—Lynn Anderson

11-21 Blow by Blow (Epic)—Jeff Beck

11-21 Wired (Epic)—Jeff Beck

11-21 Blood, Sweat & Tears Greatest Hits (Columbia)—Blood, Sweat & Tears

11-21 Blood, Sweat & Tears (Columbia)—Blood, Sweat & Tears

11-21 The Byrds Greatest Hits (Columbia)—Byrds

11-21 Switched On Bach (CBS)—Wendy Carlos

11-21 Johnny Cash's Greatest Hits (Columbia)—Johnny Cash

11-21 Johnny Cash at San Quentin (Columbia)—Johnny Cash

11-21 Johnny Cash at Folsom Prison (Columbia)—Johnny Cash

11-21 Chicago Transit Authority (Columbia)—Chicago

11-21 Chicago at Carnegie Hall I–IV (Columbia)—Chicago

11-21 Chicago III (Columbia)—Chicago

11-21 Chicago V (Columbia)—Chicago

11-21 Chicago VI (Columbia)—Chicago

11-21 Chicago VII (Columbia)—Chicago

11-21 Chicago VIII (Columbia)—Chicago

11-21 Chicago IX—Chicago's Greatest Hits (Columbia)—Chicago

11-21 Somewhere My Love (Columbia)—Ray Conniff

11-21 Baby, Don't Get Hooked on Me (Columbia)—Mac Davis

11-21 Serenade (Columbia)—Neil Diamond

11-21 Bob Dylan's Greatest Hits (Columbia)—Bob Dylan

11-21 Bob Dylan's Greatest Hits Volume II (Columbia)—Bob Dylan

11-21 Nashville Skyline (Columbia)—Bob Dylan

11-21 Gratitude (Columbia)—Earth, Wind & Fire

11-21 Open Our Eyes (Columbia)—Earth, Wind & Fire

11-21 That's the Way of the World (Columbia)—Earth, Wind & Fire

11-21 Souvenirs (Epic)—Dan Fogelberg

11-21 Breakaway (Columbia)—Art Garfunkel

11-21 Head Hunters (Columbia)—Herbie Hancock

11-21 Johnny Horton's Greatest Hits (Columbia)—Johnny Horton

11-21 Between the Lines (Columbia)—Janis Ian

11-21 Piano Man (Columbia)—Billy Joel

11-21 Cheap Thrills (Columbia)—Janis Joplin

11-21 Pearl (Columbia)—Janis Joplin

11-21 Janis Joplin's Greatest Hits (Columbia)—Janis Joplin

11-21 Loggins and Messina (Columbia)—Loggins and Messina

11-21 All-Time Greatest Hits (Columbia)—Johnny Mathis

11-21 Heavenly (Columbia)—Johnny Mathis

11-21 Johnny's Greatest Hits (Columbia)—Johnny Mathis

11-21 Merry Christmas (Columbia)—Johnny Mathis

11-21 Red Headed Stranger (Columbia)—Willie Nelson

11-21 Ted Nugent (Epic)—Ted Nugent

11-21 Family Reunion (Philadelphia International)—O'Jays

11-21 My Fair Lady (Columbia)—original cast

11-21 Sesame Street Original TV Cast Album (Columbia)—original cast

11-21 Wish You Were Here (Columbia)—Pink Floyd

11-21 Gary Puckett & the Union Gap's Greatest Hits (Columbia)—Gary Puckett & the Union Gap

11-21 Behind Closed Doors (Epic)—Charlie Rich

11-21 Gunfighter Ballads & Trail Songs (Columbia)—Marty Robbins

11-21 Abraxas (Columbia)—Santana

11-21 Caravanserai (Columbia)—Santana

11-21 Santana's Greatest Hits (Columbia)—Santana

11-21 Santana (Columbia)—Santana

11-21 Carlos Santana & Buddy Miles 'Live' (Columbia)—Carlos Santana and Buddy Miles

11-21 Parsley, Sage, Rosemary & Thyme (Columbia)—Simon and Garfunkel

11-21 Bookends (Columbia)—Simon and Garfunkel

11-21 Bridge over Troubled Water (Columbia)—Simon and Garfunkel

11-21 Simon and Garfunkel's Greatest Hits (Columbia)—Simon and Garfunkel

11-21 Paul Simon (Columbia)—Paul Simon

11-21 There Goes Rhymin' Simon (Columbia)—Paul Simon

11-21 Stand! (Epic)—Sly and the Family Stone

11-21 Sly and the Family Stone's Greatest Hits (Epic)—Sly and the Family Stone

11-21 Funny Girl (Columbia)—soundtrack

11-21 Jonathan Livingston Seagull (Columbia)—soundtrack

11-21 West Side Story (Columbia)—soundtrack

11-21 Born to Run (Columbia)—Bruce Springsteen

11-21 Christmas Album (Columbia)—Barbra Streisand

11-21 Greatest Hits (Columbia)—Barbra Streisand

11-21 Live in Concert at the Forum (Columbia)—Barbra Streisand

11-21 My Name Is Barbra, Two (Columbia)—Barbra Streisand

11-21 Stoney End (Columbia)—Barbra Streisand

11-21 The Way We Were (Columbia)—Barbra Streisand

11-21 A Space in Time (Columbia)—Ten Years After

11-21 Love Story (Columbia)—Andy Williams

11-21 The Andy Williams Christmas Album (Columbia)—Andy Williams

11-21 They Only Come Out at Night (Epic)—Edgar Winter Group

11-24 True Colors (Portrait)—Cyndi Lauper

11-25 Third Stage (MCA)—Boston

12-4 Fore! (Chrysalis)—Huey Lewis & the News

12-8 Give Me the Reason (Epic)—Luther Vandross

12-8 Never Too Much (Epic)—Luther Vandross

12-9 Word Up (Atlanta Artists)—Cameo

12-9 Night Songs (Mercury)—Cinderella

12-9 The Way It Is (RCA)—Bruce Hornsby & the Range

12-15 Skeletons from the Closet (Warner Bros.)—Grateful Dead

12-15 Speaking in Tongues (Sire)—Talking Heads

12-16 Different Light (Columbia)—Bangles

12-22 Graceland (Warner Bros.)—Paul Simon

12-22 Decade (Reprise)—Neil Young

1987

1-6 The Touch (RCA)—Alabama

1-13 Whiplash Smile (Chrysalis)—Billy Idol
1-13 Every Breath You Take The Singles (A&M)—Police
1-15 Then & Now . . . The Best of the Monkees (Arista)—Monkees
1-20 Just Like the First Time (Capitol)—Freddie Jackson
1-20 Notorious (Capitol)—Duran Duran
2-2 Licenced to Ill (Columbia)—Beastie Boys
2-2 Bruce Springsteen & the E Street Band Live 1975–85 (Columbia)—Bruce Springsteen
2-3 The Last in Line (Warner Bros.)—Dio
2-10 Storms of Life (Warner Bros.)—Randy Travis
2-18 King of Rock (Profile)—Run–D.M.C.
2-19 7800° Fahrenheit (Mercury)—Bon Jovi
2-26 Dancing under Cover (Atlantic)—Ratt
2-26 George Strait's Greatest Hits (MCA)—George Strait
3-24 Who Made Who (Atlantic)—AC/DC
4-7 Life, Love & Pain (Warner Bros.)—Club Nouveau
4-14 Bon Jovi (Mercury)—Bon Jovi
4-14 Under Lock and Key (Elektra)—Dokken
4-23 Look What the Cat Dragged In (Capitol)—Poison
5-13 The Joshua Tree (Island)—U2
5-22 Escape (Jive)—Whodini
6-1 Morning Dance (MCA)—Spyro Gyra
6-8 Into the Fire (A&M)—Bryan Adams
6-10 L.A. Woman (Elektra)—Doors
6-10 The Best of the Doors (Elektra)—Doors
6-10 13 (Elektra)—Doors
6-10 The Soft Parade (Elektra)—Doors
6-10 The Doors (Elektra)—Doors
6-10 Waiting for the Sun (Elektra)—Doors
6-12 Duotones (Arista)—Kenny G
7-1 Tango in the Night (Warner Bros.)—Fleetwood Mac
7-1 Whitesnake (Geffen)—Whitesnake
7-2 Sign o' the Times (Warner Bros.)—Prince
7-8 The Joker (Capitol)—Steve Miller Band
7-14 Bad Animals (Capitol)—Heart
7-14 Trio (Warner Bros.)—Dolly Parton, Linda Ronstadt, Emmylou Harris
7-14 Always and Forever (Warner Bros.)—Randy Travis
7-15 Girls, Girls, Girls (Elektra)—Motley Crue
7-21 Nuthin' Fancy (MCA)—Lynyrd Skynyrd
7-21 Pronounced Leh-nerd Skin-nerd (MCA)—Lynyrd Skynyrd
7-21 Second Helping (MCA)—Lynyrd Skynyrd
7-22 Too Fast for Love (Elektra)—Motley Crue
7-28 Whitney (Arista)—Whitney Houston
7-30 The Jets (MCA)—Jets

8-11 The Final Countdown (Epic)—Europe
8-11 Bigger and Deffer (Columbia)—L.L. Cool J
8-11 Spanish Fly (Columbia)—Lisa Lisa and Cult Jam
8-11 Can't Hold Back (Columbia)—Eddie Money
8-11 No Control (Columbia)—Eddie Money
8-11 Beverly Hills Cop II (MCA)—soundtrack
8-19 Christmas Wishes (Capitol)—Anne Murray
8-19 New Kind of Feeling (Capitol)—Anne Murray
8-24 Georgia Satellites (Elektra)—Georgia Satellites
9-2 Barry Manilow II (Arista)—Barry Manilow
9-2 Tryin' to Get the Feeling (Arista)—Barry Manilow
9-15 La Bamba (Slash/Warner Bros.)—soundtrack
9-16 Crushin' (Polydor/Polygram)—Fat Boys
9-18 In the Dark (Arista)—Grateful Dead
9-29 Who's That Girl (Sire)—Madonna (soundtrack)
10-7 Hysteria (Mercury)—Def Leppard
10-22 The Lonesome Jubilee (Mercury)—John Cougar Mellencamp
10-22 Exposure (Arista)—Expose
10-22 Dirty Dancing (RCA)—soundtrack
11-9 Bad (Epic)—Michael Jackson
11-9 A Momentary Lapse of Reason (Columbia)—Pink Floyd
11-9 Exit . . . Stage Left (Mercury)—Rush
11-9 Permanent Waves (Mercury)—Rush
11-10 Slide It In (Geffen)—Whitesnake
11-13 Greatest Hits (MCA)—Patsy Cline
12-1 Ocean Front Property (MCA)—George Strait
12-3 Tiffany (MCA)—Tiffany
12-7 Jody Watley (MCA)—Jody Watley
12-8 Permanent Vacation (Geffen)—Aerosmith
12-15 Nothing Like the Sun (A&M)—Sting
12-15 A Very Special Christmas (A&M)—various artists
12-17 Autumn (Windham Hill)—George Winston
12-17 Winter into Spring (Windham Hill)—George Winston
12-22 Kick (Atlantic)—Inxs
12-31 Tunnel of Love (Columbia)—Bruce Springsteen

1988

1-6 To Hell with the Devil (Enigma)—Stryper

9-27 Small World (Chrysalis)—Huey Lewis and the News

9-27 Cocktail (Elektra)—soundtrack

9-28 Don't Be Cruel (MCA)—Bobby Brown

9-28 Lap of Luxury (Epic)—Cheap Trick

9-28 Heart Break (MCA)—New Edition

10-31 And Justice for All (Elektra)—Metallica

11-1 Mannheim Steamroller Christmas (AMG)—Mannheim Steamroller

11-3 Heavy Nova (EMI America)—Robert Palmer

11-7 Tell It to My Heart (Arista)—Dayne Taylor

11-14 How Ya Like Me Now (Jive)—Kool Moe Dee

11-18 New Jersey (Mercury)—Bon Jovi

11-21 Diesel and Dust (Columbia)—Midnight Oil

11-29 Silhouette (Arista)—Kenny G

11-30 Oooh Yeah! (Arista)—Hall & Oates

12-5 Cats (Geffen)—Original Cast

12-6 Out of Order (Warner Bros.)—Rod Stewart

12-6 Rattle and Hum (Island)—U2

12-12 Giving You the Best that I Got (Elektra)—Anita Baker

12-19 Any Love (Epic)—Luther Vandross

12-21 Till I Loved You (Columbia)—Barbra Streisand

1989

1-4 Traveling Wilburys (Warner Bros.)—Traveling Wilburys

1-10 Kokomo (S) (Elektra)—The Beach Boys

1-17 Up Where We Belong (S) (Island)—Joe Cocker & Jennifer Warnes

1-20 Hold An Old Friend's Hand (MCA)—Tiffany

1-23 A Decade of Hits (Epic)—Charlie Daniels Band

1-23 Greatest Hits (Columbia)—Journey

1-23 Delicate Sound of Thunder (Columbia)—Pink Floyd

1-25 Heartland (RCA)—The Judds

1-27 American Dream (Atlantic)—Crosby, Stills Nash & Young

2-1 Shooting Rubberbands at the Stars (Geffen)—Edie Brickell & New Bohemians

2-1 19 (RPS)—Chicago

2-1 Greatest Hits (Warner Bros.)—Fleetwood Mac

2-1 Smashes, Thrashes & Hits (Mercury)—Kiss

2-3 Wild Things (S) (Broadway)—Tone Loc

2-13 I Wanna Dance With Somebody (Who Loves Me) (S) (Arista)—Whitney Houston

2-13 Tell It to My Heart (S) (Arista)—Dayne Taylor

2-14 10 from 6 (Atlantic)—Bad Company

2-14 The Music Machine (BRD)—Candle

2-14 Out of This World (Epic)—Europe

2-14 Beat It (S) (Epic)—Michael Jackson

2-14 Billie Jean (S) (Epic)—Michael Jackson

2-14 Don't Stop 'Til You Get Enough (S) (Epic)—Michael Jackson

2-14 Rock With You (S) (Epic)—Michael Jackson

2-14 Enjoy Yourself (S) (Epic)—Michael Jackson

2-14 Aldo Nova (Portrait)—Aldo Nova

2-14 Green (Warner Bros.)—R.E.M.

2-17 Up Your Alley (CBS)—Joan Jett & the Blackhearts

2-22 Upstairs at Eric's (Sire)—Yaz

3-1 G 'N R Lies (Geffen)—Guns 'N Roses

3-7 Guy (MCA)—Guy

3-9 Forever Your Girl (Virgin)—Paula Abdul

3-16 Tooth and Nail (Elektra)—Dokken

3-16 Electric Youth (Atlantic)—Debbie Gibson

3-21 Holy Diver (Warner Bros.)—Dio

3-29 Straight Up (S) (Virgin)—Paula Abdul

3-29 Hangin' Tough (Columbia)—New Kids on the Block

3-29 Mystery Girl (Virgin)—Roy Orbison

4-4 Girl You Know It's True (Arista)—Milli Vanilli

4-4 Karyn White (Warner Bros.)—Karyn White

4-12 Retrospect (Atco)—Buffalo Springfield

4-17 Everything (Columbia)—Bangles

4-17 Girls Just Want to Have Fun (S) (Portrait)—Cyndi Lauper

4-17 Vivid (Epic)—Living Colour

4-17 No Rest for the Wicked (CBS)—Ozzy Osbourne

4-17 Keep on Loving You (S) (Epic)—R.E.O. Speedwagon

4-17 Ridin' the Storm Out (Epic)—R.E.O. Speedwagon

4-21 The Raw & the Cooked (I.R.S.)—Fine Young Cannibals

5-4 Standing on a Beach—The Singles (Elektra)—The Cure

5-5 Greatest Hits Volume 2 (RCA)—Ronnie Millsap

5-8 Perhaps Love (CMA)—Placido Domingo

5-9 On Through the Night (Mercury)—Def Leppard

5-9 Funky Cold Medina (S) (DEL)—Tone Loc

5-9 Loc'ed After Dark (DEL)—Tone Loc

APPENDIX B

National Academy of Recording Arts and Sciences

Grammy Winner by Category (Selected Categories)

Over the years, various award categories have been added and/or dropped by the National Academy of Recording Arts and Sciences (NARAS) since the awards were first presented for the year 1958. In some categories, awards are variously given to singles, albums, and album tracks. These distinctions are noted (S), (A), and (T), respectively, whenever they can be determined from information provided by NARAS.

RECORD OF THE YEAR
(single)

1958 Nel Blu Dipinto Di Blu (Volare)—Domenico Modugno

1959 Mack the Knife—Bobby Darin; A&R: Ahmet Ertegun

1960 Theme from *A Summer Place*—Percy Faith; A&R: Ernest Altschuler

1961 Moon River—Henry Mancini; A&R: Dick Pierce

1962 I Left My Heart in San Francisco—Tony Bennett; A&R: Ernest Altschuler

1963 The Days of Wine and Roses—Henry Mancini; A&R: Steve Sholes

1964 The Girl from Ipanema—Stan Getz and Astrud Gilberto; A&R: Creed Taylor

1965 A Taste of Honey—Herb Albert & the Tijuana Brass; A&R: Herb Alpert and Jerry Moss

1966 Strangers in the Night—Frank Sinatra; A&R: Jimmy Bowen

1967 Up, Up and Away—5th Dimension; A&R: Marc Gordon and Johnny Rivers

1968 Mrs. Robinson—Simon and Garfunkel; A&R: Paul Simon, Art Garfunkel, and Roy Halee

1969 Aquarius/Let the Sunshine In—5th Dimension; A&R: Bones Howe

1970 Bridge over Troubled Water—Simon and Garfunkel; A&R: Paul Simon, Art Garfunkel, and Roy Halee

1971 It's Too Late—Carole King; A&R: Lou Adler

1972 The First Time Ever I Saw Your Face—Roberta Flack; A&R: Joel Dorn

1973 Killing Me Softly with His Song—Roberta Flack

1974 I Honestly Love You—Olivia Newton-John; prod.: John Farrar

1975 Love Will Keep Us Together—Captain & Tennille; prod.: Daryl Dragon

1976 This Masquerade—George Benson; prod.: Tommy Lipuma

1977 Hotel California—Eagles; prod.: Bill Szymczyk

1978 Just the Way You Are—Billy Joel; prod.: Phil Ramone

1979 What a Fool Believes—Doobie Brothers; prod.: Ted Templeman

1980 Sailing—Christopher Cross; prod.: Michael Omartian

1981 Bette Davis Eyes—Kim Carnes; prod.: Val Garay

1982 Rosanna—Toto; prod.: Toto

1983 Beat It—Michael Jackson; prod.: Quincy Jones and Michael Jackson

1984 What's Love Got to Do with It—Tina Turner; prod.: Terry Britten

1985 We Are the World—USA for Africa; prod.: Quincy Jones

1986 Higher Love—Steve Winwood; prod.: Russ Titelman and Steve Winwood

1987 Graceland—Paul Simon; prod.: Paul Simon

1988 Don't Worry Be Happy—Bobby McFerrin; prod: Linda Goldstein

ALBUM OF THE YEAR

1958 The Music from "Peter Gunn"—Henry Mancini

1959 Come Dance with Me—Frank Sinatra; A&R: Dave Cavanaugh

1960 Button-Down Mind—Bob Newhart; A&R: George Avakian

1961 Judy at Carnegie Hall—Judy Garland; A&R: Andrew Wiswell

1962 The First Family—Vaughn Meader; A&R: Bob Booker and Earle Doud

1963	The Barbra Streisand Album—Barbra Streisand; A&R: Mike Berniker
1964	Getz/Gilberto—Stan Getz and Joao Gilberto; A&R: Creed Taylor
1965	September of My Years—Frank Sinatra; A&R: Sonny Burke
1966	Sinatra: A Man & His Music—Frank Sinatra; A&R: Sonny Burke
1967	Sgt. Pepper's Lonely Hearts Club Band—Beatles; A&R: George Martin
1968	By the Time I Get to Phoenix—Glen Campbell; A&R: Al de Lory
1969	Blood, Sweat & Tears—Blood, Sweat & Tears; A&R: James Guercio
1970	Bridge over Troubled Water—Simon and Garfunkel; A&R: Paul Simon, Art Garfunkel, and Roy Halee
1971	Tapestry—Carole King; A&R: Lou Adler
1972	The Concert for Bangla Desh—George Harrison, Ravi Shankar, Bob Dylan, Leon Russell, Ringo Starr, Billy Preston, Eric Clapton, and Klaus Voormann; A&R: George Harrison and Phil Spector
1973	Innervisions—Stevie Wonder; prod.: Stevie Wonder
1974	Fulfillingness First Finale—Stevie Wonder; prod.: Stevie Wonder
1975	Still Crazy after All These Years—Paul Simon; prod.: Paul Simon and Phil Ramone
1976	Songs in the Key of Life—Stevie Wonder; prod.: Stevie Wonder
1977	Rumours—Fleetwood Mac; prod.: Fleetwood Mac, Richard Dashut, and Ken Caillat
1978	Saturday Night Fever—Bee Gees, David Shire, Yvonne Elliman, Tavares, Kool & the Gang, K.C. and the Sunshine Band, MFSB, Trammps, Walter Murphy, and Ralph MacDonald; prod.: Bee Gees, Karl Richardson, Albhy Galuten, Freddie Perren, Bill Oakes, David Shire, Arif Mardin, Thomas J. Valentino, Ralph MacDonald, W. Salter, K.G. Production, H.W. Casey, Richard Finch, Bobby Martin, Broadway Eddie, and Ron Kersey
1979	52nd Street—Billy Joel; prod.: Phil Ramone
1980	Christopher Cross—Christopher Cross; prod.: Michael Omartian
1981	Double Fantasy—John Lennon and Yoko Ono; prod.: John Lennon, Yoko Ono, and Jack Douglas
1982	Toto IV—Toto; prod.: Toto
1983	Thriller—Michael Jackson; prod.: Quincy Jones
1984	Can't Slow Down—Lionel Richie; prod.: Lionel Richie and James Anthony Carmichael
1985	No Jacket Required—Phil Collins; prod.: Phil Collins and Hugh Padgham
1986	Graceland—Paul Simon; prod.: Paul Simon
1987	The Joshua Tree—U2; prod.: Daniel Lanois and Brian Eno
1988	Faith—George Michael; prod: George Michael

SONG OF THE YEAR
(Songwriter's Award)

1958	Nel Blu Dipinto Di Blu (Volare)—Domenico Modugno
1959	The Battle of New Orleans—Jimmy Driftwood
1960	Theme from *Exodus*—Ernest Gold
1961	Moon River—Henry Mancini and Johnny Mercer
1962	What Kind of Fool Am I—Leslie Bricusse and Anthony Newley
1963	The Days of Wine and Roses—Henry Mancini and Johnny Mercer
1964	Hello, Dolly!—Jerry Herman
1965	The Shadow of Your Smile (Love Theme from *The Sandpiper*)—Paul Francis Webster and Johnny Mandel
1966	Michelle—John Lennon and Paul McCartney
1967	Up, Up and Away—Jim Webb
1968	Little Green Apples—Bobby Russell
1969	Games People Play—Joe South
1970	Bridge over Troubled Water—Paul Simon
1971	You've Got a Friend—Carole King
1972	The First Time Ever I Saw Your Face—Ewan MacColl
1973	Killing Me Softly with His Song—Norman Gimbel and Charles Fox
1974	The Way We Were—Marilyn and Alan Bergman and Marvin Hamlisch
1975	Send in the Clowns—Stephen Sondheim
1976	I Write the Songs—Bruce Johnston
1977	(tie) Love Theme from *A Star Is Born* (Evergreen)—Barbra Streisand and Paul Williams; You Light Up My Life—Joe Brooks
1978	Just the Way You Are—Billy Joel
1979	What a Fool Believes—Kenny Loggins and Michael McDonald
1980	Sailing—Christopher Cross
1981	Bette Davis Eyes—Donna Weiss and Jackie DeShannon
1982	Always on my Mind—Johnny Christopher, Mark James, and Wayne Carson
1983	Every Breath You Take—Sting
1984	What's Love Got To Do with It—Graham Lyle and Terry Britten

1985	We Are the World—Michael Jackson and Lionel Richie
1986	That's What Friends Are For—Burt Bacharach and Carole Bayer Sager
1987	Somewhere out There—James Horner, Barry Mann, and Cynthia Weil
1988	Don't Worry Be Happy—Bobby McFerrin

BEST NEW ARTIST OF THE YEAR

1959	Bobby Darin
1960	Bob Newhart
1961	Peter Nero
1962	Robert Goulet
1963	Swingle Singers
1964	Beatles
1965	Tom Jones
1966	No award
1967	Bobbie Gentry
1968	Jose Feliciano
1969	Crosby, Stills & Nash
1970	Carpenters
1971	Carly Simon
1972	America
1973	Bette Midler
1974	Marvin Hamlisch
1975	Natalie Cole
1976	Starland Vocal Band
1977	Debby Boone
1978	A Taste of Honey
1979	Rickie Lee Jones
1980	Christopher Cross
1981	Sheena Easton
1982	Men at Work
1983	Culture Club
1984	Cyndi Lauper
1985	Sade
1986	Bruce Hornsby and the Range
1987	Jody Watley
1988	Tracy Chapman

BEST VOCAL PERFORMANCE, FEMALE

1958	Ella Fitzerald Sings the Irving Berlin Songbook—Ella Fitzgerald (A)
1959	But Not for Me—Ella Fitzgerald
1960	Mack the Knife (S), Ella in Berlin (A)—Ella Fitzgerald
1961	Judy at Carnegie Hall—Judy Garland (A)
1962	Ella Swings Brightly with Nelson Riddle—Ella Fitzgerald (A)
1963	The Barbra Streisand Album—Barbra Streisand (A)
1964	People—Barbra Streisand (S)
1965	My Name Is Barbra—Barbra Streisand (A)

| 1966 | If He Walked into My Life—Eydie Gorme (S) |
| 1967 | Ode to Billie Joe—Bobbie Gentry (S) |

BEST VOCAL PERFORMANCE, MALE

1958	Catch a Falling Star—Perry Como (S)
1959	Come Dance with Me—Frank Sinatra (S)
1960	Genius of Ray Charles (A), Georgia on my Mind (S)—Ray Charles
1961	Lollipops and Roses—Jack Jones (S)
1962	I Left My Heart in San Francisco—Tony Bennett (A)
1963	Wives and Lovers—Jack Jones (S)
1964	Hello, Dolly!—Louis Armstrong (S)
1965	It Was a Very Good Year—Frank Sinatra (S)
1966	Strangers in the Night—Frank Sinatra (S)
1967	By the Time I Get to Phoenix—Glen Campbell (S)

BEST PERFORMANCE BY A VOCAL GROUP

1958	That Old Black Magic—Louis Prima and Keely Smith
1959	No award
1960	We Got Us—Eydie Gorme and Steve Lawrence
1961	High Flying—Lambert, Hendricks and Ross
1962	If I Had a Hammer—Peter, Paul and Mary (S)
1963	Blowin' in the Wind—Peter, Paul and Mary (S)
1964	A Hard Day's Night—Beatles (S)
1965	We Dig Mancini—Anita Kerr Singers (A)
1966	A Man and a Woman—Anita Kerr Singers (A)
1967	Up, Up and Away—5th Dimension

BEST MUSICAL COMPOSITION FIRST RECORDED AND RELEASED (over 5 minutes)

| 1958 | Cross Country Suite—Nelson Riddle |
| 1959 | Anatomy of a Murder—Duke Ellington |

BEST PERFORMANCE BY A CHORUS

| 1959 | Battle Hymn of the Republic—Mormon Tabernacle Choir |
| 1960 | Songs of the Cowboy—Norman Luboff Choir (A) |

849

1961 Great Band with Great Voices (Si Zentner Orchestra)—Johnny Mann Singers (A)
1962 Presenting the New Christy Minstrels—The New Christy Minstrels (A)
1963 Bach's Greatest Hits—Swingle Singers (A)
1964 The Swingle Singers Going Baroque—Swingle Singers (A)
1965 Anyone for Mozart?—Swingle Singers (A)
1966 Somewhere, My Love (Lara's Theme from *Dr. Zhivago*)—Ray Conniff & Singers
1967 Up, Up and Away—Johnny Mann Singers
1968 Mission Impossible/Norwegian Wood—Alan Copeland Singers
1969 Love Theme from *Romeo & Juliet*—Percy Faith Orchestra and Chorus

BEST CONTEMPORARY
(Rock & Roll) RECORDING

1959 Midnight Flyer—Nat "King" Cole
1960 Georgia on My Mind—Ray Charles (S)
1961 Let's Twist Again—Chubby Checker
1962 Alley Cat—Bent Fabric
1963 Deep Purple—Nino Tempo and April Stevens
1964 Downtown—Petula Clark
1965 King of the Road—Roger Miller (S)
1966 Winchester Cathedral—New Vaudeville Band
1967 Sgt. Pepper's Lonely Hearts Club Band—Beatles; A&R: George Martin (A)
1967 Up, Up and Away—5th Dimension; A&R: Marc Gordon and Johnny Rivers (S)

BEST CONTEMPORARY POP VOCAL
PERFORMANCE, FEMALE

1965 I Know a Place—Petula Clark (S)
1966 No award
1967 Ode to Billie Joe—Bobbie Gentry
1968 Do You Know the Way to San Jose—Dionne Warwick (S)
1969 Is That All There Is—Peggy Lee (S)
1970 I'll Never Fall in Love Again—Dionne Warwick (A)
1971 Tapestry—Carole King (A)
1972 I Am Woman—Helen Reddy (S)
1973 Killing Me Softly with His Song—Roberta Flack (S)
1974 I Honestly Love You—Olivia Newton-John (S)
1975 At Seventeen—Janis Ian (S)
1976 Hasten Down the Wind—Linda Ronstadt (A)
1977 Love Theme from *A Star Is Born* (Evergreen)—Barbra Streisand (S)

1978 You Needed Me—Anne Murray (S)
1979 I'll Never Love This Way Again—Dionne Warwick (S)
1980 The Rose—Bette Midler (S)
1981 Lena Horne: The Lady and Her Music Live on Broadway—Lena Horne (A)
1982 You Should Hear How She Talks about You—Melissa Manchester (S)
1983 Flashdance . . . What a Feeling—Irene Cara (S)
1984 What's Love Got to Do with It—Tina Turner (S)
1985 Saving All My Love for You—Whitney Houston (S)
1986 The Broadway Album—Barbra Streisand (A)
1987 I Wanna Dance with Somebody (Who Loves Me)—Whitney Houston (S)
1988 Fast Car—Tracy Chapman (S)

BEST CONTEMPORARY POP VOCAL
PERFORMANCE, MALE

1965 King of the Road—Roger Miller (S)
1966 Eleanor Rigby—Paul McCartney (S)
1967 By the Time I Get to Phoenix—Glen Campbell (S)
1968 Light My Fire—Jose Feliciano (S)
1969 Everybody's Talkin'—Nilsson (S)
1970 Everything Is Beautiful—Ray Stevens (S)
1971 You've Got a Friend—James Taylor (S)
1972 Without You—Nilsson (S)
1973 You Are the Sunshine of My Life—Stevie Wonder (S)
1974 Fullfillingness First Finale—Stevie Wonder (A)
1975 Still Crazy after All These Years—Paul Simon (A)
1976 Songs in the Key of Life—Stevie Wonder (A)
1977 Handy Man—James Taylor (S)
1978 Copacabana (at the Copa)—Barry Manilow (S)
1979 52nd Street—Billy Joel (A)
1980 This Is It—Kenny Loggins (T)
1981 Breakin' Away—Al Jarreau (A)
1982 Truly—Lionel Richie (S)
1983 Thriller—Michael Jackson (A)
1984 Against All Odds (Take a Look at Me Now)—Phil Collins (S)
1985 No Jacket Required—Phil Collins (A)
1986 Higher Love—Steve Winwood (S)
1987 Bring on the Night—Sting (A)
1988 Don't Worry Be Happy—Bobby McFerrin

BEST POP DUO OR GROUP WITH VOCAL PERFORMANCE

1965 Flowers on the Wall—Statler Brothers (S)
1966 Monday, Monday—Mamas and the Papas (S)
1967 Up, Up and Away—5th Dimension
1968 Mrs. Robinson—Simon and Garfunkel (S)
1969 Aquarius/Let the Sunshine In—5th Dimension (S)
1970 Close to You—Carpenters
1971 Carpenters—Carpenters (A)
1972 Where Is the Love—Roberta Flack and Donny Hathaway (S)
1973 Neither One of Us—Gladys Knight & the Pips (S)
1974 Band on the Run—Paul McCartney and Wings (S)
1975 Lyin' Eyes—Eagles (S)
1976 If You Leave Me Now—Chicago (S)
1977 How Deep Is Your Love—Bee Gees (S)
1978 Saturday Night Fever—Bee Gees (A)
1979 Minute by Minute—Doobie Brothers (A)
1980 Guilty—Barbra Streisand and Barry Gibb (T)
1981 Boy from New York City—Manhattan Transfer (S)
1982 Up Where We Belong—Jennifer Warnes and Joe Cocker (S)
1983 Every Breathe You Take—Police (S)
1984 Jump (for My Love)—Pointer Sisters (S)
1985 We Are the World—USA for Africa (S)
1986 That's What Friends Are For—Dionne (Warwick) & Friends Featuring Elton John, Gladys Knight, and Stevie Wonder (S)
1987 (I've Had) The Time of My Life—Bill Medley and Jennifer Warnes (A)
1988 Brasil—The Manhattan Transfer (A)

BEST POP INSTRUMENTAL PERFORMANCE

1958 *orchestra:*—Billy May's Big Fat Brass—Billy May (A)
dance band:—Basie—Count Basie (A)
1959 *orchestra:*—Like Young—David Rose & His Orchestra with Andre Previn
dance band:—Anatomy of a Murder—Duke Ellington
1960 *orchestra:*—Mr. Lucky—Henry Mancini
for dancing:—Dance with Basie—Count Basie (A)
1961 Breakfast at Tiffany's—Henry Mancini
for dancing:—Up a Lazy River—Si Zentner
1962 The Colorful Peter Nero—Peter Nero (A)

for dancing:—Fly Me to the Moon Bossa Nova—Joe Harnell
1963 Java—Al Hirt
for dancing:—This Time by Basie! Hits of the 50's and 60's—Count Basie (A)
1964 Pink Panther—Henry Mancini
1965 A Taste of Honey—Herb Alpert & the Tijuana Brass
1966 What Now My Love—Herb Alpert & the Tijuana Brass
1967 Chet Atkins Picks the Best—Chet Atkins (A)
1968 Classical Gas—Mason Williams
1969 Variations On a Theme by Eric Satie—Blood, Sweat & Tears
1970 Theme from Z and Other Film Music—Henry Mancini (A)
1971 Smackwater Jack—Quincy Jones (A)
1972 Outa-Space—Billy Preston (S); Black Moses—Isaac Hayes (A)
1973 Also Sprach Zarathustra (2001)—Eumir Deodata (S)
1974 The Entertainer—Marvin Hamlisch (S)
1975 The Hustle—Van McCoy and the Soul City Symphony (S)
1976 Breezin'—George Benson (A)
1977 Star Wars—John Williams conducting London Symphony Orchestra (A)
1978 Children of Sanchez—Chuck Mangione Group (A)
1979 Rise—Herb Alpert (S)
1980 One on One—Bob James and Earl Klugh (A)
1981 The Theme from "Hill Street Blues"—Mike Post Featuring Larry Carlton S)
1982 Chariots of Fire (Theme), dance version—Ernie Watts (T)
1983 Being with You—George Benson (T)
1984 Ghostbusters—Ray Parker, Jr. (T)
1985 Miami Vice Theme—Jan Hammer (S)
1986 Top Gun Anthem—Harold Faltermeyer and Steve Stevens (T)
1987 Minute By Minute—Larry Carlton (S)
1988 Close-Up—David Sanborn (A)

BEST ROCK VOCAL PERFORMANCE, SOLO

1987 Tunnel of Love—Bruce Springsteen (A)

BEST ROCK VOCAL PERFORMANCE, FEMALE

1979 Hot Stuff—Donna Summer (S)
1980 Crimes of Passion—Pat Benatar (A)
1981 Fire and Ice—Pat Benatar (S)
1982 Shadows of the Night—Pat Benatar (S)

1983 Love Is a Battlefield—Pat Benatar (S)
1984 Better Be Good to Me—Tina Turner (S)
1985 One of the Living—Tina Turner (S)
1986 Back Where You Started—Tina Turner (T)
1987 No award
1988 Tina Live In Europe–Tina Turner (A)

BEST ROCK VOCAL PERFORMANCE, MALE

1979 Gotta Serve Somebody—Bob Dylan (S)
1980 Glass Houses—Billy Joel (A)
1981 Jessie's Girl—Rick Springfield (S)
1982 Hurts So Good—John Cougar (S)
1983 Beat It—Michael Jackson (S)
1984 Dancing in the Dark—Bruce Springsteen (S)
1985 The Boys of Summer—Don Henley (S)
1986 Addicted to Love—Robert Palmer (S)
1987 No award
1988 Simply Irrestistible—Rober Palmer (S)

BEST ROCK PERFORMANCE BY A DUO OR GROUP WITH VOCAL

1979 Heartache Tonight—Eagles (S)
1980 Against the Wind—Bob Seger & the Silver Bullet Band (A)
1981 Don't Stand So Close to Me—Police (S)
1982 Eye of the Tiger—Survivor (S)
1983 Synchronicity—Police (A)
1984 Purple Rain—Music from the Motion Picture—Prince & the Revolution
1985 Money for Nothing—Dire Straits (S)
1986 Missionary Man—Eurythmics (S)
1987 The Joshua Tree—U2 (A)
1988 Desire—U2 (S)

BEST ROCK INSTRUMENTAL PERFORMANCE

1979 Rockestra Theme—Wings (T)
1980 Reggatta De Blanc—Police (T)
1981 Behind My Camel—Police (T)
1982 D.N.A.—A Flock of Seagulls (T)
1983 Brimstone & Treacle—Sting (T)
1984 Cinema (track)—Yes (T)
1985 Escape—Jeff Beck (T)
1986 Peter Gunn—Art of Noise Featuring Duane Eddy (T)
1987 Jazz from Hell—Frank Zappa (A)
1988 Blues for Salvador—Carlos Santana (A)

BEST RHYTHM & BLUES RECORDING

1958 Tequila—Champs (S)
1959 What a Diff'rence a Day Makes—Dinah Washington (S)
1960 Let the Good Times Roll—Ray Charles (S)

1961 Hit the Road Jack—Ray Charles (S)
1962 I Can't Stop Loving You—Ray Charles (S)
1963 Busted—Ray Charles (S)
1964 How Glad I Am—Nancy Wilson (S)
1965 Papa's Got a Brand New Bag—James Brown (S)
1966 Crying Time—Ray Charles (S)
1967 Respect—Aretha Franklin; A&R: Jerry Wexler (S)

BEST RHYTHM & BLUES VOCAL PERFORMANCE, FEMALE

1967 Respect—Aretha Franklin (S)
1968 Chain of Fools—Aretha Franklin (S)
1969 Share Your Love with Me—Aretha Franklin (S)
1970 Don't Play That Song—Aretha Franklin (S)
1971 Bridge over Troubled Water—Aretha Franklin (S)
1972 Young, Gifted and Black—Aretha Franklin (A)
1973 Master of Eyes—Aretha Franklin (S)
1974 Ain't Nothing Like the Real Thing—Aretha Franklin (S)
1975 This Will Be—Natalie Cole (S)
1976 Sophisticated Lady (She's a Different Lady)—Natalie Cole (S)
1977 Don't Leave Me This Way—Thelma Houston (S)
1978 Last Dance—Donna Summer (S)
1979 Déjà Vu—Dionne Warwick (T)
1980 Never Knew Love Like This Before—Stephanie Mills (S)
1981 Hold On I'm Comin'—Aretha Franklin (T)
1982 And I Am Telling You I'm not Going—Jennifer Holiday (S)
1983 Chaka Khan—Chaka Khan (A)
1984 I Feel for You—Chaka Khan (S)
1985 Freeway of Love—Aretha Franklin (S)
1986 Rapture—Anita Baker (A)
1987 Aretha—Aretha Franklin (A)
1988 Giving You the Best That I Got—Anita Baker (S)

BEST RHYTHM & BLUES VOCAL PERFORMANCE, MALE

1966 Crying Time—Ray Charles (S)
1967 Dead End Street—Lou Rawls (S)
1968 (Sittin' on) The Dock of the Bay—Otis Redding (S)
1969 The Chokin' Kind—Joe Simon (S)
1970 The Thrill Is Gone—B.B. King (S)
1971 A Natural Man—Lou Rawls (S)

1972	Me & Mrs. Jones—Billy Paul (S)
1973	Superstition—Stevie Wonder (T)
1974	Boogie on Reggae Woman—Stevie Wonder (T)
1975	Living for the City—Ray Charles (S)
1976	I Wish—Stevie Wonder (T)
1977	Unmistakably Lou—Lou Rawls (A)
1978	On Broadway—George Benson (S)
1979	Don't Stop 'Til You Get Enough—Michael Jackson (S)
1980	Give Me the Night—George Benson (A)
1981	One Hundred Ways, (track from Quincy Jones' LP *The Dude*)—James Ingram
1982	Sexual Healing—Marvin Gaye (S)
1983	Billie Jean—Michael Jackson (S)
1984	Caribbean Queen (No More Love on the Run)—Billy Ocean (S)
1985	In Square Circle—Stevie Wonder (A)
1986	Living in America—James Brown (S)
1987	Just to See Her—Smokey Robinson (S)
1988	Introducing the Hardline According to Terence Trent D'Arby—Terence Trent D'Arby (A)

BEST RHYTHM & BLUES PERFORMANCE BY A DUO OR GROUP WITH VOCAL

1966	Hold It Right There—Ramsey Lewis (S)
1967	Soul Man—Sam and Dave (S)
1968	Cloud Nine—Temptations (S)
1969	It's Your Thing—Isley Brothers (S)
1970	Didn't I (Blow Your Mind This Time)—Delfonics (S)
1971	Proud Mary—Ike and Tina Turner (S)
1972	Papa Was a Rolling Stone—Temptations (S)
1973	Midnight Train to Georgia—Gladys Knight & the Pips (S)
1974	Tell Me Something Good—Rufus (S)
1975	Shining Star—Earth, Wind & Fire (S)
1976	You Don't Have to Be a Star (to Be in My Show)—Marilyn McCoo and Billy Davis, Jr. (S)
1977	Best of My Love—Emotions (T)
1978	All'n'All—Earth, Wind & Fire (A)
1979	After the Love Has Gone—Earth, Wind & Fire (T)
1980	Shining Star—Manhattans (S)
1981	The Dude—Quincy Jones (A)
1982	Let It Whip—Dazz Band (S); tied with Wanna Be with You—Earth, Wind & Fire (S)
1983	Ain't Nobody—Rufus & Chaka Khan (S)
1984	Yah Mo B There—James Ingram and Michael McDonald (S)

1985	Nightshift—Commodores (S)
1986	Kiss—Prince & the Revolution (S)
1987	I Knew You Were Waiting (for Me)—Aretha Franklin and George Michael (T)
1988	Love Overboard—Gladys Knight & The Pips (S)

BEST RHYTHM & BLUES INSTRUMENTAL

1969	Games People Play—King Curtis
1972	Papa Was a Rolling Stone—The Temptations
1973	Hang On Snoopy—Ramsey Lewis (S)
1974	TSOP (The Sound of Philadelphia)—MFSB (S)
1975	Fly, Robin, Fly—Silver Convention (S)
1976	Theme from Good King Bad—George Benson (T)
1977	Q—Brothers Johnson (T)
1978	Runnin'—Earth, Wind & Fire (T)
1979	Boogie Wonderland—Earth, Wind & Fire (S)
1980	Off Broadway—George Benson (T)
1981	All I Need Is You—David Sanborn (S)
1982	Sexual Healing—Marvin Gaye (instrumental version) (S)
1983	Rockit—Herbie Hancock (S)
1984	Sound System—Herbie Hancock (A)
1985	Musician—Ernie Watts (A)
1986	And You Know That—Yellowjackets (T)
1987	Chicago Song—David Sanborn (S)
1988	Light Years—Chick Corea (Track from GRP Super Live in Concert, Vols. 1 & 2

BEST RHYTHM & BLUES SONG (Songwriter's Award)

1968	(Sittin' on) The Dock of the Bay—Otis Redding and Steve Cropper
1969	Color Him Father—Richard Spencer
1970	Patches—Ronald Dunbar and General Johnson
1971	Ain't No Sunshine—Bill Withers
1972	Papa Was a Rolling Stone—Barrett Strong and Norman Whitfield
1973	Superstition—Stevie Wonder
1974	Living for the City—Stevie Wonder
1975	Where Is the Love—Harry Wayne Casey, Richard Finch, Willie Clarke and Betty Wright
1976	Lowdown—Boz Scaggs and David Paich
1977	You Make Me Feel Like Dancing—Leo Sayer and Vini Poncia
1978	Last Dance—Paul Jabara

1979 After the Love Has Gone—David Foster, Jay Graydon and Bill Champlin
1980 Never Knew Love Like This Before—Reggie Lucas and James Mtume
1981 Just the Two of Us—Bill Withers, William Salter and Ralph MacDonald
1982 Turn Your Love Around—Jay Graydon, Steve Lukather and Bill Champlin
1983 Billie Jean—Michael Jackson
1984 I Feel for You—Prince
1985 Freeway of Love—Narada Michael Walden and Jeffrey Cohen
1986 Sweet Love—Anita Baker, Louis A. Johnson, and Gary Bias
1987 Lean on Me—Bill Withers
1988 Giving You the Best That I Got—Anita Baker, Skip Scarborough & Randy Holland

BEST JAZZ FUSION PERFORMANCE, VOCAL OR INSTRUMENTAL

1980 Birdland—Manhattan Transfer (S)
1981 Winelight—Grover Washington, Jr. (A)
1982 Offramp—Pat Metheny Group (A)
1983 Travels—Pat Metheny Group (A)
1984 First Circle—Pat Metheny Group (A)
1985 Straight to the Heart—David Sanborn (A)
1986 Double Vision—Bob James and David Sanborn (A)
1987 Still Life (Talking)—Pat Metheny Group (A)
1988 Politics—Yellowjackets (A)

BEST NEW AGE PERFORMANCE

1986 Down to the Moon—Andreas Vollenweider (A)
1987 Yusef Lateef's Little Symphony—Yusef Lateef (A)
1988 Folksongs for a Nuclear Village—Shadowfax (A)

BEST NEW COUNTRY ARTIST

1964 Roger Miller
1965 Statler Brothers

BEST COUNTRY ALBUM

1964 Dang Me/Chug-a-Lug—Roger Miller
1965 The Return of Roger Miller—Roger Miller

BEST COUNTRY SINGLE

1964 Dang Me—Roger Miller
1965 King of the Road—Roger Miller

BEST COUNTRY & WESTERN PERFORMANCE

1958 Tom Dooley—Kingston Trio (S)
1959 The Battle of New Orleans—Johnny Horton
1960 El Paso—Marty Robbins (S)
1961 Big Bad John—Jimmy Dean (S)
1962 Funny Way of Laughin'—Burl Ives (S)
1963 Detroit City—Bobby Bare
1964 no award
1965 no award
1966 Almost Persuaded—David Houston
1967 Gentle on My Mind—Glen Campbell; A&R: Al de Lory

BEST COUNTRY VOCAL PERFORMANCE, FEMALE

1964 Here Comes My Baby—Dottie West (S)
1965 Queen of the House—Jody Miller
1966 Don't Touch Me—Jeannie Seely (S)
1967 I Don't Wanna Play House—Tammy Wynette
1968 Harper Valley P.T.A.—Jeannie C. Riley (S)
1969 Stand by Your Man—Tammy Wynette (A)
1970 Rose Garden—Lynn Anderson (S)
1971 Help Me Make It through the Night—Sammie Smith (S)
1972 Happiest Girl in the Whole USA—Donna Fargo (S)
1973 Let Me Be There—Olivia Newton-John (S)
1974 Love Song—Anne Murray (A)
1975 I Can't Help It (If I'm Still in Love with You)—Linda Ronstadt (S)
1976 Elite Hotel—Emmylou Harris (A)
1977 Don't It Make My Brown Eyes Blue—Crystal Gayle (S)
1978 Here You Come Again—Dolly Parton (A)
1979 Blue Kentucky Girl—Emmylou Harris (A)
1980 Could I Have This Dance—Anne Murray (S)
1981 9 to 5—Dolly Parton (S)
1982 Break It to Me Gently—Juice Newton (S)
1983 A Little Good News—Anne Murray (S)
1984 In My Dreams—Emmylou Harris (S)
1985 I Don't Know Why You Don't Want Me—Rosanne Cash (S)
1986 Whoever's in New England—Reba McEntire (S)
1987 80's Ladies—K.T. Oslin (T)
1988 Hold Me—K.T. Oslin (Track from This Woman)

BEST COUNTRY VOCAL PERFORMANCE, MALE

1964 Dang Me—Roger Miller (S)
1965 King of the Road—Roger Miller (S)
1966 Almost Persuaded—David Houston (S)

1967 Gentle on My Mind—Glen Campbell (S)
1968 Folsom Prison Blues—Johnny Cash (S)
1969 A Boy Named Sue—Johnny Cash (S)
1970 For the Good Times—Ray Price (S)
1971 When You're Hot, You're Hot—Jerry Reed (S)
1972 Charley Pride Sings Heart Songs—Charley Pride (A)
1973 Behind Closed Doors Charlie Rich (S)
1974 Please Don't Tell Me How the Story Ends—Ronnie Milsap (S)
1975 Blue Eyes Crying in the Rain—Willie Nelson (S)
1976 (I'm a) Stand by My Woman Man—Ronnie Milsap (S)
1977 Lucille—Kenny Rogers (S)
1978 Georgia on My Mind—Willie Nelson (S)
1979 The Gambler—Kenny Rogers (S)
1980 He Stopped Loving Her Today—George Jones (S)
1981 (There's) No Gettin' over Me—Ronnie Milsap (S)
1982 Always on My Mind—Willie Nelson (S)
1983 I.O.U.—Lee Greenwood (S)
1984 That's the Way Love Goes—Merle Haggard (S)
1985 Lost in the Fifties Tonight (in the Still of the Night)—Ronnie Milsap (S)
1986 Lost in the Fifties Tonight—Ronnie Milsap (A)
1987 Always & Forever—Randy Travis (A)
1988 Old 8 × 10—Randy Travis (A)

BEST COUNTRY PERFORMANCE BY A DUO OR GROUP WITH VOCAL

1967 Jackson—Johnny Cash and June Carter
1968 no award
1969 MacArthur Park—Waylon Jennings and the Kimberlys
1970 If I Were a Carpenter—Johnny Cash and June Carter
1971 After the Fire Is Gone—Conway Twitty and Loretta Lynn (S)
1972 Class of '57—Statler Brothers (S)
1973 From the Bottle to the Bottom—Kris Kristofferson and Rita Coolidge (T)
1974 Fairytale—Pointer Sisters (T)
1975 Lover Please—Kris Kristofferson and Rita Coolidge (S)
1976 The End Is Not in Sight (The Cowboy Tune)—Amazing Rhythm Aces (S)
1977 Heaven's Just a Sin Away—Kendalls (S)
1978 Mamas Don't Let Your Babies Grow Up to Be Cowboys—Waylon Jennings and Willie Nelson (S)
1979 The Devil Went Down to Georgia—Charlie Daniels Band (S)
1980 That Lovin' You Feelin' Again—Roy Orbison and Emmylou Harris (S)
1981 Elvira—Oak Ridge Boys (S)
1982 Mountain Music—Alabama (A)
1983 The Closer You Get—Alabama (A)
1984 Mama He's Crazy—Judds (S)
1985 Why Not Me—Judds (A)
1986 Grandpa (Tell Me 'bout the Good Old Days)—Judds (S)
1987 Trio—Dolly Parton, Linda Ronstadt, and Emmylou Harris (A)
1988 Give a Little Love—The Judds (Track from Greatest Hits)

BEST COUNTRY VOCAL PERFORMANCE, DUET

1987 Make No Mistake, She's Mine—Ronnie Milsap and Kenny Rogers (S)
1988 Crying—Roy Orbison & K. D. Lang (S)

BEST COUNTRY INSTRUMENTAL PERFORMANCE

1968 Foggy Mountain Breakdown—Flatt & Scruggs
1969 The Nashville Brass Featuring Danny Davis/Play More Nashville Sounds—Danny Davis & the Nashville Brass (A)
1970 Me & Jerry—Chet Atkins and Jerry Reed (A)
1971 Snowbird—Chet Atkins (S)
1972 Charlie McCoy/The Real McCoy—Charlie McCoy (A)
1973 Dueling Banjos—Eric Weissberg and Steve Mandell (T)
1974 The Atkins-Travis Traveling Show—Chet Atkins and Merle Travis (A)
1975 The Entertainer—Chet Atkins (T)
1976 Chester & Lester—Chet Atkins and Les Paul (A)
1977 Country Instrumentalist of the Year—Hargus "Pig" Robbins (A)
1978 One O'Clock Jump—Asleep at the Wheel (T)
1979 Big Sandy/Leather Britches—Doc & Merle Watson (T)
1980 Orange Blossom Special/Hoedown—Gilley's "Urban Cowboy" Band (T)
1981 Country—After All These Years—Chet Atkins

1982   Alabama Jubilee—Roy Clark (T)
1983   Fireball—New South (Ricky Skaggs, Jerry Douglas, Tony Rice, J.D. Crowe and Todd Phillips) (T)
1984   Wheel Hoss—Ricky Skaggs (T)
1985   Cosmic Square Dance—Chet Atkins and Mark Knopfler (T)
1986   Raisin' the Dickens—Ricky Skaggs (T)
1987   String of Pars—Asleep at the Wheel (T)
1988   Sugarfoot Rag—Asleep at the Wheel (Track from Western Standard Time)

BEST COUNTRY SONG
(Songwriter's Award)

1964   Dang Me—Roger Miller
1965   King of the Road—Roger Miller
1966   Almost Persuaded—Billy Sherrill and Glen Sutton
1967   Gentle on My Mind—John Hartford
1968   Little Green Apples—Bobby Russell
1969   A Boy Named Sue—Shel Silverstein
1970   My Woman, My Woman, My Wife—Marty Robbins
1971   Help Me Make It through the Night—Kris Kristofferson
1972   Kiss an Angel Good Mornin'—Ben Peters
1973   Behind Closed Doors—Kenny O'Dell
1974   A Very Special Love Song—Norris Wilson and Billy Sherrill
1975   (Hey Won't You Play) Another Somebody Done Somebody Wrong Song—Chips Moman and Larry Butler
1976   Broken Lady—Larry Gatlin
1977   Don't It Make My Brown Eyes Blue—Richard Leigh
1978   The Gambler—Don Schlitz
1979   You Decorated My Life—Debbie Hupp and Bob Morrison
1980   On the Road Again—Willie Nelson
1981   9 to 5—Dolly Parton
1982   Always on My Mind—Johnny Christopher, Mark James and Wayne Carson
1983   Stranger in My House—Mike Reid
1984   City of New Orleans—Steve Goodman
1985   Highwayman—Jimmy L. Webb
1986   Grandpa (Tell Me 'bout the Good Old Days)—Jamie O'Hara
1987   Forever and Ever, Amen—Paul Overstreet and Don Schlitz
1988   Hold Me—K.T. Oslin

BEST CONTEMPORARY FOLK RECORDING

1986   Tribute to Steve Goodman—Arlo Guthrie, John Hartford, Richie Havens, Bonnie Koloc, Nitty Gritty Dirt Band, John Prine, and others; prod.: Hank Neuberger, Al Buneta, and Dan Einstein (A)
1987   Unfinished Business—Steve Goodman (A)
1988   Tracy Chapman—Tracy Chapman (A)

BEST FOLK PERFORMANCE

1959   The Kingston Trio at Large—Kingston Trio (A)
1960   Swing Dat Hammer—Harry Belafonte
1961   Belafonte Folk Singers at Home and Abroad—Belafonte Folk Singers (A)
1962   If I Had a Hammer—Peter, Paul and Mary (S)
1963   Blowin' in the Wind—Peter, Paul and Mary (S)
1964   We'll Sing in the Sunshine—Gale Garnett
1965   An Evening with Belafonte/Makeba—Harry Belafonte and Miriam Makeba (A)
1966   Blues in the Street—Cortelia Clark (A)
1967   Gentle on My Mind—John Hartford
1968   Both Sides Now—Judy Collins (S)
1969   Clouds—Joni Mitchell

BEST TRADITIONAL FOLK RECORDING

1970   Good Feelin'—T-Bone Walker
1971   They Call Me Muddy Waters—Muddy Waters (A)
1972   The London Muddy Waters Session—Muddy Waters (A)
1973   Then and Now—Doc Watson (A)
1974   Two Days in November—Doc & Merle Watson (A)
1975   The Muddy Waters Woodstock Album—Muddy Waters (A)
1976   Mark Twain—John Hartford (A)
1977   Hard Again—Muddy Waters (A)
1978   I'm Ready—Muddy Waters (A)
1979   Muddy Mississippi Waters Live—Muddy Waters (A)
1980   Rare Blues—Dr. Isaiah Ross, Maxwell Street Jimmy, Big Joe Williams, Son House, Rev. Robert Wilkins, Little Brother Montgomery, and Sunnyland Slim (A)
1981   There Must Be a Better World Somewhere—B.B. King (A)
1982   Queen Ida and the Bon Temps Zydeco Band on Tour—Queen Ida (A)

1983 I'm Here—Clifton Chenier and His Red Hot Louisiana Band (A)
1984 Elizabeth Cotten Live—Elizabeth Cotten (A)
1985 My Toot Toot—Rockin' Sidney (S)
1986 Riding the Midnight Train—Doc Watson (A)
1987 Shaka Zulu—Ladysmith Black Mambazo (A)
1988 Folkways: A Sharper Vision—A Tribute to Woody Guthrie and Leadbelly—Don De-Vito, Joe McEwen, Harold Leventhal & Ralph Rinzler, album producers.

BEST TRADITIONAL BLUES RECORDING

1982 Alright Again—Clarence Gatemouth Brown (A)
1983 Blues 'N' Jazz—B.B. King (A)
1984 Blues Explosion—John Hammond, Stevie Ray Vaughn and Double Trouble, Sugar Blue, Koko Taylor and the Blues Machine, Luther "Guitar Junior" Johnson, and J.B. Hutto and the New Hawks (A)
1985 My Guitar Sings the Blues—B.B. King (T)
1986 Showdown!—Albert Collins, Robert Cray, and Johnny Copeland (A)
1987 Houseparty New Orleans Style—Professor Longhair (A)
1988 Hidden Charms—Willie Dixon (A)

BEST CONTEMPORARY BLUES RECORDING

1987 Strong Persuader—Robert Cray Band (A)
1988 Don't be Afraid of the Dark—The Robert Cray Band (S)

BEST REGGAE RECORDING

1984 Anthem—Black Uhuru (A)
1985 Cliff Hanger—Jimmy Cliff (A)
1986 Babylon the Bandit—Steel Pulse (A)
1987 No Nuclear War—Peter Tosh (A)
1988 Conscious Party—Ziggy Marley and the Melody Makers (A)

BEST LATIN RECORDING

1979 Irakere—Irakere (A)
1980 La Onda Va Bien—Cal Tjader (A)
1981 Guajira Pa La Jeva—Clare Fischer (T)
1982 Machito and His Salsa Big Band—Machito (A)

BEST LATIN POP PERFORMANCE

1983 Me Enamore—Jose Feliciano (A)
1984 Always in My Heart (Siempre en Mi Corazon)—Placido Domingo (A)
1985 Es Facil Amar—Lani Hall (A)
1986 Lelolai—Jose Feliciano (T)
1987 Un Hombre Solo—Julio Iglesias (A)
1988 Roberto Carlos—Roberto Carlos (A)

BEST TROPICAL LATIN PERFORMANCE

1983 On Broadway—Tito Puente and His Latin Ensemble (A)
1984 Palo Pa Rumba—Eddie Palmieri (A)
1985 Mambo Diablo—Tito Puente and His Latin Ensemble (A) tied with Solito—Eddie Palmieri (A)
1986 Escenas—Ruben Blades (A)
1987 La Verdad—The Truth—Eddie Palmieri (A)
1988 Antecedente—Ruben Blades (A)

BEST MEXICAN/AMERICAN PERFORMANCE

1983 Anselma—Los Lobos (T)
1984 Me Gustas Tal Come Eres—Sheena Easton and Luis Miguel (S)
1985 Simplemente Mujer—Vikki Carr (A)
1986 Ay te Dejo en San Antonio—Flaco Jimenez (A)
1987 Gracias! America sin Fronteras—Los Tigres del Norte (A)
1988 Canciones de Mi Padre—Linda Ronstadt (A)

BEST GOSPEL OR OTHER RELIGIOUS RECORDING

1961 Everytime I Feel the Spirit—Mahalia Jackson
1962 Great Songs of Love and Faith—Mahalia Jackson (A)
1963 Dominique—Soeur Sourire
1964 Great Gospel Songs—Tennessee Ernie Ford (A)
1965 Southland Favorites—George Beverly Shea and the Anita Kerr Singers (A)

BEST GOSPEL PERFORMANCE

1967 More Grand Old Gospel—Porter Wagoner & the Blackwood Brothers Quartet
1968 The Happy Gospel of the Happy Goodmans—Happy Goodman Family (A)

1969 In Gospel Country—Porter Wagoner & the Blackwood Brothers
1970 Talk about the Good Times—Oak Ridge Boys
1971 Let Me Live—Charley Pride
1972 L-O-V-E—Blackwood Brothers
1973 Release Me—Blackwood Brothers (A)
1974 The Baptism of Jesse Taylor—Oak Ridge Boys (S)
1975 No Shortage—Imperials (A)
1976 Where the Soul Never Dies—Oak Ridge Boys (S)

BEST GOSPEL PERFORMANCE, CONTEMPORARY OR INSPIRATIONAL

1977 Sail On—Imperials (A)
1978 What a Friend—Larry Hart (T)
1979 Heed the Call—Imperials (A)
1980 The Lord's Prayer—Reba Rambo, Dony McGuire, B.J. Thomas, Andrae Crouch, The Archers, Walter and Tramaine Hawkins, and Cynthia Clawson (A)
1981 Priority—Imperials (A)
1982 Age to Age—Amy Grant (A)

BEST GOSPEL PERFORMANCE, TRADITIONAL

1977 Just a Little Talk with Jesus—Oak Ridge Boys (T)
1978 Refreshing—Happy Goodman Family (A)
1979 Lift up the Name of Jesus—Blackwood Brothers (A)
1980 Welcome to Worship—Blackwood Brothers (A)
1981 The Masters V—J.D. Sumner, James Blackwood, Hovie Lister, Rosie Rozell, and Jake Hess (A)
1982 I'm Following You—Blackwood Brothers (A)

BEST GOSPEL PERFORMANCE, FEMALE

1983 Ageless Medley—Amy Grant (S)
1984 Angels—Amy Grant (T)
1985 Unguarded—Amy Grant (A)
1986 Morning Like This—Sandi Patti (A)
1987 I Believe in You—Deniece Williams (T)
1988 Lead Me On—Amy Grant (A)

BEST GOSPEL PERFORMANCE, MALE

1983 Walls of Glass—Russ Taff (A)
1984 Michael W. Smith—Michael W. Smith (A)
1985 How Excellent Is Thy Name—Larnelle Harris (T)

1986 Triumph—Philip Bailey (A)
1987 The Father Hath Provided—Larnelle Harris (A)
1988 Christmas—Larnelle Harris (A)

BEST GOSPEL PERFORMANCE, DUO, GROUP, CHOIR, OR CHORUS

1983 More Than Wonderful—Sandi Patti and Larnelle Harris (T)
1984 Keep the Flame Burning—Debby Boone and Phil Driscoll (T)
1985 I've Just Seen Jesus—Larnelle Harris and Sandi Patti (T)
1986 They Say—Sandi Patti and Deniece Williams (T)
1987 Crack the Sky—Mylon Lefevre and Broken Heart (A)
1988 The Winans Live at Carnegia Hall—The Winans (A)

BEST SOUL GOSPEL

1968 The Soul of Me—Dottie Rambo
1969 Oh Happy Day—Edwin Hawkins Singers
1970 Every Man Wants to Be Free—Edwin Hawkins Singers
1971 Put Your Hand in the Hand of the Man from Galilee—Shirley Caesar
1972 Amazing Grace—Aretha Franklin (S)
1973 Loves Me Like a Rock—Dixie Hummingbirds (with Paul Simon) (S)
1974 In the Ghetto—James Cleveland and the Southern California Community Choir (A)
1975 Take Me Back—Andrae Crouch and the Disciples (A)
1976 How I Got Over—Mahalia Jackson (A)
1977 *Contemporary:* Wonderful—Edwin Hawkins and the Edwin Hawkins Singer (A)
Traditional: James Cleveland Live at Carnegie Hall—James Cleveland (A)
1978 *Contemporary:* Live in London—Andrae Crouch and the Disciples (A)
Traditional: Live and Direct—Mighty Clouds of Joy (A)
1979 *Contemporary:* I'll be Thinking of You—Andrae Crouch (A)
Traditional: Changing Times—Mighty Clouds of Joy (A)
1980 *Contemporary:* Rejoice—Shirley Caesar (A)
Traditional: Lord, Let Me Be an Instrument—James Cleveland and the Charles Fold Singers (A)
1981 *Contemporary:* Don't Give Up—Andrae Crouch (A)

Traditional: The Lord Will Make a Way—Al Green (A)
1982 *Contemporary:* Higher Plane—Al Green (A)
Traditional: Precious Lord—Al Green (A)

BEST SOUL GOSPEL PERFORMANCE, FEMALE

1983 We Sing Praises—Sandra Crouch (A)
1984 Sailin'—Shirley Caesar (A)
1985 Martin—Shirley Caesar (S)
1986 I Surrender All—Deniece Williams (T)
1987 For Always—Cece Winans (T)
1988 One Lord, One Faith, One Baptism—Aretha Franklin (A)

BEST SOUL GOSPEL PERFORMANCE, MALE

1983 I'll Rise Again—Al Green (A)
1984 Always Remember—Andrae Crouch (T)
1985 Bring Back the Days of Yea and Nay—Marvin Winans (T)
1986 Going Away—Al Green (S)
1987 Everything's Gonna Be Alright—Al Green (T)
1988 Abundant Life—Bebe Winans (Track from Ron Winans Family & Friends Choir)

BEST SOUL GOSPEL PERFORMANCE, DUO, GROUP, CHOIR, OR CHORUS

1983 I'm So Glad I'm Standing Here Today—Bobby Jones with Barbara Mandrell (T)
1984 Sailin' on the Sea of Your Love—Shirley Caesar and Al Green (T)
1985 Tomorrow—Winans (A)
1986 Let My People Go—Winans (A)
1987 Ain't No Need to Worry—Winans and Anita Baker (S)
1988 Take Six—Take 6 (A)

BEST MUSICAL CAST SHOW ALBUM (awards have variously gone to performers, composers, and album producers)

1958 The Music Man—comp.: Meredith Willson
1959 Gypsy—perf.: Ethel Merman; tied with Redhead—perf.: Gwen Verdon
1960 The Sound of Music—comp.: Richard Rodgers and Oscar Hammerstein
1961 How to Succeed in Business without Really Trying—comp.: Frank Loesser
1962 No Strings—comp.: Richard Rodgers

1963 She Loves Me—comp.: Jerry Bock and Sheldon Harnick
1964 Funny Girl—comp.: Jule Styne and Bob Merrill
1965 On a Clear Day—comp.: Alan Lerner and Burton Lane
1966 Mame—comp.: Jerry Herman
1967 Cabaret—comp.: Fred Ebb and John Kander; prod.: Goddard Lieberson
1968 Hair—comp.: Gerome Ragni, James Rado, and Galt MacDermott; prod.: Andy Wiswell
1969 Promises, Promises—comp.: Burt Bacharach and Hal David; prod.: Henry Jerome and Phil Ramone
1970 Company—comp.: Stephen Sondheim; prod.: Thomas Z. Shepard
1971 Godspell—comp. and prod.: Stephen Schwartz
1972 Don't Bother Me, I Can't Cope—comp.: Micki Grant; prod.: Jerry Ragavoy
1973 A Little Night Music—comp.: Stephen Sondheim; prod.: Goddard Lieberson
1974 Raisin—comp.: Judd Woldin and Robert Brittan; prod.: Thomas Z. Shepard
1975 The Wiz—comp.: Charlie Smalls; prod.: Jerry Wexler
1976 Bubbling Brown Sugar—comp.: various; prod.: Hugo & Luigi
1977 Annie—comp.: Charles Strouse and Martin Charnin; prod.: Larry Morton and Charles Strouse
1978 Ain't Misbehavin'—prod.: Thomas Z. Shepard
1979 Sweeney Todd—comp.: Stephen Sondheim; prod.: Thomas Z. Shepard
1980 Evita—Premier American Recording—comp. and prod.: Andrew Lloyd Webber and Tim Rice
1981 Lena Horne: The Lady and Her Music Live on Broadway—comp.: various; prod.: Quincy Jones
1982 Dreamgirls—comp.: Henry Krieger and Tom Eyen; prod.: David Foster
1983 Cats—prod.: Andrew Lloyd Webber
1984 Sunday in the Park with George—comp.: Stephen Sondheim; prod.: Thomas Z. Shepard
1985 West Side Story—prod.: John McClure
1986 Follies in Concert—prod.: Thomas Z. Shepard
1987 Les Miserables—comp.: Herbert Kretzmer and Claude-Michel Schonberg; prod.: Alain Boublil and Claude-Michel Schonberg
1988 Into the Woods—comp.: Stephen Sondheim; prod.: Jay David Saks

BEST ALBUM OF ORIGINAL INSTRUMENTAL BACKGROUND SCORE WRITTEN FOR A MOTION PICTURE OR TELEVISION
(Composer's Award)

1982 Dreamgirls—Henry Krieger
1983 Cats (Complete original Broadway Cast Recording)—Andrew Lloyd Webber
1984 Sunday in the Park with George—Stephen Sondheim
1985 No award
1986 No award
1987 The Untouchables—Ennio Morricone
1988 The Last Emperor—Ryuichi Sakamoto, David Byrne, Kong Su

BEST ORIGINAL SCORE FROM A MOTION PICTURE OR TV SHOW
(Composer's Award)

1963 Tom Jones—John Addison
1964 Mary Poppins—Richard M. and Robert B. Sherman
1965 The Sandpiper—Johnny Mandel
1966 Dr. Zhivago—Maurice Jarre
1967 Mission: Impossible—Lalo Schifrin
1968 The Graduate—Paul Simon and Dave Grusin
1969 Butch Cassidy & the Sundance Kid—Burt Bacharach
1970 Let It Be—Beatles
1971 Shaft—Isaac Hayes
1972 The Godfather—Nino Rota
1973 Jonathan Livingston Seagull—Neil Diamond
1974 The Way We Were—Marvin Hamlisch and Alan and Marilyn Bergman
1975 Jaws—John Williams
1976 Car Wash—Norman Whitfield
1977 Star Wars—John Williams
1978 Close Encounters of the Third Kind—John Williams
1979 Superman—John Williams
1980 The Empire Strikes Back—John Williams
1981 Raiders of the Lost Ark—John Williams
1982 E.T. The Extra-Terrestrial—John Williams
1983 Flashdance—Giorgio Moroder, Keith Forsey, Irene Cara, Shandi Sinnamon, Ronald Magness, Douglas Cotler, Richard Gilbert, Michael Boddicker, Jerry Hey, Phil Ramone, Michael Sembello, Kim Carnes, Duane Hitchings, Craig Kampf and Dennis Matkosky
1984 Purple Rain—Prince, John L. Nelson, and Lisa & Wendy

1985 Beverly Hills Cop—Sharon Robinson, John Gilutin, Bunny Hull, Hawk, Howard Hewett, Micki Free, Sue Sheridan, Howie Rice, Keith Forsey, Harold Faltermeyer, Allee Willis, Dan Sembello, Marc Benno, and Richard Theisen

BEST ENGINEERED RECORDING
(Other than Classical)
(Engineer's Award)

1958 The Chipmunk Song (David Seville)—eng.: Ted Keep
1959 Belafonte at Carnegie Hall (Harry Belafonte)—eng.: Robert Simpson (A)
novelty: Alvin's Harmonica (David Seville)—eng.: Ted Keep
1960 Ella Fitzgerald Sings George & Ira Gershwin's Song Book—eng.: Luis P. Valentin (A)
novelty: The Old Payola Roll Blues (Stan Freberg)—eng.: John Kraus
1961 Judy at Carnegie Hall (Judy Garland)—eng.: Robert Arnold (popular) (A)
novelty: Stan Freberg Presents the United States of America—eng.: John Kraus (A)
1962 Hatari!—Al Schmitt
novelty: The Civil War, Vol. I (Fennell) (Henry Mancini)—eng.: Robert Fine
1963 Charade (Mancini Orchestra & Chorus)—eng.: James Malloy
novelty: Civil War Vol II (Frederick Fennell)—eng.: Robert Fine
1964 Getz/Gilberto (Stan Getz and Joao Gilberto)—eng.: Phil Ramone (A)
novelty: The Chipmunks Sing the Beatles (Chipmunks)—eng.: Dave Hassinger
1965 A Taste of Honey (Herb Alpert & the Tijuana Brass)—eng.: Larry Levine
1966 Strangers in the Night (Frank Sinatra)—eng.: Eddie Brackett and Lee Herschberg
1967 Sgt. Pepper's Lonely Hearts Club Band (Beatles)—eng.: G.E. Emerick (A)
1968 Wichita Lineman (Glen Campbell)—eng.: Joe Polito and Hugh Davies
1969 Abbey Road (Beatles)—eng.: Geoff Emerick and Phillip McDonald (A)
1970 Bridge over Troubled Water (Simon and Garfunkel)—eng.: Roy Halee
1971 Theme from Shaft (Isaac Hayes)—eng.: Dave Purple, Ron Capone, and Henry Bush (S)
1972 Moods (Neil Diamond)—eng.: Armin Steiner (A)

1973 Innervisions (Stevie Wonder)—eng.: Robert Margouleff and Malcolm Cecil (A)
1974 Band on the Run (Paul McCartney & Wings)—eng.: Geoff Emerick (A)
1975 Between the Lines (Janis Ian)—eng.: Brooks Arthur, Larry Alexander, and Russ Payne
1976 Breezin' (George Benson)—eng.: Al Schmitt
1977 Aja (Steely Dan)—eng.: Roger Nichols, Elliott Scheiner, Bill Schnee, and Al Schmitt
1978 FM (No Static at All) (Steely Dan)—eng.: Roger Nichols and Al Schmitt (T)
1979 Breakfast in America (Supertramp)—eng.: Peter Henderson (A)
1980 The Wall (Pink Floyd)—eng.: James Guthrie (A)
1981 Gaucho (Steely Dan)—eng.: Roger Nichols, Elliot Scheiner, Bill Schnee, and Jerry Garszva (A)
1982 Toto IV (Toto)—eng.: Al Schmitt, Tom Knox, Greg Ladanyi and David Leonard (A)
1983 Thriller (Michael Jackson)—eng.: Bruce Swedlen (A)
1984 17 (Chicago)—eng.: Humberto Gatica (A)
1985 Brothers in Arms (Dire Straits)—eng.: Neil Dorfsman (A)
1986 Back in the High Life (Steve Winwood)—eng.: Tom Lord Alge and Jason Corsaro (A)
1987 Bad (Michael Jackson)—eng.: Bruce Swedien and Humberto Gatica (A)
1988 Roll With It (Steve Winwood)—eng. Tom Lord Alge

BEST HARD ROCK/METAL PERFORMANCE VOCAL OR INSTRUMENTAL

1988 Crest of a Knave—Jethro Tull (A)

BEST RAP PERFORMANCE

1988 Parents Just Don't Understand—D.J. Jazzy Jeff & The Fresh Prince (Track from He's the DJ and I'm the Rapper)

BEST BLUEGRASS RECORDING (Vocal or Instrumental)

1988 Southern Flavor—Bill Monroe (A)

APPENDIX C

Academy of Motion Pictures Arts and Sciences

Award Nominations and *Winners in Music

BEST SONG

1958
ALMOST IN YOUR ARMS (Love Song from *Houseboat*) from *Houseboat*. Paramount and Scribe, Paramount.
Music and lyrics by Jay Livingston and Ray Evans.
A CERTAIN SMILE from *A Certain Smile*. 20th Century-Fox.
Music by Sammy Fain
Lyrics by Paul Francis Webster.
*GIGI from *Gigi*. Arthur Freed Prods., M-G-M.
Music by Frederick Loewe.
Lyrics by Alan Jay Lerner.
TO LOVE AND BE LOVED from *Some Came Running*. Sol C. Siegel Prods., M-G-M.
Music by James Van Heusen.
Lyrics by Sammy Cahn.
A VERY PRECIOUS LOVE from *Marjorie Morningstar*. Beachwold Pictures, Warner Bros.
Music by Sammy Fain.
Lyrics by Paul Francis Webster.

1959
THE BEST OF EVERYTHING from *The Best of Everything*. Company of Artists, 20th Century-Fox.
Music by Alfred Newman.
Lyrics by Sammy Cahn.
THE FIVE PENNIES from *The Five Pennies*. Dena Prod., Paramount.
Music and Lyrics by Sylvia Fine.
THE HANGING TREE from *The Hanging Tree*. Baroda Prods., Warner Bros.
Music by Jerry Livingston.
Lyrics by Mack David.
*HIGH HOPES from *A Hole in the Head*. Sincap Prods., United Artists.
Music by James Van Heusen.
Lyrics by Sammy Cahn.
STRANGE ARE THE WAYS OF LOVE from *The Young Land*. C.V. Whitney Pictures, Columbia.
Music by Dimitri Tiomkin.
Lyrics by Ned Washington

1960
THE FACTS OF LIFE from *The Facts of Life*. Panama & Frank Prod., United Artists.
Music and lyrics by Johnny Mercer.
FARAWAY PART OF TOWN from *Pepe*. G. S.-Posa Films International Prod., Columbia.
Music by Andre Previn.
Lyrics by Dory Langdon.
THE GREEN LEAVES OF SUMMER from *The Alamo*. Batjac Prod., United Artists.
Music by Dimitri Tiomkin.

Lyrics by Paul Francis Webster.

*NEVER ON SUNDAY from *Never on Sunday*. Melinafilm Prod., Lopert Pictures Corp. (Greek).
Music and lyrics by Manos Hadjidakis.

THE SECOND TIME AROUND from *High Time*. Bing Crosby Prods., 20th Century-Fox.
Music by James Van Heusen.
Lyrics by Sammy Cahn.

1961

BACHELOR IN PARADISE from *Bachelor in Paradise*. Ted Richmond Prod., M-G-M.
Music by Henry Mancini.
Lyrics by Mack David.

LOVE THEME FROM EL CID ("The Falcon and the Dove") from *El Cid*. Samuel Bronston Prod. in association with Dear Film Prod., Allied Artists.
Music by Miklos Rozsa.
Lyrics by Paul Francis Webster.

*MOON RIVER from *Breakfast at Tiffany's*. Jurow-Shepherd Prod., Paramount.
Music by Henry Mancini.
Lyrics by Johnny Mercer.

POCKETFUL OF MIRACLES from *Pocketful of Miracles*. Franton Prod., United Artists.
Music by James Van Heusen.
Lyrics by Sammy Cahn.

TOWN WITHOUT PITY from *Town without Pity*. Mirisch Company in association with Gloria Films, United Artists.
Music by Dimitri Tiomkin.
Lyrics by Ned Washington.

1962

*DAYS OF WINE AND ROSES from *Days of Wine and Roses*. Martin Manulis-Jalem Prod., Warner Bros.
Music by Henry Mancini.
Lyrics by Johnny Mercer.

LOVE SONG FROM MUTINY ON THE BOUNTY ("Follow Me") from *Mutiny on the Bounty*. Arcola Prod., M-G-M.
Music by Bronislau Kaper.
Lyrics by Paul Francis Webster.

SONG FROM TWO FOR THE SEESAW ("Second Chance") from *Two for the Seesaw*. Mirisch-Argyle-Talbot Prod. in association with Seven Arts Productions, United Artists.
Music by Andre Previn.
Lyrics by Dory Langdon.

TENDER IS THE NIGHT from *Tender Is the Night*. 20th Century-Fox.
Music by Sammy Fain.
Lyrics by Paul Francis Webster.

WALK ON THE WILD SIDE from *Walk on the Wild Side*. Famous Artists Prods., Columbia.
Music by Elmer Bernstein.
Lyrics by Mack David.

1963

*CALL ME IRRESPONSIBLE from *Papa's Delicate Condition*. Amro Prods., Paramount.
Music by James Van Heusen.
Lyrics by Sammy Cahn.

CHARADE from *Charade*. Universal–Stanley Donen Prod., Universal.
Music by Henry Mancini.
Lyrics by Johnny Mercer.

IT'S A MAD, MAD, MAD, MAD WORLD from *It's a Mad, Mad, Mad, Mad World*. Casey Prod., United Artists.
  Music by Ernest Gold.
  Lyrics by Mack David.
MORE from *Mondo Cane*. Cineriz Prod., Times Film.
  Music by Riz Ortolani and Nino Oliviero.
  Lyrics by Norman Newell.
SO LITTLE TIME from *55 Days at Peking*. Samuel Bronston Prod., Allied Artists.
  Music by Dimitri Tiomkin.
  Lyrics by Paul Francis Webster.

1964

*CHIM CHIM CHER-EE from *Mary Poppins*. Walt Disney Prods., Buena Vista Distribution Co.
  Music and lyrics by Richard M. Sherman and Robert B. Sherman.
DEAR HEART from *Dear Heart*. A W. B.–Out-of-Towners Production, Warner Bros.
  Music by Henry Mancini.
  Lyrics by Jay Livingston and Ray Evans.
HUSH . . . HUSH, SWEET CHARLOTTE from *Hush . . . Hush, Sweet Charlotte*. An Associates & Aldrich Production, 20th Century-Fox.
  Music by Frank DeVol.
  Lyrics by Mack David.
MY KIND OF TOWN from *Robin and the 7 Hoods*. A P-C Production, Warner Bros.
  Music by James Van Heusen.
  Lyrics by Sammy Cahn.
WHERE LOVE HAS GONE from *Where Love Has Gone*. A Paramount-Embassy Pictures Production, Paramount.
  Music by James Van Heusen.
  Lyrics by Sammy Cahn.

1965

THE BALLAD OF CAT BALLOU from *Cat Ballou*. Harold Hecht Prod., Columbia.
  Music by Jerry Livingston.
  Lyrics by Mack David.
I WILL WAIT FOR YOU from *The Umbrellas of Cherbourg*. Parc-Madeleine Films Prod., American Intl.
  Music by Michel Legrand.
  Lyrics by Jacques Demy.
*THE SHADOW OF YOUR SMILE from *The Sandpiper*. Filmways-Venice Prod., M-G-M.
  Music by Johnny Mandel.
  Lyrics by Paul Francis Webster.
THE SWEETHEART TREE from *The Great Race*. Patricia-Jalem-Reynard Prod., Warner Bros.
  Music by Henry Mancini.
  Lyrics by Johnny Mercer.
WHAT'S NEW PUSSYCAT? from *What's New Pussycat?* Famous Artists–Famartists Prod., United Artists.
  Music by Burt Bacharach.
  Lyrics by Hal David.

1966

ALFIE from *Alfie*. Sheldrake Films, Ltd. Prod., Paramount.
  Music by Burt Bacharach.
  Lyrics by Hal David.
*BORN FREE from *Born Free*. Open Road Films, Ltd.–Atlas Films, Ltd. Prod., Columbia.
  Music by John Barry.
  Lyrics by Don Black.

GEORGY GIRL from *Georgy Girl*. Everglades Prods., Ltd., Columbia.
  Music by Tom Springfield.
  Lyrics by Jim Dale.
MY WISHING DOLL from *Hawaii*. Mirisch Corp. of Delaware Prod., United Artists.
  Music by Elmer Bernstein.
  Lyrics by Mack David.
A TIME FOR LOVE from *An American Dream*. Warner Bros.
  Music by Johnny Mandel.
  Lyrics by Paul Francis Webster.

1967

THE BARE NECESSITIES from *The Jungle Book*. Walt Disney Prods., Buena Vista Distribution Co.
  Music and lyrics by Terry Gilkyson.
THE EYES OF LOVE from *Banning*. Universal.
  Music by Quincy Jones.
  Lyrics by Bob Russell.
THE LOOK OF LOVE from *Casino Royale*. Famous Artists Prods., Ltd., Columbia.
  Music by Burt Bacharach.
  Lyrics by Hal David.
*TALK TO THE ANIMALS from *Doctor Dolittle*. Apjac Prods., 20th Century-Fox.
  Music and lyrics by Leslie Bricusse.
THOROUGHLY MODERN MILLIE from *Thoroughly Modern Millie*. Ross Hunter–Universal Prod., Universal.
  Music and lyrics by James Van Heusen and Sammy Cahn.

1968

CHITTY CHITTY BANG BANG from *Chitty Chitty Bang Bang*. Warfield Prods., United Artists.
  Music and lyrics by Richard M. Sherman and Robert B. Sherman.
FOR LOVE OF IVY from *For Love of Ivy*. American Broadcasting Companies–Palomar Pictures International Prod., Cinerama.
  Music by Quincy Jones.
  Lyrics by Bob Russell.
FUNNY GIRL from *Funny Girl*. Rastar Prods., Columbia.
  Music by Jule Styne.
  Lyrics by Bob Merrill.
STAR! from *Star!* Robert Wise Prod., 20th Century-Fox.
  Music by Jimmy Van Heusen.
  Lyrics by Sammy Cahn.
*THE WINDMILLS OF YOUR MIND from *The Thomas Crown Affair*. Mirisch-Simkoe-Solar Prod., United Artists.
  Music by Michel Legrand.
  Lyrics by Alan and Marilyn Bergman.

1969

COME SATURDAY MORNING from *The Sterile Cuckoo*. Boardwalk Prods., Paramount.
  Music by Fred Karlin.
  Lyrics by Dory Previn.
JEAN from *The Prime of Miss Jean Brodie*. 20th Century-Fox Prods., Ltd., 20th Century-Fox.
  Music and lyrics by Rod McKuen.
*RAINDROPS KEEP FALLIN' ON MY HEAD from *Butch Cassidy and the Sundance Kid*. George Roy Hill–Paul Monash Prod., 20th Century-Fox.
  Music by Burt Bacharach.
  Lyrics by Hal David.
TRUE GRIT from *True Grit*. Hal Wallis Prod., Paramount.

Music by Elmer Bernstein.

Lyrics by Don Black.

WHAT ARE YOU DOING THE REST OF YOUR LIFE? from *The Happy Ending*. Pax Films Prod., United Artists.

Music by Michel Legrand.

Lyrics by Alan and Marilyn Bergman.

1970

*FOR ALL WE KNOW from *Lovers and Other Strangers*. ABC Pictures Prod., Cinerama.

Music by Fred Karlin.

Lyrics by Robb Royer and James Griffin aka Robb Wilson and Arthur James.

PIECES OF DREAMS from *Pieces of Dreams*. RFB Enterprises Prod., United Artists.

Music by Michel Legrand.

Lyrics by Alan and Marilyn Bergman.

THANK YOU VERY MUCH from *Scrooge*. Waterbury Films, Ltd. Prod., Cinema Center Films Presentation, National General.

Music and lyrics by Leslie Bricusse.

TILL LOVE TOUCHES YOUR LIFE from *Madron*. Edric-Isracine-Zev Braun Prods., Four Star–Excelsior Releasing.

Music by Riz Ortolani.

Lyrics by Arthur Hamilton.

WHISTLING AWAY THE DARK from *Darling Lili*. Geoffrey Prods., Paramount.

Music by Henry Mancini.

Lyrics by Johnny Mercer.

1971

THE AGE OF NOT BELIEVING from *Bedknobs and Broomsticks*. Walt Disney Prods., Buena Vista Distribution.

Music and lyrics by Richard M. and Robert B. Sherman.

ALL HIS CHILDREN from *Sometimes a Great Notion*. A Universal-Newman-Foreman Company Prod., Universal.

Music by Henry Mancini.

Lyrics by Alan and Marilyn Bergman.

BLESS THE BEASTS & CHILDREN from *Bless the Beasts & Children*. Columbia.

Music and lyrics by Barry DeVorzon and Perry Botkin, Jr.

LIFE IS WHAT YOU MAKE IT from *Kotch*. A Kotch Company Production, ABC Pictures Presentation, Cinerama.

Music by Marvin Hamlisch.

Lyrics by Johnny Mercer.

*THEME FROM *SHAFT* from *Shaft*. Shaft Prods., Ltd., M-G.M.

Music and lyrics by Isaac Hayes.

1972

BEN from *Ben*. BCP Productions, Cinerama.

Music by Walter Scharf.

Lyrics by Don Black.

COME FOLLOW, FOLLOW ME from *The Little Ark*. Robert Radnitz Productions, Ltd., Cinema Center Films Presentation, National General.

Music by Fred Karlin.

Lyrics by Marsha Karlin.

MARMALADE, MOLASSES & HONEY from *The Life and Times of Judge Roy Bean*. A First Artists Production Company, Ltd. Production, National General.

Music by Maurice Jarre.

Lyrics by Marilyn and Alan Bergman.

*THE MORNING AFTER from *The Poseidon Adventure*. An Irwin Allen Production, 20th Century-Fox.
Music and lyrics by Al Kasha and Joel Hirschhorn.
STRANGE ARE THE WAYS OF LOVE from *The Stepmother*. Magic Eye of Hollywood Productions, Crown International.
Music by Sammy Fain.
Lyrics by Paul Francis Webster.

1973

ALL THAT LOVE WENT TO WASTE from *A Touch of Class*. Brut Prods., Avco Embassy.
Music by George Barrie.
Lyrics by Sammy Cahn.
LIVE AND LET DIE from *Live and Let Die*. Eon Prods., United Artists.
Music and lyrics by Paul and Linda McCartney.
LOVE from *Robin Hood*. Walt Disney Prods., Buena Vista Distribution Co.
Music by George Bruns.
Lyrics by Floyd Huddleston.
*THE WAY WE WERE from *The Way We Were*. Rastar Prods., Columbia.
Music by Marvin Hamlisch.
Lyrics by Alan and Marilyn Bergman.
NICE TO BE AROUND from *Cinderella Liberty*. A Sanford Prod., 20th Century-Fox.
Music by John Williams.
Lyrics by Paul Williams.

1974

BENJI'S THEME (I FEEL LOVE) from *Benji*. Mulberry Square.
Music by Euel Box.
Lyrics by Betty Box.
BLAZING SADDLES from *Blazing Saddles*. Warner Bros.
Music by John Morris.
Lyrics by Mel Brooks.
LITTLE PRINCE from *The Little Prince*. Stanley Donen Enterprises, Ltd., Paramount.
Music by Frederick Loewe.
Lyrics by Alan Jay Lerner.
*WE MAY NEVER LOVE LIKE THIS AGAIN from *The Towering Inferno*. An Irwin Allen Production, 20th Century-Fox/Warner Bros.
Music and lyrics by Al Kasha and Joel Hirschhorn.
WHEREVER LOVE TAKES ME from *Gold*. Avton Film Productions, Ltd., Allied Artists.
Music by Elmer Bernstein.
Lyrics by Don Black.

1975

HOW LUCKY CAN YOU GET from *Funny Lady*. A Rastar Pictures Production, Columbia.
Music and lyrics by Fred Ebb and John Kander.
*I'M EASY from *Nashville*. An ABC Entertainment–Jerry Weintraub–Robert Altman Production, Paramount.
Music and lyrics by Keith Carradine.
NOW THAT WE'RE IN LOVE from *Whiffs*. Brut Productions, 20th Century-Fox.
Music by George Barrie.
Lyrics by Sammy Cahn.
RICHARD'S WINDOW from *The Other Side of the Mountain*. A Filmways–Larry Peerce–Universal Production, Universal.
Music by Charles Fox.
Lyrics by Norman Gimbel.

THEME FROM MAHOGANY ("DO YOU KNOW WHERE YOU'RE GOING TO") from *Mahogany*. A Jobete Film Production, Paramount.
Music by Michael Masser.
Lyrics by Gerry Goffin.

1976

AVE SATANI from *The Omen*. 20th Century-Fox Productions, Ltd., 20th Century Fox.
Music and lyrics by Jerry Goldsmith.
COME TO ME from *The Pink Panther Strikes Again*. Amjo Productions, Ltd., United Artists.
Music by Henry Mancini.
Lyrics by Don Black.
*EVERGREEN (Love Theme from *A STAR IS BORN*) from *A Star Is Born*. A Barwood/Jon Peters Production, First Artists Presentation, Warner Bros.
Music by Barbra Streisand.
Lyrics by Paul Williams.
GONNA FLY NOW from *Rocky*. A Robert Chartoff–Irwin Winkler Production, United Artists.
Music by Bill Conti.
Lyrics by Carol Connors and Ayn Robbins.
A WORLD THAT NEVER WAS from *Half a House*. Lenro Productions, First American Films.
Music by Sammy Fain.
Lyrics by Paul Francis Webster.

1977

CANDLE ON THE WATER from *Pete's Dragon*. Walt Disney Prods., Buena Vista Distribution Co.
Music and lyrics by Al Kasha and Joel Hirschhorn.
NOBODY DOES IT BETTER from *The Spy Who Loved Me*. Eon Productions, United Artists.
Music by Marvin Hamlisch.
Lyrics by Carole Bayer Sager.
THE SLIPPER AND THE ROSE WALTZ (HE DANCED WITH ME/SHE DANCED WITH ME) from *The Slipper and the Rose—The Story of Cinderella*. Paradine Co-Productions, Ltd., Universal.
Music and lyrics by Richard M. and Robert B. Sherman.
SOMEONE'S WAITING FOR YOU from *The Rescuers*. Walt Disney Prods., Buena Vista Distribution Co.
Music by Sammy Fain.
Lyrics by Carol Connors and Ayn Robbins.
*YOU LIGHT UP MY LIFE from *You Light Up My Life*. The Session Company Production, Columbia.
Music and lyrics by Joseph Brooks.

1978

HOPELESSLY DEVOTED TO YOU from *Grease*. A Robert Stigwood/Allan Carr Production, Paramount.
Music and lyrics by John Farrar.
*LAST DANCE from *Thank God It's Friday*. A Casablanca-Motown Production, Columbia.
Music and lyrics by Paul Jabara.
THE LAST TIME I FELT LIKE THIS from *Same Time, Next Year*. A Walter Mirisch–Robert Mulligan Production, Mirisch Corporation/Universal Pictures Presentation, Universal.
Music by Marvin Hamlisch.
Lyrics by Alan and Marilyn Bergman.
READY TO TAKE A CHANCE AGAIN from *Foul Play*. A Miller-Milkis/Colin Higgins Picture Production, Paramount.
Music by Charles Fox.
Lyrics by Norman Gimbel.
WHEN YOU'RE LOVED from *The Magic of Lassie*. Lassie Productions, International Picture Show Company.
Music and lyrics by Richard M. and Robert B. Sherman.

1979

*IT GOES LIKE IT GOES from *Norma Rae*. A 20th Century-Fox Production, 20th Century-Fox.
Music by David Shire.
Lyrics by Norman Gimbel.
THE RAINBOW CONNECTION from *The Muppet Movie*. A Jim Henson Production, Lord Grade/Martin Starger presentation, Associated Film Distribution.
Music and lyrics by Paul Williams and Kenny Ascher.
IT'S EASY TO SAY from *10*. Geoffrey Productions, Orion.
Music by Henry Mancini.
Lyrics by Robert Wells.
THROUGH THE EYES OF LOVE from *Ice Castles*. An International Cinemedia Center Production, Columbia.
Music by Marvin Hamlisch.
Lyrics by Carole Bayer Sager.
I'LL NEVER SAY "GOODBYE" from *The Promise*. A Fred Weintraub–Paul Heller Present/Universal Production, Universal.
Music by David Shire.
Lyrics by Alan and Marilyn Bergman.

1980

*FAME from *Fame*. A Metro-Goldwyn-Mayer Production, M-G-M.
Music by Michael Gore.
Lyrics by Dean Pitchford.
9 TO 5 from *9 to 5*. A 20th Century-Fox Production, 20th Century-Fox.
Music and lyrics by Dolly Parton.
ON THE ROAD AGAIN from *Honeysuckle Rose*. A Warner Bros. Production, Warner Bros.
Music and lyrics by Willie Nelson.
OUT HERE ON MY OWN from *Fame*. A Metro-Goldwyn-Mayer Production, M-G-M.
Music by Michael Gore.
Lyrics by Lesley Gore.
PEOPLE ALONE from *The Competition*. A Rastar Films Production, Columbia.
Music by Lalo Schifrin.
Lyrics by Wilbur Jennings.

1981

*ARTHUR'S THEME (Best That You Can Do) from *Arthur*. A Rollins, Joffe, Morra and Brezner production, Orion.
Music and lyrics by Burt Bacharach, Carole Bayer Sager, Christopher Cross, and Peter Allen.
ENDLESS LOVE from *Endless Love*. A Polygram/Universal Pictures/Keith Barish/Dyson Lovell Production, Universal.
Music and lyrics by Lionel Richie.
THE FIRST TIME IT HAPPENS from *The Great Muppet Caper*. A Jim Henson/ITC Film Entertainment Limited Production, Universal.
Music and lyrics by Joe Raposo.
FOR YOUR EYES ONLY from *For Your Eyes Only*. An EON Production, United Artists.
Music by Bill Conti.
Lyrics by Mick Leeson.
ONE MORE HOUR from *Ragtime*. A Ragtime Production, Paramount.
Music and lyrics by Randy Newman.

1982

EYE OF THE TIGER from *Rocky III*. A Robert Chartoff–Irwin Winkler/United Artists Production, M-G-M/United Artists.

Music and lyrics by Jim Peterik and Frankie Sullivan III.

HOW DO YOU KEEP THE MUSIC PLAYING? from *Best Friends*. A Timberlane Films Production, Warner Bros.
Music by Michel Legrand.

Lyrics by Alan and Marilyn Bergman.

IF WE WERE IN LOVE from *Yes, Giorgio*. A Metro-Goldwyn-Mayer Production, M-G-M/United Artists.
Music by John Williams.

Lyrics by Alan and Marilyn Bergman.

IT MIGHT BE YOU from *Tootsie*. A Mirage/Punch Production, Columbia.
Music by Dave Grusin.

Lyrics by Alan and Marilyn Bergman.

*UP WHERE WE BELONG from *An Officer and a Gentleman*. A Lorimar Production in association with Martin Elfand, Paramount.
Music by Jack Nitzsche and Buffy Sainte-Marie.

Lyrics by Will Jennings.

1983

*FLASHDANCE . . . WHAT A FEELING from *Flashdance*. A Polygram Pictures Production, Paramount.
Music by Giorgio Moroder.

Lyrics by Keith Forsey and Irene Cara.

MANIAC from *Flashdance*. A Polygram Pictures Production, Paramount.
Music and lyrics by Michael Sembello and Dennis Matkowsky.

OVER YOU from *Tender Mercies*. An EMI Presentation of an Antron Media Production, Universal/AFD.
Music and lyrics by Austin Roberts and Bobby Hart.

PAPA, CAN YOU HEAR ME? from *Yentl*. A United Artists/Ladbroke Feature/Barwood Production, M-G-M/United Artists.
Music by Michael Legrand.

Lyrics by Alan and Marilyn Bergman.

THE WAY HE MAKES ME FEEL from *Yentl*. A United Artists/Ladbroke Feature/Barwood Production, M-G-M/United Artists.
Music by Michel Legrand.

Lyrics by Alan and Marilyn Bergman.

1984

AGAINST ALL ODDS (TAKE A LOOK AT ME NOW) from *Against All Odds*. A New Visions Production, Columbia.
Music and lyrics by Phil Collins.

FOOTLOOSE from *Footloose*. A Daniel Melnick Production, Paramount.
Music and lyrics by Kenny Loggins and Dean Pitchford.

GHOSTBUSTERS from *Ghostbusters*. A Columbia Pictures Production, Columbia.
Music and lyrics by Ray Parker, Jr.

*I JUST CALLED TO SAY I LOVE YOU from *The Woman in Red*. A Woman in Red Production, Orion.
Music and lyrics by Stevie Wonder.

LET'S HEAR IT FOR THE BOY from *Footloose*. A Daniel Melnick Production, Paramount.
Music and lyrics by Tom Snow and Dean Pitchford.

1985

MISS CELIE'S BLUES (SISTER) from *The Color Purple*. A Warner Bros. Production, Warner Bros.
Music by Quincy Jones and Rod Temperton.

Lyrics by Quincy Jones, Rod Temperton, and Lionel Richie.

THE POWER OF LOVE from *Back to the Future*. An Amblin Entertainment/Universal Pictures Production, Universal.
Music by Chris Hayes and Johnny Colla.

Lyrics by Huey Lewis.

*SAY YOU, SAY ME from *White Nights*. A New Visions Production, Columbia.
  Music and lyrics by Lionel Richie.
SEPARATE LIVES from *White Nights*. A New Visions Production, Columbia.
  Music and lyrics by Stephen Bishop.
SURPRISE, SURPRISE from *A Chorus Line*. An Embassy Films Associates and Polygram Pictures Production,
  Columbia.
  Music by Marvin Hamlisch.
  Lyrics by Edward Kleban.

1986

GLORY OF LOVE from *The Karate Kid Part II*. A Columbia Pictures Production, Columbia.
  Music by Peter Cetera and David Foster.
  Lyrics by Peter Cetera and Diane Nini.
LIFE IN A LOOKING GLASS from *That's Life*. A Paradise Cove/Ubilam Production, Columbia.
  Music by Henry Mancini.
  Lyrics by Leslie Bricusse.
MEAN GREEN MOTHER FROM OUTER SPACE from *Little Shop of Horrors*. A Geffen Company Production,
  Geffen Company through Warner Bros.
  Music by Alan Menken.
  Lyrics by Howard Ashman.
SOMEWHERE OUT THERE from *An American Tail*. An Amblin Entertainment Production, Universal.
  Music by James Horner and Barry Mann.
  Lyrics by Cynthia Weil.
*TAKE MY BREATH AWAY from *Top Gun*. A Don Simpson/Jerry Bruckheimer Production, Paramount.
  Music by Giorgio Moroder.
  Lyrics by Tim Whitlock.

1987

CRY FREEDOM from *Cry Freedom*. A Marble Arch Production, Universal.
  Music and lyrics by George Fenton and Jonas Gwangwa.
*(I'VE HAD) THE TIME OF MY LIFE from *Dirty Dancing*. A Vestron Pictures Production in association with
  Great American Films Limited Partnership, Vestron.
  Music by Franke Previte, John DeNicola, and Donald Markowitz.
  Lyrics by Franke Previte.
NOTHING'S GONNA STOP US NOW from *Mannequin*. A Gladden Entertainment Production, 20th
  Century Fox.
  Music and lyrics by Albert Hammond and Diane Warren.
SHAKEDOWN from *Beverly Hills Cop II*. A Don Simpson/Jerry Bruckheimer Production, in association with
  Eddie Murphy Productions, Paramount.
  Music by Harold Faltermeyer and Keith Forsey.
  Lyrics by Harold Faltermeyer, Keith Forsey, and Bob Seger.
STORYBOOK LOVE from *The Princess Bride*. An Act III Communications Production, 20th Century Fox.
  Music and lyrics by Willy DeVille.

1988

CALLING YOU from *Bagdad Cafe*. A Pelemere Film Production, Island Pictures.
  Music and Lyrics by Bob Telson.
*LET THE RIVER RUN from *Working Girl*. A 20th Century Rox Production, 20th Century Fox.
  Music and lyrics by Carly Simon.
TWO HEARTS (ONE MIND) from *Buster*. A NFH Production, Hemdale Releasing.
  Music by Lamont Dozier.
  Lyrics by Phil Collins.

SCORING AWARDS

1958

Scoring of a Dramatic or Comedy Picture

THE BIG COUNTRY. Anthony-Worldwide Prods., United Artists. Jerome Moross.

*THE OLD MAN AND THE SEA. Leland Hayward, Warner Bros. Dimitri Tiomkin.

SEPARATE TABLES. Clifton Prods., Inc., United Artists. David Raksin.

WHITE WILDERNESS. Walt Disney Prods., Buena Vista Film Distribution Co. Oliver Wallace.

THE YOUNG LIONS. 20th Century-Fox. Hugo Friedhofer.

Scoring of a Musical Picture

THE BOLSHOI BALLET. A Rank Organization Presentation/Harmony Film, Rank Film Distributors of America (British). Yuri Faier and G. Rozhdestvensky.

DAMN YANKEES. Warner Bros. Ray Heindorf.

*GIGI. Arthur Freed Prods., M-G-M. Andre Previn.

MARDI GRAS. Jerry Wald Prods., 20th Century-Fox. Lionel Newman.

SOUTH PACIFIC. South Pacific Enterprises, Magna Theatre Corp. Alfred Newman and Ken Darby.

1959

Scoring of a Dramatic or Comedy Picture

*BEN-HUR. M-G-M. Miklos Rozsa.

THE DIARY OF ANNE FRANK. 20th Century-Fox. Alfred Newman.

THE NUN'S STORY. Warner Bros. Franz Waxman.

ON THE BEACH. Lomitas Prods., United Artists. Ernest Gold.

PILLOW TALK. Arwin Prods., U-1. Frank DeVol.

Scoring of a Musical Picture

THE FIVE PENNIES. Dena Prod., Paramount. Leith Stevens.

LI'L ABNER. Panama and Frank, Paramount. Nelson Riddle and Joseph J. Lilley.

*PORGY AND BESS. Samuel Goldwyn Prods., Columbia. Andre Previn and Ken Darby.

SAY ONE FOR ME. Bing Crosby Prods., 20th Century-Fox. Lionel Newman.

SLEEPING BEAUTY. Walt Disney Prods., Buena Vista Film Distribution Co., George Bruns.

1960

Scoring of a Dramatic or Comedy Picture

THE ALAMO. Batjac Prod., United Artists. Dimitri Tiomkin.

ELMER GANTRY. Burt Lancaster/Richard Brooks Prod., United Artists. Andre Previn.

*EXODUS. Carlyle-Alpina S.A. Prod., United Artists. Ernest Gold.

THE MAGNIFICENT SEVEN. Mirisch-Alpha Prod., United Artists. Elmer Bernstein.

SPARTACUS. Bryna Prods., U-1. Alex North.

Scoring of a Musical Picture

BELLS ARE RINGING. Arthur Freed Prod., M-G-M. Andre Previn.

CAN-CAN. Suffolk-Cummings Prods., 20th Century-Fox. Nelson Riddle.

LET'S MAKE LOVE. Company of Artists, 20th Century-Fox. Lionel Newman and Earle H. Hagen.

PEPE. G.S.-Posa Films International Prod., Columbia. Johnny Green.

*SONG WITHOUT END (The Story of Franz Liszt). Goetz-Vidor Pictures Prod., Columbia. Morris Stoloff and Harry Sukman.

1961

Scoring of a Dramatic or Comedy Picture

*BREAKFAST AT TIFFANY'S. Jurow-Shepherd Prod., Paramount. Henry Mancini.

EL CID. Samuel Bronston Prod. in association with Dear Film Prod., Allied Artists. Miklos Rozsa.

FANNY. Mansfield Prod., Warner Bros. Morris Stoloff and Harry Sukman.
THE GUNS OF NAVARONE. Carl Foreman Prod., Columbia. Dimitri Tiomkin.
SUMMER AND SMOKE. Hal Wallis Prod., Paramount. Elmer Bernstein.

Scoring of a Musical Picture
BABES IN TOYLAND. Walt Disney Prods., Buena Vista Distribution Co. George Bruns.
FLOWER DRUM SONG. Universal-International–Ross Hunter Prod. in association with Joseph Fields, U-1. Alfred Newman and Ken Darby.
KHOVANSHCHINA. Mosfilm Studios, Artkino Pictures (Russian). Dimitri Shostakovich.
PARIS BLUES. Pennebaker, United Artists. Duke Ellington.
*WEST SIDE STORY. Mirisch Pictures and B and P Enterprises, United Artists. Saul Chaplin, Johnny Green, Sid Ramin, and Irwin Kostal.

1962
(NOTE: Title of awards changed)
Music Score—Substantially Original
FREUD. Universal-International–John Huston Prod., U-1. Jerry Goldsmith.
*LAWRENCE OF ARABIA. Horizon Pictures (G.B.), Ltd.–Sam Spiegel-David Lean Prod., Columbia. Maurice Jarre.
MUTINY ON THE BOUNTY. Arcola Prod., M-G-M. Bronislau Kaper.
TARAS BULBA. Harold Hecht Prod., United Artists. Franz Waxman.
TO KILL A MOCKINGBIRD. Universal-International–Pakula-Mulligan-Brentwood Prod., U-I. Elmer Bernstein.

Scoring of Music—Adaptation or Treatment
Billy Rose's JUMBO. Euterpe-Arwin Prod., M-G-M. George Stoll.
GIGOT. Seven Arts Prods., 20th Century-Fox. Michel Magne.
GYPSY. Warner Bros. Frank Perkins.
*Meredith Wilson's THE MUSIC MAN. Warner Bros. Ray Heindorf.
THE WONDERFUL WORLD OF THE BROTHERS GRIMM. M-G-M & Cinerama. Leigh Harline.

1963
Music Score—Substantially Original
CLEOPATRA. 20th Century-Fox Ltd.–MCL Films S.A.–WALWA Films S.A. Prod., 20th Century-Fox. Alex North.
55 DAYS AT PEKING. Samuel Bronston Prod., Allied Artists. Dimitri Tiomkin.
HOW THE WEST WAS WON. M-G-M & Cinerama. Alfred Newman and Ken Darby.
IT'S A MAD, MAD, MAD, MAD WORLD. Casey Prod., United Artists. Ernest Gold.
*TOM JONES. Woodfall Prod., United Artists–Lopert Pictures. John Addison.

Scoring of Music—Adaptation or Treatment
BYE BYE BIRDIE. Kohlmar-Sidney Prod., Columbia. John Green.
*IRMA LA DOUCE. Mirisch-Phalanx Prod., United Artists. Andre Previn.
A NEW KIND OF LOVE. Llenroc Prods., Paramount. Leith Stevens.
SUNDAYS AND CYBELE. Terra-Fides-Orsay-Films Trocadero Prod., Columbia. Maurice Jarre.
THE SWORD IN THE STONE. Walt Disney Prods., Buena Vista Distribution Co. George Bruns.

1964
Music Score—Substantially Original (for which only the composer shall be eligible)
BECKET. A Hal Wallis Production, Paramount. Laurence Rosenthal.
THE FALL OF THE ROMAN EMPIRE. A Bronston-Roma Production, Paramount. Dimitri Tiomkin.
HUSH . . . HUSH, SWEET CHARLOTTE. An Associates & Aldrich Production, 20th Century-Fox. Frank DeVol.

MARY POPPINS. Walt Disney Prods., Buena Vista Distribution Co. Richard M. and Robert B. Sherman.
THE PINK PANTHER. A Mirisch–G-E Production, United Artists. Henry Mancini.

Scoring of Music—Adaptation or Treatment (for
which only the adapter and/or music director shall be
eligible)
A HARD DAY'S NIGHT. A Walter Shenson Production, United Artists. George Martin.
MARY POPPINS. Walt Disney Prods., Buena Vista Distribution Co. Irwin Kostal.
MY FAIR LADY. Warner Bros. Andre Previn.
ROBIN AND THE 7 HOODS. A P-C Production, Warner Bros. Nelson Riddle.
THE UNSINKABLE MOLLY BROWN. A Marten Production, M-G-M. Robert Armbruster, Leo Arnaud, Jack
Elliott, Jack Hayes, Calvin Jackson, and Leo Shuken.

1965
Music Score—Substantially Original
THE AGONY AND THE ECSTASY. International Classics Prod., 20th Century-Fox. Alex North.
*DOCTOR ZHIVAGO. Sostar S.A.–Metro-Goldwyn-Mayer British Studios, Ltd. Prod., M-G-M.
Maurice Jarre.
THE GREATEST STORY EVER TOLD. George Stevens Prod., United Artists. Alfred Newman.
A PATCH OF BLUE. Pandro S. Berman—Guy Green Prod., M-G-M. Jerry Goldsmith.
THE UMBRELLAS OF CHERBOURG. Parc-Madeleine Films Prod., American International. Michel Legrand
and Jacques Demy.

Scoring of Music—Adaptation or Treatment
CAT BALLOU. Harold Hecht Prod., Columbia. DeVol.
THE PLEASURE SEEKERS. 20th Century-Fox. Lionel Newman and Alexander Courage.
*THE SOUND OF MUSIC. Argyle Enterprises Prod., 20th Century-Fox. Irwin Kostal.
A THOUSAND CLOWNS. Harrell Prod., United Artists. Don Walker.
THE UMBRELLAS OF CHERBOURG. Parc-Madeleine Films Prod., American International. Michel Legrand.

1966
Original Music Score
THE BIBLE. Thalia-A.-G. Prod., 20th Century-Fox. Toshiro Mayuzumi.
*BORN FREE. Open Road Films, Ltd.–Atlas Films, Ltd., Prod., Columbia. John Barry.
HAWAII. Mirisch Corp. of Delaware Prod., United Artists. Elmer Bernstein.
THE SAND PEBBLES. Argyle-Solar Prod., 20th Century-Fox. Jerry Goldsmith.
WHO'S AFRAID OF VIRGINIA WOOLF? Chenault Prod., Warner Bros. Alex North.

Scoring of Music—Adaptation or Treatment
*A FUNNY THING HAPPENED ON THE WAY TO THE FORUM. Melvin Frank Prod., United Artists. Ken
Thorne.
THE GOSPEL ACCORDING TO ST. MATTHEW. Arco-Lux Cie Cinematografique de France Prod., Walter
Reade–Continental Distributing. Luis Enrique Bacalov.
RETURN OF THE SEVEN. Mirisch Prods., United Artists. Elmer Bernstein.
THE SINGING NUN. M-G-M. Harry Sukman.
STOP THE WORLD—I WANT TO GET OFF. Warner Bros. Prods., Ltd., Warner Bros. Al Ham.

1967
Original Music Score
COOL HAND LUKE. Jalem Prod., Warner Bros.–Seven Arts. Lalo Schifrin.
DOCTOR DOLITTLE. Apjac Prods., 20th Century-Fox. Leslie Bricusse.
FAR FROM THE MADDING CROWD. Appia Films, Ltd. Prod., M-G-M. Richard Rodney Bennett.
IN COLD BLOOD. Pax Enterprises Prod., Columbia. Quincy Jones.
*THOROUGHLY MODERN MILLIE. Ross Hunter–Universal Prod., Universal. Elmer Bernstein.

Scoring of Music—Adaptation or Treatment
*CAMELOT. Warner Bros.–Seven Arts. Alfred Newman and Ken Darby.
DOCTOR DOLITTLE. Apjac Productions, 20th Century-Fox. Lionel Newman and Alexander Courage.
GUESS WHO'S COMING TO DINNER. Columbia. DeVol.
THOROUGHLY MODERN MILLIE. Ross Hunter–Universal Production, Universal. Andre Previn and Joseph Gershenson.
VALLEY OF THE DOLLS. Red Lion Prods., 20th Century-Fox. John Williams.

1968

Best Original Score—for a Motion Picture (Not a Musical)
THE FOX. Raymond Stross–Motion Pictures International Prod., Claridge Pictures. Lalo Schifrin.
*THE LION IN WINTER. Haworth Prods., Ltd., Avco Embassy. John Barry.
PLANET OF THE APES. APJAC Prods., 20th Century-Fox. Jerry Goldsmith.
THE SHOES OF THE FISHERMAN. George Englund Prod., M-G-M. Alex North.
THE THOMAS CROWN AFFAIR. Mirisch-Simkoe-Solar Prod., United Artists. Michel Legrand.

Best Score of a Musical Picture: Original or Adaptation
FINIAN'S RAINBOW. Warner Bros.–Seven Arts. Adapted by Ray Heindorf.
FUNNY GIRL. Rastar Prods., Columbia. Adapted by Walter Scharf.
*OLIVER! Romulus Films, Columbia. Adapted by John Green.
STAR! Robert Wise Prod., 20th Century-Fox. Adapted by Lennie Hayton.
THE YOUNG GIRLS OF ROCHEFORT. Mag Bodard-Gilbert de Goldschmidt-Parc Film–Madeleine Films Prod., Warner Bros.–Seven Arts. Michel Legrand and Jacques Demy.

1969

Best Original Score—for a Motion Picture (Not a Musical)
ANNE OF THE THOUSAND DAYS. Hal B. Wallis—Universal Pictures, Ltd. Prod., Universal. Georges Delerue.
*BUTCH CASSIDY AND THE SUNDANCE KID. George Roy Hill–Paul Monash Prod., 20th Century-Fox. Burt Bacharach.
THE REIVERS. Irving Ravetch–Arthur Kramer–Solar Prods. Cinema Center Films Presentation, National General. John Williams.
THE SECRET OF SANTA VITTORIA. Stanley Kramer Company Prod., United Artists. Ernest Gold.
THE WILD BUNCH. Phil Feldman Prod., Warner Bros. Jerry Fielding.

Best Score of a Musical Picture: Original or Adaptation
GOODBYE, MR. CHIPS. APJAC Prod., M-G-M. Music and lyrics by Leslie Bricusse. Adapted by John Williams.
*HELLO, DOLLY! Chenault Prods., 20th Century-Fox. Adapted by Lennie Hayton and Lionel Newman.
PAINT YOUR WAGON. Alan Jay Lerner Prod., Paramount. Adapted by Nelson Riddle.
SWEET CHARITY. Universal. Adapted by Cy Coleman.
THEY SHOOT HORSES, DON'T THEY? Chartoff-Winkler-Pollack Prod., ABC Pictures Presentation, Cinerama. Adapted by John Green and Albert Woodbury.

1970

Best Original Score
AIRPORT. Ross Hunter–Universal Prod., Universal.
CROMWELL. Irving Allen, Ltd. Prod., Columbia. Frank Cordell.
*LOVE STORY. The Love Story Company Prod., Paramount. Francis Lai.
PATTON. 20th Century-Fox. Jerry Goldsmith.

SUNFLOWER. Sostar Prod., Avco Embassy. Henry Mancini.

Best Original Song Score
THE BABY MAKER. Robert Wise Prod., National General. Music by Fred Karlin. Lyrics by Tylwyth Kymry.
A BOY NAMED CHARLIE BROWN. Lee Mendelson-Melendez Features Prod., Cinema Center Films Presentation, National General. Music by Rod McKuen and John Scott Trotter. Lyrics by Rod McKuen, Bill Melendez, and Al Shean. Adapted by Vince Guaraldi.
DARLING LILI. Geoffrey Prod., Paramount. Music by Henry Mancini. Lyrics by Johnny Mercer.
*LET IT BE. Beatles-Apple Prod., United Artists. Music and lyrics by the Beatles.
SCROOGE. Waterbury Films, Ltd. Prod., Cinema Center Films Presentation, National General. Music and lyrics by Leslie Bricusse. Adapted by Ian Fraser and Herbert W. Spencer.

1971

Best Original Dramatic Score
MARY, QUEEN OF SCOTS. A Hal Wallis–Universal Pictures, Ltd. Prod., Universal. John Barry.
NICHOLAS AND ALEXANDRA. A Horizon Pictures Prod., Columbia. Richard Rodney Bennett.
SHAFT. Shaft Prods., Ltd., M-G-M. Isaac Hayes.
STRAW DOGS. A Talent Associates, Ltd.–Amerbroco Films, Ltd. Prod., ABC Pictures Presentation, Cinerama. Jerry Fielding.
*SUMMER OF '42. A Robert Mulligan–Richard Alan Roth Prod., Warner Bros. Michel Legrand.

Best Scoring: Adaptation and Original Song Score
BEDKNOBS AND BROOMSTICKS. Walt Disney Prods., Buena Vista Distribution Co. Song score by Richard M. and Robert B. Sherman. Adapted by Irwin Kostal.
THE BOY FRIEND. A Russflix, Ltd. Prod., M-G-M. Adapted by Peter Maxwell Davies and Peter Greenwell.
*FIDDLER ON THE ROOF. Mirisch-Cartier Prods., United Artists. Adapted by John Williams.
TCHAIKOVSKY. A Dimitri Tiomkin–Mosfilm Studios Prod. Adapted by Dimitri Tiomkin.
WILLY WONKA AND THE CHOCOLATE FACTORY. A Wolper Pictures, Ltd. Prod., Paramount. Song score by Leslie Bricusse and Anthony Newley. Adapted by Walter Scharf.

1972

Best Original Dramatic Score
IMAGES. A Hemdale Group, Ltd.–Lion's Gate Films Prod., Columbia. John Williams.
*LIMELIGHT. A Charles Chaplin Prod., Columbia. Charles Chaplin, Raymond Rasch, and Larry Russell.
NAPOLEON AND SAMANTHA. Walt Disney Prods., Buena Vista Distribution Co. Buddy Baker.
THE POSEIDON ADVENTURE. An Irwin Allen Prod., 20th Century-Fox. John Williams.
SLEUTH. A Palomar Pictures International Prod., 20th Century-Fox. John Addison.

Best Scoring: Adaptation and Original Song Score
*CABARET. An ABC Pictures Prod., Allied Artists. Adapted by Ralph Burns.
LADY SINGS THE BLUES. A Motown-Weston-Furie prod., Paramount. Adapted by Gil Askey.
MAN OF LA MANCHA. A PEA Produzioni Europee Associate Prod., United Artists. Adapted by Laurence Rosenthal.

1973

Best Original Dramatic Score
CINDERELLA LIBERTY. A Sanford Prod., 20th Century-Fox. John Williams.
THE DAY OF THE DOLPHIN. Icarus Prods., Avco Embassy. Georges Delerue.
PAPILLON. A Corona–General Production Company Prod., Allied Artists. Jerry Goldsmith.
A TOUCH OF CLASS. Brut Prods., Avco Embassy. John Cameron.
*THE WAY WE WERE. Rastar Prods., Columbia. Marvin Hamlisch.

Best Scoring: Original Song Score and/or Adaptation

Jesus Christ Superstar. A Universal–Norman Jewison–Robert Stigwood Prod., Universal. Adapted by Andre Previn, Herbert Spencer, and Andrew Lloyd Webber.
*The Sting. A Universal-Bill/Phillips-George Roy Hill Film Prod., Zanuck/Brown Presentation, Universal. Adapted by Marvin Hamlisch.
Tom Sawyer. An Arthur P. Jacobs Prod., Reader's Digest Presentation, United Artists. Song score by Richard M. and Robert B. Sherman. Adapted by John Williams.

1974

Best Original Dramatic Score
Chinatown. A Robert Evans Prod., Paramount. Jerry Goldsmith.
*The Godfather Part II. A Coppola Company Prod., Paramount. Nino Rota and Carmine Coppola.
Murder on the Orient Express. A G.W. Films, Ltd. Prod., Paramount. Richard Rodney Bennett.
Shanks. William Castle Prods., Paramount. Alex North.
The Towering Inferno. An Irwin Allen Prod., 20th Century-Fox/Warner Bros. John Williams.

Best Scoring: Original Song Score and/or Adaptation
*The Great Gatsby. A David Merrick Prod., Paramount. Adapted by Nelson Riddle.
The Little Prince. A Stanley Donen Enterprises, Ltd. Prod., Paramount. Song score by Alan Jay Lerner and Frederick Loewe. Adapted by Angela Morley and Douglas Gamley.
Phantom of the Paradise. Harbor Prods., 20th Century-Fox. Song score by Paul Williams. Adapted by Paul Williams and George Aliceson Tipton.

1975

Best Original Score
Birds Do It, Bees Do It. A Wolper Pictures Production, Columbia. Gerald Fried.
Bite the Bullet. A Pax Enterprises Production, Columbia. Alex North.
*Jaws. A Universal–Zanuck/Brown Production, Universal. John Williams.
One Flew over the Cuckoo's Nest. A Fantasy Films Production, United Artists. Jack Nitzsche
The Wind and the Lion. A Herb Jaffe Production, M-G-M. Jerry Goldsmith

Best Scoring: Original Song Score and/or Adaptation
*Barry Lyndon. A Hawk Films, Ltd. Production, Warner Bros. Adapted by Leonard Rosenman.
Funny Lady. A Rastar Pictures Production, Columbia. Adapted by Peter Matz.
Tommy. A Robert Stigwood Organization, Ltd. Production, Columbia. Adapted by Peter Townshend.

1976

Best Original Score
Obsession. George Litto Productions, Columbia Pictures. Bernard Herrmann.
*The Omen. 20th Century-Fox Productions, Ltd., 20th Century-Fox. Jerry Goldsmith.
The Outlaw Josey Wales. A Malpaso Company Production, Warner Bros. Jerry Fielding.
Taxi Driver. A Bill/Phillips Production of a Martin Scorsese Film, Columbia Pictures. Bernard Herrmann.
Voyage of the Damned. An ITC Entertainment Production, Avco Embassy. Lalo Schifrin.

Best Original Song Score and Its Adaptation or Best Adaptation Score
*Bound for Glory. Bound for Glory Company Production, United Artists. Adapted by Leonard Rosenman.
Bugsy Malone. A Goodtimes Enterprises, Ltd. Production, Paramount. Song score and its adaptation by Paul Williams.
A Star Is Born. A Barwood/Jon Peters Production, First Artists Presentation, Warner Bros. Adapted by Roger Kellaway.

1977

Best Original Score

CLOSE ENCOUNTERS OF THE THIRD KIND. A Julia Phillips/Michael Phillips—Steven Spielberg Film Production, Columbia. John Williams.

JULIA. A 20th Century-Fox Production, 20th Century-Fox. Georges Delerue.

MOHAMMAD—MESSENGER OF GOD. A Filmco International Production, Irwin Yablans Company. Maurice Jarre.

THE SPY WHO LOVED ME. Eon Productions, United Artists. Marvin Hamlisch.

*STAR WARS. A Lucasfilm, Ltd. Production, 20th Century-Fox. John Williams.

Best Original Song Score and Its Adaptation or Best
Adaptation Score

*A LITTLE NIGHT MUSIC. A Sascha-Wien Film Production in association with Elliott Kastner, New World Pictures. Adapted by Jonathan Tunick.

PETE'S DRAGON. Walt Disney Prod., Buena Vista Distribution Co. Song score by Al Kasha and Joel Hirschhorn. Adapted by Irwin Kostal.

THE SLIPPER AND THE ROSE—THE STORY OF CINDERELLA. Paradine Co-Productions, Ltd., Universal. Song score by Richard M. and Robert B. Sherman. Adapted by Angela Morley.

1978

Best Original Score

THE BOYS FROM BRAZIL. An ITC Entertainment Production, 20th Century-Fox. Jerry Goldsmith.

DAYS OF HEAVEN. An OP Production, Paramount. Ennio Morricone.

HEAVEN CAN WAIT. Dogwood Productions, Paramount. Dave Grusin.

*MIDNIGHT EXPRESS. A Casablanca Filmworks Production, Columbia. Giorgio Moroder.

SUPERMAN. A Dovemead Ltd. Production, Alexander Salkind Presentation, Warner Bros. John Williams.

Best Adaptation Score

*THE BUDDY HOLLY STORY. An Innovisions-ECA Production, Columbia. Joe Renzetti.

PRETTY BABY. A Louis Malle Film Production, Paramount. Jerry Wexler.

THE WIZ. A Motown/Universal Pictures Production, Universal. Quincy Jones

1979

Best Original Score

THE AMITYVILLE HORROR. An American International/Professional Films Production, American International Pictures. Lalo Schifrin.

THE CHAMP. A Metro-Goldwyn-Mayer Production, M-G-M. Dave Grusin.

*A LITTLE ROMANCE. A Pan Arts Associates Production, Orion. Georges Delerue.

STAR TREK—THE MOTION PICTURE. A Century Associates Production, Paramount. Jerry Goldsmith.

10. Geoffrey Productions, Orion. Henry Mancini.

Best Original Song Score and Its Adaptation or Best
Adaptation Score

*ALL THAT JAZZ. A Columbia/20th Century-Fox Production, 20th Century-Fox. Adaptation score by Ralph Burns.

BREAKING AWAY. A 20th Century-Fox Production, 20th Century-Fox. Adaptation score by Patrick Williams.

THE MUPPET MOVIE. A Jim Henson Production, Lord Grade/Martin Starger Presentation, Associated Film Distribution. Song score by Paul Williams and Kenny Ascher. Adapted by Paul Williams.

1980

Best Original Score

ALTERED STATES. A Warner Bros. Production, Warner Bros. John Corigliano.

THE ELEPHANT MAN. A Brooksfilms, Ltd. Production, Paramount. John Morris.

THE EMPIRE STRIKES BACK. A Lucasfilm, Ltd. Production, 20th Century-Fox. John Williams

*FAME. A Metro-Goldwyn-Mayer Production, M-G-M. Michael Gore.

TESS. A Renn-Burrill Co-production with the participation of the Societe Francaise de Production, Columbia. Philippe Sarde.

Best Adaptation Score
No award given this year due to insufficient eligible films.

1981

Best Original Score
*CHARIOTS OF FIRE. Enigma Productions Limited, The Ladd Company/Warner Bros. Vangelis.

DRAGONSLAYER. A Barwood/Robbins Production, Paramount. Alex North.

ON GOLDEN POND. An ITC Films/IPC Films Production, Universal. Dave Grusin.

RAGTIME. A Ragtime Production, Paramount. Randy Newman.

RAIDERS OF THE LOST ARK. A Lucasfilm Production, Paramount. John Williams.

Best Original Song Score and Its Adaptation or Adaptation Score
No award given this year due to insufficient eligible films.

1982

Best Original Score
*E.T. THE EXTRA-TERRESTRIAL. A Universal Pictures Production, Universal. John Williams

GANDHI. An Indo-British Films Production, Columbia. Ravi Shankar and George Fenton.

AN OFFICER AND A GENTLEMAN. A Lorimar production in association with Martin Elfand, Paramount. Jack Nitzsche.

POLTERGEIST. A Metro-Goldwyn-Mayer/Steven Spielberg Production, M-G.M/United Artists. Jerry Goldsmith.

SOPHIE'S CHOICE. An ITC Entertainment Presentation of a Pakula-Barish Production, Universal/A.F.D. Marvin Hamlisch.

Best Original Score and Its Adaptation or Adaptation Score
ANNIE. A Rastar Films Production, Columbia. Adaptation score by Ralph Burns.

ONE FROM THE HEART. A Zoetrope Studios Production, Columbia. Song score by Tom Waits.

*VICTOR/VICTORIA. A Metro-Goldwyn-Mayer Production, M-G-M/United Artists. Song score by Henry Mancini and Leslie Bricusse. Adapted by Henry Mancini.

1983

Best Original Score
CROSS CREEK. A Robert B. Radnitz/Martin Ritt/Thorn EMI Films Production, Universal. Leonard Rosenman.

RETURN OF THE JEDI. A Lucasfilm Production, 20th Century-Fox. John Williams.

*THE RIGHT STUFF. A Robert Chartoff–Irwin Winkler Production, The Ladd Company through Warner Bros. Bill Conti.

TERMS OF ENDEARMENT. A James L. Brooks Production, Paramount. Michael Gore.

UNDER FIRE. A Lions Gate Films Production, Orion. Jerry Goldsmith.

Best Original Song Score or Adaptation Score
THE STING II. A Jennings Lang/Universal Pictures Production, Universal. Adaptation score by Lalo Schifrin.

TRADING PLACES. An Aaron Russo Production, Paramount. Adaptation score by Elmer Bernstein.

*YENTL. A United Artists/Ladbroke Feature/Barwood Production, M-G-M/United Artists. Original song score by Michel Legrand, Alan Bergman, and Marilyn Bergman.

1984

Best Original Score
INDIANA JONES AND THE TEMPLE OF DOOM. A Lucasfilm Production, Paramount. John Williams.
THE NATURAL. A Tri-Star Pictures Production, Tri-Star. Randy Newman.
*A PASSAGE TO INDIA. A G.W. Films Limited Production, Columbia. Maurice Jarre.
THE RIVER. A Universal Pictures Production, Universal. John Williams.
UNDER THE VOLCANO. An Ithaca Enterprises Production, Universal. Alex North.

Best Original Song Score
THE MUPPETS TAKE MANHATTAN. A Tri-Star Pictures Production, Tri-Star. Jeff Moss.
*PURPLE RAIN. A Purple Films Company Production, Warner Bros. Prince.
SONGWRITER. A Tri-Star Pictures Production, Tri-Star. Kris Kristofferson.

1985

Best Original Score
AGNES OF GOD. A Columbia Pictures Production, Columbia. Georges Delerue.
THE COLOR PURPLE. A Warner Bros. Production, Warner Bros. Quincy Jones, Jeremy Lubbock, Rod Temperton, Caiphus Semenya, Andrae Crouch, Chris Boardman, Jorge Calandrelli, Joel Rosenbaum, Fred Steiner, Jack Hayes, Jerry Hey, and Randy Kerber.
*OUT OF AFRICA. A Universal Pictures Limited Production, Universal. John Barry.
SILVERADO. A Columbia Pictures Production, Columbia. Bruce Boughton.
WITNESS. An Edward S. Feldman Production, Paramount. Maurice Jarre.

1986

Best Original Score
ALIENS. A 20th Century Fox Film Production, 20th Century Fox. James Horner.
HOOSIERS. A Carter De Haven Production, Orion. Jerry Goldsmith.
THE MISSION. A Warner Bros./Goldcrest and Kingsmere Production, Warner Bros. Ennio Morricone.
*'ROUND MIDNIGHT. An Irwin Winkler Production, Warner Bros. Herbie Hancock.
STAR TREK IV: THE VOYAGE HOME. A Harve Bennett Production, Paramount. Leonard Rosenman.

1987

Best Original Score
CRY FREEDOM. A Marble Arch Production, Universal. George Fenton and Jonas Gwangwa.
EMPIRE OF THE SUN. A Warner Bros. Production, Warner Bros. John Williams.
*THE LAST EMPEROR. A Hemdale Film Production, Columbia. Ryuichi Sakamoto, David Byrne, and Cong Su.
THE WITCHES OF EASTWICK. A Warner Bros. Production, Warner Bros. John Williams.
THE UNTOUCHABLES. An Art Linson Production, Paramount. Ennio Morricone.

1988

Best Original Score
ACCIDENTAL TOURIST. A Warner Bros. Production, Warner Bros. John Williams.
DANGEROUS LIAISONS. A Lorimar Film Entertainment Co. Production, Warner Bros. George Fenton.
GORILLAS IN THE MIST. A Warner Bros. Production, Warner Bros. and Universal. Maurice Jarre.
*THE MILAGRO BEANFIELD WAR. A Milagro Productions Production, Universal. Dave Frusin.
RAIN MAN. A Guber-Peters Co. Production, United Artists. Hans Zimmer.

Bibliography

Aaron, John, "Gordon Lightfoot," *Guitar Player,* December 1973, p. 20.

Alexander, Jeffry C., "The Buffalo Springfield Message," *Los Angeles Times,* calendar, September 17, 1967.

Appelo, Tim, "Steve Miller Comes Home," *Pacific Northwest,* March 1987, pp. 23–25.

Arnold, Thomas K., "Jefferson Airplane Still Flying After All These Years," *Kicks,* April 1980, pp. 14–18.

Bailey, Andrew, "Alone Together, Mason and Cass," *Rolling Stone,* September 17, 1970.

Baker, Robb, "Remembering Janis" (Janis Joplin), *After Dark,* November 1973, pp. 66–67.

Barol, Bill, "Myths Keep Us Strangers" (Bruce Springsteen), *Newsweek,* November 2, 1987.

Barrios, Gregg, "Ritchie Valens' Roots," *Los Angeles Times,* Calendar, July 19, 1987, pp. 3–5.

Bashe, Philip, "Loverboy Get Twice Lucky," *Circus,* April 30, 1982.

Beatles Press Book, London, Apple Press Office, 1971.

"Beatledammerung," *Time,* January 25, 1971, p. 55.

"Benson and Klugh," *Jazziz,* July 1987.

Belz, Carl, *The Story of Rock,* New York, Oxford University Press, 1969.

Bernstein, Paul, "From Shore to Shore with the Beach Boys," *Los Angeles Times,* Calendar, June 17, 1973, p. 50.

Berry, Leonard J., "Murder Is Done for the Rolling Stones Cameras" (Altamont, California), *Los Angeles Times,* Calendar, December 27, 1970.

Bentley, Jack, "The Starmaker Steps Forward" (Alexis Korner), *London Sunday Mirror,* October 25, 1970.

Billboard, New York, Billboard Publications, various issues.

"Black Moses" (Isaac Hayes), *Time,* December 20, 1970, p. 55.

"Blues Boy" (B.B. King), *Time,* January 10, 1969, pp. 42–43.

"Blues for Janis" (Janis Joplin), *Time,* October 19, 1970, pp. 54–55.

Broeske, Pat H., "After Death, It Was War" (Elvis Presley), *Los Angeles Times,* Calendar, August 16, 1987, pp. 4–5, 100–102.

Bronson, Fred, *The Billboard Book of Number One Hits,* New York, Billboard Publications, 1985.

Caine, Sammy, "Complexity in the HEART of Rock," *Modern Recording & Music,* December 1985.

Canby, Vincent, "In Search of Madonna's Persona," *The New York Times,* Arts & Leisure, August 23, 1987, pp. 17, 26.

Cannon, Geoffrey, "Frank Zappa's Steady Rise from Civilization's Ash Can," *Los Angeles Times,* Calendar, September 27, 1970, p. 16.

———, "Rolling Stones and a Rocky Night in Paris," ibid, November 15, 1970.

———, "An Unalienated Interlude With Ike, Tina Turner," ibid, May 30, 1971, p. 10.

Cash Box, New York, Cash Box Publishing Co., various issues.

Carr, Roy, "Alexis Korner Couldn't Afford Jagger as Radio Vocalist—So Mick Started Stones!" *New Musical Express,* October 3, 1970.

Cartnal, Alan, "Kinks Rock the Establishment," *Los Angeles Times,* part 4, March 10, 1972, p. 8.

Cerf, Martin, "The New Elton" (Elton John), *Phonograph,* pp. 32–37.

Charters, Samuel, *The Country Blues,* New York, Rinehart, Winston & Co., 1959.

———, *The Bluesmen,* New York, Oak Publications, 1968.

Cocks, Jay, "The Best Gang in Town" (The Clash), *Time,* March 5, 1979, p. 68.

Cohen, Barney, "Sting, Every Breath He Takes," New York, *Berkley Books,* 1984.

Cohen, Debra Rae, "Hall and Oates: A Question of Balance," *Rolling Stone,* March 22, 1979, p. 26.

———, "Marianne Faithfull: Younger than Yesterday," ibid, April 17, 1980, pp. 14, 19.

Cohen, Scott, "Is There Life After 'Double Live Gonzo'" (Ted Nugent), *Circus,* March 16, 1978.

Connelly, Christopher, "Steppin Out!" (Mick Jagger), *Rolling Stone,* February 14, 1985.

Cook, Richard, "The Foolish Heart of Tom Verlaine," *New Musical Express,* September 1, 1984.

Crawford, Wayne, "There's Much More Now for Dion DiMucci," *Chicago Daily News,* February 28, 1970.

Cromelin, Richard, "Has Genesis' Music Overcome Its Theatre?" *Los Angeles Times,* Calendar, October 13, 1974, p. 64.

———, "KC & the Sunshine Band," *Phonograph Record,* October 1975.

———, "Strummer on Man, God—and the Clash,"

Los Angeles Times, Calendar, January 31, 1988, pp. 61–62.

Crowe, Cameron, "Deep Purple Self Evaluation Times Again, *Rolling Stone*, June 21, 1973, p. 26.

———, "E.C.'s Been Here, There and Everywhere" (Eric Clapton), *Los Angeles Times*, Calendar, November 16, 1975, p. 64.

———, "Jethro Tull: Waves Over Oiled Water," ibid, December 22, 1974, pp. 68, 91.

———, "Led Zeppelin—the Hammer of the Gods," ibid, January 4, 1981, pp. 64–65.

———, "Lynyrd Skynyrd: Hell on Wheels Puts on the Brakes," ibid, October 24, 1976, p. 68.

———, "No Upper-Crust Pretensions for Humble Pie's Steve Marriott," ibid, September 9, 1971, p. 49.

Darling, Cary, "Only 8 Lads: Oingo Boingo's Difficult Teen Years," *BAM*, May 8, 1987, pp. 25–28.

Davis, Bob, "The Cars Elliot Easton," *Guitar World*, September 1984, pp. 34–38.

Diehl, Digby, "Jim Morrison: Love & the Demonic Psyche," *Eye*, April 1968.

DeMuir, Harold, "Kinks Konfessions—Ray Davies Tells All," *BAM*, February 13, 1987, pp. 19–21.

Doerschuk, Bob, "Kerry Livgren & Steve Walsh of Kansas," *Contemporary Keyboard*, August 1977.

Du Moyer, Paul, "The End of the Longest Night" (Chrissie Hynde & the Pretenders), *New Musical Express*, November 26, 1983, pp. 26–27, 46.

Eliezer, Christie, "The New Spirit of Oz Rock" (Men at Work), *Record*, July 1983.

Elliott, Susan, "Billy Joel: Up from Piano Man," *High Fidelity*, January 1978, pp. 110–113, 121.

Everett, Todd, "He's Only the Piano Player" (Elton John), *Los Angeles Herald Examiner*, July 11, 1987.

Farber, Jim, "Tom Verlaine: Looking for Life," *Rolling Stone*, March 20, 1980, pp. 28–29.

Feather, Leonard, "Esther Phillips Raises Her Voice," *Los Angeles Times*, Calendar, March 15, 1970.

———, "Hancock: Master of Electric Music," ibid, May 29, 1983.

———, "John Mayall—Still a Blues Crusader," ibid, part 4, October 27, 1969.

———, "Lou Rawls: Up from Ghetto But Still Involved," ibid, Calendar, April 20, 1969.

Firestone, Dan, "Former Toledoan Engineers Success of Rock's Boston," *Toledo Blade*, Section E, June 21, 1987.

Flanagan, Bill, "The Cars," *Music and Sound Output*, February 1984.

———, "The Return of Robbie Robertson," *Musician*, September 1987.

"Folk Hero Speaks" (Bob Dylan), *Time*, November 14, 1968, p. 58.

Fong-Torres, Ben, "Jefferson Starship Changes Orbit," *Rolling Stone*, April 17, 1980, pp. 9–10, 24.

———, "Natalie Cole," ibid, June 16, 1977.

Fricke, David, "King Crimson Hits the Road," *Trouser Press*, March 1982, pp. 23–25.

Gaines, Steven, "Abba: The Band That Won't Tour the States," *Circus*, March 30, 1978.

———, "Lou Reed and the Pain of 'Berlin,'" *New York Sunday News*, Leisure, January 6, 1974, p. 6.

Gambaccini, "The Boomtown Rats: Bound for Glory," *Rolling Stone*, March 8, 1979.

———, "Paul McCartney's One-Man Band," *Rolling Stone*, June 26, 1980, pp. 11, 20.

Garcia, Bob, "Jethro Tull," *World Countdown*, Vol. 5–6, 1969, p. 2.

Gardner, Edgar, "Sammy Hagar—Just Another Punk from Fontana," *Rock-N-Roll News*, April 15, 1976.

Garland, Phyl, *The Sound of Soul*, Chicago, Regnery, 1969.

George, Nelson, *Where Did Our Love Go?* New York, St. Martin's Press, 1985.

Gillett, Charlie, *The Sound of the City: The Rise of Rock and Roll*, New York, Outerbridge & Dienstery, 1970.

Gilmore, Mikal, "Bruce Springsteen," *Rolling Stone*, November 5, 1987.

———, "John Lydon Improves His Public Image," ibid, May 1, 1980, pp. 11, 20.

———, "Lou Reed's Heart of Darkness," ibid, March 22, 1979, pp. 8, 12–18.

———, "Petty Damns the Torpedoes Again," *Los Angeles Herald Examiner*, Style, 1987, pp. B–1, B–3.

———, "Terence Trent D'Arby Makes American Debut," *Rolling Stone*, November 19, 1987.

Gold, Todd, "Out of the East L.A. Barrio Stalks Los Lobos," *People*, March 4, 1985.

Goldberg, Michael, "Bangles: A Female Fab Four?" *Rolling Stone*, September 13, 1984.

———, "George Clinton: The Return of Dr. Funkenstein," ibid, June 23, 1983.

———, "The Motels Tread Where Nightmare and Reality Merge," *San Francisco Examiner/Chronicle*, August 19, 1979.

Goldman, Albert, "Chicago and the Great Dream Machine," *Life*, May 28, 1971.

Goldstein, Patrick, "Can Rap Survive Gang War?" (Run-D.M.C.), *Los Angeles Times*, Calendar, August 24, 1986, p. 5.

Goldstein, Richard, *The Poetry of Rock*, New York, Bantam Books, 1969.

Graustark, Barbara, "The Real John Lennon," *Newsweek,* September 29, 1980, pp. 76–77.

Grein, Paul, "Bacharach's Back on Key After 10-Year Slump," *Los Angeles Times,* Calendar, July 13, 1986, pp. 63–66.

———, "Houston Hits: Master Plan, Blind Luck" (Whitney Houston), *Los Angeles Times,* Calendar, June 8, 1986, p. 60.

Green, Jim, "The Pluck of the Irish" (U2), *Trouser Press,* March 1982.

Guitar Player, Los Gatos, California, various issues.

"Gunmen Kill Peter Tosh, Reggae Star, in Jamaica," *The New York Times,* September 13, 1987, p. Y-9.

Halbersberg, Elianne, "Night Ranger," *Rock Fever,* 1987, pp. 66–71.

Heilpern, John, "The Why and the How of the Who," *Los Angeles Times,* Calendar, January 14, 1968, pp. 1, 26–27.

Henderson, David, *'Scuse Me While I Kiss the Sky—The Life of Jimi Hendrix,* New York, Doubleday, 1978.

Henke, James, "The Clash," *Rolling Stone,* April 17, 1980, pp. 39–41.

———, "Middle Class Heroes" (Duran Duran), ibid, February 2, 1984.

Hewitt, Paolo, "The Mad Professor" (George Clinton), *Melody Maker,* January 8, 1983.

Hilburn, Robert, "Abba to Embark on First U.S. Tour," *Los Angeles Times,* Part IV, July 17, 1979.

———, "Aerosmith Draws the Line Against Nostalgia," ibid, Part VI, January 29, 1988.

———,"All Systems Go-Go," ibid, Calendar, June 17, 1984, pp. 1, 56–57.

———, "Allman—Blues Everyman" (Gregg Allman), ibid, Part VI, May 9, 1987, pp. 1, 9.

———, "Beatles Breakup: An Assessment of Their Future as Individuals," ibid, Calendar, April 26, 1970.

———, "Blood, Sweat & Tears All Smiles," ibid, Calendar, January 18, 1970.

———, "Big Mack Is Back" (Fleetwood Mac), ibid, Calendar, June 14, 1987, pp. 60–61.

———, "Blasting Off with the Blasters," ibid, Calendar, January 17, 1982.

———, "Carlisle Set to Go-Go It Alone," ibid, Part VI, November 10, 1986, pp. 1, 4.

———, "Creedence—A Rock Group That Means Business," ibid, Calendar, August 30, 1970.

———, "Dylan Making It on His Own Terms," ibid, Part IV, February 12, 1974, p. 1.

———, "Bob Dylan at 42—Rolling Down Highway 61 Again," ibid,Calendar, October 30, 1983, pp. 3–4.

———, "Dylan Rocks the Holy Land," ibid, Calendar, September 20, 1987, pp. 70–73.

———, "Elton John New Rock Talent," ibid, part IV, August 27, 1970, p. 22.

———, "Eurythmics: A Tune Played to Tension," ibid, Calendar, August 3, 1986, pp. 5, 73.

———, "Farewell to Bill Haley, Rock's First Big Star," ibid, Calendar, February 15, 1981, p. 71.

———, "Feisty Ronnie Lane on the Road Again," ibid, Part VI, June 13, 1986, pp. 1, 4.

———, "Fleetwood Mac's Mammoth Gamble with Tusk," ibid, Calendar, December 2, 1979, pp. 5–6.

———, "Go-Go's: Rock's New Darlings," ibid, Calendar, March 7, 1982, pp. 64–66.

———, "Greatest Show on Earth" (the Who), ibid, Part IV, December 10, 1971, pp. 1, 30.

———, "The Growing Up of Mr. Mellencamp," ibid, Calendar, February 28, 1988, pp. 68–70.

———, "James Brown Coming in Loud and Clear," ibid, Calendar, December 7, 1969.

———, "Jimi Hendrix: Quality Made Him Something Else," ibid, Calendar, October 4, 1970, p. 1.

———, "Joan Jett: Running Away from a Bad Reputation," ibid, Calendar, August 19, 1984, pp. 60–64.

———, "Life and Death with the Pretenders," ibid, Calendar, March 4, 1984, pp. 62–64.

———, "Mayfield's Message: 'Singing What All the Brothers Feel,'" ibid, Calendar, January 30, 1972.

———, "McCartney: He's at Ease at Last," ibid, Part VI, August 26, 1986, pp. 1, 44.

———, "Motown's Berry Gordy Looks Back, on 25 Years," ibid, Part VI, March 22, 1983, pp. 1, 3.

———, "Ozzy: Why Does This Guy Scare People?" (Ozzy Osbourne), ibid, Calendar, May 1, 1983, pp. 1, 54–55, 64.

———, "Tom Petty: Plugging In to the Glory of Rock," ibid,Calendar, June 4, 1978, p. 76.

———, "Pretenders Become Contenders," ibid, Calendar, pp. 66–67.

———, "A Re-Formed Clash Is Back on the Attack," ibid, Calendar, January 22, 1984, pp. 52–58.

———, "A Revamped Mack Plots Fall Tour" (Fleetwood Mac), ibid, Part VI, August 12, 1987, pp. 1, 2.

———, "The Sweet Sting of Success," ibid,Calendar, August 11, 1985, pp. 56–57, 60, 64.

———, "Tough Boy George" (Culture Club), ibid, Calendar, February 19, 1984, pp. 1, 68–69.

———, "The Tragic Elvis," ibid, Calendar, July 12, 1987, pp. 3, 92.

———, "U2 at Home in Dublin," ibid, Calendar, April 12, 1987, pp. 52–53, 56–62.

"Hochman, Steve, "Marley's Son Carries on Tradition," *Los Angeles Times,* Part VI, February 10, 1987, p. 4.

———, "Randy Rhoads—Memories of a Guitar Hero," ibid, Calendar, May 10, 1987, p. 70.

———, "Ventures Ride on Endless '60s Wave," ibid, Part VI, August 27, 1987, p. 8.

Holden, Stephen, "Billy Joel Reaches Out to Embrace Pop," *The New York Times,* Arts & Leisure, August 3, 1986, pp. 21–22.

———, "Ellie Greenwich, Her Life and Her Songs at the Bottom Line," ibid, Sect. Y, January 20, 1984, p. 18.

———, "Paul Simon Brings Home the Music of Black South Africa," ibid, Arts & Leisure, August 24, 1986, pp. 1, 18.

———, "Smokey Robinson, Motown to Broadway," ibid, Arts & Leisure, February 25, 1985, p. 16.

Hopkins, Jerry, *The Rock Story,* New York, Signet Books, 1970.

——— and Sugerman, Daniel, *No One Here Gets Out Alive* (Jim Morrison), New York, Warner Books, 1980.

Hunt, Dennis, "Ann Wilson and Her Resuscitated Heart," *Los Angeles Times,* Calendar, August 11, 1985, p. 5.

———, "Ashford & Simpson—Together—On and Off the Record," ibid, Calendar, August 8, 1981, p. 70.

———, "Billy Idol—A Rebel on a Roll," ibid, Calendar, March 18, 1984, p. 64.

———, "Bruce Dickinson Doesn't Fit Heavy Metal Mold" (Iron Maiden), ibid, Part VI, July 1984.

———, "Crosby Singing Those Old Jail Blues Again" (David Crosby), ibid, Part VI, June 30, 1985, p. 62.

———, "Faces: Pride, Prejudice for Foreigner," ibid, Calendar, January 13, 1980, p. 72.

———, "Foreigner Says Pease Was Foreign," ibid, Calendar, September 6, 1981, p. 56.

———, "Foreigner's Lou Gramm—the Unknown Agent," ibid, Calendar, February 3, 1985, p. 55.

———, "He May Be Heavy Metal, But He's Not Twisted" (Dee Snyder, Twisted Sister), ibid, Calendar, September 9, 1984.

———, "Huey Lewis—A Mr. Nice Guy Makes News," ibid, Calendar, January 11, 1987, p. 64.

———, "Huey Lewis' News Is Good," ibid, Calendar, April 25, 1982, pp. 65–66.

———, "Hungry for a Hit Record—A Boomtown Rat Tries It Solo," ibid, Calendar, November 30, 1986, p. 80.

———, "Steve Jones Takes a Solo Shot," ibid, Calendar, May 31, 1987, pp. 84–85.

———, "Julian Lennon Taking the Expressway," ibid, Calendar, April 6, 1986, p. 70–71.

———, "KC, the King of Disco, Is Staging a Comeback," ibid, Part VI, March 15, 1984, pp. 1, 6.

———, "Kahn Turns from Drugs to Books" (Chaka Khan), ibid, Calendar, March 6, 1983, p. 59.

———, "Pat Benatar: The Three Phases of Eve," ibid, Calendar, March 13, 1983, p. 55.

———, "Police, Where Is Thy Sting?" ibid, Calendar, June 12, 1983, pp. 58, 66.

———, "Vandross: Big Man with a Small Ego," ibid, Calendar, May 6, 1984, p. 68.

———, "When Rick James Talks, the Fur and the Funk Fly," ibid, Calendar, August 7, 1983, p. 64.

Hunt, James, "The Moonglows," *Record Exchanger,* March 1970.

"Into the Pain of the Heart" (Joni Mitchelll), *Time,* April 1970.

Jahn, Mike, *Jim Morrison and the Doors: An Unauthorized Book,* New York, Grosset & Dunlap.

"James Taylor: One Man's Family of Rock," *Time,* March 1, 1971, pp. 45–53.

"Janis Joplin," *Village Voice,* February 22, 1968.

Jerome, Jim, "Robby Steinhardt Is Kansas Rock Fiddler But Lately His Fur's Been Flying in Florida," *People Weekly.*

Johnson, Connie, "Aretha Back to Her Soul," *Los Angeles Times,* Part VI, December 16, 1981, pp. 1, 3.

———, "The Golden Days for Maze," *Black Stars,* October 1978.

Johnston, Pete, "The Bee Gees Learn ABC's of Pop Success," *Los Angeles Times,* Calendar, January 21, 1968, p. 9.

———, "Cream Guitarist a Reluctant Idol" (Eric Clapton), ibid, October 13, 1968, p. 1.

———, "The Man the Motown Sound Revolves Around" (Berry Gordy, Jr.), ibid, August 18, 1968, p. 1.

———, "Revere's Raiders Attack the Treasury," ibid, Calendar, August 18, 1968, p. 1.

———, "Up, Up and Away with Jefferson Airplane," ibid, Calendar, February 25, 1968, p. 13.

Jones, Allan, "Cover Lines" (Tom Verlaine), *Melody Maker,* September 1, 1984.

———, "The Elvis (Costello, that is) Interview," ibid, June 25, 1977, p. 14.

———, "Hey Lord! G.P.'s Got the Answers" (Graham Parker), ibid, March 17, 1979, pp. 17–20.

Klein, Howard, "Mink DeVille: Slick Fur Fury," *Creem,* October 1977.

———, "Sammy Hagar," *BAM,* March 1977.

Kloman, William, "Laura Nyro: She's the Hippest—and Maybe the Hottest?" *The New York Times,* October 6, 1968.

Knapp, Dan, "Morrison's Last Days in L.A.: Hope for the Future," *Los Angeles Times,* Calendar, July 25, 1971, p. 14.

———, "Tom Jones, the Singer, Is Also a Human Being," ibid, June 21, 1970.

Kociela, Ed, "Pretty: New Wave—with a Twist," *Los Angeles Herald Examiner,* Style, June 12, 1978, pp. B–1, B–2.

Kofsky, Frank,"After Bathing at Baxter's Revisited . . ." (Jefferson Aireplane), *Jazz & Pop,* March 1968, pp. 33–35.

Kozinn, Allan, "A New Lennon Mystery Tour" (John Lennon), *The New York Times,* Arts & Leisure, March 20, 1988, pp. 25, 34.

"Lady Soul Singing It Like It Is" (Aretha Franklin), *Time,* June 28, 1968, pp. 62–66.

Lanham, Tom, "No-Cal Metal Tips the Scales of Success" (Night Ranger), *BAM,* August 23, 1985, pp. 29–30.

"Latin Rock" (Santana), *Time,* September 21, 1970, p. 68.

London, Michael, "Oingo Boingo Poles Back," *Los Angeles Times,* Calendar, July 4, 1982, p. 59.

"Looking Back on Rick Nelson," *San Francisco Chronicle,* Date Book, January 1, 1987, p. 1.

Lydon, Michael, "Good Old Grateful Dead," *Rolling Stone,* August 23, 1969.

———, Rock Folk: *Portraits from the Rock Pantheon,* New York, Dial Press, 1971.

Mandell, Ellen, "Dolenz, Jones, Boyce & Hart: Prime-Mates Monkeeing Again," *The Good Times,* April 13, April 26, 1976.

Marcus, Greil, "Elvis Costello Repents," *Rolling Stone,* September 2, 1982.

———, (ed.), *Rock Will Stand,* New York, Beacon Press, 1970.

Marsh, Dave, *Botn to Run: The Bruce Springsteen Story,* New York, Dell, 1979.

———, "From the Beginning" (Smokey Robinson & The Miracles), *Creem,* April 1972, pp. 40–41.

———, *Glory Days: Bruce Springsteen in the 1980s,* New York, Pantheon, 1987.

———, and Swenson, John, *The New Rolling Stone Record Guide,* New York, Random House/Rolling Stone Press, 1983.

McDonough, Jack, "Pink Floyd—The Interstellar Band," *Rolling Stone,* November 26, 1970.

McDougal, Dennis, "Rick Nelson's Big Plans for '86 Cut Short by Fatal Crash," *Los Angeles Times,* Part II, pp. 1, 2.

McKaie, "The Band: Beyond Superstardom," *The Good Times,* January 1974.

McKenna, Kristine, "High Flying with the B-52's," *Los Angeles Times,* Part VI, October 10, 1980.

———, "The Melancholy Refrain of Roxy's Bryan Ferry," ibid, Calendar, July 25, 1982, p. 56.

———, "XTC and the ABC's of Topical Pop," ibid, Calendar, April 4, 1982, p. 73.

McLane, Daisann, "Heart Attack," *Rolling Stone,* May 1, 1980, pp. 11–13.

Mendelsohn, John, "A New Blues Boy Blows in from Britain" (Joe Cocker), *Los Angeles Times,* Calendar, August 3, 1969.

Miller, Jim, "No More Mr. Bad Guy" (Elvis Costello), *Newsweek,* August 9, 1982.

Oberbeck, S.K., "The Dada Rockers" (Alice Cooper), *Newsweek,* December 15, 1969, p. 106.

Ochs, Michael, *Rock Archives,* New York, Doubleday Dolphin, 1984.

O'Connor, John J., "When Elvis Was Still a Rockabilly Singer," *Los Angeles Times,* August 16, 1987, p. 26.

O'Hallaren, Bill, "We Love You Elvis (Still)," *West,* June 7, 1970, pp. 69–71.

Oliver, Paul, *The Story of the Blues,* London, Barrie & Rockcliffe/Grosset, 1969.

Otis, Johnny, *Listen to the Lambs,* New York, W.W. Norton, 1968.

Palmer, Robert, "Black Flag Adds a Soupçon of Sophistication to Punk Rock," *The New York Times,* February 23, 1986.

———, "Bryan Ferry's Scenes of Obsession and Consequences," ibid, Arts & Leisure, November 29, 1987, p. 27.

———, "Elvis Costello—Is He Pop's Top," ibid, Arts & Leisure, June 27, 1982.

———, "Hancock Nails Down His Direction," ibid, Section Y, August 29, 1984, p. 21.

———, "New Album of Geils Band," ibid, October 31, 1984.

———, "O'Jays Create an 80's Sound," ibid, Arts & Leisure, September 11, 1985, p. 22.

———, "One from the Flip Side of David Johansen," ibid, 1987.

———, "Records from the Roadhouse" (Jerry Lee Lewis), ibid, Arts & Leisure, April 26, 1987, p. 23.

———, "Pop's Plucky Hero" (Tom Verlaine), ibid, March 15, 1987, pp. H26, 28.

Pareles, Jon, "Chrissie Hynde Makes Peace with the Past and Moves On," *The New York Times,* Section H, January 22, 1984, pp. 21, 25.

———, "Elvis Costello on Betrayal and the Many Troubles of Love," ibid, Arts & Leisure, October 19, 1986, p. 25.

———, "The Grateful Dead, Most Alive on Stage," ibid, Section H, July 26, 1987, p. 24.

———, "Power Steering" (The Cars), *Rolling Stone,* January 25, 1979.

———, "Can Robert Plant Find a New Style After

Led Zeppelin," *The New York Times,* Arts & Leisure, July 26, 1985, p. 19.

———, "A Smaller Duran Duran Finds Disillusionment," ibid, Arts & Leisure, December 7, 1986, pp. 27, 32.

———, "Talking Heads Confronts the Modern World, ibid, March 30, 1988.

———, "Whitney Houston: She's Singing by Formula," ibid, Arts & Leisure, June 7, 1987, p. 29.

"Passionate and Sloppy" (Janis Joplin), *Time,* August 9, 1968, p. 71.

"Paul Butterfield Blues Band," *Pop/Rock Music,* December 1968.

Phillips, John (with Jim Jerome), *Papa John,* New York, Dell Books, 1987.

"Pink Floyd—Future Rock," *Los Angeles Free Press,* October 30, 1970.

Pond, Steve, "Devo Finds It's Not Easy Starting a Devolution," *Los Angeles Times,* Part VI, December 9, 1982.

———, "Huey Lewis Did It His Way—Unweird," ibid, Calendar, January 8, 1984, p. 68.

———, "Johnny Rivers, 'Crazy as Eve,'" ibid, Part VI, January 21, 1984, pp. 1, 4.

Puterbaugh, Parke, "Duran Duran: The Little Girls Understand," *Rolling Stone,* May 12, 1983.

Reber, Pat and Toepfer, Susan, "Kraftwerk, Rock Robots," *Gallery,* October 1978.

"Return of Satan's Jesters" (Rolling Stones), *Time,* May 17, 1971, p. 60.

Rhodewell, Bruce D., "The Bangles: They've Got the Best, Too," *Los Angeles Herald Examiner,* July 15, 1984, p. E-7.

Richmond, Dick, "Sammy Hagar," *St. Louis Post Dispatch,* March 8, 1979.

Robbins, Ira, "Smart, Sleek and Debonair" (Cheap Trick), *Trouser Press,* February 1978.

Robins, Wayne, "A Thriller: Pop Battles Race Barrier" (Michael Jackson), *Los Angeles Times,* Calendar, August 7, 1983, pp. 56–57.

Robinson, Lisa, "Back on the Road Again" (Boston), *New York Post,* July 1, 1987.

Rockwell, John, "Abba—Today the World, Tomorrow the U.S.," *The New York Times,* March 5, 1978.

———, "McCartney's Tour Starts Triumphantly," ibid, May 5, 1976.

———, "Tracing Little Richard to the Source," ibid, Arts & Leisure, February 1, 1987, pp. 29, 36.

———, "U2 Makes a Bid for 'Great Band' Status," ibid, Arts & Leisure, March 29, 1987, p. 23.

Rohde, H. Kandy, *The Gold of Rock & Roll, 1955–67,* New York, Arbor House, 1970.

Rosen, Steve, "Jeff Beck," *Guitar Player,* December 1973, p. 22.

Rosenthal, Jack, "Roberta's a Capital Find" (Roberta Flack), *The New York Times Magazine,* March 29, 1970.

Ruby, Jay, "Frank Zappa," *Jazz & Pop,* August 1970.

Ryan, Michael, "Darryl Hall—John Oates," *People,* April 15, 1985, pp. 50–54.

Sander, Ellen, "Crosby, Stills and Nash: Renaissance Fare," *Saturday Review,* May 31, 1969.

———, "An Interview with Paul Butterfield," *Hit Parader,* 1968, pp. 12–14.

Schneider, Steve, "Replaying the '60s Motown Sound," *The New York Times,* Arts & Leisure, August 26, 1986, p. 24.

Schruers, Ted, "The Ted (Nugent) Offensive," *Rolling Stone,* March 8, 1979, pp. 42–47.

Schwann Record & Tape Guide, Boston, W. Schwann, Inc., various issues.

Secher, Andy, "Mötley Crüe Out for blood," *Hit Parader,* December 1983.

Shaw, Arnold, *The World of Soul,* New York, Cowles Book Co., 1970.

Silverton, Pete, "B-52's," *Sounds,* May 26, 1979, pp. 16–17.

"Simon Says" (Paul Simon), *Time,* January 31, 1972, p. 36.

Snowden, Don, "Fighting Back from Real-Life Blues" (Paul Butterfield), *Los Angeles Times,* Part VI, June 26, 1986, p. 2.

———, "Lobos Takes Tex-Mex to the Max," ibid, Part V, December 18, 1982, pp. 1, 2.

———, "UB40 Digs into Roots of Reggae," ibid, Part V, February 16, 1985, p. 5.

Snyder, Michael, "Rock & Roll Will Never Die, It'll Just Devolve" (Devo), *Berkeley Barb,* October 21, 27, 1977.

Snyder, Patrick, "The Band—Drifting Toward the Last Waltz," *Rolling Stone,* December 16, 1976.

Soocher, Stan, "Sunshine Superstars" (KC & the Sunshine Band), *Circus,* October 17, 1978.

Stark, Annette, "Idol Chatter" (Billy Idol), SPIN, June 1986, pp. 44–50.

Steffens, Roger, "Rita Marley Carries on Bob's Beat," *Los Angeles Times,* Calendar, March 21, 1982, p. 67.

Synthetic, Hal, "New Musick: Kraftwerk," *Sounds,* November 26, 1977.

Tallion, Michael, "Judas Priest, the Metal Machine," *Hit Parader,* May 1984, pp. 16–18.

Tayelor, Barry, "Heart—Supergroup from Vancouver," *Record World,* October 30, 1976, p. 15.

Thompson, Tony, *Positively Main Street: An Unorthodox View of Bob Dylan,* New York, Coward-McCann, 1971.

Turner, Colin, "Board with Groups? Join a Rock

Pool" (Al Kooper), *The New York Times,* September 29, 1968.

Tuirner, Tina (with Kent Loder), *I, Tina,* New York, Morrow, 1986.

Tyler, T., "Jackson 5 at Home," *Time,* June 14, 1971, p. 64.

Valle, Victor, "The American Dream Lives in Los Lobos," *Los Angeles Times,* Calendar, January 25, 1987, p. 62.

Various writers, "Beatles Anniversary Issue," *Rolling Stone,* February 16, 1984.

Waller, Don, "The Punk Meets the Godfather" (James Brown), *Los Angeles Weekly,* April 13, 19, 1984, pp. 38, 42.

———, "Van Halen: Life with the Top Down," *Los Angeles Times,* Calendar, February 5, 1984, pp. 62–63.

Wang, Jo-Ann, "John Cougar Group Rates Raves," *Deseret News,* November 16, 1979.

Weinstein, Bob, "Kansas is Sitting on Top of the World," *Circus,* November 10, 1977

Whitburn, Joel, various editions of *Top LPs, Top Pop Records, Top R&B Records,* Menominee Falls, Wisconsin, Record Research.

Whitcomb, Ian, "Haley Was Still Vibrant Force in Britain," *Los Angeles Times,* Calendar, February 15, 1981, pp. 69–72.

White, Charles, *The Life and Times of Little Richard, The Quasar of Rock,* New York, Harmony, 1984.

Williams, Stephen, "Bee Gees New Album Stumbles Off Billboard Chart," *Los Angeles Times,* January 8, 1988, p. 11.

Willman, Chris, "Quiet Beatle with Something to Say" (George Harrison), *Los Angeles Times,* Part VI, October 6, 1987, pp. 1, 4.

———, "The Replacements—Still Standing on the Ledge," ibid, Calendar, July 26, 1987.

———, "Robbie Robertson Rides AGain," ibid, Calendar, November 1, 1987, pp. 72–74.

Wilson, Mary, *Dreamgirl: My Life as a Supreme,* New York, St. Martin's, 1986.

Winner, Langdon, "The Odyssey of Captain Beefheart," *Rolling Stone,* May 14, 1970, pp. 36–40.

Wolf, William, "James Brown Has Mutual Admiration," *Los Angeles Times,* Part IV, July 10, 1969, p. 23.

Wolfe, Tom, *Kandy Kolored Tangerine Flake Streamline Baby,* New York, Noonday, 1965.

Yorke, Ritchie, "Aretha's Comeback Anchored in the Gospel Truth" (Aretha Franklin), *Los Angeles Times,* Calendar, February 8, 1970, pp. 1, 42, 52.

———, "Cat Stevens Refueled His Rocket," ibid, September 27, 1970.

———, "George Harrison Assesses the Beatles' Past, Present, Future," ibid, December 31, 1969.

Young, Charles H., "George Thorogood and the Destroyers Play Hardball," *Rolling Stone,* March 22, 1979, pp. 8, 28–29.

———, "The Pretenders Change Diapers and Wrestle Death to a Draw," *Musician,* March 1984.

Young, Jim, "The Genesis Autodiscography," *Trouser Press,* March 1982, pp. 16–21.

Zappa, Frank, "Rock Family Affair," *Life,* September 24, 1971, pp. 46–47.

Zimmer, Dave, "The Dual Life of the Motels' Martha Davis," *BAM,* November 18, 1983.

———, "Graham Nash, The Winds of Change," ibid, February 1, 15, 1980.

Zimmerman, Deane, "Kraftwerk's Serious Synthesizer Sound, *Hit Parader,* August 1978.

Zipkin, Michael, "Herbie Hancock—Reaching for Sunlight," *BAM,* June 2, 1978.

Zito, Tom, "Boston Group and How It Grew," *Los Angeles Times,* Part IV, December 13, 1976, p. 20.